ISBN 978-1-5284-8229-5
PIBN 10136934

This book is a reproduction of an important historical work. Forgotten Books uses
state-of-the-art technology to digitally reconstruct the work, preserving the original format
whilst repairing imperfections present in the aged copy. In rare cases, an imperfection in
the original, such as a blemish or missing page, may be replicated in our edition. We do,
however, repair the vast majority of imperfections successfully; any imperfections that
remain are intentionally left to preserve the state of such historical works.

HISTORY
FOR READY REFERENCE

FROM THE BEST
HISTORIANS, BIOGRAPHERS, AND SPECIALISTS

THEIR OWN WORDS IN A COMPLETE

SYSTEM OF HISTORY

FOR ALL USES, EXTENDING TO ALL COUNTRIES AND SUBJECTS,
AND REPRESENTING FOR BOTH READERS AND STUDENTS THE BETTER AND
NEWER LITERATURE OF HISTORY IN THE
ENGLISH LANGUAGE

BY

J. N. LARNED

WITH NUMEROUS HISTORICAL MAPS FROM ORIGINAL STUDIES AND DRAWINGS BY

ALAN C. REILEY

REVISED AND ENLARGED EDITION

IN SIX VOLUMES

VOLUME VI — RECENT HISTORY
(1894–5 TO 1901)
A TO Z

SPRINGFIELD, MASS.
THE C. A. NICHOLS CO., PUBLISHERS
1901

The Riverside Press, Cambridge, Mass., U. S. A.
Printed by H. O. Houghton & Company.

PREFACE TO THE SIXTH VOLUME.

THE six years that have passed since the original five volumes of this compilation were published, in 1894-5, have been filled with events so remarkable and changes so revolutionary in political and social conditions that the work has seemed to need an extension to cover them. The wish for such an extension, expressed by many people, led to the preparation of a new volume, in which all the lines of the historical record are taken from the points at which they were dropped in the early volumes, and are carried to the end of the Nineteenth Century, and beyond it, into the opening months of the present year.

In plan and arrangement this additional volume is uniform with the preceding ones; but the material used in it is different from that dealt with before, and a quite different character is given consequently to the book. The former compilation represented closet-studies of History—perspective views of a past more or less remote from those who depicted it. This one, on the contrary, exhibits History in the making, —the day by day evolution of events and changes as they passed under the hands and before the eyes and were recorded by the pens of the actual makers and witnesses of them. If there is crudeness in the story thus constructed, there is life in it, to quite make good the lack of literary finish; and the volume is expected to prove as interesting and as useful as its predecessors. It sets forth, with the fulness which their present-day interest demands, all the circumstances that led to the Spanish-American war; the unforeseen sequences of that war, in the Philippine Islands, in Cuba, in Porto Rico, and in American politics; the whole controversy of Great Britain with the South African Boers and the resulting war; the shameful dealings of western nations with China, during late years, which provoked the outbreak of barbaric hostility to foreigners, and the dreadful experiences of the siege and relief of Peking; the strange Dreyfus agitations in France; the threatening race-conflicts in Austria; the change of sovereign in England; the Peace Conference at The Hague and its results; the federation of the Australian colonies; the development of industrial combinations or trusts in the United States; the archæological discoveries of late years in the East, and the more notable triumphs of achievement in the scientific world. On these and other occurrences of the period surveyed, the record of .fact is quoted from sources the most responsible and authentic now available, and always with the endeavor to present both sides of controverted matters with strict impartiality.

For purposes of reference and study, a large number of important documents—laws, treaties, new constitutions of government, and other state papers—are given in full, and, in most instances, from officially printed texts.

BUFFALO, N. Y., May, 1901.

ACKNOWLEDGMENTS.

I AM indebted to the following named authors, editors, and publishers, for permission kindly given me to quote from books and periodicals, all of which are duly referred to in connection with the passages severally borrowed from them:

The manager of The American Catholic Quarterly Review; the editor of The American Journal of Archæology; the editor of The American Monthly Review of Reviews; General Thomas F. Anderson; Messrs. D. Appleton & Company; Messrs. Wm. Blackwood's Sons (Blackwood's Magazine); Mr. Andrew Carnegie; Messrs. Chapman & Hall (The Fortnightly Review); Mr. Samuel L. Clemens (Mark Twain); Hon. W. Bourke Cockran; the editor of The Contemporary Review; Prof. John Franklin Crowell; the G. W. Dillingham Company; Messrs. Dodd, Mead & Company; Messrs. Doubleday, Page & Company; The Ecumenical Conference on Foreign Missions; Mr. J. Foreman; The Forum Publishing Company; Harper & Brothers (Harper's Magazine); Mr. Howard C. Hillegas; Prof. H. V. Hilprecht; Hon. Frederick W. Holls; Messrs. Houghton, Mifflin & Company (The Atlantic Monthly); Mr. George Iles; the editor of The Independent; Prof. John H. Latané; Messrs. Longmans, Green & Company (The Edinburgh Review); Mr. Charles F. Lummis; Messrs. McClure, Philips & Company (The Popular Science Monthly); Messrs. MacMillan & Company (London); The New Amsterdam Book Company; the editor of The Nineteenth Century Review; the editor of The North American Review; the editors of The Outlook; the managing editor of The Political Science Quarterly; Mr. Edward Porritt; Messrs. G. P. Putnam's Sons; Messrs. Charles Scribner's Sons; George M. Sternberg, Surgeon-General, U. S. A.; The Frederick A. Stokes Company; the managing editor of The Sunday School Times; Prof. F. W. Taussig; Prof. Elihu Thomson; the manager of The Times, London; The University Press, Cambridge; Mr. Herbert Welsh; the editors of The Yale Review.

My acknowledgments are likewise due to the Hon. D. S. Alexander, Representative in Congress, and to many officials at Washington, for courteous assistance in procuring publications of the national government for my use.

LIST OF MAPS.

Map of Asia, ... Preceding the title page
Map of Africa, ... Following page   2
Map of Alaska, ... Following page   8
Map of Australia, ... Following page 30
Map of Central America, showing the Isthmian Canal routes, ... Following page 66
Map of the East Coast of China, ... Following page 76
Map of Cuba and the West Indies, ... Following page 170
Map of Hawaii, ... Following page 254
Map of the Philippine Islands, and of the seat of war in Luzon, ... Following page 368
Map of Porto Rico, ... Following page 410
Map of the Boer Republics and their surroundings, ... Following page 492
Map illustrating the Santiago campaign in the Spanish-American war, ... On page 603

LIST OF TABLES.

The descendants of Queen Victoria, ... Page 215
Protestant foreign missions and missionary societies, ... Pages 311–313
Navies of the Sea Powers, ... Page 318
Philippine Islands, area and population, ... Pages 367–369
The Shipping of the World in 1900, ... Page 452
British military forces in South African war, ... Pages 509–510
Statistics of the Spanish-American War, ... Pages 628–631
Twelfth Census of the United States (1900), ... Pages 645–646
Revenues and expenditures of the government of the United States for the fiscal
  year ended June 30, 1900, ... Page 666
Losses from all causes in the armies of the United States from May 1, 1898, to May
  20, 1900, ... Pages 666–667
Qualifications of the elective franchise in the several States of the United States, . Pages 676–677
Military and naval expenditures of the greater Powers, ... Pages 694–697
Chronological record of events, 1895 to 1901, ... Pages 702–720

HISTORY FOR READY REFERENCE.

ABORIGINES, American. See (in this vol.) INDIANS, AMERICAN.

ABRUZZI, the Duke of: Arctic expedition. See (in this vol.) POLAR EXPLORATION, 1899-1900, 1901.

ABYDOS, Archæological exploration at. See (in this vol.) ARCHÆOLOGICAL RESEARCH : EGYPT : RESULTS.

ABYSSINIA: A. D. 1895-1896.—Successful war with the Italians. See (in this vol.) ITALY : A. D. 1895-1896.

A. D. 1897.—Treaty with Great Britain. —A treaty between King Menelek of Abyssinia and the British Government was concluded in May, 1897. It gives to British subjects the privileges of the most favored nations in trade ; opens the port of Zeyla to Abyssinian importations ; defines the boundary of the British Somali Protectorate, and pledges Abyssinia to be hostile to the Mahdists.

ACETYLENE GAS, Production of. See (in this vol.) SCIENCE, RECENT : CHEMISTRY AND PHYSICS.

ADOWA, Battle of. See (in this vol.) ITALY : A. D. 1895-1896.

AFGHANISTAN: A. D. 1893-1895.—Relinquishment of claims over Swat, Bajaur and Chitral. See (in this vol.) INDIA : A. D. 1895 (MARCH—SEPTEMBER).

A. D. 1894.—The Waziri War. See (in this vol.) INDIA : A. D. 1894.

A. D. 1895.—Anglo-Russian Agreement.— Determination of the northern frontier.— The joint Anglo-Russian Commission for fixing the northern frontier of Afghanistan, from Zulfikar on the Heri-Rud to the Pamirs, finished its work in July, 1895. This was consequent upon an Agreement between the governments of Great Britain and Russia which had been reduced to writing on the previous 11th of March. In part, that Agreement was as follows : "Her Britannic Majesty's Government and the Government of His Majesty the Emperor of Russia engage to abstain from exercising any political influence or control, the former to the north, the latter to the south, of the above line of demarcation. Her Britannic Majesty's Government engage that the territory lying within the British sphere of influence between the Hindu Kush and the line running from the east end of Lake Victoria to the Chinese frontier shall form part of the territory of the Ameer of Afghanistan, that it shall not be annexed to Great Britain, and that no military posts or forts shall be established in it. The execution of this Agreement is contingent upon the evacuation by the Ameer of Afghanistan of all the territories now occupied by His Highness on the right bank of the Panjah, and on the evacuation by the Ameer of Bokhara of the portion of Darwaz which lies to the south of the Oxus, in regard to which Her Britannic Majesty's Government and the Government of His Majesty the Emperor of Russia have agreed to use their influence respectively with the two Ameers."—*Great Britain, Papers by Command : Treaty Series, No. 8, 1895.*

A. D. 1896.—Conquest of Kafiristan.— By the agreement of 1893, between the Ameer of Afghanistan and the government of India (see, in this vol., INDIA : A. D. 1895—MARCH— SEPTEMBER), the mountain district of Kafiristan was conceded to the former, and he presently set to work to subjugate its warlike people, who had never acknowledged his yoke. By the end of 1896 the conquest of these Asiatic Kafirs was believed to be complete.

A. D. 1897-1898.—Wars of the British with frontier tribes. See (in this vol.) INDIA : A. D. 1897-1898.

A. D. 1900.—Russian railway projects. See (in this vol.) RUSSIA-IN-ASIA : A. D. 1900.

AFRICA.

A. D. 1891-1900 (Portuguese East Africa). —Delagoa Bay Railway Arbitration. See (in this vol.) DELAGOA BAY ARBITRATION.

A. D. 1893 (Niger Coast Protectorate).— Its growth.—See (in this vol.) NIGERIA : A. D. 1882-1899.

A. D. 1894 (The Transvaal).—The Commandeering question. See (in this vol.) SOUTH AFRICA (THE TRANSVAAL) : A. D. 1894.

A. D. 1894 (The Transvaal).—Dissatisfaction of the Boers with the London Convention of 1884. See (in this vol.) SOUTH AFRICA (THE TRANSVAAL) : A. D. 1884-1894.

A. D. 1894-1895 (British South Africa Company).—Extension of charter and enlargement of powers.—Influence of Cecil J.

Rhodes.—Attitude towards the Transvaal. See (in this vol.) SOUTH AFRICA (BRITISH S. A. COMPANY) : A. D. 1894-1895.

A. D. 1894-1895 (Rhodesia).—Extended territory and enlarged powers of the British South Africa Company.—Ascendancy of Cecil J. Rhodes. See (in this vol.) SOUTH AFRICA (BRITISH S. A. COMPANY): A. D. 1894-1895.

A. D. 1894-1898 (British Central Africa Protectorate : Nyassaland).—Administrative separation from British South Africa Company's territory.—Conflicts with natives.— Resources and prospects. See (in this vol.) BRITISH CENTRAL AFRICA PROTECTORATE.

A. D. 1895 (Bechuanaland).—Partial conveyance to British South Africa Company.

—Several Bechuana chiefs visited England to urge that their country should not be absorbed by Cape Colony or the British South Africa Company. An agreement was made with them which reserved certain territories to each, but yielded the remainder to the administration of the British South Africa Company.

A. D. 1895 (British East Africa).—Transfer of territory to the British Government.—The territories previously administered by the Imperial British East Africa Company (excepting the Uganda Protectorate, which had been transferred in 1894) were finally transferred to the British Government on the 1st of July. At the same time, the dominion of the Sultan of Zanzibar on the mainland came under the administrative control of the British consul-general at Zanzibar.

A. D. 1895 (Cape Colony).—Annexation of British Bechuanaland.—Proceedings for the annexation of British Bechuanaland to Cape Colony were adopted by the Cape Parliament in August.

A. D. 1895 (French West Africa).— Appointment of a Governor-General.—In June, M. Chaudie was appointed Governor-General of French West Africa, his jurisdiction extending over Senegal, the Sudan possessions of France, French Guinea, Dahomey, and other French possessions in the Gulf of Benin.

A. D. 1895 (Orange Free State).— Proposed federal union of the Free State with the Transvaal.—A resolution making overtures for a federal union with the Transvaal was passed by the Volksraad of the Orange Free State in June.

A. D. 1895 (Sierra Leone).—Establishment of a British Protectorate over the Hinterland of Sierra Leone. — Anglo-French boundary agreement. See (in this vol.) SIERRA LEONE PROTECTORATE.

A. D. 1895 (Transvaal).—Action in Swaziland.—By a proclamation in February, the Transvaal Government assumed the administration of Swaziland and installed King Buna as paramount chief.

A. D. 1895 (The Transvaal). — Closing of the Vaal River Drifts. See (in this vol.) SOUTH AFRICA (THE TRANSVAAL): A. D. 1895 (SEPTEMBER—DECEMBER).

A. D. 1895 (The Transvaal).—Discontent of the Uitlanders.—The Franchise question. See (in this vol.) SOUTH AFRICA (THE TRANSVAAL): A. D. 1895 (NOVEMBER).

A. D. 1895 (The Transvaal).—Opening of Delagoa Bay Railway. See (in this vol.) SOUTH AFRICA (THE TRANSVAAL): A. D. 1895 (JULY).

A. D. 1895 (Zululand). — Extension of Boundary. — A strip of territory west of Amatongaland, along the Pondoland River to the Maputa was formally added to Zululand in May, the South African Republic protesting.

A. D. 1895-1896 (Portuguese East Africa).—War with Gungunhana.—The Portuguese were involved in a war with Gungunhana, king of Gazaland, which lasted from September, 1895, until the following spring, when Gungunhana was captured and carried a prisoner, with his wives and son, to Lisbon.

A. D. 1895-1896 (The Transvaal).—Revolutionary conspiracy of Uitlanders at Johannesburg.— The Jameson raid. See (in this

vol.) SOUTH AFRICA (THE TRANSVAAL): A. D. 1895-1896.

A. D. 1895-1897 (British East Africa Protectorate).—Creation of the Protectorate.—Territories included.—Subjugation of Arab chiefs. — Report of commissioner. See (in this vol.) BRITISH EAST AFRICA PROTECTORATE: A. D. 1895-1897.

A. D. 1896 (Ashanti).—British conquest and occupation. See (in this vol.) ASHANTI.

A. D. 1896 (British South Africa Company).—Resignation of Mr. Rhodes.—Parliamentary movement to investigate. See (in this vol.) SOUTH AFRICA (BRITISH SOUTH AFRICA COMPANY): A. D. 1896 (JUNE); and (JULY).

A. D. 1896 (Cape Colony).—Investigation of the Jameson raid. See (in this vol.) SOUTH AFRICA (CAPE COLONY): A. D. 1896 (JULY).

A. D. 1896 (Rhodesia).—Matabele revolt. See (in this vol.) SOUTH AFRICA (RHODESIA): A. D. 1896 (MARCH—SEPTEMBER).

A. D. 1896 (Zanzibar).—Suppression of an usurper by the British.—On the sudden death (supposed to be from poison) of the Sultan of Zanzibar, August 25, his cousin, Said Khalid, seized the palace and proclaimed himself sultan. Zanzibar being an acknowledged protectorate of Great Britain, the usurper was summoned by the British consul to surrender. He refused, and the palace was bombarded by war vessels in the harbor, with such effect that the palace was speedily destroyed and about 500 of its inmates killed. Khalid fled to the German consul, who protected him and had him conveyed to German territory. A new sultan, Said Hamud-bin-Mahomed was at once proclaimed.

A. D. 1896-1899 (The Transvaal).—Controversies with the British Government. See (in this vol.) SOUTH AFRICA (THE TRANSVAAL): A. D. 1896 (JANUARY—APRIL), to 1899 (SEPTEMBER—OCTOBER).

A. D. 1897 (Congo Free State).—Mutiny of troops.—The Congo troops of an expedition led by Baron Dhanis mutinied and murdered a number of Belgian officers. Subsequently they were attacked in the neighborhood of Lake Albert Edward Nyanza and mostly destroyed.

A. D. 1897 (Dahomey and Tongoland).—Definition of boundary.—By a convention concluded in July between Germany and France, the boundary between German possessions in Tongoland and those of France in Dahomey and the Sudan was defined.

A. D. 1897 (Nigeria).—Massacre at Benin.—British expedition.—Capture of the town. See (in this vol.) NIGERIA: A. D. 1897.

A. D. 1897 (Nigeria).—Subjugation of Fulah slave-raiders.—In January and February, the forces of the Royal Niger Company successfully invaded the strong Fulah states of Nupé and Ilorin, from which slave raiding in the territory under British protection was carried on. Bida, the Nupé capital, was entered on the 27th of January, after a battle in which 800 Hausa troops, led by European officers, and using heavy artillery, drove from the field an army of cavalry and foot estimated at 30,000 in number. The Emir of Nupé was deposed, another set up in his place, and a treaty signed which established British rule. The Emir of Ilorin submitted after his town had been bombarded, and bowed himself to British authority in his government. At the same time, a treaty settled the Lagos fron-

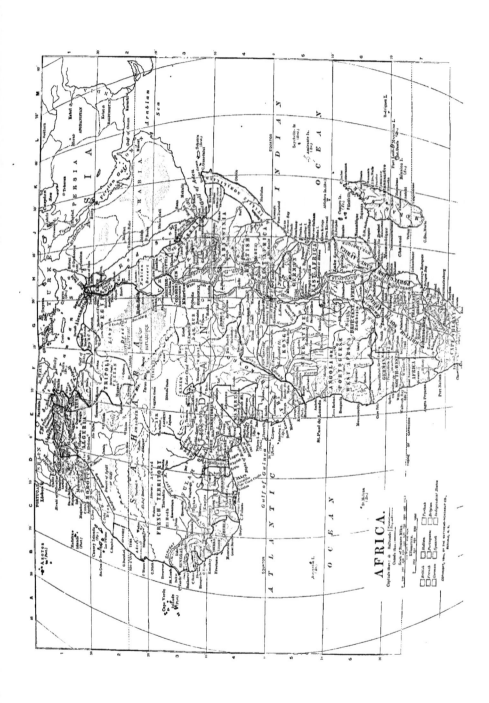

AFRICA.

tier. Later in the year, the stronghold at Kiffi of another slave-raider, Arku, was stormed and burned.

A. D. 1897 (Orange Free State and Transvaal).—Treaty defensive between the **two** republics. See (in this vol.) SOUTH AFRICA (ORANGE FREE STATE AND TRANSVAAL): A. D. 1897 (APRIL).

A. D. 1897 (Sudan).—Beginning of **the** Anglo-Egyptian conquest. See (in this vol.) EGYPT: A. D. 1885–1896.

A. D. 1897 (Zanzibar).—Abolition **of** slavery.—Under pressure from the British government, the Sultan of Zanzibar issued a decree, on the 6th of April, 1897, terminating the legal status of slavery, with compensation to be awarded on proof of consequent loss.

A. D. 1897 (Zululand).—Annexation **to** Natal.—By act of the Natal Parliament in December, 1897, Zululand (with Amatongaland already joined to it) was annexed to Natal Colony, and Dinizulu, son of the last Zulu king, was brought from captivity in St. Helena and reinstated.

A. D. 1897-1898 (Sudan).—Completion of the Anglo-Egyptian conquest. See (in this vol.) EGYPT: A. D. 1897–1898.

A. D. 1897-1898 (Uganda).—Native insurrections and mutiny of Sudanese troops **in** Uganda. See (in this vol.) UGANDA: A. D. 1897-1898.

A. D. 1898 (Abyssinia).—Treaty of King Menelek with Great Britain. See (in this vol.) ABYSSINIA: A. D. 1898.

A. D. 1898 (British South Africa Co.).—Reorganization. See (in this vol.) SOUTH AFRICA (RHODESIA): A. D. 1898 (FEBRUARY).

A. D. 1898 (Egypt).—The Nile question between England and France.—Marchand's expedition at Fashoda. See (in this vol.) EGYPT: A. D. 1898 (SEPTEMBER—NOVEMBER).

A. D. 1898 (Nigeria and the French Sudan).—Definition of French and English possessions in West and North Africa. See (in this vol.) NIGERIA: A. D. 1882–1899.

A. D. 1898 (Rhodesia).—Reorganization of the British South Africa Company and the administration of its territories. See (in this vol.) SOUTH AFRICA (RHODESIA AND THE BRITISH SOUTH AFRICA COMPANY): A. D. 1898 (FEBRUARY).

A. D. 1898 (Tunis).—Results of the French Protectorate. See (in this vol.) TUNIS: A. D. 1881–1898.

A. D. 1899.—Railway development.—"Railroad development in Africa has been rapid in the past few years and seems but the beginning of a great system which must contribute to the rapid development, civilization, and enlightenment of the Dark Continent. Already railroads run northwardly from Cape Colony about 1,400 miles, and southwardly from Cairo about 1,100 miles, thus making 2,500 miles of the 'Cape to Cairo' railroad complete, while the intermediate distance is about 3,000 miles. Mr. Rhodes, whose recent visit to England and Germany in the interest of the proposed through line from the Cape to Cairo is a matter of record, and whose visit to Germany was made necessary by the fact that in order to pass from the southern chain of British territory to the northern chain he must cross German or Belgian territory, is reported as confident that the through line

will be completed by the year 1910. Certainly it may reasonably be assumed that a continuous railway line will be in operation from the southern to the northern end of Africa in the early years of the twentieth century. Toward this line, present and prospective, which is to stretch through the eastern part of the continent, lateral lines from either coast are beginning to make their way. A line has already been constructed from Natal on the southeast coast; another from Lourenço Marquez in Portuguese territory and the gold and diamond fields; another from Beira, also in Portuguese territory, but considerably farther north, and destined to extend to Salisbury in Rhodesia, where it will form a junction with the 'Cape to Cairo' road; still another is projected from Zanzibar to Lake Victoria Nyanza, to connect, probably, at Tabora, with the transcontinental line; another line is under actual construction westward from Pangani just north of Zanzibar, both of these being in German East Africa; another line is being constructed northwestwardly from Mombasa, in British territory, toward Lake Victoria Nyanza, and is completed more than half the distance, while at the entrance to the Red Sea a road is projected westwardly into Abyssinia, and is expected to pass farther toward the west and connect with the main line. At Suakim, fronting on the Red Sea, a road is projected to Berber, the present terminus of the line running southwardly from Cairo. On the west of Africa lines have begun to penetrate inward, a short line in the French Sudan running from the head of navigation on the Senegal eastwardly toward the head of navigation on the Niger, with the ultimate purpose of connecting navigation on these two streams. In the Kongo Free State a railway connects the Upper Kongo with the Lower Kongo around Livingstone Falls; in Portuguese Angola a road extends eastwardly from Loanda, the capital, a considerable distance, and others are projected from Benguela and Mossamedes with the ultimate purpose of connecting with the 'Cape to Cairo' road and joining with the lines from Portuguese East Africa, which also touch that road, thus making a transcontinental line from east to west, with Portuguese territory at either terminus. Farther south on the western coast the Germans have projected a road from Walfisch Bay to Windhoek, the capital of German Southwest Africa, and this will probably be extended eastwardly until it connects with the great transcontinental line from 'Cape to Cairo,' which is to form the great nerve center of the system, to be contributed to and supported by these branches connecting it with either coast. Another magnificent railway project, which was some years ago suggested by M. Leroy Beaulieu, has been recently revived, being no less than an east and west transcontinental line through the Sudan region, connecting the Senegal and Niger countries on the west with the Nile Valley and Red Sea on the east and penetrating a densely populated and extremely productive region of which less is now known, perhaps, than of any other part of Africa. At the north numerous lines skirt the Mediterranean coast, especially in the French territory of Algeria and in Tunis, where the length of railway is, in round numbers, 2,250 miles, while the Egyptian railroads are, including those now under construction, about 1,500

3

miles in length. Those of Cape Colony and Natal are nearly 3,000 miles, and those of Portuguese East Africa and the South African Republic another thousand. Taking into consideration all of the roads now constructed, or under actual construction, their total length reaches nearly 10,000 miles, while there seems every reason to believe that the great through system connecting the rapidly developing mining regions of South Africa with the north of the continent and with Europe will soon be pushed to completion. A large proportion of the railways thus far constructed are owned by the several colonies or States which they traverse, about 2,000 miles of the Cape Colony system belonging to the Government, while nearly all that of Egypt is owned and operated by the State."—U. S. Bureau of Statistics, *Monthly Summary, August*, 1899.—See, also, (in this vol.), RAILWAY, CAPE TO CAIRO.

A. D. **1899** (June).—International **Conven**tion respecting the liquor **traffic.**—Representatives of the governments of Great Britain, Germany, Belgium, Spain, the Congo State, France, Italy, the Netherlands, Portugal, Russia, Sweden and Norway, and Turkey, assembled at Brussels, in June, 1899, with due authorization, and there concluded an international convention respecting the liquor traffic in Africa. Subsequently the governments of Austria-Hungary, the United States of America, Liberia and Persia, gave their adhesion to the Convention, and ratifications were deposited at Brussels in June, 1900. The Convention is, in a measure, supplemental to what is known as "the General Act of Brussels," relative to the African slave trade, which was framed at a conference of the representatives of European, American, African, and Asiatic states, at Brussels. The treaty known as the General Act of Brussels was signed July 2, 1890, but did not come into force until April 2, 1894. The text of it may be found in (U. S.) House Doc. No. 276, 56th Congress, 3d Sess. The Convention of 1899 provides :

"Article I. From the coming into force of the present Convention, the import duty on spirituous liquors, as that duty is regulated by the General Act of Brussels, shall be raised throughout the zone where there does not exist the system of total prohibition provided by Article XCI. of the said General Act, to the rate of 70 fr. the hectolitre at 50 degrees centigrade, for a period of six years. It may, exceptionally, be at the rate of 60 fr. only the hectolitre at 50 degrees centigrade in the Colony of Togo and in that of Dahomey. The import duty shall be augmented proportionally for each degree above 50 degrees centigrade ; it may be diminished proportionally for each degree below 50 degrees centigrade. At the end of the above-mentioned period of six years, the import duty shall be submitted to revision, taking as a basis the results produced by the preceding rate. The Powers retain the right of maintaining and increasing the duty beyond the minimum fixed by the present Article in the regions where they now possess that right. Article II. In accordance with Article XCIII. of the General Act of Brussels, distilled drinks made in the regions mentioned in Article XCII. of the said General Act, and intended for consumption, shall pay an excise duty. This excise duty, the collection of which the Powers undertake to insure as far

as possible, shall not be lower than the minimum import duty fixed by Article I. of the present Convention. Article III. It is understood that the Powers who signed the General Act of Brussels, or who have acceded to it, and who are not represented at the present Conference, preserve the right of acceding to the present Convention." — *Great Britain, Parliamentary Publications (Papers by Command : Treaty Series, No. 13*, 1900).

A. D. **1899.**—Progress of the Telegraph line from the Cape to Cairo. See (in this vol.) TELEGRAPH, CAPE TO CAIRO.

A. D. **1899** (German Colonies).—Cost to Germany, trade, etc. See (in this vol.) GERMANY : A. D. 1899 (JUNE).

A. D. **1899** (Nigeria).—Transfer of territory to the British Crown. See (in this vol.) NIGERIA : A. D. 1899.

A. D. **1899** (Orange Free State).—Treaty of alliance with the Transvaal.—Making common cause. See (in this vol.) SOUTH AFRICA (ORANGE FREE STATE) : A. D. 1897 (APRIL) ; and 1899 (SEPTEMBER—OCTOBER).

A. D. **1899** (The Sudan).—Anglo-Egyptian Condominium established. See (in this vol.) ÆGYPT : A. D. 1899 (JANUARY).

A. D. **1899** (Transvaal and Orange Free State).—Outbreak of war with Great Britain. See (in this vol.) SOUTH AFRICA (TRANSVAAL AND ORANGE FREE STATE) : A. D. 1899 (SEPTEMBER—OCTOBER).

A. D. **1899** (West Africa). — Definition of British and German frontiers. See (in this vol.) SAMOAN ISLANDS.

A. D. **1899** (Zanzibar). — Renunciation of rights of extra-territoriality by Germany. See (in this vol.) SAMOAN ISLANDS.

A. D. **1899-1900.**—Summary of the partition of the Continent.—"Seven European nations, as before remarked, now control territories in Africa, two of them having areas equal in each case to about the entire land area of the United States, while a few small territories remain as independent States. Beginning at the northeast, Egypt and Tripoli are nominally at least tributaries of Turkey, though the Egyptian Government, which was given large latitude by that of Turkey, has of late years formed such relations with Great Britain that, in financial matters at least, her guidance is recognized ; next west, Algeria, French ; then Morocco on the extreme northwest, an independent Government and an absolute despotism ; next on the south, Spain's territory of Rio de Oro ; then the Senegal territories, belonging to the French, and connecting through the desert of Sahara with her Algeria ; then a group of small divisions controlled by England, along the Gulf of Guinea ; then Liberia, the black Republic ; Togoland, controlled by the Germans ; Dahomey, a French protectorate ; the Niger territory, one-third the size of the United States, controlled by England ; Kamerun, controlled by Germany ; French Kongo ; then the Kongo Free State, under the auspices of the King of Belgium, and occupying the very heart of equatorial Africa ; then Portuguese Angola ; next, German Southwest Africa ; and finally in the march down the Atlantic side, Cape Colony, British. Following up the eastern side comes the British colony of Natal ; then just inland from this the two Boer Republics, the Orange Free State and the South African Republic, both of which are entirely in the interior, without ocean frontage; next, Portuguese Africa, and west of this the great territory known as 'Rhodesia'; then German Africa, which extends almost to the equator; north of these, British East Africa, fronting on the Indian Ocean, and merging northwardly with the Egyptian Sudan, which was recently recovered from the Mahdi by the joint operation of British and Egyptian troops, and the British flag placed side by side with that of Egypt; next north, upon the coast, Italian territory and a small tract opposite the entrance to the Red Sea controlled by England; and a few hundred miles west of the entrance to the Red Sea, the independent Kingdom of Abyssinia. This division of African territory, nearly all of it made within the memory of the present generation, forms the present political map of Africa. With England and France controlling an area equal in each case to that of the United States; Germany, a territory one-third the size of the United States; Portugal, with an area somewhat less; the Kongo Free State in the great equatorial basin, but

having a frontage upon the Atlantic with an area nearly one-third that of the United States; Italy and Spain, each with a comparatively small area of territory; Egypt, with relations quite as much British as Turkish; Tripoli, Turkish, and the five independent States of Morocco, Liberia, Abyssinia, and the two Boer Republics—nothing remains unclaimed, even in the desert wastes, while in the high altitudes and subtropical climate of southeast Africa civilization and progress are making rapid advancement."—U. S. Bureau of Statistics, *Monthly Summary, August,* 1899.

The following table, given in an article in "The Forum," December, 1899, by Mr. O. P. Austin, Chief of the U. S. Bureau of Statistics, shows the area, total population, foreign population, and imports and exports of the territory in Africa held by each European Government and by the independent States of that continent, at the time of its compilation so far as could be ascertained; but the statistics of area and population, especially the latter, are in many cases necessarily estimates:

	AREA.	TOTAL POPULATION.	FOREIGN POPULATION.	POP. PER SQ. MILE.	IMPORTS.	EXPORTS.
French Africa....................	3,028,000	28,155,000	922,000	9.3	$70,116,000	$69,354,000
British "	2,761,000	35,160,000	455,000	12.8	131,398,000	131,885,000
Turkish "	1,750,000	21,300,000	113,000	12.2	54,091,000	62,548,000
German "	944,000	11,270,000	4,000	12.0	4,993,000	2,349,000
Belgian "	900,000	30,000,000	2,000	33.3	4,522,000	3,309,000
Portuguese"	790,000	8,059,000	3,000	10.2	11,863,000	6,730,000
Spanish "	243,000	36,000	....	0.5	....	....
Italian "	188,000	850,000	....	4.5	....	....
Independent States.						
Morocco............................	219,000	5,000,000	....	22.8	6,402,000	6,261,000
Abyssinia..........................	150,000	3,500,000	....	23.3	....	....
South African Republic...........	120,000	1,096,000	346,000	9.2	104,703,000	53,532,000
Orange Free State.................	48,500	208,000	78,000	4.3	5,994,000	8,712,000
Liberia............................	48,000	1,500,000	25,000	31.3	1,217,000	1,034,000
Total.........................	11,189,500	146,133,000	1,948,000	....	$395,299,000	$345,714,000

According to a statistical table in the twentieth volume of Meyer's Konversations-Lexicon (third annual supplement), based upon the latest data furnished by the boundary treaties between the Powers, it would appear that all but about one-seventh of the African continent is now (A. D. 1900) included in some "protectorate" or "sphere of influence." The French sphere is the largest, comprising about 3,700,000 square miles (about the extent of Europe) out of a total area of 11,600,000. England comes next with 2,400,000 (including the Boer territories). Then follow in order Germany, Belgium (Congo Free State), and Portugal, each with somewhat less than a million square miles. The Egyptian sphere (about 400,000 square miles) may properly be regarded as part of the British. The extent of the French sphere will appear less imposing on consulting the map of Africa here given, which shows that it takes in the greater part of the sands of the Sahara. The British sphere (including Egypt and her depencies) is estimated to contain in round numbers about 50,000,000 souls; the French, 35,000,000; the Belgian, 17,-000,000; the German, 9,000,000; the Portuguese, 8,000,000.

A. D. 1900 (Ashanti). — Revolt of the tribes. — Siege and relief of Kumassi. See (in this vol.) ASHANTI.

A. D. 1900 (Togoland and Gold Coast).— Demarcation of the Hinterland.—Late in November it was announced from Berlin that conferences regarding the British and German boundaries in West Africa were then in progress in the Colonial Department of the German Foreign Office, their principal object being the demarcation of the Hinterland of Togoland and of the Gold Coast, and in particular the partition of the neutral zone of Salaga as arranged in Article 5 of the Samoa Agreement between Great Britain and Germany. See (in this vol.) SAMOAN ISLANDS.

AFRIDIS, British Indian war with the. See (in this vol.) INDIA : A. D. 1897–1898.

AFRIKANDER BUND, The. Sec (iu this vol.) SOUTH AFRICA (CAPE COLONY): A. D. 1881–1888; 1898; and 1898 (MARCH—OCTOBER).

AFRIKANDER CONGRESS. See (in this vol.) SOUTH AFRICA (Cape Colony): A. D. 1900 (DECEMBER).

AFRIKANDERS: Joining the invading Boers. See (in this vol.) SOUTH AFRICA (THE FIELD OF WAR): A. D. 1899 (OCT. —NOV.).
Opposition to the annexation of the Boer Republics. See (in this vol.) SOUTH AFRICA (CAPE COLONY): A. D. 1900 (MAY).

AGRARIAN PROTECTIONISTS, The German. See (in this vol.) GERMANY: A. D. 1895-1898; 1899 (AUGUST); and 1901 (FEBRUARY).

AGRICULTURAL LAND BILL, The. See (in this vol.) ENGLAND: A. D. 1896.

AGUINALDO y FAMY, Emilio. — First appearance in the Filipino insurrection. — His treaty with the Spaniards and departure from the Islands. See (in this vol.) PHILIPPINE ISLANDS: A. D. 1896-1898.
Circumstances in which he went to Manila to co-operate with American forces. See (in this vol.) UNITED STATES OF AM.: A. D. 1898 (APRIL—MAY: PHILIPPINES).
Arrival at Manila, May 19, 1898. — His organization of insurgent forces. — His relations with Admiral Dewey. See (in this vol.) UNITED STATES OF AM.: A. D. 1898 (APRIL—JULY).
Correspondence with General Anderson. See (in this vol.) UNITED STATES OF AM.: A. D. 1898 (JULY—AUGUST: PHILIPPINES).
Relations with American commander at Manila. — Declared President of the Philippine Republic. See (in this vol.) UNITED STATES OF AM.: A. D. 1898 (JULY—SEPTEMBER).
Conflict of his army with American forces. See (in this vol.) PHILIPPINE ISLANDS: A. D. 1898 (AUGUST—DECEMBER), and after.

ALABAMA: A. D. 1899. — Dispensary Laws. — Acts applying the South Carolina "dispensary" system of regulation for the liquor traffic (see, in this vol., SOUTH CAROLINA: A. D. 1892-1899) to seventeen counties, but not to the State at large, were passed by the Legislature.

ALASKA: A. D. 1898-1899.—Discovery of the Cape Nome gold mining region.—"The Cape Nome mining region lies on the western coast of Alaska, just beyond the military reservation of St. Michael and about 120 miles south of the Arctic Circle. It can be reached by an ocean voyage of ten or twelve days from Seattle. It has long been known that gold exists in the general vicinity of Cape Nome, and during the last five or six years a few adventurous miners have done more or less prospecting and claim staking throughout the district lying between Norton and Kotzebue sounds. During the winter of 1898-99, a large number of miners entered the Kotzebue country, while others spent the season in the vicinity of Golofnin Bay." On the 15th of October, 1898, a party of seven men reached Snake River in a schooner. "Between that date and the 18th a miners' meeting was held, the boundaries of a district 25 miles square were established, local mining regulations were formulated, and Dr. Kittleson was elected recorder for a term of two years. After organizing the district natives were hired to do the necessary packing, and a camp was established on Anvil Creek. The prospecting outfits were quickly brought into service. In one afternoon $76 was panned out on Snow Creek. Encouraged by this showing lumber was carried up from the schooner and two rockers were constructed. . . . In four or five days over $1,800 was cleaned up with these two rockers. . . The weather turned cold and the water was frozen up. As it was impossible to do any more work with the rockers the party broke camp on the 3d of November and returned to

the schooner, which they found frozen solid in 2 feet of ice. They then made their way in a small boat to an Indian village, near Cape Nome, where they obtained dogs and sleds, and a little farther on they were met by reindeer from the Swedish Mission, with which they returned to Golofnin Bay.
"The lucky miners had agreed among themselves that their discovery should be held secret, but the news was too good to keep, and soon leaked out. A general stampede commenced at once and continued all winter. Every available dog and reindeer was pressed into the service, and they were soon racing with each other for the valuable claims which had been left unstaked in the vicinity of Anvil Creek. As soon as that creek had been all taken up the stampede extended to the neighboring streams and gulches, and Glacier and Dexter creeks, as well as many others which have not proved equally valuable, were quickly staked and recorded. By the 25th of December a large party armed with numerous powers of attorney had entered the district, and as the local regulations allowed every man to stake on each creek one claim of the full legal dimensions (660 by 1,320 feet), it was not long until the whole district had been thoroughly covered, and nearly every stream had been staked with claims, which in some cases were 'jumped' and the right of possession disputed.
"The news of a rich strike at Nome worked its way up the Yukon River during the winter, and as soon as the ice broke in June a large crowd came down from Rampart City, followed by a larger crowd from Dawson. The 'Yukoners,' as these people were called, were already disgusted with the hardships, disappointments, and Canadian misgovernment which they had met with on the upper river. . . . Those to whom enough faith had been given to go over to Cape Nome were disgusted and angered to find that pretty much the whole district was already staked, and that the claims taken were two or three times as large as those commonly allowed on the upper river. Another grievance was the great abuse of the power of attorney, by means of which an immense number of claims had been taken up, so that in many cases (according to common report) single individuals held or controlled from 50 to 100 claims apiece. . . .
"A miners' meeting was called by the newcomers to remedy their grievances. Resolutions were prepared, in which it was represented that the district had been illegally organized by men who were not citizens of the United States and who had not conformed with the law in properly defining the boundaries of the district with reference to natural objects, in enacting suitable and sufficient mining regulations, and in complying with any of the details of organization required by law. It was intended by the promoters of this meeting to reorganize the district in such a way as would enable them to share the benefits of the discovery of a new gold field with the men who had entered it the previous winter, and, as they expressed it, 'gobbled up the whole country.' It is, of course, impossible to say what would have been the result if their attempt had not been interfered with. . . . On the 28th of June Lieutenant Spaulding and a detachment of 10 men from the Third Artillery had been ordered to the vicinity of Snake River, and on the 7th of July their numbers were increased by the

addition of 15 more. As soon as it was proposed to throw open for restaking a large amount of land already staked and recorded an appeal was made to the United States troops to prevent this action by prohibiting the intended meeting, which was called to assemble July 10. It was represented to them that if the newcomers should attempt, under the quasi-legal guise of a miners' meeting, to take forcible possession of lands already claimed by others, the inevitable consequence would be a reign of disorder and violence, with the possibility of considerable bloodshed. On the strength of this representation and appeal the army officers decided to prevent the adoption of the proposed resolutions. The miners were allowed to call their meeting to order, but as soon as the resolutions were read Lieutenant Spaulding requested that they be withdrawn. He allowed two minutes for compliance with his request, the alternative being that he would clear the hall. The resolutions were not withdrawn, the troops were ordered to fix bayonets, and the hall was cleared quietly, without a conflict. Such meetings as were subsequently attempted were quickly broken up by virtue of the same authority. The light in which this action is regarded by the people at Nome depends, of course, upon the way in which their personal interests were affected. . . .

"The great discontent which actually did exist at this time found sudden and unexpected relief in the discovery of the beach diggings. It had long been known that there was more or less gold on the seashore, and before the middle of July it was discovered that good wages could be taken out of the sand with a rocker. Even those who were on the ground could hardly believe the story at first, but its truth was quickly and easily demonstrated. Before the month was over a great army of the unemployed was engaged in throwing up irregular intrenchments along the edge of the sea, and those who had just been driven nearly to the point of desperation by the exhaustion of all their resources were soon contentedly rocking out from $10 to $50 each per day and even more than that. This discovery came like a godsend to many destitute men, and was a most fortunate development in the history of the camp.

"Meantime the men who were in possession of claims on Anvil and Snow creeks were beginning to sluice their ground and getting good returns for their work, while others were actively making preparations to take out the gold which they knew they had discovered. More sluice boxes were constructed and put into operation as rapidly as possible. A town site was laid off at the mouth of Snake River, and on the 4th of July a post-office was established. The town which has sprung so suddenly into existence is called 'Nome' by the Post-Office Department, but at a miners' meeting held February 28, it was decided to call it 'Anvil City,' and this is generally done by the residents of the district, as well as in all official records. At a meeting held in September, however, the name was again changed to 'Nome.'" — *United States, 56th Cong., 1st sess., Senate Doc. No. 357, pp. 1–4.*

"A year ago [that is, in the winter of 1898–9] a few Eskimo huts and one or two sod houses of white men were the only human habitations along 60 miles of the present Nome coast. Last June [1899] a dozen or score of tents contained the whole population. By October a town of 5,000 inhabitants fronting the ocean was crowded for a mile or more along the beach. Hundreds of galvanized-iron and wooden buildings were irregularly scattered along two or three thoroughfares, running parallel with the coast line. There is every description of building, from the dens of the poor prospectors, built of driftwood, canvas, and sod, to the large companies' warehouses, stores, and the army barracks — a city, as it were, sprung up in the night, built under the most adverse circumstances on the barren seacoast, a coast without harbor, all the supplies being landed through the surf. . . . The country contributes nothing toward the support of the population except a few fish and a limited supply of driftwood.

"The city is of the most cosmopolitan type and contains representatives of almost every nationality on the globe : Germans, Canadians, Frenchmen, Englishmen, Russians, Swedes, Norwegians, Poles, Chinese, negroes, Italians, Spaniards, Greeks, Jews, and Americans. The dominant type is the American, through whose efforts, with that inherent talent of the Anglo-Saxon race for self-government, this isolated community at once organized a city government. Before the close of the summer Nome had a mayor, councilmen, a police force, a deputy United States marshal, a United States post-office, a fire department with town well, a board of health, a hospital corps, and charitable organizations. A majority of the people consists of the shifting population of the Yukon country, which, upon hearing the news of the discovery of gold, poured itself into Nome. . . . Along with the shifting population of the Yukon from Dawson and other camps came also many would-be explorers, adventurers, and especially gamblers, but good order prevails throughout. Drunkenness, disorderly conduct, and theft are promptly tried before the police justice and punished by fine and imprisonment. Copies of the official rules and regulations are kept posted before the city hall and in other conspicuous places, as a warning to all : 'Ignorance of the law is no excuse.' Some of the well-known 'toughs' and most undesirable characters are reported to have been rounded up by the authorities late in the fall and exported to the States. . . . There are several printing presses and three newspapers — the Nome News, Nome Herald, and Nome Gold Digger. . . . There are at least 2,500 people now [February, 1900] wintering at Nome, and, by estimate, at least several thousand are on their way there by winter routes. . . .

"Since, according to the conservative estimate of those who are best situated to judge, it is believed that the Nome region will have a population of at least 30,000 or 40,000 people this year (1900), some public improvements there seem not only commendable but urgently necessary. Among these the most important are : Some municipal form of government, water supply, land-office service, and harbor facilities. As the General Government had never made provision for any form of municipal government in Alaska, the people of Nome, in response to the urgency of the hour, called a mass meeting, and organized the present government of Nome, with a complete corps of city officers, as aforesaid, though they were conscious at the time that it was without authority from the United States

Government."—F. C. Schrader and A. H. Brooks, *Preliminary Report on the Cape Nome Gold Region, Alaska* (*U. S. Geological Survey*), pp. 45–47.

A. D. 1900. — Civil Government. — Better provision for the civil government of Alaska was made by an Act which passed Congress after much debate and was approved by the President on the 6th of June, 1900. It constitutes Alaska a civil and judicial district, with a governor who has the duties and powers that pertain to the governor of a Territory, and a district court of general jurisdiction, civil and criminal, and in equity and admiralty, the court being in three divisions, each with a district judge. The act provides a civil code for the district.

A. D. 1900. — Exploration of Seward peninsula. See (in this vol.) POLAR EXPLORATION, 1900.

ALASKA BOUNDARY QUESTION, The.—The boundary between Alaska, when it was Russian territory, and the British possessions on the western side of the American continent, was settled by an Anglo-Russian treaty in 1825. The treaty which ceded the Russian territory to the United States, in 1867, incorporated the definition of boundary given in Articles III. and IV. of the above-mentioned convention, which (translated from French to English) read as follows:

"III. The line of demarcation between the possessions of the High Contracting Parties upon the Coasts of the Continent and the Islands of America to the North-West, shall be drawn in the following manner : Commencing from the southernmost point of the Island called Prince of Wales Island, which point lies in the parallel of 54 degrees 40 minutes, North Latitude, and between the 131st and 133d Degree of West Longitude (Meridian of Greenwich), the said line shall ascend to the North along the Channel called Portland Channel, as far as the Point of the Continent where it strikes the 56th Degree of North Latitude ; from this last mentioned Point the line of demarcation shall follow the summit of the mountains situated parallel to the coast, as far as the point of intersection of the 141st Degree of West Longitude (of the same meridian), and, finally, from the said point of intersection, the said Meridian Line of the 141st Degree, in its prolongation as far as the Frozen Ocean, shall form the limit between the Russian and British Possessions on the Continent of America to the North West.

"IV. With reference to the line of demarcation laid down in the preceding Article, it is understood : 1st. That the Island called Prince of Wales Island shall belong wholly to Russia. 2d. That wherever the summit of the mountains which extend in a direction parallel to the Coast, from the 56th Degree of North Latitude to the point of intersection of the 141st Degree of West Longitude, shall prove to be at the distance of more than ten marine leagues from the Ocean, the limit between the British Possessions and the Line of Coast which is to belong to Russia, as above mentioned, shall be formed by a line parallel to the windings of the Coast, and which shall never exceed the distance of ten marine leagues therefrom."

When attempts to reduce this description in the treaty to an actually determined boundary-line were begun, disagreements arose between Canada and the United States, which became exceedingly troublesome after the Klondike gold discoveries had given a new importance to that region and to its communications with the outside world. The Alaska boundary question proved, in fact, to be considerably the most difficult of settlement among all the many subjects of disagreement between the United States and Canada which a Joint High Commission was created in 1898 (see—in this vol.—CANADA : A. D. 1898–1900) to adjust. It was the one question on which no ground of compromise could then be found, and which compelled the Commission to adjourn in February, 1899, with its labors incomplete. The disputable points in the definition of the boundary by the Anglo-Russian treaty of 1825 are explained as follows by Prof. J. B. Moore, ex-Assistant Secretary of State, in an article contributed to the "North American Review" of October, 1899: "An examination of the boundary defined in Articles III. and IV. of the convention of 1825 shows," says Prof. Moore, "that it is scientifically divisible into two distinct sections, first, the line from the southernmost point of Prince of Wales Island, through Portland Channel and along the summit of the mountains parallel to the coast, to the point of intersection of the 141st meridian of longitude ; and, second, the line from this point to the Arctic Ocean. With the latter section, which is merely a meridian line, and as to which the United States and Canadian surveys exhibit no considerable difference, we are not now concerned. The section as to which material differences have arisen is the first. The principal differences in this quarter are two in number, first, as to what channel is meant by Portland Channel (sometimes called Portland Canal) ; and, second, as to what is the extent of the line or strip of coast (la lisière de côte) which was assigned to Russia."

The following is an English statement of the situation of the controversy at the time the Joint High Commission adjourned : "The adjournment of the Commission with nothing accomplished is fresh in all our memories. Nor is it easy to determine on whose shoulders lies the blame of this unfortunate break down. America has been blamed for her stubbornness in refusing to submit to an arbitration which should take into consideration the possession of the towns and settlements under the authority of the United States and at present under their jurisdiction ; while they have also been charged with having made no concessions at all to Canada in the direction of allowing her free access to her Yukon possessions. I am enabled to say, however, in this latter respect the Americans have not been so stiff-necked as has been made to appear. Although it was not placed formally before the Commission, it was allowed clearly to be understood by the other side, that in regard to Skagway, America was prepared to make a very liberal concession. They were ready, that is, to allow of the joint administration of Skagway, the two flags flying side by side, and to allow of the denationalisation, or internationalisation as it might otherwise be termed, of the White Pass and the Yukon Railroad, now completed to Lake Bennett, and the only railroad which gives access to the Yukon. They were even prepared to admit of the passage of troops and munitions of war over this road, thus doing away with the

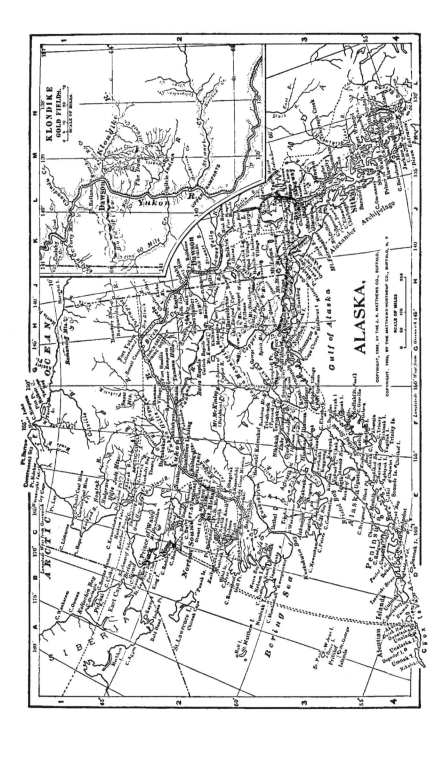

Canadian contention that, should a disturbance occur in the Yukon, they are at present debarred from taking efficient measures to quell it. This proposition, however, does not commend itself to the Canadians, whose main object, I think I am justified in saying, is to have a railroad route of their own from beginning to end, in their own territory, as far north as Dawson City. At one time, owing to insufficient information and ignorance of the natural obstacles in the way, they thought they could accomplish this by what was known as the Stikine route. They even went so far as to make a contract with Messrs. McKenzie and Mann to construct this road, the contractors receiving as part of their payment, concessions and grants of territory in the Yukon, which would practically have given them the absolute and sole control of that district. The value of this to the contractors can hardly be overestimated. However, not only did the natural obstacles I have referred to lead to the abandonment of the scheme, but the Senate at Ottawa threw out the Bill which had passed through the Lower House, affording a striking proof that there are times when an Upper House has its distinct value in legislation. It has been suggested (though I am the last to confirm it) that it was the influence of the firm of railroad contractors, to whose lot it would probably fall to construct any new line of subsidised railway, which caused the Canadian Commission to reject the tentative American proposal regarding Skagway, and to put forward the counter claim to the possession of Pyramid Harbour (which lies lower down upon the west coast of the Lynn Canal), together with a two mile wide strip of territory reaching inland, containing the Chilcat Pass, and through it easy passage through the coast ranges, and so by a long line of railroad to Fort Selkirk, which lies on the Yukon River, to the south and east of Dawson City. It is said also, though of this I have no direct evidence, that the Canadians included the right to fortify Pyramid Harbour. It is not surprising that the Americans rejected this proposal, for they entered into the discussion convinced of the impossibility of accepting any arrangement which would involve the surrender of American settlements, and though it is not so large or important as Skagway or Dyea, Pyramid Harbour is nevertheless as much an American settlement as the two latter. I am bound to point out that just as the Dominion of Canada, as a whole, has a keener interest in this dispute than has the Home Government, so the Government of British Columbia is more closely affected by any possible settlement than is the rest of the Dominion. And British Columbia is as adverse to the Pyramid Harbour scheme as the United States themselves. This is due to the fact that when finished the Pyramid Harbour and Fort Selkirk railroad would afford no access to the British Columbia gold fields on Atlin Lake, which would still be reached only by way of Skagway and the White Pass, or by Dyea and the Chilcat Pass. But quite apart from this view of the matter, we may take it for granted that the United States will never voluntarily surrender any of their tide-water settlements, while the Canadian Government, on the other hand, are no more disposed to accept any settlement based on the internationalisation of Skagway, their argument probably being that, save as a temporary 'modus vivendi,' this would be giving away their whole case to their opponents."—H. Townsend, *The Alaskan Boundary Question* (*Fortnightly Rev.*, *Sept.*, 1899).

Pending further negotiations on the subject, a "modus vivendi" between the United States and Great Britain, "fixing a provisional boundary line between the Territory of Alaska and the Dominion of Canada about the head of Lynn Canal," was concluded October 20, 1899, in the following terms : "It is hereby agreed between the Governments of the United States and of Great Britain that the boundary line between Canada and the territory of Alaska in the region about the head of Lynn Canal shall be provisionally fixed as follows without prejudice to the claims of either party in the permanent adjustment of the international boundary : In the region of the Dalton Trail, a line beginning at the peak West of Porcupine Creek, marked on the map No. 10 of the United States Commission, December 31, 1895, and on Sheet No. 18 of the British Commission, December 31, 1895, with the number 6500 ; thence running to the Klehini (or Klaheela) River in the direction of the Peak north of that river, marked 5020 on the aforesaid United States map and 5025 on the aforesaid British map; thence following the high or right bank of the said Klehini river to the junction thereof with the Chilkat River, a mile and a half, more or less, north of Klukwan, — provided that persons proceeding to or from Porcupine Creek shall be freely permitted to follow the trail between the said creek and the said junction of the rivers, into and across the territory on the Canadian side of the temporary line wherever the trail crosses to such side, and, subject to such reasonable regulations for the protection of the Revenue as the Canadian Government may prescribe, to carry with them over such part or parts of the trail between the said points as may lie on the Canadian side of the temporary line, such goods and articles as they desire, without being required to pay any customs duties on such goods and articles; and from said junction to the summit of the peak East of the Chilkat river, marked on the aforesaid map No. 10 of the United States Commission with the number 5410 and on the map No. 17 of the aforesaid British Commission with the number 5490. On the Dyea and Skagway Trails, the summits of the Chilcoot and White Passes. It is understood, as formerly set forth in communications of the Department of State of the United States, that the citizens or subjects of either Power, found by this arrangement within the temporary jurisdiction of the other, shall suffer no diminution of the rights and privileges which they now enjoy. The Government of the United States will at once appoint an officer or officers in conjunction with an officer or officers to be named by the Government of Her Britannic Majesty, to mark the temporary line agreed upon by the erection of posts, stakes, or other appropriate temporary marks."

In his Annual Message to Congress, December 3, 1900, the President of the United States stated the situation as follows : "The work of marking certain provisional boundary points, for convenience of administration, around the head of Lynn Canal, in accordance with the temporary arrangement of October, 1899, was completed by a joint survey in July last. The modus vivendi has so far worked without friction, and the Dominion Government has provided rules and regulations for securing to our citizens the benefit of the reciprocal stipulation that the citizens or subjects of either Power found by that arrangement within the temporary jurisdiction of the other shall suffer no diminution of the rights and privileges they have hitherto enjoyed. But however necessary such an expedient may have been to tide over the grave emergencies of the situation, it is at best but an unsatisfactory makeshift, which should not be suffered to delay the speedy and complete establishment of the frontier line to which we are entitled under the Russo-American treaty for the cession of Alaska. In this relation I may refer again to the need of definitely marking the Alaskan boundary where it follows the 141st meridian. A convention to that end has been before the Senate for some two years, but as no action has been taken I contemplate negotiating a new convention for a joint determination of the meridian by telegraphic observations. These, it is believed, will give more accurate and unquestionable results than the sidereal methods heretofore independently followed, which, as is known, proved discrepant at several points on the line, although not varying at any place more than seven hundred feet."

ALEXANDRIA: Discovery of the Serapeion. See (in this vol.) ARCHÆOLOGICAL RESEARCH: EGYPT: DISCOVERY OF THE SERAPEION.
Patriarchate re-established. See (in this vol.) PAPACY: A. D. 1896 (MARCH).

ALIENS IMMIGRATION LAW, The Transvaal. See (in this vol.) SOUTH AFRICA (THE TRANSVAAL): A. D. 1896–1897 (MAY—APRIL).

ALPHABET, Light on the origin of the. See (in this vol.) ARCHÆOLOGICAL RESEARCH: CRETE.

AMATONGALAND: Annexed, with Zululand, to Natal. See (in this vol.) AFRICA: A. D. 1897 (ZULULAND).

AMERICA: The Projected Intercontinental Railway. See (in this vol.) RAILWAY, THE INTERCONTINENTAL.

AMERICA, Central. See (in this vol.) CENTRAL AMERICA.

AMERICAN ABORIGINES. See (in this vol.) INDIANS, AMERICAN.

AMERICAN REPUBLICS, The Bureau of the. "The idea of the creation of an international bureau, or agency, representing the Republics of the Western Hemisphere, was suggested to the delegates accredited to the International American Conference held in Washington in 1889–90, by the conference held at Brussels in May, 1888, which planned for an international union for the publication of customs tariffs, etc. . . . On March 29, 1890, the International American Conference, by a unanimous vote of the delegates of the eighteen countries there represented, namely: The Argentine Republic, Bolivia, Brazil, Chile, Colombia, Costa Rica, Ecuador, Guatemala, Haiti, Honduras, Mexico, Nicaragua, Paraguay, Peru, Salvador, United States, Uruguay, and Venezuela, provided for the establishment of an association to be known as 'The International Union of American Republics for the Prompt Collection and Distribution of Commercial Information,' which should be repre-

sented at the capital of the United States by a Bureau, under the title of 'The Bureau of the American Republics.' This organ, so to speak, of the independent governments of the New World was placed under the supervision of the Secretary of State of the United States, and was to continue in existence for a period of ten years, and, if found profitable to the nations participating in its advantages, it was to be maintained for successive periods of ten years indefinitely. At the first session of the Fifty-first Congress of the United States, that body, in an 'Act making appropriations for the support of the Diplomatic and Consular Service, etc.,' approved July 14, 1890, gave the President authority to carry into effect the recommendations of the Conference so far as he should deem them expedient, and appropriated $36,000 for the organization and establishment of the Bureau, which amount it had been stipulated by the delegates in the Conference assembled should not be exceeded, and should be annually advanced by the United States and shared by the several Republics in proportion to their population. . . . . The Conference had defined the purpose of the Bureau to be the preparation and publication of bulletins concerning the commerce and resources of the American Republics, and to furnish information of interest to manufacturers, merchants, and shippers, which should be at all times available to persons desirous of obtaining particulars regarding their customs tariffs and regulations, as well as commerce and navigation."—*Bulletin of the Bureau of American Republics*, June, 1898.

A plan of government for the International Union, by an executive committee composed of representatives of the American nations constituting the Union, was adopted in 1896, but modified at a conference held in Washington, March 18, 1899. As then adopted, the plan of government is as follows: "The Bureau of the American Republics will be governed under the supervision of the Secretary of State of the United States, with the coöperation and advice of four representatives of the other Republics composing the International Union, the five persons indicated to constitute an Executive Committee, of which the Secretary of State is to be ex-officio Chairman, or, in his absence, the Acting Secretary of State. The other four members of the Executive Committee shall be called to serve in turn, in the alphabetical order of the official names of their nations in one of the four languages of the Union, previously selected by lot at a meeting of the representatives of the Union. At the end of each year the first of these four members shall retire, giving place to another representative of the Union, in the same alphabetical order already explained, and so on until the next period of succession."

"The interest taken by the various States forming the International Union of American Republics in the work of its organic bureau is evidenced by the fact that for the first time since its creation in 1890 all the republics of South and Central America are now [1899] represented in it. The unanimous recommendation of the International American Conference, providing for the International Union of American Republics, stated that it should continue in force during a term of ten years from the date of its organization, and no country becoming a member of the union should cease to be a member until the end of said period of ten years, and unless twelve months before the expiration of said period a majority of the members of the union had given to the Secretary of State of the United States official notice of their wish to terminate the union at the end of its first period, that the union should continue to be maintained for another period of ten years, and thereafter, under the same conditions, for successive periods of ten years each. The period for notification expired on July 14, 1899, without any of the members having given the necessary notice of withdrawal. Its maintenance is therefore assured for the next ten years." — *Message of the President of the U. S. Dec.* 5, 1899.

AMERICANISM : Pope Leo XIII. on opinions so called. See (in this vol.) PAPACY : A. D. 1899 (JANUARY).

AMNESTY BILL, The French. See (in this vol.) FRANCE : A. D. 1900 (DECEMBER).

ANARCHIST CRIMES: Assassination of Canovas del Castillo. See (in this vol.) SPAIN : A. D. 1897 (AUGUST—OCTOBER).
Assassination of the Empress of Austria. See (in this vol.) AUSTRIA-HUNGARY : A. D. 1898 (SEPTEMBER).
Assassination of King Humbert. See (in this vol.) ITALY : A. D. 1899-1900 ; and 1900 (JULY—SEPTEMBER).

ANATOLIAN RAILWAY, The. See (in this vol.) TURKEY : A. D. 1899 (NOVEMBER).

ANCON, The Treaty of. See (in this vol.) CHILE : A. D. 1894-1900.

ANDERSON, General Thomas M.: Correspondence with Aguinaldo. See (in this vol.) UNITED STATES OF AM.: A. D. 1898 (JULY—AUGUST : PHILIPPINES).

ANDRÉE, Salamon August : Arctic balloon voyage. See (in this vol.) POLAR EXPLORATION, 1897, 1898, 1899, 1900-.

ANGLO-AMERICAN POPULATION. See (in this vol.) NINETEENTH CENTURY : EXPANSION.

ANGONI-ZULUS, The. See (in this vol.) BRITISH CENTRAL AFRICA PROTECTORATE.

ANTARCTIC EXPLORATION. See (in this vol.) POLAR EXPLORATION.

ANTEMNÆ, Excavations at. See (in this vol.) ARCHÆOLOGICAL RESEARCH : ITALY.

ANTIGUA : Industrial condition. See (in this vol.) WEST INDIES, THE BRITISH : A. D. 1897.

ANTITOXINE, Discovery of. See (in this vol.) SCIENCE, RECENT : MEDICAL AND SURGICAL.

ANTI-IMPERIALISTS, The League of American. See (in this vol.) UNITED STATES OF AM.: A. D. 1900 (MAY—NOVEMBER).

ANTI-REVOLUTIONARY BILL, The German. See (in this vol.) GERMANY : A. D. 1894-1895.

ANTI-SEMITIC AGITATIONS. See (in this vol.) AUSTRIA-HUNGARY : A. D. 1895-1896, and after ; and FRANCE : A. D. 1897-1899, and after.

ANTI-SEMITIC LEAGUE, Treasonable conspiracy of the. See (in this vol.) FRANCE : A. D. 1899-1900 (AUGUST—JANUARY).

APPORTIONMENT ACT. See (in this vol.) UNITED STATES OF AM.: A. D. 1901 (JANUARY).

ARBITRATION, Industrial: In New Zealand. See (in this vol.) NEW ZEALAND : A. D. 1891-1900.
In the United States between employees and employers engaged in inter-state commerce. See (in this vol.) UNITED STATES OF AM.: A. D. 1898 (JUNE).

ARBITRATION, International: A. D. 1896-1900.—Boundary dispute between Colombia and Costa Rica. See (in this vol.) COLOMBIA : A. D. 1893-1900.
A. D. 1897.—Nicaragua and Costa Rica. See (in this vol.) CENTRAL AMERICA (NICARAGUA—COSTA RICA): A. D. 1897.
A. D. 1897-1899.—Venezuela and Great Britain.—Guiana boundary. See (in this vol.) VENEZUELA : A. D. 1896-1899.
A. D. 1898.—Argentine Republic and Chile. See (in this vol.) ARGENTINE REPUBLIC : A. D. 1898.
A. D. 1898.—Treaty between Italy and the Argentine Republic. See (in this vol.) ARGENTINE REPUBLIC : A. D. 1898.
A. D. 1899.—The Treaty for the Pacific Settlement of International Disputes concluded at the Peace Conference at the Hague (Text).—The Permanent Court created. See (in this vol.) PEACE CONFERENCE.
A. D. 1900.— Brazil and French Guiana boundary dispute. See (in this vol.) BRAZIL : A. D. 1900.
A. D. 1900.—Compulsory arbitration voted for at Spanish-American Congress. See (in this vol.) SPAIN : A. D. 1900 (NOVEMBER).

ARBITRATION TREATY, Great Britain and the United States.— Its defeat. See (in this vol.) UNITED STATES OF AM.: A. D. 1897 (JANUARY—MAY).

ARCHÆOLOGICAL RESEARCH.

The Oriental Field.—Recent achievements and future prospects. — "Three successive years have just added to the realm of Egyptian archaeology, not only the period of the first two dynasties, hitherto absolutely unrecognized from contemporary remains, but also a long prehistoric period. Assyriology likewise has lately been pushed back into antiquity with almost equal rapidity. Though the subjects will probably always have their limitations, yet the insight of scholars and explorers is opening up new vistas on all sides. . . . Our prospect for the future is bright. Egypt itself seems inexhaustible. Few of the cities of Babylonia and Assyria have yet been excavated, and each of them had its library and record office of clay-tablets as well as monuments in stone and bronze. In Northern Mesopotamia are countless sites still untouched ; in Elam and in Armenia monuments are only less plentiful. In Arabia inscriptions are now being read which may perhaps date from 1000 B. C. The so-called Hittite hieroglyphs still baffle the decipherer; but as more of the documents become known these will in all likelihood prove a fruitful source for the history of North Syria, of Cappadocia, and of Asia Minor throughout. Occasionally, too, though it is but rarely, an inscription in the Phaenician type of alphabet yields up important historical facts. When all is done, there is but scant hope that we shall be able to construct a consecutive history of persons and events in the ancient world. All that we can be confident of securing, at any rate in Egypt, is the broad outline of development and change, chronologically graduated and varied by occasioual pictures of extraordinary minuteness and brilliancy."— F. LL. Griffith, *Authority and Archaeology Sacred and Prdfane, pt.* 2, *pp.* 218-219 (*N. Y.: Chas. Scribner's Sons*).

In Bible Lands: General results as affecting our knowledge of the ancient Hebrews.— "The general result of the archaeological and anthropological researches of the past half-century has been to take the Hebrews out of the isolated position which, as a nation, they seemed previously to hold, and to demonstrate their affinities with, and often their dependence upon, the civilizations by which they were surrounded. Tribes more or less closely akin to themselves in both language and race were their neighbours alike on the north, on the east, and on the south; in addition to this, on each side there towered above them an ancient and imposing civilization, — that of Babylonia, from the earliest times active, enterprising, and full of life, and that of Egypt, hardly, if at all, less remarkable than that of Babylonia, though more self-contained and less expansive. The civilization which, in spite of the long residence of the Israelites in Egypt, left its mark, however, most distinctly upon the culture and literature of the Hebrews was that of Babylonia. It was in the East that the Hebrew traditions placed both the cradle of humanity and the more immediate home of their own ancestors; and it was Babylonia which, as we now know, exerted during many centuries an influence, once unsuspected, over Palestine itself.

"It is true, the facts thus disclosed, do not in any degree detract from that religious pre-eminence which has always been deemed the inalienable characteristic of the Hebrew race : the spiritual intuitions and experiences of its great teachers retain still their uniqueness ; but the secular institutions of the nation, and even the material elements upon which the religious system of the Israelites was itself constructed, are seen now to have been in many cases common to them with their neighbours. Thus their beliefs about the origin and early history of the world, their social usages, their code of civil and criminal law, their religious institutions, can no longer be viewed, as was once possible, as differing in kind from those of other nations, and determined in every feature by a direct revelation from Heaven; all, it is now known, have substantial analogies among other peoples, the distinctive character which they exhibit among the Hebrews consisting in the spirit with which they are infused and the higher principles of which they are made the exponent. . . .

"What is called the 'witness of the monuments' is often strangely misunderstood. The monuments witness to nothing which any reasonable critic has ever doubted. No one, for instance, has ever doubted that there were kings of Israel (or Judah) named Ahab and Jehu and Pekah and Ahaz and Hezekiah, or that Tiglath-Pileser and Sennacherib led expeditions into Palestine; the mention of these (and such like) persons and events in the Assyrian annals has brought to light many additional facts about them which it is an extreme satisfaction to know : but it has only 'confirmed' what no critic had questioned. On the other hand, the Assyrian annals have shewn that the chronology of the Books of Kings is, in certain places, incorrect : they have thus confirmed the conclusion which critics had reached independently upon internal evidence, that the parts of these books to which the chronology belongs are of much later origin than the more strictly historical parts, and consequently do not possess equal value.

"The inscriptions, especially those of Babylonia, Assyria, and Egypt, have revealed to us an immense amount of information respecting the antiquities and history of these nations, and also, in some cases, respecting the peoples with whom, whether by commerce or war, they came into contact : but (with the exception of the statement on the stele of Mcrenptah that 'Israel is desolated') the first event connected with Israel or its ancestors which they mention or attest is Shishak's invasion of Judah in the reign of Rehoboam ; the first Israelites whom they specify by name are Omri and his son Ahab. There is also indirect illustration of statements in the Old Testament relating to the period earlier than this ; but the monuments supply no 'confirmation' of any single fact recorded in it, prior to Shishak's invasion."—S. R. Driver, *Authority and Archaeology Sacred and Prdfane, pt.* 1, *pp.* 150-151 (*N. Y. : Chas. Scribner's Sons*).

Babylonia: Earlier explorations in.—For some account of the earlier archæological explorations in Babylonia and their results, see (in vol. 1) BABYLONIA, PRIMITIVE ; and (in vol. 4) SEMITES.

Babylonia: American exploration of the ruins of ancient Nippur.*—" In the summer of 1888, the University of Pennsylvania fully equipped and sent out the first American expedition to the northern half of the plains of Babylonia to effect a thorough exploration of the ruins of Nippur—the modern Niffer, or, more correctly, Nuffar—on the border of the unwholesome swamps of the Affej, and to undertake extensive excavations. A few intelligent citizens of Philadelphia had met in the house of Ex-Provost Dr. William Pepper, and formed 'The Babylonian Exploration Fund,' a short time before this with the purpose of effecting a systematic exploration of ancient Babylonia. What science owes to this unselfish undertaking can be adequately estimated only by posterity. . . . Two professors, Peters and Hilprecht, were entrusted with the management of the expedition, Dr. Peters as director, and Dr. Hilprecht as Assyriologist."—H. V. Hilprecht, *ed., Recent Research in Bible Lands, p.* 47.

---

* Quotations in this account from Professor Hilprecht's copyrighted reports in the "Sunday School Times" are used with permission from the publishers of that journal.

Professor Hilprecht, who conducts for the "Sunday School Times" a most interesting and important department, in which the proceedings and principal results of archæological exploration in Bible Lands have been currently chronicled during several years past, gave, in that journal of December 1, 1900, the following description of the scene and the historical importance of the ruins in which the excavations above mentioned have been carried on : "Nuffar is the modern Arabic name of an old Babylonian ruin situated about half-way between the Euphrates and Tigris, at the northeastern boundary of the great Affej swamps, which are formed by the regular annual inundations of the Euphrates. In a straight line, it is nearly eighty miles to the southeast from Baghdad. A large canal, now dry, and often for miles entirely filled with rubbish and sand, divides the ruins into two almost equal parts. On an average about fifty or sixty feet high, these ruins are torn up by frequent gulleys and furrows into a number of spurs and ridges, from the distance not unlike a rugged mountain range on the bank of the upper Tigris. In the Babylonian language, the city buried here was called Nippur. According to Jewish tradition, strongly supported by arguments drawn from cuneiform texts and archaeological objects found at the ruins themselves, Nippur was identical with the Biblical Calneh, mentioned in Genesis 10 : 10, as one of the four great cities of the kingdom of Nimrod. It was therefore natural that the public in general should take a warm interest in our excavations at Nuffar. This interest grew considerably in religious circles when, a few years ago, I announced my discovery of the name of the 'river Chebar' in two cuneiform texts from the archives of Nippur. It became then evident that this 'river Chebar,' which hitherto could not be located, was one of the four or five large canals once bringing life and fertility to the fields of Nippur ; that, furthermore, a large number of the Jewish captives carried away by Nebuchadrezzar after the destruction of Jerusalem were settled in the plains around this city ; and that even Ezekiel himself, while admonishing and comforting his people, and holding out to them Jehovah's mercy and never-failing promise of a brighter future, stood in the very shadow of Babylonia's ancient national sanctuary, the crumbling walls of the great temple of Bêl at Nippur. The beginning and end of Old Testament history thus point to Nippur as the background and theater for the first and final acts in the great drama of divine selection and human rejection in which Israel played the leading rôle."

In the same article, Professor Hilprecht indicated in a few words what was done at Nuffar by the first three of the four expeditions sent out from Philadelphia since 1888. "It was comparatively easy," he said, "to get a clear idea of the extent of the city and the life in its streets during the last six centuries preceding our era. Each of the four expeditions to Nuffar contributed its peculiar share to a better knowledge of this latest period of Babylonian history, particularly, however, the third and the present campaigns. But it was of greater importance to follow up the traces of a very early civilization, which, accidentally, we had met during our first brief campaign in 1889. By means of a few deep trenches, the second expedition, in the following

year, had brought to light new evidence that a considerable number of ancient monuments still existed in the lower strata of the temple mound. The third expedition showed that the monuments, while numerous, are mostly very fragmentary, thereby offering considerable difficulties to the decipherer and historian. But it also showed that a number of platforms running through the temple mound, and made of baked bricks, frequently bearing inscriptions, enable us to fix the age of the different strata of this mound with great accuracy. The two lowest of these platforms found were the work of kings and patesis (priest-kings) of 4000–3800 B. C., but, to our great astonishment, they did not represent the earliest trace of human life at Nippur. There were not less than about thirty feet of rubbish below them, revealing an even earlier civilization, the beginning and development of which lie considerably before the times of Sargon the Great (3800 B. C.) and Narâm-Sin, who had been generally regarded as half-mythical persons of the first chapter of Babylonian history."

Of the results of the work of those three expeditions of the University of Pennsylvania, and of the studies for which they furnished materials to Professor Hilprecht, Professor Sayce wrote with much enthusiasm in the "Contemporary Review" of January, 1897, as follows : " In my Hibbert Lectures on the 'Religion of the Ancient Babylonians' I had been led by a study of the religious texts of Babylonia to the conclusion that Nippur had been a centre from which Babylonian culture was disseminated in what we then regarded as prehistoric times. Thanks to the American excavations, what were prehistoric times when my Hibbert Lectures were written have now become historic, and my conclusion has proved to be correct. . . . For the first time in Babylonia they have systematically carried their shafts through the various strata of historical remains which occupy the site, carefully noting the objects found in each, and wherever possible clearing each stage away when once it had been thoroughly examined. The work began in 1888, about two hundred Arabs being employed as labourers. . . . The excavations at Nippur were carried deeply and widely enough not only to reveal the history of the city itself but also to open up a new vista in the forgotten history of civilised man. The history of civilisation has been taken back into ages which a short while since were still undreamed of. Professor Hilprecht, the historian of the expedition, upon whom has fallen the work of copying, publishing, and translating the multitudinous texts discovered in the course of it, declares that we can no longer 'hesitate to date the founding of the temple of Bel and the first settlements in Nippur somewhere between 6000 and 7000 B. C., possibly even earlier.' At any rate the oldest monuments which have been disinterred there belong to the fifth or sixth millennium before the Christian era. Hitherto we have been accustomed to regard Egypt as the land which has preserved for us the earliest written records of mankind, but Babylonia now bids fair to outrival Egypt. The earliest fixed date in Babylonian history is that of Sargon of Akkael and his son Naram-Sin. It has been fixed for us by Nabonidos, the royal antiquarian of Babylonia. In one of his inscriptions he describes the excavations he made in order to discover the memorial cylinders of Naram-Sin, who had lived '3200 years' before his own time. In my Hibbert Lectures I gave reasons for accepting this date as approximately correct. The recent discoveries at Niffer, Telloh, and other places have shown that my conclusion was justified. . . .

"Assyriologists have long had in their possession a cuneiform text which contains the annals of the reign of Sargon, and of the first three years of the reign of his son. It is a late copy of the original text, and was made for the library of Nineveh. Our 'critical' friends have been particularly merry over the credulity of the Assyriologists in accepting these annals as authentic. . . . So far from being unhistorical, Sargon and Naram-Sin prove to have come at the end of a long-preceding historical period, and the annals themselves have been verified by contemporaneous documents. The empire of Sargon, which extended from the Persian Gulf to the Mediterranean, was not even the first that had arisen in Western Asia. And the art that flourished under his rule, like the art which flourished in Egypt in the age of the Old Empire, was higher and more perfect than any that succeeded it in Babylonia. . . . Henceforward, Sargon and Naram-Sin, instead of belonging to 'the grey dawn of time,' must be regarded as representatives of 'the golden age of Babylonian history.' That they should have undertaken military expeditions to the distant West, and annexed Palestine and the Sinaitic Peninsula to the empire they created need no longer be a matter of astonishment. Such campaigns had already been undertaken by Babylonian kings long before; the way was well known which led from one extremity of Western Asia to the other. . . .

' It is Mr. Haynes [Director of the explorations from 1893] who tells us that we are henceforth to look upon Sargon of Akkad as a representative of 'the golden age of Babylonian history,' and his assertion is endorsed by Professor Hilprecht. In fact, the conclusion is forced upon both the excavator and the palæographist. Professor Hilprecht, who, thanks to the abundant materials at his disposal, has been able to found the science of Babylonian palæography, tracing the development of the cuneiform characters from one stage of development to another, and determining the age of each successive form of writing, has made it clear to all students of Assyriology that many of the inscriptions found at Niffer and Telloh belong to a much older period than those of the age of Sargon. The palæographic evidence has been supplemented by the results of excavation. . . . As far back as we can penetrate, we still find inscribed monuments and other evidences of civilisation. It is true that the characters are rude and hardly yet lifted above their pictorial forms. They have, however, ceased to be pictures, and have already become that cursive script which we call cuneiform. For the beginnings of Babylonian writing we have still to search among the relics of centuries that lie far behind the foundation of the temple of Nippur.

"The first king whom the excavations there have brought to light is a certain En-sag(sak)-ana who calls himself 'lord of Kengi' and conqueror of Kis 'the wicked.' Kengi—'the land of canals and reeds,' as Professor Hilprecht interprets the word—was the oldest name of Babylonia, given to it in days when it was still

wholly occupied by its Sumerian population, and when as yet no Semitic stranger had ventured within it. The city of Kis (now El-Hymar) lay outside its borders to the north, and between Kis and Kengi there seems to have been constant war. . . . Nippur was the religious centre of Kengi, and Mul-lil, the god of Nippur, was the supreme object of Sumerian worship. . . . A king of Kis made himself master of Nippur and its sanctuary, and the old kingdom of Kengi passed away. The final blow was dealt by the son of the Sumerian high priest of the 'Land of the Bow.' Lugai-zaggi-si was the chieftain who descended from the north upon Babylonia and made it part of his empire. . . . Lugal-zaggi-si lived centuries before Sargon of Akkad in days which, only a year ago, we still believed to lie far beyond the horizon of history and culture. We little dreamed that in that hoar antiquity the great cities and sanctuaries of Babylonia were already old, and that the culture and script of Babylonia had already extended far beyond the boundaries of their motherland. The inscriptions of Lugal-zaggi-si are in the Sumerian language, and his name, like that of his father, is Sumerian also. . . . The empire of Lugal-zaggi-si seems to have passed away with his death, and at no long period subsequently a new dynasty arose at Ur. . . . According to Professor Hilprecht, this would have been about 4000 B. C. How long the first dynasty of Ur lasted we cannot tell. It had to keep up a perpetual warfare with the Semitic tribes of northern Arabia, Ki-sarra, 'the land of the hordes,' as it was termed by the Sumerians. Meanwhile a new state was growing up on the eastern side of the Euphrates in a small provincial city called Lagas, whose ruins are now known as Telloh. Its proximity to Eridu, the seaport and trading depot of early Babylonia, had doubtless much to do with its rise to power. At all events the kings of Telloh, whose monuments have been brought to light by M. de Sarzec, became continually stronger, and the dynasty of Lagas took the place of the dynasty of Ur. One of these kings, E-Anna-gin, at length defeated the Semitic oppressors of northern Chaldæa in a decisive battle and overthrew the 'people of the Land of the Bow.' . . .

"The kings of Lagas represent the closing days of Sumerian supremacy. With Sargon and his empire the Semitic age begins. The culture of Chaldæa is still Sumerian, the educated classes are for the most part of Sumerian origin, and the literature of the country is Sumerian also. But the king and his court are Semites, and the older culture which they borrow and adopt becomes Semitised in the process. . . . For many generations Sumerians and Semites lived side by side, each borrowing from the other, and mutually adapting and modifying their own forms of expression. . . . Sumerian continued to be the language of religion and law—the two most conservative branches of human study—down to the age of Abraham. . . . The new facts that have been disinterred from the grave of the past furnish a striking confirmation of Professor Hommel's theory, which connects the culture of primitive Egypt with that of primitive Chaldæa, and derives the language of the Egyptians, at all events in part, from a mixed Babylonian language in which Semitic and Sumerian elements alike claimed a share. We now know that such a mixed language did once exist, and we also know that this language and the written characters by which it was expressed were brought to the shores of the Mediterranean and the frontiers of Egypt in the earliest age of Egyptian history."—A. H. Sayce, *Recent Discoveries in Babylonia* (*Contemporary Review*, Jan., 1897).

The third of the Pennsylvania expeditions closed its work at Nippur in February, 1896. There was then an interval of three years before a fourth expedition resumed work at the ruins in February, 1899. In the "Sunday School Times" of April 29 and May 27, 1899, Professor Hilprecht (who did not go personally to Nuffar until later in the year) gave the following account of the friendly reception of the exploring party by the Arabs of the district, from whom there had been formerly much experience of trouble: "The Affej tribes, in whose territory the large mounds are situated, had carefully guarded the expedition's stronghold, —a mud castle half-way between the ruins and the marshes, which had been sealed and entrusted to their care before we quitted the field some years ago. They now gave to the expedition a hearty welcome, accompanied by shooting, shouting, dancing, and singing, and were evidently greatly delighted to have the Americans once more in their midst. In the presence of Haji Tarfa, their commander-in-chief, who was surrounded by his minor shaykhs and other dignitaries of the El-Hamza tribes, the former arrangements with the two shaykhs Hamid el-Birjud and Abud el-Hamid were ratified, and new pledges given for the security and welfare of the little party of explorers, the question of guards and water being especially emphasized. In accordance with the Oriental custom, the expedition showed its appreciation of the warm reception by preparing for their hosts in return a great feast, at which plenty of mutton and boiled rice were eaten by some fifty Arabs, and the old bond of friendship was cemented anew with 'bread and salt.'" . . .

"Doubtless all the advantages resulting for the Affej Bed'ween and their allies from the presence of the Americans were carefully calculated by them in the three years (February, 1896–1899) that we had withdrawn our expedition from their territory. They have apparently found out that the comparatively large amount of money brought into their country through the wages paid to many Arabs employed as workmen, and through the purchase of milk, eggs, chicken, mutton, and all the other material supplied by the surrounding tribes for our camp, with its about two hundred and fifty persons, has done much to improve their general condition. The conviction has been growing with them that we have not come to rob them of anything to which they attach great value themselves, nor to establish a new military station for the Turkish government in order to gather taxes and unpaid debts. Every Arab engaged by the Expedition has been fairly treated, and help and assistance have always been given cheerfully and gratis to the many sick people who apply daily for medicine, suffering more or less during the whole year from pulmonary diseases, typhoid and malarial fevers, easily contracted in the midst of the extended marshes which they inhabit."

In the "Sunday School Times" of August 5, in the same year, Professor Hilprecht reported: "The mounds of Nippur seem to conceal an al-

most inexhaustible treasure of inscribed cuneiform tablets, by means of which we are enabled to restore the chronology, history, religion, and the high degree of civilization, obtained at a very early date by the ancient inhabitants between the lower Euphrates and Tigris. More than 33,000 of these precious documents were found during the previous campaigns. Not less than 4,776 tablets have been rescued from February 6 to June 10 this year, averaging, therefore, nearly 1,200 'manuscripts in clay,' as we may style them, per month. About the fourth part of these tablets is in perfect condition, while a very large proportion of the remaining ones are good-sized fragments or tablets so fortunately broken that their general contents and many important details can be ascertained by the patient decipherer."

In November, 1899, Professor Hilprecht started for the field, to superintend the explorations in person, and on the way he wrote to the "S. S. Times" (published December 13): "The deeper the trenches of the Babylonian Expedition of the University of Pennsylvania descend into the lower strata of Nippur, the probable site of the biblical Calneh, the more important and interesting become the results obtained. The work of clearing the northeastern wall of the high-towering temple of Bel was continued with success during the summer months. Particularly numerous were the inscribed vase fragments brought to light, and almost exclusively belonging to the pre-Sargonic period,—3800 B. C. and before. As I showed in the second part of Volume I of our official University publication, this fragmentary condition of the vases is due to the wilful destruction of the temple property by the victorious Elamitic hordes, who, towards the end of the third pre-Christian millennium, ransacked the Babylonian cities, extending their conquest and devastation even as far as the shores of the Mediterranean Sea (comp. Gen. 14). From the earliest historical period down to about 2200 B. C., when this national calamity befell Babylonia, the large temple storehouse, with its precious statues, votive slabs and vases, memorial stones, bronze figures, and other gifts from powerful monarchs and governors, had practically remained intact. What, therefore, is left of the demolished and scattered contents of this ancient chamber as a rule is found above the platform of Ur-Ninib (about 2500 B. C.), in a layer several feet thick and about twenty-five feet wide, surrounding the front and the two side walls of the temple. The systematic clearing and examination of this layer, and of the huge mass of ruins lying above it, occupied the attention of the expedition considerably in the past years, and was continued with new energy during the past six months."

At the end of January, 1900, Professor Hilprecht arrived in Babylonia, and wrote some weeks later to the "Sunday School Times" (May 3): "As early as eleven years ago, the present writer pointed out that the extensive group of hills to the southwest of the temple of Bel must be regarded as the probable site of the temple library of ancient Nippur. About twenty-five hundred tablets were rescued from the trenches in this hill during our first campaign. Later excavations increased the number of tablets taken from these mounds to about fifteen thousand. But it was only within the last six weeks that my old theory could be established beyond any reasonable doubt. During this brief period a series of rooms was exposed which furnished not less than over sixteen thousand cuneiform documents, forming part of the temple library during the latter half of the third millennium B. C. In long rows the tablets were lying on ledges of unbaked clay, serving as shelves for these imperishable Old Babylonian records. The total number of tablets rescued from different parts of the ruins during the present campaign amounts even now to more than twenty-one thousand, and is rapidly increased by new finds every day. The contents of this extraordinary library are as varied as possible. Lists of Sumerian words and cuneiform signs, arranged according to different principles, and of fundamental value for our knowledge of the early non-Semitic language of the country, figure prominently in the new 'find.' As regards portable antiquities of every description, and their archeological value, the American expedition stands readily first among the three expeditions at present engaged in the exploration of Ancient Babylonia and the restoration of its past history."

Three weeks later he added : " The Temple Library, as indicated in the writer's last report, has been definitely located at the precise spot which, in 1889, the present writer pointed out as its most probable site. Nearly eighteen thousand cuneiform documents have been rescued this year from the shelves of a series of rooms in its southeastern and northwestern wings. The total number of tablets (mostly of a didactic character) obtained from the library up to date is from twenty-five thousand to twenty-six thousand tablets (whole and broken). In view, however, of more important other duties to be executed by this expedition before we can leave Nippur this year, and in consideration of the enormous amount of time and labor required for a methodical exploration of the whole mound in which it is concealed, I have recently ordered all the gangs of Arabic workmen to be withdrawn from this section of ancient Nippur, and to be set at work at the eastern fortification line of the city, close to the temple-complex proper. According to a fair estimate based upon actual finds, the unique history of the temple, and topographical indications, there must be hidden at least from a hundred thousand to a hundred and fifty thousand tablets more in this ancient library, which was destroyed by the invading Elamites about the time of Abraham's emigration from Ur of the Chaldees. Only about the twentieth part of this library (all of Dr. Haynes's previous work included) has so far been examined and excavated."

In the same letter the Professor described the uncovering of one façade of a large pre-Sargonic palace—"the chief discovery," in his opinion, " of this whole campaign." " A thorough excavation of this large palace," he wrote, " will form one of the chief tasks of a future expedition, after its character, age, and extent have been successfully determined by the present one. Important art treasures of the Tello type, and literary documents, may reasonably be expected to be unearthed from the floor-level of its many chambers. It has become evident, from the large number of pre-Sargonic buildings, walls, and other antiquities discovered on both sides of the Shatt-en-Nil, that the pre-Sargonic Nippur was of by far greater extent than had been anticipated. This discovery, however, is only in strict accord with what we know from the cuneiform documents as to the important historical rôle which the temple of Bel ('the father of the gods'), as the central national sanctuary of ancient Babylonia, played at the earliest period, long before Babylon, the capital of the later empire, achieved any prominence."

The work at Nippur was suspended for the season about the middle of May, 1900, and Professor Hilprecht,after his return to Philadelphia, wrote of the general fruits of the campaign, in the "Sunday School Times" of December 1: " As the task of the fourth and most recent expedition, just completed, I had mapped out, long before its organization, the following work. It was to determine the probable extent of the earliest pre-Sargonic settlement at ancient Nippur ; to discover the precise form and character of the famous temple of Bêl at this earliest period ; to define the exact boundaries of the city proper ; if possible, to find one or more of the great city gates frequently mentioned in the inscriptions ; to locate the great temple library and educational quarters of Nippur ; to study the different modes of burial in use in ancient Babylonia ; and to study all types and forms of pottery, with a view to finding laws for the classification and determination of the ages of vases, always excavated in large numbers at Nuffar. The work set before us has been accomplished. The task was great,—almost too great for the limited time at our disposal. . . . But the number of Arab workmen, busy with pickax, scraper, and basket in the trenches for ten to fourteen hours every day, gradually increased to the full force of four hundred. . . . In the course of time, when the nearly twenty-five thousand cuneiform texts which form one of the most conspicuous prizes of the present expedition have been fully deciphered and interpreted ; when the still hidden larger mass of tablets from that great educational institution, the temple library of Calneh-Nippur, discovered at the very spot which I had marked for its site twelve years ago, has been brought to light,— a great civilization will loom up from past millenniums before our astonished eyes. For four thousand years the documents which contain this precious information have disappeared from sight, forgotten in the destroyed rooms of ancient Nippur. Abraham was about leaving his ancestral home at Ur when the great building in which so much learning had been stored up by previous generations collapsed under the ruthless acts of the Elamite hordes. But the light which begins to flash forth from the new trenches in this lonely mound in the desert of Irâq will soon illuminate the world again. And it will be no small satisfaction to know that it was rekindled by the hands of American explorers."

Babylonia : German exploration of the ruins of Babylon.—An expedition to explore the ruins of Babylon was sent out by the German Orient Society, in 1899, under the direction of Dr. Koldewey, an eminent architect and archæologist, who had been connected with previous works of excavation done in Babylonia and northern Syria. In announcing the project, in the "Sunday School Times" of January 28, 1899, Professor Hilprecht remarked : " These extended ruins will require at least fifty years of labor if they are to be excavated as thoroughly and systematically as the work is done by the American expedition at Nippur, which has employed in its trenches never less than sixty, but frequently from two hundred to four hundred, Arabic workmen at the same time during the last ten years. Certain parts of the ruins of Babylon have been previously explored and excavated by Layard, Rawlinson, and the French expedition under Fresnel and Oppert, to which we owe the first accurate details of the topography of this ancient city." Writing somewhat more than a year later from Nippur, after having visited the German party at Babylon, Professor Hilprecht said of its work : "The chief work of the expedition during the past year was the exploration of the great ruin heap called El-Kasr, under which are hidden the remains of the palace of Nebuchadrezzar, where Alexander the Great died after his famous campaign against India. Among the few important antiquities so far obtained from this imposing mound of Ancient Babylon is a new Hittite inscription and a neo-Babylonian slab with an interesting cuneiform legend. Very recently, Dr. Koldewey, whose excellent topographical surveys form a conspicuous part of the results of the first year, has found the temple of the goddess Nin-Makh, so often mentioned in the building inscriptions of the neo-Babylonian rulers, and a little terra-cotta statue of the goddess. The systematic examination of the enormous mass of ruins covering Ancient Babylon will require several decenniums of continued hard labor. To facilitate this great task, a bill has been submitted to the German Reichstag requesting a yearly government appropriation of over fifteen thousand dollars, while at the same time application has been made by the German Orient Committee to the Ottoman Government for another firman to carry on excavations at Warka, the biblical Erech, whose temple archive was badly pillaged by the invading Elamites at about 2280 B. C."

Some account of results from the uncovering of the palace of Nebuchadrezzar are quoted from "Die Illustrirte Zeitung" in the "Scientific American Supplement," December 16, 1899, as follows: "According to early Babylonian records, Nebuchadnezzar completed the fortifications of the city, begun by his father Narbolpolassar, consisting of a double inclosure of strong walls, the inner called Imgur-Bel ('Bel is gracions'), the outer Nemitti-Bel ('foundation of Bel'). The circumference of the latter according to Herodotus was 480 stades (55 miles), its height 340 feet, and its thickness 85 feet. At the inner and outer peripheries, one-story houses were built, between which was room enough for a chariot drawn by four horses harnessed abreast. When Koldewey cut through the eastern front of Al Kasr, he came upon a wall which was undoubtedly that described by Herodotus. The outer eastern shell was composed of burnt brick and asphalt, 24 feet in thickness; then came a filling of sand and broken stone 70½ feet in thickness, which was followed by an inner western shell of 43 feet thickness. The total thickness was, therefore, 137.5 feet. By dint of hard work this wall was cut through and the entrance to Nebuchadnezzar's palace laid bare. Koldewey and his men were enabled to verify the description given by Diodorus of the polychromatic reliefs which graced the walls of the royal towers and palaces. It still remains to

be seen how trustworthy are the statements of other ancient historians. The city itself, as previons investigators have found, was adorned with many temples, chief among them Esaglia ('the high towering house'), temple of the city, and the national god Marduk (Merodach) and his spouse Zirpanit. Sloping toward the river were the Hanging Gardens, one of the world's séven wonders, located in the northern mound of the ruins of Babel. The temple described by Herodotus is that of Nebo, in Borsippa, not far from Babylon, which Herodotus included under Babylon and which the cuneiform inscriptions term 'Babylon the Second.' This temple, which in the mound of Birs Nimrûd is the most imposing ruin of Babylon, is called the 'eternal house' in the inscriptions; it was restored by Nebuchadnezzar with great splendor. In form, it is a pyramid built in seven stages, for which reason it is sometimes referred to as the 'Temple of the Seven Spheres of Heaven and Earth.' The Tower of Babel, described in Gen. x., is perhaps the same structure. It remains for the German expedition to continue its excavations in Nebuchadnezzar's palace."

Babylonia: Discovery of an inscription of Nabonidós, the last of the Babylonian kings.—"A discovery of the greatest importance has just been made by Father Scheil, who has for some time been exploring in Babylonia. In the Mujelibeh mound, one of the principal heaps of ruins in the 'enciente' of Babylon, he has discovered a long inscription of Nabonidos, the last of the Babylonian Kings (B. C. 555-538), which contains a mass of historical and other data which will be of greatest value to students of this important period of Babylonian history. The monument in question is a small 'stela' of diorite, the upper part of which is broken, inscribed with eleven columns of writing, and which appears to have been erected early in the King's reign. It resembles in some measure the celebrated India-House inscription of Nebuchadnezzar, but is much more full of historical matter. Its value may be estimated when it is stated that it contains a record of the war of revenge conducted by the Babylonians and their Mandian allies against Assyria, for the destrution of the city by Sennacherib, in B. C. 698; an account of the election and coronation of Nabonidos in B. C. 555, and the wonderful dream in which Nebuchadnezzar appeared to him; as well as an account of the restoration of the temple of the Moon god at Kharran, accompanied by a chronological record which enables us to fix the date of the so-called Scythian invasion. There is also a valuable reference to the murder of Sennacherib by his son in Tebet, B. C. 681."—*Am. Journal of Archæology, January—March, 1896.*

Persia: French exploration of the ruins of Susa, the capital of ancient Elam.—"In 1897 an arrangement was completed between the French Government and the Shah of Persia by which the former obtained the exclusive right of archeological explorations in the latter's empire, coupled with certain privileges for the exportation of different kinds of antiquities that might be unearthed. Soon afterwards, M. J. de Morgan, late director of excavations in Egypt, who had made archeological researches in the regions east of the Tigris before, was placed at the head of a French expedition to Susa, the ancient capital of Elam, the upper strata of

6–2

which had been successfully explored by M. Dieulafoy. In the Babylonian cuneiform inscriptions Elam appears as the most terrible foe of the Babylonian empire from the earliest time; and the name of its capital, Susa, or Shûsha, was discovered by the present editor several years ago on a small votive object in agate, originally manufactured and inscribed in southern Babylonia, in the first half of the third pre-christian millennium, several hundred years afterwards carried away as part of their spoil by the invading Elamites, and in the middle of the fourteenth century B. C. recaptured, reinscribed, and presented to the temple of Nippur by King Kurigalzu, after his conquest of Susa. It was therefore evident that, if the same method of excavating was applied to the ruins of Susa as had been applied so successfully by the University of Pennsylvania's expedition in Nippur, remarkable results would soon be obtained, and amply repay all labor and money expended. M. de Morgan, accompanied by some engineers and architects, set hopefully to work, cutting his trenches more than fifty feet below the ruins of the Achæmenian dynasty. The first campaign, 1897–98, was so successful, in the discovery of buildings and inscribed antiquities, that in October of last year the French government despatched the Assyriologist Professor Seheil, in order to decipher the new cuneiform documents, and to report on their historical bearings.

"Among the more important finds so far made, but not yet published, may be mentioned over a thousand cuneiform tablets of the earlier period, a beautifully preserved obelisk more than five feet high, and covered with twelve hundred lines of Old Babylonian cuneiform writing. It was inscribed and set up by King Manishtusu, who left inscribed vases in Nippur and other Babylonian cities. A stele of somewhat smaller size, representing a battle in the mountains, testifies to the high development of art at that remote period. On the one end it bears a mutilated inscription of Narâm-Sin, son of Sargon the Great (3800 B. C.); on the other, the name of Shimti-Shilkhak, a well-known Elamitic king, and grandfather of the biblical Ariokh (Gen. 14). These two monuments were either left in Susa by the two Babylonian kings whose names they bear, after successful operations against Elam, or they were carried off as booty at the time of the great Elamitic invasion, which proved so disastrous to the treasure-houses and archives of Babylonian cities and temples [see above: BABYLONIA]. The latter is more probable to the present writer, who in 1896 ('Old Babylonian Inscriptions,' Part II, p. 33) pointed out, in connection with his discussion of the reasons of the lamentable condition of Babylonian temple archives, that on the whole we shall look in vain for well-preserved large monuments in most Babylonian ruins, because about 2280 B. C. 'that which in the eyes of the national enemies of Babylonia appeared most valuable was carried to Susa and other places; what did not find favor with them was smashed and scattered on Babylonian temple courts.'"—Prof. H. V. Hilprecht. *Oriental Research (Sunday School Times, Jan.* 28, 1899).

Egypt: Earlier explorations.—For some account of earlier archæological explorations in Egypt, see, in vol. 1, EGYPT.

Egypt: Results of recent exploration.—

The **opening** up of **prehistoric Egypt.**— The tomb of **Mena.**—The funeral temple of **Merenptah.**—Single mention of the people of Israel.—"During all this century in which Egyptian history has been studied at first hand, it has been accepted as a sort of axiom that the beginnings of things were quite unknown. In the epitome of the history which was drawn up under the Greeks to make Egypt intelligible to the rest of the world, there were three dynasties of kings stated before the time of the great pyramid builders; and yet of those it has been commonly said that no trace remained. Hence it has been usual to pass them by with just a mention as being half fabulous, and then to begin real history with Senefern or Khufu (Cheops), the kings who stand at the beginning of the fourth dynasty, at about 4000 B. C. The first discovery to break up this habit of thought was when the prehistoric colossal statues of Min, the god of the city of Koptos, were found in my excavations in his temple. These had carvings in relief upon them wholly different from anything known as yet in Egypt, and the circumstances pointed to their being earlier than any carvings yet found in that country. In the same temple we found also statues of sacred animals and pottery which we now know to belong to the very beginning of Egyptian history, many centuries before the pyramids, and probably about 5000 B. C. or earlier.

"The next step was the finding of a new cemetery and a town of the prehistoric people, which we can now date to about 5000 B. C., within two or three centuries either way. This place lay on the opposite side of the Nile to Koptos—that is to say, about 20 miles north of Thebes. At first we were completely staggered by a class of objects entirely different from any yet known in Egypt. We tried to fit them into every gap in Egyptian history, but found that it was impossible to put them before 3000 B. C. Later discoveries prove that they are really as old as 5000 B. C. They show a very different civilization from that of the Egyptians whom we already know—far less artistic, but in some respects even more skillful in mechanical taste and touch than the historical Egyptians. They built brick houses to live in, and buried their dead in small chambers sunk in the gravels of the water courses, lined with mats, and roofed over with beams. They show several points of contact with the early Mediterranean civilization, and appear to have been mainly north African tribes of European type. Their pottery, in its patterns and painting, shows designs which have survived almost unchanged unto the present day among the Kabyles of the Algerian Mountains. And one very peculiar type of pottery is found spread from Spain to Egypt, and indicates a widespread commercial intercourse at that remote day. The frequent figures upon the vases of great galley ships rowed with oars show that shipping was well developed then, and make the evidences of trading between different countries easy to be accepted.

"All of the above belongs to the age probably before 4700 B. C., which is the age given for the first historical king of Egypt by the Greek history of Manetho. A keystone of our knowledge of the civilization is the identification of the tomb of Mena, the first name in Egyptian history, the venerated founder of all the long series of hundreds of historic kings. This tomb, about

15 miles north of Thebes, was found by some Arabs, and shown to M. De Morgan, the director of the Department of Antiquities. It was a mass of about thirty chambers, built of mud brick and earth. Each chamber contained a different class of objects, one of stone vases, one of stone dishes, one of copper tools, one of water jars, etc. And among the things are carvings of lions and vases in rock crystal and obsidian, large hard-stone vases. slate palettes for grinding paint, pottery vases, and, above all, an ivory tablet with relief carvings which show the names of the king. Besides this, M. Amelineau has found sixteen tombs of this same general character at Abydos, which we can hardly now doubt belong to the early kings of the first three dynasties, and some four or five have been actually identified with the names of these kings in the Greek history. So now instead of treating the first three dynasties as half fabulous and saying that Egyptian art and civilization begin full blown at 4000 B. C., we have the clear and tangible remains of much of these early kings back to 4700 B. C., and a stretch of some centuries of the prehistoric period with a varied and distinctive civilization, well known and quite different from anything later, lying before 4700 B. C. To put the earlier part of this to 5500 B. C. is certainly no stretch of probability. . . .

"We now pass entirely from these early times, with their fascinating insight into the beginnings of things, long before any other human history that we possess, until we reach down to what seems quite modern times in the record of Egypt, where it comes into contact with the Old Testament history. On clearing out the funereal temple of King Merenptah I found in that the upper half of a fine colossal statue of his, with all the colors still fresh upon it. As this son of Rameses the Great is generally believed to be the Pharaoh of the exodus, such a fine portrait of him is full of interest. Better even than that—I found an immense tablet of black granite over 10 feet high and 5 feet wide. It had been erected over two centuries before and brilliantly carved by an earlier king, whose temple was destroyed for materials by Merenptah. He took this splendid block and turned its face inward against the wall of his temple and carved the back of it with other scenes and long inscriptions. Most of it is occupied with the history of his vanquishing the Libyans, or North African tribes, who were then invading Egypt. But at the end he recounts his conquests in Syria, among which occurs the priceless passage : 'The people of Israel are spoiled ; they have no seed.' This is the only trace yet found in Egypt of the existence of the Israelites, the only mention of the name, and it is several centuries earlier than the references to the Israelite and Jewish kings in the cuneiform inscriptions of Assyria.

"What relation this has to our biblical knowledge of the Israelites is a wide question, that has several possible answers. Without entering on all the openings, I may here state what seems to me to be the most probable connection of all the events, though I am quite aware that fresh discoveries might easily alter our views. It seems that either all the Israelites did not go into Egypt or else a part returned and lived in the north of Palestine before the exodus that we know, because we here find Merenptah defeating Israelites at about 1200 B. C. Of his conquest and of those of Rameses III in Palestine there are no traces in the biblical accounts, the absence of which indicates that the entry into Canaan took place after 1160 B. C., the last war of Rameses III. Then the period of the Judges is given in a triple record—(1) of the north, (2) of the east of the Jordan, (3) of Ephraim and the west ; and these three accounts are quite distinct and never overlap, though the history passes in succession from one to another. Thus the whole age of Judges is but little over a century. And to this agree the priestly genealogies stretching between the tabernacle and temple periods.

"Leaving now all the monumental age, we come lastly to the evidences of the Christian period, preserved in the papyri or miscellaneous waste papers left behind in the towns of the Roman times. Last winter my friends, Mr. Grenfell and Mr. Hunt, cleared out the remains of the town Behnesa, about 110 miles south of Cairo. There, amid thousands of stray papers, documents, rolls, accounts, and all the waste sweepings out of the city offices, they found two leaves which are priceless in Christian literature—the leaf of Logia, or sayings of Jesus, and the leaf of Matthew's Gospel. The leaf of the Logia is already so widely known that it is needless for me to describe it. . . . The leaf of Matthew's Gospel is of great interest in the literary history of the Gospels. Hitherto we have had no manuscripts older than the second great ecclesiastical settlement under Theodosius. Now we have a piece two ages earlier—before the first settlement of things under Constantine at the council of Nicea. Here, in the middle of the third century, we find that the beginning of the Gospel, the most artificial, and probably the latest, part, the introductory genealogy and account of the Nativity, was exactly in its present form. This gives us the greatest confidence that the Gospel as we have it dates from the time of the great persecutions. Such are some of the astonishing and far-reaching results that Egypt has given us within three years past."—W. M. Flinders Petrie, *Recent Research in Egypt (Sunday School Times*, Feb. 19, 1898.)

In a later article, contributed to the "Popular Science Monthly," Professor Petrie has described more fully the results of recent exploration in Egypt, especially with reference to the discovery and study of prehistoric remains. The following are passages from the article : "The great stride that has been made in the last six years is the opening up of prehistoric Egypt, leading us back some 2000 years before the time of the pyramid builders. Till recently nothing was known before the age of the finest art and the greatest buildings, and it was a familiar puzzle how such a grand civilization could have left no traces of its rise. This was only a case of blindness on the part of explorers. Upper Egypt teems with prehistoric remains, but. as most of what appears is dug up by plunderers for the market, until there is a demand for a class of objects, very little is seen of them. Now that the prehistoric has become fashionable, it is everywhere to be seen. The earlier diggers were dazzled by the polished colossi, the massive buildings, the brilliant sculptures of the well-known historic times, and they had no eyes for small graves, containing only a few jars or, at best, a flint knife.

"The present position of the prehistory of Egypt is that we can now distinguish two separate cultures before the beginning of the Egyptian dynasties, and we can clearly trace a sequence of manufactures and art throughout long ages before the pyramid builders, or from say 6000 B. C., giving a continuous history of 8000 years for man in Egypt. Continuous I say advisedly, for some of the prehistoric ways are those kept up to the present time. In the earliest stages of this prehistoric culture metal was already used and pottery made. Why no ruder stages are found is perhaps explained by the fact that the alluvial deposits of the Nile do not seem to be much older than 8000 years. The rate of deposit is well known — very closely one metre in a thousand years — and borings show only eight metres thick of Nile mud in the valley. Before that the country had enough rain to keep up the volume of the river, and it did not drop its mud. It must have run as a rapid stream through a barren land of sand and stones, which could not support any population except paleolithic hunters. With the further drying of the climate, the river lost so much velocity that its mud was deposited, and the fertile mud flats made cultivation and a higher civilization possible. At this point a people already using copper came into the country. . . .

"The second prehistoric civilization seems to have belonged to a people kindred to that of the first age, as much of the pottery continued unchanged, and only gradually faded away. But a new style arose of a hard, buff pottery, painted with patterns and subjects in red outline. Ships are represented with cabins on them, and rowed by a long bank of oars. The use of copper became more general, and gold and silver appear also. . . . Though this civilization was in many respects higher than that which preceded it, yet it was lower artistically, the figures being ruder and always flat, instead of in the round. . . .

"The separation of these two different ages has been entirely reached by the classification of many hundreds of tombs, the original order of which could be traced by the relation of their contents. . . . The material for this study has come entirely from excavations of my own party at Nagada (1895), Abadiyeh, and Hu (1899); but great numbers of tombs of these same ages have been opened without record by M. de Morgan (1896–'97), and by French and Arab speculators in antiquities. The connection between these prehistoric ages and the early historic times of the dynastic kings of Egypt is yet obscure. The cemeteries which would have cleared this have unhappily been looted in the last few years without any record, and it is only the chance of some new discoveries that can be looked to for filling up the history.

"We can at least say that the pottery of the early kings is clearly derived from the later prehistoric types, and that much of the civilization was in common. But it is clear that the second prehistoric civilization was degrading and losing its artistic taste for fine work before the new wave of the dynastic or historic Egyptians came in upon it. These early historic people are mainly known by the remains of the tombs of the early kings, found by M. Amelineau at Abydos (1896–'99), and probably the first stage of the same race is seen in the rude colossi of the god Min, which I found at Koptos (1894). . . . In these great discoveries of the last few years we can trace at least three successive peoples, and see the gradual rise of the arts, from the man who was buried in his goat skins, with one plain cup by him, up to the king who built great monuments and was surrounded by most sumptuous handiwork. We see the rise of the art of exquisite flint flaking, and the decline of that as copper came more commonly into use. We see at first the use of signs, later on disused by a second race, and then superseded by the elaborate hieroglyph system of the dynastic race. . . .

"Turning now to the purely classical Egyptian work, the principal discoveries of the last few years have given us new leading examples in every line. The great copper statue of King Pepy, with his son, dates from before 3000 B. C. It is over life size, and entirely wrought in hammered copper, showing a complete mastery in metal work of the highest artistic power. . . . Many of the royal temples of the 19th dynasty at Thebes were explored by the English in 1896. The Ramessoum was completely examined, through all the maze of stone chambers around it. But the most important result was the magnificent tablet of black granite, about 10 feet high and 5 wide, covered on one side with an inscription of Amen Hotep III, and on the other side with an inscription of Merenptah. The latter account, of about 1200 B. C., mentions the war with the 'People of Israel'; this is the only naming of Israel on Egyptian records, and is several centuries earlier than any Assyrian record of the Hebrews. . . .

"One of the most important results of historical Egyptian times is the light thrown on prehistoric Greek ages. The pottery known as 'Mykenæan' since the discoveries of Schliemann in the Peloponnesus was first dated in Egypt at Gurob in 1889; next were found hundreds of vase fragments at Tell el Amarna in 1892; and since then several Egyptian kings' names have been found on objects in Greece, along with such pottery. The whole of this evidence shows that the grand age of prehistoric Greece, which can well compare with the art of classical Greece, began about 1600 B. C., was at its highest point about 1400 B. C., and became decadent about 1200 B. C., before its overthrow by the Dorian invasion. Besides this dating, Greece is indebted to Egypt for the preservation of the oldest texts of its classics." — W. M. Flinders Petrie, *Recent Years of Egyptian Exploration (Appleton's Popular Science Monthly*, Apr., 1900).

Still later, in an address at the annual meeting of the Egypt Exploration Fund, November 7, 1900, Professor Petrie summed up with succinctness the gains to our knowledge of a man from the later researches in Egypt rly How many controversies," he said, "had waged over Manetho! And now from the Royal tombs of Abydos we had seen and handled this summer the drinking bowls and furniture of the Kings of the first dynasty, even the property of Menes himself, the first King of United Egypt. The early Kings, whom we had scarcely believed in, even Mena who had been proclaimed a mythical version of the Cretan Minos and the Indian Manu, came now before us as real and as familiarly as the Kings of the 30th dynasty or of Saxon England; and never before had so remote a period been brought so completely before us as it had been in the work this year at Abydos. And how did Manetho and the State history of Seti bear the test? Five Kings we could already identify out of the eight recorded for the first dynasty. Those five are proved to have been recorded in their correct order, although the time of the first dynasty was so remote from even that of Seti that all the names had become slightly altered by transmission. It was to be remembered that the first dynasty was older to Seti than the Exodus was to us. Now that we were no longer afraid of our own rashness in assigning anything to a date before the fourth dynasty, and could deal with the earliest periods back to the first entry of agricultural man into Egypt, we could see more of the perspective of history. We saw palæolithic man scattering his massive flint weapons until the age of Nile mud (beginning about 7000 B. C.) made agriculture possible, and a Caucasian race ousted the palæolithic folks, whose portraits were left us in the figures found in the earliest graves. We saw this oldest race of man to have been of the Hottentot type, but even more hairy than the Hottentot, with the traces of his original Northern habitation not yet wiped off by tropical suns. Then we saw a rapidly rising civilization already knowing metals linked with the modern Kabyle both by bodily formation and by existing products. Next after some dozen generations we could trace strong Eastern or Semitic influence, which carried on this civilization to a higher point in many respects; and then decay set in and the first cycle that we could trace was completed. The next cycle began with the entry of the dynastic race from the Red Sea, possessing the elements of hieroglyphic writing and far more artistic sense and power than the earlier people. In some three or four centuries they had gradually conquered and invaded all the races scattered through Egypt — long-haired, short-haired, bearded and unbearded, clothed and unclothed; and the first King of all Egypt, who founded his new capital at the mouth of the valley, was Mena. The era of consolidation which preceded him was stated by Manetho as the dynasty of ten Kings of Abydos, who reigned for 800 years; it was a time of rapidly increasing civilization, during which most of the main features of Egyptian language, life, and art were stamped for 5,000 years to come. From the Royal tombs of Abydos we could see now how this art rose to its finest age in the middle of the first dynasty, and was decaying and becoming cheaper and more common by the end of that time. Probably we should see that this cycle was fading when some new impetus gave birth to the colossal ages of the pyramid builders. That grand period we now see to have been the third cycle of civilization and art, which was renewed again and again until we might see in the brilliance of the Fatimite dynasty the seventh of the great eras of Egypt. Such was the wider aspect of human history which the work solely of English exploration in Egypt now put before us. It might be safely said that there had never been a greater extension of knowledge of man's past in any decade than the discoveries of the last five years had unfolded. Details yet awaited us, but the main lines were all marked out, and their work of the future was to complete the picture of which we now had the full extent before us. What, now, would occupy the com-

ing winter was the exploration of the remaining Royal tombs."

Egypt: Discovery of a fragment of the Logia, or Sayings of Jesus.—During the winter of 1896-7, Messrs. Bernard P. Grenfell and Arthur S. Hunt conducted excavations for the Egypt Exploration Fund on the site of Oxyrhynchus, which was a flourishing city in the time of Roman rule in Egypt. Large quantities of papyri were found in the rubbish heaps of the town, and among them one fragment of special and remarkable interest,—as thus described by the discoverers, in a brief report, entitled "Sayings of Our Lord," published by the Egypt Exploration Fund in 1897 : "The document in question is a leaf from a papyrus book containing a collection of Logia or Sayings of our Lord, of which some, though presenting several novel features, are familiar, others are wholly new. It was found at the very beginning of our work upon the town, in a mound which produced a great number of papyri belonging to the first three centuries of our era, those in the immediate vicinity of our fragment belonging to the second and third centuries. This fact, together with the evidence of the handwriting, which has a characteristically Roman aspect, fixes with certainty 300 A. D. as the lowest limit for the date at which the papyrus was written. The general probabilities of the case, the presence of the usual contractions found in biblical MSS., and the fact that the papyrus was in book, not roll, form, put the first century out of the question, and made the first half of the second unlikely. The date therefore probably falls within the period 150–300 A. D. More than that cannot be said with any approach to certainty. . . . The fragment measures 5¾×3¾ inches, but its height was originally somewhat greater, as it is unfortunately broken at the bottom."

The following is a translation of the fragmentary sayings inscribed on the leaf :

" . . . and then shalt thou see clearly to cast out the mote that is in thy brother's eye."

"Jesus saith, Except ye fast to the world, ye shall in no wise find the kingdom of God ; and except ye keep the sabbath, ye shall not see the Father."

"Jesus saith, I stood in the midst of the world, and in the flesh was I seen of them, and I found all men drunken, and none found I athirst among them, and my soul grieveth over the sons of men, because they are blind in their heart. . . ."

"Jesus saith, Wherever there are . . . and there is one . . . alone, I am with him. Raise the stone and there thou shalt find me, cleave the wood and there am I."

"Jesus saith, A prophet is not acceptable in his own country, neither doth a physician work cures upon them that know him."

"Jesus saith, A city built upon the top of a high hill, and stablished, can neither fall nor be hid."

Egypt: New discoveries in the tombs of the Valley of the Kings.—In the Valley of the Kings, which extends along the west bank of the Nile, in the Libyan Mountains, opposite Luxor, M. Loret, director of the Egyptian explorations, discovered in 1898 the tombs of Thutmosis III. and Amenophis II., and in the following year made the more important discovery of the tomb of Thutmosis I., "the real founder of the eighteenth dynasty, who made Egypt one of the great empires of the ancient world." Professor Steindorf of the University of Leipsic, writing of this discovery to Professor Hilprecht of the University of Pennsylvania, remarked that its special importance "lies in the fact that Thutmosis I, the earliest king of the eighteenth dynasty, was also the first ruler to depart from the ancient custom of the Pharaohs, that of building in the desert lowland pyramidal tombs. For himself he had a tomb hewn out of rock in the mountains. His predecessor, Amenophis I, according to custom, built his tomb in the plain, near the present site of Drah-abul-negge, as we know from written records. Thutmosis I, on the contrary, chose for his last dwelling-place the lonely and majestic valley in the Libyan Mountains. For centuries the Pharaohs followed his example, and during the eighteenth, nineteenth, and twentieth dynasties were built those magnificent sepulchers which in Roman times were still among the greatest curiosities of ancient Thebes. . . .

"Chief among the articles that Mr. Loret found in the tomb is a remarkably well-preserved papyrus containing texts from the Book of the Dead, with colored pictures finely executed; also a chest in which were kept a draught-board, with a full set of draughtmen, and some garlands; likewise fruit, food, poultry, and beef. The last-mentioned articles, being intended for the sustenance of the dead, each one was wrapped in linen and enclosed in a wooden case, exactly corresponding to its form. Thirteen large earthen beer jars, most of which, with their seals, stood there unmarred, and a large number of other vessels, had contained the beverages necessary for the refreshment of the dead. Weapons, among others two artistically wrought leathern quivers containing arrows, and two beautiful armchairs, completed this strange stock of equipments. The most remarkable piece of all is a large and beautifully preserved couch, the like of which has never been found in any other tomb. It consists of a quadrangular wooden frame, overspread with a thick rush mat, and over this were stretched three layers of linen with a life-size figure of the god of death, Osiris, drawn upon the outer layer. The figure itself was smeared with some material intended to make the under layer waterproof. Over this, mingled with some adhesive substance, soil had been spread, in which barley was planted. The grains had sprouted, and had grown to the height of from two and a half to three inches. The whole, therefore, represented a couch whereon the dead Osiris lay figured in greensward. Verily, a striking poetical idea, the resurrection of the dead symbolized by the picture of the barley springing up. The whole tomb, with its numerous equipments, furnishes a very important contribution to the history of the methods of burial among the ancient Egyptians."—*Sunday School Times, July 8, 1899.*

Egypt: Fall of eleven columns of the great temple at Karnak.—"From Professor Georg Steindorff, of the University of Leipsic, comes the following: ' In the covered colonnade of the great temple at Karnak extensive restorations have lately been undertaken, rendered necessary by a most deplorable accident, which, about a year ago, befell this grandest of all Egyptian edifices. It occurred on the morning of October 3, 1899, in the colonnade which was built by Ramses I, Sethos I, and Ramses II, and which is doubtless familiar to all in engravings and photographs. In the northeastern part of this structure as many as eleven immense columns fell, and were totally wrecked, while several others are leaning over so that they might fall at any time. By this event the magnificent structure has been utterly ruined, and it now presents a dreary aspect. The cause of this catastrophe has not been definitely ascertained. The first thought was of an earthquake, but nothing of the sort was experienced elsewhere in Egypt on the morning of the day above mentioned. It is more likely that during the thirty-two hundred years of the building's existence, the material used in its construction had greatly deteriorated, and that this fact increased the possibility of a collapse. Then, also, in the main hall during recent years, the work of excavation and restoration was carried on with little regard for the dilapidated condition of the temple, which was weakened rather than strengthened by this work. But especially for the last four years, during the inundation of the Nile, the hall, by artificial means, has been flooded in order to extract and remove the salt which had formed. By this periodical flooding and drying of the ground the foundations have been very badly damaged. This, according to Dr. Borchardt, is the prime cause of the ruin. First the ground gave way under a column, which then toppled, and, in falling, brought down the others with it.

" ' We must recognize the zeal with which the Egyptian Government, especially the department of Egyptian Antiquities, with its Director-General, Professor Maspero, came to the rescue of the ill-fated edifice. To prevent further catastrophe, they first proceeded to remove the architraves from five of the endangered columns, and to reduce the height of the columns to about twenty feet. This was accomplished by filling with sand that portion of the hall in which the columns stood, and then rolling the separate parts down the inclined plane formed by the sand. The north portion of the pylon terminating the colonnade toward the east—that is, toward the Nile—had badly suffered by the disaster. There were cracks in it so large as to cause the fear that it might some day collapse. After prompt and thorough work this danger also was obviated. Later on the ruins of the eleven fallen columns are to be removed, and the foundations of the hall examined. Then everything possible will be done to make the ground solid, and the attempt will be made to erect again the ruined columns. But whether the beautiful colonnade will ever resume its former appearance, whether it will ever again make upon the visitor such an overpowering impression as formerly, may well be a matter of serious doubt. Ancient Thebes has lost one of its most beautiful monuments.' "
—*Sunday School Times, Dec. 1, 1900.*

Egypt: Discovery of the Serapeion at Alexandria.—"The excavations by Dr. Botti, the Director of the Alexandrian Museum, in the neighbourhood of Pompey's Pillar, have resulted in the discovery of the Serapeion, where the last of the great libraries of Alexandria was preserved. An elaborate account of his researches, with an admirable plan, has been given by the discoverer in a memoir on 'L'Acropole d'Alexandrie et le Sérapeum,' presented to the Archæological Society of Alexandria. . . . Dr. Botti was first led to make his explorations by a passage in the orator Aphthonios, who visited Alexandria about A. D. 315."—*Am. Journal of Archæology, January—March,* 1896.

Crete : Recent explorations.—Supposed discovery of the Palace of Minos and the Cretan Labyrinth.—Fresh light on prehistoric Greece and the origin of the alphabet.—Results of extraordinary importance have been already obtained from explorations in Crete, carried on during 1899 and 1900 by the British School at Athens, under the direction of Mr. D. G. Hogarth, and by Mr. Arthur J. Evans, of the Ashmolean Museum, working with the aid of a small Cretan Exploration Fund, raised in England. The excavations of both parties were carried on at Knossos, but the latter was the most fortunate, having opened the site of a prehistoric palace which is yielding remarkable revelations of the legendary age in Crete. In a communication to the "London Times" of October 31, 1900, Mr. Evans gave the following account of the results so far as then obtained :

"The discoveries that at Knossos throw into the shade all the other exploratory campaigns of last season in the Eastern Mediterranean, by whatever nationality conducted. It is not too much to say that the materials already gathered have revolutionized our knowledge of prehistoric Greece, and that to find even an approach to the results obtained we must go back to Schliemann's great discovery of the Royal tombs at Mycenae. The prehistoric site, of which some two acres have now been uncovered at Knossos, proves to contain a palace beside which those of Tiryns and Mycenae sink into insignificance. By an unhoped-for piece of good fortune the site, though in the immediate neighbourhood of the greatest civic centres of the island in ancient, medieval, and modern times, had remained practically untouched for over 3,000 years. At but a very slight depth below the surface of the ground the spade has uncovered great courts and corridors, propylaea, a long succession of magazines containing gigantic store jars that might have hidden the Forty Thieves, and a multiplicity of chambers, pre-eminent among which is the actual throne-room and council-chamber of Homeric kings. The throne itself, on which (if so much faith be permitted to us) Minos may have declared the law, is carved out of alabaster, once brilliant with coloured designs and relieved with curious tracery and crocketed arcading which is wholly unique in ancient art and exhibits a strange anticipation of 13th century Gothic. In the throne-room, the western entrance gallery, and elsewhere, partiy still adhering to the walls, partly in detached pieces on the floors, was a series of fresco paintings, excelling any known examples of the art in Mycenaean Greece. A beautiful life-size painting of a youth, with a European and almost classically Greek profile, gives us the first real knowledge of the race who produced this mysterious early civilization. Other frescoes introduce us to a lively and hitherto unknown miniature style, representing, among other subjects, groups of women engaged in animated conversation in the courts and on the balconies of the Palace. The monuments of the sculptor's art are equally striking. It may be sufficient to mention here a marble fountain in the shape of a

lioness's head with enamelled eyes, fragments of a frieze with beautifully cut rosettes, superior in its kind to anything known from Mycenae ; an alabaster vase naturalistically copied from a Triton shell ; a porphyry lamp with graceful foliation supported on an Egyptianising lotus column. The head and parts of the body of a magnificent painted relief of a bull in gesso duro are unsurpassed for vitality and strength.

"It is impossible here to refer more than incidentally to the new evidence of intercourse between Crete and Egypt at a very remote period supplied by the Palace finds of Knossos. It may be mentioned, however, as showing the extreme antiquity of the earlier elements of the building that in the great Eastern Court was found an Egyptian seated figure of diorite, broken above, which can be approximately dated about 2000 B. C. Below this again extends a vast Stone Age settlement which forms a deposit in some places 24 ft. in thickness.

"Neither is it possible here to dwell on the new indications supplied by some of the discoveries in the 'House of Minos' as to the cult and religious beliefs of its occupants. It must be sufficient to observe that one of the miniature frescoes found represents the façade of a Mycenaean shrine and that the Palace itself seems to have been a sanctuary of the Cretan God of the Double Axe, as well as a dwelling place of prehistoric kings. There can be little remaining doubt that this huge building with its maze of corridors and tortuous passages, its medley of small chambers, its long succession of magazines with their blind endings, was in fact the Labyrinth of later tradition which supplied a local habitation for the Minotaur of grisly fame. The great figures of bulls in fresco and relief that adorned the walls, the harem scenes of some of the frescoes, the corner stones and pillars marked with the labrys or double axe—the emblem of the Cretan Zeus, explaining the derivation of the name 'Labyrinth' itself—are so many details which all conspire to bear out this identification. In the Palace-shrine of Knossos there stands at last revealed to us the spacious structure which the skill of Daedalus is said to have imitated from the great Egyptian building on the shore of Lake Moeris, and with it some part at least of his fabled masterpieces still clinging to the walls.

"But, brilliant as are the illustrations thus recovered of the high early civilization of the City of Minos and of the substantial truth of early tradition, they are almost thrown into the shade by a discovery which carries back the existence of written documents in the Hellenic lands some seven centuries beyond the first known monuments of the historic Greek writing. In the chambers and magazines of the Palace there came to light a series of deposits of clay tablets, in form somewhat analogous to the Babylonian, but inscribed with characters in two distinct types of indigenous prehistoric script—one hieroglyphic or quasi-pictorial, the other linear. The existence of a hieroglyphic script in the island had been already the theme of some earlier researches by the explorer of the Palace, based on the more limited material supplied by groups of signs on a class of Cretan seal-stones, and the ample corroboration of the conclusions arrived at was, therefore, the more satisfactory. These Cretan hieroglyphs will be found to have a special importance in their bearing on the origin of the Phoenician alphabet.

"But the great bulk of the tablets belonged to the linear class, exhibiting an elegant and much more highly-developed form of script, with letters of an upright and singularly European aspect. The inscriptions, over 1,000 of which were collected, were originally contained in coffers of clay, wood, and gypsum, which had been in turn secured by clay seals impressed with finely-engraved signets and counter-marked and counter-signed by controlling officials in the same script while the clay was still wet. The clay documents themselves are, beyond doubt, the Palace archives. Many relate to accounts concerning the Royal Arsenal, stores, and treasures. Others, perhaps, like the contemporary cuneiform tablets, refer to contracts or correspondence. The problems attaching to the decipherment of these clay records are of enthralling interest, and we have here locked up for us materials which may some day enlarge the bounds of history."

In an earlier communication to "The Times" (September 15), Mr. Evans had explained more distinctly the importance of the clay tablets found at Knossos, as throwing light on the origin of the alphabet: "In my excavation of the prehistoric Palace at Knossos," he wrote, "I came upon a series of deposits of clay tablets, representing the Royal archives, the inscriptions on which belong to two distinct systems of writing — one hieroglyhic and quasi-pictorial; the other for the most part linear and much more highly developed. Of these the hieroglyphic class especially presents a series of forms answering to what, according to the names of the Phoenician letters, we must suppose to have been the original pictorial designs from which these, too, were derived. A series of conjectural reconstructions of the originals of the Phoenician letters on this line were in fact drawn out by my father, Sir John Evans, for a lecture on the origin of the alphabet given at the Royal Institution in 1872, and it may be said that two-thirds of these resemble almost line for line actual forms of Cretan hieroglyphics. The oxhead (Aleph), the house (Beth), the window (He), the peg (Vau), the fence (Cheth), the hand (Yod) seen sideways, the open palm (Kaph), the fish (Nun), the post or trunk (Samekh), the eye (Ain), the mouth, (Pe), the teeth (Shin), the cross-sign (Tau), not to speak of several other probable examples, are all literally reproduced.

"The analogy thus supplied is indeed overwhelming. It is impossible to believe that, while on one side of the East Mediterranean basin these alphabetic prototypes were naturally evolving themselves, the people of the opposite shore were arriving at the same result by a complicated process of selection and transformation of a series of hieratic Egyptian signs derived from quite different objects. The analogy with the Cretan hieroglyphic forms certainly weighs strongly in favour of the simple and natural explanation of the origin of the Phoenician letters which was held from the time of Gesenius onwards, and was only disturbed by the extremely ingenious, though over-elaborate, theory of De Rougé."

At the annual meeting of the subscribers to the British School at Athens, held in London, October 30, 1900, Mr. Hogarth, the Director, spoke with great enthusiasm of the significance of the Cretan discoveries already made, and of the promise of enlarged knowledge which they gave. He said: "The discovery made 25 years ago [by Schliemann] that no barbarians, but possessors of a very high and individual culture, preceded the Hellenic period in Greece — a culture which could not but have affected the Hellenic — had been developed in various ways since. It had been established that this culture had had a very long existence and development; it covered completely a large geographical area; it developed various local characteristics in art production which seemed to be gathered again into one by the typical art of Mycenae. But the most important historical points remained obscure. Where was the original home of this new civilization; what family did the race or races belong to; of what speech were they and what religions; what was the history of their societies and art during their dominance, and what became of them after? Neither mainland Greece nor the Aegean islands answered these. But there were two unknown quantities, Crete and Asia Minor, with Rhodes. One of these we have now attacked. Crete by its great size and natural wealth, its position, and its mythologic fame was bound to inform us of much. It is too early to say that the questions will all be answered by Crete, but already we have much light. The discovery of written documents and of shrines has told us more than any other evidence of the origin and family. The Knossos frescoes show us the racial type; the Dictaean, Cave, and Knossos houses illuminate the religion. New arts have been discovered, and the relation to Egypt and Asia are already far better understood. It remains now to find the early tombs, and clear the lower stratum of the Palace ruins at Knossos, to know more of the earliest Cretan race, to explore the east or 'Eteocretan' end of the island, to obtain light on the language and relations to Egypt and Asia, and to investigate the 'Geometric' period, which is the transition to the Hellenic."

Commenting in another place on the discoveries in Crete, Mr. Hogarth has pointed out their effect in modifying the ideas heretofore entertained of the importance of Phoenician influence in the rise of European civilization. "For many years now," he writes, "we have had before our eyes two standing protests against the traditional claim of Phoenicia to originate European civilization, and those protests come from two regions which Phoenician influence, travelling west, ought first to have affected, namely, Cyprus and Asia Minor. In both these regions exist remains of early systems of writing which are clearly not of Phoenician descent. Both the Cypriote syllabic script and the 'Hittite' symbols must have been firmly rooted in their homes before ever the convenient alphabet of Sidon and Tyre was known there. And now, since Mr. Evans has demonstrated the existence of two non-Phoenician systems of writing in Crete also, the use of one of which has been proved to extend to the Cyclades and the mainland of Greece, it has become evident that we have to deal in south-eastern Europe, as well as in Cyprus or Asia Minor, with a non-Phoenician influence of civilization which, since it could originate that greatest of achievements, a local script, was quite powerful enough to account by itself also for the local art.

"Those who continue to advocate the Phoenician claim do not seem sufficiently to realize that nowadays they have to take account neither only of the Homeric age nor only of even half a millennium before Homer, but of an almost geologic antiquity. Far into the third millennium B. C. at the very least, and more probably much earlier still, there was a civilization in the Aegean and on the Greek mainland which, while it contracted many debts to the East and to Egypt, was able to assimilate all that it borrowed, and to reissue it in an individual form, expressed in products which are not of the same character with those of any Eastern civilization that we know." — D. G. Hogarth, *Authority and Archaeology Sacred and Profane, pt. 2, pp. 237-238 (N. Y.: Chas. Scribner's Sons).*

" During the past season, Evans, discoverer of the now famous early Cretan systems of writing, Halbherr and other Italians, as well as the French, have been proving what was already foreshadowed, that in Crete we find in its purest form and in [all its historic and racial phases that Mediterranean civilization, — Pelasgic and Achæan,—that culminated in Tiryns and Mykenae. We now see that Homer sings of the closing years of a culture that dates back of the ' Trojan War' at least for fifteen hundred years. Crete is found to be covered with ruined Pelasgic cities, surrounded by gigantic polygonal walls, crowned by acropoli, adorned with royal palaces, defended by forts, connected by artificial highways, and with necropoli of vaulted tombs like those discovered by Schliemann at Mykenae. Already the royal palaces and libraries are being unearthed at Cnossos and ' Goulâs' with sculptures and decoration of the most novel description and early date. A literature in an unknown tongue and in undeciphered scripts is being found, to puzzle scholars as much perhaps as the Hittite and Etruscan languages. Some day these ' Pelasgic' documents will disclose the secrets of a neglected civilization and fill up the gap between early Eastern and Hellenic cultures." — A. L. Frothingham, Jr., *Archæological Progress (International Monthly, Dec.,* 1900).

India : Discovery of the birthplace, tomb and relics of Gautama Buddha. See (in this vol.) BUDDHA.

Troy : Later researches on the site.—" Dr. Doerpfeld finished in 1894 the exploration which he had begun in 1893 on the site of the excavations of Schliemann at Hissarlik (Troia). It appears to be established that Schliemann, carried away by his zeal, had overlooked the very end which he wished to attain, and that the burnt city, which he thought to be the real Troia, is a more ancient foundation going back beyond the year 2000 B. C. M. Doerpfeld discerned, in one of the layers of ruins (discovered but disregarded by Schliemann), a city which must be the Ilios of Priam contemporaneous with the Mykenai of Agamemnon ; he removed the surrounding walls, the towers, and some of the houses that filled it. It is to be understood that this little acropolis, analogous to that of Tiryns, is not the whole of the city but simply its citadel, which Homer called ' Pergamos.' It was surrounded, lower down, by a city reserved for the habitation of the common people, some traces of which also have) been found."—*Am. Journal of Archæology,* 1896.

Italy : Excavations at Antemnæ disclose what early Rome was probably like.—" We can show what the earliest Rome was, the Rome

of Romulus on the Palatine, and how it grew to be the City of the Seven Hills. The City itself, crowded with the wrecks of twenty-five centuries, preserves to-day few memorials of its earliest age ; but excavations made on two sites, one close to Rome, one a little further north in Etruria, explain the process very clearly. The traveller who approaches Rome by the Via Salaria sees, just where Tiber and Anio join, a modern fort on an isolated rock. Here was Antemnae, destroyed (according to legend) by Roman jealousy very soon after Rome itself was founded. The legend seems to be true, at least in substance. On this hilltop excavations have shown a little village within a wall of stone : it had its temple and senate-house, its water-cistern, and square huts, thatched or timbered, for dwelling-houses. The relics found there shew that the site was abandoned, never to be again inhabited, about the time at which the legend fixes the fall of Antemnae. Here we have Rome's earliest rival. From the rival we may guess what the earliest Rome was like on the Palatine rock, and what all the little Italian towns were in their infancy."—*F. Haverfield, Authority and Archaeology Sacred and Profane, pt. 2, pp.* 302-303 *(N. Y.: Chas. Scribner's Sons).*

Italy : The Etruscans.—" During the decade which is now ending, archaeology has thrown some light on this strange people. Researches in North Italy prove that it never entered the Peninsula from the north. Researches in Etruria itself prove that the earliest Etruscan civilization resembled that which prevailed in the Eastern Mediterranean in the last days of the Aegean period. After all, the old legends were right. The ancients told how the Etruscans came from the east : archaeological evidence is now accumulating to confirm the legends. Precisely when they came or why is still obscure, nor can we identify them yet with any special tribe in prehistoric Greece, Pelasgian or other. Probably they were driven from their old homes, like the Phoenicians who built Carthage and the Phocaeans who built Marseilles."—*F. Haverfield, Authority and Archaeology Sacred and Profane, pt. 2, p.* 305 *(N. Y.: Chas. Scribner's Sons).*

Italy : Sunken Roman vessels in Lake Nemi.—" A discovery during 1895 which made a great sensation throughout Italy, was that of the famous Roman vessels which had been sunk for so many centuries at the bottom of Lake Nemi, the existence of which has been known or suspected ever since the fifteenth century, notwithstanding many sceptics."—*Am. Journal of Archæology, July—September,* 1896.

Syria : Ruined cities of the Roman Province.—An important exploration of ruined cities in the old Roman provinces of Syria and Arabia was conducted by an American archæological expedition organized in 1899. Mr. Howard Crosby Butler, of Princeton, was in charge of the studies made in architecture, sculpture and archæological matters generally ; Professor William K. Prentice devoted attention to classical inscriptions, of which a great number were found, while Semitic inscriptions were the subjects of the study of Dr. Enno Littmann, of the University of Halle. The ruins of thirty-three cities, nearly all of them evident places of large population in their day, were visited in regions now too bare of productive soil to support even the small nomadic population of the present day.

"The desert conditions have preserved the cities intact as they stood at the time when they appear to have been abandoned, in the beginning

ARCTIC EXPLORATION, Recent. See (in this vol.) POLAR EXPLORATION.

ARGENTINE REPUBLIC: A. D. 1895.— Census.—"According to the census, the number of persons in the Argentine Republic on May 10, 1895, was 4,042,990; the estimated number of Argentines outside the boundaries of the Republic on that day is placed at 50,000, thus making the total population 4,092,990." Of this population 663,854 is in the city of Buenos Ayres. "The increase in the population between September 15, 1869 (the last census), and May 10, 1895 (the date on which the present census was taken), has been 2,218,776, equivalent to an increase of 120 per cent, or an annual increase of 4.6 per cent. The urban population of the Republic has increased 1,045,944. . . . It is estimated that there are 345,393 foreigners in the city of Buenos Ayres, and that the total number of foreigners in the Republic is about 1,000,000. . . . Among the Argentine portion of the population, the females exceed the males in number, while it is estimated that two-thirds of the foreign population are males."—*United States Consular Rep'ts, Nov.*, 1896, *p.* 438.

A. D. 1895.—Resignation of President Peña.—President Saenz Peña having refused to issue, at the request of Congress, a decree of amnesty, extended to all persons implicated in the last revolution, his Cabinet resigned (January 16), and he found it impossible to form another. Thereupon the President himself resigned his office, on the 22d of January, and his resignation was accepted by the Congress. Señor Uriburu was elected President on the following day, and promptly issued the desired decree.

A. D. 1898.—Settlement of boundary dispute with Chile.—Election of President.—"A long unsettled dispute as to the extended boundary between the Argentine Republic and Chile, stretching along the Andean crests from the southern border of the Atacama Desert to Magellan Straits, nearly a third of the length of the South American continent, assumed an acute stage in the early part of the year, and afforded to this Government occasion to express the hope that the resort to arbitration, already contemplated by existing conventions between the parties, might prevail despite the grave difficulties arising in its application. I am happy to say that arrangements to this end have been perfected, the questions of fact upon which the respective commissioners were unable to agree being in course of reference to Her Britannic Majesty for determination. A residual difference touching the northern boundary line across the Atacama Desert, for which existing treaties provided no adequate adjustment, bids fair to be settled in like manner by a joint commission, upon which the United States Minister at Buenos Aires has been invited to serve as umpire in the last resort."—*Message of the President of the U. S. of Am., Dec.*, 1898.—The arbitration of the United States Minister, Hon. William I. Buchanan, proved successful in the matter last referred to, and the Atacama boundary was quickly determined.

In June, 1898, General Julio Roca was elected

of the seventh century." Some account of the expedition and its work is given in the "New York Tribune" of February 3, 1901.

President and assumed the office in October. In July a treaty of arbitration was concluded with the government of Italy, which provides that there shall be no appeal from the decision of the arbitrators.

ARGON, The Discovery of. See (in this vol.) SCIENCE, RECENT : CHEMISTRY AND PHYSICS.

ARICA, The question concerning. See (in this vol.) CHILE : A. D. 1894–1900.

ARMENIA: A. D. 1895-1899.—Revolt against Turkish oppression.—Massacres and atrocities of the conflict.—Final concessions. See (in this vol.) TURKEY: A. D. 1895 ; 1896 (JANUARY—MARCH) ; 1896 (AUGUST) ; 1899 (OCTOBER).

A. D. 1896.—Attack of Armenian revolutionists on the Ottoman Bank and subsequent massacre of Armenians in Constantinople. See (in this vol.) TURKEY : A. D. 1896 (AUGUST).

ARMIES, European and American: Their numbers and cost compared. See (in this vol.) WAR BUDGETS.

ARMY ADMINISTRATION, American: Investigation of. See (in this vol.) UNITED STATES OF AM. : A. D. 1898–1899.

ARMY CANTEEN, Abolition of the American. See (in this vol.) UNITED STATES OF AM. : A. D. 1901 (FEBRUARY).

ARMY, United States: Act to increase to 100,000 men. See (in this vol.) UNITED STATES OF AM.: A. D. 1901 (FEBRUARY).

ASHANTI: British occupation of the country.—Rising of the tribes.—Siege and relief of Kumassi.—In 1895, King Prempeh, of Ashanti, provoked a second expedition of British troops against his capital, Kumassi, or Coomassie (for some account of the former expedition see, in vol. 2, ENGLAND : A. D. 1873–1880), by persistence in slave-catching raids and in human sacrifices, and by other violations of his treaty engagements. Late in the year a strong force was organized in Gold Coast Colony, mostly made up of native troops. It marched without resistance to Kumassi, which it entered on the 17th of January, 1896. Prempeh made complete submission, placing his crown at the feet of the Governor of the Gold Coast ; but he was taken prisoner to Sierra Leone. A fort was built and garrisoned in the center of the town, and the country was then definitely placed under British protection, politically attached to the Gold Coast Colony. It submitted quietly to the practical conquest until the spring of 1900, when a fierce and general rising of the tribes occurred. It was said at the time that the outbreak was caused by efforts of the British to secure possession of a "golden stool" which King Prempeh had used for his throne, and which had been effectually concealed when Kumassi was taken in 1896 ; but this has been denied by Sir Frederic Hodgson, the Governor of the Gold Coast. "The 'golden stool,'" he declared, "was only an incident in the affair and had nothing to do with the cause of the rising, which had been brewing for a long time. In his opinion the Ashantis had been preparing ever since the British occupation in 1896 to reassert their independence." The Governor was, himself, in Kumassi when the Ashantis first attacked it, on the 25th of March, and he has given an account of the desperate position in which the few British officials, with their small native garrison and the refugees whom they tried to protect, were placed. "Our force," said Sir Frederic Hodgson, "consisted of only some 200 Hausas, while there is reason to believe that we had not less than 15,000 Ashantis surrounding us. In addition to our own force we had to protect some 3,500 refugees, chiefly Mahomedan traders, Fantis, and loyal Kumassis, none of whom we were able to take into the fort, where every available bit of space was required for military purposes. It was heartrending to see the efforts of these poor people to scale the walls or break through the gate of the fort, and we had to withdraw the Hausas from the cantonments and draw a cordon round the refugees. It is impossible to describe the horror of the situation with these 3,500 wretched people huddled together without shelter under the walls of the fort. That same night a tornado broke over Kumassi, and the scene next morning with over 200 children was too terrible for words. Afterwards they were able to arrange shelters for themselves." Near the end of April, two small reinforcements from other posts reached Kumassi; but while this strengthened the numbers for defence, it weakened the food supply. Taking stock of their food, the besieged decided that they could hold out until June 23, and that if the main body then marched out, to cut, if possible, their way through the enemy, leaving a hundred men behind, the latter might keep the fort until July 15. This, accordingly, was done. On the 23d of June Governor Hodgson, with all but 100 men, stole away from Kumassi, by a road which the Ashantis had not guarded, and succeeded in reaching the coast, undergoing great hardships and dangers in the march. Meantime, an expedition from Cape Coast Castle was being energetically prepared by Colonel Sir J. Willcocks, who overcame immense difficulties and fought his way into Kumassi on July 15, the very day on which the food-supply of the little garrison was expected to give out. The following account of his entry into Kumassi is from Colonel Willcocks' official report : "Forming up in the main road, we marched towards Kumassi, a mile distant, the troops cheering wildly for the Queen and then followed silence. No sound came from the direction of the fort, which you cannot see till quite close. For a moment the hideous desolation and silence, the headless bodies lying everywhere, the sickening smell, &c., almost made one shudder to think what no one dared to utter—'Has Kumassi fallen ? Are we too late ?' Then a bugle sound caught the ear —'the g   salute'—the tops of the towers appeared and again every man in the column, white and black, broke into cheers long sustained. The brave defenders had at last seen us ; they knew for hours past from the firing growing ever nearer that we were coming, yet they dared not open their only gate ; they perforce must wait, for even as we appeared the enemy were making their last efforts to destroy the outlying buildings, and were actually setting them on fire until after dark, when a party of 100 men went out and treated them to volleys and cleared

them out. If I have gone too fully into details of the final scene, the occasion was one that every white man felt for him comes perhaps but once, and no one would have missed it for a kingdom."

ASPHYXIATING SHELLS: Declaration against. See (in this vol.) Peace Conference.

ASSASSINATIONS : Of President Barrios. See (in this vol.) Central America (Guatemala): A. D. 1897–1898.
Of President Borda. See (in this vol.) Uruguay : A. D. 1896–1899.
Of Canovas del Castillo. See (in this vol.) Spain: A. D. 1897 (August—October).
Of Empress Elizabeth of Austria. See (in this vol.) Austria-Hungary : A. D. 1898 (September).
Of Governor Goebel. See (in this vol.) Kentucky: A. D. 1895–1900.
Of President Heureaux. See (in this vol.) Dominican Republic : A. D. 1899.
Of King Humbert. See (in this vol.) Italy : A. D. 1899–1900; and 1900 (July—September).
Of Professor Mihaileano. See (in this vol.) Balkan and Danubian States.
Of Nâsr-ed-din, Shah of Persia. See (in this vol.) Persia : A. D. 1896.
Of M. Stambouloff. See (in this vol.) Balkan and Danubian States (Bulgaria).

ASSIOUT, Nile barrage at. See (in this vol.) Egypt: A. D. 1898–1901.

ASSOCIATIONS BILL, The French. See (in this vol.) France: A. D. 1901.

ASSOUAN, Nile barrage at. See (in this vol.) Egypt: A. D. 1898–1901.

ASSUMPTIONIST FATHERS, Dissolution of the Society of the. See (in this vol.) France : A. D. 1899–1900 (August—January).

ATACAMA, The question concerning. See (in this vol.) Chile : A. D. 1894–1900.

ATBARA, Battle of the. See (in this vol.) Egypt: A. D. 1897–1898.

ATHENS: A. D. 1896.—The revival of Olympic games.—As the result of a movement instituted in France by the Baron de Coubertin, an interesting attempt to give athletic sports the spirit and semblance of the ancient Olympic games was made at Athens in the spring of 1896. A number of wealthy Greeks in different parts of the world joined generously in the undertaking, one gentleman especially, M. Averoff, of Alexandria, bearing the cost of a restoration in marble of the stadium at Athens, for the occasion. The games were held in April, from the 6th to the 15th, and were witnessed by a great number of people. Besides Greek competitors, there were 42 from Germany, 23 from England, 21 from America, 15 from France. The great event of the occasion was the long foot-race from Marathon to Athens, which was won by a young Greek.

The U. S. Consul at Athens, writing of the reconstruction of the ancient stadium for the games, described the work as follows :
"The stadium may be described as an immense open air amphitheater constructed in a natural ravine, artificially filled in at the end. It is in the shape of an elongated horseshoe. The spectators, seated upon the sloping sides of the ravine,

look down into the arena below, which is a little over 600 feet in length and about 100 feet wide at the widest part. . . . The stadium, as rebuilt for the games, will consist of (1) the arena, bounded by a marble curbing, surmounted by an iron railing adorned with Athenian owls; (2) a walk between this curbing and the first row of seats; (3) a low retaining wall of marble on which rests the first row of seats, the entire row being of marble; (4) the seats; (5) the underground tunnel. In addition to these features there will be an imposing entrance, a surrounding wall at the top of the hill, and two supporting walls at the entrance. As far as possible, in the reconstruction of the stadium, the old portions will be used, where these are in a sufficient state of preservation, and an effort will be made to reproduce, as nearly as practicable, the ancient structure. The seats at present will not all be made of pentelic marble, as there is neither time nor money for such an undertaking. At the closed end of the arena, seventeen rows will be made of pentelic marble, as well as the first row all the way around. The remaining rows up to the first aisle are being constructed of Piræus stone. These will accommodate 25,000 seated spectators. From this aisle to the top

will be placed wooden benches for 30,000 seated spectators. Add to these standing room for 5,000, and we have the holding capacity of the stadium 60,000 without crowding." — *United States Consular Reports, March*, 1896, *pp.* 353-54.

ATLANTA: A. D. 1895.—The Cotton States and International Exposition.—An important exposition, named as above, was held with great success at Atlanta, Georgia, from the 18th of September until the end of the year 1895. The exhibits from Mexico and many of the Central and South American States were extensive and interesting; but the main interest and value of the exposition were in its showing of the industrial resources of the Southern States of the American Union, and of the recent progress made in developing them.

AUSGLEICH, The. See (in this vol.) Aus-TRIA-HUNGARY: FINANCIAL RELATIONS; and A. D. 1897 (OCTOBER—DECEMBER).

AUSTRAL ISLANDS: Annexation to France.—The Austral or Tubuai Islands were formally annexed to France by the Governor of Tahiti, on the 21st of August, 1900.

AUSTRALIA.

Recent extensions of Democracy in the Australian Colonies and New Zealand.—Social experiments.—"The five colonies of the Australian continent, Tasmania, and New Zealand constitute seven practically independent commonwealths under the British crown. Australians and New Zealanders have therefore been able to develop their countries along their own lines, and have surpassed all other Anglo-Saxon nations in the number and variety of functions which the state is called upon to perform. . . . The railways almost without exception, and all the telegraph and telephone lines, are in the hands of the community. In the few cases in which there is private ownership of railways, a particular line was demanded at a certain time, and the government were not then in a position to borrow the funds required for its construction. Western Australia has recently purchased the entire property of one of the two private undertakings in the colony. A mass of sanitary and industrial legislation also has been placed upon the statute book. "Again, South Australia, Victoria, Western Australia, and New Zealand lend money to settlers at low rates of interest; South Australia sells its wines in London; Queensland facilitates the erection of sugar mills; Victoria and South Australia have given a bonus upon the exportation of dairy produce; South Australia, New Zealand, and Victoria receive the produce, grade and freeze it free of charge, or at a rate which barely covers the expenses; Victoria contributes toward the erection of butter factories; Victoria and New Zealand have subsidized the mining industry; and Western Australia has adopted a comprehensive scheme for the supply of water to the Coolgardie gold fields. In all the colonies the national system of primary education is compulsory and undenominational. In South Australia, Victoria, Queensland, and New Zea-

land it is also free. In the other colonies fees are charged, which may be remitted wholly or partly if parents are unable to pay them. Assistance is given in most cases for the promotion of secondary, technical, and university education. New Zealand and South Australia have appointed public trustees. New Zealand has long possessed a department of life insurance. "Finally, . . . New Zealand has adopted a system of old-age pensions. A pension of seven shillings a week is to be given to every person above the age of sixty-five years, provided he or she has lived in the colony for twenty-five years, and is able to pass a certain test in regard to sobriety and general good conduct. . . . In South Australia direct taxation takes two forms. There is an income tax at the rate of four and a half pence in the pound up to £800, and of sixpence in the pound above £800 of taxable amount resulting from personal exertions, and at the rate of ninepence and one shilling in the pound respectively on incomes from property. Incomes between £125 and £425 enjoy exemption on £125 of the amount. Again, there is a tax on the unimproved value of land of one halfpenny in the pound up to, and one penny above, the capital value of £5000. . . . "Similar taxation is to be found in New Zealand, and includes both a progressive income tax and a tax on land values which is more highly graduated than that of South Australia. . . . All improvements are excluded from the assessment of the taxable amount. . . . If the owner of the property is dissatisfied with the assessment of the government, he can call upon them to buy it of him at their own valuation. In only one case has such an extreme step been taken; and it is pleasant to find that it has resulted in an annual profit of nearly five per cent upon the outlay, and that the land which formerly gave employment to a few shepherds is now occupied by a large number of thriving settlers. I may add that when the government deem that an estate is not being developed as it should be by its owners, they are authorized by statute to purchase it—by negotiation if possible, otherwise at a price paid by an impartial tribunal—with a view to its subdivision into small holdings suitable to the requirements of the community. This system of taxation, it will be said with some truth, is based upon the teachings of Henry George. He travelled in Australia and New Zealand, and was listened to with attention ; but, while he looked to the ultimate absorption of the whole unearned increment, his hearers in the antipodes dissociated themselves from his conclusions, though they appreciated the value of his premises. Consequently, while accepting his principles, they did not hesitate to exempt small properties from the tax, and to increase its rate progressively in relation to the amount of the unimproved value. . . .

"One of the most hopeful signs of the day is that, with the help of the representatives of labor in Parliament, Australian governments have done much within recent years to mitigate the excess of population in the large towns, and to replace the unemployed upon the land. Of course mistakes have been made. In some cases settlers have failed through lack of agricultural knowledge ; in others, on account of the barrenness of the soil. In South Australia, the village settlements, which were avowedly started as an alternative to relief works, have been only a modified success. In New Zealand, village settlements have produced very satisfactory results. . . . In Victoria, a labor colony has been established, with the entire support of the trades-unionists, to which the unemployed may be sent, and at which they receive, at a very low rate of wages, a course of instruction in agricultural pursuits which enables them subsequently to obtain private employment with farmers or others. In New Zealand, I found a very strong feeling among trades-unionists that it would be to the interest of the workingmen themselves if a penal colony were established, on the lines of those which exist in Germany, to which loafers might be sent, and at which they would be compelled to work, with the alternative of starvation."—H. De R. Walker, *Australasian Extensions of Democracy* (*Atlantic Monthly*, May, 1899).—See also (in this vol.), NEW ZEALAND : A. D. 1891-1900.

Western Australia: The Outlander problem in Australia.—"Here we have a problem in many respects similar to that which has distracted South Africa. In several particulars the resemblance is startlingly close. . . . Many of the elements of disorder in the two continents are the same. In Western Australia, as in the Transvaal, there is a large population of mining residents, who complain that they are treated like 'helots'—to use Sir Alfred Milner's term—by the privileged agricultural burghers. They urge that they are denied fair representation, so that the burghers monopolise political power ; that the administration is in the hands of a knot of politicians and place-hunters at Perth—I had almost written Pretoria ; that they have made the colony wealthy by their enterprise and capital, only to see a large part of the fruits of their industry drawn from them by excessive taxation, which is expended mainly outside their

own district; that they are burdened by oppressive railway rates and denied access to the port which is the natural outlet to the Goldfields, and so on. The Kalgoorlie 'Uitlanders,' like the Johannesburgers, have sent a petition to the Queen, signed by a larger number of persons than those who forwarded the famous memorial which set the ball rolling in South Africa and led to the Bloemfontein Conference. The case is fully and temperately set forth in this petition, and in the Manifesto of the Eastern Goldfields Reform League of Western Australia, both of which documents are in the last Bluebook relating to Australian Federation. The same official compilation contains a statement to Mr. Chamberlain from Dr. Paget Thurston, in which the parallel between West Australia and the Transvaal is asserted with the most uncompromising directness. 'We have here,' says the writer, 'a Boer and Outlander question almost parallel to that in the Transvaal. As an Outlander I appeal to you.' Dr. Thurston adds : 'The old West Australians openly speak as if the colony was theirs, and we were interlopers who have no course open to us but to leave the colony if we are dissatisfied.' This has a very familiar sound, and so has the following : 'The great bulk of the taxation is levied through duties on food and drink. As the Boer party includes all the agricultural producers, and the Outlanders include the great bulk of the consumers, this acts injuriously on us in two ways. It puts a frightful load on the Outlander taxpayer, and enables the Boer producer to command a very high price for his food-stuffs. Owing to the limitation of the market by excessive protection, many articles of common use reach famine prices at times. In the three years I have been here, for instance, potatoes have been £22 10s. a ton ; apples, 2s. 6d. a pound ; oranges, 5s. a dozen ; new-laid eggs, 4s. a dozen (at the time of writing, 3s. 6d.). Fresh butter is practically unobtainable for ten months in the year, and common country wine (such as I used to buy for 3d. and 4d. a bottle in the Canary Islands) is here 2s. a bottle. I ask you, Sir, whether any other place in Her Majesty's Empire (not physically inaccessible) can show prices one half as high during the past three years ?'

"Nor does the ominous kind of hint that preceded the Jameson Raid fail to be uttered. Only three terminations, according to Dr. Thurston, are possible if Sir John Forrest does not modify his Krugerite policy towards the mining settlers : '(1) Separation of the goldfields.—This would be only fair to the goldfields ; but thousands of Outlanders have settled in the other parts of the colony, and this step would not redress their wrongs. The practical result of this step would be prosperity for the goldfields, but almost ruin for the rest of the colony. (2) Revolution.—I fear this is much more probable than is generally thought. Unless a material change takes place quickly there will be bloodshed in this colony. (3) General depression, practically equivalent to bankruptcy.' Separation, however, and the creation of a new colony, which would include the Goldfields district and come down to the sea, and would immediately join the Australian Federation, is the remedy officially proposed by the representatives of the Outlanders. . . .

"The Colonial Secretary has deferred his final

answer to the Goldfields Petition until the comments of the Perth Ministry upon that document have been received and considered. But he has sent a provisional reply to the representatives of the petitioners in London. He sees the solution of the matter in getting Western Australia somehow into the new Commonwealth. In a communication to Mr. Walter Griffiths, one of the Goldfields delegates, the Colonial Secretary says: 'The decision of the Government of Western Australia to summon Parliament immediately with the view to the passing of a measure for the submission of the Commonwealth Bill to the electors of the colony has removed the chief of the grievances put forward in the petition and has opened up an early prospect of obtaining the object which the petitioners had in view. An answer will be returned to the petition after a careful consideration of its terms and of the comments of the Government of the colony thereon, but Mr. Chamberlain trusts that before an answer can be returned the people of the colony will have decided to join the Commonwealth, for the government of which, in that event, it will be to deal with the grievances alleged in the petition in so far as they are not exclusively within the province of the Parliament and Government of Western Australia.' In other words, let the Federation dispose of the matter. But the delegates point out that this might not remove their grievances. The Federal Parliament would have no power to compel the dominant party in the Perth Assembly either to redistribute seats fairly, or divide the colony, so as to create 'Home Rule for the Rand.' True, we should have washed our hands of the affair, and could tell the malcontent Uitlanders that it was none of our business. But if Perth still remained obstinate, and Coolgardie in consequence began to carry out some of those ugly projects hinted at by Dr. Thurston, it might become our business in an embarrassing fashion. At any rate, it does not seem quite fair to the new Commonwealth to start it in life with this grave question, still unsettled, upon its hands."—S. Low, *Enigmas of Empire* (*Nineteenth Century, June*, 1900).

New South Wales: **A. D. 1894-1895.**—Defeat of the Protectionist policy.—Adoption of a liberal **tariff.**—At the general elections of July, 1894, in New South Wales, the tariff issue was sharply defined. "'Protection' was inscribed on the banners of the ministerial party, led by the then Premier, Sir George Dibbs, while the aggressive opposition, led by Mr. Reid, . . . fought under the banner of 'free trade.' The Free Traders won the battle in that election, as there were 63 Free Traders, 40 Protectionists, and 22 labor members, mostly with free-trade leanings, returned. On the reassembling of Parliament, Sir George Dibbs was confronted with a large majority, and Mr. George H. Reid was called to form a government on the lines suggested by the issues of the campaign. The Council or 'upper house,' consisting of Crown nominees for life, rejected the measures suggested by Mr. Reid and passed by the Assembly by an overwhelming majority, and Mr. Reid dissolved Parliament on July 6, 1895, and appealed to the country. The election was held on July 24, and again the issues, as set forth in the measures, were fought out vigorously. The great leader of protection, Sir George Dibbs, with several

of his ablest followers, was defeated, and the so-called Free Trade party came back, much stronger than before. Thus, it was claimed that the mandate of the people, declaring for free trade and direct taxation, had been reaffirmed, and on the reassembling of Parliament, on August 13, the same measure, as passed by the Assembly and rejected by the Council, was again presented and passed by the Assembly by a majority of 50 to 26, and again went to the upper house. Again it was met with great hostility, but the Government party in that chamber, having been augmented by ten new appointments, the temper of the house was softened and the bill was passed with some two hundred and fifty amendments. As the Assembly could only accept some eighty of these without yielding material points . . . a conference was suggested, which, after several days of discussion, agreed to a modified measure, embracing the principle of free trade, as interpreted in this colony, and direct taxation, and the new law goes into effect as above stated, on January 1, 1896.

" It may be well here to remark that there are a few articles, notably raw sugar, glucose, molasses, and treacle, upon which the duty will be removed gradually, so as not to wantonly disturb vested interests, but, with these exceptions, the change is a very sweeping one."—*United States Consular Reports, June*, 1896, *p.* 299.

New South Wales: **A. D. 1896.**—Change in the government of Norfolk Island.—Its reannexation to **New** South Wales.—A change in the government of Norfolk Island was proclaimed in November, 1896, by the Governor of New South Wales, who came to the island, acting under directions from the British Colonial Office, and announced that "Her Majesty's Government has decided to appoint a resident magistrate. The object sought is to secure the impartial administration of justice, while leaving the local and municipal affairs of the island to be conducted by a council representing the inhabitants. In consideration of the fact that the Norfolk Island settlement originally formed part of the administrative colony of New South Wales, and that the legal business of the island and the registration of all land titles and transfers have uniformly been conducted by the Government departments at Sydney, Her Majesty's Government has decided to transfer the administration of the island to the Government of New South Wales. The Government of New South Wales has accepted the charge and as soon as the necessary arrangements have been completed Norfolk Island will be administered by the governor of New South Wales in council." " It will thus be seen that the Pitcairn community, which, for more than one hundred years, has governed itself by its own laws, is now abolished and that a new era has begun. The governor's legal right to annul the constitution given by the Queen when the community emigrated from Pitcairn was questioned. A deputation was appointed to wait on the governor, but he refused to discuss the subject further."—*United States Consular Reports, May*, 1897, *p.* 37.

A. D. 1897.—Conference of colonial premiers with the British Colonial Secretary. See (in this vol.) ENGLAND: A. D. 1897 (JUNE—JULY).

A. D. 1900.—Federation of the Australian Colonies.—The steps by which the Union

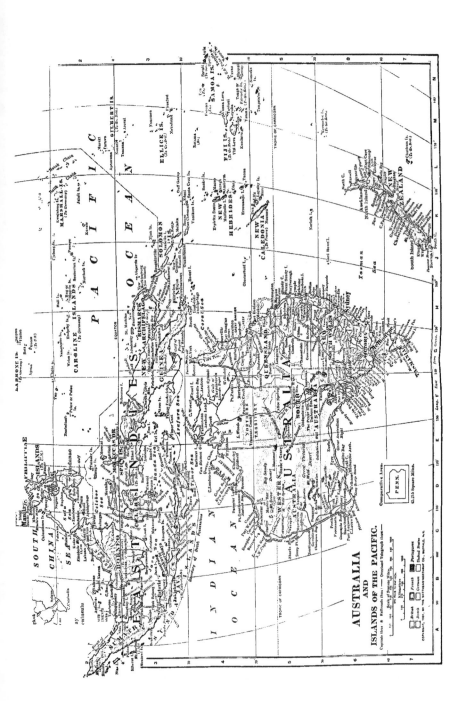

AUSTRALIA
AND
ISLANDS OF THE PACIFIC.

was accomplished.—**Passage of the " Commonwealth of Australia Constitution Act "** by the Imperial Parliament.—" The first indication of a plan for united action among the colonies is to be found in a proposal of Earl Grey in 1850. The main object of the proposal was to bring about uniformity in colonial tariffs; but, though partially adopted, it came to nothing. From 1850 to 1860 the project of federation was discussed from time to time in several of the colonial legislatures, and committees on the subject were appointed. But there seems to have been little general interest in the question, and up to 1860 all efforts in the direction of federation met with complete failure. Shortly after, however, a new form of united action, less ambitious but more likely of success, was suggested and adopted. From 1863 to 1883 conferences of colonial ministers were held at various times to discuss certain specified topics, with a view to introducing identical proposals in the separate colonial legislatures. Six of these conferences were held at Melbourne and three at Sydney; and one also was held at Hobart in 1895, though the period of the real activity of the conference scheme practically closed in 1883. The scheme proved a failure, because it was found impossible to carry out the measures concerted in the conferences. But material events were doing more than could any public agitation to draw attention to the advantages of closer union. The colonies were growing in population and wealth, railroads were building and commerce was extending. The inconveniences of border customs duties suggested attempts at something like commercial reciprocity between two or more colonies. New political problems also helped to arouse public interest. Heretofore there had been little fear of foreign aggression and, hence, no feeling of the need of united action for common defense; nor had there been any thought of the extension of Australian power and interests beyond the immediate boundaries of the different colonies. But the period from 1880 to 1890 witnessed a change in this respect. It was during this period that much feeling was aroused against the influx of French criminals, escaped from the penal settlements in New Caledonia. The difficulties in regard to New Guinea belong also to this decade. Suspicion of the designs of Germany upon that part of the island of New Guinea nearest the Dutch boundary led to the annexation of its eastern portion by the Queensland government. This action was disavowed by the British government under Gladstone, and the fears of the colonists were ridiculed; but almost immediately after the northern half of New Guinea was forcibly taken possession of by Germany. The indignation of Australians was extreme, and the opinion was freely expressed that the colonies would have to unite to protect their own interests. Finally, this was the time of the French designs on the New Hebrides Islands and of German movements with reference to Samoa. These conditions, economic and political, affected all the colonies more or less intimately and resulted in the first real, though loose, form of federal union. At the instigation of the Honorable James Service, premier of Victoria, a convention met at Sydney, November, 1883, composed of delegates from all the colonial governments. This convention adopted a bill providing for the

establishment of a Federal Council, with power to deal with certain specified subjects and with such other matters as might be referred to it by two or more colonies. . . . New South Wales and New Zealand refused to agree to the bill, but it was adopted by the other colonies; and the Imperial Parliament, in 1885, passed an act permitting such a Council to be called into existence at the request of any three colonies, to be joined by other colonies as they saw fit. Meetings of the Council took place in 1886, 1888, 1889 and 1891, but very little was accomplished. That the Federal Council was a very weak affair is obvious. . . . Meanwhile, interest in a more adequate form of federation was growing. In 1890 Sir Henry Parkes proposed a plan for federal union of a real and vigorous sort. At his suggestion, a conference met at Melbourne, February 6, 1890, to decide on the best method of getting the question into definite shape for consideration. . . . Provision was made . . . for the calling of a convention to draw up a constitution. . . . In accordance with the decision of the conference, delegates from the several colonies convened at Sydney, March 2, 1891; and with the work of this convention began the third and final stage in the federation movement. The Sydney convention formulated a bill, embodying a draft of a federal constitution, and then resolved that provision should be made by the several parliaments to submit it to the people in such manner as each colony should see fit. . . . But there was no sufficient external pressure to bring about an immediate discussion and an early settlement. . . . The result was that nothing was done. . . . Meanwhile, federation leagues had been organized in different colonies, and in 1893 delegates from a number of these leagues met at Bendigo, Victoria. . . . After adopting the bill of 1891 as a basis of discussion, the Bendigo conference resolved to urge the colonial governments to pass uniform enabling acts for a new convention—its members to be elected by popular vote—to frame a constitution which should be submitted to the people for approval. This proposal met with general favor and resulted in the calling of a meeting of the premiers of all the colonies at Hobart in January, 1895. There an enabling bill was drafted which five premiers agreed to lay before their respective parliaments. . . . It took two years to get this machinery into working order. At length, however, the requisite authority was granted by five colonies : New South Wales, Victoria, South Australia, Western Australia and Tasmania, Queensland and New Zealand declining to participate. On March 22, 1897, the second constitutional convention assembled at Adelaide. This convention drew up a new federal constitution, based upon the draft of 1891. Between May 5 and September 2 the constitution was discussed in each of the parliaments. When the convention reassembled at Sydney on March 2, as many as 75 amendments were reported as suggested by the different colonies. Many were of an insignificant character and many were practically identical. The constitution and proposed amendments were discussed in two sessions of the convention, which finally adjourned March 16, 1898, its work then being ready to submit to the people. In June a popular vote resulted in the acceptance of the constitution by Victoria, Tasmania, and South

Australia; but the failure of the parent colony, New South Wales, to adopt it blocked all hope of federal union for the moment. Recently, however, at a conference of colonial premiers certain amendments demanded by New South Wales were agreed to in part, and upon a second vote the constitution, as amended, was accepted by that colony."—W. G. Beach, *The Australian Federal Constitution (Pol. Science Quarterly, Dec., 1899)*.

In August, 1899, the draft of a Constitution thus agreed upon was transmitted to England, with addresses from the provincial legislatures, praying that it be passed into law by the Imperial Parliament. Early in the following year delegates from the several colonies were sent to England to discuss with the Colonial Office certain questions that had arisen, and to assist in procuring the passage by Parliament of the necessary Act. Looked at from the Imperial standpoint, a number of objections to the draft Constitution were found, but all of them were finally waived excepting one. That one related to a provision touching appeals from the High Court of the Australian Commonwealth to the Queen in Council. As framed and adopted in Australia, the provision in question was as follows: "74. No appeal shall be permitted to the Queen in Council in any matter involving the interpretation of this Constitution or of the Constitution of a State, unless the public interests of some part of Her Majesty's Dominions, other than the Commonwealth or a State, are involved. Except as provided in this section, this Constitution shall not impair any right which the Queen may be pleased to exercise, by virtue of Her Royal Prerogative, to grant special leave of appeal from the High Court to Her Majesty in Council. But The Parliament may make laws limiting the matters in which such leave may be asked." This was objected to on several grounds, but mainly for the reasons thus stated by Mr. Chamberlain: "Proposals are under consideration for securing a permanent and effective representation of the great Colonies on the Judicial Committee, and for amalgamating the Judicial Committee with the House of Lords, so as to constitute a Court of Appeal from the whole British Empire. It would be very unfortunate if Australia should choose this moment to take from the Imperial Tribunal the cognizance of the class of cases of greatest importance, and often of greatest difficulty. Article 74 proposes to withdraw from the Queen in Council matters involving the interpretation of the Constitution. It is precisely on questions of this kind that the Queen in Council has been able to render most valuable service to the administration of law in the Colonies, and questions of this kind, which may sometimes involve a good deal of local feeling, are the last that should be withdrawn from a Tribunal of appeal with regard to which there could not be even a suspicion of prepossession. Questions as to the constitution of the Commonwealth or of a State may be such as to raise a great deal of public excitement as to the definition of the boundaries between the powers of the Commonwealth Parliament and the powers of the State Parliaments. It can hardly be satisfactory to the people of Australia that in such cases, however important and far-reaching in their consequences, the decision of the High Court should be absolutely final. Before long the necessity for alter-

ing the Constitution in this respect would be felt, and it is better that the Constitution should be enacted in such a form as to render unnecessary the somewhat elaborate proceedings which would be required to amend it."—*Great Britain, Parliamentary Publications (Papers by Command, April and May*, 1900, *Australia — Cd.* 124 *and* 158). — In reply, the Australian delegates maintained that they had no authority to amend, in any particular, the instrument which the people of the several colonies had ratified by their votes; but the Imperial authorities were inflexible, and the article 74 was modified in the Act which passed Parliament, on the 7th of July, 1900, "to constitute the Commonwealth of Australia," as may be seen by reference to the text, published elsewhere — see (in this vol.) CONSTITUTION OF AUSTRALIA.

A. D. 1900. — The question of the Federal Capital.—By the Constitution of the Commonwealth, it is required that the seat of government "shall be determined by the Parliament, and shall be within territory which shall have been granted to or acquired by the Commonwealth, and shall be vested in and belong to the Commonwealth, and shall be in the State of New South Wales, and be distant not less than one hundred miles from Sydney;" and "such territory shall contain an area of not less than one hundred square miles." "New South Wales," says a correspondent, writing from Sydney, "is naturally anxious to get the question decided as quickly as possible; but Victoria will equally be inclined to procrastinate, and the new Parliament — which cannot be more comfortable than it will be at Melbourne—will not be in a hurry to shift. The necessity for a new and artificial capital arises entirely out of our provincial jealousies, and it would have been a great saving of initial expense and a great diminution of inconvenience if we could have used one of the old capitals for a quarter of a century." To remove preliminary difficulties and avoid delay, the government of New South Wales appointed a commissioner to visit and report on the most likely places. The report of this commissioner, made early in October, "reduces the possible positions to three— one near Bombala in the south-east corner of the colony at the foot of the Australian Alps, one near Yass on the line of the railway between Sydney and Melbourne, and one near Orange on our western line. On the whole he gives the preference to the first named."

New South Wales: A. D. 1900.—Old-Age Pension Act.—A letter from Sydney, Nov. 29, 1900, announced: "The question of the establishment of an old age pension system, similar to that now in successful operation in New Zealand [see (in this vol.) NEW ZEALAND: A. D. 1899], has been agitating New South Wales for several months, and to-day the bill for that purpose became a law. There has been a desire on the part of some members of the Legislature to hold over the bill until the convening of the Federal Parliament, in the hope that the measure would become universal throughout the continent, but the majority, including the Premier, wished the bill to be pushed through without loss of time. There is no opposition worth mentioning. . . . At a mass meeting in favor of the bill representatives of every political party, of every Church and of every profession and trade in the community were present. The sentiment of the colony has never been more unanimous. . . . The estimated cost of the scheme is something like £250,000 or £300,000 a year, but this does not take into consideration the amount which will be saved by doing away with the charitable institutions now drafuing the pockets alike of the state and of the individual. Private contributions alone amount to £600,000 a year ; all this will be saved, together with a part of the Government's annual expenditure—about £400,000—for public institutions. Not all pauper institutions can be abolished, for many of the aged and friendless poor are ailing or slightly feeble minded, and will continue to need medical attention."

A. D. 1900 (March).—New Zealand looking toward federation with the Australian Commonwealth. See (in this vol.) NEW ZEALAND : A. D. 1900 (MARCH).

West Australia : A. D. 1900 (August).— Vote to join the Commonwealth.—The question of union with the other colonies in the Commonwealth, from which the West Australians had previously held aloof, was submitted to them in August (women voting for the first time), and decided affirmatively by 44,704 against 19,691. Adding the West Australian totals to the aggregate vote at the decisive referendum in each of the other federating colonies, the following is the reported result:

For federation 422,647
Against federation 161,024

Majority 261,623

A. D. 1900 (September—December.—The Queen's Proclamation of the Australian Commonwealth.—Contemplated visit of the Duke and Duchess of York to open the first session of the Federal Parliament.—Appointment of Lord Hopetoun to be Governor-General.—The first Federal Cabinet.—On the 17th of September the following proclamation of the Australian Commonwealth was issued by the Queen: "Whereas by an Act of Parliament passed in the sixty-third and sixty-fourth years of Our reign, intituled ' An Act to constitute the Commonwealth of Australia,' it is enacted that it shall be lawful for the Queen, with the advice of the Privy Council, to declare by Proclamation that, on and after a day therein appointed, not being later than one year after the passing of this Act, the people of New South Wales, Victoria, South Australia, Queensland, and Tasmania, and also, if Her Majesty is satisfied that the people of Western Australia have agreed thereto, of Western Australia, shall be united in a Federal Commonwealth, under the name of the Commonwealth of Australia. And whereas We are satisfied that the people of Western Australia have agreed thereto accordingly. We therefore, by and with the advice of Our Privy Council, have thought fit to issue this Our Royal Proclamation, and We do hereby declare that on and after the first day of January, one thousand nine hundred and one, the people of New South Wales, Victoria, South Australia, Queensland, Tasmania, and Western Australia shall be united in a Federal Commonwealth under the name of the Commonwealth of Australia. Given at Our Court at Balmoral, this seventeenth day of September, in the year of our Lord one thousand nine hundred, and in the sixty-fourth year of Our reign. God save the Queen."

6–3

At the same time, the following announcement, which caused extreme delight in Australia, was published officially from the Colonial Office : " Her Majesty the Queen has been graciously pleased to assent, on the recommendation of the Marquis of Salisbury, to the visit of their Royal Highnesses the Duke and Duchess of York to the colonies of Australasia in the spring of next year. His Royal Highness the Duke of York will be commissioned by her Majesty to open the first Session of the Parliament of the Australian Commonwealth in her name. Although the Queen naturally shrinks from parting with her grandson for so long a period, her Majesty fully recognizes the greatness of the occasion which will bring her colonies of Australia into federal union, and desires to give this special proof of her interest in all that concerns the welfare of her Australian subjects. Her Majesty at the same time wishes to signify her sense of the loyalty and devotion which have prompted the spontaneous aid so liberally offered by all the colonies in the South African war, and of the splendid gallantry of her colonial troops. Her Majesty's assent to this visit is, of course, given on the assumption that at the time fixed for the Duke of York's departure the circumstances are as generally favourable as at present and that no national interests call for his Royal Highness's presence in this country."

To manifest still further the interest taken by the British government in the event, it was made known in October that " when the Duke of York opens the new Commonwealth Parliament, the guard of honour, it is directed, shall be so made up as to be representative of every arm of the British Army, including the Volunteers. To the Victoria and St. George's Rifles has fallen the honour of being selected to represent the entire Volunteer force of the country. A detachment of the regiment, between 50 and 60 strong, will accordingly leave for Australia in about a month and will be absent three or four months."

The honor of the appointment to be the first Governor-General of the new Commonwealth fell to a Scottish nobleman, John Adrian Louis Hope, seventh Earl of Hopetoun, who had been Governor of Victoria from 1889 to 1895, and had held high offices at home, including that of Lord Chamberlain in the household of the Queen. Lord Hopetoun landed at Sydney on the 15th of December and received a great welcome. On the 30th, his Cabinet was formed, and announced, as follows : Mr. Barton, Prime Minister and Minister for External Affairs ; Mr. Deakin, Attorney-General ; Sir William Lyne, Minister for Home Affairs ; Sir George Turner, Treasurer ; Mr. Kingston, Minister of Trade and Commerce ; Mr. Dickson, Minister of Defence ; Sir John Forrest, Postmaster-General.

A. D. 1901 (January).—Inauguration of the Federal Government.—The government of the Commonwealth was inaugurated with splendid ceremonies on the first day of the New Year and the New Century, when the Governor-General and the members of the Federal Cabinet were sworn and assumed office. Two messages from the British Secretary of State for the Colonies were read, as follows:

" The Queen commands me to express through you to the people of Australia her Majesty's heartfelt interest in the inauguration of the

Commonwealth, and her earnest wish that, under divine Providence, it may ensure the increased prosperity and well-being of her loyal and beloved subjects in Australia."

"Her Majesty's Government send cordial greetings to the Commonwealth of Australia. They welcome her to her place among the nations united under her Majesty's sovereignty, and confidently anticipate for the new Federation a future of ever-increasing prosperity and influence. They recognize in the long-desired consummation of the hopes of patriotic Australians a further step in the direction of the permanent unity of the British Empire, and they are satisfied that the wider powers and responsibilities henceforth secured to Australia will give fresh opportunity for the display of that generous loyalty and devotion to the Throne and Empire which has always characterized the action in the past of its several States."

A. D. **1901 (May).**—Opening of the first Parliament of the **Commonwealth** by the heir to the British crown.—The programme of the Federal Government.—The Duke of Cornwall and York, heir to the British crown (but not yet created Prince of Wales), sailed, with his wife, from England in March, to be present at the opening of the first Parliament of the federated Commonwealth of Australia, which is arranged to take place early in May. He makes the voyage in royal state, on a steamer specially fitted and converted for the occasion into a royal yacht, with an escort of two cruisers.

Preliminary to the election and meeting of Parliament, the new federal government has much organizing work to do, and much preparation of measures for Parliament to discuss. The Premier, Mr. Barton, in a speech made on the 17th of January, announced that the Customs were taken over from the several States on January 1, and the defences and post-offices

would be transferred as soon as possible. "Probably the railways would be acquired by the Commonwealth at an early date. Whether the debts of the several States would be taken over before the railways was a matter which had to be decided, and was now engaging the attention of the Treasurer. The Ministry would not consider the appointment of a Chief Justice of the High Court until Parliament had established that tribunal." In the same speech, the main features of the programme and policy of the federal government were indicated. "The Commonwealth," said the Premier, "would have the exclusive power of imposing Customs and excise duties, and it would, therefore, be necessary to preserve the States' power of direct taxation. There must be no direct taxation by the Commonwealth except under very great pressure. Free trade under the Constitution was practically impossible; there must be a very large Customs revenue. . . . The policy of the Government would be protective, not prohibitive, because it must be revenue-producing. No one colony could lay claim to the adoption of its tariff, whether high or low. The first tariff of Australia ought to be considerate of existing industries. The policy of the Government could be summed up in a dozen words. It would give Australia a tariff that would be Australian. Regarding a preferential duty on British goods, he would be glad to reciprocate where possible, but the question would have to receive very serious consideration before final action could be taken. Among the legislation to be introduced at an early date, Mr. Barton continued, were a Conciliation and Arbitration Bill in labour disputes, and a Bill for a transcontinental railway, which would be of great value from the defence point of view. He was in favour of womanhood suffrage. Legislation to exclude Asiatics would be taken in hand as a matter of course."

AUSTRIA-HUNGARY.

Financial relations of the **two** countries forming the dual Empire.—"The financial relations of Austria and Hungary fall under three main heads. Firstly, the Quota, or proportionate contribution to joint expenditure. The Quota is an integral portion of the compact of 1867 [see—in vol. 1—AUSTRIA: A. D. 1866–1867], but is revised every ten years. Failing agreement on the proportion to be paid by each half of the monarchy, the Quota is fixed from year to year by the Emperor till an agreement is arrived at. Secondly, the so-called commercial 'Ausgleich' treaty, which provides for a customs union, postal and telegraphic union, commercial equality of citizens of one state in the other, identical excise duties, &c. Thirdly, the Bank Union, by which Austria and Hungary have a common Austro-Hungarian bank, and common paper money. The Ausgleich and Bank Union are not essential parts of the 1867 compact; they are really only treaties renewable every ten years, and if no agreement is come to, they simply lapse, and each state makes its own arrangements, which seems very likely to be the fate of the Ausgleich unless the present crisis can be got over. The proceeds of the joint customs are applied directly to common expenses,

and only the difference is made up by Quota. But if the Ausgleich falls through, the whole of the joint expenditure will have to be settled by quota payments. The joint expenditure goes almost wholly to the up-keep of the army, navy, and consular and diplomatic services. It amounts on an average to about 150 million florins or 12½ million £, falling as low as 124½ million florins in 1885 and rising to nearly 167 million in 1888. Of this total the customs revenues have, in the last few years, accounted for nearly a third, usually about 31 per cent. The Quota was fixed in 1867 at 70 per cent. for Austria and 30 per cent. for Hungary, based on a very rough calculation from the yield of common taxation in the years 1860–1865. the last few years preceding the restoration of Hungarian independence. On the incorporation of the so-called Military Frontier in Hungary, the Hungarian proportion was increased to 31.4. Hitherto the Hungarians have resisted any attempt to increase their quota. This 'non possumus' attitude has provoked great resentment in Austria, especially when it is compared with the self-complacent tone with which the Magyars dwell on the enormous progress made by Hungary since 1867. That progress is indubitable. Hungary has not only developed as an agricultural state, but is in a very fair way of becoming an industrial and manufacturing state as well. . . .

"On all these grounds the Austrians declare that they can no longer go on paying the old Quota of 68.6 per cent. The Hungarians admit the great progress made by Hungary, but with some qualifications. In spite of the growth of Budapest, Fiume, and a few other towns, Hungary is still, on the whole, very backward when compared with Austria. The total volume of her manufactures is very small, in spite of the rapid increase of recent years. Hungary is still, to all intents and purposes, an agricultural country, and as such, has suffered largely from the fall in prices."—L. S. Amery, *Austro-Hungarian Financial Relations* (*Economic Journal, Sept.*, 1898).

A. D. 1894-1895.—The Hungarian Ecclesiastical Laws.—Conflict with the Church.—Resignation of Count Kalnoky.—In the last month of 1894 royal assent was given to three bills, known as the Ecclesiastical Laws, which marked an extraordinary departure from the old subserviency of the State to the Church. The first was a civil marriage law, which made civil marriage compulsory, leaving religious ceremonies optional with the parties, and which modified the law of divorce; the second annulled a former law by which the sons of mixed marriages were required to follow the father's religion, and the daughters to follow that of the mother; the third established an uniform State registration of births, deaths and marriages, in place of a former registration of different creeds, and legalized marriages between Christians and Jews without change of faith. These very radical measures, after passing the lower house of the Hungarian legislature, were carried with great difficulty through the aristocratic and clerical upper house, and only by a strong pressure of influence from the emperor-king himself. They were exceedingly obnoxious to the Church, and the Papal Nuncio became active in a hostility which the Hungarian premier, Baron Banffy, deemed offensive to the State. He called upon the Imperial Minister of Foreign Affairs, Count Kalnoky, to address a complaint on the subject to the Vatican. This led to disagreements between the two ministers which the Emperor strove without success to reconcile, and Count Kalnoky, in the end, was forced to retire from office. The Pope was requested to recall the offending Nuncio, and declined to do so.

A. D. 1895-1896.—Race-jealousies and conflicts.—The position of Bohemia in the part of the dual Empire called Austria.—Anti-Semitic agitation in Vienna.—Austrian Ministry of Count Badeni.—Enlarged parliamentary franchise.—In the constitutional reconstruction of the Empire after the war of 1866, almost everything was conceded to the Magyars of Hungary, who acquired independence in matters of· internal administration, and ascendancy over the other races subject to the Hungarian crown. "On the other hand, absolute equality was established between the different countries that are not connected with Hungary. No greater privileges were granted to an ancient historical kingdom such as Bohemia than were given, for instance, to the small Alpine district situated between the Tyrol and the Boden See (Lake of Constance) known as Vorarl-

berg. . . . The representatives of these countries were to meet at Vienna, and a ministry for 'Cisleithania' was appointed. That these measures were injudicious is now the opinion of almost all Austrians. Beust [the Saxon statesman who was called in to conduct the political reconstruction of 1867—see, in vol. 1, AUSTRIA: A. D. 1866-1867; and 1866-1887], created a new agglomeration of smaller and larger countries, entirely different as regards race, history, and culture. It is characteristic of the artificiality of Count Beust'a new creation that up to the present day no real and generally accepted name for it has been found. The usual designation of Cisleithania is an obvious absurdity. A glance at the map will suffice to show how senseless such a name is when applied, for instance, to Dalmatia, one of the countries ruled from Vienna. The word 'Austria' also can correctly be applied only either to all the countries ruled by the house of Habsburg-Lorraine or to the archduchies of Upper and Lower Austria, which are the cradle of the dynasty. The official designation of the non-Hungarian parts of the empire is 'the kingdoms and lands represented in the parliament' (of Vienna)—'Die im Reichsrathe vertretenen Königreiche und Länder.'

"Though the Germans willingly took part in the deliberations of the Parliament of 'Cisleithania,' the Slavs of Bohemia and Poland were at first violently opposed to the new institution. They might perhaps have willingly consented to take part in a Vienna parliament that would have consisted of representatives of the whole empire. But when the ancient historical rights of Hungary were fully recognized, countries such as Bohemia and Poland . . . naturally felt offended. Count Benat dealt differently with these two divisions of the empire. The partly true, partly imaginary, grievances of the Poles were more recent and better known thirty years ago than they are now. Beust was impressed by them and considered it advisable to make large concessions to the Poles of Galicia with regard to autonomy, local government, and the use of the national language. The Poles, who did not fail to contrast their fate with that of their countrymen who were under Russian or Prussian rule, gratefully accepted these concessions, and attended the meetings of the representative assembly at Vienna. Other motives also contributed to this decision of the Galician Poles. Galicia is a very poor country, and the Germans who then ruled at Vienna, naturally welcoming the representatives of a large Slav country in their Parliament, proved most generous in their votes in favour of the Galician railways. Matters stood differently in Bohemia, and the attitude of Count Beust and the new 'Cisleithanian' ministers was also here quite different. They seem to have thought that they could break the resistance of the Bohemians by military force, and with the aid of the German minority of the population. A long struggle ensued. . . . Bohemia is . . . the 'cockpit' of Austrian political warfare, and almost every political crisis has been closely connected with events that occurred in Bohemia. The Bohemian representatives in 1867 refused to take part in the deliberations of the Vienna Parliament, the existence of which they considered contrary to the ancient constitution of their country. In 1879 they finally decided to take part in the deliberations of the Vienna assembly. . . . The Bohemians, indeed, entered the Vienna Parliament under protest, and declared that their appearance there was by no means to be considered as a resignation of the special rights that Bohemia had formerly possessed. The Bohemian deputies, however, continued henceforth to take part in the deliberations of the Cisleithanian Parliament and loyally supported those of the many Austrian ministers who were not entirely deaf to their demands. Some of these demands, such as that of the foundation of a national university at Prague, were indeed granted by the Vienna ministers. Though a German university continued to exist at Prague, this concession was vehemently opposed by the Germans, as indeed every concession to appease the Bohemian people was."—Francis Count Lutzow, *Austria at the End of the Century* (*Nineteenth Century Rev.*, Dec., 1899).

During recent years, government in the dual empire has been made increasingly difficult, especially on the Austrian side, by the jealousy, which grows constantly more bitter, between the German and Slavic elements of the mixed population, and by the rising heat of the Anti-Semitic agitation. The latter was brought to a serious crisis in Vienna during 1895 by the election of Dr. Lueger, a violent leader of Anti-Semitism, to the office of First Vice-Burgomaster, which caused the resignation of the Burgomaster, and led to such disorders in the municipal council that the government was forced to intervene. The council was dissolved and an imperial commissioner appointed to conduct the city administration provisionally; but similar disorders, still more serious, recurred in October, when elections were held and the Anti-Semites won a majority in the council. Dr. Lueger was then elected Burgomaster. The government, supported by a majority in the Austrian Reichsrath, still refused to confirm the election. A second time Dr. Lueger was elected; whereupon the municipal council was again dissolved and the municipal administration transferred to an imperial commissioner. This measure was followed by scenes of scandalous turbulence in the Reichsrath and riotous demonstrations in the streets, which latter were vigorously suppressed by the police. Some considerable part of the temper in these demonstrations was directed against the Austrian premier, Count Badeni, and still more against the Polish race, to which he belonged. Count Badeni, who had been Governor of Galicia, had just been called to the head of affairs, and gave promise of an administration that would be strong ; but several other members of his cabinet were Poles, and that fact was a cause of offense. He gave an early assurance that the demand for an enlargement of the parliamentary franchise should be satisfactorily met, and that other liberal measures should be promptly taken in hand. These promises, with the show of firmness in the conduct of the government, produced a wide feeling in its favor. The promise of an enlargement of the parliamentary franchise in Austria was redeemed the following February (1896), by the introduction and speedy passage of a parliamentary reform bill, which embodied an important revision of the Austrian constitution. Seventy-two new members were added to the 353 which formerly constituted the lower or Abgeordneten House of the Austrian Reichsrath. The original body of 353 remained

as it had been, made up in four sections, elected by four classes in the community, namely : owners of large estates, electing 85 members ; doctors of the universities and town taxpayers who pay five florins of direct taxation yearly, these together electing 115 ; chambers of commerce and industry, electing 22 ; country taxpayers who pay five florins of direct taxation yearly, electing 131. The number of voters in these four privileged classes were said to number 1,782,000 when the Reform Bill passed. The new voters added by the bill were estimated to number about 3,600,000. But the latter would elect only the 72 new members added to the House, while the former continued to be exclusively represented by the 353 members of its former constitution. In other words, though the suffrage was now extended to all male adults, it was not with equality of value to all. For about one-third of the political community, the franchise was given five times the weight and force that it possessed for the remaining two-thirds. Nevertheless, the bill seems to have been accepted and passed with no great opposition. In Vienna, the Anti-Semitic agitation was kept up with violence, Dr. Lueger being elected four times to the chief-burgomastership of the city, in defiance of the imperial refusal to sanction his election. Finally the conflict was ended by a compromise. Lueger resigned and was permitted to take the office of Vice Burgomaster, while one of his followers was chosen to the Chief Burgomaster's seat.

A. D. 1896.—**Celebration of the Millennium of the Kingdom of Hungary.**—The millennial anniversary of the Kingdom of Hungary was celebrated by the holding of a great national exposition and festival at Buda-Pesth, from the 2d of May until the end of October, 1896. Preparations were begun as early as 1893, and were carried forward with great national enthusiasm and liberality, the government contributing nearly two millions of dollars to the expense of the undertaking. The spirit of the movement was expressed at the beginning by the Minister of Commerce, Bela Lukács, by whose department it was specially promoted. "The government," he said, "will take care that the national work be exhibited in a worthy frame, so as to further the interests of the exhibitors. May every one of you, its subjects, therefore show what he is able to attain by his diligence, his taste, and his inventive faculty. Let us all, in fact, compete—we who are working, some with our brains, others with our hands, and others with our machines—like one man for the father-land. Thus the living generation will be able to see what its forefathers have made in the midst of hard circumstances, and to realize what tasks are awaiting us and the new generations in the path which has been smoothed by the sweat, labor, and pain of our ancestors. This will be a rare family festival, the equal of which has not been granted to many nations. Let the people gather, then, round our august ruler, who has guided our country with fatherly care and wisdom in the benevolent ways of peace to the heights which mark the progress of to-day, and who—a faithful keeper of the glorious past of a thousand years—has led the Hungarian people to the threshold of a still more splendid thousand years to come!"

Writing shortly before the opening, the United States Consul at Buda-Pesth, Mr. Hammond, gave the following description of the plans and preparations then nearly complete: "The series of official festivities will be diversified by those of a social and popular character. These will be the interparliamentary conference for international courts of arbitration; the congress of journalists, with the view to constitute an international journalistic union; international congresses of art and history, of actors, tourists, athletes, etc.; numerous national congresses embracing every intellectual and material interest of the country, in which the leading personages of all groups and branches of national production, the highest authorities in the field of commerce, industry, communication, etc., as well as those who are in the forefront of the literary, spiritual, and philanthropic movements of the country will take part.

"There is activity in all classes of Hungarian society, with a view to carrying out the ingenious project of the artist Paul Vágó—the great historical pageant. Several municipal bodies have already promised their coöperation, while scores of men and women, bearers of historic names, have declared their readiness to take part at their own expense. All the costumes of all the races and social classes who have inhabited this country during ten centuries will pass before our eyes in this beautiful cortége. The genius of the artist will call into life in their descendants the warriors who conquered Pannonia under Arpad, and, during the reign of Louis the Great, annexed to this realm all the neighboring countries; all the dignitaries, both civil and ecclesiastical, who, under Stephen the Saint, King Kálman, and Mathias Corvinus, spread Christianity, enlightenment, liberty, and wealth to the extreme confines of this part of Europe; all the crusaders of Joannes Hunyady, who drove back the Crescent for a century and thus defended western civilization against eastern fanaticism; all the kings, princes, noblemen, and poets of modern times who have led the nation in her struggle for modern ideas. These historical figures will be followed by their retainers or surrounded by the popular types of the respective epochs. To judge by the sketches of the artist, this pageant promises to surpass anything that has hitherto been offered on similar occasions.

"All these festivals will move, as it were, within the fixed frame of the Millennial National Exhibition, which will cover an area of 500,000 square meters (5,382,100 square feet) and consist of 169 buildings and pavilions, erected at a total cost (including private expenses) of 10,000,000 florins ($4,020,000). This exhibition is divided into two sections, viz: (1) The historical section, containing art treasures, relics, and antiquities of the past, which will illustrate the political, religious, military, and private life of each principal period in the history of the nation. . . . (2) The section of modern times will embrace everything offered by similar exhibitions. Nevertheless, the visitor's mind will here, too, be impressed with the solemnity of the millennium and the enthusiasm inspiring the nation at this momentous period of its history. The programme embraces the national life in all its manifestations. Not only will the present condition of Hungary be laid open to general view, but the world will also be impressed with the great progress Hungary has made since the reëstablishment of her constitution in 1867."—*U. S. Consular Reports, April,* 1896.

By every possible arrangement of facilitation and cheapening, admission to the Exposition was placed within the means of all the inhabitants of the kingdom; and especial provision was made for bringing schools and teachers to receive the object-lessons which it taught.

Among the ceremonies which attended the ending of the great national festival, was the formal opening, at Orsova, of a ship channel through the rocky obstructions that have been known since the days when they troubled the Romans as the "Iron Gates of the Danube."

A. D. 1897.—Industrial combinations. See (in this vol.) TRUSTS: IN EUROPEAN COUNTRIES.

A. D. 1897.—The forces of feudalism and clericalism in Austria.—Austrian parties in the Reichsrath.—Their aims, character and relative strength.—Count **Badeni's** language decrees for Bohemia.—"In no European country have the forces of feudalism and clericalism such an enormous influence as they have in Austria. The Austrian nobility is supreme at Court and in the upper branches of the Administration. In Hungary the small nobility and landed gentry exercise a preponderating influence, but they are a wide class and filled with the national spirit. The Austrian nobility forms a narrow, intensely exclusive and bigoted caste, whose only political interest is the maintenance of its own class supremacy. The large Protestant element in Hungary has in no small degree contributed to the success of the Magyars, both in its effect on the national character and by the secondary position to which the mixture of creeds has relegated the Church. In Austria the Church of Rome is all-powerful. The House of Habsburg has always been bigotedly Catholic: Francis Joseph himself was a pupil of the Jesuits. The triumph of the reaction after 1848 was the establishment in 1855 of that 'written Canossa' the Concordat, which made the Church absolute in all matters relating to education and marriage. And even though the Concordat was got rid of in 1870, the energies of the clerical party have been but little weakened. The real explanation of the whole course of Austrian polities lies in the interaction of the two conflicts—of reaction, clerical or aristocratic, against liberalism, and of Slav against German. . . .

"In March 1897 came the general elections, to which a special interest was lent by the first appearance of the fifth class of voters. The most striking feature of the elections was the complete and final break up of the German Liberal party. . . . The history of the German Liberal party has been one of a continuous decline both in numbers and importance. It counted 200 members in 1873, 170 in 1879, 114 in 1885-1891, and only 77 out of a total of 425 in 1897. . . . Their political theories are those of moderate constitutional liberalism as understood on the Continent in the middle of the century—i. e. belief in the efficacy of parliamentary government, in commercial and industrial freedom, hostility to military bureaucracy and clericalism. . . . The most radical group among them, the Progressists, an offshoot of the last election, is about as radical as the ordinary English Conservative of to-day. The views of the Verfassungstreue Grossgrundbesitz are those of the English Tory of fifty years ago.

"Of the fractions into which the Liberal party is now divided the most important is the

Deutsch Fortschrittliche, or Progressive, which split off from the main body in November 1896. Its chief object was to direct a stronger opposition on national and liberal lines to Count Badeni. Its 35 members are almost exclusively recruited from Bohemia and Moravia. They differ from the German 'Volkspartei' mainly in their refusal to accept anti-Semitism, which would be both against their liberal professions and their economic convictions as representatives of the commercial and manufacturing classes. The constitutional landowners (Verfassungstreue Grossgrundbesitz, 30 seats) represent the most conservative element of the old Liberal party. . . . The 12 members of the Free German Union (Freie Deutsche Vereinigung) may perhaps consider themselves the most authentic remnant of the great Liberal party—it is their chief claim to distinction. The German National or People's party (Deutsche Volkspartei, 43 seats) first made its appearance at the elections of 1885. It rejected the old idea of the Liberals that the Germans were meant, as defenders of the State, to look to State interests alone without regard to the fate of their own nationality, and took up a more strictly national as well as a more democratic attitude. It has also of late years included anti-Semitism in its programme. Its main strength lies in the Alpine provinces, where it heads the German national and Liberal opposition to the Slovenes on the one side, and the German clericals on the other. It is at present the largest of the German parties. . . .

" Least but not last of the German parties comes the little group of five led by Schönerer and Wolf. Noisy, turbulent, and reckless, this little body of extremists headed the obstruction in the Reichsrath, the disorganised larger German parties simply following in its wake. The object these men aim at is the incorporation of German Austria in the German Empire, the non-German parts being left to take care of themselves. Both the German National party and Schönerer's followers are anti-Semitic, but anti-Semitism only plays a secondary part in their programme. The party that more specially claims the title of anti-Semite is the Christian Social (Christlich-Soziale, 27 seats). The growth of this party in the last few years has been extraordinarily rapid. In Dr. Lueger and Prince Alois Liechtenstein it has found leaders who thoroughly understand the arts of exciting or humouring the Viennese populace. . . . The characteristic feature of Austrian anti-Semitism, besides the reaction against the predominance of the ubiquitous Jew in commerce, journalism, and the liberal professions, is that it represents the opposition of the small tradesman or handicraftsman to the increasing pressure of competition from the large Jewish shops and the sweating system so frequently connected with them. The economic theories of the party are of the crudest and most mediæval kind ; compulsory apprenticeship, restricted trade guilds, penalties on stock exchange speculation, &c., form the chief items of its programme. . . .

"The German Clericals and the Clerical Conservatives (Katholische Volkspartei and Centrum) number some 37 votes together ; but their importance has always been increased by the skilful and unscrupulous parliamentary tactics of the party. The strength of the Clerical party lies in the ignorant and devotedly pious peas-

autry of Upper Austria and the Alpine provinces. The defence of agrarian interests is included in its programme ; but its only real object is the maintenance of the moral and material power of the Church. Its policy looks solely to the interests of the Vatican. . . .

" The best organised of the national parties is the Polish Club (59 seats). It represents the national and social interests of the Polish nobility and landed gentry. . . . Standing outside of Austrian interests, they exercise a controlling voice in Austrian affairs. The three-score well-drilled Polish votes have helped the Government again and again to ride roughshod over constitutional opposition. The partition of Poland has thus avenged itself on one at least of its spoilers. The Germans have long resented this outside interference which permanently keeps them in a minority. . . . The Czechs are a party of 60, and together with the 19 representatives of the Czech landed aristocracy, form the largest group in the Reichsrath. The Young Czech party began in the seventies as a reaction against the Old Czech policy of passive resistance. In contra-distinction to the Old Czechs, they also professed radical and anti-clerical views in politics generally. . . . In 1897 the Old Czechs finally withdrew from the contest or were merged in the victorious party. . . . Of the other nationalist parties the most important is the Slav National Christian Union (35 seats), comprising the Slovenes, Croatians, and some of the more moderate Ruthenians from Galicia. Their programme is mainly national, though tinged with clericalism ; equality of the Slav languages with German and Italian in mixed districts ; and ultimately a union of the southern Slavs in an autonomous national province. The Italians are divided into 5 Clerical Italians from the Tirol and 14 Liberals from Trieste, Istria, &c. The Tirolese Italians desire a division of the Tirol into a German and an Italian part. . . .

" The most interesting, and in some ways the most respectable, of all Austrian parties is the Socialist or Social Democratic party (15 seats). It is the only one that fights for a living political theory—German liberalism being to all intents and purposes defunct—and not for mere national aggression. The Social Democrats hold the whole national agitation to be an hysterical dispute got up by professors, advocates, and other ne'er-do-weels of the unemployed upper classes. . . . Their support is derived from the working classes in the industrial districts, and not least from the poorer Jews, who supply socialism with many of its keenest apostles. . . .

" Altogether a most hopeless jumble of incoherent atoms is this Austrian Reichsrath. The chariots driving four-ways on the roof of the Houses of Parliament are a true symbol of the nature of Austrian politics. To add to the confusion, all the parties are headless. Able men and men of culture, there are a good many in the House ; but political leaders there are none. The general tone of the House is undignified, and has been so for some time. . . .

" On April 5, 1897, Count Badeni published the notorious language decrees for Bohemia. This ordinance placed the Czech language on an absolute equality with the German in all governmental departments and in the law courts all over Bohemia. . . . After 1901 all officials in every part of Bohemia were to be obliged to know both languages. The refusal of the Germans to admit the language spoken by 62 per cent. of the population of Bohemia to an equality with their own is not quite so preposterous as would at first sight appear. Without subscribing to Professor Mommsen's somewhat insolent dicta about 'inferior races,' one must admit that the Czech and German languages do not stand on altogether the same footing. German is a language spoken by some 60,000,000 of people, the language of a great literature and a great commerce. Czech is difficult, unpronounceable, and spoken by some 5,000,000 in all. It must be remembered, too, that the two nations do not really live together in Bohemia, but that the Germans live in a broad belt all round the country, while the Czechs inhabit the central plain. There is no more reason for a German Bohemian to acquire Czech than there is for a citizen of Edinburgh to make himself master of Gaelic. On the other hand, every educated Czech naturally learns German, even in a purely Czech-speaking district. . . . It must also be remembered that the decrees, as such, were of doubtful constitutionality; the language question was really a matter for the Legislature to settle. The decrees at once produced a violent agitation among the Germans, which rapidly spread from Bohemia over the whole Empire."—*The Internal Crisis in Austria-Hungary* (*Edinburgh Review, July*, 1898).

A. D. 1897 (October—December).—Scenes in the Austrian Reichsrath described by Mark Twain.—"Here in Vienna in these closing days of 1897 one's blood gets no chance to stagnate. The atmosphere is brimful of political electricity. All conversation is political; every man is a battery, with brushes overworn, and gives out blue sparks when you set him going on the common topic. . . . Things have happened here recently which would set any country but Austria on fire from end to end, and upset the government to a certainty; but no one feels confident that such results will follow here. Here, apparently, one must wait and see what will happen, then he will know, and not before; guessing is idle; guessing cannot help the matter. This is what the wise tell you; they all say it; they say it every day, and it is the sole detail upon which they all agree. There is some approach to agreement upon another point: that there will be no revolution. . . . Nearly every day some one explains to me that a revolution would not succeed here. 'It could n't, you know. Broadly speaking, all the nations in the empire hate the government—but they all hate each other too, and with devoted and enthusiastic bitterness; no two of them can combine; the nation that rises must rise alone; then the others would joyfully join the government against her, and she would have just a fly's chance against a combination of spiders. This government is entirely independent. It can go its own road, and do as it pleases; it has nothing to fear. In countries like England and America, where there is one tongue and the public interests are common, the government must take account of public opinion; but in Austria-Hungary there are nineteen public opinions—one for each state. No—two or three for each state, since there are two or three nationalities in each. A government cannot satisfy all these public opinions; it can only go through the mo-

tions of trying. This government does that. It goes through the motions, and they do not succeed; but that does not worry the government much.' . . .

"The recent troubles have grown out of Count Badeni's necessities. He could not carry on his government without a majority vote in the House at his back, and in order to secure it he had to make a trade of some sort. He made it with the Czechs—the Bohemians. The terms were not easy for him: he must pass a bill making the Czech tongue the official language in Bohemia in place of the German. This created a storm. All the Germans in Austria were incensed. In numbers they form but a fourth part of the empire's population, but they urge that the country's public business should be conducted in one common tongue, and that tongue a world language—which German is. However, Badeni secured his majority. The German element was apparently become helpless. The Czech deputies were exultant. Then the music began. Badeni's voyage, instead of being smooth, was disappointingly rough from the start. The government must get the 'Ausgleich' through. It must not fail. Badeni's majority was ready to carry it through; but the minority was determined to obstruct it and delay it until the obnoxious Czech-language measure should be shelved.

"The 'Ausgleich' is an Adjustment, Arrangement, Settlement, which holds Austria and Hungary together [see above; also, in vol. 1, AUSTRIA: A. D. 1866–1867]. It dates from 1867, and has to be renewed every ten years. It establishes the share which Hungary must pay toward the expenses of the imperial government. Hungary is a kingdom (the Emperor of Austria is its King), and has its own parliament and governmental machinery. But it has no foreign office, and it has no army—at least its army is a part of the imperial army, is paid out of the imperial treasury, and is under the control of the imperial war office. The ten-year rearrangement was due a year ago, but failed to connect. At least completely. A year's compromise was arranged. A new arrangement must be effected before the last day of this year. Otherwise the two countries become separate entities. The Emperor would still be King of Hungary—that is, King of an independent foreign country. There would be Hungarian custom-houses on the Austrian frontier, and there would be a Hungarian army and a Hungarian foreign office. Both countries would be weakened by this, both would suffer damage. The Opposition in the House, although in the minority, had a good weapon to fight with in the pending 'Ausgleich.' If it could delay the 'Ausgleich' a few weeks, the government would doubtless have to withdraw the hated language bill or lose Hungary.

"The Opposition began its fight. Its arms were the Rules of the House. It was soon manifest that by applying these Rules ingeniously, it could make the majority helpless, and keep it so as long as it pleased. It could shut off business every now and then with a motion to adjourn. It could require the ayes and noes on the motion, and use up thirty minutes on that detail. It could call for the reading and verification of the minutes of the preceding meeting, and use up half a day in that way. It could require that several of its members be entered upon the list of permitted speakers previously to the opening of a sitting ; and as there is no time limit, further delays could thus be accomplished. These were all lawful weapons, and the men of the Opposition (technically called the Left) were within their rights in using them. They used them to such dire purpose that all parliamentary business was paralyzed. The Right (the government side) could accomplish nothing. Then it had a saving idea. This idea was a curious one. It was to have the President and the Vice-Presidents of the parliament trample the Rules under foot upon occasion ! . . .

"And now took place that memorable sitting of the House which broke two records. It lasted the best part of two days and a night, surpassing by half an hour the longest sitting known to the world's previous parliamentary history, and breaking the long-speech record with Dr. Lecher's twelve-hour effort, the longest flow of unbroken talk that ever came out of one mouth since the world began. At 8.45, on the evening of the 28th of October, when the House had been sitting a few minutes short of ten hours, Dr. Lecher was granted the floor. . . . Then burst out such another wild and frantic and deafening clamor as has not been heard on this planet since the last time the Comanches surprised a white settlement at midnight. Yells from the Left, counter-yells from the Right, explosions of yells from all sides at once, and all the air sawed and pawed and clawed and cloven by a writhing confusion of gesturing arms and hands. Out of the midst of this thunder and turmoil and tempest rose Dr. Lecher, serene and collected, and the providential length of him enabled his head to show out above it. He began his twelve-hour speech. At any rate, his lips could be seen to move, and that was evidence. On high sat the President imploring order, with his long hands put beseechingly as in prayer, and his lips visibly but not bearably speaking. At intervals he grasped his bell and swung it up and down with vigor, adding its keen clamor to the storm weltering there below. Dr. Lecher went on with his pantomime speech, contented, untroubled. . . . One of the interrupters who made himself heard was a young fellow of slight build and neat dress, who stood a little apart from the solid crowd and leaned negligently, with folded arms and feet crossed, against a desk. Trim and handsome ; strong face and thin features ; black hair roughed up ; parsimonious mustache ; resonant great voice, of good tone and pitch. It is Wolf, capable and hospitable with sword and pistol. . . . Out of him came early this thundering peal, audible above the storm :

"'I demand the floor. I wish to offer a motion.'

"In the sudden lull which followed, the President answered, 'Dr. Lecher has the floor.'

"*Wolf.* 'I move the close of the sitting !'

"*P.* 'Representative Lecher has the floor.' [Stormy outburst from the Left — that is, the Opposition.]

"*Wolf.* 'I demand the floor for the introduction of a formal motion. [Pause.] Mr. President, are you going to grant it, or not ? [Crash of approval from the Left.] I will keep on demanding the floor till I get it.'

"*P.* 'I call Representative Wolf to order. Dr. Lecher has the floor.' . . .

"Which was true ; and he was speaking, too,

calmly, earnestly, and argumentatively ; and the official stenographers had left their places and were at his elbows taking down his words, he leaning and orating into their ears—a most curious and interesting scene. . . . At this point a new and most effective noisemaker was pressed into service. Each desk has an extension, consisting of a removable board eighteen inches long, six wide, and a half-inch thick. A member pulled one of these out and began to belabor the top of his desk with it. Instantly other members followed suit, and perhaps you can imagine the result. Of all conceivable rackets it is the most ear-splitting, intolerable, and altogether fiendish. . . . Wolf went on with his noise and with his demands that he be granted the floor, resting his board at intervals to discharge criticisms and epithets at the Chair. . . . By-and-by he struck the idea of beating out a tune with his board. Later he decided to stop asking for the floor, and to confer it upon himself. And so he and Dr. Lecher now spoke at the same time, and mingled their speeches with the other noises, and nobody heard either of them. Wolf rested himself now and then from speech-making by reading, in his clarion voice, from a pamphlet.

"I will explain that Dr. Lecher was not making a twelve-hour speech for pastime, but for an important purpose. It was the government's intention to push the 'Ausgleich' through its preliminary stages in this one sitting (for which it was the Order of the Day), and then by vote refer it to a select committee. It was the Majority's scheme—as charged by the Opposition—to drown debate upon the bill by pure noise—drown it out and stop it. The debate being thus ended, the vote upon the reference would follow—with victory for the government. But into the government's calculations had not entered the possibility of a single-barrelled speech which should occupy the entire time-limit of the sitting, and also get itself delivered in spite of all the noise. . . . In the English House an obstructionist has held the floor with Bible-readings and other outside matters ; but Dr. Lecher could not have that restful and recuperative privilege—he must confine himself strictly to the subject before the House. More than once, when the President could not hear him because of the general tumult, he sent persons to listen and report as to whether the orator was speaking to the subject or not.

"The subject was a peculiarly difficult one, and it would have troubled any other deputy to stick to it three hours without exhausting his ammunition, because it required a vast and intimate knowlege—detailed and particularized knowledge—of the commercial, railroading, financial, and international banking relations existing between two great sovereignties, Hungary and the Empire. But Dr. Lecher is President of the Board of Trade of his city of Brünn, and was master of the situation. . . . He went steadily on with his speech ; and always it was strong, virile, felicitous, and to the point. He was earning applause, and this enabled his party to turn that fact to account. Now and then they applauded him a couple of minutes on a stretch, and during that time he could stop speaking and rest his voice without having the floor taken from him. . . .

"The Minority staid loyally by their champion. Some distinguished deputies of the Majority staid by him too, compelled thereto by admiration of his great performance. When a man has been speaking eight hours, is it conceivable that he can still be interesting, still fascinating ? When Dr. Lecher had been speaking eight hours he was still compactly surrounded by friends who would not leave him and by foes (of all parties) who could not ; and all hung enchanted and wondering upon his words, and all testified their admiration with constant and cordial outbursts of applause. Surely this was a triumph without precedent in history. . . .

"In consequence of Dr. Lecher's twelve-hour speech and the other obstructions furnished by the Minority, the famous thirty-three-hour sitting of the House accomplished nothing. . . . Parliament was adjourned for a week—to let the members cool off, perhaps—a sacrifice of precious time, for but two months remained in which to carry the all-important 'Ausgleich' to a consummation. . . .

"During the whole of November things went from bad to worse. The all-important 'Ausgleich' remained hard aground, and could not be sparred off. Badeni's government could not withdraw the Language Ordinance and keep its majority, and the Opposition could not be placated on easier terms. One night, while the customary pandemonium was crashing and thundering along at its best, a fight broke out. . . . On Thanksgiving day the sitting was a history-making one. On that day the harried, bedeviled and despairing government went insane. In order to free itself from the thraldom of the Opposition it committed this curiously juvenile crime : it moved an important change of the Rules of the House, forbade debate upon the motion, put it to a stand-up vote instead of ayes and noes, and then gravely claimed that it had been adopted. . . . The House was already standing up; had been standing for an hour ; and before a third of it had found out what the President had been saying, he had proclaimed the adoption of the motion ! And only a few heard that. In fact, when that House is legislating you can't tell it from artillery-practice. You will realize what a happy idea it was to sidetrack the lawful ayes and noes and substitute a stand-up vote by this fact: that a little later, when a deputation of deputies waited upon the President and asked him if he was actually willing to claim that that measure had been passed, he answered, 'Yes—and unanimously.' . . .

"The 'Lex Falkenhayn,' thus strangely born, gave the President power to suspend for three days any deputy who should continue to be disorderly after being called to order twice, and it also placed at his disposal such force as might be necessary to make the suspension effective. So the House had a sergeant-at-arms at last, and a more formidable one, as to power, than any other legislature in Christendom had ever possessed. The Lex Falkenhayn also gave the House itself authority to suspend members for thirty days. On these terms the 'Ausgleich' could be put through in an hour—apparently. The Opposition would have to sit meek and quiet, and stop obstructing, or be turned into the street, deputy after deputy, leaving the Majority an unvexed field for its work.

"Certainly the thing looked well. . . . [But next day, when the President attempted to open the session, a band of the Socialist members made a sudden charge upon him, drove him and the Vice President from the House, took possession of the tribune, and brought even the semblance of legislative proceedings to an end. Then a body of sixty policemen was brought in to clear the House.] Some of the results of this wild freak followed instantly. The Badeni government came down with a crash ; there was a popular outbreak or two in Vienna ; there were three or four days of furious rioting in Prague, followed by the establishing there of martial law ; the Jews and Germans were harried and plundered, and their houses destroyed ; in other Bohemian towns there was rioting—in some cases the Germans being the rioters, in others the Czechs—and in all cases the Jew had to roast, no matter which side he was on. We are well along in December now; the new Minister-President has not been able to patch up a peace among the warring factions of the parliament, therefore there is no use in calling it together again for the present ; public opinion believes that parliamentary government and the Constitution are actually threatened with extinction, and that the permanency of the monarchy itself is a not absolutely certain thing!

"Yes, the Lex Falkenhayn was a great invention, and did what was claimed for it—it got the government out of the frying-pan."—S. L. Clemens (Mark Twain), *Stirring Times in Austria* (*Harper's Magazine*, March, 1898).

A. D. 1897 (December).—Imperial action.— On the last day of the year the Emperor closed the sittings of the Austrian Reichsrath by proclamation and issued a rescript continuing the "Ausgleich" provisionally for six months.

A. D. 1898.—Prolongation of factious disorders.—Paralysis of constitutional government.—Though scenes in the Austrian Chamber were not quite so violent, perhaps, as they had become near the close of 1897, the state of factious disorder continued much the same throughout the year, and legislation was completely stopped. The work of government could be carried on only by imperial decrees. The ministry of Baron von Gautsch, which had succeeded that of Count Badeni, attempted a compromise on the language question in Bohemia by dividing the country into three districts, according to the distribution of the several races, in one of which German was to be the official tongue, in another Czech, while both languages were to be used in the third. But the Germans of the empire would accept no such compromise. In March, Baron von Gautsch retired, and Count Thun Hohenstein formed a Ministry made up to represent the principal factions in the Reichsrath ; but the scheme brought no peace. Nor did appeals by Count Thun, "in the name of Austria," to the patriotism and the reason of all parties, to suspend their warfare long enough for a little of the necessary work of the state to be done, have any effect. The turbulence in the legislature infected the whole community, and especially, it would seem, the students in the schools, whose disorder caused many lectures to be stopped. In Hungary, too, there was an increase of violence in political agitation. A party, led by the son of Louis Kossuth, struggled to improve what seemed to be an opportunity for breaking the political union of Hungary with Austria, and realizing the old ambition for an independent Hungarian state. The ministry of

Baron Banffy had this party against him, as well as that of the clericals, who resented the civil marriage laws, and legislation came to a deadlock nearly as complete in the Hungarian as in the Austrian Parliament. There, as well as in Austria, the extension of the Ausgleich, provisionally for another year, had to be imposed by imperial decree.

A. D. 1898 (April).—Withdrawal from the blockade of Crete and the "Concert of Europe." See (in this vol.) TURKEY: A. D. 1897-1899.

A. D. 1898 (June).—The Sugar Conference at Brussels. See (in this vol.) SUGAR BOUNTIES.

A. D. 1898 (September).—Assassination of the Empress.—Jubilee of the Emperor's reign.—On the 10th of September, Elizabeth, Empress of Austria and Queen of Hungary, was assassinated at Geneva by an Italian anarchist, named Luigi Luccheni, who stabbed her with a small stiletto, exceedingly thin and narrow in the blade. The murderer rushed upon her and struck her, as she was walking, with a single attendant, on the quay, towards a lake steamer on which she intended to travel to Montreux. She fell, but arose, with some assistance, and walked forward to the steamer, evidently unaware that she had suffered worse than a blow. On the steamer, however, she lost consciousness, and then, for the first time, the wound was discovered. It had been made by so fine a weapon that it showed little external sign, and it is probable that the Empress felt little pain. She lived nearly half an hour after the blow was struck. The assassin attempted to escape, but was caught. As Swiss law forbids capital punishment, he could be only condemned to solitary confinement for life. This terrible tragedy came soon after the festivities in Austria which had celebrated the jubilee year of the Emperor Francis Joseph's reign. The Emperor's marriage had been one of love; he had suffered many afflictions in his later life; the state of his realm was such as could hardly be contemplated without despair; men wondered if he could bear this crowning sorrow and live. But he had the undoubted affection of his subjects, much as they troubled him with their miserably factious quarrels, and that consciousness seems to have been his one support.

A. D. 1899 (May—July).— Representation in the Peace Conference at The Hague. See (in this vol.) PEACE CONFERENCE.

A. D. 1899-1900.—Continued obstruction by the German parties in Austria.—Extensive secession of German Catholics from their Church, and its significance.—Withdrawal of the Bohemian language decrees.—Obstruction taken up by the Czechs.—During most of the year the German parties in the Austrian Reichsrath continued to make legislation impossible by disorderly obstruction, with the avowed purpose of compelling the government to withdraw the language decrees in Bohemia. A still more significant demonstration of German feeling and policy appeared, in a wide-spread and organized movement to detach German Roman Catholics from their church, partly, it would seem, as a proceeding of hostility to the Clerical party, and partly as a means of recommending the Germans of the Austrian states to the sympathy of the German Empire, and smoothing the approach to

an ultimate union of some of those states with the Germanic federation. The agitation against the Catholic Church is called "Los von Rom," and is said to have had remarkable results. "Those acquainted with the situation in Austria," says a writer in the "Quarterly Review," "do not wonder that in various parts of the Empire there is a marked tendency among the German Catholics to join Christian communions separated from Rome. Many thousand Roman Catholics have recently renounced their allegiance to the Holy See. Further secessions are announced as about to take place. The movement is especially strong in great centres like Eger, Asch, and Saatz, but has made itself felt also in Carinthia, and even in coast districts. This is a grave political fact, for it is a marked indication of serious discontent, and a sure sign that some arrangement under which certain districts of Austria might be joined to Germany would not be unwelcome to a section of the people." — Quarterly Rev., January, 1899. — In September the Austrian Ministry of Count Thun resigned, and was succeeded by one formed under Count Clary-Aldingen. The new premier withdrew the language decrees, which quieted the German obstructionists, but provoked the Czechs to take up the same rôle. Count Clary-Aldingen resigned in December, and a provisional Ministry was formed under Dr. Wettek, which lasted only until the 19th of January, 1900, when a new Cabinet was formed by Dr. von Körber. In Hungary, Baron Banffy was driven from power in February, 1899, by a state of things in the Hungarian Parliament much like that in the Austrian. M. Koloman Szell, who succeeded him, effected a compromise with the opposition which enabled him to carry a measure extending the Ausgleich to 1907. This brought one serious difficulty of the situation to an end.

A. D. 1899-1901.—Attitude towards impending revolt in Macedonia. See (in this vol.) TURKEY: A. D. 1899-1901; and BALKAN AND DANUBIAN STATES.

A. D. 1900.—Military and naval expenditure. See (in this vol.) WAR BUDGETS.

A. D. 1900 (February).—Attempted pacification of German and Czech parties by a Conciliation Board.—"On Monday last [February 5] the German and Czech Conciliation Board met for the first time in Vienna, under the presidency of the Austrian Premier, Dr. von Körber, and conferred for two hours. . . . Dr. von Körber is at the head of what may be called a 'business' Ministry, composed largely of those who had filled subordinate offices in previous Ministries. It was hoped, perhaps, that, since the leading politicians with a political 'past' could apparently do nothing to bring about a settlement, men with no past, but with a capacity for business, and in no way committed on the racial question, might do better in effecting a working arrangement. The appointment of this Conciliation Board seemed a promising way of attempting such a settlement. Dr. von Körber opened Monday's proceedings with a strong appeal to both sides, saying: 'Gentlemen, the Empire looks to you to restore its happiness and tranquillity.' It cannot be said that the Empire is likely to find its wishes fulfilled, for when the Board came down to hard business, the old troubles instantly revealed themselves. The Premier recommended a committee for Bohemia of twenty-two members, and one for Moravia of fifteen members, the two sitting in joint session in certain cases. Dr. Engel then set forth the historical claims of the Czechs, which immediately called forth a demand from Dr. Funke, of the German party, that German should be declared the official language throughout Austria. Each speaker seems to have been supported by his own party, and so no progress was made, and matters remain in 'statu quo ante.' The singularly deficient constitution of this Board makes against success, for it seems that the German Nationalists and Anti-Semites have only one delegate apiece, the Social Democrats were not invited at all, while the extreme Germans and extreme Czechs, apparently regarding the Board as a farce, declined to nominate delegates to its sittings. . . . There is unhappily little reason for believing that the Board of Conciliation will effect what the Emperor himself has failed to accomplish."—*Spectator (London), Feb.* 10, 1900.

A. D. 1900 (June—December).—Co-operation with the Powers in China. See (in this vol.) CHINA.

A. D. 1900 (September — December). — Warnings by the Emperor.—Clerical interference in politics.—The attitude of Hungary.—Economic decline of Austria.—Pessimistic views in Vienna. — The pending elections.—The Vienna correspondence of the "London Times" seems to be the best source of information concerning the critical conditions that are prevailing in the composite Empire, as the Nineteenth Century closes, and the events by which those conditions are from time to time revealed. The writer, whose reports we shall quote, is evidently well placed for observation, and well prepared for understanding what he sees.

In a dispatch of September 14, he notes the significance of a reprimand which the Emperor had caused to be administered to the Archbishop of Sarajevo, for interference in political affairs: "The chief of the Emperor's Cabinet called the Archbishop's attention to newspaper reports of a speech made by him at the close of the Catholic Congress recently held at Agram, in which he was represented to have expressed the hope that Bosnia would be incorporated with Croatia at the earliest possible date. As that question was a purely political one and foreign to the sacred vocation of the Archbishop, and as its solution fell exclusively within the jurisdiction of certain lay factors, and more especially within the Sovereign prerogatives of his Majesty, the chief of the Cabinet was instructed, in case the reports were correct, to communicate to his Grace the serious warning and firm expectation of the Emperor that his Grace would abstain in future, both in word and deed, from interference in political questions. As was to be expected, this sharp reprimand to an ecclesiastic of such high position and repute has made a great sensation. It meets with warm approval from the entire Hungarian Press. . . . There is, on the other hand, bitter mortification in Clerical circles. It is evidently felt that the warning to abstain from politics may be of more than mere local and individual significance."

In another dispatch on the same day the correspondent reported a still more significant imperial utterance, this time from the Emperor's own lips: "Yesterday the Emperor, who is at-

tending the manœuvres in Galicia, received the Polish Parliamentary Deputation and, addressing their president, informed him that the dissolution of the Reichsrath and the coming elections were the last constitutional means which would be employed by his Government. That implies that, if the new Parliament will not work, the Constitution will be suspended. . . . The dissolution of the Reichsrath takes place in opposition to the wish of the moderate element of all parties, who did their utmost to dissuade the Prime Minister from taking such a drastic measure. The opinion of those who did not approve of dissolution is that in the absence of a new suffrage the next Parliament will prove more unruly than the last. . . . Yesterday's Imperial warning requires no comment. It means no more than it says—namely, an eventual suspension of the Constitution. It does not point to any alternative régime in case the Parliamentary system should break down. Indeed, there is nothing to show that any such alternative has been under the consideration of the Emperor and his Ministers. No less an authority than Dr. Lueger, the Anti-Semitic burgomaster of Vienna, has just expressed his opinion on the subject to a local journalist in the following words:—'I am firmly convinced that nobody, not a single man in Austria, including all statesmen and Parliamentary politicians, has the faintest idea of how the situation will develop.'"

A few days later (Sept. 25) the "Times" correspondence summarized an important speech by the Hungarian statesman, Count Apponyi, to his constituents, in which the same forecast of a political catastrophe in Austria was intimated. Count Apponyi,—"after dwelling upon the importance of maintaining the Ausgleich, remarked that affairs in Austria might take a turn which would render its revision indispensable owing either to a complete suspension of the constitutional system in Austria, the maintenance of which was one of the conditions of the arrangement of 1867, or such modifications thereof as would make the existing form of union between the two countries technically untenable or politically questionable. In either case the revision could only confirm the independence of Hungary. But even then Count Apponyi believed that by following the traditions of Francis Deák it would be possible to harmonize the necessary revision with the fundamental principles of the Dual Monarchy. It would, however, be a great mistake to raise that question unless forced to do so by circumstances. Count Apponyi went on to say that the importance of Hungary, not only in the Monarchy but throughout the civilized world, was enormously increased by the fact that it secured the maintenance of Austria-Hungary, threatened by the destructive influence of the Austrian chaos, and thus constituted one of the principal guarantees of European tranquillity. The peace-abiding nations recognized that this service to the dynasty, the Monarchy, and the European State system was only possible while the constitutional independence and national unity of Hungary was maintained. It was clear to every unprejudiced mind that Hungarian national independence and unity was the backbone of the Dual Monarchy and one of the most important guarantees of European peace. But the imposing position attained by Hungary through the European sanction of her national ideal would be imperilled if they were of their own initiative to raise the question of the union of the two countries and thus convert the Austrian crisis into one affecting the whole Monarchy."

An article in the "Neue Freie Presse," of Vienna, on the hostility of the Vatican to Austria and Hungary was partially communicated in a despatch of October 11. The Vienna journal ascribes this hostility in part to resentment engendered by the alliance of Catholic Austria with Italy, and in part to the Hungarian ecclesiastical laws (see above: A. D. 1894-1895). It remarked: "Never has clericalism been so influential in the legislation and administration of this Empire. The most powerful party is the one that takes its 'mot d'ordre' from the Papal Nunciature. It guides the feudal nobility, it is the thorn in the flesh of the German population, it has provoked a 20 years' reaction in Austria, and, unhindered and protected, it scatters in Hungary that seed which has thriven so well in this half of the Monarchy that nothing is done in Austria without first considering what will be said about it in Rome." A day or two later some evidence of a growing resentment in Austria at the interference of the clergy in politics was adduced: "Thus the Czech organ, inspired by the well-known leader of the party, Dr. Stransky, states that a deputation of tradespeople called on the editor and expressed great indignation at the unprecedented manner in which the priests were joining in electoral agitation. They added that they 'could no longer remain members of a Church whose clergy took advantage of religious sentiment for political purposes.' The Peasants' Electoral Association for Upper Austria has just issued a manifesto in which the following occurs:—'We have for more than 20 years invariably elected the candidates proposed by the Clerical party. What has been done during that long period for us peasants and small tradespeople? What have the Clerical party and the Clerical members of Parliament done for us? How have they rewarded our long fidelity? By treason. . . . We have been imposed upon long enough. It is due to our self-respect and honour to emancipate ourselves thoroughly from the mamelukes put forward by the Clerical wirepullers. We must show that we can get on without Clerical leadingstrings.'"

On the 26th of October the writer summarized a report that day published by the Vienna Stock Exchange Committee, as furnishing "fresh evidence of the disastrous effects of the prolonged internal political crisis." "The report begins by stating that the Vienna Stock Exchange, formerly the leading and most important one in Europe, and which, in consequence of the geographical situation of the town, was called upon to be the centre of financial operations with the Near East, has for years past been steadily declining. Every year the number of those frequenting the Bourse diminishes, and there has been an annual decrease in the amount of capital that has changed hands. Of late years, and particularly within the last few months, this has assumed such dimensions that it has become of an imperative duty for the competent authorities to investigate the causes of the evil and to seek a remedy. It is recognized that the deplorable domestic situation has largely contributed to the decline of the Bourse. The deadlock in the Legislative Assembly has occasioned stagnation in Industry and commerce, whereas outside the Monarchy there has been an unprecedented development of trade. Further prejudice has been caused by what is called in the report the anti-capitalist tendencies, which represent all gains and profits to be ill-gotten. The profession of merchant has been held up by unprincipled demagogues as disreputable. The authorities are reproached with having encouraged those tendencies by undue tolerance."

Early in November, the Vienna letters began accounts of the electioneering campaign then opening, though elections for the new House were not to take place until the following January: "Every day," wrote the correspondent, "brings its contingent of electoral manifestoes, and all parties have already had their say. Unfortunately, nothing could be less edifying. It may be said of them all that they have profited little by experience, and it is vain to search for any indication of a conciliatory disposition among Czechs or Germans, Liberals or Clericals. One and all are as uncompromising as ever, and neither the leaders nor the rank and file are prepared to reckon with the real exigencies of the situation, even to save their own Parliamentary existence. The feudal nobility, who stand aloof from Parliamentary strife, have alone lost nothing of their position and influence. They disdainfully refuse to take either the requirements of the State or the legitimate wishes of the Crown into account. They are preparing in alliance with Ultramontanism to hold their own against the coming storm. Their action in the pending electrical campaign is of an occult nature; their proceedings are seldom reported by the newspapers, and when they meet it is by groups and privately.

"The political speeches which have hitherto been delivered in various parts of the country are bewildering. The Germans are split up into several fractions, and even on the other side there have been separate manifestoes from the Young Czechs and also from the Old Czechs, who have long ceased to play a part in the Reichsrath. It is confusion worse confounded, in fact complete chaos. The prospect of a rallying of the heterogeneous and mutually antagonistic groups on the basis of resistance to Hungarian exigencies, though possible, is not yet at hand, whatever the future may reserve. . . . The words of warning that came from the Crown as to this being the last attempt that would be made to rule by constitutional methods has clearly failed to produce that impression among Parliamentary politicians which might justly have been anticipated. Not even the most experienced and best informed among the former members of the Reichsrath are disposed to make any prophecy as to what will follow the dissolution of the next Chamber."

In the following month, a significant speech in the Reichsrath at Buda-Pesth, by the very able Hungarian Prime Minister, M. Szell, was reported. "He foreshadowed the possibility of a situation in which Austria would not be able to fulfil the conditions prescribed in the Ausgleich Act of 1867 with regard to the manner of dealing with the affairs common to both halves of the Monarchy. He himself had, however, made up his mind on the subject, and was convinced that even in those circumstances the Hungarians would by means of provisional measures regulate the common affairs and interests of the two States, 'while specially asserting the rights of Hungary and its independence.' Another version of this somewhat oracular statement runs as follows : — ' Hungary, without infringing the Ausgleich law, will find ways and means of regulating those affairs which, in virtue of the Pragmatic sanction, are common to both States, while at the same time protecting her own interests and giving greater emphasis to her independence.' M. Szell added : — ' When the right-time comes I shall explain my views, and eventually submit proposals to the House. Meanwhile, let us husband our strength and keep our powder dry.' The self-confident and almost defiant tone of this forecast, coming from a responsible statesman accustomed to display such prudence and moderation of language as M. Szell, has made a profound impression in Austria. It assumes the breakdown of the Austrian Parliamentary system to be a certainty, and anticipates the adoption by Hungary of one-sided measures which, according to M. Szell, will afford more effective protection to its interests and confirm its independence. This seems to be interpreted in Vienna as an indication that the Hungarian Premier has a cut and dry scheme ready for the revision of the Ausgleich in a direction which bodes ill for Austria. The gravity of the Ministerial statement is recognized by journals of such divergent views as the semi-official ' Fremdenblatt,' the pan-Germanic and Anti-Semitic ' Deutsche Zeitung,' and the ' Neues Wiener Tagblatt,' which is the organ of the moderate German element. The ' Neues Wiener Tagblatt' frankly acknowledges that, in addition to all her other cares, Austria has now to consider the crucial question of the form which her relations with Hungary will assume at no distant date. Commercial severance and declarations of independence are, it says, being discussed by the initiated sections of the community in both countries, as if it were a matter of merely economic concern, instead of the greatest and most perilous political problem that the Monarchy has been called upon to solve since the establishment of the Dual system, which, in spite of its complexity, has worked well for such a long period. The ' Neues Wiener Tagblatt,' nevertheless, admits that things have now reached a stage at which economic severance is no longer impossible." In a subsequent speech on New Year's Day, M. Szell declared that it " would be a fatal mistake to sever the ties which had so long connected the two countries, as the objects for which they were called into existence still remained and their fundamental basis was not shaken."

The Vienna journals, on that New Year's Day of 1901, reviewed the past and surveyed the prospects of the future in gloomy and pessimistic tones. Heading its article " Progress Backward," the " Wiener Allgemeine Zeitung " said: "It is true that Austria has at her disposal a larger and more efficiently trained army than ever. The natural resources of the country have been better developed than in the past. The progress of the century has not been without influence upon ourselves. But, whereas other nations are more vigorous, greater, and mightier, we have become weaker, smaller, and less important. The history of the world during the second half of the past century has been made at our expense. . . . In the new partition of the world no room has been reserved for Austria. The most important events which will perhaps give the world a new physiognomy are taking place without Austria's being able to exercise the slightest influence thereon. We are living upon our old reputation, but in the long run that capital will prove insufficient."

A. D. 1900 (December).—Census of Vienna. See (in this vol.) VIENNA : A. D. 1900.

A. D. 1901.—Parliamentary elections.— Weakening of the Clerical and Anti-Semitic parties.—Gains for the ultra-radical German parties.—Disorderly opening of the Reichsrath.—Speech of the Emperor from the throne. —From the parliamentary elections held in January the Clerical and Anti-Semitic parties came back to the Reichsrath shorn of about one-third of their strength, while the various radical factions, especially those among the Germans, appear to have made considerable gains. Even in the Tyrol, one of the strongest of the Clerical leaders, Baron Di Pauli, was defeated, and in Vienna the Anti-Semitic majority was cut to less than one-fourth of what it had been three years before. "The Pan-Germanic group," writes "The Times" correspondent from Vienna, "which only numbered five in the last Parliament, now musters 21. It will be remembered that it openly advocates incorporation with the German Empire, and as a preparatory measure the wholesale conversion of the German population of Austria to Protestantism. It has hitherto been to a certain extent boycotted by the other German parties, being excluded from their so-called union for mutual defence and joint action." "But the programme which had thus been boycotted by the bulk of the German members has been the most successful of all in the recent general election. The position of its leading representative, Herr Schönerer, has been so strengthened that he has been able to impose upon the whole group the title of Pan-Germanic Union, and to enforce the acceptance of the principle of ' emancipation from Rome.' The latter demand caused a certain hesitation on the part of some of his new followers, who, however, ultimately decided to adopt it, although not to the full extent of renouncing the Roman Catholic faith, as Herr Schönerer and his principal lieutenant, Herr Wolf, themselves had done. At a conference of the party its programme was declared to be the promotion of such a federal connexion of the German provinces of Austria with the German Empire as would furnish a permanent guarantee for the maintenance of the German nationality in this country. The party would oppose every Government that resisted the realization of that object, and it could not participate in any manifestations of loyalty while such a Government policy was maintained. At the same time, the party regarded it as their obvious duty to emancipate themselves from Rome in a political but not religious sense—that is to say, to free themselves from the influence of the Roman Curia in affairs of State.

"This boycotted party and programme now threatens to win the voluntary or enforced adherence of the advanced section of the other German groups which had hitherto declined to commit themselves to such an extreme policy. The most moderate of all the German parties, that of the constitutional landed proprietors, has felt called upon to enter an energetic and indignant protest against the foregoing Pan-Germanic programme. While they are convinced supporters of the Austro-German alliance, they unconditionally reject aspirations which they hold to be totally inconsistent with the tried and reliable basis of that agreement, and which would constitute an undignified sacrifice of the independence of the Monarchy. They further decline to make their manifestations of loyalty to the Sovereign dependent upon any condition; and they strongly condemn the emancipation from Rome movement as a culpable confusion of the spheres of religion and politics, and an infringement of the liberty of conscience which is calculated to sow dissension among the German nationality in Austria.

"It now remains to be seen to which side the bulk of the German representatives will rally ; to that of the Moderates, who have re-affirmed their devotion to the Dynasty and the existing Constitution, or to that of the Pan-Germanic revolutionaries, who have decided to make their manifestations of loyalty dependent upon the adoption by the Crown of their programme.

"The outlook has thus undergone, if anything, a change for the worse since the last Reichsrath was dissolved. The only reassuring feature of the situation is that the fall of the Ministry is not a primary end with any of the parties in the Reichsrath. Dr. von Körber, who is a politician of great tact and experience, has avoided friction on all sides."

The opening session of the newly elected Reichsrath was held on the 31st of January, and the disorderly temper in it was manifested upon a reference by the President to the death of Queen Victoria, which called out cries of hostility to England from both Germans and Czechs. " In the course of the proceedings some of the members of the Extreme Czech fraction warned the Prime Minister in threatening terms against introducing a single word hostile to the Czech nation in the coming Speech from the Throne. They also announced their intention of squaring accounts with him so soon as the Speech from the Throne should be delivered. The whole sitting did not last an hour, but . . . what happened suffices to show that not only the Pan-Germanic Union, but also the Extreme section of the German People's party and a couple of Radical Czechs, are ready at a moment's notice to transform the Reichsrath into a bear garden."

On the 4th of February the two Houses of the Reichsrath were assembled at the Palace and addressed by the Emperor, in a speech from the throne of which the following is a partial report : "His Majesty referred to various features of legislation, including the Budget, the revision of the Customs tariff, the promotion of trade, industry, and navigation, the protection of the working classes and the regulation of the hours of labour, the Government railway projects and the Bosnian lines, and Bills for the regulation of emigration, the construction of dwellings for the lower classes, the repression of drunkenness, the development of the University system and other educational reforms, and a revision of the Press laws—in fact a whole inventory of the important legislative arrears consequent upon the breakdown of Parliament.

"The following passage occurs in the further course of the speech : 'The Constitution which I bestowed upon my dominions in the exercise of my free will ought to be an adequate guarantee for the development of my people. The finances of the State have been put in order in exemplary fashion and its credit has been raised to a high level. The freedom of the subject reposes upon a firm foundation, and thanks to the scholastic organization and the extraordinary increase of educational establishments general culture has reached a gratifying standard, which has more especially contributed to the efficiency and intelligence of my army. The Provincial Diets have been able to do much within the limits of their jurisdiction. The beneficial influence of the constitutional system has penetrated as far as the communal administrations. I am thus justified in saying that the fundamental laws of the State are a precious possession of my loyal people. Notwithstanding the autonomy enjoyed by certain kingdoms and provinces, they constitute for foreigners the symbol of the strength and unity of the State. I was, therefore, all the more grieved that the last sessions of the Legislature should have had no result, even if I am prepared to acknowledge that such business as affected the position of the Monarchy was satisfactorily transacted by all parties.'

"The Emperor then expressed his regret that other matters of equal importance affecting the interests of Austria had not been disposed of. His Majesty made an appeal to the representatives of the Reichsrath to devote their efforts to the necessary and urgent work awaiting them, and assured them that they might count upon the Government. All attempts at the moral and material development of the Empire were, he said, stultified by the nationality strife. Experience had shown that the efforts of the Government to bring about a settlement of the principal questions involved therein had led to no result and that it was preferable to deal with the matter in the Legislature. The Government regarded a generally satisfactory solution of the pending language question as being both an act of justice and a necessity of State. Trusting in the good will manifested by all parties, the Ministry would do its utmost to promote a settlement which would relieve the country of its greatest evil. At the same time, the Cabinet was under the obligation of maintaining intact the unity of language in certain departments of the Administration, in which it constituted an old and well-tested institution. Success must never again be sought through paralysing the popular representation. The hindrance of Parliamentary work could only postpone or render quite impossible the realization of such aspirations as most deeply affected the public mind. The Sovereign then referred to the damage done to the interests of the Empire by the obstacles placed in the way of the regular working of the Constitution, and pointed to the indispensable necessity of the vigorous co-operation of Parliament in the approaching settlement of the commercial relations between the two halves of the Monarchy. The speech concluded with a warmly-worded appeal to the representatives to establish a peace which would correspond to the requirements of the time and to defend as their fathers had defended ' this venerable State which accords equal protection to all its peoples.'"

A. D. 1901 (March).—Continued turbulence of the factions in the Austrian Reichsrath.—Outspoken aim of the Pan-Germans.—At this writing (late in March), the disgraceful and destructive conflict of reckless factions is still raging in the Austrian Reichsrath, and the parties have come to blows several times. The hope of the German extremists for a dissolution of the Empire seems to be more and more openly avowed. On one occasion, "a Czech member, Dr. Sieleny, having accused the Pan-Germans of wistfully glancing across the frontier, Herr Stein, a member of the Pan-Germanic group, replied, 'We do not glance, we gaze.' Being reproached with looking towards Germany with an ulterior motive, the same gentleman answered, 'You Czechs want to go to Russia, and we Germans want to go to Germany.' Again, on being told that he would like to become a Prussian, he exclaimed, 'I declare openly that we want to go to the German Empire.' Finally, in reply to another remark, Herr Stein observed that everybody in the country who was an Austrian patriot was stupid."

AUTONOMY, Constitutional: Granted by Spain to Cuba and Porto Rico. See (in this vol.) CUBA : A. D. 1897 (NOVEMBER); and 1897–1898 (NOVEMBER—FEBRUARY).

AYUNTAMIENTOS.—Town councillors in Spain and in the Spanish American states. See (in this vol.) CUBA : A. D. 1901 (JANUARY).

B.

BABYLON: Exploration of the ruins of the city. See (in this vol.) ARCHÆOLOGICAL RESEARCH : BABYLONIA : GERMAN EXPLORATION.
Railway to the ruins. See (in this vol.) TURKEY : A. D. 1899 (NOVEMBER).

BABYLONIA: Archæological Exploration in. See (in this vol.) ARCHÆOLOGICAL RESEARCH : BABYLONIA : AMERICAN EXPLORATION.

BACHI, or BASHEE ISLANDS, The American acquisition of. See (in this vol.) UNITED STATES OF AM. : A. D. 1898 (JULY—DECEMBER).

BACTERIAL SCIENCE, Recent. See (in this vol.) SCIENCE, RECENT : MEDICAL AND SURGICAL.

BADENI, Count : Austrian ministry. See (in this vol.) AUSTRIA-HUNGARY : A. D. 1895–1896.

BADEN-POWELL, General **R. S. S. :** Defense of Mafeking. See (in this vol.) SOUTH AFRICA (THE FIELD OF WAR) : A. D. 1899 (OCTOBER—NOVEMBER); and 1900 (MARCH—MAY).

BAGDAD, Railways to. See (in this vol.) TURKEY : A. D. 1899 (NOVEMBER); and JEWS : A. D. 1899.

BAJAUR. See (in this vol.) INDIA : A.D. 1895 (MARCH—SEPTEMBER).

BALFOUR, Arthur J. : First Lord of the Treasury in the British Cabinet. See (in this vol.) ENGLAND : A. D. 1894–1895 ; and 1900 (NOVEMBER—DECEMBER).
Tribute to Queen Victoria. See (in this vol.) ENGLAND : A. D. 1901 (JANUARY).

BALKAN AND DANUBIAN STATES, The.—"The States of the Balkan Peninsula, ever since the practical disruption of European Turkey after the war of 1877–78, have been in a condition of chronic restlessness. Those who desire the repose of Europe have hoped against hope that the new communities which were founded or extended on the ruins of the Ottoman dominion in Europe would be able and willing to keep the peace among themselves and to combine in resisting the intrusion of foreign influences. These expectations have been too frequently disappointed. The lawlessness of Bulgaria and the unsettled state of Servia, more especially, continue to constitute a periodical cause of anxiety to the diplomacy of Europe. The recent murder at Bukharest of Professor Mihaileano, a Macedonian by birth and a Rumanian by extraction, appears to be a shocking example of the teaching of a school of political conspirators who have their centre of operations at Sofia. These persons had already combined to blackmail and terrorise the leading Rumanian residents in the capital of Bulgaria, where the most abominable outrages are stated to have been committed with impunity. Apparently, they have now carried the war, with surprising audacity, into the Rumanian capital itself. Two persons marked out for vengeance by the terrorists of Sofia had previously been murdered in Bukbarest, according to our Vienna Correspondent, but these were Bulgarians by birth. It is a further step in this mischievous propaganda that a Rumanian subject, the occupant of an official position at the seat of the Rumanian government, should be done to death by emissaries from the secret society at Sofia. His crime was that, born of Rumanian parents in Macedonia, he had the boldness to controvert in the Press the claims of the Bulgarians to obtain the upper hand in a Turkish province, where Greeks, Turks, Bulgarians, Albanians, and Serbs are inextricably mixed up. Professor Mihaileano had probably very good reasons for coming to the conclusion that, whatever may be the evils of Ottoman rule, they are less than those which would follow a free fight in the Balkans, ending, it may be, in the ascendency of Bulgarian ruffianism.
"It is for this offence that M. Mihaileano suffered the penalty of death by the decree of a secret tribunal, and at the hands of assassins sent out to do their deadly work by political intriguers who sit in safety at Sofia. The most serious aspect of the matter, however, is the careless and almost contemptuous attitude of the Bulgarian Government. The reign of terror at Sofia and the too successful attempts to extend it to Rumania have provoked remonstrances not only from the government at Bukharest, but from some of the Great Powers, including Austria-Hungary, Germany, and Italy. . . . There is only too much reason to fear, even now, that both the Bulgarian Government and the ruler of the Principality are afraid to break with the terrorists of Sofia. Political assassination is unfor-

tunately among the traditions of the Bulgarian State, but it has never been practised with such frequency and impunity as under the rule of Prince Ferdinand. . . . His own conduct as a ruler, coupled with the lamentable decline of the spirit of Bulgarian independence, which seemed to be vigorous and unflinching before the kidnapping of Prince Alexander, has steadily lowered his position. The Bulgarian agitation — to a large extent a sham one — for the 'redemption,' as it is called, of Macedonia is a safety-valve that relieves Prince Ferdinand and those who surround him from much unpleasant criticism. . . .

"The situation in the Balkans is in many respects disquieting. The Bulgarian agitation for the absorption of Macedonia is not discouraged in high quarters. The hostility of the Sofia conspirators to the Koutzo-Wallachs, the Rumanians of Macedonia, is due to the fact that the latter, being a small minority of the population, are ready to take their chance of equal treatment under Turkish rule, subject to the supervision of Europe, rather than to be swallowed up in an enlarged Bulgaria, dominated by the passions that now prevail in the Principality and that have been cultivated for obvious reasons. Russia, it is believed, has no wish to see Bulgarian aspirations realized, and would much rather keep the Principality in a state of expectant dependence. Servia and Greece would be as much embarrassed as Rumania by the success of the Bulgarian propaganda, and Austria-Hungary would regard it as a grave menace. Of course the Turkish government could not be expected to acquiesce in what would in fact, be its knell of doom. . . . In Greece, the insubordination in certain sections of the army is a symptom not very alarming in itself, but unpleasantly significant of latent discontent. In Turkey, of course, the recrudescence of the fanaticism which periodically breaks out in the massacres of the Armenians cannot be overlooked. A more unfortunate time could not be chosen for endeavouring to reopen the Eastern question by pressing forward the Bulgarian claim to Macedonia. Nor could a more unfortunate method be adopted of presenting that claim than that of the terrorists who appear to be sheltered or screened at Sofia."— *London Times, August* 23, 1900.—See, also (in this vol.), TURKEY: A. D. 1899-1901.

Bulgaria.—On the 15th of July, 1895, M. Stambouloff, lately the powerful chief minister in the Bulgarian government, but now overthrown and out of favor, was attacked by four assassins, in the streets of Sofia, and received wounds from which he died three days afterwards.

The increasing influence of Russia in Bulgaria was manifested unmistakably on the 14th of February, 1896, when Prince Boris, the infant son and heir of the reigning Prince Ferdinand, was solemnly baptised into the Orthodox Greek Church, the Tzar of Russia, represented by proxy at the ceremony, acting as sponsor. This is understood to have been done in opposition to the most earnest remonstrances of the mother of the child, who is an ardent Roman Catholic, the father being nominally the same.

Montenegro: Recent changes.—"The accession of territory obtained under the Berlin Treaty has already begun to alter the character of the country. The area of the Principality has been almost doubled, and fertile valleys, tracts of rich woodland and a strip of sea-coast have been added to the realm of Prince Nikolas. Montenegro is now something more than the rocky eyrie of a warlike clan, and the problem of its commercial development constantly occupies the mind of its ruler. The state of transition is reflected in the aspect of the capital. A tiny hamlet in 1878, Tzetinye now bears witness to the growth of civilisation and to the beneficent influence of a paternal despotism. . . . Nikolas I., 'Prince and Gospodar of free Tzrnagora and the Berda,' is the most picturesque and remarkable figure in the South Slavonic world. Descended from a long line of heroes, the heir of the Vladikas, he has, like them, distinguished himself in many a hard-fought conflict with the hereditary foe. In the field of poetry he has also won his triumphs; like his father Mirko, 'the Sword of Montenegro,' he has written lyric odes and ballads; like his ancestor, the Vladika Petar II., he has composed historical dramas, and his poems and plays hold a recognised place in contemporary Slavonic literature. The inheritor of a splendid tradition, a warrior and a bard, gifted by nature with a fine physique and a commanding presence, he forms the impersonation and embodiment of all that appeals most to the imagination of a romantic and impressionable race, to its martial instinct, its poetic temperament, and its strange—and to us incomprehensible—yearning after long-vanished glories. . . . Any attempt to describe Prince Nikolas' work as an administrator and a reformer would lead me too far. The codification of the law, which was begun by his ancestors, Danilo I. and Petar I., has been almost completed under his supervision. . . . The suppression of the vendetta is one of the greatest of the Prince's achievements. . . . Crime is now rare in the Principality, except in the frontier districts, where acts of homicide are regarded as justifiable, and indeed laudable, if perpetrated in payment of old scores, or if the victim is an Albanian from over the border. Primary education has been made universal, schools have arisen in every village, and lecturers have been appointed to explain to the peasants the advantages of learning. Communications are being opened up, and the Principality, which a few years since possessed nothing but mule-tracks, can now boast of 138 miles of excellent carriage-road, better engineered and maintained than any I have seen in the Peninsula. The construction of roads is viewed with some apprehension by the more conservative Montenegrins, who fear that their mountain stronghold may lose its inaccessible character. But the Prince is determined to keep abreast of the march of civilisation. Nine post-offices and thirteen telegraph stations have been established. The latter, which are much used by the people, will play an important part in the next mobilization of the Montenegrin army. Hitherto the forces of the Principality have been called together by stentorian couriers who shouted from the tops of the mountains. A great reform, however, still remains to be attempted—the conversion of a clan of warriors into an industrial nation. The change has been rendered inevitable by the enlargement of the bounds of the Principality, and its necessity is fully recognised by the Prince. Once the future of the country is assured, his order will be 'à bas les armes.' He is aware that such an edict would be intensely unpopular, but he will not flinch when the time for issuing it arrives. Every Montenegrin has been taught from his cradle to regard warfare as his sole vocation in life, and to despise industrial pursuits. The tradition of five hundred years has remained unbroken, but the Prince will not hesitate to destroy it. So enormous is his influence over the people, that he feels confident in his ability to carry out this sweeping reform."— J. D. Bourchier, *Montenegro and her Prince* (*Fortnightly Rev., Dec.*, 1898).

Montenegro: New title of the Prince.— On the 19th of December, 1900, at Tzetinye, or Cettigne, "the President of the Council of State, in the presence of the other Ministers and dignitaries and of the members of the Diplomatic Corps, presented an address to the Prince of Montenegro praying him, in token of the gratitude of the Montenegrin people for the benefits which he had conferred on them during his 40 years' reign, to take the title of Royal Highness. The Prince acceded to the request, and, replying to the President, thanked all the European rulers who on this occasion had given him a fresh proof of their friendship by their recognition of his new title. After the ceremony a Te Deum was celebrated in the Cathedral, and the Prince subsequently reviewed the troops, receiving a great welcome from the people."—*Telegram, Reuter's Agency.*

Servia.—In January, 1894, the young king, Alexander, called his father, the ex-king, Milan (abdicated in 1889—see, in vol. 1, BALKAN AND DANUBIAN STATES: A. D. 1879–1889), to Belgrade to give him help against his Radical ministers, who had been taking, the latter thought, too much into their own hands. The first result was a change of ministry, soon followed by a decision from the synod of Servian bishops annulling the divorce of ex-King Milan and Queen Natalie; by a public announcement of their reconciliation, and by an ukase from King Alexander, cancelling all laws and resolutions which touched his parents and restoring to them their rights and privileges as members of the royal house. This, again, was followed, on the 21st of May, by a royal proclamation which abolished the constitution of December, 1888, and restored the old constitution of 1869. This was a tremendous step backward, to a state of things in which almost no protection against arbitrary kingship could be found.

For some years the ex-king exercised considerable influence over his son, and was again an uncertain and much distrusted factor in the troubled politics of southeastern Europe. In 1898 the son appointed him commander-in-chief of the Servian army, and he is said to have ably and energetically improved its efficiency during the brief period of his command. A breach between father and son was brought about before long, however, by the determination of the latter to marry a lady, Madame Draga Maschin, considerably older than himself, who had been lady-in-waiting to his mother; while the father was arranging a political marriage for him with a German princess. The young king married his chosen bride in August, 1900, and guarded his frontier with troops to bar the return of his father, then sojourning at a German watering place, to the kingdom. It was a final exile for

the ex-king. He visited Paris for a time; then went to Vienna, and there, on the 11th of February, 1901, he died, at the age of 47.

BALLOONS, Declaration against explosives from. See (in this vol.) PEACE CONFERENCE.

BALTIC and NORTH SEA CANALS. See (in this vol.) GERMANY: A. D. 1895 (JUNE); and 1900 (JUNE).

BANK OF FRANCE: Renewal of privileges. See (in this vol.) MONETARY QUESTIONS: A. D. 1897.

BANKING: Its effect on the Nineteenth Century. See (in this vol.) NINETEENTH CENTURY: THE TREND.

BANKRUPTCY LAW, National. See (in this vol.) UNITED STATES OF AM.: A. D. 1898 (JULY 1).

BARBADOS: Condition and relief measures. See (in this vol.) WEST INDIES, THE BRITISH: A. D. 1897.

BARCELONA: A. D. 1895. — Student riots. See (in this vol.) SPAIN: A. D. 1895–1896.

BAROTSILAND: British Protectorate proclaimed. See (in this vol.) SOUTH AFRICA (RHODESIA): A. D. 1900 (SEPTEMBER).

BARRAGE WORKS, Nile. See (in this vol.) EGYPT: A. D. 1898–1901.

BARRIOS, President: Assassination. See (in this vol.) CENTRAL AMERICA (GUATEMALA): A. D. 1897–1898.

BARTON, Miss Clara, and the Red Cross Society.—Relief work in Armenia and Cuba. See (in this vol.) ARMENIA: A. D. 1896 (JANUARY—MARCH); and CUBA: A. D. 1896–1897.

BASHEE, or BACHI ISLANDS, The American acquisition of. See (in this vol.) UNITED STATES OF AM.: A. D. 1898 (JULY—DECEMBER).

BECHUANALAND, British: Annexation to Cape Colony. See (in this vol.) AFRICA: A. D. 1895 (CAPE COLONY).
Partial conveyance to the British South Africa Company. See (in this vol.) AFRICA: A. D. 1895 (BECHUANALAND).

BEEF INVESTIGATION, The American Army. See (in this vol.) UNITED STATES OF AM.: A. D. 1898–1899.

BEET SUGAR. See (in this vol.) GERMANY: A. D. 1896 (MAY); and SUGAR BOUNTIES.

BEHRING SEA. See (in this vol.) BERING SEA.

BÊL, Temple of: Exploration of its ruins at Nippur. See (in this vol.) ARCHÆOLOGICAL RESEARCH: BABYLONIA: AMERICAN EXPLORATION.

BELGIAN ANTARCTIC EXPEDITION. See (in this vol.) POLAR EXPLORATION, 1897–1899.

BELGIUM: A. D. 1894-1895.—The first election under the new constitution.—Victory of the Catholics and surprising Socialist gains.—Elsewhere in this work (see—in vol. 1—CONSTITUTION OF BELGIUM) will be found

6-4　　　　　　　49

the full text of the Belgian constitution as it was revised in 1893; while in volume 3 (see NETH-ERLANDS (BELGIUM): A. D. 1892-1893), the peculiar features of the new constitution, especially in its provision of a system of cumulative or plural voting, are described. The singularity of the experiment thus introduced caused the elections that were held in Belgium in 1894 and 1895 to be watched with an interest widely felt. Elections for the Chamber of Representatives and the Senate occurred on the same day, Oct. 14, 1894. Previously the Belgian suffrage had been limited to about 130,000 electors. Under the new constitution the electors numbered no less than 1,370,000, and the working of the plural system gave them 2,111,000 votes. The result was a more crushing victory for the Catholics than they had ever won before. Of 152 Representatives they elected no less than 104. The Liberal party was almost annihilated, securing but 20 seats in the Chamber; while the Socialists rose to political importance, winning 28 seats. This representation is said to be not at all proportioned to the votes cast by the several parties, and it lent force to the demand for a system of proportional representation, as the needed accompaniment of plural voting, which had been urged when the constitution was revised. In the Senate the Conservatives obtained 52 seats and the Liberals 24. In the next year an electoral law relating to communal councils was passed. In this law, the principle of proportional representation was introduced, along with that of cumulative or plural voting. Compulsory voting, enforced by penalties more or less severe, was also a feature of the law. In November, the first election under it was held, and again the Socialists made surprising gains, at the expense of the Radical party, the Catholics and Liberals generally holding their ground.

A. D. **1895.**—**New** School **Law.**—Compulsory religions teaching restored. See (in this vol.) EDUCATION: A. D. 1895 (BELGIUM).

A. D. **1897.**—Industrial combinations. See (in this vol.) TRUSTS: IN EUROPEAN COUNTRIES.

A. D. **1897** (July).—British notice to terminate existing commercial treaties. See (in this vol.) ENGLAND: A. D. 1897 (JUNE—JULY).

A. D. **1898** (June).—The Sugar Conference at Brussels. See (in this vol.) SUGAR BOUNTIES.

A. D. **1898** (July—December).—In the Chinese "battle of concessions." See (in this vol.) CHINA: A. D. 1898 (FEBRUARY—DECEMBER).

A. D. **1899** (**May**—July).—Representation in the Peace Conference at The Hague. See (in this vol.) PEACE CONFERENCE.

A. D. **1899-1900.**—Threatened revolution. —An explosion of discontent with the working of the electoral provisions of the new constitution (see above) occurred in June, and created for a time an exceedingly dangerous situation. It was precipitated by an attempt on the part of the government to pass a bill providing for proportional representation in certain districts, which was expected to increase the advantage already possessed by the Clerical or Catholic party. Excitement in the Chamber of Deputies reached such a height on the 28th of June that fighting among the members occurred, and soldiers were called in. That night and the next day there was serious rioting in Brussels; bar-

ricades were built; sharp battles between citizens and soldiers were fought, and a general strike of working men was proposed. On the 30th, the government arranged a compromise with the Socialist and Liberal leaders which referred the question of proportional representation to a committee in which all parties were represented. This quieted the disorder. In due time the committee reported against the measure which the government had proposed; whereupon a change of ministry was made, the new ministry being expected to bring forward a more satisfactory plan of proportional representation. It produced a bill for that purpose, the provisions of which failed to give satisfaction. but which was passed, nevertheless, near the end of the year.

Commenting, in July, on the disturbances then just quieted in Belgium, the "Spectator," of London, remarked: "The recent explosion of political feeling in Belgium was a much more serious event than was quite understood in this country. It might have involved all Europe, as, indeed, it may even yet. There was revolution in the air, and a revolution in Belgium would gravely affect the military position both of France and Germany, would rouse keen suspicions and apprehensions in this country, and would perturb all the dynasties with fears of coming change. The new electoral bill drove the Liberals and Socialists of the little kingdom into one another's arms—both believing that it would give the Clericals a permanent hold on power—and whenever these two parties are united they control the majority of the Belgian people. That majority is a most dangerous one. It controls all the cities, and it includes hundreds of thousands of men who resent their economic condition with justifiable bitterness, and who are penetrated with a tradition of victories achieved by insurrection. At the same time they have no pacific vent for their discontents, for the suffrage gives double votes to the well-to-do, and secures to both Liberals and laborers on all economic or religious questions a certainty of defeat. With the inhabitants of the cities all rioting and killing the officials, the government would have been compelled to resort to force, and it is by no means clear that force was decidedly on their side. The Belgian army is not a caste widely separated in feeling from the people; it has no instinctive devotion to the Clerical party, and it has no great soldier whom it admires or to whom it is attached. The king is distrusted and disliked both personally and politically; and the dynasty, which has no historic connection with Belgium, has never taken root in the soil as the Bernadottes, for example, have done in Sweden. If the revolutionists had been beaten, they would have appealed to France, where Belgium is regarded as a reversionary estate; while if they had been victorious, they might—in our judgment, they certainly would—have proclaimed a republic. . . . The danger has, we suppose, for the moment been smoothed away; but it has not been removed, probably can not be removed, while the conditions which produce it continue to exist. The Belgians, who are commonly supposed to be so prosperous and pacific, are divided by differences of race, creed, and social condition more violent than exists in Ireland, where at all events, all alike, with insignificant exceptions, speak one tongue. The French-speaking Belgians despise the Flemish-speaking Belgians, and the Flemish-speaking Belgians detest the French-speaking Belgians, with a rancor only concealed by the long habit of living and acting together,—a habit which, remember, has not prevented the same contempts and aversions from continuing to exist in Ireland. The Clericals and the Secularists hate each other as only religious parties can hate ; far more than Catholics and Protestants in any of the countries where the two creeds stand side by side. The Secularist seems to the Clerical a blasphemer, against whom almost all devices are justifiable, while the Clerical is held by the Secularist to be a kind of evil fool, from whom nothing is to be expected except cunningly concealed malignity. The possessors of property expect that the ‘ugly rush’ which used to be talked of in England will occur tomorrow, while the wage receivers declare that they are worked to death for the benefit of others, who will not leave them so much as a living wage. All display when excited to a noteworthy fierceness of temper, a readiness to shed blood, and a disposition to push every quarrel into a sort of war,—tendencies visible throughout the history of the country."

At the parliamentary election in June, 1900, under the new law providing for proportional representation, the Socialists gained seventeen seats from the Clerical party.

A. D. 1900.—Relations with the Congo State. See (in this vol.) CONGO FREE STATE: A. D. 1900.

BELL TELEPHONE SYSTEM, Recent development of. See (in this vol.) SCIENCE, RECENT : ELECTRICAL.

BELMONT, Battle of. See (in this vol.) SOUTH AFRICA (THE FIELD OF WAR): A. D. 1899 (OCTOBER—DECEMBER).

BENIN : Massacre of British officials.— Capture of the town. See (in this vol.) NIGERIA : A. D. 1897.

BERGENDAL FARM, Battle of. See (in this vol.) SOUTH AFRICA (THE FIELD OF WAR): A. D. 1900 (JUNE—DECEMBER).

BERING SEA QUESTIONS.—"Several vexatious questions were left undetermined by the decision of the Bering Sea Arbitration Tribunal [see, in vol. 5, UNITED STATES OF AM.: A. D. 1886–1893]. The application of the principles laid down by that august body has not been followed by the results they were intended to accomplish, either because the principles themselves lacked in breadth and definiteness or because their execution has been more or less imperfect. Much correspondence has been exchanged between the two Governments [of Great Britain and the United States] on the subject of preventing the exterminating slaughter of seals. The insufficiency of the British patrol of Bering Sea under the regulations agreed on by the two Governments has been pointed out, and yet only two British ships have been on police duty during this season in those waters. The need of a more effective enforcement of existing regulations as well as the adoption of such additional regulations as experience has shown to be absolutely necessary to carry out the intent of the award have been earnestly urged upon the British Government, but thus far without effective results. In the meantime the deple-

tion of the seal herds by means of pelagic hunting [that is, in the open sea] has so alarmingly progressed that unless their slaughter is at once effectively checked their extinction within a few years seems to be a matter of absolute certainty. The understanding by which the United States was to pay and Great Britain to receive a lump sum of $425,000 in full settlement of all British claims for damages arising from our seizure of British sealing vessels unauthorized under the award of the Paris Tribunal of Arbitration was not confirmed by the last Congress, which declined to make the necessary appropriation. I am still of the opinion that this arrangement was a judicious and advantageous one for the Government, and I earnestly recommend that it be again considered and sanctioned. If, however, this does not meet with the favor of Congress, it certainly will hardly dissent from the proposition that the Government is bound by every consideration of honor and good faith to provide for the speedy adjustment of these claims by arbitration as the only other alternative. A treaty of arbitration has therefore been agreed upon, and will be immediately laid before the Senate, so that in one of the modes suggested a final settlement may be reached."—*Message of the President of the United States to Congress, December,* 1895.

The treaty thus referred to by the President was signed at Washington, February 8, 1896, and ratifications were exchanged at London on the 3d of June following. Its preamble set forth that, whereas the two governments had submitted certain questions to a tribunal of arbitration, and "whereas the High Contracting Parties having found themselves unable to agree upon a reference which should include the question of the liability of each for the injuries alleged to have been sustained by the other, or by its citizens, in connection with the claims presented and urged by it, did, by Article VIII of the said Treaty, agree that either party might submit to the Arbitrators any questions of fact involved in said claims, and ask for a finding thereon, the question of the liability of either Government on the facts found to be the subject of further negotiation : And whereas the Agent of Great Britain did, in accordance with the provisions of said Article VIII, submit to the Tribunal of Arbitration certain findings of fact which were agreed to as proved by the Agent of the United States, and the Arbitrators did unanimously find the facts so set forth to be true, as appears by the Award of the Tribunal rendered on the 15th day of August, 1893 : And whereas, in view of the said findings of fact and of the decision of the Tribunal of Arbitration concerning the jurisdictional rights of the United States in Behring Sea, and the right of protection of property of the United States in the fur-seals frequenting the islands of the United States in Behring Sea, the Government of the United States is desirous that, in so far as its liability is not already fixed and determined by the findings of fact and the decision of said Tribunal of Arbitration, the question of such liability should be definitely and fully settled and determined, and compensation made, for any injuries for which, in the contemplation of the Treaty aforesaid, and the Award and findings of the Tribunal of Arbitration, compensation may be due to Great Britain from the United States : And whereas it is claimed by

Great Britain, though not admitted by the United States, that prior to the said Award certain other claims against the United States accrued in favour of Great Britain on account of seizures of or interference with the following named British sealing-vessels, to wit: the 'Wanderer,' the 'Winifred,' the 'Henrietta,' and the 'Oscar and Hattie,' and it is for the mutual interest and convenience of both the High Contracting Parties that the liability of the United States, if any, and the amount of compensation to be paid, if any, in respect to such claims, and each of them should also be determined under the provisions of this Convention — all claims by Great Britain under Article V of the modus vivendi of the 18th April, 1892, for the abstention from fishing of British sealers during the pendency of said arbitration having been definitely waived before the Tribunal of Arbitration"—therefore the two nations have concluded the Convention referred to, which provides that "all claims on account of injuries sustained by persons in whose behalf Great Britain is entitled to claim compensation from the United States, and arising by virtue of the Treaty aforesaid, the Award and the findings of the said Tribunal of Arbitration, as also the additional claims specified in the 5th paragraph of the preamble hereto, shall be referred to two Commissioners, one of whom shall be appointed by Her Britannic Majesty, and the other by the President of the United States, and each of whom shall be learned in the law." — *Great Britain, Parliamentary Publications (Papers by Command: Treaty Series, No. 10, 1896).*

Judges William L. Putnam, of the United States, and George E. King, of Canada, were subsequently appointed to be the two commissioners provided for in the treaty. Meantime each government had appointed a number of men of science to investigate the condition of the herds of fur-seals on Pribilof Islands, President David S. Jordan, of Leland Stanford Junior University being director of the American investigation and Professor D'Arcy W. Thompson having charge of the British. The two bodies of investigators reached quite different conclusions. Professor Jordan, in a preliminary statement, announced: "There is still a vast body of fur seals on the islands, more than the commissioners were at first led to expect, but the number is steadily declining. The only cause of this decline is the killing of females through pelagic sealing. The females are never molested on the islands, but three-fourths of those killed in Bering sea are nursing females. The death of the mother causes the death of the young on shore, so that for every four fur seals killed at sea three pups starve to death on shore. As each of those females is also pregnant, a like number of unborn pups is likewise destroyed." His formal report, made in January, 1897, was to the same effect, and led to the following conclusion: "The ultimate end in view should be an international arrangement whereby all skins of female fur seals should be seized and destroyed by the customs authorities of civilized nations, whether taken on land or sea, from the Pribilof herd, the Asiatic herds, or in the lawless raiding of the Antarctic rookeries. In the destruction of the fur seal rookeries of the Antarctic, as well as those of the Japanese islands and of Bering sea, American enterprise has taken a leading part. It would be well for America to lead the way in

stopping pelagic sealing by restraining her own citizens without waiting for the other nations. We can ask for protection with better grace when we have accorded, unasked, protection to others." The report of Professor Thompson, made three months later, agreed but partially with that of the American experts. He admitted the extensive starving of the young seals, caused by the killing of the mothers, but contended that the herd was diminishing slightly, if at all, and he did not favor drastic measures for the suppression of pelagic sealing.

The government of the United States adopted measures in accordance with the views of Professor Jordan, looking to an international regulation of the killing of seals. Hon. John W. Foster was appointed a special ambassador to negotiate arrangements to that effect. Through the efforts of Mr. Foster, an international conference on the subject was agreed to on the part of Russia and Japan, but Great Britain declined to take part. While these arrangements were pending, the American Secretary of State, Mr. Sherman, addressed a letter to the American Ambassador at London, Mr. Hay, criticising the conduct of the British government and its agents in terms that are not usual among diplomats, and which excited much feeling when the letter was published in July. This called out a reply from the British Colonial Secretary, Mr. Chamberlain, in which he wrote: "When Her Majesty's government sent their agents to inquire into the actual facts in 1896, it was found that, in spite of the large catch of 1895, the herd actually numbered more than twice as many cows as it had been officially asserted to contain in 1895. The result of these investigations, as pointed out in Lord Salisbury's dispatch of May 7, has further been to show that pelagic sealing is much less injurious than the practice pursued by the United States' lessees of killing on land every male whose skin was worth taking. If the seal herd to-day is, as Professor Jordan estimates, but one-fifth of what it was in 1872–74, that result must be, in great measure, due to the fact that, while the islands were under the control of Russia, that power was satisfied with an average catch of 33,000 seals; subsequently under the United States' control more than three times that number have been taken every year, until the catch was, perforce, reduced because that number of males could no longer be found.

" Last year, while the United States government were pressing Her Majesty's government to place further restrictions on pelagic sealing, they found it possible to kill 30,000 seals on the islands, of which Professor Jordan says (in one place in his report) 22,000 were, to the best of his information, three-year-olds, though (in another place) he estimated the total number of three-year-old males on the islands as 15,000 to 20,000. If such exhaustive slaughter is continued, it will, in the light of the past history of the herd, very quickly bring about that commercial extermination which has been declared in the United States to be imminent every year for the last twelve years. Enough has perhaps been said to justify the refusal of Her Majesty's government to enter on a precipitate revision of the regulations."

The two countries were thus being carried into serious opposition, on a matter that looks contemptible when compared with the great common interests which ought to bind them in firm friendship together. But, while the government of Great Britain declined to enter into conference with those of Russia, Japan and the United States, on general questions relating to the seals, it assented at length to a new conference with the United States and Canada, relative to the carrying out of the regulations prescribed by the Paris tribunal of 1893. Both conferences were held at Washington in October and November of 1897. The first resulted in a treaty (November 6) between Russia, Japan, and the United States, providing for a suspension of pelagic sealing during such time as might be determined by experts. The other conference led, after some interval, to the creation of a Joint High Commission for the settlement of all questions in dispute between the United States and Canada, the sealing question included. See (in this vol.) CANADA: A. D. 1898-1899.

So far as concerned its own citizens, the American government adopted vigorous measures for the suppression of pelagic sealing. An Act of Congress, approved by the President on the 29th December, 1897, forbade the killing of seals, by any citizen of the United States, in any part of the Pacific Ocean north of 35 degrees north latitude. The same act prohibited the importation into the United States of sealskins taken elsewhere than in the Pribilof Islands, and very strict regulations for its enforcement were issued by the Treasury Department. No sealskins, either in the raw or the manufactured state, might be admitted to the country, even among the personal effects of a traveller, unless accompanied by an invoice, signed by an United States Consul, certifying that they were not from seals killed at sea. Skins not thus certified were seized and destroyed.

In his annual report for 1898, the U. S. Secretary of the Treasury stated that no pelagic sealing whatever had been carried on by citizens of the United States during the season past; but that 30 British vessels had been engaged in the work, against 32 in the previous year, and that their total catch had been 10,581, against 6,100 taken by the same fleet in 1897. The number of seals found on the Islands was reported to be greatly reduced.

BERLIN: A. D. 1895.— Census. See (in this vol.) GERMANY: A. D. 1895 (JUNE—DECEMBER).

A. D. 1896.—Industrial exposition.—An exposition of German industries and products was opened at Berlin on the 1st of May, 1896, which excited wide interest and had an important stimulating effect in Germany.

A. D. 1900.—Growth shown by the latest census. See (in this vol.) GERMANY: A. D. 1900 (DECEMBER).

A. D. 1901.—The Berlin and Stettin Ship Canal. See GERMANY: A. D. 1901 (JANUARY).

BETHLEHEM, Capture of. See (in this vol.) SOUTH AFRICA (THE FIELD OF WAR): A. D. 1900 (JUNE—DECEMBER).

BIAC-NA-BATO, Treaty of. See (in this vol.) PHILIPPINE ISLANDS: A. D. 1896-1898.

BIBLE LANDS, Archæological exploration in. See (in this vol.) ARCHÆOLOGICAL RESEARCH: BABYLONIA: AMERICAN EXPLORATION.

BICOLS, The. See (in this vol.) PHILIPPINE ISLANDS: THE NATIVE INHABITANTS.

BIDA, British subjugation of. See (in this vol.) AFRICA: A. D. 1897 (NIGERIA).

BIG SWORD, or BIG KNIFE SOCIETY. See (in this vol.) CHINA: A. D. 1900 (JANUARY—MARCH).

BISMARCK, Prince Otto von: Death. See (in this vol.) GERMANY: A. D. 1898 (JULY).

BLACK FLAG REBELLION. See (in this vol.) CHINA: A. D. 1898 (APRIL—JULY).

BLANCO, General Ramon, Captain-General of Cuba. See (in this vol.) CUBA: A. D. 1896-1897.

BLANCOS. See (in this vol.) URUGUAY: A. D. 1896-1899.

BLOEMFONTEIN: Taken by the British. See (in this vol.) SOUTH AFRICA (THE FIELD OF WAR): A. D. 1900 (MARCH—MAY).

BLOEMFONTEIN CONFERENCE, The. See (in this vol.) SOUTH AFRICA (THE TRANSVAAL): A. D. 1899 (MAY—JUNE).

BLUEFIELDS INCIDENT, The. See (in this vol.) CENTRAL AMERICA (NICARAGUA): A. D. 1894-1895.

BOARD SCHOOLS, English. See (in this vol.) ENGLAND: A. D. 1896-1897.

BOERS. See (in this vol.) SOUTH AFRICA (THE TRANSVAAL).

BOHEMIA: Recent situation in the Austro-Hungarian Empire. See (in this vol.) AUSTRIA-HUNGARY: A. D. 1895-1896, and after.

A. D. 1897.—The language decrees. See (in this vol.) AUSTRIA-HUNGARY: A. D. 1897; and 1898.

BOLIVIA: A. D. 1894-1900.—The dispute with Chile concerning Atacama. See (in this vol.) CHILE: A. D. 1894-1900.

A. D. 1899.—Revolution.—The government of President Alonzo (elected in 1896) was overthrown in April, 1899, by a revolutionary movement conducted by General José Manuel Pando, who was elected President by the legislative chambers in the following October.

BOMBAY: A. D. 1896-1901.—The Bubonic Plague. See (in this vol.) PLAGUE.

A. D. 1901.—Census returns.—Decrease of population.—A telegram from Bombay, March 6, 1901, reports that "the census returns show the city of Bombay has 770,000 inhabitants, a decrease of over fifty thousand in ten years, mainly due to the exodus of the last two months on account of the plague. Partial returns from the rural districts show terrible decreases in population through famine."

BORDA, President: Assassination. See (in this vol.) URUGUAY: A. D. 1896-1899.

BORIS, Prince: Conversion. See (in this vol.) BALCAN AND DANUBIAN STATES (BULGARIA).

BOSTON: A. D. 1895-1899.—The municipal experiments of Mayor Quincy.—First elected Mayor of Boston in 1895, and reëlected in 1897, the two terms of the administration of Mayor

53

Josiah Quincy were made remarkable by the number, the originality and the boldness of the experiments which he introduced in extension of the functions of municipal government. They consisted on the one hand in the substitution, in certain branches of public work, of direct labor for the contract system, and on the other in the provision of new facilities for promoting popular health, recreation, and instruction. He established a municipal printing office, a municipal department of electrical construction, and another municipal department which conducts every kind of repairing work that the city requires; all of these to supersede the old system of contracts and jobs. He instituted a great number and variety of public baths,—floating baths, beach baths, river baths and swimming pools. He opened playgrounds and gymnasiums, both outdoor and in-door. He carried the city into the work of the fresh air missions for poor children. He reorganized the administration of public charities. He placed the artistic undertakings of the city under the supervision of a competent board. He instituted cheap concerts of a high order, as well as popular lectures. Boston at length took alarm at the extent of the ventures of Mayor Quincy, complained of the cost, and refused him reëlection for a third term. But the Boston correspondent of a New York journal opposed in politics to Mayor Quincy, writing on the 15th of December, 1900, testifies that "most of the experiments are working well, and a study of them cannot fail to be beneficial to those who have the government of other cities in their hands. . . . The madness of Mayor Quincy had evidently a method. It seems to have made permanent a good many excellent institutions. Some good citizens say that things were done too quickly, that they cost too much money, that the Mayor was always robbing Peter to pay Paul, as it were. But, after all, it seems cause for thankfulness that they were done at all."

A. D. 1899.—Completion of the Subway.— In this year the city of Boston completed a very important public improvement, undertaken in 1895, and carried out under the direction of a commission appointed that year. This was the construction of a Subway under Boylston and Tremont streets, and under various streets in the northern district, for the transit of electric cars through the crowded central parts of the city. The section of Subway from Park Square to Park Street was finished in the fall of 1897; the remainder in 1899. The entire length of underground road is one and two-thirds miles. The cost of work done was $4,686,000; cost of real estate taken, $1,100,000. The legislative Act authorizing the work provided further for the construction of a tunnel to East Boston, and for the purchase of rights of way for an elevated road to Franklin Park, with new bridges to Charlestown and West Boston.

BOWER, Sir Graham: Testimony before British Parliamentary Committee on the Jameson Raid. See (in this vol.) SOUTH AFRICA (THE TRANSVAAL): A. D. 1897 (FEBRUARY—JULY).

BOXERS, The Chinese: The secret society and the meaning of its name. See (in this vol.) CHINA: A. D. 1900 (JANUARY—MARCH), and after.

BRADFORD'S HISTORY: Return of the

manuscript to Massachusetts. See (in this vol.) MASSACHUSETTS: A. D. 1897.

BRAZIL: A. D. 1897.—Conflict with the "Fanatics."—A religious enthusiast, called Conselheiro (Counsellor), who had made his appearance in the State of Bahia and gathered a great number of followers, began in 1897 to become dangerous to the government, which he denounced as atheistic; his following grew disorderly, and political malcontents were taking advantage of the disturbance which he caused. Attempts on the part of the government to stop the disorder were fiercely resisted, and its conflict with "the Fanatics," as Conselheiro and his followers were known, soon became a very serious war, demanding many thousands of troops, and spreading over wide regions of the country. Amazonian bands of women fought with "the Fanatics," and were among the most dreaded forces on their side. The headquarters and stronghold of the movement were finally taken in July, after an obstinate defense, and in October Conselheiro was killed; after which the rebellion came to an end.

A. D. 1898.—Election of Dr. Campos Salles to the Presidency.—The nomination and election of Dr. M. F. de Campos Salles, who was inaugurated President of the United States of Brazil on the 15th of November, 1898, "marks the decided distinction of parties in Brazil. Previously, there had been various divergencies among the Republicans, but no distinct party differences. But at that time there arose a party advocating the selection of a candidate who would favor the national against the foreign (naturalized) element; one who would have influence with the few remaining advocates of the monarchical government; who would give preference to a military over a civil government; finally, one who would introduce into the government the system called 'Jacobinism,' a designation which the new party did not refuse to accept. Dr. Campos Salles was the candidate of the moderate Republicans or Conservatives, who were organized under the name of the Republican party, with a platform demanding respect for the constitution and declaring for the institution of such reforms as only reason and time should dictate. The sympathies of the conservative element and of foreigners who had interests in the country were with the candidate of this party and gave him their support. The election of Dr. Campos Salles inspired renewed confidence in the stability of Brazil, a confidence which was at once manifested by the higher quotation of the national bonds, by an advance in the rate of exchange, and by greater activity in business throughout the country. Brazil, in spite of all hindrances, has prospered since 1889."—*Bulletin of the Bureau of Am. Republics, Dec.*, 1898.

A. D. 1900.—Arbitration of the French Guiana boundary dispute.—Award of the Swiss Government.—A dispute with France concerning the boundary of the French possessions in Guiana, which Brazil inherited from Portugal, and which dates back to the 17th century, was submitted at last to the Swiss Federal Council, as a tribunal of arbitration, and settled by the award of the Council on December 1, 1900. The decision fixes the River Oyapok and the watershed of the Tumuc Humac Mountains as the boundary. It is practically in favor of

Brazil, for France had claimed, a year before, a territory of not less than 400,000 square kilomètres, ten times the area of Switzerland itself. Even after a large abatement had been made, the claim was still for 260,000 square kilomètres, or 100,000 square miles, much more than the area of Great Britain. The actual territory allotted to France by the Federal Government of Switzerland is about 8,000 square miles. The arbitrators had no excuse for saying that the case was not brought before them in all its length and breadth. The documents presented by France formed four large volumes, supplemented by an atlas of 35 maps, while Brazil, not to be outdone, put in 13 volumes of documents and three atlases, with about 200 maps.

BRITISH CENTRAL AFRICA PROTECTORATE: Administrative separation from British South Africa Company's territory.—Conflicts with natives.—Resources and prospects of the country.—Until 1894, the territory north of the Zambezi over which the British South Africa Company claimed a "sphere of influence," and the region covered by the British Protectorate that was declared in 1889-90 over Nyassaland and the Shiré Highlands, were administered together by Sir Harry Johnston. But in that year the South Africa Company undertook the administration of its own portion of British Central Africa, and Commissioner Johnston became the Administrator of the remaining "British Central Africa Protectorate." In his report for 1895-6 (April to April) the Commissioner estimated the native population of the Protectorate at 844,420; British subjects, 259; other Europeans, 30; Indians, 263; half-castes, 23. Of hostilities with the natives, Commissioner Johnston gave the following report:

"In the autumn of 1895, ... a campaign lasting four months was commenced and carried to a successful conclusion against all the independent Yao Chiefs who dwelt on the south-eastern border of the Protectorate, and who continued to raid our territories for slaves. This campaign culminated in the complete defeat and death or expulsion of those Arabs who had created an independent power in the North Nyasa district. Action was also taken against the Angoni Chief, Mwasi Kazungu, in the interior of the Marimba district, who had made common cause with the Arabs, and was attempting to form against us a league of the Angoni-Zulus. ... The only people likely now to give trouble in any way are the Angoni-Zulus, who are to the west of the Protectorate what the Yaos and Arabs have been to the north. For the past 40 years the western portions of the Protectorate have been the happy hunting-ground of the descendants of the Zulu bands who quitted Matabeleland at various periods during the last 70 years, and who penetrated into Central Africa as far as the eastern part of Tanganyika and the south shores of the Victoria Nyanza. They established themselves strongly as a ruling caste on the high plateaux to the west and to the north-east of Lake Nyasa. From these plateaux they raided perseveringly for slaves, chiefly in the regions of the Great Luangwa valley, but also to some extent the coast lands of Lake Nyasa.

"Not a few of the Angoni Chiefs are friendly and well disposed towards the British, and seem likely to settle down quietly as they appreciate

the futility of continued defiance of our power; but we may have yet a little trouble from the Western Angoni, and also from an ill-conditioned young Chief ordinarily known by his father's name, Chikusi, but whose private appellation is Gomanikwenda. Chikusi lives on the wedge of Portuguese territory which penetrates the south-western part of the Protectorate. Secure in the knowledge that our forces cannot infringe the Portuguese border, he occasionally makes raids for slaves into the Upper Shiré and Central Angoniland districts."—Sir Harry Johnston, *Report* (*Great Britain, Parliamentary Publications: Papers by Command, Africa, No. 5,* 1896), *pp.* 12-13.—In the autumn of 1896, Chikusi raided one of the mission stations at Ntonda, killing many native Christians. An expedition was then sent against him, which pursued him to his chief kraal, and took him prisoner. He was tried for murder, condemned and shot.

"Nyasaland, or British Central Africa as it is officially called, is now [1898] in a fair way of becoming one of the richest coffee and tobacco growing districts of the world. It enjoys the immense advantage of direct water communication with the coast and, with the exception of a stretch of one hundred miles, the River Shiré, which runs out of Lake Nyasa, is navigable along its whole course. Before long the Upper and Lower Shiré will be connected by a railway line, and goods will then be landed at the northern extremity of Lake Nyasa—a distance of 700 miles from the mouth of the Zambezi—at a trifling cost. At present the journey can already be accomplished in a week. Ten steamers navigate Lake Nyasa, and double that number run on the Zambezi and the Shiré Rivers. This mighty task—accomplished, we must not forget it, without the cost of a single penny to the British tax-payer—did not benefit Great Britain alone. The Portuguese, who, for the last three centuries were slumbering in their East African possessions, were aroused by the extraordinary activity which was displayed at their door. At first they raised objections, but they soon understood what advantages they would derive from the situation, and gave their hearty co-operation to Great Britain. It brought more wealth than they had ever dreamt of to their Zambezi provinces, now a busy centre of trade, in telegraphic communication with the Cape in the South and Lake Nyasa in the North. The Portuguese port of Beira, a sandbank some years ago, has become the most important harbour between Zanzibar and Delagoa Bay, and owes its present position to the railway line which runs to Mashonaland."—L. Decle, *The Fashoda Question* (*Fortnightly Rev., Nov.,* 1898).

BRITISH COLUMBIA. See (in this vol.) CANADA.

BRITISH EAST AFRICA PROTECTORATE, The: A. D. 1895. — Territory transferred to the British Government. See (in this vol.) AFRICA: A. D. 1895 (BRITISH EAST AFRICA).

A. D. 1895-1897. — Its creation and extent. — Existence of slavery. — War in the Province of **Seyyidieh.**—Report of the commissioner.—"The British East Africa Protectorate is bounded on the east by the Indian Ocean, on the west by the Uganda Protectorate, and on the south-west by the Anglo-German frontier, which, starting from the mouth of the River Umba, runs in a generally north-west direction till it strikes the eastern shore of Lake Victoria Nyanza at the point at which it is intersected by the 1st parallel of south latitude. To the north and north-east it is bounded by the Italian sphere of influence from which it is divided by the River Juba up to parallel 6° of north latitude, and thence by a line running along that parallel until it reaches the Blue Nile. The frontier between the East Africa and Uganda Protectorates is only partially defined : starting from the German frontier, it follows the Guaso Masai River as far as Sosian, thence strikes north-east to the Kedong River, which it follows to its source, and thence runs in a northerly direction along the Likipia escarpment or eastern lip of the great ' meridional rift.' It is, however, still undecided whether or not it should be deflected, for greater convenience in dealing with the Uganda Masai, so as to leave to Uganda the region between the southern portion of the Likipia escarpment and the so-called Aberdare range. In view of the uncertainty existing as to the inland boundaries, it is impossible to give the exact area of the territory, though it may be estimated roughly at 280,000 square miles. It will be sufficient here to state that its coast-line, including in the term the Islands of Lamu, Manda, and Patta, which are separated from the mainland by narrow channels, is 405 miles long, whilst its greatest breadth, measured from the centre of the district of Gosha on the Juba to the Likipia escarpment, is 460 miles.

''The Protectorate in its present form was constituted on the 1st July, 1895. Previous to that date a Protectorate had been declared on the 4th November, 1890, over those portions of the territory which formed part of the Zanzibar Sultanate, and on the 19th November of the same year over Witu and the whole of the coast between the Tana and Juba Rivers. The administration of this second Protectorate was confided in 1893, with the exception of those portions of the coast between the Tana and Juba which belonged to the Zanzibar Sultanate and were rented by the Imperial British East Africa Company from him, to the Sultan of Zanzibar, but without being fused in or united to the Sultanate. In September, 1894, a Protectorate was established under an independent Commissioner over Uganda, and was subsequently defined as extending over the whole of the intervening territory from which the Imperial British East Africa Company had withdrawn its effective control, that is, as far as the western limits of its district of Kikuyu, which still constitutes the frontier between the East Africa and Uganda Protectorates. The remainder of the British sphere between the Zanzibar and Uganda boundaries and the Tana River and German frontier was placed under Her Majesty's protection on the 1st July, 1895, and the whole of the above-described territories to the east of the Uganda Protectorate were at the same time fused into one administrative whole under the title of the ' East Africa Protectorate.'

''British East Africa includes three district sovereignties, i. e. : 1. The mainland territories of the Sultan of Zanzibar. 2. The Sultanate of Witu. 3. The remainder of the Protectorate consisting of the old ' chartered territory ' of the Imperial British East Africa Company and of the region between the Tana and the Juba not included either in Zanzibar or Witu. This division, which I propose for the sake of convenience to style British East Africa proper, is not, of course, technically under Her Majesty's sovereignty, and is divided among a number of tribes and races under our Protectorate, but it differs from Zanzibar and Witu in that the status of the Chiefs exercising authority there is not recognized by international law or at least by any international engagement.

''The mainland dominions of the Sultan of Zanzibar included in the Protectorate (for he possesses certain coast ports to the north of it now leased to Italy) consist—(1.) Of a strip of coast 10 miles deep from high-water mark, extending from the mouth of the River Umba on the south to Kipini on the Ozi on the north ; and (2.) Of a series of islands off the coast between the Ozi and the Juba and of the mainland town of Kismayu with a radius of 10 miles around it. . . . The State of Witu extends along the coast from Kipini to Kwyhoo, its northern boundary being a straight line drawn in 1887 by Commissioners representing the German and Zanzibar Governments due west from Kwyhoo to a point a few miles east of the Ozi River. It was founded, or rather gradually grew up, in the years from 1860 to 1885, round a colony of outlaws. . . . When the German Government first interested itself, about a decade ago, in East African affairs, it recognized the little colony of outlaws and refugees from the coast towns which had grown up in Witu, as an independent State. . . . Accordingly, on transferring this Protectorate by the Treaty of 1890 to Great Britain, it stipulated by Article II of that Agreement, that the sovereignty of the Sultan of Witu over the territory formally defined as his in 1887 should be recognized by the new Protecting Power. . . .

'' Beyond the Zanzibar and Witu limits, the territories comprised in the Protectorate are ruled directly under Her Majesty by the British officers in charge of them. All the various tribes, Mahommedan and heathen, retain, however, their respective native Rulers and institutions. . . . For a period of ten months from the transfer from the Imperial British East Africa Company to Her Majesty's Government, the country now forming the Province of Seyyidieh, was the theatre of disturbances, which for a time retarded the development of the territory, and diverted the attention of the Administration from useful schemes of improvement that might otherwise have been immediately set on foot. These disturbances began under the Administration of the Imperial British East Africa Company, their immediate cause being a dispute over the succession to the Chieftainship of Takaungu between Rashid-bin-Salim, the son, and Mubarak-bin-Rashid, the nephew of the former Chief. . . . The Company supported Rashid, who, though younger in years than Mubarak, was friendly to the English. . . . Though the rebellion of the Mazrui Chiefs retarded to some extent the development of the province, and entailed in its suppression considerable expense, its occurrence, under the special circumstances which attended it, has not been an unmixed evil. We have broken once for all the power of several influential Arab potentates, who were never thoroughly subjugated either by the Sultans or the Company, and whose ambitions and semi-independent position would sooner or later have involved us in trouble with them had we attempted to make the authority of our Administration effective, and to interfere with the slavery, and even Slave Trade, which flourished under their protection."—Sir A. Hardinge, *Report (Great Britain, Parliamentary Publications: Papers by Command, Africa, No. 7, 1897), pp. 1-3, and 65.*

A. D. 1900-1901.—Rising of Ogaden Somalis.—In the later part of November, 1900, news reached Zanzibar of a rising of the Somali tribe called Ogadens in the Jubaland province of the British East Africa Protectorate, and that the British Sub-Commissioner, Mr. Jenner, had probably been killed. The Somalis are a very warlike race, supposed to be Gallas by descent, with an admixture of Arab blood. In the following February it was announced that Aff-Madu, the headquarters of the Ogaden Somalis, had been occupied without opposition by the British punitive expedition sent to exact reparation for the murder of Mr. Jenner, and that the Ogaden Sultan was a prisoner.

BRITISH EMPIRE, Penny postage in. See (in this vol.) ENGLAND : A. D. 1898 (DECEMBER).

BRITISH SOUTH AFRICA COMPANY: A. D. 1889.—The founding of the Company. See (in vol. 4) SOUTH AFRICA : A. D. 1885-1893.

A. D. 1894-1895.—Extended charter and enlarged powers.—Its master spirit, Mr. Rhodes. See (in this vol.) SOUTH AFRICA (BRITISH SOUTH AFRICA COMPANY): A. D. 1894-1895.

A. D. 1895.—Arrangements in Bechuanaland. See (in this vol.) AFRICA : A. D. 1895 (BECHUANALAND).

A. D. 1896.—Revocation of the Company's charter called for by President Kruger. See (in this vol.) SOUTH AFRICA (THE TRANSVAAL): A. D. 1896 (JANUARY—APRIL).

A. D. 1896.—Resignation of Mr. Rhodes. See (in this vol.) SOUTH AFRICA (BRITISH SOUTH AFRICA COMPANY): A. D. 1896 (JUNE).

A. D. 1896.—Parliamentary investigation of its administration. See (in this vol.) SOUTH AFRICA (BRITISH SOUTH AFRICA COMPANY): A. D. 1896 (JULY).

A. D. 1896.—Complicity of officials in the Jameson Raid. See (in this vol.) SOUTH AFRICA (CAPE COLONY): A. D. 1896 (JULY).

A. D. 1896-1897.—Demands from President Kruger for proceedings against the Directors. See (in this vol.) SOUTH AFRICA (THE TRANSVAAL): A. D. 1896-1897 (MAY—APRIL).

A. D. 1897.—Convicted of subjecting natives to forced labor. See (in this vol.) SOUTH AFRICA (BRITISH SOUTH AFRICA COMPANY): A. D. 1897 (JANUARY).

A. D. 1898.—Reorganization. See (in this vol.) SOUTH AFRICA (RHODESIA AND THE BRITISH SOUTH AFRICA COMPANY): A. D. 1898 (FEBRUARY).

A. D. 1900.—Administration extended over Barotsiland. See (in this vol.) SOUTH AFRICA (RHODESIA): A. D. 1900 (SEPTEMBER).

BRONX, The Borough of the. See (in this vol.) NEW YORK CITY: A. D. 1896-1897.

BROOKE, General John R. : Military Governor of Cuba.—Report. See (in this vol.) CUBA: A. D. 1898-1899 (DECEMBER—OCTOBER).

Commanding in Porto Rico. See (in this vol.) PORTO RICO : A. D. 1898-1899 (OCTOBER—OCTOBER).

BROOKLYN : Absorption in Greater New York. See (in this vol.) NEW YORK CITY : A. D. 1896-1897.

Tunnel from New York. See (in this vol.) NEW YORK CITY: A. D. 1900 (JANUARY—SEPTEMBER).

BRUGES: A. D. 1900.—The new canal from the city to the sea.—"On the 25th day of February, the inauguration of the new canal was celebrated at Bruges. . . . The canal runs from Zeebrugge, a port on the North Sea 14.29 miles north of Ostend, to the city of Bruges, a total distance of 7.46 miles. The work is now so far completed that vessels of a draft of 25 feet can enter and pass to the port of Bruges. The locks are fully completed, as well as three-fifths of the wharf wall at Bruges ; when finished, the wharf wall will have a total length of 1,575 feet. The canal has a width of 72 feet 6 inches at the bottom and 229 feet 4 inches at the water level and will have, when completed, a depth of 26 feet 3 inches ; this will also be the depth of the interior port and of the great basin of Bruges. Bruges is an old, inland deep-water port, having connection with the sea by canal from Ostend, but this only for vessels of very light draft."— *United States Consular Rep'ts, July,* 1900, *p.* 346.

BRUSSELS: A. D. 1898.—Sugar Conference. See (in this vol.) SUGAR BOUNTIES.

The General Act of. See (in this vol.) AFRICA: A. D. 1899 (JUNE).

BRYAN, William J. : Candidacy for the American Presidency.—His speech of acceptance, 1900. See (in this vol.) UNITED STATES OF AM. : A. D. 1896 (JUNE—NOVEMBER) ; and 1900 (MAY–NOVEMBER).

BUBONIC PLAGUE, The. See (in this vol.) PLAGUE.

BUDA-PESTH : A. D. 1896.—Celebration of the Hungarian Millennium. See (in this vol.) AUSTRIA-HUNGARY : A. D. 1896.

BUDDHA, Gautama: Discovery of his birthplace and his tomb, with personal relics. —"Mr. Vincent Smith, of the Bengal Civil Service, a learned antiquary, has published in the Allahabad 'Pioneer' a statement as to the nature and significance of recent discoveries of Buddhist antiquities in India. The first of these is the home of Gautama Buddha, who lived about 500 B. C., and who is known to have been the son of the Raja of Kapilavastu, a small state in the Nepal Terai, bordering on the modern Oudh. The site of Kapilavastu has long been eagerly sought for, and it is only within the past three years that the accidental discovery of an inscribed pillar erected by the Emperor Asoka, in the third century B. C., fixed with certainty the site of the city. The ruins, which were lately visited by Mr. Smith, are, so far as is yet known, all of brick ; they are for the most part buried in jungle, and are so extensive that many years would be required for their exploration. The city was destroyed during the lifetime of Gautama, and when the first of the famous Chinese pilgrims visited the place, in 410 A. D., it was a mass of desolate ruins, and there is no indication that it has since been occupied. This fact gives exceptional interest to the excavations now in progress, for they are bringing to light buildings more ancient than any previously known in India. More interesting even than Kapilavastu is the discovery of the Lumbini Garden, the traditional birthplace of Gautama. The sacred spot has been found marked by another of Asoka's pillars, on which the inscription is perfeet. This is also in Nepalese territory, five miles from the British frontier. The pillar stands on the western edge of a mound of ruins, about a hundred yards in diameter, and on the south side of the mound is the tank in which the child's mother bathed after his birth. Another discovery which was made in a stupa, or brick tumulus, close to the British frontier, is that of relics of Buddha himself. These consist only of fragments of bone, which were deposited in a wooden vessel that stood on the bottom of a massive coffer, more than four feet long and two feet deep, cut out of a solid block of fine sandstone. This coffer was buried under eighteen feet of masonry, composed of huge bricks, each sixteen inches long. The wooden vessel was decayed, and with it was an exquisitely finished bowl of rock crystal, the largest yet discovered in India, and also five small vases of soapstone. All these vessels were partially filled, in honor of the relics, with a marvellous collection of gold stars, pearls, topazes, beryls, and other jewels, and of various objects delicately wrought in crystal, agate, and other substances. An inscription on the lid of one of the soapstone vases declares the relics to be those of Buddha himself, and the characters in which the inscription is written are substantially the same as those of the Asoka inscriptions, and indicate that the tumulus was constructed between 300 and 250 B. C."—*London Times, May,* 1898.—The relics discovered, as described above, were presented by the Indian government to the King of Siam, he being the only existing Buddhist monarch, with the proviso that he offer a portion of them to Buddhists of Ceylon and Burmah.

BUENOS AYRES: A. D. 1895.—Population. See (in this vol.) ARGENTINE REPUBLIC: A. D. 1895.

BUFFALO: A. D. 1896.—First reception of electric power from Niagara Falls. See SCIENCE, RECENT: ELECTRICAL.

A. D. 1901.—The Pan-American Exposition. —As this volume goes to press, the preparations are about completed for holding a great Exposition at Buffalo, which promises to be second in importance only to the Columbian Exposition at Chicago, in 1893, so far as concerns undertakings of like character in America. The Columbian Exposition was a "World's Fair"; this at Buffalo is "Pan-American,"—an exhibition, that is, of the arts, the industries, and all the achievements in civilization of the peoples of the Western hemisphere, from Bering Strait to Cape Horn. Very nearly every country in North, South and Central America has taken a warmly interested part in the preparations for the Exposition, and many have erected special buildings for their exhibits. The States of the Union have likewise been active, and few of them will be unrepresented in the numerous buildings on the grounds. Cuba, Porto Rico, and the West Indies generally, as well as Hawaii and the Philippine Islands, in

their new character as dependencies of the United States, are brought importantly into the scheme.

The enterprise received official endorsement from the Federal Government when Congress in July, 1898, by resolution declared that "A Pan-American Exposition will undoubtedly be of vast benefit to the commercial interests of the countries of North, South and Central America, and it merits the approval of Congress, and of the people of the United States." In March, 1899, Congress appropriated $500,000, and declared that "it is desirable to encourage the holding of a Pan-American Exposition on the Niagara Frontier in the City of Buffalo, in the year 1901, fittingly to illustrate the marvelous development of the Western Hemisphere during the Nineteenth Century, by a display of the arts, industries, manufactures and the products of the soil, mine and sea," and also declared that "the proposed Pan-American Exposition being confined to the Western Hemisphere, and being held in the near vicinity of the great Niagara Cataract, within a day's journey of which reside forty million people, would unquestionably be of vast benefit to the commercial interests, not only of this country, but of the entire hemisphere, and should therefore have the sanction of the Congress of the United States."

The grounds of the Exposition are in the northern part of the city of Buffalo, taking in a portion of its most beautiful public park. They extend about one mile in length, from north to south, and about half a mile in width, containing 350 acres. A general plan of landscape and building architecture, with which every detail of form and color should be made to harmonize, was worked out at the beginning by a board of the leading architects of the United States, and has been adhered to with beautifully harmonious effects.

In one of the circular announcements of the Exposition it is said: "In planning the Exposition the management early decided upon giving to electricity special homage. The progress of the electrical science has been so marked in recent years as to excite the wonderment of the scientific world. Buffalo is, perhaps, more than any other city on the globe, interested in this science, owing to the nearness of Niagara Falls, where the greatest electric power plants known to this class of engineering have been installed. In fact the electrical displays here contemplated would be impossible except where a large volume of power is available, such as Buffalo receives from the great Falls of Niagara. . . . The Pan-American Exposition will far surpass former enterprises of this kind in six important features: First, the electrical effects; second, the hydraulic and fountain effects; third, the horticultural, floral and garden effects; fourth, the original sculptural ornamentation; fifth, the color decorations; sixth, the court settings. Particular attention has been given by the designers in the arrangement of its court settings, to provide unusually large vistas, both for the purpose of providing a memorable picture and for the utility reason of accommodating large crowds of people."

The Pan-American Exposition is under the management of a strong company of professional and business men in Buffalo, with Mr. John G. Milburn for its President. The Director-General is Hon. William I. Buchanan, former United States Minister to the Argentine Republic.

BULGARIA: A. D. 1895-1900.—Condition. See (in this vol.) BALKAN AND DANUBIAN STATES; and TURKEY: A. D. 1899-1901.

A. D. 1899 (May—July).—Representation in the Peace Conference at The Hague. See (in this vol.) PEACE CONFERENCE.

BULLER, General Sir Redvers: In the South African War. See (in this vol.) SOUTH AFRICA (THE FIELD OF WAR): A. D. 1899 (OCTOBER—DECEMBER), and after.

BULLETS, Declaration against certain. See (in this vol.) PEACE CONFERENCE.

Dum-dum. See (in this vol.) DUM-DUM BULLET.

BUREAU OF THE AMERICAN REPUBLICS. See (in this vol.) AMERICAN REPUBLICS, BUREAU OF THE.

BURMAH: A. D. 1897.—Raised in status as a British dependency.—Burmah was raised in status as a British dependency, under the government of India, by royal proclamation in 1897. The chief commissioner became lieutenant-governor, and a local legislative council was to be created.

C.

CAGAYAN, or KAGAYAN: The American acquisition. See (in this vol.) UNITED STATES OF AM.: A. D. 1898 (JULY—DECEMBER).

CAGAYANS, The. See (in this vol.) PHILIPPINE ISLANDS: THE NATIVE INHABITANTS.

CALCIUM CARBIDE, The production of. See (in this vol.) SCIENCE, RECENT: CHEMISTRY AND PHYSICS.

CALNEH, The ancient city of: Its identity with Nippur.—Exploration of its ruins. See (in this vol.) ARCHÆOLOGICAL RESEARCH: BABYLONIA: AMERICAN EXPLORATION.

CAMBON, M. Jules: Action for Spain in making overtures for peace with the United States. See (in this vol.) UNITED STATES OF AM.: A. D. 1898 (JULY—DECEMBER).

CAMEROONS, or KAMERUNS, The: Cost of maintenance. See (in this vol.) GERMANY: A. D. 1899 (JUNE).

CANADA.

A. D. 1890-1896.—The Manitoba School Question.—" When Manitoba in 1870 passed from the position of a Crown territory, managed by the Hudson's Bay Company, into that of a province of Canada, its area, which is considerably greater than that of England and Wales, was peopled by about 12,000 persons, whites and half-breeds. In religion this population was about equally divided into Catholics and Protestants. Previous to the Union there was no State system of education. A number of elementary schools existed, but they owed their foundation entirely to voluntary effort, and were supported exclusively by private contributions, either in the form of fees paid by some of the parents or of funds supplied by the Churches. In every case these schools were conducted and managed on strictly denominational lines. When the Act of Union was passed it was sought to secure the continuance of this state of things, and to safeguard the rights of whichever Church should in the hereafter be in the minority by the following sub-sections in the 22nd section, which gave to the legislature of the province the power to make laws in relation to education : '(1) Nothing in any such law shall prejudicially affect any right or privilege with respect to denominational schools which any class of persons have by law or practice in the province at the Union. (2) An appeal shall lie to the Governor-General in Council from any act or decision of the legislature of the province, or of any provincial authority, affecting any right or privilege of the Protestant or Roman Catholic minority of the Queen's subjects in relation to education.' Those two clauses of the Manitoba Act, 1870, govern the whole situation.

"The attention of the new provincial legislature was at once directed to the condition of the elementary schools. The Government decided to supersede the old voluntary system by one of State-aided schools, which, however, were still to be scrupulously denominational in character. The legislature simply took the educational system as it found it and improved it by assistance from public funds. Thus it was arranged that the annual public grant for common school education was to be appropriated equally between the Protestant and the Catholic schools. . . . The only important amendment to this Act was passed in 1875, and provided that the legislative grant, instead of being divided between the Protestant and Catholic schools as heretofore, should in future be distributed in proportion to the number of children of school age in the Catholic and Protestant districts. Already immigration had begun to upset the balance of numbers and power, and as the years went on it became evident that the Catholics were destined to be in a permanent minority in Manitoba. This trend of immigration, which in 1875 made legislation necessary, has continued ever since ; and to-day the Catholics of the province number only 20,000 out of a total population of 204,000. No further change was made in the educational system of Manitoba until the memorable year of 1890. In that year the provincial legislature boldly broke all moorings with the past, and, abolishing the separate denominational schools, introduced a system of free compulsory and unsectarian schools, for the support of which the whole community was to be taxed. . . . To test the legality of the change, what is known as Barrett's case was begun in Winnipeg. It was carried to the Supreme Court of Canada, and the Canadian judges by a unanimous decision declared that the Act of 1890 was ultra vires and void. The city of Winnipeg appealed to the Privy Council, and that tribunal in July 1892 reversed the decision of the Canadian Court and affirmed that the Act was valid and binding. . . . The second subsection of the 22nd section of the Manitoba Act already quoted says : ' An appeal shall lie to the Governor-General in Council from any Act or decision of the legislature of the province, or of any provincial authority, affecting any right or privilege of the Protestant or Roman Catholic minority of the Queen's subjects in relation to education.' But if the legislation of 1890 was intra vires, and expressly declared to be so on the ground that it had not prejudicially affected the position which the minority held at the time of the Union, how could there be an appeal from it ? . . . The Governor-General, however, consented to refer the question as to his jurisdiction to the courts of justice. What is known as Brophy's case was begun, and in due course was carried to the Supreme Court of Canada. The decision of that tribunal, though not unanimous, was in accord with public expectation. The majority of the judges felt that the previous judgment of the Privy Council had settled the matter beforehand. The Act of 1890 had been declared intra vires on the ground that it had not interfered with the rights which the minority possessed before the Union, and therefore there could be no appeal from it. . . .

"Still the undaunted Archbishop of St. Boniface went on, and for a last time appealed to that Judicial Committee of the Privy Council which two years and a half before had so spoiled and disappointed the Catholic hopes. In January 1894 the final decision in Brophy's case was read by the Lord Chancellor. For a second time the Lords of the Council upset the ruling of the Supreme Court of Canada, and treated their reasoning as irrelevant. It will be remembered that both the appellant prelates and the Canadian judges had assumed that the clause in the Manitoba Act, which conferred the right of appeal to the Governor-General, was limited to one contingency, and could be invoked only if the minority were robbed at any time of the poor and elementary rights which they had enjoyed before the Act of Union. But was the clause necessarily so limited? Could it not be used to justify an appeal from legislation which affected rights acquired after the Union? . . . In the words of the judgment : ' The question arose : Did the sub-section extend to the rights and privileges acquired by legislation subsequent to the Union? It extended in terms to " any " right or privilege of the minority affected by any Act passed by the legislature, and would therefore seem to embrace all the rights and privileges existing at the time when such Act was passed. Their lordships saw no justification for putting a limitation on language thus unlimited. There was nothing in the surrounding circumstances or in the apparent intention of the legislature to warrant any such limitation.'. . . In other words, the dispute was referred to a new tribunal, and one which was free to consider and give effect to the true equities of the case. The Governor-General and his responsible advisers, after considering all the facts, found in favour of the Catholic minority, and at once issued a remedial Order to the Government of Manitoba, which went far beyond anything suggested in the judgment in Brophy's case. The province was called upon to repeal the legislation of 1890, so far as it interfered with the right of the Catholic minority to build and maintain their own schools,

to share proportionately in any public grant for the purposes of education, and with the right of such Catholics as contributed to Catholic schools to be held exempt from all payments towards the support of any other schools. In a word, the Governor-General and Sir Mackenzie Bowell's Administration, exercising, as it were, appellate jurisdiction, decided that the minority were entitled to all they claimed. The Government of Manitoba, however, had hardened their hearts against the minority in the province, and refused to obey the remedial Order. . . .

" The refusal of the provincial Government ' to accept the responsibility of carrying into effect the terms of the remedial Order ' for the first time brought the Parliament of Canada into the field, and empowered them to pass coercive legislation. A remedial Bill was accordingly, after an inexplicable delay, brought into the Federal Parliament to enforce the remedial Order. . . . The Cabinet recognised that the Federal Parliament had no power to spend the money of the province, and so all they could do was to exempt the minority from the obligation to contribute to the support of schools other than their own. The Bill bristled with legal and constitutional difficulties ; it concerned the coercion of a province ; it contained no less than 116 clauses ; it was introduced on the 2nd of March 1896, when all Canada knew that the life of the Federal Parliament must necessarily expire on the 24th of April. Some fifteen clauses had been considered when the Government admitted, what all men saw, the impossibility of the task, and abandoned the Bill. . . . While the fate of the remedial Bill was still undecided, Sir Donald Smith and two others were commissioned by the Federal Government to go to Winnipeg and see if by direct negotiations some sort of tolerable terms could be arranged. . . . Sir Donald Smith proposed that the principle of the separate school should be admitted wherever there were a reasonable number of Catholic children—thus, wherever in towns and villages there are twenty-five Catholic children of school age, and in cities where there are fifty such children, they should have ' a school-house or school-room for their own use,' with a Catholic teacher. . . . In the event the negotiations failed ; the baffled Commissioners returned to Ottawa, and on the 24th of April 1896 Parliament was dissolved. The Government went to the country upon the policy of the abandoned Bill. On the other hand, many of the followers of Mr. Laurier in the province of Quebec pledged themselves to see justice done to the Catholics of Manitoba, and let it be understood that they objected to the remedial Bill only because it was not likely to prove effective in the face of the combined hostility of the legislature and the municipalities of the province. . . . Catholic Quebec gave Mr. Laurier his majority at Ottawa.

" When the Liberal party for the first time for eighteen years found itself in power at Ottawa, Mr. Laurier at once opened negotiations with Manitoba. The result was a settlement which, although it might work well in particular districts, could not be accepted as satisfactory by the Catholic authorities. It arranged that where in towns and cities the average attendance of Catholic children was forty or upwards, and in villages and rural districts the average attendance of such children was twenty-five or upwards, one Catholic teacher should be employed. There were various other provisions, but that was the central concession. . . . Leo the Thirteenth, recognising the difficulties which beset Mr. Laurier's path, mindful, perhaps, also that it is not always easy immediately to resume friendly conference with those who have just done their best to defeat you, has sent to Canada an Apostolic Commissioner."—J. G. Snead Cox, *Mr. Laurier and Manitoba (Nineteenth Century, April*, 1897).

A. D. 1895.—Northern territories formed into provisional districts.—"The unorganized and unnamed portion of the Dominion this year was set apart into provisional districts. The territory east of Hudson's Bay, having the province of Quebec on the south and the Atlantic on the east, was to be hereafter known as Ungava. The territory embraced in the islands of the Arctic Sea was to be known as Franklin, the Mackenzie River region as Mackenzie, and the Pacific coast territory lying north of British Columbia and west of Mackenzie as Yukon. The extent of Ungava and Franklin was undefined. Mackenzie would cover 538,600 square miles, and Yukon 225,000 square miles, in addition to 143,500 square miles added to Athabasca and 470,000 to Keewatin. The total area of the Dominion was estimated at 3,456,383 square miles."—*The Annual Register*, 1895, *p.* 391.

A. D. 1895.—Negotiations with Newfoundland.—Negotiations for the entrance of Newfoundland into the federation of the Dominion of Canada proved ineffectual and were abandoned in May. The island province refused the terms proposed.

A. D. 1896 (June—July).—Liberal triumph in Parliamentary elections.—Formation of Ministry by Sir Wilfred Laurier.—General elections held in Canada on the 23d of June, 1896, gave the Liberal Party 113 seats out of 213 in the Dominion House of Commons; the Conservatives securing 88, and the Patrons of Industry and other Independents 12. Much to the general surprise, the scale was turned in favor of the Liberals by the vote of the province of Quebec, notwithstanding the Manitoba school question, on which clerical influence in the Roman church was ranged against that party. The effect of the election was to call the Liberal leader, Sir Wilfred Laurier, of Quebec, to the head of the government, the Conservative Ministry, under Sir Charles Tupper, retiring on the 8th of July.

A. D. 1896–1897.—Policy of the Liberal Government.—Revision of the tariff, with discriminating duties in favor of Great Britain, and provisions for reciprocity.—"The position of the Canadian Liberals, when they came into power after the General Election of 1896, was not unlike that of the English Liberals after the General Election of 1892. Both Liberal parties had lists of reforms to which they were committed. The English measures were in the Newcastle Programme. Those of the Canadian Liberals were embodied in the Ottawa Programme, which was formulated at a convention held at the Dominion Capital in 1893. . . . A large part of the Ottawa Programme was set out in the speech which the Governor-General read in the Senate when the session of 1897 commenced. There was then promised a measure for the revision of the tariff; a bill provid-

ing for the extension of the Intercolonial railway from Levis to Montreal; a bill repealing the Dominion Franchise Act and abolishing the costly system of registration which goes with it; and a measure providing for the plebiscite on the Prohibition question. Neither of these last two measures was carried through Parliament. Both had to be postponed to another session; and the session of 1897 was devoted, so far as legislation went, chiefly to the tariff, and to bills, none of which were promised in the Speech from the Throne, in retaliation for the United States Contract Labor Laws, and the new United States tariff. . . .

"The new tariff was a departure from the tariffs of the Conservative régime in only one important direction. Protective duties heretofore had been levied on imports from England, in the same way as on imports from the United States or any other country. The 'National Policy' had allowed of no preferences for England; and during the long period of Conservative rule, when the Conservatives were supported by the Canadian manufacturers in much the same way as the Republican party in the United States is supported by the manufacturing interests, the Canadian manufacturers had been as insistent for adequate protection against English-made goods, as against manufactured articles from the United States or Germany. The Conservative party had continuously claimed a monopoly of loyalty to England; but in its tariffs had never dared to make any concession in favour of English goods. In the new tariff, preferences for England were established; and with these openings in favour of imports from Great Britain, there came a specific warning from the Minister of Finance that Canadian manufacturers must not regard themselves as possessing a vested interest in the continuance of the protective system. . . .

"When the Minister of Finance laid the tariff before the House of Commons, he declared that the 'National Policy,' as it had been tried for eighteen years, was a failure; and . . . claimed that lowering the tariff wall against England was a step in the direction of a tariff 'based not upon the protective system but upon the requirements of the public service.' During the first fifteen months of the new tariff, the concession to England consists of a reduction by one-eighth of the duties chargeable under the general list. At the end of that time, that is on the last of July, 1898, the reduction will be one-fourth. The reductions do not apply to wines, malt liquors, spirits and tobacco, the taxes on which are essentially for revenue. While England was admitted at once to the advantages of the reduced tariff, this tariff is not to be applicable to England alone. In July, it was extended to the products of New South Wales, the free-trade colony of the British Australasian group; and any country can come within its provisions whose government can satisfy the Comptroller of Customs at Ottawa, that it is offering favourable treatment to Canadian exports, and is affording them as easy an entrance through its customs houses as the Canadians give by means of the reciprocal tariff. It is also possible, under a later amendment to the Tariff Act, for the Governor in Council to extend the benefits of the reciprocal tariff to any country entitled thereto by virtue of a treaty with Great Britain. Numerous alterations were made in the general list of import duties. Some of these involved higher rates; others lowered the duties. But if the changes in the fiscal system had been confined to these variations, the new tariff would not have been noteworthy, and it would have fulfilled few of the pledges made by the Liberals when they were in Opposition. It owes its chief importance to the establishment of an inner tariff in the interests of countries which deal favourably with Canada."—E. Porritt, *The New Administration in Canada* (*Yale Review, August,* 1897).

A. D. 1897 (June—July).—Conference of colonial premiers with the British Colonial Secretary. See (in this vol.) ENGLAND : A. D. 1897 (JUNE—JULY).

A. D. 1897 (October).—Self-government for the Northwestern Territories.—By an Act passed in October, a system of self-government, going far towards the full powers of a provincial government, but having some limitations, was provided for the Northwest Territories.

A. D. 1898 (January).—Encyclical Letter of the Pope on the Manitoba School Question.—On the report made by his delegate, Monsignor Merry del Val, Pope Leo XIII. addressed an encyclical letter to the Roman Church in Canada, concerning the duty of Catholics in the matter of the Manitoba schools (see above : A. D. 1890-1896), which was made public at Quebec on the 9th of January, 1898. The letter has great general importance, as defining with precision the attitude of the Church towards all secular school systems. With a few unessential passages it is given in what follows : " It was with extreme solicitude," wrote the Pope, "that we turned our mind to the unhappy events which in these later years have marked the history of Catholic education in Manitoba. . . . And since many expected that we should make a pronouncement on the question, and asked that we should trace a line of conduct and a way to be followed, we did not wish to decide anything on this subject before our Apostolic delegate had been on the spot, charged to proceed to a serious examination of the situation, and to give an account to us of the state of affairs. He has faithfully and diligently fulfilled the command which we had given him. The question agitated is one of great and exceptional importance. We speak of the decision taken seven years ago by the parliament of Manitoba on the subject of education. The act of Confederation had secured to Catholic children the right of education in public schools in keeping with their conscientious convictions. The parliament of Manitoba abolished this right by contrary law. By this latter law a grave injury was inflicted, for it was not lawful for our children to seek the benefits of education in schools in which the Catholic religion is ignored or actively combated, in schools where its doctrine is despised and its fundamental principles repudiated. If the Church has anywhere permitted this, it was only with great reluctance and in self-defense, and after having taken many precautions, which, however, have too often been found unequal to parrying the danger. In like manner one must at all cost avoid, as most pernicious, those schools wherein every form of belief is indifferently admitted and placed on an equal footing — as if in what regards God and Divine

things, it was of no importance whether one believed rightly or wrongly, whether one followed truth or falsehood. You well know, venerable brothers, that all schools of this kind have been condemned by the Church, because there can be nothing more pernicious nor more fitted to injure the integrity of faith and to turn away the tender minds of youth from the truth. . . . For the Catholic there is but one true religion, the Catholic religion ; hence in all that concerns doctrine, or morality, or religion, he cannot accept or recognize anything which is not drawn from the very sources of Catholic teaching. Justice and reason demand, then, that our children have in their schools not only scientific instruction but also moral teachings in harmony, as we have already said, with the principles of their religion, teachings without which all education will be not only fruitless but absolutely pernicious. Hence the necessity of having Catholic teachers, reading books, and textbooks approved of by the bishops, and liberty to organize the schools, that the teaching therein shall be in full accord with Catholic faith as well as with all the duties that flow therefrom. For the rest, to decide in what institutions their children shall be instructed, who shall be their teachers of morality, is a right inherent to parental authority. When, then, Catholics demand, and it is their duty to demand, and to strive to obtain, that the teaching of the masters shall be in conformity with the religion of their children, they are only making use of their right ; and there can be nothing more unjust than to force on them the alternative of allowing their children to grow up in ignorance, or to expose them to manifest danger in what concerns the supreme interests of their souls. It is not right to call in doubt or to abandon in any way these principles of judging and acting which are founded on truth and justice, and which are the safe-guards both of public and private interests. Therefore, when the new law in Manitoba struck a blow at Catholic education, it was your duty, venerable brothers, to freely protest against the injury and disaster inflicted ; and the way in which you all fulfilled that duty is a proof of your common vigilance, and of a spirit truly worthy of bishops ; and, although each one of you will find on this point a sufficient approbation in the testimony of his own conscience, learn, nevertheless, that you have also our conscience and our approbation, for the things which you sought and still seek to protect and defend are most sacred. The difficulties created by the law of which we speak by their very nature showed that an alleviation was to be sought for in a united effort. For so worthy was the Catholic cause that all good and upright citizens, without distinction of party, should have banded themselves together in a close union to uphold it. Unfortunately for the success of this cause, the contrary took place. What is more deplorable still, is that Catholic Canadians themselves failed to unite as they should in defending those interests which are of such importance to all—the importance and gravity of which should have stilled the voice of party politics, which are of much less importance. We are not unaware that something has been done to amend that law. The men who are at the head of the federal government and of the Province of Manitoba have already taken certain measures with a view to decreasing the difficulties of which the Catholics of Manitoba complain, and against which they rightly continue to protest. We have no reason to doubt that these measures were taken from love of justice and from a laudable motive. We cannot, however, dissimulate the truth; the law which they have passed to repair the injury is defective, unsuitable, insufficient. The Catholics ask—and no one can deny that they justly ask—for much more. Moreover, in the remedial measures that have been proposed there is this defect, that in changes of local circumstances they may easily become valueless. In a word, the rights of Catholics and the education of their children have not been sufficiently provided for in Manitoba. Everything in this question demands, and is conformable to justice, that they should be thoroughly provided for, that is, by placing in security and surrounding with due safe-guards those unchangeable and sacred principles of which we have spoken above. This should be the aim, this the end to be zealously and prudently sought for. Nothing can be more injurious to the attainment of this end than discord; unity of spirit and harmony of action are most necessary. Nevertheless since, as frequently happens in things of this nature, there is not only one fixed and determined but various ways of arriving at the end which is proposed and which should be obtained, it follows that there may be various opinions equally good and advantageous. Wherefore let each and all be mindful of the rules of moderation, and gentleness, and mutual charity; let no one fail in the respect that is due to another; but let all resolve in fraternal unanimity, and not without your advice, to do that which the circumstances require and which appears best to be done. As regards especially the Catholics of Manitoba, we have every confidence that with God's help they will succeed in obtaining full satisfaction. This hope is founded, in the first place, in the righteousness of the cause, next in the sense of justice and prudence of the men at the head of the government, and finally in the good-will of all upright men in Canada. In the meantime, until they are able to obtain their full rights, let them not refuse partial satisfaction. If, therefore, anything is granted by law to custom, or the good-will of men, which will render the evil more tolerable and the dangers more remote, it is expedient and useful to make use of such concessions, and to derive therefrom as much benefit and advantage as possible. Where, however, no remedy can be found for the evil, we must exhort and beseech that it be provided against by the liberality and munificence of their contributions, for no one can do anything more salutary for himself or more conducive to the prosperity of his country, than to contribute, according to his means, to the maintenance of these schools. There is another point which appeals to your common solicitude, namely, that by your authority, and with the assistance of those who direct educational institutions, an accurate and suitable curriculum of studies be established, and that it be especially provided that no one shall be permitted to teach who is not amply endowed with all the necessary qualities, natural and acquired, for it is only right that Catholic schools should be able to compete in bearing, culture, and scholarship with the best in the country. As concerns intellectual culture and the progress of civilization, one can only recognize as praiseworthy and noble the desire of the provinces of Canada to develop public instruction, and to raise its standard more and more, in order that it may daily become higher and more perfect. Now there is no kind of knowledge, no perfection of learning, which cannot be fully harmonized with Catholic doctrine."

A. D. **1898** (September).—Popular vote on the question of Prohibition.—Pursuant to a law passed by the Dominion Parliament the previous June, a vote of the people in all the Provinces of the Dominion was taken, on the 29th of September, 1898, upon the following question: "Are you in favor of the passing of an act prohibiting the importation, manufacture or sale of spirits, wine, ale, beer, cider, and all other alcoholic liquors for use as beverages?" The submitting of this question to a direct vote of the people was a proceeding not quite analogous to the Swiss Referendum, since it decided the fate of no pending law; nor did it imitate the popular Initiative of Swiss legislation, since the result carried no mandate to the government. It was more in the nature of a French Plébiscite, and many called it by that name; but no Plébiscite in France ever drew so real an expression of popular opinion on a question so fully discussed. The result of the voting was a majority for prohibition in every Province except Quebec, Ontario pronouncing for it by more than 39,000, Nova Scotia by more than 29,000, New Brunswick by more than 17,000, Manitoba by more than 9,000, Prince Edward's Island by more than 8,000, and the Northwest Territories by more than 3,000, while British Columbia gave a small majority of less than 600 on the same side. Quebec, on the other hand, shouted a loud "No" to the question, by 93,000 majority. The net majority in favor of Prohibition was 107,000. The total of votes polled on the question was 540,000. This was less than 44 per cent of the total registration of voters; hence the vote for Prohibition represented only about 23 per cent of the electorate, which the government considered to offer too small a support for the measure asked for.

A. D. **1898-1899.**—The Joint High Commission for settlement of all unsettled questions between Canada and the United States.—As the outcome of negotiations opened at Washington in the previous autumn by the Canadian Premier, relative to the seal-killing controversy, an agreement between Great Britain, Canada and the United States was concluded on the 30th of May, 1898, for the creation of a Joint High Commission to negotiate a treaty, if possible, by which all existing subjects of controversy between the United States and Canada should be settled with finality. Appointments to the Commission by the three governments were made soon afterwards, Great Britain being represented by the Lord High Chancellor, Baron Herschell; Canada by Sir Wilfred Laurier, Premier, Sir Richard Cartwright, Minister of Trade and Commerce, and Sir Louis Henry Davies, Minister of Marine and Fisheries; the United States by Hon. John W. Foster, ex-Secretary of State, Senator Charles W. Fairbanks, Senator George Gray, Representative Nelson Dingley, and the Hon. John A. Kasson, Reciprocity Commissioner. Senator Gray having been subsequently appointed on the Commission to negotiate peace with Spain, his place on the Anglo-American Commission was taken by Senator Faulkner. The Joint Commission sat first in Quebec and later in Washington. Among the questions referred to it were those relating to the establishment of the boundary between Alaska and British Columbia; the issues over Bering Sea and the catch of fur seals; the unmarked boundary between Canada and the United States near Passamaquoddy Bay in Maine and at points between Wisconsin and Minnesota and Canada; the northeast fisheries question, involving the rights of fishing in the North Atlantic off Newfoundland and other points; the regulation of the fishing rights on the Great Lakes; alien-labor immigration across the Canadian-American border; commercial reciprocity between the two countries; the regulation of the bonding system by which goods are carried in bond across the frontier and also the regulation of traffic by international railways and canals of the two countries; reciprocal mining privileges in the Klondyke, British North America and other points; wrecking and salvage on the ocean and Great Lakes coasting waters; the modification of the treaty arrangement under which only one war vessel can be maintained on the Great Lakes, with a view to allowing warships to be built on the lakes and then floated out to the ocean. The sessions of the Joint Commission were continued at intervals until February, 1899, when it adjourned to meet at Quebec in the following August, unless further adjournment should be agreed upon by the several chairmen. Such further adjournment was made, and the labors of the Joint Commission were indefinitely suspended, for reasons which the President of the United States explained in his Message to Congress, December, 1899, as follows: "Much progress had been made by the Commission toward the adjustment of many of these questions, when it became apparent that an irreconcilable difference of views was entertained respecting the delimitation of the Alaskan boundary. In the failure of an agreement as to the meaning of articles 3 and 4 of the treaty of 1825 between Russia and Great Britain, which defined the boundary between Alaska and Canada, the American Commissioners proposed that the subject of the boundary be laid aside and that the remaining questions of difference be proceeded with, some of which were so far advanced as to assure the probability of a settlement. This being declined by the British Commissioners, an adjournment was taken until the boundary should be adjusted by the two Governments. The subject has been receiving the careful attention which its importance demands, with the result that a modus vivendi for provisional demarcations in the region about the head of Lynn Canal has been agreed upon [see (in this vol.) ALASKA BOUNDARY QUESTION] and it is hoped that the negotiations now in progress between the two Governments will end in an agreement for the establishment and delimitation of a permanent boundary."

A. D. 1899 (October).—Modus Vivendi, fixing provisional boundary line of Alaska. See (in this vol.) ALASKA BOUNDARY QUESTION.

A. D. 1899-1900.—Troops to reinforce the British army in South Africa.—A proposal from the Canadian government to assist that of the Empire in its South African War was gratefully accepted in the early stages of the war, and

a regiment of infantry called the Royal Canadian, numbering a little more than 1,000 men, sailed from Quebec, October 30. In the following January a second contingent of more than 1,000 men was sent to the field. This latter comprised squadrons of mounted rifles and rough-riders, and three batteries of field artillery. In the same month the Canadian government accepted an offer from Lord Strathcona to raise, equip and transport at his own expense a body of 500 mounted men from the Northwest.

A. D. 1900 (November).—General election.—The general election of members of the Dominion House of Commons was held November 7, resulting as follows:

PROVINCES.	Liberal.	Conservative.	Independent.	Total.
Nova Scotia....................	15	5	–	20
New-Brunswick...............	9	5	–	14
Prince Edward Island.......	3	2	–	5
Quebec........................	57	8	–	65
Ontario........................	33	54	5	92
Manitoba......................	2	3	2	7
Northwest Territories........	2	–	2	4
British Columbia..............	3	2	1	6
Totals....................	124	79	10	213

As in the election of 1896, the Liberal Ministry of Sir Wilfred Laurier found its strong support in the province of Quebec. Its party suffered unexpected losses in Ontario. The slight meaning of the election was summed up by Professor Goldwin Smith as follows: "The net result of the elections seems to be a Government resting on French Quebec and an Opposition resting on British Ontario. The minor provinces have been carried, as usual, by local interests rather than on general questions. Apart from the distinction of race between the two great provinces and the antagonism, before dormant but somewhat awakened by the war, there was no question of importance at issue between the parties. Both concurred in sending contingents to South Africa. The Liberals, though they went in at first on the platform of free trade—at least, of a tariff for revenue only—have practically embraced protection under the name of stability of the tariff, and are believed to have received from the protected manufacturers contributions to their large election fund. The other special principles, such as the reduction of expenditure and discontinuance of the bonus to railways, proclaimed by Liberals before the last election, have been dropped. So has reform of the Senate. It is not likely that the Liberal victory will be followed by any change either in legislation or government, or by any special reform. Mr. Bourassa and Monet, of the French-Canadian members who protested against the contingent, have been re-elected. Great as may be the extent and warmth of British feeling, the statement that Canadians were unanimously in favour of participation in the war must not be taken without qualification. For myself, I felt that so little principle was at stake that I voted for two Conservatives on their personal merits."

CANAL, The new Bruges. See (in this vol.) BRUGES : A. D. 1900.

CANAL, The Chicago Drainage. See (in this vol.) CHICAGO : A. D. 1900.

CANAL, City of Mexico Drainage. See (in this vol.) MEXICO : A. D. 1898.

CANAL, The Elbe and Trave. See (in this vol.) GERMANY : A. D. 1900 (JUNE).

**CANAL, Interoceanic, The Project of the :
A. D. 1581-1892.**—The early inception of the project.—Movements towards its realization.—" The thought of uniting the two great oceans by means of a canal across the American isthmus sprang up, as is known, from the moment the conviction was reached that the passage which, from the days of Columbus, was thought to exist towards the Southern Sea, was not a reality. . . . Nevertheless the first survey of the land was not carried out until the year 1581, when, in obedience to superior instructions, Capt. Antonio Pereira, Governor of Costa Rica, organized an expedition and explored the route by way of the San Juan river, the lake, and the rivers emptying into Gulf Nicoya, Costa Rica. Thirty-nine years later Diego de Mercado submitted to King Philip III his famous report of January 23, 1620, suggesting the route by the river and lake, and thence through Costa Rican territory along the Quebrada or Barranca Honda to Salinas Bay, then called ·Puerto del Papagayo. Either because the magnitude of the undertaking was at that time superior to the necessities of trade, or, as was said, because Spain considered the canal antagonistic to her interests, the era of independence arrived without the execution of the project ever having been entered upon. After independence the Congress of Central America, in which Costa Rica and Nicaragua were represented as States of the Federation which succeeded the Colonial Government, enacted on June 16, 1825, a decree providing for the construction of the canal, and in that same year Don Antonio José Cañas, Diplomatic Representative of Central America in Washington, addressed the Secretary of State, Mr. Henry Clay, informing him of this resolution and stating that : 'A company formed of American citizens of respectability was ready to undertake the work as soon as a treaty with the United States insuring the coöperation of the latter was signed ; that he was ready to enter into negotiations for the treaty, and that nothing would be more pleasant for Central America than to see the generous people of the United States joining her in the opening of the canal, sharing the glory of the enterprise, and enjoying the great advantages to be derived from it.' The Government of Central America could not carry the undertaking into effect, notwithstanding that among the means employed to reach the desired result there figures the arrangement concluded with the King of Holland in October, 1830. But, though the hopes centered in the undertaking were frustrated, to the honor of Central America the declarations of that Congress, which constitute, like the concession for the canal itself, one of the loftiest public documents ever issued by any nation of the earth, have become a matter of record. The Central American Federation dissolved, this important matter attached to Nic-

aragua and Costa Rica directly, and the boundary line between the two republics having been determined by the treaty of April 15, 1858, as were also the points relative to the canal, the two governments jointly granted a concession on May 1 of that same year to Mr. Felix Belly, a distinguished French writer, to whom the Emperor Napoleon gave his support to carry forward the undertaking. This failing of accomplishment, the two governments, in perfect accord, concluded the contract known as the Ayon-Chevalier, signed by Nicaragua on October 16, 1868, and by Costa Rica on June 18, 1869, which, it is unnecessary to say, also failed to produce any results whatever. Some years after the expiration of this last contract Nicaragua promoted a discussion as to the validity of the treaty and the meaning of some of its stipulations, which Costa Rica upheld in its original form, and the question was submitted to the decision of the President of the United States, Mr. Cleveland, who in his award of March 22, 1888, accepted by both parties, declared the treaty valid and binding upon each Republic and interpreted the points which in the opinion of Nicaragua were doubtful. According to the provisions of both of these documents, the treaty and award, even in the remote event that the natural rights of Costa Rica should not be injured, Nicaragua is bound not to make any grants for canal purposes across her territory without first asking the opinion of the Republic of Costa Rica. Three years prior, and while this question was still pending, Nicaragua concluded the treaty known as the Zavala-Frelinghuysen, signed in Washington on December 1, 1884, whereby the title to the canal was conveyed to the United States, and Costa Rica adhered to this treaty under date of February 23, 1885 ; but the negotiations remained without effect, because, ratification having been denied in the Senate, although a reconsideration of the subject had been agreed to, President Cleveland, on inaugurating his first administration, withdrew the document from the Senate. Things then returned to the status they formerly maintained, and Nicaragua in April, 1887, and Costa Rica in July, 1888, respectively granted the concessions pursuant to which the construction of the American waterway has been pending of late years. The Congress of the United States has been giving special attention to this important matter since the year 1892, and commissions have been created charged with the survey and location of the route, as well as the study of the influence of the canal in its different aspects. Recently the investigation is not limited to the route by Nicaragua and Costa Rica alone, but extends to Panama."—*Speech of Señor Calvo, Costa Rican Minister, at the International Commercial Congress, Philadelphia, Oct. 24, 1899.*

A. D. 1889-1899.—The Maritime Canal Company. — Investigation of Nicaragua routes.—" The failure of the Frelinghuysen-Zavala treaty [see above] was a severe disappointment to the friends of the canal project, but it did not discourage them. A company of private citizens, capitalists and promoters, was organized, which at length took the name of the Maritime Canal Company. Fair and full concessions were secured from the government of Nicaragua, while similar articles were also signed with the Republic of Costa Rica on account of imagined ownership of a portion of the territory through which the canal was to pass, though it has been shown subsequently, in the settlement of the boundary dispute between those two governments, that Costa Rica's rights in the matter were solely riparian. In due time Congress was called upon to grant a charter to the Maritime Company, which asked nothing more than this." The chartering act was passed by Congress in 1889, with an important amendment proposed by Judge Holman of Indiana, providing that "nothing in this act contained shall be so construed as to commit the United States to any pecuniary liability whatever for any account of said company, nor shall the United States be held in any wise liable or responsible in any form or by any implication for any debt or liability in any form which said company may incur, nor as guaranteeing any engagement or contract of said company." But two years afterwards, the company having failed to enlist the necessary capital for its undertaking, an attempt was made to set aside the above provision and to persuade Congress to guarantee $100,000,000 of bonds, taking $70,-000,000 of stock and making the government a partner in the enterprise. The proposal was rejected. Congress "did not guarantee the company's bonds. The company, without such guarantee, was unable to raise the necessary capital, either in the United States or abroad, and the financial crisis of 1893 so overwhelmed it that all active operations on the isthmus were suspended, and they have never been resumed. The same issue, the guaranteeing of bonds, has come up from time to time in succeeding Congresses, but not until the second session of the Fifty-fourth [1897] did it appear to have much chance of being decided in favor of the company. The opposition in the Senate, where it was first considered, was strong, and the arguments advanced against the bill were clear, sound and forceful. The advocates of the measure were pressing for a vote, but almost at the supreme moment a note was received from the State Department, accompanied by a communication from Minister Rodriguez, the representative of the Greater Republic of Central America, setting forth several unassailable objections of his government to the methods of procedure. This final thrust determined the fate of the bill, and a vote on it was not taken. . . . The material points of Minister Rodriguez's criticism, which caused the Senate bill in 1897 to be withdrawn, were that some of the vital provisions of the cessions under which the Maritime Canal Company had the right to construct the canal were violated."—C. M. Stadden, *Latest Aspects of the Nicaragua Canal Project* (*N. Am. Rev.*, *Dec.*, 1898).—Congress now (June 4, 1897) passed an Act which created a commission to examine all practicable routes for a canal through Nicaragua, and report its judgment as to the best, with an estimate of the cost of the work on such route. The commissioners appointed were Admiral Walker, Professor Haupt, and Colonel Hains. Their report, submitted to the President in May, 1899, unanimously recommended the route described as follows: "This line, leaving Brito, follows the left bank of the Rio Grande to near Bueno Retiro, and crosses the western divide to the valley of the Lajas, which it follows to Lake Nicaragua. Crossing the

lake to the head of the San Juan river, it follows the upper river to near Boca San Carlos; thence, in excavation, by the left bank of the river to the San Juanillo and across the low country to Greytown, passing to the northward of Lake Silico." But while the commissioners agreed in finding this route preferable to any others in the Nicaragua region, they disagreed seriously in their estimates of cost, Colonel Hains, putting it at nearly $185,000,000, while Admiral Walker and Professor Haupt placed the cost at little more than $118,000,000. Before the report of this Nicaragua Canal Commission was made, however, Congress (March 3, 1899) had directed the appointment of another commission to examine and report upon all possible routes for an interoceanic canal, in the Panama region and elsewhere, as well as through Nicaragua and to determine the cost of constructing such a canal and "placing it under the control, management and ownership of the United States." This later commission, known as the Isthmian Canal Commission, was made up as follows: Rear-Admiral John G. Walker, U. S. N.; Samuel Pasco, of Florida; Alfred Noble, C. E., of Illinois; George S. Morrison, C. E., of New York; Colonel Peter C. Hains, U. S. A.; Prof. William H. Burr, of Connecticut; Lieutenant-Colonel Oswald H. Ernst, U. S. A.; Prof. Lewis M. Haupt, C. E., of Pennsylvania; Prof. Emory R. Johnston, of Pennsylvania.

In his Message to Congress the next December, President McKinley stated: "The contract of the Maritime Canal Company of Nicaragua was declared forfeited by the Nicaraguan Government on the 10th of October, on the ground of nonfulfillment within the ten years' term stipulated in the contract. The Maritime Canal Company has lodged a protest against this action, alleging rights in the premises which appear worthy of consideration. This Government expects that Nicaragua will afford the protestants a full and fair hearing upon the merits of the case." But another company had been put into the place of the Maritime Canal Company, by action of President Zelaya, of Nicaragua, who, in 1898, granted to Edward Eyre and E. F. Cragin, who represented an American Syndicate, the right to construct the canal when the contract with the Maritime should have lapsed. This transaction, however, lacked confirmation by Costa Rica and the United States.

A. D. 1893-1900.—The Panama Canal Concession twice extended.—Formation of new company. See (in this vol.) COLOMBIA: A. D. 1893-1900.

A. D. 1899 (December).—Transfer of the Panama Canal to an American company.— The transfer of the Panama Canal from the later French company to an American company, chartered in New Jersey, was accomplished in December, 1899. The new company received all the property, rights, and powers of its French predecessor, the consideration to be paid to the latter being mainly in the form of shares in the American company.

A. D. 1900 (November).—**Preliminary report** of the Isthmian Canal Commission in favor of the Nicaragua route.—The preliminary report of the Isthmian Canal Commission, appointed under the Act of March 3, 1899, was presented to the President on the 30th November,

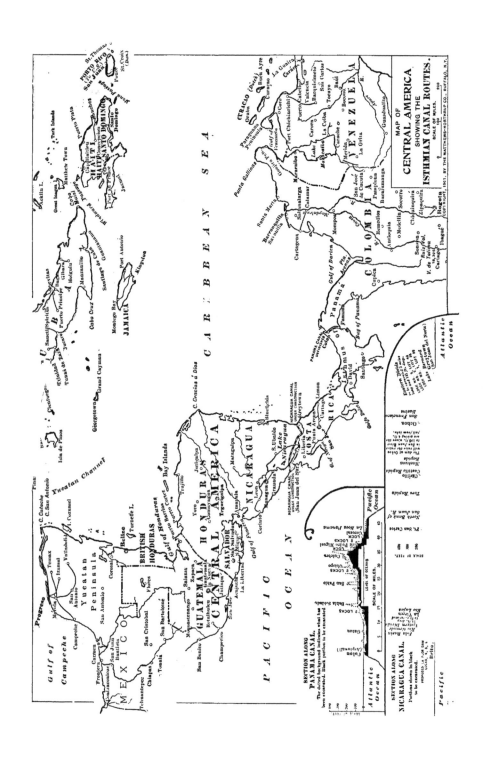

MAP OF
CENTRAL AMERICA
SHOWING THE
ISTHMIAN CANAL ROUTES.
SCALE OF MILES.

COPYRIGHT, 1901, BY THE MATTHEWS-NORTHRUP CO., BUFFALO, N.Y.

1900, and communicated to Congress at the opening of the session. The Commission reported in favor of the Nicaragua route, essentially on the lines laid down by the previous Nicaragua Canal Commission, as defined above. It found that the choice of routes lies between this and the route of the partly constructed Panama Canal, and its discussion of the question presented the following views: "(a) Between New York and San Francisco, the Nicaragua Canal route would be 377 nautical miles shorter than the Panama route. Between New Orleans and San Francisco 579 miles would be saved, and, in general, the distances between the Atlantic and Pacific ports of the United States are less by way of Nicaragua. Between our east coast and Yokohama and Shanghai the Nicaragua route is somewhat shorter, but for the trade of our eastern ports with the west coast of South America the Panama route is not so long as the Nicaragua. (b) A part of the saving in distance effected by using a Nicaragua canal instead of one at Panama would be offset by the longer time of transit at Nicaragua. An average steamer would require twelve hours to make the passage through the Panama Canal, and thirty-three through one across Nicaragua. For a 10-knot steamer this difference of twenty-one hours would be equivalent to 210 knots difference in distance, and for a 13-knot steamer, the difference in time of transit would be equivalent to 273 knots. (c) The Nicaragua route would be the more favorable one for sailing vessels because of the uncertain winds in the bay of Panama. It would not be impossible for sailing vessels to use the Panama Canal, but for average voyages between the two seaboards of the United States, a sailing vessel would require about nine days additional time to make the passage by way of the Panama Canal. However, neither route would be much used by sailing vessels, because of their inability to compete with steamers. They would certainly not be able to compete with steamers, both using the Panama Canal. (d) For the promotion of the domestic trade of the United States, the Nicaragua route would possess advantages over the Panama route, because the distance between our two seaboards is less. For our trade with Japan, China, the Philippines, and Australia, the advantages of the two routes are nearly equal, the distance by way of the Nicaragua route being slightly less. For our trade with South America the Panama route is shorter and more direct. (e) The industrial changes which the Nicaragua Canal would produce in the countries through which it will pass would be great. Nicaragua and Costa Rica comprise a region capable of producing a large amount of tropical products for which there is a demand in Europe and the United States. A canal across their territory would give a great impetus to their economic development.

"A careful examination has been made of all the rights, privileges, and franchises held and owned by corporations, associations, and individuals at the different canal routes. This necessarily included a study of the treaties relating to the establishment of an interoceanic communication made by the Republics, whose territory is to be occupied, and by the United States, with one another, and also with foreign governments. The treaties heretofore made exclude all idea of a relinquishment of sovereignty over any of the proposed routes. In most of them the right of transit and the innocent use of the communication, whether by railway or canal, is granted to the other contracting party, its citizens and subjects, to be enjoyed upon equal terms with other governments and people ; and the leading commercial nations of the world have committed themselves to the policy of neutrality at the different routes, and some of them have obligated themselves to use their influence to induce other nations to agree to the same policy. No existing treaties between the United States and the Republics of Nicaragua and Costa Rica, or of Colombia, give our Government the right to excavate and operate a maritime canal through any of these countries. The concessions granted by the different Republics through whose territory the lines of the projected canals extend, in terms, exclude the right of the companies holding them to transfer them to any foreign government, and further treaty rights must be acquired to enable the United States to undertake the excavation of a navigable waterway between the two oceans in a governmental capacity. The only prior obligations to corporations, associations, or individuals in the way of a direct agreement between the United States and Nicaragua authorizing our Government to construct a canal across the territory of the latter, to be under its control, management, and ownership, have been eliminated by the forfeiture and termination of the contracts with the Maritime Canal Company of Nicaragua and the Interoceanic Canal Company. In view of this declaration the Commission has not made any effort to ascertain the cost at which the concessions of these companies can be purchased, for if these forfeitures are final the rights formerly granted to these companies are not in the way of diplomatic negotiations with the Government interested to acquire the consent and authority necessary for the construction of a canal by this route. The situation in Costa Rica is practically the same.

" The situation at Panama is different. The Republic of Colombia first granted a concession to the Panama Railroad Company, giving it exclusive privileges on the Isthmus, which will continue according to modifications afterwards made for ninety-nine years from August 16, 1867. A later concession to the Panama Canal Company required it to enter into some amicable arrangement with the railroad company under which the former might occupy the territory along or near its line. The canal company acquired by purchase a majority of the railroad stock and the necessary arrangements were made. This stock is now under the control of the New Panama Canal Company, which gives it a directing influence in both organizations. The canal concession is to continue according to its latest extension for ninety-nine years from the day on which the canal shall be wholly or partially opened to public service, and the date fixed for this in the contract is October 31, 1910. Should it fail and the concession be forfeited the company will still have exclusive control of the territory through which its line extends till 1966 under the railroad concession. The canal company is absolutely prohibited to cede or mortgage its rights under any consideration whatever to any nation or foreign government under penalty of forfeiture. The contract with the railroad company contains a like prohibition and declares further that the pain of forfeiture will be incurred by the mere act of attempting to cede or transfer its privilege to a foreign government and such an act is declared absolutely null and of no value or effect. These concessions, if acquired by the United States, would not give to the Government the control and ownership evidently contemplated by the law, that is, an absolute ownership in perpetuity. The right under the contract with the railroad company is designated as ' the use and possession' of the property for ninety-nine years, and it is provided that ' at the expiration of the term of the privilege' and by the sole fact of the expiration, the Government of Colombia shall be substituted in all the rights of the company and shall immediately enter into the enjoyment of the line of communication, its fixtures, dependencies and all its products. The right of the canal company is substantially of the same character. . . . An examination of the charter rights of the New Panama Canal Company under the general incorporation laws of France and the special legislation in its behalf resulted in finding an enactment, included in a law passed June 8, 1888, requiring that all the plant necessary for the construction of the canal shall be manufactured in France and that the material must be of French origin. This being the situation, it was manifest that, even if the privileges of the companies could be purchased by and transferred to the United States, they were encumbered with charges and conditions that would not permit this Government to exercise all the rights of complete ownership over a canal constructed by it at the Panama route. A new arrangement is necessary if the United States is to undertake such a work. The relinquishment by the canal company, with the consent of Colombia, of the privileges it has under existing concessions, for a consideration to be agreed upon with the United States, would leave the way open for treaty negotiations between the two governments to ascertain whether Colombia will consent to the occupation of its territory by the United States for the construction of a canal to be under Government control, management, and ownership, and, if so, whether they can agree upon terms mutually satisfactory. The situation is peculiar, as there are three parties in interest. The United States can enter into no agreement with Colombia that does not have the approval of the company, and the concessions do not permit the company to transfer or attempt to transfer its rights to a foreign government.

"The Commission has, however, attempted to ascertain the views of the New Panama Canal Company with reference to a disposition and transfer of its rights. Interviews were had with its president and other officers during the visit to Paris and on several occasions from time to time since then, and on the 10th day of April last a formal letter was addressed to Mr. Maurice Hutin, the president and director-general, asking whether he was in a position to name terms upon which the company would dispose of its property and interests to the United States. At different times since then the subject has been discussed by the representatives of the company with the Commission and its committee on rights, privileges, and franchises, but no formal reply to the letter was received until this report was being closed. These conferences and correspondence have resulted in no offer to dispose of the property and privileges of the company to the United States upon any terms, even with the consent of the Colombian Government, nor has the company expressed any desire or wish to enter into any negotiations with the United States with reference to such a disposition of its property and rights. It was proposed by President Hutin that the United States might obtain control of the canal scheme as a majority stockholder of a new organization to which the present company could contribute its concession, plant, unfinished work, and other property, at a valuation to be determined by arbitration, and he expressed the opinion that such an arrangement could be made without violating the concessions. But this must include some plan for the protection of the minority stockholders in the financial management, for they would favor a policy that would realize liberal dividends in proportion to the commercial value of the canal, while the policy of this Government might be to reduce tolls and charges to the cost of maintenance or even below it, if the interests of the people would be thereby advanced. The plan, however, which the company prefers is that outlined in its letter of February 28, 1899, addressed to the President of the United States, which has been published in Senate Document No. 188, Fifty-Sixth Congress, first session, pages 41 and 42. This was to reincorporate under the laws of New York or some other State, and accord to the United States such representation in its board of directors and such opportunity to acquire an interest in its securities as its concessions permitted. And an assurance was added to the effect that if the United States should desire to perpetuate or enlarge its existing rights and privileges acquired under the treaty of 1846, the company would conform to such supplemental treaty as might be entered into between the United States and Colombia. The Commission having no other authority than to make investigations and obtain information submits this result of its efforts to ascertain upon what terms the rights and privileges at the Panama route can be obtained. It is proper to add that the examination of the title of the present company to the canal property under the laws of France and Colombia has satisfied this Commission that the New Panama Canal Company has the entire control and management of the canal property. . . .

"The estimated cost of building the Nicaragua Canal is about $58,000,000 more than that of completing the Panama Canal, leaving out the cost of acquiring the latter property. This measures the difference in the magnitude of the obstacles to be overcome in the actual construction of the two canals, and covers all physical considerations such as the greater or less height of dams, the greater or less depth of cuts, the presence or absence of natural harbors, the presence or absence of a railroad, the exemption from or liability to disease, and the amount of work remaining to be done. The New Panama Canal Company has shown no disposition to sell its property to the United States. Should that company be able and willing to sell, there is reason to believe that the price would not be such as would make the total cost to the United States less than that of the Nicaragua Canal. . . . In view of all the facts, and particularly in view of all the difficulties of obtaining the necessary rights, privileges, and franchises on the Panama route, and assuming that Nicaragua and Costa Rica recognize the value of the canal to themselves and are prepared to grant concessions on terms which are reasonable and acceptable to the United States, the Commission is of the opinion that 'the most practicable and feasible route for' an isthmian canal to be 'under the control, management, and ownership of the United States' is that known as the Nicaragua route."—*United States, 56th Cong., 2d Sess., Senate Doc. No. 5.*

A. D. **1900** (December).—The **Hay**-Pauncefote Treaty between the United States and Great Britain, to facilitate the construction of the Canal, as amended by the U. S. Senate.— In his annual Message to Congress, December 3, 1900, President McKinley had the following to say on the subject of the Interoceanic Canal: "The all important matter of an interoceanic canal has assumed a new phase. Adhering to its refusal to reopen the question of the forfeiture of the contract of the Maritime Canal Company, which was terminated for alleged non-execution in October, 1899, the Government of Nicaragua has since supplemented that action by declaring the so-styled Eyre-Cragin option void for nonpayment of the stipulated advance. Protests in relation to these acts have been filed in the State Department, and are under consideration. Deeming itself relieved from existing engagements, the Nicaraguan Government shows a disposition to deal freely with the canal question either in the way of negotiations with the United States or by taking measures to promote the waterway. Overtures for a convention to effect the building of a canal under the auspices of the United States are under consideration. In the mean time, the views of the Congress upon the general subject, in the light of the report of the Commission appointed to examine the comparative merits of the various trans-isthmian ship canal projects, may be awaited. I commend to the early attention of the Senate the convention with Great Britain to facilitate the construction of such a canal, and to remove any objection which might arise out of the convention commonly called the Clayton-Bulwer Treaty." (On the terms of the Clayton-Bulwer Treaty see, in vol. 4, NICARAGUA: A. D. 1850.)

The Convention thus referred to was negotiated by the Secretary of State of the United States, Mr. John Hay, with the British Ambassador to the United States, Lord Pauncefote. It was signed at Washington on the 5th of February, 1900, and communicated by the President to the Senate on the same day. The action of the Senate on the Convention was not taken until after the opening of the session of Congress in December. It was then ratified (December 20), but with three amendments which seriously changed its character. The following is the text of the Convention as ratified, with the Senate amendments indicated :

"ARTICLE I. It is agreed that the canal may be constructed under the auspices of the Government of the United States, either directly at its own cost, or by gift or loan of money to individuals or corporations or through subscription to or purchase of stock or shares, and that, subject to the provisions of the present Convention, the said Government shall have and enjoy all the rights incident to such construction, as well as the exclusive right of providing for the regulation and management of the canal.

"ARTICLE II. The High Contracting Parties, desiring to preserve and maintain the 'general principle' of neutralization established in Article VIII of the Clayton-Bulwer Convention, * which convention is hereby superseded, adopt, as the basis of such neutralization, the following rules, substantially as embodied in the convention between Great Britain and certain other Powers, signed at Constantinople, October 29, 1888, for the Free Navigation of the Suez Maritime Canal, that is to say: 1. The canal shall be free and open, in time of war as in time of peace, to the vessels of commerce and of war of all nations, on terms of entire equality, so that there shall be no discrimination against any nation or its citizens or subjects in respect of the conditions or charges of traffic, or otherwise. 2. The canal shall never be blockaded, nor shall any right of war be exercised nor any act of hostility be committed within it. 3. Vessels of war of a belligerent shall not revictual nor take any stores in the canal except so far as may be strictly necessary ; and the transit of such vessels through the canal shall be effected with the least possible delay, in accordance with the regulations in force, and with only such intermission as may result from the necessities of the service. Prizes shall be in all respects subject to the same rules as vessels of war of the belligerents. 4. No belligerent shall embark or disembark troops, munitions of war or warlike materials in the canal except in case of accidental hindrance of the transit, and in such case the transit shall be resumed with all possible despatch. 5. The provisions of this article shall apply to waters adjacent to the canal, within three marine miles of either end. Vessels of war of a belligerent shall not remain in such waters longer than twenty-four hours at any one time except in case of distress, and in such case shall depart as soon as possible ; but a vessel of war of one belligerent shall not depart within twenty-four hours from the departure of a vessel of war of the other belligerent. * It is agreed, however, that none of the immediately foregoing conditions and stipulations in sections numbered one, two, three, four and five of this article shall apply to measures which the United States may find it necessary to take for securing by its own forces the defense of the United States and the maintenance of public order. 6. The plant, establishments, buildings, and all works necessary to the construction, maintenance and operation of the canal shall be deemed to be part thereof, for the purposes of this Convention, and in time of war as in time of peace shall enjoy complete immunity from attack or injury by belligerents and from acts calculated to impair their usefulness as part of the canal. 7. No fortifications shall be erected commanding the canal or the waters adjacent. The United States, however, shall be at liberty to maintain such military police along the canal as may be necessary to protect it against lawlessness and disorder.

"ARTICLE III. The High Contracting Parties will, immediately upon the exchange of the ratifications of this Convention, bring it to the notice of the other Powers [and invite them to adhere to it].†

"ARTICLE IV. The present Convention shall be ratified by the President of the United States, by and with the advice and consent of the Senate thereof, and by Her Britannic Majesty ; and the

---

* Added by the Senate.
† Stricken out by the Senate.

ratifications shall be exchanged at Washington or at London within six months from the date hereof, or earlier if possible."—*United States, 56th Cong., 1st Sess., Senate Doc. No.* 160.

Anticipating the ratification of the above Treaty with Great Britain, the President of the United States, in December, 1900, concluded agreements with the governments of Costa Rica and Nicaragua, both of which were in the following terms: "It is agreed between the two Governments that when the President of the United States is authorized by law to acquire control of such portion of the territory now belonging to [Costa Rica and Nicaragua] as may be desirable and necessary on which to construct and protect a canal of depth and capacity sufficient for the passage of vessels of the greatest tonnage and draft now in use from a point near San Juan del Norte, on the Caribbean Sea, via Lake Nicaragua, to Brito, on the Pacific Ocean, they mutually engage to enter into negotiations with each other to settle the plan and the agreements, in detail, found necessary to accomplish the construction and to provide for the ownership and control of the proposed canal. As preliminary to such future negotiations it is forthwith agreed that the course of said canal and the terminals thereof shall be the same that were stated in a treaty signed by the plenipotentiaries of the United States and Great Britain on February 5, 1900, and now pending in the Senate of the United States for confirmation, and that the provisions of the same shall be adhered to by the United States and [Costa Rica and Nicaragua]." No action on these agreements was taken in the Senate.

A. D. 1901 (March).—Rejection by the British Government of the Hay-Pauncefote Treaty as amended by the U. S. Senate.— Early in March, soon after the adjournment of Congress, a communication from Lord Lansdowne, the British Secretary of State for Foreign Affairs, declining with courtesy and in friendly terms to accept the Senate amendments to the Hay-Pauncefote Treaty, was received by Lord Pauncefote, the British Ambassador at Washington. The objections urged most strongly are against those amendments which touch the neutrality of the proposed canal and its unimpeded use in time of war as well as in time of peace. "The first of them," said Lord Lansdowne, "which reserves to the United States the right of taking any measures which they may find necessary to secure by their own forces the defence of the United States, appears to His Majesty's government to involve a distinct departure from the principle which has until now found acceptance with both governments; the principle, namely, that in time of war, as well as in time of peace, the passage of the canal is to remain free and unimpeded, and is to be so maintained by the power or powers responsible for its control. Were this amendment added to the convention the United States would, it is presumed, be within their rights, if, at any moment when it seemed to them that their safety required it, in view of warlike preparations not yet commenced, but contemplated or supposed to be contemplated by another power, they resorted to warlike acts in or near the canal — acts clearly inconsistent with the neutral character which it has always been sought to give it, and which would deny the free use of it to the commerce and navies of the world. . . . If the new clause were to be added, the obligation to respect the neutrality of the canal in all circumstances would, so far as Great Britain is concerned, remain in force; the obligation of the United States, on the other hand, would be essentially modified. The result would be a onesided arrangement, under which Great Britain would be debarred from any warlike action in or around the canal, while the United States would be liable to resort to such action to whatever extent they might deem necessary to secure their own safety."

To the contention that there is a specific prohibition in the Hay-Pauncefote treaty against the erection of fortifications, and that this would sufficiently insure the free use of the canal, Lord Lansdowne replies that this "contention is one which His Majesty's government are quite unable to admit." He notes the vagueness of language in the amendment, and says: "Even if it were more precisely worded it would be impossible to determine what might be the effect if one clause permitting defensive measures and another forbidding fortifications were allowed to stand side by side in the convention. To His Majesty's government it seems, as I have already said, that the amendment might be construed as leaving it open to the United States at any moment, not only if war existed, but even if it were anticipated, to take any measures, however stringent or far-reaching, which in their own judgment might be represented as suitable for the purpose of protecting their national interests. Such an enactment would strike at the very root of that 'general principle' of neutralization upon which the Clayton-Bulwer treaty was based, and which was reaffirmed in the convention as drafted."

As to the third Senate amendment, which struck out the provision inviting the adherence of other powers, Lord Lansdowne says: "The amendment not only removes all prospect of the wider guarantee of the neutrality of the canal, but places this country in a position of marked disadvantage compared with other powers which would not be subject to the self-denying ordinance which Great Britain is desired to accept. It would follow, were His Majesty's government to agree to such an arrangement, that while the United States would have a treaty right to interfere with the canal in time of war, or apprehended war, and while other powers could with a clear conscience disregard any of the restrictions imposed by the convention, Great Britain alone, in spite of her enormous possessions on the American Continent, in spite of the extent of her Australasian colonies and her interests in the East, would be absolutely precluded from resorting to any such action or from taking measures to secure her interests in and near the canal."

The British Minister closes his communication to Lord Pauncefote as follows: "I request that your excellency will explain to the Secretary of State the reasons, as set forth in this dispatch, why His Majesty's government feel unable to accept the convention in the shape presented to them by the American Ambassador, and why they prefer, as matters stand at present, to retain unmodified the provisions of the Clayton-Bulwer Treaty. His Majesty's government have throughout these negotiations given evidence of their earnest desire to meet the views of the United

States. They would on this occasion have been ready to consider in a friendly spirit any amendments of the convention not inconsistent with the principles accepted by both governments which the government of the United States might have desired to propose, and they would sincerely regret a failure to come to an amicable understanding in regard to this important subject."

CANAL, The Kaiser Wilhelm Ship. See (in this vol.) GERMANY : A. D. 1895 (JUNE).

CANAL, Manchester Ship.—On the 1st of January, 1894, the ship canal from Liverpool to Manchester, which had been ten years in course of construction and cost £15,000,000, was formally opened, by a long procession of steamers, which traversed it in four and a half hours.

CANAL : The Rhine-Elbe, the Dortmund-Rhine, and other Prussian projects. See (in this vol.) GERMANY : A. D. 1899 (AUGUST) ; and 1901 (JANUARY).

CANDIA: A. D. 1898 (September).—Fresh outbreak. See (in this vol.) TURKEY : A. D. 1897-1899.

CANEA : Christian and Moslem conflicts at. See (in this vol.) TURKEY : A. D. 1897 (FEBRUARY—MARCH).

CANOVAS DEL CASTILLO, Antonio: Formation of Spanish Cabinet. See (in this vol.) SPAIN : A. D. 1895-1896.
Assassination. See (in this vol.) SPAIN : A. D. 1897 (AUGUST—OCTOBER).

CANTEEN, The Army. See (in this vol.) UNITED STATES OF AM. : A. D. 1900 (MAY—NOVEMBER), THE PROHIBITION PARTY ; and 1901 (FEBRUARY).

CANTON: A. D. 1894. — The Bubonic Plague. See (in this vol.) PLAGUE.
A. D. 1899.—Increasing piracy in the river. See (in this vol.) CHINA : A. D. 1899.

CAPE COLONY. See (in this vol.) SOUTH AFRICA (CAPE COLONY).

CAPE NOME, Gold discovery at. See (in this vol.) ALASKA : A. D. 1898-1899.

CAPE SAN JUAN, Engagement at. See (in this vol.) UNITED STATES OF AM. : A. D. 1898 (JULY—AUGUST : PORTO RICO).

CARNEGIE, Andrew: Gifts and offers to public libraries. See (in this vol.) LIBRARIES ; and LIBRARY, NEW YORK PUBLIC.

CARNEGIE COMPANY, Sale of the interests of the. See (in this vol.) TRUSTS: UNITED STATES.

CAROLINE and **MARIANNE ISLANDS :** Their sale by Spain to Germany. — By a treaty concluded in February, 1899, the Caroline Islands, the Western Carolines or Pelew Islands, and the Marianne or Ladrone Islands (excepting Guam), were sold by Spain to Germany for 25,000,000 pesetas — the peseta being equivalent to a fraction less than twenty cents. Spain reserved the right to establish and maintain naval and mercantile stations in the islands, and to retain them in case of war. Spanish trade and privileges for the Spanish religious orders are guaranteed against interference.

CARROLL, Henry K.: Report on Porto Rico. See (in this vol.) PORTO RICO: A. D. 1898-1899 (AUGUST—JULY).

CASSATION, The Court of. — The French Court of Appeals. See (in this vol.) FRANCE : A. D. 1897-1899.

CASTILLO, Pedro Lopez de : Letter to the soldiers of the American army. See (in this vol.) UNITED STATES OF AM. : A. D. 1898 (AUGUST 21).

CATALOGUE, International, of Scientific Literature. See (in this vol.) SCIENCE, RECENT : SCIENTIFIC LITERATURE.

CATALONIA: Independent aspirations in. See (in this vol.) SPAIN : A. D. 1900 (OCTOBER—NOVEMBER).

CATASTROPHES, Natural: A. D. 1894. — Late in December, the orange groves of Florida were mostly destroyed or seriously injured by the severest frost known in more than half a century.
1896.—On Jan. 8, a severe earthquake shock was felt at Meshed, Kelat and other Persian towns, causing over 1,100 deaths.
1896.—In March, the Tigris overflowed its banks, causing incalculable loss of life and property in Mesopotamia.
1896. — A succession of earthquake shocks in March, 1896, did great damage at Santiago, Valparaiso, and other parts of Chile.
1896.—On May 15, a cyclone destroyed part of the town of Sherman, in Texas, killing more than 120 persons, mostly negroes. The same day a waterspout burst over the town of Howe in the same state, killing 8 people.
1896.—On May 27, a fierce cyclone swept the city of St. Louis, Mo., completely devastating a large part of the city, and causing great loss of life and property.
1896.—A destructive wave swept the Japanese coast in June. See (in this vol.) JAPAN : A. D. 1896.
1896.—On July 26, a tidal wave, 5 miles in width, inundated the coast of Kiangsu, in China, destroying many villages and more than 4,000 inhabitants.
1896-1897.—A severe famine prevailed in India from the spring of 1896 until the autumn of 1897. See (in this vol.) INDIA : A. D. 1896-1897.
1897.—A severe earthquake occurred at the island of Kishm in the Persian Gulf, in January, causing great loss of life.
1897.—In March and April of this year the floods along the Mississippi river and its tributaries reached the highest level ever recorded. In extent of area and loss of property these floods were the most remarkable in the history of the continent. The total area under water on April 10 was about 15,800 square miles, containing about 39,500 farms, whose value was close upon $65,000,000. The loss of life was small. Congress gave relief to the extent of $200,000, besides appropriating $2,583,300 for the improvement of the Mississippi.
1897.—Extensive floods occurred in Galatz, Moldavia, in June, rendering 20,000 people homeless.
1897.—The islands of Leyte and Samar, in the Visayas group, were swept by an immense

71

wave, caused by a cyclone, in October, thousands of natives being killed, and much property destroyed.

1897.—On October 6, the Philippine Islands were swept by a typhoon, which destroyed several towns. The loss of life was estimated at 6,000, of whom 400 were Europeans. This was followed on October 12 by a cyclone which destroyed several villages and caused further loss of life.

1897.—By an eruption of the Mayon volcano in the island of Luzon, Philippine Islands, four hundred persons were buried in the lava, and the large town of Libog completely destroyed.

1898.—A series of earthquake shocks in Asia Minor during the month of January occasioned considerable loss of life and property.

1898.—In January, Amboyna, in the Molucca Islands, was almost destroyed by an earthquake, in which about 50 persons were killed and 200 injured.

1898.—On January 11, a tornado wrecked many buildings in Fort Smith, Ark. The loss of life was reported as 50, with hundreds injured.

1898.—A disastrous blizzard occurred in New England, January 31 and February 1. Fifty lives were reported as lost, and the damage in Boston alone amounted to $2,000,000. Many vessels were driven ashore or foundered, with further loss of life.

1898.—Floods on the Ohio river in March and April caused much loss of life and property. Shawneetown, Ill., on the Ohio river, was almost entirely destroyed by the flood, more than 60 lives being lost.

1898.—On the night of September 10, the island of Barbados was swept by a tornado which destroyed 10,000 houses and damaged 5,000 more. Three-fourths of the inhabitants were left homeless, and about 100 were killed. The islands of St. Vincent and St. Lucia also suffered great losses of life and property.

1898.—A typhoon swept the central provinces of Japan in September, causing heavy floods, and destroying 100 lives.

1899.—Severe floods on the Brazos river, in Texas, occasioned the death of about 100 people, and property losses to the extent of $15,000,000.

1899.—A destructive tornado in Northern Missouri, in April, did much damage in the towns of Kirksville and Newtown. Over fifty persons were killed.

1899.—An almost unprecedented failure of crops in eastern Russia caused famine, disease and awful destruction of life.

1899.—A terrific hurricane visited the West Indies August 7 and 8. Of the several islands affected, Porto Rico suffered most, three-fourths of the population being left homeless. The total loss of life in the West Indies was estimated at 5,000. See (in this vol.) PORTO RICO: A. D. 1899 (AUGUST).

1899.—About 1,500 people lost their lives in an earthquake around Aidin, Asia Minor, September 3.

1899.—The island of Ceram, in the Moluccas, was visited by an earthquake and tidal wave, November 2. Many towns were destroyed, and 5,000 people killed.

1899-1900.—Recurrence of famine in India. See (in this vol.) INDIA A. D. 1899-1900.

1900.—The city of Galveston, Texas, was overwhelmed and mostly destroyed, on the 9th of September, by an unprecedented hurricane, which drove the waters of the Gulf upon the low-lying town. See (in this vol.) GALVESTON.

1901.—Famine in China. See (in this vol.) CHINA : A. D. 1901 (JANUARY—FEBRUARY).

CATHOLICS, Roman : Protest of British peers against the declaration required from the **sovereign**. See (in this vol.) ENGLAND : A. D. 1901 (FEBRUARY).

Victory in Belgium. See (in this vol.) BELGIUM : A. D. 1894–1895.

See, also, PAPACY.

CEBU : The American occupation of **the** island. See (in this vol.) PHILIPPINE ISLANDS : A. D. 1899 (JANUARY—NOVEMBER).

CENSUS : Of the United States, A. D. **1900.** See (in this vol.) UNITED STATES OF AM. : A. D. 1900 (MAY—OCTOBER).

CENTRAL AFRICA PROTECTORATE, British. See (in this vol.) BRITISH CENTRAL AFRICA PROTECTORATE.

CENTRAL AMERICA, A. D. 1821-1898.—Unsuccessful attempts to unite the republics.—"In 1821, after numerous revolutions, Central America succeeded in throwing off the yoke of Spain. A Congress assembled at Guatemala in March, 1822, and founded the Republic of Central America, composed of Guatemala, Salvador, Honduras, Nicaragua, and Costa Rica. The new Republic had but a short existence ; after numerous civil wars the Union was dissolved, October 26, 1838, and the five States of the Republic became so many independent countries. Several attempts toward a reorganization of the Constitution of the Republic of Central America remained fruitless and had cost the lives of certain of their authors, when, through the influence of Dr. P. Bonilla, President of the Republic of Honduras, a treaty was concluded between Nicaragua and Salvador, according to which the three Republics constituted a federation under the name of the Greater Republic of Central America. The three Republics became States, and the sovereignty of the federation was exercised by a Diet composed of three members, one for each State, and which convened every year in the capital of the Federal States.

"On the invitation of this Diet, the three States appointed a delegation which met as a Constituent Assembly at Managua, Nicaragua, and established a constitution, according to the terms of which the three States took the name of the United States of Central America, November 1, 1898. This Constitution, grand and patriotic, which, in the minds of those who had elaborated it, meant a complete consolidation of the three Federal States and a speedy realization of a reorganization of the Grand Republic of Central America, dreamed of by Morazan, had a sad ending. The day after the meeting of the Constituent Assembly a revolutionary movement hostile to the new federation broke out in Salvador and gave a new administration to this State. Its first act was to retire from the Union, and this secession brought about the dissolution of the United States of Central America ; for, following the example of Salvador, Honduras and

Nicaragua took back their absolute sovereignty."
—H. Jalhay, quoted in *Bulletin of American Republics, March*, 1899.

The secession of Salvador was brought about by a revolutionary movement, which overthrew the constitutional government of President Gutierrez and placed General Tomas Regolado at the head of a provisional government, which issued the following manifesto on the 25th of November, 1898 : "Considering—That the compact of Amapala, celebrated in June, 1895, and all that proceeds therefrom, has not obtained the legitimate sanction of the Salvadorean people, and, moreover, has been a violation of the political constitution of Salvador; That in the assembled Constituent Assembly of Managua, reunited in June of the present year, the deputies of Salvador were not directly elected by the Salvadorean people, and for that reason had no legal authority to concur to a constituent law that could bind the Republic; That the union with the Republics of Honduras and Nicaragua under the contracted terms will seriously injure the interests of Salvador : Decrees. ART. 1. The Republic of Salvador is not obliged by the contract of Amapala to acknowledge any authority in the constitution of Managua of the 27th August of the current year, and it is released from the contract of union with the Republics of Honduras and Nicaragua. ART. 2. The Republic of Salvador assumes in full its self-government and independence, and will enter the union with the sister Republics of Central America when same is convenient to its positive interests and is the express and free will of the Salvadorean people."—*United States, 55th Cong., 3d Sess., Senate Doc. No.* 50.

A. D. **1884-1900.**—Interoceanic Canal measures of later years. See (in this vol.) CANAL, INTEROCEANIC, with accompanying map.

Nicaragua : A. D. **1894-1895.**—**Insurrection in the Mosquito Indian Strip. — The Bluefields Incident.**—In his Annual Message to Congress, December, 1894, President Cleveland referred as follows to disturbances which had occurred during the year at Bluefields, the principal town of the Mosquito district of Nicaragua, and commonly known as "the Bluefields Incident :" "By the treaty of 1860 between Great Britain and Nicaragua, the former Government expressly recognized the sovereignty of the latter over the strip, and a limited form of self-government was guaranteed to the Mosquito Indians, to be exercised according to their customs, for themselves and other dwellers within its limits, The so-called native government, which grew to be largely made up of aliens, for many years disputed the sovereignty of Nicaragua over the strip and claimed the right to maintain therein a practically independent municipal government. Early in the past year efforts of Nicaragua to maintain sovereignty over the Mosquito territory led to serious disturbances, culminating in the suppression of the native government and the attempted substitution of an impracticable composite administration in which Nicaragua and alien residents were to participate. Failure was followed by an insurrection, which for a time subverted Nicaraguan rule, expelling her officers and restoring the old organization. This in turn gave place to the existing local government established and upheld by Nicaragua. Although the alien interests arrayed against Nic-

aragua in these transactions have been largely American and the commerce of that region for some time has been and still is chiefly controlled by our citizens, we can not for that reason challenge the rightful sovereignty of Nicaragua over this important part of her domain."—*United States, Message and Documents (Abridgment, 1894-5).*—In his Message of 1895 the President summarized the later history of the incident as follows: "In last year's message I narrated at some length the jurisdictional questions freshly arisen in the Mosquito Indian Strip of Nicaragua. Since that time, by the voluntary act of the Mosquito Nation, the territory reserved to them has been incorporated with Nicaragua, the Indians formally subjecting themselves to be governed by the general laws and regulations of the Republic instead of by their own customs and regulations, and thus availing themselves of a privilege secured to them by the treaty between Nicaragua and Great Britain of January 28, 1860. After this extension of uniform Nicaraguan administration to the Mosquito Strip, the case of the British vice-consul, Hatch, and of several of his countrymen who had been summarily expelled from Nicaragua and treated with considerable indignity, provoked a claim by Great Britain upon Nicaragua for pecuniary indemnity, which, upon Nicaragua's refusal to admit liability, was enforced by Great Britain. While the sovereignty and jurisdiction of Nicaragua was in no way questioned by Great Britain, the former's arbitrary conduct in regard to British subjects furnished the ground for this proceeding. A British naval force occupied without resistance the Pacific seaport of Corinto, but was soon after withdrawn upon the promise that the sum demanded would be paid. Throughout this incident the kindly offices of the United States were invoked and were employed in favor of as peaceful a settlement and as much consideration and indulgence toward Nicaragua as were consistent with the nature of the case."— *United States, Message and Documents (Abridgment,* 1895-6).

Guatemala : A. D. **1895.**—**Mex**ican bound**ary** dispute. See (in this vol.) MEXICO : A. D. 1895.

Nicaragua : A. D. **1896-1898.**—Revolutionary conflicts.—Vice-President Baca of Nicaragua joined a revolutionary movement which was set on foot in February, 1896, by the Clericals, for the overthrow of President Zelaya, and was declared Provisional President. The rebellion had much support from exiles and friends in Honduras; but the government of that State sustained and assisted Zelaya. The insurgents were defeated in a number of battles, and gave up the contest in May. During the civil war American and British marines were landed on occasions at Corinto to protect property there. In 1897, and again in 1898, there were renewed insurrections, quickly suppressed.

Costa Rica : A. D. **1896-1900.**—Boundary dispute with Colombia settled by arbitration. See (in this vol.) COLOMBIA : A. D. 1893-1900.

Nicaragua—Costa Rica : A. D. **1897.**—A dispute between Nicaragua and Costa Rica, as to the eastern extremity of their boundary line, was decided by General Alexander, a referee accepted by the two republics. The boundary had not been well defined in a treaty negotiated for its settlement in 1858. According to the terms of the treaty, the line was to start from the Atlantic at the mouth of the San Juan river; but changes of current and accumulation of river drift, etc., gave ground for dispute as to where the river actually made its exit. President Cleveland in 1888, acting as arbitrator at the request of the two countries, decided that the treaty of 1858 was valid, but was not clear as to which outlet of the delta was the boundary. Finally, in 1896, an agreement was reached for a final survey and marking of the boundary line, and President Cleveland, on request, appointed General Alexander as arbitrator in any case of disagreement between the surveying commissions. The decision gives to Nicaragua the territory upon which Greytown is situated, and practical control of the mouth of the canal.

Guatemala: A. D. 1897-1898.—Dictatorship of President Barrios.—His assassination.—In June, 1897, President José M. Reyna Barrios, whose six years term in the presidency would expire the next March, fearing defeat in the approaching election, forcibly dissolved the National Assembly and proclaimed a dictatorship. Three months later a revolt was organized by General Prospero Morales; but Barrios crushed it with merciless energy, and a veritable reign of terror ensued. In February, 1898, the career of the Dictator was cut short by an assassin, who shot him to avenge the death of a wealthy citizen, Don Juan Aparicio, whom Barrios had executed for expressing sympathy with the objects of the rebellion of the previous year. Control of the government was then taken by Dr. Cabrera, who had been at the head of the party which supported Barrios. A rising under Morales was again attempted, but failed. Morales, in a dying condition at the time, was betrayed and captured. Cabrera, with no more opposition, was elected President for six years.

Nicaragua—Costa Rica: A. D. 1900.—Agreements with the United States respecting the control of territory for interoceanic canal. See (in this vol.) CANAL, INTEROCEANIC, A. D. 1900 (DECEMBER).

CENTURY, The Nineteenth: Date of its ending.—Its character and trend.—Comparison with preceding ages.—Its failures. See (in this vol.) NINETEENTH CENTURY.

CERVERA, Rear-Admiral, and the Spanish Squadron at Santiago de Cuba. See (in this vol.) UNITED STATES OF AM.: A. D. 1898 (APRIL—JUNE); and (JULY 3).

CHAFFEE, General Adna R.: At Santiago. See (in this vol.) UNITED STATES OF AM.: A. D. 1898 (JUNE—JULY).
Commanding American forces in China. See (in this vol.) CHINA: A. D. 1900 (JUNE—AUGUST); (JULY); and (AUGUST).
Report of the allied movement to Peking and the capture of the city. See (in this vol.) CHINA: A. D. 1900 (AUGUST 4-16).

CHAKDARRA, Defense of. See (in this vol.) INDIA: A. D. 1897-1898.

CHALDEA, New light on ancient. See (in this vol.) ARCHÆOLOGICAL RESEARCH: BABYLONIA.

CHAMBERLAIN, Joseph: Appointed British Secretary of State for the Colonies.

See (in this vol.) ENGLAND: A. D. 1894-1895; and 1900 (NOVEMBER—DECEMBER).
Conference with Colonial Premiers. See (in this vol.) ENGLAND: A. D. 1897 (JUNE—JULY).
Controversies with the government of the South African Republic. See (in this vol.) SOUTH AFRICA (THE TRANSVAAL): A. D. 1896 (JANUARY—APRIL); 1896-1897 (MAY—APRIL), and after.
Testimony before British Parliamentary Committee on the Jameson Raid. — Remarks in Parliament on Mr. Rhodes. See (in this vol.) SOUTH AFRICA (THE TRANSVAAL): A. D. 1897 (FEBRUARY—JULY).
Instructions to the Governor of Jamaica. See (in this vol.) JAMAICA: A. D. 1899.
Reassertion of British suzerainty over the South African Republic.—Refusal to arbitrate questions of disagreement. See (in this vol.) SOUTH AFRICA (THE TRANSVAAL): A. D. 1897 (MAY—OCTOBER); and 1898-1899.
Declaration of South African policy. See (in this vol.) SOUTH AFRICA (THE FIELD OF WAR): A. D. 1901.

CHANG CHIH-TUNG, Viceroy: Admirable conduct during the Chinese outbreak. See (in this vol.) CHINA: A. D. 1900 (JUNE—DECEMBER).

CHEMICAL SCIENCE, Recent advances in. See (in this vol.) SCIENCE, RECENT: CHEMISTRY AND PHYSICS.

CHEROKEES, United States agreement with the. See (in this vol.) INDIANS, AMERICAN: A. D. 1893-1899.

CHICAGO: A. D. 1894.—Destruction of the Columbian Exposition buildings.—By a succession of fires, January 9, February 14, most of the buildings of the Exposition, with valuable exhibits not yet removed, were destroyed.

A. D. 1896.—Democratic National Convention. See (in this vol.) UNITED STATES OF AM.: A. D. 1896 (JUNE—NOVEMBER).

A. D. 1899.—Significance of the municipal election.—The municipal election of April 4, 1899, in Chicago, resulted in the reëlection of Mayor Carter H. Harrison, Democrat, by 149,000 votes, against 107,000 cast for Zina R. Carter, Republican, and 46,000 for Ex-Governor Altgeld, radical Democrat, running independently. In the opinion of a correspondent of the "Review of Reviews," "The campaign disclosed three interesting results — namely: (1) the growth of independence and of attention to local issues; (2) the dominance of the street-railroad issue; and (3) the growth of sentiment in favor of municipal ownership. Nearly two-thirds of all the votes cast were against the Republican candidate, and our correspondent regards this as largely due to the belief that he, more than any of the others, represented the interests of the street-railroad corporations." This writer holds that "in all probability any practical proposition for municipal ownership and operation of the street-railroads would to-day be approved by a popular vote in Chicago."

A. D. 1900.—Opening of the Drainage Canal.—An extraordinary public work was brought into use early in the year, by the opening of what is known as the Chicago Drainage Canal. This was constructed for the purpose of turning the natural flow of water in Chicago River backward, away from Lake Michigan, its natural embouchure, into the small Des Plaines River, which runs to the Illinois, and the Illinois to the Mississippi, — the object being to carry the sewage of Chicago away from the Lake, where it contaminates the water supply of the city. Part of the city sewage was already being sent in that direction by a pumping system which carried it over the divide; the purpose of the canal is to take the whole. The work was begun in September, 1892, and practically finished, so far as concerns the canal, in little more than seven years, at a cost of about $34,500,000. Changes in the city sewage system, to fully utilize the object of the canal, were still to be completed. When the full use is realized, there is said to be provision in the canal for a maximum discharge of 600,000 cubic feet of water per minute. Some have anticipated that such an outflow would seriously lower the level of the lakes; but there were no signs of that effect in the season of 1900. Nor did it seem to appear that the sewage then passing by river flow westward was doing harm to towns on the Illinois and Mississippi, as they had apprehended; but the discharge was, as yet, far short of what it is intended to be. It is possible that ultimately the Chicago Drainage Canal may become part of a navigable water-way from the lakes to the Mississippi, realizing an old project of water transportation in that direction to compete with the rails. The canal has been constructed upon a scale to suffice for that use; but the river-improvement called for is one of formidable cost.

About the time of the opening of the canal, the State of Missouri, by its Attorney-General, moved in the Supreme Court of the United States for leave to file a bill of complaint against the State of Illinois and the Sanitary District of Chicago, the purpose of which was to enjoin the defendants from discharging the sewage and noxious filth of the Sanitary District of Chicago into the Mississippi River by artificial methods. The complaint alleged that unless the relief sought is granted the water of the Mississippi, which is used for drinking and other domestic purposes by many thousands of inhabitants of the State, will be polluted, and that the public health will be endangered. The Court granted leave to file the bill. The defendants then interposed a demurrer, claiming that the controversy, not being in reality between two States, but between two cities, was one over which the Supreme Court has no jurisdiction. On the 28th of January, 1901, the Court rendered its decision, overruling the demurrer to its jurisdiction. The effect of the opinion is that the Drainage Canal attorneys now must answer the complaint that the sewage and noxious filth of the sanitary district are contaminating the waters of the Mississippi River at St. Louis. No evidence of the facts will be taken in court. On the request of the parties to the suit, a commission will be appointed to take testimony and make a report.

CHICAGO UNIVERSITY: Dedication of the Yerkes Observatory. See (in this vol.) YERKES OBSERVATORY.

CHICKASAWS, United States agreement with the. See (in this vol.) INDIANS, AMERICAN: A. D. 1893–1899.

CHIH-LI, The "Boxer" outbreak in. See (in this vol.) CHINA: A. D. 1900 (JANUARY—MARCH).

CHILE: A. D. 1894-1900.—The questions with Bolivia and Peru concerning Atacama, Tacna and Arica. — Of the treaties which closed the war of 1879–84 between Chile, Bolivia and Peru (see, in vol. 1, CHILE: A. D. 1833–1884), that between Chile and Bolivia contained the following curious provision, of "indefinite truce," as it has been called: "Until the opportunity presents itself of celebrating a definite treaty of peace between the Republics of Chile and Bolivia, both countries duly represented by . . . have agreed to adjust a treaty of truce in accordance with the following bases: First, the Republics of Chile and Bolivia agree to celebrate an indefinite truce; and, in consequence, declare at an end the state of war, which will not be renewed unless one of the contracting parties should inform the other, with at least a year's notification, of its intention to recommence hostilities. In this case the notification will be made directly, or through the diplomatic representative of a friendly nation. Second, the Republic of Chile, while this truce is in force, shall continue to rule, in accordance with the political and administrative system established by Chilian law, the territories situated between parallel 238 and the mouth of the Loa in the Pacific, such territories having for their eastern boundary a straight line." Under this agreement Chile has held ever since the territory in question (which is the province of Atacama) and has claimed that her possession of it should be made conclusive and permanent by such a "definite treaty" as the "treaty of truce" in 1884 contemplated. In her view it was taken in lieu of a war indemnity. Bolivia has disputed this view, maintaining that a permanent cession of the province, which was her only seaboard, and without which she has no port, was not intended. The Bolivian government has continually urged claims to the restoration of a seaport for Bolivian trade, which Chile has refused.

At the same time when Atacama was taken from Bolivia, the provinces of Tacna and Arica were taken by Chile from Peru, with a stipulation in the peace treaty of Ancon (1884) that she should hold them for ten years, pending the payment by Peru of a war indemnity, and that the inhabitants should then decide by vote to which country they would belong. But, down to the close of the year 1900, the Chilian government had not allowed the vote to be taken.

In September, 1900, the dispute, as between Chile and Bolivia, was brought to what seemed to be an ultimate stage by an incisive note from the Chilian to the Bolivian government, proposing to grant to the latter "in exchange for a final cancelling of all claims to the littoral, three compensations, viz.: First, to pay all obligations contracted by the Bolivian Government with the mining enterprises at Huaichaca, Corocoro and Oruro, and the balance of the Bolivian loan contracted in Chile in 1867; second, an amount of money, to be fixed by mutual agreement, for the construction of a railroad connecting any port on the Chilian coast with the interior of Bolivia, or else to extend the present Oruro Railway; and, third, to grant free transit for all products and merchandise passing into and out of Bolivia through the port referred to." Bolivia has not seemed to be disposed to accept this proposal, and the situation is likely to become more strained than before.

A. D. 1896.—Presidential election.—An excited but orderly presidential election held in June, 1896, without government interference, resulted in the choice of Señor Errazuriz, to succeed Admiral Jorge Montt, who had been at the head of the government since the overthrow and death of Balmaceda in 1891.

A. D. 1898.—Settlement of boundary dispute with Argentine Republic. See (in this vol.) ARGENTINE REPUBLIC : A. D. 1898.

A. D. 1900. —Adoption of compulsory military service. — The " Diario Oficial " of Chile of September 5, 1900, published a decree of the Chilian Government establishing compulsory military service in Chile. By the decree all Chilians will be liable to military service from their 20th to their 45th year. Every man on completing his 20th year will be liable to be

chosen by lot to serve one year with the colors, after which, if so chosen, he will pass into the first reserve, where he will remain for nine years. Those not chosen by lot to serve one year with the colors will pass directly into the first reserve. The second reserve will consist of men of from 30 to 45 years of age. Among those who will be exempt from compulsory military service are the members of the Government, members of Congress, State and municipal councillors, Judges, the clergy, including all those who wear the tonsure, or belong to any religious order, the directors and teachers of public schools and colleges, and the police. The last, however, will be liable to military duty if called upon by the President. Various civil servants and every only son, or every one of two only sons of a family which he assists to maintain, may be excused service under certain conditions.

A. D. 1900.—Vote against compulsory arbitration at Spanish-American Congress. See (in this vol.) SPAIN : A. D. 1900 (NOVEMBER).

CHINA.

A. D. 1894-1895.—The war with japan.—The peace treaty of Shimonoseki.—Recognition of Korean independence.—Cession of part of Fêng-tien, of Formosa, and of the Pescadores Islands to Japan.—Relinquishment of Fêng-tien by Japan.—In the original edition of this work, the causes of the war of 1894-5 between China and Japan will be found stated in the Supplement (vol. 5), under "Corea." In the new, revised edition, the same appears in vol. 3, under "Korea." At the close of the year 1894 the Japanese were pressing their campaign, with little heed to the cold of winter, for which they seemed to be well prepared. They had won, almost with ease, every serious engagement of the war. They had half destroyed the Chinese navy, on the 18th of September, in a great battle at the mouth of the Yalu River, and, on the 21st-22d of November, they had captured Port Arthur, the strongest fortress in China, with costly dockyards and great stores of the munitions of war. In the first month of the new year the successes of the Japanese were renewed. Kaiphing was taken on the 10th ; a vigorous Chinese attack was repulsed, near Niuchuang, on the 16th ; a landing of 25,000 troops on the Shantung Peninsula was effected on the 20th, and a combined attack by army and navy on the strong forts which protected the important harbor of Wei-hai-wei, and the Chinese fleet sheltered in it, was begun on the 30th of the month. The attack was ended on the 13th of February, when the Chinese admiral Ting-Juchang gave up the remnant of his fleet and then killed himself. The Chinese general, Tai, had committed suicide in despair on the third night of the fighting. There was further fighting around Niuchuang and Yingkow during February and part of March, while overtures for peace were being made by the Chinese government. At length the famous viceroy, Li Hung-chang, was sent to Japan with full powers to conclude a treaty. Negotiations were interrupted at the outset by a foul attack on the Chinese ambassador by a Japanese ruffian, who shot and seriously wounded him in the cheek. But the Mikado or-

dered an armistice, and the Treaty of Shimonoseki was concluded and signed on the 17th of April. The essential provisions of the treaty are as follows :

" Article I. China recognizes definitely the full and complete independence and autonomy of Corea, and, in consequence, the payment of tribute and the performance of ceremonies and formalities by Corea to China in derogation of such independence and autonomy shall wholly cease for the future.

" Article II. China cedes to Japan in perpetuity and full sovereignty the following territories, together with all fortifications, arsenals, and public property thereon : — (a.) The southern portion of the Province of Fêng-tien, within the following boundaries— The line of demarcation begins at the mouth of the River Yalu, and ascends that stream to the mouth of the River An-Ping ; from thence the line runs to Fêng Huang ; from thence to Haicheng ; from thence to Ying Kow, forming a line which describes the southern portion of the territory. The places above named are included in the ceded territory. When the line reaches the River Liao at Ying Kow it follows the course of that stream to its mouth, where it terminates. The mid-channel of the River Liao shall be taken as the line of demarcation. This cession also includes all islands appertaining or belonging to the Province of Fêng-tien situated in the eastern portion of the Bay of Liao Tung, and in the northern part of the Yellow Sea. (b.) The Island of Formosa, together with all islands appertaining or belonging to the said Island of Formosa. (c.) The Pescadores Group, that is to say, all islands lying between the 119th and 120th degrees of longitude east of Greenwich and the 23rd and 24th degrees of north latitude. . . .

" Article IV. China agrees to pay to Japan as a war indemnity the sum of 200,000,000 Kuping taels. The said sum to be paid in eight instalments. The first instalment of 50,000,000 taels to be paid within six months, and the second instalment of 50,000,000 taels to be paid within twelve months after the exchange of the ratifica-

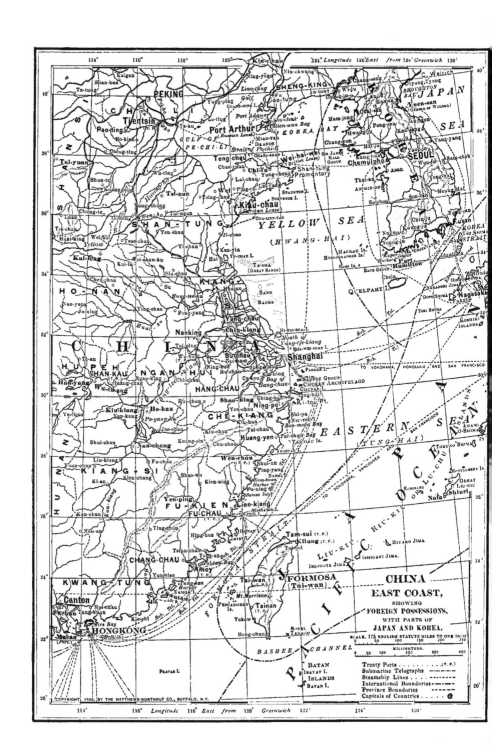

CHINA
EAST COAST,
SHOWING
FOREIGN POSSESSIONS,
WITH PARTS OF
JAPAN AND KOREA.

SCALE, 175 ENGLISH STATUTE MILES TO ONE INCH

Treaty Ports	(T. P.)
Submarine Telegraphs	
Steamship Lines	
International Boundaries	
Province Boundaries	
Capitals of Countries	

tions of this Act. The remaining sum to be paid in six equal annual instalments as follows: the first of such equal annual instalments to be paid within two years, the second within three years, the third within four years, the fourth within five years, the fifth within six years, and the sixth within seven years after the exchange of the ratifications of this Act. Interest at the rate of 5 per cent. per annum shall begin to run on all unpaid portions of the said indemnity from the date the first instalment falls due. China shall, however, have the right to pay by anticipation at any time any or all of said instalments. In case the whole amount of the said indemnity is paid within three years after the exchange of the ratifications of the present Act, all interest shall be waived, and the interest for two years and a half, or for any less period if then already paid, shall be included as a part of the principal amount of the indemnity.

"Article V. The inhabitants of the territories ceded to Japan who wish to take up their residence outside the ceded districts shall be at liberty to sell their real property and retire. For this purpose a period of two years from the date of the exchange of the ratifications of the present Act shall be granted. At the expiration of that period those of the inhabitants who shall not have left such territories shall, at the option of Japan, be deemed to be Japanese subjects. Each of the two Governments shall immediately upon the exchange of the ratifications of the present Act, send one or more Commissioners to Formosa to effect a final transfer of that province, and within the space of two months after the exchange of the ratifications of this Act such transfer shall be completed.

"Article VI. All Treaties between Japan and China having come to an end in consequence of war, China engages, immediately upon the exchange of the ratifications of this Act, to appoint Plenipotentiaries to conclude with the Japanese Plenipotentiaries a Treaty of Commerce and Navigation, and a Convention to regulate frontier intercourse and trade. The Treaties, Conventions, and Regulations now subsisting between China and European Powers shall serve as a basis for the said Treaty and Convention between Japan and China. From the date of the exchange of the ratifications of this Act until the said Treaty and Convention are brought into actual operation the Japanese Government, its officials, commerce, navigation, frontier intercourse and trade, industries, ships and subjects, shall in every respect be accorded by China most-favoured-nation treatment. China makes, in addition, the following concessions to take effect six months after the date of the present Act :— 1. The following cities, towns, and ports, in addition to those already opened, shall be opened to the trade, residence, industries, and manufactures of Japanese subjects under the same conditions, and with the same privileges and facilities as exist at the present open cities, towns, and ports of China. (1.) Shashih, in the Province of Hupeh. (2.) Chung King, in the Province of Szechuan. (3.) Suchow, in the Province of Kiang Su. (4.) Hangchow, in the Province of Chekiang. The Japanese Government shall have the right to station Consuls at any or all of the above-named places. 2. Steam navigation for vessels under the Japanese flag for the conveyance of passengers and cargo shall be extended to the following places :—(1.) On the

Upper Yangtsze River, from Ichang to Chung King. (2.) On the Woosung River and the Canal, from Shanghae to Suchow and Hangchow. The Rules and Regulations which now govern the navigation of the inland waters of China by foreign vessels, shall, so far as applicable, be enforced in respect of the above-named routes, until new Rules and Regulations are conjointly agreed to. 3. Japanese subjects purchasing goods or produce in the interior of China or transporting imported merchandize into the interior of China, shall have the right temporarily to rent or hire warehouses for the storage of the articles so purchased or transported, without the payment of any taxes or exactions whatever. 4. Japanese subjects shall be free to engage in all kinds of manufacturing industries in all the open cities, towns, and ports of China, and shall be at liberty to import into China all kinds of machinery, paying only the stipulated import duties thereon. All articles manufactured by Japanese subjects in China, shall in respect of inland transit and internal taxes, duties, charges, and exactions of all kinds and also in respect of warehousing and storage facilities in the interior of China, stand upon the same footing and enjoy the same privileges and exemptions as merchandize imported by Japanese subjects into China. In the event additional Rules and Regulations are necessary in connection with these concessions, they shall be embodied in the Treaty of Commerce and Navigation provided for by this Article.

"Article VII. Subject to the provisions of the next succeeding Article, the evacuation of China by the armies of Japan, shall be completely effected within three months after the exchange of the ratifications of the present Act.

"Article VIII. As a guarantee of the faithful performance of the stipulations of this Act, China consents to the temporary occupation by the military forces of Japan, of Wei-hai-wei, in the Province of Shantung. Upon the payment of the first two instalments of the war indemnity herein stipulated for and the exchange of the ratifications of the Treaty of Commerce and Navigation, the said place shall be evacuated by the Japanese forces, provided the Chinese Government consents to pledge, under suitable and sufficient arrangements, the Customs Revenue of China as security for the payment of the principal and interest of the remaining instalments of said indemnity. In the event no such arrangements are concluded, such evacuation shall only take place upon the payment of the final instalment of said indemnity. It is, however, expressly understood that no such evacuation shall take place until after the exchange of the ratifications of the Treaty of Commerce and Navigation.

"Article IX. Immediately upon the exchange of the ratifications of this Act, all prisoners of war then held shall be restored, and China undertakes not to ill-treat or punish prisoners of war so restored to her by Japan. China also engages to at once release all Japanese subjects accused of being military spies or charged with any other military offences. China further engages not to punish in any manner, nor to allow to be punished, those Chinese subjects who have in any manner been compromised in their relations with the Japanese army during the war.

"Article X. All offensive military operations

shall cease upon the exchange of the ratifications of this Act."

When the terms of the treaty were made known, Russia, Germany and France entered such protests against the cession of a portion of the Fêng-tien peninsula, on the main land, and brought such pressure to bear on Japan, that the latter was compelled to yield, and relinquished the districts in question by the following imperial proclamation, dated May 10, 1895:

"We recently, at the request of the Emperor of China, appointed Plenipotentiaries for the purpose of conferring with the Ambassadors sent by China, and of concluding with them a Treaty of Peace between the two Empires. Since then the Governments of the two Empires of Russia and Germany and of the French Republic, considering that the permanent possession of the ceded districts of the Feng-tien Peninsula by the Empire of Japan would be detrimental to the lasting peace of the Orient, have united in a simultaneous recommendation to our Government to refrain from holding those districts permanently.

"Earnestly desirous as we always are for the maintenance of peace, nevertheless we were forced to commence hostilities against China for no other reason than our sincere desire to secure for the Orient an enduring peace. The Governments of the three Powers are, in offering their friendly recommendation, similarly actuated by the same desire, and we, out of our regard for peace, do not hesitate to accept their advice. Moreover, it is not our wish to cause suffering to our people, or to impede the progress of the national destiny by embroiling the Empire in new complications, and thereby imperilling the situation and retarding the restoration of peace.

"China has already shown, by the conclusion of the Treaty of Peace, the sincerity of her repentance for her breach of faith with us, and has made manifest to the world our reasons and the object we had in view in waging war with that Empire. Under these circumstances we do not consider that the honour and dignity of the Empire will be compromised by resorting to magnanimous measures, and by taking into consideration the general situation of affairs. We have therefore accepted the advice of the friendly Powers, and have commanded our Government to reply to the Governments of the three Powers to that effect.

"We have specially commanded our Government to negotiate with the Chinese Government respecting all arrangements for the return of the peninsular districts. The exchange of the ratifications of the Treaty of Peace has now been concluded, the friendly relations between the two Empires have been restored, and cordial relations with all other Powers have been strengthened. We therefore command all our subjects to respect our will, to take into careful consideration the general situation, to be circumspect in all things, to avoid erroneous tendencies, and not to impair or thwart the high aspirations of our Empire."—*Great Britain, Parliamentary Publications: Papers by Command, Japan, No. 1, 1895.*

A. D. 1894-1895 (March—July).—Cession of Kiang-Hung to France protested against by Great Britain.—In March, 1894, the government of China entered into a treaty with that of Great Britain, for the settlement of boundaries of Burmah, in which it agreed to make no cession of the district of Kiang-Hung, or any part of it, to any other Power. Notwithstanding this agreement, the eastern part of Kiang-Hung was ceded to France in July, 1895; for which proceeding the British Government promptly called China to account.

A. D. 1895.—Treaty with Russia, giving railway privileges and other rights in Manchuria.—On the 28th of October, 1896, the "North China Daily News," the leading English newspaper in China, published what purports to be, and is believed to be, the text of a secret treaty, concluded in the previous year, between Russia and China, under which the former is extending her Trans-Siberian railway system through Manchuria, and is practically in possession of that province. The preamble of the treaty declares that the Emperor of China has specially appointed the princes and great officers of the Crown composing the Imperial Chinese Ministry of War to confer with the Russian Minister concerning the connecting of the railway system of the Three Eastern Provinces with the Trans-Siberian Railway, "with the object of facilitating the transport of goods between the two empires and strengthening the frontier defences and sea coasts. And, furthermore, to agree upon certain special privileges to be conceded by China to Russia as a response to the loyal aid given by Russia in the retrocession of Liaotung and its dependencies." The articles of the convention relating to the route of the railway are as follows:

"I. Owing to the fact that the Russian Great Siberian Railway is on the point of completion, China consents to allow Russia to prolong her railway into Chinese territories (a) from the Russian port of Vladivostok into the Chinese city of Hunch'un, in the province of Kirin, from thence north-westwards to the provincial capital of Kirin, and (b) from a railway station of some city in Siberia to the Chinese town of Aiyun, in Heilungchiang province, from thence southwestwards to the provincial capital of Tsitsihar, and from thence to the town of Petuné, in Kirin province, and from thence south-eastwards to the provincial capital of Kirin.

"II. All railways built by Russia into the Chinese provinces of Heilungchiang and Kirin shall be built at the sole expense of Russia, and the regulations and building thereof shall be solely on the Russian system, with which China has nothing to do, and the entire control shall be in the hands of Russia for the space of thirty years. At the end of the said period China shall be allowed to prepare the necessary funds wherewith, after proper estimation of the value of the said railways, she shall redeem them, the rolling stock, machine shops, and buildings connected therewith. But as to how China will at that date redeem these railways shall be left for future consideration.

"III. China is now in the possession of a railway which she intends to extend from Shanhaikuan into the provincial capital of Fêngtien—namely, Mukden (Shenking), and from Mukden to the provincial capital of Kirin. If China should hereafter find it inconvenient to build this road, she shall allow Russia to provide the funds to build the railway from the city of Kirin on behalf of China, the redemption of which road shall be permissible to China at the end of ten years. With reference to the route to be taken by this railway, Russia shall follow the surveys already made by China in connection therewith, from Kirin to Mukden, Newchwang, &c.

"IV. The railway to be built by China, beginning from Shanhaikuan, in Fêngtien, to Newchwang, to Kaiping, to Chinchou, to Lushunk'ou (Port Arthur), and to Talienwan and their dependencies, shall follow the Russian railway regulations, in order to facilitate the commercial intercourse between the respective empires."

Article V. authorizes Russia to place special battalions of horse and foot soldiers at the various important stations for the better protection of railway property. Article VII. "permits" Russians and Chinese to exploit and open any mines in the Amur and Kirin provinces, and in the Long White Mountain range in the north of Korea. Article VIII. "permits" Chinese to engage Russian military officers to reform the whole army organization of the three Eastern provinces in accordance with the Western system. The next three Articles are as follows:

"IX. Russia has never possessed a seaport in Asia which is free from ice and open all the year round. If, therefore, there should suddenly arise military operations in this continent, it will naturally be difficult for the Russian Eastern seas and Pacific fleets to move about freely and at pleasure. As China is well aware of this, she is willing to lease temporarily to Russia the port of Kiaochou (Chiaochou), in the province of Shantung, the period of such lease being limited to fifteen years. At the end of this period China shall buy all the barracks, godowns, machine shops, and docks built there by Russia (during her occupation of the said port). But should there be no danger of military operations, Russia shall not enter immediately into possession of the said port or hold the important points dominating the port in order to obviate the chance of exciting the jealousy and suspicions of other Powers. With reference to the amount of rent and the way it is to be paid, this shall form the subject of consideration in a protocol at some future date.

"X. As the Liaotung ports of Lushunk'ou (Port Arthur) and Talienwan and their dependencies are important strategical points, it shall be incumbent upon China to properly fortify them with all haste and to repair all their fortifications, &c., in order to provide against future dangers. Russia shall therefore lend all necessary assistance in helping to protect these two ports, and shall not permit any foreign Power to encroach upon them. China, on her part, also binds herself never to cede them to another country; but, if in future the exigencies of the case require it, and Russia should find herself suddenly involved in a war, China consents to allow Russia temporarily to concentrate her land and naval forces within the said ports in order the better to enable Russia to attack the enemy or to guard her own position.

"XI. If, however, there be no dangers of military operations in which Russia is engaged, China shall have entire control over the administration of the said ports of Lushunk'ou and Talienwan, nor shall Russia interfere in any way therein. But as regards the building of the railways in the three Eastern Provinces and the exploitation and opening of the mines therein, they shall be permitted to be proceeded with immediately after the ratification of this convention and at the pleasure of the people concerned therein. With reference to the civil and military officers of Russia and Russian merchants and traders travelling (in any part of the territories herein mentioned), wherever they shall go, they shall be given all the privileges of protection and facilities within the power of the local authorities, nor shall these officials be allowed to put obstructions in the way or delay the journeys of the Russian officers and subjects herein mentioned."—Henry Norman, *Russia and England* (*Contemporary Review, Feb.*, 1897).

A. D. 1895 (August).—**Massacre of missionaries at Hua Sang.**—In the fall of 1894 the English and American missionaries at Ku Cheng, in the Chinese province of Fu Kien, of which Foochow is the capital, began to be threatened by a sect or party called the "Vegetarians" (Siah Chai), who were violently hostile to foreigners, and said to be revolutionary in their aims. The hostile demonstrations were repeated in the following April, and the missionary party started upon a retreat to Foochow, but were stopped on the way by news that the Mandarin at Ku Cheng had pacified the Vegetarians and that they might safely return. They did so and were apparently secure for some months. In July they retired from the city to a mountain sanatorium, named Hua Sang, 12 miles from Ku Cheng, and there, on the 1st day of August, without warning, they were surrounded by a Vegetarian band of some eighty savage men, armed with swords and spears, who performed a rapid work of murder, killing eleven persons, including six women and two children, and then disappeared. "These men did not belong either to Hua Sang or Ku Cheng, but came from some villages at a considerable distance. . . . The city authorities at Ku Cheng had no hand in the outrage. It was evidently the work of a band of marauders, and the district magistrate seems to have done all that could be done under the circumstances."—D. M. Berry, *The Sister Martyrs of Ku Cheng.*—The British and American governments joined in sending a consular commission to investigate the crime, and with difficulty compelled the Chinese government to execute twenty of the ringleaders of the attack. At Fatshan, near Canton, there had been mob attacks on the missionary station, with destruction of buildings, but no murders, during the same month in which the massacre at Hua Sang occurred.

A. D. 1896.—**Tour of Li Hung-chang in Europe and America.**—"Li Hung Chang, the Chinese statesman, left Shanghai with a numerous suite, March 28, on board a French mail steamer for Europe, to represent the Emperor of China at the coronation of the Czar of Russia, and afterwards to visit other countries. He declared that his object was to see Europe for himself, in order to report to the Emperor as to feasible reforms for China. A great reception was offered to him at Hong-kong, but he refused to land by the advice of the European physician of the embassy, who feared lest any member of the suite, by catching the plague, would render the party liable to quarantine elsewhere. Proceeding to Singapore, via Saigon, he visited the Governor of the Straits Settlements. At Colombo he was received on landing by a guard of honour. After the Russian Coronation he visited Germany, Holland, Belgium and France, and arrived in London early in August. Wherever he went he was lionised, and he lost no opportunity of asking questions and informing himself concerning the manufactures and armaments of the several countries he visited. He returned to China via New York and the Canadian Pacific Railway, sailing from Vancouver (September 14) for Yokohama and Tien-tsin, where he arrived October 3. Thence he proceeded to Peking (October 20), where he was received by the Emperor, and appointed a member of the Tsung-li-Yamen. At the same time for presuming to enter the precincts of the ruined Summer Palace while visiting the Empress Dowager after his return home, his enemies took occasion of the slight trespass to insult him, and proposed that he should be stripped of all his titles and honours, with the exception of the earldom, which is confirmed to the Li family for twenty-nine generations. The case was referred to the Board of Civil Appointments, and the Controller-General, Chang-chih-wan, decided that 'according to precedent' the ex-Viceroy should be cashiered, but on account of his life-long and distinguished services to the imperial dynasty he should be recommended to the clemency of the Throne, which took the form of a loss of one year's salary. He took over his seals of office in the Tsung-li-Yamen on November 1, but none of his colleagues were present to welcome him."—*Annual Register*, 1896, *pp.* 349–50.

A. D. **1897.**—The condition of Manchuria and Mongolia. See (in this vol.) MANCHURIA AND MONGOLIA.

A. D. **1897.**—Foreigners resident in China.—Ports open to them.—" In the 'Bulletin de la Société de Géographie Commerciale,' Paris, Vol. XIX, a report is published from which the following extracts are taken : There are over ten thousand Europeans and Americans resident in China. The English head the list with 4,000; the Americans number 1,325; Germans, 882; French, 875; Portuguese, 805; Spaniards, 461; Norwegians, 375; Russians, 116; Italians, 108, etc. There are 669 Japanese. Twenty-two ports are open to foreign residence, that is to say, that Europeans are allowed to acquire conditional title to certain lands, on which they live, govern themselves, and have special privileges in judicial matters. The ports are Mengtz, Lung Chow, Pakhoi, King Chow, Lappa, Canton, Kowlon, Swatow, Amoy, Fuchau, Winchow, Ningpo, Shanghai, Chinkiang, Wuhu, Kiukiang, Hankow, Ichang, Chungking, Chefoo, Tientsin, and Niuchwang. It is to be noted that Peking does not appear on this list, although the embassies and legations are established there. The Chinese who find themselves under foreign jurisdiction appear more than contented with the situation, because, although taxes are high, they are fixed. Two hundred thousand natives live in the European settlements of Shanghai. Besides the foreign residents of China, a large number live in ports that have been ceded to other nations. For instance, Hongkong comprises in its civil population 4,195 Europeans and Americans. With the troops and sailors, this number is raised to 8,545. Hongkong is the actual capital of foreign industry in the far East. More than 8,000 vessels, with a tonnage of nearly 4,000,000 touch there annually. The same spirit which caused the development of Singapore, Colombo, and Hongkong is to be found in the foreign settle-

ments of the open ports of China."—*U. S. Consular Reports*, Oct., 1897, *p.* 315.

A. D. **1897 (May—June).**—Cessions and concessions to England and France.—In May, the Chinese government sanctioned an extension of the British settlement at Tien-tsin from 65 acres to about 300. In the next month, it satisfied the complaints of Great Britain concerning the cession of Kiang-Hung to France (see above :

A. D. 1894–1895, MARCH—JULY), by ceding to that Power the Shan district of Kokang, about 400 square miles in extent, and leasing to Great Britain in perpetuity a considerable tract at the south of the Namwan River. The same treaty opened new routes to trade across the frontier between Burmah and China, and admitted British consuls and merchants to two new ports. At about the same time France secured mining privileges on the Tonquin frontier and rights for the extension of a railway into Chinese territory.

A. D. **1897 (November).**—Germany opens the attack of European Powers on the integrity of the Chinese Empire.—Seizure of the port of Kiao-Chau.—Concessions obtained as reparation for the murder of German missionaries.—" Among the recent events that have attracted especial attention to China is the lease to foreign nations of important strategic or commercial ports on the coast of the Empire. While the Portuguese have controlled the island of Macao, near Canton, since 1537, and the English became owners of the island of Hongkong, in the same vicinity, by the treaty of 1842, no other nation had possessions on or near the coast of China until within a comparatively recent date. One result of the war between China and Japan was that Japan obtained the island of Formosa, lying 90 miles off the coast of central China. By this treaty Japan was also to have certain territory on the peninsula of Liaotung, which commands from the north the entrance to the Gulf of Pechili, the gateway to the capital of China ; but on the urgent protest of Russia, France, and Germany this was abandoned, and the mainland of China up to that time thus remained intact. On November 4, 1897, however, the German Government seized the port of Kiao-chau, on the northeastern coast of China, asserting as the cause of its action the desire to obtain satisfaction for the murder of [two] German missionaries by Chinese on November 1 of that year. This port was held by a German war ship until the announcement of a treaty with China by which the port of Kiaochau and adjacent territory were leased to Germany for a term of ninety-nine years, the German Government being given the right to land troops, construct fortifications, and establish a coaling and naval station, while German subjects were to have the right to construct railways, open mines, and transact business in the rich mineral and agricultural province of Shantung, in which Kiaochau is located, Chinese vessels, however, to have the same privileges in the port of Kiaochau that the German Government might decide to give to other nations."—*U. S. Bureau of Statistics, Monthly Summary of Commerce and Statistics, March*, 1899.

The terms of the German acquisition of Kiao-chau, as officially communicated to the Reichstag by Herr von Bülow, Foreign Secretary of the German Empire, on the 8th of February, 1898, were as follows: "The Imperial

Chinese Government, in fulfilment of the legitimate wish of the German Government to possess, in common with other Powers, a point in the matters [waters?] of Eastern Asia, where German vessels may be fitted out and repaired, where the necessary materials can be deposited, and other arrangements made in connection with that object, cedes to the German Government in the form of a lease, to run, as at present fixed, for a period of ninety-nine years, the territory situated on both sides of the entrance to the Bay of Kiao-chau, in South Shantung, more accurately described below, in such a manner that the German Government will be at liberty to erect all necessary buildings, &c., within the territory, and take all the measures required for their defence. According to the English chart of Kiao-chau Bay of 1863, the district leased to the German Government consists of the following : — 1. The promontory north of the entrance to the bay, bounded on the north-east by a straight line drawn from the extreme north-eastern point of Potato Island to the sea-coast in the direction of Zoshan. 2. The promontory south of the entrance to the bay, bounded on the south-west by a straight line drawn from the southernmost point of the inlet situated to the south-west of Tschiposan, in the direction of the Tolosan Islands (Weber chart), to the sea-coast. 3. The Island of Tschiposan and Potato Island, as well as all the islands lying at the entrance to the bay, inclusive of Tolosan and Seslien. Further, the Chinese Government undertake not to frame any Regulations within a zone of 50 kilom. round the bay without the consent of the German Government, and, in particular, to offer no resistance to any measures necessary for regulating the course of the rivers. The Chinese Government also grant to German troops the right of passage across the zone above described. With the object of avoiding every possibility of collision, the Chinese Government will exercise no rights of sovereignty within the leased territory during the period of the lease, but they cede these rights as well as those over the entire water-surface of the Bay of Kiao-chau to the German Government. The German Government will erect sea-marks on the islands and shallows at the entrance to the bay. 4. In the event of the territory leased not proving to be adapted to the requirements of the German Government, the Government of China will cede to Germany a more suitable district, and will take back the Bay of Kiao-chau, paying compensation for any improvements or constructions the Germans may have made there. 5. A more accurate delimitation of the boundaries of the district leased will take place in accordance with the local conditions, and will be carried out by Commissioners from both Governments."

The Foreign Secretary added the following particulars respecting the area, &c., of the territory and the character of the lease : — "The territory leased, the boundaries of which are not yet accurately determined, will cover an area of 30 to 50 square kilom. Consequently, it is materially larger than the British possession at and opposite Hong Kong. For military reasons, the northern boundary had been pushed a little further forward than is shown on the map presented to the Budget Commission. The number of inhabitants is calculated at a few thousand. As regards the size of the bay, accurate details

6—6

are as yet wanting. It runs about 20 geographical miles into the mainland. At its narrowest point, the entrance to the bay is about 3,000 metres broad. Two-thirds of the bay afford harbour accommodation. The rent payable to China, the exact amount of which has not yet been determined, is an unimportant point, as it possesses a nominal character merely representing the continuation in theory of the proprietorship of China over the territory ceded. The following stipulations have been secured respecting railway and mining concessions : — The Chinese Government have consented to hand over to a German-Chinese Railway Company, to be formed hereafter, the construction of a railway from Kiao-chau, which will run first in a northerly and then in a westerly direction, to be subsequently connected with the projected great railway system of China. The railway will serve the coalfields of Weih-sien and Poshan, situated to the north of Kiao-chau, which will be exploited by German capital. The Chinese Government have further pledged themselves to accord to the Railway Company to be thus formed, conditions at least as favourable as those granted to any other European Chinese Railway Company in China."

The Foreign Secretary concluded his speech with an exposition of the motives which had induced the German Government to occupy Kiao-chau in preference to other places. Its proximity to the scene of the massacre had been the first consideration. Secondly, it was favourably situated from a political point of view, being removed from the French and British spheres in Southern China and from the Russian base of operations in the north. Lastly, the spacious, ice-free harbour, the climate, which is probably the best to be met with in China, and the existence of coalfields in the vicinity of the coast, offered sufficient grounds for the choice of Kiao-chau. Herr von Bülow might have quoted in this connection a candid remark which had been made not long before by the "Kolonial Zeitung:" "The principal point is that the Power which possesses Kiao-chau will control the coal supply in northern Chinese waters." — *Great Britain, Papers by Command: China, No. 1,* 1898.

A. D. **1898** (February).—British diplomacy in China.—The tone in which foreign demands were made on the Tsung-li Yamên.—Agreement not to alienate the Yang-tsze region.—Early in 1898 the Chinese government was in need of money for the final payment of indemnity to Japan, and opened negotiations with the British government for the guarantee of a loan. Her Majesty's Ministers were quite ready to give the needed financial aid, for a consideration, requiring, in return, that Ta-lien-wan should be opened to trade as a treaty port. But Russia was then scheming to secure possession of Ta-lien-wan, and interfered with the British negotiation so vigorously that the Chinese were frightened into breaking it off, even after they had practically accepted the offered loan. Not daring, however, to take from Russia the financial guarantee which they rejected at British hands, they thought to balance themselves between these jealous rivals by borrowing without help from either. Both the Powers were thus offended, England especially showing stern resentment on account of the slight with which she had been treated. The following report by

Sir Claude MacDonald, the British Minister at Peking, of his interviews with the Tsung-li Yamên on the subject, is very interesting, as showing the tone in which the European Powers were making demands on the government of China at that time. The despatch of Sir Claude MacDonald is dated at Peking, February 20, 1898.

"Since the 4th of February," he wrote. "I have had four interviews with the Yamên for the purpose of extracting some concessions in return for the rejection of the offer of a guaranteed loan from Great Britain after it had in principle been accepted. At the first of these, on the 5th February, the Yamên refused to recognize that we had any claim to compensation, declaring that the refusal of a Russian as well as a British guarantee left no ground for complaint. I told them that this argument might have had some plausibility if the two offers had been equally advantageous, or if the Chinese Government had not committed themselves to serious negotiations with us. The British Government had at China's own request reluctantly agreed to do her a very exceptional favour, and the Yamên could not suppose that we should accept with equanimity a brusque intimation that the Chinese Government had changed its mind.

"The Yamên abounded in protestations of their readiness at some future date to give proofs of their gratitude to Great Britain in the shape of encouragement to commerce, but they insisted that the loan negotiations must first be dismissed, and all demands for compensation in connection with them dropped. I refused to telegraph such a suggestion to your Lordship, and as after long debate they still refused to bind themselves by any promises, I reminded them that at an earlier interview they had asked me whether the action threatened by Great Britain in the event of their accepting a Russian guarantee would equally be taken if they borrowed from neither Power. I could not at the time answer the question, but I could now tell them that Her Majesty's Government had a right to feel deeply affronted by what had occurred, and I would not be answerable for the consequences if they declined to make to Great Britain even such concessions as they had frequently admitted to be in China's own interests.

"The Yamên begged me to smooth matters for them, to which I answered that their present attitude made it impossible for me to do so. Let them permit me to report that China was ready to open inland navigation to steamers ; to establish Treaty ports at Nanning and Hsiang T'an; and to give reasonable security to trade by a pledge against alienation of the Yang-tsze region to another Power, and the rejection of our loan might be forgiven. All these were matters within the Yamên's power.

"The Ministers did not deny the feasibility of what I had asked (except as regarded the opening of Nanning), but objected to these measures being tacked on to the loan, for if that were done, Russia would at once demand counter-concessions for the rejection of her loan, and China would be placed in a very difficult position. On this they laid much stress. I said I did not insist on the concessions being formally announced as made to England in connection with the loan, and should be prepared to move Her Majesty's Government to treat them as steps taken spon-

taneously by China, but that I absolutely refused to treat the loan account as settled until I had some definite assurance that these measures would be carried out within a fixed time. The Yamên again attempted to persuade me to leave the carrying out of the measures indicated entirely to the Chinese Government, and it was only after the usual prolonged argument that they consented to open internal waters to steam navigation within four months; to let me know at an early date when they would open a port in Hunan, and to give me a written guarantee against the alienation of the Yang-tsze region to a foreign Power."

After reporting conversation on other matters, the Minister recounted his action on the subject of the Yang-tsze region, and on that of the opening of inland waterways to steam navigation, at an interview with the Tsung-li Yamên on the 9th. "I then produced," he said, "a draft of the note I intended addressing to them with regard to non-alienation of the Yang-tsze region. This was accepted with little demur, with the insertion of the words 'now entirely in China's possession,' which, as recording an undeniable fact, I agreed to put in. Copies of the notes subsequently exchanged are inclosed. I have not thought it necessary to narrate the arguments by which I supported the demand for this pledge at both these interviews. My chief ground was that we could not afford to find one morning that by reason of the murder of a foreign subject, or the refusal of some demand by a foreign Power, some place on the Yang-tsze had been seized and was to be retained on a ninety-nine years' lease. I then handed to the Ministers the despatch . . . recording their assurance with regard to steam navigation of inland waterways. They read it with attention, and accepted it as satisfactory."

Of the notes thus passed between the British Minister and the Tsung-li Yamên, that of the former, dated February 9, was as follows: "Your Highnesses and your Excellencies have more than once intimated to me that the Chinese Government were aware of the great importance that has always been attached by Great Britain to the retention in Chinese possession of the Yang-tsze region, now entirely hers, as providing security for the free course and development of trade. I shall be glad to be in a position to communicate to Her Majesty's Government a definite assurance that China will never alienate any territory in the provinces adjoining the Yang-tsze to any other Power, whether under lease, mortgage, or any other designation. Such an assurance is in full harmony with the observations made to me by your Highnesses and your Excellencies."

On the 11th, the Yamên returned the following reply : "The Yamên have the honour to acknowledge the receipt of the British Minister's despatch of the 9th February, stating that the Yamên had more than once intimated to him that the Chinese Government were aware of the great importance that has always been attached by Great Britain to the retention in Chinese possession of the Yang-tsze region, now entirely hers, as providing security for the free course and development of trade. The British Minister would be glad to be in a position to communicate to Her Majesty's Government a definite assurance that China would never alienate (any territory) in the provinces adjoining the Yang-tsze to any other Power, whether under lease, mortgage, or any other designation. The Yamên have to observe that the Yang-tsze region is of the greatest importance as concerning the whole position (or interests) of China, and it is out of the question that territory (in it) should be mortgaged, leased, or ceded to another Power. Since Her Britannic Majesty's Government has expressed its interest (or anxiety), it is the duty of the Yamên to address this note to the British Minister for communication to his Government."

The despatch recording the Chinese concession of steam navigation on inland waters was in the following terms : "It was . . . with great pleasure that I learnt from your Highnesses and your Excellencies at a recent interview that the Chinese Government had determined that wherever the use of native boats is now by Treaty permitted to foreigners, they shall equally be permitted to employ steamers or steam-launches, whether Chinese or foreign-owned, or their own boats, and, further, that this arrangement would come into effect before the end of the 4th Chinese moon. I shall have great pleasure in communicating the Chinese Government's decision to my Government, for it is an indication that China is prepared to take every step open to her to increase the volume of trade, and so add to her resources and the wealth of the people." — *Great Britain, Papers by Command : China, No. 1, 1899, pp.* 13–18.

A. D. 1898 (February—December).—The "Battle of Concessions," for railway building and mining.—By summer-time in 1898 the scramble among the Powers for footholds of territory on the Chinese coast seemed to be giving way to what Lord Salisbury described as "the battle of concessions," for the building of railways and the opening of mines. This newer battle gave his lordship much anxiety. On the 13th of July he cabled to Sir Claude MacDonald : "It does not seem that the battle of Concessions is going well for us, and that the mass of Chinese railways, if they are ever built, will be in foreign hands is a possibility that we must face. One evil of this is, that no orders for materials will come to this country. That we cannot help. The other evil is, that by differential rates and privileges the Managers of the railways may strangle our trade. This we ought to be able to prevent, by pressing that proper provisions for equal treatment be inserted in every Concession."

The British Minister at Peking, in reply, dissented warmly from Lord Salisbury's opinion. "The battle of Concessions is not, in my opinion," he cabled on the 23d of July, "going against us. . . . Up to the present, any concessions granted to other nationalities are far out-balanced in financial value by the Shansi and Honan mining and railway concession, with its possible extensions. I have consistently informed the Chinese government that, as to differential rates and privileges, we want none ourselves, and cannot admit that other nationalities have a claim to them." In due time, as will appear, Sir Claude was able to furnish very good evidence in support of his contention that the "battle of concessions" was not going against Great Britain, by forwarding a list of all the concessions granted to clamoring capitalists and promoters of the several nationalities. Meantime, he gave close attention to the varying fortunes of the battle.

A concession for the Peking-Hankow Railway was the one which interested the English most. Its line would traverse the rich and populous provinces of Chi-li, Honan, and Hoa-Pé, and be connected by another line, for which the Russo-Chinese Bank held concessions, with the valuable coal-mining basin of Ping-ting. Early in August, the British found reason to believe that the pending agreement with a Belgian syndicate for the building of this road was one that would give control of it to the Russo-Chinese Bank, — which meant Russian, or Russian and French control. He promptly remonstrated to the Yamên, and was assured that the agreement had not yet been submitted to the throne, and would not be ratified if the effect were such as he had described. He cabled this assurance to Lord Salisbury on the 6th of August. On the 13th he had a very different report to make. " I learnt on the 9th," he says, "that the Yamên had, under the influence of Li Hung-chang, abandoned this position [that they would not ratify the Belgian agreement if its effect was to give control of the Peking-Hankow line of railway to the Russo-Chinese Bank], and intended to ratify the agreement immediately. In view of the urgency of the matter, I addressed a note on the same day to the Yamên, in which I asked for an interview on the 10th or 11th instant, and informed them that the Chinese text of the Contract had reached me, warning them at the same time that if they did not give me another interview before they ratified the Agreement Her Majesty's Government would look upon their action as unfriendly, and would probably insist on the same rights being given to Great Britain in all the provinces adjoining the Yang-tsze.

"On the evening of the 10th the Yamên answered that they would appoint a day for an interview when they had received the Contract, which, they said, had not yet reached Peking for ratification. On the 11th I replied that I understood from this communication that they undertook not to ratify until they had seen me. To this they returned an evasive answer to the effect that they were all engaged by ceremonies at the Palace connected with the Emperor's birthday, which would last some days. I should add that I had already, on the 10th, sent them a note in which I criticized the Contract in detail, stating finally that I should have further objections to bring forward at my interview with them. I now hear on good authority that the Contract was ratified yesterday, the 12th. That the ratification has thus been rushed through is undoubtedly due to the influence of Li Hung-chang, combined with strong pressure on the part of the Representatives of Russia, France, and Belgium, and if heavy payment is not exacted from the Chinese Government for their bad faith, Li will persuade his colleagues that it is safer to slight England than any other Power, and any pressure which we may want to bring to bear in other matters will be without weight. I therefore think that Her Majesty's Government should insist either : —

"1. On a written assurance from the Yamên that if British Syndicates apply for any railway concessions in the Yang-tsze provinces, they shall be given on the same terms as those which France, under cover of the Belgian Syndicate, has received in the Peking-Hankow Contract, and that no mining or railway concessions will be granted in those provinces unless they have been previously declined by British Syndicates; or

"2. On a written assurance that all railways for which British Syndicates are now in Treaty, that is to say — (a.) The Shan-hai-Kuan-Niu-chwang line; (b.) The line from Tien-tsin to Chinkiang (the latter, as I understand, in conjunction with Germans and Americans); (c.) The line from Shanghae to Nanking with its continuations and branches; (d.) The lines in Honan and Shansi should be granted without any further delay on terms identical with those contained in the Contract for the Peking-Hankow line. The latter consist, so far as I can learn, in complete control over the construction, choice of material, working, and personnel of the line, together with an Imperial guarantee for the repayment of the loan. The second demand seems to me to be preferable on the whole; it will be impossible to obtain either demand without bringing great pressure to bear, and I consider that the demand should be made not as a compensatory concession, but as a punishment for bad faith."

On the 17th the reply of the British Foreign Office was sent by Mr. Balfour, as follows: "With reference to your telegram of the 13th instant, inform Yamên that they must assent to your proposal No. 2 without delay, omitting from it the Shankaikuan-Newchwang Railway, which we must deal with as a separate question. You are authorized to inform them, if you have any reason to apprehend that they will delay compliance, that, unless they agree at once, we shall regard their breach of faith concerning the Peking-Hankow Railway as an act of deliberate hostility against this country, and shall act accordingly. After consultation with the Admiral, you may give them the number of days or hours you think proper within which to send their reply. The delay should not be of too long duration. It should be noted, on face of your demand, that Chingkiang Concession is for Americans and Germans, if they desire a share, as well as ourselves. Also make it clear that your ultimatum has nothing to do with the line to Newchwang."

The tone of these demands made them effectual. On the 4th of September, Sir Claude MacDonald was able to announce to his superiors, in London: "At an interview which I had with them yesterday, the Yamên entered into the following undertaking:— Within the next few days they will address a despatch to me, apologising for their action, and consenting to the construction of the following lines by British Syndicates: 1. A line from Shanghae to Nanking with a continuation viâ Chinkiang to Sui Yang. They said, however, that the latter route was that followed by the line from Tien-tsin to Chinkiang, for which they said that a Preliminary Agreement had been signed between Yung Wing and the Anglo-American Syndicate; and the continuation in question must be dependent on the cancellation of that Agreement. 2. A line connecting Hangchow and Soochow with Shanghae, to be continued if required to Ningpo. 3. A line from Canton to Kowloon. 4. The Peking Syndicate to be entitled to construct a railway to convey minerals from their mines to the Yang-tsze. The Yamên have also agreed to send me a Confidential note embodying a declaration that the terms accorded for the construction of these lines will not be inferior to those granted for the construction of any railways in China

proper. The Manchurian lines are excluded from the scope of this Agreement. I venture to think that this is a satisfactory settlement. I did not give them an ultimatum, confining myself to a warning of the grave consequences which would now attend any failure on their part to keep their word. The fact that the fleet is concentrating is, of course, known to them."

Before receiving this announcement, Mr. Balfour had cabled, on the 24th of August: "Negotiations with Yamên may be facilitated if you informed them at once that, unless the very moderate terms already demanded are immediately complied with, we shall, in addition, require the Concession of another line, on same conditions as those granted in case of Peking Hankow line of railway, and that additional demands will be preferred as the result of further delay. If you think it would conduce to the rapid and satisfactory termination of the negotiations, you are authorized to make a communication to them in this sense." Whether this suggestion was acted upon or not does not appear.

This transaction, connected with the project of a railway from Peking to Hankow, appears to illustrate, not unfairly, on the whole, the mode in which speculative concessions were being wrung from the Chinese government in the busiest year of oriental speculation, 1898. The outcome of the grand "battle" was communicated by Sir Claude MacDonald to Lord Charles Beresford, on the 23d of November, in a full list of the concessions then granted to British subjects, compared with the grants to other nationalities. "We do not seem," wrote Sir Claude, with pardonable complacency, "to have come out second best. . . . Not a single bona fide or approximately practical scheme which has been brought to this Legation has failed to be put through." The summarized result in railway concessions was 9 British (2,800 miles); 3 Russian (1,530 miles); 2 German (720 miles); 3 French (420 miles); 1 Belgian (650 miles); 1 American (300 miles). In detail, the railway and mining concessions were described in the list as follows:

" Railway and other Concessions obtained by British Companies: I.—Province of Shansi. The Peking Syndicate have acquired the ' sole right to open and work coal and iron mines throughout the districts of Yu Hsien and Ping Ting-chou, and the Prefectures of Lusan Fu, Tsü-chou Fu, and Ping Yang Fu, and also petroleum, wherever found.' Under their contract, the Syndicate have also the right to ' construct branch railways to connect with main lines or with water navigation, to facilitate transport of Shansi coal.' This has been interpreted officially to include the right of connecting the mines with Siang-yang in Hupeh, the nearest head of navigation giving access to the Yang-tsze. This means a railway of 250 miles. As to the value of this Concession, it is not amiss to quote the testimony of Baron von Richthofen, the great authority on the geology of China. He says that, ' in proportion to its area, Shansi has probably the largest and most easily workable coalfield of any region on the globe, and the manufacture of iron is capable of almost unlimited extension.' II.—Province of Honan. The Peking Syndicate have also acquired rights similar to those obtained in Shansi in that part of Honan north of the Yellow River. III.—Province of

Chihli. The Hong Kong and Shanghae Bank are financing and controlling the North China railways from Peking to Tien-tsin, and thence to Shanhaikuan and Newchwang. The total length of these lines is about 500 miles, of which 300 miles are completely open to traffic. IV.— This bank has also acquired a half-interest in the coal-mines at Nan P'iao, in the Ch'ao-yang district. According to experts, these mines possess the best and richest coal seams in North China, and they have the immense advantage of being close to a line of railway and the sea. V.—Provinces of Chihli and Kiangsu. The Tsung-li Yamên have undertaken officially that the construction of the Tien-tsin-Chinkiang line shall be intrusted to an Anglo-German Syndicate. The British portion of this Syndicate is represented in China by Messrs. Jardine, Matheson, and Co., and the Hong Kong and Shanghae Bank. This will be a trunk line of 600 miles, passing through more populous country than the Lu-Han Railway (the Belgian line), with which it is certain to be able to compete successfully. VI.—Province of Kiangsu. A British Syndicate, represented by Messrs. Jardine, Matheson, and Co., and the Hong Kong and Shanghae Bank, has obtained the Concession to finance and construct the Shanghae-Nanking Railway. There is no more paying district than this for a railway in China. The length of line will be 170 or 180 miles. VII.—Provinces of Kiangsu, Anhui, and Honan. The same Syndicate has the right to extend the Shanghae-Nanking Railway from P'u-k'ou, opposite Nanking, to Hsin Yang, in Honan, a distance of 270 miles. VIII.—Provinces of Kiangsu and Chêkiang. The same Syndicate has the right to construct a line from Soochow to Hangchow, with a possible extension to Ningpo. This line will run through very populous districts for over 200 miles. The last three Concessions all lie within the Yang-tsze region. IX.—Province of Chêkiang. The Peking Syndicate have also obtained mining Concessions similar to the Shansi and Honan in this province. X.—Province of Kwangtung. The Jardine Syndicate has the right to construct a railway from Kowloon to Canton. The length of line will be nearly 100 miles. XI.—Provinces of Hupei, Kiangsi, and Kwangtung. An American Syndicate signed a preliminary Agreement for the construction of a railway from Hankow to Canton in May last. Negotiations are now in progress for the amalgamation of this Concession with No. 10, Kowloon to Canton, and the working of the whole line from Hankow to Kowloon by an Anglo-American Company. This will be a trunk line of, approximately, 600 miles long. XII.—Provinces of Yünnan, Kweichow, and Ssuchuan. The right to extend the Burmah system into China as far as the Yang-tsze is admitted, and surveys are now in progress. This involves a possible railway of 700 miles. (See Remarks on French Concessions.)

"Concessions other than British. Russian. —The Manchurian Railway Concession dates from 1896. As is well known, it was obtained as recompense for help given in securing the retrocession of Liaotung. From Stretensk on the Shilka, where it leaves the main Siberian line, this railway will cross the Argun and Hingan Mountains, and reach Kirin viâ Petuna. The whole length from Stretensk to Vladivostock is estimated at 1,400 miles, of which about 1,000

will pass through Chinese territory. The Concession is purely strategical. The country traversed, though potentially rich, in great part is, and will be for long, sparsely populated, and the line cannot, in the near future at any rate, hope to pay its working expenses. 2. The Port Arthur Agreement of March 1898 arranges for the conclusion by Russia of a branch from the above line to Port Arthur or Talienwan. The length of the railway will be about 400 miles. Commercially, this branch is more promising than the first Concession. 3. The Russo-Chinese Bank has signed a contract for the construction of a branch line from T'ai-yüan Fu to connect with the Lu-Han trunk lines near Chêng-tung. Length, approximately 130 miles. They have, up to date, been unable to raise money for this line. I think it very possible that it will eventually be built by an Anglo-Russian Syndicate. I am trying to arrange this.

"French.—The French possess the right to construct three lines, but beyond acquiring this right they have done nothing. 1. From Tonquin up the Red River Valley to Yünnau Fu, say 200 miles. The impression in French railway circles is that a railway through Yünnan will not pay expenses, and if any serious attempt is made to carry out the extension of the Tonquin system, it will be merely as a stepping-stone to Ssüch'uan. Yet again, any pretensions that a railway from Yünnan to the Yang-tsze may have to rank as a commercial project have been pronounced against by every traveller in Central China. 2. Langson-Lungchow-Nanning Railway; length, about 100 miles. (There appears to be an alternative open to the French of going to Pésé instead of Nanning.) The right to build this line has been conceded, but the idea is growing amongst the French of Tonquin that, instead of diverting traffic from the West River, a line from Langson to Lungchow and Nanning would prove an additional feeder of the West River route. 3. From Pakhoi inland, presumably to Nanning; length, say 120 miles. The Tonquin press have pointed out that this line will benefit English commerce more than French. It will never, in my opinion, be built—by the French.

"German.—1. Kiao-chau-Yichow-Tsinan line; length, 420 miles. Nothing has been done towards the construction of this line, which does not promise commercially. 2. Tien-tsin-Chinkiang line to be built by an Anglo-German Company (see No. 5 of the British Concessions).

"Belgian.—The Lu-Han or Peking-Hankow Railway. A Franco-Belgian Syndicate have secured the Concession for this, a trunk line of some 650 or 700 miles, passing north and south through Chihli, Honan, and Hupeh. This railway is an old project born of Chang-Chih-Tung's objection to building lines near the coast, 'lest they should facilitate the access of an enemy.' Its prospects as a commercial enterprise are not considered so good as those of the rival Tien-tsin-Chinkiang line.

"American.—The only railway in which America is at present interested is the trunk line projected from Hankow to Canton (see British Concessions, No. 11)."

On the 18th of December the British Minister announced to Lord Salisbury: "An Imperial Decree, stating that no more railway proposals will be for the present entertained by the Chinese government, has been officially communicated to me by the Yamên." To which the response from London was: "You should inform the Chinese Government that Her Majesty's Government claim, in the event of their revoking their present resolve not to entertain any more proposals for railways, priority of consideration by the Chinese Government of all British applications already made." This notice was given, as directed, and the Yamên replied to it (December 31) with some dignity: "We have the honour to observe that the development of railways in China is the natural right and advantage of the Chinese Government. If, hereafter, in addition to the lines already sanctioned, which shall be proceeded with in order, China proposes to construct other railways, she will negotiate with the nation which she finds suitable. When the time arrives China must use her own discretion as to her course of action. The applications of British merchants can, of course, be kept on record as material for negotiation at that day, but it is not expedient to treat them as having a prior claim over all others to a settled agreement."—*Great Britain, Papers by Command: China, No. 1, 1899, pp. 164–69, 190–92, 215–16, 327, 344–47; and No. 1, 1900, p. 22.*

A. D. 1898 (March).—An intelligent Chinese view of the situation of the country.—How well the situation and the dangers of their country were understood at this period by some, at least, of the Chinese officials, and how intelligently they considered them, may be gathered from some passages in a memorial addressed by Viceroy Chang Chih-tung and another high official, Sheng Hsuan-huai, Director-General of Railways, to the Emperor, on the subject of the construction of the Hankow-Kwangtung Railway. A translation of the document was transmitted to London at the end of March. The memorialists say: "The original idea was that the construction of the Hankow-Kwangtung Southern trunk line should be postponed for a time, but now, owing to the exigencies of the present situation, this work must not be delayed. The powerful foreign nations stand around watching for their opportunity, and, making use of trivial pretexts in the conduct of international affairs, swiftly dispatch their war-ships from one end of the Empire to the other. It is impossible to say when our communication by sea may be blocked, and the establishment of internal communication by railways has become a necessity. Kwangtung is a rich province, and the defence of the southern territory and waterways must not be neglected, so that the making of the Hankow-Kwangtung line should be proceeded with at the same time as the northern road. The original intention was to construct a road from Kwangtung to Hupeh viâ Chiangsi, but this circuitous route is longer than the direct route through Hunan Province, and for many reasons it will be a source of greater prosperity and strength to the Empire if the latter route is adopted. There is, moreover, no doubt that the officials and merchants of the three provinces are in favour of this scheme. The most direct route will be to proceed viâ Ch'en-chou, Yung-chou, Feng-chou, and Ch'ang-sha to Wuch'ang, and so to Hankow. . . . Now Hankow is the central point to which all the waterways of the eighteen provinces from north, south, east, and west converge. If England is allowed to build the Hankow and Kwangtung

road, passing through this important point, afterwards when the Russian line advances southward, and the English line is continued to the north, although we shall be in possession of the Hankow-Lü Kou-chiao line, we shall be stifled and our profits curtailed, for, being between the other lines, we shall not be able to defend our own. It is also greatly to be feared that our own line would pass into either English or Russian hands. In this case not only is our throat stopped by the foreigners being in possession of our ports, but our vital parts are injuriously affected. Should we wish to raise and drill soldiers, make arms, or obtain funds for the necessities of the Empire, it will be impossible, and China not only will not make progress, but we fear she will barely be able to maintain her independence.

"Your memorialists are distressed when they consider the extreme danger of the situation, but they think that the best method of meeting it is to proceed ourselves at once with the construction of the Hankow-Kwangtung Railway. Should it be made by degrees, starting from Kwangtung through Hunan to Hankow, it will be seized forcibly before completion, and we fear sufficient funds cannot be raised for hurrying forward its construction. Your memorialist, Shêng, had the intention of employing American capital for the construction of the Lü Kou-chaio-Hankow line, but afterwards when the American, Washburn, came to China, his conditions were found to be too hard, and consequently negotiations were broken off. Your servant was thus constrained to approach Belgium. By acting thus our privileges would not be lost, nor would ill consequences follow. But Belgium is a small country, and her strength is inconsiderable, and often she has pointed out that an unfinished railroad is hardly a sufficient guarantee for the loan. Consequently she is very undecided, but we have hopes that by the adoption of some compromise terms may be arrived at, though the question is extremely difficult. Thus another scheme must be adopted for raising the capital for the southern line. There are grave objections to allowing either England, France, or Germany to undertake the work, and your memorialists suggest that Wu Ting-fang, the Minister at Washington, should be communicated with. He is a Cantonese, and will not fail to do his best to find a scheme."—*Great Britain, Papers by Command: China, No. 1, 1899, pp. 87–89.*

A. D. 1898 (March—July).—Russian acquisition of Port Arthur and Talienwan.—Ineffectual British opposition.—Consequent British demand for Wei-hai Wei.—Its lease by China.—While the British Minister at Peking was securing these assurances from the Tsung-li Yamên, concerning the non-alienation of the Yang-tsze region and the opening of inland waters to steam navigation, the Russian Minister was equally busy, extorting a cession or lease of Port Arthur and Talienwan, with privileges of railway construction through neighboring territory which gave immense value to those acquisitions. The probability of his success was soon known to the British authorities, who made no serious objection to the leasing of Talienwan, but were strongly opposed to a Russian occupation of Port Arthur. On the 22d of March, 1898, Lord Salisbury wrote to the British Ambassador at St. Petersburg: "Her Majesty's Government on their part would not regard with any dissatisfaction the lease by Russia of an ice-free commercial harbour, connected by rail with the trans-Siberian Railway which is now under construction. Questions of an entirely different kind are opened if Russia obtains control of a military port in the neighbourhood of Peking. Port Arthur is useless for commercial purposes, its whole importance being derived solely from its military strength and strategic position, and its occupation would inevitably be considered in the East as a standing menace to Peking and the commencement of the partition of China."

On the 28th of March he wrote again: "Port Arthur is not a commercial harbour. It is doubtful whether it could be converted into one. It is certain that, even if such a project were possible, it could never be worth while for the owners or lessees of Talienwan to embark upon it. But though not a commercial harbour, Port Arthur supplies a naval base, limited indeed in extent, but possessing great natural and artificial strength. And this, taken in connection with its strategic position, gives it an importance in the Gulf of Pechili and therefore at Peking, upon which, in their representations to Japan at the close of the war with China, the Russian Government laid the greatest emphasis. It is from this last point of view that the occupation of Port Arthur chiefly concerns Her Majesty's Government. It is not because a position which can easily be made a naval arsenal of great strength has been acquired by Russia that they regret its occupation by that Power. It is because the possession, even if temporary, of this particular position, is likely to have political consequences at Peking of great international importance, and because the acquisition of a Chinese harbour notoriously useless for commercial purposes by a foreign Power will be universally interpreted in the Far East as indicating that the partition of China has begun.

"As regards the second of these reasons nothing further need be said, inasmuch as Her Majesty's Government understand from Count Mouravieff's communication to you that this result is as little desired by the Russian Government as it is by that of Her Majesty. As regards the first, it may perhaps be proper to observe that a great military Power which is coterminous for over 4,000 miles with the land frontier of China, including the portion lying nearest to its capital, is never likely to be without its due share of influence on the councils of that country. Her Majesty's Government regard it as most unfortunate that it has been thought necessary in addition to obtain control of a port which, if the rest of the Gulf of Pechili remains in hands so helpless as those of the Sovereign Power, will command the maritime approaches to its capital, and give to Russia the same strategic advantage by sea which she already possesses in so ample a measure by land. Her Majesty's Government have thought it their duty thus to put on record their grave objections to the occupation of Port Arthur by Russia."

Before this despatch was written, Lord Salisbury already knew that his remonstrances had failed and that Russia was to possess Port Arthur, and he had cabled, March 25, the following instructions to Sir Claude MacDonald, the British Minister to Peking : "Balance of power in Gulf of Pechili is materially altered by surrender of Port Arthur by Yamên to Russia.

It is therefore necessary to obtain, in the manner you think most efficacious and speedy, the refusal of Wei-hai Wei on the departure of the Japanese. The terms should be similar to those granted to Russia for Port Arthur. British fleet is on its way from Hong Kong to Gulf of Pechili." The day following, Lord Salisbury advised the British Ambassador at Berlin by telegram : "Her Majesty's Government have demanded a reversionary lease of Wei-hai Wei, and it is possible that the German Government will address you with regard to our occupying territory which forms part of the Province of Shantung. Should this be the case, you are authorized to explain that Wei-hai Wei is not at present, and cannot, we believe, be made a commercial port by which access can be obtained to any part of the province. We do not wish to interfere with the interests of Germany in that region. The action, in our opinion very regrettable, of Russia with respect to Port Arthur, has compelled us to take the course we are now pursuing."

On the 29th of March the completion of the transaction by which China transferred Port Arthur and Talienwan to Russia was officially announced at St. Petersburg by the following publication in the "Official Messenger": "At Peking on the 15th (27th) March a special Agreement was signed by the Plenipotentiaries of Russia and China, by virtue of which Ports Arthur and Talienwan, with the corresponding territory and waters, have been ceded to the Imperial Government for twenty-five years — which period, by mutual agreement, may be still further prolonged — and the construction allowed of branches of railways in order to connect these ports with the main Great Siberian line. This Agreement is a direct and natural outcome of the friendly relations between great neighbouring Empires, all of whose endeavours should be directed towards the preservation of tranquillity along the vast extent of their neighbouring possessions for the common benefit of the people of both of them. The peaceful occupation, by the diplomatic Agreement of the 15th March, of the ports and territory of a friendly nation shows, in the best possible way, that the Government of China truly appreciates the meaning of the Agreement established between us.

"Securing the inviolability of the sovereign rights of China, and satisfying the daily requirements of Russia in her capacity of a great and neighbouring naval Power, this Agreement can in no way insure [injure?] the interests of any other foreign Power ; on the contrary, it gives to all nations of the world the possibility in the near future of entering into communication with this hitherto closed-up country on the coast of the Yellow Sea. The opening to the commercial fleets of all foreign nations of the port of Talienwan creates in the Pacific Ocean a new and extended centre for the commercial and trading undertakings of those nations, especially by means of the Great Siberian line, henceforth to be taken into account, and which, thanks to the friendly Treaty between Russia and China, will unite the extreme ends of the Old World. Thus, the Agreement signed at Peking has for Russia a deep historical signification, and must be joyfully welcomed by all to whom happy peace and successes, based on the mutual understandings of nations, are dear."

On the 3d of April, Sir Claude MacDonald was able to announce by cable to Lord Salisbury: "Yamên agreed yesterday to the following arrangement: China will lease Wei-hai Wei to Great Britain on the same terms as Port Arthur has been leased to Russia, but Great Britain agrees not to take possession of the place until it has been given up by Japan. The lease will continue until Russia ceases to occupy Liaotung Peninsula. Details are left for subsequent adjustment." Negotiations relative to the terms of the lease of Wei-hai Wei were protracted until the first of July, when the Convention determining them was signed at Peking. Its provisions were as follows: "The territory leased shall comprise the Island of Liu-kung and all islands in the Bay of Wei-hai Wei, and a belt of land 10 English miles wide along the entire coast line of the Bay of Wei-hai Wei. Within the above-mentioned territory leased Great Britain shall have sole jurisdiction. Great Britain shall have, in addition, the right to erect fortifications, station troops, or take any other measures necessary for defensive purposes, at any points on or near the coast of the region east of the meridian 121° 40′ east of Greenwich, and to acquire on equitable compensation with that territory such sites as may be necessary for water supply, communications, and hospitals. Within that zone Chinese administration will not be interfered with, but no troops other than Chinese or British shall be allowed therein. It is also agreed that within the walled city of Wei-hai Wei, Chinese officials shall continue to exercise jurisdiction except so far as may be inconsistent with naval and military requirements for the defence of the territory leased. It is further agreed that Chinese vessels of war, whether neutral or otherwise, shall retain the right to use the waters herein leased to Great Britain. It is further understood that there will be no expropriation or expulsion of the inhabitants of the territory herein specified, and that if land is required for fortifications, public officers, or any official or public purpose, it shall be bought at a fair price."—*Great Britain, Papers by Command: China, No. 1, 1898, and No. 1, 1899.*

A. D. 1898 (April—July).—Charges of corruption against Li Hung-chang and the Tsung-li Yamen.—'One of the censors of highest rank memorialised the Emperor early in April, accusing the whole Tsung-li Yamên of being in Russian pay, and alleging that the sum of 10,000,000 taels was paid to them. He also stated that Li Hung-chang had secured from Russia 1,500,000 taels, and he prayed for a full inquiry and for the decapitation of Li Hung-chang if the accusation were proved, or if he were found guiltless, he himself should be decapitated. Li Hung-chang was dismissed on September 6, but afterwards in November was appointed an imperial commissioner to report on the inundations of the Yellow River, an unwelcome post. . . . . A Black Flag rebellion in the southern province of Kwang-si, in which the secret society called The Triads was said to be concerned, was giving the Pekin Government great anxiety in July. The rebels, numbering about 40,000, were for a time victorious and seemed determined to overthrow the dynasty." — *Annual Register, 1898, pp. 333-4.*

A. D. 1898 (April—August).—France in the field with demands.—New demands from Great Britain.—France had now come forward to seize a place in the attacking line, preparatory to what seemed to be the impending partition of China. On the 12th of April, Sir Claude MacDonald cabled to Lord Salisbury the following despatch: "I had an interview with the Yamên yesterday, at which they informed me that China had acceded to the following demands on the part of France:—1. Kwangchow Wan [in the Lei-chau peninsula, on the southern coast, near Tonquin] to be leased as a coaling-station to France. 2. The right to construct a railway to Yünnan-fu from the Tonquin frontier. 3. The promise not to alienate any territory in the three provinces of Kwangtung, Kwangsi, and Yünnan, which border on the French frontier. 4. The Chinese Government agree that if ever they constitute a Postal Department independent of the maritime customs, and if a European is to be appointed as Director thereof, France shall have an equal right with that of other Powers to nominate a candidate for the post of Director. The Chinese Government are willing—1. To lease us as much additional territory on Kowloon promontory [opposite Hong Kong], exclusive of Kowloon city, as is required for military and naval purposes. 2. The Yamên state that China is quite willing to allow the extension into Yünnan of the Burmah Railway."

On the 13th, Mr. Balfour, in the absence of Lord Salisbury, cabled from London in reply: "Inform Yamên that, although they have not followed our advice, we are anxious to maintain, as far as possible, integrity of China, and will, therefore, not make new territorial demands upon them. It is, however, absolutely necessary, if we are to pursue this policy, that they, on their side, should first immediately conclude negotiations—(a) for giving us all the land required for military defences of Hong Kong; (b) to fulfil their promise to make Nanning a Treaty port; (c) to give some railway concession; (d) an agreement as to the non-alienation of Kuang'tung and Yünnan. In connection with condition (d), it is in the interests of the integrity of China, and is justified by the proximity of Yünnan to Burmah, and by our commercial preponderance in Kuang'tung."

On the same day (13th April) the British Minister at Paris telegraphed to the Foreign Office, London: "It is stated in to-night's papers that, at the Cabinet Council held this morning, M. Hanotaux was able to announce to his colleagues that the French demands on China had been satisfactorily met. They are stated in the semi-official 'Temps' to be:—1. Concession of a lease of a bay on the south coast of China. 2. Concession of a railway connecting Tonquin with Yünnan-fu by the Red River. 3. Engagement on the part of China never to alienate the territories of the provinces contiguous to Tonquin. 4. Engagement never to cede to any other Power the Island of Hainan. 5. Arrangement in regard to the constitution of the postal service."

Thus, for the time being, France was satisfied, and England would be, before she gave rest to the Tsung-li Yamên. Her present demands, as above specified by Mr. Balfour, were pressed without ceasing by the pertinacious Sir Claude. On the 9th of June he obtained from the Yamên a lease for the British government of about 200 square miles of territory on the mainland opposite its island crown colony of Hong Kong, and surrounding the Chinese city of Kowloon, the latter, however, to remain under Chinese jurisdiction. The term of the lease was 99 years. With regard to the opening of Nanning as a Treaty Port, he received an assurance from the Yamên in August that it should be done so soon as the Kwang-si rebellion was crushed. On the other points he had equal success. — *Great Britain, Papers by Command: China, No.* 1, 1899, *pp.* 12, 19, 98–9, 178.

A. D. 1898 (May).—**How** the murder of a missionary was made the ground of French demands for a Railway Concession.—On the 17th of May, 1898, the British Minister at Peking cabled to Lord Salisbury : " Murder of missionary in Kuang-si. French demands for compensation. . . . The Yamên . . . said they were not certain that the murdered missionary was not a Chinaman, and that the demands made by the French for compensation comprise a Concession for a railway to some point on the sea-coast not specified, a chapel to be built, and a pecuniary indemnity of 100,000 fr. to be paid. Up to the present they had refused all these demands." Later, the following particulars of the murder were received from the British Consul at Canton : " The occurrence happened about a fortnight ago at Yungan-ehou, in the P'ing-lo Prefecture. While walking through the streets the missionary noticed a placard directed against the Christian religion. Having discovered the author of the placard, the missionary, with two converts, proceeded to his house and attempted to arrest him. Out of this a disturbance arose in which the passers-by took part, and in the end the missionary and the two converts lost their lives."

On the 21st of May Sir Claude MacDonald reported to Lord Salisbury from Peking : " I am very reliably informed that the demands made at an interview with the Yamên yesterday by M. Pichon, the French Minister, in connection with this case were :— 1. A Concession to construct a railway from Pakhoi to Nanning ; 2. Construction of a chapel at Pakhoi ; 3. A pecuniary indemnity of 100,000 fr. ; and 4. The responsible officials to be punished. In response to these demands, the Yamên suggested that the Railway Concession should be granted in a document by itself, apart from the granting of the other demands, and that the chapel should be built at Yungan-chou, the scene of the murder, instead of at Pakhoi, and the French Minister undertook to refer these modifications to his Government for their favourable consideration."

On the 27th, Sir Claude reported further that he had heard on very good authority that all the French demands had been granted, and added : " The Yamên have since denied to me that they have committed themselves to granting them, but I have little doubt that they have practically done so. The reason for making the Railway Concession a separate matter is that the Chinese are anxious to avoid establishing precedents for compensation for attacks on missionaries taking the shape of commercial Concessions, and they hope, rather foolishly, to do so by nominally closing the missionary case before the other matter is taken up. They did this in the case of the German Agreement for the lease of Kiao-chau Bay, which begins by declaring that the Shantung missionary case has already been closed. The French demands are not at all excessive. I

have already expressed my belief that the proposed railway will not injure us commercially, provided, of course, that no differential rates are allowed, as to which I shall insist on specific assurances from the Yamên." — *Great Britain, Papers by Command: China, No.* 1, 1899, *pp.* 91, 146, 159.

Alluding to this incident, and to that which the German government made its pretext for seizing Kiao Chau (see, above, A. D. 1897—November), a German writer has remarked :

" Never before, perhaps, has so much material value been attached to ministers of the Gospel in foreign lands, and the manner in which, after their death, they are used to spread civilization is somewhat foreign to our older ideas of the functions of the bearers of spiritual blessings."

A. D. 1898 (June—September).—**Momentary** influence of a reform party in the palace.—Futile attempt of the young emperor to uphold it.—The decaying state of the Empire had now become so desperately plain, and the predatory swarm of governments and speculators which gathered to despoil it had grown so greedy and so bold, that a party which could see that the only hope for its salvation must be sought in some modernizing reforms, of education and administration, was able to win a momentary footing of influence in the palace at Peking. Its leading spirit appears to have been one Kang Yeu Wei, an extremely radical reformer who came from Canton. In an article which he wrote some months later, and which was published in the " Contemporary Review," Kang Yeu Wei gave this account of himself, and of the mode in which he was brought into relations with the young Emperor :

" I was always fond of studying Western learning. After the French took Foochow in 1885 there was evident danger of China's end drawing nigh. Consequently, in 1889, I memorialised about the matter in great grief. I feared Russia's advance southward, and pointed out the secret intentions of Japan and the latent danger in Corea. I thought that China had come to such a pass that if she should devote these years for the purpose of speedy reform she might become strong, but if there was delay nothing could save her. At that time the high Ministers of State were all Conservatives, and would not present my memorial to the throne. After the loss of Formosa, Wêng Tung Ho [the Emperor's tutor] was sorry that he had listened to their advice, and was very cordial to me. Then I exhorted him to reform, and I wrote a long memorial, signed by 1,300 provincial graduates, to urge reform again and again, and a Reform Club was formed in Peking, and the newspaper, ' Chinese Progress,' was started in Shanghai. At this time (1895) Wêng Tung Ho strongly urged reform on the Emperor, but was checked by the Empress-Dowager, and almost put aside then, and the Reform Club was shut up. I then returned to Canton, and founded the Ethical Society in Canton province and the Sacred Society in Kwang-Si province. My disciples, Liang Chi Chao and Tan Tze Tung, formed the Southern Learning Society in Hunan province ; Liu Shio started the Fookien Learning Society in the Fukien province ; Yang Tui the Szechuen Learning Society, in the province of Szechuen ; Yang Shin Sheu and Sung Peh

Luh opened the Pass Learning Society in the provinces of Shansi and Shensi; I and my brother K'ang Kwang In, with King Yuen Shen, opened a Chinese girls' school and formed the Anti-foot-binding Society in Shanghai; and many newspapers were started. Thus newspapers and new schools flourished in all the provinces. and all the empire knew of the reform.

"When Kiaochow was taken by the Germans I went to Peking again and sent up another memorial strongly urging reform, with the same motive as Peter the Great, and on the same political lines as have been adopted by the present Emperor of Japan. I also presented my books on the history of reform in Japan and the history of Peter the Great's reforms, and suggested that all the coast of the empire be open to international trade. Wêng Tung Ho approved of it, and strongly supported the measure at Court. But the crowd of Conservatives opposed, and he could not carry it. Then it was proposed to make an alliance with England, as was advised in the reform paper of Macao. The Government was undecided and feared that a great nation like England would not be willing. But when England asked that Port Arthur and Ta Lien Wan should be open ports I hastened to Wêng Tung Ho and said, 'China is saved and will not perish. You must grant the request. Since God gives us this opportunity, it should on no account be let slip.' But the Empress-Dowager and Li Hung Chang had made up their minds to give them to Russia. Again, England promised to lend China ten millions at 3 per cent. Russia was forcing China to borrow from her at 4 per cent. The Foreign Office was in great fear between these two great nations, and undecided. They then discussed about borrowing from both, and finally decided not to borrow from either. I said, 'You should decline Russia's offer and borrow from England. Russia, though she might threaten us, will never dare to declare war on this account.' The Empress-Dowager favoured Russia and was afraid. In the end they did not borrow from either.

"When Russia was seeking Port Arthur and Ta Lien Wan, I presented two memorials that they should be refused to Russia and both made open ports. The Emperor blamed Prince Kung and Li Hung Chang, and asked, 'What is the use of a secret treaty with Russia? Not only does Russia not protect us, but she herself takes away territory from us.' Both the Prince and Li replied: 'It is by giving Port Arthur and Ta Lien Wan to Russia that the secret treaty is preserved.' At this the Emperor was very angry. When the Empress-Dowager decided to give them to Russia, and Wêng Tung Ho found that all my prophecies came true, he strongly recommended me to the Emperor. Kao Hsueh Tseng, the Supervising Censor, Chen Pao Chen, the Governor of Hunan, Su Chih Ching, of the Hanlin College, and Li Twan Fên, President of the Board of Rites, also had recommended me from time to time. When the Emperor asked the members of the Cabinet, Wêng Tung Ho recommended me, saying, 'His abilities are a hundred times superior to my own,' and prayed the Emperor to listen to me in all matters of reform. I also presented to the Emperor a record of England, France, and Germany, a comparative diagram of all nations, and the Rev. Timothy Richard's 'History of the Nineteenth Cen-

tury' and his 'Essays for the Times,' and translations of Western books. The Emperor then understood something of the cause of the rise and fall of nations, and made up his mind to introduce great reforms. Desiring men to help him, he invited me, and acted on my former suggestions."

But the situation at Peking, as Kang Yeu Wei describes it,—the weakness of the young Emperor and the strength of the Empress-Dowager, —made the undertaking of reform hopeless from the beginning. The Empress-Dowager had professed to resign the government, but, says Kang Yeu Wei, "she really still held the reins in her hands. She made the memorials about appointments. All the Ministers of the first and second rank were her nominees. The Emperor had no voice. In all matters he had to inform her first before acting. The Emperor was only an Emperor in name.

"The Emperor was of a studious disposition. Since the loss of Formosa he has been greatly distressed about the decline of the Empire. After this his faithful tutor, Wêng Tung Ho, who was a learned man, sought foreign books for study, and presented them, with atlases, to the Emperor. These the Emperor daily studied, discovered the cause of foreign prosperity, discovered the reason of China's weakness and conservatism, and made up his mind to reform. But this was not in accordance with the view of the Empress-Dowager. At the beginning of the war with Japan the Emperor and his Ministers wanted war. The Empress-Dowager and Li Hung Chang wanted peace. The Empress-Dowager was ready to give up Manchuria and Formosa. The Emperor could not think of it for a moment without crying with distress; he wanted to make an alliance with England and to reform, while the Empress-Dowager was equally bent on alliance with Russia without reform. Thus their views diverged more and more, so that when the Emperor wanted to reform in 1895 the Empress hated him; two of his favourite Imperial ladies were beaten : the Vice-Presidents, Chang Lin, Wang Ming Luan, and Tsz Tui, a brother of one of these Imperial ladies, were driven away; and the Imperial ladies' tutor, Wên Ting Shih, was stripped of his honours, never to be employed any more. This was because all these advised the Emperor to keep the power in his own hands.

"The eunuch Kow Lang Tsai memorialised the Empress-Dowager to resign the government into the hands of the Emperor. For this he was put to death. The Emperor himself narrowly escaped being put aside then. . . . Chang Lin was a straightforward man in whom Prince Kung put great confidence. In a memorial to the Emperor he said: 'The relation of the Empress-Dowager to the late Emperor Tung Chih was that of his own mother, but her relation to you is that of the widowed concubine of a former Emperor.' When the Empress-Dowager came to know this she was in a great rage. Prince Kung was also in great fear. When the Emperor issued an edict, by command of the Empress-Dowager, to degrade Chang Lin, Prince Kung was weeping on his knees. When asked the reason of it, the Emperor waved his hand and said, 'Don't ask him.' The Emperor and the Prince wept together, and the Prince wept so bitterly that he had no strength to rise up.

The Emperor commanded the eunuchs to help him up and lead him away. Wên Ting Shih begged the Emperor to exercise his rights. The Emperor waved his hand, saying, 'Don't speak,' for the Emperor knew long ago that when he took the reins of government into his own hands the Empress hated him."

Nevertheless, in 1898, the well-meaning but weak young Emperor was moved to a spasmodic assertion of his authority, in bold strokes of reform. "Rather than lose his empire like those of the Chin and the Ming dynasties, and become a by-word of disgrace for all future generations, he would risk the dangers of reform. If he succeeded, then he would get power into his own hands and save his country. If he failed, he would greatly open the minds of the people and prepare them for the future, and thus, perhaps, preserve a remnant of China. At this time the Emperor considered the chief thing was to preserve the country from being lost to foreign nations, and looked upon his position on the throne as of little consequence in comparison—considering the welfare of the people as of supreme importance, while his own person was of little importance. He had none to consult with, but decided to risk all danger and try."—Kang Yeu Wei, *The Reform of China and the Revolution of* 1898 (*Contemporary Rev., August,* 1899).

Read with a knowledge of what came of them, the futile decrees which the helpless young Emperor issued in June, 1898, seem pathetic in the extreme. The following is a translation of the first of his reform edicts, which bears the date, "Kuang Hsu, 24th year, 4th moon, 23d day," corresponding to June 11, 1898 :

"For a long time past the condition of Imperial affairs has been a subject of discussion among the officials of the Empire, both metropolitan and provincial, with a view to bring about changes necessary for improvement. Decrees have been frequently issued by the Emperor, for a special system of examinations, for doing away with the surplus soldiery, for the alteration of the military examinations and for the institution of colleges. In spite of the fact that these things have so often been carefully thought out, and so many plans have been formed, there is no general consensus of opinion, and discussion is still rife as to which plans are best. There are some among the older officials who affirm that the old ways are best and need no alteration, and that the new plans are not required. Such babblings are vain and useless.

"The Emperor puts the question before you thus : In the present condition of Imperial affairs, with an untrained army, with limited funds, with ignorant 'literati,' and with artisans untaught because they have no fit teachers, is there any difficulty in deciding, when China is compared with foreign nations, who is the strong and who is the weak ? It is easy to distinguish between the rich and the poor. How can a man armed with a wooden stick smite his foe encased in a coat of mail ? The Emperor sees that the affairs of the Empire are in an unsettled condition, and that his various Decrees have availed nothing. Diversity of opinion, each unlike another as fire differs from water, is responsible for the spread of the existing evil. It is the same evil as that which existed in the Sung and Ming dynasties (circa A. D. 1000 and 1500). Our present system is not of the slightest use. We

cannot in these modern days adhere to the ways of the five Kings (circa B. C. 2500); even they did not continue exactly after the manner of their respective predecessors. It is like wearing thick clothes in summer and thin ones in winter.

"Now, therefore, the Emperor orders all officials, metropolitan and provincial, from prince down to 'literati,' to give their whole minds to a real endeavour to improvement. With perseverance, like that of the saints of old, do your utmost to discover which foreign country has the best system in any branch of learning and learn that one. Your great fault is the falseness of your present knowledge. Make a special effort and determine to learn the best of everything. Do not merely learn the outside covers of the books of knowledge, and do not make a loud boast of your own attainments. The Emperor's wish is to change what is now useless into something useful, so that proficiency may be attained and handed on to posterity. The Metropolitan College will be the chief one, and must be instituted at once. The Emperor orders the Grand Councillors to consult with the Tsung-li Yamên on the subject, and to come to a decision as soon as possible, and then to memorialize the Throne. Any of the compilers and graduates of the Hanlin College, the secretaries of the Boards, the officers of the Palace Guards, expectant Intendants, Prefects, district Magistrates, and subordinate officials, sons and brothers of officials, the hereditary officials of the Eight Banners, and the sons of the military officials of the Empire, can enter the College who wish to do so. By this means knowledge will be handed down from one generation to another. It will be strictly forbidden to members of the College to be careless or dilatory in their studies, or to introduce as students any of their friends without regard for the latter's capabilities ; for such things would frustrate the benefit of this excellent plan of His Imperial Majesty."

A day later he issued the following: "The Tsung-li Yamên have reported to the Throne that in obedience to instructions they have considered the requests contained in the memorial of the Vice-President Jung Hui, for the appointment of special Ministers of Commerce, and the sending of members of the Imperial family to visit foreign nations. Commercial matters are of the highest importance, and the suggestion is one which deserves to be acted upon. As the result of a former consultation of the Tsung-li Yamên on the subject, commercial bureaus have been established at the capitals of the provinces, and the officials of each province have ordered the leading gentry and merchants to elect from their numbers managers of the bureaus, who will then draw up commercial regulations. It is to be hoped that strict conformity to these Regulations will lead to a daily improvement in trade ; and the Emperor orders the Viceroys and Governors of the provinces to direct the gentry and merchants to strictly obey the official instructions, and to consult together for the most speedy and satisfactory arrangement of commercial matters : it is to be hoped that in this way the officials will be kept in touch with the merchants. We must not adhere blindly to our old customs. Let the officials of each province memorialize the Throne, and inform the Emperor how commercial affairs are managed in their respective provinces. With regard to the suggestion that members of the

Imperial Family should go abroad, this is a new departure, but is quite in accordance with modern custom. The Emperor, therefore, orders the Court of the Imperial clan to select from the Princes of the first three ranks any who are well versed in modern affairs and ideas, and who are on the side of modern improvement, and to inform the Emperor of their selection. The selected Princes will then await the Emperor's orders with regard to their journey."

On the 15th the following imperial mandate was published: "Wêng T'ung-ho, Assistant Grand Secretary and President of the Board of Revenue, has of late made many errors in the conduct of business, and has forfeited all confidence; on several occasions he has been impeached to the Throne. At his private audiences of the Emperor he has replied to His Majesty's questions with no regard for anything except his own personal feeling and opinion, and he has made no attempt to conceal his pleasure or displeasure either in his speech or in his countenance. It has gradually become clear that his ambition and rebellious feeling have led him to arrogate to himself an attempt to dictate to the Emperor. It is impossible to permit him to remain in the responsible position of a Grand Councillor. In former days a strict inquiry would have been held, and his crime punished with the utmost rigour of the law. Taking into consideration, however, his long service as tutor to the Emperor, His Majesty cannot bring himself to mete out to him such a severe penalty. Let Wêng T'ung-ho vacate his posts, and retire into private life, as a warning that he is preserved (from a worse fate)."

In transmitting this mandate to the British Foreign Office, Sir Claude MacDonald explained that Wêng T'ung-ho was a "reactionary," whose "influence was invariably against innovation and progress," but personally "prepossessing, courteous, and scholarly — an excellent type of the Conservative Chinese statesman." But that the dismissal of Wêng T'ung-ho did not signify the triumph of the reform party was shown the same day by a decree commanding special honors to the Empress Dowager, who seemed to be losing no time in reasserting herself. "In future," said the edict, "whenever officials receive favours or gifts from the Empress Dowager, or receive promotion to the highest civil or military rank or to the Vice-Presidency of a Board, they must (after thanking the Emperor) present themselves before the Empress Dowager and thank her; and in similar cases all provincial Tartar-Generals, Lieutenant-Generals, Viceroys, Governors, and Commanders-in-chief must write their thanks to the Empress Dowager (as well as to the Emperor)."

Other radically reforming decrees that were issued by the Emperor during June and early in July were described by the British Minister in a despatch dated July 9, as follows: "To effect a change in the agricultural methods of an ancient Eastern nation would seem a very hopeless task, but from a Decree published on the 4th instant, it appears that a censor has made proposals for the establishment of a school of agriculture, on which the Tsung-li Yamên were asked to report. The Decree founded on their Report states that agriculture is the basis of the States' wealth, and that measures for its revival are urgently needed. The provincial authorities

are, therefore, directed to examine all methods of cultivation, whether Chinese or foreign, with a view to their adoption by the people. . . . The Decree proceeds to promise rewards for successful treatment of agricultural problems, and to direct the translation and circulation in provincial Colleges of foreign works on the subject.

"Two Decrees, published on the 27th June and 5th July, have reference to reforms in the Chinese army, but they throw no light on the nature of them, and merely refer certain suggestions to various Departments for examination. The last Decree I shall mention, which appeared on the 5th instant, contains a very frank admission of the need of reforms. It states that in foreign countries commerce and industry thrive and progress, while in China, though there is no lack of ability, it is fettered in the bonds of ancient custom, and cannot free itself. As one means of assisting in its liberation it is ordained that any persons producing ' new books' (presumably books that show originality of thought), or being the first to use new methods, or to produce new instruments or appliances suitable for use, are to receive rewards from the State in the shape either of official employment, if they are fitted for it, or of some other distinction. In the case of inventions a certificate will be given, and the profits secured to the inventor for a fixed term of years—in fact patent rights will be granted. Rewards will also be given to those who, with their own resources, establish colleges, open up mines, or set up arsenals for the manufacture of rifles and cannon. In conclusion, the Tsung-li Yamên are directed to draw up Regulations for effecting the above objects."

The zeal of the reforming movement was kept alive and its authors held their ground throughout the summer, and nearly to the end of September. On the 17th of that month, Sir Claude MacDonald wrote to Lord Salisbury: "Imperial Decrees intended to launch China on the path of reform continue to appear, though there are few signs of any of them taking practical effect. The Emperor is evidently learning that it is one thing to issue a reform Edict and another to get it obeyed. Not long ago a Decree was issued, the object of which was to make the Throne more accessible to the subordinate portion of the official world. At the beginning of this month a case was brought to His Majesty's notice, in which the Board of Ceremonies disobeyed this Decree by refusing to transmit a Memorial sent in by a Secretary. He was much enraged, and forthwith cashiered the six head officials of the Board, that is to say, the two Presidents and four Vice-Presidents.

"On the 12th instant he followed this up by a fresh Decree dwelling on the circumstances and reiterating his previous instructions. Memorials were to be presented as they came in, it being of the highest importance, in the present critical state of public affairs, that all such communications should be examined as soon as possible. Obstruction and delay were to be punished with the utmost rigour, and special commands were given that the previous Edicts on reform, all of which were enumerated, were to be hung up in a public place in each Yamên throughout the Empire, so that no one should be ignorant of their contents. Not satisfied with all this, he issued, also on the 12th instant, a long and remarkable Decree calling attention to the advantages of Western methods, and inveighing against degenerate officials and conservative Ministers, who not only could not assist him in adopting their methods, but spread reports instead calculated to disturb the minds of the people. He wanted his subjects to know that they 'could depend on their Prince,' and appealed to them to make China powerful by working for reform with 'united minds.' The previous orders were amplified, and the privilege of memorializing the Throne, which formerly stopped at officers of a high rank, is now extended to practically every soul in the Empire.

"Next day, the 13th September, another Decree repeated the terms of the above in clearer detail, and laid down precisely the procedure each class was to observe in making itself heard. The severest penalties were threatened should there be any interference with the free exercise of this privilege by the high officers of Government, who were commanded to report by telegram the steps they were taking to fulfil the Imperial wishes. The series of Decrees above quoted are naturally creating a great commotion in the Chinese official world, and it will be interesting to note their effect."—*Great Britain, Papers by Command: China, No.* 1, 1899, *pp.* 179–279.

The effect was soon known. It was one which brought the reformers to grief and their reforms to an end.

A. D. 1898 (September).—Overthrow of the Reformers.—Subjugation of the Emperor by the Empress-Dowager.—His countermanding decrees.—The Imperial reformer announced the downfall of his own authority on the 21st of September, in the following significant decree: "The affairs of the nation are at present in a difficult position, and everything awaits reform. I, the Emperor, am working day and night with all my powers, and every day arrange a multitude of affairs. But, despite my careful toil, I constantly fear to be overwhelmed by the press of work. I reverently recall that Her Majesty the Empress Dowager has on two occasions since the reign of Tung Chih (1861) assumed the reins of Government with great success in critical periods. In all she did Her Majesty showed perfection. Moved by a deep regard for the welfare of the nation, I have repeatedly implored Her Majesty to be graciously pleased to advise me in government, and have received her assent. This is an assurance of prosperity to the whole nation, officials and people. Her Majesty will commence to transact business from to-day in the side Hall. On the 23rd of September, I, the Emperor, will lead my princes and high officials to make obeisance in the Ch'in Chêng Hall. Let the proper officials reverently and carefully prepare the fitting programme of the ceremony."

On the 25th he announced: "Since the 4th moon, I, the Emperor, have been frequently ailing in health, and in spite of long-continued treatment there is still no great improvement. Should there be any persons, either in the capital or the provinces, who are highly skilled in the treatment of disease, let the officials at once recommend them to the throne and await our orders. Should such men be in the provinces l t them be sent to the capital without the least delay."

On the 26th the unfortunate Emperor was made to send forth another decree, countermand-

ing the greater part of the orders he had been giving, on the pretext that they had been misunderstood and badly carried out. The obstructive offices which he had abolished were restored; the permission given to scholars and people to present memorials was withdrawn. "The original purpose," said the decree, "was that we should see with the eyes and hear with the ears of everybody, but the Court has now opened wide the path of access to the throne, and if there are useful proposals for reform made in the statements of any of the different classes of officials they are bound to be observed at once and set into operation. At present, careless documents all alike in character pour in. All are full of frivolous statements, some even touch on the extravagant, and all are much wanting in order. Hereafter all officers whose duty it is to speak shall say what they have to say in fitting language. In accordance with the prescribed rules, persons or officers who are not competent to memorialize the throne are not permitted to submit sealed documents. The 'Times,' official newspaper, is of no benefit to good government and will vainly disturb men's minds; let it be abolished at once. The Imperial colleges will be ground for the cultivation of talent. Apart from those which are already being gradually established in Peking and the provincial capitals, let the local officials in all prefectures and districts where it is proposed to establish minor colleges consider the local conditions and the convenience of the people. Let the temples [which were to have been turned into colleges] in the provinces remain as before; there is no need to make colleges of them and disturb the feelings of the people. Over and above the matters above mentioned, there are others which have been duly considered and put into operation, and others which are under consideration, such as trade, agriculture, reorganization of the army, and the development of resources, all of which are of undoubted consequence to the State and the people, and must imperatively be introduced gradually. Those measures which are of no benefit to the present system of government, and are detrimental to the Constitution, need not be discussed. Let the six Boards and the Tsung-li Yamên make an investigation of these matters, consider them with special care, and submit a report to the throne so that they may be dealt with."

The events which attended and followed these decrees were reported by Sir Claude MacDonald on September 28, as follows: "The Decree [of the 21st] naturally created much excitement in Peking, and rumours of impending disaster to the most prominent of the advocates of reform were prevalent. Subsequent proceedings justified the alarm and assumed the character of a coup d'état. The same day the house of Chang Yin-huan was surrounded by the police in search of one K'ang Yu-wei. This K'ang Yu-wei is a Chinese scholar of high repute who was, until lately, editor of a Chinese newspaper in Shanghae known as 'Progress.' He was a strong advocate of reform, and was this year recommended to the Emperor, and on his arrival in Peking was given a position of Secretary in the Board of Works. He is said to have acquired great influence over the Emperor, and to have been his adviser in his recent reform measures. K'ang Yu-wei could not be found, and it has subsequently transpired that he has escaped and left Shanghae on the 27th in the English mail for Hong Kong. So keen was the hunt for him that on the 22nd all traffic was stopped on the Tien-tsin Railway line to prevent his passage. On the 24th instant orders were issued for the arrest of several officials who had been in relation with him, including Chang Yin-huan and Hsü Chih-ch'ing. The latter had recommended K'ang to the throne, and had been recently appointed President of the Board of Rites. Chang Yin-huan went to the Board of Punishments and has remained a prisoner since. The precise charge against K'ang and his friends has not transpired, but it is supposed to be one of conspiracy against the liberty and even the life of the Empress Dowager.

"It was reported on the 25th that Chang was to be executed the same evening or early next morning, and I thought it advisable to make an appeal on his behalf for at least due consideration of any charge brought against him. The report reached me late in the afternoon, and it was therefore necessary to take prompt measures. It was supposed that Li Hung-chang had been consulted by the Empress Dowager in the matter. I accordingly addressed a letter to his Excellency pointing out the horror with which such sudden executions were regarded by all Western nations, and the bad effect the secret and hasty condemnation of an official of Chang's rank, who was so well known in Europe, would produce, and begged his Excellency to use what influence he possessed to prevent such hurried action. I concluded my letter by saying that I appealed to him, Li, because he was the only Statesman now in Peking who was conversant with European methods, and would, therefore, thoroughly realize the disastrous impression which such a summary execution would produce throughout the Western world. It is well known that Li Hung-chang and Chang Yin-huan are deadly enemies, and it was generally reported that Chang's imprisonment was due to Li. The Grand Secretary replied saying that he highly respected my generous and humane motives, and he assured me that no summary action would be taken."

On the 30th Sir Claude reported : "Six of the reformers referred to in my despatch of the 28th September were executed on the 28th instant. They included a brother of K'ang Yu-wei, the chief reformer, and, though subordinates, all were graduates and men of standing. Chang Yin-huan has been banished to Chinese Turkestan, where he is to be kept under rigorous surveillance. No precise crime is charged against him. The Edict announcing his punishment accuses him vaguely of being treacherous, fickle, and a sycophant. Last night a long Decree appeared dealing with the so-called conspiracy. K'ang Yu-wei is declared to have taken advantage of the Emperor's leaning towards beneficial reforms to plot a revolution, which was to be opened by surrounding the Palace at Wan Shou-shan and seizing the Empress-Dowager and the Emperor. The haste in executing K'ang's chief accomplices, for it appears that the legal formalities had not been observed, is admitted to have been caused by Memorials, whose dominant note was fear of a revolution if punishment was delayed."—*Great Britain, Papers by Command: China, No. 1, 1899, pp. 291-4.*

A. D. **1898** (October).—The **Empress-Dow-** ager.—Her past career.—Her character.— The Empress-Dowager, so called, who now recovered her ascendancy over the weak young Emperor, which the reformers had momentarily overcome, and who became again the real Sovereign of the Empire, as she had been for the past thirty years, "was never Empress, not even as imperial consort, having been but the secondary wife of Hsien-fêng, the Emperor who fled from his capital on the approach of the Anglo-French forces in 1860 [see, in vol. 1. CHINA : A. D. 1856-1860]. But she took the title as the mother of that ill-starred monarch's heir, in which capacity she was allowed to share with the widow proper the regency during the minority of the Emperor Tung-Chih (or Che, for there is no agreement as to the transliteration of Chinese sounds). . . . The female duumvirate was not what was intended—was in fact an unforeseen result of the last will and testament of the Emperor Hsien-fêng, who died at his hunting lodge at Jêho, whither he himself had been hunted by the victorious invaders. . . .

"The fundamental law of the Ta-tsing dynasty is the Salic law. No woman and no eunuch can ever reign or rule. Conforming to the laws of his house, the Emperor in his will nominated a Council of Regency during the minority of his infant son, afterwards known as the Emperor Tung-Chih. The Council was composed of two imperial princes and the Minister Sun-che. To his two wives, the true but childless one and the secondary one who was mother of the Prince Imperial, he bequeathed the guardianship of the infant. The Emperor placed his real confidence in the first, the legal wife ; but he was fond of the other, the mother of his heir. A serious dilemma thus confronted him, which he thought to evade by placing in the hands of the Empress a private and personal testament, giving her absolute authority over her colleague, only to be exercised, however, in certain emergencies. As a matter of fact, the power was never called into exercise.

"The Empress-mother was twenty-seven years old, clever, ambitious, and apparently fearless. . . . She conceived a scheme by which the position might be reversed, and confided it to her brother-in-law, Prince Kung. . . . The ambition which the Empress-mother confided to Prince Kung was nothing less than to suppress the Council of Regency, and set up in its place the authority of the two Empresses. Inasmuch, however, as they were ignorant of affairs, and women to boot, the Prince himself was to be the real executive and de facto ruler of the empire. Prince Kung yielded to the seduction, and thus became accessory to the violation of the dynastic law. . . . The Regents were returning from the obsequies of the deceased Emperor when Prince Kung launched trumped-up charges against them of neglect of certain funeral rites, had them arrested on the road, and executed. By this summary violence the two Empresses were securely established as Regents, with Prince Kung as Chancellor of the empire. For a few years things went smoothly. . . . The two Regents seldom met. . . . From the relative position of the buildings in which they had their respective apartments, the ladies were known as the Eastern and Western Empresses, the former being the title commonly applied to the one whom we have termed the true Empress. . . .

"The 'Eastern Empress' was full of gentleness, meditation, and widowhood. . . . She was, therefore, unequally yoked with her sterner sister, and the pair could never have really worked together to any practical end. The eclipse of the weaker luminary was only a question of time. . . . The life and death of the young Emperor Tung-Chih, the son of Hsien-fêng and the presént Empress-regnante, seems little more than an episode in the career of his imperial—and imperious—mother. He died within two years of his full accession, removed by his own mother as some would have us believe, but by quite other agencies as others no less boldly affirm. . . . With the disappearance of her son, the last plank in the legal platform of the Empress-mother disappeared. But her appetite had grown by what it fed upon. She had now had fourteen years' schooling in statecraft, and she resolved that, 'per fas et nefas,' reign who might, she would govern. . . . The story of her second coup d'état of January, 1875, has been often related,—how the Empress so-called caused her own sister's child to be snatched out of its warm bed on a bitter night and conveyed into the Palace, whence he was proclaimed Emperor at daybreak. By this stroke the Regent at once aggrandised her own family, made a friend of a younger brother-in-law, the father of the child, to replace the elder who had become an enemy, and, to sum up all, secured for herself a new lease of power. For she who could thus make an emperor could also make a regent."—*The Empress-Regent of China (Blackwood's Magazine, Nov., 1898)*.

A. D. **1898**. (October—November).—Outbreaks of popular hostility to foreigners.—Guards for the Legations sent to Peking.—Chinese troops removed.—The palace revolution which overthrew the reforming party was followed quickly by outbreaks of popular hostility to foreigners. Two messages were cabled to Lord Salisbury from Peking October 1st. One informed him: "A Chinese mob at a point between Peking and the railway station yesterday afternoon violently assaulted several foreigners who had to pass that way from the train. Among those assaulted was Mr. Mortimore of his Legation, and an English lady, who were severely attacked with mud and stones; a member of the United States' Legation had one of his ribs broken. There is a decided spirit of disturbance among the Chinese, though the fact that many bad characters were about yesterday in consequence of the mid-autumn festival may go some way towards accounting for these outrages. I have requested Admiral Seymour by telegraph to despatch a vessel to Taku, in case a guard should be required for the protection of this Legation, and I am making strong representations to the Tsung-li Yamên."

In his second despatch the British Minister announced: "I do not anticipate any danger, but a good and reassuring effect will be produced, as after the Japanese war, by the presence of a guard. The foreign Representatives decided this morning to send for a small guard to protect the respective Legations. I have asked Admiral Seymour to send me twenty-five marines with a machine-gun. The German, Russian, Japanese, and Italian Representatives had previously arranged for their guards."

On the 5th, Sir Claude MacDonald reported:

"A meeting of foreign Representatives yesterday decided to notify the Chinese Government of the proposed departure from Tien-tsin for Peking to-morrow of bodies of British, German, and Russian marines, and to ask that all facilities, including a special train, should be extended to them by the Chinese authorities; the French, American, Japanese, and Italian marines to come straight on to Peking on their arrival at Tien-tsin. The meeting was held in consequence of the refusal of the Viceroy of Chihli to permit any foreign soldiers to leave Tien-tsin for Peking without special permission from the Tsung-li Yamên. It is very likely that the Chinese Government will make a protest similar to that of 1895, but it would be very ill-advised at the present crisis to give way to their protests, and it is absolutely necessary that the decision of the foreign Representatives should be put into effect."

The Chinese government did protest, but without effect. The legation guards were insisted upon, and, as speedily as possible, they were provided from the war-ships of the several powers, and quartered in Peking. Then the Chinese authorities brought troops to the capital, and the sense of danger at the legations grew. On the 25th of October Minister Mac-Donald cabled to London: "A serious menace to the safety of Europeans is the presence of some 10,000 soldiers, who have come from the Province of Kansu, and are to be quartered in the hunting park, two miles south of Peking. A party of these soldiers made a savage assault on four Europeans (including Mr. C. W. Campbell, of this Legation), who were last Sunday visiting the railway line at Lukou Chiao. The foreign Ministers will meet this morning to protest against these outrages. I shall see the Yamên to-day, and propose to demand that the force of soldiers shall be removed to another province, and that the offenders shall be rigorously dealt with."

On the 29th he telegraphed again: "The Foreign Representatives met yesterday, and drafted a note to the Yamên demanding that the Kansu troops should be withdrawn at once. The troops in question have not been paid for some months, and are in a semi-mutinous state. They have declared their intention to drive all Europeans out of the north of China, and have cut the telegraph wires and destroyed portions of the railway line between Lukouchiao and Paoting Fu. Some disturbances have been caused by them on the railway to Tien-tsin, but the line has not been touched, and traffic has not been interrupted. In the city here all is quiet. The presence of these troops in the immediate vicinity of Peking undoubtedly constitutes a serious danger to all Europeans. The Yamên gave me a promise that the force should be removed, but have not yet carried it into effect."

On the 6th of November he reported that the Yamên had replied to the note of the Diplomatic Body, acknowledging that the troops lacked discipline and were a source of danger, and again promising their removal, but that nothing had been done. He added: "It was decided unanimously to address a note to the Yamên, stating that if the troops in question were not withdrawn by the 15th instant, our respective Governments would adopt such measures as they considered necessary for the protection during the winter months of foreigners in Peking and Tien-tsin."

After several more exchanges of notes between the Diplomatic Body and the Yamên, peremptory on one side, apologetic on the other, the troops were removed to Chi-chow, about 80 miles east of Peking, beginning their march November 15. A few days previously Sir Claude Mac-Donald had been able to report "That two of the ringleaders in the attack on Mr. Campbell and other Europeans at Lu Kow-chiao [announced in despatch of Oct. 25] were brought into Peking and flogged in Mr. Campbell's presence at the Yamên of the Governor of the city on the 29th October. The men were sentenced to 1,000 blows each, but Mr. Campbell, after eighty blows had been inflicted, begged that the flogging might cease. It turned out that two other soldiers were struck by bullets from a small revolver, which was used by one of the railway engineers in self-defence, and, chiefly for this reason, I did not press for more floggings.

"I attached more importance to the punishment of the officer in command, who, it appears, had been warned beforehand by the railway authorities to keep his men away from the railway bridge, but had refused to do so. I consider him the person really responsible for what happened, and at an interview on the 31st October I told the Yamên that I should not be satisfied, and the incident would not be closed, until I saw his degradation published in the official Gazette. On the 4th November an Imperial Decree was issued ordering this officer, a Colonel named Chu Wan-jung, to be handed over to the Board of War for punishment. The Ministers inform me that this is likely to mean his degradation. I have, however, again warned their Excellencies that nothing short of this punishment will be satisfactory to Her Majesty's Government."—*Great Britain, Papers by Command: China, No. 1, 1899, pp. 258–79, and 332.*

A. D. **1898** (December).—**Reorganization of Chinese armies.—Reception by the Empress-Dowager to the ladies of the Legations.**—On the 20th of December Sir Claude MacDonald reported: "The reorganization of the land forces in the north appears to be occupying the serious attention of the Central Government. In the early half of this month Edicts were issued by the Empress Dowager approving proposals made by Jung Lu, who was appointed Generalissimo of northern armies immediately after the K'ang Yü-wei conspiracy. The following are the principal features of these proposals. The armies under the command of Sung Ch'ing and others, that is to say all the brigaded troops in North China, are to be organized in four corps—front, rear, right, and left—to occupy different strategical points. In addition, Jung Lu will raise a centre corps of 10,000 men, to be stationed presumably in or about Peking. . . . The importance of bringing the other four corps into an efficient state is dwelt upon, and the Edicts are stern in demanding the production of sufficient funds for the purpose. The Viceroy of Chihli is also instructed to closely scrutinize the condition of the Peiyang drilled troops—formerly Li Hung-chang's army—and bring them into order. They are to be under the orders of Jung Lu, instead of the Viceroy.

"The Viceroys responsible for the Arsenals of North and Mid China are also commanded to see

to the immediate construction of quick-firing guns and Mauser rifles and other war material, and to the preparation of maps of the coast-line for military purposes. Jung Lu has done nothing yet towards raising the centre corps beyond calling in the assistance of a German-educated officer named Yin Ch'ang, who holds a post in the Tien-tsin Military Academy. He is reputedly able, and probably one of the best Chinese available for the work, but I question whether he will be given sufficient powers of control. He is now engaged in drawing up a scheme."

Bearing the same date as the above, we find a despatch from Sir Claude MacDonald descriptive of a reception given by the Empress-Dowager, on the 13th, to the wives of the foreign representatives at Peking, "to accept their congratulations on the occasion of Her Imperial Majesty's birthday." "The ceremony," said the British Minister, "passed off extremely well. The Empress Dowager made a most favourable impression by her courtesy and affability. Those who went to the Palace under the idea that they would meet a cold and haughty person of strong imperious manners were agreeably surprised to find Her Imperial Majesty a kind and courteous hostess, who displayed both the tact and softness of a womanly disposition." "Thus ended," writes Sir Claude, in closing his despatch, "the incident which may be considered to mark another step in the nearer relations of China and foreign nations."—*Great Britain, Papers by Command: China, No. 1, 1900, pp. 12–15.*

A. D. **1898-1899.**—**Rioting in Shanghai consequent on French desecration of a cemetery.—French demand for extension of settlement ground in Shanghai.—English and American protests.**—The outcome.—On the 18th of July, 1898, the following was reported by the British Consul-General at Shanghai: "Serious rioting took place in the French Settlement on the 16th and the morning of 17th instant, in the course of which some fifteen natives lost their lives. The disturbance was due to an attempt of the French authorities to take possession of certain temple land known as the Ningpo Joss-house Cemetery. The ground is full of graves, and it is also used for depositing coffins until a favourable opportunity presents itself for removing them to the native districts of the deceased. The cemetery is within the limits of the French Settlement; originally it was far removed from the inhabited portion of the Settlement, but by degrees new streets have been laid out, and houses have been built, until the cemetery is surrounded by dwellings.

"Twenty-four years ago the French Municipality attempted to make a road through the cemetery, but such serious rioting broke out that the French Consul thought it prudent to abandon his claim to the ground, and gave the Ningpo Guild to understand that they would be left in undisturbed possession. As years have gone on, the nuisance of having a cemetery in the midst of a crowded Settlement has made itself more and more felt, and some months ago the French Municipal Council decided to expropriate the owners and to pay them compensation. The Ningpo Guild and the Chinese authorities were duly apprised of the intention, and they were urged to make their own arrangements for removing the coffins to some other site. They would not admit that the French had any right to dispossess them, and they refused to vacate the land. The French Consuls then gave the Chinese officials notice that the Municipal Council would take possession on a certain day; and as the day drew near the Taotai became very uneasy, and appealed to the Foreign Consuls to interfere in the matter, giving hints that serious rioting and loss of life would result if the French Consul persisted in his intentions.

"On the morning of the 16th, the day appointed for taking possession of the cemetery, a detachment from the French cruiser 'Éclaireur' and a strong body of police marched to the cemetery, and afforded protection to the workmen who were told off to make a breach in the cemetery wall by way of taking possession. . An angry mob watched these operations, and, as time went on, the streets filled with crowds of men, who moved about making hostile demonstrations, but the French showed great self-restraint, and no serious collision took place on that day. All night long the crowds filled the streets, and many lamps were smashed and lamp-posts uprooted.

"Early on Sunday morning a determined attack was made by the mob on one of the French police-stations, and when the small body of men within saw that their lives were in danger, they opened fire. About the same time the police and the 'Éclaireur's' men attacked bands of rioters in other quarters, with the result that on Sunday morning, as far as can be ascertained, fifteen men were shot dead or bayoneted, and about forty were seriously wounded. After that the rioters seemed to have become intimidated for a time, and the streets were left to the police. Meanwhile many of the shops in both Settlements were closed, and orders were sent to all Ningpo men—and they form 50 per cent. of the population—to go out on strike.

"Some of the principal Ningpo merchants came forward in the afternoon, and through the good offices of a peacemaker came to an understanding with the French Consul, under which it was agreed that the French should postpone taking possession of the cemetery for one month, during which time the Ningpo Guild trust to come to some amicable arrangement. The French Consul has given them to understand that he will not recede from his position; the cemetery must be given up, but he is willing that this should be done in any way that will be most pleasing to the Ningpo residents."

On the 23d of August it was announced by telegram from Shanghai that "the dispute arising out of the Ningpo Josshouse is about to be settled by French withdrawing their claims to remove the buildings in consideration for an extension of their concession as far as Si-ca Wei, an addition of 20 square miles." This raised protests from Great Britain and the United States, many of whose citizens owned property within the area thus proposed to be placed under French jurisdiction; and the distracted Tsung-li Yamên was threatened and pulled about between the contending parties for months. The final outcome was an extension of the general Foreign Settlement at Shanghai (principally British and American) and a limited extension of that especially controlled by the French. The adjustment of the question was not reached until near the end of 1899.—*Great Britain, Papers by Command: China, No. 1, 1899, and No. 1, 1900.*

A. D. **1898-1899** (June—january).—Anti-mis-

6–7

sionary insurrection at Shun-ch'ing, in Central Szechuan.—The following is from a communication addressed by the British Minister to the Tsung-li Yamên, August 2, 1898: "At Shun-ch'ing Fu the local officials, with a few of the gentry, have for years shown themselves determinedly hostile to foreigners, and have refused to allow houses to be let to missionaries. British missionaries have in consequence been forced to quarter themselves in an inn for the last six years, but even that was apparently objected to; in 1893 there was a riot, and in 1895 another, in which two missionaries were treated with brutal violence. In May of this year a house was finally rented; the District Magistrate was notified, but neither he nor the Pao-ning Taotai issued proclamations or gave protection, though requested by the missionaries to do so. The Shun-ch'ing Prefect, instead of giving protection, connived at the local opposition, and with the usual results. On the 15th June three missionaries were attacked and stoned, and one severely wounded, while passing through the city, and though protection was asked of the Prefect, he gave none, and later he and the other officials repeatedly refused to issue a Proclamation or to take any measures whatever to avert disturbances. On the 20th the Prefect feigned sickness, and could not be appealed to, and on the 27th the house leased by the missionaries was destroyed, with all the property it contained. The Roman Catholic establishment was also gutted.

"As usual the disturbance did not end at Shunch'ing. Later on a Roman Catholic Chapel at Yung ch'ang Hsien was attacked and looted, two native Christians killed, 10,000 taels of silver stolen, and a French priest [Father Fleury] seized and held to ransom by a band of rioters. I am also informed that other acts of brigandage have occurred, and that the Protestant missions at Pao-ning and Shê-Hung are in grave danger. The Provincial Government appears to absolutely ignore the recent Imperial Decrees for the prevention of missionary troubles. All the conditions point to this, or to an utter incapacity on the part of those officers to exercise satisfactory control. Her Majesty's Consul, indeed, informs me that there is one band of brigands, led by an outlaw known as Yü Mau Tzu, which is able to terrorise two important districts in the centre of Szechuan and even to overawe the Chêngtu authorities. In connection with the Shun-ch'ing affair Her Majesty's Consul has made the following demands:—1. Immediate restoration of their house to the missionaries, the officers to pay the whole cost of repairs; 2. Punishment of the ringleaders; 3. The local headmen to give security for future good conduct; 4. Compensation for all property destroyed; 5. Punishment of officials in fault. I shall look to the Yamên and see that these demands are fully satisfied and with the least possible delay."

But urgency from both England and France failed to stimulate action on the part of the Chinese government, energetic enough to stop this anti-missionary movement in Central Szechuan. What seems to have been a riot at first became a formidable revolt. "The action of the Provincial Government was paralysed by the fact that Father Fleury was still in Yü's hands, and would be killed if a move was made against the brigands. On the other side the Viceroy was informed by M. Haas, the French Consul, that if anything happened to the Father the consequences to China would be disagreeable. The Taotai was in consequence making efforts to secure the release of the prisoners by paying blackmail." In September it was reported that "Yü's power was increasing, his emissaries were scattered about in places beyond his immediate sphere of influence, and were attempting to stir up Secret Societies, and he had issued a manifesto. A riot took place at Ho Chou, 60 miles north of Chungking, on the 14th September, the American mission hospital being partially looted and a Roman Catholic establishment destroyed by fire. The Provincial Government was acting weakly and unprofitably."

Towards the end of September, "Yü marched with about 2,000 uniformed men and took up a position on the Ch'êng-tu road; thence he moved east to Tung-Liang, pillaging and burning the houses of Christians, and levying contributions on the rich. The Viceroy, at the request of the Consuls, was said to have sent 4,000 troops from Ch'êng-tu, Lu-chou, and Ho-chiang to converge on Chungking. Twelve of the rebels, who had been seized at a place only 30 miles south of the port, were publicly executed with torture in Chungking on the 30th September." In October the report was that "fresh troops were arriving, and were taking up positions along the Ch'êng-tu road, and the passes north of Chungkiug. Further executions had taken place. . . . The Procureur of the French Mission estimated that up to date the total damage done by Yü Mau-tzu was twenty persons killed, the houses of 6,000 Christians burned and their property stolen, and twelve Missions destroyed."—*Great Britain, Papers by Command: China, No. 1, 1899, p. 249, and No. 1, 1900, p. 152.*

On the 12th of October the United States Minister, Mr. Conger, sent to the State Department at Washington the following translation of a decree issued by the Empress Dowager on the 6th:
"From the opening of ports to foreign trade to the present time, foreigners and Chinese have been as one family, with undivided interests, and since missionaries from foreign countries are living in the interior, we have decreed, not three or four times, but many times, that the local officials must protect them; that the gentry and people of all the provinces must sympathize with our desire for mutual benevolence; that they must treat them truthfully and honestly, without dislike or suspicion, with the hope of lasting peaceful relations.

"Recently, there have been disturbances in the provinces which it has been impossible to avoid. There have been several cases of riot in Szechuan, which have not been settled. The stupid and ignorant people who circulate rumors and stir up strife, proceeding from light to grave differences, are most truly to be detested. On the other hand, the officials, who have not been able at convenient seasons to properly instruct the people and prevent disturbances, can not be excused from censure.

"We now especially decree again that all high provincial officials, wherever there are churches, shall distinctly instruct the local officials to most respectfully obey our several decrees, to recognize and protect the foreign missionaries as they go to and fro, and to treat them with all courtesy. If lawsuits arise between Chinese and na-

tive Christians, they must be conducted with justice and speedily concluded. Moreover, they must command and instruct the gentry and people to fulfill their duties, that there may be no quarrels or disagreements. Wherever there are foreigners traveling from place to place, they must surely be protected and the extreme limit of our hospitality extended. After the issue of this decree, if there is any lack of preparation and disturbances should arise, the officials of that locality will be severely dealt with; whether they be viceroys or governors or others they shall be punished, and it will not avail to say we have not informed you."—*U. S. Consular Reports, Feb., 1899, p. 299.*

On the 1st of November the British Consul at Chungking announced "an alarming extension of the rebellion. Flourishing communities of Christians in four districts were destroyed, and heavy contributions were laid on non-Christians. The continued inactivity of the Government troops was chiefly attributable to orders from the Yamên to the effect that the first and foremost consideration was the rescue of Père Fleury. Negotiations were being carried on by the Chungking Taotai and the Chinese Generals for the Father's release; a ransom of 100,000 taels was offered, presents were sent to Yü and his mother, and he and his lieutenants were given buttons of the third rank." The next month, however, brought on the scene a new Viceroy who really wished to suppress the insurrection, though he "complained that his hands were tied by the Yamên's instructions, which urged him to come to terms with Yü." At last this singularly energetic Viceroy got permission to fight the rebels. On arriving in front of the terrible Yü he "found that the troops who had been stationed there previously were quite untrustworthy, and that the Generals and local officials were all more or less in league with the rebels. However, as soon as it was learnt that the Treasurer meant business, a number of the rebels dispersed. The main band, under Yü Mau-tzu, about 6,000 in number, was then surrounded in Ta Tsu Hsien, after a preliminary encounter in which the rebels lost some 100 men. By the 19th January, a Maxim was brought to bear on Yü's camp, and the rebels fled like rabbits. Yü begged Père Fleury to save his life, and next day released the Father, who found his way to the Treasurer, after some narrow escapes. Yü then surrendered."

It was said at the time that the French government was demanding an indemnity in this case to the amount of £150,000. Later it was understood that the French Minister at Peking "had taken advantage of the pending missionary case to revive an old request for a Mining Concession."—*Great Britain, Papers by Command: China, No. 1, 1900.*

A. D. 1899.—Anti-missionary outbreaks, increasing piracy, and other signs of growing disorder in the country.—During 1899 there was a notable relaxation of the hard and ceaseless pressure upon China which governments, capitalists and speculators had been keeping up of late, in demands more or less peremptory for harbor leases, settlement grounds, railway franchises, mining privileges, and naval, military and commercial advantages of every possible sort. But the irritation of the country under the bullying and "nagging" of the treatment it had received from the European nations revealed itself in increasing outbreaks of popular hostility to foreigners; and these called out threats and demands, for indemnity and punishment, which were made, as a rule, in the truculent tone that had become habitual to western diplomacy in dealing with the people of the East. It was a tone which the Chinese provoked, by the childish evasions and treacherous deceptions with which their officials tried to baffle the demands made on them; but it gave no less offense, and is no less plainly to be counted among the causes of what afterwards occurred.

Throughout most of the year, the British Legation at Peking and the Consulate at Chungking were busied in obtaining satisfaction for the murder of Mr. Fleming, a missionary in the China Inland Mission, stationed at Pang Hai, near Kwei-Yang. He had been killed and the mission looted in November, 1898. The Chinese authorities claimed that he had been killed by a band of rebels. The British Consul investigated and became convinced that the missionary had been the victim of a deliberate plot, directed by the headman of the village of Chung An Chiang, where the murder occurred, and connived at by the military official Liu. The Chinese government, yielding to this conviction, caused two of the murderers to be executed, degraded and exiled all of the local officials who were involved in the crime, except the headman, and paid an indemnity of $30,000. But the headman escaped, and it was claimed by the governor of the province that he could not be found. The British authorities found evidence that he was being shielded by the governor, and demanded the dismissal of the governor, which was persistently refused. Finally, in October, 1899, the guilty headman was hunted down.

On the 18th of February, the British Minister complained energetically to the Tsung-li Yamên of the rapid increase of piracy on the Canton River. "Since November, 1898," he wrote, "that is in three months, no less than forty-seven cases of piracy in the Canton waters have been reported in the papers. In several of these cases life was taken, and it may almost be said that a reign of terror exists on the waterways of the Two Kuang. Cargo boats are afraid to travel at night, or to move about except in company, and trade is becoming to a certain extent paralysed. The Viceroy is always ailing, and it is difficult to obtain an interview with him. Her Majesty's Consul has repeatedly addressed him on the subject of these piracies in the strongest terms, but can only obtain the stereotyped reply that stringent instructions have been sent to the officials concerned. Admiral Ho, who should properly be the officer to inaugurate a vigorous campaign against the pirates, appears absolutely supine and incapable of dealing with the evil. The complaints of the Hong Kong Government and Her Majesty's Consuls show a state of affairs in Canton waters which is quite intolerable. There is no security for life or property, and as British subjects are closely concerned, it is my duty to inform your Highness and your Excellencies that unless measures are immediately taken to prevent such outrages, I shall have to report, for the consideration of Her Majesty's Government, the advisability of taking steps to protect British lives and property, either by patrolling the waterways or by placing guards on the steamers, the expense of which

would be the subject of a claim on the Chinese Government."

On the 28th of February, Herr von Bülow, the German Imperial Secretary of State for Foreign Affairs, announced in the Reichstag, at Berlin, the reception of a telegram from Tien-tsin, reporting that several Germans had been attacked and insulted in that town on the 24th, and had been compelled to take refuge in the side streets and narrow alleys. The Imperial Government, he said, had been already aware for some weeks past that a considerable feeling of irritation had manifested itself against foreigners in China, especially in the southern portion of the Province of Shantung. The Chinese Government were thereupon warned of the necessity of maintaining order and securing public safety, and, upon the receipt of the telegram above referred to, the German Minister at Peking was instructed to impress upon the Chinese Government that, if such incidents were permitted to recur, or the perpetrators allowed to escape unpunished, the consequences for China would be very serious. "We have," Herr von Bülow declared, "neither the occasion nor the desire to interfere in the internal affairs of China. But it is our duty to watch lest the life and property of our fellow subjects, whether missionaries or traders, should be made to suffer through the internal complications in China."

In March, however, the state of things at and near Peking was so far improved that the Legation guards were being withdrawn. Sir Claude MacDonald obtained leave of absence and left Peking on the 23d for a visit to England, and the business of the Legation was conducted for a time by Mr. Bax-Ironside, the Chargé d'Affaires.

In June there was an anti-missionary riot at Kienning, in the neighborhood of Foochow, excited by the murder of a boy, popular rumor ascribing the murder to foreigners. "In all directions," wrote one of the threatened missionaries, who gave an account of the occurrence, "murders were said to be taking place, though no bodies were ever found; that seemed of no consequence to the people, and the story was current, and was apparently generally believed, that these murders were done by men in our employ, and that we used the eyes and legs to make medicine. There were endless stories of people being kidnapped, chloroformed in the road by a bottle being held out to their nose, and the day I arrived it was said that eyes had been found at Tai-lui, a suburb of Kienning, and as I passed a crowd was actually on the spot seeking for the said eyes." The missionaries succeeded in escaping from the mob; but one native convert was killed, and the mission hospital and other premises were looted.

The ideas and the state of feeling out of which this attack on the missionaries and their converts grew are revealed in the following translation of a placard that was posted in Kienning in June: "We of this region have hitherto led a worthy life. All the four castes (scholars, agriculturists, artizans, traders) have kept the laws and done their duty. Of late foreigners have suddenly come among us in a disorderly march and preaching heretical doctrines. They have had from us indulgent treatment, but they have repaid us by endangering our lives. This year, in town and country, people have been hewn in two, men and women in numbers have fallen upon evil days.

Everywhere the perpetrators have been seized, and every one of them has confessed that it was by the missionary chapels they were ordered to go forth and slay men and women; to cut out their brains and marrow to make into medicine. The officials deliberately refrained from interfering. They garbled the evidence and screened the malefactors. The whole country side is filled with wrath; the officials then posted Proclamations, and arrested spreaders of false reports. The hewing down of men is hateful; but they issued no Proclamations forbidding that. Now fortunately the people is of one mind in its wrath. They have destroyed two chapels. The Ou-ning ruffian has issued another Proclamation, holding this to be the work of local rowdies. He little knows that our indignation is righteous, and that it is a unanimous expression of feeling. If the officials authorize the police to effect unjust arrests, the people will unite in a body, in every street business will be stopped, and the Wu-li missionary chapel will be destroyed, while the officials themselves will be turned out of the city, and the converts will be slain and overthrown. When cutting grass destroy the roots at the same time. Do not let dead ashes spring again into flame."

A settlement of the Kienning case was arranged locally between the British Consul at Foochow, Mr. Playfair, and the Viceroy of the province. The views of the Consul were expressed in a communication to Mr. Bax-Ironside as follows: "Since the missionaries established themselves there it is the sixth attempt made to drive them out of the region. The common people (from what I can gather) have no animus against the foreign preacher of the Gospel, and show none. On the contrary, whether moved to accept Christianity or not, they appear to recognize that missionaries are in any case there for benevolent and beneficial objects. Schools and hospitals are independent of proselytizing, and, even if the missionaries were never to make another convert, they would be doing good and useful work in spreading Western knowledge and healing the sick. In addition to this, the presence of missionaries in out-of-the-way places in China has one unquestionable advantage. To use the phrase of Sir Thomas Wade, they 'multiply the points of contact,' and familiarize the Chinese with the sight of the European. To the missionary, either as a preacher of the Gospel or as a dispenser of benefits, the populace at Kienning does not seem to have shown any aversion; yet six times this populace has risen and tried to drive the missionaries from the place. The logical inference is that the Kienning peasant, though tolerant by nature, is subject to some outside influence. He is moved, not by what he sees, but by what he is told exists beyond his range of vision; and these things are pointed out to him by such as he believes to be his intellectual superiors, and as have, therefore, the faculty of perceiving what is hid from himself. The history of almost every anti-missionary movement in China points to the same process. Why the educated classes of this land should be so inveterately hostile to the foreigner is a difficult question to answer. It has been suggested that the Chinese of this type have an ineradicable conviction that every European is at heart a 'land-grabber'; that missionaries are the advance agents of their Governments; that the Bible is

the certain forerunner of the gun-boat; and that where the missionary comes as a sojourner he means to stay as a proprietor; consequently, that the only hope of integrity for China is that her loyal sons should on every occasion destroy the baneful germ. Extravagant and (in the instance of Kienning) far-fetched as these notions may seem, I am convinced that the literati and gentry have been at the root not only of the present outbreak, but of the others which have preceded it. While, therefore, I have insisted throughout that Kienning must be made a place of safe residence for the British missionary, I have considered that the only way to attain that result will be to shackle the hands of the gentry by making any further breach of the peace a sure precursor of punishment."

To this end, Mr. Playfair's exactions included, not only the trial and punishment of those guilty of the riot and the murder, but the signing of a bond by twenty-four leading notables of Kienning, binding them, with penalties, to protect the missionaries. His demand was complied with, and, on the 29th of September, he reported that the required bond had been given. He added: "Before accepting it, however, I required the authorities to inform me officially that the terms, which to me seemed somewhat vague, were understood by the authorities to extend the responsibility of the gentry to any outbreak of the populace. I received this intimation and I consider that it supplements the original wording effectually."

In November the German government made public the substance of an official telegram received from Peking, reporting a serious state of disturbance in the German missionary districts of Shantung: "It appears from this communication that the followers of the sects of the 'Red Fist' and the 'Great Knife' are in a state of revolt against the Administration and the people in that province, and are engaged in plunder and rapine in many places. The native Christians suffer no less than the rest of the population by this revolt. Money was usually extorted from them, and their dwellings were pillaged or destroyed. The Italian Mission, situated in the adjoining district, were faring no better, and their chapel had just been burned down. Owing, however, to the unremitting representations of the German Minister, the Chinese Government have caused several of the agitators to be arrested by the local authorities, and they are taking further steps in this direction, with the result that order is gradually being restored. At several places the native Christians, with their non-Christian fellow-countrymen, repulsed the rebels by force of arms. The Provincial Governor has promised the authorities of the Mission a full indemnity for the losses suffered by them and by the other Christians, and several payments have already been made."

On the 4th of December, the following despatch was sent to London from the British Legation at Peking: "During the delimitation of French leased territory at Kwang-chou-wan on the 13th November, Chinese villagers seized two French officers and decapitated them. The execution of a dignitary—the Prefect concerned in the murder—has been demanded by the French Minister, as well as the dismissal of the Canton Viceroy, who is also implicated. The Chinese Commissioner engaged in the delimitation and the gunboat in which he travelled are held by the French as hostages."

A. D. 1899 (March).—The Tsung-li Yamên. — Its character and position. — The power of the Empress Dowager. — The Tsung-li Yamên is a small body of Councillors who form a species of Cabinet, with a special obligation to advise the Emperor on foreign affairs. "They have no constitutional position whatever, they have no powers except those derived from the Emperor, and they are very much afraid for themselves. He may by mere fiat deprive them of their rank, which is high ; he may 'squeeze' them of their wealth, which is often great ; he may banish them from the delights of Pekin to very unpleasant places; or he may order them to be quietly decapitated or cut slowly into little pieces. At such times their preoccupation is neither their country nor their immediate business, nor even their own advancement, but to avoid offending the irritable earthly deity who holds their lives and fortunes in his hands. Such a time it is just now. The Empress-Dowager is Emperor in all but name, she has ideas and a will, and she is suspicious to the last degree. There is no possibility of opposing her, for she has drawn together eighty thousand troops round Pekin, who while she pays their Generals will execute anybody she pleases; there is no possibility of appeal from her, for she represents a theocracy ; and there is no possibility of overpowering her mind, for she is that dreadful phenomenon four or five times revealed in history, an Asiatic woman possessed of absolute power, and determined to sweep away all who oppose, or whom she suspects of opposition, from her path. Under her régime the members of the Tsung-li Yamên are powerless nonentities, trembling with fear lest, if they make a blunder, they may awaken the anger of their all-powerful and implacable Sovereign, whose motives they themselves often fail to fathom."—*The Spectator (London), March* 18, 1899.

A. D. 1899 (March—April). — Agreement between England and Russia concerning their railway interests in China.—On the 28th of April, 1899, the governments of Great Britain and Russia exchanged notes, embodying an agreement (practically arrived at in the previous month) concerning their respective railway interests in China, in the following terms : "Russia and Great Britain, animated by the sincere desire to avoid in China all cause of conflict on questions where their interests meet, and taking into consideration the economic and geographical gravitation of certain parts of that Empire, have agreed as follows : 1. Russia engages not to seek for her own account, or on behalf of Russian subjects or of others, any railway concessions in the basin of the Yang-tsze, and not to obstruct, directly or indirectly, applications for railway concessions in that region supported by the British Government. 2. Great Britain, on her part, engages not to seek for her own account, or on behalf of British subjects or of others, any railway concessions to the north of the Great Wall of China, and not to obstruct, directly or indirectly, applications for railway concessions in that region supported by the Russian Government. The two contracting parties, having nowise in view to infringe in any way the sovereign rights of China or of ex-

isting treaties, will not fail to communicate to the Chinese Government the present arrangement, which, by averting all cause of complication between them, is of a nature to consolidate peace in the far East, and to serve the primordial interests of China herself."

Second Note. "In order to complete the notes exchanged this day respecting the partition of spheres for concessions for the construction and working of railways in China, it has been agreed to record in the present additional note the arrangement arrived at with regard to the line Shanghaikuan-Newchwang, for the construction of which a loan has been already contracted by the Chinese Government with the Shanghai-Hongkong Bank, acting on behalf of the British and Chinese corporation. The general arrangement established by the above-mentioned notes is not to infringe in any way the rights acquired under the said loan contract, and the Chinese Government may appoint both an English engineer and a European accountant to supervise the construction of the line in question, and the expenditure of the money appropriated to it. But it remains understood that this fact can not be taken as constituting a right of property or foreign control, and that the line in question is to remain a Chinese line under the control of the Chinese Government, and can not be mortgaged or alienated to a non-Chinese Company. As regards the branch line from Siaoheichan to Sinminting, in addition to the aforesaid restrictions, it has been agreed that it is to be constructed by China herself, which may permit European— not necessarily British—engineers to periodically inspect it, and to verify and certify that the work is being properly executed. The present special agreement is naturally not to interfere in any way with the right of the Russian Government to support, if it thinks fit, applications of Russian subjects or establishments for concessions for railways, which, starting from the main Manchurian line in a southwesterly direction, would traverse the region in which the Chinese line terminating at Sinminting and Newchwang is to be constructed."—*Great Britain, Papers by Command, Treaty Series, No.* 11, 1899.

A. D. 1899 (April).—Increasing ascendancy of Manchus in the **government.**—On the 17th of April, Mr. Bax-Ironside reported to Lord Salisbury : "There has been no change of importance to note in the political situation. The tendency to replace Chinese by Manchus in the important political posts of the Empire is increasing. There are sixty-two Viceroys, Governors, Treasurers, and Judges of the eighteen provinces and the New Dominion. Twenty-four of these posts are now held by Manchus, whereas before the coup d'état only thirteen of them were so occupied. So large a percentage of Manchus in the highest positions tends to indicate a retrograde administration, as the Manchus are, as a race, very inferior to the Chinese in intelligence and capacity, and their appointment to important positions is viewed with disfavour by the Chinese themselves. The Dowager-Empress has sent special instructions both to Moukden and Kirin to raise the present standard of the Manchu schools in those towns to that existing in the ordinary schools in Peking."— *Great Britain, Papers by Command : China, No.* 1, 1900, *p.* 129.

A. D. 1899 (May—July).—Representation

in the Peace Conference at The Hague. See (in this vol.) PEACE CONFERENCE.

A. D. 1899 (August).—Talienwan declared a free port.—"The Emperor of Russia in a quaintly worded Imperial Order issued on Sunday last [August 13] and addressed to the Minister of Finance, has declared that after the completion of the railway Talienwan shall be a free port during the whole duration of the lease from China. In the course of the Order the Emperor says : 'Thanks to the wise decision of the Chinese Government, we shall through the railway lines in course of construction be united with China,—a result which gives to all nations the immeasurable gain of easy communication and lightens the operations of the world's trade.' The Emperor also speaks of 'a rapprochement between the peoples of the West and East' (brought about apparently by obtaining an outlet for the great Siberian railway) as 'our historic aim.'"—*Spectator (London), Aug.* 19, 1899.

A. D. 1899 (December). — Li Hung-chang appointed Acting Viceroy at Canton.—On the 20th of December it was announced that the Viceroy at Canton had been ordered to Peking and that Li Hung-chang had been appointed Acting Viceroy of Kwangtung and Kwangsi —the provinces of which Canton is the Viceroyal seat.

A. D. 1899-1900 (September—February).— Pledges of an "open-door" commercial policy in China obtained by the government of the United States from the governments of Great Britain, Russia, France, Germany, Italy and Japan.—On the 6th of September, 1899, the American Secretary of State, Mr. John Hay, despatched to the United States Ambassador at Berlin the following instructions, copies of which were forwarded at the same time to the Ambassadors at London and St. Petersburg, to be communicated to the British and Russian governments :

"At the time when the Government of the United States was informed by that of Germany that it had leased from His Majesty the Emperor of China the port of Kiao-chao and the adjacent territory in the province of Shantung, assurances were given to the ambassador of the United States at Berlin by the Imperial German minister for foreign affairs that the rights and privileges insured by treaties with China to citizens of the United States would not thereby suffer or be in anywise impaired within the area over which Germany had thus obtained control. More recently, however, the British Government recognized by a formal agreement with Germany the exclusive right of the latter country to enjoy in said leased area and the contiguous 'sphere of influence or interest' certain privileges, more especially those relating to railroads and mining enterprises ; but, as the exact nature and extent of the rights thus recognized have not been clearly defined, it is possible that serious conflicts of interest may at any time arise, not only between British and German subjects within said area, but that the interests of our citizens may also be jeopardized thereby. Earnestly desirous to remove any cause of irritation and to insure at the same time to the commerce of all nations in China the undoubted benefits which should accrue from a formal recognition by the various powers claiming 'spheres of interest,' that they shall enjoy perfect equality

of treatment for their commerce and navigation within such 'spheres,' the Government of the United States would be pleased to see His German Majesty's Government give formal assurances and lend its coöperation in securing like assurances from the other interested powers that each within its respective sphere of whatever influence—

"First. Will in no way interfere with any treaty port or any vested interest within any socalled 'sphere of interest' or leased territory it may have in China.

"Second. That the Chinese treaty tariff of the time being shall apply to all merchandise landed or shipped to all such ports as are within said 'sphere of interest' (unless they be 'free ports'), no matter to what nationality it may belong, and that duties so leviable shall be collected by the Chinese Government.

"Third. That it will levy no higher harbor duties on vessels of another nationality frequenting any port in such 'sphere' than shall be levied on vessels of its own nationality, and no higher railroad charges over lines built, controlled, or operated within its 'sphere' on merchandise belonging to citizens or subjects of other nationalities transported through such 'sphere' than shall be levied on similar merchandise belonging to its own nationals transported over equal distances.

"The liberal policy pursued by His Imperial German Majesty in declaring Kiao-chao a free port and in aiding the Chinese Government in the establishment there of a custom-house are so clearly in line with the proposition which this Government is anxious to see recognized that it entertains the strongest hope that Germany will give its acceptance and hearty support. The recent ukase of His Majesty the Emperor of Russia declaring the port of Ta-lien-wan open during the whole of the lease under which it is held from China, to the merchant ships of all nations, coupled with the categorical assurances made to this Government by His Imperial Majesty's representative at this capital at the time, and since repeated to me by the present Russian ambassador, seem to insure the support of the Emperor to the proposed measure. Our ambassador at the Court of St. Petersburg has, in consequence, been instructed to submit it to the Russian Government and to request their early consideration of it. A copy of my instruction on the subject to Mr. Tower is herewith inclosed for your confidential information. The commercial interests of Great Britain and Japan will be so clearly served by the desired declaration of intentions, and the views of the Governments of these countries as to the desirability of the adoption of measures insuring the benefits of equality of treatment of all foreign trade throughout China are so similar to those entertained by the United States, that their acceptance of the propositions herein outlined and their coöperation in advocating their adoption by the other powers can be confidently expected. I inclose herewith copy of the instruction which I have sent to Mr. Choate on the subject. In view of the present favorable conditions, you are instructed to submit the above considerations to His Imperial German Majesty's minister for foreign affairs, and to request his early consideration of the subject. Copy of this instruction is sent to our ambassadors at London and at St. Petersburg for their information." Subsequently the same proposal was addressed to the governments of France, Italy and Japan.

On the 30th of November, Lord Salisbury addressed to Ambassador Choate the reply of his government, as follows: "I have the honor to state that I have carefully considered, in communication with my colleagues, the proposal contained in your excellency's note of September 22 that a declaration should be made by foreign powers claiming 'spheres of interest' in China as to their intentions in regard to the treatment of foreign trade and interest therein. I have much pleasure in informing your excellency that Her Majesty's Government will be prepared to make a declaration in the sense desired by your Government in regard to the leased territory of Wei-hai Wei and all territory in China which may hereafter be acquired by Great Britain by lease or otherwise, and all spheres of interest now held or that may hereafter be held by her in China, provided that a similar declaration is made by other powers concerned."

Ambassador Porter, at Paris, received a prompt reply, December 16, from the French Minister for Foreign Affairs, M. Delcassé, in the following note: "The declarations which I made in the Chamber on the 24th of November last, and which I have had occasion to recall to you since then, show clearly the sentiments of the Government of the Republic. It desires throughout the whole of China and, with the quite natural reservation that all the powers interested give an assurance of their willingness to act likewise, is ready to apply in the territories which are leased to it, equal treatment to the citizens and subjects of all nations, especially in the matter of customs duties and navigation dues, as well as transportation tariffs on railways."

Viscount Aoki, Minister for Foreign Affairs, replied for the government of Japan, December 26, in the following note to Minister Buck: "I have the happy duty of assuring your excellency that the Imperial Government will have no hesitation to give their assent to so just and fair a proposal of the United States, provided that all the other powers concerned shall accept the same."

The reply of the Russian government was addressed to Ambassador Tower by Count Mouravieff, on the 30th of December, in the following terms: "In so far as the territory leased by China to Russia is concerned, the Imperial Government has already demonstrated its firm intention to follow the policy of 'the open door' by creating Dalny (Ta-lien-wan) a free port; and if at some future time that port, although remaining free itself, should be separated by a customs limit from other portions of the territory in question, the customs duties would be levied, in the zone subject to the tariff, upon all foreign merchandise without distinction as to nationality. As to the ports now opened or hereafter to be opened to foreign commerce by the Chinese Government, and which lie beyond the territory leased to Russia, the settlement of the question of customs duties belongs to China herself, and the Imperial Government has no intention whatever of claiming any privileges for its own subjects to the exclusion of other foreigners. It is to be understood, however, that this assurance of the Imperial Government is given upon condition that a similar declaration shall be made by other Powers having interests in China.

With the conviction that this reply is such as to satisfy the inquiry made in the aforementioned note, the Imperial Government is happy to have complied with the wishes of the American Government, especially as it attaches the highest value to anything that may strengthen and consolidate the traditional relations of friendship existing between the two countries."

On the 7th of January the reply of the Italian government was addressed to Minister Draper, at Rome, by the Marquis Visconti Venosta, as follows: "Supplementary to what you had already done me the honor of communicating to me in your note of December 9, 1899, your excellency informed me yesterday of the telegraphic note received from your Government that all the powers consulted by the cabinet of Washington concerning the suitability of adopting a line of policy which would insure to the trade of the whole world equality of treatment in China have given a favorable reply. Referring to your communications and to the statements in my note of December 23 last, I take pleasure in saying that the Government of the King adheres willingly to the proposals set forth in said note of December 9."

Finally, on the 19th of February, Count von Bülow wrote to Ambassador White, at Berlin: "As recognized by the Government of the United States of America, according to your excellency's note, . . . the Imperial Government has from the beginning not only asserted but also practically carried out to the fullest extent in its Chinese possessions absolute equality of treatment of all nations with regard to trade, navigation, and commerce. The Imperial Government entertains no thought of departing in the future from this principle, which at once excludes any prejudicial or disadvantageous commercial treatment of the citizens of the United States of America, so long as it is not forced to do so, on account of considerations of reciprocity, by a divergence from it by other governments. If, therefore, the other powers interested in the industrial development of the Chinese Empire are willing to recognize the same principles, this can only be desired by the Imperial Government, which in this case upon being requested will gladly be ready to participate with the United States of America and the other powers in an agreement made upon these lines, by which the same rights are reciprocally secured."

Having, now, the assent of all the Powers which hold leased territory or claim "spheres of interest" in China, Secretary Hay sent instructions to the Ambassadors and Ministers representing the government of the United States at the capital of each, in the following form: "The —— Government having accepted the declaration suggested by the United States concerning foreign trade in China, the terms of which I transmitted to you in my instruction No. —— of ——, and like action having been taken by all the various powers having leased territory or so-called 'spheres of interest' in the Chinese Empire, as shown by the notes which I herewith transmit to you, you will please inform the government to which you are accredited that the condition originally attached to its acceptance—that all other powers concerned should likewise accept the proposals of the United States—having been complied with, this

Government will therefore consider the assent given to it by —— as final and definitive."— *United States, 56th Cong., 1st Sess., House Doc. No. 547.*

A. D. 1900 (January).—**Imperial** Decree relative to the succession to the Throne.—The following is a translation of an Imperial Decree, "by the Emperor's own pen," which appeared in the "Peking Gazette," January 24, 1900:

"When at a tender age we entered into the succession to the throne, Her Majesty the Empress-Dowager graciously undertook the rule of the country as Regent, taught and guided us with diligence, and managed all things, great and small, with unremitting care, until we ourself assumed the government. Thereafter the times again became critical. We bent all our thoughts and energies to the task of ruling rightly, striving to requite Her Majesty's loving kindness, that so we might fulfil the weighty duties intrusted to us by the late Emperor Mu Tsung Yi (T'ung Chih). But since last year we have suffered from ill-health, affairs of State have increased in magnitude and perplexity, and we have lived in constant dread of going wrong. Reflecting on the supreme importance of the worship of our ancestors and of the spirits of the land, we therefore implored the Empress-Dowager to advise us in the government. This was more than a year ago, but we have never been restored to health, and we have not the strength to perform in person the great sacrifices at the altar of Heaven and in the temples of the spirits of the land. And now the times are full of difficulties. We see Her Gracious Majesty's anxious toil by day and by night, never laid aside for rest or leisure, and with troubled mind we examine ourself, taking no comfort in sleep or food, but ever dwelling in thought on the labours of our ancestors in founding the dynasty, and ever fearful lest our strength be not equal to our task.

"Moreover, we call to mind how, when we first succeeded to the throne, we reverently received the Empress-Dowager's Decree that as soon as a Prince should be born to us he should become the heir by adoption to the late Emperor Mu Tsung Yi (T'ung Chih). This is known to all the officials and people throughout the Empire. But we suffer from an incurable disease, and it is impossible for us to beget a son, so that the Emperor Mu Tsung Yi has no posterity, and the consequences to the lines of succession are of the utmost gravity. Sorrowfully thinking on this, and feeling that there is no place to hide ourself for shame, how can we look forward to recovery from all our ailments? We have therefore humbly implored Her Sacred Majesty carefully to select from among the near branches of our family a good and worthy member, who should found a line of posterity for the Emperor Mu Tsung Yi (T'ung Chih), and to whom the Throne should revert hereafter. After repeated entreaties, Her Majesty has now deigned to grant her consent that P'u Chün, son of Tsai Yi, Prince Tuan, should be adopted as the son of the late Emperor Mu Tsung Yi (T'ung Chih). We have received Her Majesty's Decree with unspeakable joy, and in reverent obedience to her gracious instruction we appoint P'u Chün, son of Tsai Yi, as Prince Imperial, to carry on the dynastic succession. Let this Decree be made known to all men." — *Great Britain, Parliamentary Pub-*

lications (*Papers by Command: China, No. 3, 1900, pp.* 15–16).

A. D. 1900 (January—March).—First **ac**counts **of** the secret society of "the Boxers" and their bloody work.—The murder of **Mr.** Brooks, the missionary.—Prolonged **effort of** foreign Ministers to procure an Imperial Edict for the suppression of the hostile secret societies.—A naval demonstration **recom**mended.—Testimony of **Sir Robert Hart** as to the causes and the patriotic inspiration of the Boxer movement.—The year 1900 opened with news of the murder of Mr. Brooks, of the Church of England Mission in northern Shantung, who was wounded and captured December 30 and beheaded the day following, by a band of marauders belonging to a secret organization which soon became notorious under the name of the society of " the Boxers." The British Minister at Peking reported it to London on the 4th of January, and on the 5th he gave the following account of the state of affairs in northern Shantung, where the outrage occurred: "For several months past the northern part of the Province of Shantung has been disturbed by bands of rebels connected with various Secret Societies, who have been defying the authorities and pillaging the people. An organization known as the 'Boxers' has attained special notoriety, and their ravages recently spread over a large portion of Southern Chihli, where the native Christians appear to have suffered even more than the rest of the inhabitants from the lawlessness of these marauders. The danger to which, in both provinces, foreign missionary establishments have been thus exposed, has been the subject of repeated representations to the Chinese Government by others of the foreign Representatives—especially the German and United States' Ministers—and myself. Early last month the Governor of Shantung, Yü Hsien, was ordered to vacate his post and come to Peking for audience, and the General Yüan Shih-K'ai was appointed Acting Governor in his place. In Southern Chihli the task of dealing with the disturbances was entrusted to the Viceroy at Tien-tsin. Her Majesty's Consul at Tientsin has had repeatedly to complain to the latter of the inadequacy of the protection afforded to British life and property in the districts affected by the rebellion; and in consequence of these representations and of my own communications to the Tsung-li Yamên, guards of soldiers have been stationed for the special protection of the missionary premises which were endangered. On the 29th ultimo I took occasion to warn the Yamên by letter that if the disorder were not vigorously quelled, international complications were likely to ensue."

After narrating an interview with the Tsung-li Yamên on the subject of the murder of Mr. Brooks, and repeating the assurances he had received of vigorous measures to punish the murderers, Minister MacDonald concluded his despatch by saying: "In a note which I addressed to the Yamên this morning I took occasion to remind the Ministers that there were other British missionaries living in the district where Mr. Brooks was killed, and to impress upon their Excellencies the necessity of securing efficient protection to these. I do not, however, entertain serious apprehensions as to their safety, because guards of soldiers have been for some time past stationed to protect the various missionary residences. The unfortunate man who was murdered was seized when he was travelling by wheel-barrow, without escort, through the country infested by the rebels."

A few days later, Bishop Scott, of the Church of England Mission, at Peking, received from Mr. Brown, another missionary in Shantung province, the following telegram: "Outlook very black; daily marauding; constant danger; Edict suppressing published; troops present, but useless; officials complete inaction; T'ai An Prefect blocks; secret orders from Throne to encourage." On this Sir Claude again called upon the Yamên, and "spoke to them," he says, "in terms of the gravest warning. While I could not believe it possible, I said, that the rumours of secret orders from the Throne were true, the mere fact of the currency of such rumours showed the impression which the conduct of the Prefect conveyed to the public. So much was I impressed by this, that I had come to-day especially to protest against the behaviour of the Shantung officials. The whole of the present difficulty could be traced to the attitude of the late Governor of Shantung, Yü Hsien, who secretly encouraged the seditious Society known as 'the Boxers.' I had again and again pointed out to the Ministers that until China dealt with the high authorities in such cases these outrages would not cease. I asked the Ministers to telegraph to the new Governor Yüan that I had called at the Yamên that day to complain of the conduct of the Prefect of T'ai An. The Ministers attempted to excuse the inertia of the local officials on the plea that their difficulties were very great. The primary cause of the trouble was the bad feeling existing between the converts and the ordinary natives. This had developed until bands of marauders had formed, who harassed Christians and other natives alike. The local officials had hitherto not had sufficient force to cope with so widespread a rising, but now that Yüan and his troops had been sent to the province they hoped for the speedy restoration of order. I impressed upon the Ministers in the most emphatic manner my view of the gravity of the situation. The Imperial Edict expressing sorrow for what had occurred and enjoining strong measures was satisfactory so far as it went; but Her Majesty's Government required something more than mere words, and would now await action on the part of the Chinese Government in conformity with their promises."

On the day of this interview (January 11), an Imperial Decree was issued by the Chinese government, opening in ambiguous terms and decreeing nothing. "Of late," it said, "in all the provinces brigandage has become daily more prevalent, and missionary cases have recurred with frequency. Most critics point to seditious Societies as the cause, and ask for rigorous suppression and punishment of these. But reflection shows that Societies are of different kinds. When worthless vagabonds form themselves into bands and sworn confederacies, and relying on their numbers create disturbances, the law can show absolutely no leniency to them On the other hand, when peaceful and law-abiding people practise their skill in mechanical arts for the self-preservation of themselves and their families, or when they combine in village communities for the mutual protection of the rural population, this is in accordance with the public-spirited principle (enjoined by Mencius) of 'keeping mutual watch and giving mutual help.' Some local authorities, when a case arises, do not regard this distinction, but, listening to false and idle rumours, regard all alike as seditious Societies, and involve all in one indiscriminate slaughter. The result is that no distinction being made between the good and the evil, men's minds are thrown into fear and doubt. This is, indeed, 'adding fuel to stop a fire,' 'driving fish to the deep part of the pool to catch them.' It means, not that the people are disorderly, but that the administration is bad."

The foreign ministers at Peking soon learned that this ambiguous decree had given encouragement to the "Boxers," and the British, American, German, French and Italian representatives, by agreement, addressed an "identic note" to the Yamên, dated January 27, in which, referring to the state of affairs in north Shantung and in the centre and south of Chihli, each one said: "This state of affairs, which is a disgrace to any civilized country, has been brought about by the riotous and lawless behaviour of certain ruffians who have banded themselves together into two Societies, termed respectively the 'Fist of Righteous Harmony' and the 'Big Sword Society,' and by the apathy, and in some instances actual connivance and encouragement of these Societies by the local officials. The members of these Societies go about pillaging the homes of Christian converts, breaking down their chapels, robbing and ill-treating inoffensive women and children, and it is a fact, to which I would draw the special attention of your Highness and your Excellencies, that on the banners which are carried by these riotous and lawless people are inscribed the words, 'Exterminate the Foreigners.'

"On the 11th January an Imperial Decree was issued drawing a distinction between good and bad Societies. The wording of this Decree has unfortunately given rise to a widespread impression that such Associations as the 'Fist of Righteous Harmony' and the 'Big Sword Society' are regarded with favour by the Chinese Government, and their members have openly expressed their gratification and have been encouraged by the Decree to continue to carry on their outrages against the Christian converts. I cannot for a moment suppose that such was the intention of this Decree. These Societies are, as I have shown, of a most pernicious and rebellious character.

"I earnestly beg to draw the serious attention of the Throne to the circumstances above described: the disorders have not reached such a stage that they cannot be stamped out by prompt and energetic action: but if such action be not immediately taken, the rioters will be encouraged to think that they have the support of the Government and proceed to graver crimes, thereby seriously endangering international relations. As a preliminary measure, and one to which I attach the greatest importance, I have to beg that an Imperial Decree be published and promulgated, ordering by name the complete suppression and abolition of the 'Fist of Righteous Harmony' and the 'Big Sword Societies,' and I request that it may be distinctly stated in the Decree that to belong to either of these Societies, or to harbour any of its members, is a criminal offence against the laws of China."

In communicating the above note to Lord Salisbury, Sir Claude MacDonald explained : "The name of the Society given in the note as 'The Fist of Righteous Harmony' is the same as the 'Boxers.' The latter name was given in the first instance, either by missionaries or newspapers, but does not convey the meaning of the Chinese words. The idea underlying the name is that the members of the Society will unite to uphold the cause of righteousness, if necessary by force."

On the 2ist of February no reply to the identic note had been given, and the five foreign Ministers then wrote again. This brought an answer so evasive that they asked for an interview with the Yamên,and it was appointed for March 2d. On the evening of the 1st they received copies of a proclamation which the Governor-General of Chihli had been commanded to issue. The proclamation embodied an Imperial Decree, transmitted to the Governor-General on the 21st of February, which said : "Last year the Govcruor of Shantung telegraphed that the Society known as 'the Fist of Righteous Harmony' in many of his districts, under the plea of enmity to foreign religions, were raising disturbances in all directions, and had extended their operations into the southern part of Chihli. We have repeatedly ordered the Governor-General of Chihli and the Governor of Shantung to send soldiers to keep the peace. But it is to be feared that if stern measures of suppression of such proceedings as secretly establishing societies with names and collecting in numbers to raise disturbances be not taken, the ignorant populace will be deluded and excited, and as time goes on things will grow worse, and when some serious case ensues we shall be compelled to employ troops to extirpate the evil. The sufferers would be truly many, and the throne cannot bear to slay without warning. Let the Governor-General of Chihli and the Governor of Shantung issue the most stringent Proclamations admonishing the people and strictly prohibiting (the societies) so that our people may all know that to secretly establish societies is contrary to prohibition and a breach of the law."

To this the Governor-General of Chihli added, in his own name : " I (the Governor-General) find it settled by decided cases that those people of no occupation, busybodies who style themselves Professors, and practise boxing, and play with clubs, and teach people their arts; those also who learn from these men, and those who march about and parade the villages and marts flourishing tridents, and playing with sticks, hoodwinking the populace to make a profit for themselves, are strictly forbidden to carry on such practices. Should any disobey, on arrest the principals will receive 100 blows with the heavy bamboo, and be banished to a distance of 1,000 miles. The pupils will receive the same beating, and be banished to another province for three years, and on expiration of that period and return to their native place be subjected to strict surveillance. Should any inn, temple or house harbour these people without report to the officials, or should the police and others not search them out and arrest them, the delinquents will be sentenced to eighty blows with the heavy bamboo for improper conduct in the higher degree.

" From this it appears that teaching or prsc-

tising boxing and club play, and deluding the people for private gain are fundamentally contrary to law. But of late some of the ignorant populace have been deluded by ruffians from other parts of the Empire who talk of charms and incantations and spiritual incarnations which protect from guns and cannon. They have dared to secretly establish the Society of the Fist of Righteous Harmony and have practised drill with fists and clubs. The movement has spread in all directions, and under the plea of hatred of foreign religions these people have harried the country. When soldiers and runners came to make arrests, turbulent ruffians had the audacity to defy them, relying on their numbers, thereby exhibiting a still greater contempt for the law. . . .

"In addition to instructing all the local officials to adopt strict measures of prohibition and to punish without fail all offenders, I hereby issue this most stringent admonition and notify all people in my jurisdiction, gentry and every class of the population, that you should clearly understand that the establishment and formation of secret societies for the practice of boxing and club exercises are contrary to prohibition and a breach of the law. The assembly of mobs to create disturbances and all violent outrages are acts which the law will still less brook. . . . The converts and the ordinary people are all the subjects of the throne, and are regarded by the Government with impartial benevolence. No distinction is made between them. Should they have lawsuits they must bow to the judgments of the officials. The ordinary people must not give way to rage, and by violent acts create feuds and trouble. The converts on the other hand must not stir up strife and oppress the people or incite the missionaries to screen them and help them to obtain the upper hand."

According to appointment, the interview with the Yamên took place on the 2d of March : " Mr. Conger, United States' Minister, Baron von Ketteler, German Minister, Marquis Salvago, Italian Minister, Baron d'Anthouard, French Chargé d'Affaires, and myself," writes Sir Claude MacDonald, " were received at the Yamên by Prince Ch'ing and nearly all the Ministers. On behalf of myself and my colleagues I recapitulated the circumstances, as detailed above, which had led to the demand which we now made. My colleagues all expressed to the Prince and Ministers their entire concurrence with the language I used. Mr. Conger reminded the Yamên of the incredulity with which they had listened to his representations regarding these disturbances over three months ago, and the promises they had been making ever since, from which nothing had resulted. Baron von Ketteler laid special stress on the fact that in the Decree just communicated no mention was made of the 'Ta Tao Hui,' or 'Big Knife Society,' the denunciation of which, equally with that of the ' I-Ho-Ch'uan,' or ' Fist of Righteous Harmony,' had been demanded. The Prince and Ministers protested emphatically that the Throne was earnest in its determination to put a stop to the outrages committed by these Societies. They maintained that the method adopted for promulgating the Imperial Decree, that of sending it to the Governors of the provinces concerned, to be embodied in a Proclamation and acted upon, was much speedier and more effective than that of publishing a Decree in the ' Peking Gazette,' as suggested by us. With regard to the omission of the term 'Ta Tao Hui' from the Decree, they declared that this Society was now the same as the 'I-Ho-Ch'uan.'"

At the close of the interview the five Ministers presented identic notes to the Yamên, in which each said : "I request that an Imperial Decree may be issued and published in the 'Peking Gazette' ordering by name the complete suppression and abolition of the 'Fist of Righteous Harmony' and 'Big Sword Societies,' and I request that it may be distinctly stated in the Decree that to belong to either of these societies or to harbour any of its members is a criminal offence against the law of China. Nothing less than this will, I am convinced, put an end to the outrages against Christians which have lately been so prevalent in Chihli and Shantung. Should the Chinese Government refuse this reasonable request I shall be compelled to report to my Government their failure to take what may be called only an ordinary precaution against a most pernicious and anti-foreign organization. The consequences of further disorder in the districts concerned cannot fail to be extremely serious to the Chinese Government."

The reply of the Yamên to this "identic note" was a lengthy argument to show that publication in the "Peking Gazette" of the Imperial Edict against "Boxers" would be contrary to "an established rule of public business in China which it is impossible to alter"; and that, furthermore, it would be useless, because the common people of the provinces would not see it. Not satisfied with this reply, the Ministers, on the 10th of March, addressed another identic note to the Yamên, in the following words : "Acknowledging receipt of your Highness' and your Excellencies' note of the 7th March, I regret to say that it is in no way either an adequate or satisfactory reply to my notes or my verbal requests concerning the suppression of the two Societies known as the 'Big Sword' and 'Fist of Righteous Harmony.' I therefore am obliged to repeat the requests, and because of the rapid spread of these Societies, proof of which is accumulating every day, and which the Imperial Decree of the 11th January greatly encouraged, I insist that an absolute prohibitive Decree for all China, mentioning these two Societies by name, be forthwith issued and published in the 'Peking Gazette,' as was done with the Decree of the 11th January. Should I not receive a favourable answer without delay, I shall report the matter to my Government, and urge strongly the advisability of the adoption of other measures for the protection of the lives and property of British subjects in China."

On the same day, each of the Ministers cabled the following recommendation to his government : "If the Chinese Government should refuse to publish the Decree we have required, and should the state of affairs not materially improve, I would respectfully recommend that a few ships of war of each nationality concerned should make a naval demonstration in North Chinese waters. Identic recommendations are being telegraphed home by my four colleagues above-mentioned."

On the 16th, Sir Claude wrote: "No reply has yet been received from the Tsung-li Yamên to the note of the 10th March, and it was with serious misgivings as to the attitude of the Chinese Government on this question that I read yesterday the official announcement of the appointment of Yü Hsien, lately Governor of Shantung, to the post of Governor of Shansi. The growth and impunity of the anti-Christian Societies in Shantung has been universally ascribed to the sympathy and encouragement accorded to them by this high officer, and his conduct has for some time past formed the subject of strong representations on the part of several of the foreign Representatives."—*Great Britain, Papers by Command : China, No. 3, 1900, pp. 3–26.*

"The foundation of the 'Boxers' can be traced to one man, Yü Hsien, who, when Prefect of Tsao-chau, in the south-west corner of Shan-tung, organized a band of men as local militia or trainbands. For them he revived the ancient appellation of 'I-Ho-Ch'üan,' the Patriotic Harmony Fists. Armed with long swords, they were known popularly as the Ta-tao-huei, or Big Knife Society. After the occupation of Kiao-chan Bay the society grew in force, the professed objects of its members being to oppose the exactions of native Catholics and to resist further German aggression. They became anti-Christian and anti-foreign. They became a religious sect, and underwent a fantastic kind of spiritual training of weird incantations and grotesque gymnastics, which they professed to believe rendered them impervious to the sword and to the bullet of the white man. Three deities they specially selected as their own—namely, Kwanti, the God of War and patron deity of the present dynasty, Kwang Chêng-tze, an incarnation of Laotze, and the Joyful Buddha of the Falstaffian Belly. They made Taoist and Buddhist temples their headquarters. Everywhere they declared that they would drive the foreigner and his devilish religion from China. To encourage this society its founder, Yü Hsien, was in March, 1899, appointed by the Throne Governor of Shan-tung. In four years he had risen from the comparatively humble post of Prefect to that of the highest official in the province."—*Peking Correspondence London Times, Oct. 13, 1900.*

Sir Robert Hart, an English gentleman who had been in the service of the Chinese government at Peking for many years, administering its maritime customs, is the author of an account of the causes and the character of the Boxer movement, written since its violent outbreak, from which the following passages are taken : "For ages China had discountenanced the military spirit and was laughed at by us accordingly, and thus, ever since intercourse under treaties has gone on, we have been lecturing the Government from our superior standpoint, telling it that it must grow strong—must create army and navy—must adopt foreign drill and foreign weapons—must prepare to hold its own against all comers—must remember 'Codlin' is its friend, not 'Short': our words did not fall on closed ears—effect was given to selected bits of advice—and various firms did a very remarkable and very remunerative trade in arms. But while the Chinese Government made a note of all the advice its generous friends placed at its disposal, and adopted some suggestions because they either suited it or it seemed polite and harmless to do so, it did not forget its own thirty centuries of historic teaching, and it looked at affairs abroad through its own eyes and the eyes of its representatives at foreign Courts, studied their reports and the printed utterances of books, magazines, and newspapers, and the teaching thus received began gradually to crystallise in the belief that a huge standing army on European lines would be wasteful and dangerous and that a volunteer association—as suggested by the way all China ranged itself on the Government side in the Franco-Chinese affair—covering the whole Empire, offering an outlet for restless spirits and fostering a united and patriotic feeling, would be more reliable and effective, an idea which seemed to receive immediate confirmation from without in the stand a handful of burghers were making in the Transvaal: hence the Boxer Association, patriotic in origin, justifiable in its fundamental idea, and in point of fact the outcome of either foreign advice or the study of foreign methods.

"In the meanwhile the seeds of other growths were being sown in the soil of the Chinese mind, private and official, and were producing fruit each after its kind: various commercial stipulations sanctioned by treaties had not taken into full account Chinese conditions, difficulties, methods, and requirements, and their enforcement did not make foreign commerce more agreeable to the eye of either provincial or metropolitan officials,—missionary propagandism was at work all over the country, and its fruits, Chinese Christians, did not win the esteem or goodwill of their fellows, for, first of all, they offended public feeling by deserting Chinese for foreign cults, next they irritated their fellow villagers by refusing, as Christians, to take part in or share the expenses of village festivals, and lastly, as Christians again, they shocked the official mind, and popular opinion also, by getting their religious teachers, more especially the Roman Catholics, to interfere on their behalf in litigation, &c., a state of affairs which became specially talked about in Shantung, the native province of the Confucius of over 2,000 years ago and now the sphere of influence of one of the Church's most energetic bishops,—the arrangement by which missionaries were to ride in green chairs and be recognised as the equals of Governors and Viceroys had its special signification and underlined missionary aspiration telling people and officials in every province what they had to expect from it: on the top of this came the Kiao Chow affair and the degradation and cashiering of a really able, popular, and clean-handed official, the Governor Li Ping Hêng, succeeded by the cessions of territory at Port Arthur, Wei-Hai-Wei, Kwang Chow Wan, &c., &c., &c., and these doings, followed by the successful stand made against the Italian demand for a port on the Coast of Chekiang, helped to force the Chinese Government to see that concession had gone far enough and that opposition to foreign encroachment might now and henceforth be the key-note of its policy.

"Li Ping Hêng had taken up his private residence in the southeastern corner of Pecheli, close to the Shantung frontier, and the Boxer movement, already started in a tentative way in the latter province, now received an immense impetus from the occurrences alluded to and was carefully nurtured and fostered by that cashiered official—more respected than ever by his countrymen. Other high officials were known to be in sympathy with the new departure and to give it their strongest approval and support, such as

Hsü Tung, Kang I, and men of the same stamp and standing, and their advice to the throne was to try conclusions with foreigners and yield no more to their demands. However mistaken may have been their reading of foreigners, and however wrong their manner of action, these men—eminent in their own country for their learning and services—were animated by patriotism, were enraged at foreign dictation, and had the courage of their convictions: we must do them the justice of allowing they were actuated by high motives and love of country—but that does not always or necessarily mean political ability or highest wisdom. . . .

"The Chinese, an intelligent, cultivated race, sober, industrious, and on their own lines civilised, homogeneous in language, thought, and feeling, which numbers some four hundred millions, lives in its own ring fence, and covers a country which—made up of fertile land and teeming waters, with infinite variety of mountain and plain, hill and dale, and every kind of climate and condition—on its surface produces all that a people requires and in its bosom hides untold virgin wealth that has never yet been disturbed—this race, after thousands of years of haughty seclusion and exclusiveness, has been pushed by the force of circumstances and by the superior strength of assailants into treaty relations with the rest of the world, but regards that as a humiliation, sees no benefit accruing from it, and is looking forward to the day when it in turn will be strong enough to revert to its old life again and do away with foreign intercourse, interference, and intrusion: it has slept long, as we count sleep, but it is awake at last and its every member is tingling with Chinese feeling—'China for the Chinese and out with the foreigners!'

"The Boxer movement is doubtless the product of official inspiration, but it has taken hold of the popular imagination and will spread like wildfire all over the length and breadth of the country: it is, in short, a purely patriotic volunteer movement, and its object is to strengthen China—and for a Chinese programme. Its first experience has not been altogether a success as regards the attainment through strength of proposed ends—the rooting up of foreign cults and the ejection of foreigners, but it is not a failure in respect of the feeler it put out—will volunteering work?—or as an experiment that would test ways and means and guide future choice: it has proved how to a man the people will respond to the call, and it has further demonstrated that the swords and spears to which the prudent official mind confined the initiated will not suffice, but must be supplemented or replaced by Mauser rifles and Krupp guns: the Boxer patriot of the future will possess the best weapons money can buy, and then the ' Yellow Peril ' will be beyond ignoring."—Robert Hart, *The Peking Legations* (*Fortnightly Review, Nov.*, 1900).

A. D. 1900 (March—April).—Proposed joint naval demonstration of the Powers in Chinese waters.—On receipt of the telegram from Peking (March 10) recommending a joint naval demonstration in North Chinese waters, the British Ambassador at Paris was directed to consult the Government of France on the subject, and did so. On the 13th, he reported M. Delcassé, the French Minister for Foreign Affairs, as saying that "he could not, of course, without reflection and without consulting his colleagues, say what the decision of the French Government would be as to taking part in a naval demonstration, but at first sight it seemed to him that it would be difficult to avoid acting upon a suggestion which the Representatives of Five Powers, who ought to be good judges, considered advisable." On the 16th, he wrote to Lord Salisbury : "M. Delcassé informed me the day before yesterday that he had telegraphed to Peking for more precise information. I told him that I was glad to hear that no precipitate action was going to be taken by France, and that I believed that he would find that the United States' Government would be disinclined to associate themselves with any joint naval demonstration. I added that, although I had no instructions to say so, I expected that Her Majesty's Government would also adhere to their usual policy of proceeding with great caution, and would be in no hurry to take a step which only urgent necessity would render advisable."

On the 23d of March, Sir Claude MacDonald telegraphed to Lord Salisbury : "I learn that the Government of the United States have ordered one ship-of-war to go to Taku for the purpose of protecting American interests, that the Italian Minister has been given the disposal of two ships, and the German Minister has the use of the squadron at Kiao-chan for the same purpose. With a view to protect British missionary as well as other interests, which are far in excess of those of other Powers, I would respectfully request that two of Her Majesty's ships be sent to Taku."

On the 3d of April, the Tsung-li Yamên communicated to the British Ambassador the following information, as to the punishment of the murderers of Mr. Brooks, and of the officials responsible for neglect to protect him : "Of several arrests that had been made of persons accused of having been the perpetrators of the crime or otherwise concerned in its committal, two have been brought to justice and, at a trial at which a British Consul was present, found guilty and sentenced to be decapitated—a sentence which has already been carried into effect. Besides this, the Magistrate of Feichen, and some of the police authorities of the district, accounted to have been guilty of culpable negligence in the protection of Mr. Brooks, have been cashiered, or had other punishments awarded them of different degrees of severity."

For some weeks after this the Boxer movement appears to have been under constraint. Further outrages were not reported and no expressions of anxiety appear in the despatches from Peking. The proposal of a joint naval demonstration in the waters of Northern China was not pressed.—*Great Britain, Papers by Command : China, No. 3, 1900, pp. 6–17.*

A. D. 1900 (May—June).—Renewed activity of the "Boxers" and increasing gravity of the situation at Peking.—Return of Legation guards.—Call upon the fleets at Taku for reinforcement and rescue.—About the middle of May the activity of the "Boxers" was renewed, and a state of disorder far more threatening than before was speedily made known. The rapid succession of startling events during the next few weeks may be traced in the following series of telegrams from the British Minister at Peking to his chief :

"May 17.—The French Minister called to-day to inform me that the Boxers have destroyed three villages and killed 61 Roman Catholic Christian converts at a place 90 miles from Peking, near Paoting-fu. The French Bishop informs me that in that district, and around Tientsin and Peking generally, much disorder prevails."

"May 18.—There was a report yesterday, which has been confirmed to-day, that the Boxers have destroyed the London Mission chapel at Kung-tsun, and killed the Chinese preacher. Kung-tsun is about 40 miles south-west of Peking."

"May 19.—At the Yamên, yesterday, I reminded the Ministers how I had unceasingly warned them during the last six months how dangerous it was not to take adequate measures in suppression of the Boxer Societies. I said that the result of the apathy of the Chinese Government was that now a Mission chapel, a few miles distant from the capital, had been destroyed. The Ministers admitted that the danger of the Boxer movement had not previously appeared to them so urgent, but that now they fully saw how serious it was. On the previous day an Imperial Decree had been issued, whereby specified metropolitan and provincial authorities were directed to adopt stringent measures to suppress the Boxers. This, they believed, would not fail to have the desired effect."

"May 21.—All eleven foreign Representatives attended a meeting of the Diplomatic Body held yesterday afternoon, at the instance of the French Minister. The doyen was empowered to write, in the name of all the foreign Representatives, a note to the Yamên to the effect that the Diplomatic Body, basing their demands on the Decrees already issued by the Palace denunciatory of the Boxers, requested that all persons who should print, publish, or disseminate placards which menaced foreigners, all individuals aiding and abetting, all owners of houses or temples now used as meeting places for Boxers, should be arrested. They also demanded that those guilty of arson, murder, outrages, &c., together with those affording support or direction to Boxers while committing such outrages, should be executed. Finally, the publication of a Decree in Peking and the Northern Provinces setting forth the above. The foreign Representatives decided at their meeting to take further measures if the disturbances still continued, or if a favorable answer was not received to their note within five days. The meeting did not decide what measures should be taken, but the Representatives were generally averse to bringing guards to Peking, and, what found most favour, was as follows :—With the exception of Holland, which has no ships in Chinese waters, it was proposed that all the Maritime Powers represented should make a naval demonstration either at Shanhaikuan, or at the new port, Chingwangtao, while, in case of necessity, guards were to be held ready on board ship. My colleagues will, I think, send these proposals as they stand to their governments. As the Chinese Government themselves seem to be sufficiently alarmed, I do not think that the above measure will be necessary, but, should the occasion arise, I trust that Her Majesty's Government will see fit to support it. . . . I had a private interview with my Russian colleague, who came to see me before the matter reached its acute stages. M. de Giers said that there were only two countries with serious interests in China : England and Russia. He thought that both landing guards and naval demonstrations were to be discouraged, as they give rise to unknown eventualities. However, since the 18th instant, he admits that matters are grave, and agreed at once to the joint note."

"May 24.—Her Majesty's Consul at Tien-tsin reported by telegraph yesterday that a Colonel in charge of a party of the Viceroy's cavalry was caught, on the 22nd instant, in an ambuscade near Lai-shui, which is about 50 miles south-west of Peking. The party were destroyed."

"May 25.—Tsung-li Yamên have replied to the note sent by the doyen of the Corps Diplomatique, reported in my telegram of the 21st May. They state that the main lines of the measures already in force agree with those required by the foreign Representatives, and add that a further Decree, which will direct efficacious action, is being asked for. The above does not even promise efficacious action, and, in my personal opinion, is unsatisfactory."

"May 27.—At the meeting of the Corps Diplomatique, which took place yesterday evening, we were informed by the French Minister that all his information led him to believe that a serious outbreak, which would endanger the lives of all European residents in Peking, was on the point of breaking out. The Italian Minister confirmed the information received by M. Pichon. The Russian Minister agreed with his Italian and French colleagues in considering the latest reply of the Yamên to be unsatisfactory, adding that, in his opinion, the Chinese Government was now about to adopt effective measures. That the danger was imminent he doubted, but said that it was not possible to disregard the evidence adduced by the French Minister. We all agreed with this last remark. M. Pichon then urged that if the Chinese Government did not at once take action guards should at once be brought up by the foreign Representatives. Some discussion then ensued, after which it was determined that a precise statement should be demanded from the Yamên as to the measures they had taken, also that the terms of the Edict mentioned by them should be communicated to the foreign Representatives. Failing a reply from the Yamên of a satisfactory nature by this afternoon, it was resolved that guards should be sent for. Baron von Ketteler, the German Minister, declared that he considered the Chinese Government was crumbling to pieces, and that he did not believe that any action based on the assumption of their stability could be efficacious. The French Minister is, I am certain, genuinely convinced that the danger is real, and owing to his means of information he is well qualified to judge. . . . I had an interview with Prince Ch'ing and the Yamên Ministers this afternoon. Energetic measures are now being taken against the Boxers by the Government, whom the progress of the Boxer movement has, at last, thoroughly alarmed. The Corps Diplomatique, who met in the course of the day, have decided to wait another twenty-four hours for further developments."

"May 29.—Some stations on the line, among others Yengtai, 6 miles from Peking, together with machine sheds and European houses, were burnt yesterday by the Boxers. The line has also been torn up in places. Trains between this and Tien-tsin have stopped running, and traffic has not been resumed yet. The situation here is serious, and so far the Imperial troops have done nothing. It was unanimously decided, at a meeting of foreign Representatives yesterday, to send for guards for the Legations, in view of the apathy of the Chinese Government and the gravity of the situation. Before the meeting assembled, the French Minister had already sent for his."

"May 30.—Permission for the guards to come to Peking has been refused by the Yamên. I think, however, that they may not persist in their refusal. The situation in the meantime is one of extreme gravity. The people are very excited, and the soldiers mutinous. Without doubt it is now a question of European life and property being in danger here. The French and Russians are landing 100 men each. French, Russian, and United States' Ministers, and myself, were deputed to-day at a meeting of the foreign Representatives to declare to the Tsung-li Yamên that the foreign Representatives must immediately bring up guards for the protection of the lives of Europeans in Peking in view of the serious situation and untrustworthiness of the Chinese troops. That the number would be small if facilities were granted, but it must be augmented should they be refused, and serious consequences might result for the Chinese Government in the latter event. In reply, the Yamên stated that no definite reply could be given until to-morrow afternoon, as the Prince was at the Summer Palace. As the Summer Palace is within an hour's ride we refused to admit the impossibility of prompt communication and decision, and repeated the warning already given of the serious consequences which would result if the Viceroy at Tien-tsin did not receive instructions this evening in order that the guards might be enabled to arrive here to-morrow. The danger will be greatest on Friday, which is a Chinese festival."

"May 31.—Provided that the number does not exceed that of thirty for each Legation, as on the last occasion, the Yamên have given their consent to the guards coming to Peking. . . . It was decided this morning, at a meeting of the foreign Representatives, to at once bring up the guards that are ready. These probably include the British, American, Italian, and Japanese."

"June 1.—British, American, Italian, Russian, French and Japanese guards arrived yesterday. Facilities were given, and there were no disturbances. Our detachment consists of three officers and seventy-five men, and a machine gun."

"June 2.—The city is comparatively quiet, but murders of Christian converts and the destruction of missionary property in outlying districts occur every day, and the situation still remains serious. The situation at the Palace is, I learn from a reliable authority, very strained. The Empress-Dowager does not dare to put down the Boxers, although wishing to do so, on account of the support given them by Prince Tuan, father of the hereditary Prince, and other conservative Manchus, and also because of their numbers. Thirty Europeans, most of whom were Belgians, fled from Paoting-fu viâ the river to Tien-tsin. About 20 miles from Tien-tsin they were attacked by Boxers. A party of Europeans having gone to their rescue from Tientsin severe fighting ensued, in which a large number of Boxers were killed. Nine of the party are still missing, including one lady. The rest have been brought into Tien-tsin. The Russian Minister, who came to see me to-day, said he thought it most imperative that the foreign Representatives should be prepared for all eventualities, though he had no news confirming the above report. He said he had been authorized by his Government to support any Chinese authority at Peking which was able and willing to maintain order in case the Government collapsed."

"June 4.—I am informed by a Chinese courier who arrived to-day from Yung-Ching, 40 miles south of Peking, that on the 1st June the Church of England Mission at that place was attacked by the Boxers. He states that one missionary, Mr. Robinson, was murdered, and that he saw his body, and that another, Mr. Norman, was carried off by the Boxers. I am insisting on the Chinese authorities taking immediate measures to effect his rescue. Present situation at Peking is such that we may at any time be besieged here with the railway and telegraph lines cut. In the event of this occurring, I beg your Lordship will cause urgent instructions to be sent to Admiral Seymour to consult with the officers commanding the other foreign squadrons now at Taku to take concerted measures for our relief. The above was agreed to at a meeting held to-day by the foreign Representatives, and a similar telegram was sent to their respective Governments by the Ministers of Austria, Italy, Germany, France, Japan, Russia, and the United States, all of whom have ships at Taku and guards here. The telegram was proposed by the French Minister and carried unanimously. It is difficult to say whether the situation is as grave as the latter supposes, but the apathy of the Chinese Government makes it very serious."

"June 5.—I went this afternoon to the Yamên to inquire of the Ministers personally what steps the Chinese Government proposed to take to effect the punishment of Mr. Robinson's murderers and the release of Mr. Norman. I was informed by the Ministers that the Viceroy was the responsible person, that they had telegraphed to him to send troops to the spot, and that that was all they were able to do in the matter. They did not express regret or show the least anxiety to effect the relief of the imprisoned man, and they displayed the greatest indifference during the interview. I informed them that the Chinese Government would be held responsible by Her Majesty's Government for the criminal apathy which had brought about this disgraceful state of affairs. I then demanded an interview with Prince Ching, which is fixed for to-morrow, as I found it useless to discuss the matter with the Yamên. This afternoon I had an interview with the Prince and Ministers of the Yamên. They expressed much regret at the murder of Messrs. Robinson and Norman, and their tone was fully satisfactory in this respect. . . . No attempt was made by the Prince to defend the Chinese Government, nor to deny what I had said. He could say nothing to reassure me as to the safety of the city, and admitted that the Government was reluctant to deal harshly with the movement, which, owing to its anti-foreign character, was popular. He stated that they were bringing

6,000 soldiers from near Tien-tsin for the protection of the railway, but it was evident that he doubted whether they would be allowed to fire on the Boxers except in the defence of Government property, or if authorized whether they would obey. He gave me to understand, without saying so directly, that he has entirely failed to induce the Court to accept his own views as to the danger of inaction. It was clear, in fact, that the Yamên wished me to understand that the situation was most serious, and that, owing to the influence of ignorant advisers with the Empress-Dowager, they were powerless to remedy it."

"June 6.—Since the interview with the Yamên reported in my preceding telegram I have seen several of my colleagues. I find they all agree that, owing to the now evident sympathy of the Empress-Dowager and the more conservative of her advisers with the anti-foreign movement, the situation is rapidly growing more serious. Should there be no change in the attitude of the Empress, a rising in the city, ending in anarchy, which may produce rebellion in the provinces, will be the result, 'failing an armed occupation of Peking by one or more of the Powers.' Our ordinary means of pressure on the Chinese Government fail, as the Yamên is, by general consent, and their own admission, powerless to persuade the Court to take serious measures of repression. Direct representations to the Emperor and Dowager-Empress from the Corps Diplomatique at a special audience seems to be the only remaining chance of impressing the Court."

"June 7.—There is a long Decree in the 'Gazette' which ascribes the recent trouble to the favour shown to converts in law suits and the admission to their ranks of bad characters. It states that the Boxers, who are the objects of the Throne's sympathy equally with the converts, have made use of the anti-Christian feeling aroused by these causes, and that bad characters among them have destroyed chapels and railways which are the property of the State. Unless the ringleaders among such bad characters are now surrendered by the Boxers they will be dealt with as disloyal subjects, and will be exterminated. Authorization will be given to the Generals to effect arrests, exercising discrimination between leaders and their followers. It is probable that the above Decree represents a compromise between the conflicting opinions which exist at Court. The general tone is most unsatisfactory, though the effect may be good if severe measures are actually taken. The general lenient tone, the absence of reference to the murder of missionaries, and the justification of the proceedings of the Boxers by the misconduct of Christian converts are all dangerous factors in the case."

"June 8.—A very bad effect has been produced by the Decree reported in my immediately preceding telegram. There is no prohibition of the Boxers drilling, which they now openly do in the houses of the Manchu nobility and in the temples. This Legation is full of British refugees, mostly women and children, and the London and Church of England Missions have been abandoned. I trust that the instructions requested in my telegrams of the 4th and 5th instant have been sent to the Admiral. I have received the following telegram, dated noon to-day, from Her Majesty's Consul at Tien-tsin:—'By now the

Boxers must be near Yang-tsun. Last night the bridge, which is outside that station, was seen to be on fire. General Nich's forces are being withdrawn to Lutai, and 1,500 of them have already passed through by railway. There are now at Yang-tsun an engine and trucks ready to take 2,000 more men.' Lutai lies on the other side of Tien-tsin, and at some distance. Should this information be correct, it means that an attempt to protect Peking has been abandoned by the only force on which the Yamên profess to place any reliance. The 6,000 men mentioned in my telegram of the 5th instant were commanded by General Nieh."

"Tong-ku, June 10.—Vice-Admiral Sir E. Seymour to Admiralty. Following telegram received from Minister at Peking:—'Situation extremely grave. Unless arrangements are made for immediate advance to Peking it will be too late.'

"In consequence of above, I am landing at once with all available men, and have asked foreign officers' co-operation."—*Great Britain, Papers by Command: China, No. 3, 1900, pp. 26-45.*

A. D. 1900 (June 10-26).—Bombardment and capture of Taku forts by the allied fleets.—Failure of first relief expedition started for Peking.—The following is from an official report by Rear-Admiral Bruce of the British Navy, dated at Taku June 17, 1900: "On my arrival here on the 11th inst. I found a large fleet, consisting of Russian, German, French, Austrian, Italian, Japanese, and British ships. In consequence of an urgent telegram from Her Majesty's Minister at Peking, Vice-Admiral Sir Edward H. Seymour, K. C. B., Commander-in-Chief, had started at 3 o'clock the previous morning (10th June), taking with him a force of 1,375 of all ranks, being reinforced by men from the allied ships as they arrived, until he commanded not less than 2,000 men. At a distance of some 20 to 30 miles from Tientsin—but it is very difficult to locate the place, as no authentic record has come in—he found the railway destroyed and sleepers burned, &c., and every impediment made by supposed Boxers to his advance. Then his difficulties began, and it is supposed that the Boxers, probably assisted by Chinese troops, closed in on his rear, destroyed railway-lines, bridges, &c., and nothing since the 13th inst. has passed from Commander-in-Chief and his relief force and Tientsin, nor vice versa up to this date. . . .

"During the night of the 14th inst. news was received that all railway-carriages and other rolling stock had been ordered to be sent up the line for the purpose of bringing down a Chinese army to Tong-ku. On receipt of this serious information a council of Admirals was summoned by Vice-Admiral Hiltebrandt, Commander-in-Chief of the Russian Squadron, and the German, French, United States Admirals, myself, and the Senior Officers of Italy, Austria, and Japan attended; and it was decided to send immediate orders to the captains of the allied vessels in the Peiho River (three Russian, two German, one United States, one Japanese, one British—'Algerine') to prevent any railway plant being taken away from Tong-ku, or the Chinese army reaching that place, which would cut off our communication with Tientsin; and in the event of either being attempted they were to use force to prevent it, and to destroy the Taku Forts. By the evening,

and during the night of 15th inst., information arrived that the mouth of the Peiho River was being protected by electric mines. On receipt of this, another council composed of the same naval officers was held in the forenoon of 16th June on board the 'Rossia,' and in consequence of the gravity of the situation, and information having also arrived that the forts were being provisioned and reinforced, immediate notice was sent to the Viceroy of Chili at Tientsin and the commandant of the forts that, in consequence of the danger to our forces up the river, at Tientsin, and on the march to Peking by the action of the Chinese authorities, we proposed to temporarily occupy the Taku Forts, with or without their good will, at 2 a.m. on the 17th inst." Early on Sunday, 17th June, "the Taku Forts opened fire on the allied ships in the Peiho River, which continued almost without intermission until 6.30 a.m., when all firing had practically ceased and the Taku Forts were stormed and in the hands of the Allied Powers, allowing of free communication with Tientsin by water, and rail when the latter is repaired."

The American Admiral took no part in this attack on the forts at Taku, "on the ground that we were not at war with China and that a hostile demonstration might consolidate the anti-foreign elements and strengthen the Boxers to oppose the relieving column."

From the point to which the allied expedition led by Admiral Seymour fought its way, and at which it was stopped by the increasing numbers that opposed it, it fell back to a position near Hsiku, on the right bank of the Peiho. There the allies drove the Chinese forces from an imperial armory and took possession of the buildings, which gave them a strong defensive position, with a large store of rice for food, and enabled them to hold their ground until help came to them from Tientsin, on the 25th. They were encumbered with no less than 230 wounded men, which made it impossible for them, in the circumstances, to fight their way back without aid; though the distance was so short that the return march was accomplished, on the 26th, between 3 o'clock and 9 of the same morning. In his report made the following day Admiral Seymour says: ",The number of enemy engaged against us in the march from Yungtsin to the Armoury near Hsiku cannot be even estimated; the country alongside the river banks is quite flat, and consisted of a succession of villages of mud huts, those on the outskirts having enclosures made of dried reeds; outside, high reeds were generally growing in patches near the village, and although trees are very scarce away from the River, alongside it they are very numerous; these with the graves, embankments for irrigation and against flood, afforded cover to the enemy from which they seldom exposed themselves, withdrawing on our near approach. Had their fire not been generally high it would have been much more destructive than it was. The number of the enemy certainly increased gradually until the Armoury near Hsiku was reached, when General Nieh's troops and the Boxers both joined in the attack. In the early part of the expedition the Boxers were mostly armed with swords and spears, and not with many firearms; at the engagement at Langfang on 18th, and afterwards, they were armed with rifles of late pattern; this together with banners captured and uniform worn, shows that they had either the active or covert support of the Chinese Government, or some of its high officials."

A. D. 1900 (June 11-29).—Chinese Imperial Edicts.—"On June 11 Mr. Sugiyama, the Chancellor of the Japanese Legation, was brutally murdered [in Peking] by the soldiers of General Tung-fuh-siang. Two days later the following Imperial edict was published in the 'Peking Gazette': 'On June 11 the Japanese Chancellor was murdered by brigands outside the Yung-ting Mên. On hearing this intelligence we were exceedingly grieved. Officials of neighbouring nations stationed in Peking ought to be protected in every possible way, and now, especially, extra diligence ought to be displayed to prevent such occurrences when banditti are as numerous as bees. We have repeatedly commanded the local officials to ensure the most efficient protection in their districts, yet, in spite of our frequent orders, we have this case of the murder of the Japanese Chancellor occurring in the very capital of the Empire. The civil and military officials have assuredly been remiss in not clearing their districts of bad characters, or immediately arresting such persons, and we hereby order every Yamên concerned to set a limit of time for the arrest of the criminals, that they may suffer the extreme penalty. Should the time expire without any arrest being effected, the severest punishment will assuredly be inflicted upon the responsible persons.' It is needless to add that the 'criminals' were never arrested and the 'responsible persons' were never punished. In the same 'Gazette' another decree condemns the 'Boxer brigands' who have recently been causing trouble in the neighbourhood of the capital, who have been committing arson and murder and revenging themselves upon the native converts. Soldiers and 'Boxers', it says, have leagued together to commit acts of murder and arson, and have vied with one another in disgraceful acts of looting and robbery. The 'Boxers' are to disband, desperadoes are to be arrested, ringleaders are to be seized, but the followers may be allowed to disband.

"Similar decrees on the 14th and 15th show alarm at the result of the 'Boxer' agitation and lawlessness within the city. Nothing so strong against the 'Boxers' had previously been published. Fires were approaching too closely to the Imperial Palace. No steps had been taken by the Court to prevent the massacre and burning of Christians and their property in the country, but on the 16th the great Chien Mên gate fronting the Palace had been burned and the smoke had swept over the Imperial Courts. Yet even in these decrees leniency is shown to the 'Boxers,' for they are not to be fired upon, but are, if guilty, to be arrested and executed. On June 17th the edict expresses the belief of the Throne that:—'All foreign Ministers ought to be really protected. If the Ministers and their families wish to go for a time to Tien-tsin, they must be protected on the way. But the railroad is not now in working order. If they go by the cart road it will be difficult, and there is fear that perfect protection cannot be offered. They would do better, therefore, to abide here in peace as heretofore and wait till the railroad is repaired, and then act as circumstances render expedient.'

"Two days later an ultimatum was sent to the Ministers ordering them to leave Peking within 24 hours. On the 20th Baron von Ketteler was

6–8

murdered and on June 21 China published, having entered upon war against the whole world, her Apologia :—'Ever since the foundation of the Dynasty, foreigners coming to China have been kindly treated. In the reigns Tao Kuang, and Hsien Fêng, they were allowed to trade and they also asked leave to propagate their religion, a request that the Throne reluctantly granted. At first they were amenable to Chinese control, but for the past 30 years they have taken advantage of China's forbearance to encroach on China's territory and trample on Chinese people and to demand China's wealth. Every concession made by China increased their reliance on violence. They oppressed peaceful citizens and insulted the gods and holy men, exciting the most burning indignation among the people. Hence the burning of chapels and slaughter of converts by the patriotic braves. The Throne was anxious to avoid war, and issued edicts enjoining the protection of Legations and pity to the converts. The decrees declaring 'Boxers' and converts to be equally the children of the State were issued in the hope of removing the old feud between people and converts. Extreme kindness was shown to the strangers from afar. But these people knew no gratitude and increased their pressure. A despatch was yesterday sent by Du Chaylard, calling us to deliver up the Ta-ku Forts into their keeping, otherwise they would be taken by force. These threats showed their aggressive intention. In all matters relating to international intercourse, we have never been wanting in courtesies to them, but they, while styling themselves civilized States, have acted without regard for right, relying solely on their military force. We have now reigned nearly 30 years, and have treated the people as our children, the people honouring us as their deity, and in the midst of our reign we have been the recipients of the gracious favour of the Empress-Dowager. Furthermore, our ancestors have come to our aid, and the gods have answered our call, and never has there been so universal a manifestation of loyalty and patriotism. With tears have we announced war in the ancestral shrines. Better to enter on the struggle and do our utmost than seek some measures of self-preservation involving eternal disgrace. All our officials, high and low, are of one mind, and there have assembled without official summons several hundred thousand patriotic soldiers (I Ping "Boxers"). Even children carrying spears in the service of the State. Those others relying on crafty schemes, our trust is in Heaven's justice. They depend on violence, we on humanity. Not to speak of the righteousness of our cause, our provinces number more than 20, our people over 400,000,000, and it will not be difficult to vindicate the dignity of our country.' The decree concludes by promising heavy rewards to those who distinguish themselves in battle or subcribe funds, and threatening punishment to those who show cowardice or act treacherously.

"In the same 'Gazette' Yü Lu reports acts of war on the part of the foreigners, when, after some days' fighting, he was victorious. 'Perusal of his memorial has given us great comfort,' says the Throne. Warm praise is given to the 'Boxers,' 'who have done great service without any assistance either of men or money from the State. Marked favour will be shown them later on, and they must continue to show their devotion.' On the 24th presents of rice are sent to the

'Boxers.' Leaders of the 'Boxers' are appointed by the Throne—namely, Prince Chuang, and the Assistant Grand Secretary Kang-Yi to be in chief command, and Ying Nien and Duke Lan (the brother of Prince Tuan, the father of the Crown Prince) to act in coöperation with them, while another high post is given to Wen Jui."—*London Times, Oct.* 16, 1900 (*Peking Correspondence*).

Very different in tone to the imperial decree of June 21, quoted above, was one issued a week later (June 29), and sent to the diplomatic representatives of the Chinese government in Europe and America. As published by Minister Wu Ting-fang, at Washington, on the 11th of July, it was in the following words: "The circumstances which led to the commencement of fighting between Chinese and foreigners were of such a complex, confusing and unfortunate character as to be entirely unexpected. Our diplomatic representatives abroad, owing to their distance from the scene of action, have had no means of knowing the true state of things, and accordingly cannot lay the views of the government before the ministers for foreign affairs of the respective Powers to which they are accredited. Now we take this opportunity of going fully into the matter for the information of our representatives aforesaid.

"In the first place there arose in the provinces of Chih Li and Shantung a kind of rebellious subjects who had been in the habit of practicing boxing and fencing in their respective villages, and at the same time clothing their doings with spiritualistic and strange rites. The local authorities failed to take due notice of them at the time. Accordingly the infection spread with astonishing rapidity. Within the space of a month it seemed to make its appearance everywhere, and finally even reached the capital itself. Everyone looked upon the movement as supernatural and strange, and many joined it. Then there were lawless and treacherous persons who sounded the cry of 'Down with Christianity!' About the middle of the fifth moon these persons began to create disturbances without warning. Churches were burned and converts were killed. The whole city was in a ferment. A situation was created which could not be brought under control. At first the foreign Powers requested that foreign troops be allowed to enter the capital for the protection of the legations. The imperial government, having in view the comparative urgency of the occasion, granted the request as an extraordinary mark of courtesy beyond the requirements of international intercourse. Over five hundred foreign troops were sent to Pekin. This shows clearly how much care China exercised in the maintenance of friendly relations with other countries.

"The legations at the capital never had much to do with the people. But from the time foreign troops entered the city the guards did not devote themselves exclusively to the protection of their respective legations. They sometimes fired their guns on top of the city walls and sometimes patrolled the streets everywhere. There were repeated reports of persons being hit by stray bullets. Moreover they strolled about the city without restraint, and even attempted to enter the Tung Hua gate (the eastern gate of the palace grounds). They only desisted when admittance was positively forbidden. On this account, both the soldiers and the people were provoked to resentment, and voiced their indignation with one accord. Lawless persons then took advantage of the situation to do mischief, and became bolder than ever in burning and killing Christian converts. The Powers thereupon attempted to reinforce the foreign troops in Pekin, but the reinforcements encountered resistance and defeat at the hands of the insurgents on the way and have not yet been able to proceed. The insurgents of the two provinces of Chih Li and Shantung had by this time effected a complete union and could not be separated. The imperial government was by no means reluctant to issue orders for the entire suppression of this insurgent element. But as the trouble was so near at hand there was a great fear that due protection might not be assured to the legations if the anarchists should be driven to extremities, thus bringing on a national calamity. There also was a fear that uprisings might occur in the provinces of Chih Li and Shantung at the same time, with the result that both foreign missionaries and Chinese converts in the two provinces might fall victims to popular fury. It was therefore absolutely necessary to consider the matter from every point of view.

"As a measure of precaution it was finally decided to request the foreign ministers to retire temporarily to Tien-Tsin for safety. It was while the discussion of this proposition was in progress that the German minister, Baron Von Ketteler, was assassinated by a riotous mob one morning while on his way to the Tsung-Li-Yamen. On the previous day the German minister had written a letter appointing a time for calling at the Tsung-Li-Yamen. But the Yamen, fearing he might be molested on the way, did not consent to the appointment as suggested by the minister. Since this occurrence the anarchists assumed a more bold and threatening attitude, and consequently it was not deemed wise to carry out the project of sending the diplomatic corps to Tien-Tsin under an escort. However, orders were issued to the troops detailed for the protection of the legations to keep stricter watch and take greater precaution against any emergency.

"To our surprise, on the 20th of the fifth moon (June 16th), foreign (naval ?) officers at Taku called upon Lo Jung Kwang, the general commanding, and demanded his surrender of the forts, notifying him that failing to receive compliance they would at two o'clock the next day take steps to seize the forts by force. Lo Jung Kwang, being bound by the duties of his office to hold the forts, how could he yield to the demand? On the day named they actually first fired upon the forts, which responded, and kept up fighting all day and then surrendered. Thus the conflict of forces began, but certainly the initiative did not come from our side. Even supposing that China were not conscious of her true condition, how could she take such a step as to engage in war with all the Powers simultaneously? and how could she, relying upon the support of anarchistic populace, go into war with the Powers?

"Our position in this matter ought to be clearly understood by all the Powers. The above is a statement of the wrongs we have suffered, and how China was driven to the unfortunate position from which she could not escape. Our several ministers will make known accurately and in detail the contents of this decree and the policy of China to the ministers of foreign affairs in their respective countries, and assure them that military authorities are still strictly enjoined to afford protection to the legations as hitherto to the utmost of their power. As for the anarchists they will be as severely dealt with as circumstances permit. The several ministers will continue in the discharge of the duties of their office as hitherto without hesitation or doubt. This telegraphic decree to be transmitted for their information. Respect this."

A. D. 1900 (June—July). — Failure of attempt to entrust Japan with the rescuing of the Legations at Peking. — A British Blue Book, issued on the 18th of February, 1901, contains correspondence that took place between the Powers late in June and early in July, looking to an arrangement for the immediate sending of a large force from Japan to the rescue of the beleaguered Legations in Peking. As summarized in the "London Times," this correspondence showed that "the necessity of asking the help of the only Power that was near enough to intervene promptly was strongly pressed by Lord Salisbury on the other Powers in the beginning of July. M. Delcassé fell in entirely with the scheme and insisted on the need of putting aside all jealousies or afterthoughts which might hinder unity of action on the spot. The Russian Government, however, seems to have misunderstood Lord Salisbury's meaning and to have conceived him to wish Japan to settle the Chinese crisis by herself and with a view to her own interests, a misunderstanding which it required a whole series of despatches to clear up completely. The Japanese Government itself showed the most commendable readiness to act, and on July 11 Mr. Whitehead telegraphed from Tokio, in reply to an appeal from Lord Salisbury to the Japanese Government, that 'in consequence of the friendly assurances' given by Lord Salisbury the Japanese Government had decided to send one or two more divisions to China. To this Lord Salisbury replied on July 13 that her Majesty's Government were willing to assist the Japanese Government up to £1,000,000 if they at once mobilized and despatched an additional 20,000 men to Peking. But the latter, in the absence of any definite scheme of operations on the part of the Powers, showed an unwillingness to accede to this proposal, which thus fell through."

A. D. 1900 (June—August). — The siege of the Foreign Legations at Peking. — The story of two dreadful months as told by one of the besieged. — The most detailed and altogether best account of the dreadful experience which the foreigners besieged in the quarter of the Legations at Peking underwent, from the first week in June until the 14th day of August, when a rescuing army forced its way into the city, is that furnished to the "London Times" by its Peking correspondent, who was one of the besieged. His narrative, forwarded immediately upon the opening of communication with the outer world, was published in "The Times" of October 13 and 15. With some abridgment it is given here under permission from the Manager of "The Times."

"Missionaries in Peking began collecting together into the larger mission compounds for common protection. Many ladies went for safety into the British Legation. Railway communication was now severed and the telegraph communication threatened. Our isolation was being completed. In the country disaffection spread

to the districts to the east of Peking, and the position of the American missionaries at Tung-chau became one of great danger. It was decided to abandon their great missionary establishments, and with the native Christians that could follow them to come into Peking. They asked for an escort, but Mr. Conger felt himself compelled to decline one, on the ground that he did not venture to send the small body of men that he could spare from the Legation through so dangerous a district. Protection must be looked for from the Chinese Government. What soldiers could not be sent to do one fearless American missionary succeeded in doing. Late in the evening of June 7 the Rev. W. S. Ament, of the Board Mission, left Peking in a cart, and with 20 other carts journeyed 14 miles to Tung-chau through a country palpitating with excitement. It was an act of courage and devotion that seemed to us who knew the country a deed of heroism. His arrival was most opportune. He brought safely back with him to Peking the whole missionary body then in Tung-chau—five men, including the author of 'Chinese Characteristics,' 11 ladies, and seven children, together with their Christian servants. . . .

"More troops were sent for to reinforce the Legation guards in Peking, but they were sent for too late. Already many miles of the railway had been torn up, and it was hopeless to expect an early restoration of communication. . . . The Empress-Dowager and the Emperor, who had been for some time past at the Summer Palace, returned to Peking, entering the city at the same hour by different gates. Large escorts of cavalry and infantry accompanied them; Manchu bannermen in large numbers were posted on the walls. It was noticeable that the body-guard of the Empress was provided by the renegade Mahomedan rabble of Tung-fuh-siang, who had long been a menace to foreigners in the province. The return of the Court was expected to have a tranquillizing effect upon the populace. But this was not the case. Students were attacked when riding in the country; our race-course grand stand, and stables were burnt by 'Boxers' armed with knives; Europeans could not venture along the streets outside the foreign quarter without being insulted. People were saying everywhere, 'The foreigners are to be ended.' Streets were being patrolled by cavalry, but there was every fear that the patrols were in league with the 'Boxers,' who were marching through the streets bearing banners inscribed 'Fu Ching Mieh Yang.' 'Protect Pure (the Dynasty), exterminate the foreigner.'

"The London Mission and the Society for the Propagation of the Gospel handed over their buildings to the Chinese authorities, holding them responsible for their safe keeping, and all missionaries and their families went to the British Legation. The American Board Mission likewise delivered over their valuable property to the Government and fell back upon the great Methodist Episcopalian Mission near the Hata Mên Gate, beyond the foreign quarter. Tung-chau missionaries and their families and several hundred Christian converts were already gathered there. Steps were at once taken to fortify the compound. Under the direction of Mr. F. D. Gamewell deep trenches were cut, earthworks thrown up, and barbed-wire entanglements laid down. Watch was kept and sentries posted, provisions laid in, and all preparations made to withstand a siege. Twenty marines and a captain from the American Legation were sent as a guard, and some spare rifles were obtained from the British Legation. Converts were armed with pikes and knives, and a determined effort was to be made in case of attack. The mission was, however, absolutely at the mercy of any force holding the high city wall and Hata Mên Gate. Without the power of reply the small garrison could have been shot down from the wall, which is little more than a stone's throw from the nearest point of the compound. Shell-fire such as was subsequently used against the Legations would have smashed the buildings into fragments. All the Maritime Customs staff and their families living in the East City, a mile or more beyond the foreign quarter, the professors and teachers of the Tung-wen-Kuan, Dr. Dudgeon, Mr. Pethick, the secretary of Li Hung Chang, and others, were forced to abandon their homes and come in for protection. Preparations for defence went on at all the Legations, for it was now inevitable that we should have to fight. A 'conseil de guerre' was held, attended by all the military officers, and a plan of defence determined. The palace and grounds of Prince Su, opposite the British Legation, were to be held for the Christian refugees, and an area was to be defended some half a mile long by half a mile broad, bounded by the Austrian and Italian Legations to the east, the street running over the north bridge of the canal to the north, the British, Russian, and American Legations to the west, while the southern boundary was to be the street running at the foot of the great City Wall from the American Legation on the west, past the German Legation on the east, to the lane running from the Wall north past the French Legation, the buildings of the Inspectorate General of Customs, and the Austrian Legation. All women and children and non-combatants were to come into the British Legation. Each position was to be held as long as possible, and the final stand was to be made at the British Legation. No question of surrender could ever be entertained, for surrender meant massacre.

"On the 10th it was announced that reinforcements were on the way and that they were coming with the approval of the Viceroy and of the Chinese Government, an approval more readily accorded since it was known to the Viceroy that the troops could not come by train. More than one of the Ministers was so confident that they were coming that carts were sent to await their arrival at Machia-pu, the terminal railway station at Peking. . . . Then Government gave its first public official recognition of the 'Boxers' by announcing that the notorious chief of the 'Boxers,' Prince Tuan, had been appointed President of the Tsung-li-Yamên. Prince Ching was superseded but was not removed from the Yamên. One harmless old Chinese, Liao Shou-hêng was sent into retirement while four rabidly anti-foreign Manchus entirely ignorant of all foreign affairs were appointed members. The last hope of any wisdom springing from the Yamên disappeared with the supersession of Prince Ching by the anti-foreign barbarian who, more than any other man in China, was responsible for the outbreak. The following morning most of the Europeans rode to Machia-pu to await the arrival of the foreign troops. They waited, but

no troops came, and then rode back past the jeering faces of hordes of Chinese soldiers. Our security was not increased by this fiasco.

"Soldiers sent to guard the summer residences of the British Legation in the Western Hills left their posts during the night. The buildings had been officially placed under the protection of the Imperial Government. In the pre-arranged absence of the soldiers the buildings were attacked by 'Boxers' and entirely burnt to the ground; the soldiers witnessed if they did not assist in the burning. But worse events were to happen that day. In the afternoon news passed through Peking that Mr. Sugiyama, the Chancellor of the Japanese Legation, had been murdered by soldiers. He had been sent by his Minister a second time to Machia-pu to await the arrival of the troops. Passing unarmed and alone in his cart beyond the Yung-ting Mên, the outer gate on the way to the station, he was seized by the soldiers of Tung-fub-siang, dragged from his cart, and done to death in the presence of a crowd of Chinese who witnessed his struggles with unpitying interest and unconcealed satisfaction. . . .

"On the 12th a deputation, consisting of Chi Hsiu, a member of the Grand Council and newly appointed to the Yamên, Hsu Ching-chêng, the ex-Minister, the 'Boxer' leader Chao Shu-chiao, and another Manchu, called upon the British Minister. Chi'Hsiu made a long address, his theme being the enduring nature of the friendship between China and England and the duty which China has always recognized as a sacred obligation to protect the members of the Legations who were her guests and the strangers within her walls. Chi Hsiu assured the Minister that the movement was at an end, that all was now tranquil, and that there was no more reason to fear. Yet the very next day Baron von Ketteler himself captured a 'Boxer' from amid the crowd in Legation-street. He carried the consecrated headpiece, and was armed with a sword. Round his waist he had a belt containing a talisman of yellow paper smeared with mystic red symbols by which he was rendered 'impermeable to foreign bullets.' And in the afternoon the 'Boxers' came down in force from the north of the city and the burning of foreign buildings began. The cry arose that the 'Boxers' were coming. Every man ran to his post, a cordon was established round the foreign quarter and no one was allowed to pass. Guards were on watch at all the Legations, but their numbers, spread over so many posts, were very inadequate, and they were still further reduced by the guards detached for duty at the Pei-tang Cathedral, where, three miles distant within the Imperial City, were gathered in the one great compound Mgr. Favier, the Bishop, his coadjutor, Mgr. Jarlin, the missionaries and lay brothers, the sisters of charity, and a vast concourse of Christian refugees, estimated at 2,000, who had fled from the massacre in the country. A guard of five Austrians was sent to the Belgian Legation. The Austrians with their machine gun commanded the Customs-street leading to the north; the Italians with a one pounder commanded the Legation-street to the east. The British with their Nordenfeldt swept the Canal-street to the north and the North-bridge, the Russians were on the South-bridge, while the Americans with their Colt machine gun had command of Legation-street to the west as far as the court facing the Imperial Palace. The Russians, having no gun, dropped their heavy ammunition down the well.

"As darkness came on the most awful cries were heard in the city, most demoniacal and unforgettable, the cries of the 'Boxers,' 'Sha kweitze'—'Kill the devils'—mingled with the shrieks of the victims and the groans of the dying. For 'Boxers' were sweeping through the city massacring the native Christians and burning them alive in their homes. The first building to be burned was the chapel of the Methodist Mission in the Hata Mên-street. Then flames sprang up in many quarters of the city. Amid the most deafening uproar the Tung-tang, or East Cathedral, shot flames into the sky. The old Greek Church in the north-east of the city, the London Mission buildings, the handsome pile of the American Board Mission, and the entire foreign buildings belonging to the Imperial Maritime Customs in the East City burned throughout the night. It was an appalling sight. Late in the night a large party of 'Boxers' bearing torches were seen moving down Customs-street towards the Austrian Legation. The machine gun mounted was in waiting for them. They were allowed to come within 150 yards in the open street near the great cross road, and then the order was given and the gun rained forth death. It was a grateful sound. The torches disappeared. They had come within a restricted space, and none, we thought, could have escaped. Eagerly we went forth to count the dead, expecting to find them in heaps. But there was not one dead. The gun had been aimed very wide of the mark. Two hundred yards north of the 'Boxers' there is a place where 30 ft. above the level road the telegraph wires crossed to the station. Next morning they were found to have been cut by the Austrian fire. The only persons who suffered injury were possible wayfarers two miles up the street. There can be little doubt that this fiasco helped to confirm the Boxers in a belief in their invulnerability.

"The Tung-tang, or East Cathedral, having been burned, it was clear that the Nan-tang, the South Cathedral, was in danger. Père Garrigues, the aged priest of the Tung-tang, had refused to leave his post and had perished in the flames. But the fathers and sisters at the Nan-tang might yet be saved. Their lives were in great peril; it was necessary to act quickly. A party of French gentlemen, led by M. Fliche of the French Legation and accompanied by M. and Mme. Chamot, rode out at night, and early the following morning safely escorted to the hotel every member of the mission—Père d'Addosio and his two colleagues, a French brother, five sisters of charity, and some twenty native nuns of the Order of Josephine. They were rescued just in time. Scarcely had they reached a place of safety when the splendid edifice they had forsaken was in flames. . . . It continued burning all day, the region round it, the chief Catholic centre of Peking, being also burnt. Acres of houses were destroyed and the Christians in thousands put to the sword. . . .

"On the 15th rescue parties were sent out by the American and Russian Legations in the morning, and by the British and German Legations in the afternoon, to save if possible native Christians from the burning ruins around the Nan-tang. Awful sights were witnessed. Wo-men and children hacked to pieces, men trussed like fowls, with noses and ears cut off and eyes gouged out. Chinese Christians accompanied the reliefs and ran about in the labyrinth of network of streets that formed the quarter, calling upon the Christians to come out from their hiding-places. All through the night the massacre had continued, and 'Boxers' were even now shot redhanded at their bloody work. But their work was still incomplete, and many hundreds of women and children had escaped. They came out of their hiding-places crossing themselves and pleading for mercy. It was a most pitiful sight. Thousands of soldiers on the wall witnessed the rescue; they had with callous hearts witnessed the massacre without ever raising a hand to save. During the awful nights of the 13th and 14th Duke Lan, the brother of Prince Tuan, and Chao Shu-Chiao, of the Tsung-li-Yamên, had followed round in their carts to gloat over the spectacle. Yet the Chinese Government were afterwards to describe this massacre done under official supervision under the very walls of the Imperial Palace as the handiwork of local banditti. More than 1,200 of the poor refugees were escorted by the 'foreign devils' to a place of safety. Many were wounded, many were burnt beyond recognition. All had suffered the loss of every thing they possessed in the world. They were given quarters in the palace grounds of Prince Su, opposite the British Legation. Among them was the aged mother and the nephew of Ching Chang, recently Minister to France, and now Chinese Commissioner to the Paris Exhibition. The nephew was cruelly burnt; nearly every other member of the family was murdered. A Catholic family of much distinction—a family Catholic for seven generations—was thus almost exterminated and its property laid in ashes. It was announced this day that only 'Boxers' might enter the Imperial City. The Government was rushing headlong to its ruin.

"On June 16 a party of twenty British, ten Americans, and five Japanese, with some Volunteers, and accompanied by Lieutenant-Colonel Shiba, the Japanese military attaché, patrolled the East City, visiting the ruins in the hopes that some Christians might yet be in hiding. But to our calls everywhere no reply was given. Refugees, however, from the East City had managed to escape miraculously and find their way, many of them wounded, to the foreign Legations, seeking that protection and humanity that was denied them by their own people. As the patrol was passing a Taoist temple on the way, a noted 'Boxer' meeting place, cries were heard within. The temple was forcibly entered. Native Christians were found there, their hands tied behind their backs, awaiting execution and torture. Some had already been put to death, and their bodies were still warm and bleeding. All were shockingly mutilated. Their fiendish murderers were at their incantations burning incense before their gods, offering Christians in sacrifice to their angered deities. They shut themselves within the temple, but their defence availed them nothing. Every one of them, 46 in all, was in 'Boxer' uniform armed with sword and lance. Retribution was swift; every man was shot to death without mercy. In the afternoon a fire broke out in the foreign drug store in the native city outside the great gate of the Chien Mên. It was the work of 'Boxers,' done while the soldiers were looking on. In order to burn the foreign drug store and do the foreigners a few pounds worth of damage, they did not hesitate to jeopardize by fire property worth millions of pounds, and that is what happened. Adjoining buildings took fire, the flames spread to the booksellers' street, and the most interesting street in China, filled with priceless scrolls, manuscripts, and printed books, was gutted from end to end. Fire licked up house after house, and soon the conflagration was the most disastrous ever known in China, reducing to ashes the richest part of Peking, the pearl and jewel shops, the silk and fur, the satin and embroidery stores, the great curio shops, the gold and silver shops, the melting houses, and nearly all that was of the highest value in the metropolis. Irreparable was the damage done. . . .

"During the night the Americans, fearing an attack from the street at the back of their Legation, kept the street clear till daybreak. During one of the volleys four of the Tsung-li-Yamên Ministers called upon the American Minister. They were blandly assuring him that all was now quiet, that there was no need for further alarm, that great was the tenderness of the Throne for men from afar, when a rattle of musketry was heard which rendered them speechless with fear. They hurriedly went away. Assurances of the Throne's tenderness did not deceive us. Our barricades were everywhere strengthened and defences systematically planned, for rumour was quick to reach us that the relief forces had been driven back to Tien-tsin, and this did not add to the security of our position. Inside the Imperial City wall, within one hundred yards of the British picket on the north bridge a large Chinese camp was formed. Peking was in a state of panic, all the streets near the foreign quarters were empty, and people were fleeing from the city. There was a run on the banks, and the Ssu-ta-hêng, the four great banks, the leading banks of Peking, closed their doors, and paper money was not in circulation. The Palace of Prince Su was occupied by the refugees, and its defence, the most important of all and a vital one to the British Legation, was entrusted to Colonel Shiba and Japanese marines and volunteers.

"The crisis was approaching. On the morning of June 19 Mr. Cordes, the Chinese Secretary of the German Legation, was at the Yamên, when the secretaries told him that the allied fleets had taken the Ta-ku forts on June 17. This was remembered when at 4.30 in the afternoon an ultimatum was sent to the foreign Ministers. It was a bolt from the blue. They were to leave Peking within 24 hours. 'A despatch,' they wrote, 'has arrived from the Viceroy Yu Lu, forwarding a note which he has received from the doyen of the Consular body in Tien-tsin, the French Comte du Chaylard, to say that, unless foreign troops are at once permitted to land at Tien-tsin, the allied fleets will bombard the Ta-ku forts. As this is equivalent to a declaration of war, the Tsung-li-Yamên herewith notify the foreign Ministers that they must leave Peking within 24 hours, otherwise protection cannot be guaranteed to them. They will be given safe conduct and transport.' It was quite in accordance with Chinese custom that a despatch saying that the seizure of the Ta-ku forts had been threatened

should be sent after the seizure had been effected. What is distasteful to them to say they avoid saying. A meeting of the diplomatic body was at once held. It was decided to accept the ultimatum. They had been given their passports by the Chinese Government; what other course was open to them ? . . . Word was passed round that preparation had to be made to leave Peking the following day. Mr. Conger, the American Minister, asked for 100 carts; and his Legation spent most of the night making preparations. No packing was done at the British Legation, for it was there considered inconceivable that China should insist upon sending the Ministers their passports. Only two days before, in the 'Peking Gazette' of June 17, it had been officially announced that the road to Tien-tsin was unsafe. . . . When the decision of the Diplomatic Body became known in Peking the most profound indignation was everywhere expressed at so unworthy a decision and the most profound astonishment that such a course of action should have received the support of M. Pichon, the French Minister 'Protecteur des Missions Catholiques en Chine,' and of so humane a man as Mr. Conger, the American Minister; for to leave Peking meant the immediate abandonment to massacre of the thousands of native Christians who had trusted the foreigner and believed in his good faith.

"Early on the morning of the 20th a meeting of the Diplomatic Body was held at the French Legation. No reply had been received from the Tsung-li-Yamên to the request for an audience, and the proposition that all the Ministers should go to the Yamên found no seconder. Had it been carried out, there would have occurred one of the most appalling massacres on record. Two chairs later left for the Yamên. In the first was the German Minister, Baron von Ketteler, who had this advantage over the other Ministers, that he spoke Chinese fluently. In the second was the Chinese Secretary of the German Legation, Mr. Cordes. News travels quickly in Peking. Not many minutes later my boy burst into my office —'Any man speakee have makee kill German Minister !' It was true. The German Minister had been assassinated by an Imperial officer. The Secretary had been grievously wounded, but, running for his life, shot at by a hundred rifles, had escaped as if by a miracle. A patrol of 15 men under Count Soden, the commander, went out to recover the body. Fired on by Chinese soldiers from every side, they were forced to retire. . . . There was no more question about leaving for Tien-tsin. Later in the day the Yamên, evidently indifferent to the gravity of the position created by the Government, sent an impudent despatch to the German Legation to the effect that two Germans had been proceeding in chairs along the Hata Mên-street, and at the month of the street leading to the Tsung-li-Yamên one of them had fired upon the crowd. The Chinese had retaliated and he had been killed. They wished to know his name. No reply was sent, for it was felt to be a mockery. Only too well the Yamên knew whom they had murdered. Weeks passed before the body was recovered, and it was not until July 18 that any official reference was made to the murder. In the course of the morning a despatch was sent to the Diplomatic Body in reply to the answer they had sent to the ultimatum of yesterday. The country, it said, between Peking and Tien-tsin was overrun with brigands, and it would not be safe for the Ministers to go there. They should therefore remain in Peking. It is difficult to write with calmness of the treachery with which the Chinese were now acting. Four p. m. was the hour given in the ultimatum for the Ministers to vacate their Legations, but the ultimatum had been rescinded, and the Ministers invited to remain in Peking. Thus it was hoped that they would be lulled into a false security. Chinese soldiers were secretly stationed under cover at every vantage point commanding the outposts. At 4 p. m. precisely to the minute, by preconcerted signal, they opened fire upon the Austrian and French outposts. A French marine fell shot dead through the forehead. An Austrian was wounded. The siege had begun.

" At this time (June 20), at the opening of the siege, the total strength of the combined Legation guards consisted of 18 officers and 389 men, distributed as follows :—

"American.—Three officers, Captain Myers in command, Captain Hall, Surgeon Lippett, and 53 marines from the Newark.

" Austrian.—Five officers, Captain Thomann, the Commander of the Zenta, Flag-Lieutenant von Winterhalder, Lieutenant Kollar, two midshipmen, and 30 marines from the Zenta.

"British.—Three officers, Captain B. M. Strouts in command, Captain Halliday, Captain Wray, and 79 men R. M. L. I.—30 from H. M. S. Orlando and 49 from Wei-hai-wei.

"French.—Two officers, Captain Darcy and Midshipman Herbert, and 45 marines from the D'Entrecasteaux and Descartes.

"German.—Lieutenant Graf Soden and 51 marines of the 3rd Battalion Kiao-chau.

" Italian.—Lieutenant Paolini and 28 blue-jackets from the Elba.

" Japancae.—Lieutenant Hara and 24 marines from the Atago.

" Russian.—Two officers, Lieutenant Baron von Rahden and Lieutenant von Dehn, and 79 men—72 marines from the Sissoi Veliki and Navarin and seven Legation Cossacks.

"Total, 18 officers and 389 men.

" In addition the French sent Lieutenant Henry and 30 men to guard the Pei-tang Cathedral, and the Italians detached one officer, Lieutenant Cavalieri, and 11 men for the same humane mission. To this insignificant force of 18 officers and 389 men of eight nationalities the entire foreign quarter had to trust for its defence. Fortunately several visitors or residents had received military training, and they at once went on the active list and rendered invaluable service. . . . A volunteer force numbering altogether 75 men, of whom 31 were Japanese, was enrolled and armed with all available rifles. They added greatly to the strength of the garrison, taking watch and watch like the Regulars, fighting behind the barricades, and never shrinking from any duty imposed upon them. There was also an irregular force of 50 gentlemen of many nationalities, who did garrison guard duty in the British Legation and were most useful. They were known, from the gentleman who enrolled them, as 'Thornbill's Roughs,' and they bore themselves as the legitimate successors on foot of Roosevelt's Roughriders. Armed with a variety of weapons, from an elephant rifle to the 'fusil de chasse' with a picture of the Grand Prix,

to all of which carving knives had been lashed as bayonets, they were known as the 'Carving Knife Brigade.'. . . Such were the effective forces. They were provided with four guns, an Italian one-pounder with 120 rounds, an American Colt with 25,000 rounds, an Austrian machine gun, and a British five-barrel Nordenfelt, pattern 1887. Rifle ammunition was very scanty. The Japanese had only 100 rounds apiece, the Russians 145, and the Italians 120, while the best provided of the other guards had only 300 rounds per man, none too many for a siege the duration of which could not be foreseen.

"Punctually, then, at 4 o'clock Chinese soldiers began firing upon us whom they had requested to remain in peace at Peking. And immediately after the Austrian Legation was abandoned. No sufficient reason has been given for its abandonment, which was done so precipitately that not an article was saved. It was left to the mercy of the Chinese, and the guard retired to the corner of Customs-lane, leading west to the Prince's Palace. This involved the sacrifice of Sir Robert Hart's and all the Customs buildings, and hastened the advance of the Chinese westward. As previously arranged, the American mission buildings had been abandoned in the morning, for they were quite untenable. All the missionaries, their wives, and families crossed over to the British Legation. Converts to the number of several hundreds joined the other refugees. The captain and 20 American marines returned to the American Legation. By an error of judgment on the part of the captain the mission was finally left in a panic. Almost nothing was saved, and nearly all the stores accumulated for a siege were lost. The British Legation was now thronged. Rarely has a more cosmopolitan gathering been gathered together within the limits of one compound. All the women and children were there, all the missionaries, American, British, French, and Russian, all the Customs staff, the French, Belgian, Russian, American, Spanish, Japanese, and Italian Ministers, and their families, the entire unofficial foreign community of Peking, with the exception of M. Chamot, who remained in his hotel throughout, though it was in the hottest corner of the besieged area. . . . French volunteers bravely stood by their own Legation, and the Austrian Chargé d'Affaires and Mme. von Rosthorn remained there as long as there was a room habitable. Mr. Squiers, the first Secretary of the American Legation, with Mr. Cheshire, the Chinese Secretary, and Mr. Pethick, the well-known private secretary of Li Hung Chang, stayed by the United States Legation, and the staff of the German Legation also kept stanchly to their posts. . . . At the British Legation fortification began in real earnest, the refugees working like coolies. Sand-bags were made by the thousand, and posts mounted round the Legation. A way was knocked through the houses to the Russian Legation, so that the Americans, if they had to fall back, could pass through to the British Legation. During the day every Legation was exposed to a continuous fire from surrounding house-tops, and in the case of the British Legation from the cover in the Imperial Carriage Park. Chinese put flames to the abandoned buildings, and the Belgian Legation, the Austrian Legation, the Methodist Mission, and some private houses were burned.

"June 22 opened disastrously. The evening before, Captain Thomann, the Austrian commander, announced that as the senior officer he had taken command in Peking. This morning, hearing from an irresponsible American that the American Legation was abandoned, he, without taking steps to verify the information, ordered the abandonment of all the Legations east of Canal-street, the detachments to fall back upon the British Legation. There had been no casualties to speak of, none of the Legations had been attacked, and every commander who received the order to retreat regarded the action as madness. Peremptory orders were sent to the Japanese to abandon the Prince's Palace or Fu (as I shall henceforth call it), and they retired to their Legation. In the British Legation nothing was known of the order when, to the amazement of all, the Italians, Austrians, and French came running down Legation-street, followed a little later by the Japanese, and subsequently by the Germans, who recalled their post on the wall and marched without a shot being fired at them down under the wall to Canal-street. Americans and Russians, learning that all east of Canal-street had been abandoned, saw themselves cut off, though their communications had not even been menaced, and retreated precipitately into the British Legation. It was a veritable stampede—a panic that might have been fraught with the gravest disaster. Prompt action was taken. Captain Thomann was relieved of his command, and Sir Claude MacDonald, at the urgent instance of the French and Russian Ministers, subsequently confirmed by all their colleagues, assumed the chief command. The French and Austrians reoccupied the French Legation, but the barricade in Customs-street was lost. One German only was killed and the position was saved, but the blunder might have been disastrous.

"It was obvious from the first that the great danger at the British Legation was not so much from rifle-fire as from incendiarism, for on three sides the compound was surrounded by Chinese buildings of a highly inflammable nature. Before time could be given to clear an open space round the Legation, the buildings to the rear of Mr. Cockburn's house were set on fire, and as the wind was blowing strongly towards us it seemed as if nothing could prevent the fire from bursting into the Legation. Water had to be used sparingly, for the wells were lower than they had been for years, yet the flames had to be fought. Bullets were whistling through the trees. Private Scadding, the first Englishman to fall, was killed while on watch on the stables near by. Men and women lined up, and water passed along in buckets to a small fire engine that was played upon the fire. Walls were broken through, trees hastily cut down, and desperate work saved the building. It was the first experience of intense excitement. Then the men set to with a will, and till late at night were demolishing the temple and buildings outside the wall of the Legation. Work was continued in the morning, but when it was proposed to pull down an unimportant building in the Hanlin Academy that abuts upon the Legation to the North, the proposition was vetoed. Such desecration, it was said, would wound the susceptibilities of the Chinese Government. It was 'the most sacred building in China.' To lay hands upon it, even

to safeguard the lives of beleaguered women and children, could not be thought of, for fear of wounding the susceptibilities of the Chinese Government! So little do the oldest of us understand the Chinese.

"A strong wind was blowing from the Hanlin into the Legation, the distance separating the nearest building from the Minister's residence being only a few feet. Fire the one and the Minister's residence would have been in danger. Suddenly there was the alarm of fire. Smoke was rising from the Hanlin. The most venerated pile in Peking, the great Imperial Academy, centre of all Chinese learning, with its priceless collection of books and manuscripts, was in flames. Every one who was off duty rushed to the back of the Legation. The Hanlin had been occupied during the night by Imperial soldiers, who did not hesitate, in their rage to destroy the foreigners, to set fire to the buildings. It was first necessary to clear the temple. A breach was made in the wall, Captain Poole headed a force of Marines and volunteers who rushed in, divided, searched the courts, and returned to the main pavilion with its superb pillars and memorial tablets. Chinese were rushing from other burning pavilions to the main entrance. They were taken by surprise and many were killed, but they had done their evil deed. . . . To save the Legation it was necessary to continue the destruction and dismantle the library buildings. With great difficulty, with inadequate tools, the buildings were pulled down. Trees endangering our position were felled. An attempt was made to rescue specimens of the more valuable manuscripts, but few were saved for the danger was pressing. Sir Claude MacDonald, as soon as the fire was discovered, despatched a messenger to the Tsung-li-Yamên, telling them of the fire and urging them to send some responsible officials to carry away what volumes could be rescued, but no attention was given to his courteous communication. The Dutch Legation was burned on the 22nd, and next day Chinese soldiers set fire to the Russo-Chinese Bank, and a greater part of the buildings were destroyed, involving in danger the American Legation. Chinese volunteers were called for. They responded readily, worked with much courage exposed to fire from the wall, and the Legation was saved. All the buildings back from the bank to the Chien Mên (the main gate between the Chinese and Tartar cities facing the entrance to the Forbidden City) seemed to be on fire. Then all the Customs buildings were fired, so that flames were on every side, and the smoke was tremendous, while the fusillade was incessant. An Italian and a German died of their wounds. The first American was killed, shot from the wall, then a Russian fell. They were dropping off one by one, and already we were well accustomed to the sight of the stretcher and the funeral. Wounded were being brought in from every Legation to the hospital in the British Legation. . . .

"Then a new terror was added to the fears of the besieged, for the Imperial troops mounted a 3 in. Krupp gun on the Chien Mên, the gate opposite to the Forbidden City, and began throwing segment shells from a distance of 1,000 yards into the crowded Legation. The first shell struck the American Legation, others burst over the British compound, while others crashed into the upper rooms of the German Legation. It was known that the Chinese had ten similar guns in Peking, while we had nothing with which to answer their fire, and no one ever knew where the next gun might be mounted. Immediately all hands dug bomb-proof shelters for the women and children. Rifle fire also played on the Americans from the wall quite close to them at a distance of a few hundred feet only, whence, safely sheltered by the parapet of the wall, men could enfilade the barricade which was held by the Americans on the street running east and west under the wall. The barricade became untenable, and to occupy the wall was a paramount necessity which could no longer be delayed. . . . Down in the besieged area the enemy pressed upon every side. Again they attempted to fire the British Legation from the Mongol market on the west; but a sortie was made by British Marines and Volunteers, and the Chinese were driven from house to house out of the market. The work was dangerous, and Captain Halliday was dangerously wounded, while Captain Strouts had an extraordinary escape, the bullet grazing the skin above the carotid artery. The sortie was entirely successful; some rifles were captured, and ammunition, which was more precious than silver. The buildings were then fired by us, the fire being kept under control, which cleared a long distance round the west of the Legation. Fortification proceeded without intermission and all the defences of the besieged area quickly gathered strength. For the first time in war, art was a feature in the fortification. Sandbags were of every colour under the sun and of every texture. Silks and satins, curtains and carpets and embroideries were ruthlessly cut up into sandbags. In the Prince's Fu the sandbags were made of the richest silks and satins, the Imperial gifts and accumulated treasures of one of the eight princely families of China. In the Prince's Fu the Chinese made a determined attempt to force their way into the Palace in their frenzy to slaughter the native Christians. In the angle of the wall in the northeastern court of the Palace they made a breach in the wall and rushed wildly in. But the Japanese were waiting for them and from loopholes they had made opposite rolled them over like rabbits, driving them helter-skelter back again. Some 20 were killed, and but for the unsteadiness of the Italians who were assisting the Japanese the execution would have been greater. The Chinese were driven back, but the same evening they threw fireballs of petroleum over the wall and set fire to the building. Flames spread to the splendid main pavilion of the Palace. The Japanese in their turn were driven back, and the Christians escaping from the burning building overflowed from the Fu into all that quarter lying between the Palace grounds and Legation-street.

"On June 25 a truly Oriental method of weakening our defence was attempted by the Chinese. Up to 4 o'clock in the afternoon the shooting of rifles and field guns had been continuous, when suddenly bugles were sounded north, east, south, and west, and, as if by magic, the firing ceased. It was under perfect control—Imperial control commanded by responsible central authority. The silence abruptly following the fusillade was striking. Then an official of low rank was seen .to affix to the parapet of the north bridge near the British Legation a board inscribed with 18 Chinese characters :—'Imperial command to protect Ministers and stop firing. A despatch will be handed at the Imperial Canal Bridge.' A placard whereon was written 'Despatch will be received' was sent by one of the Chinese clerks employed in the Legation, but when he approached the bridge a hundred rifles from the Imperial Palace gate were levelled at him. The despatch was never received. The artifice deceived no one. Treachery was feared, vigilance was redoubled. Sandbags were thrown on positions which during fire were untenable. So that when at midnight the general attack was made upon us we were prepared, and every man was at his post. The surprise had failed. As firing had ceased so it began. Horns were sounded, and then from every quarter a hail of bullets poured over us, sweeping through the trees and striking with sharp impact the roofs of the pavilions. No harm was done though the noise was terrific. Great steadiness was shown by the men. They lay quietly behind the sandbags and not a shot was fired in reply. It was suggested as an explanation of this wild firing that the shots were to kill the guardian spirits which were known to hover over us. Similar fusillades took place at the American Legation and at the French Legation, and with the same result. During the armistice the Chinese had availed themselves of the quiet to throw up earthworks in the Carriage Park alongside the British Legation, in the Mongol market between the British and Russian Legations, and at both ends of Legation-street facing the Americans on the west and facing the French Legation corner on the east.

"Our isolation was now complete, and the enemy's cordon was constantly drawing closer. Every wall beyond the lines was loopholed. Not only was the besieged area cut off from all communication with the world outside Peking, but it was cut off from all communication with the Pei-tang. No messenger could be induced for love or money to carry a message there. Bishop Favier and his guards must have been already hard pressed, for they were exposed to the danger not only of rifle and cannon, but of fire and starvation. The small garrison detached from the guards was known to be inadequately supplied with ammunition. It was known, however, that the danger of the situation had long been foreseen by Monseigneur Favier, who, speaking with unequalled authority, had weeks before the siege vainly urged his Minister to bring troops to Peking. When the crisis became inevitable and Christian refugees poured into the city the Bishop endeavoured to buy arms and ammunition, so that there was a hope, though a faint one, that the Chinese themselves had assisted in the defence. So with stores. Large quantities of grain were stored in the Pei-tang, but whether sufficient for a siege for a garrison of 3,000 souls was not known. Their condition was a constant source of anxiety to the Europeans within the Legations, who were powerless to help them. Watch was kept unceasingly for any sign of the disaster that seemed inevitable—the massacre and the conflagration.

"Towards evening of the 28th a Krupp gun was mounted in the Mongol market, not 300 yards from the British Legation, and fire was opened upon a storeyed building occupied by marines in the south court of the Legation.

Fired at short range, the shells crashed through the roof and walls. For an hour the bombardment continued, but no one was injured, though a crack racing pony in the stables below was killed, and next day eaten. It was determined to capture this gun, so in the early morning a force consisting of 26 British, ten Germans, ten Russians, five French, and five Italians, and about 20 volunteers made a sortie from the Legation to try and capture the gun and burn the houses covering it; but the attempt was a fiasco. The men got tangled up in the lanes so that the reserve line with the kerosene marched ahead of the firing line; there was a Babel of voices, no one knew where to go, the captain lost his head and set fire to the houses in the rear and the men retreated pell-mell. . . . The Chinese, however, were alarmed and removed the gun. Meanwhile both French and German Legations had suffered heavily. . . .

"On the 29th the French Legation was hard pressed. One of their officers, the midshipman Herbert, was shot. Reinforcements were hastily sent from the Fu, and the attack was repulsed; but some of the outer buildings of the Legation were burned, and the French had to retire further into the Legation. In this siege it was striking what a powerful part petroleum was made to play. Already the French Legation had suffered more severely than any other Legation; of their 45 men 16 had been killed or wounded. Krupp guns had been mounted not 50 yards to the eastward, and the eastern walls of the pavilions were being gradually and systematically battered into ruins. All day now and until the cessation of hostilities shells were pounding into the French Legation, into Chamot's hotel, and from the Chien Mên on the wall, promiscuously, everywhere. Much property was destroyed, but, though the shells burst everywhere and escapes were marvellous, few people were hit. Bullets whistled in the Legation compounds. Surgeon Lippett was talking to Mr. Conger in the American Legation when he was hit by a bullet that smashed the thigh bone. Had the bullet not struck the surgeon it would have hit the Minister. Mr. Pethick was sitting at a window of the American Legation fanning himself when a bullet pierced the fan. A civilian was wounded in the British Legation, and a marine, Phillips, was killed while walking in the compound. A fragment of shell fell on a patient inside the hospital.

"The cordon was drawing closer. In the Fu nearly one-third of the buildings had been abandoned and the Japanese retired to a second line of defence. Shells were fired by the hundred. On the 29th 70 shells were thrown into the British Legation. The difficulty of holding the American and German barricades on the city wall was increasing. The positions were very much exposed. A Krupp gun was brought close to the American barricade. The Russo-Chinese Bank and all the buildings near were occupied by Chinese troops, the walls being loopholed and lanes barricaded. And all were so close that you could not look through a loophole without being shot at. Yet the American barricade, with its mixed guard of Americans, Russians, and British, had to be held at all hazards; otherwise the Krupp gun could be brought down the wall and play havoc upon the Legations, the furthest of which—the British—

was at its nearest point not 400 yards distant. Still more exposed than the American barricade was the outpost on the wall held by the Germans. At first they had been reinforced by the French and Austrians, but the needs of the French Legation were equally pressing and the guards were withdrawn and a small picket of British sent to aid the Germans. . . . In the morning of July 1 the Chinese climbed up the ramp and surprised the guard. The order was hastily given to retire, and the picket, shaken by its losses of yesterday, left the wall. The German non-commissioned officer who gave the order was severely blamed for thus abandoning a position that he had been ordered to hold. Withdrawal left the Americans exposed in the rear. They saw the Germans retire, and in a panic fell back to the Legation, rushing pell-mell down the ramp. Nothing had occurred at the barricade itself to justify the retreat, although two men had fallen within a few hours before. Yet the wall was the key of the position and had to be maintained. A conference was held at the British Legation, and as a result orders were given to return to the post. Captain Myers at once took back a strong detachment of 14 Americans, ten British, and ten Russians, and reoccupied the barricade as if nothing had happened. The Chinese, ignorant that the post had been evacuated, lost their opportunity. Then the guard in the French Legation was driven a stage further back and M. Wagner, a volunteer, was killed by the bursting of a shell. . . .

"It was a day of misfortunes. In the afternoon the most disastrous sortie of the siege was attempted. A Krupp gun, firing at short range into the Fu (i. e., the Prince's Palace), was a serious menace to our communications. Captain Paolini, the Italian officer, conceived the idea that he could capture the gun if volunteers could be given him and if the Japanese could assist. . . . By this ineffective sortie our small garrison was reduced by three men killed, one officer and four men and one volunteer wounded. Fortunately it was no worse. The gun that was not captured was brought up again next day into play and continued battering down the Fu walls. The enemy were working their way ever nearer to the refugee Christians. Their rage to reach the Christians was appalling. They cursed them from over the wall, hurled stones at them, and threw shells to explode overhead. Only after the armistice, when we received the 'Peking Gazette,' did we find that word to burn out and slaughter the converts had come from the highest in the land. The Japanese were driven still further back. Already they had lost heavily, for upon them had fallen the brunt of a defence the gallantry of which surpassed all praise. When the siege was raised it was found that of the entire force of marines only five men had escaped without wounds; one was wounded five times. Colonel Shiba early raised a force of 'Christian volunteers,' drilled them, instructed them, and armed them with rifles captured from the enemy. They made an effective addition to the Japanese strength. . . .

"At daybreak on July 3, the Chinese barricade on the top of the wall near the American outpost was successfully stormed by a party of British, Americans, and Russians, under the leadership of Captain Myers, Captain Vroublevsky, and Mr. Nigel Oliphant. . . . The position was intolerable. It was imperative to rush the barricade and drive out the Chinese; nothing else could be done. An attack was planned for 3 in the morning, and before that hour a strong force of British was sent over from the Legation. The combined force assembled for the attack consisted of 26 British marines under Sergeant Murphy and Corporal Gregory, with Mr. Nigel Oliphant as volunteer, 15 Russians under Captain Vroublevsky, and 15 Americans, all being under the command of Captain Myers. When asked if they came willingly one American begged to be relieved and was sent below. This left the total force at 56, of whom 14 were Americans. So close were the Chinese that it was only a couple of jumps from our barricade to their fort. There was a rush to be first over, the fort was stormed, and dashing round the covering wall the 'foreign devils' charged behind the barricade. Taken by surprise the Chinese fired in the air, fled incontinently, and were shot down as they ran along the open surface of the wall. Captain Vroublevsky and his detachment acted with especial gallantry, for their duty it was to attack the Chinese barricade in the front, while the British and Americans took it in the rear. Two banners marked 'General Ma' were captured. Fifteen Chinese soldiers of Tung-fuh-siang were killed outright and many more must have been wounded. Some rifles and ammunition were captured. Then the allied forces, exposed to a heavy fire, retired within what had been the Chinese barricade and employed it against the enemy who had built it. Captain Myers was wounded in the knee by tripping over a fallen spear, two Americans, Turner and Thomas—one having accidentally jumped on the wrong side of the barricade—were killed, and Corporal Gregory was wounded in the foot. News of the successful sortie gave much pleasure to the community. Chinese coolies were sent on the wall, and a strongly intrenched redoubt was built there; the camp was made safe by traverses. Unfortunately, the wound of Captain Myers proved more serious than was at first suspected, and he was not again able to return to duty. The services of a brave and capable officer were lost to the garrison; his post on the wall was taken most ably by Captain Percy Smith and other officers in turn.

"Most of the shelling was now directed against the French and German Legations and Chamot's Hotel. The hotel was struck 91 times and was several times set on fire, but the flame was extinguished. Work continued there, however hot the shelling, for food had to be prepared there for half the community in Peking, Russians, French, Germans, and Austrians. The energy of Chamot was marvellous. He fed the troops and a crowd of Christian refugees, killed his own mules and horses, ground his own wheat, and baked 300 loaves a day. Shelled out of the kitchen he baked in the parlour. His courage inspired the Chinese, and they followed him under fire with an amazing confidence.

"Then suddenly a new attempt was made to reduce the British Legation. Guns firing round shot, eight-pounders and four-pounders, were mounted on the Imperial City wall overlooking from the north the Hanlin and the British Legation. With glasses—the distance was only 350 yards—one could clearly see the officers and distinguish their Imperial Peacock feathers and Mandarin hats. . . . Three batteries in all, carrying five guns, were mounted on the Imperial City wall where the bombardment could be witnessed by the Empress Dowager and her counsellors, and day after day round shot were thrown from them into the British Legation, into a compound crowded with women and children. . . . On July 5 Mr. David Oliphant, of the British Legation, was killed. He was felling a tree by the well in the Hanlin when he was shot by a sniper concealed in a roof in the Imperial Carriage Park, and died within an hour. Only 24 years of age, he was a student of exceptional promise and ability. . . .

"Day by day the Chinese were pressing us more closely. In the Fu they were gradually wedging their way in from the north-east so as to cut the communications between the British and the Legations to the east. They burned their way from house to house. Keeping under cover, they set alight the gables within reach by torches of cloth soaked in kerosene held at the end of long poles. If the roof were beyond reach they threw over fireballs of kerosene, or, if still further, shot into them with arrows freighted with burning cloth. In this way and with the use of the heavy gun they battered a way through the houses and courtyards of the Prince's Palace. A daring attempt made by the Japanese to capture the gun resulted in failure. Coolies failed them when they were within four yards of success, and they were forced to retire. Their gallant leader Captain Ando was shot in the throat while waving on his men, one marine was seriously wounded, and one Christian volunteer killed. . . . By the 8th the position in the Fu was alarming, for the Japanese force had been reduced to 13 marines and 14 volunteers; yet with decreasing numbers they were constantly called upon to defend a longer line. Reinforcements were sent them of half-a-dozen Customs and student volunteers and of six British marines. Nothing can give a better indication of the smallness of our garrison than the fact that throughout the siege reinforcements meant five men or ten men. Strong reinforcements meant 15 men. Our reinforcements were counted by ones, not by companies. With this force a line of intrenchments stretching from the outer court of the Fu on the east across the grounds to near the extreme northwest corner was held till the end. . . . The position was one of constant solicitude, for the loss of the Fu would have imperilled the British Legation. A Krupp gun, mounted 50 yards away, had the range and raked the post with shell and shrapnel. To strengthen the breastwork exposure to rifle fire was incurred from 20 yards' distance, while to reach the post required crossing a zone of fire which was perhaps the hottest in the whole of the defences. Many men were wounded there, and one Italian had his head blown off. Shell fire finally made it impossible to live there. The advanced posts were abandoned, and the sentries fell back to the main picket. No sooner was the advanced post abandoned than it was occupied by the Chinese, and the defences we had made were turned against us.

"Meanwhile, the French and German Legations were being roughly handled, and men were falling daily. At the German Legation shells burst through the Minister's drawing-room. Most of the other buildings conspicuous by their height were uninhabitable, but every member of the Legation remained at his post. So, too, in the French Legation, where the Austrians were, Dr. and Madame von Rosthorn remained by the side of their men. The French volunteers and Dr. Matignon stood stanchly by their Legation, although it was fast tumbling into ruins, their coolness and resolution being in curious contrast to the despair of their Minister, who, crying, 'Tout est perdu,' melodramatically burned the French archives in a ditch at the British Legation. Chinese and French were so close that the voices of the Chinese officers could be heard encouraging their men. Chinese were within the Legation itself. Their guns literally bombarded the Minister's residence 'à bout portant,' and the noise of the exploding shells was terrific. Yet the men never flinched. . . . July 11 was a day of many casualties. One German was mortally wounded ; one Englishman, one Italian, and one Japanese were seriously wounded. Mr. Nigel Oliphant, a volunteer, received a bullet wound in the leg, while Mr. Narahara, the well-known secretary of the Japanese Legation, wounded by the bursting of a shell, suffered a compound fracture of the leg, which from the first gave cause for anxiety. He gradually sank and died on July 24. . . .

"On the 11th 18 prisoners were captured by the French in a temple near the Legation. They were soldiers, and a Chinese Christian gave information as to their whereabouts. Every one of them was put to death without mercy in the French Legation, bayoneted by a French corporal to save cartridges. Questioned before death they gave much information that was obviously false. One man, however, declared that a mine was being dug under the French Legation. His story had quick corroboration. As the afternoon of the 13th was closing a feint attack was made on the Japanese intrenchments in the Fu. Then the sound of many bugles was heard from the camps round the French Legation, to be followed in a few minutes by a terrific explosion, and in a moment or two by another; and bricks and débris were hurled into the air. It was a dull roar in the midst of the devilish cries of hordes of Chinese, shrieking like spirits in hell, the rattle of musketry, and the boom of heavy guns. The mine of which the prisoner had warned us had exploded and burst an entrance into the French Legation. When the first mine exploded the French Captain Darcy, the Austrian Chargé d'Affaires, two French marines, and Mr. Destelan of the Customs were standing over the death-trap. Mr. Destelan was buried up to the neck, but was rescued unhurt, the two marines were engulfed and their bodies were never recovered, Captain Darcy and Dr. von Rosthorn escaped miraculously. The latter was buried by the first explosion and released unhurt a moment or two later by the second. Driven out of the main buildings, the small garrison (it consisted only of 17 Austrians with three officers, 27 French with two officers, and nine volunteers) fell back a few paces to a line of defence, part of which had only been completed in the afternoon, and securely held the position.

"Simultaneously with this attack upon the French Legation the Chinese made a determined assault upon the German Legation, the effective strength of whose garrison numbered only one officer and 31 men. They broke into the Club alongside the Legation and were on the tennis ground when Count Soden and a handful of German soldiers gallantly charged them at the point of the bayonet and drove them out headlong. . . . Uniforms on the dead Chinese showed that the attack had been carried out by the troops of Yung Lu, reinforced by the savages of Tung-fuh-siang. Some of the dead were armed with the latest pattern Mauser and the newest German army revolver. Some ammunition, of which the guards were in much need, was recovered and distributed among the Japanese and Italians. Firing continued round the other Legations ; every battery opened fire ; the air hissed with bullets. There was momentary darkness, then flames broke out from the large foreign houses between the German Legation and Canal-street. It seemed at one time as if the whole of the quarter would be burned, but the fire did not spread. Heavy rain came on, and the rest of the night passed in quiet.

"On July 14, a messenger, sent out on the 10th, with a letter for the troops, returned to the British Legation. He had been arrested by the Chinese, cruelly beaten, and taken, he said, to the yamên of Yung Lu, and there given the following letter, purporting to be written by Prince Ching 'and others,' addressed to the British Minister. It was the first communication of any kind whatsoever that had reached us from outside for nearly one month. ' For the last ten days the soldiers and Militia have been fighting, and there has been no communication between us, to our great anxiety. Some time ago we hung up a board, expressing our intentions, but no answer has been received, and contrary to expectation the foreign soldiers made renewed attacks, causing alarm and suspicion among soldiers and people. Yesterday the troops captured a convert named Chin Ssu-hei and learnt from him that all the foreign Ministers were well, which caused us very great satisfaction. But it is the unexpected which happens. The reinforcements of foreign troops were long ago stopped and turned back by the "Boxers," and if, in accordance with previous agreement, we were to guard your Excellencies out of the city, there are so many "Boxers" on the road to Tien-tsin and Ta-ku that we should be apprehensive of misadventure. We now request your Excellencies to first take your families and the various members of your staffs, and leave your Legations in detachments. We should select trustworthy officers to give close and strict protection, and you should temporarily reside in the Tsung-li-Yamên, pending future arrangements for your return home, in order to preserve friendly relations intact from beginning to end. But at the time of leaving the Legations there must on no account whatever be taken any single armed soldier, in order to prevent doubt and fear on the part of the troops and people, leading to untoward incidents. If your Excellencies are willing to show this confidence, we beg you to communicate with all the foreign Ministers in Peking, to-morrow at noon being the limit of time, and to let the original messenger deliver the reply in order that we may settle the day for leaving the Legations. This is the single way of preserving relations which we have been able to devise in the face of innumerable difficulties. If no reply is received by the time fixed, even our affection will not enable us to help you. Compliments. (Signed) Prince Ching and others. July 14, 1900.'

"Following as it did immediately after the attack on the French Legation, which reduced it to ruins, the letter did not lack for impudence. 'Boxers' had driven back our troops, 'Militia,' not 'Boxers,' had been attacking us in Peking. The letter was read with derision. It was interpreted as a guileless attempt to seduce the Ministers away from their Legations and massacre them at ease. News we heard subsequently had just reached the Chinese of the taking of Tientsin city. . . . On the 15th a reply was sent declining on the part of the foreign representatives the invitation to proceed to the Tsung-li-Yamên, and pointing out that no attacks had been made by our troops, who were only defending the lives and property of foreigners against the attacks of Chinese Government troops. The reply concluded with a statement that if the Chinese Government wished to negotiate they should send a responsible official with a white flag. . . .

"The morning of the 16th opened with a disaster. Captain Strouts, the senior British officer, was shot while returning from the outposts in the Fu. He was struck in the upper part of the left thigh by an expanding bullet, and died an hour after being brought into the hospital, to the grief of the entire community. . . . While shells were bursting in the trees, and amid the crack of rifle bullets, the brave young fellow to whose gallant defence we all owed so much was laid to rest. . . . While the service was proceeding a messenger bearing a flag of truce was approaching the gate. . . The letter was from 'Prince Ching and others.' It explained that the reason for suggesting the removal of the Legations to the Tsung-li-Yamên was that the Chinese Government could afford more efficient protection to the members of the Legations if concentrated than if scattered as at present. As the foreign Ministers did not agree, however, the Chinese would as in duty bound do their utmost to protect the Legations where they were. (While the latter sentence was being read the translator had to raise his voice in order that it should be heard above the crack of the Imperial rifle bullets.) They would bring reinforcements and continue their endeavours to prevent the 'Boxers' from firing, and they trusted that the foreign Ministers on their part would restrain their troops also from firing.

' By the same messenger a cipher message was brought to Mr. Conger, the American Minister. It said :—'Communicate tidings bearer.' It was in the State Department cipher and had no date or indication by whom it had been sent. Mr. Conger replied in the same cipher :—'For one month we have been besieged in British Legation under continued shot and shell from Chinese troops. Quick relief only can prevent general massacre.' When forwarding his reply he asked that it should be sent to the address from which the other had come, which address had not been communicated to him. Next day the Yamên sent him an answer saying that his message had been forwarded and explaining that the telegram sent to him had been contained in a telegram from Wu Ting Fang, the Chinese Minister at Washington, dated July 11. This telegram read :—' The United States cheerfully aid China, but it is thinking of Mr. Minister Conger. The Hon. Secretary of State inquires after him by

telegram, which I beg to be transmitted to him and get his reply.' From this we could well imagine what specious assurances had been given to Mr. Hay by Wu Ting Fang's bland assurances that there had been a most regrettable outbreak on the part of lawless bands in the north of China which the Government was vainly struggling to cope with. . . . From July 17 there was a cessation of hostilities ; not that men were not wounded afterwards and Christian coolies fired upon whenever they showed themselves, but the organized attacks ceased and the Krupp guns were muzzled. Fearing treachery, however, we relaxed none of our vigilance. Trenches were cut where mines might have been driven. All walls and shelters were so strengthened as to be practically shell-proof. Our preparations were purely defensive. On their part the Chinese also continued work at their barricades. From their barricade on the top of the wall near the German Legation they advanced westward so that they could fire directly down into the German Legation and pick off men going up the steps of the Minister's house. They built a wall with loop-holes across Legation-street not 20 yards from the Russian barricade. In nearly every position the enemy were so close that you could shoot into the muzzles of their rifles thrust through the loop-holes. The cordon was still drawn tightly round us, and we were penned in to prevent our acting in co-operation with the troops who were coming to our relief. No provisions were permitted to reach us, but a few eggs for the women and children were surreptitiously sold us by Chinese soldiers. All were on reduced rations, the allowance for the 2,750 native Christians whom we had to provide for being barely sufficient to save them from starvation. Their sufferings were very great, the mortality among the children and the aged pitiful. No one could have foreseen that within the restricted limits of the besieged area, with the food supply therein obtainable, 473 civilians (of these 414—namely, 191 men, 147 women, 76 children—were inside the British Legation), a garrison of 400 men, 2,750 refugees, and some 400 native servants could have sustained a siege of two entire months. Providentially in the very centre of Legation-street there was a mill with a large quantity of grain which turned out 900 lb. of flour a day divided between the hotel and the Legation. One day the Tsung-li-Yamên insultingly sent us a present of 1,000 lb. of flour and some ice and vegetables, but no one would venture to eat the flour, fearing that it might be poisoned. Communications now passed almost daily with the Tsung-li-Yamên or with the officials whose despatches were signed 'Prince Ching and others.' On July 17, Sir Claude Mac-Donald replied to the suggestion that the Ministers would restrain their troops from firing upon the Chinese. He said that from the first the foreign troops had acted entirely in self-defence, and would continue to do so. But the Chinese must understand that previous events had led to a want of confidence and that if barricades were erected or troops moved in the vicinity of the Legations the foreign guards would be obliged to fire. In the afternoon the Chinese replied, reviewing the situation and ascribing the hostilities to the attacks previously made by the Legation guards. They noted with satisfaction that a cessation of firing was agreed to on both sides, but suggested that as foreign soldiers had been firing from the city wall east of the Chien Mên, they should be removed from that position. Next day, Sir Claude MacDonald replied with a review of the situation from the forcign point of view. . . . He hoped that mutual confidence would gradually be restored, but meanwhile he again pointed out that cessation of hostile preparations as well as firing was necessary on the part of the Chinese troops to secure that the foreign troops should cease firing. As for the suggestion that the foreign troops should leave the city wall, it was impossible to accede to it, because a great part of the attacks on the Legations had been made from the wall. He concluded by suggesting that sellers of fruit and ice should be allowed to come in. They were never permitted to come in. It was clear, however, that events were happening elsewhere to cause alarm in the Imperial Court. On the afternoon of the first day of what might be called the armistice M. Pelliot, a French gentleman from Tongking, entered the Chinese lines and to the great anxiety of all was absent five hours. He was taken by soldiers to a yamên of one of the big generals—he knew not which—was plied with questions which, speaking some Chinese, he could answer, and was sent back unmolested with an escort of 15 soldiers ' to protect him against the Boxers.' This unusual clemency was interpreted favourably. It was clear that the Chinese had sustained a severe defeat and that relief was coming. Next day direct communication was for the first time held with an official of the Tsung-li-Yamên. A secretary named Wen Jui came to the Legation to see Sir Claude MacDonald and was received by the Minister outside the gate, not being permitted to enter. He said that the regrettable occurrences were due to ' local banditti,' that the Government had great concern to protect the foreigners, that Baron von Ketteler's body had been recovered from the hands of the ' local banditti ' who had murdered him and been enclosed in a valuable coffin. He urged that the maintenance of foreign troops on the city wall was unnecessary and that they should be withdrawn. It was pointed out to him that, as we had been very continuously shelled from the city wall both from the Ha-ta Mên and the Chien Mên, it would be inadvisable to retire. Asked to send copies of the ' Peking Gazette,' he hesitated a moment and then stammered that he really had not himself seen the ' Peking Gazette ' for a long time, but he would inquire and see if they could be bought. He never came back and never sent a ' Gazette.' His name was Wen Jui. When we did obtain copies of the ' Gazette' it was interesting to find two items that must have been especially unpleasant for him to have us know. On June 24, by Imperial decree, leaders were appointed to the ' Boxers.' or ' patriotic militia.' Among the chiefs was Wen Jui.

" The visit of Wen Jui was on the 18th. Up to the time of his visit, though more than four weeks had passed since the assassination, no allusion of any kind whatever had been made in any ' Peking Gazette ' to the murder of Baron von Ketteler. Then the Empress-Dowager, yielding to her fears, published an allusion to the murder. Will the German Emperor rest satisfied with the tardy official reference to the brutal assassination of his Minister by an Imperial officer ? ' Last month

the Chancellor of the Japanese Legation was killed. This was, indeed, most unexpected. Before this matter had been settled the German Minister was killed. Suddenly meeting this affair caused us deep grief. We ought vigorously to seek the murderer and punish him.' No more. The date July 18 ; the murder June 20 I

" Yet even in this decree there was a complete ' volte-face.' Missionaries who were by the decree of July 2 ' to be at once driven away to their own countries' were by the decree of July 18 ' to be protected in every province,' ' to be proteeted without the least carelessness.' The trueulence and belligerence of the decrees issued when our troops had been driven back had disappeared ; the tone now was one of justification and conciliation. Only one interpretation was possible—that the Chinese had been defeated. Confirmation came the same day. A messenger sent out by the Japanese successfully passed the enemy's lines and brought us the news that we had so long awaited. . . . By the same messenger a letter was received by the French Minister. . . . The same messenger also brought to the Belgian Minister a despatch from his Consul at Tien-tsin. . . . Days followed quietly now, though ' sniping' did not cease. Several casualties occurred among the garrison. A Russian was killed and an Austrian wounded ; an Italian wounded and also a Japanese. In the Fu it was still dangerous for the Christian refugees to move about, and several were hit and two killed. But the Yamên became more and more conciliatory, until we could gauge the advance of the reliefs by the degree of apology in their despatches. But all supplies were rigorously cut off, and the sufferings of the Christians were acute. . . .

" On the 22nd Sir Robert Hart received a despatch from the Tsung-li-Yamên. They naïvely remarked that it was now one month since they had heard from him, and his silence gave them concern for his welfare. Moreover, a report had just reached them that his house had been burned, but they expressed the hope that he and all his staff were well. Another despatch requested his advice upon a Customs question that had arisen in Shanghai. Sir Robert Hart wrote a dignified reply. For more than a month, he said, he had been a refugee in the British Legation with all his staff, having had to flee from his house without warning ; that all Customs records and papers, and every paper and letter of value that he had accumulated during a lifetime, had been destroyed ; that not only his house, but some 19 other buildings in the occupation of his staff had been burned with all their contents ; that the acting postal secretary had been killed by a shell, and two other members of his staff—Mr. Richardson and Mr. Macoun—had been wounded by bullets. . . .

" Meanwhile, the armistice continued, if armistice it can be called where true armistice there was none. Desultory firing continued, and sniping was still the chief pastime at the Chinese outposts. Friendly relations were, however, opened with some Chinese soldiers in the Fu. A Japanese Volunteer established a bureau of intelligence to which the enemy's soldiers had access. One soldier was especially communicative, and earned high reward for the valuable information that he conveyed to us. For a week from July 26 to August 2 daily bulletins based upon this information of the advance of the relief column were posted on the bell tower of the British Legation. An unbroken series of victories was attending our relief forces. . . . Letters were given to the soldier to take to the general of the relief column, and a reward offered if an answer should be brought next day, but no answer was ever brought. Our informant had brought the armies along too quickly. He was compelled to send them back. Accordingly on the 31st he made the Chinese recapture Chang-chia-wan, killing 60 of the foreigners ; advancing upon Matou he killed 70 foreigners more, and drove them back to An-ping. Next day he drove the foreigners disastrously back to Tien-tsin with a loss of 1,000. The day was equally disastrous to himself. Our informant had killed the goose that lay the golden egg. For a messenger arrived on that day with letters from Tien-tsin, dated July 30, informing us that a large force was on the point of leaving for our relief. . . . Meanwhile, while our informant was marching our relief backwards and forwards to Tien-tsin, Prince Ching and others were vainly urging the Ministers to leave Peking, but whether they left Peking or not they were to hand over the Christian refugees now under the protection of the Legations to the mercies of the Government, which had issued a decree commanding that they be exterminated unless they recanted their errors. In other communications Prince Ching 'and others' urged that the foreign Ministers should telegraph to their Government 'en clair' lying reports of the condition of affairs in Peking.

"Two days after the cessation of hostilities Prince Ching 'and others' sent a despatch to Sir Claude MacDonald to the effect that it was impossible to protect the Ministers in Peking because 'Boxers' were gathering from all points of the compass, and that nothing would satisfy them (the 'Boxers') but the destruction of the Legations, and that the Ministers would be given safe conduct to Tien-tsin. Sir Claude, in reply, asked why it was that protection could be given to the Ministers on the way to Tien-tsin and yet could not be given to them while in the Legations in Peking. Prince Ching 'and others' replied :— 'July 25, 1900. . . . As to the inquiry what difference there is between giving protection in the city or on the road, and why it is possible to give it in the latter, there is only an apparent discrepancy. For the being in the city is permanent, the being on the road is temporary. If all the foreign Ministers are willing to temporarily retire we should propose the route to Tung-chau and thence by boat down stream to Tien-tsin, which could be reached in only two days. No matter what difficulties there might be a numerous body of troops would be sent, half by water to form a close escort, half by road to keep all safe for a long way on both banks. Since the time would be short we can guarantee that there would be no mishap. It is otherwise with a permanent residence in Peking, where it is impossible to foretell when a disaster may occur.' . . . In the envelope which brought this letter were two other communications of the same guileless nature. 'On July 24,' said the first, 'we received a telegram from Mr. Warren, British Consul-General in Shanghai, to the effect that while China was protecting the Legations no telegram had been received from the British Minister, and asking the Yamên to transmit Sir C. M. MacDonald's telegram to Shanghai. As in

duty bound we communicate the above, and beg you to send a telegram "en clair" to the Yamên for transmission.' Tender consideration was shown for us in the second letter : — 'For the past month and more military affairs have been very pressing. Your Excellency and other Ministers ought to telegraph home that your families are well in order to soothe anxiety, but at the present moment peace is not yet restored, and your Legation telegrams must be wholly "en clair," stating that all is well, without touching on military affairs. Under those conditions the Yamên can transmit them. The writers beg that your Excellency will communicate this to the other foreign Ministers.'

"Evasive replies were given to these communications. . . . Our position at this time compelled us to temporize. We knew from the alteration in tone of the Chinese despatches that they had suffered defeats and were growing alarmed, but we did not know how much longer international jealousies or difficulties of obtaining transport were to delay the departure of the troops for Tien-tsin. . . . Though now nominally under the protection of an armistice sniping still continued, especially in the Fu, into any exposed portion of the besieged area. . . . The Chinese worked on continuously at their fortifications. . . . Finding that the Ministers declined to telegraph to their Governments 'en clair' that all was well with the Legations, the Tsung-li-Yamên wrote to Sir Robert Hart asking him to send home a telegram in the sense they suggested. Sir Robert replied diplomatically, 'If I were to wire the truth about the Legations I should not be believed.'

"A malevolent attempt was next made by the Chinese to obtain possession of the refugees who were in our safe keeping. On July 27 they wrote to Sir Claude MacDonald saying that 'they hear that there are lodged at the Legations a considerable number of converts, and that, as the space is limited and weather hot, they suggest that they must be causing the Legations considerable inconvenience. And now that people's minds are quieted, these converts can all be sent out and go about their ordinary avocations. They need not have doubts or fears. If you concur, an estimate should be made of the numbers and a date fixed for letting them out. Then all will be in harmony.' The reply of the diplomatic body was to the effect that while they were considering the two last letters—one offering safe conduct to Tien-tsin and the other declaring that the converts might leave the Legations in perfect security—heavy firing was heard in the direction of the Pei-tang, which was evidently being attacked in force; that yesterday and last night a barricade was built across the North Bridge, from behind which shots are being continuously fired into the British Legation. The French and Russian Legations are also being fired upon. As all this seems inconsistent with the above letters, an explanation is asked for before further consideration is given to the offer. Promptly the Yamên sent its explanation. The Pei-tang refugees, it seemed, who were starving, had made a sortie to obtain food. And they had fired upon the people. 'A decree,' it went on to say, 'has now been requested to the effect that if the converts do not come out to plunder they are to be protected and not to be continually attacked,' for they also are the children of the State. This practice (of continually tiring upon the converts) will thus be gradually stopped.' Such a callous reply was read with indignation, and there was not the slightest intention on the part of any Minister to leave Peking. Yet on the 4th of August a decree was issued appointing Yung Lu to conduct the foreign Ministers safely to Tien-tsiu ' in order once more to show the tenderness of the Throne for the men from afar.' . . .

"On August 10, Friday, a messenger succeeded in passing the enemy's lines, and brought us letters from General Gaselee and General Fukushima. A strong relief force was marching to Peking, and would arrive here if nothing untoward happened on the 13th or 14th. Our danger then was that the enemy would make a final effort to rush the Legations before the arrival of reinforcements. And the expected happened. . . .

"Yesterday [August 13] passed under a continuous fusillade which increased during the night. Then at 3 on this morning we were all awakened by the booming of guns in the east and by the welcome sound of volley firing. Word flew round that 'the foreign troops are at the city wall and are shelling the East Gate.' At daylight most of us went on to the wall, and witnessed the shelling of the Great East Gate. We knew that the allies would advance in separate columns, and were on the qui vive of excitement, knowing that at any moment now the troops might arrive. Luncheon, the hard luncheon of horseflesh, came on, and we had just finished when the cry rang through the Legation, 'The British are coming,' and there was a rush to the entrance and up Canal-street towards the Water Gate. The stalwart form of the general and his staff were entering by the Water Gate, followed by the 1st Regiment of Sikhs and the 7th Rajputs. They passed down Canal-street, and amid a scene of indescribable emotion marched to the British Legation. The siege has been raised.

"Peking, Aug. 15. On reading over my narrative of the siege I find that in the hurry and confusion of concluding my report I have omitted one or two things that I had wished to say. In the first place, I find that I have not in any adequate way expressed the obligation of all those confined in the British Legation to the splendid services done by the Rev. F. D. Gamewell, of the American Episcopal Mission [who was educated as a civil engineer at Troy and Cornell], to whom was due the designing and construction of all our defences, and who carried out in the most admirable manner the ideas and suggestions of our Minister, Sir Claude MacDonald. To the Rev. Frank Norris, of the Society for the Propagation of the Gospel, our thanks are also specially due. He superintended, often under heavy fire, the construction of defences in the Prince's Fu and in other exposed places, working always with a courage and energy worthy of admiration. He was struck in the neck once by a segment of a shell, but escaped marvellously from serious injury. He speaks Chinese well, and Chinese worked under him with a fearlessness that few men can inspire. In the second place, I noticed that I have not sufficiently recorded the valuable services rendered by Mr. H. G. Squiers, the First Secretary of the American Legation, who on the death of Captain

Strouts became Chief of the Staff to Sir Claude MacDonald. He had been for 15 years in the United States cavalry, and his knowledge and skill and the resolution with which he inspired his small body of men will not readily be forgotten. . . .

"To-day the Pei-tang Cathedral was relieved. Bishops, priests, and sisters had survived the siege and, thanks to the wonderful foresight of Bishop Favier, the Christians had been spared from starvation. Japanese coming down from the north of the city relieved the cathedral; French, British, and Russians from the south arrived as the siege was raised. Mines had been employed with deadly effect. The guards had lost five French killed and five Italians. Some 200 of the Christians had perished." — *London Times, Oct.* 13 *and* 15, 1900.

A. D. 1900 (June—December).—Upright conduct of the Chinese Viceroys in the Yang-tsze provinces.—In his annual message of December 3, 1900, to Congress, referring to the occurrences in China, the President of the United States remarked with much justice: "It is a relief to recall and a pleasure to record the loyal conduct of the viceroys and local authorities of the southern and eastern provinces. Their efforts were continuously directed to the pacific control of the vast populations under their rule and to the scrupulous observance of foreign treaty rights. At critical moments they did not hesitate to memorialize the Throne, urging the protection of the legations, the restoration of communication, and the assertion of the Imperial authority against the subversive elements. They maintained excellent relations with the official representatives of foreign powers. To their kindly disposition is largely due the success of the consuls in removing many of the missionaries from the interior to places of safety." The viceroys especially referred to in this are Chang Chih-tung and Liu Kun-yi, often referred to as "the Yang-tsze viceroys."

A. D. 1900 (July).—Speech of German Emperor to troops departing to China, commanding no quarter. See (in this vol.) GERMANY: A. D. 1900 (OCTOBER 9).

A. D. 1900 (July).—American troops sent to co-operate with those of other Powers.—Capture of Tientsin by the allied forces.—Death of Colonel Liscum.—Reported massacre of foreign Ministers and others in Peking.—The long month of dread suspense.—Overtures from Earl Li Hung-chang for negotiation.— "On the 26th of June Maj. Gen. Adna R. Chaffee, U. S. V., was appointed to the command of the American forces in China. He embarked from San Francisco on the 1st of July, reached Nagasaki on the 24th, and Taku, China, on the 28th. . . . On reaching Nagasaki he received the following instructions, dated, . . . July 19: 'Secretary War directs that you proceed at once with transport Grant, Sixth Cavalry, and Marines to Taku, China, and take command of American land forces, which will be an independent command known as the China relief expedition. You will find there the Ninth and Fourteenth Infantry, one battery of the Fifth Artillery, and one battalion of Marines. Sumner sailed from San Francisco July 17 with Second Battalion of Fifteenth Infantry and recruits to capacity of vessel. Reinforcements will follow to make your force in the immediate future up to

5,000, and very soon to 10,000. . . . Reports now indicate that American Minister with all the legation have been destroyed in Pekin. Chinese representatives here, however, insists to the contrary, and there is, therefore, a hope which you will not lose sight of until certainty is absolute. It is the desire of this Government to maintain its relations of friendship with the part of Chinese people and Chinese officials not concerned in outrages on Americans. Among these we consider Li Hung Chang, just appointed viceroy of Chili. You will to the extent of your power aid the Government of China, or any part thereof, in repressing such outrages and in rescuing Americans, and in protecting American citizens and interests, and wherever Chinese Government fails to render such protection you will do all in your power to supply it. Confer freely with commanders of other national forces, act concurrently with them, and seek entire harmony of action along the lines of similar purpose and interest. There should be full and free conference as to operations before they are entered upon. You are at liberty to agree with them from time to time as to a common official direction of the various forces in their combined operations, preserving, however, the integrity of your own American division, ready to be used as a separate and complete organization. Much must be left to your wise discretion and that of the admiral. At all times report fully and freely to this Department your wants and views. The President has to-day appointed you major-general of volunteers.' . . .

"In the meantime the Ninth Infantry, from Manila, reached Taku on the 6th of July. Two battalions of that regiment, under Colonel Liscum, pressed forward to Tientsin, reaching that point on the 11th, and on the 13th took part with the British, French, and Japanese forces in an attack upon the southwest part of the walled city of Tientsin, which had been rendered necessary by the persistent shelling of the foreign quarters, outside of the walls, on the part of the Chinese troops occupying the city. Colonel Liscum's command formed part of a brigade under General Dorward, of the British army, and was assigned to the duty of protecting the flank of the allied forces. In the performance of that duty it maintained a position under heavy fire for fifteen hours, with a loss of 18 killed and 77 wounded. Among the killed was the gallant Colonel Liscum, who thus ended an honorable service of nearly forty years, commencing in the ranks of the First Vermont Infantry at the outbreak of the civil war, and distinguished by unvarying courage, fidelity, and high character. The regiment was withdrawn from its position on the night of the 13th, and on the morning of the 14th the native city was captured, and the southeast quarter was assigned to the American forces for police and protection. . . .

"At the time of the capture of Tientsin the most positive and circumstantial accounts of the massacre of all the ministers and members of the legations in Pekin, coming apparently from Chinese sources, had been published, and were almost universally believed. The general view taken by the civilized world of the duty to be performed in China was not that the living representatives of the Western powers in Pekin were to be rescued, but that their murder was to be avenged and their murderers punished. In

the performance of that duty time and rapidity of movement were not especially important. The resolution of the commanders of the allied forces, communicated by Admiral Kempff on the 8th of July, to the effect that 80,000 men would be required—20,000 to hold the position from Taku to Tientsin and 60,000 to march to Pekin, while not more than 40,800 troops were expected to have arrived by the middle of August, practically abandoned all expectation of rescuing the ministers and members of the legations alive, for it proposed that after the middle of August any forward movement should be still deferred until 40,000 more troops had arrived. On the 11th of July, however, the American Secretary of State secured, through the Chinese minister at Washington, the forwarding of a dispatch in the State Department cipher to the American minister at Pekin, and on the 20th of July, pursuant to the same arrangement, an answer in cipher was received from Minister Conger, as follows : 'For one month we have been besieged in British legation under continued shot and shell from Chinese troops. Quick relief only can prevent general massacre.' This dispatch from Mr. Conger was the first communication received by any Western power from any representative in Pekin for about a month, and although it was at first received in Europe with some incredulity, it presented a situation which plainly called for the urgency of a relief expedition rather than for perfection of preparation. It was made the basis of urgent pressure for an immediate movement upon Pekin, without waiting for the accumulation of the large force previously proposed."— *United States, Secretary of War, Annual Report, Nov.* 30, 1900, *pp.* 14–16, 19–20.

As mentioned above, in the instructions of the American government to General Chaffee, the veteran Chinese statesman and diplomat, Earl Li Hung-chang, well known in Europe and America, had now been recalled by the Peking government to the viceroyalty of Chili, from which he was removed six years before, and had been given the authority of a plenipotentiary to negotiate with the allied Powers. He addressed a proposal to the latter, to the effect that the Ministers in Peking would be delivered, under safe escort, at Tientsin, if the allies would refrain from advancing their forces to Peking. The reply from all the governments concerned was substantially the same as that made by the United States, in the following terms : "The government will not enter into any arrangement regarding disposition or treatment of legations without first having free communication with Minister Conger. Responsibility for their protection rests upon Chinese government. Power to deliver at Tientsin presupposes power to protect and to open communication. This is insisted on." Earl Li then asked whether, "if free communication were established, it could be arranged that the Powers should not advance pending negotiations," and was told in reply : "Free communication with our representatives in Peking is demanded as a matter of absolute right, and not as a favor. Since the Chinese government admits that it possesses the power to give communication, it puts itself in an unfriendly attitude by denying it. No negotiations seem advisable until the Chinese government shall have put the diplomatic representatives of the Powers in full and free communication with their respective governments, and removed all danger to their lives and liberty."

A. D. **1900 (July—August).**—Boxer attack on the Russians in Manchuria, and Russian retaliation.—See (in this vol.) MANCHURIA: A. D. 1900.

A. D. **1900 (August).**—Appointment of Count **Waldersee** to command the allied forces.—Field-Marshal Count von Waldersee, appointed to command the German forces sent to China, being of higher military rank than any other of the commanding officers in that country, was proposed for the general command of the allied armies, and accepted as such. Before his arrival in China, however, many of the American, Russian, and some other troops, had been withdrawn.

A. D. **1900 (August 4-16).**—The advance of the allied forces on Peking and the capture of the city.—The following is from the report of General Chaffee, commanding the American forces in the allied movement from Tientsin, to rescue the beleaguered Legations at Peking: "On my arrival at Tientsin I called on the various generals commanding troops, and on August 1 a conference of generals was held at the headquarters of Lieutenant-General Linivitch, of the Russian army. Present at the conference were the commanding general of the Russian army and his chief of staff; Lieutenant-General Yamagutcbi and his chief of staff; Major-General Fukushima, of the Japanese army; Lieutenant-General Gaselee, of the British army, and his chief of staff, General Barrow; General Frey, of the French army; the Germans were also represented by an officer of the German navy; myself and Maj. Jesse M. Lee, Ninth Infantry, and Lieut. Louis M. Little, of the marines, who speaks French. The purpose of this conference was to decide whether the armies were ready to make a movement for the relief of Pekin. It was disclosed in the conference that the Japanese, whose forces occupied the right bank of the river in and about Tientsin, where also were located the British and American forces, had by various patrols determined that the Chinese were in considerable force in the vicinity of Pei-tsang, about 7 miles distance up the river from Tientsin, and that they were strengthening their position by earthworks extending from the right bank of the river westward something like 3 miles, and from the left bank east to the railroad embankment was also being strengthened. The forces were variously estimated, from reports of Chinese, at from 10,000 to 12,000 men in the vicinity of Pei-tsang, with large bodies to the rearward as far as Yangtsun, where it was reported their main line of defenses would be encountered.

"The first question submitted for decision was 'whether a movement should be made at once,' which was decided in the affirmative, two Powers only dissenting, and these not seriously, as their doubt seemed to be that the force we could put in movement was not sufficiently strong to meet the opposition that might be expected. The decision was that the attack should be made on Sunday, August 5, and as the Japanese, British, and American forces occupied the right bank of the river, the Russians the left, the attack should be made without change of situation of the troops, the British to send four heavy guns to aid the Russian column. The strategy on the right bank of the river was left to the determination of the British, American, and Japanese

generals. The force reported to the conference as available for the movement was: Japanese, about 8,000 ; Russian, 4,800 ; British, about 3,000 ; American, 2,100 ; French, 800. With special effort on the part of Captains Byron and Wood, Reilly's battery was gotten to Tientsin August 3 and assembled. We were also able to make one pack train available on the 4th, just in time to march with the column. The marines and Sixth Cavalry were gotten off the 'Grant' and to Tientsin August 3. The presence of the Sixth Cavalry at Tientsin, dismounted, enabled me to take all available men of the Ninth and Fourteenth, also all the marines except one company 100 strong, left to assist the civil government of the city. By arrangement prior to my arrival the officers selected to establish a civil government for Tientsin were to be allowed a military force, of which the United States should furnish 100. I was compelled, of course, to leave the Sixth Cavalry, because the horses had not arrived. . . . The troops moved out from the city of Tientsin during the afternoon and night of August 4 and bivouacked in the vicinity of Si-ku that was taken by Admiral Seymour in his retrograde movement."

The Chinese were driven from the Arsenal by the Japanese, before whom they also fell back from Pei-tsang, and the first serious battle was fought at Yang-tsun, on the 6th. Having rested at Yang-tsun and cared for its sick and wounded, on the 7th, the army moved forward on the 8th, encountered slight resistance at Shang-shia-wan on the 11th, found Tong-chow abandoned, on the 12th, and reached Pekin on the 14th, having suffered more from heat, fatigue, and the want of potable water on the march, than from "Boxers" or imperial troops.

Returning now to the report of General Chaffee, we take from it his account of the final movement to the walls of Pekin, of the forcing of the gates and of the clearing of Chinese troops from the city : ' The Japanese when taking possession of Tong-Chow in the morning [of the 12th] advanced troops toward Pekin for a distance of 6½ miles. It was finally agreed that the next day, the 13th, should be devoted to reconnoissance ; the Japanese should reconnoiter on the two roads to the right or north of the paved road which is just north of the canal ; the Russians on the paved road, if at all; the Americans to reconnoiter on the road just south of the canal; the British a parallel road 1½ miles to the left of the road occupied by the Americans. On the 14th the armies should be concentrated on the advance line headed by the Japanese, and that that evening a conference should be held to determine what the method of attack on Pekin should be. On the morning of the 13th I reconnoitered the road to be occupied by the Americans with Troop M, Sixth Cavalry, Reilly's battery, and the Fourteenth Infantry up to the point specified in our agreement, or about 7 miles from Tong-Chow. Finding no opposition, I directed the remainder of my force to march out and close in on the advance guard. This force arrived at midnight. The British reconnoitered their road with some cavalry. The Japanese reconnoitered their front and also the front which properly belonged to the Russians.

"For reasons unknown to me the Russians left their camp at Tong-Chow about the time that my troops were marching to close on my advance guard. They followed the road which had been assigned to them, and about nine o'clock heavy firing was heard in the vicinity of Pekin. It was the next day ascertained that they had moved forward during the previous evening and had attacked the 'Tong-pien-men Gate,' an east gate of the city near where the Chinese wall joins the Tartar wall. Very heavy artillery and considerable small-arm firing was continued throughout the night. At the time of the occurrence I supposed the firing to be the last efforts of the Chinese troops to destroy the legations. . . .

"The 14th being the day decided upon for the concentration on the line 7 miles from Tong-Chow, I made no preparations for carrying on any operations beyond a small reconnoissance by a troop of cavalry to my front, which duty I assigned to Captain Cabell. . . . My cavalry had been absent not more than an hour, when Mr. Lowry, the interpreter who had accompanied it, raced back and informed me that Captain Cabell was surrounded by Chinese cavalry. I immediately ordered a battalion of the Fourteenth Infantry to fall in, and we went forward about a mile and a half and found Captain Cabell occupying some houses, firing from the roofs on a village in his front. I insisted on the French troops giving me the road, which they reluctantly did. Having joined Cabell, I continued the reconnoissance to my front, wishing to get as near the wall of the city as I could, but not expecting to move my whole force, which was contrary to the agreement at Tong-Chow on the evening of August 12. Without serious opposition we arrived at the northeast corner of the Chinese city, having brushed away some Chinese troops or 'Boxers' that fired from villages to our left and front. About 10 o'clock I saw the advantage of holding the ground that I had obtained, and directed all my force to move forward, as I had then become aware of Russian troops being in action on my right, and could also hear the Japanese artillery farther to the right. My left flank at this time was uncovered, except by a small force of British cavalry. The British troops did not advance from Tong-Chow until the 14th, owing to the agreement previously referred to. On that day they marched for the line of concentration and found my force advancing on Pekin. At noon a British battery was at work a mile to my left and rear.

"At 11 a. m. two companies of the Fourteenth Infantry, under the immediate command of Colonel Daggett, had scaled the wall of the Chinese city at the northeast corner, and the flag of that regiment was the first foreign colors unfurled upon the walls surrounding Pekin. The two companies on the wall, with the assistance of the troops facing the wall, drove away the Chinese defenders from the corner to the east gate of the Chinese city, where the British entered without opposition later in the day. About noon it was reported to me that the Russians had battered open 'Tung-pien-men gate' during the night and had effected an entrance there. I arrived at the gate soon afterwards and found in the gate some of the Fourteenth Infantry, followed by Reilly's battery. The Russian artillery and troops were in great confusion in the passage, their artillery facing in both directions, and I could see no effort being made to extricate themselves and give passage into the city. One company of the

Fourteenth Infantry deployed itself in the buildings to the right of the gate and poured effective fire onto the Tartar wall. Captain Reilly got two guns through a very narrow passage to his left, tearing down a wall to do so, and found a position a few yards to the left of the road where he could enfilade the Tartar wall, section by section, with shrapnel. The Fourteenth Infantry crossed the moat and, taking position paralleling the moat, deployed along a street facing the Tartar wall, and with the aid of the artillery swept it of Chinese troops. In this way, gradually working to the westward, the Tartar wall was cleared of opposition to the 'Hait-men gate' and beyond.

"Orders were sent to the Ninth to follow up the movement of the Fourteenth Infantry and Reilly's battery as soon as the wall was cleared of Chinese ; also to follow the movement to the 'Chien-men' gate of the Tartar city. The marines were to follow the general movement, but later were ordered to protect the train. At about 3 o'clock p. m. our advance had arrived opposite the legations, the fire of the Chinese having practically ended, and we drew over to the Tartar wall and entered the legation grounds with the Fourteenth Infantry by the 'water gate or moat,' Reilly's battery passing through the 'Chien-men' gate, which was opened by the American and Russian marines of the besieged force. The Fourteenth Infantry was selected on this occasion in recognition of gallantry at Yang-tsun and during this day. The British troops entered at the 'Shahuo' gate of the Chinese city, and following a road through the center of the city to opposite the legations, arrived there through the 'water gate or moat' in advance of the United States troops. Having communicated with Minister Conger, I withdrew the troops from the legation and camped just outside near the Tartar wall for the night. My casualties during the day were 8 enlisted men wounded in the Fourteenth Infantry, 1 enlisted man wounded of Battery F, Fifth Artillery, and 1 officer and 2 enlisted men wounded of the marines. . . .

"I was informed by Mr. Conger that a portion of the imperial city directly in front of the Chien-men gate had been used by Chinese to fire on the legations, and I determined to force the Chinese troops from this position. On the morning of the 15th I placed four guns of Reilly's battery on the Tartar wall at Chien-men gate and swept the walls to the westward to the next gate, there being some slight opposition in that direction, supported by poor artillery. About 8 o'clock a. m. the Chinese opened fire on us at Chien-men gate, from the second gate of the imperial city north of Chien-men gate, whereupon I directed an attack on the first gate to be made, and in a short while Lieut. Charles P. Summerall, of Reilly's battery, had opened the door of this gate. Our troops entered, and were met with a severe fire from the next gate, about 600 yards distant. Fire was directed upon the second gate with the battery and such of the infantry as could be elevated on the Tartar wall and side walls of the imperial city and act effectively. In the course of half an hour the Chinese fire was silenced, and Colonel Daggett led forward his regiment to the base of the second gate. Lieutenant Summerail was directed to open this gate with artillery, which he did. The course just indicated was pursued for four gates, the Chinese troops being driven from each gate in succession, the fourth gate being near what is known as the 'palace grounds,' which is surrounded by the 'imperial guards.'

"At a conference that afternoon it was decided not to occupy the imperial city, and I withdrew my troops into the camp occupied the night before, maintaining my position on the Tartar wall at Chien-men gate. The idea of not occupying the imperial city was not concurred in by the ministers in a conference held by them the next day. In their opinion the imperial city should be occupied. It was later decided by the generals to occupy the imperial grounds, and in consequence of this decision I reoccupied the grounds we had won on the 15th, placing the Ninth Infantry within as guard at the gate where our attack ceased.

"During the 15th and the attack upon the gates referred to our losses were 2 enlisted men killed and 4 wounded, Ninth Infantry; 3 enlisted men killed and 14 wounded, Fourteenth Infantry; 1 enlisted man, Battery F, Fifth Artillery, wounded. At 8.50 o'clock a. m. of this date Capt. Henry J. Reilly, Fifth Artillery, was struck in the mouth and almost instantly killed when standing at my left elbow observing the effect of a shot from one of his guns by his side.

"At a conference of the generals on the afternoon of the 16th the Chinese and Tartar cities were divided to the various forces for police and protection of the inhabitants. The United States troops were assigned to the west half of the Chinese city and to that section of the Tartar city lying between the Chien-men gate and Shun-chin gate of the south wall of the Tartar city and north to the east and west street through the Tartar city, being bounded upon the east by the wall of the imperial city."— *United States, Secretary of War, Annual Report, Nov. 30, 1900, pp. 61–71.*

A. D. 1900 (August 5-16).—The horrors of the allied invasion.—Barbarity of some divisions of the army in the march from Tien-tsin to Peking.—Murder, rape, pillage and destruction.—Of the conduct of some divisions of the allied army which advanced from Tien-tsin, and which represented to "the heathen Chinee" the civilized and Christian nations of Europe and the Western world, a writer in "Scribner's Magazine," who evidently shared the experience and witnessed the scenes of the march, gives the following account : " The dreary stretches through which the Pei-ho flows, never attractive to the Western eye, presented, as the allied armies slowly traversed them, a scene of indescribable desolation. . . . In a region which usually contained a population of many millions, scarcely a human being, besides those attached to the allied armies, was to be seen. Towns and villages were completely deserted. In China an ordinary town will have from one to three hundred thousand inhabitants, while villages not of sufficient importance to be designated on the maps, have populations varying from ten to thirty thousand. These villages line the banks of the Pei-ho and the main road to Peking by hundreds. The troops were never entirely clear of them. . . . So hurried had been the flight of the inhabitants that hundreds of houses were left open, such household possessions that could not be carried away being tousled about in great disorder. Of all that dense population, only a few scattered hundreds of aged, decrepit men and women, and some unfortunate

cripples and abandoned children, remained. A great majority of these were ruthlessly slain. The Russians and Japanese shot or bayoneted them without compunction. Their prayers for mercy availed not. If these miserable unfortunates chanced to fall into the hands of American or British troops they had a chance for their lives, but even our armies are not free from these wanton sacrifices. Every town, every village, every peasant's hut in the path of the troops was first looted and then burned. A stretch of country fully ten miles in width was thus swept. Mounted 'flanks in the air' scoured far and wide, keen on the scent of plunder, dark columns of smoke on the horizon attesting their labors. In this merry task of chastising the heathen Chinese, the Cossacks easily excelled. . . . Like an avenging Juggernaut the Army of Civilization moved. Terror strode before it; Death and Desolation sat and brooded in its path. Through such scenes as these, day after day, the army glided. A spirit of utter callousness took root, and enveloped officers and men alike. Pathetic scenes passed without comment or even notice. Pathos, involved in a riot of more violent emotions, had lost its power to move."—T. F. Millard, *A Comparison of the Armies in China* (*Scribner's Magazine, Jan.*, 1901).

Another eye witness, writing in the "Contemporary Review," tells the same sickening and shameful story, with more vividness of description and detail: "As a rule," he remarks, "the heathen Chinee suffers silently, and dies calmly. He has, it is true, a deep-rooted hatred of war, and sometimes a paralysing fear of being shot down in battle. But he takes beheading, hanging, or death by torture with as much resignation as did Seneca, and a great deal less fuss. And he bears the loss of those near and dear to him with the same serenity, heroism, or heartlessness. But he does not often move to pity, and very seldom yearns for sympathy. The dire sights which anyone might have witnessed during the months of August and September in Northern China afforded admirable illustrations of this aspect of the national character. The doings of some of the apostles of culture were so heinous that even the plea of their having been perpetrated upon wild savages would not free them from the nature of crimes. I myself remember how profoundly I was impressed when sailing on one calm summer's day up to the bar of Taku towards the mouth of the river Pei-ho. Dead bodies of Chinamen were floating seawards, some with eyes agape and aghast, others with brainless skulls and eyeless sockets, and nearly all of them wearing their blue blouses, baggy trousers, and black glossy pigtails. Many of them looked as if they were merely swimming on their backs. . . .

"The next picture that engraved itself upon my memory had for its frame the town of Tong-kew. . . . On the right bank [of the Pei-ho] naked children were amusing themselves in the infected water which covered them to the arm-pits, dancing, shouting, splashing each other, turning somersaults, and intoxicating themselves with the pure joy of living. A few yards behind them lay their fathers, mothers, sisters, brothers, dead, unburied, mouldering away. On the left bank, which was also but a few yards off, was the site of Tongkew: a vast expanse of smoking rubbish heaps. Not a 'roof was left standing;

hardly a wall was without a wide breach; formless mounds of baked mud, charred woodwork, and half-buried clothes were burning or smouldering still. Here and there a few roofless dwellings were left, as if to give an idea of what the town had been before the torch of civilisation set it aflame. Every one of these houses, one could see, had been robbed, wrecked, and wantonly ruined. All the inhabitants who were in the place when the troops swept through had been swiftly sent to their last account, but not yet to their final resting-place. Beside the demolished huts, under the lengthening shadows of the crumbling walls, on the thresholds of houseless doorways, were spread out scores, hundreds of mats, pieces of canvas, fragments of tarpaulin, and wisps of straw, which bulged suspiciously upwards. At first one wondered what they could have been put there for. But the clue was soon revealed. In places where the soldiers had scamped their work, or prey birds had been busy, a pair of fleshless feet or a plaited pigtail protruding from the scanty covering satisfied any curiosity which the passer-by could have felt after having breathed the nauseating air. Near the motionless plumage of the tall grass happy children were playing. Hard by an uncovered corpse a group of Chinamen were carrying out the orders they had received from the invaders. None of the living seemed to heed the dead. . . .

"Feeling that I never know a man until I have been permitted to see somewhat of his hidden springs of action and gauge the depth or shallowness of his emotion, I set myself to get a glance at what lay behind the mask of propriety which a Chinaman habitually wears in Tongkew as in every other town and village in the Empire. As soon as the ice seemed broken I asked one smiling individual: 'Why do you stay here with the slayers of your relatives and friends?' 'To escape their fate, if we can,' was the reply. 'We may be killed at any time, but while we live we must eat, and for food we have to work.' 'Were many of your people killed?' I inquired. 'Look there,' he answered, pointing to the corpses in the vast over-ground churchyard, 'and in the river there are many more. The Russians killed every Chinaman they met. Of them we are in great fear. They never look whether we have crosses or medals; they shoot everyone.' 'You are a Christian, then?' I queried. 'Yes, a Christian,' he eagerly answered. 'And I,' 'And I,' chimed in two others. Ten minutes' further conversation, however, brought out the fact that they were Christians not for conscience' sake but for safety, and they were sorely afraid that they were leaning on a broken reed. The upshot of what they had to tell me was that the Europeans, mainly the Russians, looked upon them all as legitimate quarry, and hounded them down accordingly. They and theirs, they declared, had been shot in skirmishes, killed in sport, and bayoneted in play.

"But the ever-recurring refrain of their narrative was the massacre in cold blood of the three hundred coolies of Taku. . . . The story has been often told since then, not merely in the north but throughout the length and breadth of China. The leading facts, as narrated on the spot, are these: Some three hundred hard-working coolies eked out a very cheerless existence by loading and unloading the steamers of all nations which touched at Taku. For the conven-

ience of both sides they all cooped themselves up in one boat, which served them as a permanent dwelling. When times were slack they were huddled together there like herrings in a barrel, and when work was brisk they toiled and moiled like galley slaves. Thus they managed to get along, doing harm to no man and good to many. The attack of the foreign troops upon Taku was the beginning of their end. Hearing one day the sharp reports of rifle shots, this peaceable and useful community was panic-stricken. In order to save their dreary lives they determined to go ashore. Strong in their weakness, and trusting in their character of working men who abhorred war, they steered their boat landwards. In an evil hour they were espied by the Russian troops, who at that time had orders, it is said, to slay every human being who wore a pigtail. Each of the three hundred defenceless coolies at once became a target for Muscovite bullets. It must have been a sickening sight when it was all done. . . .

"The river Pei-ho, could it bear witness in words to the dramas of blood enacted on its banks by Europeans, would have many a tale to tell as grewsome as that of the slaughter of the three hundred coolies. . . . I lived for twelve or thirteen days on that foul river, and never was I more profoundly impressed than by what I saw in its waters and on its banks. The first day after I had left Tientsin I was towed by untiring coolies through a land thickly studded over with what had once been human dwellings, but were now high heaps of smouldering rubbish. . . . A wave of death and desolation had swept over the land, washing away the vestiges of Chinese culture. Men, women, boys, girls, and babes in arms had been shot, stabbed, and hewn to bits in this labyrinth of streets, and now, on both banks of the river, reigned the peace described by Tacitus. . . .

"Fire and sword had put their marks upon this entire country. The untrampled corn was rotting in the fields, the pastures were herdless, roofless the ruins of houses, the hamlets devoid of inhabitants. In all the villages we passed the desolation was the same. . . . The streets and houses of war-blasted cities were also the scenes of harrowing tragedies, calculated to sear and scar the memory even of the average man who is not given to 'sickly sentimentality.' In war they would have passed unnoticed; in times of peace (hostilities were definitely over) they ought to have been stopped by drastic measures, if mild means had proved ineffectual. I speak as an eye-witness when I say, for example, that over and over again the gutters of the city of Tungtschau ran red with blood, and I sometimes found it impossible to go my way without getting my boots bespattered with human gore. There were few shops, private houses and courtyards without dead bodies and pools of dark blood. . . . The thirst of blood had made men mad. The pettiest and most despicable whipper-snapper who happened to have seen the light of day in Europe or Japan had uncontrolled power over the life and limbs, the body and soul, of the most highly-cultivated Chinaman in the city. From his decision there was no appeal. A Chinaman never knew what might betide him an hour hence, if the European lost his temper. He might lie down to rest after having worked like a beast of burden for twelve or fourteen hours only to be suddenly awakened out of his sleep, marched a few paces from his hard couch, and shot dead. He was never told, and probably seldom guessed, the reason why. I saw an old man and woman who were thus hurriedly hustled out of existence. Their day's work done they were walking home, when a fire broke out on a little barge on the river. They were the only living beings found out of bed at the time, and in the pockets of the woman a candle and some matches were stowed away. Nobody, not even the boat-watchman, had seen them on or near the boat. They were pounced upon, taken to the river's edge, shot and buried. It was the work of fifteen minutes or less. . . .

"The circumstantial tales told of the dishonouring of wives, girls, children, in Tientsin, Tungtschau, Pekin, are such as should in normal beings kindle some sparks of indignation without the aid of 'sickly sentimentality.' . . . I knew well a man whose wife had been dealt with in this manner, and then killed along with her child. He was one of the 'good and loyal people' who were on excellent terms with the Christians; but, if ever he gets a chance of wreaking vengeance upon the foreigners, he will not lightly let it slip. I knew of others whose wives and daughters hanged themselves on trees or drowned themselves in garden-wells in order to escape a much worse lot. Chinese women honestly believed that no more terrible fate could overtake them than to fall alive into the hands of Europeans and Christians. And it is to be feared that they were right. Buddhism and Confucianism have their martyrs to chastity, whose heroic feats no martyrology will ever record. Some of these obscure, but rightminded, girls and women hurled themselves into the river, and, finding only three feet of water there, kept their heads under the surface until death had set his seal on the sacrifice of their life. This suicidal frenzy was catching. . . . So far as I have been able to make out, and I have been at some pains to investigate the subject, no officers or soldiers of English or German-speaking nationalities have been guilty of these abominations against defenceless women."—E. J. Dillon, *The Chinese Wolf and the European Lamb* (*Contemporary Review, Jan.*, 1901).

A. D. 1900 (August 15-28).—Occupation of Peking by the allied forces.—International jealousies.—License to some of the soldiery.—Shameful stories of looting and outrage.—Formal march through the "Forbidden City."—"Early on the morning of the 15th [of August]—the day after the siege of the Legations was raised—General Chaffee [the American commander] advanced his men from the Chien Mên, which he had held overnight, and drove the Chinese from gateway to gateway back along the wide-paved approach to the far-famed 'Forbidden City.' From the wall at the Chien Mên the American field battery shelled each of the great gateways before the infantry advanced, and Captain Reilly, who commanded the battery, was killed while directing the operations—a bullet striking him full in the face and passing out through the|back of his head. In him was lost a popular and efficient officer. The movements of the Americans were watched with no little anxiety by certain of the allies, who evidently feared that General Chaffee was about to enter and seize the Forbidden City itself. The French, who had only

that morning arrived, were apparently very keen to establish a claim by joining in the attack, for they took their mountain guns to the top of the wall opposite the Legations, and began blazing away in the direction of the approaches to the Palace. It so happened that by this time the Americans had penetrated nearly to the gateway of the Palace itself, and this French fire, so suddenly opened, was directed upon them, instead of, as the French General thought, upon the enemy. General Chaffee rode down himself from the Chien Mên to where the guns were placed on the wall, and from below conducted a spirited conversation with the French General and M. Pichon. 'Stop firing those guns,' the General shouted up from 60 ft. below, 'you are killing my men.' Not understanding, the French General replied to the effect that he was firing for the honour of France, and M. Pichon joined in with similar protestations. General Chaffee's protests increased in vigour, and the force, perhaps, rather than the lucidity of them eventually induced the French General to desist from firing upon the Americans for the honour and glory of 'la patrie.' The Russians also displayed a marked desire to participate in the operations in front of the Palace, coming up after the fighting was practically finished and attempting to occupy a part of the position won by the Americans. Again General Chaffee had to speak forcibly to persuade the Russians to retire. General Chaffee cleared and occupied the whole length of the approaches—a series of noble paved courtyards—from the Chien Mên to the south gate of the Palace, before which he set a strong guard. His doings were quite evidently being watched with suspicion, and in the afternoon a conference was held, at which it was solemnly agreed by the representatives of the allies that in the meantime, pending the arrangement of some concerted plan, the Forbidden City should not be entered. In other parts of the city the work of clearing out the enemy was meanwhile progressing, the Japanese and Russians operating on the east and to the north, and the British to the south in the Chinese city.

"It was thought that an expedition would have been undertaken by the French to relieve the besieged in the Pei-tang. Help could have been obtained for the asking, and it is difficult to understand why no effort was made to reach the unfortunate people, who, be it noted, were still being attacked, and whose position, for all that was known, might have been desperate to the last degree. The story of the long and weary weeks of fighting round the stately cathedral pile—alas, now, how battered and rent!—must be written by no outsider from hearsay, but first hand by a survivor. As heard from the lips of Père Favier, it is, indeed, a thrilling narrative in many respects, surpassing in wonder even its sister story of the defence of the Legations. . . . The relief was effected the following morning by a combined force of French and Russians, with whom also were the British Marines under Major Luke, R. M. L. I., the whole under the command of the French general. When this force arrived it was found that the Japanese had already practically raised the siege, having started earlier and worked along on the north-west of the Imperial City, driving the Chinese before them. However, the Japanese had not actually penetrated into the Pei-tang defences, and the French had the satisfaction, after all, of being first in to receive a joyful welcome from their long-suffering fellow-countrymen. The raising of the siege was signalized by the slaughter of a large number of Chinese who had been rounded up into a cul de sac and who were killed to a man, the Chinese Christian converts joining in with the French soldiers of the relieving force, who lent them bayonets, and abandoning themselves to the spirit of revenge. Witnesses describe the scene as a sickening sight, but in judging such acts it is necessary to remember the provocation, and these people had been sorely tried. . . .

"The French general had given orders to Major Luke to remain with his men to guard a bridge in the rear while the relief of the Pei-tang was being effected. Afterwards the main body of the relieving force was pushed on through the Imperial City, leaving the British contingent behind. After waiting some time Major Luke came to the conclusion that he must have been forgotten, and, leaving a guard on the bridge, followed on in the track of the French troops, to find that they had penetrated into the Imperial City along the wall of the Palace as far as the Meishan (Coal Hill), from the pagodas on which the tri-colour was flying. The Russians had taken up a position near the North Gate of the Palace, and he was only just in time to secure the temple building at the foot of the Meishan, and the camping-ground alongside of it. There was great enthusiasm between the Russians and French, who cheered each other as their forces appeared, in marked contrast to the coolness with which the arrival of Major Luke and his men was received. . . . The Russians are camped round the old place and will permit no one in to see over it ; in fact, in this part of the city French or Russian sentries make it difficult to see most of the many objects of art or interest. . . .

"Now that the common bond of interest in the success of the relief expedition was removed, the points of difference at once began to appear, and the underlying jealousy and suspicion with which it seems each nation regards almost every other manifested itself in various ways, particularly in the unseemly race for loot and the game of general grab that now started up, the methods of which were indicated above with regard to the seizure of the Meishan. The Japanese seized the Board of Revenue and must have found a huge amount of money there, to judge by the length of the line of pack mules that it took to carry it away. Through a mistake, it is said, on the part of the Americans, the French got possession of the Palace of Prince Li, said to contain treasure to the extent of many millions of dollars. The Russians also got some treasure, seizing on a large bank.

"Inside the Forbidden City, the Chinese say, there is fabulous wealth in treasure stowed away or buried, and it is principally lest this should prove true that so much jealousy exists about the privilege of entering. Of course, the question is also of great importance politically, and after several diplomatic conferences it was eventually decided that, on a date still to be arranged, the Ministers and Generals of all the Powers should enter at the same time and proceed together through the Palace, ascertaining the nature and value of its contents and then sealing the whole place up and withdrawing to await instructions from the home Governments. . . . As regards the larger game of grab, the Russians

succeeded in winning the last large prize, the Wan Shen Shan, or new Summer Palace, seven miles out near the western hills, racing for it against a body of Japanese and coming in a quarter of an hour ahead, having had a long start. So the story goes, but it is not easy to check such stories, both Japanese and Russians being very reticent about their relations with each other. One thing only is certain, that the Russians are in jealous possession of the Wan Shen Shan. Two British officers who rode out there a couple of days ago in uniform were refused admission to the grounds.

"Alongside of this official looting, private looting on the part of the foreign soldiers was freely permitted during the first few days ; in fact, the city was abandoned for the most part to the soldiery, and horrible stories of the kind common in war, but nevertheless and everlastingly revolting, were current—stories of the ravishing of women in circumstances of great savagery, particularly by the rough Russian soldiers and their following of French. The number of Chinese women who committed suicide rather than submit to dishonour was considerable. A British officer of standing told me he had seen seven hanging from the same beam in the house of apparently a well-to-do Chinaman. These stories, and I heard of many more, reflect credit upon Chinese womanhood and something very different upon the armies of Europe, which are supposed to be the forerunners and upholders of civilization in this particular campaign. However, this period of licence was not of long duration. The soldiers having had their fling, the city was divided, by arrangement, into districts, each under the control of one of the Powers, proclamations were issued reassuring the remaining peaceable citizens and encouraging others to return, and gradually the work of restoring law and order and confidence is progressing. . . .

"Where is the Chinese Government? Fled to Je-hol ? No one seems to know for certain. It is only certain that on the morning of the 14th the Empress-Dowager and her following, and the Imperial Court, fled by the west gate of the city and disappeared. This flight took place while the Japanese were actually engaged in shelling the Tse-kwa Mên and the city wall. If they had succeeded in their first attempt on the gate in the morning, the flight of the Court might have been prevented. The Empress and her advisers had a narrow escape. . . .

"August 28. After deliberations occupying a full fortnight the question of what was to be done with the Forbidden City has been settled, at any rate, for the time being. The main problem presented was not new ; Lord Elgin had to face it forty years ago. Considerations of immediate political expediency guided his action then, as they have dictated the course adopted now. He spared the Imperial Palace, and burnt instead the Yuen Ming Yuen, or Summer Palace, seven miles from Peking. As a result the fact that British troops ever entered Peking does not appear in Chinese history, indeed the idea is ridiculed by Mandarindom. Remembering this, many people here thought it would be desirable in the present instance to burn the Imperial Palace, after carefully removing the art treasures, and thus, if possible, impress upon the whole Chinese nation some idea of the enormity of the crime which their Government has committed against civilization at large. On the other hand, it was held that if this were done the Imperial Court, through loss of 'face,' could never return to Peking, and this contingency appealed strongly to the representatives of both Russia and Japan, who conceived that the interests of their respective countries demanded the retention of Peking as the capital. What the representatives of the other Powers thought has not transpired, nor does it matter much at present, the overwhelming position of Russia and Japan combined making all opposition to their proposals futile. Germany may insist upon burning the Palace when her forces have all arrived, and those who think it ought to be done hope that she will ; but in the meantime the conference of commanding officers, in consultation with the Ministers, decided not to do more than march a small force of foreign troops through the 'sacred precincts' from the South Gate to the North, after which these were to be again closed, leaving the Palace intact. There was to be no looting. Everything was to be done to provide against the idea arising that the place had been desecrated. The ceremony was merely to be a display of military power. . . .

"Arrangements were made for certain Chinese officials to be present during the ceremony and also for a number of attendants to open up the various halls through which the troops would require to pass, and to close the doors behind the 'barbarians' when they finally withdrew. Yesterday there were reports of further friction and possible further postponement of the ceremony, but by evening these had died away and the programme had assumed at last a definite shape. According to it the various troops were to parade this morning between 7 and 8 outside the Tien-an Mên, the Inner Gate of the Imperial City. There at the time appointed they were drawn up, and the interest of a great historic event began. The Imperial Palace, or Forbidden City, is an enclosure about two-thirds of a mile long from north to south and about half a mile broad from east to west. It is surrounded by a high wall. Outside this wall on the west, north, and east lies a broad moat. From the south it is approached by a series of immense paved courtyards divided one from the other by high and massive gateways, above which rise imposing pavilions with yellow-tiled overhanging roofs, flanked by great towers built in the same style and similarly roofed with Imperial yellow. This Forbidden City or Imperial Palace enclosure is situated within the Imperial City, a larger enclosure, also surrounded by a high tile-topped wall. It was outside the Inner Gateway to this Imperial City that the troops were drawn up. The Russians took up their position on the centre, close to the stone bridge in front of the Tien-an Mên ; the Japanese were opposite the gateway on the left : the British to the right of the Russians in a wide paved avenue running east and west outside the inner wall of the Imperial City. The remainder of the allies were drawn up to the rear of the Russians and Japanese in the wide avenue running north and south from the Outer Gateway (Ta-ching Mên). As a pageant it was not a success. Soldiers on service do not make a fine show. . . . Inside the Tien-an Mên the central stone road continues for about half a mile down a broad, flagged avenue running between handsome temple buildings on either hand, until the Wu Mên, or south gate, of the Forbidden City is reached. It is an imposing entrance. The gateway itself is high and massive, and the towers on top are particularly fine. Thus far, on the morning of the 15th, the American troops fought, driving the Chinese before them into the city. The self-denial displayed by General Chaffee on that occasion has not, perhaps, received proper recognition. There was at that time no agreement to hold him back, and he might have pressed on and taken the palace and hoisted the Stars and Stripes over it. It would have been a fine prize, and the temptation must have been great, but General Chaffee, acting, possibly, under the advice of Mr. Conger, the United States Minister, refrained—a noteworthy act. This gateway has been held by an American guard ever since, and American troops have been quartered in the approach to it. . . .

"After it was over the generals and staff officers and the Ministers and other privileged persons returned by the way we had come through the Forbidden City. Tea was provided by the Chinese officials in the summer-house of the palace garden, the quaint beauties of which there was now time to appreciate. Beautiful stone carvings and magnificent bronzes claimed attention. The march through had occupied about an hour, and another was spent sauntering back through the various halls and courtyards. As the halls were cleared the Chinese attendants hastily closed the doors behind us with evident relief at our departure. A few jade ornaments were pocketed by quick-fingered persons desirous of possessing souvenirs, but on the whole the understanding that there was to be no looting was carried out. Arrived at the courtyard where their horses had been left, the generals and staff officers mounted and rode out of the palace, and the rest of us followed on foot. The gates were once more closed and guards were stationed outside to prevent any one from entering. The Forbidden City resumed its normal state, inviolate, undesecrated. The honour of the civilized world, we were told, had been thus vindicated. But had it ?"—*London Times, Peking Correspondence.*

A. D. 1900 (August—September).—The flight of the Imperial Court.—The following account of the flight of the Court from Peking to Tai-yuen-fu was given to a newspaper correspondent, in October, by Prince Su, who accompanied the fugitive Emperor and Dowager-Empress, and afterwards returned to Peking: "The day the Court left Peking they travelled in carts to Kuan-shi, 20 miles to the north, escorted by 3,000 soldiers of various commands. This composite army pillaged, murdered, and outraged along the whole route. At Kuan-shi the Imperial cortége was supplied with mule litters. The flight then continued at the rate of 20 miles daily to Hsuan-hua-fu, where a halt was made for three days. This place is 120 miles from Peking. Up to this time the flight had been of a most panic-stricken nature. So little authority was exerted that the soldiers even stole the meals which had been prepared for the Emperor and the Dowager-Empress. Some improvement was effected by the execution of several for murder and pillaging, and gradually the various constituents of the force were brought under control. Many of the Dowager-Empress's advisers were in favour of remaining at Hsuan-hua-fu, on account of the comparatively easy means of communication with the capital. The majority, however, were in such fear of pursuit by the foreign troops that the proposition was overruled. The flight was then resumed towards Tai-yuen-fu. Before leaving Hsuan-hua-fu, 10,000 additional troops under Tung-fuh-siang joined the escort. The newcomers, however, only added to the discord already prevailing. The Dowager-Empress did little else but weep and upbraid those whose advice had brought them into such a position. The Emperor reviled every one irrespective of his opinions. The journey to Tai-yuen-fu took 26 days, the longest route being taken for fear of pursuit. On arriving there the formation of some kind of Government was attempted, but owing to the many elements of discord this was found to be next to impossible. Though many edicts were issued they could not be enforced. Neither party cared for an open rupture, and affairs rapidly assumed a state of chaos. Prince Su further said that the Emperor did not desire to leave Peking, preferring to trust himself to the allies, but his objections were not listened to and he was compelled to accompany the flight."

The final resting-place of the fugitive Imperial Court for some months was Si-ngan-fu, or Sin-gan Fu, or Segan Fu, or Sian Fu (as it is variously written), a large city, the capital of the western province of Shensi.

A. D. 1900 (August—December).—Discussions among "the Powers" as to the terms to be made with the Chinese Government.— Opening of negotiations with Prince Ching and Li Hung-chang.—Immediately upon the capture of Peking, Li Hung-chang addressed appeals to the Powers for a cessation of hostilities, for the withdrawal of troops from Peking, and for the appointment of envoys to negotiate a permanent peace. Discussion among the governments followed, the first definite outcome of which appeared in the announcement of an intention on the part of Russia to withdraw her troops from Peking as soon as order had been re-established there, and of a disposition on the part of the United States to act with Russia in that procedure. This substantial agreement between the two governments was made public by the printing of the following dispatch, dated August 29, from Mr. Adee, the American Acting Secretary of State, to the representatives of the United States in London, Paris, Vienna, Berlin, Rome, and Tokio:

"The Russian Chargé d'Affaires yesterday afternoon made me an oral statement regarding Russia's purposes in China to the following effect:—'That, as she has already repeatedly declared, Russia has no designs of territorial acquisition in China; that, equally with the other Powers now operating there, Russia sought the safety of her Legation in Peking and to help the Chinese Government to repress the troubles that arose; that incidentally to the necessary defensive measures on the Russian border, Russia has occupied Niu-chwang for military purposes, and as soon as order is re-established she will withdraw her troops from the town if the action of the other Powers be no obstacle; that the purpose for which the various Governments have co-operated for the relief of the Legations in Peking has been accomplished; that taking the

position that as the Chinese Government has left Peking there is no need for the Russian representative to remain, Russia has directed her Minister to retire with his official personnel from China; that the Russian troops will likewise be withdrawn, and that when the Government of China shall regain the reins of government and can afford an authority with which the other Powers can deal, and will express a desire to enter into negotiations, the Russian Government will also name its representative.' Holding these views and purposes, Russia has expressed the hope that the United States will share the same opinion.

"To this declaration our reply has been made by the following memorandum:—'The Government of the United States has received with much satisfaction the reiterated statement that Russia has no designs of territorial acquisition in China and that, equally with the other Powers now operating in China, Russia has sought the safety of her Legation and to help the Chinese Government to repress the existing troubles. The same purposes have moved, and will continue to control, the Government of the United States, and the frank declarations of Russia in this regard are in accord with those made to the United States by the other Powers. All the Powers, therefore, having disclaimed any purpose to acquire any part of China, and now that the adherence thereto has been renewed since relief reached Peking, it ought not to be difficult by concurrent action through negotiations to reach an amicable settlement with China whereby the treaty rights of all the Powers shall be secured for the future, the open door assured, the interests and property of foreign citizens conserved, and full reparation made for the wrongs and injuries suffered by them.

"So far as we are advised, the greater part of China is at peace and earnestly desires to protect the life and property of all foreigners, and in several of the provinces active and successful efforts to suppress the 'Boxers' have been taken by the Viceroys, to whom we have extended encouragement through our Consuls and naval officers. This present good relation should be promoted for the peace of China. While we agree that the immediate object for which the military forces of the Powers have been co-operating—the relief of the Ministers in Peking—has been accomplished, there still remain other purposes which all the Powers have in common, which have been referred to in the communication of the Russian Chargé d'Affaires, and which were specifically enumerated in our Note to the Powers.

"These are:—To afford all possible protection everywhere in China to foreign life and property; to guard and protect all legitimate foreign interests; to aid in preventing the spread of disorders to the other provinces of the Empire and the recurrence of such disorders; to seek a solution which may bring about permanent safety and peace in China; to preserve the Chinese territorial and administrative entity; to protect all rights guaranteed by treaty and international law to friendly Powers; and to safeguard for the world the principle of equal and impartial trade with all parts of the Chinese Empire. In our opinion, these purposes could best be attained by the joint occupation of Peking under a definite understanding between the Powers until the Chinese Government shall have been re-established and shall be in a position to enter into new treaties containing adequate provisions for reparation and guarantees for future protection.

"With the establishment and recognition of such authority the United States would wish to withdraw its military forces from Peking and remit to the processes of peaceful negotiation our just demands. We consider, however, that the continued occupation of Peking would be ineffective to produce the desired result unless all the Powers unite therein with entire harmony of purpose. Any Power which determines to withdraw its troops from Peking will necessarily proceed thereafter to protect its interests in China by its own method, and we think this would make a general withdrawal expedient. As to the time and manner of withdrawal, we think that, in view of the imperfect knowledge of the military situation resulting from the interruptions of telegraphic communication, the several military commanders in Peking should be instructed to confer and to agree together upon the withdrawal as a concerted movement, as they agreed upon in advance.

"The result of these considerations is that, unless there is such a general expression by the Powers in favour of the continued occupation as to modify the views expressed by the Russian Government and lead to a general agreement for continued occupation, we shall give instructions to the commander of the American forces in China to withdraw our troops from Peking after due conference with the other commanders as to the time and manner of withdrawal.

"The Government of the United States is much gratified by the assurance given by Russia that the occupation of Niu-chwang is for military purposes incidental to the military steps for the security of the Russian border provinces menaced by the Chinese, and that as soon as order is established Russia will withdraw her troops from those places if the action of the other Powers is not an obstacle thereto. No obstacle in this regard can arise through any action of the United States, whose policy is fixed and has been repeatedly proclaimed."

Even before the communication received from Russia, the government of the United States had taken steps to withdraw the greater part of its troops. "On the 25th of August," says the American Secretary of War, in his annual report, November 30, 1900, "General Chaffee was directed to hold his forces in readiness for instructions to withdraw, and on the 25th of September he was instructed to send to Manila all the American troops in China with the exception of a legation guard, to consist of a regiment of infantry, a squadron of cavalry, and one light battery."

The expressions from Russia and the United States in favor of an early withdrawal of foreign troops from Peking, and the opening of pacific negotiations with the Chinese government, were unsatisfactory to several of the concerted Powers, and were sharply criticised in the British and German press. The German government, especially, was disposed to insist upon stern and strenuous measures in dealing with that of China, and it addressed the following circular note, on the 18th of September, to all the Powers: "The Government of the Emperor holds as preliminary

to entering upon diplomatic relations with the Chinese Government that those persons must be delivered up who have been proved to be the original and real instigators of the outrages against international law which have occurred at Peking. The number of those who were merely instruments in carrying out the outrages is too great. Wholesale executions would be contrary to the civilized conscience, and the circumstances of such a group of leaders cannot be completely ascertained. But a few whose guilt is notorious should be delivered up and punished. The representatives of the powers at Peking are in a position to give or bring forward convincing evidence. Less importance attaches to the number punished than to their character as chief instigators or leaders. The Government believes it can count on the unanimity of all the Cabinets in regard to this point, insomuch as indifference to the idea of just atonement would be equivalent to indifference to a repetition of the crime. The Government proposes, therefore, that the Cabinets concerned should instruct their representatives at Peking to indicate those leading Chinese personages from whose guilt in instigating or perpetrating outrages all doubt is excluded."

The British government was understood to be not unwilling to support this demand from Germany, but little encouragement seems to have been officially given to it from other quarters, and the government of the United States was most emphatic in declining to approve it. The reply of the latter to the German circular note was promptly given, September 21, as follows : "The government of the United States has, from the outset, proclaimed its purpose to hold to the uttermost accountability the responsible authors of any wrongs done in China to citizens of the United States and their interests, as was stated in the Government's circular communication to the Powers of July 3 last. These wrongs have been committed not alone in Peking, but in many parts of the Empire, and their punishment is believed to be an essential element of any effective settlement which shall prevent a recurrence of such outrages and bring about permanent safety and peace in China. It is thought, however, that no punitive measures can be so effective by way of reparation for wrongs suffered and as deterrent examples for the future as the degradation and punishment of the responsible authors by the supreme Imperial authority itself, and it seems only just to China that she should be afforded in the first instance an opportunity to do this and thus rehabilitate herself before the world.

"Believing thus, and without abating in anywise its deliberate purpose to exact the fullest accountability from the responsible authors of the wrongs we have suffered in China, the Government of the United States is not disposed, as a preliminary condition to entering into diplomatic negotiations with the Chinese Government, to join in a demand that said Government surrender to the Powers such persons as, according to the determination of the Powers themselves, may be held to be the first and real perpetrators of those wrongs. On the other hand, this Government is disposed to hold that the punishment of the high responsible authors of these wrongs, not only in Peking, but throughout China, is essentially a condition to be embraced and provided for in the negotiations for a final settlement. It is the purpose of this Government, at the earliest practicable moment, to name its plenipotentiaries for negotiating a settlement with China, and in the mean time to authorize its Minister in Peking to enter forthwith into conference with the duly authorized representatives of the Chinese Government, with a view of bringing about a preliminary agreement whereby the full exercise of the Imperial power for the preservation of order and the protection of foreign life and property throughout China, pending final negotiations with the Powers, shall be assured."

On the same day on which the above note was written the American government announced its recognition of Prince Ching and Li Hung-chang, as plenipotentiaries appointed to represent the Emperor of China, in preliminary negotiations for the restoration of the imperial authority at Peking and for a settlement with the foreign Powers.

Differences between the Powers acting together in China, as to the preliminary conditions of negotiation with the Chinese government, and as to the nature and range of the demands to be made upon it, were finally adjusted on the lines of a proposal advanced by the French Foreign Office, in a note dated October 4, addressed to the several governments, as follows : " The intention of the Powers in sending their forces to China was, above all, to deliver the Legations. Thanks to their union and the valour of their troops this object has been attained. The question now is to obtain from the Chinese Government, which has given Prince Ching and Li Hung-chang full powers to negotiate and to treat in its name, suitable reparation for the past and serious guarantees for the future. Penetrated with the spirit which has evoked the previous declarations of the different Governments, the Government of the Republic has summarized its own sentiments in the following points, which it submits as a basis for the forthcoming negotiations after the customary verification of powers : — (1) The punishment of the chief culprits, who will be designated by the representatives of the Powers in Peking. (2) The maintenance of the embargo on the importation of arms. (3) Equitable indemnity for the States and for private persons. (4) The establishment in Peking of a permanent guard for the Legations. (5) The dismantling of the Ta-ku forts. (6) The military occupation of two or three points on the Tientsin-Peking route, thus assuring complete liberty of access for the Legations should they wish to go to the coast and to forces from the sea-board which might have to go up to the capital. It appears impossible to the Government of the Republic that these so legitimate conditions, if collectively presented by the representatives of the Powers and supported by the presence of the international troops, will not shortly be accepted by the Chinese Government."

On the 17th of October, the French Embassy at Washington announced to the American government that "all the interested powers have adhered to the essential principles of the French note," and added : " The essential thing now is to show the Chinese Government, which has declared itself ready to negotiate, that the powers are animated by the same spirit ; that they are decided to respect the integrity of China and the independence of its Government, but that they are none the less resolved to obtain the satisfaction to which they have a right. In this regard it would seem that if the proposition which has been accepted as the basis of negotiations were communicated to the Chinese plenipotentiaries by the Ministers of the powers at Peking, or in their name by their Dean, this step would be of a nature to have a happy influence upon the determinations of the Emperor of China and of his Government." The government of the United States approved of this suggestion from France, and announced that it had "instructed its Minister in Peking to concur in presenting to the Chinese plenipotentiaries the points upon which we are agreed." Other governments, however, seem to have given different instructions, and some weeks were spent by the foreign Ministers at Peking in formulating the joint note in which their requirements were to be presented to Prince Ching and Earl Li.

The latter, meantime, had submitted, on their own part, to the allied plenipotentiaries, a draft of what they conceived to be the just preliminaries of a definitive treaty. They prefaced it with a brief review of what had occurred, and some remarks, confessing that " the throne now realizes that all these calamities have been caused by the fact that Princes and high Ministers of State screened the Boxer desperados, and is accordingly determined to punish severely the Princes and Ministers concerned in accordance with precedent by handing them over to their respective Yaméns for the determination of a penalty." The "draft clauses" then submitted were as follows:—

" The siege of the Legations was a flagrant violation of the usages of international law and an utterly unpermissible act. China admits the gravity of her error and undertakes that there shall be no repetition of the occurrence. China admits her liability to pay an indemnity, and leaves it to the Powers to appoint officers who shall investigate the details and make out a general statement of claims to be dealt with accordingly.

" With regard to the subsequent trade relations between China and the foreign Powers, it will be for the latter to make their own arrangements as to whether former treaties shall be adhered to in their entirety, modified in details, or exchanged for new ones. China will take steps to put the respective proposals into operation accordingly.

" Before drawing up a definitive treaty it will be necessary for China and the Powers to be agreed as to general principles. Upon this agreement being arrived at, the Ministers of the Powers will remove the seals which have been affixed to the various departments of the Tsung-li-Yamén and proceed to the Yamén for the despatch of business in matters relating to international questions exactly as before.

" So soon as a settlement of matters of detail shall have been agreed upon between China and the various nations concerned in accordance with the requirements of each particular nation, and so soon as the question of the payment of an indemnity shall have been satisfactorily settled, the Powers will respectively withdraw their troops. The despatch of troops to China by the Powers was undertaken with the sole object of protecting the Ministers, and so soon as peace negotiations between China and the Powers shall have been opened there shall be a cessation of hostilities.

"The statement that treaties will be made with each of the Powers in no way prejudices the fact that with regard to the trade conventions mentioned the conditions vary in accordance with the respective powers concerned. With regard to the headings of a definitive treaty, questions of nomenclature and precedence affecting each of the Powers which may arise in framing the treaty can be adjusted at personal conferences."

Great Britain and Germany were now acting in close accord, having, apparently, been drawn together by a common distrust of the intentions of Russia. On the 16th of October, Lord Salisbury and Count Hatzfeldt signed the following agreement, which was made known at once to the other governments concerned, and its principles assented to by all :

"Her Britannic Majesty's Government and the Imperial German Government, being desirous to maintain their interests in China and their rights under existing treaties, have agreed to observe the following principles in regard to their mutual policy in China : —

"1. It is a matter of joint and permanent international interest that the ports on the rivers and littoral of China should remain free and open to trade and to every other legitimate form of economic activity for the nationals of all countries without distinction ; and the two Governments agree on their part to uphold the same for all Chinese territory as far as they can exercise influence.

"2. The Imperial German Government and her Britannic Majesty's Government will not, on their part, make use of the present complication in order to obtain for themselves any territorial advantages in Chinese dominions, and will direct their policy towards maintaining undiminished the territorial condition of the Chinese Empire.

"3. In case of another Power making use of the complications in China in order to obtain under any form whatever such territorial advantages, the two Contracting Parties reserve to themselves to come to a preliminary understanding as to the eventual steps to be taken for the protection of their own interests in China.

"4. The two Governments will communicate this Agreement to the other Powers interested, and especially to Austria-Hungary, France, Italy, Japan, Russia, and the United States of America, and will invite them to accept the principles recorded in it."

The assent of Russia was no less positive than that of the other Powers. It was conveyed in the following words : "The first point of this Agreement, stipulating that the ports situated on the rivers and littoral of China, wherever the two Governments exercise their influence, should remain free and open to commerce, can be favorably entertained by Russia, as this stipulation does not infringe in any way the 'status quo' established in China by existing treaties. The second point corresponds all the more with the intentions of Russia, seeing that, from the commencement of the present complications, she was the first to lay down the maintenance of the integrity of the Chinese Empire as a fundamental principle of her policy in China. As regards the third point relating to the eventuality of an infringement of this fundamental principle, the Imperial Government, while referring to their Circular of the 12th (25th) August, can only renew the declaration that such an infringement would oblige Russia to modify her attitude according to circumstances."

On the 13th of November, while the foreign plenipotentiaries at Peking were trying to agree in formulating the demands they should make, the Chinese imperial government issued a decree for the punishment of officials held responsible for the Boxer outrages. As given the Press by the Japanese Legation at Washington, in translation from the text received there, it was as follows :

"Orders have been already issued for the punishment of the officials responsible for opening hostilities upon friendly Powers and bringing the country into the present critical condition by neglecting to suppress and even by encouraging the Boxers. But as Peking and its neighborhood have not yet been entirely cleared of the Boxers, the innocent people are still suffering terribly through the devastation of their fields and the destruction of their houses, a state of affairs which cannot fail to fill one with the bitterest feelings against these officials. And if they are not severely punished, how can the anger of the people be appeased and the indignation of the foreign Powers allayed ?

"Accordingly, Prince Tuan is hereby deprived of his title and rank, and shall, together with Prince Chwang, who has already been deprived of his title, be delivered to the Clan Court to be kept in prison until the restoration of peace, when they shall be banished to Sheng-King, to be imprisoned for life. Princes Yi and Tsai Yung, who have both been already deprived of their titles, are also to be delivered to the Clan Court for imprisonment, while Prince Tsai Lien, also already deprived of title and rank, is to be kept confined in his own house. Duke Tsai Lan shall forfeit his ducal salary, but may be transferred with the degradation of one rank. Chief Censor Ying Nien shall be degraded two ranks and transferred. As to Kang Yi, Minister of the Board of Civil Appointment, upon his return from the commission on which he had been sent for the purpose of making inquiries into the Boxer affair he memorialized the Throne in an audience strongly in their favor. He should have been severely punished but for his death from illness, and all penalties are accordingly remitted. Chao Shuy Yao, Minister of the Board of Punishment, who had been sent on a mission similar to that of Kang Yi, returned almost immediately. Though such conduct was a flagrant neglect of his duties, still he did not make a distorted report to the Throne, and therefore he shall be deprived of his rank, but allowed to retain his present office. Finally, Yu Hsien, ex-Governor of Shan-Se, allowed, while in office, the Boxers freely to massacre the Christian missionaries and converts. For this he deserves the severest punishment, and therefore he is to be banished to the furthermost border of the country, and there to be kept at hard labor for life.

"We have a full knowledge of the present trouble from the very beginning, and therefore, though no impeachment has been brought against Chinese officials at home or abroad against Princes Yi, Tsai Lien and Tsai Yung, we order them to be punished in the same manner as those who have been impeached. All who see this edict will thus perceive our justice and impartiality in inflicting condign penalties upon these officials "

It was not until the 20th of December that the

joint note of the plenipotentiaries of the Powers, after having been submitted in November to the several governments represented, and amended to remove critical objections, was finally signed and delivered to the Chinese plenipotentiaries. The following is a précis of the requirements set forth in it:

"(1) An Imperial Prince is to convey to Berlin the Emperor's regret for the assassination of Baron von Ketteler, and a monument is to be erected on the site of the murder, with an inscription, in Latin, German, and Chinese, expressing the regret of the Emperor for the murder.

"(2) The most severe punishment fitting their crimes is to be inflicted on the personages designated in the Imperial decree of September 21, whose names—not mentioned—are Princes Tuan and Chuang and two other princes, Duke Lan, Chao Shu-chiao, Yang-yi, Ying-hien, also others whom the foreign Ministers shall hereafter designate. Official examinations are to be suspended for five years in those cities where foreigners have been assassinated or cruelly treated.

"(3) Honourable reparation is to be made to Japan for the murder of M. Sugiyama.

"(4) Expiatory monuments are to be erected in all foreign cemeteries where tombs have been desecrated.

"(5) The importation of arms or 'materiel' and their manufacture are to be prohibited.

"(6) An equitable indemnity is to be paid to States, societies, and individuals, also to Chinese who have suffered injury because of their employment by foreigners. China will adopt financial measures acceptable to the Powers to guarantee the payment of the indemnity and the service of the loans.

"(7) Permanent Legation guards are to be maintained, and the diplomatic quarter is to be fortified.

"(8) The Ta-ku forts and those between Peking and the sea are to be razed.

"(9) There is to be a military occupation of points necessary to ensure the safety of the communications between Peking and the sea.

"(10) Proclamations are to be posted during two years throughout the Empire threatening death to any person joining an anti-foreign society and enumerating the punishment inflicted by China upon the guilty ringleaders of the recent outrages. An Imperial edict is to be promulgated ordering Viceroys, Governors, and Provincial officials to be held responsible for anti-foreign outbreaks or violations of treaties within their jurisdiction, failure to suppress the same being visited by the immediate cashiering of the officials responsible, who shall never hold office again.

"(11) China undertakes to negotiate a revision of the commercial treaties in order to facilitate commercial relations.

"(12) The Tsung-li-Yamên is to be reformed, and the Court ceremonial for the reception of foreign Ministers modified in the sense indicated by the Powers.

"Until the foregoing conditions are complied with ('se conformer à') the Powers can hold out no expectation of a limit of time for the removal of the foreign troops now occupying Peking and the provinces."

A. D. 1900 (November).—Russo-Chinese agreement relating to Manchuria. See (in this vol.) MANCHURIA.

A. D. 1900 (December).—Russo-Chinese agreement concerning the Manchurian province of Fêng-tien. See (in this vol.) MANCHURIA: A. D. 1900.

A. D. 1900-1901 (November—February).—Seizure of grounds at Peking for a large Legation Quarter.—Extensive plans of fortification.—In February, 1901, the following from a despatch written in the previous November by Mr. Conger, the American Minister at Peking, was given to the Press by the State Department at Washington: "I have the honor to report that in view of the probability of keeping large legation grounds in the future, and because of the general desire on the part of all the European representatives to have extensive legations, all of the Ministers are taking possession of considerable areas adjoining their legations—property belonging either to the Chinese Government or to private citizens, and having been abandoned by the owners during the siege—with the intention to claim them as conquest, or possibly credit something for them on their account for indemnity. I have as yet not taken formal possession of any ground for this purpose, nor shall I without instructions, but I shall not for the present permit any of the owners or other persons to reoccupy any of the property between this legation and the canal to the east of it. While this area will be very small in comparison with the other legations, yet it will be sufficient to make both the legation personnel and the guard very comfortable, and will better comport with our traditional simplicity vis-a-vis the usual magnificence of other representatives.

"It is proposed to designate the boundaries of a legation quarter, which shall include all the legations, and then demand the right to put that in a state of defence when necessary, and to prohibit the residence of Chinese there, except by permission of the Ministers. If, therefore, these ideas as to guards, defence, etc., are to be carried out, a larger legation will be an absolute necessity. In fact, it is impossible now to accommodate the legation and staff in our present quarters without most inconvenient crowding.

"There are no public properties inside the legation quarter which we could take as a legation. All the proposed property to be added, as above mentioned, to our legation, is private ground, except a very small temple in the southeast corner, and I presume, under our policy, if taken, will be paid for either to the Chinese owners or credited upon account against the Chinese Government for indemnity, although I suspect most of the other Governments will take theirs as a species of conquest. The plot of ground adjoining and lying to the east of the legation to which I have made reference is about the size of the premises now occupied by us."

Before its adjournment on the 4th of March, 1901, the Congress of the United States made an appropriation for the purchase of grounds for its Legation at Peking, and instructions were sent to make the purchase.

By telegram from Peking on the 14th of February it was announced that a formidable plan of fortification for this Legation Quarter had been drawn up by the Military Council of the Powers at Peking, and that work upon it was to begin at once. The correspondent of the "London Times" described the plan and wrote satirically of it, as follows: "From supreme contempt for the weakness of China armed we have swayed to exaggerated fear of the strength of China disarmed. The international military experts have devised a scheme for putting the Legation quarter in a state of defence which is equivalent to the construction of an International fortress alongside the Imperial Palace. The plan requires the breaching of the city wall at the Water-gate, the levelling of the Ha-ta Mên and Chien Mên towers, the demolition of the ramparts giving access to them, the sweeping clear of a space 150 to 300 yards wide round the entire Legation area, and the construction of walls, glacis, moats, barbed wire defences, with siege guns, Maxims, and barracks capable of holding 2,000 troops, with military stores and equipment sufficient to withstand a siege of three months. All public buildings, boards, and civil offices between the Legations and the Imperial walls are to be levelled, while 11,000 foreign troops are to hold the communications between Peking and the sea, so that no Chinese can travel to Peking from the sea without the knowledge of the foreign military authorities.

" The erection of the defences is to begin at once, before the return of the Court to Peking. They are no doubt devised to encourage the Court to return to Peking, it being apparently the belief of the foreign Ministers that an Imperial Court governing an independent empire are eager to place themselves under the tutelage of foreign soldiers and within the reach of foreign Maxims.

" Within the large new Legation area all the private property of Chinese owners who years before sought the advantages of vicinity to the Legations has been seized by the foreign Legations. France and Germany, with a view to subsequent commercial transactions, have annexed many acres of valuable private property for which no compensation is contemplated, while the Italian Legation, which boasts a staff of two persons, carrying out the scheme of appropriation to a logical absurdity, has, in addition to other property, grabbed the Imperial Maritime Customs gardens and buildings occupied for so many years by Sir Robert Hart and his staff."

A. D. 1901 (January—February).—Famine in Shensi.—A Press telegram from Peking, late in January, announced a fearful famine prevailing in the province of Shensi, where thousands of natives were dying. The Chinese government was distributing rice, and there was reported to be discrimination against native Christians in the distribution. Mr. Conger, Sir E. Satow, and M. Pichon protested to Prince Ching and Li Hung-chang against such discrimination. A Court edict was therefore issued on the 26th instant ordering all relief officials and Chinese soldiers to treat Christians in exactly the same way as all other Chinese throughout the Empire, under penalty of decapitation. Another despatch, early in February, stated : " Trustworthy reports received here from Singan-fu [the temporary residence of the fugitive Chinese court] all agree that the famine in the provinces of Shen-si and Shan-si is one of the worst in the history of China. It is estimated that two-thirds of the people are without sufficient food or the means of obtaining it. They are also suffering from the bitter cold. As there is little fuel in either province the woodwork of the houses is being used to supply the want. Oxen, horses, and dogs have

been practically all sacrificed to allay hunger. Three years of crop failures in both provinces and more or less of famine in previous seasons had brought the people to poverty when winter began. This year their condition has rapidly grown worse. Prince Ching stated to Mr. Conger, the United States Minister, that the people were reduced to eating human flesh and to selling their women and children. Infanticide is alarmingly common."

A. D. 1901 (January—February).—Submission to the demands of the Powers by the Imperial Government.—Punishments inflicted and promised.—A new Reform Edict.—With no great delay, the Chinese plenipotentiaries at Peking were authorized by the Emperor and Empress to agree to the demands of the Powers, which they did by formally signing the Joint Note. Prince Ching gave his signature on the 12th of January, 1901, and Li Hung-chang, who was seriously ill, signed on the following day. Discussion of the punishments to be inflicted on guilty officials was then opened, and went on for some time. On the 5th of February, the foreign Ministers submitted the names of twelve leading officials, against whom formal indictments were framed, and who were considered to be deserving of death. Three of them, however (Kang Yi, Hsu Tung, and Li Ping Heng), were found to be already deceased. The remaining nine were the following : Prince Chuang, commander-in-chief of the Boxers ; Prince Tuan, who was held to be the principal instigator of the attack on foreigners ; Duke Lan, the Vice-President of Police, who admitted the Boxers to the city ; Yu Iisien, who was the governor of Shan-Si Province, promoter of the Boxer movement there, and director of the massacres in that province ; General Tung Fu Siang, who led the attacks on the Legations, Ying Nien, Chao Hsu Kiao, Hsu Cheng Yu, and Chih Siu, who were variously prominent in the murderous work. In the cases of Prince Tuan and Duke Lan, who were related to the Imperial family, and in the case of General Tung Fu Siang, whose military command gave him power to be troublesome, the Chinese court pleaded such difficulties in the way of executing a decree of death that the Ministers at Peking were persuaded to be satisfied with sentences of exile, or degradation in rank, or both. On the 21st of February the Ministers received notice that an imperial edict had been issued, condemning General Tung Fu Siang to be degraded and deprived of his rank ; Prince Tuan and Duke Lan to be disgraced and exiled ; Prince Chuang, Ying Nien and Chao Hsu Kiao to commit suicide ; Hsu Cheng Yu, Yu Hsien and Chih Siu to be beheaded. Hsu Cheng Yu and Chih Siu were then prisoners in the hands of the foreign military authorities at Peking, and the sentence was executed upon them there, on the 26th of February, in the presence of Japanese, French, German and American troops. A despatch from Peking reporting the execution stated that, while it was being carried out, " the ministers held a meeting and determined on the part of the majority to draw a curtain over further demands for blood. United States Special Commissioner Rockhill sided strongly with those favoring humane methods, who are Sir Ernest Satow and MM. Komura, De Cologan and De Giers, respectively British, Japanese, Spanish and Russian ministers. Others believe that China has not been sufficiently punished, and that men should be executed in every city, town and village where foreigners were injured."

While the subject of punishments was pending, and with a view, it was said, of quickening the action of the Chinese government, Count von Waldersee, the German Field-Marshal commanding the allied forces in China, ordered preparations to be made for an extensive military expedition into the interior. The government of the United States gave prompt directions that its forces at Peking should not take part in this movement, and the remonstrances of other Powers more pacifically inclined than the Germans caused the project to be given up.

Meantime, three Imperial edicts of importance, if faithfully carried out, had been issued. One, on the 5th of February, commanded new undertakings of reform, accounting for the abandonment of the reform movement of 1898 by declaring that it was seditionary and would have resulted in anarchy, and that it was entered upon when the Emperor was in bad health; for all which reasons he had requested the Empress Dowager to resume the reins of government. Now, it was declared, since peace negotiations were in progress, the government should be formed on a basis for future prosperity. Established good methods of foreign countries should be introduced to supply China's deficiencies. "China's greatest difficulty," said the edict, "is her old customs, which have resulted in the insincere dispatch of business and the promoting of private gain. Up to the present time those who have followed the Western methods have had only superficial knowledge, knowing only a little of foreign languages and foreign inventions, without knowing the real basis of the strength of foreign nations. Such methods are insufficient for real reform."

In order to obtain a true basis, the Emperor commanded a consultation between the ministers of the privy council, the six boards, nine officers, the Chinese ministers to foreign countries and all the viceroys and governors. Those were instructed to recommend reforms in the seven branches of government, namely, the central government, ceremonies, taxation, schools, civil-service examinations, military affairs and public economies. They were also to recommend what part of the old system can be used and what part needs changing. Two months were given them in which to prepare their report.

On the following day, two edicts, in fulfilment of demands made in the Joint Note of the Powers, were promulgated. The first provided, in accordance with article 3 of the Joint Note, for the suspension of official examinations for five years in places where foreigners are killed. The second edict forbade anti-foreign societies, recited the punishment of guilty parties and declared that local officials will be held responsible for the maintenance of order. If trouble occurs the officials would be removed without delay and never again allowed to hold office.

A. D. 1901 (March).—The murdered Christian missionaries and native converts.— Varying statements and estimates of their number.—To the time of this writing (March, 1901), no complete enumeration of the foreign Christian missionaries and members of missionary families who were killed during the Boxer outbreak of the past year has been made. Varying

estimates have appeared, from time to time, and it is possible that one of the latest among these, communicated from Shanghai on the 1st of March, may approach to accuracy. It was published in the "North China Daily News," and said to be founded on the missionary records, according to which, said the "News," "a total of 134 adults and 52 children were killed or died of injuries in the Boxer rising of 1899 and 1900."

On the 13th of March, the "Lokal Anzeiger," of Berlin, published a statistical report from its Peking correspondent of "foreign Christians killed during the troubles, exclusive of the Peking siege," which enumerated 118 Englishmen, 79 Americans, Swedes and Norwegians, 26 Frenchmen, 11 Belgians, 10 Italians and Swiss, and 1 German. The total of these figures is largely in excess of those given by the "North China Daily News," but they cover, not missionaries alone, but all foreign Christians. It is impossible, however, not to doubt the accuracy of both these accounts. Of native Christians, the German writer estimated that 30,000 had perished.

In September, 1900, the United States Consul-General at Shanghai, Mr. Goodnow, "after making inquiries from every possible source," placed the number of British and American missionaries who had probably been killed at 93, taking no account of a larger number in Chih-li and Shan-si whose fate was entirely unknown. Of those whose deaths he believed to be absolutely proved at that time, 34 were British, including 9 men, 15 women and 10 children, and 22 were American, 8 of these being men, 8 women and 6 children.

In December, 1900, a private letter from the "Association for the Propagation of the Faith, St. Mary's Seminary," Baltimore, Md., stated that up to the end of September 48 Catholic missionaries were known to have been murdered. A pastoral letter issued in December by Cardinal Vaughan, in London, without stating the numbers killed, declared that all work of the Catholic church, throughout the most of China, where 942 European and 445 native priests had been engaged, was practically swept away.

A private letter, written early in January, 1901, by the Rev. Dr. Judson Smith, one of the corresponding secretaries of the American Board of Commissioners for Foreign Missions, contains the following statement: "The American Board has lost in the recent disturbances in China 13 missionaries, 6 men and 7 women, and 5 children belonging to the families who perished. The number of native converts connected with the mission churches of the American Board who have suffered death during these troubles cannot be stated with accuracy. It undoubtedly exceeds 1,000; it may reach a much larger figure; but some facts that have come to light of late imply that more of those who were supposed to be lost have been in hiding than was known. If we should reckon along with native converts members of their families who have suffered death, the number would probably be doubled."

There seems to be absolutely no basis of real information for any estimate that has been made of the extent of massacre among the native Christian converts. Thousands perished, without doubt, but how many thousands is yet to be learned. As intimated by Dr. Smith, larger numbers than have been supposed may have escaped, and it will probably be long before the true facts are gathered from all parts of the country.

In any view, the massacre of missionaries and their families was hideous enough; but fictions of horror were shamefully added, it seems, in some of the stories which came from the East. At Pao-Ting Fu, where women were said to have suffered indescribable brutalities before being slain, investigation by an American military officer convinced him that "there is no evidence of any peculiar atrocities committed upon the persons of those who were slain"; and the American Board of Commissioners for Foreign Missions has publicly announced: "While forced to believe that our missionaries in Shan Si and at Pao Ting Fu were put to death by the Chinese, we have never credited the published reports concerning atrocities connected with their slaughter."

A. D. 1901 (March).—Withdrawal of American troops, excepting a Legation guard.— The following order was sent by cable from the War Department at Washington to General Chaffee, commanding the United States forces in China, on the 15th of March: "In reply to your telegram Secretary of War directs you complete arrangements sail for Manila with your command and staff officers by end April, leaving as legation guard infantry company composed of 150 men having at least one year to serve or those intending re-enlist, with full complement of officers, medical officer, sufficient hospital corps men and, if you think best, field officer especially qualified to command guard. Retain and instruct officer quartermaster's department proceed to erect necessary buildings for guard according to plan and estimates you approve."

A. D. 1901 (March—April).—Discussion of the question of indemnity.—Uneasiness concerning rumored secret negotiations of Russia with the Chinese government relative to Manchuria.—As we write this (early in April), the reckoning of indemnities to be demanded by the several Powers of the Concert in China is still under discussion between the Ministers at Peking, and is found to be very difficult of settlement. There is understood to be wide differences of disposition among the governments represented in the discussion, some being accused of a greed that would endeavor to wring from the Chinese government far more than the country can possibly pay; while others are laboring to reduce the total of exactions within a more reasonable limit. At the latest accounts from Peking, a special committee of the Ministers was said to be engaged in a searching investigation of the resources of China, in order to ascertain what sum the Empire has ability to pay, and in what manner the payment can best be secured and best made. It seems to be hoped that when those facts are made clear there may be possibilities of an agreement as to the division of the total sum between the nations whose legations were attacked, whose citizens were slain, and who sent troops to crush the Boxer rising.

Meantime grave anxieties are being caused by rumors of a secret treaty concerning Manchuria which Russia is said to be attempting to extort from the Chinese government [see, in this vol., MANCHURIA], the whispered terms of which would give her, in that vast region, a degree of control never likely to become less. The most positive remonstrance yet known to have been made, against any concession of that nature, was addressed, on the 1st of March, by the government of the United States, to its representatives at St. Petersburg, Berlin, London, Paris, Vienna, Rome, and Tokio, as follows: "The following memorandum, which was handed to the Chinese Minister on February 19, is transmitted to you for your information and communication to the government to which you are accredited:

"The preservation of the territorial integrity of China having been recognized by all the powers now engaged in joint negotiation concerning the injuries recently inflicted upon their ministers and nationals by certain officials and subjects of the Chinese Empire, it is evidently advantageous to China to continue the present international understanding upon this subject. It would be, therefore, unwise and dangerous in the extreme for China to make any arrangement or to consider any proposition of a private nature involving the surrender of territory or financial obligations by convention with any particular power; and the government of the United States, aiming solely at the preservation of China from the danger indicated and the conservation of the largest and most beneficial relations between the empire and other countries, in accordance with the principles set forth in its circular note of July 3, 1900, and in a purely friendly spirit toward the Chinese Empire and all the powers now interested in the negotiations, desires to express its sense of the impropriety, inexpediency and even extreme danger to the interests of China of considering any private territorial or financial arrangements, at least without the full knowledge and approval of all the powers now engaged in negotiation. HAY."

CHINESE TAXES. See (in this vol.) LIKIN.

CHING, Prince: Chinese Plenipotentiary to negotiate with the allied Powers. See (in this vol.) CHINA: A. D. 1900 (AUGUST—DECEMBER).

CHITRAL: A. D. 1895.—The defense and relief of. See (in this vol.) INDIA: A. D. 1895 (MARCH—SEPTEMBER).

A. D. 1901.—Included in a new British Indian province. See (in this vol.) INDIA: A. D. 1901 (FEBRUARY).

CHOCTAWS, United States agreements with the. See (in this vol.) INDIANS, AMERICAN: A. D. 1893-1899.

CHRISTIAN ENDEAVOR, The Young People's Society of.—The nineteenth annual international convention of Young People's Societies of Christian Endeavor was held in the Alexandra Palace, London, England, from the 13th to the 20th of July, 1900, delegates being present from most countries of the world. Reports presented to the convention showed a total membership of about 3,500,000, in 59,712 societies, 43,262 of which were in the United States, 4,000 in Canada, some 7,000 in Great Britain, 4,000 in Australia, and smaller numbers in Germany, India, China, Japan, Mexico, and elsewhere.

The first society, which supplied the germ of organization for all succeeding ones, was formed in the Williston Congregational Church of Portland, Maine, on the 2d of February, 1881, by the Rev. Francis E. Clark, the pastor of the church. The object, as indicated by the name of the society, was to organize the religious energies of the young people of the church for Christian life and work. The idea was caught and imitated in other churches—Congregational, Presbyterian, Methodist, Baptist, and others— very rapidly, and the organization soon became, not only widely national, but international. In 1898, it was reported that Russia then remained the only country in the world without a Christian Endeavor Society, and the total was 54,191. In the next year's report Russia was announced to have entered the list of countries represented, and the number of societies had advanced to 55,813. In 1900, the numbers had risen to the height stated above. The Epworth League is a kindred organization of young people in the Methodist Church. See (in this vol.) EPWORTH LEAGUE.

CHRISTIANS AND MOSLEMS: Conflicts in Armenia. See (in this vol.) TURKEY: A. D. 1895.

CONFLICTS IN CRETE. See (in this vol.) TURKEY: A. D. 1897 (FEBRUARY—MARCH).

CHUNGKING.—"Chungking, which lies nearly 2,000 miles inland, is, despite its interior position, one of the most important of the more recently opened ports of China. Located at practically the head of navigation on the Yangtze, it is the chief city of the largest, most populous, and perhaps the most productive province of China, whose relative position, industries, population, and diversified products make it quite similar to the great productive valley of the upper Mississippi. The province of Szechuan is the largest province of China, having an area of 166,800 square miles, and a population of 67,000,000, or but little less than that of the entire United States. Its area and density of population may be more readily recognized in the fact that its size is about the same as that of the States of Ohio, Indiana, Illinois, and Kentucky combined, but that its population is six times as great as that of those States. Its productions include wheat, tobacco, buckwheat, hemp, maize, millet, barley, sugar cane, cotton, and silk."—*United States, Bureau of Statistics, Monthly Summary, March,* 1899, *p.* 2196.

CHURCH OF ENGLAND: A. D. 1896.— Papal declaration of the invalidity of its ordinations. See (in this vol.) PAPACY: A. D. 1896 (SEPTEMBER).

CIVIL CODE: Introduction in Germany. See (in this vol.) GERMANY: A. D. 1900 (JANUARY).

CIVIL - SERVICE REFORM IN THE UNITED STATES: A. D. 1893-1896.— Extensions of the Civil-Service rules by President Cleveland.—"Through the extensions of the Federal classification during President Cleveland's second administration, the number of positions covered by the civil-service rules was increased two-fold. On March 3, 1893, the number classified was 42,928. By a series of executive orders ranging from March 20, 1894, to June 25. 1895, 10,000 places were added to the list, bringing the total, approximately, to 53,000. Meanwhile, the Civil Service Commission had recommended to the President a general

6-10

revision that would correct the imperfections of the original rules and extend their scope to the full degree contemplated by the Pendleton Act. After much correspondence and consultation with department officers, and careful work on the part of the Commission, the rules of May 6 [1896] were promulgated. They added to the classification about 29,000 more places, and by transferring to the control of the Commission the system of Navy Yard employment, established by Secretary Tracy, brought the total number in the classified service to 87,117. The positions in the Executive branch unaffected by these orders included those classes expressly excluded by the statute—persons nominated for confirmation by the Senate and those employed 'merely as laborers or workmen'—together with the fourth-class postmasters, clerks in post-offices other than free delivery offices and in Customs districts having less than five employees, persons receiving less than $300 annual compensation, and about 1,000 miscellaneous positions of minor character, not classified for reasons having to do with the good of the service—91,600 in all. Within the classified service, the list of positions excepted from competitive examination was confined to the private secretaries and clerks of the President and Cabinet officers, cashiers in the Customs Service, the Internal Revenue Service and the principal post-offices, attorneys who prepare cases for trial, principal Customs deputies and all assistant postmasters—781 in all. The new rules provided for a general system of promotion, based on competitive examinations and efficiency records, and gave the Commission somewhat larger powers in the matter of removals by providing that no officer or employee in the classified service, of whatever station, should be removed for political or religious reasons, and that in all cases like penalties should be imposed for like offenses. They created an admirable system, a system founded on the most sensible rules of business administration, and likely to work badly only where the Commission might encounter the opposition of hostile appointing officers. President Cleveland's revised rules were promulgated before the Convention of either political party had been held, and before the results of the election could be foreshadowed. The extensions were practically approved, however, by the Republican platform, which was adopted with full knowledge of the nature of the changes, and which declared that the law should be 'thoroughly and honestly enforced and extended wherever practicable.' . . . Mr. McKinley, in his letter of acceptance and in his inaugural address, repeated the pledge of the Republican party to uphold the law, and during the two months of his administration now past he has consistently done so. He has been beset by many thousands of place-seekers, by Senators and Representatives and by members of his own Cabinet, all urging that he undo the work of his predecessor, either wholly or in part, and so break his word of honor to the nation, in order that they may profit. . . . At least five bills have been introduced in Congress, providing for the repeal of the law. . . . Finally, the Senate has authorized an investigation, by the Committee on Civil Service and Retrenchment, with the view of ascertaining whether the law should be 'continued, amended or repealed,' and sessions of this Committee are now in progress. . . . Mr.

McKinley, by maintaining the system against these organized attacks, will do as great a thing as Mr. Cleveland did in upbuilding it."—*Report of the Executive Committee of the New York Civil Service Reform Association*, 1897.

In his annual Message to Congress, December, 1896, President Cleveland remarked on the subject: "There are now in the competitive classified service upward of eighty-four thousand places. More than half of these have been included from time to time since March 4, 1893. . . . If fourth-class postmasterships are not included in the statement, it may be said that practically all positions contemplated by the civil-service law are now classified. Abundant reasons exist for including these postmasterships, based upon economy, improved service, and the peace and quiet of neighborhoods. If, however, obstacles prevent such action at present, I earnestly hope that Congress will, without increasing post-office appropriations, so adjust them as to permit in proper cases a consolidation of these post-offices, to the end that through this process the result desired may to a limited extent be accomplished. The civil-service rules as amended during the last year provide for a sensible and uniform method of promotion, basing eligibility to better positions upon demonstrated efficiency and faithfulness."—*United States, Message and Documents (Abridgment)*, 1896–7, *p.* 33.

A. D. **1894.**—Constitutional provision in New York. See (in this vol.) CONSTITUTION OF NEW YORK.

A. D. **1897-1898.**—Onslaught of the spoilsmen at Washington.—Failure of the Congressional attack.—"During the four months following the inauguration [of President McKinley] the onslaught of place-seekers was almost unprecedented. Ninety-nine out of every hundred of them discovered that the office or position he desired was classified and subject to competitive examination. The tenure of the incumbent in each case was virtually at the pleasure of the department officers; removals might easily be made: but appointments to the places made vacant could be made only from the eligible lists, and the lists were fairly well filled. It is true that the rules permitted the reinstatement without examination of persons who had been separated from the service without personal fault within one year, or of veterans who had been in the service at any time. and that some removals were made to make room for these. But the appointments in such cases went but a very little way toward meeting the demand. The result was that almost the whole pressure of the office-hunting forces and of their members of Congress was directed for the while toward one end—the revocation or material modification of the civil service rules. President McKinley was asked to break his personal pledges, as well as those of his party, and to take from the classified service more than one half of the 87,000 offices and positions it contained. . . . But the President yielded substantially nothing. . . . The attack of the spoils-seekers was turned at once from the President to Congress. It was declared loudly that the desired modifications would be secured through legislation, and that it might even be difficult to restrain the majority from voting an absolute repeal. In the House the new movement was led by General Grosvenor of Ohio; in the Senate by Dr. Gallinger of New

Hampshire. . . . The first debates of the session dealt with civil service reform. The House devoted two weeks to the subject in connection with the consideration of the annual appropriation for the Civil Service Commission. . . . The effort to defeat the appropriation ended in the usual failure. It was explained, however, that all of this had been mere preparation for the proposed legislation. A committee was appointed by the Republican opponents, under the lead of General Grosvenor, to prepare a bill. The bill appeared on January 6, when it was introduced by Mr. Evans of Kentucky, and referred to the Committee on Reform in the Civil Service. It limited the application of the civil service law to clerical employees at Washington, letter carriers and mail clerks, and employees in principal Post Offices and Customs Houses, proposing thus to take from the present classified service about 55,000 positions. A series of hearings was arranged by the Civil Service Committee, at which representatives of this and other Associations, and of the Civil Service Commission, were present. A sub-committee of seven, composing a majority of the full committee, shortly afterward voted unanimously to report the bill adversely. About the same time, the Senate Civil Service Committee, which had been investigating the operation of the law since early summer, presented its report. Of the eight members, three recommended a limited number of exceptions, amounting in all to probably 11,000; three recommended a greatly reduced list of exceptions, and two proposed none whatever. All agreed that the President alone had authority to act, and that no legislation was needed. . . . The collapse of the movement in Congress has turned the attention of the spoilsmen again toward the President. He is asked once more to make sweeping exceptions."—*Report of the Executive Committee of the New York Civil Service Reform Association*, 1898.

A. D. **1897-1899.**—Temporary check in New York.—Governor Black's law.—Restoration of the merit system under Governor Roosevelt.—"In June [1897]—after the Court of Appeals . . . had declared that the constitutional amendment was self-executing, and that appointments made without competitive examination, where competitive examinations were practicable, must be held to be illegal—steps were taken to secure a reduction of the exempt and non-competitive positions in the State Service. A letter was addressed to Governor Morton, by the officers of the Association, on June 8, asking that the service be reclassified, on a basis competitive as far as practicable. The Governor replied that he had already given the subject some thought, and that he would be glad to give our suggestions careful consideration. On the 4th of August he instructed the Civil Service Commission to prepare such a revision of the rules and classification as had been proposed. On the 11th of November this revision, prepared by Commissioner Burt, was adopted by the full Commission, and on the 9th of December the new rules were formally promulgated by the Governor and placed in immediate operation. . . . The Governor, earlier in the year, had reversed his action in the case of inspectors and other employees of the new Excise Department, by transferring them from the non-competitive to the competitive class. . . . This marked the beginning of a vigorous movement against the competitive system led by chairmen of district committees, and other machine functionaries. Governor Morton's sweeping order of December completed the discomfiture of these people and strengthened their purpose to make a final desperate effort to break the system down. The new Governor, of whom little had been known prior to his unexpected nomination in September, proved to be in full sympathy with their plan. In his message to the legislature, Mr. Black, in a paragraph devoted to 'Civil Service,' referred to the system built up by his predecessor in contemptuous language, and declared that, in his judgment, 'Civil service would work better with less starch.' He recommended legislation that would render the examinations 'more practical,' and that would permit appointing officers to select from the whole number on an eligible list and not confine them to selections 'from among those graded highest.' Such legislation, he promised, would 'meet with prompt executive approval.' Each house of the legislature referred this part of the message to its Judiciary Committee, with instructions to report a bill embodying the Governor's ideas. . . . Within a few days of the close of the legislative session, the measure currently described as 'Governor Black's bill was introduced. . . . The bill provided that in all examinations for the State, county or municipal service, not more than 50 per cent. might be given for 'merit,' to be determined by the Examining Boards, and that the rest of the rating, representing 'fitness,' was to be given by the appointing officer, or by some person or persons designated by him. All existing eligible lists were to be abolished in 30 days, and the new scheme was to go into operation at once. . . . A hearing was given by the Senate Committee on the following day, and one by the Assembly Committee a few days later. . . . The bill, with some amendments, was passed in the Senate, under suspension of the rules, and as a party measure. . . . It was passed in the Assembly also as a caucus measure."—*Report of the Executive Committee of the New York Civil Service Reform Association,* 1897.

"Early [in 1898] after time had been allowed for the act to prove its capabilities in practice, steps were taken toward commencing a suit to test its constitutionality in the courts. . . . Pending the bringing of a test suit, a bill was prepared for the Association and introduced in the Legislature on March 16th, last, one of the features of which was the repeal of the unsatisfactory law. . . . The bill . . . was passed by the Senate on March 29th. On the 31st, the last day of the session, it was passed by the Assembly. . . . On the same date it was signed by the Governor and became a law. This act has the effect of exempting the cities from the operation of the act of 1897, restoring the former competitive system in each of them."—*The Same,* 1898.

"As a result of the confusing legislation of [1897 and 1898] at least four systems of widely differing character had come into existence by the first of [1899]. New York city had its charter rules, . . . the state departments were conducted under two adaptations of the Black law, and in the smaller cities the plan of the original law of 1883 was followed. In his first annual message, Governor Roosevelt directed the atten-

tion of the Legislature to this anomalous condition and strongly urged the passage of an act repealing the Black law and establishing a uniform system, for the state and cities alike, subject to state control. Such an act was prepared with the co-operation of a special committee of the Association. . . . After some discussion it was determined to recast the measure, adopting a form amounting to a codification of all previously existing statutes, and less strict in certain of its general provisions. . . . The bill was . . . passed by the Senate by a majority of two. . . . In the Assembly it was passed with slight amendments. . . . On the . . . 19th of April the act was signed by the Governor, and went into immediate effect. . . . The passage of this law will necessitate the complete recasting of the civil service system in New York, on radically different lines."

A. D. 1899.—Modification of Civil Service Rules by President **McKinley.**—Severe criticism of the order by the National Civil Service Reform **League.**—On the 29th of May, 1899, President McKinley was persuaded to issue an order greatly modifying the civil service rules, releasing many offices from their operation and permitting numerous transfers in the service on a non-competitive examination. This presidential order was criticised with severity in a statement promptly issued by the Executive Committee of the National Civil Service Reform League, which says: "The National Civil Service Reform League, after mature consideration, regards the order of President McKinley, of May 29, changing the Civil Service rules, as a backward step of the most pronounced character. The order follows a long succession of violations, of both the spirit and the literal terms of the law and rules, in various branches of the service, and must be considered in its relations to these. Its immediate effects, which have been understated, may be set forth as follows: (1) It withdraws from the classified service not merely 3,000 or 4,000 offices and positions, but, as nearly as can be now estimated, 10,109. It removes 3,693 from the class of positions filled hitherto either through competitive examination or through an orderly practice of promotion, and it transfers 6,416 other positions in the War Department, filled hitherto through a competitive registration system, under the control of the Civil Service Commission, to a system to be devised and placed in effect by the present Secretary of War. (2) It declares regular at least one thousand additional appointments made temporarily, without examination—in many cases in direct disregard of the law—in branches that are not affected by the exceptions, but that remain nominally competitive. (3) It permits the permanent appointment of persons employed without examination, for emergency purposes during the course of war with Spain, thus furnishing a standing list of many thousands from which positions in the War Department may be filled, without tests of fitness, for a long time to come. (4) It alters the rules to the effect that in future any person appointed with or without competitive examination, or without any examination, may be placed by transfer in any classified position without regard to the character or similarity of the employments interchanged, and after non-competitive examination only. (5) It permits the reinstatement, within the discretion of the respective department officers, of persons separated from the service at any previous time for any stated reason. The effect of these changes in the body of the rules will be of a more serious nature than that of the absolute exceptions made. It will be practicable to fill competitive positions of every description either through arbitrary reinstatement—or through original appointment to a lower grade, or to an excepted position without tests of any sort, or even by transfer from the great emergency force of the War Department, to be followed in any such case by a mere 'pass' examination. As general experience has proven, the 'pass' examinations, in the course of time, degenerate almost invariably into farce. It will be practicable also to restore to the service at the incoming of each new administration those dismissed for any cause during the period of any administration preceding. That such a practice will lead to wholesale political reprisals, and, coupled with the other provisions referred to, to the re-establishment on a large scale of the spoils system of rotation and favoritism, cannot be doubted."

In his next succeeding annual Message to Congress the President used the following language on the subject: "The Executive order [by President Cleveland] of May 6, 1896, extending the limits of the classified service, brought within the operation of the civil-service law and rules nearly all of the executive civil service not previously classified. Some of the inclusions were found wholly illogical and unsuited to the work of the several Departments. The application of the rules to many of the places so included was found to result in friction and embarrassment. After long and very careful consideration it became evident to the heads of the Departments, responsible for their efficiency, that in order to remove these difficulties and promote an efficient and harmonious administration certain amendments were necessary. These amendments were promulgated by me in Executive order dated May 29, 1899. All of the amendments had for their main object a more efficient and satisfactory administration of the system of appointments established by the civil-service law. The results attained show that under their operation the public service has improved and that the civil-service system is relieved of many objectionable features which heretofore subjected it to just criticism and the administrative officers to the charge of unbusinesslike methods in the conduct of public affairs. It is believed that the merit system has been greatly strengthened and its permanence assured."— *United States. Message and Documents (Abridgment),* 1899–1900, *v.* 1.

At its next annual meeting, December 14, 1900, in New York, the National Civil Service Reform League reiterated its condemnation of the order of President McKinley, declaring: "The year has shown that the step remains as unjustified in principle as ever and that it has produced, in practical result, just the injuries to the service that were feared, as the reports of our committee of various branches of the service have proved. The league, therefore, asserts without hesitancy that the restoration of very nearly all places in every branch of the service exempted from classification by this deplorable order is demanded by the public interest and

that the order itself should be substantially revoked."

A. D. 1900.—Civil Service Rules in **the** Philippine Islands.—"An Act for the establishment and maintenance of an efficient and honest civil service in the Philippine Islands" was adopted, on the 19th of September, by the Commission which now administers the civil government of those islands. The bill is founded on the principles of the American civil service in their stricter construction, and its provisions extend to all the executive branches of the government. The framing of rules and regulations for the service are left to the Civil Service Board provided for in the act. A correspondent of the "New York Tribune," writing from Manila on the day after the enactment, states: "W. Leon Pepperman, who has long been connected with the civil service in the United States, and who has made a personal study of the systems maintained by Great Britain, France, and Holland in their Eastern colonies, will be on this board, as will be F. W. Kiggins of the Washington Civil Service Commission. The third member probably will be a Filipino. President Taft had selected for this post Dr. Joaquin Gonzalez, an able man, but that gentleman's untimely death on the eve of his appointment has forced President Taft to find another native capable of meeting the necessary requirements. Mr. Kiggins probably will act as Chief Examiner, and Mr. Pepperman as Chairman of the board." According to the same correspondent: "Examinations for admittance to the service will be held in Manila, Iloilo, and Cebu, in the Philippines, and in the United States under the auspices and control of the Federal Civil Service Commission." At the annual meeting of the National Civil Service Reform League of the United States held in New York, December 13, 1900, the above measure was commended highly in the report of a special committee appointed to consider the subject of the civil service in our new dependencies, as being one by which, "if it be persevered in, the merit system will be established in the islands of that archipelago, at least as thoroughly and consistently as in any department of government, Federal, State or municipal, in the Union. This must be, in any case, regarded as a gratifying recognition of sound principles of administration on the part of the commission and justifies the hope that, within the limits of their jurisdiction at least, no repetition of the scandals of post-bellum days will be tolerated. The ruling of the several departments that the provisions of the Federal offices established in the dependencies which would be classified if within the United States is also a matter to be noted with satisfaction by the friends of good government."

A. D. 1901.—The "spoils system" of service in the House of Representatives.—The "spoils system" maintained by Congressmen among their own immediate employees, in the service of the House of Representatives, was depicted in a report, submitted February 28, 1901, by a special committee which had been appointed to investigate the pay of the House employees. The report, presented by Mr. Moody, of Massachusetts, makes the following general statements, with abundance of illustrative instances, few of which can be given here: "The four officers elected by the House, namely, the Clerk, Sergeant-at-Arms,

Doorkeeper, and Postmaster, appoint the employees of the House, except the clerks and assistant clerks of members and committees, four elevator men, the stenographers, and those appointed by House resolutions. The appointments, however, are made on the recommendation of members of the House, and very largely, though not entirely, of members of the dominant party in the House. If a member upon whose recommendation an appointment is made desires the removal of his appointee and the substitution of another person, the removal and substitution are made without regard to the capacity of either person. In case a member upon whose recommendation an appointment has been made ceases to be a member of the House, an employee recommended by him ordinarily loses his place. Thus the officers of the House, though responsible for the character of the service rendered by the employees, have in reality little or no voice in their selection, and, as might reasonably be expected, the results obtained from the system which we have described are in some cases extremely unsatisfactory. This method of appointing House employees has existed for many years, during which the House has been under the control of each party alternately. We believe that candor compels us to state at the outset that some of the faults in administration which we have observed are attributable to the system and to the persistence of members of the House in urging upon the officers the appointment of their constituents and friends to subordinate places, and that such faults are deeply rooted, of long standing, and likely to continue under the administration of any political party as long as such a system is maintained."

The committee found nothing to criticise in the administration of the offices of the House Postmaster or Sergeant-at-Arms. With reference to the offices of the Clerk and the Doorkeeper they say: "We have found in both departments certain abuses, which may be grouped under three heads, namely : Transfers of employees from the duties of the positions to which they were appointed to other duties, unjustifiable payments of compensation to employees while absent from their posts of duty, and divisions of salary.

"First. Transfers of employees from the duties to which they were appointed to other duties.—Some part of this evil is doubtless attributable to the fact that the annual appropriation acts have not properly provided for the necessities of the House service. An illustration of this is furnished by the case of Guy Underwood, who is carried on the rolls as a laborer at \$720 per annum, while in point of fact he performs the duty of assistant in the Hall Library of the House and his compensation is usually increased to \$1,800 per annum by an appropriation of \$1,080 in the general deficiency act. Again, a sufficient number of messengers has not been provided for the actual necessities of the service, while more folders have been provided than are required. As a result of this men have been transferred from the duties of a folder to those of a messenger, and the compensation of some has been increased by appropriation in deficiency acts. But evils of another class result from transfers, some examples of which we report. They result in part, at least, from an attempt to adjust salaries so as to satisfy the members that their appointees obtain a just share of the whole appropriation, instead of attempting to apportion the compensation to the merits of the respective employees and the character of the services which they render. . . .

"Second. Payments of compensation to employees while absent.—The duty of many of the employees of the House ceases with the end of a session, or very soon thereafter. Such is the case with the reading clerks, messengers, enrolling clerks, and many others who might be named. Their absence from Washington after a session of Congress closes and their duties are finished is as legitimate as the absence of the members themselves. But many employees who should be at their posts have been from time to time absent without justification, both during sessions and between sessions. In the absence of any record it is impossible for the committee to ascertain with anything like accuracy the amount of absenteeism, but in our opinion it is very considerable.

"Some of those employed in the library service have been absent for long periods between the sessions of Congress, although the House library is in a condition which demands constant attention for years to come in order to bring it up to a proper condition of efficiency. The pay roll of the librarian, his assistants, and those detailed to the library service, including deficiency appropriations, amounts to \$9,200 per annum. No one of the employees of the library, with the exception of a \$600 deficiency employee and Guy Underwood, who in his freshman year at college was librarian part of one session at the Ohio State University, has ever had any library experience, although they all appear to be capable, intelligent men. The House library is said to consist of 300,000 volumes, many of which are duplicates, and is scattered from the Dome to the basement of the Capitol, in some instances, until recently, books being piled in unused rooms, like so much wood or coal. The present librarian testified as follows: 'Q. It would be difficult to describe a worse condition than existed ?' 'A. It would, for the condition of books. It would be all right for a barnyard, but for books it was terrible.' It is just to say that under the present administration of the library some attempt has been made at improvement, but the effect of fifty years' neglect can not be remedied in a day. We can not think that any absenteeism, beyond a reasonable vacation, on the part of those employed in the library is justifiable in view of the foregoing facts.

"The folders, taking the orders of members rather than those of the Doorkeeper, are absent a great deal during the vacation, and in some cases persons are employed by resolution to do their work. The Doorkeeper testified as follows: 'I think Mr. Lyon told me where members requested they had three months at home during this last Congress.' 'Q. Drawing their pay in the meantime ?' 'A. Yes, sir; they had three months'.' 'Q. That is not in the interest of your service, is it ?' 'A. No, sir.' 'Q. Have you been able to prevent it ?' 'A. No, sir.' 'Q. Why ?' 'A. They would go to the superintendent of the folding room and say to him, "My man has got to go home." ' 'Q. You mean the members would go ?' 'A. Yes, sir. I do not like to criticise members, but that is the situation. They go and say, "I have got to have my man home, and he must go home ; it is absolutely necessary ;" and he has been permitted to go.'

"We have been unable to inquire as much into specific instances of absenteeism as we desired, but it may be said generally that absenteeism on the folders' force is very general. . . .

"Third, division of salaries.—According to the testimony of Thomas H. McKee, the Journal clerk, the custom of dividing salaries is an old one and has existed for at least twenty years. We are satisfied that we are unable to report all the instances of divisions of salaries which have occurred : but we submit the following facts, which were clearly proved before us: On the organization of the House in the Fifty-fourth Congress it appears that more places, or places with higher salaries, were promised than the officers of the House were able to discover under the law. It does not appear by whom these promises were made. There began at once a system whereby the employees agreed to contribute greater or less portions of the salaries they received for the purpose either of paying persons not on the roll or of increasing the compensation of persons who were on the roll. Of the latter class, the increases were not proportioned to the character of the services rendered or the merit of the employees, but to the supposed rights of the States or Congressional districts from which the recipients came. Some of these contributions were made voluntarily and cheerfully ; others we believe to have been made under a species of moral duress."—*Congressional Record, Feb. 28, 1901, p. 3597.*

CLERICAL PARTY: Austria. See (in this vol.) AUSTRIA-HUNGARY : A. D. 1897, and after.

Belgium. See (in this vol.) BELGIUM : A. D. 1899-1900.

CLEVELAND, Grover: President of the United States. See (in vol. 5 and in this vol.) UNITED STATES OF AM.: A. D. 1893, to 1897.

Extensions of Civil Service Rules. See (in this vol.) CIVIL SERVICE REFORM : A. D. 1893-1896.

Message to Congress on the Boundary Dispute between Great Britain and Venezuela. See (in this vol.) VENEZUELA: A. D. 1895 (DECEMBER).

On Cuban affairs. See (in this vol.) CUBA: A. D. 1896-1897.

CLEVELAND, OHIO: A. D. 1896.—The centennial anniversary of the founding of the city was celebrated with appropriate ceremonies on the 22d of July, 1896, and made memorable by a gift to the city, by Mr. John D. Rockefeller, of 276 acres of land for a public park.

COAL MINERS, Strikes among. See (in this vol.) INDUSTRIAL DISTURBANCES.

COAMO, Engagement at. See (in this vol.) UNITED STATES OF AM.: A. D. 1898 (JULY—AUGUST): PORTO RICO).

COLENSO, Battle of. See (in this vol.) SOUTH AFRICA (THE FIELD OF WAR): A. D. 1899 (OCTOBER—DECEMBER).

COLLEGES. See (in this vol.) EDUCATION.

COLOMBIA : A. D. 1893-1900.—Resumption of work on the Panama Canal.—Revolutionary movements.—Prolonged Civil War.—Boundary dispute with Costa Rica.—Panama Canal concession twice extended.—In 1893 the receiver or liquidator of the affairs of the bankrupt Panama Canal Company of De Lesseps

(see, in vol. 4, PANAMA CANAL) obtained from the government of Colombia an extension of the terms of the concession under which that company had worked, provided that work on the canal should be resumed before November 1, 1894. He succeeded in forming in France a new company which actually made a beginning of work on the canal before the limit of time expired. But this attempted revival of the undertaking was quickly harassed, like everything else in Colombia, by an outbreak of revolt against the clerical control of government under President Caro. The revolutionary movement was begun late in 1894, receiving aid from exiles and sympathizers in Venezuela, Ecuador and Central America. It had no substantial success, the revolutionists being generally defeated in the pitched battles that were fought; but after a few months they were broken into guerilla bands and continued warfare in that method throughout most of the year 1895. They were still threatening in 1896, but the activity and energy of President Caro prevented any serious outbreak. A boundary dispute between Colombia and Costa Rica, which became considerably embittered in 1896, was finally referred to the President of the French Republic, whose decision was announced in September, 1900.

Colombia began a fresh experience of civil war in the autumn of 1899, when an obstinate movement for the overthrow of President Saclemente (elected in 1898) was begun. General Herrera was said, at the outset, to be in the lead, but, as the struggle proceeded, General Rafael Uribe-Uribe seems to have become its real chief. It went on with fierce fighting, especially in the isthmus, and with varying fortunes, until near the close of 1900, when the insurgents met with a defeat which drove General Uribe-Uribe to flight. He made his escape to Venezuela, and thence to the United States, arriving at New York early in February, 1901. In conversation with representatives of the Press he insisted that there was no thought in his party or in his own mind of abandoning the revolutionary attempt. The cause of the revolution, he said, was due to the oppression of the government, which was in the hands of the Conservative party. "They have not governed according to the constitution," he said, "and while taxing the Liberals, will not allow them to be adequately represented in the government. For fifteen years the Liberal party has been deprived of all its rights. I have been the only representative of the party in Congress. We tried every peaceable method to obtain our rights before going to war, but could not get anything from the government. The government did not want to change anything, because it did not want to lose any of its power. I, as the only representative of the Liberal party, made up my mind to fight, and will fight to the end."

By what is said to have been a forced resignation, some time in the later part of the year 1900, President Saclemente, a very old man, retired from the active duties of the office, which were taken in hand by the Vice-President, Dr. Manoquin.

During the year 1900, the government signed a further extension of the concession to the Panama Canal Company, prolonging the period within which the canal must be completed six years from April, 1904.

COLORADO: A. D. 1897.—Abolition of the death penalty.—By an Act of the Legislature of Colorado which became law in March, 1897, the death penalty was abolished in that state.

COLORADOS. See (in this vol.) URUGUAY: A. D. 1896-1899.

COLUMBUS, Christopher: Removal of remains from Havana to Seville. See (in this vol.) CUBA: A. D. 1898 (DECEMBER).

COMBINATIONS, Industrial. See (in this vol.) TRUSTS.

COMMANDO.—Commandeering. See (in this vol.) SOUTH AFRICA (THE TRANSVAAL): A. D. 1894.

COMMERCIAL CONGRESS, International. See (in this vol.) INTERNATIONAL COMMERCIAL CONGRESS.

COMMERCIAL MUSEUM, Philadelphia. See (in this vol.) PHILADELPHIA: A. D. 1897.

COMPULSORY INSURANCE: The State System in Germany. See (in this vol.) GERMANY: A. D. 1897-1900.

COMPULSORY VOTING. See (in this vol.) BELGIUM: A. D. 1894-1895.

CONCERT OF EUROPE.—Concert of the Powers.—"We have heard of late so much about 'the Concert'. that the man in the street talks of it as if it were a fact of nature like the Bosphorus or the Nile ; and he assumes that he and all his neighbours understand exactly what it means. Yet it may be doubted whether even persons so omniscient as the politician and the journalist could describe it with any approach to truth or even to common sense. An energetic newspaper lately described the Concert as 'Three Despots, two Vassals, and a Coward.' This doubtless was a libel. An Olympian Under-Secretary called it 'the Cabinet of Europe.' Lord Salisbury himself, impatient of facile caricatures, insisted that it was a 'Federation.' It has also, to Sir William Harcourt's wrath, been spoken of as an 'Areopagus' having 'legislative' powers. All these phrases are mere nonsense ; and yet they have profoundly influenced the action of this country and the course of recent history. The patent fact of the hour is that six powerful States are pleased to interest themselves in the Eastern Question—which is the question of the dissolution of Turkey [see, in this vol., TURKEY : A. D. 1895, and after]. They base their claim to take exceptional steps in the matter on the plea that there is imminent risk of a general European war if they do not act. . . . What is the Concert of Europe? It is not a treaty, still less a federation. If it is anything, it is a tacit understanding between the 'six Powers' that they will take common action, or abstain from 'isolated action,' in the Eastern question [see, in this vol., TURKEY: A. D. 1897 (FEBRUARY—MARCH); and 1897-1899]. Whether it is even that, in any rational sense of the word 'understanding,' is more than doubtful. For there has been much and very grave 'isolated action,' even in pending troubles."—*The Concert of Europe* (*Contemporary Rev.*, May, 1897).

The joint action of the leading European Powers in dealing with Turkish affairs, between 1896

and 1899, which took the name of "The Concert of Europe," was imitated in 1900, when the more troublesome "Far Eastern Question" was suddenly sprung upon the world by the "Boxer" rising in China (see, in this vol., CHINA: A. D. 1900, JANUARY—MARCH, and after). The United States and Japan were then associated in action with the European nations, and the "Concert of Europe" was succeeded by a larger "Concert of the Powers."

CONCESSIONS, The battle of, in China. See (in this vol.) CHINA: A. D. 1898 (FEBRUARY—DECEMBER).

CONDOMINIUM, Anglo-Egyptian, in the Sudan. See (in this vol.) EGYPT: A. D. 1899 (JANUARY).

CONFEDERATE DISABILITIES, Removal of. See (in this vol.) UNITED STATES OF AM.: A. D. 1896 (MARCH).

CONGER, Edwin H.: United States Minister to China. See (in this vol.) CHINA.

CONGO FREE STATE: A. D. 1897.—Mutiny of troops of Baron Dhanis's expedition. See (in this vol.) AFRICA: A. D. 1897 (CONGO FREE STATE).

A. D. 1899.—Results of the King of Belgium's attempt to found an African Empire.—Contradictory representations.—"The opening in the first few days of July [1898] of the railway through the District of the Cataracts, from Matadi to Stanley Pool, has turned public attention to Central Africa, where the genius and courage of the King of the Belgians have created a Black Empire within the short space of twelve years. It is the special pride of its founder that the vast state of the Congo has been formed without bloodshed, except at the cost of the cruel Arab slave-hunters, and of the not less cruel cannibals like Msiri or the Batetelas, that a thousand treaties have been signed without a gunshot, and that from the commencement the highest ideals of modern civilisation have been aimed at, and, considering the stupendous difficulties of the task, practically attained in the administration. The standard of humanity and progress has been firmly planted in the midst of a population of thirty millions, the decadence of those millions has been arrested, peace exists where there was only slaughter and savagery, and prosperity is coming in the train of improved communications, and of the development of the natural resources of a most promising region. In the history of Empires that of the Congo State is unique. . . .

"The Berlin Conference [see, in vol. 1, CONGO FREE STATE] did nothing for the Congo State beyond giving it a being and a name. On the other hand it imposed upon it some onerous conditions. There was to be freedom of trade—an excellent principle, but not contributory to the State exchequer—it was to employ all its strength in the suppression of the slave trade— 'a gigantic task, undertaken with the resources of pygmies,' as some one has said—and the navigation of the Congo was to be free to all the world without a single toll. The sufficiently ample dimensions marked out for the State in the Conventional limits attached to the Berlin General Act had to be defined and regulated by subsequent negotiation with the neighbouring Powers. France attenuated the northern pos-

151

sessions of the State at every possible opportunity, but at length, in February, 1895, she was induced to waive in favour of Belgium the right of pre-emption which the Congo Association had given her in April, 1884, over its possessions, at the moment when the Anglo-Portuguese Convention threatened that enterprise with extinction. . . . Four years after the meeting at Berlin it was found necessary to convene another conference of the Powers, held on this occasion at Brussels, under the presidency of Baron Lambermont, whose share in the success of the earlier conference had been very marked and brilliant. The chief object set before the new Conference was to devise means for the abolition of the Slave Trade in Central Africa. . . . The Conference lasted more than seven months, and it was not until July, 1890, that the General Act bearing the signatures of the Powers was agreed upon. It increased the obligations resting on the State; its decisions, to which the Independent State was itself a party, made the task more onerous, but at the same time it sanctioned the necessary measures to give the State the revenue needed for the execution of its new programme. . . .

"Fresh from the Brussels Conference the Congo State threw itself into the struggle with the Arabs. . . . Thanks to the skill and energy with which the campaign was conducted the triumph of the State was complete, and the downfall of the Arabs sounded the knell of the slave trade, of which they were the principal, and indeed the sole, promoters. The Arab campaign did not conclude the military perils that beset the nascent State. The Batetela contingent of the Public Force or native army of the Congo mutinied in January, 1897, while on the march to occupy the Lado district of the Upper Nile, and the episode, ushered in in characters of blood by the assassination of many Belgian officers, seemed to shake the recently-constructed edifice to its base. But if the ordeal was severe, the manner in which the authorities have triumphed over their adversaries and surmounted their difficulties, furnishes clear evidence of the stability of their power. The Batetela mutineers have been overthrown in several signal encounters, a mere handful of fugitives still survive, and each mail brings news of their further dispersal. Even at the moment of its occurrence the blow from the Batetela mutiny was tempered by the success of the column under Commandant Chaltin in overthrowing the Dervishes at Redjaf and in establishing the State's authority on the part of the Nile assigned to it by the Anglo-Congolese Convention of 1894. The triumphs of the Congo State have, however, been those of peace and not of war. With the exception of the operations named and the overthrow of the despotism of the savage Msiri, the State's record is one of unbroken tranquillity. These wars, little in magnitude but great in their consequences, were necessary for the suppression of the slave trade as well as for the legitimate assertion of the authority of the Congo Government. But their immediate consequence was the effective carrying out of the clauses in the Penal Code making all participation in the capture of slaves or in cannibalism a capital offence. That was the primary task, the initial step, in the establishment of civilisation in Central Africa, and of the credit for this the Congo State

cannot be deprived. When this was done there remained the still more difficult task of saving the black races from the evils which civilisation brings in its train among an ignorant population incapable of self-control. The import of firearms had to be checked in order to prevent an untamed race indulging in internecine strife, or turning their weapons upon the mere handful of Europeans engaged in the task of regenerating the negroes. The necessary measures inspired by the double motives of self-preservation and the welfare of the blacks have been taken, and the State controls in the most complete and effectual manner the importation of all weapons and munitions of war. Nor has the success of the administration been less clear or decisive in its control of the liquor traffic."—Demetrius C. Boulger, *Twelve Years' Work on the Congo* (*Fortnightly Review, Oct.*, 1898).

To a considerable extent this favorable view of the work of the Belgians in the Congo State is sustained by the report which a British Consul, Mr. Pickersgill, made to his government in 1898. He wrote admiringly of the energy with which the Belgians had overcome enormous difficulties in their undertaking, and then asked : "Has this splendid invasion justified itself by benefiting the aborigines? Equatorial Africa is not a white man's country. He can never prove his claim to sole possession of it by surviving as the fittest ; and without the black man's co-operation it can serve no useful purpose to anybody. Has the welfare of the African, then, whose prosperous existence is thus indispensable, been duly cared for in the Congo State ?" By way of answer to these questions, his report sets forth, with apparently strict fairness, the conditions produced in the country as he carefully observed them. He found that much good had been done to the natives by restrictions on the liquor trade, by an extensive suppression of inter-tribal wars, and by a diminution of cannibalism. Then comes a rehearsal of facts which have a different look.

"The yoke of the notorious Arab slave-traders has been broken, and traffic in human beings amongst the natives themselves has been diminished to a considerable degree. Eulogy here begins with a spurt and runs out thin at the end. But there is no better way of recording the facts concisely. To hear, amidst the story's wild surroundings, how Dhanis and Hinde, and their intrepid comrades, threw themselves, time after time, upon the strongholds of the banded menstealers, until the Zone Arabe was won in the name of freedom, is to thrill with admiration of a gallant crusade. . . . But it is disappointing to see the outcome of this lofty enterprise sink to a mere modification of the evil that was so righteously attacked. Like the Portuguese in Angola, the Belgians on the Congo have adopted the system of requiring the slave to pay for his freedom by serving a new master during a fixed term of years for wages merely nominal. On this principle is based the 'serviçal' system of the first-named possession, and the 'libéré' system of the latter ; the only difference between the two being that the Portuguese Government permits limited re-enslavement for the benefit of private individuals, but does not purchase on its own account ; while the Government of the Independent State retains for itself an advantage which it taboos to everybody else

"The State supports this system because labour is more easily obtainable thereby than by enforcing corvée amongst the free people, and less expensively than by paying wages. The slave so acquired, however, is supposed to have undergone a change of status, and is baptized officially as a free man. After seven years' service under the new name he is entitled to his liberty complete. In Angola the limit is five years. The natives are being drilled into the habit of regular work. . . . The first Europeans who travelled inland of Matadi had to rely entirely on porters from the coast, and it was not until the missionaries had gained the confidence of the people, and discovered individuals amongst them who could be trusted as gangers, that the employment of local carriers became feasible. The work was paid for, of course, and it is to the credit of the State that the remuneration continued, undiminished, after compulsion was applied. But how, it cannot fail to be asked, did the necessity for compulsion arise ? In the same way that it has since arisen in connection with other forms of labour : the State wished to get on faster than circumstances would permit. Accordingly the Government authorities prohibited the missionaries from recruiting where porters were most easily obtained, and under the direction of their military chief, the late Governor-General Wahis, initiated a rigorous system of corvée. In spite of the remuneration this was resisted, at first by the men liable to serve absenting themselves from home, and afterwards, when the State Officers began to seize their women and children as hostages, by preparations for war. Deserting their villages, the people of the caravan route took to the bush, and efforts were made by the chiefs to bring about a general uprising of the entire Cataract district. Things were in so critical a condition that Colonel Wahis had to leave unpunished the destruction of a Government station and the murder of the officer in charge. Mainly through the influence of the missionaries the general conflagration was prevented, but the original outbreak continued to smoulder for months, and transport work of all kinds had to be discontinued until means were devised of equalising the burden of the corvée, and of enlisting the co-operation of the chiefs in its management. That was in 1894. Three years later the system appeared to be working with remarkable smoothness. . . . Whatever views may be held respecting the influence of the State at the present stage of its schoolmaster task, there can be no doubt that the condition, a year or two hence, of those sections of the population about to be relieved from the transport service, will afford conclusive evidence, one way or the other, of the Government's civilising ability. . . . It needs no great knowledge of coloured humanity to foresee that such pupils will quickly relapse into good-for-nothingness more than aboriginal, unless their education be continued. . . .

"One of the most obvious duties of an European Government standing in 'loco parentis' to savage tribes, and exercising 'dominatio parentis' with an unspared rod, is to educate the juvenile pagan. Since 1892 the Congo State has disbursed, according to the published returns, taking one year with another, about 6,000 l. per annum, on this department of its enterprise. It cannot be said, therefore, to have neglected the duty entirely A school for boys has been estab lished at Boma, and another at Nouvelle Anvers ; while large numbers of children of both sexes have been placed with the Roman Catholic missionaries, in the same and other districts. Except in one direction, however, the movement has not been very successful. The young Africans thus blessed with a chance of becoming loyal with intelligence are all waifs and strays, who have been picked up by exploring parties and military expeditions. Their homes are at the points of the compass, and their speech is utter bewilderment. . . .

"A word must be said as to the employment of what are known as 'sentries.' A 'sentry' on the Congo is a dare-devil aboriginal, chosen, from troops impressed outside the district in which he serves, for his loyalty and force of character. Armed with a rifle and a pouch of cartridges, he is located in a native village to see that the labour for which its inhabitants are responsible is duly attended to. If they are indiarubber collectors, his duty is to send the men into the forest and take note of those who do not return with the proper quantity. Where food is the tax demanded, his business is to make sure that the women prepare and deliver it ; and in every other matter connected with the Government he is the factotum, as far as that village is concerned, of the officer of the district, his power being limited only by the amount of zeal the latter may show in checking oppression. When Governor-General Wahis returned from his tour of inspection he seemed disposed to recommend the abolition of this system, which is open to much abuse. But steps have not yet been taken in that direction."—*Great Britain. Parliamentary Publications* (*Papers by Command: No.* 459, *Miscellaneous Series*, 1898, *pp.* 7–12).

From this account of things it would seem that Mr. Boulger, in the view quoted above from his article on the work of King Leopold in the Congo country, had chosen to look only at what is best in the results. On the other hand, the writer of the following criticism in the "Spectator" of London may have looked at nothing but the blacker side : "King Leopold II., who, though he inherits some of the Coburg kingcraft, is not a really able man, deceived by confidence in his own great wealth and by the incurable Continental idea that anybody can make money in the tropics if he is only hard enough, undertook an enterprise wholly beyond his resources, and by making revenue instead of good government his end, spoiled the whole effect of his first successes. The Congo Free State, covering a million square miles, that is, as large as India, and containing a population supposed to exceed forty-two millions, was committed by Europe to his charge in absolute sovereignty, and at first there appeared to be no resistance. Steamers and telegraphs and stations are trifles to a millionaire, and there were any number of Belgian engineers and young officers and clerks eager for employment. The weak point of the undertaking, inadequate resources, soon, however, became patent to the world. The King had the disposal of a few white troops, but they were only Belgians, who suffer greatly in tropical warfare, and his agents had to form an acclimatised army 'on the cheap.' They engaged, therefore, the fiercest blacks they could find, most of them cannibals, paid them by tolerating license, and then endeavoured to maintain their own authority by savage discipline. The result was that the men, as events have proved, and as the King seems in his apologia to admit, were always on the verge of mutiny, and that the native tribes, with their advantages of position, numbers, and knowledge of the forest and the swamps, proved at least as good fighters as most of the forces of the Congo State. So great, however, is the intellectual superiority of white men, so immeasurable the advantage involved in any tincture of science, that the Belgians might still have prevailed but for the absolute necessity of obtaining money. They could not wait for the growth of resources under scientific taxation such as will follow Mr. Mitchell Innes's financial reforms in Siam, but attempted to obtain them from direct taxation and monopolies, especially that of rubber. Resistance was punished with a savage cruelty, which we are quite ready to believe was not the original intention of the Belgians, but which could not be avoided when the only mode of punishing a village was to let loose black cannibals on it to work their will, and which gradually hardened even the Europeans, and the consequence was universal disloyalty. The braver tribes fought with desperation, the black troops were at once cowed and attracted by their opponents, the black porters and agriculturists became secret enemies, all were kept in order by terror alone, and we all see the result. The Belgians are beaten ; their chiefs, Baron Dhanis and Major Lothaire, are believed to be prisoners ; and the vast territories of the far interior, whence alone rubber can now be obtained, are already lost. . . . The administration on the spot is tainted by the history of its cruelties and its failures, and there are not the means in Brussels of replacing it by competent officials, or of supplying them with the considerable means required for what must now be a deliberate reconquest."—*Spectator* (*London*), *Feb.* 4, 1899.

A. D. 1900.—Expiration of the Belgian Convention of 1890.—King Leopold's will.—

Three days after the close of the year 1900, the Convention of 1890, which regulated for a period of ten years the relations between Belgium and the Congo State, expired by lapse of time, but was likely to be renewed. The chief provisions of the Convention were (1) that Belgium should advance to the Congo State a loan of 25,000,000f. (£1,000,000), free of interest, of which one-fifth was payable at sight and the balance in ten yearly instalments of 2,000,000f. each; (2) Belgium acquired within six months of the final payment the option of annexing the Congo State with all the rights and appurtenances of sovereignty attaching thereto; or (3) if Belgium did not avail herself of this right the loan was only redeemable after a further period of ten years, but became subject to interest at the rate of 3½ per cent. per annum. The will of King Leopold, executed in 1889, runs as follows: "We bequeath and transmit to Belgium, after our death, all our Sovereign rights to the Congo Free State, such as they have been recognized by the declarations, conventions, and treaties, drawn up since 1884, on the one hand between the International Association of the Congo, and on the other hand the Free State, as well as all the property, rights, and advantages, accruing from such sovereignty. Until such time as the Legislature of Belgium shall have stated its intentions as to the acceptation of these dispositions, the sovereignty shall be exercised collectively by the Council of three administrators of the Free State and by the Governor-General."

CONGRESS : Of the United States.—Reapportionment of Representatives. See (in this vol.) UNITED STATES OF AM.: A. D. 1901 (JANUARY).

CONSTANTINOPLE : A. D. 1896.—Attack of Armenian revolutionists on the Ottoman Bank, and subsequent Turkish massacre of Armenians. See (in this vol.) TURKEY : A. D. 1896 (AUGUST).

CONSTITUTION OF AUSTRALIA.

The following is the "Act to constitute the Commonwealth of Australia," as passed by the Imperial Parliament, July 9, 1900 (63 & 64 Vict. ch. 12)—see (in this vol.) AUSTRALIA: A. D. 1900. The text is from the official publication of the Act:

Whereas the people of New South Wales, Victoria, South Australia, Queensland, and Tasmania, humbly relying on the blessing of Almighty God, have agreed to unite in one indissoluble Federal Commonwealth under the Crown of the United Kingdom of Great Britain and Ireland, and under the Constitution hereby established: And whereas it is expedient to provide for the admission into the Commonwealth of other Australasian Colonies and possessions of the Queen: Be it therefore enacted by the Queen's most Excellent Majesty, by and with the advice and consent of the Lords Spiritual and Temporal, and Commons, in this present Parliament assembled, and by the authority of the same, as follows:—

1. This Act may be cited as the Commonwealth of Australia Constitution Act.

2. The provisions of this Act referring to the

Queen shall extend to Her Majesty's heirs and successors in the sovereignty of the United Kingdom.

3. It shall be lawful for the Queen, with the advice of the Privy Council, to declare by proclamation that, on and after a day therein appointed, not being later than one year after the passing of this Act, the people of New South Wales, Victoria, South Australia, Queensland, and Tasmania, and also, if Her Majesty is satisfied that the people of Western Australia have agreed thereto, of Western Australia, shall be united in a Federal Commonwealth under the name of the Commonwealth of Australia. But the Queen may, at any time after the proclamation, appoint a Governor-General for the Commonwealth.

4. The Commonwealth shall be established, and the Constitution of the Commonwealth shall take effect, on and after the day so appointed. But the Parliaments of the several colonies may at any time after the passing of this Act make any such laws, to come into operation on the day so appointed, as they might have made if the

Constitution had taken effect at the passing of this Act.

5. This Act, and all laws made by the Parliament of the Commonwealth under the Constitution, shall be binding on the courts, judges, and people of every State and of every part of the Commonwealth, notwithstanding anything in the laws of any State; and the laws of the Commonwealth shall be in force on all British ships, the Queen's ships of war excepted, whose first port of clearance and whose port of destination are in the Commonwealth.

6. "The Commonwealth" shall mean the Commonwealth of Australia as established under this Act. "The States" shall mean such of the colonies of New South Wales, New Zealand, Queensland, Tasmania, Victoria, Western Australia, and South Australia, including the northern territory of South Australia, as for the time being are parts of the Commonwealth, and such colonies or territories as may be admitted into or established by the Commonwealth as States; and each of such parts of the Commonwealth shall be called "a State." "Original States" shall mean such States as are parts of the Commonwealth at its establishment.

7. The Federal Council of Australasia Act, 1885, is hereby repealed, but so as not to affect any laws passed by the Federal Council of Australasia and in force at the establishment of the Commonwealth. Any such law may be repealed as to any State by the Parliament of the Commonwealth, or as to any colony not being a State by the Parliament thereof.

8. After the passing of this Act the Colonial Boundaries Act, 1895, shall not apply to any colony which becomes a State of the Commonwealth; but the Commonwealth shall be taken to be a self-governing colony for the purposes of that Act.

9. The Constitution of the Commonwealth shall be as follows:—

THE CONSTITUTION.

This Constitution is divided as follows:—

Chapter   I.—The Parliament:
Part   I.—General:
Part   II.—The Senate:
Part   III.—The House of Representatives:
Part   IV.—Both Houses of the Parliament:
Part   V.—Powers of the Parliament:
Chapter   II.—The Executive Government:
Chapter   III.—The Judicature:
Chapter   IV.—Finance and Trade:
Chapter   V.—The States:
Chapter   VI.—New States:
Chapter   VII.—Miscellaneous:
Chapter   VIII.—Alteration of the Constitution.

The Schedule.

CHAPTER I. THE PARLIAMENT: PART I.—GENERAL.

1. The legislative power of the Commonwealth shall be vested in a Federal Parliament, which shall consist of the Queen, a Senate, and a House of Representatives, and which is herein-after called "The Parliament," or "The Parliament of the Commonwealth."

2. A Governor-General appointed by the Queen shall be Her Majesty's representative in the Commonwealth, and shall have and may exercise in the Commonwealth during the Queen's pleasure, but subject to this Constitution, such powers and functions of the Queen as Her Majesty may be pleased to assign to him.

3. There shall be payable to the Queen out of the Consolidated Revenue fund of the Commonwealth, for the salary of the Governor-General, an annual sum which, until the Parliament otherwise provides, shall be ten thousand pounds. The salary of a Governor-General shall not be altered during his continuance in office.

4. The provisions of this Constitution relating to the Governor-General extend and apply to the Governor-General for the time being, or such person as the Queen may appoint to administer the Government of the Commonwealth; but no such person shall be entitled to receive any salary from the Commonwealth in respect of any other office during his administration of the Government of the Commonwealth.

5. The Governor-General may appoint such times for holding the sessions of the Parliament as he thinks fit, and may also from time to time, by Proclamation or otherwise, prorogue the Parliament, and may in like manner dissolve the House of Representatives. After any general election the Parliament shall be summoned to meet not later than thirty days after the day appointed for the return of the writs. The Parliament shall be summoned to meet not later than six months after the establishment of the Commonwealth.

6. There shall be a session of the Parliament once at least in every year, so that twelve months shall not intervene between the last sitting of the Parliament in one session and its first sitting in the next session.

PART II.—THE SENATE.

7. The Senate shall be composed of senators for each State, directly chosen by the people of the State, voting, until the Parliament otherwise provides, as one electorate. But until the Parliament of the Commonwealth otherwise provides, the Parliament of the State of Queensland, if that State be an Original State, may make laws dividing the State into divisions and determining the number of senators to be chosen for each division, and in the absence of such provision the State shall be one electorate. Until the Parliament otherwise provides there shall be six senators for each Original State. The Parliament may make laws increasing or diminishing the number of senators for each State, but so that equal representation of the several Original States shall be maintained and that no Original State shall have less than six senators. The senators shall be chosen for a term of six years, and the names of the senators chosen for each State shall be certified by the Governor to the Governor-General.

8. The qualification of electors of senators shall be in each State that which is prescribed by this Constitution, or by the Parliament, as the qualification for electors of members of the House of Representatives; but in the choosing of senators each elector shall vote only once.

9. The Parliament of the Commonwealth may make laws prescribing the method of choosing senators, but so that the method shall be uniform for all the States. Subject to any such law, the Parliament of each State may make laws prescribing the method of choosing the senators

for that State. The Parliament of a State may make laws for determining the times and places of elections of senators for the State.

10. Until the Parliament otherwise provides, but subject to this Constitution, the laws in force in each State, for the time being, relating to elections for the more numerous House of the Parliament of the State shall, as nearly as practicable, apply to elections of senators for the State.

11. The Senate may proceed to the despatch of business, notwithstanding the failure of any State to provide for its representation in the Senate.

12. The Governor of any State may cause writs to be issued for elections of senators for the State. In case of the dissolution of the Senate the writs shall be issued within ten days from the proclamation of such dissolution.

13. As soon as may be after the Senate first meets, and after each first meeting of the Senate following a dissolution thereof, the Senate shall divide the senators chosen for each State into two classes, as nearly equal in number as practicable; and the places of the senators of the first class shall become vacant at the expiration of the third year, and the places of those of the second class at the expiration of the sixth year, from the beginning of their term of service; and afterwards the places of senators shall become vacant at the expiration of six years from the beginning of their term of service. The election to fill vacant places shall be made in the year at the expiration of which the places are to become vacant. For the purposes of this section the term of service of a senator shall be taken to begin on the first day of January following the day of his election, except in the cases of the first election and of the election next after any dissolution of the Senate, when it shall be taken to begin on the first day of January preceding the day of his election.

14. Whenever the number of senators for a State is increased or diminished, the Parliament of the Commonwealth may make such provision for the vacating of the places of senators for the State as it deems necessary to maintain regularity in the rotation.

15. If the place of a senator becomes vacant before the expiration of his term of service, the Houses of Parliament of the State for which he was chosen shall, sitting and voting together, choose a person to hold the place until the expiration of the term, or until the election of a successor as hereinafter provided, whichever first happens. But if the Houses of Parliament of the State are not in session at the time when the vacancy is notified, the Governor of the State, with the advice of the Executive Council thereof, may appoint a person to hold the place until the expiration of fourteen days after the beginning of the next session of the Parliament of the State, or until the election of a successor, whichever first happens. At the next general election of members of the House of Representatives, or at the next election of senators for the State, whichever first happens, a successor shall, if the term has not then expired, be chosen to hold the place from the date of his election until the expiration of the term. The name of any senator so chosen or appointed shall be certified by the Governor of the State to the Governor-General.

16. The qualifications of a senator shall be the same as those of a member of the House of Representatives.

17. The Senate shall, before proceeding to the despatch of any other business, choose a senator to be the President of the Senate; and as often as the office of President becomes vacant the Senate shall again choose a senator to be the President. The President shall cease to hold his office if he ceases to be a senator. He may be removed from office by a vote of the Senate, or he may resign his office or his seat by writing addressed to the Governor-General.

18. Before or during any absence of the President, the Senate may choose a senator to perform his duties in his absence.

19. A Senator may, by writing addressed to the President, or to the Governor-General if there is no President or if the President is absent from the Commonwealth, resign his place, which thereupon shall become vacant.

20. The place of a senator shall become vacant if for two consecutive months of any session of the Parliament he, without the permission of the Senate, fails to attend the Senate.

21. Whenever a vacancy happens in the Senate, the President, or if there is no President or if the President is absent from the Commonwealth the Governor-General, shall notify the same to the Governor of the State in the representation of which the vacancy has happened.

22. Until the Parliament otherwise provides, the presence of at least one-third of the whole number of the senators shall be necessary to constitute a meeting of the Senate for the exercise of its powers.

23. Questions arising in the Senate shall be determined by a majority of votes, and each senator shall have one vote. The President shall in all cases be entitled to a vote; and when the votes are equal the question shall pass in the negative.

PART III.—THE HOUSE OF REPRESENTATIVES.

24. The House of Representatives shall be composed of members directly chosen by the people of the Commonwealth, and the number of such members shall be, as nearly as practicable, twice the number of the senators. The number of members chosen in the several States shall be in proportion to the respective numbers of their people, and shall, until the Parliament otherwise provides, be determined, whenever necessary, in the following manner :—(i.) A quota shall be ascertained by dividing the number of the people of the Commonwealth, as shown by the latest statistics of the Commonwealth, by twice the number of the senators. (ii.) The number of members to be chosen in each State shall be determined by dividing the number of the people of the State, as shown by the latest statistics of the Commonwealth, by the quota; and if on such division there is a remainder greater than one-half of the quota, one more member shall be chosen in the State. But notwithstanding anything in this section, five members at least shall be chosen in each Original State.

25. For the purposes of the last section, if by the law of any State all persons of any race are disqualified from voting at elections for the more numerous House of the Parliament of the State, then, in reckoning the number of the people of the State or of the Commonwealth, persons of that race resident in that State shall not be counted.

26. Notwithstanding anything in section

twenty-four, the number of members to be chosen in each State at the first election shall be as follows :—New South Wales, twenty-three; Victoria, twenty; Queensland, eight; South Australia, six; Tasmania, five; provided that if Western Australia is an Original State, the numbers shall be as follows :—New South Wales, twenty-six; Victoria, twenty-three; Queensland, nine; South Australia, seven; Western Australia, five; Tasmania, five.

27. Subject to this Constitution, the Parliament may make laws for increasing or diminishing the number of the members of the House of Representatives.

28. Every House of Representatives shall continue for three years from the first meeting of the House, and no longer, but may be sooner dissolved by the Governor-General.

29. Until the Parliament of the Commonwealth otherwise provides, the Parliament of any State may make laws for determining the divisions in each State for which members of the House of Representatives shall be chosen, and the number of members to be chosen for each division. A division shall not be formed out of parts of different States. In the absence of other provision, each State shall be one electorate.

30. Until the Parliament otherwise provides, the qualification of electors of members of the House of Representatives shall be in each State that which is prescribed by the law of the State as the qualification of electors of the more numerous House of Parliament of the State; but in the choosing of members each elector shall vote only once.

31. Until the Parliament otherwise provides, but subject to this Constitution, the laws in force in each State for the time being relating to elections for the more numerous House of the Parliament of the State shall, as nearly as practicable, apply to elections in the State of members of the House of Representatives.

32. The Governor-General in Council may cause writs to be issued for general elections of members of the House of Representatives. After the first general election, the writs shall be issued within ten days from the expiry of a House of Representatives or from the proclamation of a dissolution thereof.

33. Whenever a vacancy happens in the House of Representatives, the Speaker shall issue his writ for the election of a new member, or if there is no Speaker or if he is absent from the Commonwealth the Governor-General in Council may issue the writ.

34. Until the Parliament otherwise provides, the qualifications of a member of the House of Representatives shall be as follows :—(i.) He must be of the full age of twenty-one years, and must be an elector entitled to vote at the election of members of the House of Representatives, or a person qualified to become such elector, and must have been for three years at the least a resident within the limits of the Commonwealth as existing at the time when he is chosen : (ii.) He must be a subject of the Queen, either natural-born or for at least five years naturalized under a law of the United Kingdom, or of a Colony which has become or becomes a State, or of the Commonwealth, or of a State.

35. The House of Representatives shall, before proceeding to the despatch of any other business, choose a member to be the Speaker of the House,

and as often as the office of Speaker becomes vacant the House shall again choose a member to be the Speaker. The Speaker shall cease to hold his office if he ceases to be a member. He may be removed from office by a vote of the House, or he may resign his office or his seat by writing addressed to the Governor-General.

36. Before or during any absence of the Speaker, the House of Representatives may choose a member to perform his duties in his absence.

37. A member may by writing addressed to the Speaker, or to the Governor-General if there is no Speaker or if the Speaker is absent from the Commonwealth, resign his place, which thereupon shall become vacant.

38. The place of a member shall become vacant if for two consecutive months of any session of the Parliament he, without the permission of the House, fails to attend the House.

39. Until the Parliament otherwise provides, the presence of at least one-third of the whole number of the members of the House of Representatives shall be necessary to constitute a meeting of the House for the exercise of its powers.

40. Questions arising in the House of Representatives shall be determined by a majority of votes other than that of the Speaker. The Speaker shall not vote unless the numbers are equal, and then he shall have a casting vote.

PART IV.—BOTH HOUSES OF THE PARLIAMENT.

41. No adult person who has or acquires a right to vote at elections for the more numerous House of the Parliament of a State shall, while the right continues, be prevented by any law of the Commonwealth from voting at elections for either House of the Parliament of the Commonwealth.

42. Every senator and every member of the House of Representatives shall before taking his seat make and subscribe before the Governor-General, or some person authorised by him, an oath or affirmation of allegiance in the form set forth in the schedule to this Constitution.

43. A member of either House of the Parliament shall be incapable of being chosen or of sitting as a member of the other House.

44. Any person who—(i.) Is under any acknowledgment of allegiance, obedience, or adherence to a foreign power, or is a subject or a citizen or entitled to the rights or privileges of a subject or a citizen of a foreign power : or (ii.) Is attainted of treason, or has been convicted and is under sentence, or subject to be sentenced, for any offence punishable under the law of the Commonwealth or of a State by imprisonment for one year or longer : or (iii.) Is an undischarged bankrupt or insolvent : or (iv.) Holds any office of profit under the Crown, or any pension payable during the pleasure of the Crown out of any of the revenues of the Commonwealth : or (v.) Has any direct or indirect pecuniary interest in any agreement with the Public Service of the Commonwealth otherwise than as a member and in common with the other members of an incorporated company consisting of more than twenty-five persons : shall be incapable of being chosen or of sitting as a senator or a member of the House of Representatives. But sub-section iv. does not apply to the office of any of the Queen's Ministers of State for the Commonwealth, or of any of the Queen's Ministers for a State, or to the re-

ceipt of pay, half pay, or a pension by any person as an officer or member of the Queen's navy or army, or to the receipt of pay as an officer or member of the naval or military forces of the Commonwealth by any person whose services are not wholly employed by the Commonwealth.

45. If a senator or member of the House of Representatives—(i.) Becomes subject to any of the disabilities mentioned in the last preceding section: or (ii.) Takes the benefit, whether by assignment, composition, or otherwise, of any law relating to bankrupt or insolvent debtors: or (iii.) Directly or indirectly takes or agrees to take any fee or honorarium for services rendered to the Commonwealth, or for services rendered in the Parliament to any person or State: his place shall thereupon become vacant.

46. Until the Parliament otherwise provides, any person declared by this Constitution to be incapable of sitting as a senator or as a member of the House of Representatives shall, for every day on which he so sits, be liable to pay the sum of one hundred pounds to any person who sues for it in any court of competent jurisdiction.

47. Until the Parliament otherwise provides, any question respecting the qualification of a senator or of a member of the House of Representatives, or respecting a vacancy in either House of the Parliament, and any question of a disputed election to either House, shall be determined by the House in which the question arises.

48. Until the Parliament otherwise provides, each senator and each member of the House of Representatives shall receive an allowance of four hundred pounds a year, to be reckoned from the day on which he takes his seat.

49. The powers, privileges, and immunities of the Senate and of the House of Representatives, and of the members and the committees of each House, shall be such as are declared by the Parliament, and until declared shall be those of the Commons House of Parliament of the United Kingdom, and of its members and committees, at the establishment of the Commonwealth.

50. Each House of the Parliament may make rules and orders with respect to—(i.) The mode in which its powers, privileges, and immunities may be exercised and upheld: (ii.) The order and conduct of its business and proceedings either separately or jointly with the other House.

PART V.—POWERS OF THE PARLIAMENT.

51. The Parliament shall, subject to this Constitution, have power to make laws for the peace, order, and good government of the Commonwealth with respect to:—(i.) Trade and commerce with other countries, and among the States: (ii.) Taxation ; but so as not to discriminate between States or parts of States : (iii.) Bounties on the production or export of goods, but so that such bounties shall be uniform throughout the Commonwealth: (iv.) Borrowing money on the public credit of the Commonwealth : (v.) Postal, telegraphic, telephonic, and other like services: (vi.) The naval and military defence of the Commonwealth and of the several States, and the control of the forces to execute and maintain the laws of the Commonwealth : (vii.) Lighthouses, lightships, beacons and buoys : (viii.) Astronomical and meteorological observations : (ix.) Quarantine : (x.) Fisheries in Australian waters beyond territorial limits : (xi.) Census and statis-

tics: (xii.) Currency, coinage, and legal tender : (xiii.) Banking, other than State banking ; also State banking extending beyond the limits of the State concerned, the incorporation of banks, and the issue of paper money : (xiv.) Insurance, other than State insurance ; also State insurance extending beyond the limits of the State concerned: (xv.) Weights and measures: (xvi.) Bills of exchange and promissory notes: (xvii.) Bankruptcy and insolvency: (xviii.) Copyrights, patents of inventions and designs, and trade marks : (xix.) Naturalization and aliens : (xx.) Foreign corporations, and trading or financial corporations formed within the limits of the Commonwealth : (xxi.) Marriage : (xxii.) Divorce and matrimonial causes ; and in relation thereto, parental rights, and the custody and guardianship of infants : (xxiii.) Invalid and old-age pensions : (xxiv.) The service and execution throughout the Commonwealth of the civil and criminal process and the judgments of the courts of the States : (xxv.) The recognition throughout the Commonwealth of the laws, the public Acts and records, and the judicial proceedings of the States : (xxvi.) The people of any race, other than the aboriginal race in any State, for whom it is deemed necessary to make special laws : (xxvii.) Immigration and emigration : (xxviii.) The influx of criminals: (xxix.) External affairs : (xxx.) The relations of the Commonwealth with the islands of the Pacific: (xxxi.) The acquisition of property on just terms from any State or person for any purpose in respect of which the Parliament has power to make laws : (xxxii.) The control of railways with respect to transport for the naval and military purposes of the Commonwealth : (xxxiii.) The acquisition, with the consent of a State, of any railways of the State on terms arranged between the Commonwealth and the State : (xxxiv.) Railway construction and extension in any State with the consent of that State : (xxxv.) Conciliation and arbitration for the prevention and settlement of industrial disputes extending beyond the limits of any one State : (xxxvi.) Matters in respect of which this Constitution makes provision until the Parliament otherwise provides: (xxxvii.) Matters referred to the Parliament of the Commonwealth by the Parliament or Parliaments of any State or States, but so that the law shall extend only to States by whose Parliaments the matter is referred, or which afterwards adopt the law : (xxxviii.) The exercise within the Commonwealth, at the request or with the concurrence of the Parliaments of all the States directly concerned, of any power which can at the establishment of this Constitution be exercised only by the Parliament of the United Kingdom or by the Federal Council of Australasia : (xxxix.) Matters incidental to the execution of any power vested by this Constitution in the Parliament or in either House thereof, or in the Government of the Commonwealth, or in the Federal Judicature, or in any department or officer of the Commonwealth.

52. The Parliament shall, subject to this Constitution, have exclusive power to make laws for the peace, order, and good government of the Commonwealth with respect to—(i.) The seat of government of the Commonwealth, and all places acquired by the Commonwealth for public purposes: (ii.) Matters relating to any department of the public service the control of which is by

this Constitution transferred to the Executive Government of the Commonwealth : (iii.) Other matters declared by this Constitution to be within the exclusive power of the Parliament.

53. Proposed laws appropriating revenue or moneys, or imposing taxation, shall not originate in the Senate. But a proposed law shall not be taken to appropriate revenue or moneys, or to impose taxation, by reason only of its containing provisions for the imposition or appropriation of fines or other pecuniary penalties, or for the demand or payment or appropriation of fees for licences, or fees for services under the proposed law. The Senate may not amend proposed laws imposing taxation, or proposed laws appropriating revenue or moneys for the ordinary annual services of the Government. The Senate may not amend any proposed law so as to increase any proposed charge or burden on the people. The Senate may at any stage return to the House of Representatives any proposed law which the Senate may not amend, requesting, by message, the omission or amendment of any items or provisions therein. And the House of Representatives may, if it thinks fit, make any of such omissions or amendments, with or without modifications. Except as provided in this section, the Senate shall have equal power with the House Representatives in respect of all proposed bfws.

54. The proposed law which appropriates revenue or moneys for the ordinary annual services of the Government shall deal only with such appropriation.

55. Laws imposing taxation shall deal only with the imposition of taxation, and any provision therein dealing with any other matter shall be of no effect. Laws imposing taxation, except laws imposing duties of customs or of excise, shall deal with one subject of taxation only ; but laws imposing duties of customs shall deal with duties of customs only, and laws imposing duties of excise shall deal with duties of excise only.

56. A vote, resolution, or proposed law for the appropriation of revenue or moneys shall not be passed unless the purpose of the appropriation has in the same session been recommended by message of the Governor-General to the House in which the proposal originated.

57. If the House of Representatives passes any proposed law, and the Senate rejects or fails to pass it, or passes it with amendments to which the House of Representatives will not agree, and if after an interval of three months the House of Representatives, in the same or the next session, again passes the proposed law with or without any amendments which have been made, suggested, or agreed to by the Senate, and the Senate rejects or fails to pass it, or passes it with amendments to which the House of Representatives will not agree, the Governor-General may dissolve the Senate and the House of Representatives simultaneously. But such dissolution shall not take place within six months before the date of the expiry of the House of Representatives by effluxion of time. If after such dissolution the House of Representatives again passes the proposed law, with or without any amendments which have been made, suggested, or agreed to by the Senate, and the Senate rejects or fails to pass it, or passes it with amendments to which the House of Representatives will not agree, the

Governor-General may convene a joint sitting of the members of the Senate and of the House of Representatives. The members present at the joint sitting may deliberate and shall vote together upon the proposed law as last proposed by the House of Representatives, and upon amendments, if any, which have been made therein by one House and not agreed to by the other, and any such amendments which are affirmed by an absolute majority of the total number of the members of the Senate and House of Representatives shall be taken to have been carried, and if the proposed law, with the amendments, if any, so carried is affirmed by an absolute majority of the total number of the members of the Senate and House of Representatives, it shall be taken to have been duly passed by both Houses of the Parliament, and shall be presented to the Governor-General for the Queen's assent.

58. When a proposed law passed by both Houses of the Parliament is presented to the Governor-General for the Queen's assent, he shall declare, according to his discretion, but subject to this Constitution, that he assents in the Queen's name, or that he withholds assent, or that he reserves the law for the Queen's pleasure. The Governor-General may return to the house in which it originated any proposed law so presented to him, and may transmit therewith any amendments which he may recommend, and the Houses may deal with the recommendation.

59. The Queen may disallow any law within one year from the Governor-General's assent, and such disallowance on being made known by the Governor-General by speech or message to each of the Houses of the Parliament, or by Proclamation, shall annul the law from the day when the disallowance is so made known.

60. A proposed law reserved for the Queen's pleasure shall not have any force unless and until within two years from the day on which it was presented to the Governor-General for the Queen's assent the Governor-General makes known, by speech or message to each of the Houses of the Parliament, or by Proclamation, that it has received the Queen's assent.

CHAPTER II. THE EXECUTIVE GOVERNMENT.

61. The executive power of the Commonwealth is vested in the Queen and is exerciseable by the Governor-General as the Queen's representative, and extends to the execution and maintenance of this Constitution, and of the laws of the Commonwealth.

62. There shall be a Federal Executive Council to advise the Governor-General in the government of the Commonwealth, and the members of the Council shall be chosen and summoned by the Governor-General and sworn as Executive Councillors, and shall hold office during his pleasure.

63. The provisions of this Constitution referring to the Governor-General in Council shall be construed as referring to the Governor-General acting with the advice of the Federal Executive Council.

64. The Governor-General may appoint officers to administer such departments of State of the Commonwealth as the Governor-General in Council may establish. Such officers shall hold office during the pleasure of the Governor-General. They shall be members of the Federal Executive Council, and shall be the Queen's

159

Ministers of State for the Commonwealth. After the first general election no Minister of State shall hold office for a longer period than three months unless he is or becomes a senator or a member of the House of Representatives.

65. Until the Parliament otherwise provides, the Ministers of State shall not exceed seven in number, and shall hold such offices as the Parliament prescribes, or, in the absence of provision, as the Governor-General directs.

66. There shall be payable to the Queen, out of the Consolidated Revenue Fund of the Commonwealth, for the salaries of the Ministers of State, an annual sum which, until the Parliament otherwise provides, shall not exceed twelve thousand pounds a year.

67. Until the Parliament otherwise provides, the appointment and removal of all other officers of the Executive Government of the Commonwealth shall be vested in the Governor-General in Council, unless the appointment is delegated by the Governor-General in Council or by a law of the Commonwealth to some other authority.

68. The command in chief of the naval and military forces of the Commonwealth is vested in the Governor-General as the Queen's representative.

69. On a date or dates to be proclaimed by the Governor-General after the establishment of the Commonwealth the following departments of the public service in each State shall become transferred to the Commonwealth :—Posts, telegraphs, and telephones : Naval and military defence : Lighthouses, lightships, beacons, and buoys : Quarantine. But the departments of customs and of excise in each State shall become transferred to the Commonwealth on its establishment.

70. In respect of matters which, under this Constitution, pass to the Executive Government of the Commonwealth, all powers and functions which at the establishment of the Commonwealth are vested in the Governor of a Colony, or in the Governor of a Colony with the advice of his Executive Council, or in any authority of a Colony, shall vest in the Governor-General, or in the Governor-General in Council, or in the authority exercising similar powers under the Commonwealth, as the case requires.

CHAPTER III. THE JUDICATURE.

71. The judicial power of the Commonwealth shall be vested in a Federal Supreme Court, to be called the High Court of Australia, and in such other federal courts as the Parliament creates, and in such other courts as it invests with federal jurisdiction. The High Court shall consist of a Chief Justice, and so many other Justices, not less than two, as the Parliament prescribes.

72. The Justices of the High Court and of the other courts created by the Parliament — (i.) Shall be appointed by the Governor-General in Council : (ii.) Shall not be removed except by the Governor-General in Council, on an address from both Houses of the Parliament in the same session, praying for such removal on the ground of proved misbehaviour or incapacity : (iii.) Shall receive such remuneration as the Parliament may fix ; but the remuneration shall not be diminished during their continuance in office.

73. The High Court shall have jurisdiction, with such exceptions and subject to such regulations as the Parliament prescribes, to hear and determine appeals from all judgments, decrees, orders, and sentences — (i.) Of any Justice or Justices exercising the original jurisdiction of the High Court : (ii.) Of any other federal court, or court exercising federal jurisdiction; or of the Supreme Court of any State, or of any other court of any State from which at the establishment of the Commonwealth an appeal lies to the Queen in Council : (iii.) Of the Inter-State Commission, but as to questions of law only : and the judgment of the High Court in all such cases shall be final and conclusive. But no exception or regulation prescribed by the Parliament shall prevent the High Court from hearing and determining any appeal from the Supreme Court of a State in any matter in which at the establishment of the Commonwealth an appeal lies from such Supreme Court to the Queen in Council. Until the Parliament otherwise provides, the conditions of and restrictions on appeals to the Queen in Council from the Supreme Courts of the several States shall be applicable to appeals from them to the High Court.

74. No appeal shall be permitted to the Queen in Council from a decision of the High Court upon any question, howsoever arising, as to the limits inter se of the Constitutional powers of the Commonwealth and those of any State or States, or as to the limits inter se of the Constitutional powers of any two or more States, unless the High Court shall certify that the question is one which ought to be determined by Her Majesty in Council. The High Court may so certify if satisfied that for any special reason the certificate should be granted, and thereupon an appeal shall lie to Her Majesty in Council on the question without further leave. Except as provided in this section, this Constitution shall not impair any right which the Queen may be pleased to exercise by virtue of Her Royal prerogative to grant special leave of appeal from the High Court to Her Majesty in Council. The Parliament may make laws limiting the matters in which such leave may be asked, but proposed laws containing any such limitation shall be reserved by the Governor-General for Her Majesty's pleasure.

75. In all matters — (i.) Arising under any treaty : (ii.) Affecting consuls or other representatives of other countries : (iii.) In which the Commonwealth, or a person suing or being sued on behalf of the Commonwealth, is a party : (iv.) Between States, or between residents of different States, or between a State and a resident of another State : (v.) In which a writ of Mandamus or prohibition or an injunction is sought against an officer of the Commonwealth: the High Court shall have original jurisdiction.

76. The Parliament may make laws conferring original jurisdiction on the High Court in any matter—(i.) Arising under this Constitution, or involving its interpretation : (ii.) Arising under any laws made by the Parliament : (iii.) Of Admiralty and maritime jurisdiction : (iv.) Relating to the same subject-matter claimed under the laws of different States.

77. With respect to any of the matters mentioned in the last two sections the Parliament may make laws—(i.) Defining the jurisdiction of any federal court other than the High Court : (ii.) Defining the extent to which the jurisdiction of any federal court shall be exclusive of

that which belongs to or is invested in the courts of the States : (iii.) Investing any court of a State with federal jurisdiction.

78. The Parliament may make laws conferring rights to proceed against the Commonwealth or a State in respect of matters within the limits of the judicial power.

79. The federal jurisdiction of any court may be exercised by such number of judges as the Parliament prescribes.

80. The trial on indictment of any offence against any law of the Commonwealth shall be by jury, and every such trial shall be held in the State where the offence was committed, and if the offence was not committed within any State the trial shall be held at such place or places as the Parliament prescribes.

CHAPTER IV. FINANCE AND TRADE.

81. All revenues or moneys raised or received by the Executive Government of the Commonwealth shall form one Consolidated Revenue Fund, to be appropriated for the purposes of the Commonwealth in the manner and subject to the charges and liabilities imposed by this Constitution.

82. The costs, charges, and expenses incident to the collection, management, and receipt of the Consolidated Revenue Fund shall form the first charge thereon ; and the revenue of the Commonwealth shall in the first instance be applied to the payment of the expenditure of the Commonwealth.

83. No money shall be drawn from the Treasury of the Commonwealth except under appropriation made by law. But until the expiration of one month after the first meeting of the Parliament the Governor-General in Council may draw from the Treasury and expend such moneys as may be necessary for the maintenance of any department transferred to the Commonwealth and for the holding of the first elections for the Parliament.

84. When any department of the public service of a State becomes transferred to the Commonwealth, all officers of the department shall become subject to the control of the Executive Government of the Commonwealth. Any such officer who is not retained in the service of the Commonwealth shall, unless he is appointed to some other office of equal emolument in the public service of the State, be entitled to receive from the State any pension, gratuity, or other compensation, payable under the law of the State on the abolition of his office. Any such officer who is retained in the service of the Commonwealth shall preserve all his existing and accruing rights, and shall be entitled to retire from office at the time, and on the pension or retiring allowance, which would be permitted by the law of the State if his service with the Commonwealth were a continuation of his service with the State. Such pension or retiring allowance shall be paid to him by the Commonwealth ; but the State shall pay to the Commonwealth a part thereof, to be calculated on the proportion which his term of service with the State bears to his whole term of service, and for the purpose of the calculation his salary shall be taken to be that paid to him by the State at the time of the transfer. Any officer who is, at the establishment of the Commonwealth, in the public service of a State, and who is, by consent of the

Governor of the State with the advice of the Executive Council thereof, transferred to the public service of the Commonwealth, shall have the same rights as if he had been an officer of a department transferred to the Commonwealth and were retained in the service of the Commonwealth.

85. When any department of the public service of a State is transferred to the Commonwealth — (i.) All property of the State of any kind, used exclusively in connexion with the department, shall become vested in the Commonwealth ; but, in the case of the departments controlling customs and excise and bounties, for such time only as the Governor-General in Council may declare to be necessary: (ii.) The Commonwealth may acquire any property of the State, of any kind used, but not exclusively used in connexion with the department : the value thereof shall, if no agreement can be made, be ascertained in, as nearly as may be, the manner in which the value of land, or of an interest in land, taken by the State for public purposes is ascertained under the law of the State in force at the establishment of the Commonwealth : (iii.) The Commonwealth shall compensate the State for the value of any property passing to the Commonwealth under this section ; if no agreement can be made as to the mode of compensation, it shall be determined under laws to be made by the Parliament : (iv.) The Commonwealth shall, at the date of the transfer, assume the current obligations of the State in respect of the department transferred.

86. On the establishment of the Commonwealth, the collection and control of duties of customs and of excise, and the control of the payment of bounties, shall pass to the Executive Government of the Commonwealth.

87. During a period of ten years after the establishment of the Commonwealth and thereafter until the Parliament otherwise provides, of the net revenue of the Commonwealth from duties of customs and of excise not more than one-fourth shall be applied annually by the Commonwealth towards its expenditure. The balance shall, in accordance with this Constitution, be paid to the several States, or applied towards the payment of interest on debts of the several States taken over by the Commonwealth.

88. Uniform duties of customs shall be imposed within two years after the establishment of the Commonwealth.

89. Until the imposition of uniform duties of customs — (i.) The Commonwealth shall credit to each State the revenues collected therein by the Commonwealth. (ii.) The Commonwealth shall debit to each State — (a) The expenditure therein of the Commonwealth incurred solely for the maintenance or continuance, as at the time of transfer, of any department transferred from the State to the Commonwealth ; (b) The proportion of the State, according to the number of its people, in the other expenditure of the Commonwealth. (iii.) The Commonwealth shall pay to each State month by month the balance (if any) in favour of the State.

90. On the imposition of uniform duties of customs the power of the Parliament to impose duties of customs and of excise, and to grant bounties on the production or export of goods, shall become exclusive. On the imposition of uniform duties of customs all laws of the several

6–11

States imposing duties of customs or of excise, or offering bounties on the production or export of goods, shall cease to have effect, but any grant of or agreement for any such bounty lawfully made by or under the authority of the Government of any State shall be taken to be good if made before the thirtieth day of June, one thousand eight hundred and ninety-eight, and not otherwise.

91. Nothing in this Constitution prohibits a State from granting any aid to or bounty on mining for gold, silver, or other metals, nor from granting, with the consent of both Houses of the Parliament of the Commonwealth expressed by resolution, any aid to or bounty on the production or export of goods.

92. On the imposition of uniform duties of customs, trade, commerce, and intercourse among the States, whether by means of internal carriage or ocean navigation, shall be absolutely free. But notwithstanding anything in this Constitution, goods imported before the imposition of uniform duties of customs into any State, or into any Colony which, whilst the goods remain therein, becomes a State, shall, on thence passing into another State within two years after the imposition of such duties, be liable to any duty chargeable on the importation of such goods into the Commonwealth, less any duty paid in respect of the goods on their importation.

93. During the first five years after the imposition of uniform duties of customs, and thereafter until the Parliament otherwise provides—(i.) The duties of customs chargeable on goods imported into a State and afterwards passing into another State for consumption, and the duties of excise paid on goods produced or manufactured in a State and afterwards passing into another State for consumption, shall be taken to have been collected not in the former but in the latter State : (ii.) Subject to the last subsection, the Commonwealth shall credit revenue, debit expenditure, and pay balances to the several States as prescribed for the period preceding the imposition of uniform duties of customs.

94. After five years from the imposition of uniform duties of customs, the Parliament may provide, on such basis as it deems fair, for the monthly payment to the several States of all surplus revenue of the Commonwealth.

95. Notwithstanding anything in this Constitution, the Parliament of the State of Western Australia, if that State be an Original State, may, during the first five years after the imposition of uniform duties of customs, impose duties of customs on goods passing into that State and not originally imported from beyond the limits of the Commonwealth ; and such duties shall be collected by the Commonwealth. But any duty so imposed on any goods shall not exceed during the first of such years the duty chargeable on the goods under the law of Western Australia in force at the imposition of uniform duties, and shall not exceed during the second, third, fourth, and fifth of such years respectively, four-fifths, three-fifths, two-fifths, and one-fifth of such latter duty, and all duties imposed under this section shall cease at the expiration of the fifth year after the imposition of uniform duties. If at any time during the five years the duty on any goods under this section is higher than the duty imposed by the Commonwealth on the im-

portation of the like goods, then such higher duty shall be collected on the goods when imported into Western Australia from beyond the limits of the Commonwealth.

96. During a period of ten years after the establishment of the Commonwealth and thereafter until the Parliament otherwise provides, the Parliament may grant financial assistance to any State on such terms and conditions as the Parliament thinks fit.

97. Until the Parliament otherwise provides, the laws in force in any Colony which has become or becomes a State with respect to the receipt of revenue and the expenditure of money on account of the Government of the Colony, and the review and audit of such receipt and expenditure, shall apply to the receipt of revenue and the expenditure of money on account of the Commonwealth in the State in the same manner as if the Commonwealth, or the Government or an officer of the Commonwealth, were mentioned whenever the Colony, or the Government or an officer of the Colony, is mentioned.

98. The power of the Parliament to make laws with respect to trade and commerce extends to navigation and shipping, and to railways the property of any State.

99. The Commonwealth shall not, by any law or regulation of trade, commerce, or revenue, give preference to one State or any part thereof over another State or any part thereof.

100. The Commonwealth shall not, by any law or regulation of trade or commerce, abridge the right of a State or of the residents therein to the reasonable use of the waters of rivers for conservation or irrigation.

101. There shall be an Inter-State Commission, with such powers of adjudication and administration as the Parliament deems necessary for the execution and maintenance, within the Commonwealth, of the provisions of this Constitution relating to trade and commerce, and of all laws made thereunder.

102. The Parliament may by any law with respect to trade or commerce forbid, as to railways, any preference or discrimination by any State, or by any authority constituted under a State, if such preference or discrimination is undue and unreasonable, or unjust to any State ; due regard being had to the financial responsibilities incurred by any State in connexion with the construction and maintenance of its railways. But no preference or discrimination shall, within the meaning of this section, be taken to be undue and unreasonable, or unjust to any State, unless so adjudged by the Inter-State Commission.

103. The members of the Inter-State Commission—(i.) Shall be appointed by the Governor-General in Council : (ii.) Shall hold office for seven years, but may be removed within that time by the Governor-General in Council, on an address from both Houses of the Parliament in the same session praying for such removal on the ground of proved misbehaviour or incapacity : (iii.) Shall receive such remuneration as the Parliament may fix ; but such remuneration shall not be diminished during their continuance in office.

104. Nothing in this Constitution shall render unlawful any rate for the carriage of goods upon a railway, the property of a State, if the rate is deemed by the Inter-State Commission to be nec-

essary for the development of the territory of the State, and if the rate applies equally to goods within the State and to goods passing into the State from other States.

105. The Parliament may take over from the States their public debts as existing at the establishment of the Commonwealth, or a proportion thereof according to the respective numbers of their people as shown by the latest statistics of the Commonwealth, and may convert, renew, or consolidate such debts, or any part thereof ; and the States shall indemnify the Commonwealth in respect of the debts taken over, and thereafter the interest payable in respect of the debts shall be deducted and retained from the portions of the surplus revenue of the Commonwealth payable to the several States, or if such surplus is iusufficient, or if there is no surplus, then the deficiency or the whole amount shall be paid by the several States.

CHAPTER V. THE STATES.

106. The Constitution of each State of the Commonwealth shall, subject to this Constitution, continue as at the establishment of the Commonwealth, or as at the admission or establishment of the State, as the case may be, until altered in accordance with the Constitution of the State.

107. Every power of the Parliament of a Colony which has become or becomes a State, shall, unless it is by this Constitution exclusively vested in the Parliament of the Commonwealth or withdrawn from the Parliament of the State, continue as at the establishment of the Commonwealth, or as at the admission or establishment of the State, as the case may be.

108. Every law in force in a Colony which has become or becomes a State, and relating to any matter within the powers of the Parliament of the Commonwealth, shall, subject to this Constitution continue in force in the State ; and, until provision is made in that behalf by the Parliament of the Commonwealth, the Parliament of the State shall have such powers of alteration and of repeal in respect of any such law as the Parliament of the Colony had until the Colony became a State.

109. When a law of a State is inconsistent with a law of the Commonwealth, the latter shall prevail, and the former shall, to the extent of the inconsistency, be invalid.

110. The provisions of this Constitution relating to the Governor of a State extend and apply to the Governor for the time being of the State, or other chief executive officer or administrator of the government of the State.

111. The Parliament of a State may surrender any part of the State to the Commonwealth ; and upon such surrender, and the acceptance thereof by the Commonwealth, such part of the State shall become subject to the exclusive jurisdiction of the Commonwealth.

112. After uniform duties of customs have been imposed, a State may levy on imports or exports, or on goods passing into or out of the State, such charges as may be necessary for executing the inspection laws of the State ; but the net produce of all charges so levied shall be for the use of the Commonwealth ; and any such inspection laws may be annulled by the Parliament of the Commonwealth.

113. All fermented, distilled, or other intoxi-cating liquids passing into any State or remaining therein for use, consumption, sale, or storage, shall be subject to the laws of the State as if such liquids had been produced in the State.

114. A State shall not, without the consent of the Parliament of the Commonwealth, raise or maintain any naval or military force, or impose any tax on property of any kind belonging to the Commonwealth, nor shall the Commonwealth impose any tax on property of any kind belonging to a State.

115. A State shall not coin money, nor make anything but gold and silver coin a legal tender in payment of debts.

116. The Commonwealth shall not make any law for establishing any religion, or for imposing any religious observance, or for prohibiting the free exercise of any religion, and no religious test shall be required as a qualification for any office or public trust under the Commonwealth.

117. A subject of the Queen, resident in any State, shall not be subject in any other State to any disability or discrimination which would not be equally applicable to him if he were a subject of the Queen resident in such other State.

118. Full faith and credit shall be given, throughout the Commonwealth to the laws, the public Acts and records, and the judicial proceedings of every State.

119. The Commonwealth shall protect every State against invasion and, on the application of the Executive Government of the State, against domestic violence.

120. Every State shall make provision for the detention in its prisons of persons accused or convicted of offences against the laws of the Commonwealth, and for the punishment of persons convicted of such offences, and the Parliament of the Commonwealth may make laws to give effect to this provision.

CHAPTER VI. NEW STATES.

121. The Parliament may admit to the Commonwealth or establish new States, and may upon such admission or establishment make or impose such terms and conditions, including the extent of representation in either House of the Parliament, as it thinks fit.

122. The Parliament may make laws for the government of any territory surrendered by any State to and accepted by the Commonwealth, or of any territory placed by the Queen under the authority of and accepted by the Commonwealth, or otherwise acquired by the Commonwealth, and may allow the representation of such territory in either House of the Parliament to the extent and on the terms which it thinks fit.

123. The Parliament of the Commonwealth may, with the consent of the Parliament of a State, and the approval of the majority of the electors of the State voting upon the question, increase, diminish, or otherwise alter the limits of the State, upon such terms and conditions as may be agreed on. and may, with the like consent. make provision respecting the effect and operation of any increase or diminution or alteration of territory in relation to any State affected.

124. A new State may be formed by separation of territory from a State, but only with the consent of the Parliament thereof, and a new State may be formed by the union of two or more States or parts of States, but only with the consent of the Parliaments of the States affected.

CHAPTER VII. MISCELLANEOUS.

125. The seat of Government of the Commonwealth shall be determined by the Parliament, and shall be within territory which shall have been granted to or acquired by the Commonwealth, and shall be vested in and belong to the Commonwealth, and shall be in the State of New South Wales, and be distant not less than one hundred miles from Sydney. Such territory shall contain an area of not less than one hundred square miles, and such portion thereof as shall consist of Crown lands shall be granted to the Commonwealth without any payment therefor. The Parliament shall sit at Melbourne until it meet at the seat of Government.

126. The Queen may authorise the Governor-General to appoint any person, or any persons jointly or severally, to be his deputy or deputies within any part of the Commonwealth, and in that capacity to exercise during the pleasure of the Governor-General such powers and functions of the Governor-General as he thinks fit to assign to such deputy or deputies, subject to any limitations expressed or directions given by the Queen; but the appointment of such deputy or deputies shall not affect the exercise by the Governor-General himself of any power or function.

127. In reckoning the numbers of the people of the Commonwealth, or of a State or other part of the Commonwealth, aboriginal natives shall not be counted.

CHAPTER VIII. ALTERATION OF THE CONSTITUTION.

128. This Constitution shall not be altered except in the following manner:—The proposed law for the alteration thereof must be passed by an absolute majority of each House of the Parliament, and not less than two nor more than six months after its passage through both Houses the proposed law shall be submitted in each State to the electors qualified to vote for the election of members of the House of Representatives. But if either House passes any such proposed law by an absolute majority, and the other House rejects or fails to pass it or passes it with any amendment to which the first-mentioned House will not agree, and if after an interval of three months the first-mentioned House in the same or the next session again passes the proposed law by an absolute majority with or without any amendment which has been made or agreed to by the other House, and such other House rejects or fails to pass it or passes it with any amendment to which the first-mentioned House will not agree, the Governor-General may submit the proposed law as last proposed by the first-mentioned House, and either with or without any amendments subsequently agreed to by both Houses, to the electors in each State qualified to vote for the election of the House of Representatives. When a proposed law is submitted to the electors the vote shall be taken in such manner as the Parliament prescribes. But until the qualification of electors of members of the House of Representatives becomes uniform throughout the Commonwealth, only one-half the electors voting for and against the proposed law shall be counted in any State in which adult suffrage prevails. And if in a majority of the States a majority of the electors voting approve the proposed law, and if a majority of all the electors voting also approve the proposed law, it shall be presented to the Governor-General for the Queen's assent. No alteration diminishing the proportionate representation of any State in either House of the Parliament, or the minimum number of representatives of a State in the House of Representatives, or increasing, diminishing, or otherwise altering the limits of the State, or in any manner affecting the provisions of the Constitution in relation thereto, shall become law unless the majority of the electors voting in that State approve the proposed law.

CONSTITUTION OF AUSTRIA: Parliamentary reform of, 1896. See (in this vol.) AUSTRIA-HUNGARY: A. D. 1895–1896.

CONSTITUTION OF BELGIUM: The working of its electoral provisions. See (in this vol.) BELGIUM: A. D. 1894–1895; and 1899–1900.

CONSTITUTION OF CUBA: The grant of autonomous government by Spain in 1897. See (in this vol.) CUBA: A. D. 1897 (NOVEMBER); and 1897–1898 (NOVEMBER—FEBRUARY).

Outline of the draft reported to the Convention of 1900-1901. See (in this vol.) CUBA: A. D. 1901 (JANUARY).

CONSTITUTION OF DELAWARE, New. See (in this vol.) DELAWARE: A. D. 1897.

CONSTITUTION OF IDAHO: Adoption of Woman Suffrage. See (in this vol.) IDAHO: A. D. 1896.

CONSTITUTION OF LOUISIANA: Its discriminating educational qualification. See (in this vol.) LOUISIANA: A. D. 1898.

CONSTITUTION OF MEXICO: Amendments.—The text of the constitution of Mexico, as published in 1891, will be found in volume 1 of this work, under the same heading as above.

In 1896, the Constitution received two amendments promulgated by decrees published in the "Diario Official" on the 24th of April and the 1st of May in that year. Translations of these decrees were transmitted to the State Department at Washington by the United States Minister to Mexico and published in U. S. Consular Reports, July, 1896, from which source they are copied below. That of April 24 was as follows:

The Congress of the United Mexican States, in the exercise of the power which article 127 of the federal constitution concedes to it, and with the previous approbation of the majority of the legislatures of the States, declares articles 79, 80, 82, and 83 of the constitution to be amended and an addition to article 72 of the same, in the following tenor:

ART. 72. Congress has power:

XXXI. To appoint, both houses of Congress being assembled for such purpose, a President of the Republic, either with the character of substitute or with that of ad interim, to act in the absolute or temporary defaults of the constitutional President. Likewise, to replace in the respective cases and in equal form the substitute as well as the ad interim, if these in their turn should default.

XXXII. To qualify and to decide upon the petition for leave of absence that the President of the Republic may make. It is the exclusive faculty of the House of Deputies — II. To qualify and decide upon the resignations of the President of the Republic and of the magistrates of the supreme court of justice.

ART. 79. I. In the absolute defaults of the President, excepting that arising from resignation, and in the temporary defaults, excepting that proceeding from permission, the Secretary of Foreign Relations, and in case there be none or if there exists an impediment, the Secretary of Government shall take immediate charge of the Executive power.

II. The Congress of the union shall assemble in an extraordinary session the following day, in the Chamber of Deputies, more than half of the total number of members of both houses being present, the officers of the House of Deputies acting. If no session can be had on account of no quorum or for other cause, those present shall compel, from day unto day, the presence of the absentees, in accordance with the law, so as to hold the session as soon as possible.

III. In this session, the substitute President shall be elected by the absolute majority of those present, and in a nominal and public vote, without any proposition being discussed therein nor anything else done but to take in the votes, publish them, and make a close examination and publish the name of the one elected.

IV. If no one of the candidates should have received the absolute majority of the votes, the election shall be repeated as to the two who had the greater number of votes, and the one receiving the majority will be elected. If the competitors should have received an equal number of votes, and on a repetition of the election an equal result shall be obtained, then the drawing of lots shall decide the one who must be elected.

V. If there be an equality of votes for more than two candidates, the election as to which of these shall be made, but if at the same time there is another candidate who may have obtained a majority of votes, he shall be considered as first competitor, and the second shall be chosen by votes out of the first mentioned.

VI. If Congress be not in session, it shall meet, without the necessity of a convocation, on the fourteenth day following that of the default, under the direction of the board of permanent commission which may be in duty, and shall proceed as already stated.

VII. In case of absolute default caused by the renouncement of the President, Congress shall convene in the form set forth for the appointment of the substitute, and the resignation shall not take effect until the appointment of the subatitute and of the legal protest by him.

VIII. In relation to temporary defaults, from whatever cause, Congress shall appoint an ad interim President, observing for this purpose the same procedure as prescribed for the cases of absolute default. Should the President ask for leave of absence, he will, at the time of so doing, propose the citizen who must take his place ; the permission being granted, it will not take effect until the ad interim (President) shall have protested, it being within the President's faculty to make use or not of said leave, or to lessen its duration. The ad interim shall only exercise the functions during the time of temporary default. The petition for permission shall be addressed to the House of Deputies, who shall at once deliver it to the proper commission for its perusal, at the same time summoning the Senate for an extraordinary session of Congress, before which the commission shall render its decision. The proposition with which the decision may end, if favorable, shall comprise in a decree of a sole article the granting of the permission and the approval of the proposition, which shall be decided upon only by one ballot.

IX. If, on the day appointed by the constitution, the people's President-elect shall not enter into the discharge of his office, Congress shall at once appoint an ad interim President. If the cause of the impediment be transitory, the ad interim shall cease in the Presidential functions when said cause ceases and the President-elect enters into the discharge of his functions. But, should the cause be of that kind that produces absolute impossibility, so that the President-elect cannot enter into the exercise of power during the four years, Congress, after appointing the ad interim President, shall, without delay, convoke the extraordinary elections. The ad interim President shall cease in his functions as soon as the new President-elect protests, and this shall complete the constitutional period. Should the impediment arise from the fact that the election be not made or published on the 1st of December, a President ad interim shall also be appointed, who will discharge the Presidential duties until those requisites are complied with and the President-elect takes due protest.

X. The defaults of the substitute President and those of the ad interim shall also be remedied in the manner prescribed, except in regard to the second, in the case when the constitutional President, who, having temporarily separated himself, may again assume the exercise of his duties.

ART. 80. Should the default of the President be absolute, the substitute appointed by Congress shall terminate the constitutional period.

ART. 82. The President, upon taking possession of his office, shall swear before Congress under the following formula : " I protest to perform loyally and patriotically the functions of President of the United Mexican States ; to keep and cause to be kept, without any reserve, the constitution of 1857, with all its additions and reforms, the laws of reform, and all those laws emanating therefrom, watching everything for the good and prosperity of the union." The Secretary of Department, who may take provisional charge of the Executive power, in its case, is exempted from this requisite.

The decree of May 1, 1896, was as follows :

The Congress of the Union has decreed the following : The General Congress of the United Mexican States, in conformity with the provisions of article 127 of the federal constitution, and with the previous approbation of the State legislatures, declares articles 111 and 124 of said constitution amended and an addition made to same in the following terms :

First. Section III. of article 111 of the federal constitution is amended, and an addition made to the said article in the following terms : The States shall not—

III. Coin money, issue paper money, stamps, or stamped paper.

IV. Obstruct the transit of persons or goods crossing its territory.

V. Prohibit or molest, either directly or indirectly, the entrance or exit, to or from its territory, of national or foreign merchandise.

VI. Obstruct the circulation or consumption of national or foreign goods by means of imposts or taxes that may be exacted through local custom-houses, by requiring the inspection or registration of packages, or by requiring the documentation to accompany the merchandise.

VII. Decree or maintain in force laws or fiscal decrees which may cause differences of taxes or requisites, by reason of the source of national or foreign merchandise, whether these differences be established in regard to a like production in that locality or on account of like production from different sources.

Second. Article 124 of the federal constitution is amended in the following terms:

ART. 124. It is the exclusive faculty of the federation to obstruct merchandise, imported or exported, or which passes in transit through the national territory, likewise to regulate at all times, and even to prohibit for reasons of policy and security, the circulation within the Republic of all merchandise from whatever source; but the said federation cannot establish or decree in the district or federal territories the taxes and laws expressed in Sections VI. and V. of Article 111.

Transitory article. — These amendments and additions shall take effect on the 1st of July, 1896.

CONSTITUTION OF MINNESOTA:
Amendments. See (in this vol.) MINNESOTA: A. D. 1896.

CONSTITUTION OF MISSISSIPPI:
Amendment. See (in this vol.) MISSISSIPPI: A. D. 1890–1892.

CONSTITUTION OF NEW JERSEY:
Proposed Amendments. See (in this vol.) NEW JERSEY: A. D. 1897.

CONSTITUTION OF NEW YORK.—
The constitution of the State of New York, as revised by the Convention of 1894 (see, in vol. 4, NEW YORK: A. D. 1894), was submitted to the people at the election in November that year and adopted. The important features of the revision were set forth in an address by the Convention to the people, as follows: "We seek to separate, in the larger cities, municipal elections from State and national elections to the end that the business affairs of our great municipal corporations may be managed upon their own merits, uncontrolled by national and State politics. . . . We have provided further safeguards against abuses in legislative procedure, by requiring that all bills shall be printed in their final form at least three days before their passage, prohibiting riders on appropriation bills, providing for notice to municipal authorities before special acts relating to the larger cities can take effect, prohibiting the issue of passes by railroad, telegraph and telephone companies to public officers, enlarging the express constitutional powers of the President of the Senate. . . . We have extended the prohibition against lotteries so as to include all pool-selling, book-making and other forms of gambling. . . . We have sought to throw greater safeguards around the elective franchise by prescribing a period of ninety instead of ten days of citizenship before that right can be exercised, so

that naturalization may be taken out of the hands of campaign committees and removed from the period immediately before election. . . . We have modified the language relating to election so that if any mechanical device for recording and counting votes is so perfected as to be superior to the present system, the Legislature may make trial of it. We have established in the Constitution the well-tried and satisfactory system of registration of votes, forbidding, however, any requirement of personal attendance on the first day of registration in the thinly-settled regions outside of the cities and large villages, where voters would have long distances to travel to the place of registration, and we have provided for securing an honest and fair election by requiring that on all election boards election officers shall equally represent the two principal political parties of the State. We have provided for a new appointment of Senate and Assembly districts. . . . Attack has been made upon two rules laid down in the proposed measure for the guidance of the Legislature in future apportionments. One of these is the rule that no county shall have more than three Senators unless it shall have a full ratio for each Senator, although smaller counties may receive a Senator or an additional Senator on a major fraction of a ratio. . . . The other rule attacked is that no one county shall have more than one-third of all the Senators, and that New York and Kings county together shall not have more than one-half of all the Senators. . . . We have declared in the Constitution the principle of civil service reform, that appointments and promotions are to be based upon merit and ascertained so far as practicable by competitive examination. We have sought by this to secure not merely the advantage derived from declaring the principle, but the practical benefit of its extension to the State prisons, canals and other public works of the State, to which, under the existing Constitution, the court of last resort has decided that civil service rules cannot be applied. . . . We have prohibited the contract system of convict labor. . . . We have authorized the Legislature to provide for the improvement of the canals, without, however, borrowing money for that purpose unless the people expressly authorize it. . . . We have required the Legislature to provide for free public schools, in which all the children of the State may be educated, and we have prohibited absolutely the use of public money in aid of sectarian schools. . . . We have so amended the present Constitution as to provide for a naval as well as a land force of militia. . . . In order to allow every voter to exercise a choice in voting on some of the important proposed amendments, we have provided that the Revised Constitution shall be submitted to the people in three parts, viz.: 1. That making an apportionment of Senators and members of the Assembly. 2. That pertaining to the improvements of the canals. 3. All the remainder of the proposed amendments as a whole."—*Journal of the Constitutional Convention, State of New York, 1894, pp. 839–46.*

CONSTITUTION OF NORTH CAROLINA:
Amendment qualifying the **suffrage**. See (in this vol.) NORTH CAROLINA: A. D. 1900.

CONSTITUTION (GRONDWET) OF THE SOUTH AFRICAN REPUBLIC.

The following are the Articles of main importance in the Grondwet or Constitution of the South African Republic:

ART. 1.—This State shall bear the name of the South African Republic.

ART. 2.—The form of government of this State shall be that of a republic.

ART. 3.—It desires to be recognized and respected by the civilized world as an independent and free people.

ART. 4.—The people seek for no extension of territory, and desire it only in accordance with just principles, when the interest of the Republic makes such extension desirable.

ART. 5.—The people desire to retain and maintain their territory in South Africa unimpaired. The boundaries thereof are fixed by proclamation.

ART. 6.—Its territory is open for every foreigner who obeys the laws of this Republic. All who are within the territory of this Republic have equal claims to protection of person and property.

ART. 7.—The land or farms situate in this territory which have not yet been given out, are declared to be the property of the State.

ART. 8.—The people claim the utmost social freedom, and expect the result from the maintenance of their religious belief, from the observance of their obligations, from submission to law, order and right, and the maintenance of the same. The people permit the spread of the Gospel among the heathen under fixed precautions against deceit or misleading.

ART. 9.—The people will not allow any equalization of the coloured inhabitants with the white.

ART. 10.—The people will not suffer any slave trade or slavery in this Republic.

ART. 11.—The people reserve to themselves the protection and defence of the independence and inviolability of the State, subject to the laws.

ART. 12.—The people entrust the legislation to a Volksraad—the highest authority in the land—consisting of representatives or deputies of the people, chosen by the enfranchised burghers; but with the reservation that a period of three months shall be left to the people to enable them if they so wish to communicate to the Volksraad their verdict on a proposed law; except those laws which can suffer no delay.

ART. 13.—The people charge the President with the task of proposing and executing the laws; he also brings before the Volksraad the appointments of all civil servants for ratification.

ART. 14.—The people entrust the maintenance of order to the military force, the police, and other persons appointed by the law for that purpose.

ART. 15.—The people place the judicial power in the hands of a Supreme Court, Circuit Court, Landrosts, Juries, and such other persons as shall be entrusted with judicial powers, and leave all these free to discharge their function according to their judgment and consciences, according to the laws of the land.

ART. 16.—The people shall receive from the Volksraad an estimate of the general income and expenses of the State, and learn therefrom how much every man's taxes shall amount to.

ART. 17.—Potchefstrom, situated on the Mooi River, shall be the capital of the Republic, and Pretoria the seat of Government.

ART. 18.—All services rendered on behalf of the public are remunerated by the public.

ART. 19.—Freedom of the press is granted provided the printer and publisher remain responsible for all the documents which contain defamation, insult, or attacks against any one's character.

ART. 20.—The people shall only appoint as representatives in the Volksraad those who are members of a Protestant Church.

ART. 21.—The people desire the growth, prosperity, and welfare of the State, and with this view provision for suitable school teachers.

ART. 22.—Providing also that in time of peace precautionary measures are taken to enable the State to wage or withstand a war.

ART. 23.—In case of a hostile attack from outside, everyone, without distinction, shall be held bound to lend his assistance on the promulgation of martial law. . . .

ART. 26.—The Volksraad shall be the highest authority of the country, and the legislative power.

ART. 27.—No civil servants are to be representatives of the people.

ART. 28.—The Volksraad shall consist of at least twelve members, who must possess the following qualifications:—They must have attained the age of thirty years, and be born in the Republic, or have for fifteen consecutive years been burghers entitled to vote, be members of a Protestant Church, reside, and possess immovable property, in the Republic. No persons of notoriously bad character, or who have had a dishonouring sentence pronounced against them, and no uncertified or unrehabilitated insolvents shall be eligible. They may not be related to each other in the relationship of father and son or stepson. No coloured persons or bastards shall be admitted into our Assemblies. In like manner no military officer or official of the State, who draws a fixed annual or monthly salary, shall be eligible as member of the Volksraad.

ART. 29.—The members of the Volksraad are elected by a majority of votes from among the electors of each district. No one shall be considered as elected who has not obtained at least sixty votes. Every one who is born in the country and has attained the age of twenty-one years, or has become naturalized, shall be a burgher qualified to vote. The members of the Volksraad are elected for the period of four years. . . .

[The above provisions of the Constitution, relating to the Volksraad and the representation of the people, were modified by the following among other provisions of an Act of the Volksraad passed in 1891:—

ART. 1.—The legislative power shall rest with a representation of the people, which shall consist of a First Volksraad and a Second Volksraad.

ART. 2.—The First Volksraad shall be the highest authority in the State, just as the Volksraad was before this law came into operation. The First Volksraad shall be the body named the Volksraad until this law came into operation. From the period of this law coming into operation, the name of that body shall be altered from the Volksraad to the First Volksraad. The persons forming that body as members shall, however, remain the same, only they shall, from the said period, be named members of the First Volksraad instead of members of the Volksraad. All laws and resolutions having reference to the Volksraad and the members thereof shall remain in force and apply to the First Volksraad and the members thereof, except in so far as a change is or shall be made by this and later laws. . . .

ART. 4.—The number of the members of the Second Volksraad shall be the same as of the First Volksraad. This number shall be fixed later by the First Volksraad for both Volksraads. . . .

ART. 9.—The members of the First Volksraad are chosen by those enfranchised burghers who have obtained the burgher right, either before this law came into operation, or thereafter by birth, and have reached the age of sixteen years. The franchise for the First Volksraad can besides also be obtained by those who have during ten years been eligible for the Second Volksraad, by resolution of the First Volksraad, and according to rules to be fixed later by law.

ART. 10.—The members of the Second Volksraad are chosen by all enfranchised burghers who have reached the age of sixteen years. . . .

ART. 27.—The Second Volksraad shall have the power to pass further regulations on the following subjects as is necessary, either by law or resolution :—(1) The department of mines. (2) The making and support of wagon and post roads. (3) The postal department. (4) The department of telegraphs and telephones. (5) The protection of inventions, samples and trademarks. (6) The protection of the right of the author. (7) The exploitation and support of the woods and salt-pans. . (8) The prevention and coping with contagious diseases. (9) The condition, the rights, and obligations of companies. (10) Insolvency. (11) Civil procedure. (12) Criminal procedure. (13) Such other subjects as the First Volksraad shall decide later by law or resolution, or the First Volksraad shall specially refer to the Second Volksraad.

ART. 28.—All laws or resolutions accepted by the Second Volksraad are as soon as possible, that is to say at the outside within forty-eight hours, communicated both to the First Volksraad and to the President.

ART. 29.—The President has the right, when he has received notice from the Second Volksraad of the adoption of a law or a resolution, to bring that law or resolution before the First Volksraad for consideration within fourteen days after the receipt of such notice. The President is in any case bound, after the receipt of such a notice, to communicate it to the First Volksraad within the said time.

ART. 30.—If the President has not brought the law or resolution as communicated before the First Volksraad for consideration, and the First Volksraad has not on its own part thought it necessary to take said law or resolution into consideration, the President shall, unless with the advice and consent of the Executive Council he thinks it undesirable in the interests of the State, be bound to have that law or resolution published in the first succeeding Volksraad, unless within the said fourteen days the First Volksraad may be adjourned, in which case the publication in

the "Staats Courant" shall take place after the lapse of eight days from the commencement of the first succeeding session of the First Volksraad.

ART. 31.—The law or resolution adopted by the Second Volksraad shall have no force, unless published by the President in the "Staats Courant."]

ART. 43.—The President shall bring forward for discussion the proposals for laws which have come in before the Volksraad, whether the latter have been made known to the public three months before the commencement of the session, or whether the same have come in during the session of the Volksraad.

ART. 44.—When the notices of laws and Government notices to the public have not been given in time, the President shall examine with whom the blame of that delay lies. A Landrost found guilty hereof shall have a fine of Rds. 50 inflicted and a Field-Cornet or lesser official of Rds. 25. . . .

ART. 56.—The executive power resides in the State President, who is responsible to the Volksraad. He is chosen by a majority of the burghers entitled to vote, and for the term of five years. He is eligible for reelection. He must have attained the age of thirty years, and need not be a burgher of the State at the time of his nomination, and must be a member of a Protestant Church, and have no dishonouring sentence pronounced against him. [By a subsequent law the President must be chosen from among the burghers.]

ART. 57.—The President is the first or highest official of the State. All civil servants are subordinate to him ; such, however, as are charged with exercise of the judicial power are left altogether free and independent in its exercise.

ART. 58.—As long as the President holds his position as such he shall fill no other, nor shall he discharge any ecclesiastical office, nor carry on any business. The President cannot go outside the boundaries of the State without consent of the Volksraad. However, the Executive Council shall have the power to grant him leave to go outside the boundaries of the State upon private affairs in cases of necessity. . . .

ART. 60.—The President shall be discharged from his post by the Volksraad after conviction of misconduct, embezzlement of public property, treachery, or other serious crimes, and be treated further according to the laws.

ART. 61.—If in consequence of transgression of the Constitution or other public misdemeanors the Volksraad resolve that the President shall be brought to trial, he shall be tried before a special court composed of the members of the High Court, the President and another member of the Volksraad, while the State Attorney acts as Public Prosecutor. The accused shall be allowed to secure assistance of a lawyer at his choice.

ART. 62.—The President is charged with the proposing of laws to the Volksraad, whether his own proposals or others which have come in to him from the people ; he must make these proposals known to the public by means of the "Staats Courant" three months before presenting them to the Volksraad, together with all such other documents as are judged useful and necessary by him.

ART. 63.—All proposals for a law sent in to

the President shall, before they are published, be judged by the President and Executive Council as to whether publication is necessary or not.

ART. 64.—The President submits the proposals for laws to the Volksraad, and charges the official to whose department they belong first and foremost, with their explanation and defence.

ART. 65.—As soon as the President has received the notice of the Volksraad that the proposed law is adopted, he shall have that law published within two months, and after the lapse of a month, to be reckoned from the publication, he shall take measures for the execution of the same.

ART. 66.—Proclamation of martial law, as intended in Article 23, shall only be made by the President with the assent of the members of the Executive Council. . . .

ART. 67.—The President, with advice of the Executive Council, declares war and peace, with reference to Article 66 of the Constitution ; the Government having first, if possible, summoned the Volksraad before the declaration of war. Treaties of peace require the ratification of the Volksraad, which is summoned as soon as possible for that purpose. . . .

ART. 70.—The President shall submit, yearly, at the opening of the Volksraad, estimates of general outgoings and income, and therein indicate how to cover the deficit or apply the surplus.

ART. 71.—He shall also give a report during that session of that Volksraad, of his actions during the past year, of the condition of the Republic and everything that concerns its general interest. . . .

ART. 75.—The President and one member of the Executive Council shall, if possible, visit the towns and villages of the Republic where Landrost's officers are, once in the year ; he shall examine the state of those offices, inquire into the conduct of the officials, and on these circuits give the inhabitants during their stay an opportunity to bring before him anything they are interested in. . . .

ART. 82´.—The President exercises his power along with the Executive Council. An Executive Council shall be joined to the President, consisting of the Commandant-General, two enfranchised burghers, a Secretary, and a Notekeeper (notulenhouder), who shall have an equal vote, and bear the title of members of the Executive Council. The Superintendent of Native Affairs and the Notekeeper shall be ex-officio members of the Executive Council. The President and members of the Executive Council shall have the right to sit, but not to vote, in the Volksraad. The President is allowed, when important affairs arise, to invite the head official to be present in the Executive Council whose department is more directly concerned with the subject to be treated of. The said head official shall then have a vote in the Executive Council, be

equally responsible for the resolution taken, and sign it along with the others.

ART. 83.—According to the intention of Article 82 the following shall be considered "Head Officials": The State Attorney, Treasurer, Auditor, Superintendent of Education, Orphan-Master, Registrar of Deeds, Surveyor-General, Postmaster-General, Head of the Mining Department, Chief Director of the Telegraph Service, and Chief of Public Works.

ART. 84.—The President shall be Chairman of the Executive Council, and in case of an equal division of votes have a casting vote. For the ratification of sentences of death, or declarations of war, the unanimous vote of the Executive Council shall be requisite for a decision. . . .

ART. 87.—All resolutions of the Executive Council and official letters of the President must, besides being signed by him, also be signed•by the Secretary of State. The latter is at the same time responsible that the contents of the resolution, or the letter, is not in conflict with the existing laws.

ART. 88.—The two enfranchised burghers or members of the Executive Council contemplated by Article 82 are chosen by the Volksraad for the period of three years, the Commandant-General for ten years ; they must be members of a Protestant Church, have had no sentence in a criminal court to their discredit, and have reached the age of thirty years.

ART. 89.—The Secretary of State is chosen also by the Volksraad, but is appointed for the period of four years. On resignation or expiration of his term he is re-eligible. He must be a member of a Protestant Church, have had no sentence in a criminal court to his discredit, possess fixed property in the Republic, and have reached the age of thirty years. . . .

ART. 93.—The military force consists of all the men of this Republic capable of bearing arms, and if necessary of all those of the natives within its boundaries whose chiefs are subject to it.

ART. 94.—Besides the armed force of burghers to be called up in times of disturbance or war, there exists a general police and corps of artillery, for which each year a fixed sum is drawn upon the estimates.

ART. 95.—The men of the white people capable of bearing arms are all men between the ages of sixteen and sixty years : and of the natives, only those which are capable of being made serviceable in the war.

ART. 96.—For the sub-division of the military force the territory of this Republic is divided into field-cornetcies and districts. . . .

ART. 97.—The men are under the orders of the following officers, ascending in rank : Assistant Field-Cornets, Field-Cornets, Commandants, and a Commandant-General. — *Selected Official Documents of the South African Republic and Great Britain* (Supplement to the *Annals of the Am. Academy of Pol. and Soc. Science, July,* 1900).

CONSTITUTION OF SOUTH CAROLINA: The revision of 1895-6. — Disfranchisement provision. See (in this vol.) SOUTH CAROLINA: A. D. 1896.

CONSTITUTION OF SOUTH DAKOTA: Amendment introducing the Initia-

tive and Referendum. See (in this vol.) SOUTH DAKOTA: A. D. 1898..

CONSTITUTION OF SWITZERLAND: Amendments. See (in this vol.) SWITZERLAND: A. D. 1897.

CONSTITUTION OF UTAH. See (in this vol.) UTAH: A. D. 1895–1896.

CONWAY, Sir W. Martin: **Explorations** of Spitzbergen. See (in this vol.) POLAR EXPLORATION, 1896, 1897.

COOK, or HERVEY ISLANDS: Annexation to New Zealand. See (in this vol.) NEW ZEALAND: A. D. 1900 (OCTOBER).

COOMASSIE, or KUMASSI: Occupation by the British.—Siege and relief. See (in this vol.) ASHANTI.

COPTIC CHURCH: Authority of the Pope re-established. See (in this vol.) PAPACY: A. D. 1896 (MARCH).

COREA. See (in this vo.l) KOREA.

CORNWALL AND YORK, The Duke of. See (in this vol.) WALES, THE PRINCE OF.

COSTA RICA. See (in this vol.) CENTRAL AMERICA.

COTTON-MILL STRIKE, New England. See (in this vol.) INDUSTRIAL DISTURBANCES: A. D. 1898.

COTTON STATES EXPOSITION, The. See (in this vol.) ATLANTA: A. D. 1895.

COURT OF ARBITRATION, The Permanent. See (in this vol.) PEACE CONFERENCE.

CREEKS, United States agreement with the. See (in this vol.) INDIANS, AMERICAN: A. D. 1893–1899.

CRETE: Recent archæological explorations.—Supposed discovery of the Palace of Minos and the Cretan Labyrinth.—Fresh light on the origin of the Alphabet. See (in this vol.) ARCHÆOLOGICAL RESEARCH: CRETE.
A. D. 1896.—Conflict between Christians and Mussulmans, and its preceding causes. See (in this vol.) TURKEY: A. D. 1896.

A. D. 1897.—Fresh conflicts.—Reports of the British Consul-General and others.—Greek interference and demands for annexation to Greece.—Action of the Great Powers.—Blockade of the island. See (in this vol.) TURKEY: A. D. 1897 (JANUARY—FEBRUARY).
A. D. 1897.—Withdrawal of Greek troops.—Acceptance of autonomy by the Greek government. See (in this vol.) TURKEY: A. D. 1897 (MARCH—SEPTEMBER).
A. D. 1897–1898.—Prolonged anarchy, and blockade by the Powers.—Final departure of Turkish troops and officials.—Government established under Prince George of Greece. See (in this vol.) TURKEY: A. D. 1897–1898.
A. D. 1901.—Successful administration of Prince George of Greece. See (in this vol.) TURKEY: A. D. 1901.

CRISPI, Signor: Ministry. See (in this vol.) ITALY: A. D. 1895–1896.
Parliamentary investigation of charges against. See (in this vol.) ITALY: A. D. 1898 (MARCH—JUNE).

CROKER, "Boss." See (in this vol.) NEW YORK CITY: A. D. 1894–1895; and 1897.

CROMER, Viscount: Administration in Egypt. See (in this vol.) EGYPT: A. D. 1898.

CROMWELL, Oliver, Proposed statue of.—A proposal in the English House of Commons, in 1895, to vote £500 for a statue of Cromwell was so violently opposed by the Irish members that the government was compelled to withdraw the item from the estimates.

CRONJE, General Piet: In the South African war. See (in this vol.) SOUTH AFRICA (THE FIELD OF WAR): A. D. 1899 (OCTOBER—DECEMBER); and 1900 (JANUARY—FEBRUARY).

CROZIER, Captain William: American Commissioner to the Peace Conference at The Hague. See (in this vol.) PEACE CONFERENCE.

CUBA.

A. D. 1868–1885.—Ten years of insurrection.—The United States and Spain.—The Affair of the Virginius.—End of Slavery.—"The abolition of slavery in the southern states left the Spanish Antilles in the enjoyment of a monopoly of slave labor, which, in the production of sugar, especially, gave them advantages which overcame all competition. This led to the formation of a strong Spanish party, for whom the cause of slavery and that of Spanish dominion were identical. These were known as Peninsulars or Spanish immigrants. They were the official class, the wealthy planters and slave-owners, and the real rulers of Cuba. Their central organization was the Casino Espagñol of Havana, which was copied in all the towns of the island, and through these clubs they controlled the volunteers, who at times numbered 60,000 or 70,000. . . . These volunteers never took the field, but held possession of all the cities and towns, and thus were able to defy even the captain-general. They were obedient to his orders only so long as he was acting in close accord with the wishes of their party. On the other hand, there was a party composed of Creoles, or native Cubans, whose cry was 'Cuba for the Cubans!' and who hoped to effect the complete separation of the island from Spain, either through their own efforts or through the assistance of the United States. . . .

"The Spanish revolution of September, 1868, was the signal for an uprising of the native or Creole party in the eastern part of the island under the leadership of Cespedes. This movement was not at first ostensibly for independence, but for the revolution in Spain, the cries being, 'Hurrah for Prim!' 'Hurrah for the Revolution!' Its real character was, however, apparent from the first, and its supporters continued for a period of ten years, without regard to the numerous vicissitudes through which the Spanish Government passed — the provisional government, the regency, the elective monarchy, the republic, and the restored Bourbon dynasty — to wage a dogged, though desultory warfare against the constituted authorities of the island. This struggle was almost conterminous with President Grant's Administration of eight years."

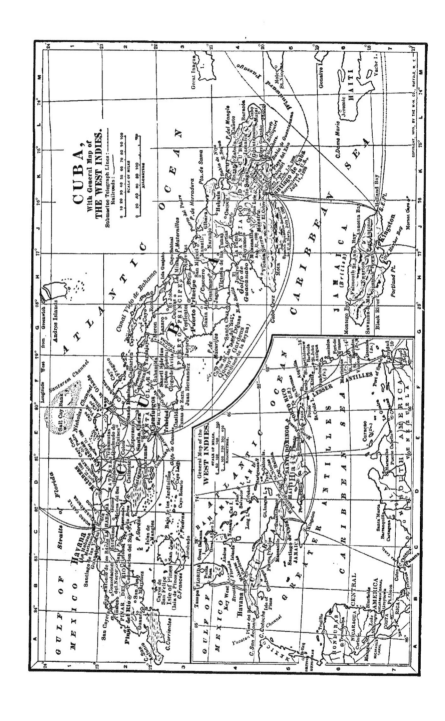

CUBA,
With General Map of
THE WEST INDIES.

President Grant made early offers of mediation between Spain and the insurgents, but no agreement as to terms could be reached. An increasing sympathy with the Cubans raised demands in the United States for their recognition as belligerents, with belligerent rights, and the President is said to have been ready to yield to the demand, but was deterred by the influence of his Secretary of State, Mr. Fish, who contended that the insurgents had established no government that could claim such rights. The Cuban sympathizers in Congress were accordingly checked by an opposing message (June 13, 1870), and no interference occurred.

"In February, 1873, when King Amadeus resigned his crown and a republic was proclaimed in Spain, the United States made haste to give the new government recognition and support, which led to friendly relations between the two countries for a time, and promised happy results. The Spanish republicans were being urge to give the Cubans self-government and end slavery in the whole Spanish domain, and they were lending, at least, a considerate ear to the advice. But negotiation on that topic was soon disturbed. On October 31, 1873, the steamer 'Virginius,' sailing under American colors and carrying a United States registry, was captured on the high seas by the 'Tornado,' a Spanish war vessel, and on the afternoon of the first of November taken into the port of Santiago de Cuba. The men and supplies she bore were bound for the insurgents, but the capture did not occur in Cuban waters. General Burriel, the commandant of the city, summoned a court-martial, and, in spite of the protests of the American consul, condemned to death—at the first sitting—four of the passengers—General W. A. C. Ryan, an Irish patriot, and three Cubans. They were shot on the morning of November 4. On the 7th twelve other passengers were executed, and on the 8th Captain Fry and his entire crew, numbering 36, making the total number of executions 53." This barbarous procedure caused hot excitement in the United States, and demands for reparation were made so sharply that the two countries came near to war. In the end it was shown that the "Virginius" was sailing under the American flag without right, being owned by Cubans and controlled by them. The vessel was surrendered, however, but foundered off Cape Fear, while being conveyed to the United States. Her surviving passengers were released, and an indemnity was paid for all who were put to death. The brutal officer who took their lives was never brought to justice, though his punishment was promised again and again. On the settlement of the Virginius question, the government of the United States resumed its efforts to wring concessions to the Cubans from Spain, and sought to have its efforts supported by Great Britain and other European powers. Cold replies came from all the cabinets that were approached. At the same time, the Spanish government met the demand from America with promises so lavish (April, 1876), going so far in appearance towards all that had been asked, that no ground for intervention seemed left. The act of Secretary Fish, in proposing intervention to foreign powers, was sharply criticised as a breach of the Monroe doctrine; but he made no defense.

"The Cuban struggle continued for two years

longer. In October, 1877, several leaders surrendered to the Spanish authorities and undertook the task of bringing over the few remaining ones. Some of these paid for their efforts with their lives, being taken and condemned by court-martial, by order of the commander of the Cuban forces. Finally, in February, 1878, the terms of pacification [under an agreement called the Treaty of El Zanjon] were made known. They embraced representation in the Spanish Cortes, oblivion of the past as regarded political offences committed since the year 1868, and the freedom of slaves in the insurgent ranks. In practice, however, the Cuban deputies were never truly representative, but were men of Spanish birth, designated usually by the captain-general. By gradual emancipation, slavery ceased to exist in the island in 1885. The powers of the captain-general, the most ·objectionable feature of Spanish rule, continued uncurtailed." —J. H. Latané, *The Diplomatic Relations of the U. S. and Spanish America*, ch. 3.

A. D. 1895.—Insurrection renewed.—Early in 1895 a new uprising of the oppressed Cubans was begun, and on the 7th of December, in that year, T. Estrada Palma, writing as their authorized representative, presented to the State Department at Washington a statement setting forth the causes of the revolt and describing its state of organization at that time. The causes, he wrote, " are substantially the same as those of the former revolution, lasting from 1868 to 1878, and terminating only on the representation of the Spanish Government that Cuba would be granted such reforms as would remove the grounds of complaint on the part of the Cuban people. Unfortunately the hopes thus held out have never been realized. The representation which was to be given the Cubans has proved to be absolutely without character ; taxes have been levied anew on everything conceivable ; the offices in the island have increased, but the officers are all Spaniards ; the native Cubans have been left with no public duties whatsoever to perform, except the payment of taxes to the Government and blackmail to the officials, without privilege even to move from place to place in the island except on the permission of the governmental authority. Spain has framed laws so that the natives have substantially been deprived of the right of suffrage. The taxes levied have been almost entirely devoted to support the army and navy in Cuba, to pay interest on the debt that Spain has saddled on the island, and to pay the salaries of the vast number of Spanish officeholders, devoting only $746,000 for internal improvements out of the $26,000,000 collected by tax. No public schools are within reach of the masses for their education. All the principal industries of the island are hampered by excessive imposts. Her commerce with every country but Spain has been crippled in every possible manner, as can readily be seen by the frequent protests of shipowners and merchants. The Cubans have no security of person or property. The judiciary are instruments of the military authorities. Trial by military tribunals can be ordered at any time at the will of the Captain-General. There is, beside, no freedom of speech, press, or religion. In point of fact, the causes of the Revolution of 1775 in this country were not nearly as grave as those that have driven the Cuban people to the various insurrections which culminated in the present revolution. . . .

171

"Years before the outbreak of the present hostilities the people within and without the island began to organize, with a view of preparing for the inevitable revolution, being satisfied, after repeated and patient endeavors, that peaceful petition was fruitless. In order that the movement should be strong from the beginning, and organized both as to civil and military administration, the Cuban Revolutionary party was founded, with José Marti at its head. The principal objects were by united efforts to obtain the absolute independence of Cuba, to promote the sympathy of other countries, to collect funds with these objects in view, and to invest them in munitions of war. The military organization of this movement was completed by the election of Maximo Gomez as commander in chief. This election was made by the principal officers who fought in the last revolution. The time for the uprising was fixed at the solicitation of the people in Cuba, who protested that there was no hope of autonomy, and that their deposits of arms and ammunition were in danger of being discovered and their leaders arrested. A large amount of war material was then bought by Marti, and vessels chartered to transport it to Cuba, where arrangements were made for its reception in the provinces of Santiago, Puerto Principe, and Santa Clam; but at Fernandina, Fla., it was seized by the United States authorities. Efforts were successfully made for the restitution of this material; nevertheless valuable time and opportunity was thus lost. The people in Cuba clamored for the revolution to proceed immediately, and in consequence the uprising was not further postponed. The date fixed for the uprising was the 24th of February. The people responded in Santiago, Santa Clara, and Matanzas. The provinces of Puerto Principe and Pinar del Rio did not respond, owing to lack of arms. In Puerto Principe rigorous search had previous to the 24th been instituted, and all arms and ammunition confiscated by the Government. The leaders in the provinces of Matanzas and Santa Clara were imprisoned, and so the movement there was checked for the time being. . . . In the province of Santiago the revolution rapidly increased in strength under the leadership of Bartolome Masso; one of the most influential and respected citizens of Manzanillo; Guillermo Moncada, Jesus Rabi, Pedro Perez, José Miro, and others. It was characterized by the Spanish Government as a negro and bandit movement, but many of the most distinguished and wealthy white citizens of the district flocked to the insurgent camp. . . .

"On the 1st of April, Generals Antonio and José Maceo, Flor Crombet, and Augustin Cebreco, all veteran leaders in the former revolt, landed at Duaba, in the province of Santiago, and thousands rose to join them. Antonio Maceo then took command of the troops in that province, and on the 11th of April a detachment received Generals Maximo Gomez, José Marti, Francisco Borrerro, and Angel Guerra. Captain-General Calleja was, on the 16th of April, succeeded by Gen. Arsenio Martinez Campos, the present commander in chief of the Spanish forces, who has the reputation of being Spain's greatest living general. . . . The military organization of the Cubans is ample and complete. Maj. Gen. Maximo Gomez is the commander in chief, as we have said, of all the forces, a veteran of the last revolution, as indeed are all the generals

almost without exception. Maj. Gen. Antonio Maceo is second in command of the army of liberation, and was, until called upon to cooperate with the commander in chief in the late march to the western province, in command of Santiago. The army is at present divided into five corps—two in Santiago, one in Puerto Principe, and two in Santa Clara and Matanzas. . . .

"As above indicated, José Marti was the head of the preliminary civil organization, and he, immediately upon landing with Gomez in Cuba, issued a call for the selection of representatives of the Cuban people to form a civil government. His death [in an engagement at Boca de Dos Rios, May 19] postponed for a time the selection of these men, but in the beginning of September the call previously issued was complied with. Representatives from each of the provinces of Santiago, Puerto Principe, Santa Clara, and the western part of the island, comprising the provinces of Matanzas and Havana, making twenty in all, were elected to the constituent assembly, which was to establish a civil government, republican in form. . . . A constitution of the Republic of Cuba was adopted on the 16th of September. . . . On the 18th of September . . . officers of the Government were elected by the constituent assembly in accordance with the terms of the constitution. . . .

"The Spaniards charge, in order to belittle the insurrection, that it is a movement of negroes. It should be remembered that not more than one-third of the entire population are of the colored race. As a matter of fact, less than one-third of the army are of the colored race. Take, for instance, the generals of corps, divisions, and brigades; there are but three of the colored race, namely, Antonio and José Maceo and Augustin Cebreco, and these are mulattoes whose deeds and victories have placed them far above the generals of those who pretend to despise them. None of the members of the constituent assembly or of the government are of the colored race. The Cubans and the colored race are as friendly in this war as they were in times of peace. . . .

"The subject . . . which has caused probably the most discussion is the order of General Gomez to prevent the grinding of sugar cane and in case of the disobedience of said order the destruction of the crop. . . . The reasons underlying this measure are the same which caused this country to destroy the cotton crop and the baled cotton in the South during the war of the secession. The sugar crop is a source of large income to the Spanish Government, directly by tax and export duty, as well as indirectly. The action of the insurgents is perfectly justified, because it is simply a blockade, so to speak, on land—a prevention of the gathering, and hence the export, of the commodity with, naturally, a punishment for the violation thereof. . . .

"In view of the history of this revolution as herein stated, in view of the causes which led to it, its rapid growth, its successes in arms, the establishment, operation, and resources of the Government of the Cuban Republic, the organization, number, and discipline of its army, the contrast in the treatment of prisoners to that of the enemy, the territory in its control and subject to the carrying out of its decrees, of the futility of the attempts of the Spanish Government to crush the revolution, in spite of the immense increase of its army in Cuba and of its blockade and the many millions spent for that purpose, the cruelties which on the part of the Spanish have especially characterized this sanguinary and fiercely conducted war, and the damage to the interests of the citizens of this country under the present conditions, I, as the duly accredited representative, in the name of the Cuban people in arms who have fought singly and alone against the monarchy of Spain for nearly a year, in the heart of a continent devoted to republican institutions, in the name of justice, in the name of humanity, in the name of liberty, petition you, and through you the Government of the United States of America, to accord the rights of belligerency to a people fighting for their absolute independence."— *United States, 54th Cong., 1st Sess., Senate Doc. No.* 166.

A. D. 1896-1897.—Captain-General Campos succeeded by General Weyler. — Weyler's Concentration Order and other edicts.— Death of Antonio Maceo.—Weyler succeeded by Blanco.— In January, 1896, Governor and Captain-General Campos, whose policy had been as humane and conciliatory as his Spanish surroundings would permit it to be, was recalled, and Don Valeriano Weyler y Nicolau, Marquis of Teneriffe, and lately Captain-General of Catalonia, was sent to take his place. General Weyler arrived at Havana on the 10th of February, and six days later, before he could possibly have acquired any personal knowledge of the conditions with which he had to deal, he issued three military edicts, in which a policy of merciless ruin to the island was broadly set forth. The first of these edicts or proclamations commanded as follows :

" Article 1. All inhabitants of the district of Sancti Spiritus and the provinces of Puerto Principe and Santiago de Cuba will have to concentrate in places which are the headquarters of a division, a brigade, a column, or a troop, and will have to be provided with documentary proof of identity, within eight days of the publication of this proclamation in the municipalities.

" Art. 2. To travel in the country in the radius covered by the columns in operation, it is absolutely indispensable to have a pass from the mayor, military commandants, or chiefs of detachments. Any one lacking this will be detained and sent to headquarters of divisions or brigades, and thence to Havana, at my disposition, by the first possible means. Even if a pass is exhibited, which is suspected to be not authentic or granted by authority to person with known sympathy toward the rebellion, or who show favor thereto, rigorous measures will result to those responsible.

" Art. 3. All owners of commercial establishments in the country districts will vacate them, and the chiefs of columns will take such measures as the success of their operations dictates regarding such places which, while useless for the country's wealth, serve the enemy as hiding places in the woods and in the interior.

" Art. 4. All passes hitherto issued hereby become null and void."

The order of "concentration" contained in the first article of this decree was slowly executed, but ultimately it produced horrors of suffering and death which words could hardly describe. The second of Weyler's edicts delegated his own unlimited "judicial attributes," for the enforcement of the "military code of justice," to certain

subordinate commanders, and gave sharp directions for their exercise. The third specified a large number of offenses as being "subject to military law," including in the category every use of tongue or pen that could be construed as "favorable to the rebellion," or as injurious to the "prestige" of the Spanish army, or "the volunteers, or firemen, or any other force that co-operates with the army." It is said to have been nearly a year before the Weyler policy of "concentration" was generally carried out; but even before that occurred the misery of the country had become very great. Both parties in the war were recklessly laying waste the land. The insurgent leaders had published orders for a total destruction of sugar factories and plantations, because the product supplied revenues to Spain ; and now the Spanish governor struck all traffic and industry down in the rural districts, by driving the inhabitants from their homes and fields, to concentrate and pen them up in certain prescribed places, with practically no provision for employment, or shelter or food. At the close of the year 1896 the state of suffering in the island was not yet at its worst ; but already it was riveting the attention of the neighboring people of the United States, exciting a hot feeling against Spain and a growing desire for measures on the part of the American government to bring it to an end. Repeated attempts had already been made by frothy politicians in Congress to force the country into an attitude toward Spain that would challenge war ; but the Executive, supported by a congressional majority, and by the better opinion of the American public, adhered with firmness to a policy which aimed at the exhausting of pacific influences in favor of the Cuban cause. In his annual message to Congress at the opening of the session in December, 1896, President Cleveland set forth the situation in the following words :

"It is difficult to perceive that any progress has thus far been made towards the pacification of the island. . . . If Spain still holds Havana and the seaports and all the considerable towns, the insurgents still roam at will over at least two-thirds of the inland country. If the determination of Spain to put down the insurrection seems but to strengthen with the lapse of time, and is evinced by her unhesitating devotion of largely increased military and naval forces to the task, there is much reason to believe that the insurgents have gained in point of numbers, and character, and resources, and are none the less inflexible in their resolve not to succumb, without practically securing the great objects for which they took up arms. If Spain has not yet re-established her authority, neither have the insurgents yet made good their title to be regarded as an independent state. Indeed, as the contest has gone on, the pretense that civil government exists on the island, except so far as Spain is able to maintain it, has been practically abandoned. Spain does keep on foot such a government, more or less imperfectly, in the large towns and their immediate suburbs. But, that exception being made, the entire country is either given over to anarchy or is subject to the military occupation of one or the other party. . . . In pursuance of general orders, Spanish garrisons are now being withdrawn from plantations and the rural population required to concentrate itself in the towns. The sure result would seem to be that the industrial value of the island is fast diminishing, and that unless there is a speedy and radical change in existing conditions, it will soon disappear altogether. . . .

"The spectacle of the utter ruin of an adjoining country, by nature one of the most fertile and charming on the globe, would engage the serious attention of the Government and people of the United States in any circumstances. In point of fact, they have a concern with it which is by no means of a wholly sentimental or philanthropic character. It lies so near to us as to be hardly separated from our territory. Our actual pecuniary interest in it is second only to that of the people and Government of Spain. It is reasonably estimated that at least from $30,000,000 to $50,000,000 of American capital are invested in plantations and in railroad, mining, and other business enterprises on the island. The volume of trade between the United States and Cuba, which in 1889 amounted to about $64,000,000, rose in 1893 to about $103,000,000, and in 1894, the year before the present insurrection broke out, amounted to nearly $96,000,000. Besides this large pecuniary stake in the fortunes of Cuba, the United States finds itself inextricably involved in the present contest in other ways both vexatious and costly. . . . These inevitable entanglements of the United States with the rebellion in Cuba, the large American property interests affected, and considerations of philanthropy and humanity in general, have led to a vehement demand in various quarters, for some sort of positive intervention on the part of the United States. . . .

"It would seem that if Spain should offer to Cuba genuine autonomy — a measure of home rule which, while preserving the sovereignty of Spain, would satisfy all rational requirements of her Spanish subjects — there should be no just reason why the pacification of the island might not be effected on that basis. Such a result would appear to be in the true interest of all concerned. . . . It has been objected on the one side that Spain should not promise autonomy until her insurgent subjects lay down their arms; on the other side, that promised autonomy, however liberal, is insufficient, because without assurance of the promise being fulfilled. . . . Realizing that suspicions and precautions on the part of the weaker of two combatants are always natural and not always unjustifiable—being sincerely desirous in the interest of both as well as on its own account that the Cuban problem should be solved with the least possible delay— it was intimated by this Government to the Government of Spain some months ago that, if a satisfactory measure of home rule were tendered the Cuban insurgents, and would be accepted by them upon a guaranty of its execution, the United States would endeavor to find a way not objectionable to Spain of furnishing such guaranty. While no definite response to this intimation has yet been received from the Spanish Government, it is believed to be not altogether unwelcome, while, as already suggested, no reason is perceived why it should not be approved by the insurgents. . . .

"It should be added that it can not be reasonably assumed that the hitherto expectant attitude of the United States will be indefinitely maintained. While we are anxious to accord all due respect to the sovereignty of Spain, we can not

view the pending conflict in all its features, and properly apprehend our inevitably close relations to it, and its possible results, without considering that by the course of events we may be drawn into such an unusual and unprecedented condition, as will fix a limit to our patient waiting for Spain to end the contest, either alone and in her own way, or with our friendly co-operation." — *President Cleveland's Message to Congress, Dec. 7, 1896.*

Just at this time (Dec. 7, 1896) the Cuban insurgents suffered a serious calamity, in the death of Antonio Maceo, the heroic mulatto, who seems to have been the most soldierly and inspiring of their leaders. He had broken through the "trocha," or fortified line across the island, by which the Spaniards were endeavoring to hold its western part, and had been troubling them in the province of Pinar del Rio for some months. At length he was killed in an unimportant skirmish, and much of the vigor of the insurrection appears to have gone out of it when he died. The obstinacy of spirit remained, nevertheless, and all the merciless energy of Weyler only spread death and misery, without opening any prospect of an end to the state of war. Spain was being utterly exhausted by the immense cost of the struggle; Cuba was being ruined and depopulated; yet neither would yield. The oppressors would not set their victims free; the oppressed would not submit. But, politically, the situation continued for another year as it had been when described by President Cleveland at the close of 1896. The only visible authority was that which the Spaniards maintained here and there. The revolutionists established no government that could reasonably be given the name, and their "Republic of Cuba," which foolish people in the United States were clamoring to have recognized, existed on paper alone. To concede "belligerent rights" to the scattered bands of insurgents would only bring them under crippling rules of international law, and do no good to their cause. President McKinley, who succeeded President Cleveland in March, 1897, made no change in the policy which the latter had pursued. He continued the insistent pressure by which it was sought to persuade the Spanish government to give a satisfying measure of free government to its great dependency. After some months there appeared to be a fair promise of success. The Liberal party had come into power at Madrid, with Sagasta at its head. In October, Weyler was recalled, General Blanco took his place, and a new constitution for Cuba was announced, giving the colony what seemed to be a fairly autonomous government, under a parliament of its own. In his message to Congress the following December, President McKinley was able to meet the continued clamor for more violent measures of interference by saying: "It is honestly due to Spain, and to our friendly relations with Spain, that she should be given a reasonable chance to realize her expectations, and to prove the asserted efficacy of the new order of things to which she stands irrevocably committed. She has recalled the commander whose brutal orders inflamed the American mind and shocked the civilized world. She has modified the horrible order of concentration, and has undertaken to care for the helpless and permit those who desire to resume the cultivation of their fields to do so, and assures them the protection of the Spanish Government in their lawful occupations." But the awful tragedy of suffering among the "reconcentrados" had excited lookers-on to such a pitch that the conduct of Spain in any new line of policy could no longer be fairly judged. There had been attempts on the part of the Spanish authorities to give some relief to the starved and perishing multitude, and help to that end had been accepted from the United States. The American Red Cross Society, with Miss Clara Barton at its head, entered the island in December, with vast stores of food and hospital supplies, and a strong force of generous workers; but the need was far beyond their means. The tale of death and misery in the stricken country seemed to grow more sickening every day.

A. D. 1897 (November).—Constitution establishing self-government in the islands of Cuba and Porto Rico, promulgated by Royal Decree.—The following is a translation of the text of the Constitution establishing self-government in the islands of Cuba and Porto Rico which was promulgated by royal decree at Madrid on the 25th of November, 1897:

Upon the proposition of my Prime Minister, and with the concurrence of the Council of Ministers in the name of my august son, King Alfonso XIII, and as Queen Regent of the Kingdom, I hereby decree as follows:

TITLE I.* GOVERNMENT AND CIVIL ADMINISTRATION IN THE ISLANDS OF CUBA AND PORTO RICO.

ARTICLE 1. The system of government and civil administration in the islands of Cuba and Porto Rico shall hereafter be carried on in conformity with the following provisions:

ART. 2. Each island shall be governed by an insular parliament, consisting of two chambers, and by the Governor-General, representing the mother country, who shall exercise supreme authority.

TITLE II. THE INSULAR CHAMBERS.

ART. 3. The legislative power as to colonial matters in the shape and manner prescribed by law, shall be vested in the insular chambers conjointly with the Governor-General.

ART. 4. Insular representation shall consist of two bodies of equal powers, which shall be known as chamber of representatives and council of administration.

* EXPLANATORY NOTE.—To facilitate the understanding of this decree and to avoid confusion as to the legal value of the terms employed therein the following definitions are to be observed:

Central Executive Power: The King with his Council of Ministers.
The Spanish Parliament: The Cortes with the King.
The Spanish Chambers: The Congress and the Senate.
The Central Government: The Council of Ministers of the Kingdom.
The Colonial Parliament: The two Chambers with the Governor-General.
The Colonial Chambers: The Council of Administration and the Chamber of Representatives.
Colonial Legislative Assemblies: The Council of Administration and the Chamber of Representatives.
Governor-General in Council: The Governor-General with the Secretaries of his Cabinet.
Instructions of the Governor-General: Those which he may have received when named for his office.
Statute: Colonial measure of a legislative character.
Colonial Statutes: Colonial Legislation.
Legislation or General Laws: Legislation or laws of the Kingdom.

TITLE III. COUNCIL OF ADMINISTRATION.

ART. 5. The council shall be composed of thirty-five members, of whom eighteen shall be elected in the manner directed by the electoral law and seventeen shall be appointed by the Governor-General acting for the Crown, from among such persons as have the qualifications specified in the following articles:

ART. 6. To be entitled to sit in the council of administration it is necessary to be a Spanish subject; to have attained the age of thirty-five years; to have been born in the island, or to have had four years' constant residence therein; not to be subject to any pending criminal prosecution; to be in the full enjoyment of his political rights; to have his property free from attachment; to have had for two or more years previous an annual income of four thousand dollars; to have no interest in any contract with either the insular or the home government. The shareholders of a stock company shall not be considered as government contractors, even if the company has a contract with the government.

ART. 7. Persons are also qualified to serve as councilors who, besides the above-stated requirements, have any of the following qualifications: 1. To be or to have been a senator of the Kingdom, or to possess the requirements for being a senator, in conformity with Article III of the constitution. 2. To have held for a period of two years any of the following offices: President, or prosecuting attorney of the pretorian court of Havana; rector of the University of Havana; councilor of administration in the council formerly thus designated; president of the Havana Chamber of Commerce; president of the Economic Society of Friends of the Country; president of the Sugar Planters' Association; president of the Tobacco Manufacturers' Union; president of the Merchants, Tradesmen's, and Agriculturalists' League; dean of the bar of Havana; mayor of Havana; president of the provincial assembly of Havana during two terms or of any provincial assembly during three terms; dean of either of the chapters of the two cathedrals. 3. Likewise may be elected or appointed as councilor any property owner from among the fifty taxpayers paying the highest taxes, either on real estate or on industries, commerce, arts, and the professions.

ART. 8. The councilors appointed by the Crown shall be appointed by special decrees, stating the qualification entitling the appointee to serve as councilor. Councilors thus appointed shall hold office for life. One-half the number of elective councilors shall be elected every five years, and the whole number shall be elected whenever the council of administration shall be dissolved by the Governor-General.

ART. 9. The qualifications required in order to be appointed or elected councilor of administration may be changed by a national law, at the request or upon the proposition of the insular chambers.

ART. 10. No councilor shall, during the session of the council, accept any civil office, promotion (unless it be strictly by seniority), title, or decoration; but any councilor may be appointed by either the local or the home government to any commission within his own profession or category, whenever the public service shall require it. The secretaries of the insular government shall be excepted from the foregoing rule.

TITLE IV. THE CHAMBER OF REPRESENTATIVES.

ART. 11. The chamber of representatives shall be composed of members named by the electoral boards in the manner prescribed by law and in the proportion of one for every twenty-five thousand inhabitants.

ART. 12. To be elected as representative the candidate must have the following requirements: To be a Spanish citizen, to be a layman, to have attained his majority, to be in full enjoyment of civil rights, to have been born in the island or to have had four years' constant residence therein, and not to be subject to any pending criminal prosecution.

ART. 13. Representatives shall be elected every five years, and any representative may be re-elected any number of times. The insular chamber shall determine what classes of offices are incompatible with the office of representative, as well as the cases governing re-election.

ART. 14. Any representative upon whom either the local or home government shall confer a pension, or any employment, promotion (unless it be by strict seniority), paid commission, title, or decoration, shall cease to be such without necessity of any declaration to that effect, unless he shall within fifteen days of his appointment notify the chamber of his having declined the favor. The provisions of the preceding paragraph shall not include the representatives who shall be appointed members of the cabinet.

TITLE V. PROCEEDINGS OF THE INSULAR CHAMBERS AND THEIR RELATIONS TO EACH OTHER.

ART. 15. The chambers will meet every year. The King, the Governor-General acting in his name, shall convene, suspend, and adjourn the sessions and dissolve the chamber of representatives and the council of administration, either separately or simultaneously, under the obligation to call them together again or renew them within three months.

ART. 16. Each of the two legislative bodies shall determine the rules of their proceedings and shall be the judges of the qualifications of their respective members and the legality of their election. Until the chamber and the council shall pass their own rules, they shall be governed by the rules of the national house of representatives and of the senate, respectively.

ART. 17. Each chamber shall choose its president, vice-president and secretaries.

ART. 18. Neither chamber shall sit unless the other be sitting also, except when the council exercises judicial functions.

ART. 19. The two insular chambers shall not deliberate together nor in the presence of the Governor-General. The sessions shall be public, but either chamber may hold secret sessions whenever business of a private nature shall require it.

ART. 20. To the Governor-General, through his secretaries, as well as to either of the two chambers, belongs the power to initiate and propose colonial statutes.

ART. 21. All colonial statutes in regard to taxes and the public credit shall originate in the chamber of representatives.

ART. 22. Resolutions may be passed by either chamber by a plurality of votes; but in order to pass a measure of a legislative character a majority of all the members constituting the body must be present. Nevertheless, one-third of the members shall constitute a quorum for deliberation.

ART. 23. No resolution or law shall be considered passed by the insular parliament unless it has had the concurrence of the chamber of representatives and the council of administration.

ART. 24. Every colonial statute, as soon as it has been approved in the form prescribed in the preceding article, shall be presented to the Governor-General by the officers of both chambers for his sanction and proclamation of the same.

ART. 25. Members of the council and the chamber of representatives shall have immunity for any speech or vote in either chamber.

ART. 26. No councilor or representative shall be indicted or arrested without a previous resolution of the council, unless he shall be found "in flagranti" or the council shall not be in session, but in every case notice shall be given to that body as soon as possible, that it may determine what should be done. Nor shall the representatives be indicted or arrested during the sessions without the permission of the chamber unless they are found "in flagranti," but in this last case, or in case of indictment or arrest when the chamber is not sitting, notice shall be given as soon as possible to the chamber of representatives for its information and action. All proceedings against councilors and representatives shall be brought before the pretorian court at Havana in the cases and manner that shall be prescribed by colonial statutes.

ART. 27. The guarantees established in the foregoing section shall not apply to a councilor or representative who shall himself admit that he is the author of any article, book, pamphlet, or printed matter wherein military sedition is incited or invoked, or the Governor-General is insulted and maligned, or national sovereignty is assailed.

ART. 28. The relations between the two chambers shall be governed, until otherwise provided, by the act of July 19, 1837, regulating the relations between the two legislative houses of the Cortes.

ART. 29. Besides the power of enacting laws for the colony the insular chambers shall have power: 1. To receive the oath of the Governor-General to preserve the constitution and the laws which guarantee the autonomy of the colony. 2. To enforce the responsibility of the secretaries of the executive. who shall be tried by the council, whenever impeached by the chamber of representatives. 3. To address the home government through the Governor-General, proposing the abrogation or modification of existing laws of the Kingdom; to invite the home government to present bills as to particular matters, or to ask a decision of an executive character on matters which interest the colony.

ART. 30. The Governor-General shall communicate to the home government before presenting to the insular parliament any bill originating in the executive government of the island whenever, in his judgment, said bill may affect national interests. Should any such bill originate in the insular parliament, the government of the island shall ask for a postponement of the debate until the home government shall have given its opinion. In either case the correspondence passing between the two governments shall be laid before the chambers and published in the official Gazette.

ART. 31. All differences of jurisdiction between the several municipal, provincial, and insular assemblies, or between any of them and the executive, which by their nature may not be referred to the home government, shall be submitted to the courts of justice in accordance with the rules herein prescribed.

TITLE VI. POWERS VESTED IN THE INSULAR PARLIAMENT.

ART. 32. The insular chambers shall have power to pass upon all matters not specially and expressly reserved to the Cortes of the Kingdom or to the central government as herein provided, or as may be provided hereafter, in accordance with the prescription set forth in additional Article 2. In this manner, and without implying that the following enumeration presupposes any limitation of their power to legislate on other subjects, they shall have power to legislate on all matters and subjects concerning the departments of justice, interior, treasury, public works, education, and agriculture.

They shall likewise have exclusive cognizance of all matters of a purely local nature which may principally affect the colonial territory; and to this end they shall have power to legislate on civil administration; on provincial, municipal, or judicial apportionment; on public health, by land or sea, and on public credit, banks, and the monetary system. This power, however, shall not impair the powers vested in the colonial executive according to the laws in connection with the matters above mentioned.

ART. 33. It shall be incumbent upon the colonial parliament to make regulations under such national laws as may be passed by the Cortes and expressly intrusted to it. Especially among such measures parliament shall legislate, and may do so at the first sitting, for the purpose of regulating the elections, the taking of the electoral census, qualifying electors, and exercising the right of suffrage; but in no event shall these dispositions affect the rights of the citizens, as established by the electoral laws.

ART. 34. Notwithstanding that the laws governing the judiciary and the administration of justice are of a national character, and therefore obligatory for the colony, the insular parliament may, within the provisions of said laws, make rules or propose to the home government such measures as shall render easier the admission, continuance, or promotion in the local courts of lawyers, natives of the island, or practicing therein.

The Governor-General in council shall have, as far as the island of Cuba is concerned, the same power that has been vested heretofore in the minister for the colonies for the appointment of the functionaries and subordinate and auxiliary officers of the judicial order and as to the other matters connected with the administration of justice.

ART. 35. The insular parliament shall have exclusive power to frame the local budget of expenditures and revenues, including the revenue corresponding to the island as her quota of the national budget. To this end the Governor-General shall present to the chambers every year before the month of January the budget for the next fiscal year, divided in two parts, as follows: The first part shall state the revenues needed to defray the expenses of sovereignty, and the second part shall state the revenues and expenditures estimated for the maintenance of the colonial administration. Neither chamber shall take up the budget of the colonial government without having finally voted the part for the maintenance of sovereignty.

ART. 36. The Cortes of the Kingdom shall determine what expenditures are to be considered by reason of their nature as obligatory expenses inherent to sovereignty, and shall fix the amount every three years and the revenue needed to defray the same, the Cortes reserving the right to alter this rule.

ART. 37. All treaties of commerce affecting the island of Cuba, be they suggested by the insular or by the home government, shall be made by the latter with the co-operation of special delegates duly authorized by the colonial government, whose concurrence shall be acknowledged upon submitting the treaties to the Cortes. Said treaties, when approved by the Cortes, shall be proclaimed as laws of the Kingdom and as such shall obtain in the colony.

ART. 38. Notice shall be given to the insular government of any commercial treaties made without its participation as soon as said treaties shall become laws, to the end that, within a period of three months, it may declare its acceptance or nonacceptance of their stipulations. In case of acceptance the Governor-General shall cause the treaty to be published in the Gazette as a colonial statute.

ART. 39. The insular parliament shall also have power to frame the tariff and fix the duties to be paid on merchandise as well for its importation into the territory of the island as for the exportation thereof.

ART. 40. As a transition from the old régime to the new constitution, and until the home and insular governments may otherwise conjointly determine hereafter, the commercial relations between the island and the metropolis shall be governed by the following rules: 1. No differential duty, whether fiscal or otherwise, either on imports or exports, shall be imposed to the detriment of either insular or peninsular production. 2. The two governments shall make a schedule of articles of direct national origin to which shall be allowed by common consent preferential duty over similar foreign products. In another schedule made in like manner shall be determined such articles of direct insular production as shall be entitled to privileged treatment on their importation into the peninsula and the amount of preferential duties thereon. In neither case shall the preferential duty exceed 35 per cent. Should the home and the colonial government agree upon the schedules and the preferential duties, they shall be considered final and shall be enforced at once. In case of disagreement the point in dispute shall be submitted to a committee of representatives of the Cortes, consisting of an equal number of Cubans and Peninsulars. The committee shall appoint its chairman, and in case of disagreement the eldest member shall preside. The chairman shall have the casting vote. 3. The valuation tables concerning the articles in the schedules above mentioned shall be fixed by mutual agreement, and shall be revised after discussion every two years. The modifications which may thereupon become necessary in the tariff duties shall be carried out at once by the respective governments.

TITLE VII. THE GOVERNOR-GENERAL.

ART. 41. The supreme authority of the colony shall be vested in a Governor-General, appointed by the King on the nomination of the council of ministers. In his capacity he shall have as viceroyal patron the power inherent in the patronate of the Indies; he shall have command of all military and naval forces in the island; he shall act as delegate of the departments of state, war, navy, and the colonies; all other authorities in the island shall be subordinate to his, and he shall be responsible for the preservation of order and the safety of the colony. The Governor-General shall, before taking possession of his office, take an oath in the presence of the King to discharge his duties faithfully and loyally.

ART. 42. The Governor-General, representing the nation, will discharge by himself and with the aid of his secretaries all the functions indicated in the preceding articles and such others as may devolve upon him as direct delegate of the King in matters of a national character. It shall be incumbent upon the Governor-General as representing the home government: 1. To appoint without restriction the secretaries of his cabinet. 2. To proclaim, execute, and cause to be executed in the island all laws, decrees, treaties, international covenants, and all other acts emanating from the legislative branch of the government, as well as all decrees, royal commands, and other measures emanating from the executive which shall be communicated to him by the departments of which he acts as delegate. Whenever in his judgment and in that of his secretaries he considers the resolutions of the home government as liable to injure the general interests of the nation or the special interests of the island, he shall have power to suspend the publication and execution thereof, and shall so notify the respective department, stating the reasons for his action. 3. To grant pardons in the name of the King, within the limitations specially prescribed to him in his instructions from the government, and to stay the execution of a death sentence whenever the gravity of the circumstances shall so demand or the urgency of the case shall allow of no time to solicit and obtain His Majesty's pardon; but in either case he shall bear the counsel of his secretaries. 4. To suspend the guarantees set forth in articles 3, 5, 6, and 9, and in the first, second, and third paragraphs of article 13 of the constitution; to enforce legislation in regard to public order, and to take all measures which he may deem necessary to preserve the peace within and the safety without for the territory entrusted to him after hearing the counsel of his cabinet. 5. To take care that in the colony justice be promptly and fully administered, and that it shall always be administered in the name of the King. 6. To hold direct communication on foreign affairs with the ministers, diplomatic agents, and counsels of Spain throughout America. A full copy of such correspondence shall be simultaneously forwarded to the home Department of State.

ART. 43. It behooves the Governor-General, as the superior authority in the colony and head of its administration: 1. To take care that the rights, powers, and privileges now vested or that may henceforth be vested in the colonial admin-

istration be respected and protected. 2. To sanction and proclaim the acts of the insular parliament, which shall be submitted to him by the president and secretaries of the respective chambers. Whenever, in the judgment of the Govcruor-General, an act of the insular parliament goes beyond its powers or impairs the rights of the citizens as set forth in Article I of the constitution, or curtails the guarantees prescribed by law for the exercise of said rights, or jeopards the interest of the colony or of the nation, he shall forward the act to the council of ministers of the Kingdom, which, within a period that shall not exceed two months, shall either assent to it or return it to the Governor-General with the objections to its sanction and proclamation. The insular parliament may, in view of the objections, reconsider or modify the act, if it deems fit, without a special proposition. If two months shall elapse without the central government giving any opinion as to a measure agreed upon by the chambers which has been transmitted to it by the Governor-General, the latter shall sanction and proclaim the same. 3. To appoint, suspend, and discharge the employees of the colonial administration, upon the suggestion of the secretaries of the departments and in accordance with the laws. 4. To appoint and remove, without restriction, the secretaries of his cabinet.

ART. 44. No executive order of the Governor-General, acting as representative and chief of the colony, shall take effect unless countersigned by a secretary of the cabinet, who by this act alone shall make himself responsible for the same.

ART. 45. There shall be five secretaries of department, to wit: Grace and justice and interior; finance; public education, public works and posts and telegraphs; agriculture, industry, and commerce. The Governor-General shall appoint the president of the cabinet from among the secretaries, and shall also have power to appoint a president without a secretaryship. The power to increase or diminish the number of secretaries composing the colonial cabinet, and to determine the scope of each department, is vested in the insular parliament.

ART. 46. The secretaries of the cabinet may be members of either the chamber of representatives or the council of administration and take part in the debates of either chamber, but a secretary shall only vote in the chamber of which he is a member.

ART. 47. The secretaries of the cabinet shall be responsible to the insular parliament.

ART. 48. The Governor-General shall not modify or abrogate his own orders after they are assented to by the home government, or when they shall declare some rights, or when a sentence by a judicial court or administrative tribunal shall have been based upon said orders, or when they shall deal with his own competency.

ART. 49. The Governor-General shall not turn over his office when leaving the island except by special command from the home government. In case of absence from the seat of government which prevents his discharging the duties of his office or of disability to perform such duties, he can appoint one or more persons to take his place, provided the home government has not previously done so or the method of substitution shall not be stated in his instructions.

178

ART. 50. The supreme court shall have the sole power to try the Governor-General when impeached for his responsibilities as defined by the Penal Code. The council of ministers shall take cognizance of his other responsibilities.

ART. 51. The Governor-General shall have the power, in spite of the provisions of the different articles of this decree, to act upon his own responsibility, without consulting his secretaries, in the following cases: 1. When forwarding to the home government a bill passed by the insular parliament, especially when, in his opinion, it shall abridge the rights set forth in Article 1 of the constitution of the monarchy or the guarantees for the exercise thereof vouchsafed by the laws. 2. When it shall be necessary to enforce the law or public order, especially if there be no time or possibility to consult the home government. 3. When enforcing the national laws that shall have been approved by the Crown and made applicable to all of the Spanish or to the colony under his government. The proceedings and means of action which the Govcruor-General shall employ in the above cases shall be determined by a special law.

TITLE VIII. MUNICIPAL AND PROVINCIAL GOVERNMENT.

ART. 52. Municipal organization shall be compulsory for every group of population of more than one thousand inhabitants. Groups of less number of inhabitants may organize the service of their community by special covenants. Every legally constituted municipality shall have power to frame its own laws regarding public education; highways by land, river, and sea; public health; municipal finances, as well as to freely appoint and remove its own employees.

ART. 53. At the head of each province there shall be an assembly, which shall be elected in the manner provided for by the colonial statutes, and shall be composed of a number of members in proportion to the population.

ART. 54. The provincial assembly shall be autonomous as regards the creation and maintenance of public schools and colleges; charitable institutions and provincial roads and ways by land, river, or sea; also as regards their own budgets and the appointment and removal of their respective employees.

ART. 55. The municipalities, as well as the provincial assemblies, shall have power to freely raise the necessary revenue to cover their expenditures, with no other limitation than to make the means adopted compatible with the general system of taxation which shall obtain in the island. The resources for provincial appropriations shall be independent of municipal resources.

ART. 56. The mayors and presidents of boards of aldermen shall be chosen by their respective boards from among their members.

ART. 57. The mayors shall discharge without limitation the active duties of the municipal administration, as executors of the resolutions of the board of aldermen or their representatives.

ART. 58. The aldermen and the provincial assemblymen shall be civilly responsible for the damages caused by their acts. Their responsibility shall be exacted before the ordinary courts of justice.

ART. 59. The provincial assemblies shall freely choose their respective presidents.

ART. 60. The elections of aldermen and assemblymen shall be conducted in such manner as to allow for a legitimate representation of the minorities.

ART. 61. The provincial and municipal laws now obtaining in the island shall continue in vogue, wherever not in conflict with the provisions of this decree, until the insular parliament shall legislate upon the matter.

ART. 62. No colonial statute shall abridge the powers vested by the preceding articles in the municipalities and the provincial assemblies.

TITLE IX. AS TO THE GUARANTEES FOR THE FULFILLMENT OF THE COLONIAL CONSTITUTION.

ART. 63. Whenever a citizen shall consider that his rights have been violated or his interests injured by the action of a municipality or a provincial assembly he shall have the right to apply to the courts of justice for redress. The department of justice shall, if so required by the agents of the executive government of the colony, prosecute before the courts the boards of aldermen or provincial assemblies charged with breaking the laws or abusing their power.

ART. 64. In the cases referred to in the preceding article, the following courts shall have jurisdiction: The territorial audiencia shall try all claims against municipalities; and the pretorian court of Havana shall try all claims against provincial assemblies. Said courts, when the charges against any of the above-mentioned corporations shall be for abuse of power, shall render their decisions by a full bench. From the decision of the Territorial audiencia an appeal shall be allowed to the pretorian court of Havana, and from the decisions of the latter an appeal shall be allowed to the supreme court of the Kingdom.

ART. 65. The redress of grievances which Article 62 grants to any citizen can also be had collectively by means of public action, by appointing an attorney or representative claimant.

ART. 66. Without in any way impairing the powers vested in the Governor-General by Title V of the present decree, he may, whenever he deems fit, appear before the pretorian court of Havana in his capacity as chief of the executive government of the colony, to the end that said court shall finally decide any conflict of jurisdiction between the executive power and the legislative chambers of the colony.

ART. 67. Should any question of jurisdiction be raised between the insular parliament and the Governor-General in his capacity as representative of the home government, which shall not have been submitted to the council of ministers of the Kingdom by petition of the insular parliament, either party shall have power to bring the matter before the supreme court of the Kingdom, which shall render its decision by a full bench and in the first instance.

ART. 68. The decisions rendered in all cases provided for in the preceding articles shall be published in the collection of colonial statutes and shall form part of the insular legislation.

ART. 69. Every municipal measure for the purpose of contracting a loan or a municipal debt shall be without effect, unless it be assented to by a majority of the townspeople whenever one-third of the number of aldermen shall so demand. The amount of the loan or debt which, according to the number of inhabitants of a

179

township, shall make the referendum proceeding necessary, shall be determined by special statute.

ART. 70. All legislative acts originating in the insular parliament or the Cortes shall be compiled under the title of colonial statutes in a legislative collection, the formation and publication of which shall be entrusted to the Governor-General as chief of the colonial executive.

ADDITIONAL ARTICLES.

ART. 1. Until the colonial statutes shall be published in due form, the laws of the Kingdom shall be deemed applicable to all matters reserved to the jurisdiction of the insular government.

ART. 2. When the present constitution shall be once approved by the Cortes of the Kingdom for the islands of Cuba and Porto Rico, it shall not be amended except by virtue of a special law and upon the petition of the insular parliament.

ART. 3. The provisions of the present decree shall obtain in their entirety in the island of Porto Rico; they shall, however, be ordained by special decree in order to conform them to the population and nomenclature of said island.

ART. 4. Pending contracts for public services affecting in common the Antilles and the Peninsula shall continue in their present shape until termination, and shall be entirely governed by the conditions and stipulations therein made.

As regards other contracts already entered into, but not yet in operation, the Governor-General shall consult the home government, or the colonial chambers, as the case may be, and the two governments shall by mutual accord decide as between themselves the final form of such contract.

TRANSITORY PROVISIONS.

ART. 1. With a view to carry out the transition from the present régime to the system hereby established with the greatest possible dispatch and the least interruption of the public business, the Governor-General shall, whenever he deems it timely and after consulting the home government, appoint the secretaries of the executive office as per Article 45 of this decree, and with their aid he shall conduct the local government of the island until the insular chambers shall have been constituted. The secretaries thus appointed shall vacate their offices as soon as the Governor-General shall take his oath of office before the insular chambers, and the Governor-General shall immediately appoint as their successors the members of parliament who, in his judgment, most fully represent the majorities in the chamber of representatives and the council of administration.

ART. 2. The manner of meeting the expenditures occasioned by the debt now weighing upon the Spanish and Cuban treasuries, and the debt that may be contracted until the termination of the war, shall be determined by a law fixing the share that shall be borne by each treasury, and the special ways and means for the payment of the interest, and the sinking fund, and for refunding the principal in due time. Until the Cortes of the Kingdom shall decide this point no changes shall be made in the conditions under which said debts were contracted, nor in the payment of the interest, nor provisions for a sinking fund, nor in the guarantees which they enjoy, nor in the actual terms of payment. When the Cortes shall have apportioned the shares, each of

the two treasuries shall take upon itself the payment of the share allotted. In no event shall the obligations contracted towards the lenders on the faith of the Spanish nation cease to be scrupulously respected. Issued in the Palace, Madrid, November 25, 1897. MARIA CRISTINA.

The President of the Council of Ministers, PRÁXEDES MATEO SAGASTA.

A. D. 1897-1898 (November—February).— The experiment of autonomy or home rule.— It cannot be said that the Constitution of 1897 was given a fair trial. In the circumstances, one may doubt whether a fair trial of its working was possible. It came too late for advantageous testing or unprejudiced judging of its practicability. The autonomist party, which might once have been able to make Cuba a constitutional dependency, like Canada, had been discouraged and broken up. Weyler's policy had excited a feeling in the United States which was too impatient to wait for new experiments in Spanish dealing with Cuba to be worked out, or to estimate reasonably the chances of their success. The first showing of results from the scheme of autonomy was unpromising, as it could hardly have failed to be, and that was readily taken as conclusive in condemnation of it. The judgment of General Fitzhugh Lee, Consul-General of the United States at Havana, had great influence in America, and he saw nothing to expect from the Constitution. In an article contributed subsequently to the "Fortnightly Review," June, 1898, he wrote:

"It [the Constitution] was an elaborate system of 'Home Rule' with a string to every sentence; so that I soon became satisfied that, if the insurrection against the Spanish throne on the island ceased, the condition of the Cubans would speedily be the same as it was at the commencement of the war. I gave the reasons therefor in a paper now on file in the State Department which clearly proved that the Spaniards could easily control one of the legislative chambers, and that behind any joint action on the part of both was the veto of the Governor-General, whose appointment was made from the throne in Madrid.

"This system of autonomy, however, was gravely proceeded with. An Autonomistic Cabinet was seriously formed, composed in part of Cubans who, though at one time in favour of a government of the island free from Spanish control, had given satisfactory intimations that, if they were appointed to cabinet offices, their former opinions could be modified to suit existing circumstances. Blanco's Autonomistic Government was doomed to failure from its inception. The Spanish soldiers and officers scorned it, because they did not desire Cuban rule, which such autonomy, if genuine, would insure. The Spanish merchants and citizens were opposed to it, because they too were hostile to the Cubans having control of the island, and if the question could be narrowed down to Cuban control or annexation to the United States, they were all annexationists, believing that they could get a better government and one that would protect, in a greater measure, life and property under the United States flag than under the Cuban banner. On the other hand, the Cubans in arms would not touch it, because they were fighting for Free Cuba; and the Cuban citizens and sympathizers, or the non-arm-bearing population, were distinctly opposed to it also; while those in favour of it seemed to consist of the Autonomistic Cabinet,

General Blanco, his Secretary-General and Staff, and a few followers elsewhere."—Fitzhugh Lee, *Cuba and her Struggle for Freedom* (*Fortnightly Review*, June, 1898).

A. D. 1897-1898 (December—March).—**Condition of the Reconcentrados.**—On the 14th of December, 1897, General Fitzhugh Lee, Consul-General of the United States at Havana, reported to the Department of State as follows: "I have the honor to report that I have received information that in the Province of Havana reports show that there have been 101,000 'reconcentrados,' and that out of that 52,000 have died. Of the said 101,000, 32,000 were children. This excludes the city of Havana and seven other towns from which reports have not yet been made up. It is thought that the total number of 'reconcentrados' in Havana Province will amount to 150,-000, nearly all women and children, and that the death rate among their whole number from starvation alone will be over 50 per cent. For the above number of 'reconcentrados' $12,500, Spanish silver, was set aside out of the $100,000 appropriated for the purpose of relieving all the 'reconcentrados' on the island. Seventy-five thousand of the 150,000 may be still living, so if every dollar appropriated of the $12,500 reaches them the distribution will average about 17 cents to a person, which, of course, will be rapidly exhausted, and, as I can hear of no further succor being afforded, it is easy to perceive what little practical relief has taken place in the condition of these poor people."

On the 8th of January, 1898, General Lee made another report on the same subject as follows: "I have the honor to state, as a matter of public interest, that the 'reconcentrado order' of General Weyler, formerly Governor-General of this island, transformed about 400,000 self-supporting people, principally women and children, into a multitude to be sustained by the contributions of others or die of starvation or of fevers resulting from a low physical condition and being massed in large bodies without change of clothing and without food. Their houses were burned, their fields and plant beds destroyed, and their live stock driven away or killed. I estimate that probably 200,000 of the rural population in the Provinces of Pinar del Rio, Havana, Matanzas, and Santa Clara have died of starvation, or from resultant causes, and the deaths of whole families almost simultaneously, or within a few days of each other, and of mothers praying for their children to be relieved of their horrible sufferings by death, are not the least of the many pitiable scenes which were ever present. In the Provinces of Puerto Principe and Santiago de Cuba, where the 'reconcentrado order' could not be enforced, the great mass of the people are self-sustaining. A daily average of ten cents' worth of food to 200,000 people would be an expenditure of $20,000 per day, and of course the most humane efforts upon the part of our citizens can not hope to accomplish such a gigantic relief, and a great portion of these people will have to be abandoned to their fate."

A little later, Senator Proctor, of Vermont, visited Cuba, for personal observation of the condition of things in the island, and, on his return, made a statement of what he had seen and learned, in a speech to the Senate, which made an impression on the country much deeper than any previous testimony on the subject that had reached the public eye or ear. The following is a part of the account that he gave: "My observations were confined to the four western provinces, which constitute about one-half of the island. The two eastern ones are practically in the hands of the insurgents, except the few fortified towns. These two large provinces are spoken of to-day as 'Cuba Libre.' Outside Habana all is changed. It is not peace nor is it war. It is desolation and distress, misery and starvation. Every town and village is surrounded by a 'trocha' (trench), a sort of rifle pit, but constructed on a plan new to me, the dirt being thrown up on the inside and a barbed-wire fence on the outer side of the trench. These trochas have at every corner and at frequent intervals along the sides what are there called forts, but which are really small blockhouses, many of them more like large sentry boxes, loopholed for musketry, and with a guard of from two to ten soldiers in each.

"The purpose of these trochas is to keep the reconcentrados in as well as to keep the insurgents out. From all the surrounding country the people have been driven in to these fortified towns and held there to subsist as they can. They are virtually prison yards, and not unlike one in general appearance, except that the walls are not so high and strong; but they suffice, where every point is in range of a soldier's rifle, to keep in the poor reconcentrado women and children. Every railroad station is within one of these trochas and has an armed guard. Every train has an armored freight car, loopholed for musketry and filled with soldiers, and with, as I observed usually, and was informed is always the case, a pilot engine a mile or so in advance. There are frequent blockhouses inclosed by a trocha and with a guard along the railroad track. With this exception there is no human life or habitation between these fortified towns and villages, and throughout the whole of the four western provinces, except to a very limited extent among the hills where the Spaniards have not been able to go and drive the people to the towns and burn their dwellings. I saw no house or hut in the 400 miles of railroad rides from Pinar del Rio Province in the west across the full width of Habana and Matanzas provinces, and to Sagua La Grande on the north shore, and to Cienfuegos on the south shore of Santa Clara, except within the Spanish trochas.

"There are no domestic animals or crops on the rich fields and pastures except such as are under guard in the immediate vicinity of the towns. In other words, the Spaniards hold in these four western provinces just what their army sits on. Every man, woman, and child, and every domestic animal, wherever their columns have reached, is under guard and within their so-called fortifications. To describe one place is to describe all. To repeat, it is neither peace nor war. It is concentration and desolation. This is the 'pacified' condition of the four western provinces. West of Habana is mainly the rich tobacco country; east, so far as I went, a sugar region. Nearly all the sugar mills are destroyed between Habana and Sagua. Two or three were standing in the vicinity of Sagua, and in part running, surrounded, as are the villages, by trochas and 'forts' or palisades of the royal palm, and fully guarded. Toward and near Cienfuegos there were more mills running, but all with the same protection. . . . All the country people in the four western provinces, about 400,000 in number, remaining outside the fortified towns when Weyler's order was made were driven into these towns, and these are the reconcentrados. They were the peasantry, many of them farmers, some landowners, others renting lands and owning more or less stock, others working on estates and cultivating small patches; and even a small patch in that fruitful clime will support a family. It is but fair to say that the normal condition of these people was very different from what prevails in this country. Their standard of comfort and prosperity was not high, measured by ours. But according to their standards and requirements their conditions of life were satisfactory. They lived mostly in cabins made of palms or in wooden houses. Some of them had houses of stone, the blackened walls of which are all that remain to show the country was ever inhabited.

" The first clause of Weyler's order [renewing that of Feb. 16, 1896] reads as follows: ' I Order and Command. First. All the inhabitants of the country or outside of the line of fortifications of the town shall, within the period of eight days, concentrate themselves in the towns occupied by the troops. Any individual who, after the expiration of this period, is found in the uninhabited parts will be considered a rebel and tried as such.' . . . Many, doubtless, did not learn of this order. Others failed to grasp its terrible meaning. Its execution was left largely to the guerrillas to drive in all that had not obeyed, and I was informed that in many cases the torch was applied to their homes with no notice, and the inmates fled with such clothing as they might have on, their stock and other belongings being appropriated by the guerrillas. When they reached the towns, they were allowed to build huts of palm leaves in the suburbs and vacant places within the trochas, and left to live, if they could.

" Torn from their homes, with foul earth, foul air, foul water, and foul food or none, what wonder that one-half have died and that one-quarter of the living are so diseased that they cannot be saved ? . . . Deaths in the streets have not been uncommon. I was told by one of our consuls that they have been found dead about the markets in the morning, where they had crawled, hoping to get some stray bits of food from the early hucksters, and that there had been cases where they.had dropped dead inside the market surrounded by food. These people were independent and self-supporting before Weyler's order. . . . I went to Cuba with a strong conviction that the picture had been overdrawn; that a few cases of starvation and suffering had inspired and stimulated the press correspondents, and that they had given free play to a strong, natural, and highly cultivated imagination. . . . I could not believe that, out of a population of 1,600,000, 200,000 had died within these Spanish forts, practically prison walls, within a few months past from actual starvation and diseases caused by insufficient and improper food. My inquiries were entirely outside of sensational sources. They were made of our medical officers, of our consuls, of city alcaldes (mayors), of relief committees, of leading merchants and bankers, physicians, and lawyers. Several of my informants were Spanish born, but every

time the answer was that the case had not been overstated. What I saw I cannot tell so that others can see it. It must be seen with one's own eyes to be realized. . . .

" The dividing lines between parties are the most straight and clear cut that have ever come to my knowledge. The division in our war was by no means so clearly defined. It is Cuban against Spaniard. It is practically the entire Cuban population on one side and the Spanish army and Spanish citizens on the other. I do not count the autonomists in this division, as they are so far too inconsiderable in numbers to be worth counting. General Blanco filled the civil offices with men who had been autonomists and were still classed as such. But the march of events had satisfied most of them that the chance for autonomy came too late. . . . There is no doubt that General Blanco is acting in entire good faith; that he desires to give the Cubans a fair measure of autonomy, as Campos did at the close of the ten-year war. He has, of course, a few personal followers, but the army and the Spanish citizens do not want genuine autonomy, for that means government by the Cuban people. And it is not strange that the Cubans say it comes too late."—*Congressional Record, March 17, 1898.*

A. D. 1898 (February).—Destruction of **the** U. S. Battleship Maine in Havana harbor. See (in this vol.) UNITED STATES OF AM. : A. D. 1898 (FEBRUARY—MARCH).

A. D. 1898 (March—April).—Discussion of Cuban affairs between Spain and the United States.—Message of the President to Congress asking for authority to intervene. See (in this vol.) UNITED STATES OF AM.: A. D. 1898 (MARCH—APRIL).

A. D. 1898 (April).—Demand of the U. S. Government for the withdrawal of Spain from the island, and its result in a state of war. See (in this vol.) UNITED STATES OF AM. : A. D. 1898 (APRIL).

A. D. 1898 (April—December).—Operations of war between the United States and Spain. —Suspension of hostilities.—Negotiation of treaty of peace.—Relinquishment of sovereignty by Spain. See (in this vol.) UNITED STATES OF AM.: A. D. 1898 (APRIL) to 1898 (JULY—DECEMBER).

A. D. 1898 (December).—Removal of the remains of Columbus to Spain.—The remains of Columbus were taken from the Cathedral in Havana, on the 12th of December, for transfer to the cathedral at Seville, in Spain.

A. D. 1898-1899 (December—October).— Organization of military government under United States authority.—Report of the military governor, on conditions prevailing, measures adopted, and results obtained.—On the 13th of December, 1898, the following General Order was issued by the Secretary of War: " By direction of the President, a division to be known as the Division of Cuba, consisting of the geographical departments and provinces of the island of Cuba, with headquarters in the city of Habana, is hereby created, under command of Maj. Gen. John R. Brooke, U. S. A., who, in addition to command of the troops in the division, will exercise the authority of military governor of the island. Maj. Gen. Fitzhugh Lee, U. S. V., commanding the Seventh Army Corps, is assigned to the immediate command of all the troops in the province of Habana. Maj. Gen. William Ludlow, U. S. V., is designated as the military governor of the city of Habana, and will report direct to the division commander. He is charged with all that relates to collection and disbursement of revenues of the port and city, and its police, sanitation, and general government, under such regulations as may be prescribed by the President."

General Brooke arrived at Havana on the 28th of December and assumed the command of the troops and the military governorship of the island. In his subsequent report (October 1, 1899) of conditions then existing, proceedings taken, events occurring and results attained, he wrote: "It was found that considerable confusion incident to the withdrawal of the Spanish troops and replacing them with the United States troops existed, but no untoward event occurred, however, as every precaution was taken to maintain order. The gradual withdrawal of the Spanish troops and the advance of the United States troops continued, until the morning of the 1st of January, 1899, found but few Spanish troops in the city, and these went on board transports, which movement was completed about 12.30 p. m. Outside of the principal towns the retiring Spanish army was closely followed by the Cuban army, which took charge of the towns and country, maintaining order, and, generally, performing police duty. This state of affairs continued, substantially, until the final disbandment of that army. The disbandment of the Cuban army was commenced in November, 1898, but only such as could procure work, or were anxious to resume their former vocations, seem to have taken advantage of the 'licencia' (furlough) which was given to many. A large part of the army was held together on various pretexts until the distribution of the $3,000,000 [allotted for distribution to the Cuban army, to enable the soldiers to return to their homes], and the giving up of their arms effected a final disbandment. During the time the army was held together as an organized body the police duties performed seemed to be well done and order was preserved. The spectacle of an army of, according to the rolls, 48,000 men being peacefully dispersed among the people has for its prototype the disappearance of the great volunteer army of the United States in 1865. In neither case has there been any great disturbance, as was feared in both cases, and particularly so as regards the Cuban army. The small attempts at brigandage were quickly suppressed, the lawbreakers placed in prison, and the courts are now hearing their cases.

"On January 1, 1899, a division of the Seventh Army Corps, under the command of General Fitzhugh Lee, General Keifer's division, was brought to the city, and, with the regiments on duty in Habana under the command of Gen. William Ludlow, were so placed as to insure good order during the ceremonies of the relinquishment of sovereignty by Spain, which occurred in the Governor-General's palace at 12 o'clock noon, where were assembled the Captain-General and his staff, the United States commission with its officers, the American military governor with his staff, Maj. Gen. Fitzhugh Lee, Maj. Gen. William Ludlow, Maj. Gen. J. Warren Keifer, and their staffs, and nine Cuban gen-

erals as his guests. This ceremony was simple in its character, though very impressive, consisting of a formal speech by the Spanish Governor-General, which was replied to by General Wade, the chairman of the United States evacuation commission, who, in concluding his remarks, turned to the military governor and transferred the island of Cuba to him, who, thereupon, entered upon the full exercise of his duty as the military governor of Cuba. Of course, the gathering into his hands of all the duties of his office took time. The desire of a large body of the Cuban army to take part on the 1st of January in the ceremonies of the relinquishment of sovereignty by Spain was reported verbally, by General Ludlow, and he was informed that the danger to life and property was too great, and that the celebration must be postponed to a time when the excitement had cooled off and the passions of the people could be under control. This celebration afterwards took place on the arrival in the city of Gen. Maximo Gomez, Commander in Chief of the Cuban forces, on February 24. General Ludlow was directed to meet General Gomez at the city limits and show him every courtesy possible. The Quinta de los Molinos, the summer residence of the Governor-General, was placed at his disposal, and for several months he, with his staff and escort, occupied the houses and grounds as the guests of this Government. The civil bureaus of the Governor-Generalcy were taken over by officers of the military governor's staff, and held by them until the proper civil officials could be selected and appointed. . . .

"In reaching this stage on the highway of progress toward the establishment of government through civil channels, many obstacles have been overcome, the most serious being the very natural distrust of the people, which was born and nurtured under the system of the preceding government, and was particularly the effect of the wars which these people waged in their effort to improve their condition. It is believed that this distrust has given way to confidence in the minds of a majority of the people, and that they are generally beginning to see that the government, as administered by the United States, is for them and for their benefit. It is proper at this time to speak of the condition of the people and the country as it existed at the time of the relinquishment of sovereignty by Spain. A large number of the people were found to be actually starving. Efforts were immediately made to supply food, which the War Department sent, all told, 5,493,500 Cuban rations, in addition to the 1,000,000 rations distributed by Mr. Gould, and these were sent into the country and distributed under the direction of the commanding generals of departments, through such agencies as they established; while in the cities the distribution was generally conducted by an officer of the Army. The result of this action was the immediate lowering of the death rate, the restoration to health of the sick, and a general change for the better was soon apparent. Medicines were also supplied for the sick with most beneficial results. Employment was given to those who could work, and they were paid weekly, so that they might have money to buy food. In fact, no effort was spared to relieve the terrible condition in which so many thousand people were found. . . .

"Turning to the present conditions, we have in view such a change that the progress seems incredible. A great part of the improvement dates from the month of May, when the muster out of the Cuban army removed a great source of distrust. The extent to which have been carried the cultivation of the fields, the reconstruction of homes, the re-establishment of order and public service, especially in the matter of hygiene in the towns, is something wonderful. . . . The question of finance, as relates to the restoration of crippled and destroyed agricultural industries, is one which has occupied a great deal of attention on the part of this government. It is evident that assistance in the way of repairing the roads and bridges, as well as to municipalities in their present impoverished conditions, is a necessity, and the most pressing wants in this direction have been met by granting money from the revenues of the island. There is every reason to hope that the municipal revenues will meet all requirements as soon as agriculture is again on its feet, and there will, doubtless, be some changes in the present tax law made. In this connection, it is well to know that planters and small farmers in the tobacco growing districts are rapidly recovering from their forlorn condition. The quick growing crop and the remunerative prices have enabled them to restore, in a measure, the lost cattle, mules, and implements necessary to the farmers. There is, also, a desire to use labor-saving devices, which are now being slowly introduced. . . .

"The quiet severance of church and state has been effected by the fact of the Government of the United States being in control. Certain changes have already been made in the laws, and others will follow in due course ; this without violating the legal rights of the Roman Catholic Church, which was the only religious denomination tolerated in the island, except a small body of Baptists. The important subject of schools is now approaching a solution. The present system will be improved upon, but it will require time to develop fully a good school system throughout the island. There are no school-houses, and under present conditions there can be none built for some time to come. It is hoped that a manual training school will be opened as soon as certain repairs and changes can be made in the Spanish barracks at Santiago de las Vegas, a short distance south of Habana, in which about 600 of both sexes can receive instruction at one time. This form of instruction is more important, under the conditions found to exist, than the ordinary instruction given in the other schools. As conditions improve, an opportunity can be given to increase the number of these schools, and by their means introduce modern methods more rapidly than by other systems."—Gen. John R. Brooke, *Civil Report, Oct.* 1, 1899 (*Message and Documents : Abridgment,* 1899–1900, *v.* 2, *pp.* 1266–76).

General Fitzhugh Lee reported, Sept. 19, 1899, on the state of things in the province of Havana. as follows : " I assumed command of the department of the province of Habana January 1, 1899, and of the province of Pinar del Rio April 19, 1899. The deplorable condition of the land after it was evacuated by the Spanish is well known. Business of all sorts was suspended. Agricultural operations had ceased ; large sugar estates, with their enormous and expensive ma-

chinery, were destroyed ; houses burned : stock driven off for consumption by the Spanish troops, or killed. There was scarcely an ox left to pull a plow, had there been a plow left. Not a pig had been left in the pen, nor a hen to lay an egg for the poor, destitute people who still held on to life, most of them sick, weary, and weak. Miles and miles of country uninhabited either by the human race or domestic animals was visible to the eye on every side. The great fertile island of Cuba in some places resembled an ash pile ; in others, the dreary desert. The ' reconcentrado ' order of the former Captain-General. Weyler, it will be remembered, drove from their houses and lands all the old men, women, and children who had remained at their homes because they were not physically able to bear the burdens of war. The wheels of the former government had ceased to revolve. Chaos, confusion, doubt, and uncertainty filled with apprehension the minds of the Cubans, who, for the first time, had been relieved of the cruel care of those who for centuries controlled their country and their destiny. . . . The railroads on the island were in bad order, having been used to the extent of their endurance conveying Spanish troops and Spanish supplies over them, while the great calzadas or turnpikes were filled with holes, for the war prevented repairs to either railroads or roads. Municipalities were all greatly in debt. None of the civil officers had been paid, and school-teachers had large amounts of back salary due. Judicial officers were discharging their duties as far as they could—for there was really no law in the island except the mandate of the Captain-General—without pay, and many months of back pay was due to the professors in the colleges of the largest cities. The whole framework of the government had to be rebuilt, and its machinery carefully and gradually reconstructed. Important government problems had to be promptly solved, which involved social, economic, commercial, agricultural, public instruction, support of eleemosynary institutions of all kinds, means of communications, reorganization of municipalities, with the necessary town and city police, including a mounted force to patrol the adjoining rural districts within the limits, and subject to the authorities of the mayors and council of their respective municipalities : the appointment of new alcaldes and other officers to replace those left in authority by the Spanish Government, and who would be more in accord with the inhabitants whose local affairs they directed. Many trying and troublesome questions arose, and many difficulties environed on either side of the situation.

"Of the Cuban rural population, less than 20 per cent of them were able to read and write, resembling children awaking the first time to the realities of life. They were in the main obedient, docile, quiet, and inoffensive, and anxious to adapt themselves as soon as possible to the new conditions which confronted them. The Cuban soldiers, black and white, who had been in the fields and woods for four years defying the Spanish banner, still kept their guns, and were massing around the cities and towns, producing more or less unrest in the public mind with the fear that many of them, unaccustomed to work so long, would be transformed into brigands, and not become peaceful, law-abiding citizens. In eight months wonderful progress has been made. The arms of the Cuban soldiers have been stacked, and they have quietly resumed peaceful vocations. Brigandage, which partially flourished for a time, has been stamped out, tillage everywhere has greatly increased, many houses rebuilt, many huts constructed, fences are being built, and more and more farming lands are gradually being taken up, and municipalities reorganized with new officers representing the wishes of the majority of the inhabitants. Municipal police have been appointed who are uniformed and under the charge of, in most cases, efficient officers."—Gen. Fitzhugh Lee, *Report, Sept.* 19, 1899.

General Leonard Wood, commanding in the province of Santiago, reported at the same time as follows : "On the assumption of control by the American Government, July 17, 1899, of that portion of the province of Santiago included in the surrendered territory, industries were practically at a standstill. In the rural districts all industries were at an end. The estates, almost without exception, have been destroyed, and no work is being done. . . . In the towns the effect of reconcentration was shown by large crowds of women and children and old men who were practically starving. They were thin, pale, and barely able to drag themselves about. The merchants and a few planters were the only prosperous people in the province. . . . A feeling of bitter hostility existed between the Cubans and Spaniards, and also a very ugly feeling between the Cubans who had acted in harmony with the autonomists in the latter days of the Spanish occupation and those who had been in the Cuban army. At first there was a good deal of talk of a threatening character in regard to what the Cubans would do to the Spaniards, now that they were in a position to avenge themselves for some of the many injuries received in the past. This, however, soon passed over, and much more friendly and sensible ideas prevailed. There were no schools and no material for establishing them. All officers of the civil government had resigned and left their posts, with the exception of one judge of the first instance and several municipal judges and certain police officers. The prisons were full of prisoners, both Spanish and Cuban, many of them being Spanish military and political prisoners. The administration of justice was at a standstill. The towns all presented an appearance of greatest neglect, and showed everywhere entire disregard of every sanitary law. The amount of clothing in the possession of the people was very limited, and in many of the interior villages women were compelled to keep out of sight when strangers appeared, as they had only skirts and waists made of bagging and other coarse material. Many of the children were absolutely without clothing. Evidences of great suffering were found on every hand. A very large proportion of the population was sick in the country districts from malaria and in the seaboard towns from lack of food and water. . . .

"The first two and a half months after the surrender were devoted almost entirely to the distribution of food and to supplying hospitals and charities with such limited quantities of necessary material as we were able to obtain. Commanding officers in all parts of the island were busily engaged in cleaning up towns and carrying out all possible sanitary and adminis-

trative reforms. Schools were established, some 60 in the city of Santiago and over 200 in the province as a whole. Affairs have continued to improve slowly but surely, until at the present time we find the towns, generally speaking, clean, the death rate lower than the people have known before, some public improvements under way in all the large towns, the amount of work done being limited only by the amount of money received. . . . Industries of all kinds are springing up. New sugar plantations are being projected ; hospitals and charitable institutions are being regularly supplied, and all are fairly well equipped with necessary articles. The death rate among the native population is very much lower than in former years. The people in the towns are quiet and orderly, with the exception of a few editorial writers, who manage to keep up a certain small amount of excitement, just enough to give the papers in question a fair sale. The people are all anxious to work. The present currency is American currency. A condition of good order exists in the rural districts. The small planters are all out on their farms and a condition of security and good order prevails. The issue of rations has been practically stopped and we have few or almost no applications for food." — Gen. Leonard Wood, *Report, Sept.* 20, 1899.

A. D. **1899** (October).—**Census of the Island.**—Statistics of population, nativity, illiteracy, etc.—" The total population of Cuba on October 16, 1899, determined by the census taken [under the direction of the War Department of the United States] as of that date, was 1,572,797. This was distributed as follows among the six provinces : Habana, 424,804 ; Matanzas, 202,444 ; Pinar del Rio, 173,064 ; Puerto Principe, 88,234 ; Santa Clara, 356,536 ; Santiago, 327,715. The latest census taken under Spanish authority was in 1887. The total population as returned by that census was 1,631,687, and the population by provinces was as follows : Habana, 451,928 ; Matanzas, 259,578 ; Pinar del Rio, 225,891 ; Puerto Principe, 67,789 ; Santa Clara, 354,122 ; Santiago, 272,379. Whether that census was correct may be a matter of discussion, but if incorrect, the number of inhabitants was certainly not overstated. Comparing the total population at these two censuses, it is seen that the loss in the 12 years amounted to 58,890, or 3.6 per cent of the population in 1887. This loss is attributable to the recent civil war and the reconcentration policy accompanying it, but the figures express only a part of the loss from this cause. Judging from the earlier history of the island and the excess of births over deaths, as shown by the registration records, however imperfect they may be, the population probably increased from 1887 up to the beginning of the war and at the latter epoch reached a total of little less than 1,800,000. It is probable, therefore, that the direct and indirect losses by the war and the reconcentration policy, including a decrease of births and of immigration and an increase of deaths and of emigration reached a total of approximately 200,000. . . .

"The area of Cuba is approximately 44,000 square miles, and the average number of inhabitants per square mile 35.7, about the same as the State of Iowa. . . . Habana, with the densest population, is as thickly populated as the State of Connecticut, and Puerto Principe, the most sparsely populated, is in this respect comparable with the State of Texas. . . .

"The total number of males of voting age in Cuba was 417,993, or 26 per cent of the total population. This is a little less than the proportion, in 1890, in the United States, where it was 27 per cent. . . . Classifying the potential voters of Cuba by birthplace and race, it is seen that 44.9 per cent were whites, born in Cuba ; that 30.5 per cent were colored, and as nearly all the colored were born in the island it is seen that fully seven-tenths of the potential voters of Cuba were native born, 23 per cent were born in Spain, and 1.6 per cent in other countries. Classifying the whole number of potential voters by citizenship it is seen that 70 per cent were Cuban citizens, 2 per cent were Spanish citizens, 18 per cent were holding their citizenship in suspense, and 10 per cent were citizens of other countries, or their citizenship was unknown. . . .

"The Cuban citizens, numbering 290,905, were composed almost entirely of persons born in Cuba, there being among them but 220 white persons, and probably not more colored, of alien birth. The white Cuban citizens, who were natives of the island, numbered 184,471, and of these 94,301, or 51 per cent, were unable to read. The colored Cuban citizens numbered 106,214, of which not less than 78,279, or 74 per cent, were unable to read. The people of Cuba who claimed Spanish citizenship numbered 9,500, and of these nearly all were born in Spain, there being but 159 born elsewhere. Those whose citizenship was in suspense numbered 76,669. These also were nearly all of Spanish birth, the number born elsewhere being but 1,420. The number of persons of other or unknown citizenship was 40,919. Of these fully one-half were colored, most of them being Chinese, and much the larger proportion of the remaining half were of Spanish birth.

"Summing up the situation, it appears that the total number of males of voting age who could read was 200,631, a little less than half the total number of males of voting age. Of these 22,629 were of Spanish or other foreign citizenship or unknown citizenship. The number whose citizenship was in suspense was 59,724, and the number of Cuban citizens able to read was 118,-278, or 59 per cent of all Cuban citizens of voting age."—*Census of Cuba, Bulletins Nos. I and III.*

A. D. **1899** (December).—Appointment of General Leonard Wood to the military command and Governorship.—On the 6th of December General Leonard Wood was commissioned major-general of volunteers, and was assigned to command of the Division of Cuba, relieving General Brooke as division commander and military governor of Cuba. On the 30th, Governor Wood announced the appointment of the following Cuban ministers, to form his cabinet : Secretary of State and Government, Diego Tamayo ; Secretary of Justice, Luis Estevoz ; Secretary of Education, Juan Bautista Hernandez ; Secretary of Finance, Enrique Varona ; Secretary of Public Works, José Ramon Villalon ; Secretary of Agriculture, Industry, and Commerce, Rius Rivera.

A. D. **1900**.—Organization of a school system.—Teachers at Harvard Summer School.—"Especial attention has been given by the military government to the development of primary education. The enrollment of the

public schools of Cuba immediately before the last war shows 36,306 scholars, but an examination of the reports containing these figures indicates that probably less than half the names enrolled represented actual attendance. There were practically no separate school buildings, but the scholars were collected in the residences of the teachers. There were few books, and practically no maps, blackboards, desks or other school apparatus. . . . Even these poor apologies for public schools were, to a great extent, broken up by the war, and in December, 1899, the entire public-school enrollment of the island numbered 21,435. The following table shows the advance in school during the half year ending June 30 facilities

	School rooms.	Enroll-ment.
January, 1900............................	635	37,995
February, 1900...........................	1,338	69,476
March, 1900..............................	3,126	127,881
April, 1900...............................	3,126	127,426
May, 1900.................................	3,313	139,616
June, 1900................................	3,550	143,120

"This great development was accomplished under the Cuban secretary of public instruction and the Cuban commissioner of public schools, with the able and experienced assistance of Mr. Alexis E. Frye as superintendent. It is governed by a school law modeled largely upon the law of Ohio. . . . The schools are subject to constant and effective inspection and the attendance is practically identical with the enrollment.

"The schools are separated from the residences of the teachers, and each schoolroom has its separate teacher. The courses and methods of instruction are those most approved in this country. The text-books are translations into Spanish of American text-books. For the supply of material $150,000 were, in the first instance, appropriated from the insular treasury, and afterwards, upon a single order, 100,000 full sets of desks, text-books, scholars' supplies, etc., were purchased upon public advertisement in this country at an expense of about three-quarters of a million dollars. All over the island the old Spanish barracks, and barracks occupied by the American troops which have been withdrawn, are being turned into schoolrooms after thorough renovation. The pressure for education is earnest and universal. The appropriations of this year from the insular treasury for that purpose will amount to about four and a half million dollars ; but great as the development has been it will be impossible, with the resources of the island for a long time yet to come, to fully meet the demand for the learning so long withheld. The provincial institutions and high schools and the University of Habana have been reorganized.

"During the past summer, through the generosity of Harvard University and its friends, who raised a fund of $70,000 for that purpose, 1,281 Cuban teachers were enabled to attend a summer school of instruction at Cambridge, designed to fit them for their duties. They were drawn from every municipality and almost every town in the island. They were collected from the different ports of the island by five United States transports, which carried them to Boston, and, at the expiration of their visit, took them to New York and thence to Habana and to their homes. They were lodged and boarded in and about the University at Cambridge, and visited the libraries and museums and the educational institutions and manufacturing establishments in the neighborhood of Boston. Through the energy of Mr. Frye money was raised to enable them to visit New York and Washington. They were returned to their homes without a single accident or loss, full of new ideas and of zeal for the educational work in which they had found so much sympathy and encouragement." — *United States, Secretary of War, Annual Report, Nov.* 30, 1900, *pp.* 32–33.

A. D. 1900 (June—November).—**Municipal elections and election of a Constitutional Convention.—Meeting of the Convention.— Statement of the Military Governor.**—"The census having been completed and the period given for Spanish residents to make their election as to citizenship having expired on the 11th of April, 1900, steps were immediately taken for the election of municipal governments by the people. In view of the fact that 66 per cent of the people could not read and write, it was not deemed advisable that absolutely unrestricted suffrage should be established, and, after very full conference with leading Cubans, including all the heads of the great departments of state, a general agreement was reached upon a basis of suffrage, which provided that every native male Cuban or Spaniard who had elected to take Cuban citizenship, of full age, might vote if he either could read and write, or owned real estate or personal property to the value of $250, or had served in and been honorably discharged from the Cuban army; thus according a voice in the government of the country to every one who had the intelligence to acquire the rudiments of learning, the thrift to accumulate property, or the patriotism to fight for his country. On the 18th of April an election law, which aims to apply the best examples of our American election statutes to the existing conditions of Cuba, was promulgated for the guidance of the proposed election. On the 16th of June an election was held throughout the island in which the people of Cuba in all the municipalities, which include the entire island, elected all their municipal officers. The boards of registration and election were composed of Cubans selected by the Cubans themselves. No United States soldier or officer was present at or in the neighborhood of any polling place. There was no disturbance. After the newly elected municipal officers had been installed and commenced the performance of their duties an order was made enlarging the powers of the municipal governments and putting into their hands as much of the government of the people as was practicable.

"As soon as the new municipal governments were fairly established the following call for a constitutional convention was issued: 'Habana, July 25, 1900. The military governor of Cuba directs the publication of the following instructions: Whereas the Congress of the United States by its joint resolution of April 20, 1898, declared That the people of the island of Cuba are, and of right ought to be, free and independent: That the United States hereby disclaims any disposition or intention to exercise sovereignty, jurisdiction, or control over said island except for the pacification thereof, and asserts its determination, when that is accomplished, to leave the govern-

ment and control of the island to its people; And whereas the people of Cuba have established municipal governments, deriving their authority from the suffrages of the people given under just and equal laws, and are now ready, in like manner, to proceed to the establishment of a general government which shall assume and exercise sovereignty, jurisdiction, and control over the island: Therefore

"'It is ordered, That a general election be held in the island of Cuba on the third Saturday of September, in the year nineteen hundred, to elect delegates to a convention to meet in the city of Habana, at twelve o'clock noon on the first Monday of November, in the year nineteen hundred, to frame and adopt a constitution for the people of Cuba, and, as a part thereof, to provide for and agree with the Government of the United States upon the relations to exist between that Government and the Government of Cuba, and to provide for the election by the people of officers under such constitution and the transfer of government to the officers so elected.

"'The election will be held in the several voting precincts of the island under and pursuant to the provisions of the electoral law of April 18, 1900, and the amendments thereof. The people of the several provinces will elect delegates in number proportionate to their populations as determined by the census, viz: The people of the province of Pinar del Rio will elect three (3) delegates. The people of the province of Habana will elect eight (8) delegates. The people of the province of Matanzas will elect four (4) delegates. The people of the province of Santa Clara will elect seven (7) delegates. The people of the province of Puerto Principe will elect two (2) delegates. The people of the province of Santiago de Cuba will elect seven (7) delegates.'

"Under this call a second election was held on the 15th of September, under the same law, with some slight amendments, and under the same conditions as the municipal elections. The election was wholly under the charge of Cubans, and without any participation or interference whatever by officers or troops of the United States. The thirty-one members of the constitutional convention were elected, and they convened at Habana at the appointed time. The sessions of the convention were opened in the city of Habana on the 5th of November by the military governor, with the following statement: 'To the delegates of the Constitutional Convention of Cuba. Gentlemen: As military governor of the island, representing the President of the United States, I call this convention to order. It will be your duty, first, to frame and adopt a constitution for Cuba, and, when that has been done, to formulate what, in your opinion, ought to be the relations between Cuba and the United States. The constitution must be adequate to secure a stable, orderly, and free government.

"'When you have formulated the relations which, in your opinion, ought to exist between Cuba and the United States, the Government of the United States will doubtless take such action on its part as shall lead to a final and authoritative agreement between the people of the two countries for the promotion of their common interests.

"'All friends of Cuba will follow your deliberations with the deepest interest, earnestly desiring that you shall reach just conclusions, and that, by the dignity, individual self-restraint, and wise conservatism which shall characterize your proceedings, the capacity of the Cuban people for representative government may be signally illustrated. The fundamental distinction between true representative government and dictatorship is that in the former every representative of the people, in whatever office, confines himself strictly within the limits of his defined powers. Without such restraint there can be no free constitutional government. Under the order pursuant to which you have been elected and convened you have no duty and no authority to take part in the present government of the island. Your powers are strictly limited by the terms of that order.'"—*United States, Secretary of War, Annual Report, Nov.* 30, 1900, *pp.* 24–32.

A. D. 1900 (December).—Measures for the destruction of the mosquito, as a carrier of yellow fever. See (in this vol.) SCIENCE, RECENT: MEDICAL AND SURGICAL.

A. D. 1900-1901.—Frauds by American officlais in the Havana post office.—Question of the extradition of C. F. W. Neely.—Decision of the Supreme Court of the United States as to the independent status of Cuba in its relations to the United States.—In the spring of 1900 a discovery was made of extensive frauds committed by American officials who had been placed, by U. S. military authority, in the post office at Havana. One of the persons accused, named C. F. W. Neely, having returned to the United States, his extradition, for trial in Cuba, was demanded, and a question thereon arose as to the status of the island of Cuba in its relations to the United States. The case (Neely vs. Henkel) was taken on appeal to the Supreme Court of the United States, and Neely was subjected to extradition by the decision of that tribunal, rendered in January, 1901. The status of Cuba, as an independent foreign territory, was thus defined in the opinion of the Court :

"The legislative and executive branches of the Government, by the joint resolution of April 20, 1898, expressly disclaimed any purpose to exercise sovereignty, jurisdiction, or control over Cuba, 'except for the pacification thereof,' and asserted the determination of the United States, that object being accomplished, to leave the government and control of Cuba to its own people. All that has been done in relation to Cuba has had that end in view, and so far as the court is informed by the public history of the relations of this country with that island, nothing has been done inconsistent with the declared object of the war with Spain. Cuba is none the less foreign territory, within the meaning of the act of Congress, because it is under a military governor appointed by and representing the President in the work of assisting the inhabitants of that island to establish a government of their own, under which, as a free and independent people, they may control their own affairs without interference by other nations. The occupancy of the island by troops of the United States was the necessary result of the war. That result could not have been avoided by the United States consistently with the principles of international law or with its obligations to the people of Cuba. It is true that as between Spain and the United States—indeed, as between the United States and all foreign nations—Cuba, upon the cessation of hostilities with Spain and after the treaty of

Paris, was to be treated as if it were conquered territory. But—as between the United States and Cuba, that island is territory held in trust for the inhabitants of Cuba, to whom it rightfully belongs and to whose exclusive control it will be surrendered when a stable government shall have been established by their voluntary action."

A. D. 1901 (January).—Draft of Constitution reported to the Convention by its Central Committee.—Public sessions of the Constitutional Convention were not opened until the middle of January, 1901, when the draft of a Constitution was reported by its Central Committee, and the text given to the Press. By subsequent action of the Convention, various amendments were made, and the instrument, at this writing (early in April), still awaits finish and adoption. The amendments have been reported imperfectly and the text of the Constitution, even in its present state, cannot be authentically given. It is probable, however, that the structure of government provided for in the draft reported to the Convention stands now and will remain substantially unchanged. An outline of its features is the most that we will venture to give in this place.

The preamble is in these words : "We, the delegates of the Cuban people, having met in assembly for the purpose of agreeing upon the adoption of a fundamental law, which, at the same time that it provides for the constitution into a sovereign and independent nation of the people of Cuba, establishes a solid and permanent form of government, capable of complying with its international obligations, insuring domestic tranquillity, establishing justice, promoting the general welfare, and securing the blessings of liberty to the inhabitants, we do agree upon and adopt the following constitution, in pursuance of the said purpose, invoking the protection of the Almighty, and prompted by the dictates of our conscience."

The form of government is declared to be republican. The guarantees of the Constitution, defined with precision and at length, include "equal rights under the law," protection from arbitrary arrest and imprisonment, freedom of thought, speech, writing and publication, freedom of worship, freedom of association and meeting, freedom of teaching, freedom of travel, inviolability of private dwellings and private papers, "except by order of a competent authority and with the formalities prescribed by the laws."

Legislative powers are to be exercised by two elective bodies, to be named House of Representatives and Senate, and conjointly known as Congress. The Senate to be composed of six senators elected from each of the six departments of the republic; the boundaries and names of the departments to be those of the present provinces "as long as not modified by the laws." The terms of the senators to be six years, one third of their number to be elected every two years. The House of Representatives to be composed of "one representative for every 25,000 inhabitants or fraction of more than 12,000, elected for a period of four years, by direct vote, and in the manner prescribed by law"; one half to be elected every two years. Representatives and Senators not to be held responsible for opinions expressed in the exercise of their duties, and not to be arrested nor tried without the consent of the body to which they belong, "except in case of being discovered in the act of committing some crime." Congress to meet in regular session every year on the first Monday in November, and to remain in session for at least ninety consecutive days, excepting holidays and Sundays. Its powers to be substantially the same as those exercised by the Congress of the United States.

The executive power to be exercised by the President of the republic, who "shall be elected by direct votes, and an absolute majority thereof, cast on one single day, in accordance with the provisions of the law." The term of the President to be four years, and none to be elected for three consecutive terms. A Vice-President to be elected "in the same manner as the President, conjointly with the latter and for a like term."

The judicial power to be "exercised by the Supreme Court of Justice and such other courts as may be established by law." The Supreme Court, like that of the United States, "to decide as to the constitutionality of legislative acts that may have been objected to as unconstitutional," and to have an appellant jurisdiction corresponding to that of the Supreme Court of the United States.

Over each of the six departments or provinces it is provided that there shall be a governor, "elected by a direct vote for a period of three years," and a Departmental Assembly, "to consist of not less than eight or more than twenty, elected by direct vote for a like period of three years." The Departmental Assemblies to "have the right of independent action in all things not antagonistic to the constitution, to the general laws nor to international treaties, nor to that which pertains to the inherent rights of the municipalities, which may concern the department, such as the establishment and maintenance of institutions of public education, public charities, public departmental roads, means of communication by water or sea, the preparation of their budgets, and the appointment and removal of their employés."

The "municipal terminos" are to be governed by "Ayuntamientos," composed of Councilmen elected by a direct vote in the manner prescribed by law, and by a Mayor, elected in like manner. The Ayuntamientos to be self-governing, free to "take action on all matters that solely and exclusively concern their municipal termino, such as appointment and removal of employés, preparation of their budgets, freely establishing the means of income to meet them without any other limitation than that of making them compatible with the general system of taxation of the republic."

The provision for amendment of the Constitution is as follows: "The constitution cannot be changed in whole or part except by two-thirds vote of both legislative bodies. Six months after deciding on the reform, a Constitutional Assembly shall be elected, which shall confine itself to the approval or disapproval of the reform voted by the legislative bodies. These will continue in their functions independently of the Constitutional Assembly. The members in this Assembly shall be equal to the number of the members in the two legislative bodies together."

A. D. 1901 (February—March).—Conditions on which the government of the island will be yielded to its people prescribed by the **Congress of the United States.**—In the call for a Constitutional Convention issued by the military governor on the 25th of July, 1900 (see above), it was set forth that the duty of the Convention would be "to frame and adopt a constitution for the people of Cuba, and, as a part thereof, to provide for and agree with the government of the United States upon the relations to exist between that government and the government of Cuba." This intimated an intention on the part of the government of the United States to attach conditions to its recognition of the independent government for which the Convention was expected to provide. The intimation was conveyed still more plainly to the Constitutional Convention by Military Governor Wood, at the opening of its sessions, when he said: "When you have formulated the relations which, in your opinion, ought to exist between Cuba and the United States, the government of the United States will doubtless take such action on its part as shall lead to a final and authoritative agreement between the two countries for the promotion of their common interests." The Convention, however, gave no sign of a disposition to act as desired by the government of the United States, and seemed likely to finish its work, either without touching the subject of relations between the Cuban and American Republics, or else offering proposals that would not meet the wishes of the latter. Those wishes were made known to the Convention in flat terms, at length, by the military governor, and its prompt action was urged, in order that the judgment of the Congress of the United States might be pronounced on what it did. But the day on which the session of Congress would expire drew near, and still nothing came from the Cubans, who seem to have understood that they were exempted from such dictation by the resolution which Congress adopted on the 18th of April, 1898, when it took up the Cuban cause [see (in this vol.) UNITED STATES OF AM.: A. D. 1898 (APRIL)], declaring that "the United States hereby disclaims any disposition or intention to exercise sovereignty, jurisdiction, or control over said island [of Cuba], except for the pacification thereof, and asserts its determination when that is accomplished to leave the government and control of the island to its people."

Unwilling to be left to deal, alone, with the question thus arising between the Cubans and their liberators, President McKinley caused it to be understood that he should call an extra session of Congress, if no Congressional expression on the subject of Cuban relations was found practicable before the 4th of March. This stimulated action in the expiring Congress, and the Army Appropriation Bill, then pending in the Senate, was made the vehicle of legislation on the subject, by the hasty insertion therein of the following amendment, offered by Senator Platt, of Connecticut:

"In fulfillment of the declaration contained in the joint resolution approved April 20, 1898, entitled 'For the recognition of the independence of the people of Cuba, demanding that the Government of Spain relinquish its authority and government in the island of Cuba, and to withdraw its land and naval forces from Cuba and Cuban waters, and directing the President of the United States to use the land and naval forces of the United States to carry these resolutions into effect,' the President is hereby authorized to ' leave the government and control of the island of Cuba to its people,' so soon as a government shall have been established in said island under a constitution which, either as a part thereof or in an ordinance appended thereto, shall define the future relations of the United States with Cuba, substantially as follows :

I.

"That the government of Cuba shall never enter into any treaty or other compact with any foreign power or powers which will impair or tend to impair the independence of Cuba, nor in any manner authorize or permit any foreign power or powers to obtain by colonization or for military or naval purposes or otherwise, lodgment in or control over any portion of said island.

II.

"That said government shall not assume or contract any public debt, to pay the interest upon which, and to make reasonable sinking fund provision for the ultimate discharge of which, the ordinary revenues of the island, after defraying the current expenses of government, shall be inadequate.

III.

"That the government of Cuba consents that the United States may exercise the right to intervene for the preservation of Cuban independence, the maintenance of a government adequate for the protection of life, property, and individual liberty, and for discharging the obligations with respect to Cuba imposed by the treaty of Paris on the United States, now to be assumed and undertaken by the government of Cuba.

IV.

"That all acts of the United States in Cuba during its military occupancy thereof are ratified and validated, and all lawful rights acquired thereunder shall be maintained and protected.

V.

"That the government of Cuba will execute,

and as far as necessary extend, the plans already devised or other plans to be mutually agreed upon, for the sanitation of the cities of the island, to the end that a recurrence of epidemic and infectious diseases may be prevented, thereby assuring protection to the people and commerce of Cuba, as well as to the commerce of the Southern ports of the United States and the people residing therein.

VI.

"That the Isle of Pines shall be omitted from the proposed constitutional boundaries of Cuba, the title thereto being left to future adjustment by treaty.

VII.

"That to enable the United States to maintain the independence of Cuba, and to protect the people thereof, as well as for its own defence, the government of Cuba will sell or lease to the United States lands necessary for coaling or naval stations at certain specified points, to be agreed upon with the President of the United States.

VIII.

"That by way of further assurance the government of Cuba will embody the foregoing provisions in a permanent treaty with the United States."

The Platt Amendment, as it is known, was adopted by the Senate on the 27th of February (yeas 43, nays 20, not voting 25), and concurred in by the House on the 1st of March (yeas 161, nays 136, not voting 56). The opponents of the amendment were weakened by their dread of an extra session of Congress, and by their knowledge that the party of the administration would be still stronger in the new Congress than in that which expired on the 4th of March. Otherwise, no vote on the measure could have been reached before that date.

At the time of this writing, the effect in Cuba of the declarations of the Congress of the United States remains in doubt. The Constitutional Convention has taken no action upon them.

CULEBRA. See (in this vol.) PORTO RICO: AREA AND POPULATION.

CUMULATIVE VOTING. See (in this vol.) BELGIUM : A. D. 1894–1895.

CURTIS ACT, The. See (in this vol.) INDIANS, AMERICAN : A. D. 1893–1899.

CURZON, George N., Baron: Appointed Viceroy of India. See (in this vol.) INDIA : A. D. 1898 (SEPTEMBER).

CZECH PARTIES. See (in this vol.) AUSTRIA-HUNGARY : A. D. 1897.

D.

DAHOMEY: A. D. 1895.—Under a Governor-General of French West Africa. See (in this vol.) AFRICA: A. D. 1895 (FRENCH WEST AFRICA).

A. D. 1897.—Settlement of Tongaland boundary. See (in this vol.) AFRICA: A. D. 1897 (DAHOMEY AND TONGALAND).

DAMASCUS, Railway to. See (in this vol.) JEWS: A. D. 1899.

DARGAI, Battle of. See (in this vol.) INDIA: A. D. 1897–1898.

"DARKEST ENGLAND" SCHEME, Results from General Booth's. See (in this vol.) SALVATION ARMY.

DAVIS, General George W.: Military Governor of Porto Rico. See (in this vol.) PORTO RICO: A. D. 1898–1899 (OCTOBER—OCTOBER).

Report on the Civil Government of Porto Rico. See (in this vol.) PORTO RICO: A. D. 1898–1899 (AUGUST—JULY).

DAWES COMMISSION, The work of the. See (in this vol.) INDIANS, AMERICAN : A. D. 1893–1899.

DE BEERS CONSOLIDATED MINING COMPANY: Complicity in the Jameson Raid. See (in this vol.) SOUTH AFRICA (CAPE COLONY): A. D. 1896 (JULY).

DECLARATION AGAINST TRANSUBSTANTIATION, The English King's. See (in this vol.) ENGLAND: A. D. 1901 (FEBRUARY).

DELAGOA BAY, and the railway to Pretoria. See (in this vol.) SOUTH AFRICA (THE TRANSVAAL): A. D. 1895 (JULY) and (SEPTEMBER—DECEMBER).

DELAGOA BAY ARBITRATION.—"On December 11th, 1875, Portugal concluded a treaty with the Transvaal Government under which the latter Government bound itself to continue the line of railway — which the Portuguese Government proposed to build from Lourenço-Marques to the Transvaal frontier — 'up to a centre of production and consumption which should insure the traffic of the line and the development of international commerce.' The Portuguese Government then began to look about for a concessionaire and contractor for this line, and after some research, eventually came to terms with one Colonel Edward McMurdo, a citizen of the United States of America, who undertook to build the line without any Government subvention, — a matter of some importance to the Portuguese Government, — but upon certain conditions, of which the most important was that the concessionaire should have the right to fix the tariffs without any State interference. A contract . . . was drawn up and executed in Lisbon on December 14th, 1883." The government bound itself to grant no concession for a rival railway from the coast to the Transvaal boundary, and gave the contractor certain valuable mining rights and grants of land. On his part he was to complete the road within three years. He formed a Portuguese company for the purpose, and seems to have been prepared for success in his undertaking, when rumors began to circulate that the Transvaal government had secured from that of Portugal the right to build a steam tramway from the eastern terminus of its own line to the coast. These rumors were contradicted by the Portuguese government; but are said to have been eventually confirmed. Five months after the signing of the contract with Colonel McMurdo, the Portuguese authorities, it seems, had actually violated it in the manner described. Henceforth the contractor appears to have had every possible embarrassment thrown in his way by combined action of the Portuguese and Boer governments. His Portuguese company was broken down, but he organized another in England, which struggled on with the enterprise until 1889, when a decree from Lisbon rescinded the concession, declared the railway forfeited, and ordered military possession of it to be taken. The sufferers in the matter, being British and American citizens, appealed then to their respective governments. and both intervened in their behalf. The result was a reference of the matter to the arbitration of Switzerland. So much was settled in June, 1891 ; but it was not until March, 1900, that the judgment of the arbitrators was pronounced. They awarded to the Delagoa Bay Company, as its due on the railway, 13,980,000 francs. "To this is added a sum of fr. 2,000,000 as an indemnity for the land grant, which brings

the total award (less £28,000 paid by Portugal on account in 1890) to fr. 15,314,000 (or about £612,560), with interest at 5 per cent. from June 25th, 1889, to the date of payment. The amount of this award came as a considerable shock to the claimants, as well it might. It was insufficient to pay even the bonds in full (including interest at 7 per cent.), and left nothing whatever for the shareholders, while even the expenses are to be borne by each party equally." — M. McIlwraith, *The Delagoa Bay Arbitration (Fortnightly Rev., Sept., 1900).*

DELAWARE: A. D. 1897.—A new Constitution.—A new constitution for the State of Delaware, which went into effect June 10, 1897, provides that after January 1, 1900, no citizen shall vote who cannot write his name and read the constitution in the English language. It also provides a registration fee of one dollar as a qualification to vote.

DEMOCRACY: In the Nineteenth Century. See (in this vol.) NINETEENTH CENTURY : THE TREND.
Pope Leo's Encyclical concerning. See (in this vol.) PAPACY: A. D. 1901.

DEMOCRATIC EXPERIMENTS, New Zealand. See (in this vol.) NEW ZEALAND : A. D. 1891–1900.

DEMOCRATIC PARTY, and the Silver Question in the United States. See (in this vol.) UNITED STATES OF AM. : A. D. 1896 (JUNE—NOVEMBER); and 1900 (MAY—NOVEMBER).

DENMARK: A. D. 1899.—Complaints from Danish Sleswick of German treatment. See (in this vol.) GERMANY : A. D. 1899.
A. D. 1899.—Representation in the Peace Conference at The Hague. See (in this vol.) PEACE CONFERENCE.

DÉROULÈDE, Paul: Trial and conviction for treasonable conspiracy. See (in this vol.) FRANCE : A. D. 1899 (FEBRUARY—JUNE); and 1899–1900 (AUGUST—JANUARY).

DERVISHES, of the Sudan, The. See (in this vol.) EGYPT : A. D. 1885–1896 ; 1897–1898 ; and 1899–1900.

DEVIL'S ISLAND. See (in this vol.) FRANCE : A. D. 1897–1899.

DEWEY, Admiral George : Destruction of Spanish fleet in Manila Bay. See (in this vol.) UNITED STATES OF AM. : A. D. 1898 (APRIL—JULY).

DIAMOND JUBILEE, Queen Victoria's. See (in this vol.) ENGLAND : A. D. 1897 (JUNE).

DIAZ, Porfirio : The results of twenty years of his Presidency in Mexico. See (in this vol.) MEXICO : A. D. 1898–1900.

DINGLEY TARIFF, The. See (in this vol.) UNITED STATES OF AM. : A. D. 1897 (MARCH—JULY) ; and 1899–1901.

DIPHTHERIA : Discovery of antitoxine treatment of. See (in this vol.) SCIENCE, RECENT : MEDICAL AND SURGICAL.

DIR : Inclusion in a new British Indian province. See (in this vol.) INDIA : A. D. 1901 (FEBRUARY).

DISCOVERIES, Scientific: Comparison of the Nineteenth Century with preceding ages. See (in this vol.) NINETEENTH CENTURY: COMPARISON.

DISFRANCHISEMENT OF THE NE-GRO. See (in this vol.) MISSISSIPPI; LOUISIANA; NORTH CAROLINA: A. D. 1900; SOUTH CAROLINA: A. D. 1896; MARYLAND; and UNITED STATES OF AM.: A. D. 1901 (JANUARY).

DISPENSARY LAWS. See (in this vol.) SOUTH CAROLINA: A. D. 1892-1899; NORTH CAROLINA: A. D. 1897-1899; SOUTH DAKOTA: A. D. 1899; and ALABAMA: A. D. 1899.

DIVINE RIGHT, Kingship by: German revival of the doctrine. See (in this vol.) GERMANY: A. D. 1894-1899.

DOMINICA: Condition and relief measures. See (in this vol.) WEST INDIES, THE BRITISH: A. D. 1897.

DOMINICAN REPUBLIC: A. D. 1899. —Assassination of President Heureaux.—Revolution.—Election of President Jiminez. —General D. Ulises Heureaux, President of the Republic, was shot through the heart by an assassin and instantly killed, on the 26th of July. "He was in his fourth consecutive term as president, and had occupied that position for fifteen years, although still a young man. San Domingo had been more free from revolution, more prosperous, better inclined toward outside capital and enterprise, and more disposed toward the ways of modern civilization under Heureaux, than at any previous time for many decades. Although nominally a republic, San Domingo was ruled by this iron-willed and resolute negro with a stern despotism hardly matched by any other contemporary government on earth. He was superior to all law. He constantly made use of the practice of executing officials, generals, and well-known public men with his own hand whenever dissatisfied with them. Still more frequently, when the objects of his disapproval were not within easy traveling distance, he gave orders to some officer or subordinate, dependent upon his favor, to undertake an assassination. Failure to comply promptly and successfully with such a mandate meant death to the men who failed. These statements convey no exaggerated impression of the way in which Heureaux has ruled San Domingo, nipped insurrection in the bud, and kept himself in power. . . . He always excused his ruthlessness on the ground of public necessity. Of course, it was inevitable that such a man should sooner or later be assassinated himself."—*Am. Review of Reviews, Sept.,* 1899.

According to the provisions of the constitution, the Vice-President, General Figuereo, succeeded to the presidency; but an insurrection against his government was so rapidly successful that he resigned his office on the 31st of August, and a provisional government was created, pending arrangements for an election. The recognized leader of the revolutionary movement was Juan Isidro Jiminez, who had been compelled, some years before, to quit San Domingo, on account of his opposition to Heureaux, leaving a large property behind. Since that time he had been a successful and well-known merchant in New York. Latterly, Jiminez had

established himself in Cuba, whence he attempted to assist as well as direct the revolution in the neighboring island; but the United States authorities objected to such use being made of neutral territory, and he was placed for a time under arrest. When released, however, he was permitted to proceed to San Domingo, without men or arms, and there he was elected President, assuming the office on the 14th of November.

A. D. 1900.—Commercial Convention with the United States. See (in this vol.) UNITED STATES OF AM.: A. D. 1899-1901.

DOMOKO, Battle of. See (in this vol.) TURKEY: A. D. 1897 (MARCH—SEPTEMBER).

DONGOLA, Expedition to. See (in this vol.) EGYPT: A. D. 1885-1896.

DREYFUS AFFAIR, The. See (in this vol. FRANCE: A. D. 1897-1899.

Closed by the Amnesty Bill. See (in this vol.) FRANCE: A. D. 1900 (DECEMBER).

DRIEFONTEIN, Battle of. See (in this vol.) SOUTH AFRICA (THE FIELD OF WAR): A. D. 1900 (MARCH—MAY).

DRIFTS, Closing of the Vaal River. See (in this vol.) SOUTH AFRICA (THE TRANSVAAL): A. D. 1895 (SEPTEMBER—DECEMBER).

DUM-DUM BULLET, The.—The dum-dum bullet, about which there was much discussion at The Hague Peace Conference, is constructed to spread slightly at the point. All modern rifle bullets have an outer jacket of hard metal, to take the grooving of the gun-barrel. "Originally the jacket was thickest at the point, and so strong that, while penetration was enormous, stopping power was wanting; in other words, one bullet might easily go through half a dozen men, yet, unless it happened to hit a vital spot or a bone, they need not be disabled, and might therefore continue to fight. This was amply illustrated in the Chitral campaign, during which our soldiers began to lose confidence in their weapon, while the enemy, quick to recognize the different effect of volleys, were inclined to attack British infantry armed with the Lee-Metford rather than native infantry armed with the Martini-Henry. The Indian military authorities at once set about designing a bullet which, while maintaining range, should have the required stopping power. The result was the dum-dum bullet—so named after the place near Calcutta where it is made—of which much has been heard. The difference in appearance between it and the original pattern is comparatively slight. The shape is exactly the same, but the jacket is differently arranged; instead of having its greatest strength at the point, it is weakest there—indeed, at the apex a small part of the core is uncovered, but does not project." —*Quarterly Review, July,* 1899.

DUTCH EAST INDIES: A. D. 1894.—Revolt in Lombok.—A rising in the island of Lombok, one of the Lesser Sunda group, which began in August, proved a troublesome affair. "The cause of the rebellion was the concession made to the Sassaks, to be henceforth governed by their own chiefs, instead of by the Balinian chiefs, who had hitherto been all-powerful. During the continuance of the hostilities, the Sassaks remained constantly faithful to the

Dutch, and fought against the Balinians, who, although far inferior in numbers, had, nevertheless, oppressed their fellow-islanders for many years; but the courage, energy and audacity of the Balinians were well known, and as early as 1868 the Dutch troops had been in serious conflict with them. The news of this disaster aroused in Holland great excitement, and public opinion was unanimous in its demand for speedy and energetic reprisals. Several severe and bloody encounters took place, but finally the Dutch troops, under the orders of General Vetter, succeeded in making the Rajah of Lombok prisoner, his immense wealth falling at the same time into the hands of the victors."—*Annual Register*, 1894, *p.* 308.

DYNAMITE MONOPOLY, The Boer. See (in this vol.) SOUTH AFRICA (THE TRANSVAAL): A. D. 1895 (NOVEMBER).

E.

EAGAN, General Charles P. : The case of. See (in this vol.) UNITED STATES OF AM.: A. D. 1899 (JANUARY).

EAST AFRICA, German: Trade, etc. See (in this vol.) GERMANY : A. D. 1899 (JUNE).

EAST AFRICA PROTECTORATE, British. See (in this vol.) BRITISH EAST AFRICA PROTECTORATE : A. D. 1895-1897.

EAST INDIES, Dutch. See (in this vol.) DUTCH EAST INDIES.

ECCLESIASTICAL LAWS, The Hungarian. See (in this vol.) AUSTRIA-HUNGARY : A. D. 1894-1895.

ECUADOR: A. D. 1894-1899.—Successful Revolution.—**Government** measures against the Church.—In the fall of 1894 the government of Chile sold ostensibly to that of Ecuador a war vessel, which the latter at once transferred to Japan, then at war with China. The round-about transaction was regarded with suspicion, the Ecuadorian government being accused of a corrupt agency in it, to cover the Chilian breach of neutrality. Much feeling on the subject was excited in the country, and this gave to the Radical party an opportunity to stir up revolt. They improved it with success. After an obstinate civil war of more than six months the government of President Cordero was overthrown, and General Aloy Alfaro, the revolutionist leader, was inaugurated Executive Chief of the, Republic on the 4th of November, 1895. The defeated Conservatives, stimulated by the clergy, were quickly in arms again, in the summer of 1896, but again they were overcome, and the government of Alfaro began to deal severely with the religious orders and the Church. Much of the Church property was confiscated, and the inmates of religious houses are said to have fled in considerable numbers to other countries. In October, 1896, a National Convention was held and the constitution revised. Among other changes, it imposed limitations on the former power of the Church, and extended religious freedom to other sects. In 1897 the Indians who had supported Alfaro two years before were admitted to citizenship. A renewed attempt at revolution, that year, organized and armed in Colombia, was suppressed with the help of the Colombian government. The same fate attended another undertaking of rebellion in January, 1899 ; but it was overcome only after a hard fought battle.

A. D. 1900.—Commercial Convention with the United States. See (in this vol.) UNITED STATES OF AM.: A. D. 1899-1901.

ECUMENICAL CONFERENCE ON MISSIONS. See (in this vol.) MISSIONS.

6–13

EDUCATION: Australia and New Zealand.—Progress of educational work. See (in this vol.) AUSTRALIA : RECENT EXTENSIONS OF DEMOCRACY.

Birth of educational systems in the Nineteenth Century. See (in this vol.) NINETEENTH CENTURY: THE TREND.

Canada : A. D. 1890-1896.—The Manitoba School Question. See (in this vol.) CANADA: A. D. 1890–1896.

Canada: A. D. 1898.—Encyclical Letter of Pope Leo XIII. on the Manitoba School Question. See (in this vol.) CANADA : A. D. 1898 (JANUARY).

Belgium : A. D. 1895.—Religious teaching restored.—A new school law was carried in Belgium, against fierce opposition from the Liberals and Socialists, which restores obligatory religious teaching in both public and private schools. Parents are permitted, however, to withhold their children from the instruction that is given during school hours by Catholic priests, on attesting in writing that it is their wish to do so.

Congo State: The Belgian provision of schools. See (in this vol.) CONGO FREE STATE : A. D. 1899.

Cuba: A. D. 1898.—As left by the Spaniards. See (in this vol.) CUBA: A. D. 1898–1899 (DECEMBER—OCTOBER).

Cuba: A. D. 1900.—Organization of public schools. See (in this vol.) CUBA: A. D. 1900.

Egypt: Gordon Memorial College at Khartoum. See (in this vol.) EGYPT: A. D. 1898–1899.

England: A. D. 1896-1897.—" The Voluntary Schools Act " and " The Elementary Education Act." See (in this vol.) ENGLAND: A. D. 1896–1897.

England: A. D. 1899.—Creation of a Board of Education. See (in this vol.) ENGLAND: A. D. 1899 (AUGUST).

England: A. D. 1900.—Age at which children may leave school raised from eleven to twelve years. See (in this vol.) ENGLAND: A. D. 1900 (FEBRUARY).

Hawaii: Progress of educational work. See (in this vol.) HAWAII : A. D. 1900.

Japan : 1897.—Restriction of religious teaching. See (in this vol.) JAPAN: A. D. 1899 (AUGUST).

Japan: A. D. 1899.—A Japanese injunction to students concerning behavior to foreigners. See (in this vol.) JAPAN : A. D. 1899 (JULY).

Mexico: Progress of educational work. See (in this vol.) MEXICO: A. D. 1898–1900.

Philippine Islands: A. D. 1898.—Schools and colleges under the Spanish régime.— " The only educational advantages attainable by the common people of the archipelago are those afforded by the primary schools. The Spanish regulations provided that there should be one male and one female primary school teacher for each 5,000 inhabitants, instruction being given separately to the two sexes. This wretchedly inadequate provision was, as a matter of fact, never carried out. . . . From [a table showing the relation between number of primary school teachers and population in the several provinces, etc.] it appears that the number of teachers of each sex required by law for a population of 6,709,810 is 1,342, making a total of 2,684 teachers, whereas there are in reality but, 991 male teachers and 923 female teachers, giving a total of 1,914. Disregarding the question of sex, we see that while there should be one teacher for each 2,500 inhabitants, there is in reality but one to each 3,500, even if we include only that portion of the population sufficiently civilized to be taken account of in the above enumeration. Taking the entire population at 8,000,000, we find that there is but one teacher to each 4,179 individuals. Examination of the . . . table further shows that in many instances the lack of teachers is greater in those provinces which are most thickly populated and whose people are most highly civilized. . . .

"While most of the small towns have one teacher of each sex, in the larger towns and cities no adequate provision is made for the increased teaching force necessary; so that places of 30,000 or 40,000 inhabitants are often no better off as regards number of teachers than are other places in the same province of but 1,500 or 2,000 souls. The hardship thus involved for children desiring a primary education will be better understood if one stops to consider the nature of the Philippine 'pueblo,' which is really a township, often containing within its limits a considerable number of distinct and important villages or towns, from the most important of which the township takes its name. The others, under distinct names, are known as 'barrios,' or wards. It is often quite impossible for small children to attend school at the particular town which gives its name to the township on account of their distance from it. . . .

"The character and amount of the instruction which has heretofore been furnished is also worthy of careful consideration. The regulations for primary schools were as follows: 'Instruction in schools for natives shall for the present be reduced to elementary primary instruction and shall consist of — 1. Christian doctrine and principles of morality and sacred history suitable for children. 2. Reading. 3. Writing. 4. Practical instruction in Spanish, including grammar and orthography. 5. Principles of arithmetic. comprising the four rules for figures, common fractions, decimal fractions, and instruction in the metric system with its equivalents in ordinary weights and measures. 6. Instruction in general geography and Spanish history. 7. Instruction in practical agriculture as applied to the products of the country. 8. Rules of deportment. 9. Vocal music.'

"It will be noted that education in Christian doctrine is placed before reading and writing, and, if the natives are to be believed, in many of the more remote districts instruction began and ended with this subject and was imparted in the local native dialect at that. It is further and

persistently charged that the instruction in Spanish was in very many cases purely imaginary, because the local friars, who were formerly 'ex officio' school inspectors, not only prohibited it, but took active measures to enforce their dictum. . . . Ability to read and write a little of the local native language was comparatively common. Instruction in geography was extremely superficial. As a rule no maps or charts were available, and such information as was imparted orally was left to the memory of the pupil, unaided by any graphic method of presentation. The only history ever taught was that of Spain, and that under conventional censorship. The history of other nations was a closed volume to the average Filipino. . . . The course as above outlined was that prescribed for boys. Girls were not given instruction in geography, history, or agriculture, but in place of these subjects were supposed to receive instruction 'in employments suitable to their sex.'

"It should be understood that the criticisms which have been here made apply to the provincial schools. The primary instruction given at the Ateneo Municipal at Manila, under the direction of the Jesuits, fulfilled the requirements of the law, and in some particulars exceeded them. . . . The only official institution for secondary education in the Philippines was the College of San Juan de Letran, which was in charge of the Dominican Friars and was under the control of the university authorities. Secondary education was also given in the Ateneo Municipal of Manila, by the Jesuit Fathers, and this institution was better and more modern in its methods than any other in the archipelago. But although the Jesuits provided the instruction, the Dominicans held the examinations. . . . There are two normal schools in Manila, one for the education of male and the other for the education of female teachers. . . . The only institutions for higher education in the Philippines have been the Royal and Pontifical University of Santo Tomas, and the Royal College of San-José, which has for the past twenty-five years been under the direction of the university authorities."—*Report of the Philippine Commission, Jan. 1, 1900, v. 1, pt. 3.*

Porto Rico: A. D. **1898.**—Spanish schools and teachers. See (in this vol.) PORTO RICO: A. D. 1898–1899 (AUGUST—JULY).

Porto Rico: A. D. **1900.**—First steps in the creation of a public school system. See (in this vol.) PORTO RICO: A. D. 1900 (AUGUST—OCTOBER).

Russia: Student troubles in the universities. See (in this vol.) RUSSIA: A. D. 1899 (FEBRUARY—JUNE); 1900; and 1901.

Tunis: Schools under the French **Protectorate.** See (in this vol.) TUNIS: A. D. 1881–1898.

United States: Indian schools. See (in this vol.) INDIANS, AMERICAN: A. D. 1899–1900.

United States: A. D. **1896.**—Princeton University.—The one hundred and fiftieth anniversary of the founding of the institution at Princeton, N. J., which had borne the name of "The College of New Jersey," was celebrated on the 20th, 21st, and 22d of October, 1896, with ceremonies in which many representatives from famous seats of learning in Europe and America took part. The proceedings included a formal change of name, to Princeton University.

United States: A. D. **1900.**—Women **as** students **and as** teachers. See (in this vol.) NINETEENTH CENTURY : THE WOMAN'S CENTURY.

EDWARD VII., King of England.—Ac-

cession.—English estimate of his character See (in this vol.) ENGLAND: A. D. 1901 (JANUARY—FEBRUARY).

Opening of his first Parliament.—The Royal Test Oath. See (in this vol.) ENGLAND: A. D. 1901 (FEBRUARY).

EGYPT.

Recent Archæological Explorations and their result.—Discovery of prehistoric remains.—Light on the first dynasties. See (in this vol.) ARCHÆOLOGICAL RESEARCH : EGYPT : RESULTS.

A. D. **1885-1896.** — Abandonment of the Egyptian Sudan to the Dervishes.—Death of the Mahdi and reign of the Khalifa.—Beginning of **a new** Anglo-Egyptian movement for the recovery of the Sudan.—The expedition to Dongola.—After the failure to rescue General Gordon from the Mahdists at Khartoum (see, in vol. 1, EGYPT : A. D. 1884-1885), the British government, embarrassed in other quarters, felt compelled to evacuate the Sudan. Before it did so the Mahdi had finished his career, having died of small-pox in June, 1885, and one of his three chief commanders, styled khalifas, had acquired authority over the Dervish army and reigned in his place. This was the Khalifa Abdullah, a chieftain of the Baggara tribe. Khartoum had been destroyed, and Omdurman, on the opposite side of the river, became his capital. The rule of the Khalifa was soon made so cruelly despotic, and so much in the interest of his own tribe, that incessant rebellions in many parts of his dominions restrained him from any vigorous undertaking of the conquest of Egypt, which was the great object of Dervish desire. But his able and energetic lieutenant in the Eastern Sudan, Osman Digna, was a serious menace to the Egyptian forces holding Suakin, under Major Watson, at first, and afterwards Colonel Kitchener, were holding command, under General Grenfell, who was then the Egyptian Sirdar, or military chief. Osman Digna, however, was defeated in all his attempts. At the same time the Khalifa was desperately at war with the Negus, John, of Abyssinia, who fell in a great battle at Galabat (March, 1889), and whose death at the crisis of the battle threw his army into confusion and caused its defeat. Menelek, king of the feudatory state of Shoa, acquired the Abyssinian crown, and war with the Dervishes was stopped. Then they began an advance down the Nile, and suffered a great defeat from the British and Egyptian troops, at Toski, on the 17th of August, 1889. From that time, for several years, "there was no real menace to Egypt," and little was heard of the Khalifa. "His territories were threatened on all sides: on the north by the British in Egypt ; on the south by the British in Uganda; on the west by the Belgians in the Congo Free State, and by the French in the Western Soudan ; whilst the Italians held Kassala on the east ; so that the Khalifa preferred to husband his resources until the inevitable day should arrive when he would have to fight for his position."

A crisis in the situation came in 1896. The Egyptian army, organized and commanded by British officers, had become a strong fighting force, on which its leaders could depend. Its Sirdar was now Major-General Sir Herbert Kitchener, who succeeded General Grenfell in 1892. Suddenly there came news, early in March, 1896, of the serious reverse which the Italians had suffered at Adowa, in their war with the Abyssinians (see, in this vol., ITALY : A. D. 1895–1896). " The consternation felt in England and Egypt at this disaster deepened when it became known that Kassala, which was held by the Italian forces, was hemmed in, and seriously threatened by 10,000 Dervishes, and that Osman Digna was marching there with reinforcements. If Kassala fell into the hands of the Dervishes, the latter would be let loose to overrun the Nile valley on the frontier of Egypt, and threaten that country itself. As if in anticipation of these reinforcements, the Dervishes suddenly assumed an offensive attitude, and it was rumoured that a large body of Dervishes were contemplating an immediate advance on Egypt. . . . A totally new situation was now created, and immediate action was rendered imperative. Everything was ripe for an expedition up the Nile. Whilst creating a diversion in favour of the Italians besieged at Kassala, it afforded an opportunity of creating a stronger barrier than the Wady Halfa boundary between Egypt and the Dervishes, and it would moreover be an important step towards the long-wished-for recovery of the Soudan. The announcement of the contemplated expedition was made in the House of Commons on the 17th of March, 1896, by Mr. Curzon, Under-Secretary for Foreign Affairs. It came as a great surprise to the whole country, which, having heard so little of the Dervishes of late years, was not prepared for a recrudescence of the Soudan question. [But a vote of censure on the Egyptian policy of the government, moved by Mr. John Morley in the House of Commons, was rejected by 288 to 145.] . . .

"An unexpected difficulty arose in connection with the financing of the expedition. This is explained very plainly and concisely in the 'Annual Register,' 1896, which we quote at length: —' In order to defray the cost of the undertaking, it being obviously desirable to impose as little strain as possible on the slowly recovering finances of Egypt, it was determined by the Egyptian Government to apply for an advance of £500,000 from the General Reserve Fund of the Caisse de la Dette, and the authorities of the Caisse obligingly handed over the money. . . . However, the French and Russian members of the Caisse de la Dette protested against the loan which the Caisse had made. . . . In December (1896) the International Court of Appeal required the Egyptian Government to refund to the Caisse the £500,000 which they had secured. The very next day Lord Cromer offered an English loan to make good the advance. The Egyptian Government accepted his offer, and repaid immediately the £500,000 to the Caisse, and the result of this somewhat absurd transaction is that England has thus strengthened her hold in another small point on the Government of Egypt.'"—H. S. L. Alford, and W. D. Sword, *The Egyptian Soudan, its Loss and Recovery, ch.* 4 (*London: Macmillan & Co.*).

On the 21st of March, the Sirdar left Cairo for Assouan and Wady Halfa, and various Egyptian battalions were hurried up the river. Meantime, the forces already on the frontier had moved forward and taken the advanced post of the Dervishes, at Akasheh. From that point the Sirdar was ready to begin his advance early in June, and did so with two columns, a River Column and a Desert Column, the latter including a camel corps and a squadron of infantry mounted on camels, besides cavalry, horse artillery and Maxim guns. Ferket, on the east bank of the Nile, 16 miles from Akasheh, was taken after hard fighting on the 7th of June, many of the Dervishes refusing quarter and resisting to the death. They lost, it was estimated, 1,000 killed and wounded, and 500 were taken prisoners. The Egyptian loss was slight. The Dervishes fell back some fifty miles, and the Sirdar halted at Suarda during three months, while the railroad was pushed forward, steamers dragged up the cataracts and stores concentrated, the army suffering greatly, meantime, from an alarming epidemic of cholera and from exhausting labors in a season of terrific heat. In the middle of September the advance was resumed, and, on the 23d, Dongola was reached. Seeing themselves outnumbered, the enemy there retreated, and the town, or its ruins, was taken with only a few shots from the steamers on the river. "As a consequence of the fall of Dongola every Dervish fled for his life from the province. The mounted men made off across the desert direct to Omdurman, and the foot soldiers took the Nile route to Berber, always being careful to keep out of range of the gunboats, which were prevented by the Fourth Cataract from pursuing them beyond Merawi." — C. Royle, *The Egyptian Campaigns, new and revised ed., to December,* 1899, *ch.* 70-71.

The Emir who commanded at Dongola was a comparatively young man, Mohammed Wad el Bishara, who seems to have been possessed by a very genuinely religious spirit, as shown in the following letter, which he had written to the Dervish commander at Ferket, just before the battle there, and which was found by the British officers when they entered that place: "You are, thank God, of good understanding, and are thoroughly acquainted with those rules of religion which enjoin love and unison. Thanks be to God that I hear but good reports of you. But you are now close to the enemy of God, and have with you, with the help of God, a sufficient number of men. I therefore request you to unite together, to have the heart of a single man founded on love and unity. Consult with one another, and thus you will insure good results, which will strengthen the religion and vex the heathen, the enemies of God. Do not move without consulting one another, and such others, also, in the army who are full of sense and wisdom. Employ their plans and tricks of war, in the general fight more especially. Your army, thank God, is large ; if you unite and act as one hand, your action will be regular ; you will, with the help of God, defeat the enemies of God and set

at ease the mind of the khalifa, peace be on him ! Follow this advice, and do not allow any intrigues to come between you. Rely on God in all your doings ; be bold in all your dealings with the enemy ; let them find no flaw in your disposition for the fight. But be ever most vigilant, for these enemies of God are cunning, may God destroy them! Our brethren, Mohamed Koku, with two others, bring you this letter; on their return they will inform me whether you work in unison or not. Let them find you as ordered in religion, in good spirits, doing your utmost to insure the victory of religion. Remember, my brethren, that what moves me to urge on you to love each other and to unite is my love for you and my desire for your good. This is a trial of war ; so for us love and amity are of utmost necessity. You were of the supporters of the Mahdi, peace be on him ! You were as one spirit occupying one body. When the enemy know that you are quite united they will be much provoked. Strive, therefore, to provoke these enemies of religion. May God bless you and render you successful."

A. D. 1895.—New anti-slavery law.—A convention to establish a more effective anti-slavery law in Egypt was signed on the 21st of November, 1895, "by the Minister of Foreign Affairs, representing the Khedival Government, and the British diplomatic agent and consul-general. . . . This new convention will supplant that of August 4, 1877, which . . . was found to be defective, inasmuch as it provided no penalty for the purchaser of a slave, but for the seller only. An Egyptian notable, Ali Pasha Cherif, at that time president of the Legislative Council, was tried for buying slaves for his household, but escaped punishment through a technicality of the law hitherto escaping notice. . . . Under the existing regulations, every slave in the Egyptian dominions has the right to complete freedom, and may demand his certificate of manumission whenever he chooses. Thus, all domestic slaves, of whom there are thousands in Cairo, Alexandria, and the large towns, may call upon their masters to set them free. Many choose to remain in nominal bondage, preferring the certainty of food and shelter to the hardships and uncertainty of looking after themselves." — *United States, Consular Reports, March,* 1896, *p.* 370.

A. D. 1897.—Italian evacuation of Kassala, in the eastern Sudan. See (in this vol.) ITALY: A. D. 1897.

A. D. 1897 (June).—Census.—A census of Egypt, taken on the 1st of June, 1897, showed a population of 9,700,000, the area being Egypt up to Wady Halfa. In 1882 an imperfect census gave six and three-quarter millions. Twelve per cent. of the males can write, the rest are totally illiterate. There are, it is said, about 40,-000 persons not really Egyptians, but who come from other parts of the Ottoman Empire. The Bedouin number 570,000, but of these only 89,-000 are really nomads, the rest being semi-sedentary. Of foreign residents there are 112,500, of whom the Greeks, the most numerous, number 38,000. Then come the Italians, with 24,500. The British (including 6,500 Maltese and 5,000 of the Army of Occupation) are 19,500 ; and the French (including 4,000 Algerians and Tunisians), 14,000. The Germans only number 1,300. The classification according to religion shows nearly

9,000,000 Moslems, 730,000 Christians, and 25,-000 Jews. The Christians include the Coptic race, numbering about 608,000. Only a very small proportion profess the Roman Catholic and Protestant faiths. Amongst the town populations Cairo contains 570,000, Alexandria 320,000.

A. D. 1897-1898.—The final campaigns of the Anglo-Egyptian conquest of the Eastern Sudan.—Desperate battles of the Atbara and of Omdurman.—"The winter of 1896-1897 was passed, undisturbed by the enemy. The extended and open front of the Egyptian army imperatively called for fresh guarantees against a Dervish invasion. The important strategic position of Abu Hamed was then held by the enemy, to dislodge whom was the objective of the 1897 campaign. The railway was boldly launched into the Nubian Desert; the rail-head crept rapidly and surely towards the Dervish post, until within striking distance of Abu Hamed : when the river-column, by a forced march, through difficult country, delivered an attack on 7th August. Abu Hamed was taken by the Egyptian army under Major-General (now Sir Archibald) Hunter, with trifling loss : and the effect of this victory caused the precipitate evacuation of Berber. The Dervishes withdrew : the Egyptians—not to lose so favourable an opening—advanced. Berber, the key to the Sudan, was promptly re-occupied. The railway was hastened forward; reinforcements were detrained, before the close of the year, at a short distance from Berber : and the Anglo-Egyptian authorities gathered force for the last heat. British troops were called up. In this final struggle [1898] nothing could be risked. An Egyptian reverse would have redoubled the task on the accomplishment of which, having deliberately accepted it, we had pledged our honour. Mahmud, the Dervish emir, and that ubiquitous rascal Osman Digna, with their united forces, were marching on Berber. They, however, held up at the confluence of the Atbara, and comfortably intrenched themselves in a 'zariba.' Here the Sirdar came out to have a look at them. The Dervish force numbered about 19,000 men. The Anglo-Egyptian army was composed of 13,000 men. The odds were good enough for the Sirdar : and he went for them. Under the demoralization created by some sharp artillery practice, the Anglo-Egyptians stormed the 'zariba,' killed three-fourths of the defenders, and chased the remainder away. This victory [April 8, 1898], which cost over 500 men in killed and wounded, broke the Dervish power for offence and seriously damaged the Khalifa's prestige. With reinforcements, bringing his army up to 22,-000 men, including some picked British regiments, the Sirdar then advanced slowly up the river. It was a pilgrimage to the Mahdi's tomb, in sight of which Cross and Crescent combined to overthrow the false prophet. This sanguinary and decisive engagement [before Omdurman] took place on 2nd September, 1898. The Khalifa was put to flight : his forces were scattered and ridden down. On the same evening, the Sirdar entered Omdurman, and released the European captives. Subsequently, the British and Egyptian flags were hoisted together at Khartum ; and divine service was celebrated at the spot where Gordon fell."—A. S. White, *The Expansion of Egypt*, pp. 383-4 (*N. Y. : New Amsterdam Book Co.*).

"The honour of the fight [at Omdurman] must still go with the men who died. Our men were perfect, but the dervishes were superb—beyond perfection. It was their largest, best, and bravest army that ever fought against us for Mahdism, and it died worthily of the huge empire that Mahdism won and kept so long. Their riflemen, mangled by every kind of death and torment that man can devise, clung round the black flag and the green, emptying their poor, rotten, home-made cartridges dauntlessly. Their spearmen charged death at every minute hopelessly. Their horsemen led each attack, riding into the bullets till nothing was left but three horses trotting up to our line, heads down, saying, 'For goodness' sake, let us in out of this.' Not one rush, or two, or ten—but rush on rush, company on company, never stopping, though all their view that was not unshaken enemy was the bodies of the men who had rushed before them. A dusky line got up and stormed forward : it bent, broke up, fell apart, and disappeared. Before the smoke had cleared, another line was bending and storming forward in the same track.

"It was over. The avenging squadrons of the Egyptian cavalry swept over the field. The Khalifa and the Sheikh-ed-Din had galloped back to Omdurman. Ali Wad Helu was borne away on an angareb with a bullet through his thigh-bone. Yakub lay dead under his brother's banner. From the green army there now came only death-enamoured desperadoes, strolling one by one towards the rifles, pausing to shake a spear, turning aside to recognise a corpse, then caught by a sudden jet of fury, bounding forward, checking, sinking limply to the ground. Now under the black flag in a ring of bodies stood only three men, facing the three thousand of the Third Brigade. They folded their arms about the staff and gazed steadily forward. Two fell. The last dervish stood up and filled his chest; he shouted the name of his God and hurled his spear. Then he stood quite still, waiting. It took him full; he quivered, gave at the knees, and toppled with his head on his arms and his face towards the legions of his conquerors. Over 11,000 killed, 16,000 wounded, 4,000 prisoners,—that was the astounding bill of dervish casualties officially presented after the battle of Omdurman. Some people had estimated the whole dervish army at 1,000 less than this total: few had put it above 50,000. The Anglo-Egyptian army on the day of battle numbered, perhaps, 22,000 men : if the Allies had done the same proportional execution at Waterloo, not one Frenchman would have escaped. . . . The dervish army was killed out as hardly an army has been killed out in the history of war. It will shock you, but it was simply unavoidable. Not a man was killed except resisting—very few except attacking. Many wounded were killed, it is true, but that again was absolutely unavoidable. . . . It was impossible not to kill the dervishes: they refused to go back alive."

The same brilliant writer gives the following description of Omdurman, as the British found it on entering the town after the victory: "It began just like any other town or village of the mean Sudan. Half the huts seemed left unfinished, the other half to have been deserted and fallen to pieces. There were no streets, no doors or windows except holes, usually no roofs. As for a garden, a tree, a steading for a beast—any evidence of thrift or intelligence, any attempt at comfort or amenity or common cleanliness,—not a single trace of any of it. Omdurman was just planless confusion of blind walls and gaping holes, shiftless stupidity, contented filth and beastliness. But that, we said, was only the outskirts: when we come farther in we shall surely find this mass of population manifesting some small symbols of a great dominion. And presently we came indeed into a broader way than the rest—something with the rude semblance of a street. Only it was paved with dead donkeys, and here and there it disappeared in a cullender of deep holes where green water festered. . . . Omdurman was a rabbit-warren—a threadless labyrinth of tiny huts or shelters, too flimsy for the name of sheds. Oppression, stagnation, degradation, were stamped deep on every yard of miserable Omdurman.

"But the people! We could hardly see the place for the people. We could hardly hear our own voices for their shrieks of welcome. We could hardly move for their importunate greetings. They tumbled over each other like ants from every mud heap, from behind every dunghill, from under every mat. . . . They had been trying to kill us three hours before. But they salaamed, none the less, and volleyed, 'Peace be with you' in our track. All the miscellaneous tribes of Arabs whom Abdullahi's fears or suspicions had congregated in his capital, all the blacks his captains had gathered together into franker slavery—indiscriminate, half-naked, grinning the grin of the sycophant, they held out their hands and asked for backsheesh. Yet more wonderful were the women. The multitude of women whom concupiscence had harried from every recess of Africa and mewed up in Baggara harems came out to salute their new masters. There were at least three of them to every man. Black women from Equatoria and almost white women from Egypt, plum-skinned Arabs and a strange yellow type with square, bony faces and tightly-ringleted black hair, . . . the whole city was a huge harem, a museum of African races, a monstrosity of African lust."— G. W. Steevens, *With Kitchener to Khartum, ch.* 32-34 (*copyright, Dodd, Mead & Co., quoted with permission*).

"Anyone who has not served in the Sudan cannot conceive the state of devastation and misery to which that unfortunate country has been brought under Dervish rule. Miles and miles of formerly richly cultivated country lies waste; villages are deserted; the population has disappeared. Thousands of women are without homes or families. Years must elapse before the Sudan can recover from the results of its abandonment to Dervish tyranny; but it is to be hoped and may be confidently expected, that in course of time, under just and upright government, the Sudan may be restored to prosperity; and the great battle of September will be remembered as having established peace, without which prosperity would have been impossible; and from which thousands of misguided and wretched people will reap the benefits of civilization."—E. S. Wortley, *With the Sirdar (Scribner's Magazine,* Jan., 1899).

A. D. 1898.—The country and its people after 15 years of British occupation.—"The British occupation has now lasted for over fifteen years. During the first five, comparatively little

was accomplished, owing to the uncertain and provisional character of our tenure. The work done has been done in the main in the last ten years, and was only commenced in earnest when the British authorities began to realise that, whether we liked it or not, we had got to stay; and the Egyptians themselves came to the conclusion that we intended to stay. . . . Under our occupation Egypt has been rendered solvent and prosperous; taxes have been largely reduced; her population has increased by nearly 50 per cent.; the value and the productiveness of her soil has been greatly improved; a regular and permanent system of irrigation has been introduced into Lower Egypt, and is now in the course of introduction into Upper Egypt; trade and industry have made giant strides; the use of the Kurbash [bastinado] has been forbidden; the Corvée has been suppressed; regularity in the collection of taxes has been made the rule, and not the exception; wholesale corruption has been abolished; the Fellaheen can now keep the money they earn, and are better off than they were before; the landowners are all richer owing to the fresh supply of water, with the consequent rapid increase in the saleable price of land; justice is administered with an approach to impartiality; barbarous punishments have been mitigated, if not abolished; and the extraordinary conversion of Cairo into a fair semblance of a civilised European capital has been repeated on a smaller scale in all the chief centres of Egypt. To put the matter briefly, if our occupation were to cease to-morrow, we should leave Egypt and the Egyptians far better off than they were when our occupation commenced.

"If, however, I am asked whether we have succeeded in the alleged aim of our policy, that of rendering Egypt fit for self-government, I should be obliged honestly to answer that in my opinion we have made little or no progress towards the achievement of this aim. The one certain result of our interference in the internal administration of Egypt has been to impair, if not to destroy, the authority of the Khedive; of the Mudirs, who, as the nominees of the Effendina, rule over the provinces; and of the Sheiks, who, in virtue of the favour of the Mudirs, govern the villages. We have undoubtedly trained a school of native officials who have learnt that it is to their interest to administer the country more or less in accordance with British ideas. Here and there we may have converted an individual official to a genuine belief in these ideas. But I am convinced that if our troops were withdrawn, and our place in Egypt was not taken by any other civilised European Power, the old state of things would revive at once, and Egypt would be governed once more by the old system of Baksheesh and Kurbash."—E. Dicey, *Egypt, 1881 to 1897 (Fortnightly Rev., May,* 1898).

Reviewing the report, for 1898, of Lord Cromer, the British Agent and Consul-General, who is practically the director of the government of Egypt, "The Spectator" (London) has noted the principle of Lord Cromer's administration to be that of "using English heads but Egyptian hands. In practice this means the policy of never putting an Englishman into any post which could be just as well filled by a native. In other words, the Englishman is only used in the administration where he is indispensable. Where he is not, the native, as is only just and right, is employed. The outcome of this is that Lord Cromer's work in Egypt has been carried out by 'a body of officials who certainly do not exceed one hundred in number, and might possibly, if the figures were vigorously examined, be somewhat lower.' Lord Cromer adds, however, that ' these hundred have been selected with the greatest care.' In fact, the principle has been, —never employ an Englishman unless it is necessary in the interests of good government to do so, but then employ a first-class man.   The result is that the inspiring force in every Department of the Egyptian State is a first-class English brain, and yet the natives are not depressed by being deprived of their share of the administration. The Egyptians, that is, do not feel the legitimate grievance that is felt by the Tunisians and Algerians when they see even little posts of a couple of hundred a year filled by Frenchmen."—*Spectator, April* 15, 1899.

A. D. **1898** (September—November).—**The French expedition of M. Marchand at Fashoda.** —On the 10th of September, eight days after destroying the power of the Khalifa at Omdurman, the Sirdar, Lord Kitchener, left that fallen capital with five gunboats and a considerable force of Highlanders, Sudanese and Egyptians, to take possession of the Upper Nile. At Fashoda, in the Shilluk country, a little north of the junction of the Sobat with the White Nile, he found a party of eight French officers and about a hundred Senegalese troops, commanded by M. Marchand, entrenched at the old government buildings in that place and claiming occupation of the country. It had been known for some time that M. Marchand was leading an expedition from the French Congo towards the Nile, and the British government had been seeking an explanation of its objects from the government of France, uttering warnings, at the same time, that England would recognize no rights in any part of the Nile Valley except the rights of Egypt, which the evacuation of the Egyptian Sudan, consequent on the conquests of the Mahdi and the Dervishes, had not extinguished. Even long before the movements of M. Marchand were known, it had been suspected that France entertained the design of extending her great possessions in West Africa eastward, to connect with the Nile, and, as early as the spring of 1895, Sir Edward Grey, speaking for the British Foreign Office, in reply to a question then asked in the House of Commons, concerning rumors that a French expedition from West Africa was approaching the Nile, said with unmistakable meaning: "After all I have explained about the claims we consider we have under past Agreements, and the claims which we consider Egypt may have in the Nile Valley, and adding to that the fact that those claims and the view of the Government with regard to them are fully and clearly known to the French Government, I cannot think it is possible that these rumours deserve credence, because the advance of a French expedition under secret instructions right from the other side of Africa into a territory over which our claims have been known for so long would be not merely an inconsistent and unexpected act, but it must be perfectly well known to the French Government that it would be an unfriendly act, and would be so viewed by England." In December, 1897, the British Ambassador at Paris had called the attention of the French government to Sir Edward Grey's declaration,

adding that "Her Majesty's present Government entirely adhere to the language that was on this occasion employed by their predecessors."

As between the two governments, then, such was the critical situation of affairs when the Sirdar, who had been already instructed how to act if he found intruders in the Nile Valley, came upon M. Marchand and his little party at Fashoda. The circumstances and the results of the meeting were reported by him promptly as follows: "On reaching the old Government buildings, over which the French flag was flying, M. Marchand, accompanied by Captain Germain, came on board. After complimenting them on their long and arduous journey, I proceeded at once to inform M. Marchand that I was authorized to state that the presence of the French at Fashoda and in the Valley of the Nile was regarded as a direct violation of the rights of Egypt and Great Britain, and that, in accordance with my instructions, I must protest in the strongest terms against their occupation of Fashoda, and their hoisting of the French flag in the dominions of His Highness the Khedive. In reply, M. Marchand stated that as a soldier he had to obey orders; the instructions of his Government to occupy the Bahr-el-Ghazal and the Mudirieh of Fashoda were precise, and, having carried them out, he must await the orders of his Government as to his subsequent action and movements. I then pointed out that I had the instructions of the Government to re-establish Egyptian authority in the Fashoda Mudirieh, and I asked M. Marchand whether he was prepared— on behalf of the French Government—to resist the execution of these orders; he must be fully aware, I said, that the Egyptian and British forces were very much more powerful than those at his disposal, but, at the same time, I was very averse to creating a situation which might lead to hostilities. I therefore begged M. Marchand to most carefully consider his final decision on this matter. I further informed him that I should be pleased to place one of the gun-boats at his disposal to convey him and his expedition north. In answer to this, M. Marchand did not hesitate to admit the preponderating forces at my disposal, and his inability to offer effective armed resistance; if, however, he said, I felt obliged to take any such action, he could only submit to the inevitable, which would mean that he and his companions would die at their posts. He begged, therefore, that I would consider his position, and would allow the question of his remaining at Fashoda to be referred to his Government, as, without their orders, he could not retire from his position or haul down his flag; at the same time, he said he felt sure that, under the circumstances, the orders for his retirement would not be delayed by his Government, and that then he hoped to avail himself of the offer I had made him. I then said to him : ' Do I understand that you are authorized by the French Government to resist Egypt in putting up its flag and reasserting its authority in its former possessions—such as the Mudirieh of Fashoda ?' M. Marchand hesitated, and then said that he could not resist the Egyptian flag being hoisted. I replied that my instructions were to hoist the flag, and that I intended to do so. . . . The Egyptian flag was hoisted . . . at 1 P. M. with due ceremony in the presence of the British and Egyptian troops, and a salute of twenty-one guns was fired. I should add that, in the course of the conversation, I informed M.

Marchand that, in addition to my verbal protest, I intended to make a formal protest in writing, and this I duly handed him before leaving Fashoda. During these somewhat delicate proceedings nothing could have exceeded the politeness and courtesy of the French officers. Having officially appointed Major Jackson Commandant of the Fashoda district, and leaving with him a battalion of infantry, four guns, and a gun-boat, I proceeded south with the remainder of the troops and four gun-boats. . . .

"I had no opportunity for a further interview with M. Marchand, who, I venture to think, holds at Fashoda a most anomalous position—encamped with 120 men on a narrow strip of land, surrounded by marshes, cut off from access to the interior, possessing only three small boats without oars or sails and an inefficient steam-launch which has lately been dispatched on a long journey south, short of ammunition and supplies, his followers exhausted by years of continuous hardship, yet still persisting in the prosecution of his impracticable undertaking in the face of the effective occupation and administration of the country I have been able to establish. It is impossible not to entertain the highest admiration for the courage, devotion, and indomitable spirit displayed by M. Marchand's expedition, but our general impression was one of astonishment that an attempt should have been made to carry out a project of such magnitude and danger by the dispatch of so small and ill-equipped a force which—as their Commander remarked to me, was neither in a position to resist a second Dervish attack nor to retire—indeed, had our destruction of the Khalifa's power at Omdurman been delayed a fortnight, in all probability he and his companions would have been massacred. The claims of M. Marchand to have occupied the Bahr-el-Ghazal and Fashoda Provinces with the force at his disposal would be ludicrous did not the sufferings and privations his expedition endured during their two years' arduous journey render the futility of their efforts pathetic."— *Great Britain, Parliamentary Publications* (*Papers by Command: Egypt, Nos. 2 and 3*, 1898).

The "Fashoda incident," as it was described, caused great excitement in both England and France, and threatened for some weeks to involve the two countries in war. Both army feeling and popular feeling in France very nearly forced the government to persist in what was plainly an ill-considered and inopportune movement, and to hold untenable ground. But better sense prevailed, and, on the 2d of November, when the Sirdar, Lord Kitchener, who had visited England, was being feasted and given the freedom of London, at Guildhall, Lord Salisbury was able to make a dramatic announcement of the closing of the dispute. "I received," he said, speaking at the banquet, "from the French ambassador this afternoon the information that the French Government had come to the conclusion that the occupation of Fashoda was of no sort of value to the French Republic, and they thought that, under those circumstances, to persist in an occupation which only cost them money and did them harm, merely because some people—some bad advisers —thought it might be disagreeable to an unwelcome neighbor, would not show the wisdom with which, I think, the French Republic has been uniformly guided, and they have done what I believe many other governments would have

done in the same position—they have resolved that the occupation must cease."

A. D. 1898–1899.—The Gordon Memorial College at Khartoum. — On an appeal from Lord Kitchener, funds were raised in Great Britain for the founding of a Gordon Memorial College, to be, in the first instance, a school for elementary instruction to the sons of the heads of districts and villages.

A. D. 1898–1901.—The Barrage and Reservoir works on the Nile.—In February, 1898, the Khedive in Council approved a contract concluded with the British firm of John Aird & Co., for the construction of a dam or "barrage" across the Nile at Assouan, drowning the cataracts and turning the river above into a vast storage reservoir; with another dam at Assiout, for the irrigation of Middle Egypt and the Fayum. In the report of Lord Cromer for 1898, Sir William Garstein, at the head of the Egyptian Public Works Department, gave the following description of the plan of the works, then fairly under way: "The dam which is to form the reservoir will be built at the first cataract, a few miles south of Assouan. It is designed to hold up water to a level of 106 metres above mean sea level, or rather more than 20 metres above the low-water level of the Nile at site. Its total length will be 2,156 yards with a width at crest of 26·4 feet. The width of base at the deepest portion will be 82·5 feet, and the height of the work at the deepest spot will be 92·4 feet. The dam will be pierced by 180 openings, or under-sluices (140 of which are 23·1 feet by 6·6 feet and 40 are 18·2 feet by 6·6 feet) provided with gates. These sluices will pass the flood and surplus water through the dam, and by them the reservoir will be emptied when water is required for irrigation in Middle and Lower Egypt. Three locks will be built, and a navigation channel made on the west of the river to enable boats to pass up and down.

"The dam at Assiout will be what is called an open Barrage, and will be similar in construction to the existing Barrages on the Rosetta and Damietta branches. The new work will consist of 111 bays or openings, each 16·5 feet wide, and each bay will be provided with regulating gates. The total length of the work will be 903 yards. A lock 53 feet in width will be constructed on the west bank, large enough to pass the largest tourist boat plying on the river. By regulating on this Barrage water will be supplied in spring and summer to the Ibrahimieh Canal, which irrigates Middle Egypt. At present this canal has to be dredged to a depth of some 2 metres below the lowest summer level in the river, and even with these the crops suffer in years of low summer supply. A regulation bridge with a look will be built at the head of the Ibrahimieh Canal in order to allow of the supply being reduced, if necessary, in flood." — *Great Britain, Papers by Command: Egypt, No. 3, 1899.*

By a singular happening, the Nile flood of 1899 was the lowest recorded in the century, and gave an opportunity for the barrage and irrigation works, barely begun as they were, to give a convincing foretaste of their value. According to the report of that year, "the distress was enormously less than on all previous occasions of a failure of the flood. The area of 'sharaki,' or land unirrigated and therefore untaxed, which had been 900,000 feddans in 1877 was only one-third of this in 1899. Even in this area, which lay principally in Upper Egypt, 'distress,' says Sir William Garstein, 'was hardly felt at all by the people. The immense amount of contract work in progress in the country enabled them to obtain a good daily wage and tided over the interval between the two crops.' In Lower Egypt ' the situation was saved by the Barrage, which, for the first time in its history, was regulated upon throughout the flood. Had it not been for the work done by this structure, there is little doubt that large areas of crop would have been lost. As it is, the cotton crop is very nearly the largest on record, and the maize crop was up to the average.'" Of the progress of the work at Assouan it is said: "After nearly a year had been spent in accumulation of material and various preparations, the foundation stone of the dam was laid by H. R. H. the Duke of Connaught on February 12; and from that date the work was carried on with less interruption than must have been necessitated by a normal flood. Beginning on the east bank, masonry was carried on throughout a length of 620 mètres, and of these, 360 mètres were brought up to within two mètres of their full height. . . . Not less satisfactory progress was made with the weir at Assiut, although the original design had to be considerably altered."

On the 7th of February, 1901, a Press despatch from Cairo reported: "Sir John Aird and Sir Benjamin Baker start for England on Sunday next, having completed their visit of inspection to the great engineering works at Assuan, where the immense dam to hold up the waters of the Nile is being constructed. The total extent of the dam is one mile and a quarter, of which one mile and an eighth of the foundation is finished. Temporary dams enabling the remaining section to be put in are now carried across the channel. Pumps for getting in the permanent dam foundations will be started next week. The whole of the granite masonry required for the dam is cut and ready to be laid in its place. The parapet alone remains to be prepared. The portion of the dam remaining to be built is that across the well-known deep western channel. The work is of considerable difficulty, but the experience gained last season in dealing with other channels has rendered the engineers and contractors confident that equal success will be obtained this year in the western channel. The dam is pierced with 180 openings, about 23ft. high and 7ft. wide, which openings are controlled by steel sluices. The work for the latter is now well advanced. The discharge through these sluices at high Nile may reach 15,000 tons of water per second. The navigation channel and chain of locks are equally advanced with the dam itself, and the lock gates will also be in course of construction in about three months. Unless anything unforeseen occurs the reservoirs will be in operation for the Nile flood of 1903. This will be well within the contract time, although owing to the increased depth of the foundations the work done by the contractors has been largely increased.

"At Assiut the great regulating dam across the Nile approaches completion, the foundations being practically all in position, leaving a portion of the superstructure to be completed. The sluice openings here number 119, all 16ft. wide. This dam is somewhat similar in principle to the well-known barrage near Cairo, but the details of construction are entirely different, as the foundations are guarded against undermining by a complete line of cast iron and steel-piling above and below the work. The barrage itself is constructed of high-class masonry instead of brickwork as at the old barrage. Although the Assiut barrage is overshadowed by the greater magnitude of the Assuan dam, it will, doubtless, rank second as the monumental work of Egypt."

A. D. 1899 (January).—The Anglo-Egyptian Condominium established in the Sudan. —The following agreement between the British government and that of the Khedive of Egypt, relative to the future administration of the Sudan, establishing a condominium or joint dominion therein, was signed at Cairo on the 19th of January, 1899, and made public the same day:

Whereas certain provinces in the Sudan which were in rebellion against the authority of His Highness the Khedive have now been reconquered by the joint military and financial efforts of Her Britannic Majesty's Government and the Government of His Highness the Khedive; and whereas it has become necessary to decide upon a system for the administration of and for the making of laws for the said reconquered provinces, under which due allowance may be made for the backward and unsettled condition of large portions thereof, and for the varying requirements of different localities; and whereas it is desired to give effect to the claims which have accrued to Her Britannic Majesty's Government by right of conquest, to share in the present settlement and future working and development of the said system of administration and legislation; and whereas it is conceived that for many purposes Wadi Halfa and Suákin may be most effectively administered in conjunction with the reconquered provinces to which they are respectively adjacent; now, it is hereby agreed and declared by and between the Undersigned, duly authorized for that purpose, as follows:

ART. I. The word "Sudan" in this Agreement means all the territories South of the 22nd parallel of latitude, which: 1. Have never been evacuated by Egyptian troops since the year 1882; or 2. Which, having before the late rebellion in the Sudan been administered by the Government of His Highness the Khedive, were temporarily lost to Egypt, and have been reconquered by Her Majesty's Government and the Egyptian Government acting in concert; or 3. Which may hereafter be reconquered by the two Governments acting in concert.

ART. II. The British and Egyptian flags shall be used together, both on land and water, throughout the Sudan, except in the town of Suákin, in which locality the Egyptian flag alone shall be used.

ART. III. The supreme military and civil command in the Sudan shall be vested in one officer, termed the "Governor-General of the Sudan." He shall be appointed by Khedivial Decree on the recommendation of Her Britannic Majesty's Government, and shall be removed only by Khedivial Decree, with the consent of Her Britannic Majesty's Government.

ART. IV. Laws, as also Orders and Regulations with the full force of law, for the good government of the Sudan, and for regulating the holding, disposal, and devolution of property of every kind therein situate, may from time to time be made, altered, or abrogated by Proclamation of the Governor-General. Such Laws, Orders, and Regulations may apply to the whole or any named part of the Sudan, and may, either explicitly or by necessary implication, alter or abrogate any existing Law or Regulation. All such Proclamations shall be forthwith notified to Her Britannic Majesty's Agent and Consul-General in Cairo, and to the President of the Council of Ministers of His Highness the Khedive.

ART. V. No Egyptian Law, Decree, Ministerial Arrêté, or other enactment hereafter to be made or promulgated shall apply to the Sudan or any part thereof, save in so far as the same shall be applied by Proclamation of the Governor-General in manner hereinbefore provided.

ART. VI. In the definition by Proclamation of the conditions under which Europeans, of whatever nationality, shall be at liberty to trade with or reside in the Sudan, or to hold property within its limits, no special privileges shall be accorded to the subjects of any one or more Power.

ART. VII. Import duties on entering the Sudan shall not be payable on goods coming from Egyptian territory. Such duties may, however, be levied on goods coming from elsewhere than Egyptian territory, but in the case of goods entering the Sudan at Suákin, or any other port on the Red Sea Littoral, they shall not exceed the corresponding duties for the time being leviable on goods entering Egypt from abroad. Duties may be levied on goods leaving the Sudan at such rates as may from time to time be prescribed by Proclamation.

ART. VIII. The jurisdiction of the Mixed Tribunals shall not extend, nor be recognized for any purpose whatsoever, in any part of the Sudan, except in the town of Suákin.

ART. IX. Until, and save so far as it shall be otherwise determined, by Proclamation, the Sudan, with the exception of the town of Suákin, shall be and remain under martial law.

ART. X. No Consuls, Vice-Consuls, or Consular Agents shall be accredited in respect of nor allowed to reside in the Sudan, without the previous consent of Her Britannic Majesty's Government.

ART. XI. The importation of slaves into the Sudan, as also their exportation, is absolutely prohibited. Provision shall be made by Proclamation for the enforcement of this Regulation.

ART. XII. It is agreed between the two Governments that special attention shall be paid to the enforcement of the Brussels Act of the 2nd July 1890, in respect to the import, sale, and manufacture of fire-arms and their munitions, and distilled or spirituous liquors. Done in Cairo, the 19th January, 1899. (Signed) Boutros Ghali-Cromer.—A. S. White, *The Expansion of Egypt*, App. V. (*N. Y. : New Amsterdam Book Co.*)

By a subsequent agreement signed July 10, the exceptions in the above relative to Suákin were abrogated.

A. D. 1899-1900.—Final defeat and death of the Khalifa.—Capture of Osman Digna.—Condition of the Sudan.—The Khalifa, who escaped from the scene of his overthrow at Omdurman, in 1898, kept a following of his own tribe, the Baggaras, sufficient to give trouble for

more than another year. At length, late in November, 1899, he was overtaken by Sir Francis Wingate, who succeeded General Kitchener as Governor-General of the Sudan, and was killed in a battle fought near Gedil. Again Osman Digna, his able lieutenant, escaped ; but in January of the following year the latter was captured and taken to Suez.

In a report to Lord Salisbury, made on the 20th of February, 1900, Lord Cromer, British Agent and Consul-General in Egypt, gave the following account of the general state of affairs in the Sudan : "The territorial situation may be briefly described as follows :—The frontier between the Soudan and the Italian Colony of Erythræa has now been delimitated from Ras Kasar, on the Red Sea, to Sabderat, a few miles east of Kassala. Negotiations are proceeding which will, without doubt, result before long in the delimitation of the small remaining portion of the Italian frontier from Sabderat up to the point where it strikes Abyssinian territory. The most friendly relations exist between the British and Abyssinian Governments. The general basis of a frontier arrangement in respect to the country lying west of the Blue Nile has already been settled with the Emperor Menelek. When the survey party, now being employed, has finished its work, it may confidently be expected that the detailed delimitation will be carried out without much difficulty.

"An endeavour is being made to cut through the sudd which obstructs the White Nile, and thus open up communication with Uganda. To a certain extent this communication may be said to be already established, for a mixed party, consisting of British, French, and Belgian officers, with their followers, arriving from the South, recently succeeded in getting through and joining the Egyptian party, under Major Peake, which was engaged in cutting the sudd. . . . From the moment of the Khalifa's crushing defeat at Omdurman, the desert and Kordofan tribes, with the exception of a certain number of Baggaras who still adhered to the cause of their Chief, threw in their lot with the Government. Most of these tribes, however, rendered but little active assistance to the Government in the subsequent operations against the Khalifa. Omdurman and the Ghezireh [the tract of country lying south of Khartoum, between the White and Blue Niles] were found to be full of Arabs belonging to the Kordofan and far western tribes, who had been brought from their homes by the Khalifa. They were without any regular means of subsistence, but, in the existing state of insecurity, it was for the time being impossible for them to return to their own districts. . . . The inhabitants of the districts which were raided by the Dervishes were obliged to take refuge in the Ghezireh, with the result that the situation remained practically unchanged until the Khalifa's overthrow and death. Since then, the main objects of the Government have been to send back to their homes the inhabitants of the gum producing region, and to get rid of the useless mouths from the Ghezireh. In respect to the first point, some success has attended their efforts, but many thousands of Arabs belonging to tribes whose homes are in Kordofan and Darfour, still remain in the Ghezireh. . . . The attitude of the Nubas and of other tribes in Central and Southern Kordofan has, since the battle of Omdurman, been perfectly satisfactory. . . . Some long time must certainly elapse before prosperity returns to the tribes in the Soudan. The population has

ELAM. See (in vol. 1) BABYLONIA, PRIMITIVE ; (in vol. 4) SEMITES ; and (in this vol.) ARCHÆOLOGICAL RESEARCH : BABYLONIA, and PERSIA.

ELANDSLAAGTE, Battle of. See (in this vol.) SOUTH AFRICA (THE FIELD OF WAR) : A. D. 1899 (OCTOBER—DECEMBER).

ELBE - RHINE CANAL PROJECT, The. See (in this vol.) GERMANY : A. D. 1899 (AUGUST) ; and 1901 (JANUARY).

EL CANEY, Battle of. See (in this vol.) UNITED STATES OF AM. : A. D. 1898 (JUNE—JULY).

ELECTRICAL SCIENCE, Recent advances in. See (in this vol.) SCIENCE, RECENT: ELECTRICAL.

ELIZABETH, Empress of Austria: As-

wasted away under Dervish rule."—*Great Britain, Papers by Command: Egypt, No.* 1, 1900, *pp.* 43–44.

sassination. See (in this vol.) AUSTRIA-HUNGARY : A. D. 1898 (SEPTEMBER).

EL ZANJON, Treaty of. See (in this vol.) CUBA : A. D. 1868–1885.

EMPLOYERS' FEDERATION, British. See (in this vol.) INDUSTRIAL DISTURBANCES : A. D. 1897.

EMPLOYERS' LIABILITY BILL, The English. See (in this vol.) ENGLAND : A. D. 1897 (MAY—JULY).

EMPRESS-DOWAGER, of China, The. See (in this vol.) CHINA : A. D. 1898 (OCTOBER), and after.

ENGINEERS, Strike and lockout of British. See (in this vol.) INDUSTRIAL DISTURBANCES : A. D. 1897.

ENGLAND (GREAT BRITAIN).

A. D. 1894.—The commandeering question with the South African Republic. See (in this vol.) SOUTH AFRICA (THE TRANSVAAL): A. D. 1894.

A. D. 1894-1895.—Retirement of Mr. Gladstone from public life.—Earl of Rosebery Prime Minister.—His speech on the "predominant member" and Home Rule. — Weakening and overthrow of the Liberal Government.—Dissolution of Parliament.— Conservative and Unionist triumph.—Third Ministry of Lord Salisbury.—Mr. Gladstone, who had passed his 84th year, whose health was failing, and who might justly consider that his public work was done, resigned his post as Prime Minister, on the 2d of March, 1894, and the Earl of Rosebery, on his recommendation, was called by the Queen to take his place. Slight changes, otherwise, were made in the cabinet, but the spirit in the Liberal government was no longer the same. The new Premier soon signified that his disposition in the matter of Home Rule for Ireland was not quite what Mr. Gladstone's had been, by using the following language in a speech (March 13) in the House of Lords : "Before Irish Home Rule is conceded by the Imperial Parliament England, as the predominant member of the partnership of the three kingdoms, will have to be convinced of its justice. That may seem to be a considerable admission to make, because your lordships will know that the majority of English members of Parliament, elected from England proper, are hostile to Home Rule. But I believe that the conviction of England in regard to Home Rule depends on one point alone, and that is the conduct of Ireland herself. I believe that if we can go on showing this comparative absence of agrarian crime; if we can point to the continued harmony of Ireland with the great Liberal party of this country; if we can go on giving proofs and pledges that Ireland is entitled to be granted that boon which she has never ceased to demand since the Act of Union was passed, I believe that the conversion of England will not be of a slow or difficult charac-

ter. My lords, the question of Home Rule is one that I regard not from the point of view of Ireland only. It has for me a triple aspect. It has, in the first place, the aspect that I believe that Ireland will never be contented until this measure of Home Rule be granted to her; and that, though you may come in on other issues and succeed us who sit here, your policy of palliatives is bound to fail. In the second place, I believe that not merely have we in our Irish policy to satisfy those who live in the island of Ireland itself, encompassed, as Mr. Disraeli once said, by that melancholy ocean, we have not merely to satisfy the Irish themselves within Ireland, but, for the good of our Empire and for the continuity and solidarity of our relations with our brethren across the Atlantic, it is uecessary that we should produce an Irish policy which shall satisfy the Irish people. And, lastly, I view it from the highest Imperial grounds, because I believe that the maintenance of this Empire depends, not on centralization, but on decentralization, and that if you once commence to tread this path, you will have to give satisfaction under the same conditions certainly to Scotland, and possibly to Wales, not in the same degree or possibly in the same way, but so as to relieve this groaning Imperial Parliament from the burden of legislation under which it labours. I will not detain you further on this subject to-night. I did not mean to dilate so much on the question of Home Rule."

His remarks seemed to show an intention to postpone the pressing of the measure. Distrust arose among the Irish and uncertainty was created in the mind of the Liberal party. It became evident very quickly that the Liberals, with the loss of their old leader, had lost heart and faith in the policy to which he had committed them, and that a serious weakening of the political energies of the party had been produced. No measures which raised troublesome issues were undertaken in Parliament during the year of Mr. Gladstone's retirement; but, at the session which opened in the following February (1895), the government brought forward a number of highly important bills.

The first to be introduced was a bill " to terminate the Establishment of the Church of England in Wales and Monmouth." The bill made provision for the creation of a representative Church body, giving power to the bishops, clergy and laity to hold synods and to legislate on ecclesiastical matters. It entrusted ecclesiastical revenues to a commission ; provided for the transfer of churches and parsonages to the representative body of the Church, and of burial grounds and glebes to parish, district, and town councils ; other property of the Church to be vested in the commission before mentioned, which should also have the charge of cathedrals, to keep them in repair. The bill had its first reading on the 28th of February, and its second on the 1st of April, but went no further. It shared the fate of the other measures of the Government, including a bill to establish local control of the liquor traffic, and others for the remedying of defects in the Irish Land Law, and for the abolition of plural voting, all of which were extinguished by the sudden and unexpected overthrow of the Government on the 21st of June. It was defeated on a motion to reduce the salary of the Secretary for War, which was made for no purpose but to start a question as to the adequacy of the provision of certain ammunition stored for use. When the vote was found to be against the Government there was great surprise in both parties. But the Ministry had been steadily losing support and was quite willing to resign, which it did the next day.

Lord Salisbury was sent for by the Queen and accepted the task of forming a new Government, with the understanding that Parliament should be dissolved as soon as practicable, and the will of the country ascertained. In the new Government, Lord Salisbury filled the office of Secretary of State for Foreign Affairs, with that of Prime Minister ; Mr. A. J. Balfour became First Lord of the Treasury ; Sir Michael Hicks-Beach Chancellor of the Exchequer ; Mr. Joseph Chamberlain Secretary of State for the Colonies ; Mr. G. J. Goschen First Lord of the Admiralty. Before the dissolution of Parliament, which occurred on the 6th of July, a bill for the amendment of the Factories Act, on which both parties agreed, was passed. The elections that followed, beginning July 13, resulted in the return of a majority of 152 in favor of the new Ministry, which represented the coalition of Conservatives and Liberal Unionists. The majority of the popular vote on the same side in the three kingdoms was a little more than 30,000, in a total poll of 4,792,512 ; but in England the new Government received a majority of some 300,-000. In Ireland the vote went heavily against them, and in Wales and Scotland to a lighter extent. Of the Irish members elected, 12 were of the Parnell faction and 69 Anti-Parnell. The new Parliament came together August 12, and, after a brief session, at which little was done, was prorogued September 5.

A. D. 1895.—Enforcement of claims against Nicaragua. See (in this vol.) CENTRAL AMERICA (NICARAGUA) : A. D. 1894-1895.

A. D. 1895.—The question of Chitral. See (in this vol.) INDIA : A. D. 1895 (MARCH—SEPTEMBER).

A. D. 1895 (January). — Agreement with

France defining the boundaries of the Hinterland of Sierra Leone. See (in this vol.) SIERRA LEONE PROTECTORATE.

A. D. 1895 (March — July).—Agreement with Russia concerning the northern Afghan frontier and spheres of influence in the Pamir region. See (in this vol.) AFGHANISTAN : A. D. 1895.

A. D. 1895 (July—November).—Correspondence with the Government of the United States on the Venezuela boundary question. See (in this vol.) VENEZUELA : A. D. 1895 (JULY) and (NOVEMBER).

A. D. 1895 (November).—Action on the closing of the Vaal River Drifts by the South African Republic. See (in this vol.) SOUTH AFRICA (THE TRANSVAAL) : A. D. 1895 (SEPTEMBER — DECEMBER).

A. D. 1895 (December).—Message of the President of the United States to Congress on the British Guiana-Venezuela boundary dispute. See (in this vol.) VENEZUELA : A. D. 1895 (DECEMBER).

A. D. 1895-1896 (November—January). — Discontent and revolutionary conspiracy of Uitlanders in the Transvaal.—The Jameson Raid. See (in this vol.) SOUTH AFRICA (THE TRANSVAAL) : A. D. 1895 (NOVEMBER); and A. D. 1895-1896.

A. D. 1895-1896 (December—January).—The feeling in England and America over the Venezuela boundary dispute. See (in this vol.) UNITED STATES OF AM. : A. D. 1895-1896 (DECEMBER—JANUARY).

A. D. 1896.—Establishment of the Sierra Leone Protectorate. See (in this vol.) SIERRA LEONE PROTECTORATE.

A. D. 1896.—Report on Old-Age Pensions. —The question of the practicability and expediency of a national system of pensions for old age, which had been agitated in England for some years, and which a royal commission, appointed in 1893, had already examined with great thoroughness and no definite result, was referred in 1896 to a committeee of financial experts, with Lord Rothschild at their head. This committee reported that it could recommend no scheme as satisfactory, though it put forward that of Sir Spencer Walpole as open to less objection than others. The scheme in question was as follows : " 1. Any person at 65 having an assured income of not less than 2s. 6d. and not more than 5s. may apply for a pension. 2. If the pensioning authority is satisfied as to the income a pension may be granted. 3. The applicant must not be physically or mentally infirm. 4. To an income of 2s. 6d. 2s. 6d. is to be added. To an income of 3s. 0d. 2s. 0d. is to be added. To an income of 4s. 0d. 1s. 0d. is to be added. 5. ' Assured income' includes real estate, leasehold property, securities, or annuities (Government, friendly society, or insurance office), but not out-relief. 6. The guardians are to be the pensioning authority. 7. Not more than half of the pension is to be paid out of Imperial taxation, the remainder out of local rates. 8. The pension is not to involve disenfranchisement."

The committee, however, pointed out some very strong objections to this scheme, which they roughly estimated as likely to apply to 443,333 persons, and to cost £2,300,000 a year. On the whole, while they regarded the Walpole scheme as the best suggested, the Rothschild committee held that, like the rest, its inherent disadvantages outweighed its merits. In effect, they pronounced the establishment of old-age pensions to be impracticable.

A. D. 1896.—Report of Royal Commission on the financial relations between Great Britain and Ireland. See (in this vol.) IRELAND: A. D. 1896–1897.

A. D. 1896 (January).— Agreement with France concerning Siam. See (in this vol.) SIAM: A. D. 1896–1899.

A. D. 1896 (January).—Excitement over the German Emperor's message to President Kruger on the Jameson Raid. See (in this vol.) SOUTH AFRICA (THE TRANSVAAL): A. D. 1896 (JANUARY).

A. D. 1896 (January—February).—Appointment of United States Commission to investigate the Venezuela boundary.—Reopening of discussion with the government of the United States on the arbitration of the dispute. See (in this vol.) VENEZUELA: A. D. 1896–1899.

A. D. 1896 (February).—New treaty with the United States for arbitration of Bering Sea claims. See (in this vol.) BERING SEA QUESTIONS.

A. D. 1896 (March—September).—Expedition to Dongola.—Beginning of an Anglo-Egyptian movement for the recovery of the Sudan. See (in this vol.) EGYPT: A. D. 1885–1896.

A. D. 1896 (May).—The New Radical party. —A New Radical party, under the leadership of Sir Charles Dilke and Mr. Labouchere, issued a statement of its policy (May 19), setting forth as its chief aim "the democritisation and devolution of Parliament."

A. D. 1896 (June).—The Agricultural Land Bill.—Among the measures brought forward in Parliament this year and carried by the Conservative government was one which aroused bitter feeling and was sharply denounced, as being legislation in the interest of the landholding class, at the expense of the community at large. A ground of justice for it was found by its supporters, however, in the extreme agricultural depression of the time. This Agricultural Land Bill, as it was styled, provided that, in the case of every rate to which it applied, agricultural land should be assessed in future on half its ratable value, while houses and buildings would still be assessed on the whole of their ratable value. The bill passed the Commons near the end of June, and went speedily through the House of Lords.

A. D. 1896 (July).—Parliamentary movement to investigate the British South Africa Company. See (in this vol.) SOUTH AFRICA (BRITISH SOUTH AFRICA COMPANY); A. D. 1896 (JULY).

A. D. 1896 (August).—Suppression of an usurper in Zanzibar. See (in this vol.) AFRICA: A. D. 1896 (ZANZIBAR).

A. D. 1896 (September).—Papal Bull declaring Anglican orders invalid. See (in this vol.) PAPACY: A. D. 1896 (SEPTEMBER).

A. D. 1896 (November).—Agreement with the United States for the settlement of the Venezuela dispute. See (in this vol.) VENEZUELA: A. D. 1896–1899.

A. D. 1896-1897.—"The Voluntary Schools Act" and "The Elementary Education Act." —The Conservative Ministry of Lord Salisbury

came to power, in England, in 1895, under pledges to the Church that it would revise the educational system in the interest of the "Voluntary Schools" (mostly Church schools), as against the secular or non-sectarian "Board Schools" (see, in vol. 1, EDUCATION, MODERN: ENGLAND: A. D. 1699–1870), which were steadily gaining ground from the former, and proving superior efficiency. A bill to that end, for England and Wales, was introduced at the end of March, 1896. In support of the bill it was stated that, in the previous year, the voluntary schools educated 2,445,812 children, as against 1,879,218 educated in the board schools, though the voluntary schools were, as a rule, "understaffed," had less qualified teachers, and labored generally under financial difficulties; but that a large proportion of the members of the Church of England, as well as Roman Catholics, made it a point of conscience that their children should be educated by teachers of their own denomination, and could not be forced to send them to board schools without a gross exercise of religious intolerance; that, finally, it would cost £25,345,635 to replace the voluntary schools, and £2,250,000 yearly to maintain board schools in their place, if they were not kept up. Therefore, it was contended that they should receive a more liberal allowance of state aid by parliamentary grant, to keep them alive and improve their efficiency. Connected with provisions to that effect were others which would completely reorganize the system of school administration and control. They proposed to take the administration to a great extent from the Committee of Council on Education, where it had been centralized, and to place it in the County Councils, to be exercised by statutory educational committees appointed by each Council. By what was called a "conscience clause," the bill required separate religious instruction to be given to children in schools (board or voluntary) wherever a "reasonable number of parents" required it. The measure was strenuously opposed on the ground that its aim was the extinction of the board schools; that it would give them only £17,000 out of £500,000, and give it, said Lord Rosebery, "without any vestige of control, so that in 8,000 places where only Church of England schools existed the Nonconformists would have only the vague protection of the conscience clause." So much debate was provoked by the bill, and so much time was being consumed by it, that the Government was forced to drop the measure in June, in order to save the other business of the session from being spoiled,—promising, however, to bring it forward again the next January. The promise was redeemed, on the convening of Parliament in January, 1897, in so far that a new Education Bill was brought forward by the government; but the measure was very different from that of the previous session. It was addressed solely to the end of strengthening the voluntary or Church schools against the board schools, firstly by increasing the aid to them from public funds, and secondly by uniting them in organized associations, under stronger governing bodies. The main provisions of the bill were as follows:

"(1.) For aiding voluntary schools there shall be annually paid out of moneys provided by Parliament an aid grant, not exceeding in the aggregate five shillings per scholar for the whole number of scholars in those schools.

"(2.) The aid grant shall be distributed by the Education Department to such voluntary schools and in such manner and amounts, as the Department think best for the purpose of helping necessitous schools and increasing their efficiency, due regard being had to the maintenance of voluntary subscriptions.

"(3.) If associations of schools are constituted in such manner in such areas and with such governing bodies representative of the managers as are approved by the Education Department, there shall be allotted to each association while so approved, (a) a share of the aid grant to be computed according to the number of scholars in the schools of the association at the rate of five shillings per scholar, or, if the Department fix different rates for town and country schools respectively (which they are hereby empowered to do) then at those rates; and (b) a corresponding share of any sum which may be available out of the aid grant after distribution has been made to unassociated schools.

"(4.) The share so allotted to each such association shall be distributed as aforesaid by the Education Department after consulting the governing body of the association, and in accordance with any scheme prepared by that body which the Department for the time being approve.

"(5.) The Education Department may exclude a school from any share of the aid grant which it might otherwise receive, if, in the opinion of the Department, it unreasonably refuses or fails to join such an association, but the refusal or failure shall not be deemed unreasonable if the majority of the schools in the association belong to a religious denomination to which the school in question does not itself belong.

"(6.) The Education Department may require, as a condition of a school receiving a share of the aid grant, that the accounts of the receipts and expenditure of the school shall be annually audited in accordance with the regulations of the Department.

"(7.) The decision of the Education Department upon any question relating to the distribution or allotment of the aid grant, including the question whether an association is or is not in conformity with this Act, and whether a school is a town or a country school, shall be final."

The passage of the bill was resisted strenuously by the Liberals in the House of Commons. "Whether they regarded the bill from an educational, a constitutional, a parliamentary, or a social aspect," said Mr. John Morley, in his concluding speech in the debate, "he and his friends regarded it as a mischievous and reactionary measure." But the opposition was of no avail. The bill passed its third reading in the House of Commons, on the 25th of March, with a majority of 200 in its favor, the Irish Nationalists giving it their support. In the House of Lords it was ruled to be a money bill, which their lordships could not amend, and they passed it with little debate. In April, the government brought forward a second school bill, which increased the parliamentary grant to Board schools by £110,000. The sum was so trivial that it excited the scorn of the friends of the Board schools, and did nothing towards conciliating them. It became a law on the 3d of June.

A. D. 1896-1897 (May—April).—Continued controversies with the South African Repub-

lic. See (in this vol.) SOUTH AFRICA (THE TRANSVAAL): A. D. 1896-1897 (MAY—APRIL).

A. D. 1897 (January—May).—Arbitration Treaty with the United States defeated in the U. S. Senate. See (in this vol.) UNITED STATES OF AM.: A. D. 1897 (JANUARY—MAY).

A. D. 1897 (February).—Indemnity for Jameson Raid claimed by the South African Republic. See (in this vol.) SOUTH AFRICA (THE TRANSVAAL): A. D. 1897 (FEBRUARY).

A. D. 1897 (February).—Loan for national defense.—Purchase of 60 square miles on Salisbury Plain.—A bill which authorized a loan of £5,458,000 for purposes of national defense was passed rapidly through both Houses of Parliament in February. It included an item of £450,000 for the purchase of 40,000 acres (60 square miles) on Salisbury Plain, for military manœuvres.

A. D. 1897 (February).—Punitive expedition against Benin. See (in this vol.) NIGERIA: A. D. 1897.

A. D. 1897 (February—July).—Parliamentary investigation of the Jameson Raid. See (in this vol.) SOUTH AFRICA (THE TRANSVAAL): A. D. 1897 (FEBRUARY—JULY).

A. D. 1897 (April).—Increase of armament in South Africa.—The Government accused of a war policy. See (in this vol.) SOUTH AFRICA (THE TRANSVAAL): A. D. 1897 (APRIL).

A. D. 1897 (May).—Treaty with Menelek of Abyssinia. See (in this vol.) ABYSSINIA: A. D. 1897.

A. D. 1897 (May—June).—New cessions and concessions from China. See (in this vol.) CHINA: A. D. 1897 (MAY—JUNE).

A. D. 1897 (May—July).—The Workmen's Compensation Act.—A subject which had grown urgent, in England, for parliamentary attention, was that of a better provision in law for securing proper compensation to workmen for accidental injuries suffered in the course of their employment. The measure was not one that a Conservative government would be likely, under ordinary circumstances, to take up; since the class of large employers of labor, from which opposition to it came, were mostly in the Conservative ranks. But the Liberal Unionists, now in parliamentary coalition with the Conservatives, were called upon to favor such a piece of legislation by their creed, and rumor said that they bargained for it with their political partners, in exchange for the support they gave unwillingly to the Voluntary Schools Bill. At all events, a bill which was first called the Employers' Liability Bill, but finally named the Workmen's Compensation Bill, was brought in to the House of Commons, by the government, in May, and was carried, after much debate, through both Houses in July. The essential provisions of the Act as passed are the following:

"1.—(1.) If in any employment to which this Act applies personal injury by accident arising out of and in the course of the employment is caused to a workman, his employer shall, subject as herein-after mentioned, be liable to pay compensation in accordance with the First Schedule to this Act. (2.) Provided that:—(a.) The employer shall not be liable under this Act in respect of any injury which does not disable the workman for a period of at least two weeks from earning full wages at the work at which he was employed; (b.) When the injury was caused by the personal negligence or wilful act of the employer, or of some person for whose act or default the employer is responsible, nothing in this Act shall affect any civil liability of the employer, but in that case the workman may, at his option, either claim compensation under this Act, or take the same proceedings as were open to him before the commencement of this Act; but the employer shall not be liable to pay compensation for injury to a workman by accident arising out of and in the course of the employment both independently of and also under this Act, and shall not be liable to any proceedings independently of this Act, except in case of such personal negligence or wilful act as aforesaid; (c.) If it is proved that the injury to a workman is attributable to the serious and wilful misconduct of that workman, any compensation claimed in respect of that injury shall be disallowed. (3.) If any question arises in any proceedings under this Act as to the liability to pay compensation under this Act (including any question as to whether the employment is one to which this Act applies), or as to the amount or duration of compensation under this Act, the question, if not settled by agreement, shall, subject to the provisions of the First Schedule to this Act, be settled by arbitration, in accordance with the Second Schedule to this Act. . . .

"2.—(1.) Proceedings for the recovery under this Act of compensation for an injury shall not be maintainable unless notice of the accident has been given as soon as practicable after the happening thereof and before the workman has voluntarily left the employment in which he was injured, and unless the claim for compensation with respect to such accident has been made within six months from the occurrence of the accident causing the injury, or, in case of death, within six months from the time of death. . . .

"3.—(1.) If the Registrar of Friendly Societies, after taking steps to ascertain the views of the employer and workmen, certifies that any scheme of compensation, benefit, or insurance for the workmen of an employer in any employment, whether or not such scheme includes other employers and their workmen, is on the whole not less favourable to the general body of workmen and their dependants than the provisions of this Act, the employer may, until the certificate is revoked, contract with any of those workmen that the provisions of the scheme shall be substituted for the provisions of this Act, and thereupon the employer shall be liable only in accordance with the scheme, but, save as aforesaid, this Act shall apply notwithstanding any contract to the contrary made after the commencement of this Act. . . .

"7.—(1.) This Act shall apply only to employment by the undertakers as herein-after defined, on or in or about a railway, factory, mine, quarry, or engineering work, and to employment by the undertakers as herein-after defined on, in or about any building which exceeds thirty feet in height, and is either being constructed or repaired by means of a scaffolding, or being demolished, or on which machinery driven by steam, water, or other mechanical power, is being used for the purpose of the construction, repair, or demolition thereof. (2.) In this Act— . . . 'Undertakers' in the case of a railway

means the railway company; in the case of a factory, quarry, or laundry means the occupier thereof within the meaning of the Factory and Workshop Acts, 1878 to 1895; in the case of a mine means the owner thereof within the meaning of the Coal Mines Regulation Act, 1887, or the Metalliferous Mines Regulation Act, 1872, as the case may be, and in the case of an engineering work means the person undertaking the construction, alteration, or repair; and in the case of a building means the persons undertaking the construction, repair, or demolition. . . . 'Workman' includes every person who is engaged in an employment to which this Act applies, whether by way of manual labour or otherwise, and whether his agreement is one of service or apprenticeship or otherwise, and is expressed or implied, is oral or in writing."

The "First Schedule" referred to in the first section of the Act prescribes rules for determining compensation, those principally important being as follows: "The amount of compensation under this Act shall be—(a) where death results from the injury—(i) if the workman leaves any dependants wholly dependent upon his earnings at the time of his death, a sum equal to his earnings in the employment of the same employer during the three years next preceding the injury, or the sum of one hundred and fifty pounds, whichever of those sums is the larger, but not exceeding in any case three hundred pounds, provided that the amount of any weekly payments made under this Act shall be deducted from such sum, and if the period of the workman's employment by the said employer has been less than the said three years, then the amount of his earnings during the said three years shall be deemed to be 156 times his average weekly earnings during the period of his actual employment under the said employer; (ii) if the workman does not leave any such dependants, but leaves any dependants in part dependent upon his earnings at the time of his death, such sum, not exceeding in any case the amount payable under the foregoing provisions, as may be agreed upon, or, in default of agreement, may be determined, on arbitration under this Act, to be reasonable and proportionate to the injury to the said dependants; and (iii) if he leaves no dependants, the reasonable expenses of his medical attendance and burial, not exceeding ten pounds; (b) where total or partial incapacity for work results from the injury, a weekly payment during the incapacity after the second week not exceeding fifty per cent. of his average weekly earnings during the previous twelve months, if he has been so long employed, but if not, then for any less period during which he has been in the employment of the same employer, such weekly payment not to exceed one pound." —60 & 61 *Victoria, ch.* 37.

A. D. 1897 (May—October).—Reassertion of suzerainty over the South African Republic.—Refusal of arbitration. See (in this vol.) SOUTH AFRICA (THE TRANSVAAL): A. D. 1897 (MAY—OCTOBER); and 1898–1899.

A. D. 1897 (June).—The "Diamond Jubilee" of Queen Victoria.—The sixtieth anniversary of the coronation of Queen Victoria was celebrated in London on the 20th of June, by religious services of great solemnity and impressiveness, and, two days later, by pageants of extraordinary pomp and magnificence, in which representatives of every people who acknowledge the queen's supremacy bore a part. Numerous functions and ceremonies followed, to many of which the aged sovereign was able to lend her presence. At the end of all, on the 15th of July, she addressed the following letter to the millions of her subjects throughout the world: "I have frequently expressed my personal feelings to my people, and though on this memorable occasion there have been many official expressions of my deep sense of the unbounded loyalty evinced I cannot rest satisfied without personally giving utterance to these sentiments. It is difficult for me on this occasion to say how truly touched and grateful I am for the spontaneous and universal outburst of loyal attachment and real affection which I have experienced on the completion of the sixtieth year of my reign. During my progress through London on the 22nd of June this great enthusiasm was shown in the most striking manner, and can never be effaced from my heart. It is indeed deeply gratifying, after so many years of labour and anxiety for the good of my beloved country, to find that my exertions have been appreciated throughout my vast empire. In weal and woe I have ever had the true sympathy of all my people, which has been warmly reciprocated by myself. It has given me unbounded pleasure to see so many of my subjects from all parts of the world assembled here, and to find them joining in the acclamations of loyal devotion to myself, and I would wish to thank them all from the depth of my grateful heart. I shall ever pray God to bless them and to enable me still to discharge my duties for their welfare as long as life lasts. VICTORIA. R. I."

A. D. **1897** (June—July).—Conference of **colonial** premiers with the **Secretary of State** for the Colonies.—Discussion of important questions.—Denunciation of commercial treaties with Germany and **Belgium.**—"On Thursday, the 24th of June, the Prime Ministers of Canada, New South Wales, Victoria, New Zealand, Queensland, Cape Colony, South Australia, Newfoundland, Tasmania, Western Australia, and Natal, assembled at the Colonial Office, Downing Street, for the discussion of certain Imperial questions with the Secretary of State for the Colonies. It was decided that the proceedings should be informal and that the general results only should be published. With the view of giving a definite direction to the discussion, the Secretary of State, in opening the proceedings, set forth the subjects which he considered might usefully be discussed, so as to secure an interchange of views upon them, and where they were ripe for a statement of opinion, a definite resolution in regard to them. [He did so in a speech of some length, after which the several questions brought forward in his remarks were discussed in succession at a series of meetings in the Colonial Office.] The commercial relations of the United Kingdom and the self-governing Colonies were first considered, and the following resolutions were unanimously adopted:— 1. That the Premiers of the self-governing Colonies unanimously and earnestly recommend the denunciation, at the earliest convenient time, of any treaties which now hamper the commercial relations between Great Britain and her Colonies. 2. That in the hope of improving the trade relations between the mother country and the Colonies, the Premiers present undertake to confer with their colleagues with the view to seciug whether such a result can be properly secured by a preference given by the Colonies to the products of the United Kingdom. Her Majesty's Government have already [July 31, 1897] given effect to the first of these resolutions by formally notifying to the Governments concerned their wish to terminate the commercial treaties with Germany and Belgium, which alone of the existing commercial treaties of the United Kingdom are a bar to the establishment of preferential tariff relations between the mother country and the Colonies. From and after the 30th July 1898, therefore, there will be nothing in any of Her Majesty's treaty obligations to preclude any action which any of the Colonies may see fit to take in pursuance of the second resolution. It is, however, right to point out that if any Colony were to go farther and to grant preferential terms to any Foreign Country, the provisions of the most favoured nation clauses in many treaties between Her Majesty and other powers, in which the Colonies are included, would necessitate the concession of similar terms to those countries.

"On the question of the political relations between the mother country and the self-governing Colonies, the resolutions adopted were as follows:— 1. The Prime Ministers here assembled are of opinion that the present political relations between the United Kingdom and the self-governing Colonies are generally satisfactory under the existing condition of things. Mr. Seddon and Sir E. N. C. Braddon dissented. 2. They are also of opinion that it is desirable, whenever and wherever practicable, to group together under a federal union those colonies which are geographically united. Carried unanimously. 3. Meanwhile, the Premiers are of opinion that it would be desirable to hold periodical conferences of representatives of the Colonies and Great Britain for the discussion of matters of common interest. Carried unanimously. Mr. Seddon and Sir E. N. C. Braddon dissented from the first resolution because they were of opinion that the time had already come when an effort should be made to render more formal the political ties between the United Kingdom and the Colonies. The majority of the Premiers were not yet prepared to adopt this position, but there was a strong feeling amongst some of them that with the rapid growth of population in the Colonies, the present relations could not continue indefinitely, and that some means would have to be devised for giving the Colonies a voice in the control and direction of those questions of Imperial interest in which they are concerned equally with the mother country. It was recognised at the same time that such a share in the direction of Imperial policy would involve a proportionate contribution in aid of Imperial expenditure, for which at present, at any rate, the Colonies generally are not prepared.

"On the question of Imperial defence, the various points raised in the speech of the Secretary of State were fully discussed;" but on this, and on some questions of minor importance, no conclusions were definitely formulated.—*Great Britain, Parliamentary Publications (Papers by Command, C.—8596, 1897).*

The following reference to the "denunciation" of the treaties appeared in the "London Statist" of August 7, 1897: "Last week the

British Government gave notice to Germany and Belgium of its intention to terminate the commercial treaties with those countries at the end of July next year, at the same time expressing its willingness to conclude fresh treaties. This important step is a fitting sequel to the jubilee festivities. It is a graceful recognition of the great loyalty displayed by our colonies toward the mother country and prepares the way to that closer union which this paper has strongly advocated. In twelve months' time, therefore, we shall be free from our embarrassing engagements not to permit our colonies to place higher or other import duties on the produce of Germany and Belgium than upon the produce of the United Kingdom. Our colonies will thus have complete freedom to place what duties they choose on any produce they care to purchase from the United Kingdom or from any other country, and if they so desire they may place discriminating duties on their own exports. The action taken indicates no change in the policy of this country, and foreign nations need have no fear that British markets will be closed to their produce. It is quite possible that at some future time, when the colonies have much further developed their resources and the struggle for existence becomes still keener, we may be disposed to give a greater preference to colonial than to foreign produce, but that period has not yet come. Of course, the time may be greatly hastened by the attitude of foreign countries. The unfriendliness of Germany last year caused a wave of feeling in this country in favor of a duty upon German goods, and the Canadian offer of preferential duties to the mother country has created a responsive desire to assist Canadian trade. Should our other colonies follow the lead of Canada, which, from Mr. Chamberlain's statement, appears most likely, a strong movement might arise for giving them preferential treatment, especially if, at the same time, Germany, Belgium, or any one else were disposed to raise their duties on British goods."

A. D. 1897 (July—October).—Discussion with American envoys of a bi-metallic agreement. See (in this vol.) MONETARY QUESTIONS: A. D. 1897 (APRIL—OCTOBER).

A. D. 1897 (August).—Report on condition and prospects of West India colonies, and Parliamentary action. See (in this vol.) WEST INDIES, THE BRITISH: A. D. 1897.

A. D. 1897-1898.—Campaigns on the Nile. —Anglo-Egyptian conquest of the Sudan. See (in this vol.) EGYPT: A. D. 1897-1898.

A. D. 1897-1898.—Insurrections and mutiny in Uganda. See (in this vol.) UGANDA: A. D. 1897-1898.

A. D. 1897-1898 (June—April).—Wars on the Afghan frontier of India. See (in this vol.) INDIA: A. D. 1897-1898.

A. D. 1897-1898 (July—January).—The great strike and lock-out in the engineering trades. See (in this vol.) INDUSTRIAL DISTURBANCES: A. D. 1897 (GREAT BRITAIN).

A. D. 1898.—Alleged treaty with Portugal. See (in this vol.) PORTUGAL: A. D. 1898.

A. D. 1898.—Results of British occupation of Egypt. See (in this vol.) EGYPT: A. D. 1898.

A. D. 1898 (February).—British troops fighting in eight regions of the world.—"We are a people of peaceful traders—shopkeepers, our rivals of the Continent affirm—and are consequently at war on only eight points of the globe,

with forces which in the aggregate only just exceed sixty thousand men. There are thirty-five thousand on the Indian Frontier fighting the clansmen of the Northern Himalayas, who, according to the Afridi sub-officers interrogated by Sir Henry Havelock-Allan, are all eager to enter our service; twenty-five thousand about to defeat the Khalifa at Omdurman; a thousand doing sentry duty in Crete; four hundred putting down an outbreak in Mekran; three hundred crushing a mutiny in Uganda; and some hundreds more restoring order in Lagos, Borneo, and Basutoland. All these troops, though of differeat nationalities—Englishmen, Sikhs, Ghoorkas, Rajpoots. Malays, Egyptians, Soudanese, Haussas, and Wagandas—are under British officers, are paid from funds under British control, and are engaged in the self-same work, that of solidifying the 'Pax Britannica,' so that a commercial civilisation may have a fair chance to grow."—The Spectator (London), Feb. 5, 1898.

A. D. 1898(February).—Resentment shown to China for rejection of a loan, through Russian influence.—Chinese agreement not to alienate the Yang-tsze region and to open internal waters to steam navigation. See (in this vol.) CHINA: A. D. 1898 (FEBRUARY).

A. D. 1898 (February—May).—Native revolt in the Sierra Leone Protectorate. See (in this vol.) SIERRA LEONE PROTECTORATE.

A. D. 1898 (March—April).—Unsuccessful opposition to Russian lease of Port Arthur and Talienwan from China.—Compensatory British lease of Wei-hai Wei. See (in this vol.) CHINA: A. D. 1898 (MARCH—JULY).

A. D. 1898 (April—August).—Further exactions from China.—Lease of territory opposite Hong Kong, etc. See (in this vol.) CHINA: A. D. 1898 (APRIL—AUGUST).

A. D. 1898 (May).—Death of Mr. Gladstone.—After a long and painful illness, the great statesman and leader of the Liberal party in England, William Ewart Gladstone, died on the 19th of May. His death drew tributes in Parliament from his political opponents which exalted him quite to the height of great distinction that those who followed him would claim. It was said by Lord Salisbury that "the most distinguished political name of the century had been withdrawn from the roll of Englishmen." Mr. Balfour described him as "the greatest member of the greatest deliberative assembly that the world had yet seen"; and expressed the belief that "they would never again have in that assembly any man who could reproduce what Mr. Gladstone was to his contemporaries."

Lord Rosebery paid an eloquent tribute to the dead statesman. "This country," he said, "this nation, loves brave men. Mr. Gladstone was the bravest of the brave. There was no cause so hopeless that he was afraid to undertake it; there was no amount of opposition that would cowe him when once he had undertaken it. My lords, Mr. Gladstone always expressed a hope that there might be an interval left to him between the end of his political and of his natural life. That period was given to him, for it is more than four years since he quitted the sphere of politics. Those four years have been with him a special preparation for his death, but have they not also been a preparation for his death with the nation at large? Had he died in the plenitude of his power as Prime Minister, would

It have been possible for a vigorous and convinced Opposition to allow to pass to him, without a word of dissent, the honours which are now universally conceded? Hushed for the moment are the voices of criticism, hushed are the controversies in which he took part; hushed for the moment is the very sound of party faction. I venture to think that this is a notable fact in our history. It was not so with the elder Pitt. It was not so with the younger Pitt. It was not so with the elder Pitt, in spite of his tragic end, of his unrivalled services, and of his enfeebled old age. It was not so with the younger Pitt, in spite of his long control of the country and his absolute and absorbed devotion to the State. I think that we should remember this as creditable not merely to the man, but to the nation." With the consent of Mrs. Gladstone and family, a public funeral was voted by Parliament, and the remains of the great leader were laid, with simple but impressive ceremonies, in Westminster Abbey, on the 28th of May.

A. D. **1898** (June).—The Sugar Conference at Brussels. See (in this vol.) SUGAR BOUNTIES.

A. D. **1898** (July).—The Local Government Act for Ireland. See (in this vol.) IRELAND: A. D. 1898 (JULY).

A. **D. 1898** (July—December).—In the Chinese " Battle of Concessions." See (in this vol.) CHINA: A. D. 1898 (FEBRUARY—DECEMBER).

A. D. **1898** (September—November).—The Nile question with France.—Marchand's expedition at Fashoda. See (in this vol.) EGYPT: A. D. 1898 (SEPTEMBER—NOVEMBER).

A. D. **1898** (December).—Imperial Penny Postage.—On Christmas Day, 1898, the Imperial penny postage came into operation, — i. e., it became possible to send for a penny a letter not above half an ounce in weight to all places in the British Empire, except the Australasian Colonies and the Cape. "Thousands of small orders and business transactions and millions of questions and answers will fly round the world at a penny which were too heavily weighted at twopence halfpenny. The political effect of the fact that it will not now be necessary to think whether an address is outside the United Kingdom, but only whether it is inside the British Empire, will be by no means insignificant. If people will only let the Empire alone we shall ultimately weave out of many varied strands—some thick, some thin—a rope to join the Motherland and the Daughter States which none will be able to break. Not an unimportant thread in the hawser will be,—letters for a penny wherever the Union Jack is flown."—*The Spectator (London)*, Dec. 31, 1898.

A. D. **1898-1899**.—Joint High Commission for settlement of pending questions between the United States and Canada. See (in this vol.) CANADA: A. D. 1898–1899.

A. D. **1898-1899** (June—June).—Convention with France defining West African and Sudan possessions. See (in this vol.) NIGERIA: A. D. 1882–1899.

A. D. **1899**.—Dealings with anti-missionary demonstrations in China. See (in this vol.) CHINA: A. D. 1899.

A. D. **1899** (January).—Agreement with Egypt, establishing the Anglo-Egyptian Condominium in the Sudan. See (in this vol.) EGYPT: A. D. 1899 (JANUARY).

A. D. **1899** (March—April).—Agreement with Russia concerning railway interests in China. See (in this vol.) CHINA: A. D. 1899 (MARCH—APRIL).

A. D. **1899** (May—June).—The Bloemfontein Conference with President Kruger. See (in this vol.) SOUTH AFRICA (THE TRANSVAAL): A. D. 1899 (MAY—JUNE).

A. D. **1899** (May—July).—Representation in the Peace Conference at The Hague. See (in this vol.) PEACE CONFERENCE.

A. D. **1899** (June—October).—Arbitration and settlement of the Venezuela boundary question. See (in this vol.) VENEZUELA: A. D. 1896–1899.

A. D. **1899** (July).—Passage of the London Government Act. See (in this vol.) LONDON: A. D. 1899.

A. D. **1899** (July—September).—Discussion of proposed amendments to the Franchise Law of the South African Republic. See (in this vol.) SOUTH AFRICA (THE TRANSVAAL): A. D. 1899 (JULY—SEPTEMBER).

A. D. **1899** (August).—The Board of Education Act.—An Act of Parliament which became law on the 9th of August, 1899, and operative on the 1st of April, 1900, created a national Board of Education, "charged with the superintendance of matters relating to education in England and Wales," and taking the place of the Committee of the Privy Council on Education, by which that function had previously been performed. The Act provided that the Board "shall consist of a President, and of the Lord President of the Council (unless he is appointed President of the Board), Her Majesty's Principal Secretaries of State, the First Commissioner of Her Majesty's Treasury, and the Chancellor of Her Majesty's Exchequer. . . . The President of the Board shall be appointed by Her Majesty, and shall hold office during Her Majesty's pleasure." The Act provided further for the creation by Her Majesty in Council of "a Consultative Committee consisting, as to not less than two-thirds, of persons qualified to represent the views of Universities and other bodies interested in education, for the purpose of—(a) framing, with the approval of the Board of Education, regulations for a register of teachers, . . . with an entry in respect to each teacher showing the date of his registration, and giving a brief record of his qualifications and experience ; and (b) advising the Board of Education on any matter referred to the committee by the Board."—62 & 63 *Victoria, ch.* 33.

A. D. **1899** (August).—Instructions to the Governor of Jamaica. See (in this vol.) JAMAICA : A. D. 1899.

A. D. **1899** (September—October).—Preparations for war in South Africa.—The Boer Ultimatum. See (in this vol.) SOUTH AFRICA (THE TRANSVAAL AND ORANGE FREE STATE): A. D. 1899 (SEPTEMBER—OCTOBER).

A. D. **1899** (October—November).—Opening circumstances of the war in South Africa. — Want of preparation. See (in this vol.) SOUTH AFRICA (THE FIELD OF WAR): A. D. 1899 (OCTOBER—NOVEMBER).

A. D. **1899** (November).—Adhesion to the arrangement of an "open door" commercial policy in China. See (in this vol.) CHINA : A. D. 1899-1900 (SEPTEMBER—FEBRUARY).

A. D. **1899** (November).—Withdrawal from

the Samoan Islands, with compensations in the Tonga and Solomon Islands and in Africa. See (in this vol.) SAMOAN ISLANDS.

A. D. 1899-1900.—Renewed investigation **of the Old-Age** Pension question.—On the initiative of the government, a fresh investigation of the question of old-age pensions was opened in 1899 by a select committee of the House of Commons, under the chairmanship of Mr. Chaplin. The report of the Committee, made in the following year, suggested the following plan: Any person, aged 65, whether man or woman, who satisfied the pension authority that he or she "(1) Is a British subject; (2) Is 65 years of age; (3) Has not within the last 20 years been convicted of an offence and sentenced to penal servitude or imprisonment without the option of a fine; (4) Has not received poor relief, other than medical relief, unless under circumstances of a wholly exceptional character, during twenty years prior to the application for a pension; (5) Is resident within the district of the pension authority; (6) Has not an income from any source of more than 10s. a week; and (7) Has endeavoured to the best of his ability, by his industry or by the exercise of reasonable providence, to make provision for himself and those immediately dependent on him—" should receive a certificate to that effect and be entitled to a pension. The amount of pension to be from 5s. to 7s. a week.

As a means of ascertaining approximately the number of persons in the United Kingdom who would be pensionable under this scheme, a test census was taken in certain districts made as representative as possible by the inclusion of various kinds of population. In each of the selected areas in Great Britain a house-to-house visitation was made with a view of ascertaining how many of the aged would satisfy the conditions of the scheme. In Ireland a similar census had to be abandoned as impracticable because "the officials, although they proceeded courteously, were received with abuse"; but the Poor Law inspectors framed some rough estimates after consultation with local authorities. Altogether the inquiry in Great Britain extended to a population of rather over half a million persons. From facts thus obtained the following estimate of the cost of the proposed pensioning project was deduced:

Estimated number of persons over 65 years of age in 1901	2,016,000
Deduct:—	
1. For those whose incomes exceed 10s. a week	741,000
2. For paupers	515,000
3. For aliens, criminals, and lunatics	32,000
4. For inability to comply with thrift test	72,700
Total deductions	1,360,700
Estimated number of pensionable persons	655,000
Estimated cost (the average pension being taken at 6s. a week)	£9,976,000
Add administrative expenses (3 per cent.)	299,000
Total estimated cost	£10,275,000
In round figures	£10,300,000

The Committee estimated, still further, that the cost would rise to £15,650,000 by 1921. No legislative action was taken on the report.

A. D. 1899-1900 (October—January).—Troops from Canada for the South African War. See (in this vol.) CANADA: A. D. 1899-1900.

A. D. 1899-1901.— The Newfoundland French Shore question. See (in this vol.) NEWFOUNDLAND: A. D. 1899-1901.

A. D. 1900.—Industrial combinations. See (in this vol.) TRUSTS: IN ENGLAND.

A. D. 1900.—Naval strength. See (in this vol.) NAVIES OF THE SEA POWERS.

A. D. 1900 (January—March).—The outbreak of the "Boxers" in northern China.—See (in this vol.) CHINA: A. D. 1900 (JANUARY —MARCH).

A. D. 1900 (February).—Compulsory education.—A bill introduced in Parliament by a private member, unsupported by the government, providing that the earliest date at which a child should be permitted to leave school should be raised from 11 to 12 years, was passed, only one member of the Cabinet voting for it.

A. D. 1900 (February).—Negotiation of a convention with the United States relative to the projected Interoceanic Canal. See (in this vol.) CANAL, INTEROCEANIC: A. D. 1900 (DECEMBER).

A. D. 1900 (March).—Overtures of peace from the Boer Presidents.—Reply of Lord Salisbury. See (in this vol.) SOUTH AFRICA (THE FIELD OF WAR): A. D. 1900 (MARCH).

A. D. 1900 (May).—Annexation of Orange Free State by right of conquest. See (in this vol.) SOUTH AFRICA (ORANGE FREE STATE): A. D. 1900 (MAY).

A. D. 1900 (June—December).—Co-operation with the Powers in China. See (in this vol.) CHINA.

A. D. 1900 (July).—Passage of the "Commonwealth of Australia Constitution Act," federating the Australian Colonies. See (in this vol.) AUSTRALIA: A. D. 1900; and CONSTITUTION OF AUSTRALIA.

A. D. 1900 (September).—Proclamation of the Commonwealth of Australia. See (in this vol.) AUSTRALIA: A. D. 1900 (SEPTEMBER—DECEMBER).

A. D. 1900 (September—October).—Dissolution of Parliament.—Election of a new Parliament.—Victory for the Conservatives and Liberal Unionists.—By royal proclamation, September 17, the existing Parliament was dissolved and order given for the issue of writs calling a new Parliament, the elections for which were held in October, concluding on the 24th of that month. The state of parties in the House of Commons resulting from the election was as follows: Conservatives, 334, Liberal Unionists, 68; total supporters of the Unionist Ministry, 402. Liberals and Labor members, 186, Nationalists (Irish), 82; total opposition, 268. Unionist majority, 134, against 128 in the preceding Parliament. The issues in the election were those growing out of the South African War. Although most of the Liberals upheld the war, and the annexation of the South African republics, they sharply criticised the prior dealings of the Colonial Secretary, Mr. Chamberlain, with the Transvaal Boers, and the general conduct of the war. A number of the leading Liberals were uncompromising in condemnation of the war, of the policy which caused it, and of the proposed extinction of Boer independence. The sentiment of the country was shown by the election to be strongly against all questioning of the righteousness of the war or of the use to be made of victory in it.

A. D. 1900 (October). — Anglo-German agreement concerning policy in China. See (in this vol.) CHINA : A. D. 1900 (AUGUST—DECEMBER).

A. D. 1900 (October).—Annexation of the Transvaal. See (in this vol.) SOUTH AFRICA (THE TRANSVAAL): A. D. 1900 (OCTOBER).

A. D. 1900 (November—December).—The Fourth Ministry of Lord Salisbury.—Brief session of Parliament.—For the fourth time, Lord Salisbury was called to the lead in government, and formed his Ministry anew, making considerable changes. He relieved himself of the conduct of Foreign Affairs (which was transferred to the Marquis of Lansdowne), and took, with the office of Prime Minister, that of Lord Privy Seal. Mr. Brodrick, who had been an Under Secretary, succeeded Lord Lansdowne as Secretary of State for War. Mr. Balfour continued to be First Lord of the Treasury, and Leader of the House; Mr. Chamberlain remained in the Colonial Office. Mr. Goschen retired.

Parliament met on the 6th of December, for the purpose set forth in a remarkably brief "Queen's Speech," as follows : "My Lords, and Gentlemen, It has become necessary to make further provision for the expenses incurred by the operations of my armies in South Africa and China. I have summoned you to hold a Special Session in order that you may give your sanction to the enactments required for this purpose. I will not enter upon other public matters requiring your attention until the ordinary meeting of Parliament in the spring." The estimates of the War Office called for £16,000,000, and it was voted after a few days of debate, in which the causes and conduct of the war were criticised and defended by the two parties, and, on the 15th, Parliament was prorogued to the 14th of February, 1901, by the Queen's command.

A. D. 1900 (December).—Fall of stones at Stonehenge. See (in this vol.) STONEHENGE.

A. D. 1900 (December). — Parliamentary statements of the number of men employed in the South African War, and the number dead and disabled.—In the House of Commons, December 11, Mr. Brodrick, Secretary of State for War, moved a vote of £16,000,000, required for the current year, to meet additional expenditure in South Africa and China. In the course of his remarks, explanatory of the need for this supplementary supply, he made the following statement: "When the war broke out we had in South Africa in round figures 10,000 men, all Regular troops. We have in the 14 months which have since elapsed sent to this country and landed in South Africa 175,000 Regular soldiers, a number which exceeds by far any number which any Minister from this bench or any gentleman sitting behind these benches or in front of them ever suggested that this country ought to be in a position to ship to any part of the world, and a number far in excess of that which during any period that I have sat in the house any member of the House, except an official, would have been willing to believe that the War Office could find to dispose of. But they are not the only troops. We have called on them, I will not say to the extreme limit of our power, but, at all events, with an unsparing hand. But you have in addition, as this return will show, some 40,000 Volunteers of various descriptions from the United Kingdom—40,000 including the Im-

perial Yeomanry, whose service is spoken of by every officer under whom they have served with such satisfaction ; 30 Militia regiments, who are also Volunteers, since their term of service was only for the United Kingdom and who have gone abroad at great personal sacrifice to themselves ; and the Volunteer companies who have joined the Regular battalions. You have also got 40,000 colonial troops, to a large extent, no doubt, men raised in the colonies affected, and as everybody knows to a still larger extent consisting of men who have gone for a year from Australia, Canada, and other places."

Sir William Harcourt replied to Mr. Brodrick, not in opposition to the motion, but in criticism of the conduct of the war. Referring to a return submitted by the War Office, he analyzed its showing of facts, thus : "Now just let us look at this table. By some accident it only gives the rank and file and non-commissioned officers. It is a very terrible return, and I think it is worthy of the attention of the men who delight in war, of whom, I am afraid, there are unhappily not a few. I have made a short analysis of the paper. It shows that the garrison at the Cape before the war was 9,600. Reinforcements of 6,300 men were sent out in October last year and from India 5,600, which with the former garrison made up 21,000 in all when the war broke out. Up to August, that is, after the last estimate for 1900, according to this table 267,000 men had been in arms in South Africa—that is without the officers. Therefore I will call it 270,000 men in round numbers. I think the right hon. gentleman made a mistake when he said that the colonial troops were more numerous from beyond the seas than they were in the Cape. This return shows that the men raised in South Africa were 30,000, and, apart from them, the colonials from beyond the seas were 11,000. According to your last return there were 210,000 men in South Africa. You will observe there is a balance of some 60,000 or 70,000 men. What has become of those men ? You would find from this return, one would suppose, that a good many of these have returned safe and sound to England. No, Sir ; the men who have returned to England according to this paper, not invalids, are 7,500 and to the colonies 3,000 more. That makes 10,000 men, or with the officers about 11,-000 men. But since July you have sent out 13,000 men to South Africa, more, in fact, than you have been bringing home, and yet you have only 210,000 men there. Now, Sir, how is this accounted for ? First of all you have the heading, 'killed or died of wounds,' 11,000 men. You have 'wounded,' 13,000, you have 'in hospital in South Africa,' 12,000, and you have 'returned to England, sick, wounded, or died on passage,' 36,000 men. That is the balance. Seventy thousand men have been killed, wounded, or disabled, or have died in this war. And now what is the prospect that is held before us with this force, once 270,000 men, and now 210,000, in South Africa? Lord Roberts has declared that the war is over, yet you hold out to us no prospect of diminishing the force you have in South Africa of 210,000 men."

A. D. 1901 (January).—Death of Queen Victoria.—The following notice, which appeared in the "Court Circular," on the 18th of January, dated from the winter residence of the Queen at Osborne House, in the Isle of Wight, seems to have been the first intimation to the country of its sovereign's failing health: "The Queen has not lately been in her usual health and is unable for the present to take her customary drives. The Queen during the past year has had a great strain upon her powers, which has rather told upon her Majesty's nervous system. It has, therefore, been thought advisable by her Majesty's physicians that the Queen should be kept perfectly quiet in the house and should abstain for the present from transacting business." It was subsequently found, as stated in an "authoritative account" by the "British Medical Journal," and the "Lancet," that "the Queen's health for the past 12 months had been failing, with symptoms mainly of a dyspeptic kind, accompanied by impaired general nutrition, periods of insomnia, and later by occasional slight and transitory attacks of aphasia, the latter suggesting that the cerebral vessels had become damaged, although her Majesty's general arterial system showed remarkably few signs of age. . . . The dyspepsia which tended to lower her Majesty's original robust constitution was especially marked during her last visit to Balmoral. It was there that the Queen first manifested distinct symptoms of brain fatigue and lost notably in weight. These symptoms continued at Windsor, where in November and December, 1900, slight aphasic symptoms were first observed, always of an ephemeral kind, and unattended by any motor paralysis. . . . A few days before the final illness transient but recurring symptoms of apathy and somnolence, with aphasic indications and increasing feebleness, gave great uneasiness to her physician." Before the publication of the cautious announcement quoted above, the symptoms had become too grave to leave any doubt as to the near approach of death. It came on Tuesday, the 22d of January, at half past six o'clock in the evening, the dying Queen being then surrounded by a large number of her many children, grandchildren and great grandchildren, whom she recognized, it is said, within a few moments of the end. The eldest of the Queen's children, the Empress Frederick, was kept from her mother's side at this last hour by serious illness of her own; but the Emperor William, of Germany (son of the Empress Frederick and eldest grandson of Queen Victoria) had hastened to the scene and showed a filial affection which touched English hearts.

On Friday, the first day of February, the remains of the Queen were borne from the island where she died to Portsmouth, between long lines of battle-ships and cruisers—British, German, French, Italian, Japanese, Belgian and Portuguese. The scene of the funeral voyage was impressively described by a correspondent of the New York "Sun," as follows: "Nature was never kindlier. The smiling waters of the Solent were as calm as on a summer's morning. It was 'Queen's weather' to the very last. The cavalcade which wended slowly through the narrow lane, green even in midwinter, down through the streets of the little town of Cowes to the Trinity pier was a funeral procession such as the world had never seen before. Kings and princes, a Queen and princesses, walked humbly between black lines of mourning islanders, escorting the coffin of the dead sovereign. Then followed a sight far more notable and more impressive, indeed, than the great tribute the great capital of

the empire will pay to-morrow. It was the transit of the funeral yacht across the waters between lines of steel which are England's bulwarks against the world. Battleship after battleship thundered its grief, band after band wailed its dirge and crew after crew bowed low their heads as the pigmy yacht swept past, bearing no passengers save an admiral on the bridge and four red-coated guards at the corners of the simple, glowing white bier resting amidships. It was a picture neither a painter's brush nor an orator's eloquence could reproduce. . . . The boat slowly glided on in the mellow light of the afternoon sun, herself almost golden in hue, sharply contrasting with the black warships. The ears also were assailed in strange contrast, the sad strains of Beethoven's funeral march floating over the water being punctuated by the roar of minute guns from each ship. Somehow it was not incongruous and one felt that it was all a great and majestic tribute to a reign which was an era and to a sovereign to whom the world pays its highest honors."

On the following day the remains were conveyed by railway from Portsmouth to London, carried in solemn procession through the streets of the capital, and thence by railway to Windsor, where the last rites were performed on Monday, the 4th. The Queen was then laid to rest, by the side of her husband, in the mausoleum which she had built at Frogmore.

Of the sincerity with which Queen Victoria had been loved by her own people and respected and admired by the world at large, and of the genuineness of sorrow that was manifested everywhere at her death, there can be no doubt. To the impressiveness of the ending of an unexampled period of history there was added a true sense of loss, from the disappearance of a greatly important personage, whose high example had been pure and whose large influence had been good.

Among all the tributes to the Queen that were called out by her death none seem so significant and so fully drawn from knowledge of what she was in her regal character, as the words that were spoken by Lord Salisbury in the House of Lords, at the meeting of Parliament on the Friday following her death. "My lords," he said, "the late Queen had so many titles to our admiration that it would occupy an enormous time to glance at them even perfunctorily; but that on which I think your lordships should most reflect, and which will chiefly attach to her character in history, is that, being a constitutional monarch with restricted powers, she reigned by sheer force of character, by the lovableness of her disposition, over the hearts of her subjects, and exercised an influence in moulding their character and destiny which she could not have done more if she had had the most despotic power. She has been a great instance of government by example, by esteem, by love; and it will never be forgotten how much she has done for the elevation of her people, not by the exercise of any prerogative, not by the giving of any commands, but by the simple recognition and contemplation of the brilliant qualities which she has exhibited in her exalted position. My lords, it may be, perhaps, proper that those who, like noble lords opposite and myself, have had the opportunity of seeing the close workings of her character in the discharge of her duties as Sovereign, should take this opportunity of testifying to the great admiration she inspired and the great force which her distinguishing characteristics exercised over all who came near her. The position of a Constitutional Sovereign is not an easy one. Duties have to be reconciled which sometimes seem far apart. Much has to be accepted which it may not be always pleasant to accept; but she showed a wonderful power, on the one hand, of observing with the most absolute strictness, the limits of her action which the Constitution draws, and, on the other hand, of maintaining a steady and persistent influence on the action of her Ministers in the course of legislation and government which no one could mistake. She was able to accept some things of which, perhaps, she did not entirely approve, but which she thought it her duty in her position to accept.

"She always maintained and practised a rigorous supervision over public affairs, giving to her Ministers her frank advice and warning them of danger if she saw there was danger ahead; and she certainly impressed many of us with a profound sense of the penetration, almost intuition, with which she saw the perils with which we might be threatened in any course it was thought expedient to adopt. She left upon my mind, she left upon our minds, the conviction that it was always a dangerous matter to press on her any course of the expediency of which she was not thoroughly convinced; and I may say with confidence that no Minister in her long reign ever disregarded her advice, or pressed her to disregard it, without afterwards feeling that he had incurred a dangerous responsibility. She had an extraordinary knowledge of what her people would think. I have said for years that I always thought that when I knew what the Queen thought I knew certainly what view her subjects would take, and especially the middle classes of her subjects. Such was the extraordinary penetration of her mind. Yet she never adhered to her own conceptions obstinately. On the contrary, she was full of concession and consideration; and she spared no effort—I might almost say she shrank from no sacrifice—to make the task of conducting this difficult Government more easy to her advisers than it would otherwise have been. My lords, I feel sure that the testimony I have borne will be abundantly sustained by all those who have been called to serve her.

"We owe her gratitude in every direction—for her influence in elevating the people, for her power with foreign Courts and Sovereigns to remove difficulties and misapprehension which sometimes might have been dangerous; but, above all things, I think, we owe her gratitude for this, that by a happy dispensation her reign has coincided with that great change which has come over the political structure of this country and the political instincts of its people. She has bridged over that great interval which separates old England from new England. Other nations may have had to pass through similar trials, but have seldom passed through them so peaceably, so easily, and with so much prosperity and success as we have. I think that future historians will look to the Queen's reign as the boundary which separates the two states of England—England which has changed so much—and recognize that we have undergone the change with constant increase of public prosperity, without any friction to endanger the peace or stability of our

civil life, and at the same time with a constant expansion of an Empire which every year grows more and more powerful. We owe all these blessings to the tact, the wisdom, the passionate patriotism, and the incomparable judgment of the Sovereign whom we deplore."

In the House of Commons, on the same day, Mr. Balfour, the leader of the House, spoke with fine feeling, partly as follows: "The reign of Queen Victoria is no mere chronological landmark. It is no mere convenient division of time, useful for the historian or the chronicler. No, Sir, we feel as we do feel for our great loss because we intimately associate the personality of Queen Victoria with the great succession of events which have filled her reign and with the development of the Empire over which she ruled. And, associating her personality with those events, surely we do well. In my judgment, the importance of the Crown in our Constitution is not a diminishing, but an increasing, factor. It is increasing, and must increase, with the growth and development of those free, self-governing communities, those new commonwealths beyond the sea, who are bound to us by the person of the Sovereign, who is the living symbol of the unity of the Empire. But, Sir, it is not given, it cannot, in ordinary course, be given, to a Constitutional Monarch to signalize his reign by any great isolated action. The effect of a Constitutional Sovereign, great as it is, is produced by the slow, constant, and cumulative results of a great ideal and a great example; and of that great ideal and that great example Queen Victoria surely was the first of all Constitutional Monarchs whom the world has yet seen. Where shall we find that ideal so lofty in itself, so constantly and consistently maintained, through two generations, through more than two generations, of her subjects, through many generations of her public men and members of this House?

"Sir, it would be almost impertinent for me were I to attempt to express to the House in words the effect which the character of our late Sovereign produced upon all who were in any degree, however remote, brought in contact with her. The simple dignity, befitting a Monarch of this realm, in that she could never fail, because it arose from her inherent sense of the fitness of things. It was no trapping put on for office, and therefore it was that this dignity, this Queenly dignity, only served to throw into stronger relief and into a brighter light those admirable virtues of the wife, the mother, and the woman with which she was so richly endowed. Those kindly graces, those admirable qualities, have endeared her to every class in the community, and are known to all. Perhaps less known was the life of continuous labour which her position as Queen threw upon her. Short as was the interval between the last trembling signature affixed to a public document and final rest, it was yet long enough to clog and hamper the wheels of administration; and I remember when I saw a vast mass of untouched documents which awaited the hand of the Sovereign of this country to deal with it was brought vividly before my mind how admirable was the unostentatious patience with which for 63 years, through sorrow, through suffering, in moments of weariness, in moments of despondency, it may be, she carried on without intermission her share in the

DESCENDANTS OF QUEEN VICTORIA

And of the Prince Consort, Albert, second son of the Duke of Saxe-Coburg-Gotha, whom she married on the 10th of February, 1840, and who died December 14, 1861.

CHILDREN.	GRANDCHILDREN.	GREAT-GRANDCHILDREN.
Victoria, Born 1840, Married 1858, to Frederick, Crown Prince of Prussia, afterwards German Emperor.	William, German Emperor, Born 1859, Married 1881, to Augusta of Schleswig-Holstein.	William, Born 1882. Eitel, Born 1883. Adalbert, Born 1884. Augustus, Born 1887. Oscar, Born 1888. Joachim, Born 1890. Victoria, Born 1892.
	Charlotte, Born 1860, Married 1878, to the Prince of Saxe-Meiningen.	Feodora, Born 1879, Married 1893, to Henry, Prince Reuss.
	Albert William Henry,* Born 1862, Married 1888, to Princess Irene of Hesse.	Waldemar, Born 1889. Sigismund, Born 1896. Henry, Born 1900.
	Francis Frederick Sigismund, b. 1864 — d. 1866.	
	Frederika Victoria, Born 1866, Married 1890.	
	Ernest Waldemar, b. 1868 — d. 1879.	
	Sophie Dorothea, Born 1870, Married 1889, to the Duke of Sparta.	George, Born 1890. Alexander, Born 1893. Helena, Born 1896.
	Margaretta Beatrice, Born 1872, Married 1893, to Frederick Charles of Hesse-Cassel.	Frederick, Born 1893. Maximilian, Born 1894. Philippe, Born 1896. Wolfgang, Born 1896.
EDWARD VII., King of England, Born 1841, Married 1863, to Princess Alexandra of Denmark.	Albert Victor, Duke of Clarence, b. 1864 — d. 1892.	
	George, Duke of York, Born 1865, Married 1893, to Princess Victoria Mary of Teck.	Edward Albert, Born 1894. Albert Frederick, Born 1895. Victoria Alexandra, Born 1897. Henry William, Born 1900.
	Louise, Born 1867, Married 1889, to the Duke of Fife.	Alexandra, Born 1891. Maud, Born 1893.
	Victoria, Born 1868.	
	Maud, Born 1869, Married 1896.	
	Alexander, b. 1871 — d. 1871.	
Alice, Born 1843, Married 1862, to Grand Duke of Hesse. Died 1878.	Victoria, Born 1863, Married 1884, to Prince Louis of Battenberg.	Alice, Born 1885. Louise, Born 1889. George, Born 1892. Albert, Born 1900.

CHILDREN.	GRANDCHILDREN.	GREAT-GRANDCHILDREN.
Alice — continued	Elizabeth, Born 1864, Married 1884.	
	Irene,* Born 1866, Married 1888, to Prince Henry of Prussia.	
	Ernest Louis,* Born 1868, Married 1894.	Elizabeth, Born 1895.
	Frederick William, b. 1870 — d. 1873.	
	Alix Victoria, Born 1872, Married 1894, to Nicholas II., Tsar of Russia.	Olga, Born 1895. Tatiana, Born 1897. Marie, Born 1899.
	Maria Victoria, b. 1874 — d. 1878.	
Alfred, Duke of Saxe-Coburg and Gotha, Born 1844, Married 1874, to Grand Duchess Marie of Russia. Died 1900.	Alfred, b. 1874 — d. 1899.	
	Marie, Born 1875, Married 1893, to Ferdinand, Crown Prince of Roumania.	Carol, Born 1893. Elizabeth, Born 1894. Marie, Born 1900.
	Victoria Melita,* Born 1876, Married 1894.	Godefroy, Born 1897. Marie, Born 1899.
	Alexandra, Born 1878, Married 1896.	
	Beatrice, Born 1884.	
Helena, Born 1846, Married 1866, to Prince Christian of Schleswig-Holstein.	Christian Victor, b. 1867 — d. 1900.	
	Albert John, Born 1869.	
	Victoria Louise, Born 1870.	
	Louise Augusta, Born 1872, Married 1891.	
	Harold Frederick, b. 1876 — d. 1876.	
Louise, Born 1848, Married 1871, to the Marquis of Lorne.		
Arthur, Duke of Connaught, Born 1850, Married 1879, to Princess Margaret of Prussia.	Louise Margaret, Born 1882. Arthur Patrick, Born 1883. Victoria Patricia, Born 1886.	
Leopold, Duke of Albany, Born 1853, Married 1882, Died 1884.	Alice Mary, Born 1883. Leopold, Born 1884.	
Beatrice, Born 1857, Married 1885, to Prince Henry of Battenberg.	Alexander Albert, Born 1886. Victoria Eugénie, Born 1887. Leopold, Born 1889. Maurice, Born 1891.	

* These are marriages of first cousins, or cousins-german.

government of this great Empire. For her there was no holiday, to her there was no intermission of toil. Domestic sorrow, domestic sickness, made no difference in her labours, and they were continued from the hour at which she became our Sovereign to within a very few days of her death. It is easy to chronicle the growth of Empire, the progress of trade, the triumphs of war, all the events that make history interesting or exciting; but who is there that will dare to weigh in the balance the effect which such an example continued over 63 years has produced on the highest life of the people? It is a great life, and had a fortunate, and, let me say, in my judgment, a happy ending."

The especial and peculiar importance which Queen Victoria had acquired in the political world, and the weight in its councils which England owed to her personality, were impressively suggested by Lord Rosebery, in a speech which he made at a special court of the Governors of the Corporation of the Royal Scottish Hospital, when he said: "We hear much in these days of the life of the Queen and of what we owe her. But I sometimes wonder if we all realize how much we do owe her, for you would have had to know much about the Queen to realize adequately the debt which the nation was under to her. Probably every subject in Great Britain realizes that he has lost his greatest and his best friend. But they do not understand of what enormous weight in the councils of the world we are deprived by the death of our late Sovereign. She gave to the councils of Great Britain an advantage which no talents, no brilliancy, no genius, could supply. Think of what her reign was! She had reigned for 63 years. For 63 years she had known all that was to be known about the political condition of her country. For 63 years she had been in communication with every important Minister and with every important public man. She had received reports, daily reports almost, from her successive Ministers, or their deputies in the House of Commons. She had, therefore, a fund of knowledge which no constitutional historian has ever had at his command. That by the stroke of death is lost to us to-day. All that was of incalculable advantage to our Monarchy. But have you realized what the personal weight of the late Queen was in the councils of the world? She was by far the senior of all the European Sovereigns. She was, it is no disparagement to other Kings to say, the chief of all the European Sovereigns. The German Emperor was her grandson by birth. The Emperor of Russia was her grandson by marriage. She had reigned 11 years when the Emperor of Austria came to his throne. She had seen two dynasties pass from the throne of France. She had seen, as Queen, three Monarchs of Spain, and four Sovereigns of the House of Savoy in Italy. In all those kingdoms which have been carved out of the Turkish Empire she had seen the foundation of their reigning dynasties. Can we not realize, then, what a force the personal influence of such a Sovereign was in the troubled councils of Europe? And when, as we know, that influence was always given for peace, for freedom, and for good government, we feel that not merely ourselves but all the world has lost one of its best friends."

A statement in the "London Times" of January 26 shows the descendants of Queen Victoria to

be in number as follows: "The Queen has had

9 children	of whom	6 survive
40 grandchildren . .	of whom	31 survive
37 great-grandchildren	of whom	37 survive
86		74

"Of the great-grandchildren 22 are boys and 15 are girls; 6 are grandchildren of the Prince of Wales; 18 are grandchildren of the Empress Frederick; 11 are grandchildren of the late Princess Alice; 6 are grandchildren of the late Duke of Saxe-Coburg and Gotha. This would appear to make a total of 41, but three of them are grandchildren of both the Empress Frederick and Princess Alice, while one is grandchild of both the Princess Alice and the Duke of Saxe-Coburg and Gotha.

"It will be seen that in the course of nature the future rulers of Great Britain, Germany, Russia, Greece, and Rumania will be descendants of her Majesty."

A. D. 1901 (January—February).—**Ceremonies of the accession of King Edward VII.—His speech in Council and his messages to the people of the British Empire.**—On Wednesday, the 23d of January—the day following the death of the Queen—her eldest son, Albert Edward, long known as Prince of Wales, went from Osborne to London to take up the sceptre of sovereignty which his mother had laid down. The proceedings in Council which took place thereupon were officially reported in the "London Gazette" as follows:

"At the Court at Saint James's, the 23rd day of January, 1901. Present,

"The King's Most Excellent Majesty in Council. His Majesty being this day present in Council was pleased to make the following Declaration:—

"'Your Royal Highnesses, My Lords, and Gentlemen, This is the most painful occasion on which I shall ever be called upon to address you. My first and melancholy duty is to announce to you the death of My beloved Mother the Queen, and I know how deeply you, the whole Nation, and I think I may say the whole world, sympathize with Me in the irreparable loss we have all sustained. I need hardly say that My constant endeavour will be always to walk in Her footsteps. In undertaking the heavy load which now devolves upon Me, I am fully determined to be a Constitutional Sovereign in the strictest sense of the word, and as long as there is breath in My body to work for the good and amelioration of My people.

"'I have resolved to be known by the name of Edward, which has been borne by six of My ancestors. In doing so I do not undervalue the name of Albert, which I inherit from My ever to be lamented, great and wise Father, who by universal consent is I think deservedly known by the name of Albert the Good, and I desire that his name should stand alone.

"'In conclusion, I trust to Parliament and the Nation to support Me in the arduous duties which now devolve upon Me by inheritance, and to which I am determined to devote My whole strength during the remainder of My life.'

"Whereupon the Lords of the Council made it their humble request to His Majesty that His Majesty's Most Gracious Declaration to their

Lordships might be made public, which His Majesty was pleased to Order accordingly."

The King then "caused all the Lords and others of the late Queen's Privy Council, who were then present, to be sworn of His Majesty's Privy Council." Orders had been previously given for proclaiming "His present Majesty," in the following form: "Whereas it has pleased Almighty God to call to His Mercy Our late Sovereign Lady Queen Victoria, of Blessed and Glorious Memory, by whose Decease the Imperial Crown of the United Kingdom of Great Britain and Ireland is solely and rightfully come to the High and Mighty Prince Albert Edward: We, therefore, the Lords Spiritual and Temporal of this Realm, being here assisted with these of Her late Majesty's Privy Council, with Numbers of other Principal Gentlemen of Quality, with the Lord Mayor, Aldermen, and Citizens of London, do now hereby, with one Voice and Consent of Tongue and Heart, publish and proclaim, That the High and Mighty Prince, Albert Edward, is now, by the Death of our late Sovereign of Happy Memory, become our only lawful and rightful Liege Lord Edward the Seventh, by the Grace of God, King of the United Kingdom of Great Britain and Ireland, Defender of the Faith, Emperor of India: To whom we do acknowledge all Faith and constant Obedience, with all hearty and humble Affection; beseeching God, by whom Kings and Queens do reign, to bless the Royal Prince Edward the Seventh, with long and happy Years to reign over Us."

The proclamation was made in London, with antique and picturesque ceremony on the succeeding day, January 24, and the following official report of it, from "Earl Marshal's Office," published in the "London Gazette":

"This day His Most Gracious Majesty King Edward VII. was, in pursuance of an Order in Council of the 23rd instant, proclaimed with the usual ceremonies. At 9 o'clock in the forenoon, the Officers of Arms habited in their tabards, the Serjeants-at-Arms, with their maces and collars; and Deputy-Serjeant Trumpeter in his collar; the Trumpeters, Drum Major, and Knight Marshalmen being assembled at St James's Palace, the Proclamation was read in the Grand Court by William H. Weldon, Esq., Norroy King of Arms, Deputy to Sir Albert W. Woods, Garter Principal King of Arms, in the presence of the Earl Marshal of England, the Lord Steward, the Lord Chamberlain, the Master of the Horse, and many other Members of Her late Majesty's Household, with Lords and others of the Privy Council and several personages of distinction. Deputy Garter read the Proclamation. Then the Officers of Arms having entered Royal Carriages, a procession was formed in the following order:—

The High Bailiff of Westminster, in his carriage.
Horse Guards.
Trumpeters.
A Royal Carriage containing
The four Serjeants-at-Arms, bearing their maces.
A Royal Carriage containing
Pursuivants.
Rouge Dragon:
Everard Green.

Bluemantle: Rouge Croix:
G. Ambrose Lee.   G. W. Marshall.

Heralds.
Windsor:
W. A. Lindsay, Esq.
York: Somerset:
A. S. Scott-Gatty, Esq., H. Farnham Burke, Esq., in a Royal Carriage.
A Detachment of Horse Guards.

"The Procession, flanked by the Horse Guards, moved from St. James's Palace to Temple Bar, and Rouge Dragon Pursuivant of Arms, alighting from the carriage, advanced between two trumpeters, preceded by two of the Horse Guards, to the barrier, and after the trumpets had sounded thrice, demanded in the usual form admission into the City to proclaim His Royal Majesty King Edward VII.; and being admitted, and the barrier again closed, Rouge Dragon was conducted by the City Marshal and his Officers to the Lord Mayor, who was in attendance in his State Carriage, when Rouge Dragon delivered to his Lordship the Order in Council, which the Lord Mayor, having read, returned, and directed the barrier to be opened; and Rouge Dragon being reconducted to his place in the Procession it then moved into the City; the High Bailiff of Westminster filing off at Temple Bar.

"At the corner of Chancery-lane York Herald read the Proclamation; then the Lord Mayor, Aldermen, Recorder, Sheriffs, Chamberlain, Common Serjeant, Town Clerk, and City Officers fell into the procession immediately after the Officers of Arms, and the procession moved on to the Royal Exchange, where it was lastly read by Somerset Herald, when the guns in St. James's Park and at the Tower of London were fired. A multitude of spectators filled the streets through which the procession passed, the windows of which were crowded; and the acclamations were loud and general."

As described more fully by the "London Times," the interesting proceeding, according to ancient custom, at Temple Bar—the site of the old city gate—was as follows: "Temple Bar has passed away, but not so the privileges associated with it, although they have ceased to have more than an historical, ceremonial, and picturesque interest. In accordance, therefore, with ancient custom, the Lord Mayor yesterday proceeded in State to the site of Temple Bar to grant entrance to the King's Officer of Arms, who was about to proclaim his Majesty King within the City. The gates of Temple Bar were formerly closed for a short time before this ceremony, to be opened, upon demand of the Officer of Arms, by the direction of the Lord Mayor. As there are now no gates, a barrier was made for the occasion by the holding of a red silken rope across the street on either side of the Griffin which commemorates the spot upon which Temple Bar formerly stood. A strong force of burly constables was entrusted with this duty, and the barrier thus created answered every practical purpose, although there must have been lingering in the minds of some of the venerable City Fathers some little regret that stern necessity had occasioned the removal of the historic landmark which stood there when Queen Victoria was proclaimed and remained for many a long year afterwards, one of the most interesting features of the ancient City.

"The Pursuivant (Rouge Dragon), the heralds, the officials of Westminster, and the cavalcade halted a short distance to the west of the barrier, and the Pursuivant then advanced between two trumpeters, and the trumpets sounded thrice. Upon this the City Marshal, on horseback, in scarlet tunic and cocked hat with plumes, advanced to the barrier to meet the Pursuivant, and in a loud voice, which could be heard by those at a considerable distance, asked, 'Who comes there?' The Pursuivant replied, 'The Officer of Arms, who demands entrance into the City to proclaim his Royal Majesty, Edward the Seventh.' Thereupon the barrier was opened so as to admit the Pursuivant without escort, and immediately closed again. The Pursuivant was then conducted by the City Marshal to the Lord Mayor, who, being made acquainted with the object of the Pursuivant's visit, directed the opening of the barrier, and the Pursuivant returned to his cavalcade. There was a fanfare of trumpets, and York Herald, Mr. A. S. Scott-Gatty, between two trumpeters, approached the Lord Mayor, and presented to his lordship the Order in Council requiring him to proclaim his Majesty. The Lord Mayor replied:—'I am aware of the contents of this paper, having been apprised yesterday of the ceremony appointed to take place, and I have attended to perform my duty in accordance with ancient usages and customs of the City of London.'

"The Lord Mayor then read aloud the Order in Council requiring the herald to proclaim his Majesty within the jurisdiction of the City, and returned it to the herald. . . . The trumpets sounded and, the officials of Westminster having filed off, the cavalcade advanced into the City as far as the corner of Chancery-lane. There was another fanfare of trumpets, and the herald then made the proclamation, reading it with admirable clearness. When it was over the spectators, who had listened with bared heads, cried 'God Save the King.' The trumpets were again sounded, and a military band stationed to the west of Temple Bar played the National Anthem. This was followed by cheering, which lasted while the Lord Mayor and his retinue resumed their places in the carriages which had brought them, and the procession made its way to the Royal Exchange, the route being down Fleet-street, up Ludgate-hill, through St. Paul's Churchyard, and along Cheapside.

"Thus ended a ceremony which impressed all who saw it by its solemnity, its dignity, and its significance. It brought home vividly to the mind of every spectator the continuity which exists amid all the changes of our national life, and the very strangeness of the quaint heraldic garb worn by the heralds and pursuivants, which at another time might have provoked a smile, was felt to be an object-lesson for all, telling of unbroken tradition reaching far back into the glorious history of our country. On turning away from the site of Temple Bar after the Proclamation had been made and the procession had disappeared, one felt that the seriousness of the occasion had impressed itself on every mind and that from every heart there rose a common prayer—God Save the King!"

With somewhat less ceremony, on the same day, the same proclamation was read in many parts of the United Kingdom.

On Friday, the 25th, both Houses of Parliament met (the members having, one by one, taken the oath of allegiance to the new sovereign

on the two preceding days) to receive a message from the King and to adopt an address in reply. The royal message was as follows : "The King is fully assured that the House of Commons will share in the deep sorrow which has befallen his Majesty and the nation by the lamented death of his Majesty's mother, the late Queen. Her devotion to the welfare of her country and her people and her wise and beneficent rule during the sixty-four years of her glorious reign will ever be held in affectionate remembrance by her loyal and devoted subjects throughout the dominions of the British Empire."

The Marquis of Salisbury, in the House of Lords, and Mr. Balfour, in the House of Commons, moved the following Address, in speeches from which some passages have been quoted above: "That an humble Address be presented to his Majesty to assure his Majesty that this House deeply sympathizes in the great sorrow which his Majesty has sustained by the death of our beloved Sovereign, the late Queen, whose unfailing devotion to the duties of her high estate and to the welfare of her people will ever cause her reign to be remembered with reverence and affection ; to submit to his Majesty our respectful congratulations on his accession to the Throne ; to assure his Majesty of our loyal attachment to his person ; and, further, to assure him of our earnest conviction that his reign will be distinguished under the blessing of Providence by an anxious desire to maintain the laws of the kingdom and to promote the happiness, the welfare, and the liberty of his subjects." Speeches in support of the motion were made by the leaders of the Opposition party, the Earl of Kimberley, in the House of Lords, and Sir H. Campbell-Bannerman, in the House of Commons, and by the Archbishop of Canterbury, also, in the former chamber. The Address was then adopted, and Parliament was adjourned until February 14.

On the 4th of February, the new King addressed the following messages to his subjects in the British Empire at large, to the Colonies, and to the princes and people of India:

"To My People. Now that the last Scene has closed in the noble and ever glorious life of My beloved Mother, The Queen, I am anxious to endeavour to convey to the whole Empire the extent of the deep gratitude I feel for the heart-stirring and affectionate tributes which are everywhere borne to Her Memory. I wish also to express My warm recognition of those universal expressions of what I know to be genuine and loyal sympathy with Me and with the Royal Family in our overwhelming sorrow. Such expressions have reached Me from all parts of My vast Empire, while at home the sorrowful, reverent and sincere enthusiasm manifested in the magnificent display by sea and land has deeply touched Me. The consciousness of this generous spirit of devotion and loyalty among the millions of My Subjects and of the feeling that we are all sharing a common sorrow, has inspired Me with courage and hope during the past most trying and momentous days. Encouraged by the confidence of that love and trust which the nation ever reposed in its late and fondly mourned Sovereign, I shall earnestly strive to walk in Her Footsteps, devoting Myself to the utmost of My powers to maintaining and promoting the highest interests of My People, and to the diligent and zealous fulfilment of the great and sacred responsibilities which, through the Will of God, I am now called to undertake. ED-WARD, R. I."

"To My People Beyond the Seas. The countless messages of loyal sympathy which I have received from every part of My Dominions over the Seas testify to the universal grief in which the whole Empire now mourns the loss of My Beloved Mother. In the welfare and prosperity of Her subjects throughout Greater Britain the Queen ever evinced a heartfelt interest. She saw with thankfulness the steady progress which, under a wide extension of Self-Government, they had made during Her Reign. She warmly appreciated their unfailing loyalty to Her Throne and Person, and was proud to think of those who had so nobly fought and died for the Empire's cause in South Africa. I have already declared that it will be My constant endeavour to follow the great example which has been bequeathed to Me. In these endeavours I shall have a confident trust in the devotion and sympathy of the People and of their several Representative Assemblies throughout My vast Colonial Dominions. With such loyal support I will, with God's blessing, solemnly work for the promotion of the common welfare and security of the great Empire over which I have now been called to reign. EDWARD, R. I."

"To the Princes and People of India. Through the lamented death of My beloved and dearly mourned Mother, I have inherited the Throne, which has descended to Me through a long and ancient lineage. I now desire to send My greeting to the Ruling Chiefs of the Native States, and to the Inhabitants of My Indian Dominions, to assure them of My sincere good will and affection, and of My heartfelt wishes for their welfare. My illustrious and lamented Predecessor was the first Sovereign of this Country who took upon Herself the direct Administration of the Affairs of India, and assumed the title of Empress in token of Her closer association with the Government of that vast Country. In all matters connected with India, the Queen Empress displayed an unvarying deep personal interest, and I am well aware of the feeling of loyalty and affection evinced by the millions of its peoples towards Her Throne and Person. This feeling was conspicuously shown during the last year of Her long and glorious reign by the noble and patriotic assistance offered by the Ruling Princes in the South African War, and by the gallant services rendered by the Native Army beyond the limits of their own Country. It was by Her wish and with Her sanction that I visited India and made Myself personally acquainted with the Ruling Chiefs, the people, and the cities of that ancient and famous Empire. I shall never forget the deep impressions which I then received, and I shall endeavour to follow the great example of the first Queen Empress to work for the general well being of my Indian subjects of all ranks, and to merit, as She did, their unfailing loyalty and affection. EDWARD, R. et I."

English feeling toward the new sovereign of the British Empire, and the English estimate of his character and promise, are probably expressed quite truly, for the general mass of intelligent people, by the following remarks of "The Times:" "In the whole range of English social and political life there is no position more difficult to fill satisfactorily and without reproach than that of Heir Apparent to the Throne, and it may be justly said that the way in which that position has been filled for more than the ordinary lifetime of a generation has contributed to the remarkable increase of devotion to the Throne and the dynasty which is one of the most striking characteristics of Queen Victoria's reign. In the relations of private life, from his childhood upwards, 'the Prince' has been universally and deservedly popular. Cheerful and amiable, kind and generous, ever ready to sympathize with the joys and sorrows of those around him, a true friend, and a loyal antagonist, possessing considerable mental culture and wide intellectual sympathies without any tinge of pedantry, he has represented worthily the type of the genuine English gentleman. Though a lover of sport, like most of his countrymen, he differed from some of them in never regarding it as the chief interest and occupation in life. If he had been born in a humbler station he might have become a successful business man or an eminent administrator, for he possesses many of the qualities which command success in such spheres of action. He is a quick and methodical worker, arranges his time so as never to be hurried, is scrupulously conscientious in fulfilling engagements, great and small, with a punctuality which has become proverbial, never forgets to do anything he has undertaken, and never allows unanswered letters to accumulate. Few men have a larger private correspondence, and his letters have the clearness, the directness, the exquisite tactfulness, and the absolute freedom from all affectation which characterize his conversation. . . .

"In public life he has displayed the same qualities and done a great deal of very useful work. The numerous and often irksome ceremonial duties of his position have been invariably fulfilled most conscientiously and with fitting dignity. Of the remainder of his time a considerable part has been devoted to what might be called semi-official activity. In works of benevolence and public utility and in efforts to promote the interests of science and art he was ever ready and anxious to lend a helping hand. He never forgot, however, that in his public appearances he had not the liberty of speech and action enjoyed by the ordinary Englishman. Whilst taking the keenest interest in public affairs of every kind, he carefully abstained from overstepping in the slightest degree the limits imposed on him by constitutional tradition and usage. No party clique or Court camarilla ever sheltered itself behind him, and no political intrigue was ever associated with his name. Throughout her dominions Queen Victoria had no more loyal, devoted subject than her own eldest son. If this strictly correct attitude had been confined to his relations with the Head of the State we might have supposed that it proceeded from a feeling of deep filial affection and reverence, but, as it was displayed equally in his relations with Parliament and politicians, we must assume that it proceeded also from a high and discriminating sense of duty. Of the Prime Ministers, leaders of her Majesty's Opposition, and politicians of minor degree with whom he came in contact, he may have found some more sympathetic than others, but such personal preferences were carefully concealed in his manner, which was invariably courteous and considerate, and were not allowed to influence his conduct."

In another article, the same journal again re-marked that "there is no position more difficult to fill than that of Heir Apparent to the Throne." and added: "It is beset by more than all the temptations of actual Royalty, while the weight of counteracting responsibility is much less directly felt. It must be with a feeling akin to hopelessness that a man in that position offers up the familiar prayer, ' Lead us not into temptation.' Other men may avoid much temptation if they honestly endeavour to keep out of its way, but the heir to a Throne is followed, dogged, and importuned by temptation in its most seductive forms. It is not only the obviously bad that he has to guard against; he must also steel himself against much that comes in the specious garb of goodness and almost with the imperious command of necessity. The King has passed through that tremendous ordeal, prolonged through youth and manhood to middle age. We shall not pretend that there is nothing in his long career which those who respect and admire him could not wish otherwise. Which of us can say that with even approximate temptations to meet he could face the fierce light that beats upon an heir apparent no less than upon the Throne?"

The King was in his sixtieth year when he succeeded to the throne, having been born on the 9th of November, 1841. "By inheritance under a patent of Edward III., he became at once Duke of Cornwall, and a month later he was created, by patent, Prince of Wales and Earl of Chester—titles which do not pass by descent." He was married to the Princess Alexandra, of Denmark, on the 10th of March, 1863. The children born of the marriage have been six in all—three sons and three daughters. Of the former only one survives, Prince George, Duke of York, the second son, who will no doubt be created Prince of Wales. The eldest son, Prince Albert Victor, Duke of Clarence and Avondale, died in his 27th year, on the eve of his marriage. The third son, Alexander, born in 1871, died an infant. The Duke of York is married to Princess Victoria Mary, daughter of the late Duke of Teek and of his wife, Princess Mary of Cambridge. There are four children of the marriage, three sons and a daughter, the eldest son, in direct succession to the Throne, bearing the name of Prince Edward Albert. Of the daughters of the new Sovereign the eldest, Princess Louise, is the wife of the Duke of Fife and has two daughters. Of her two sisters, the Princess Victoria is unmarried. The Princess Maud became in 1896 the wife of Prince Charles of Denmark.

A. D. 1901 (February).—The opening of Parliament by King Edward VII.—The royal declaration against transubstantiation and the invocation of saints.—Protest of Roman Catholic peers.—Parliament, reassembling on the 14th of February, was formally opened by the King in person, with a degree of pomp and ceremony which had been made strange by half a century of disuse. King and Queen were escorted in procession, with all possible state, from Buckingham Palace to Westminster. Received there, at the royal entrance, by the great officers of state, they were conducted, by a still more imposing procession of dignitaries, to the "robing room." "His Majesty being robed and the Imperial Crown borne by the Duke of Devonshire (Lord President of the Council), the Procession advanced into the House of Peers in the

same order, except that the Cap of Maintenance [a mediæval symbol of dignity] was borne immediately before His Majesty, on the right hand of the Sword of State, by the Marquess of Winchester. The King being seated on his Throne, the Lord bearing the Cap of Maintenance stood on the Steps of the Throne, on the right, and the Peer bearing the Sword of State, on the left, of His Majesty. The Lord Chancellor, the Lord President and the Earl Marshal stood on the right, and the Lord Privy Seal on the left, of His Majesty; the Lord Great Chamberlain stood on the Steps of the Throne on the left hand of His Majesty, to receive the Royal Commands. The Lord Steward and the other officers of His Majesty's Household arranged themselves on each side of the Steps of the Throne, in the rear of the Great Officers of State."

By hereditary right, the ceremonial arrangements of the occasion were controlled by the Duke of Norfolk, as Earl Marshal, and the Marquess of Cholmondeley, as Lord Great Chamberlain, and they are said to have followed ancient precedent with a strictness which became very offensive to modern democratic feeling. The small chamber of the House of Lords was so filled with peeresses as well as peers that next to no room remained for the House of Commons when its members were summoned to it, to meet the King. What should have been a dignified procession behind the Speaker became, in consequence, a mob-like crush and scramble, and only some fifty out of five hundred Commoners are said to have succeeded in squeezing themselves within range of his Majesty's eye.

The King, then, as required by laws of the seventeenth century (the Bill of Rights and the Test Act—see, in vol. 2, ENGLAND: A. D. 1689, OCTOBER, and 1672–1673) signed and made oath to the following Declaration against the doctrine of transubstantiation, the invocation of the Virgin and the invocation of saints : "I doe solemnely and sincerely in the presence of God professe testifie and declare that I doe believe that in the sacrament of the Lord's Supper there is not any transubstautiation of the elements of bread and wine into the body and blood of Christ at or after the consecration thereof by any person whatsoever; and that the invocation or adoration of the Virgin Mary or any other saint and the sacrifice of the masse are now used in the Church of Rome are superstitious and idolatrous, and I doe solemnely in the presence of God professe testifie and declare that I doe make this declaration and every part thereof in the plaine and ordinary sence of the words read unto me as they are commonly understood by English Protestants without any evasion, equivocation or mentall reservation whatsoever and without any dispensation already granted me for this purpose by the Pope or any other authority or person whatsoever or without any hope of any such dispensation from any person or authority whatsoever or without thinking that I am or can be acquitted before God or man or absolved of this declaration or any part thereof although the Pope or any other person or persons or power whatsoever should dispence with or annull the same, or declare that it was null and void from the beginning."

Having thus submitted to the old test of a Protestant qualification for the Throne, the King read his Speech to Parliament, briefly stating the general posture of public affairs and setting forth the business which the two Houses were asked by government to consider. The war in South Africa was dealt with by the royal speaker in a very few words, as follows: "The war in South Africa has not yet entirely terminated; but the capitals of the enemy and his principal lines of communication are in my possession, and measures have been taken which will, I trust, enable my troops to deal effectually with the forces by which they are still opposed. I greatly regret the loss of life and the expenditure of treasure due to the fruitless guerrilla warfare maintained by Boer partisans in the former territories of the two Republics. Their early submission is much to be desired in their own interests, as, until it takes place, it will be impossible for me to establish in those colonies a government which will secure equal rights to all the white inhabitants, and protection and justice to the native population." In a later paragraph of the Speech he said: "The prolongation of hostilities in South Africa has led me to make a further call upon the patriotism and devotion of Canada and Australasia. I rejoice that my request has met with a prompt and loyal response, and that large additional contingents from those Colonies will embark for the seat of war at an early date." The Speech concluded with the following announcement of subjects and measures to be brought before Parliament:

"Gentlemen of the House of Commons, The Estimates for the year will be laid before you. Every care has been taken to limit their amount, but the naval and military requirements of the country, and especially the outlay consequent on the South African war, have involved an inevitable increase.

"The demise of the Crown renders it necessary that a renewed provision shall be made for the Civil List. I place unreservedly at your disposal those hereditary revenues which were so placed by my predecessor; and I have commanded that the papers necessary for a full consideration of the subject shall be laid before you.

"My Lords and Gentlemen, Proposals will be submitted to your judgment for increasing the efficiency of my military forces.

"Certain changes in the constitution of the Court of Final Appeal are rendered necessary in consequence of the increased resort to it, which has resulted from the expansion of the Empire during the last two generations.

"Legislation will be proposed to you for the amendment of the Law relating to Education.

"Legislation has been prepared, and, if the time at your disposal shall prove to be adequate, will be laid before you, for the purpose of regulating the voluntary sale by landlords to occupying tenants in Ireland, for amending and consolidating the Factory and Workshops Acts, for the better administration of the Law respecting Lunatics, for amending the Public Health Acts in regard to Water Supply, for the prevention of drunkenness in Licensed Houses or Public Places, and for amending the Law of Literary Copyright.

"I pray that Almighty God may continue to guide you in the conduct of your deliberations, and may bless them with success."

Dated from the House of Lords, on the day of the opening, the following protest, signed by Roman Catholic peers (of whom there are thirty),

against the continued requirement from the British sovereign of the Declaration quoted above, was laid before the Lord Chancellor:

"My Lord,—On the opening of his first Parliament to-day his Majesty was called upon to make and subscribe the so-called Declaration against Transubstantiation, which was framed during the reign of Charles II., at a moment when religious animosities were unusually bitter.

"Some days ago we addressed ourselves to your lordship, as the chief authority on English law, to ascertain whether it was possible to bring about any modification of those parts of the Declaration which are specially provocative to the religious feelings of Catholics. We received from your lordship the authoritative assurance that no modification whatever was possible, except by an Act of Parliament, and that no action of ours would therefore be of the slightest use to effect the pacific purpose we had in view. The Sovereign himself has, it appears, no option, and is obliged by statute to use the very words prescribed, although we feel assured that his Gracious Majesty would willingly have been relieved (as all his subjects have for many years been relieved by Act of Parliament) from the necessity of branding with contumelious epithets the religious tenets of any of his subjects.

"While we submit to the law, we cannot be wholly silent on this occasion. We desire to impress upon your lordship that the expressions used in this Declaration made it difficult and painful for Catholic peers to attend to-day in the House of Lords in order to discharge their official or public duties, and that those expressions cannot but cause the deepest pain to millions of subjects of his Majesty in all parts of the Empire, who are as loyal and devoted to his Crown and person as any others in his dominions.

"We are, my lord, your lordship's most obedient and faithful servants."—*London Times, Feb. 15*, 1901.

In the House of Lords, on the 22d of February, the Marquis of Salisbury made the following reply to Lord Braye, who asked if the Prime Minister could hold out hope of an early measure to abolish the oath so offensive to Catholic subjects of the King: "Though I am very anxious to give an answer which would be satisfactory to the noble lord and his co-religionists, I do not wish to leave on his mind an impression that there are any doubts in the matter. We all of us deplore the language in which that declaration is couched, and very much wish it could be otherwise expressed; but when it comes to altering an enactment which has now lasted, as far as I know, without serious question, 200 years, and which was originally included in the Bill of Rights, it is a matter which cannot be done without very considerable thought. We must remember that an enactment of that kind represents the passions, feelings, and sensibilities of the people by whom it was originally caused; and that these have not died out. They are not strong within these walls; but there are undoubtedly parts of the country where the controversies which the declaration represents still flourish, and where the emotions which it indicates have not died out. Before an enactment is proposed, with all the discussion which must precede such an enactment, we shall have to consider how far it is desirable to light again passions which sleep at this moment, for an occasion which is not now urgent, and which we all earnestly hope may not be urgent in our lives. I do not wish to dchar the noble lord from any action which he may think it right to take; but I wish to point out to him the extreme difficulties and anxieties which would accompany any such attempt. With respect to the actual question of legislation, I need hardly observe that it is rather a question for the House of Commons than for us, because here I do not imagine there would be any doubt whatever about the result of such attempted legislation. But I could not be certain that a very strong feeling might not be excited elsewhere; and I notice that, possibly with a view to that consideration, the leader of the other House, in answer to a question, said that, at all events for the present year, he did not see the possibility of having the requisite opportunity of bringing the question before the House. I am afraid, therefore, however deeply I sympathize with the feelings of the noble lord and wish there had been no cause for their being appealed to, that my answer would have to be of a discouraging character."

Notwithstanding this discouraging reply to the question, Lord Salisbury, on the 21st of March, moved the following resolution in the House of Lords : "To resolve that it is desirable that a Joint Committee of both Houses be appointed to consider the declaration required of the Sovereign, on his accession, by the Bill of Rights ; and to report whether its language can be modified advantageously, without diminishing its efficacy as a security for the maintenance of the Protestant succession." On introducing the resolution he said : "The only thing that it is necessary I should mention is that something has been said with respect to referring the Coronation Oath to the same committee and making in it alterations which undoubtedly will have to be made. But the two subjects are not at all similar, and it would have been impossible to put the Coronation Oath into this reference. If, later, it should be thought wise to use the same committee for the purpose of considering the matter of the Coro-

nation Oath, I probably shall see no difficulty in that."

A. D. 1901 (February).—Attitude of the Liberal party towards the South African War.—At the annual meeting of the general committee of the National Liberal Federation, held at Rugby, February 27, 1901, more than 400 affiliated Liberal Associations in England and Wales being represented by about 500 delegates, including many eminent men, the following resolution was adopted : "That this committee records its profound conviction that the long continuance of the deplorable war in South Africa, declared for electioneering purposes to be over last September, is due to the policy of demanding unconditional surrender and to a want of knowledge, foresight, and judgment on the part of the Government, who have neither demonstrated effectively to the Boers the military supremacy of Great Britain, nor so conducted the war as to induce them to lay down their arms; this committee bitterly laments the slaughter of thousands of brave men on both sides, the terrible loss of life from disease, owing in no small degree to the scandalous inadequacy of sanitary and hospital arrangements provided for our forces, and the enormous waste of resources in actual expenditure upon the war, in the devastation of territory, and in the economic embarrassments which must inevitably follow ; the committee calls upon the Government to announce forthwith, and to carry out, on the cessation of hostilities, a policy for the settlement of South African affairs which will secure equal rights to the white races, just and humane treatment of natives, and such a measure of self-government as can honourably be accepted by a brave and high-spirited people."

A. D. 1901 (February).—Emphatic declaration of the policy of the government in dealing with the Boers. See (in this vol.) SOUTH AFRICA (THE FIELD OF WAR) : A. D. 1901.

A. D. 1901 (March).—Rejection of the Interoceanic Canal Treaty as amended by the U. S. Senate. See (in this vol.) CANAL, INTEROCEANIC : A. D. 1901 (MARCH).

ENSLIN, Battle of. See (in this vol.) SOUTH AFRICA (THE FIELD OF WAR) : A. D. 1899 (OCTOBER—DECEMBER).

EPWORTH LEAGUE, The.—The Epworth League, an organization of young people in the Methodist Episcopal Church, on lines and with objects kindred to those of the "Young People's Society of Christian Endeavor" (see, in this vol., CHRISTIAN ENDEAVOR), was instituted by a convention of representatives from various societies of young people in that church, held at Cleveland, Ohio, May 14-15, 1889. It was officially adopted by the General Conference of the M. E. Church in 1892. The Year-book of the League for 1901 says : — "A dozen years ago the Epworth League had no regularly organized Chapter. To-day it has almost twenty-one thousand. Twelve years ago it had a total membership of twenty-seven. To-day it has a million and a half. Twelve years ago the Junior League had scarcely been dreamed of. To-day it is the most promising division of the great Epworth army, having a membership of tens of thousands. Twelve years ago a suggestion to establish a newspaper organ was looked upon as a most

doubtful experiment, and predictions of failure were freely made. To-day the organization has an official journal whose circulation exceeds that of any Church weekly in the world."

ETRUSCANS, The: Fresh light on their origin. See (in this vol.) ARCHÆOLOGICAL RESEARCH : ITALY.

EUPHRATES, Valley of the: Recent archæological exploration. See (in this vol.) ARCHÆOLOGICAL RESEARCH : BABYLONIA.

EUROPEAN RACES, The expansion of the. See (in this vol.) NINETEENTH CENTURY : EXPANSION.

EVOLUTION, The doctrine of: Its influence on the Nineteenth Century. See (in this vol.) NINETEENTH CENTURY : DOMINANT LINES.

EXCAVATIONS, Recent archæological. See (in this vol.) ARCHÆOLOGICAL RESEARCH.

EXPLOSIVES FROM BALLOONS, Declaration against. See (in this vol.) PEACE CONFERENCE.

EXPOSITION, The Cotton States and International. See (in this vol.) ATLANTA : A. D. 1895.

National Export. See (in this vol.) INTERNATIONAL COMMERCIAL CONGRESS.

Pan-American. See (in this vol.) BUFFALO : A. D. 1901.

Paris. See (in this vol.) FRANCE : A. D. 1900 (APRIL—NOVEMBER).

Scandinavian. See (in this vol.) STOCKHOLM.

Tennessee Centennial, at Nashville. See (in this vol.) TENNESSEE : A. D 1897.

Trans-Mississippi. See (in this vol.) OMAHA : A. D. 1898.

EXTERRITORIAL RIGHTS. See (in this vol.) JAPAN : A. D. 1899 (JULY).

F.

FAMINE : In China. See (in this vol.) CHINA : A. D. 1901 (JANUARY—FEBRUARY).

In India. See (in this vol.) INDIA : A. D. 1896–1897 ; and 1899–1900.

In Russia. See (in this vol.) RUSSIA : A. D. 1899.

"**FANATICS,**" The. See (in this vol.) BRAZIL : A. D. 1897.

FAR EASTERN QUESTION, The. See (in this vol.) CONCERT OF EUROPE.

FARM BURNING, In the South African War. See (in this vol.) SOUTH AFRICA (THE FIELD OF WAR) : A. D. 1900 (AUG.—DEC.).

FARMERS' ALLIANCE, and Industrial Union, The.—The Supreme Council of the Farmers' Alliance and Industrial Union held its fourth annual session at Washington, February 6–8, 1900, and pledged support to whatever candidates should be named by the national convention of the Democratic Party, making, at the same time, a declaration of principles analogous to those maintained by the People's Party.

FASHODA INCIDENT, The. See (in this vol.) EGYPT : A. D. 1898 (SEPT.—NOV.).

FAURE, François Felix, President of the French Republic.—Sudden death. See (in this vol.) FRANCE : A. D. 1899 (FEBRUARY—JUNE).

FEDERAL STEEL COMPANY, The. See (in this vol.) TRUSTS : UNITED STATES.

FÊNG-TIEN PENINSULA : A. D. 1894-1895.—Cession in part to Japan and subsequent relinquishment. See (in this vol.) CHINA : A. D. 1894–1895.

A. D. 1900.—Russian occupation and practical Protectorate. See (in this vol.) MANCHURIA : A. D. 1900.

FILIPINOS. See (in this vol.) PHILIPPINE ISLANDS.

FINLAND : A. D. 1898-1901.—A blow at the constitutional rights of the country.—Attempt to Russianize the Finnish army.—Possible defeat of the measure.—"In July, 1898, just one month before the publication of the Czar's Peace Manifesto, the Diet of Finland was summoned to meet in extraordinary session during January, 1899, in order to debate upon the new Army Bill submitted by the Russian Government. Hitherto, the army of Finland has been strictly national in character, and has served solely for the defence of the province. The standing army has been limited to 5,600 men, 1,920 of whom are annually selected to bear arms during a period of three years. This has now been changed; the main features of the new Army Bill

being as follows: 1. Finnish troops may be requisitioned for service beyond the confines of the Grand Duchy. 2. Russians may serve in the Finnish, and Finlanders in the Russian, Army. 3. A lightening of the duties of military service upon the ground of superior education will be granted to those only who can speak, read, and write Russian. 4. The period of active service under the flag is increased from three years to five. 5. The annual contingent of soldiers in active service is increased from 1,920 men to 7,200. We at once perceive the fundamental nature of these changes, which threaten to impose a far heavier burden upon Finland, and to Russify her army. Naturally, the new law met with the most determined opposition. But while the bill was still in committee there appeared on February 15, 1899, an Imperial ukase, whereby the entire situation was radically changed, and the independence of Finland seriously threatened. This ukase decrees that while the internal administration and legislation of Finland are to remain unimpaired, matters affecting the common interests of Finland and Russia are to be no longer submitted solely to the jurisdiction of the Grand Duchy. Furthermore, the Emperor reserves to himself the final decision as to which matters are to be included in the above category. . . .

"The document is couched in terms expressing good-will for Finland. In effect, however, it signifies the complete demolition of the constitutional rights of that country. For in all matters involving the interests of both countries, or affecting in any way those of Russia, Finland will hereafter be confined to a mere expression of opinion: she will no longer be able to exercise the privilege of formulating an independent resolution. The definition of 'common interests' as furnished by the ukase is so vague as to make the exercise of any form of self-government on the part of the Finlanders a matter of uncertainty, if not of serious difficulty. Not only the interpretation of 'common interests,' but also the designation of the law governing them, is primarily in the hands of the Russian authorities. Finland, an independent, constitutional state [see, in vol. 4, SCANDINAVIAN STATES: A. D. 1807–1810], has been, or, at all events, is to be, converted into a province of Russia. . . .

"The conviction is general that the Czar, who had formerly manifested such good-will toward the country, and who had abrogated the enactments curtailing its constitutional rights, could not possibly have so completely changed his views within so short a time. Consequently, it was decided to address a monster petition in behalf of the people directly to the ruler himself. This plan met with the enthusiastic approval of the entire nation, and the document was signed by no fewer than 523,931 men and women of Finland. A deputation of five hundred was elected to present this petition, which so eloquently voiced the conviction of the whole nation. These five hundred representatives went to St. Petersburg, and requested an audience with the Czar. But their efforts were unavailing. They were not received; and it appeared as if the united voice of a peaceful and loyal people could not penetrate to the ear of the ruler. "In the meantime the attention of all Europe was directed to the matter; and everywhere the liveliest sympathy was manifested for that little Nation in the Northeast. . . . There now arose —entirely from private initiative, and without the exercise of any influence on the part of Finland—a general movement among European nations to select prominent scholars and artists; i. e, men entirely removed from the political arena, to act as representatives of the popular sentiment, and to speak a good word with the Czar in behalf of Finland. . . . Addresses of sympathy for Finland were formulated in England, France, Germany, Austria, Hungary, Italy, Switzerland, Belgium, Holland, Denmark, Sweden, and Norway; and these addresses were signed by over one thousand and fifty scholars and artists. . . . All the addresses together were to be presented to the Czar by a small deputation; and for this purpose the Commission mentioned at the beginning of this article proceeded to St. Petersburg. The gentlemen took great pains to secure an audience; they went from one minister to another, and avoided every appearance of unfriendliness. Nevertheless, their request was politely declined; and the acceptance of the document bearing the signatures of over one thousand notabilities firmly refused."—R. Eucken, *The Finnish Question (Forum, Nov.,* 1899).

A correspondent of the "London Times," writing from Helsingfors, December 28, 1900, reported: "The situation in Finland at the end of the year is by no means improved, notwithstanding a few gratifying events, such as the permission granted by General Bobrikoff for a new daily paper to be published in Helsingfors. . . . Two papers, one published in a provincial town, and a weekly journal in Helsingfors, have been suppressed for ever, and the preventive censorship is applied with the utmost rigour. The Governor-General has displayed great energy in enforcing the restrictions on the right to hold meetings, and he has in circulars to the provincial Governors issued instructions for the introduction of Russian as the language of the Provincial Government offices even earlier, and more fully, than is provided for in the language ordinance promulgated last autumn. Denunciations of private persons to General Bobrikoff by secret agents, as well as public authorities, are events of wellnigh daily occurrence, and one consequence of these secret reports is that five University professors are threatened with summary dismissal unless they 'bind themselves to mix themselves up no longer in any sort of political agitation.' . . .
"The question of the new military law will in all probability come before the Russian Imperial Council in January, all authorities concerned having had an opportunity of expressing their views on the report made on the question by the Finnish Diet in 1899, including the Minister of War, General Kuropatkin. In conformity with the manifesto of February 15, 1899, this report

will be regarded merely as an 'opinion' given by that body, in no way binding when the matter comes up for further consideration. This scheme, it will be remembered, not only imposes on Finland a military burden beyond the powers of the country, but has the political aim of denationalizing the Finnish army, and is thus intended to serve as a potent lever in the Russification of the Grand Duchy. The main features of the Bill were rejected by the Finnish Diet, but, although several members of the Imperial Council are opposed to the new scheme, it is believed that it will gain the majority in the Council in all its more salient points."

Three months later (Feb. 26, 1901), an important change in the situation was reported from St. Petersburg by the same correspondent. The project of Russifying the Finnish army had suffered defeat, he learned, in the Council of State, by a large majority. "But," he added, "this does not by any means imply that the military reform scheme in Finland, which has been the chief cause of all the harm done to the Finnish Constitution during the last three years, has been finally upset. A similar procedure in any other European civilized country would mean as much, but it is not so in Russia. It simply means that the Russification of Finland is still being prosecuted by a small powerful minority, who will probably gain their point in spite of the vast majority of his Majesty's councillors. The Council of State, the highest institution in the sphere of supreme administration, is merely a consultative body, whose opinion can be, and often has been, set aside by the Sovereign without the least difficulty. A mere stroke of the pen is necessary.

"In the present case the Finnish military project was discussed by the four united departments of the Council. It is stated that M. Pobiedonostzeff and the Minister of War said nothing, being, perhaps, either too much impressed by the speech of M. Witte against the project, or feeling sure of their ground without the need of entering into useless discussion. M. Witte, whose influence is gradually embracing every branch of government, is also looming big in this question. He is reported to have made a speech on the occasion which carried over 40 members of the Council with him in opposition to the project. He attacked it principally on financial grounds, and declared that nobody could advise his Majesty to adopt it. The rejection of the proposal by the four departments is preliminary to its discussion by a plenary assembly of the Council, and only after that has taken place will the opinion of the majority be laid before the Emperor."

FIST OF RIGHTEOUS HARMONY, Society of the. See (in this vol.) CHINA: A. D. 1900 (JANUARY—MARCH).

FIVE CIVILIZED TRIBES, The. See (in this vol.) INDIANS, AMERICAN: A. D. 1893–1899.

FORBIDDEN CITY, March of allied forces through the. See (in this vol.) CHINA: A. D. 1900 (AUGUST 15–28).

FORMOSA: A. D. 1895.—Cession by China to Japan. See (in this vol.) CHINA: A. D. 1894–1895.

A. D. 1896.—Chinese risings against the Japanese. See (in this vol.) JAPAN: A. D. 1896.

FRANCE.

A. D. 1894-1896.—Final subJugation and annexation of Madagascar. See (in this vol.) MADAGASCAR.

A. D. 1895.—Cession of Kiang-Hung by China. See (in this vol.) CHINA : A. D. 1894-1895 (MARCH—JULY).

A. D. 1895.—Ministerial changes.—The alliance with Russia.—On the resignation of the presidency of the Republic by M. Casimir-Perier (see, in vol. 2, FRANCE : A. D. 1894-1895), and the election of M. Felix Faure to succeed him (January 15-17), a ministry was formed which represented the moderate republican groups, with M. Ribot at its head, as President of the Council and Minister of Finance, and with M. Hanotaux as Minister of Foreign Affairs. The most important work of the new government was the arrangement of an alliance with Russia, which was conspicuously signified to the world by the union of the French and Russian fleets when they entered the German harbor of Kiel, on the 17th of June, to take part in the celebration of the opening of the Kaiser Wilhelm Ship Canal, between the Baltic and North Seas (see, in this vol., GERMANY : A. D. 1895, JUNE). This gave the greatest possible satisfaction to the nation, and powerfully strengthened the ministers for a time ; but they were discredited a little later in the year by disclosures of waste, extravagance and peculation in the military department. Early in the autumn session of the Chamber of Deputies a vote was carried against them, and they resigned. A more radical cabinet was then formed, under M. Leon Bourgeois, President of the Council and Minister of the Interior ; with M. Berthelot holding the portfolio of foreign affairs, M. Cavaignac that of war, and M. Lockroy that of the marine.

A. D. 1896 (January). — Agreement with Great Britain concerning Siam. See (in this vol.) SIAM : A. D. 1896-1899.

A. D. 1896 (March).—Census of the Republic.—Returns of a national census taken in March showed a population in France of 38,228,969, being an increase in five years of only 133,919. The population of Paris was 2,511,955.

A. D. 1896 (April—May).—Change of Ministry.—Socialist gains.—After a long conflict with a hostile Senate, the Radical Ministry of M. Bourgeois gave way and was succeeded, April 30, by a Cabinet of Moderate Republicans, in which M. Méline presided, holding the portfolio of Agriculture, and with M. Hanotaux returned to the direction of Foreign Affairs. At municipal elections in the following month the Socialists made important gains. " The elections of May, 1896, revealed the immense progress that socialism had made in all lands since the year 1893. Towns as important as Lille, Roubaix, Calais, Montluçon, Narbonne, re-elected socialist majorities to administer their affairs ; and even where there was only a socialist minority, a socialist mayor was elected, as in the case of Dr. Flaissières at Marseilles, and Cousteau at Bordeaux. But in the small towns and the villages our victories have been especially remarkable. The Parti Ouvrier alone can reckon more than eighteen hundred municipal councillors elected upon its collectivist programme ; and at the Lille Congress, which held a few days before the International Congress in London, thirty-eight socialist municipal councils and twenty-one socialist minorities of municipal councils were represented by their mayors or by delegates chosen by the party."—P. Lafargue, *Socialism in France* (*Fortnightly Rev., Sept.*, 1897).

A. D. 1897.—Industrial combinations. See (in this vol.) TRUSTS : IN EUROPEAN COUNTRIES.

A. D. 1897 (May—June).—Cessions and concessions from China. See(in this vol.) CHINA : A. D. 1897 (MAY—JUNE).

A. D. 1897 (June). —Renewal of the privileges of the Bank of France. See (in this vol.) MONETARY QUESTIONS : A. D. 1897.

A. D. 1897 (July).—Co-operation with American envoys in negotiations for a bi-metallic agreement with Great Britain. See (in this vol.) MONETARY QUESTIONS : A. D. 1897 (APRIL—OCTOBER).

A. D. 1897-1899.—The Dreyfus Affair.—Although Captain Alfred Dreyfus, of the French army, was arrested, tried by court-martial, convicted of treasonable practices, in the betrayal of military secrets to a foreign power, and thereupon degraded and imprisoned, in 1894, it was not until 1897 that his case became historically important, by reason of the unparalleled agitations to which it gave rise, threatening the very life of the French Republic, and exciting the whole civilized world. Accordingly we date the whole extraordinary story of Captain Dreyfus and his unscrupulous enemies in the French Army Staff from that year, in order to place it in its proper chronological relations with other events. As told here, the story is largely borrowed from a singularly clear review of its complicated incidents by Sir Godfrey Lushington, formerly Permanent Under Secretary in the British Home Office, which appeared in the "London Times," while the question of a revision of the Dreyfus trial was pending in the Court of Cassation. We are indebted to the publisher of "The Times" for permission to make use of it :

"In October, 1894, Captain Alfred Dreyfus, an artillery officer on the staff, was arrested for treason. He belonged to a respected and highly loyal Jewish family in Alsace, his military character was unblemished, and he was in easy circumstances. At this time General Mercier was Minister of War, General de Boisdeffre Chief of the Staff (practically Commander-in-Chief of the French army), General Gonse, Assistant-Chief. Colonel Sandherr, well known as an Anti-Semite, was head of the Intelligence Department, under him were Commandants Picquart, Henry, and Lauth, and the Archivist Griblin. Commandant Du Paty de Clam was an officer attached to the general staff. Commandant Esterhazy was serving with his regiment. On October 15, on the order of the Minister of War, Captain Dreyfus was arrested by Commandant Du Paty de Clam, and taken in the charge of Commandant Henry to the Cherche-Midi Prison, of which Commandant Forzinetti was governor. For a fortnight extraordinary precautions were taken to keep his arrest an absolute secret from the public and even from his own family. His wife alone knew of it, but dared not speak. . . . So harsh was his treatment that Commandant Forzinetti felt it his duty to take the strong step of making a formal representation to the Minister of War and also to the Governor of Paris, at the same time declaring his own conviction that Captain Dreyfus was an innocent man. On October 31 Commandant Du Paty de Clam made his report, which has not seen the light, and on November 3 Commandant d'Ormescheville was appointed 'rapporteur' to conduct a further inquiry, and in due course to draw up a formal report, which practically constitutes the case for the prosecution. Not till then was Captain Dreyfus informed of the particulars of the charge about to be laid against him. From this report of Commandant d'Ormescheville's we learn that the basis of the accusation against Captain Dreyfus was a document known by the name of the 'bordereau' [memorandum]. Neither Commandant d'Ormescheville's report nor the 'bordereau' has been officially published by the Government, but both ultimately found their way into the newspapers. The bordereau was a communication not dated, nor addressed, nor signed. It began:—'Sans nouvelles m'indiquant que vous désirez me voir, je vous adresse cependant, Monsieur, quelques renseignements intéressants.' ['Without news indicating that you wish to see me, I send you, nevertheless, monsieur, some important information.'] (Then followed the titles of various military documents, 1, 2, &c.) The report stated that the bordereau had fallen into the hands of the Minister of War, but how the Minister declined to say, beyond making a general statement that the circumstances showed that it had been sent to an agent of a foreign Power. It is now generally accepted that it had been brought to the War Office by a spy—an Alsatian porter who was in the service of Colonel von Schwarzkoppen, then the military attaché to the German Embassy in Paris. The report contained nothing to show that Captain Dreyfus had been following treasonable practices or to connect him in any manner with the bordereau. The sole question for the Court-martial was whether the bordereau was in his handwriting. On this the experts were divided, three being of opinion that it was, two that it was not, in his handwriting.

"The Court-martial was duly held, and Captain Dreyfus had the aid of counsel, Maitre Demange; but the first act of the Court was, at the instance of the Government representative, to declare the 'huis clos,' so that none but those concerned were present. After the evidence had been taken the Court, according to custom, adjourned to consider their verdict in private. Ultimately they found Captain Dreyfus guilty, and he was sentenced to be publicly expelled from the army and imprisoned for life. Not till after his conviction was he allowed to communicate with his wife and family. The sentence has been carried out with the utmost rigour. Captain Dreyfus was transported to the Isle du Diable [off the coast of French Guiana], where he lives in solitary confinement. . . . The Court-martial having been held within closed doors, the public at large knew nothing . . . beyond the fact that Captain Dreyfus had been convicted of betraying military secrets to a foreign Power, and they had no suspicion that there had been any irregularity at the Court-martial or that the verdict was a mistaken one. . . . For two years the Dreyfus question may be said to have slumbered. In the course of this time Colonel Sandherr, who died in January, 1897, had been compelled to retire from ill-health, and Commandant Picquart became head of the Intelligence Department. . . . In May, 1896, there were brought

to the Intelligence Department of the War Office some more sweepings from Colonel von Schwarzkoppen's waste-paper basket by the same Alsatian porter who had brought the bordereau. These were put by Commandant Henry into a packet, and given by him (according to the usual custom) to Commandant Picquart. Commandant Picquart swears that amongst these were about 60 small pieces of paper. These (also according to custom) he gave to Commandant Lauth to piece together. When pieced together they were found to constitute the document which is known by the name of 'Petit bleu, à carte télégramme' for transmission through the Post-office, but which had never been posted. It was addressed to Commandant Esterhazy, and ran as follows:—

"'J'attends avant tout une explication plus détaillée que celle que vous m'avez donnée, l'autre jour, sur la question en suspens. En conséquence, je vous prie de me la donner par écrit, pour pouvoir juger si je puis continuer mes relations avec la maison R . . . ou non. [I await, before anything farther, a more detailed explanation than you gave me the other day on the question now in suspense. In consequence, I request you to give this to me in writing, that I may judge whether I can continue my relations with the house of R. or not.] M. le Commandant Esterhazy, 27, Rue de la Bienfaisance, Paris.'

"At this time Commandant Esterhazy was a stranger to Commandant Picquart, and the first step which Commandant Picquart took was to make inquiry as to who and what he was. His character proved most disreputable, and he was in money difficulties. The next was to obtain a specimen of his handwriting in order to compare it with other writings which had been brought by spies to the office and were kept there. In this way it came about that it was compared with the facsimile of the bordereau, when, lo and behold, the writings of the two appeared identical. It was Commandant Esterhazy, then, who had written the bordereau, and if Commandant Esterhazy, then not Captain Dreyfus. . . . Commandant Picquart acquainted his chiefs with what had been done—namely, General de Boisdeffre in July, and his own immediate superior, General Gonse, in September. . . .

"On September 15 of the same year, 1896, took place the first explosion. This solely concerned the Dreyfus trial. On that day the 'Éclair,' an anti-Semite newspaper, published an article headed 'Le Traitre,' in which they stated that at the Court-martial the 'pièce d'accusation' on which Captain Dreyfus was tried was the bordereau; but that after the Court had retired to the 'chamber of deliberation,' there was communicated to them from the War Office, in the absence of the prisoner and his counsel, a document purporting to be addressed by the German military attaché to his colleague at the Italian Embassy in Paris, and ending with a postscript, 'Cet animal de Dreyfus devient trop exigeant'; further, that this document was the only one in which appeared the name Dreyfus. This at once had removed all doubts from the minds of the Court-martial, who thereupon had unanimously brought the prisoner in guilty; and the 'Éclair' called upon the Government to produce this document and thus satisfy the public conscience. This document has, for sufficient reasons hereinafter appearing, come to be known as 'le document libérateur,' and by this name we will distinguish it. As to the article in the 'Éclair,' it must have proceeded either from a member of the Court-martial or from some one in the War Office ; but whether its contents were true is a matter which to this day has not been fully cleared up. This much, however, is known. We have the authority of Maitre Demange (Captain Dreyfus's advocate) that no such document was brought before the Court-martial during the proceedings at which he was present. On the other hand, it has now been admitted that at the date of Captain Dreyfus's trial there was, and that there had been for some months previously, in the archives of the War Office a similar document, not in the Dreyfus 'dossier' proper, but in a secret dossier, only that the words therein are not 'Cet animal de Dreyfus,' but ' Ce (sic) canaille de D——' (initial only) 'devient trop exigeant.' . . . The Government have never yet either admitted or denied that General Mercier went down to the Court-martial and made to them a secret communication. . . .

"As might have been expected, the article in the 'Éclair' occasioned a considerable stir ; both parties welcomed it, the one as showing Captain Dreyfus to have been really a traitor and therefore justly deserving his sentence ; the other as a proof that whether guilty or not he had been condemned illegally on a document used behind his back. The public excitement was increased when on the 10th of November the 'Matin'— a War Office journal—published what purported to be a fac-simile of the bordereau, and a host of experts and others set to work to compare it with the accused's handwriting. The reproduction was no doubt made, not from the original bordereau, which was in the sealed-up Dreyfus dossier, but from a photograph of it. And the photograph must have been obtained surreptitiously from some one in the War Office or from some one who had attended the secret Court-martial. . . . The natural sequel to these revelations was an interpellation in the Chamber — the ' interpellation Castelin' of November 18, 1896. On that day, M. Castelin, an anti-Semite deputy, by asking some question as ·to the safe custody of Dreyfus, gave the Government an opportunity. General Billot, then Minister of War, replied in general terms:— 'L'instruction de l'affaire, les débats, le jugement, ont eu lieu conformément aux règles de la procédure militaire. Le Conseil de Guerre regulièrement composé, a regulièrement déliberé,' &c. ['The instructions, the debates, the verdict, have all taken place conformably to the rules of military procedure. The Court-martial, regularly composed, has deliberated regularly,' etc.] . . . On November 14, 1896, on the eve of the Interpellation Castelin, Commandant Picquart was sent on a secret mission, which has not been disclosed. He left his duties as head of the Intelligence Department nominally in the hands of General Gonse, his superior, but practically to be discharged by Commandant Henry, who was Commandant Picquart's subordinate. He requested his family to address their private letters for him to the War Office, whence they would be forwarded. His secret mission, took him first to Nancy, then to Besançon (permission being refused to him to return to Paris even for a night to renew his wardrobe), later on to Algeria and Tunisia, with instructions to proceed to the fron-

tier. . . . In March, 1897, Commandant Picquart was appointed Lieutenant-Colonel of the 4th Tirailleurs, the appointment being represented to him as a favour. He was the youngest Colonel in the service. In his stead Commandant Henry became Chief of the Intelligence Department. . . . From the first Colonel Picquart had, of course, felt some uneasiness at being sent on these missions away from his ordinary duties, and various little circumstances occurred to increase it, and in May, 1897, having occasion to write unofficially to Commandant Henry, now Chief of the Intelligence Department, he expressed himself strongly as to the mystery and falsities with which his departure had been surrounded ; and he received a reply dated June 3, in which Commandant Henry said that the mystery he could well enough explain by what had come to his knowledge after some inquiry, and he alluded in general to three circumstances— (1) Opening letters in the post ; (2) attempt to suborn two officers in the service to speak to a certain writing as being that of a certain person ; and (3) the opening of a secret dossier. The first Colonel Picquart knew to refer to his having intercepted Commandant Esterhazy's letters ; the other two allusions he did not at the time (June, 1897) fully understand ; but the letter, couched in such terms and coming from one who had until lately been his subordinate, and was now the head of the Department, convinced him that he was the object of serious and secret machinations in the War Office. He immediately applied for leave and came to Paris. There he determined, with a view to his self-defence, to obtain legal advice from an advocate, M. Leblois ; saw him, and showed him Colonel Henry's letter, and, whilst abstaining (according to his own account and that of M. Leblois) from touching on the third matter, the secret dossier, spoke freely on the other two—on the 'affaires' Dreyfus and Esterhazy generally ; also, in order to explain how far he had acted with the sanction or cognizance of his superiors, he placed in his hands the correspondence—not official but confidential— about Commandant Esterhazy which he had had with General Gonse in 1896. He left it to M. Leblois to take what course he might think necessary, and returned to Sousse. In the course of the autumn he was summoned to Tunis and asked by the military authority there whether he had been robbed of a secret document by a woman. The question seemed a strange one and was answered by him with a simple negative. Later on he received at Sousse two telegrams from Paris, dated November 10. One:—'Arretez Bondieu. Tout est découvert. Affaire très grave. Speranza.' This was addressed to Tunis and forwarded to Sousse. The other:—'On a des preuves que le bleu est fabriqué par Georges. Blanche.' This was addressed to Sousse. And two days after he received a letter, likewise of November 10, from Esterhazy, an abusive one, charging him with conspiring against him, &c. He felt certain that the telegrams were sent in order to compromise him. . . . Colonel Picquart suspected Commandant Esterhazy to be the author of the telegrams, the more so that in Commandant Esterhazy's letter and in one of the telegrams his own name Picquart was spelt without a c. He at once telegraphed to Tunis for leave to come and see the General there. He did see him and through him forwarded to the

Minister of War the three documents, with a covering letter in which he demanded an inquiry. He then obtained leave to go to Paris, but the condition was imposed on him that he should see no one before presenting himself to General de Pellieux. When he saw the General he learnt for the first time and to his surprise that ever since he left Paris in November, 1896, his letters had been intercepted and examined at the War Office and he was called upon to explain various letters and documents. . . .

"Before June, 1897, Commandant Esterhazy's name had not been breathed to the public ; it is now to come out, and from two independent sources. Some little time after seeing Colonel Picquart, in June, 1897, M. Leblois had determined, in his interest, to consult M. Scheurer-Kestner, who was well known to have taken an interest in the 'affaire Dreyfus,' because of the suspicion that Captain Dreyfus had been condemned on a document which he had never seen and because of the discrepancies between Captain Dreyfus's handwriting and that of the bordereau. He was Vice-President of the Senate and a personal friend of General Billot, the Minister of War. M. Leblois communicated to him what he knew about Commandant Esterhazy and showed him General Gonse's letters to Colonel Picquart. In October M. Scheurer-Kestner communicated on the subject both with General Billot and with the President of the Council, M. Méline. He was now to learn the name of Commandant Esterhazy from another quarter. One afternoon in the end of October a M. de Castro, a stock-broker, was seated in a café in Paris, and a boy from the street came up with copies of the facsimile of the bordereau, which had then been on sale for more than a year. M. de Castro bought a copy, and at once recognized, as he thought, the handwriting of the bordereau to be that of Commandant Esterhazy, who was a client of his. He took the copy home, compared it with letters of Commandant Esterhazy, and all doubts vanished. His friends told M. Matthieu Dreyfus, who begged him to take the letters to M. Scheurer-Kestner, and he did so on November 12, 1897, and M. Scheurer-Kestner advised that M. Matthieu Dreyfus should go to General Billot and denounce Commandant Esterhazy as the author of the bordereau. And now to turn to Commandant Esterhazy. His own statement is this. In the month of October, 1897, when in the country, he received a letter from 'Speranza' giving minute details of a plot against himself, the instigator of which was, Speranza said, a colonel named Picquart (without the c). He at once went to Paris, saw the Minister of War, and gave him Speranza's letter. Shortly afterwards he received a telegram asking him to be behind the palisades of the bridge Alexander III. at 11.30 p.m. He would there meet a person who would give him important information. He kept his appointment, met a veiled woman, who, first binding him over under oath to respect her incognito, gave him long details of the plot of the 'band' against himself. Afterwards he had three similar interviews, but not at the same place. At the second of these four interviews the unknown woman gave him a letter, saying :—' Prenez la pièce contenue dans cette euveloppe, elle prouve votre innocence, et si le torchon brûle, n'hésitez pas à vous en servir.' ['Take the piece contained in this enve-

lope, it proves your innocence, and if there is trouble do not hesitate to use it.'] This document, henceforward called 'le document libérateur,' was no other than the letter referred to in the 'Éclair' (ce canaille de D.), which, of course, ought to have been safe in the archives of the Intelligence Department. On November 14 Commandant Esterhazy returned this document to the Minister of War under a covering letter in which he called upon his chief to defend his honour thus menaced. The Minister of War sent Commandant Esterhazy a receipt. The next day the Minister received a letter from M. Matthieu Dreyfus denouncing Commandant Esterhazy as the author of the bordereau. The letter of Speranza to Commandant Esterhazy has not yet been divulged to the public; and the War Office, after diligent inquiries, have not been able to find the veiled woman. Very different was the interpretation put on this narrative by M. Trarieux, ex-Minister of Justice, and others interested in revision. Their suggestion was that Commandant Esterhazy was in the first instance apprised beforehand by his friends in the War Office of the coming danger and was for flying across the frontier, but that subsequently these same friends, finding that the chiefs of the army were fearful of being compromised by his flight from justice and would make common cause with him, wished to recall him, and with this view, took from the archives the 'document libérateur,' and sent it to him as an assurance that he might safely return and stand his trial, and also with a view to his claiming the credit of having restored to the office a document which it was now intended to charge Colonel Picquart with abstracting. On November 16, 1897, on a question being asked in the Chamber, General Billot, Minister of War, replied that he had made inquiries, and the result 'n'ébranlait nullement dans mon esprit l'autorité de la chose jugée,' but that as a formal denunciation of an officer of the army had been made by the 'famille Dreyfus,' there would be a military investigation. A fortnight or so afterwards he repeated that the Government considered the 'affaire Dreyfus comme régulièrement et justement jugée.' Here; as elsewhere, the reader will remember that the question at issue was who was the author of the bordereau, and that if Captain Dreyfus was, Commandant Esterhazy could not be. Consequently, a public declaration by the Minister of War that Captain Dreyfus had been justly condemned was as much as to say that Commandant Esterhazy must be acquitted. . . . Commandant Esterhazy was acquitted.

"On the morrow of Commandant Esterhazy's acquittal M. Zola launched his letter of January 13, 1898, which was addressed to the President of the Republic, and wound up with a series of formal accusations attributing the gravest iniquities to all concerned in either of the Courts-martial, each officer being in turn pointedly mentioned by name. M. Zola's avowed object was to get himself prosecuted for defamation and so obtain an opportunity for bringing out 'la lumière' on the whole situation. The Minister of War so far accepted the challenge as to institute a prosecution at the Assizes ; but resolving to maintain the 'chose jugée' as to the 'affaire Dreyfus,' he carefully chose his own ground so as to avoid that subject, selecting from the whole letter only 15 lines as constituting the defamation. In particular as to one sentence, which ran :—['J'accuse enfin le Premier Conseil de Guerre d'avoir violé le droit en condamnant un accusé sur une pièce restée secrète, et] j'accuse le Second Conseil de Guerre d'avoir couvert cette illegalité par ordre, en commettant à son tour le crime juridique d'acquitter sciemment un coupable'; ['I accuse, finally, the first Court-martial of having violated the law in its conviction of the accused on the strength of a document kept secret; and I accuse the second Court-martial of having covered this illegality, acting under orders and committing in its turn the legal crime of knowingly acquitting a guilty person.']

"The prosecution omitted the first half of the sentence, the part within brackets. By French law it is for the defendants to justify the defamatory words assigned, and to prove their good faith. But this was a difficult task even for M. Labori, the counsel for M. Zola. There were several notable obstacles to be passed before light could reach the Court:—1. The 'chose jugée' as applicable to the 'affaire Dreyfus.' 2. The 'huis clos'; the whole proceedings at the Dreyfus trial, and all the more important part of the proceedings at the Esterhazy trial, having been conducted within closed doors. 3. The 'secret d'État' excluding all reference to foreign Governments. 4. The 'secret professionnel,' pleaded not only by officers civil and military, but even by the experts employed by the Court for the identification of handwriting. 5. To these may be added the unwillingness of a witness for any reason whatever. Thus Colonel Du Paty de Clam was allowed to refuse to answer questions as to his conduct in family affairs; and, as for Commandant Esterhazy, he turned his back on the defendants and refused to answer any question whatever suggested by them, although it was put to him by the mouth of the Judge. . . . Of the above-mentioned obligations to silence, three were such as it was within the competence of the Government to dispense from. No dispensation was given, and hence it was that the Minister of War was seen as prosecutor pressing his legal right to call upon the defendants, under pain of conviction, to prove the truth of the alleged libel, and at the same time, by the exercise or non-exercise of his official authority, preventing the witnesses for the defence from stating the facts which were within their knowledge and most material to the truth. But the 'chose jugée' was a legal entity by which was meant not merely that the sentence could not be legally disputed, but that it was to be accepted as 'la vérité légale'; no word of evidence was to be admitted which in any way referred to any part of the proceedings—the whole affair was to be eliminated. The bar thus raised was very effectual in shutting out of Court large classes of witnesses who could speak only to the 'affaire Dreyfus' . . . whatever was the rule as to the 'chose jugée,' it should have been enforced equally on both parties. This was not always the case. One single example of the contrary shall be given, which, as will be shown hereafter, events have proved to be of the utmost significance. General de Pellieux had completed his long evidence, but having received from 'a Juror' a private letter to the effect that the jury would not convict M. Zola unless they had some further

proof of the guilt of Captain Dreyfus, on a subsequent day he asked leave to make a supplementary deposition and then said:—

"'Au moment de l'interpellation Castelin [i. e., in 1896] il s'est produit un fait que je tiens à signaler. On a eu au Ministère de la Guerre (et remarquez que je ne parle pas de l'affaire Dreyfus) la preuve absolue de la culpabilité de Dreyfus, et cette preuve je l'ai vue. Au moment de cette interpellation, il est arrivé au Ministère de la Guerre un papier dont l'origine ne peut être contestée, et qui dit—je vous dirai ce qu'il y a dedans—"Il va se produire une interpellation sur l'affaire Dreyfus. Ne dites jamais les relations que nous avons eues avec ce juif."' ['At the time of the Castelin interpellation (1896) there was a fact which I want to point out. The Ministry of War held—remark that I am not speaking of the Dreyfus case—absolute proof of the guilt of Dreyfus; and this proof I have seen. At the moment of that interpellation there arrived at the Ministry of War a paper the origin of which is incontestable, and which says,—I will tell you what it says,—"There is going to be an interpellation about the Dreyfus affair. You must never disclose the relations which we had with that Jew."'] And General de Pellieux called upon General de Boisdeffre and General Gonse to confirm what he said, and they did so. But when M. Labori asked to see the document and proposed to cross-examine the generals upon it, the Judge did not allow him, 'Nous n'avons pas à parler de l'affaire Dreyfus.' It may be conceived what effect such a revelation, made by the chiefs of the French army in full uniform, had upon the jury. They pronounced M. Zola guilty and found no extenuating circumstances; and he was sentenced by the Judge to the maximum penalty, viz., imprisonment for a year and a fine of 3,000 francs.

"On April 2 the Zola case is brought up before the Court of Cassation [the French Court of Appeals] and the Court quashes the verdict of the Assizes, on the technical ground that the prosecution had been instituted by the wrong person. The Minister of War was incompetent to prosecute; the only persons competent were those who could allege they had been defamed—in this instance the persons constituting the Esterhazy Court-martial. . . . The officers who had sat at the Esterhazy Court-martial were then called together again in order to decide whether M. Zola should be reprosecuted. To put a stop to any unwillingness on their part, M. Zola published in the 'Siècle' of April 7 a declaration of Count Casella, which the Count said he would have deposed to on oath at the former trial if the Judge had allowed him to be a witness. This declaration gave a detailed history of various interviews in Paris with Count Panizzardi, the military attaché at the Italian Embassy, and at Berlin with Colonel von Schwarzkoppen, who had been the military attaché at the German Embassy. According to Count Casella, both these officers had declared positively to him that they had had nothing to do with Captain Dreyfus, but Colonel von Schwarzkoppen much with Commandant Esterhazy. It will be said that this declaration of Count Casella had not been sifted by cross-examination; but it is understood that at the end of 1896, immediately after the 'Éclair' made the revelation of 'le document libérateur,' both the German and Italian Governments made a diplomatic representation to the French Government, denying that they had had anything to do with Captain Dreyfus. At all events, in January, 1898, official denials had been publicly made by the German Minister of Foreign Affairs to the Budget Commission of the Reichstag and by the Italian Under-Secretary for Foreign Affairs to the Parliament at Rome. The officers of the Court-martial resolve to reprosecute, and the case is fixed for the May Assizes at Versailles. When the case comes on, M. Zola demurs to its being tried outside Paris; the demurrer is overruled by the Court of Cassation, and ultimately, on July 18, the case comes on again at the Versailles Assizes. The charge, however, is now cut down from what it had been on the first trial in Paris. Of the whole letter of M. Zola now only three lines are selected as defamatory — viz.: — 'Un conseil de guerre vient par ordre d'oser acquitter un Esterhazy, soufflet suprême à toute vérité, à toute justice.' ['The Court-martial has by order dared to acquit an Esterhazy, supreme blow to all truth, to all justice.'] This selection was manifestly designed to shut out any possibility of reference to the 'affaire Dreyfus,' and M. Labori, finding that any attempt to import it would be vain, allowed the case to go by default, and M. Zola was condemned and, as before, sentenced to a year's imprisonment and a fine of 3,000f. He has appealed to the Cour de Cassation, and the appeal may be heard in the course of the autumn. To secure his own liberty in the meantime, M. Zola has avoided personal service of the order of the Assizes by removing beyond the frontier.

"We will now go back to Colonel Picquart. During the year 1897 he had become aware that in the Intelligence Department suspicions were expressed that the 'petit-bleu' was not a genuine document and insinuations made that Colonel Picquart had forged it. . . . The ground on which this imputation was rested came out clearly in the evidence which was subsequently in the Zola trial, to which reference may now be made. The sweepings of Colonel von Schwarzkoppen's basket had been brought by a spy to the Intelligence Department, and were given first into the hands of Commandant Henry, who put them into a packet or 'cornet' and passed them on to Colonel Picquart to examine. Colonel Picquart swore that on examination he had found amongst the papers a large number of fragments, fifty or sixty. These he gave to Commandant Lauth to piece together and photograph. When pieced together they were found to constitute the 'petit-bleu' addressed to Commandant Esterhazy, who at that time was a perfect stranger to Colonel Picquart. At the Zola trial Colonel Henry had sworn that the pieces were not in the 'cornet' when he gave it to Colonel Picquart, and the insinuation was that Colonel Picquart had forged the document, torn it in pieces, and put the pieces into the 'cornet.' . . . Commandant Esterhazy was acquitted by the Court-martial, and on the very next day Colonel Picquart was himself summoned to submit to a military inquiry. The Court-martial sat with closed doors, so that neither the charges nor the proceedings nor the findings would be known to the public, but the findings have found their way into the newspapers. [Picquart cleared himself on the main charges.] . . . But as to the charge (which had never been disputed) that in 1897

Colonel Picquart had communicated General Gonse's letters to M. Leblois, this the Court found to be proved; and for this military offence Colonel Picquart was removed from the army upon a pension of a little more than 2,000f., or £80, per annum. Other chastisements have followed. . . .

"We now come to the famous declaration of July 7 (1898), made by M. Cavaignac, Minister of War. On an interpellation by M. Castelin, the Minister of War replied that hitherto the Government had respected the 'chose jugée,' but now considerations superior to reasons of law made it necessary for them to bring before the Chamber and the country all the truth in their possession, the facts which had come to confirm the conviction of Captain Dreyfus. He made this declaration because of the absolute certainty he had of his guilt. He based his declaration first on documents in the Intelligence Department, and then on Captain Dreyfus's own confessions. The latter will here be dealt with first. The Minister relied on two witnesses. One was Captain d'Attel, who on the day of Captain Dreyfus's resignation had told Captain Anthoine that Captain Dreyfus had just said in his presence, 'As to what I have handed over, it was worth nothing. If I had been let alone I should have had more in exchange.' Captain Anthoine had, according to the Minister, immediately repeated these words to Major de Mitry. But Captain d'Attel is dead, and M. Cavaignac did not state to the Chamber at what date or on whose authority this information came to the War Office. The other witness was a Captain Lebrun-Renault, still alive, who had acted as captain of the escort on the day of degradation, January 5, 1895. . . . The Minister omits to specify the date at which Captain Lebrun-Renault first communicated to the War Office. It is believed to be in November, 1897; and against these allegations may be set the testimony of Commandant Forzinetti, the governor of the prison in which Captain Dreyfus was confined, to the effect that there is no record of confession in the official report made at the time by Captain Lebrun-Renault, as Captain of the escort, and that within the last year the Captain had denied to him (Commandant Forzinetti) that there had been any confession. Further we know that throughout his imprisonment before trial, at the trial, at the scene of his degradation, and in his letter written immediately afterwards to his wife, and to the Minister of War, Captain Dreyfus protested his innocence and that he had never committed even the slightest imprudence.

"Then as to the documents confirmatory of the conviction of Captain Dreyfus. M. Cavaignac did not say whether by this term 'guilt' he meant that Captain Dreyfus had been guilty of writing the bordereau, or had been guilty otherwise as a traitor. Indeed it was remarked that he never so much as mentioned the bordereau. Was, then, the bordereau dropped, as a document no longer recognized to be in the handwriting of Captain Dreyfus? But he informed the Chamber that the Intelligence Department had during the last six years accumulated 1,000 documents and letters relating to espionage, of the authorship of which there was no reasonable doubt. He would call the attention of the Chamber to only three, all of which, he said, had passed between the persons who had been mentioned

(Colonel von Schwarzkoppen and M. Panizzardi). Here again it was noticed that the ' document libérateur ' (ce canaille de D.) was not mentioned. Had this, too, been dropped as no longer to be relied upon, because ' D.' did not mean Dreyfus, or was it now omitted because it had been produced at the Court-martial by General Mercier and therefore could not be said to be confirmatory of his conviction ? Of the three documents which M. Cavaignac specified, the first, dated in March, 1894, made reference to a person indicated as D. ; the second, dated April 16, 1894, contained the expression ' cette canaille de D.,' the same as that used in the ' document libérateur.' The third was no other than 'la preuve absolue ' which General de Pellieux had imported into his evidence in the Zola trial as having been in the hands of the Government at the time of the Castelin interpellation in November, 1896. M. Cavaignac read out its contents, of which the following is an exact transcript :—'J'ai lu qu'un député va interpeller sur Dreyfus. Si— je dirai que jamais j'avais des relations avec ce Juif. C'est entendu. Si on vous demande, dites comme ça, car il faut pas que on sache jamais personne ce qui est arrivé avec lui.' [' I read that a deputy is going to question concerning Dreyfus. I shall say that I never had relations with that Jew. If they ask you, say the same, for it is necessary that we know no one who approaches him.'] M. Cavaignac went on to say that the material authenticity of this document depended not merely on its origin, but also on its similarity with a document written in 1894 on the same paper and with the same blue pencil, and that its moral authenticity was established by its being part of a correspondence exchanged between the same persons in 1896. ' The first writes to the other, who replies in terms which left no obscurity on the cause of their common uneasiness.' The Chamber was transported with the speech of the Minister of War, and, treating it as a ' coup de grâce ' to the ' affaire Dreyfus,' decreed by a majority of 572 to two that a print of it should be placarded in the 36,000 communes of France. On the next day Colonel Picquart wrote a letter to the Minister of War undertaking to prove that the first two documents had nothing to do with Captain Dreyfus, and that the third, 'la preuve absolue,' was a forgery. Within six weeks his words as to 'la preuve absolue' come true. On August 31 the public are startled with the announcement that Colonel Henry has confessed to having forged it himself, and has committed suicide in the fortress Mont Valérien, being found with his throat cut and a razor in his left hand. The discovery of the forgery was stated to have arisen from a clerk in the Intelligence Department having detected by the help of a specially strong lamp that the blue paper of 'la preuve absolue' was not identical with the blue paper of a similar document of 1894 which M. Cavaignac had relied upon as a proof of its material authenticity. . . . As a sequel to this confession, General de Boisdeffre, chief of the staff, has resigned, feeling he could not remain after having placed before the Minister of War as genuine a document proved to be a forgery. Commandant Esterhazy has been removed from the active list of the army, having been brought by M. Cavaignac before a Court-martial sitting with closed doors—his offence not disclosed, but conceived to be his anti-patriotic correspondence

with a Mme. de Boulancy. A like fate has befallen Colonel Du Paty de Clam from a similar Court-martial instituted by M. Cavaignac's successor, his offence likewise not disclosed, but presumed to be improper communication of official secrets to Commandant Esterhazy. . . .

"However, notwithstanding the confession of Colonel Henry, M. Cavaignac insisted that Captain Dreyfus was guilty, and refused consent to revision. The Cabinet not acceding to this view, M. Cavaignac resigns the Ministry of War, and is succeeded by General Zurlinden, then military Governor of Paris. General Zurlinden asks first to be allowed time to study the dossier, and after a week's study and communication with the War Office staff he also declares his opposition to revision, retires from the Ministry of War, and resumes his post of Governor of Paris. With him also retires one other member of the Cabinet. Then the Minister of Justice takes the first formal step in referring the matter to a legal Commission, the technical question at issue appearing to be whether the confession by Colonel Henry—a witness in the case—of a forgery committed by him subsequently to the conviction with a view to its confirmation might be considered either as a new fact in the case or as equivalent to a conviction for forgery, so as to justify an application to the Cour de Cassation for revision. The Commission were divided in opinion, and the matter would have fallen to the ground if the Cabinet had not decided to take the matter into their own hands and apply to the Court direct. This has now been done; the Court is making preliminary inquiries, and will then decide whether revision in some form may be allowed or a new trial ordered.

"With regard to Colonel Picquart, his public challenge of the documents put forward in the speech of the Minister of War was followed three days afterwards by an order of the Cabinet directing the Minister of War to set the Minister of Justice in motion with a view that he should be criminally prosecuted in a non-military Court for communication of secret documents—the same offence as that for which he had been punished by the Court-martial early in the year by removal from the active list of the army—and M. Leblois was to be prosecuted with him as an accomplice. On the 13th of July Colonel Picquart is put into prison to await his trial, M. Leblois being left at large. The prison was a civil prison, where he was allowed to communicate with his legal advisor. . . . On September 21 Colonel Picquart is taken from his prison to the Court for his trial. The Government Prosecutor rises and asks for an indefinite postponement on the ground that the military authorities are about to bring him before a military Court for forgery. . . . The military prosecution for forgery was ordered, and on the strength of it the Correctional Court acceded to the application for indefinite postponement of the other case of which it was seised; the military authorities claimed to take the prisoner out of the hands of the Civil authorities, and the Correctional Court acquiesced. Then it was that Colonel Picquart broke out—'This, perhaps, is the last time my voice will be heard in public. It will be easy for me to justify myself as to the petit-bleu. I shall perhaps spend to-night in the Cherche-Midi (military) Prison, but I am anxious to say if I find in my cell the noose of Lemercier-Picard, or the razor of Henry, it will be an assassination. I have no intention of committing suicide.' The same or the next day Colonel Picquart was removed to the Cherche-Midi Prison, there to await his Court-martial, which is not expected yet for some weeks. He is not permitted to communicate with his legal advisor or any one else."—G. Lushington, *The Dreyfus Case* (*London Times, Oct.* 13, 1898).

Late in October (1898) the Court of Cassation decided that it found ground for proceeding to a supplementary investigation in the case of Captain Dreyfus, but not for the suspension meantime of the punishment he was undergoing. On the 15th of November it decided that the prisoner should be informed by telegraph of the pending revision proceedings, in order that he might prepare his defense. The Court was now endeavoring to secure possession of the secret documents (known as the "Dreyfus dossier") on which the conviction of the accused was said to have been really founded. For some time the war office seemed determined to withhold them; but at length, late in December, the dossier was turned over, under pledges of strict secrecy as to the documents contained. Showing still further a disposition to check the doings of the military authorities, the Court of Cassation, in December, ordered a suspension of proceedings in the military court against Colonel Picquart, and demanded all documents in his case for examination by itself.

Attacks were now made on the Court which had thus ventured to interfere with the secret doings of the army chiefs. Suddenly, on the 8th of January (1899), the president of the civil section of the Court, M. Quesnay de Beaurepaire, resigned his office and denounced his recent colleagues as being in a conspiracy to acquit Dreyfus and dishonor the army. This, of course, was calculated to stimulate anti-Dreyfus excitement and furnish ground for challenging the final decision of the Court, if it should be favorable to a new trial for the imprisoned Captain. It also delayed proceedings in the case, leading to the enactment of a law requiring all cases of revision to be tried by the united sections of the Court of Cassation. This act took the Dreyfus case from the 16 judges of the criminal section and committed it to the whole 48 judges of the Court.

Major Esterhazy had taken refuge in England. On the 2d of June he went to the office of the London "Chronicle" and made the following confession for publication: "The chiefs of the army have disgracefully abandoned me. My cup is full, and I shall speak out. Yes, it was I who wrote the bordereau. I wrote it upon orders received from Sandherr. They (the chiefs of the general staff) will lie, as they know how to lie; but I have them fast. I have proofs that they knew the whole thing and share the responsibility with me, and I will produce the proofs." Immediately it was said that he had been bribed by the friends of Dreyfus to take the crime upon himself.

On the day following this confession, the decision of the Court of Cassation was announced. Meantime, the newspaper "Figaro" had, by some means, been able to obtain and publish the testimony which the Court had taken with closed doors, and had thus revealed the flimsiness and the contradictoriness of the grounds on which the officers of the Army Staff based their strenu-

ous assertions that they had positive knowledge of the guilt of Dreyfus. This had great influence in preparing the public mind for the decision of the Court when announced. On grounds relating to the bordereau, to the document which contained the expression "ce canaille de D.," and to the alleged confession of Dreyfus,—leaving aside all other questions of evidence,—the judgment as delivered declared that "the court quashes and annuls the judgment of condemnation pronounced on December 22, 1894, against Alfred Dreyfus by the first court-martial of the Military Government of Paris, and remits the accused to the court-martial of Rennes, named by special deliberation in council chamber, to be tried on the following question :—Is Dreyfus guilty of having in 1894 instigated machinations or held dealings with a foreign power or one of its agents in order to incite it to commit hostilities or undertake war against France by furnishing it with the notes and documents enumerated in the bordereau? and orders the prescribed judgment to be printed and transcribed on the registers of the first court-martial of the Military Government of Paris in the margin of the decision annulled." Captain Dreyfus was taken immediately from his prison on Devil's Island and brought by a French cruiser to France, landing at Quiberon on the 1st of July and being taken to Rennes, where arrangements for the new military trial were being made.

The new court-martial trial began at Rennes on the 7th of August. When it had proceeded for a week, and had reached what appeared to be a critical point—the opening of a cross-examination of General Mercier by the counsel for Dreyfus—M. Labori, the leading counsel for the defense, was shot as he walked the street, by a would-be assassin who escaped. Fortunately, the wound he received only disabled him for some days, and deprived the accused of his presence and his powerful service in the court at a highly important time. The trial, which lasted beyond a month, was a keen disappointment in every respect. It probed none of the sinister secrets that are surely hidden somewhere in the black depths of the extraordinary case. In the judgment of all unimpassioned watchers of its proceeding, it disclosed no proof of guilt in Dreyfus. On the other hand, it gave no opportunity for his innocence to be distinctly shown. Apparently, there was no way in which the negative of his non-guiltiness could be proved except by testimony from the foreign agents with whom he was accused of having treasonable dealings; but that testimony was barred out by the court, though the German and Italian governments gave permission to the counsel for Dreyfus to have it taken by commission. Outside of France, at least, the public verdict may be said to have been unanimous, that the whole case against Captain Dreyfus, as set forth by the heads of the French army, in plain combination against him, was foul with forgeries, lies, contradictions and puerilities, and that nothing to justify his condemnation had been shown. But the military court, on the 9th of September, by a vote of five judges against two, brought in a verdict of Guilty, with "extenuating circumstances" (as though any circumstances could extenuate the guilt of an actual crime like that of which Dreyfus was accused), and sentenced him to imprisonment in a fortress for ten years, from which term the years of his past imprisonment would be taken out. Mr. G. W. Steevens, the English newspaper correspondent, who attended the trial and has written the best account of it, makes the following comment on the verdict, which sums up all that needs to be said : "In a way, the most remarkable feature about the verdict of Rennes was the proportion of the votes. When it had been over a few hours, and numb brains had relaxed to thought again, it struck somebody that on the very first day the very first motion had been carried by five to two. The next and next and all of them had been carried by five to two. Now Dreyfus was condemned by five to two. The idea—the staggering idea—dropped like a stone into the mind, and spread in widening circles till it filled it with conviction. Every one of the judges had made up his mind before a single word of evidence had been heard. The twenty-seven days, the hundred-and-something witnesses, the baskets of documents, the seas of sweat and tears—they were all utterly wasted. . . . The verdict was, naturally, received with a howl of indignation, and to endeavour to extenuate the stupid prejudiec—that at least, if not cowardly dishonesty—of the five who voted against the evidence is not likely to be popular with civilized readers. Yet it may be said of them in extenuation—if it is any extenuation—that they only did as almost any other five Frenchmen would have done in their place. Frenchmen are hypnotized by the case of Dreyfus, as some people are hypnotized by religion ; in its presence they lose all mental power and moral sense." The army chiefs had had their way ; the stain of their condemnation had been kept upon Dreyfus ; but the government of France was magnanimous enough to punish him no more. His sentence was remitted by the President, and he was set free, a broken man.

A. D. 1898.—State of the French Protectorate of Tunis. See (in this vol.) TUNIS : A. D. 1881-1898.

A. D. 1898 (April).—Lease of Kwangchow Wan from China.—Railway and other concessions exacted. See (in this vol.) CHINA : A. D. 1898 (APRIL—AUGUST).

A. D. 1898 (April—December).—In the Chinese "Battle of Concessions." See (in this vol.) CHINA : A. D. 1898 (FEBRUARY—DECEMBER).

A. D. 1898 (May).—Demands on China consequent on the murder of a missionary. See (in this vol.) CHINA : A. D. 1898 (MAY).

A. D. 1898 (May—November).—General Elections.—Fall of the Ministry of M. Meline. —Brief Ministry of M. Brisson, struggling with the Dreyfus question.—Coalition Cabinet of M. Dupuy.—General elections for a new Chamber of Deputies were held throughout France on Sunday, May 8, with a second balloting on Sunday, May 22, in constituencies where the first had resulted in no choice. Of the 584 seats to be filled, the Progressive Republicans secured only 225, so that the Ministry of M. Méline could count with no certainty on the support of a majority in the Chamber. It was brought to a downfall in the following month by a motion made by M. Bourgeois, in the following words: "The Chamber determines to support only a Ministry relying exclusively on a Republican majority." This was carried by

a majority of about fifty votes, and on the next day the Ministry resigned. It was succeeded by a Radical cabinet, under M. Henri Brisson, after several unsuccessful attempts to form a Conservative government. By announcing that it would not attempt to carry out a Radical programme in some important particulars, the Brisson Ministry secured enough support to maintain its ground for a time; but there were fatal differences in its ranks on the burning Dreyfus question, as well as on other points. M. Cavaignac, Minister of War, was bitterly opposed to a revision of the Dreyfus case, which the Premier and M. Bourgeois (now Minister of Public Instruction) were understood to favor. M. Cavaignac soon placed himself in an extremely embarrassing position by reading to the Chamber certain documents which he put forward as absolute proofs of the guilt of Dreyfus, but of which one was shown presently to have been forged, while another had no relation to the case. He accordingly resigned (September 4), and General Zurlinden took his place. But Zurlinden, too, resigned a few days later, when a determination to revise the trial of Dreyfus was reached. The government was then exposed to a new outburst of fury in the anti-Dreyfus factions, and all the enemies of the Republic became active in new intrigues. The Orleanists bestirred themselves with fresh hopes, and the old Boulangist conspirators revived their so-called Patriotic League, with M. Déroulède at its head. At the same time dangerous labor disturbances occurred in Paris, threatening a complete paralysis of railway communications as well as of the industries of the capital. The Ministry faced its many difficulties with much resolution; but it failed of support in the Chamber, when that body met in October, and it resigned. A coalition cabinet was then formed, with M. Charles Dupuy in the presidency of the council, and M. de Freycinet as Minister of War.

A. D. 1898 (June).—The Sugar Conference at Brussels. See (in this vol.) SUGAR BOUNTIES.

A. D. 1898 (September—November).—The Nile question with England.—Marchand's expedition at Fashoda. See (in this vol.) EGYPT : A. D. 1898 (SEPTEMBER—NOVEMBER).

A. D. 1898-1899.—Demands upon China for attacks on Missions in Szechuan. See (in this vol.) CHINA : A. D. 1898-1899 (JUNE—JANUARY).

A. D. 1898-1899.—Demand on China for extension of settlement at Shanghai. See (in this vol.) CHINA : A. D. 1898-1899.

A. D. 1898-1899 (June—June).—Convention with England defining possessions in West and North Africa.—The great Empire in the Sudan and Sahara. See (in this vol.) NIGERIA : A. D. 1882-1899.

A. D. 1899 (February—June).—Death of President Faure.—Election of President Loubet.—Revolutionary attempts of "Nationalist" agitators.—The Ministry of M. Waldeck-Rousseau.—Felix Faure, President of the French Republic, died suddenly on the 16th of February,—a victim, it is believed, of the excitements and anxieties of the Dreyfus affair. The situation thus produced was so sobering in its effect that the Republican factions were generally drawn together for the moment, and acted promptly in filling the vacant executive. The Senate and the Chamber of Deputies were convened in joint session, as a National Assembly, at Versailles, on the 18th, and Émile Loubet, then President of the Senate, was chosen to the presidency of the Republic on its first ballot, by 483 votes, against 279 for M. Méline, and 45 for M. Cavaignac. At the funeral of the late President Faure, which occurred on the 23d, the pestilential Déroulède and his fellow mis-chief-makers, with their so-called "League of Patriots," "League de Patrie Française," and party of "Nationalists," attempted to excite the troops to revolt, but without success. Dérou-lède and others were arrested for this treasonable attempt. During some months the enemies of the Republic were active and violent in hostility to President Loubet, and the cabinet which he inherited from his predecessor was believed to lack loyalty to him. On the 4th of June, while attending the steeple-chase races at Auteuil, he was grossly insulted, and even struck with a cane, by a party of young royalists, the leader of whom, Count Christiani, who struck the shame-ful blow, was sentenced afterwards to imprison-ment for four years. The Ministry of the day was considered to be responsible for these dis-orders, and, on the 12th of June, a resolution was passed in the Chamber to the effect that it would support only a government that was de-termined to defend republican institutions with energy and preserve public order. Thereupon the Ministry of M. Dupuy resigned, and a new cabinet was formed with much difficulty by M. Waldeck-Rousseau. It included a radical Social-ist, M. Millerand, who became Minister of Com-merce, and a resolute and honest soldier, the Marquis de Gallifet, as Minister of War. The latter promptly cleared the way for more inde-pendent action in the government, by remov-ing several troublesome generals from impor-tant commands. The new Ministry assumed the name of the "Government of Republican De-fense," and offered a front to the enemies of the Republic which plainly checked their attacks. M. Déroulède and some of his fellow conspirators were brought to trial before the Court of Assizes, and acquitted.

A. D. 1899 (May).—New Convention with Siam. See (in this vol.) SIAM: A. D. 1896–1899.

A. D. 1899 (May—July).—Representation in the Peace Conference at The Hague. See (in this vol.) PEACE CONFERENCE.

A. D. 1899 (July).—Reciprocity Treaty with the United States. See (in this vol.) UNITED STATES OF AM.: A. D. 1899–1901.

A. D. 1899 (December).—Adhesion to the arrangement of an "open door" commercial policy in China. See (in this vol.) CHINA: A. D. 1899–1900 (SEPTEMBER—FEBRUARY).

A. D. 1899-1900 (August—January).—Arrest and trial of revolutionary conspirators.—In August, 1899, the government, having obtained good evidence that treasonable plans for the over-throw of the Republic had been under organiza-tion for several months, in the various royalist, anti-Semitic, and so-called "Patriotic" leagues, caused the arrest of a number of the leaders im-plicated, the irrepressible Paul Déroulède being conspicuous among them. The president of the Anti-Semitic League, M. Guérin, with a number of his associates, barricaded themselves at the headquarters of the League and defied arrest,

evidently expecting a mob rising in Paris if they were attacked. Serious rioting did occur on the 20th of August; but the government prudently allowed Guérin and his party to hold their citadel until the ending of the excitements of the Dreyfus trial; then, on the showing of a serious determin-ation to take it by force, they gave themselves up. The trial of the conspirators was begun in September, before the Senate, sitting as a high court of Justice, and continued at intervals un-til the following January. Déroulède conducted himself with characteristic insolence, and received two sentences of imprisonment, one for three months and the other for two years, on account of outrageous attacks on the Senate and on the President of the Republic. These were additional to a final sentence to ten years of banishment for his treasonable plotting, which he shared with one fellow conspirator. Guérin was condemned to ten years imprisonment in a fortified place. The remainder of the accused were discharged with the exception of one who had escaped arrest, and who was convicted in his absence. The trial, wrote the Paris correspondent of the "London Times," "showed how strange a thing was this motley conspiracy between men who had but one common bond of sympathy, namely, the desire to upset the Republic,—men from whom the Bonapartist, another variety of anti-Republi-can conspirators, had held aloof. The latter fancied themselves sufficiently represented in the conspiracy by the plebiscitary party [of Dérou-lède] whose accession to office would have been tantamount to the success of Imperialism. . . . The condemnation of these conspirators of varied aspirations proved that the Nationalist party was a mere conglomeration of ambitions which would end in every form of violence if ever the conspir-ators were called upon to share the booty. The harm that they have already done, even before they have made themselves masters of France, shows that the danger which they constitute to their country is infinitely greater than the danger with which it was menaced by Boulangism, for then at least at the moment of victory all the ambitions would have been concentrated round a single will, however mediocre that will, and General Boulanger would at all events have been a rallying flag for the conspirators visible all over France. The Nationalism condemned by the Court in its various personifications has not even a head around which at the moment of action the accomplices could be grouped. It is confusion worse confounded. If it succeeded in its aims it could only avoid at home the couse-quences of its incoherent policy by some desper-ate enterprise abroad. The judgment of the High Court, by restoring tranquillity in the streets, preserved France from the dangers towards which she was hastening, and which were increased, consciously or unconsciously, by auxiliaries at the head of the executive office. But owing to the verdict of the High Court France had time to pull herself together, to breathe more easily, and to take the necessary resolutions to secure tranquillity. The approach of the Exhibition imposed upon every one a kind of truce, and M. Déroulède himself, with an imprudence of which he is still feeling the consequences, declared that he would return to France when once the Exhibition was over."

In a speech which he made subsequently, at San Sebastian, his place of exile, Déroulède declared that the "coup d'état" prepared by his party of revolutionists for the 23d of February, 1899, on the occasion of the funeral of President Faure (see above), was frustrated because he refused, at the last moment, to permit it to be used in the interest of the Duke of Orleans. "The following day," he said, "between midday and 4 o'clock in the afternoon, a mysterious hand had upset all the preparations made, the position of the troops, their dislocation, their order and the officers commanding them, and the same evening Marcel Habert and myself were arrested." The intimation of his speech seemed to be that the hand in the government which changed the position of the troops and upset the revolutionary plot would not have done so if the royalists had been taken into it.

Soon after the conclusion of the conspiracy trials, the superior and eleven monks of the Order of the Assumptionist Fathers, who had appeared to be mixed up in the plot, were brought to account as an illegal association, and their society was dissolved.

A. D. 1899-1901.—The Newfoundland French Shore question. See (in this vol.) NEWFOUNDLAND: A. D. 1899-1901.

A. D. 1900.—Military and naval expendi- ture. See (in this vol.) WAR BUDGETS.

A. D. 1900.—Naval strength. See (in this vol.) NAVIES OF THE SEA POWERS.

A. D. 1900 (January).—Elections to the Senate.—Elections to the French Senate, on the 28th of January, returned 61 Republicans, 6 Liberal Republicans, 18 Radicals, 7 Socialists, 4 Monarchists, and 3 Nationalists. "The Radicals are as they were. The Socialists have just gained an entrance to the Senate, and to this they were entitled by the large and solid Socialist vote throughout France. The great mass of solid and sensible Republicans have not only held their ground, but have increased and solidified their position. The reactionaries, whether avowed Monarchists, or supporters of the Déroulède movement, have made one or two merely formal gains, but have really fallen back, from the point of view of their pretensions, and the long list of candidates they put forward. On the whole, we may fairly say that the solid, sober Republican vote of France has proved that it is in the ascendant. Once more, in a deeper sense than he meant, the verdict of M. Thiers has, for the moment at any rate, been verified,—that France is really at bottom Left Centre. That is to say, the nation is for progress, but for progress divested of vague revolutionary pretensions, of mere a priori dogmas as to what Republican progress involves. In the main the nation seems to have supported the Government in repelling the aggressive attacks of unbridled Clericalism, and in rejecting the pretensions of the Army to dictate French politics. On the other hand, the mass of the French electors do not desire a crusade against the Roman Catholic Church, and they do not care for an indiscriminate attack on the French Army."—*The Spectator* (*London*), *Feb.* 3, 1900.

A. D. 1900 (January—March).—The outbreak of the "Boxers" in northern China. See (in this vol.) CHINA: A. D. 1900 (JANUARY—MARCH).

A. D. 1900 (April—November).—The Paris Exposition.—The Paris Exposition of 1900, which exceeded all previous "world's fairs" in extent and in the multitude of its visitors, was formally opened on the 14th of April, but with unfinished preparations, and closed on the 12th of November. The reported attendance during the whole period of the Exposition was 48,130,301, being very nearly double the attendance at the Exposition of 1889. The total receipts of money were 114,456,213 francs, and total expenditures 116,500,000 francs, leaving a deficit of 2,044,787 francs. But France and Paris are thought to have profited greatly, notwithstanding. Forty countries besides France took part in the preparations and were officially represented. The number of exhibitors was 75,531; the awards distributed were 42,790 in number. The buildings erected for the Exposition numbered more than 200, including 36 official pavilions erected by foreign governments. The ground occupied extended on each side of the Seine for a distance of nearly two miles, comprising, besides the quays on each side of the river, the Champ de Mars, the Esplanade des Invalides, the Trocadero Gardens, and part of the Champs Elysées.

A. D. 1900 (June—December).—Co-opera- tion with the Powers in China. See (in this vol.) CHINA.

A. D. 1900 (August).—Annexation of the Austral Islands. See (in this vol.) AUSTRAL ISLANDS.

A. D. 1900 (September).—The centenary of the Proclamation of the French Republic.— A gigantic banquet.—On the 22d of September, the centenary of the proclamation of the French Republic was celebrated in Paris by a gigantic banquet given by President Loubet, accompanied by his Ministers, to the assembled Mayors of France, gathered from near and far. Some 23,000 guests sat down to the déjeuner, for which a temporary structure had been prepared in the Tuileries Gardens. It was a triumphant demonstration of the culinary resources of Paris; but it had more important objects. It was a political demonstration, organized by the President of the Republic, in concert with the Cabinet of M. Waldeck-Rousseau, as a check to certain schemes of the Paris Nationalists, against the government. It brought the municipal representatives of the provinces to the capital to show the array of their feeling for the Republic against that of the noisy demagogues of the capital. It was a striking success.

A. D. 1900 (October).—Proposal of terms for negotiation with the Chinese government. See (in this vol.) CHINA : A. D. 1900 (AUGUST—DECEMBER).

A. D. 1900 (December).—The Amnesty Bill. —With the object of making it impossible for the enemies of the Republic to find such opportunity for a revival of the dangerous Dreyfus controversy as any new trial of its issues would give them, the French government, in December, accomplished the passage of an amnesty bill. which purges everybody connected with the affair. so far as legal proceedings are concerned. The measure was strenuously opposed by the friends of Dreyfus, Picquart and Zola, none of whom are willing to be left unvindicated by law, nor willing to be barred from future proceedings against some of the army staff. It was also fought by the mischievous factions which wish to keep the Dreyfus quarrel alive for purposes of disorderly excitement. The policy of the measure, from the govermental standpoint, was thus described at the time it was pending: The Cabinet "felt that this affair had done great injury to France, that it was a dangerous weapon in the hands of all the conspirators against the Republic, that no Court-martial would agree to acquit Dreyfus, even though convinced of his innocence, and that, in view of the futility of any attempt to secure an acquittal, it was necessary to avoid danger to the Republic by reopening the affair. France had already suffered irreparable mischief from it. . . . The affair has falsified the judgment and opinion of the army, so that it has no longer a clear notion of its duty at home. In external affairs it is still always ready to march to the defence of the country, but as to its duties at home it is in a state of deplorable confusion. . . . Considering that the Dreyfus affair has so armed the adversaries of the Government that it cannot be sure of the army in internal matters, the Cabinet, it is evident, could not allow that affair to remain open and produce anarchy. On the other hand, there was a prosecution pending against M. Zola, who, it was clearly proved to all, was right in his famous letter 'J'accuse.' There was a prosecution against Colonel Picquart, who had sacrificed a brilliant future in the defence of truth against falsehood. There was likewise a prosecution against M. Joseph Reinach, who had accused Henry of having been a traitor or the accomplice of a traitor. I do not know how far M. Reinach had proofs of his allegations, but these three prosecutions were so closely connected with the Dreyfus case that, if they had been allowed to go on, that affair, which was so dangerous to tranquillity, security, and order, would be reopened. Now the Government will not at any cost allow the affair to be reopened. The whole Amnesty Bill hinges on this question. The Government agrees to amnesty everybody except the persons condemned by the High Court, and who continue to defy it. . . . It insists on these three prosecutions being struck off the rolls of the Tribunals. This is the whole question. Nothing else in the eyes of the Government is essential, but it will not allow the further serious mischief which would result from the reopening of the affair. The Bill will not stop the civil proceedings against MM. Zola, Picquart, and Reinach, but such proceedings do not cause the same excitement as criminal prosecutions. If the latter are stopped, the dangers occasioned by the confusion in the spirit of the army will disappear, and it may then be hoped that the excitement will calm down."

M. Zola protested vigorously against the Amnesty Bill, and, on its passage, wrote an open letter to the President in which he said: "I shall not cease repeating that the affair cannot cease as long as France does not know and repair the injustice. I said that the fourth act was played at Rennes and that there would have to be a fifth act. Anxiety remains in my heart. The people of France always forget that the Kaiser is in possession of the truth, which he may throw in our face when the hour strikes. Perhaps he has already chosen his time. This would be the horrible fifth act which I have always dreaded. The French Government should not for one hour accept such a terrible contingency."

A. D. 1900 (December).—Award in the arbitration of French Guiana boundary dis-

pute with **Brazil**. See (in this vol.) BRAZIL: A. D. 1900.

A. D. 1901.—The Bill on Associations.—A measure to place the Religious Orders under strict regulations of law, and to limit their possession of property.—In a speech delivered at Toulouse on the 28th of October, 1900, the French Prime Minister, M. Waldeck-Rousseau, announced the intention of the government to bring forward, at the next session of the Chambers, a measure of critical importance and remarkable boldness, being no less than the project of a law (called in general terms a "Bill on Associations") for the stringent regulation and restriction of the religious orders in France,—especially for the restriction of their acquisition and ownership of property. Forecasting the measure in that speech, he said: "The question is the rendering free, and subject only to the common law, all the associations which are in themselves lawful as regards the safety of the State. Another object of the same Bill is to cope with the peril which arises from the continuous development in a Democratic society of an organism which, according to a famous definition, the merit of which is due to our old Parliaments, 'tends to introduce into the State under the specious veil of a religious institution a political corporation the object of which is to arrive first at complete independence and then at the usurpation of all authority.' I am filled with no sectarian spirit, but merely with the spirit which dominated as well the policy of the Revolution as the entire historical policy of France. The fundamental statute determining the relations between the churches and the State should be exactly applied so long as it has not been altered, and we have always interpreted its spirit with the broadest tolerance. But as things are now going, what will remain of this pact of reciprocal guarantees? It had been exclusively confined to the secular clergy owing hierarchic obedience to their superiors and to the State and to questions of worship, the preparation for ecclesiastical functions and preaching in the churches. And, now, lo and behold, we find religious orders teaching in the seminaries, the pulpit usurped by the missions, and the Church more and more menaced by the chapel. The dispersed but not suppressed religious communities cover the territory with a close network, which has been evidenced in a recent trial, and have been so bold as to defy the Church dignitaries not accepting their vassalage. In pointing to the peril of increasing mortmain threatening the principle of the free circulation of property, it is sufficient to say that we are influenced by no vain alarms, that the value of the real property occupied or owned by the communities was in 1880 as much as 700,000,000f., and that it now exceeds a milliard. Starting from this figure, what may be the value of mortmain personalty? Yet the real peril does not arise from the extension of mortmain. In this country, whose moral unity has for centuries constituted its strength and greatness, two youths are growing up ignorant of each other until the day when they meet, so unlike as to risk not comprehending one another. Such a fact is explained only by the existence of a power which is no longer even occult and by the constitution in the State of a rival power. All efforts will be fruitless as long as a rational, effective legislation has not superseded a legislation at once illogical, arbitrary, and inoperative. If we attach so much importance to a Law on Association it is also because it involves the solution of at least a portion of the education question. This Bill is the indispensable guarantee of the most necessary prerogatives of modern society."

This pre-announcement of the intentions of the government gave rise, as it must have been intended to do, to a warm discussion of the project in advance, and showed something of the strength of the antagonists with whom its supporters must make their fight. At length, late in December—a few days before the opening of debate on the bill in the Chambers—the attitude of the Church upon it was fully declared by the Pope, in a lengthy interview which M. Henri des Houx, one of the members of the staff of the "Matin," was permitted to publish in that Paris journal. "After M. Waldeck-Rousseau's Toulouse speech, and in presence of the Associations Bill," said the Pope, "I can no longer keep silent. It is my Apostolic duty to speak out. French Catholics will know that their father does not abandon them, that he suffers with them in their trials, and that he encourages their generous efforts for right and liberty. They are well aware that the Pope has unceasingly laboured in their behalf and for the Church, adapting the means to the utility of the ends. The pilot is the judge of the manœuvre at the bar. At one moment he seems to be tacking before the tempest; at another he is bound to sail full against it. But his one aim ever is to make the port. Now, the Pope cannot consent to allow the French Government to twist the Concordat from its real intent and transform an instrument of peace and justice into one of war and oppression. The Concordat [see, in vol. 2, FRANCE: A. D. 1801-1804] established and regulated in France the exercise of Catholic worship and defined, between the Church and the French State, mutual rights and duties. The religious communities form an integral part of the Apostolic Church as much as the secular clergy. They exercise a special and a different mission, but one not less sacred than that of the pastors recognized by the State To try to destroy them is to deal a blow at the Church; to mutilate it, and to restrain its benefits. Such was not the intent of the Concordat. It would be a misconstruction of this treaty to declare illegal and to interdict whatever it was not able to settle or foresee. The Concordat is silent as to religious communities. This means that the regular clergy has no share in the special rights and relative privileges granted by the Concordat to the members of the secular ecclesiastical hierarchy. It does not mean that religious orders are to be excluded from the common law and put outside the pale of the State. . . . There was no need of mentioning the religious communities in the Concordat because these pious bodies were permitted to live under the shelter of the equal rights accorded to men and citizens by the fundamental clauses of your Constitution. But if an exception is to be made to these solemn declarations in the case of certain citizens it is an iniquity towards the Church, an infraction of the intentions of the negotiators of 1801. Look at the countries with which the Holy See has signed no Concordat, and even at Protestant countries like England, the United States, and many another.

Are religious communities there excluded from the liberties recognized as belonging to other citizens? Do they not live there without being harrassed? And thither, perhaps, these communities would take refuge, as in the evil days of the Terror, from the iniquity of Catholic France! But since then France has become bound by the Concordat, and she seems to forget it. . . .

"Why does France figure to-day by the side of the great nations in the concert of the Powers settling the Chinese question? Whence have your Ministry for Foreign Affairs and your representative in Peking the authority which gives weight to their opinion in the assembly of plenipotentiaries? What interest have you in the north of China? Are you at the head there in trade and industry? Have you many traders there to protect? No. But you are there the noblest champions of Christian civilization, the protectors of the Catholic missions. Your foreign rivals are envious of this privileged situation. They are seeking to dispute your rights laid down in treaties that assign to you the rôle of defenders of native missions and Christian settlements. . . . Hitherto your Governments had had a better notion of the importance of their rights. It is in the name of treaties guaranteeing them that they protested to me when the Chinese Emperor asked me to arrange diplomatic relations directly with the Holy See. Upon the insistence of M. de Freycinet, the then Minister, I refused, so fearful was I that France might believe, even wrongfully, that I wished in any way to diminish her prestige, her influence, and her power. In the Levant, at Constantinople, in Syria, in the Lebanon, what will remain of the eminent position held by your Ambassador and Consuls if France intends to renounce representing there the rights of Christianity? . . .

"M. Waldeck-Rousseau, in his Toulouse speech, spoke of the moral unity of France. Who has laboured more than I for it? Have I not energetically counselled Catholics to cease all conflict against the institutions which your country has freely chosen and to which it remains attached? Have I not urged Catholics to serve the Republic instead of combating it? I have encountered warm resistance among them, but I believe that their present weakness arises from their very lack of union and their imperfect deference to my advice. The Republican Government at least knows in what degree my authority has been effective towards bringing about that public peace and moral unity which is proclaimed at the very moment when it is seriously menaced. It has more than once thanked me. If the Pontifical authority has not been able entirely to accomplish the union so much desired I at least have spared no effort for it. Is there now a desire to reconstitute the union of Catholics against the Republic? How could I prevent this if, instead of the Republic liberal, equitable, open to all, to which I have invited Catholics to rally, there was substituted a narrow, sectarian Republic, governed by an inflamed faction governed by laws of exception and spoliation, repugnant to all honest and upright consciences, and to the traditional generosity of France? Is it thought that such a Republic can obtain the respect of a single Catholic and the benediction of the Supreme Pontiff? I still hope that France will spare herself such crises, and that her Government will not renounce the services which I have been able to render and can still render it. On several occasions, for instance, and quite recently, I have been asked by the head of a powerful State to allow disregard of the rights of France in the East and Far East. Although compensations were offered to the Church and the Holy See, I resolved that the right of France should remain intact, because it is an unquestionable right, which France has not allowed to become obsolete. But if in your country the religious orders, without which no Catholic expansion is possible, are ruined and suppressed, what shall I answer whenever such requests are renewed to me? Will the Pope be alone in defending privileges the possessors of which prize them so little?"

Of the seriousness of the conflict thus opening between the French Republicans and the Roman Catholic Church there could be no doubt.

The threatened bill was brought forward by the government and debate upon it opened on the 15th of January, 1901. The most stringent clauses of the measure were translated and communicated to the "London Times" by its Paris correspondent, as follows:

"II. Any association founded on a cause, or for an illicit end, contrary to the laws, to public order, to good manners, to the national unity, and to the form of the Government of the Republic, is null and void.

"III. Any member of an association which has not been formed for a determined time may withdraw at any term after payment of all dues belonging to the current year, in spite of any clauses to the contrary.

"IV. The founders of any association are bound to publish the covenants of the association. This declaration must be made at the prefecture of the Department or at the sub-prefecture of the district which is the seat of the association. This declaration must reveal the title and object of the association, the place of meeting and the names, professions, and domiciles of the members or of those who are in any way connected with its administration. . . . The founders, directors, or administrators of an association maintained or reconstituted illegally after the verdict of dissolution will be punished with a fine of from 500f. to 5,000f. and imprisonment ranging from six days

to a year. And the same penalty will apply to all persons who shall have favoured the assemblage of the members of the dissolved association by the offer of a meeting place. . . .

"X. Associations recognized as of public utility may exercise all the rights of civil life not forbidden in their statutes, but they cannot possess or acquire other real estate than that necessary for the object which they have in view. All personal property belonging to an association should be invested in bonds bearing the name of the owner. Such associations can receive gifts and bequests on the conditions defined by Clause 910 of the Civil Code. Real estate included in an act of donation or in testamentary dispositions, which is not necessary for the working of the association, is alienated within the period and after the forms prescribed by the decree authorizing acceptance of the gift, the amount thereby represented becoming a part of the association's funds. Such associations cannot accept a donation of real estate or personal property under the reserve of usufruct for the benefit of the donor.

"XI. Associations between Frenchmen and foreigners cannot be formed without previous authorization by a decree of the Conseil d'Etta. A special law authorizing their formation and determining the conditions of their working is necessary in the case, first of associations between Frenchmen, the seat or management of which is fixed or emanates from beyond the frontiers or is in the hands of foreigners; secondly, in the case of associations whose members live in common. . . .

"XIV. Associations existing at the moment of the promulgation of the present law and not having previously been authorized or recognized must, within six months, be able to show that they have done all in their power to conform to these regulations."

Discussion of the Bill in the Chamber of Deputies was carried on at intervals during ten weeks, the government defeating nearly every amendment proposed by its opponents, and carrying the measure to its final passage on the 29th of March, by a vote of 303 to 220. Of the passage of the bill by the Senate there seems to be no doubt.

After disposing of the Bill on Associations, on the 27th of March, the Chamber adjourned to May 14.

FRANCHISE LAW, The Boer. See (in this vol.) SOUTH AFRICA (THE TRANSVAAL): A. D. 1899 (MAY—JUNE); and (JULY—SEPTEMBER).

FRANCHISES, Taxation of public. See (in this vol.) NEW YORK STATE: A. D. 1899 (MAY).

FRANKLIN, The Canadian district of. See (in this vol.) CANADA: A. D. 1895.

FRANZ JOSEF LAND: Exploration of. See (in this vol.) POLAR EXPLORATION, 1896; 1897; 1898–1899; 1900–; and 1901.

FREE SILVER QUESTION, The. See (in this vol.) UNITED STATES OF AM.: A. D. 1896 (JUNE—NOVEMBER); and 1900 (MAY—NOVEMBER).

FREE SPEECH: Restrictions on, in Germany. See (in this vol.) GERMANY: A. D. 1898; and 1900 (OCTOBER 9).

FREE TRADE. See (in this vol.) TARIFF LEGISLATION.

FREE ZONE, The Mexican. See (in this vol.) MEXICAN FREE ZONE.

FRENCH SHORE QUESTION, The. Newfoundland. See (in this vol.) NEWFOUNDLAND: A. D. 1899–1901.

FRENCH WEST AFRICA. See (in this vol.) AFRICA: A. D. 1895; and NIGERIA: A. D. 1882–1899.

FRIARS, Spanish, in the Philippines. See (in this vol.) PHILIPPINE ISLANDS: A. D. 1900 (NOVEMBER).

G.

GALABAT, Battle of. See (in this vol.)
EGYPT : A. D. 1885-1896.

**GALVESTON : A. D. 1900.—The city over-
whelmed by wind and waves.**—"The southern coast of the United States was visited by a
tropical hurricane on September 6-9, the fury of
which reached its climax at and near Galveston,
Texas, 1 : 45 A. M., on Sunday, the 9th. Galveston is built upon the east end of a beautiful but
low-lying island some thirty miles long and six
or seven miles wide at the point of greatest extent, though only a mile or two wide where the
city is built. The pressure of the wind upon the
waters of the Gulf was so powerful and so continuous that it lifted the waves on the north
coast many feet above the ordinary high-tide
level, and for a short time the entire city was
submerged. . . . The combined attack of hurricane and tidal-wave produced indescribable horrors—the destruction of property sinking into
insignificance when compared with the appalling
loss of life. The new census taken in June accredited Galveston with a population of 37,789.
The calamity of a few hours seems to have reduced that number by 20 per cent. The loss of
life in villages and at isolated points along the
coast-line will probably bring the sum total of
deaths caused by this fatal storm up to 10,000.
The condition of the survivors for two or three
days beggars description. The water had quickly
receded, and all means of communication had been
destroyed, including steamships, railroads, telephone and telegraph lines, and public highways.
Practically all food supplies had been destroyed,
and the drinking-water supply had been cut off
by the breaking of the aqueduct pipes. The
tropical climate required the most summary
measures for the disposition of the bodies of the
dead. Military administration was made necessary, and many ghoulish looters and plunderers
were summarily shot, either in the act of robbing
the dead or upon evidence of guilt. . . .
"Relief agencies everywhere set to work
promptly to forward food, clothing, and money
to the impoverished survivors. Great corporations like the Southern Pacific Railroad made
haste to restore their Galveston facilities, and ingenious engineers brought forward suggestions
for protection of the city against future inundations. These suggestions embraced such improvements as additional break-waters, jetties,
dikes, and the filling in of a portion of the bay,
between Galveston and the mainland. The
United States Government in recent years has
spent $8,000,000 or $10,000,000 in engineering
works to deepen the approach to Galveston harbor. The channel, which was formerly only 20
or 21 feet deep across the bar, is now 27 feet deep,
and the action of wind and tide between the jetties cuts the passage a little deeper every year.
The foreign trade of Galveston, particularly in
cotton, has been growing by leaps and bounds."
—*Am. Review of Reviews, Oct.*, 1900, *p.* 398.

GARCIA, General : Commanding Cuban
forces at Santiago. See (in this vol.) UNITED
STATES OF AM. : A. D. 1898 (JUNE—JULY).

**GENEVA CONVENTION: Adaptation to
maritime warfare.** See (in this vol.) PEACE
CONFERENCE.

**GEORGE, Henry : Candidacy for Mayor of
Greater New Yor , and death.** See (in this
vol.) NEW YORK CITY : A. D. 1897 (SEPTEMBER
—NOVEMBER).

**GERMAN ORIENT SOCIETY : Explo-
ration of the ruins of Babylon.** See (in this
vol.) ARCHÆOLOGICAL RESEARCH : BABYLONIA :
GERMAN EXPLORATION.

GERMAN PARTIES, in Austria. See (in
this vol.) AUSTRIA-HUNGARY.

GERMANY.

**A. D. 1891—1899.—Recent commercial trea-
ties.—Preparations for forthcoming treaties.**
—"The new customs tariff of July 15, 1879 [see,
in vol. 4, TARIFF LEGISLATION (GERMANY):
A. D. 1853—1892] exhibited the following characteristics : An increase of the existing duties
and the introduction of new protective duties in
the interests of industrial and agricultural prod-
nets. The grain and wood duties, abolished in
1864, were reintroduced, and a new petroleum
duty was adopted. Those on coffee, wine, rice,
tea, tobacco, cattle, and textiles were raised.
Those on iron were restored ; and others were
placed on many new articles formerly admitted
free. In 1885 the tariff was again revised, especially in the direction of trebling the grain and
of doubling the wood duties. Those on cattle,
brandy, etc., were raised at the same time. The
year 1887 saw another general rise of duties.
But, on the other hand, some reductions in the
tariff for most-favored nations came about in
1883 and in 1889 in consequence of the tariff
treaties made with Switzerland and Spain.
Other reductions were made by the four tariff
treaties of 1891 with Belgium, Italy, Austria-
Hungary, and Switzerland, and again in 1892 and
1893, when like treaties were respectively made
with Servia and Roumania. Increases in some
duties took place in 1894 and 1895, such as those
on cotton seeds, perfumes, ether, and honey. . . .
In consequence of the higher price, rendered
possible at home from the protective duty, the
German manufacturer can afford to sell abroad
the surplus of his output at a lower price than he
could otherwise do. His average profit on his
whole output is made up of two parts : Firstly,
of a rather high profit on the sales in Germany ;
and, secondly, of a rather low profit on the sales
abroad. The net average profit is, however,
only an ordinary one ; but the larger total quantity sold (which he could not dispose of without
the foreign market, combined with the extra low
price of sale abroad) enables him to produce the
commodity in the larger quantities at a lower
cost of production than he otherwise could if he
had only the German market to manufacture for.
He thereby obtains abroad, when selling against
an Englishman, an indirect advantage from his

home protection, which stands him in good stead and is equivalent to a small indirect benefit (which the Englishman has not) on his foreign sales, which is, however, paid for by the German consumer through the higher sale price at home.

"The customs tariff now in force provides one general or 'autonomous' rate of duty for all countries, from which deviations only exist for such nations as have tariff treaties or treaties containing the most-favored-nation clause. Such deviations are 'treaty' or 'conventional' duties. At the present moment treaties of one kind or another exist with most European powers (excepting Great Britain, Spain, and Portugal) and with the majority of extra-European countries. So that, with few exceptions, the German Empire may now be said to trade with the world on the basis of the lower 'conventional' or 'treaty' tariff. Most of the tariff treaties existing in Europe expired early in 1892, whereupon many countries prepared higher customs tariffs in order to be prepared to grant certain concessions reciprocally when negotiating for the new treaties. Germany, therefore, under the auspices of General Caprivi, set to work to make a series of special tariff treaties with Belgium, Italy, Austria-Hungary, and Switzerland, which were all dated December 6, 1891. Later additions of the same class were those with Servia in 1892, with Roumania in 1893, and with Russia in 1894.

"Perhaps almost the greatest benefit conferred upon the country by these seven tariff treaties was the fact of their all being made for a long period of years and not terminable in any event before December 31, 1903. This secured for the mercantile classes the inestimable benefit of a fixed tariff for most of the important commodities of commerce over a long period of time—a very valuable factor in trade, which has in this case greatly assisted the development of commerce. The reductions in Germany granted by these treaties were not great except on imported grains, and those in the various foreign countries were not very considerable either. . . . The preparations for the negotiation of the new commercial treaties which are to replace those which expire on January 1, 1904, were begun in Germany as early as 1897. Immense trouble has been and is being taken by the Government to obtain thoroughly reliable data on which to work, as they were by no means content merely to elaborate a new tariff on the wide experience already gained from the working of the seven commercial treaties of 1891 to 1893."—*Diplomatic and Consular Reports of the British Gov't, Jan., 1899 (quoted in Monthly Summary of Commerce and Finance of the U. S., Jan.,* 1899).

A. D. 1894-1895.—The Emperor and the Social Democrats.—His violent and autocratic speeches.—Failure of the Anti-Revolutionary Bill.—Socialist message to France.
—At the opening of the winter session of the Reichstag, in December, 1894, the Emperor, speaking in person, declared it to be "necessary to oppose more effectually than hitherto the pernicious conduct of those who attempt to disturb the executive power in the fulfilment of its duty," and announced that a bill to that end, enlarging the penal provisions of law, would be introduced without delay. This was well understood to be aimed at the Social Democrats, against whom the Emperor had been making savagely violent speeches of late. At Potsdam,

in addressing some recruits of the Foot Guards, he had gone so far as to say: "You have, my children, sworn allegiance to me. That means that you have given yourselves to me body and soul. You have only one enemy, and that is my enemy. With the present Socialist agitation I may order you,—which God forbid!—to shoot down your brothers, and even your parents, and then you must obey me without a murmur." In view of these fierce threatenings of the Emperor, and the intended legislative attack upon their freedom of political expression and action, six members of the Social Democratic party, instead of quitting the House, as others did, before the customary cheers for his Imperial Majesty were called for, remained silently sitting in their seats. For that behaviour they were not only rebuked by the president of the Reichstag, but a demand for proceedings against them was made by the public prosecutor, at the request of the Imperial Chancellor. The Reichstag valued its own rights too highly to thus gratify the Emperor, and the demand was refused, by a vote of three to one. His Imperial Majesty failed likewise to carry the bill—the Anti-Revolutionary Bill, as it was called —on which he had set his heart, for silencing critical tongues and pens. The measure was opposed so stoutly, in the Reichstag and throughout the Empire, that defeat appeared certain, and in May (1895) it was dropped. The Emperor did not take his defeat quietly. Celebrating the anniversary of the battle of Sedan by a state dinner at the palace, he found the opportunity for a speech in which the Socialists were denounced in the following terms: "A rabble unworthy to bear the name of Germans has dared to revile the German people, has dared to drag into the dust the person of the universally honoured Emperor, which is to us sacred. May the whole people find in themselves the strength to repel these monstrous attacks; if not, I call upon you to resist the treasonable band, to wage a war which will free us from such elements." The Social Democrats replied by despatching the following telegram to the Socialists in Paris: "On the anniversary of the battle of Sedan we send, as a protest against war and chauvinism, our greeting and a clasp of the hand to our French comrades. Hurrah for international solidarity!" Prosecutions followed. The editor of "Vorwärts" got a month's imprisonment for saying the police provoked brawls to make a pretext for interference; Liebknecht, four, for a caustic allusion to the Emperor's declarations against Socialism, and for predicting the collapse of the Empire; and Dr. Forster, three, for lèse-majesté.

A. D. 1894-1899.—The Emperor's claim to Kingship by Divine Right."—A great sensation was produced in Germany by a speech addressed on September 6, 1894, by the German Emperor to the chief dignitaries and nobles of East Prussia in the Royal Palace at Königsberg. The following are the principal passages of this speech: "Agriculture has been in a seriously depressed state during the last four years, and it appears to me as though, under this influence, doubts have arisen with regard to the fulfilment of my promises. Nay, it has even been brought home to me, to my profound regret, that my best intentions have been misunderstood and in part disputed by members of the nobility with whom I am in close personal relation. Even the word 'opposition' has reached my ears. Gentlemen, an Opposition of Prussian noblemen, directed against their king, is a monstrosity. Such an Opposition would be justifiable only when the king was known to be at its head. The history of our House teaches us that lesson. How often have my predecessors had to oppose misguided members of a single class on behalf of the whole community! The successor of him who became Sovereign Duke in Prussia in his own right will follow the same path as his great ancestor. The first King of Prussia once said, 'Ex me mea nata corona,' and his great son 'set up his authority as a rocher de bronze.' I, in my turn, like my imperial grandfather, hold my kingship as by the grace of God. . . . We witnessed an inspiring ceremony the day before yesterday. Before us stands the statue of the Emperor William, the imperial sword uplifted in his right hand, the symbol of law and order. It exhorts us all to other duties, to the serious combating of designs directed against the very basis of our political and social fabric. To you, gentlemen, I address my summons to the fight for religion, morality, and order against the parties of revolution. Even as the ivy winds round the gnarled oak, and, while adorning it with its leaves, protects it when storms are raging through its topmost branches, so does the nobility of Prussia close round my house. May it, and with it the whole nobility of the German nation, become a brilliant example to those sections of the people who still hesitate. Let us enter into this struggle together. Forward with God, and dishonor to him who deserts his king."

Time has wrought no change in these extraordinary ideas of the German Emperor. Speaking at Hamburg, October 19, 1899, on the necessity of strengthening the naval forces of the Empire, in order to afford protection to trade over the sea, he said: "The feeling for these things is only slowly gaining ground in the German fatherland, which, unfortunately, has spent its strength only too much in fruitless factional strife. Germans are only slowly beginning to understand the questions which are important to the whole world. The face of the world has changed greatly during the last few years. What formerly required centuries is now accomplished in a few months. The task of Kaiser and government has consequently grown beyond measure, and a solution will only be possible when the German people renounce party divisions. Standing in serried ranks behind the Kaiser, proud of their great fatherland, and conscious of their real worth, the Germans must watch the development of foreign states. They must make sacrifices for their position as a world power, and, abandoning party spirit, they must stand united behind their prince and emperor." Commenting on this utterance, a recent writer has said: "This ideal of a docile nation led by a triumphant emperor whose intelligence embraces everything throws considerable light on the relations of imperialism to party government and parliamentary institutions. . . . There are many other expressions of the emperor which indicate an almost medieval conception of his office, a revival of the theory of divine right. The emperor believes that his grandfather, had he lived in the Middle Ages, would have been canonized, and that his tomb would have become a cynosure of pilgrimages from all parts of the world. . . . In a speech delivered at Coblenz

on August 31, 1897, he speaks of the 'kingship by the grace of God, with its grave duties, its tremendous responsibility to the Creator alone, from which no man, no minister, no parliament can release the monarch.'"

A. D. 1895 (June).—Opening of the Kaiser Wilhelm Ship Canal.—The opening of the new ship canal (named the Kaiser Wilhelm Canal) between the Baltic and the North Sea was made the occasion of a great celebration, on the 21st of June, in which the navies of Great Britain, Russia, France, Austria and Italy took part, steaming in procession with the German squadron through the canal. It was also made the occasion for an exhibition of the newly-formed alliance between Russia and France, the Russian and French fleets entering the harbor of Kiel together. (See, in this vol., FRANCE: A. D. 1895.) The canal had been eight years in building, the first spadeful of earth in the excavation having been turned by Emperor William I. at Holtenau, near Kiel, on the 3d of June, 1887. The canal is thus described: It is "98.6 kilometers (61.27 miles) in length. It begins at Holtenau, on the Bay of Kiel, and terminates near Brunsbüttel, at the mouth of the River Elbe, thus running clear through the province of Schleswig-Holstein from northeast to southwest. Both openings are provided with huge locks. Near Rendsburg, there is a third lock connecting the canal with the old Eider Canal. The medium water level of the canal will be about equal to the medium water level of Kiel harbor. At the lowest tide the profile of the canal has, in a depth of 6.17 meters (20 feet 6 inches) below the surface of the water, a navigable width of 36 meters (118.11 feet), so as to allow the largest Baltic steamers to pass each other. For the navy, 22 meters (72.18 feet) of canal bottom are provided, at least 58 meters (190.29 feet) of water surface, and 8½ meters (27 feet 9 inches) depth of water. The greatest depth for merchant vessels was calculated at 6.5 meters (21 feet 3 inches). The estimated cost was $37,128,000. Two-thirds of the cost is defrayed by Germany; the remaining one-third by Russia. The time saved by a steamship sailing from Kiel to Hamburg via the canal, instead of through the Skaugh (the strait between Jutland and Sweden), is estimated at 2½ days. The time of passage through the canal, including stoppages and delays, will be about thirteen hours. In time of peace, the canal is to be open to men-of-war, as well as merchant vessels of every nation, but in time of war, its use will be restricted to vessels of the German navy. Many vessels have been wrecked and many lives lost on the Danish and Swedish coasts, in waters which need not be navigated after the canal is opened to traffic. Its strategic importance to Germany will also be great, as it will place that country's two naval ports, Kiel on the Baltic, and Wilhelmshafen on the North Sea, within easy access of each other."—U. S. Consular Report, No. 175, p. 603.

A. D. 1895 (June—December).—Census of the Empire and census of Prussia.—"The results of the last census of the German Empire (the census being taken every five years in December) . . . have produced some surprise in that, notwithstanding the alleged depression of agriculture and manufactures, the tables show an increase greater than any census since the formation of the Empire. The population, according to the official figures, is 52,244,503, an increase since December, 1890, of 2,816,027, or 1.14 per cent increase per year. The percentages of the previous censuses was : In 1871–1875, 1 per cent; 1875–1880, 1.14 per cent; 1880–1895, 0.7 per cent; 1885–1890, 1.06 per cent. A striking illustration is given by a comparison with the figures of the French census. The increase in France for the same period (1890–1895) was but 124,000, an annual average of 0.07 per cent of its population, and Germans see in this proportionally smaller increase a reason for certain classes in France entertaining a less warlike feeling toward Germany, and thereby assuring general European peace.

"In 1871, at the foundation of the German Empire, its population was 40,997,000. [In 1890, it was 49,428,470.] The percentage of increase differs vastly in northern and southern Germany. In the former, the annual increase was 1.29 per cent; in the latter, only 0.71 per cent. This must be attributed in a great measure to the highly developed mining industries of the Rhineland and Westphalia, where the soil, besides its hidden mineral wealth, is devoted to agriculture. The southern states — Bavaria, Baden, and Würtemberg—being more mountainous, offer less opportunities for agricultural pursuits and are favored with less natural riches. It is again noticeable that those provinces which are ultra-agrarian show a very favorable increase. It would seem that it is not the peasant, but the great landowner, whose condition is undesirable and that this condition is due less to the present low prices of cereals and the customs-revenue policy of the Government than to the heavily mortgaged estates and lavish style of living which is not in keeping with their revenues. . . .

"The number of marriages, which showed a decrease from the middle of the eighties, has increased since 1892. An unlooked-for increase is shown in the country population." — United States, *Consular Reports, June*, 1896, *pp.* 245–46.

"Some of the results of the last census of Prussia, taken on the 14th of June, 1895, with special regard to trades and professions, have appeared in an official journal devoted to statistics. . . . The entire population of Prussia, which includes the provinces wrested from Poland, Denmark, and Saxony, as well as the seized Kingdom of Hanover, counts up for both sexes on the 14th of June, 1895, 31,491,209 ; by the last census (December 1, 1890), it was 29,955,281, an increase of 1,335,928, or 5.13 per cent. Of males, June 14, 1895, there were 15,475,202; December 1, 1890, 14,702,151, an increase of 773,051 ; females, June 14, 1895, 16,016,007 ; December 1, 1890, 15,253,130, an increase of 762,877. The relatively small surplus in Prussia of females over males, viz, 540,805, may . . . be ascribed in part to the stoppage of emigration to the United States since 1892. This affects more men than women, since men emigrate more readily than women.

"The population of Rhineland is the largest unit in Prussia. This year it is 5,043,979, against 4,710,391 in 1890, an increase of 333,588 ; that of Silesia is 4,357,555, against 4,224,458 in 1890, an increase of only 133,097, notwithstanding the temporary harvest hands in summer. Posen, its neighbor province, has the lowest increase of all —about 20,000 souls. All parts of Prussia, however, show some increase. The largest increase

of population—that of Rhineland or the Rhenish provinces (333,588)—may be safely ascribed to the flourishing manufactures of that district, while the low figures in Posen, Silesia, and East Prussia are due to the depression in agriculture produced by the rivalry of the United States, Argentina, and Australia, as well as by the unprotected state of the laborer in his relations with the landed proprietors.

"One of the surprises of the new census is the small increase of Berlin's population, all the more remarkable owing to the unprecedented increase of Berlin for the years between 1870 and 1890. It is only 36,288, or 2.2 per cent for the past four years and a half. By the census of 1895, it was 1,615,082; 1890, 1,578,794; increase, 36,288."—United States, *Consular Reports, Jan.*, 1896, *pp.* 75–76.

A. D. 1895–1898.—The Agrarian Protectionists and their demands.—"The depression of agriculture in Germany was the subject which most occupied German politicians throughout the year [1895]. The policy favoured by the Agrarian League was that advocated by Count Kanitz, of which the following were the chief points: (1) That the State should buy and sell the foreign grain, flour, and meal destined for consumption in Germany ; (2) that the average selling price in Germany from 1850 to 1890 should be fixed as the selling price of grain, and that the price of flour and meal should be determined by the proportion they bear to the unground grain and the said selling price, provided that the buying price is covered thereby ; while in the case of higher buying prices, the selling prices must be proportionally raised ; (3) that the profit obtained be spent, so that a part at least equal to the amount of the present grain duty flows into the Imperial Treasury ; (4) that steps should be taken for the accumulation of stocks to be used in extraordinary time of need, as, for instance, in the event of war; and (5) that a reserve should be formed when prices are higher at home and abroad, to secure the payment of the above-mentioned annual amount to the Treasury. The Emperor, however, repeatedly expressed his disapproval of this policy, and Prince Bismarck is said to have remarked that if he were a deputy he would vote for it, but as Chancellor he would reject it. . . . The Agrarians now started an agitation all over the country in favour of Count Kanitz's proposal, and even threatened to refuse the supplies required for the navy if the Government should not accept it. In March, the Emperor referred the question to the committee of the Federal State Council, which passed a resolution declaring the proposals of Count Kanitz for establishing a State monopoly in cereals to be incompatible with the correct interpretation of the present position of the State in regard to industry and international trade, and irreconcilable with Germany's commercial treaties."—*Annual Register*, 1895, *pp.* 256–7.

"The agrarian protectionists control the Conservative party in Parliament completely; they are strongly represented in the Center, or Catholic, party, and are not without a considerable following among the National Liberals. The Antisemitic party, the Poles, and other small parties are all infected with the agrarian protectionist ideas. The only decided opponents, as well as the only decided free-traders, are to be found among the three Liberal sections and the Social Democrats. The agrarian protectionists not only wish to annul the commercial treaties, because these hinder them from raising the protective duties on agricultural imports (these duties are by no means low—for instance, 35 marks per ton on rye or wheat), but the extreme members of the party advocate the abolition of the gold standard and the adoption of a so-called bimetallic—in reality a silver—standard. The most rabid among them oppose the cutting of canals, because foreign produce would thus enter Germany on cheaper terms. In short, the agrarian protectionists oppose the natural evolution of all economic progress. . . .

"The old Prussian feudal aristocracy (Junkerthum), forming the pith and marrow of the agrarian movement, has never been well off; but for the last twenty years they have suffered from the competition with the whole world, which is felt so keenly in all old countries, in the reduction of the rent of land. They have sunk deeper and deeper into debt, while the standard of material comfort has risen throughout all classes in Germany. The 'Junker' has long since given up the hope of making both ends meet by his own industry, and while endeavoring to raise the rent of land by various kinds of protective measures, he is really at the same time struggling for bread-and-butter and upholding a tradition of political supremacy.

"No government can really satisfy these claims, and hence each in turn is compelled, sooner or later, to oppose the agrarian movement. However, considering the strong influence the Prussian 'Junker' exerts in the army, in the ranks of government officials, and at court, practical statesmen deem it advisable to avoid any open rupture with the pack of famished wolves."—T. Barth, *Political Germany* (*Am. Review of Reviews, April*, 1898).

A. D. 1896 (January).—Emperor William's congratulations to the President of the South African Republic on the defeat of the Jameson Raid. See (in this vol.) SOUTH AFRICA (THE TRANSVAAL): A. D. 1896 (JANUARY).

A. D. 1896 (May).—The Berlin Industrial Exposition. See (in this vol.) BERLIN INDUSTRIAL EXPOSITION.

A. D. 1896 (May).—Sugar bounty and sugar tax legislation.—"The sugar-tax amendment law, over which has been waged in the German Parliament one of the longest and most-determined battles of recent years, was finally enacted as a concession to the agrarian interest, and went into effect [May, 1896]. Its influence will be to increase the sugar production of Germany, and, to that extent, exert a depressing effect upon the general market and the interests of producers in other beet-growing countries. The circumstances which have led to the present situation are, briefly, these: From the time when the Prussian Government began the systematic encouragement of the beet-sugar industry down to 1887, the tax on sugar for home consumption was calculated upon the quantity of beets worked up by each separate factory, it being assumed that the quantity of roots required to produce a given weight of sugar would be uniform and invariable. The proportion adopted was 20 units of raw beet root to 1 unit of sugar, which, at the time when the law was enacted, was approximately correct. . .

"But, under the stimulus of the export bounties provided by the same law, the German beet growers and sugar makers worked hard and intelligently to improve and increase their product. By careful selection and cultivation, the beets were so improved that from 12 to 14 tons of roots would yield a ton of sugar. Great advance was also made in the machinery and processes employed in the sugar factories, so that, as a final result, the German Government, which paid nearly 12 cents per cwt. bounty on all sugar exported, and charged a tax of the same amount on all sugar for home consumption that could be made from 20 cwts. of beets, found that the export bounties completely absorbed the revenue derived from the sugar tax. This tendency of the system had become apparent as early as 1869, and an attempt was made at that time to revise the law, but the sugar-producing interest was powerful enough to resist this effort. . . . Sugar growing still continued to be the most profitable form of culture for German farmers, the area of cultivation and number of sugar factories continued to increase, loud complaints were heard against a system that favored one class of farmers at the expense of the entire population, and, in 1891, the Imperial Diet reduced the sugar export bounty by half, that is, to 29.7 cents per 100 kilograms, and decreed that such bounty should entirely cease on the 31st of July, 1897, provided that, in the meantime, Austria, France, and other bounty-paying countries should likewise reduce their bounties on exported sugar. Several attempts have been made to reach such an international agreement, but without successful result, and under cover of this failure to secure a general reduction or abolition of bounties, the German Agrarians have rallied and secured the adoption of the present law, which restores the export bounty of 1887 (59.5 cents per 220.46 pounds) and raises the tax on sugar for home consumption from .18 marks ($4.28) to 21 marks ($4.99) per 100 kilograms, or about 2.2 cents per pound. This increased tax will, of course, be added to the retail price of sugar, already very high, and tend to still further retard the increase of sugar consumption in Germany, which is now only 28.8 pounds per capita, against 73.68 pounds per capita in England and 77 pounds in the United States. . . .

"From the statistics that were brought out in the recent debate, it appears that the whole system of beet culture and sugar manufacture in Germany has reached a higher standard of scientific perfection than has been attained in any other European country. Every step, from the preparation and fertilization of the land to the smallest detail in the factory process, has been reduced as nearly as possible to exact scientific methods. . . . Statistics were cited to prove that the German sugar producers are safe from all European competition and do not need the protection of an increased export bounty; but nothing could withstand the demand of the Agrarians, and their victory is one of the most significant events in recent German legislation."— *U. S. Consular Reports, July*, 1896, *p.* 512. — See, also, (in this vol.) SUGAR BOUNTIES.

A. D. 1897.—Industrial combinations.—Trusts. See (in this vol.) TRUSTS: IN EUROPEAN COUNTRIES.

A. D. 1897 (July).—Defeat in Prussia of a bill to restrict the right of political association and meeting.—In July, the government in Prussia suffered a significant defeat in the Prussian Landtag on an attempt to give the police new powers for interference with political meetings and associations. The bill was especially aimed at the Social Democrats, enacting in its first clause that "agents of the police authorities have power to dissolve meetings in which anarchist or Social Democratic movements are manifest, having for their object the overthrow of the existing order of state or of society, and finding an expression in a manner which endangers public security, and in particular the security of the state." It passed the upper house overwhelmingly, but was rejected in the lower by 209 votes to 205.

A. D. 1897 (July).—British notice to terminate existing commercial treaties. See (in this vol.) ENGLAND: A. D. 1897 (JUNE—JULY).

A. D. 1897 (September—December).—Demand for indemnity enforced against Hayti. See (in this vol.) HAYTI: A. D. 1897.

A. D. 1897 (November—December).—Seizure and acquisition of Kiao-chan Bay.—Naval expedition to China.—Speeches of the Emperor and Prince Henry.—The murder of two German missionaries in Shantung province, China, gave the German government a pretext, in November, 1897, for the seizure of the port of Kiao-chan, on demands for indemnity which were not satisfied until the Chinese government had consented to lease that port, with adjacent territory, to Germany, for 99 years, with extensive rights and privileges in the whole rich province of Shantung — see (in this vol.) CHINA: A. D. 1897 (NOVEMBER). To support this opening of an "imperial policy" in the East, a German naval expedition was despatched to China, in December, under the command of the Emperor's brother, Prince Henry, and its departure was made the occasion for speeches by the Emperor and Prince Henry, at a royal banquet, at Kiel, which caused much remark, and some smiling, in Europe and America. Said the Emperor, addressing his brother, at the end of some remarks in a similar strain : "As a sign of imperial and of naval power, the squadron, strengthened by your division, will now have to act in close intercourse and good friendship with all the comrades of the foreign fleets out there, for the protection of our home interests against everybody who tries to injure Germany. That is your vocation and your task. May it be clear to every European out there, to the German merchant, and above all, to the foreigner whose soil we may be on, and with whom we shall have to deal, that the German Michael has planted his shield, adorned with the eagle of the empire, firmly on that soil. in order, once for all, to afford protection to those who apply to him for it. May our countrymen abroad, whether priests or merchants, or of any other calling, be firmly convinced that the protection of the German Empire, as represented by the imperial ships, will be constantly afforded them. Should, however, any one attempt to affront us, or to infringe our good rights, then strike out with mailed fist, and if God will, weave round your young brow the laurel which nobody in the whole German Empire will begrudge you."

The Prince in reply said : "Most Serene Emperor, most powerful King and Lord, illustrious brother, — As children we grew up together.

Later on it was granted to us as men to look into each other's eyes and stand faithfully at each other's side. To your Majesty the imperial crown has come with thorns. I have striven in my restricted sphere and with my scanty strength, as man, soldier, and citizen, to help your Majesty. We have reached a great epoch, an important epoch for the nation — an important epoch for your Majesty and the Navy. Your Majesty has made a great sacrifice, and has shown great favour to myself in entrusting this command to me. I thank your Majesty from the bottom of a loyal, brotherly and humble heart. I well understand your Majesty's feelings. I know what a heavy sacrifice you made in giving me so fine a command. It is for this reason, your Majesty, that I am so much moved, and that I so sincerely thank you. I am further deeply indebted for the confidence which your Majesty reposes in my weak person, and I can assure your Majesty of this—I am not allured by hopes of winning glory or laurels, I am only animated by one desire—to proclaim and preach abroad to all who will hear, as well as to those who will not, the gospel of your Majesty's anointed person. This I will have inscribed on my banner, and will bear it wherever I go. These sentiments with which I set out are shared by my comrades. I raise my glass and call upon those who with me enjoy the happy privilege of being permitted to go forth, to remember this day, to impress the person of the Emperor on their minds, and to let the cry resound far out into the world—Our most Serene, Mighty, Beloved Emperor, King and Master, for ever and ever. Hurrah, hurrah, hurrah!"

A. D. 1897-1900.—Practical operation of the state system of workingmen's insurance.—Enlargement of its provisions.—By a series of laws enacted in 1883, 1884, and 1889, a system of compulsory state insurance of workingmen was established in Germany, applying in the first instance to sickness, then to accidents, and finally becoming a pensioning insurance for old age and permanent invalidity. These laws establish a compulsion to be insured, but leave freedom of choice as to the associations in which the insurance shall be maintained, all such associations being under the surveillance of the state. In a report from U. S. Consul J. C. Monaghan, Chemnitz, made July, 1898, the practical working of the system to that time is thus described : "Time is proving the practical value of the German workingmen's insurance system. . . . The social and economic influence of so gigantic a system must be very great.

" The object of the system is to alleviate the sufferings of workmen and their families : (1) In cases of sickness (sick insurance); (2) in cases of accidents incurred at work (accident insurance); (3) in cases of feebleness, wasting diseases, decreased capacity to work, and old age (invalid and old-age insurance). In cases coming under No. 1 there is given free medical treatment; sick money—that is, money during period of sickness with which to obtain medicine, nourishment, etc.—or, if desired, free treatment in a hospital and support for the family ; and money, in case of death, is supplied the family. The fund is furnished by employers and employed—the former paying one-third, the latter two-thirds. In cases of accident insurance the parties receive support during convalescence, from the fourteenth week after the accident happens. Money is given the wounded person from the fifth week. Rents are paid from the first day of the fourteenth week after the accident. The rents amount to two-thirds, and in some cases to three-fifths, of the workman's yearly salary. The fund for burial expenses is furnished by the employers. In cases coming under invalid and old-age insurance, the parties receive rents from the time they are unable to work, without regard to age; old-age rents, from the seventieth year, even if they can work and do not draw invalid rent; and assistance against disease so as to prevent incapacity. In case of his death or marriage, the full sum paid by the party is returned. "The following amounts were paid out in the years given:

Year.	Sick in- surance.	Accident insurance.	Invalid and old-age in- surance.
1885–86	$23,905,005	$460,625	
1887	13,138,099	1,412,030	
1888	14,651,637	2,304,173	
1889	16,892,097	3,442,503	
1890	20,013,420	4,835,041	
1891	21,243,594	6,289,483	$3,643,089
1892	22,433,499	7,696,967	5,344,742
1893	24,269,264	9,082,984	6,700,509
1894	23,702,063	10,539,044	8,332,475
1895	24,947,731	11,929,940	10,221,647
1896	26,114,026	13,602,747	12,293,533
1897	26,207,417	15,252,301	14,161,000
Total	257,517,856	86,847,842	60,696,997

"During the years from 1885 to 1897 employers had paid in 1,337,741,176 marks ($318,382,399), and workmen 1,173,449,805 marks ($279,281,-053), a total of 2,511,190,981 marks ($597,663,452). Of this amount 1,702,184,100 marks ($405,121,-816) have been paid out. Thus the workmen have already received 528,700,000 marks ($125,830,-600) more than they have paid in. The annual amount paid out is increasing at the rate of 15,000,000 marks ($3,570,000) per annum. The reserve fund at the end of 1897 was, in round numbers, 850,000,000 marks ($202,500,000). For every twentieth person of the Empire's population, one has been paid insurance.

"Besides this system, there are others by which workingmen are aided. There are State and private insurance and pension systems. One alone, the Miners' and Smelters' Union, paid out in the years 1895–1897, inclusive, 320,000,000 marks ($76,160,000). From 1900 on, the annual amount to be paid out will be upwards of 300,-000,000 marks ($71,400,000), or 100 marks ($23.80) for every working-day in the year. Whether a system which makes so much for paternalism is one to commend, I can not say. Its effects here have been anything but bad. Poverty, in spite of poor wages, is practically unknown."—*U. S. Consular Reports, Sept.*, 1898, *p.* 51.

A revision of the accident insurance law in 1900 extended the compulsory insurance to laborers in breweries and in the shops of blacksmiths, locksmiths and butchers, and to window cleaners. It raised the amount of assistance provided for the injured in many cases, making it in some instances of permanent disability equal to the wages previously earned. It also fixed more sharply the responsibility for carelessness on the part of an employer.

A. D. 1898.—Lèse-majesté.—"In 1898 there were 246 convictions for 'lèse-majesté,' and the punishments inflicted amounted to a total of 83 years imprisonment, in addition to various terms of confinement in a fortress."—*Annual Register*, 1899, *p.* 273.

A. D. 1898 (March—December).—In the Chinese "Battle of Concessions." See (in this vol.) CHINA: A. D. 1898 (FEBRUARY—DECEMBER).

A. D. 1898 (April).—The new naval policy. —"One of the most important economic movements taking place in Germany is the development of her maritime interests. The mercantile marine and 'over-sea' interests had developed to such an extent that recently the Government obtained the consent of the nation to add largely to its navy. During the year 1897 continuous efforts had been made to bring this question prominently before the public, and to point out the absolute necessity of a large increase of the navy in order to adequately protect Germany's growing maritime interests. The introductory statement of the bill presented to the Reichstag in November gave great prominence to the following considerations of general interest in connection with the new programme, namely, that during the last twenty years the increase of imports and exports, the rapid investment of capital abroad, the acquisition of colonies, the flourishing fisheries, and the rapidly-increasing population had greatly added to German 'oversea' interests, but that at the same time this expansion had brought with it the danger of a conflict with the interests of foreign nations, which must be provided against by an increase of the navy, for any injury to these maritime interests would entail serious consequences on the whole country.

"The bill, as eventually passed on April 10, 1898, provided that the nonrecurring expenditure should not exceed £20,445,000, of which £17,-835,000 was to be devoted to the construction of ships and their armaments. The German fleet will then be brought up to a total strength of 17 battle ships of the line, 8 coast-defense vessels, 9 large and 26 small cruisers, besides a variety of torpedo and other small craft. It is thought and hoped that, in consequence of the favorable state of the revenues of the Empire, a total sum of £5,876,274 a year can easily be devoted exclusively to the annual naval budget of the next six years, by which time the additions to the fleet are to be completed."—*U. S. Bureau of Statistics, Monthly Summary of Commerce and Finance, Jan.*, 1899.—See, also, below: A. D. 1900 (JUNE).

A. D. 1898 (April).—Withdrawal from the blockade of Crete and the "Concert of Europe." See (in this vol.) TURKEY: A. D. 1897-1899.

A. D. 1898 (June).—Elections to the Imperial Parliament, and their significance.— Elections to the Parliament of the Empire (the Reichstag) took place in June, and resulted in the following distribution of seats: Conservatives, 52; Imperialists, 22; National Liberals, 48; Liberal Unionists, 12; Liberal Democrats, 29; German Democrats, 8; Social Democrats, 56; Centre (Catholic), 106; Poles, 14; Anti-Semites, 10; Independents, 40;—Total, 397. "The elections as a whole show the growing power of German manufactures and the decline of German agriculture. Germany has become already, in far less time than it took England, a great urban community. That appears to us the most prominent fact in German life, and it was therefore bound to make itself manifest in German politics. In spite of Imperial patronage, the rural parties have lost. Both the Conservative sections have indeed lost rather heavily; the Conservatives proper standing in the new Reichstag at sixty-two instead of at seventy-two, as in the Reichstag of 1893, and the Free Conservatives at twenty instead of twenty-seven. The losses of the National Liberals, who usually vote solidly with the Conservatives, are smaller, but still they have lost. Though they represent 'Particularism,' yet the Poles are a peasant party, and they have lost, standing as they do at fourteen as compared with nineteen in 1893. The Anti-Semites, who under clerical guidance draw their strength largely from country districts, have also lost. On the other hand, those parties which have gained are the parties which hold the German cities,—the Centre, the Radicals, and the Social Democrats. The Centre, as we have said, represents the nascent Rhenish and Bavarian industrialism, the Radicals have made significant gains in Berlin, and the Social Democrats have gained in nearly all the towns except Berlin, where they have lost seats to the Radicals,—on what ground does not seem clear, unless it is that the more Anarchical section, which has all along been strong in Berlin Socialism, has rebelled against the centralised dictatorship of the party. We imagine that the urban professional and trading classes, dependent for their position on the growth of industry, have mainly voted Radical, and that the working classes have, on the whole, voted Socialist, except in those cases where they have, as devout Catholics, supported the Centre party. It will be seen, therefore, that what we may call Toryism (of an extreme and fanatical type, practically unknown in England), representing rural proprietorial interests, has lost; and that the forces of democracy, whether Liberal of the 'Manchester' type, Socialist, or Catholic, but all representing the growth of industrialism and urban life, have gained. In short, what strikes us as the most obvious moral of the elections is that the old forces and forms of German life are weakening, that the ancient Conservative entrenchments are being destroyed, and that we now have to deal with a modernised Germany.

"It may perhaps be asked why we place the Centre party in the same category with the Radicals and Social Democrats, since the last-named party is avowedly anti-religious, and the Radicals are largely indifferent on the religious question. We reply that the Centre party is essentially a democratic party, and a party, moreover, committed to reforms only less far-reaching than those of the Social Democrats, for whose candidates the Catholic democratic electors have often voted on the second ballots. The Centre party embodies to a large extent the spirit of Bishop Ketteler of Mainz, the chief founder of German Catholic 'Christian Socialism'; its organs in the Press are democratic in tone; and so far as the present Pope has advanced in the direction of wide Catholic social reform, he has had no stronger supporters than the members of the German Centre party, with the possible exception of the democratic American Catholic prelates, with whom the Centre party has much in common. This being the case, it is clear that democracy, in some or other of its varied forms, controls a majority of votes in the Reichstag; a small majority, it is true."— *The Spectator (London), July 2, 1898.*

A. D. 1898 (June).—The Sugar Conference at Brussels. See (in this vol.) SUGAR BOUNTIES.

A. D. 1898 (July).—Death of Prince Bismarck.—Prince Otto von Bismarck, whose importance in German history is comparable only with that of Charlemagne, Luther, and Frederick the Great, died on the 31st of July, at the age of 83. Immediately upon his death his confidential secretary, Dr. Moritz Busch, made public the full text of the letter of resignation which Bismarck addressed to the Emperor, William II., when he withdrew—practically dismissed—from the public service, in 1890. It showed that the immediate cause of his resignation was an order from the new sovereign which repealed an arrangement established by the latter's grandfather, in 1852, whereby a responsible ministry was created in Prussia, through the giving of responsible authority to a prime minister at its head. For nearly half a century that constitutional usage had been maintained. William II. appears to have made his first grasp at absolutism by setting it aside, and thereupon Bismarck resigned, as he was undoubtedly expected to do.

A. D. 1898 (October—November).—The Emperor's visit to Palestine.—A journey made by the Emperor and Empress, with a large retinue and considerable state, first to Constantinople, and then to Palestine, in October and November, was suspected of having some other motive than a love of travel and an interest in seeing the Holy Land. Looked at in connection with some other movements, it was supposed to indicate a policy aiming at the establishment of German influence in the realm of the Turk.

A. D. 1899.—Complaints from Danish Sleswick.—"It can never be anything but an encroachment and a cruelty to insist, as is now being done in Danish North Sleswick, that all teaching in the schools, with the exception of two miserable hours a week of religious lessons, shall be carried on in German, and to forbid even private instruction in the Danish language. It can never be called anything but brutality and meanness to punish young men who go into Danish territory for the purpose of study by depriving their parents of their parental rights, or by expelling innocent persons from the country. These methods, too, are beside the purpose. The Germans complain that Danes who have become Prussian subjects against their will do not feel like Prussians. They are tortured and annoyed, subjected to the most minute espionage and the most contemptible police reports, with the persecution connected therewith, and then it is considered amazing that they are not changed into enthusiastic admirers of Prussia. . . . The Danish language, in spite of its small area, is a language of culture. And only the same undue self-admiration which the Germans are in the habit of criticising in the French can look upon the forcible extermination of Danish culture, for the sake of spreading German, as a worthy act, an end that justifies the means. . . .

"Some years ago the actors of the Royal Theatre were forbidden to produce some innocent old vaudevilles in Sleswick towns (although permission had already been given to the owner of a theatre in Haderslev); indeed, they were not even allowed to remain over night at an hotel. Intense indignation was roused in Denmark by this narrow-minded police rule, which used as a pretext the danger to the peace and quietness of Germany of a scenic representation in Danish. This, however, was nothing compared with recent events, which, however, will in South Jutland only have a stimulating effect on the self-respect and patriotism of the people; while in Denmark those who have hitherto tried to bring about a better understanding between Danes and Germans will throw up the game, and without superfluous words take their stand on the side of the oppressed. The Danes can and must submit to humiliations, which the stronger nation again and again puts upon the weaker, humiliations which itself would never stand from any other Power. But one thing they cannot do. They cannot give up exerting all their power to preserve their language and culture within the Sleswick territory, which for a thousand years has been Danish, and is so still. They would be miserable creatures if they could. From the Danish side no attempt has been made, nor can be made, to regain politically what has been lost. No political agitation has been undertaken, nor can it be undertaken, to excite the South Jutlanders against the conditions which by ill-fate have once been legally imposed upon them. But the alliance of hearts and minds cannot be broken even by a great Power like Germany.

"How insecure this Prussian rule feels in North Sleswick in spite of its mailed fist! Everything alarms it. It dares not allow Danish actors to play an old vaudeville dating from 1830. It fears the storm of applause which would break loose as soon as the first unimportant, but Danish, words were heard from the stage. It feels obliged to forbid a Danish orator from holding any discourse whatsoever on South Jutland territory. He is not even allowed to speak on literature—not on German literature, not even on Goethe. For one can really never know!—One cannot be sure that the audience, in spite of the subject being of no political significance whatever, though even it be a German national topic, might not seize the opportunity to applaud a speaker from Denmark. And in Heaven's name that must not happen! On such fragile feet of clay does the Prussian Colossus stand in Sleswick that it cannot bear a hand-clap after a Danish lecture on Goethe. Still less can it endure Danish reading-books and Danish songbooks in the hands of little children, or Danish colours in a lady's gown or upon a house; Danish songs it fears even behind closed doors. What is the use of gendarmes if not to wage war against colours and songs? Such is the measure of the anxiety of Prussia, equipped with all the instruments of power, as to whether German might, German wealth, German military glory, German science and art, and half a hundred million of German people will exercise so great an attraction on the inhabitants of North Sleswick as the important miniature State which bears the name of Denmark."—G. Brandes, *Denmark and Germany* (*Contemporary Rev.*, July, 1899).

A. D. 1899.—Foreign interests of the German people.—United States Consul J. C. Monaghan wrote from Chemnitz in 1899:—" German economists are not exaggerating when they say this

Empire's people and capital are operating in every part of the world. Not only Hamburg, Bremen, Stettin, Lübeck, and Kiel—i. e., the seaport cities—but towns far inland, have invested millions in foreign enterprises. In the Americas, North and South, in Australia, in Asia, in a large part of Africa, German settlements, German factories, German merchants, and German industrial leaders are at work. Nor is it always in settlements under the Empire's control that this influence is strongest. In Senegambia, on the Gold Coast, the Slave Coast, in Zanzibar and Mozambique, in Australia, Samoa, the Marshall Islands, Tahiti, Sumatra, and South and Central America, there are powerful commercial organizations aiding the Empire. From Vladivostock to Singapore, on the mainland of Asia, and in many of the world's most productive islands, the influence of German money and thrift is felt. In Central America and the West Indies, millions of German money are in the plantations; so, too, in the plantations along the Gold Coast. In Guatemala, Honduras, Mexico, the Dominican Republic, Cuba, Puerto Rico, Trinidad, Venezuela, Brazil, etc., German capital plays a very important part in helping to develop the agricultural and in some cases the manufacturing and commercial interests. A consequence of this development is seen in the numerous banking institutions whose fields of operation show that German commerce is working more and more in foreign parts. These banks look after and aid foreign investment as well as the Empire's other commercial relations. They help the millions of Germans in all parts of the world to carry on trade relations, not only with the Fatherland, but with other countries.

"These are the links in a long and very strong chain of gold uniting the colonies with the Mother Country. Quite recently, large quantities of German capital have been invested in various industries. The Empire's capital in United States railroads is put down at $180,000,000. In America, Germans have undertaken manufacturing. They have used German money to put up breweries, bat factories, spinning, weaving, and paper mills, tanneries, soap-boiling establishments, candle mills, dye houses, mineral-water works, iron foundries, machine shops, dynamite mills, etc. Many of these mills use German machinery, and not a few German help. The Liebig Company, the Chilean saltpeter mines, the Chilean and Peruvian metal mines, many of the mines of South Africa, etc., are in large part controlled by German money and German forces. Two hundred different kinds of foreign bonds or papers are on the Berlin, Hamburg, and Frankfort exchanges. Germany has rapidly risen to a very important place in the financial, industrial, and mercantile world. Will she keep it? Much will depend on her power to push herself on the sea."—*U. S. Consular Reports, Sept.*, 1899, *p.* 127.

A. D. 1899.—Military statistics.—A report presented to the Reichstag showed the total number of men liable for service in 1899, including the surplus from previous years, was 1,696,760. Of these 716,998 were 20 years of age, 486,978 of 21 years, 362,568 of 22 years, and 130,216 of more than 22 years. The whereabouts of 94,224 was unknown, and 97,800 others failed to appear and sent no excuse; 427,586 had already undertaken military duties, 579,429 cases were either adjourned or the men rejected (for physical reasons), 1,245 were excluded from the service,

43,196 were exempt, 112,839 were incorporated in the naval reserve, 226,957 were called upon to join the colors, leaving a surplus of 5,187; there were 23,266 volunteers for the army and 1,222 for the navy. Of the 226,957 who joined the colors 216,880 joined the army as combatants and 4,591 as non-combatants, and 5,486 joined the navy. Of the 5,486 the maritime population furnished 3,132 and the inland 2,354. There were 21,189 men who entered the army before attaining the regulation age, and 1,480 under age who entered the navy; 33,652 of the inland population and only 189 of the maritime were condemned for emigrating without leave; while 14,150 inland and 150 maritime cases were still under consideration at the end of the year.

A. D. **1899** (February).—Chinese anti-missionary demonstrations in Shantung. See (in this vol.) CHINA: A. D. 1899.

A. D. **1899** (February).—Purchase of Caroline, Pelew and Marianne Islands from Spain. See (in this vol.) CAROLINE AND MARIANNE ISLANDS.

A. D. **1899** (May—July).—Representation in the Peace Conference at The Hague. See (in this vol.) PEACE CONFERENCE.

A. D. **1899** (May—August).—Advice to the South African Republic. See (in this vol.) SOUTH AFRICA (THE TRANSVAAL): A. D. 1899 (MAY—AUGUST).

A. D. **1899** (June).—State of German colonies.—The following report on German colonies for the year ending June 30, 1899, was made to the British Foreign Office by one of the secretaries of the Embassy at Berlin: "The number of Europeans resident in the German African Protectorates, viz, Togoland, Cameroons, South-West Africa, and East Africa, at the time of the issue of the latest colonial reports in the course of 1899 is given as 4,522 men, women, and children, of whom 3,228 were Germans. The expense to the home government of the African colonies, together with Kiao-chao in the Far East, the Caroline and Samoa Islands in the South Seas, and German New Guinea and its dependencies, is estimated at close upon £1,500,000 for 1900, the Imperial Treasury being asked to grant in subsidies a sum nearly double that required last year. Kiao-chao is included for the first time in the Colonial Estimates, and Samoa is a new item. The Imperial subsidy has been increased for each separate Protectorate, with the single exception of the Caroline Islands, which are to be granted £5,000 less than last year. East Africa receives about £33,000 more; the Cameroons, £10,000; South-West Africa, £14,000; Togoland, £800; New Guinea, £10,000; and the new items are: £489,000 for Kiao-chao (formerly included in the Naval Estimates), and £2,500 for Samoa. A Supplementary Vote of £43,265 for the Protectorate troops in the Cameroons is also now before the Budget Committee. . . .

"Great efforts have been made to encourage German trade with the African colonies, and it is shown that considerable success has been attained in South-West Africa, where the total value of goods imported from Germany amounted to £244,187, as against £181,961 in the previous year, with an appreciable falling-off in the value of imports from other countries. In East Africa the greater part of the import trade still comes from India and Zanzibar—about £450,000 worth of goods out of the gross total of £592,630, hav-

ing been imported thence. The export trade is also largely carried on through Zanzibar."—*Great Britain, Parliamentary Publications (Papers by Command: Miscellaneous Series, No 528, 1900, pp. 3–5).*

A. D. **1899** (August).—Defeat of the Rhine-Elbe Canal Bill.—**Resentment** of the Emperor.—**An** extraordinary edict.—Among several new canal projects in Germany, those of "the Dortmund-Rhine Canal and the Great Midland Canal (joining from the east to west the rivers Elbe, Weser, and Rhine) are the most important. The first involves an expenditure of over £8,000,000 altogether, and the second is variously estimated at from £10,000,000 to £20,000,000, according to its eventual scope. The latter is intended to amalgamate the eastern and western waterways of the nation and to join the Dortmund-Ems Canal to the Rhine system, in order to give the latter river an outlet to the sea via a German port, instead of only through ports in the Netherlands. It will also place the Rhine-Main-Danube connection in direct communication with all the streams of North Germany."—*U. S. Bureau of Statistics, Monthly Summary of Commerce and Finance, Jan., 1899.*—The Rhine-Elbe canal project is one which the Emperor has greatly at heart, and when, in August, 1899, a bill to promote it was defeated in the Prussian Landtag by the Agrarians, who feared that canal improvements would promote agricultural competition, his resentment was expressed in an extraordinary edict, which said: "The royal government, to its keen regret, has been compelled to notice that a number of officials, whose duty it is to support the policy of His Majesty the King, and to execute and advance the measures of His Majesty's government, are not sufficiently conscious of this obligation. . . . Such conduct is opposed to all the traditions of the Prussian administration, and cannot be tolerated." This was followed by an extensive dismissal of officials, and excited strong feeling against the government in a class which is nothing if not loyal to the monarchy.

A. D. **1899** (November).—Railway concession in Asia Minor, to the Persian Gulf. See (in this vol.) TURKEY: A. D. 1899 (NOVEMBER).

A. D. **1899** (November).—Re-arrangement of affairs in the Samoan Islands.—Partition of the islands with the United States.—Withdrawal of England, with compensations in the Tonga **and** Solomon Islands **and** in Africa. See (in this vol.) SAMOAN ISLANDS.

A. D. **1900.**—Military and naval **expenditure.** See (in this vol.) WAR BUDGETS.

A. D. **1900.**—Naval strength. See (in this vol.) NAVIES OF THE SEA POWERS.

A. D. **1900** (January).—Introduction of **the** Civil Code.—On the first day of the year 1900 a great revolution was effected in the laws of Germany, by putting into operation the new German Civil Code. "Since the close of the fifteenth century Germany has been the land of documentary right. The Roman judicial code was recognized as common law; while all legal procedure distinctly native in its origin was confined to certain districts and municipalities, and was, therefore, entirely devoid of Imperial signification in the wider sense. The Civil Code of the land was represented by the Corpus Juris Civilis, a Latin work entirely incomprehensible to the layman. This very remarkable circumstance can be accounted for only by the weakness of mediæval German Imperialism. In England and France royalty itself had, since the fourteenth century, assumed control of the laws in order that a homogeneous national code might be developed. German Imperialism of the fourteenth and fifteenth centuries, however, was incapable of such a task. . . .

"An incessant conflict has been waging in Germany between the Roman law of the Empire and the native law as perpetuated in the special enactments of the separate provinces and municipalities. During the sixteenth and seventeenth centuries the preponderance of power lay with the Roman system, which was further supported by the German science of jurisprudence— a science identified exclusively with the common law of Rome. Science looked upon the native systems of legal procedure as irrational and barbarous; and as Roman judicature exercised complete dominion over all legislation, the consequence was that it steadily advanced, while native and local law was gradually destroyed. Only within the eighteenth and nineteenth centuries has the native law of Germany been aroused to the defence of its interests, . . . the signal for the attack upon Roman law being given by King Frederick William I, of Prussia. As early as 1713 this monarch decreed that Roman law was to be abrogated in his dominions, and replaced by the native law of Prussia. The movement became general; and the era of modern legal codes was ushered in. The legal code of Bavaria was established in 1756; Prussia followed in 1794; France, in 1804 (Code Civil); Baden, in 1809; Austria, in 1811 (Das Oesterreichische Buergerliche Gesetzbuch); and finally Saxony, in 1863 (the designation here being similar to that adopted by Austria). Everywhere the motto was the same; viz., 'Emancipation from the Latin Code of Rome.' The native code was to supplant the foreign, obscure, and obsolete Corpus Juris. But the success of these newly established codes was limited; each being applicable to its own particular province only. Moreover, many of the German states had retained the Roman law; confining their reforms to a few modifications. . . .

"The reëstablishment of the German Empire was, therefore, essential also to the reëstablishment of German law. As early as 1874 the initial steps for the incorporation of a new German Civil Code had already been taken; and this work has now at last been completed. On August 18, 1896, the new system, together with a 'Law of Introduction,' was promulgated by Emperor William II. It will become effective on January 1, 1900, a day which will ever be memorable as marking the climax of a development of four centuries. At the close of the fifteenth century Roman law was accepted in Germany; and now, at the end of the nineteenth, this entire system is to be completely abolished throughout the Empire. As a means of education, and solely for this purpose, the Roman Code will be retained in the universities. As a work of art it is immortal; as a system of laws, perishable. The last relic of that grand fabric of laws, which once dominated the whole world, crumbles to-day. The national idea is victorious; and German law for the German Empire is at last secured."—R. Sohm, *The Civil Code of Germany* (*Forum, October*, 1899).

A. D. 1900 (January—March).—The outbreak of the "Boxers" in northern China. See (in this vol.) CHINA: A. D. 1900 (JANUARY— MARCH).

A. D. 1900 (February).—Adhesion to the arrangement of an "open door" commercial policy in China. See (in this vol.) CHINA: A. D. 1899–1900 (SEPTEMBER—FEBRUARY).

A. D. 1900 (February—June).—Increased naval programme.—With much difficulty, and as the result of strenuous pressure, the Emperor succeeded in carrying through the Reichstag, in June, a bill which doubles the programme of naval increase adopted in 1898—see above: A. D. 1898 (APRIL). "After the way had been prepared by a speech of the Emperor to the officers of the Berlin garrison on January 7, 1900, and by a vigorous Press agitation, this project was brought before the Reichstag on February 8. In form it was an amendment of the Sexennate, or Navy Law of 1898, which had laid down a six years' programme of naval construction. By the new measure this programme was revised and extended over a period of 20 years. Instead of the double squadron of 19 battleships, with its complement of cruisers and other craft, it was demanded that the Government should be authorized to build two double squadrons, or 38 battleships and the corresponding number of cruisers. The Bill also provided for a large increase in the number of ships to be employed in the protection of German interests in foreign waters. The Centre party, both through its speakers in the Reichstag and through its organs in the Press, at first took up a very critical attitude towards the Bill. Its spokesmen dwelt especially upon the breach of faith involved in the extension of the programme of naval construction so soon after the compromise of 1898 had been accepted, and upon the difficulty of finding the money to pay for a fleet of such magnitude. The Clerical leaders, however, did not persist in their opposition, and finally agreed to accept the main provisions of the Bill, with the exception of the proposed increase in the number of ships employed in foreign waters. They made it a condition that the Government should incorporate with the Bill two financial projects designed to provide the money required without burdening the working classes. Both the Stamp Duties Bill and the Customs Bill were adopted by the Government, and the Navy Bill was carried with the aid of the Centre."—*Berlin Cor. London Times.*

A. D. 1900 (May).—The **Lex** Heinze.—The Socialists won a notable triumph in May, when they forced the Reichstag to adopt their views in the shaping of a measure known as the Lex Heinze. This Bill, as introduced by the Government, gave the police increased powers in dealing with immorality. The Clericals and the Conservatives sought to extend its scope by amendments which were denounced by the Radicals and Socialists as placing restrictions upon the "liberty of art and literature." After a prolonged struggle, in which the Socialists resorted to the use of obstruction, the most obnoxious amendments were withdrawn.

A. D. 1900 (May).—Passage of the Meat Inspection Bill.—A much discussed and sharply contested bill, providing for a stringent inspection of imported meats, and aimed especially at the obstructing of the American meat trade, was passed by the Reichstag on the 23d of May. It prohibits the importation of canned or sausage meat entirely, and imposes conditions on the introduction of other meats which are thought to be, in some cases, prohibitory. The measure was originally claimed to be purely one of sanitary precaution. It "had been introduced in the Reichstag early in 1899, but the sharp conflict of interests about it kept it for more than a year in committee. When the bill finally emerged for discussion in the Reichstag, it was found that the Agrarian majority had distorted it from a sanitary to a protective measure. Both in the new form they gave the bill and in their discussions of it in the Reichstag, the Agrarians showed that it was chiefly the exclusion of foreign meats, rather than a system of sanitary inspection, that they wanted. As finally passed in May the bill had lost some of the harsh prohibitory features given it by the Agrarians, the latter contenting themselves with the exclusion of canned meats and sausages. To the foreign student of German politics, the Meat Inspection Law is chiefly interesting as illustrating the tendency of the general government to seize upon functions which have hitherto been in the hands of the individual states and municipalities, as well as of bringing the private affairs of the people under the control of governmental authority. It is another long step of the German government away from the principle of 'laissez-faire.' The task undertaken by the government here is itself a stupendous one. There is certainly no other great government in the world that would endeavor to organize the administrative machinery for inspecting every pound of meat that comes upon the markets of the country."—W. C. Dreher, *A Letter from Germany* (*Atlantic Monthly, March*, 1901).

A. D. 1900 (June).—Opening of the Elbe and Trave Canal.—"The new Elbe and Trave Canal, which has been building five years and has been completed at a cost of 24,500,000 marks ($5,831,000)—of which Prussia contributed 7,500,-000 marks ($1,785,000) and the old Hansa town of Lübeck, which is now reviving, 17,000,000 marks ($4,046,000)—was formally opened by the German Emperor on the 16th [of June]. The length of the new canal—which is the second to join the North Sea and the Baltic, following the Kaiser Wilhelm Ship Canal, or Kiel Canal, which was finished five years ago at a cost of 156,000,-000 marks ($37,128,000)—is about 41 miles. The available breadth of the new canal is 72 feet; breadth of the lock gates, 46 feet; length of the locks, 87 yards; depth of the locks, 8 feet 2 inches. The canal is crossed by twenty-nine bridges, erected at a cost of $1,000,000. The span of the bridges is in all cases not less than 30 yards and their height above water level about 15 feet. There are seven locks, five being between Lübeck and the Möllner See—the highest point of the canal—and two between Möllner See and Lauenburg-on-the-Elbe."—*United States, Consular Reports, Sept.*, 1900, *p.* 8.

A memorandum by the British Chargé d'Affaires in Berlin on the Elbe-Trave Canal says that the opening of the Kaiser Wilhelm Canal injuriously affected the trade of Lübeck. This was foreseen, and in 1894 a plan was sanctioned for the widening of the existing canal, which only allowed of the passage of vessels of about thirty tons. The direction of the old canal was followed only to some extent, as it had immense

curves, while the new bed was fairly straight from Lübeck to Lauenburg, on the Elbe above Hamburg. The memorandum states that the undertaking is of great importance to the States along the Elbe, as well as to Sweden, Norway, Denmark, and Russia. It will to some extent divert traffic from Hamburg, and possibly reduce somewhat the revenue of the Kaiser Wilhelm Canal.

A. D. 1900 (June—December).—Co-operation with the Powers in China. See (in this vol.) CHINA.

A. D. 1900 (September).—Government loan placed in America.—Great excitement and indignation was caused in September by the action of the imperial government in placing a loan of 80,000,000 marks (about $20,000,000) in the American money market. On the meeting of the Reichstag, the finance minister, Dr. von Miquel, replying to attacks upon this measure, explained that in September the state of the German market, was such that if they had raised the 80,000,000 marks at home the bank discount rate would have risen above the present rate of 5 per cent. before the end of the year. In the previous winter the bank rate had been at 6 per cent. for a period of 90 days, and during three weeks it had stood at 7 per cent. The government had been strongly urged to do everything in its power to prevent the recurrence of such high rates of discount. The London rate was rapidly approaching the German, and there was reason to fear that there would be a serious flow of gold from Germany. It was therefore urgently desirable to attract gold from abroad, and there was no country where money was so easy at the time as in the United States. This was due to the extraordinarily favorable balance of American trade and the remarkable increase in exports out of all proportion to the development of imports. Another reason was the American Currency Law, which enabled the national banks to issue as much as 100 per cent. of their capital in loans, whereas they formerly issued only 90 per cent. There was no doubt that the 80,000,000 marks could have been obtained in Germany, but the public must have been aware that other loans of much greater extent were impending. There was going to be a loan of about 150,000,000 marks for the expedition to China, and it was certain that before the end of the year 1901 considerable demands would be made upon the public.

A. D. 1900 (September).—Proposal to require leaders of the Chinese attack on foreigners to be given up. See (in this vol.) CHINA: A. D. 1900 (AUGUST—DECEMBER).

A. D. 1900 (October). — Anglo-German agreement concerning policy in China. See (in this vol.) CHINA : A. D. 1900 (AUGUST—DECEMBER).

A. D. 1900 (October 9).—Lèse-majesté in criticism of the Emperor's speech to soldiers departing for China, enjoining no quarter and commending the Huns as a military example. —Increasing prosecutions for lèse-majesté.— On the 9th of October, a newspaper correspondent wrote from Berlin : "The Berlin newspapers of yesterday and to-day chronicle no fewer than five trials for 'lèse-majesté.' The most important case was that of Herr Maximilian Harden, the editor of the weekly magazine 'Zukunft.' Herr Harden, who enjoyed the confidence of the late Prince Bismarck, wields a very satirical pen, and has been designated 'The Junius of modern Germany.' In 1898 Herr Harden was convicted of lèse-majesté and was sentenced to six months' incarceration in a fortress. In the present instance he was accused of having committed lèse-majesté in an article, 'The Fight with the Dragon,' published in the 'Zukunft' of August 11. The article dealt with the speech delivered by the Emperor at Bremerhaven on July 27, 'the telegraphic transmission of which, as was asserted at the time, had been forbidden by Count von Bülow.' The article noted as a fact that the Emperor had commanded the troops who were leaving for China to give no quarter and to make no prisoners, but, imitating the example of Attila and the Huns, to excite a terror in East Asia which would last for a thousand years. The Emperor had added, 'May the blessing of God attend your flags and may this war have the blessed result that Christianity shall make its way into China.' Herr Harden in his comments on this speech had critically examined the deeds of the historic Attila and had contrasted him with the Attila of popular story in order to demonstrate that he was not a proper model to set up for the imitation of German soldiers. The article in the 'Zukunft' had also maintained that it was not the mission of the German Empire to spread Christianity in China, and, finally, had described a war of revenge as a mistake." No publicity was allowed to be given to the proceedings of the trial. "Herr Harden was found guilty not only of having been wanting in the respect due to the Emperor but of having actually attacked his Majesty in a way that constituted lèse-majesté. The Court sentenced him to six months' incarceration in a fortress and at the same time directed that the incriminated number of the 'Zukunft' should be destroyed.

"The 'Vossische Zeitung' remarks:—'We read in the newspapers to-day that a street porter in Marburg has been sentenced to six months' imprisonment for insulting the Empress, that in Hamburg a workman has been sentenced to five months' imprisonment for lèse-majesté, that in Beuthen a workman has been sentenced to a year's imprisonment for lèse-majesté, and that in Dusseldorf a man who is deaf and dumb has been sentenced to four months' imprisonment for the same offence. The prosecutions for lèse-majesté are multiplying at an alarming rate. We must emphatically repeat that such proceedings appear to us to be in the last degree unsuited to promote the principles of Monarchy. . . . The greater the number of political prosecutions that are instituted the more accustomed, under force of circumstances, does the Press become to the practice of writing so that the reader may read between the lines. And this attitude is to the advantage neither of public morals nor of the Throne. . . . We regret in particular that the case of yesterday (that of Herr Harden) was tried 'in camera.' . . . It has justly been said that publicity is more indispensable in political trials than in prosecutions against thieves and murderers. . . . If there is no prospect of an improvement in this respect the Reichstag will have to devote its serious attention to the question how the present administration of justice is to be dealt with, not only in the interest of freedom of speech and of the Press, but also for the good of the Crown and the well-being of the State.' "

A. D. **1900** (October **18**).—Change in **the** Imperial Chancellorship.—On the 18th of October it was announced in the "Imperial Gazette" that "His Majesty the Emperor and King has been graciously pleased to accede to the request of the Imperial Chancellor, the President of the Ministry and Minister for Foreign Affairs, Prince Hohenlohe-Schillingsfürst, Prince of Ratibor and Corvey, to be relieved of his offices, and has at the same time conferred upon him the high Order of the Black Eagle with brilliants. His Majesty has further been graciously pleased to appoint Count von Bülow, Minister of State and Secretary of State to the Foreign Office, to be Imperial Chancellor and Minister for Foreign Affairs." Count von Bülow is the third of the successors of Prince Bismarck in the high office of the Imperial Chancellor. The latter was followed by Count von Caprivi, who gave way to Prince Hohenlohe in 1894. Prince Hohenlohe had nearly reached the age of 82 when he is said to have asked leave to retire from public life.

A. D. **1900** (November).—Withdrawal of legal tender silver coins. — "Germany has lately taken a step to clear off the haze from her financial horizon by calling in the outstanding thalers which are full legal tender, and turning them into subsidiary coins of limited legal tender —a process which will extend over ten years. At the end of that time, if no misfortune intervenes, she will be on the gold standard as surely and safely as England is. Her banks can now tender silver to their customers when they ask for gold, as the Bank of France can and does occasionally. When this last measure is carried into effect the only full legal-tender money in Germany will be gold, or Government notes redeemable in gold." —*N. Y. Nation, Nov.* 29, 1900.

A. D. **1900** (November—December).—The Reichstag and the Kaiser.—His speeches and his system of personal government.—In the Reichstag, which reassembled on the 14th of November, "the speeches of the Kaiser were discussed by men of all parties, with a freedom that was new and refreshing in German political debates. Apart from the Kaiser's speeches in connection with the Chinese troubles, the debates brought out some frank complaints from the more 'loyal' sections of German politics, that the Kaiser is surrounded by advisers who systematically misinform him as to the actual state of public opinion. It has long been felt, and particularly during the past few years, that the present system of two cabinets—one of which is nominally responsible to the Reichstag and public opinion, while the other is merely a personal cabinet, responsible to neither, and yet exercising an enormous influence in shaping the monarch's policies—has been growing more and more intolerable. This system of personal government is becoming the subject of chronic disquietude in Germany, and even the more loyal section of the press is growing restive under it. Bismarck's wise maxim, 'A monarch should appear in public only when attired in the clothing of a responsible ministry,' is finding more and more supporters among intelligent Germans."— W. C. Dreher, *A Letter from Germany (Atlantic Monthly, March,* 1901).

A. D. **1900** (December).—Census of **the** Empire.—Growth of Berlin and other cities. —Urban population compared with that in the United States.—A despatch from Berlin,

February 26, announced the results of the census of December, 1900, made public that day. The population of the German Empire is shown to have increased from 52,279,901 in 1895 to 56,345,014. Of this population 27,731,067 are males and 28,613,947 females. Over 83 per cent. of the whole population is contained in the four kingdoms; of these Prussia comes first with (in round figures) 34,500,000 inhabitants, and Bavaria second with 6,200,000. The figures for Saxony and Würtemberg are 4,200,000 and 2,300,000 respectively. More than 16 per cent. of the population is resident in the 33 towns of over 100,000 inhabitants. Of these 33 towns the largest is Berlin, while the smallest is Cassel, of which the inhabitants number 106,001.

The Prussian Statistical Office had already published the results of the census, so far as they concern Berlin and its suburbs. It appears that the population of the German capital now amounts to 1,884,151 souls, as against 1,677,304 in 1895 and 826,341 in 1871. The population of the suburbs has increased from 57,735 in 1871 and 435,236 in 1895, to 639,310 in 1900. The total population of the capital, including the suburbs, is given as 2,523,461 souls, as against 2,112,540 in 1895, an increase of over 19 per cent. Some figures relating to other cities had previously appeared, going to show "an acceleration of the movement of population from the country toward the great cities. The growth of the urban population in five years has been astonishing. The population of Berlin, for example, increased more than twice as much in the last five years as in the preceding five. The fourteen German cities now having a population of above 200,000 have increased more than 17 per cent since 1895. . . . No other European capital is growing so fast in wealth and numbers as Berlin; and the city is rapidly assuming a dominant position in all spheres of German life."
—W. C. Dreher, *A Letter from Germany* (*Atlantic Monthly, March*, 1901).

The percentage of growth in Berlin "has been far outstripped by many other cities, especially by Nuremberg; and so far as our own census shows, no American city of over 50,000 inhabitants can match its increase. In five years it has grown from 162,000 to 261,000—60 per cent increase. That would mean 120 per cent in a decade.

"But though Germany has only one city of more than one million, and one more of more than half a million, and the United States has three of each class, Germany has, in proportion to its population rather more cities of from 50,-000 to 100,000 inhabitants, and decidedly more of from 100,000 to 500,000, than the United States. In the United States 8,000,000 people live in cities of over 500,000 inhabitants, against some 3,000,000 in Germany; yet in the United States a larger percentage of the population lives in places which have under 50,000 inhabitants."—*The World's Work, March*, 1901.

A. D. 1901 (January).—Celebration of the Prussian Bicentenary. See (in this vol.) PRUSSIA: A. D. 1901.

A. D. 1901 (January).—**Promised** increase of protective duties.—In the Reichstag—the Parliament of the Empire—on the 26th of January, the Agrarians brought in a resolution demanding that the Prussian Government should "in the most resolute manner" use its influence to secure a "considerable increase" in the protective duties on agricultural produce at the approaching revision of German commercial policy, and should take steps to get the new Tariff Bill laid before the Reichstag as promptly as possible. In response, the Imperial Chancellor, Count von Bülow, made the following declaration of the policy of the government, for which all parties had been anxiously waiting: "Fully recognizing the difficult situation in which agriculture is placed, and inspired by the desire effectively to improve that situation, the Prussian Government is resolved to exert its influence in order to obtain adequate protection for agricultural produce by means of the Customs duties, which must be raised to an extent calculated to attain that object."

A. D. 1901 (January).—**The** Prussian Canal scheme enlarged.—The canal scheme which suffered defeat in the Prussian diet in 1899 (see above), and the rejection of which by his dutiful agrarian subjects roused the wrath of the emperor-king, was again brought forward, at the opening of the session of the Diet, or Landtag, in January, 1901, with a great enlargement of its scope and cost, and with an emphatic expression of the expectation of his Majesty that the bill providing for it should be passed. The bill covered no less than seven different projects, of which the total cost to the State was estimated at about 389,010,700 marks, or nearly $100,000,000. These include the Rhine-Elbe Canal, which is calculated to cost 260,784,700 marks; a ship canal between Berlin and Stettin, to cost 41,500,000 marks; a waterway connecting the Oder and the Vistula, of which the cost, together with that of a channel rendering the Warthe navigable for ships from Posen to the junction of the Netze, is estimated at 22,631,000 marks, and a canal connecting the province of Silesia with the canal joining the Oder to the Spree. The bill further proposed that the State should participate in the work of improving the flow of water in the Lower Oder and the Upper Havel to the extent of 40,989,000 marks and 9,670,000 marks respectively, and should contribute the sum of 9,336,000 marks towards the canalization of the Spree.

A. D. 1901 (February).—Annual meeting of the Husbandists.—The annual meeting of the Husbandists, one of the organizations of German agrarian interests, held at Berlin on the 11th of February, is reported to have been attended by some 8,000 delegates. The official report of the organization showed a membership of 232,000, or an increase of 26,000 over that of the previous year. Large gains were made during the year in the southern section of the Empire. It also appeared that no fewer than 202,000 members represented small farmers. A resolution was adopted demanding that the Government grant such protection to agriculture as would enable it to form prices independent of the Bourse, fixing the duties high enough to make it possible for tillers of the soil to reap as large profits for their products as from 1870 to 1890. "Above all," said the resolution, "Germany must not grant the same tariffs to countries discriminating in their tariffs, as in the case of the United States."

GERRYMANDERING: Legislation against by the Congress of the United States. See (in this vol.) UNITED STATES OF AM.: A. D. 1901 (JANUARY).

GLADSTONE, William Ewart: Retirement from public life. See (in this vol.) ENGLAND: A. D. 1894–1895.
Death and burial. See (in this vol.) ENGLAND: A. D. 1898 (MAY).

GOEBEL, Governor William E.: Assassination. See (in this vol.) KENTUCKY: A. D. 1895–1900.

GOLD COAST COLONY. See (in this vol.) ASHANTI ; and AFRICA: A. D. 1900.

GOLD DEMOCRATS. See (in this vol.) UNITED STATES OF AM.: A. D. 1896 (JUNE—NOVEMBER).

GOLD FIELDS, The Witwatersrand. See (in this vol.) SOUTH AFRICA (THE TRANSVAAL): A. D. 1885–1890.

GOLD MINING: Cape Nome discovery See (in this vol.) ALASKA: A. D. 1898–1899

GOLD STANDARD. See (in this vol.) MONETARY QUESTIONS AND MEASURES.

GOLDEN STOOL, King Prempeh's. See (in this vol.) ASHANTI.

GORDON MEMORIAL COLLEGE, at Khartoum. See (in this vol.) EGYPT: A. D. 1898–1899.

GOSCHEN, George J.: First Lord of the Admiralty in the British Cabinet. See (in this vol.) ENGLAND: A. D. 1894–1895.

GOSPODAR. See (in this vol.) BALKAN AND DANUBIAN STATES (MONTENEGRO).

GOTHENBURG SYSTEM, The.—Dispensary Laws. See (in this vol.) SOUTH CAROLINA: A. D. 1892–1899; NORTH CAROLINA: A. D. 1897–1899; SOUTH DAKOTA: A. D. 1899; and ALABAMA: A. D. 1899.

GRASPAN, Battle of. See (in this vol.) SOUTH AFRICA (THE FIELD OF WAR): A. D. 1899 (OCTOBER—DECEMBER).

GREAT BRITAIN. See ENGLAND.

GREATER NEW YORK. See (in this vol.) NEW YORK CITY: A. D. 1896–1897.

GREECE: Light on prehistoric times.— Recent explorations in Crete and Egypt. See (in this vol.) ARCHÆOLOGICAL RESEARCH: CRETE; and same: EGYPT.
A. D. 1896 (April).—Revival of Olympic Games. See (in this vol.) ATHENS: A. D. 1896.
A. D. 1897 (February—March).—Interference in Crete.—Expedition of Colonel Vassos.—Appeal for the annexation of the island. —Action of the Great Powers. See (in this vol.) TURKEY: A. D. 1897 (FEBRUARY—MARCH).

A. D. 1897 (March—June).—Disastrous war with Turkey.—Appeal for peace.—Submission to the Powers on the Cretan question. See (in this vol.) TURKEY: A. D. 1897 (MARCH—SEPTEMBER).
A. D. 1899 (May—July).—Representation in the Peace Conference at The Hague. See (in this vol.) PEACE CONFERENCE.
A. D. 1899–1900.—Attitude towards impending revolt in Macedonia. See (in this vol.) TURKEY: A. D. 1899–1901; and BALKAN AND DANUBIAN STATES.

GREENBACKS. See (in this vol.) UNITED STATES OF AM.: A. D. 1895 (JANUARY—FEBRUARY); 1895–1896 (DECEMBER—FEBRUARY) ; 1896–1898 ; and 1900 (MARCH—DECEMBER)

GREENLAND, Recent exploration of See (in this vol.) POLAR EXPLORATION, 1895–1896, 1896, 1897, 1898–1899, 1898–, 1899, 1899–, 1900.

GREYTOWN : Possession given to Nicaragua. See (in this vol.) CENTRAL AMERICA (NICARAGUA—COSTA RICA): A. D. 1897.

GRONDWET (CONSTITUTION), of the South African Republic. See (in this vol.) CONSTITUTION (GRONDWET) OF THE SOUTH AFRICAN REPUBLIC.

GUAM, The island of: A. D. 1898 (June).— Seizure by the U. S. S. Charleston. See (in this vol.) UNITED STATES OF AM.: A. D. 1898 (JUNE), THE WAR WITH SPAIN.
A. D. 1898 (December).—Cession to the United States. See (in this vol.) UNITED STATES OF AM.: A. D. 1898 (JULY—DECEMBER)
A. D. 1900.—Naval station.—Work planned for the creation of an U. S. naval station at Guam is expected to cost, it is said, about $1,000,000.

GUANTANAMO: Capture of harbor by American navy. See (in this vol.) UNITED STATES OF AM.: A. D. 1898 (JUNE—JULY).

GUATEMALA. See (in this vol.) CENTRAL AMERICA.

GUAYAMA, Engagement at. See (in this vol.) UNITED STATES OF AM.: A. D. 1898 (JULY—AUGUST : PORTO RICO).

GUÉRIN, M.: The barricade of. See (in this vol.) FRANCE: A. D. 1899–1900 (AUGUST—JANUARY).

GUIANA, British: A. D. 1895–1899.— Venezuela boundary question. See (in this vol.) VENEZUELA.

GUIANA, French : Boundary dispute with Brazil.—Award of Swiss arbitrators. See (in this vol.) BRAZIL : A. D. 1900.

GUINEA, French. See (in this vol.) AFRICA: A. D. 1895 (FRENCH WEST AFRICA).

GUNGUNHANA, Portuguese war with. See (in this vol.) AFRICA: A. D. 1895–1896 (PORTUGUESE EAST AFRICA).

H.

HABANA, or HAVANA. See (in this vol.) CUBA.

HAFFKINE'S PROPHYLACTIC. See (in this vol.) PLAGUE.

HAGUE, The, Peace Conference at. See (in this vol.) PEACE CONFERENCE.

HALEPA, The Pact of. See (in this vol.) TURKEY: A. D. 1896.

HALL OF FAME, for Great Americans, The.—In the designing of new buildings for the New York University College of Arts and Science, at University Heights. certain exigencies of art led to the construction of a stately colonnade, surrounding a high terrace which overlooks Harlem River, and the happy idea was conceived by Chancellor MacCracken of evolving therefrom a "Hall of Fame for Great Americans." The idea has been carried out, by providing for the inscription of carefully chosen names on panels of stone, with a further provision of space for statues, busts, portraits, tablets, autographs, and other memorials of those whose names are found worthy of the place. For the selection of names thus honored, a body of one hundred electors, representing all parts of the country, was appointed by the Senate of the University. These electors were apportioned to four classes of citizens, in as nearly equal numbers as possible, namely : (A) University or college presidents and educators. (B) Professors of history and scientists. (C) Publicists, editors, and authors. (D) Judges of the Supreme Court, State or National. It was required of the electors that they should consider the claims of eminent citizens in many classes, not less than fifteen, and that a majority of these classes should be represented among the first fifty names to be chosen. They were, furthermore, restricted in their choice to native-born Americans, a rule which had some reasons in its favor, though it excluded from the Hall such shining names in American history as those of John Winthrop, Roger Williams, and Alexander Hamilton.

As the result of the votes given by 97 electors, in the year 1900, 29 names were found to have received the approval of 51 or more of the electors, and these were ordered to be inscribed in the Hall of Fame. The 29 names are as follows, in the order of preference shown them by the 97 electors, as indicated by the number of votes given to each:

GEORGE WASHINGTON	97
ABRAHAM LINCOLN	96
DANIEL WEBSTER	96
BENJAMIN FRANKLIN	94
ULYSSES S. GRANT	92
JOHN MARSHALL	91
THOMAS JEFFERSON	90
RALPH WALDO EMERSON	87
HENRY WADSWORTH LONGFELLOW	85
ROBERT FULTON	85
WASHINGTON IRVING	83
JONATHAN EDWARDS	81
SAMUEL F. B. MORSE	80
DAVID GLASGOW FARRAGUT	79
HENRY CLAY	74
NATHANIEL HAWTHORNE	73
GEORGE PEABODY	72

ROBERT E. LEE	69
PETER COOPER	69
ELI WHITNEY	67
JOHN JAMES AUDUBON	67
HORACE MANN	67
HENRY WARD BEECHER	66
JAMES KENT	65
JOSEPH STORY	64
JOHN ADAMS	61
WILLIAM ELLERY CHANNING	58
GILBERT STUART	52
ASA GRAY	51

Resolutions by the Senate of the University have determined the action to be taken for the selection of further names, as follows : " The Senate will take action in the year 1902, under the rules of the Hall of Fame, toward filling at that time the vacant panels belonging to the present year, being 21 in number." " Each nomination of the present year to the Hall of Fame that has received the approval of ten or more electors, yet has failed to receive a majority, will be considered a nomination for the year 1902. To these shall be added any name nominated in writing by five of the Board of Electors. Also other names may be nominated by the New York University Senate in such way as it may find expedient. Any nomination by any citizen of the United States that shall be addressed to the New York University Senate shall be received and considered by that body." Furthermore : " Every five years throughout the twentieth century five additional names will be inscribed, provided the electors under the rules can agree by a majority upon so many."

The Senate further took note of the many requests that foreign-born Americans should be considered, by adopting a memorial to the University Corporation, to the effect that it will welcome a similar memorial to foreign-born Americans, for which a new edifice may be joined to the north porch of the present hall, containing one fifth of the space of the latter, providing thirty panels for names. — Chancellor H. M. MacCracken, *The Hall of Fame* (*Am. Rev. of Reviews*, Nov., 1900, *p.* 563).

HANKOW. See (in this vol.) SHANGHAI.

HART, Sir Robert: Testimony as to the causes and character of the " Boxer " movement in China. See (in this vol.) CHINA : A. D. 1900 (JANUARY—MARCH).

HARVARD UNIVERSITY: Summer School for Cuban Teachers. See (in this vol.) CUBA : A. D. 1900.

HAVANA. See (in this vol.) CUBA.

HAWAII.—Names and areas of the islands. — " For practical purposes, there are eight islands in the Hawaiian group. The others are mere rocks, of no value at present. These eight islands, beginning from the northwest, are named Niihau, Kauai, Oahu, Molokai, Lanai, Kahoolawe, Maui, and Hawaii. The areas of the islands [in square miles] are : Niihau, 97 ; Kauai, 590 ; Oahu, 600 ; Molokai, 270 ; Maui, 760 ; Lanai, 150 ; Kahoolawe, 63 ; Hawaii, 4,210. Total, 6,740. As compared with States of the Union, the total area of the group approximates most nearly to

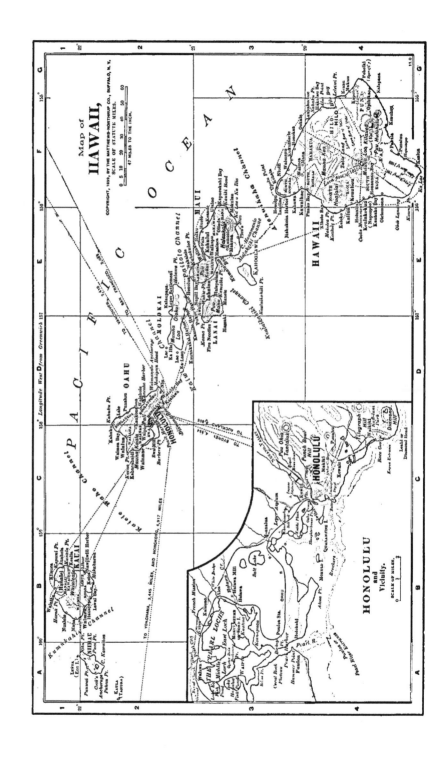

Map of
HAWAII,

COPYRIGHT, 1899, BY THE MATTHEWS-NORTHRUP CO., BUFFALO, N.Y.

SCALE OF STATUTE MILES.

47 MILES TO THE INCH.

HONOLULU
and
Vicinity.

SCALE OF MILES.

that of the State of New Jersey—7,185 square miles. It is more than three times that of Delaware—2,050 square miles."—*Bulletin of the Bureau of Am. Republics, Aug.*, 1898.

Annexation to the United States.—On the 16th of June, 1897, the President of the United States transmitted to Congress a new treaty for the annexation of the Republic of Hawaii to the United States, signed that day by representatives of the governments of the two countries, appointed to draft the same. With the treaty he submitted a report from his Secretary of State, Mr. Sherman, in which the latter said : " The negotiation which has culminated in the treaty now submitted has not been a mere resumption of the negotiation of 1893 (see HAWAIIAN ISLANDS, in vol. 3), but was initiated and has been conducted upon independent lines. Then an abrupt revolutionary movement had brought about the dethronement of the late queen and set up instead of the theretofore titular monarchy a provisional government for the control and management of public affairs and the protection of the public peace, such government to exist only until terms of union with the United States should have been negotiated and agreed upon. Thus self-constituted, its promoters claimed for it only a de facto existence until the purpose of annexation in which it took rise should be accomplished. As time passed and the plan of union with the United States became an uncertain contingency, the organization of the Hawaiian commonwealth underwent necessary changes, the temporary character of its first Government gave place to a permanent scheme under a constitution framed by the representatives of the electors of the Islands, administration by an executive council not chosen by suffrage, but self-appointed, was succeeded by an elective and parliamentary régime, and the ability of the new Government to hold—as the Republic of Hawaii—an independent place in the family of sovereign States, preserving order at home and fulfilling international obligations abroad, has been put to the proof. Recognized by the powers of the earth, sending and receiving envoys, enforcing respect for the law, and maintaining peace within its island borders, Hawaii sends to the United States, not a commission representing a successful revolution, but the accredited plenipotentiary of a constituted and firmly established sovereign State. However sufficient may have been the authority of the commissioners with whom the United States Government treated in 1893, and however satisfied the President may then have been of their power to offer the domain of the Hawaiian Islands to the United States, the fact remains that what they then tendered was a territory rather than an established Government, a country whose administration had been cast down by a bloodless but complete revolution and a community in a state of political transition. Now, however, the Republic of Hawaii approaches the United States as an equal, and points for its authority to that provision of article 32 of the constitution, promulgated July 24, 1894, whereby—' The President, with the approval of the cabinet, is hereby expressly authorized and empowered to make a treaty of political or commercial union between the Republic of Hawaii and the United States of America, subject to the ratification of the Senate.' " The essential articles of the treaty thus submitted were the following :

ART. I. The Republic of Hawaii hereby cedes absolutely and without reserve to the United States of America all rights of sovereignty of whatsoever kind in and over the Hawaiian Islands and their dependencies ; and it is agreed that all the territory of and appertaining to the Republic of Hawaii is hereby annexed to the United States of America under the name of the Territory of Hawaii.

ART. II. The Republic of Hawaii also cedes and hereby transfers to the United States the absolute fee and ownership of all public, government or crown lands, public buildings or edifices, ports, harbors, military equipments and all other public property of every kind and description belonging to the Government of the Hawaiian Islands, together with every right and appurtenance thereunto appertaining. The existing laws of the United States relative to public lands shall not apply to such lands in the Hawaiian Islands ; but the Congress of the United States shall enact special laws for their management and disposition, Provided : that all revenue from or proceeds of the same, except as regards such part thereof as may be used or occupied for the civil, military or naval purposes of the United States, or may be assigned for the use of the local government, shall be used solely for the benefit of the inhabitants of the Hawaiian Islands for educational and other public purposes.

ART. III. Until Congress shall provide for the government of such Islands all the civil, judicial and military powers exercised by the officers of the existing government in said Islands, shall be vested in such person or persons and shall be exercised in such manner as the President of the United States shall direct ; and the President shall have power to remove said officers and fill the vacancies so occasioned. The existing treaties of the Hawaiian Islands with foreign nations shall forthwith cease and determine, being replaced by such treaties as may exist, or as may be hereafter concluded between the United States and such foreign nations. The municipal legislation of the Hawaiian Islands, not enacted for the fulfilment of the treaties so extinguished, and not inconsistent with this treaty nor contrary to the Constitution of the United States, nor to any existing treaty of the United States, shall remain in force until the Congress of the United States shall otherwise determine. Until legislation shall be enacted extending the United States customs laws and regulations to the Hawaiian Islands, the existing customs relations of the Hawaiian Islands with the United States and other countries shall remain unchanged.

ART. IV. The public debt of the Republic of Hawaii, lawfully existing at the date of the exchange of the ratifications of this Treaty, including the amounts due to depositors in the Hawaiian Postal Savings Bank, is hereby assumed by the Government of the United States ; but the liability of the United States in this regard shall in no case exceed $4,000,000. So long, however, as the existing Government and the present commercial relations of the Hawaiian Islands are continued, as hereinbefore provided, said Government shall continue to pay the interest on said debt.

ART. V. There shall be no further immigration of Chinese into the Hawaiian Islands, except upon such conditions as are now or may hereafter be allowed by the laws of the United States, and no Chinese by reason of anything herein contained shall be allowed to enter the United States from the Hawaiian Islands.

ART. VI. The President shall appoint five commissioners, at least two of whom shall be residents of the Hawaiian Islands, who shall as soon as reasonably practicable, recommend to Congress such legislation concerning the Territory of Hawaii as they shall deem necessary or proper."— *United States, 55th Cong., 1st Sess., Senate Executive Document E.*

A determined opposition to the renewed proposal of Hawaiian annexation was manifested at once, in Congress and by many expressions of public opinion at large. It condemned the measure on grounds of principle and policy alike. It denied the right of the existing government at Honolulu to represent the Hawaiian people in such disposal of their country. It denied the constitutional right of the government of the United States to annex territory in the circumstances and the manner proposed. It denied, too, the expected advantages, whether naval or commercial, that the annexation of the islands would give to the United States. A protest against the annexation came also from the deposed Hawaiian queen, Liliuokalani, and another from a party in the island which attempted to rally round the presumptive heiress to the overturned Hawaiian throne, the Princess Kaiulani. The government of Japan also entered a protest, apprehending some disturbance of rights which it had acquired for its emigrating subjects, by treaty with the Republic of Hawaii ; but this protest was ultimately withdrawn. The array of opposition sufficed, however, to hold the question of annexation in abeyance for more than a year. No action was taken on the treaty during the special session of the Senate. When Congress assembled in December, 1897, President McKinley repeated his expressions in its favor, and the treaty was reported to the Senate, from the committee on foreign relations, early in the following year ; but the two-thirds majority needed for its ratification could not be obtained.

Attempts to accomplish the annexation by that method were given up in March, 1898, and the advocates of the acquisition determined to gain their end by the passage of a joint resolution of Congress, which required no more than a majority of each House. Over the question in this form the battle was fiercely fought, until the 15th of June in the House of Representatives and the 6th of July in the Senate, on which dates the following "joint resolution to provide for annexing the Hawaiian Islands to the United States" was passed. It was signed by the President the following day :

"Whereas the Government of the Republic of Hawaii having, in due form, signified its consent, in the manner provided by its constitution, to cede absolutely and without reserve to the United States of America all rights of sovereignty of whatsoever kind in and over the Hawaiian Islands and their dependencies, and also to cede and transfer to the United States absolute fee and ownership of all public, Government, or Crown lands, public buildings or edifices, ports, harbors, military equipment, and all other public property of every kind and description belonging to the Government of the Hawaiian Islands, together with every right and appurtenance thereunto appertaining : Therefore.

"Resolved by the Senate and House of Representatives of the United States of America in Congress assembled, That said cession is accepted, ratified, and confirmed, and that the said Hawaiian Islands and their dependencies be, and they are hereby, annexed as a part of the territory of the United States and are subject to the sovereign dominion thereof, and that all and singular the property and rights hereinbefore mentioned are vested in the United States of America. The existing laws of the United States relative to public lands shall not apply to such lands in the Hawaiian Islands; but the Congress of the United States shall enact special laws for their management and disposition : Provided, That all revenue from or proceeds of the same, except as regards such part thereof as may be used or occupied for the civil, military, or naval purposes of the United States, or may be assigned for the use of the local government, shall be used solely for the benefit of the inhabitants of the Hawaiian Islands for educational and other public purposes.

"Until Congress shall provide for the government of such islands all the civil, judicial, and military powers exercised by the officers of the existing government in said islands shall be vested in such person or persons and shall be exercised in such manner as the President of the United States shall direct ; and the President shall have power to remove said officers and fill the vacancies so occasioned. The existing treaties of the Hawaiian Islands with foreign nations shall forthwith cease and determine, being replaced by such treaties as may exist, or as may be hereafter concluded, between the United States and such foreign nations. The municipal legislation of the Hawaiian Islands, not enacted for the fulfillment of the treaties so extinguished, and not inconsistent with this joint resolution nor contrary to the Constitution of the United States nor to any existing treaty of the United States, shall remain in force until the Congress of the United States shall otherwise determine. Until legislation shall be enacted extending the United States customs laws and regulations to the Hawaiian Islands the existing customs relations of the Hawaiian Islands with the United States and other countries shall remain unchanged. The public debt of the Republic of Hawaii, lawfully existing at the date of the passage of this joint resolution, including the amounts due to depositors in the Hawaiian Postal Savings Bank, is hereby assumed by the Government of the United States; but the liability of the United States in this regard shall in no case exceed four million dollars. So long, however, as the existing Government and the present commercial relations of the Hawaiian Islands are continued as hereinbefore provided said Government shall continue to pay the interest on said debt.

"There shall be no further immigration of Chinese into the Hawaiian Islands, except upon such conditions as are now or may hereafter be allowed by the laws of the United States; and no Chinese, by reason of anything herein contained, shall be allowed to enter the United States from the Hawaiian Islands.

"The President shall appoint five commissioners, at least two of whom shall be residents of the Hawaiian Islands, who shall, as soon as reasonably practicable, recommend to Congress such legislation concerning the Hawaiian Islands as they shall deem necessary or proper.

"SECT. 2. That the commissioners hereinbefore provided for shall be appointed by the President, by and with the advice and consent of the Senate.

"SECT. 3. That the sum of one hundred thousand dollars, or so much thereof as may be necessary, is hereby appropriated, out of any money in the Treasury not otherwise appropriated, and to be immediately available, to be expended at the discretion of the President of the United States of America, for the purpose of carrying this joint resolution into effect."

There was no strict division of parties on the passage of the resolution; but only three Republicans in the House voted against it. Speaker Reed, who had strenuously opposed the measure, was absent. Two Republican senators voted against the resolution and three who opposed it were paired. A large majority of the Democrats in both Houses were in opposition.

The policy advocated by the opponents of annexation was set forth in the following resolution, which was brought to a vote in the House, and which was defeated by 205 to 94: '1. That the United States will view as an act of hostility any attempt upon the part of any government of Europe or Asia to take or hold possession of the Hawaiian islands or to account upon any pretext or under any conditions sovereign authority therein. 2. That the United States hereby announces to the people of those islands and to the world the guarantee of the independence of the people of the Hawaiian islands and their firm determination to maintain the same."

Immediately upon the passage of the resolution of annexation, preparations were begun at Honolulu for the transfer of sovereignty to the United States, which was performed ceremoniously August 12. Meantime, the President had appointed, as commissioners to recommend legislation for the government of the Islands, Messrs. Shelby M. Cullom, John T. Morgan, Robert R. Hitt, Sanford B. Dole, and Walter F. Frear. In the following November the Commission presented its report, with a draft of several bills embodying the recommended legislation. When the subject came into Congress, wide differences of opinion appeared on questions concerning the relations of the new possession to the United States and the form of government to be provided for it. As the consequence, more than a year passed before Congress reached action on the subject, and Hawaii was kept in suspense for that period, provisionally governed under the terms of the resolution of annexation. The Act which, at last, determined the status and the government of Hawaii, under the flag of the United States, became law by the President's signature on the 30th of April, 1900, and Sanford B. Dole, formerly President of the Republic of Hawaii, was appointed its governor.

The fundamental provisions of the "Act to provide a government for the Territory of Hawaii" are the following:

SEC. 2. That the islands acquired by the United States of America under an Act of Congress entitled "Joint resolution to provide for annexing the Hawaiian Islands to the United States," approved July seventh, eighteen hundred and ninety-eight, shall be known as the Territory of Hawaii.

SEC. 3. That a Territorial government is here-

by established over the said Territory, with its capital at Honolulu, on the island of Oahu.

SEC. 4. That all persons who were citizens of the Republic of Hawaii on August twelfth, eighteen hundred and ninety-eight, are hereby declared to be citizens of the United States and citizens of the Territory of Hawaii. And all citizens of the United States resident in the Hawaiian Islands who were resident there on or since August twelfth, eighteen hundred and ninety-eight, and all the citizens of the United States who shall hereafter reside in the Territory of Hawaii for one year shall be citizens of the Territory of Hawaii.

SEC. 5. That the Constitution, and, except as herein otherwise provided, all the laws of the United States which are not locally inapplicable, shall have the same force and effect within the said Territory as elsewhere in the United States: Provided, that sections eighteen hundred and fifty and eighteen hundred and ninety of the Revised Statutes of the United States shall not apply to the Territory of Hawaii.

SEC. 6. That the laws of Hawaii not inconsistent with the Constitution or laws of the United States or the provisions of this Act shall continue in force, subject to repeal or amendment by the legislature of Hawaii or the Congress of the United States. . . .

SEC. 12. That the legislature of the Territory of Hawaii shall consist of two houses, styled, respectively, the senate and house of representatives, which shall organize and sit separately, except as otherwise herein provided. The two houses shall be styled "The legislature of the Territory of Hawaii.". . .

SEC. 17. That no person holding office in or under or by authority of the Government of the United States or of the Territory of Hawaii shall be eligible to election to the legislature, or to hold the position of a member of the same while holding said office. . . .

SEC. 55. That the legislative power of the Territory shall extend to all rightful subjects of legislation not inconsistent with the Constitution and laws of the United States locally applicable. . . .

SEC. 66. That the executive power of the government of the Territory of Hawaii shall be vested in a governor, who shall be appointed by the President, by and with the advice and consent of the Senate of the United States, and shall hold office for four years and until his successor shall be appointed and qualified, unless sooner removed by the President. He shall be not less than thirty-five years of age ; shall be a citizen of the Territory of Hawaii ; shall be commander in chief of the militia thereof ; may grant pardons or reprieves for offences against the laws of the said Territory and reprieves for offences against the laws of the United States until the decision of the President is made known thereon. . . .

SEC. 68. That all the powers and duties which, by the laws of Hawaii, are conferred upon or required of the President or any minister of the Republic of Hawaii (acting alone or in connection with any other officer or person or body) or the cabinet or executive council, and not inconsistent with the Constitution or laws of the United States, are conferred upon and required of the governor of the Territory of Hawaii, unless otherwise provided. . . .

6-17   257

SEC. 80. That the President shall nominate and, by and with the advice and consent of the Senate, appoint the chief justice and justices of the supreme court, the judges of the circuit courts, who shall hold their respective offices for the term of four years, unless sooner removed by the President. . . .

SEC. 81. That the judicial power of the Territory shall be vested in one supreme court, circuit courts, and in such inferior courts as the legislature may from time to time establish. . . .

SEC. 85. That a Delegate to the House of Representatives of the United States, to serve during each Congress, shall be elected by the voters qualified to vote for members of the legislature ; such Delegate shall possess the qualifications necessary for membership of the senate of the legislature of Hawaii. . . . Every such Delegate shall have a seat in the House of Representatives, with the right of debate, but not of voting.

SEC. 86. That there shall be established in said Territory a district court to consist of one judge, who shall reside therein and be called the district judge. The President of the United States, by and with the advice and consent of the Senate of the United States, shall appoint a district attorney, and a marshal of the United States for the said district, and said judge, attorney, and marshal shall hold office for six years unless sooner removed by the President. Said court shall have, in addition to the ordinary jurisdiction of district courts of the United States, jurisdiction of all cases cognizable in a circuit court of the United States, and shall proceed therein in the same manner as a circuit court. . . .

SEC. 88. That the Territory of Hawaii shall comprise a customs district of the United States, with ports of entry and delivery at Honolulu, Hilo, Mahukona, and Kahului.

A. D. 1900.—Census of the Islands.—Progress of educational work.—"The last Hawaiian census, taken in the year 1896, gives a total population of 109,020, of which 31,019 were native Hawaiians. The number of Americans reported was 8,485. The results of the Federal census taken this year [1900] show the islands to have a total population of 154,001, an increase over that reported in 1896 of 44,981, or 41.2 per cent. The total land surface of the Hawaiian Islands is approximately 6,449 square miles ; the average number of persons to the square mile at the last three censuses being as follows : For 1890, 13.9 ; 1896, 16.9 ; 1900, 23.8.

"Education in Hawaii is making favorable progress. In Honolulu two large schoolhouses have recently been erected at a cost of $24,778 and $20,349, respectively. The department of education is under the management of a superintendent of public instruction, assisted by six commissioners of public instruction, two of whom are ladies. The tenure of office of the commissioners is six years, the term of two of them expiring each year. They serve without pay. The system is the same as that existing under the Republic of Hawaii. In the biennial period ending December 31 there were 141 public and 48 private schools in the Hawaiian Islands ; 344 teachers in the public schools, of whom 113 were men and 231 were women, and 200 teachers in the private schools, of whom 79 were men and 121 were women. In the same period there were

11,436 pupils in the public schools, of whom 6,395 were boys and 5,041 were girls, and 4,054 pupils in the private schools, of whom 2,256 were boys and 1,798 were girls. This gives a total of 15,490 pupils, of whom 8,651 were boys and 6,839 were girls. . . . Of the 15,490 pupils, 5,045 were Hawaiian, 2,721 part Hawaiian, 601 American, 213 British, 337 German, 3,882 Portuguese, 84 Scandinavian, 1,141 Japanese, 1,314 Chinese, 30 South Sea Islanders, and 124 other foreigners. Each nationality had its own teacher. The expenditures for the two years ending December 31, 1899, were $575,353. Since the year 1888 nearly all the common schools, in which the Hawaiian language was the medium of instruction, have been converted into schools in which English alone is so employed, 98 per cent. of the children being at present instructed by teachers who use English."—*United States, Secretary of the Interior, Annual Report, Nov. 30, 1900.*

HAY-PAUNCEFOTE TREATY, The. See (in this vol.) CANAL, INTEROCEANIC : A. D. 1900 (DECEMBER) ; and 1901 (MARCH).

HAYTI : A. D. 1896.—Election of President **Sam.**—Hayti elected a new President, General Theresias Simon Sam, to succeed General Hippolyte, who died suddenly on the 24th of March.

A. D. 1897.—Quarrel with Germany.—The government of Hayti came into conflict with that of Germany, in September, 1897, over what was claimed to be the illegal arrest of a Haytien-born German, named Lueders, who had secured German citizenship. Germany demanded his release, with an indemnity at the rate of $1,000 per day for his imprisonment. The demand not being acceded to promptly, the German consul at Port-au-Prince hauled down his flag. Then the United States Minister persuaded the Haytien President, General Simon Sam, to set Lueders free. But the demand for indemnity, still pending, brought two German war-ships to Port-au-Prince on the 6th of December, with their guns ready to open fire on the town if payment were not made within eight hours. For Hayti there was nothing possible but submission, and $30,000 was paid, with apologies and expressions of regret.

HEBREWS, The ancient : Their position in history as affected by recent archæological research. See (in this vol.) ARCHÆOLOGICAL RESEARCH : IN BIBLE LANDS.

HECKER, Father Isaac Thomas, and the opinions called "Americanism." See (in this vol.) PAPACY : A. D. 1899 (JANUARY).

HELIUM, The discovery of. See (in this vol.) SCIENCE, RECENT : CHEMISTRY AND PHYSICS.

HENRY, General Guy V. : Military Governor of Porto Rico. See (in this vol.) PORTO RICO : A. D. 1898–1899 (OCTOBER—OCTOBER).

HERVEY, or COOK, ISLANDS : Annexation to New Zealand. See (in this vol.) NEW ZEALAND : A. D. 1900 (OCTOBER).

HEUREAUX, President : Assassination. See (in this vol.) DOMINICAN REPUBLIC : A. D. 1899.

HICKS-BEACH, Sir Michael, Chancellor of the Exchequer, in the British Cabinet. See (in this vol.) ENGLAND: A. D. 1894-1895.

HILPRECHT, Professor H. V.: Re- searches on the site of ancient Nippur. See (in this vol.) ARCHÆOLOGICAL RESEARCH: BABYLONIA: AMERICAN EXPLORATION.

HINTCHAK, The. See (in this vol.) TURKEY: A. D. 1895.

HINTERLAND.—A German word which has come into general use to describe unnamed and poorly defined regions lying behind, or on the inland side, of coast districts, in Africa more especially, which have been occupied or claimed by European powers.

HISTORICAL DISCOVERIES, Recent. See (in this vol.) ARCHÆOLOGICAL RESEARCH.

HOAR, Senator George F.: Action to recover the manuscript of Bradford's History. See (in this vol.) MASSACHUSETTS: A. D. 1897.
Speech in opposition to the retention of the Philippine Islands as a subject State. See (in this vol.) UNITED STATES OF AM.: A. D. 1900 (APRIL).

HOBART, Garret A.: Vice President of the United States.—Death. See (in this vol.) UNITED STATES OF AM.: A. D. 1899 (Nov.).

HOBOKEN, Great fire at.—On the 30th of June, 1900, between 200 and 300 people lost their lives in a fire which destroyed the pier system of the North German Lloyd steamship line, at Hoboken, N. J. The fire wrecked three of the large ships of the company, and is said to have been the most destructive blaze that ever visited the piers and shipping of the port of New York. An estimate placed the loss of life at nearly 300, and the damage to property at about $10,000,000, but the company's estimate of the loss of life and the value of the property wiped out was considerably less. The fire started in some cotton on one of the four large piers at 4 o'clock in the afternoon. In a few minutes the pier on which it broke out was enveloped in flames, and in six minutes the whole pier system was burning. The flames spread so quickly that many men on the piers and on the vessels, lighters and barges were hemmed in before they realized that their lives were in danger.

HOBSON, Lieutenant Richmond Pearson: The sinking of the collier Merrimac at Santiago. See (in this vol.) UNITED STATES OF AM.: A. D. 1898 (APRIL—JUNE).

HOLLAND. See (in this vol.) NETHERLANDS, THE KINGDOM OF THE.

HOLLS, Frederick W.: American Commissioner to the Peace Conference at The Hague. See (in this vol.) PEACE CONFERENCE.

HOLY YEAR 1900, Proclamation of the Universal Jubilee of the, Its extension. See (in this vol.) PAPACY: A. D. 1900-1901.

HONDURAS. See (in this vol.) CENTRAL AMERICA.

HONG KONG: A. D. 1894.—The Bubonic Plague. See (in this vol.) PLAGUE.
A. D. 1898.—British lease of territory on the mainland. See (in this vol.) CHINA: A. D. 1898 (APRIL—AUGUST).

HORMIGUEROS, Engagement at. See (in this vol.) UNITED STATES OF AM.: A. D. 1898 (JULY—AUGUST: PORTO RICO).

HOUSE OF REPRESENTATIVES, The United States: The "Spoils System" in its service. See (in this vol.) CIVIL SERVICE REFORM: A. D. 1901.

HOVA, The. See (in this vol.) MADAGASCAR.

HUA SANG, Massacre of missionaries at. See (in this vol.) CHINA: A. D. 1895 (AUGUST).

HUDSON BAY, Investigation of. See (in this vol.) POLAR EXPLORATION, 1897.

HUMBERT I, King of Italy: Assassination. See (in this vol.) ITALY: A. D. 1899-1900; and 1900 (JULY—SEPTEMBER).

HUNGARY. See (in this vol.) AUSTRIA-HUNGARY.

HUSBANDISTS, The. See (in this vol.) GERMANY: A. D. 1901 (FEBRUARY).

I.

ICELAND, Recent exploration of. See (in this vol.) POLAR EXPLORATION, 1898-1899.

IDAHO: A. D. 1896.—Adoption of Woman Suffrage.—On the 11th of December, 1896, an amendment of the constitution of Idaho, extending the suffrage to women, was submitted to the then voters of the State, and carried by 12,126, against 6,282. Though carried by a large majority of the votes given on the suffrage issue, it did not receive a majority of the whole vote cast on other questions at the same election; but the supreme court of the State decided that the amendment had been adopted.

I-HO-CH'UAN, The. See (in this vol.) CHINA: A. D. 1900 (JANUARY—MARCH).

ILLINOIS: A. D. 1898.—Strike of coal miners.—Bloody conflict at Virden. See (in this vol.) INDUSTRIAL DISTURBANCES: A. D. 1898.

ILOCANOS, The. See (in this vol.) PHILIPPINE ISLANDS: THE NATIVE INHABITANTS.

ILOILO: The American occupation of the city. See (in this vol.) PHILIPPINE ISLANDS: A. D. 1899 (JANUARY—NOVEMBER).

ILORIN, British subjugation of. See (in this vol.) AFRICA: A. D. 1897 (NIGERIA).

IMPERIAL BRITISH EAST AFRICA COMPANY: Transfer of territory to the British Government. See (in this vol.) AFRICA: A. D. 1895 (BRITISH EAST AFRICA).

IMPERIAL CONFERENCE: Meeting of British Colonial Prime Ministers at the Colonial Office, London. See (in this vol.) ENGLAND: A. D. 1897 (JUNE—JULY).

IMPERIALISM: The question in American politics. See (in this vol.) UNITED STATES OF AM.: A. D. 1900 (APRIL); and (MAY—NOVEMBER).

INCOME TAX: Decision against by U. S. Supreme Court. See (in this vol.) UNITED STATES OF AM. : A. D. 1895 (APRIL—MAY).

INDIA: A. D. 1894.—The Waziri War.— A fierce attempt to interrupt the demarcation of the Afghan boundary was made by the Waziris. The escort of 5,000 troops, consisting mainly of Sikhs and Goorkhas, was desperately attacked in camp at Wano, November 3. The attack was repulsed, but with heavy loss on the British side. It became afterwards necessary to send three strong columns into the country, under Sir William Lockhart, in order to carry out the work.

A. D. 1895 (March—September).—The defense and relief of Chitral.—The British frontier advanced.—At the extreme northwestern limit of British-Indian dominion and semi-dominion, under the shadow of the lofty Hindu-Kush mountains, lie a group of quasi-independent tribal states over which the Amir of Afghanistan claimed at least a "sphere of influence" until 1893. In that year the Amir and the Government of India agreed upon a line which defined the eastern and southern frontier of Afghanistan, "from Wakhan to the Persian border," and agreed further as follows: "The Government of India will at no time exercise interference in the territories lying beyond this line on the side of Afghanistan, and his Highness the Amir will at no time exercise interference in the territories lying beyond this line on the side of India. The British Government thus agrees to his Highness the Amir retaining Asmar and the valley above it, as far as Chanak. His Highness agrees, on the other hand, that he will at no time exercise interference in Swat, Bajaur, or Chitral, including Arnawai or Bashgal valley." Under this agreement, the Indian Government prepared itself to be watchful of Chitral affairs. The little state was notoriously a nest of turbulence and intrigue. Its rulers, who bore the Persian title of Mehtar, signifying "Greater," can never have expected to live out their days. Changes of government were brought about commonly by assassination. The reigning prince, Nizam-ul-Mulk, owed his seat to the murder of his father, Aman-ul-Mulk, though not by himself. In turn, he fell, on New Year's day, 1895, slain at the instigation of his half-brother, Amir-ul-Mulk, who mounted the vacant chair of state. The usurper was then promptly assailed by two rivals, one of them his brother-in-law, Umra Khan, a mountain chieftain of Bajaur, the other an uncle, Sher Afzul, who had been a refugee at Kabul. On the news of these occurrences at Chitral, the Government of India sent thither, from Gilgit, its political agent, Surgeon-Major Robertson, with a small escort, to learn the state of affairs.

The result of Dr. Robertson's attempt to settle matters was an alliance of Umra Khan and Sher Afzul in a desperate attempt to destroy him and his small force of native troops, which had five English officers at its head. The latter took possession (March 1) of the fort at Chitral, a structure about 80 yards square, walled partly with wood, and so placed in a valley that it was commanded from neighboring hills. In this weak fortification the little garrison held off a savage swarm of the surrounding tribes during 46 days of a siege that is as thrilling in the story of it as any found in recent history. The first reinforcements sent to Dr. Robertson,

from near Gilgit, were disastrously beaten back, with the loss of the captain in command and 50 of his men. As speedily as possible, when the situation was known in India, an army of about 14,000 men was made ready at Peshawur, under the command of Major-General Sir Robert Low, and relieving columns were pushed with great difficulty through the Malakand Pass, then filled deep with snow. A smaller force, of 600 men, under Colonel Kelly, fought its way from Gilgit, struggling through the snows of a pass 12,000 feet above the level of the sea. Colonel Kelly was the first to reach Chitral, which he did on the 20th of April. The besiegers had fled at his approach. The beleaguered garrison was found to have lost 40 killed and 70 wounded, out of its fighting force of about 370 men. Sher Afzul was caught by the Khan of Dir, who led 2,000 of his followers to the help of the British. Umra Khan escaped to Kabul, where he was imprisoned by the Amir. Shuja-ul-Mulk, a younger brother of Amir-ul-Mulk was declared Mehtar. The question whether British authority should be maintained in Chitral or withdrawn was now sharply debated in England; but Lord Salisbury and his party, coming into power at that moment, decided that the advanced frontier of Indian Empire must be held. The young Mehtar was installed in the name of the Maharaja of Kashmir as his suzerain, and the terms under which his government should be carried on were announced at his installation (Sept. 2, 1895) by the British Agent, as follows:

"The general internal administration of the country will be left in the hands of the Mehtar and of his advisers. The Government of India do not intend to undertake themselves the management of the internal affairs of Chitral, their concern being with the foreign relations of the State, and with its general welfare. It, however, has to be remembered that Shuja-ul-Mulk is only a boy, and that, at an age when other boys are engaged in education and amusement, he has been called upon to hold the reins of State. Bearing this fact in mind, the Government of India recognise the necessity of his receiving some help during the time of his minority, and it has consequently been decided to leave at Chitral an experienced Political Officer upon whom the Mehtar may always call for advice and assistance, while it is proposed to appoint three persons, Raja Bahadur Khan, the Governor of Mastuj, Wazir Inayat Khan and Aksakal Fateh Ali Shah, to give him help, instruction and advice in the management of his State and in the laws and customs of the people. Ordinarily the entire country will be governed in accordance with their experience and judgment; but nevertheless the Assistant British Agent, if he thinks it necessary to do so, may, at any time, ask the Mehtar to delay action recommended by his three advisers, until the opinion of the British Agent at Gilgit has been obtained, whose decision shall be final and authoritative.

"The desirability of abolishing traffic in slaves is a matter to which the Government of India attach much importance, and that they have lately interested themselves with some success in procuring the release of Natives of Kashmir and her dependencies, including Chitralis, who are held in bondage in Chinese Turkistan. It is in accordance therefore with the general policy of the Government of India that in Chitral also all buying and selling of slaves, whether for disposal in the country or with the intention of sending them abroad, should be altogether prohibited. Any such selling of slaves is therefore from this time forward absolutely illegal."— *Great Britain, Parliamentary Publications: Papers by Command,* 1896 (*C.*—8037). Also in: C. Lowe, *The Story of Chitral* (*Century Mag.,* v. 55, p. 89).

A. D. **1895** (April).—Report of the Opium Commission.—"The long-deferred publication of the report of this commission was made in April, and the report was signed by eight out of nine members of the commission. The commissioners declared that it had not been shown to be necessary, or to be demanded by the people, that the growth of the poppy and the manufacture of opium in British India should be prohibited. Such a prohibition, if extended to the protected States, would be an unprecedented act of interference on the part of the paramount Power, and would be, sure to be resisted by the chiefs and their people. The existing treaties with China in regard to the importation of Indian opium into that country had been admitted by the Chinese Government to contain all they desired. The evidence led the commissioners to the conclusion that the common use of opium in India is moderate, and its prohibition is strongly opposed by the great mass of native opinion."— *Annual Register,* 1895, *pp.* 337–8.

A. D. **1896-1897.**—Famine in northwestern and central provinces.—A failure of rains, especially in northwestern and central India, produced the inevitable consequence of famine, lasting with awful severity from the spring of 1896 until the autumn of 1897. In December of the former year there were 561,800 persons employed on relief works which the Indian government organized. In the following March the number had risen to more than three millions, and in June it exceeded four millions. Rain fell in July, and August, and the distress began soon afterwards to grow less. In addition to the heavy expenditures of the government, the charitable contributions for the relief of sufferers from this famine were officially reported to have amounted to 1,750,000 pounds sterling ($8,750,000).

A. D. **1896-1900.**—The Bubonic Plague. See (in this vol.) PLAGUE.

A. D. **1897.**—Change in the government of Burmah. See (in this vol.) BURMAH: A. D. 1897.

A. D. **1897.**—Rejection of American proposals for a reopening of mints to silver. See (in this vol.) MONETARY QUESTIONS: A. D. 1897 (APRIL—OCTOBER).

A. D. **1897-1898.**—Frontier wars.—From the early summer of 1897 until beyond the close of the year, the British were once more seriously in conflict with the warlike tribes of the Afghan frontier. The risings of the latter were begun in the Tochi Valley, on the 10th of June, when a sudden, treacherous attack was made by Waziri tribesmen on the escort of Mr. Gee, the political agent, at the village of Maizar. A number of officers and men were killed and wounded, and the whole party would have been destroyed if timely reinforcements had not reached them. Over 7,000 troops were subsequently employed in the suppression and punishment of this revolt. The next outbreak, in the Swat Valley, was

more extensive. It was ascribed to the preaching of a fanatical Mohammedan priest, known as "the mad mullah," who labored to excite a religious war, and was opened, July 26, by a night attack on the British positions at Malakand and Chakdarra. The latter outpost, guarding the bridge over the Swat river, on the road to Chitral, was held by a small garrison of less than 300 men, who were beleaguered for a considerable time before relief came. According to an official return of "wars and military operations on or beyond the borders of British India in which the Government of India has been engaged," made to Parliament on the 30th of January, 1900, there were 11,826 troops employed in the operations immediately consequent on this rising, with the result that "the insurgents were defeated and the fanatical gatherings were dispersed; large fines were taken in money and arms." But other neighboring tribes either gave help to the Swats or were moved to follow their example, and required to be subdued, their countries traversed by punitive expeditions and "fines of money and arms" collected. Before the year closed, these tasks employed 6,800 men in the Mohmand country, 3,200 in the Utman Khel country, 7,300 in the Buner country, 14,231 in the Kurram Valley; and then came the most serious business of all. The Afridis, who had been subsidized by the government of India for some years, as guardians of the important Khyber Pass, were suddenly in arms against their paymasters, in August, destroying the Khyber posts. This serious hostility called nearly 44,000 British-Indian troops into the field, under General Sir William Lockhart, whose successful campaign was not finished until the following spring. The most serious engagement of the war with the Afridis was fought at the village of Dargai, October 18. The final results of the campaign are thus summarized in the return mentioned above: "British troops traversed the country of the tribes, inflicting severe loss on the tribesmen, who were ultimately reduced to submission; they paid large fines in money and arms, and friendly relations have since been restored."— *Great Britain, House of Commons Reports and Papers,* 1900, 13.

A. D. **1898.**—Discovery of the birthplace and the tomb of Gautama Buddha. See (in this vol.) BUDDHA.

A. D. **1898** (September).—Appointment of Lord Curzon to the Viceroyalty.—In September, 1898, the Right Hon. George N. Curzon, lately Under Secretary of State for Foreign Affairs, was appointed Viceroy and Governor-General of India, to succeed the Earl of Elgin. In the following month, Mr. Curzon was raised to the peerage, as Baron Curzon of Kedleston.

A. D. **1899-1900.**—Famine again.—There was a recurrence of drought and famine in 1899, far more extensive than that of 1896–7, producing more death and suffering, and calling out more strenuous exertions for its relief. The regions afflicted were largely the same as two years before, embracing much of northwestern and central India. The relief measures which it demanded were carried far into the summer of 1900. In October of the latter year Lord Curzon, the Viceroy, addressing the Legislative Council at Simla, and reviewing the experience through which the government and the country had passed, made some important statements of fact:

"In a greater or less degree," he said, "nearly one-fourth of the entire population of the Indian continent came within the range of the relief operations. The loss occasioned may be roughly put in this way. The annual agricultural production of India and Burma averages in value between 300 and 400 crores of rupees [the crore being ten millions, and the rupee equivalent to about one-third of a dollar]. On a very cautious estimate the production of 1899-1900 must have been at least one-quarter, if not one-third, below the average, or at normal prices 75 crores, or £50,000,000 sterling. If to this be added the value of some millions of cattle, some conception may be formed of the destruction of property which great drought occasions. There have been many great droughts in India, but no other of which such figures could be predicated as these. . . .

"If a special characteristic can be attributed to our campaign of famine relief in the past year, it has been its unprecedented liberality. There is no parallel in the history of India or any country of the world to the total of over 6,000,000 persons who, in British India and the native States for weeks on end, have been dependent upon the charity of the Government. The famine cost ten crores in direct expenditure, while 238 lakhs were given to landholders and cultivators on loans and advances, besides loans to native States. . . . There has never been a famine when the general mortality has been less, when the distress has been more amply or swiftly relieved, or when the Government and its officers have given themselves with more whole-hearted devotion to the saving of life and the service of the people. It is impossible to tell the actual mortality, but there has apparently been an excess of mortality over the normal of 750,000, Cholera and smallpox have accounted for 230,000, which is probably below the mark, so that the excess in British India has equalled 500,000 during the year. To say that the greater part of these died of starvation or even of destitution would be an unjustifiable exaggeration, since many other contributory causes have been at work."

Referring to the charitable help received from various parts of the world, Lord Curzon said: "In 1896-97 the total collections amounted to 170 lakhs [the lakh being 100,000 rupees] of which 10 lakhs remained over at the beginning of the recent famine. In the present year the Central Relief Committee has received a sum of close upon 140 lakhs, not far short of £1,000,000 sterling. To analyze the subscriptions: India has contributed about the same amount to the fund as in 1896-97—namely, 32 lakhs. If the contributions from the European community are deducted, India may be considered to have contributed less than one-fifth of the total collections of 140 lakhs. More might have been expected from the native community as a whole, notwithstanding individual examples of remarkable generosity. The little colony of the Straits Settlements, which has no connexion with India beyond that of sentiment, has given more than the whole Punjab. A careful observation of the figures and proceedings in each province compels me to say that native India has not yet reached as high a standard of practical philanthropy and charity as might reasonably be expected. . . . The collections from abroad amounted to 108 lakhs, as

against 137 in 1896-97. The United Kingdom's contribution of 88½ lakhs compared indifferently with its contribution of 123 lakhs in 1896-97, but in the circumstances of the year it is a noble gift. Glasgow has been especially generous with a donation of 8½ lakhs and Liverpool with 4½, in addition to nearly 16 lakhs from the rest of Lancashire. Australasia has given nearly 8 lakhs in place of 2 lakhs. The Straits Settlements, Ceylon, and Hong-kong have also been extremely generous. Even the Chinese native officials have collected handsome sums. The liberal donation of Germany at the instigation of the Emperor has already been publicly acknowledged. The United States, both through direct contributions to the fund and by means of privately-distributed gifts of money and grain, have once more shown their vivid sympathy with England's mission and India's need."

A. D. 1901.—Census of the Empire.—Decrease of population in several of the Native States.—The Indian census, begun on the 1st of March, 1901, was completed for the entire empire in fourteen days, the result being announced on the 15th. It showed a total population in British territory of 231,085,000, against 221,266,000 in 1891 ; in Native States 63,181,000, against 66,050,000 in 1891 ; total for all India, 294,266,000, against 287,317,000 in 1891. The Native States, it will be seen, have declined in population to the extent of nearly 3,000,000, showing greater severity in those states of the effects of famine and disease. In several provinces, however, of the British territory, a decrease of population appears : Berar declining from 2,897,-000 in 1891 to 1,491,000 in 1901 ; Bombay (British Presidency) from 15,957,000 to 15,330,000 ; Central Provinces from 10,784,000 to 9,845,000 ; Aden from 44,000 to 41,000 ; Coorg from 173,000 to 170,000. Of the Native States the greatest loss of population was suffered in Rajputana, which sank from 12,016,000 to 9,841,000 ; in Central India, where the numbers fell from 10,318,000 to 8,501,000 ; and in the Bombay States, which were reduced in population from 8,059,000 to 6,891,000. The provinces in British India which show the greatest percentage of gain are Upper and Lower Burma, Assam and Sind. The present population of the greater British provinces is as follows : Bengal, 74,713,000 ; Madras, 38,-208,000 ; Northwest provinces, 84,812,000 ; Punjab, 22,449,000.

A. D. 1901 (February).—Continued famine.—On the 24th of January, 1901, the Viceroy of India reported to the British Government, by telegram, that the winter rainfall had been unusually good in Upper India, Rajputana, Central Provinces, and Central India, and agricultural prospects were very favorable ; but that in Gujarat, Deccan, and the Karnatik districts of Bombay, through the early cessation of the monsoon in September and the absence of rain, the crop prospects were bad and serious distress was expected between then and August. Relief measures would be required. The affected district included Baroda and part of Haidarabad. On the 14th of February the Viceroy reported further that the number on the relief works and gratuitous relief showed little increase, but greater pressure was expected in the affected area after the reaping of the scanty harvests there. In Upper and Central India some damage by storm and damp had been done to crops which promised to be very good. The number of persons then in receipt of relief was :—Bombay, 176,000 ; Bombay Native States, 17,000 ; Baroda, 15,000 ; Haidarabad, 2,000 ; Madras, 3,000 ; Central India States, 1,000. Total, 214,000.

A. D. **1901** (February).—Creation of a **new** administrative province on the northwestern frontier.—A despatch from Calcutta, February 13, announced the determination of the government of India to create " a new frontier agency or province, formed out of the four trans-Indus districts of the Punjab, under an Agent to the Governor-General of similar status to the Agent in Baluchistan, with revenue and judicial commissioners, all the officers being under the Supreme Government and enrolled in the Political Department. The districts which form the new province will be Peshawar, Kohat, Bannu, and Dera Ismail Khan, with the tribal country beyond their limits, and also the existing political agencies of Dir, Swat, Chitral, the Khaibar, the Kuram, Tochi, and Wana. The scheme takes as little as possible away from the Punjab, while making a compact charge, easily controllable by one officer."

A. D. **1901** (February).—**Message of King Edward VII. to the princes and people.** See (in this vol.) ENGLAND : A. D. 1901 (JANUARY—FEBRUARY).

INDIANAPOLIS CONVENTION, and **Monetary** Commission, The. See (in this vol.) UNITED STATES OF AM. : A. D. 1896-1898.

INDIANS, The American : A. D. **1893-1899.**—Negotiations and agreements with the Five Civilized Tribes.—**Work of the Dawes Commission.**—In his annual Message to the Congress of the United States, December 7, 1896, President Cleveland made the following reference to the work of a commission created in 1893, for negotiating with what are known as the Five Civilized Tribes of Indians : "The condition of affairs among the Five Civilized Tribes, who occupy large tracts of land in the Indian Territory and who have governments of their own, has assumed such an aspect as to render it almost indispensable that there should be an entire change in the relations of these Indians to the General Government. This seems to be necessary in furtherance of their own interests, as well as for the protection of non-Indian residents in their territory. A commission organized and empowered under several recent laws is now negotiating with these Indians for the relinquishment of their courts and the division of their common lands in severalty, and are aiding in the settlement of the troublesome question of tribal membership. The reception of their first proffers of negotiation was not encouraging, but through patience and such conduct on their part as demonstrated that their intentions were friendly and in the interest of the tribes the prospect of success has become more promising. The effort should be to save these Indians from the consequences of their own mistakes and improvidence and to secure to the real Indian his rights as against intruders and professed friends who profit by his retrogression. A change is also needed to protect life and property through the operation of courts conducted according to strict justice and strong enough to enforce their mandates. As a sincere friend of the Indian, I am exceedingly anxious that these reforms should

be accomplished with the consent and aid of the tribes and that no necessity may be presented for radical or drastic legislation."—*United States, Message and Documents (Abridgment,* 1896-7).

The Act of March 3, 1893, by which the commission was created, set forth its character, its duties and its powers, as follows: "The President shall nominate and, by and with the advice and consent of the Senate, shall appoint three commissioners to enter into negotiations with the Cherokee Nation, the Choctaw Nation, the Chickasaw Nation, the Muscogee (or Creek) Nation, the Seminole Nation, for the purpose of extinguishment of the national or tribal title to any lands within that territory now held by any and all of such nations or tribes, either by cession of the same or some part thereof to the United States, or by the allotment and division of the same in severalty among the Indians of such nations or tribes, respectively, as may be entitled to the same, or by such other method as may be agreed upon between the several nations and tribes aforesaid, or each of them, with the United States, with a view to such an adjustment, upon the basis of justice and equity, as may, with the consent of such nations or tribes of Indians, so far as may be necessary, be requisite and suitable to enable the ultimate creation of a State or States of the Union which shall embrace the lands within said Indian Territory. . . .

"Such commissioners shall, under such regulations and directions as shall be prescribed by the President, through the Secretary of the Interior, enter upon negotiation with the several nations of Indians as aforesaid in the Indian Territory, and shall endeavor to procure, first, such allotment of lands in severalty to the Indians belonging to each such nation, tribe, or band, respectively, as may be agreed upon as just and proper to provide for each such Indian a sufficient quantity of land for his or her needs, in such equal distribution and apportionment as may be found just and suited to the circumstances; for which purpose, after the terms of such an agreement shall have been arrived at, the said commissioners shall cause the land of any such nation, or tribe, or band to be surveyed and the proper allotment to be designated; and, secondly, to procure the cession, for such price and upon such terms as shall be agreed upon, of any lands not found necessary to be so allotted or divided, to the United States; and to make proper agreements for the investment or holding by the United States of such moneys as may be paid or agreed to be paid to such nation, or tribes, or bands, or to any of the Indians thereof, for the extinguishment of their [title ?] therein. But said commissioners shall, however, have power to negotiate any and all such agreements as, in view of all the circumstances affecting the subject, shall be found requisite and suitable to such an arrangement of the rights and interests and affairs of such nations, tribes, bands, or Indians, or any of them, to enable the ultimate creation of a Territory of the United States with a view to the admission of the same as a State in the Union."

A subsequent Act, of March 2, 1895, authorized the appointment of two additional members of the commission ; and an Act of June 10, 1896, provided that " said commission is further authorized and directed to proceed at once to hear and determine the application of all persons who may apply to them for citizenship in any of said nations, and after said hearing they shall determine the right of said applicant to be so admitted and enrolled. . . . That the said commission . . . shall cause a complete roll of citizenship of each of said nations to be made up from their records, and add thereto the names of citizens whose right may be conferred under this act, and said rolls shall be, and are hereby, made rolls of citizenship of said nations or tribes, subject, however, to the determination of the United States courts, as provided herein."

A further Act of Congress, known as the Curtis Act, June 28, 1898, ratified, with some amendments, an agreement made by the commission with the Choctaws and Chickasaws, in April, 1897, and with the Creeks in September of that year, to become effective if ratified by a majority of the voters of those tribes at an election held prior to December 1, 1898. In the annual report, for 1899, made by the commission (of which the Hon. Henry L. Dawes, of Massachusetts, is chairman, and which is often referred to as "the Dawes Commission,") the following account of results is given: "A special election was called by the executives of the Choctaw and Chickasaw nations to be held August 24, and the votes cast were counted in the presence of the Commission to the Five Civilized Tribes at Atoka, August 30, resulting in the ratification of the agreement by a majority of seven hundred ninety-eight votes. Proclamation thereof was duly made, and the 'Atoka agreement,' so called, is therefore now in full force and effect in the Choctaw and Chickasaw nations. Chief Isparhecher of the Creeks was slow to call an election, and it was not until November 1, 1898, that the agreement with that tribe was submitted in its amended form for ratification. While no active interest was manifested, the full-bloods and many of the freedmen were opposed to the agreement and it failed of ratification by about one hundred and fifty votes. . . .

"The Cherokees now began to realize the sensations of 'a man without a country,' and again created a commission at a general session of the national council in November, 1898, clothed with authority to negotiate an agreement with the United States. The earlier efforts of this commission to conclude an agreement with that tribe were futile, owing to the disinclination of the Cherokee commissioners to accede to such propositions as the Government had to offer. The commission now created was limited in its power to negotiate to a period of thirty days. The United States Commission had advertised appointments in Mississippi extending from December 19, 1898, to January 7, 1899, for the purpose of identifying the Mississippi Choctaws, a duty imposed upon the commission by the act of June 28, 1898, but on receiving a communication from the chairman of the Cherokee Commission requesting a conference it was deemed desirable to postpone the appointments in Mississippi and meet the Cherokee Commission, which it did on December 19, 1898, continuing negotiations until January 14, 1899, producing the agreement which is appended hereto. In the meantime the Creeks had, by act of council, created another commission with authority to negotiate an agreement with the United States, and a conference was accorded it immediately upon conclusion of the negotiations with the Cherokees, continuing to

February 1, 1899, when an agreement was concluded. The agreement with the Cherokees was ratified by the tribe at a special election held January 31, 1899, by a majority of two thousand one hundred six votes, and that with the Creeks on February 18, 1899, by a majority of four hundred eighty-five.

"While these agreements do not in all respects embody those features which the commission desired, they were the best obtainable, and the result of most serious, patient, and earnest consideration, covering many days of arduous labor. The commissions were many times on the point of suspending negotiations, there having arisen propositions upon the part of one of the commissions which the other was unwilling to accept. Particularly were the tribal commissioners determined to fix a maximum and minimum value for the appraisement of lands, while this commission was equally vigorous in its views that the lands should be appraised at their actual value, excluding improvements, without limitations in order that an equal division might be made. The propositions finally agreed upon were the result of a compromise, without which no agreement could have been reached. The desirability, if not the absolute necessity, of securing a uniform land tenure among the Five Tribes leads the commission to recommend that these agreements, with such modifications and amendments as may be deemed wise and proper, be ratified by Congress. . . .

"The Choctaw and Chickasaw governments, in a limited way, are continued, by agreement, to March 4, 1906, and certain of their laws are therefore effective within the territory of those tribes. A similar condition exists as to the Seminoles, with which an agreement was concluded at the close of the year 1897. To supply needed laws to replace various tribal statutes which had by Congress been made inoperative, the laws of Arkansas pertaining to certain matters have been extended over Indian Territory. The Federal laws have been made to apply to still other subjects, and officials under the Interior Department are charged with the enforcement of rules and regulations governing still further matters, and so on. So complicated and complex a state of affairs does this system of jurisprudence present that the people are dazed and often unable to determine what is law and who is authorized to enforce it. Indeed, none other than an able lawyer can reasonably hope to understand the situation, and even he must be content to look upon certain phases of it as not being susceptible of solution.

"Conditions are not yet ripe for the immediate installation of a Territorial or State government. 'T is a consummation devoutly to be wished,' but wholly impracticable at this time for various reasons, not the least of which is found in the fact that there are four non-citizens in Indian Territory to every citizen. The non-citizen does not own a foot of soil, save as provisions have recently been made for the segregation and sale of town sites, and with a voice in legislation, the non-citizen would soon legislate the Indian into a state of innocuous desuetude. On the other hand, it would be manifestly unjust and at ill-accord with the spirit of our institutions to deny the right of franchise to so great a number of people, in all respects otherwise entitled to enjoy that prerogative. Another very serious obstacle to the establishment of a territorial form of government is the lack of uniform land tenures. The commission indulges in the hope and belief that at no great distant date some method may be devised whereby the lands of all the Five Tribes may be subjected to a uniform tenure. It will be seen that the legislative feature of the popular form of government is not possible at this time, and while legislation by Congress for all the petty needs of the Territory is impracticable in the highest degree, the more urgent requirements of the people must be met by this means for the present. The judicial branch is well represented by the United States courts. . . .

"The commission, in conclusion, most earnestly urges the importance of adequate appropriations for pushing to an early completion the work contemplated by the various laws and agreements under which a transformation is to be wrought in Indian Territory. The all-important and most urgent duty now devolving upon the Government of the United States incident to the translation of conditions among the Five Tribes is the allotment of lands in severalty, and the most pressing and essential preliminary steps toward that end are the completion of citizenship rolls, the appraisement of lands, and the subdivision of sections into forty-acre tracts, all of which have been already discussed in detail in this report. The commission believes that the enrollment of citizens is progressing as rapidly as the nature of the work will permit, and unless some unforeseen obstacle arises to prevent, the rolls in four of the nations will be completed and delivered to the Secretary during the fiscal year ending June 30, 1900, and very material progress made in the fifth."—*Sixth Annual Report of the Commission to the Five Civilized Tribes, 1899, pp. 66–7, and 9–29.*

A. D. 1898.—Outbreak in northern Minnesota.—An alarming outbreak of hostility on the part of some of the Indians of the Leech Lake Reservation in northern Minnesota occurred in October, 1898, provoked, as was afterwards shown, by gross frauds and abuses on the part of certain of the officials with whom they had to deal. They had been shamefully defrauded in the sale of their timber lands, which the government assumed to undertake for their benefit; but the immediate cause of trouble appeared to be a scandalous practice on the part of deputy marshals, who made arrests among them for trivial reasons, conveyed prisoners and witnesses to the federal court at St. Paul, in order to obtain fees and mileage, and left them to make their way home again as they could. The outbreak began on the arrest of a chief of the Pillager band of Chippewas, on Bear Island. He was to be taken to St. Paul as a witness in a case of alleged whiskey-selling; but his followers rescued him. The marshal, thereupon, called for military aid, and a company of U. S. infantry was sent to the Reservation. They were ambuscaded by the Indians and suffered a loss of 5 killed and 16 wounded. The Pillager band was joined by Indians from neighboring tribes, and all in the region were dangerously excited by the event, while the whites were in great dread of a general Indian war. But reinforcements of troops were promptly sent to the scene, and peace was soon restored. —measures being taken to remedy the wrongs of which the Indians complained.

A. D. 1899-1900.—The recent Indian policy of the government, and its results.—Indian schools and education.—Present Indian population.—"This, then, is the present Indian policy of the nation, — to fit the Indian for civilization and to absorb him into it. It is a national work. It is less than twenty-five years since the government turned from the policy of keeping him on reservations, as quiet as possible, out of the way of civilization, waiting, with no excess of patience, for the race to fade out of existence and to cease from troubling. It was in 1877 that the nation made the first appropriation from its own treasury to fit for its own citizenship this portion of the human race living under its own flag and constitution, but without legal status or constitutional immunities. . . . The first appropriation was a mere pittance of $20,000 ; it was given only after a hard struggle. But the first step met with encouragement, and the next year the sum was increased to $30,000, and then to $60,000, and in two years more it became $125,000. The policy has at last so grown in public confidence that, while there is still much discussion of the best methods of expenditure, not a word is heard among the lawgivers for its abandonment. It has in the meantime so broadened in its scope that the appropriations for this work have increased from year to year, till this year (1899) it has risen to $2,638,390. . . . There are now 148 well-equipped boarding schools and 295 day schools, engaged in the education of 24,004 children, with an average attendance of 19,671. How near this comes to including the whole number of children of school age, in a total population of a quarter of a million of Indians, every inquirer can form a pretty close estimate for himself. No one will deny that, at this rate of progress, the facilities for the education of Indian children will soon reach, if they have not already reached, those enjoyed by their white neighbors in the remote regions of the West. The results thus far are of a most encouraging character.

"But the work does not stop with the rising generation of the race ; it embraces also the adult Indian. . . . Soon after the beginning of appropriations for Indian schools, Congress, in what is called the Severalty Act, provided for every Indian capable of appreciating its value, and who chose to take it, a homestead of one hundred and sixty acres to heads of families, and a smaller number to other members, inalienable and untaxable for twenty-five years, to be selected by him on the reservation of his tribe. If he prefer to abandon his tribe and go elsewhere, he may take his allotment anywhere on the public domain, free of charge. No English baron has a safer title to his manor than has each Indian to his homestead. He cannot part with it for twenty-five years without the consent of Congress, nor can the United States, without his consent, be released from a covenant to defend his possession for the same period. This allotment carries with it also all the rights, privileges, and immunities of an American citizen ; opens to these Indians, as to all other citizens, the doors of all the courts; and extends to them the protection of all the laws, national and state, which affect any other citizen. Any Indian, if he prefers not to be a farmer, incumbered with one of these homesteads, may become a citizen of the United States, and reside and prosecute any calling in any part of the United States, as securely under this law as any one else by taking up his residence separate and apart from his tribe, and adopting the habits of civilized life. Thus every door of opportunity is thrown wide open to every adult Indian, as well as to those of the next generation.

"This recognition of the home and family as a force in Indian civilization became a part of the present policy of dealing with the race only twelve years ago. These are some of its results: 55,467 individual Indians, including a few under former treaty stipulations, have taken their allotments, making an aggregate of 6,708,628 acres. Of these, 30,000 now hold complete patents to their homes, and the rest are awaiting the perfection and delivery of their title deeds. . . . Not alone in these statistics are manifest the evidences of permanent advance of the race toward the goal of orderly, self-supporting citizenship. Bloody Indian wars have ceased. The slaughter of warring clans and the scalping of women and children fleeing from burning wigwams are no longer recorded. Geronimo himself has become a teacher of peace. The recent unfortunate difficulty with the Chippewas in Minnesota, caused more by lack of white than of red civilization, is no exception. We are at peace with the Indian all along the border, and the line between the Indian and the white settlements is fast fading out."— H. L. Dawes, *Have we Failed with the Indian?* (*Atlantic Monthly, August,* 1899).

"Indian education is accomplished through the means of nonreservation boarding schools, reservation boarding schools, and reservation and independent day schools, all under complete Government control, State and Territorial public schools, contract day and boarding schools, and mission day and boarding schools. The Indian school system aims to provide a training which will prepare the Indian boy or girl for the every day life of the average American citizen. It does not contemplate, as some have supposed on a superficial examination, an elaborate preparation for a collegiate course through an extended high-school curriculum. The course of instruction in these schools is limited to that usually taught in the common schools of the country. Shoe and harness making, tailoring, blacksmithing, masonry work, plastering, brick making and laying, etc., are taught at the larger nonreservation schools, not, it is true, with the elaborateness of special training as at the great polytechnic institutions of the country, but on a scale suited to the ability and future environment of the Indian. There are special cases, however, where Indian boys are, and have been, trained so thoroughly that their work compares favorably with that of the white mechanic. . . . Phoenix, Haskell, Albuquerque, and other institutions, have well-organized schools of domestic science, where the girls are practically taught the art of preparing a wholesome meal, such as appears on the tables of persons of moderate means. . . .

"Nonreservation schools . . . are as a rule the largest institutions devoted to Indian education. As indicated by their designation, they are situated off the reservations and usually near cities or populous districts, where the object lessons of white civilization are constantly presented to the pupils. They are recruited principally from the day and boarding schools on the reservations. The majority are supported by special appropriations made by Congress, and are adapted to the teaching of trades, etc., in a more extended degree than are schools on the reservations. The largest of these schools is situated at Carlisle, Pa., where there are accommodations for 1,000 pupils; the next largest is at Phoenix, Ariz., with a capacity for 700; the third, at Lawrence, Kans., and known as Haskell Institute, accommodating 600 pupils. These three large schools are types of their class, and are not restricted in territory as to collection of pupils. Chemawa school, near Salem, Oreg., and Chilocco school, near Arkansas City, Okla., are types of the medium-sized schools, and each has a capacity of 400 pupils. The remainder of the schools are of less capacity and have not been developed so highly. There are altogether 25 of these schools. . . .

"There are 81 boarding schools located on the different reservations, an increase of 11 over last year. At these institutions the same general line of policy is pursued as at the nonreservation schools. Frequently located far from the centers of civilization, conditions are different, and their conduct must be varied to suit their own special environment. Many were formerly mission schools and army posts, unsuited to Indian school purposes, but by constant modification are being brought into general harmony with the system. . . . Government day schools are small schools with capacity for 30 or 40 pupils each. As a rule they are located at remote points on the reservations, and are conducted by a teacher and a housekeeper. A small garden, some stock, and tools are furnished, and the rudiments of industrial education are given the boys; and the girls are taught the use of the needle in mending and sewing, and of the washtub in cleanliness. . . . There were 147 day schools in operation during the year, an increase of 5 over last year."

The number of government schools reported for the year 1900 was 253, total enrollment, 22,-124, average attendance, 17,860; contract schools, 32, with an enrollment of 2,806, average attendance, 2,451; public and mission schools, 22, with an enrollment of 1,521, and an average attendance of 1,257; the aggregate being 307 schools, with an enrollment of 26,451, and an average attendance of 21,568. "Statistics of the schools for the New York Indians are not included in the above, for the reason that as they are cared for by the State of New York this office has no jurisdiction over them. . . . The Indian population of the United States under the control of the Indian Office (excluding the Five Civilized Tribes) was 187,312 in 1899, which would give a scholastic population of between 45,000 and 47,000. Deduct 30 per cent for the sick and otherwise disabled, and those in white schools or away from the direct control of the office, and it would leave about 34,000 children for whom educational facilities should be provided. There are now 26,000 of them in school, leaving about 8,000 unprovided for."—*Annual Report of the Commissioner of Indian Affairs,* 1900, pp. 15–23.

"Taking the concurrent facts of history and experience into consideration, it can, with a great degree of confidence, be stated that the Indian population of the United States has been very little diminished from the days of Columbus, Coronado, Raleigh, Capt. John Smith, and other early explorers." The number of Indians in the United States in the year 1900, according to the report of the Indian Office, was 272,023. This excludes "the Indians of Alaska, but includes the New York Indians (5,334) and the Five Civilized Tribes in Indian Territory (84,750)—a total population of 90,084. These Indians are often separated from the others in statistics because they have separate school and governmental systems."—*Annual Report of the Commissioner of Indian Affairs, 1900, pp. 47–49.*

INDONESIAN RACE. See (in this vol.) PHILIPPINE ISLANDS: THE NATIVE INHABITANTS.

INDUSTRIAL ARBITRATION. See (in this vol.) NEW ZEALAND: A. D. 1891–1900 ; and UNITED STATES OF AM.: A. D. 1898 (JUNE).

INDUSTRIAL COMBINATIONS. See (in this vol.) TRUSTS; UNITED STATES.

INDUSTRIAL COMMISSION, The United States. See (in this vol.) UNITED STATES OF AM.: A. D. 1898 (JUNE).

INDUSTRIAL DISTURBANCES, Wide-spread: A. D. 1895-1896.—Strike of glassworkers in France.—A great strike of French glassworkers, beginning in the summer of 1895, ended the following January in a lockout of the men, leaving thousands without means of subsistence.

A. D. 1897.—The great dispute in the British engineering trades.—"The strike originated in an effort on the part of some of the men employed in London to introduce the eight-hour day. As a consequence of this movement, the Employers' Federation voted, on July 1st, that in case the threatened movement in favor of eight hours should be carried out 'notices will immediately be given by the members of the associations affiliated to the federation that a reduction of hands of 25 per cent. will take place of the members of such unions in their employment.' This challenge of the employers was quickly taken up by the Unionists. The Amalgamated Society at once gave instructions that in all cases in which notices of lockout were issued to 25 per cent. of their members, the remaining 75 per cent. should hand in notices to cease work at the same time. The result was the inauguration of a dispute, which took in part the form of a lockout, in part that of a strike, but which from the beginning was carried on with an ominous display of bitterness and obstinacy on both sides. The membership of the different societies concerned in the dispute was estimated, by the Labor Gazette in July, at over 109,000. All of these were not, of course, actually on strike. . . . It seems as if the employers had been quite ready to enter into this contest with the view of crushing the union, or at least of teaching it a lesson; but the result is a very widespread industrial conflict, which is producing results far beyond those immediately concerned."—*Yale Review (November, 1897).*

"The number of workpeople directly affected by the dispute was about 25,000 at the outset, but as the area of the dispute widened the number of firms and of workmen involved gradually increased, until the lock-out involved 702 firms and 35,000 workmen directly and 12,500 indirectly. . . . Though the immediate cause of the

general dispute was the demand for an eight hours' day in London, the real questions at issue between the parties had become of a much more far-reaching kind, and now involved the questions of workshop control and the limits of trade union interference. During October and November negotiations under the Conciliation Act took place between the Board of Trade and the representatives of the parties with a view to arrange a conference between them. As a result of the correspondence both sides assented to the following basis for a conference suggested by the Board of Trade :—1. The Federated Employers, while disavowing any intention of interfering with the legitimate action of trade unions, will admit no interference with the management of their business. The Trade Unions on their part, while maintaining their right of combination, disavow any intention of interfering with the management of the business of the employers. 2. The notices demanding a 48 hours' week served on the Federated Employers in London without previous request for a conference are withdrawn. 3. A conference between representatives of the Federated Employers and the Trade Unions concerned in the dispute shall be held forthwith. . . . Pending the conference the employers agreed to suspend all pending lock-out notices, and the Unions not to interfere in any way with men in employment. . . .

"The sittings were held on November 24th and two following days, and again on November 30th and three following days, after which an adjournment took place until December 14th in order to allow the men to vote as to the acceptance or otherwise of the proposals made by the employers. . . . When the Conference resumed its sittings on December 14th the result of the ballot of the men was declared to be :—For the terms, 752; against, 68,966. Discussion of the proposals was, however, resumed and continued over four days by a sub-committee of three representatives on each side, who consulted with their colleagues when necessary. The terms were somewhat amended. . . . On submitting these amended conditions to the vote of the men 1,041 voted in favour of their acceptance and 54,933 against. The truce which had been arranged over the period of negotiations was brought to an end by this vote, and fresh notices of lock-out were given in various centres, which considerably increased the numbers affected. . . .

"On January 13th, however, an important change was made in the position of the men. The London Joint Committee, the body which took the first actual step in the dispute by ordering strike notices to be given in certain London shops, passed the following resolution:—That we intimate to the Employers' Federation that the demand for an eight hours' day, or forty-eight hours' week be withdrawn. That before such intimation is given the above resolution is to be sent to the Executive Councils of the Societies represented on the Joint Committee for their approval or otherwise. . . . This resolution received the approval of the trade unions concerned, and the withdrawal of the demand for a 48 hours' week was intimated to the Employers' Federation. which, however, still insisted on the acceptance by the unions of the 'conditions of management mutually adjusted at the recent Westminster Conference' as a condition of returning to work. The men asked that the employers' notes and explanations should be read as part of the proposed agreement, and eventually, after renewed negotiations between the parties, a provisional agreement was arrived at and submitted to the votes of the men, who ratified it by 28,598 to 13,727. The final agreement was signed in London on January 28th, and work was resumed in the following week. . . .

"Naturally, after so long a stoppage the resumption of work by the men was a gradual process, but the number unemployed owing to the dispute, including those indirectly affected, sank from 44,500 at the close of the lock-out to 7,500 at the end of February, 2,000 at the end of April, 1,500 at the end of May, and 1,000 at the end of June. . . . Some idea of the indirect effects of the stoppage on trades related to those engaged in the struggle may be formed from the fact that the percentage of unemployed members in trade unions of the ship-building group rose from 4.4 per cent. in July, to 14.1 per cent. in December."— *Great Britain, Board of Trade (Labour Department), Report on the Strikes and Lock-outs of* 1897.

A. D. 1897.—Great coal miners' strike in the United States.—A general strike of the coal miners in the various districts of the United States began in July, 1897. The territory covered five states and involved about 157,000 men. The strikers asked for an advance in wages on the ground that it was their right to share in the increase of business prosperity and advanced prices. A grievance for which redress was asked was that of being obliged to buy at the company stores, paying in company's orders, to be deducted from their wages. The principal grievance was the 54-cent rate, paid by Mr. W. P. De Armitt of the New York and Cleveland Gas Coal Company. The men employed by Mr. De Armitt had signed a contract to accept a rate 10 cents below that of other operators, in return for which he had abolished company stores, gave steady employment, and paid promptly in cash. His men were satisfied with the arrangement, although the prevailing price for mining coal was 64 cents a ton. Most of them, however, were finally forced by the organization to join the strikers. The strike lasted until September 12, when matters were arranged in a convention at Columbus, Ohio, when a uniform rate of 65 cents was adopted.

A tragic feature of the strike occurred at Lattimer, Penn., where a mob of marching miners, resisting the sheriff and handling him roughly, were fired upon by armed deputies. Eighteen were killed and about forty wounded.

A. D. 1898.—New England cotton mill strike.—In January a general strike, affecting 125,000 operatives, resulted from a reduction in wages in 150 cotton mills of New England. By April most of the strikers returned to work at the manufacturers' terms.

A. D. 1898.—Coal miners' strike in Illinois.—This strike, beginning in May, originated in the refusal of the mine operators to grant the rate of 40 cents a ton, agreed upon after the strike of 1897. The operators refused to compromise and the miners were upheld by the United Mine Workers. Riots arose in the towns of Pana and Virden upon the attempt of the mine owners to import negro workers from the south. Governor Tanner, in sending troops to restore order, enjoined upon them to protect citizens, but on no

account to assist mine owners to operate their mines with imported labor. The governor's attitude provoked much criticism. A serious outbreak occurred on October 12, at Virden, when 14 persons were killed and 25 wounded. The strike at Virden was settled in November, the mine owners agreeing to the demands of the miners. The trouble at Pana lasted until April, when a settlement was arrived at.

A. D. 1900.—Anthracite coal miners' strike in Pennsylvania.—A great strike of the anthracite mine workers of Pennsylvania, which began September 17, practically ended October 17, when the Philadelphia and Reading Coal and Iron Company and the Lehigh Valley Coal Company agreed to abolish the sliding scale in their respective regions and to grant an advance in wages of 10 per cent. net, the advance to remain in operation until April 1, 1901, and thereafter till further notice. Mr. John Mitchell, president of the Mine Workers' National Union, in a speech soon after the end of the strike, said that of the 142,000 men concerned "at first only 8,000 men were in the union or organized. Nevertheless, the day the strike began, 112,000 men laid down their tools; and when the strike ended, after 39 days of non-employment, all but 2,000 of them had joined the ranks of the union."

INDUSTRIAL REVOLUTION, in the United States. See (in this vol.) UNITED STATES OF AM.: A. D. 1897.

INITIATIVE IN SWITZERLAND, The. See (in this vol.) SWITZERLAND: A. D. 1894–1898.

INSURANCE, Compulsory, in Germany. See (in this vol.) GERMANY: A. D. 1897–1900.

INTERCONTINENTAL RAILWAY, The. See (in this vol.) RAILWAY, INTERCONTINENTAL.

INTERNATIONAL ARBITRATION. See (in this vol.) ARBITRATION, INTERNATIONAL.

INTERNATIONAL CATALOGUING, of Scientific Literature. See (in this vol.) SCIENCE, RECENT: SCIENTIFIC LITERATURE.

INTERNATIONAL COMMERCIAL CONGRESS.—An important step in promotion of the development of international commerce was taken at Philadelphia, in October, 1899, by the assembling of an International Commercial Congress, under the auspices of the Philadelphia Commercial Museum and the Franklin Institute, with the co-operation, not only of the city and the State, but also of the Congress of the United States. Some forty governments, and a great number of chambers of commerce and other business organizations were represented, and much good was expected from the meeting. It adopted resolutions urging co-operative and assimilated action by all nations, in the registration of trade marks, in the preparation of trade statistics and agricultural reports, and in the establishing of the parcels post. It commended the Philadelphia Commercial Museum as an example to be imitated ; urged the construction of an interoceanic canal, recommended free trade in artistic works, and pleaded for the pacific settlement of international disputes by arbitration. At the time of the session of the Congress, a

National Export Exposition was being held at Philadelphia, under the same auspices, with great success.

INTEROCEANIC CANAL. See (in this vol.) CANAL, INTEROCEANIC.

INTEROCEANIC RAILWAY, The Tehuantepec. See (in this vol.) MEXICO : A. D. 1898-1900.

INTER-STATE COMMERCE, American.—Arbitration of industrial disputes. See (in this vol.) UNITED STATES OF AM.: A. D. 1898 (JUNE).

INVENTIONS: Comparison of the Nineteenth Century with preceding ages. See (in this vol.) NINETEENTH CENTURY : COMPARISON.

IRADE. See (in this vol.) TURKEY: A. D. 1895.

IRELAND.

A. D. 1890-1900.—Hopeful work in the organization and systematization of Irish agriculture.—"Can nothing be made of an essentially food-producing country situated at the very door of the greatest market for food-stuffs that the world has ever seen ? Government has at last moved in this matter, but, as usual, not before private initiation had shamed them into action. Mr. Horace Plunkett and his friends went to work ten years ago, pointing out that Ireland had natural resources equal or superior to those of countries which were driving her few products out of the English market, and preached the organisation, the co-operation, and the scientific methods of agriculture which in those other countries were inculcated and subsidised by state agencies. Then the Congested Districts Board, under the auspices of Mr. Arthur Balfour, began its beneficent work. Then came in 1895 the Recess Committee, on Mr. Plunkett's suggestion ; and finally, in 1899, the recommendations of that Committee's invaluable Report were practically embodied in the creation of a Board of Agriculture and Technical Instruction. This body has scarcely as yet begun its work, but its main business will be to do throughout the whole of Ireland what has been done in the least hopeful districts by the Congested Districts Board, and over a larger area, but with very inadequate means, by the Irish Agricultural Organisation Society, of which Mr. Plunkett has been the moving spirit. Things are therefore only at their beginning. . . . The main purpose of the Irish Agricultural Organisation Society has been not to create new industries but to organize and systematise the one already existing — the characteristic Irish industry of agriculture. It has done the work which in France, Denmark, Canada, and a dozen other countries that can be named, is being done by a State department; and the efforts of its promoters have brought into being such a department for Ireland also. The Society spent in nine years £15,000 of subscriptions. This neither can last nor ought to last. It is the business 'of the Department, if it does not supersede the Society, to subsidise it." —Stephen Gwynn, *A Month in Ireland* (*Blackwood's Magazine*, Oct., 1900, p. 573).—The most effective work done thus far, by the official and private agencies above mentioned, appears to have been in the organization of co-operative creameries and dairies.

A. D. 1894.—Cooling of the Liberal party towards Irish Home Rule. See (in this vol.) ENGLAND : A. D. 1894-1895.

A. D. 1896.—A new Land Act.—"The celebrated Land Act of 1881, supplemented by Acts in the same direction, placed the land of

Ireland, as everyone knows, under a system of perpetual leases, at State-settled rents, renewable every fifteen years ; and, in 1896, the time was at hand for revising the rents fixed from 1881 onwards, and for renewing the leases made during this interval of time. An Act, accordingly, was passed through Parliament in order fully to accomplish this end; and, incidentally, it dealt with many other things connected with the Irish Land System, and with the legislation inaugurated in 1881. It enlarged the sphere of State-settled rent, bringing within it certain classes of tenants which, hitherto, had been excluded from it ; it placed the law for exempting tenants' improvements from rent, to a considerable extent, on a new basis ; and it introduced, for the first time, what is called the principal of 'compulsory purchase' into the system of 'Land Purchase,' so named in Ireland, always a favourite policy of Lord Salisbury's Governments." —Judge O'Connor Morris, *The Report of the Fry Commission* (*Fortnightly Rev., Nov.*, 1898).—The new bill (59 & 60 Vict. ch. 47) was carried successfully through Parliament by the Government, with skillful management on the part of Mr. Gerald Balfour, the Secretary for Ireland, after many amendments and much debate. It was a compromise measure, reluctantly accepted and satisfying no interest or party. The general feeling with which it was passed is described as follows : " The practical result of the discussion was to show that the bill did not go so far as Mr. T. W. Russell, a member of the Government and the representative of the Ulster farmers, wished ; that the section of the Nationalists headed by Mr. Dillon were anxious to throw cold water upon it, but afraid to oppose it openly ; and that Mr. Healy and his friends, as well as the Parnellites, were ready to do their best to ensure its passing. But while the representatives of the tenants were ready to accept the bill as an installment of their claims, they at the same time pronounced it to be inadequate. . . . The Dillonites were unwilling to give the Healyites and the Parnellites the chance of taunting them with having lost the bill, whilst the landlords hoped for an improvement of the purchase clauses and a reform of procedure in the law courts. . . . The debate on the third reading, although not forced to a division, was spirited ; the landlords opposing it because it was too much of a tenant's bill, and Mr. Davitt opposing it because it was too much of a landlords' bill. Mr. Dillon and his followers voted for it, but in their speeches did all they could to run it down, while the Parnellites and Healyites did all in their power to support it."—*Annual Register*, 1896, *pp.* 160-61.

1896-1897.—Report of a Royal Commission on the Financial Relations between Great Britain and Ireland.—"At various times since the passing of the Act of Legislative Union between Great Britain and Ireland, complaints have been made that the financial arrangements between the two countries were not satisfactory, or in accordance with the principles of that Act, and that the resources of Ireland have had to bear an undue pressure of taxation. Inquiries into the truth of these allegations have frequently been called for"; but it was not until 1894 that provision was made for a thorough investigation of the subject. In that year a Royal Commission was appointed, with Mr. Childers, ex-Chancellor of the Exchequer, at its head, "to inquire into the financial relations between Great Britain and Ireland, and their relative taxable capacity, and to report :—(1.) Upon what principles of comparison, and by the application of what specific standards, the relative capacity of Great Britain and Ireland to bear taxation may be most equitably determined. (2.) What, so far as can be ascertained, is the true proportion, under the principles and specific standards so determined, between the taxable capacity of Great Britain and Ireland. (3.) The history of the financial relations between Great Britain and Ireland at and after the Legislative Union, the charge for Irish purposes on the Imperial Exchequer during that period, and the amount of Irish taxation remaining available for contribution to Imperial expenditure; also the Imperial expenditure to which it is considered equitable that Ireland should contribute."

The Commission made its "Final Report" in 1896, submitting the conclusions on which its members were unanimously agreed, and presenting, further, no less than seven differing reports on other points upon which agreement could not be reached. The summary of conclusions in the unanimous joint report was as follows : "In carrying out the inquiry we have ascertained that there are certain questions upon which we are practically unanimous, and we think it expedient to set them out in this joint report. Our conclusions on these questions are as follows :— I. That Great Britain and Ireland must, for the purpose of this inquiry, be considered as separate entities. II. That the Act of Union imposed upon Ireland a burden which, as events showed, she was unable to bear. III. That the increase of taxation laid upon Ireland between 1853 and 1860 was not justified by the then existing circumstances. IV. That identity of rates of taxation does not necessarily involve equality of burden. V. That whilst the actual tax revenue of Ireland is about one-eleventh of that of Great Britain the relative taxable capacity of Ireland is very much smaller, and is not estimated by any of us as exceeding one-twentieth."—*Great Britain, Parliamentary Publications (Papers by Command : C.—8262, pp. 1–2).*

The report was keenly criticised in England, and the fact that it emanated from a Commission in which the majority were partisans of Irish Home Rule was used by the Conservatives to disparage its conclusions. A new investigation of the subject was called for. The subject came before Parliament in the session of 1897,—first in the Lords, and later in the Commons. On the 30th of March, Mr. Blake, a member from Ireland, moved a resolution in the House of Commons, to the effect that the report of the Commission had established the existence of an undue burden of taxation on Ireland and made it the duty of the Government to propose remedial legislation at an early day. The debate which this opened was continued during three nights, at the end of which the motion was negatived by a vote of 317 to 157.

A. D. **1898** (July).—The Local Government Act.—A bill which had great success, so far as it went, in satisfying the representatives of Ireland in the Parliament of the United Kingdom, was brought forward there, by the Conservative Government, in February, 1898, and carried through both Houses in July. It was accepted by the Irish as "no substitute for Home Rule," but as a recognized "step in that direction." It had been foreshadowed in the Queen's Speech at the opening of Parliament, and described as a measure "for the organisation of a system of local government in Ireland substantially similar to that which, within the last few years, has been established in Great Britain." This important Act established County Councils, Urban District Councils, Rural District Councils, and Boards of Guardians, all elected by ballot every three years, on a franchise broader than the Parliamentary franchise, since it gave the local suffrage to women. The same Act extended to Ireland the provisions of the Act for the relief of agricultural land, and contained some other welcome provisions of financial relief.— 61 & 62 *Vict. ch. 37.*

"To understand the extent of the change which is now determined on . . . it is necessary first to describe the system of Irish Local Government which is about to pass away forever. Broadly speaking, that system consisted of three parts, viz.: the Grand Jury, the Poor Law Boards, and various forms of Municipal Government in towns and cities. . . . The Grand Jury was about the most anomalous and indefensible institution which can be conceived. It consisted, usually, of a couple of dozen persons chosen from a larger number selected by the High Sheriff for the county or the city, as the ease might be, the High Sheriff himself being the nominee of the Lord Lieutenant, who acted on the recommendation of the Superior Court Judges, who, in their turn, always recommended some leading landlord and magistrate. . . . The Grand Jury in every Irish county, down even to the present year, has always consisted almost entirely of members of the landlord class, and mainly of Protestants also. To bodies thus constituted was entrusted the control of all public roads and other public works of the county, the contracts therefor, the management of the prisons, the care of the public buildings, the power to contribute to infirmaries, lunatic asylums and fever hospitals, the appointment of all the paid officials of the county, and the right to levy a tax called the county cess, which, of late years, has produced considerably more than a million pounds sterling annually. Associated with the Grand Juries were smaller bodies, the members of which met at 'Presentment Sessions' once or twice a year to initiate county works. Those bodies also were non-elective, and represented mainly the landlords and magistrates of the respective counties. In the old days, these Grand Juries became— not unnaturally — not merely nests of jobbery and corruption, but an agency of social and political oppression. . . .

For many years past, indeed, the Grand Juries have not been open to all those charges. They have not, as a rule, been the corrupt jobbers they were forty or fifty years ago. Their administration of the business entrusted to them has been fairly honest and efficient. But in their constitution they have, on the whole, continued to be what they were. . . .

"The Boards of Poor Law Guardians have in the course of time become more or less popular bodies, and, besides their original function of dispensing relief out of the rates to the destitute poor, have been invested with the management of so many other matters in recent years that their title is now really a misnomer. They are, for instance, the sanitary authorities in all rural and in some urban districts; they have to do with the registration of births, deaths, and marriages, and—not to go through the whole list of their powers and duties—they have had the administration of the Laborers' Acts, under which a good deal has been done, since the year 1883, to improve the homes of agricultural laborers.

"It remains to notice the system of Government in the towns and cities. In this case there has been some degree of reality in the phrase, 'local self-government'—at least, for the last forty or fifty years. Down to 1840 there was no really representative system of government in any Irish town or city. . . . Since the year mentioned the corporations have been more or less representative, and since 1854 the smaller towns in Ireland have been allowed the right to possess municipal institutions of a less important, but still representative, character. In respect, however, of both the corporations of the cities and of the town boards of the smaller civic communities, the franchise for municipal purposes has been ridiculously restricted. In Dublin, the population exceeds 300,000; the Parliamentary electorate is upwards of 40,000; but the municipal electorate amounts to only about 8,000 or 9,000; and the same story is true of all the other municipalities, except a few which, like Belfast, have by special acts of Parliament obtained extensions of the suffrage peculiar to themselves.

"Here, then, was a state of things which, assuredly, required mending, and, as I have said, innumerable efforts to mend it had been made up to last year with no result. Last summer, however, the reform now virtually accomplished was announced to the House of Commons one afternoon by Mr. Arthur Balfour, without anyone having asked for it and without any warning whatever. The chief features of the measure may be briefly described. In the first place, the ground is cleared by absolutely sweeping away the Grand Juries for fiscal purposes. Those bodies are still retained for their original purpose—that, namely, of dealing with indictments. . . . With them go the Boards of Guardians as they are at present constituted. Bodies will still continue to exist under that name, but they will be no longer constituted as they are now. . . . In the place of the Grand Juries and the Boards of Guardians there has been set up a rather complicated system of County Councils and District Councils, these latter being sub-divided into two classes—Urban District Councils and Rural District Councils; and at this point one provision applicable to all those bodies, and also to every Corporation and Town Board in the country, may be conveniently mentioned. It is that which

enacts that the electorate in each case shall be the Parliamentary electorate, in addition to peers and to such women as would, if they were men, be qualified for the Parliamentary franchise. Here is manifestly a great reform in itself. . . . The change is a vast one, in view of the narrow foundation on which even the most popular Irish local institutions have hitherto rested. It means the transfer of power from a class to the people. It means the ousting of what used to be the English garrison in Ireland from what it had come to regard as its inalienable heritage. It marks the entry of the Irish Nation, after ages of weary waiting, into at least a considerable portion of its birthright. To the County Councils, which will thus repose on a thoroughly popular basis, and one of which will be established in every county, will be entrusted all the fiscal business of the Grand Juries, with one exception. The excepted business is that of assessing compensation for malicious injuries."—J. J. Clancy, *The Latest Reform in Ireland* (*North American Review, Sept.*, 1898).

A. D. 1900 (April). — Visit of Queen Victoria.—For the first time in nearly forty years, Queen Victoria paid a visit to Ireland in April, and held court in Dublin for three weeks, being cordially received and treated throughout with respect by well-mannered crowds. Apparently the visit gave satisfaction to most of the Irish people.

A. D. 1900-1901.—Parliamentary elections. —Triumph of the United Irish League.—Its absorption of the Nationalist party.—Its programme.—The elections to a new Parliament (see, in this vol., ENGLAND: A. D. 1900, SEPTEMBER—OCTOBER), held in October, resulted in a sweeping victory for the United Irish League, a new organization formed by Mr. William O'Brien, which, according to the "London Times," "has practically absorbed the whole of the Irish Nationalist party" and "is the successor in title of the old Land League." "Mr. William O'Brien," says the "Times," "returned his own followers to Parliament from practically every Nationalist constituency in Ireland. . . . For the moment at least all the other successors of Mr. Parnell are vanquished or in captivity, and Mr. O'Brien finds himself at the head of a party which for the first time in ten years has the right to call itself 'united.'"

On the opening of the Parliament, in the following February, the new League was soon brought to its attention by Mr. O'Brien, who moved, on the 22d, to amend the Address to the King, which was then under discussion, by adding to it the following : "Humbly to represent to your Majesty that this House has observed that a combination of the agricultural classes in Ireland has been formed, under the name of the United Irish League, with the object of accomplishing reforms which alone, in the opinion of nine-tenths of the constitutional representatives of Ireland, can arrest the continued depopulation of that country and the decay of its only great national industry. These reforms being, first, the creation of an occupying proprietary in substitution for the present unsettled and vexatious system of dual ownership of land; and, secondly, the utilization of extensive tracts, at present lying practically waste in the congested districts, for the purpose of supplying holdings of sufficient extent to a hard-working

271

and deserving population, who for want of land are compelled to live in a condition of chronic privation and even famine on the borders of those fertile depopulated areas; that the movement which has been carried on for the past three years for the promotion of these objects has been marked by the disappearance of those crimes of violence and secret conspiracies which were used to the discredit of all former agrarian combinations in Ireland, and the league, basing itself on the principle that its struggle is in the nature of a great economic industrial dispute between the tillers of the soil on the one side and the rent-owners, supported by a vast capital and territorial influence, on the other, has relied for success upon those combinations for mutual protection and appeals to public opinion which the trade union laws have expressly authorized in the cause of disputes between capital and labour of a non-agricultural character; that, nevertheless, this House has observed that the forces of the Crown have been unconstitutionally employed, and public justice has been polluted in the interest of one of the parties to the dispute; that the right of public meeting has been capriciously suppressed; that prosecutions for conspiracy and Whiteboyism have been instituted in reference to open and advised appeals to public opinion and measures of mutual protection, which are indisputably within the right of trade unions in ordinary industrial struggles; that the power of contempt of Court has been unconstitutionally and oppressively abused for the purpose of inflicting prolonged sentences of imprisonment without trial; that the right of trial by jury has been outraged by the systematic exclusion from the jury-box of all jurors sharing the politics or creed of the accused, and the empanelling of juries composed exclusively of sympathizers with the territorial class, that the liberty of the Press in Ireland has been assailed, and influential organs of opinion prosecuted in the endeavour to silence public comment on this iniquitous system; that grievous and vindictive fines have been exacted from districts obnoxious to the landlord interest by means of charges for extra police quartered upon peaceful populations, and that the people of Ireland have been subjected to divers others the like cruel oppressions and provocations; and humbly to represent to your Majesty that, it being of the highest constitutional import to encourage the Irish people to seek the redress of their grievances by the fullest freedom of speech and of combination which is warranted by the example of the trade unions of

Great Britain, this House is of opinion that the attacks at present directed by the Executive against the rights of free speech and of combination in Ireland should cease, and that the legislation protecting the trade unions in the exercise of their rights of combination against capital and non-union labour should be extended to all agricultural combinations of a similar character in that country."

In his speech supporting the amendment Mr. O'Brien charged that, "there being no real crime in Ireland, the Executive there had made crime of perfectly legitimate actions, treating the people as if the object was to goad them into conspiracy and violence. The record of the league was virtually a crimeless one, it had carried on its work now for three years without any of those blood-curdling incidents which coercion Ministers used to smack their lips over in that House. . . . The league, which had been tested by time and had proved its power at the general election, had started and carried on in Ireland an irresistible agitation for the suppression, for the abolition of landlordism, and had elicited in the King's first Speech a promise, such as it was, of another land Bill, although two years ago that House was assured that there was no longer an Irish land question."

An extensive combination, he said, was going on in Ireland against the taking of evicted farms, and "what form of trade unionism could be more legitimate?" But charges of intimidation and conspiracy, he claimed, were trumped up, and juries were packed, for the suppression of this movement, though it went no farther than trades unions in England could go with no interference. "The Irish people exercised the right of combination in the United Irish League, and they would continue to exercise it whether the Government liked it or not, in order to obtain the land on conditions that would give its cultivators a living wage. In the ranks of the organization were 500,000 farmers and labourers, representing with their families three-fourths of the population of Ireland. Their object was to parcel out the vast grazing lands lying derelict among the cottagers who were starving on their verge. A department of the Government was actually engaged in carrying out the programme of the league, but at such a snail's pace that it would take centuries to make any impression upon the mass of misery which existed in the country."

After several hours of debate the amendment to the Address was rejected by 203 votes against 109.

IRON, Combinations in the production of. See (in this vol.) TRUSTS: UNITED STATES.

IRON GATES OF THE DANUBE, Opening of the. See (in this vol.) AUSTRIA-HUNGARY: A. D. 1896.

ISLE DU DIABLE. See (in this vol.) FRANCE: A. D. 1897-1899.

ISRAEL, The People of: Discovery of the sole mention of them in Egyptian inscriptions.

See (in this vol.) ARCHÆOLOGICAL RESEARCH: EGYPT: RESULTS.

ISTHMIAN CANAL, The. See (in this vol.) CANAL, INTEROCEANIC.

ISTHMIAN RAILWAY, The Tehuantepec. See (in this vol.) MEXICO: A. D. 1898-1900.

ITAGAKI, Count: Leader of the Japanese Liberal party. See (in this vol.) JAPAN: A. D. 1890-1898.

ITALY.

Recent archæological explorations. See (in this vol.) ARCHÆOLOGICAL RESEARCH : ITALY.

A. D. 1895-1896.—Accusations against the Crispi Ministry.—Fresh offense to the Vatican.—Disastrous war with Abyssinia.—Fall of Crispi.—In elections to the Italian Chamber of Deputies, which took place in May, 1895, the government, under Signor Crispi, was accused of audacious practices, striking the names of opposed electors from the voting lists, to the number, it is said, of several hundreds of thousands, and contriving otherwise to paralyze the opposition to itself. The result of the elections was the return of 336 government candidates, against 98 of other parties. An attempt to obtain an official return of all the deputies who were receiving pay from the State, directly or indirectly, was skilfully baffled by Signor Crispi, and remained a matter of rumor and guess. In September, the government gave fresh offense to the Vatican by an imposing celebration of the 25th anniversary of the entry of the Italian troops into Rome, with a display of the flag of free-masonry.

Hostility of France and Russia to Italy was made acute "by the renewal, on the return of Lord Salisbury to office in 1895, of an agreement between England, Austria and Italy for common action in the Eastern question, originally made in 1887. In virtue of this agreement Italy sent her fleet to the Aegean to support Great Britain at the opening of the Armenian question [see, in this vol., TURKEY : A. D. 1895, and after], and the consequence was that France and Russia put pressure on Abyssinia to renew hostilities against Italy. This new campaign Crispi was ill-prepared to meet, as he had detailed a corps d'armée for an expedition to Asia Minor in conjunction with the naval preparations, and the strength of the forces under arms did not enable the minister of war to detach another corps to Erythrea. To complete the difficulties of the position, a coolness arose between the Emperor of Germany and the government of Crispi, the latter having notified the German government that he should at the proper time denounce the Treaty of the Triple Alliance with the object of providing better security for Italian interests in Africa. The Emperor in reply advised the King of Italy that Crispi was becoming importunate and must be got rid of. This defection probably determined the fall of Crispi. It gave such strength to the opposition at home, that the intrigues of the Court and military circles succeeded in paralyzing all his military plans, and especially in preventing him from superseding Baratieri, now recognized as incompetent for the enlarged operations which were in view. The King refused to consent to the suppression until it became imperative through the increase of the force to a point at which a superior officer was necessitated by the regulations, when Baldissera was appointed to the superior command. But before Baldissera could enter on his command, Baratieri, against the distinct orders of the government, attacked with a force of 14,000 men the impregnable positions near Adowah which Menelek held with 80,000. He was met by the most crushing defeat that Italy has had to undergo in modern times. Out of the total force no less than 6,000 perished.

"The history of this affair still remains more or less a secret, the court-martial which followed being rather calculated to bury than expose the facts of the case, but the immediate effect was to induce the ministry to resign without waiting for the assembling of parliament. The magnitude of the disaster made it evident that, considering the Italian temperament and its tendency to panic, the responsibility for it would be visited on the ministry, though it was only responsible in so far as it had submitted to the Royal decision deferring the recall of Baratieri. The King, unwilling to accept the programme of Rudini, gave the formation of the new ministry to General Ricotti, a Senator, Rudini taking the portfolio of home affairs (March, 1896). . . . The scheme of army reorganization proposed by Ricotti, which aimed at improving the efficiency of the force by devoting money rather to the instruction of the rank and file than to the maintenance of superfluous officers, was opposed, . . . the law was defeated in the chamber, and Ricotti gave place to Rudini as President of the Council. The rejection of Ricotti's plan was a triumph for the Franco-Russian party, which had re-assumed the direction of foreign affairs. Africa, under this policy, being excluded from the Italian sphere of action, peace was made with Menelek [October 26, 1896] on terms which practically implied withdrawal from Erythrea to the port of Massowah. This measure satisfied the exigencies of the old Right, while the Radicals were conciliated by the exclusion and proscription of Crispi and by the understanding with France, as well as by the reversal of the repressive policy towards the extreme members of their party. Thus the year 1897 saw Italy reduced to inertia abroad and apathy within."—W. J. Stillman, *The Union of Italy, ch.* 15 (*Cambridge : University Press*).

The peace made with King Menelek in 1896 ended the Italian claim to a protectorate over Abyssinia, which seems never to have had any basis of right. It started from a treaty negotiated in 1889, known as the Treaty of Uchali, which purported to be no more than an ordinary settlement of friendly relations, commercial and political. But the convention contained a clause which is said to have read in the Amharic (the court and official language of Abyssinia), "the King of Abyssinia may make use of the government of the King of Italy in all matters whereon he may have to treat with other governments." In the Italian version of the treaty, the innocent permissive phrase, "may make use," became, it is said, an obligatory "agrees to make use," &c., and was so communicated to foreign governments, furnishing grounds for a claim of "protection" which the Abyssinians rejected indignantly. Hence the wars which proved disastrous to Italy.

A. D. 1897.—Dissolution of the Chamber.—Election of Deputies.—Reconstruction of the Ministry.—Early in the year a royal decree dissolved the Chamber of Deputies, and elections held in March gave the Rudini Ministry a large majority. The Catholic party refrained almost entirely from voting. But divisions arose in the course of the year which brought about a reconstruction of the Cabinet in December, Signor Rudini still being at the head. An important event of the year was the resolution of the Italian

6–18

government to evacuate Kassala, on the Abyssinian frontier, directly eastward from Khartum. The Italians had taken it from the Mahdists in 1894. It now became part of the Anglo-Egyptian territory.

A. D. 1898.—Arbitration Treaty with Argentine Republic. See (in this vol.) ARGENTINE REPUBLIC: A. D. 1898.

A. D. 1898 (March—June).—Report on charges against Signor Crispi.—His resignation from Parliament and re-election.— Change of Ministry.—In March, a special commission, appointed the previous December, to investigate certain serious charges against the ex-Premier, Signor Crispi, reported his culpability, but that nothing in his conduct could be brought for trial before the High Court. The charges were connected with a scandalous wrecking of several banks, at Rome, Naples, and elsewhere, which had occurred during Signor Crispi's administration, and which was found to be due to political extortions practiced on those institutions by members and agents of the government. Personally, it did not appear that the ex-Premier had profited by what was done ; but his wife seemed to have been a large recipient of gain, and moneys wrung from the banks had been used for party political purposes and for the government secret service fund. On the report made by the commission Signor Crispi resigned his seat in Parliament, and was promptly re-elected from Palermo by an overwhelming majority. In May, the Ministry of the Marquis di Rudini, much weakened by the troubled state of the country, was reconstructed, but only to hold its ground for another month. On the 17th of June, upon a threatened vote of want of confidence, it resigned, and, on the 28th, a new Liberal Ministry took office, with General Pelloux at its head.

A. D. 1898 (April—May).—Bread riots in the south and revolutionary outbreaks in the north.—"May 1898 will be remembered for a long time in Italy, and one may wish that the eventful month may mark the turning-point in political life of the new kingdom. The revolt was general, the explosion broke out almost suddenly, but long was the period of preparation. 'Malcontento' is quite a household word in Italy—and the Italians had more than one reason to be dissatisfied with their national government. The rise in the price of bread, as a consequence of the Hispano-American war, was the immediate, but by no means the only, cause of the uprising which darkened the skies of sunny Italy for several days. The enormous taxation imposed upon a people yet young in its national life, in order to carry out a policy far too big for the financial means of the country ; the failure in the attempt to establish a strong colony in the Red Sea ; the economic war with France ; the scanty help Italy received from her allies in time of need ; the political corruption, unchecked when not encouraged by those who stood at the helm of the State ; the impotence of the Chambers of Deputies to deal with the evil-doers as the claims of justice and the voice of the people required, all these evils have prepared a propitious ground for the agitators both of the radical and reactionary parties.

"The Bread Riots began towards the end of April, and in a few days they assumed a very alarming aspect, especially in the small towns of the Neapolitan provinces, inhabited by people ordinarily pacific and law-abiding. The destruction of property was wanton and widespread, women careless of their lives leading the men to the assault. In many cases the riots soon came to an end ; in others the immediate abolition of the 'octroi' did not produce the desired effect. . . . There was no organization in the Neapolitan provinces ; the riots were absolutely independent of one another, but they were originated by the same cause—misery ; they aimed at the same object—a loud protest by means of devastation ; they all ended in the same way—viz., after two or three days the soldiers restored order, the dead were buried, and the ringleaders taken to prison to be dealt with by the military court. In the north, at Milan, the uprising was of quite a different character. In the south of Italy it was truly a question of bread and bread alone. In Central Italy it was a question of work, in Lombardy a truly revolutionary movement. The Neapolitan mob shouted for bread and bread alone, some asking for cheaper bread, some others for 'free bread.' In Tuscany the cry was, 'Pane o Lavoro!' (bread or work). In Lombardy quite another trumpet was sounded : 'Down with the Government ! Down with the Dynasty !'

"The Milanese, of all the people of Italy, have plenty of work and bread, and it is admitted by all that bread had nothing to do with the revolt of Milan. I have studied this movement from its inception, and my conclusion is that the revolt broke out long before it was expected, thus making the discomfiture more certain. The great majority of the population of Milan was, and is, conservative and loyal to the King, although not pleased with the doings of the Government. Only a minority, but a very noisy and active minority, is against monarchical institutions. For some time past the revolutionary party of Milan have made no mystery of their political aspirations towards the establishment of a Milanese republic, to be called 'Republica Ambrogiana.' . . . Milan is also the headquarters of Socialism and Anarchism. Socialists and Republicans once upon a time were implacable foes. Many a battle they fought one against the other ; but since 1886 the two have come to love each other more, or to hate each other less, whichever it may be : and towards the end of 1895 they entered into partnership against their common enemy—Crispi ! Then the Anarchists came in. Decent Republicans and timid Socialists were rather averse to ally themselves with anarchy ; the very name was loathsome to them. However, this natural mistrust soon disappeared, and the Anarchists were welcomed into the dual alliance. Still another element was to enter— the clerical party. . . . The clericals have not a special cry of their own. They satisfied themselves by rubbing their hands and saying : 'Down it goes at last.' Little they knew that not the dynasty, not united Italy was then going down, but society itself. . . . A friend of mine, who was in the midst of the revolt, assures me that its importance has been very much exaggerated in the first reports sent abroad ; and from the official documents, since published, it appears that about 90 barricades were erected, and some 20 houses ransacked to provide the necessary material to build them. The number of the killed amounted to 72, and that of the seriously wounded to 63. On Monday evening [May 9] order was restored in Milan. . . . On Wednesday morning shops and factories were reopened, but it will take years to undo the mischief done on May 7, 8, and 9, 1898. All are sadder now ; one may hope that they will be wiser also. The agitators, the deluded, the masses, the governing classes, the Government, all have had their lesson."— G. D. Vecchia, *The Revolt in Italy* (*Contemporary Review, July*, 1898).

A. D. 1899 (May—July).—Representation in the **P**eace Conference at The Hague. See (in this vol.) PEACE CONFERENCE.

A. D. 1899-1900.—Parliamentary disorder, leading to arbitrary government.—**Assassi**nation of King Humbert.—Much feeling was excited in Italy by the agreement between Great Britain and France which practically awarded most of the Sahara Hinterland of Tripoli (a possession long hoped for and expected by the Italians), as well as that of Tunis, Algiers, and Morocco, to France (see, in this vol., NIGERIA). The government was accused of want of vigor in opposing this, and was held responsible, at the same time, for the humiliating failure of an attempt to secure a share of spoils in China, by lease of Sammun Bay. The resignation of the Ministry was consequent, early in May ; but the King retained General Pelloux at the head of the government, and new associates in his cabinet were found. The Chamber of Deputies became unmanageable ; obstruction, very much in the Austrian manner, was carried to such an extent that Parliament was prorogued. The King then, by royal decree, conferred extraordinary powers on the Ministry, suspending, at the same time, rights of meeting and association, to suppress political agitation, and taking, in fact, a serious backward step, toward government outside of constitutional law. Liberals of all shades, and, apparently, many constitutional Conservatives, were alarmed and outraged by this threatening measure, and, when Parliament was reconvened, the proceedings of obstruction were renewed with more persistency than before. The government then attempted an arbitrary adoption of rules to prevent obstruction ; whereupon (April 3, 1900) the entire Opposition left the House in a body. The situation at length became such that the King adjourned the Parliament sine die, on the 16th of May, and a new Chamber of Deputies was elected on the 3d of the month following. The Opposition was considerably strengthened in the election, and the Ministry of General Pelloux, finding itself more helpless in Parliament than ever, resigned on the 18th of June. A new Cabinet under Signor Saracco was formed.

On the 29th of July, 1900, King Humbert was assassinated by an Italian anarchist, named Angelo Bresci, who went to Italy for the purpose, from Paterson, N. J., in the United States, where he had latterly been living. The King was at Monza, and had been distributing prizes at a gymnasium. At the close of the ceremony, as he entered his carriage, the assassin fired three shots at him, inflicting wounds from which the King died within an hour. The murderer was seized on the spot, tried and convicted of the crime. He received the severest penalty that Italian law could inflict, which was imprisonment for life. The son who succeeds King Humbert, Victor Emmanuel III., was in his

thirty-first year when thus tragically raised to the throne. He is weak in body, but is reputed to have an excellent mind. He was wedded in 1896 to Princess Helene of Montenegro.

A. D. 1900.—Military and naval expenditure. See (in this vol.) WAR BUDGETS.

A. D. 1900.—Naval strength. See (in this vol.) NAVIES OF THE SEA POWERS.

A. D. 1900 (January).—Adhesion to the arrangement of an "open door" commercial policy in China. See (in this vol.) CHINA : A. D. 1899–1900 (SEPTEMBER—FEBRUARY).

A. D. 1900 (January).—Exposure of the Mafia.—Circumstances came to light in the course of the year 1899 which compelled the government to enter upon an investigation of the doings of the Sicilian secret society known as the Mafia. This resulted in the arrest of a number of persons, including a Sicilian member of the Chamber of Deputies, named Palizzolo, charged with complicity in the murder, seven years before, of the Marquis Notarbartolo, manager of the Bank of Sicily at Palermo. The accused were brought to Milan for trial, which took place in January, 1900, and the disclosures then made showed that Sicily had long been térrorized and tyrannized, in all departments of affairs, by a few men who controlled this murderous secret organization, Palizzolo being, apparently, the head of the fiendish crew. One of the ministers in the Italian government, General Mirri, Secretary of War, was found to have had, at least, some scandalous understandings with the Mafia, and he was forced to resign.

A. D. 1900 (January—March).—The outbreak of the "**B**oxers" in northern China. See (in this vol.) CHINA : A. D. 1900 (JANUARY—MARCH).

A. D. 1900 (June—December).—Co-operation with the Powers in China. See (in this vol.) CHINA.

A. D. 1900 (July—September).—An Italian view of the state of the country.—"Appearances, it is well known, are often deceptive, and the present condition of Italy is a case in point. Discontent is not a new thing for the Italian mind to be agitated by, but there is an enormous difference between being discontented with the Government of the day and being dissatisfied with the national institutions. Italians have a quick perception and are extremely impulsive ; they often act suddenly and on the impression of the moment, but they are also apt to fall into a state of lethargy, during which the will of the nation is very weak, both as a stimulus to good government and as repressive of that which is bad. There are, however, times in which this will asserts itself. Italy is just passing through one of these lucid intervals.

" The assassination of King Humbert seems to have awakened the whole nation from a long sleep. Those who thought there was no affection left for monarchical institutions in Italy must have experienced a very depressing disappointment. For forty-eight hours there was no king at all in Italy. King Humbert was dead and his successor was somewhere on the high seas, but nobody knew exactly where, yet not a single disorderly movement was noticed anywhere. Clericals, Socialists, Republicans, the three declared enemies of the monarchy, entirely disappeared from the scene during the crisis. If any one of these parties, which during the last period of national lethargy had grown more audacious and bolder, had only attempted to assert itself, the Italian public 'en masse' would have revolted against it, and performed one of those acts of summary justice of which the history of Italy furnishes abundant examples. I think this absence of disorder of any kind is the most convincing proof that can be adduced in favour of the present state of things in Italy. Surely, if the people had been nursing in their hearts a general revolt, that was the moment for action.

"Of course a few anarchists here and there have rejoiced over the crime of their comrade; however, I venture to assert that it is not quite correct to call Italy the hotbed of anarchy. It is true that many of the most fierce anarchists are Italian by birth; but anarchism did not originate in Italy, it was imported there. France and Russia had—under another name—anarchists long before the name of any Italian was ever connected with anarchism. . . . Political education is still in Italy of very poor quality—truthfully speaking, there is none. Even the anarchists go elsewhere to perfect their education. The assassins of Carnot, of the Empress Elizabeth, and of Canovas, had their political education perfected in Paris or in London. Italy does not export political murderers, as was very unkindly said on the occasion of the assassination of the Empress of Austria. Italy at the worst exports only the rough material for the making of anarchical murderers. Even the assassin of King Humbert belongs to this category. He left Italy with no homicidal mania in him. He was not then a wild beast with a human face, to make use of an expression uttered by Signor Saracco, the Premier of Italy. The anarchist clubs of Paris, London, and New York were his university colleges."—G. D. Vecchia, *The Situation in Italy* (*Nineteenth Century Rev.*, *Sept.*, 1900).

A. D. **1901.**—Fall of the Saracco Ministry. —Formation of a Liberal Cabinet under Signor **Zanardelli.**—Census of the kingdom.— The Saracco Ministry, which took direction of the government in June, 1900, was defeated on the 6th of February, 1901, and compelled to resign. An extraordinarily heavy vote (318 to 102) was cast against it in condemnation of its conduct in matters relating to a "Chamber of Labor" at Genoa. First, it had ordered the dissolution of that body, as being subversive in influence, and then, when a "strike" occurred in Genoa, as the consequence, it receded from its action and reconstituted the Chamber. By the first proceeding it had disgusted the Conservatives; by the second the Radicals, and by its indecision the Moderates. They combined to overthrow it. With some difficulty a new Cabinet was formed containing Liberals of various shades, with Signor Zanardelli, a veteran republican of the Garibaldi generation, at its head. A writer who has frequently discussed foreign politics with a good deal of knowledge in the columns of the "New York Tribune," over the signature "Ex-Attaché," believes that Zanardelli is committed "to anti-clerical legislation of the most drastic and far reaching character," and "may be depended upon to proceed against the Vatican with a vigor unprecedented in the annals of united Italy. And there will be," he thinks, "no attempt on the part of Victor Emmanuel to hold him in leash. Existing laws will be enforced to the utmost against the Papacy, while new measures may be looked for to restrict further the activity of the Church as a factor in political life, to extend the control of the government over all ecclesiastical enterprises and undertakings and to emphasize the fact that all Italians, no matter whether they form part of the Papal Court or not, are Italian citizens, as well as subjects of the Italian crown, and required to obey the laws and to fulfil their obligations as such."

A Press despatch from Rome, in February, announced that "the result of the first Italian census in 20 years has proved a surprise. It shows that the population is 35,000,000, while it was not expected that it would exceed 31,000,000. The ratio of increase is greater than in any other European country. This is ascribed to improved sanitation. The birthrate continues high. It is estimated that 5,000,000 Italians have gone to the United States and South America."

ITO, Marquis: Administration and political experiments. See (in this vol.) JAPAN: A. D.

1890–1898; 1898–1899; and 1900 (AUGUST—OCTOBER).

J.

JACKSON-HARMSWORTH EXPEDITION, Return of the. See (iu this vol.) POLAR EXPLORATION, 1897.

JAMAICA: A. D. **1898.**—Industrial condition. See (in this vol.) WEST INDIES, THE BRITISH: A. D. 1897.

A. D. **1899.**—Financial crisis and conflict between the Governor and the Legislative Assembly.—A crisis in the financial circumstances of the Colony, consequent on expenditures exceeding revenue for several years, was reached in 1899, and led to a serious conflict of views between the Governor and the Legislative Assembly. The latter is constituted of members partly elected and partly appointed by the Governor. The elected members of the Assembly had been in the majority, hitherto, but the Governor possessed authority to add to the nominated membership, and he exercised that authority, as a means of obtaining action on a tariff bill which he held to be a necessary measure. He did so under instructions from the British Colonial Secretary. Before this occurred, an agent of the Colonial Office, Sir David Barbour, had been sent to Jamaica to report on the financial situation. His report, submitted in June, besides recommending financial remedies, contained some references to the political constitution of the colony—among them these:

"The peculiar constitution of the Government had . . . an influence in bringing about or aggravating the present financial difficulties. When it was apparent that either more revenue must be raised or expenditure must be reduced, the Government was in favour of increasing taxation, while the elected members of the Legislative Council pressed for reductions of expenditure.

From the nature of the Constitution, the Government was practically unable to carry proposals for increased taxation in opposition to the votes of nine elected members, while the elected members could not in any satisfactory manner enforce reduction of expenditure. The present state of things shows that both increase of taxation and reduction of expenditure were necessary, but though there has been much friction in recent years, and great loss of time in the Legislative Council, neither increase of taxation nor reduction of expenditure was effected in any degree at all adequate to avert the difficulties which were approaching. . . . The Home Government are, in the last resort, responsible for the financial condition of Jamaica, while, under ordinary circumstances, the Colonial Office exercises at present no real direct and immediate control over the finances. . . . It may be taken for granted that under any circumstances Her Majesty's Government would be unwilling to see the Colony sink into a condition of insolvency without an effort for its relief, and as the ultimate responsibility must, therefore, rest on Her Majesty's Government it would seem better to exercise the power of control, while it is still possible to apply a remedy, rather than to wait until the mischief can only be redressed at the cost of the British taxpayer. On the other hand, as no real responsibility can be enforced on the Elected Members, it seems necessary to give the Governor some practicable means of enforcing his policy, and I would suggest that this might be done by keeping the number of nominated Members at its full strength so that in case of need the Governor would only have to make the necessary declaration, and would not have to go through the preliminary operation of adding to the number of nominated Members."

On the 22d of August, the report of Sir David Barbour was reviewed at length by the Colonial Secretary, Mr. Chamberlain, in a despatch to Governor Hemming, and the above recommendations were substantially approved and made instructions to the Governor. "Two plain facts in connection with this matter," said the Colonial Secretary, "must force themselves upon the attention of all who study the question, still more of all who are called upon to find a solution of it. The first is, that 'the Home Government,' in Sir David Barbour's words, 'are in the last resort responsible for the financial condition of Jamaica.' The second is that as a 'working compromise,' the existing system has failed. It

is a compromise, but it has not worked. I am not now so much concerned with principle as with practice. As a machine for doing the work which has to be done the present system has failed. It is in fact impossible, except where tact and goodwill and friendly feeling exist in an unusual degree, for the government of a country to be carried on when those who are responsible for it are in a permanent minority in the Legislature. I decline to allow the Jamaica Government to remain in that position any longer, not merely because it is unfair to them, but also because, recognizing the ultimate responsibility of Her Majesty's Government for the solvency of the Colony, I must ensure that the measures which they may consider necessary are carried out. I must instruct you, therefore, before the Legislative Council is again summoned, to fill up the full number of nominated members and to retain them, using at your discretion the power given you by the Constitution to declare measures to be of paramount importance. You will give the Council and the public to understand that this step is taken by my express instructions. It is my hope that the Elected Members will recognise that my decision is based on public grounds, and has become inevitable, that they will loyally accept it, and co-operate with me and with you for the good of the Colony."—*Great Britain, Parliamentary Publications (Papers by Command: Jamaica*, 1899 [*C.—9412] and* 1900 [*Cd.—125]*).

JAMESON, Dr. Leander S. : Administrator of Rhodesia. See (in this vol.) SOUTH AFRICA (BRITISH SOUTH AFRICA COMPANY): A. D. 1894–1895.

Raid into the Transvaal.—Surrender.—Trial in England.—Imprisonment. See (in this vol.) SOUTH AFRICA (THE TRANSVAAL): A. D. 1895–1896.

The German Emperor's message to President Kruger concerning the Jameson Raid. See (in this vol.) SOUTH AFRICA (THE TRANSVAAL): A. D. 1896 (JANUARY).

Investigation of the Raid by the Cape Colony Assembly. See (in this vol.) SOUTH AFRICA (CAPE COLONY): A. D. 1896 (JULY).

Indemnity for the Raid claimed by South African Republic. See (in this vol.) SOUTH AFRICA (THE TRANSVAAL): A. D. 1897 (FEBRUARY).

British Parliamentary investigation of the Raid. See (in this vol.) SOUTH AFRICA (THE TRANSVAAL): A. D. 1897 (FEBRUARY—JULY).

JAPAN.

A. D. 1890-1898.—Rise of Parliamentary parties.—Working of Constitutional Government.—"When the Emperor's nominal authority was converted into a reality by the overthrow of the Shogun in 1868, the work was largely due to the four clans of Satsuma, Choshu, Hizen, and Tosa. Their aim was to destroy the Shogunate and to create an Imperial Government, and though many other motives actuated them, these were the two main ideas of the revolution which grew in importance and left political results. No sooner, however, was the Imperial Government established than it was found that the Satsuma clan was strongly divided. There were

within it a party in favour of reform, and another party, led by Shimazu Saburo and Saigo Takamori, who clung to old traditions. The sword had not yet given place to the ballot-box, and the result of a bloody contest was the annihilation of the reactionaries. There remained, therefore, the Satsuma men loyal to the Emperor and to the absolute government of 1868, and with them the Choshu, Hizen, Tosa, and other clans. Some of these clans had not always been friendly in the past. They found it difficult to work together now. Marquis Ito has observed that Japanese politicians are more prone to destroy than to construct, and an opportunity to indulge this proclivity soon presented itself. Although the four clans were equally pledged to secure representative government eventually, jealousy of one another drove two of them to take up this cry as a pretext for dissolving the alliance. The Tosa clan, now represented by Count Itagaki, seceded accordingly in 1873. and the Hizen clan, represented by Count Okuma, followed its example eight years afterwards. The former organised a party called the Fuyu-to. or Liberals, and the latter the Kaishin-to, or Progressives. The two remaining clans of Satsuma and Choshu were called for shortness the Sat-Cho. Such was the origin of parliamentary parties in Japan. There was no political issue at stake ; the moving cause was simply clan jealousy, and hence it was that Hizen and Tosa did not join hands, though both strenuously opposed the Sat-Cho Government and each posed as the friend of the people. Consequently, when the first Diet met, in November, 1890, the Sat-Cho Ministry, with Marquis Yamagata as Premier, found itself face to face with a bitter and, it must be added, an unscrupulous opposition."—H. N. G. Bushby, *Parliamentary Government in Japan* (*Nineteenth Century, July*, 1899).

" The history of the Japanese Parliament [see CONSTITUTION OF JAPAN, in vol. 1], briefly told, is as follows: The first Diet was opened in November, 1890, and the twelfth session in May, 1898. In this brief space of time there have been four dissolutions and five Parliaments. From the very first the collision between the Government and the Diet has been short and violent. In the case of the first dissolution, in December, 1891, the question turned on the Budget estimate, the Diet insisting on the bold curtailment of items of expenditure. In the second dissolution, in December. 1893, the question turned on the memorial to be presented to the Throne, the Opposition insisting in very strong terms on the necessity of strictly enforcing the terms of treaties with Western Powers, the Diet regarding the Cabinet as too weak-handed in foreign politics. The third dissolution, in June, 1894, was also on the same question. The Cabinet, in these two latter cases, was under the presidency of Marquis Ito (then Count), and was vigorously pushing forward negotiations for treaty revision, through the brilliant diplomacy of Count Mutsu, the Foreign Minister. This strict-enforcement agitation was looked upon by the Government as a piece of anti-foreign agitation—a Jingo movement—and as endangering the success of the treaty-revision negotiations. In fact, the revised treaty with Great Britain was on the latter date well-nigh completed, it being signed in July following by Lord Kimberley and Viscount Aoki. It was at this stage that the scepticism of foreign observers as to the final success of representative institutions in Japan seemed to reach its height. . . . Marquis Ito and some of the most tried statesmen of the time were out of office, forming a sort of reserve force, to be called out at any grave emergency. But great was the disappointment when it was seen that after Marquis Ito, with some of the most trusted statesmen as his colleagues, had been in office but little over a year, dissolution followed dissolution, and it seemed that even the Father of the Constitution was unable to manage its successful working. . . . There is no question that the Constitutional situation was at that time exceedingly critical.

" But when the war broke out the situation was completely changed. In the August following the whole nation spoke and acted as if they were one man and had but one mind. In the two sessions of the Diet held during the war the Government was most ably supported by the Diet, and everybody hoped that after the war was over the same good-feeling would continue to rule the Diet. On the other hand, it was well known that the Opposition members in the Diet had clearly intimated that their support of the Government was merely temporary, and that after the emergency was over they might be expected to continue their opposition policy. Sure enough, many months before the opening of the ninth session, mutterings of deep discontent, especially with reference to the retrocession of the Liaotung peninsula, began to be widely heard, and it was much feared that the former scenes of fierce opposition and blind obstruction would be renewed. However, as the session approached (December, 1896), rumours were heard of a certain ' entente' between the Government and the Liberal party, at that time the largest and the best organised in the country. And in the coming session the Government secured a majority, through the support of the Liberals, for most of its important Bills.

"Now this ' entente' between Marquis Ito and the Liberals was a great step in advance in the constitutional history of the country, and a very bold departure in a new direction on the part of the Marquis. He was known to be an admirer of the German system, and a chief upholder of the policy of Chozen Naikaku, or the Transcendental Cabinet policy, which meant a Ministry responsible to the Emperor alone. Marquis Ito saw evidently at this stage the impossibility of carrying on the Government without a secure parliamentary support, and Count Itagaki, the Liberal leader, saw in the Marquis a faithful ally, whose character as a great constructive statesman, and whose history as the author of the Constitution. both forbade his ever proving disloyal to the Constitution. The 'entente' was cemented in May following by the entrance of Count Itagaki into the Cabinet as the Home Minister. On the other hand, this ' entente' led to the formation of the Progressist party by the union of the six Opposition parties, as well as to the union of Count Okuma, the Progressist leader, and Count Matsugata, leader of the Kagoshima statesmen. Their united opposition was now quite effective in. harassing the administration. At this stage certain neutral men, particularly Count Inouye, suggested compromise, offering a scheme of a Coalition Cabinet. . . . But Count Itagaki was firm in opposing such a compromise, saying it was tantamount to the ignoring of party distinction, and as such was a retrogression instead of being a forward step in the constitutional history of the country. He finally tendered his resignation. When Marquis Ito saw that the Count was firm in his determination, he, too, resigned, saying that he felt so deeply obliged to the Liberals for their late parliamentary support that he would not let the Count go out of office alone. Thus fell the Ito Ministry after five years' brilliant service.

" The new Cabinet, formed in September, 1896, had Count Matsukata for Premier and Treasury Minister ; Count Okuma for Foreign Minister ; and Admiral Kabayama, the hero of the Yaloo battle, for Home Minister. There were at this time three things that the nation desired. It wanted to be saved from the impending business depression. It wished 'to see Japanese Chauvinism installed at the Foreign Office, and the shame of the retrocession of the Liaotung peninsula wiped off. It hoped, lastly, to see a Parliamentary Government inaugurated and all the evils of irresponsible bureaucracy removed. The statesmen now installed in office aspired to satisfy all these desires, and they were expected to work wonders. But, unfortunately, the Cabinet lacked unity. . . . Early in the fall [of 1897] Count Okuma resigned office, saying that he felt like a European physician in consultation over a case with Chinese doctors. . . . Count Okuma led away the majority of the Progressist party, and the Government was left with but an insignificant number of supporters. As soon as the Diet met, the spirit of opposition manifested was so strong that the Ministers asked the Emperor to issue an edict for dissolution. It was expected that the government would at once appeal to the country with some strong programme. But to the astonishment of everybody the Ministry resigned the very next day. In the midst of the general confusion which followed, Marquis Ito's name was in the mouth of everybody. He was unanimously hailed as the only man to bring order into the political situation. In January following [1898] the new Cabinet was announced with Ito for Premier, Count Inouye for the Treasury, and Marquis Saionji, one of the best cultured, most progressive, and, perhaps, also most daring of the younger statesmen, for Education Minister."—Tokiwo Yokoi, *New Japan and her Constitutional Outlook (Contemporary Review, Sept., 1898).*

A. D. 1895.—The war with China.—Treaty of Shimonoseki.—Korean independence secured.—Part of Feng-tien, Formosa and the Pescadores ceded by China.—Relinquishment of Feng-tien by Japan. See (in this vol.) CHINA: A. D. 1894-1895.

A. D. 1896.—Affairs in Formosa.—Retirement of Marquis Ito.—Progressists in power.—Destructive sea-wave.—Serious risings of the Chinese in Formosa against the newly established Japanese rule in that island were said to have been caused by insolent and atrocious conduct on the part of the Japanese soldiery. Possibly a decree which prohibited the importation of opium into Formosa, and which placed the medicinal sale of the drug under close restrictions, had something to do with the discontent. In Japan, the able statesman, Marquis Ito, was made unpopular by his yielding of the Liao Tung peninsula (in the Feng-tien province of China,—see, in this vol., CHINA: A. D. 1894-1895), under pressure from Russia, Germany and France. He retired from the government, and Count Matsukata became Premier in September, with a cabinet of the Progressist (Kaishinto) party, which advocated resistance to Russia, and opposition generally to the encouragement of foreign enterprises in Japan. A frightful calamity was suffered in June, when a prodigious wave, probably raised by some submarine volcano, overwhelmed a long stretch of northeastern coast, destroying some 30,000 people, and sweeping out of existence a number of considerable towns.—*Annual Register, 1896.*

A. D. 1897.—New tariff.—A new tariff, regu-

lating the customs duties levied in all cases wherein Japan is not bound by treaty stipulations, was adopted in March, 1897. The duties imposed range from 5 to 40 per cent., ad valorem, the higher being laid upon liquors and tobacco. The "Japan Gazette" is quoted as saying in explanation: "The statutory tariff fixes the duties to be collected on every article imported into Japan from countries that have not concluded tariff conventions with her, or that are not entitled to the most-favored-nation treatment in regard to the tariff, in their new treaties with this country. Spain, Portugal, Greece, and many other countries have no tariff conventions with Japan and no favored-nation clause, in regard to tariff, in their new treaties with this country. The United States, Belgium, Holland, Russia, and others have the favored-nation clause and will get the benefit of the lesser duties on items named in the different mentioned tariffs. There will, therefore, be two columns of figures in the printed general tariff list, showing in the first column the duties on the articles named in the conventional tariffs, and in the second column the duties on the same articles imported from countries that have no tariff convention with Japan, and that are not entitled to favored-nation treatment. For instance, most textile articles are subject to a duty of 10 per cent in the conventional tariff column and to a duty of 15 per cent in the statutory column."—*U. S. Consular Reports, July and September, 1897, pp. 475 and 91.*

A. D. 1897 (October).—Introduction of the gold standard. See (in this vol.) MONETARY QUESTIONS: A. D. 1897 (MARCH).

A. D. 1897 (November).—Treaty with the United States and Russia to suspend pelagic sealing. See (in this vol.) BERING SEA QUESTIONS.

A. D. 1897-1898.—Contentions with Russia in Korea. See (in this vol.) KOREA: A. D. 1895-1898.

A. D. 1898-1899.—The struggle between clan government and party government.— "When, in January 1898, Marquis Ito made an attempt to win the country back to non-party government and efficiency by forming an independent Ministry in defiance of the Liberal demands, he was acting no doubt from no mere clan instinct, but, as he conceived, in the highest interests of the realm. His experiment was not destined to succeed. In the general election of March 1898, 109 Progressives and 94 Liberals were returned as Representatives in a House of 300. A common hunger for office and a common sense of humiliation at their treatment by the greater statesmen of the clans united the two parties under one banner as they had not been united since 1873. At last they took up in earnest the crusade against clan government, which, logically, they should have commenced together exactly a quarter of a century before. They called their coalition the 'Kensei-to,' or Constitutional Party. Japan is a country of rapid progress, but she is lucky that for twenty-five years the formation of the Kensei-to was deferred while she was content to be guided through difficult times by clansmen more skilled in statecraft than the usurient nobodies who were kicking at the heels of Counts Okuma and Itagaki.

"Meanwhile Marquis Ito had to decide how he would act. He had tried to govern with the help of a party and had partially succeeded. He had tried to govern without one, and had discovered that it was impossible. The two parties could no longer be played off one against the other. They were united, and with fifty new recruits formed the Kensei-to, 253 strong. There remained only nineteen clan government sympathisers, calling themselves National Unionists, and twenty-eight Independents. In these difficult circumstances Marquis Ito's decision was a bold one, and in its consequences far-reaching. He advised that Count Okuma, the Progressive leader of the Kensei-to should be summoned to form a Cabinet in conjunction with his Liberal colleague, Count Itagaki. His advice was followed by the Emperor, but with the significant condition that the Ministries of War and the Navy were to be retained by clansmen. The Emperor was not disposed to allow constitutional experiments in these departments. On the 28th of June 1898, Marquis Ito resigned, and on the 30th the Okuma-Itagaki Cabinet was formed.

" It now seemed to many that the death-blow had been given to clan government, and that at last the era of government by party had commenced. . . . The elements of which the Kensei-to was composed were the two great ones of the Progressives, led by Count Okuma, and the Liberals, led by Count Itagaki. These two parties acted together in a condition of veiled ¡hostility. There was coalition without any approach to amalgamation. A common hunger for office, a common dislike for clan government, obscured for a little while a mutual jealousy and distrust. Meanwhile the Kensei-to as a whole, and both wings of it, were divided into endless clubs, cliques, and associations. Our own Temperance, Colonial, Church, and China parties are affable and self-effacing in comparison. Thus, to name only a few of the political divisions of the Kensei-to, there were the territorial associations of the Kwanto-kai (led by Mr. Hoshi), the Hokuriku-kai (led by Mr. Sugita), the Kyushu Kurabu (led by Mr. Matsuda), the Tohoku-dantai, the Chugoku-kai, and the Shigoku-kai ; there were the Satsuma section, the Tosa section, the Kakushinto, the Young Constitutionalists, the Senior Politicians (such as Baron Kusumoto, Mr. Hiraoka, the chief organiser of the coalition, and others), the Central Constitutionalist Club, and so forth. Each clique had its private organisation and animosities ; each aspired to dictate to the Cabinet and secure portfolios for its members in the House. They combined and recombined among themselves. . . . Clearly, however loyally the two leaders wished to work together, each must find it impossible in such circumstances to preserve discipline among his own followers. Indeed, the leaders scarcely tried to lead. . . . It was impossible to carry on the Government under such conditions. The Okuma-Itagaki Cabinet fell, and Field Marshal the Marquis Yamagata, Premier of the first Japanese Ministry, was summoned by the Emperor. Once more a clan Ministry, independent of party, was formed ; once more it seem.ed as though party government was to be indefinitely postponed. . . . Marquis Yamagata formed his Ministry in November 1898, on strictly clan lines. . . . Being an old soldier, he wisely determined to profit by experience and seek an ally. No one knew

better than himself the need of passing the Land Tax Bill, on which the efficiency of the national defence and the future of Japan depended. . . . It was natural, therefore, for him to approach the Liberals, who had shown themselves favourable to an increase of the Land Tax. . . . On the 27th of November the support of the Liberals was assured, an event which prompted the 'Jiji' to express its joy that Marquis Yamagata had become a party man, leaving ' the mouldy, effete cause of the non-partisan Ministry.' The Government party consisted now of the National Unionists (in favour of clan government and loyal followers of Marquis Yamagata), the Liberals, and a few so-called Independents (who, of course, speedily formed themselves into a club), giving the Government a majority of about fifteen or twenty votes in the House. . . .

" The first session of Marquis Yamagata's second Ministry will always be remembered in Japan because the Land Tax Bill was successfully passed through both Houses. . . . But the most important episode of the session, from a parliamentary point of view, was a remarkable act of self-denial on the part of the Liberals. In March of this year [1899] they agreed not to demand office from Marquis Yamagata for any of their number, though they were to be free to accept such offices as he might of his own bounty from time to time be able to offer them. If this unprecedented pledge be loyally adhered to, it marks a very great stride towards effective party government in the future. . . . The hope of the Liberals now lies, not in the immediate enjoyment of the sweets of office, but in winning over Marquis Ito to their party. If he were to show the way, it is probable that many more of the leading clan statesmen would take sides, in which case, to adopt Mr. Bodley's phrase, political society would be divided vertically as in England, not horizontally as in France, and either party on obtaining a majority in the House would be able to find material in its own ranks for an efficient Cabinet. At present neither is in that happy position."—H. N. G. Bushby, *Parliamentary Government in Japan (Nineteenth Century, July,* 1899).

A. D. 1899 (May—July).—**Representation** in the Peace Conference at The Hague. See (in this vol.) PEACE CONFERENCE.

A. D. 1899 (July).—Release from the treaties with Western Powers which gave them exterritorial rights.—Consular jurisdictions abolished.—"Japan has been promoted. The great sign that Europe regards a Power as only semi-civilised is the demand that all who visit it, or trade in it, should be exempted from the jurisdiction of the local Courts, the Consuls acting when necessary as Judges. This rule is maintained even when the Powers thus stigmatised send Ambassadors, and is, no doubt, very keenly resented. It seems specially offensive to the Japanese, who have a high opinion of their own merits, and they have for seventeen years demanded the treatment accorded to fully civilised States. As the alliance of Japan is now earnestly sought by all Europe this has been conceded, and on Monday, July 17th, the Consular jurisdiction ceased. (Owing to some blunder, the powers of the French and Austrian Consuls last a fortnight longer, but the difference is only formal.) The Japanese are highly delighted, and the European traders are not displeased, as with the Consular jurisdictions all restrictions on trading with the interior disappear."—*The Spectator (London), July* 22, 1899.—The early treaties of Japan with Western Powers, which gave the latter what are called rights of extra-territoriality, or exterritoriality, for all their subjects (the right, that is, to administer their own laws, by their own consular or other courts, upon their own subjects, within a foreign country), were modified in 1894. Japan then became free to extinguish the foreign courts on her soil at the end of five years, upon giving a year's notice, which she did as stated above. Her government has thus attained a recognized peerage in sovereignty with the governments of the Western world. At the same time, the whole country has been thrown open to foreign trade—restricted previously to certain ports.

In careful preparation of the Japanese people for this important change in their relations with the foreign world, the following imperial rescript was issued at the end of June, 1899: "The revision of the treaties, our long cherished aim, is to-day on the eve of becoming an accomplished fact; a result which, while it adds materially to the responsibilities of our Empire, will greatly strengthen the basis of our friendship with foreign countries. It is our earnest wish that our subjects, whose devoted loyalty in the discharge of their duties is conspicuous, should enter earnestly into our sentiments in this matter, and, in compliance with the great policy of opening the country, should all unite with one heart to associate cordially with the peoples from afar, thus maintaining the character of the nation and enhancing the prestige of the Empire. In view of the responsibilities that devolve upon us in giving effect to the new treaties, it is our will that our ministers of state, acting on our behalf, should instruct our officials of all classes to observe the utmost circumspection in the management of affairs, to the end that subjects and strangers alike may enjoy equal privileges and advantages, and that, every source of dissatisfaction being avoided, relations of peace and amity with all nations may be strengthened and consolidated in perpetuity."

Obedient to this command, the Minister President of State, Marquis Yamagata, published the following instruction on the 1st of July: "The work of revising the treaties has caused deep solicitude to His August Majesty since the centralization of the Government, and has long been an object of earnest desire to the people. More than twenty years have elapsed since the question was opened by the dispatch of a special embassy to the West in 1871. Throughout the whole of that interval, numerous negotiations were conducted with foreign countries and numerous plans discussed, until finally, in 1884, Great Britain took the lead in concluding a revised treaty, and the other powers all followed in succession, so that now the operation of the new treaties is about to take place on the 17th of July and the 4th of August.

"The revision of the treaties in the sense of placing on a footing of equality the intercourse of this country with foreign states was the basis of the great liberal policy adopted at the time of the restoration, and that such a course conduces to enhance the prestige of the Empire and to promote the prosperity of the people is a proposition not requiring demonstration. But if there should

be anything defective in the methods adopted for giving effect to the treaties, not merely will the object of revision be sacrificed, but also the country's relations with friendly powers will be impaired and its prestige may be lowered. It is, of course, beyond question that any rights and privileges accruing to us as a result of treaty revision should be duly asserted. But there devolves upon the Government of this Empire the responsibility, and upon the people of this Realm the duty, of protecting the rights and privileges of foreigners, and of sparing no effort that they may one and all be enabled to reside in the country confidently and contentedly. It behooves all officials to clearly apprehend the august intentions and to pay profound attention to these points."

With still finer care for the honor and good name of Japan, the following instruction to schools was published on the same day by Count Kabayma, the Minister of State for Education: "The schools under the direct control of the Government serve as models to all the public and private educational institutions throughout the country. It is therefore my earnest desire that the behavior of the students at such schools should be regulated with notably strict regard to the canons of propriety, so that they may show themselves worthy of the station they occupy. The date of the operation of the revised treaties is now imminent, and His Imperial Majesty has issued a gracious rescript. It may be expected that the coming and going of foreigners in the interior of the country will henceforth grow more frequent, and if at such a time students be left without proper control, and suffered to neglect the dictates of propriety by cherishing sentiments of petty arrogance and behaving in a violent, outrageous, or vulgar manner, not only will the educational systems be brought into discredit, but also the prestige of the country will be impaired and its reputation may even be destroyed. For that reason I have addressed an instruction to the local governors urging them to guard against any defects in educational methods, and I am now constrained to appeal to the Government schools which serve for models. I trust that those upon whom the functions of direction and teaching devolve, paying respectful attention to the august intention, will discharge their duties carefully towards the students, and, by securing the latter's strict adherence to rules, will contrive that they shall serve as a worthy example to the schools throughout the country."—*U. S. Consular Reports, Oct.,* 1899, *p.* 285.

A. D. 1899 (August). — Prohibition of religious instruction in the government schools. — Some important regulations for the national schools were promulgated in August by the Minister of Education, having the effect, probably intended, of discouraging attendance at the Christian mission schools, and stimulating a preference for the schools of the national system. They forbade religious exercises or instruction in any schools that adopt the curriculum of the national schools, while, at the same time, they allow admission from no others to the higher schools of the national system without examination. Students in the middle schools of the national system are exempted from conscription, while others are not. That the aim in this policy is to strengthen the national schools, rather than to interfere with religious freedom, seems probable.

A. D. **1899** (December). — Adhesion to the arrangement of an " open door " commercial policy in China. See (in this vol.) CHINA: A. D. 1899-1900 (SEPTEMBER—FEBRUARY).

A. D. **1900.**—Naval strength. See (in this vol.) NAVIES OF THE SEA POWERS.

A. D. **1900** (June—December).—Co-operation with the Powers in China. See (in this vol.) CHINA.

A. D. **1900** (July).—Failure of attempts to entrust the Japanese government with the rescue of the foreign Legations at Peking. See (in this vol.) CHINA: A. D. 1900 (JUNE—JULY).

A. D. **1900** (August—October).—The **new** party of Marquis Ito.—The letters of the Tokio correspondent of the London "Times" describe interestingly the genesis of a new party of which Marquis Ito has taken the lead, and which took control of the government in October, 1900. Various parties, the career of which the writer reviews, had been formed in opposition to the veteran statesmen who continued to hold the reins of government after constitutional forms were introduced in 1889. But very few of the party politicians who constructed these parties, says the writer, had held high office. "They were without the prestige of experience. To put such men on the administrative stage while the gallery was occupied by the greybeards—the ' Meiji statesmen,' as they are called—who had managed the country's affairs since the Restoration, would have seemed a strange spectacle in the eyes of the nation. The Meiji statesmen, however, persistently declined to be drawn into the ranks of the political parties. They gave the latter plenty of rope; they even allowed them to administer the State, which essay ended in a fiasco; and they took them into alliances which served chiefly to demonstrate the eagerness of these politicians for office and emoluments. But there was no amalgamation. The line of demarcation remained indelible. . . .

"The political parties, discovering the impossibility of becoming a real power in the State without the coöperation of the Meiji statesmen, asked Marquis Ito to assume their leadership. Marquis Ito may be said to possess everything that his country can give him. He has the unbounded confidence of his Sovereign and his countrymen; he is loaded with titles and honours, and a word from him can make or mar a Ministry. It seems strange that such a man should step down from his pedestal to become a party leader; to occupy a position which can bring no honour and must at once create enemies. Yet Marquis Ito has consented. He issued his manifesto. It is in two respects a very remarkable document. First, it tells the politicians that their great fault has been self-seeking; that they have set party higher than country; office and emolument above public duty and political responsibility. Secondly, it informs them in emphatic terms that Parliamentary Cabinets are unconstitutional in Japan; that Ministers and officials must be appointed by the Sovereign without any reference to their party connexions. The politicians who place themselves under Marquis Ito's leadership must eschew the former failing and abandon the latter heresy. It would be impossible to imagine a more complete reversal of

the tables. The men who, ten years ago, asked the nation to condemn the Meiji statesmen on a charge of political self-seeking are now publicly censured by the chief of these statesmen for committing the very same sin in their own persons; and the men who for ten years have made Parliamentary Cabinets the text of their agitation now enrol themselves in a party which openly declares such Cabinets to be unconstitutional."

The new party calls itself the "Association of Friends of the Constitution" (Rikken Seiyukai). "In its ranks are found the whole of the Liberals, and many members of the Diet who had hitherto maintained an independent attitude, so that it can count on 152 supporters among the 300 members of the Lower House. . . . The Opposition, the Progressists, command only 90 votes, and the remainder of the House is composed mainly of men upon whose support the Cabinet can always reckon. In fact, now for the first time since the Diet opened, does the direction of State affairs come into the hands of Ministers who may rest assured of Parliamentary coöperation."

Marquis Yamagata, who had conducted the administration for nearly two years, resigned in October, and Marquis Ito brought his new party into power. His Cabinet "does not include one of the elder statesmen—the 'clan statesmen'—except the marquis himself. Among the seven portfolios that have changed hands—those of War and of the Navy are still held as before—three have been given to unequivocal party politicians, leaders of the Liberals, and four to men who may be regarded as Marquis Ito's disciples. . . . The Yamagata Cabinet consisted entirely of clan statesmen and their followers. The Ito Cabinet has a clan statesman for leader and his nominees for members. It may be called essentially a one man Ministry, so far does the Premier tower above the heads of his colleagues."

A. D. **1900-1901.**—Strategic importance of Korea.—Interest in the designs of Russia. See (in this vol.) KOREA: A. D. 1900.

A. D. **1901.**—Movement to erect a monument to commemorate the visit of Commodore Perry.—A movement in Japan to erect a monument at Kurihama, the landing place of the American expedition, commanded by Commodore Matthew C. Perry, which visited Japan in 1853 and brought about the opening of that country to intercourse with the western world (see, in vol. 3, JAPAN: A. D. 1852–1888), was announced to the State Department at Washington by the U. S. Consul-General at Yokohama, in March, 1901. The undertaking is directed by the "American Association of Japan," of which the Japanese Minister of Justice is President, and its purpose is to commemorate an event which the Association, in a published circular, declares to be "the most memorable" in the annals of Japan. The language of the circular, in part, is as follows: "This visit of Commodore Perry was in a word the turning of the key which opened the doors of the Japanese Empire to friendly intercourse with the United States, and subsequently to the rest of the nations of Europe on similar terms, and may in truth be regarded as the most memorable event in our annals — an event which paved the way for and accelerated the introduction of a new order of things, an event that enabled the country to enter upon the uprecedented era of National ascendancy in which we are now living. Japan has not forgotten—nor will she ever forget—that next to her reigning and most beloved sovereign, whose high virtues and great wisdom are above all praise, she owes, in no small degree, her present prosperity to the United States of America, in that the latter rendered her a great and lasting service already referred to.

After the lapse of these forty-eight years, her people, however, have come to entertain but an uncertain memory of Kurihama, and yet it was there that Commodore Perry first trod on the soil of Japan and for the first time awoke the country from a slumberous seclusion of three centuries — there it was where first gleamed the light that has ever since illumined Japan's way in her new career of progress."

JESUS, Discovery of a fragment of the Logia or Sayings of. See (in this vol.) ARCHÆ- OLOGICAL RESEARCH : EGYPT : DISCOVERY OF A FRAGMENT.

JEWS.

Discovery of the sole mention of the people of Israel in Egyptian inscriptions. See (in this vol.) ARCHÆOLOGICAL RESEARCH : EGYPT : RESULTS.

General results of recent archæological research as affecting our knowledge of the ancient Hebrews. See (in this vol.) ARCHÆOLOGICAL RESEARCH : IN BIBLE LANDS.

A. D. 1897 : Freedom of residence in Russia given to the university educated. See (in this vol.) RUSSIA : A. D. 1897.

A. D. 1897-1901.—The Zionist movement. — " The three closing days of August [1897] saw a congress at Basle concerning the significance of which friends and foes alike seem already pretty well agreed. It was the Congress of Zionists. Zionists ! Until then that word was almost unknown to the public at large. Zionism virtually made its bow to the Gentile world at Basle, and disclosed for the first time what its aims and its needs were. . . . It was in my work, 'The Jewish State,' which appeared a year and a half ago, that I first formulated what the Congress at Basle virtually adopted as an axiom. In the terms of that definition : ' Zionism has for its object the creation of a home, secured by public rights, for those Jews who either cannot or will not be assimilated in the country of their adoption.'

"Nothing was more instructive at the Basle Congress than the vigour—I might almost say violence—with which the representatives of the great Jewish strata of population resisted any attempt to limit the guarantees for a State based on public rights. The executive appointed to draw up a programme had proposed ' a legally secured home.' The delegates, however, were not satisfied, and clamoured for an alteration to ' secured on the basis of international rights.' It was only by adopting the intermediary expression ' public rights' that an agreement was arrived at. The significance of this logomachy is, that what the Jews desire is not to acquire more tracts of land, but a country for the Jewish people, and to emphasise that desire in terms as plain as possible without wounding certain legitimate and sovereign susceptibilities. We can acquire land any day in our private right everywhere. But that is not the point with Zionists. In our case we have nothing to do with private rights. That will come later—as well as the land speculators—once our movement has achieved success. What the Zionists are alone directing their attention to is the ' public rights' idea. In that they hope to find a remedy for the old evil. Were I to

express myself paradoxically, I should say that a country belonging to the Jews on the basis of public rights, even though down to the very last parcel it was the legally secured property of non-Jews, would mean the final solution of the Jewish question. . . . We have held a gathering at Basle before the whole world, and there we saw the national consciousness and the popular will break forth, at times like a convulsive upheaval. To Basle came Jews of all countries, of all tongues, of all parties, and of all forms of religious confession. There were more than 200 representatives of the Jewish people—most of them delegates for hundreds and thousands. Men from Roumania alone brought over 50,000 signatures of those who had sent them there. There surely was never such a motley assembly of opinions in such a narrow space before. On the other hand, there would certainly have been more conflict of opinion in any other deliberative assembly than there was in this. . . .

"It would . . . appear to be to the interest of Turkey to come to an arrangement with the Jews. But what are the interests which other Governments would have in assisting the realisation of a legally guaranteed Jewish home ? The interest would vary with each country, but it is present in some form or other everywhere. It would mean the drawing off of an unhappy and detested element of population which is reduced more and more to a condition of despair, and which, scattered over the face of the earth, and in a state of unrest, must perforce identify itself with the most extreme parties everywhere. Governments and all friends of the existing order of things cannot bring themselves to believe that, by helping us in the solution we propose, they could give peace to an element which has been driven to revolution and rendered dangerous through its dispersion. That a highly conservative people, like the Jews, have always been driven into the ranks of revolutionists is the most lamentable feature in the tragedy of our race. Zionism would mean an end to all that. We should see results accrue for the general condition of mankind, the full benefits of which we cannot even guess. There are, of course, a great number of existing political difficulties to be overcome, but these, given the necessary good will, might be surmounted."—Theodor Herzl, *The Zionist Congress (Contemporary Review, Oct.,* 1897).

" The programme of the Philo-Zionists as defined in their printed constitution is as follows : — (a) To foster the national idea in Israel. (b) To promote the colonization of Palestine and

283

neighbouring territories by Jews, by establishing new colonies and assisting those already established. (c) To diffuse the knowledge of Hebrew as a living language. (d) To further the moral, intellectual, and material status of Israel. The English Association, known as the Chovevi Zion, is presided over by Colonel Albert Edward Goldsmid, Assistant Adjutant-General of Her Majesty's Forces ; it has 35 established 'Tents' spread through the length and breadth of the United Kingdom. . . . Similar associations have been established in America, Germany, France, Russia, Austria, Denmark, Switzerland, and other countries ; and there is a central committee meeting at Paris, where the organisation of new colonies and development of existing ones in the Holy Land is systematically carried out. Even before these associations had been called into existence Baron Edmond de Rothschild of Paris, encouraged by the success of the agricultural schools at Jaffa, founded by the late Charles Netter, had devoted his vast influence and his open purse to the work ; and there is a separate administration in Palestine charged with the control and management of what are known as 'the Baron's colonies.'

"To-day we have in Palestine between twenty and thirty distinct colonies or communities spreading along the coast from Askalon in the south to Carmel in the north, and along the Jordan from the Waters of Meron to the Sea of Galilee in the east. The population of these colonies varies from 100 to 700 souls, and they may safely be estimated to number 10,000 souls in all, independently of the large number of Jewish day labourers from neighbouring towns and villages, to whom they give occasional employment. There are 50,000 more Jews—mostly refugees—in the various Holy Cities, and the immediate problem is to get these—or the better part of them—also on the land. The current language of the colonists is the Hebrew of the Bible, although many of them have acquired the native Arabic, and also French, which is taught in their schools. They have their places of worship, their houses of study, their modest institutes, their public baths, and in fact the counterpart in small of all the features of the model European village : and they have, thanks to the Baron and the Philo-Zionists' Associations, the most modern appliances and complete installations for the prosecution of their agricultural works."—Herbert Bentwich, *Philo-Zionists and Anti-Semites* (*Nineteenth Century*, Oct., 1897).

"At the beginning of March, 1898, an important Conference was held in London, attended by delegates from nearly 50 societies, representing 10,000 English Zionists, and resolutions were passed adopting the International programme, and making provisions for a federation of all the English Zionist bodies. Similar conferences were held in New York, in Berlin, in Galatz (Roumania), and other great centres ; and local federations were everywhere formed to give greater strength and solidity to the general organization. At the second International Congress, which was held at Basle in August, 1898, and was attended by an imposing body of more than 500 delegates, the Executive Committee were able to report that the 'Basle programme' had received the support of 913 Zionist organizations (out of which over 700 had sprung up since the first Congress), it being calculated that these represented at least a quarter

of a million of active members. The Congress had become the authorised representative and exponent of the people's wishes, and the Zionists had become a power to be reckoned with in any settlement of the Jewish question. Prominent among the attendants at this world gathering were the Rabbis—crown officials from orthodox Russia and Poland, as well as the elect of reform congregations from America—who took an active interest in the settlement of the programme of work for the ensuing year, which was the main business of the meeting."—H. Bentwich, *The Progress of Zionism* (*Fortnightly Rev.*, Dec., 1898).

At the International Zionist Congress which assembled in London on the 13th of August, 1900, the report of the executive committee on the progress which the movement has made showed as follows : ' In Russia there are at least 100,000 members of Zionist societies ; in England the movement is supported by 38 societies, as against 16 last year, and all these societies have increased membership. Thanks to the work of the English Zionist Federation Zionism has made great headway in England. In the United States there are 135 societies, as against 102 last year. Notwithstanding the war in South Africa, the contributions towards the expenses of the movement have been well maintained. Having regard to the returns received by the executive committee the reporter felt no hesitation in saying that to-day the vast majority of the Jewish nation were in favour of Zionism."—*London Times*, Aug. 15, 1900.

Late in December, 1900, it was announced at Vienna that the Sultan had issued or renewed a decree, according to which the Jews are forbidden to remain in Palestine for longer than three months. This measure, which applies both to traders and pilgrims, further prohibits the acquisition by Jews of landed property. It was suggested that the wholesale exodus of Jews from Russia and their recent emigration from Rumania gave rise to the apprehension that they might overcrowd Palestine. This apprehension is said to have been strengthened by the increasing activity of the Zionists, who are suspected in certain circles in Constantinople of pursuing distinct political ends. According to another suggestion, Russia had grown jealous of the Jewish colonization of Palestine, fearing it to be in the interest of German policy, and had used influence to check it.

" Viewed merely on its prosaic side, Zionism is by no means a visionary scheme. The aggregation of Jews in Palestine is only a matter of time, and it is better that they should be aggregated there under their own laws and religion, and the mild suzerainty of the Sultan, than under the semi-barbarous restrictions of Russia or Roumania, and exposed to recurrent popular outbreaks. True, Palestine is a ruined country, and the Jews are a broken people, but neither is beyond recuperation. Palestine needs a people, Israel needs a country. If, in regenerating the Holy Land, Israel could regenerate itself, how should the world be other than the gainer ? In the solution of the problem of Asia, which has just succeeded the problem of Africa, Israel might play no insignificant part. Already the colony of Rishon le Zion has obtained a gold medal for its wines from the Paris Exposition, which is not prejudiced in the Jew's favor. We may be sure the spiritual wine of Judæa would again pour forth likewise that precious vintage which the world has drunk for so many centuries. And as the unscientific activities of the colonization societies would have paved the way for the pastoral and commercial future of Israel in its own country, so would the rabbinical sing-song in musty rooms prove to have been but the unconscious preparation of the ages for the Jerusalem University.

"But Palestine belongs to the Sultan, and the Sultan refuses to grant the coveted Judæan Charter, even for dangled millions. Is not this fatal? No, it matters as little as that the Zionists could not pay the millions, if suddenly called upon. They have barely collected a quarter of a million (in English pounds). But there are millionaires enough to come to the rescue, once the charter was dangled before the Zionists. It is not likely that the Rothschilds would see themselves ousted from their familiar headship in authority and well-doing, nor would the millions left by Baron Hirsch be altogether withheld. And the Sultan's present refusal is equally unimportant, because a national policy is independent of transient moods and transient rulers. The only aspect that really matters is whether Israel's face be, or be not, set steadily Zionwards,—for decades and even for centuries. Much less turns on the Sultan's mind than on Dr. Herzl's. Will he lose patience? for leaders like Herzl are not born in every century."
—I. Zangwill, *The Wandering Jew and the New Century (Sunday School Times, Jan. 12, 1901).*

A. D. 1899.—In Palestine.—"In view of the impetus given the Zionist movement by the second Zionist congress, held at Basel in September, and also by the Palestine journey of Emperor Wilhelm II, the present status of Jews in Palestine becomes a matter of general interest. Out of a total population in Palestine of some 200,000 souls, about 40,000 are Jews, as against 14,000 twenty years ago. In Jerusalem, there are 22,-000 Jews, half of whom have immigrated from Europe and America and are called Aschkenazim to distinguish them from the oriental Israelites, the Sephardists. Nine hundred and sixty families, numbering about 5,000 souls, inhabit the twenty-two Jewish colonies in Palestine which have been founded and subsidized by Europeans —ten by Baron Edmond de Rothschild, representing the Alliance Israélite Universelle; the rest by the Jewish Colonization Association and by the Odessa Company.

'The idea of gathering in Palestine homeless Jews scattered all over the globe was championed in the forties by Moses Montefiore, but with indifferent success. In the eighties, however, the immigration of Jews to Palestine assumed significant proportions. Of the twenty-two present colonies, the 'Jacob Memorial' is the largest, supporting more than 1,000 souls. It boasts a graded school (five teachers), a synagogue, etc., and 4,000 acres of land under cultivation, on which are raised fruit (chiefly grapes), honey, and mulberry leaves, the rearing of silkworms being a leading industry. The 'First to Zion' is another quite important colony, owning 2,000 acres of land. Some forty two-storied stone dwelling houses greet the eye of the approaching stranger; also a school house with a Hebrew library, a synagogue, and a hospital. One million five hundred thousand vines and 25,000 olive, almond, orange, and mulberry trees belong to this

colony, which also possesses famous wine cellars. The 'Hope of Israel,' a mile beyond Yafa, in the plains of Sharon, is perhaps best known for its agricultural school, in which one hundred or more pupils are taught gardening. Recently, a high school for Jewish girls was established in Yafa. The 'Head Corner Stone,' amid the hills beyond Tiberias, with snow-capped Hermon in the background, is another quite prosperous Jewish colony in Palestine. Being near the source of the Jordan, water is plentiful; and its situation, high up above the level of Lake Gennesareth, insures fair climatic conditions. In the 'Door of Hope,' dairy farming is profitably followed and experiments made in tea planting. This colony is said to have 1,000,000 vines.

"Entirely irrespective of whether or not the Zionists will succeed in awakening in the Jewish people a national spirit and forming a Judean monarchy or republic, with its parliament in Jerusalem and its representation in foreign capitals, the present agitation makes for the development of a country which is but a shadow of its former self, and which will generously respond to modern influences. The Sultan seems quite disposed to grant railway, harbor, and other franchises, and it is possible that the new Jewish Colonial Bank, the organization of which was decided upon in Basel, will be permitted, under certain guaranties, to play an important part in the industrial advancement and growth of Palestine. The movement is furthermore bringing out new qualities in the Jews residing in Palestine. They are no longer content with studying the Talmud and living on charity, but are waking to the fact, as the Hebrew would put it, that to till the ground is worship of God.

"It should not be inferred from statements here made that peace and prosperity have suddenly become the lot of the Jews in Palestine. Only a few days ago, Rev. William King Eddy, of Sidon, returned from beyond the Jordan, and he informs me that a Jewish colony situated not far from El Mzerib (on the caravan route from Damascus to Mekka) was recently attacked by predatory Bedouin tribes. The settlers were all driven away, their gardens and crops destroyed. Even a road built by the Jews to connect their frontier colony with older ones in Galilee, west of the river, was at least partially obliterated. Taxes are more oppressive than ever, officials are corrupt, and prohibitive measures regarding immigration are still in force, although inadequate. I think, however, I am justified in saying that the prospects are brighter than ever for the Jews in Palestine and for Palestine itself. European influence has obtained a foothold in the country, and the tide of modern ideas can not be long debarred. Only four or five weeks ago, an English company announced its determination to build a broad-gauge railway from the sea at Haifa through the very heart of Samaria and Galilee to Damascus and on to Bagdad, and active operations have already commenced."—G. B. Ravndal, U. S. Consul at Beirut (*U. S. Consular Reports, April, 1899, p. 691*).

A. D. 1901.—Turkish order regulating visits to Palestine.—A Press telegram from Washington, February 16, 1901, states that "Consul Merrill, at Jerusalem, has reported to the State Department that the Turkish Minister of the Interior at Constantinople has issued an order relative to Jews who visit Palestine, which went into effect on January 29. The order applies to all Jews who come to Palestine from other countries as pilgrims or visitors. The conditions of the order are as follows : On arriving at Joppa the visitor must deliver his passport to the Turkish authorities and receive therefor a Turkish

document. The visitor is allowed to stay in the country three months, when he must leave, surrendering the Turkish permit and receiving his own. Foreign consuls are to compel the Jews who overstay the three months' period to leave Turkey."

JOAN OF ARC, The Beatification of.— The beatification of Joan of Arc, recommended by the Congregation of Rites, at Rome, was pronounced by the Pope, January 28, 1894.

JOHANNESBURG: Origin. See (in this vol.) SOUTH AFRICA (THE TRANSVAAL): A. D. 1885–1890.
A. D. **1895-1896.**—Revolutionary conspiracy of Uitlanders. See (in this vol.) SOUTH AFRICA (THE TRANSVAAL) : A. D. 1895–1896.
A. D. **1900.**—Taken by the British forces. See (in this vol.) SOUTH AFRICA (THE FIELD OF WAR) : A. D. 1900 (MAY–JUNE).

JOINT HIGH COMMISSION, Anglo-American. See (in this vol.) CANADA : A. D. 1898–1899.

JOLO, The Sultan of. See (in this vol.)

PHILIPPINE ISLANDS: A. D. 1899 (MAY—AUGUST).

JONES, Samuel M., Mayor of Toledo. See (in this vol.) TOLEDO, O. : A. D. 1899–1901.

JOUBERT, General **Pietrus** Jacobus : In the South African **War.** See (in this vol.) SOUTH AFRICA (THE FIELD OF WAR): A. D. 1899 (OCTOBER—DECEMBER).
Death. See (in this vol.) SOUTH AFRICA (THE FIELD OF WAR) : A. D. 1900 (MARCH).

JUBILEE, The Diamond, of Queen Victoria. See (in this vol.) ENGLAND: A. D. 1897 (JUNE).

JUBILEE OF THE HOLY YEAR 1900, Proclamation of the Universal. See (in this vol.) PAPACY: A. D. 1900-1901.

JU JU SACRIFICE. See (in this vol.) NIGERIA : A. D. 1897.

K.

KAFIRISTAN: Its conquest by the Afghans. See (in this vol.) AFGHANISTAN: A. D. 1896.

KAGAYAN, or **CAGAYAN,** The American acquisition of. See (in this vol.) UNITED STATES OF AM. : A. D. 1898 (JULY—DECEMBER).

KAIRWAN: Opened to tourists. See (in this vol.) TUNIS: A. D. 1881–1898.

KAISER WILHELM II. See (in this vol.) GERMANY.

KAISER WILHELM SHIP CANAL, The. See (in this vol.) GERMANY: A. D. 1895 (JUNE).

KAMERUNS, The: Cost of maintenance. See (in this vol.) GERMANY: A. D. 1899 (JUNE).

KANG YEU-WEI, Chinese reformer. See (in this vol.) CHINA: A. D. 1898 (JUNE—SEPTEMBER), and after.

KAPILAVASTU, Discovery of the ruins of. See (in this vol.) BUDDHA.

KARNAK, Fall of eleven columns of the temple of. See (in this vol.) ARCHÆOLOGICAL RESEARCH: EGYPT: FALL OF KARNAK COLUMNS.

KASSALA, Italian evacuation of. See (in this vol.) ITALY: A. D. 1897.

KATIPUNAN, The. See (in this vol.) PHILIPPINE ISLANDS: A. D. 1896–1898.

KEARSARGE, Loss of the.—The U. S. cruiser Kearsarge, destroyer of the Alabama, was totally wrecked, Feb. 2, 1894, on Roncadore Reef, off the Mosquito coast, her crew being saved.

KENGI. See (in this vol.) ARCHÆOLOGICAL RESEARCH: BABYLONIA: AMERICAN EXPLORATION.

KENTUCKY: A. D. 1895-1900.—Political conflicts.—Assassination of Governor Goebel. —In 1895 a Republican Governor, William O. Bradley, was elected in Kentucky by a majority of nearly 9,000 votes. In 1896 the conflict of political parties became fierce and dangerous, on the occasion of the election of an United States Senator to succeed the Democratic incumbent, J. C. S. Blackburn, whose term would expire March 3d, 1897. On joint ballot in the Legislature the Republicans and Democrats had 68 votes each, and the Populists had 2,—the latter thus holding a balance of power. But the two Populist members were divided, and the Democrats could not act together, owing to the division in their party on the money question. The "sound-money" Democrats refused support to Senator Blackburn, who obtained the caucus nomination of his party for re-election, and their votes were scattered. The Republicans were united on a candidate, and secured one of the Populist votes, but needed one more to give them a majority. They attempted to win the needed vote by unseating a Democrat in the Lower House whose seat was contested; but the Democrats promptly neutralized their move by unseating two Republicans in the Upper House. The passions excited by the factious contest had by this time become so violent and threatening that in March, 1897, the Governor of the State deemed it necessary to call out several companies of militia to preserve peace at Frankfort. In the end, the Legislature adjourned without electing an United States Senator; but a special session was called and the election accomplished, on the 28th of April, William J. Deboe, Republican, winning the senatorial seat.
In the following year (1898) the Democrats secured strong majorities in both branches of the Legislature, and, under the lead of Senator William Goebel, passed an election bill which was bitterly denounced as a contrivance for fraud.

It created a State election board, appointed by the existing Legislature for four years, which board should name three commissioners in each county, by whom all election and registration officers should be chosen. Notwithstanding this provision of partisan returning officers, the Democrats were so divided on the silver question in the gubernatorial election of 1899, and further weakened by personal hostilities which Goebel, who became their candidate for governor, had stirred up, that the official returns of the election gave William S. Taylor, the Republican candidate, a plurality of more than 2,000 votes over Goebel. There had been fear of riot in Louisville on election day, and the Governor had called out State troops, to preserve order. The defeated party claimed that military interference in that city had made the election illegal, and demanded that the returns from Louisville should be thrown out. On both sides there were accusations of fraud, and a dangerous state of political excitement ensued again. But two of the three members (all Democrats) of the State Board of Election Commissioners decided that Taylor, the Republican candidate, had been lawfully elected, and he was inaugurated Governor on the 12th of December. Goebel and his partisans, refusing to accept the decision, determined to unseat Governor Taylor, by authority of the Legislature, in which they controlled a considerable majority of votes.

The Legislature met and organized on the 1st of January, 1900. The Governor prepared to defend his possession of the office by summoning troops of the State Guard from the strong Republican districts of the mountain region, and 1,000 or more armed men arrived in Frankfort on the 25th. There had been fighting between the two parties already, and the situation now became desperately strained. Some kind of a bloody outcome seemed inevitable, but no one could anticipate the barbarous tragedy which ensued. As Senator Goebel was walking to the state house, on the 30th of January, he was shot from one of its windows, by a hidden assassin, receiving a wound from which he died February 3d. The Legislature at once closed its investigation of the election, and voted to recognize the dying William E. Goebel as Governor, with J. C. W. Beckham as his Lieutenant and the successor to the office in the event of his death. Governor Taylor issued an address to the people of the State, denouncing the murder and enjoining the preservation of order. At the same time he proclaimed an adjournment of the Legislature, closed the State House against it, and summoned its members to reassemble on the 6th of February, not at Frankfort, but at the distant small mountain town of London. Goebel, on his death-bed, took the oath of office, and issued orders dismissing Governor Taylor's Adjutant-General, appointing another in his place, and commanding the force at Frankfort to return to their homes.

The President of the United States was applied to by Governor Taylor for recognition and support, but decided that he had no authority to interfere. The supporters of Goebel applied with more effect to the Circuit Court of Kentucky, which issued a writ enjoining Governor Taylor from the use of armed force to prevent the Legislature from meeting. A clerk who succeeded in serving the writ by tacking it on the door of the Governor's office was seized and held

prisoner by the military, and a writ of habeas corpus requiring his deliverance was disobeyed for several days. All authority was breaking down, and a state of political chaos being produced. To save the State from actual anarchy and civil war, a conference of leaders in both parties was held at Louisville, February 5, and an agreement reached to withdraw troops from the capital, allow the Legislature to meet there, and abide by its action, with promise to repeal the obnoxious election law. Governor Taylor refused acceptance of the agreement. He dismissed the troops, however, on the 12th, and called the Legislature to meet at the capital. The Democratic members of that body were holding meetings at Louisville, the Republican members at London. The latter obeyed the call to Frankfort, while the former continued at Louisville, both fragments claiming to be the Legislature of the State. A petition to the United States Circuit Court, for injunctions against the Democratic claimants for certain of the minor State offices, was denied by Judge Taft on the 14th.

On the 21st, Republican and Democratic leaders came to another agreement, that the gubernatorial question should be settled in the courts,— first in those of the State, and then carried by appeal to the Supreme Court of the United States. This agreement prevailed, and the case, as between Governor Taylor and Governor Beckham (declared to be Governor by a majority of the members of the Legislature after Governor Goebel's death) was peacefully adjudicated in favor of the latter. The Circuit Court of the State recognized the Legislature's decision of the election as final; the Court of Appeals, with only one of three Republican judges dissenting, did the same, April 6. On April 30 the case was argued, on appeal, before the Supreme Court of the United States, and on the 21st of May that tribunal decided that it had no jurisdiction. This ended attempts to dispute the authority of Governor Beckham.

Strenuous efforts were being made to implicate his competitor, Mr. Taylor, as accessory to the murder of Goebel. Several persons had been arrested and put on trial for that crime, including Caleb Powers, the Secretary of State in Governor Taylor's fallen government, from the window of whose office it was claimed that the cowardly shot had been fired. The trials were scandalized by confessions of perjury and charges and counter-charges of subornation on the part of witnesses. In August, Powers was found guilty and sentenced to imprisonment for life. Subsequently, Henry E. Youtsey received the same sentence, while James Howard was condemned to death. Appeals were taken in each case. Mr. Taylor, under indictment as an accomplice, had left the State, and a requisition for his rendition was refused by the Governor of Indiana, where he sojourned. He indignantly denied all knowledge of the alleged conspiracy to kill his competitor, but claimed that a fair trial could not be secured to him if he was placed in the power of his political enemies.

In October, a new election law was passed by the Legislature and signed by the Governor. It provides that, of the three State Election Commissioners, one is to be taken from each of the dominant parties, upon the recommendation of the State Central Committee, and the Clerk of the Court of Appeals, an elective officer, is to act as umpire. The Commissioners are to be appointed by the Governor. They are to appoint the county boards, one from each party, with the Sheriff as umpire. All the boards are to have only ministerial powers, and the law gives the right of appeal in all cases of contests to the courts except in the case of Governor and Lieutenant-Governor, which must be tried by the Legislature, as the constitution prescribes. The Goebel law made the boards supreme. The new law also provides for an equitable division of election officers.

KHAIBAR: Inclusion in a **new** British Indian province. See (in this vol.) INDIA: A. D. 1901 (FEBRUARY).

KHALIFA, The. See (in this vol.) EGYPT: A. D. 1885-1896; 1897-1898; and 1899-1900.

KHARTUM, Destruction of. See (in this vol.) EGYPT: A. D. 1885-1896.
Gordon Memorial College. See (in this vol.) EGYPT: A. D. 1898-1899.

KIANG-HUNG: Cession to France. See (in this vol.) CHINA: A. D. 1894-1895 (MARCH—JULY).

KIAO-CHAU: A. D. **1897**.—Seizure by Germany. See (in this vol.) CHINA: A. D. 1897 (NOVEMBER).
A. D. **1899**.—Cost of maintenance. See (in this vol.) GERMANY: A. D. 1899 (JUNE).

KIEL: Opening of the Baltic Canal. See (in this vol.) GERMANY: A. D. 1895 (JUNE).

KIENNING, Anti-missionary riot at. See (in this vol.) CHINA: A. D. 1899.

KIMBERLEY, Siege of. See (in this vol.) SOUTH AFRICA (THE FIELD OF WAR): A. D. 1899 (OCTOBER—NOVEMBER); (OCTOBER—DECEMBER); and 1900 (JANUARY—FEBRUARY).

KINGSHIP BY DIVINE RIGHT: German revival **of** the doctrine. See (in this vol.) GERMANY: A. D. 1894-1899.

KIS, The city of. See (in this vol.) ARCHÆOLOGICAL RESEARCH: BABYLONIA: AMERICAN EXPLORATION.

KITCHENER, Major-General Sir Herbert (afterwards Lord): Sirdar of the Egyptian army.—**Expedition** to Dongola. See (in this vol.) EGYPT: A. D. 1885-1896.
Final campaigns against the Dervishes. See (in this vol.) EGYPT: A. D. 1897-1898.
Dealing with the French expedition at Fashoda. See (in this vol.) EGYPT: A. D. 1898 (SEPTEMBER—NOVEMBER).
In the South African **War**. See (in this vol.) SOUTH AFRICA (THE FIELD OF WAR): A. D. 1900 (JANUARY—FEBRUARY), and after.

KLONDIKE GOLD FIELDS, The.—
"Many years ago gold was known to exist on the Yukon. The Hudson Bay Company's men tested the bars of the main river, and found 'the color,' but not in sufficient quantity to warrant working. The reason is, that, in the disintegration of the rocks by the smaller streams and the action of frost and melting snow, the metallic burden of the waters is dropped in the causeway of the smaller tributaries; only the finest float gold and the lighter sand and gravel being carried

as far as the Yukon itself. In 1880, after years of fruitless search on the main stream, a body of prospectors under the protection of Captain (now Admiral) Beardsley, U. S. N., landed at the head of Lynn Canal, crossed the divide, and proceeded to explore the head-waters. Not much being found at first in Canadian territory, the prospectors descended the river to the region near the lower end of the Upper Ramparts. In this region lies the boundary, formed by the one hundred and forty-first degree of west longitude from Greenwich. Here the Yukon receives from the southwest a tributary called Forty-Mile Creek. A few miles of the lower part of this creek, including its mouth, are on the Canadian side of the line: the head-waters—on which the gold is chiefly found—are, for the most part, on the American side. In this vicinity the first substantial deposits were discovered, many of which are still worked. . . .

"The site of the new diggings—which have produced an excitement recalling the 'Fraser River rush' of 1857—is on a stream tributary to the Yukon from the northeast, wholly in Canadian territory, and entering the main river about fifty miles eastward from the boundary. Here a mining camp, called Dawson City,—after the head of the Dominion Geological Survey,—has been established. . . . The stream above referred to has been named the Klondyke,—signifying 'reindeer': on some of the older maps it is designated Reindeer River. It is said however that the name should really be Throndak,—a Tinneh term meaning 'plenty of fish.' The existence of gold on this stream and its branches appears to have been first made known by Indians. One of the first prospectors to locate upon it with success was J. A. Carmich, who staked out his claim in August, 1896, and with two helpers, in a few weeks, washed out over $14,000."—W. H. Dall, *Alaska and the New Gold-Field* (*Forum*, Sept., 1897).

KNIGHTHOOD: Victorian Order. See (in this vol.) VICTORIAN ORDER.

KNOSSOS, Archæological excavations at. See (in this vol.) ARCHÆOLOGICAL RESEARCH: CRETE.

KOKANG: Cession to Great Britain. See (in this vol.) CHINA: A. D. 1897 (MAY—JUNE).

KOREA: A. D. **1895-1898**.—Nominal independence **of** Korea.—Japanese **influence** supplanted by Russian.—On the 7th of January, 1895, the independence of Korea (see, in this vol., CHINA: A. D. 1894-1895) was formally proclaimed at Seoul. For a time, Japanese influence prevailed, and the party favorable to it controlled affairs. But Russian jealousy gave encouragement to the opposing faction, headed by the queen, and the latter succeeded at length in thwarting most of the aims of the Japanese. The result was a revolutionary conspiracy in October, carried out by a murderous band which broke into the palace and killed three women, one of whom was supposed to be the queen. The assassins were dressed in Japanese costume, and were said to belong to the "soshi," or hireling cutthroats, of that country; but the Japanese government indignantly repudiated the crime, recalled and arrested its Minister, who was suspected of complicity, and forbade its subjects to enter Korea without special permission. Russian influence, nevertheless, became dominant soon after; the king yielded to it completely, and obtained riddance of opposing ministers with Russian support. In the end, Russia and Japan came to an agreement, nominally establishing a joint protectorate over Korea; but practically the Japanese seemed to be fairly shouldered out.

In the later part of 1897, the Russian Minister to Korea brought about the dismissal of an English official, Mr. Brown, who had been the financial adviser of the Korean government and its commissioner of customs, putting a Russian in his place, and secured a written agreement that none but Russians or Koreans should fill that important post in future. The vigorous remonstrance of the British government, however, caused this action to be reversed.

Russia and Japan came to a new understanding in 1898, more favorable to the interests of the latter in Korea. This was embodied in a protocol, signed at Tokyo on the 25th of April, 1898, in terms as follows: "I. That the Governments of Japan and Russia, recognizing the sovereignty and complete independence of Korea, shall in no way directly interfere with the domestic government of that country. II. That in order to avoid misunderstandings in the future, whenever either Japan or Russia is applied to by Korea for advice or assistance, neither contracting party shall take any steps toward the appointment of military instructors or financial advisers without previous consultation with the other. III. That Russia, recognizing the great progress made in commercial and industrial enterprises by Japan in Korea, and the great number of Japanese subjects residing in the settlements, will do nothing to injure the development of the commercial and industrial relations between Japan and Korea."— *U. S. Consular Reports, Aug.,* 1898, *p.* 591.

A reform party had begun to manifest influence at this time, even aspiring to representative institutions in the government. Various progressive measures were undertaken in 1898; the gold monetary standard was adopted; American engineers were engaged to plan roads, bridges, etc., and new ports were opened.

A. D. 1900.—Strategic importance of Korea to Russia and Japan.—Japanese jealousy of Russian encroachments in Manchuria and its grounds.—"Considerable as are the material interests which Japan is building up in Korea, it is still from the strategical point of view that she is most deeply concerned with the future of the Korean peninsula, which, in the hands of a great military Power like Russia, would be a permanent threat to her safety. And the Japanese appear to be firmly convinced that, when once Russia is firmly seated in Northern China, she must inevitably seek to absorb Korea. In any other hands but her own the Korean peninsula would always be a wedge inconveniently driven in between her older acquisitions on the Pacific seaboard and her more recent acquisitions in the Gulf of Chi-li, nor could she regard her strategi-

cal position in the Far East as thoroughly secured so long as she did not command one shore of the straits through which lies the natural waterway between her two naval bases at Vladivostok and at Port Arthur. . . . Port Arthur is situated practically on an inland sea to which the approaches can be dominated not only by positions already in the hands of other European Powers, such as Wei-hai-wei and Kiaochau, but by the Korean peninsula and islands as well as by the Japanese archipelago, from Tsushima down to Formosa. With Port Arthur as her main base Russia's position as a naval Power in the Far East would be subject to natural limitations not altogether unlike those which hamper her in the Black Sea and the Baltic.

"Considered in this light the question of Russian aggrandisement in Northern China is so closely interwoven with that of the future of Korea that it must necessarily wear a much more serious aspect for Japan than for any other Power —so serious, indeed, that not a few Japanese deem the time to be close at hand when Japan should retort upon Russia in precisely the same terms which the latter used in 1895 and demand the evacuation of territories where her presence must be a permanent threat to the independence of the Chinese Empire and the peace of the Far East."—*London Times, Tokio Correspondence, Dec.* 27, 1900.

KOTZE, Chief-Justice: Conflict with President Kruger of the Transvaal. See (in this vol.) SOUTH AFRICA (THE TRANSVAAL): A. D. 1897 (JANUARY—MARCH); and 1898 (JANUARY—FEBRUARY).

KROONSTAD: Temporary seat of Orange Free State government. See (in this vol.) SOUTH AFRICA (THE FIELD OF WAR): A. D. 1900 (MARCH—MAY).

KRUGER: President Stephanus Johannes Paulus. See (in this vol.) SOUTH AFRICA (THE TRANSVAAL): A. D. 1885–1890, and after.

KUANG HSU, Emperor of China. See (in this vol.) CHINA: A. D. 1898 (JUNE—SEPTEMBER), and after.

KUMASSI, or **COOMASSIE:** Occupation by the British.—Siege and relief. See (in this vol.) ASHANTI.

KURAM, The: Inclusion in a new British Indian province. See (in this vol.) INDIA: A. D. 1901 (FEBRUARY).

KURRAM VALLEY, British-Indian war with tribes in the. See (in this vol.) INDIA: A. D. 1897–1898.

KWANGCHOW WAN, Lease of, to France. See (in this vol.) CHINA: A. D. 1898 (APRIL—AUGUST).

KWANG-SI, Rebellion in. See (in this vol.) CHINA: A. D. 1898 (APRIL—JULY).

L.

LABOR COLONIES: In Australia. See (in this vol.) AUSTRALIA : RECENT EXTENSIONS OF DEMOCRACY.

LABOR CONFLICTS. See (in this vol.) INDUSTRIAL DISTURBANCES.

LABOR LEGISLATION: Compulsory insurance in Germany. See (in this vol.) GERMANY : A. D. 1897-1900.

Eight-hours day in Utah. See (in this vol.) UTAH : A. D. 1895-1896.

New Zealand Labor Laws. See (in this vol.) NEW ZEALAND : A. D. 1891-1900.

Workmen's Compensation Act in Great Britain. See (in this vol.) ENGLAND : A. D. 1897 (MAY—JULY).

The United States Industrial Commission. See (in this vol.) UNITED STATES OF AM. : A. D. 1898 (JUNE).

LABRADOR, Recent exploration of. See (in this vol.) POLAR EXPLORATION, 1893-1900, 1896.

LABYRINTH, The Cretan : Its supposed discovery. See (in this vol.) ARCHÆOLOGICAL RESEARCH : CRETE.

LADRONE ISLANDS: Sale by Spain to Germany. See (in this vol.) CAROLINE AND MARIANNE ISLANDS.

LADYSMITH, Siege of. See (in this vol.) SOUTH AFRICA (THE FIELD OF WAR) : A. D. 1899 (OCTOBER—DECEMBER) ; and 1900 (JANUARY—FEBRUARY).

LAGAS, The ancient city of. See (in this vol.) ARCHÆOLOGICAL RESEARCH : BABYLONIA : AMERICAN EXPLORATION.

LAGOS. See (in this vol.) NIGERIA : A. D. 1899.

LA GUASIMA, Battle at. See (in this vol.) UNITED STATES OF AM. : A. D. 1898 (JUNE—JULY).

LAKE SUPERIOR CONSOLIDATED IRON MINES: In the United States Steel Corporation. See (in this vol.) TRUSTS : UNITED STATES : THE CLIMAX.

LAND BILL, Irish (1896). See (in this vol.) IRELAND : A. D. 1896.

LAND SYSTEM, The New Zealand. See (in this vol.) NEW ZEALAND : A. D. 1891-1900.

LAND TAXATION: In Australia and New Zealand. See (in this vol.) AUSTRALIA : RECENT EXTENSIONS OF DEMOCRACY.

LANDLORDS, Irish, New League against. See (in this vol.) IRELAND : A. D. 1900-1901.

LATTIMER, Conflict of striking coal miners with sheriffs' deputies at. See (in this vol.) INDUSTRIAL DISTURBANCES : A. D. 1897.

LAURIER, Sir Wilfrid : Prime Minister of Canada. See (in this vol.) CANADA : A. D. 1890-1896, and after.

LAWS OF WAR. See (in this vol.) PEACE CONFERENCE.

LAWTON, General Henry **W. :** Command at Santiago de Cuba. See (in this vol.) UNITED STATES OF AM. : A. D. 1898 (JULY—AUGUST CUBA).

Military operations in the Philippine Islands. See (in this vol.) PHILIPPINE ISLANDS A. D. 1899 (JANUARY—NOVEMBER).

Death. See (in this vol.) PHILIPPINE ISLANDS : A. D. 1899-1900.

LECHER, Dr. : Twelve-hours speech. See (in this vol.) AUSTRIA-HUNGARY : A. D. 1897 (OCTOBER—DECEMBER).

LEE, General Fitzhugh : U. S. Consul-General at Havana. See (in this vol.) CUBA A. D. 1897-1898 (NOVEMBER—FEBRUARY) ; and (DECEMBER—MARCH).

Command at Havana. — Report. See (in this vol.) CUBA : A. D. 1898-1899 (DECEMBER—OCTOBER).

LEICHAU PENINSULA, Leases in, to France. See (in this vol.) CHINA : A. D. 1898 (APRIL—AUGUST).

LEO XIII., Pope. See PAPACY.

LÈSE MAJESTÉ.—A hurt to Majesty. Any offense or crime against the sovereign. For lèse majesté in Germany, see (in this vol.) GERMANY : A. D. 1898; and 1900 (OCTOBER).

LEX FALKENHAYN, The. See (in this vol.) AUSTRIA-HUNGARY : A. D. 1897 (OCTOBER—DECEMBER).

LEX HEINZE, The. See (in this vol.) GERMANY : A. D. 1900 (MAY).

LEXOW INVESTIGATION, The. See (in this vol.) NEW YORK CITY : A. D. 1894-1895.

LIAOTUNG PORTS: A. D. 1895.—Russo-Chinese Treaty relating to. See (in this vol.) CHINA : A. D. 1895. See, also, references from PORT ARTHUR; TALIENWAN; and FÊNG-TIEN PENINSULA.

LIBRARIES, The gifts of Mr. Andrew Carnegie to.—Of neither the manifold items nor the stupendous total of the gifts made by Mr. Andrew Carnegie for the founding or assistance of public libraries in America and Great Britain is there any authentic account; but a tentative record of them, compiled mainly from the news columns of the "Library Journal," and published, on the 17th of March, 1901, in the "Buffalo Illustrated Express," is probably not far from correct. It begins in 1881, with the founding of a public library at Dunfermline, Scotland, the birthplace of Mr. Carnegie, who then gave for it $40,000. Two years later, he is said to have given $50,000 to a library at Inverness. In 1885 the New York Free Circulating Libraries were helped by him to the extent of $5,000. In the following year his benefactions were raised to their larger scale by his gift of $250,000 to the Free Public Library of Edinburgh; besides which he gave $28,000 to the Workmen's Library of the Keystone Bridge Works, and smaller donations elsewhere. In 1889 he founded the Carnegie Library at Braddock, Pa., at a cost of $300,000. In 1890 he con-

290

tributed $325,000 to the founding of the Carnegie Free Public Library at Allegheny, Pa., which the city undertook to support; be replaced the Cambria Library, which the great flood at Johnstown had destroyed, expending $65,000 in that kindly work; gave $40,000 to a library at Fairfield, Iowa, and $9,000 to another at Augusta, Me. Five thousand dollars to a library in Airdrie, $50,000 to one in Ayr, and $2,500 to a third at Jedburgh, all three in Scotland, are the gifts recorded in 1893 and 1894.

In 1895 Mr. Carnegie seemed to be crowning his munificence by the creation, at Pittsburg, of the great institution, combining library, art gallery, and museum, on which, between that year and 1899 he is said to have expended no less than $3,860,000. In the same year he founded a small library at Wick, in Scotland. In 1897 the donations appear to have been small. In 1898 Dumfries, in Scotland, received for a public library $50,000 from his open purse, and $250,000 went from it to the creation of the Carnegie Library at Homestead, Pa., the seat of the Carnegie works.

Hitherto the stream of Mr. Carnegie's bounty to public libraries had been a rivulet: it now, in 1899, began to pour like the fertilizing flood of the Nile, and that first twelvemonth of the amazing tide was celebrated by American librarians, at the annual meeting of their Association, as "the Carnegie year." In reality, it but opened a series of "Carnegie years," which have filled the period since, and may still go on. As compiled by the "Express," supplemented by a later record in the "Library Journal" for April, 1901, the list of the library gifts and offers of Mr. Carnegie, from the beginning of 1899 until March, 1901, includes $5,200,000, tendered to the city of New York for branches to its Public Library (see below); $1,000,000 tendered to St. Louis; $350,000 to the city of Washington; $260,000 to Syracuse; $125,000 each to Atlanta and Louisville; $100,000, or $150,000 (there seems to be uncertainty as to the sum) to Seattle; $100,000 each to Richmond, Conneaut, Grand Rapids, Ottawa, Ont., and the State College in Pennsylvania ; $75,000 each to Lincoln, Neb., Springfield, Ill., Davenport, Ia., Tacoma, Wash., and the Bellevue Medical College, N. Y.; $50,000 each to San Diego, Oakland, Duluth, Sedalia, East Liverpool, O., Steubenville, Sandusky, Connellsville, McKeesport, Beaver, Beaver Falls, Tyrone, Pa., Clarion, Oil City, Fort Worth, Dallas, Cheyenne, Dubuque, Ottumwa, Emporia College, East Orange, York, Coal Center and Wilkinsburg, Pa., Chattanooga, Houston, San Antonio, Vancouver, B. C., Aurora, Ill., Lewiston, Me., Niagara Falls, Yonkers, Canton, O., Montgomery, Ala., Marion, Ind., Galesburg, Ill., Schenectady, N. Y., and Hawick, Scotland; besides a great number of lesser sums, ranging from a few hundred dollars to $40,000. The total of the library gifts and proffers of Mr. Carnegie, from the beginning to March, 1900, is thought to exceed $23,000,000.

To many other educational institutions Mr. Carnegie has been munificently generous, giving, for example, $500,000 for the Manual Training School of Cooper Institute, New York; $250,-000 to Birmingham University; $50,000 to the engineering laboratory of Stevens Institute, Hoboken; $50,000 to the Edinburgh Technical School, and making other gifts of like kind.

LIBRARY, New York Public, Astor, Lenox and Tilden Foundations.—Andrew Carnegie's offered gift.—" The New York Public Library, Astor, Lenox and Tilden Foundations, was formed by the consolidation, on the 23d of May, 1895, of the three corporations, ' The Trustees of the Astor Library,' originally incorporated January 18, 1849, ' The Trustees of the Lenox Library,' originally incorporated January 20, 1870, and ' The Tilden Trust,' originally incorporated March 26, 1887. . . . In the agreement for consolidation it was provided that the name of the new corporation should be 'The New York Public Library, Astor, Lenox and Tilden Foundations'; that the number of its trustees should be twenty-one, to be selected from the thirty-three members of the separate boards ; and that ' the said new corporation shall establish and maintain a free public library and reading room in the city of New York, with such branches as may be deemed advisable, and shall continue and promote the several objects and purposes set forth in the respective acts of incorporation of ' The Trustees of the Astor Library,' ' The Trustees of the Lenox Library,' and the 'Tilden Trust.' . . . In December, Dr. John Shaw Billings, U. S. A. (retired), was chosen Director, but he did not enter fully upon his duties until June, 1896. . . .

"At the time of the consolidation the Astor library owned its site and buildings, had an endowment fund of about $941,000, producing an annual income of about $47,000, and contained 267,147 volumes. The Lenox library owned its site and building, had an endowment fund of $505,500, producing an annual income of $20,500, and contained about 86,000 volumes. The Tilden Trust possessed Mr. Tilden's private library, containing about 20,000 volumes, and an endowment fund estimated at $2,000,000, making the total number of volumes in the New York Public Library 373,147, and the total endowment fund about $3,446,500. . . . The joint libraries now contain about 500,000 volumes and 175,000 pamphlets."

Immediately upon the completion of the consolidation of the three libraries, the city of New York was asked to provide a suitable building for the great institution contemplated, and the ground covered by the old reservoir, on Fifth Avenue, between Fortieth and Forty-second Streets, was suggested as an advantageous site. "The result of this appeal, which met with cordial public support, was that an act was passed by the legislature and approved May 19, 1897, giving the necessary authority to the city to issue bonds for the construction of a library building, the result of which was that on November 10, 1897, the plans prepared by Messrs. Carrère & Hastings, of New York City, were selected and approved, and were laid before the Board of Estimate and Apportionment of the City of New York on December 1, 1897. These plans were approved by the Board of Estimate and on December 8 a contract was entered into between the City of New York and the New York Public Library, by which the library building to be erected upon Bryant Park was leased to the New York Public Library. . . . The sketch plans provide for a building about 350 feet in length and about 250 feet in width from east to west, giving shelving for about 1,500,000 volumes and seating capacity for about 800 readers in the main reading room. . . .

291

"Plans and specifications for the removal of the Forty-second Street reservoir and laying the foundations for the new building having been approved the contract for this work was awarded to Mr. Eugene Lentilhon, and the work of removing was begun on June 6th, 1899."—*Handbook to the New York Public Library*, 1900.

In October, 1900, it was stated in the newspapers of the city that Mayor Van Wyck, Controller Coler, and the other members of the Board of Estimate had come to an understanding regarding the consolidation of all the libraries of the Greater New York under the New York Public Library. "It was announced officially that all the smaller libraries would be allowed about the same amount of money for maintenance this year as was allowed last year. A practical plan of consolidation will be perfected, and when the matter comes up before the Board of Estimate next year it was agreed that the libraries would be put under one head. . . . It is proposed to spend $5,000,000 on the New York Public Library now in course of erection in Bryant Park on the site of the old reservoir. It will be four years before the building can be completed. Controller Coler's idea is to gradually merge the smaller libraries so that when the new building is completed New York will have the largest and best equipped library for sending out books of any city in the world."

On the 12th of March, 1901, Mr. Andrew Carnegie addressed the following letter to Dr. Billings, the Director of the New York Public Library, making a proposal of unparalleled munificence : "Dear Dr. Billings : Our conferences upon the needs of greater New-York for branch libraries to reach the masses of the people in every district have convinced me of the wisdom of your plans. Sixty-five branches strike one at first as a very large order, but as other cities have found one necessary for every sixty thousand or seventy thousand of population, the number is not excessive. You estimate the average cost of these libraries at, say, $80,000 each, being $5,200,000 for all. If New-York will furnish sites for these branches for the special benefit of the masses of the people, as it has done for the central library, and also agree in satisfactory form to provide for their maintenance as built, I should esteem it a rare privilege to be permitted to furnish the money as needed for the buildings, say, $5,200,000. Sixty-five libraries at one stroke probably breaks the record, but this is the day of big operations, and New-York is soon to be the biggest of cities. Very truly yours, ANDREW CARNEGIE."

In communicating this extraordinary proposal to the New York Public Library Board, Dr. Billings made the following statement of the plan contemplated in the suggestions he had made : "In the conferences referred to by Mr. Carnegie the suggestions which I have made have related mainly to a free public library system for the boroughs of Manhattan and The Bronx. I have stated that such a system should include the great central reference library in Forty-second-st. and Fifth-ave., about forty branch libraries for circulation, small distributing centres in those public school buildings which are adapted to such purpose, and a large travelling library system operated from the central building. Each of the branch libraries should contain reading rooms for from 50 to 100 adults and for from 75 to 125 children, and in these reading rooms should be about

500 volumes of encyclopædias, dictionaries, atlases and large and important reference books. There should be ample telephone and delivery arrangements between the branches and the central library.

"To establish this system would require at least five years. The average cost of the branch libraries I estimated at from $75,000 to $125,000, including sites and equipment. The cost of maintaining the system when completed I estimated at $500,000 a year. The circulation of books for home use alone in these boroughs should amount to more than 5,000,000 of volumes a year, and there should be at least 500,000 volumes in the circulation department, with additions of new books and to replace worn out books of at least 40,000 a year.

"With regard to the other boroughs of greater New-York I have made no special plans or estimates, but have said that about twenty-five libraries would be required for them."

LIBRARY, The Temple, of ancient Nippur. See (in this vol.) ARCHÆOLOGICAL RESEARCH : BABYLONIA : AMERICAN EXPLORATION.

LIBRARY, The U. S. House of Representatives : Its management under the spoils system. See (in this vol.) CIVIL SERVICE REFORM : A. D. 1901.

LIBRARY OF CONGRESS, at Washington.—The **new** building.—"By the act of April 15, 1886, the present site, one-quarter of a mile south of east from the Capitol, was selected, its acquisition by the United States provided for, and the construction of a building authorized. During this long period of discussion many schemes for attaining the desired end, including a variety of plans for enlarging and occupying the Capitol and many different sites in the city of Washington, were considered. Several times did the legislation reach an advanced stage and fail through the pressure of more absorbing interests. Finally the law referred to adopted sketch plans that had been prepared by Messrs. Smithmeyer and Pelz, a firm of Washington architects, but it fixed no limit of cost, nor did it specify the materials of construction or character of execution of the design other than to stipulate that the building should be fireproof. A commission, composed of the Secretary of the Interior, the Librarian of Congress, and the Architect of the Capitol, was designated to conduct the construction of the building. The site, comprising two city squares—nearly nine acres, within the city building lines and with the included streets—was purchased of the private owners, the ground cleared of some seventy buildings occupying it, and by the summer of 1888 about one-half of the foundation footings for the building were laid. During that year, however, Congress became dissatisfied with the progress that had been made and the uncertainties involved in the operation of the inadequate original law, and accordingly, on October 2, modified it and lodged the entire control of the work, including the preparation of new plans at a limited cost, in the hands of Brig. Gen. Thomas Lincoln Casey, Chief of Engineers of the United States Army. He immediately placed the writer in local charge. On March 2, 1889, Congress enacted that the building should be erected at a total cost of $6,500,000, including previous expenditures, according to a plan that had been prepared and submitted by General Casey, pursuant to the previous act of October 2, 1888. This plan was based on that adopted by the original act, and provided a building of similar form, dimensions, and architecture. The project embodied the principal materials of construction and a detailed estimate of the cost. Under these auspices operations were begun in the spring of 1889 where the operations had left off the year before, and the construction thence proceeded without interruption until the building was finally completed, in the spring of 1897. It was 470 feet in length by 340 feet in width, having three stories and a subbasement, and fronts west—toward the Capitol. . . . The foundations of the building are of hydraulic cement concrete, 6 feet deep in ground which is a mixture of clay and sand of very uniform character. The cellar walls are of hard red brick ; the exterior face of the superstructure of a fine grained light blue granite from Concord, N. H. ; the stone of the rotunda and the trimmings of the court walls a light blue granite from near Woodstock, Md. ; the facing of the court walls enamcled brick from Leeds, England ; and the backing and interior walls as well as all of the vaulting of the basement and first stories are of hard red brick. Most of the floors that are flat ceiled are of terra cotta, and this material also forms the covering and filling of the roofs and main dome, of which the supporting members are of rolled steel in beams, girders, and trusses. All of the floors are leveled up with concrete and surfaced with tiles, terrazzo, or mosaic in the public spaces, while in the office and working rooms they are covered with a carpet of southern pine boards. The most important of the strictly useful features of the building are the book stacks, of which the design is largely original. The problem was new, not only through the capacity to be provided but the numerous other conditions to be met, such as light, ventilation, adjustability to several uses, communication, immunity from fire, cleanliness, durability, and simplicity. It was also necessary that rapid mechanical transmission of books between the shelving and the reading room should be provided, coupled with a quick and reliable means of communication, both written and oral. . . . The book carrier is a pair of parallel, endless chains, running in a vertical shaft in the middle of the stack ; thence in a horizontal duct in the cellar to a point below the central desk of the reading room, where it turns upward and ascends vertically to the delivery outlet at the desk. A series of equidistant book trays, eighteen in number, are suspended between the chains. The machine runs continuously and automatically takes on and delivers books of the size of a quarto or less at its reading room terminal and at each of the stack stories. The speed of the carrier is about 100 feet per minute. The pneumatic message tube is also convenient as a speaking tube. The great rotunda or public reading room of the building, the main staircase hall or foyer, the private reading rooms for the members of Congress, the Librarian's office, the corridors communicating with these, and the exhibition halls as well as many portions of the exterior walls, especially the west main pavilion, have received a good degree of artistic treatment and embellishment, but all within strict architec-

tural requirements. Some forty sculptors and mural painters, about equally divided in numbers, furnished the principal works of art under the architects' supervision and direction. Many appropriate quotations and names are inscribed on the walls in the architectural tablets, friezes and panels, adding to the general impressiveness and interest of the building. In all ways and from all points of view the library building is eminently instructive as an example of good design, good appointment for its great purpose, good building and good administration in the execution, and therefore the more appropriate to house the nation's library. The unusual success of the undertaking under Government auspices is almost wholly due to the selection of a known competent, sturdy, and faithful individual such as General Casey was, and giving him the sole charge directly under Congress without an executive superior liable to interfere and cause delays. The work went on quietly, but with energy, and was completed within the originally estimated time and well within the legal limit of cost. The total cost of the building was $6,344,-585.34—that of the site, $585,000."—Bernard R. Green, *The Building for the Library of Congress* (*Annual Report Smithsonian Institution*, 1897, p. 625).

LI HUNG-CHANG : Negotiation of peace with Japan. See (in this vol.) CHINA: A. D. 1894–1895.

Tour in Europe and America. See (in this vol.) CHINA : A. D. 1896.

Charged with being in Russian pay. See (in this vol.) CHINA : A. D. 1898 (APRIL—JULY).

Acting Viceroy at Canton. See (in this vol.) CHINA : A. D. 1899 (DECEMBER).

Attempt to open negotiations with allied Powers. See (in this vol.) CHINA : A. D. 1900 (JULY).

Chinese Plenipotentiary to negotiate with the allied Powers. See (in this vol.) CHINA: A. D. 1900 (AUGUST—DECEMBER).

LIKIN, The Chinese taxes called.—" Chinese tariff rates, where they exist, average about 5 per cent ad valorem. Many articles are admitted free of duty, and on some the rates are higher than 5 per cent, but in general terms this is about the average rate. To this, however, there is a material addition where the goods are intended for interior points. The Chinese Government, while it collects a part of its revenue from customs, relies largely upon the provinces to supply revenue, and arbitrarily names each year the sum which each province must supply, leaving to the officers of that province the methods by which this is obtained. The consequence is that each province is permitted to collect a tax on goods entering it from the adjacent provinces, and this custom has been extended to the subdivision of the provinces, so that goods in transit are frequently compelled to pay taxes every few miles. As a consequence, the interior taxes, known as 'likin,' became not only the terror of importers, but sometimes almost prohibitory. So serious was this system in its effects upon attempts to introduce foreign goods that, upon the insistence of foreign ministers, the Chinese Government announced that an addition of 50 per cent to the rates paid at the custom-houses would insure passage of the goods to any point in the interior without the exaction of likin taxes. This was gladly accepted by foreigners desiring to do business in the interior of China. The additional 50 per cent on duties was paid and 'transit passes' issued for the goods in question, purporting to authorize their free transit to any point in the Empire. Actual experience, however, shows that these transit passes do not always accomplish what was expected. . . . Every 8 or 10 miles along the principal waterways or caravan routes a likin station is found, where a tax is levied upon some article or articles carried through by boat, pack animal, or wheelbarrow. At some points every article is taxed. This is the usual rule at the gates of cities. In some cases the tax is as little as 2 per cent ad valorem; in others, such as silk, satin, and native opium, much more, amounting at times to 6, 8, or even 10 per cent. Between Shanghai and Soochow, a distance of 84 miles, there are 8 likin stations. At the first and last stations all goods are dutiable; at the rest all goods must be examined, and there is scarcely a single article that does not in that distance pay at least three taxes. It is easily seen that under such a system foreign goods cannot be carried very far from the coast before their prices become prohibitive for ordinary people."—*United States, Bureau of Statistics, Monthly Summary, March, 1899, pp. 2188, 2231.*

LINCOLN PARTY, The. See (in this vol). UNITED STATES OF AM.: A. D. 1900 (MAY—NOVEMBER), SILVER REPUBLICAN.

LIQUID AIR, The production of. See (in this vol.) SCIENCE, RECENT: CHEMISTRY AND PHYSICS.

LIQUOR SELLING, The regulation of.—Abolition of the Army Canteen. See (in this vol.) UNITED STATES OF AM.: A. D. 1901 (FEBRUARY).

Dispensary Laws. See (in this vol.) SOUTH CAROLINA: A. D. 1892–1899; NORTH CAROLINA: A. D. 1897–1899; SOUTH DAKOTA: A. D. 1899; and ALABAMA: A. D. 1899.

International convention respecting the liquor traffic in Africa. See (in this vol.) AFRICA: A. D. 1899 (JUNE).

The question in American politics. See (in this vol.) UNITED STATES OF AM.: A. D. 1896 (JUNE—NOVEMBER); and 1900 (MAY—NOVEMBER).

The Raines Liquor Law. See (in this vol.) NEW YORK STATE: A. D. 1896–1897.

LISCUM, Colonel Emerson H.: Death. See (in this vol.) CHINA: A. D. 1900 (JULY).

LITTLE ENGLAND PARTY.—A name given by its opponents to the section of the Liberal party in Great Britain which condemns the boundless enlargement of British annexations, protectorates and spheres of influence in all parts of the world, and which is critical of expansive and imperialistic wars.

LIU KUN-YI, Viceroy at Nanking: Admirable conduct during the Chinese outbreak. See (in this vol.) CHINA: A. D. 1900 (JUNE—DECEMBER).

LOCH, Sir H. B.: British High Commissioner in South Africa. See (in this vol.) SOUTH AFRICA (THE TRANSVAAL): A. D. 1894.

LOCKOUTS. See (in this vol.) INDUSTRIAL DISTURBANCES.

LOG OF THE MAYFLOWER, The so-called. See (in this vol.) MASSACHUSETTS: A. D. 1897.

LOGIA, Discovery of a fragment of the. See (in this vol.) ARCHÆOLOGICAL RESEARCH: EGYPT; DISCOVERY OF A FRAGMENT.

LOMBOK. See (in this vol.) DUTCH EAST INDIES.

LONDON: A. D. 1894.—The Tower Bridge.—The Tower Bridge was formally opened on the 30th of June, eight years after the beginning of the work. Its cost was £1,250,000.

A. D. 1897.—Great fire.—On November 19, 1897, occurred one of the largest fires in London since 1666. Beginning in Aldersgate, it spread over six acres of a densely populated quarter, destroying over 100 warehouses and buildings. The loss was estimated at £2,000,000.

A. D. 1899.—The London Government Act. —" The London Government Act is the most important measure passed by Lord Salisbury's Government during the year 1899 ; indeed, in some respects it is the most valuable reform carried by the Parliament which [expired in 1900]. There was urgent need for such a measure. The machinery of London Government was hopelessly out of gear. It was both cumbrous and intricate; it was controlled by a network of small local authorities whose duties were ill-defined and often clashed with each other. There was no uniformity or harmony in the system." The old Roman wall, "built somewhere between A. D. 350 and A. D. 370 . . . played a most important part in the history of London ; and, indeed, it had a large share in creating the problems with which Mr. Balfour had to deal in 1899. Little did its unknown builder dream that his wall, so admirable in itself, would cause us trouble fifteen centuries after his death. But such is the fact. He was a wise man, this nameless benefactor of the infant municipality ; he took care that the wall should be thoroughly well built ; and he allowed, as he thought, ample room for later growth. The exact position of this wall is well known to antiquaries. Many portions of it still remain ; it included in its ambit about a square mile of territory, with wells and trees, gardens and pastures, bordering on the great Roman roads. For a thousand years or more this area was sufficient for all purposes. . . . So far as we now can gness, it was not till the 16th century that any Londoner felt cramped within the wall and craved more elbow-room. Gradually the City expanded, and at first it incorporated its extra-mural parishes, such as Bishopsgate and Farringdon Without. The borough of Southwark was supposed for some purposes to be annexed to the City; it was till last year by a fiction regarded as a ward of the City—the ward of Bridge Without. To this extent, then, the City spread outside its wall. But here its natural expansion stopped. . . . The City proper remained a compact town, well organized and well governed, but the suburbs were treated as mere country villages ; their only local authority was the parish vestry, and its only officers the churchwardens and the overseers.

"This state of things obviously could not last. It soon became impossible for the parishioners to assemble in the vestry; no room, indeed, would hold them. First one parish and then another applied to Parliament for an Act creating what was called a 'select vestry,' and many representative bodies were thus formed with diverse and very miscellaneous powers. . . . Where the parishes were small, instead of a select vestry a district board was formed, under which several small parishes were grouped. And so when the London Government Act was passed there were 78 parishes and extra-parochial places within the county, but outside the City of London. . . . These vestries and boards were the sanitary authorities for their respective areas; they superintended the removal of nuisances, and the lighting, paving, watering, and cleansing of the streets; they also attended to some minor works of drainage, ancillary to the main system. . . . In 1855, the Metropolitan Board of Works was created to control the main drainage, to carry out improvements, to regulate the streets and bridges, and to maintain and manage the Fire Brigade. But its members were elected on a vicious system—by the various vestries and boards, and not directly by the ratepayers. . . . Its place was taken [in 1888] by the London County Council. But besides these vestries, local boards, district boards, and the Metropolitan Board, it was deemed necessary from time to time to create many minor authorities to meet various pressing needs ; such were the Metropolitan Asylums Board, the Thames Conservators, the Lee Conservators, the commissioners of baths and washhouses, the commissioners of free libraries, the burial boards, &c., in addition to 30 boards of guardians and the London School Board. As the population of London outgrew its existing institutions, the defeets and shortcomings were remedied by patchwork. . . .

"From this position of affairs we have been rescued by two important measures, . . . the Local Government Act, 1888, and the London Government Act, 1899. . . . The Local Government Act of 1888 abolished the Metropolitan Board of Works ; it created the administrative county of London; it called into existence the London County Council. The London Government Act of 1899 has done still more for London. It has abolished some 127 local authorities, whose place will be taken by the 28 borough councils which must be elected on November 1. The London County Council, the City Corporation, the Metropolitan Asylums Board, the boards of guardians, and the London School Board remain practically untouched. But 78 vestries, 12 district boards, the Woolwich Local Board of Health (the last of its race), 12 burial boards, 19 boards of library commissioners, and 10 boards of baths and washhouses commissioners, for all purposes of civic government, cease to exist."—*London Times, Oct.* 16, 1900.

LONDON CONVENTION (British-Boer), of **1884.** See (in this vol.) SOUTH AFRICA (THE TRANSVAAL) : A. D. 1884–1894.

LONGEVITY, Human: The Nineteenth Century increase of. See (in this vol.) NINETEENTH CENTURY: THE LENGTHENED AVERAGE.

LOOTING, in China. See (in this vol.) CHINA : A. D. 1900 (AUGUST 5-16, and 15-28).

"LOS VON ROM" MOVEMENT, The. See (in this vol.) AUSTRIA-HUNGARY : A. D. 1899–1900.

LOUBET, Émile : Election to the Presidency of the French Republic. See (in this vol.) FRANCE : A. D. 1899 (FEBRUARY—JUNE).

LOUISIANA: A. D. 1898.—New State Constitution.—An educational qualification of the suffrage which applies to all negroes and few whites.—The framing of a new constitution for the State was completed in May. Its distinctive feature is an educational qualification of the suffrage which does not apply to men who were qualified in any State to vote at the beginning of the year 1867, nor to the sons and grandsons of such men, nor to foreigners naturalized before the 1st of January, 1898. The amendment is as follows :

"SEC. 3. He (the voter) shall be able to read and write, and shall demonstrate his ability to do so when he applies for registration, by making, under oath administered by the registration officer or his deputy, written application therefor, in the English language, or his mother tongue, which application shall contain the essential facts necessary to show that he is entitled to register and vote, and shall be entirely written, dated, and signed by him, in the presence of the registration officer or his deputy, without assistance or suggestion from any person or memorandum whatever, except the form of application hereinafter set forth : Provided, however, That if the applicant be unable to write his application in the English language, he shall have the right, if he so demands, to write the same in his mother tongue from the dictation of an interpreter; and if the applicant is unable to write his application by reason of physical disability, the same shall be written at his dictation by the registration officer or his deputy, upon his oath of such disability. The application for registration, above provided for, shall be a copy of the following form, with the proper names, dates, and numbers substituted for the blanks appearing therein, to wit :

"I am a citizen of the State of Louisiana. My name is ——. I was born in the State (or country) of ——, parish (or county) of ——, on the day of ——, in the year——. I am now —— years —— months and —— days of age. I have resided in this State since ——, and am not disfranchised by any provision of the constitution of this State.

"SEC. 4. If he be not able to read and write, as provided by section 3 of this article, then he shall be entitled to register and vote if he shall, at the time he offers to register, be the bona fide owner of property assessed to him in this State at a valuation of not less than $300 on the assessment roll of the current year, if the roll of the current year shall then have been completed and filed, and on which, if such property be personal only, all taxes due shall have been paid.

"SEC. 5. No male person who was on January 1, 1867, or at any date prior thereto, entitled to vote under the constitution or statute of any State of the United States, wherein he then resided, and no son or grandson of any such person not less than 21 years of age at the date of the adoption of this constitution, and no male person of foreign birth, who was naturalized prior to the first day of January, 1898, shall be denied the right to register and vote in this State by reason of his failure to possess the educational or property qualifications prescribed by this constitution:

Provided, He shall have resided in this State for five years next preceding the date at which he shall apply for registration, and shall have registered in accordance with the terms of this article prior to September 1, 1898; and no person shall be entitled to register under this section after said date."

LOW, Seth: Citizens' Union candidate for Mayor of Greater New York. See (in this vol.) NEW YORK CITY: A. D. 1897 (SEPTEMBER —NOVEMBER.)

American commissioner to the Peace Conference at The Hague. See (in this vol.) PEACE CONFERENCE.

LÜBECK: A. D. 1900.—The Elbe and Trave Canal. See (in this vol.) GERMANY: A. D. 1900 (JUNE).

LUDLOW, General William: Military Governor of Havana. See (in this vol.) CUBA: A. D. 1898–1899 (DECEMBER—OCTOBER).

LUEGER, Dr.: Anti-Semitic agitation in Vienna. See (in this vol.) AUSTRIA-HUNGARY: A. D. 1895–1896.

LUXEMBOURG: A. D. 1899 (May—July). —Representation in the Peace Conference at The Hague. See (in this vol.) PEACE CONFERENCE.

LUZON. See (in this vol.) PHILIPPINE ISLANDS.

LYNCH LAW, in the United States.— Statistics, compiled by the "Chicago Tribune," of the cases of mob-murder, called "lynchings," which were reported in the newspapers as having occurred in the United States during the year 1899, showed a total of 107, being 20 less than a similar record for 1898 had shown. Of the reported cases, 8 were in Kansas, 1 in Pennsylvania, and 103 in Southern States. Georgia led in the latter list, being credited with 20 executions under lynch law. Mississippi followed with 14, Louisiana with 13, Arkansas with 11, and other States of the South with lesser numbers. Of the victims (mostly colored) 44 were accused of murder; 11 of complicity in murder; 11 with rape or attempted rape; 1 with rape and murder.

The "Political Science Quarterly," in its Record of Political Events between November 11, 1897, and May 10, 1898, cites 31 incidents of lynching, exclusive of a mob-murder committed at Lake City, South Carolina, where a negro postmaster and one of his children were killed, his wife and three other children wounded, and their house burned down. Of these incidents, 23 were reported from the South, the victims in every case being black; 8 were from northwestern States, the victims being white.

For 1897, the "Buffalo Express" compiled statistics of reported l nchings from its news columns, which showed 38 between January 1 and June 8, and 77 during the remainder of the year, making a total of 115.

M.

MacARTHUR, General: Military operations in the Philippine Islands. See (in this vol.) PHILIPPINE ISLANDS: A. D. 1899 (JANUARY—NOVEMBER).

MacDONALD, Sir Claude: British Minister at Peking. See (in this vol.) CHINA: A. D. 1898 (FEBRUARY), and after.

MACEDONIA, Impending revolt in. See (in this vol.) TURKEY: A. D. 1899–1901 ; and BALKAN AND DANUBIAN STATES.

MACEO, Antonio: Death of the Cuban leader. See (in this vol.) CUBA: A. D. 1896–1897.

MACHADADORP: Temporary seat of Transvaal government. See (in this vol.) SOUTH AFRICA (THE FIELD OF WAR): A. D. 1900 (MAY—JUNE).

MACKENZIE, The district of. See (in this vol.) CANADA: A. D. 1895.

McKINLEY, William: Election and re-election to the Presidency of the United States. See (in this vol.) UNITED STATES OF AM.: A. D. 1896 (JUNE—NOVEMBER) ; and 1900 (MAY—NOVEMBER).

Administration. See (in this vol.) UNITED STATES OF AM. : A. D. 1897 (MARCH), and after.

Message on the condition of Cuba in 1897. See (in this vol.) CUBA : A. D. 1896–1897.

Message on the destruction of the battleship Maine. See (in this vol.) UNITED STATES OF AM.: A. D. 1898 (FEBRUARY—MARCH).

Message asking for power to intervene in Cuba. See (in this vol.) UNITED STATES OF AM.: A. D. 1898 (MARCH—APRIL).

Message announcing state of war with Spain. See (in this vol.) UNITED STATES OF AM.: A. D. 1898 (APRIL).

Civil Service order in 1899. See (in this vol.) CIVIL SERVICE REFORM : A. D. 1899.

Negotiation of peace with Spain.—Instructions to and correspondence with Commissioners at Paris. See (in this vol.) UNITED STATES OF AM.: A. D. 1898 (JULY—DECEMBER).

Instructions to the military commander and to the two commissions in the Philippines. See (in this vol.) PHILIPPINE ISLANDS: A. D. 1898–1899 (DECEMBER—JANUARY); 1899 (JANUARY) ; and 1900 (APRIL).

MADAGASCAR.—The island of Madagascar, which stretches through more than thirteen degrees of latitude, in close neighborhood to the eastern African coast, opposite Mozambique, though often called "the great African island," is more Malayan than African in its population. The dominant tribe is the Hova. For more than a century the French have been covetous of the island, and since 1883, when they opened a war with its Hova rulers, they have pursued a steady policy toward the end of making it their own. The result of the war of 1886 was a treaty under which the French claimed a certain protectorate or control of Malagasy foreign relations,—a claim concerning which there remained much dispute. In 1890 the British government recognized the French protectorate, but the native government continued steadily to refuse acknowledgment that the treaty had given any such rights.

Subjugation of the island by the French.— Anti-foreign and anti-Christian risings.—**Revival** of idolatry. — Final possession of the island by France proclaimed. — Submissive Declaration of the Queen.—In 1894 the French government took decisive measures looking toward the subjugation of the island, and, early in 1895, a strong expedition under General Duchesne was landed on the coast. The Malagasy were much divided among themselves, and they were poorly prepared for war. They made feeble resistance to the invaders; but the latter had a difficult and costly campaign, notwithstanding, on account of the nature of the country and the absence of roads, which they were obliged to construct as they advanced. They are said to have lost only 20 men killed in action, but 6,000 by disease. They reached Antananarivo, the Hova capital, at the end of September. "Immediately on the arrival of General Duchesne a treaty was signed by the Malagasy authorities, by which the whole power of the country was ceded to the French. The queen remained in her place, and the Hova Prime Minister was also allowed to be nominally at the head of affairs. Part of this arrangement was found impracticable after a short time; the Prime Minister had enjoyed unlimited power for too long a period to accept a subordinate position, and General Duchesne was forced to remove him. Accordingly, he was taken to a house of his own at a short distance from the capital, where he was kept under surveillance for two or three months, but as he was still supposed to be plotting he was deported to Algiers, in which country he died after a very short exile.

"It seemed at first as if the change of masters in the island was to be accomplished without any serious disturbance. . . . In the early part of November (1895), however, this satisfactory state of affairs was rudely interrupted. A paltry quarrel between two clans about a piece of ground, which each claimed, gradually developed into a serious rising. The two parties came to an understanding by agreeing to make an attack upon the Europeans. As soon as General Duchesne was informed of what had been happening to the south-west of the capital, he sent a column . . . with orders to punish the insurgents and to pacify the district. . . . The resistance on the part of the natives was vigorous, and, for a time well sustained. . . . Discipline and Lebel rifles, however, were more than a match for all their efforts, and after a loss of about 150 men they desisted. . . . One distressing feature in the insurrection was the revival of idolatry, which was thought to be extinct in Imerina, but which evidently has been scotched and not killed. Almost the first move on the part of the rebels had been to reinstate a local idol called Ravololona, and the performance of certain acts of worship in the presence of the idol was considered the mark of a good patriot. Naturally under these circumstances the teachers and the more prominent Christians in the various churches and chapels were objects of dislike and hatred, and in the disaffected district these men with their wives and families had to fly for their lives. It is useless to shut one's eyes to facts; a considerable number of those who were held in esteem by the missionaries failed to stand the test of persecution, and if not guilty of actually worshipping idols were actively in league with those who did

so. . . . After the suppression of this first outbreak matters remained quiet in Imerina for some months. . . .

"The next serious event in the island was an outbreak of a different character. With the exception of the Hova, few if any of the tribes were thought to be opposed to French rule. . . . The Hova were as much hated as they were feared, and, from whatever quarter it might come, release from their rule would be welcome. The arrival of the French was the long-wished-for moment; but news spreads slowly in Madagascar, and though the Hova power came to an end at the beginning of October, it was not realised on the coast until the new year [1896]. When, however, it was known that the French were masters of the country the explosion came. The two large tribes of the Betsimisaraka and the Taimoro on the east rose against the Hova, and ruthlessly killed them wherever they could catch them. . . . The buildings used as churches and schools were also burnt, for, as the greater part of the teachers came from Imerina, religion and education were associated with the Hova. In one or two instances Europeans were murdered, but only when they were mixed up with the Hova."— F. A. Gregory, *The French in Madagascar* (*Nineteenth Century, Jan.*, 1897).

Formal possession of the island was now proclaimed, and, on the 18th of January, 1896, the submissive queen signed the following "Declaration": "Her Majesty the Queen of Madagascar, having been made acquainted with the Proclamation taking possession of the Island of Madagascar by the French Government, declares her acceptance of the following conditions:—

"ART. I. The Government of the French Republic shall be represented at the Court of Her Majesty the Queen of Madagascar by a Resident-General.

"ART. II. The Government of the French Republic shall represent Madagascar in all relations with foreign Powers. The Resident-General shall be intrusted with the conduct of relations with the Agents of foreign Powers; and all questions affecting foreigners in Madagascar shall be dealt with through him. The French Diplomatic and Consular Agents abroad shall be charged with the protection of Malagasy subjects and interests.

"ART. III. The Government of the French Republic reserve to themselves the right of maintaining in Madagascar the armed forces necessary for the exercise of their authority.

"ART. IV. The Resident-General shall control the internal administration of the island. Her Majesty the Queen of Madagascar undertakes to introduce such reforms as the French Government shall deem expedient for the economic development of the island, and for the advancement of civilization.

"ART. V. The Government of Her Majesty the Queen of Madagascar undertake to contract no loan without the authorization of the Government of the French Republic. (Signed) RANAVALOMANJAKA, *Mpanjakany Madagascar*."

On the 11th of February the following "Notification" was officially communicated to all the Powers: "In consequence of difficulties which have arisen in Madagascar, the Government of the Republic, in the exercise of their Protectorate, have been obliged to intervene by force of arms in order to make their rights respected, and to obtain guarantees for the future. They have thus been obliged to occupy the island with their troops, and to take final possession thereof."—*Great Britain, Parliamentary Publications (Papers by Command: Africa, No. 8, 1897).*

About this time. "M. Laroche, the first Resident-General, arrived at the capital and began to organise the government of the country. A new Prime Minister was appointed,.in whose name laws might be issued, for it had been settled that the administration should be indirect, that is to say conducted through the medium of the natives. A considerable number of regulations were promulgated, affecting the development of the industries of the country, the granting of concessions, and the education of the natives. Most of these were much too elaborate to be useful, and up to the present time nearly all of them have remained a dead letter. Some may be useful when the insurrection has been quelled, when the country is such as to invite capitalists, and when schools have been re-established. In March there were again signs of trouble, though at first these were faint and perhaps too far off to attract the serious attention of the authorities. . . .

" A petty disturbance in the beginning, fomented for private purposes and fostered by an appeal to patriotic feeling, has developed into a formidable insurrection. I say formidable, but I do not mean to give the idea that the insurrection is formidable from a military point of view. . . . But from industrial, educational, and religious points of view, the rebellion has been a complete success, and however soon it may be suppressed, the progress of the country in some parts has been thrown back for years, a large tract reduced to desolation, and the inhabitants to little better than savages. This destruction has been effected in five months, for, beginning in May, it has spread over the whole of Avaradrano, Vonizongo, part of Imarovatana, and Vakin 'Ankaratoa, four out of the six divisions of Imerina. . . . To mark the anti-European character of the rising, the churches were burnt without distinction, and in some places leper hospitals were destroyed, and their unhappy inmates rendered houseless. The English and Norwegian missions have suffered the most severely. It is impossible to estimate correctly the number of churches and chapels that have been burnt, but at the lowest computation it must amount to 600. . . . As in the West, idol-worship was practised, the idol in this case being Ramahavaly, the war-god or goddess; the pillaging of houses and property became almost universal, and soon it came to pass that no one was safe unless he either joined the insurgents or paid them to leave him unmolested. . . .

" The greatest move in the organisation of the country is the abolition of slavery throughout the island. This was proclaimed in the official gazette issued on the 27th of September [1896] by decree of the Resident-General. It was wholly unexpected at the time, though there had been rumours two or three months previously to the effect that the step was contemplated, but would be effected gradually. Naturally, it fell upon the Hova like a clap of thunder, and, as the law was published on a Sunday, some worthy folk found themselves, on their return from service, without a slave to cook the dinner. . . . It would have been bet'er to have proceeded more slowly

to the desired end ; to have made all children born after a fixed day free ; and to have made the redemption of the rest, either by themselves or by others, cheap and easy. However, it has been decided otherwise, and certainly the state of the country is such as to justify any measure, for, when everything is in a state of upheaval the exact amount of pressure is of small importance. In addition to this it must be remembered that in consequence of the outbreak Madagascar has been declared a French colony, and that this carries with it the abolition of the status of slavery. While, then, the greater number of Europeans who know Madagascar would have preferred that slavery should have been abolished by degrees, few would be prepared to say that it was altogether a mistake "—F. A. Gregory, *The French in Madagascar (Nineteenth Century, Jan., 1897).*

An Act for the annexation of Madagascar was passed by the French Chamber and Senate in the early summer of 1896, with a declaration for the immediate abolition of slavery. In the following year Queen Ranavalomanjaka was banished to the French Island of Réunion, and in 1899 she was removed to a more distant and more cruel exile in Algiers.

MAFEKING, Siege of. See (in this vol.) SOUTH AFRICA (THE FIELD OF WAR): A. D. 1899 (OCTOBER—NOVEMBER); and 1900 (MARCH —MAY).

MAFIA, Exposure in Italy of the. See (in this vol.) ITALY: A. D. 1900 (JANUARY).

MAHAN, Captain Alfred T.: American Commissioner to the Peace Conference at The Hague. See (in this vol.) PEACE CONFERENCE.

MAHDI, The death of the. See (in this vol.) EGYPT: A. D. 1885–1896.

MAINE, The battle-ship: Destruction in Havana harbor. See (in this vol.) UNITED STATES OF AM.: A. D. 1898 (FEBRUARY— MARCH).

MAJESFONTEIN, Battle of. See (in this vol.) SOUTH AFRICA (THE FIELD OF WAR): A. D. 1899 (OCTOBER—DECEMBER).

MALAGASY, The. See (in this vol.) MADAGASCAR.

MALAKAND, Attack by **Swat** tribes on. See (in this vol.) INDIA: A. D. 1897–1898.

MALARIA, Discovery of the secret of. See (in this vol.) SCIENCE, RECENT: MEDICAL AND SURGICAL.

MALAYAN RACE. See (in this vol.) PHILIPPINE ISLANDS: THE NATIVE INHABITANTS.

MALOLOS : The seat of Aguinaldo's government in the Philippines. See (in this vol.) UNITED STATES OF AM.: A. D. 1898 (JULY—SEPTEMBER).

MANCHESTER SHIP CANAL. See (in this vol.) CANAL, MANCHESTER SHIP.

MANCHURIA: A. D. 1895-1900.—Trans-Siberian Railway.—Russo-Chinese Treaty. See (in this vol.) CHINA: A. D. 1895; and RUSSIA IN ASIA; A. D. 1891–1900.

A. D. 1900-1901.—Chinese Boxer attack on the Russians and savage Russian retaliation. —Russian occupation of Niu-chwang.—Russo-Chinese negotiations concerning the province. —Distrust of Russian designs.—The Boxer outbreak in and around Peking, in the early summer (see, in this vol., CHINA: A. D. 1900—MAY—JUNE, and after), was followed, in July, by an attack on the Russians in Manchuria, along the line of the Manchurian branch of their Trans-Siberian Railway (see, in this vol., RUSSIA IN ASIA), and on the Amur. The retaliation of the Russians appears to have been simply ferocious. Professor G. Frederick Wright, who was travelling in Manchuria at the time, gives a sickening account of what he saw on the Amur, above Blagovestchensk, in a letter written, August 6, from Stretensk, Siberia, to "The Nation," of New York. The Chinese fort at Aygun, on the Manchurian side of the Amur, began, without warning, on the 14th of July, he writes, "to fire upon passing steamboats, and, on the 15th, fire was opened upon Blagovestchensk, and some Russian villages were burned opposite the fort. The actual injury inflicted by the Chinese was slight; but the terror caused by it was indescribable, and it drove the Cossacks into a frenzy of rage. The peaceable Chinese, to the number of 3,000 or 4,000, in the city were expelled in great haste, and, being forced upon rafts entirely inadequate, were most of them drowned in attempting to cross the river. The stream was fairly black with their bodies. Three days after, we counted hundreds of them in the water. In our ride through the country to reach the city on Thursday, the 19th, we saw as many as thirty villages and hamlets of the Chinese in flames. One of them was a city of 8,000 or 10,000 inhabitants. We estimated that we saw the dwellings of 20,000 peaceable Chinese in flames that awful day, while parties of Cossacks were scouring the fields to find Chinese, and shooting them down at sight. What became of the women and children no one knew; but there was apparently no way for them to escape to a place of safety. On our way up the river for 500 miles above the city, every Chinese hamlet was a charred mass of ruins. The large village of Motcha was still smoking, and we were told that 4,000 Chinese had been killed. We do not mention these facts to excite prejudice against the Russian authorities or against the Cossacks. This work of devastation has not been ordered by those high in authority. It is rather the result of mob violence such as instigates the promoters of lynch law in the Southern States, or, more nearly, such as has from time immemorial animated the pioneers in America against the Indians. The wholesale destruction, both of property and of life, was thought to be a military necessity. The wives and children of the Cossacks were in terror."

Russian troops were poured into Manchuria in vast numbers, and however much or little there may have been of the Boxer movement, it was crushed with merciless rigor. A letter from the Manchurian treaty port of Niu-chwang, on the Liao-tung Gulf, written August 13, to the "London Times," describes the Russian occupation of that town and region, in the previous week. After some 1,500 or 2,000 Chinese soldiers and civilians, in flight from the town, had been intercepted and killed, "the Russian general," says the writer, "was about to order a general assault on the town when the foreign residents interceded,

as there were no longer any soldiers or 'Boxers' left. He declared his intention was to kill all, as it was impossible to distinguish between soldiers, 'Boxers,' and civilians. Some foreigners then went down into the city and brought up the principal merchants, who were given until 10 a. m. to deliver up all the guns in the town. This, of course, they could not and did not do, so some foreign residents offered to enter the city with the Russian soldiers, and guaranteed peaceful occupation. This offer was accepted, and the town was spared enormous loss of life, though there was a certain amount of looting, and a few people were bayoneted in the outlying houses. Outside the walls men, women, and children were killed, and from all sides came reliable reports of violation of women. There is no possible doubt about the truth of these reports. The Russians are carrying out a policy of destruction of property and extermination of the people. Kai-chan, the district city, 24 miles south of this port, and nearly all the villages have been burnt and the inhabitants killed. The soldiers, both infantry and Cossacks, have been allowed to do what they like for some days."

The same correspondent goes on to say: "The Russians hoisted their naval flag over the Custom-house at 7.30 p. m. on August 4. Neither in the attack and bombardment of the town nor in hoisting their flag did they consult any of the foreign Consuls or the commanders of the two Japanese gunboats in port. Admiral Alexeieff arrived on the 5th and issued a circular announcing the occupation of the treaty port by Russian military forces. . . . What the other Powers will say to the seizure of a treaty port and hoisting of only one flag remains to be seen." The "one flag" seems to have been still waving over Niu-chwang as late as the 15th of February, 1901, since a member in the British House of Commons, on that day, arraigning his government for want of vigor in China, said that "though British people traded with Niu-chwang to the extent of three millions sterling a year, the port was now under the civil and military administration of Russia alone. He should like to know what undertaking his Majesty's Government had obtained that Russia would speedily evacuate Niu-chwang, and that the administration of the port would revert to the hands of the Chinese Government."

A few days later, the Under Secretary of State for Foreign Affairs, Viscount Cranborne, said in reply to this statement: "We made proper inquiry from our representative, and he assured us that any agreement which exists between Russia and China in respect to Manchuria is in the nature of a 'modus vivendi,' consisting merely in the simultaneous presence of the Russian and Chinese forces in Manchuria, and in order to prevent disturbances on their frontier. He assured us that the occupation of the railway is of a purely temporary character, and that, although a guarantee is expected by the Russian Government that upon their withdrawal the disturbances shall not break out again, yet that guarantee will not take the form of an acquisition of territory or of a virtual or actual protectorate in Manchuria. . . . In respect to Niu-chwang we have received assurances at least equal to those which have been given us in respect to the province of South Manchuria. We understand the Russians are prepared to restore Niu-chwang at the end of their occupation precisely to its former condition."

For the time being, however, the Russians seem to have established in practice a very real protectorate over the province of Fêng-tien, in Southern Manchuria, by an agreement between the Russian governor of the territory leased from China in the Liao-tung peninsula and the Chinese Tartar general of Fêng-tien, signed on the 11th of November, 1900. The general terms of this agreement were reported late in December, and excited much uneasiness as to Russian designs. The full text was communicated to the "London Times," in the February following, by its Peking correspondent, with the information that the Tartar general who signed it, in transmitting a copy to Li Hung-chang, "states that grief pierces his very soul, but what alternative has he ?" The agreement required the Tartar general to disband his troops and disarm them, on account of the rebellions which had occurred among them; to deliver up all munitions of war and dismantle all forts and defences, and to give full information of all important measures taken by him to a Russian resident who should be stationed at Mukden, with "general powers of control."

Late in February, 1901, it was ascertained that the Russian Minister at Peking, M. de Giers, was negotiating a more definite and binding convention relative to Manchuria with the Chinese imperial government, as represented by Li Hung-chang; and, on the 7th of March, the Peking correspondent of the "London Times" telegraphed to that journal what claimed to be a translation of the full text of the treaty, as follows:

"I. The Emperor of Russia, being desirous to manifest his friendly feelings, agrees to restore Manchuria completely to China without keeping in mind the fact of the recent warfare in that province. The Chinese administration shall be restored in all respects to the 'status quo ante.'

"II. China granted to the railway company, as stipulated in Article VI. of the Eastern China Railway Concession, the right of guarding the line with troops, but the country being still in disorder and the number of troops being insufficient, it has been found necessary to station a body of troops in the province, which will be withdrawn as soon as peace and order are restored and the provisions of the last four articles of the present convention are carried out.

"III. In case of emergency, the Russian troops stationed in the province shall render all possible assistance to China to suppress any disturbances.

"IV. The recent attacks against Russia having been conducted principally by regular troops, China agrees not to organize any army before the completion of the railway and the opening thereof for traffic. When China subsequently organizes her military forces, the number of troops shall be fixed in consultation with Russia. The importation of arms and ammunition into Manchuria is prohibited.

"V. In order to safeguard the province, China shall immediately dismiss such Governors-General and high local officials as have committed improper acts in connexion with foreign relations against which Russia would protest. China can organize infantry and cavalry in Manchuria for police purposes, but the number shall be fixed in consultation with Russia. Artillery should be excluded, and arms given to no subjects of any other Power employed in connexion with the exercise of functions.

"VI. China, as previously agreed, shall not employ the subjects of any other Power for training her naval and military forces in the northern provinces.

"VII. In order to maintain peace and order, the local authorities, residing in the vicinity of the neutral zone provided for by the fifth article of the convention relating to the lease of the territory of Leao-tong, shall establish special regulations suitable to the circumstances, and shall relinquish the administrative autonomy of Kin-chau, which is reserved to China by Article IV. of the special convention.

"VIII. China shall not grant, without the consent of Russia, to any other Power or their subjects advantages relative to mines, railways, or other matters in the Russo-Chinese Frontier provinces—namely, Manchuria, Mongolia, Kash-.gar, Yarkand, Khotan, and Turkestan; neither shall she construct her own railways in those provinces without the consent of Russia. Leases of land outside Niu-chwang shall not be granted to the subjects of any other Power.

"IX. China being under obligations to pay the war expenses of Russia and the claims of the various other Powers, the amount of Russia's indemnity, and the terms of payment and the security for it, shall be adjusted conjointly with the other Powers.

"X. Indemnities shall be paid and compensation granted for the destruction of railway property and to the employés of the company. Losses accruing from delay in the work shall be adjusted between China and the railway company.

"XI. When the indemnities for the various damages shall have been agreed upon between China and the company the whole or part of the amount of such indemnities should be met by advantages other than pecuniary compensation—that is, either by revision of the existing agreement relating to the railway or by the grant of new advantages.

"XII. China shall, as previously agreed, grant to Russia a concession for the construction of a railway from the main or branch line of the Manchuria Railway towards Peking and to the Great Wall."

Notwithstanding the very positive agreement contained in the first article of this treaty, that the Emperor of Russia will "restore Manchuria completely to China," the publication of its terms excited new and greater distrust of the designs and the action of the Muscovite Power. It was seen that Chinese authority, for the time being, would be pushed out of Manchuria so completely, and that of Russia would be established so firmly, that any future restoration of the former was improbable, to say the least. Moreover, the entire exclusion of all people except Russians from any share in the development of Manchurian resources was exceedingly offensive to the money-making desires with which the whole western world is looking toward the great decaying empire of the East. That such an exclusion should extend beyond Manchuria, even to Mongolia, Kashgar, Yarkand, Khotan and Turkestan, as set forth in the above report of the pending treaty, was an idea at which capitalistic circles in Europe and America stood aghast. Very soon there was denial that the exclusiveness asked

for by the modest Russian went farther than the
bounds of Manchuria; but, even as thus limited,
it roused strenuous protest from the Press of the
western world, if not from the governments.
What diplomatic action was taken by the Powers
in general is not known at the time of this writing; but the United States remonstrated to China
(see CHINA : A. D. 1901, MARCH—APRIL), and,
as stated by the British Foreign Minister, Lord
Lansdowne, in Parliament, on the 28th of March,
the British and German governments did the
same. The Chinese government was nerved accordingly to resist the Russian demands, though
Li Hung-chang appears to have urged submission to them. The contemplated treaty was not
signed.

Before and after this determination the Russian government maintained that it had no ulterior designs in the arrangement it sought with
China. Lord Lansdowne, in the speech to Parliament referred to above, spoke as follows of the
assurances he had received from Count Lams-
dorff, the Russian Foreign Minister : "He told
us that it was the object of the Russian Government 'to arrange with the local civil authorities
the terms of a "modus vivendi" between them
for the duration of the simultaneous presence of
Russian and Chinese authorities in Southern
Manchuria, the object being to prevent the recurrence of disturbances in the vicinity of the
Russian frontier and to protect the railway from
the Russian frontier to Port Arthur.' And he
told us that his government had 'no intention of
seeking this guarantee in any acquisition of territory or of an actual or virtual protectorate over
Manchuria.'"

Similar assurances are reported to have been
given to the American government, on the 4th
of April; and, for the time being at least, the
Manchurian question has ceased to be disturbing
to the "Concert of the Powers."

MANCHURIA AND MONGOLIA.—The
following information concerning Manchuria and
Mongolia is taken from notes made in 1897 by
Colonel Browne, Military Attaché to the British
Legation at Peking : "The area of Manchuria is
computed to contain no less than 362,310 square
miles, or just three times as large as that of
Great Britain and Ireland. It is divided into
three provinces, of which the most southerly,
Fêng-tien or Shên-king, with its capital at Mukden, has for several hundred years formed an integral part of the Chinese Empire, and is consequently more opened up and more densely
inhabited than the two northern provinces, which
were regarded until the beginning of this century as waste lands, outside the pale of civilization, fit only for the transportation of criminals.
Though the old palisades have long disappeared,
their trace still marks the boundary between
Manchuria and Mongolia, and the gateways on the
main roads are still used as posts for the collection of transit dues. These places may be recognized by the termination 'mên' (a gate), such as
Fa-k'u-mên, Fa-ta-ha-mên. The province of Kirin
and its capital bear the same name, while the huge
northern province of Hei-lung-chiang has its seat
of government at Tsi-tsi-har. It is generally said
that the Governor of Fêng-tien (Mukden) occupies somewhat the position, as regards the two
northern provinces, as a viceroy in China holds
towards the provinces comprised in his Viceroy-

alty, but this does not appear to be so, except in
his capacity as High Commissioner for the defence of the three Manchurian provinces. The
Governors of the three provinces are styled in
the official Gazette by the same title of Military
Governor of the. Provincial Capital and Tartar
General of the Province, but the Governor of
Fêng-tien holds the more honourable post, because Mukden is an Imperial city, within its walls
is an Imperial Palace, without its walls the tombs
of the founders of the Manchu dynasty. It has
also, in miniature, Boards similar to those at the
capital for regulating ceremonies, punishments,
and civil appointments ; in short, all the theoretical paraphernalia to carry on the government of
the country, should the Emperor visit this quarter of his dominions. . . . The great grain and
bean producing area in the three provinces is
contained in a strip of country, extending from
the Treaty Port of Newchwang to 30 miles north
of Pei-tuan-lin-tzu. To the west of this belt of
arable are the Mongolian steppes, all in grass,
but fading away into sand as they merge in the
great desert of Gobi ; to the east is a hilly or
mountainous region, in which the only large cultivated area is that watered by the River
Hwei-fa, an affluent of the Upper Sungari ; elsewhere the cultivated areas are small, such as those
at Mergen, Tsi-tsi-har, the Valley of the Yen,
and at Sansing, Ninguta, Hun-chun, and Omoso.
Exclusive of patches of cultivation in remote
districts and valleys, the great cultivated area
may be estimated to amount to 16,000 square
miles, or about one twenty-fourth of the total
area of the country. To what extent under improved communications, drainage, and more favourable conditions generally, the cultivated
area is capable of expansion, it is difficult to
say. . . . The population of Manchuria has been
variously estimated from a few millions by the
Chinese to as much as 25,000,000 by Europeans.
A Russian engineer, who has travelled all over
the country, estimates it as between 10,000,000
and 15,000,000. . . . Before I received these
figures I had arrived at a somewhat similar result by taking the cultivated area at 700 per
square mile which gives a population of 11,250,-
000, and assuming 2,500,000 scattered throughout the more remote districts, or a population in
all of about 14,000,000. What proportion of these
are Manchus is also a vexed question to which
no definite answer can be given. Certainly the
Manchus are in the minority, for though there
are several towns almost wholly Chinese, I know
of no town in which it is not acknowledged that
the Chinese form more than half the population.
The Manchus are nearly all concentrated in
towns ; there are Manchu villages, but they are
small, possibly their numbers amount to between
2,000,000 and 3,000,000, or about 20 per cent. of
the population. The chief appointments in
Manchuria are, without exception, held by Manchus, the descendants of the conquerors of China.
In four centuries of ease and sloth they have lost
the wild courage, the spirit of adventure that inspired them to overrun China, and the hardihood
and skill at arms that brought success to their
venture. But if they have lost the warlike instincts of their savage ancestors, they have retained all their pride, their ignorance, their cruelty, and their superstition. All these qualities a
Manchu possesses far in excess of the liberal share
that nature has bestowed on the Chinese. It is true

that skill at arms still nominally opens the door to military preferment, but such arms and such skill! Shooting arrows from a moderately strung bow when cantering on a pony is a test which displays neither skill, strength, nor endurance. Even according to Chinese ideas they are ignora . . . As regards their privileges, the Manchus pay no land tax; but in so far as I have been able to ascertain, the opinion generally held, that they are all pensioned by Government, is erroueous. . . . But though the mass of the Manchus receive no pension, nearly all are in pay as hangers-on at Yamêns, body-guard to officials, soldiers, care-takers at the Palace or Imperial tombs, and similar posts. The emoluments are small, just sufficient to enable the man to support his family without working, or making his way in the world as an ordinary Chinese must do. Formerly the Manchus did not intermarry with Chinese women, but at the present time this custom is frequently broken through, though of course no Chinese would be permitted to marry a Manchu woman. The Manchus, especially the dependents, hangers-on, and soldiers, are great opium smokers, and a very worthless class; probably intermarriage with the Chinese will prevent the extinction of the race, which, were the present dynasty to fall, would be speedily absorbed, for, without being propped up with State assistance, it could not on its merits hold the position it does at present. As regards the Chinese, few of the rich merchants make Manchuria their home. They come to the country for a definite number of years, and the same applies to their agents, managers, and staff generally, who leave their families in China. The settlers, on the contrary, have made the country their home. They are a fine, healthy, and vigorous race. Driven from China by poverty or famine, they regard Manchuria as a land flowing with milk and honey. . . . Whether it be the rigour of the climate which softens their manners, or the absence of the Chinese Mandarin, or living under the sway of an alien race which humbles their pride, or a combination of all these elements, it is difficult to say, but the people are far less hostile to the foreigner than those in China proper. . . .

"Mongolia extends for 1,500 miles along the northern frontier of China, and as its eastern border is coterminous with Manchuria, a few words regarding the Mongols may not be out of place in these notes. The race is said to come with the Manchus from a common Tartar stock, but, except in colour and features, there is little resemblance between the two races. The Mongol is essentially a nomad, hating towns and houses. He prefers to wander about the steppes, pitching his 'yourt,' or felt tent; wherever water and pasture are for the time most plentiful. As the nature of the country they inhabit prohibits agriculture, the art is unknown among his people, who are entirely engaged in tending their flocks and herds, ponies, and camels. They are mere children in the hands of the Chinese, who can outwit them as easily as a member of the 'confidence trick' fraternity outwits a rustic from the shires. . . . A small portion of their territory is rented by the Chinese on the west of the Provinces of Kirin and Fêng-tien, of which it has now become an integral part. Kuan-cheng-tzu was originally in Mongolia, and so are all the towns and villages to the west of the palisade,

of which the principal are Mai-mai-kai (Feng-hua), Ch'ang-tu, and Cheng-chia-tun. Mongolia is the great breeding land for horses and cattle. At first sight when travelling through the country one is astonished at the enormous size of the troops of ponies; but when one considers that this territory supplies Siberia, China, and Manchuria with animals, it is easy to see that the supply is not greater than the demand. . . . The Mongols are governed by their hereditary Princes, Chinese authority being maintained by Imperial Residents at Ching-hai, in Western Mongolia (Ko-ko-nor), and at Urga, in the north."—*Great Britain, Parliamentary Publications (Papers by Command, China, No.* 1, 1899, *pp.* 34–37).

MANCHUS: Increasing ascendancy in Chinese Government. See (in this vol.) CHINA: A. D. 1899 (APRIL).

MANETHO, Vindication of the list of. See (in this vol.) ARCHÆOLOGICAL RESEARCH: EGYPT: RESULTS.

MANHATTAN BOROUGH. See (in this vol.) NEW YORK CITY: A. D. 1896–1897.

MANILA.—The capital city of the Philippine Islands. See (in this vol.) PHILIPPINE ISLANDS.

A. D. **1898** (April—July).—Destruction of the Spanish fleet in Manila Bay.—Blockade and siege. See (in this vol.) UNITED STATES OF AM.: A. D. 1898 (APRIL—JULY).

A. D. **1898** (July—September).—Capture by the Americans. — Relations of Americans with Filipino insurgents.—General Merritt's report. See (in this vol.) UNITED STATES OF AM.: A. D. 1898 (JULY—SEPTEMBER).

A. D. **1900.**—Regulation of the sale of liquors. See (in this vol.) PHILIPPINE ISLANDS: A. D. 1900 (SEPTEMBER—NOVEMBER).

MANITOBA SCHOOL QUESTION. See (in this vol.) CANADA: A. D. 1890–1896; and 1898 (JANUARY).

MARCHAND'S EXPEDITION. See (in this vol.) EGYPT: A. D. 1898 (SEPTEMBER—NOVEMBER).

MARCONI, Guglielmo: Development of wireless telegraphy. See (in this vol.) SCIENCE, RECENT: ELECTRICAL.

MARIANNE ISLANDS: Sale by Spain to Germany. See (in this vol.) CAROLINE AND MARIANNE ISLANDS.

MARITIME CANAL COMPANY. See (in this vol.) CANAL, INTEROCEANIC.

MARITIME POWERS. See (in this vol.) NAVIES; and WAR BUDGETS.

MARITIME WARFARE, Convention relative to. See (in this vol.) PEACE CONFERENCE.

MARRIAGE LAWS, Hungarian. See (in this vol.) AUSTRIA-HUNGARY: A. D. 1894–1895.

MARYLAND: New election **law,** establishing a qualification of the **suffrage.**—A new election law, said to have been driven through the Legislature by partisan pressure, and for the purpose of disfranchising the majority of colored citizens, was passed by both houses on the

20th of March, 1901. It is said to be "considerably more fair than the North Carolina and similar laws in States farther south. It disfranchises by means of regulations which practically make it necessary for a voter to be able to read his ballot. The illiterate are denied any assistance when they go into the booths, and all emblems are omitted from the ticket. The color line is not drawn. It is believed that there are about 32,000 negroes and 16,000 whites who will not be able to vote under this law. Practically all of the negroes are supposed to be Republicans, while it is estimated that the whites are divided about evenly between the parties."

MASHONALAND: Embraced in Rhodesia. See (in this vol.) SOUTH AFRICA (BRITISH SOUTH AFRICA COMPANY): A. D. 1894–1895.

MASSACHUSETTS: A. D. 1897.—Recovery of the original manuscript of Governor Bradford's History of Plymouth Colony, sometimes called "The Log of the Mayflower."—"It has long been well known that Governor Bradford wrote and left behind him a history of the settlement of Plymouth. It was quoted by early chroniclers. There are extracts from it in the records at Plymouth. Thomas Prince used it when he compiled his annals, Hubbard depended on it when he wrote his 'History of New England,' Cotton Mather had read it, or a copy of a portion of it, when he wrote his 'Magnalia,' Governor Hutchinson had it when he published the second volume of his history in 1767. From that time it disappeared from the knowledge of everybody on this side of the water. All our historians speak of it as lost, and can only guess what had been its fate. . . .

"In 1844 Samuel Wilberforce, Bishop of Oxford, afterward Bishop of Winchester, one of the brightest of men, published one of the dullest and stupidest of books. It is entitled 'The History of the Protestant Episcopal Church in America.' It contained extracts from manuscripts which he said he had discovered in the library of the Bishop of London at Fulham. The book attracted no attention here until, about twelve years later, in 1855, John Wingate Thornton . . . happened to pick up a copy of it while he was lounging in Burnham's book store. He read the bishop's quotations, and carried the book to his office, where he left it for his friend, Mr. Barry, who was then writing his 'History of Massachusetts,' with passages marked, and with a note which is not preserved, but which, according to his memory, suggested that the passages must have come from Bradford's long-lost history. That is the claim for Mr. Thornton. On the other hand, it is claimed by Mr. Barry that there was nothing of that kind expressed in Mr. Thornton's note, but in reading the book when he got it an hour or so later, the thought struck him for the first time that the clue had been found to the precious book which had been lost so long. He at once repaired to Charles Deane, then and ever since, down to his death, as President Eliot felicitously styled him, 'the master of historical investigators in this country.' Mr. Deane saw the importance of the discovery. He communicated at once with Joseph Hunter, an eminent English scholar. Hunter was high authority on all matters connected with the settlement of New England. He visited the palace at Fulham, and established beyond question the identity of the manuscript with Governor Bradford's history, an original letter of Governor Bradford having been sent over for comparison of handwriting.

"How the manuscript got to Fulham nobody knows. Whether it was carried over by Governor Hutchinson in 1774; whether it was taken as spoil from the tower of the Old South Church in 1775; whether, with other manuscripts, it was sent to Fulham at the time of the attempts of the Episcopal churches in America, just before the Revolution, to establish an episcopate here, —nobody knows."—George F. Hoar, *address, May 26, 1897, on the Return of the Manuscript to Massachusetts.*

After the discovery of the manuscript, several attempts to bring about its return to America were made: by Justin Winsor, in 1860, and again in 1877; by Mr. Motley, in 1869; and by others. At length, Senator Hoar, after delivering an address at Plymouth, in 1895, on the anniversary of the landing of the Pilgrims, went abroad, with his interest in the matter warmly stirred up, and took steps, in concurrence with Ambassador Bayard, which led to the enlistment of potent influences on both sides of the sea in favor of the restoration of the precious piece of writing to its proper home. There were many difficulties in procuring the necessary legal authority for the surrender of the manuscript by the Bishop of London,—difficulties not created wilfully, but by questions and processes of law; but they were all overcome, with kindly help from everybody concerned, and, on the 12th of April, 1897, the coveted manuscript book was formally delivered to the United States Ambassador, Mr. Bayard, for conveyance to the Governor of the Commonwealth of Massachusetts. It was delivered by Mr. Bayard in person, on the 26th of May following, in the presence of the Senate and the House of Representatives of Massachusetts, sitting together in the chamber of the latter, with many guests invited for the occasion. The ceremonies of the occasion included the address by Senator Hoar from which the above account is taken.

The manuscript volume is now deposited in the State Library of Massachusetts at Boston. A new edition, carefully reproducing the text of the history from it, with a full report of the proceedings incident to its return to Massachusetts, was printed in 1900, under the direction of the Secretary of the Commonwealth, by order of the General Court. The following remarks on the manuscript are from the Introduction to that edition: "By very many it has been called, incorrectly, the log of the 'Mayflower.' Indeed, that is the title by which it is described in the decree of the Consistorial Court of London. The fact is, however, that Governor Bradford undertook its preparation long after the arrival of the Pilgrims, and it cannot be properly considered as in any sense a log or daily journal of the voyage of the 'Mayflower.' It is, in point of fact, a history of the Plymouth Colony, chiefly in the form of annals, extending from the inception of the colony down to the year 1647. The matter has been in print since 1856, put forth through the public spirit of the Massachusetts Historical Society, which secured a transcript of the document from London, and printed it in the Society's Collections of the above-named year."

MASSACRES, of Armenians in Constantinople. See (in this vol.) TURKEY: A. D. 1896 (AUGUST).

Of Chinese by the allied troops. See (in this vol.) CHINA: A. D. 1900 (AUGUST 5–16).

Of Chinese in Manchuria by the Russians. See (in this vol.) MANCHURIA: A. D. 1900.

Of Christian missionaries and converts in China. See (in this vol.) CHINA: A. D. 1895 (AUGUST); 1898 (MAY); 1898–1899 (JUNE—JANUARY); 1899; 1900 (JANUARY—MARCH), (MAY—JUNE); and 1901 (MARCH).

MATABELES.—Matabeleland. See (in this vol.) SOUTH AFRICA (BRITISH SOUTH AFRICA COMPANY): A. D. 1894–1895; and (RHODESIA); 1896 (MARCH—SEPTEMBER).

MATTHEW, The Gospel of: Discovery of a fragment of an early copy. See (in this vol.) ARCHÆOLOGICAL RESEARCH: EGYPT: RESULTS.

MAYFLOWER, The so-called Log of the. See (in this vol.) MASSACHUSETTS: A. D. 1897.

MAZET INVESTIGATION, The. See (in this vol.) NEW YORK CITY: A. D. 1899 (APRIL—DECEMBER).

MEAT INSPECTION BILL, The German. See (in this vol.) GERMANY: A. D. 1900 (MAY).

MEDICAL SCIENCE, Recent advances in. See (in this vol.) SCIENCE, RECENT: MEDICAL AND SURGICAL.

MEHTAR OF CHITRAL, The. See (in this vol.) INDIA: A. D. 1895 (MARCH—SEPTEMBER).

MEIJI STATESMEN. See (in this vol.) JAPAN: A. D. 1900 (AUGUST—OCTOBER).

MENA, The tomb of. See (in this vol.) ARCHÆOLOGICAL RESEARCH: EGYPT: RESULTS.

MENELEK II., King of Shoa and Negus of Abyssinia. See (in this vol.) EGYPT: A. D. 1885–1896.

MERENPTAH I., The funeral temple of. See (in this vol.) ARCHÆOLOGICAL RESEARCH: EGYPT: RESULTS.

MERRIMAC, The sinking of the collier, at Santiago. See (in this vol.) UNITED STATES OF AM.: A. D. 1898 (APRIL—JUNE).

MERRITT, General: Report of capture of Manila. See (in this vol.) UNITED STATES OF AM.: A. D. 1898 (JULY—SEPTEMBER).

MESOPOTAMIA, Recent archæological research in. See (in this vol.) ARCHÆOLOGICAL RESEARCH: BABYLONIA.

Projected railways. See (in this vol.) TURKEY: A. D. 1899 (NOVEMBER); and JEWS: A. D. 1899.

MEXICAN FREE ZONE, The.—"The Department of State has received through Consul-General Barlow a report of the Free Zone, compiled by the Secretary of the Treasury of Mexico, giving a history of the original creation of the zone and defining its limits, and the privileges and restrictions applicable thereto. The Free Zone is a narrow strip of territory extending along the northern border from the Gulf of Mexico to the Pacific Ocean, with a latitudinal area of about 12½ miles to the interior, and embracing a portion of the States of Tamaulipas, Coahuila, Chihuahua, Sonora, and the territory of Lower California. It was established many years ago [1861] by the Central Government, as a compromise or concession to the States bordering the Rio. Grande, as a protection against smuggling from the United States. The principal cities of the zone are Matamoras, Camargo, Mier, Guerrero, Laredo, Porfirio Diaz (Piedras Negras), Juarez, and Nogales. The total population does not exceed 100,000 people. According to the official reports, there exist within the limits of the free zone no industries worth mentioning, which is explained by the fact that all industrial products manufactured in the zone when sent into the interior of the country are required to pay the regular duties charged on imports into the country; and, on account of the protective tariff of the United States, it is impracticable to export such products to that country. Thus the manufacturing industries would have to depend upon the home consumption, which is not sufficient to maintain them. All merchandise imported into the zone destined for consumption therein is admitted on a basis of 10 per cent of the regular tariff duties, but such merchandise when reshipped into the interior of Mexico is required to pay an additional duty of 90 per cent, making, in connection with the 10 per cent already paid, the regular tariff duty of Mexico. In his report the secretary of the treasury, Senor Limantour, makes this statement: 'Many distinguished financiers and eminent statesmen are opposed to the Free Zone, but all recognize the fact that, on account of existing circumstances in the northern frontier, its sparse population, without resources in agriculture, industry, or mining, the privilege could not be abolished without compensation, and the problem lies in choosing some other advantage without prejudice to the rest of the country.'"—*Bulletin of the Am. Republics, Aug.*, 1898.

"The franchise granted the Free Zone consisted, in the beginning, in not levying any duty upon imported articles; afterwards, however, some small duties, purely local, were established, and the ordinance of 1887 established as a fixed basis 3 per cent on the value of the duties according to tariff—a basis which was raised to 10 per cent by the ordinance of 1891. By subsequent decrees the duties were raised 1½ per cent for the municipality and 7 per cent for stamps for internal revenue, the result of all this being that the merchandise introduced into the Free Zone from abroad now paid 18½ per cent upon the importation duties according to tariff.
. . . As the records of the frontier custom-houses of the north make no distinction in the duties, those for the Free Zone as well as those for the interior appearing in the same classification, it is impossible to know exactly what the treasury loses by the 90 per cent rebate on the duties of the merchandise destined for consumption in the Free Zone; but, admitting as an exaggerated estimate that the total consumption of the Free Zone represents in duties $400,000 ($177,600) a year, with the 10 per cent charge on this amount, the average annual loss would be $365,000 ($162,060).

"The institution of the Free Zone obliges the Mexican Government, in order to prevent the introduction clandestinely into the interior of merchandise proceeding therefrom, to maintain a body of fiscal guards at an annual expense of $562,525.95 ($249,762). The guards of the custom-houses must not be reckoned in this account; for these, with or without the Free Zone, are necessary to prevent the smuggling which would be carried on from the United States, and which is even now done. In case of abolishing the Free Zone, it would not be possible to completely suppress the fiscal guards; lessened in number and with a distinct organization, they would have to be maintained, especially since in case of their abolition the entire duties would be charged (that is to say, 90 per cent more than is now levied), and this would be inducement enough to provoke attempts at smuggling. This body of guards, fiscal as well as administrative, supplies the place of an interior custom-house (although it does not levy duties), as it reviews in certain instances the merchandise shipped through the frontier custom-houses and in a military capacity guards the roads leading to and from the frontier to prevent smuggling. It has a system of fixed sections situated at convenient locations between the Gulf of Mexico and the Pacific, and of flying detachments continually patrolling the strip of territory named. Experience has demonstrated the usefulness of the body, for instances of smuggling by wagons, carts, or animals can be said to no longer exist."

Of smuggling, "there are two divisions to be made, as follows: Smuggling to the interior of the Republic and smuggling to the United States of America. The first was at one time of importance, since it was practiced on a large scale. Bands of smugglers, resorting at times to violence, conducted merchandise to the interior, but since the Republic entered the period of peace the Government has been able to take measures to end this illegal traffic. The custom-houses, which formerly scarcely produced enough to pay the employees, now render from $4,000,000 to $5,000,000 annually from import duties.

"Smuggling from Mexico to the United States of America has never been practiced to any great extent." — *U. S. Consular Reports*, *August*, 1898, p. 619.

MEXICO.

A. D. 1892–1895.—Boundary surveys.— The international commission which had been engaged since 1892 in resurveying the incorrectly marked boundary between Mexico and the United States from San Diego, California, to El Paso, Texas, finished its work in 1895. Another commission began in the same year to resurvey the remainder of the boundary, along the Río Grande from El Paso to the Gulf.

A. D. 1895.—Boundary dispute with Guatemala.—There was a quite serious threatening of war between Mexico and Guatemala in 1895, consequent upon a disputed boundary line. The mediation of the United States brought about a settlement, which gave the disputed district to Guatemala, and provided for an arbitration of indemnities, the United States Minister to Mexico being selected as arbitrator.

A. D. 1895.—Census of population.—Its distribution.—"The population of Mexico appears to be, from our . . . census . . . in 1895, 12,570,195, which would give 16.38 for each square mile; but from my personal knowledge of the country, I am quite sure that it is not less than 15,000,000. It is very difficult to take a correct census in Mexico, because there is not the proper machinery in operation for that purpose, and especially because a great many districts are inhabited by Indians, who are impressed with the fear that if they inscribe themselves in the census they will be taxed or drafted into the military service, and they try to avoid registration.

"A great many of our people live in such remote districts that they are practically cut off from communication with other portions of the country, and in fact are almost isolated; and this constitutes still another difficulty in the way of taking a correct census. . . . The upper lands being the healthiest, most of the population in Mexico is settled in the central plateau; a relatively small portion lives in the temperate zone, while the torrid zone is very thinly populated. I imagine, at a rough calculation, that about 75 per cent. of the population make their abode in the cold zone, from 15 to 18 per cent. in the temperate zone, and from 7 to 10 per cent. in the torrid zone.

"From the synopsis of our censuses, . . . it appears that the population in Mexico has duplicated during the last century, and although that increase does not keep pace with the increase in the United States, because this has been really wonderful, it compares favorably with the increase in other countries."—M. Romero, *Mexico and the United States*, *v.* 1, *pp.* 89–90 (*N. Y.: G. P. Putnam's Sons*).

A. D. 1896. Amendments to the Constitution. See (in this vol.) CONSTITUTION OF MEXICO.

A. D. 1896.—Re-election of President Diaz. —By a popular election held on the 28th of June, 1896, followed by a vote of "electors" cast July 13, Porfirio Diaz was chosen President of the Republic of Mexico for a fifth term of four years, to begin December 1, 1896.

A. D. 1896 (July).—Abolition of inter-state taxes.—The following announcement was reported in May, 1896, by the U. S. Consul-General at the City of Mexico: "'All the States and Territories having approved the amendment to the constitution prohibiting any interstate tax on commerce (alcabalas), Congress has passed the bill, the President has signed it, the Diario Oficial has published it, and it will soon be promulgated by "bando," as the Vice-Presidency was the other day. The law takes effect July 1.' This tax has been in existence for many years in Mexico, and has been a source of much embarrassment to internal and external trade. Its repeal meets with general approval, although some of the States will be compelled to seek other modes of taxation to replace the money heretofore obtained by this interstate tax."— *U. S. Consular Reports, June*, 1896, *p.* 354.

A. D. 1896–1899.—Revolts of the Yaquis.— The Yaquis, one of the native tribes of northwestern Mexico, taking their name from the river, in Sonora, on which they dwell, have been in frequent revolt. In 1896, and again in 1899, some of the tribe were fiercely in arms, excited, it was said, by a religious enthusiast, Teresa Urrea, who claimed a divine mission and obtained boundless influence over her tribe, as a saint. She was expelled from the country by the Mexican government, but stayed on the border, in United States territory, and continued to stir up hostilities. Though repeatedly beaten by the government troops, with heavy loss, their late rising was obstinately persisted in for many months; but early in 1900 their chief, Tetabiate, was slain, and a few sharp engagements after that time seems to have brought the revolt, practically, to an end. A writer in the California magazine, entitled "The Land of Sunshine" (July, 1899), says of the Yaquis that they are "the backbone of the population of Sonora. They are the best workmen in the republic, commanding from 10 to 20 per cent. higher wages in many localities than Mexican or other Indian labor. There is not a lazy bone in the Yaqui body. They are a peaceable, law-abiding people when justly treated. From time immemorial they have been hunters, miners, and tillers of the soil. They have the nomad instinct in less degree than almost any other Indian tribe."

Another writer makes this statement: "There are about three hundred wild and rebellious Yaqui Indians hidden in the fastnesses of the Bacatete Mountains, and some thirty thousand peaceful Yaquis working all over Sonora—among the best workers, the most successful farmers, and the quietest citizens in the whole state. . . . There are few things in the history of the native races of North America of such absorbing interest as the career of the Yaqui Indians. The Spanish conquistadores found them living in this country three hundred and fifty years ago. They were a strong and stalwart race. Put a Yaqui by the side of an Iroquois and you can hardly tell them apart. Put a Yaqui and an Iroquois by the side of any other Indians in North America, and their physical superiority is seen at once. Compare them physically with all the other races of the earth and you will find that they have few, if any, superiors. The Yaquis were not, however, like their prototypes, the Iroquois, dependent upon the chase for their food. From the beginning they were not woodsmen, but farmers. Cabeza de Vaca, after his long, romantic and perilous journey across the continent, found great fields of Indian corn waving on the Yaqui River as far back as 1636. When the early Spanish missions were established in the Californias they obtained their supplies from the agricultural Indians in the Yaqui Valley, and many are the Spanish armies that have been saved from starvation in times past by the Yaqui corn fields."—W. S. Logan, *Yaqui, the Land of Sunshine and Health, pp.* 15, 17.

A. D. **1898.**—Completion of the great drainage tunnel and canal of the City of Mexico.—"Mexico is finishing a great work, the drainage of the valley where the capital city is located, which has required for its completion nearly three hundred years and many millions of dollars, and has cost the lives of hundreds of thousands of men. . . . The Valley of Mexico is an immense basin, of approximately circular shape, with one extreme diameter of about 60 miles, completely bounded by high mountains,

and having only two or three quite high passes out of it. No water drains out of the basin. The surface of this valley has a mean altitude above the sea of 7,413 feet and an area of about 2,220 square miles. Mountain ranges rise on every side, making a great corral of rock containing dozens of villages and hamlets, with the ancient capital in the centre. . . . Evaporation is so excessive at certain periods of the year that malaria, consequent on drouth, was far more dreaded by the inhabitants than the periodical floods, and thousands perished annually, so that proper drainage was an absolute necessity for the preservation of health. Nearly fifty years before the discovery of America, which took place in 1492, Netzahualcoyotl saw the necessity for a drainage canal, and commenced the work in 1450." The Spaniards, throughout their rule, labored at projects to the same end, and sacrificed the lives of vast numbers of the natives in the work, without much result.

"Frequent floodings of the old Aztec city and of the Spanish capital, situated almost at the lowest point of the valley, were sure to come in times of unusually heavy rains. In early days, when the Aztecs lived in the middle of Lake Mexico, when their temples and wigwams were built on piles and the streets were often only canals, the periodical overflows from the upper lakes were a matter of small concern, though even then the Nahua engineers were called upon to protect the city by dykes. But when by evaporation, by filling in at the site of the city, by lessened waters, due to the fissures caused by earthquakes, Lake Mexico had disappeared, and the city had come to be built on the spongy soil, above all, when the short-sighted choice of Cortez had been confirmed and the capital of New Spain had come to stand on the ruins of the Aztec town, increasing rapidly in population and wealth,—it became a serious matter that on an average of once in twenty-five years the streets should be from two to six feet under water for an indefinite time. . . .

"In 1866 the works now [1895] nearing completion were commenced. A project proposed by Señor Don Francisco de Garay, a well-known engineer of the city of Mexico, was pronounced the most feasible. But the revolutionary struggle succeeded, and for many years the work was relegated to the background. . . . The present gigantic work cannot have been considered to have been seriously undertaken, with a view of completion at any cost, until the year 1885, when the City Council of Mexico submitted a project to the Government to which they offered to contribute largely in the event of its being adopted. A special commission, with ample authority to deal with the funds set aside for the work, was appointed by President Porfirio Diaz. . . .

"The drainage works, when carried out, will receive the surplus waters and sewage of the City of Mexico and carry them outside of the valley, and will also control the entire waters of the valley, affording an outlet, whenever found necessary, to those which might otherwise overflow fields and towns, rendering the soil stagnant and marshy. The work consists of three parts— 1st, the tunnel; 2d, a canal starting from the gates of San Lázaro, and having a length of 47 1-2 kilometres, or 43 miles; . . . and 3d, the sewage of the City of Mexico. . . . As this paper goes to press, the drainage works of the Valley

of Mexico are practically finished, as the waters of the valley have been for several years passing through the canal and the tunnel to their outlet in the river which takes them to the Gulf of Mexico, and the company with whom the canal was contracted is now giving the finishing touches to the sides and bottom of the canal and will deliver it to the Government Board of the Drainage Directors in January, 1898. . . .
"The canal and six-mile tunnel through the mountain range have a total length approaching (50) miles. The present works will take rank with the great achievements of modern times, just as the immense 'cut' of Nochistongo, their unsuccessful predecessor, was the leader among ancient earthworks in all the world. The completed system will have cost $20,000,000."—M. Romero, *Mexico and the United States, pp.* 266-280 (*N. Y.: G. P. Putnam's Sons*).

A. D. 1898-1900.—The results of twenty years of the presidency of **Porfirio Diaz.**—The wonderful advance of the Republic.—In his interesting book on Mexico, entitled "The Awakening of a Nation," written in 1898, Mr. Charles F. Lummis expresses the opinion that, under the Presidency of Porfirio Diaz, that country "has graduated to be the most compact and unified nation in the New World"; that "she has acquired not only a government which governs, but one which knows how to govern— and contemporaneously a people which has learned how to be ruled"; and he characterizes its government as "logical paternalism — a scheme frightfully dangerous under a bad father, incalculably beneficial under a good one." Two years later, in a contribution to an elaborate "Review of the Nineteenth Century," by many writers, which was published by the "New York Evening Post," January 12, 1901, Mr. Lummis wrote: "Before Diaz, the rich and ancient capital had spent two and a half centuries and ten millions in vain attempts to relieve its recurrent floods. Sewerage was unknown. To-day the valley is drained and sewered by a system nowhere surpassed. Electric lighting, transit, and power-transmission are in vogue. Law and order are of a proportion we may well envy. Public education and individual scholarship have no call to blush in any fair comparison with any land. Business is prosperous, almost without individual exceptions. Factories of all sorts — and some of the costliest and finest factories in the world—have sprung up by the thousand. The comminuted bones of a national spirit have knit as they never were before. Nowadays, it is not Mexico, but we, who are 'fooled' when we omit her from the category of the nations that count. She does count; she will count far more. She has mastered anarchy, she has triumphed even over free silver. She is busily engaged in practising one of the first gospels and mottoes of the American colonies—'Mind Your Own Business'—and is making a magnificent success at it. It is a curious problem in the philosophies of history, what shall be the outcome of a nation which instead of being born rugged and growing old and easy, was born old and in the last quarter-century has come into the heritage of sturdy youth. For it is as a young nation, with results still growing, that we must think of new Old Mexico."

Hon. John W. Foster, writing to the "New York Tribune," on the 9th of January, 1901, from the City of Mexico, where he formerly resided for some years as United States Minister, has borne similar testimony to the astonishing progress of the country. "Since the advent of General Porfirio Diaz to power in 1876," writes Mr. Foster, "there has been no foreign war and no serious disturbance of an internal character, the only exception being the outbreak of certain semi-independent Indian tribes. In the previous fifty years of the existence of the republic there had been as many presidents, the majority of whom owed their existence to revolutionary movements. The wretched story of Mexican history of that period is too familiar to be repeated here. . . . In his inaugural address to Congress last month, on being again installed as President, he [President Diaz] referred to the achievements of Mexico in the last twenty-five years, and modestly said that in it there were no brilliant deeds to chronicle. From that notable address I make this extract: 'If it were true that a peaceful and laborious people have no history, the administration period I am about to review would almost be devoid of history. But, on the contrary, those nations that deserve to be called happy in the only intelligible sense of the word, far from being without a history, have a very glorious and interesting one, if, besides being peaceful and laborious, they are also progressive. That history is the history of their progress, their achievements, their growing prosperity, of the improvements of every kind which they have introduced—a history which, in this modern age and the present constitution of civilized societies, is as interesting as that of their past and just as deserving of attention.'"

A report for 1900 by the British Consul at Vera Cruz is to the same effect. The result of the recent elections he describes as an assurance of prosperity and a guarantee of the foreign capital invested in the country. Few countries, the Consul observes, can boast of such rapid and beneficial reforms as Mexico; these have, in a short time, prepared the way for the development of her extensive resources, which are themselves a sufficient assurance of the future. The finances have of recent years been brought to a high state of excellence, and commerce throughout the Republic has flourished. Foreign capital has flowed in steadily, railway construction has progressed, and other modes of communication have improved, the telegraph and postal service have been reformed. The improvement of interoceanic communication across the Tehuantepec isthmus, with the harbors now being constructed on both coasts, will revolutionize the foreign trade of Mexico. It will take more than three years to complete the reconstruction of the railway and to put the ports in a condition to enable freight to be taken from the ship's side at one port and placed alongside the ship at the other within 24 hours. The Consul thinks the route is destined to become one of the principal thoroughfares of the world, competing with all other routes between Europe and the Far East.

Of what has been done for public education in Mexico under the Diaz government the following account is given in one of the publications (1900) of the Bureau of the American Republics: "Education in Mexico has been for many years the subject of serious consideration on the part of the Government, on account of the difficulty experienced in combating the conservative ideas prevailing in the Republic. The main obstacles have, however, been overcome, and the country to-day enjoys the benefit of a liberal system of education, which is administered under three branches—gratuitous, lay, and obligatory. . . . The law making education compulsory was promulgated March 23, 1888, but its enforcement was not decreed at that time, and the first Congress of Public Education was convened for the purpose of adopting such measures as should tend to establish an efficient and uniform system of education. This congress met on December 1, 1889, and closed its sessions on March 31, 1890. . . . A second congress was convened on December 1, 1890, which solved certain problems on compulsory elemental education, fixed the methods to be followed in the schools of superior primary education, and settled matters pertaining to normal schools, preparatory education, and special schools. As the result of this congress, the law of March 21, 1891, was enacted, regulating compulsory education in the Federal District and the Territories of Tepic and Lower California, which law became effective on January 17, 1892. . . .

"On May 19, 1896, the law of public education was promulgated, its salient points being as follows: Official primary elemental education in the Federal Districts and Federal Territories was placed under the exclusive control of the Executive; primary superior education was organized as an intermediate educational system between elementary and preparatory instruction. A general board of primary education was created, charged to develop and maintain the same under a scientific and administrative plan. Preparatory education was decreed to be uniform for all professions, its extent being limited to the study of such matters as are necessary to the development of the physical and intellectual faculties and the morals of youth, it being further directed that professional education be reorganized, limiting it to technical matters which pertain to the profession or professions to which each particular school is devoted.

"By virtue of this law public education ceased to be in charge of the Board of Aldermen (ayuntamientos) of the above-mentioned sections. At the time of its promulgation the municipality of Mexico contained 113 schools, supported by the Board of Aldermen, 14,246 students being entered on the rolls, with an average attendance of 9,798. Each State defrays the expenses of public education, either with funds specially appropriated for that purpose or with the municipal funds.

"According to statistical data, in 1876, there were throughout the country 8,165 primary schools, with 368,754 students of both sexes. In 1895 Government schools reached the number of 4,056, of which 2,189 were for males, 1,119 for females, and 748 for both sexes; municipal schools numbered 8,394—for males, 1,754; females, 932; both sexes, 708. These comprised 7,380 primary, 32 secondary, and 35 professional schools, the number of students enrolled being 310,496 males and 181,484 females (a total of 491,980), and the mean attendance 338,066. The total cost to the Government and the municipalities for the maintenance of these institutions was $3,973,738. In the same year private schools to the number of 1,816 were being conducted, 659 for males, 460 for females, and the remainder under a coeduca-

tional system. In addition, 276 were supported by the clergy and 146 by associations, the total number of students enrolled being 68,879, of which 40,135 were males and 38,744 females. The total number of private schools was accordingly 2,238, of which 2,193 were devoted to primary education, 34 to secondary instruction, and 11 to professions.

"The statistics for 1897, which are the latest available, give the following figures : ·

SCHOOLS.	1896.	1897.
Federal and State Governments....	5,852	6,141
Municipal.............................	3,218	1,953
Private institutions.................	1,953	1,797
Supported by the clergy...........	303	285
Supported by associations.........	186	122

"Using the figures given in 1896 for Vera Cruz and the Federal District as identical for 1897, it may be safely assumed that on December 31, 1897, the public schools in Mexico (Federal, State, and municipal) stood as follows:

Number of schools	9,065
Students enrolled	666,787
Average monthly attendance . . .	458,035
Private institutions	2,361
Number of students	92,387
Average attendance	75,857

"The total expenditures for the support of Federal, State, and municipal schools amounted in 1897 to $6,291,000. In addition to the normal and primary schools, the Government also supports the following institutions: School of jurisprudence, school of medicine, school of agriculture and veterinary instruction, school of engineers, school of fine arts, school of arts and trades for men, and a similar institution for women, school of commerce and administration, National conservatory of music, preparatory school, schools for the blind, for deaf-mutes, reform schools, etc., also 9 museums, and 17 libraries containing from 400 to 159,000 volumes. Beside the Government institutions above mentioned, there are throughout the country 26 museums, 83 libraries, 32 scientific and literary associations, and 457 periodical publications."—*Bureau of Am. Republics, Mexico : a Geographical Sketch, p. 313.*

A. D. 1899 (May—July).—**Representation in the Peace Conference at The Hague.** See (in this vol.) PEACE CONFERENCE.

A. D. 1900 (January).—**Re-election of President Diaz.**—President Porfirio Diaz was re-elected on January 1, for a sixth term of four years.

A. D. 1900 (October).—**Census of the Republic.**—Gains shown in five years.—Announcement was made from Washington, on the 24th of February, 1901, that "complete official returns of the census taken on October 28, 1900, received by the Bureau of American Republics, shows that the population of Mexico is 13,570,545, against a population of 12,632,427 [given by M. Romero as 12,570,195—see above] in 1895. The gain in five years was 938,118, or 7.43 per cent. due in part to the greater accuracy of the latest enumeration. The Federal District, in which is located the City of Mexico, is the most densely populated portion of the republic, and contains

530,723 people. The City of Mexico increased about 20,000 in five years, and now has nearly 357,000 inhabitants. The population of seven States, Jalisco, Guanajuato, Puebla, Vera Cruz, Oaxaca, Michoacan and Mexico, is 6,995,880, or a little more than one-half of the entire population of the country. The population of the States of Sonora, Tamaulipas, Tlaxcala, Morelos, Tabasco, Aguas Calientes, Campeche, Colima, and the territories of Tepic and Lower California, the total area of which is more than one-fourth the entire country, is slightly in excess of 1,380,000, or a density of only about 2.7 inhabitants to the square kilometre. The central and southern portions of the republic are the most thickly populated, the Western and Northern States being the most sparsely settled, and the Gulf region, or eastern coast, contains a larger number of inhabitants than the Pacific Coast region. . . . The greatest percentage of increase is noted in the northern States. These States, in addition to being good agricultural districts, are enormously rich in mineral wealth, and the large increase in population in this part of the country is chiefly due to the rapid development of the mines of the republic, the erection of smelters and manufacturing plants, and to the general stimulus given to trade and commerce by the construction of railroads and the heavy investments of foreign capital in the republic."

MIDDLE-OF-THE-ROAD POPULISTS, The. See (in this vol.) UNITED STATES OF AM.: A. D. 1896 (JUNE—Nov.); and 1900 (MAY—Nov.).

MILAN, Ex-King: His later years and death. See (in this vol.) BALKAN AND DANUBIAN STATES (SERVIA).

MILAN: A. D. 1898.—Revolutionary outbreak. See (in this vol.) ITALY: A. D. 1898 (APRIL—MAY).

MILES, General Nelson A.: Operations against Santiago de Cuba. See (in this vol.) UNITED STATES OF AM.: A. D. 1898 (JUNE—JULY).

Commanding expedition against Porto Rico. See (in this vol.) UNITED STATES OF AM.: A. D. 1898 (JULY—AUGUST: PORTO RICO).

Charges aga the Commissary Department, U. S. Army. See (in this vol.) UNITED STATES OF AM.: A. D. 1898–1899.

MILITARY ESTABLISHMENTS: Armies of Europe and America and their cost. See (in this vol.) WAR BUDGETS.

MILLENNIUM, The Hungarian. See (in this vol.) AUSTRIA-HUNGARY: A. D. 1896.

MILNER, Sir Alfred: Governor of Cape Colony and High Commissioner for South Africa. See (in this vol.) SOUTH AFRICA: A. D. 1897 (FEBRUARY), and after.

Governor of the Transvaal and British High Commissioner. See (in this vol.) SOUTH AFRICA (BRITISH COLONIES): A. D. 1901 (JANUARY).

MINDANAO. See (in this vol.) PHILIPPINE ISLANDS.

MINERS, Strikes among. See (in this vol.) INDUSTRIAL DISTURBANCES.

MINNESOTA: A. D. 1896.—Constitutional amendments.—Use of the Referendum.—Several constitutional amendments were submitted to the voters of the State and adopted; among them one requiring citizenship of the United States for three months and residence in the State for six months before permitting a new-comer to vote ; another vesting the pardoning power in a Board of Pardons; another empowering cities to frame their own charters, subject to the State laws. At the same time, the Referendum was brought into practical use, by the submission of several legislative acts to the popular vote. One of the acts thus submitted, providing for the holding of a constitutional convention, was rejected.

A. D. 1898.—Outbreak of Pillager Indians. See (in this vol.) INDIANS, AMERICAN: A. D. 1898.

MINOS, The Palace of: Its supposed discovery. See (in this vol.) ARCHÆOLOGICAL RESEARCH: CRETE.

MISSIONARIES, Christian: The outbreak against in China. See (in this vol.) CHINA: A. D. 1895 (AUGUST) ; 1898 (MAY); 1898–1899 (JUNE—JANUARY); 1899; 1900 (JANUARY—MARCH), (MAY—JUNE) ; and 1901 (MARCH).

Outbreak against in Madagascar. See (in this vol.) MADAGASCAR.

MISSIONS, Christian: The Ecumenical Conference of 1900 in New York.—Statistics of the Protestant foreign missionary work of the world.—The third Ecumenical Conference on Protestant foreign missions (the second having been held in London in 1888) was assembled at New York on the 21st of April, 1900, under circumstances related as follows in vol. I. of the official report: "The immediate origin of the Ecumenical Conference of 1900 was the discussion of a question put in the 'question box' at the Annual Conference of Foreign Missions Boards of the United States and Canada, which met in New York in January, 1896, as to whether it would be advisable to invite the secretaries or representatives of societies from the other side of the Atlantic to meet with the Annual Conference of the American societies as it was then held, consisting chiefly of the officers of the Boards. The Rev. F. F. Ellinwood, D. D., speaking to the question, said : 'I have had a hope that in the year 1898, ten years from the great London Conference, we might invite our brethren from all lands to a great Ecumenical Conference on Missions.'

"Following this suggestion, a committee of five, consisting of the Rev. Drs. Judson Smith, F. F. Ellinwood, A. B. Leonard, S. W. Duncan, and William S. Langford was appointed 'to consider the advisability of calling an Ecumenical Missionary Conference, to meet in this country within the next four years, to make preliminary preparation therefor, if deemed advisable, and to report at the Conference of the following year.' This committee corresponded with missionary societies throughout the world, and at the next Annual Conference recommended that such a Conference be held in New York City in April of the year 1900 ; that this recommendation be communicated to the societies, and a final date agreed upon. In January, 1898, after further correspondence, the place and date were finally decided." Measures were taken to raise a guarantee fund of $30,000 for expenses, and other preparations were made. Then "under date of

June 1, 1899, a general invitation was sent to every missionary whose name and address could be secured, to attend the Conference and participate in the discussions."

The Conference was opened in Carnegie Hall, New York, on the 21st of April, 1900, and continued its sessions, there and in neighboring churches, until the 1st of May. "The personnel of the Conference was broadly representative. It consisted (1) of delegates appointed by organizations conducting foreign missions outside of Europe and America; (2) the missionaries of such organizations, and (3) members elected by the Executive Committee. The British and Continental and other foreign societies were invited to send as many delegates as possible. The American and Canadian societies were limited in the number of their delegates; the total from both countries, being fixed at 1,666, was apportioned among the societies on the basis of their expenditures in foreign missions. All foreign missionaries in active service or retired were received as full members. Some of the honorary members and vice-presidents who were unable to attend desired to have their names connected with so historic a gathering. Members of committees and speakers, who were not already delegates, were by a general act of the Executive Committee, constituted 'special members.' In addition to the members of the Conference a large number of persons came from far and near to attend the meetings. Over fifty thousand tickets to the Carnegie Hall and alternate meetings were distributed among this class of visitors. Many thousands more attended the sectional and overflow meetings where no tickets were required. The Hon. Benjamin Harrison, for four years President of the United States of America, occupied the chair, and made an opening speech."

The magnitude of the organizations of missionary work, all the interests, needs and fruits of which were discussed in the Conference, is most succinctly represented in the subjoined tables, prepared by Dr. James S. Dennis, which are given in the appendix to the official report (pp. 424–6, vol. 2). The classification appearing in the tables is explained as follows :

"The Bible Societies, the Tract and Literature Societies, the United Society of Christian Endeavor, the Epworth Leagues, and similar organizations, philanthropic specialties like that of the Pundita Ramabai in India, with a considerable number of organizations, foreign missionary in title and purpose, but simply rendering financial or other aid to existing societies—demand recognition, and yet should they be counted as strictly and technically foreign missionary societies? It was chosen for the present purpose, to differentiate and classify, naming three classes of societies as follows : Class I. Societies directly engaged in conducting foreign missions. Class II. Societies indirectly co-operating or aiding in foreign missions. Class III. Societies or Institutions independently engaged in specialized effort in various departments of foreign missions."

MISSISSIPPI: A. D. 1890-1892.—New State Constitution.—Qualification of the suffrage.—A new State Constitution, framed and put in force in 1890 by a constitutional convention, without submission to the people, established a qualification of the suffrage which heavily diminished the negro vote by its effect. It im-

posed a poll tax of two dollars per head, to which any county might add a further tax not exceeding one dollar per head, which poll tax for the year every voter must have paid before his ballot would be received at any election. A further clause of the Constitution on the subject was as follows: "On and after the first day of January, A. D. 1892, the following qualifications are added to the foregoing : Every qualified elector shall be able to read any section of the Constitution of this State, or he shall be able to understand the same when read to him, or to give a reasonable interpretation thereof. A new registration shall be made before the next ensuing election after these qualifications are established. Electors in municipal elections shall possess all the qualifications herein prescribed, and such additional qualifications as may be prescribed by law." In 1892 the Supreme Court of the State affirmed the validity of the Constitution, which had been challenged on two grounds, namely: that it had not been submitted to the vote of the people, and that it was in conflict with the Fourteenth Amendment of the Constitution of the United States.

So far, the disfranchisement of the mass of blacks seems to have had an unlooked for evil effect. "The Negro eliminated, only one political party remains, and political stagnation has followed. In Mississippi, the requirement that a poll tax be paid long before the election deprives many white men also of their votes. But it does not bar them out of nominating conventions. Many communities are ruled by a mere handful of whites who cannot even cast a ballot. For instance, there are 320,000 males of voting age in Mississippi, but the whole vote cast in the State in November was only 59,000. This is 11,000 votes less than were cast four years ago under the same restrictions of suffrage. In other words, the whole State of Mississippi cast practically no more ballots to elect seven members of Congress than were cast in a single congressional district in New York. (The fourteenth New York district cast 58,000 votes.) In the town of Eudora, where a mayor, a marshal, a treasurer, and four aldermen were elected, only eight votes were cast, and of the eight voters seven are said to have been candidates for office.

"'The same men,' says a trustworthy despatch from New Orleans, 'were voters, candidates for office, and judges of election to pass as judges on their own votes as voters for themselves; and in spite of all their efforts they could get only one outsider to come to the polls and cast his ballot.' This is an extreme case ; but in every State that has disfranchised the Negro (making a discrimination between him and the ignorant white man, in the white man's favor) political activity has constantly disappeared, the vote has shrunk, public spirit in politics has died. In Louisiana the total vote in November fell from 99,000 in 1896 to 61,000 ; of Mississippi, from 69,000 to 59,000 ; of South Carolina, from 69,000 to 50,000 — the shrinkage in four years in these three States being nearly 68,000 votes, in spite of the increase of population."—*The World's Work*, Feb., 1901.

MODDER RIVER, Military operations on. See (in this vol.) SOUTH AFRICA (THE FIELD OF WAR): A. D. 1899 (OCTOBER—DECEMBER) ; and 1900 (JANUARY—FEBRUARY).

NATIONAL OR CONTINENTAL DIVISIONS.	Number of Societies.	Income from Home and Foreign Sources.	FOREIGN MISSIONARIES.							NATIVE WORKERS.		
			Ordained Missionaries.	Physicians.		Lay Missionaries (Men), not Physicians.	Married Women, not Physicians.	Unmarried Women, not Physicians.	Total of Foreign Missionaries.	Ordained Natives.	Unordained Natives, Preachers, Teachers, and other Helpers.	Total of Ordained and Unordained Native Helpers.
				Men.	Women.							
CLASS I. Societies directly engaged in conducting Foreign Missions.												
United States	49	$5,403,048	1,352	160	114	109	1,274	1,006	4,110	1,575	15,013	16,605
Canada	8	352,743	69	17	9	24	64	59	236	39	677	716
England	42	6,843,031	1,747	139	47	664	958	1,407	5,136	1,665	25,980	27,795
Scotland	7	1,280,684	188	52	23	88	161	230	653	52	2,909	3,026
Ireland	4	101,930	32	11	4	13	29	25	112	5	397	419
Wales	1	40,729	17	3	......	......	13	6	36	7	493	500
Denmark	3	42,770	18	......	......	......	11	3	32	1	35	36
Finland	1	28,860	10	......	......	......	10	......	20	......	......	8
France	2	268,191	48	1	......	17	43	15	123	42	300	342
Germany	15	1,430,151	731	10	......	91	609	76	1,515	160	6,284	6,464
Netherlands	10	124,126	65	2	......	2	12	......	81	30	220	250
Norway	4	158,328	49	3	......	9	37	17	113	78	1,806	1,884
Sweden	7	166,036	85	2	2	14	49	37	187	5	217	222
Switzerland	2	34,337	15	1	......	2	13	11	41	......	31	31
Australasia and Oceania	26	309,234	96	11	......	57	64	91	313	152	4,771	4,923
Asia	29	97,569	48	6	4	104	39	81	282	15	298	313
Africa	28	216,705	217	3	......	33	......	31	347	98	4,400	4,507
West Indies	11	262,620	166	......	......	17	64	24	270	105	5,469	5,574
Totals for Class I	249	$17,161,092	4,953	421	203	1,244	3,450	3,119	13,607	4,029	60,300	73,615

NATIONAL OR CONTINENTAL DIVISIONS.	STATIONS.		CHURCHES.			SUNDAY SCHOOLS.		CONTRIBUTIONS.	NATIVE CHRISTIANS.
	Principal Stations.	All other Sub-stations.	Organized Churches.	Total Number of Communicants.	Additions during the Last Year.	Sunday Schools.	Total Sunday-School Membership.	Total of Native Contributions.	Total of Native Christian Community, including, besides Communicants, Non-communicants of all Ages.
CLASS I. Societies directly engaged in conducting Foreign Missions.									
United States	1,038	6,291	4,107	421,597	31,970	7,231	344,385	$628,717	1,257,425
Canada	73	230	80	9,987	985	402	12,731	1,377	32,925
England	1,810	12,158	4,744	278,548	20,093	2,875	171,247	580,855	1,081,384
Scotland	243	841	195	40,247	4,179	437	26,257	206,240	91,667
Ireland	23	93	21	4,588	652	95	4,816	5,160	14,421
Wales	15	393	140	3,596	365	410	11,615	5,100	16,561
Denmark	11	10	....	361	54	......	....	75	890
Finland	3	3	3	240	18	6	300	....	676
France	40	......	......	14,788	388	......	......	......	......
Germany	499	1,320	564	154,356	7,064	330	35,979	161,705	357,436
Netherlands	56	174	10	5,041	110	12	2,620	40	32,667
Norway	41	903	204	35,289	4,545	......	......	2,000	50,811
Sweden	49	108	10	3,447	1,027	22	953	....	2,639
Switzerland	8	18	8	749	151	26	1,394	182	2,463
Australasia and Oceania	276	344	218	71,637	1,904	1,921	58,241	21,112	162,332
Asia	71	46	69	9,993	183	103	2,020	3,888	14,042
Africa	689	1,961	62	132,280	3,881	326	26,988	34,618	202,984
West Indies	291	693	558	102,554	6,326	744	65,138	182,912	1,005,960
Totals for Class I	5,233	25,586	10,993	1,289,298	83,895	14,940	764,684	$1,833,981	4,327,283

NATIONAL OR CONTINENTAL DIVISIONS.	Number of Societies.	Income from Home and Foreign Sources.	FOREIGN MISSIONARIES.							NATIVE WORKERS.		
			Ordained Missionaries.	Physicians.		Lay Missionaries, not Physicians (Men).	Married Women, not Physicians.	Unmarried Women, not Physicians.	Total of Foreign Missionaries.	Ordained Natives.	Unordained Natives—Preachers, Teachers, Bible-women, and other Helpers.	Total of Ordained and Unordained Native Helpers.
				Men.	Women.							
CLASS II. Societies indirectly co-operating or aiding in Foreign Missions.												
United States	16	$171,607	18	......	......	19	12	1	50	......	243	243
Canada	1	13,832	15	1	......	2	14	6	37	1	......	1
England	30	784,122	18	3	......	19	6	26	959	4	2,478	2,482
Scotland	10	103,032	14	5	......	11	8	17	53	1	382	383
Ireland	1	20,402	4	......	......	......	2	4	10	3	42	45
Germany	3	9,795	......	......	......	9	2	13	24	......	11	11
Netherlands	4	5,200	......	......	......	......	......	......	......	......	......	......
Norway	4	1,352	......	......	......	2	3	4	9	......	1	1
Sweden	1	8,750	4	2	......	5	6	14	31	......	14	14
Switzerland	1	3,000	......	......	......	......	......	......	......	......	......	......
Australasia and Oceania	3	28,645	......	......	......	......	......	......	78	......	......	......
Asia	24	77,944	1	......	......	2	1	......	4	......	36	36
Totals for Class II...	98	$1,227,731	74	11	......	69	54	85	1,255	9	3,207	3,216

NATIONAL OR CONTINENTAL DIVISIONS.	STATIONS.		CHURCHES.			SUNDAY SCHOOLS.		CONTRIBUTIONS.	NATIVE CHRISTIANS.
	Principal Stations.	All other Sub-stations.	Organized Churches.	Total Number of Communicants.	Additions during the Last Year.	Sunday Schools.	Total Sunday-School Membership.	Total of Native Contributions.	Total of Native Christian Community, including, besides Communicants, Non-communicants of all Ages.
CLASS II. Societies indirectly co-operating or aiding in Foreign Missions.									
United States	14	......	......	......	......	......	......	......	......
England	102	503	9	25,078	......	4	190	$ 100	75,243
Scotland	12	1	......	......	......	9	960	1,125	......
Ireland	1	11	......	203	37	......	......	......	545
Germany	6	3	......	45	......	......	......	......	......
Norway	1	2	1	35	......	1	......	......	40
Sweden	6	5	7	200	......	......	......	......	500
Asia	3	16	......	......	......	......	......	......	......
Totals for Class II...	145	541	17	25,561	37	14	1,150	$1,225	76,328

312

NATIONAL OR CONTINENTAL DIVISIONS.	Number of Societies.	Income from Home and Foreign Sources.	FOREIGN MISSIONARIES.							NATIVE WORKERS.		
			Ordained Missionaries.	Physicians.		Lay Missionaries, not Physicians (Men).	Married Women, not Physicians.	Unmarried Women, not Physicians.	Total of Foreign Missionaries.	Md Natives.	Unordained Preachers, Teachers, Bible-Women, and their Helpers.	Total of Med and Native Helpers.
				Men.	Women.							
CLASS III. Societies or Institutions independently engaged in specialized effort in various departments of Foreign Missions.												
United States	28	$253,661	26	27	7	101	40	30	304	7	63	70
England	33	245,465	1	5	2	34	8	26	76	1	115	116
Scotland	13	96,520	1	5	......	2	3	6	20	......	48	48
Ireland	1	4,125	......	......	......	......	......	......	......	......	4	4
Wales	1	10,956	......	......	......	......	......	......	......	6	200	206
Germany	4	101,440	5	7	......	16	8	115	151	1	11	12
Holland	1	1,452	1	......	......	1	......	......	2	......	......	......
Norway	2	497	......	1	......	......	......	2	3	......	......	......
Sweden	1	......	......	......	......	......	......	7	7	......	3	3
Australasia	2	......	......	......	......	......	......	......	......	......	......	......
Asia	14	23,083	2	7	6	3	4	13	35	......	48	48
Africa	2	98	......	......	......	......	......	......	......	......	......	......
Totals for Class III.	102	$737,297	36	52	15	157	63	199	598	15	492	507

NATIONAL OR CONTINENTAL DIVISIONS.	STATIONS.		CHURCHES.			SUNDAY SCHOOLS.		CONTRIBUTIONS.	NATIVE CHRISTIANS.
	Principal Stations.	All other Sub-stations.	Organized Churches.	Total Number of Communicants.	Additions during the Last Year.	Sunday Schools.	Total Sunday-School Membership.	Total of Native Contributions.	Total of Native Christian Community, including, besides Communicants, Non-communicants of all Ages.
CLASS III. Societies or Institutions independently engaged in specialized effort in various departments of Foreign Missions.									
United States	53	4	......	......	......	4	474	$102	120
England	23	110	9	190	40	27	1,498	24	505
Scotland	10	......	......	......	......	5	246	......	......
Ireland	1	......	......	......	......	......	......	......	......
Wales	11	......	17	2,500	200	30	3,000	4,655	10,000
Germany	24	2	1	95	......	9	733	270	......
Holland	1	......	......	......	......	......	......	......	......
Asia	70	4	2	40	14	3	143	1,500	......
Totals for Class III.	193	120	29	2,825	254	78	6,094	$6,551	10,625

MODUS VIVENDI, Alaskan Boundary. See (in this vol.) ALASKA BOUNDARY QUESTION.

MODUS VIVENDI, The Newfoundland. See (in this vol.) NEWFOUNDLAND: A. D. 1899–1901.

MOMBASA-VICTORIA RAILWAY, The. See (in this vol.) UGANDA RAILWAY.

MONETARY QUESTIONS AND MEASURES: A. D. 1895.—The situation of the Treasury of the United States.—Contract for replenishing its gold reserve. See (in this vol.) UNITED STATES OF AM. : A. D. 1895 (JANUARY—FEBRUARY).

A. D. 1895-1896.—The gold reserve in the U. S. Treasury again imperilled.—Refusal of relief by the Senate. See (in this vol.) UNITED STATES OF AM. : A. D. 1895–1896 (DECEMBER—FEBRUARY).

A. D. 1896-1900.—The Silver Question in the United States Presidential elections. See (in this vol.) UNITED STATES OF AM. : A. D. 1896 (JUNE—NOVEMBER); and 1900 (MAY—NOVEMBER).

A. D. 1896-1898.—Movements for monetary reforms in the United States. See (in this vol.) UNITED STATES OF AM. : A. D. 1896–1898.

A. D. 1897.—Renewal of the privileges of the Bank of France.—The privileges of the Bank of France, as the fiscal agent of the French Government, expired with the close of the year 1897, and renewal of them was opposed by the Radicals and Socialists, who demanded the creation of a State Bank. The government succeeded, however (June, 1897), in carrying the measure necessary for continuing the existing system, on terms somewhat more favorable to the state than before.

A. D. 1897 (March).—Adoption of the gold standard in Japan.—By a law of the Japanese Parliament, passed in March, 1897, to come into force October 1, a gold monetary standard was adopted, at the ratio of 32½ to 1, the silver dollar to be legal tender until six months after notice given of its withdrawal.

A. D. 1897 (April—October).—Negotiation by American Commissioners in Europe for an international bi-metallic agreement.—In fulfilment of the pledge given by the Republican party, at its national convention, in 1896, that it would use efforts to bring about an international agreement for free coinage of gold and silver at some common ratio, the following Act was passed by the two Houses of Congress in January and February, 1897: "That whenever after March 4, 1897, the president of the United States shall determine that the United States should be represented at any international conference called by the United States or any other country with a view to securing by international agreement a fixity of relative value between gold and silver as money by means of a common ratio between these metals, with free mintage at such ratio, he is hereby authorized to appoint five or more commissioners to such international conference; and for compensation of said commissioners, and for all reasonable expenses connected therewith, to be approved by the secretary of state, including the proportion to be paid by the United States of the joint expenses of any such conference, the sum of $100,000, or so much thereof as may be necessary, is hereby appropriated. That the

president of the United States is hereby authorized, in the name of the government of the United States, to call, in his discretion, such international conference, to assemble at such point as may be agreed upon. And he is further authorized, if in his judgment the purpose specified in the first section hereof can thus be better attained, to appoint one or more special commissioners or envoys to such of the nations of Europe as he may designate, to seek by diplomatic negotiations an international agreement for the purpose specified in the first section hereof. And in case of such appointment so much of the appropriation herein made as shall be necessary shall be available for the proper expenses and compensation of such commissioners or envoys." Pursuant to this Act, President McKinley, on the 12th of April, appointed Senator Edward O. Wolcott, of Colorado, ex-Vice-President Adlai E. Stevenson, of Illinois, and General Charles J. Paine, of Massachusetts, to be commissioners for the purpose which the bill describes. The commissioners first visited Paris, and there obtained assurances from the French government of cordial coöperation and support. They then proceeded to London, for negotiation with the British authorities, on whose attitude towards the movement for international action in the matter its success was well known to depend. Some members of the British government, conspicuously Mr. Balfour, were outspoken advocates of bi-metallism, and much was hoped from the discussion to be opened with them. The American commissioners were cordially received, and they were invited to a formal meeting, on the 12th of July, with Lord Salisbury, the Prime Minister, Mr. Balfour, First Lord of the Treasury, Sir Michael Hicks-Beach, Chancellor of the Exchequer, and Lord George Hamilton, Secretary of State for India. The American Ambassador, Mr. Hay, accompanied them to the conference, which was held at the Foreign Office. A memorandum of the conversation at this meeting, and at a second one held on the 15th, together with a correspondence which followed, were published later in a parliamentary "blue book," from which the following account is drawn. Mr. Wolcott explained the wish of the American envoys to obtain the views of several governments, preliminary to the inviting of an international bi-metallic conference. He added that they expected to have, in England, the full coöperation of the Ambassador of the French Republic, who happened, for the moment, to be absent from the country, but who had requested them to proceed with the meeting in his absence. "Mr. Wolcott then presented some reasons which, in the opinion of the Special Envoys, rendered it desirable that some international agreement for the restoration of bimetallism should be reached, and explained why, in their opinion, the success of this effort depended upon the attitude which England would take regarding the question. He then stated that the Special Envoys requested that England should agree to open English mints as its contribution to an attempt to restore bimetallism by international agreement, and dwelt upon the importance of the fact that France and the United States were together engaged in an attempt to bring about such an agreement, and were coöperating together to that end. Lord Salisbury desired to know if the French Government would co-operate upon the basis of opening their mints to the free and unlimited coinage of silver. Mr. Wolcott answered in the affirmative. Lord Salisbury then asked at what ratio, and was informed by Mr. Wolcott that the French Government preferred the ratio of 15½ to 1, and that the United States were inclined to yield this point and accept this as a proper ratio. Considerable discussion on the question of the ratio and the method by which it should be settled then took place. . . . It was then suggested that further proceedings should be deferred until the French Ambassador might be also present. The Chancellor of the Exchequer, in further conversation, said that if the suggestion of opening the English mints was to be made, he thought an answer in the negative would undoubtedly be given. The First Lord of the Treasury asked whether, assuming this request for opening English mints to be refused, it was desired that the subject be discussed upon the basis of something different and less than the opening of English mints. Upon a mutual understanding that in the absence of the French Ambassador, anything said should be considered as said informally, a discussion then took place as to the concessions that England might make towards an international solution of the question, if it should refuse to open English mints. Mr. Wolcott, for the Special Envoys, presented the following as a list of contributions which, among others, England might make towards bimetallism if an international agreement could be effected:—1. Opening of the Indian mints. Repeal of the order making the sovereign legal tender in India. 2. Placing one-fifth of the bullion in the Issue Department of the Bank of England in silver. 3.—(a.) Raising the legal tender limit of silver to, say, £10. (b.) Issuing the 20s. notes based on silver, which shall be legal tender. (c.) Retirement, gradual or otherwise, of the 10s. gold pieces, and substitution of paper based on silver. 4. Agreement to coin annually £   of silver [present silver coinage average for five years about £1,000,000, less annual withdrawal of worn and defaced coin for recoinage, £350,000]. 5. Opening of English mints to coinage of rupees, and for coinage of British dollar, which shall be full tender in Straits Settlements and other silver standard Colonies, and tender in the United Kingdom to the limit of silver legal tender. 6. Colonial action, and coinage of silver in Egypt. 7. Something having the general scope of the Huskisson plan. Some general conversation followed in regard to the preceding suggestions, and the interview terminated, to be resumed on the 15th July, 1897, when it was understood that the French Ambassador would also be present."

At the second meeting, July 15, Baron de Courcel, Ambassador of the French Republic, and M. L. Geoffray, French Minister Plenipotentiary, were present, and the former spoke at length, stating the position of the French government on the question of the free coinage of silver. He said : " ' Our population, notably the agricultural population, finds that it has not at its disposition sufficient resources in currency, in metallic money. On the other hand, if the Government in the actual state of affairs reopens the mints to the free coinage of silver, we would be flooded by the abundance of this metal coming from all other countries of the world, and we could not resist the even greater evil of the inevitable depreciation of one of our precious metals,

that is to say, of the effective destruction of the legal ratio upon which our monetary system is based. . . . In other words, we think that the production of silver, more active in certain quarters of the globe in the last quarter of a century, is not of itself considerable enough to change in an enduring manner the normal ratio between gold and silver after these two metals will have been scattered over the entire surface of the world among all nations who are called upon to absorb them. There is, then, in our eyes, a need which is perhaps transitory, but which is actually common to all the commercial nations, of taking measures adequate for assuring, by a common understanding, the re-establishment of the normal ratio of 15½ between silver and gold. If measures of this kind should be adopted by all the commercial nations, we would be able to reopen our mints to the free coinage of silver without fear of being submerged by an excessive influx of this metal. The reopening of the mints of all the commercial countries to the free coinage of silver in the ratio of 15½ with gold would be the most natural and the most efficacious means of arriving at the result sought for. This is the desideratum which I am instructed to bring forward here, and which I am particularly to urge upon the English Government as a primordial condition of the success of the common understanding. If the Government of the Queen, even in consenting to reopen the mints in India, should refuse to adopt the same measure for England, at least would they not be able to take certain measures which would be, up to a certain point, equivalent, in order to maintain the full value of silver, and to prevent India from being the victim of a depreciation of this metal in consequence of an unlimited coinage ? . . . By way of suggestion, I would indicate, as one of the measures which the English Government might usefully adopt, the annual purchase of a certain quantity of silver metal, which might afterwards be disposed of as seemed best—either it might be preserved in ingots, or it might be used for regular consumption, or it might be sent to India. This quantity might be fixed approximately, at least, for a number of years, at a sum of £10,000,000 in nominal value. This is, perhaps, only a palliative ; it is, in any event, only one of the expedients which would be deemed necessary. But I am to urge strongly that the English Government determine to take measures of this kind, or other equivalent measures, if, as I believe, it recognizes with us the necessity of improving the monetary situation in a great part of its Empire—I may say, in a great part of the entire world.' Lord Salisbury then asked whether the French Government would decline to open its mints unless England would also open her mints. The French Ambassador replied that he preferred to discuss the subject upon the basis that France would go to open mints if England would consent to open her mints, but that he would not exclude from his view the question of contributions by England towards maintaining the value of silver, short of open mints. The Chancellor of the Exchequer. in response to this, stated definitely that the English Government would not agree to open English mints to the unlimited coinage of silver, and that, whatever views he and his colleagues might separately hold on the question of bimetallism, he thought he could say they were united upon this point. . . . The suggestions made by the Special Envoys at the interview on the 12th July were again read, and the Special Envoys accepted also as important and desirable the proposal that the English Government should purchase annually, say, £10,000,000 of silver, with proper safeguards and provisions as to the place and manner of its use. The French Ambassador expressed his approval generally of the suggestions of the Special Envoys, as being serviceable in the consideration of the question. It was then understood that the proposals submitted by the French Ambassador and by the Special Envoys of the United States should be considered, and due notice given when a reply could be made."

The proposal for the reopening of the Indian mints to silver was submitted at once by the home authorities of the India Office, at London, to the government of India, and the reply of the latter was not received until the following October. When the reply came, it extinguished hopes of the arrangement which the American and French governments desired. In a long despatch, the Indian government explained with clearness the monetary situation in that country, and discussed the effect which a return to the unrestricted mintage of silver would have upon it, under the circumstances and prospects of the time. "The currency system of India," said the despatch, "is in a transition state; the Government of India in 1893 decided to establish a gold standard, and the first step towards that object was the closing of the mints to silver by Act VIII of 1893. The silver rupee is still the sole legal tender coin, though the Government has by Executive orders undertaken to receive gold and sovereigns under certain restrictions, . . . the rate of exchange adopted being 16d. the rupee or 15 rupees=£1. The measures to be taken when the transition period has passed have not been laid down, but it is probable that the Indian mints will be opened to gold, and gold coins will be made legal tender to an unlimited amount; silver rupees would also continue to be legal tender to an unlimited amount, and the ratio between the rupee and the gold coins as legal tender would at the same time be finally settled. The system towards which India is moving is thus a gold standard of the same kind as that which now exists in France and the United States, but with a different ratio for legal tender; but for the present the mints are closed both to gold and silver. The transition period has lasted for more than four years, but there is ground for hope that it is now drawing to a close. The changes which are involved in the arrangements proposed to Her Majesty's Government are the following. France and the United States are to open their mints to the free coinage of silver, continuing the free coinage of gold and the unlimited legal tender of coins of both metals, the ratio remaining unchanged in France and being altered to the French ratio of 15½ to 1 in the United States. India is to open her mints to silver, to keep them closed to gold, and to undertake not to make gold legal tender. France and the United States would thus be bimetallic; India would be monometallic (silver); while most of the other important countries of the world would be monometallic (gold). The object which the proposers have in view is the establishment of a stable relation between the

values of gold and of silver. This would include the establishment of a stable exchange between the rupee and sterling currency, which was the object of the Government of India in the proposals made in our financial despatch of the 21st June, 1892, which proposals ultimately resulted in the adoption, in view to the attainment of that object, of the policy of a gold standard, and in the closing of the mints to the free coinage of silver. If, then, it were certain that the suggested measures would result in the establishment of a stable ratio, the Government of India might well consider whether their adoption would not be preferable to the policy to which they committed themselves in 1893 in the hope of attaining the same result by isolated action on the part of India alone. The principal questions therefore for us to consider are whether the measures are more likely to succeed than the policy of 1893, and what consequences to India may be apprehended if the measures should fail of success after being brought into operation. . . . The first result of the suggested measures, if they even temporarily succeed in their object, would be an intense disturbance of Indian trade and industry by the sudden rise in the rate of exchange, which, if the ratio adopted were 15½ to 1, would be a rise from about 16d. to about 23d. the rupee. Such a rise is enough to kill our export trade, for the time at least. If the public were not convinced that the arrangement would have the effect intended, or believed that it would not be permanent, the paralysis of trade and industry would be prolonged and accompanied by acute individual suffering, none of the advantages expected would be attained, and the country would pass through a critical period which would retard its progress for years. How long the crisis would last before normal or stable conditions were restored it is not possible to conjecture. It would be long even if the mercantile and banking community saw that silver was being steadily maintained at the prescribed ratio, while any indication of unsteadiness would greatly prolong the period by giving foundation for doubt. If the doubt should happen to be justified by the results, the position would be disastrous alike to the State, to individuals, and to trade generally. . . . We cannot help seeing that if the policy of 1893 is now abandoned, and if the triple union now proposed as a substitute should fail in its operation or should terminate, and in its failure subject Indian trade to the violent shocks we have described, the Government of India could not, as a responsible Government, call upon the commercial public to face another prolonged period of doubt, suspense, agitation, and difficulties. For it must be clearly and fully recognized that if India joins in the proposed measures, we shall be left dependent, as the sole means of attaining stability in exchange, on the success of those measures, and that if they should fail, India must be content to remain permanently under the silver standard with all its admitted disadvantages. . . . We have given very careful consideration to the question whether France and the United States are likely, with the help of India, to be able to maintain the relative value of gold and silver permanently at the ratio they intend to adopt, and have come to the conclusion that while we admit a possibility of the arrangements proposed resulting in the permanent maintenance of the value of gold and silver at the ratio of 15½ to 1, the probability is that they will fail to secure that result, and that it is quite impossible to hold that there is anything approaching a practical certainty of their doing so. One reason for this conclusion is, that the arrangement would rest on too narrow a basis. A union consisting of two countries, with a third lending assistance, is a very different thing from the general international union of all or most of the important countries of the world, which was advocated by the Government of India in the despatches of March and June 1892 and of February and September 1886. To afford a hope that a monetary union will succeed in establishing stability in the relative value of gold and silver, it is essential that the nations adhering to it should be of such number and importance that the metallic currency of the whole body shall be of sufficient extent to allow of the exercise of adequate influence on the value of the two metals. We doubt whether any two, or even three, nations in the world, unless, indeed, one of them was Great Britain, could comply with this condition, and we have no hesitation in saying that France and the United States and India certainly could not. . . . We have no hesitation in recommending your Lordship to refuse to give the undertaking desired by the Governments of France and the United States. We are quite clearly of opinion that the interests of India demand that her mints shall not be opened as part of an arrangement to which two or three countries only are parties, and which does not include Great Britain." Immediately on receiving this reply, Lord Salisbury informed Ambassador Hay that "Her Majesty's Government feel it their duty to state that the first proposal of the United States Representatives is one which they are unable to accept," and expressing a wish to know "how far the views of the American and French Governments are modified by the decision now arrived at, and whether they desire to proceed further with the negotiations at the present moment."—*Great Britain, Parliamentary Publications (Papers by Command: Commercial, No. 8, 1897).*

In the view of the American envoys, it seemed useless to proceed, with no hope of coöperation from Great Britain, and they returned to America with a discouraging report.

A. D. **1897** (December).—Adoption of the gold standard in Russia.—An imperial ukase declared the adoption of the .gold standard in Russia, authorizing the issue of a new five-rouble gold piece.

A. D. **1900**.—Settlement of the monetary system in the United States. See (in this vol.) UNITED STATES OF AM.: A. D. 1900 (MARCH—DECEMBER).

A. D. **1900** (November).—Withdrawal of legal tender silver coins in Germany. See (in this vol.) GERMANY: A. D. 1900 (NOVEMBER).

MONGOLIA. See (in this vol.) MANCHURIA AND MONGOLIA.

MONOPOLIES. See (in this vol.) TRUSTS: UNITED STATES.

MONROE DOCTRINE, The: As emphasized in the Treaty of International Arbitration. See (in this vol.) PEACE CONFERENCE.

Its discussion as involved in the Venezuela Boundary Question. See (in this vol.) VENEZUELA: A. D. 1895 (JULY) and (NOVEMBER).

MONTAUK POINT, Removal of troops from Santiago de Cuba to. See (in this vol.) UNITED STATES OF AM.: A. D. 1898 (JULY—AUGUST: CUBA).

MONTENEGRO. See (in this vol.) BALKAN AND DANUBIAN STATES.

MOROS, The. See (in this vol.) PHILIPPINE ISLANDS: THE NATIVE INHABITANTS; and A. D. 1899 (MAY—AUGUST).

MORTMAIN, Proposed restrictions on, in France. See (in this vol.) FRANCE: A. D. 1901 (JANUARY).

MOSLEMS AND CHRISTIANS: Conflicts in Armenia. See (in this vol.) TURKEY: A. D. 1895.

Conflicts in Crete. See (in this vol.) TURKEY: A. D. 1897 (FEBRUARY—MARCH).

MOSQUITO, The, as a carrier of disease. See (in this vol.) SCIENCE, RECENT: MEDICAL AND SURGICAL.

MUKDEN. See (in this vol.) MANCHURIA AND MONGOLIA; also, RUSSIA IN ASIA: A. D. 1891–1900.

MUNICIPAL EVENTS, Notable. See (in this vol.) BOSTON, CHICAGO, NEW YORK, TOLEDO, LONDON.

MUNICIPAL GOVERNMENTS: Institution in Cuba. See (in this vol.) CUBA: A. D. 1900 (JUNE—NOVEMBER).

Institution in the Philippines. See (in this vol.) PHILIPPINE ISLANDS: A. D. 1900 (MARCH).

MUSIC: In the Nineteenth Century. See (in this vol.) NINETEENTH CENTURY: THE MUSICAL CENTURY.

N.

NABONIDOS, Discovery of an inscription of. See (in this vol.) ARCHÆOLOGICAL RESEARCH: BABYLONIA: DISCOVERY OF AN INSCRIPTION.

NANSEN'S EXPEDITION, Return of. See (in this vol.) POLAR EXPLORATION, 1896.

NASHVILLE EXPOSITION. See (in this vol.) TENNESSEE: A. D. 1897.

NATAL. See (in this vol.) SOUTH AFRICA.

NATIONAL DEMOCRATIC PARTY OF 1896. See (in this vol.) UNITED STATES OF AM.: A. D. 1896 (JUNE—NOVEMBER.)

NATIONAL PARTY, The. See (in this vol.) UNITED STATES OF AM.: A. D. 1896 (JUNE—NOVEMBER); and 1900 (MAY—NOVEMBER).

NATIONAL SILVER PARTY. See (in this vol.) UNITED STATES OF AM.: A. D. 1896 (JUNE—NOVEMBER).

NATIONAL STEEL COMPANY, The. See (in this vol.) TRUSTS: UNITED STATES.

NATIONALISTS, FRENCH, Revolutionary conspiracy of. See (in this vol.) FRANCE: A. D. 1899-1900 (AUGUST—JANUARY).

NAVAL POLICY, German. See (in this vol.) GERMANY: A. D. 1900 (FEBRUARY—JUNE).

NAVIES OF THE SEA POWERS: A. D. 1900.—The following tables are compiled from a return issued by the British Admiralty in the spring of 1900, showing the state of the fleets of Great Britain, France, Russia, Germany, Italy, the United States, and Japan, including vessels then built and in progress of construction.

Of battle-ships, there were built and building in the several navies:

Great Britain	70,	with a displacement of	821,605
France	35,	" "	339,599
Russia	24,	" "	262,912
Germany	25,	" "	191,259
Italy	19,	" "	193,004
United States	16,	" "	184,144
Japan	7,	" "	92,420

Of armored and protected cruisers, there were built and building:

Great Britain	147,	with a displacement of	827,430
France	60,	" "	297,486
Russia	23,	" "	144,673
Germany	22,	" "	107,844
Italy	25,	" "	93,673
United States	26,	" "	140,274
Japan	23,	" "	114,479

Of unprotected cruisers, armored coast-defence vessels, and special vessels there were built and building:

Great Britain	31,	with a displacement of	104,250
France	29,	" "	93,385
Russia	26,	" "	66,886
Germany	35,	" "	59,617
Italy	3,	" "	13,821
United States	30,	" "	77,150
Japan	13,	" "	24,065

Of torpedo vessels and torpedo-boat destroyers the number built and building was:

Great Britain	238,	with a displacement of	70,311
France	305,	" "	34,002
Russia	233,	" "	37,735
Germany	130,	" "	20,094
Italy	180,	" "	24,863
United States	50,	" "	12,121
Japan	71,	" "	9,537

A consolidation of the above figures shows a total of ships in the principal navies as follows: Great Britain, 486; France, 429; Russia, 306; Germany, 212; Italy, 227; United States, 122; Japan, 114.

A writer in the "Fortnightly Review," discussing the above returns, points out the imperfectness of the representation which such gross figures give of the actual naval strength of the several Powers, and he has undertaken to correct them by a calculation of what he calls the "fighting weight" of the ships, based on the age of each and its displacement in tons. He says: "The scale of depreciation for age that I have used is as follows: Ships, built and now building, that were launched, or which will be launched, during 1895-1899 (and later), are reckoned at their full value of fighting weight; i. e., at 100 per cent. Ships launched during 1890-1894 are reckoned as now worth only 80 per cent. of their fighting weight. The other depreciations being: Ships launched 1885-1889 are valued at 60 per cent. of their nominal fighting weight;

1880-1884, at 40 per cent.; before 1880, at 20 per cent."

By this mode of reckoning, the table of battle-ships is converted to the following exhibit of estimated "naval strength":

Great Britain	70,	adjusted fighting weight	604,141
France	35,	" "	220,635
Russia	24,	" "	221,988
Germany	25,	" "	152,929
Italy	19,	" "	112,899
United States	16,	" "	176,708
Japan	7,	" "	88,088

This method of depreciating the tonnage on the basis of the age of a ship causes the respective proportions of Great Britain, France and Italy, in battle-ships, to become smaller, while the respective proportions of Russia, Germany, United States and Japan become larger. The United States lose but 4 per cent. of the nominal value of their battle-ships; Japan, 5 per cent.; Russia, 16; Germany, 20; Great Britain, 26; France, 35; Italy, 42.

Applying the same arithmetic to the returns of armored and protected cruisers, the writer shows that Japan suffers a loss of 10 per cent. of their nominal fighting weight, France 14, United States 14, Italy 18, Great Britain 21, Russia 23, Germany 24.

Reducing in like manner all the remaining returns, he arrives at the following summary of "the seven navies arranged in the order of their strength"—taking the navy of Japan as the unit: Great Britain, Degree of strength, 6.38; France, 2.57; Russia, 1.88; United States, 1.65; Germany, 1.34; Italy, 1.03; Japan, 1.00. Stated in "tons of fighting weight," his comparison stands: Great Britain, 1,347,000; France, 543,000; Russia, 397,000; United States, 349,000; Germany, 282,000; Italy, 218,000; Japan, 211,000.

Turning next to the consideration of armaments, the writer has compiled the following table, which shows "for each class of gun separately, and for all classes of guns combined, the number of these guns that are possessed by the seven naval powers":

POWER.	Breech-Loading Guns.	Quick-Firing Guns.	Muzzle-Loading Guns.	Torpedo Tubes.	All classes of Guns.
Great Britain	912	7,454	340	1,534	10,240
France	471	3,653	–	928	5,052
Russia	393	2,589	–	625	3,607
Germany	258	1,995	–	611	2,864
Italy	140	1,791	4	573	2,508
United States	303	1,791	–	230	2,324
Japan	110	1,168	–	314	1,592
All the Powers combined	2,587	20,441	344	4,815	28,187

In this comparison the United States drops from the fourth rank to the sixth.

For a comparison of the naval expenditure of the Powers, see (in this vol.) WAR BUDGETS.

NEBUCHADREZZAR, Exploration of the ruins of the palace of. See (in this vol.) ARCHÆOLOGICAL RESEARCH: BABYLONIA; GERMAN EXPLORATION.

NEELY EXTRADITION CASE, The. See (in this vol.) CUBA: A. D. 1900-1901.

NEGRITOS. See (in this vol.) PHILIPPINE ISLANDS : THE NATIVE INHABITANTS.

NEGRO, Disfranchisement of the. See (in this vol.) MARYLAND, MISSISSIPPI, NORTH CAROLINA : A. D. 1900 ; SOUTH CAROLINA : A. D. 1896 ; LOUISIANA : A. D. 1898 ; and UNITED STATES OF AM. : A. D. 1901 (JANUARY).

NEGROS, The island of: American occupation. See (in this vol.) PHILIPPINE ISLANDS : A. D. 1899 (JANUARY—NOVEMBER).

Acceptance of American sovereignty.—Establishment of provisional government. See (in this vol.) PHILIPPINE ISLANDS: A. D. 1899 (MARCH—JULY).

NEMI, Lake: Sunken Roman vessels found in. See (in this vol.) ARCHÆOLOGICAL RESEARCH : ITALY.

NETHERLANDS, The Kingdom of the (Holland): A. D. **1894.—War in Lombok.** See (in this vol.) DUTCH EAST INDIES : A. D. 1894.

A. D. 1896.—Electoral Reform Act.—A notable extension of the franchise was accomplished by an Act passed this year by the States General, to have effect in the elections of 1897. It made voters of all Dutch citizens not under 25 years of age who present " certain outward and positive signs of capacity and well-being. The chief sign is the fact of payment of one or more direct State taxes (for the land tax an amount of 1 florin is sufficient). Besides these, the Reform Act admits as electors all those who can prove that they are householders, and have paid rent of houses or lodgings during a fixed term, or that they are owners or tenants of boats of not less than 24 tons capacity, or that they have been during a fixed term in employment with an annual wage or salary of at least £22 18s. 4d., or possess a certificate of State interest of at least 100 florins, or a State savings bank deposit of at least 50 florins, or the legal qualifications for any profession or employment."—*Statesman's Year-Book*, 1899, *p.* 807.

A. D. 1897.—First election under the **new Franchise Law.**—The first election in Holland under the new franchise law, held June 15-25, 1897, returned to the Chamber 47 Liberals, 22 Catholics, 22 Protestant anti-Revolutionists, 4 Radicals, and one deputy who is styled an Historic Christian.

A. D. 1898.—Enthronement of Queen Wilhelmina.—Queen Wilhelmina, who succeeded to the crown on the death of her father, William III., in 1890, reached the age of 18 on the 31st of August, 1898, and received the reins of government from her mother, Queen Emma, who had acted as Regent until that time. The young Queen was enthroned September 6 in the New Church at Amsterdam, where she delivered, with a simplicity and fervor which impressed those present, her address to the States-General and took her oath of allegiance to the Constitution. "I am happy and thankful," the Queen said, "to rule over the people of the Netherlands, who, although small in numbers, are great in virtue and strong by nature and character. I esteem it a great privilege that it is my life's task and duty to dedicate all my powers to the prosperity and interests of my dear fatherland ; and I adopt the words of my beloved father,—' Yes, Orange can never do enough for the Nether-

lands.' " After the Queen and the Queen-Mother, the most striking figures at the ceremony were the Princes from the Dutch Indies.

A. D. 1898 (June).—The Sugar Conference at Brussels. See (in this vol.) SUGAR BOUNTIES.

A. D. 1899 (April).—Invitation to the Peace Conference to be held at The Hague. See (in this vol.) PEACE CONFERENCE.

A. D. 1899 (May—July).—Representation in the Peace Conference at The Hague. See (in this vol.) PEACE CONFERENCE.

A. D. 1899 (May—August).—Advice to President Kruger of the South African Republic. See (in this vol.) SOUTH AFRICA (THE TRANSVAAL): A. D. 1899 (MAY—AUGUST).

A. D. 1901.—Marriage of Queen Wilhelmina.—Queen Wilhelmina was married, on the 7th of February, to Duke Henry of Mecklenburg-Schwerin, who received the title of Prince of the Netherlands by proclamation on the same day. Both civil and religious ceremonies of marriage were performed.

NEW BRUNSWICK. See (in this vol.) CANADA.

NEWEL, Stanford: American Commissioner to the Peace Conference at The Hague. See (in this vol.) PEACE CONFERENCE.

NEWFOUNDLAND: A. D. 1895.—Union with Canada refused.—Terms proposed for the union of Newfoundland with the Dominion of Canada were rejected, and negotiations abandoned.

A. D. 1897.—Conference of colonial premiers with the British Colonial Secretary. See (in this vol.) ENGLAND : A. D. 1897 (JUNE—JULY).

A. D. 1897-1900.—The Reid contract.—The question in politics.—In the fall of 1897 a line of narrow-gauge railway, with branches over six hundred miles in total length, was completed and opened to traffic. The main line of rail extends from the capital, St. Johns, to Port-aux-Basques, at the southwestern extremity of the island, and is expected to produce an important development of resources from the forests and mines, as well as from agricultural lands. The railway was constructed by a contractor, Mr. Reid, who agreed to operate it for seven years at his own expense, receiving therefor a land grant of 5000 acres per mile. In 1898 a new contract was made with Mr. Reid, which placed most of the resources of the island under his control. For an additional land-grant of 2500 acres per mile of road he undertook to operate the road for fifty years. By a present cash payment of $1,000,000 to the colony treasury, he purchased the reversion of its right to the possession of the road at the end of that period. At the same time he secured the right to purchase from the government its telegraph lines and the dry-dock at St. Johns, for half a million of dollars, and was given a monopoly for 30 years of the coast mail steam service, with an annual subsidy of $150,000, he undertaking to maintain in it eight steamers, well equipped. This remarkable contract was bitterly denounced by a large party in the island, and the Imperial government was strongly petitioned to nullify the whole transaction : but the British Colonial Secretary, Mr. Chamberlain, while he characterized the contract as representing " the most unparalled abrogation of its functions by a responsible government," decided that he could not properly interfere. The "Reid Deal," as it was known, then became a burning issue in Newfoundland politics, and the Ministry responsible for it, led by Sir James Winter, was ousted from the government in February, 1900. Mr. Reid was then arranging to transfer his Newfoundland contract and franchises to a company, which required the sanction of the colonial government. The new (Liberal) Ministry, of which Mr. Robert Bond was Premier, refused consent to the transfer unless Mr. Reid would amend his bargain with the colony in several very important particulars. He offered some concessions, but not to the extent demanded ; and so the question between him and the Bond Ministry went into the canvass of 1900, for the election of a new Assembly, and the Conservatives, heavily backed by Mr. Reid, were defeated overwhelmingly, winning but 4 seats out of 36 in the Lower House of the Legislature. On this result of the elections the "London Times" of Nov. 26, 1900, comments as follows: "The course which the victorious Bond Ministry will now take must be awaited with interest. . . . A policy of compromise would certainly appear to be the wisest and the safest for all parties. Mr. Reid, it seems to be acknowledged, has carried out his part of the bargain of 1898 fully and even generously, and the colony, it is stated, has profited largely in consequence. In the absence of actual fraud or corruption it would be difficult in these circumstances to justify the rescission or even the material modification of the agreement, on the faith of which he has spent his money, without his assent. A repeal of the Act of 1898 against him will would savour of repudiation. It would assuredly damage the credit of the colony very seriously."

A. D. 1899-1901.—The French Shore Question.—The Modus Vivendi.—"At the period of the negotiation of the Treaty of Utrecht, in 1713, by which the rights of the French fishermen were regulated [see, in vol. 4, NEWFOUNDLAND: A. D. 1713], thousands of French fishing vessels availed themselves of the inshore fisheries about the island; and that they might be not altogether without facilities for the drying and curing of their fish, they were granted under the Treaty the 'right to use a strip of the coast seven hundred miles long and half a mile wide.' Accompanying the Treaty, but, be it noted, not a part of it, was a declaration of King George, that British subjects on the island were not to interfere with these French coast rights by erecting permanent structures upon it, calculated to obstruct the operations of the French fishermen. This Royal declaration was harmless and unimportant when the population of the island was very small, and the French fishermen resorted to the inshore fisheries of Newfoundland. But to-day, a different condition exists. The French fishermen no longer use the inshore fisheries of the island, but prosecute, instead, their fishing operations on the Grand Banks, several hundred miles distant, drying their product either at the French islands of St. Pierre and Miquelon, which are more adjacent to the Banks, or transporting the fish direct to France. . . . The need for which the French shore right was granted has practically ceased to exist; and inasmuch as the prohibition to the people of the island from erecting permanent structures on the

island was merely a mandate emanating from the King, and not an integral part of the Treaty itself; and because the reason for the observance of the mandate has thus ceased to exist, it is imperative that, in the interests of the prosperity of the island, this Royal concession should be revoked. . . . But what, it may be asked, on a perusal of the whole case, has caused the Newfoundland question to suddenly become paramount ? Why is its urgency greater in 1899 than it was in 1889 ? Is there not some concentrated force, some propelling power, at work behind the scenes ? There is —and that power is a millionaire. The name of this millionaire is Robert Gillespie Reid, who, having voluntarily assumed, by means of the measure known as the Reid contract, the responsibility of developing the island's resources, finds himself, at the outset, confronted by a situation which precludes all present enterprise. This gentleman has acquired, in fee simple, some three or four million acres of land in Newfoundland; and where the islanders were content to wait patiently for justice, he, as a business-man, eager to exploit his mines and timber, can hardly be expected to pin his faith to assurances so frail, and of fulfilment so remote."—B. Wilson, *Newfoundland's Opportunity* (*Fortnightly Rev., Feb., 1899*).

A royal commission which lately investigated the situation of affairs on the Treaty Coast of Newfoundland found that the coast "is 800 miles in extent, with a permanent population of 13,300, all but 76 of whom are native-born, while the total of French frequenting the territory during the fishing season does not exceed 600 men. The French, last year, according to the official reports furnished to the Admiralty, ocenpied only eight cod and nine lobster stations, with a personnel as above, while their catch of cod was but 18,000 qtls., worth about 36,000 dollars, and their pack of lobsters about 7,000 cases, of about equal value. And is it not monstrous that, in order to satisfy vexatious French claims and perpetuate obsolete treaty claims, the people of the Treaty Coast should be coerced and victimised, and the development of the whole colony retarded, as has been the case ? The Commissioners found that, despite the liberal bounties given by France for fishing on the Treaty Coast, the allowance of 50 francs per head by the St. Pierre municipality for the same purpose, and the special appropriation the past two seasons in the French colonial grant 'for extending operations on the Newfoundland coast, 4,000 francs,' the number of men frequenting there and the number of stations operated are steadily declining every year, and in ten years' time it is doubtful if there would be a Frenchman on the coast. Still, so powerful is the French fetish that the shore is tabooed as far as industrial development is concerned, and the hinterland likewise. No grant of land can be given there except with the stipulation that it is subject to French rights. No permanent building can be erected within half a mile of high-water mark, because the French claim the strand for drying their fish. No wharves can be built by which to load minerals, because they will interfere with the French fishery. (Only last year they stopped the erection of one which was twenty-two miles from their nearest station, and Mr. Reid, the railway contractor, when he wanted to build a wharf at Bay St. George to land construction materials, had to seize the opportunity of the French war-ship in the Bay leaving to coal and renew stores, and put an army of men to work, who built it in seventeen days, so that it was completed when the Frenchmen returned.) No mineral develop-ments are permitted because they may hamper the French. Competition on near-by fishing grounds is prohibited for the same reason. Il-licit (?) lobster packers are hunted like malefac-tors for disregarding a 'modus vivendi' as un-just as it is ridiculous. Bait-selling is only pos-sible by permission of the French and on their terms. The railway was deflected 120 miles out of its proper course because of French objection to a terminus on the shore. In fact, fishing is only pursued with the greatest difficulty, while the land is closed to agricultural settlement and mining enterprise. And that, too, in the face of the fact that the French 'army of occupation' consists of about one vessel, one station, and about sixty fishermen on every 100 miles of coast, whose annual catch is worth about 10,000 dollars."—P. T. McGrath, *France in Newfoundland* (*Nineteenth Century, Jan.*, 1899).

In 1890, a temporary agreement ("modus vi-vendi") concerning the lobster packing and other questions, was arranged between the British and French governments, which has been extended from time to time, very much to the dissatisfac-tion of the Province. The last extension expired at the end of the year 1900, and the Newfound-landers showed a strong disposition to resist any renewal of it. A letter from St. Johns, in De-cember, 1900, stated the feeling of the colony as follows : "Last year the term of the 'modus vivendi' was allowed to run out, and a dead-lock, such as now seems inevitable, would doubt-less have been created; but when the end of December came the reverses in South Africa appealed to our patriotism as the oldest British colony, and the Legislature unanimously passed at one sitting a Bill renewing the arrangement for another year. The colony was unable to afford any more substantial aid at the time, as her naval reserve had not then been inaugurated, but this course on her part testified to her sym-pathy with the Imperial mother, and her readi-ness to relieve her from other difficulties. This year Newfoundland is taking the bit between her teeth, and the result must be a complication which, however unwelcome to the Imperial Cabi-net, cannot but have been regarded as inevitable sooner or later. If our case is as strong as we are led to believe that the Royal Commission represents it to be, there is certainly good ground for our insisting upon remedial measures. It must not be forgotten that the French now keep up less than 15 cod and lobster stations alto-gether on the treaty coast, and that about 550 men is the number they had there last season. As against this the resident population is nearly 14,000, and the objections which they urged against the 'modus vivendi' in its early days apply with equal strength now. These people are shamefully treated, the colony as a whole is humiliated, and the recognition of such condi-tions by England without making an attempt to get rid of them is a cause of reproach which she should remove without delay."

Much newspaper discussion of the subject has been going on in both England and France, with an apparent showing of readiness on the part of the latter country to bargain with the British for

cessions in West Africa or elsewhere. How much of a price Great Britain is willing to pay for release from the treaty of Utrecht is a question the answer to which cannot be forever post-poned.

Despite its reluctance, the Newfoundland Leg-islature was prevailed upon, in February, 1901, to pass an Act renewing the "modus vivendi" for another year. Several members who sup-ported the measure declared that they did so for the last time, and only because of an unwilling-ness to embarrass the British government during the continuance of the South African war.

A. D. 1901.—Change of Government.—Early in the year, Sir Henry McCallum was transferred from the governorship of Newfoundland to that of Natal, and Sir Cavendish Boyle was appointed to succeed him.

NEW JERSEY: A. D. 1897.—Constitu-tional Amendments.—On the 28th of September, several proposals of constitutional amendment were voted on in New Jersey. One prohibitory of gambling was adopted by a small majority. Another, that would give the suffrage in school elections to women, was rejected by about 10,000 majority.

NEW SOUTH WALES. See (in this vol.) AUSTRALIA ; and CONSTITUTION OF AUS-TRALIA.

NEW YORK CITY: A. D. 1894-1895.—The Lexow Investigation of Tammany gov-ernment.—Election of Mayor Strong.—" On the second Sunday in February 1892 the minister of a wealthy Presbyterian church, Dr. Charles Parkhurst, startled his congregation by preach-ing an outspoken political sermon, in which he attacked the Tammany administration in most unmeasured language. 'The mayor and those associated with him are polluted harpies [be de-clared]. Under the pretence of governing this city they are feeding day and night on its quiv-ering vitals. They are a lying, perjured, rum-soaked, and libidinous lot. . . . Every effort to make men respectable, honest, temperate, and sexually clean is a direct blow between the eyes of the mayor and his whole gang of lecherous subordinates, in the sense that while we fight iniquity they shield and patronise it ; while we try to convert criminals they manufacture them, and they have a hundred dollars invested in the manufacturing business to every one invested in converting machinery. . . . Police and criminals all stand in with each other. It is simply one solid gang of criminals, one half in office and the other half out.' This sermon was the starting point of the new anti-Tammany movement. Dr. Parkhurst was called before the grand jury to prove his words, but he was obliged to admit that all he knew was the repeated accusations that appeared in almost every local newspaper. Thereupon the grand jury publicly rebuked him, and sent a formal presentment to the Recorder declaring their 'disapproval and condemnation' of the sermon. Every one at once concluded that no more would be heard of Parkhurst in politics, but they did not know the man. The clergy-man called a couple of detectives to his aid, and personally visited the lowest resorts, to obtain the necessary evidences of corruption. A month later he preached a second political sermon, and this time he took into the pulpit with him a bundle of affidavits. He repeated and emphasised his former accusations, and again he was summoned before the grand jury. This time the result was different. ' The police are either incompetent or corrupt,' the jury declared, and citizens generally agreed. . . .

" In 1894, the State Senate . . . appointed a committee, this time under Senator Lexow, to inquire into New York municipal affairs. Soon after the committee was appointed Mr. Croker found it convenient to hastily resign the leadership of Tammany and go to Europe. The worst accusations of the bitterest enemies of Crokerism were almost all more than substantiated by the evidence given before the committee. It was found that the police were utterly corrupt, that they extorted blackmail from gambling house keepers, women of ill fame, saloon keepers, and others, and in return gave them their protection. Even thieves, in some instances, were found to be regularly paying their police dues in return for immunity from arrest. One police justice had to admit that he received a hundred dollars from a keeper of a disorderly house. Everywhere that the Lexow Committee probed, or that other competent critics examined, the same thing was found. For several years New York had been living under a system of universal blackmail. Saloon keepers had to pay Tammany to be allowed to evade the Sunday closing law, merchants to be granted the simplest conveniences for getting their goods into their premises. But in the case of Mr. Croker no dishonesty could be proved. It was known that he had in a few years risen from a poor man to a millionaire, but in no instance could it be shown that he had acquired this wealth by corruption. His friends said he had made his money by horse-racing and real estate speculation, but unfortunately Mr. Croker did not go before the witness stand to finally clear up the matter. While the committee was sitting he remained in Europe.

"The usual storm of indignation followed the ' Lexow' exposure, and most reputable citizens united once more to overthrow Tammany. Colonel Strong, a well-known banker, was chosen reform candidate for mayor, and secured a majority of fifty thousand. In 1895 he began his administration, and initiated a vigorous reform movement. The police force was entirely reorganised; municipal offices were given for merit rather than political reward; the streets, for the first time in the memory of the oldest inhabitant, were really kept clean, and the whole local government was taken out of politics. Mayor Strong's time of office has not been without its faults, but among those faults dishonesty has not been one. Rather the mistake has been to enforce all laws too rigidly, and make too few allowances for the weaknesses of human nature in a cosmopolitan resort. Police President Roosevelt's strict enforcement of the Sunday closing and social purity laws was only his duty, but yet it cost the reformers many votes. Although the report of the ' Lexow ' Committee did Tammany much temporary harm, it recovered quickly. After the mayoral defeat of 1894 it pulled its forces together again, and rallied around it all the ambitious men who were disappointed in Mayor Strong's bestowal of his patronage. In the autumn of 1895 it was able to score a minor victory at the polls, and it carefully nursed its strength for the election of November 1897. Mr. Croker,

notwithstanding his repeated declarations that he was ' out of politics,' came back to New York, and at once took over command of his party."
—F. A. McKenzie, *Tammany (Nineteenth Century, Dec.*, 1897).

A. D. 1895.—Consolidation of the Astor, Lenox and Tilden foundations to form the New York Public Library. See (in this vol.) LIBRARY, NEW YORK PUBLIC.

A. D. 1896-1897.—Consolidation of New York, Brooklyn, and neighboring towns, in the Greater New York.—"The project of uniting the cities of New York, Brooklyn, and the cities, towns and villages contiguous to the same, into one great municipality, although long mooted before 1890, first took definite form in that year, by the passage on May 8th, by the Legislature, of Laws 1890, Chap. 11, entitled ' An Act to create a commission to inquire into the expediency of consolidating the various municipalities in the State of New York, occupying the several islands in the harbor of New York.' . . . Pursuant to the provisions of this act, a commission consisting of the following members was appointed, viz.: Andrew H. Green, Frederick W. Devoe, John L. Hamilton, J. Seaver Page of New York; J. S. T. Stranahan, Edward F. Linton, William D. Veeder of Brooklyn; John H. Brinkerhoff of Queen's county; George G. Greenfield of Richmond county; Charles P. McClelland of Westchester county; and Campbell W. Adams, State Engineer and Surveyor, ex officio, and Albert E. Henschel acting as secretary. In 1893, the commission presented to the Legislature a bill providing for the submission of the question of consolidation to a vote of the residents of the various municipalities proposed to be united into one city. The following year the Legislature provided for the referendum suggested by the commission. . . . The following vote was cast upon the question of consolidation in the ensuing election on November 6, 1894 : New York, for consolidation, 96,938 ; against, 59,959 ; Kings, for, 64,744 ; against, 64,467 ; Queens, for, 7,712 ; against, 4,741 ; Richmond, for, 5,531 ; against, 1,505 ; Mount Vernon, for, 873 ; against, 1,603 ; Eastchester, for, 374 ; against, 260 ; Westchester, for, 620 ; against, 621 ; Pelham, for, 261 ; against, 153. At the opening of the Legislature in 1895, the Commission of Municipal Consolidation Inquiry presented a report with a proposed bill declaring the entire district before mentioned (with the exception of the city of Mount Vernon) consolidated with the city of New York. The bill, however, failed of passage because of the addition of an amendment of refercudum in the last hours of the session of 1895, too late for further action. The Legislature, as a result no doubt of this vote on consolidation, did annex to New York city the towns of Westchester, Eastchester, Pelham and other parts of Westchester county.

"Early in January, 1896, the Legislature appointed a joint sub-committee of the Cities Committees of both Houses to inquire into the subject of the proposed consolidation and report March 1, 1896. The committee made a report and submitted a bill favoring consolidation. The bill as reported was passed by the Legislature and was submitted to the Mayors of the cities of New York and Brooklyn, and to the Mayor and Common Council of Long Island City pursuant to the provisions of the Constitution. The bill was returned to the Legislature without the acceptance of the cities of New York and Brooklyn. The Legislature repassed the bill over the vetoes of the Mayors of New York and Brooklyn, and it became a law May 11, 1896, with the approval of the Governor. This act (L. 1896, ch. 488) is entitled, 'An Act consolidating the local governments of the territory within the city and county of New York, the counties of Kings and Richmond and Long Island City and the towns of Newtown, Flushing and Jamaica and part of the town of Hempstead, in the county of Queens, and providing for the preparation of bills for enactment into laws for the government thereof.' . . . Pursuant to the act of consolidation, the Governor (Levi P. Morton) appointed on June 9, 1896, the following members of the commission to draft the proposed charter viz.: Seth Low, Benjamin F. Tracy, John F. Dillon, Ashbel P. Fitch, Stewart L. Woodford, Silas B. Dutcher, Wm. C. De Witt, George M. Pinney, Jr, Harrison S. Moore. Mr. Fitch having resigned from the commission, the Governor appointed Thomas F. Gilroy in his place. By virtue of the act, the following gentlemen were members of the commission: Andrew H. Green, president of the commission appointed by L. 1890, ch. 311; Campbell W. Adams, State Engineer; Theodore E. Hancock, Attorney-General; William L. Strong, Mayor of New York; Frederick W. Wurster, Mayor of Brooklyn; and Patrick Jerome Gleason, Mayor of Long Island City. The commission organized on June 25, 1896, appointed Benjamin F. Tracy as president and George M. Pinney, Jr., as secretary, and named William C. De Witt, John F. Dillon, Thomas F. Gilroy, Seth Low, Andrew H. Green, Benjamin F. Tracy, and George M. Pinney, Jr., as a committee on draft of proposed charter."—M. Ash, *The Greater New York Charter, introd.*

The committee submitted a draft charter to the commission on the 24th of December, with a report in which a fundamental feature of its plan is thus set forth: "It is clear that the work of administering all of the Departments over so large a space of territory, situated on three islands and partly on the main land, must be subdivided in order to be successfully done. The draft, therefore, proposes to divide the city into the five Boroughs which nature and history have already formed; that is to say: (1.) Manhattan, which consists of the island of Manhattan and the outlying islands naturally related to it. (2.) The Bronx; that is to say, all that part of the present City of New York lying north of the Harlem, a territory which comprises two-thirds of the area of the present City of New York. (3.) Brooklyn. (4.) Queens, consisting of that portion of Queens County to be incorporated into the Greater New York. (5.) Richmond, that is, Staten Island. Power is given to the Municipal Assembly to subdivide these Boroughs still further, in case of need. The Greater New York will start with these five Boroughs for administrative purposes. Your Committee have reconstructed the Borough system, as submitted in the tentative draft, upon lines which we are of one accord in believing to be a better and more appropriate development of the plan for the Greater New York. These lines give to each Borough various boards through which the prosecution of local improvements may be facilitated within the limits of small districts, but reserve to the Municipal Assembly the

right to incur indebtedness and to authorize the making of contracts."

The draft thus prepared was subjected to criticism in the commission and in public hearings, and, after amendment and revision, was reported to the Legislature in February, 1897, as the charter recommended by the Commission for the consolidated city called "The Greater New York." It received some amendment and was passed. On submission, as required by the State constitution, to the mayors of New York and Brooklyn and the mayor and Common Council of Long Island City, ' was approved in Brooklyn and Long Island City, but returned without approval by the mayor of New York. The Legislature then re-enacted the bill, and it was made law, by the governor's signature, on the 4th of May, 1897.

A. D. 1897 (September—November).—Election of the first Mayor of Greater New York. —The first municipal election in Greater New York excited a passion of interest that was natural in the city itself, but extraordinary in the degree and the extent to which it spread, not only throughout the United States, but widely in the foreign world. The election was looked upon as the test of a vastly important experiment in the democratic government of an enormous city. The charter of the great consolidated municipality had lodged tremendous, unprecedented power and responsibility in the office of its mayor. The people were given an opportunity to determine by a single act of suffrage— by their choice of a single man—the character of their government. Would they choose that man, at the beginning of the new system, in the interest of the corrupting organization in party politics which had misruled the old city of New York for years, or would they rise to the grand opportunity afforded them, and set a strong, free, independently honest man at the head of their local government. Democracy in municipal affairs, at least, had never been put on trial so sharply before. To a great number of the citizens of New York the duty of the hour was plain, and they promptly set their hands to it. Many months before the election they began the organization of a Citizens' Union, in which men of all political parties, sinking every other difference, should join for the defeat of Tammany and "Boss" Croker, and for the election to the mayor's office of the best mayor to be found. With remarkable unanimity, their thought of the man turned to Seth Low, President of Columbia University, but one time mayor of Brooklyn, where his vigor, his firmness and his independence had been conspicuously proved. An extensive canvass of the city showed so widely spread a feeling in favor of Mr. Low that he was named at the beginning of September as the candidate of the non-partisan Citizens' Union.

It was hoped that the whole opposition to Tammany Hall could be united in support of Mr. Low, representing as he did no partisan hostility to any organization in national or state politics. It was especially hoped and believed that the Republican party organization would endorse the choice of the Citizens' Union and make Mr. Low (himself a strong Republican) its own candidate. By nothing less than a general combination could the compact forces of Tammany Hall be overcome, and that fact was well understood. It was a fact so plain, indeed, that when the head of the Republican organization in New York persisted in setting a party candidate in the field, to divide the opposing voters of the city, there seemed to be small doubt of the intention with which it was done. The master politicians of the party were evidently more willing that the vast powers of the mayoralty, in the organization of the government of Greater New York, should be wielded by their prototypes of Tammany than that they should be given to independent hands. The party was obedient to them, and General Benjamin F. Tracy was put forward, by a Republican convention held September 28, in opposition to Mr. Low. The night previous, another candidate had appeared, in the person of Mr. Henry George, author of the economic doctrine of the "single tax," supported ardently by a large following, especially in the Democratic party. A section of that party, organized under the name of the United Democracy, had nominated Mr. George, and his nomination was endorsed a week later by a great assembly which claimed to represent the Jeffersonian Democracy of New York. On the 30th of September the nomination of the Tammany Democracy was given to Judge Robert A. Van Wyck. Between these four principal candidates, the result of the election was only put in doubt by some question as to the strength of the Democratic vote which Mr. George would draw away from Judge Van Wyck. It was a question extinguished sadly, three days before the election, by the sudden death of Mr. George. He had not been in good health, and the strain of the exciting canvass broke him down. His followers made a hasty nomination of his son, Henry George, Jr., in his place; but the personal prestige which might have carried a large vote with them was lost. Of the triumph of Tammany there was no longer any doubt, and no surprise was felt (though abundant grief and anger found expression) when the returns of the voting on November 2d were announced. Judge Van Wyck was elected by the ballots of 233,997 citizens, against 151,540 cast for Mr. Low, 102,-873 for General Tracy, 21,693 for the younger Mr. George. Tammany would have been beaten if the Republican vote had gone to Mr. Low. Besides the four principal candidates here named, there were four other nominees who received small numbers of votes. Lucien Sanial, put forward by the Social Democrats, received 14,467; William T. Wardwell, named by the Prohibitionists, received 1,359; Patrick J. Gleason and Alfred B. Cruikshank, running with little more than some personal support, received a few hundreds of votes each.

A. D. 1899 (April—December).—The Mazet Investigation.—An investigation of charges against the city government, by a committee of the Legislature, Mr. Robert Mazet, chairman, was opened in April, 1899, the examination of witnesses being conducted by Mr. Frank Moss. The investigation followed lines much the same as those pursued by the Lexow committee, in 1894, and revealed much the same foul state of things, especially in the department of police. But there was evidently less earnestness in the committee; the probing of iniquities was far less thorough, and the whole proceeding was stopped with suspicious suddenness as soon as it drew near to prominent members of the party by which it was controlled. It called fresh atten-

tion to the rottenness in municipal politics, and it led to the creation of a new commission for the revision of the Greater New York charter; but otherwise it was most unsatisfactory.

A. D. 1899-1900.—The Ramapo Water Contract.—In August, 1899, Bird S. Coler, Controller of the City, exposed a gigantic scheme of plunder involved in a contract with the Ramapo Water Company, which Tammany officials, assisted, it was said, by some interested Republicans, were attempting to crowd through the Board of Public Improvements. The contract would have bound the city for forty years to pay to the Ramapo Company $70 per million gallons for 200,000,000 gallons of water daily. In his Message to the State Legislature, January 2, 1901, Governor Odell thus referred to the matter: "Under chapter 985 of the laws of 1895, as amended, the Ramapo Water Company was given the power of condemnation for the purpose of securing to it the water and lands necessary for its purposes. During the year 1899 an attempt was made to enter into a contract with this company by the municipal board empowered to make such contracts. This proposition, when presented to the citizens of New York, was severely criticised by them, and the question of continued municipal ownership of their water supply was thus brought to their attention. The Legislature of 1900 enacted a law which made the consummation of such a contract impossible without the unanimous consent of those empowered to make such contract. The ownership of water rights sufficient to provide the city of New York with an ample supply of pure and wholesome water should be entirely under the control and direction of the municipality." Action on the subject was taken by the Legislature, which, in March, repealed the Act of 1895, thus stripping the Ramapo Company of its extraordinary powers.

A. D. 1900 (January—September).— The Rapid Transit Tunnel Contract.—Projected Tunnel to Brooklyn.—"The great project of underground rapid transit is now an assured thing. A few months ago the prospect seemed very dark. It is true that the rapid transit commissioners, a very able and upright body of men, with the invaluable aid of a distinguished engineer, Mr. Parsons, had a good while ago decided on the route and the plans; but the way seemed blocked by a series of semi-political and semi-legal difficulties. . . . Suddenly these difficulties began to disappear. . . . The financial plan adopted was that the city should provide the money which a contractor would expend in building the road, the contractor following the plans furnished by the city, submitting to municipal inspection, and agreeing upon his part to pay the interest on the bonds sold by the city to obtain the money, and also to pay enough into a sinking fund to provide for the ultimate redemption of the bonds. Bids were called for on November 15, to be opened on January 15. . . . It turned out that two well-known contractors were the only bidders, and the award was given to Mr. John B. McDonald. His bid was $35,000,-000. The theory of this contract is that the road is to be the property of the city, leased for fifty years to the contractor, who is to pay a rental that will be large enough so that the taxpayers will not have expended a penny. . . . The main trunk line will start at the post-office (City Hall

Square) on the south and proceed northward along the spine of Manhattan Island, following the general direction of Broadway to Kingsbridge, a distance from the point of beginning of twelve or thirteen miles. Near the upper end of Central Park, at a distance of six or seven miles from the point of beginning, a branch of the tunnel road will take a northeasterly direction, terminating at Bronx Park, which is about the same distance north as Kingsbridge, but several miles further east. The road will have four tracks for six miles of main line, two of which will be used for local trains and two for express trains."—*Am. Rev. of Reviews, Feb.*, 1900.

Work on the great undertaking was begun promptly, and had made great progress within the first twelve months.

In September, 1900, preliminary steps were taken toward the construction of a connecting tunnel, under the East River, to Brooklyn, and through the congested districts of the latter borough. "At least three years will be necessary for the preliminary work and actual construction before trains are running. . . . Tentative estimates have been made, and these are said to be from $8,000,000 to $10,000,000. . . . The route as contemplated . . . starts in connection with the Manhattan proposed tunnel at a point at or near the intersection of Broadway and Park Row; thence under Broadway and Bowling Green to Whitehall Street; under Whitehall Street to South Street; thence under South Street to the East River, and under the river, striking the Brooklyn shore at a point in Joralemon Street between the East River and Furman Street, under Joralemon Street to Fulton Street, to the Borough Hall, out Fulton Street to Flatbush Avenue, and under this thoroughfare to the railroad station. On the New York side the route includes a loop to be built whose debouching point shall lie between Bowling Green and Exchange Place in Broadway, running under Broadway to Bowling Green, and thence under Bowling Green to State Street, to and under Battery Park to Whitehall Street, thence returning under Whitehall Street and Battery Park to State Street and to Broadway. The construction calls for two tracks, and avoids all grade crossings, each track to have a separate tubular tunnel."—*N. Y. Times, Sept.* 28, 1900.—On the 25th of January, 1901, announcement was published that the Board of Rapid Transit Commissioners had adopted a resolution definitely providing for the extension of the Rapid Transit Railroad to Brooklyn. The original plan of route in Brooklyn had been chosen. The only change made was in Manhattan. The trains would be run through State St. instead of Whitehall, as formerly planned, with a loop at the Battery for Manhattan trains.

A. D. 1900 (April—May).—Ecumenical Conference on Missions. See (in this vol.) MISSIONS.

A. D. 1900 (June).—Great fire at the Hoboken piers. See (in this vol.) HOBOKEN.

A. D. 1900-1901.—Revision of the charter. —Carefully as the Greater New York charter had been drawn, it proved unsatisfactory in the working, in various respects, and a commission to revise it was appointed in 1900. The report of the commission was submitted to the Governor on the 1st of December, and transmitted, with his approval, to the Legislature in the following month. In the hands of the Legislature,

the bill embodying the revised charter underwent considerable amendment, very much, it would seem, to its detriment. It was passed by the Senate on the 3d of April and by the Assembly on the 4th, and went to the Mayor of New York for the submission to his judgment which the State Constitution of New York requires.

Some of the more important changes in the charter made by the revision, as passed, are the shortening of the mayor's term of office from four years (which the revision commission had advised retaining) to two years, with eligibility for re-election (which the commission had advised against); an increase of the administrative powers of the presidents of boroughs; abolition of the municipal Council and creation of a Board of Aldermen of 73 members; reorganization of various departments of the municipal administration.

A. D. 1901 (March).—Offered gift of $5,200,-000 to the Public Library by Andrew Carnegie. See (in this vol.) LIBRARY, NEW YORK PUBLIC.

NEW YORK STATE: A. D. 1894.—The revised Constitution. See (in this vol.) CONSTITUTION OF NEW YORK.

A. D. 1896-1897.—Passage of the Raines Liquor Law.—An Act for the regulation of the liquor traffic, which was and is the subject of much controversy, was passed in March, 1896, by the Legislature of the State of New York. From its author, Senator John Raines, it has borne the name of the Raines Law. It heavily increased the tax on the selling of liquor, raising it to $800 on common "saloons" in the city of New York; to $650 in Brooklyn; to $500 in other cities having more than 50,000 and not more than 500,000 inhabitants; and to rates in lesser cities and towns which ranged from $100 to $350. It forbade the licensing of any liquor shop within 200 feet of a schoolhouse or a church, and also forbade the opening of any new shop of that character in a residence district without consent of two-thirds of the property owners. It prohibited the sale of liquor on Sundays, except in hotels and clubs; but this provision furnished a means of evasion which was speedily brought into use. "Raines hotels" and "Raines Clubs," as they were called, sprang into existence everywhere, sufficiently answering the requirements of the law to escape its penalties. These and other defects were considerably remedied by amendments of the Act in April, 1897. It survived a powerful attack in the Legislature at that time, the whole strength of the leading cities in the State being brought against the law. The country districts were generally united in supporting it, partly on principle, and partly because of the extent to which it lightened the burdens of taxation. By apportioning two-thirds of the enormous revenue raised under the Act to the towns, counties and cities in which it is collected, and one-third to the state treasury, the Raines Law fortified itself strongly in more than the moral sentiment of the people. Under the Raines Law all local excise boards are abolished, and the whole licensing and regulating of the liquor traffic is placed under the supervision of a State commissioner.

A. D. 1897.—The Black Civil Service Law. See (in this vol.) CIVIL SERVICE REFORM: A. D. 1897-1899.

A. D. **1898.**—Primary Election **Law.**—An Act which aims to make the political party caucus for nominating candidates, and for choosing delegates to nominating conventions, a "primary election," conducted under strict regulations of law and guarded by registration, was passed by the New York State Legislature and signed by the Governor March 23, 1898.

A. D. **1899.**—**New** Civil Service Enactment. See (in this vol.) CIVIL SERVICE REFORM: A. D. 1897-1899.

A. D. **1899 (May).**—Taxation of public franchises.—A measure of great importance, introducing a new and eminently just principle in taxation, was carried through the Legislature of New York in May, by the energetic influence of Governor Roosevelt. Recommended by the Governor in a special message on the 27th of March and passed in an unsatisfactory form, a bill to provide for the taxing of public franchises which did not promise successful working was being left on his hands when the Legislature adjourned. He promptly called a special session and renewed to it his urgent recommendations. "I recommend," he said, "the enactment of a law which shall tax all these franchises as realty, which shall provide for the assessment of the tax by the Board of State Tax Commissioners, and which shall further provide that from the tax thus levied for the benefit of each locality, there shall be deducted the tax as now paid by the corporation in question. Furthermore, as the time for assessing the largest and wealthiest corporations, those of New York and Buffalo, has passed for this year, and as it will be preferable not to have the small country corporations taxed before the larger corporations of the city are taxed, I suggest that the operations of the law be deferred until October 1, of this year."

Within a few days, the desired bill was passed by both Houses of the Legislature, signed by the Governor and became a law. The public franchises to which it relates are defined in its first section, as follows:

"The terms 'land,' 'real estate,' and 'real property,' as used in this chapter, include the land itself above and under water, all buildings and other articles and structures, substructures, and superstructures, erected upon, under or

above, or affixed to the same; all wharves and piers, including the value of the right to collect wharfage, cranage, or dockage thereon; all bridges, all telegraph lines, wires, poles, and appurtenances; all supports and inclosures for electrical conductors and other appurtenances upon, above, and underground; all surface, underground, or elevated railroads, including the value of all franchises, rights, or permission to construct, maintain, or operate the same in, under, above, on, or through streets, highways, or public places; all railroad structures, substructures, and superstructures, tracks, and the iron thereon, branches, switches, and other fixtures permitted or authorized to be made, laid, or placed on, upon, above, or under any public or private road, street, or grounds; all mains, pipes, and tanks laid or placed in, upon, above, or under any public or private street or place for conducting steam, heat, water, oil, electricity, or any property, substance or product capable of transportation or conveyance therein, or that is protected thereby, including the value of all franchises, rights, authority, or permission to construct, maintain, or operate in, under, above, upon, or through any streets, highways, or public places, any mains, pipes, tanks, conduits, or wires, with their appurtenances, for conducting water, steam, heat, light, power, gas, oil, or other substance, or electricity for telegraphic, telephonic, or other purposes; all trees and underwood growing upon land, and all mines, minerals, quarries, and fossils in and under the same, except mines belonging to the state. A franchise, right, authority, or permission, specified in this subdivision, shall, for the purpose of taxation, be known as a special franchise. A special franchise shall be deemed to include the value of the tangible property of a person, copartnership, association, or corporation, situated in, upon, under, or above any street, highway, public place, or public waters in connection with the special franchise. The tangible property so included shall be taxed as a part of the special franchise."

NEW YORK UNIVERSITY: The Hall of Fame for Great Americans. See (in this vol.) HALL OF FAME.

NEW ZEALAND.

A. D. **1891-1900.**—Democratic experiments. —Labor laws and the land system.—Compulsory industrial arbitration and its working.— "I have been a studious observer of every phase of social life and legislative change that has taken place in this colony during the past seven years," wrote U. S. Consul Connolly, at Auckland, in July, 1896. "I arrived at the very beginning of the experimental era—and it is no misnomer to call much of the legislation of the past few years experimental in the truest sense [see, also (in this vol.), AUSTRALIA : RECENT EXTENSIONS OF DEMOCRACY]. But while it is so, there is a most gratifying feature which compensates for the violence done to the feelings of those whose motto has been ' let us permit matters to remain as they are, they suit us well enough.' That the legislative innovations of the immediate past have shocked the sensibilities of a large number

of prominent and well-to-do colonists is unquestionably true, but, at the same time, as against any inconvenience they may have experienced on this account, there is the fact of increased prosperity in nearly every branch of trade and industrial life throughout the country, farm products are fetching satisfactory prices, manufacturing industries are running full time and paying good wages and fair interest on the capital invested, labor is remuneratively employed, interest on money has fallen from 6 and 7 per cent to 4 and 5 per cent (this of itself, is sufficient to prove that money is abundant). Millions of English capital are flowing in for the development of the gold fields of the colony, and the credit of the country at no period of its history stood so high on the English market as it does to-day. I may also mention that, through the genuine encouragement given by the Government to the small-farmer class, the waste lands of the country are being rapidly taken up wherever land is found suitable for farming or grazing purposes. Notwithstanding the admitted prosperity of the colony and the fact that the Government have had a substantial surplus over expenditure now for a number of years, the national debt continues to increase. But the increased indebtedness is not of the usual character, for the reason that the country has security for nearly all the money borrowed in recent years. Money had to be borrowed under Government guaranty to save the Bank of New Zealand from closing its doors. This was done to avert financial disaster. . . .

"Money has been borrowed to purchase large estates for the purposes of settlement. Those who take up land under this system, as already stated, pay an annual rental sufficient to cover the interest on the purchase money and the cost of administration. The land is always vested in the Government and this must be regarded as a good asset. One million and a half sterling was borrowed last year in England at 3 per cent per annum. This £1,500,000 loan is called the 'advances to settlers loan.' This money is lent out to farmers at 4 per cent per annum. . . . I need scarcely add that the large landholders, the mortgage companies, and the money lenders generally did not favor this kind of legislation, particularly the cheap advances to settlers, but their opposition was utterly futile. With the advent of the one-man-one-vote and the extension of the franchise to women, the power of corporate wealth in this country appears to have been irrevocably destroyed. Whether this be for good or evil, I am not, of course, in a position to say. I can say, however, that no ill effects of the change are apparent up to the present; on the contrary, the country is more prosperous and at least as honestly and as economically administered as it was under the old régime.

"To say that this country is, in my opinion, more truly democratic than any country in the world would be merely stating a simple truth; and to say that the present Government is a workingman's Government is equally true. A great deal of the legislation of recent years, however, is in advance of the requirements and ideas of the people, with the result that some of it has proved to be annoying and irksome to many. This is especially true of some of the labor laws. The Government are honestly endeavoring to place the masses in possession of their legitimate rights with as little friction as possible, and at the same time with due regard to vested interests and the propriety of things generally. But while struggling thus with the duties and responsibilities of their official positions, the members of the Ministry are torn asunder by the clamorous and impracticable demands of the unreasonable and irresponsible. The sympathies of the Government are unmistakably with the people, but the honor, the dignity, and the welfare of the country will not permit them to depart from a course too inconsistent with the sense of obligation, fair dealing, integrity, and responsibility which are the admitted characteristics and duty of all civilized governments. The great danger at the present moment is too much legislation in one direction. This is the one thing wherein the Government find it really hard to resist the demands of organized labor. There is, however,

a very gratifying disposition manifesting itself among the more reasonable members of the labor societies to let well enough alone for the present —a disposition it is much to be hoped may extend throughout the whole body of the workers. If not, I have no hesitation in predicting a serious revulsion of public sentiment and sympathy within the next few years."—*U. S. Consular Reports, January,* 1897, *p.* 35.

"Australian experience seems in many ways to prove the value of our system of written constitutions. to be construed and enforced by the courts. The effect on the minds of ill-informed legislators of the knowledge that they can do anything for which they can get a majority, is naturally to beget extravagance and an overweening sense of power, and lead to excessive experimentation. . . . It is in devices for the protection of labor that most of this experimentation occurs. New Zealand affords the best example of it. It provides elaborate legal protection for the eight-hour day. A workman cannot consent to work overtime without extra pay. The state sees that he gets the extra pay. It looks closely after the condition of women and children in the factories. It sees that servant girls are not overcharged by the registry offices for getting them places. It prescribes one half-holiday a week for all persons employed in stores and offices, and sees that they take it. It will not allow even a shopkeeper who has no employees to dispense with his half-holiday; because if he does not take it, his competition will injure those who do. The 'labor department' of the government has an army of inspectors, who keep a close watch on stores and factories, and prosecute violations of the law which they themselves discover. They do not wait for complaints; they ferret out infractions, so that the laborer may not have to prejudice himself by making charges. The department publishes a 'journal' once a month, which gives detailed reports of the condition of the labor market in all parts of the colony, and of the prosecutions which have taken place anywhere of employers who have violated the law. It provides insurance for old age and early death, and guarantees every policy. It gives larger policies for lower premiums than any of the private offices, and depreciates the private offices in its documents. It distributes the profits of its business as bonuses among the policy-holders, and keeps a separate account for teetotalers, so that they may get special advantages from their abstinence. The 'journal' is, in fact, in a certain sense a labor manual, in which everything pertaining to the comfort of labor is freely discussed. The poor accommodation provided for servants in hotels and restaurants is deplored, and so is the difficulty which middle-aged men have in finding employment. More attention to the morals and manners of nursemaids is recommended. All the little dodges of employers are exposed and punished. If they keep the factory door fastened, they are fined. If housekeepers pretend that their servants are lodgers, and therefore not liable to a compulsory half-holiday, they are fined. If manufacturers are caught allowing g   to take their meals in a workshop, they are fined.

"As far as I can make out, too, without visiting the country, there is as yet no sign of reaction against this minute paternal care of the laborer. The tendency to use the powers of the government chiefly for the promotion of the comfort of the working classes, whether in the matter of land settlement, education, or employment, seems to undergo no diminution. The only thing which has ceased, or slackened, is the borrowing of money for improvements. The results of this borrowing have been so disastrous that the present generation, at least, will hardly try that experiment again."—E. L. Godkin, *The Australian Democracy* (*Atlantic Monthly, March*, 1898).

Labor Laws.—Compulsory industrial arbitration.—"There is not in any other country in the world a more valuable or more enlightened body of Labour laws than those now upon the statute book of this progressive colony. They cover almost every risk to life, limb, health, and interest of the industrial classes. They send the law, as it were, everywhere a worker is employed for daily wages to fling the shield of the state over him or her in the labour of livelihood. The bare enumeration of these laws will indicate the far-reaching ground they cover:—The Coal Mines Act, the Master and Apprentices Act, the Conspiracy Law Amendment Act, the Trade Union Act, the Servant's Registry Offices Act (for the protection of servant girls against the risks of dishonest offices of that kind), Contractors and Workmen's Lien Act, three amended Employer's Liability Acts, three amended Shipping and Seamen's Acts, two Shops and Shop-assistants Acts, the Factories Act, and the Industrial Conciliation and Arbitration Act of 1894. . . . The Industrial Conciliation and Arbitration Act, passed in 1894 . . . has attracted much attention outside New Zealand. An Act with a similar purpose, but permissive in its operations, was passed . . . in the New South Wales Legislature in 1892. It was limited in duration to four years, and was not a success. The New Zealand bill was more skilfully drawn, and, possessing the element of a gentle compulsion, has so far achieved its aim. The Act begins by inviting all parties to join 'in lawful association for the purpose of protecting or furthering the interests of employers or workmen in, or in connection with, any industry in the colony.' Such parties as accept the legal invitation are allowed to register themselves as 'an industrial union,' and this step once taken they are enticed on through a network of solicitations, provisions, and safeguards, until they find themselves, almost without knowing it, agreeing to everything that follows. Trades Unions, or any other labour organization, or any combination of employers, can register as individual bodies without a mixed association of workers and employers. Once registered, they are in the network of arbitration:—'The effect of registration shall be to render the industrial union, and all persons who may be members of any society or trade union, so registered as an industrial union at the time of registration, or who after such registration may become members of any society or trade union so registered, subject to the jurisdiction by this Act given to a Board and the Court respectively, and liable to all the provisions of this Act, and all such persons shall be bound by the rules of the industrial union during the continuance of the membership.' . . . 'Every industrial agreement duly made and executed shall be binding on the parties thereto, and on every person who at any time during the term of such agreement is a member of any industrial union, trade union, or association party thereto, and on every employer who shall in the prescribed manner signify to the Registrar of the Supreme Court where such agreement is filed concurrence therein, and every such employer shall be entitled to the benefit thereof, and be deemed to be a party thereto.' . . . 'In and for every district there shall be established a Board of Conciliation, to have jurisdiction for the settlement of industrial disputes occurring in such district, which may be referred to it by one or more of the parties to an industrial dispute, or by industrial agreement.' . . . 'Every Board shall consist of such equal number of persons as the Governor may determine, being not more than six nor less than four persons, who shall be chosen by the industrial unions of employers and of workmen in the industrial district respectively, such unions voting separately, and electing an equal number of such members.' . . . Should this body itself be unable to come to a satisfactory decision it may refer the matter in question to a small committee of its members fairly representing each side. If a settlement or reconciliation be unattainable in this way, either party to the dispute can appeal to the Court of Arbitration, which is constituted as follows:—'There shall be one Court of Arbitration for the whole colony for the settlement of industrial disputes pursuant to this Act. . . . The Court shall consist of three members to be appointed by the Governor, one to be so appointed on the recommendation of the councils or a majority of the councils of the industrial associations of workmen in the colony, and one to be so appointed on the recommendation of the councils or a majority of the councils of the industrial associations of employers of the colony.' . . . 'No recommendation shall be made as to the third member, who shall be a Judge of the Supreme Court, and shall be appointed from time to time by the Governor, and shall be President of the Court.' "—M. Davitt, *Life and Progress in Australasia, ch.* 68.

Hon. W. P. Reeves, lately Agent-General of New Zealand in England, but who was Minister of Education and Labor in New Zealand from 1891 to 1896, and who is looked upon as the principal author of the industrial arbitration laws in that colony, wrote, during the summer of 1900, on the working of those laws, in an article contributed to the "London Express," as follows: "The arbitration law has been in constant use in New Zealand for about four years and a half. During those years there has never been a time when there has not been a dispute pending before one or other of the Conciliation Boards or the Central Arbitration Court. Writing, as I do, at some distance from London, I cannot say from memory what the exact number of disputes finally adjusted has been; but, so far, they cannot be less than sixty or seventy. Most of these have been carried, on appeal from some Conciliation Board, to the Arbitration Court and settled there. In about two cases out of seven the Conciliation Boards have been able successfully to arrange the disputes. Even where they have not done so, it by no means follows that their labors have been useless. Very often the appeal to the Arbitration Court is merely on one or two points out of many involved, and the advice of the Conciliation Board is accepted on the others. Often, too, most of the parties to a dispute have been ready to accept a board's suggestions, but it has needed the firm hand of the Arbitration Court to bring one or two stubborn men to acquiescence.

"The process may be tedious, but it is not costly. Lawyers are not employed as counsel before either the boards or the court unless all parties to the action agree thereto, and they very seldom do agree. A firm of employers may appear by a manager or accredited representative, a trade union is usually represented by its Secretary or other official. During the hearing, of course, the factories concerned remain open, and work goes on as usual. Employers are secured not only against a dead stop of business, but against the meaner kinds of competition of undercutting rivals. In the organized trades all the shops of a district have to keep the same hours and pay the same wages. No man may filch trade from a neighbor by sweating his own people. The fair-minded employer now knows where he is, and is freed from many anxieties.

"For six years there has virtually been neither strike nor lockout in New Zealand. All these, except the first, have been years of remarkable and increasing prosperity. During the time of depression which came before them, wages had fallen. With improving times employers would have been faced by resolute demands from trade unions for a return to former high rates of pay, and had there been no arbitration system in working order a series of very bitter conflicts must have ensued. This has been avoided. Workmen and workwomen have gained notable advances of pay, and also improved conditions as to hours of labor and otherwise. But this has come about gradually, and only after careful and painstaking inquiry. Many of the demands of labor have been refused; many more have been modified. In no case has an industry been throttled or crippled. Not only can we claim that no factory has been closed for a single day in New Zealand by labor war, but we can claim that the peace thus obtained has not been bought at the dear price of hampered industry and discouraged enterprise.

"When the Arbitration act came into operation the number of hands returned as employed in the registered factories was about 26,000. It is now not far short of 50,000. A percentage of this striking increase may be due to more thorough registration. Far the larger part of it represents an actual increase of industry. During these years the imports and exports of the colony have grown apace. The revenue received from the customs, from the income tax, from the stamps, and the railways has risen in each case rapidly. Employment from being scarce has grown plentiful. Building has been brisk in all centres of population. The marriage rate has gone up. In a word, New Zealand shows all the signs which we connect with a highly prosperous country. It would be too much to claim that this is chiefly due to the working of the Arbitration act. It is perfectly fair, however, to claim that the Arbitration act and the improved condition of labor, and of confidence which it has brought about, have had some share in leading up to this happy state of things.

"It is frequently asked, How could you possibly enforce an award of the Arbitration Court upon an employer or a union stubbornly determined to go to all lengths rather than obey it? In the first place, for nearly five years the law has been in constant use without a single exhibition of this desperate resistance. That alone

should be evidence of some weight that such a duel is not likely in a British community. It is quite true that an employer could go out of business rather than obey an award, and that the court could not prevent him from doing so. But employers are not given to ruining themselves merely because they may not like the decision of an impartial tribunal. It is suggested that the decision itself might be ruinous. There need be no fear of that. Experience has shown that if arbitrators err at all it is almost invariably in the direction of overcaution. They may show too great a desire to 'split the difference'; they are not in the least likely to impose intolerable conditions either upon masters or men. An employer who has the choice between accepting a legal decision arrived at after painstaking inquiry, and being taken into court and fined, will almost always accept the decision. In a very few cases he may run the risk of being fined once, but he will not lay himself open to a second penalty. That is the New Zealand experience.

"On the other hand, it has been flatly declared that the court cannot coerce trade unions. Vivid pictures have been painted of the tragic absurdity of endeavoring to collect fines from trade unionists by distraining on the goods of poor workmen whose union is without funds, and who are themselves penniless. The answer to that is that poverty-stricken unions, composed of penniless workers, are only too thankful to accept the decision of a State tribunal. They cannot strike against a powerful employer; much less can they hope to starve out a court of arbitration. Its decision may not altogether please them, but it is all they are likely to get. The Arbitration Court, therefore, is as potent to deal with trade unions as with employers. Wealthy unions it can fine. Penniless unions are helpless to fight it. Finally, at its back is the mighty force of public opinion, which is sick of labor wars and determined that the experiment of judicial adjustment shall have a full and fair trial."

The full text of the New Zealand "Industrial Conciliation and Arbitration Act" is published in pamphlet form by the United States Department of Labor, and appeared also in one of the Bulletins of the Department, in 1900.

Land system.—"The Crown lands of New Zealand are administered under 'the land act, 1892,' and the regulations made thereunder. The distinguishing features of the present land system are the outcome of ideas which have been gradually coming to maturity for some years past in this colony. These features involve the principle of State ownership of the soil, with a perpetual tenancy in the occupier. This, whatever may be the difference in detail, is the prevailing characteristic of the several systems under which land may now be selected. In New Zealand, this tendency to State ownership has taken a more pronounced form than in any other of the Australasian colonies, and the duration of the leases has become so extended as to warrant the name, frequently given to them, of 'everlasting leases.' In point of fact, most of the Crown lands are now disposed of for terms of 999 years. The rentals are based on the assessed value of the land at the time of disposal, without increase or recurring valuations. Under this system there is a fixity of tenure practically equal to freehold, and which, like freehold, necessarily carries with it the power of sale, sublease, mortgage, or disposition by will. Since all lands held under the Crown 'by lease in perpetuity' are subject to the land tax, the necessity for the periodical revaluations under the perpetual-lease system is done away with, the State reaping the advantage of the unearned increment through the before-mentioned tax. At the same time, the improvements made in the soil by cultivation, etc., are secured to the tenant.

"The advantages of this system to the selector are manifest. When it is taken into consideration that, with few exceptions, the Crown lands are, in their prairie condition, incapable of producing anything until brought into cultivation, the advantage to the settler of setting free his capital to develop the capabilities of the soil, rather than having to expend it in the purchase of a freehold, is very apparent. One of the most striking benefits of this system is the advantage it gives to the poor man, who, with little more capital than his strong right arm, is enabled to make a home for himself, which, under the freehold system, he is frequently unable to accomplish. The values placed on the Crown lands are, as a rule, low, for the State does not so much seek to raise a revenue directly therefrom as to encourage the occupation of the lands by the people; this secures indirectly an increased revenue, besides other advantages, resulting from a numerous rural population.

"Again, underlying the whole of the New Zealand land system is a further application of the principle of 'the land for the people,' viz, the restriction in area which any man may hold. This subject has been forced upon the attention of the legislature by defects in former systems, under which one individual with means at his command could appropriate large areas, to the exclusion of his poorer fellow-settler. Under conditions where the price at which the land is offered is fixed and where choice of selection is by ballot, the poor settler has the same chance as the rich one and may, should he wish it, hold as much land. The limit that a selector may hold is so fixed as to encourage the class of small farmers, and up to that limit the amount he may select is left entirely to himself. The act defines the amount of land anyone may select at 640 acres of first-class or 2,000 acres of second-class land, inclusive of any land he may already hold. These limits apply to lands which are thrown open for 'free selection,' as it is termed, but in some cases, where found desirable, the limit is by regulation made much smaller.

"In addition to the many advantages offered by the 'lease-in-perpetuity' system, the land act provides others to meet the wants of different classes. The rule is almost invariable that land thrown open for so-called 'free selection' is offered to the public under three different tenures, and the choice left entirely to the would-be settler. The three tenures are: (1) For cash, in which one-fourth of the purchase-money is paid down at once, and the remainder within thirty days. The title does not issue until certain improvements have been made on the land. (2) Lease with a purchasing clause, at a 5-per-cent rental on the value of the land; the lease being for twenty-five years, with the right to purchase at the original upset price at any time after the first ten years. (3) Lease in perpetuity, at a rental of 4 per cent on the capital value, as already described above.

"The present [1895] land laws have been in force since the 1st of November, 1892, and, therefore, the returns of the Department of Lands and Survey for the year ending the 31st of March, 1895, will give a fair idea of the proportions in which lands are selected under the three tenures above described during the past two and a half years. The figures given below include the 'special settlements,' all of which must by law be held on lease in perpetuity: (1) Selected for cash, 1,542; area, 110,570 acres. (2) Occupation with right of purchase, 1,060; area, 236,270 acres. (3) Lease in perpetuity, 3,224; area, 634,086 acres.

"'The land act, 1892,' provides for a special class of settlement, which has found favor with the public to a very considerable extent during the last two years. This is known as the 'small-farm association' system. It provides that, where not less than twelve individuals have associated themselves together for mutual help, such an association can, with the approval of the Minister of Lands, select a block of land of not more than 11,000 acres, but there must be a selector to each 200 acres in the block. The extreme limit that one person may hold is fixed at 320 acres. Settlements of this class are held on 'lease in perpetuity' for 999 years, in the same way as lands under the same tenure when thrown open for free selection. The conditions of residence and improvements are the same."—S. Percy Smith, *in New Zealand Official Year-Book*, 1895 (*reprinted in U. S. Consular Reports, Jan.*, 1897, *p.* 4).

A. D. 1899.—Old-Age Pension Act.—In the winter of 1899 an old-age pension act was added to the radical legislation of New Zealand. The Agent-General for New Zealand in England has described the measure in a review article, as follows: "As finally licked into shape, the act is one for giving a small pension to the poorest section of aged colonists without any contribution on their part whatever. Briefly summarized, its effect will be that any New Zealander—man or woman—who has come to the age of sixty-five, after living not less than twenty-five years in New Zealand, shall be entitled to 6s. 11d. a week, or £18 a year. The full pension is to be paid to those whose income from any source is less than £34. When the private income is above £34 a year £1 is deducted from the pension for every £1 of such excess income. When, therefore, the private income is large enough to be £18 a year in excess of £34 no state pension is paid. In other words, no one who has an income of £52 a year is entitled to even a fraction of the pension. A rather more elaborate portion of the act deals with deductions to be made from the pension where the applicant for it is possessed of accumulated property. Under this the applicant's real and personal property are assessed, and his debts, if any, are subtracted from the total value thereof. Then he is allowed to own £325 without suffering any deduction therefor. After that he loses £1 of pension for every £15 worth of accumulated property. The result is that any one possessed of £600 worth of accumulated property ceases to be entitled to any allowance whatever. Men and women are equally entitled to the pension, and where a husband and wife are living together their property or income is divided by two for the purpose of the calculations above mentioned. That is to say, their united income must amount to £104 or their united property to £1,200 before they are altogether disentitled to any part of the pension. They may have, between them, an income of £68, or as much as £650 of property, and yet be entitled to draw their respective pensions in full."

The government is only authorized to pay the required amounts during three years from the passage of the Act, after which Parliament will have to decide on its continuance or amendment. Mr. Reeves expects that "the opposition will, more or less in unison, submit a rival old-age pension scheme to the constituencies. One of their prominent members, Mr. George Hutchison, indicated in the debate on the third reading of the measure a scheme which some think will be generally adopted by his party. This is to draw a distinction between the older poor of the colony now living and the younger generation of colonists. All now over fifty years of age are to be permitted as they attain sixty-five to take advantage of Mr. Seddon's act without let or hindrance. But for the younger people a contributory scheme is to be drawn up, under which they would have to pay some such sum as sixpence a week, to go in aid of a substantial pension in their old age. Whatever may be thought of the economic merits of such a scheme, it might conceivably be expected at election-time to disarm the hostility of the aged poor to any such interference with their prospects under the present system as would be entailed by a complete repeal of the Seddon act."—*National Review, February*, 1899.

A. D. 1900 (March).—Looking towards federation with Australia.—New Zealand did not take part in the movements which led to the federation of the Australian colonies in the Commonwealth of Australia, but watched them with evident interest and a final wakening of inclination to be joined in union with them. When the Act of the Imperial Parliament "to constitute the Commonwealth of Australia" was under discussion in England (see, in this vol., AUSTRALIA : A. D. 1900), the Agent-General for New Zealand in London addressed to the Colonial Office (March 30, 1900) the following Memorandum, which explains the attitude of that colony towards the federation movement in Australia : "The Government of New Zealand desires to secure the insertion of certain amendments in the Commonwealth of Australia Constitution Bill shortly to be laid before the Imperial Parliament. These amendments are three in number. The first of them is, in effect, that New Zealand should preserve the right of joining the proposed Commonwealth of Australia on the same terms as the original States now about to be united in such Commonwealth. The second is, that while New Zealand remains outside the Commonwealth, litigants in her higher Courts, though reserving the right they now possess to appeal to the Queen in Council, should, as an alternative, have the right to appeal to the High Court of Australia on paying the fees and complying with the rules of that tribunal. The third amendment is, that the Australian Commonwealth and the Colony of New Zealand should be empowered to make the necessary arrangements to employ their naval and military forces for mutual aid and defence, including operations outside their own boundaries, and for that purpose to co-operate in forming a homogeneous Australasian force.

"The importance of the first amendment to New Zealand is great. The Colony is divided from Australia by 1,200 miles of unbroken sea. It still takes from four to five days for persons quitting New Zealand to reach any port in Australia. Though a large and valuable trade is carried on between the two countries, and though New Zealand is linked to Australia, not merely by financial ties, but by bonds of intercourse, cordial friendship, and sympathy, she has also vital and separate interests. Many, also, of the leading matters on which the discussions on Federation in Australia during the last 12 years have turned are topics with which the New Zealand people is almost unacquainted. It is therefore only to be expected that the Colony should watch the Federal movement with caution and reserve. It is also true that, until June of last year, New Zealand was unable to judge as to the intentions of the great Colony of New South Wales with regard to the Commonwealth Bill. It was not until the month of September that Queensland decided to enter the Commonwealth ; Western Australia has not even yet done so. And it was directly after the decision of Queensland had become known that, in response to a request from Sir John Forrest, the leading statesmen of Australia intimated that, in their opinion, it was impossible to consider any further amendments of the Commonwealth Bill. From that moment the only course left open to New Zealand has been that now taken. About that time there appeared in New Zealand evidences of the growth of a feeling in the Colony in favour of a closer union with Australia. This was on the eve of the general elections, and Mr. Seddon, the Prime Minister, then defined his position, stating that the future relations of New Zealand with Australia were a matter for education and careful examination : that for himself he kept an open mind, but that prudent deliberation was advisable. At the general elections which took place in December last, Mr. Seddon was returned to power with an unusually large majority. It may therefore very safely be assumed that this cautious but not hostile attitude fairly represents the present view of the people of the Colony. Some stress may be laid on the foregoing facts in view of the possible objection that New Zealand's action now comes too late. The Colony virtually asks that, in view of its position of distance and difficulty, it should have more time given it to make up its mind than has been found necessary by colonies which are contiguous or almost so. If it should be proposed to fix a limit of time to this, that would clearly be a matter for reasonable consideration.

"In so far as the second amendment would give certain New Zealand litigants a right of resort to the High Court of Australia, it is scarcely likely to meet with objection in Australia unless on the general ground that no amendment whatever of the Commonwealth Bill is now desirable. In the event of the amendment being admitted, it is obvious that certain precautions might have to be taken to conserve the existing rights of New Zealand litigants, and also to prevent clashing of appeals, but doubtless these could be provided for. The third amendment, that providing for a species of partial federation for purposes of defence and mutual assistance, seems not only desirable but unobjectionable in every way. It does not propose that any kind of compulsion should be applied to either the Commonwealth or New Zealand : it merely empowers them to make such arrangements as may be deemed mutually advantageous. At present it seems more than doubtful whether either the Commonwealth or the Colony has the power to make simple, binding and effective arrangements which would involve operations and expenditure outside their own boundaries, and under which each would have to act so as to affect colonists not subject to their respective jurisdictions. Recent events have clearly shown that the time has passed by for regarding the military forces of a colony as something never to be employed outside of its own boundaries. I need not point out that such a co-operation would be of value not only to Australia and New Zealand, but to the Empire which both are so anxious to serve."

The reply of the Colonial Office to this Memorandum set forth that its suggestions had been submitted to the delegates of the federating colonies and did not meet their approval. "They pointed out that during the period of grace proposed to be allowed circumstances might arise which would cause grave embarrassment to the Commonwealth if it were open to New Zealand to claim admission on the same terms as the original States, and that Article 121 of the draft Bill provided sufficiently for the admission of New Zealand at any time upon such conditions as might be found mutually acceptable to the Colony and the Commonwealth." It was added that "the suggested amendments as to the appeal from New Zealand Courts to the High Court of Australia, and the arrangements for mutual defence, would, if undertaken now, lead to great delay, and involve a fresh referendum to the people of the Federating Colonies, while there does not appear to be any probability that the Federation would not favourably entertain any proposals of the kind, if put forward after Federation."

In the Constitution Act as passed, however, New Zealand is mentioned specifically among the "States" to which its provisions may apply, though not included in what relates to the "Original States." See (in this vol.) CONSTITUTION OF AUSTRALIA.—*Great Britain, Parliamentary Publications (Papers by Command: Cd. 158, 1900, pp. 30–31, and 51).*

A. D. 1900 (October).—**Annexation of the Cook Islands.**—A correspondent of the "London Times," writing from Rarotonga, the largest of the Cook (or Hervey) Islands, on the 10th of October, 1900, reported the arrival there of the Earl of Ranfurly, Governor of New Zealand, for the purpose of effecting the annexation of the islands to that colony, in accordance with the expressed wish of the natives. "Lord Ranfurly," he writes, "landed this morning, and, as the representative of her Majesty, addressed the Arikis, or high chiefs, on the question of annexation, for which they had asked. This is his second visit to the island, and he congratulated the people on now finding such a satisfactory condition of affairs in Rarotonga. He expressed pleasure at their liberality in subscribing so large a sum of money for the relief of those families who, in the fortunes of the war in South Africa, might lose their main support, and in sending one of their representative residents to represent them on the field of battle. All this and much more about the interest they took in the British Empire the Queen was aware of, and their petition for annexation had been laid at the foot of the Throne and duly considered. He urged them, however, to consider carefully their decision in this matter, and, further, that it should be arrived at of their own free and untrammelled will. He had heard from the British Resident that the high chiefs and all the people wanted annexation, but he wished to hear it from their own lips. It would then remain but for them to perform the act of cession to her Majesty, and for him formally to annex the group, hoisting the British flag, and proclaiming that from henceforth they were part of the British Empire whose prestige and honour they would from that moment share. The high chiefs unanimously agreed to annexation. . . . There are 2,300 Maoris on this island and 70 Europeans. All are intensely loyal to Queen Victoria. The island was discovered in 1823 by Messrs. Williams and Bourne, two officers of the London Mission Society, which for many years has had its headquarters for the Eastern Pacific located here. The volcanic soil of the island is marvellously fertile, coffee, cocoa, cotton, oranges, limes, cocoanuts and many other tropic fruits and trees growing without almost any cultivation. A British protectorate was declared over the group by Captain Bourke, of H. M. S. Hyacinth, in 1888. Since 1892 the interests of the protectorate have been guarded and directed by a British Resident, paid by the New Zealand Government, so that the islands will now probably be included within the boundaries of that colony. Nearly the whole of the trade is with New Zealand. There are six islands in the group annexed [700 miles southeast of Samoa] the total population of which is about 4,500." The "Times," commenting on the annexation, remarked: "The New Zealand Legislature has passed resolutions expressing its desire that the Suwaroff Island, to the north of the Cook group and about half-way to the Penrhyn group, should also be annexed to the colony. This island, although thinly inhabited, is said to possess one of the best ports in that part of the Pacific. The only quarter from which any protest against the acquisition of the Cook Islands has come so far seems to be New South Wales, which fears the influence of the introduction of the New Zealand tariff on its trade with that place."

NIAGARA, Electric power at. See (in this vol.) SCIENCE, RECENT : ELECTRICAL.

NICARAGUA.—**Nicaragua Canal.** See (in this vol.) CENTRAL AMERICA ; also, CANAL, INTEROCEANIC ; and UNITED STATES OF AM. : A. D. 1899–1901.

NICHOLAS II. OF RUSSIA: Coronation. See (in this vol.) RUSSIA : A. D. 1896 (MAY—JUNE).

NICHOLSON'S NEK, Battle of. See (in this vol.) SOUTH AFRICA (THE FIELD OF WAR): A. D. 1899 (OCTOBER—DECEMBER).

NIFFER, or NUFFAR, Explorations at. See (in this vol.) ARCHÆOLOGICAL RESEARCH: BABYLONIA: AMERICAN EXPLORATION.

NIGERIA: A. D. 1882–1899.—History of the formation of the Niger Coast Protectorate.—Conventions of Great Britain with

Germany and France.—Settlement **of the** boundary of the French Sudan and Sahara Sphere.—The following "Notes on the Niger Districts and Niger Coast Protectorates, 1882–1893," tracing the several steps by which the existing Protectorate was formed, appear in a paper "presented to both Houses of Parliament by command of Her Majesty, 1899 (C.—9372)" : "In 1882 a Company, entitled the 'National African Company, Limited,' was formed to take over the business of the 'United Africa Company, Limited,' in Central Africa and in the Niger Regions. In October, 1884, the Company purchased the business and objects of the 'Compagnie Française de l'Afrique Equatoriale.' In the same year various treaties were concluded between Consul Hewett and native chiefs of the Niger Districts, by which these territories were placed under British protection. On the 26th February, 1885, the General Act of the Berlin Conference was signed, Chapter V. of which contained an 'Act of Navigation for the Niger,' which applied, generally, to the Niger and its affluents the free navigation articles of the Final Act of the Congress of Vienna of 1815. In April–June, 1885, the British and German Governments entered into an Agreement, by an exchange of Notes, defining their respective spheres of action in the Gulf of Guinea. By this Agreement Germany engaged not to make acquisition, accept Protectorates, or interfere with the extension of British influence in that part of the Gulf of Guinea lying between the right river bank of the mouth of the Rio del Rey entering the sea between 8° 42' and 8° 46' long. east of Greenwich and the British colony of Lagos, nor in the interior, to west of a line following the right river bank of the Rio del Rey from the said mouth to its source, thence striking direct to the left river bank of the Old Calabar or Cross River, and terminating, after crossing that river, at the point about 9° 8' of long. east of Greenwich, marked 'Rapids' on the English Admiralty chart.

" On the 5th June, 1885, a Notification was inserted in the 'London Gazette' to the effect that a British Protectorate had been established over the Niger Districts; the territories comprised within the Protectorate were defined to be—the line of coast between the British Protectorate of Lagos, and the right or western bank of the mouth of the Rio del Rey ; and also the territories on both banks of the Niger, from its confluence with the River Benuê at Lukoja to the sea, as well as the territories on both banks of the River Benué, from the confluence up to and including Ibi. On the 10th July, 1886, a Royal Charter was granted to the 'National African Company, Limited.' In July–August, 1886, a Supplementary Agreement was entered into between the British and German Governments defining their respective spheres of action in the Gulf of Guinea from the Rio del Rey to a point to the east and near to Yola. On the 18th October, 1887, another Notification was inserted in the 'London Gazette,' in which it was stated that the British Protectorate of the Niger Districts then comprised the following territories :—On the line of coast between the British Protectorate of Lagos and the right or western river bank of the mouth of the Rio del Rey, and all territories in the basin of the Niger and its affluents, which were or might be for the time being subject to

the government of the 'National African Company, Limited' (then called the 'Royal Niger Company'), in accordance with the provisions of the Charter of the said Company, dated 10th July, 1886.

"On the 5th August, 1890, a Declaration was signed by the British and French Governments, which contained the following clause:—'The Government of Her Britannic Majesty recognises the sphere of influence of France to the south of her Mediterranean Possessions up to a line from Say on the Niger to Barrawa on Lake Tchad, drawn in such manner as to comprise in the sphere of action of the Niger Company all that fairly belongs to the kingdom of Sokoto ; the line to be determined by Commissioners to be appointed.' On the 1st July, 1890, another Agreement was entered into between the British and German Governments defining their spheres of influence in the Gulf of Guinea and in other parts of Africa. On the 18th June, 1892, that portion of the Niger Protectorate which lies on, or to the north of, the 7 degree of north latitude was, by notification to the Signatory Powers of the Brussels Act, placed under the terms of Art. 91 of that Act, within the zone of prohibition of alcoholic liquors. On the 14th April, 1893, an agreement was signed between the British and German Governments, in which it was declared that the right bank of the Rio del Rey waterway should be the boundary between the Oil Rivers Protectorate and the Colony of the Cameroons.

"On the 13th May, 1893, a Notification was inserted in the 'London Gazette,' announcing that the portion of the British Protectorate of the Niger Districts which was under the administration of Her Majesty's Commissioner and Consul would, from the date of that Notification, be administered under the name of the 'Niger Coast Protectorate,' and would cease to be known as the 'Oil Rivers Protectorate.' And on the 15th November, 1893, a further Agreement was signed between the British and German Governments defining the boundary between their respective spheres of influence in the region extending from the Rio del Rey to 'a point to the east of, and close to Yola,' and on Lake Chad.

"Between 1884 and 1893 numerous Treaties were concluded by the National Africa Company and by the Royal Niger Company with native Chiefs and others possessing territories in the basin of the Niger districts, by which they engaged to make no cession of territory or to enter into any Treaty negotiations with Foreign States without the previous consent of the British Government, and in return for which they were placed under British protection."—*Great Britain, Parliamentary Publications (Papers by Command, C.*—9372).

In October, 1897, after a number of threatening collisions between English and French claims and undertakings had occurred in the Niger region, representatives of the two nations met in Paris to negotiate an agreement concerning boundaries. The result of their work was embodied in a convention signed June 14, 1898, but not ratified by both governments until June 13, 1899. By this agreement, the frontiers separating the British colony of the Gold Coast from the French colonies of the Ivory Coast and Sudan, and the British colony of Lagos from the French colony of Dahomey, were defined with precision, and the British and French possessions east of the Niger were then in the IVth article of the Convention, delimited as follows : Starting from a point on the left bank of the Niger which is fixed by the median line of the Dallul Mauri at its mouth, "the frontier shall follow this median line until it meets the circumference of a circle drawn from the centre of the town of Sokoto with a radius of 100 miles (160·932 metres). From this point it shall follow the northern arc of this circle as far as its second intersection with the 14th parallel of north latitude. From this second point of intersection it shall follow this parallel eastward for a distance of 70 miles (112·652 metres); then proceed due south until it reaches the parallel of 13° 20' north latitude, then eastward along this parallel for a distance of 250 miles (402·230 metres); then due north until it regains the 14th parallel of north latitude ; then eastwards along this parallel as far as its intersection with the meridian passing 35° east of the centre of the town of Kuka, and thence this meridian southward until its intersection with the southern shore of Lake Chad. The Government of the French Republic recognizes, as falling within the British sphere, the territory to the east of the Niger, comprised within the above-mentioned line, the Anglo-German frontier, and the sea. The Government of Her Britannic Majesty recognizes, as falling within the French sphere, the northern, eastern, and southern shores of Lake Chad, which are comprised between the point of intersection of the 14th degree of north latitude, with the western shore of the lake and the point of incidence on the shore of the lake of the frontier determined by the Franco-German Convention of the 15th March, 1894."

On the 21st of March, 1899, the following Declaration was added to the Convention, and ratified with it in the following June : "The IVth Article of the Convention of the 14th June, 1898, shall be completed by the following provisions, which shall be considered as forming an integral part of it :—

"1. Her Britannic Majesty's Government engages not to acquire either territory or political influence to the west of the line of frontier defined in the following paragraph, and the Government of the French Republic engages not to acquire either territory or political influence to the east of the same line.

"2. The line of frontier shall start from the point where the boundary between the Congo Free State and French territory meets the water-parting between the watershed of the Nile and that of the Congo and its affluents. It shall follow in principle that water-parting up to its intersection with the 11th parallel of north latitude. From this point it shall be drawn as far as the 15th parallel in such manner as to separate, in principle, the Kingdom of Wadai from what constituted in 1882 the Province of Darfur ; but it shall in no case be so drawn as to pass to the west beyond the 21st degree of longitude east of Greenwich (18° 40' east of Paris), or to the east beyond the 23rd degree of longitude east of Greenwich (20° 40' east of Paris).

"3. It is understood, in principle, that to the north of the 15th parallel the French zone shall be limited to the northeast and east by a line which shall start from the point of intersection of the Tropic of Cancer with the 16th degree of

longitude east of Greenwich (13° 40' east of Paris), shall run thence to the south-east until it meets the 24th degree of longitude east of Greenwich (21° 40' east of Paris), and shall then follow the 24th degree until it meets, to the north of the 15th parallel of latitude, the frontier of Darfur as it shall eventually be fixed.

"4. The two Governments engage to appoint Commissioners who shall be charged to delimit on the spot a frontier-line in accordance with the indications given in paragraph 2 of this Declaration. The result of their work shall be submitted for the approbation of their respective Governments.

"It is agreed that the provisions of Article IX of the Convention of the 14th June, 1898, shall apply equally to the territories situated to the south of the 14° 20' parallel of north latitude, and to the north of the 5th parallel of north latitude, between the 14° 20' meridian of longitude east of Greenwich (12th degree east of Paris) and the course of the Upper Nile."—*Great Britain, Papers by Command : Treaty Series, No.* 15, 1899.

Of the territorial partition in West Africa which this important treaty as first signed in 1898 determined, and of the magnitude of the empire which it conceded to France, a striking English view was given at the time in the following article : "Though we are perfectly satisfied with the agreement, and though we believe that the country as a whole will be perfectly satisfied, we do not disguise from ourselves the fact that under the Convention France receives the full title-deeds for the most magnificent piece of empire obtained this century by any European Power,—a dominion which, though 'in partibus infidelium,' is yet within easy reach of both the western and the southern shores of France. We do not grudge France the great possession that was finally rounded off and consolidated on Tuesday ; nay, rather we are glad to see it in her hands, for we want monopoly neither in trade nor in empire. We see, however, no good in pretending that she has not obtained the most magnificent opportunity for over-sea development which has fallen to any Power within recent times. The best way of understanding the Convention is to realise what it is that France now possesses in West Africa. Let our readers look at a map of Africa, and first fix their eyes on Algiers and Tunis, with their rich soil and splendid harbours and their remains of an ancient and splendid civilisation,—Phœnician, Greek, Roman, Christian, and Arab. Then let them allow their eyes to travel downwards to the right bank of the greatest river of Africa, the Congo. From Constantine, with its great memories and its scenery almost European in charm and splendour, to Brazzaville and Stanley Pool, with their tropical vegetation and savage life, there is a continuous and uninterrupted stretch of French territory. As they say in our country districts, the French President might now ride on his own land from Tunis to Loango. The French dominion of West Africa (as says an official 'communiqué' to the Paris Press with very natural exultation) now extends over a space as great as that from Paris to Moscow. From Algeria to the Congo, from Senegal to Lake Chad—i. e., almost to the centre of Africa—stretches this vast tract of French territory. 'At the present moment,' to quote the words of the 'communiqué,' 'all our West African colonies—Algeria, Tunis, Senegal, Futa-

Jallon, the Ivory Coast, the Soudan, and the Congo—are in communication by their respective Hinterlands.'

"But probably this will not convey much to the ordinary English reader. Perhaps we can best make him realise the immensity of the French West African Empire by pointing out that, with the exception of certain great German and English and other 'enclaves' the whole of the huge piece of Africa which bulges out on the map towards the west now belongs to France. She has all the connecting links, all that does not specifically belong to some one else, and she cuts off short the Hinterlands of all the Powers with possessions on the West African coast. Let us begin at the most western point of the coast-line of Tripoli in the Mediterranean, and travel round the coast, marking off all that is not French.

"First, we come to Tunis,—that is in the possession of France just as Egypt is in our possession. Algiers comes next,—that is French. Then Morocco. Morocco is at present independent, but at the back of Morocco all the land, be it desert or cultivate, is French. Next comes a strip of Spanish coast, but it goes only a very little way inland, and all the back country is French. Next come the great French colonies of Senegambia and Futa-Jallon, with two little colonies embedded in them, one belonging to us—the Gambia—and the other belonging to Portugal. Next come our Sierra Leone and independent Liberia, but here again the Hinterlands are all French. Next comes the French Ivory Coast colony, then the British Gold Coast, then German Togoland, and then French Dahomey. Here again all the Hinterlands beyond, say, four hundred miles inland, belong, since the signing of the Convention, to France. After that comes our Colony of Lagos, then the German Cameroons, and finally the French Congo—the last French possession in West Africa. Here, too, the Hinterlands have been cut off by the French, and our Colonies have been made into 'enclaves' in the mighty French dominion. It is true that the Niger or Lagos 'enclave' is a very vast one, and stretches now up to Lake Chad, which becomes henceforth as international a sheet of water as the Lake of Constance. Still, it is an 'enclave,' for, as we read the Convention, who embarks upon Lake Chad from the British shore and steers eastward will land on French territory. In other words, Nigeria cannot now cross Lake Chad and expand beyond it. We should be glad to hear that this is not the true reading of the Convention, but we fear it is. We have travelled, then, round the map of Africa, from Tunis to the Congo, and found that France is everywhere the chief owner, —that hers is the great estate, and that the other Powers only have odd bits of land here and there. We do not say this in any grumbling spirit, for our odd bit—Nigeria—is very possibly worth as much as the great estate if Algiers and Tunis are not counted. We merely wish to make the public understand clearly that West Africa as a political and geographical expression has finally passed to France, though we no doubt have carved one very valuable piece out of it."—*The Spectator* (*London*) *June* 18, 1898.

Nine months later, when the agreement embodied in the Declaration of March 21, 1899, had been added to the original convention, the "Spectator" explained its effect as follows: "It will be remembered that last year we and the French

agreed upon a delimitation of 'spheres' in West Africa which extended as far as Lake Chad. As to the country east of Lake Chad nothing was said. It was left as a kind of No-man's Land. What has now been done is to extend the area of the French 'sphere' eastward beyond Lake Chad till it reaches Darfur and the Bahr-el-Ghazel. Darfur and the region of the Bahr-el-Ghazel are declared to be in the English 'sphere.' All the rest of Northern Central Africa is to become French. France, that is, is to have the great Mahommedan State of Wadai as well as Baghirmi and Kanem. In the territory between Lake Chad and the Nile each Power, however, is to allow the other equality of treatment in matters of commerce. This will no doubt allow France to have commercial establishments on the Nile and its affluents, but it will also allow us to have similar privileges for trade on the eastern shore of Lake Chad. But as our system of giving equal trading rights to all foreigners would in any case have secured commercial rights to France, we are not in the least hampered by this provision, while the concession to us of equal rights on the eastern shore of Lake Chad will improve our position in the face of French Colonial Protection. . . .

"The first thing that strikes one in considering the French possessions in Africa, after this latest addition, is their vastness. Practically, France will now have all North-Western, and all Northern, and all North Central Africa, except Morocco, our West African Colonies, Tripoli, Darfur, and the Valley of the Nile,—giving that phrase its widest interpretation, and regarding it as the whole of the country whence water flows into the Nile. . . . That, if she plays her cards properly, she ought to make a success of her African Empire we cannot doubt, for she starts with immense advantages. To begin with, she is nearer her African possessions than any other Power. You can go in a couple of days from Marseilles to Algiers and Tunis. Next, in Algiers and Tunis she has rich colonies with a temperate climate which may be made the basis for great developments in the way of railway extension. Lastly, her African possessions are conterminous, or, at any rate, connected with each other by land. She owns, that is, Northern Africa, and the rest of the Powers have only, as it were, enclaves—very large enclaves, no doubt, in many cases—in her territory. At present this advantage may not seem very great owing to the vast distances and the desert character of many of the French Hinterlands, but if and when France completes her Soudan railways, the strength of this continuity of territory will become apparent. But though France has many advantages, it would be foolish to deny that she has also many serious problems to solve. We shall perhaps be stating the most dangerous of them when we say that France now becomes the undisputed master of the great sect of El Senoussi. There are reported to be over twenty million followers of El Senoussi in North Africa, and, except in Tripoli, all these may now be said to be within the French 'sphere of influence.' The Sultanate of Wadai —which, be it remembered, is a very formidable State, and one which has never yet come into contact with any European Power—is a Senoussi State. But the followers of the Senoussi, besides being numerous, are extremely fanatical. Though practising a much purer form of Mahommedanism than the Dervishes, they hate Europeans quite as ardently, and if once their religious zeal were to be thoroughly roused they would prove most formidable foes. We do not envy the French their task if they attempt to conquer Wadai."—*The Spectator, March* 25, 1899.

A. D. **1897**: Massacre of British officials near Benin.—Capture of Benin.—An unarmed expedition from the Niger Coast Protectorate, going, in January, on a peaceful mission to the King of Benin, led by Acting Consul-General Phillips, was attacked on the way and the whole party massacred excepting two, who were wounded, but who hid themselves in the bush and contrived to make their way back. The Consul-General had been warned that the king would not allow the mission to enter Benin, but persisted in going on. A "punitive expedition" was sent against Benin the following month, and the town was reached and taken on the 18th, but the king had escaped.

"The city presented the most appalling sight, particularly around the King's quarters, from which four large main roads lead to the compounds of the bigger Chiefs, the city being very scattered. Sacrificial trees in the open spaces still held the corpses of the latest victims [of 'Ju Ju' sacrifice]—seven in all were counted—and on every path a freshly-sacrificed corpse was found lying, apparently placed there to prevent pursuit. One large open space, 200 to 300 yards in length, was strewn with human bones and bodies in all stages of decomposition. Within the walls, the sight was, if possible, more terrible. Seven large sacrifice compounds were found inclosed by walls 14 to 16 feet high, each 2 to 3 acres in extent; against the end wall in each, under a roof, was raised a dais with an earthen (clay) sacrificial altar about 50 feet long close against the wall on which were placed the gods to whom sacrifice is made — mostly being carved ivory tusks, standing upright, mounted at base, in hideously-constructed brass heads. In front of each ivory god was a small earthen mound on which the victim's forehead would apparently be placed. The altars were covered with streams of dried human blood and the

stench was too frightful. It would seem that the populace sat around in these huge compounds while the Ju Ju priests performed the sacrifices for their edification. In the various sacrifice compounds were found open pits filled with human bodies giving forth most trying odours. The first night several cases of fainting and sickness occurred owing to the stench, which was equally bad everywhere. In one of the pits, partially under other bodies, was found a victim, still living, who, being rescued, turned out to be a servant of Mr. Gordon's, one of the members of Mr. Phillips' ill-fated expedition. At the doors and gates of houses and compounds were stinking goats and fowls, sacrificed apparently to prevent the white man entering therein. The foregoing is but a feeble attempt to describe the horrors of this most terrible city, which after five days' continuous fatigue, working with about 1,000 natives, still presents most appalling and frightful sights. In the outlying parts of the city the same sights are met and the annual expenditure of human life in sacrifice must have been enormous. Most of the wells were also found filled with human bodies."—*Great Britain, Papers by Command: Africa, No.* 6, 1897, *p.* 28.

A. D. **1897**: Subjugation of Fulah slave-raiders. See (in this vol.) AFRICA : A. D. 1897 (NIGERIA).

A. D. **1899**: Transfer to the British Crown. The Royal Niger Company transferred its territories to the crown in July, 1899, receiving the sum of £865,000. It was announced to Parliament that three governments would be formed, named North Nigeria, South Nigeria, and Lagos.

NILE, Barrage and reservoir works on the. See (in this vol.) EGYPT : A. D. 1898–1901.

NILE VALLEY: The question of possession. See (in this vol.) EGYPT : A. D. 1898 (SEPTEMBER—NOVEMBER).

NINETEEN HUNDRED, The Universal Jubilee of. See (in this vol.) PAPACY : A. D. 1900.

THE NINETEENTH CENTURY.

The date of the ending of the Century.— Controversy as to whether the Nineteenth Century came to its end at the ending of the year 1899 or the year 1900 seems nearly incomprehensible to one who takes the trouble to begin a counting of years from the beginning of the Christian Era, and so reaches in his reckoning the fact that the first century did not end until the 100th year was ended. That seems to clear all confusion from the question, since the 200th, 300th, 400th, and so on up to the 1900th, must be the closing years of the successive centuries, just as certainly as the 100th is the last year of the first century. Arithmetically, there is no question left ; but some minds refuse to recognize the century as a merely arithmetical fact. They see in it an entity of time with which the counting of years has little to do. Their somewhat mystical view is set forth in the following, which we quote from a communication that appeared in the "New York Times" :

"The centurial figures are the symbol, and

the only symbol, of the centuries. Once every hundred years there is a change in the symbol, and this great secular event is of startling prominence. What more natural than to bring the century into harmony with its only visible mark ? What more consonant with order than to make each group of a hundred years correspond with a single centennial emblem ? Be it noticed that, apart from the centennial emblems, there is absolutely nothing to give the centuries any form. The initial figures 18 are time's standard which the earth carries while it makes 100 trips around the sun. Then a new standard, 19, is put up. Shall we wait now a whole year for 1901, at the behest of the abacists ? No, we will not pass over the significant year 1900, which is stamped with the great secular change, but with cheers we will welcome it and the new century. The 1900 men, who compose the vast majority of the people, say to their opponents : 'We freely admit that the century you have in your mind, the artificial century, begins in **1901**, but the natural century (which we prefer) begins in 1900.'"

A consistent application of this view to the defining and naming of the centuries would seem to require that the years which carry the initial figures 18 should make up the Eighteenth, not the Nineteenth Century, and that we should turn back our centurial nomenclature a whole round.

The epoch of a transformation of the world.—In the last years of the Eighteenth Century a new epoch in history was entered,—an epoch marked by many distinctions, but most strikingly by what may be called the transformation of the world. The earlier great ages had been ages of simple expansion,—of a widening theatre for the leading races,—of a widening knowledge of the earth and the heavens,—a widening range for human thought; but those expansive movements in civilization led up, at last, to more wonderful processes of transformation, which were just in their beginning when the Nineteenth Century dawned. For all the generations of mankind that had lived before this century, the earth, as a dwelling place, remained nearly unchanged. They had cleared some forests from its face, and smoothed some paths; but, in every substantial feature, the France, for example, of Napoleon was the unaltered Gaul that Julius Cæsar knew. Everywhere the material conditions of life were essentially the same for the man of the Eighteenth Century that they had been for the man of the First. Then began the amazing work of the brain and hand of man, by which he has been refashioning and refitting the planet he inhabits, and making a new world for his dwelling. As a habitable earth, to-day, it bears no likeness to the earth on which the first day of this century dawned. Its distances mean nothing that they formerly did; its dividing seas and mountains have nothing of their old effect; its pestilences have lost half their terror; its very storms are sentinelled and rarely surprise us in our travels or our work. Netted with steam and electric railways, seamed with canals, wire-strung with telegraphic and telephonic lines, its ocean-voyages made holiday excursions, its every-day labors, of the forge, the plough, the sickle, the spindle, the loom, the needle, and even of the pen, done with magical deftness by machines, which its coal mines and its waterfalls lend forces to move, it is nothing less than a new world that men are making for themselves, out of that in which they lived at the beginning of the era of mechanism and electricity and steam.

"Yet these are but outward features of the transformation that is being wrought in the world. Socially, politically, and morally, it has been undergoing a deeper change. A growth of fellow-feeling which began in the last century has been an increasing growth. It has not ended war, nor the passions that cause war, but it is rousing an opposition which gathers strength every year. It has made democratic institutions of government so common that the few arbitrary governments now remaining in civilized countries seem disgraceful to the people who endure them so long. It has broken old yokes of conquest, and revived the independence of long subjugated states. It has swept away unnatural boundary lines, which separated peoples of kindred language and race. It is pressing long-neglected questions of right and justice on the attention of all classes of men, everywhere, and requiring that answers shall be found.

"And, still, even these are but minor effects of the prodigious change which the Nineteenth Century has brought into the experience of mankind." Beyond them all in importance are the new conceptions of the universe, and of the method of God's working in it, which can, with no exaggeration, be said to have imparted a wholly new spirit and quality to the human mind. By what it learned from Copernicus, it was given a new standpoint in thinking. By what it learned from Newton, it was given a new and larger grasp. By what it has learned from Darwin and Spencer it has been equipped with a new insight, and looks at even the mystery of life as a problem to be solved. "If we live in a world that is different from that which our ancestors knew, it is still more the fact that we think of a different universe, and feel differently in all our relations to it."—J. N. Larned, *Hist. of England for the Use of Schools, p.* 561.

Comparison of the Century with all preceding ages, as regards man's power over Nature.—"No one, so far as I am aware, has yet pointed out the altogether exceptional character of our advance in science and the arts, during the century which is now so near its close. In order to estimate its full importance and grandeur—more especially as regards man's increased power over nature, and the application of that power to the needs of his life to-day, with unlimited possibilities in the future—we must compare it, not with any preceding century, or even with the last millennium, but with the whole historical period,—perhaps even with the whole period that has elapsed since the stone age."

Such a comparison is made in the following lists of "the great inventions and discoveries of the two eras":

"Of the Nineteenth Century.	"Of all Preceding Ages.
1. Railways.	1. The Mariner's Compass.
2. Steam-ships.	2. The Steam Engine.
3. Electric Telegraphs.	3. The Telescope.
4. The Telephone.	4. The Barometer and Thermometer.
5. Lucifer Matches.	5. Printing.
6. Gas illumination.	6. Arabic numerals.
7. Electric lighting.	7. Alphabetical writing.
8. Photography.	8. Modern Chemistry founded.
9. The Phonograph.	9. Electric science founded.
10. Röntgen Rays.	10. Gravitation established.
11. Spectrum-analysis.	11. Kepler's Laws.
12. Anæsthetics.	12. The Differential Calculus.
13. Antiseptic Surgery.	13. The circulation of the blood.
14. Conservation of energy.	14. Light proved to have finite velocity.
15. Molecular theory of Gases.	15. The development of Geometry.
16. Velocity of Light directly measured, and Earth's Rotation experimentally shown.	
17. The uses of Dust.	
18. Chemistry, definite proportions.	
19. Meteors and the Meteoritic Theory.	
20. The Glacial Epoch.	
21. The Antiquity of Man.	
22. Organic Evolution established.	
23. Cell theory and Embryology.	
24. Germ theory of disease, and the function of the Leucocytes.	

"Of course these numbers are not absolute. Either series may be increased or diminished by taking account of other discoveries as of equal importance, or by striking out some which may be considered as below the grade of an important or epoch-making step in science or civilization. But the difference between the two lists is so large, that probably no competent judge would bring them to an equality. Again, it is noteworthy that nothing like a regular gradation is perceptible during the last three or four centuries. The eighteenth century, instead of showing some approximation to the wealth of discovery in our own age, is less remarkable than the seventeenth, having only about half the number of really great advances."—A. R. Wallace, *The Wonderful Century*, ch. 15 (*copyright. Dodd, Mead & Co., N. Y., quoted with permission*).

Difference of the Century from preceding ages.—"In the last 100 years the world has seen great wars, great national and social upheavals, great religious movements, great economic changes. Literature and art have had their triumphs and have permanently enriched the intellectual inheritance of our race. Yet, large as is the space which subjects like these legitimately fill in our thoughts, much as they will occupy the future historian, it is not among these that I seek for the most important and the most fundamental differences which separate the present from preceding ages. Rather is this to be found in the cumulative products of scientific research, to which no other period offers a precedent or a parallel. No single discovery, it may be, can be compared in its results to that of Copernicus; no single discoverer can be compared in genius to Newton; but, in their total effects, the advances made by the 19th century are not to be matched. Not only is the surprising increase of knowledge new, but the use to which it has been put is new also. The growth of industrial invention is not a fact we are permitted to forget. We do, however, sometimes forget how much of it is due to a close connection between theoretic knowledge and its utilitarian application which, in its degree, is altogether unexampled in the history of mankind. I suppose that, at this moment, if we were allowed a vision of the embryonic forces which are predestined most potently to affect the future of mankind, we should have to look for them not in the Legislature, nor in the Press, nor on the platform, nor in the schemes of practical statesmen, nor the dreams of political theorists, but in the laboratories of scientific students whose names are but little in the mouths of men, who cannot themselves forecast the results of their own labors, and whose theories could scarcely be understood by those whom they will chiefly benefit. . . .

"Marvellous as is the variety and ingenuity of modern industrial methods, they almost all depend in the last resort upon our supply of useful power; and our supply of useful power is principally provided for us by methods which, so far as I can see, have altered not at all in principle, and strangely little in detail, since the days of Watt. Coal, as we all know, is the chief reservoir of energy from which the world at present draws, and from which we in this country must always draw; but our main contrivance for utilizing it is the steam engine and, by its essential nature, the steam engine is extravagantly wasteful. So that, when we are told, as if it was something to be proud of, that this is the age of steam, we may admit the fact, but can hardly share the satisfaction. . . . We have, in truth, been little better than brilliant spendthrifts. Every new invention seems to throw a new strain upon the vast but not illimitable, resources of nature. Lord Kelvin is disquieted about our supply of oxygen; Sir William Crookes about our supply of nitrates. The problem of our coal supply is always with us. Sooner or later the stored-up resources of the world will be exhausted. Humanity, having used or squandered its capital, will thenceforth have to depend upon such current income as can be derived from that diurnal heat of the sun and the rotation of the earth till, in the sequence of the ages, these also begin to fail. . . .

"After all, however, it is not necessarily the material and obvious results of scientific discoveries which are of the deepest interest. They have affected changes more subtle and perhaps less obvious which are at least as worthy of our consideration and are at least as unique in the history of the civilized world. No century has seen so great a change in our intellectual apprehension of the world in which we live. Our whole point of view has changed. The mental framework in which we arrange the separate facts in the world of men and things is quite a new framework. The spectacle of the universe presents itself now in a wholly changed perspective. We not only see more, but we see differently. The discoveries in physics and in chemistry, which have borne their share in thus re-creating for us the evolution of the past, are in process of giving us quite new ideas as to the inner nature of that material whole of which the world's traversing space is but an insignificant part. Differences of quality once thought ultimate are constantly being resolved into differences of motion or configuration. What were once regarded as things are now known to be movement. . . . Plausible attempts have been made to reduce the physical universe, with its infinite variety, its glory of color and of form, its significance and its sublimity, to one homogeneous medium in which there are no distinctions to be discovered but distinction of movement or of stress. And although no such hypothesis can, I suppose, be yet accepted, the gropings of physicists after this, or some other not less audacious unification, must finally, I think, be crowned with success. The change of view which I have endeavored to indicate is purely scientific, but its consequences cannot be confined to science. How will they manifest themselves in other regions of human activity, in literature, in art, in religion?"—A. J. Balfour, *The Nineteenth Century* (*Address before the University Extension Students at Cambridge, Aug. 2, 1900*).

The intellectual and social trend of the Century.—"The two influences which have made the nineteenth century what it is seem to me to be the scientific spirit and the democratic spirit. Thus, the nineteenth century, singularly enough, is the great interpretative century both of nature and of the past, and at the same time the century of incessant and uprooting change in all that relates to the current life of men. It is also the century of national systems of popular education, and at the same time of nation-great armies; the century that has done more than any other to scatter men over the face of the earth, and to concentrate them in cities; the century of a universal suffrage that is based upon a belief in the inherent value of the individual; and the century of the corporation and the labor union, which in the domain of capital and of labor threaten to obliterate the individual. . . .

"The mind has been active in all fields during this fruitful century; but, outside of politics, it is to science that we must look for the thoughts that have shaped all other thinking. When von Helmholtz was in this country, a few years ago, he said that modern science was born when men ceased to summon nature to the support of theories already formed, and instead began to question nature for her facts, in order that they might thus discover the laws which these facts reveal. I do not know that it would be easy to sum up the scientific method, as the phrase runs, in simpler words. It would not be correct to say that this process was unknown before the present century; for there have been individual observers and students of nature in all ages. . . . But it is true that only in this century has this attitude toward nature become the uniform attitude of men of science. . . .

"One of the chief results of the scientific method as applied to nature and the study of the past is the change that it has wrought in the philosophic conception of nature and of human society. By the middle of the century, Darwin had given what has been held to be substantial proof of the theory of the development of higher forms out of lower in all living things; and since then, the doctrine of evolution, not as a body of exact teaching, but as a working theory, has obtained a mastery over the minds of men which has dominated all their studies and all their thinking. . . .

"Every public educational system of our day, broadly speaking, is the child of the nineteenth century. The educational system of Germany, which in its results has been of hardly less value to mankind than to Germany itself, dates from the reconstitution of the German universities after the battle of Jena. Whatever system France may have had before the Revolution went down in the cataclysm that destroyed the ancient régime, so that the educational system of France also dates from the Napoleonic period. In the United States, while the seeds of the public school system may have been planted in the eighteenth, or perhaps even in the seventeenth century, it has only been in the nineteenth century, with the development of the country, that our public school system has grown into what we now see; while in England, the system of national education, in a democratic sense, must be dated from 1870. . . . Out of the growth of the democratic principle has come the belief that it is worth while to educate all the children of the state; and out of the scientific method, which has led to the general acceptance of the evolutionary theory, has been developed the advance in educational method which is so marked a feature of the last decades of the century. . . .

"Not only has the scientific method furnished a philosophy of nature and of human life, but, by the great increase in man's knowledge of natural law to which it has led, it has resulted in endless inventions, and these, in turn, have changed the face of the world. . . . The rapid progress of invention during the century has been concident with one far-reaching change in the habits of society, the importance of which is seldom recognized. I refer to deposit banking. Of all the agencies that have effected the world in the nineteenth century, I am sometimes inclined to think that this is one of the most influential. If deposit banking may not be said to be the result of democracy, it certainly may be said that it is in those countries in which democracy is most dominant that deposit banking thrives best. . . . Some one has said that it would have been of no use to invent the railroad, the submarine cable, or the telephone at an earlier period of the world's history, for there would have been no money at command to make any one of them available before this modern banking system had made its appearance. If this be so, then indeed the part that has been played by deposit banking in the developments of the century cannot be overestimated.

"During the century the conditions of the world's commerce have been radically altered. It is not simply that the steamboat and the locomotive have taken the place of the sailing-ship and the horse; that the submarine cable has supplanted the mails; nor even that these agencies have led to such improvements in banking facilities that foreign commerce is done, for the most part, for hardly more than a brokerage upon the transaction. These are merely accidents of the situation. The fundamental factors have been the opening up of virgin soil in vast areas to the cultivation of man, and the discovery of how to create artificial cold, which makes it possible to transport for long distances produce that only a few years ago was distinctly classed as perishable. The net result of these influences has been to produce a world competition at every point of the globe. . . .

"Democracy, as a political theory, emphasizes the equality of men and the equal rights and privileges of all men before the law. The tendency of it has been, in this country, to develop in multitudes of men great individuality and self-reliance. Side by side with this tendency, however, we see the corporation supplanting the individual capitalist, and the trade union obliterating the individual laborer, as direct agents in the work of the world. Strange as this contrast is, both tendencies must be consistent with democracy, for the corporation and the trade union flourish most where democracy is most developed. Indeed, they seem to be successful and powerful just because democracy pours into them both its vital strength. . . .

"The tendency to democracy in politics is unquestionably the dominant political fact of the century. . . . Outside of Russia, and possibly even there, monarchical government in Europe is obliged to depend for its support upon the great body of the nation, instead of upon the power of the great and the noble. . . . In the United States, the century, though it began with a limited suffrage, ends with universal manhood suffrage, and even with woman suffrage in some of the Western States. . . . Undoubtedly, universal suffrage and the large immigration of people without any experience in self-government have given form to many of our problems; but I often think there is far too great a disposition among us to magnify the difficulties which these conditions present. . . . The fact is, in my judgment, that our problems arise not so much from universal suffrage as from the effect of the multiplication table applied to all the problems of life. . . . Any one building a house in the country, when he has dug a well has solved the problem of his water supply ; but to supply water for a great city calls for the outlay of millions of dollars, and for the employment of the best engineering talent in the land. Yet nothing has happened except that the problem has been magnified. Thus the difficulties created by the multiplication table are real ; so that the very enlargement of opportunity that democracy has brought with it has faced democracy with problems far harder than were formerly presented to any government. . . .

" To sum up, therefore, I should say that the trend of the century has been to a great increase in knowledge, which has been found to be, as of old, the knowledge of good and evil ; that this knowledge has become more and more the property of all men rather than of a few ; that, as a result, the very increase of opportunity has led to the magnifying of the problems with which humanity is obliged to deal ; and that we find ourselves, at the end of the century, face to face with problems of world-wide importance and utmost difficulty, and with no new means of coping with them other than the patient education of the masses of men."—Seth Low, *The Trend of the Century* (*Atlantic Monthly, August*, 1898).

Dominant lines in the intellectual development of the Century.—"The future historian of thought will no doubt regard the promulgation and the rapid triumph of evolutionist doctrines as the most remarkable phenomenon in the intellectual development of the nineteenth century."—Leslie Stephen, *Evolution and Religious Conceptions* (*Review of the Nineteenth Century, in New York Evening Post, Jan.* 12, 1901).

" In the briefest sketch of what the nineteenth century has done in literature, it is absolutely imperative to mention the publication of ' The Origin of Species ' [Darwin, 1859] and ' Principles of Psychology ' [Spencer, 1855], because, although neither work is written with an attractive elegance, each is the starting point of an intellectual and moral revolution so vast that every branch of life is affected by it, and literature itself—in its lightest forms—can no longer ignore the germinal forces with which evolution has quickened all our emotions."—Edmund Gosse, *A Century of English Literature* (*in the same*).

"To an earlier age knowledge was power, merely that and nothing more ; to us it is life and the 'summum bonum.' Emancipation from the bonds of self, of one's own prepossessions, importunately sought at the hands of that rational power before which all must ultimately bow—this is the characteristic that distinguishes all the great figures of nineteenth-century science from those of former periods."—Prof. Charles S. Peirce, *The Century's Great Men in Science* (*in the same*).

"The mark of the century has been a continuous attempt at a comprehensive understanding of nature, after the manner of Newton, but not limited or governed solely by his dynamical ideas. . . . The Newtonian laws of dynamics as applied to matter still hold, and will always hold, but they may no longer be fundamental or ultimate, they may be derivatives from a still deeper scheme : and it is towards this deeper scheme that physicists at present are groping. The realization of a need for some such scheme constitutes the chief philosophic feature of the latter part of the century."—Oliver J. Lodge, *The Scope and Tendencies of Physics* (*in the same*).

The failures of the Century.—Its sinful mismanagement of the powers which Science has given it.—"The Nineteenth Century . . . has been characterised by a marvellous and altogether unprecedented progress in knowledge of the universe and of its complex forces ; and also in the application of that knowledge to an infinite variety of purposes, calculated, if properly utilized, to supply all the wants of every human being, and to add greatly to the comforts, the enjoyments, and the refinements of life. The bounds of human knowledge have been so far extended that new vistas have opened to us in directions where it had been thought that we could never penetrate, and the more we learn the more we seem capable of learning in the ever-widening expanse of the universe. . . .

" But the more we realize the vast possibilities of human welfare which science has given us, the more we must recognise our total failure to make any adequate rational use of them. With ample power to supply to the fullest extent necessaries, comforts, and even luxuries for all, and at the same time allow ample leisure for intellectual pleasures and æsthetic enjoyments, we have yet so sinfully mismanaged our social economy as to give unprecedented and injurious luxury to the few, while millions are compelled to suffer a lifelong deficiency of the barest necessaries for a healthy existence. Instead of devoting the highest powers of our greatest men to remedy these evils, we see the governments of the most advanced nations arming their people to the teeth, and expending much of their wealth and all the resources of their science, in preparation for the destruction of life, of property, and of happiness.

" With ample knowledge of the sources of health, we allow, and even compel, the bulk of our population to live and work under conditions which greatly shorten life ; while every year we see from 50,000 to 100,000 infants done to death by our criminal neglect. In our mad race for wealth, we have made gold more sacred than human life ; we have made life so hard for the many, that suicide and insanity and crime are alike increasing. With all our labour-saving machinery and all our command over the forces of nature, the struggle for existence has become more fierce than ever before ; and year by year an ever-increasing proportion of our people sink into paupers' graves.

"Even more degrading, and more terrible in its consequences, is the unblushing selfishness of the greatest civilized nations. While boasting of their military power, and loudly proclaiming their Christianity, not one of them has raised a finger to save a Christian people, the remnant of an ancient civilization, from the most barbarous persecution, torture, and wholesale massacre. A hundred thousand Armenians murdered or starved to death while the representatives of the great powers coldly looked on—and prided themselves on their unanimity in all making the same useless protests—will surely be referred to by the historian of the future, as the most detestable combination of hypocrisy and inhumanity that the world has yet produced, and as the crowning proof of the utter rottenness of the boasted civilization of the Nineteenth Century. When the brightness of future ages shall have dimmed the glamour of our material progress, the judgment of history will surely be, that the ethical standard of our rulers was a deplorably low one, and that we were unworthy to possess the great and beneficent powers that science had placed in our hands.

"But although this century has given us so many examples of failure, it has also given us hope for the future. True humanity, the determination that the crying social evils of our time shall not continue; the certainty that they can be abolished; an unwavering faith in human nature, have never been so strong, so vigorous, so rapidly growing as they are to-day."—A. R. Wallace, *The Wonderful Century, ch.* 21 *(copyright, Dodd, Mead & Co., N. Y., quoted with permission).*

Expansion of the European races during the Century.—Changes in the distribution of political power.—Dominance of the Anglo-American peoples.—Rise of the United States of America to the highest rank.—At a dinner given by the Manchester Statistical Society, October 17, 1900, Sir Robert Giffen, the eminent statistician, made a notable speech on the political ideas which the statistics of the Nineteenth Century suggest. "The first of these was the prodigious rate at which the civilized world—the community of European nations and nations of European origin—was growing. The population of Europe and of nations of European origin like the United States might now be put at something over 500,000,000. The United States themselves might be put at nearly 80 millions; Russia in its recent census showed a population which must already have grown to about 135 millions; Germany about 55 millions; the United Kingdom, with the self-governing colonies of Canada and Australasia and the white population of South Africa, 55 millions; Austria-Hungary, 45 millions; France, 40 millions; Italy, 32 millions; Spain and Portugal, 25 millions; Scandinavian countries, ten millions; Holland and Belgium, ten millions; and other European countries, 20 millions. A century ago the corresponding figure to this 500,000,000 would not have been more than about 170,000,000. The economic development of the people had been even more marvellous. The wealth of the people all told, which would probably not have been reckoned at more than £5,000,000,000 at the beginning of the century, must be reckoned now by tens of thousands of millions.

"Again the development was for the most part not uniform among the European populations. It was most marked in the Anglo-American section. The increase here was from a population of not more than about 20 millions, which was the population of the United States and the United Kingdom together 100 years ago, to a population of not less than 130 millions at the present time. Russia and Germany also showed remarkable increases, but nothing like this. This astonishing growth of population meant a great change in the relative position of the European nations in the world—their relative weight in international politics. Practically the non-European races of the world had all the time been stationary, except in India, where the 'pax Bri-

tannica' had permitted the native population to expand. The result was that the forces of civilization, as against those of the black and yellow races, had become practically irresistible. The numbers were relatively far greater than ever they were before, and the economic force was indefinitely greater. A great change in the distribution of political power among European nations themselves was also indicated. The existence alone of the United States implied an immense change. If we considered that an empire like that of Britain had its strength rather diminished than increased by the possession of territories like India, then the United States having a larger European population than that of the British Empire might be considered the most powerful State in the world as far as population and resources were concerned. No doubt Russia had a much larger population, but the inferiority of the units was so great that the preeminence of the United States was not in question. Germany, Russia, and the United Kingdom had all grown, while France and Austria had by comparison remained stationary, so that now the great world Powers were four only—the United States, Britain, Russia, and Germany, with France a doubtful fifth. The extent of the revolution that had taken place in a century was evident, and obviously accounted for much that was going on in international politics.

"If the forces now in existence continue to operate as they had done in the past century for only a few more generations, the close of the coming century must witness a further transformation, whose beginnings would be apparent in the lifetime of some amongst us. It was a reasonable probability that unless some great internal change should take place in the ideas and conduct of the European races themselves, the population of 500 millions would in another century become one of 1,500 to 2,000 millions. The black and yellow races still remaining, as far as one could see, comparatively stationary, this would make a greatly changed world. The yellow peril, for instance, of which we heard so much, would have vanished, because the yellow races themselves would be so much outnumbered. What would be the 400 millions of China compared with 1,500 or 2,000 millions of Aryan race? Further progress must also be made in the redistribution of power among European nations. International politics would be more and more limited to the affairs of what were already the four great Powers—the United States, the United Kingdom, Germany, and Russia. The most serious problem would of course arise whether the dilemma stated by Malthus and hitherto put aside by the occupation of new lands, would at length become an urgently practical question. It was impossible not to wonder which of the two forces—the growth of population and the increase of the needs of the growing population on the one side, and the growth of invention and mechanical power in supplying human wants on the other side —would gain as time went on. Referring to the desire to secure new markets abroad, Sir Robert Giffen said that the figures with which he had been dealing pointed to quite another source of new markets. Surely there could be no lack of new customers if the 500 millions of the advanced races themselves were to be doubled in from 30 to 50 years and trebled or quadrupled in a century."—*London Times, Oct.* 18, 1900.

The lengthened average of human life.—" What has been the chief characteristic of the nineteenth century? No two critics agree, nor can they, because each prefers a different quality. One singles out science, another, invention, as the dominant trait. A third, who looks mainly at the political aspect of life, says democracy. Others, again, say pessimism, philanthropy, doubt, or toleration. So many features, so much diversity, argue at least for many-sidedness.

"There is one characteristic, however, which distinguishes the nineteenth century from all previous centuries—a characteristic which has become too common to attract the attention it deserves, although it really measures all the rest: this is longevity. During the past one hundred years the length of life of the average man in the United States and in the more civilized parts of Europe has increased from a little over 30 to about 40 years. A multitude of causes, mostly physical, have contributed to this result. Foremost among these should be placed (1) whatever may be included under the general term sanitation; (2) improved methods in medicine; and (3) the more regular habits of living which are the direct outcome of industrial life on a large scale.

"These are some of the evident means by which life has been lengthened. Inventions, which have made production cheap and the transportation of all products both cheap and easy, have had an influence too great to be computed. And no doubt much has been due to a general improvement in methods of government; although, in the main, there has been much less progress in practical government than is commonly supposed. No great railroad company or banking house or manufacturing corporation could prosper if its officers and employees were chosen and kept in office according to the system by which political offices, almost everywhere, are filled. 'None but experts wanted,' is the sign written over the entrance to every profession, trade, and occupation — except government.

"But, whatever governments have done or left undone, the fact to be insisted on here is, that the average man to-day lives almost ten years longer than his grandfather lived."—W. R. Thayer, *Longevity and Degeneration* (*Forum*, Feb., 1900).

The Musical Century.—"Music is the only one of the fine arts of which it can be said that it reached its highest development in the nineteenth century. It is the modern art par excellence; and while everybody has been told that it is the youngest of the arts, few realize how much is implied in that assertion."—Henry T. Finck, *The Musical Century* (*N. Y. Evening Post, Jan.* 12, 1901).

The Woman's Century.—"Victor Hugo predicted that the nineteenth century would be known as Woman's Century. The comparison of the woman of 1800 and the woman of 1900 offers abundant proof of the correctness of the prophecy."—Mrs. Carrie C. Catt, *Women in the Industries and Professions* (*N. Y. Evening Post, Jan.* 12, 1901).—"In 1900 a third of all the college students in the United States are women. Sixty per cent. of the pupils in the secondary schools, both public and private, are girls—i. e., more girls are preparing for college than boys. Women having in general more leisure than men, there is reason to expect that there will soon be more women than men in our colleges and graduate schools. The time, too, has passed when girls went to college to prepare themselves solely for teaching or for other bread-winning occupations. In considerable numbers they now seek intellectual resources and the enrichment of their private lives. Thus far between 50 and 60 per cent. of women college graduates have at some time taught. In the country at large more than 70 per cent. of the teaching is done by women, in the North Atlantic portion over 80 per cent. Even in the secondary schools, public and private, more women than men are teaching, though in all other countries the advanced instruction of boys is exclusively in the hands of men. Never before has a nation intrusted all the school training of the vast majority of its future population, men as well as women, to women alone."—Mrs. Alice F. Palmer, *The Higher Education of Women* (*in the same*).

The Age of Steel succeeding the Age of Iron.—"The age of iron, which passed away during the last century, was succeeded by the age of Bessemer steel, which enjoyed a reign of only thirty-six years, beginning, as it did, in 1864, and is in turn now passing away to be succeeded by the age of Siemens open-hearth steel. Already the product of open-hearth is far beyond that of Bessemer in Britain, and such the writer ventures to predict will soon be the case in the United States."—Andrew Carnegie, *The Development of Steel Manufacture* (*N. Y. Evening Post, Jan.* 12, 1901).

As the "Age of Steam." See (in vol. 4) STEAM ENGINE, STEAM LOCOMOTION, etc.; and (in this vol.) SCIENCE, RECENT: MECHANICAL.

As the "Electric Age." See (in vol. 2) ELECTRICAL DISCOVERY; and (in this vol.) SCIENCE, RECENT: ELECTRICAL.

NIPPUR, Explorations of the ruins of. See (in this vol.) ARCHÆOLOGICAL RESEARCH: BABYLONIA: AMERICAN EXPLORATION.

NIUCHWANG.—"Niuchwang, while a comparatively small city of but 60,000 population, is of especial importance to the United States as a treaty port. It is located at the extreme north of the Gulf of Pechili, considerably farther north than Tientsin, and is of especial importance to the United States because of the demand for goods from this country in that section. . . . The proposed Russian railway line, which is projected through Manchuria and the province of Shingking to the port of Port Arthur, passes near Niuchwang and is to be connected by a short line.

Another line, to be built by British capital, will connect Niuchwang with Shanhaikwan, which is already in railway connection with Peking, the capital of the Empire."—*United States, Bureau of Statistics, Monthly Summary, March,* 1899, *p.* 2196.

Russian occupation. See (in this vol.) MANCHURIA: A. D. 1900.

NORFOLK ISLAND: Change of government. See (in this vol.) AUSTRALIA (NEW SOUTH WALES): A. D. 1896.

NORTH CAROLINA: A. D. 1897-1899.—Local Dispensary Laws.—An Act applying the South Carolina "dispensary" system of regulation for the liquor traffic (see, in this vol., SOUTH

CAROLINA: A. D. 1892–1899) to Fayetteville was passed by the Legislature in 1897, and several smaller towns secured local legislation to the same effect in 1899; but attempts to carry a general dispensary law for the State were defeated.

A. D. 1898.—Race war in Wilmington.— Wilmington, N. C., was the scene, in November, of what can only be called a fierce revolution, whereby the city government, dominated by the colored population, which outnumbered the white, was violently overturned by the latter. The race conflict was precipitated by an article in a Republican newspaper, edited by a negro, which reflected on the honor of some of the white women, and caused wild excitement among the white men. The offending newspaper office was destroyed and its editor fled. Resistance being offered, furious fighting occurred, in which a considerable number of negroes was killed, many were wounded, and hundreds were driven by terror from the town. White Republican officials were also expelled or took to flight, and their opponents secured control of city affairs.

A. D. 1900.—Constitutional amendment for the qualification of the suffrage.—By a constitutional amendment, adopted in August, 1900, the following qualification of the suffrage was established:

"SEC. 4. Every person presenting himself for registration shall be able to read and write any section of the constitution in the English language : and, before he shall be entitled to vote, he shall have paid, on or before the 1st day of May of the year in which he proposes to vote, his poll tax for the previous year as prescribed by Article V, section 1, of the constitution. But no male person who was, on January 1, 1867, or at any time prior thereto, entitled to vote under the laws of any State in the United States wherein he then resided, and no lineal descend-

ant of any such person, shall be denied the right to register and vote at any election in this State by reason of his failure to possess the educational qualification herein prescribed, provided he shall have registered in accordance with the terms of this section prior to December, 1908. The general assembly shall provide for the registration of all persons entitled to vote without the educational qualifications herein prescribed, and shall, on or before November 1, 1908, provide for the making of a permanent record of such registration, and all persons so registered shall forever thereafter have the right to vote in all elections by the people in this State, unless disqualified under section 2 of this article : Provided, Such person shall have paid his poll tax as above required."

NORTHWEST TERRITORIES, Canadian: Self-government granted. See (in this vol.) CANADA : A. D. 1897 (OCTOBER).

NORWAY. See (in this vol.) SWEDEN AND NORWAY.

NOVA SCOTIA. See (in this vol.) CANADA.

NOVA ZEMBLA, Recent exploration of. See (in this vol.) POLAR EXPLORATION, 1895, 1896, 1897, 1900.

NUFFAR, or NIFFER, Explorations at. See (in this vol.) ARCHÆOLOGICAL RESEARCH : BABYLONIA : AMERICAN EXPLORATION.

NUPÉ, British subjugation of. See (in this vol.) AFRICA : A. D. 1897 (NIGERIA).

NUREMBERG: A. D. 1900.—Remarkable growth in five years. See (in this vol.) GERMANY : A. D. 1900 (DECEMBER).

NYASSALAND. See (in this vol.) BRITISH CENTRAL AFRICA PROTECTORATE.

O.

OIL RIVERS PROTECTORATE, The. See (in this vol.) NIGERIA : A. D. 1882–1899.

OLD-AGE INSURANCE: In Germany. See (in this vol.) GERMANY : A. D. 1897–1900.

OLD-AGE PENSIONS: In New South Wales. See (in this vol.) AUSTRALIA (NEW SOUTH WALES): A. D. 1900.
In New Zealand. See (in this vol.) NEW ZEALAND : A. D. 1899 ; and AUSTRALIA : RECENT EXTENSIONS OF DEMOCRACY.
The question in England. See (in this vol.) ENGLAND : A. D. 1896 ; and 1899–1900.

OLNEY, Richard: Correspondence with Lord Salisbury on the Venezuela boundary question. See (in this vol.) VENEZUELA : A. D. 1895 (JULY), and (NOVEMBER).

OLYMPIC GAMES, Revival of. See (in this vol.) ATHENS : A. D. 1896.

OMAHA : A. D. 1898.—The Trans-Mississippi Exposition.—A highly successful Trans-Mississippi Exposition was opened on the 1st of June and closed on the last day of October, having been attended by 2,600,000 people. Buildings and grounds were prepared with beautiful effect, at a cost of $2,500,000.

OMDURMAN : Capital of the Khalifa.— Capture by the Anglo-Egyptian Army. See (in this vol.) EGYPT : A. D. 1885–1896 ; and 1897–1898.

ONTARIO. See (in this vol.) CANADA.

"OPEN DOOR," The commercial policy of the. See (in this vol.) CHINA : A. D. 1899–1900 (SEPTEMBER—FEBRUARY).

OPIUM COMMISSION, Report of the. See (in this vol.) INDIA : A. D. 1895 (APRIL).

ORANGE FREE STATE: A. D. 1895.— Proposed federal union with the Transvaal. See (in this vol.) AFRICA : A. D. 1895 (ORANGE FREE STATE).
A. D. 1897.—Treaty with the South African Republic. See (in this vol.) SOUTH AFRICA (ORANGE FREE STATE AND TRANSVAAL): A. D. 1897 (APRIL).
A. D. 1899-1900.—Making common cause with the South African Republic.—War with Great Britain. See (in this vol.) SOUTH AFRICA (ORANGE FREE STATE): A. D. 1899 (SEPTEMBER —OCTOBER), and after.
A. D. 1900 (May.)—Proclamation of annexation to the British dominions. See (in this vol.) SOUTH AFRICA (ORANGE FREE STATE): A. D. 1900 (MAY).

OSMAN DIGNA. See (in this vol.) EGYPT: A. D. 1885–1896; 1897–1898; and 1899–1900.

OTIS, General: Reports **as** Military Governor of the Philippines. See (in this vol.) PHILIPPINE ISLANDS: A. D. 1898 (AUGUST—DECEMBER).

OTTAWA: A. D. 1900.—Great **fire.**—The city of Ottawa, capital of the Dominion of Canada, and the lumber manufacturing town of Hull, on the opposite side of the Ottawa River, were both devastated, on the 26th of April, by one of the most destructive fires of the century. It originated in the upsetting of a lamp in a dwelling in Hull. This was at half-past ten o'clock in the morning. A big gale blowing from the northeast made quick work of the in-flammable houses in Hull, and by twelve o'clock the flames had reached the river-bank and leaped across to the Ottawa side. The fire then retraced its steps in Hull, and destroyed a group of factories. It "blazed a crescent-shaped path five miles long and a mile wide, destroying in its journey the public buildings and the residential part of Hull, the industrial area of the Chaudiere, and the suburbs of the Ottawa laboring classes at Mechanicsburg, Rochesterville, and Hintonburg. Fully 15,000 people were rendered homeless, and $15,000,000 worth of property was annihilated."— *Canadian Magazine, July,* 1900.

OTTOMAN BANK: Attack **of** Armenian revolutionists at Constantinople. See (in this vol.) TURKEY: A. D. 1896 (AUGUST).

P.

PAARDEBERG, Battle of. See (in this vol.) SOUTH AFRICA (THE FIELD OF WAR): A. D. 1900 (JANUARY—FEBRUARY).

PACT OF HALEPA, The. See (in this vol.) TURKEY: A. D. 1896.

PAGO PAGO: Acquisition by **the** United States. See(in this vol.) SAMOAN ISLANDS.

PALESTINE: A. D. 1897-1901.—The Zionist movement for **Jewish** colonization. See (in this vol.) JEWS: A. D. 1897–1901.
A. D. **1898.**—Visit of **the** German Emperor. See (in this vol.) GERMANY: A. D. 1898 (OCTOBER—NOVEMBER).
A. D. **1901.**—Turkish restriction **on** Jewish visits. See (in this vol.) JEWS: A. D. 1901.

PALMER, General John M.: Candidacy for the American Presidency in **1896.** See (in this vol.) UNITED STATES OF AM.: A. D. 1896 (JUNE—NOVEMBER).

PAMIR REGION, The: Anglo-Russian agreement concerning. See (in this vol.) AFGHANISTAN: A. D. 1895.

PAMPANGAS, The. See (in this vol.) PHILIPPINE ISLANDS: THE NATIVE INHABITANTS.

PANA, Riotous coal-mining strike **at.** See (in this vol.) INDUSTRIAL DISTURBANCES: A. D. 1898.

PANAMA CANAL, The: A. D. 1900. See (in vol. 4.) PANAMA CANAL; and (in this vol.) CANAL, INTEROCEANIC: A. D. 1900 (NOVEMBER).

PAN-AMERICAN EXPOSITION, The. See (in this vol.) BUFFALO: A. D. 1901.

PANGASINANS, The. See (in this vol.) PHILIPPINE ISLANDS: THE NATIVE INHABITANTS.

PAN-GERMANIC UNION. See (in this vol.) AUSTRIA-HUNGARY: A. D. 1901.

PAPACY.

A. D. 1894.—Conference with **Eastern Patriarchs.**—A conference of Eastern Patriarchs to consider the reunion of the Eastern Churches (Armenian, Maronite, Melchite, etc.) with the Church of Rome was opened at the Vatican, in October, under the presidency of the Pope. The meeting had no result.
A. D. 1894-1895.—The Hungarian **Ecclesiastical Laws.** See (in this vol.) AUSTRIA-HUNGARY: A. D. 1894–1895.
A. D. 1896 (March).—Resumption of **authority** over the Coptic Church.—The authority of the Pope over the Coptic Church was resumed on the 30th of March, 1896, after a suspension of four centuries, by the re-establishment of the Catholic Patriarchate of Alexandria. Bishop Macarius was appointed Patriarch and two bishops were appointed for Upper and Lower Egypt.
A. D. 1896 (September).—Decision on the invalidity of Anglican orders.—In September, 1896, the final decision of the Vatican, on a re-opened question as to the validity of ordinations under the ritual of the Church of England, was announced by Pope Leo XIII. in a bull which declares: "After long study, I must confirm the decree of my predecessors, that all ordinations made under the Anglican rite are absolutely invalid." Soon after the decision was announced, a writer in the "Contemporary Review" gave the following account of circumstances connected with it:

"The question of Anglican Orders was taken up in connection with the appeal for union made by Leo XIII. in the Encyclical 'Præclara' of 1894, and more particularly in his letter to the English people. The group of Anglicans of whom Lord Halifax is the spokesman took this appeal seriously, and ever since that time negotiations have been going on more or less continuously between them and the Vatican. . . . The idea of an incorporate union, so dear to Lord Halifax, and so much favoured in the first instance by the Pope, could only be carried out on the basis of a prior admission that the Anglican Church had an existence as a Church, and was therefore in a position to discuss a union with the Roman Church. Once recognise the validity of her Orders, and it would be possible to go into conference as to the points of difference between the two Churches, and the means of coming to an agreement. It is quite certain that the Pope entered heartily into these views. The Abbé Duchesne was accordingly deputed to inquire into the validity of the Anglican Orders, and was well aware that a favourable conclusion would be very well received. This was before the Abbé was put at the head of the French College at Rome. He made his investigation, arrived at the conclusion that the Orders were valid, sent his report to the Vatican, and received from Cardinal Rampolla a letter of thanks and congratulations, together with a grand silver medal, which the Holy Father sent him as a sign of his satisfaction and particular goodwill. All this happened in the winter of 1894-95.

"In the autumn of 1895 the idea of union was in higher favour at the Vatican than ever. Cardinal Rampolla encouraged the foundation of the 'Revue Anglo-Romaine,' a journal devoted to the treatment of problems concerning the union of Churches, and particularly the re-union of the Anglican Church, and edited by the Abbé Portal, a French priest, and a personal friend of Lord Halifax. This movement in favour of union was, however, regarded by the Catholics in England with no little apprehension and mistrust, and their opposition alone would have been sufficient to wreck it for the time being. Cardinal Vaughan viewed the idea of incorporate union as a chimera, but treated the efforts to realise it as a real danger. . . . Leo, who would fain have maintained an attitude of judicial impartiality, soon found out that he must take a side: he must either definitely encourage the hopes of the Anglicans, or he must do something to calm the excited fears of the Catholics. Even at Rome, if we except the Pope and Cardinal Rampolla, who for a long time fondly hoped that they could make this policy of union a means of accomplishing very large results, theological opinion was adverse to the validity. Were there not, indeed, decisions of the Sacred Congregations which settled the dispute? There were, but in spite of them all the Pope was not disabused of his fancy. Compelled at last to take some action, he named a Commission of theologians, which sat at Rome in the spring of the present year [1896], under the presidency of Cardinal Mazzella. . . . The theologians set forth the arguments which favoured their respective views; papers were written, and, after a series of deliberations, a report was placed in the hands of the Pope. No conclusion was arrived at; none could be come to in this preliminary assembly. Only the materials for a judgment were worked out, in case his Holiness should think fit to pronounce a decision. . . . The Pope himself tells us, in the Bull Apostolicæ Curæ, that he left the final examination of the question to the congregation of cardinals called 'Suprema.' . . . The 'Suprema' met on July 16, under the presidency of the Pope. All the cardinals were of opinion that the matter had been long since decided, and that the debates in the preliminary commission had served to show how wise the decision had been. . . . The Bull declaring Anglican Orders null and void was published about the middle of September." — Catholicus, *The Pope and the Anglicans: The Policy of the Bull* (*Contemporary Review*, Dec., 1896).

A. D. 1897.—Influence in Austria. See (in this vol.) AUSTRIA-HUNGARY: A. D. 1897.

A. D. 1898 (January).—Encyclical Letter of Pope Leo XIII. on the Manitoba School Question. See (in this vol.) CANADA: A. D. 1898 (JANUARY).

A. D. 1899.—Secession of German Catholics in Austria from the Church. See (in this vol.) AUSTRIA-HUNGARY: A. D. 1899-1900.

A. D. 1899 (Jannary).—Encyclical Letter of Pope Leo XIII. condemning certain opinions "called by some 'Americanism.'"—The following passages are from the translation of an encyclical letter addressed, on the 22d of January, 1899, by Pope Leo XIII. to Cardinal Gibbons, for communication to the bishops and clergy of the Catholic Church in America:

"To Our Beloved Son, James, Cardinal Gibbons, Cardinal Priest of the Title Sancta Maria, Beyond the Tiber, Archbishop of Baltimore: . . . We have often considered and admired the noble gifts of your nation which enable the American people to be alive to every good work which promotes the good of humanity and the splendor of civilization. Although this letter is not intended, as preceding ones, to repeat the words of praise so often spoken, but rather to call attention to some things to be avoided and corrected; still because it is conceived in that same spirit of apostolic charity which has inspired all our letters, we shall expect that you will take it as another proof of our love; the more so because it is intended to suppress certain contentions which have arisen lately among you to the detriment of the peace of many souls.

"It is known to you, beloved son, that the biography of Isaac Thomas Hecker, especially through the action of those who undertook to translate or interpret it in a foreign language, has excited not a little controversy, on account of certain opinions brought forward concerning the way of leading Christian life. We, therefore, on account of our apostolic office, having to guard the integrity of the faith and the security of the faithful, are desirous of writing to you more at length concerning this whole matter.

"The underlying principle of these new opinions is that, in order to more easily attract those who differ from her, the Church should shape her teachings more in accord with the spirit of the age and relax some of her ancient severity and make some concessions to new opinions. Many think that these concessions should be made not only in regard to ways of living, but even in regard to doctrines which belong to the deposit of the faith. They contend that it would be opportune, in order to gain those who differ from us, to omit certain points of her teaching which are of lesser importance, and to tone down the meaning which the Church has always attached to them. It does not need many words, beloved son, to prove the falsity of these ideas if the nature and origin of the doctrine which the Church proposes are recalled to mind. The Vatican Council says concerning this point: 'For the doctrine of faith which God has revealed has not been proposed, like a philosophical invention to be perfected by human ingenuity, but has been delivered as a divine deposit to the Spouse of Christ to be faithfully kept and infallibly declared. Hence that meaning of the sacred dogmas is perpetually to be retained which our Holy Mother, the Church, has once declared, nor is that meaning ever to be departed from under the pretense or pretext of a deeper comprehension of them.'—Constitutis de Fide Catholica, Chapter iv. . . .

"Let it be far from anyone's mind to suppress for any reason any doctrine that has been handed down. Such a policy would tend rather to separate Catholics from the Church than to bring in those who differ. There is nothing closer to our heart than to have those who are separated from the fold of Christ return to it, but in no other way than the way pointed out by Christ.

"The rule of life laid down for Catholics is not of such a nature that it cannot accommodate itself to the exigencies of various times and places. The Church has, guided by her Divine Master, a kind and merciful spirit, for which reason from the very beginning she has been what St. Paul said of himself: 'I became all things to all men that I might save all.'

"History proves clearly that the Apostolic See, to which has been intrusted the mission not only of teaching but of governing the whole Church, has continued 'in one and the same doctrine, one and the same sense, and one and the same judgment.'—Const. de fide, Chapter iv.

"But in regard to ways of living she has been accustomed to so yield that, the divine principle of morals being kept intact, she has never neglected to accommodate herself to the character and genius of the nations which she embraces. Who can doubt that she will act in this same spirit again if the salvation of souls requires it? In this matter the Church must be the judge, not private men who are often deceived by the appearance of right. In this, all who wish to escape the blame of our predecessor, Pius the Sixth, must concur. He condemned as injurious to the Church and the spirit of God who guides her the doctrine contained in proposition lxxviii of the Synod of Pistoia, 'that the discipline made and approved by the Church should be submitted to examination, as if the Church could frame a code of laws useless or heavier than human liberty can bear.'

"But, beloved son, in this present matter of which we are speaking, there is even a greater danger and a more manifest opposition to Catholic doctrine and discipline in that opinion of the lovers of novelty, according to which they hold such liberty should be allowed in the Church, that her supervision and watchfulness being in some sense lessened, allowance be granted the faithful, each one to follow out more freely the leading of his own mind and the trend of his own proper activity. They are of opinion that such liberty has its counterpart in the newly given civil freedom which is now the right and the foundation of almost every secular state.

"In the apostolic letters concerning the constitution of states, addressed by us to the bishops of the whole Church, we discussed this point at length; and there set forth the difference existing between the Church, which is a divine society, and all other social human organizations which depend simply on free will and choice of men. It is well, then, to particularly direct attention to the opinion which serves as the argument in behalf of this greater liberty sought for and recommended to Catholics.

"It is alleged that now the Vatican decree concerning the infallible teaching authority of the Roman Pontiff having been proclaimed that nothing further on that score can give any solicitude, and accordingly, since that has been safeguarded and put beyond question a wider and freer field both for thought and action lies open to each one. But such reasoning is evidently faulty, since, if we are to come to any conclusion from the infallible teaching authority of the Church, it should rather be that no one should wish to depart from it and moreover that the minds of all being leavened and directed thereby, greater security from private error would be enjoyed by all. And further, those who avail themselves of such a way of reasoning seem to depart seriously from the over-ruling wisdom of the Most High—which wisdom, since it was pleased to set forth by most solemn decision the authority and supreme teaching rights of this Apostolic See—willed that decision precisely in order to safeguard the minds of the Church's children from the dangers of these present times.

"These dangers, viz., the confounding of license with liberty, the passion for discussing and pouring contempt upon any possible subject, the assumed right to hold whatever opinions one pleases upon any subject and to set them forth in print to the world, have so wrapped minds in darkness that there is now a greater need of the Church's teaching office than ever before, lest people become unmindful both of conscience and of duty.

"We indeed, have no thought of rejecting everything that modern industry and study has produced; so far from it that we welcome to the patrimony of truth and to an ever-widening scope of public well-being whatsoever helps toward the progress of learning and virtue. Yet all this, to be of any solid benefit, nay, to have a real existence and growth, can only be on the condition of recognizing the wisdom and authority of the Church. . . .

"From the foregoing it is manifest, beloved son, that we are not able to give approval to those views which, in their collective sense, are called by some 'Americanism.' But if by this name are to be understood certain endowments of mind which belong to the American people, just as other characteristics belong to various other nations, and if, moreover, by it is designated your political condition and the laws and customs by which you are governed, there is no reason to take exception to the name. But if this is to be so understood that the doctrines which have been adverted to above are not only indicated, but exalted, there can be no manner of doubt that our venerable brethren, the bishops of America, would be the first to repudiate and condemn it as being most injurious to themselves and to their country. For it would give rise to the suspicion that there are among you some who conceive and would have the Church in America to be different from what it is in the rest of the world.

"But the true church is one, as by unity of doctrine, so by unity of government, and she is catholic also. Since God has placed the centre and foundation of unity in the chair of Blessed Peter, she is rightly called the Roman Church, for 'where Peter is, there is the church.' Wherefore, if anybody wishes to be considered a real Catholic, he ought to be able to say from his heart the self-same words which Jerome addressed to Pope Damasus; 'I, acknowledging no other leader than Christ, am bound in fellowship with Your Holiness: that is, with the chair of Peter. I know that the church was built upon him as its rock, and that whosoever gathereth not with you, scattereth.' . . ."—*American Catholic Quarterly Review, April*, 1899.

A. D. 1900 (September—October).—Church and State in Austria. See (in this vol.) AUSTRIA-HUNGARY : A. D. 1900 (SEPTEMBER—DECEMBER).

A. D. 1900 (December).—Pope Leo XIII. on the French Associations Bill. See (in this vol.) FRANCE : A. D. 1901 (JANUARY).

A. D. 1900-1901.—Proclamation of the Universal Jubilee of the Holy Year Nineteen Hundred.—Its extension for six months.—The following is the text of the Papal proclamation of the Universal Jubilee, in its English translation, as published in the "American Catholic Quarterly Review " :

" To all the Faithful of Christ who shall read these Letters, Health and Apostolic Benediction. The century, which, by the grace of God, we have ourselves seen almost from its commencement, draws rapidly to its close. Willingly have we followed the institutions of our predecessors in so ordering things that they may redound in the good of all Christian peoples, and which may be perhaps for them the last proof of our care to the government of the Sovereign Pontificate. We speak of the Great Jubilee introduced in ancient times among Christian customs and observed by our predecessors, who bestowed upon the years of general jubilee the title of the Holy Year, because it was usual for such a year to be blessed by a greater number of holy ceremonies, as these furnish the most copious means of help for the correction of morals and the leading of souls to sanctity.

" We have ourselves seen with our own eyes the fruitful result of the last solemn celebration of the Holy Year. It was in the Pontificate of Leo XII, and we were as yet in the years of our youth. It was truly a grand sight to see then the manifestations of religious fervor in Rome. We can remember as if the scene were still before our eyes, the immense concourse of pilgrims, the multitudes which flocked processionally to one or other of the great basilicas, the sacred orators who preached in the public streets, and the most frequented quarters of the city resounding with the Divine praises. The Sovereign Pontiff himself, with a numerous suite of Cardinals and in the sight of all the people, gave a noble example of piety and charity.

" From such thoughts as these we turn with renewed sorrow to the times in which we now live ; for such practices of piety, when without hindrance they were fulfilled under the eyes of all the citizens, augmented admirably the fervor and piety of the whole people ; but now, on account of the changed condition of Rome, it is impossible to renew them, for in order to do so in any measure we must depend upon the arbitration of others., But however that may be, God, who ever blesses salutary counsels, will concede—such is our hope—success to this our design, undertaken solely for Him and for His glory. At what do we aim or what do we wish? Nothing else truly than to render more easy the way of eternal salvation to the souls confided to us, and for this end to administer to the infirm of spirit those remedies which it has pleased our Lord Jesus Christ to place in our hands. This administration seems to us not alone a duty of our apos-

tolic office, but a duty which is peculiarly necessary to our times. The present age, however, cannot be said to be sterile, either in regard to good works or to Christian virtues. Thanks be to God, we have examples of both in abundance, nor is there any virtue, however lofty and arduous its attainment and practice, in which many are not found to signalize themselves, because it is a power proper to the Christian religion, Divinely founded, inexhaustible and perpetual, to generate and nourish virtue. Yet, casting our eyes around, we see, on the other hand, with what blindness, with what persistent error, whole peoples are hurrying to eternal ruin. And this thought strikes bitterly to our heart—how many Christians, led away by the license of hearing and of thought, absorbing with avidity the intoxicating errors of false doctrine, go on day by day dissipating and destroying the grand gift of the faith. Hence arise repugnance to Christian living, that insatiable appetite for the things of this world, and hence cares and thoughts alienated from God and rooted in the world. It is almost impossible to express in words the damage which has already accrued from this iniquitous source to the very foundations of society. The minds of men ordinarily rebellious, the blind tendency of popular cupidity, hidden perils, tragical crimes, are nothing more to those who seek their source and cause than the unrestrained strife to possess and enjoy the goods of this world.

" It is of supreme importance, therefore, to public no less than private life, to admonish men as to the duties of their state, to arouse souls steeped in forgetfulness of duty, to recall to the thought of their own salvation those who run imminent risk of perishing and of losing through their negligence and pride those celestial and unchangeable rewards for the possession of which we are born. This is the aim of the Holy Year. The Church, mindful only of her intrinsic benignity and mercy as a most tender Mother, studies at this time, with love and by every means within her ample power, to re-conduct souls to better counsels and to promote in each works of expiation by means of penance and emendation of life. To this end, multiplying prayers and augmenting the fervor of the faithful, she seeks to appease the outraged majesty of God and to draw down His copious and celestial gifts. She opens wide the rich treasury of indulgences, of which she is the appointed dispenser, and exhorts the whole of Christianity to the firm hope of pardon. She is purely intent upon vanquishing with unconquerable love and sweetness the most rebellious wills. How, then, may we not hope to obtain, with God's help, rich fruits and profuse, and such as are most adapted to the present needs ?

" Several extraordinary solemnities, the notices of which we believe to be already sufficiently diffused, and which will serve in some manner to consecrate the end of the nineteenth century and the beginning of the twentieth, greatly increase the advantage of the opportunity now given. We speak of the honors to be rendered at this time in every part of the world to Jesus Christ as our Redeemer. On this account we were profuse in our approbation and praise of a project which had its source in the piety of private individuals, and, in fact, what could be more holy and salutary? All that which man should hope for and desire is contained in the

347

only-begotten Son of God, our Salvation, Life, and Resurrection. To desire to abandon Him is to desire eternal perdition. We could never silence adoration, praise, thanksgiving due to our Lord Jesus Christ, and without intermission they should be repeated everywhere, for in every place no thanksgiving, no honor, can be so great but that it may be increased. Our age produces perhaps many men who are forgetful and ungrateful, who ordinarily respond to the mercy of their Divine Saviour with disdain and to His gifts with offenses and injuries. Certainly the lives of many are so far removed from His laws and His precepts as to argue in themselves ungrateful and malicious souls. And what shall we say to see renewed again in these times and not once alone, the blasphemy of the Arian heresy regarding the Divinity of Jesus Christ. Courage, then, and to work, all you who with this new and most beautiful proposition seek to excite the piety of the people to new fervor. Do what you can in such manner that you impede not the course of the Jubilee and the appointed solemnities. Let it be added that in the forthcoming manifestations of faith and religion this special intention shall be kept in view—hatred of all that which within our memory has been impiously said or done, especially against the Divine Majesty of our Lord Jesus Christ, and to satisfy publicly for the injuries publicly inflicted upon Him. Now if we are really in earnest, we must know that to repent of evil done, and, having implored peace and pardon of God, to exercise ourselves with great diligence, in the duties necessary to virtue, and to assume those we have cast aside, is the means of satisfaction most desirable and assured, and which bears upon it the impress of truth. Since the Holy Year offers to all the opportunities which we have touched on in the beginning, it is a necessary provision that the Christian people enter upon it full of courage and of hope.

"For which reason, raising our eyes to heaven and praying from our heart that God, so rich in mercy, would vouchsafe to concede benignly His blessing and favor to our desires and works, and would illuminate with His Divine light the minds of all men, and move their souls to conform with His holy will and inestimable goodness, We, following in this the example of the Roman Pontiffs, our predecessors, with the assent of the Cardinals of the Holy Roman College, our Venerable Brethren, in virtue of these letters, with the authority of Christ, of the blessed Peter and Paul, and with our own authority, order and promulgate from this hour the great and universal jubilee, which will commence in this holy city of Rome at the first Vespers of the Nativity of our Lord Jesus Christ of the year 1899, and which will close at first Vespers of the Nativity of our Lord of the year 1900. May all redound to the glory of God, the salvation of souls, and the good of the Church. During this year of jubilee we concede and impart mercifully in our Lord full indulgence, remission and pardon of sin to all faithful Christians of either sex, who, being truly penitent shall confess and communicate, visiting devoutly the Roman basilicas of SS. Peter and Paul, St. John Lateran, and St. Mary Major, at least once a day for twenty days continuously or at intervals; that is, the obligation is to be fulfilled between the first Vespers of each day and the last Vespers of the day following, whether the Faithful be citizens of Rome or not, if they are residing permanently in Rome. If they come to Rome as pilgrims, then they must visit the said basilicas in the same manner for ten days, praying devoutly to God for the exaltation of Holy Church, for the extirpation of heresies, for peace and concord amongst Christian princes, and for the salvation of the whole Christian people.

"And since it may happen to many that with all their good-will they cannot or can only in part carry out the above, being either, while in Rome or on their journey, impeded by illness or other legitimate causes, we, taking into account their good-will, can, when they are truly repentant and have duly confessed and communicated, concede to them the participation in the same indulgences and remission of sins as if they had actually visited the basilicas on the days appointed. Rome, therefore, invites you lovingly to her bosom, beloved children, from all parts of the world, who have means of visiting her. Know also that to a good Catholic in this sacred time it is fitting that he come to Rome guided purely by Christian faith, and that he should renounce especially the satisfaction of sight-seeing merely idle or profane, turning his soul rather to those things which predispose him to religion and piety. And that which tends greatly so to predispose him, if he look within, is the natural character of the city, a certain character divinely impressed upon her, and not to be changed by human means, nor by any act of violence. For Jesus Christ, the Saviour of the world, chose only, amongst all its cities, that of Rome to be the centre of an action more than earthly, cousecrating it to Himself. Here He placed, and not without long and careful preparation, the throne of His own empire; here He commanded that the see of His Vicar should be raised to the perpetuity of time; here He willed that the light of revealed truth should be jealously and inviolably guarded, and that from here light should be diffused throughout the whole earth in such a manner that those who are alienated from the faith of Rome are alienated from Christ. The religious monuments raised by our fathers, the singular majesty of her temples, the tomb of the Apostles, the Catacombs of the martyrs, all serve to increase the aspect of holiness and to impress those who visit her in the spirit of faith. Whosoever knows the voice of such monuments feels that he is no pilgrim in a foreign city, but a citizen in his own, and by God's grace he will realize this fact at his going, more forcibly than at his coming.

"We wish, in order that these present letters may be brought more easily under the notice of all, that printed copies, signed by a public notary and furnished with the seal of some ecclesiastical dignitary, shall be received with the same faith as would be given to the original by those who have heard or read it.

"To no one will it be lawful to alter any word of this our disposition, promulgation, concession, and will, or to rashly oppose it. If any should presume to make any such attempt, let them know that they incur thereby the indignation of God Almighty and of His Apostles Peter and Paul.

"Given at St. Peter's, Rome, on the 11th of May, in the year of the Incarnation of our Lord 1899, and the 22d of our Pontificate. C. Card. ALOISI-MASELLA, Pro-Datory. L. Card. MACCHI.

"Witnessed on behalf of the Curia: G. DELL' AQUILA VISCONTI. Registered in the Secretariate of Briefs, J. CUGNONI. In the year of the Nativity of our Lord 1899, on the 11th day of May, feast of the Ascension of our Lord Jesus Christ, in the 22d year of the Pontificate of our Holy Father and Lord in Christ, Leo XIII, by Divine Providence Pope, I have read and solemnly promulgated the present apostolical letters in the presence of the people, in the porch of the Holy Patriarchal Vatican Basilica. GIUSEPPE DELL' AQUILA VISCONTI, Official of the Curia."

On the termination of the "holy year," by a letter "given at Rome in the year of Our Lord 1901," the Pope announced : "We do, therefore, by the authority of Almighty God, of the Blessed Apostles Peter and Paul, and by our own, extend and prorogue, for a period of six months, the Great Jubilee which has just been celebrated in the Holy City. Wherefore, to all the faithful of both sexes, in all parts of the earth, including even those that have come to Rome during the past year and there or elsewhere gained the Jubilee under any conditions, we grant and accord mercifully in the Lord, for once, the fullest indulgence, remission and pardon of their sins, the annual Paschal confession and communion being, however, not valid as conditions for gaining the Jubilee, provided that within six months from the date of the publication in each diocese of this letter they visit the cathedral in the episcopal city or the principal church in other parts of the different dioceses, together with three other churches in the same place, as appointed by the Ordinary either directly or through his officials, the parish priests or Vicar Foran, at least once a day for fifteen continuous or uninterrupted days, natural or ecclesiastical (the ecclesiastical day being that which commences with the first vespers of one day and ends with the dusk of the day following), and pray devoutly to God for the exaltation of the Church, the extirpation of heresy, the concord of Catholic princes and the salvation of the Christian people. In places where there are not four churches, power is granted in the same way to the Ordinaries to fix a smaller number of churches, or even one church where there is only one, in which the faithful may make the full number of visits, separate and distinct, on the same natural or ecclesiastical day, in such a way that the sixty visits be distributed through fifteen continuous or interrupted days."

Provisions relating to the circumstances of persons at sea or traveling, or in religious community, or in prison, are prescribed in the papal letter, and special privileges and powers are granted to "Jubilee confessors."

A. D. 1901.—Encyclical Letter of Pope Leo XIII. concerning Social and Christian Democracy.—In a letter dated January 18, 1901, addressed "to the Patriarchs, Primates, Archbishops, Bishops, and other Local Ordinaries in communion with the Apostolic See," the Pope has discussed the subjects of Democracy and Socialism, with reference to controverted views and opinions "defining what Catholics ought to think," and giving them "some injunctions so as to make their own action larger in scope and more beneficial to the commonwealth." The letter opens with these words: "Venerable Brethren—Grave economical disputes in more than one country have long been raging ; peace and concord are affected ; the violence of the disputants grows

every day, insomuch that the thoughts of the wiser part are laden with doubt and apprehension. These disputes arise in the first instance from widespread philosophical and moral error. The scientific resources belonging to the age, increased facilities of communication and appliances of all kinds for economizing labor and making it more productive have resulted in a keener struggle for existence. Through the malefic influence of agitators the gulf between rich and poor has been widened, so that frequent disturbances arise and even great calamities seem impending such as would bring ruin on a country."

The Pope then refers to his early encyclicals ("Quod Apostolici Muneris," issued in 1878, on the error in socialistic opinions, and "Rerum Novarum," issued in 1891, on "the rights and duties binding together the two classes of capitalists and laborers"), and to the good influence which he finds reason to believe they have had, and says further : "Thus, therefore, under the guidance of the Church, some sort of concerted action and institutional provision has been set up among Catholics for the protection of the lower classes, who are very often as much the victims of dangerous machinations and snares as they are suffering from hardship and poverty. The creed of the benefactor of the people had originally no name of its own ; that of Christian Socialism and its derivatives, which some brought in, has not undeservedly grown obsolete. Afterward many wanted, very rightly, to name it Popular Christianity. In some places those who devote themselves to such work are called Christian Socialists ; elsewhere it is called Christian Democracy, and its supporters Christian Democrats, as opposed to the Social Democracy, which Socialists uphold. Of these two appellations, certainly that of Christian Socialists, if not also of Christian Democracy, is offensive to many right-minded people, inasmuch as they think there is a perilous ambiguity attaching to it. They are afraid of the name for several reasons—popular government may be covertly promoted or preferred to other forms of political constitution ; the influence of Christianity may seem to be confined to the benefit of the common people, all other ranks being as it were left out in the cold ; beneath the specious designation may lurk some design or other of subverting all legitimate authority, being civil and religious.

"There is now commonly much dispute, and sometimes over-bitter dispute, on this topic, and we deem it our duty to put an end to the controversy by defining what Catholics ought to think ; moreover we intend to give them some injunctions so as to make their own action larger in scope and more beneficial to the commonwealth.

"What Social Democracy means, and what Christian ought to mean, does not surely admit of doubt. The former, more or less extreme, as the case may be, is by many carried to such extravagance of wickedness as to reckon human satisfaction supreme and acknowledge nothing higher, to pursue bodily goods and those of the natural world, and to make the happiness of man consist in attaining and enjoying them. Hence they would have the supreme power in a state to be in the hands of the common people, in such sort that all distinctions of rank being abolished and every citizen made equal to every other, all might have equal access also to the good things of life ; the law of lordship is to be abolished, private fortunes confiscated and even socialization of the appliances of labor carried out. But Christian Democracy, as Christian, ought to have as its foundation the principles laid down by divine faith, having regard, indeed, to the temporal advantage of the lower orders, but designing therewith to fit their minds for the enjoyment of things eternal. Accordingly, to Christian Democracy, let there be nothing more sacred than law and right ; let it bid the right of having and holding be kept inviolate ; let it maintain the diversity of ranks which properly belong to a well-ordered state ; in fine, let it prefer for human association that form and character which its divine author has imposed upon it. Clearly, therefore, Social and Christian Democracy can have nothing in common ; the difference between them is no less than that between the sectarianism of socialism and the profession of the Christian law.

"Far be it from any one to pervert the name of Christian Democracy to political ends. For although democracy by its very name and by philosophical usage denotes popular rule, yet in this application it must be employed altogether without political significance, so as to denote nothing whatever besides this beneficent Christian action upon the people. For natural morality and the precepts of the Gospel, for the very reason that they transcend the chances of human existence, must necessarily be independent of any particular form of civil government and adapt themselves to all, so long as there is nothing to conflict with virtue and right. They are, therefore, and remain in themselves, absolutely external to all conflict of parties and vicissitudes of occurrence, so that, under whatever kind of government, people may and ought to abide by these precepts, which bid them love God above all and their neighbors as themselves. This has ever been the morality of the Church : by it Roman Pontiffs have constantly dealt with states whatever might be their executive government. And this being so, the mind and action of Catholics, when devoted to promoting the good of the lower orders, cannot by any possibility aim at embracing and introducing any one form of government in preference to another.

"Just in the same way must Christian Democracy repudiate the other ground of offense, which arises from paying so much regard to the interests of the lower classes as to seem to pass over the higher, who are nevertheless of equal importance to the preservation and development of the State. The Christian law of charity, which we have just mentioned, forbids this. It is large enough to embrace all ranks as the aim and the task of those who would have the common people in a Christian spirit on the one hand suitably relieved, and, on the other, preserved against the contagion of socialism. . . .

"We have recalled these various topics on which we have before this found occasion to dilate according to our ability, and we trust that all dispute over the name of Christian Democracy may now be laid aside, as well as any suspicion of dangerous signification attaching to it. This trust we rightly cherish. For making exception of the ideas of certain persons regarding the force and virtue of this kind of Christian Democracy, ideas which are not free from extravagance or error, surely there will be no single

person to find fault with an endeavor, conformably to the law of nature and of God, to do merely this, to make the lives of laborers and artisans more tolerable, and gradually to give them the opportunity of self-culture, so that at home and in the world they may freely fulfil the obligations of virtue and religion, may feel themselves to be men, and not mere animals, Christian men, not pagans, and so strive with more felicity and earnestness to attain that 'one thing needful,' that final good, for which we came into the world. This is belonging to one and the same family, the offspring of the same all-beneficent Father, redeemed by one Saviour and called to the same eternal inheritance. . . .

"God forbid that under the name of Christian democracy should lie the surreptitious aim of throwing off all obedience and turning away from those in lawful authority. The law of nature, no less than that of Christ, enjoins respect for all such as in their several degree hold office in the State, and further enjoins obedience to their lawful commands. This is the only attitude worthy of a man and a Christian, and ought to be taken up heartily and as a matter of duty, 'for conscience's sake,' as the Apostle himself has admonished, when he ordained: 'Let every soul be subject to the highest powers.' . . .

"We spoke just now advisedly of virtue and religion. For it is the opinion of some, which is caught up by the masses, that the social question, as they call it, is 'economical' merely. The precise opposite is the truth—that it is first of all moral and religious, and for that reason its solution is to be expected mainly from the moral law and the pronouncements of religion. . . . Without the instincts which Christian wisdom implants and keeps alive, without providence, self-control, thrift, endurance and other natural qualities, you may try your hardest, but prosperity you cannot provide. That is the reason why we have never encouraged Catholics to form associations for the assistance of the poor, or introduce other schemes of the kind, without at the same time warning them that such things must not be attempted without the sanction of religion, without its inclusion and aid. . . . It is a laudable charity not merely to relieve the temporary needs of the poor, but to have an organized system of relief; this will be a more real and reliable assistance. It must be considered still more laudable to desire to instill into the minds of the mechanic and of the laborer notions of thrift and prudence, so that they may at least in part make provision for their declining years. It is an aim which not only relieves the cost of the wealthy, but it is a moral step for the poor themselves; it encourages them to approve their position, while it keeps them away from temptations, checks self-indulgence and leads them on to virtuous behavior. . . .

"Finally, we again enjoin with greater insistence that whatever schemes people take up in the popular cause, whether individually or in association, they should remember that they must be entirely submissive to episcopal authority. Do not let them be beguiled by an excessive ardor for charitable enterprise, which, if it induces any relaxation of due obedience, is itself false, unproductive of solid benefit and displeasing to God. Those who please God are those who are ready to give up their own ideas and listen to the bidding of the rulers of the Church, absolutely as to His own." . . . *Catholic Union and Times, Feb.* 21, 1901.

PARIS: A. D. 1897.—Burning of the Charity Bazaar.—An awful destruction of life was caused on the 4th of May by fire breaking out in a charity bazaar, held in the Rue Jean Gonjon, at Paris. Temporary structures had been erected, of wood and other combustible materials, to represent a street of Old Paris shops, and the flames ran through them like wildfire. The place was thronged with people, mostly of the aristocratic class and more than 200 are said to have perished.

A. D. 1900 (April—November).—Exposition. See (in this vol.) FRANCE : A. D. 1900 (APRIL—NOVEMBER).

A. D. 1900 (September).—Gigantic banquet to the Mayors of France. See (in this vol.) FRANCE : A. D. 1900 (SEPTEMBER).

PARIS, Treaty of **(1898),** between the United States and Spain. See (in this vol.) UNITED STATES OF AM. : A. D. 1898 (JULY—DECEMBER).

PARKHURST, Rev. Dr. Charles: His attack on the Tammany administration of New York City. See (in this vol.) NEW YORK CITY : A. D. 1894–1895.

PARLIAMENT, The British : Ceremonions opening by King Edward VII. See (in this vol.) ENGLAND : A. D. 1901 (FEBRUARY).

PARLIAMENTARY REFORM, Austrian. See (in this vol.) AUSTRIA-HUNGARY : A. D. 1895–1896.

PARTIES AND FACTIONS, POLITICAL AND POLITICO-RELIGIOUS.—Afrikander Bund, or Bondsmen. See (in this vol.) SOUTH AFRICA (CAPE COLONY) : A. D. 1881–1888 ; 1898 ; 1898 (MARCH—OCTOBER) ; and 1900 (DECEMBER). . . . .Agrarian Protectionists, German. See (in this vol.) GERMANY : A. D. 1895–1898. . . . . Anti-Imperialists. See (in this vol.) UNITED STATES OF AM. : A. D. 1900 (MAY—NOVEMBER). . . . . Anti-Semites. See (in this vol.) AUSTRIA-HUNGARY : A. D. 1895–1896, and after ; FRANCE : A. D. 1897–1899, and after ; GERMANY : A. D. 1898 (JUNE). . . . . Blancos, or Whites. See (in this vol.) URUGUAY : A. D. 1896–1899. . . . . The Bond. See above, AFRIKANDER BUND. . . . . Centre (Catholic, of Germany). See (in this vol.) GERMANY : A. D. 1898 (JUNE). . . . . Christian Social party. See (in this vol.) AUSTRIA-HUNGARY : A. D. 1897. . . . . Clerical party, Austria. See (in this vol.) AUSTRIA-HUNGARY : A. D. 1897. . . . . Colorados, or Reds. See (in this vol.) URUGUAY : A. D. 1896–1899. . . . . Deutsch Fortschrittliche. See (in this vol.) AUSTRIA-HUNGARY : A. D. 1897. . . . . "Fanatics." See (in this vol.) BRAZIL : A. D. 1897. . . . . "Free Silver" Democracy. See (in this vol.) UNITED STATES OF AM. : A. D. 1896 (JUNE—NOVEMBER) ; and 1900 (MAY—NOVEMBER). . . . . Fuyu-to (Liberals). See (in this vol.) JAPAN : A. D. 1890–1898. . . . . German Democrats. See (in this vol.) GERMANY : A. D. 1898 (JUNE). . . . . German Liberal party, Austria. See (in this vol.) AUSTRIA-HUNGARY : A. D. 1897. . . . . German People's party. See (in this vol.) AUSTRIA-HUNGARY : A. D. 1897. . . . . Gold Democrats. See (in this vol.) UNITED STATES OF AM. : A. D. 1896 (JUNE—NOVEMBER). . . . . Hintchak, The. See (in this vol.) TURKEY : A. D.

1895. . . . .Historic Christian party. See (in this vol.) NETHERLANDS : A. D. 1897. . . . .Kaishin-to (Progressives). See (in this vol.) JAPAN : A. D. 1890–1898. . . . .Kensei-to (Constitutional party). See (in this vol.) JAPAN : A. D. 1898–1899. . . . .Labor party, French (Parti Ouvrier). See (in this vol.) FRANCE : A. D. 1896 (APRIL—MAY). . . . .Liberal Democrats (German). See (in this vol.) GERMANY : A. D. 1898 (JUNE). . . . .Liberal Unionists (German). See (in this vol.) GERMANY : A. D. 1898 (JUNE). . . . .Lincoln party. See (in this vol.) UNITED STATES OF AM.: A. D. 1900 (MAY—NOVEMBER), SILVER REPUBLICAN. . . . . Little England party. See (in this vol.) LITTLE ENGLAND PARTY. . . .Middle-of-the-Road Populists. See (in this vol.) UNITED STATES OF AM.: A. D. 1896 (JUNE—NOVEMBER) ; and 1900 (MAY—NOVEMBER). . . . .National Democratic party. See (in this vol.) UNITED STATES OF AM. : A. D. 1896 (JUNE—NOVEMBER). . . . . National Liberals (German). See (in this vol.) GERMANY : A. D. 1898 (JUNE). . . . .National party, 1896 and 1900. See (in this vol.) UNITED STATES OF AM. : A. D. 1896 (JUNE—NOVEMBER) ; and 1900 (MAY—NOVEMBER). . . . .National Silver party. See (in this vol.) UNITED STATES OF AM. : A. D. 1896 (JUNE—NOVEMBER). . . . .New Radical party. See (in this vol.) ENGLAND : A. D. 1896 (MAY). . . . .Old Czechs. See (in this vol.) AUSTRIA-HUNGARY : A. D. 1897. . . . .Pan-Germanic Union. See (in this vol.) AUSTRIA-HUNGARY : A. D. 1901. . . . .Patriotic League. See (in this vol.) FRANCE : A. D. 1898 (MAY—NOVEMBER). . . . .Polish Club. See (in this vol.) AUSTRIA-HUNGARY : A. D. 1897. . . . .Progressives (Kaishin-to). See (in this vol.) JAPAN : A. D. 1890–1898. . . . . Progressives (Cape). See (in this vol.) SOUTH AFRICA (CAPE COLONY): A. D. 1898 ; and 1898 (MARCH—OCTOBER). . . . . Protestant Anti-Revolutionists. See (in this vol.) NETHERLANDS : A. D. 1897. . . . .Rikken Seiyu-kai (Association of Friends of the Constitution. See (in this vol.) JAPAN : A. D. 1900 (AUGUST—OCTOBER). . . . .Siah Chai, The. See (in this vol.) CHINA : A. D. 1895 (AUGUST). . . . . Silver Republicans. See (in this vol.) UNITED STATES OF AM. : A. D. 1896 (JUNE—NOVEMBER) ; and 1900 (MAY—NOVEMBER). . . . .Socialist parties. See (in this vol.) AUSTRIA-HUNGARY : A. D. 1897 ; FRANCE : A. D. 1896 (APRIL—MAY) ; GERMANY : A. D. 1894–1895, and 1898 (JUNE) ; UNITED STATES OF AM. : A. D. 1896 (JUNE—NOVEMBER), and 1900 (MAY—NOVEMBER). . . . . "Sound Money" Democrats. See (in this vol.) UNITED STATES OF AM. : A. D. 1896 (JUNE—NOVEMBER). . . . .United Christian party. See (in this vol.) UNITED STATES OF AM. : A. D. 1900 (MAY—NOVEMBER). . . . .United Irish League. See (in this vol.) IRELAND : A. D. 1900–1901. . . . ."Vegetarians." See (in this vol.) CHINA : A. D. 1895 (AUGUST). . . . .Verfassungstreue Grossgrundbesitz. See (in this vol.) AUSTRIA-HUNGARY : A. D. 1897. . . . . Volkspartei. See (in this vol.) AUSTRIA-HUNGARY : A. D. 1897. . . . .Young Czechs. See (in this vol.) AUSTRIA-HUNGARY : A. D. 1897.

PATRIARCHATE: Re-established at Alexandria. See (in this vol.) PAPACY : A. D. 1896 (MARCH).

PATRIOTIC LEAGUE. See (in this vol.) FRANCE : A. D. 1898 (MAY—NOVEMBER).

351

PAUNCEFOTE, Sir Julian: British commissioner to the Peace Conference at The Hague. See (in this vol.) PEACE CONFERENCE.

PEACE CONFERENCE.

On the 24th of August, 1898, without previous heralding or intimation, Count Mouravieff, the Russian Minister for Foreign Affairs, placed copies of the following momentous proposal from the Tsar in the hands of all the foreign representatives attending his weekly reception at St. Petersburg: "The maintenance of universal peace and a possible reduction of the excessive armaments which weigh upon all nations represent, in the present condition of affairs all over the world, the ideal towards which the efforts of all Governments should be directed. This view fully corresponds with the humane and magnanimous intentions of His Majesty the Emperor, my august Master. Being convinced that this high aim agrees with the most essential interests and legitimate aspirations of all the Powers, the Imperial Government considers the present moment a very favourable one for seeking, through international discussion, the most effective means of assuring to all peoples the blessings of real and lasting peace, and above all of limiting the progressive development of existing armaments. During the last twenty years aspirations towards general pacification have particularly asserted themselves in the consciences of civilized nations. The preservation of peace has been made the aim of international policy; for the sake of peace the Great Powers have formed powerful alliances, and for the purpose of establishing a better guarantee of peace they have developed their military forces in an unprecedented degree, and continue to develop them without hesitating at any sacrifice. All these efforts, however, have not yet led to the beneficent results of the desired pacification. The ever increasing financial burdens strike at the root of public prosperity. The physical and intellectual forces of the people, labour and capital, are diverted for the greater part from their natural application and wasted unproductively. Hundreds of millions are spent in acquiring terrible engines of destruction which are regarded to-day as the latest inventions of science, but are destined to-morrow to be rendered obsolete by some new discovery. National culture, economical progress, and the production of wealth are either paralysed or developed in a wrong direction. Therefore, the more the armaments of each Power increase, the less they answer to the objects aimed at by the Governments. Economic disturbances are caused in great measure by this system of excessive armaments, and the constant danger involved in this accumulation of war material renders the armed peace of to-day a crushing burden more and more difficult for the nations to bear. It consequently seems evident that if this situation be prolonged, it will inevitably lead to that very disaster which it is desired to avoid, and the horrors of which make every humane mind shudder by anticipation. It is the supreme duty, therefore, at the present moment of all States to put some limit to these unceasing armaments, and to find means of averting the calamities which threaten the whole world. Deeply impressed by this feeling, His Majesty the Emperor has been pleased to command me to propose to all Governments who have Representatives at the Imperial Court the meeting of a Conference to discuss this grave problem. Such a Conference, with God's help, would be a happy augury for the opening century. It would concentrate in one powerful effort the strivings of all States which sincerely wish to bring about the triumph of the grand idea of universal peace over the elements of trouble and discord. It would, at the same time, cement their agreement by a united affirmation of the principles of law and equity on which rest the security of States and the welfare of peoples."—*Great Britain, Parliamentary Publications* (*Papers by Command: Russia, No.* 1, 1899).

Having allowed his supremely noble proposition to stand before the world for consideration during a period of four months, and having received from almost every governing authority a formal expression of willingness to join in the Conference recommended, the sovereign of Russia pursued his grand design, on the 11th of January, 1899, by the following communication to the foreign representatives at his court: "When, in the month of August last, my august master instructed me to propose to the Governments which have Representatives in St. Petersburg the meeting of a Conference with the object of seeking the most efficacious means for assuring to all peoples the blessings of real and lasting peace, and, above all, in order to put a stop to the progressive development of the present armaments, there appeared to be no obstacle in the way of the realization, at no distant date, of this humanitarian scheme. The cordial reception accorded by nearly all the Powers to the step taken by the Imperial Government could not fail to strengthen this expectation. While highly appreciating the sympathetic terms in which the adhesions of most of the Powers were expressed, the Imperial Cabinet has been able also to collect, with lively satisfaction, evidence of the warmest approval which has reached it, and continues to be received, from all classes of society in various parts of the globe. Notwithstanding the strong current of opinion which set in in favour of the ideas of general pacification, the political horizon has recently undergone a sensible change. Several Powers have undertaken fresh armaments, striving to increase further their military forces, and in the presence of this uncertain situation, it might be asked whether the Powers considered the present moment opportune for the international discussion of the ideas set forth in the Circular of the 12th (24th) August. In the hope, however, that the elements of trouble agitating political centres will soon give place to a calmer disposition of a nature to favour the success of the proposed Conference, the Imperial Government is of opinion that it would be possible to proceed forthwith to a preliminary exchange of ideas between the Powers, with the object:—(a.) Of seeking without delay means for putting a limit to the progressive increase of military and naval armaments, a question the solution of which becomes evidently more and more urgent in view of the fresh extension given to these armaments; and (b.) Of preparing the way for a discussion of the questions relating to the possibility of preventing armed conflicts by the pacific means at the disposal of international diplomacy. In the event of the Powers considering the present moment favourable for the meeting of a Conference on these bases, it would certainly be useful for the Cabinets to come to an understanding on the subject of the programme of their labours. The subjects to be submitted for international discussion at the Conference could, in general terms, be summarized as follows:—

"1. An understanding not to increase for a fixed period the present effective of the armed military and naval forces, and at the same time not to increase the Budgets pertaining thereto; and a preliminary examination of the means by which a reduction might even be effected in future in the forces and Budgets above-mentioned.

"2. To prohibit the use in the armies and fleets of any new kind of fire-arms whatever and of new explosives, or any powders more powerful than those now in use either for rifles or cannon.

"3. To restrict the use in military warfare of the formidable explosives already existing, and to prohibit the throwing of projectiles or explosives of any kind from balloons or by any similar means.

"4. To prohibit the use in naval warfare of submarine torpedo-boats or plungers, or other similar engines of destruction; to give an undertaking not to construct vessels with rams in the future.

"5. To apply to naval warfare the stipulations of the Geneva Convention of 1864, on the basis of the Additional Articles of 1868.

"6. To neutralize ships and boats employed in saving those overboard during or after an engagement.

"7. To revise the Declaration concerning the laws and customs of war elaborated in 1874 by the Conference of Brussels, which has remained unratified to the present day.

"8. To accept in principle the employment of good offices, of mediation and facultative arbitration in cases lending themselves thereto, with the object of preventing armed conflicts between nations; to come to an understanding with respect to the mode of applying these good offices, and to establish a uniform practice in using them.

"It is well understood that all questions concerning the political relations of States and the order of things established by Treaties, as generally all questions which do not directly fall within the programme adopted by the Cabinets, must be absolutely excluded from the deliberations of the Conference. In requesting you, Sir, to be good enough to apply to your Government for instructions on the subject of my present communication, I beg you at the same time to inform it that, in the interest of the great cause which my august master has so much at heart, His Imperial Majesty considers it advisable that the Conference should not sit in the capital of one of the Great Powers, where so many political interests are centred which might, perhaps, impede the progress of a work in which all the countries of the universe are equally interested."

General assent being given to the suggestions here offered, the next step toward realization of the grand project was taken, by an arrangement with the government of the Kingdom of the Netherlands, in accordance with which an invitation was addressed from The Hague, in April, to many governments, both the greater and the less of the political world, in the following terms: "For political reasons the Imperial Russian Government considered that it would not be desirable that the meeting of the Conference should take place in the capital of one of the Great Powers, and after securing the assent of the Governments interested, it addressed the Cabinet of The Hague with a view of obtaining its consent to the choice of that capital as the seat of the Conference in question. The Minister for Foreign Affairs at once took the orders of Her Majesty the Queen in regard to this request, and I am happy to be able to inform you that Her Majesty, my august Sovereign, has been pleased to authorize him to reply that it will be particularly agreeable to her to see the proposed Conference meet at The Hague. Consequently, my Government, in accord with the Imperial Russian Government, charges me to invite [the Government named] to be good enough to be represented at the above-mentioned Conference, in order to discuss the questions indicated in the second Russian Circular of the 30th December, 1898 (11th January, 1899), as well as all other questions connected with the ideas set forth in the Circular of the 12th (24th) August, 1898, excluding, however, from the deliberations everything which refers to the political relations of States or the order of things established by Treaties. My Government trusts, that [the Government named] will associate itself with the great humanitarian work to be entered upon under the auspices of His Majesty the Emperor of All the Russias, and that it will be disposed to accept this invitation, and to take the necessary steps for the presence of its Representatives at The Hague on the 18th May next for the opening of the Conference, at which each Power, whatever may be the number of its Delegates, will only have one vote."—*Great Britain, Parliamentary Publications (Papers by Command: Miscellaneous, No.* 1, 1899, *pp. 3-4 and* 8).

In response to this definite invitation, the governments of Austria-Hungary, Belgium, Bulgaria, China, Denmark, France, Germany, Great Britain, Greece, Italy, Japan, Luxembourg, Mexico, Montenegro, the Netherlands, Persia, Portugal, Roumania, Russia, Servia, Siam, Spain, Sweden and Norway, Switzerland, Turkey, and the United States of America, appointed representatives who met at The Hague, on the 18th of May, 1899, and organized the Conference by electing M. de Staal, Russian Ambassador, to preside. The United States was represented by the Hon. Andrew D. White, Ambassador to Berlin, the Hon. Seth Low, President of Columbia University, the Hon. Stanford Newel, Envoy Extraordinary, &c., to The Hague, Capt. Alfred T. Mahan, U. S. N., Capt. William Crozier, U. S. A., and the Hon. Frederick W. Holls, of New York. The representatives of Great Britain were Sir Julian Pauncefote, Ambassador to the United States, Sir Henry Howard, Envoy Extraordinary, &c., to The Hague, Vice-Admiral Sir John A. Fisher, Major-General Sir J. C. Ardagh, and Lieutenant-Colonel C. à Court.

"The Conference at The Hague was a Parliament of Man representing, however imperfectly, the whole human race. The only independent ones not represented at the Huis ten Bosch were the South American republics, the Emperor of Morocco, the King of Abyssinia, and the Grand Lama of Tibet. That the South American republics were not represented is not the fault of the Russian Emperor. Mexico received and accepted an invitation. Brazil received, but rejected, the invitation to be present, and so did one other South American republic. The original Russian idea was to assemble representatives from every independent government in the world; nor did they even confine themselves to the secular governments. They were very anxious that the Pope should also be directly represented in this supreme assembly. Even with the Pope and South America left out, the Congress represented more of the world and its inhabitants than any similar assembly that has ever been gathered together for the work of international legislation. That circumstance in itself is sufficient to give distinction to the Conference at The Hague, which, it is expected, will be the forerunner of a series of conferences, each of which will aim at being more and more universally representative. On the eve of the twentieth century the human race has begun to federate itself. That is the supreme significance of the assembly which has just spent two months in the capital of Holland."—W. T. Stead, *The Conference at The Hague* (*Forum, Sept.*, 1899).

To systematize and facilitate the discussions of the Conference, three Commissions or Committees were appointed, between which the several subjects suggested in the Russian circular of January 11 (as given above), and agreed to by the several governments, were distributed. The 1st, 2d, 3d and 4th propositions of the programme were referred to the First Commission, the 5th, 6th and 7th to the Second, the 8th (concerning mediation and arbitration) to the Third. This was done on the 23d of May, after which the general Conference was held only at intervals, to receive and consider reports from the several Commissions, of agreements reached or disagreements ascertained. This went on until the 29th of July, when the several Conventions, Declarations, and Recommendations agreed upon for submission to the governments represented were summarized in the following "Final Act," signed by all : "In a series of meetings, between the 18th May and the 29th July, 1899, in which the constant desire of the Delegates above mentioned has been to realize, in the fullest manner possible, the generous views of the august Initiator of the Conference and the intentions of their Governments, the Conference has agreed, for submission for signature by the Plenipotentiaries, on the text of the Conventions and Declarations enumerated below and annexed to the present Act :—

"I. Convention for the pacific settlement of international conflicts.

"II. Convention regarding the laws and customs of war by land.

"III. Convention for the adaptation to maritime warfare of the principles of the Geneva Convention of the 22nd August, 1864.

"IV. Three Declarations :—1. To prohibit the launching of projectiles and explosives from balloons or by other similar new methods. 2. To prohibit the use of projectiles, the only object

of which is the diffusion of asphyxiating or deleterious gases. 3. To prohibit the use of bullets which expand or flatten easily in the human body, such as bullets with a hard envelope, of which the envelope does not entirely cover the core, or is pierced with incisions.

"These Conventions and Declarations shall form so many separate Acts. These Acts shall be dated this day, and may be signed up to the 31st December, 1899, by the Plenipotentiaries of the Powers represented at the International Peace Conference at The Hague.

"Guided by the same sentiments, the Conference has adopted unanimously the following Resolution : — 'The Conference is of opinion that the restriction of military budgets, which are at present a heavy burden on the world, is extremely desirable for the increase of the material and moral welfare of mankind.'

"It has, besides, formulated the following wishes :—

"1. The Conference, taking into consideration the preliminary steps taken by the Swiss Federal Government for the revision of the Geneva Convention, expresses the wish that steps may be shortly taken for the assembly of a Special Conference having for its object the revision of that Convention. This wish was voted unanimously.

"2. The Conference expresses the wish that the questions of the rights and duties of neutrals may be inserted in the programme of a Conference in the near future.

"3. The Conference expresses the wish that the questions with regard to rifles and naval guns, as considered by it, may be studied by the Governments with the object of coming to an agreement respecting the employment of new types and calibres.

"4. The Conference expresses the wish that the Governments, taking into consideration the proposals made at the Conference, may examine the possibility of an agreement as to the limitation of armed forces by land and sea, and of war budgets.

"5. The Conference expresses the wish that the proposal, which contemplates the declaration of the inviolability of private property in naval warfare, may be referred to a subsequent Conference for consideration.

"6. The Conference expresses the wish that the proposal to settle the question of the bombardment of ports, towns, and villages by a naval force may be referred to a subsequent Conference for consideration.

" The last five wishes were voted unanimously, saving some abstentions.

"In faith of which, the Plenipotentiaries have signed the present Act, and have affixed their seals thereto. Done at The Hague, 29th July, 1899, in one copy only, which shall be deposited in the Ministry for Foreign Affairs, and of which copies, duly certified, shall be delivered to all the Powers represented at the Conference."—*Great Britain, Parliamentary Publications* (*Papers by Command: Miscellaneous, No.* 1, 1899, *pp.* 3–4, 8 *and* 288–9).

The accompanying Conventions and Declarations were in no case unanimously signed, several delegations, in each case, claiming time for the governments they represented to consider certain questions involved. The most important of the proposed Conventions, namely, that "For the

Pacific Settlement of International Disputes," was signed at The Hague by the delegates from Belgium, Denmark, Spain, the United States of America, Mexico, France, Greece, Montenegro, the Netherlands, Persia, Portugal, Roumania, Russia, Siam, Sweden and Norway, and Bulgaria; but not by Austria-Hungary, Germany, Italy, Japan, Great Britain, Luxembourg, Switzerland, Servia, Turkey, or China. Ultimately, however, the great Treaty of Arbitration was signed by every one of the Powers represented. The signature of the delegates of the United States was given under reserve of a declaration which will be found in the following excerpt from the general report of the American Commission. The full text of each of the Conventions is given below.

" The entire plan for the tribunal and its use is voluntary, so far as sovereign States are concerned. The only seeming exceptions to this rule are contained in Article 1, which provides that the Signatory Powers agree to employ their efforts for securing the pacific regulation of international differences; and Article 27, which says that the Signatory Powers consider it to be a duty, in the case where an acute conflict threatens to break out between two or more of them, to remind those latter that the permanent court is open to them. The obligation thus imposed is not legal or diplomatic in its nature. These articles merely express a general moral duty for the performance of which each State is accountable only to itself. In order, however, to make assurance doubly sure and to leave no doubt whatever of the meaning of the Convention, as affecting the United States of America, the Commission made the following declaration in the full session of the Conference, held July 25:—
' The Delegation of the United States of America, in signing the Convention regulating the peaceful adjustment of international differences, as proposed by the International Peace Conference, make the following declaration:—Nothing contained in this Convention shall be so construed as to require the United States of America to depart from its traditional policy of not intruding upon, interfering with, or entangling itself in the political questions or policy or internal administration of any foreign State; nor shall anything contained in the said Convention be construed to imply a relinquishment by the United States of America of its traditional attitude toward purely American questions.' Under the reserve of this declaration the United States delegates signed the Arbitration Convention itself. Article 8 of the Convention, providing for a special form of Mediation, was proposed individually by Mr. Holls of the United States Commission. . . . It is hoped that in particular crises, when the other means provided by the Convention for keeping or restoring peace have failed, it may prove to have real and practical value. It is certain that, by the Continental States of Europe, it has been exceedingly well received."—*General Report of the American Commission.*

" Objection has been made to [the International Court of Arbitration] on the ground that submission to it is purely voluntary and that no executive authority has been provided to carry out its decrees. The answer to all such objections is simply that the power of enlightened public opinion is relied upon to be amply sufficient for the purpose of insuring obedience to

every just mandate of this Court. In the case of the United States of America the judgments of the Court, according to the decisions now in force, will have a peculiarly binding force. An agreement to submit a case to the Court cannot be made by the United States, except by way of a treaty, which, when ratified by the Senate, becomes the supreme law of the land. In the case of La Ninfa, Whitelaw v. The United States (75 Fed. Rep., 513), it was decided by the United States Circuit Court of Appeals in California that by virtue of the treaty the judgment of the Court of Arbitration provided for by the terms of the treaty has all the force of a federal statute, and it is itself the supreme law of the land, binding upon every individual citizen of the United States, including all federal and State authorities. For us, at least, the International Court of Arbitration at The Hague will, if this view prevails, in reality be the highest possible tribunal, with an authority binding even on our own United States Supreme Court.

"Article 27 aims, in a measure, to supply the deficiency of the provision for obligatory arbitration, in that it declares it to be the duty of all Signatory Powers to remind any one or more of themselves, in case of a threatened dispute, that the permanent Court of Arbitration is open to them. What particular effect this particular article will have must be left to the future. Without modification or reservation the article, when ratified by the United States, would have constituted a complete abandonment of the time-honored Monroe Doctrine. Accordingly the representatives of the United States declined to sign the treaty, except under a reservation or declaration, which was solemnly accepted by the Peace Conference, thus materially modifying the jurisdiction of the Court [see above]. . . . By this declaration the Monroe Doctrine was not only self-guarded, but it was stated and vindicated more emphatically than ever before in our history, and the people of this country are, therefore, in a position to cordially support the International Court of Arbitration, without the fear that the Court itself, or the fact of its establishment, may ever be used against this country, or to the embarrassment of its diplomacy and traditional policy. . . .

" The effect of the establishment of the Court upon European diplomacy is necessarily surrounded by great uncertainty. In a recent review of the work of the Peace Conference I ventured to use this language : 'It is most encouraging and of the highest importance that upon the whole Continent the governments are apparently in advance of public opinion upon the entire subject of the Peace Conference. The reason is not far to seek. No man who is fit for the position can to-day hold a place involving the direction of his country's international policy without feeling an almost intolerable pressure of responsibility. To him every remote chance of a lightening of his burden comes as a promise of blessed relief. It is a historical fact that none of the obstacles to success which the Peace Conference had to overcome originated in the mind of any sovereign or of any high minister of State. In every case they were raised by underlings without responsibility and anxious to show superior wisdom by finding fault. So long as this favorable governmental attitude continues there is every reason for encouragement.' 'Continental public opinion, especially in questions of foreign policy, seems more pliable than ever before, and is as clay in the hands of a potter, so far as alliances and sympathies are concerned, when following a popular monarch or foreign minister.' I have since been assured by the highest officials of at least two great European Powers, that this statement meets with their unqualified approval. The sneers of irresponsible journals and politicieiaus cannot and will not affect the deliberate purposes of a high-minded and serious minister of State."—F. W. Holls, *The International Court of Arbitration at The Hague ; a paper read before the N. Y. State Bar Association, Jan. 15, 1901.*

Convention for the Pacific Settlement of International Disputes.

TITLE I.—On the Maintenance of the General Peace.

ARTICLE I. With a view to obviating, as far as possible, recourse to force in the relations between States, the Signatory Powers agree to use their best efforts to insure the pacific settlement of international differences.

TITLE II.—On Good Offices and Mediation.

ARTICLE II. In case of serious disagreement or conflict, before an appeal to arms, the Signatory Powers agree to have recourse, as far as circumstances allow, to the good offices or mediation of one or more friendly Powers.

ARTICLE III. Independently of this recourse, the Signatory Powers recommend that one or more Powers, strangers to the dispute, should, on their own initiative, and as far as circumstances may allow, offer their good offices or mediation to the States at variance. Powers, strangers to the dispute, have the right to offer good offices or mediation, even during the course of hostilities. The exercise of this right can never be regarded by one or the other of the parties in conflict as an unfriendly act.

ARTICLE IV. The part of the mediator consists in reconciling the opposing claims and appeasing the feelings of resentment which may have arisen between the States at variance.

ARTICLE V. The functions of the mediator are at an end when once it is declared, either by one of the parties to the dispute, or by the mediator himself, that the means of reconciliation proposed by him are not accepted.

ARTICLE VI. Good offices and mediation, either at the request of the parties at variance, or on the initiative of Powers strangers to the dispute, have exclusively the character of advice and never have binding force.

ARTICLE VII. The acceptance of mediation can not, unless there be an agreement to the contrary, have the effect of interrupting, delaying, or hindering mobilization or other measures of preparation for war. If mediation occurs after the commencement of hostilities it causes no interruption to the military operations in progress, unless there be an agreement to the contrary.

ARTICLE VIII. The Signatory Powers are agreed in recommending the application, when circumstances allow, for special mediation in the following form :—In case of a serious difference endangering the peace, the States at variance choose respectively a Power, to whom they intrust the mission of entering into direct communication with the Power chosen on the other side,

with the object of preventing the rupture of pacific relations. For the period of this mandate, the term of which, unless otherwise stipulated, cannot exceed thirty days, the States in conflict cease from all direct communication on the subject of the dispute, which is regarded as referred exclusively to the mediating Powers, who must use their best efforts to settle it. In case of a definite rupture of pacific relations, these Powers are charged with the joint task of taking advantage of any opportunity to restore peace.

TITLE III.—On International Commissions of Inquiry.

ARTICLE IX. In differences of an international nature involving neither honour nor vital interests, and arising from a difference of opinion on points of fact, the Signatory Powers recommend that the parties, who have not been able to come to an agreement by means of diplomacy, should as far as circumstances allow, institute an International Commission of Inquiry, to facilitate a solution of these differences by elucidating the facts by means of an impartial and conscientious investigation.

ARTICLE X. The International Commissions of Inquiry are constituted by special agreement between the parties in conflict. The Convention for an inquiry defines the facts to be examined and the extent of the Commissioners' powers. It settles the procedure. On the inquiry both sides must be heard. The form and the periods to be observed, if not stated in the inquiry Convention, are decided by the Commission itself.

ARTICLE XI. The International Commissions of Inquiry are formed, unless otherwise stipulated, in the manner fixed by Article XXXII of the present Convention.

ARTICLE XII. The powers in dispute engage to supply the International Commission of Inquiry, as fully as they may think possible, with all means and facilities necessary to enable it to be completely acquainted with and to accurately understand the facts in question.

ARTICLE XIII. The International Commission of Inquiry communicates its Report to the conflicting Powers, signed by all the members of the Commission.

ARTICLE XIV. The Report of the International Commission of Inquiry is limited to a statement of facts, and has in no way the character of an Arbitral Award. It leaves the conflicting Powers entire freedom as to the effect to be given to this statement.

TITLE IV.—On International Arbitration.

CHAPTER I.—On the System of Arbitration.

ARTICLE XV. International arbitration has for its object the settlement of differences between States by judges of their own choice, and on the basis of respect for law.

ARTICLE XVI. In questions of a legal nature, and especially in the interpretation or application of International Conventions, arbitration is recognized by the Signatory Powers as the most effcetive, and at the same time the most equitable, means of settling disputes which diplomacy has failed to settle.

ARTICLE XVII. The Arbitration Convention is concluded for questions already existing or for questions which may arise eventually. It may embrace any dispute or only disputes of a certain category.

ARTICLE XVIII. The Arbitration Convention implies the engagement to submit loyally to the Award.

ARTICLE XIX. Independently of general or private Treaties expressly stipulating recourse to arbitration as obligatory on the Signatory Powers, these Powers reserve to themselves the right of concluding, either before the ratification of the present Act or later, new Agreements, general or private, with a view to extending obligatory arbitration to all cases which they may consider it possible to submit to it.

CHAPTER II.—On the Permanent Court of Arbitration.

ARTICLE XX. With the object of facilitating an immediate recourse to arbitration for international differences, which it has not been possible to settle by diplomacy, the Signatory Powers undertake to organize a permanent Court of Arbitration, accessible at all times and operating, unless otherwise stipulated by the parties, in accordance with the Rules of Procedure inserted in the present Convention.

ARTICLE XXI. The Permanent Court shall be competent for all arbitration cases, unless the parties agree to institute a special Tribunal.

ARTICLE XXII. An International Bureau, established at The Hague, serves as record office for the Court. This Bureau is the channel for communications relative to the meetings of the Court. It has the custody of the archives and conducts all the administrative business. The Signatory Powers undertake to communicate to the International Bureau at The Hague a duly certified copy of any conditions of arbitration arrived at between them, and of any award concerning them delivered by special Tribunals. They undertake also to communicate to the Bureau the Laws, Regulations, and documents eventually showing the execution of the awards given by the Court.

ARTICLE XXIII. Within the three months following its ratification of the present Act, each Signatory Power shall select four persons at the most, of known competency in questions of international law, of the highest moral reputation, and disposed to accept the duties of Arbitrators. The persons thus selected shall be inscribed, as members of the Court, in a list which shall be notified by the Bureau to all the Signatory Powers. Any alteration in the list of Arbitrators is brought by the Bureau to the knowledge of the Signatory Powers. Two or more Powers may agree on the selection in common of one or more Members. The same person can be selected by different Powers. The Members of the Court are appointed for a term of six years. Their appointments can be renewed. In case of the death or retirement of a member of the Court, his place shall be filled in accordance with the method of his appointment.

ARTICLE XXIV. When the Signatory Powers desire to have recourse to the Permanent Court for the settlement of a difference that has arisen between them, the Arbitrators called upon to form the competent Tribunal to decide this difference, must be chosen from the general list of members of the Court. Failing the direct agreement of the parties on the composition of the Arbitration Tribunal, the following course shall be pursued :—Each party appoints two Arbitrators, and these together choose an Umpire. If the votes are equal, the choice of the Umpire is intrusted to a third Power, selected by the parties by common accord. If an agreement is not arrived at on this subject, each party selects a different Power, and the choice of the Umpire is made in concert by the Powers thus selected. The Tribunal being thus composed, the parties notify to the Bureau their determination to have recourse to the Court and the names of the Arbitrators. The Tribunal of Arbitration assembles on the date fixed by the parties. The Members of the Court, in the discharge of their duties and out of their own country, enjoy diplomatic privileges and immunitica.

ARTICLE XXV. The Tribunal of Arbitration has its ordinary seat at The Hague. Except in cases of necessity, the place of session can only be altered by the Tribunal with the assent of the parties.

ARTICLE XXVI. The International Bureau at The Hague is authorized to place its premises and its staff at the disposal of the Signatory Powers for the operations of any special Board of Arbitration. The jurisdiction of the Permanent Court, may, within the conditions laid down in the Regulations, be extended to disputes between non-Signatory Powers, or between Signatory Powers and non-Signatory Powers, if the parties are agreed on recourse to this Tribunal.

ARTICLE XXVII. The Signatory Powers consider it their duty, if a serious dispute threatens to break out between two or more of them, to remind these latter that the Permanent Court is open to them. Consequently, they declare that the fact of reminding the conflicting parties of the provisions of the present Convention, and the advice given to them, in the highest interests of peace, to have recourse to the Permanent Court, can only be regarded as friendly actions.

ARTICLE XXVIII. A Permanent Administrative Council, composed of the Diplomatic Representatives of the Signatory Powers accredited to The Hague and of the Netherland Minister for Foreign Affairs, who will act as President, shall be instituted in this town as soon as possible after the ratification of the present Act by at least nine Powers. This Council will be charged with the establishment and organization of the International Bureau, which will be under its direction and control. It will notify to the Powers the constitution of the Court and will provide for its installation. It will settle its Rules of Procedure and all other necessary Regulations. It will decide all questions of administration which may arise with regard to the operations of the Court. It will have entire control over the appointment, suspension or dismissal of the officials and employés of the Bureau. It will fix the payments and salaries, and control the general expenditure. At meetings duly summoned the presence of five members is sufficient to render valid the discussions of the Council. The decisions are taken by a majority of votes. The Council communicates to the Signatory Powers without delay the Regulations adopted by it. It furnishes them with an annual Report on the labours of the Court, the working of the administration, and the expenses.

ARTICLE XXIX. The expenses of the Bureau shall be borne by the Signatory Powers in the proportion fixed for the International Bureau of the Universal Postal Union.

CHAPTER III.   On Arbitral Procedure.

ARTICLE XXX.   With a view to encourage the development of arbitration, the Signatory Powers have agreed on the following Rules which shall be applicable to arbitral procedure, unless other Rules have been agreed on by the parties.

ARTICLE XXXI.   The Powers who have recourse to arbitration sign a special Act ("Compromis"), in which the subject of the difference is clearly defined, as well as the extent of the Arbitrators' powers. This Act implies the undertaking of the parties to submit loyally to the award.

ARTICLE XXXII.   The duties of Arbitrator may be conferred on one Arbitrator alone or on several Arbitrators selected by the parties as they please, or chosen by them from the members of the Permanent Court of Arbitration established by the present Act. Failing the constitution of the Tribunal by direct agreement between the parties, the following course shall be pursued: Each party appoints two Arbitrators, and these latter together choose an Umpire. In case of equal voting, the choice of the Umpire is intrusted to a third Power, selected by the parties by common accord. If no agreement is arrived at on this subject, each party selects a different Power, and the choice of the Umpire is made in concert by the Powers thus selected.

ARTICLE XXXIII.   When a Sovereign or the Chief of a State is chosen as Arbitrator, the arbitral procedure is settled by him.

ARTICLE XXXIV.   The Umpire is by right President of the Tribunal. When the Tribunal does not include an Umpire, it appoints its own President.

ARTICLE XXXV.   In case of the death, retirement, or disability from any cause of one of the Arbitrators, his place shall be filled in accordance with the method of his appointment.

ARTICLE XXXVI.   The Tribunal's place of session is selected by the parties. Failing this selection the Tribunal sits at The Hague. The place thus fixed cannot, except in case of necessity, be changed by the Tribunal without the assent of the parties.

ARTICLE XXXVII.   The parties have the right to appoint delegates or special agents to attend the Tribunal, for the purpose of serving as intermediaries between them and the Tribunal. They are further authorized to retain, for the defense of their rights and interests before the Tribunal, counsel or advocates appointed by them for this purpose.

ARTICLE XXXVIII.   The Tribunal decides on the choice of languages to be used by itself, and to be authorized for use before it.

ARTICLE XXXIX.   As a general rule the arbitral procedure comprises two distinct phases; preliminary examination and discussion. Preliminary examination consists in the communication by the respective agents to the members of the Tribunal and to the opposite party of all printed or written Acts and of all documents containing the arguments invoked in the case. This communication shall be made in the form and within the periods fixed by the Tribunal in accordance with Article XLIX. Discussion consists in the oral development before the Tribunal of the arguments of the parties.

ARTICLE XL.   Every document produced by one party must be communicated to the other party.

ARTICLE XLI.   The discussions are under the direction of the President. They are only public if it be so decided by the Tribunal, with the assent of the parties. They are recorded in the "procès-verbaux" drawn up by the Secretaries appointed by the President. These "procès-verbaux" alone have an authentic character.

ARTICLE XLII.   When the preliminary examination is concluded, the Tribunal has the right to refuse discussion of all fresh Acts or documents which one party may desire to submit to it without the consent of the other party.

ARTICLE XLIII.   The Tribunal is free to take into consideration fresh Acts or documents to which its attention may be drawn by the agents or counsel of the parties. In this case, the Tribunal has the right to require the production of these Acts or documents, but is obliged to make them known to the opposite party.

ARTICLE XLIV.   The Tribunal can, besides, require from the agents of the parties the production of all Acts, and can demand all necessary explanations. In case of refusal, the Tribunal takes note of it.

ARTICLE XLV.   The agents and counsel of the parties are authorized to present orally to the Tribunal all the arguments they may think expedient in defence of their case.

ARTICLE XLVI.   They have the right to raise objections and points. The decisions of the Tribunal on those points are final, and cannot form the subject of any subsequent discussion.

ARTICLE XLVII.   The members of the Tribunal have the right to put questions to the agents and counsel of the parties, and to demand explanations from them on doubtful points. Neither the questions put nor the remarks made by members of the Tribunal during the discussions can be regarded as an expression of opinion by the Tribunal in general, or by its members in particular.

ARTICLE XLVIII.   The Tribunal is authorized to declare its competence in interpreting the "Compromis" as well as the other Treaties which may be invoked in the case, and in applying the principles of international law.

ARTICLE XLIX.   The Tribunal has the right to issue Rules of Procedure for the conduct of the case, to decide the forms and periods within which each party must conclude its arguments, and to arrange all the formalities required for dealing with the evidence.

ARTICLE L.   When the agents and counsel of the parties have submitted all explanations and evidence in support of their case, the President pronounces the discussion closed.

ARTICLE LI.   The deliberations of the Tribunal take place in private. Every decision is taken by a majority of members of the Tribunal. The refusal of a member to vote must be recorded in the "procès-verbal."

ARTICLE LII.   The award, given by a majority of votes, is accompanied by a statement of reasons. It is drawn up in writing and signed by each member of the Tribunal. Those members who are in the minority may record their dissent when signing.

ARTICLE LIII.   The award is read out at a public meeting of the Tribunal, the agents and counsel of the parties being present, or duly summoned to attend.

ARTICLE LIV. The award, duly pronounced and notified to the agents of the parties at variance, puts an end to the dispute definitely and without appeal.

ARTICLE LV. The parties can reserve in the "Compromis" the right to demand the revision of the award. In this case, and unless there be an agreement to the contrary, the demand must be addressed to the Tribunal which pronounced the award. It can only be made on the ground of the discovery of some new fact calculated to exercise a decisive influence on the award, and which, at the time the discussion was closed, was unknown to the Tribunal and to the party demanding the revision. Proceedings for revision can only be instituted by a decision of the Tribunal expressly recording the existence of the new fact, recognizing in it the character described in the foregoing paragraph, and declaring the demand admissible on this ground. The "Compromis" fixes the period within which the demand for revision must be made.

ARTICLE LVI. The award is only binding on the parties who concluded the "Compromis." When there is a question of interpreting a Convention to which Powers other than those concerned in the dispute are parties, the latter notify to the former the "Compromis" they have concluded. Each of these Powers has the right to intervene in the case. If one or more of them avail themselves of this right, the interpretation contained in the award is equally binding on them.

ARTICLE LVII. Each party pays its own expenses and an equal share of those of the Tribunal.

General Provisions.

ARTICLE LVIII. The present Convention shall be ratified as speedily as possible. The ratification shall be deposited at The Hague. A "procès-verbal" shall be drawn up recording the receipt of each ratification, and a copy duly certified shall be sent, through the diplomatic channel, to all the Powers who were represented at the International Peace Conference at The Hague.

ARTICLE LIX. The non-Signatory Powers who were represented at the International Peace Conference can adhere to the present Convention. For this purpose they must make known their adhesion to the Contracting Powers by a written notification addressed to the Netherland Government, and communicated by it to all the other Contracting Powers.

ARTICLE LX. The conditions on which the Powers who were not represented at the International Peace Conference can adhere to the present Convention shall form the subject of a subsequent Agreement among the Contracting Powers.

ARTICLE LXI. In the event of one of the High Contracting Parties denouncing the present Convention, this denunciation would not take effect until a year after its notification made in writing to the Netherland Government, and by it communicated at once to all the other Contracting Powers. This denunciation shall only affect the notifying Power. In faith of which the Plenipotentiaries have signed the present Convention and affixed their seals to it. Done at The Hague, the 29th July, 1899, in a single copy, which shall remain in the archives of the Netherland Government, and copies of it, duly certified, be sent through the diplomatic channel to the Contracting Powers. — *United States*, 56*th Cong.*, 1*st Sess.*, *Senate Doc.* 159.

The Permanent Court of Arbitration.—The following is the membership of the Permanent Court of Arbitration, as finally organized, in January, 1901, and announced to be prepared for the consideration of any international dispute that may be submitted to it. Fifteen of the greater nations of the world are represented in this most august tribunal that has ever sat for judgment of the disputes of men :

Austria-Hungary. His Excellency Count Frederic Schonborn, LL. D., president of the Imperial Royal Court of Administrative Justice, former Austrian Minister of Justice, member of the House of Lords of the Austrian Parliament, etc. His Excellency Mr. D. de Szilagyi, ex-Minister of Justice, member of the House of Deputies of the Hungarian Parliament. Count Albert Apponyi, member of the Chamber of Magnates and of the Chamber of Deputies of the Hungarian Parliament, etc. Mr. Henri Lammasch, LL. D., member of the House of Lords of the Austrian Parliament, etc.

Belgium. His Excellency Mr. Beernaert, Minister of State, member of the Chamber of Representatives, etc. His Excellency Baron Lambermont, Minister of State, Envoy Extraordinary and Minister Plenipotentiary, Secretary-General of the Ministry of Foreign Affairs. The Chevalier Descamps, Senator. Mr. Rolin Jacquemyns, ex-Minister of the Interior.

Denmark. Professor H. Matzen, LL. D., Professor of the Copenhagen University, Counsellor Extraordinary of the Supreme Court, President of the Landsthing.

France. M. Leon Bourgeois, Deputy, ex-President of the Cabinet Council, ex-Minister for Foreign Affairs. M. de Laboulaye, ex-Ambassador. Baron Destournelles de Constant, Minister Plenipotentiary, Deputy. M. Louis Renault, Minister Plenipotentiary, Professor in the Faculty of Law at Paris, Law Office of the Department of Foreign Affairs.

Germany. His Excellency Mr. Bingner, LL. D., Privy Councillor, Senate President of the Imperial High Court at Leipsic. Mr. von Frantzius, Privy Councillor, Solicitor of the Department of Foreign Affairs at Berlin. Mr. von Martitz, LL. D., Associate Justice of the Superior Court of Administrative Justice in Prussia, Professor of Law at the Berlin University. Mr. von Bar, LL. D., Judicial Privy Councillor, Professor of Law at the Göttingen University.

Great Britain. His Excellency the Right Honorable Lord Pauncefote of Preston, G. C. B., G. C. M. G., Privy Councillor, Ambassador at Washington. The Right Honorable Sir Edward Baldwin Malet, ex-Ambassador. The Right Honorable Sir Edward Fry, member of the Privy Council, Q. C. Professor John Westlake, LL. D., Q. C.

Italy. His Excellency Count Constantin Nigra, Senator of the Kingdom, Ambassador at Vienna. His Excellency Commander Jean Baptiste Pagano Guarnaschelli, Senator of the Kingdom, First President of the Court of Cassation at Rome. His Excellency Count Tornielli Brusati di Vergano, Senator of the Kingdom, Ambassador at Paris. Commander Joseph Zanardelli, Attorney at Law, Deputy to the National Parliament.

Japan. Mr. I. Motono, Envoy Extraordinary and Minister Plenipotentiary at Brussels. Mr. H. Willard Denison, Law Officer of the Minister for Foreign Affairs at Tokio.

Netherlands. Mr. T. M. C. Asser, LL. D., member of the Council of State, ex-Professor of the University of Amsterdam. Mr. F. B. Coninck Liefsting, LL. D., President of the Court of Cassation. Jonkheer A. F. de Savornin Lohman, LL. D., ex-Minister of the Interior, ex-Professor of the Free University of Amsterdam, member of the Lower House of the States-General. Jonkheer G. L. M. H. Ruis de Beerenbrouck, ex-Minister of Justice, Commissioner of the Queen in the Province of Limbourg.

Portugal. Count de Macedo, Peer of the Realm, ex-Minister of Marine and Colonies, Envoy Extraordinary and Minister Plenipotentiary at Madrid.

Rumania. Mr. Theodore Rosetti, Senator, ex-President of the High Court of Cassation and Justice. Mr. Jean Kalindero, Administrator of the Crown Domain, ex-Judge of the High Court of Cassation and Justice. Mr. Eugene Statsco, ex-President of the Senate, ex-Minister of Justice and Foreign Affairs. Mr. Jean N. Lahovari, Deputy, ex-Envoy Extraordinary and Minister Plenipotentiary, ex-Minister of Foreign Affairs.

Russia. Mr. N. V. Mouravieff, Minister of Justice, Active Privy Councillor, Secretary of State of His Majesty the Emperor. Mr. C. P. Pobedonostzeff, Attorney-General of the Most Holy Synod, Active Privy Councillor, Secretary of State of His Majesty the Emperor. Mr. E. V. Frisch, President of the Department of Legislation of the Imperial Council, Active Privy Councillor, Secretary of State of His Majesty the Emperor. Mr. de Martens, Privy Councillor, permanent member of the Council of the Ministry of Foreign Affairs.

Spain. His Excellency the Duke of Tetuan, ex-Minister of Foreign Affairs, Senator of the Kingdom, Grandee of Spain. Mr. Bienvenido Oliver, Director-General of the Ministry of Justice, ex-Delegate of Spain to the Conference on Private International Law at The Hague. Dr. Manuel Torres Campos, Professor of international law at the University of Grenada, associate member of the Institute of International Law.

Sweden and Norway. Mr. S. R. D. K. D'Olivecrona, member of the International Law Institute, ex-Associate Justice of the Supreme Court of the Kingdom of Sweden, Doctor of Laws and Letters at Stockholm. Mr. G. Gram, ex-Minister of State of Norway, Governor of the Province of Hamar, Norway.

United States. Mr. Benjamin Harrison, ex-President of the United States. Mr. Melville W. Fuller, Chief Justice of the United States. Mr. John W. Griggs, Attorney-General of the United States. Mr. George Gray, United States Circuit Judge.

First Secretary of the Court—J. J. Rochussen. Second Secretary of the Court—Jonkheer W. Roell.

The Administrative Council consists of the Minister of Foreign Affairs of the Netherlands and the diplomatic representatives at The Hague of the ratifying Powers.

Secretary-General—Mr. R. Melvil, Baron Van Leyden, Judge of the District Court of Utrecht and a member of the First Chamber of the States-General.

Convention with respect to the Laws and Customs of War on Land.

ARTICLE I. The High Contracting Parties shall issue instructions to their armed land forces, which shall be in conformity with the "Regulations respecting the Laws and Customs of War on Land" annexed to the present Convention.

ARTICLE II. The provisions contained in the Regulations mentioned in Article I. are only binding on the Contracting Powers, in case of war between two or more of them. These provisions shall cease to be binding from the time when, in a war between Contracting Powers, a non-Contracting Power joins one of the belligerents.

ARTICLE III. The present Convention shall be ratified as speedily as possible. The ratifications shall be deposited at The Hague. A "procès-verbal" shall be drawn up recording the receipt of each ratification, and a copy, duly certified, shall be sent through the diplomatic channel, to all the Contracting Powers.

ARTICLE. IV. Non-Signatory Powers are allowed to adhere to the present Convention. For this purpose they must make their adhesion known to the Contracting Powers by means of a written notification addressed to the Netherland Government, and by it communicated to all the other Contracting Powers.

ARTICLE V. In the event of one of the High Contracting Parties denouncing the present Convention, such denunciation would not take effect until a year after the written notification made to the Netherland Government, and by it at once communicated to all the other Contracting Powers. This denunciation shall affect only the notifying Power.

In faith of which the Plenipotentiaries have signed the present Convention and affixed their seals thereto.

[Signed by representatives of Belgium, Denmark, Spain, Mexico, France, Greece, Montenegro, the Netherlands, Persia, Portugal, Roumania, Russia, Siam, Sweden and Norway, and Bulgaria.]

REGULATIONS.

SECTION I.—On Belligerents.— CHAPTER I.—On the qualifications of Belligerents.

ARTICLE I. The laws, rights, and duties of war apply not only to armies, but also to militia and volunteer corps, fulfilling the following conditions:—1. To be commanded by a person responsible for his subordinates; 2. To have a fixed distinctive emblem recognizable at a distance; 3. To carry arms openly; and, 4. To conduct their operations in accordance with the laws and customs of war. In countries where militia or volunteer corps constitute the army, or form part of it, they are included under the denomination "army."

ARTICLE II. The population of a territory which has not been occupied who, on the enemy's approach, spontaneously take up arms to resist the invading troops without having time to organize themselves in accordance with Article I., shall be regarded a belligerent, if they respect the laws and customs of war.

ARTICLE III. The armed forces of the belligerent parties may consist of combatants and non-combatants. In case of capture by the enemy both have a right to be treated as prisoners of war.

CHAPTER II.—On Prisoners of War.

ARTICLE IV. Prisoners of war are in the power of the hostile Government, but not in that of the individuals or corps who captured them. They must be humanely treated. All their personal belongings, except arms, horses, and military papers remain their property.

ARTICLE V. Prisoners of war may be interned in a town, fortress, camp, or any other locality, and bound not to go beyond certain fixed limits ; but they can only be confined as an indispensable measure of safety.

ARTICLE VI. The State may utilize the labour of prisoners of war according to their rank and aptitude. Their tasks shall not be excessive, and shall have nothing to do with the military operations. Prisoners may be authorized to work for the Public Service, for private persons, or on their own account. Work done for the State shall be paid for according to the tariffs in force for soldiers of the national army employed on similar tasks. When the work is for other branches of the Public Service or for private persons, the conditions shall be settled in agreement with the military authorities. The wages of the prisoners shall go towards improving their position, and the balance shall be paid them at the time of their release, after deducting the cost of their maintenance.

ARTICLE VII. The Government into whose hands prisoners of war have fallen is bound to maintain them. Failing a special agreement between the belligerents, prisoners of war shall be treated as regards food, quarters, and clothing, on the same footing as the troops of the Government which has captured them.

ARTICLE VIII. Prisoners of war shall be subject to the laws, regulations, and orders in force in the army of the State into whose hands they have fallen. Any act of insubordination warrants the adoption, as regards them, of such measures of severity as may be necessary. Escaped prisoners, recaptured before they have succeeded in rejoining their army, or before quitting the territory occupied by the army that captured them, are liable to disciplinary punishment. Prisoners who, after succeeding in escaping, are again taken prisoners, are not liable to any punishment for the previous flight.

ARTICLE IX. Every prisoner of war, if questioned, is bound to declare his true name and rank, and if he disregards this rule, he is liable to a curtailment of the advantages accorded to the prisoners of war of his class.

ARTICLE X. Prisoners of war may be set at liberty on parole if the laws of their country authorize it, and, in such a case, they are bound, on their personal honour, scrupulously to fulfil, both as regards their own Government and the Government by whom they were made prisoners, the engagements they have contracted. In such cases, their own Government shall not require of nor accept from them any service incompatible with the parole given.

ARTICLE XI. A prisoner of war cannot be forced to accept his liberty on parole; similarly the hostile Government is not obliged to assent to the prisoner's request to be set at liberty on parole.

ARTICLE XII. Any prisoner of war, who is liberated on parole and recaptured, bearing arms against the Government to whom he had pledged his honour, or against the allies of that Government, forfeits his right to be treated as a prisoner of war, and can be brought before the Courts.

ARTICLE XIII. Individuals who follow an army without directly belonging to it, such as newspaper correspondents and reporters, sutlers, contractors, who fall into the enemy's hands, and whom the latter think fit to detain, have a right to be treated as prisoners of war, provided they can produce a certificate from the military authorities of the army they were accompanying.

ARTICLE XIV. A Bureau for information relative to prisoners of war is instituted, on the commencement of hostilities, in each of the belligerent States and, when necessary, in the neutral countries on whose territory belligerents have been received. This Bureau is intended to answer all inquiries about prisoners of war, and is furnished by the various services concerned with all the necessary information to enable it to keep an individual return for each prisoner of war. It is kept informed of internments and changes, as well as of admissions into hospital and deaths. It is also the duty of the Information Bureau to receive and collect all objects of personal use, valuables, letters, &c., found on the battlefields or left by prisoners who have died in hospital or ambulance, and to transmit them to those interested.

ARTICLE XV. Relief Societies for prisoners of war, which are regularly constituted in accordance with the law of the country with the object of serving as the intermediary for charity, shall receive from the belligerents for themselves and their duly accredited agents every facility, within the bounds of military requirements and Administrative Regulations, for the effective accomplishment of their humane task. Delegates of these Societies may be admitted to the places of internment for the distribution of relief, as also to the halting places of repatriated prisoners, if furnished with a personal permit by the military authorities, and on giving an engagement in writing to comply with all their Regulations for order and police.

ARTICLE XVI. The Information Bureau shall have the privilege of free postage. Letters, money orders, and valuables, as well as postal parcels destined for the prisoners of war or despatched by them, shall be free of all postal duties, both in the countries of origin and destination, as well as in those they pass through. Gifts and relief in kind for prisoners of war shall be admitted free of all duties of entry and others, as well as of payments for carriage by the Government railways.

ARTICLE XVII. Officers taken prisoners may receive, if necessary, the full pay allowed them in this position by their country's regulations, the amount to be repaid by their Government.

ARTICLE XVIII. Prisoners of war shall enjoy every latitude in the exercise of their religion, including attendance at their own church services, provided only they comply with the regulations for order and police issued by the military authorities.

ARTICLE XIX. The wills of prisoners of war are received or drawn up on the same conditions as for soldiers of the national army. The same rules shall be observed regarding death certificates, as well as for the burial of prisoners of war, due regard being paid to their grade and rank.

ARTICLE XX. After the conclusion of peace, the repatriation of prisoners of war shall take place as speedily as possible.

CHAPTER III.—On the Sick and Wounded.

ARTICLE XXI. The obligations of belligerents with regard to the sick and wounded are governed by the Geneva Convention of the 22d August, 1864, subject to any modifications which may be introduced into it.

SECTION II.—On Hostilities.—CHAPTER I.—On means of injuring the Enemy, Sieges, and Bombardments.

ARTICLE XXII. The right of belligerents to adopt means of injuring the enemy is not unlimited.

ARTICLE XXIII. Besides the prohibitions provided by special Conventions, it is especially prohibited:—(a.) To employ poison or poisoned arms; (b.) To kill or wound treacherously individuals belonging to the hostile nation or army; (c.) To kill or wound an enemy who, having laid down arms, or having no longer means of defence, has surrendered at discretion; (d.) To declare that no quarter will be given; (e.) To employ arms, projectiles, or material of a nature to cause superfluous injury; (f.) To make improper use of a flag of truce, the national flag, or military ensigns and the enemy's uniform, as well as the distinctive badges of the Geneva Convention; (g.) To destroy or seize the enemy's property, unless such destruction or seizure be imperatively demanded by the necessities of war.

ARTICLE XXIV. Ruses of war and the employment of methods necessary to obtain information about the enemy and the country, are considered allowable.

ARTICLE XXV. The attack or bombardment of towns, villages, habitations or buildings which are not defended, is prohibited.

ARTICLE XXVI. The Commander of an attacking force, before commencing a bombardment, except in the case of an assault, should do all he can to warn the authorities.

ARTICLE XXVII. In sieges and bombardments all necessary steps should be taken to spare as far as possible edifices devoted to religion, art, science, and charity, hospitals, and places where the sick and wounded are collected, provided they are not used at the same time for military purposes. The besieged should indicate these buildings or places by some particular and visible signs, which should previously be notified to the assailants.

ARTICLE XXVIII. The pillage of a town or place, even when taken by assault, is prohibited.

CHAPTER II.—On Spies.

ARTICLE XXIX. An individual can only be considered a spy if, acting clandestinely, or on false pretences, he obtains, or seeks to obtain information in the zone of operations of a belligerent, with the intention of communicating it to the hostile party. Thus, soldiers not in disguise who have penetrated into the zone of operations of a hostile army to obtain information are not considered spies. Similarly, the following are not considered spies : soldiers or civilians, carry-

ing out their mission openly, charged with the delivery of despatches destined either for their own army or for that of the enemy. To this class belong likewise individuals sent in balloons to deliver despatches, and generally to maintain communication between the various parts of an army or of a territory.

ARTICLE XXX. A spy taken in the act cannot be punished without previous trial.

ARTICLE XXXI. A spy who, after rejoining the army to which he belongs, is subsequently captured by the enemy, is treated as a prisoner of war, and incurs no responsibility for his previous acts of espionage.

CHAPTER III.—On Flags of Truce.

ARTICLE XXXII. An individual is considered as bearing a flag of truce who is authorized by one of the belligerents to enter into communication with the other, and who carries a white flag. He has a right to inviolability, as well as the trumpeter, bugler, or drummer, the flag-bearer, and the interpreter who may accompany him.

ARTICLE XXXIII. The Chief to whom a flag of truce is sent is not obliged to receive it in all circumstances. He can take all steps necessary to prevent the envoy taking advantage of his mission to obtain information. In case of abuse, he has the right to detain the envoy temporarily.

ARTICLE XXXIV. The envoy loses his rights of inviolability if it is proved beyond doubt that he has taken advantage of his privileged position to provoke or commit an act of treachery.

CHAPTER IV.—On Capitulations.

ARTICLE XXXV. Capitulations agreed on between the Contracting Parties must be in accordance with the rules of military honour. When once settled, they must be scrupulously observed by both the parties.

CHAPTER V.—On Armistices.

ARTICLE XXXVI. An armistice suspends military operations by mutual agreement between the belligerent parties. If its duration is not fixed, the belligerent parties can resume operations at any time, provided always the enemy is warned within the time agreed upon, in accordance with the terms of the armistice.

ARTICLE XXXVII. An armistice may be general or local. The first suspends all military operations of the belligerent States ; the second, only those between certain fractions of the belligerent armies and in a fixed radius.

ARTICLE XXXVIII. An armistice must be notified officially, and in good time, to the competent authorities and the troops. Hostilities are suspended immediately after the notification, or at a fixed date.

ARTICLE XXXIX. It is for the Contracting Parties to settle, in the terms of the armistice, what communications may be held, on the theatre of war, with the population and with each other.

ARTICLE XL. Any serious violation of the armistice by one of the parties gives the other party the right to denounce it, and even, in case of urgency, to recommence hostilities at once.

ARTICLE XLI. A violation of the terms of the armistice by private individuals acting on their own initiative, only confers the right of demanding the punishment of the offenders, and, if necessary, indemnity for the losses sustained.

SECTION III.—On Military Authority over Hostile Territory.

ARTICLE XLII.   Territory is considered occupied when it is actually placed under the authority of the hostile army.   The occupation applies only to the territory where such authority is established, and in a position to assert itself.

ARTICLE XLIII.   The authority of the legitimate power having actually passed into the hands of the occupant, the latter shall take all steps in his power to re-establish and insure, as far as possible, public order and safety, while respecting, unless absolutely prevented, the laws in force in the country.

ARTICLE XLIV.   Any compulsion of the population of occupied territory to take part in military operations against its own country is prohibited.

ARTICLE XLV.   Any pressure on the population of occupied territory to take the oath to the hostile Power is prohibited.

ARTICLE XLVI.   Family honours and rights, individual lives and private property, as well as religious convictions and liberty, must be respected.   Private property cannot be confiscated.

ARTICLE XLVII.   Pillage is formally prohibited.

ARTICLE XLVIII.   If, in the territory occupied, the occupant collects the taxes, dues, and tolls imposed for the benefit of the State, he shall do it, as far as possible, in accordance with the rules in existence and the assessment in force, and will in consequence be bound to defray the expenses of the administration of the occupied territory on the same scale as that by which the legitimate Government was bound.

ARTICLE XLIX.   If, besides the taxes mentioned in the preceding Article, the occupant levies other money taxes in the occupied territory, this can only be for military necessities or the administration of such territory.

ARTICLE L.   No general penalty, pecuniary or otherwise, can be inflicted on the population on account of the acts of individuals for which it cannot be regarded as collectively responsible.

ARTICLE LI.   No tax shall be collected except under a written order and on the responsibility of a Commander-in-chief.   This collection shall only take place, as far as possible, in accordance with the rules in existence and the assessment of taxes in force.   For every payment a receipt shall be given to the taxpayer.

ARTICLE LII.   Neither requisitions in kind nor services can be demanded from communes or inhabitants except for the necessities of the army of occupation.   They must be in proportion to the resources of the country, and of such a nature as not to involve the population in the obligation of taking part in military operations against their country.   These requisitions and services shall only be demanded on the authority of the Commander in the locality occupied.   The contributions in kind shall, as far as possible, be paid for in ready money ; if not, their receipt shall be acknowledged.

ARTICLE LIII.   An army of occupation can only take possession of the cash, funds, and property liable to requisition belonging strictly to the State, depôts of arms, means of transport, stores and supplies, and, generally, all movable property of the State which may be used for military operations.   Railway plant, land telegraphs,

telephones, steamers, and other ships, apart from cases governed by maritime law, as well as depôts of arms and, generally, all kinds of war material, even though belonging to Companies or to private persons, are likewise material which may serve for military operations, but they must be restored at the conclusion of peace, and indemnities paid for them.

ARTICLE LIV.   The plant of railways coming from neutral States, whether the property of those States, or of Companies, or of private persons, shall be sent back to them as soon as possible.

ARTICLE LV.   The occupying State shall only be regarded as administrator and usufructuary of the public buildings, real property, forests, and agricultural works belonging to the hostile State, and situated in the occupied country.   It must protect the capital of these properties, and administer it according to the rules of usufruct.

ARTICLE LVI.   The property of the communes, that of religious, charitable, and educational institutions, and those of arts and science, even when State property, shall be treated as private property.   All seizure of, and destruction, or intentional damage done to such institutions, to historical monuments, works of art or science, is prohibited, and should be made the subject of proceedings.

SECTION IV.—On the Internment of Belligerents and the Care of the Wounded in Neutral Countries.

ARTICLE LVII.   A neutral State which receives in its territory troops belonging to the belligerent armies shall intern them, as far as possible, at a distance from the theatre of war.   It can keep them in camps, and even confine them in fortresses or localities assigned for this purpose.   It shall decide whether officers may be left at liberty on giving their parole that they will not leave the neutral territory without authorization.

ARTICLE LVIII.   Failing a special Convention, the neutral State shall supply the interned with the food, clothing, and relief required by humanity.   At the conclusion of peace, the expenses caused by the internment shall be made good.

ARTICLE LIX.   A neutral State may authorize the passage through its territory of wounded or sick belonging to the belligerent armies, on condition that the trains bringing them shall carry neither combatants nor war material.   In such a case, the neutral State is bound to adopt such measures of safety and control as may be necessary for the purpose.   Wounded and sick brought under these conditions into neutral territory by one of the belligerents, and belonging to the hostile party, must be guarded by the neutral State, so as to insure their not taking part again in the military operations.   The same duty shall devolve on the neutral State with regard to wounded or sick of the other army who may be committed to its care.

ARTICLE LX.   The Geneva Convention applies to sick and wounded interned in neutral territory.

The Convention establishing these regulations was not signed by the delegates from the United States, nor by those of Great Britain.   The reasons for abstention on the part of the latter were stated in a communication from the British War Office, as follows : "Lord Lansdowne . . . considers it essential that the revised Articles, together with the Preamble and final dispositions, should be submitted to the most careful examination by the high military authorities and by the legal advisers of Her Majesty's Government, before he can pronounce a definitive opinion on the three points raised. Subject to such reserves as may result from this examination, Lord Lansdowne is of opinion that the Project of Convention is in general of such a nature that it may, in principle, be accepted as a basis of instructions for the guidance of the British army, but he is unable, until that examination has been completed, to offer an opinion as to whether it is desirable to enter into an international engagement. Lord Lansdowne would therefore suggest, for Lord Salisbury's consideration, that instructions should be given to Sir Julian Pauncefote to reserve full liberty for Her Majesty's Government, to accept only such Articles as, after mature examination by their military and legal advisers, they may approve of." Probably the delegates from the United States were similarly instructed by their government.

Added to the Convention relative to Laws and Customs of War were three Declarations, separately signed, as follows:

1. "The contracting powers agree to prohibit, for a term of five years, the launching of projectiles and explosives from balloons, or by other new methods of a similar nature."

2. "The contracting parties agree to abstain from the use of bullets which expand or flatten easily in the human body, such as bullets with a hard envelope which does not entirely cover the core, or is pierced with incisions."

3. "The contracting parties agree to abstain from the use of projectiles the object of which is the diffusion of asphyxiating or deleterious gases."

The first of these Declarations was signed by the delegates from the United States, but not by those from Great Britain. The second and third were signed by neither British nor American representatives. In the discussion that preceded the adoption of the second Declaration by a majority of the Conference, Captain Crozier, of the American delegation, presented the objections to it, on which he and his colleagues were in agreement with the British representatives. He said "there was a great difference of opinion as to whether the bullets of small calibre rifles sufficed to put men 'hors de combat,' which was admitted on all sides to be the object which rifle fire was expected to achieve. He considered the proposition before the Conference to be unsatisfactory, since it limited the prohibition to details of construction which only included a single case, and left all others out of consideration. He would not enter into a recapitulation of all the advantages of small calibre rifles, since they were perfectly well known ; but he felt sure that certain Powers might adopt calibres even smaller than those at present in use, and, in this case, he maintained that they would be compelled to secure increased shock by some new method of construction of the projectile. He considered that it would be perfectly easy to devise such projectiles while keeping within the terms of the proposed interdiction, and he thought that the result might be the ultimate adoption of a bullet of an even less humane character than those aimed at by the Resolution. He declared that

he had nothing to say for or against the Dum-Dum bullet [see, in this vol, Dum-Dum Bullet], of which he knew nothing except what had been stated during the meetings of the First Commission, but that he was not disposed to make any condemnation without proofs, and these proofs had not been forthcoming."

As for the third Declaration, it was opposed by Captain Mahan, who spoke for the Americans, because "he considered the use of asphyxiating shell far less inhuman and cruel than the employment of submarine boats, and as the employment of submarine boats had not been interdicted by the Conference (though specially mentioned with that object in the Mouravieff Circular), he felt constrained to maintain his vote in favour of the use of asphyxiating shell on the original ground that the United States' Government was averse to placing any restriction on the inventive genius of its citizens in inventing and providing new weapons of war."

Convention for the adaptation to maritime warfare of the principles of the Geneva Convention of August 22, 1864.

ARTICLE I. Military hospital-ships, that is to say, ships constructed or assigned by States specially and solely for the purpose of assisting the wounded, sick, or shipwrecked, and the names of which shall have been communicated to the belligerent Powers at the commencement or during the course of hostilities, and in any case before they are employed, shall be respected and cannot be captured while hostilities last. These ships, moreover, are not on the same footing as men-of-war as regards their stay in a neutral port.

ARTICLE II. Hospital-ships, equipped wholly or in part at the cost of private individuals or officially recognized relief Societies, shall likewise be respected and exempt from capture, provided the belligerent Power to whom they belong has given them an official commission and has notified their names to the hostile Power at the commencement of or during hostilities, and in any case before they are employed. These ships should be furnished with a certificate from the competent authorities, declaring that they had been under their control while fitting out and on final departure.

ARTICLE III. Hospital-ships, equipped wholly or in part at the cost of private individuals or officially recognized Societies of neutral countries, shall be respected and exempt from capture, if the neutral Power to whom they belong has given them an official commission and notified their names to the belligerent Powers at the commencement of or during hostilities, and in any case before they are employed.

ARTICLE IV. The ships mentioned in Articles I, II, and III shall afford relief and assistance to the wounded, sick, and shipwrecked of the belligerents independently of their nationality. The Governments engage not to use these ships for any military purpose. These ships must not in any way hamper the movements of the combatants. During and after an engagement they will act at their own risk and peril. The belligerents will have the right to control and visit them ; they can refuse to help them, order them off, make them take a certain course, and put a Commissioner on board; they can even detain them, if important circumstances require it. As far as possible the belligerents shall inscribe in the sailing papers of the hospital-ships the orders they give them.

ARTICLE V. The military hospital-ships shall be distinguished by being painted white outside with a horizontal band of green about a metre and a half in breadth. The ships mentioned in Articles II and III shall be distinguished by being painted white outside with a horizontal band of red about a metre and a half in breadth. The boats of the ships above mentioned, as also small craft which may be used for hospital work, shall be distinguished by similar painting. All hospital-ships shall make themselves known by hoisting, together with their national flag, the white flag with a red cross provided by the Geneva Convention.

ARTICLE VI. Neutral merchantmen, yachts, or vessels, having, or taking on board, sick, wounded, or shipwrecked of the belligerents, cannot be captured for so doing, but they are liable to capture for any violation of neutrality they may have committed.

ARTICLE VII. The religious, medical, or hospital staff of any captured ship is inviolable, and its members cannot be made prisoners of war. On leaving the ship they take with them the objects and surgical instruments which are their own private property. This staff shall continue to discharge its duties while necessary, and can afterwards leave when the Commander-in-chief considers it possible. The belligerents must guarantee to the staff that has fallen into their hands the enjoyment of their salaries intact.

ARTICLE VIII. Sailors and soldiers who are taken on board when sick or wounded, to whatever nation they belong, shall be protected and looked after by the captors.

ARTICLE IX. The shipwrecked, wounded, or sick of one of the belligerents who fall into the hands of the other, are prisoners of war. The captor must decide, according to circumstances, if it is best to keep them or send them to a port of his own country, to a neutral port, or even to a hostile port. In the last case, prisoners thus repatriated cannot serve as long as the war lasts.

ARTICLE X. The shipwrecked, wounded, or sick, who are landed at a neutral port with the consent of the local authorities, must, failing a contrary arrangement between the neutral State and the belligerents, be guarded by the neutral State, so that they cannot again take part in the military operations. The expenses of entertainment and internment shall be borne by the State to which the shipwrecked, wounded, or sick belong.

ARTICLE XI. The rules contained in the above Articles are binding only on the Contracting Powers, in case of war between two or more of them. The said rules shall cease to be binding from the time when, in a war between the Contracting Powers, one of the belligerents is joined by a non-Contracting Power.

ARTICLE XII. The present Convention shall be ratified as soon as possible. The ratifications shall be deposited at The Hague. On the receipt of each ratification a "procès-verbal" shall be drawn up, a copy of which, duly certified, shall be sent through the diplomatic channel to all the Contracting Powers.

ARTICLE XIII. The non-Signatory Powers who accepted the Geneva Convention of the 22d August, 1864, are allowed to adhere to the present Convention. For this purpose they must make their adhesion known to the Contracting Powers by means of a written notification addressed to the Netherland Government, and by it communicated to all the other Contracting Powers.

ARTICLE XIV. In the event of one of the High Contracting Parties denouncing the present Convention, such denunciation shall not take effect until a year after the notification made in writing to the Netherland Government, and forthwith communicated by it to all the other Contracting Powers. This denunciation shall only affect the notifying Power.

In faith of which the respective Plenipotentiaries have signed the present Convention and affixed their seals thereto.

[Signed by the representatives of Belgium, Denmark, Spain, Mexico, France, Greece, Montenegro, the Netherlands, Persia, Portugal, Roumania, Russia, Siam, Sweden and Norway, and Bulgaria]

PEARY'S EXPLORATIONS. See (in this vol.) POLAR EXPLORATION, 1895, 1896, 1897, 1898–.

PEKING: A. D. 1900.—The siege of the Foreign Legations and their rescue.—Occupation of the city by the allied forces.—Looting and outrage.—March through the "Forbidden City." See (in this vol.) CHINA: A. D. 1900 (JUNE—AUGUST); and (AUGUST 4–16, and 15–28).

A. D. 1900–1901.—Seizure of grounds for a fortified Legation Quarter. See (in this vol.) CHINA: A. D. 1900–1901 (NOVEMBER—FEBRUARY).

PEKING SYNDICATE, Chinese concessions to the. See (in this vol.) CHINA: A. D. 1898 (FEBRUARY—DECEMBER).

PELAGIC SEAL KILLING, The question of. See (in this vol.) BERING SEA QUESTIONS.

PELEW ISLANDS: Sale by Spain to Germany. See (in this vol.) CAROLINE AND MARIANNE ISLANDS.

PENNSYLVANIA: A. D. 1897.—Great strike of coal miners.—**Conflict at Lattimer.** See (in this vol.) INDUSTRIAL DISTURBANCES: A. D. 1897.

A. D. 1900.—Strike of anthracite coal miners. See (in this vol.) INDUSTRIAL DISTURBANCES: A. D. 1900.

PENNSYLVANIA, University of: Expeditions to explore the ruins of Nippur. See (in this vol.) ARCHÆOLOGICAL RESEARCH: BABYLONIA: AMERICAN EXPLORATION.

PENNY POSTAGE, British Imperial. See (in this vol.) ENGLAND: A. D. 1898 (DECEMBER).

PENSIONS, Old-Age. See references (in this vol.) under OLD-AGE PENSIONS.

PEONES. See (in this vol.) PORTO RICO: A. D. 1898–1899 (AUGUST—JULY).

PEOPLE'S PARTY, The. See (in this vol.) UNITED STATES OF AM.: A. D. 1896 (JUNE—NOVEMBER); and 1900 (MAY—NOVEMBER).

PERRY'S EXPEDITION TO JAPAN,
Proposed monument to commemorate. See
(in this vol.) JAPAN: A. D. 1901.

PERSIA: A .D. 1896.—Assassination of
the Shah.—The Shah of Persia, Nâsr-ed-din,
was shot, on the 1st day of May, when entering
the mosque of Shah Abdul Azim, by one Mirza
Mahomed Reza, said to be of the Babi sect.
Nâsr-ed-din had reigned since 1848. He was
succeeded by his son, Muzaffar-ed-din, who was
forty-three years old at his accession.

A. D. 1897-1899.—Recent exploration of
the ruins of Susa. See (in this vol.) ARCHÆO-
LOGICAL RESEARCH: PERSIA.

A. D. 1899 (May—July).—Representation
in the Peace Conference at The Hague. See
(in this vol.) PEACE CONFERENCE.

A. D. 1900.—Russian railway projects. See
(in this vol.) RUSSIA IN ASIA: A. D. 1900.

PERSIAN GULF, Railways to the. See
(in this vol.) TURKEY: A. D. 1899 (NOVEMBER);
and RUSSIA IN ASIA: A. D. 1900.

PERU: A. D. 1894-1899.—Overthrow of
an unconstitutional government.—Legitimate
authority restored.—The death of President
Bermudez, in March, 1894, brought about a revolutionary movement in the interest of ex-President Caceres. Constitutionally, the First Vice-
President, Dr. del Solar, would have succeeded
the deceased President, until a new election was
held; but the Second Vice-President, who was a
partisan of Caceres, and who had the army with
him, seized control of the government. In May,
Caceres was proclaimed Provisional President,
and in August it was claimed for him that he
had been elected by Congress; but the election
was not recognized by his opponents. A formidable rebellion was organized, under the lead
of ex-President Pierola, who had been in exile
and now returned. Civil war raged for nearly a
year, Pierola gaining steadily. In February, 1895,
his forces reached the capital and laid siege to it.
On the 17th of March they entered the city, and
there was desperate fighting in the streets of
Lima for three days, nearly 2,000 of the combatants being killed and more than 1,500 wounded.
Chiefly through the efforts of the Papal delegate,
the bloody conflict was finally stopped and terms
of peace arranged. A provisional government,
made up from both parties, was formed, under
which a peaceable election was held in the following July. Pierola was then elected President. Caceres and his partisans attempted a
rising the next year (1896), but it had no success.
In the northern department of Loreto, on the
border of Ecuador, an abortive movement for
independence was set on foot by an ambitious
official, who gave the government considerable
trouble, but accomplished nothing more. In
1899, President Pierola was succeeded by Eduar-
do L. de Romana, elected in May. A rebellion
attempted that year by one General Durand was
promptly suppressed.

A. D. 1894-1900.—The dispute with Chile
concerning Tacna and Arica. See (in this
vol.) CHILE: A. D. 1884-1900.

PESCADORES ISLANDS: Cession by
China to Japan. See (in this vol.) CHINA:
A. D. 1894-1895.

PHILADELPHIA: A. D. 1897.—Opening
of the Commercial Museum.—A Commercial
Museum which has acquired great importance
was opened in Philadelphia on the 2d of June,
1897. " In both aim and results the institution
is unique. Other countries, also, have their commercial museums, which are doing excellent
work. Their scope, however, is much more
limited; the Museum of Philadelphia differing
from them in that it is an active, not merely a
passive, aid to the prospective exporter. The
foreign museums, situated in London, Bremen,
Hamburg, Stuttgart, Vienna, Havre, Brussels,
and various other commercial centres, do not extend active aid, but content themselves with
more or less complete displays of samples of
domestic and foreign competitive goods sold in
export markets. The theory of their organization is, that the manufacturer, contemplating a
foreign business campaign, will be enabled to
pursue it intelligently through the study of these
samples. The initiative is left to the exporter
himself, who must discover what opportunities
exist for him abroad; and it is also left to him
to take advantage of his opportunities in the way
that may seem best to him. The display of manufactured samples is only a small part of the
work of the Philadelphia Museum. This institution shows not only what goods are sold in foreign markets, but also where those markets are,
what commercial conditions obtain in connection
with them, what particular kinds of goods they
demand, how these markets may be best com-
peted for, and where the raw material may be
most profitably purchased. It furnishes information, furthermore, as to business connections as
well as the credit ratings of the agents or firms
recommended. To secure specific information it
is not necessary to visit the institution itself; for
reports of trade opportunities abroad are distributed by the Museum to its members; and
these reports are provided with photographs of
many of the articles which, at that particular
time, are in demand, in certain parts of the
world. Under these circumstances, the exporter
is practically provided with a staff of expert,
foreign representatives, without any expense to
himself beyond the merely nominal fee for membership. While its activities are dependent to
a certain extent upon the income derived from
subscribers, the Museum is not a money-making
institution. Indeed, its income from this source
does not cover half the expenditures. It is enabled to carry on its work only by reason of the
generous, annual appropriation provided for it
by the City Councils of Philadelphia. But a
very large income is required to maintain a staff
of 150 employees in Philadelphia, as well as 500
regular and several thousand occasional correspondents scattered throughout the world. The
only advantage which the city itself derives
from the Museum is that resulting indirectly
from the presence of foreign buyers attracted to
Philadelphia by the Museum's work."—W. P.
Wilson, *The Phila. Commercial Museum* (*Forum*,
Sept., 1899).

A. D. 1899.—National Export Exposition
and International Commercial Congress.
See (in this vol.) INTERNATIONAL COMMERCIAL
CONGRESS.

PHILIPPINE ISLANDS.

Number, area, shore line, and population.— "In regard to the number and areas of the islands in the archipelago there must necessarily be a certain inaccuracy, because the group has never been properly surveyed, and the only method of determining the number and areas is by counting and measuring on the charts. The following figures are probably the best ever compiled. They are drawn from enumeration and mensuration on maps recently obtained by the United States commissioners to the Philippines and which are without doubt the most complete and the most thorough ever made. The following is quoted from the introduction to these maps, which are being published by the United States Coast and Geodetic Survey. All the islands or groups having an area of over 20 square miles have been measured, and the areas are here given in square miles and square kilometers. Many different statements have been made in regard to the number of the islands composing the archipelago. The cause for this must be attributed to the scale of the charts on which the count was made and the difficulty of distinguishing between rocks and formations of sufficient area to dignify them by the name of islands. Thus on a small-scale Spanish chart of the entire group 948 islands were counted; on various large-scale charts of the same area there were found 1,725. The principal islands, with the extent of shore line of some of them and their area, are given on the following lists. The areas were carefully measured, but are subject to the inaccuracy of the charts.

Name.	Square miles.	Square kilometers.	Name.	Square miles.	Square kilometers.
Babuyan	36	93	GROUPS.		
Bagata, or Quinalasag	27	70			
Balabac	38	98	Alabat		
Basilan	350	907	Jomalig	76	197
Batan	21	54	Banton		
Bantayan	26	67	Simara	44	114
Bohol	1,439	3,727	Romblon		
Bucas	41	106	Daram		
Burias	163	422	Buad	41	106
Busuanga	328	850	Camotes group:		
Calayan	37	96	Ponson		
Calamian	117	303	Poro	74	192
Camiguin (Babuyanes group)	54	140	Pasijan		
Camiguin	71	184	Calaguas group:		
Catanduanes	680	1,761	Tinagua	19	49
Cebu	1,742	4,512	Guintinua		
Dalupiri	20	53	Cuyos group:		
Dinagat	259	671	Cuyos		
Dumaran	95	246	Cugo		
Fuga	21	54	Agutaya	28	73
Guimaras	176	456	Hamipo		
Leite (Leyte)	2,713	7,027	Bisukei		
Linapacan	40	104	Laguan		
Luzon	47,238	122,346	Batag	23	60
Mactan	20	52	Limbancauyan		
Malhou (Homonkon)	35	91	Mesa, or Talajit		
Marindugua	287	743	Maripipi	184	477
Masbate	1,290	3,341	Balupiri		
Mindanao	36,237	93,854	Biliran		
Mindoro	3,972	10,987	Lubang		
Negros	4,854	12,571	Ambil	63	163
Olutanga	71	184	Golo		
Panaon	57	148	San Miguel		
Panay	4,708	12,194	Batan	82	212
Panglao	24	62	Cacraray		
Pangutaran	32	85	Rapurrapu		
Paragua, or Palawan	3,937	10,197	Tawi Tawi group:		
Polillo	231	598	Tawi Tawi		
Samal	105	272	Tabulinga	183	474
Samar	5,040	13,054	Tandubato		
Saranguani	36	93	Others of the Tawi Tawi group.	54	140
Semerara	23	60			
Siargao	134	347	Total measured	118,542	307,025
Sibuyan	131	339	Estimated area of unmeasured islands	1,000	2,590
Siquijor	83	215			
Sulu, or Jolo	241	624	Total area	119,542	309,615
Tablas	250	648			
Ticao	94	243			
Ybayat, or Ibayat	22	57			
Ylin	24	62			

Length of general shore line.

Name.	Statute miles.	Kilometers.	Name.	Statute miles.	Kilometers.
Bohol	161	259	Mindoro	322	518
Cebu	310	499	Negros	386	621
Jolo Archipelago	858	1,381	Palawan	644	1,036
Kalamines	126	203	Panay	377	607
Leite	363	584	Samar	412	663
Luzon	2,144	3,450	Minor islands	3,505	5,641
Masbate	244	393			
Mindanao	1,592	2,562	Total	11,444	18,417

"The following [as to population] is a quotation from an article by W. F. Wilcox, of the United States Census Bureau. It is well to notice that the last official census was in 1887 and that the figures of that census, though probably underestimating the population of the islands, are the ones which, in default of better, we are obliged to take as final. It is probable that these are an understatement of the true population of the Philippines for several reasons, among which is one not observed by Mr. Wilcox, and which is therefore mentioned. It is, of course, only supposition, but is at least suggestive. For every adult counted in the census the officials were obliged to return a poll tax. Thus, for instance, if 100,000 persons were counted 100,000 pesetas would have to be returned to the treasury. It has therefore been supposed that the officials counted, say, 150,000 and returned only 100,000 pesetas and 100,000 names. Mr. Wilcox says (Am. Statistical Assoc. Publ., Sept., 1899): 'The population of the islands in 1872 was stated in a letter to Nature (6:162), from Manila, by Dr. A. B. Meyer, who gives the latest not yet published statistics as his authority. The letter gives the population of nine islands, as follows:

Luzon	4,467,111
Panay	1,052,586
Cebu	427,356
Leite	285,495
Bohol	283,515
Negros	255,873
Samar	250,062
Mindanao	191,802
Mindoro	70,926

"It also gives the population of each of the 43 provinces of the Philippines. The population was not counted, but estimated. The number who paid tribute was stated as 1,232,544. How this was ascertained we are not informed. The total population, 7,451,352, was approximated 'on the supposition that about the sixth part of the whole has to pay tribute.' In reality this population is 6.046 times the assigned tribute-paying population. But Dr. Meyer adds: 'As there exist in all the islands, even in Luzon, independent tribes and a large number in Mindanao, the number of 7,451,352 gives no correct idea of the real population of the Philippines. This is not known at all and will not be known for a long time to come.'

"Since 1872 there have been actual enumerations of the Philippines, but authorities differ as to the time when they occurred and the detailed results. These enumerations were usually confined to the subject and Catholic population, and omitted the heathen, Mohammedan, and independent tribes. Four reports of the entire population have been printed : 1. A report made by the religious orders in 1876 or 1877, in which the nationalities and creeds of the population were distinguished. 2. A manuscript report to Professor Blumentritt of the enumeration made by the religious orders in December, 1879. 3. The official report of the civil census of December 31, 1877, contained in Reseña geog. y estad. de España, 1888, p. 1079. 4. The official report upon the census taken by the civil officers December 31, 1887, and printed in the first volume of Censo de la Poblacion de España, at Madrid, in 1891. The first two may be compared, and tend somewhat to corroborate each other, as follows :

1. Tribute-paying natives	5,501,356
2. Army	14,545
3. Navy	2,924
4. Religious officers (Geistlichkeit)	1,962
5. Civil officers	5,552
6. Other Spaniards	13,265
Total Spaniards	38,248

	1876-77.	1879.
Total Catholics	5,539,604	5,777,522
Heathen and Mohammedan natives	602,853	632,645
Foreigners (in 1876 there were : British, 176 ; German, 109 ; Americans, 42 ; French, 30)...	378	592
Chinese	30,797	39,054
Total	6,173,632	6,449,813

"The third enumeration reported 5,567,685 as the tribute-paying population. To this number should be added the estimated number of the independent tribes, 'Indios no sometidos'; this according to the missionaries' count was about 600,000, making a total of 6,167,685. Most experts agree that this official report is untrustworthy and involves serious omissions, but believe that the facts are so imperfectly known that they are unable to correct it. One author, del Pac, writing in 1882, started from the missionaries' census of 1876-77, viz, 6,173,632, assumed that this omitted as many as 600,000 members of independent tribes and that the increase of 1876-1882 would be 740,000. In this way he got 7,513,632. A second writer, Sanciano, estimated the population in 1881 as 10,260,249. The missionaries made an estimate of their own in 1885 which showed 9,529,841.

"The fourth enumeration of those mentioned above showed a population of 5,985,123 in 1887, and the totals both for the group as a whole and for the fifty odd provinces tend to confirm and to be confirmed by the civil count of 1877. This number, however, represents only the nominally Catholic or tribute-paying population. To it

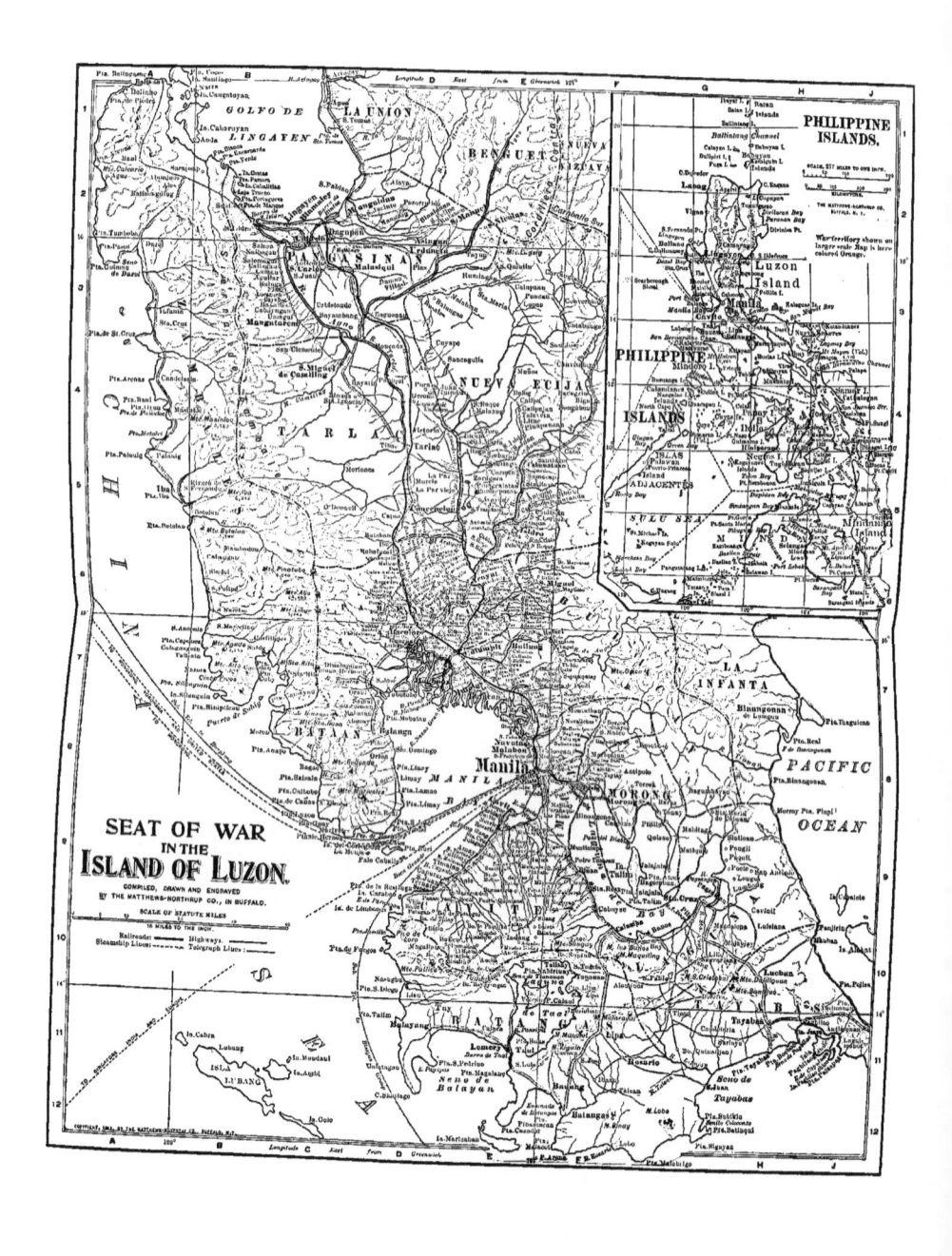

SEAT OF WAR
IN THE
ISLAND OF LUZON.

PHILIPPINE
ISLANDS.

must be added the Mohammedan or heathen tribes set down by clerical authorities as about 600,000. Perhaps the highest authority in this field, Professor Blumentritt, is confident that this number does not include all the independent tribes, but only those in the mountains who have a special arrangement freeing them from all the dues of the subject tribes. On the whole, therefore, Prof. H. Wagner is inclined to estimate these omissions of independent or non-Christian tribes at about 1,000,000 and the population of the group at about 7,000,000. This result is indorsed by the latest German authority, Hübner's Geographisch-Statistische Tabellen for 1898, which gives the population as 5,985,124 + 1,000,-000=6,985,124, as follows :

	Spanish census.	Estimated number not counted.
Luzon and adjacent islands....	3,443,000	150,000
Mindoro and Masbate..........	126,000	100,000
Visayas Archipelago...........	2,181,000	200,000
Mindanao	209,000	400,000
Calamianes and Palawan......	22,000	50,000
Jolo (Sulu) Islands............	4,000	100,000
Total	5,985,000	1,000,000

"Personally I am disposed to suspect that this number, although called by Professor Wagner an outside estimate, is below rather than above the truth. In favor of this position it may be urged that Professor Wagner's estimate makes no allowance either for the natural increase of population, 1887–1898, or for the fact that the first careful census of densely populated regions, like India and Japan, usually reveals a larger population than had been previously estimated. This analogy might reasonably be applied to Luzon and the Visayas."—*United States, 56th Cong., 1st Sess., Senate Doc. No. 171, pp. 4–7.*

The native inhabitants.—"The inhabitants of the Philippines belong to three sharply distinct races—the Negrito race, the Indonesian race, and the Malayan race. It is universally conceded that the Negritos of to-day are the disappearing remnants of a people which once populated the entire archipelago. They are, physically, weaklings of low stature, with black skin, closely-curling hair, flat noses, thick lips, and large, clumsy feet. In the matter of intelligence they stand at or near the bottom of the human series, and they are believed to be incapable of any considerable degree of civilization or advancement. Centuries ago they were driven from the coast regions into the wilder interior portions of the islands by Malay invaders, and from that day to this they have steadily lost ground in the struggle for existence, until but a few scattered and numerically insignificant groups of them remain. . . . It is believed that not more than 25,000 of them exist in the entire archipelago, and the race seems doomed to early extinction. . . .

"So far as is at present known, the Philippine tribes belonging to the Indonesian race are confined to the great island of Mindanao, the surface of which constitutes about one-third of the total land area of the archipelago. . . . The Philippine representatives of this race are physically superior not only to the Negritos, but to the more numerous Malayan peoples as well. They are tall and well developed, with high foreheads, aqui-

line noses, wavy hair, and often with abundant beards. The color of their skins is quite light. Many of them are very clever and intelligent. None of the tribes have been Christianized. Some of them have grown extremely fierce and warlike as a result of their long struggle with hostile Malayan peoples. Others, more happy in their surroundings, are pacific and industrious.

"The great majority of the inhabitants of the Philippines are of Malayan extraction, although the race is not found pure in any of the islands, but is everywhere more or less modified through intermarriage with Chinese, Indonesians, Negritos, Arabs, and, to a limited extent, Spaniards and other Europeans. The individuals belonging to these Malayan tribes are of medium size, with straight black hair. As a rule the men are beardless, and when they have a beard it is usually straggling, and appears late in life. The skin is brown and distinctly darker than that of the Indonesians, although very much lighter than that of the Negritos. The nose is short and frequently considerably flattened. The representatives of these three races are divided into numerous tribes, which often differ very greatly in language, manners, customs, and laws, as well as in degree of civilization. . . .

"Any estimate of the total population must manifestly depend on the number of inhabitants assigned to the various wild tribes, of which there are no less than 69. For the purposes of this report the commission has adopted as the total figure 8,000,000, considering this a conservative estimate. Baranera, whose figures are believed to be carefully prepared, places the total at 9,000,000. The extent of territory occupied in whole or in part by each of the more important civilized tribes can be estimated with a greater degree of accuracy, and is approximately as follows: Visayans (occupying 28,100 square miles) 2,601,600 ; Tagalogs (15,380 sq. miles) 1,663,900; Bicols (6,900 sq. miles) 518,100 ; Ilocanos (6,170 sq. miles) 441,700 ; Pangasinans (1,950 sq. miles) 365,500 ; Pampangas (1,950 sq. miles) 337,900 ; Moros (12,860 sq. miles) 268.000 ; Cagayans (11,500 sq. miles) 166,300. All of these peoples, although ignorant and illiterate, are possessed of a considerable degree of civilization, and, with the exception of the Mohammedan Moros, are Christianized."—*Philippine Commission, Report, Jan. 31, 1900, v. 1, pp. 11–15.*

A. D. 1896-1898.—The Katipunan and the rising against Spanish rule.—Appearance of Aguinaldo as a leader.—Dr. José Rizal.—The Treaty of Biac-na-bato.—Departure of Aguinaldo and his return with the American forces.—The Philippine Islands, discovered in 1521 by Magellan (or Maghallanes or Magalhaes), and occupied by the Spaniards in 1565, seems, for a long period, to have interested that people more as a missionary than as a commercial field. Indeed, the doings of the church and of the religious orders, and the acceptance of Roman teachings of Christianity by the greater part of the native population, make up the essential history of the Philippines until quite recent times. If the islands had offered gold mines, or pearl fisheries, or spice forests to their European discoverers, the story would certainly have been different. As it was, the Spaniards were not moved to much eagerness in exploiting such resources of commerce as they found; and so, through fortunate circumstances, the

6-24

natives were made converts instead of slaves. By missionaries. more than by soldiers, they were subdued ; by the church, more than by the Spanish state, they were ruled. It is certain that there were great corruptions and oppressions in the government, and it follows that a large share of responsibility for them rests on those who controlled the affairs of the church. For the past hundred years, at least, the more spirited part of the native population has been restive under the misrule and its burdens, and frequent attempts at insurrection have been made. Such an outbreak in 1872 was suppressed and punished with a vengefulness, in executions and banishment, which rankled ever afterwards in the hearts of the people.

A secret society, called the "Katipunan," or League, was then formed, which became a revolutionary organization, and from which sprang the most serious of Filipino rebellions, in 1896. The province of Cavite was the center of revolt, and it was there that Emilio Aguinaldo, then the schoolmaster at Silan, came into prominence as a leader. Mr. John Foreman, who was in the Philippines at the time of the insurrection, states that Aguinaldo was personally humane, but fearful atrocities were committed in the first months of the rising by some of the insurgents of his band. One captured priest, according to Mr. Foreman's account, "was cut up piecemeal ; another was saturated with petroleum and set on fire ; and a third was bathed in oil and fried on a bamboo spit run through the length of his body." The Spaniards, on their side, were equally inhuman in their treatment of captured rebels and "suspects." Says Mr. Foreman : "About 600 suspects were confined in the dungeons of Fort Santiago at the mouth of the Pasig River. Then occurred a frightful tragedy. The dungeons are below water-mark at high tide ; the river filtered in through the crevices in the ancient masonry ; thus twice a day these unfortunates were up to their waists or necks in water, according to the height of the men. The Spanish sergeant on duty threw his rug over the only light and ventilating shaft, and, in a couple of days, carts were seen by many citizens carrying away the dead, calculated to number 70. Provincial governors and parish priests seemed to regard it as a duty to supply the capital with batches of 'suspects' from their localities. In Vigan, where nothing had occurred, many of the heads of the best families and monied men were arrested and brought to Manila in a steamer. They were bound hand and foot, and carried like packages of merchandise in the hold. I happened to be on the quay when the steamer discharged her living freight, with chains and hooks to haul up and swing out the bodies like bales of hemp. . . .

"Thousands of peaceful natives were treated with a ferocity which would have shocked all Europe. . . . Within three months of the outbreak, hundreds of the richest natives and half-castes in Manila were imprisoned for a few days and released conditionally"—the condition being a payment of ransom, sometimes said to be as high as $40,000. But General Blanco, the then Governor-General, was not vigorous enough in his measures to satisfy the all-powerful clerical party in the islands, and he was replaced by General Polaveja, who received large reinforce-

ments from Spain, and who succeeded in breaking the strength of the rebellion to a great extent. But the character of Polaveja's administration is thus described by Mr. Foreman : "Apart from the circumstances of legitimate warfare, in which probably neither party was more merciful than the other, he initiated a system of striking terror into the non-combatant population by barbarous tortures and wholesale executions. . . . Men were escorted to the prisons by pure caprice and subjected to horrible maltreatment. Many of them were liberated in the course of a few days, declared innocent, but maimed for life and forever unable to get a living. . . . The only apparent object in all this was to disseminate broadcast living examples of Spanish vengeance." The most notable victim at this period was Dr. José Rizal, a physician, highly educated in Europe, distinguished as an oculist, and the author of certain novels in which the condition of things in his native country was set forth. On his return to the Islands, Dr. Rizal incurred the enmity of the friars by opposing them, and was pursued by their hostility. From 1893 to 1896 he was kept in banishment, closely watched, at a small town in the island of Mindanao. Then he sought and obtained permission to go to Cuba in the medical staff of the Spanish army ; but, just as he arrived at Manila, on his way to Spain, the insurrection of 1896 broke out, and though he was suffered to depart, his enemies pursued him with accusations of complicity in the rising and caused him to be brought back. Says Mr. Foreman, who was an eye-witness of what occurred : "Not a few of us who saw the vessel leave wished him 'God speed.' But the clerical party were eager for his extermination. . . . The lay authorities always had to yield to the monks, and history herein repeated itself. Dr. Rizal was cabled for to answer certain accusations, and so on his landing in the Peninsula he was incarcerated in the celebrated fortress of Montjuich (the scene of so many horrors), pending his re-shipment by the returning steamer. He reached Manila as a state prisoner in the Colon, isolated from all but his jailors. It was materially impossible for him to have taken any part in the rebellion, whatever his sympathies may have been." Nevertheless, he was tried by court-martial for sedition and rebellion, condemned and shot ; and his memory is cherished in the islands as that of a martyred patriot. "The decree of execution was one of Polaveja's foulest acts."

Having scotched but not killed the insurrection, Polaveja went home, with broken health, in the spring of 1897, and was succeeded by General Primo de Rivera, who, after some months of continued warfare, opened negotiations with Aguinaldo, the recognized leader of the revolt. The result was a treaty, known as the "Pacto de Biac-na-bato, signed December 14. By this treaty "the rebels undertook to deliver up their arms and ammunition of all kinds to the Spaniards ; to evacuate the places held by them ; to conclude an armistice for three years for the application and development of the reforms to be introduced by the other part, and not to conspire against Spanish sovereignty in the Islands, nor aid or abet any movement calculated to counteract the reforms. Emilio Aguinaldo and 34 other leaders undertook to quit the Philippine Islands, and not to return to them until so authorised by the Spanish Government. On behalf of the Spanish Government it was agreed to pay, through the medium of Pedro A. Paterno, to the rebels the sum of $1,000,000, and to the families who had sustained loss by reason of the war $700,000, in instalments and conditionally,"—the condition being that no renewal of rebellion or conspiracy occur. Aguinaldo and other chiefs of the insurrection left the Islands, accordingly; but they are said to have been utterly duped. One instalment, only ($400,000), of the promised money was ever paid; the promised reforms were not carried out, and persecution of those who had been in sympathy with the rising was renewed.—J. Foreman, *The Philippine Islands, ch. 26 (N. Y. : Chas. Scribner's Sons).*

"Aguinaldo and his associates went to Hongkong and Singapore. A portion of the money, $400,000, was deposited in banks at Hongkong, and a lawsuit soon arose between Aguinaldo and one of his subordinate chiefs named Artacho, which is interesting on account of the very honorable position taken by Aguinaldo. Artacho sued for a division of the money among the insurgents according to rank. Aguinaldo claimed that the money was a trust fund, and was to remain on deposit until it was seen whether the Spaniards would carry out their promised reforms, and if they failed to do so, it was to be used to defray the expenses of a new insurrection. The suit was settled out of court by paying Artacho $5,000. No steps have been taken to introduce the reforms, more than 2,000 insurgents, who had been deported to Fernando Po and other places, are still in confinement, and Aguinaldo is now using the money to carry on the operations of the present insurrection."—F. V. Greene, *Memorandum concerning the Situation in the Philippines, Aug. 30, 1898 (Treaty of Peace and Accompanying Papers : 55th Cong., 3d Sess., Senate Doc. No. 62, pt. 1, p. 421.*

A. D. 1897.—Refusal of United States Government to negotiate with the insurgent republic. See (in this vol.) UNITED STATES OF AM.: A. D. 1897 (NOVEMBER).

A. D. 1898 (April—May).—Circumstances in which Aguinaldo was brought to Manila to co-operate with American forces. See (in this vol.) UNITED STATES OF AM.: A. D. 1898 (APRIL—MAY: PHILIPPINES).

A. D. 1898 (April—July).—Destruction of the Spanish fleet in Manila Bay.—Blockade and siege of the city.—Co-operation of insurgents under Aguinaldo. See (in this vol.) UNITED STATES OF AM.: A. D. 1898 (APRIL—JULY).

A. D. 1898 (May—August).—Conduct of English and German naval officers at Manila. See (in this vol.) UNITED STATES OF AM.: A. D. 1898 (MAY—AUGUST).

A. D. 1898 (July—August).—Correspondence between the American commander and Aguinaldo.—This is fully given (showing the relations between the American and Filipino forces, before the capture of Manila), in the general account of the Spanish-American War. See (in this vol.) UNITED STATES OF AM.: A. D. 1898 (JULY—AUGUST : PHILIPPINES).

A. D. 1898 (July—September).—American capture of Manila.—Relations with the Filipino insurgents.—General Merritt's report.

—Aguinaldo declared President of the Philippine Republic. See (in this vol.) UNITED STATES OF AM.: A. D. 1898 (JULY—SEPTEMBER).

A. D. 1898 (August).—Suspension of hostilities between the United States and Spain.—Manila held by the former pending the conclusion of a treaty of peace. See (in this vol.) UNITED STATES OF AM.: A. D. 1898 (JULY—DECEMBER).

A. D. 1898 (August).—Losses of the American army during the war with Spain. See (in this vol.) UNITED STATES OF AM.: A. D. 1900 (JUNE).

A. D. 1898 (August—December).—The state of things following the occupation of Manila by American forces.—Growing distrust and unfriendliness of the Tagalos.—General Otis's report.—Of the state of things which followed the departure of General Merritt, August 30, General Otis, who succeeded him in command, reported subsequently as follows:

"Until October 14 [1898], the United States troops in the Philippines remained stationed at Manila and Cavite, as provided in General Merritt's orders of August 23, with very slight exceptions, Major-General Anderson retaining supervision of the district of Cavite and Major-General MacArthur of the troops stationed in Manila, the three organizations composing the provost guard continuing, however, under the control of Brigadier-General Hughes. They were most bountifully supplied with subsistence and medicines, but light clothing suited to the climate and facilities necessary for occupying and messing in barracks were needed. These were soon obtained through contract and purchase from the merchants of Hongkong and Manila and by shipment from the United States. The troops received tactical instructions daily, but the weather was too hot for much physical exertion, and time hung heavily upon them. They entertained the impression that the Spanish war had terminated, and the volunteers appeared to believe that they should be recalled to the United States at once and regular troops sent out to perform the monotonous garrison duties which were about to follow the victory of Manila. Many became ill from too free indulgence in the fruits and manufactured drinks of the country, and indifference to that care and attention of person which a tropical climate makes necessary. Homesickness alone produced illness in numerous cases, so that early in September the hospitals began to be rapidly filled. This led to the adoption of judicious precautionary measures. . . . In November improvement was noticeable, and in January the health of this army would compare favorably with those of any concentrated army of like proportions in existence. To be sure the men had become by this time fairly acclimatized, and new troops arriving here will be obliged to pass through this period of acclimatization before they become properly efficient for prolonged service in the field.

"During my first weeks of duty here I was impressed with the spirit of suspicion and the partially concealed unfriendly feeling manifested by the Tagalos toward the American forces. That they either had very little confidence in our promises or were then forming conclusions to oppose any establishment of United

States authority in Luzon was apparent, however loudly they might disclaim hostile intent or declare as an excuse for their attitude fear of the return of Spain. I saw, however, with satisfaction, their ablest men by education and mental equipment taking part in their authoritative deliberations, and I had considerable confidence in the efficacy of their suggestions and advice. Still, after carefully weighing conditions, I was unable to arrive at any satisfactory conclusions. . . .

"Measures were being applied constantly to improve the sanitary condition of the city, to increase the efficiency of the troops, and to meet any emergency which might develop from an uprising of the inhabitants, or from hasty action by any portion of our or the insurgent forces, which, though maintaining amicable intercourse, were, in fact, in an attitude of resistance and hostility upon all questions involving the right of armed occupation of the suburbs and defenses of Manila. The insurgent soldiers had looted extensively the portions of the city to which they gained access, and were greatly disappointed that this privilege over other parts of the same was not accorded them. Their enforced withdrawal to outer lines was the cause of discontent, and augmented any desire which they may have formerly entertained to resist or attack the American troops. This growing discontent was observable among the lower classes of the city's inhabitants, from whom a considerable share of Aguinaldo's army was drawn, and was undoubtedly increased by the reprehensible conduct and illegal actions of some of our own men, who were severely punished for their misdeeds when detected. Outwardly, however, relations of the most friendly character were maintained. The officers and enlisted men of the two armies mingled in friendly social intercourse. To the casual observer the only discordant element in this dense complex population, made up of every nation and tongue in existence, were the hated Spanish prisoners, whom the Filipinos still longed to persecute and kill, and who were obliged to keep within the walls of Old Manila for safety. Repeated conferences were held with influential insurgents, whose chief aim appeared to be to obtain some authoritative expression on the intent of the United States with regard to the Philippines, and complained that they were unable to discover any one who could speak ex cathedra. They asserted that the Malolos arrangement was a government de facto, which had the right to ask an expression of intent from the United States Government. . . .

"My own confidence at this time in a satisfactory solution of the difficulties which confronted us may be gathered from a dispatch sent to Washington on December 7, wherein I stated that conditions were improving and that there were signs of revolutionary disintegration; that I had conferred with a number of the members of the revolutionary government and thought that the most of them would favor peaceful submission to United States authority. I had strong reasons for this expressed confidence from assurances made to me by some of the ablest Filipinos who had occupied positions of importance in the insurgent government and had signified their intention to withdraw from it."—*Report of General Otis, Aug. 31, 1899 (Message and Documents: Abridgment, 1899–1900, v. 2, pp. 1048–52).*

A. D. 1898 (August—December).—The state of things following the occupation of Manila, as represented by English witnesses.—The writer of the following remarks, in an interesting book on "The Inhabitants of the Philippines," published late in 1900, is an English civil engineer, who had resided in Luzon for fourteen years and knew the country and people thoroughly well: "Personally, I think that if a sympathetic and conciliatory attitude had been adopted, had the local government established been recognized, had Aguinaldo and his staff been given commissions in the Native Army or Civil Service, and the flower of the Tagal Army taken into the service of the United States, a peaceful settlement could have been made on the lines of a Protectorate. I therefore look upon the war as unnecessary, and consider the lives already sacrificed, and that will have to be sacrificed, as absolutely thrown away. The tragical side of American unpreparedness is manifest in the state of anarchy in which the whole Archipelago has been plunged by the American unreadiness to occupy the military posts as soon as they were vacated by the Spanish garrisons. A hideous orgy of murder, plunder, and slave-raiding has prevailed in Visayas, and especially in Mindanao.

"Three conditions were essential to a peaceful settlement: First.—A broad-minded and sympathetic representative of America, fully authorized to treat, and a lover of peace. Second.—A strict discipline amongst the American forces. Third.—The principal aim and object of the Tagal insurrection must be secured.

"General Otis does not seem to me to fulfil the first condition, he lacked prestige and patience, and he showed that he had an insufficient conception of the magnitude of his task by occupying himself with petty details of all kinds and by displaying an ill-timed parsimony. Apparently he had no power to grant anything at all, and only dealt in vague generalities which the Tagals could not be expected to accept.

"As regards the second point, I regret that I am not personally acquainted with the gentlemen from Nebraska, Colorado, Dakota and other states serving in the United States Army or volunteers. I have no doubt that they are good fighting-men, but from all I can hear about them they are not conspicuous for strict military discipline, and too many of them have erroneous ideas as to the most suitable drink for a tropical climate. Manila was in the time of the Spaniards a most temperate city; a drunken man was a very rare sight, and would usually be a foreign sailor. Since the American occupation, some hundreds of drinking saloons have been opened, and daily scenes of drunkenness and debauchery have filled the quiet natives with alarm and horror. When John L. Motley wrote his scathing denunciation of the army which the great Duke of Alva led from Spain into the Low Countries, to enforce the high religious purposes of Philip II., he could not foresee that his words would be applicable to an American Army sent to subjugate men struggling to be free ' for their welfare, not our gain,' nor that this army, besides bringing in its train a flood of cosmopolitan harlotry, would be allowed by its commander to inaugurate amongst a strictly temperate people a mad saturnalia of drunkenness that has scarcely a parallel. Such, however, is undoubtedly the case, and I venture to think that these occurrences have confirmed many of the Tagals in their resolve rather to die fighting for their independence than to be ruled over by such as these."—F. H. Sawyer, *The Inhabitants of the Philippines*, p. 113–114 (*N. Y. : Chas. Scribner's Sons*).

Substantially the same account of things at Manila in this period has been given in a magazine article by Mr. John Foreman, the well known writer on the Philippine Islands. "The conduct," he declares, " of the boisterous, undisciplined individuals who formed a large percentage of the first volunteer contingents sent to Manila had had an ineffaceably demoralizing effect on the proletariat, and has inspired a feeling of horror and loathful contempt in the affluent and educated classes who guide the Philippine public opinion. From the outset it was a mistake to treat the Christian Philippine population like savages ignorant of western civilization, considering that there are thousands of Filipinos mentally equal to the invading forces, and comparable, in intellectual training, with the average middle-class Europeans.

" Within a fortnight after the capitulation of Manila the drinking saloons had increased fourfold. According to the latest advices, there are at least twenty to one existing in the time of the Spaniards. Drunkenness, with its consequent evils, is rife all over the city among the new white population. The orgies of the new-comers, the incessant street brawls, the insults offered with impunity to natives of both sexes, the entry with violence into private houses by the soldiery, who maltreated the inmates and laid hands on what they chose, were hardly calculated to arouse in the natives admiration for their new masters. Brothels were absolutely prohibited under the Spanish rule, but since the evacuation there has been a great influx of women of ill fame, whilst native women have been pursued by lustful tormentors. During a certain period after the capitulation there was indiscriminate shooting, and no peaceable native's life was safe in the suburbs. Adventurers of all sorts and conditions have flocked to this centre of vice, where the sober native is not even spoken of as a man by many of the armed rank and file, but, by way of contempt, is called a *yuyu*. A few miles from Manila, the villages of Mandaloyan and Sant Ana were looted by the victors, much of the spoil being brought up to the capital and included in auction sales or sold to the Chinese. In Taal the houses of families, with whom I have been long acquainted, were ransacked, effects of little value, or too difficult to transport, being carelessly strewn about from sheer wantonness. And presumably no greater respect for private property was shown in the other numerous villages overrun by the invaders. . . .

"The situation then during this period was somewhat as follows : The Filipinos, aided by Dewey's victory, had driven the Spaniards from practically the whole Archipelago except the city of Manila, they had established a government of their own, and they looked upon the country as belonging both by nature and by right of conquest to them. We upon the other hand, having destroyed the Spanish fleet and captured the city of Manila, and being in the process of acquiring by treaty the Spanish title to the whole country regarded it as belonging to us. The situation was therefore critical."—J. Foreman, *Will the United States withdraw from the Philippines? (National Rev., Sept.,* 1900).

A. D. 1898 (September—December).—**Instructions** from the President of the United States to the Commissioners for the negotiation of peace with Spain concerning the Philippine Archipelago.—Cession of the Islands to the United States. See (in this vol.) UNITED STATES OF AM.: A. D. 1898 (JULY—DECEMBER).

A. D. 1898 (October—November).—**State of the country under the native government of Aguinaldo, as witnessed by two U. S. naval officers who traversed it.—Conflicting opinions as to the fitness of the Filipinos for self-government.**—During October and November, 1898, while the only authority in Luzon, outside of Manila and Cavite, was that exercised by the native government organized under Aguinaldo, two American naval officers, Paymaster W. B. Wilcox and Cadet Leonard R. Sargent, with permission from Admiral Dewey, made a tour of observation through seven provinces of the island, and rendered a report of what they saw and what they experienced, which Admiral Dewey sent to Washington, commending it to the attention of the government as containing " the most complete and reliable information obtainable in regard to the present state of the northern part of Luzon Island." Subsequently Mr. Sargent wrote articles descriptive of the journey, which were published in "The Outlook" and " The Independent," and which were reprinted, with the official report, in a document compiled for the U. S. Senate. The following is from the article in " The Outlook," September 2, 1899 :

"Although this government has never been recognized, and in all probability will go out of existence without recognition, yet it cannot be denied that, in a region occupied by many millions of inhabitants, for nearly six months it stood alone between anarchy and order. The military forces of the United States held control only in Manila, with its environs, and in Cavite, and had no authority to proceed further ; while in the vast remaining districts the representatives of the only recognized power on the field were prisoners in the hands of their despised subjects. It was the opinion at Manila during this anomalous period in our Philippine relations, and possibly in the United States as well, that such a state of affairs must breed something akin to anarchy. I can state unreservedly, however, that Mr. Wilcox and I found the existing conditions to be much at variance with this opinion. During our absence from Manila we travelled more than 600 miles in a very comprehensive circuit through the northern part of the island of Luzon, traversing a characteristic and important district. In this way we visited seven provinces, of which some were under the immediate control of the central government at Malolos, while others were remotely situated, separated from each other and from the seat of government by natural divisions of land, and accessible only by lengthy and arduous travel. As a tribute to the efficiency of Aguinaldo's government and to the law-abiding character of his subjects, I offer the fact that Mr. Wilcox and I pursued our journey throughout in perfect security, and returned to Manila with only the most pleasant recollections of the quiet and orderly life which we found the natives to be leading under the new régime."

The following is from the official report, jointly made by Cadet Sargent and Paymaster Wilcox : " The Philippine officers, both military and civil, that we have met in all the provinces we have visited, have, with very few exceptions, been men of intelligent appearance and conversation. The same is true of all those men who form the upper class in each town. The education of most of them is limited, but they appear to seize every opportunity to improve it. They have great respect and admiration for learning. Very many of them desire to send their children to schools in the United States or Europe. Many men of importance in different towns have told us that the first use to be made of the revenues of their government, after there is no more danger of war, will be to start good schools in every village. The poorer classes are extremely ignorant on most subjects but a large percentage of them can read and write. . . .

" Of the large number of officers, civil and military, and of the leading townspeople we have met, nearly every man has expressed in our presence his sentiment on this question [of independence]. It is universally the same. They all declare that they will accept nothing short of independence. They desire the protection of the United States at sea, but fear any interference on land. . . .

" There is much variety of feeling among the Philippines with regard to the debt of gratitude they owe the United States. In every town we found men who said that our nation had saved them from slavery, and others who claimed that without our interference their independence would have been recognized before this time. On one point they are united, however, viz., that whatever our Government may have done for them it has not gained the right to annex them. They have been prejudiced against us by the Spaniards. The charges made have been so numerous and so severe that what the natives have since learned has not sufficed to disillusion them. With regard to the record of our policy toward a subject people, they have received remarkable information on two points,— that we have mercilessly slain and finally exterminated the race of Indians that were natives of our soil, and that we went to war in 1861 to suppress an insurrection of negro slaves, whom we also ended by exterminating. Intelligent and well-informed men have believed these charges. They were rehearsed to us in many towns in different provinces, beginning at Malolos. The Spanish version of our Indian problem is particularly well known."— *United States, 56th Congress, 1st Sess., Senate Doc.* 66.

In the third number of the first series of its publications, the Philippine Information Society—see below: A. D. 1899 (JANUARY—FEBRUARY)—has brought together a number of conflicting opinions expressed by various persons concerning the capacity of the Filipinos for self-government, among them the following :

" The population of Luzon is reported to be something over 3,000,000, mostly natives. These are gentle, docile, and under just laws and with the benefits of popular education would soon make good citizens. In a telegram sent to the department on June 23 I expressed the opinion that 'these people are far superior in their

intelligence and more capable of self-government than the natives of Cuba, and I am familiar with both races.' Further intercourse with them has confirmed me in this opinion."—Admiral Dewey, *Letter, Aug.* 29, 1898, *replying to inquiry of War Dept.*

" They [the natives] would have to be educated up to it [self-government]. They want a protectorate, but they do not exactly understand what that means. Their idea is that they should collect the revenues and keep them in their treasury, and that we should be at the expense of maintaining an army and a navy there for their protection, which is the kind of a protectorate they would like very much."—General Merritt, *statement before U. S. Peace Commission at Paris, Oct.* 4, 1898.

" If the United States should evacuate these islands, anarchy and civil war will immediately ensue and lead to foreign intervention. The insurgents were furnished arms and the moral support of the navy prior to our arrival, and we cannot ignore obligations, either to the insurgents or to foreign nations, which our own acts have imposed upon us. The Spanish Government is completely demoralized, and Spanish power is dead beyond all possibility of resurrection. . . . On the other hand, the Filipinos cannot govern the country without the support of some strong nation. They acknowledge this themselves, and say their desire is for independence under American protection, but they have only vague ideas as to what our relative positions would be—what part we should take in collecting and expending the revenue, and administering the government." —General F. V. Greene, *Memorandum concerning the Philippine Islands, made Aug.* 27, 1898.

" The capability of the Filipinos for self-government cannot be doubted. Such men as Arellano, Aguinaldo, and many others whom I might name are highly educated ; nine tenths of the people can read and write, all are skilled artisans in one way or another ; they are industrious, frugal, temperate, and, given a fair start, could look out for themselves infinitely better than our people imagine. In my opinion they rank far higher than the Cubans or the uneducated negroes to whom we have given right of suffrage."—General Charles King, *Letter to Milwaukee Journal, June* 22, 1899.

" Concerning the capacity of the Filipinos to govern themselves I regret to say that I see no reason to change the opinion previously expressed, that they are unfit. I wish my opinion might be otherwise, for I prefer to believe them capable of self-government. There are a number of Filipinos whom I have met, among them General Aguinaldo and a few of his leaders, whom I believe thoroughly trustworthy and fully capable of self-government, and the main reliance for small official positions and many larger ones would be upon people who know no standard of government other than that the Spaniards have furnished. Their sense of equity and justice seems not fully developed, and their readiness to coerce those who come under their power has been strongly illustrated in this city since our occupation. A regularly organized system of blackmail has been instituted under the guise of making subscriptions to the insurgent cause."—Major J. F. Bell [of Engineers, on " secret service "], *Letter to General Merritt, Manila, Aug.* 29, 1898.

"The people are the most enlightened and vigorous branch of the Malay race, and have been Christians for centuries, in fact longer than the principles of the Reformation were established in Great Britain, and are the nearest akin to European people of any alien race, and it is simply ridiculous to imagine that eight to ten millions of such people can be bought and sold as an article of commerce without first obtaining their consent. Let all those who are greedy for a slice of the archipelago ponder well over this before burning their fingers."—H. W. Bray [merchant and planter in the islands for fifteen years], *Letter to Singapore Free Press, June 8, 1898.*

"The native has no expansive ideas; he cannot go far enough to understand what it is to rule matters for the benefit of the common weal; he cannot get past his own most personal interest, or his town, at the most. I think the greatest length he would go would be his own town. But constructing laws, and obeying them, for the benefit of the commonwealth, I do not think he is capable of it at all. I think an attempt at a native government would be a fiasco altogether." —John Foreman, *Testimony before U. S. Peace Commission at Paris.*

"The excuse that they [the Filipinos] are not ripe for independence is not founded on facts. The Filipinos number more educated people than the kingdom of Servia and the principalities of Bulgaria and Montenegro. They have fewer illiterates than the states of the Balkan peninsula, Russia, many provinces of Spain and Portugal, and the Latin republics of America. There are provinces in which few people can be found who do not at least read. They pay more attention to education than Spain or the Balkan states do. There is no lack of trained men fit to govern their own country, and indeed in every branch, because under the Spanish rule the official business was entirely transacted by the native subalterns. The whole history of the Katipunan revolt and of the war against Spain and America serves to place in the best light the capability of the Filipinos for self-government."—F. Blumentritt, *The Philippine Islands, p. 61.*

A. D. 1898-1899 (December—January).— Instructions by the President of the United States to General Otis, Military Governor and Commander in the Philippines.—Their proclamation to the people of the Islands as modified by General Otis.—The effect.—On the 27th of December, 1898, the following instructions, dated Dec. 21, and signed by the President, were cabled by the Secretary of War to General Otis, in command of the United States forces in the Philippines. They were not made public in the United States until the 5th of January following, when they appeared in the newspapers of that day: "The destruction of the Spanish fleet in the harbor of Manila by the United States naval squadron commanded by Rear Admiral Dewey, followed by the reduction of the city and the surrender of the Spanish forces, practically effected the conquest of the Philippine Islands and the suspension of Spanish sovereignty therein. With the signature of the treaty of peace between the United States and Spain by their respective plenipotentiaries at Paris, on the 10th inst., and as the result of victories of the American arms, the future control, disposition and government of the Philippine Islands are ceded to the United States. In ful-

filment of the offices of the sovereignty thus acquired, and the responsible obligations of government thus assumed, the actual occupation and administration of the entire group becomes immediately necessary, and the military government heretofore maintained by the United States in the city, harbor and bay of Manila is to be extended with all possible despatch to the whole of the ceded territory. In performance of this duty, the military commander of the United States is enjoined to make known to the inhabitants of the Philippine Islands that in succeeding to the sovereignty of the islands, in severing the former political relations of the inhabitants and in establishing a new political power, the authority of the United States is to be exerted for the security of the persons and property of the people of the islands and for the confirmation of all their private rights. It will be the duty of the commander of the forces of occupation to announce and proclaim in the most public manner that we come, not as invaders or conquerors, but as friends, to protect the natives in their homes, in their employments and in their personal and religious rights. All persons who, either by active aid or by honest submission, cooperate with the government of the United States to give effect to these beneficent purposes, will receive the reward of its support and protection. All others will be brought within the lawful rule we have assumed, with firmness if need be, but without severity so far as may be possible.

"Within the absolute domain of military authority, which necessarily is and must remain supreme in the ceded territory until the government of the United States shall otherwise provide, the municipal laws of the territory in respect to private interests and property and the repression of crime are continued in force, the authority to be administered by the ordinary tribunals so far as practicable. The operations of civil and municipal government are to be performed by such officers as may accept the supremacy of the United States by taking the oath of allegiance, or by officers chosen, as far as may be practicable, from the inhabitants of the islands. While the control of all the public property and the revenues of the state passes with the cession, and while the use and management of all public means are of necessity reserved to the authority of the United States, private property, whether belonging to individuals or corporations, is to be respected except for cause duly established. The taxes and duties heretofore payable by the inhabitants to the late government become payable to the authorities of the United States, unless it be seen fit to substitute for them other reasonable rates or modes of contribution to the expenses of government, whether general or local. If private property be taken for military use, it shall be paid for when possible in cash at a fair valuation, and when payment in cash is not practicable receipts are to be given.

"All ports and places in the Philippine Islands in the actual possession of the land and naval forces of the United States will be opened to the commerce of all friendly nations. All goods and wares not prohibited for military reasons by due announcement of the military authority will be admitted upon payment of such duties and other charges as shall be in force at the time of their importation. Finally, it should be the earnest and paramount aim of the military administration to win the confidence, respect and affection of the inhabitants of the Philippines by assuring to them in every possible way that full measure of individual rights and liberties which is the heritage of free peoples, and by proving to them that the mission of the United States is one of benevolent assimilation, substituting the mild sway of justice and right for arbitrary rule. In the fulfilment of this high mission, supporting the temperate administration of affairs to the greatest good of the governed, there must be sedulously maintained the strong arm of authority, to repress disturbance and to overcome all obstacles to the bestowal of the blessings of good and stable government upon the people of the Philippine Islands under the free flag of the United States. WILLIAM MCKINLEY."

On receiving President McKinley's "proclamation," as the instructions of December 21 were commonly described, General Otis promptly forwarded a copy to General Miller, who had been sent to occupy the city of Iloilo, and the latter made it public. Meantime General Otis had studied the document with care and arrived at conclusions which he sets forth in his subsequent annual report as follows: "After fully considering the President's proclamation and the temper of the Tagalos with whom I was daily discussing political problems and the friendly intentions of the United States Government toward them, I concluded that there were certain words and expressions therein, such as 'sovereignty,' 'right of cession,' and those which directed immediate occupation, etc., though most admirably employed and tersely expressive of actual conditions, might be advantageously used by the Tagalo war party to incite widespread hostilities among the natives. The ignorant classes had been taught to believe that certain words, as 'sovereignty,' 'protection,' etc., had peculiar meaning disastrous to their welfare and significant of future political domination, like that from which they had recently been freed. It was my opinion, therefore, that I would be justified in so amending the paper that the beneficent object of the United States Government would be brought clearly within the comprehension of the people, and this conclusion was the more readily reached because of the radical change [a change of cabinet] of the past few days in the constitution of Aguinaldo's government, which could not have been understood at Washington at the time the proclamation was prepared. . . .

"The amended proclamation of January 4 appeared in the English, Spanish, and Tagalo languages, and was published in Manila through newspapers and posters. The English text is as follows: 'To the people of the Philippine Islands: Instructions of His Excellency the President of the United States relative to the administration of affairs in the Philippine Islands have been transmitted to me by direction of the honorable the Secretary of War, under date of December 28, 1898. They direct me to publish and proclaim, in the most public manner, to the inhabitants of these islands that in the war against Spain the United States forces came here to destroy the power of that nation and to give the blessings of peace and individual freedom to the Philippine people; that we are here as friends of the Filipinos; to protect them in their homes, their employments, their individual and religious

liberty, and that all persons who, either by active aid or honest endeavor, co-operate with the Government of the United States to give effect to these beneficent purposes, will receive the reward of its support and protection. The President of the United States has assumed that the municipal laws of the country in respect to private rights and property and the repression of crime are to be considered as continuing in force in so far as they be applicable to a free people, and should be administered by the ordinary tribunals of justice, presided over by representatives of the people and those in thorough sympathy with them in their desires for good government; that the functions and duties connected with civil and municipal administration are to be performed by such officers as wish to accept the assistance of the United States, chosen in so far as it may be practicable from the inhabitants of the islands; that while the management of public property and revenues and the use of all public means of transportation are to be conducted under the military authorities, until such authorities can be replaced by civil administration, all private property, whether of individuals or corporations, must be respected and protected. If private property be taken for military uses it shall be paid for at a fair valuation in cash if possible, and when payment in cash is not practicable at the time, receipts therefor will be given to be taken up and liquidated as soon as cash becomes available. The ports of the Philippine Islands shall be open to the commerce of all foreign nations, and goods and merchandise not prohibited for military reasons by the military authorities shall be admitted upon payment of such duties and charges as shall be in force at the time of importation. The President concludes his instructions in the following language: "Finally, it should be the earnest and paramount aim of the Administration to win the confidence, respect, and affection of the inhabitants of the Philippines by insuring to them in every possible way the full measure of individual rights and liberty which is the heritage of a free people, and by proving to them that the mission of the United States is one of beneficent assimilation, which will substitute the mild sway of justice and right for arbitrary rule. In the fulfilment of this high mission, while upholding the temporary administration of affairs for the greatest good of the governed, there will be sedulously maintained the strong arm of authority to repress disturbance, and to overcome all obstacles to the bestowal of the blessings of good and stable government upon the people of the Philippine Islands."

"'From the tenor and substance of the above instructions of the President, I am fully of the opinion that it is the intention of the United States Government, while directing affairs generally, to appoint the representative men now forming the controlling element of the Filipinos to civil positions of trust and responsibility, and it will be my aim to appoint thereto such Filipinos as may be acceptable to the supreme authorities at Washington. It is also my belief that it is the intention of the United States Government to draw from the Filipino people so much of the military force of the islands as is possible and consistent with a free and well-constituted government of the country, and it is my desire to inaugurate a policy of that character. I am also convinced that it is the intention of the

United States Government to seek the establishment of a most liberal government for the islands, in which the people themselves shall have as full representation as the maintenance of law and order will permit, and which shall be susceptible of development, on lines of increased representation and the bestowal of increased powers, into a government as free and independent as is enjoyed by the most favored provinces of the world. It will be my constant endeavor to coöperate with the Filipino people, seeking the good of the country, and I invite their full confidence and aid. E. S. OTIS, Major-General, U. S. V., Military Governor.'

''Before publication of this proclamation I endeavored to obtain from able Filipino residents of the city an expression of opinion as to its probable effect upon the population, but was not much encouraged. A few days thereafter they declared the publication to have been a mistake, although the foreign residents appeared to believe the proclamation most excellent in tone and mod·cration, offered everything that the most hostile of the insurgents could expect, and undoubtedly would have a beneficial influence. It was received by the better classes of natives with satisfaction, as it was the first authoritative announcement of the attitude which the United States assumed toward the islands and declared the policy which it intended to pursue, and because the declared policy was one which, in their opinion, conditions imperatively demanded should be imposed for the interests of the Filipino people who were incapable of self-government. The publication separated more widely the friendly and war factions of the inhabitants and was the cause of exciting discussion. The ablest of insurgent newspapers, which was now issued at Malolos and edited by the uncompromising Luna, . . . attacked the policy of the United States as declared in the proclamation, and its assumption of sovereignty over the islands, with all the vigor of which he was capable. . . .

''Aguinaldo met the proclamation by a counter one in which he indignantly protested against the claim of sovereignty by the United States in the islands, which really had been conquered from the Spaniards through the blood and treasure of his countrymen, and abused me for my assumption of the title of military governor. Even the women of Cavite province, in a document numerously signed by them, gave me to understand that after all the men were killed off they were prepared to shed their patriotic blood for the liberty and independence of their country. The efforts made by Aguinaldo and his assistants made a decided impression on the inhabitants of Luzon outside of Manila. . . . Shortly before this time the insurgents had commenced the organization of clubs in the city, membership in which now, I was informed, amounted to 10,000. The chief organizer was a shrewd mestizo, a former close companion of Aguinaldo, by whom he had been commissioned to perform this work. He was a friend and associate of some of our officers; was engaged in organizing the clubs only, as he stated, to give the poorer classes amusement and education; held public entertainments in athletics to which our officers were invited, and in which our soldiers were asked to participate. Gradually arms were being secretly introduced and bolos were being manufactured and distributed. The arms were kept concealed in buildings, and many of them were subsequently captured. The Chinamen were carrying on a lucrative business in bolo making, but the provost-marshal had cruelly seized considerable of their stock. These clubs had received military organization and were commanded by cunning Filipino officers regularly appointed by the Malolos government. The chief organizer departed after organization had been perfected and thereafter became a confidential adviser in Malolos affairs. This organization was the subject of grave apprehension, as it was composed of the worst social element of the city, and was kept under police supervision as closely as possible. . . . The streets of the city were thronged with unarmed insurgent officers and enlisted men from the numerically increasing insurgent line on the outskirts, proud of their uniforms and exhibiting matchless conceit, amusing to our men, who were apparently unconcerned observers, but who were quick to take in the rapidly changing conditions. . . .

''Greater precautionary measures were directed and taken in the way of redistributing organizations throughout the city, in advancing and strengthening (though still far within our own mutually conceded military lines) our posts of observation, and for the quick response of the men if summoned for defensive action. Otherwise no change in the conduct, condition, or temper of the troops was observable. So quietly were these precautions effected that Filipino citizens, noticing the apparent indifference of our men, warned me repeatedly of the danger to be apprehended from a sudden simultaneous attack of the insurgents within and without the city, and were quietly informed that we did not anticipate any great difficulty. Another very noticeable proof of premeditated intent on the part of the insurgents was perceived in the excitement manifested by the natives and their removal in large numbers from the city. All avenues of exit were filled with vehicles transporting families and household effects to surrounding villages. The railway properties were taxed to their utmost capacity in carrying the fleeing inhabitants to the north within the protection of the established insurgent military lines. Aguinaldo, by written communications and messages, invited his old-time friends to send their families to Malolos, where their safety was assured, but Hongkong was considered a more secure retreat and was taken advantage of. A carefully prepared estimate showed that 40,000 of the inhabitants of the city departed within the period of fifteen days."—*Report of General Otis, Aug. 31, 1899 (Message and Documents: Abridgment, 1899-1900, v. 2, pp. 1075-88)*.

The counter-proclamation of Aguinaldo, referrred to above by General Otis, was issued on the 5th of January, 1899, from Malolos, addressed to ''My brothers, the Filipinos, all the honorable consuls, and other foreigners.'' It said : ''Maj. Gen. E. S. Otis's proclamation published yesterday in the Manila papers obliges me to circulate the present one, in order that all who read and understand it may know of my most solemn protest against said proclamation, for I am moved by my duty and my conscience before God, by my political obligations with my beloved country, by my official and private relations to the North American nations. In the above mentioned proclamation, General Otis calls himself

'Military Governor in the Philippines,' and I protest once and a thousand times, with all the energy in my soul, against such an authority. I solemnly proclaim that I have never had, either at Singapore or here in the Philippines, any verbal or written contract for the recognition of American sovereignty over this cherished soil. . . . Our countrymen and foreigners are witnesses that the land and naval forces of the United States existing here have recognized by act the belligerency of the Philippines, not only respecting but also doing public honor to the Filipino banner, which triumphantly traversed our seas in view of foreign nations represented here by their respective consuls.

" As in his proclamation General Otis alludes to some instructions issued by His Excellency the President of the United States relating to the administration of affairs in the Philippines, I solemnly protest in the name of God, root and source of all justice and all right, who has visibly acceded me the power to direct my dear brethren in the difficult task of our regeneration, against this intrusion of the United States Government in the administration of these islands. In the same manner I protest against such an unexpected act which treats of American sovereignty in these islands in the face of all antecedents that I have in my possession referring to my relations with the American authorities, which are unequivocal testimony that the United States did not take me out of Hong Kong to make war against Spain for their own benefit, but for the benefit of our liberty and independence, to which end said authorities verbally promised me their active support and efficacious co-operation. So that you all may understand it, my beloved brothers, it is the principle of liberty and absolute independence that has been our noble ambition for the purpose of obtaining the desired object, with a force given by the conviction, now very widespread, not to retrace the path of glory that we have passed over."— *United States, 56th Congress, 1st Sess., Senate Doc. 208, p. 103.*

A. D. **1899** (January).—Appointment of the First Commission to the Philippines and the President's instructions to it.—On the 20th of January, 1899, the President of the United States addressed the following communication to the Secretary of State : " My communication to the Secretary of War, dated December 21, 1898, declares the necessity of extending the actual occupation and administration of the city, harbor, and bay of Manila to the whole of the territory which by the treaty of Paris, signed on December 10, 1898, passed from the sovereignty of Spain to the sovereignty of the United States, and the consequent establishment of military government throughout the entire group of the Philippine Islands. While the treaty has not yet been ratified, it is believed that it will be by the time of the arrival at Manila of the commissioners named below. In order to facilitate the most humane, pacific, and effective extension of authority throughout these islands, and to secure, with the least possible delay, the benefits of a wise and generous protection of life and property to the inhabitants, I have named Jacob G. Schurman, Rear-Admiral George Dewey, Maj. Gen. Elwell S. Otis, Charles Denby, and Dean C. Worcester to constitute a commission to aid in the accomplishment of these results. In

the performance of this duty, the commissioners are enjoined to meet at the earliest possible day in the city of Manila and to announce, by a public proclamation, their presence and the mission intrusted to them, carefully setting forth that, while the military government already proclaimed is to be maintained and continued so long as necessity may require, efforts will be made to alleviate the burden of taxation, to establish industrial and commercial prosperity, and to provide for the safety of persons and of property by such means as may be found conducive to these ends.

" The commissioners will endeavor, without interference with the military authorities of the United States now in control of the Philippines, to ascertain what amelioration in the condition of the inhabitants and what improvements in public order may be practicable, and for this purpose they will study attentively the existing social and political state of the various populations, particularly as regards the forms of local government, the administration of justice, the collection of customs and other taxes, the means of transportation, and the need of public improvements. They will report through the Department of State, according to the forms customary or hereafter prescribed for transmitting and preserving such communications, the results of their observations and reflections, and will recommend such executive action as may from time to time seem to them wise and useful. The commissioners are hereby authorized to confer authoritatively with any persons resident in the islands from whom they may believe themselves able to derive information or suggestions valuable for the purposes of their commission, or whom they may choose to employ as agents, as may be necessary for this purpose.

" The temporary government of the islands is intrusted to the military authorities, as already provided for by my instructions to the Secretary of War of December 21, 1898, and will continue until Congress shall determine otherwise. The commission may render valuable services by examining with special care the legislative needs of the various groups of inhabitants, and by reporting, with recommendations, the measures which should be instituted for the maintenance of order, peace, and public welfare, either as temporary steps to be taken immediately for the perfection of present administration, or as suggestions for future legislation. In so far as immediate personal changes in the civil administration may seem to be advisable, the commissioners are empowered to recommend suitable persons for appointment to these offices from among the inhabitants of the islands who have previously acknowledged their allegiance to this Government.

" It is my desire that in all their relations with the inhabitants of the islands the commissioners exercise due respect for all the ideals, customs, and institutions of the tribes which compose the population, emphasizing upon all occasions the just and beneficent intentions of the Government of the United States. It is also my wish and expectation that the commissioners may be received in a manner due to the honored and authorized representatives of the American Republic, duly commissioned on account of their knowledge, skill, and integrity as bearers of the good will, the protection, and the richest blessings of a liberating rather than a conquering nation. WILLIAM MCKINLEY." — *Report of the Philippine Commission, Jan.* 31, 1900, *v.* 1, *exhibit* 2 (*p.* 185).

A. D. **1899** (January—February).—Causes **of and** responsibility for the outbreak of hostilities between the Americans and the Filipinos.—"The Philippine Information Society," organized for the purpose of "placing within reach of the American people the most reliable and authoritative evidence attainable in regard to the people of the Philippine Islands and our relations to them," has published in No. VII of the First Series of its pamphlets a carefully made collection of information, from official and other sources, relative to the circumstances in which hostilities between the American and Filipino forces came about. On this as on other subjects which the society has investigated it seems to have pursued its inquiries with no aim but to learn and set forth the truth. Its conclusions, resting on the evidence which it submits, are stated in an introduction to the pamphlet as follows:

"It will presumably be admitted that the important question with regard to the Outbreak of Hostilities, February 4, 1899, is not; who fired the first shot, but who was responsible for the conditions that made it evident to every observer weeks before the clash came that a single shot might bring on war. . . . The situation may be briefly explained as follows: We believed that the Philippine Archipelago was and ought to be ours, and we were moving to take possession as rapidly as possible. The Filipinos, or at least Aguinaldo's government and followers, believed that the country was theirs and they resented every effort on our part to occupy it. We considered it ours through cession from Spain and right of conquest. They claimed that Spain no longer held possession of the country and therefore had no right to cede it to us; moreover, that by right of conquest we were entitled only to temporary occupation of Manila. We wished to extend our sovereignty throughout the Archipelago with all possible dispatch. They desired independence, or at least a protectorate which, while securing them from foreign aggression, should leave them control of their internal affairs. While a discussion of the justice of either position does not come within the limits of the present inquiry, it is important to remember that from the first a minority in this country urged that the Filipinos were entitled to a promise of ultimate independence, and that a resolution of Congress, similar to that passed in the case of Cuba, would avert all occasion for war. This course having been rejected by our country, the question arises, did the assertion of United States sovereignty render war inevitable? . . .

"No doubt most Americans believe that left to themselves the Filipinos would soon have lapsed into anarchy, while a few maintain that with temporary assistance in international affairs they would have developed a government better suited to their peculiar needs than we can ever give them. Still others who are familiar with the Filipinos and kindred races believe that their aspiration for an independent national existence was not deep rooted, that had we adopted an affectionate, admiring tone to their leaders, had we recognized their government and approved of it, we could soon have made their government our

government, could have been as sovereign as we pleased, and had the people with us. Whatever view one may hold, it must be admitted that if we were to establish our sovereignty by peaceful methods it was essential to win the confidence and affection of the Filipinos. . . . There is every indication that the Filipinos were prepared, at first, to treat us as friends and liberators. General Anderson tells the following interesting story: The prevailing sentiment of the Filipinos towards us can be shown by one incident. About the middle of July the insurgent leaders in Cavite invited a number of our army and navy officers to a banquet. There was some post-prandial speech-making, the substance of the Filipino talk being that they wished to be annexed but not conquered. One of our officers in reply assured them that we had not come to make them slaves, but to make them free men. A singular scene followed. All the Filipinos rose to their feet, and Buencomeno, taking his wine-glass in his hand, said: We wish to be baptized in that sentiment. Then he and the rest poured the wine from their glasses over their heads. After the very first, however, the cultivation of intimate relations with the Filipino leaders seems to have been considered unimportant or inadvisable. General Merritt states that we never saw Aguinaldo. Social intercourse between our officers and the Filipinos was discouraged by General Otis. In fact after the surrender of Manila General Whittier seems to have been the only one of our superior officers who ever had a personal interview with Aguinaldo.

"Certainly after the proclamation of January 4, [see above : A. D. 1898—1899 (JANUARY—FEBRUARY)] war could only have been avoided by a decisive action of Congress promising ultimate independence to the Filipinos. That proclamation of January 4 raised the issue and provoked the counter proclamation of January 5, which so stirred the people against us—a proclamation in which Aguinaldo once and a thousand times and with all the energy of his soul protested against American sovereignty, and which closed with the words, 'upon their heads be all the blood which may be shed.' . . .

"Aguinaldo's proclamation was followed by a series of conferences of which General Otis reports 'It was one continued plea for some concession that would satisfy the people.' On January 16th he cabled to Washington, 'Aspiration Filipino people is independence with restrictions resulting from conditions which its government agree with American when latter agree to officially recognize the former.' Finally on January 25th he sent word to the insurgent commissioners that 'To this dispatch no reply has been received.' From this time General Otis states, the insurgents hurried forward preparations for war. Contemporaneous with these events in the Philippines the Treaty of Peace was pending in the United States Senate where it had been assigned for a vote on February 6th.

"With regard to the actual outbreak of hostilities, there is a sharp difference of opinion. The United States press dispatches announcing the outbreak, and the contemporaneous newspaper statements by the Filipinos . . . are of interest as evidence that from the very first each side claimed the other to be the aggressor. As to which of these opposing claims is borne out by the facts, the editors would say that after careful study of all the accessible evidence they find that according to the most authoritative statements the outbreak occurred as the result of a trespass by four armed Filipinos on territory admitted by the Filipino in command to be within the jurisdiction of the United States. The number of Filipinos has been variously estimated. The editors follow the report of General MacArthur in command of the division in which the firing began, which agrees with the report of Second-Lieutenant Wbeedon of the First Nebraska U. S. Volunteer Infantry, stationed at Santa Mesa. The action of the Filipino trespassers seems to have been an instance of bad discipline in the insurgent army. Certainly it was not ordered on that date by the insurgent leaders, although there are some indications that the leaders had planned to attack in a few days. The claim that our forces instigated the attack for the purpose of securing the votes necessary to ratify the treaty is absolutely unsupported by any evidence which has come to the attention of the editors."—Philippine Information Society, *Publications, First Series, VII., Introduction.*

A. D. 1899 (January—November).—Attack on American forces by the Tagalos.—Continued hostilities.—Progress of American conquest.—"No definite date had been set for the attack [by the hostile Tagalos], but a signal by means of rockets had been agreed upon, and it was universally understood that it would come upon the occurrence of the first act on the part of the American forces which would afford a pretext; and in the lack of such act, in the near future at all events. Persistent attempts were made to provoke our soldiers to fire. The insurgents were insolent to our guards and made persistent and continuous efforts to push them back and advance the insurgent lines farther into the city of Manila. . . . With great tact and patience the commanding general had held his forces in check, and he now made a final effort to preserve the peace by appointing a commission to meet a similar body appointed by Aguinaldo and to 'confer with regard to the situation of affairs and to arrive at a mutual understanding of the intent, purposes, aims, and desires of the Filipino people and of the people of the United States.' Six sessions were held, the last occurring on January 29, six days before the outbreak of hostilities. No substantial results were obtained, the Filipino commissioners being either unable or unwilling to give any definite statements of the 'intent, purposes, and aims of their people.' At the close of the last session they were given full assurances that no hostile act would be inaugurated by the United States troops. The critical moment had now arrived. Aguinaldo secretly ordered the Filipinos who were friendly to him to seek refuge outside the city. The Nebraska regiment at that time was in camp on the east line at Santa Mesa, and was guarding its front. For days before the memorable 4th of February, 1899, the outposts in front of the regiment had been openly menaced and assaulted by insurgent soldiers; they were attempting to push our outposts back and advance their line. They made light of our sentinels and persistently ignored their orders. On the evening of the 4th of February, an insurgent officer came to the front with a detail of men and attempted to pass the guard on the San Juan Bridge, our guard being stationed at the west end of the bridge. The

Nebraska sentinel drove them back without firing, but a few minutes before 9 o'clock that evening a large body of insurgent troops made an advance on the South Dakota outposts, which fell back rather than fire. About the same time the insurgents came in force to the east end of the San Juan Bridge, in front of the Nebraska regiment. For several nights prior thereto a lieutenant in the insurgent army had been coming regularly to our outpost No. 2, of the Nebraska regiment, and attempting to force the outpost back and insisting on posting his guard within the Nebraska lines; and at this time and in the darkness he again appeared with a detail of about six men and approached Private Grayson, of Company D, First Nebraska Volunteers, the sentinel on duty at outpost No. 2. He, after halting them three times without effect, fired, killing the lieutenant, whose men returned the fire and then retreated. Immediately rockets were sent up by the Filipinos, and they commenced firing all along the line, . . . and continued to fire until about midnight; and about 4 o'clock on the morning of February 5 the insurgents again opened fire all around the city and kept it up until the Americans charged them and drove them with great slaughter out of their trenches."—*Philippine Commission, Preliminary Report (Exhibit 1.—Report, January 31, 1900, v. 1, pp. 174–5).*

"They [the insurgents] were promptly repulsed in a series of active engagements which extended through the night of the 4th, and the 5th, 6th, and 10th days of February. Our lines were extended and established at a considerable distance from the city in every direction. On the 22d of February a concerted rising of the Tagalogs in the city of Manila, of whom there are about 200,000, was attempted, under instructions to massacre all the Americans and Europeans in the city. This attempt was promptly suppressed and the city was placed under strict control. The troops composing the Eighth Army Corps under General Otis's command at that time were of regulars 171 officers and 5,201 enlisted men and of volunteers 667 officers and 14,831 enlisted men, making an aggregate of 838 officers and 20,032 enlisted men. All of the volunteers and 1,650 of the regulars were, or were about to become, entitled to their discharge, and their right was perfected by the exchange of ratifications of the treaty on the 11th of April. . . .

"The months of the most intense heat, followed by the very severe rainy season of that climate, were immediately approaching, and for any effective occupation of the country it was necessary to await both the close of the rainy season and the supply of new troops to take the place of those about to be discharged. Practically all the volunteers who were then in the Philippines consented to forego the just expectation of an immediate return to their homes, and to remain in the field until their places could be supplied by new troops. They voluntarily subjected themselves to the dangers and casualties of numerous engagements, and to the very great hardships of the climate. They exhibited fortitude and courage, and are entitled to high commendation for their patriotic spirit and soldierly conduct. . . .

"No attempt was . . . made to occupy the country, except in the vicinity of Manila, and at such points as were important for the protection of our lines. Such movements as passed beyond this territory were designed primarily to break up threatening concentrations of insurgent troops, and to prevent undue annoyance to the positions which we occupied. On the 11th of February the city of Iloilo, on the island of Panay, the second port of the Philippines in importance, was occupied. After the capture of Iloilo the navy took possession of the city of Cebu, on the island of Cebu, and on the 26th of February a battalion of the 23d Infantry was dispatched to that port for the protection of the inhabitants and property. On the 1st of March a military district comprising the islands of Panay, Negros, and Cebu, and such other Visayan islands as might be thereafter designated, to be known as the 'Visayan Military District,' was established and placed under the supervision of Brig. Gen. Marcus P. Miller, commanding 1st Separate Brigade, Eighth Army Corps, with headquarters at Iloilo. The 3d Battalion of the 1st California Volunteer Infantry was thereupon ordered to the island of Negros, under the command of Col. (now Brig. Gen.) James F. Smith, and took possession of the city of Bacolod, on that island, without resistance. On the 5th of May Brig. Gen. James F. Smith assumed temporary command of the Visayan military district, and on the 25th of May Brig. Gen. R. P. Hughes, United States Volunteers, was assigned to the command of the district. On the 19th of May the Spanish garrison at Jolo, in the Sulu Archipelago, was replaced by American troops. By the 31st of August the number of troops stationed at Jolo and the Visayan Islands, including a small guard at the Cavite Arsenal, amounted to 4,145. . . .

"All of the forces who were entitled to be discharged as above mentioned have now [Nov. 29, 1899] been returned to this country and mustered out. The new troops designed to take the place of those returning to this country, and to constitute an effective army for the occupation of the Philippines, have been transported to Manila. . . . The troops now in the Philippines comprise 905 officers and 30,578 men of the regular force, and 594 officers and 15,388 men of the volunteer force, making an aggregate of 1,499 officers and 45,966 men, and when the troops on the way have arrived the total force constituting the Eighth Army Corps will be 2,051 officers and 63,483 men.

"By the 10th of October the process of changing armies and the approach of the dry season had reached a point where an advance toward the general occupation of the country was justified. At that time the American lines extended from the Bay of Manila to Laguna de Bay, and included considerable parts of the provinces of Cavite, Laguna, and Morong to the south and east of Manila, substantially all of the province of Manila and the southern parts of Bulacan and Pampanga, dividing the insurgent forces into two widely separated parts. To the south and east of our lines in Cavite and Morong were numerous bands occasionally concentrating for attack on our lines, and as frequently dispersed and driven back toward the mountains. On the 8th of October, the insurgents in this region having again gathered and attacked our lines of communication, General Schwan with a column of 1,726 men commenced a movement from Bacoor, in the province of Cavite, driving the enemy through

Old Cavite, Noveleta, Santa Cruz, San Francisco de Malabon, Saban, and Perez das Marinas, punishing them severely, scattering them and destroying them as organized forces, and returning on the 13th to Bacoor. On the north of our lines stretched the great plain of central Luzon extending north from Manila about 120 miles. This plain comprises parts of the provinces of Manila, Pampanga, Bulacan, Tarlac, Nueva, Ecija, and Pangasinan. It is, roughly speaking, bounded on the south by the Bay of Manila; on the east and west by high mountain ranges separating it from the sea coasts, and on the north by mountains and the Gulf of Lingayen. Through the northeast and central portion flows the Rio Grande from the northern mountains southwesterly to the Bay of Manila, and near the western edge runs the only railroad on the island of Luzon, in a general southeasterly direction from Dagupan, on the Bay of Lingayen, to Manila. In this territory Aguinaldo exercised a military dictatorship, and with a so-called cabinet imitated the forms of civil government, having his headquarters at Tarlac, which he called his capital, and which is situated near the center of the western boundary of the plain.

"The operations commenced in October involved the movement of three separate forces : (1) A column proceeding up the Rio Grande and along the northeastern borders of the plain and bending around to the westward across the northern boundary toward the Gulf of Lingayen, garrisoning the towns and occupying the mountain passes which gave exit into the northeastern division of the island. (2) An expedition proceeding by transports to the Gulf of Lingayen, there to land at the northwestern corner of the plain and occupy the great coast road which from that point runs between the mountains and the sea to the northern extremity of the island, and to proceed eastward to a junction with the first column. (3) A third column proceeding directly up the railroad to the capture of Tarlac, and thence still up the road to Dagupan, driving the insurgent forces before it toward the line held by the first two columns. These movements were executed with energy, rapidity, and success, notwithstanding the exceedingly unfavorable weather and deluges of rain, which rendered the progress of troops and transportation of subsistence most difficult. On the 12th of October a strong column under General Lawton, with General Young commanding the advance. commenced the northerly movement up the Rio Grande from Arayat, driving the insurgents before it to the northward and westward. On the 18th the advance reached Cabiao. On the 19th San Isidro was captured, and a garrison established ; on the 27th Cabanatuan was occupied, and a permanent station established there. On the 1st of November Aliaga and Talavera were occupied. In the meantime detachments, chiefly of Young's cavalry, were operating to the west of the general line of advance, striking insurgent parties wherever they were found and driving them toward the line of the railroad. By the 13th of November the advance had turned to the westward, and our troops had captured San Jose, Lupao, Humingan, San Quintin, Tayug, and San Nicolas. By the 18th of November the advance had occupied Asingan and Rosales, and was moving on Pozorrubio, a strongly intrenched post about 12 miles east of San Fabian. General Lawton's forces now held a line of posts extending up the eastern side of the plain and curving around and across the northern end to within a few miles of the Gulf of Lingayen.

"On the 6th of November a force of 2,500, under command of General Wheaton, sailed from Manila for the Gulf of Lingayen, convoyed by ships of the Navy, and on the 7th the expedition was successfully landed at San Fabian with effective assistance from a naval convoy against spirited opposition. On the 12th the 33d Volunteers, of Wheaton's command, under Colonel Hare, proceeded southeastward to San Jacinto, attacked and routed 1,200 intrenched insurgents, with the the loss of the gallant Maj. John A. Logan and 6 enlisted men killed, and one officer and 11 men wounded. The enemy left 81 dead in the trenches and suffered a total loss estimated at 300. In the meantime, on the 5th of November, a column under General McArthur advanced up the railroad from Angeles to Magalang, clearing the country between Angeles and Arayat, encountering and routing bodies of the enemy at different points, and capturing Magalang. On the 11th it took Bamban, Capas, and Concepcion, and on the 12th of November entered Tarlac, from which the enemy fled on its approach. Meantime, parties, mainly of the 36th Volunteers, under Col. J. F. Bell, cleared the country to the right of the line of advance as far east as the points reached by General Lawton's flanking parties. On the 17th of November McArthur's column had occupied Gerona and Panique, to the north of Tarlac. On the 19th, Wheaton's troops, and on the 20th, McArthur's troops, entered Dagupan.

"On the 24th of November General Otis was able to telegraph to the Department as follows: 'Claim to government by insurgents can be made no longer under any fiction. Its treasurer, secretary of the interior, and president of congress in our hands; its president and remaining cabinet officers in hiding, evidently in different central Luzon provinces; its generals and troops in small bands scattered through these provinces, acting as banditti, or dispersed, playing the rôle of " Amigos," with arms concealed.' Since that time our troops have been actively pursuing the flying and scattered bands of insurgents, further dispersing them, making many prisoners, and releasing many Spanish prisoners who had been in the insurgents' hands. On the 23d General Young's column had reached Namacpacan, 30 miles north of San Fernando, in the province of Union, and passed north into the mountains; and on the 24th Vigan, the principal port of the northwest coast, was occupied by a body of marines landed from the battle ship Oregon. Wherever the permanent occupation of our troops has extended in the Philippine Islands civil law has been immediately put in force. The courts have been organized and the most learned and competent native lawyers have been appointed to preside over them. A system of education has been introduced and numerous schools have been established."—*Annual Report of the Secretary of War, 1899 (Message and Documents; Abridgment, 1899–1900. v. 2, pp. 735–41).*

General Young, whose movement is referred to above, reported to General Otis from Pozorrubio, on the 17th of November: "Aguinaldo is now a fugitive and an outlaw, seeking security in escape to the mountains or by sea. My cavalry have ridden down his forces wherever found, utterly routing them in every instance, killing some, capturing and liberating many prisoners, and destroying many arms, ammunition, and other war impediments." On the 30th, Major March was sent by General Young, as he expresses it, "on Aguinaldo's trail," and encountered the forces of the Filipino General Pilar in the Tila Pass. The following is Major March's report of the fight which then occurred, and in which the Filipino commander fell: "The trail winds up the Tila Mountains in a sharp zigzag. The enemy had constructed a stone barricade across the trail at a point where it commanded the turns of the zigzag for a considerable distance. The barricade was loopholed for infantry fire and afforded head cover for the insurgents. On passing on beyond Lingey the advance was checked by a heavy fire from this barricade, which killed and wounded several men, without having its position revealed. I brought up the remainder of the command at double time, losing two men wounded during the run up. On arriving at the point, I located the insurgents' position with my glasses—their fire being entirely Mauser and smokeless powder—by the presence of the insurgent officer who showed himself freely and directed the fire. On pushing forward, the number of my men who were hit increased so rapidly that it was evident that the position could not be taken by a front attack, when the trail only allowed the men to pass one at a time. On the left of the barricade was a gorge several hundred feet deep. On its right, as we faced it, was a precipitous mountain which rose 1,500 feet above the trail. Across the gorge and to the left front of the barricade was a hill, which, while it did not permit of flank fire into the barricade, commanded the trail in its rear, and this point I occupied with ten sharpshooters in command of Sergeant-Major McDougall. He lost one man wounded in getting to the top, and when there rendered most effective assistance. I then ordered Lieutenant Tompkins to take his company (H) and proceeding back on the trail to ascend the slope of the mountain under cover of a slight ridge which struck the face of the mountain about 150 feet from the summit. From there he had a straight-up climb to the top, where the men pulled themselves up by twigs and by hand. The ascent took two hours, during which the enemy kept up an incessant and accurate fire, which they varied by rolling down stones on our heads. When Tompkins' men appeared upon the crest of the hills over their heads, he had the command of the two other trenches which were constructed in rear of the barricade, I have described, around a sharp turn in the trail, and which were also held by the insurgents. He opened fire upon them and I charged the first barricade at the same time, and rushed the enemy over the hill. We found eight dead bodies on the trail, and the bushes which grew at the edge of the gorge were broken and blood-stained where dead or wounded men fell through. Among the dead bodies was that of Gregorio del Pilar, the general commanding insurgent forces. I have in my possession his shoulder straps; French field glasses, which gave the range of objects; official and private papers, and a mass of means of identification. He was also recognized personally by Mr. McCutcheon and Mr. Keene, two newspaper correspondents who had met him before. The insurgents' report of their loss in this fight is 52, given to me after I reached Cervantes. My loss was 2 killed and 9 wounded. I reached the summit at 4.30 P. M. and camped there for the night. ... At Cervantes I learned that the force at Tila Pass was a picked force from Aguinaldo's body guard, and that it was wiped out of existence. Aguinaldo with his wife and two other women and a handful of men were living in a convent at Cervantes, perfectly secure in his belief that Tila Pass was an impregnable position. It was the insurgents' Thermopylæ." — *Report of Lieutenant-General Commanding the Army*, 1900, *pt.* 4, *p.* 331.

Mr. McCutcheon, one of the newspaper correspondents referred to by Major March, gave to the "Chicago Record" a graphic account of the fight in Tila Pass, and wrote feelingly of the death to the young Filipino General Pilar:

"Gen. Gregorio del Pilar," wrote Mr. McCutcheon, "was the last man to fall. He was striving to escape up the trail and had already received a wound in the shoulder. A native was holding his horse for him and just as he was preparing to mount a Krag-Jorgensen bullet caught him in the neck, and passing through came out just below his mouth. The men of Company E, rushing up the trail, caught the native, who was endeavoring to secure the papers which the general had in his pockets, and a moment later captured the horse. At that time no one knew who the dead man was, but from his uniform and insignia they judged that he was an officer of high rank. The souvenir fiend was at once at work and the body was stripped of everything of value from the diamond ring to the boots. . . . Many letters were found, most of them from his sweetheart, Dolores Jose, who lived in Dagupan. A handkerchief bearing her name was also found in his pocket. One letter was found from the president of Lingay and gave the exact number of soldiers in March's command. Pilar's diary, which ran from November 19 on to the day of his death, was of remarkable interest, for it detailed many things regarding the wild flight of himself and Aguinaldo's party up the coast. The last words written in it were pathetic and indicated something of the noble character of the man. The passage, which was written only a few minutes previously, while the fight was on and while death even then was before him, said: 'I am holding a difficult position against desperate odds, but I will gladly die for my beloved country.'

"Pilar alive and in command, shooting down good Americans, was one thing, but Pilar lying in that silent mountain trail, his body half denuded of its clothes, and his young, handsome, boyish face discolored with the blood which saturated his blouse and stained the earth, was another thing. We could not help but feel admiration for his gallant fight, and sorrow for the sweetheart whom he left behind. The diary was dedicated to the girl, and I have since learned that he was to have married her in Dagupan about two weeks before. But the Americans came too soon. Instead of wedding bells there sounded the bugle calls of the foe and he was hurriedly ordered to accompany his chief, Aguinaldo, on that hasty retreat to the mountains. The marriage was postponed, and he carried out his orders by leaving for the north. Pilar was one of the best types of the Filipino soldier. He was only 23 years old, but he had been through the whole campaign in his capacity as brigadier-general. It was he who commanded the forces at Quingua the day that Col. Stotsenberg was killed, and it may be remembered that the engagement that day was one of the most bloody and desperate that has occurred on the island. He was a handsome boy, and was known as one of the Filipinos who were actuated by honestly patriotic motives, and who fought because they believed they were fighting in the right and not for personal gain or ambition." — *Chicago Record's Stories of Filipino Warfare, p.* 14.

A. D. 1899 (March—July).—The establishment of a provisional government in the island of Negros.—Negros "was the first island to accept American sovereignty. Its people unreservedly proclaimed allegiance to the United States and adopted a constitution looking to the establishment of a popular government. It was impossible to guarantee to the people of Negros that the constitution so adopted should be the ultimate form of government. Such a question, under the treaty with Spain and in accordance with our own Constitution and laws, came exclusively within the jurisdiction of the Congress. The government actually set up by the inhabitants of Negros eventually proved unsatisfactory to the natives themselves. A new system was put into force by order of the Major-General Commanding the Department [July 22, 1899], of which the following are the most important elements:

"It was ordered that the government of the island of Negros should consist of a military governor appointed by the United States military governor of the Philippines, and a civil governor and an advisory council elected by the people. The military governor was authorized to appoint secretaries of the treasury, interior, agriculture, public instruction, an attorney-general, and an auditor. The seat of government was fixed at Bacolod. The military governor exercises the supreme executive power. He is to see that the laws are executed, appoint to office, and fill all vacancies in office not otherwise provided for, and may, with the approval of the military governor of the Philippines, remove any officer from office. The civil governor advises the military governor on all public civil questions and presides over the advisory council. He, in general, performs the duties which are performed by secretaries of state in our own system of government. The advisory council consists of eight members elected by the people within territorial limits which are defined in the order of the commanding general. The times and places of holding elections are to be fixed by the military governor of the island of Negros. The qualifications of voters are as follows: (1) A voter must be a male citizen of the island of Negros. (2) Of the age of 21 years. (3) He shall be able to speak, read, and write the English, Spanish, or Visayan language, or he must own real property worth $500, or pay a rental on real property of the value of $1,000. (4) He must have resided in the island not less than one year preceding, and in the district in which he registers as a voter not less than three months immediately preceding the time he offers to register. (5) He must register at a time fixed by law before voting. (6) Prior to such registration he shall have paid all taxes due by him to the Government. Provided, that no insane person shall be allowed to register or vote. The military governor has the right to veto all bills or resolutions adopted by the advisory council, and his veto is final if not disapproved by the military governor of the Philippines. The advisory council discharges all the ordinary duties of a legislature. The usual duties pertaining to said offices are to be performed by the secretaries of the treasury, interior, agriculture, public instruction, the attorney-general, and the auditor. The judicial power is vested in three judges, who are to be appointed by the military governor of the island. Inferior courts are to be established. Free public schools are to be established throughout the populous districts of the island, in which the English language shall be taught, and this subject will receive the careful consideration of the advisory council. The burden of government must be distributed equally and equitably among the people. The military authorities will collect and receive the customs revenue, and will control postal matters and Philippine inter-island trade and commerce. The military governor, subject to the approval of the military governor of the Philippines, determines all questions not specifically provided for and which do not come under the jurisdiction of the advisory council."— *Message of the President, Dec. 5, 1899 (Message and Documents: Abridgment, 1899–1900, v. 2, p. 47).* Also in: *Report of General Otis (Message and Documents, v. 2, pp. 1131–37).*

A. D. 1899 (May—August).—Agreement of terms with the Sultan of Jolo, concerning the Sulu Archipelago.—On the 19th of May, a detachment of U. S. troops took the place of the Spanish garrison at Jolo, the military station in the Sulu Archipelago. On the 3d of July, General Otis, Military Governor of the Philippines, issued orders as follows to General J. C. Bates, U. S. V.: "You will proceed as soon as practicable to the United States military station of Jolo, on the island of that name, and there place yourself in communication with the Sultan of Jolo, who is believed to be at Siassi, where he was sojourning when the last information concerning him was received. You are hereby appointed and constituted an agent on the part of the United States military authorities in the Philippines to discuss, enter into negotiations, and perfeet, if possible, a written agreement of character and scope as hereinafter explained, with the Sultan, which upon approval at these headquarters and confirmation by the supreme executive authority of the United States, will prescribe and control the future relations, social and political, between the United States Government and the inhabitants of the archipelago. . . . In your discussions with the Sultan and his datos the question of sovereignty will be forced to the front, and they will undoubtedly request an expression of opinion thereon, as they seem to be impressed apparently with the belief that the recent Spanish authorities with whom they were in relationship have transferred full sovereignty of the islands to them. The question is one which admits of easy solution, legally considered, since by the terms of treaties or protocols between Spain and European powers Spanish sovereignty over the archipelago is conceded. Under the agreement between Spain and the Sultan and datos of July, 1878, the latter acknowledged

Spanish sovereignty in the entire archipelago of Jolo and agreed to become loyal Spanish subjects, receiving in consideration certain specific payments in money. The sovereignty of Spain, thus established and acknowledged by all parties in interest, was transferred to the United States by the Paris treaty. The United States has succeeded to all the rights which Spain held in the archipelago, and its sovereignty over the same is an established fact. But the inquiry arises as to the extent to which that sovereignty can be applied under the agreement of 1878 with the Moros. Sovereignty, of course, implies full power of political control, but it is not incompatible with concessionary grants between sovereign and subject. The Moros acknowledged through their accepted chiefs Spanish sovereignty and their subjection thereto, and that nation In turn conferred upon their chiefs certain powers of supervision over them and their affairs. The kingly prerogatives of Spain, thus abridged by solemn concession, have descended to the United States, and conditions existing at the time of transfer should remain. The Moros are entitled to enjoy the identical privileges which they possessed at the time of transfer, and to continue to enjoy them until abridged or modified by future mutual agreement between them and the United States, to which they owe loyalty, unless it becomes necessary to invoke the excreise of the supreme powers of sovereignty to meet emergencies. You will therefore acquaint yourself thoroughly with the terms of the agreement of 1878, and take them as a basis for your directed negotiations. . . .

"It is greatly desired by the United States for the sake of the individual improvement and social advancement of the Moros, and for the development of the trade and agriculture of the islands in their interests, also for the welfare of both the United States and Moros, that mutual friendly and well-defined relations be established. If the Sultan can be made to give credit to and fully understand the intentions of the United States, the desired result can be accomplished. The United States will accept the obligations of Spain under the agreement of 1878 in the matter of money annuities, and in proof of sincerity you will offer as a present to the Sultan and datos $10,000, Mexican, with which you will be supplied before leaving for Jolo—the same to be handed over to them, respectively, in amounts agreeing with the ratio of payments made to them by the Spanish Government for their declared services. From the 1st of September next, and thereafter, the United States will pay to them regularly the sums promised by Spain in its agreement of 1878, and in any subsequent promises of which proof can be furnished. The United States will promise, in return for the concessions to be hereinafter mentioned, not to interfere with, but to protect the Moros in the free exercise of their religion and customs, social and domestic, and will respect the rights and dignities of the Sultan and his advisers."

Of the results of the mission of General Bates, General Otis reported subsequently as follows: "General Bates had a difficult task to perform and executed it with tact and ability. While a number of the principal datos were favorably inclined, the Sultan, not responding to invitations, kept aloof and was represented by his secretary, until finally, the general appearing at Maibung, the Moro capital, a personal interview was secured. He being also Sultan of North Borneo and receiving large annual payments from the North Borneo Trading Company, expected like returns from the United States, and seemed more anxious to obtain personal revenue than benefits for his people. Securing the port of Siassi from the Spaniards, establishing there his guards and police, he had received customs revenues from the Sandaken trade which he was loath to surrender. Negotiations continued well into August, and finally, after long conferences, an agreement was reached by which the United States secured much more liberal terms than the Spaniards were ever able to obtain."—*Report of Gen. Otis, Aug.* 31, 1899 (*Message and Documents: Abridgment,* 1899-1900, *v.* 2, *pp.* 1162–64).

"By Article I the sovereignty of the United States over the whole archipelago of Jolo and its dependencies is declared and acknowledged. The United States flag will be used in the archipelago and its dependencies, on land and sea. Piracy is to be suppressed, and the Sultan agrees to co-operate heartily with the United States authorities to that end and to make every possible effort to arrest and bring to justice all persons engaged in piracy. All trade in domestic products of the archipelago of Jolo when carried on with any part of the Philippine Islands and under the American flag shall be free, unlimited, and undutiable. The United States will give full protection to the Sultan in case any foreign nation should attempt to impose upon him. The United States will not sell the island of Jolo or any other island of the Jolo archipelago to any foreign nation without the consent of the Sultan. Salaries for the Sultan and his associates in the administration of the islands have been agreed upon to the amount of $760 monthly. Article X provides that any slave in the archipelago of Jolo shall have the right to purchase freedom by paying to the master the usual market value. The agreement by General Bates was made subjcet to confirmation by the President and to future modifications by the consent of the parties in interest. I have confirmed said agreement, subject to the action of the Congress, and with the reservation, which I have directed shall be communicated to the Sultan of Jolo, that this agreement is not to be deemed in any way to authorize or give the consent of the United States to the existence of slavery in the Sulu archipelago." —*Message of the President, Dec.* 5, 1899 (*Message and Documents: Abridgment,* 1899-1900, *v.* 2, *pp.* 47–48).

"The population of the Sulu Archipelago is reckoned at 120,000, mostly domiciled in the island of Jolo, and numbers 20,000 fighting men. Hostilities would be unfortunate for all parties concerned, would be very expensive to the United States in men and money, and destructive of any advancement of the Moros for years to come. Spain's long struggle with these people and their dislike for the former dominant race in the Philippines, inherited, it would seem, by each rising generation during three centuries, furnishes an instructive lesson. Under the pending agreement General Bates, assisted by the officers of the Navy, quietly placed garrisons of one company each at Siassi and at Bongao, on the Tawai Tawai group of islands, where they were well received by the friendly natives. With the ap-

proval of the agreement, the only difficulty to a satisfactory settlement of the Sulu affairs will arise from discontent on the part of the Sultan personally because of a supposed decrease in anticipated revenues or the machinations of the insurgents of Mindanao, who are endeavoring to create a feeling of distrust and hostility among the natives against the United States troops.

"The Sultan's government is one of perfect despotism, in form at least, as all political power is supposed to center in his person; but this does not prevent frequent outbreaks on the part of the datos, who frequently revolt, and are now, in two or three instances, in declared enmity. All Moros, however, profess the Mohammedan religion, introduced in the fourteenth century, and the sacredness of the person of the Sultan is therefore a tenet of faith. This fact would prevent any marked success by a dato in attempting to secure supreme power. Spain endeavored to supplant the Sultan with one of his most enterprising chiefs and signally failed. Peonage or a species of serfdom enters largely into the social and domestic arrangements and a dato's following or clan submits itself without protest to his arbitrary will. The Moro political fabric bears resemblance to the state of feudal times—the Sultan exercising supreme power by divine right, and his datos, like the feudal lords, supporting or opposing him at will, and by force of arms occasionally, but not to the extent of dethronement, as that would be too great a sacrilege for a Mohammedan people to seek to consummate. The United States must accept these people as they are, and endeavor to ameliorate their condition by degrees, and the best means to insure success appears to be through the cultivation of friendly sentiments and the introduction of trade and commerce upon approved business methods. To undertake forcible radical action for the amelioration of conditions or to so interfere with their domestic relations as to arouse their suspicions and distrust would be attended with unfortunate consequences."—*Report of Gen. Otis, Aug.* 31, 1899 (*Message and Documents: Abridgment,* 1899-1900, *v.* 2, *p.* 1165).

A. D. **1899-1900.**—Military operations against the insurgents.—Death of General Lawton.—"The enlargement of the field of operations and government in the Philippine Islands made it impracticable to conduct the business under the charge of the army in those islands through the machinery of a single department, and by order made April 7, 1900, the Philippine Islands were made a military division, consisting of four departments: The Department of Northern Luzon, the Department of Southern Luzon, the Department of the Visayas, and the Department of Mindanao and Jolo. The Department of Northern Luzon is subdivided into six, the Department of Southern Luzon into four, the Department of the Visayas into four, and the Department of Mindanao and Jolo into four military districts. . . .

"At the date of the last report (November 29, 1899 [see above]) the government established by the Philippine insurgents in central Luzon and the organized armed forces by which it was maintained had been destroyed, and the principal civil and military leaders of the insurrection, accompanied by small and scattered bands of troops, were the objects of pursuit in the western and the northern parts of the island. That pursuit was prosecuted with vigor and success, under conditions of extraordinary difficulty and hardship, and resulted in the further and practically complete disintegration of the insurrectionary bands in those regions, in the rescue of nearly all the American prisoners and the greater part of the Spanish prisoners held by the insurgents, in the capture of many of the leading insurgents, and in the capture and destruction of large quantities of arms, ammunition, and supplies. There still remained a large force of insurgents in Cavite and the adjacent provinces south of Manila, and a considerable force to the east of the Rio Grande de Pampanga, chiefly in the province of Bulacan, while in the extreme southeastern portions of Luzon, and in the various Visayan islands, except the island of Negros, armed bodies of Tagalogs had taken possession of the principal seacoast towns, and were exercising military control over the peaceful inhabitants. Between the insurgent troops in Bulacan and the mountains to the north, and the insurgents in the south, communication was maintained by road and trail, running along and near the eastern bank of the Mariquina River, and through the towns of Mariquina, San Mateo, and Montalban and the province of Morong. This line of communication, passing through rough and easily defended country, was strongly fortified and held by numerous bodies of insurgents.

"On the 18th of December, 1899, a column, under the command of Maj. Gen. Henry W. Lawton, proceeded from Manila, and between that date and the 29th of December captured all the fortified posts of the insurgents, took possession of the line of communication, which has ever since been maintained, and destroyed, captured, or dispersed the insurgent force in that part of the island. In the course of this movement was sustained the irremediable loss of General Lawton, who was shot and instantly killed while too fearlessly exposing his person in supervising the passing of his troops over the river Mariquina at San Mateo.

"On the 4th of January, 1900, Gen. J. C. Bates, U. S. V., was assigned to the command of the First Division of the Eighth Army Corps, and an active campaign under his direction was commenced in Southern Luzon. The plan adopted was to confront and hold the strong force of the enemy near Imus and to the west of Bacoor by a body of troops under General Wheaton, while a column, under General Schwan, should move rapidly down the west shore of the Laguna de Bay to Biñang, thence turn southwesterly and seize the Silang, Indang, and Naic road, capture the enemy's supplies supposed to be at the towns of Silang and Indang, and arrest the retreat of the enemy, when he should be driven from northern Cavite by our troops designated to attack him there, and thus prevent his reassembling in the mountains of southern Cavite and northern Batangas. This plan was successfully executed. General Schwan's column moved over the lines indicated with great rapidity, marching a distance of over 600 miles, striking and defeating numerous bodies of insurgents and capturing many intrenched positions, taking possession of and garrisoning towns along the line, and scattering and demoralizing all the organized forces of the enemy within that section of country. From these operations and the simultaneous attacks by

our troops under General Wheaton in the north the rebel forces in the Cavite region practically disappeared, the members either being killed or captured or returning to their homes as unarmed citizens, and a few scattered parties escaping through General Schwan's line to the south. By the 8th of February the organized forces of the insurgents in the region mentioned had ceased to exist. In large portions of the country the inhabitants were returning to their homes and resuming their industries, and active trade with Manila was resumed. In the course of these operations about 600 Spanish prisoners were released from the insurgents, leaving about 600 more still in their hands in the extreme southeastern provinces of Camarines and Albay, nearly all of whom were afterwards liberated by our troops. In the meantime an expedition was organized under the command of Brig. Gen. William A. Kobbé, U. S. V., to expel the Tagalogs who had taken possession of the principal hemp ports of the islands situated in Albay, the extreme southeastern province of Luzon, and in the islands of Leyte, Samar, and Catanduanes. This expedition sailed from Manila on the 18th of January and accomplished its object. All of the principal hemp ports were relieved from control of the insurgents, garrisoned by American troops, and opened to commerce by order of the military governor of the islands on the 30th of January and the 10th and 14th of February. The expedition met with strong resistance at Legaspi by an intrenched force under the Chinese general, Paua. He was speedily overcome and went into the interior. After a few days he reassembled his forces and threatened the garrisons which had been left in Albay and Legaspi, whereupon he was attacked, and defeated, and surrendered. Thirty pieces of artillery, a large quantity of ammunition, a good many rifles, and a considerable amount of money were captured by this expedition.

"On the 15th of February an expedition, under the supervision of Major-General Bates and under the immediate command of Brig. Gen. James M. Bell, U. S. V., sailed from Manila to take possession of the North and South Camarines provinces and Western Albay, in which the insurgent forces had been swelled by the individuals and scattered bands escaping from our operations in various sections of the north. The insurgent force was defeated after a sharp engagement near the mouth of the Bicol River, pursued, and scattered. Large amounts of artillery and war material were captured. The normal conditions of industry and trade relations with Manila were resumed by the inhabitants. On the 20th of March the region covered by the last-described operations was created a district of southeastern Luzon, under the command of Gen. James M. Bell, who was instructed to proceed to the establishment of the necessary customs and internal-revenue service in the district. In the meantime similar expeditions were successfully made through the mountains of the various islands of the Visayan Group, striking and scattering and severely punishing the bands of bandits and insurgents who infested those islands. In the latter part of March General Bates proceeded with the Fortieth Infantry to establish garrisons in Mindanao. The only resistance was of a trifling character at Cagayan, the insurgent general in northeastern Mindanao surrendering and turning over the ordnance in his possession. With [the execution of these movements] all formal and open resistance to American authority in the Philippines terminated, leaving only an exceedingly vexatious and annoying guerilla warfare of a character closely approaching brigandage, which will require time, patience, and good judgment to finally suppress. As rapidly as we have occupied territory, the policy of inviting inhabitants to return to their peaceful vocations, and aiding them in the reëstablishment of their local governments, has been followed, and the protection of the United States has been promised to them. The giving of this protection has led to the distribution of troops in the Philippine Islands to over 400 different posts, with the consequent labor of administration and supply. The maintenance of these posts involves the continued employment of a large force, but as the Tagalogs who are in rebellion have deliberately adopted the policy of murdering, so far as they are able, all of their countrymen who are friendly to the United States, the maintenance of garrisons is at present necessary to the protection of the peaceful and unarmed Filipinos who have submitted to our authority; and if we are to discharge our obligations in that regard their reduction must necessarily be gradual."—*United States, Secretary of War, Annual Report, Nov.* 30, 1900, *pp.* 5-10.

A. D. 1900 (January).—Report of the First Philippine Commission.—The First Commission to the Philippines returned to the United States in the autumn of 1899, and then submitted to the President a brief preliminary statement of its proceedings in the Islands and the opinions its members had formed, concerning the spirit and extent of the Tagalo revolt, the general disposition of the people at large, their capacity for independent self-government, etc. On the 31st of January following the commissioners presented a report which deals extensively with many subjects of investigation and deliberation. In Part I., it sets forth the efforts made by the commission "toward conciliation and the establishment of peace," through interviews with various emissaries of Aguinaldo, and others, and by means of a proclamation to the people. In Part II., it gives an extended account of the races and tribes of which the native population of the Islands is composed. In Part III., it details the provision that has heretofore been made for education, and states the conclusions of the commission as to the capacity of the people and their fitness for a popular government. In Part IV., a very full account of the Spanish organization of government in the Philippines, general, provincial and municipal, is given, and the reforms that were desired by the Filipino people are ascertained. From this the commission proceeds to consider the question of a plan of government for the Islands under the sovereignty of the United States, and concludes that the Territorial system of the United States offers all that can be desired. "What Jefferson and the nation did for Louisiana," says the report, "we are . . . free to-day to do for the Philippines. The fact that Bonaparte had provided in the treaty that Louisiana should in due time be admitted as a State in the Union, and that in the meantime its inhabitants should have protection in the free enjoyment of their liberty, property, and religion, made no difference in the relation

of Louisiana to the Constitution of the United States so long as Louisiana remained a Territory ; and, if it had made a difference, it should have constituted something of a claim to the immediate enjoyment of some or all of the benefits of the Constitution. Unmoved by that consideration, however, the Jeffersonian policy established once for all the subjection of national domain outside the States to the absolute and unrestricted power of Congress. The commission recommends that in dealing with the Philippines this vast power be exercised along the lines laid down by Jefferson and Madison in establishing a government for Louisiana, but with . . . deviations in the direction of larger liberty to the Filipinos. . . . The result would be substantially the transformation of their second-class Territorial government of Louisiana into a Territorial government of the first-class for the Philippine Islands." To this recommendation of the Territorial system of government the commission adds a strenuous plea for a closely guarded civil service. "It is a safe and desirable rule," says the report, "that no American should be appointed to any office in the Philippines for which a reasonably qualified Filipino can, by any possibility, be secured. Of course the merit or business system must be adopted and lived up to; the patronage or spoils system would prove absolutely fatal to good government in this new Oriental territory." Further parts of the report are devoted to the Philippine judicial system, as it has been and as it should be; to "the condition and needs of the United States in the Philippines from a naval and maritime standpoint"; to the secular clergy and religious orders; to registration laws ; to the currency ; to the Chinese in the Philippines; and to public health. Among the exhibits appended in volume 1 of the published Report are the constitution of Aguinaldo's Philippine Republic (called the Malolos constitution), and several other constitutional drafts and proposals from Filipino sources, indicating the political ideas that prevail.—*Report of the Philippine Commission, Jan.* 31, 1900, *v.* 1. —See, also (in this vol.), EDUCATION : A. D. 1898 (PHILIPPINE ISLANDS).

A. D. 1900 (March).—Institution of municipal governments.—By General Orders, on the 29th of March, 1900, the Military Governor of the Islands promulgated a law providing for the election and institution of municipal governments, the provisions of which law had been framed by a board, appointed in the previous January, under the presidency of Don Cayetano Arellano, chief justice of the Philippines. The first chapter of the law reads as follows :

"ART. 1. The towns of the Philippine Islands shall be recognized as municipal corporations with the same limits as heretofore established, upon reorganizing under the provisions of this order. All property vested in any town under its former organization shall be vested in the same town upon becoming incorporated hereunder.

"ART. 2. Towns so incorporated shall be designated as 'municipios,' and shall be known respectively by the names heretofore adopted. Under such names they may, without further authorization, sue and be sued, contract and be contracted with, acquire and hold real and personal property for the general interests of the town, and exercise all the powers hereinafter conferred. The city of Manila is exempt from the provisions of this order.

"ART. 3. The municipal government of each town is hereby vested in an alcalde and a municipal council. The alcalde and councilors, together with the municipal lieutenant, shall be chosen at large by the qualified electors of the town, and their term of office shall be for two years from and after the first Monday in January next after their election and until their successors are duly chosen and qualified: Provided, That the alcalde and municipal lieutenant elected in 1900 shall hold office until the first Monday in January, 1902, only; and that the councilors elected in 1900 shall divide themselves, by lot, into two classes; the seats of those of the first class shall be vacated on the first Monday of January, 1901, and those of the second class one year thereafter, so that one-half of the municipal council shall be chosen annually.

"ART. 4. Incorporated towns shall be of four classes, according to the number of inhabitants. Towns of the first class shall be those which contain not less than 25,000 inhabitants and shall have 18 councilors; of the second class, those containing 18,000 and less than 25,000 inhabitants and shall have 14 councilors; of the third class, those containing 10,000 and less than 18,000 inhabitants and shall have 10 councilors; of the fourth class, those containing less than 10,000 inhabitants and shall have 8 councilors. Towns of less than 2,000 inhabitants may incorporate under the provisions of this order, or may, upon petition to the provincial governor, signed by a majority of the qualified electors thereof, be attached as a barrio to an adjacent and incorporated town, if the council of the latter consents.

The qualifications of voters are defined in the second chapter as follows:

"ART. 5. The electors charged with the duty of choosing elective municipal officers must be male persons, 23 years of age or over, who have had a legal residence in the town in which they exercise the suffrage for a period of six months immediately preceding the election, and who are not citizens or subjects of any foreign power, and who are comprised within one of the following three classes: 1. Those who, prior to the 13th of August, 1898, held the office of municipal captain, gobernadorcillo, lieutenant or cabeza de barangay. 2. Those who annually pay 30 pesos or more of the established taxes. 3. Those who speak, read, and write English or Spanish."

Succeeding articles in this chapter prescribe the oath to be taken and subscribed by each elector before his ballot is cast, recognizing and accepting "the supreme authority of the United States of America"; appoint the times and places for holding elections, and set forth the forms to be observed in them. In the third chapter, the qualifications of officers are thus defined:

"ART. 13. An alcalde, municipal lieutenant, or councilor must have the following qualifications: 1. He must be a duly qualified elector of the municipality in which he is a candidate, of 26 years of age or over, and have had a legal residence therein for at least one year prior to the date of election. 2. He must correctly speak, read, and write either the English language or the local dialect.

"ART. 14. In no case can there be elected or appointed to municipal office ecclesiastics, soldiers in active service, persons receiving salary from municipal, provincial or government funds; debtors to said funds, whatever the class of said funds; contractors of public works and their bondsmen; clerks and functionaries of the administration or government while in said capacity; bankrupts until discharged, or insane or feeble-minded persons.

"ART. 15. Each and every person elected or appointed to a municipal office under the provisions of this order shall, before entering upon the duties thereof, take and subscribe before the alcalde or town secretary"—an oath analogous to that required from the electors.

Further articles in this chapter and the next define the duties of the alcalde, the municipal lieutenant, municipal attorney, municipal secretary, municipal treasurer, and the municipal councilors. The fifth chapter relates to taxation and finances; the sixth and seventh contain provisions as follows:

"ART. 53. The governor of the province shall be ex officio president of all municipal councils within the province and shall have general supervisory charge of the municipal affairs of the several towns and cities therein organized under the provisions of this order, and in his said supervisory capacity may inspect or cause to be inspected, at such times as he may determine, the administration of municipal affairs and each and every department thereof, and may hear and determine all appeals against the acts of municipal corporations or their officers. He, or those whom he may designate in writing for that duty, shall at all times have free access to all records, books, papers, moneys, and property of the several towns and cities of the province, and may call upon the officers thereof for an accounting of the receipts and expenditures, or for a general or special report of the official acts of the several municipal councils or of any and every of them, or of any and every of the officers thereof, at any time, and as often as he may consider necessary to inform himself of the state of the finances or of the administration of municipal affairs, and such requests when made must be complied with without excuse, pretext, or delay. He may suspend or remove municipal officers, either individually or collectively, for cause, and appoint substitutes therefor permanently, for the time being or pending the next general election, or may call a special election to fill the vacancy or vacancies caused by such suspension or removal, reporting the cause thereof with a full statement of his action in the premises to the governor of the islands without delay. He shall forward all questions or disputes that may arise over the boundaries or jurisdictional limits of the city, towns, or municipalities to the governor of the islands for final determination, together with full report and recommendations relative to the same. He may, with the approval of the governor of the islands, authorize the cities and towns to form among themselves associations or communities for determined ends, such as the construction of public works, the creation and foundation of beneficent, charitable, or educational institutions, for the better encouragement of public interests or the use of communal property.

"ART. 54. It shall be the duty of commanding officers of military districts, immediately after the publication of this order, to recommend to the office of the military governor in which towns within their commands municipal governments shall be established, and upon approval of recommendations, either personally or through subordinate commanders designated by them, to issue and cause to be posted proclamations calling elections therein. Such proclamations shall fix the time and place of election and shall designate three residents of the town who shall be charged with the duty of administering electors' oaths; of preparing, publishing, and correcting, within specified dates, a list of electors having the qualifications hereinbefore set forth, and of presiding at and making a due return of the election thus appointed. The proclamation shall specify the offices to be filled, and in order to determine the number of councilors the commanders charged with calling the election shall determine, from the best available evidence, the class to which the town belongs, as hereinbefore defined; the classification thus made shall govern until the taking of an official census. The first alcaldes appointed under the provisions of this order shall take and subscribe the oath of office before the commanding officer of the military district or some person in the several towns designated by said commanding officer for the said purpose; whereupon the alcalde so sworn shall administer the said oath of office to all the other officers of the municipio there elected and afterwards appointed. The election returns shall be canvassed by the authority issuing the election proclamation, and the officers elected shall assume their duties on a date to be specified by him in orders.

"ART. 55. Until the appointment of governors of provinces their duties under this order will be performed by the commanding officers of the military districts. They may, by designation, confer on subordinate commanding officers of subdistricts or of other prescribed territorial limits of their commands the supervisory duties herein enumerated, and a subordinate commander so designated shall perform all and every of the duties herein prescribed for the superior commanding officer.

"ART. 56. For the time being the provisions of this order requiring that alcaldes be elected, in all cases shall be so far modified as to permit the commanding officers of military districts, in their discretion, either to appoint such officers or to have them elected as hereinbefore prescribed. The term of office of alcaldes appointed under this authority shall be the same as if they had been elected; at the expiration of such term the office shall be filled by election or appointment.

"ART. 57. The governments of towns organized under General Orders. No. 43, Headquarters Department of the Pacific and Eighth Army Corps, series 1899, will continue in the exercise of their functions as therein defined and set forth until such time as municipal governments therefor have been organized and are in operation under this order."—*United States, 56th Congress, 1st Sess., House Doc. No.* 659.

A. D. 1900 (April).—Appointment of the Second Commission to the Philippines and the President's instructions to it.—Steps to be taken towards the establishment of civil government, and the principles to be observed. —On the 7th of April, 1900, the President of the United States addressed the following communication to the Secretary of War, appointing a Second Commission to the Philippines, "to continue and perfect the work of organizing and establishing civil government" in the Islands, and defining the principles on which that work should proceed : "In the message transmitted to the Congress on the 5th of December, 1899, I said, speaking of the Philippine Islands: 'As long as the insurrection continues the military arm must necessarily be supreme. But there is no reason why steps should not be taken from time to time to inaugurate governments essentially popular in their form as fast as territory is held and controlled by our troops. To this end I am considering the advisability of the return of the commission, or such of the members thereof as can be secured, to aid the existing authorities and facilitate this work throughout the islands.'

"To give effect to the intention thus expressed I have appointed the Hon. William H. Taft of Ohio, Prof. Dean C. Worcester of Michigan, the Hon. Luke I. Wright of Tennessee, the Hon. Henry C. Ide of Vermont, and Prof. Bernard Moses of California, Commissioners to the Philippine Islands to continue and perfect the work of organizing and establishing civil government already commenced by the military authorities, subject in all respects to any laws which Congress may hereafter enact. The Commissioners named will meet and act as a board, and the Hon. William H. Taft is designated as President of the board. It is probable that the transfer of authority from military commanders to civil officers will be gradual and will occupy a considerable period. Its successful accomplishment and the maintenance of peace and order in the meantime will require the most perfect co-operation between the civil and military authorities in the island, and both should be directed during the transition period by the same executive department. The commission will therefore report to the Secretary of War, and all their action will be subject to your approval and control.

"You will instruct the commission to proceed to the City of Manila, where they will make their principal office, and to communicate with the Military Governor of the Philippine Islands, whom you will at the same time direct to render to them every assistance within his power in the performance of their duties. Without hampering them by too specific instructions, they should in general be enjoined, after making themselves familiar with the conditions and needs of the country, to devote their attention in the first instance to the establishment of municipal governments, in which the natives of the islands, both in the cities and in the rural communities, shall be afforded the opportunity to manage their own local affairs to the fullest extent of which they are capable, and subject to the least degree of supervision and control which a careful study of their capacities and observation of the workings of native control show to be consistent with the maintenance of law, order, and loyalty. The next subject in order of importance should be the organization of government in the larger administrative divisions corresponding to counties, departments, or provinces, in which the common interests of many or several municipalities falling within the same tribal lines, or the same natural geographical limits, may best be subserved by a common administration. Whenever the commission is of the opinion that the condition of affairs in the islands is such that the central administration may safely be transferred from military to civil control, they will report that conclusion to you, with their recommendations as to the form of central government to be established for the purpose of taking over the control.

"Beginning with the 1st day of September, 1900, the authority to exercise, subject to my approval, through the Secretary of War, that part of the power of government in the Philippine Islands which is of a legislative nature is to be transferred from the Military Governor of the Islands to this commission, to be thereafter exercised by them in the place and stead of the Military Governor, under such rules and regulations as you shall prescribe, until the establishment of the civil central government for the islands contemplated in the last foregoing paragraph, or until Congress shall otherwise provide. Exercise of this legislative authority will include the making of rules and orders, having the effect of law, for the raising of revenue by taxes, customs duties, and imposts ; the appropriation and expenditure of public funds of the islands ; the establishment of an educational system throughout the islands ; the establishment of a system to secure an efficient civil service ; the organization and establishment of courts ; the organization and establishment of municipal and departmental governments, and all other matters of a civil nature for which the Military Governor is now competent to provide by rules or orders of a legislative character. The commission will also have power during the same period to appoint to office such officers under the judicial, educational, and civil service systems and in the municipal and departmental governments as shall be provided for. Until the complete transfer of control the Military Governor will remain the chief executive head of the Government of the islands, and will exercise the executive authority now possessed by him and not herein expressly assigned to the commission, subject, however, to the rules and orders enacted by the commission in the exercise of the legislative powers conferred upon them. In the meantime the municipal and departmental governments will continue to report to the Military Governor, and be subject to his administrative supervision and control, under your direction, but that supervision and control will be confined within the narrowest limits consistent with the requirement that the powers of government in the municipalities and departments shall be honestly and effectively exercised and that law and order and individual freedom shall be maintained. All legislative rules and orders, establishments of Government, and appointments to office by the commission will take effect immediately, or at such times as it shall designate, subject to your approval and action upon the coming in of the commission's reports, which are to be made from time to time as its action is taken. Wherever civil Governments are constituted under the direction of the commission, such military posts, garrisons, and forces will be continued for the suppression of insurrection and brigandage, and the maintenance of law and order, as the military commander shall deem requisite, and the military forces shall be at all times subject under his orders to the call of the civil authorities for the maintenance of law and order and the enforcement of their authority.

"In the establishment of Municipal Governments the commission will take as the basis of its work the Governments established by the Military Governor under his order of Aug. 8, 1899, and under the report of the board constituted by the Military Governor by his order of Jan. 29, 1900, to formulate and report a plan of Municipal Government, of which his Honor Cayetano Arellano, President of the Audencia, was Chairman, and it will give to the conclusions of that board the weight and consideration which the high character and distinguished abilities of its members justify. In the constitution of Departmental or Provincial Governments it will give especial attention to the existing Government of the Island of Negros, constituted, with the approval of the people of that island, under the order of the Military Governor of July 22, 1899, and after verifying, so far as may be practicable, the reports of the successful working of that Government, they will be guided by the experience thus acquired, so far as it may be applicable to the conditions existing in other portions of the Philippines. It will avail itself, to the fullest degree practicable, of the conclusions reached by the previous commissions to the Philippines. In the distribution of powers among the Governments organized by the commission, the presumption is always to be in favor of the smaller sub-division, so that all the powers which can properly be exercised by the Municipal Government shall be vested in that Government, and all the powers of a more general character which can be exercised by the Departmental Government shall be vested in that Government, and so that in the governmental system, which is the result of the process, the Central Government of the islands, following the example of the distribution of the powers between the States and the National Government of the United States, shall have no direct administration except of matters of purely general concern, and shall have only such supervision and control over local Governments as may be necessary to secure and enforce faithful and efficient administration by local officers.

"The many different degrees of civilization and varieties of custom and capacity among the people of the different islands preclude very definite instruction as to the part which the people shall take in the selection of their own officers ; but these general rules are to be observed : That in all cases the municipal officers, who administer the local affairs of the people, are to be selected by the people, and that wherever officers of more extended jurisdiction are to be selected in any way, natives of the islands are to be preferred, and if they can be found competent and willing to perform the duties, they are to receive the offices in preference to any others. It will be necessary to fill some offices for the present with Americans which after a time may well be filled by natives of the islands. As soon as practicable a system for ascertaining the merit and fitness of candidates for civil office should be put in force. An indispensable qualification for all offices and positions of trust and authority in the islands must be absolute and unconditional loyalty to the United States, and absolute and unhampered authority and power to remove and punish any officer deviating from that standard must at all times be retained in the hands of the central authority of the islands. In all the forms of government and administrative provisions which they are authorized to prescribe, the commission should bear in mind that the government which they are establishing is designed not for our satisfaction, or for the expression of our theoretical views, but for the happiness, peace, and prosperity of the people of the Philippine Islands, and the measures adopted should be made to conform to their customs, their habits, and even their prejudices, to the fullest extent consistent with the accomplishment of the indispensable requisites of just and effective government.

"At the same time the commission should bear in mind, and the people of the islands should be made plainly to understand, that there are certain great principles of government which have been made the basis of our governmental system which we deem essential to the rule of law and the maintenance of individual freedom, and of which they have, unfortunately, been denied the experience possessed by us; that there are also certain practical rules of government which we have found to be essential to the preservation of these great principles of liberty and law, and that these principles and these rules of government must be established and maintained in their islands for the sake of their liberty and happiness, however much they may conflict with the customs or laws of procedure with which they are familiar. It is evident that the most enlightened thought of the Philippine Islands fully appreciates the importance of these principles and rules, and they will inevitably within a short time command universal assent. Upon every division and branch of the government of the Philippines, therefore, must be imposed these inviolable rules: That no person shall be deprived of life, liberty, or property without due process of law; that private property shall not be taken for public use without just compensation; that in all criminal prosecutions the accused shall enjoy the right to a speedy and public trial, to be informed of the nature and cause of the accusation, to be confronted with the witnesses against him, to have compulsory process for obtaining witnesses in his favor, and to have the assistance of counsel for his defense; that excessive bail shall not be required, nor execssive fines imposed, nor cruel and unusual punishment inflicted; that no person shall be put twice in jeopardy for the same offense, or be compelled in any criminal case to be a witness against himself; that the right to be secure against unreasonable searches and seizures shall not be violated; that neither slavery nor involuntary servitude shall exist except as a punishment for crime; that no bill of attainder or ex post facto law shall be passed; that no law shall be passed abridging the freedom of speech or of the press, or the rights of the people to peaceably assemble and petition the Government for a redress of grievances; that no law shall be made respecting an establishment of religion, or prohibiting the free exercise thereof, and that the free exercise and enjoyment of religious profession and worship without discrimination or preference shall forever be allowed.

"It will be the duty of the commission to make a thorough investigation into the titles to the large tracts of land held or claimed by individuals or by religious orders; into the justice of the claims and complaints made against such landholders by the people of the island or any

part of the people, and to seek by wise and peaceable measures a just settlement of the controversies and redress of wrongs which have caused strife and bloodshed in the past. In the performance of this duty the commission is enjoined to see that no injustice is done; to have regard for substantial rights and equity, disregarding technicalities so far as substantial right permits, and to observe the following rules: That the provision of the treaty of Paris pledging the United States to the protection of all rights of property in the islands, and, as well, the principle of our own Government, which prohibits the taking of private property without due process of law, shall not be violated; that the welfare of the people of the islands, which should be a paramount consideration, shall be attained consistently with this rule of property right; that if it becomes necessary for the public interest of the people of the islands to dispose of claims to property which the commission finds to be not lawfully acquired and held, disposition shall be made thereof by due legal procedure, in which there shall be full opportunity for fair and impartial hearing and judgment; that if the same public interests require the extinguishment of property rights lawfully acquired and held, due compensation shall be made out of the public Treasury therefor; that no form of religion and no minister of religion shall be forced upon any community or upon any citizen of the islands; that, upon the other hand, no minister of religion shall be interfered with or molested in following his calling, and that the separation between State and Church shall be real, entire, and absolute.

"It will be the duty of the commission to promote and extend, and, as it finds occasion, to improve, the system of education already inaugurated by the military authorities. In doing this it should regard as of first importance the extension of a system of primary education which shall be free to all, and which shall tend to fit the people for the duties of citizenship and for the ordinary avocations of a civilized community. This instruction should be given in the first instance in every part of the islands in the language of the people. In view of the great number of languages spoken by the different tribes, it is especially important to the prosperity of the islands that a common medium of communication may be established, and it is obviously desirable that this medium should be the English language. Especial attention should be at once given to affording full opportunity to all the people of the islands to acquire the use of the English language. It may be well that the main changes which should be made in the system of taxation and in the body of the laws under which the people are governed, except such changes as have already been made by the military Government, should be relegated to the civil Government which is to be established under the auspices of the commission. It will, however, be the duty of the commission to inquire diligently as to whether there are any further changes which ought not to be delayed, and, if so, it is authorized to make such changes, subject to your approval. In doing so it is to bear in mind that taxes which tend to penalize or to repress industry and enterprise are to be avoided; that provisions for taxation should be simple, so that they may be understood by the people; that they should affect the fewest practicable subjects of taxation which will serve for the general distribution of the burden.

"The main body of the laws which regulate the rights and obligations of the people should be maintained with as little interference as possible. Changes made should be mainly in procedure, and in the criminal laws to secure speedy and impartial trials, and at the same time effective administration and respect for individual rights. In dealing with the uncivilized tribes of the islands the commission should adopt the same course followed by Congress in permitting the tribes of our North American Indians to maintain their tribal organization and government, and under which many of those tribes are now living in peace and contentment, surrounded by a civilization to which they are unable or unwilling to conform. Such tribal governments should, however, be subjected to wise and firm regulation; and, without undue or petty interference, constant and active effort should be exercised to prevent barbarous practices and introduce civilized customs. Upon all officers and employés of the United States, both civil and military, should be impressed a sense of the duty to observe not merely the material but the personal and social rights of the people of the islands, and to treat them with the same courtesy and respect for their personal dignity which the people of the United States are accustomed to require from each other. The articles of capitulation of the City of Manila on the 13th of August, 1898, concluded with these words: 'This city, its inhabitants, its churches and religious worship, its educational establishments, and its private property of all descriptions, are placed under the special safeguard of the faith and honor of the American Army.' I believe that this pledge has been faithfully kept. As high and sacred an obligation rests upon the Government of the United States to give protection for property and life, civil and religious freedom, and wise, firm, and unselfish guidance in the paths of peace and prosperity to all the people of the Philippine Islands. I charge this commission to labor for the full performance of this obligation, which concerns the honor and conscience of their country, in the firm hope that through their labors all the inhabitants of the Philippine Islands may come to look back with gratitude to the day when God gave victory to American arms at Manila and set their land under the sovereignty and the protection of the people of the United States. WILLIAM McKINLEY."

A. D. 1900 (April).—Speech of Senator Hoar against the subjugation and retention of the Islands by the United States. See (in this vol.) UNITED STATES OF AM.: A. D. 1900 (APRIL).

A. D. 1900 (May).—Filipinos killed, captured and surrendered from the breaking out of hostilities with them to May, 1900.—Losses of American army.—In response to a resolution of the United States Senate, May 17, 1900, the following report, by cable, from Manila, was made by General MacArthur: "Filipinos killed, 10,780; wounded, 2,104; captured and surrendered, 10,425; number prisoners in our possession, about 2,000. No systematic record Filipino casualties these headquarters. Foregoing, compiled from large number reports made immediately after engagements, is as close an approximation as now possible, owing to wide distribution of troops. More accurate report would take weeks to prepare. Number reported killed probably in excess of accurate figures; number reported wounded probably much less, as Filipinos managed to remove most wounded from field, and comparatively few fell into our hands. Officers high rank and dangerous suspicious men have been retained as prisoners; most other men discharged on field as soon as disarmed. Propose to release all but very few prisoners at early date."—*56th Congress, 1st Sess., Senate Doc.* 435.—For returns of casualties in the American army during the same period, see (in this vol.) UNITED STATES OF AM.: A. D. 1900 (JUNE).

A. D. 1900 (May—November).—The question in American politics. See (in this vol.) UNITED STATES OF AM.: A. D. 1900 (MAY—NOVEMBER).

A. D. 1900 (July).—**Appeal** of citizens of Manila to the Congress of the United States.—An appeal "to the Congress of the United States," dated at Manila, July 15, 1900, and signed by 2,006 of the inhabitants of the city, who were said by Senator Hoar and Senator Teller to be "the leading people of that section of country—lawyers and bankers and professional men generally" was presented to the Senate on the 10th of January, 1901. It opens as follows: "The undersigned, Filipinos and peaceful inhabitants of this city, in their own name and in the name of the misnamed 'irreconcilables,' respectfully present themselves and submit to the worthy consideration of the Congress of the United States of America the following appeal:

"The people of the Philippine Islands, in view of their calamitous condition, demand in the name of her sons, in the name of all races, in the name of humanity, that an end be put to the misfortunes which afflict them which, while they distress and agonize her, compel her to struggle for the rights that are hers, and for the maintenance whereof she must, if necessary, continue to pour out her blood as she has so constantly and generously done on battlefields, in the woods, on the mountains, in the city, everywhere! The blood which has been shed and that is still being shed, and which will continue to be shed until she has secured her rights, is not shed because of the intrigues of a few who, according to misinformed persons, desire to exploit the people and enrich themselves at the cost of their brother's blood. It has, gentlemen, sprung from the hearts of the people, who alone are the real strength of nations, the sovereign king of races, the producers of the arts, of science, of commerce, of wealth, of agriculture, of civilization, of progress, and of all the productions of human labor and intelligence, in all of which the people of the Philippine Islands had made great progress. The Filipinos were not sunk in lethargy, as some untruthfully assert. They suffered, but the hour to break their chains came to them in August, 1896, and they proclaimed to the world their emancipation."

The paper proceeds to review the circumstances of the revolt against Spanish rule which broke out in 1896, and the later circumstances of the conflict between Filipinos and Americans at such length that it cannot be given in full. Its aim and its spirit may be sufficiently shown by quotation of the following passages from the closing parts of the appeal: "Even supposing that America should force us to submit, and after many years of war the country should submit, as the lesser evil, to the proclamation of an ample autonomy, that autonomy would not produce a sincere bond of friendship between the two people, because, having sacrificed herself for her independence, the country could not look with affection upon those who would be the only obstacle to her happiness. She would always retain her aspirations, so that autonomy would be a short 'interregnum' which the country would necessarily take advantage of to regain new strength to be used in the attainment of her high political ideals, happen what may, and perhaps in some hour of peril strike a fatal blow at a hated oppressor. . . . In giving this warning we do not forget the good Americans whom we sincerely respect; we are mindful of the rupture of our good relations with the United States; we are mindful of the blood which will again run on the soil of our country. We see in that autonomy a new and sorrowful page in the history of the Philippines, and therefore we can not but look upon it with horror. Our people have had enough of suffering. . . . They steadfastly believe that their independence is their only salvation. Should they obtain it, they would be forever grateful to whomsoever shall have helped them in their undertaking; they would consider him as their redeemer, and his name will be engraved with bright letters in the national history, that all the generations to come may read it with sublime veneration. America, consistent with her tradition, is the only one which could play that great rôle in the present and future of the Philippines. If she recognizes their independence, they could offer her a part of the revenues of the Philippine state, according to the treaty which shall be stipulated; the protection in the country of the merchandise of the United States, and a moral and material guarantee for American capital all over the archipelago; finally, whatever may bring greater prosperity to America and progress to the country will, we doubt not, be taken into account in the treaty which shall be celebrated.

"That the independence of the country will be attended with anarchy is asserted only by those who, offending the truth and forgetting their dignity, represent the Filipinos under horrible colors, comparing them to beasts. Their assertions are backed by isolated acts of pillage and robbery. What revolution of the world was free from such deeds? At this epoch passions are unrestrained; vengeance finds opportunity to satisfy itself; private ambitions are often favored by the occasion. Could such criminal deeds be avoided? Pythagoras said: 'If you like to see monsters, travel through a country during a revolution.' . . .

"In order to end our appeal we will say, with the learned lawyer, Senor Mabini: 'To govern is to study the wants and interpret the aspirations of the people, in order to remedy the former and satisfy the latter.' If the natives who know the wants, customs, and aspirations of the people are not fit to govern them, would the Americans, who have had but little to do with the Filipinos, be more capable to govern the latter? We have, therefore, already proven—1. That the revolution was the exclusive work of the public; 2.

That in preparing it they were moved by a great ideal, the ideal of independence; 3. That they are ready to sacrifice their whole existence in order to realize their just aspirations; 4. That in spite of the serious difficulties through which they are passing, they still expect from America that she will consider them with impartiality and justice, and will recognize what by right belongs to them, and thus give them an opportunity to show their boundless gratitude; 5. That the annexation of the Philippines to America is not feasible; 6. That the American sovereignty is not favored by the Philippine people; 7. That an ample autonomy can not be imposed without violating the Filipino will; 8. That the Filipinos are firm for self-government.

"From this it results that the only admissible solution for the present difficulties is the recognition by America of the independence of the Filipinos. In saying this we do not consider either the nullity or the legality of the Paris treaty on our country, but the well-known doctrine of the immortal Washington, and of the sons of the United States of America, worthy champions of oppressed people. Therefore we, in the name of justice and with all the energies of our souls, demand—1. That the independence of the Filipinos be recognized; 2. That all the necessary information regarding the events which are taking place, concerning the peaceful towns and places which are supporting the arms of the revolution, be obtained from Filipinos who, by their antecedents and by their actual conduct, deserve the respect and confidence of the Filipino people."—*Congressional Record, Jan. 10, 1901, p. 850.*

A. D. 1900 (September).—Adoption of civil service rules. See (in this vol.) CIVIL SERVICE REFORM: A. D. 1900.

A. D. 1900 (September—November).—**Civil government of the Islands by the President's Commission.—Legislative measures.—Report of the Commission.**—"In April of this year the second Philippine commission, of which Hon. William H. Taft, of Ohio, Prof. Dean C. Worcester, of Michigan, Hon. Luke I. Wright, of Tennessee, Hon. Henry C. Ide, of Vermont, and Prof. Bernard Moses, of California, were members, sailed for Manila with the powers of civil government prescribed in the instructions of April 7, 1900 [see above]. After devoting several months to familiarizing themselves with the conditions in the islands, this commission on the 1st of September, 1900, entered upon the discharge of the extensive legislative powers and the specific powers of appointment conferred upon them in the instructions, and they have since that time continued to exercise all that part of the military power of the President in the Philippines which is legislative in its character, leaving the military governor still the chief executive of the islands, the action of both being duly reported to this Department for the President's consideration and approval. . . . On consultation with the commission, and with the President's approval, a note of amnesty was issued by the military governor, dated June 21, 1900, and supplemented by a public statement by the military governor, under date of July 2, 1900, based, in the main, upon the instructions to the commission. . . . In pursuance of them something over 5,000 persons, of all grades of the civil and military service of the insurrection, presented themselves and took the following oath: ' I hereby renounce all allegiance to any and all so-called revolutionary governments in the Philippine Islands and recognize and accept the supreme authority of the United States of America therein; and I do solemnly swear that I will bear true faith and allegiance to that government; that I will at all times conduct myself as a faithful and law-abiding citizen of said islands, and will not, either directly or indirectly, hold correspondence with or give intelligence to an enemy of the United States. neither will I aid, abet, harbor, or protect such enemy. That I impose upon myself this voluntary obligation without any mental reservation or purpose of evasion, so help me God.' This number included many of the most prominent officials of the former Tagalog government. . . .

"The commission in its legislative action is following the ordinary course of legislative procedure. Its sessions are open, and its discussion and the proposed measures upon which it is deliberating are public, while it takes testimony and receives suggestions from citizens as if it were a legislative committee. Its first legislative act was the appropriation, on the 12th of September, of $2,000,000 (Mexican), to be used in the construction and repair of highways and bridges in the Philippine Islands. The second act, on the same day, was an appropriation of $5,000 (Mexican) for a survey of a railroad to the mountains of Benguet, in the island of Luzon. The proposed railroad. about 45 miles in length, extending from the Manila and Dagupan road, near the Gulf of Lingayen, to the interior, will open, at a distance of about 170 miles from Manila, a high tableland exceedingly healthy, well wooded with pine and oak, comparatively dry and cool, and where the mercury is said to range at night in the hottest season of the year between 50° and 60° F. The value of such a place for the recuperation of troops and foreign residents will be very great. The third act of the commission was an appropriation for the payment of a superintendent of public instruction. They have secured for that position the services of Frederick W. Atkinson, recently principal of the high school of Springfield, Mass., who was selected by the commission for that purpose before their arrival in Manila.

"Before the 1st of September a board of officers had been engaged upon the revision of the tariff for the islands in the light of such criticisms and suggestions as had been made regarding the old tariff. The commission has considered the report of this board, and after full public hearings of business interests in the island has formulated a tariff law which has been transmitted to the Department. . . . A civil-service board has been constituted by the commission [see, in this vol., CIVIL SERVICE REFORM: A. D. 1900]. They have secured from the United States Civil Service Commission the experienced and capable services of Mr. Frank M. Kiggins, and a civil-service law has been enacted by the commission providing for the application of the merit system to appointments in the island."— *United States, Secretary of War, Annual Report, Nov.* 30, 1900, *pp.* 25–27.

A report by the Commission, dated November 30, was received at Washington late in January, 1901. Of the legislative work on which it entered September 1st. and which, at the time of reporting, it had prosecuted during three months, the

Commission speaks as follows: "It adopted the policy of passing no laws, except in cases of emergency, without publishing them in the daily press after they had passed a second reading, and giving to the public an opportunity to come before the Commission and suggest objections or amendments to the bills. The Commission has likewise adopted as part of its regular procedure the submission of all proposed bills to the Military Governor for his consideration and comment before enactment. We think that the holding of public sessions furnishes instructive lessons to the people, as it certainly secures to the Commission a means of avoiding mistakes. . . . The Commission has now passed forty-seven laws of more or less importance. . . . A municipal code has been prepared and forwarded to you for the consideration of one or two critical matters, and has not yet been adopted, pending your consideration of it. A tariff bill . . . has been prepared. . . . A judicial and civil procedure bill is nearly completed. The same thing is true of a bill for provincial government organization. A new internal tax law must then be considered. The wealth of this country has largely been in agricultural lands, and they have been entirely exempt. This enabled the large landowners to escape any other taxation than the urbana, a tax which was imposed upon the rental value of city buildings only, and the cedula tax, which did not in any case exceed $37.50 (Mexican) a person. We think that a land tax is to be preferred, but of this there will be found more detailed discussion below. . . .

"The only legislation thus far undertaken by the Commission which bears directly on the conduct of municipal affairs in the city of Manila is a law regulating the sale of spirituous, malt, vinous or fermented liquors. It is provided that none of the so-called native 'wines' [said to be concocted by mixing alcohol with oils and flavoring extracts] shall be sold except by holders of native wine licenses, and that such holders shall not be allowed to sell intoxicants of any other sort whatever. . . . The selling of native wines to soldiers of the United States under any circumstances is strictly prohibited, because the soldiers are inclined to indulge in those injurious beverages to excess, with disastrous results. . . . The Filipino ordinarily uses them moderately, if at all. Fortunately, he does not, to any considerable extent, frequent the American saloon. With a view to preventing his being attracted there, the playing of musical instruments or the operation of any gambling device, phonograph, slot machine, billiard or pool table or other form of amusement in saloons, bars or drinking places is prohibited."

The report of the Commission urged strongly the establishing of a purely civil government in the Islands, for reasons thus stated: "The restricted powers of a military government are painfully apparent in respect to mining claims and the organization of railroad, banking and other corporations and the granting of franchises generally. It is necessary that there be some body or officer vested with legislative authority to pass laws which shall afford opportunity to capital to make investment here. This is the true and most lasting method of pacification. Now the only corporations here are of Spanish or English origin with but limited concessions, and American capital finds itself completely obstructed. Such difficulties would all be removed by the passage of the Spooner bill [see below : A. D. 1901 (FEB-RUARY—MARCH)] now pending in both houses. The far reaching effect upon the feeling of the people of changing the military government to one purely civil, with the Army as merely auxiliary to the administration of civil law, cannot be too strongly emphasized. Military methods in administering quasi-civil government, however successful in securing efficiency and substantial justice, are necessarily abrupt and in appearance arbitrary, even when they are those of the Army of the Republic; and until a civil government is established here it will be impossible for the people of the Philippine Islands to realize the full measure of the difference between a government under American sovereignty and one under that of Spain."

Another subject of great importance dealt with in the November report of the Commission was that concerning the employment of native troops and police, on which it was said : "The question as to whether native troops and a native constabulary are at present practicable has received much thought and a careful investigation by the Commission. . . . We have sought and obtained the opinions of a large number of Regular and volunteer officers of all rank, having their fields of operation in all parts of the islands, and there appears to be a general consensus of opinion among them that the time is ripe for these organizations, and this is also our conclusion. Assuming that Congress at its next session will provide for an increase of the Regular Army, it by no means follows that a large part thereof will, or should, be stationed here permanently. Considerations of public policy and economy alike forbid such a programme, nor in our judgment is it necessary.

"While the American soldier is unsurpassed in war, as it is understood among civilized people, he does not make the best policeman, especially among a people whose language and customs are new and strange to him, and in our opinion should not be put to that use when, as we believe, a better substitute is at hand. We therefore earnestly urge the organization of ten regiments of native troops of infantry and cavalry, the proportion between the two arms of the service to be fixed by competent military judges. These troops should in the main be officered by Americans. Certainly this should be the case as to their field officers and company commanders. Lieutenants might be Filipinos, judicially selected, and provision might be made for their promotion in the event of faithful or distinguished service.

"We further recommend that a comprehensive scheme of police organization be put in force as rapidly as possible ; that it be separate and distinct from the army, having for its head an officer of rank and pay commensurate with the importance of the position, with a sufficient number of assistants and subordinates to exercise thorough direction and control. This organization should embrace every township in the islands, and should be so constituted that the police of several contiguous townships could be quickly mobilized. The chief officers of this organization should be Americans, but some of the subordinate officers should be natives, with proper provision for their advancement as a reward for loyal and efficient services. The main

duty of the police would, of course, be to preserve the peace and maintain order in their respective townships, but occasion would, no doubt, frequently arise when it would be necessary to utilize the forces of several townships against large bands of ladrones."

With regard to the organization of municipal government in the townships (pueblos) of the Islands the report of the Commission says, in part : "The 'pueblos' of these islands sometimes include a hundred or more square miles. They are divided into so-called 'barrios' or wards, which are often very numerous and widely separated. In order that the interests of the inhabitants of each ward may be represented in the Council, on the one hand, and that the body may not become so numerous as to be unwieldy, on the other, it is provided that the Councillors shall be few in number (eighteen to eight, according to the number of inhabitants), and shall be elected at large; that where the wards are more numerous than are the Councillors the wards shall be grouped into districts, and that one Councillor shall be in charge of each ward or district, with power to appoint a representative from among the inhabitants of every ward thus assigned to him, so that he may the more readily keep in touch with conditions in that portion of the township which it is his duty to supervise and represent. . . .

"In order to meet the situation presented by the fact that a number of the pueblos have not as yet been organized since the American occupation, while some two hundred and fifty others are organized under a comparatively simple form of government and fifty-five under a much more complicated form on which the new law is based, the course of procedure which must be followed in order to bring these various towns under the provisions of the new law has been prescribed in detail, and every effort has been made to provide against unnecessary friction in carrying out the change.

"In view of the disturbed conditions which still prevail in some parts of the archipelago it has been provided that the military government should be given control of the appointment and arming of the municipal police and that in all provinces where civil provincial government has not been established by the Commission the duties of the Provincial Governor, Provincial Treasurer and Provincial 'Fiscal' (prosecuting attorney) shall be performed by military officers assigned by the Military Governor for these purposes. It has been further provided that in these provinces the Military Governor shall have power through such subordinates as he may designate for the purpose to inspect and investigate at any time all the official books and records of the several municipalities, and to summarily suspend any municipal officer for inefficiency, misconduct or disloyalty to the United States. If upon investigation it shall prove that the suspended officer is guilty, the Military Governor has power to remove him and to appoint his successor, should he deem such a course necessary in the interest of public safety. It is thought that where the necessity still exists for active intervention on the part of the Military Governor it will ordinarily be desirable to allow the towns to retain their existing organization until such time as conditions shall improve ; but, should it prove necessary or desirable in individual instances to put the new law into operation in such provinces, it is felt that the above provisions will give to the Military Governor ample power to deal with any situation which can arise, and he has expressed his satisfaction with them.

"There are at the present time a considerable number of provinces which, in the judgment of the Commission, are ready for a provincial civil government. It is believed that in the majority of cases it will be possible to organize all the municipalities of a province, creating at the same time a civil provincial government. So soon as civil government is established in any province, power to remove officials for inefficiency, misconduct or disloyalty, and, should public safety demand it, to fill the offices thus made vacant, is vested in the civil authorities. The law does not apply to the city of Manila or to the settlements of non-Christian tribes, because it is believed that in both cases special conditions require special legislation. The question as to the best methods of dealing with the non-Christian tribes is one of no little complexity. The number of these tribes is greatly in excess of the number of civilized tribes, although the total number of Mahometans and pagans is much less than the number of Christianized natives. Still, the non-Christian tribes are very far from forming an insignificant element of the population. They differ from each other widely, both in their present social, moral and intellectual state and in the readiness with which they adapt themselves to the demands of modern civilization."

A. D. 1900 (October).—United States military forces in the Islands.—"At the date of my last annual report there were in the Philippine Islands 971 officers and 31,344 enlisted men; and there were en route for service in those islands 546 officers and 16,553 enlisted men—the latter force being principally in California. Since that time an additional force ordered to the Philippine Islands was diverted to the Philippine Islands, making a total of 98,668 men sent to the archipelago. Of this number 15,000 volunteers, first sent to that country in 1898, together with the sick and disabled, have been returned to the United States, leaving at the present time in the islands, according to last report, 2,367 officers and 69,161 enlisted men. Fifteen hundred men have been left in China to act as a guard for the American legation in that country and for other purposes."
—*United States, Annual Report of Lieut.-Gen. Commanding the Army, Oct. 29, 1900.*

A. D. 1900 (November).—The problem of the Spanish Friars.—**Two** contradictory representations of their **work** and **influence.**—Views and recommendations of the United States Commission.—Of the character, work and influence of the Spanish religious orders in the Philippine Islands there are two diametrically opposite accounts given by different writers. Both are represented in two of the quotations below, and those are followed by extracts from a report made by the U. S. Commission, November 30, 1900, on the subject of the problem they present to the new government of the Islands. The first writer is condemnatory. He says:

"The better classes [of the Filipinos] have absorbed much of Spanish civilization in their three-century-old apprenticeship. They show extraordinary talent for music. The church of the mother land of Spain is much in evidence among them. It brought to them its blessings,

but also incidentally a terrible curse. The mendicant orders—the Franciscans, the Dominicans, the Augustinians, no longer poor preachers, thinking only of serving, blessing, loving men, but grown rich, domineering, and, in many cases, sadly corrupt in morals—ate up the land. They added field to field, house to house, till there was but little space left for the people. They charged enormous rents to those who to put bread in their mouths must till their fields. Just such cause for revolt existed as that which in France aroused the storm of the great revolution; the people taxed without mercy, the clergy untaxed, reaping the benefit. Had the Christ-like St. Francis of Assisi been endowed with the gift of prophetic vision to see this gross degeneracy of his followers, more than ever would he have felt the soundness of his intuition which made him set his face like flint against the acquisition of any property by his order. His beloved fair Lady of Poverty would have seemed to him more beautiful than ever. He would have been horrified with the knowledge of the cruel rapacity of monks bearing his name, who, nevertheless, grossly oppressed the Philippine peasantry in rents and taxes,—the very poor whom St. Francis founded his order to serve.

"Perhaps the most deep-seated cause of Filipino insurrection against Spanish authority was this unchecked growth of ignorant, cruel, and oppressive ecclesiasticism. It was this which weighed most heavily upon the people. It made the mere question of gaining a livelihood difficult, but especially did it strangle intellectual and moral growth. It not only oppressed the Filipinos, but it overawed and dominated the Spanish authorities. It was the power of the mendicant orders which drove out the just Condé de Caspe, and later the well-disposed and clement Blanco, which stimulated and supported the frightful atrocities of the cruel Polavieja during the revolution of 1896. Archbishop Nozaleda, a Spanish monk of the Dominican order, was a leader in urging wholesale and often wholly unjustifiable arrests, which were succeeded by the torture and execution of hundreds of persons. It is difficult for a mind reared in the freedom and culture of modern Europe, or still freer America, to realize the horrible excesses and actual mediæval cruelties which were committed in the prisons of Manila and elsewhere in the islands upon Filipino insurgents, or those accused of being in league with them, during the revolution of 1896. The actual story of these things as it is unfolded, not only from Filipino sources, but from the Spanish archives of Manila, is like a scene evoked from the long-buried and forgotten past in the middle ages. Indeed, the only intelligible interpretation of events which cast shame on the name of Spanish authority and Spanish Christianity is found by reflecting that affairs in the Philippines, just previous to the battle of Manila, were controlled by ideas and forces which existed generally in Europe previous to the Reformation,—ideas which slowly retreated before the dawn of the new learning and the liberation of the individual conscience."—H. Welsh, *The Other Man's Country, ch.* 1 (*Phil. : J. B. Lippincott Co.*).

In the other view there is an appeal to results which cannot easily be divested of force. They are set forth in the following :

"The ideals of civilization for the Spanish

missionary priests in the Philippines were substantially the same as those of Bacon and Raleigh, of the founders of New England and the founders of New York. In the mind of all, a civilized people was one which lived under settled laws by steady labor, which was more or less acquainted with the material progress made amongst the races of Europe, and, as all would say, which was Christian. The Spanish friars undertook the task of giving such a civilization to the Malays of the Philippines, and no other body of men of any race or any faith have accomplished what they have done. A task of somewhat similar kind has been attempted by others in our own day in the name of Christian civilization but not the Catholic Church. Hawaii has been under control of missionaries from New England for seventy-five years more completely than the Philippines were ever under that of the Spanish friars. The native kings adopted the new creed and enforced its adoption on their subjects by vigorous corporal punishments. The missionaries were abundantly supplied with such resources of civilization as money could buy, and they have grown wealthy on their mission; but what has been the fate of the natives? They have dwindled in numbers to a fourth of what they were when Messrs. Bingham and Thurston entered their islands, their lands have been taken by strangers, their government overthrown by brute force, and the scanty remnant has dropped the religion imposed on them. In the Philippines in a hundred and forty years a million of Catholic natives has grown seven fold. In Hawaii under missioners of the world's manufacture a hundred and forty thousand of the same race has shrunk to thirty-eight thousand. Have the promises of the Spanish friars or those of the American ministers been the most truthfully kept? The actual condition of the Catholic population formed by the work of the religious orders should not be judged by the excesses which have marked the present revolution. Many old Christian nations have gone through similar experiences. It would be as unreasonable to judge the Christianity of France by the Reign of Terror as to condemn the Filipino population for the atrocities sanctioned by Aguinaldo. The mass of the country population has taken no part in these deeds of blood which are the work of a small number of political adventurers and aspirants for office by any means. Until lately revolutionary disturbance was unknown in the Philippines. During three centuries there was only one serious Indian rebellion, that of Silan, in the province of Illocos, at the time of the English invasion. The Spanish military force was always too small to hold the islands had there been any real disaffection to the Government. The whole force at Manila in the present war, as given by General Otis, was only fifty-six hundred, and about as many more represented the entire Spanish force among a population of seven millions.

"The disposition of the Catholic Filipinos is essentially law abiding. One of the friars lately driven from the islands by the revolution assured the writer that in Panay, an island with a population of half a million, a murder did not occur more often than once or twice in a year. In our own country last year the proportion was more than fifty times as great. There is no forced labor as in the Dutch Indian colonies to compel the native Filipinos to work, yet they support themselves in content without any of the famines so common in India under the boasted rule of civilized England. A sure evidence of material prosperity is the growth of the population, and of its religion a fair test is the proportion of Catholic marriages, baptisms and religious interments to the whole number. The proportion of marriages in 1896 to the population among the natives administered by the friars was one to every hundred and twenty, which is higher than England, Germany, or any European country. The number of baptisms exceeded the deaths by more than two and a half per cent, a greater proportion than in our own land. Compare this with Hawaii and one feels what a farce is the promise of increased prosperity held out by the American Press as the result of the expulsion of the Spanish friars. It is not easy to compare accurately the intellectual development of the Catholic Filipinos with American or European standards. The ideals of civilization of the Catholic missioners were different from those popular with English statesmen and their American admirers. The friars did not believe that the accumulation of wealth was the end of civilization, but the support of a large population in fair comfort. There are no trusts and few millionaires in the islands, but their population is six times greater than that of California after fifty years of American government. The test so often applied of reading and writing among the population finds the Filipinos fairly up to the standard of Europe at least. Of highly educated men the proportion is not so large as in Europe, but it is not inconsiderable, and neither in science nor in literature are the descendants of the Malay pirates unrepresented in their remote islands. The native languages have developed no important literature of their own, but they have a fair supply of translations from Spanish works in history, poetry, and philosophy. In that they are superior to the Hindoo of British India, though spoken by nearly a hundred millions. These are facts that throw a strange light on the real meaning of civilization as planted by the Spanish friars among a barbarian race. Compare them with the fate of the Indian races on our own territory and say what benefit the Filipinos may expect from the advent of 'Anglo-Saxon' civilization." — Bryan J. Clinch (*American Catholic Quarterly Rev., v. 24, p. 15*).

These opposing views are suggestive of the seriousness of the problem which the subject offers to the new authority in the Philippines. The American Commission now studying such problems in those islands has presented its first views concerning the Spanish friars in a lengthy report, written by Judge Taft, and transmitted to Washington as part of the general report of the Commission, bearing date November 30, 1900. The passages quoted below contain what is most essential in the interesting document: "Ordinarily, the Government of the United States and its servants have little or no concern with religious societies or corporations and their members. With us, the Church is so completely separated from the State that it is difficult to imagine cases in which the policy of a Church in the selection of its ministers and the assignment of them to duty can be regarded as of political moment, or as a proper subject of comment in the report of a public officer. In the pacification of the Philippines by our Government, however, it is impossible to ignore the very great part which such a question plays. Excepting the Moros, who are Moslems, and the wild tribes, who are pagans, the Philippine people belong to the Roman Catholic Church. The total number of Catholic souls shown by the Church registry in 1898 was 6,559,998. To care for these in that year there were in the archipelago 746 regular parishes, 105 mission parishes and 116 missions, or 967 in all. Of the regular parishes all save 150 were administered by Spanish monks of the Dominican, Augustinian, or Franciscan orders. Natives were not admitted to these orders. There were two kinds of Augustinians in these islands, the shod and the unshod. The latter are called Recolletos, and are merely an offshoot from the original order of St. Augustine.

"By the revolutions of 1896 and 1898 against Spain, all the Dominicans, Augustinians, Recolletos, and Franciscans acting as parish priests were driven from their parishes to take refuge in Manila. Forty were killed and 403 were imprisoned, and were not all released until by the advance of the American troops it became impossible for the insurgents to retain them. Of the 1,124 who were in the islands in 1896, only 472 remain. The remainder were either killed or died, returned to Spain, or went to China or South America. There were also in the islands engaged in missions and missionary parishes, 42 Jesuits, 16 Capuchins, and six Benedictines, and while many of these left their missions because of disturbed conditions they do not seem to have been assaulted or imprisoned for any length of time. In addition to the members of the monastic orders, there were 150 native secular clergymen in charge of small parishes who were not disturbed. There were also many native priests in the larger parishes who assisted the friar curates and they have remained, and they have been and are acting as parish priests. The burning political question, discussion of which strongly agitates the people of the Philippines, is whether the members of the four great orders of St. Dominic, St. Augustine, St. Francis, and the Recolletos shall return to the parishes from which they were driven by the revolution. Colloquially the term 'friars' includes the members of these four orders. The Jesuits, Capuchins, Benedictines, and the Paulists, of whom there are a few teachers here, have done only mission work or teaching, and have not aroused the hostility existing against the four large orders to which we are now about to refer. . . .

"The truth is that the whole government of Spain in these islands rested on the friars. To use the expression of the Provincial of the Augustinians, the friars were 'the pedestal, or foundation, of the sovereignty of Spain in these islands,' which being removed, 'the whole structure would topple over.' . . . Once settled in a parish, a priest usually continued there until superannuation. He was, therefore, a constant political factor for a generation. The same was true of the Archbishop and the bishops. The civil and military officers of Spain in the island were here for not longer than four years, and more often for a less period. The friars, priests, and bishops, therefore, constituted a solid, powerful, permanent, well organized political force in the islands which dominated policies. The stay of those officers who attempted to pursue a course at variance with that deemed wise by the orders was invariably shortened by monastic influence. Of the four great orders, one, the Franciscans, is not permitted to own property, except convents and schools. This is not true of the other three. They own some valuable business property in Manila, and have large amounts of money to lend. But the chief property of these orders is in agricultural land. The total amount owned by the three orders in the Philippines is approximately 403,000 acres. Of this 121,000 acres is in the Province of Cavité alone. The whole is distributed as follows: Cavité, Province of Luzon, 121,747 acres ; Laguna, Province of Luzon, 62,172 acres ; Manila, Province of Luzon, 50,145 ; Bulacan, Province of Luzon, 39,341 ; Morong, Province of Luzon, 4,940 ; Bataan, Province of Luzon, 1,000 ; Cagayan, Province of Luzon, 49,-400, Island of Cebu, 16,413 ; Island of Mindoro, 58,455. Total, 403,713. . . .

"It cannot admit of contradiction that the autocratic power which each friar curate exercised over the people and civil officials of his parish gave them a most plausible ground for belief that nothing of injustice, of cruelty, of oppression, of narrowing restraint of liberty, was imposed on them for which the friar was not entirely responsible. His sacerdotal functions were not in their eyes the important ones, except as they enabled him to clinch and make more complete his civil and political control. The revolutions against Spain's sovereignty began as movements against the friars. . . . Having in view these circumstances, the statement of the bishops and friars that the mass of the people in these islands, except only a few of the leading men of each town and the native clergy, are friendly to them cannot be accepted as accurate. All the evidence derived from every source but the friars themselves shows clearly that the feeling of hatred for the friars is well nigh universal and permeates all classes. In the provinces of Cavité, Laguna, and Bulacan, as well as in the country districts of Manila, the political feeling against the friars has in it also an element of agrarianism. For generations the friars have been lords of these immense manors, upon which, since 1880, they have paid no taxes, while every 'hombre' living on them paid his cedula, worked out a road tax, and, if he were in business of any kind, paid his industrial impost. . . .

"In the light of these considerations it is not wonderful that the people should regard the return of the friars to their parishes as a return to the conditions existing before the revolution. The common people are utterly unable to appreciate that under the sovereignty of the United States the position of the friar as curate would be different from that under Spain. This is not a religious question, though it concerns the selection of religious ministers for religious communities. The Philippine people love the Catholic Church. . . . The depth of their feeling against the friars may be measured by the fact that it exists against those who until two years ago administered the sacraments of the Church upon which they feel so great dependence and for which they have so profound a respect. The feeling against the friars is solely political. The people would gladly receive as ministers of the Roman Catholic religion any save those who are to them the embodiment of all in the Spanish rule that was hateful. If the friars return to their parishes, though only under the same police protection which the American Government is bound to extend to any other Spanish subjects in these islands, the people will regard it as the act of that Government. They have so long been used to have every phase of their conduct regulated by governmental order that the coming again of the friars will be accepted as an executive order to them to receive the friars as curates with their old, all-absorbing functions. It is likely to have the same effect on them that the return of General Weyler under an American Commission as Governor of Cuba would have had on the people of that island.

"Those who are charged with the duty of pacifying these islands may therefore properly have the liveliest concern in a matter which, though on its surface only ecclesiastical, is, in the most important phase of it, political, and fraught with the most critical consequences to the peace and good order of the country, in which it is their duty to set up civil government. . . . It is suggested that the friars, if they returned, would uphold American sovereignty and be efficient instruments in securing peace and good order, whereas the native priests who now fill the parishes are, many of them, active insurgent agents or in strong sympathy with the cause. It is probably true that a considerable number of the Filipino priests are hostile to American sovereignty, largely because they fear that the Catholic Church will deem it necessary, on the restoration of complete peace, to bring back the friars or to elevate the moral tone of the priesthood by introducing priests from America or elsewhere. But it is certain that the enmity among the people against the American Government caused by the return of the friars would far outweigh the advantage of efforts to secure and preserve the allegiance of the people to American Sovereignty which might be made by priests who are still subjects of a monarchy with which the American Government has been lately at war, and who have not the slightest sympathy with the political principles of civil liberty which the American Government represents.

"We have set forth the facts upon this important issue because we do not think they ought to be or can be ignored. We earnestly hope that those who control the policy of the Catholic Church in these islands with the same sagacity and prevision which characterize all its important policies, will see that it would be most unfortunate for the Philippine Islands, for the Catholic Church and for the American Government to attempt to send back the friars, and that some other solution of the difficulties should be found. . . . The friars have large property interests in these islands which the United States Government is bound by treaty obligations and by the law of its being to protect. It is natural and proper that the friars should feel a desire to remain where so much of their treasure is. . . . It would avoid some very troublesome agrarian disturbances between the friars and their quondam tenants if the Insular Government could buy these large haciendas of the friars, and sell them out in small holdings to the present tenants, who, forgiven for the rent due during the two years of war, would recognize the title of

the Government without demur, and gladly accept an opportunity, by payment of the price in small instalments, to become absolute owners of that which they and their ancestors have so long cultivated. With the many other calls upon the insular treasury a large financial operation like this could probably not be conducted to a successful issue without the aid of the United States Government, either by a direct loan or by a guaranty of bonds to be issued for the purpose. The bonds or loans could be met gradually from the revenues of the islands, while the proceeds of the land, which would sell readily, could be used to constitute a school fund. This object, if declared, would make the plan most popular, because the desire for education by the Filipinos of all tribes is very strong, and gives encouraging promise of the future mental development of a now uneducated and ignorant people. The provincials of the orders were understood in their evidence to intimate a willingness on the part of the orders to sell their agricultural holdings if a satisfactory price should be paid. What such a price would be we are unable without further investigation to state. If an agreement could not be reached it is probable, though upon this we express no definite opinion, that there would be ground in the circumstances for a resort to condemnation proceedings."

A. D. 1901.—Act of the United States Congress increasing army and authorizing the enlistment of native troops.— Rejection of the proviso of Senator Hoar. See (in this vol.) UNITED STATES OF AM. : A. D. 1901 (FEBRUARY).

A. D. 1901 (February—March).—Congressioual grant of military, civil and judicial powers for the government of the Islands to persons whom the President may appoint.— The so-called "Spooner Amendment."—During the first session of the 56th Congress the following bill was introduced in the U. S. Senate by Mr. Spooner, of Wisconsin, but received no action : "Be it enacted, etc., That when all insurrection against the sovereignty and authority of the United States in the Philippine Islands, acquired from Spain by the treaty concluded at Paris on the 10th day of December, 1898, shall have been completely suppressed by the military and naval forces of the United States, all military, civil, and judicial powers necessary to govern the said islands shall, until otherwise provided by Congress, be vested in such person and persons, and shall be exercised in such manner as the President of the United States shall direct for maintaining and protecting the inhabitants of said islands in the free enjoyment of their liberty, property, and religion."

Half the following session of Congress passed before any disposition to take the action proposed by Senator Spooner was shown. Then the matter was brought to notice and pressed by the following communication to the Secretary of War, from the Commission in the Philippines : "If you approve, ask transmission to proper Senators and Representatives of following : Passage of Spooner bill at present session greatly needed to secure best result from improving conditions. Until its passage no purely central civil government can be established, no public franchises of any kind granted, and no substantial investment of private capital in internal improvements possible." This was repeated soon afterwards more urgently by cable in the message following : "Sale of public lands and allowance of mining claims impossible until Spooner bill. Hundreds of American miners on ground awaiting law to perfect claims. More coming. Good element in pacification. Urgently recommend amendment Spooner bill so that its operation be not postponed until complete suppression of all insurrection, but only until in President's judgment civil government may be safely established."

The request of the Philippine Commission, endorsed by the Secretary of War, was communicated to Congress by the President, who said in doing so : " I earnestly recommend legislation under which the government of the islands may have authority to assist in their peaceful industrial development." Thereupon the subject was taken up in Congress, not as formulated in Senator Spooner's bill of the previous session, but in the form of an amendment to the Army Appropriation Bill, then pending in the Senate. The amendment, as submitted to discussion in the Senate on the 25th of February, 1901, was in the following terms :

" All military, civil, and judicial powers necessary to govern the Philippine Islands, acquired from Spain by the treaties concluded at Paris on the 10th day of December, 1898, and at Washington on the 7th day of November, 1900, shall, until otherwise provided by Congress, be vested in such person and persons and shall be exercised in such manner as the President of the United States shall direct, for the establishment of civil government and for maintaining and protecting the inhabitants of said islands in the free enjoyment of their liberty, property, and religion : Provided, That all franchises granted under the authority hereof shall contain a reservation of the right to alter, amend, or repeal the same. Until a permanent government shall have been established in said archipelago full reports shall be made to Congress, on or before the first day of each regular session, of all legislative acts and proceedings of the temporary government instituted under the provisions hereof, and full reports of the acts and doings of said government and as to the condition of the archipelago and its people shall be made to the President, including all information which may be useful to the Congress in providing for a more permanent government."

Strenuous opposition was made, firstly to the hasty grafting of so profoundly important a measure of legislation on an appropriation bill, and secondly to the measure itself, as being a delegation of powers to the President which did violence to the Constitution and to all the precedents and principles of the American government, and also as having objects which would not only do flagrant wrong to the people of the Philippine Islands, but bring dishonor on those of the United States. The military authority already exercised by the President in the Philippines sufficed fully, it was contended, for every purpose of temporary or provisional government there, except in its lack of ability to grant franchises and to dispose of the public lands. Hence it was freely charged that the controlling influences which pressed this measure on the government came from capitalists and speculators who were reaching after valuable franchises, mining rights and land grants in the archipelago. Said

Senator Daniel in the debate : " So far as any legislation which looks forward to the opening of the way to civil government may be involved to the softening of the conditions which exist, to the amelioration of the distresses which are upon the Philippine people, I would give most cheerful acquiescence. But because we desire to do these things in a good spirit, in a resolute and patriotic spirit, let us not permit the provocation of difficult conditions to lead us into enacting any kind of provision of law that is not necessary to these ends. Let us not undertake to give to the President of the United States any power of disposing of the permanent assets of the Philippine people ; let us not put him in the attitude of being a franchise giver or a franchise seller or a franchise lessor. The franchises of those islands—their rivers, their ferries, their streets, their roads, the thousand and one privileges which are granted by public authority—are as important and as valuable to that people and as permanently associated with their happiness and their prosperity as are their fields or their mines or their fisheries or anything else which belongs to their country. . . . It is true there is the reservation of the right to alter, amend, or repeal, but while that is legally broad enough for any remedial legislation whatsoever to follow, we know that practically it is of very small consequence. If capital goes in and invests itself in improvements which are in themselves of a permanent nature, if railroads are constructed, telegraph lines run, telephones established, ferries built, steamers and boats, gas establishments, electrical establishments—if those things are disposed of, the man who once gets in will never be gotten out. In all such affairs possession is nine points of the law before they get into court, where it is generally made the tenth."

Senator Hoar called attention "to the fact that the report of the Taft commission urges that power be given to sell the public lands at once, as it is necessary for their development, and a large amount of capital is there now clamoring to be invested," and he remarked : "So I suppose that one of the chief purposes of this is that the public lands in the Philippine Islands may be sold before the people of the islands have any chance whatever to have a voice in their sale." He then quoted the following passages from the report of the Taft commission : " The commission has received a sufficient number of applications for the purchase of public land to know that large amounts of American capital are only awaiting the opportunity to invest in the rich agricultural field which may here be developed. In view of the decision that the military government has no power to part with the public land belonging to the United States, and that the power rests alone in Congress. it becomes very essential, to assist the development of these islands and their prosperity, that Congressional authority be vested in the government of the islands to adopt a proper public-land system, and to sell the land upon proper terms. There should, of course, be restrictions preventing the acquisition of too large quantities by any individual or corporation, but those restrictions should only be imposed after giving due weight to the circumstances that capital can not be secured for the development of the islands unless the investment may be sufficiently great to justify the expenditure of large amounts for expensive machinery and equipments. Especially is this true in the cultivation of sugar land. . . . Restricted powers of a military government referred to in discussing the public lands are also painfully apparent in respect to mining claims and the organization of railroad, banking, and other corporations, and the granting of franchises generally. It is necessary that there be some body or officer vested with legislative authority to pass laws which shall afford opportunity to capital to make investment here. This is the true and most lasting method of pacification." "In other words," said Senator Hoar, "the leading, principal, bald proposal on which this amendment rests is that before those 10,000,000 people are allowed any share in their own government whatever their property is to be sold by Americans to Americans in large quantities, as on the whole the best means of pacification — that the best way to pacify a man is to have one foreign authority to sell his property and another to buy it."

An amendment to the amendment, offered by Senator Bacon, reserving to Congress the right to annul any grant or concession made, or any law enacted, by any governmental authority created under the powers proposed to be conferred on the President; another offered, by Senator Vest, providing that "no judgment, order, nor act by any of said officials so appointed shall conflict with the Constitution and laws of the United States," and still others of somewhat kindred aims, were voted down; but the influence of Senator Hoar prevailed with the Senate so far as to induce its acceptance of the following important modification of the so-called "Spooner Amendment":

"Provided, That no sale or lease or other disposition of the public land, or the timber thereon, or the mining rights therein, shall be made: And provided further, That no franchise shall be granted which is not approved by the President of the United States, and is not, in his judgment, clearly necessary for the immediate government of the islands and indispensable for the interests of the people thereof, and which can not, without great public mischief, be postponed until the establishment of a permanent civil government, and all such franchises shall terminate one year after the establishment of such civil government."

With this proviso added, the "Spooner amendment" was adopted by the Senate on the 26th of February (yeas 45, nays 27, not voting 16), and agreed to by the House on the 1st of March (yeas 161, nays 136, not voting 56).—*Congressional Record, Feb. 25—March 1*, 1901.

A. D. 1901 (March).—Organization of provincial governments.—Establishment of a department of public education.—Proposed tariff.—Date fixed for cessation of military régime.—On the 3d of March, the President of the Philippine Commission, Judge Taft, addressed a cable despatch to the U. S. Secretary of War in which he reported: "Commission has last three weeks organized five provincial governments—Pampanga, Pangasinan, Tarlac, Bulacan, Bataan—last two are Tagalog provinces. Attended each provincial capital in a body; met by appointment Presidentes, Councillors, and principal men of towns; explained provisions general provincial act and special bill for particular province and invited discussion natives present of both

6-26

bills. Conventions thus held very satisfactory; amendments suggested, considered, special bills enacted, appointments followed. . . . In three large provinces natives appointed provisional Governors. In Bataan, on petition, eight out of nine towns, volunteer officer appointed. In Tarlac feeling between loyal factions required appointment American. . . . In compliance with urgent native invitations leave March 11 for south to organize provinces Tayabas, Romblon, Iloilo, Capiz, Zamboanga, such others are ready. Returning shall organize Zambales, Union, Cagayan, Ilocos Norte. Military Governor has recommended organization Batangas, Cavité, Laguna, Nueva Ecija, but shall delay action as to these until return from northern and southern trips."

On the 18th of March it was announced from Washington that a number of recent Acts of the Philippine Commission had been received at the War Department, among them one which establishes a general department of public instruction, with a central office at Manila, under the direction of a general superintendent, to be appointed by the commission, at a salary of $6,000 a year. "Schools are to be established in every pueblo in the archipelago where practicable, and those already established shall be reorganized where necessary. There are to be ten school divisions in the archipelago, each with a division superintendent, and there is to be a superior advisory board, composed of the general superintendent and four members to be appointed by the Philippine Commission, to consider the general subject of education in the islands and make regulations. The English language, as soon as practicable, shall be made the basis of all public instruction, and soldiers may be detailed as instructors until replaced by trained teachers. Authority is given to the general superintendent to obtain from the United States 1,000 trained teachers, at salaries of not less than $75 nor more than $100 a month, the exact salary to be fixed according to the efficiency of the teacher. The act provides that no teacher or other person "shall teach or criticise the doctrines of any church, religious sect or denomination or shall attempt to influence the pupils for or against any church or religious sect in any public school." Violation of this section is made punishable by summary dismissal from the public service. It is provided, however, that it may be lawful for the priest or minister of the pueblo where the school is situated to teach religion for half an hour three times a week in the school building to pupils whose parents desire it. But if any priest, minister or religious teacher use this opportunity "for the purpose of arousing disloyalty to the United States or of discouraging the attendance of pupils or interfering with the discipline of schools," the division superintendent may forbid such offending priest from entering the school building thereafter. The act also provides for a normal school at Manila for the education of natives in the science of teaching. It appropriates $400,000 for school buildings, $220,000 for text books and other supplies for the current calendar year, $25,000 for the normal school, $15,000 for the organization and maintenance of a trade school in Manila and the same amount for a school of agriculture.

The new tariff for the Islands, which the Commission had been long engaged in framing, was submitted, in March, to the government at Washlugton for approval. "In his letter of transmittal Judge Taft says that the proposed bill follows largely the classification of the Cuban tariff, 'but has been considerably expanded by the introduction of articles requiring special treatment here by reason of different surroundings and greater distance from the markets.' Judge Taft says also that the disposition of the business interests of the islands is to accept any tariff the commission proposes, provided only that the duties are specific and not ad valorem. The question of revenue was kept steadily in view in the preparation of the schedules, but it was not the only consideration. Raw materials of Philippine industries, tools, implements and machinery of production, materials of transportation, the producers and transmitters of power and food products are taxed as lightly as possible. . . . Export duties are levied on only six articles—hemp, indigo, rice, sugar, cocoanuts, fresh or as copra, and tobacco. The free list admits natural mineral waters, trees, shoots and plants, gold, copper and silver ores, fresh fruits, garden produce, eggs, milk, ice and fresh meat, except poultry and game. There is also a list of articles conditionally free of duty. The importation of explosives is prohibited, but that of firearms is not."

It is announced from Washington that "Judge Taft and General MacArthur have agreed upon July 1 as the date for the establishment of civil government in the Philippines. The military régime in the islands will therefore cease on June 30, when General Chaffee will relieve General MacArthur of the command, and Governor Taft will be inaugurated the next day with considerable ceremony."

A. D. 1901 (March—April).—Capture of Aguinaldo.—His oath of allegiance to the United States.—His address to his countrymen, counselling peace.—A stratagem, executed with great daring by General Funston of the American forces, accomplished the capture of the Filipino leader, Aguinaldo, on the 23d of March. From intercepted correspondence, it had been learned that Aguinaldo, then occupying his headquarters at Palanan, Isabela Province, was expecting to be joined by some riflemen, whom his brother had been ordered to send to him from central Luzon. On this, General Funston conceived the plan of equipping a number of native troops who should pass themselves off as the expected reinforcements, several American officers going with them ostensibly as prisoners, the hope being that Aguinaldo might thus be reached and taken by surprise. Gen. MacArthur approved the scheme, and it was carried out with success. The party was made up of 78 Macabebe scouts, four Tagalogs who had formerly been officers in the insurgent army, and General Funston, Captain Newton, Lieutenants Hazzard and Mitchel, who acted the part of prisoners. They were taken by gunboat from Cavite to a point above Baler, whence they made their way on foot, sending a message in advance that the expected reinforcements were on the way and had captured some prisoners en route. The following brief narrative of what occurred subsequently is taken from a newspaper account of the expedition:

"For six days the expedition marched over an exceedingly difficult country, covering 90 miles.

When the men reached a point eight miles from Aguinaldo's camp they were almost exhausted from lack of food and the fatigue of the march. They stopped at this place and sent a message to Aguinaldo, requesting him to send food to them. The ruse thus far had worked with the greatest success, and on March 22d, when Aguinaldo sent provisions, it was seen that he did not have the slightest suspicion. With the food he sent word that the Americans were not wanted in his camp, but instructing their supposed captors to treat them kindly. On March 23d the march was resumed, the Macabebe officers starting an hour ahead of the main body of the expedition. The 'prisoners,' under guard, followed them. When the party arrived at Aguinaldo's camp a bodyguard of 50 riflemen was paraded, and the officers were received at Aguinaldo's house, which was situated on the Palanan River. After some conversation with him, in which they gave the alleged details of their suppositious engagement with an American force, they made excuses and quietly left the house. They at once gave orders in an undertone for the Macabebes to get in position and fire on the bodyguard. The order was obeyed with the greatest rapidity, and three volleys were delivered. The insurgents were panic-stricken by the sudden turn in affairs, and they broke and ran in consternation. Two of them, however, were killed and eighteen wounded. Simultaneously with the delivery of the volleys the American officers rushed into Aguinaldo's house. Maj. Alhambra, one of Aguinaldo's staff, had been shot in the face. He, however, was determined not to be captured and he jumped from a window into the river and disappeared. Two captains and four lieutenants made their escape in a similar manner. Aguinaldo, Col. Villa, his chief of staff, and Santiago Barcelona, the insurgent treasurer, did not have time to make an attempt to get away before Gen. Funston and the others were upon them, demanding their surrender. Seeing that the situation was hopeless, they gave themselves up. Aguinaldo was furious at having been caught, but later he became philosophical and declared that the ruse by which he had been captured was the only one which would have proved successful if the Americans had tried for 20 years. One of the Macabebes was wounded. The party stayed two days at the camp and then marched overland to the coast, where the Vicksburg, whose arrival was excellently timed, picked them up and brought them back to Manila."

On the 2d of April, a despatch from General MacArthur to the War Department announced that Aguinaldo, on the advice of Chief Justice Arellano, had taken the following oath of allegiance to the United States : "I hereby renounce all allegiance to any and all so-called revolutionary governments in the Philippine Islands, and recognize and accept the supreme authority of the United States of America therein ; I do solemnly swear that I will bear true faith and allegiance to that government ; that I will at all times conduct myself as a faithful and law abiding citizen of the said islands, and will not, either directly or indirectly, hold correspondence with or give intelligence to an enemy of the United States, nor will I abet, harbor or protect such enemy ; that I impose upon myself these voluntary obligations without any mental reservations or purpose of evasion, so help me God."

On the 19th of April, Aguinaldo issued the following address to his countrymen : "I believe I am not in error in presuming that the unhappy fate to which my adverse fortune has led me is not a surprise to those who have been familiar with the progress of the war. The lessons taught with a full meaning, and which have recently come to my knowledge, suggest with irresistible force that a complete termination of hostilities and lasting peace are not only desirable, but absolutely essential to the welfare of the Philippine Islands. The Filipinos have never been dismayed at their weakness, nor have they faltered in following the path pointed out by their fortitude and courage. The time has come, however, in which they find their advance along this path to be impeded by an irresistible force, which, while it restrains them, yet enlightens their minds and opens to them another course, presenting them the cause of peace. This cause has been joyfully embraced by the majority of my fellow countrymen who already have united around the glorious sovereign banner of the United States.

In this banner they repose their trust and believe that under its protection the Filipino people will attain all those promised liberties which they are beginning to enjoy. The country has declared unmistakably in favor of peace. So be it. There has been enough blood, enough tears and enough desolation. This wish cannot be ignored by the men still in arms, if they are animated by a desire to serve our noble people, which has thus clearly manifested its will. So do I respect this will, now that it is known to me. After mature deliberation, I resolutely proclaim to the world that I cannot refuse to heed the voice of a people longing for peace, nor the lamentations of thousands of families yearning to see their dear ones enjoying the liberty and the promised generosity of the great American Nation. By acknowledging and accepting the sovereignty of the United States throughout the Philippine Archipelago, as I now do, and without any reservation whatsoever, I believe that I am serving thee, my beloved country. May happiness be thine."

PHŒNICIANS, The: Modified estimates of their influence upon early European civilization. See (in this vol.) ARCHÆOLOGICAL RESEARCH: CRETE.

PILLAGER INDIAN OUTBREAK. See (in this vol.) INDIANS, AMERICAN: A. D. 1898.

PLAGUE, The Bubonic.—For years the plague has "continued to breed in various inner parts of Asia, and in 1894, coming from the Chinese province of Yunnan, it invaded Canton, taking there 60,000 victims in a few weeks. Thence it spread to Hong Kong, reached next year the island of Haïnan and Macao, invaded Formosa in 1896, and in the autumn of the same y appeared at Bombay. In the big city of India it found all necessary conditions for breeding, unchecked, for several months in succession: famine, overcrowding, and the absence of all preventive measures; and from Bombay it was carried by rail and road, to different parts of India. . . . Happily enough, the plague is no longer the mysterious, revengeful being which it used to be for our ancestors. Its cause and modes of propagation are well known. It is an infectious disease with a short period of incubation. From four to six days after infection takes place, a sudden loss of forces—often a full prostration, accompanied by a high fever—sets in. A bubo appears, and soon grows to the size of an egg. Death soon follows. If not—there is a chance of slow and painful recovery; but that chance is very small, because even under the best conditions of nursing, the mortality is seldom less than four out of each five cases of illness. As to the means of propagation of the plague, they are many. The poison may infect a wound or a scratch; it may be ingested in food; it may be simply inhaled. Dust from an infected house was sufficient to infect healthy rats; and when healthy rats were shut up in one cage with unhealthy ones, all caught the disease and died. Already in 1881 Netten Redcliffe and Dr. Pichon indicated that before the plague attacks men it destroys mice and rats. This was fully confirmed in 1894 by the Japanese and French bacteriologists Kitasato and Yersin, at Hong Kong, and by Dr. Rennie, of the Chinese Customs, at Canton. Masses of dead rats were seen in the streets of the infested parts of Hong Kong, and the

keeper of the west gates of Canton collected and buried 24,000 of these animals. Dr. Rennie also pointed out that among those inhabitants of Canton who lived in boats on the river there were no cases of plague, except a few imported from town, so that even rich Cantonese took to living in boats; and he explained the immunity of the boat-dwellers by the absence of infection through rats. The worst is, however, that swine, and even goats and buffaloes, snakes and jackals, are attacked by the plague. . . .

"As soon as the plague broke out at Hong Kong, the great Japanese bacteriologist Kitasato and the French doctor Yersin, who is well known for his work with Roux on the serum treatment of diphtheria, were already on the spot. Yersin obtained from the English authorities permission to erect a small straw hut in the yard of the chief hospital, and there he began his researches. Both Kitasato and Yersin had no difficulty in ascertaining that the plague buboes teemed with special bacteria, which had the shape of tiny microscopic sticklets, thickened at their ends. To isolate these bacteria, to cultivate them in artificial media, and to ascertain the deadly effects of these cultures upon animals, was soon done by such masters in bacteriology as Kitasato and Yersin. The cause of the plague was thus discovered. It was evident that infected rats and swine—especially swine with the Chinese, who keep them in their houses—were spreading the disease, in addition to men themselves. The same bacteria teemed in the dead animals. As to men, the discharges from their buboes, and even, in many cases, their expectorations, were full of plague bacteria. Besides, Yersin soon noticed that in his 'laboratory,' where he was dissecting animals killed by the plague, the flies died in numbers. He found that they were infested with the same bacteria, and carried them about: inoculations of bacteria obtained from the flies at once provoked the plague in guinea-pigs. Ants, gnats, and other insects may evidently spread infection in the same way, while in and round the infested houses the soil is impregnated with the same bacteria. As soon as the pest microbe became known, experiments were begun, at the Paris Institut Pasteur, for finding the means to combat it; and in July 1895 Yersin, Calmette, and Borel could already announce that some very promising results had been obtained."—P. Kropotkin, *Recent Science* (*Nineteenth Century, July,* 1897).

Of the first appearance of the plague in India, at Bombay, and the early stages of its spread in that country, the Viceroy, Lord Elgin, made the following report to the Secretary of State for India, on the 27th of January, 1897: "The first official intimation of the outbreak which reached us was in a telegram from the Government of Bombay, dated the 29th September 1896. The disease was then reported to be of a mild type, and at first it showed no tendency to increase. . . . Throughout the months of October and November the disease made little or no progress, and the number of deaths reported a day averaged nine. Early in December there was a marked increase, and the number of deaths reported daily from the 2nd to the 23rd (inclusive) was about 32. From the 24th December onwards there was another marked increase, and the number of deaths reported from that date to the 14th January (inclusive) averaged about 51. The next week shows a further increase, the reported number of deaths averaging 74 a day. The total number of deaths reported during October was 276; during November, 268; during December, 1,160; and from the 1st to the 25th January, 1,444. The total number of deaths reported from the beginning of the outbreak thus amounts to 3,148. We have reason to fear that all deaths from the plague have not been reported as such, and that the true mortality from the disease is higher than is shown by the above figures. . . . For a considerable time, except for a few imported cases in some towns in Gujarat, the outbreak was confined to Bombay itself, but on the 23rd of December we learnt from the Government of Bombay that the plague had broken out in Karachi. . . . The total number of deaths that have been reported in Karachi, from the beginning of the outbreak up to the 24th January, is 608. It will be observed that the disease has been very malignant in Karachi, and that almost all the cases reported have been fatal. As soon as the Surgeon General with the Government of Bombay reported to that Government that he had seen cases of a mild type of bubonic plague in the city, preventive measures were adopted and a Committee of medical experts were appointed to report on the disease and the situation. The Municipal Corporation have from the outset required the infected quarters to undergo a thorough and systematic cleaning and disinfection; and they have also pushed on vigorously other sanitary measures, such as the improvement of house connections and the construction of surface drains in quarters where the drainage was defective. A house-to-house visitation by medical officers has also been instituted. The Corporation have sanctioned liberal measures towards these ends, and the executive officers have displayed great energy in carrying them out. . . . We have informed the Government of Bombay that we consider it necessary that the plan of removing all persons from infected houses, and thoroughly cleansing and disinfecting the buildings, should be carried out, and we have asked His Excellency in Council, if he agrees, to report the measures that are adopted to bring the plan into general effect."

To the above suggestion that all persons be removed from infected houses, the government of Bombay replied, on the 12th of February: "His Excellency is advised that, to give full effect to such a proposal, at the lowest computation, 30,000 persons belonging to different races, castes, and creeds would need to be provided with temporary dwellings. There is no site within the limits of the Bombay municipality which would accommodate a tenth of this number. Great difficulty has attended all attempts at the segregation of healthy inmates of infected houses hitherto made, and very limited success has been achieved. From the beginning of the outbreak of this disease it has been found that the native inhabitants of the city are very reluctant to leave their houses or to allow any member of their family afflicted with the disease to be taken away. Indeed, their dread of the disease itself appears to be hardly so powerful as their horror of being removed from their houses. Ignorance and superstition prevent them from discerning either that removal to a hospital is good for the sick or removal [from] infected dwellings good for the healthy, and they are far more easily moved by fear of the municipal and police authorities than by any realisation of the benefits that will accrue from a sensible course of action. It is estimated that not less than 300,000 persons have already fled from Bombay, moved so to do, not only by fear of the plague, but quite as much, if not more, by an unfounded and unreasonable fear of what might happen to them at the hands of the police and municipal authorities were they to remain."

Contending with such obstacles to the use of the most effective measures for checking the spread of the disease, the authorities at Bombay and elsewhere, who seem to have worked with energy, saw little to encourage their efforts for some time. In a second report to the Secretary of State for India, made February 10, Lord Elgin was compelled to write: "We much regret that we are unable to report that the plague shows any signs of abating. In both Bombay and Karachi there has been an increase in the daily number of seizures and deaths since the beginning of the current month." But, a month later, on the 10th of March, the Viceroy reported that "the position of affairs in Bombay is distinctly better. There has been a decrease in the reported number of plague seizures and deaths, and the total daily mortality from all causes shows a marked diminution. During the week ending the 22nd February, the average daily number of seizures and deaths was 115 and 117, respectively; during the following week the daily average fell to 107 and 99, whilst during the period March 2nd to March 8th it has been 99 and 84. . . . Persons are now returning to the quarters of Bombay, which are comparatively free from plague, from the more infected outlying suburbs, and the Government of Bombay have therefore found it necessary to watch persons entering as well as those leaving Bombay. In the suburbs of Kurla, Bandora, and Bhiwandi the plague continues to be severe. Outside Bombay in the Presidency proper the number of indigenous cases has increased, and the disease shows a tendency to spread, especially in the Thana and Surat districts. . . . Outside Karachi the plague shows no tendency to spread in Sind, and Sukkur is the only other place from which indigenous cases have been reported."—*Great Britain, Parliamentary Pub-*

lications (Papers by Command: C.—8386, 1897; and C.—8511, 1897).

From that time there appears to have been a nearly steady subsidence of the disease until the following September, when it showed renewed virulence at Poona, and began to be newly spread, invading districts in the Punjab and elsewhere outside of the Bombay Presidency. By the middle of November Poona was substantially empty of inhabitants, except those stricken with the disease and those who bravely cared for the sick and dying. In December there was a fresh outbreak in Bombay, which soon became more deadly than that of the previous winter and spring. By the beginning of February, 1898, and through March, the deaths from plague alone in Bombay had risen above a thousand a week. Then another subsidence occurred, followed by another recrudescence of the disease in August, and another decline in October. But the variations in other districts were not uniform with those in Bombay. At the end of 1898, the total of mortality from plague in all the afflicted districts of India, reckoning from the beginning, was believed to exceed 100,000, including 70,000 in the Bombay Presidency and Sind (28,000 in the city of Bombay), and 2,000 in the Punjab. In Calcutta there had been but 150 deaths. Although the measures taken for checking the spread of the pestilence were far less stringent than they would have been among people more capable of understanding what they meant and what their importance was, they alarmed the religious jealousies of both the Hindus and the Mohammedans, and were resisted and resented with dangerous fury at a number of times. At Poona, in June, 1897, two British officials were murdered by young Brahmins, who had been excited to the deed by native journals, the language of which was so violent that the government found it necessary to prosecute several for sedition. At Bombay, in March, 1898, when the plague was at its worst, there were very serious riots, in which a number of Europeans were killed. and troops were called to the help of the police before the frenzied mob could be overcome.

Again, in 1899, there was a revival of the disease in India, especially at Bombay, during the winter, with a decline in April and fresh virulence in September. At the end of the year the estimate of total mortality from plague in India since the beginning was 250,000.

Of the wider spreading of the pestilence during 1900 the following summary of information is given in the annual report of the United States Secretary of the Treasury, in connection with details of quarantine measures: "The Surgeon-General reports that plague has been more widely distributed during the year than was ever known in history, and for the first time obtained lodgment in the Western Hemisphere, at Santos, Brazil, in October, 1899. By this it is not meant that the disease has been actually more prevalent than before, but that its points of contact have embraced nearly every civilized country in the world, though its prompt recognition and application of modern methods have either entirely prevented its spread or have caused it to disappear after a short period of infection. The scientific knowledge of the disease renders it far less to be dreaded than before, but increase in rapid communication between different parts of the world facilitates its transportation. In illustra-

tion, the fact is cited that 20 vessels have been reported. arriving at as many principal seaports in different parts of the world, on which plague was discovered on arrival or had manifested itself during the voyage. As heretofore, its chief ravages have been in India, where preventive measures have been hindered by religious fanaticism. In India during the year there were 66,294 deaths. Notable outbreaks of the disease occurred in Kobé and in Formosa, Japan, at Oporto, Santos, Rio de Janeiro, Honolulu, Sydney, Mauritius, Hongkong, and Glasgow.

"In December, 1899, on account of the apparent spread of this disease, 12 commissioned officers were detailed by order of the President for duty in the offices of the United States consuls at the principal ports in England and on the Continent. In June, the disease fortunately not having become as widespread as anticipated, they were recalled, with the exception of five, who are still retained for the purpose of furnishing information and for service at any needed point. Two of those thus retained, when the plague was announced at Glasgow, Scotland, on August 28, 1900, were immediately sent to that point and began inspection of vessels for the United States and also for Canada, by request of that Government, thus enabling vessels to be entered at ports on this side without undue restraint. In the laboratory of the Service, scientific investigations as to the viability of the plague bacillus and the methods and efficiency of disinfection have been conducted, and the results, together with excerpts from all available literature bearing upon the prevention of plague, have been published in the Public Health Reports, forming, for this year, a volume containing most complete information upon this disease. About 700,000 doses of Haffkine's prophylactic were also prepared in the laboratory and sent to the United States quarantine officers at home and abroad, together with large quantities of Yersin's serum, purchased early in the year from the Pasteur Institute in Paris. In these two preparations, the one (Haffkine) a prophylactic and the other (Yersin) both prophylactic and a cure, the Surgeon-General says that science has effective methods of combating the spread of this disease."—*United States, Secretary of the Treasury, Annual Report, Dec. 4, 1900.*

The "antitoxin, or serum, first prepared by Professor Haffkine as a plague inoculation, called Haffkine's prophylactic, is now being used in Bombay and western India with remarkable results. This prophylactic is prepared by first taking the plague bacilli, or the young germs, from a person affected with the plague and cultivating them. These microbes are killed by artificial means and a high degree of heat. From these dead germs and their poisonous excrements is produced a fluid that is believed to have acquired the power, when injected into the human system, to render the blood immune from the attack of plague germs and to neutralize their effect. The injection of such a poison has the effect of an antitoxin and prevents the system from nourishing plague. A dead plague germ being inoculated into a person, plague will not follow. A person after having one attack of the disease is rarely liable to a second. The person first inoculated is subject to symptoms of the plague. In vaccination for smallpox a living germ is dealt with, whereas in plague inoculation dead seed only are injected. . . . Inoculation is exceedingly unpopular among the natives. The government has had great labor in persuading the Hindoo mind of the efficacy of Haffkine's prophylactic against plague and at the same time of its utter harmlessness in every other respect. The Hindoo is suspicious that the dead germs and their toxic excreta may be of animal rather than vegetable substance, which would make the injection of the fluid into their body a religious offense."—*United States Consular Reports, Jan.,* 1900, *p.* 101.

"In the present epidemic, plague-spots are scattered over the whole face of the globe from Sydney to Santos and Hongkong, and recently from San Francisco suspicious cases have been reported. The annual pilgrimage of Moslems to worship at the shrines of Mecca and Medina is now, as in the past, of all human agencies, the most active in spreading the pest. . . . Since Egypt is nearest, plague first appears there in the seaport towns, particularly Alexandria. Sanitary conditions have improved vastly, like economics, under British control; and, last year, what in other times might have been a devastating epidemic was limited to relatively a few scattered cases. Recognizing the danger to themselves, the European powers have been led to take steps, under the Venice Convention, for their own protection. An international quarantine, under the control of the Egyptian Sanitary, Maritime, and Quarantine Council, in which the powers have one vote each and Egypt three, has established stations at two points on the Red Sea."—*American Review of Reviews, May,* 1900.

PLATT AMENDMENT, The. See (in this vol.) CUBA : A. D. 1901 (FEBRUARY—MARCH).

PLURAL VOTING. See (in this vol.) BELGIUM : A. D. 1894–1895.

PLYMOUTH COLONY: Return of the manuscript of Bradford's History to Massachusetts. See (in this vol.) MASSACHUSETTS: A. D. 1897.

POET LAUREATE.—To the line of English Poets Laureate (see, in vol. 3, LAUREATE. ENGLISH POETS), there was added on the 1st of January. 1896, the name of Alfred Austin, succeeding Tennyson, who died October 6, 1892.

POLAND, Russian : Relaxation of oppres- sions. See (in this vol.) RUSSIA : A. D. 1897.

POLAR EXPLORATION, Arctic and Antarctic: A chronological record.—Until quite recent years, the antarctic region had had few explorers. In 1598–9 Dirk Gerritz was carried south by a storm and found land, probably the South Shetlands, at 64° S. lat. Capt. Cook made two antarctic voyages. in the second one reaching lat. 71° 10′ S., at long. 106° 54′ W., sailing entirely around the southern ocean in a high latitude, and discovering many islands. In a Russian expedition. 1819–21, Bellinghausen discovered Peter I. Island and Alexander I. Land. Enderby Land was discovered by John Biscoe in 1831–2. In 1840–3 the great English expedition under Capt. (afterward Sir) James Ross, in the Erebus and Terror, discovered and named Victoria Land, and reached lat. 78° 11′, Feb. 23, 1842. The continent which Capt. Wilkes claimed to have discovered in 1840 has not been found by

later explorers. In 1874 the Challenger was turned back by the ice in lat. 66° 43′ S.

1892-1893.—Whaling voyage of the Dundee vessels, the Balæna, Active, Diana and Polar Star, equipped for geographical observation by the Royal Geographical Society and others interested, carrying Wm. S. Bruce, C. W. Donald, and W. G. Burn Murdoch. Accompanied by the Norwegian sealer Jasen, under Capt. Larsen. South Shetlands and Graham Land visited and valuable observations made.

1893-1900.—Scientific exploration of Labrador by A. P. Low. Operations still in progress.

1894-1895.—Commercial voyage of the Norwegian whaler Antarctic, under Capt. Kristensen, sent by Capt. Svend Foyn, fitted out by H. J. Bull, and carrying the scientist C. E. Borchgrevinck. The valuable right whale was not found, but large beds of guano were discovered in Victoria Land, where a landing was made near Cape Adare.

1895.—Return of Peary relief expedition with Lieut. Robert E. Peary and his companions. In spite of great difficulties Lieut. Peary had again crossed the ice-sheet to Independence Bay, determined the northern limits of Greenland, charted 1,000 miles of the west coast, discovered eleven islands and the famous Iron Mountain (three great meteorites), and obtained much knowledge of the natives. The purely scientific results of the expedition are of great value. The relief expedition was organized by Mrs. Peary.

1895.—Cruise of Mr. Pearson and Lieut. Feilden in Barents Sea.

1895.—Return of Martin Ekroll from Spitzbergen after s winter's study of the ice conditions there. Convinced that his plan of reaching the pole by a sledge journey had little chance of success.

1895.—Survey of the lower Yenesei River and Obi Bay by Siberian hydrographic expedition.

1895.—Commercial expedition of Capt. Wiggins from England to Golchika, at the mouth of the Yenesei.

1895.—Russian geological expedition to Nova Zembla.

1895-.—Russian expedition under the geologist Bogdanovich to the Sea of Okhotsk and Kamchatka.

1895-1896.—Two scientific voyages of the Danish cruiser Ingolf in the seas west and east of Greenland.

1896.—Summer expedition of naturalists and college students to the northern coast of Labrador.

1896.—Attempt of Lieut. Peary to remove the great meteorite discovered by him at Cape York, Greenland. After dislodging it he was compelled by the ice to leave it. Small parties from Cornell University and Massachusetts Institute of Technology and one under Mr. George Bartlett. left by Peary at different points to make scientibe observations and collections, returned with him.

1896.—Hydrographical survey of the Danish waters of Greenland and Iceland.

1896.—Hansen sent to Siberia to look for traces of Nansen.

1896.—Return of Dr. Nansen from voyage begun in 1893. After skirting the coast of Siberia almost to the Lena delta. the Fram was enclosed by the ice and drifted with it north and northwest. On March 14, 1895, in 84° 4′ N. lat.,

102° E. long., Nansen and Johansen left the Fram and pushed northward with dogs and sledges across an ice floe till they reached lat. 86° 13.6', at about 95° W. long., on April 8, within 261 statute miles of the pole. With great difficulty they made their way to Franz Josef Land, where they wintered, and in June met explorer Jackson. Returning on the Jackson supply steamer Windward, they reached Vardö Aug. 13. The Fram drifted to lat. 85° 57' N., 66° E. long., then southwestward, reaching Tromsoë Aug. 20, 1896. Nansen demonstrated the existence of a polar sea of great depth, comparatively warm below the surface, apparently with few islands ; though he did not find the trans-polar current he sought.

1896.—Spitzbergen crossed for the first time, by Sir W. Martin Conway and party.

1896.—Many parties visit the northern coast of Norway and Nova Zembla to view the total eclipse of the sun, Aug. 8–9.

1896.—Expedition sent by Russian Hydrographic Department to find site for a sealers' refuge in Nova Zembla. Bielusha Bay, on the southwest coast, chosen.

1897.—Expedition sent by Canadian government to investigate Hudson Bay and Strait as a route to Central Canada. Passage found to be navigable for at least sixteen weeks each summer.

1897.—Seventh Peary expedition to Greenland. Accompanied by parties for scientific research. Preliminary arrangements made with the Eskimos for the expedition of 1898, and food-stations established. Relics of Greeley's expedition found on Cape Sabine, and the great meteorite at Cape York brought away at last.

1897.—Second expedition of Sir Martin Conway for the exploration of Spitzbergen.

1897.—A summer resort established on west coast of Spitzbergen, with regular steamer service for tourists during July and August.

1897.—Cruise of Mr. Arnold Pike and Sir Savile Crossley among the islands east of Spitzbergen.

1897.—Cruise of Mr. Pearson and Lieut. Feilden in the Laura in the Kara Sea and along the east coast of Nova Zembla, for the purpose of studying the natural history of the region.

1897.—Expedition of F. W. L. Popham with a fleet of steamers through Yugor Straits to the Yenesei.

1897.—Hydrological and commercial expedition, comprising seven steamers, under Rear-Admiral Makaroff, sent by the Russian government to the north Siberian sea.

1897.—Balloon voyage of Salamon August Andrée and two companions, Mr. Strindberg and Mr. Fraenkel, starting from Danes' Island, north of Spitzbergen, in the hope of being carried to the pole. Four buoys from the balloon have been found. The first, found in Norway in June, 1899, and containing a note from Andrée, was thrown out eight hours after his departure. The "north pole buoy," to be dropped when the pole was passed, was found empty on the north side of King Charles Island, north-east of Spitzbergen, Sept. 11, 1899. A third buoy, also empty, was found on the west coast of Iceland July 17, 1900. Another, reported from Norway, Aug. 31, 1900, contained a note showing that the buoy was thrown out at 10 P. M., July 11, 1897, at an altitude of 250 metres (820 ft.), moving N.

45 E., with splendid weather. Many search expeditions, some equipped at great expense, have returned unsuccessful. In spite of many rumors nothing definite is known of the fate of any of the party. One message from Andrée was brought back by a carrier pigeon. It was dated July 13, 12.30 P. M., in lat. 82° 2', long. 12° 5' E., and stated that the balloon was moving eastward.

1897.—New islands on the southern coast of Franz Josef Land discovered by Capt. Robertson of the Dundee whaler Balæna.

1897.—Return of Jackson-Harmsworth expedition from three years' exploration of Franz Josef Land and the region north of it. Franz Josef Land was resolved into a group of islands and almost entirely mapped. Small parties journeying northward over the ice, establishing depots of supplies, the most northern in latitude 81° 21', discovered and named Victoria Sea, the most northern open sea in the world.

1897.—Anglo-Australasian antarctic conference in London.

1897-1899.—Journey of Andrew J. Stone through the Canadian Rockies, down Mackenzie River and along the arctic coast, in search of rare mammals and information concerning the native tribes. Mr. Stone often had only one companion. He traveled rapidly, in one period of five months covering 3,000 miles of arctic coast and mountains, between 70° and 72° N. lat. and between 117½° and 140° W. long.

1897-1899.—Belgian antarctic expedition under Capt. Adrien de Gerlache to lands south of America. Sailed from Antwerp to explore and chart coast line, expecting to leave party to winter at Cape Adare and explore interior. Near Alexander I. Land the Belgica caught in the ice pack and held for a year, drifting as far south as lat. 71° 36', in long. 87° 39' W. Finally released by the cutting of a canal through the ice. This dreary winter the first spent by men far enough south to lose sight of the sun. The continent found to be mountainous, glaciated, and without land animals except a few insects, though sea fowl abounded. One flowering grass, and a few mosses, rock lichens, and fresh-water algæ constitute the flora. Some 500 miles of coast chartered.

1898.—Expedition of Dr. K. J. V. Steenstrup to Greenland to study the glaciers of Disko island.

1898.—Completion by Dr. Thoroddsen of his systematic exploration of Iceland, begun in 1881.

1898.—Spitzbergen circumnavigated and surveyed by Dr. A. G. Nathorst. Coast mapped and important scientific observations made.

1898.—Pendulum observations made in Spitzbergen by Prof. J. H. Gore, with instruments of the United States Coast and Geodetic Survey, for the determination of the force of gravity in that latitude.

1898.—Cruise of Prince Albert of Monaco, on coast of Spitzbergen, for the purpose of making scientific observations.

1898.—Some claim to Spitzbergen made by Russia. Never before claimed by any nation.

1898.—German arctic expedition under Theodor Lerner to the islands east of Spitzbergen, for scientific purposes and to obtain news of Andrée if possible.

1898.—Andrée search expedition under J. Stadling sent to the Lena delta, the mouth of the Yenesei and the islands of New Siberia by the Swedish Anthropological and Geographical Society.

1898.—Conference on antarctic exploration held in the rooms of the Royal Society, London, Feb. 24.

1898-1899.—Reconnoitring expedition by Danish party under Lieut. G. C. Amdrup, to east coast of Greenland. Coast explored and mapped from Angmagsalik, 65⅘° N. lat., to 67° 22′. Remains of a small extinct Eskimo settlement found.

1898-1899.—Second attempt by Walter Wellman to reach the north pole. Wintered in Franz Josef Land, establishing an outpost, called Fort McKinley, in lat. 81° N. In February Mr. Wellman, with three companions, started northward and seemed likely to succeed in their undertaking, but a serious accident befalling Mr. Wellman, and an icequake destroying many dogs and sledges, a hurried return to headquarters was necessary. Here important scientific observations were made. The 82d parallel was reached by the explorer.

1898-1899.—German expedition for deep-sea exploration in antarctic waters, in charge of Prof. Carl Chun, on the Valdivia. Southern ocean found to be of great depth.

1898-1900.—British antarctic expedition under Borchgrevinck to Victoria Land; the funds provided by Sir George Newnes. Lat. 78° 50′ S. reached, and the present position of the southern magnetic pole determined.

1898-.—Carefully planned expedition of Lieut. Peary, purposing to advance toward the pole by west coast of Greenland, establishing food stations and depending upon picked Eskimos for co-operation with his small party. In the last dash for the pole, supply sledges to be sent back as emptied, and the returning explorer, with two companions only, to be met by a relief party of Eskimos. The Windward was presented by Mr. Harmsworth for this expedition. Lieut. Peary was disabled for several weeks in 1898-9 by severe frost-bites, causing the loss of seven toes. The Greeley records were found at Fort Conger and sent back by the annual supply vessel. Sextant and record of the Narcs expedition found and sent back; presented by Lieut. Peary to the Lords of the Admiralty of Great Britain and placed in the museum of the Royal Naval College at Greenwich. Vessel sent to Greenland each summer to carry supplies and bring back letters, carrying also small parties of explorers, scientists, university students and hunters, to be left at various points and picked up by the vessel on its return.

1898-.—Expedition of Capt. Sverdrup to northern Greenland — Lieut. Peary's especial field. Having planned a polar expedition similar to Peary's he sailed up the west coast, but the Fram was frozen in near Cape Sabine. Sverdrup therefore explored the western part of Ellesmere Land, then sailed again in an attempt to round the northern coast of Greenland.

1899.—International conference held at Stockholm in June recommended a program for hydrographical and biological work in the northern parts of the Atlantic ocean, the North Sea, the Baltic, and adjoining seas.

1899-.—Scientific expedition of Edward Bay, a Dane, to Melville Bay, Greenland.

1899.—Swedish expedition under Dr. A. G. Nathorst to search for Andrée in eastern Green-

land. Valuable observations made and fjord-systems of King Oscar Fjord and Kaiser Franz Josef Fjord mapped.

1899.—Explorations in Iceland by F. W. W. Howell and party.

1899.—Hydrographic surveys on the coasts of Iceland and the Färoe Islands by MM. Holm and Hammer in the Danish guard-ship Diana.

1899.—Joint Russian and Swedish expedition to Spitzbergen, for the measurement of a degree of the meridian. Owing to the condition of the ice, the northern and southern surveying parties unable to connect their work.

1899.—Explorations in Spitzbergen by the Prince of Monaco, with a scientific staff.

1899.—Successful experimental voyage of the Russian Vice-Admiral Makaroff in his ice-breaking steamer, the Yermak, north of Spitzbergen.

1899.—Russian government expedition, to cost £5,400, to explore northern shores of Siberia to mouths of the Obi and Ycnesei.

1899-1900.—Arctic expedition of the Duke of the Abruzzi. His ship, the Stella Polare, was left at Crown Prince Rudolf Land during the winter. The Duke became incapacitated by a fall and by the loss of two joints from the fingers of his left hand, incurably frost-bitten; but a small party under Capt. Cagni pushed northward till provisions were exhausted. Nansen's record was beaten, the Italian party reaching lat. 86° 33′, at about 56° E. long. No land was found north or northwest of Spitzbergen. Three men were lost from Cagni's party.

1899-.—Exploration of Ellesmere Land, Greenland, by Dr. Robert Stein, of the United States Geological Survey, Dr. Leopold Kann of Cornell, and Samuel Warmbath of Harvard, who took passage in the Peary supply ship Diana, trusting to chance for conveyance home. Their totally inadequate outfit was generously augmented by Peary's friends of the Diana. Dr. Kann returned in 1900, leaving Dr. Stein.

1900.—Seward peninsula, the most westward extension of Alaska, explored and surveyed by five government expeditions.

1900.—Exploration of the interior of northern Labrador by a party from Harvard University. Soundings along the coast by schooner Brave.

1900.—Second Danish expedition under Lieut. Amdrup to east Greenland, completing the work of 1898-9 by mapping the coast between 67° 20′ N. and Cape Gladstone, about 70° N., and making valuable scientific collections.

1900.—Swedish expedition, under Gustav Kolthoff, to eastern Greenland, for study of the arctic fauna.

1900.—Swedish scientific expedition of Prof. G. Kolthoff to Spitzbergen and Greenland.

1900.—Exploration of Spitzbergen by a Russian expedition under Knipovich.

1900.—Russian expedition to east coast of Nova Zembla by Lieut. Borissoff to complete survey of the islands.

1900-.—Dr. Nansen's expedition under the leadership of Dr. J. Hjort, for the physical and biological examination of the sea between Norway, Iceland, Jan Mayen and Spitzbergen.

1900-.—German expedition, under Capt. Bade, to explore East Spitzbergen, King Charles' Land and Franz Josef Land, and to look for traces of Andrée.

1900-.—Attempt of a German, Capt. Bauendahl, to reach the north pole, leaving his vessel in the ice north of Spitzbergen and traveling over the ice with provisions for two years, weighing ten tons.

1900-.—Scientific expedition of Baron E. von Toll to the unexplored Sannikoff Land, sighted in 1805 from the northern coast islands of New Siberia. Preceded by a party which established food depots at various places months before.

1901.—Three exploring parties sent to Alaska by the United States Geological Survey.

1901.—Expedition sent by the Duke of the Abruzzi to Franz Josef Land to search for the three men lost from his party in 1900.

1901.—North polar expedition under Mr. Evelyn B. Baldwin of the United States Weather Bureau; splendidly equipped by Mr. Wm. Ziegler of New York. Mr. Baldwin, who has had arctic experience with Lieut. Peary and Mr. Wellman, will probably proceed by way of Franz Josef Land.

1901-.—Several expeditions to co-operate in exploration of the antarctic region and to reach the south pole if possible. The British expedition, long striven for by the Royal Geographical Society and the Royal Society and made possible by L. W. Longstaff's contribution of £25,000, to be under the command of Capt. Robert Scott and to explore the Victoria (90°–180° E.) and Ross (180°–90° W.) quadrants, — in the main the region south of the Pacific. The Weddell (90° W.–0°, Greenwich) and Enderby (0°–90 E.) quadrants assigned to the finely equipped German expedition, under Drygalski, which will first explore south of the Indian Ocean. The Swedish expedition under Dr. Nordenskïold to explore the lands south of America. A private Scottish expedition under Wm. S. Bruce to explore the Weddell Sea region south of the Atlantic Ocean. An Argentine expedition to visit the South Shetlands.

1901-.—Projected expedition of Capt. J. E. Bernier of Quebec, on Nansen's principle, with a specially built vessel, to sail through Bering Strait, coast Siberia to long. 170° or 165° E., then enter the ice. Sledging parties to push toward the pole, marking the route with hollow signal poles (of aluminum) packed with records and provisions, and maintaining communication with the ship by wireless telegraphy. This is one of two plans which has before the Canadian government. The other contemplates a movement, with dogs and reindeers, from Franz Josef Land, coming back to Spitzbergen, taking 12 or 14 men, all scientists.

1901-.—Projected expedition of Herr Annschütz-Kämpfe, of Munich, to the north pole, in a submarine boat capable of carrying five men and remaining under water for fifteen hours at a time.

1901-.—As this goes to press (April, 1901), a national antarctic expedition is being fitted out, jointly, by the Royal Geographical Society and the Royal Society of Great Britain, assisted by a subsidy of £45,000 from the British government. A steamer named the "Discovery," built especially for the expedition, at Dundee, was launched in March, and is being equipped with remarkable completeness. Special arrangements, says "The Times," will be made for magnetic work, while meteorology, geology and biology will be well cared for. "The staff of navigating officers and of scientific specialists has been carefully selected, and under Commander Robert Scott, R. N., who will be in command of the expedition, their work, we may be sure, will be so well organized that nothing of importance will be neglected. There will be five navigating officers, three of them belonging to the Royal Navy and two others to the Royal Naval Reserve, while the special scientific staff, including the two medical officers, will be of equal strength. . . . Captain Scott is at present investigating the question of the utility of balloons."

POLISH PARTY, in Austria. See (in this vol.) AUSTRIA-HUNGARY: A. D. 1895–1896, and after.

POONA, The Plague at. See (in this vol.) PLAGUE.

POPE LEO XIII. See PAPACY.

POPULATION: Of Europe and countries peopled from Europe. See (in this vol.) NINETEENTH CENTURY: EXPANSION.

POPULIST PARTY, The. See (in this vol.) UNITED STATES OF AM.: A. D. 1896 (JUNE—NOVEMBER); and 1900 (MAY—NOVEMBER.)

PORT ARTHUR: A. D. 1894.—Capture by Japanese. See (in this vol.) CHINA: A. D. 1894–1895.

A. D. 1895.—Trans-Siberian Railway.—Russo-Chinese Treaty. See (in this vol.) RUSSIA IN ASIA: A. D. 1891–1900.

A. D. 1898.—Lease to Russia. See (in this vol.) CHINA: A. D. 1898 (MARCH—JULY).

PORTO RICO.

Area and Population.—In the testimony given, Jan. 13, 1900, before the U. S. Senate Committee on Pacific Islands and Porto Rico, General George W. Davis, Military Governor of Porto Rico, gave the following information: " The island of Puerto Rico has an area of about 3,600 square miles, according to the best information that now exists, but that area has to be verified, and it is doubted if the area is quite so large. It has a population of about a million, perhaps—certainly one of the most densely populated areas of 3,000 or 4,000 square miles on the face of the earth, approximating the density of population of Belgium, I think, and considerably greater than that of any of our thickly settled agricultural

regions in the United States. New England has about 200 to the square mile while Puerto Rico has nearly 300. The inhabitants are mostly of Spanish origin—emigrants from Spain during the last 400 years and their descendants. There is a large representation from the Canary Islands and the Balearic group in the Mediterranean, a large number of Corsicans and their descendants, and consequently they are French subjects, a few Germans, a few English, and very few Americans before the occupation ; a few Venezuelans, a few from Santo Domingo, and a few Cubans, but the most of the population is Spanish. Included in that million are about 300,000 negroes and mulattoes, approximately a little more than that number. About one-third of the entire population is of the negro or mixed race, what would be called in the United States 'colored' people. Of pure-blood negroes there are about 70,000, the remainder mulattoes, and all speaking Spanish, and largely the slaves liberated in 1874. The number of slaves liberated at that time was considerably less than the number of negroes in Puerto Rico, the number being only about 30,000, for whom some $11,000,000 was paid the owners. That statement gives a fair idea of the character of the population as respects numbers and race." Several small adjacent islands are regarded as belonging to Porto Rico and were included in the cession to the United States. One of these, named Vieques, about 15 miles long and 3 or 4 miles wide, is very fertile, and has about 7,000 inhabitants. On another, called Culebra, there are some 600 or 700 people. The remaining islands are smaller and unimportant.—*56th Congress, 1st Sess., Senate Doc. No. 147, pp. 1-2.*

The government as it **was** under Spanish rule.—"The civil government of the island was the Governor-General, and the Governor-General was the civil government. All power was lodged in his hands and he was accountable only to Madrid. He was at once the executive, the legislative, and the judicial head. As Captain-General, he had chief command of the military forces, and made such disposition of them as he chose; as Governor-General, he conducted civil affairs, whether insular or municipal, according to his own pleasure. . . . If, as occasionally happened, he was a wise and good man, seeking the welfare of the people rather than his own personal enrichment or the advancement of his political friends, there was less cause for complaint from the people, who were completely ignored. As the position was one of great power and of large opportunities for pecuniary profit, it not infrequently went to those who were prepared to exploit it in their own interests. . . .

"The system of autonomy, which was proclaimed November 25, 1897 [see, in this vol., CUBA: A. D. 1897 (NOVEMBER)], was never fully installed. The war intervened, and the provincial legislature, which was its most important feature, was dissolved when Sampson's fleet appeared, and the Governor-General conducted the government practically on the old plan, except that the ministry, as provided by the autonomistic law, was retained, as follows: Secretary of government or of state, secretary of the treasury, secretary of the fomento or interior, including public works, public instruction, public lands, mines, etc., agriculture and commerce, and secretary of justice and worship. The last three secretaries were subordinate to the secretary of government, through whom all orders from the Governor-General and all communications to or from him must pass. The autonomist law allowed the secretaries or ministers to be members of one or the other of the two legislative chambers. The Governor-General with his council constituted the executive power. No act of his was valid unless approved by one of the secretaries, and the secretaries could issue no order which he had not countersigned. He had the power to convoke or dissolve the chambers, to refer objectionable bills to Madrid for approval or disapproval, and to appoint or remove the secretaries. All matters of a diplomatic character

were in his hands exclusively, and, constituted by the Pope patronato real, he was the head of the church in the island and practical director of ecclesiastical affairs. The legislature consisted of two chambers, the council and the house of representatives. The council was composed of fourteen members, eight of whom were elected, and six appointed by the Crown; the house of representatives of one representative for each 25,000 inhabitants, elected by the people. The liberality of this law is further indicated by the fact that it gave the right of suffrage to all males of 25 years of age and over. The two chambers were empowered to legislate on all insular questions, such as the estimates, which must be adopted by the Cortes at Madrid, public instruction, public works, sanitation, charities, etc. It will be seen that the reforms granted by this autonomistic decree were large in the letter, taking powers which the Governor-General had exercised unquestioned and giving them to the people, who had never been allowed to participate in the government of their own country. Whether it would have proved liberal in practical operation is not so certain. The Government invariably discriminated against Porto Ricans in favor of Spaniards, and it is also to be remembered that Spanish laws as written and Spanish laws as administered are not always identical." H. K. Carroll (Special Commissioner), *Report on Porto Rico, 1899, pp. 15-16.*

A. D. 1898 (May).—American bombardment of forts at San Juan. See (in this vol.) UNITED STATES OF AM.: A. D. 1898 (APRIL—JUNE).

A. D. 1898 (July—August).—American conquest of. See (in this vol.) UNITED STATES OF AM.: A. D. 1898 (JULY—AUGUST: PORTO RICO).

A. D. 1898 (July—December).—Suspension of hostilities.—Cession to the United States. See (in this vol.) UNITED STATES OF AM.: A. D. 1898 (JULY—DECEMBER).

A. D. 1898-1899 (August—July).—Popular feeling in the Island on the American occupation. — Welcome to the Stars and Stripes. — Expectations and desires of the people. — Their character. — Extent of illiteracy.—The Peones.—"All classes of natives of the island welcomed the American Army, American occupation, and American methods, and accepted without hesitation the Stars and Stripes in place of the red and yellow bars. They had not been disloyal to the old flag; but it had come to represent to them, particularly during the present century, in which a class feeling developed between the insular and the peninsular Spaniard, partiality and oppression. In the short war, some of the natives occupying official positions made demonstrations of loyalty to the Crown of Spain, as was perfectly natural, but they were among the first to submit to American rule when the protocol promised cession of the island to the United States. On the other hand, as the commissioner is informed, a Porto Rican who had hoped and prayed for American intervention for fifty years enrolled himself as a Spanish citizen some months after the war was concluded, and his hopes had been realized. Porto Ricans generally complained that the former Government discriminated in favor of the Spaniard, who, in the distribution of the offices, was preferred to the native, and who, aided by the powerful influence of the authorities, prospered in business as

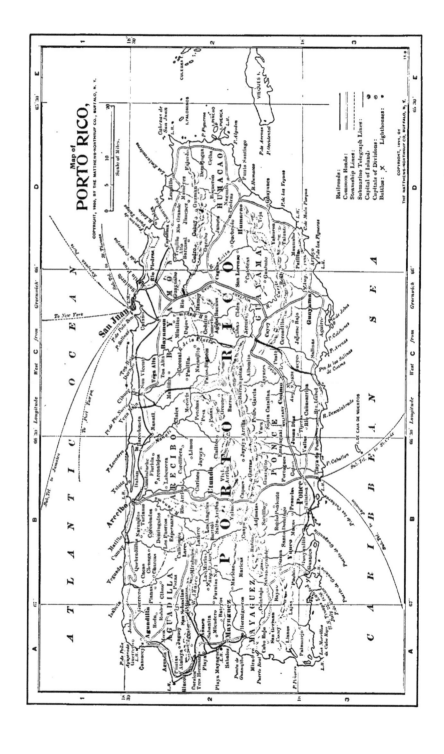

Map of
PORTO RICO,

COPYRIGHT, 1899, BY THE MATTHEWS-NORTHRUP CO., BUFFALO, N. Y.

Scale of Miles.

Railroads:
Common Roads:
Steamship Lines:
Submarine Telegraph Lines:
Capital of Island:
Capital of Divisions:
Battles: X
Lighthouses:

COPYRIGHT, 1899, BY
THE MATTHEWS-NORTHRUP CO., BUFFALO, N. Y.

banker, merchant, manufacturer, or agriculturist. They also insist that the internal improvement of the island was neglected; that agriculture bore more than its share of the burden of taxation; that the assessments were very inequitable and unequal; that education was not fostered, and that in general the welfare of the people was not the first concern of their rulers.

"They expect under American sovereignty that the wrongs of centuries will be righted; that they will have an honest and efficient government; the largest measure of liberty as citizens of the great Republic under the Constitution; home rule as provided by the Territorial system; free access to the markets of the United States and no customs duties on goods coming from our ports; a school system modeled after that of the United States; the adoption of the English language in due time and the general adaptation to the island of all those institutions which have contributed to the prosperity, progress, and happiness of the American people. The largest and most representative gathering, since American occupation, was held in San Juan, October 30, 1898, without distinction of party or class with the object of consultation and formulation of a programme for the future. In brief, the propositions of the congress as submitted to the commissioner for presentation to the President of the United States were these: Immediate termination of military and inauguration of civil government; establishment of the Territorial system, with laws common to other Territories of the Union; a legislature in two branches; suffrage for all male citizens of 21 years of age or over, the right to be surrendered at the end of the first two years by those who do not then know how to read and write; judicial reform; introduction of the jury system; autonomy for municipal governments; taxation on the basis of valuation; free and reciprocal commerce with the ports of the United States; aid for agriculture; obligatory and universal education; trade schools; savings banks. This programme of reforms seems to have very general support, although there is a difference of opinion on certain points. Many Porto Ricans urged the commissioner to represent them as desiring that the military régime be made as short as possible, not because the military governors were in any way objectionable or their rule oppressive, but because the civil status of the island should be fixed with no unnecessary delay. There was no other opinion except among foreign subjects, many of whom thought that the people were not yet ready for self-government, and that the firm hand of military power would be needed for probably two years. . . .

"If the desire to assume the burdens of local self-government may be taken as indicating some degree of capacity for self-government, the people of Porto Rico certainly have the desire. They may be poor, but they are proud and sensitive, and would be bitterly disappointed if they found that they had been delivered from an oppressive yoke to be put under a tutelage which proclaimed their inferiority. Apart from such qualifications as general education and experience constitute, the commissioner has no hesitation in affirming that the people have good claims to be considered capable of self-government. Education and experience, although too high a value can hardly

be set upon them, do not necessarily make good citizens. . . . The unswerving loyalty of Porto Rico to the Crown of Spain, as demonstrated by the truth of history, is no small claim to the confidence and trust of the United States. The people were obedient under circumstances which provoked revolt after revolt in other Spanish colonies. The habit of obedience is strong among them. Their respect for law is another notable characteristic. They are not turbulent or violent. Riots are almost unknown in the island; so is organized resistance to law; brigandage flourished only for a brief period after the war and its object was revenge rather than rapine. They are not a criminal people. The more violent crimes are by no means common. Burglary is almost unknown. There are many cases of homicide, but the number in proportion to population is not as large as in the United States. Thievery is the most common crime, and petty cases make up a large part of this list of offenses. The people as a whole are a moral, law-abiding class, mild in disposition, easy to govern, and possess the possibilities of developing a high type of citizenship."—H. K. Carroll (Special Commissioner), *Report on Porto Rico*, 1899, *pp.* 55–57.

"On the 25th day of July, 1899, an election was held in Adjuntas for municipal officers, and the registration was made in conformity to General Orders, No. 112, c. s., Headquarters Department of Puerto Rico. The order imposed the following qualifications for electors: Men over 21 years old, able to read and write, or who were taxpayers of record, who had been actual residents of the island for at least two years, and of the municipality for six months preceding the date of the election. The number who proved these qualifications before the board of registration was 906, out of a population, according to the census of 1897, of 18,505; that is, less than 5 per cent could vote under the conditions stated. There was much public interest in this election, and it is believed that about all who were eligible were registered. This incident indicated that in the whole island there may be approximately 45,000 who could vote under the conditions of the order above referred to. The class who can not fulfill these conditions, say 75 per cent of the males over 21 years of age, are usually in a state of abject poverty and ignorance, and are assumed to include one-fifth of the inhabitants. They are of the class usually called peones. This word in Spanish America, under old laws, defined a person who owed service to his creditor until the debt was paid. While those laws are obsolete, the condition of these poor people remains much as before. So great is their poverty that they are always in debt to the proprietors or merchants. They live in huts made of sticks and poles covered with thatches of palm leaves. A family of a dozen may be huddled together in one room, often with only a dirt floor. They have little food worthy of the name and only the most scanty clothing, while children of less than 7 or 8 years of age are often entirely naked. A few may own a machete or a hoe, but more have no worldly possessions whatever. Their food is fruit, and if they are wage-earners, a little rice and codfish in addition. They are without ambition and see no incentive to labor beyond the least that will provide the barest sustenance. All over the island they can be seen to-day sitting beside their ruined huts, thinking naught of to-morrow, making no effort to repair and restore their cabins nor to replant for future food.

" The remarks of Mr. James Anthony Froude in his work on ' The English in the West Indies' apply with full force to these people : ' Morals in the technical sense they have none, but they can not be said to sin because they have no knowledge of law, and therefore they can commit no breach of the law. They are naked and not ashamed. They are married but not parsoned. The women prefer the looser tie, that they may be able to lose the man if he treats her unkindly. Yet they are not licentious. . . . The system is strange, but it answers. . . . There is evil, but there is not the demoralizing effect of evil. They sin, but they sin only as animals, without shame, because there is no sense of doing wrong. They eat the forbidden fruit, but it brings with it no knowledge of the difference between good and evil. . . . They are innocently happy in the unconsciousness of the obligations of morality. They eat, drink, sleep, and smoke, and do the least in the way of work they can. They have no ideas of duty, and therefore are not made uneasy by neglecting it.' Between the negro and the peon there is no visible difference. It is hard to believe that the pale, sallow, and often emaciated beings are the descendants of the conquistadores who carried the flag of Spain to nearly all of South America, and to one-third of North America."—General George W. Davis, *Report on the Civil Government of Puerto Rico, Sept. 30, 1899 (Message and Documents: Abridgment, 1899-1900, v. 2, pp. 1293-4).*—" The educated class of Puerto Ricans are as well educated and accomplished as the educated men of any country. They have had the benefit of a liberal education, a few in the United States, a good many in France, and a great many in Madrid and Habana, where they have passed through the universities. The lawyers and doctors are all graduates of either the university in Habana or some university in Spain, with very few exceptions. The merchants are largely Spanish, many of whom will probably preserve their nationality under the provision of the Treaty of Paris which gives them that right. A few may adopt American citizenship, and ultimately possibly all will, but many of the merchants who conduct the largest part of the business of Puerto Rico will retain their Spanish citizenship. There are a number of merchants who are natives, a few Germans, and a few English. I do not remember any American merchant in business there before the occupation. The schools in Puerto Rico conducted under the Spanish system were few in number. The amount allotted for education by the insular budget was something like 300,000 pesos a year, as I now recall the figures. The teachers were officers of the government, holding life positions and receiving pensions when superannuated. They belong to a civil-service class which is not dependent upon any change of administration, only being removed for cause. The lawyers, or judges, rather, of the island, occupy a similar position."—General George W. Davis, *Testimony before Senate Com. (56th Cong., 1st Sess., Senate Doc. No. 147).*

A. D. **1898-1899** (October—October).—The military government instituted by the United States.—"The government of the island, its various civil institutions, its codes and its courts, the systems of taxation, etc., have been modified in very important particulars since the American occupation began, October 18, 1898. It will be useful, perhaps, to indicate the more important changes. Under General John R. Brooke [in command of the Department, October 18 to December 5, 1898] orders were issued declaring —(1) That the political relations of Porto Rico with Spain were at an end ; that provincial and municipal laws were in force in so far as not incompatible with the changed conditions, and that they would be enforced substantially as they were before. (2) Abolishing the use of all stamped paper and stamps of every kind for documents, public and private. (3) Exempting all conveyances and contracts from the payment of royal dues. (4) Discontinuing the diputacion provincial, and distributing its duties among the secretaries or ministers. (5) Directing that appeals should not be sent to the supreme court in Madrid, but should be heard by the superior court at San Juan. (6) Abolishing the subdelegation of pharmacy which gave degrees to pharmacists. (7) Making the fisheries free to all. Appropriations for the support of the church ceased with American occupation, and the Government lottery was discontinued.

" Under the military government of Gen. Guy V. Henry [December 6, 1898 to May 8, 1899], orders were issued—(1) Appointing military commissions to try cases of arson and murder which had accumulated in the civil courts. (2) Closing public offices on Sunday, as far as possible. (3) Suspending the municipal tax on fresh beef for use of the Army. (4) Making Christmas and New Year's holidays. (5) Forbidding grants or concessions of public or corporate rights or franchises without the approval of the commanding general and the Secretary of War. (6) Abolishing the municipal consumo tax on articles of food, fuel, and drink, and providing for additional assessments on the sale of liquors and tobacco. (7) Separating the collection of customs duties from that of direct taxes. (8) Establishing a new system of land taxation, by which agricultural lands should be taxed according to the several classes instituted, from 1 peso down to 25 centavos per cuerda, and levying 50 per cent additional on lands whose owners reside abroad. (9) Providing for the free vaccination of the people of the island. (10) Prohibiting the exhumation of bodies in the cemeteries, recognizing the right of priests to control burials in consecrated grounds, and requiring municipalities to keep cemeteries in repair. (11) Reducing notarial fees from $1.88 to $1, from $4.50 to $1, from $11 to $1, and from $1 to 50 cents, according to class of document, and canceling others. (12) Reorganizing the cabinet, so as to make all the secretaries directly responsible to the governor-general. (13) Suspending the foreclosure of mortgages on agricultural property and machinery for one year. (14) Appointing February 22 a holiday. (15) Prohibiting the sale of liquor to children under 14 years of age. (16) Modifying the civil marriage law. (17) Declaring that eight hours shall constitute a day's work. (18) Creating an insular police.

"Under the military government of Gen. George W. Davis [May 8, 1899, to May 1, 1900], orders were issued—(1) Modifying the order of

General Henry concerning hours of labor, so as to allow agreements between employer and employee for longer or shorter hours. (2) Naming May 30 as a holiday. (3) Allowing the writ of habeas corpus to be issued. (4) Constituting a board of prison control and pardon. (5) Continuing the observance as a holiday of June 24. (6) Creating a provisional court on the basis of circuit and district courts of the United States for the hearing of cases not falling within the jurisdiction of local insular courts. (7) Creating a superior board of health for the island. (8) Reorganizing the bureau of public instruction and the system of education. (9) Relieving the judiciary from all control by the department of justice, discontinuing the office of secretary of justice, and appointing a solicitor-general. (10) Abolishing the sale at auction of the privilege of slaughter of cattle, and making it free. (11) Reorganizing the judicial system of the island, with a supreme court in San Juan and district courts in San Juan, Ponce, Mayaguez, Arecibo, and Humacao, and with modifications of civil and criminal procedure. (12) Discontinuing the departments of state, treasury, and interior, and creating bureaus of state and municipal affairs, of internal revenue, and of agriculture, to be placed under the direction of a civil secretary, responsible to the governor-general, and continuing the bureaus of education and public works, with an insular board of nine members to advise the governor-general on matters of public interest referred to them.

" The reductions in the budget of expenditures have been extensive. That of 1898–99, adopted in June, 1898, amounted to $4,781,920, native money. The appropriations for 'general obligations,' which went to Madrid, $498,502, for the clergy, $197,945; for the army, $1,252,378; for the navy, $222,668, making a total of $2,171,493, ceased to be obligations, leaving $2,610,428 for the fiscal year. A new budget was adopted for the calendar year 1899, which still further reduces expenditures, calling only for $1,462,276. This budget, if carried out, would have involved a reduction from the proposed budget of 1898–99 of $3,319,644; but a new budget was formed, as already stated, for 1899–1900, which appears to call for an increase over this very moderate sum. The revenues were reduced by the abolition of stamped paper, personal passports, export duties, royal dues on conveyances, the lottery system, and other sources of income, amounting, all told, to less probably than a million of pesos."—H. R. Carroll (Special Commissioner), *Report on Porto Rico, October* 6, 1899, *pp.* 53–55.

A. D. **1899** (August).—Destructive cyclone. —" On the morning of the 7th of August, 1899, the United States Weather Bureau, through its branch establishment here, announced the approach of a cyclonic disturbance, and the danger signal was ordered to be hoisted at substations of the Bureau at Ponce and Mayaguez. At the same time I directed that the danger be reported to all commanding officers of posts throughout the island. There had been no serious or destructive storm in Puerto Rico since 1867, and the inhabitants had ceased to feel great concern on account of tropical tempests. Except at seaports, little heed was given to the caution, and in some cases the telegraph operators failed to receive or to promptly deliver the warning messages. The vortex of the cyclone appears to

have traversed the island throughout its whole length, from about Humacao to Mayaguez, and its path was a scene of very great devastation. . . . The gale struck the island at Humacao about midnight of August 7, and furiously blew all the rest of that night and well into the next day, while at Mayaguez the violence was not great until 9 o'clock on the morning of the 8th. But as the latter town was under the lee of high mountains, it suffered much less than it would have done had it been higher or not thus protected. Most of the habitations in the track of the center of the cyclone were entirely smashed and the débris strewn all over the country. The full reports of the loss of life bring the number of deaths up to 2,700. The wind worked dreadful havoc with nearly everything useful to man. Besides the mortality, which was appalling, the material damage was almost beyond belief. But the greatest loss of life resulted, not from the wind, but from the terrible downfall of rain that immediately followed. . . . Added to the horror of the situation there came with the gale on the southern coast a tidal wave, which submerged large areas with sea water and swept away what the wind and rain had spared, in some places completing the destruction. Every river bed or bottom of a land depression was a roaring torrent. The wind uprooted myriads of trees, and the rain, entering and permeating the soil, loosened it, and on steep declivities resulted in avalanches of earth, mud, and water, covering wide areas and piling up the débris in the ravines and gorges. . . . The material loss to the coffee growers can as yet only be estimated, but the most conservative figures received place this year's crop at one-third of the normal. . . . Regard being had to the fact that five years must elapse before the coffee trees and their shade can be replanted and reach a normal bearing condition, the total loss can not be safely placed below 25,000,000 pesos for Puerto Rico on account of this hurricane."—Gen. George W. Davis, *Report* (*Message and Documents: Abridgment*, 1899–1900, *v.* 2, *pp.* 1343–4).

A. D. **1899** (October).—Census of the Island taken under the direction of the War Department of the United States.—" The population of Porto Rico shown by the schedules of the present census taken with reference to the date of October 16, 1899, was 953,243. This was about nine-tenths of the population of Maryland in 1890, the State whose population is nearest to that of Porto Rico. . . . If the figures for . . . earlier censuses may be accepted, it appears that the population of Porto Rico has been growing through the last twelve years with greater rapidity than before since 1860. Its present rate of increase is about the same as that of Ohio, Tennessee, or the Carolinas during the decade between 1880 and 1890. . . . It appears that the average increase of population in the interior has been more rapid than that on the coast. If the figures for the coast cities of San Juan, Ponce, and Mayaguez had been excluded, the difference would be yet more marked. The depressed condition of sugar-cane growing in the West Indies of recent years may have played an important part in producing this difference, for the growing of sugar cane is prevalent in the coast plains of Porto Rico.

"The area of Porto Rico, including the adjacent and dependent islands of Vieques, Culebra,

413

Mona, and Muertos, has been measured in connection with this census and found to be 3,606 square miles. But owing to the imperfect surveys on which all maps of Porto Rico are based there must be a considerable and indeterminate margin of possible error in any such measurement. The island is about three times the size of Long Island, which was in 1890 perhaps the largest insular division of the United States. It is also slightly greater than the eastern shore of Maryland (3,461 square miles). . . . Porto Rico has 264 persons to a square mile. This density of population is about the same as in Massachusetts, twice that in New York State, and thrice that in Ohio. It is more than seven times that of Cuba and not much less than twice that of Habana province. . . .

"The people of Porto Rico are, in the main, a rural community. There are no large cities in the island, the two largest being San Juan, which, regarding the entire municipal district as a city, had a population of 32,048, and Ponce, which with its port constituted practically one city, with a population of 27,952. These are the only two cities exceeding 25,000 inhabitants. The next city of magnitude is Mayaguez, on the west coast, with a population of 15,187. The only other city exceeding 8,000 inhabitants is Arecibo, with a population of 8,008. The total urban population of the island contained in cities exceeding 8,000 inhabitants each is 83,195, or only 8.7 per cent of the population of the island. This is a much smaller proportion than in Cuba, where the corresponding figures are 32.3 per cent, or in the United States, where the corresponding proportion in 1890 was 29 2 per cent. There are in Porto Rico 57 cities, each having a population of 1,000 or more. The total urban population of the island, under this definition, numbers 203,792, or 21.4 per cent of the total number of inhabitants of the island. Similar figures for Cuba show 47.1 per cent of the population of that island."—*Census of Porto Rico, Bulletin No.* 1.

A. D. 1899-1900.—The question of the tariff treatment of its new Territory by the United States Government.—Writing in "The Forum," November, 1899, Mr. H. K. Carroll, who had investigated the conditions in Porto Rico as a Special Commissioner of the United States government, described the obligation which, in his view, they imposed on the latter as follows: "The only free market the Puertorican has for his products is the island market. All the rest of the world is closed to him. He cannot even buy in a free market ; everything he buys as well as everything he sells being subject to duties. This is the penalty of independence ; but Puerto Rico is not, and does not want to be, independent. She wants such commercial relations with us as Alaska, New Mexico, and Arizona have, and desires a territorial form of government. I am of the opinion that we cannot refuse these reasonable requests without doing great injustice to Puerto Rico. It must be remembered that we sought Puerto Rico; for Puerto Rico did not seek us. We wrested her from the sovereignty of Spain, without asking her if she desired to change her allegiance. We were of the opinion that she was not justly treated by Spain ; that she was governed in the interests of the mother country solely ; that she was oppressed and overtaxed and denied a proper

measure of home rule ; and that in consequence we were serving the cause of humanity in breaking the chains that bound her. This was what the Puertoricans thought also. They welcomed our troops and our control. They were glad to turn their backs on the history of the past, and begin under the glorious Republic of the North a new and more prosperous career. They are disappointed, perhaps unreasonably, that their new life has not already begun ; they are eagerly expectant. They look to the President to recommend, and to Congress to adopt, a system of government which will make the island a Territory, equal in rank and rights and privileges to existing Territories. They ought not to be disappointed without the best and strongest of reasons. Three reasons are mentioned in opposition to the granting of territorial government to Puerto Rico. First, admission as a Territory implies ultimate admission to statehood ; and statehood for islands separated as Hawaii and Puerto Rico are by from 1,200 to 2,500 miles from the United States is not to be thought of for a moment. Second, territorial organization involves the relinquishment of customs duties ; and the cane- and tobacco-growers of our West India possession would have free access to the markets of the United States, and thus come into injurious competition with our own farmers. Third, the people of Puerto Rico are not competent for the measure of self-government which the territorial system provides."

This most reasonable and just view of the duty of the American people to their new fellow citizens received strong endorsement from higher official authority in the subsequent annual report of the Secretary of War, who said : "It is plain that it is essential to the prosperity of the island that she should receive substantially the same treatment at our hands as she received from Spain while a Spanish colony, and that the markets of the United States should be opened to her as were the markets of Spain and Cuba before the transfer of allegiance. Congress has the legal right to regulate the customs duties between the United States and Porto Rico as it pleases ; but the highest considerations of justice and good faith demand that we should not disappoint the confident expectation of sharing in our prosperity with which the people of Porto Rico so gladly transferred their allegiance to the United States, and that we should treat the interests of this people as our own ; and I wish most strongly to urge that the customs duties between Porto Rico and the United States be removed."—*Message and Documents: Abridgment,* 1899–1900, v. 2, p. 757.

And, finally, the President of the United States, in his Message to Congress, December 5, 1899, gave his high authority to the declaration that this duty of his government to Porto Rico was "plain" : "It must be borne in mind," he said, "that since the cession Porto Rico has been denied the principal markets she had long enjoyed and our tariffs have been continued against her products as when she was under Spanish sovereignty. The markets of Spain are closed to her products except upon terms to which the commerce of all nations is subjected. The island of Cuba, which used to buy her cattle and tobacco without customs duties, now imposes the same duties upon these products as from any other country entering her ports. She has therefore lost her free intercourse with Spain and Cuba, without any compensating benefits in this market. Her coffee was little known and not in use by our people, and therefore there was no demand here for this, one of her chief products. The markets of the United States should be opened up to her products. Our plain duty is to abolish all customs tariffs between the United States and Porto Rico and give her products free access to our markets."—*Message and Documents: Abridgment, v. 1, p. 53.*

Notwithstanding all which high official acknowledgments and declarations of obligation and duty, on the part of the Republic of the United States to the people of the island which it had wrested from Spain, certain interests in the former that objected to competition from the latter were able to secure legislation which deferred the performance of the "plain duty" required. An Act of Congress which the President approved on the 12th of April, 1900, "temporarily to provide revenues and a civil government for Porto Rico and for other purposes," enacted as follows:

"SEC. 3. That on and after the passage of this Act all merchandise coming into the United States from Porto Rico and coming into Porto Rico from the United States shall be entered at the several ports of entry upon payment of fifteen per centum of the duties which are required to be levied, collected, and paid upon like articles of merchandise imported from foreign countries; and in addition thereto upon articles of merchandise of Porto Rican manufacture coming into the United States and withdrawn for consumption or sale upon payment of a tax equal to the internal-revenue tax imposed in the United States upon the like articles of merchandise of domestic manufacture; such tax to be paid by internal-revenue stamp or stamps to be purchased and provided by the Commissioner of Internal Revenue and to be procured from the collector of internal revenue at or most convenient to the port of entry of said merchandise in the United States, and to be affixed under such regulations as the Commissioner of Internal Revenue, with the approval of the Secretary of the Treasury, shall prescribe; and on all articles of merchandise of United States manufacture coming into Porto Rico in addition to the duty above provided upon payment of a tax equal in rate and amount to the internal-revenue tax imposed in Porto Rico upon the like articles of Porto Rican manufacture: Provided, That on and after the date when this Act shall take effect, all merchandise and articles, except coffee, not dutiable under the tariff laws of the United States, and all merchandise and articles entered in Porto Rico free of duty under orders heretofore made by the Secretary of War, shall be admitted into the several ports thereof, when imported from the United States, free of duty, all laws or parts of laws to the contrary notwithstanding; and whenever the legislative assembly of Porto Rico shall have enacted and put into operation a system of local taxation to meet the necessities of the government of Porto Rico, by this Act established, and shall by resolution duly passed so notify the President, he shall make proclamation thereof, and thereupon all tariff duties on merchandise and articles going into Porto Rico from the United States or coming into the United States from Porto Rico shall cease, and from and after

such date all such merchandise and articles shall be entered at the several ports of entry free of duty; and in no event shall any duties be collected after the first day of March, nineteen hundred and two, on merchandise and articles going into Porto Rico from the United States or coming into the United States from Porto Rico.

"SEC. 4. That the duties and taxes collected in Porto Rico in pursuance of this Act, less the cost of collecting the same, and the gross amount of all collections of duties and taxes in the United States upon articles of merchandise coming from Porto Rico, shall not be covered into the general fund of the Treasury, but shall be held as a separate fund, and shall be placed at the disposal of the President to be used for the government and benefit of Porto Rico until the government of Porto Rico herein provided for shall have been organized, when all moneys theretofore collected under the provisions hereof, then unexpended, shall be transferred to the local treasury of Porto Rico, and the Secretary of the Treasury shall designate the several ports and sub-ports of entry in Porto Rico, and shall make such rules and regulations and appoint such agents as may be necessary to collect the duties and taxes authorized to be levied, collected, and paid in Porto Rico by the provisions of this Act, and he shall fix the compensation and provide for the payment thereof of all such officers, agents, and assistants as he may find it necessary to employ to carry out the provisions hereof: Provided, however, That as soon as a civil government for Porto Rico shall have been organized in accordance with the provisions of this Act and notice thereof shall have been given to the President he shall make proclamation thereof, and thereafter all collections of duties and taxes in Porto Rico under the provisions of this Act shall be paid into the treasury of Porto Rico, to be expended as required by law for the government and benefit thereof instead of being paid into the Treasury of the United States."

A. D. 1900 (April).—Act to provide temporarily for the civil government of the Island. —The fundamental provisions of the act of the Congress of the United States to provide temporarily for the civil government of Porto Rico, which the President approved April 12, 1900, are the following:

"SEC. 6. That the capital of Porto Rico shall be at the city of San Juan and the seat of government shall be maintained there.

"SEC. 7. That all inhabitants continuing to reside therein who were Spanish subjects on the eleventh day of April, eighteen hundred and ninety-nine, and then resided in Porto Rico, and their children born subsequent thereto, shall be deemed and held to be citizens of Porto Rico, and as such entitled to the protection of the United States, except such as shall have elected to preserve their allegiance to the Crown of Spain on or before the eleventh day of April, nineteen hundred, in accordance with the provisions of the treaty of peace between the United States and Spain entered into on the eleventh day of April, eighteen hundred and ninety-nine; and they, together with such citizens of the United States as may reside in Porto Rico, shall constitute a body politic under the name of The People of Porto Rico, with governmental powers as hereinafter conferred, and with power to sue and be sued as such.

"SEC. 8. That the laws and ordinances of Porto Rico now in force shall continue in full force and effect, except as altered, amended, or modified hereinafter, or as altered or modified by military orders and decrees in force when this Act shall take effect, and so far as the same are not inconsistent or in conflict with the statutory laws of the United States not locally inapplicable, or the provisions hereof, until altered, amended, or repealed by the legislative authority hereinafter provided for Porto Rico or by Act of Congress of the United States : Provided, That so much of the law which was in force at the time of cession, April eleventh, eighteen hundred and ninety-nine, forbidding the marriage of priests, ministers, or followers of any faith because of vows they may have taken, being paragraph four, article eighty-three, chapter three, civil code, and which was continued by the order of the secretary of justice of Porto Rico, dated March seventeenth, eighteen hundred and ninety-nine, and promulgated by Major-General Guy V. Henry, United States Volunteers, is hereby repealed and annulled, and all persons lawfully married in Porto Rico shall have all the rights and remedies conferred by law upon parties to either civil or religious marriages : And provided further, That paragraph one, article one hundred and five, section four, divorce, civil code, and paragraph two, section nineteen, of the order of the minister of justice of Porto Rico, dated March seventeenth, eighteen hundred and ninety-nine, and promulgated by Major-General Guy V. Henry, United States Volunteers, be, and the same hereby are, so amended as to read : ' Adultery on the part of either the husband or the wife.' . . .

"SEC. 14. That the statutory laws of the United States not locally inapplicable, except as hereinbefore or hereinafter otherwise provided, shall have the same force and effect in Porto Rico as in the United States, except the internal-revenue laws, which, in view of the provisions of section three, shall not have force and effect in Porto Rico.

"SEC. 15. That the legislative authority hereinafter provided shall have power by due enactment to amend, alter, modify, or repeal any law or ordinance, civil or criminal, continued in force by this Act, as it may from time to time see fit.

"SEC. 16. That all judicial process shall run in the name of ' United States of America, ss : the President of the United States,' and all criminal or penal prosecutions in the local courts shall be conducted in the name and by the authority of ' The People of Porto Rico' ' ; and all officials authorized by this Act shall before entering upon the duties of their respective offices take an oath to support the Constitution of the United States and the laws of Porto Rico.

"SEC. 17. That the official title of the chief executive officer shall be ' The Governor of Porto Rico.' He shall be appointed by the President, by and with the advice and consent of the Senate ; he shall hold his office for a term of four years and until his successor is chosen and qualified unless sooner removed by the President ; he shall reside in Porto Rico during his official incumbency, and shall maintain his office at the seat of government ; he may grant pardons and reprieves, and remit fines and forfeitures for offenses against the laws of Porto Rico, and respites for offenses against the laws of the United States, until the decision of the President can be ascertained ; he shall commission all officers that he may be authorized to appoint, and may veto any legislation enacted, as hereinafter provided ; he shall be the commander in chief of the militia, and shall at all times faithfully execute the laws, and he shall in that behalf have all the powers of governors of the Territories of the United States that are not locally inapplicable ; and he shall annually, and at such other times as he may be required, make official report of the transactions of the government in Porto Rico, through the Secretary of State, to the President of the United States : Provided, That the President may, in his discretion, delegate and assign to him such executive duties and functions as may in pursuance with law be so delegated and assigned.

" SEC. 18. That there shall be appointed by the President, by and with the advice and consent of the Senate, for the period of four years, unless sooner removed by the President, a secretary, an attorney-general, a treasurer, an auditor, a commissioner of the interior, and a commissioner of education, each of whom shall reside in Porto Rico during his official incumbency and have the powers and duties hereinafter provided for them, respectively, and who, together with five other persons of good repute, to be also appointed by the President for a like term of four years, by and with the advice and consent of the Senate, shall constitute an executive council, at least five of whom shall be native inhabitants of Porto Rico, and, in addition to the legislative duties hereinafter imposed upon them as a body, shall exercise such powers and perform such duties as are hereinafter provided for them, respectively, and who shall have power to employ all necessary deputies and assistants for the proper discharge of their duties as such officials and as such executive council. . . .

" SEC. 27. That all local legislative powers hereby granted shall be vested in a legislative assembly which shall consist of two houses ; one the executive council, as hereinbefore constituted, and the other a house of delegates, to consist of thirty-five members elected biennially by the qualified voters as hereinafter provided ; and the two houses thus constituted shall be designated ' The legislative assembly of Porto Rico.'

"SEC. 28. That for the purposes of such elections Porto Rico shall be divided by the executive council into seven districts, composed of contiguous territory and as nearly equal as may be in population, and each district shall be entitled to five members of the house of delegates.

"SEC. 29. That the first election for delegates shall be held on such date and under such regulations as to ballots and voting as the executive council may prescribe. . . . At such elections all citizens of Porto Rico shall be allowed to vote who have been bona fide residents for one year and who possess the other qualifications of voters under the laws and military orders in force on the first day of March, 1900, subject to such modifications and additional qualifications and such regulations and restrictions as to registration as may be prescribed by the executive council. . . .

" SEC. 32. That the legislative authority herein provided shall extend to all matters of a legislative character not locally inapplicable, including power to create, consolidate, and reorganize the municipalities, so far as may be necessary, and to provide and repeal laws and ordinances therefor; and also the power to alter, amend, modify, and repeal any and all laws and ordinances of every character now in force in Porto Rico, or any municipality or district thereof, not inconsistent with the provisions hereof : Provided, however, That all grants of franchises, rights, and privileges or concessions of a public or quasipublic nature shall be made by the executive council, with the approval of the governor, and all franchises granted in Porto Rico shall be reported to Congress, which hereby reserves the power to annul or modify the same.

"SEC. 33. That the judicial power shall be vested in the courts and tribunals of Porto Rico as already established and now in operation, including municipal courts. . . .

"SEC. 34. That Porto Rico shall constitute a judicial district to be called 'the district of Porto Rico.' The President, by and with the advice and consent of the Senate, shall appoint a district judge, a district attorney, and a marshal for said district, each for a term of four years, unless sooner removed by the President. The district court for said district shall be called the district court of the United States for Porto Rico.

"SEC. 35. That writs of error and appeals from the final decisions of the supreme court of Porto Rico and the district court of the United States shall be allowed and may be taken to the Supreme Court of the United States in the same manner and under the same regulations and in the same cases as from the supreme courts of the Territories of the United States. . . .

"SEC. 39. That the qualified voters of Porto Rico shall, on the first Tuesday after the first Monday of November, anno Domini nineteen hundred, and every two years thereafter, choose a resident commissioner to the United States, who shall be entitled to official recognition as such by all Departments, upon presentation to the Department of State of a certificate of election of the governor of Porto Rico, and who shall be entitled to a salary, payable monthly by the United States, at the rate of five thousand dollars per annum : Provided, That no person shall be eligible to such election who is not a bona fide citizen of Porto Rico, who is not thirty years of age, and who does not read and write the English language.

"SEC. 40. That a commission, to consist of three members, at least one of whom shall be a native citizen of Porto Rico, shall be appointed by the President, by and with the advice and consent of the Senate, to compile and revise the laws of Porto Rico; also the various codes of procedure and systems of municipal government now in force, and to frame and report such legislation as may be necessary to make a simple, harmonious, and economical government, establish justice and secure its prompt and efficient administration, inaugurate a general system of education and public instruction, provide buildings and funds therefor, equalize and simplify taxation and all the methods of raising revenue, and make all other provisions that may be necessary to secure and extend the benefits of a republican form of government to all the inhabitants of Porto Rico."

A. D. 1900 (May).—Organization of civil government.—Appointment of Governor Allen.—Under the Act to establish civil government in Porto Rico, Hon. Charles H. Allen, formerly a representative in Congress from Massachusetts, and lately Assistant-Secretary of the

6–27

Navy, was appointed to the governorship of the island. Mr. J. H. Hollander, of Maryland, was appointed Treasurer, and Mr. John R. Garrison, of the District of Columbia, Auditor. Governor Allen was inducted into office with considerable ceremony, at San Juan, on the 1st of May.

A. D. 1900 (August—October).—First steps in the creation of a public school system.—"The report of M. G. Brumbaugh, commissioner of education, on education in Porto Rico, dated October 15, 1900, shows what has been accomplished in the short time that elapsed after the commissioner entered upon his duties on August 4, 1900. . . . The people want schools . . . and the pupils will attend them. In 1899, 616 schools were opened in Porto Rico. In 1900 the department will maintain at least 800 schools, an increase of 30 per cent, which will provide for nearly 9,000 additional pupils.

"In 1899 there were 67 Americans in the teaching force of the island. Since October 1, 1900, the number has increased to 100. The commissioner criticises one class of teachers who are 'seekers after novelty and new experiences, who imposed upon the administration and the children, and who used the salary and position of teacher solely to see a new country for a year and then return. . . . The people of Porto Rico have patiently borne with these adventurers, and quietly longed for their departure.' This class of teachers is now gone and the newly selected American teachers have some knowledge of Spanish and are graduates of universities, colleges, and normal schools in the States, and are for the most part young men and women of ability and discretion. The salaries of American teachers were fixed by law at $40 per month for nine months in cities of less than 5,000 population. In cities of larger population the salary was $50 per month for nine months and both are inadequate, although at the time the salaries were fixed the War Department provided free transportation from and to the United States. This transportation may now be withdrawn at any time, and the small inducement held out by the meager salary offered to teachers is not calculated to invite the best class of them to the island.

"The new normal and industrial school at Fajardo, which was to have been established by the joint efforts of the local municipality and the American Government, was only so far advanced that the land had been purchased by the end of September, 1900. The normal department was opened October 1, in a rented building, while the industrial department cannot be opened until suitable quarters are provided. The commissioner recommends that the United States make this place the site of an agricultural experiment station for which it is pre-eminently fitted. On account of the industries of the country—coffee, sugar, tobacco, and fruit—agriculture could be well studied here, and free boarding, lodging, and tuition would be given the students, who would be for the most part poor boys and girls.

"As to the school accommodation, the commissioner states that there are no public school buildings in Porto Rico. The schools are conducted in rented houses or rooms which are often unfit for the purpose, and the hygienic conditions are bad. There is a wide field, or rather a demand, for improvement in this direction, as well as in the school equipment and material.

In 1899, $33,000 was expended for school-books, and in 1900, $20,000 will be expended for books and supplies, which shall be free. In the United States ' free books' means usually their purchase by local boards and free use by the pupils. In Porto Rico the books and supplies will be free to the pupils without expense to the local boards. A pedagogical museum and library has been established for the benefit of teachers and others. About 300 volumes have been contributed to the library from friends in the States, and the Department will make the number up to 500 by purchase. A library of 5,000 volumes of standard Spanish and American literature was found in a building in San Juan, which has been installed in suitable rooms as a public library.

"Many of the leading institutions of the United States have responded cordially to the application of the Department of Education on behalf of young Porto Ricans who wish to prosecute their studies in colleges and universities. Some have offered free tuition, some have added free lodging, while others have offered even free living to all such students as wish to avail themselves of their instruction. Many young Porto Ricans have availed themselves of these generous offers.

"There are now 800 schools in Porto Rico, and 38,000 pupils attending them, while there are 300,000 children of school age for whom there are no accommodations. But the commissioner expresses the hope that gradually the great illiteracy in Porto Rico will be reduced, and the people prepared for the duties of citizenship in a democracy by means of the schools that shall be established. . . . The total expenditure for education in Porto Rico from the 1st of May to the end of September was $91,057.32."—*United States, Secretary of the Interior, Annual Report, Nov. 28, 1900, p. 116.*

A. D. 1900 (November—December).—The first election under U. S. law.—Meeting of the Legislative Assembly.—The first election in the Island under the provisions of the Act recited above occurred on the 6th of November simultaneously with the elections in the United States. It seems to have been almost entirely a one-sided vote. "About two weeks before election day," says a despatch from San Juan, November 7, "the Federal Party, which carried the island at the election of less than a year ago by a majority of 6,500 votes, suddenly withdrew from the electoral contest. The Federal leaders sent instruction to their followers not to appear at the polls, but the Federal Election Judges were instructed to appear and watch the proceedings until the elections were concluded in order to gather evidence of any unfairness in the registration and any irregularity in the voting. The Federal Party intends to institute court proceedings after the election in the hope of nullifying it, claiming that gross irregularities in the registration and voting will be shown, and alleging that the districting was not done according to law." Only about 200 Federals voted, it is stated, while some 60,000 votes were cast for the candidates of the Republicans. Governor Allen cabled the following announcement of the election to President McKinley : "I am gratified and delighted. The outcome in Porto Rico is a guarantee of the island's future. To bring people who had long been under different rules and conditions to their first general election, to have

the election pass off as quietly and orderly as in any State of the North conducted by the people without let or hindrance, and without a soldier or armed force of any sort, and to have nearly 60,000 men march to the polls to deposit their first ballot for self-government in such a manner, are good reasons for congratulation, not only to the people of the island, but to the painstaking members of the Administration, who had worked diligently and patiently to this end. This overwhelming Republican victory also means legislation for the good of the island in line with the American Administration. It means stable government and the protection of property interests, with which prospective investors in Porto Rico are deeply concerned. It means education, public works, and all the beneficent works which follow legislation wisely and conscientiously undertaken. It is an emphatic declaration of unqualified loyalty to the United States."

The newly elected Legislative Assembly met and the House of Delegates was organized Dec. 3. A correspondent of the "New York Tribune," writing a week later, said : "Already nineteen bills have been introduced. To introduce nineteen bills in six days after organizing, as well as forming the regular committees, is not bad work when it is considered that not one of the members had the slightest idea of parliamentary procedure. During the session one of the members may be seen making frequent trips to the Executive Mansion, where he confers with Secretary Hunt in regard to some doubtful point. It is said by some that in a short time the lower house will be controlled entirely by the portfolio members of the Council. It is known that the five Porto Rican members of the Council, when considering the question of franchises, etc., often vote contrary to their own ideas in order that the Council may continue harmonious. But it is not likely that the heads of departments will be able to control the thirty-five members of the House. The House, although regularly elected, is not representative of the island ; the Federals refraining from voting kept over half the natives from the polls. The Federal party, it is asserted, is made up of the richest and best element of Porto Rico. The Republicans, though in power, do not feel that they are able to run things alone, so the majority is willing to be dictated to by the Council. Nevertheless there is a certain element in the House which will not be dictated to. So soon as any really important bill comes up for debate it is predicted that the House will divide against itself. And a little later, when the House passes some pet bill and the Council rejects it, the House will probably resign in a body. It is a natural trait of the people."

After another fortnight had passed, the same correspondent wrote very discouragingly of the disposition shown by a majority of the members of the House of Delegates, and their conduct of business, and stated : "The popular opinion among the Americans, even among some of the higher officials, is that if the House continues as it is Congress will abolish it altogether, and govern the island through a Governor and Cabinet. Such irregular procedure has been followed that it is a question here whether any business has been legally done."

A. D. 1901 (January).—Close of the first session of the Legislative Assembly.—The first session of the first Legislative Assembly of the island came to a close on the 31st of January, 1901, and the following remarks on its work were made in a newspaper despatch of that date from San Juan : " Over one hundred bills have been introduced in the House of Delegates, and dozens have been passed by both houses, and are awaiting the Governor's approval. . . . Committees have a hard day's work if they get together and agree to pass the bills on hand before midnight to-night. Ever since the House of Delegates resumed business after the new year, eight or nine members have been continually absent. There are only thirty-five members altogether, and the island is small, yet twenty-six has been the average attendance. A full attendance for even one day is not recorded. It was predicted that a number of the members would resign; they did not. They simply remained away, like truant schoolboys. A bill has been passed providing for the education of certain young Porto Rican men and women in the United States, about two hundred of them having petitioned the House of Delegates to be sent north at the island's expense. It is not known on what ground these petitions have been made. The island expends about $400,000 yearly on education, and excellent educational facilities are offered. But the people, in a way, seem to discredit the value of the opportunities at hand."

A. D. 1901 (April).—Distress of the **workingmen** of the Island.—Their appeal to the President of the United States.—The following petition, signed by 6,000 of the workingmen of Porto Rico, was brought to the United States by a delegate from the Federation of Labor in Porto Rico and presented to President McKinley on the 15th of April : " The undersigned, workers of Porto Rico, without distinction of color, political or religious creed, have the honor to bring to your attention the following facts : Misery, with all its horrible consequences, is spreading in our homes with wonderful rapidity. It has already reached such an extreme that many workers are starving to death while others, that have not the courage to see their mothers, wives, sisters and children perish of hunger, commit suicide by drowning themselves in the rivers or hanging themselves from branches of trees. All this, honorable sir, is due to the scarcity of work, which keeps us in enforced idleness, the mother of our misery. Our beautiful estates are idle; our lands are not being cultivated; our shops remain closed ; and our Chambers do absolutely nothing to prevent our misery on this once so rich an island. The Government and municipality do not undertake any public works to keep us out of idleness. The emigration of workers, unknown in this island before, increases day by day, in proportion as misery increases. Under these trying conditions we are no longer a happy and contented people. We therefore, beg of you, honorable sir, to interest yourself in our cause, leading us, as the father of our country, in the path that will bring us work, and with it the means of subsistence. We want work; nothing but work. We want to earn the means of subsistence by the sweat of our brows; and nobody better than our Chief Magistrate can help us by lending ear to our appeals."

PORTUGAL : A. D. 1891-1900.—Delagoa Bay Arbitration. See (in this vol.) DELAGOA BAY ARBITRATION.

A. D. 1898.—Alleged Treaty with Great Britain.—There is said to be knowledge in diplomatic circles of a treaty between Great Britain and Portugal, concluded in 1898, which has never been made public, but which is understood to engage the former to assist the latter financially and to protect the kingdom as against dangers both external and internal. In return it is believed that England received the right to embark and disembark troops, stores and ammunitions at any point on Portuguese territory in Africa, to keep them there, or to convey them across Portuguese territory to any point she might see fit, irrespective as to whether she was at war with any third Power. Circumstances have given some support to this rumor, but it has no positive confirmation.

A. D. 1899.—Reciprocity Treaty with the United States. See (in this vol.) UNITED STATES OF AM. : A. D. 1899-1901.

A. D. 1899 (May—July).—Representation in the Peace Conference at The Hague. See (in this vol.) PEACE CONFERENCE.

PORTUGUESE EAST AFRICA: A. D. 1895-1896.—War with Gungunhana. See (in this vol.) AFRICA : A. D. 1895–1896 (PORTUGUESE EAST AFRICA).

POSTAGE, British Imperial Penny. See (in this vol.) ENGLAND : A. D. 1898 (DECEMBER).

POWERS, Concert of the. See (in this vol.) CONCERT OF EUROPE.

POWERS, The four great. See (in this vol.) NINETEENTH CENTURY : EXPANSION.

PRATT, Consul: Interviews with Aguinaldo at Singapore. See (in this vol.) UNITED STATES OF AM. : A. D. 1898 (APRIL—MAY: PHILIPPINES).

" PREDOMINANT MEMBER," Remarks of Lord Rosebery on the. See (in this vol.) ENGLAND : A. D. 1894-1895.

PREHISTORIC DISCOVERIES. See (in this vol.) ARCHÆOLOGICAL RESEARCH.

PREMPEH, Overthrow of King. See (in this vol.) ASHANTI.

PRESBYTERIAN CHURCHES: Union in Scotland. See (in this vol.) SCOTLAND : A. D. 1900.

PRESS, The : Relaxation of restrictions in Poland. See (in this vol.) RUSSIA : A. D. 1897.

Prosecutions in Germany. See (in this vol.) GERMANY : A. D. 1900 (OCTOBER 9).

PRETORIA: A. D. 1894.—Demonstration of British residents. See (in this vol.) SOUTH AFRICA (THE TRANSVAAL) : A. D. 1894.

A. D. 1900.—Taken by the British forces. See (in this vol.) SOUTH AFRICA (THE FIELD OF WAR): A. D. 1900 (MAY—JUNE).

PRIMARY ELECTION LAW. See (in this vol.) NEW YORK STATE : A. D. 1898.

PRINCE EDWARD'S ISLAND. See (in this vol.) CANADA.

PRINCETON UNIVERSITY: Celebration of 150th anniversary.—Assumption of

new name. See (in this vol.) EDUCATION (UNITED STATES): A. D. 1896.

PRINSLOO, Commandant: Surrender. See (in this vol.) SOUTH AFRICA (THE FIELD OF WAR): A. D. 1900 (JUNE—DECEMBER).

PROCTOR, Senator Redfield: Account of the condition of the Cuban Reconcentrados. See (in this vol.) CUBA: A. D. 1897-1898 (DECEMBER—MARCH).

PROGRESSISTS, or PROGRESSIVES. See (in this vol.) AUSTRIA-HUNGARY: A. D. 1897; JAPAN: A. D. 1890-1898, and after; SOUTH AFRICA (CAPE COLONY): A. D. 1898, and 1898 (MARCH—OCTOBER).

PROHIBITION PARTY, The. See (in this vol.) UNITED STATES OF AM. : A. D. 1896 (JUNE—NOVEMBER); and 1900 (MAY—NOVEMBER).

PROHIBITION PLEBISCITE, Canadian. See (in this vol.) CANADA: A. D. 1898 (SEPTEMBER).

PROTECTIVE TARIFFS. See (in this vol.) TARIFF LEGISLATION.

PROTOCOL, for suspension of **Spanish**-American War. See (in this vol.) UNITED STATES OF AM. : A. D. 1898 (JULY—DECEMBER).

PRUSSIA: Census, **1895.** See (in this vol.) GERMANY: A. D. 1895 (JUNE—DECEMBER).

A. D. **1899-1901.**—Canal projects. See (in this vol.) GERMANY : A. D. 1899 (AUGUST); and 1901 (JANUARY).

A. D. **1901.**—Bicentenary celebration.—The bicentenary of the coronation of the first King of Prussia was celebrated with much ceremony and festivity on the 18th of January, 1901.

PULLMAN.—A decision of the Supreme Court of Illinois, rendered early in 1899, deprives the Pullman Car Company of the legal right to own and conduct the affairs of the town of Pullman, Ill. The effect is understood to be that the town will be incorporated with Chicago.

PUNJAB, Formation of a **new** province from districts of the. See (in this vol.) INDIA : A. D. 1901 (FEBRUARY).

PUPIN, Dr. Michael I.: Improvement in long-distance telephony. See (in this vol.) SCIENCE, RECENT : ELECTRICAL.

Q.

QUEBEC, Province. See (in this vol.) CANADA.

QUEENS COUNTY: Incorporation in Greater **New** York. See (in this vol.) NEW YORK CITY: A. D. 1896-1897.

QUEENSLAND. See (in this vol.) AUSTRALIA ; and CONSTITUTION OF AUSTRALIA.

QUINCY, Josiah: Progressive measures as Mayor of Boston. See (in this vol.) BOSTON : A. D. 1895-1899.

R.

RACES, European, The expansion of. See (in this vol.) NINETEENTH CENTURY : EXPANSION.

RAILWAY, The Anatolian.—Extension to the Persian Gulf. See (in this vol.) TURKEY : A. D. 1899 (NOVEMBER).

RAILWAY, Cape to Cairo.—"A line now [1899] runs northward from Cape Town to Bulawayo, in Rhodesia, a distance of 1,360 miles, and is being pushed still farther northward. From Bulawayo to Lake Tanganyika is about 1,000 miles; and this Mr. Rhodes hopes to reach by 1905. Lake Tanganyika is 410 miles long; and it is likely that its waters will be utilized for a time at least for transferring northwardly the freights and passengers reaching its southern end. Meantime the railroad from Cairo is being pushed southwardly to meet the line which is coming from the Cape northwardly. It has already been constructed to Atbara, where American contractors have just finished the steel bridge in a time which British bridge-builders considered impossible; and the line is being pushed forward to Khartoum from that point. Khartoum is 1,300 miles from Cairo; so that when work on the section from Atbara to Khartoum is completed, as it will be within a few months, the two gaps to be filled in will be from Khartoum to the north end of Lake Tanganyika, a distance of 1,700 miles, and the 950 miles from the south end of Lake Tanganyika to Bulawayo; i. e., 2,700 miles in all. Thus, of the necessary

land length, assuming that at least the 410 miles length of Lake Tanganyika will be at first utilized, about one-half will be finished on the completion of the section from Atbara to Khartoum, within the next few months. The remaining 2,700 miles will, it is estimated, cost $60,000,000; and Mr. Rhodes confidently predicts its completion before the year 1910."—O. P. Austin, *Africa: Present and Future (Forum, Dec.,* 1899).—See, also (in this vol.), AFRICA: A. D. 1899.

Of course, the plans and calculations of Mr. Cecil Rhodes have been seriously interfered with by the South African War. He may have anticipated the war, but not the length nor the effects of it.

RAILWAY, Haifa to Damascus and **Bag**-dad. See (in this vol.) JEWS : A. D. 1899.

RAILWAY, The Intercontinental, or "Three Americas."—"One of the important results of the International American Conference, held in Washington in 1889-90, was its recommendation that an International Commission be created to ascertain the feasibility, the cost, and the available location for a railroad connecting the countries of South and Central America with Mexico and the United States. This recommendation was cordially indorsed by Secretary Blaine in submitting the report to President Harrison, who transmitted it to Congress, asking that an appropriation be made to commence the surveys. In the same act which authorized the establishment of the Bureau of the American

420

Republics—the Diplomatic and Consular Appropriation Act of July 14, 1890—the Intercontinental Railway Commission was created. In this act it was provided that three Commissioners on the part of the United States should be appointed by the President, with the advice and consent of the Senate, who were to act with representatives of the other American Republics to devise plans for carrying out the objects recommended by the International American Conference. The Commission organized December 4, 1890, and at once set about the equipping of the surveying parties to make the necessary topographical examination. The United States representatives on the Commission were practical railroad men—A. J. Cassatt, Henry G. Davis, and R. C. Kerens, and eleven other Republics were represented on the Commission. The report just issued [March, 1899] is in four volumes, with four sets of maps and profiles, exhibiting the surveys and examination of the country that were made from Mexico through Central America to Colombia, Ecuador, and Peru, in South America. In addition to the personal observations in South America, the officers making the reports also gathered from the best obtainable sources geographical, railroad, and other information relating to Bolivia, Argentina, Brazil, Paraguay, Uruguay, Chile, and Venezuela. The report gives the proposed distances as follows: Central American division, from Ayutla, Guatemala, on the Mexican border, to Rio Golfito, Colombia, 1,043 miles; from Rio Golfito to Buenos Aires, Argentina, 5,446.76 miles; through the United States from New York to Laredo, Tex., 2,094 miles; and from that point, through Mexico to Ayutla, Guatemala, 1,644.3 miles; making a total of 10,228.06 miles, including the lines already in operation in the different countries. The extent of railway to be constructed is a little over one-half the total, being 5,456.13 miles. An estimate is given of the cost for grading, masonry, and bridges of that portion of the line which must be constructed to complete the connections, which amounts to $174,290,271.84."—*Bureau of American Republics, Bulletin, March,* 1899.

As now surveyed, from New York City to Buenos Ayres, it will be 10,221 miles long, and to finish and equip it will cost at least $200,000,-000. This length and cost will also be increased when the line is extended through Patagonia to the southern limits of South America. The complete surveys . . . prove that a practicable route can be found and the road built within a reasonable time. The route of this road can be traced on the map, while the following table shows the distances, the miles built, and the gaps to be filled:

	Built.	Proposed.	Total.
United States	2,094	....	2,094
Mexico	1,183	461	1,644
Total North America	3,277	461	3,738
Guatemala	43	126	169
San Salvador	64	166	230
Honduras	....	71	71
Nicaragua	103	106	209
Costa Rica	....	360	360
Total Central America	210	829	1,039

	Built.	Proposed.	Total.
Colombia	....	1,354	1,354
Ecuador	....	658	658
Peru	151	1,633	1,784
Bolivia	195	392	587
Argentina	936	125	1,061
Total South America	1,282	4,769	5,444
Grand total	4,769	5,452	10,221

" The demands of trade may compel early construction of this railroad. It is doubtful if a remunerative commerce can be built up between North and South America by ship. The conformation of the eastern coast of South America compels a long detour to the east, and brings a ship almost as near to the ports of Europe as to the ports of the United States. The exports of South America, being mainly agricultural, will find a readier sale in Europe than in this country, and when they are exchanged for the cheap manufactured goods of that continent the conditions for trade are supplied. If, for these reasons, this country can not build up a commerce with South America by water, a quicker means of transit must be had, such as the Pan-American Railway would provide. The obstacles to be overcome are great. They surpass the difficulties in the way of the Siberian or the 'Cape to Cairo' road, but the results will be correspondingly greater.

" South America has greater undeveloped resources than any other continent. Its agricultural possibilities are boundless. It has the greatest rivers in the world; its soil can produce any crop grown on the earth, and its mines of gold, silver, and coal have been scarcely touched. A railroad which would traverse the coffee lands of the Central American States, pass through the mines of Peru, and penetrate the rich pampas of Brazil and Argentina, must have great possibilities before it. The products of the three great valleys of the Orinoco, the Amazon, and the Paraguay rivers would find a market by means of it, and the riches of the mines of the Incas be shown to surpass those of California and South Africa."—*Bureau of American Republics, Bulletin, Dec.,* 1899.

RAILWAY, The Tehuantepec. See (in this vol.) MEXICO : A. D. 1898–1900.

RAILWAY, The Three Americas. See, above, RAILWAY, INTERCONTINENTAL.

RAILWAY, Trans-Siberian. See (in this vol.) RUSSIA IN ASIA: A. D. 1891–1900.

RAILWAY, The Uganda, or Mombasa-Victoria. See (in this vol.) UGANDA RAILWAY.

RAILWAYS : in Africa. See (in this vol.) AFRICA: A. D. 1899.

American Inter-State.—Arbitration of industrial disputes. See (in this vol.) UNITED STATES OF AM. : A. D. 1898 (JUNE).

Concessions in China. See (in this vol.) CHINA: A. D. 1895; 1897 (MAY—JUNE); 1897 (NOVEMBER); 1898 (FEBRUARY—DECEMBER); 1898 (MARCH); 1898 (APRIL—AUGUST); 1898 (MAY) ; 1899 (MARCH—APRIL).

Russian projects in Persia. See (in this vol.) RUSSIA IN ASIA : A. D. 1900.

State purchase in Switzerland. See (in this vol.) SWITZERLAND: A. D. 1894-1898.

RAINES LAW, The. See (in this vol.) NEW YORK STATE: A. D. 1896-1897.

RAMAPO WATER CONTRACT, The. See (in this vol.) NEW YORK CITY: A. D. 1899-1900.

RANAVALOMANJAKA, Queen. See (in this vol.) MADAGASCAR.

RAND, Gold fields of the. See (in this vol.) SOUTH AFRICA (THE TRANSVAAL): A. D. 1885-1890.

RECIPROCITY: Treaties under the Dingley Tariff Act. See (in this vol.) UNITED STATES OF AM.: A. D. 1899-1901.

RECONCENTRADOS. (See in this vol.) CUBA: A. D. 1896-1897; and 1897-1898 (DECEMBER—MARCH).

RED CROSS SOCIETY, The: Relief work in Armenia and Cuba. See (in this vol.) TURKEY: A. D. 1896 (JANUARY—MARCH); and CUBA: A. D. 1896-1897.

REFERENDUM, The: In Minnesota. See (in this vol.) MINNESOTA: A. D. 1896.
Introduction in South Dakota. See (in this vol.) SOUTH DAKOTA: A. D. 1898.
Its exercise in Switzerland. See (in this vol.) SWITZERLAND: A. D. 1894-1898.

REID CONTRACT, The. See (in this vol.) NEWFOUNDLAND: A. D. 1897-1900; and 1899-1901.

REITFONTEIN, Battle of. See (in this vol.) SOUTH AFRICA (THE FIELD OF WAR): A. D. 1899 (OCTOBER—DECEMBER).

RELIGIOUS ORDERS, Bill to regulate, in France. See (in this vol.) FRANCE: A. D. 1901 (JANUARY).

REPRESENTATIVES: Reapportionment in the Congress of the United States. See (in this vol.) UNITED STATES OF AM.: A. D. 1901 (JANUARY).

REPUBLICAN PARTY, The, in the U. S. Presidential elections, 1896 and 1900. See (in this vol.) UNITED STATES OF AM.: A. D. 1896 (JUNE—NOVEMBER); and 1900 (MAY—NOVEMBER).

RESERVOIRS, Nile. See (in this vol.) EGYPT: A. D. 1898-1901.

RHINE-ELBE CANAL PROJECT, The. See (in this vol.) GERMANY: A. D. 1899 (AUGUST); and 1901 (JANUARY).

RHODE ISLAND: A. D. 1900.—Newport no longer a capital city.—At the election in November, 1900, a constitutional amendment was adopted which makes Providence alone the capital city of Rhode Island. Newport had been one of the capitals since the colonies of Rhode Island and Providence Plantations were united.

RHODES, Cecil John: Founder of the British South Africa Company. See (in this vol.) SOUTH AFRICA (THE TRANSVAAL): A. D. 1884-1894.
Master spirit of the British South Africa Company.—His name given to its dominions.

See (in this vol.) SOUTH AFRICA (BRITISH SOUTH AFRICA COMPANY): A. D. 1894-1895.
Participation in Uitlander revolutionary conspiracy at Johannesburg, leading to Jameson Raid.—Resignation of Cape Colony premiership. See (in this vol.) SOUTH AFRICA (THE TRANSVAAL): A. D. 1895-1896.
Dealing with Matabele revolt. See (in this vol.) SOUTH AFRICA (RHODESIA): A. D. 1896 (MARCH—SEPTEMBER).
Resignation from the Board of the British South Africa Company. See (in this vol.) SOUTH AFRICA (BRITISH SOUTH AFRICA COMPANY): A. D. 1896 (JUNE).
Accused by the Cape Colony Assembly of complicity in the Jameson Raid. See (in this vol.) SOUTH AFRICA (CAPE COLONY): A. D. 1896 (JULY).
Testimony before British Parliamentary Committee on the Jameson Raid.—The Committee's report. See (in this vol.) SOUTH AFRICA (THE TRANSVAAL): A. D. 1897 (FEBRUARY—JULY).
In Cape Colony politics. See (in this vol.) SOUTH AFRICA (CAPE COLONY): A. D. 1898.
Projection of a Cape to Cairo Railway. See (in this vol.) RAILWAY, CAPE TO CAIRO; and AFRICA: A. D. 1899.
Beleaguered in Kimberley. See (in this vol.) SOUTH AFRICA (THE FIELD OF WAR): A. D. 1899 (OCTOBER—NOVEMBER).
Projection of a Cape to Cairo Telegraph. See (in this vol.) TELEGRAPH, CAPE TO CAIRO.

RHODESIA: A. D. 1896 (March—September).—Revolt of the Matabeles. See (in this vol.) SOUTH AFRICA (RHODESIA): A. D. 1896 (MARCH—SEPTEMBER).
A. D. 1896 (July).—Parliamentary investigation of British South Africa Company. See (in this vol.) SOUTH AFRICA (BRITISH SOUTH AFRICA COMPANY): A. D. 1896 (JULY).
A. D. 1897.—Report on compulsory native labor. See (in this vol.) SOUTH AFRICA (BRITISH AFRICA COMPANY): A. D. 1897 (JANUARY).
A. D. 1898.—Reorganized administration. See (in this vol.) SOUTH AFRICA (RHODESIA AND THE BRITISH SOUTH AFRICA COMPANY): A. D. 1898 (FEBRUARY).
A. D. 1900.—Protectorate proclaimed over Barotsiland. See (in this vol.) SOUTH AFRICA (RHODESIA): A. D. 1900 (SEPTEMBER).

RIO PRIETO, Engagement at the. See (in this vol.) UNITED STATES OF AM.: A. D. 1898 (JULY—AUGUST; PORTO RICO).

RIZAL, Dr. José. See (in this vol.) PHILIPPINE ISLANDS: A. D. 1896-1898.

ROBERTS, Field Marshal, Lord (Sir Frederick Sleigh): In the South African War. See (in this vol.) SOUTH AFRICA (THE FIELD OF WAR): A. D. 1900 (JANUARY—FEBRUARY), and after.

ROBINSON, Sir Hercules: British High Commissioner in South Africa. See (in this vol.) SOUTH AFRICA (THE TRANSVAAL): A. D. 1896 (JANUARY—APRIL).

ROMAN CATHOLIC CHURCH, The. See PAPACY.

ROMAN CATHOLICS: Protest of British Peers against the Declaration required from the Sovereign. See (in this vol.) ENGLAND: A. D. 1901 (FEBRUARY).

Victory in Belgium. See (in this vol.) BELGIUM: A. D. 1894–1895.

ROMAN LAW: Superseded in Germany. See (in this vol.) GERMANY: A. D. 1900 (JANUARY).

ROME: The likeness of its early settlement shown by excavations at Antemnæ. See (in this vol.) ARCHÆOLOGICAL RESEARCH: ITALY.

RÖNTGEN, Wilhelm Konrad: Discovery of the X rays. See (in this vol.) SCIENCE, RECENT: CHEMISTRY AND PHYSICS.

ROOSEVELT, Theodore: Lieutenant-Colonel of the Regiment of Rough Riders. See (in this vol.) UNITED STATES OF AM.: A. D. 1898 (APRIL—MAY).

Elected Vice President of the United States. See (in this vol.) UNITED STATES OF AM.: A. D. 1900 (MAY—NOVEMBER).

ROSEBERY, Earl of: Prime minister.— Remarks on the "predominant member." See (in this vol.) ENGLAND: A. D. 1894–1895.

Tribute to Mr. Gladstone. See (in this vol.) ENGLAND: A. D. 1898 (MAY).

Tribute to Queen Victoria. See (in this vol.) ENGLAND: A. D. 1901 (JANUARY).

ROUGH RIDERS, The. See (in this vol.) UNITED STATES OF AM.: A. D. 1898 (APRIL—MAY).

At Santiago. See (in this vol.) UNITED STATES OF AM.: A. D. 1898 (JUNE—JULY).

ROUMANIA. See (in this vol.) BALKAN AND DANUBIAN STATES; and TURKEY: A. D. 1899–1901.

ROYAL NIGER COMPANY, The. See (in this vol.) NIGERIA: A. D. 1882–1899.

Transfer of territories to the British crown. See (in this vol.) NIGERIA: A. D. 1899.

RUDINI, Marquis di: Resignation of Ministry. See (in this vol.) ITALY: A. D. 1898 (MARCH—JUNE).

RUMANIA. See (in this vol.) BALKAN AND DANUBIAN STATES; and TURKEY: A. D. 1899–1901.

RUSSIA: A. D. 1895.—Agreement with Great Britain concerning the frontier of Afghanistan and spheres of influence in the Pamir region. See (in this vol.) AFGHANISTAN: A. D. 1895.

A. D. 1895.—Alliance with France. See (in this vol.) FRANCE: A. D. 1895.

A. D. 1895.—Treaty with China giving railway and other privileges and rights in Manchuria. See (in this vol.) CHINA: A. D. 1895.

A. D. 1896 (May—June).—Coronation of the Tzar.—The Tzar Nicholas II., who succeeded his father, Alexander III., on the death of the latter, November 1, 1894, was not formally crowned until May 26, 1896. The splendid festivities of the occasion lasted from May 18 until June, and were attended by a brilliant assembly of princes and high officials from all parts of the world. They were saddened by a frightful calamity on the 31st of May, when an attempt was made to distribute gifts of food and drink to

a vast multitude of nearly half a million people, on Khodynskoye plain. Adequate measures for controlling the pressure of the crowd had not been taken, and nearly 3,000 were suffocated or trampled to death.

A. D. 1897.—Relaxations of oppressive laws.—Several important relaxations of oppressive laws were commanded by the Tzar in the course of the year. By one, sons of the marriage of an orthodox Russian with one of another creed were allowed to be brought up in the religion of the father and daughters in that of the mother. By another, Jews having an university education were allowed freedom of residence in any part of the empire. By others, greater freedom was given to the Polish press, formerly forbidden to discuss political questions; local assemblies of Polish nobles were organized; permission was given to restore Roman Catholic churches in Poland, and certain special Polish taxes were removed.

A. D. 1897 (February).—Census of the Empire.—"For the first time in the history of the Hyperborean Empire, a general, and if I may use the expression, scientific, census has been taken of the various tongues and tribes, religions and sects, cultured races and nomadic hordes who acknowledge the sway of the Tsar. It was a Herculean labour, without precedent in history and without a formula in statistics. . . . On June 5, 1895, the reigning Tsar gave his sanction to a scheme which was both conformable to the exigencies of modern statistics and suitable to the various conditions peculiar to Russia. . . . The general plan of operations was simple, and calculated as far as possible to impose a large portion of the task upon officials of the Administration, and obviate the necessity of paying for it. Thus there was a Committee in every Government or Province of the Empire, presided over by the actual Governor; and there were sub-committees in every district under the direction of the Marshal of the Nobility. . . . The task undertaken by the Central Committee was in the highest degree formidable: rooted prejudices had to be overcome, inarticulate suspicions removed—the half-civilised nomads have an insuperable dislike to answer questions of the 'Tshinovniks'—the confidence of the people gained, languages mastered, routes studied, badges prepared for the officials, millions upon millions of census papers printed and distributed over the length and breadth of the Empire, &c. . . .

"In order that the work might be finished as early as possible at the same time, the cantonal sections were split up into divisions, which had to be more or less equal. In country places the division was not usually allowed to exceed 400 households, or say, 2,000 souls; in cities 150 flats, or about 750 souls. The registrars, who were answerable for the census in these districts, were chosen from all classes of society, the only condition being that they must be persons of some education, and calculated to inspire the population with confidence—a very important consideration in Russia. Thus, there were priests, officers, school-teachers, students, merchants, landowners, and in some cases peasants. The remuneration fixed for the work, which was sometimes attended with danger and in almost every case with very disagreeable experiences, was 1½ roubles, or about £1 4s. 6d., in rural districts, and 7 roubles in towns. Labour is still cheap in Russia, but even there this modest sum was found insufficient to tempt the competent persons, who in out-of-the-way districts were few and far between. When this had become painfully evident, it was too late to set the clumsy machinery in motion through which alone it might have been possible to obtain a higher rate of remuneration. As the registrars were, in many places, not to be had, it seemed likely that the census would prove a lamentable failure. Then the Tsar appeared as a 'deus ex machinâ,' and instituted a special medal for all those who should agree to undertake the work gratis. Like most Continental peoples, Russians have a hankering after 'ribbons to stick in their coats,' and the moment the medal was promised for gratuitous services there was no lack of willing workmen. Thousands of volunteers presented themselves, and the authorities selected the most competent. . . . On January 28 [Old Style, being, N. S. February 9, 1897], . . . at break of day an army of 150,000 individuals left their homes to count the number of people inhabiting an empire which occupies one-sixth of the globe. . . .

"The first Russian census . . . may be considered to have proved a brilliant success. The results may be summed up very briefly as follows : The population of the Russian Empire and the Grand Duchy of Finland numbers 129,-211,114 souls, of whom

94,188,750 inhabit the 50 Governments of European Russia
9,442,590 inhabit the 10 Governments of Poland
9,723,553 inhabit the 11 Governments of the Caucasus
5,731,732 inhabit the 9 Governments of Siberia
3,415,174 inhabit the 5 Governments of the Steppe regions
4,175,101 inhabit the Provinces of Transcaspia and of Turkestan
6,413 inhabit Khiva and Boukhara
2,527,801 inhabit Finland
_____
129,211,114

"Compared with the figures of former years, as given by the partial official returns and the tables of the statistician Köppen, we find that the population has increased since the year 1851 by 96·2 per cent ; since 1858 by 73·2 per cent; since 1885 by 18·1 per cent. The average density of the population is 8·8 persons to the square verst [the verst equalling 1166.66 yards], but it naturally varies a good deal in the different districts and Provinces. Thus, in the 10 Governments of Poland it amounts to 84.6 to the sq. verst. In the 50 Governments of European Russia it amounts to 22·2 to the sq. verst. In the Governments of the Caucasus it amounts to 23·6 to the sq. verst. In Siberia it amounts to 0·5 to the sq. verst. In the Steppe region it amounts to 1·6 to the sq. verst.

"Even in the different Governments of European Russia the density varies considerably. . . . "There are 19 cities in Russia, with a population of more than 100,000 souls each, and 35 which have from 50,000 to 100,000. In fifteen cities the number of females exceeds that of the males, whereas in all the others it is smaller. . . . The natural increase of the population is kept down to a relatively low figure by an abnormally large death-rate, which is mainly due to avoidable causes. Infectious diseases and insufficiency of medical help are among the most obvious. . . . In no country in the world are infectious diseases so frequently mortal as in Russia. Chil-

dren especially suffer, and diphtheria, measles, scarlatina, smallpox, &c., literally decimate villages and country towns, It has been stated by the statistician Ekk, with the help of official figures, that about 1,900,000 persons, chiefly children, die every year who might, with a little care, be preserved to the Empire. The difference which this loss makes to the population in fifty years is enormous."—E. J. Dillon, *The First Russian Census (Contemporary Review, Dec.*, 1897).

A. D. 1897 (November).—Treaty with the United States and Japan, to suspend pelagic sealing. See (in this vol.) BERING SEA QUESTIONS.

A. D. 1897 (December).—Adoption of the gold monetary standard. See (in this vol.) MONETARY QUESTIONS : A. D. 1897 (DECEMBER).

A. D. 1897-1898.—Contentions with Japan in Korea. See (in this vol.) KOREA : A. D. 1895-1898.

A. D. 1898 (March).—Increase of naval armament.—On the 10th of March an imperial ukase ordered an addition of 90,000,000 roubles to the expenditure on war ships already provided for, the extra disbursement to be spread over seven years.

A. D. 1898 (March).—Lease of Port Arthur, Talienwan and the Liaotung Peninsula from China. See (in this vol.) CHINA : A. D. 1898 (MARCH—JULY).

A. D. 1898 (May—December).—In the Chinese "Battle of Concessions." See (in this vol.) CHINA : A. D. 1898 (FEBRUARY—DECEMBER).

A. D. 1898-1899.—The Tzar's proposal to check the increase of armaments.—The resulting Peace Conference at The Hague. See (in this vol.) PEACE CONFERENCE.

A. D. 1898-1901.—The question of sugar bounties.—U. S. countervailing duties and Russian retaliation. See (in this vol.) SUGAR BOUNTIES.

A. D. 1898-1901.—The Russianizing of Finland.—Overthrow of the constitutional rights of the Finns. See (in this vol.) FINLAND: A. D. 1898-1901.

A. D. 1899.—Famine.—A fearful famine in eastern Russia, within and beyond the valley of the Volga, was caused in 1899 by an almost unprecedented failure of crops. With the famine came typhus fever, and the tale of suffering and death was one of the most heart-rending of the century.

A. D. 1899 (February—June.)—Disorder among the students.—For some months, the universities and most of the higher schools of Russia were in a state of disorder, and in conflict with the police authorities. Many of the institutions were closed and a great number of the students were under arrest. The students complained of the statutes of the universities, and of the general treatment to which they were subjected, and were bitterly hostile to the police. The Tzar seems to have given personal attention to their grievances, which he appointed a commission to investigate. On the report of the commission he issued an imperial order severely censuring the administration of the universities, and also reproving the police, while, at the same time, he addressed some serious admonitions to the students.

A. D. 1899 (March—April).—Agreement with Great Britain concerning railway inter-

424

ests in China. See (in this vol.) CHINA : A. D. 1899 (MARCH—APRIL).

A. D. 1899 (May).—Steps toward the abolition of transportation to Siberia.—On the 18th of May, the Tzar issued the following order : "A commission of the officers of the ministry of justice and representatives of the respective departments under the auspices of the minister of justice shall be formed. The commission is to work out the following : To replace transportation of criminals by punishment by courts; to abolish or limit administrative transportation by peasant boards; to reorganize penal servitude and the deportation which follows; to better the condition of the convicts now in Siberia; to improve prisons where criminals are confined awaiting transportation and deportation; to establish compulsory public labor and workhouses as penal measures; to provide means for carrying out the measures necessary for the reorganization of the transportation of criminals and of penal establishments. The minister of justice is to ask direct, and not through any department, for the imperial sanction of the committee's recommendations." The British Commercial Agent in Russia, reporting to the Foreign Office in June, 1900, stated in allusion to the above order : "The State Council is reported to have just decided, by a majority of votes, to introduce at once the necessary changes, as the Central Prisons Administration has declared that the gaol accommodation is sufficient. The number of exiles to Siberia from 1823 to 1898 is given as 908,266, mostly to Eastern Siberia."

A. D. 1899 (May—July).—Representation in the Peace Conference at The Hague. See (in this vol.) PEACE CONFERENCE.

A. D. 1899 (December).— Adhesion to the arrangement of an "open door" commercial policy in China. See (in this vol.) CHINA : A. D. 1899–1900 (SEPTEMBER—FEBRUARY).

A. D. 1899–1901.—Attitude towards impending revolt in Macedonia. See (in this vol.) TURKEY : A. D. 1899–1901 ; and BALKAN AND DANUBIAN STATES.

A. D. 1900.—Military and naval expenditure. See (in this vol.) WAR BUDGETS.

A. D. 1900.—Naval strength. See (in this vol.) NAVIES OF THE SEA POWERS.

A. D. 1900 (June—December).—Co-operation with the Powers in China. See (in this vol.) CHINA.

A. D. 1900 (August).—Proposal to withdraw troops from Peking. See (in this vol.) CHINA : A. D. 1900 (AUGUST—DECEMBER.)

A. D. 1900–1901.—Student outbreaks.— Serious demonstrations of discontent.—Severe measures of repression.—Action of the Tzar.—A fresh outbreak of revolt among the students in the Russian universities, more serious in its nature, apparently, than that of 1899 (see above: A. D. 1899, FEBRUARY—JUNE), was started at Kieff, in December, 1900, by a remonstrance on the part of the students against the retention of a professor whom they deemed incompetent. The rector of the university refused to dismiss the objectionable professor; whereupon the g   -general of the province intervened and ofortmade him to lecture. The rector and the council of the university could not resist the authority of the governor-general, but they are said to have revenged themselves on the students by requiring seven of the latter to choose

between three days of imprisonment and three years of expulsion from the university. They chose the latter and were expelled. Then the students as a body began to be troublesome, especially after the rector had refused to meet them for a discussion of their grievances. Finally the police and the military authorities were called in; a large number of the students were arrested and brought to trial before a special court which had been created for dealing with the student troubles of the year before. According to subsequent reports, more than two hundred of them were condemned to be sent into the ranks of the army—which seems to be a punishment newly devised for such cases, and not likely to improve the loyal spirit of the army.

This hard treatment of the students at Kieff inflamed their sympathetic fellows in all the universities of the empire, and became the immediate cause of disorderly demonstrations, which began, in January or early in February, to be made at St. Petersburg, Moscow, Odessa, and elsewhere; but there cannot be a doubt that the disturbances since occurring represent an instigation deeper, more revolutionary, more serious, than the resentment of students misused by their teachers. The students persisted resolutely in attempts to hold meetings which were prohibited as seditious; to make appeals to the people; to circulate forbidden literature; while the authorities struck them, at every movement they made, with a relentless hand. As usual, the oppressive violence of government provoked desperate crime. On the 27th of February, the Minister of Public Instruction, Privy Councillor Bogoliepoff, was shot by an expelled student, who approached him, in his official apartments, under pretense of presenting a petition. He died of the wound on the 15th of March. Meantime, the conduct of students, at St. Petersburg and Moscow especially, became more and more riotous and revolutionary in spirit. There were signs, too, of an understanding between them and the discontented workingmen of the cities, which caused anxiety. A Vienna journal claims to have knowledge that, after the troubles at Kieff, a widespread movement of alliance between secret associations of students and workmen was set on foot, and that it threatened to be the most formidable revolutionary organization that the government had yet faced.

That the sympathy of literary circles in Russia is with the students appears to be proved by the following manifesto, which was published in Paris on the 22d of March, signed, it is said, by forty-five Russian men of letters: "We, the undersigned Russian men of letters, deprived of the possibility of freely expressing our ideas on the needs of our poor Fatherland, prevented by the censorship from speaking of what happens before our eyes or indicating an outlet from the terrible situation of our country, and conscious of our duty towards the people, resort to our foreign brethren for the purpose of informing the civilized world of the atrocities now being committed among us. On March 17, in the Kazan Square at St. Petersburg, the police fell on an inoffensive and unarmed crowd of several thousand persons, men, women, and children, and without any provocation showed unexampled brutality and ferocity. Cossacks, surrounding the crowd and preventing it from dispersing, charged without warning the compact mass, which had mostly been drawn together by curiosity. The police seized at random the people who fell into their hands, striking them without mercy with their fists or swords. Those of the public, even officers in uniform, who begged for a cessation of the carnage, were maltreated or even arrested. Such are the facts of which several of us have been eye-witnesses. Similar atrocities have recently been committed in other Russian towns. Full of terror and anguish at the future in store for our country, thus given up to the whips of Cossacks and the swords of the police, convinced that our indignation is shared by those of our Russian brethren whose signatures we have not had time to obtain, by all the intellectual society of Russia, and by all those from whom feelings of self-respect and humanity have not yet been eradicated, convinced also that our foreign brethren will not remain indifferent to what passes among us, we appeal to the Press of the world to give the utmost publicity to the attestation of the lamentable facts of which we have been witnesses." A despatch from St. Petersburg on the 26th reported that the Mutual Aid Association of Russian writers attached to the St. Petersburg Literary Society, from which this protest emanated, had been suppressed, as the consequence of its publication.

A more significant expression, and one from which a more definite idea of the nature and causes of the discontent among the students may be obtained, is the following petition, addressed to the Tzar by a number of Russian professors and Senators in March. The St. Petersburg correspondent of the "London Times," who sent a translation of the paper to that journal on the 18th of March, remarked that "it is very doubtful if it will have any real effect, and its contents may very possibly be regarded by the red-tape officials into whose hands it may fall, if not by the Emperor himself, as implying a request for something like a Constitution. Apart from that consideration a collective petition in Russia is illegal." The translation of the document is as follows:—"Your Imperial Majesty,—We, the undersigned loyal subjects, consider it our patriotic duty to address you, Sire, with the present humble petition on the subject of the recent agitation among the students. We desire to express in this paper the thoughts that have long been a matter of painful reflection to every Russian conscious of the life which he is living. This perturbation among the students, which has been of periodical recurrence for the last 40 years, has ruined the careers of thousands of young men and women animated by the most ardent aspirations for the good and happiness of their native country. It would undoubtedly be most unjust to lay all the blame for these disorders on the students themselves. The causes of this state of things lie much deeper. They are connected with many of the general conditions of the life of our State and society; they are to a great extent rooted in the want of organization of academical centres. This want of organization was explained by the special commission appointed by your Majesty's command two years ago. But the labours of that body failed to have the practical result which was apparently expected of it; public opinion was not permitted to take part in its deliberations, either by means of the Press or in any other way. The matter was treated according to the usual official routine, and in the

Ministry of Public Instruction the magnanimous intentions of your Majesty were not only rendered colourless, but deprived of all their real significance. Instead of properly carrying out your Majesty's indications in regard to closer communion between the students and professors of the higher educational establishments, the Ministry dismissed those among the latter whose moral qualities and devotion to duty were calculated to exercise the most beneficial influence over their scholars.

"Those among the students who took part in the disturbances, and who should have been worked upon by moral persuasion, were expelled from the Universities, and the force of inspectors, otherwise the University police, was increased for the purpose of controlling those who remained. The temporary law of June 29, 1899, against further disorders threatened the agitators with the punishment of being drafted into the ranks of the army. This measure, which has now been enforced, will, of course, put down the movement at least for a time; but it is impossible to ignore its moral effect. It only represses, but does not thoroughly convince. By this means the more hot-headed among the students, inspired by the most respectable aspirations and feelings, will be weeded out of the scholastic ranks, and their parents will be suddenly deprived of all hope and consolation in their children perhaps for years; while on the rest this measure can only have the effect which is always produced by terror and fear for the future. It oppresses them, extinguishes their best impulses, and tends to bring the weaker ones beneath the influence of those petty egotistical motives which are already so powerful in our daily life. To bring up an entire generation in such conditions is to create and support an oppressive state of things in the life of the nation which must finally lead to downfall and decay.

"The oppressiveness of this environment is felt not only by the young, but also by their elders. Is it normal that in an autocratic State the voice of loyal subjects should be unable to reach their Sovereign? And yet at the present moment many persons regard the signature of this loyal petition as almost an act of the greatest civil courage. In order to loyally and honestly bring their wants and traditional desires to the notice of their Monarch (Lord), the subjects of your Majesty are obliged to act in the dark for fear that the police will seize hold on the petition and intercept it before it can reach your Majesty's hands. Many who fully agree with all that is here expressed will certainly be deterred from signing the petition because of the unpleasant consequences to themselves which they fear may follow. In such conditions life becomes intolerable. A deadening apathy spreads over every one, all interest in public activity is lost, and in all spheres of the Government and society there is a decided feeling of the want of men. Put an end, Sire, by your magnanimous initiative to this oppressive situation! Show confidence in your faithful subjects, and, while discontinuing repression, accord us the possibility of freely expressing the voice of public opinion, which is now stifled. The agitation among the students will cease of itself, and the young men will quietly turn to their studies as soon as their youthful minds are no longer excited by the disagreeable conditions which surround them, when they see the prospect on finishing their education of being allowed to take a free and useful part in the affairs of their native land."

An attempt on the life of a Minister far more important and more obnoxious than M. Bogolie-poff was made on the 22d of March. This was M. Pobiedonostzeff, Procurator of the Holy Synod, who has long been credited with being the master-spirit of evil influence in Russian councils,—a Torquemada of the nineteenth century, responsible for all the mediævalism in Russian policy for the past twenty years. Three shots were fired at the Procurator from the street, through the windows of his study, and he was missed by them all. The would-be assassin, named Lagofsky, was promptly seized, and it is claimed to have been found that he was chosen by lot to execute an avenging decree. On the other hand, it is reported that he was moved to the deed by the excommunication of Count Tolstoi, which the Russian Church had lately pronounced.

If reports are to be credited, the Tzar, at length, took the direction of measures relating to the disturbances into his own hands, and began by putting a stop to the forcing of condemned students into the army. He then appointed to the Ministry of Public Education General Vannovsky, who had investigated the student disorders of 1899 for him, and who seems to have recognized that the disaffection of the students was not without grounds. It is rumored that unlimited powers for two years have been given to the new Minister, so that he cannot be interfered with by the powerful reactionaries who evidently stand between the best intentions of the Tzar and their execution. The obvious difficulty of the autocrat is to learn the truth of things and to know what is being done by those who ostensibly obey his commands. Apparently he is striving to be served faithfully and intelligently in this case, and it is to be hoped that he may have success. He addressed a rescript to General Vannovsky, in which he said : "The regular organization of popular education has always formed one of the chief cares of the Russian rulers, who have striven, surely but gradually, to perfect it in accordance with the fundamental principles of Russian life and the requirements of the times. The experiences of recent years, however, have shown the existence of defects so material in our scholastic system that I think that the time has come to undertake an immediate and thorough revision and improvement. Highly valuing your experience as a statesman and your enlightenment, I have chosen you to co-operate with me in the work of renovating and reorganizing Russian schools ; and, in appointing you to the now specially important office of Minister of Public Instruction, I am firmly convinced that you will unswervingly endeavour to attain the goal indicated by me, and that you will bring into the work of educating the Russian youth your cordial sympathy and sagacity ripened by experience. May God bless our work, and may parents and families, who above all are bound to care for their children, help us in our work, and then the time will soon come when I with all my people shall see in the young generation, with pride and encouragement, the firm and sure hope of the Fatherland and its strong protection for the future."

The Russian "Official Messenger," St. Petersburg, announced on the 14th of April that "in consequence of the recent student disturbances many of the high schools were closed before the Easter holidays, and the young men were compelled either to lose a year of their studies or even to leave the college altogether. In view of the serious consequences which this measure involved for the career of the students, a special conference of the principals of the higher colleges was called to deliberate, under the presidency of the Minister of Public Instruction, upon the situation thus created. The conference decided that the following measures were indispensably necessary for the re-establishment of the regular course of study at the institutions concerned :—1. Lectures to be renewed in the higher colleges in the course of April and intermediate examinations under the direction of the scholastic authorities to be held under the usual regulations at the customary intervals. 2. The lectures and examinations to be continued during the summer vacation, should they not have been completed during the preceding term. 3. All those who without sufficient reason did not attend the examinations or failed to pass them to be liable to all the legal consequences thereof. 4. In particularly important cases autumn and supplementary examinations to be permitted in the higher schools exceptionally this year."

According to a later despatch from St. Petersburg to the Associated Press, April 23d, the students of the university at the capital were informed that day by the rector that "Gen. Vannoffsky, the Russian Minister of Public Instruction, had refused to defer the examinations until autumn or make further concessions to the students. Although the popular professor, M. Petrozicky, pleaded against an action which would make it difficult for a liberal minister to carry through his benevolent intentions, the students decided by a vote of 684 to 649 against participating in the examinations. They resolved, however, not to create obstruction and the minority agreed to submit to the will of the majority. The electro-technical, the civil engineering, the women's medical and the women's academic institutions also will decide against taking the examinations. The sincere friends of the students regret the step in this respect, believing the students should allow the recall of the absentees to come as an act of grace from the Government and should not attempt to force concessions."

A. D. 1900-1901.—Operations in Manchuria.—Practical possession of the country.—Refusal of Chinese government to sign a demanded treaty. See (in this vol.) MANCHURIA: A. D. 1900–1901.

A. D. 1900-1901.—Strategic importance of Korea.—Ground of Japanese jealousy. See (in this vol.) KOREA : A. D. 1900.

A. D. 1901 (April).—Expulsion of Count Tolstoi.—His reply to the decree of excommunication.—A reply by Count Tolstoi to the decree of excommunication pronounced against him by the Russian Church, some weeks before, written at Moscow on the 13th of April, was published in Paris on the 30th. As reported to the Associated Press, he states in his reply that, in consequence of the decree, he has received letters from ignorant people menacing him with death. "He characterizes the decree as illegal or intentionally equivocal, arbitrary, unjustified and full of falsehoods. Moreover, he says, it constitutes an instigation to evil sentiments and deeds. Count Tolstoi denounces the practices of the church, and says he is convinced that the teaching of the church, theoretically astute, is injurious, is a lie in practice and is a compound of vulgar superstitions and sorcery, under which entirely disappears the sense of Christian doctrine."

By Press despatch from Vienna, April 23, it was reported that a decree expelling Count Tolstoi from Russia had been signed by the Tzar, and carried into execution.

RUSSIA IN ASIA: A. D. 1891-1900.—The Trans-Siberian Railway.—Resources of Siberia and the Amur country.—The following account was reported to the British Foreign Office in June, 1900: "For over 30 years the question of constructing this line had been a theme of interminable discussions and reports. Finally, the following unmistakeably emphatic note of its Imperial founder, the Emperor Alexander III., appended to a report on the general condition of Siberia, moved the whole project definitely forward as a thing that was to be and at once: 'How many of these reports of the Governors-General of Siberia have I perused, and with sorrow and shame must own that the Government has hitherto hardly done anything to satisfy the demands of this rich but neglected region! It is time, indeed time!' A further equally emphatic and still briefer note, added to a report of the Minister of Ways with regard to the projected Ussuri route, is to form the appropriate inscription to the monument to be erected at Vladivostock, the terminus of his great work, to his late Imperial Majesty : 'The construction of this railway must be begun forthwith.' The first stone was laid at Vladivostock on May 19, 1891, by the then Grand Duke Nicholas, now the reigning Emperor. . . . A Siberian railway committee was formed under the presidency of the then Grand Duke Nicholas Alexandrovich, whose duties were (1) to construct the main and necessary feeding lines; (2) to take measures for the general commercial and industrial development of Siberia; and (3) to direct and control the colonisation movement.

"Taking the direction of the route, not as it was to have been, but as it is or will be, we see that with Moscow as the European centre point, and the Moscow-Samara-Cheliabinsk line as its principal feeder, the main road runs from Cheliabinsk, whence it really starts eastward, direct through mid-Siberia to Lake Baikal, and thence, viâ Chita, to Stretensk on the Shilka, a navigable tributary of the Amur. At present, the projected course of the railway viâ the Amur has been arrested, owing on the one hand to various technical difficulties, and on the other to the facilities, political and otherwise, conceded by China, and another direction, in the nature of a short cut through Manchuria, has been entered upon. The well-known agreement with China [see, in this vol., CHINA: A. D. 1895] and the formation of the Chinese Eastern Railway Company, rendering the original continuation of the line from Stretensk less urgent, it has been resolved, instead, to construct two direct lines to the Chinese frontiers, from Kaidalovo on the main Siberian route on the one side, and from the Ussuri or Habarovsk-Vladivostock line on the

other. These two lines, traversing Manchuria from opposite directions, are to meet at Khulan-Chan (Khaorbin), thence running southwards to Dalni and Port Arthur. Thus, we see the three lines, the main Siberian road, which, except for the brief stoppage at Lake Baikal, will run in a practically straight and uninterrupted course from Cheliabinsk to Vladivostock; the Ussuri line running northward through Russian territory from Vladivostock to Habarovsk; and the branch section from Khulan-Chan (Khaorbin), on the main line, striking out southward through Eastern China to Dalni and Port Arthur.

"As far as Russia is concerned, it may be said that her portion of the work is practically ready, though much re-laying and reconstruction may at any time be necessary. The main line is open for regular traffic from Cheliabinsk to Lake Baikal, and for provisional traffic to Stretensk. According to the latest telegrams, regular traffic from Lake Baikal to Stretensk is to be commenced on July 1/14, 1900. Thus, there is now a direct run (excepting only the lake crossing of 60 versts (about 40 miles), from Moscow, viâ Samara, Cheliabinsk, Omsk, and Irkutch, to Kaidalovo (252 versts—168 miles—this side of Stretensk), whence the rail will turn off to Nagodan on the Chinese frontier. This latter stretch, a distance of 325 versts (216 miles), will complete the work as regards Russia. The Ussuri line, from Habarovsk to Vladivostock, has been open for traffic since 1897. The Circum-Baikal connecting line, round the southern bend of the lake, a distance of 292 versts (195 miles), remains to be laid, the lake being crossed at present by steam ferries or ice-breakers. A new ice-breaker, built in England, is now on its way in pieces to Lake Baikal. It is the Manchurian sections, therefore, that at present retard the consummation of the complete overland track to Vladivostock. Nor, from recent accounts, does it seem likely that the Chinese engaged in the work will bring it to a conclusion much before 1902, if then. Even now, however, goods can make their way through Siberia to Stretensk by rail, and thence down the Shilka and the Amur to Habarovsk, or further on, by the Ussuri line, to Vladivostock. As regards the railroad from Port Arthur northward, the latest news brings it to Telin, north of Mukden, trains with workmen running this distance, some 500 versts. The Chinese Eastern Railway Company promise to join Port Arthur to Vladivostock by October next, it is said, but, even on the route already temporarily in rough working order, dwellings, stations and permanent bridges have yet to be built. Thus, there is now direct communication between Moscow and Stretensk by rail, a distance of 6,471 versts (4,214 miles), and from Stretensk to Habarovsk and Nikolaieff by the Shilka and Amur rivers, a further distance to Habarovsk of about 2,000 versts (1,332 miles), and to Nikolaieff, the mouth of the Amur, of over 3,000 versts (2,000 miles). The Amur is navigable from May to September, but for shallow-draft vessels only.

"Various important European feeding lines have been constructed, and others, partaking more of the character of huge main thoroughfares are projected. Cheliabinsk, the starting-point eastwards, is connected with Moscow by the Zlatoust-Samara-Moscow Railway, which, touching the Volga at Samara, crosses it at Sisran. Two northern branches, the Tiumen-Perm, and Kotlass-Viatka-Perm. meeting at Ekaterinburg, the capital of the rich Ural mineral district, run into the main Siberian line at Cheliabinsk. From this latter point, too, a new route has long been projected direct to St. Petersburg, viâ Viatka and Vologda. So that, while the future will connect Cheliabinsk, and with it the main Siberian railway, in a direct line with the Baltic, not as now viâ Moscow, the present joins it on the one side with that city, the business-centre of Russia, and on the other to the new northern through route, which, viâ Kotlass and Archangel, is this year to bring the cereals of Siberia to London."—*Great Britain, Parliamentary Publications (Papers by Command: Miscellaneous Series No. 533, 1900, pp. 5-7).*

"It may be a wild idea, but Russian engineers are actually talking of a railroad from Stryetensk to Bering Strait, over a comparatively easy route that does not enter the Arctic Circle. This imaginary line, they hope, would connect with the American line which is now being built to Dawson City, the distance from which to Stryetensk is about three thousand miles. If this road ever is completed they figure that New York will be placed in railroad connection with London, Calcutta and Cape Town."—A. H. Ford, *The Warfare of Railways in Asia (Century, March, 1900).*

"Siberia and the Amur lands are rich beyond belief. . . . This vast territory, long looked upon as a barren waste, is destined to be one of the world's richest and most productive sections. In northern France, wheat ripens in 137 days; in Siberia, in 107. Even heavy night frosts do not injure the young seed. Under such conditions, the possibilities of agriculture are practically unlimited. I may add that oats require, in Siberia and in the Amur country, only 96 days, and in the regions of the Yenisei only 107. The frost period lasts only 97 days in the Irkutsk country. Transbaikalja lies entirely within the agricultural regions; so, too, almost the entire territory traversed by the Amur as far north as it runs. Efforts are being made to obtain along the Amur at least 300,000 square kilometers (115,835 square miles) for the higher forms of northern agriculture. Climatically, the best of northern Asia's territory, for planting purposes, is the Usuri country, which, in spite of its vast tracts of wood and grazing lands, has 195,000 square kilometers (75,292 square miles) of arable ground. The building of the Trans-Siberian Railroad has already added to the Empire's wheat product.

"The mineral resources of western Siberia are vast. Between Tomsk and Kooznesk lie 60,000 square kilometers (23,167 square miles) of coal lands which have never been touched. The coal is said to be excellent. In eastern Siberia, with its 280,000 square kilometers (108,112 square miles) of fruitful soil, there are 400 places yielding gold. Rich mineral deposits — graphite, lapis lazuli; iron mines, particularly rich in quality (as high as 60 per cent); hard and soft coals, i. e., black and brown coals—await hands willing to work for them. To-day, thousands of colonists are hurrying to these promising lands. Russia's output in gold and silver is already very large, and is constantly increasing.

"The industries of Siberia are in their infancy; still, they are growing and are bound to grow, so rich are the rewards promised. Chemical,

sugar, and paper mills have been put up in several places and are paying well. Even Manchuria, a province so vast that it might make an empire, is looking to Russia for its future development. The wealth of this province, like that of Siberia and all eastern Russia, is ripe for harvesting. The traffic in Siberia and eastern Russia is increasing faster than even the advocates of the great Trans-Siberian road anticipated. The Ob, one of the world's big rivers, emptying through the Gulf of Ob into the Arctic Ocean, has 102 steamers and 200 tugs running already. On the Yenisei, 10 steamers carry the mails regularly. The mouths of both these rivers were visited last summer by English and Russian ships. This proves the practicability of connecting eastern and western Siberia with Europe by water."— *U. S. Consular Reports, Nov.,* 1899, *p.* 411.

An official publication of the year 1900 from St. Petersburg, furnished to American journals by the Russian embassy at Washington, is the source of the following statements relative to the rapid development of the vast Siberian country along the line of the great railway: "When viewed with reference to colonization Siberia divides itself naturally into two zones, extending east and west, and differing essentially from one another. The first of these embraces the region traversed by the new Siberian railway, the more populous southern portion of Siberia, in which the conditions of climate and soil are favorable to the development of agriculture and colonization. The other zone occupies the extensive, deserted northern region, the land of tundras, or polar marshes, with a constantly frozen subsoil and a severe climate, a dreary tract of land totally unfit for agriculture. Between these two zones stretches a broad belt of forests of tall trees, partly primeval pine and fir, partly leafy trees. The wealth of these broad agricultural and timber areas is, moreover, augmented by mineral deposits of every conceivable nature, as abundant and diversified as those of America, and into this whole region immigration is pouring in volume unequalled except in the history of American colonization. Ever since the serfs were emancipated in 1861 they have formed the bulk of the emigrants from the thickly populated agricultural districts of European Russia, but the great tide of settlers in the new territory is only now assuming tremendous proportions. During the twenty years' period of 1860 to 1880 about 110,000 persons emigrated to Siberia, while for the thirteen years from 1880 to 1892 there were over 440,000, and for the succeeding years since the great railway has been building the number of immigrants of both sexes has been as follows: 1893, 65,000; 1894, 76,000; 1895, 109,000; 1896, 203,000; 1897, 87,000; 1898, 206,000; 1899, 225,000. Total, 971,000. According to the census of 1897, the population of Siberia had risen to 8,188,368 inhabitants, of which the Russian peasantry formed over 25 per cent."

A. D. **1899 (May).**—Steps toward the abolition of transportation. See (in this vol.) Russia: A. D. 1899 (MAY).

A. D. **1900.**—Russian railway building and railway projects in Persia and Afghanistan. —By several writers who seem to have knowledge of what is doing in those parts of the eastern world, it was reported in the spring of 1900 that an active projection, planning, and building (to some extent) of railroads in Persia and

Afghanistan was on foot among the Russians. From Tiflis, it was said, their plans contemplated a line of rail to Teheran; thence to be extended by one branch, southward, via Ispahan, to the Persian Gulf, and by another branch westward to Herat, in Afghanistan. From their Central Asian acquisitions they had advanced their railway to within 70 miles of Herat, and were said to be confidently expecting to push it on, through Kandahar and through Baluchistan, to the Arabian Sea. If these extensive plans could be carried out, and if Russian influence in Persia, said to be growing fast, should become actually controlling, the Muscovite Power would have made an enormous gain, by planting itself on the shores of the Indian Ocean. How far Russia can continue to press forward in this line of policy without collision with Great Britain and with Germany—which seems to have aims in the same direction, through Asiatic Turkey—is an interesting question for the future.

The following is from a despatch to the "London Times" from its correspondent at Vienna, Feb. 24, 1901: "According to trustworthy information from Teheran, Russia is particularly active just now in Persia and the Persian Gulf. . . . The road from Resht to Teheran, which has been built by a Russian company, is of no value for European trade in the absence of an agreement with Russia respecting the transit traffic through that country. European commerce is dependent upon the long and expensive caravan routes via Trebizond, Bushire, Baghdad, Mochamera, &c. These occupy from four to six months."

RUSSO-CHINESE BANK, Concessions to the. See (in this vol.) CHINA: A. D. 1898 (FEBRUARY—DECEMBER).

S.

SAGASTA, Señor Praxedes Mateo: Resignation from **Spanish Ministry.** See (in this vol.) SPAIN: A. D. 1895–1896.

Return to power. See (in this vol.) SPAIN: A. D. 1897 (AUGUST—OCTOBER).

Resignation. See (in this vol.) SPAIN: A. D. 1899.

SAGHALIEN. See (in this vol.) SAKHALIN.

SAHARA, The: French possessions. See (in this vol.) NIGERIA: A. D. 1882–1899.

ST. KITTS: Industrial condition. See (in this vol.) WEST INDIES, THE BRITISH: A. D. 1897.

ST. LOUIS: A. D. 1896.—Republican National Convention. See (in this vol.) UNITED STATES OF AM.: A. D. 1896 (JUNE—NOVEMBER).

ST. VINCENT, The British colony of. See (in this vol.) WEST INDIES, THE BRITISH: A. D. 1897.

SAKHALIN.—"Of late years . . . its increasing importance as a place of exile for Russian political and criminal offenders has invested Sakhalin with a certain interest, derived, perhaps, more from penal associations than physical resources, which latter may, when fully developed, materially affect trade and commerce in the far East. The island of Sakhalin is 584 miles in length, its breadth varying from 18 to 94 miles. The southern extremity is separated from the island of Yezo, twenty miles distant, by the Straits of La Perouse, and its western coast by the shallow Gulf of Tartary (at one point barely five miles across) from the mainland of Siberia. Although Dutch explorers are said to have landed here in 1643, the first reliable survey of the island was probably obtained in the year 1787 by La Perouse. Russian fur traders followed in the early part of the present century, but it was only in 1853 that, disturbances having occurred with the natives, a score or so of Cossacks were stationed at Dui on the west coast. In 1867 negociations were entered into by the Russian and Japanese Governments for joint occupation of Sakhalin, but the subsequent discovery of coal, and consequent influx of Russian convicts, rendered this arrangement highly unsatisfactory. Further negotiations, therefore, ensued, with the result that, in 1875, the island was formally ceded to Russia, Japan receiving, in exchange, the entire Kurile Archipelago.

"Sakhalin is by no means easy of access. Even during the open season (from May to September) but very few vessels visit the island, and, with the exception of the monthly arrival of convict-ships from Europe, and a couple of small Russian trading steamers, there is no fixed service with Vladivostok, which, with the exception of Nikolaefsk, is the only Siberian port whence Sakhalin may, in three days, be reached. During the winter months the island is completely ice-bound and unapproachable by water. Communication with the mainland is then maintained by means of dog-sledges, and the mails for Europe are dispatched across the frozen Gulf of Tartary—a journey, under favourable circumstances, of about three months. . . .

"Sakhalin is, for administrative purposes, divided into three districts, viz.: Korsakovsky-Post in the south, Tymovsk in the north, and Alexandrovsky-Post on the western coast. The latter, which is situated in the centre of the coal district, is a picturesque, straggling town of about 7,000 inhabitants, consisting almost entirely of officials and convicts. This is the most important penal settlement on the island, contains the largest prison, and is, moreover, the residence of the Governor of Sakhalin, a subordinate of the Governor-General of Eastern Siberia. Alexandrovsky is garrisoned by about 1,500 men, and contains large foundries and workshops for convict labour, but most of the prisoners are employed in the adjacent coal mines of Dui. . . . Korsakovsky-Post, on the south coast, is the next largest settlement, containing about 5,000 convicts who are chiefly employed in agricultural pursuits. Although it may seem a paradox, the remaining prisons in the interior of the island, Derbynskaya, Rykovskaya, and Onor are not prisons at all, but huge wooden barracks, innocent of bolts and bars. Here, also, the work done is solely agricultural."—Harry de Windt, *The Island of Sakhalin* (*Fortnightly Review*, *May,* 1897).

SALISBURY, Lord Robert Cecil, Marquis of: Third Ministry. See (in this vol.) ENGLAND: A. D. 1894–1895.

Correspondence with the Government of the United States on the Venezuela boundary question. See (in this vol.) VENEZUELA: A. D. 1895 (JULY) and (NOVEMBER).

Fourth Ministry. See (in this vol.) ENGLAND: A. D. 1900 (NOVEMBER—DECEMBER).

Tribute to Queen Victoria. See (in this vol.) ENGLAND: A. D. 1901 (JANUARY).

SALISBURY PLAIN: Purchase by Government. See (in this vol.) ENGLAND : A. D. 1897 (FEBRUARY).

SALVADOR. See (in this vol.) CENTRAL AMERICA.

SALVATION ARMY, The: Secession of the American Volunteers.—Late account of the Army's work.—Much feeling in the American branch of the Salvation Army, and among those who valued its work, was caused in January, 1896, by an order from the London headquarters of the Army recalling Mr. Ballington Booth, who had been its American Commander for nine years. Commander Booth and Mrs. Booth had been remarkably successful in their organization and direction of the Salvation Army work, and had won a high place in the esteem, not only of their own followers, but of the American public at large. A wide and strong movement of protest against their removal from the field failed to change the London order, which was said to be made in obedience to a necessary rule of the Army against long service in any one post. Miss Eva Booth, representing her father, General Booth, with Colonel Nicol, from London, and Commandant Herbert Booth, from Canada, came to New York as mediators, endeavoring to heal a threatened breach in the ranks; but their mission failed. Commander Ballington Booth resigned his office, and withdrew from the Salvation Army service, declining to return to London. After a time, he and Mrs. Booth became the heads of a new organization called the "Volunteers of America," for religious work, not in rivalry with that of the Salvation Army, but directed more towards the awakening of the interest of the working people, Mr. Ballington Booth was succeeded as Commander in America by a son-in-law of General Booth, Commissioner Frederick St. Clair Tucker. —For an account of the origin and growth of the Salvation Army see, under that heading, in the Supplement (vol. 5) of the original edition of this work, or in vol. 4 of the revised edition.

Of results accomplished in that part of the work of the Salvation Army known as the "Darkest England Scheme," General Booth wrote, early in 1900, an extended account in the "Sunday Strand." He stated that the public had subscribed altogether for his scheme about $1,300,000. "It is a debated point," he wrote, "with the intelligent admirers of the scheme and the careful observers of its progress whether the benefits bestowed on the wretched classes for whom it was originated have been greater within than without our borders. The copyists of our plan have been legion, both at home and abroad, in church and state. The representatives of the different governments specially charged with the responsibility for the outcast classes have been gradually coming to appreciate the principles and methods involved in the scheme, and to show willingness to coöperate in giving it a chance. They have done this in two ways: (1) In attempt-

ing similar tasks themselves; (2) in using and subsidizing the army for doing the work for them. Many governments make grants to our various institutions in varying amounts toward the cost of dealing with different classes of the submerged."

The following is a summary of the agencies which have been set at work by the general: "We have now 158 shelters and food depots for homeless men and women, 121 slum posts, each with its own slum sisters, 37 labor bureaus, 60 labor factories for the unemployed, 11 land colonies, 91 rescue homes for women, 11 labor homes for ex-criminals, several nursing institutions, 2 maternity hospitals for deserted women, an institution with branches in forty-five countries and colonies for finding lost and missing persons, together with a host of allied and minor agencies which I am not able here to enumerate. The total number of institutions named above is now 545, under the care of more than 2,000 trained officers and others wholly employed, all working in harmony with the principles I have laid down for helping the poorest and most unfortunate of their fellows, and all more or less experts at their work.

"Nearly 20,000 destitute men and women are in some way or other touched by the operations of the scheme every day. No less than 15,000 wretched and otherwise homeless people are housed under our roofs every night, having their needs met, at least in part, with sympathy and prayer and the opportunity for friendly counsel. More than 300 ex-criminals are to-day in our houses of reformation, having before them another chance for this life, and in many cases the first they have ever had for preparing for the life to come. More than 5,000 women taken from lives of darkness and shame are safely sheltered in our homes each year, on the way—as we have abundantly proved in the ease of others, in respect of a large proportion of them—to a future of virtue, goodness, and religion. Over 1,000 men are employed on the land colonies. Many of them are working out their own deliverance, and at the same time helping to solve one of the most difficult problems of modern times, and proving that many of the helpless loafers of the great cities can be made useful producers on the soil. Over the gates of every one of these homes, elevators, labor factories, and colonies there might be written: 'No man or woman need starve, or beg, or pauperize, or steal, or commit suicide. If willing to work, apply within. Here there is hope for all.'" General Booth adds that he has always 2,000 women in the rescue homes of the army.

SAMOAN ISLANDS, The : Ending of the joint control of the Islands by Germany, England and the United States.—Partition between Germany and the United States.— Retirement of England.—Said President Cleveland, in his annual Message to the Congress of the United States, December 4, 1893 : "Led by a desire to compose differences and contribute to the restoration of order in Samoa, which for some years previous had been the scene of conflicting foreign pretensions and native strife, the United States, departing from its policy consecrated by a century of observance, entered [in 1889] . . . into the treaty of Berlin [see, in vol. 4, SAMOA], thereby becoming jointly bound with England

and Germany to establish and maintain Malietoa Laupepa as King of Samoa. The treaty provided for a foreign court of justice ; a municipal council for the district of Apia, with a foreign president thereof, authorized to advise the King ; a tribunal for the settlement of native and foreign land titles, and a revenue system for the Kingdom. It entailed upon the three powers that part of the cost of the new Government not met by the revenue of the islands. Early in the life of this triple protectorate the native dissensions it was designed to quell revived. Rivals defied the authority of the new King, refusing to pay taxes and demanding the election of a ruler by native suffrage. Mataafa, an aspirant to the throne, and a large number of his native adherents were in open rebellion on one of the islands. Quite lately, at the request of the other powers and in fulfillment of its treaty obligation, this Government agreed to unite in a joint military movement of such dimensions as would probably secure the surrender of the insurgents without bloodshed. The war ship Philadelphia was accordingly put under orders for Samoa, but before she arrived the threatened conflict was precipitated by King Malietoa's attack upon the insurgent camp. Mataafa was defeated and a number of his men killed. The British and German naval vessels present subsequently secured the surrender of Mataafa and his adherents. The defeated chief and ten of his principal supporters were deported to a German island of the Marshall group, where they are held as prisoners under the joint responsibility and cost of the three powers. This incident and the events leading up to it signally illustrate the impolicy of entangling alliances with foreign powers."— *United States, Message and Documents (Abridgment)*, 1893-4.

In his next annual Message, December 3, 1894, the President thus summarized the later situation in the islands : "The suppression of the Mataafa insurrection by the powers and the subsequent banishment of the leader and eleven other chiefs, as recited in my last message, did not bring lasting peace to the islands. Formidable uprisings continued, and finally a rebellion broke out in the capital island, Upolu, headed in Aana, the western district, by the younger Tamasese, and in Atua, the eastern district, by other leaders. The insurgents ravaged the country and fought the Government's troops up to the very doors of Apia. The King again appealed to the powers for help, and the combined British and German naval forces reduced the Atuans to apparent subjection, not, however, without considerable loss to the natives. A few days later Tamasese and his adherents, fearing the ships and the marines, professed submission. Reports received from our agents at Apia do not justify the belief that the peace thus brought about will be of long duration. It is their conviction that the natives are at heart hostile to the present Government, that such of them as profess loyalty to it do so from fear of the powers, and that it would speedily go to pieces if the war ships were withdrawn. . . . The present Government has utterly failed to correct, if indeed it has not aggravated, the very evils it was intended to prevent. It has not stimulated our commerce with the islands. Our participation in its establishment against the wishes of the natives was in plain defiance of the conservative teachings and warnings of the wise and patriotic men who laid the foundations of

our free institutions, and I invite an expression of the judgment of Congress on the propriety of steps being taken by this Government looking to the withdrawal from its engagements with the other powers on some reasonable terms not prejudicial to any of our existing rights."— *United States, Message and Documents (Abridgment*, 1894-5).—In the Message of 1895 the subject was again pressed on the attention of Congress without result.

In August, 1898, Malietoa Laupepa died. By the Berlin Treaty of 1889 "it was provided that in case any question should arise in Samoa, respecting the rightful election of King, or of any other Chief claiming authority over the islands, or respecting the validity of the powers which the King or any Chief might claim in the exercise of his office, such question should not lead to war, but should be presented for decision to the Chief Justice of Samoa, who should decide it in writing, conformably to the provisions of the Act, and to the laws and customs of Samoa not in conflict therewith, and that the Signatory Governments would accept and abide by such decision. After the death of Malietoa an exchange of views took place between the Powers, and it was agreed that there should be no interference with the right of the Samoans to elect a King, and that the election should proceed strictly in accordance with the provisions of the Final Act. Some time elapsed before any action was taken, pending the completion of certain ceremonial usages customary in Samoa on the death of a High Chief. . . . As soon as the funeral ceremonies were at an end, deliberation and discussion among the Chiefs ensued. There were in the first instance several candidates for the succession. Their number was eventually reduced to two: 1. Malietoa Tanu, the son of the late King. 2. The High Chief Mataafa. This Chief had been in rebellion against Malietoa Laupepa, but had suffered defeat, and with other Chiefs had been deported, by agreement between the three Powers, to the Marshall Islands. On the recommendation of the Consular officers at Apia, the Powers, in July 1898, consented to his return. . . . On the 19th September, Mataafa and the other exiled Chiefs landed in Samoa. It does not appear that he took any overt steps to claim the vacant throne, but a section of the natives pronounced in his favour and announced on the 12th November to the Consuls and to the Chief Justice that he had been duly elected King. On the 13th November the opposing faction declared that the real election of a King had not taken place, and on the following day announced that their choice had fallen upon Malietoa Tanu. Both parties appealed to Mr. Chambers, the Chief Justice, who considered himself then in a position to take cognisance of the matter, according to the provisions of the Final Act, a question having arisen 'in Samoa respecting the rightful election or appointment of King.'"—*Great Britain, Parliamentary Publications (Papers by Command: Samoa, No.* 1, 1899).

The decision of the Chief Justice was in favor of Malietoa Tanu, and the adherents of Mataafa took up arms, defeating those of the favored candidate and driving many of them to take refuge on British and German ships of war. Subsequent events were related by the President of the United States in his Message to Congress, Dec. 5, 1899, as follows : " In this emergency a

432

joint commission of representatives of the United States, Germany, and Great Britain was sent to Samoa to investigate the situation and provide a temporary remedy. By its active efforts a peaceful solution was reached for the time being, the kingship being abolished and a provisional government established. Recommendations unanimously made by the commission for a permanent adjustment of the Samoan question were taken under consideration by the three powers parties to the General Act. But the more they were examined the more evident it became that a radical change was necessary in the relations of the powers to Samoa. The inconveniences and possible perils of the tripartite scheme of supervision and control in the Samoan group by powers having little interest in common in that quarter beyond commercial rivalry had been once more emphasized by the recent events. The suggested remedy of the Joint Commission, like the scheme it aimed to replace, amounted to what has been styled a 'tridominium,' being the exercise of the functions of sovereignty by an unanimous agreement of three powers. The situation had become far more intricate and embarrassing from every point of view than it was when my predecessor, in 1894, summed up its perplexities and condemned the participation in it of the United States. The arrangement under which Samoa was administered had proved impracticable and unacceptable to all the powers concerned. To withdraw from the agreement and abandon the islands to Germany and Great Britain would not be compatible with our interests in the archipelago. To relinquish our rights in the harbor of Pago Pago, the best anchorage in the Pacific, the occupancy of which had been leased to the United States in 1878 by the first foreign treaty ever concluded by Samoa, was not to be thought of either as regards the needs of our Navy or the interests of our growing commerce with the East. We could not have considered any proposition for the abrogation of the tripartite control which did not confirm us in all our rights and safeguard all our national interests in the islands. Our views commended themselves to the other powers. A satisfactory arrangement was concluded between the Governments of Germany and of England, by virtue of which England retired from Samoa in view of compensations in other directions, and both powers renounced in favor of the United States all their rights and claims over and in respect to that portion of the group lying to the east of the one hundred and seventy-first degree of west longitude, embracing the islands of Tutuila, Ofoo, Olosenga, and Manua."—*United States, Message and Documents (Abridgment), 1899–1900, v. 1.*

The compensations to England "in other directions" were given by Germany, in the following provisions of a treaty signed at London, November 14, 1899:

"ART. II. Germany renounces in favour of Great Britain all her rights over the Tonga Islands, including Vavau, and over Savage Island, including the right of establishing a naval station and coaling station, and the right of extra-territoriality in the said islands. . . . She recognizes as falling to Great Britain those of the Solomon Islands, at present belonging to Germany, which are situated to the east and southeast of the Island of Bougainville, which

latter shall continue to belong to Germany, together with the Island of Buka, which forms part of it. The western portion of the neutral zone in West Africa, as defined in Article V of the present Convention, shall also fall to the share of Great Britain. . . .

"ART. IV. The arrangement at present existing between Germany and Great Britain and concerning the right of Germany to freely engage labourers in the Solomon Islands belonging to Great Britain shall be equally extended to those of the Solomon Islands mentioned in Article II, which fall to the share of Great Britain.

"ART. V. In the neutral zone the frontier between the German and English territories shall be formed by the River Daka as far as the point of its intersection with the 9th degree of north latitude, thence the frontier shall continue to the north, leaving Morozugu to Great Britain, and shall be fixed on the spot by a Mixed Commission of the two Powers, in such manner that Gambaga and all the territories of Mamprusi shall fall to Great Britain, and that Yendi and all the territories of Chakosi shall fall to Germany.

"ART. VI. Germany is prepared to take into consideration, as much and as far as possible, the wishes which the Government of Great Britain may express with regard to the development of the reciprocal Tariffs in the territories of Togo and of the Gold Coast.

"ART. VII. Germany renounces her rights of extra-territoriality in Zanzibar, but it is at the same time understood that this renunciation shall not effectively come into force till such time as the rights of extra-territoriality enjoyed there by other nations shall be abolished."

To the treaty was appended the following "Declaration": "It is clearly understood that by Article II of the Convention signed to-day, Germany consents that the whole group of the Howe Islands, which forms part of the Solomon Islands, shall fall to Great Britain. It is also understood that the stipulations of the Declaration between the two Governments signed at Berlin on the 10th April, 1886, respecting freedom of commerce in the Western Pacific, apply to the islands mentioned in the aforesaid Convention. It is similarly understood that the arrangement at present in force as to the engagement of labourers by Germans in the Solomon Islands permits Germans to engage those labourers on the same conditions as those which are or which shall be imposed on British subjects nonresident in those islands."—*Great Britain, Parliamentary Publications (Papers by Command: Treaty Series, No. 7, 1900).*

Article III of the general treaty between the United States, Germany and Great Britain stipulated: "It is understood and agreed that each of the three signatory Powers shall continue to enjoy, in respect to their commerce and commercial vessels, in all the islands of the Samoan group, privileges and conditions equal to those enjoyed by the sovereign Power, in all ports which may be open to the commerce of either of them."—*United States, 56th Cong., 1st Sess., Senate Doc. No. 157.*

On the 17th of April, 1900, an "instrument of cession" was signed by the marks of twenty-two chiefs, conveying to the United States the islands of the Samoan group lying east of the 171st degree of west longitude, and the American flag was raised over the naval station at Pago-Pago.

6–28

From Pago-Pago, March 27, 1901, a Press despatch announced : " The natives under the United States Government number 5,800, according to a census just taken, while the natives in the other islands under German rule number 32,000. The population has increased very slightly in the last thirty years, and the main cause of this failure to increase is the infant mortality, due to the violation of the simplest health principles in the care and diet of children. . . . Reports from the six islands under United States control show that the natives are improving in general conditions, and that they show a desire to keep their houses neat and to educate their children. Not a single native has been arrested for drunkenness since the Americans assumed control of Tutuila island."

SAMPSON, Rear-Admiral William T.: Commanding North Atlantic Station.— Blockade of Cuban ports. See (in this vol.) UNITED STATES OF AM. : A. D. 1898 (APRIL— MAY : CUBA).

Operations at Santiago de Cuba. See (in this vol.) UNITED STATES OF AM.: A. D. 1898 (APRIL—JUNE).

Destruction of Spanish squadron. See (in this vol.) UNITED STATES OF AM.: A. D. 1898 (JULY 3).

SAN DOMINGO. See (in this vol.) DOMINICAN REPUBLIC.

SAN FRANCISCO: A. D. 1898.—New city charter.—A city charter of a quite new and experimental character was adopted by popular vote in May, to go into effect at the beginning of the year 1900. Its main features were described at the time by the " New York Tribune," as follows : " The formation of this charter is an advanced example of the exercise of municipal home rule. The constitution of California gives the cities of the state the uncommon privilege of framing their own charters subject simply to the veto power of the legislature. Exercising that right, the people, acting through fifteen freeholders, elected for that purpose, have drawn up the new charter. . . . If the legislature approves, it will become the local constitution. The charter provides for its own amendment by the people without appeal to the legislature. So the present provisions of that instrument may be only a form to be entirely remodeled by the city at its own pleasure until it has no resemblance to the laws to which the state authorities gave approval. That is an extreme delegation of powers, such as we think has never before been made in an American state. The mayor has large powers of appointment and removal. He can suspend all elected officers except the supervisors—the city legislators—who may remove those whom he suspends, and he may remove at any time for cause all appointive officers. The elective list is large, for, though there are only eighteen supervisors, the number of places filled by election each year is thirty. This is a great departure

from the charter-making practice recently prevalent, which has tended to the election of only a few administrative officers who are responsible for the selection of agents in different departments. Attempt is made to centre responsibility in the mayor, but the supervisors and the people both can pass ordinances likely to interfere with that responsibility. So the charter is as far as possible from inaugurating the one-man power, which has been much advocated as the cure for the ills which spring from a municipal administration animated by no uniform purpose or intelligence."

SAN JUAN HILL, Battle of. See (in this vol.) UNITED STATES OF AM. : A. D. 1898 (JUNE —JULY).

SAND RIVER CONVENTION, The. See (in this vol.) SOUTH AFRICA (THE TRANSVAAL): A. D. 1884–1894.

SANTIAGO DE CUBA: A. D. 1898 (May —June).—Blockade of Spanish squadron in the Bay. See (in this vol.) UNITED STATES OF AM. : A. D. 1898 (APRIL—JUNE).

A. D. 1898 (June—July).—Attack and investment by American army. See (in this vol.) UNITED STATES OF AM. : A. D. 1898 (JUNE —JULY).

A. D. 1898 (July 3).—Destruction of Spanish fleet. See (in this vol.) UNITED STATES OF AM. : A. D. 1898 (JULY 3).

A. D. 1898 (July 4-17).—Surrender of the city and Spanish forces. See (in this vol.) UNITED STATES OF AM. : A. D. 1898 (JULY 4–17).

A. D. 1898 (August).—Sickness in the American army.—Withdrawal of troops. See (in this vol.) UNITED STATES OF AM. : A. D. 1898 (JULY—AUGUST: CUBA).

SARGON OF AKKAD. See (in this vol.) ARCHÆOLOGICAL RESEARCH : BABYLONIA : AMERICAN EXPLORATION.

SAYINGS OF OUR LORD, Discovery of a fragment of the. See (in this vol.) ARCHÆOLOGICAL RESEARCH : EGYPT: DISCOVERY OF A FRAGMENT.

SCHLEY, Admiral W. S.: In operations at Santiago de Cuba. See (in this vol.) UNITED STATES OF AM. : A. D. 1898 (APRIL—JUNE).

Destruction of Spanish squadron. See (in this vol.) UNITED STATES OF AM.: A. D. 1898 (JULY 3).

SCHOOLS. See EDUCATION.

SCHREINER, W. P.: Resignation of the Premiership of Cape Colony. See (in this vol.) SOUTH AFRICA (CAPE COLONY): A. D. 1900 (APRIL—JUNE).

SCHWAN, General: Military operations in the Philippine Islands. See (in this vol.) PHILIPPINE ISLANDS: A. D. 1899 (JANUARY— NOVEMBER).

SCIENCE, RECENT.

NOTABLE ACHIEVEMENTS.

Archæological discovery. See (in this vol.) ARCHÆOLOGICAL RESEARCH.

Chemistry and Physics: Acetylene Gas.—Acetylene gas has been known since 1832, when it was discovered by Edmund Davy; but it remained a mere laboratory product until 1892, when two experimenters, in America and France, stumbled accidentally on the production, in an electric furnace, of calcium carbide, which water decomposes, readily yielding the gas in question. The American discoverer was Mr. Thomas Willson, a Canadian electrician, residing at Spray, North Carolina; his French rival was Professor Henry Moisson, of Paris. The priority of Mr. Willson in the discovery, or in the announcement of it, is most generally recognized, and he secured patents in the United States and elsewhere. Electrical developments since 1892 have economized the manufacture of calcium carbide, by electric heat acting on a mixture of lime and coke, and it has become an important commercial product, at Niagara Falls and other seats of electric power, bringing acetylene gas into extensive use as an illuminant. There have been dangers and difficulties in the use, however, not easily overcome.

Chemistry and Physics: Discovery of Argon and Helium. "After Lord Rayleigh, in 1892, had proved that nitrogen obtained from chemical combinations was about one-half per cent lighter than that obtained from the atmosphere, a determination that was again verified in 1894, Lord Rayleigh and Professor Ramsay separated from atmospheric nitrogen an elementary gas of great density which, by reason of its chemical indifference, they called argon. They proved that this gas formed about 0.8 or 0.9 per cent of the volume of nitrogen, from which it could be separated either by incandescent magnesium or by the continued action of the electric spark. It was established beyond doubt that Cavendish produced this gas a hundred years ago by the use of the electric spark. Argon, either alone or accompanied by helium, has also been found in natural waters as well as in minerals. Its discovery in a meteorite of Augusta County, Virginia, United States of America, may perhaps lead us to ascribe to it an extra-terrestrial origin.

"The physical properties of argon are very distinct, and its characteristic spectrum enables us to at once distinguish it with certainty from any other substance, but from a chemical point of view this gas is most extraordinarily inactive, and we have not yet succeeded in making it form combinations as the other elements do. This peculiarity, and also the impossibility of finding a place in the periodic system for a simple body having the molecular weight of argon (39.88), have given rise to all sorts of hypotheses relative to the nature of this gas. . . .

"Another most interesting discovery was that of helium, made by Professor Ramsay. In 1891 Hillebrand showed that uranium ore and ores of the same family when dissolved in acids or fused with alkaline carbonates, or even merely heated in a vacuum, may give off as much as 3 per cent of nitrogen. Professor Ramsay obtained this gas from cleveite and by means of spectroscopic examination demonstrated the presence of argon; and in the course of his experiments—in March, 1895—he observed beside the spectrum of argon another bright, yellow line that did not belong to that spectrum, and which Crookes recognized as identical with the line D that Lockyer had already observed in 1868 in the spectrum of the solar chromosphere, and which he had attributed to an element as yet unknown upon the earth—helium. The same line had also been distinguished in the spectra of other fixed stars, particularly in the spectrum of Orion, so that it may be admitted that helium exists in large quantities extra-terrestrially. . . . On our planet it appears, on the contrary, to be very rare, and may be ranked among the rarest of elements. . . .

"Helium is the lightest of all the gases except hydrogen; Stoney deduces from this fact an explanation of the existence of these two elements in but very small quantities in a free state upon the face of the earth, while they are distributed in enormous masses throughout the universe. The comparatively small force of the earth's gravitation does not form a sufficient counterpoise to the velocity of their molecules, which therefore escape from the terrestrial atmosphere unless restrained by chemical combination. They then proceed to reunite around great centres of attraction, such as the fixed stars, in whose atmospheres these elements exist in large quantities."—*C. Winkler, The Discovery of new Elements within the last twenty-five years* (Annual Report of Smithsonian Institution, 1897, p. 237, trans. from Revue Scientifique, 4th ser., vol. 8).

Chemistry and Physics: Liquefaction of Oxygen, Hydrogen and Air.—"The most remarkable recent work in refrigeration is that of Professor James Dewar, of the Royal Institution in London. The feat of liquefying oxygen by a succession of approaches to its critical temperature has been thus described by him, in an interview which appeared in 'McClure's Magazine,' November, 1893: 'The process of liquefying oxygen, briefly speaking, is this: Into the outer chamber of that double compressor I introduce, through a pipe, liquid nitrous oxide gas, under a pressure of about 1,400 pounds to the square inch. I then allow it to evaporate rapidly, and thus obtain a temperature around the inner chamber of −90° C. Into this cooled inner chamber I introduce liquid ethylene, which is a gas at ordinary temperatures, under a pressure of 1,800 pounds to the square inch. When the inner chamber is full of ethylene, its rapid evaporation under exhaustion reduces the temperature to −135° C. Running through this inner chamber is a tube containing oxygen gas under a pressure of 750 pounds to the square inch. The critical point of oxygen gas—that is, the point above which no amount of pressure will reduce it to a liquid—is −115° C., but this pressure, at the temperature of −145° C., is amply sufficient to cause it to liquefy rapidly.'

"In May, 1898, Professor Dewar, by the use of liquid oxygen, succeeded in liquefying hydrogen, producing a liquid having but one-fourteenth the specific gravity of water; this exploit brought him within 21° of the absolute zero of centigrade. He afterward reduced the liquid to solid form, attaining a temperature estimated at four to five degrees lower. Faraday and other investigators of an earlier day surmised that hydrogen, when solidified, would prove to be a metal ; now that the feat of solidification has been accomplished, hydrogen astonishes the physicist by displaying itself as non-metallic. . . .

"For some years the plan was to employ a series of chemical compounds, each with a lower boiling-point than its predecessor in the process, and all troublesome and hazardous in manipulation. A better method has been developed by keeping to simple air from first to last, as in the apparatus of Dr. Linde, of Dr. Hampson, and of Mr. Charles E. Tripler.

"As the Tripler machine does its work on a bolder scale than either of the others, let its operation be briefly outlined : Air is first compressed to 65 pounds pressure to the square inch ; through a second pump this pressure is exalted to 400 pounds, and with a third pump the pressure is carried to 2,500 pounds. After each compression the air flows through jacketed pipes, where it is cooled by a stream of water. At the third condensation a valve, the secret of whose construction Mr. Tripler keeps to himself, permits part of the compressed air to flow into a pipe surrounding the tube through which the remainder is flowing. This act of expansion severely chills the imprisoned air, which at last discharges itself in liquid form—much as water does from an ordinary city faucet."—G. Iles, *Flame, Electricity and the Camera, ch.* 6 (*N. Y. : Doubleday, Page & Co.*).

Chemistry and Physics: Smokeless Powders.—"In recent years smokeless powders have largely superseded all others. These contain usually nitro-cellulose (gun cotton), or nitro-glycerine, or both, made up into a plastic, coherent, and homogeneous compound of a gluey nature, and fashioned into horn-like sticks or rods by being forced under pressure, through a die plate having small holes, through which the plastic material is strained into strings like macaroni, or else is molded into tablets, pellets, or grains of cubical shape. Prominent among those who have contributed to this art are the names of Turpin, Abel and Dewar, Nobel, Maxim, Munroe, Du Pont, Bernadou and others. In the recent years of the Nineteenth Century great activity has been manifest in this field of invention. In the United States more than 600 different patents have been granted for explosives, the larger portion of them being for nitro-compounds which partake in a greater or less degree of the qualities of gun cotton or nitro-glycerine." — E. W. Byrn, *Progress of Invention in the 19th Century, p.* 419.

Chemistry and Physics : X Rays.—The Discovery of Professor Rontgen.—"Fresh proofs await us of the supreme rank of both electricity and photography as resources of art and science as we observe the transcendent powers evoked by their union. From this union no issue is more extraordinary, more weighty with meaning and promise, than the X-ray pictures due to Professor Wilhelm Konrad Röntgen. In these pictures he has but crowned labours which began when Sir John Herschel noticed that a peculiar blue light was diffused from a perfectly colourless solution of quinine sulphate. Professor (now Sir) George Stokes explained the phenomenon by showing that this blue light consists of vibrations originally too rapid to be visible, which are slowed down within the limits of perceptibility as they pass through the liquid. . . .

"One path of approach to the achievement of Professor Röntgen was opened by Sir John Herschel ; another, as important, was blazed and broadened by Professor (now Sir) William Crookes. In 1874 and 1875 he was engaged upon the researches which gave the world the radiometer, the tiny mill whose vanes rotate with rays of light or heat. The action of this mill depends upon its being placed in a glass bulb almost vacuous. When such a bulb incloses rubies, bits of phenakite, or other suitable objects, and electrical discharges are directed upon them, they glow with the most brilliant luminescence known to art. Excited by a cathode ray, that is, a ray from the negative pole of an electrical machine, a Crookes bulb itself shines with a vivid golden green ray which reminds the onlooker of the fluorescence of earlier experiments. . . .

"Year by year the list of substances excitable to luminosity in a Crookes bulb has been lengthened, and in 1894 it was the good fortune of Professor Philipp Lenard to discover a wonderful power of such a bulb. Emerging from it was a cathode ray which passed nearly as freely through a thin plate of aluminium as common sunshine does through a pane of glass. Hertz had, a few years previously, discovered that metals in very thin sheets were virtually transparent (or, to use Mr. Hyndman's term, transradiable) to his electric waves. This property was found by Professor Lenard to extend to the cathode ray and in a much higher degree. . . . The ultra-violet ray of ordinary light has the singular power of causing the gases which it may traverse to become conductors of electricity, with the effect of discharging an electrified metallic plate ; this property is shared by cathode rays. Associated with them are the rays of still more extraordinary powers, discovered by Professor Röntgen. In his own words let his achievement be recounted, as published in 'McClure's Magazine,' April, 1896.

"'I have been for a long time interested in the problem of the cathode rays from a vacuum tube as studied by Hertz and Lenard. I had followed their and other researches with great interest, and determined, as soon as I had the time, to make some researches of my own. This time I found at the close of last October. I had been at work for some days when I discovered something new.' 'What was the date?' 'The 8th of November.' 'And what was the discovery?' 'I was working with a Crookes tube covered by a shield of black cardboard. A piece of barium platino-cyanide paper lay on the bench there. I had been passing a current through the tube, and I noticed a peculiar black line across the paper.' 'What of that?' 'The effect was one which could only be produced, in ordinary parlance, by the passage of light. No light could come from the tube, because the shield which covered it was impervious to any light known, even that of the electric arc.' 'And what did you think?' 'I did not think ; I investigated. I assumed that the effect must have come from the tube, since its character indicated that it could come from nowhere else. I tested it. In a few minutes there was no doubt about it. Rays were coming from the tube which had a luminescent effect upon the paper. I tried it successfully at greater and greater distances, even at two metres. It seemed at first a new kind of invisible light. It was clearly something new, something unrecorded.' 'Is it light?' 'No.' 'Is it electricity?' 'Not in any known form.' 'What is it?' 'I don't know.' And the discoverer of the X rays thus stated as calmly his ignorance of their essence as has everybody else who has written on the phenomena thus far.

" 'Having discovered the existence of a new kind of rays, I of course began to investigate what they would do.' He took up a series of cabinet-sized photographs. 'It soon appeared from tests that the rays had penetrative power to a degree hitherto unknown. They penetrated paper, wood, and cloth with ease; and the thickness of the substance made no perceptible difference, within reasonable limits.' He showed photographs of a box of laboratory weights of platinum, aluminium, and brass, they and the brass hinges all having been photographed from a closed box, without any indication of the box. Also a photograph of a coil of fine wire, wound on a wooden spool, the wire having been photographed and the wood omitted.

" 'The rays,' he continued, 'passed through all the metals tested, with a facility varying, roughly speaking, with the density of the metal. These phenomena I have discussed carefully in my report to the Würzburg Society, and you will find all the technical results therein stated.' He showed a photograph of a small sheet of zinc. This was composed of smaller plates soldered laterally with solders of different metallic proportions. The differing lines of shadow caused by the difference in the solders were visible evidence that a new means of detecting flaws and chemical variations in metals had been found. A photograph of a compass showed the needle and dial taken through the closed brass cover. The markings of the dial were in red metallic paint, and thus interfered with the rays, and were reproduced. 'Since the rays had this great penetrative power, it seemed natural that they should penetrate flesh, and so it proved in photographing the hand, as I showed you.'" . . .

"Provided with a Röntgen bulb, the photographer passes from the exterior to the interior of an object, almost as if he were a sorcerer with power to transmute all things to glass. Equipped with a simple X-ray apparatus, dislocations and fractures are detected by the surgeon, diseases of bones are studied, and shot, needles, and bits of glass or corroding wire within the muscles of a patient are located with exactitude. Thanks to the work of Mr. Mackenzie Davidson, the like detection of renal calculi can be looked forward to with a fair degree of certainty. The same means of exploration offers equal aid to medicine: it demonstrates the calcification of arteries, and aneurisms of the heart or of the first part of the aorta; with improved methods it may be possible to study fatty degenerations of the arteries and larger blood-vessels. Dr. C. M. Mouillin, addressing the Röntgen Society of London as its president, states that the fluorescent screen has now reached such a degree of perfection that the minutest movement of the heart and lungs, and the least change in the action of the diaphragm, can be watched and studied at leisure in the living subject. He considers it probable that the examination of a patient's chest with this screen may become as much a matter of common routine as with the stethoscope to-day. . . .

"Manifestly, the unseen universe which enfolds us is steadily being brought to the light of day. The investigations of Hertz established that the light-waves which affect the eye are but one octave in a gamut which sweeps indefinitely far both above and below them. In his hands, as in those of Joseph Henry long before, electric waves found their way through the walls and floors of a house; in the Marconi telegraph these waves pass through the earth or a fog, a mist or a rain-storm, with little or no hindrance. What does all this mean? Nothing less than that, given its accordant ray, any substance whatever is permeable, and that, therefore, to communicate between any two places in the universe is simply a question of providing the right means."
—G. Iles, *Flame, Electricity and the Camera, ch. 24 (N. Y.: Doubleday, Page & Co.).*

In an article made public in the "New York Tribune" of January 6, 1901, Professor John Trowbridge, of Harvard University, expressed his anticipations from the further improvement of the use of the X rays, as follows: "At present all of the great hospitals of the world examine injuries of the extremities of the human body by means of these rays. In some cases the thicker portions of the body can be studied by their means. There is, however, much to be desired in the method, for in general the rays exhibit only the shadows of the bones of the extremities, or reveal at most the regions of greatest density in the body. If the muscles and tendons or the veins and arteries could be studied by means of these rays, an immense aid to surgery would result. Some experiments I have conducted with currents of great strength, lead me to believe that much can be done in this direction, for I have in certain cases obtained unmistakable traces of muscles and tendons, and the direction in which to advance is becoming clearer. The use of the X rays is not confined to the examination of the body. Together with the ultra violet rays, the X rays are used to cure cutaneous disorders. We are realizing that electricity is an important factor in health and disease. The investigations which have resulted from the discovery of these rays have opened wide vistas in the molecular world."

Electrical Science: Power.—Lighting.— Electro-chemical and Electro-metallurgical works.—The development at Niagara Falls. —"There were perhaps not more than twenty trolley cars in actual service in 1887, and these were of doubtful success. There were no regularly constituted electric railways worthy of the name. The telephone and electric-lighting wires were largely overhead, and frequently the construction was of the most imperfect and temporary character. . . . Within the past eight or ten years much has been done in the perfection of thoroughly practical forms of meters and other instruments for the measurement of electric forces and quantities. While such work resembles in its delicacy that demanded by watch mechanism, on the other hand the large station dynamos are examples of the heaviest machine construction. . . . A few years ago a dynamo was large if it demanded 100 or 200 horsepower to drive it, while now such machines are diminutive when compared with those of 2,000 horsepower commonly constructed. Dynamos are in use at Niagara of 5,000 horsepower capacity. A single one of these would supply more than 50,000 incandescent lights such as are ordinarily used, or would give motion to 500 trolley cars. The period since 1887 has been marked by great extension in electric lighting by both arc and incandescent lamps. . . . One of the chief factors in this great extension has been the application of alternating electric currents, or currents of wave-like nature, reversing their direction many times in each second. The direct or continuous current had previously occupied the field alone. But the alternating current possessed the advantage of readily permitting the sending out over a long distance of a high pressure current with but little loss and by means of comparatively small and inexpensive lines. This current, relatively dangerous, could then be exchanged for a safe low-pressure current on the house mains for working the lights. The device which makes the exchange is called a transformer. It is in reality a modified induction coil—a simple structure of copper wire, sheet-iron, and insulating materials, with no moving parts to need attention or to get out of order. The properties and use of the transformer in an alternating-current system were comparatively unknown before 1887, but since that time it has played a part in electric development the importance of which cannot easily be overestimated. It has been, furthermore, brought to a high degree of perfection by the persistent and painstaking effort of numerous workers. In transforming a current of high pressure to one of lower pressure, or the reverse, only a very slight loss of power or energy is suffered. On a large scale, this loss is barely 3 per cent of the energy of the transformed current. The larger sizes of transformers now in use have capacities equivalent to considerably over 1,000 horsepower. Some of these structures are employed at Niagara and others at Buffalo. As in the case of the apparatus just mentioned, the effort spent in the perfection of the huge dynamo-electric generators used in lighting and power stations has resulted in machines so perfect as to leave but little chance of further increase of effectiveness. They waste only a small percentage in converting mechanical power into electrical energy, and run for years with but little attention or need of repairs. Along with all this improvement has gone a like betterment in the thousand and one details and minor devices which go to make up an electric system. . . .

" Perhaps . . . no better example of the varied application of electric energy exists than at Niagara. Certainly no grander exemplification of the way in which electric forces may be called into play, to replace other and unlike agencies, can be cited. Here at Niagara we may forcibly realize the importance of cheap and unfailing power developed from water in its fall. We find the power of huge water wheels delivered to the massive dynamos for giving out electric energy. This energy is variously employed. The electric lighting of the city of Niagara and surroundings and the electric railways naturally depend upon the water power. Besides these, which may be termed the ordinary applications of electricity, there are clustered at Niagara a number of unique industrial establishments, the importance of which will undoubtedly increase rapidly. In the carborundum factory we find

huge furnaces heated by the passage of electric current, and attaining temperatures far beyond those of the ordinary combustion of fuel. These electric furnaces produce carborundum, a new abrasive nearly as hard as the diamond, which is a combination of carbon and silicon, unknown before the electric furnace gave it birth. Sand and coke are the raw substances for its production, and these are acted upon by the excessively high heat necessary to form the new product, already in extensive use for grinding hard materials. The metal aluminum, which not many years ago cost $2 an ounce, is now produced on a large scale at Niagara, and sold at a price which makes it, bulk for bulk, cheaper than brass. Here, again, electricity is the agent ; but in this case its power of electrolyzing or breaking up strong chemical unions is employed. . . . Works for the production of metallic sodium and other metals similarly depend upon the decompositions effected by the electric current. Solutions of ordinary salt or brine are electrolyzed on a large scale in extensive works established for the purpose. . . . The very high temperature which exists in an electric arc, or between the carbons of an arc lamp, has in recent years found application in the manufacture of another important compound, which was formerly but slightly known as a chemical difficult to prepare. Carbide of calcium is the compound referred to, and large works for its production exist at Niagara. Here again, as in the carborundum works, raw materials of the simplest and cheapest kind are acted upon in what may be termed an electric-arc furnace. Coke, or carbon, and lime are mixed and charged into a furnace in which an enormous electric arc is kept going. . . . The importance of carbide of calcium rests in the fact that, by contact with water, it produces acetylene gas. The illuminating power of this gas, when burned, is its remarkable property.

" It will be seen that the metallurgical and chemical developments at Niagara are the direct outgrowth of electrical utilization of water power. With many water powers, however, the outlet for the application of the electrical energy exists many miles away from the place at which the water power is found. Even at Niagara there is an example of the beginning of long-distance transmission, by a high-pressure line extending to Buffalo and delivering electric energy to an electric station there. In this case ' step-up' transformers, as they are called, are employed at the Niagara power plant to step up or raise the electrical pressure or potential from that given by the dynamos to that required for the transmission to Buffalo. This transformation is from about 2,500 up to 10,000 volts. At the Buffalo end the reverse process is carried on by ' step-down' transformers, and the energy is delivered to the trolley lines at about 500 volts. . . . The whole Niagara plant has grown into existence within the past five years, and as a consequence of the technical advances within the period of the past ten years. There are, however, in active operation, besides the Niagara power plant, several other water-power transmissions, some of them far exceeding in distance that between Niagara and Buffalo, and some in which the amount of power conveyed, as well as the pressure of the current used upon the line, is much greater than is yet to be found at Niagara. . . . No limit can as yet be definitely set as to the distance which can be covered in an electrical transmission. . . . It may be said that at present the range of distances is between 30 and 100 miles. . . .

"Electricity seems destined at no distant day to play an important part in revolutionizing passenger traffic between large centers of population. The facility with which electric service may be superposed on ordinary steam roads will greatly further this development. The work with the third-rail system, undertaken by one of our prominent railway organizations, has abundantly demonstrated the practicability of such superposition. The future will witness the growing substitution of either single motor cars or two or three coupled cars for long, heavy trains drawn by locomotives, and a more frequent service will result. There is an eventual possibility of higher average speeds, since stops will not consume much time, and the time required to recover the speed after a stop will be much less than at present. . . . The heating power of the electric current is now utilized in a variety of ways. Electric welding machinery has been put into service either for accomplishing results which were not possible to be obtained before its development, or to improve the work and lessen the cost."— Elihu Thomson, *Electrical Advance in Ten Years* (*Forum, Jan.*, 1898).

Electrical Science : Development of Power at Niagara Falls.—The following description of the engineering work by which Niagara was harnessed to turbines and dynamos, for an enormous development of electrical power, is taken from a paper read by Mr. Thomas Commerford Martin, of New York, at a meeting of the Royal Institution of Great Britain, June 19, 1896, and printed in the Proceedings of the Institution, Vol. 15 ; reprinted in the Annual Report of the Smithsonian Institution, 1896, p. 223 : "Niagara is the point at which are discharged, through two narrowing precipitous channels only 3,800 feet wide and 160 feet high, the contents of 6,000 cubic miles of water, with a reservoir area of 90,000 square miles, draining 300,000 square miles of territory. The ordinary overspill of this Atlantic set on edge has been determined to be equal to about 75,000 cubic feet per second, and the quantity passing is estimated as high as 100,000,000 tons of water per hour. The drifting of a ship over the Horse Shoe Fall has proved it to have a thickness at the center of the crescent of over 16 feet. Between Lake Erie and Lake Ontario there is a total difference of level of 300 feet, and the amount of power represented by the water at the falls has been estimated on different bases from 6,750,000 horsepower up to not less than 16,800,000 horsepower, the latter being a rough calculation of Sir William Siemens, who, in 1877, was the first to suggest the use of electricity as the modern and feasible agent of converting into useful power some of this majestic but squandered energy. . . .

"It was Mr. Thomas Evershed, an American civil engineer, who unfolded the plan of diverting part of the stream at a considerable distance above the falls, so that no natural beauty would be interfered with, while an enormous amount of power would be obtained with a very slight reduction in the volume of the stream at the crest of the falls. Essentially scientific and correct as the plan now shows itself to be, it found

prompt criticism and condemnation, but not less quickly did it rally the able and influential support of Messrs. W. B. Rankine, Francis Lynde Stetson, Edward A. Wickes, and Edward D. Adams, who organized the corporate interests that, with an expenditure of £1,000,000 in five years, have carried out the present work. So many engineering problems arose early in the enterprise that after the survey of the property in 1890 an International Niagara Commission was established in London, with power to investigate the best existing methods of power development and transmission, and to select from among them, as well as to award prizes of an aggregate of £4,400. This body included men like Lord Kelvin, Mascart, Coleman Sellers, Turrettini, and Dr. Unwin, and its work was of the utmost value. Besides this the Niagara Company and the allied Cataract Construction Company enjoyed the direct aid of other experts, such as Prof. George Forbes, in a consultative capacity ; while it was a necessary consequence that the manufacturers of the apparatus to be used threw upon their work the highest inventive and constructive talent at their command.

"The time-honored plan in water-power utilization has been to string factories along a canal of considerable length, with but a short tail race. At Niagara the plan now brought under notice is that of a short canal with a very long tail race. The use of electricity for distributing the power allows the factories to be placed away from the canal, and in any location that may appear specially desirable or advantageous. The perfected and concentrated Evershed scheme comprises a short surface canal 250 feet wide at its mouth, 1¼ miles above the falls, far beyond the outlying Three Sisters Islands, with an intake inclined obliquely to the Niagara River. This canal extends inwardly 1,700 feet, and has an average depth of some 12 feet, thus holding water adequate to the development of about 100,000 horsepower. The mouth of the canal is 600 feet from the shore line proper, and considerable work was necessary in its protection and excavation. The bed is now of clay, and the side walls are of solid masonry 17 feet high, 8 feet at the base, and 3 feet at the top. The northeastern side of the canal is occupied by a power house, and is pierced by ten inlets guarded by sentinel gates, each being the separate entrance to a wheel pit in the power house, where the water is used and the power is secured. The water as quickly as used is carried off by a tunnel to the Niagara River again. . . .

"The wheel pit, over which the power house is situated, is a long, deep, cavernous slot at one side, under the floor, cut in the rock, parallel with the canal outside. Here the water gets a fall of about 140 feet before it smites the turbines. The arrangement of the dynamos generating the current up in the power house is such that each of them may be regarded as the screw at the end of a long shaft, just as we might see it if we stood an ocean steamer on its nose with its heel in the air. At the lower end of the dynamo shaft is the turbine in the wheel pit bottom, just as in the case of the steamer shaft we find attached to it the big triple or quadruple expansion marine steam engine. . . . The wheel pit which contains the turbines is 178 feet in depth, and connects by a lateral tunnel with the main tunnel running at right angles. This main tunnel is no less than 7,000 feet in length, with an average hydraulic slope of 6 feet in 1,000. It has a maximum height of 21 feet, and a width of 18 feet 10 inches, its net section being 386 square feet. The water rushes through it and out of its mouth of stone and iron at a velocity of $26\frac{1}{2}$ feet per second, or nearly 20 miles an hour. More than 1,000 men were employed continuously for more than three years in the construction of this tunnel. . . .

"The American Company has also pre-empted the great utilization of the Canadian share of Niagara's energy. The plan for this work proposes the erection of two power houses of a total ultimate capacity of 125,000 horsepower. . . . With both the Canadian and American plants fully developed, no less than 350,000 horsepower will be available."

"Within the last five years," said the "Electrical Review," in a "historical number" issued at the beginning of 1901, "there have been built in many parts of the world electrical installations of great magnitude, transmitting the power of cataracts for considerable distances. The longest of these, in California, operates over a distance of 115 miles. Perhaps the largest of them is that at Niagara, where 105,000 horse power is developed, and much of it transmitted . . . to the city of Buffalo"—20 miles.

The first transmission of power from Niagara Falls to Buffalo was made at midnight, November 15–16, 1896, when 1,000 horsepower was sent over the wires to the power-house of the Buffalo Railway Company. The important event was signalled to the citizens by the firing of cannon, the ringing of bells and sounding of steam whistles.

Electrical Science: The rotary magnetic field.—Polyphased currents.—Nikola Tesla's inventions.—"At about the same time [1888], Galileo Ferraris, in Italy, and Nikola Tesla, in the United States, brought out motors operating by systems of alternating currents displaced from one another in phase by definite amounts and producing what is known as the rotating magnetic field. This invention seems destined to be one of the most important that has been made in the history of electricity. The result of the introduction of polyphase systems has been the ability to transmit power economically for considerable distances, and, as this directly operated to make possible the utilization of water-power in remote places and the distribution of power over large areas, the immediate outcome of the polyphase system was power transmission; and the outcome of power transmission almost surely will be the gradual supersession of coal and the harnessing of the waste forces of Nature to do useful work."—Electrical Review, Jan. 12, 1901.

The following description of Tesla's invention was given by N. W. Perry in the "Engineering Magazine": "If the north and south poles of a small horseshoe magnet be suspended over a bar of soft iron free to revolve in a horizontal plane, or be placed over an ordinary compass-needle, the latter will be attracted at either end by the poles of the magnet and take up a position parallel to a straight line drawn between the two poles of the magnet. Now if the latter be revolved through any angle the soft iron or needle will follow, being dragged around by the magnet, and if the magnet be caused to revolve regularly

the iron will also revolve, being pulled around by the full force of the magnet. It was not feasible, however, to cause the magnet to revolve in this way, and Tesla's invention consisted in obviating this trouble and, in fact, greatly simplifying the problem. He conceived the idea that if he took an iron ring and used two alternating currents, one of which had its maximum value at the instant that the other had a zero value—or, in other words, two currents whose periods were such that one waned as the other increased—he could produce in that iron ring by winding these circuits in alternate coils surfaces that without any mechanical movement of the parts would travel around that ring with a rapidity equal to the number of changes of direction of the currents employed. He thus had a ring, the north and south poles of which were rapidly revolving just as would the poles of the horseshoe magnet were it tied at its middle to a twisted string and allowed to revolve. A piece of iron pivoted at its middle placed concentric with this ring would therefore be dragged around by the changing poles of the ring. He had thus discovered what is somewhat awkwardly expressed by the expression, 'the rotary magnetic field,' and also the use of what have been termed 'polyphased currents'—the one referring to the magnetism and the other to the combination of currents by which this changing magnetism was produced. This discovery is undoubtedly one of the most important that has ever been made within the domain of alternating currents."—Engineering Magazine, v. 7, p. 780.

Another of Tesla's inventions or discoveries which excited greater popular interest was that which produced what were called "high frequency effects," first publicly shown in connection with a lecture at Columbia College, in the spring of 1890. "Mr. Tesla started with the idea of setting matter into vibration at a rate approximating that of light (some two and a half millions a second), with the expectation that under such violent molecular agitation it would emit light. He has not as yet succeeded in obtaining so high a rate, but a much lower one produced some very surprising luminous effects. . . . The dynamo method for getting very high frequencies was soon abandoned as inadequate, and the oscillatory discharge of a Leyden jar or plate condensers was substituted. . . . Perhaps the most surprising of the new facts elicited from his investigations is that the shock due to these very high voltage and high frequency currents can be supported by a person without any serious inconvenience. He passes a current of two hundred thousand volts through his body with perfect impunity."—F. J. Patten, New Science Review, v. 1, p. 84.

Electrical Science: Development of the Telephone System.—The annual report of the American Telephone and Telegraph Company (by which the property and business of the American Bell Telephone Company were taken over at the close of the year 1899) for the year ending December 31, 1900, contains the following brief review of the development and growth of the telephone system, especially in the United States: "The year just passed rounds out the quarter century, within which is compassed the discovery and application of the art of transmitting speech by telephone. A brief review of the development and growth of this new industry, which has become so important a factor in commercial and social life, seems appropriate at this time. Twenty-five years ago the wonderful invention of Professor Bell was made known to the world. Twenty-three years ago the first telephone exchange in the world was established in the United States, and from that beginning has been built up the great system of exchanges, and the network of connecting lines over which conversation can be held between points over a thousand miles apart. Twenty years ago there were 47,880 telephone subscribers in the United States, and 29,714 miles of wire in use for telephonic purposes. At the end of last year, there were 800,880 exchange stations equipped with our instruments, and 1,961,801 miles of wire were employed for exchange and toll line service. The United States has, from the beginning, held the leading place among nations in respect not only of the extensive development of the business, but in the employment of modern and improved appliances, tending to greater efficiency of service.

"In connection with the record of development of telephone service in this country, some comparison of the systems of foreign countries is of interest. The latest reports that can be obtained, part of which are for the year 1899, others to the close of 1900, show the countries next in order to the United States, as respects the development of telephone service, to be the German Empire, having 229,391 stations ; Great Britain, 171,660 ; Sweden, 73,500 ; France, 59,927 ; Switzerland, 38,864 ; Austria, 32,255 ; Russia, 31,376 ; Norway, 29,446.

"As before stated, there were, at the close of last year, more than 800,000 stations connected with the exchanges of our licensee companies, which exceeds the aggregate number of subscribers in all the countries of Continental Europe. In addition to this, there were over 40,000 private line stations equipped with our telephones. The number of exchange and toll line connections in the United States now reaches almost two thousand millions yearly."

More detailed and precise statistics of the telephone service in the United States are given in the report as follows :

	Jan. 1, 1892.	Jan. 1, 1901.
Exchanges.........................	788	1,348
Branch offices....................	509	1,427
Miles of wire on poles............	180,139	627,897
Miles of wire on buildings........	14,954	16,833
Miles of wire underground.........	70,334	705,269
Miles of wire submarine...........	1,029	4,203
Total miles of wire...............	266,456	1,354,202
Total circuits....................	186,462	508,262
Total employés....................	8,376	32,837
Total stations....................	216,017	800,880

The estimated number of exchange connections daily in the United States, made up from actual count in most of the exchanges, is 5,668,986. Or a total per year of about 1,825,000,000. The number of daily calls per station varies in different exchanges from 1 to $15\frac{7}{10}$, the average throughout the United States being $7\frac{1}{10}$. The average cost to the subscriber varies according to the size of the exchange and character of the service, from less than 1 to 9 cents per connection.

Electrical Science : Dr. Pupin's revolutionary improvement in long-distance Telephony. —The most important advance in telephonic science that has been made since the invention of the Bell instrument was announced at about the beginning of the new century, as the result of studies pursued by Dr. Michael I. Pupin, of Columbia University, New York. Mathematical and experimental investigations which Dr. Pupin had been carrying on, for several years, led him to a determination of the precise intervals at which, if inductance coils are inserted in a long conductor, an electric current in traversing it may be made to travel far without much loss of force. He is said to have taken a hint from seeing how waves of vibration in a cord are strengthened by lightly "loading" it at certain exact points, determined by the wave lengths. It is probably correct to describe his invention as being a scientific ascertainment of the points in a long telephonic circuit at which to load the electric current in it, and the precise loading to be applied.

In a paper published in the "Western Electrician," describing his investigations mathematically, Dr. Pupin wrote: "If an increase in efficiency of wave transmission over a cord thus loaded is to be obtained, it is evident that the load must be properly subdivided and the fractional parts of the total load must be placed at proper distances apart along the cord, otherwise the detrimental effects due to reflections resulting from the discontinuities thus introduced will more than neutralize the beneficial effects derived from the increased mass. . . . The insertion of inductance coils at periodically recurring points along the wave conductor produces the same effect upon electrical wave transmission as the distribution of the small loads along the stretched cord . . . produces upon mechanical wave transmission along the cord."

The result is said to be that conversation by telephone over a distance of 3,000 miles is made not only practicable but easy, and that it is believed to be as practicable through submarine cables as through overland wires. If it does not make the telephone a common instrument of communication from continent to continent, it will, at least, improve oceanic telegraphy beyond measure. According to newspaper report, Dr. Pupin's invention has been sold to the Bell Telephone Company for a very large sum.

Electrical Science : Wireless Telegraphy. —"In 1864 Maxwell observed that electricity and light have the same velocity, 186,400 miles a second, and he formulated the theory that electricity propagates itself in waves which differ from those of light only in being longer. This was proved to be true by Hertz, in 1888, who showed that where alternating currents of very high frequency were set up in an open circuit, the energy might be conveyed entirely away from the circuit into the surrounding space as electric waves. . . . He demonstrated that electric waves move with the speed of light, and that they can be reflected and refracted precisely as if they formed a visible beam. At a certain intensity of strain the air insulation broke down, and the air became a conductor. This phenomenon of passing quite suddenly from a non-conductive to a conductive state is . . . also to be noted when air or other gases are exposed to the X ray.

"Now for the effect of electric waves such as Hertz produced, when they impinge upon substances reduced to powder or filings. Conductors, such as the metals, are of inestimable service to the electrician ; of equal value are non-conductors, such as glass and gutta-percha, as they strictly fence in an electric stream. A third and remarkable vista opens to experiment when it deals with substances which, in their normal state, are non-conductive, but which, agitated by an electric wave, instantly become conductive in a high degree. As long ago as 1866 Mr. S. A. Varley noticed that black lead, reduced to a loose dust, effectually intercepted a current from fifty Daniell cells, although the battery poles were very near each other. When he increased the electric tension four- to sixfold, the black-lead particles at once compacted themselves so as to form a bridge of excellent conductivity. On this principle he invented a lightning-protector for electrical instruments, the incoming flash causing a tiny heap of carbon dust to provide it with a path through which it could safely pass to the earth. Professor Temistocle Calzecchi Onesti of Fermo, in 1885, in an independent series of researches, discovered that a mass of powdered copper is a non-conductor until an electric wave beats upon it; then, in an instant, the mass resolves itself into a conductor almost as efficient as if it were a stout, unbroken wire. Professor Edouard Branly of Paris, in 1891, on this principle devised a coherer, which passed from resistance to invitation when subjected to an electric impulse from afar. He enhanced the value of his device by the vital discovery that the conductivity bestowed upon filings by electric discharges could be destroyed by simply shaking or tapping them apart. . . .

"The coherer, as improved by Marconi, is a glass tube about $1\frac{1}{4}$ inches long and about $\frac{1}{12}$ of an inch in internal diameter. The electrodes are inserted in this tube so as almost to touch; between them is about $\frac{1}{30}$ of an inch filled with a pinch of the responsive mixture which forms the pivot of the whole contrivance. This mixture is 90 per cent. nickel filings, 10 per cent. hard silver filings, and a mere trace of mercury; the tube is exhausted of air to within $\frac{1}{10000}$ part. . . . The coherer, when unexcited, forms a link which obstructs the flow of a current eager to leap across. The instant that an electric wave from the sending-station impinges upon the coherer it becomes conductive; the current instantly glides through it, and at the same time a current, by means of a relay, is sent through [a] powerful voltaic battery, so as to announce the signal through an ordinary telegraphic receiver.

"An electric impulse, almost too attenuated for computation, is here able to effect such a change in a pinch of dust that it becomes a free avenue instead of a barricade. Through that avenue a powerful blow from a local store of energy makes itself heard and felt. No device of the trigger class is comparable with this in delicacy. An instant after a signal has taken its way through the coherer a small hammer strikes the tiny tube, jarring its particles asunder, so that they resume their normal state of high resistance. We may well be astonished at the sensitiveness of the metallic filings to an electric wave originating many miles away, but let us remember how clearly the eye can see a bright lamp at the same distance as it sheds a sister beam. Thus far no substance has been discovered with a mechanical responsiveness to so feeble a ray of light; in the world of nature and art the coherer stands alone. . . .

"An essential feature of this method of etheric

telegraphy, due to Marconi himself, is the suspension of a perpendicular wire at each terminus, its length twenty feet for stations a mile apart, forty feet for four miles, and so on, the telegraphic distance increasing as the square of the length of suspended wire. In the Kingstown regatta, July, 1898, Marconi sent from a yacht under full steam a report to the shore without the loss of a moment from start to finish. This feat was repeated during the protracted contest between the 'Columbia' and the 'Shamrock' yachts in New York Bay, October, 1899. On March 28, 1899, Marconi signals put Wimereux, two miles north of Boulogne, in communication with the South Foreland Lighthouse, thirty-two miles off. In August, 1899, during the manœuvres of the British navy, similar messages were sent as far as eighty miles. . . .

"A weak point in the first Marconi apparatus was that anybody within the working radius of the sending-instrument could read its message. To modify this objection secret codes were at times employed, as in commerce and diplomacy. A complete deliverance from this difficulty is promised in attuning a transmitter and a receiver to the same note, so that one receiver, and no other, shall respond to a particular frequency of impulses. The experiments which indicate success in this vital particular have been conducted by Professor Lodge."—G. Iles, *Flame, Electricity and the Camera*, ch. 16 (*N. Y.: Doubleday, Page & Co.*).

"Shall we not," said Professor John Trowbridge, in an article published in the "New York Tribune," January 6, 1901, "in the next hundred years dispense with the limitations of wires and speak boldly through space, reaching some expectant human ear hundreds of miles away with the same ease that we now converse in a room? It is already possible to send messages by dots and dashes sixty to seventy miles without the use of wires. In the early days of the telephone this was the practical limit of that instrument, and we are all familiar with the immense extension which has taken place. Shall we not see a similar extension in the field of wireless telegraphy? Some late experiments which I have made lead me·to be optimistic in regard to a possible great extension of the methods of wireless telegraphy.

"In the first place, I believe that these experiments prove that wireless telegraphy is not necessarily or merely accomplished through the air, but, on the contrary, that the earth plays the controlling part, and that the message flows, so to speak, through the earth or over its surface rather than through the air. The most striking experiment was as follows: The poles of a storage battery of twenty thousand cells were connected with the ground at the Jefferson Laboratory, and I was enabled to receive the message in a room three quarters of a mile from the laboratory without the use of masts or wires of any sort. The earth was the medium of communication, and it seems possible, by arranging the sending and receiving apparatus suitably in connection with the electrical capacity of the earth, that we may dispense with lofty masts and overcome in this way the curvature of the earth."

Extensive experiments in wireless telegraphy are being conducted by the United States Weather Bureau, of which the following is a recent report: "Recognizing the advantage that would result to commerce and navigation by the establishment of wireless electrical communication between vessels at sea and exposed points on our lake and sea coasts, and also between islands along said coasts and the mainland, the Weather Bureau was directed to systematically investigate the various methods of electrical communication without wires. The progress made is eminently satisfactory. New appliances have been devised for the transmission of signals, and receivers have been constructed that probably are more delicate than any heretofore made. Messages already have been successfully transmitted and received over 50 miles of land, which presented a rough and irregular surface, conditions most unfavorable for the transmission of electro-magnetic waves. It is believed that the efficiency indicated by such transmission overland is sufficient to operate successfully over several hundred miles of water. The apparatus used is capable of further improvement. I hope the time is near at hand when the great number of craft employed in the coastwise commerce of the United States and over its great inland seas will be placed in instantaneous communication with the numerous stations of our Weather Bureau, which are located at all important ports. The matter is one of such great importance to our commerce that I have authorized extensive experimentation, which, from the success so far attending our efforts, will be vigorously prosecuted."—*United States, Annual Report of the Secretary of Agriculture, Nov.* 24, 1900, *p.* 12.

On the 12th of March, 1901, the chief of the Weather Bureau, Professor Moore, gave to the Press the following statement as to experiments in progress along the Virginia and North Carolina coast: "The most efficient method of long distance transmission has been found to be from wire cylinders. The new coast stations are being equipped with cylinders of sixteen wires each and 140 feet in length. From these cylinders it is expected to cover a magnetic field of not less than five hundred miles. The stations now in operation are at Hatteras and at Roanoke Island, in Pamlico Sound, North Carolina. Workmen are beginning the construction of a station at Cape Henry, which will be the third station. When this is finished the two remote stations will be 127 miles apart."

Mechanics: Steam turbines.—"The latest form of steam-engine recalls the first. The steam-turbines of De Laval and of Parsons turn on the same principle as the æolipile of Hero. That simple contrivance was a metallic globe mounted on axes, and furnished through one of its trunnions with steam from a boiler near by. As steam rushed out from two nozzles diametrically opposite to each other, and at tangents to the globe, there resulted from the relieved pressure a swift rotation which might have done useful work. . . . Before the steam-turbine could be invented, metallurgists and mechanics had to become skilful enough to provide machinery which may with safety rotate 10,000 times in a minute ; Watt had to invent the separate condenser; means had to be devised for the thorough expansion of high-pressure steam ; and the crude device of Hero had to be supplanted by wheels suggested by the water-turbine.

"The feature which gives the Parsons steam-turbine its distinction is the ingenious method by which its steam is used expansively. In a piston-engine the cylinder is filled to one-twelfth or one-fifteenth of its capacity with high-pressure steam, when communication with the boiler is cut off ; during the remainder of its stroke the piston is urged solely by the steam's elasticity. In the Parsons turbine, by arranging what is practically a series of wheels on the same shaft, the steam passes from one wheel to the next, and at each wheel parts with only a fraction of its pressure and velocity. . . .

"The 'Turbinia,' a torpedo-boat of 44½ tons displacement, 100 feet in length, and 9 feet in beam, driven by this turbine, has consumed but 14½ pounds of steam an hour per indicated horse-power. The 'Viper,' a torpedo-boat destroyer of 325 tons, and provided with a turbine capable of developing as much as 12,000 horse-power, ran at the rate of 37 knots in a rough sea during her trial trip in November, 1899."—G. Iles, *Flame, Electricity and the Camera, ch.* 5 (*N. Y. : Doubleday, Page & Co.*).

Medical and Surgical: The determination of germ diseases.—"Since 1880 it has been proved that anthrax, Asiatic cholera, cerebrospinal meningitis, diphtheria, one form of dysentery, erysipelas, glanders, gonorrhœa, influenza, certain epidemics of meat poisoning, pyæmia and suppuration in general, pneumonia, tetanus, relapsing fever, tuberculosis, bubonic plague, and typhoid fever are due to minute vegetable organisms known as bacteria ; that malarial fevers, Texas cattle fever, and certain forms of dysentery are due to forms of microscopic animal organisms known as microzoa; and for most of these diseases the mode of development and means of introduction of the micro-organism into the body are fairly well understood. To the information thus obtained we owe the triumphs of antiseptic and aseptic surgery, a great increase of precision in diagnosis, the use of specific antitoxins as remedies and as preventives, and some of the best practical work in public hygiene."— Dr. John S. Billings, *Progress of Medicine in the Nineteenth Century* (*N. Y. Evening Post, Jan.* 12, 1901).

Medical and Surgical: Antitoxine.—Treatment of diphtheria.—"In the early study of germs and their relation to disease it was supposed that the symptoms of the disease depended directly upon the germs themselves. This, however, has been proven to be false with reference to most of the infectious diseases studied. Thus, in diphtheria, the bacilli were found, as a rule, only in the throat or upper air passages, while the effects of the disease were far-reaching, involving the heart, the nerves, and other distant parts of the body. This, and other like observations, led to the careful study of the products produced by the growth of bacteria. As the result of the work of Roux in Paris, and Brieger in Berlin, the exact nature of the toxic products of the diphtheria bacillus was discovered. It was found that this bacillus produces in its growth a poison which is known as the diphtheria 'toxine.' This was isolated and injected into animals with the reproduction of all the symptons of diphtheria excepting the membrane in the throat. . . .

"In his early work upon splenic fever and chicken-cholera Pasteur, having established the causes of these diseases, set himself the task of discovering means of preventing them. After very many experiments he found that animals inoculated with the germs of splenic fever, when these germs had been cultivated at a relatively high temperature, were protected against the disease itself, while these inoculations themselves were harmless. . . . These methods of producing immunity have been extensively used in Europe for the past twenty years and have been of immense practical value.

"With the discovery that it was not the bacteria themselves which produced most of the symptoms, but their poisonous products or toxines, new experiments in immunity were made by injecting these toxines into animals. It was found that if the quantity of the diphtheria toxine introduced was at first so small as not to kill the animal, the dose could gradually be increased until finally such a tolerance was established that the animal could resist enormous doses of it. Many theories were advanced as to the manner in which this tolerance was established. The conclusion was finally reached that it was due to the gradual production in the blood of larger and larger quantities of some substance which neutralized the toxine, i. e., an 'antitoxine.' . . . Later experiments showed that if some of the blood of an animal, which in this way had been made insusceptible to diphtheria, was injected into another animal, the latter likewise became to a certain degree and for a certain time insusceptible; that is to say, became 'immunized.' . . .

"The present plan of producing antitoxine is somewhat as follows. Large animals, such as the horse or cow, are usually employed for purposes of injection. In the beginning as large a quantity of the toxine of diphtheria is injected as the animal will bear without danger to life. . . . It is found that the dose of the toxine can gradually be increased with each injection until enormous quantities can be tolerated. When this point is reached at which the injection of large amounts of the toxine produces no reaction, the animal is said to possess a high degree of immunity. At this time the blood-serum contains a very large amount of the antitoxine. A long time is required for the production of this condition, the period being from three to twelve months, according to the size of the animal, its susceptibility, and many other conditions. . . . The antitoxine is obtained from the blood of the animal, generally by bleeding from the jugular vein. . . . After standing for a few hours this blood separates into a clot and a clear portion above which is known as the serum. The antitoxine is contained in the blood-serum."—L. E. Holt, *The Antitoxine Treatment of Diphtheria* (*Forum, March*, 1895).—See, also (in this vol.), PLAGUE.

Medical and Surgical: Discovery of the secret of malaria.—Detection of the mosquito as a carrier of disease.—"Twenty-five years ago the best-informed physicians entertained erroneous ideas with reference to the nature of malaria and the etiology of the malarial fevers. Observation had taught them that there was something in the air in the vicinity of marshes in tropical regions, and during the summer and autumn in semi-tropical and temperate regions, which gave rise to periodic fevers in those exposed in such localities, and the usual inference was that this something was of gaseous form — that it was a special kind of bad air generated in swampy localities under favorable meteorological conditions. It was recognized at the same time that there are other kinds of bad air, such as the offensive emanations from sewers and the products of respiration of man and animals, but the term malaria was reserved especially for the kind of bad air which was supposed to give rise to the so-called malarial fevers. In the light of our present knowledge it is evident that this term is a misnomer. There is no good reason for believing that the air of swamps is any more deleterious to those who breathe it than the air of the sea coast or that in the vicinity of inland lakes and ponds. Moreover, the stagnant pools, which are covered with a 'green scum' and from which bubbles of gas are given off, have lost all terrors for the well-informed man, except in so far as they serve as breeding places for mosquitoes of the genus Anopheles. The green scum is made up of harmless algæ such as Spirogyra, Zygnema Protococcus, Euglena, etc. ; and the gas which is given off from the mud at the bottom of such stagnant pools is for the most part a well-known and comparatively harmless compound of hydrogen and carbon-methane or 'marsh-gas.'

"In short, we now know that the air in the vicinity of marshes is not deleterious because of any special kind of bad air present in such localities, but because it contains mosquitoes infected with a parasite known to be the specific cause of the so-called malarial fevers. This parasite was discovered in the blood of patients suffering from intermittent fevers by Laveran, a surgeon in the French army, whose investigations were conducted in Algiers. This famous discovery was made toward the end of the year 1880 ; but it was several years later before the profession generally began to attach much importance to the alleged discovery."—G. M. Sternberg, *Malaria* (*Popular Science Monthly, Feb.*, 1901).

"It was the French doctor Laveran who, after a stay in a deadly malarial region of Algeria, discovered the malaria parasite in 1880. True, that pigment-cells, which we should now describe as malaria-parasites, were observed in human blood as early as 1835, among others by Virchow ; but their relation to the disease was not known. In 1881, Laveran embodied his researches in a book, but its importance was overlooked. Bacteria attracted then general attention, and Laveran's parasite, not being a bacterium, was little thought of. He stuck, nevertheless, to his discovery, and was soon joined in his researches by Golgi (the Italian professor to whom we owe the method that led to the discovery of the neurons), as also by Marchiafava, Celli, Councilman, Sternberg, and the Viennese doctor Mannaberg who published in 1893 a full compendium of these researches. Dr. Mannaberg proved in this book that the real cause of malaria is Laveran's parasite, and he told its most interesting life-history so far as it was then known.

"The parasite of malaria is not a bacterium. It is one of the protozoa—namely, as it appeared later on, a coccidium, which, like all other members of that family, undergoes in its development a series of transformations. . . . Laveran saw that some parasites ('corps à flagelles') would send out thin and long flagella which soon parted company with the mother body, and, owing to a proper helicoidal movement, disappeared in the plasm of the blood. This never happened, however, in the body of man, but only when a drop of his infected blood was drawn and placed on the glass plate under the microscope. Laveran noticed, moreover, minute 'crescent-shaped bodies' which adhered to the red corpuscles and looked very much like cysts, protected by a harder envelope. From fifteen to twenty minutes after these bodies had been placed under the microscope, they also gave origin to a great number of 'flagella' ; and this evolution, too, he remarked, seemed to be accomplished only when the cysts were taken out of the human body.

"It was only natural to conclude from these observations that the further development of the flagella may take place in the body of some other animal than man, and this consideration brought Laveran, in a book which he published in 1884, to the idea that, taking into consideration the quantities of mosquitoes in malarial countries, they may be the agents of transition of malaria. This remark passed, however, unperceived. Many had the suspicion that gnats may play some part in the inoculation of malaria : the Italian peasants always thought so, and in the medical literature an American doctor, Mr. King, had advocated the same idea. But the complete life-history of the malaria parasite being not yet known fifteen years ago, the necessity of the mosquito or of some other living being serving as a host for the completion of the reproduction - cycle was not understood."—P. Kropotkin, *Recent Science* (*Nineteenth Century Rev.*, Dec., 1900).

Dr. Patrick Manson, of London, is credited with the final formulation of the mosquito-malarial theory ; but the proofs by which it has been established have come from a number of investigators, who have patiently traced the singular life-history of the parasite, throughout its passage from man to the mosquito and from the mosquito back to man, as a vehicle of disease. Among the latter, prominence is given to Major Ronald Ross, who lectured on the subject in London in September, 1900, and was reported in "The Times" as follows:

"They first carried on their life in man—the intermediary host—and later in the mosquito, the definitive host. These Hæmamœbidæ began as spores which entered a blood corpuscle, grew and became amœbæ. The nuclear matter divided, the corpuscle containing it burst, the spores scattered, and each spore then attached itself to a fresh corpuscle. The access of the typical fever began with this scattering of the spores, and thus the periodicity of the fever was accounted for. Besides this neutral proliferation there was proliferation by gametes. The blood of a fever patient exhibited the first forms of the gametocytes. The spore grew inside the blood corpuscle, and in that species which caused malignant fever it had almost eaten the whole of the host. It was then technically called a crescent. If this crescent were examined under the microscope a wonderful development might be observed to take place in a few moments. The crescent swelled and became first oval, then spherical, and in about 15 minutes after the drawing of the blood the microgametes made their escape and were to be seen wriggling about in the 'liquor sanguinis.' Ultimately they entered the macrogametocytes and produced zygotes, which was nothing but a perfect example of the sperm and the ovum process.

"The whole process could be watched under the microscope. The mosquito, having bitten a person in whose blood these gametocytes were present, would take perhaps 100 of them into its own system, where the zygotes acquired a power of movement, edging towards the wall of the mosquito's stomach. About 12 hours afterwards they would be found adhering to the walls of the stomach, through which they passed and to which they finally attached themselves on the outside. This process was accomplished in about 36 hours. The zygotes then grew until they had increased to about eight times their original diameter and were almost visible to the naked eye. As the zygote increased it divided into meres containing nuclear matter, which went to the surface. The process here seemed to be closely similar to spermato-genesis, and Professor Ray Lankester declared that the process was the first known example of androcratic parthenogenesis. When the final development was reached the cells burst and the blasts escaped and were immediately carried into all parts of the insect. They made their way to the salivary gland, with the evident purpose of seeking the blood of a fresh human host; and the injection of the secretion of the mosquito's salivary gland caused the bump which marked the mosquito's bite. A very large series of experiments had shown conclusively that malarial infection was caused by the bite of the mosquito.

"The parasites which infested human blood were carried only by one genus of mosquito—'Anopheles'; the genus 'Culex' was harmless. The two genera could be readily distinguished. For example, 'Anopheles' rested on walls with their tails stuck out perpendicular to the wall ; 'Culex' attached themselves with tails hanging downwards. 'Culex' bred in the water in pots and tubs; 'Anopheles' in pools. The larvæ of 'Culex,' if disturbed, sank to the bottom; the larvæ of 'Anopheles' skimmed along the surface. It was doubtful whether the eggs of 'Anopheles' would live for more than a few days after desiccation. The eggs were laid in an equilateral triangular pattern ; they were soon hatched, and the larvæ then began to feed on the green scum in the water. A still evening, just before or after rain, was the time most favourable for the hatching out from the pupæ. As to the adults, he believed that they could live for a year; at any rate, they had been kept alive in tubes for more than a month; and it was certain that in England and Italy they hibernated. The female of 'Anopheles' alone was the biter, and though the favourite feeding time was at night, in West Africa the insects had been found to bite all day. While 'Culex' could be detected by its humming, 'Anopheles' was silent, and it was possible to be bitten without knowing of it at the moment. He had found that a blood diet was always necessary to the maturing of the eggs. He had kept many thousands of mosquitoes under observation and had never known one to lay eggs except after a meal of blood. Malarial infection was derived chiefly from the native children, who swarmed everywhere, and whose blood was full of the infecting parasites."

An expedition sent out to West Africa by the Liverpool School of Tropical Medicine, to pursue investigations there, reported in December, 1900, that its observations confirm the conclusion "that the blood parasite which gives rise to malarial fever in man is carried by the mosquito from the native to the European—and more especially from the native children. The examination of the blood of hundreds of native children revealed the interesting fact that between 50 and 80 per cent. of those under five years, between 20 and 30 per cent. of ages between five and ten years, and a small percentage over ten years contained malarial parasites, often in very large numbers. The breeding places of the 'Anopheles' were found to be chiefly the dug-out native canoes in the regions of the mangrove swamps, claypits and puddles in the forested district, and at Lokoja puddles and ditches on and alongside the roads and footpaths. It was particularly noticed everywhere how carelessness in the construction of roads and footpaths, and more especially in the laying out of the areas surrounding the factories of the European traders, was accountable for the production of a large number of breeding places for mosquitoes, which could easily have been avoided. In fact, it is certain that in West Africa such conditions are far more dangerous and more common than the proximity of a marsh or swamp, which is often noted as a cause of fever. . . . The two methods upon which alone any reliance can be placed as measures for prevention are—(1) segregation of Europeans from natives of all sorts, at a distance of about half a mile; and (2) complete and efficient surface drainage of the whole district in the immediate neighbourhood of European quarters."

The detection of the mosquito as a carrier of one disease drew suspicion on the pestilent insect of other kindred crimes, and strong evidence of its agency in propagating yellow fever has been gathered already. A board of medical officers, which went from the United States to Cuba in the summer of 1900 to study the matter, reported in October that their investigations tended quite positively to that conclusion. The board was composed of Dr. Walter Reed, surgeon, United States Army, and Dr. James Carroll, Dr. A. Agramonte, and Dr. Jesse W. Lazear, all acting assistant surgeons of the United States Army. Two months later, so much confirmation had been obtained that Major-General Wood, Military-Governor of Cuba (himself a medical man) was reported, on the 29th of December, to have issued a general order directed to his post commanders, "reciting that the chief surgeon of the Department of Cuba has reported that it is now well-established that malaria, yellow fever and filarial infection are transmitted by the bites of mosquitoes. Therefore the troops are enjoined to observe carefully two precautions: First—they are to use mosquito bars in all barracks, hospitals and field service whenever practicable. Second —They are to destroy the 'wigglers,' or young mosquitoes, by the use of petroleum on the water where they breed. Permanent pools or puddles are to be filled up. To the others is to be applied one ounce of kerosene to each fifteen square feet of water twice a month, which will destroy not only the young but the old mosquitoes. This does not injure drinking water if drawn from below and not dipped out. Protection is thus secured, according to the order, because the mosquito does not fly far, but seeks shelter when the wind blows, and thus each community breeds its own mosquitoes."

This was followed in April, 1901, by an order from the chief surgeon at Havana, approved by Surgeon-General Sternberg, U. S. A., which says: "The recent experiments made in Havana by the Medical Department of the Army having proved that yellow fever, like malarial fever, is conveyed chiefly, and probably exclusively, by the bite of infected mosquitoes, important changes in the measures used for the prevention and treatment of this disease have become uccessary. So far as yellow fever is concerned, infection of a room or building simply means that it contains infected mosquitoes, that is mosquitoes which have fed on yellow fever patients. Disinfection, therefore, means the employment of measures aimed at the destruction of these mosquitoes. The most effective of these measures is fumigation, either with sulphur, formaldehyds or insect powder. The fumes of sulphur are the quickest and the most effective insecticide, but are otherwise objectionable. Formaldehyde gas is quite effective if the infected rooms are kept closed and sealed for two or three hours. The smoke of insect powder has also been proved useful; it readily stupefies mosquitoes, which drop to the floor and can then be easily destroyed. The washing of walls, floors, ceilings and furniture with disinfectants is unnecessary."

Medical and Surgical: Recent advances in surgery.—"In no department of surgery has greater progress been made than in the treatment of diseases of the abdominal organs. . . . At the present time no abdominal organ is sacred from the surgeon's knife. Bowels riddled with bullet-holes are stitched up successfully; large pieces of gangrenous or cancerous intestine are cut out, the ends of the severed tube being brought into continuity by means of ingenious appliances; the stomach is opened for the removal of a foreign body, for the excision of a cancer, or for the administration of nourishment to a patient unable to swallow; stones are extracted from the substance of the kidneys, and these organs when hopelessly diseased are extirpated; the spleen, when enlarged or otherwise diseased, is removed bodily; gall-stones are cut out, and even tumours of the liver are excised. The kidney, the spleen, and the liver, when they cause trouble by unnatural mobility, are anchored by stitches to the abdominal wall; and the stomach has been dealt with successfully in the same way for the cure of indigestion. Besides all this, many cases of obstruction of the bowels, which in days not very long gone by would have been doomed to inevitable death, are now cured by a touch of the surgeon's knife. The perforation of the intestine, which is one of the most formidable complications of typhoid fever, has in a few cases been successfully closed by operation; and inflammation of the peritoneum, caused by the growth of tuberculous masses upon it, has been apparently cured by opening the abdominal cavity. Among the most useful advances of this department of surgery must be accounted the treatment of the condition known as 'appendicitis,' which has been to a large extent rescued from the physician, with his policy of 'laissez faire,' and placed under the more resolute and more efficient government of the surgeon. A New York surgeon not long ago reported a series of 100 cases of operation for appendicitis, with only two deaths. . . .

"That surgery could ever deal with the abdominal organs in the manner just described would have seemed to our predecessors in the earlier part of the Queen's reign the baseless fabric of a vision. But the modern surgeon, clad in antisepsis, as the Lady in 'Comus' was 'clothed round with chastity,' defies the 'rabble rout' of microbes and dares things which only a short time ago were looked upon as beyond the wildest dreams of scientific enthusiasm. It is scarcely twenty years since the late Sir John Erichsen declared in a public address that operative surgery had nearly reached its furthest possible limits of development. He pointed out that there were certain regions of the body into which the surgeon's knife could never penetrate, naming the brain, the heart, and the lung as the most obvious examples of such inviolable sanctuaries of life. Within the last fifteen years the surgeon has brought each of these organs, which constitute what Bichat called the 'tripod of life,' within his sphere of conquest. . . . It must, however, be admitted that the results of brain surgery, though brilliant from the operative point of view, have so far been somewhat disappointing as regards the ultimate cure of the disease. In certain forms of epilepsy, in particular, which at first seemed to be curable by removal of the 'cortical discharging centre' in the brain which is the source of the mischief, the tendency to fits has been found to return after a time, and the last state of the patient has been worse than the first. Still, the mere fact that the brain has been proved to be capable of being dealt with surgically with perfect safety is in itself a very distinct progress. . . .

"Other parts of the nervous system have been brought within the range of surgical art. The vertebral column has been successfully trephined, and fragments of bone pressing on the cord have been taken away in cases of fractured spine; tumours have also been removed from the spinal cord by Mr. Horsley and others. There is a steadily increasing record of cures of intractable neuralgia, especially of the face, by division or removal of the affected nerve trunks. . . .The ends of cut nerves have also been re-united, and solutions of their continuity have been filled up with portions of nerve taken from animals. . . . The heart naturally cannot be made so free with, even by the most enterprising surgeon, as the brain or the lung. Yet within the past twelve months a Norwegian practitioner has reported a case which encourages a hope that even wounds of the heart may not be beyond surgical treatment. . . . Tuberculous and inflammatory diseases of bones and joints, formerly intractable except by the 'ultima ratio' of the amputating knife, are now cured without mutilation. Deformities are corrected by division of tendons, the excision of portions of bone, and the physiological exercise of muscles, without complicated apparatus. The healing of large wounds is assisted by the grafting of healthy skin on the raw surface; wide gaps in bones and tendons are filled up with portions of similar structures obtained from animals." . . . Malcolm Morris, *The Progress of Medicine during the Queen's Reign* (*Nineteenth Century*, May, 1897).—See, also, X RAYS, below.

Scientific Literature: International cataloguing.—On the 22d of March, 1894, the Secretaries of the Royal Society of London addressed the following communication to various institutions and societies : "The Royal Society of London, as you are probably aware, has published nine quarto volumes of 'The catalogue of scientific papers,' the first volume of the decade 1874–83 having been issued last year. This catalogue is limited to periodical scientific literature, i. e., to papers published in the transactions, etc., of societies, and in journals; it takes no account whatever of monographs and independent books, however important. The titles, moreover, are arranged solely according to authors' names ; and though the Society has long had under consideration the preparation of, and it is hoped may eventually issue, as a key to the volumes already published, a list in which the titles are arranged according to subject-matter, the catalogue is still being prepared according to authors' names. Further, though the Society has endeavored to include the titles of all the scientific papers published in periodicals of acknowledged standing, the catalogue is, even as regards periodical literature, confessedly incomplete, owing to the omission of the titles of papers published in periodicals of little importance, or not easy of access.

"Owing to the great development of scientific literature, the task of the Society in continuing the catalogue, even in its present form, is rapidly increasing in difficulty. At the same time it is clear that the progress of science would be greatly helped by, indeed, almost demands, the compilation of a catalogue which should aim at completeness, and should contain the titles of scientific publications, whether appearing in periodicals or independently. In such a catalogue the titles should be arranged not only according to authors' names, but also according to subject-matter, the text of each paper and not the title only being consulted for the latter purpose. And the value of the catalogue would be greatly enhanced by a rapid periodical issue, and by publication in such a form that the portion which pertains to any particular branch of science might be obtained separately. It is needless to say that the preparation and publication of such a complete catalogue is far beyond the power and means of any single society. . . .

"Led by the above considerations, the president and council of the Royal Society have appointed a committee to inquire into and report upon the feasibility of such a catalogue being compiled through international co-operation."— *Library Journal, March*, 1895.

The movement thus initiated received cordial support and led to the convening of an International Conference in London, in 1896. The Conference was opened on Tuesday, July 14, at Burlington House. "The 42 delegates, representing nearly all the governments of civilized countries and most of the leading scientific societies of the world, were welcomed by Sir John Gorst, as provisional president. . . . It was decided that English, German and French should be the official languages of the conference. . . . The conference closed on Friday, July 17, the need of an international catalogue having been fully recognized, and a plan for its preparation mapped out. It was decided 'That it is desirable to compile and publish by means of some international organization a complete catalogue of scientific literature, arranged according both to subject-matter and to authors' names. That in preparing such a catalogue regard shall, in the first instance, be had to the requirements of scientific investigators, to the end that these may, by means of the catalogue, find out most easily what has been published concerning any particular subject of inquiry.'

"The preparation of the catalogue is to be in charge of an international council, is to be appointed, and the final editing and publication shall be conducted by a central international bureau, under the direction of the international council. Any country that is willing to do so shall be entrusted with the task of collecting, provisionally classifying, and transmitting to the central bureau, in accordance with rules laid down by the international council, all the entries belonging to the scientific literature of that country. 'In indexing according to subject-matter regard shall be had, not only to the title (of a paper or book), but also to the nature of the contents.' The catalogue shall comprise all published original contributions—periodical articles, pamphlets, memoirs, etc.—to the mathematical, physical, or natural sciences, . . . 'to the exclusion of what are sometimes called the applied sciences—the limits of the several sciences to be determined hereafter.'. . .

"The central bureau shall issue the catalogue in the form of 'slips' or 'cards,' the details of the cards to be hereafter determined, and the issue to take place as promptly as possible. . . . It was also decided that the central bureau shall be located in London, and that the Royal Society appoint a committee to study all undecided questions relating to the catalogue and to report later. . . . No system of classification was adopted and the subject was turned over for consideration to the committee of organization, which should also suggest 'such details as will render the catalogue of the greatest possible use to those unfamiliar with English.' January 1, 1900, is fixed as the date for the beginning of the catalogue."—*Library Journal, August,* 1896.

A second international conference, to consider further the plans previously outlined, was held Oct. 11-13, 1898, at Burlington House, London. "The attendance was a representative one, including delegates from Austria, Belgium, France, Germany, Hungary, Japan, Mexico, Netherlands, Norway, Sweden, Switzerland, the United Kingdom, the United States (represented by Dr. Cyrus Adler), Cape Colony, India, Natal, New Zealand, and Queensland. Russia, Spain and Italy were the only large continental countries unrepresented. . . .

"Professor Forster having formally presented the report of the Committee of the Royal Society, copies of which were forwarded in April last to the several governments represented at the conference, the discussion of the recommendations was opened, and it was resolved: 'That the conference confirms the principle that the catalog be published in the double form of cards and books. That schedules of classification shall be authorized for the several branches of science which it is decided to include in the catalog. That geography be defined as limited to mathematical and physical geography, and that political and general geography be excluded. That anatomy be entered on the list as a separate subject. That a separate schedule be provided for each of the following branches of science: Mathematics, Astronomy, Meteorology, Physics, Crystallography, Chemistry, Mineralogy, Geology (including Petrology), Geography, mathematical and physical, Paleontology, Anatomy, Zoölogy, Botany, Physiology (including Pharmacology and Experimental Pathology), Bacteriology, Psychology, Anthropology. That each of the sci-

ences for which a separate schedule is provided shall be indicated by a symbol.'" Resolutions were then adopted providing for the regulations to be observed in the preparation of cards or slips, and for the organization of the work through Regional Bureaus.

"The following recommendations of the Royal Society providing for international conventions in connection with the catalog were adopted: 'Each region in which a Regional Bureau is established, charged with the duty of preparing and transmitting slips to the Central Bureau for the compilation of the catalog, shall be called a constituent region. In 1905, in 1910, and every tenth year afterwards, an international convention shall be held in London (in July) to reconsider, and, if necessary, revise the regulations for carrying out the work of the catalog authorized by the international convention of 1898. Such an international convention shall consist of delegates appointed by the respective governments to represent the constituent regions, but no region shall be represented by more than three delegates. The rules of procedure of each international convention shall be the same as those of the international convention of 1898. The decisions of an international convention shall remain in force until the next convention meets.'

"The following recommendations of the Royal Society relating to the constitution of an International Council, which shall be the governing body of the catalog, were adopted: 'Each Regional Bureau shall appoint one person to serve as a member of a body to be called The International Council. The International Council shall, within the regulations laid down by the international convention, be the governing body of the catalog. The International Council shall appoint its own chairman and secretary. It shall meet in London once in three years at least, and at such other times as the chairman, with the concurrence of five other members, may specially appoint. It shall, subject to the regulations laid down by the convention, be the supreme authority for the consideration of and decision concerning all matters belonging to the Central Bureau. It shall make a report of its doings, and submit a balance sheet, copies of which shall be distributed to the several Regional Bureaus, and published in some recognized periodical or periodicals in each of the constituent regions.'"—*Library Journal, December,* 1898.

The third international conference on a catalog of scientific literature was held in London, June 12, 1900, under the auspices of the Royal Society. "Unfortunately the United States finds no place in the list [of delegates]. This is owing to the failure to secure from Congress the necessary appropriation enabling the United States to join in the enterprise; and as the call to the conference required that delegates be charged with full powers, it was impossible for any representative of the United States to be in attendance. . . .

"The general results of the conference are reviewed by Prof. Henry E. Armstrong, in 'Nature,' as follows: 'There can be little doubt that the ultimate execution of this important enterprise is now assured. . . . Every one was of opinion that if a fair beginning can once be made, the importance of the work is so great; it will be of such use to scientific workers at large; that it will rapidly grow in favor and soon secure that wide support which is not yet given to it simply because its character and value are but imperfectly understood. Therefore, all were anxious that a beginning should be made.

"'It has been estimated that if 300 sets or the equivalent are sold the expenses of publication will be fully met. As the purchase of more than half this number was guaranteed by France, Germany, Italy, Norway, Switzerland, and the United Kingdom, the conference came to the conclusion that the number likely to be taken by other countries would be such that the subscriptions necessary to cover the cost of the catalog would be obtained. The resolution arrived at after this opinion had been formed, That the catalog include both an author's and a subject index, according to the schemes of the Provisional International Committee, must, in fact, be read as a resolution to establish the catalog.

"'Of the countries represented at the various conferences, excepting Belgium, not one has expressed any unwillingness eventually to co-operate in the work. Unfortunately, neither the United States nor Russia was officially represented on the present occasion. The attempts that have been made to induce the government in the United States to directly subsidise the catalog have not been successful: but that the United States will contribute its fair share, both of material and pecuniary support, cannot be doubted. There as here private or corporate enterprise must undertake much that is done under government auspices in Europe. As to Russia, the organization of scientific workers there has been so little developed that it is very difficult to secure their attention, and probably our Russian colleagues are as yet but very imperfectly aware of what is proposed. . . . A Provisional International Committee has been appointed, which will take the steps now necessary to secure the adhesion and co-operation of countries not yet pledged to support the scheme.

"'Originally it was proposed to issue a card as well as a book catalog, but on account of the great additional expense this would involve, and as the Americans in particular have not expressed themselves in favor of a card issue, it is resolved to publish the catalog, for the present, only in the form of annual volumes.

"'From the outset great stress has been laid on the preparation of subject indexes which go behind the titles of papers and give fairly full information as to the nature of their contents. Both at the first and the second International Conference this view met with the fullest approval. Meanwhile, the action of the German government has made it necessary to somewhat modify the original plan. In Germany, a regional bureau will be established, supported by a government subvention, and it is intended that the whole German scientific literature shall be cataloged in this office; no assistance will be asked from authors or editors or corporate bodies. In such an office it will for the present be impossible to go behind titles; consequently, only the titles of German papers will be quoted in the catalog. In the first instance, some other countries may prefer to adopt this course on the ground of economy. But in this country, at least, the attempt will be made to deal fully with the literature, and the co-operation of authors and editors will be specially invited. . . .

"'The catalog is to be published annually in seventeen distinct volumes. The collection of material is to commence from January 1, 1901. As it will be impossible to print and issue so many volumes at once, it is proposed to publish them in sets of four or five at quarterly intervals.'"—*Library Journal, September,* 1900.

The fourth Conference was held at London, December 12–13, 1900, when "all arrangements were completed for the definitive commencement of the work on January 1. . . . The responsibility for publication and for the initial expenditure is undertaken by the Royal Society. . . . A comprehensive and elaborate system of classification has been devised with the assent of all the countries interested. This uniformity in a region where diversity of a perplexing kind has hitherto ruled is in itself a great boon to scientific workers everywhere. It may be anticipated that the scheme will by degrees be adopted in all collections of scientific works. As to the nothing aspects of this important undertaking, larger more need be said at present than that the scientific cataloguing of all scientific work most appropriately celebrates the opening of the twentieth century."—*London Times, Dec. 14,* 1900.

In the Nineteenth Century. See (in this vol.) NINETEENTH CENTURY: DOMINANT LINES.

SCOTLAND: A. D. 1900.—Union of the Free and United Presbyterian Churches.— "In the ecclesiastical world only one event of the first importance has happened [in Scotland, in 1900], the consummation of the union between the Free and United Presbyterian Churches, which has been the subject of negotiation for six years past. The May meetings of the leading representative courts of the two denominations were occupied almost exclusively with the final arrangements for the formal act of union, which was fixed to take place on October 31. An attempt by a number of lay office-bearers of the Free Church to postpone the final step, on the ground that the congregations had not been directly and fairly consulted, failed of its object. On October 30 the General Assembly of the Free Church and the Synod of the United Presbyterian Church held their last meetings in Edinburgh as independent bodies. On the following

day they formally constituted themselves the United Free Church of Scotland in the Waverley Market, the largest public hall in Scotland, in presence of an audience computed to number 6,000 persons. The union has, as is the rule in Scotland, been accompanied by a 'disruption.' The minority of the Free Church, which on October 30 resolved to remain outside the United Free Church, is very small in number and is financially weak, but it claims to be the true Free Church of Scotland, it is asserting itself vigorously in the Highlands and islands, where Free Church 'constitutionalism' has always been strongest, and it has taken the first step in a process of litigation for the purpose of discovering whether it or the United Free Church is legally entitled to the property of the original Free Church founded in 1843. But for this secession, the strength of which is not accurately estimable, the new denomination would, according to the latest official returns, have opposed about 1,680 congregations and about 530,000 members to the 1,450 congregations and 650,000 members of the Church of Scotland."—*London Times, Dec.* 27, 1900.

SEA POWER. See (in this vol.) NAVIES OF THE SEA POWERS.

SEAL-KILLING DISPUTES. See (in this vol.) BERING SEA QUESTIONS.

SEGAN FU, or SI-NGAN-FU, The Chinese Imperial Court at. See (in this vol.) CHINA : A. D. 1900 (AUGUST—SEPTEMBER).

SEMINOLES, United States Agreement with the. See (in this vol.) INDIANS, AMERICAN : A. D. 1893–1899.

SENEGAL : A. D. 1895.—Under a French Governor-General. See (in this vol.) AFRICA : A. D. 1895 (FRENCH WEST AFRICA).

SENOUSSI, The Sect of the. See (in this vol.) NIGERIA : A. D. 1882–1899.

SERAPEION, Discovery of the. See (in this vol.) ARCHÆOLOGICAL RESEARCH : EGYPT : DISCOVERY OF THE SERAPEION.

SERVIA : A. D. 1894-1901.—Abolition of the constitution by royal proclamation.— Final exile and death of ex-King Milan. See (in this vol.) BALKAN AND DANUBIAN STATES (SERVIA).

A. D. 1901 (April).—Promulgation of a new constitution.—A new constitution for Servia was promulgated by King Alexander, at Belgrade, on the 19th of April, 1901. Of the character of the instrument, the King had previously given intimations in an interview conceded to the editor of the "Revue d'Orient," the account of which, translated for the "London Times," is partly as follows : "Our three Constitutions of 1869, 1888, and 1901 differ from each other in important matters of principle. That of 1869 practically amounted to absolutism, if I may thus qualify any Constitution. It is true that the executive power retained but few prerogatives, but that was deceptive, as the rights of the Legislature were surrounded by exceptions and restrictions which made it easy to paralyse and annihilate them at any moment. The Constitution of 1888 had the contrary defects. It subordinated the executive power to that of the Legislature, only leaving to the former an altogether insufficient sphere of action. It had another great fault. It was excessively doctrinaire and theoretical, affecting to foresee everything and to regulate everything, so that the legislative power was bound hand and foot and could not legislate freely. The Constitution which will be promulgated on April 19, the anniversary of the day when the fortress of Belgrade was finally evacuated by the Turks in 1867, is a charter similar to those which organize the public powers in several countries of Europe, as, for instance, in England and in France. It settles the form of government, the powers of the King and of the State, the rights of subjects, the working of the national representation, &c. But it leaves to the Legislature the settlement of all details. What more particularly distinguishes the Constitution of 1901 from that of 1869 is that it prevents the use and abuse of ordinances by the Executive, which will be obliged to frame special laws in

every case—that is to say, laws accepted and approved of by the King, the Senate, and the Chamber of Deputies. Thus legality will henceforth be the regulating wheel in the machinery of government. The Chamber of Deputies will be much better organized, as the enlightened classes will be much more numerously represented. The Constitution of 1901 will also present great advantages over that of 1888. The Legislature will control the acts of the Government as far as can possibly be desired. At the same time the constitutional régime as established in the new Constitution will give the King all the power that he ought to retain in a country that is still new, like Servia, without diminishing any of the inviolable liberties of the nation.

"I attach very great importance to the new political institution with which I am going to endow Servia—namely, an Upper Chamber. Considering that it already exists, not only in monarchical countries, but also in most Republics, as, for instance, in France and the United States, I cannot admit that it should be regarded as involving the slightest aristocratic tendency or idea. I know my country well enough to be sure that I shall find a sufficient number of high-class politicians to recruit the Senate, and that enough will remain for the Chamber of Deputies. I am likewise fully persuaded that the legislative task of the Parliament will be much better performed when the Chamber of Deputies is conscious that above it there exists a Senate whose business it is to revise and improve the laws which it has elaborated, of course for the greater benefit of the nation. Then, again, the Senate will form a moderating element which was much wanting in our Legislature. What Servia is suffering from is not any lack of legislation, but from the circumstances that the existing laws were hastily framed or were the outcome of party rancour. If we had formerly had a Senate composed of men of experience and good patriots, they would never have consented to the conclusion of so many onerous loans, to the application of so many iniquitous measures, nor to the convocation of the special tribunal, 'le tribunal extraordinaire,' of 1899.

"At first the Radical party was not favourable to the institution of an Upper Chamber, but it now recognizes the great advantages it will offer, and has rallied to my project. The Progressist party has always been favourable to it. The majority of the Liberal party has also adhered to it. I therefore believe that this new institution will be of the greatest service to the country. All that is required, and with a little good will it can be easily done, is that the members of the two Chambers should endeavour honestly, sincerely, and loyally to work for the good of the State and of the nation. If I have not thought right to raise the qualification for the suffrage, as desired by some people, it is because I did not wish to disfranchise any of those who have enjoyed the right of voting during the last 35 years. I do not wish to restrict any of the rights of the nation.

"The application of the new Constitution will be the great task of my Government, in which I have every confidence. The Prime Minister, Dr. Vuitch, has the sympathy and support not only of his own party but of all who would like to see the country governed in a liberal spirit.

His presence at the head of the Ministry is a pledge for the active and sincere co-operation of all elements of order and progress. . . . As soon as the new Constitution has been promulgated, the Government will invite the co-operation of all those which admit its necessity and fitness. A large Conservative party will thus be formed which will have the requisite power and authority for all purposes of government, for the application of the Constitution, and for the elaboration of financial and economic laws necessary for the progress of the country.

"As regards the question of the succession to the Throne, I wanted to settle it finally, as the members of the reigning dynasty are not numerous unless the remote collateral lines be included, which is not possible. Moreover, everybody wished me to take in this matter such decisions as I might think proper in view of securing the continuation of the Servian Monarchy. The first thing to be done was to safeguard the rights of the direct line without seeking to bind ourselves by the Salic Law, which there is really no reason to apply in our country. I should add here that there are no anti-dynastic elements in Servia, with the exception, perhaps, of a few hare-brained individuals who really do not enter into account. My people are profoundly attached to the reigning dynasty, and never lose an opportunity of showing me their loyalty. It is the same with all the political parties.

"Before promulgating the Constitution I decided to consult the most influential members of the parties in office. They agreed with me, and promised me to assist harmoniously in the work. I have also consulted the leading members of the Liberal party, and with two or three exceptions they have given me the same assurances. Such being the case, I may say that the Constitution of 1901 is not a production of my will or of my good pleasure, but that it is the result of an understanding between the Sovereign and the leaders of the three political parties. I consequently reckon upon their sincere and active co-operation, and I trust they will not fail me. I am firmly convinced that the new Constitution will act as a fresh and vigorous stimulus to my country, and that it will bring it that calm and stability which it sorely needs. I sincerely regard it as a source of prosperity and welfare for Servia."

SEVERALTY ACT, The Indian. See (in this vol.) INDIANS, AMERICAN : A. D. 1899–1900.

SEYMOUR, Vice-Admiral Sir Edward: Expedition to relieve Peking. See (in this vol.) CHINA : A. D. 1900 (JUNE 10–26).

SEYYIDIEH, The province of. See (in this vol.) BRITISH EAST AFRICA PROTECTORATE : A. D. 1895–1897.

SHAFTER, General : Commanding the expedition against Santiago de Cuba. See (in this vol.) UNITED STATES OF AM. : A. D. 1898 (JUNE—JULY).
Surrender of Spanish forces at Santiago and all eastern Cuba. See (in this vol.) UNITED STATES OF AM.: A. D. 1898 (JULY 4–17).
Report of sickness in army.—Removal of troops to Montauk Point. See (in this vol.) UNITED STATES OF AM. : A. D. 1898 (JULY—AUGUST : CUBA).

SHANGHAI.—"Shanghai is the New York of China. It occupies a position on the coast quite similar to that of New York on our own eastern coast, and its percentage of importations into China is about the same as that which New York enjoys in the United States. The large share of the foreign trade of China which Shanghai controls is due largely to its position at the mouth of the great artery through which trade flows to and from China—the Yangtze-Kiang. Transportation in bulk in China up to the present time having been almost exclusively by water, and the Yangtze being navigable by steamers and junks for more than 2,000 miles, thus reaching the most populous, productive, and wealthy sections of the country, naturally a very large share of the foreign commerce entering or leaving that country passes through Shanghai, where foreign merchants, bankers, trade representatives, trade facilities, and excellent docking and steamship conveniences exist. The lines of no less than eight great steamship companies center at Shanghai, where they land freight and passengers from their fleets of vessels which are counted by hundreds, while the smaller vessels, for river and coastwise service, and the native junks are counted literally by thousands. The Yangtze from Shanghai westward to Hankow, a distance of 582 miles, is navigable for very large steamships and is capable of coasting as well as river service. Hankow, which with its suburbs has nearly a million people, is the most important of the interior cities, being a great distributing center for trade to all parts of central and western China and thus the river trade between Shanghai and Hankow is of itself enormous, while the coastwise trade from Shanghai, both to the north and south, and that by the Grand Canal to Tientsin, the most important city of northern China, is also very large."—*United States, Bureau of Statistics, Monthly Summary, March,* 1899, *p.* 2191.

"When the English chose this position, in 1842, for their mercantile settlement, it seemed difficult to believe that they would ever succeed in making the place a rival of Canton or of Amoy. It is true that Shanghai possessed important commercial relations already, and the great geographical advantage of commanding the entrance to the navigable river which traverses the whole empire from west to east; but the builders of the city there had to struggle with enormous difficulties of soil and climate. They had to solidify and drain the land, dig canals, dry up marshes, cleanse the air of its miasms, besides incessantly dredging and clearing the channel, to keep it open for their ships. The first European merchants established at Shanghai were favored in fortune by the national disasters of China. The Taiping war drove fugitives in multitudes to the territory conceded to foreigners, and when the town of Soutcheou was destroyed, in 1860, Shanghai succeeded it as the great city of the country."—E. Reclus, *Nouvelle géographie universelle, v.* 7, *p.* 455.

A. D. 1898.—Rioting consequent on French desecration of a cemetery.—Extension of foreign settlements. See (in this vol.) CHINA : A. D. 1898–1899.

SHANTUNG, The "Boxer" outbreak in. See (in this vol.) CHINA : A. D. 1900 (JAN.—MAR.).

SHIMONOSEKI, Text of the Treaty of. See (in this vol.) CHINA : A. D. 1894–1895.

SHIPPING OF THE WORLD: In 1900. —Statement of number and net and gross tonnage of steam and sailing vessels of over 100 tons | of the several countries of the world, as recorded in Lloyd's Register for 1900–1901 [dated July 1, 1900].

FLAG.	STEAM.			SAIL.		TOTAL.	
	No.	Net tons.	Gross tons.	No.	Net tons.	No.	Tonnage.
British:							
United Kingdom.......................	7,020	7,072,401	11,513,759	1,894	1,727,687	8,914	13,241,446
Colonies...............................	910	378,925	635,331	1,014	384,477	1,924	1,019,808
Total	7,930	7,451,326	12,149,090	2,908	2,112,164	10,838	14,261,254
American (United States):							
Sea	690	594,237	878,564	2,130	1,156,498	2,820	2,035,062
Lake.................................	242	436,979	576,402	73	138,807	315	715,209
Total	932	1,031,216	1,454,966	2,203	1,295,305	3,135	2,750,271
Argentine	95	36,938	57,239	106	30,407	201	87,646
Austro-Hungarian	214	240,808	387,471	56	28,613	270	416,084
Belgian	115	111,624	162,493	2	420	117	162,913
Brazilian.............................	215	85,799	133,507	117	29,580	332	163,087
Chilean...............................	52	38,960	62,872	75	48,106	127	110,978
Chinese...............................	48	41,847	65,721	1	573	49	66,294
Colombian	1	555	877	5	1,110	6	1,987
Danish...............................	369	240,599	412,273	433	106,738	802	519,011
Dutch................................	289	307,574	467,209	117	63,068	406	530,277
French...............................	662	542,305	1,052,193	552	298,369	1,214	1,350,562
German	1,209	1,344,605	2,159,919	501	490,114	1,710	2,650,033
Greek	139	111,797	178,137	230	65,957	369	245,094
Haitian...............................	5	912	1,750	2	414	7	2,164
Italian...............................	312	343,020	540,349	864	443,306	1,176	983,655
Japanese.............................	484	303,303	488,187	582	86,370	1,066	574,557
Mexican..............................	25	6,562	11,460	13	3,081	38	14,541
Montenegrin	1	1,064	1,857	14	3,513	15	5,370
Norwegian	806	467,123	764,683	1,574	876,129	2,380	1,640,812
Peruvian	3	3,204	4,869	33	9,607	36	14,476
Portuguese...........................	48	37,153	57,664	156	53,391	204	111,055
Roumanian............................	17	9,686	17,361	3	659	20	18,020
Russian..............................	496	292,277	469,496	750	251,405	1,246	720,901
Sarawakian...........................	2	244	418	....	....	2	418
Siamese	4	821	1,435	1	294	5	1,729
Spanish..............................	422	416,882	642,231	175	52,549	597	694,780
Swedish..............................	678	260,023	418,550	755	218,722	1,433	637,272
Turkish..............................	135	58,974	94,781	170	48,709	305	143,490
Uruguayan............................	17	6,438	10,468	19	4,032	36	14,500
Venezuelan...........................	12	2,450	4,246	8	1,185	20	5,431
Zanzibarian..........................	3	1,871	2,808	....	....	3	2,808
Other countries:							
Hawaii	23	11,185	16,922	24	29,707	47	46,629
Cuba	35	17,651	27,040	11	2,410	46	29,450
Philippine Islands	69	19,587	31,099	42	8,236	111	39,335
Various: Arabia, Salvador, Ecuador, Liberia, Samos, Nicaragua, Bulgaria, Costa Rica, Egypt, Persia, Porto Rico, etc.....	31	10,130	17,717	22	9,127	53	26,844
Total	15,898	13,856,513	22,369,358	12,524	6,674,370	28,422	29,043,728

—*United States, Commissioner of Navigation, Annual Report*, 1900, p. 125.

SHIRE HIGHLANDS, The. See (in this vol.) BRITISH CENTRAL AFRICA PROTECTORATE.

SHOA. See (in this vol.) EGYPT: A. D. 1885–1896.

SHUN-CH'ING, Anti-missionary **insurrection at.** See (in this vol.) CHINA: A. D. 1898–1899 (JUNE—JANUARY).

SIAH CHAI, or **Vegetarians,** The. See (in this vol.) CHINA: A. D. 1895 (AUGUST).

SIAM: A. D. 1896-1899.—Declaration between Great Britain and France with regard to Siam.—A declaration of agreement, in part as follows, between Great Britain and France, was signed at London, January 15, 1896: "I. The Governments of Great Britain and France engage to one another that neither of them will, without the consent of the other, in any case, or under any pretext, advance their armed forces into the region which is comprised in the basins of the Petcha

Bouri, Meiklong, Menam, and Bang Pa Kong (Petriou) Rivers and their respective tributaries, together with the extent of coast from Muong Bang Tapan to Muong Pase, the basins of the rivers on which those two places are situated, and the basins of the other rivers, the estuaries of which are included in that coast; and including also the territory lying to the north of the basin of the Menam, and situated between the Anglo-Siamese frontier, the Mekong River, and the eastern watershed of the Me Ing. They further engage not to acquire within this region any special privilege or advantage which shall not be enjoyed in common by, or equally open to, Great Britain and France, and their nationals and dependents. These stipulations, however, shall not be interpreted as derogating from the special clauses which, in virtue of the Treaty concluded on the 3rd October, 1893, between France and Siam, apply to a zone of 25 kilom. on the right bank of the Mekong and to the navigation of that river. II. Nothing in the foregoing clause shall hinder any action on which the two Powers may agree, and which they shall think necessary in order to uphold the independence of the Kingdom of Siam. But they engage not to enter into any separate Agreement permitting a third Power to take any action from which they are bound by the present Declaration themselves to abstain. III. From the mouth of the Nam Huok northwards as far as the Chinese frontier the thalweg of the Mekong shall form the limit of the possessions or spheres of influence of Great Britain and France. It is agreed that the nationals and dependents of each of the two countries shall not exercise any jurisdiction or authority within the possessions or sphere of influence of the other."

In a despatch to the British Ambassador at Paris, written on the same day, Lord Salisbury explained the intent and purpose of the agreement as follows: "It might be thought that because we have engaged ourselves, and have received the engagement of France, not under any circumstances to invade this territory, that therefore we are throwing doubt upon the complete title and rights of the Siamese to the remainder of their kingdom, or, at all events, treating those rights with disregard. Any such interpretation would entirely misrepresent the intention with which this arrangement has been signed. We have selected a particular area for the application of the stipulations of this Treaty, not because the title of the King of Siam to other portions of his dominions is less valid, but because it is the area which affects our interests as a commercial nation. The valley of the Menam is eminently fitted to receive a high industrial development. Possibly in course of time it may be the site of lines of communication which will be of considerable importance to neighbouring portions of the British Empire. There seems every prospect that capital will flow into this region if reasonable security is offered for its investment, and great advantage would result to the commerce and industry of the world, and especially of Great Britain, if capitalists could be induced to make such an application of the force which they command. But the history of the region in which Siam is situated has not in recent years been favourable to the extension of industrial enterprise, or to the growth of that confidence which is the first condition of material improvement. A large territory to the north has passed from the hands of the Burmese Government to those of Great Britain. A large territory to the east has passed from the hands of its former possessors to those of France. The events of this recent history certainly have a tendency to encourage doubts of the stability of the Siamese dominion; and without in any degree sharing in those doubts, or admitting the possibility, within any future with which we have to deal, of the Siamese independence being compromised, Her Majesty's Government could not but feel that there would be an advantage in giving some security to the commercial world that, in regard to the region where the most active development is likely to take place, no further disturbances of territorial ownership are to be apprehended." —*Great Britain, Parliamentary Publications (Papers by Command: France, No. 2, 1896, pp. 1-3).*

Perhaps the above explanation can be better understood after reading the following: "In the early eighties France commenced the subjugation of Tonquin. . . . It was not until 1893 that France openly attacked Siam. The demand was subtly formulated—on behalf, not of the Government of the French Republic, but of 'the Empire of Annam.' But even so the French had been in Annam for perhaps a quarter of a century, whereas Siam could show an undisturbed, undisputed tenure of the Mekong River's 'rive gauche' for at least ninety years. . . . The cession to France of territory amounting to rather more than one-third of the entire kingdom was insisted upon; and in March 1893 that Power sent the ship-of-war Lutin to Bangkok, where she remained for months a standing menace. A rigorous blockade of the Siamese seaboard followed, resulting in a few short days in complete surrender of the disputed territory to France and the payment of a heavy war indemnity. . . . By the Anglo-French Convention of last year [as given above] the King of Siam's position became, to say the least, slightly anomalous. That agreement practically amounted to the fair division, between France and England, of the whole of Siam save that portion situate in the fertile valley of the Meinam, whose autonomy they still guarantee to preserve. . . . France holds, in addition to the long-coveted port of Chantabûn, that part of the province of Luang Phrabang which is situate upon the right bank of the Mekong. . . . The Siamese king is 'nulli secundus' among Oriental monarchs as a progressive ruler. And fate has been unkind to him indeed! He has encouraged English customs and the English language by all the means in his power—has taken the kindliest possible interest in the introduction of electric light, electric tramways, &c., into his capital—has endeavoured to model his army and navy, his prison and other systems, upon the English method—and has in person opened the first railway (that connecting Bangkok with Pâk-nam) in Siam. It is, indeed, one of the strangest and most interesting sights, as you stroll through the streets of the capital, to witness the 'riksha and gharry of comparative barbarism travelling in juxtaposition to the electric tramcar and the bicycle! And for his broad and enlightened views the King of Siam has been requited by the wholesale and utterly unjustifiable plunder of his most fertile lands."—Percy Cross Standing. *The Significance of the Siamese Visit (Nineteenth Century, June, 1897).*

Frequent collisions between French and Siamese in the so-called "neutral zone" on the right bank of the Mekong continued, until a new convention was agreed upon in May, 1899. This gave to France the province of Luang-Phrabang, in return for which she agreed to withdraw entirely from the neutral territory and from the port of Chantabûn.

A. D. 1898.—Gift of relics of Buddha. See (in this vol.) BUDDHA.

A. D. 1899 (May—July).—**Representation in** the Peace Conference at The Hague. See (in this vol.) PEACE CONFERENCE.

SIAN FU, or SI-NGAN-FU, The Chinese Imperial Court at. See (in this vol.) CHINA: A. D. 1900 (AUGUST—SEPTEMBER).

SIBERIA. See (in this vol.) RUSSIA IN ASIA.

SIBERIAN ARCTIC EXPLORATION. See (in this vol.) POLAR EXPLORATION, 1893, 1896, 1897, 1898, 1899, 1900.

SIERRA LEONE PROTECTORATE.

—**Extension** of British authority over the Hinterland of the Colony of Sierra Leone.— The hut **tax**.—Insurrection of natives.—"Immediately adjoining the Colony of Sierra Leone, lying to the northward and eastward, is the Hinterland, the boundaries of which were defined by the Agreement between Great Britain and France which was concluded 21st January 1895. The extreme depth from south to north is about 210 miles, lying between 7° and 10° north latitude, and 180 miles from east to west, lying between 10° 40′ and 13° 20′ of west longitude. The estimated area is rather more than 30,000 square miles — about the size of Ireland. . . . Unlike many regions on the west coast of Africa, the country is, for the most part, well watered by rivers and running streams. The population of the Hinterland has not been ascertained. It has been variously estimated, before the present troubles, at from about 750,000 up to about 2,000,000. The trade and revenue of the Colony depend almost entirely on the Hinterland. A very large proportion of the goods imported into the Colony are carried into and consumed in the Hinterland. These goods are paid for by means of the products of the Hinterland, which are exported, and the profits derived from the exchange enable the merchants to pay the Customs duties, which constitute the bulk of the Colonial revenue. The territories forming the Hinterland are, according to the native organisation, ruled over by a large number of Chiefs (or Kings, as they used to be, and still in native parlance are, called). The portions of country under each Chief are well ascertained, and recognised by the various Chiefs and their subjects. . . .

"The relations between the English Government and the Chiefs at the time of the conclusion of the Agreement between France and England in 1895 was . . . that some of the Chiefs whose territories lay most adjacent to the Colony of Sierra Leone had contracted with the English Crown certain treaties of cession, and treaties directed to definite objects of amity and good offices. In addition there had sprung up by usage a limited consensual and advisory jurisdiction, under which Chiefs as well as persons not Chiefs would bring their differences (mainly as to territorial boundaries) before the Govcruor of Sierra Leone as a sort of arbitrator, and implicitly follow his awards. This jurisdiction was exercised over an area of no defined limits, so far as any rules were concerned. As a fact, it was limited by conditions of distance and facility of travel, so that whilst the usage was most established in the countries nearest to Freetown, there was none in the most distant regions, or if there was any it was at most so rudimentary as to be jurally of no account. . . . I have not been able to trace any instance in which, either under treaty or any other form of consent, or without consent, the English Government has imposed, or endeavoured to impose any direct taxation upon the Chiefs or people of the Hinterland prior to 1896.

"The agreement between France and Great Britain delimited the respective spheres of interest of the two countries south and west of the Middle or Upper Niger, and thus defined for England in the Hinterland of Sierra Leone a territory within which, so far as concerned any question between France and England, England was at liberty to exercise whatever species or extent of jurisdiction she might consider proper. It made, of course, no alteration on the existing native organisation, nor upon the existing relations between England and the native Chiefs, who were not parties to the agreement in any sense. . . . On 31st August 1896 a Proclamation was published setting forth that Her Majesty had assumed a Protectorate over the territories adjacent to the Colony of Sierra Leone in which Her Majesty had acquired power and jurisdiction. For purposes of administration the Hinterland was divided into five districts, intended to be of about equal size, avoiding severance as far as possible by the district boundary of the territories of Paramount Chiefs. These districts have been named as the Karene, Ronietta, Bandajuma, Panguma, and Koinadugu districts. In anticipation of the arrangements that might become necessary for the government of the Protectorate, an Order of the Queen in Council had been made on 24th August 1895, . . . whereby, . . . Her Majesty was pleased, by and with the advice of her Privy Council, to order that it shall be lawful for the Legislative Council, for the time being, of the Colony of Sierra Leone, by Ordinance or Ordinances, to exercise and provide for giving effect to all such jurisdiction as Her Majesty may at any time, before or after the passing of the Order in Council, have acquired in the said territories adjacent to the Colony of Sierra Leone. Following upon the Order of the Queen in Council, an Ordinance, entitled 'An Ordinance to Determine the mode of exercising Her Majesty's Jurisdiction in the Territories adjacent to the Colony of Sierra Leone,' was passed by the Legislative Council and Governor of Sierra Leone for the Government of the Protectorate, on 16th September 1896."—*Great Britain, Report and Correspondence on Insurrection in the Sierra Leone Protectorate (Parliamentary Publications: Papers by Command,* 1899, *C.* 9388, *pp.* 10–17).

The Ordinance above mentioned, which was re-enacted, with some changes, in September, 1897, provided, among other things, for the imposition of a house tax, or hut tax, upon the natives, and this proved to be the main cause of a serious native revolt in the Protectorate. "By way of asserting the Crown's ownership of all lands, whether in use and occupation or not—and also of attempting to make the people defray the cost of governing them by methods they resent—the Protectorate Ordinance imposes a 'house tax' of five shillings a year, and, in the case of 'houses with four rooms or more,' of ten shillings a year, on every 'householder'; the same to be paid in 'sterling coin' on or after the 1st January in each year, or, in default of payment on demand, to be distrained for with so much addition as will defray the cost of removing the property and disposing of it for 'the price current at the nearest market.' The absurdity of thus importing the mechanism of civilisation into 'house tax' levying among these ignorant savages matches the injustice of the tax itself. The mud hovels to be taxed are rarely worth more than the equivalent of two or three shillings apiece, and shillings or other 'sterling coin' are rarely seen or handled by the natives, such wages as they earn being generally paid in kind, and such trade as they carry on being nearly always in the way of barter. Few who are not chiefs or headmen own property worth as much as five shillings, and property for which five shillings could be obtained 'at the nearest market' might be worth the equivalent of five pounds to them. There was no attempt to raise the proposed house or hut tax before last January [1898], and perhaps none of the natives have even yet any understanding of the clauses of the Protectorate Ordinance providing them with new-fangled 'courts of justice,' and taking from them all proprietary rights in their land. But as soon as a proclamation was issued on 21st August, 1896, notifying the contemplated changes, all who heard of them were reasonably alarmed, and wherever the news spread seeds of fresh discontent were sown. . . . "There were burning of huts, buffeting of chiefs, and so forth, in the south and east, as well as in the north, where, owing to the alleged recalcitrancy of Bai Bureh and the zeal of Captain Sharpe, the District Commissioner, the havoc was greatest. Early in February several chiefs and headmen were brought to Freetown from Port Lokko in manacles, to be tried, or punished without trial, on a charge of 'refusing to comply with the provisions of the Protectorate Ordinance, and inciting their subjects to resist the law.' 'The most affecting part of the matter,' says the newspaper report, 'is that the natives all loudly affirm their unswerving loyalty to the Government, and say that they do not refuse to pay the hut tax because they do not wish to, but because they really cannot pay.' Their apologies were not listened to. Instead, a detachment of the West India Regiment was sent up to assist Captain Sharpe in the little war on which he had already embarked. A futile attempt to arrest Bai Bureh on 18th February led to a general uprising, and the first battle was fought on 3rd March, when the town of Karina was recovered from the 'insurgents' who had occupied it, and over sixty of them were killed. Another fight occurred at Port Lokko, on 5th March, when the 'insurgents' lost about forty more. These victories being insufficient, fresh troops were sent up in batches, until the entire force of conquerors numbered 800 or upwards. They found it easier to cow than to conquer the people, and the unequal struggle went on for three months. At the end of May operations had to be suspended during the rainy season, and before they can be renewed it may be hoped that peace will be patched up. Already, indeed, the 'rebellion' appears to be practically crushed, and with it all the civilisation and all the commerce that had been planted in the Karina district. Hundreds of natives have been shot down, many more hundreds have died of starvation. Nearly all the huts that it was proposed to tax have been destroyed, either by the owners themselves, or by the policemen and soldiers."—H. R. Fox Bourne, *Sierra Leone Troubles* (*Fortnightly Review*, *Aug.*, 1898).

SILVER QUESTION, The: A. D. 1895 (January—February).—Attitude of Free Silver majority in the U. S. Senate towards the Treasury gold reserve. See (in this vol.) UNITED STATES OF AM. : A. D. 1895 (JANUARY—FEBRUARY); and 1895-1896 (DECEMBER—FEBRUARY).

A. D. 1896.—In the American Presidential election. See (in this vol.) UNITED STATES OF AM.: A. D. 1896 (JUNE—NOVEMBER).

A. D. 1896-1898.—The Indianapolis Monetary Commission report and Secretary Gage's plan in Congress. See (in this vol.) UNITED STATES OF AM. : A. D. 1896-1898.

A. D. 1897.—Negotiations by envoys from the United States for an international bimetallic agreement. See (in this vol.) MONETARY QUESTIONS: A. D. 1897 (APRIL—OCTOBER).

A. D. 1900.—Practical settlement of the issue in the United States.—Attempted revival in the Presidential canvass. See (in this vol.) UNITED STATES OF AM. : A. D. 1900 (MARCH—DECEMBER), and (MAY—NOVEMBER).

SILVER REPUBLICANS. See (in this vol.) UNITED STATES OF AM. : A. D. 1896 (JUNE—NOVEMBER) ; and 1900 (MAY—NOVEMBER).

SI-NGAN-FU, or SINGAN FU, The Chinese Imperial Court at. See (in this vol.) CHINA : A. D. 1900 (AUGUST—SEPTEMBER).

SIRDAR, Egyptian. See (in this vol.) EGYPT : A. D. 1885-1896 ; and 1897-1898.

SLAVERY: A. D. 1885.—Emancipation in Cuba. See (in this vol.) CUBA : A. D. 1868-1885.

A. D. 1895.—New anti-slavery law in Egypt. See (in this vol.) EGYPT : A. D. 1895.

A. D. 1896.—Abolition in Madagascar. See (in this vol.) MADAGASCAR : A. D. 1894-1896.

A. D. 1897.—Abolished in Zanzibar. See (in this vol.) AFRICA: A. D. 1897 (ZANZIBAR).

A. D. 1897.—Compulsory labor in Rhodesia. See (in this vol.) SOUTH AFRICA (BRITISH SOUTH AFRICA COMPANY): A. D. 1897 (JANUARY).

A. D. 1897.—Subjugation of Fulah slave raiders in Nupé and Ilorin. See (in this vol.) AFRICA : A. D. 1897 (NIGERIA).

A. D. 1899.—Forced labor in Congo State. See (in this vol.) CONGO FREE STATE : A. D. 1899.

SLESWICK: Complaints of German treatment. See (in this vol.) GERMANY : A. D. 1899.

SMOKELESS POWDERS, Invention of. See (in this vol.) SCIENCE, RECENT : CHEMISTRY AND PHYSICS.

SOCIAL DEMOCRACY, Encyclical Letter of Pope Leo XIII. on. See (in this vol.) PAPACY: A. D. 1901.

SOCIALIST PARTIES. See (in this vol.) AUSTRIA-HUNGARY : A. D. 1897, and after ; BELGIUM : A. D. 1894-1895 ; FRANCE: A. D. 1896 (APRIL—MAY), and 1900 (JANUARY) ; GERMANY : A. D. 1894-1895, and 1897 (JULY); ITALY : A. D. 1898 (APRIL—MAY); SWITZERLAND: A. D. 1894-1898 ; UNITED STATES OF AM. : A. D. 1896 (JUNE—NOVEMBER), and 1900 (MAY—NOVEMBER).

SOKOTO. See (in this vol.) NIGERIA: A. D. 1882-1899.

SOLOMON ISLANDS, The: Definite division between Great Britain and Germany. See (in this vol.) SAMOAN ISLANDS.

SOMALIS, Rising of, in Jubaland. See (in this vol.) BRITISH EAST AFRICA PROTECTORATE: A. D. 1900.

SOUDAN. See (in this vol.) SUDAN.

"SOUND MONEY" DEMOCRATS. See (in this vol.) UNITED STATES OF AM. : A. D. 1896 (JUNE—NOVEMBER).

SOUTH AFRICA.

Cape Colony: A. D. **1881-1888.**—Organization of the "Afrikander Bund."—The "Afrikander Bund" or National Party was formed in Cape Colony in 1881, but held its first Congress, or convention, in 1888, at which meeting the following platform, or formal statement of objects, was adopted: "1· The Afrikander National party acknowledge the guidance of Providence in the affairs both of lands and peoples. 2. They include, under the guidance of Providence, the formation of a pure nationality and the preparation of our people for the establishment of a 'United South Africa.' 3. To this they consider belong: (a) The establishment of a firm union between all the different European nationalities in South Africa, and (b) The promotion of South Africa's independence. 4. They consider that the union mentioned in Art. 3 (a) depends upon the clear and plain understanding of each other's general interest in politics, agriculture, stock-breeding, trade, and industry, and the acknowledgment of every one's special rights in the matter of religion, education, and language; so that all national jealousy between the different elements of the people may be removed, and room be made for an unmistakable South African national sentiment. 5. To the advancement of the independence mentioned in Art. 3 (b) belong: (a) That the sentiment of national self-respect and of patriotism toward South Africa should above all be developed and exhibited in schools, and in families, and in the public press. (b) That a system of voting should be applied which not only acknowledges the right of numbers, but also that of ownership and the development of intelligence, and that is opposed, as far as possible, to bribery and compulsion at the poll. (c) That our agriculture, stock-breeding, commerce, and industries should be supported in every lawful manner, such as by a conclusive law as regards masters and servants, and also by the appointment of a prudent and advantageous system of Protection. (d) That the South African Colonies and States, either each for itself or in conjunction with one another, shall regulate their own native affairs, employing thereto the forces of the land by means of a satisfactory burgher law; and (e) That outside interference with the domestic concerns of South Africa shall be opposed. 6. While they acknowledge the existing Governments holding rule in South Africa, and intend faithfully to fulfil their obligations in regard to the same, they consider that the duty rests upon those Governments to advance the interests of South Africa in the spirit of the foregoing articles; and whilst, on the one side, they watch against any unnecessary or frivolous interference with the domestic or other private matters of the burgher, against any direct meddling with the spiritual development of the nation, and against laws which might hinder the free influence of the Gospel upon the national life, on the other hand they should accomplish all the positive duties of a good Government, among which must be reckoned: (a) In all their actions to take account of the Christian character of the people. (b) The maintenance of freedom of religion for every one, so long as the public order and honor are not injured thereby. (c) The acknowledgment and expression of religious, social, and bodily needs of the people, in

the observance of the present weekly day of rest. (d) The application of an equal and judicious system of taxation. (e) The bringing into practice of an impartial and, as far as possible, economical administration of justice. (f) The watching over the public honor, and against the adulteration of the necessaries of life, and the defiling of ground, water, or air, as well as against the spreading of infectious diseases. 7. In order to secure the influence of these principles, they stand forward as an independent party, and accept the coöperation of other parties only if the same can be obtained with the uninjured maintenance of these principles.

The Transvaal: A. D. **1884-1894.**—The restored independence of the Boers and their dissatisfaction with its terms.—Frustration of their desire for extended territory.—The London Convention of **1884.**—After the British-Boer War of 1880–81 (see, in vol. 4, SOUTH AFRICA: A. D. 1806–1881), which had been caused by an arbitrary annexation of the Transvaal State to the dominions of the British crown, the sense of justice in Mr. Gladstone led him to restore to the Transvaal Boers (by the Convention or Treaty of Pretoria, 1881) their right of internal self-government, with a reservation of "the suzerainty of Her Majesty," supposably relative to nothing but foreign affairs. The Boers were not satisfied with that concession, and began at once to strive for the complete independence they had previously possessed, under a Convention agreed upon and signed at Sand River, 1852, which guaranteed (quoting its precise terms) " in the fullest manner, on the part of the British Government, to the emigrant farmers (boers) beyond the Vaal River, the right to manage their own affairs and to govern themselves, without any interference on the part of Her Majesty the Queen's Government." To regain that status of complete independence became the first object of the Boers. They went far towards success in this endeavor, as early as 1884, when the British Colonial Secretary, Lord Derby, was induced to agree to a new Convention with the South African Republic (as it was then styled) which superseded the Convention of 1881. The terms of the later instrument are given below.

The second aim of the Boers appears to have been the widening of their territory, by advances, in the first instance, southward into Zululand and westward into Bechuanaland. In the former movement they had success; in the latter they were thwarted. English missionaries complained of their treatment of the natives, and stirred up the British government to take the Bechuana tribes under its protection. Their eastern frontier they succeeded, after long controversies with Great Britain, in stretching beyond Swaziland, but they were not allowed to push it to the sea. Northward, they would probably have gone far, had it not been for the appearance, at this time, of Mr. Cecil Rhodes, who came upon the scene of South African politics with imperial ambitions, with great energies and capabilities, with few apparent hesitations, and with a vast fortune acquired in the Kimberley diamond mines. He organized the British South Africa Company, under a royal charter, got some settlers into the country north of the Limpopo and set up a government there, in 1890, just in time, it appears, to forestall the Boers (see, in vol. 4, SOUTH AFRICA : A. D. 1885-1893).

Of the effect of the two conventions, of 1881 and 1884, on the relations of the British government to the South African Republic, the following is an English view, by a well-known publicist : "In the Treaty of Pretoria, bearing date the 5th of April, 1881, it is stated that Great Britain guarantees 'complete self-government, subject to the Suzerainty of Her Majesty, to the inhabitants of the Transvaal.' . . . Article 15 declares that 'the Resident will report to the High Commissioner, as representative of the Suzerain, as to the working and observance of the provisions of this Convention.' . . . On the 31st of March, 1881, Lord Kimberley, who was then Secretary of State for the Colonies, used these words in the House of Lords with reference to the terms of the Convention, upon which the Treaty of Pretoria was afterwards based : 'I believe the word Suzerainty expresses very correctly the relation which we intend to exist between this country and the Transvaal. Our intention is that the Transvaal shall have independent power as regards its internal government; and we shall only reserve certain powers to be exercised by the Queen. . . . With respect to our control over the relations of the Transvaal with foreign Powers, . . . it is quite clear there ought to be, as regards foreign relations, only one Government in South Africa ; that there ought to be no communication with foreign Powers upon any subject except through the representatives of the Queen.'

"On the 25th of June, 1881, Mr. Gladstone, while defending in the House of Commons an assertion he had made during the Midlothian Campaign about the blood-guiltiness of the war with the Transvaal, referred to our Suzerainty in the following words : 'I apprehend that the term which has been adopted, the Suzerainty of the Queen, is intended to signify that certain portions of Sovereignty are reserved. . . . What are these portions of Sovereignty ? The portions of Sovereignty we desire to reserve are, first, the relations between the Transvaal community and foreign governments, the whole care of the foreign relations of the Boers. The whole of these relations will remain in the hands of the Queen.'

"From these quotations it is obvious that when we agreed to restore the independence of the Transvaal, the British public were led to believe, both by the then Premier and the then Colonial Minister, that this restoration left the control of all relations between the Transvaal and foreign Powers absolutely and entirely in the hands of Her Majesty's Government. . . . It is possible, or even probable, that at the time the Treaty of Pretoria was concluded, Mr. Gladstone, or at any rate several of his colleagues, imagined that our Suzerainty would really be made effective. But, when once the treaty had been signed and sealed, and the South African Republic had been granted absolute internal independence, it became evident that our Suzerainty could only be rendered efficacious, as against the sullen resistance of the Boers, by the exercise of force—that is, by the threat of war in the event of Boer non-compliance with the demands of the Suzerain Power. . . .

"For the first two years which succeeded our surrender the Boers were too much occupied in the reorganisation of the Republic to trouble

themselves greatly about their relations to the Suzerain Power. . . . Disputes were mainly connected with the treatment of the native chiefs, residing either within, or on the borders of, the territory of the Republic, who asserted, with or without reason, that they were the objects of Boer hostility on account of the support they had given to the British authorities during the period of British rule.

"In May 1883 Mr. Gladstone stated in Parliament, in answer to certain protests about the proceedings of the Boers, that the British Government had decided to send a Commissioner to the Transvaal to investigate the working of the Convention concluded at Pretoria in 1881. This intention, however, was not carried out owing to the opposition of the South African Republic. In lieu of the despatch of a British Commissioner to the Transvaal, it was suggested at Pretoria that a Boer deputation should be sent to London. The suggestion, as usual, was accepted ; and thereupon the Africander Bond in the Cape Colony forwarded a petition to the Queen, praying Her Majesty to entertain favourably the proposals of the Boer delegates for the modification of the Treaty of Pretoria. The deputation, consisting of President Kruger and Messieurs Du Toit and Smit, arrived in London in October; and submitted to the late Lord Derby, who had succeeded Lord Kimberley as Minister for the Colonies, a statement of the modifications they were instructed to demand. The memorandum in question distinctly declared that the alleged impracticability of the Treaty of Pretoria related, amongst other matters, 'to the extent of the Suzerain rights reserved to Her Majesty by Articles 2 and 18 of the Treaty of Pretoria, and to the vague and indefinite terms in which the powers reserved to Her Majesty's Government by the Convention are indicated.'

"To this memorandum Lord Derby replied, on the 20th of November, 1883, admitting that the 'expediency of substituting a new agreement for that of 1881 might be matter for discussion, but asking for information, in what sense it is wished that in such new agreement some connection with England should be maintained, and, if it is the desire of the Transvaal people that their State should hereafter stand in any special relation to this country, what is the form of connection which is proposed ?' In reply to this request the Boer delegates answered as follows in the somewhat evasive fashion : 'In the new agreement any connection by which we are now bound to England should not be broken ; but that the relation of a dependency "publici juris" in which our country now stands to the British Crown be replaced by that of two contractive Powers.'

"The above documents were submitted to the Governor of Cape Colony, the then Sir Hercules Robinson. Characteristically enough, Sir Hercules recommended the surrender of our Suzerainty on the ground that 'The Transvaal burghers obviously do not intend to observe any condition in it (the Convention of 1881) distasteful to themselves, which Her Majesty's Government are not prepared to insist on, if necessary, by the employment of force. Her Majesty's Government, I understand, do not feel justified in proceeding to this extremity ; and no provision, therefore, of the Convention which is not agreeable to the Transvaal will be carried out.'

"A few days later the delegates submitted a draft treaty, in which the following clause stands first: 'It is agreed that Her Britannic Majesty recognises and guarantees by this treaty the full independence of the South African Republic, with the right to manage its own affairs according to its own laws, without any interference on the part of the British Government; it being understood that this system of non-interference is binding on both parties.' To the letter enclosing this draft treaty Lord Derby replied that the proposed treaty was 'neither in form nor in substance such as Her Majesty's Government could adopt.' Meanwhile the discussion between the British Government and the Boer delegates seems to have turned mainly upon the extension of the territories of the Transvaal and the relations between the Republic and the native chiefs, subjects which had only an indirect bearing on the question of Suzerainty. It was only on the 25th of January, 1884, that the Colonial Office wrote to the delegates stating that if a certain compromise with regard to the frontier line were accepted, the British Government would be prepared 'to proceed at once with the consideration of the other proposals for the modification of the Treaty of Pretoria.' The delegates replied on the next day virtually accepting the proposed frontier compromise, and requested the British Government to proceed at once with the substitution of a new Convention. . . . The draft treaty was signed on the 27th of February, 1884. . . .

"The Convention of London did not repeat the preamble of the original Convention in which the words 'subject to the Suzerainty of Her Majesty' are to be found. Nor is the word Suzerainty mentioned in the Convention of 1884, which declares that the articles contained therein, if endorsed by the Volksraad, 'shall be substituted for those of the Convention of 1881.' No formal withdrawal, however, of the Queen's Suzerainty is to be found in the Convention of 1884. On the contrary, it is distinctly affirmed in Article 4 of the modified Convention that 'the South African Republic will conclude no treaty or engagement with any State or nation, other than the Orange Free State, until the same has been approved by Her Majesty the Queen.'"—Edward Dicey, *British Suzerainty in the Transvaal* (*Nineteenth Century, Oct.*, 1897).

In its preamble, the Convention of 1884 recites that—"Whereas the Government of the Transvaal State, through its Delegates, consisting of [Kruger, Du Toit and Smit], have represented that the Convention signed at Pretoria on the 3rd day of August, 1881, and ratified by the Volksraad of the said State on the 25th of October, 1881, contains certain provisions which are inconvenient, and imposes burdens and obligations from which the said State is desirous to be relieved, and that the south-western boundaries fixed by the said Convention should be amended with a view to promote the peace and good order of the said State, . . . now, therefore, Her Majesty has been pleased to direct," &c.—substituting the articles of a new Convention for those signed and ratified in 1881.

Article I. of the new Convention describes the lines of boundary as amended. Article II. binds the two governments, respectively, to guard said boundaries against all trespassing. Article III. provides for the reception and protection, at Pre-

toria, of a resident British officer, "to discharge functions analogous to those of a consular officer."

Article IV. reads as follows: "The South African Republic will conclude no Treaty or engagement with any State or nation other than the Orange Free State, nor with any native tribe to the eastward or westward of the Republic, until the same has been approved by Her Majesty the Queen. Such approval shall be considered to have been granted if Her Majesty's Government shall not, within six months after receiving a copy of such Treaty (which shall be delivered to them immediately upon its completion), have notified that the conclusion of such Treaty is in conflict with the interests of Great Britain, or of any of Her Majesty's possessions in South Africa."

Articles V. and VI. relate to public debts. Article VII. guarantees the non-molestation of persons in the South African Republic who "remained loyal to Her Majesty during the late hostilities." Article VIII. is a declaration against slavery in the Republic. Article IX. is in language as follows: "There will continue to be complete freedom of religion and protection from molestation for all denominations, provided the same be not inconsistent with morality and good order; and no disability shall attach to any person in regard to rights of property by reason of the religious opinions which he holds." Article X. relates to graves of British soldiers; XI. to former grants of land which the present arrangement of boundary places outside of the Republic; XII. to the independence of the Swazis; XIII. to non-discrimination in import duties on both sides.

Articles XIV. and XV. read thus: Article XIV. "All persons, other than natives, conforming themselves to the laws of the South African Republic, (a) will have full liberty, with their families, to enter, travel or reside in any part of the South African Republic; (b) they will be entitled to hire or possess houses, manufactories, warehouses, shops and premises; (c) they may carry on their commerce either in person or by any agents whom they may think fit to employ; (d) they will not be subject, in respect of their persons or property, or in respect of their commerce or industry, to any taxes, whether general or local, other than those which are or may be imposed upon citizens of the said Republic." Article XV. "All persons, other than natives, who establish their domicile in the Transvaal between the 12th day of April, 1877, and the 8th day of August, 1881, and who within twelve months after such last mentioned date have had their names registered by the British resident, shall be exempt from all compulsory military service whatever." Article XVI. provides for a future extradition treaty; XVII. for the payment of debts in the same currency in which they were contracted; XVIII. establishes the validity of certain land grants; XIX. secures certain rights to the natives; XX. nullifies the Convention if not ratified by the Volksraad within six months from the date of its signature—February 27, 1884.

With considerable reluctance, the Convention was ratified by the Volksraad of the South African Republic in the following terms: "The Volksraad having considered the new Convention concluded between its deputation and the British

458

Government at London on 27th February 1884, as likewise the negotiations between the contracting parties, which resulted in the said Convention, approves of the standpoint taken by its deputation that a settlement based upon the principle of the Sand River Convention can alone fully satisfy the burghers of the Republic. It also shares the objections set forth by the deputation against the Convention of Pretoria, as likewise their objections against the Convention of London on the following points:—1st. The settlement of the boundary, especially on the western border of the Republic, in which the deputation eventually acquiesced only under the express conditions with which the Raad agree. 2nd. The right of veto reserved to the British Crown upon treaties to be concluded by the Republic with foreign powers; and 3rd. The settlement of the debt. Seeing, however, that in the said Convention of London considerable advantages are secured to the Republic, especially in the restoration of the country's independence, Resolves, With acknowledgment of the generosity of Her Britannic Majesty, to ratify, as it hereby does, the said Convention of London."— *Selected Official Documents of the South African Republic and Great Britain (Supplement to the Annals of the Am. Academy of Pol. and Soc. Science, July, 1900).*

Also in: *State Papers, British and Foreign, v. 76.*

The Transvaal: **A. D. 1885-1890.**—**The gold discoveries on the Rand and the influx of Uitlanders (Outlanders or Foreigners).**— " It was not until 1884 that England heard of the presence of gold in South Africa. A man named Fred Stuben, who had spent several years in the country, spread such marvellous reports of the underground wealth of the Transvaal that only a short time elapsed before hundreds of prospectors and miners left England for South Africa. When the first prospectors discovered auriferous veins of wonderful quality on a farm called Sterkfontein, the gold boom had its birth. It required the lapse of only a short time for the news to reach Europe, America, and Australia, and immediately thereafter that vast and widely scattered army of men and women which constantly awaits the announcement of new discoveries of gold was set in motion toward the Randt [the Witwatersrand or Whitewatersridge]. . . . In December, 1885, the first stamp mill was erected for the purpose of crushing the gneiss rock in which the gold lay hidden. This enterprise marks the real beginning of the gold fields of the Randt, which now yield one third of the world's total product of the precious metal. The advent of thousands of foreigners was a boon to the Boers, who owned the large farms on which the auriferous veins were located. Options on farms that were of little value a short time before were sold at incredible figures, and the prices paid for small claims would have purchased farms of thousands of acres two years before. In July, 1886, the Government opened nine farms to the miners, and all have since become the best properties on the Randt. . . . On the Randt the California scenes of '49 were being re-enacted. Tents and houses of sheet iron were erected with picturesque lack of beauty and uniformity, and during the latter part of 1886 the community had reached such proportions that the Government marked off a township and called it

Johannesburg. The Government, which owned the greater part of the land, held three sales of building lots, or ' stands,' as they are called in the Transvaal, and realized more than $300,000 from the sales. . . . Millions were secured in England and Europe for the development of the mines, and the individual miner sold his claims to companies with unlimited capital. The incredibly large dividends that were realized by some of the investors led to too heavy investments in the Stock Exchange in 1889, and a panic resulted. Investors lost thousands of pounds, and for several months the future of the gold fields appeared to be most gloomy. The opening of the railway to Johannesburg and the re-establishment of stock values caused a renewal of confidence, and the growth and development of the Randt was imbued with renewed vigour. Owing to the Boers' lack of training and consequent inability to share in the development of the gold fields, the new industry remained almost entirely in the hands of the newcomers, the Uitlanders [so called in the language of the Boers], and two totally different communities were created in the republic. The Uitlanders, who, in 1890, numbered about 100,000, lived almost exclusively in Johannesburg and the suburbs along the Randt. The Boers, having disposed of their farms and lands on the Randt, were obliged to occupy the other parts of the republic, where they could follow their pastoral and agricultural pursuits. The natural contempt which the Englishmen, who composed the majority of the Uitlander population, always have for persons and races not their intellectual or social equals, soon created a gulf between the Boers and the newcomers."—H. C. Hillegas, *Oom Paul's People, ch. 3 (with permission of D. Appleton & Co., copyright, 1899).*

As the influx of newcomers increased and advanced, "the Boers realized that the world and civilisation were once more upon them. In spite of all the opposition that patriarchal prejudice could muster, railways usurped the place of the slow moving ox-waggon, and in the heart of their solitude a city had arisen; while to the north and to the east between them and the sea were drawn the thin red lines of British boundary. . . . A primitive pastoral people, they found themselves isolated, surrounded— 'shut in a kraal for ever,' as Kruger is reported to have said,—while the stranger was growing in wealth and numbers within their gates. Expansion of territory, once the dream of the Transvaal Boers, as their incursions into Bechuanaland, into Zululand, and the attempted trek into Rhodesia, all testify, was becoming daily less practicable. One thing remained,—to accept their isolation and strengthen it. Wealth, population, a position among the new States of the world had been brought to them, almost in spite of themselves, by the newcomer, the stranger, the Uitlander. What was to be the attitude towards him politically ? Materially he had made the State—he developed its resources, paid nine-tenths of its revenue. Would he be a strength or a weakness as a citizen—as a member of the body politic ? Let us consider this new element in a new State—how was it constituted, what were its component parts ? Was it the right material for a new State to assimilate ? Cosmopolitan to a degree—recruited from all the corners of the earth—there was in it a strong South

African element, consisting of young colonists from the Cape Colony and Natal—members of families well known in South Africa—and many of them old schoolfellows or in some other way known to each other. Then the British contingent, self-reliant, full of enterprise and energy—Americans, for the most part skilled engineers, miners and mechanics—French, Germans, and Hollanders. A band of emigrants, of adventurers, and constituted, as I think all emigrants are, of two great classes—the one who, lacking neither ability nor courage, are filled with an ambition, characteristic particularly of the British race, to raise their status in the world, who find the conditions of their native environment too arduous, the competition too keen, to offer them much prospect, and who seek a new and more rapidly developing country elsewhere; and another, a smaller class who sometimes through misfortune, sometimes through their own fault, or perhaps through both, have failed elsewhere. "Adventurers all, one must admit; but it is the adventurers of the world who have founded States and Kingdoms. Such a class as this has been assimilated by the United States and absorbed into their huge fabric, of which to-day they form a large and substantial portion. What should the Transvaal Boers have done with this new element so full of enterprise and vigour? This had been for the last ten years the great question for them to solve. . . . Enfranchisement, participation in the political life of the State by the Uitlander,—this means, they said, a transference of all political power from our hands to those of men whom we do not trust. 'I have taken a man into my coach,' said President Kruger, 'and as a passenger he is welcome; but now he says, Give me the reins; and that I cannot do, for I know not where he will drive me.' To the Boer it is all or nothing; he knows no mean, no compromise. Yet in that very mean lies the vital spirit of republicanism. What is the position of the Boers in the Cape Colony? Are they without their share, their influence, their Africander bond in the political affairs of the country? And so it is throughout the world to-day,—in the United States, in England, in France, in the British Colonies, wherever the individual thrives and the State is prosperous—the compromise of divided political power among all classes, all factions, is the great guarantee of their well being. . . . That the enfranchisement of the Uitlander would mean a complete transference of political power into his hands involves two assumptions: the first is that the Uitlanders would form a united body in politics; the second is that their representatives would dominate the Volksraad. The most superficial acquaintance with the action of the inhabitants of the Witwatersrand district on any public matter will serve to refute the first of these. . . . The second of these assumptions—though it is continually put forward—almost answers itself. The number of representatives from the Uitlander districts under any scheme of redistribution of seats which the Boer could reasonably be expected to make would fall considerably short of those returned from the Boer constituencies. Such was the attitude of the Boers on this vital question which led to the Reform Movement of 1895; and I have stated what I believe to be the injustice of it as regards the Uitlanders and the unwisdom of it in the true interests of the Boers."—A. P.

Hillier, *Raid and Reform*, pp. 24-29 (*London: Macmillan & Co.*).

Portuguese Possessions: **A. D. 1891.**—Delagoa Bay Railway question. See (in this vol.) DELAGOA BAY ARBITRATION.

The Transvaal: **A. D. 1894.**—Estimated population.—In October, 1894, the British agent at Pretoria, J. A. de Wet, estimated the population of the Transvaal (on the basis of a census taken in 1890) as follows: "Transvaalers and Orange Free Staters, 70,861: British subjects, 62,509: other foreigners, 15,558;" total, 148,928.

The Transvaal: **A. D. 1894.**—The "Commandeering" question.—Visit of the British High Commissioner to Pretoria.—Demonstration of British residents.—The first question which came to a sharp issue between the government of the South African Republic and the British subjects resident in the gold fields related to the claim which the former made on the latter for military service in the wars of the Republic with neighboring native tribes. The demand for such service was made, in each case, by what was called a "commando," the commando being defined in the military law of the Boers as follows: "By commando is understood a number of armed burghers and subjects of the state called together to suppress rebellion amongst the natives, or disturbances amongst the white population." British residents protested against the requirement of this service from them; and the British government, in 1894, opened negotiations with that of the Boer Republic to obtain their exemption from it. It was acknowledged that there is "nothing contrary to international comity in the application of such a law as the commando law to a foreigner"; but, said the British Colonial Secretary, in a despatch (June 8, 1894) giving instructions to the British High Commissioner in South Africa, "Her Majesty's Government consider that a special reason for now claiming exemption for our people is afforded by the fact that treaties have been concluded by the South African Republic under which, as they understand, the subjects of no less than seven Powers—Portugal, Holland, Belgium, Germany, France, Italy, and Switzerland—are now exempt from this liability; and they consider that they can hardly be expected to acquiesce in a state of things under which Her Majesty's subjects, whose interests in the South African Republic are greater and more intimate than those of any other Power, should remain in a position of such marked disadvantage. I have therefore to instruct you to address, in moderate and courteous terms, a friendly representation to the Government of the South African Republic on the subject."

Negotiations on the subject were then opened, which led to a visit to the Boer capital by the British High Commissioner, Sir H. B. Loch, on invitation from President Kruger. His arrival at Pretoria (June 25) gave occasion for a demonstration on the part of British residents which showed the state of feeling existing more plainly, no doubt, than it had appeared before. The circumstances were reported a few days later by the High Commissioner, as follows: "When I entered the carriage with President Kruger, two men got on to the box with a Union Jack, and the crowd, notwithstanding the President's remonstrances, took the horses out and dragged the carriage to the hotel, a distance of nearly a mile, singing all the way 'God save the Queen,' and 'Rule Britannia.' On arrival at the hotel, the address was presented, to which I briefly replied, and then called for three cheers for the President, which were heartily given. He was then dragged in his carriage to the Government Office. I am satisfied that no personal insult was intended, by this demonstration, to the President, and any annoyance with which he viewed the occurrence seemed to be caused from the fact of the arrangements for keeping order having been so defective. The political atmosphere, however, was charged with such an amount of electricity that every moment an explosion was imminent. The Legislative and Executive enactments which press heavily on the great industry which contributes upwards of £1,000,000 annually out of a total revenue of little more than a million and a quarter, without the population that produces this wealth possessing any franchise rights, or voice in the government of the country, has created a deep-seated feeling of dissatisfaction, shared alike by the English, American, German, and other foreign residents in the country. The compulsory commandeering was the last straw that broke down the patience they had hitherto exhibited. . . . The Transvaal Government were, before my arrival, seriously alarmed at the state of feeling at Johannesburg, but when they came to consider the real meaning of the demonstration on my arrival at Pretoria, which showed to them how general the dissatisfaction was amongst all classes of British subjects, who formed the majority of the whole population of the Republic, they, for the first time, realised the imminent danger of the situation, and told me of their dread of a collision that at any moment might occur between the Boer burghers, who were in considerable numbers in the town, and the English and foreign residents."

To avoid any further excitement of feeling, the Commissioner declined to visit Johannesburg, which he had intended to do. During his stay at Pretoria, he submitted to President Kruger the draft of a Convention stipulating that "the subjects of Her Majesty the Queen whilst residing within the limits of the South African Republic, and the citizens of the South African Republic whilst residing within the dominions of Her Majesty the Queen, shall enjoy the same rights and privileges as the subjects of the most favoured nation with regard to military service and all obligations of a like nature"; and he received from President Kruger a counter proposition, for the negotiation of a new agreement, to take the place of the London Convention of 1884, embodying the desired provision concerning military service, along with other amendments of the old Convention. To this proposal, President Kruger added: "In order, however, to meet the request of Her Majesty's Government, the Government will, in the meantime, provisionally, no more commandeer British subjects for personal military service." Practically, this assurance disposed of the commandeering grievance; but no Convention on the subject was attained.—*Great Britain, Parliamentary Publications (Papers by Command, C. 8159).*

"A great mass meeting was held at Johannesburg (July 14) for the purpose of demanding that the franchise should be extended to all aliens, and insisting that the Constitution should

be amended and made more genuinely democratic. In consequence of this meeting the Volksraad passed at one sitting two readings of a bill restricting severely the right of public meeting. No outdoor meetings or addresses were to be allowed, and an assemblage of six persons would be considered a public meeting. The police were given power by this bill to order those present to disperse, and every one attending was made liable to imprisonment for two years, while the callers of any meeting that the police might consider to be against the public peace might be fined £500 or sentenced to two years hard labour. . . . On the return of the 'commandeered' men from the war [with the rebellious chief Malaboch] President Kruger welcomed them, and said that no doubt the Volksraad would bestow on them the rights of full citizenship. The effect of the Franchise Act passed in June, however, was in general to prevent any citizen from obtaining the franchise unless his father was born in the State or had been naturalized. The formation of committees by aliens for the support of political candidates was rendered penal. . . . The Volksraad postponed for one year the consideration of the Government proposal to grant the franchise to the foreign residents who had recently served in the various 'commandos' against the Kaffir rebels."—*Annual Register, 1894, p. 369.*

British South Africa Company: A. D. 1894-1895.—Extended charter and enlarged powers of the Company.—Its master spirit, Mr. Cecil J. Rhodes.—Attitude towards the South African Republic.—The British South Africa Company, royally chartered in 1889 for the promotion of "trade, commerce, civilization and good government" in "the region of South Africa lying immediately to the north of British Bechuanaland, and to the north and west of the South African Republic, and to the west of the Portuguese dominions," was now in full possession, both politically and commercially, not only of the great domain of the Matabeles and the Mashonas, stretching to the Zambesi River, but likewise of a vast territory beyond that stream. Its charter had been extended in 1891, to cover the whole sphere of British influence north of the Zambesi, except the strip of country called Nyassaland, which borders the western shore of Nyassa Lake. It had subjugated the Matabeles, extinguished their kingdom, driven its native sovereign, Lo Bengula, to exile and death (see in vol. 4, SOUTH AFRICA: A. D. 1885-1893). By a new agreement with the British Government, signed on the 23d of May, 1894, it had received political authority over this imperial domain, in addition to the powers and privileges which its broad charter gave.

The administration of the government of the region was to be conducted by the Company, under an Administrator and a Council of four members composed of a Judge and three other members. The Administrator to be appointed by the Company, with the approval of the Colonial Secretary, and to be removed either by the Secretary or by the Company, with the approval of the Secretary. The Judge, appointed by the Company, with the approval of the Colonial Secretary, and removable only by the Secretary, was to be a member of the Council ex officio. The members of the Council, other than the Judge, to be appointed by the Company, with the approval of the Secretary, and to be removable by the Company. . . . The Administrator should, as representative of the Company, administer the government, but must take the advice of his Council on all questions of importance. In cases of emergency, when he found it impracticable to assemble a quorum, the Administrator might take action alone, but must report such action to the Council at its next meeting. Moreover, he might overrule the Council, but must, in that case, report the matter forthwith to the Company, with the reasons for his action ; and the Company might rescind the decision of the Administrator, whether made with, or without, or against, the advice of the Council. With the concurrence of at least two members of the Council, and with the approval of the British High Commissioner for South Africa, the Administrator was empowered to frame and issue regulations, which should have the force of law ; but the Colonial Secretary or the Company could veto any such regulation at any time within twelve months of the date of approval by the High Commissioner. This power of making ordinances included the power to impose such taxes as might be necessary, and the right to impose and to collect customs duties. The armed forces of the Company were expressly forbidden to act outside the defined limits of its territory without the permission of Her Majesty's Government.

The master spirit of the Company which exercised these imperial powers of government over so great a dominion in Africa was Mr. Cecil J. Rhodes, Premier of Cape Colony, organizer and chief of the De Beers Consolidated Mining Co. in the diamond fields,—millionaire projector and manager of everything stupendous in the enterprises of the African world. He seemed, in fact, to be more than a master spirit in the Company. Apparently he had created it as an instrument of his ambitions, and it moved in his shadow throughout. Its Administrator, Dr. Leander S. Jameson, was his closely confidential friend. Presently it stamped his name on the broad empire which bore already the stamp of his personality and will, by proclaiming (May 1, 1895) : "The territories now or hereafter placed under the control of the British South Africa Company shall be named collectively Rhodesia. The provinces at the present time included in the territory of Rhodesia are Mashonaland, Matabeleland, and Northern Zambesia." Great ambitions —imperial ambitions—had thus come to be powerfully embodied in a corporation which practically served the will of one remarkably able man. They were ambitions which had been in conflict from the beginning with the interests as well as the ambitions of the Boers of the South African Republic, and the conflict was not to be ended by the triumph which the Rhodesians had won. Naturally the Boer was jealous and distrustful of the energetic men who had seized lands which he desired and hemmed his republic in. Naturally, too, the bold adventurers of Rhodesia, arrogant in their success and as little scrupulous as "empire-builders" are apt to be, looked with contempt and impatience at the plodding Boer, as an obstacle to their booming development in Africa of a civilization "up to date." Between the two incongruous neighbors rose the cry of the angry Uitlanders at Johannesburg, threatening the one and appealing to the sympathy of the other. The consequences soon appeared.

The Transvaal: A. D. 1895 (July).—**Opening of Delagoa Bay Railway.**—The opening of the railway to Delagoa Bay was celebrated with much ceremony at Pretoria on the 8th of July.

The Transvaal: A. D. 1895 (September— December).—**Closing of Vaal River "drifts" (fords) as ports of entry.**—**Anger in Cape Colony.**—**A threatening situation.**—In September, the government of the South African Republic adopted a measure, for the benefit of its new railway, connecting Delagoa Bay with Pretoria, and for the development of foreign trade via Delagoa Bay rather than through Cape Colony, which raised a storm of indignation at the Cape, giving birth to a grievance there which became for a time more threatening than the grievances of the Uitlanders of the Rand. The measure in question was one that closed the "drifts" or fords of the Vaal River, between Cape Colony and the Transvaal, as ports of entry for the importation of over-sea goods. As stated by the British High Commissioner, in a despatch (October 7) to Mr. Chamberlain, the British Colonial Secretary, the history of the case is as follows:

"In the year 1891 the Cape Government came to an agreement with the Transvaal Government and the Netherlands Railway Company to advance the latter £600,000 towards the construction of the railway from the Vaal river to Johannesburg, receiving in exchange for such advance Netherlands Railway Company 4 per cent. bonds at £93, guaranteed by the Transvaal Government. It was stipulated in the agreement that the Cape Government might fix the traffic rates on the Transvaal extension until the close of 1894, or until the completion of the railway from Delagoa Bay to Pretoria, if such completion should take place before that date. The railway extension from the Vaal river so provided for was opened in September, 1892, and the Cape Government secured thereby, during the continuance of the agreement, practically the monopoly of the Johannesburg traffic. The agreement terminated on the 31st December, 1894, the Delagoa Bay to Pretoria Railway having shortly before been completed and commenced working. Up to the close of the agreement the through-traffic rates from the coast to Johannesburg had been fixed by the Cape at the average rate of about 2.4d. per ton per mile. After the close of the agreement the Netherlands Railway Company raised the rates on its 52 miles of railway, from the Vaal river to Johannesburg, to an average of nearly 8d. per ton per mile. Upon this importers began to remove a portion of their goods from the railway at the Vaal river, and to send them on by road and bullock-waggon to their destination in the Transvaal, instead of by the Netherlands Railway to Johannesburg and elsewhere as before. This move has recently been met by the Transvaal Government issuing a Proclamation closing the drifts on the Vaal river alongside the railway as ports of entry for over-sea goods, leaving them open for other goods, the produce of South Africa. Importers of over-sea goods have thus only the choice between making use of the Netherlands line from the Vaal to Johannesburg at the enhanced traffic rates imposed on that line, or of importing via Delagoa Bay or Durban."

Vigorous remonstrances against this measure were made instantly by the government of Cape

Colony, not only on the ground of its unfriendliness to the Colony, but also as being an infraction of the 13th article of the London Convention of 1884 (see above: A. D. 1884–1894), and the British government was appealed to for its interference. To this appeal the British Colonial Secretary replied with much caution, on the 1st of November, in a communication cabled to the High Commissioner, as follows: "Subject to the conditions stated further on, I am prepared to authorize you to send to the Government of the South African Republic a message to the following effect:—'I am advised by the Law Officers of the Crown (who, it is hardly necessary to state, have examined the question from a purely legal standpoint) that the recent action of the South African Republic is a breach of Article XIII. of the London Convention. I am further advised that the Government of the South African Republic cannot now set itself right by making general the prohibition of entry by the drifts, so as to include Colonial goods, if and when they reissue their Proclamation, which, I am surprised to observe, they appear to have some intention of doing. Her Majesty's Government accept the legal advice which they have received; but independently of their Conventional rights they are of opinion that the closing of the drifts, and especially the extension of that measure to Colonial goods, is so unfriendly an action as to call for the gravest remonstrance on their part. While anxious for an amicable settlement of the question, they must therefore protest against what they regard as an attempt to force the hand of the Cape Government in Conference by a proceeding which almost partakes of the nature of an act of hostility.' You will communicate this message confidentially to your Ministers in writing, pointing out that when once it is sent Her Majesty's Government cannot allow the matter to drop until they have obtained a compliance with their demands, even if it should be necessary to undertake an expedition for that purpose. Her Majesty's Government do not intend that such an expedition should, like most previous Colonial wars, be conducted at the entire cost of this country; and you should explain to your Ministers that you are therefore instructed to require from them a most explicit undertaking in writing that, if it becomes necessary to send an expedition, the Cape Parliament will bear half the gross expense, and that the Local Government will furnish a fair contingent of the fighting force, so far as its resources in men may suffice, besides giving the full and free use of its railways and rolling stock for military purposes. If your Ministers cannot give you such assurances you will report fully by telegraph, and defer action pending further instructions from me; but if you obtain these assurances in writing, explicitly and without qualification, you may send the above message to the Government of the South African Republic."

This was followed by a further cautionary message, November 3, in these words: "Referring to my telegrams of the 1st November, although willing to support your Ministers on the conditions already stated, I should think it would be well, in their own interests, and those of South African commerce generally, if they will be as moderate as they can find it consistent with their duty to be in their demands as to their share of railway business. I have no doubt

that you have availed yourself of any chances you may have had of impressing such a view on them, and if you think it expedient you may tell them, confidentially, that such is my view." On the 4th, Sir Hercules Robinson replied: "My Ministers, including Schreiner and Faure, the two Dutch Members, were unanimous in their decision to accept your conditions. I am assured by Mr. Rhodes that he can count on the support of the majority in the Cape Parliament, and there are no facts before me which would lead me to a different view; but I do not think that the question will arise, as the Government of the South African Republic will not hold out against the united action of the Cape and Her Majesty's Government." On the same day he transmitted to President Kruger the message contained (as above) in Secretary Chamberlain's despatch of November 1. On the 21st of November the reply of the Transvaal Government was given, as follows:

"This Government most deeply regrets that the Cape Colony has by its own acts created a condition of things, in consequence of which it afterwards found itself compelled to invoke the intervention of the British Government, and it still more deeply regrets that Her Majesty's Government, on the 'ex parte' representations of the Cape Colony, felt itself constrained to telegraph to this Government in the terms of the communication of the 3rd instant. From the reply of this Government, it will be evident to your Excellency that it wishes to contribute in every possible way to preserve the good understanding in South Africa, and it therefore considers a passage such as occurs in your Excellency's telegram of the 3rd instant, 'An attempt to force the hand of the Cape Government at the Conference by a measure which almost resembles the nature of a hostile act,' not justified as regards this Republic. This Government adheres to its opinion and view that it has an undoubted right to regulate the ports of entrance on the borders of the Republic, and if Her Majesty's Government calls this an unfriendly act, this Government can only say that it was the consequence of an unfriendly act of the Cape Colony. In order not to be the cause of disturbance in South Africa, this Government is prepared to submit the regulating of the ports of entrance on the borders to arbitration, it being convinced of the justice of its assertion that the regulating of the ports of entrance on its borders by it is no infringement of Article 13 of the Convention of London."—*Great Britain, Papers by Command:* 1897, *C.* 8474, *pp.* 11–21.

The Transvaal: A. D. 1895 (November).—The state of discontent among the Uitlanders, and its causes.—The franchise question.—Growth of British Imperialistic designs.—The suspension of commandeering went a very little way towards removing the grievances of the British residents in the Transvaal. Underlying that and all other causes of discontent was the evident determination of the Boer inhabitants of the Republic to keep in their own hands the whole power of government, both state and municipal, and to deal with the increasing multitude of incomers from the outside world (whom they called Uitlanders, or Outlanders) permanently as aliens, excluded from citizenship by as many bars as a jealous legislature could raise. Until 1882, a foreigner, settling in the Transvaal, could become a citizen and a voter after a residence of two years. The required residence was then raised to five years, and in 1887 it was carried up to fifteen. By this time the immigrant population was growing numerous, and its complaints of disfranchisement and nonrepresentation in the Volksraad, or Legislature, soon took on angry tones. In 1890 a nominal concession was made to the discontented Uitlanders, by the creation of a Second Volksraad (see, in this vol., CONSTITUTION OF THE SOUTH AFRICAN REPUBLIC—the bracketed amendments or added articles following Article 29), to which they could elect representatives. The suffrage in elections to this new chamber was given after two years residence, on the taking of an oath of allegiance to the Republic, and qualification for sitting in it was acquired after a residence of four years. But the Second Volksraad had no independent power. It could act only on certain specified subjects, taxation not included, and all that it did was subject to overruling by the First Volksraad, while the enactments of the latter were entirely valid without its consent. The Second Volksraad, in fact, was no actual branch of the national legislature, but a powerless appendage to it, where an appearance of representation in the government could be given to the Uitlander population without the reality.

Naturally, this aggravated rather than pacified the discontent of the new comers. They were a rapidly increasing population, congregated, for the most part, in one district, where it was easy for them to feel and act in combination. By 1895 there was said to be 100,000 of them in the Witwatersrand, and some 60,000 natives were working in their mines. They were being heavily taxed, and they complained that they could get nothing adequate in return for the taxation,—neither an efficient police, nor decent sanitary regulations, nor a proper water supply, nor a safe restraint upon the sale of liquors to their native work people. At the same time it was charged that corruption prevailed in the omnipotent First Volksraad, and among public officials, and that, on the whole, the Republic was in bad as well as in ignorant hands. This was not alone the view of the complaining foreign residents, but was shared more or less by unprejudiced visitors to the country, including Mr. James Bryce, who travelled in the Transvaal in 1895, and who wrote of the grievances of the Uitlanders in quite a sympathetic vein.

Until the gold-seekers came into it, the Republic had been poor and its revenues small. Their coming gave it a full treasury. They were the principal consumers of the imported goods on which its tariff was laid. Their large use of dynamite and other explosives in mining gave the government an opportunity to make a highly profitable monopoly of the manufacture, afterwards exchanged for an equally profitable concession to a monopolistic company. Their mines were the proper subject of a tax which yielded large returns. In fact, the Republic was taking much to itself from the Uitlanders,—no more, perhaps, than it had a fair right to take,— but, according to what seems to be trustworthy testimony, it was giving them far less in return for it than they had a just right to demand, and it was offering them no prospect of anything better in time to come.

It seems to be certain that responsibility for whatever was hostile and unjust in the treatment of the foreign population rested largely upon the President of the Republic, Mr. Paul Kruger, who had been at the head of the government for many years. He exercised an influence and authority that had scarcely any limit. The Volksraad was obedient to his will, and most of its legislation was understood to emanate from him and from those whose council he took. There can be little doubt that he practically shaped the whole policy of the Boer Republic in its dealing with the Uitlanders, and that it expressed the attitude of his mind toward foreigners in general and Englishmen in particular. He distrusted even the Dutch of Cape Colony, and sought Hollanders for the public service when he needed qualifications which his own people did not possess.

"While within the Transvaal there was growing discontent, matters were so shaping themselves without as to still further complicate the situation. The idea of a Confederation of British South Africa and the extension of the British sphere to the Zambesi, had long been the dream of imperialists, and the ruling classes at the Cape had persistently urged this upon the home government. . . . After the consolidation of the diamond companies, Mr. Cecil Rhodes became the imperialist leader in South Africa and marshaled behind him all the corporate interests and combined influence of his many associates. The Boer Republics stood in the way of the success of imperialistic enterprise. Then too the 'scramble for Africa,' which began with the efforts of the King of Belgium to consolidate the native tribes of central Africa under Belgian rule and which resulted in the carving out of the Congo Free State, the assertion of German protection over Damaraland and Namaqueland, and the joint effort of European powers to check the British sphere, all lent zest to ambition and brought the English popular mind into temper for concerted action. Under such circumstances the 'little England' party lost its standing and an imperial policy gained fullest support. With such an atmosphere surrounding the Transvaal the grievances of the 'aliens' within could not long be disregarded without serious trouble."— F. A. Cleveland, *The South African Conflict* (*The American Academy of Political and Social Science, No.* 265), *pp.* 19–22.

The Transvaal: A. D. 1895–1896.—Revolutionary conspiracy of disaffected Uitlanders at Johannesburg with Rhodesians.—The Jameson Raid and its results.—In the fall of 1895, certain of the disaffected Uitlanders at Johannesburg, leaders of an organization called the Transvaal National Union, abandoned attempts to obtain what they sought from the President and the Volksraad by petition and agitation, and either invited or accepted proposals of assistance from the armed forces of the British South Africa Company, with a view to some kind of a revolutionary undertaking. The story of the plot has been told with great frankness by one of the actors in it, Mr. Alfred P. Hillier, who writes: "Mr. Cecil Rhodes, . . . accustomed as he was to success, quick movement and rapid developments, in his great career, had . . . watched with impatient eyes the setting back of the clock within the South African Republic. His chief lieutenant, Dr. Jameson, who had shared with him the labour of reclaiming from barbarism and developing Rhodesia, and whose ambition was no less than his superior's, discussed with him the desirability of some active outside pressure; and between them was evolved what is known as the Jameson plan. Mr. Beit, the capitalist most largely interested in the mines of the Rand, an old financial colleague of Mr. Rhodes, both in the De Beers amalgamation and in the establishment of the Chartered Company, promised both his influence and his purse in support of the plan. Overtures were then made to Mr. Lionel Phillips, who was at the head of the Chamber of Mines, and Mr. Charles Leonard, the Chairman of the National Union. . . . The plan at this early stage was presented in a very attractive form. A forec under Dr. Jameson was to be quietly gathered on the border. The Johannesburg agitation, reinforced with capitalist support, was to be steadily pushed forward. Rifles and ammunition were to be smuggled into Johannesburg. Both the High Commissioner and the Colonial Office might be counted on, it was said, to support a vigorous forward movement for reform. Mr. Phillips and Mr. Leonard, sick and weary of the hopelessness of unsupported constitutional action, and of the continual set back in Boer politics, already casting round in their minds for some new departure, accepted and from that time forth co-operated with Mr. Rhodes and Dr. Jameson in the development of the Jameson plan.

"In October, 1895, a meeting took place at Groote Schuur, Mr. Rhodes' residence near Cape Town, at which were present, in addition to Mr. Cecil Rhodes, Mr. Lionel Phillips, Mr. Hammond, Mr. Charles Leonard, and Colonel Frank Rhodes. At this meeting the plan was more fully discussed and matured; and in November, 1895, when Dr. Jameson visited Johannesburg, the details were finally settled. The letter of invitation was written, signed and handed to Dr. Jameson, and the date of combined action provisionally fixed for the end of December. Dr. Jameson's force was to be about 1,000 strong, and the start to be made when finally summoned by the signatories of the letter. In the meantime the Johannesburg leaders were to have sent in to them 4,500 rifles and 1,000,000 rounds of ammunition, and were, if possible, to arrange for an attack on the Pretoria Arsenal simultaneously with the move from outside. With regard to the letter of invitation which was subsequently used by Dr. Jameson as a justification for his start, . . . Mr. Leonard, Colonel Rhodes, and Mr. Phillips have all distinctly stated that this letter was never intended as an authority to Dr. Jameson to enter the Transvaal, unless and until he received a further summons from them. Such was in brief the history of the Jameson plan as far as concerned Johannesburg. And it is necessary here to refer to the position with regard to it of the bulk of the men who subsequently constituted the Reform Committee. They at this time, with the exception of a few of their number, of which I personally was one, were entirely ignorant of what was going on. . . . The Johannesburg leaders, relying on the general sentiment of the community, assumed the responsibility of arranging a basis of operations. So that the plan when it was gradually revealed to various men had either to be accepted by

them in its entirety or rejected. . . . Men demanded and received assurance that the movement was to be a republican one, and in no way to be an attempt on the independence of the country. A sufficient number of rifles were also to be forthcoming, and the High Commissioner was to be on the spot to expedite the adjustment of matters immediately disturbances arose."—A. P. Hillier, *Raid and Reform, pp. 47-53.*

The practical working of the conspiracy proved less easy than the planning of it. Arms and ammunition were smuggled into Johannesburg, but not in sufficient quantities. The time of action had been fixed for the 28th of December. When it came near there were found to be only 2,500 rifles at hand, instead of the 10,000 that were wanted. A scheme for the surprising of the Boer arsenal at Pretoria was pronounced at the last moment impracticable. Still more disconcerting to many was a report which came from Cape Town, that Jameson would require the rising to be made under and in favor of the British flag. "The movement within the Transvaal," says Mr. Hillier, "had from its outset been one in favour, not of a British Colony, but of a sound Republic. . . . Many Americans and South Africans had accorded their support only on this understanding." Until a clearer arrangement with the Rhodesians on this point could be reached, the leaders in Johannesburg determined not to act. Accordingly, on the 26th of December, two days before the appointed date of insurrection, they telegraphed to Jameson, in covert language which he understood, that it was "absolutely necessary to postpone the flotation." On the following day they issued a lengthy manifesto, setting forth all their grievances, and deferring until the 6th of January a general meeting of the National Union which had been called for the 27th of December—the eve of the intended rising. The manifesto concluded as follows: "We have now only two questions to consider: (a) What do we want? (b) how shall we get it? I have stated plainly what our grievances are, and I shall answer with equal directness the question, 'What do we want?' We want: (1) the establishment of this Republic as a true republic: (2) a Grondwet or Constitution which shall be framed by competent persons selected by representatives of the whole people and framed on lines laid down by them—a constitution which shall be safeguarded against hasty alteration; (3) an equitable franchise law, and fair representation; (4) equality of the Dutch and English languages; (5) responsibility of the Legislature to the heads of the great departments; (6) removal of religious disabilities; (7) independence of the courts of justice, with adequate and secured remuneration of the judges; (8) liberal and comprehensive education; (9) efficient civil service, with adequate provision for pay and pension; (10) free trade in South African products. That is what we want. There now remains the question which is to be put before you at the meeting of the 6th January, viz., How shall we get it?"—*Great Britain: Papers by Command, 1896, C.—7933.*

Acting, as appears, on his own responsibility, Dr. Jameson refused to be stopped by the postponement at Johannesburg, and, on the evening of December 29, he entered the Transvaal territory, from Pitsani-Pitlogo, in Bechuanaland, with a force of about 500 men. His movement

6–30

created consternation in all the circles of the conspiracy, and received no effectual support. It was promptly disavowed and condemned by the British authorities, and by the home officials of the British South Africa Company. Cecil Rhodes could do nothing but tacitly acknowledge his responsibility for what his lieutenant had done (though the precipitation of the raid was evidently a surprise and a trouble to him) by resigning the premiership of Cape Colony. Meantime, the invaders had learned that the Boers were not to be ridden over in the easy fashion they supposed. Hasty levies had intercepted their march, had repulsed them at Krugersdorp, with a heavy loss in killed and wounded, surrounded them at Doornkop, and forced them to surrender on New Year's day. A few days later, the Uitlanders at Johannesburg, some of whom had made a confused and ineffectual attempt to take arms, proclaiming a provisional government, and around whose town the excited Boers had gathered in large force, were persuaded by the British High Commissioner to submit to the Transvaal authorities, and more than fifty of the leaders were placed under arrest.

With great difficulty, President Kruger overcame the desire of his people that Jameson and his officers should be brought to trial and punished in the country they had outraged by their invasion, and they were handed over to the British government for removal to England and trial by an English court. The trial took place in July (20–28), before the Lord Chief Justice (Lord Russell of Killowen), Baron Pollock, and Justice Hawkins, with a special jury. The charge on which the prisoners were tried was that of having fitted out a warlike expedition against a friendly state, in violation of the Foreign Enlistment Act. The charge of the Lord Chief Justice gave the following questions to the jury : Were preparations for a raid made by the defendants ? Did they aid, abet, counsel, or procure such preparation ? Were they employed in the actual expedition ? Did the Queen exercise dominion and sovereignty in Pitsani-Pitlogo ? The jury returned affirmative answers, which were held to constitute a verdict of "guilty," and sentence was pronounced,—fifteen months of imprisonment for Dr. Jameson, and terms varying from five to ten months for his four subordinate officers. During the trial and after there were many demonstrations of popular sympathy with the prisoners. Meantime, in April, the Transvaal authorities had brought the imprisoned leaders of the Johannesburg "reform committee" to trial at Pretoria on charges of treason and had convicted them all. Four, namely, Colonel Rhodes (brother of Cecil), Lionel Phillips, George Farrar, and John Hays Hammond (an American), were sentenced to death ; the remainder to a payment of heavy fines. The death sentences were soon commuted, first to imprisonment for fifteen years, and subsequently to fines of $125,000 on each of four prisoners.

The Transvaal: A. D. 1896 (January).— Message of the German Emperor to President Kruger, relative to the Jameson Raid.— The critical situation of affairs produced by the Jameson raid was dangerously complicated at the beginning by the publication of the following telegram, sent to President Kruger, on the 3d of January, by the German Emperor : "I express my sincere congratulations that, supported by your people and without appealing for help to friendly powers, you have succeeded by your own energetic action against the armed bands which invaded your country as disturbers of the peace, and have thus been enabled to restore peace, and safeguard the independence of your country against attacks from without." President Kruger replied : "I testify to Your Majesty my very deep and heartfelt thanks for Your Majesty's sincere congratulations. With God's help we hope to do everything further that is possible for the holding of our dearly bought independence and the stability of our beloved republic." This kindled a white heat of indignation in England. It was supposed to signify a disposition on the part of the German Emperor to recognize the absolute independence which the South African Republic claimed, and to threaten interference as between Great Britain and the Boers. A powerful "flying squadron" was instantly put in commission, and several ships were ordered to Delagoa Bay. For some time the relations between Great Britain and Germany were seriously strained; but various influences gradually cooled the excited feeling in England, though not a little distrust of German intentions has remained.

The Transvaal: A. D. 1896 (January— April).—Urgency of the British Colonial Secretary for redress of Uitlander grievances.— Invitation to President Kruger to visit England.—His requirement that Article IV. of the London Convention shall be discussed.— Deadlock of the parties.—The complaints of the Uitlanders, effectually silenced for the time being at Johannesburg by the vigorous action of the Boers, were now taken up by the British Secretary of State for the Colonies, Mr. Chamberlain, and pressed in strenuous despatches to the High Commissioner in South Africa, Sir Hercules Robinson. On the 4th of January, 1896, four days after the surrender of Jameson and four days before the insurgent Uitlanders at Johannesburg had laid down their arms, a long despatch was cabled by Mr. Chamberlain to the High Commissioner, instructing him to make "friendly representations" to President Kruger on the subject of those complaints. "I am aware," wrote the Colonial Secretary, "that victory of Transvaal Government over Administrator of Mashonaland may possibly find them not willing to make any concessions. If this is the attitude they adopt, they will, in my opinion, make a great mistake; for danger from which they have just escaped was real, and one which, if the causes which led up to it are not removed, may recur, although in a different form. I have done everything in my power to undo and to minimise the evil caused by late unwarrantable raid by British subjects into the territory of the South African Republic, and it is not likely that such action will be ever repeated ; but the state of things of which complaint has been made cannot continue forever. If those who are now a majority of inhabitants of the Transvaal, but are excluded from all participation in its government, were, of their own initiative, and without any interference from without, to attempt to reverse that state of things, they would, without doubt, attract much sympathy from all civilised communities who themselves live under a free Government, and I cannot regard the present state of things in the South African Republic as free from danger to the stability of its institutions. The Government of the South African Republic cannot be indifferent to these considerations, and President of South African Republic himself has on more than one occasion, expressed his willingness to inquire into and to deal with just reasons for discontent; and the Volksraad have now the opportunity to show magnanimity in the hour of their success and to settle all differences by moderate concessions. They must fully admit the entire loyalty of yourself and of Her Majesty's Government to the terms of London Convention, as shown by their recent intervention, and they must recognise that their authority in crisis through which they have passed could not have been so promptly and effectively asserted without that intervention. If they will recognise this by making concessions in accordance with our friendly advice, no one will be able to suggest that they are acting under pressure, and their voluntary moderation will produce best effect among all who are interested in well-being of the Transvaal and in future of South Africa."

On the 13th of January the Colonial Secretary pursued the subject in another despatch to Sir Hercules Robinson, as follows: "Now that Her Majesty's Government have fulfilled their obligations to the South African Republic, and have engaged to bring the leaders in the recent invasion to trial, they are anxious that the negotiations which are being conducted by you should result in a permanent settlement by which the possibility of further internal troubles will be prevented. The majority of the population is composed of Uitlanders, and their complete exclusion from any share in the government of the country is an admitted grievance which is publicly recognised as such by the friends of the Republic as well as by the opinion of civilised Europe. There will always be a danger of internal disturbance so long as this grievance exists, and I desire that you will earnestly impress on President Kruger the wisdom of making concessions in the interests alike of the South African Republic and of South Africa as a whole. There is a possibility that the President might be induced to rely on the support of some foreign Power in resisting the grant of reforms or in making demands upon Her Majesty's Government; and in view of this I think it well to inform you that Great Britain will resist at all costs the interference of any foreign Power in the affairs of the South African Republic. The suggestion that such interference was contemplated by Germany was met in this country by an unprecedented and unanimous outburst of public feeling. In order to be prepared for all eventualities, it has been thought desirable by Her Majesty's Government to commission a Flying Squadron of powerful men-of-war, with twelve torpedo-ships; and many other vessels are held in reserve. Her Majesty's Government have no reason, at the present moment, to anticipate any conflict of interest with foreign Powers; but I think it right for you to know that Great Britain will not tolerate any change in her relations with the Republic, and that, while loyally respecting its internal independence, subject to the Conventions, she will maintain her position as the Paramount Power in South Africa, and especially the provisions of Article IV. of the Convention of 1884. It is my sincere hope

that President Kruger, who has hitherto shown so much wisdom in dealing with the situation, will now take the opportunity afforded to him of making of his own free will such reasonable concessions to the Uitlanders as will remove the last excuse for disloyalty, and will establish the free institutions of the Republic on a firm and lasting basis."

To this Sir Hercules replied with a remonstrance, saying: "Your telegram 13 January No. 1 only reached me last night after I had left Pretoria. I could, if you consider it desirable, communicate purport to President of South African Republic by letter, but I myself think such action would be inopportune. . . . Nearly all leading Johannesburg men are now in gaol, charged with treason against the State, and it is rumoured that Government has written evidence of a long-standing and wide-spread conspiracy to seize Government of country on the plea of denial of political privileges, and to incorporate the country with that of British South Africa Company. The truth of these reports will be tested in the trials to take place shortly in the High Court, and meanwhile to urge claim for extended political privileges for the very men so charged would be ineffectual and impolitic. President of South African Republic has already promised municipal government to Johannesburg, and has stated in a Proclamation that all grievances advanced in a constitutional manner will be carefully considered and brought before the Volksraad without loss of time; but until result of trials is known nothing, of course, will now be done." Mr. Chamberlain saw force in the High Commissioner's objections, and assented to a momentary suspension of pressure on the Transvaal President, but not for long. "I recognise," he telegraphed on the 15th, "that the actual moment is not opportune for a settlement of the Uitlanders' grievances, and that the position of the President of the South African Republic may be an embarrassing one, but I do not consider that the arrest of a few score individuals out of a population of 70,000 or more, or the supposed existence of a plot among that small minority, is a reason for denying to the overwhelming majority of innocent persons reforms which are just in themselves and expedient in the interests of the Republic. Whatever may be said about the conduct of a few individuals, nothing can be plainer than that the sober and industrious majority refused to countenance any resort to violence, and proved their readiness to obey the law and your authority. I hope, therefore, to hear at an early date that you propose to resume the discussion with President of South African Republic on lines laid down in my previous telegrams. I do not see that the matter need wait until the conclusion of the trial of the supposed plotters."

On the 28th of January the High Commissioner, under instructions from London, addressed to President Kruger the following invitation: "I am directed by Her Majesty's Government to tender to your Honour a cordial invitation to visit England, with a view to discussing with them all those questions which relate to the security of the South African Republic and the general welfare of South Africa. I am to add that, although Her Majesty's Government cannot consent to modify Article 4 of the London Convention [see above; A. D. 1884-1894], other matters are open to friendly discussion. Her Majesty's Government hope that your Honour will come as the guest of the British Government." While this invitation was being considered, and before a reply to it had been made, the British Colonial Secretary reopened his own discussion of the questions at issue, February 4, in a despatch of great length, reviewing the whole history of the relations of the Uitlanders to the government of the South African Republic, and of the recent occurrences which had been consequent upon their discontent. It praised "the spirit of wisdom and moderation" shown by President Kruger, who "kept within bounds the natural exasperation of his burghers," and it gave especial attention to a proclamation which President Kruger had addressed to the inhabitants of Johannesburg, on the 10th of January, in which he had said : "It is my intention to submit a draft Law at the first ordinary session of the Volksraad, whereby a Municipality with a Mayor at its head will be appointed for Johannesburg, to whom the whole municipal government of this town will be entrusted."

On this the Secretary made the following suggestions : "Basing myself upon the expressed desire of President Kruger to grant municipal government to Johannesburg, I suggest, for his consideration, as one way of meeting the difficulty, that the whole of the Rand district, from end to end, should be erected into something more than a municipality as that word is ordinarily understood ; that, in fact, it should have a modified local autonomy, with powers of legislation on purely local questions, and subject to the veto of the President and Executive Council ; and that this power of legislation should include the power of assessing and levying its own taxation, subject to the payment to the Republican Government of an annual tribute of an amount to be fixed at once and revised at intervals, so as to meet the case of a diminution or increase in the mining industry. As regards judicial matters in such a scheme, the Rand, like the Eastern Provinces and the Kimberley District of the Cape Colony, might have a superior court of its own. It would, of course, be a feature of this scheme that the autonomous body should have the control of its civil police, its public education, its mine management, and all other matters affecting its internal economy and well-being. The central Government would be entitled to maintain all reasonable safeguards against the fomenting of a revolutionary movement, or the storage of arms for treasonable purposes within the district. Those living in, and there enjoying a share in the government of, the autonomous district, would not, in my view, be entitled to a voice in the general Legislature or the Central Executive, or the presidential election. The burghers would thus be relieved of what is evidently a haunting fear to many of them—although I believe an unfounded one—that the first use which the enfranchised newcomers would make of their privileges would be to upset the republican form of government. Relieved of this apprehension, I should suppose that there would not be many of them who would refuse to deal with the grievances of the comparatively few Uitlanders outside the Rand on those liberal principles which characterized the earlier legislation of the Republic. The President may rest assured that in making the above suggestions I

am only actuated by friendly feeling towards himself and the South African Republic. They are not offered in derogation of his authority, but as the sincere and friendly contribution of Her Majesty's Government towards the settlement of a question which continues to threaten the tranquillity of the Republic and the welfare and progress of the whole of South Africa. A proper settlement of the questions at issue involves so many matters of detail which could be more easily and satisfactorily settled by personal conference, that I should be glad to have the opportunity of discussing the subject with the President, if it suited his convenience, and were agreeable to him, to come to this country for the purpose. Should this be impracticable, I rely upon you to make my views known to him and to carry on the negotiations."

This despatch, as soon as it had been forwarded from the Colonial Office, was published in the "London Gazette," so that a telegraphed summary of its contents reached President Kruger before it came to him officially,—which naturally added something to the irritations existing at Pretoria. However, the President, on the 8th of February, by telegram to the High Commissioner, and more fully on the 25th by letter, responded to the invitation to visit England. In his telegram he said : "In order to give me the liberty to let the Honourable Volksraad judge whether permission and power to act will be given me to go out of the country, an understanding must, of course, be come to as to what points will be discussed or not, so that I may lay those points before the Volksraad for deliberation and resolution." In his letter he wrote :

"At the commencement, I wish to observe that the object of this letter is to pave the way for a friendly discussion of the matters herein mentioned, in order to arrive at a satisfactory solution, and further that, although as yet I desire no positive and direct assent to the desires expressed herein, I would, nevertheless, to prevent a misunderstanding, desire to have an assurance that they will be taken into the most mature consideration with the earnest endeavour and the sincere desire to comply with my wishes. The desire to receive this assurance will be respected by your Excellency and Her Majesty's Government as reasonable, when I say that, considering especially my advanced age and the unavoidable delay, owing to my absence, in the transaction of matters affecting the highest State interests, I would, with difficulty, be able to make the sacrifice in going only to discuss matters without arriving at the desired result, and it is evident that if the assurance referred to by me cannot be given by Her Majesty's Government, in all probability the Honourable Volksraad would not grant its consent and commission. . . . Although, as already said, the Government could tolerate no interference in its internal relations and the official discussion of affairs with the object of requiring changes therein will have to be avoided, on the other hand I wish it to be understood that private hints given by statesmen of experience in the true interest of the country and its independence will always be warmly appreciated by me, from whatever side they may come.

"Going over to a summing up of the points which, in my opinion, should be brought under discussion, I wish to mention in the first place :—
1. The superseding of the Convention of London

with the eye, amongst others, on the violation of the territory of the South African Republic · because in several respects it has already virtually ceased to exist; because in other respects it has no more cause for existence; because it is injurions to the dignity of an independent Republic; because the very name and the continual arguments on the question of suzerainty, which since the conclusion of this Convention no longer exists, are used as a pretext, especially by a libellous press, for wilfully inciting both white and coloured people against the lawful authority of the Republic; for intentionally bringing about misunderstanding and false relations between England and the Republic, whereby in this manner the interests of both countries and of their citizens and subjects are prejudiced and the peaceful development of the Republic is opposed. In the discussion of the withdrawal of the Convention as a whole, Article IV. should naturally not be kept back. I have reason to believe that the British Government has come to the decision to make no alteration in this on account of false representations made to it and lying reports spread by the press and otherwise with a certain object, to the effect that the Government of the Republic has called in, or sought, the protection of other Powers. While I thankfully acknowledge and will ever acknowledge the sympathy of other Powers or their subjects, and the conduct of the last named has, in the light of the trials recently passed through, on the whole offered a favourable contrast to that of British subjects, there is nevertheless nothing further from my thoughts than to strive for the protection of a foreign power, which I will never even seek. Neither I nor the people of the Republic will tolerate an interference with the internal relations from any power whatever, and I am prepared, if the course proposed by me be adopted, to give the necessary assurances for this, in order that Her British Majesty's Government need have no fear that Her interests in South Africa should be injured. 2. Further should be discussed the superseding of the Convention by a treaty of peace, commerce and friendship, by which the existing privileges of England in the dominion of commerce and intercourse and the interests of British subjects in the Republic will be satisfactorily guaranteed on the footing of the most-favoured nation, and herein I would be prepared to go to the utmost of what can reasonably be asked. 3. Then the necessary guarantes will have to be given against a repetition of the violation of territory out of the territory of the Chartered Company or the Cape Colony, and of disturbing military operations and unlawful military or police or even private movements on the borders of the Republic. 4. Further should be discussed the compensation for direct and indirect injury to be given or caused to be given by England for and by reason of the incursion that recently took place. The reasons for this are evident and need no argument. The amount to be demanded it is impossible as yet to determine, but, if required, it can still be given before my departure to England. 5. I would, although in the following respects I would not insist beforehand on an assurance such as that intended with regard to the above-mentioned points, nevertheless wish to request the earnest consideration of a final settlement of the Swaziland question, in this sense, that that country shall henceforth become a part of the Republic. . . . 6. Further, I would very much like to have discussed the revocation of the charter of the Chartered Company, which, if this does not take place, will continue to be a threatening danger to the quiet and peace of the Republic and thereby also to the whole South Africa. I am of opinion that all the above desires are fair and just. . . . I will be pleased to receive the views of Her Majesty's Government on the points herein brought forward, in order that I may be enabled to bring the matter for decision before the Honourable Volksraad."

Mr. Chamberlain's reply to this communication was, in part, as follows: "Her Majesty's Government·regret that President has given no definite reply to invitation to visit England which was sent to him on 28th January. This invitation was the result of private information conveyed to Her Majesty's Government that the President was desirous of arranging with them a settlement of all differences, and of placing on a permanent and friendly basis the relations between the United Kingdom and the South African Republic. Before forwarding the invitation, Her Majesty's Government knew that his Honour was in full possession of their opinion, that no arrangement can be satisfactory or complete which does not include a fair settlement of those grievances of the Uitlander population which have been recognized by the general public opinion of South Africa, and which have been the cause of discontent and agitation in the past, and are likely—unless remedied—to lead to further disturbances in future. Her Majesty's Government also took care to satisfy themselves that the President had been made aware that they were not prepared to modify in any way the provisions of Article IV. of the Convention of 1884, and this was again made clear in the formal invitation to visit England. Under these circumstances, it was with great surprise that Her Majesty's Government learnt from the Despatch of the President of 25th February that his Honour objected to discuss the question of the reforms asked for by the Uitlanders, and that he desired to propose withdrawal of Article IV. of the Convention, and Her Majesty's Government regret that they were not informed of his Honour's views on the subject at an earlier date, as they would not have felt justified in inviting the President to encounter the fatigue of a journey to this country if they had not been led to believe that he was in agreement with them as to the general object of such a visit.

"In their view, Her Majesty's Government were able to offer a complete guarantee in the future to the South African Republic against any attack upon its independence, either from within any part of Her Majesty's dominions or from the territory of a foreign Power. In return, they assumed that the President would make known to them the measures which he proposed to take to remedy the acknowledged grievances of the Uitlanders, and to consider any suggestions which Her Majesty's Government might wish to offer as to the adequacy of these measures for the removal of all cause of internal disturbances. . . . Such a discussion as they contemplate would not involve any acknowledgment on the part of the President of a right of interference in the internal concerns of the Republic, but would only at the most amount to a recognition of the friendly interest of Her Majesty's Government in its security, and in the general welfare of South Africa. The President would be, of course, at liberty to accept or to reject any advice that might be tendered to him by Her Majesty's Government, but in the latter case the responsibility for the result would naturally rest wholly with him. Her Majesty's Government have already expressed a willingness to give full consideration to any representations which his Honour may wish to make on the other points named in his letter, although some of them are matters wholly in jurisdiction of Her Majesty's Government. But unless the President is satisfied with the explanations I have now given, Her Majesty's Government are reluctantly obliged to come to the conclusion that no good purpose can be served by the proposed visit."

In return to this despatch, President Kruger, on 17th of March, expressed his "deep disappointment" at its contents, by reason of which, he said, "it is not possible for me to proceed to convene a special session of the Volksraad at once" for the purpose of action upon the invitation of the British Government. Thereupon (April 27), the Colonial Secretary cabled to the High Commissioner in South Africa: "Her Majesty's Government have no alternative but to withdraw the invitation, which it appears from the President's message was given under a misapprehension of the facts." Thus the two parties were at a deadlock.—*Great Britain, Papers by Command : 1896, C. 7933, pp. 19–91; and C. 8063, pp. 11–17.*

Rhodesia : **A. D. 1896** (March—September). —Matabele revolt.—Taking advantage of the confusion in affairs which followed the Jameson raid, and its removal of part of the police force from the country, the Matabele rose in revolt. The main provocation of the rising appears to have been from severe measures that were adopted for stamping out rinderpest in the country Many whites were killed in the regions of scattered settlement, and Buluwayo and Gwelo, where considerable numbers had taken refuge, were in much danger for a time. But prompt and vigorous measures were taken by the colonial and imperial authorities, as well as by the officers of the South Africa Company. Troops were sent from Cape Colony, Natal, and England, and Major-General Sir Frederick Carrington was ordered from Gibraltar to take command. Cecil Rhodes hastened to Salisbury on the first news of the outbreak and organized a force of volunteers for the relief of the beleaguered towns. The Transvaal government offered help. By June, when General Carrington arrived, and Lord Grey had succeeded Dr. Jameson as Administrator, the insurgent natives had been put on the defensive and had nearly ceased their attacks. They were driven into the Matoppo hills, where their position was formidably strong. At length, in August, Mr. Rhodes opened negotiations with some of the chiefs, and went, with three companions, unarmed, into their stronghold. He there made an agreement with them, which the British military authorities and many of the Matabele warriors refused to be bound by. But the revolt had been practically broken and soon came to an end.

British South Africa Company: **A. D. 1896** (June).—Resignation of **Mr. Rhodes.**—On the 26th of June the resignations of Cecil J. Rhodes and Mr. Beit from the Board of Directors of the British South Africa Company, and of Mr. Rutherford Harris as its Secretary, were accepted by the Board.

Cape Colony: **A. D. 1896** (July).—Investigation of the Jameson Raid.—Responsibility of Cecil J. Rhodes.—On the 17th of July a Select Committee of the Cape Colony House of Assembly, appointed in the previous May "to inquire into the circumstances, as affecting this colony, in connexion with the preparations for and carrying out of the recent armed inroad into the territory of the South African Republic," made its report, rehearsing at length the facts ascertained, with evidence in full, and submitting a number of "conclusions," among them the following: "Your Committee are of opinion that no member of the then Colonial Government with the exception of the then Prime Minister [Mr. Cecil J. Rhodes], had any knowledge whatever or suspicion of the intention to send an armed force across the border of the South African Republic. . . . Your Committee is convinced that the stores and workshops of the De Beers Consolidated Mines were for some time previous to the inroad used for the storage and for the unlawful exportation of arms destined for the South African Republic, in connexion with this inroad, and also that 11 men were sent from De Beers to Johannesburg, who were afterwards allowed to resume their positions. The evidence is clear, and leaves no room for doubt on this point. The local directors give an emphatic denial to any guilty knowledge on their part, and your Committee must acquit them of anything beyond negligence, which, looking to the magnitude of the transactions and the length of time over which they extended, must have been very marked. It is not conceivable that such proceedings could have been permitted without the knowledge and approval of the Chairman and Life Governor, Mr. C. J. Rhodes. With regard to the Chartered Company, your Committee find that the principal officials in Cape Town either knew, or were in a position to have known, the existence of this plot. Two at least of the directors, Mr. Beit and the Right Hon. C. J. Rhodes, were, together with the Administrator, Dr. Jameson, and Dr. Harris, the South African Secretary of the Company, active as promoters and moving spirits throughout, and they were from time to time kept informed of the preparations. . . . The whole movement was largely financed and engineered from outside, and in both cases certain directors and officials of the Chartered Company of British South Africa were active throughout. As regards the Right Hon. C. J. Rhodes, your Committee can come to no other conclusion than that he was thoroughly acquainted with the preparations that led to the inroad. That in his capacity as controller of the three great joint-stock companies, the British South Africa Company, the De Beers Consolidated Mines, and the Gold Fields of South Africa, he directed and controlled the combination which rendered such a proceeding as the Jameson raid possible. . . . It would appear that Mr. Rhodes did not direct or approve of Dr. Jameson's entering the territory of the South African Republic at the precise time when he did do so, but your Committee cannot find that that fact relieves Mr. Rhodes from responsibility for the unfortunate occurrences which took place. Even if Dr.

Jameson be primarily responsible for the last fatal step, Mr. Rhodes cannot escape the responsibility of a movement which had been arranged, with his concurrence, to take place at the precise time it did, if circumstances had been favourable at Johannesburg."—*Great Britain, Papers by Command:* 1897, *C.* 8380, *pp.* 7–9.

British South Africa Company: A. D. 1896 (July).—Parliamentary movement to investigate its administration.—In the British House of Commons, on the 30th of July, Mr. Chamberlain, Secretary of State for the Colonies, made a motion for the appointment of a select committee of fifteen to conduct an inquiry into the administration of the British South Africa Company, and the motion was adopted.

The Transvaal: A. D. 1896–1897 (May—April).—Continued controversies between the British Colonial Secretary, Mr. Chamberlain, and the Government of the South African Republic.—Complaints and counter complaints.—Aliens Immigration Law, etc.—For a time after the abandonment of the proposed visit of President Kruger to England, the older questions at issue between Great Britain and the Transvaal fell into the background; but new ones were constantly rising. Each party watched the other with suspicious and critical eyes, sharply questioning things that would hardly have been noticed in ordinary times. The Boer authorities, on their side, were naturally disturbed and made inquisitive by every movement of troops or arms in the surrounding British territory, both of which movements were being somewhat increased by the revolt of the Matabeles. They were impatient, too, for some action on the part of the British government against the chief authors of the recent invasion,—the officials of the British South Africa Company,—and against the Company itself. On the 11th of May, 1896, the State Secretary of the Transvaal government telegraphed to the British High Commissioner as follows: "The newspapers of the last few days state that Her Majesty's Government still continue to take the part of the Directors of British South Africa Company, especially Mr. Rhodes. This Government will not believe the accuracy of these reports, but it is of opinion that the Chartered Company as administering the Government up to now is a source of danger to whole of South Africa. The inroad into this Republic was made by officers, troops, and arms of that Chartered Company, and even the explicit prohibition of Her Majesty's Government was unable to restrain them, notwithstanding the Chartered Company had taken upon itself the international obligations of Great Britain. The behaviour of the persons who knew of the scheme of the inroad beforehand and supported it is, as we see, defended by saying that they acted thus in the interests of and for the extension of Imperialism in South Africa. This Government does not believe that the end justifies the means, and is convinced that Her Majesty's Government does not wish to be served by misdeed."

When this had been communicated to the British Colonial Secretary, Mr. Chamberlain, he replied (May 13) that the President of the South African Republic "has been misinformed if he supposes that Her Majesty's Government have taken the part of any of British South Africa Company Directors, including Mr. Rhodes, with regard to any connexion which they may be here-

after proved to have had with the recent raid. . . . On the contrary, while appreciating Mr. Rhodes's services in the past, Her Majesty's Government have condemned the raid, and the conduct of all the parties implicated by the telegrams recently published. Her Majesty's Government have promised a full Parliamentary inquiry, as soon as legal proceedings against Dr. Jameson and his officers have been concluded, to examine the Charter granted to British South Africa Company and the operation of its provisions, and to consider whether any improvements in it are desirable. Such an inquiry will go into the whole subject, not only of recent events, but of the whole administration. Her Majesty's Government cannot be expected to announce any decision as to the future of the Company until the Parliamentary Committee has made its recommendations."

On the 15th President Kruger replied: "This Government is very pleased at receiving the assurance that a searching inquiry is being instituted against British South Africa Company and its Directors, and will follow its course with interest." But the following month found the authorities at Pretoria still unsatisfied as to the intention of the British government to bring Mr. Rhodes and the South Africa Company to account for what they had done. On the 19th of June, the then Acting High Commissioner (Sir Hercules Robinson having gone to England on leave) transmitted to Mr. Chamberlain two telegrams just received by him from the government of the South African Republic. The first was as follows: "Acting under instructions, I have the honour to acquaint your Excellency, for the information of Her Majesty's Government, that, with a view to the welfare and peace of South Africa, this Government is convinced that the proofs in the possession and at the disposal of Her Majesty's Government now completely justify and compel the bringing to trial of Messrs. Cecil Rhodes, Alfred Beit, and Doctor Rutherford Harris, as has already been done with Doctor Jameson and his accomplices. In the interests of all South Africa, this Government feels itself obliged to press the taking of this step upon Her Majesty's Government. I have also the honour to request your Excellency to communicate this despatch by cable to Her Majesty's Government in London."

The second was in this language: "This Government regards with great regret the delay in the matter of the inquiry with respect to the complicity and responsibility of British South Africa Company in connexion with the raid of Doctor Jameson and his band within the territory of this Republic. This Government considers it its right and duty to press for the speedy holding of the inquiry, not merely because it is the injured party but also because of its interest and share in the well-being of South Africa, whose interests, as repeatedly intimated, are also dear to Her Majesty the Queen. This Government is also convinced that it is urgently necessary that the entire control and administration, as well civil as military, be taken out of hands of British South Africa Company and transferred to Her Majesty's Government, and I am instructed to press this point on behalf of this Government. I have further the honour to request your Excellency to cable this despatch to Her Majesty's Government in London."

To these communications Mr. Chamberlain made a somewhat haughty response. "Inform the Government of the South African Republic," he cabled on the 25th of June, "that Her Majesty's Government have received their telegrams of the 19th June, which were published in London almost simultaneously with their receipt by me. Her Majesty's Government do not require to be reminded of their duty in regard to the recent invasion of the South African Republic, and they cannot admit the claim of the Government of the Republic to dictate the time and manner in which they shall fulfil their obligations. I am unable to understand the reasons which have suddenly influenced the Government of the South African Republic to make representations which are inconsistent with their previous statements. On 18th April and on 15th May the Government of the Republic appeared to be satisfied with the assurances given them by Her Majesty's Government, from which there has never been any intention of departing. It would not be in accordance with English ideas of justice to condemn the British South Africa Company and deal with its powers as proposed in the telegrams before an enquiry had been made, and before the Company had been heard in its own defence. With regard to the demand of the Government of the South African Republic that the three gentlemen specifically named shall now be placed on their trial, you will remind them that Her Majesty's Government can only act in this matter upon the advice of the Law Officers of the Crown, and in accordance with the principles of English law."

But Mr. Secretary Chamberlain, on his side, was equally—perhaps more than equally—watchful and critical of the doings and omissions of the government of the South African Republic. He kept an eye upon them that was especially alert for the detection of infractions of the London Convention of 1884 (see above: A. D. 1884-1894), with its provisions very strictly construed. He found treaties negotiated with foreign powers in contravention of Article IV. of that Convention, and laws passed which he deemed an infringement of its Article XIV. He arraigned the government of the Republic upon each as it came to his knowledge, and then, on the 6th of March, 1897, went back over the record of his complaints and summed them up, as follows: "It will be convenient if I recapitulate briefly the occasions for such complaint, beginning with the cases relating to Article IV. of the Convention. . . .

"1.—Netherlands Treaty. On the 9th November 1895, an Extradition Treaty between the South African Republic and the Netherlands was signed at the Hague, and the ratifications were exchanged on the 19th June last, without the Treaty being submitted for the approval of Her Majesty. The case was therefore one of a clear infraction of the Convention, inasmuch as the Treaty had not been submitted to Her Majesty's Government on its completion, and had been concluded by the exchange of ratifications without obtaining the previous approval of the Queen. The Government of the South African Republic, on their attention being called to the infraction, did not deny that there had been a departure from the general practice, but urged that they had made no publication of the Treaty in anticipation of the approval of Her Majesty. The

Treaty had, however, been published in the 'Netherlands Gazette' of the 3rd July, and I observed that when the Treaty was published in the 'Staats Courant' of the South African Republic after Her Majesty's approval had been given, the official notice merely stated that the Treaty was signed and ratified on certain dates, no reference being made to that approval.

"2.—The Accession of the South African Republic to the Geneva Convention. After Dr. Jameson's raid, owing to a report made by the St. John's Ambulance Association, Her Majesty's Government determined to invite the South African Republic to accede to the Geneva Convention, and the necessary instructions were sent to Sir J. de Wet, who, however, omitted to carry them out. The South African Republic, on the 30th September, formally communicated to the Swiss Government, through their Representative at the Hague, their act of accession to the Geneva Convention. Her Majesty's Government, in the circumstances, did not hesitate to convey the Queen's approval, but the action of the Government of the Republic none the less constituted a breach of the London Convention.

"3.—Portuguese Treaty. An Extradition Treaty between the South African Republic and Portugal was signed on the 3rd November 1893, but, contrary to the usual practice, has not yet been submitted for the Queen's approval, although two years have elapsed since Lord Ripon, in his Despatch of the 25th February 1895, requested your predecessor to call the attention of the President to the omission to communicate this Convention to Her Majesty's Government under the provisions of Article IV. of the London Convention. . . . I now pass to the consideration of some of the recent legislation of the Volksraad in its relation to Article XIV. It will be found that it involves in more than one case actual or possible breaches of the Convention. Article XIV. runs as follows:—'All persons, other than natives, conforming themselves to the laws of the South African Republic (a) will have full liberty, with their families, to enter, travel, or reside in any part of the South African Republic; (b) they will be entitled to hire or possess houses, manufactories, warehouses, shops, and premises; (c) they may carry on their commerce either in person or by any agents whom they may think fit to employ; (d) they will not be subject, in respect of their persons or property, or in respect of their commerce or industry, to any taxes, whether general or local, other than those which are or may be imposed upon citizens of the said Republic.'

"4.—The Aliens Immigration Law. This law imposes upon aliens conditions of a new and burthensome character in excess of the simple requirement that they must conform themselves to the laws of the Republic. . . . 2. The Aliens Expulsion Law. This law empowers the President, with the advice and consent of the Executive Council, after consulting the State Attorney, to expel, without an appeal to the Court, any foreigner who, by word or writing, excites to disobedience or transgression of the law, or takes any steps dangerous to public peace and order. . . . Her Majesty's Government . . . do not admit that the Government of the Republic have a right to expel foreigners who are not shown to have failed to conform to the laws of the Republic, and they reserve the right to object to proceedings under the Act which may amount to a breach of the Convention. 3. The Press Law. This law empowers the State President, on the advice and with the consent of the Executive, to prohibit entirely or for a time the circulation of printed or published matter the contents of which are, in his judgment, contrary to good morals or a danger to the peace and order in the Republic. The suppression of the 'Critic' newspaper, the property of a British subject, under this law, is a matter which may raise a serious question as to whether the action of the Government of the Republic has been consistent with the Convention, but as Her Majesty's Government have not yet received the explanation of the Government of the Republic in that case, it is only necessary for me to make a passing allusion to it in this Despatch.

"In several of the cases above cited, the strict letter of the Convention could apparently have been observed without any difficulty, while in others the objects which the Government of the South African Republic had in view could have been attained without any infringement of the Convention by a previous understanding with Her Majesty's Government. Her Majesty's Government therefore cannot conceal from themselves that the Government of the South African Republic have in these cases failed to give effect in practice to the intention, so frequently expressed in public and official utterances, of upholding the Convention on the part of the Republic, and of maintaining that good understanding with Her Majesty's Government which is so necessary in the interests of South Africa."

Of the laws complained of by Mr. Chamberlain, that relating to immigrant aliens had raised the most protest, because of its requirement that all such aliens who were permitted to enter and remain in the country must carry "travelling and residential passes," to be shown on demand. The Transvaal Government had met Mr. Chamberlain's first remonstrance on this subject, in January, by saying: "It is an evident fact that, especially during the last time, the immigration of aliens of the lowest class and without any means of subsistence has been increasing in a disquieting manner. These persons are dangerous to the peace of the inhabitants and of the State itself, and, in the opinion of this Government, no country whatever can be obliged to admit such undesirable persons. The regulation of unrestricted entry, as it at present takes place, is thus, from the point of view of police requirement, not only necessary but also entirely justified and constitutes no infringement of Article 14 of the Convention. This Government does not desire as yet to express any opinion on the suggestion that under the circumstances mentioned it should have approached Her Britannic Majesty's Government with a view to arriving at an understanding. In case, however, the Government of Her Britannic Majesty has another practical measure to propose whereby its abovementioned subjects, whose presence here is not desired for the reasons stated, can be prevented from seeking an outlet on the soil of the South African Republic, and that measure can be found to be applicable to the subjects of other Powers as well (since the law makes no distinction in that respect) it will be ready, with gratitude, to give its full consideration to such measure."—*Great Britain, Papers by Command:* 1897, *C.* 8423.

Cape Colony and Natal: A. D. 1897.—Conference of colonial premiers with the British Colonial Secretary. See (in this vol.) ENGLAND: A. D. 1897 (JUNE—JULY).

British South Africa Company: **A. D. 1897 (January).**—Compulsory labor in Rhodesia.—In January, 1897, the Deputy Commissioner of the British government in Rhodesia made a report to the High Commissioner on several subjects pertaining to the native administration of the British South Africa Company which he had been instructed to investigate. One question to be answered was "whether there exists a law or practice whereby compulsory labor is exacted from natives, either by the government of the British South Africa Company, or by private persons with consent of the government, or by both?" From his lengthy report on this subject the High Commissioner deduced the following summary of conclusions, which he communicated to the colonial secretary: '(1.) That compulsory labour did undoubtedly exist in Matabeleland, if not in Mashonaland. (2.) That labour was procured by the various Native Commissioners for the various requirements of the Government, mining companies, and private persons. (3.) That the Native Commissioners, in the first instance, endeavoured to obtain labour through the indunas, but, failing in this, they procured it by force.''—*Great Britain, Papers by Command:* 1897, *C.*— 8547.

The Transvaal: **A. D. 1897 (January—March).**—Conflict of the Judiciary with the Executive and the Volksraad.—The case of R. E. Brown.—In January, 1897, a decision was rendered by the High Court of the Republic which brought it into conflict with President Kruger and the Volksraad. This decision was given in connection with a suit brought against the government of the South African Republic by an American engineer, Mr. R. E. Brown, and the claim of Mr. Brown had arisen out of circumstances which were subsequently related by a speaker in the United States Senate, as follows: "Mr. R. E. Brown, a young American mining engineer, living and operating in the Cœur d'Alene district, in the State of Idaho, about eight years ago, at the invitation of English capitalists, left this country to go to the South African Republic for the purpose of assisting in the development of the gold mines of that country. It was about that time that Hammond, Clements, and other American engineers went there, and it is not too much to say that the genius and the energy of those young Americans more than anything else made that country a great gold producer and its mines the most valuable of any in the world. At that time most of the mines were held by English companies or Germans. The laws were very simple, but in some respects appear to have been drawn in the interest of the wealthy syndicates. Upon the discovery of new mines the President of the Republic by proclamation opened them to mining locations, fixing a day and hour at which they would be opened to such location. Thereafter persons desiring to stake out mines had to go to the office of the responsible clerk of the district in which the mines were located to make application for licenses to locate the mines, and thereafter they were authorized, either in person or by deputy, to go on the ground and make mining locations. Under this system most of the valuable mines of the country had been absorbed, as I said, by English and German syndicates. The mode in which they operated to absorb the mines was to place their men upon the newly opened ground and at the earliest possible moment apply for licenses to locate the mines, and then by means of couriers with swift horses, or by signals from mountain to mountain where that was possible, to convey information to their men and cause the mines to be located before their rivals could get on the ground. Mr. Brown had not been in the country very long before he learned of this antiquated system, and he determined on the next opening of mines to apply to their location some of the snap and go of American methods.

"In June, 1895, President Kruger by proclamation opened the mines on the Witfontein farm, district of Potchefstroom, the responsible clerk for which resided at Doornkop, in that district. Mr. Brown determined that he would acquire some of these mines, at least, and as large a number of them as possible. Witfontein was only 30 miles from Doornkop. The mines were known to be very valuable, because they had been prospected on each side and it was found that valuable gold-bearing reefs ran through them from end to end. Accordingly he purchased heliographic instruments and employed expert heliographic operators, and without the knowledge of his rivals established heliographic communication between Doornkop and Witfontein. Then he placed his men upon the ground, and on the 19th day of July, 1895, the earliest period at which he was permitted to do so, he appeared at the office of the responsible clerk and sought licenses to locate 1,200 mines upon this ground. However, on the day before the opening of the mines his rivals had found out about the heliographic communication, but they were beaten in the race. In that extremity they communicated with President Kruger by wire and induced him on the night of the 18th to issue a second proclamation, withdrawing the mines of Witfontein from the privilege of mining locations, and when Mr. Brown appeared at the office of the responsible clerk and tendered his money he was met with the information of this action on the part of the President of the South African Republic, and his application was refused. But nothing daunted he caused his agents on the ground to locate the mines the same as if the licenses had been granted to him, and then he brought suit before the high court of justice of the South African Republic against the Republic, alleging the facts substantially as I have stated them and praying that the authorities be compelled to issue to him licenses for the mines located, or in lieu thereof that compensation be made to him in the sum of £372,400, amounting to about $1,850,000. While this suit was pending it was sought to re-enforce the action of the President in withdrawing these lands, and the Volksraad [passed a resolution approving the withdrawal and declaring that no person should be entitled to compensation on account of it]."—*U. S. Congressional Record, Jan.* 21, 1901, *p.* 1370.

On Mr. Brown's suit, the High Court of the Republic decided that the claimant's right to the land was good, and could not be set aside by ex post facto measures of the Executive or the Legislature. The President and the Volksraad

refused to submit to this decision, and passed a law to overrule it, on the ground that, under the Grondwet (constitution), the Volksraad is the highest power in the state. In a subsequent public statement of the matter, Justice Kotze, the Chief Justice, explained the issue that was thus raised between his court and the President, and also related the circumstances of a compromise by which it was settled temporarily, as follows : "This so-called Law No. 1 of 1897 seeks to deprive the judges of the testing right, authorizes the President to put a certain question to the members of the bench that they would not arrogate to themselves the so-called testing power, and empowers him to instantly dismiss the judge or judges from whom he receives no answer, or, in his opinion, an unsatisfactory answer. The judges for the future are also subjected to a humiliating form of oath. This measure, it seems almost superfluous to observe, is no law. It alters the constitution of the country without any previous reference to the people, and for the reasons given in the Brown case it is devoid of all legal validity. The five judges, on March 1, 1897, unanimously issued a declaration, stating that by this so-called Law No. 1 of 1897 a vital violation of the independence of the bench had taken place, and that the judges were exposed in future to the suspicion of bribery. In fact, the nature and tendency of this measure are so immoral that one of the judges openly said that no honorable man can occupy a seat on the bench while Law No. 1 of 1897 remains on the statute book.

"The question above referred to was duly put by the President to the judges, who had unanimously signed a letter to the effect that they did not feel themselves at liberty to give any answer, when the chief justice of the Cape Colony arrived in Pretoria, and through his mediation a written understanding was proposed by the judges on March 19, and accepted without any qualification by the President on March 22, 1897. By the terms of this compact the judges undertook not to test laws and resolutions of the Volksraad on the distinct understanding that the President would as soon as possible submit a draft Grondwet to the Volksraad providing how alone the Grondwet can be altered by special legislation in a manner analogous to the provisions contained in the constitution of the Orange Free State on the subject, and incorporating the guaranties for the independence of the judiciary. By these means the judges intended to protect both the constitution and the bench against sudden surprises and attacks, such as, for instance, the oft-quoted measure known as Law No. 1, of 1897. They did this to avert a crisis, and, in order to help the Government and Volksraad out of a difficulty of their own creation, placed themselves under a temporary obligation upon the faith of the President as speedily as possible complying with his portion of the understanding."—*United States, 56th Congress, 1st Sess., House Doc. No.* 618.

The promised amendment of the Grondwet was not made, and the issue concerning it was brought to a crisis in the next year. See below : A. D. 1898 (JANUARY—FEBRUARY).

A. D. 1897 (February) : Appointment of Sir Alfred Milner.—In February, Sir Alfred Milner was appointed High Commissioner for South Africa and Governor of Cape Colony, to succeed

Sir Hercules Robinson, retired, and raised to the peerage as Lord Rosmead.

The Transvaal : **A. D. 1897** (February).— The franchise.—The government of the Transvaal extended the full franchise to 862 Uitlanders who supported it at the time of the Jameson raid.

The Transvaal : **A. D. 1897** (February.)— Indemnity claimed by the South African Republic for the Jameson Raid.—On the 16th of February, 1897, the State Secretary of the South African Republic, Dr. W. J. Leyds, presented to the British High Commissioner the following " specification of the compensation to which the Government of the South African Republic lays claim for and in connexion with the incursion into the Territory of the South African Republic by Dr. Jameson and the Troops of the Chartered Company at the end of December 1895 and the beginning of January 1896.

	£	s.	d.
1. Expenditure for military and commando services in connexion with the incursion, the sum of	136,733	4	3
2. Compensation to the Netherlands South African Railway Company for making use, in accordance with the concession granted to that Company, of the railway worked by it during the commando on account of the incursion of Dr. Jameson....	9,500	0	0
3. Disbursements to surviving relatives of slain and wounded	234	19	6
4. For annuities, pensions, and disbursements to widows and children of slain burghers and to relatives of unmarried slain burghers, as also to wounded burghers, a total sum of	28,243	0	0
5. Expenses of the telegraph department, for more overtime, more telegrams on service in South African communication, more cablegrams, &c................	4,692	11	9
6. Hospital expenses for the care of the wounded and sick men, &c. of Dr. Jameson	225	0	0
7. For support of members of the families of commandeered burghers during the commando......................................	177	8	8
8. Compensation to be paid to the commandeered burghers for their services and the troubles and cares brought upon them	462,120	0	0
9. Account of expenses of the Orange Free State.................................	36,011	19	1
	677,938	3	3

" Moral or intellectual compensation to which the Government of the South African Republic lays claim for and in connexion with the incursion into the Territory of the South African Republic by Dr. Jameson and the Troops of the Chartered Company at the end of December 1895 and the beginning of January 1896. One million pounds sterling (£1,000,000)."

To this claim the British colonial secretary, Mr. Chamberlain, replied on the 10th of April, saying, with reference to the specification under the second head, " for moral or intellectual damage," that " Her Majesty's Government . . . regret that they do not feel justified in presenting it to the British South Africa Company " : and adding : " Her Majesty's Government fear that they may be compelled to take similar exception to certain of the items composing the first head, especially in view of the very short period which elapsed between the crossing of the frontier by Dr. Jameson's force and its surrender ; but as it is apparent from the nature of the figures that the Government of the South African Republic have proceeded on very precise data in arriving at the various sums to which they lay claim, Her Majesty's Government, before offering any observations on this part of the claim, would ask

his Honour to be so good as to furnish them with full particulars of the way in which the different items comprised in the first head have been arrived at."—*Great Britain, Papers by Command : C.*—8404, 1897 ; *and C.*—8721, 1898.

The Transvaal : **A. D. 1897** (February— July).—British parliamentary investigation of the Jameson Raid.—A Committee of the British House of Commons, appointed " to inquire into the origin and circumstances of the incursion into the South African Republic by an armed force, and into the administration of the British South Africa Company," began its sittings on the 16th of February, 1897. Among the members of the Committee were the Chancellor of the Exchequer, the Attorney-General, Mr. Chamberlain, the Secretary of State for the Colonies, Sir William Harcourt, Sir John Lubbock, Sir H. Campbell-Bannerman, Mr. Labouchere, Mr. John Ellis, Mr. Buxton, Mr. Blake, and others. Mr. Rhodes, who was first examined by the Committee, read a statement of the circumstances leading up to the raid, in which he said that, as one largely interested in the Transvaal, he felt that the unfriendly attitude of the Boer Government was the great obstacle to common action among the various states in South Africa, and that, therefore, he had assisted the movement in Johannesburg with his purse and influence. " Further," he said, " acting within my rights, in the autumn of 1895 I placed a body of troops under Dr. Jameson, prepared to act in the Transvaal in certain eventualities." Subsequently Mr. Rhodes declared : " With reference to the Jameson raid, I may state that Dr. Jameson went in without my authority." He concluded his statement by declaring that in what he did he was greatly influenced by his belief that the policy of the Boer Government was to "introduce the influence of another foreign Power into the already complicated system of South Africa." Mr. Rhodes was kept under examination before the Committee for four days, and then "almost the next thing heard of him was that he had started for South Africa on his way back to Rhodesia." Another witness examined was Sir Graham Bower, Secretary to the High Commissioner at the Cape. " His evidence was certainly most startling, and at the same time of great importance. He stated that late in October, 1895, Mr. Rhodes came into his office and said : ' I want you to give me your word of honour that you will not say a word to any one about what I am going to tell you.' Sir Graham Bower —who, as he said, had a great many Cape secrets in his possession—pledged his word, and soon found he was in possession of a secret which it was his official duty to disclose to the High Commissioner and his private duty not to disclose. Mr. Rhodes then said that he was negotiating about the Protectorate, that there was going to be a rising in Johannesburg, and that he wished to have a police force on the border. He added in substance : ' If trouble comes I am not going to sit still. You fellows are infernally slow.' It further transpired that on the fateful Sunday (Dec. 28) Mr. Rhodes had told him that Jameson had gone in, but that he hoped that the message he had sent would stop him." When Dr. Jameson was examined he fully acknowledged his conspiracy with the Johannesburg revolutionists, and stated that he had given information of it to Mr. Rhodes, adding : " He agreed, and we arranged that when the rising took place he should go to Johannesburg or Pretoria with the High Commissioner and Mr. Hofmeyr to mediate between the Transvaal Government and the Uitlanders. With these matters settled, I left Cape Town and joined my camp at Pitsani. I required no orders or authority from Mr. Rhodes, and desired neither to receive nor to send any messages from or to Cape Town."

In the course of the inquiry, Mr. Chamberlain, the Colonial Secretary, desired to give testimony, and related that Dr. Harris, the Secretary in South Africa to the British South Africa Company, said to him, "I could tell you something in confidence," or "I could give you some confidential information"; but that he (Chamberlain) stopped him at once, saying, "I do not want to hear any confidential information. I am here in an official capacity, and I can only hear information of which I can make official use"; and adding: "I have Sir Hercules Robinson in South Africa. I have entire confidence in him, and I am quite convinced he will keep me informed of everything I ought to know." In concluding his testimony, Mr. Chamberlain said: "I desire to say, in the most explicit manner, that I did not then have, and that I never had, any knowledge or—until, I think it was, the day before the raid took place—the slightest suspicion of anything in the nature of a hostile or armed invasion of the Transvaal." The Committee having called upon Mr. Rhodes' solicitor, a Mr. Hawksley, to produce telegrams which had passed between Mr. Rhodes and himself, refused to do so.

"The proceedings which ensued were not to the credit of the Committee, for instead of reporting the matter to the House at once in a special report, they decided to refer to it in the interim report on the raid. Mr. Labouchere and Mr. Blake alone opposed this course, which was either a confession of unwillingness to reach the bottom of the business, or the suggestion that somebody was to be shielded. . . . Having devoted two days to hearing counsel on behalf of Mr. Rhodes, Mr. Beit and Dr. Harris, the Committee adjourned to consider its report. The general feeling was that the proceedings had been conducted with singular laxity or want of skill. Those interested in keeping secret the true history of the raid were entirely successful, and it was generally by the merest chance that any fact of importance was elicited from the witnesses. The representatives of the Opposition, Sir William Harcourt, Sir H. Campbell-Bannerman and Mr. Buxton, were, after Mr. Rhodes had been unaccountably permitted to quit England, willing to allow the breakdown of the proceedings; and what was even more surprising in so strict a parliamentarian as Sir William Harcourt, a witness was allowed to treat the Committee with defiance, and to pass unchecked. To a very great extent the inquiry had been obviously factitious, but in whose interest concealment was considered necessary remained undivulged. It was surmised that reasons of State had been found which outweighed party considerations, and that the leaders of the Opposition had been privately convinced that the alleged grounds were sufficient for the course adopted."

The report of the majority of the Committee, signed by all of its members except Mr. Labouchere and Mr. Blake (the former of whom submitted a minority report), was made public on

the 18th of July. The results of its inquiry were summed up under the following heads: I. "Great discontent had, for some time previous to the incursion, existed in Johannesburg, arising from the grievances of the Uitlanders. II. Mr. Rhodes occupied a great position in South Africa; he was Prime Minister of the Cape Colony, and, beyond all other persons, should have been careful to abstain from such a course of action as that which he adopted. As managing director of the British South Africa Company, as director of the De Beers Consolidated Mines and the Gold Fields of South Africa, Mr. Rhodes controlled a great combination of interests; he used his position and those interests to promote and assist his policy. Whatever justification there might have been for action on the part of the people of Johannesburg, there was none for the conduct of a person in Mr. Rhodes' position in subsidising, organising, and stimulating an armed insurrection against the Government of the South African Republic, and employing the forces and resources of the Chartered Company to support such a revolution. He seriously embarrassed both the Imperial and Colonial Governments, and his proceedings resulted in the invasion of the territory of a State which was in friendly relations with her Majesty, in breach of the obligation to respect the right to self-government of the South African Republic under the conventions between her Majesty and that State. Although Dr. Jameson 'went in' without Mr. Rhodes' authority, it was always part of the plan that these forces should be used in the Transvaal in support of an insurrection. Nothing could justify such a use of such a force, and Mr. Rhodes' heavy responsibility remains, although Dr. Jameson at the last moment invaded the Transvaal without his direct sanction. III. Such a policy once embarked upon inevitably involved Mr. Rhodes in grave breaches of duty to those to whom he owed allegiance. He deceived the High Commissioner representing the Imperial Government, he concealed his views from his colleagues in the Colonial Ministry and from the board of the British South Africa Company, and led his subordinates to believe that his plans were approved by his superiors. IV. Your committee have heard the evidence of all the directors of the British South Africa Company, with the exception of Lord Grey. Of those who were examined, Mr. Beit and Mr. Maguire alone had cognisance of Mr. Rhodes' plans. Mr. Beit played a prominent part in the negotiations with the Reform Union; he contributed large sums of money to the revolutionary movement, and must share full responsibility for the consequences. V. There is not the slightest evidence that the late High Commissioner in South Africa, Lord Rosmead, was made acquainted with Mr. Rhodes' plans. The evidence, on the contrary, shows that there was a conspiracy to keep all information on the subject from him. The committee must, however, express a strong opinion upon the conduct of Sir Graham Bower, who was guilty of a grave dereliction of duty in not communicating to the High Commissioner the information which had come to his knowledge. Mr. Newton failed in his duty in a like manner. VI. Neither the Secretary of State for the Colonies nor any of the officials of the Colonial Office received any information which made them, or should have made them or any of them, aware of the plot during its development.

VII. Finally, your committee desire to put on record an absolute and unqualified condemnation of the raid and of the plans which made it possible."

"The result caused for the time being grave injury to British influence in South Africa. Public confidence was shaken, race feeling embittered, and serious difficulties were created with neighbouring States. The course of action subsequently taken by the Government increased the suspicions which were aroused by such an emasculated report. Two days after its publication (July 15), Mr. Balfour was asked to set apart a day for the formal discussion of so important a matter. To this request Mr. Balfour, with the tacit concurrence of the front Opposition bench, replied that he saw no useful purpose to be served by such a debate."

Those who were known as the "Forward Radicals," or "Forwards," in the House, were not to be silenced in this manner, and debate was forced upon a motion expressing regret at "the inconclusive action and report of the select committee on British South Africa," and summoning Mr. Hawksley to the bar of the House, to produce "then and there," the telegrams which he had refused to the committee. In the course of the discussion which followed, Mr. Chamberlain expressed his conviction that, "while the fault of Mr. Rhodes was about as great a fault as a politician or statesman could commit, there existed nothing which affected his personal character as a man of honour." When Sir Elliott Lees, a supporter of the government, rose to protest against such a doctrine, he was met by cries which silenced his speech. The House then divided, and the resolution was defeated by 304 to 77. "It was an open secret that throughout the debate one member, unconnected with either front bench, sat with the famous telegrams in his pocket, and with them certain correspondence relating thereto which he had been instructed to read in the event of Mr. Rhodes' character being aspersed."—*Annual Register*, 1897.

"The position . . . stands thus. The Colonial Office conceals its own documents. From none of its officials have we had any detailed or frank statement as to their relations to South African affairs during the critical period. The High Commissioner himself has not been examined. Mr. Rhodes has been allowed to go without any serious inquiry into this branch of the case. The most important cables are refused by Mr. Rhodes's order, and the Committee decline to exercise their power to compel the production of them. The story, in fact, so far as it concerns this question of the truth or falsity of the allegation that Mr. Chamberlain was 'in it,' is being smothered up, with an audacious disregard of the principles which guide all ordinary tribunals. The last steps in this proceeding have been taken with the direct assent of the leader of the Opposition. Everybody, therefore, is inquiring what reason can have induced Sir William Harcourt to execute this startling change of front. There is only one reason that can, with any probability, be assigned—that is, that some member of the Government has made a 'Front Bench communication' to the leader of the Opposition, indicating to him explicitly that there are 'reasons of State' for stopping the disclosures. There can be little doubt that this is what has happened, and conjecture, not only in this country but elsewhere, will

naturally be keen to know what the nature of this momentous disclosure was.

"If Mr. Chamberlain was as absolutely free from knowledge of the Jameson plan as he has professed to be, it is hard to see how full disclosure could do any damage to the Empire, or could do anything but good to the Colonial Secretary himself. Mr. Chamberlain, of course, professes in words his private desire that everything should come out. He has not, however, assisted in the attainment of that result. The consequence is that a national and international question of very grave importance has arisen. It is said in circles usually well informed, that when the Raid occurred, it became necessary to give assurances to foreign Governments, and in particular to Germany, that the Queen's Government was in no way compromised. These assurances, it is said, were given. It is even said that they were given expressly in the name of the Queen. Something of this kind may well have happened; but it is hard to see how, if it did happen, and if the Colonial Office was as innocent as it claims to be, the disclosure of the facts can do anything but confirm the Queen's word. That documents exist which are supposed to be compromising, and which the very authors of them allege to be compromising, is a fact past hiding. It casts, unless it is cleared up, a damning doubt. Therefore it would appear to be the duty of all honest men, and, above all, of the Parliament of Great Britain, to see that an immediate end is put to a policy which may be aptly described as 'thimble-rigging,' and that the truth, whether it suits Mr. Rhodes or Mr. Chamberlain, or neither of them, must be told at last."
—*Contemporary Review, July,* 1897.

Orange Free State and Transvaal: A. D. **1897** (April).—Treaty of alliance.—In April, the two republics entered into a treaty for mutual support and defense against attacks on the independence of either, each opening its political franchises to the citizens of the other on the taking of an oath of allegiance.

The Transvaal: A. D. **1897** (April).—Military expenditure by British and Boer Governments.—The budget of the British Chancellor of the Exchequer, submitted to the House of Commons in April, contained an item of £200,000 for increased military expenditure in South Africa. This was promptly attacked by the opposition, who accused the government of pursuing a war policy in its dealings with the Transvaal. Sir William Harcourt declared that Mr. Chamberlain had, "in every utterance of his during the last few months, been endeavouring to exasperate sentiment in South Africa, and to produce what, thank God! he had failed in producing—a racial war." Mr. Chamberlain retorted that Sir William Harcourt's attitude was unpatriotic and injurious to the cause of peace. He denied aggressiveness in the policy of the government, asserting that the South African Republic had been spending millions on armaments imported from abroad, in view of which the strengthening of the British garrison at the Cape by an additional regiment and three batteries was no unreasonable measure. Mr. Balfour, also, begged the House and the country to believe that the troops were sent only as a measure of precaution, to maintain admitted rights.

The Transvaal: A. D. **1897** (May—October).—**The British assertion of suzerainty**

and declination of proposal to arbitrate disagreements.—On the 7th of May, 1897, the Acting State Secretary of the South African Republic addressed to the British Agent at Pretoria a communication of great length, reviewing the positions taken by Mr. Chamberlain in his several arraignments of the government of the Republic for alleged violation of the London Convention of 1884, and proposing an arbitration of the questions involved. "The complaint," he wrote, "which Her British Majesty's Government has advanced in an unmistakably pronounced manner over an actual or possible breach of the Convention has deeply grieved this Government, as it thinks that it has fulfilled its obligations. It sees in the fulfilment of the mutual obligations under the Convention one of the best guarantees for the maintenance of a mutual good understanding and for the promotion of reciprocal confidence. To this good understanding and that confidence, however, severe shocks have been given by events which cannot be lightly forgotten. And if it were not that this Government wishes to guard itself against adopting a recriminating tone, it might put the question whether, for example, the incursion of Dr. Jameson, whether considered as a breach of the Convention or a grievance, is not of immeasurably greater importance than the various matters adduced by Her British Majesty's Government would be, even if the contention that they constitute breaches of the Convention could be accepted. There should, in the view of this Government, be a strong mutual endeavour to restore the shocked confidence and to calm the excited spirit which this Government with sincere regret sees reigning throughout almost the whole of South Africa. This Government is anxious to co-operate for this end, for the desire of the Republic, with the maintenance of its independence and rights, is for peace, and where for the reasons given it has been unable to entertain the proposal of Her British Majesty's Government in the matter of the Aliens Law,—and it appears very difficult to arrive at a solution of the question by means of correspondence,—it wishes to come to a permanent good understanding along a peaceful course, not only with respect to its undisturbed right to make an alien law, but also with regard to all points touching the Convention which are referred to in the two Despatches under reply by Her British Majesty's Government. While it respects the opinion of Her British Majesty's Government, it takes the liberty, with full confidence in the correctness of its own views, to propose to Her British Majesty's Government the principle of arbitration with which the honourable the First Volksraad agrees, in the hope that it will be taken in the conciliatory spirit in which it is made. . . .

"Although this Government is firmly convinced that a just and impartial decision might be obtained even better in South Africa than anywhere else, it wishes, in view of the conflicting elements, interests, and aspirations, which are now apparent in South Africa, and in order to avoid even the appearance that it would be able or desire to exercise influence in order to obtain a decision favourable to it, to propose that the President of the Swiss Bondstate, who may be reckoned upon as standing altogether outside the question. and to feel sympathy or antipathy neither for the one party nor for the other, be requested to point out a competent jurist, as has already oftener been done in respect of international disputes. The Government would have no objection that the arbitrator be subject to a limitation of time, and gives the assurance now already that it will willingly subject itself to any decision if such should, contrary to its expectation, be given against it. The Government repeats the well-meant wish that this proposal may find favour with Her British Majesty's Government, and inasmuch as the allegations of breaches of the Convention find entrance now even in South Africa, and bring and keep the feelings more and more in a state of suspense, this Government will be pleased if it can learn the decision of Her Majesty's Government as soon as possible."

Mr. Chamberlain's reply to this proposal was not written until the 16th of the following October, when he, in turn, reviewed, point by point, the matters dealt with in the despatch of Mr. Van Boeschoten. With reference to the Jameson raid he said: "Her Majesty's Government note with satisfaction that the Government of the South African Republic see in the fulfilment of the mutual obligations under the London Convention one of the best guarantees for the maintenance of a mutual understanding and for the promotion of reciprocal confidence. Her Majesty's Government have uniformly fulfilled these obligations on their part, and they must strongly protest against what appears to be an implication in the Note under consideration that the incursion of Dr. Jameson can be considered as either a breach of the Convention by Her Majesty's Government or a grievance against them. That incursion was the act of private individuals unauthorised by Her Majesty's Government, and was repudiated by them immediately it became known. The immense importance to the Government of the South African Republic of that repudiation, and of the proclamation issued by the High Commissioner under instructions from Her Majesty's Government, is recognised throughout South Africa. Her Majesty's Government maintain strongly that since the Convention of 1881 there has never been any breach or even any allegation of a breach on their part of that or the subsequent Convention, and, as the subject has been raised by the implied accusation contained in the Note under consideration, Her Majesty's Government feel constrained to contrast their loyal action in the case of the Jameson raid with the cases in which they have had cause to complain that the Government of the South African Republic failed to interfere with, if they did not countenance, invasions of the adjacent territories by its burghers in violation of the Convention, and they feel bound to remind the Government of the Republic that in one of these cases Her Majesty's Government were compelled to maintain their rights by an armed expedition at the cost of about one million sterling, for which no compensation has ever been received by them."

Concerning the proposal of arbitration, the reply of the British colonial secretary was as follows: "In making this proposal the Government of the South African Republic appear to have overlooked the distinction between the Conventions of 1881 and 1884 and an ordinary treaty between two independent Powers, questions arising upon which may properly be the subject of arbitration. By the Pretoria Convention of 1881 Her Majesty, as Sovereign of the Transvaal Territory, accorded to the inhabitants of that territory complete self-government subject to the suzerainty of Her Majesty, her heirs and successors, upon certain terms and conditions and subject to certain reservations and limitations set forth in 33 articles, and by the London Convention of 1884 Her Majesty, while maintaining the preamble of the earlier instrument, directed and declared that certain other articles embodied therein should be substituted for the articles embodied in the Convention of 1881. The articles of the Convention of 1881 were accepted by the Volksraad of the Transvaal State, and those of the Convention of 1884 by the Volksraad of the South African Republic. Under these Conventions, therefore, Her Majesty holds towards the South African Republic the relation of a suzerain who has accorded to the people of that Republic self-government upon certain conditions, and it would be incompatible with that position to submit to arbitration the construction of the conditions on which she accorded self-government to the Republic. One of the main objects which Her Majesty's Government had in view was the prevention of the interference of any foreign Power between Her Majesty and the South African Republic, a matter which they then held, and which Her Majesty's present Government hold, to be essential to British interests, and this object would be defeated by the course now proposed. The clear intention of Her Majesty's Government at the time of the London Convention, that questions in relation to it should not be submitted to arbitration, is shown by the fact that when the delegates of the South African Republic, in the negotiations which preceded that Convention, submitted to Her Majesty's Government in the first instance (in a letter of the 26th of November, 1883, which will be found on page 9 of the Parliamentary Paper C. 3947 of 1884) the draft of a treaty or convention containing an arbitration clause, they were informed by the Earl of Derby that it was neither in form nor in substance such as Her Majesty's Government could adopt."—*Great Britain, Papers by Command: C.*—8721, 1898.

Natal: A. D. 1897 (December).—Annexation of Zululand. See (in this vol.) AFRICA: A. D. 1897 (ZULULAND).

Cape Colony: A. D. 1898.—The position of political parties.—The Progressives and the Afrikander Bund.—"The present position of parties at the Cape is as unfortunate and as unwarranted as any that the severest critic of Parliamentary institutions could have conjured up. . . . The Cape has always had the curse of race prejudice to contend with. Time might have done much to soften, if not to expunge it, if home-made stupidities had not always been forthcoming to goad to fresh rancour. The facts are too well known to need repetition. It is true not only of the Transvaalers that 'the trek has eaten into their souls,' and up to the time of emancipation and since, every conceivable mistake has been committed by those in authority. Thus, when the breach was, to all appearances, partly healed, the fatal winter of 1895 put back the hands of the clock to the old point of departure. As Englishmen, our sympathies are naturally with the party that is prevalently English,

and against the party that is prevalently Dutch; but to find a real line of political difference between them other than national sentiment requires fine drawing. . . . According to our lines of cleavage both Bondsmen [Afrikander Bund] and Progressives are Conservatives of a decided type. Practically they are agreed in advocating protective duties on sea-borne trade, although in degree they differ, for whilst the Bond would have imposts as they are, the Progressives wish to reduce the duties on food stuffs to meet the grievance of the urban constituencies, and might be induced to accord preferential treatment to British goods. On the native question neither party adopts what would in England be considered an 'advanced' programme, for education is not made a cardinal point, and they would equally like, if possible, to extend the application of the Glen Grey Act, which, by levying a tax on the young Kaffirs who have not a labour certificate, forces them to do some service to the community before exercising their right of ' putting the spoon,' as the phrase is, ' into the family pot.' Neither party wishes to interfere with the rights of property or the absolute tenure of land under the Roman-Dutch law. A tax on the output of diamonds at Kimberley has been advocated by some members of the Bond as a financial expedient, but it is understood to have been put forward rather as a threat against Mr. Rhodes personally than as a measure of practical politics. Questions of franchise are tacitly left as they are, for no responsible politicians wish to go back upon the enactment which restricted the Kaffir vote to safe and inconsiderable limits. The redistribution of seats was the subject of a Bill upon which the last House was dissolved, after the rebuff that the Ministry received upon a crucial division, but it has been dealt with rather for practical than theoretical reasons. Two schemes of redistribution have been formulated, and each has been proposed and opposed with arguments directed to show the party advantage to be derived. For political reform, in the abstract, with or without an extension of the suffrage, there is no sort of enthusiasm in any quarter. Railway administration furnishes, no doubt, an occasional battle-field for the two sides of the House. Roughly, the Progressives favour the northern extension, and are willing to make concessions in rates and charges to help on the new trade with Rhodesia ; whilst the Bond declare themselves against special treatment of the new interests, and would spend all the money that could be devoted to railway construction in the farming districts of the colony itself. Mr. Rhodes, however, has warned the Cape that any hostile action will be counteracted by a diversion of traffic to the East, and it is unlikely that any line of policy will be pursued that is likely to injure the carrying trade of the southern ports. Between the followers of Mr. Rhodes and the followers of Mr. Hofmeyr there is no wide divergence of principle on public affairs of the near future, so far as they have been or are to be the subject of legislation; where the difference comes in is in the attitude they severally assume towards the two republics and the territories of the north, but when talk has to yield to action it is improbable that there will be much in their disagreement."—N. L. W. Lawson, *Cape Politics and Colonial Policy (Fortnightly Rev., Nov., 1898).*

The Transvaal: A. D. 1898 (January—Feb-

ruary).—Re-election of President Kruger.—
Renewed conflict of the Executive with the
Judiciary.—Dismissal of Chief-Justice Kotze.
—The Presidential election in the South African
Republic was held in January and February, the
polls being open from the 3d of the former month
until the 4th of the latter. President Kruger was
re-elected for a fourth term of five years, by
nearly 13,000 votes against less than 6,000 divided between Mr. Schalk Burger and General
Joubert, who were opposing candidates. Soon
afterwards, the conflict of 1897 between the Judiciary and the Executive (see above: A. D.
1897, JANUARY—MANcu), was reopened by a
communication in which Chief-Justice Kotze, of
the High Court, called the attention of the President to the fact that nothing had been done in fulfilment of the agreement that the independence
of the Court and the stability of the Grondwet
should both be protected by law against arbitrary
interference, and giving notice that he considered
the compromise then arranged to be ended.
Thereupon (February 16) President Kruger removed the judge from his office and placed the
State Attorney in his seat. Justice Kotze denied
the legality of the removal, and adjourned his
court sine die. In a speech at Johannesburg,
some weeks afterwards, he denounced the action
of President Kruger with great severity, saying:
"I charge the President, as head of the State,
with having violated both the constitution and
the ordinary laws of the land; with having interfered with the independence of the High Court;
and invaded and imperilled the rights and liberties of every one in the country. The guarantees
provided by the constitution for the protection
of real and personal rights have disappeared, and
these are now dependent on the 'arbitrium' of
President Kruger."

Rhodesia and the British South Africa
Company: A. D. 1898 (February).—Reorganization.—In February, the British government
announced the adoption of plans for a reorganization of the British South Africa Company and
of the administration of its territories. The
Company, already deprived of military powers,
was to give up, in great part, but not wholly, its
political functions. It was still to appoint an
Administrator for Rhodesia south of the Zambesi,
and to name the majority of members in a council assisting him, so long as it remained responsible for the expenses of administration; but,
by the side of the Administrator was to be placed
a Resident Commissioner, appointed by the
Crown, and over both was the authority of the
High Commissioner for South Africa, to whom
the Resident Commissioner made reports. At
home the status of the Board of Directors was
to be considerably altered. The life director-
ships were to be abolished, and the whole Board
of Directors in future to be elected by the shareholders,—any official or director removed by the
Secretary of State not being eligible without his
consent. The Board of Directors was to communicate all minutes, etc., to the Secretary of State,
and he to have the power of veto or suspension.
Finally, the Secretary of State was to have full
powers to inspect and examine all documents;
Colonial Office officials named by him were, in
effect, to exercise powers like those of the old
Indian Board of Control.

Cape Colony: A. D. 1898 (March—October).
—Election in favor of the Afrikander Bund.

—Change in the government.—Elections to the
Upper House of the Cape Parliament, in March,
gave the party called the Progressives, headed
by Mr. Rhodes, a small majority over the Afrikander Bund—more commonly called the Bond.
The Parliament opened in May, and the Progressive Ministry, under Sir Gordon Sprigg, was
defeated in the Lower House in the following
month, on a bill to create new electoral divisions.
The Ministry dissolved Parliament and appealed
to the constituencies, with the result of a defeat
on that appeal. The Bond party won in the
elections by a majority of two, which barely
enabled it to carry a resolution of want of confidence in the government when Parliament was
reassembled, in October. The Ministry of Sir
Gordon Sprigg resigned, and a new one was
formed with Mr. Schreiner at its head.

The Transvaal: A. D. 1898-1899.—Continued dispute with the British Government
concerning Suzerainty.—During 1898 and half
of 1899, a new dispute, raised by Mr. Chamberlain's emphatic assertion of the suzerainty of
Great Britain over the South African Republic,
went on between the British Colonial Office and
the government at Pretoria. Essentially, the
question at issue seemed to lie between a word
and a fact, and the difference between the disputants was the difference between the meanings
they had severally drawn from the omission of the
word "suzerainty" from the London Convention
of 1884. On one side could be quoted the report
which the Transvaal deputation to London, in
1884, had made to their Volksraad, when they
brought the treaty back, and recommended
that it be approved. The treaty, they reported,
"is entirely bilateral [meaning that there were
two sides in the making of it] whereby your
representatives were not placed in the humiliating position of merely having to accept from
a Suzerain Government a one-sided document
as rule and regulation, but whereby they were
recognized as a free contracting party. It makes,
then, also an end of the British suzerainty, and,
with the official recognition of her name, also
restores her full self-government to the South
African Republic, excepting one single limitation regarding the conclusion of treaties with
foreign powers (Article 4). With the suzerainty
the various provisions and limitations of the
Pretoria Convention which Her Majesty's Government as suzerain had retained have also, of
course, lapsed."

On the other side, Mr. Chamberlain could quote
with effect from a speech which Lord Derby,
then the British Colonial Secretary, who nego-
tisted the Convention of 1884 with the Boer
envoys, made on the 17th of March, that year, in
the House of Lords. As reported in Hansard,
Lord Derby had then dealt with the very question of suzerainty, as involved in the new convention, and had set forth his own understanding of the effect of the latter in the following
words: "Then the noble Earl (Earl Cadogan)
said that the object of the Convention had been
to abolish the suzerainty of the British Crown.
The word 'suzerainty' is a very vague word,
and I do not think it is capable of any precise
legal definition. Whatever we may understand
by it, I think it is not very easy to define. But
I apprehend, whether you call it a protectorate, or
a suzerainty, or the recognition of England as a
paramount Power, the fact is that a certain con-

trolling power is retained when the State which exercises this suzerainty has a right to veto any negotiations into which the dependent State may enter with foreign Powers. Whatever suzerainty meant in the Convention of Pretoria, the condition of things which it implied still remains; although the word is not actually employed, we have kept the substance. We have abstained from using the word because it was not capable of legal definition, and because it seemed to be a word which was likely to lead to misconception and misunderstanding."—*Great Britain, Papers by Command: C.* 9507, 1899, *pp.* 24 *and* 34).

The Transvaal: A. D. **1899** (March).—Petition of British subjects to the Queen.—A fresh excitement of discontent in the Rand, due especially to the shooting of an Englishman by a Boer policeman, whom the Boer authorities seemed disposed to punish lightly or not at all, led to the preparation of a petition to the British Queen, from her subjects in the South African Republic, purporting to be signed in the first instance by 21,684, and finally by 23,000. The genuineness of many of the signatures was disputed by the Boers, but strenuously affirmed by those who conducted the circulation of the petition. It set forth the grievances of the memorialists at length, and prayed Her Majesty to cause them to be investigated, and to direct her representative in South Africa to take measures for securing from the South African Republic a recognition of their rights. The petition was forwarded to the Colonial Office on the 28th of March.—*Great Britain, Papers by Command: 1899, C.* 9345.

The Transvaal: A. D. **1899** (May—June).— The Bloemfontein Conference between President Kruger and the British High Commissioner, Sir Alfred Milner.—There seems to be no mode in which the questions at issue between the British and the Boers, and the attitude of the two parties, respectively, in their contention with each other, can be represented more accurately than by quoting essential parts of the official report of a formal conference between President Kruger and the British High Commissioner in South Africa, Sir Alfred Milner, which was held at Bloemfontein, the capital of the Orange Free State, during five days, May 31— June 5, 1899. The meeting was arranged by President Steyn, of the Orange Free State, with a view to bringing about an adjustment of differences by a free and full discussion of them, face to face. In the official report of the conversations that occurred, from which we shall quote, the remarks of President Kruger are given as being made by the "President," and those of the High Commissioner as by "His Excellency."

The latter, invited by the President to speak first, said:

' There are a considerable number of open questions between Her Majesty's Government and the Government of the South African Republic on which there is at present no sign of agreement. On the contrary, disagreements seem to increase as time goes on. . . . In my personal opinion the cause of many of the points of difference, and the most serious ones, arises out of the policy pursued by the Government of the South African Republic towards the Uitlander population of that Republic among whom many thousands are British subjects. This policy, the

bitter feeling it engenders between the Government and a section of Uitlanders, and the effect of the resulting tension in South Africa, and the feeling of sympathy in Great Britain, and even throughout the British Empire generally, with the Uitlander population, creates an irritated state of public opinion on both sides, which renders it much more difficult for the two Governments to settle their differences amicably. It is my strong conviction that if the Government of the South African Republic could now, before things get worse, of its own motion change its policy towards the Uitlanders, and take measures calculated to content the reasonable people among them, who, after all, are a great majority, such a course would not only strengthen the independence of the Republic but it would make such a better state of feeling all round that it would become far easier to settle outstanding questions between the two Governments. . . . The President, in coming here, has made a reservation as to the independence of the Republic. I cannot see that it is in any way impairing the independence of the Republic for Her Majesty's Government to support the cause of the Uitlanders as far as it is reasonable. A vast number of them are British subjects. If we had an equal number of British subjects and equally large interests in any part of the world, even in a country which was not under any conventional obligations to Her Majesty's Government we should be bound to make representations to the Government in the interests of Her Majesty's subjects, and to point out that the intense discontent of those subjects stood in the way of the cordial relations which we desire to exist between us. I know that the citizens of the South African Republic are intensely jealous of British interference in their internal affairs. What I want to impress upon the President is that if the Government of the South African Republic of its own accord, from its own sense of policy and justice, would afford a more liberal treatment to the Uitlander population, this would not increase British interference, but enormously diminish it. If the Uitlanders were in a position to help themselves they would not always be appealing to us under the Convention. . . .

"President.—I shall be brief. I have come with my commission, in the trust that Your Excellency is a man capable of conviction, to go into all points of difference. . . . I should like His Excellency to go point by point in this discussion, so that we can discuss each point that he thinks requires attention, not with a view to at once coming to a decision, but to hear each side, and we can go back on any point if necessary, and see if we can arrive at an understanding. I would like to give concessions as far as is possible and practicable, but I want to speak openly, so that His Excellency may be able to understand. I should like to say that the memorials placed before Her Majesty's Government came from those who do not speak the truth. I mean to convey that we do give concessions wherever we think it practicable to do so, and after we have discussed it in a friendly way Your Excellency will be able to judge whether I or the memorialists are right. I have said that if there are any mistakes on our side, we are willing to discuss them. Even in any matter concerning internal affairs I would be willing to listen to his advice if he said it could be removed in this way or that way. But when I show him that by the point we may be discussing our independence may be touched, I trust he will be open to conviction on that subject. . . .

"His Excellency.—I think the point which it would be best to take first, if the President agrees, . . . would be the Franchise. . . . There are a number of questions more or less resting upon that. . . . I should like to know a little more about the President's views. I want to know more because if I were to begin and say I want this, that, and the other, I know I should be told this was dictation. I do not want to formulate a scheme of my own, but I can, if necessary.

"President.—As long as I understand that it is meant in a friendly manner, and you mean to give hints, I won't take it that they are commands. It has already been arranged that you give me friendly hints and advice, and I will not take it as dictation, even though it should be on points on which I should consider you have no right to interfere. . . . I would like you to bear one point in view, namely, that all kinds of nations and languages, of nearly all powers, have rushed in at the point where the gold is to be found. In other countries . . . there are millions of old burghers, and the few that come in cannot out-vote the old burghers, but with us, those who rushed in to the gold fields are in large numbers and of all kinds, and the number of old burghers is still insignificant; therefore we are compelled to make the franchise so that they cannot all rush into it at once, and as soon as we can assure ourselves by a gradual increase of our burghers that we can safely do it, our plan was to reduce the time for anyone there to take up the franchise, and that is also my plan. . . . As His Excellency doubtless knows, I have proposed to the Volksraad that the time should be reduced by five years, and gradually as more trusted burghers join our numbers, we can, perhaps, go further. There are a number who really do not want the franchise, but they use it as pretext to egg on people with Her Majesty. . . . You must remember, also, on this subject, that the burghers in our Republic are our soldiers, who must protect the land, and that we have told these men to come and fight when we have had difficulties with the Kaffirs. They wanted the vote, but they would not come and fight. Those who were willing to help obtained the franchise, but it appears that many do not want to have it.

"His Excellency.—They did not want to take the obligations without the rights of citizenship, and in that I sympathize with them. If they should obtain that right, then naturally they would have to take those burdens upon them.

"President.—Those who want the franchise should bear the burdens.

"His Excellency.—Yes. Immediately they get the franchise they take upon themselves the obligations connected therewith."

[From this the talk wandered to the subject of commandeering, until the High Commissioner brought it back to the franchise question.]

"His Excellency.—If I made a proposal to admit strangers under such conditions as to swamp the old burghers it would be unreasonable. But the newcomers have, at present, no influence on the legislation of the Republic, which makes an enormous difference. They haven't got a single

representative. The First Volksraad consists of 28 members, and not one member represents the feelings of the large Uitlander population.

"President.—Men from any country could after two years vote for the Second Volksraad, and after two years more sit in the Second Raad. There are Englishmen who have obtained the full franchise in that way, and are eligible for the Volksraad. And now I have proposed to shorten the last ten years of the period required for the full franchise and make it five years.

"His Excellency.—There are a great many objections of the gravest kind to the process by which men may now obtain burgher rights. First of all, before he can begin the process of gradually securing burgher rights—which will be completed in 14 years at present, and in 9 years according to the President—he has to forswear his own allegiance. Take the case of a British subject, which interests me most. He takes the oath, and ceases to be a British subject by the mere fact of taking that oath; he loses all the rights of a British subject, and he would still have to wait for 12 years, and under the new plan 7 years, before he can become a full citizen of the Republic. British subjects are discouraged by such a law from attempting to get the franchise. Even if they wanted to become citizens, they would not give up their British citizenship on the chance of becoming in 12 years citizens of the Republic.

"President.—The people are the cause of that themselves. In 1870 anyone being in the land for one year had the full franchise.

"His Excellency.—That was very liberal.

"President.—In 1881, after the war of independence, some of our officials and even members of our Raad then said that they were still British subjects, although they had taken the oath of allegiance, and I had to pay back, out of the £250,000, what I had commandeered from them. That was the reason the oath had to be altered. . . .

"His Excellency.—In 1882, after all this had happened, there was a franchise law in the Transvaal, which demanded five years' residence, but it did not require the oath that is now taken. It required a simple declaration of allegiance to the State, though all this that the President refers to happened before. Why was not it necessary to introduce this alteration then?

"President.—The people who, before the annexation, had taken that oath, but had not forsworn their nationality, 1887, sent a lying memorial, as they are sending lying memorials now, to say that everybody was satisfied, as they now say that everybody is dissatisfied.

"His Excellency.—I think I must just explain a little more clearly my views on the point we are now discussing. . . . I think it is unreasonable to ask a man to forswear one citizenship unless in the very act of giving up one he gets another, and I think it is also unnecessary to ask him to do more than take an oath of fealty to the new State, of willingness to obey its laws and to defend its independence, when it is known and certain that the taking of that oath deprives him of his existing citizenship. I think the oath should be a simple oath of allegiance, and that it should not be required of a man until the moment he can get full rights in a new State. Now that was the position under the law of 1882, and all these reasons which the President has been giving are based on what happened before that. Why were they not considered and acted upon when the law of 1882 was made ? . . . As for the period required to qualify for the full franchise, I do not see why the length of time should be longer in the South African Republic than in any other South African State. They are all new countries. In the new country which is springing up in the north, and which is getting a new Constitution this year, the period is one year. The people who have conquered that country for the white race may find that the newcomers are more numerous than they are. But I do not expect that anything like that will be done in the South African Republic ; something far short of that would be reasonable. What I do think and desire, and that is the object of my suggestion, is this: that the numerous foreign population engaged in commerce and industry—to which the country, after all, owes its present great position in wealth and influence—should have a real share in the government of the Republic, not to over-rule the old burghers —not at all—but to share the work of Government with them, to give them the benefit of their knowledge and experience, which is in many cases greater than that of the old burghers, so that through their gradual co-operation a time may come when, instead of being divided into two separate communities they will all be burghers of the same State. It is not enough that a few people should be let in. It is obvious, however, that you could not let in the whole crowd, without character or anything— I do not ask it—but you want such a substantial measure that in elections of members of the Volksraad the desires of the new industrial population should have reasonable consideration. They have not got it now, and when the questions that interest them come before the Volksraad it is too evident that they are discussed from an outside point of view. The industrial population are regarded as strangers. . . . I do not want to swamp the old population, but it is perfectly possible to give the new population an immediate voice in the legislation, and yet to leave the old burghers in such a position that they cannot possibly be swamped.

"President.—I hope you will be open to conviction on that point. I would like to convince you on the subject, and to show you that it would be virtually to give up the independence of my burghers. In the Republic the majority of the enfranchised burghers consider they are the masters. Our enfranchised burghers are probably about 30,000, and the newcomers may be from 60,000 to 70,000, and if we give them the franchise to-morrow we may as well give up the Republic. I hope you will clearly see that I shall not get it through with my people. We can still consult about the form of oath, but we cannot make the time too short, because we would never get it through with the people—they have had bitter experience. I hope His Excellency will think about what I have said, and weigh it well.

"His Excellency.—I see your point, and want to meet it.

"President.—I will think over what has been said, and will try and meet every difficulty.

At the opening of the Conference on the second day the President spoke of reports of an increase of British forces in South Africa, which the High Commissioner assured him were untrue. The latter in turn referred to accounts that had appeared of an extensive purchase of arms in the Transvaal ; and was assured by the President that the armament of the burghers was only for their proper preparation to deal with the surrounding natives. The President then produced a memorial purporting to be signed by 21,000 Uitlanders, contradictory of the representations contained in the memorial sent to the Queen in March (see above). After discussion upon this, the conversation returned to the question of the franchise.

"His Excellency.—What makes this whole discussion so difficult is the intense prejudice on the side of the present burghers, and their intense suspicion of us. They think Her Majesty's Government wants to get their country back in one way or another. Her Majesty's Government does not ; but what it does desire is that it should have such a state of rest in the country as will remove causes of friction and difficulty between the Republic and Her Majesty's possessions in South Africa, and the whole of the British Empire, and my suggestions here are directed to that end. I do not want to say it over and over again, I say it once for all. . . .

"President.—I should like to make a slight explanation to His Excellency. His Excellency yesterday mentioned that in some States those going in from outside speedily got burgher rights, but he must not forget, as I said before, they are glad of the people who come in. But, here we have all nations and all kinds, and if they were to get burgher rights quickly then that would be the end of our independence, and then they could send us away where they liked. I would like His Excellency to bear that in mind.

"His Excellency.—I do not see how the old burghers can have it both ways. They cannot have a very large population streaming in to develop the resources of the country, and giving it a much higher position in the world than it would otherwise have, and at the same time exclude these people from participation in the Government of the country.

"President.—Your Excellency must bear this in mind. There is no Gold Law in the world that is so liberal as that of the Republic."

The President then recurred to the right which the Uitlanders might obtain, of voting for the Second Volksraad after two years, and becoming eligible to seats in it after four years, and said that it was in the Second Volksraad that their own interests were dealt with—not in the First. The High Commissioner asked if the Second Raad could act without consent of the First. The President acknowledged that the latter could alter any law which "appears to be against the general welfare," but contended that it had no wish to go into gold field matters, though it has the power, and that it had interfered with action of the Second Raad in but three or four instances. The High Commissioner remarked that Uitlanders who abandoned their own nationality to wait years for full citizenship in the Republic might have the latter prospect taken away from them at any moment by a single resolution of the First Raad. The President replied : " They haven't done it yet. The legislatures of all the world have the same power." To which the High Commissioner made answer: "This power existing, the new comers cannot be expected—I should not recommend one of them—to give up his present citizenship for the mere chance of becoming a citizen of the new country."

"His Excellency.—If the President thinks we are asking too much . . . I must report to Her Majesty's Government that the President rejects our friendly suggestions.

"The President.—I would be misleading you if I should tell you that I can give all the strangers the franchise in a very short time. I would consider that our independence was sacrificed thereby: but I say this, let His Excellency keep impartially in view my points of difficulty, and let him make his proposals and submit them to us, so that we can consider them and judge about them. . . . I have already said that perhaps means may be found to alter the form of oath. . . . I would now like His Excellency to propose a scheme.

"His Excellency.— . . . What I suggest is this: That every foreigner who can prove satisfactorily that he has been resident in the country for five years, and that he desires to make it his permanent place of residence, that he is prepared to take the oath to obey the laws, to undertake all the obligations of citizenship, and to defend the independence of the country, should be allowed to become a citizen on taking that oath. This should be confined to persons possessing a certain amount of property, or a certain amount of yearly wages, and who have good characters. In order to make that proposal of any real use for the new citizens who mostly live in one district in the Republic, and a district which only returns one member in 28 to the First Raad, and one in 28 to the Second Raad, I propose that there should be a certain number of new constituencies created, the number of which is a detail upon the discussion of which I will not now enter. But what is vital from my point of view is that the number of these districts should not be so small as to leave the representatives of the new population in a contemptible minority.

"President.—With us the majority of the enfranchised burghers constitutes the ruling voice, and must be listened to in the Volksraad. If the 60,000 came in immediately, they would swamp the 30,000. . . . I mean this: that if they are all enfranchised then they would at once form the majority of the whole population, and the majority of enfranchised burghers, according to our law, must be listened to by the Volksraad; since in a Republic we cannot leave the sovereign voice out of account.

"His Excellency.—This is pure theory, that the Volksraad have to do what the majority of the people desire. The Volksraad does what it considers right in its own eyes: it is elected by the people, and does what it thinks right, and the President has made it quite clear during the last year or two that anything the Volksraad does is law."

At an afternoon meeting on the same day, there was a long discussion of the dynamite grievance of the Uitlanders, and the President wished to bring up other points; but the High Commissioner objected:

"His Excellency.—I think the discussion will be of interminable length if we are to proceed in this way, and if we cannot approach one another on the point on which I have made my suggestions, and which lies outside all the pending questions between the two Governments, these other controversies may as well be allowed to go on in the usual course. If the President to-morrow will give me an answer on the first subject I raised, and then wishes to bring forward his grievances, I will consider them to-morrow. I do not want to go on with a long list of my own until I understand what is the basis on which I stand in regard to what I consider the most important question of all.

"President.—I think it would be as well if we returned in a little while to discuss our points, but I would like to give His Excellency some things to think over. The first point I would like to mention is my wish that Swaziland should now be handed over to me as a portion of my land. . . . Secondly, the demand made with regard to the damages for the Jameson Raid, Mr. Chamberlain said he was against paying the million, but he is not against paying the expenses incurred. Thirdly, that differences such as those now existing between us, should be settled by arbitration, and then no war or quarrel could arise between us. . . . These are some of the questions I wish His Excellency to think about."

At the opening of the Conference on the third day, the President sought to commit the High Commissioner to an "understanding," that "if we came," he said, "to some agreement on the franchise Her Majesty's Government then would engage not in any way to concern itself with internal affairs in the Republic any longer, and that in future questions that then may arise, whether out of the Convention or otherwise, Her Majesty would agree to have such questions referred to arbitration." The High Commissioner declined to deal with the subject of the franchise as a matter of "bargain." It was a subject of grievances and discontent, dangerous to the Republic and dangerous to the relations between the Republic and Great Britain, which ought to be dealt with on its merits alone. Nevertheless, after some controversy, he said:

"His Excellency.— . . . As far as the Jameson Indemnity is concerned I know that a despatch is on the way to me at this present moment, which forwards a statement from the British South Africa Company examining the details of the claim which has been sent in, and asking that the question of the amount payable in respect of the Raid may be submitted to arbitration. I have received a telegram that that despatch is coming. The position is this—the British Government have admitted in principle that the Company must pay what is fairly due on account of that raid; but the question of the amount is still under discussion, and I hope that this proposal will lead to a settlement. As to the question of arbitration, which I think is the matter that interests the President most, I am in so far entirely with him that I want if possible to have in future as few questions to discuss with the Government of the South African Republic, as I now have with the Government of the Orange Free State. I feel that the President will need, if he accepts my scheme of franchise, or any other similar proposal, to have some assurance that there shall not be perpetual controversies between him and England, and that if there are controversies, some regular way of dealing with them should be devised. The President once proposed that some question, or a number of questions, should be submitted to the President of the Swiss Republic. The British Government refused that on the general principle—from which I am sure they will not depart—that they will not have any foreign Government, or any foreign interference at all, between them and the South African Republic. But if some other method can be devised of submitting to an impartial tribunal questions that may in future arise between us, and perhaps even some questions which exist at present—but in any case to provide for the future—if such a plan can be devised and suggested to me, I will lay it before Her Majesty's Government and do what I can personally to assist in a satisfactory solution of the matter. The President must understand that I cannot pledge Her Majesty's Government in any way on this subject. The question has taken me by surprise; I did n't come here contemplating a discussion on it, but I must say if it could be satisfactorily arranged while excluding the interference of the foreigner, it would seem to me to open a way out of many difficulties. But all the same, I adhere firmly to my proposal that we should first try and settle on the scheme which the President would accept as regards the matter which I put forward."

At the close of the morning interview, both parties expressed hopelessness of agreement. On meeting again in the afternoon, the President submitted in writing the following proposals concerning the franchise: "As the purpose I had in view at this Conference principally consists in the removal of existing grounds of disagreement and further to provide for the friendly regulation of the way of settling future disputes by means of arbitration, the following proposals with regard to the franchise must be considered as conditional and dependent on the satisfactory settlement of the first mentioned points, and on the request that my request to incorporate Swaziland in the South African Republic shall be submitted by the High Commissioner to Her Majesty's Government. Subject to the foregoing I undertake to submit without delay to the approval of the Volksraad and the people the following proposals about the franchise:

" I. Every person who fixes his residence in the South African Republic has to get himself registered on the Field-cornets' books within fourteen days after his arrival according to the existing law ; will be able after complying with the conditions mentioned under 'A.,' and after the lapse of two years to get himself naturalised ; and will five years after naturalisation, on complying with the conditions mentioned under 'B.,' obtain the full franchise.

" A.—1. Six months' notice of intention to apply for naturalisation ; 2. Two years' continued registration ; 3. Residence in the South African Republic during that period ; 4. No dishonouring sentence ; 5. Proof of obedience to the laws ; no act against Government or independence ; 6. Proof of full State citizenship and franchise or title thereto in former country ; 7. Possession of unmortgaged fixed property to the value of £150 approximately, or occupation of house to the rental of £50 per annum, or yearly income of at least £200. Nothing, however, shall prevent the Government from granting naturalisation to persons who have not satisfied this condition ; 8. Taking of an oath similar to that of the Orange Free State.

"B.—1. Continuous registration five years after naturalisation ; 2. Continuous residence during that period ; 3. No dishonouring sentence ; 4. Proof of obedience to the laws, &c. ; 5. Proof that applicant still complies with the condition A (7).

" II. Furthermore, the full franchise shall be obtained in the following manner : — (a.) Those who have fixed their residence in the South African Republic before the taking effect of Act 4, 1890, and who get themselves naturalised within six months after the taking effect of this Act on complying with the conditions under 1A, shall obtain the full franchise two years after such naturalisation on proof of compliance with the conditions mentioned under 1B (altering the five into two years). Those who do not get themselves naturalised within six months under Article 1, (b.) Those who have been resident in the South African Republic for two years or more can get themselves immediately naturalised on compliance with the conditions under 1A., and shall five years after naturalisation obtain the full franchise on compliance with the conditions under 1B. (c.) Those who have been already naturalised shall five years after naturalisation obtain the full franchise on compliance with the conditions under 1B."

At the meeting next day, the High Commissioner presented to the President a written memorandum in reply to the proposals of the latter. He admitted that "the scheme proposed is a considerable advance upon the existing provisions as to franchise," but said that he could not recommend its acceptance as adequate to the needs of the case. "Under this plan," he continued, "no man who is not already naturalised, even if he has been in the country 13 or 14 years, will get a vote for the First Volksraad in less than 2½ years from the passing of the new law. There will be no considerable number of people obtaining that vote in less than five years, that is if they come in and naturalise. But I fear the majority of them will not come in, because the scheme retains that unfortunate provision, first introduced in 1890, by which, owing to the two stages—first, naturalisation with a partial franchise, and then, after five years, full franchise—a man has to abandon his old citizenship before he becomes a full-fledged citizen of his new country. My plan avoided this. My doctrine is that, however long a period of residence you fix before a man becomes a citizen of your State, you should admit him, once for all, to full rights on taking the oath of allegiance. And this is especially important in the South African Republic, because, owing to the facility and frequency with which laws—even fundamental laws—are altered, the man who takes the oath and thereby loses his old country will never feel quite sure that something may not happen in the interval, when he is only half a citizen, to prevent his becoming a whole one. The vote for the First Volksraad is the essential point. According to the present constitution of the Transvaal, the First Volksraad and the President really are the State. But under this scheme it will be a considerable time before any number of Uitlanders worth mentioning can vote for the First Volksraad, and even then they will only command one or two seats. My point was to give them at once a few representatives. They might be a minority, even a small minority. I have said over and over again I do not want to swamp the old burghers. But as long as the representatives of the new comers are entirely excluded from the supreme legislative council, they will, as a body, remain an inferior caste. The co-operation and gradual blending of the two sections of the population will not take place. The old separation and hostility will continue. I see no prospect here of that concord to which I had looked both to bring about a more progressive system of government, and to remove causes of friction between the Government of the South African Republic and Great Britain. For these reasons I regret to say the scheme seems to me so inadequate that I think it would be wasting the time of the Conference to discuss its details."

The President rejoined in another memorandum, which added one more to his former proposals, namely this: "I am ready to propose and to recommend to the First Volksraad to increase the number of members of the First Volksraad, whereby the Gold Fields will be represented by five, instead of as now by two, members."

The response to this by the High Commissioner was a review, at length, of all that had been proposed, leading to the conclusion which he expressed as follows: "If I am asked whether I think they will satisfy the Uitlander community, and are calculated to relieve the British Government from further solicitude on the score of its Uitlander subjects, I cannot answer in the affirmative. Still less can I encourage the idea that the British Government can be asked to give something in exchange for such legislation as the President proposes. My own proposal was put forward in no bargaining spirit. I asked myself, in advancing it, what is the smallest measure of reform that will really be of any use, that is to say, which will allay the present unrest and enable the Uitlanders to exercise within a reasonable time an appreciable influence on the Government of the country. It was in that spirit that I suggested the outline of a scheme, intentionally not working it out in detail (for I was ready to listen as to details), but indicating a certain minimum from which I am not prepared to depart. . . . When I came here I came in the hope that I might be able to report to Her Majesty's Government that measures were about to be adopted which would lead to such an improvement in the situation as to relieve Her Majesty's Government from pressing for the redress of particular grievances on the ground that the most serious causes of complaint would now gradually be removed from within. I do not feel that what His Honour has seen his way to propose in the matter of franchise or what he indicates as the extreme length to which he might, at some future time, be willing to go in the extension of local government is sufficient to justify me in reporting in that sense."

The Conference was ended by a last memorandum from the President, in which he said: "As it is my earnest wish that this Conference should not be fruitless, I wish to make the following proposal to His Excellency, viz. :—As according to his own admission my proposal about franchise is an important step in the right direction, I shall be prepared to lay my proposal before the Volksraad and to recommend it, even though His Excellency does not fully agree with it. From his side I shall then expect that His Excellency will lay before and recommend to Her Majesty's

Government my request about arbitration on future matters of difference under the Convention. His Excellency will, however, readily understand that if Her Majesty's Government should not meet me so far, so as to grant my acknowledged fair request for arbitration, it could be with difficulty expected that the people of the South African Republic would approve of my comprehensive proposal with regard to franchise."—*Great Britain, Papers by Command: 1899, C. 9404.*

The Transvaal: A. D. 1899 (May—August). —Advice to President Kruger from Cape Afrikanders, and from Holland and Germany.—Several private letters written at the time of these occurrences by Sir J. H. De Villiers, a leading Afrikander, Chief Justice of Cape Colony, and one of the Commissioners who negotiated the Convention of 1881, addressed to persons who might have influence with President Kruger, were made public a year later. In the first of these letters, written to President Steyn of the Orange Free State, on the 21st of May, 1899, Justice De Villiers used strong expressions, as follows: "On my recent visit to Pretoria I did not visit the President as I considered it hopeless to think of making any impression on him, but I saw Reitz, Smuts, and Schalk Burger, who, I thought, would be amenable to argument, but I fear that either my advice had no effect on them, or else their opinion had no weight with the President. I urged upon them to advise the President to open the Volksraad with promises of a liberal franchise and drastic reforms. It would have been so much better if these had come voluntarily from the Government instead of being gradually forced from them. In the former case they would rally the greater number of the malcontents around them, in the latter case no gratitude will be felt to the Republic for any concessions made by it. Besides, there can be no doubt that as the alien population increases, as it undoubtedly will, their demands will increase with their discontent, and ultimately a great deal more will have to be conceded than will now satisfy them. The franchise proposal made by the President seems to be simply ridiculous. I am quite certain that if in 1881 it had been known to my fellow Commissioners that the President would adopt his retrogressive policy, neither President Brand nor I would ever have induced them to consent to sign the Convention. They would have advised the Secretary of State to let matters revert to the condition in which they were before peace was concluded; in other words, to recommence the war. . . . If I had any influence with the President I would advise him no longer to sit on the boiler to prevent it from bursting. Some safety-valves are required for the activities of the new population. In their irritation they abuse the Government, often unjustly, in the press, and send petitions to the Queen; but that was only to be expected. Let the Transvaal Legislature give them a liberal franchise and allow them local self-government for their towns, and some portion of the discontent will be allayed. The enemies of the Transvaal will not be satisfied; on the contrary, the worst service that can be done to them is the redress of the grievance, but it is the friends of the country who should be considered."

On the 31st of July, the Justice wrote still more urgently and impatiently to a Mr. Fischer, who was in close relations with the Transvaal President: "I do not think that President Kruger and his friends realize the gravity of the situation. Even now the State Secretary is doing things which would be almost farcical if the times were not so serious. Some time ago I begged of him to drop the censorship of telegrams because it serves no useful purpose and only delays the publication of lies by a few days. His answer was that the Government should not disseminate lies by its own wires. He might as well have said Government should not disseminate lies by its own post-office. To crown all, I see that he has now gone so far as to stop a private telegram (which had been paid for) because it contained a lie. I really do not know where he is going to stop or whether he intends to guarantee that all telegrams allowed to pass contain the truth and nothing but the truth. Could you not induce him to stop such childish nonsense? The Transvaal will soon not have a single friend left among the cultivated classes. Then there is the Franchise Bill, which is so obscure that the State Attorney had to issue an explanatory memorandum to remove the obscurities. But surely a law should be clear enough to speak for itself, and no Government or Court of Law will be bound by the State Attorney's explanations. I do not know what those explanations are, but the very fact that they are required condemns the Bill. That Bill certainly does not seem quite to carry out the promises made to you, Mr. Hofmeyr, and Mr. Herholdt. The time really has come when the friends of the Transvaal must induce President Kruger to become perfectly frank and take the newcomers into his confidence. It may be a bitter pill to have to swallow in yielding to further demands, but it is quite clear to the world that he would not have done as much as he has done if pressure had not been applied. What one fears is that he will do things in such a way as to take away all grace from his concessions. Try to induce him to meet Mr. Chamberlain in a friendly manner and at once remove all the causes of unrest which have disturbed this unhappy country for so many years. As one who signed the Convention in 1881, I can assure you that my fellow Commissioners would not have signed it if they had not been led to believe that President Kruger's policy towards the Uitlanders would have been very different from what it has been."

Three confidential despatches sent to President Kruger, in the same period, by the Minister for Foreign Affairs in the Netherlands government were laid before the States General at The Hague, October 25, 1900, and made public through Reuter's press agency, as follows: "In the first despatch, which is dated May 13, 1899, the Minister states that news received from different capitals leads him to believe in the imminence of the danger of a violent solution of the problem in South Africa. As a faithful friend he counsels Mr. Kruger in the true interests of the Republic to show himself as conciliatory and moderate as possible, and adds that he learns from a trustworthy source that the German Government fully shares that opinion. Mr. Kruger replied that he had always been conciliatory and did not desire war, but that he could not sacrifice the independence of the Republic. He was willing enough to grant the suffrage, but he could not tolerate Englishmen remaining subjects of the Queen while receiving at the same time the right to vote in the Republic. In the second despatch, dated August 4, 1899, the Netherlands Minister for Foreign Affairs advised President Kruger, in the interests of the country, not to refuse peremptorily the British proposal for an international commission. Mr. Kruger replied that the commission would not be international, but an Anglo-Transvaal commission. He intended to ask for further information from Great Britain as to the scope and composition of the commission, and did not mean to give a decided refusal. Finally, the Netherlands Minister, in a telegram dated August 15, 1899, stated that the German Government entirely shared his opinion as to the inadvisability of declining the English proposal, adding that the German Government, like himself, was convinced that any request to one of the Great Powers at such a critical moment would be barren of result and highly dangerous to the Republic. To this Mr. Kruger replied that the British proposal would result in very direct interference by the English in the internal affairs of the Republic. He added that he had no intention of appealing to a Great Power."

Speaking in the German Reichsrath, on the 10th of December, 1900, the Imperial Chancellor, Count von Bülow, referred to the above publications by the Dutch government, and confirmed them, saying that it was in accordance with the views of the German Government that the Dutch Foreign Minister "strongly advised Mr. Kruger to maintain a moderate attitude. In June, 1899, Mr. Kruger was advised by Germany through the Dutch Government to invite mediation, but Dr. Leyds informed the Dutch Minister in Paris that Mr. Kruger did not consider 'that the moment had yet come for applying for the mediation of America.' Some time afterwards Mr. Kruger made the attempt to obtain arbitration, but 'feeling had become too heated,' and in August Mr. Kruger complained to the Dutch Government that arbitration could not be arranged. The answer to this complaint is given in the Dutch Yellow-book under the date of August 15, 1899, and points out that the German Government would at that date have regarded any appeal to a Great Power as hopeless and as very dangerous for the Republics. The German Government also shared the Dutch view that Mr. Kruger ought not to reject the English proposal then before him."

The Transvaal: A. D. 1899 (July—September).—Amendment of the Franchise Law.—After much discussion and many changes, an amended Franchise Law was adopted by the First Volksraad of the Republic and published on the 26th of July. It conceded to foreigners who had already been resident in the Republic for seven years a possibility of obtaining full burgher rights simultaneously with the taking of the oath of allegiance, but subjected the proceeding to conditions which would make it, in Uitlander opinion, of service to very few. The judgment of Sir Alfred Milner, the High Commissioner, as expressed to Secretary Chamberlain, was to the effect that "the bill, as it stands, leaves it practically in the hands of the Government of the South African Republic to enfranchise or not enfranchise the Uitlanders as it chooses. If worked in a liberal spirit, its clumsy and unreasonable provisions may be got over.

But if it is to be enforced rigidly, there will be practically unlimited opportunities of excluding persons whom the Government may consider undesirable, nor does the tone of the debate in the Raad leave much doubt as to the spirit in which some at least of the authors of the Bill would like to see it worked." His criticism applied especially to the certificate required from every applicant. " The certificate," he said, " which every applicant must obtain from three different officials, as to (a) continuous registration and domicile, (b) obedience to the laws, (c) committing no crime against the independence of the country, is one which these officials, even if well disposed, would be able in hardly any case to give. None of them can have any such knowledge of the Uitlander population as would enable them to give this comprehensive certificate; it is acknowledged that some of the Johannesburg lists have been lost; and the Field-cornet has, I believe, held his present office for less than four years." Moreover, a requirement of "continuous" registration "may mean," said the High Commissioner, "(and I cannot understand what else it could mean) registration for seven years in one ward and district ; so that a person having resided and been registered in one district and subsequently removed to another would forfeit the benefit of his first period of residence. Even if this were not so, he would doubtless have to get a double set of certificates."

Simultaneously with the publication of the new Franchise Law it was announced that the Executive Council had decided to give the Witwatersrand Gold Fields a representation of five members (out of 31) in the First Volksraad, as well as representation by the same number in the Second Volksraad. To the British Agent at Pretoria, Mr. Conyngham Greene, this seemed to be "so wholly inadequate as not to be worthy of serious consideration."

In view of the complexities and uncertainties involved in the new Franchise Law, the High Commissioner addressed the following communication to the government of the South African Republic. August 1 : " Her Majesty's Government authorize me to invite President South African Republic to appoint delegates to discuss with delegates to be appointed by me on behalf of Her Majesty's Government, whether Uitlander population will be given immediate and substantial representation by franchise law recently passed by Volksraad, together with other measures connected with it, such as increase of seats, and, if not, what additions or alterations may be necessary to secure that result. In this discussion it should be understood that the delegates of Her Majesty's Government would be free to make any suggestions calculated to improve measures in question and secure their attaining the end desired."

The reply to this proposal was given by the Boer government to the British Agent at Pretoria in two notes, the first, dated August 19, as follows : "With reference to your proposal for a joint enquiry contained in your despatches of the 2nd and 3rd August, Government of South African Republic have the honour to suggest the following alternative proposal for consideration of Her Majesty's Government, which this Government trusts may lead to a final settlement. (1.) The Government are willing to recommend

to the Volksraad and the people a 5 years' retrospective franchise, as proposed by His Excellency the High Commissioner on the 1st June, 1899. (2.) The Government are further willing to recommend to the Volksraad that 8 new seats in the First Volksraad, and, if necessary, also in the Second Volksraad, be given to the population of the Witwatersrand, thus with the 2 sitting members for the Goldfields giving to the population thereof 10 representatives in a Raad of 36, and in future the representation of the Goldfields of this Republic shall not fall below the proportion of one-fourth of the total. (3.) The new Burghers shall equally with the old Burghers be entitled to vote at the election for State President and Commandant-General. (4.) This Government will always be prepared to take into consideration such friendly suggestions regarding the details of the Franchise Law as Her Majesty's Government, through the British Agent, may wish to convey to it. (5.) In putting forward the above proposals Government of South African Republic assumes : (a) That Her Majesty's Government will agree that the present intervention shall not form a precedent for future similar action and that in the future no interference in the internal affairs of the Republic will take place. (b) That Her Majesty's Government will not further insist on the assertion of the suzerainty, the controversy on the subject being allowed tacitly to drop. (c) That arbitration (from which foreign element other than Orange Free State is to be excluded) will be conceded as soon as the franchise scheme has become law. (6.) Immediately on Her Majesty's Government accepting this proposal for a settlement, the Government will ask the Volksraad to adjourn for the purpose of consulting the people about it, and the whole scheme might become law say within a few weeks. (7.) In the meantime the form and scope of the proposed Tribunal are also to be discussed and provisionally agreed upon, while the franchise scheme is being referred to the people, so that no time may be lost in putting an end to the present state of affairs. The Government trust that Her Majesty's Government will clearly understand that in the opinion of this Government the existing Franchise Law of this Republic is both fair and liberal to the new population, and that the consideration that induces them to go further, as they do in the above proposals, is their strong desire to get the controversies between the two Governments settled, and further to put an end to present strained relations between the two Governments and the incalculable harm and loss it has already occasioned in South Africa, and to prevent a racial war from the effects of which South Africa may not recover for many generations, perhaps never at all, and therefore this Government, having regard to all these circumstances would highly appreciate it if Her Majesty's Government, seeing the necessity of preventing the present crisis from developing still further and the urgency of an early termination of the present state of affairs, would expedite the acceptance or refusal of the settlement here offered. (Signed) F. W. REITZ."—The second note, which followed on the 21st of August, was in these terms: " In continuation of my despatch of the 19th instant and with reference to the communication to you of the State Attorney this morning, I wish to forward to you the following in explanation thereof, with the request that the same may be telegraphed to His Excellency the High Commissioner for South Africa, as forming part of the proposals of this Government embodied in the above-named despatch. (1.) The proposals of this Government regarding question of franchise and representation contained in that despatch must be regarded as expressly conditional on Her Majesty's Government consenting to the points set forth in paragraph 5 of the despatch, viz.: (a) In future not to interfere in internal affairs of the South African Republic. (b) Not to insist further on its assertion of existence of suzerainty. (c) To agree to arbitration. (2.) Referring to paragraph 6 of the despatch, this Government trusts that it is clear to Her Majesty's Government as to this question that this Government has not consulted the Volksraad as to this question and will only do so when an affirmative reply to its proposals has been received from Her Majesty's Government. (Signed) F. W. REITZ."

The above notes were repeated by cable, in full, to the Colonial Secretary, at London, and, on the 28th of August, he returned by the same medium his reply, as follows: "Her Majesty's Government have considered the proposals which the South African Republic Government in their notes to the British Agent of 19th and 21st August have put forward as an alternative to those contained in my telegram of 31st July. Her Majesty's Government assume that the adoption in principle of the franchise proposals made by you at Bloemfontein will not be hampered by any conditions which would impair their effect, and that by proposed increase of seats for the Goldfields and by other provisions the South African Republic Government intend to grant immediate and substantial representation of the Uitlanders. That being so, Her Majesty's Government are unable to appreciate the objections entertained by the Government of the South African Republic to a Joint Commission of Inquiry into the complicated details and technical questions upon which the practical effect of the proposals depends. Her Majesty's Government, however, will be ready to agree that the British Agent, assisted by such other persons as you may appoint, shall make the investigation necessary to satisfy them that the result desired will be achieved and, failing this, to enable them to make those suggestions which the Government of the South African Republic state that they will be prepared to take into consideration. Her Majesty's Government assume that every facility will be given to the British Agent by the Government of the South African Republic, and they would point out that the inquiry will be both easier and shorter if the Government of the South African Republic will omit in any future Law the complicated conditions of registration, qualification and behaviour which accompanied previous proposals, and would have entirely nullified their beneficial effect. Her Majesty's Government hope that the Government of the South African Republic will wait to receive their suggestions founded on the report of the British Agent's investigation before submitting a new Franchise Law to the Volksraad and the Burghers. With regard to the conditions of the Government of the South African Republic: First, as regards intervention; Her Majesty's Government hope that the fulfilment of the promises made and the just treatment of the Uitlanders in future

will render unnecessary any further intervention on their behalf, but Her Majesty's Government cannot of course debar themselves from their rights under the Conventions nor divest themselves of the ordinary obligations of a civilized Power to protect its subjects in a foreign country from injustice. Secondly, with regard to suzerainty Her Majesty's Government would refer the Government of the South African Republic to the second paragraph of my despatch of 13th July. Thirdly, Her Majesty's Government agree to a discussion of the form and scope of a Tribunal of Arbitration from which foreigners and foreign influence are excluded. Such a discussion, which will be of the highest importance to the future relations of the two countries, should be carried on between the President and yourself, and for this purpose it appears to be necessary that a further Conference, which Her Majesty's Government suggest should be held at Cape Town, should be at once arranged. Her Majesty's Government also desire to remind the Government of the South African Republic that there are other matters of difference between the two Governments which will not be settled by the grant of political representation to the Uitlanders, and which are not proper subjects for reference to arbitration. It is necessary that these should be settled concurrently with the questions now under discussion, and they will form, with the question of arbitration, proper subjects for consideration at the proposed Conference."

On the 2d of September the Boer government replied to this at length, stating that it considered the proposal made in its note of August 19 to have lapsed; again objecting to a joint inquiry relative to the practical working of the Franchise Law, but adding: "If they [the Government] can be of assistance to Her Majesty's Government with any information or explanation they are always ready to furnish this; though it appears to it that the findings of a unilateral Commission, especially when arrived at before the working of the law has been duly tested, would be premature and thus probably of little value."

Meantime, on the 31st of August, Sir Alfred Milner had telegraphed to Mr. Chamberlain: "I am receiving representations from many quarters to urge Her Majesty's Government to terminate the state of suspense. Hitherto I have hesitated to address you on the subject, lest Her Majesty's Government should think me impatient. But I feel bound to let you know that I am satisfied, from inquiries made in various reliable quarters that the distress is now really serious. The most severe suffering is at Johannesburg. Business there is at a standstill; many traders have become insolvent; and others are only kept on their legs by the leniency of their creditors. Even the mines, which have been less affected hitherto, are now suffering owing to the withdrawal of workmen, both European and native. The crisis also affects the trading centres in the Colony. In spite of this, the purport of all the representations made to me is to urge prompt and decided action; not to deprecate further interference on the part of Her Majesty's Government. British South Africa is prepared for extreme measures, and is ready to suffer much in order to see the vindication of British authority. It is prolongation of the negotiations, endless and indecisive of result, that is dreaded."

On the 8th of September, the High Commissioner was instructed by Mr. Chamberlain to communicate the following to the government of the Transvaal : "Her Majesty's Government are still prepared to accept the offer made in paragraphs 1, 2, and 3 of the note of the 19th August taken by themselves, provided that the inquiry which Her Majesty's Government have proposed, whether joint—as Her Majesty's Government originally suggested—or unilateral, shows that the new scheme of representation will not be encumbered by conditions which will nullify the intention to give substantial and immediate representation to the Uitlanders. In this connection Her Majesty's Government assume that, as stated to the British Agent, the new members of the Raad will be permitted to use their own language. The acceptance of these terms by the Government of the South African Republic would at once remove the tension between the two Governments, and would in all probability render unnecessary any further intervention on the part of Her Majesty's Government to secure the redress of grievances which the Uitlanders would themselves be able to bring to the notice of the Executive and the Raad."

In a lengthy response to this by State Secretary Reitz, September 16, the following are the essential paragraphs: "However earnestly this Government also desires to find an immediate and satisfactory course by which existing tension should be brought to an end, it feels itself quite unable, as desired, to recommend or propose to South African Republic Volksraad and people the part of its proposal contained in paragraphs 1, 2, and 3 of its note 19th August, omitting the conditions on the acceptance of which alone the offer was based, but declares itself always still prepared to abide by its acceptance of the invitation [of] Her Majesty's Government to get a Joint Commission composed as intimated in its note of 2nd September. It considers that if conditions are contained in the existing franchise law which has been passed, and in the scheme of representation, which might tend to frustrate object contemplated, that it will attract the attention of the Commission, and thus be brought to the knowledge of this Government. This Government has noticed with surprise the assertion that it had intimated to British Agent that the new members to be chosen for South African Republic Volksraad would be allowed to use their own language. If it is thereby intended that this Government would have agreed that any other than the language of the country would have been used in the deliberations of the Volksraad, it wishes to deny same in the strongest manner."

Practically the discussion was ended by a despatch from the British Colonial Secretary, September 22d, in which he said : "Her Majesty's Government have on more than one occasion repeated their assurances that they have no desire to interfere in any way with independence of South African Republic, provided that the conditions on which it was granted are honourably observed in the spirit and in the letter, and they have offered as part of a general settlement to give a complete guarantee against any attack upon that independence, either from within any part of the British dominions or from the terri-

tory of a foreign State. They have not asserted any rights of interference in the internal affairs of the Republic other than those which are derived from the Conventions between the two countries or which belong to every neighbouring Government (and especially to one which has a largely predominant interest in the adjacent territories) for the protection of its subjects and of its adjoining possessions." Referring to his despatch of September 8, the Secretary concluded : "The refusal of the Government of the South African Republic to entertain the offer thus made, coming as it does at the end of nearly four months of protracted negotiations, themselves the climax of an agitation extending over a period of more than five years, makes it useless to further pursue a discussion on the lines hitherto followed, and Her Majesty's Government are now compelled to consider the situation afresh, and to formulate their own proposals for a final settlement of the issues which have been created in South Africa by the policy constantly followed for many years by the Government of the South African Republic. They will communicate to you the result of their deliberations in a later despatch."—*Great Britain, Papers by Command :* 1899, *C.* 9518, 9521, 9530.

Orange Free State: A. D. 1899 (September —October).—The Free State makes common cause with the South African Republic.—On the 27th of September, President Steyn communicated to the British High Commissioner a resolution adopted that day by the Orange Free State Volksraad, instructing the government to continue efforts for peaceful settlement of differences between the South African Republic and Great Britain, but concluding with the declaration that "if a war is now begun or occasioned by Her Majesty's Government against South African Republic, this would morally be a war against the whole of white population of South Africa and would in its results be calamitous and criminal, and further, that Orange Free State will honestly and faithfully observe its obligations towards South African Republic arising out of the political alliance between the two Republics whatever may happen."

On the 11th of October, the High Commissioner communicated to President Steyn the ultimatum that he received from the South African Republic, and asked: "In view of Resolution of Volksraad of Orange Free State communicated to me in Your Honour's telegram of 27th September I have the honour to request that I may be informed at Your Honour's earliest possible convenience whether this action on the part of the South African Republic has Your Honour's concurrence and support." The reply of the Orange Free State President was as follows : "The high handed and unjustifiable policy and conduct of Her Majesty's Government in interfering in and dictating the purely internal affairs of South African Republic, constituting a flagrant breach of the Convention of London, 1884, accompanied at first by preparations, and latterly followed by active commencement of hostilities against that Republic, which no friendly and well-intentioned efforts on our part could induce Her Majesty's Government to abandon, constitute such an undoubted and unjust attack on the independence of the South African Republic that no other course is left to this State than honourably to abide by its Conventional Agreements entered into with that Republic. On behalf of this Government, therefore, I beg to notify that, compelled thereto by the action of Her Majesty's Government, they intend to carry out the instructions of the Volksraad as set forth in the last part of the Resolution referred to by Your Excellency."—*Great Britain, Papers by Command:* 1899, *C.*—9530, *pp.* 38 *and* 67.

The Transvaal and Orange Free State: A. D. 1899 (September—October).—Preparations for war.—Troops massed on both sides of the frontiers.—Remonstrances of Orange Free State.—The Boer Ultimatum.—Before the controversy between Boer and Briton had reached the stage represented above, both sides were facing the prospect of war, both were bringing forces to the frontier, and each was declaring that the other had been first to take that threatening step. Which of them did first begin movements that bore a look of menace seems difficult to learn from official reports. On the 19th of September, the British High Commissioner gave notice to the President of the Orange Free State that "it has been deemed advisable by the Imperial military authorities to send detachments of the troops ordinarily stationed at Cape Town to assist in securing the line of communication between the Colony and the British territories lying to the north of it"; and "as this force, or a portion of it, may be stationed near the borders of the Orange Free State," he wished the burghers of that State to understand that the movement was in no way directed against them. Eight days later, President Steyn, of the Orange Free State, addressed a long despatch to the High Commissioner, remonstrating against the whole procedure of the British government in its dealing with the South African Republic, and alluding to the "enormous and ever increasing military preparations of the British government." On the 2d of October he announced to the Commissioner that he had "deemed it advisable, in order to allay the intense excitement and unrest amongst our burghers, arising from the totally undefended state of our border, in the presence of a continued increase and movement of troops on two sides of this State, to call up our burghers, to satisfy them that due precaution had been taken." The High Commissioner replied on the 3d: "Your Honour must be perfectly well aware that all the movements of British troops which have taken place in this country since the beginning of present troubles, which have been necessitated by the natural alarm of the inhabitants in exposed districts, are not comparable in magnitude with the massing of armed forces by government of South African Republic on the borders of Natal." Some days previous to this, on the 29th of September, Secretary Chamberlain had cabled from London to Sir Alfred Milner : "Inform President of Orange Free State that what he describes as the enormous and ever-increasing military preparations of Great Britain have been forced upon Her Majesty's Government by the policy of the South African Republic, which has transformed the Transvaal into a permanent armed camp, threatening the peace of the whole of South Africa and the position of Great Britain as the paramount State."

On the 9th of October the High Commissioner received another telegram from the President of the Orange Free State, of which he cabled the substance to London as follows: "He demurs to statement that military preparations of Her Majesty's Government have been necessitated by conversion of South African Republic into an armed camp. Her Majesty's Government must be entirely misinformed and it would be regrettable if, through such misunderstanding, present state of extreme tension were allowed to continue. Though Her Majesty's Government may regard precautions taken by South African Republic after Jameson Raid as excessive, Government of South African Republic cannot be blamed for adopting them, in view of large Uitlander population constantly being stirred up, through hostile press, to treason and rebellion by persons and organizations financially or politically interested in overthrowing the Government. Arming of Burghers not intended for any purpose of aggression against Her Majesty's dominions. People of South African Republic have, since shortly after Jameson Raid, been practically as fully armed as now, yet have never committed any act of aggression. It was not till Her Majesty's Government, with evident intention of enforcing their views on South African Republic in purely internal matters, had greatly augmented their forces and moved them nearer to borders that a single Burgher was called up for the purpose, as be firmly believed, of defending country and independence. If this natural assumption erroneous, not too late to rectify misunderstanding by mutual agreement to withdraw forces on both sides and undertaking by Her Majesty's Government to stop further increase of troops."

But, in reality, it was already too late; for, on the same day on which the above message was telegraphed from Bloemfontein, the government of the South African Republic had presented to the British Agent at Pretoria a note which ended the possibility of peace. After reviewing the issue between the two governments, the note concluded with a peremptory ultimatum, as follows:

"Her Majesty's unlawful intervention in the internal affairs of this Republic in conflict with the Convention of London, 1884, caused by the extraordinary strengthening of troops in the neighbourhood of the borders of this Republic, has thus caused an intolerable condition of things to arise whereto this Government feels itself obliged, in the interest not only of this Republic but also [?] of all South Africa, to make an end as soon as possible, and feels itself called upon and obliged to press earnestly and with emphasis for an immediate termination of this state of things and to request Her Majesty's Government to give it the assurance (a) That all points of mutual difference shall be regulated by the friendly course of arbitration or by whatever amicable way may be agreed upon by this Government with Her Majesty's Government. (b) That the troops on the borders of this Republic shall be instantly withdrawn. (c) That all reinforcements of troops which have arrived in South Africa since the 1st June, 1899, shall be removed from South Africa within a reasonable time, to be agreed upon with this Government, and with a mutual assurance and guarantee on the part of this Government that no attack upon or hostilities against any portion of the possessions of the British Government shall be made by the Republic during further negotiations within a period of time to be subsequently agreed upon between the Governments, and this Government will, on compliance therewith, be prepared to withdraw the armed Burghers of this Republic from the borders. (d) That Her Majesty's troops which are now on the high seas shall not be landed in any port of South Africa. This Government must press for an immediate and affirmative answer to these four questions, and earnestly requests Her Majesty's Government to return such an answer before or upon Wednesday the 11th October, 1899, not later than 5 o'clock p. m., and it desires further to add that in the event of unexpectedly no satisfactory answer being received by it within that interval [it] will with great regret be compelled to regard the action of Her Majesty's Government as a formal declaration of war, and will not hold itself responsible for the consequences thereof, and that in the event of any further movements of troops taking place within the above-mentioned time in the nearer directions of our borders this Government will be compelled to regard that also as a formal declaration of war."

To this ultimatum the British government gave its reply, in a despatch from Mr. Chamberlain to Sir Alfred Milner, October 10, as follows: "Her Majesty's Government have received with great regret the peremptory demands of the South African Republic conveyed in your telegram of 9th October, No. 3. You will inform the Government of the South African Republic, in reply, that the conditions demanded by the Government of the South African Republic are such as Her Majesty's Government deem it impossible to discuss."—*Great Britain, Papers by Command: 1899, C.—9530.—* Efforts which were being made at the time in Holland to assist the Boer Republic in pacific negotiations with Great Britain were suddenly frustrated by this action. A year later (in November, 1900) it was stated in the States General at The Hague that "in the autumn of 1899 the Netherlands Government offered in London its good offices for the resumption of negotiations with the Transvaal, but these efforts had no result in consequence of the sudden ultimatum of the Transvaal and the commencement of hostilities by the armies of the Republics, actions which surprised the Netherlands Government. When once the war had broken out any effort in the direction of intervention would have been useless, as was shown by the peremptory refusal given by Great Britain to the offer of the United States."

An Englishman who was in the country at the time gives the following account of the Boer preparation for war: "In the towns the feeling was strongly against war; in the country districts war was popular, as the farmers had not the slightest doubt they would be able to carry out their threat of 'driving the English into the sea.' . . . Skilled artillerymen were finding their way into the country towards the end of August last [1899]. The Boers themselves did not put much faith in their artillery, but they were reassured by the officers who told them that they would yet learn to respect its usefulness and efficiency—a prophecy which to our cost has been more than fulfilled. . . . General Joubert was always ready and willing, at any time, to inspect and test new guns or military necessaries, and no expense was spared to make the Transvaal burgher army a first-class fighting-machine. . . . Surprise has been expressed at the inaccurate statements made by colonials as to the fighting

strength of the Boers. They had not allowed for the enormous increase of population. From an absolutely reliable source the writer ascertained in September last that they could put in the field between 50 and 60 thousand men, made up as follows: Transvaal burghers, 22,000; resident foreigners, etc., 10,000; Free Staters, 16,-000; colonists who would cross the border and join, 6,000; total, 54,000. . . . As soon as war seemed likely, no time was lost in perfecting the military arrangements. Before Great Britain had thought of mobilizing a soldier, the Boer emissaries were again scouring the colonies of Natal and the Cape, sounding the farmers as to what part they were prepared to take in the coming conflict. . . . While people at home were wondering what the next move would be, the Boers were ready to answer the question. Towards the middle of September all preparations were completed, the Government had laid in large quantities of supplies (mainly of flour, Boer meal, and tinned foods), which they anticipated would tide them over twelve to eighteen months, and by that time, if they had not beaten the British, they relied on foreign intervention. They had also received large sums of money from Europe, and some additional supplies of arms and ammunition. Ammunition was distributed in large quantities throughout the country, each burgher receiving a sealed packet in addition to his ordinary supply. The last batch of the Mauser rifles was distributed, and the mobilization scheme finally arranged, by which, on a given word being telegraphed to the different centres, the first Republican army corps would be mobilized within twenty-four hours. This actually took place. . . . The British Government could hardly fail to be aware of the fact that the Transvaal was in earnest this time. A visit to the country districts towards the end of August, about the time when the Boer Executive themselves sounded the country through their private agencies, would have revealed the fact that the people were not only perfectly willing to go to war, but that they absolutely wished for it. As one Boer put it to the writer: 'We look on fighting the English as a picnic. In some of the Kaffir wars we had a little trouble, but in the Vryheids Oorlog (the Boer War of 1881) we simply potted the Rooineks as they streamed across the veld in their red jackets, without the slightest danger to ourselves.' They had the utmost contempt for Tommy Atkins and his leaders, many of them bragging that the only thing that deterred them from advocating war instanter was the thought that they would have to kill so many of the soldiers, with whom individually they said there was no quarrel. With such a state of things, which should have been perfectly clear to the Intelligence Department (and through it to the War Office) in London—because no resident with eyes to see could be deceived in the matter—we allowed the present war to find us unprepared!" —J. Scoble and H. R. Abercrombie, *The Rise and Fall of Krugerism, ch.* 16 (*N. Y.: F. A. Stokes Co.*).

The Field of **War**: A. D. 1899 (October—November).—The Boer advance.—Invasion of Cape Colony and Natal.—The invaders joined by Dutch farmers of the colony.—The British unprepared.—Investment of Kimberley and Mafeking.—In a despatch dated January 16, 1900, Sir Alfred Milner gave particulars of the

THE
BOER REPUBLICS
AND THEIR
SURROUNDINGS.

JOHANNESBURG
and Vicinity.

first advance of the Boer forces from the Orange Free State into Cape Colony, and of the extent to which they were joined by Dutch farmers in districts south of Orange River. He wrote: "The portion of the Colony with which I propose to deal is that which lies south of the Orange River. The districts north of that river have been so completely cut off, and our accounts of what has been, and is, going on there are so scanty and imperfect, that the history of their defection cannot yet be written. I shall content myself with quoting an extract from a report upon the state of affairs in that region by a gentleman lately resident in Vryburg, which undoubtedly fairly expresses the truth so far as he has been in a position to observe it:—'All the farmers in the Vryburg, Kuruman, and Taungs districts,' he says, 'have joined the Boers, and I do not believe that you will find ten loyal British subjects among the Dutch community in the whole of Bechuanaland.' . . . The districts invaded by the enemy south of the Orange River are:—Colesberg, Albert, Aliwal North, Wodehouse, and Barkly East. It was on the 12th October that the enemy committed the first act of war and of invasion near Vryburg, on the western border, but it was not till more than a month later, namely, the 14th November, that they occupied Colesberg. Apparently they were waiting for reinforcements, for when they actually did cross the frontier they were 1,100 strong. Whatever the cause of their delay, it was not due to any discouragement from the people of Colesberg. The small British garrison then in the country being engaged elsewhere, and the district being entirely unguarded save by a few policemen, people from there continually visited the river to communicate with the enemy. The Chief Constable reports that when he left the town 300 Colesberg farmers had already joined the enemy, and that 400 more were expected from the adjoining district of Philipstown. . . . On the 16th November General Grobler, the Boer Commandant, addressed the following telegram to Bloemfontein :—'Colesberg was occupied by me without opposition. . . . I was very well pleased with the conduct of the Afrikanders. We were everywhere welcomed.' . . . Eastwards along the border the tide of insurrection ran strong. In the closing days of October a Boer force assembled at Bethulie Bridge, which was guarded only by a handful of police. As the days passed and the alarm grew, the Cape police force was withdrawn from Burghersdorp, which lies south of Bethulie, down the line to Stormberg, while, in their turn, the Imperial forces abandoned the important position of Stormberg, and retired on Queenstown, thus leaving the district clear for the invaders. That they did not immediately advance was certainly not owing to any fear of resistance at Burghersdorp, the inhabitants of which fraternised with the commando stationed on the river, continually passing to and fro. Finally, on the 14th November, the date of the occupation of Colesberg, the advance was made, and on the following morning a body of 500 Boers occupied the town. . . . According to the despatch of the Boer Commandant, dated 16th November, Burghersdorp was occupied 'amidst cheers from the Afrikanders,' and 'the Colonial burghers are very glad to meet us.' Commandeering at once began throughout the district of Albert, and a Burghersdorp resident estimated that about 1,000 farmers were prepared to join at the date of his leaving the place. . . .

"Within a space of less than three weeks from the occupation of Colesberg, no less than five great districts—those of Colesberg, Albert, Aliwal North, Barkly East, and Wodehouse—had gone over without hesitation, and, so to speak, bodily, to the enemy. Throughout that region the Landdrosts of the Orange Free State had established their authority, and everywhere, in the expressive words of a Magistrate, British loyalists were 'being hunted out of town after town like sheep.' In the invaded districts, as will be seen from the above, the method of occupation has always been more or less the same. The procedure is as follows:—A commando enters, the Orange Free State flag is hoisted, a meeting is held in the Court-house or market-place, and a Proclamation is read, annexing the district. The Commandant then makes a speech, in which he explains that the people must now obey the Free State laws generally, though they are at present under martial law. A local Landdrost is appointed, and loyal subjects are given a few days or hours in which to quit, or be compelled to serve against their country. . . . The number of rebels who have actually taken up arms and joined the enemy during their progress throughout the five annexed districts can for the present only be matter of conjecture. I shall, however, be on the safe side in reckoning that during November it was a number not less than the total of the invading commandos, that is, 2,000, while it is probable that of the invading commandos themselves a certain proportion were colonists who had crossed the border before the invasion took place. And the number, whatever it was, which joined the enemy before and during November has been increased since. A well-informed refugee from the Albert district has estimated the total number of Colonial Boers who have joined the enemy in the invaded districts south of the Orange River at 3,000 to 4,000. In the districts north of that river, to which I referred at the beginning of this despatch, the number can hardly be less. Adding to these the men who became burghers of the Transvaal immediately before, or just after, the outbreak of war, with the view of taking up arms in the struggle, I am forced to the conclusion that, in round figures, not less than 10,000 of those now fighting against us in South Africa, and probably somewhat more, either are, or till quite recently were, subjects of the Queen."— *Great Britain, Papers by Command : Cd.* 264, *1900, pp.* 1–5.

The above relates to movements from the Orange Free State into Cape Colony, where the most of reinforcement from Afrikander inhabitants of British soil was to be got. From the Transvaal, the movement of Boer forces across the frontiers, both eastward and westward, was equally prompt. Early on the morning of the 12th they were in Natal, advancing in three strong columns, under General Joubert, upon Newcastle, threatening the advance posts of the British at Dundee and Glencoe (some 40 miles northeast of Ladysmith), where valuable coal mines claimed defence. At the same time, another Boer army, under General Cronje, had passed the western border and was moving upon Mafeking, where Colonel (afterwards General)

Baden-Powell, with an irregular force of about 1,200 men, was preparing for a siege. The inhabitants of the town, including refugees, numbered about 2,000 whites and 7,000 blacks. A few days later Boer forces were skirmishing with the defenders of the diamond mines at Kimberley, where Colonel Kekewich commanded about 1,000 men, and where Cecil Rhodes was among the beleaguered citizens. The population of Kimberley was 33,000, more than half blacks.

It is plain that the British were wholly unprepared for so vigorous an opening of hostilities on the part of the Boers. A military writer in the "London Times," discussing the "Lessons of the War," at the end of a year after its beginning, made the following statements and comment:—"There was no difficulty in obtaining the fullest information as to the resources of the Transvaal and the Free State, and we have been officially informed that 'the armed strength of the Boers, the number of their guns, with their character and calibre,' as laid down in the report of the Director of Intelligence, 'corresponds exactly with our recently-ascertained knowledge of what the enemy has put into the field.' Whether or not these reports ever travel from Queen Anne's-gate to Pall-mall seems uncertain, since the Commander-in-Chief publicly stated that 'We have found that the enemy . . . are much more powerful and numerous than we expected.' The report of the Intelligence Department seems, therefore, to have been as valueless for practical purposes as were those transmitted to Paris by Colonel Stoffel prior to the outbreak of the Franco-German war, and Lord Wolseley was apparently as little aware of the fighting resources of the Boers as was Marshal Lebœuf of those of the Germans. When, early in September, 1899, it became a pressing necessity to reinforce the troops in South Africa, it was painfully realized that not a single unit at home was ready to take the field. One weak battalion and three field batteries, hastily compounded by wholesale drafting from others, represented the available contribution from a standing army at home whose nominal effectives considerably exceeded 100,000. The reinforcements, totally inadequate to meet the crisis, were made up by drawing upon India and the colonial garrisons."—*London Times, Nov.* 22, 1900.

Another writer in "The Times," reviewing, at nearly the same time, the previous year of the war, gave this account of its opening circumstances:—"If the organization of the British Army had permitted the despatch at short notice of 30,000 troops from Great Britain, the whole course of the war would have been different. It was a prevailing illusion that Mr. Kruger would yield to diplomatic pressure not backed by available force, and political expediency, over-riding military considerations, led to a compromise. It was tardily decided to bring the forces in South Africa up to a total of about 22,000 by drawing on India and the colonial garrisons; mobilization was deferred till October 7. Thus the first reinforcements arrived barely in time to prevent Natal from being over-run by the Boers, and the expeditionary force did not begin to reach Durban [the port of Natal] till after Ladysmith had been closely invested. . . . There were advisers of the Cabinet who held that the military strength of the Boers was a bubble easily pricked. Thus it was widely believed that a severe repulse in

Northern Natal would suffice to break up the Boer forces, and, knowing only that a body of 4,000 British troops was assembled at Dundee and another somewhat larger at Ladysmith, we hastily assumed that these places were naturally well suited and had been specially prepared for defence. When, on the 26th, the concentration at Ladysmith was accomplished, after a painful and a hazardous march, it was imagined that our forces occupied an intrenched camp, which, if necessary, could be held with ease. Later it became clear that Ladysmith was exceedingly ill-adapted for defence, that it was practically unfortified when invested, and finally that, if the attacking force had been composed of trained troops, it must have fallen, in spite of every effort on the part of the garrison. The occupation of Dundee, it was discovered, was maintained against the military judgment of Sir G. White. . . .

"When at length the army corps and the cavalry division began, early in November, to arrive in South Africa, we believed that the bulk of this large force, which was apparently ready to take the field, would invade the Orange Free State and strike for Bloemfontein, clearing Cape Colony and inevitably drawing Boer forces away from the investments of Kimberley and of Ladysmith. This was another illusion. At least one-half of the expeditionary force was despatched to Durban and the rest was frittered away between three separate lines of advance. There were thus four separate groupings of British troops, spread over an immense front, and incapable of affording each other mutual support. Moreover, the Commander-in-Chief being involved in a difficult campaign in Natal, there was no responsible head in Cape Colony, where partial chaos soon supervened. . . . Faulty as was the strategy which substituted scattered efforts with insufficient force for a primary object, that of the Boers was happily even more ill-conceived. In place of attempting to occupy our troops in Natal and throwing their main strength into Cape Colony, where a Dutch rising on a large scale would inevitably have occurred, they also preferred to fritter away their strength, devoting their main efforts against Ladysmith, Kimberley, and Mafeking, and contenting themselves with the occupation of Colesberg and Stormberg in small force, which, however, was quickly swelled by local rebels."—*London Times, Nov.* 5, 1900.

The Field of War: A. D. 1899 (October–December).—The early battles.—British reverses.—Siege of Ladysmith.—The serious fighting of the war began in Natal, as early as the 20th of October, when three columns of the Boer forces closed in on the British advance post at Glencoe. The first of the Boer columns to arrive opened a precipitate attack, and in the hard battle which ensued (at Talana Hill) the British could claim the final advantage, though at very heavy cost. Their commander, General Sir W. Penn Symons, received a mortal wound and died three days afterwards, kindly cared for and buried by the enemy, his successor in the command, General Yule, having found it necessary to retreat from Glencoe and Dundee to Ladysmith. The Boers were already striking at the railroad between Glencoe and Ladysmith, and sharp fighting had taken place on the 21st at Elandslaagte, a station on the line only seventeen miles from the latter town. The Boers, in that encounter, had been driven from the neighboring hills, but the British had again suffered greatly, and began to realize the quality of the foe with which they had to deal. A graphic account of the battle at Elandslaagte was written by the famous newspaper correspondent, G. W. Steevens, who died shortly afterwards at Ladysmith. Two days after Elandslaagte there was another engagement at Reitfontein, still nearer to Ladysmith, fought for the purpose of keeping the Boers from intercepting the retreat of General Yule. The British forces defending Natal were now concentrated at Ladysmith, which they had chosen for their main position, and in which they had been collecting large quantities of military stores. General Sir George White was there in general command. The Boers, with General Joubert in chief command, were rapidly closing in upon the town, and, on the 29th, they had a Creusot (French) six-inch gun on a neighboring hill, within range, ready to drop shells into its streets. That night General White made an attempt to break their lines which ended in sore disaster. One column, which marched far out, to a hill called Nicholson's Nek, for a flanking attack on the enemy, lost most of its ammunition and its battery, by a stampede of mules, and then was caught in so helpless a position that it had to lay down its arms. "The cursed white flag," wrote Mr. Steevens, "was up again over a British force in South Africa. The best part of a thousand British soldiers, with all their arms and equipment and four mountain guns, were captured by the enemy. The Boers had their revenge for Dundee and Elandslaagte in war ; now they took it full measure in kindness. As Atkins had tended their wounded and succoured their prisoners there, so they tended and succoured him here. One commandant wished to send the wounded to Pretoria ; the others, more prudent as well as more humane, decided to send them back into Ladysmith. They gave the whole men the water out of their own bottles; they gave the wounded the blankets off their own saddles and slept themselves on the naked veldt. They were short of transport, and they were mostly armed with Martinis; yet they gave captured mules for the hospital panniers and captured Lee-Metfords for splints." It is consoling to come on a bit of incident like this in the generally horrid story of war.

A few days later the communications of Ladysmith southward were cut off, and the forces commanded by General White, about 10,000 in number, were hemmed in by superior numbers of the Boers. British reinforcements were now beginning to arrive in South Africa, and great numbers were at sea, not only imperial troops, coming from England, India, Ceylon and elsewhere, but colonial troops, offered by Canada, New Zealand and the Australian colonies, and accepted by the imperial government. The first operations of the British campaign were planned with three objects, more or less distinct, namely, to rescue General White's army, at Ladysmith, to relieve Kimberley, and to expel the Boers from northern Cape Colony. They were conducted on three lines, from the Natal port of Durban, towards Ladysmith, under General Clery at the beginning; from Cape Town towards Kimberley, under General Lord Methuen ; from Port Elizabeth and East London to Queenstown and the Cape districts occupied by the Boers, under General Gatacre.

In the early battles of General Methuen's campaign, fought at Belmont, November 23d, at Enslin, or Graspan, on the 25th, and at Modder River, only 25 miles from Kimberley, on the 28th, he carried his point, and kept up his advance, but at a heavy sacrifice of men. The battle with Cronje's forces at Modder River was a desperate struggle of ten hours duration, in which the British lost nearly 500 men and gained little. The Boers withdrew to an equally strong position, behind fortified lines which extended, some six miles in length, on hills between two points which bore the names of Spytfontein and Majesfontein. There General Methuen attacked them again, December 11, and met with a terrible repulse. His Highland Brigade, advancing in the darkness, before daybreak, was in the midst of the enemy's intrenchments before it knew them to be near, and was horribly cut to pieces, losing 53 officers, including its commander, General Wauchope, and 650 men. The British fell back to Modder River, leaving not less than 1,000 men behind. Just one day before this catastrophe, on the 10th, another of like nature, but little less serious, was sustained by General Gatacre's column, moving from Queenstown. He, too, attempted a night march and an early morning attack on the Boers in a fortified position at Stormberg, was misled by guides, miscalculated the distance, neglected to send scouts ahead, and so took his men to the very muzzles of waiting guns. From the storm which then opened on them there were more than 500 who did not escape. Besides the dead and wounded, many went as prisoners to Pretoria. Before the week of these defeats reached its end, another, far worse, had been added in the Natal campaign. General Sir Redvers Buller, appointed to the chief command in South Africa, had arrived at Cape Town on the last day of October, and, after some general study of the field at large, had taken personal direction of the operations in Natal, for the relief of Ladysmith. His movements were undoubtedly hurried by urgent appeals from General White. On the 15th of December he felt prepared to attempt the passage of the Tugela River, near Colenso, and did so with his full force, at two drifts, or fords, some two miles apart. Like Methuen and Gatacre, he seems to have been strangely misinformed as to the location and strength of the intrenchments of the Boers. The latter had succeeded again and again in concealing lines of deadly rifle-pits and batteries until their assailants fairly stumbled against them, within fatally close range. This happened at Colenso, as at Stormberg and Majesfontein, and the ill-managed attempt to begin an advance upon Ladysmith cost 165 men and officers killed, 670 wounded, 337 prisoners and missing, besides 11 guns.

The Field of War: A. D. 1900.—Fighting qualities of the Boers.—"Take a community of Dutchmen of the type of those who defended themselves for fifty years against all the power of Spain at a time when Spain was the greatest power in the world. Intermix with them a strain of those inflexible French Huguenots who gave up home and fortune and left their country forever at the time of the revocation of the Edict of Nantes. The product must obviously be one of the most rugged, virile, unconquerable races ever seen upon earth. Take this formidable people and train them for seven generations in

constant warfare against savage men and ferocious beasts, in circumstances under which no
weakling could survive, place them so that
they acquire exceptional skill with weapons and
in horsemanship, give them a country which is
eminently suited to the tactics of the huntsman,
the marksman, and the rider. Then, finally,
put a finer temper upon their military qualities
by a dour fatalistic Old Testament religion and
an ardent and consuming patriotism. Combine
all these qualities and all these impulses in one
individual, and you have the modern Boer—the
most formidable antagonist who ever crossed
the path of Imperial Britain."—A. C. Doyle,
The Great Boer War, ch. 1.—Count Adalbert
von Sternberg, a German officer who served
with the Boers, and who has since related his
experiences in a book, writes to the same effect.
"The Boers," he remarks, "were mounted,
whilst the English were on foot, a matter of
considerable importance in these hot countries.
Given the same or even slightly superior forces,
no Continental army would have played its part
better than the English, and I even doubt
whether, in regard to practical equipment and
technical smartness and efficiency the Continent
would have done as well. The fact is the Boer
is an enemy of quite exceptional a character,
such as never has been met before, or is likely
to be met again. Mounted sharpshooters, armed
with the very best of weapons, acclimatized,
fanatical, and accustomed to habits of war, are
terrible opponents, and cannot be dealt with off
hand as if they were hordes of savages. One
must not forget that the Boers have the keenest
eyes imaginable, and that they understand better
than any one else how to get the fullest advantage of cover. All these are advantages which
go far towards compensating defective leading
and the weakening of moral due to being always
on the defensive. . . . The Boers would have
had much greater successes if they had not
abandoned all idea of taking the offensive. They
could not be brought to that, for that they
lacked courage, and to that lack of courage they
owe their destruction."

The Field of War: A. D. 1900 (January-
February).—Continued British disasters on
the Tugela.—Lord Roberts and Lord Kitchener in the field.—Invasion of Orange Free
State. — Capture of General Cronje and
army.—Relief of Kimberley and Ladysmith.—
The dark and heavy clouds of disaster which
overhung the British in South Africa at the
close of the year shadowed England with anxiety and gloom. For the first time, the seriousness of the task of war in which the country had
become engaged was understood, and energies
corresponding to it were roused. Field-Marshal
Lord Roberts, of Indian and Afghan renown,
was sent out to take supreme command, with
the equally famous Lord Kitchener, subjugator
of the Egyptian Sudan, for his chief of staff.
Immense reinforcements of troops were provided
for with haste. On the 1st of January it was
estimated that 30,000 fresh troops were afloat
or on the point of embarkation, and that Lord
Roberts would have 200,000 men at command
when all then assigned to South Africa should
have reached Natal and the Cape. Lord Roberts landed at the Cape on the 10th of January,
and was occupied for a month in organizing
and preparing for new movements in the field.

Meantime, General Buller had made a second
attempt to turn the strongly fortified position of
his opponent on the Tugela, between his own
army and the beleaguered force at Ladysmith,
and had failed more discouragingly than before.
Crossing the Tugela, some miles west of Colenso, on the 17th, he pressed a hard-fought, up-
hill advance, from one to another of the rocky
hills (called kopjes) of the region, for several
days. On the 23d his troops stormed the fortifications of the Boers on Spion Kop, a spur of
the Drakenberg mountains, and carried them
with heavy loss, only to find that they were
commanded from other heights and could not
be held. Again he drew back to the southern
bank of the Tugela, on the 29th; but only for
a few days. On the 5th of February his army
was once more pushed beyond the river, and
entrenched in a position among the hills, which
it held until the 9th, and was then, for the third
time, withdrawn. This third movement is supposed to have been a feint, intended to detain
the Boer forces in his front, either from some
assault feared at Ladysmith or from interference
with the campaign which Lord Roberts was
about to open. The besieged at Ladysmith were
holding out with grim resolution, but they were
known to be in sore straits. Occasional messages
by the heliograph told of much sickness and
fast approaching starvation in the town. Fever
was killing more than the shells from the bombarding guns; and the chances of relief seemed
to have almost disappeared.

But a sudden change in the whole military
situation was about to be made. Lord Roberts
and Lord Kitchener had organized arrangements
of transportation and supplies for handling the
immense force now at their command, and were
ready to execute their plans. The former arrived
at Modder River on the 9th of February; two
days later his columns were set in motion, and
the Boer forces, under General Cronje, were too
greatly outnumbered to withstand the avalanche
which fell upon them. General French led
a cavalry expedition to Kimberley, reaching the
town on the 15th and raising the siege. The
next day General Cronje was in retreat towards
Bloemfontein, the Free State capital, harassed
by British cavalry, and with the main army of
Lord Roberts straining every nerve to strike him
before he reached it. On the 18th he was
brought to bay, at a point on the Modder River,
near Paardeberg, where he defended himself
for nine days, in a situation that was impregnable to assault, but terribly exposed to artillery
fire from surrounding heights. He was expecting help from the forces in Natal and elsewhere,
and several attempts were made by his associates to reach him; but the British were too
strong to be driven from their prey. After
suffering to such a degree that his men would
endure no more, the brave and stubborn Boer
surrendered on the 27th, his army, reduced to
about 4,000, laying down their arms. Some 500
had been taken in the previous fighting, and
considerable numbers in the last days of the
siege, are said to have deserted and found means
to slip through the enemy's lines. The prisoners
were sent, for convenience of custody, to the
island of St. Helena, the general being accompanied by his whole family, and treated with much
respect.

While these operations were being carried to

success by Lord Roberts, General Buller was again attacking the formidable fortifications of the enemy in his front. From the 14th of February until the 23d he sacrificed great numbers of men in assaults which failed to break a passage through the kopjes defended by Boer guns. But Lord Roberts's invasion of the Free State had, by this time, caused large withdrawals of Boers from the line of the Tugela, and they were preparing to raise the siege of Ladysmith. Consequently, when the British attack was renewed, on the 27th, it achieved success, at last. The Boers were driven from their main position and abandoned their whole line. Ladysmith was reached by a swift advance of cavalry the next day, and the half-starved garrison and citizens were soon receiving supplies.

The Field of War: A. D. 1900 (March).—Overtures of peace from Presidents Kruger and Steyn.—The reply of Lord Salisbury.—Death of General Joubert.—On the 5th of March, the Presidents of the South African Republic and the Orange Free State addressed the following telegram, jointly, to Lord Salisbury: "The blood and tears of the thousands who have suffered by this war, and the prospect of all the moral and economic ruin with which South Africa is now threatened, make it necessary for both belligerents to ask themselves dispassionately, and as in the sight of the Triune God, for what they are fighting, and whether the aim of each justifies all this devouring misery and devastation. With this object, and in view of the assertions of various members of the British Parliament to the effect that this war was begun and is being carried on with the set purpose of undermining Her Majesty's authority in South Africa, and of setting up an Administration over all South Africa independent of Her Majesty's Government, we consider it our duty solemnly to declare that this war was undertaken solely as a defensive measure for securing the threatened independence of the South African Republic, and is only continued in order to secure the incontestable independence of both Republics as sovereign international States, and to ensure that those of Her Majesty's subjects who have taken part with us in this war shall suffer no harm whatever in person or property. On these conditions, but on these conditions alone, are we now, as in the past, desirous of seeing peace reëstablished in South Africa, and of putting an end to the evil now reigning over South Africa; while, if Her Majesty's Government is determined to destroy the independence of the Republics, there is nothing left to us and our people but to persevere to the end in the course already begun, in spite of the overwhelming pre-eminence of the British Empire, confident that the God who lighted the unextinguishable fire of the love of freedom in the hearts of our fathers will not forsake us, but will accomplish His work in us and in our descendants. We hesitated to make this declaration earlier to Your Excellency, as we feared that as long as the advantage was always on our side, and as long as our forces held defensive positions far in Her Majesty's Colonies, such a declaration might hurt the feelings of honour of the British people; but now that the prestige of the British Empire may be considered to be assured by the capture of one of our forces by Her Majesty's troops, and that we are thereby forced to evacuate other positions

6–32

which our forces had occupied, that difficulty is over, and we no longer hesitate clearly to inform your Government and people in the sight of the whole civilised world why we are fighting, and on what conditions we are ready to restore peace."

On the 11th Lord Salisbury replied as follows: "I have the honour to acknowledge Your Honours' telegram, dated the 5th of March, from Bloemfontein, of which the purport is principally to demand that Her Majesty's Government shall recognise the 'incontestable independence' of the South African Republic and Orange Free State 'as sovereign international States,' and to offer, on those terms, to bring the war to a conclusion. In the beginning of October last peace existed between Her Majesty and the two Republics under the Conventions which then were in existence. A discussion had been proceeding for some months between Her Majesty's Government and the South African Republic, of which the object was to obtain redress for certain very serious grievances under which British residents in the South African Republic were suffering. In the course of those negotiations, the South African Republic had, to the knowledge of Her Majesty's Government, made considerable armaments, and the latter had, consequently, taken steps to provide corresponding reinforcements to the British garrisons of Cape Town and Natal. No infringement of the rights guaranteed by the Conventions had, up to that point, taken place on the British side. Suddenly, at two days' notice, the South African Republic, after issuing an insulting ultimatum, declared war upon Her Majesty; and the Orange Free State, with whom there had not even been any discussion, took a similar step. Her Majesty's dominions were immediately invaded by the two Republics, siege was laid to three towns within the British frontier, a large portion of the two Colonies was overrun, with great destruction to property and life, and the Republics claimed to treat the inhabitants of extensive portions of Her Majesty's dominions as if those dominions had been annexed to one or other of them. In anticipation of these operations the South African Republic had been accumulating for many years past military stores on an enormous scale, which by their character could only have been intended for use against Great Britain. Your Honours make some observations of a negative character upon the object with which these preparations were made. I do not think it necessary to discuss the questions you have raised. But the result of these preparations, carried on with great secrecy, has been that the British Empire has been compelled to confront an invasion which has entailed upon the Empire a costly war and the loss of thousands of precious lives. This great calamity has been the penalty which Great Britain has suffered for having in recent years acquiesced in the existence of the two Republics. In view of the use to which the two Republics have put the position which was given to them, and the calamities which their unprovoked attack has inflicted upon Her Majesty's dominions, Her Majesty's Government can only answer Your Honours' telegram by saying that they are not prepared to assent to the independence either of the South African Republic or of the Orange Free State." —*Great Britain, Papers by Command: Africa, No. 2, 1900.*

On the 27th of March, the Boer cause experienced a great loss, in the sudden death, from peritonitis, of General Joubert, the Commandant-General and Vice President of the South African Republic.

Orange Free State: A. D. 1900 (March).—Proclamation to the burghers by the British commander.—Soon after entering the Orange Free State, Lord Roberts issued a proclamation addressed to the burghers, assuring them that the British government did not believe them to be responsible for the aggressive act of war committed by the government of the Orange Free State, and bore them no ill-will. "I, therefore," his proclamation continued, "warn all Burghers to desist from any further hostility towards Her Majesty's Government and the troops under my command, and, I undertake that any of them, who may so desist and who are found staying in their homes and quietly pursuing their ordinary occupations, will not be made to suffer in their persons or property on account of their having taken up arms in obedience to the order of their Government. Those, however, who oppose the forces under my command, or furnish the enemy with supplies or information, will be dealt with according to the customs of war. Requisitions for food, forage, fuel, or shelter, made on the authority of the officers in command of Her Majesty's troops, must be at once complied with; but everything will be paid for on the spot, prices being regulated by the local market rates. If the inhabitants of any district refuse to comply with the demands made on them, the supplies will be taken by force, a full receipt being given. Should any inhabitant of the country consider that he or any member of his household has been unjustly treated by any officer, soldier or civilian attached to the British Army, he should submit his complaint, either personally or in writing, to my Headquarters or to the Headquarters of the nearest General Officer. Should the complaint on enquiry be substantiated, redress will be given. Orders have been issued by me, prohibiting soldiers from entering private houses, or molesting the civil population on any pretext whatever, and every precaution has been taken against injury to property on the part of any person belonging to, or connected with, the Army."

After the occupation of Bloemfontein, Lord Roberts issued a second proclamation, announcing that he had received authority from his government to offer the following terms to those "who have been engaged in the present war": "All Burghers who have not taken a prominent part in the policy which has led to the war between Her Majesty and the Orange Free State, or commanded any forces of the Republic, or commandeered or used violence to any British subjects, and who are willing to lay down their arms at once, and to bind themselves by an oath to abstain from further participation in the war, will be given passes to allow them to return to their homes and will not be made prisoners of war, nor will their property be taken from them."—*Great Britain, Papers by Command: Cd. 261, 1900, pp.* 62–3.

The Transvaal and the Free State: A. D. 1900 (March).—Boer Peace Commissioners to Europe and America.—In March, three commissioners, Messrs. Fischer, Wolmeraans and Wessels were sent to Europe and America by the two Boer governments to solicit intervention in their behalf. They visited several European countries and proceeded thence to the United States, in May. There were many demonstrations of popular sympathy in their reception, on both sides of the ocean, but they failed to obtain official recognition.

The Field of War: A. D. 1900 (March—May).—The British in Bloemfontein and Kroonstad.—The relief of Mafeking.—From the scene of the surrender of General Cronje Lord Roberts moved quickly on the Free State capital. His advance was resisted by considerable forces of the Boers, but he was able to turn most of their positions, and fought only one severe battle, at Driefontein, on the 10th of March. On the 12th his cavalry was in possession of Bloemfontein, and the Field-Marshal entered the city on the following day, receiving from the municipal officers a formal surrender of the keys of the public buildings, and being welcomed by some part of the population with demonstrations of joy. President Steyn and most of the members of the government of the Republic had retired to Kroonstad and established the seat of authority there. The fighting and the forced marches of a single month, since he began his advance, had now exhausted the mobility of Lord Roberts's army, worn out the means of transportation which Lord Kitchener had hastily organized for it,—while his troops were being stricken with fever,—and he was compelled to suspend his campaign for some weeks. The situation at that time was probably described with accuracy by a military contributor to "Blackwood's Magazine" for June, 1900, who wrote: "Lord Roberts found himself at Bloemfontein with the wreck of an army and a single narrow-gauge line of railway between himself and his base, upwards of 700 miles distant. It was very soon known in Boer headquarters at Kroonstad that he could not move beyond Bloemfontein for some weeks. The triumphal march of Generals Gatacre and Clements through the recently captured territory, accepting submissions, hoisting union-jacks and picking up rifles of antique date, afforded much amusement to the Boers, who saw their opportunity and streamed down in large numbers on the small British posts which were scattered east and south of the railway."

There was a good deal of raiding and fighting on a minor scale, with a number of mortifying mishaps to the British arms; but little of importance occurred in the military field until near the end of April, when Lord Roberts had reinforced and mobilized his army sufficiently to move forward again, towards Pretoria. On the 12th of May he entered Kroonstad, and the Free State government was again in flight. He paused at Kroonstad for some days, and while he paused there came news of the relief of Mafeking, which caused a wilder joy in England than any other event of the war. There had been painful anxiety on account of the besieged in that remote town, in the far corner of Bechuanaland, on the border of the Transvaal,—so far from help, and so stoutly defended for seven weary months by a very small force. From a point near Kimberley, a flying column of mounted men, mostly colonial troops, commanded by Colonel Mahon, had been started northward on the 4th of May, taking a route east of the railway, to avoid, as much as possible, the Boers. On the 15th they were 20 miles west of Mafeking, and there they were joined by another detachment, under Colonel Plumer, which had been operating in the northern region for some weeks without being able to break up the siege. The two advanced on the works of the besiegers, drove them out by hard fighting, and entered the town on the 18th of May. Meantime, another column, under General Hunter, had been securing and opening the railway, to bring up the sorely needed supplies for the famished and worn-out garrison and people of the town. The defense of Mafeking was one of the finest performances of the war, and gave distinction to Colonel Baden-Powell.

Cape Colony: A. D. 1900 (April—June).— The question of the treatment of Cape Colonists who had taken part with the Boers in the war.—Resignation of Premier Schreiner. —On the 28th of April, the Ministers of Cape Colony addressed to the Governor, Sir Alfred Milner, a Minute upon the subject of the treatment of those inhabitants of the Colony who had joined or given aid to the Boers in the war, and who had thus made themselves liable to the pains and penalties of high treason. "Ministers submit," they said, "that the ends of justice would be served by the selection of a certain limited number of the principal offenders, whose trials would mark the magnitude of their offence, and whose punishment, if found guilty, would act as a deterrent. For the remainder, Ministers believe that the interests both of sound policy and of public morality would be served if Her Gracious Majesty were moved to issue, as an act of grace, a Proclamation of amnesty under which, upon giving proper security for their good behaviour, all persons chargeable with high treason, except those held for trial, might be enlarged and allowed to return to their avocations. Ministers urge such a course not only on the ground of that natural desire for clemency towards her erring subjects which they feel sure would spring from Her Gracious Majesty, but from a deep sense of the importance of such a step upon the future well-being of this country."

The substance of the Minute was transmitted by cable to Mr. Chamberlain, and he replied to it on the 5th of May, objecting to the proposed proclamation of a broad amnesty, saying: "Clemency to rebels is a policy which has the hearty sympathy of Her Majesty's Government, but justice to loyalists is an obligation of duty and honour. The question is how can these two policies be harmonized. It is clear that in the interest of future peace it is necessary to show that rebellion cannot be indulged in with impunity, and above all that if unsuccessful it is not a profitable business for the rebel. Otherwise the State would be offering a premium to rebellion. The present moment, therefore, while the war is still proceeding, and while efforts may still be made to tempt British subjects into rebellions courses, is in any case not appropriate for announcing that such action may be indulged in with absolute impunity. And if, as has been suggested, a great many of the Queen's rebellious subjects are the mere tools of those who have deceived them, it is important that these should be made aware individually that whatever their leaders may tell them rebellion is a punishable offence." This attitude of the Imperial Government on the subject of amnesty occasioned differences in the Ministry of Cape Colony which led to the resignation of the Premier, Mr. W. P. Schreiner, on the 13th of June, and the appointment of a new Ministry, under Sir Gordon Sprigg.—*Great Britain, Papers by Command: July,* 1900, *Cape Colony, Cd.* 264.

The Field of War: A. D. 1900 (May).—The British army stricken with fever.—The losses of the British army in battle during this campaign of Lord Roberts had not been severe; but it had encountered a worse enemy than the Boers, and was being terribly thinned and shattered by the ravages of enteric or typhoid fever. The sanitary condition of the army in May, and the lack of due provision for dealing with the dreadful epidemic, have been graphically described by the writer already quoted, in "Blackwood's Magazine." Referring to the outset of the campaign, in February, he wrote:

"The movement of men and cattle depends on flesh and muscle—it cannot go on for ever; the strain of incessant marching on insufficient food and forage will find out the weak spot even in the most willing. General French started on his memorable ride with 4,800 horses,· of which 990 dropped by the way, though the loss in the ranks, exclusive of Paardeberg, was only fifty men,— the brunt of the battle for life lay with the horses. But not for long. The men with worn-out boots, tattered clothes, hurrying through scorching days and frosty nights, with half a biscuit and water tainted with dead Boers, to satisfy an appetite and thirst compelled by hard work at an altitude of 4,000 feet, who marched in as soldiers, proud of the victory they had won, staggered and fell out, victims to the curse that creeps in, unnoticed, wherever camps are crowded—enteric. . . . Of all things on which we prided ourselves was the care and the money we had lavished to provide comforts for our sick soldiers. The foremost surgeons of the day had volunteered; military hospitals had been arranged on the latest plan ; private benevolence had provided as many more; ladies of every rank in life had gone out to nurse ; the soldiers, at all events, would be looked after. Letters from the front had come from patients to say how well they had been treated. Mr. Treves at the Reform Club made a speech eulogizing the perfection of the hospitals in Natal, and Sir W. MacCormac spoke of the medical arrangements as admirable—our minds rested content. All this was so long ago as the 10th March, but what happened in March, for all we knew, was happening in May. Then Mr. Burdett-Coutts told us that hundreds of men were lying in the worst stages of typhoid, with only a blanket to cover them, a thin water-proof sheet (not even that for many) between them and the ground ; no milk and hardly any medicines ; without beds, stretchers, or mattresses ; without pillows, without linen of any kind, without a single nurse amongst them, with a few private soldiers as orderlies, and only three doctors to attend on 350 patients ; their faces covered with flies in black clusters, the men too weak to brush them off, trying in vain to dislodge them by painful twitching of the features—there was no one to do it for them. And this a mile from Bloemfontein, where the army had been for six weeks. It is true that a terrible epidemic had followed it from Paardeberg, to break out when it halted. Lord Roberts tells us that before he left on May 3rd the sick gradually increased to

2,000, reaching on June 4th the appalling number, in Bloemfontein, of over 5,000 suffering from typhoid alone. Such were the bare facts as stated on either side—a sudden and devastating epidemic with totally inadequate hospital arrangements to meet it. . . . Yet typhoid has always been the scourge of armies in the field,—in South Africa the water-supply, invariably surface drainage fouled by dead animals, is proverbial—that at least was known. The medical authorities on the spot were repeatedly warned by local medical men that from February onwards ten men would be down with typhoid for one with wounds. Ladysmith is in evidence of the persistent presence of typhoid—every one who has visited South Africa bears witness to the same—it can hardly be urged that an outbreak was unreasonable to expect; yet when it did occur it seems to have been taken by the medical administration at the base as an unwarrantable intrusion."—*The War Operations in South Africa (Blackwood's Magazine, Aug., 1900).*

The Transvaal: A. D. 1900 (May).—Speech of President Kruger to the Volksraads.—The following translation of a speech addressed to both Volksraads by President Kruger, in May, 1900, was published in England some months later: "It is known to you," said the President, "how, before the war started, pressure was brought to bear to obtain the franchise. It is known to you that the Government conceded, after the Raad had consented, although this body saw the difficulty in the matter, till even the burghers made petitions to the effect that we had parted with all our rights. The Government had in view the prevention of shedding blood. The Raad then consented to a seven years' franchise, and also to grant immediately the franchise to people resident here longer than seven years. There were then nearly 30,000 who would obtain the franchise immediately, and so much was conceded that when these had obtained the franchise they would have been able to out-vote the old burghers. We consented to this solely to prevent the shedding of blood. Yet they were not satisfied and they wanted the franchise after five years' residence. Our burghers were against this, and there were also members of the Raad who would not agree to this, yet, nevertheless, the Government made a proposition about it, because they had discovered that it was not about the franchise, but that it was a pretence full of Pharisaic hypocrisy, because documents had been found that in 1896 it was decided that the two independent Republics should not be allowed to exist any more. I cannot express myself otherwise than to call it a devilish fraud. Peace was spoken of while a resolution had already been passed to annihilate us. Even if we had conceded more, yea, even if we had said that the franchise could be obtained after one year, then that would not have been accepted. It was proved by documents that, as this nation could not be allowed to be a free nation, as was pointed out in the address, the Government, to prevent the further shedding of blood, made a proposition to Chamberlain and Salisbury about this matter, and what was the reply? You have, doubtless, read the paper, and, although I cannot verbally repeat the contents of the said document, it amounts to this. That they were annoyed ever to have acknowledged us as an

independent nation, and that, notwithstanding all conventions made, they would never acknowledge this nation as self-supporting. Hon. gentlemen, I had to express that which was in my mind. Psalm 83 speaks of the assault of the evil one on the Kingdom of Christ. That must not exist. The self-same words of Salisbury also appear, because he says ' this nation must not exist,' and God says, ' this nation shall exist.' Who will be victorious? Certainly the Lord. You see therein the deceit which they then already practised, even they, for though our nation did not wish to part with any rights, the Executive Council conceded so far that we nearly lost the country. The intention was not to obtain these rights. They wanted our country not to be independent any longer. Every other proposition was unsatisfactory to them.

"Let us look this matter in the face and see the cunning deceit enveloped therein. They wrote to the Orange Free State that they had nothing against them, but that they had some grievance against this Republic. Their intention was to tear the two Republics asunder, and it has been proved by documentary evidence that neither of them would be allowed to remain. You see the deception which lies therein. The documents prove that this was already decided in 1896, from the time of Jameson's invasion, and yet they maintain that if the Orange Free State had laid down their weapons that that country would remain in existence. The Orange Free State decided not to lay down their arms, and we started together. We were 40,000 men, but everywhere we had to watch the Kaffirs, and even the commander of Mafeking informed us that certain Kaffir chiefs would assist him. We know that these numbered 30,000 able-bodied men. The number of Kaffirs nearly equalled the number of our forces. Besides them, more than 200,000 English troops arrived, and against these we have to fight. Now, gentlemen, look on God's government. Is it not wonderful that 40,000 men having to fight these thousands, besides the coloured people, still live? Acknowledge therein the hand of God. The matter I wish to impress is this. It is remarkable that when we meet the enemy we stand in the proportion of 10 to 100. Yet the Lord hath spared us thus far. I do not wish to prophesy, but I wish to point out that our guidance is in the word of God. It is extraordinary, but this war is a sign of the times. What it amounts to is this. That the power of the Beast is an obstinate power to persecute the Church and will continue this until the Lord says, ' Thus far and no further,' and why? Because the Church must be tried and purified as there is so much iniquity among us. That is why the war is extraordinary and is a sign of the times. Every one will be convinced that the word of God can be plainly traced in this matter. They say that the people ' shall not exist,' but God says, ' it shall exist and be purified.' In my mind it lies clear and discernable that the day of grace is not far off. The Lord will prove to be ruler, and nothing shall take place without His will. When He allows chastisement to come upon us we must bend ourselves and humble ourselves, confess our sins and turn again to the Lord. When the whole nation has been humbled, and it is seen that we can do nothing ourselves, the Lord will help us and we shall have peace immediately. This humility has not grasped our hearts sufficiently at present, and we must perform our earnest duty as Peter says in 1 Peter, chapter v., v. 7 and 8: —'Casting all your care upon Him; for He careth for you'; but in the eighth verse it states: —'Be sober, be vigilant; because your adversary the Devil, as a roaring lion, walketh about, seeking whom he may devour.' That is the point on which we must be careful. If we fall into disbelief then we lower ourselves.

"I ask you, brothers, what is their behaviour? In an open letter Kaffirs are called up by them as at Derdepoort, and women and children are murdered. The English assert that no Kaffirs were utilized against us but only coloured people, but it is a fact that Montsioa with his Kaffirs are in Mafeking, and are employed to fight against us. Now, gentlemen, you must not come to the conclusion that every one who fights against us belongs to the Beast (vide Revelations, chap. 13). There are certainly hundreds of God's children with them who, however, through fear are the Beast's, and are forced to act with them, but God knows all hearts. We did not seek to spill the blood which lies strewn upon the earth, as we conceded nearly all our rights; but when they wanted to murder us, we could not give way any more. How did it fare with Ahab? The mighty foe came on to the walls of the city, and they lost heart. Then the prophet of God came and said, Fear nothing. Then God arose, and in that God we must put our trust, because He is the same God. Let us not, therefore, live as if no God existed; He reigns. In the beginning was the Word, and the Word was God, and the Word became flesh and lived amongst us. Look at history, it must be an example to us. He is still the same God who led out Israel and hardened the heart of Pharaoh to the end, until finally all the first-born of the Egyptians died, whereupon Pharaoh allowed the Israelites to go. He is still the same God who calmed the winds and storms on the sea, and His arm is not shortened. Some ask, 'Does not this only have reference to the Church in the two Republics?' No. See the three youths in the burning oven. Did these rejoice alone? No; but God's people of the whole earth. Was it solitary for Daniel in the lions' den? No, but all Christians on the whole earth rejoiced. So the Lord often chooses a small body to whom He shows His miracles as an example for the whole Christian world. Look upon the blood which has been spilt upon this earth. Who is the cause of it? We have wanted peace and our freedom since 1836, and the Lord has given it us, and will the Lord ever give anything and then withdraw? No. But let us humble ourselves before the Lord. There is no doubt about it that eventually the Lord will lead us to victory. The day of grace is not far from His people. Do not let us doubt but remain true to God's word and fight in His name. When the cup of humiliation is brought to our lips and we earnestly humble ourselves before the Lord, then the day of grace has arrived. Let each one then acknowledge that it is the hand of God which makes us free and nothing else, then we shall not boast. Yet He uses man as His instrument.

"I have laid my address before you, and I hope that the Raad will not sit over it longer than to-morrow morning. There are several members of the Raad who are burghers or military officers in the field, so there will be no time to treat ordinary subjects. I trust that you will only treat such subjects as I lay before you. I have appointed an acting Commandant General since I have lost my right-hand man, although I do not infer that I have not more such men. The late most noble Commandant General, Messrs. Kock and Wolmarans, members of the executive council, are lost to me. The State Secretary is a newly appointed one, and I am the only one remaining of the old members of the executive council, yet I have experienced much assistance and support from the present members, and God will also support us. The Lord is still our Commander-in-Chief; He gives orders and He knows when to say, 'Thus far and no further.' It is surprising how other Powers are unanimously with us and how the whole of Europe prays for us, and will the Lord lend a deaf ear to these prayers? Oh, no! Trust in the Lord and let us stand by Him, and He will perform miracles. Even if I have to go to St. Helena, the Lord will bring His people back and make them free, and the same judgment will fall on the present Babylon, the cause of all the spilt blood. We fight for the freedom which God granted to us. I say again, should any brothers from this Raad and private persons fall by the sword, they fought in the name of the Lord and believed, and they, so says the word of the Lord, are sacrificed on the altar for the glorification of His name and of the glorious Church, which, at this time, is to be revealed. The Church must be tried and purified, and that is why I cannot see that this extraordinary war will be allowed to destroy us. This war will be continued until the Lord says, 'Thus far and no further,' remain at that, abide by that, and fight with me. I give myself in the hands of the Lord, whatever He has destined for me, I shall kiss His rod with which He chastizes me because I am also guilty. Let every one humble himself before the Lord, I have said."

Orange Free State: A. D. 1900 (May).—Annexation by proclamation of Lord Roberts to the Dominions of the Queen.—"In view of Lord Robert's opinion that early annexation would tend towards the pacification of the country, by removing a feeling of uncertainty as to the return of President Steyn's government," the following commission by the Queen to Lord Roberts was issued on the 21st of May: "Victoria R. I., by the Grace of God of the United Kingdom of Great Britain and Ireland Queen, Defender of the Faith, Empress of India: To Our Right Trusty and Well-beloved Councillor Frederick Sleigh, Baron Roberts of Kandahar, Field Marshal of Our Forces, Knight of Our Most Illustrious Order of Saint Patrick, Knight Grand Cross of Our Most Honourable Order of the Bath, Knight Grand Commander of Our Most Exalted Order of the Star of India, Knight Grand Commander of Our Most Eminent Order of the Indian Empire, upon whom We have conferred the Decoration of the Victoria Cross. Greeting: Whereas the territories in South Africa heretofore known as the Orange Free State have been conquered by Our forces, And whereas it is expedient that such territories should be annexed to and should henceforth form part of Our Dominions: Now know you that We, reposing especial trust and confidence in you the said Frederick Sleigh, Baron Roberts of Kandahar, do hereby authorize and empower you in Our name to annex the said territories and to declare that the said territories shall henceforth form part of Our Dominions. And We do hereby constitute and appoint you to be thereupon Administrator of the said territories provisionally and until Our pleasure is more fully known. And We do authorize and empower you as such Administrator to take all such measures, and to make and enforce such laws as you may deem necessary for the peace, order, and good government of the said territories. And we do strictly charge and command all Our officers, civil and military, and all other Our faithful subjects, that in their several places, and according to their respective opportunities, they do aid and assist you in the execution of this Our Commission, and for so doing this shall be your Warrant. Given at Our Court at St. James's, this 21st day of May, One thousand nine hundred, in the Sixty-third Year of Our Reign." The commission was executed by a public reading of the proclamation of Lord Roberts at Bloemfontein on the 24th of May.—*Great Britain, Papers by Command: 1900, Cd. 261, pp. 136, 144.*

A counter-proclamation, referring to that of the British commander, was issued by President Steyn, from Reitz, on the 11th of June, declaring : " Whereas an unjust war was forced on the people of the Orange Free State and of the South African Republic by Great Britain in the month of October 1899, and whereas these two small Republics have maintained the unequal struggle with the powerful British Empire for more than eight months and still maintain it ; . . . Whereas the forces of the Orange Free State are still in the field and the Orange Free State has not been conquered and whereas the aforesaid proclamation is thus in contradiction with International Law ; Whereas the independence of the Orange Free State has been acknowledged by nearly all the civilised Powers ; Whereas it is notorious that the British authorities have lately recognised that the Orange Free State is governed in an exemplary manner, and that it is both a violation of the laws of civilization and a denial of the fundamental rights of such people to rob it on what a pretence soever, of its freedom, and whereas I consider it desirable to make known to all whom it may concern that the aforesaid Proclamation is not recognised by the Government and the people of the Orange Free State: So, therefore, I, M. T. Steyn, State President of the Orange Free State, in consultation with the Executive Council, and in the name of the independent people of the Orange Free State, do hereby proclaim that the aforesaid annexation is not recognised and is hereby declared to be null and of no avail. The people of the Orange Free State is and remains a free and independent people, and refuses to submit to British rule."—*Great Britain, Papers by Command : Cd. 261, 1900, p. 155.*

Cape Colony : A. D. **1900 (May).**—Opposition of Cape Colony Afrikanders to the **annexation** of the Republics.—A " People's Congress " of the Afrikanders, or Bondmen, of Cape Colony, was held at Graaff-Reinet, on the 30th of May, to protest against the annexation of the Boer Republics. The following resolution was adopted by acclamation : " Whereas, were the Republics to be annexed the majority of Cape Colonists would feel themselves bound morally to work unceasingly by every right and lawful means for the restoration of independence to the Republics, and to make that end their first political object ; And whereas from our knowledge of the history and character of the Republics we are convinced they would never become the willing subjects of the Empire, but would seize any and every opportunity which might offer itself to recover their independence, possibly by force of arms, once they were to be deprived of it ; And whereas instead of the annexation of the Republics tending to promote the welfare of their people, as has been claimed, it would, if successfully maintained for any long period, tend to degrade those people and their offsprings, seeing that the servitude of a self-governing State is as demoralising to its people as the more direct form of personal slavery ; And whereas, as the annexation of the Republics by Great Britain would be as great a wrong morally as the theft by a rich man of a poor man's hard-earned savings : On that general ground alone it is not believable that permanent good could result from such a policy. Therefore be it resolved now that we, on behalf of the majority of Cape Colonists, do hereby declare our solemn and profound conviction that the annexation of the two South African Republics would be disastrous to the peace and welfare of South Africa and of the Empire as a whole." Also the following : " Be it resolved that it is the opinion of the people in Congress here assembled that a settlement of the South African question on the following basis would prove a blessing to South Africa and the Empire, namely, that the two Republics should have their unqualified independence ; that the Colonies should have the right to enter into treaties of obligatory arbitration with the Republics for the settlement of all disputes affecting the internal affairs of the South African Continent, and that this colony, and any other colony so deserving it, should have a voice in the selection of its Governors. Be it further resolved that a settlement on the above basis would make the majority of the people who have made South Africa their home the warm friends and staunch allies of the British Empire, and that in no other way known to us can that end now be attained."

In transmitting a report of this meeting to Secretary Chamberlain, the High Commissioner, Sir Alfred Milner, wrote: " I do not myself take a very gloomy view of the prospect of racial relations in the Colony, much less in South Africa generally. If it is true, as the conciliators are never tired of threatening us, that race hatred will be eternal, why should they make such furious efforts to keep it up at the present moment? The very vehemence of their declarations that the Africanders will never forgive, nor forget, nor acquiesce, seems to me to indicate a considerable and well-justified anxiety on their part lest these terrible things should after all happen."—*Great Britain, Papers by Command: July, 1900, South Africa, Cd. 261, pp. 182–88.*

The Field of **War: A. D. 1900 (May—June).** —The British invasion of the Transvaal.— Occupation of Johannesburg and Pretoria.— **Expulsion** of the Boers from **Natal.**—Discussion of terms of surrender.—On the 22d of May, Lord Roberts resumed his forward movement from Kroonstad, with a strong column of cavalry, under General French, in advance on the west, and another, of mounted infantry, under General

Ian Hamilton, on the east. The Boers, under General Botha, had prepared defensive works on the Rhenoster River, but were too much endangered by the flanking column of General Hamilton to make a stand there, and fell back. Again at the Vaal River, their fortifications were untenable, as against an invasion of such numbers, with so large a mounted force. With little resistance the British army crossed the Vaal on the 26th and 27th and entered the territory of the South African Republic. On the 30th it was before Johannesburg, and the town was surrendered on the following day. Thence the invading force moved upon Pretoria,. meeting some opposition, but evidently none that was hopefully made, and the capital was surrendered unconditionally to Lord Roberts on the 5th of June. President Kruger and the officials of his government had left the town, with their archives and their treasure, and movable offices had been prepared for them in railway cars, which were transferred for the time being to Machadodorp, at some distance eastward. Most of the armed burghers had escaped from the town, and they had been able to remove about 900 of their British prisoners; but a large number of the latter were set free. General Botha gathered up his broken and discouraged forces and intrenched them in a strong position on the Lorenzo Marquez railway, only 15 miles eastward from Pretoria. Lord Roberts moved against him on the 11th and compelled him to retreat, after hard fighting for five hours. This ended important operations in that part of the field.

In Natal, General Buller, since early in May, had been pushing his army northward, in a movement co-operative with that of Lord Roberts. He had turned the flank of the Boer forces in the positions they had fortified against his advance, regained Glencoe and Dundee, and moved on to Newcastle. Then, with more serious fighting, he forced Botha's Pass through the mountains, compelled the Boers to evacuate their strongholds on Laing's Nek and Majuba Hill, and was substantially in possession of Natal.

On the 30th of May, General Buller sent word to General Chris Botha that Lord Roberts had crossed the Vaal, and suggested surrender. further resistance appearing useless. This led to a meeting of the opposed commanders, at which Botha asked what terms Lord Roberts would offer. Buller immediately referred the question to Lord Roberts, saying: "Can you let me know your terms of peace for individual and separate commandos? . . . I think they are inclined to give in, and that I have in front of me about half the Transvaal forces now in the field. If you think it worth while please let me know if I may mention any terms of peace to them. I think, even if assisted from the Orange Free State, it will cost me about 500 men killed and wounded to get out of Natal." The reply of Lord Roberts, dated June 3, 1900, was as follows: "Your telegram of yesterday. My terms with the Transvaal Government are unconditional surrender. With regard to troops, those who deliver up their arms and riding animals are allowed to go to their homes on signing pledge that they will not fight again during present war. The exceptions to this rule are those who have commanded portions of the Republican forces, or who have taken an active part in the policy which brought about the war, or who have been guilty of or been parties to wanton destruction of property, or guilty of acts contrary to the usages of civilized warfare. Principal officers should remain with you on parole until you receive instructions regarding their disposal." General Botha declined the terms.

Nine days later (June 12) Lord Roberts opened correspondence on the same subject with General Louis Botha, Acting Commandant-General of the Boer forces, endeavoring to persuade him, "in the cause of humanity, to refrain from further resistance." The Commandant-General wrote in return: "For the purpose of arriving at a decision, it is not only absolutely necessary for me to call a General Council of War of my Officers and to consult them, but above all it is necessary for me to consider the subject with my Government. I trust that for the sake of humanity your Excellency will give me the opportunity for such consideration and consultation. As some of my Officers are near the Natal Border, and I am also a long way separate from my Government, this will require some time. I ask your Excellency kindly, therefore, for an armistice for six days, beginning from to-morrow morning at sunrise, during which time no forward movement will be made on either side within the territory of the South African Republic."

Lord Roberts replied: "I am anxious to meet your wishes and to enable your Honour to communicate with the Government of the South African Republic, but as the movement of my troops in that Republic are intimately connected with operations in progress in other parts of South Africa, it is impossible for me to accede to your Honour's request that there should be an armistice for 6 days, during which time no forward movement will be made on either side within the territory of the South African Republic. I am willing, however, to refrain from making further movements in the district to the east of the Elands River Railway Station, our present most advanced post in that direction, and also in the district north of the Volksrust and Johannesburg Railway, for a period of five (5) days, commencing at dawn on the 15th June, on the condition that no movement westward or southward is made by the Army of the South African Republic during that same period. This will, I trust, give your Honour the opportunity you desire of consulting your Officers and conferring with your Government, and I sincerely hope that the result will be of such a satisfactory nature as to prevent further unnecessary loss of life."

The proposal was declined by General Botha, in the following note (June 15): "In answer to your letter, dated 14th June, just received by me, wherein your Excellency consents to an armistice for five days, but with the reservation of the right to your Excellency to move your Army in all directions within the South African Republic, except east of Elands River Station and north of the Volksrust-Johannesburg Railway line, I must, to my great regret, inform your Excellency that this reservation makes it impossible for me to accept this armistice, which I have so much desired."

The Field of War: A. D. 1900 (June—December).—Continued resistance of the Boers in guerilla warfare.—An outline of the events of seven months.—A British view of the later situation.—"After the occupation of Pretoria, exhaustion of the mounted forces and of the transport again supervened and Lord Roberts was preoccupied with the double task of bringing up large numbers of horses and masses of stores by a railway exposed to attack along a distance of 290 miles, and at the same time of dealing, as best he could, with scattered parts of the enemy, nowhere formidable in a military sense, but capable of much mischief. The period beginning with the occupation of Bloemfontein, during which the Boers developed and maintained warfare of guerilla type, imposed highly responsible duties upon British officers in charge of scattered posts and convoys. In some cases those duties were not adequately discharged, and for a time the defences of the important line of communications appeared to be somewhat imperfectly organized and supervised. There were signs of the tendency to relax precautions after a conspicuous success, which has been shown by British armies on other occasions. It was clear that the main centre of Boer activity was in the Bethlehem district, and at the end of June Lord Roberts despatched a strong column south under Lieutenant-General Hunter to co-operate with Major-Generals MacDonald, Clements, and Paget from the west. Bethlehem was captured on July 7, and by the end of the month Commandant Prinsloo, caught in the Brandwater Basin between the forces of Lieutenant-Generals Hunter and Rundle, surrendered with more than 4,000 men and a large number of horses and wagons. . . . Meanwhile, Lord Roberts, who had driven back the Boers along the Lorenzo Marques line, in two actions near Eerste Fabricken, on June 11 and 12, began an advance eastward on July 23, and on August 7 Sir R. Buller moved northwards from Paarde Kop. On August 25 the Commander-in-Chief met Sir R. Buller and Generals French and Pole-Carew at Belfast, and after the fighting of the 27th the resistance of the Boers in this district practically collapsed. Starting from Machadodorp on September 1, Sir R. Buller moved slowly towards Spitzkop, driving the enemy before him through a difficult mountainous region, and General French pressed on to Barberton, which was occupied on the 13th without opposition. On the 24th the Guards reached Komati Poort. The rugged hill country east of Belfast offered great opportunities for the tactics in which the Boers appeared to excel; but the 'natural fortress surrounded by a glacis of about 1,500 yards absolutely without cover' near Bergendal Farm was not defended with the tenacity shown on previous occasions, and the subsequent British advance led to a wholesale destruction of artillery material and to the surrender of some 3,000 men to the Portuguese. This, the third great disaster which has befallen the Boers, left them without any centre of resistance or any considerable gathering of fighting men.

"Before the outbreak of war we estimated their available strength at about 45,000, to which must be added some 10,000 colonial rebels and perhaps 5,000 mercenaries. It is doubtful whether the force actually in the field at any one time reached 45,000, and the total loss in killed, wounded and prisoners, cannot be much less than 30,000. . . . Exhaustion of supplies and of ammunition must soon begin to tell heavily upon the Boers; but it cannot be said that they have at present given evidence of personal demoralization. Comparatively small bodies, lightly equipped, still hold the field and show much activity over a wide area. It is impossible to provide British garrisons for every town and village, and wherever the roving bands of the enemy appear there is are crudescence of local hostility, even in districts which have been apparently tranquil for months. Large mobile columns are employed in pursuit, but the Boers carefully avoid general engagements and attack only when there appears to be a chance of surprising and overpowering small detachments. . . . Mounted forces, marching as light as possible and capably commanded, are the principal requirements of the situation. .It is necessary to give the roving commandos no rest and to make every effort to capture their leaders. The work is not easy, and it requires great energy and sound military judgment ; but it will be successfully accomplished, and the scale of the operations will steadily dwindle into measures of police. Meanwhile a gradual withdrawal of troops from South Africa is taking place, and progress is doubtless being made with the new organization under Lieutenant-General Baden-Powell, which will be specially fitted for the work that now lies before us. . . .

"The total casualties of the war up to the 31st ult. are estimated at about 46,000, and 'the reduction of the military forces' due to a campaign of more than a year is returned at 12,769, of which total 11,739 are accounted for by death, including 6,482 victims to disease. It is impossible to rank the Boer war among the great campaigns of the British Army; but the peculiar difficulties must never be forgotten. The closest parallel is probably that of the American Civil war, in which an armed people long resisted far superior forces and carried invasion into the territory of the stronger Power. The military potentiality of the Southern States was at first as little realized in Washington as was that of the Boers in London, and disasters therefore resulted. In both cases the issue was certain as soon as adequate force in strong hands was available. The Southern leaders, like the Boers, hoped and strove for foreign intervention in vain ; but the former were far less prepared for war than the latter. On the other hand the Boers, though ably led in a limited sense, have produced no commanders with a genius for war comparable to that of Lee and of Jackson, nor have they shown the discipline and the cohesion which characterized the Southern armies when at their best. Desultory and irregular warfare may still be prolonged for a time ; great activity and ample vigilance will still be required."—*London Times, Nov.* 5, 1900.

At the end of the year the "Times" summed up the later features of the situation as follows: "The spirit of the Boers remained unbroken, and small mobile commandos, scattered over the vast area of the countries which we had undertaken to occupy, perfectly familiar with the ground, and in close touch with the civil population, have succeeded up to the present time in making the task of the British Generals one of extreme difficulty. The Boer resistance has centered chiefly in three men, Commandants Louis Botha in the north-east, Delarey to the west of Pretoria, and De Wet in the Orange Free State. The first, who since the death of General Joubert was in chief command in Natal, and afterwards in the Eastern Transvaal, has not been conspicuously

active since September, but the other two have achieved a great deal with their very limited resources, and have earned enduring fame as guerrilla chieftains. De Wet, especially, after having been 'routed' and 'surrounded' times without number, has succeeded in giving occupation to several British Generals and their forces up to the present time, has kept the eastern part of the Orange Colony in a continual ferment, and till now has defied the energetic efforts of General Charles Knox to capture him. Delarey, after remaining fairly quiescent for several weeks, suddenly advanced through the Magaliesburg in the middle of the present month with a force variously estimated at 1,500 or 3,000 men, surrounded and captured a position held by four companies of the Northumberlands, and compelled the retreat of General Clements and the evacuation of his camp. It is true that these things are but the episodes of the later stages of a war in which there will be no more great battles, but they are exhausting, costly, and sometimes humiliating."
—*London Times, Dec.* 31, 1900.

The Field of **War: A. D. 1900** (August—December).—Farm-burning by the British troops.—Under proclamations issued by Lord Roberts in August and September, aimed at the suppression of irregular warfare, a punitive policy was adopted, which included the burning of farmhouses where guerrilla bands were sheltered, or whose inmates acted with such bands, and which soon came to be denounced as one of shameful barbarity. Such different representations have been made, as to the manner in which the orders of Lord Roberts were carried out, and as to the measure of devastation and suffering produced, that it seems to be impossible to judge whether the British farm-burning in the Transvaal and Orange Free State has or has not gone beyond the usual brutalities that belong to the very nature of war. Mr. Kruger, in speeches made after he went to Europe, represented it as monstrous beyond example. "The war waged against us," he said, on landing at Marseilles, "is a war of barbarians. I have witnessed wars of barbarians and never have I seen committed barbarities so monstrous as those committed daily among us. Our farms, which we had had so much difficulty to construct, are burned. The women whose husbands are at the war are hunted down and brutally separated from their children, who are deprived of bread and necessaries." The Afrikanders of Cape Colony held similar language. Men of conscience and heart in England were troubled by such accusations. Mr. Trevelyan, M. P., wrote to "The Times," on the 24th of November : "What so many of us feel, in the first place, is that we are not in a position to form a fair judgment from sheer lack of the most elementary reliable information of what has been done and is still doing. An officer returned from the war about two months told me the other day that he supposed only about 40 farms had been burnt. I read in the 'Westminster Gazette' from an equally honourable gentleman that it would not be an exaggeration to say that one-third of the farms in the Orange River Colony were in ashes. Clearly it is impossible for the nation to make out the truth when such contradictory statements are universally current. . . . One thing we do know for certain—that on September 2 Lord Roberts, regarding the war as having degenerated

into guerrilla fighting, proclaimed that all farms would be burnt within a radius of ten miles of any point upon the railway raided by the Boers. It is now November 24. We know that many people innocent of any dealing with De Wet have lost all they possess owing to his misguided energy. Has it diminished sensibly the Boer forces in the field? If not, what is its utility? . . . If the resistance of the Boers is being lessened by these destructions, let us at least have the poor consolation of knowing it. Again, we want to know what really happens to the women and children whom our soldiers conduct, I believe, generally to the nearest town after their homes have been burned. People whose property has been totally destroyed in a country where war has stopped all industry obviously cannot keep themselves."

When Parliament met in December the subject was brought up there, by Mr. Trevelyan and others, and debated at length, without much clearer light on it being found. The government could give no definite information as to what was being done, but stoutly upheld the course which the military leaders had taken. Mr. Balfour said : "The ordinary laws of war as practised by civilized countries depend essentially upon drawing a sharp distinction between combatant and non-combatant. The combatant has his particular privileges, the non-combatant has his particular privileges. What has been universally found intolerable is that a man should oscillate, according to his convenience, from one category to the other—be a peaceful agriculturist when it suits him and an effective combatant when circumstances seem to be favourable. That practice is so intolerable that I believe all nations have laid down the severest rules for repressing it. I have in my hands the instructions to the army of the United States in the field, dated 1898. I should like to read to the House two extracts from this document. Rule 52 says : —'If a people of a country, or any portion of same already occupied by the army, rises against it, they are violators of the laws of war, and are not entitled to their protection.' The 82nd Rule is to the effect that men, or squads of men, who take part in raids of any kind without permission, and without being part or portion of an organized hostile army, are not public enemies, and therefore if captured are not entitled to be treated as prisoners of war, but shall be treated as highway robbers or pirates."

Mr. Chamberlain said : "Lord Roberts's proclamation was to the effect that, in the first instance, general officers were authorized to burn down farmhouses as a punishment in cases in which they were used as fortified places or places for the concealment of arms, or in which the white flag had been improperly used, or where they had been the scenes of gross treachery and of acts contrary to the laws of war. As a matter of right and morality, the Government are prepared to sustain Lord Roberts absolutely. . . . Lord Roberts was placed in the most difficult position in which a general could possibly be placed. He had his base 1,500 miles away at least from his front, through a most difficult country, and he was served only by a single line of railway, and any catastrophe to the railway might have meant a catastrophe to the whole army. It is all very well to talk of humanity, but you must take first account of our own people. Now, Sir, it was of the first importance, it was the clear duty of Lord Roberts, to take any steps in his power to prevent the cutting of the line and the danger which would thereby accrue to his force, and he accordingly issued a proclamation that in the case of the destruction of the line persons in the vicinity would be held responsible, and that farmhouses in the vicinity might be destroyed. We understood his proclamation to mean that he would require evidence of some complicity on the part of the persons whose farmhouses were destroyed. . . . We inquired the other day, when the matter assumed greater importance, whether the construction we placed upon the proclamation was true, and we have a reply from Lord Kitchener, who has now taken the place of Lord Roberts, that we are perfectly right in that assumption. . . . According to the proclamation of Lord Roberts, whose humanity is proverbial, and who therefore could not under any circumstances be accused of unnecessary cruelty, cattle are always to be paid for by the troops, or a receipt given, which is as good as payment, except in those cases in which the owner of the cattle has been guilty of acts of war or of outrages which are punishable by all civilized nations who are at war. Therefore the taking of cattle does not mean necessarily that the owner of the cattle is placed in the impossibility of continuing his occupation. If he has not got the cattle he has got the money for them except in the cases in which destruction has taken place as a punitive measure. In all other cases the instructions are precise, and I believe from all the information we have obtained from the reports of the generals in the field they have been strictly carried out. Never in the history of war has war been carried out with so much humanity on the part of the officers and of the soldiers concerned as in the present war. The hon. member also spoke of the deportation of women. That sounds like something serious, but I believe it will be found that it is only for their own protection. If we are unable in this vast country to occupy and garrison every bit of it, when our troops are removed, if women and children are left alone they remain there in some danger—in danger from those marauding bands of which I have spoken and also from the vast native population. And, Sir, this native population is answerable, I believe, for every case of proved outtrage either upon women or children. I believe, and the last reports to which we have received confirm that belief, that in no case has a British soldier been justly accused of such an outrage."

The following proclamation, issued by Lord Roberts, November 18, seems to indicate that there had been practices in farm-burning, before that time, which he could not approve : "As there appears to be some misunderstanding with reference to burning of farms and breaking of dams, Commander-in-Chief wishes following to be lines on which General Officers Commanding are to act : —No farm is to be burnt except for act of treachery, or when troops have been fired on from premises, or as punishment for breaking of telegraph or railway line, or when they have been used as bases of operations for raids, and then only with direct consent of General Officer Commanding, which is to be given in writing, the mere fact of a burgher being absent on commando is on no account to be used as reason for

burning the house. All cattle, wagons, and foodstuffs are to be removed from all farms; if that is found to be impossible, they are to be destroyed, whether owner be present or not."— *Great Britain, Papers by Command: Cd.* 426, 1900, p. 23.

Rhodesia: **A. D. 1900** (September).—Protectorate over Barotsiland. — The "Cape Times" of September 19, 1900, stated that a "Government Gazette Extraordinary" had been issued containing an Order in Council proclaiming a protectorate over Barotsiland—North-Western Rhodesia. "The limits of the country included in the protectorate are the parts of Africa bounded by the River Zambesi, the German South-West African Protectorate, the Portuguese possessions, the Congo Free State, and the Kafukwe or Loengi River. The Order provides that the British South Africa Company may nominate officials to govern the territory, and that these are to be confirmed by the High Commissioner. The High Commissioner may, amongst other things, from time to time by proclamation provide for the administration of justice, the raising of revenue by the imposition of taxes (which may include a tax in respect of the occupation of native huts), and Customs duties or otherwise, and generally for the peace, order, and good government of all persons within the limits of the order, including the prohibition and punishment of acts tending to disturb the public peace. The expenses of the administration of this country, if not entirely borne by the revenues of the country, will be borne by the British South Africa Company, and if the revenue more than meet the expenses, the excess will be paid to the Chartered Company."

The Transvaal: **A. D. 1900** (September).— Leave of absence to President Kruger.—His departure for Europe.—Proclamation of Lord Roberts.—The following proclamation by the Executive Council of the Boer government was issued from Nelspruit on the 10th of September, 1900 : "Whereas the advanced age of His Honour the State President makes it impossible for His Honour further to accompany the Commandos ; and whereas the Executive Council is convinced that the highly-valued services of His Honour can still be usefully applied in the interest of Land and People, the Executive Council hereby determines to grant His Honour leave of absence to Europe for the period of six months, in order still to advance our cause there, and Mr. S. W. Burger, Vice-President, takes his place according to law. [Signed] S. W. BURGER, Vice President. F. W. REITZ, State Secretary."

Lord Roberts seems to have regarded the acceptance of this "leave of absence" by President Kruger as equivalent to a resignation of his office; for he published, on the 14th of September, a proclamation in the following words : "The late President, Mr. Kruger, and Mr. Reitz, with the archives of the South African Republic, have crossed the Portuguese frontier, and arrived at Lourenço Marques with a view to sailing for Europe at an early date. Mr. Kruger has formally resigned the position he held as President of the South African Republic, thus severing his official connection with the Transvaal. Mr. Kruger's action shows how hopeless in his opinion is the war which has now been carried on for nearly a year, and his desertion of the Boer cause should make it clear to his fellow burghers that it is useless for them to continue the struggle any longer.

"It is probably unknown to the inhabitants of the Transvaal and Orange River Colony that nearly 15,000 of their fellow-subjects are now prisoners of war, not one of whom will be released until those now in arms against us surrender unconditionally. The burghers must by this time be cognisant of the fact that no intervention on their behalf can come from any of the Great Powers, and, further, that the British Empire is determined to complete the work which has already cost her so many valuable lives, and to carry to its conclusion the war declared against her by the late Governments of the South African Republic and Orange Free State, a war to which there can be but one ending. If any further doubts remain in the minds of the burghers as to Her Britannic Majesty's intentions, they should be dispelled by the permanent manner in which the country is gradually being occupied by Her Majesty's Forces, and by the issue of the Proclamations signed by me on the 24th May and 1st September 1900, annexing the Orange Free State and the South African Republic respectively, in the name of Her Majesty.

"I take this opportunity of pointing out that, except in the small area occupied by the Boer army under the personal command of Commandant-General Botha, the war is degenerating, and has degenerated, into operations carried on in an irregular and irresponsible manner by small, and in very many cases, insignificant bodies of men. I should be failing in my duty to Her Majesty's Government and to Her Majesty's Army in South Africa if I neglected to use every means in my power to bring such irregular warfare to an early conclusion. The means which I am compelled to adopt are those which the customs of war prescribe as being applicable to such cases. They are ruinous to the country, and entail endless suffering on the burghers and their families, and the longer this guerrilla warfare continues the more vigorously must they be enforced."—*Great Britain, Papers by Command:* 1900, Cd. 420, p. 78, *and Cd.* 426, p. 17.

The Transvaal: A. D. **1900** (October).—Proclamation of annexation to the British Dominions.—In terms similar to those used in proclaiming the annexation of the Orange Free State (see above: MAY) the annexation of the Transvaal to the Dominions of Her British Majesty was proclaimed with great ceremony at Pretoria on the 25th of October.

The Field of **War**: A. D. **1900** (November).—Return of Lord Roberts to England, leaving Lord Kitchener in command.—Having been appointed Commander-in-Chief of the British Army, in the place of Lord Wolseley, Field-Marshal Lord Roberts, on the 29th of November, delivered the command in South Africa to Lord Kitchener, and returned to England. At the same time, Lord Kitchener was raised to the rank of Lieutenant-General.

Cape Colony and the Transvaal: A. D. **1900** (December).—Afrikander Congress.—Lord Kitchener to the burghers of Pretoria.—From 6,000 to 8,000 persons were reported to be in attendance at an "Afrikander Congress," held at Worcester, in Cape Colony, December 6, which adopted the following resolutions: "1. We men and women of South Africa assembled and represented here, having heard the report of the people's deputation to England, and having taken into earnest consideration the deplorable condition into which the people of South Africa have been plunged, and the grave danger threatening our civilization, record our solemn conviction that the highest interests of South Africa demand, first, the termination of the war now raging with untold misery and horror, such as the burning of houses, the devastation of the country, the extermination of the white nationality, and the treatment to which women and children are subjected, which will leave a lasting heritage of bitterness and hatred, while seriously endangering further relations between civilization and barbarism in South Africa; secondly, the retention by the Republics of their independence, whereby alone the peace of South Africa can be maintained. 2. The congress desires full recognition of the right of the people of this colony under its Constitution to settle and manage their own affairs and to express grave disapproval of the policy pursued and the attitude adopted in this matter by the Governor and High Commissioner, his Excellency Sir Alfred Milner. 3. The congress solemnly pledges itself to labour in a constitutional way unceasingly for the above resolutions, and resolves to send a deputation to his Excellency Sir Alfred Milner, asking him to bring the resolutions officially to the notice of her Majesty's Government."

On the 21st of December Lord Kitchener addressed a meeting, at Pretoria, of burghers who had surrendered to the British and who desired to bring about peace. In his remarks he was reported to have said: "The Boers had fought a good fight, but they were overpowered. There would be no dishonour in the leaders recognizing this fact. The proclamations that had been issued were of little use, as means were adopted to prevent them from reaching the burghers. He trusted that the committee would endeavour to acquaint the Boers in the field with the true position. He desired to give them every chance to surrender voluntarily, and to finish the war by the most humane means possible. If the conciliatory methods now being adopted failed he had other means which he would be obliged to exercise. He would give the committee notice if the time arrived to consider conciliation as a failure. The principal difficulties were that burghers desirous of surrendering were afraid they would not be allowed to remain in their own districts or that they would be punished for violating their oath of neutrality. Gen. Kitchener declared that he had issued instructions that burghers who surrendered would, with their families and stock, be protected in their own districts. Those who had broken the oath of neutrality under compulsion would be accorded the same treatment. Deserted women and children would be kept in laagers, where their friends could freely join them. It was essential to clear the country. While food remained the commandos were enabled to continue in the field. Gen. Kitchener added that it must be understood that the British would not be responsible for stock unless it was brought in and kept within protected limits. In conclusion Gen. Kitchener said that he had come to speak to the burghers personally in order that they might be able to tell their friends what they had heard from his own lips."

The Field of **War**: A. D. **1900** (December).—Numbers of British troops employed in the **war** from the beginning, **and** their losses. See (in this vol.) ENGLAND: A. D. 1900 (DEC.).

British Colonies: A. D. **1901** (January).— **New** heads of the Colonial Governments.— The following appointments were announced by the British Colonial Office on the 4th of January, 1901: Sir Alfred Milner to be Governor of the Transvaal and British High Commissioner. The Hon. Sir Walter Francis Hely-Hutchinson (Govcruor of Natal and Zululand since 1893) to be Governor of Cape Colony. Lieutenant-Colonel Sir Henry C. McCallum (Governor of Newfoundland since 1898, and aide-de-camp to the Queen since 1900) to be Governor of Natal. Major Hamilton John Goold-Adams (Resident Commissioner of the Bechuanaland Protectorate) to be Lieutenant-Governor of the Orange River Colony.

Cape Colony: A. D. **1901** (January).—Boer invasion.—Declaration of martial **law.**—On New Year's Day, 1901, the Cape Town correspondent of the "London Times" was compelled to write: "The immediate aspect of affairs in Cape Colony at the opening of the new year is scarcely less gloomy than at the beginning of 1900. The number of Boers invading the country to-day may be less than it was a year ago, but they have penetrated further south, and their presence near such centres of hostile Dutch feeling as Graaf Reinet constitutes an element of danger which was not present last January. The proclamation issued this morning by the High Commissioner calling for volunteers to defend the lines of communication proves that the military authorities are at last alive to the critical nature of the situation, but the measure comes very late in the day."

On the 17th of January a cable message from Cape Town announced: "An extraordinary gazette issued this afternoon contains a proclamation placing the whole of the Cape Colony under martial law, with the exception of the Cape Town, Wynberg, Simonstown, Port Elizabeth and East London districts and the territories of the Transkei, Tembuland, Griqualand and East Pondoland. The gazette also states that the peace-preservation act will be enforced in the Cape Colony, Wynberg and Simonstown districts. Under this act all the civil population will be called upon to deliver up their arms."

Orange Free State: A. D. **1901** (January). —Peace movement.—Condition of country described.—**Defiant** proclamation of Steyn and De **Wet.**—Early in January, a "Central Peace Committee," formed at Kroonstad, addressed an open letter to their fellow citizens, appealing for submission and peace, saying: "The country is literally one vast wilderness. The farmers are obliged to go to the towns for protection, and huge refugee camps have been formed by the British for them and their families. These people have lost everything, and ruin and starvation stare them in the face. All this misery is caused by a small and obstinate minority, who will not bow to the inevitable and who make the majority suffer. Any encouragement to the men still on commando to continue the hopeless struggle can only injure us and cause us further misery. We have done our best and fought to get Africa under one flag, and we have lost. Let there be no mistake about this. England has

spent millions and sacrificed thousands of lives, and no reasonable being can believe for one moment that she will now give up the fruits of victory. It is, therefore, a duty for us, her beaten foe, to accept the terms offered by our conqueror. . . . We appeal to you and ask you to appoint another congress, and nominate men of influence out of your midst to visit Mr. Steyn and General De Wet, and try to persuade them to accept the terms offered by England. These two men are the only obstacles to peace. We ask you to believe us when we say that Mr. Kruger and the late Transvaal Government have been willing twice already to accept British terms, but Mr. Steyn refused to have anything to do with surrender. He continued the war and encouraged the burghers in the hope that we should get European assistance. To-day he is cut off from all communication with the outside world. You know and we know how unfounded that hope is and it is your duty to assist us to make him understand this. We appeal to you to help us to make an end to this unhappy state of affairs, which is plunging everybody into poverty and despair."

As if in response to this cry for peace, Steyn and De Wet issued the following proclamation a few days later: "Be it known to all that the war which was forced on the Republics by the British Government still rages in the Orange Free State and in the South African Republic; and that the customs of civilized warfare and also the Conventions of Geneva and The Hague have not been observed by the enemy, who has not scrupled, contrary to the Geneva Convention, to capture doctors and ambulances and to deport them, in order to prevent our wounded from getting medical assistance. He has seized ambulances and material appertaining thereto, and has not hesitated, contrary to the recognized primitive rules of warfare, and contrary to his solemn agreement at The Hague, to arrest neutrals and deport them, and to send out marauding bands to plunder, burn, and damage the burghers' private property. He has armed Kaffirs and natives and made use of them against us in war. He has been continually busy capturing women and children, old and sickly men. Many women's deaths have been occasioned because the so-called Christian enemy had no consideration for women on a sick bed or for those whose state of health should have protected them against rough treatment. Honourable women and tender children have not only been treated roughly, but also in an insulting manner by the soldiers, by order of their officers. Moreover, old mothers and women have been raped, even wives and children. The property of prisoners of war, and even of killed burghers, has not been respected. In many instances the mother and father have been taken from the house, which was thus left unprotected, and all have been left to their fate, an easy prey to the savage. The world has been untruthfully informed by the enemy that he was obliged to carry out this destruction because the burghers blew up the line and cut the wires, or misused the white flag. Nearly all the houses in the two Republics have been destroyed, whether in the neighbourhood of the railway line or not; while with regard to the misuse of the white flag, that is simply a continuance of the everlasting calumny against which the Afrikander has had to strive since God brought him into contact with Englishmen. Robbing his opponent of his goods has not satisfied him ; he will not be satisfied till he has robbed him of his good name also.

"Then he wishes to inform the world that the Republics are conquered and the war ended, and that only here and there small plundering bands are to be found who continue the strife in an irresponsible manner. It is an untruth. The Republics are not yet conquered. The war is not finished. The burgher forces of the two Republics are still led by responsible leaders, as from the commencement of the war, under the supervision of the Governments of both Republics. The fact that Lord Roberts and Lord Kitchener choose to term the burgher forces marauding bands does not make them such. Similarly, saying that the war is over does not put an end to it while fighting still continues. When was this war over ? After the battle of Spion Kop or after Paardeberg ? After the occupation of Bloemfontein or Pretoria ? Or perhaps after the battles of Dewetsdorp or Commando Nek, in both of which irregulars were captured and the enemy totally vanquished. The burghers would be less than men if they allowed the enemy to go unpunished after ill-treating their wives and destroying their homes from sheer lust of destruction. Therefore a portion of our burghers have again been sent into Cape Colony, not only to wage war, but to be in a position to make reprisals as they have already done in the case of the ambulances.

Therefore we again warn the officers of her Majesty's troops that unless they cease the destruction of property in the Republics, we shall wreak vengeance by destroying the property of her Majesty's subjects who are unkindly disposed to us ; but at the same time, to avoid being misunderstood, we hereby openly declare that the women and children will always remain unmolested, despite anything done to ours by her Majesty's troops. We ask for nothing from our brothers in Cape Colony, but we call upon them, as well as upon the civilized world, to assist on behalf of civilization and Christianity in putting an end to the barbarous manner of the enemy's warfare. Our prayer will always be that the God of our fathers will not desert us in this unrighteous strife.   STEYN.
"On the field, January 14.   DE WET."

The Field of War : A. D. 1901 (February). —Report of British military forces in South Africa from the beginning of the war, with the number of killed and wounded and the deaths from wounds and disease.—A Parliamentary paper issued on the 26th of February, 1901, contained the following table, showing the strength of the garrison in South Africa on the 1st of August, 1899, before the beginning of the war, with the subsequent reinforcements and casualties, and the total strength of forces on the 1st of February, 1901:

	OFFICERS.	NON-COMMISSIONED OFFICERS AND MEN.					TOTAL OFFICERS AND MEN.
		Cavalry.	Artillery.	Infantry and Mounted Infantry.	Others.	Total.	
I. Garrison on Aug. 1, 1899	318	1,127	1,035	6,428	1,032	9,622	9,940
II. Reinforcements, Aug. 1, 1899, to Oct. 11, 1899 (outbreak of war) —							
(1.) From Home	280	....	743	5,620	....	6,363	6,643
(2.) From India (some of these did not reach South Africa until after the outbreak of hostilities)	259	1,564	653	3,427	....	5,644	5,903
	539	1,564	1,396	9,047	....	12,007	12,546
III. Further reinforcements from Oct. 11, 1899, to end of July, 1900 —							
Regulars —							
(1.) From Home and Colonies	5,748	11,003	14,145	110,292	14,347	149,787	155,535
(2.) From India	132	713	376	670	....	1,759	1,891
	5,880	11,716	14,521	110,962	14,347	151,546	157,426
Colonials —							
(1.) From Colonies other than South African	550	287	692	9,788	267	11,034	11,584
(2.) Raised in South Africa	1,387	....	....	....	....	28,932	30,319
	1,937	....	....	....	....	39,966	41,903
Imperial Yeomanry	536	....	....	....	....	10,195	10,731
Volunteers from United Kingdom.	342	....	358	9,995	434	10,787	11,129
Militia	831	....	617	19,753	256	20,626	21,457
Total all arms sent to, and raised in, South Africa up to Aug. 1, 1900, including garrison on Aug. 1, 1899	10,383	....	....	....	....	254,749	265,132
IV. Further reinforcements from Aug. 1, 1900, to Jan. 31, 1901 —							
(1.) Regulars	820	3,213	652	10,439	975	15,279	16,099
(2.) Militia	7	....	....	1,141	....	1,141	1,148
	11,210	....	....	....	....	271,169	282,379

	OFFICERS.	NON-COMMISSIONED OFFICERS AND MEN.					TOTAL OFFICERS AND MEN.
		Cavalry.	Artillery.	Infantry and Mounted Infantry.	Others.	Total.	
V. Numbers —							
(1.) Killed to Jan. 31, 1901	334	....	....	....	....	3,346	3,680
(2.) Wounded to Jan 31, 1901.......	1,242	....	....	....	....	14,914	16,156
(3.) Died of disease or wounds or accidentally killed in South Africa to Jan. 31, 1901........	301	....	....	....	....	9,008	9,309
(4.) Disbanded and discharged in South Africa.....	299	....	....	....	....	5,231	5,530
(5.) In hospital in South Africa on Dec. 28, 1900 (latest returns)..	415	....	....	....	....	13,716	14,131
VI. Numbers left South Africa —							
(1.) For England — not invalids....	1,214	....	....	....	....	11,109	12,323
(2.) For England — sick, wounded, and died on passage..........	1,703	....	....	....	....	39,095	40,798
(3.) Returned to India direct from South Africa..............	20	....	....	....	....	70	90
(4.) Returned to Colonies direct from South Africa —							
(a) Regulars, including two battalions to Ceylon......	98	....	....	....	....	2,041	2,139
(b) Colonials................	177	....	....	....	....	3,384	3,561
VII. Present strength of Forces in South Africa, Feb. 1, 1901 —							
(1.) Regulars......................	4,305	12,600	12,000	99,700	12,885	137,185	141,490
(2.) Colonials.....................	1,339	....	....	....	....	27,000	28,339*
(3.) Imperial Yeomanry............	495	....	....	....	....	7,500	7,995
(4.) Volunteers....................	200	....	....	....	....	7,500	7,700
(5.) Militia.......................	725	....	....	....	....	18,700	19,425
	7,064	....	....	....	....	197,885	204,949*

* Exclusive of recently raised Colonials whose numbers have not yet been reported.

On the 9th of February the following announcement was issued officially from the British War Office: "In view of recent Boer activity in various directions his Majesty's Government have decided, in addition to the large forces recently equipped locally in South Africa, to reinforce Lord Kitchener by 30,000 mounted troops beyond those already landed in Cape Colony. The recruiting for Imperial Yeomanry has proceeded so rapidly that it is anticipated not less than 10,000 will be shortly available. The South African Mounted Constabulary, including those enlisted in the colonies, may be relied upon to the extent of 8,000. The new colonial contingents to replace those withdrawn will probably reach 5,000. The remainder of the force will be made up by cavalry and mounted infantry from the home establishment. The enlistment of Volunteer companies to replace those who have served a year in South Africa is also being proceeded with. Arrangements have been made for the prompt equipment and transportation of the force."

In reply to a question in Parliament the 18th of February, 1901, Mr. Brodrick, the Secretary of State for War, stated that the total number of cases of typhoid or enteric fever in the British army, from the beginning of the war to the end of December, 1900, had been 19,101; deaths 4,233; invalided and sent home, 10,975.

The Field of War: A. D. 1901 (February). —The declared policy of the British Government.—Speaking in the House of Commons on the 18th of February, 1901, the Colonial Secretary, Mr. Chamberlain, declared the government policy of dealing with the Boers, with strong emphasis, in the following words: "From the moment when the invasion took place, and the

first shot was fired by the Boers, from that moment we declared our policy, that not one shred of the independence which the Boers had abused should ever again be conceded to them. That was the policy stated by the Prime Minister in his answer to the representations which were made to him by the Presidents of the two Republics. That was the policy, is the policy, and will be the policy of His Majesty's Government to the end. Let there be no mistake about that. It is no use arguing with us on the subject of independence. That, as far as we are concerned, is a closed question. Raise it, if you like to raise it, not in speeches, but by amendments. We are quite ready. We challenged you at the last election. You have never ceased to complain of the challenge. We challenge you in the House of Commons. If you believe the annexation we have announced ought to be repudiated; if you think, with the hon. and learned gentleman who has just spoken, that we ought to restore the independence of these two Republics, in any form, it is for you to say so in a definite amendment. It is for you to put the issue before the House of Commons and the country and we are perfectly prepared to meet you. Assuming that we are all agreed that annexation cannot be undone, then the policy of the Government is to establish equality and protection and justice for the native population and to grant the fuller liberties involved in our definition of self-government as soon as that can safely be conceded. . . . The Boers know perfectly well, they have been told again and again, directly and indirectly, and it has been repeatedly stated in this House that at the earliest possible moment they will be granted self-government."

The Liberal leader interrupted the speaker to

intimate that he understood a Crown colony government to be in contemplation, and that his objection was to that. On which Mr. Chamberlain proceeded to say: "Either the right hon. gentleman does not know what Crown colony government is or else he is quibbling about words. Will he be satisfied if I call it a civil government, with Ministers and a Governor appointed by his Majesty and a council to advise him? That is civil government, and it has this about it—that the Imperial Government has control in the last resort. That is what we mean. . . . We are quite ready to establish the civil government of which I have spoken, we are ready to maintain equality, we are ready to secure justice to all the inhabitants of the Transvaal and the Orange River Colony, but we are not prepared to put into their hands the whole control of the administration and civil government until we know it will be safe to do so. It is said that our views have not been communicated to the Boers and that a proclamation which I promised I would endeavour to have circulated has not yet been so distributed. I wish to say that, so far as the leaders are concerned, I am convinced they know perfectly well what terms we are willing to offer. There is no excuse on their part. It is possible that many of their followers, being ignorant people—when they come to us we find they have been deceived as to what is going on—do not know the terms we are willing to offer. We have by various means endeavoured to get to the rank and file a knowledge of the terms which are being offered, and we know what the result has been. The emissaries have been sent—emissaries not sent by us, permitted by us to go, who volunteered themselves in what they believed to be the interests of their countrymen, to make these representations— these emissaries have been apparently, as far as our information goes, brutally ill-used, tortured before execution, shot as spies after having been flogged."

The Field of **War: A. D. 1901** (February). —Attitude of the **English** Liberal party towards the **war.** See (in this vol.) ENGLAND: A. D. 1901 (FEBRUARY).

The Field of **War: A. D. 1901** (February— March).—Unsuccessful peace parley between Lord Kitchener and Commandant Botha.— By the intermediation of the wife of the Boer Commandant Louis Botha, an interview between that officer and Lord Kitchener was brought about, on the last day of February, for discussion "as to means of bringing the war to an end." The questions raised in the conversation were reported by Lord Brodrick to Mr. Brodrick, the British Secretary for War, in a telegram from Pretoria, March 1, as follows: "I have had a long interview with Botha, who showed very good feeling and seemed anxious to bring about peace. He asked for information on a number of subjects which he said that he should submit to his Government and people, and if they agreed he should visit Orange River Colony and get them to agree. They should all then hand in their arms and finish the war. He told me that they could go on for some time, and that he was not sure of being able to bring about peace without independence. He tried very hard for some kind of independence, but I declined to discuss such a point, and said that a modified form of independence would be most dangerous and likely to lead to war in the future. Subject was then dropped, and—

"Firstly.—The nature of future government of Colonies asked about. He wanted more details than were given by Colonial Secretary, and I said that, subject to correction from home, I understood that when hostilities ceased military guard would be replaced by Crown Colony administration, consisting of nominated Executive, with elected assembly to advise administration, to be followed after a period by representative government. He would have liked representative government at once, but seemed satisfied with above.

"Secondly.—Whether a Boer would be able to have a rifle to protect him from native? I said I thought he would be by a licence and on registration.

"Thirdly.—He asked whether Dutch language would be allowed? I said that English and Dutch would, I thought, have equal rights. He expressed hope that officials dealing with farmers would know Dutch.

"Fourthly.—The Kaffir question. This turned at once on franchise of Kaffirs, and a solution seemed to be that franchise should not be given to Kaffirs until after representative government was granted to Colonies. Orange Free State laws for Kaffirs were considered good.

"Fifthly.—That Dutch Church property should remain untouched.

"Sixthly.—Public trusts and orphan funds to be left intact. He asked whether British Government, in taking over the assets of Republics, would also take over legal debts. This he made rather a strong point of, and he intended it to include debts legally contracted since the war began. He referred to notes issued amounting to less than a million.

"Seventhly.—He asked if any war tax would be imposed on farmers? I said I thought not.

"Eighthly.—When would prisoners of war return?

"Ninthly.—He referred to pecuniary assistance to repair burnt farms, and enable farmers to start afresh. I said I thought some assistance would be given.

"Tenthly.—Amnesty to all at end of war. We spoke of Colonials who joined Republics, and he seemed not adverse to their being disfranchised.

"I arranged with him that I should write and let him know the view of the Government on these points. All I said during the interview was qualified by being subject to confirmation from home. He was anxious to get an answer soon."

Two days later, General Kitchener drafted and submitted to High Commissioner Sir A. Milner the reply which he wished to be authorized to make to the questions of Commandant Botha. This was transmitted, in turn, by the High Commissioner to Colonial Secretary Chamberlain, with approval of all the suggestions of Lord Kitchener, except on the subject of amnesty to the rebel "Afrikanders" of Cape Colony and Natal, who had joined the ranks of the Boers. Lord Kitchener wished to say that "on the cessation of hostilities and the complete surrender of arms, ammunition, cannon, and other munitions of war now in the hands of the burghers in the field or in Government depôts or elsewhere, His Majesty's Government is prepared at once to grant an amnesty in the Transvaal and Orange River Colony for all bona fide acts of war committed during the recent hostilities; as well as to move the Governments of Cape Colony and Natal to take similar action but qualified by the disfranchisement of any British subjects implicated in the recent war." Sir Alfred Milner proposed to amend the latter clause as follows: " British subjects of Cape Colony or Natal, though they will not be compelled to return to those Colonies, will, if they do so, be liable to be dealt with under the laws of those Colonies specifically passed to meet the circumstances arising out of the present war and which greatly mitigate the ordinary penalties of rebellion." "While willing," he said, " to concede much in order to strengthen Botha in inducing his people to submit, the amnesty of rebels is not, in my opinion, a point which His Majesty's Government can afford to concede. I think it would have a deplorable effect in Cape Colony and Natal to obtain peace by such a concession." Mr. Chamberlain agreed with the High Commissioner, writing in reply: " His Majesty's Government feel that they cannot promise to ask for complete amnesty to Cape and Natal rebels who are in totally different position to burghers without injustice to those who have remained loyal under great provocation, and they are prepared substantially to adopt your words, but you must consider whether your last line is strictly applicable to Natal." Mr. Chamberlain made numerous other criticisms of Lord Kitchener's suggested letter, and amended it in many particulars, the most important of which related to the form of government under which the late republics would be placed. Lord Kitchener would have said : " Military law will cease and be at once replaced by civil administration, which will at first consist of a Governor and a nominated Executive with or without an advisory elected Assembly, but it is the desire of His Majesty's Government, as soon as circumstances permit, to establish representative Government in the Transvaal and Orange River Colony." His political superior instructed him to change the statement as follows : " For ' military law will cease ' say ' military administration will cease.' It is possible that there may be disturbed districts for some time after terms have been accepted, and Governor of Colonies cannot abandon right of proclaiming martial law where necessary. In the same sentence omit the words ' at the same time' and ' at once' and substitute at the beginning the words ' at the earliest practicable date.' For ' consist of a Governor' down to ' Assembly ' read ' consist of a Governor and an Executive Council composed of the principal officials with a Legislative Council consisting of a certain number of official members to whom a nominated unofficial element will from the first be added.' In place of the words ' to establish representative government' substitute ' to introduce a representative element, and ultimately to concede to the new Colonies the privilege of self-government.' It is desirable at this stage to be quite precise in order to avoid any charge of breach of faith afterwards."

Out of the instructions he received, Lord Kitchener finally framed the following letter to Commandant Botha, sent to him on the 7th of March: " With reference to our conversation at Middelburg on 28th February, I have the honour to inform you that in the event of a general and complete cessation of hostilities and the surrender of all rifles, ammunition, cannon,

and other munitions of war in the hands of the burghers or in Government depôts or elsewhere, His Majesty's Government is prepared to adopt the following measures:

"His Majesty's Government will at once grant an amnesty in the Transvaal and Orange River Colonies for all bona fide acts of war committed during the recent hostilities. British subjects belonging to Natal and Cape Colony, while they will not be compelled to return to those Colonies, will, if they do so, be liable to be dealt with by the law of those Colonies specially passed to meet the circumstances arising out of the present war. As you are doubtless aware, the special law in the Cape Colony has greatly mitigated the ordinary penalties for high treason in the present cases.

"All prisoners of war now in St. Helena, Ceylon, or elsewhere will, on the completion of the surrender, be brought back to their country as quickly as arrangements can be made for their transport.

"At the earliest practicable date military administration will cease and will be replaced by civil administration in the form of Crown Colony Government. There will therefore be, in the first instance, in each of the new Colonies a Governor and an Executive Council, consisting of a certain number of official members, to whom a nominated unofficial element will be added. But it is the desire of His Majesty's Government, as soon as circumstances permit, to introduce a representative element and ultimately to concede to the new Colonies the privilege of self-government. Moreover, on the cessation of hostilities a High Court will be established in each of the new Colonies to administer the law of the land, and this Court will be independent of the Executive.

"Church property, public trusts, and orphans funds will be respected.

"Both the English and Dutch languages will be used and taught in public schools where parents of the children desire it, and allowed in Courts of Law.

"As regards the debts of the late Republican Governments, His Majesty's Government cannot undertake any liability. It is, however, prepared, as an act of grace, to set aside a sum not exceeding £1,000,000 to repay inhabitants of the Transvaal and Orange River Colonies for goods requisitioned from them by the late Republican Governments, or, subsequent to annexation, by Commandants in the field being in a position to enforce such requisitions. But such claims will have to be established to the satisfaction of a Judge or Judicial Commission appointed by the Government to investigate and assess them, and if exceeding in the aggregate £1,000,000, they will be liable to reduction pro rata.

"I also beg to inform your Honour that the new Government will take into immediate consideration the possibility of assisting by loan the occupants of farms who will take the oath of allegiance to repair any injury sustained by destruction of buildings or loss of stock during the war, and that no special war tax will be imposed on farmers to defray the expense of the war.

"When burghers require the protection of fire-arms such will be allowed to them by licence and on due registration, provided they take the oath of allegiance. Licences also will be issued for sporting rifles, guns, &c., but military fire-arms will only be allowed for means of protection.

" As regards the extension of the franchise to Kaffirs in the Transvaal and Orange River Colony, it is not the intention of His Majesty's Government to give such franchise before representative government is granted to these Colonies, and if then given it will be so limited as to secure the just predominance of the white races. The legal position of coloured persons will, however, be similar to that which they hold in Cape Colony.

" In conclusion, I must inform your Honour that if the terms now offered are not accepted after a reasonable delay for consideration they must be regarded as cancelled."

On the 16th of March the following reply came from the Boer Commandant: " I have the honour to acknowledge receipt of your Excellency's letter stating what steps your Excellency's Government is prepared to take in the event of a general and total cessation of hostilities. I have advised my Government of your Excellency's said letter; but, after the mutual exchange of views at our interview at Middelburg on 28th February last, it will certainly not surprise your Excellency to know that I do not feel disposed to recommend that the terms of the said letter shall have the earnest consideration of my Government. I may add also that my Government and my chief officers here entirely agree to my views." This ended the negotiations.

A discussion of the negotiations in Parliament occurred on the 28th of March, when Mr. Bryce (Liberal) said "they were agreed that the Government took an onward step when they allowed the peace negotiations to be entered into, and it was important to observe that, not only Lord Kitchener, but Sir Alfred Milner was persuaded that General Botha meant business. It was possible there were causes at work with which the House were not acquainted which caused the negotiations to be broken off. General Botha wrote to Lord Kitchener: —' You will not be surprised to hear that my answer is in the negative.' One of two things must have happened—either Lord Kitchener heard from General Botha something that the House had not heard of, or else General Botha was so much struck by the difference between the terms which Lord Kitchener had discussed and the terms contained in the letter that he conceived a distrust of us altogether and believed that the Government would not accept what Lord Kitchener had offered. He thought the Government were right in asking that the oath of allegiance should be taken, that they were entitled to insist upon the provision that all hostilities must cease, and that they could not pledge themselves as to the precise time when they would bring back the prisoners. But there were three points on which there were substantial differences between the terms Lord Kitchener appeared to have offered and the terms in the final letter. The first is the question of amnesty for the Cape rebels. Lord Kitchener and General Botha appeared to have come to an agreement on that subject. General Botha did not object to the disfranchisement of the Cape rebels, and Lord Kitchener did not appear to have conveyed any suggestion what-

ever of anything except disfranchisement. He could conceive nothing more likely to turn back the pacific desires of the Boers than the fact that they found that, instead of the Cape rebels having nothing but disfranchisement to fear, they were to be held subject to the Cape laws as to treason. He was not arguing whether that was right or wrong. The question was what the Boers would think, and he put it to the House that it was the most natural thing that they should be struck by the contrast between the terms which Lord Kitchener appeared to offer and the terms which were offered when the final letter came, and that that was just the point upon which brave men, feeling for their comrades, would be inclined to stand out. They would be told that they would displease the loyalists at the Cape if they did not exact all the penalties for treason. He hoped they would never in that House consider it any part of their business to satisfy the vindictive feeling of the colonists at the Cape."

As to the difference between the terms of future government for the inhabitants of the late republics proposed by Lord Kitchener and those laid down by the Colonial Secretary, Mr. Bryce said: " He should like to have known what the proposals were that General Botha made with regard to a modified independence, for he thought it was quite possible that it might turn out in the long run that some kind of what was called modified independence, protection, would be a great deal easier for this country to work than a system of Crown colony government. He thought the contrast between the elective assembly which Lord Kitchener offered and the purely arbitrary and despotic system which the final letter conveyed must at once have struck the Boers as indicating the difference between the views which the military man on the spot entertained and the proposal which they might expect from the Government. Of course there were objections to the immediate grant of self-government. So also there were objections to any course, and that course should be chosen which was open to the fewest objections. But the proposal of Crown colony government was, of all courses, the worst that could be suggested. It had been suggested that members of the Liberal party had asked for full-grown representative and responsible government, but they never had suggested that. What they had objected to was Crown colony government. They admitted that when the war ended there must be an intermediate period of administration, military or civil, but there was all the difference in the world between an admittedly provisional administration understood to be provisional and the creation of the whole apparatus of Crown colony government. The Boer population had an aversion to Crown colony administration, associated in their minds with the days of Sir Owen Lanyon, and an arbitrary form of government it was known to be. Of course it was arbitrary; hon. members who questioned that could not know what Crown colony administration was. The existence of a nominated council did not prevent it being arbitrary inasmuch as the members were obliged to vote as they were directed by the Governor. He could not help thinking that Lord Kitchener might, if he were asked to do so, throw some light on a remarkable expression in the letter from General Botha in which he said, after the mutual interchange of views at their meeting, Lord Kitchener would not be surprised to learn that he was not disposed to recommend the terms proposed."

The radical Mr. Labouchere was sharper in his criticism : "He held that it was nonsense to call the terms offered to the Boers liberal and lenient; they were neither. We had burnt their farms and desolated their country, and then we offered them a small gift of money to put them back on their farms while we took away their independence and their flag. He honoured the men who resisted, no matter at what cost, when the question was the independence of their native land. How right General Botha was in distrusting the alterations made by the Secretary for the Colonies in the matter of the gift was shown by the right hon. gentleman himself, when he said that, whereas the gift was to be limited to a certain sum, the loyalists were to be paid first. In that case what would remain to the burghers of the two colonies? The position of the Boers in the Empire under the terms of the Colonial Secretary would be little better than that of Kaffirs. As far as ultimate self-government was concerned, they were to put their faith in the Colonial Secretary. If he might offer them a word of advice it would be—Put no faith in the Colonial Secretary; get it in black and white. We had lost a great opportunity of ending the war and settling South Africa. Peace won by the sword would create a dependency in which racial feuds would go on and the minority would be maintained over the majority by a huge British garrison. The Dutch majority was certain to increase every decade. The Transvaal farmers lived in a poor, rude manner which English people would not accept. . . .

"He did not particularly admire the Boers. To his mind they had too much of the conservative element in them; but, judging between the Afrikanders and the English who went to South Africa, whilst fully recognizing that among the latter there were many respectable men, he thought, taking them collectively, the Boers were the better men. If we wanted to maintain our rule in South Africa the Boers were the safest men with whom to be on good terms. What were the Boers ready to do? As he read the correspondence, they were ready to enter the area of the British Empire, but only upon terms. Surely our problem was to find terms honourable to us and to them, which would lead to South Africa becoming one of those great commonwealths connected with the Empire such as existed in Australia and Canada. He suggested that, in the first place, we should offer a full and absolute amnesty. He urged that the Orange State and the Transvaal should as soon as possible be made self-governing colonies. The Orange State was regarded by every Englishman who had written about it as a model State. As to the Transvaal, he admitted there was a difficulty, but he would suggest that the main area of the country should be separated from the Rand. The Rand might be administered by a governor, a military governor if they liked, while in the rest of the country the Dutch would have a majority. If this course were adopted, instead of our giving some sort of pecuniary aid to the Transvaalers, they might be paid a reasonable rent for the Rand district, of which they would be deprived. . . . They on that side of the House

would be perfectly ready to agree to the establishment of a provisional government, military or civil—he should himself prefer Lord Kitchener to Sir Alfred Milner—to carry on the country while they were arranging for the colony to be self-governing. They were accustomed to be told that Sir Alfred Milner was a sort of divine pro-consul. He believed Sir Alfred Milner to be a most honourable man, and very intelligent in many walks of life; but the truth was that he began life as an Oxford don and then became an official in the Treasury, facts which militated against his success in practical politics. He believed that a man like Lord Dufferin would do more for the cause of peace in South Africa than all our soldiers."

The Field of War : A. D. 1901 (February—April).—The High Commissioner, Sir Alfred Milner, on the situation and prospects.— Leave of absence obtained by Sir Alfred.— A British Blue Book, made public in London on the 18th of April, contains an interesting despatch from Sir Alfred Milner, frankly reviewing the general situation in South Africa, as it appeared to him on the 6th of February, when he wrote, from Cape Town, and giving his forecast of future prospects. The following are the more important passages of the communication :

"A long time has elapsed since I have attempted to send to you any general review of South African affairs. The reason is twofold. In the first place, I am occupied every day that passes from morning till night by business, all of which is urgent, and the amount and variety of which you are doubtless able to judge from the communications on a great variety of subjects, which are constantly passing between us. In the next place, I have always hoped that some definite point would be reached at which it might be possible to sum up that chapter of our history which contained the war, and to forecast the work of administrative reconstruction which must succeed it. But I am reluctantly forced to the conclusion that there will be no such dividing line. I have not the slightest doubt of the ultimate result, but I foresee that the work will be slower, more difficult, more harassing, and more expensive than was at one time anticipated. At any rate, it is idle to wait much longer in the hope of being able to describe a clear and clean-cut situation. Despite the many other calls upon my time, and despite the confused character of the present position, I think it better to attempt to describe, however roughly and inadequately, the state of things as it exists to-day.

"It is no use denying that the last half-year has been one of retrogression. Seven months ago this Colony was perfectly quiet, at least as far as the Orange River. The southern half of the Orange River Colony was rapidly settling down, and even a considerable portion of the Transvaal, notably the south-western districts, seemed to have definitely accepted British authority, and to rejoice at the opportunity of a return to orderly government, and the pursuits of peace. To-day the scene is completely altered. It would be superfluous to dwell on the increased losses to the country caused by the prolongation of the struggle, and by the form which it has recently assumed. The fact that the enemy are now broken up into a great number of small forces, raiding in every direction, and that our troops are similarly broken up in pursuit of them, makes the area of actual fighting, and consequently of destruction, much wider than it would be in the case of a conflict between equal numbers operating in large masses. Moreover, the fight is now mainly over supplies. The Boers live entirely on the country through which they pass, not only taking all the food they can lay hands upon on the farms, grain, forage, horses, cattle, &c., but looting the small village stores for clothes, boots, coffee, sugar, &c., of all which they are in great need. Our forces, on their side, are compelled to denude the country of everything moveable, in order to frustrate these tactics of the enemy. No doubt a considerable amount of the stock taken by us is not wholly lost, but simply removed to the refugee camps, which are now being established at many points along the railway lines. But even under these circumstances, the loss is great, through animals dying on the route, or failing to find sufficient grass to live upon when collected in large numbers at the camps. Indeed, the loss of crops and stock is a far more serious matter than the destruction of farm buildings, of which so much has been heard. I say this not at all as an advocate of such destruction. I am glad to think that the measure is now seldom if ever resorted to. At the same time, the destruction of even a considerable number of farms, having regard to the very rough and inexpensive character of the majority of these structures in the Orange River Colony and Transvaal, is a comparatively small item in the total damage caused by the war to the agricultural community.

"To the losses incidental to the actual course of the campaign, there has recently been added destruction of a wholly wanton and malicious character. I refer to the injury done to the head-gear, stamps, and other apparatus of some of the outlying mines by Boer raiders, whose sole object was injury. For this destruction there is, of course, no possible excuse. . . . Fortunately the damage done to the mines has not been large, relatively to the vast total amount of the fixed capital sunk in them. The mining area is excessively difficult to guard against purely predatory attacks having no military purpose, because it is, so to speak, 'all length and no breadth'—one long thin line, stretching across the country from east to west for many miles. Still, garrisoned as Johannesburg now is, it is only possible successfully to attack a few points in it. Of the raids hitherto made, and they have been fairly numerous, only one has resulted in any serious damage. In that instance the injury done to the single mine attacked amounted to £200,000, and it is estimated that the mine is put out of working for two years. This mine is only one out of a hundred, and is not by any means one of the most important. These facts may afford some indication of the ruin which might have been inflicted, not only on the Transvaal and all South Africa, but on many European interests, if that general destruction of mine works which was contemplated just before our occupation of Johannesburg had been carried out. However serious in some respects may have been the military consequences of our rapid advance to Johannesburg, South Africa owes more than is commonly recognized to that brilliant dash forward, by which the vast mining apparatus, the foundation of all her wealth, was saved from the ruin threatening it.

"The events of the last six or seven months will involve a greater amount of repair and a longer period of recuperation, especially for agriculture, than anybody could have anticipated when the war commenced. Yet, for all that, having regard to the fact that both the Rand and Kimberley are virtually undamaged, and that the main engines of prosperity, when once set going again, will not take very long to get into working order, the economic consequences of the war, though grave, do not appear by any means appalling. The country population will need a good deal of help, first to preserve it from starvation, and then, probably, to supply it with a certain amount of capital to make a fresh start. And the great industry of the country will need some little time before it is able to render any assistance. But, in a young country with great recuperative powers, it will not take many years before the economic ravages of the war are effaced.

"What is more serious to my mind than the mere material destruction of the last six months is the moral effect of the recrudescence of the war. I am thinking especially of the Orange River Colony, and of that portion of the Transvaal which fell so easily into our hands after the relief of Mafeking, that is to say, the country lying between Johannesburg and Pretoria, and the border of Bechuanaland. Throughout this large area the feeling in the middle of last year was undoubtedly pacific. The inhabitants were sick of the war. They were greatly astonished, after all that had been dinned into them, by the fair and generous treatment they received on our first occupation, and it would have taken very little to make them acquiesce readily in the new régime. At that time too, the feeling in the Colony was better than I have ever known it. The rebellious element had blown off steam in an abortive insurrection, and was glad to settle down again. If it had been possible for us to screen those portions of the conquered territory, which were fast returning to peaceful pursuits, from the incursions of the enemy still in the field, a great deal of what is now most deplorable in the condition of South Africa would never have been experienced. The vast extent of the country, the necessity of concentrating our forces for the long advance, first to Pretoria and then to Komati Poort, resulted in the country already occupied being left open to raids, constantly growing in audacity, and fed by small successes, on the part of a few bold and skilful guerrilla leaders who had nailed their colours to the mast. The reappearance of these disturbers of the peace, first in the south-east of the Orange River Colony, then in the south-west of the Transvaal, and finally in every portion of the conquered territory, placed those of the inhabitants who wanted to settle down in a position of great difficulty. Instead of being made prisoners of war, they had been allowed to remain on their farms on taking the oath of neutrality, and many of them were really anxious to keep it. But they had not the strength of mind, nor, from want of education, a sufficient appreciation of the sacredness of the obligation which they had undertaken, to resist the pressure of their old companions in arms when these reappeared among them appealing to their patriotism and to their fears. . . .

"As the guerrilla warfare swept back over the

whole of the western Transvaal, and practically the whole of the Orange River Colony, its effect upon the Cape Colony also became very marked. There was a time, about the middle of last year, when the bulk of the Dutch population in the Cape Colony, even those who had been most bitter against us at the outset, seemed disposed to accept the 'fait accompli,' and were prepared to acquiesce in the union of all South Africa under the British flag. Some of them even began to see certain advantages in such a consummation. The irreconcilable line taken in the Cape Parliament, during its recent Session from July to October, was a desperate effort to counteract this tendency. But I doubt whether it would have succeeded to the moderate extent to which it has, had it not been for the recrudescence of the war on the borders of the Colony, and the embittered character which it assumed. Every act of harshness, however necessary, on the part of our troops, was exaggerated and made the most of, though what principally inflamed the minds of the people were alleged instances of needless cruelty which never occurred. Never in my life have I read of, much less experienced, such a carnival of mendacity as that which accompanied the pro-Boer agitation in this Colony at the end of last year. And these libels still continue to make themselves felt. . . .

"The present position of affairs, alike in the new territories and in a large portion of the Cape Colony, if by no means the most critical, is possibly the most puzzling that we have had to confront since the beginning of the war. Naturally enough the public are impatient, and those who are responsible for the government of the country are bombarded with most conflicting advice. On the one hand, there is the outcry for greater severity and for a stricter administration of Martial Law. On the other hand, there is the expression of the fear that strict measures would only exasperate the people. Personally, I am of the opinion, which I have always held, that reasonable strictness is the proper attitude in the presence of a grave national danger, and that exceptional regulations for a time of invasion, the necessity of which every man of sense can understand, if clearly explained and firmly adhered to, are not only not incompatible with, but actually conducive to, the avoidance of injustice and cruelty. I am satisfied by experience that the majority of those Dutch inhabitants of the Colony who sympathize with the Republics, however little they may be able to resist giving active expression to that sympathy, when the enemy actually appear amongst them, do not desire to see their own districts invaded, or to find themselves personally placed in the awkward dilemma of choosing between high treason and an unfriendly attitude to the men of their own race from beyond the border. There are extremists who would like to see the whole of the Cape Colony overrun. But the bulk of the farmers, especially the substantial ones, are not of this mind. . . .

"The inherent vice, if I may say so, of almost all public discussion of our South African difficulties is the tendency to concentrate attention too exclusively upon the Boers. Say what we will, the controversy always seems to relapse into the old ruts—it is the British Government on the one hand, and the Boers on the other. The question how a particular policy will affect, not merely our enemies, but our now equally numerous friends, seems seldom to be adequately considered. And yet it would seem that justice and policy alike should lead us to be as eager to consider the feelings and interests, and to retain the loyalty, of those who are fighting on our side, as to disarm the present enmity and win the future confidence of those who are fighting against us. And this principle would seem all the easier to adhere to because there is really nothing which the great body of the South African loyalists desire which it is not for the honour and advantage of the Mother Country to insist upon. Of vindictiveness, or desire to oppress the Afrikanders, there is, except in hasty utterances, inevitable in the heat of the conflict, which have no permanent significance, or in tirades which are wholly devoid of influence, no sign whatever. The attitude of almost all leading and representative men, and the general trend of public feeling among the loyalists, even in the intensity of the struggle, is dead against anything like racial exclusiveness or domination. If this were not so, it would be impossible for a section of pure bred Afrikanders, small no doubt in numbers but weighty in character and position, to take the strong line which they do in opposition to the views of the majority of their own people, based as these are, and as they know them to be, upon a misconception of our policy and intentions. These men are among the most devoted adherents to the Imperial cause, and would regard with more disfavour and alarm than any one the failure of the British nation to carry out its avowed policy in the most complete manner. They are absolutely convinced that the unquestioned establishment of the British supremacy, and the creation of one political system from Cape Town to the Zambesi, is, after all that has happened, the only salvation for men of their own race, as well as for others. Of the terms already offered, a great majority, I believe, of the South Africans at present in arms on our side entirely approve. There is, no doubt, an extreme section who would advocate a sterner attitude on our part, but they are not numerous, and their feelings are not lasting. The terms offered by Lord Kitchener, which are, in substance, identical with repeated declarations of policy on the part of His Majesty's Government, are generally regarded as a generous and statesmanlike offer, as one which, if firmly adhered to, will ultimately be accepted, but as an offer which we cannot afford to enlarge. On the other hand, there is a very general desire that no effort should be spared to make the generous character of our intentions widely known, and to encourage any disposition on the part of the enemy to parley, with the object of making them better acquainted with the terms on which we are prepared to accept their submission.

"If I might sum up the predominant, indeed, the almost unanimous feeling of those South Africans who sympathise with the Imperial Government, I should describe it as follows:—They are sick to death of the war, which has brought ruin to many of them, and imposed considerable sacrifices on almost all. But they would rather see the war continue for an indefinite time than run the risk of any compromise which would leave even the remotest chance of the recurrence of so terrible a scourge in the future. They are prepared to fight and suffer on, in order to make South Africa, indisputably and for ever, one country under one flag, with one system of government, and that system the British, which they believe to ensure the highest possible degree of justice and freedom to men of all races. But, with that object accomplished, they are willing, and, indeed, ready, to bury racial animosities. They have fought against the principle of race oligarchy in one form, and they do not wish to re-establish it in another. For the attainment of that object, they would rely for the present on the vigorous prosecution of the war in which they are prepared themselves to take the most active part, coupled with every inducement to the enemy to come in on the terms already offered, and for the future, as soon as public security is assured and the circumstances permit, on the extension to the newly acquired territories of a system of Colonial self-government. For my own part, I have no doubt that this attitude is a wise one, and that it only requires persistence in it, in spite of the discouraging circumstances of the moment, to lead us to ultimate success."—*Great Britain, Papers by Command, Cd.* 547.

The same Blue Book made known the fact that, on the 3d of April, Sir Alfred Milner applied for and obtained leave of absence for three months from his duties in South Africa.

The Field of **War: A. D. 1901** (April).—The situation.—Early in April it was announced that the seat of government of the South African Republic had been transferred from Pietersburg to Leydsdorp in the Zoutpansberg by the Vice-President, General Schalk-Burger, which seems to indicate the beginning of another stage of the South African war. The Boers are said to have been for some time past collecting great quantities of cattle and sheep in the fastnesses of the Zoutpansberg, where also they have ample supplies of ammunition, and intend making it a point of ultimate resistance as well as a base of present operations.

The Field of **War: A. D. 1901** (April).—The cost of the **war** to Great Britain as stated **by** the Chancellor of the **Exchequer.**—In his speech (April 18), on introducing the budget for 1901, in the House of Commons, the Chancellor of the Exchequer, Sir Michael Hicks-Beach, made the following statements of the cost of the war to Great Britain: "I would remind the Com-

mittee that so far we have borrowed towards the cost of the war £67,000,000—£13,000,000 Treasury bills, £10,000,000 Exchequer Bonds maturing rather less than three years hence, £14,000,000 Exchequer Bonds maturing about five years hence, and £30,000,000 War Loan maturing in 1910. Now, Sir, in what mode may we fairly borrow such a large sum as we now require? This can no longer be considered a small war. In cost it is a great war. Let me just make a statement to the Committee as to what, so far, the estimated cost of this war has been. In 1899-1900 the Estimates were £23,217,000. Last year they were £68,620,000, and this year's Estimates amount to £60,230,000, including in each case the interest on the sums borrowed. That amounts to over £152,000,000. I must ask the Committee to remember that in those figures I include the cost of both the South African and Chinese wars. Then I have to add a million and a quarter for this year's borrowing, making in all over £153,000,000. That is double the cost of the Crimean War, and when I look back at the Peninsular War I find the two most expensive years were 1813 and 1814. The forces engaged, of course, were very much smaller than those engaged now; but in those two years the total cost of our Army and Navy amounted to £144,581,000. This amount is less than the charges of the South African and Chinese wars. Therefore, I think I am justified in saying that in cost this has been a great war. I think, then, it is clear we can no longer, in borrowing towards the cost of it, rely upon temporary borrowing. We have already £67,000,000 of unfunded debt borrowed for this purpose and maturing within the next ten years. We have also some £36,000,000 of 2¾ and 2½ per cent., redeemable in 1905. Therefore, whatever may be the prosperity of the country, whatever may be the condition of our finances, it is perfectly obvious to my mind that the stanchest advocate of the redemption of the debt will have ample scope for his energies in the years that are now before us. For this reason I propose to ask the Committee to extend the powers of borrowing which they gave me in previous Acts, to Consols."

SOUTH AFRICAN REPUBLIC, The. See (in this vol.) SOUTH AFRICA (THE TRANSVAAL); also, CONSTITUTION (GRONDWET) OF THE SOUTH AFRICAN REPUBLIC.

SOUTH AUSTRALIA. See (in this vol.) AUSTRALIA; and CONSTITUTION OF AUSTRALIA.

SOUTH CAROLINA: A. D. 1892-1899.—The Dispensary Law.—In 1892 the Legislature of South Carolina passed an Act, commonly called the Dispensary Law, which caused turbulent agitations in the State, and excited much interest in the country at large. It was based upon the principle of what is known as the Gothenburg system of regulation for the sale of intoxicating liquors, making the traffic a State monopoly, carried on by officials, under rigorous restrictions, with profit to the public treasury, and none else. It provided for the creation of a State Board of Control, under the direction of which a Commissioner, appointed by the Governor, should purchase all intoxicating liquors allowed to be sold in the State, and should furnish the same to such agents (called "dispensers")

in the several counties as might be appointed by county boards to sell them, in accordance with the regulations prescribed. It required all liquors purchased by the Commissioner to be tested by an official chemist and declared to be pure and unadulterated. It allowed nobody but the official "dispensers" to deal in any manner with any kinds of intoxicating liquors after the 1st of July, 1893. It forbade the selling of such drinks by the authorized salesmen to minors and drunkards, and it required all who bought to sign and date a printed or written request, stating their residence and age.

The law was fiercely resisted in many parts of the State by mobs, and powerfully assailed in the courts; but Governor (afterwards Senator) Tillman, who then occupied the executive chair, gave it resolute enforcement and support. The attack in the courts had momentary success in 1894, the Supreme Court of the State rendering a decision adverse to the constitutionality of the law; but, meantime, the Legislature, in 1893, had made changes in the Act, and its new enactment was held to be untouched by the judgment of the court. Before a new case could be brought to issue, the retirement of one of the justices of the Supreme Court brought about a change of opinion in that tribunal, and the law in its new form was sustained. Disorderly resistance to the enforcement of the law was long kept up; but in the end such resistance seems to have been mostly overcome.

In January, 1897, however, one provision of the Act, which forbade all importation of liquors into the State by private persons, even for their own use, was declared by the Supreme Court of the United States to be an interference with inter-state commerce, and therefore unconstitutional. This breaks down the Dispensary Law, so far as concerns citizens who are able to import liquors for themselves. Otherwise the law seems to be now stoutly entrenched, and other States are being sufficiently satisfied with its success in South Carolina to adopt it. The following testimony as to its success is from the pen of a North Carolinian, who became instrumental in carrying the system into his own State.

"The familiar features of the dispensary were its closing promptly at sundown; no drinking on the premises; the sale of liquor to those only who were of age, who were not in the habit of drinking to excess, who were sober at the time of the sale, and who signed an application for what they bought on a public book; and the fact that the dispenser was a salaried officer, and thus free from pecuniary interest in stimulating sales. To this was added in South Carolina a force of constables whose special business it was to arrest those who sold liquor contrary to law.

"The fact that the dispensary law was a substitute for Prohibition made the law odious at first to those who had fought most ardently for the Prohibition cause. And the political faction over which Mr. Tillman had triumphed, containing a good proportion of the best blood and brains of the State, opposed the dispensary on personal grounds. The spy system, as it was called, and the resistance to the constables, sometimes resulting in bloodshed, set many of the more peaceable and conservative citizens against the law. Added to this, the constitutionality of the law as a whole and of important provisions separately was strenuously contested in the United States Courts, with varying success until the Supreme Court settled the matter forever in favor of the law. These difficulties are mentioned to show what the system has had to face in South Carolina, and for the purpose of remarking that the system has triumphed over all opposition. The amended Constitution of the State decrees against the re-establishment of the saloon. The Dispensary candidate for Governor in the last election defeated the Prohibition candidate. And the testimony of sober, conservative citizens of every rank and profession is now practically unanimous to the effect that drunkenness and the crimes resulting therefrom have decreased beyond expectation."—A. J. McKelway, *The Dispensary in North Carolina* (*Outlook, April* 8, 1899).

A. D. 1896.—New constitution.—Introduction of a qualified suffrage.—Practical disfranchisement of the greater part of the negroes.—On the 1st of January, 1896, a new constitution, promulgated by a constitutional convention the previous month, without submission to popular vote, came into effect. It was framed especially to accomplish a practical disfranchisement of the larger part of the negro population, which it did by the operation of an educational qualification with peculiar conditions attached. Until the first of January, 1898, it permitted the enrollment of voters who could read, or who could explain to the satisfaction of the registering officer a section of the constitution read to them; and all citizens registered before that date were to be qualified voters thereafter. But subsequent to the date specified, none could be registered except those able to read and write any required part of the constitution, or else to prove themselves owners of property and taxpayers on not less than $300. Registration to be conducted by county boards appointed by the governor.—See, also (in this vol.), MISSISSIPPI.

Speaking in the United States Senate in justification of this measure, Senator Tillman, of South Carolina, said: "We took the government away. We stuffed ballot boxes. We shot them. We are not ashamed of it. The Senator from Wisconsin would have done the same thing. I see it in his eye right now. He would have done it. With that system—force, tissue ballots, etc. —we got tired ourselves. So we called a constitutional convention, and we eliminated, as I said, all of the colored people whom we could under the fourteenth and fifteenth amendments. . . . I want to call your attention to the remarkable change that has come over the spirit of the dream of the Republicans; to remind you gentlemen from the North that your slogans of the past—brotherhood of man and the fatherhood of God—have gone glimmering down the ages. The brotherhood of man exists no longer, because you shoot negroes in Illinois, when they come in competition with your labor, as we shoot them in South Carolina when they come in competition with us in the matter of elections. You do not love them any better than we do. You used to pretend that you did, but you no longer pretend it except to get their votes. . . . You deal with the Filipinos just as we deal with the negroes, only you treat them a heap worse."— *Congressional Record, 56th Congress, 1st Sess., pp.* 2347, 2349.

SOUTH DAKOTA: A. D. 1898.—Constitutional amendment introducing the Initiative and the Referendum.—A constitutional amendment, adopted by popular vote at the November election, introduces the principle of the Swiss Initiative and Referendum, providing that the Legislature must render obedience to petitions signed by 5 per cent. of the voters of the State, which call for the enactment and submission to popular vote of any stipulated law, or which require the submission to a popular vote of any Act which the Legislature may have passed.

A. D. 1899.—Adoption of the Dispensary System.—A constitutional amendment, providing for a dispensary system of regulation for the liquor traffic (see, in this vol., SOUTH CAROLINA: A. D. 1892–1899), was adopted in 1899 by a majority of 1,613 votes. The newly adopted clause reads as follows: "The manufacture and sale of intoxicating liquors shall be under exclusive State control, and shall be conducted by duly authorized agents of the State, who shall be paid by salary and not by commission."

SOUTHWEST AFRICA, German: Trade, etc. See (in this vol.) GERMANY: A. D. 1899 (JUNE).

SPAIN: A. D. 1868-1885.—Affairs in Cuba. See (in this vol.) CUBA: A. D. 1868-1885.

A. D. 1895-1896.—Conflict between army and Press.—Change of Ministry.—Renewed insurrection in Cuba.—A violent conflict between the military authorities and the newspaper Press arose in consequence of an attack made by officers of the army on a Republican editor who had sharply criticised certain details of army administration. They not only assaulted him in person, but broke up his presses and type. This military mob outrage was resented and denounced by the whole Press, of every party; whereupon the military authorities began prosecutions in the military courts, and making arrests of publishers and editors, with a contempt for law which seemed to be ominous of some revolutionary intent. The Liberal Ministry, under Señor Sagasta, not able, apparently, to control these proceedings, resigned office, and a Conservative Cabinet was formed by Señor Canovas del Castillo. The new Ministry had many difficulties to face, the fresh outbreak of revolt in Cuba (see, in this vol., CUBA: A. D. 1895) being the most serious. But student rioting at Barcelona, caused by the dismissal of a professor whose writings were condemned at Rome, became grave enough to require the sending of the redoubtable General Weyler to the scene; and popular excitements in Madrid, growing out of exposures of corruption in the municipal council, drove two of the colleagues of Canovas from their posts. In January, 1896, Weyler was sent to Cuba, to pursue in that unhappy island a policy which produced conditions that horrified the world—see (in this vol.) CUBA: A. D. 1896-1897, and 1897-1898 (DECEMBER—MARCH). Elections held in April, 1896, gave the government of Canovas an overwhelming majority in the Cortes.

A. D. 1896-1897.—Administration of General Weyler in Cuba. See (in this vol.) CUBA: A. D. 1896-1897.

A. D. 1896-1898.—Insurrection in the Philippines. See (in this vol.) PHILIPPINE ISLANDS: A. D. 1896-1898.

A. D. 1897 (August—October).—Assassination of the Prime Minister, Canovas del Castillo.—Return of Sagasta to power.—Condition of the country.—On the 8th of August, the Spanish Prime Minister, Señor Canovas del Castillo, was shot by an Italian anarchist, a Neapolitan, named Angiolillo, while sojourning for a few days, with his wife, at the baths of Santa Aguada. He lived but two hours after receiving his wounds. General Azcarraga, Minister of War, was called by the Queen to take temporary charge of the government; but before the end of September he and his cabinet were forced to resign, and the Liberals, under the lead of Señor Sagasta, returned to power. "Canovas was the strong man of Spain. He was not the educator of the people, or the worker of the popular inclination. His vigorous understanding was their muscular master. The police were on his side; a useful portion of the press, hired judiciously for the purpose; the army; and the brains to set them all in motion; and, so equipped, Antonio Canovas del Castillo confronted the Spanish people and said, 'Come on.' It was a resolute and daring attitude, and kept the crowd triumphantly at bay for thirty years. But of late a change had taken place. A good deal of the old fire had burned out. Fifteen years of colonial revolt, again, impress even the thickest-headed Spanish peasant into conceiving that the trouble has no business to last so long, and that his rulers, if hard and exigent towards himself, are weak, extravagant, and undexterous elsewhere. And this suspicion ripens into certainty when he sees his sons torn from his side and packed over sea, and when his taxes swell and swell, and the price of bread goes up and up, and still no alteration for the better. This cumulative truth is what the Spanish plebs have learned at last, within a year ago, and if Canovas had had the foresight of the true statesman, instead of the blind egoism of the autocrat, he would have thrown up his losing cards while there was time and said, 'The Cuban War is a mistake. Forgive me.' But his unflagging obstinacy held him to his desperate and aimless course. Although his complicity with his emissary, Weyler, in sending and publishing one lying telegram after another, was manifest as day, he smiled and rubbed his hands, and vowed the war was all but over; and behind that smile he half despised and half defied the victims he invited to believe him. He made no claim to be a patriot. He knew he was unpopular. He knew that for every cottage whence a son had been torn away to that disastrous strife in Cuba the Conservative Government of the nation may count upon one bitter foe—the Republicans or the Duke of Madrid upon one sure ally. What would have happened in Spain, had he lived longer, is quite beyond the average power to say. The prospect was too horrible for words. However, he died, and his ministry, after feebly mimicking the stubborn temper of their chief, succumbed also, leaving to the Liberal Party a legacy which may be likened to a bomb with time-fuse well alight and sputtering into the explosive. In plainer words what faces Señor Sagasta is the following: Spain is a beggar. Her credit is gone. Her army, always of late years behindhand in discipline, instruction, commissariat, and the thousand and one minutiæ other nations are solicitous to attend to, is decimated by disease, dispirited, and utterly incompetent to engage in war with any civilised power. Her navy is rotten. Her people are discontented and divided into various creeds. Some are for the existing régime, some for Don Carlos, and some for the Republic."—L. Williams, *Can Sagasta save Spain?* (*Fortnightly Rev.*, Dec., 1897).

A. D. 1897 (November).—Autonomous Constitution granted to Cuba and Porto Rico. See (in this vol.) CUBA: A. D. 1897 (NOVEMBER); and 1897-1898 (NOVEMBER—FEBRUARY).

A. D. 1898.—War with the United States. See (in this vol.) UNITED STATES OF AM.: A. D. 1898 (FEBRUARY—MARCH), to 1899 (JANUARY—FEBRUARY).

A. D. 1898 (February—March).—Destruction of the U. S. battle-ship Maine in Havana harbor. See (in this vol.) UNITED STATES OF AM.: A. D. 1898 (FEBRUARY—MARCH).

A. D. 1898 (March—April).—Discussion of Cuban affairs with the Government of the United States.—Message of the President to Congress, asking for authority to intervene

in Cuba. See (in this vol.) UNITED STATES OF
AM. : A. D. 1898 (MARCH—APRIL).

A. D. 1898 (April).—Demand of the U. S.
Government that the authority and Government of Spain be withdrawn from Cuba, and
its result in a state of **war.** See (in this vol.)
UNITED STATES OF AM. : A. D. 1898 (APRIL).

A. D. 1898 (July—December).—Suspension
of hostilities and negotiations of Treaty of
Peace with the United States.—Relinquishment of sovereignty over Cuba, and cession
of Porto Rico, Guam and the Philippine Islands to the United States. See (in this vol.)
UNITED STATES OF AM. : A. D. 1898 (JULY—
DECEMBER).

A. D. 1898 (August 21).—Letter from Spanish soldiers, on their departure from Santiago
de Cuba, to the soldiers of the American
army. See (in this vol.) UNITED STATES OF
AM.: A. D. 1898 (AUGUST 21).

A. D. 1899.—Abolition of the Ministry of
the Colonies.—Resignation of the Sagasta
Cabinet.—Ratification of the Treaty of Peace.
—The new conditions in Spanish government resulting from the loss of Cuba, Porto Rico, and
the Philippines were promptly acknowledged,
in January, by the abolition of the Ministry
of Colonies, for which no sufficient duties remained. On the 20th of February the Cortes
was summoned, and on the same day the "state
of siege," declared during the war, which had
practically suspended constitutional rights, was
removed by proclamation. The Treaty of Peace
with the United States was laid before the Cortes;
but the military party, led by General Weyler,
opposed the approval of the Treaty, evidently
for the purpose of embarrassing and weakening
the government. They were so far successful
that Señor Sagasta and his cabinet were forced
to resign, on the 28th of February, and a Conservative Ministry, under Señor Silvela, was
formed. But the Cortes, which declined to support the government in accepting the Treaty of
Peace, was dismissed a few days later by the
Queen-Regent, who signed the Treaty on her
own responsibility, March 11. The Silvela Ministry proved inharmonious, made so especially
by the Minister of War, General Polavieja, and
in September it was reconstructed, with Polavieja dropped out.

A. D. 1899 (January).—Relinquishment of
sovereignty in Cuba. See (in this vol.) CUBA :
A. D. 1898–1899 (DECEMBER—OCTOBER).

A. D. 1899 (February).—Sale of the Caroline, Pelew and Marianne Islands to Germany. See (in this vol.) CAROLINE AND MARI-
ANNE ISLANDS.

A. D. 1899 (May—July).—Representation
in the Peace Conference at The Hague. See
(in this vol.) PEACE CONFERENCE.

A. D. 1900 (October—November).—Weyler
appointed Captain-General of Madrid.—Resignation of the Silvela Ministry.—The army
in control.—The army won control of the government in October, when General Linares,
Minister of War, without consulting his colleagues of the cabinet—if report be true—appointed General Weyler to be Captain-General
of Madrid. Several members of the cabinet resigned in protest, and the Premier, Señor Silvela, found it necessary to place the resignation
of the Ministry as a whole in the hands of the
Queen-Regent (October 21). A new cabinet

was formed, with General Azcarraga for its
chief, General Linares retaining the portfolio of
the War Office, and Weyler holding the military
command in Madrid. The military party appears to be fully in power, and a token of the
spirit it has carried into the government was
given within ten days after the formation of the
new Ministry, by the promulgation of a decree
suspending the guarantees of the constitution
and establishing martial law throughout the
kingdom. Some movements of Carlist agitation
and insurrection furnished a pretext for this
measure, but they appear to have had no serious
character.

It is probable that the military reaction at
Madrid will stimulate a revival of the old independent aspirations of the Catalonians, which
have been showing of late many signs of new
life. The desire for separation from Spain has
never died out in Catalonia, and a resolute new
effort to accomplish it may easily appear among
the incidents of the near future.

A. D. 1900 (November).—Spanish-American
Congress.—At the instance of the "Sociedad
Union Ibero-Americana," an unofficial organization which has been in existence for more than
15 years, a congress was held in Madrid in November, 1900, with the object of strengthening
the relations between Spain and those American peoples who are of Spanish origin. The
proposal of the "Union Ibero-Americana" met
with the approval of the Spanish Government,
and on April 16 a Royal decree was issued appointing Señor Silvela, the Prime Minister, to
be president of a congress to be held in Madrid.
The Government of Spain then issued invitations to the Spanish-American Republics, asking
them to send representatives, which invitations
were accepted by the governments of Mexico,
the Argentine Republic, Chile, Uruguay, Peru,
and other States. The list of subjects for discussion included proposals of treaties of commerce, international arbitration, the harmonizing
of the civil, penal, and administrative legal codes
of the various countries represented, emigration,
the international validity of professional diplo-
mas, the establishment of Ibero-American banks,
and others. The most important result of the
Congress was the voting of a plan of compulsory
arbitration by the South American republics.
The motion was introduced by Peru, which has
the most to gain by arbitration. Chile's was the
sole dissenting voice. "This," remarks "The
Nation," of New York, "recalls the fact that
Chile consented to take part in the Pan-American
Congress at the City of Mexico, only on condition that any arbitration there provided for
should not concern her own disputed boundaries."

A. D. 1901.—Anti-clerical agitation, directed especially against the Jesuits.—Marriage of the Princess of the Asturias.—A case
arising in Madrid in February produced excitements of feeling against the Jesuits which spread
to all parts of the country, and were the cause of
serious political demonstrations and rioting in
many cities. A wealthy young lady, Señorita
Ubao, had been persuaded by her confessor, a
priest of the Jesuit order, to enter a convent,
against the wish of her family. The family applied to the High Court for a mandate to secure
her release. The prominence of the parties drew
universal attention to the case, and it was dis-

cussed with passion throughout Spain, stirring up, as appears to be evident, a latent anti-clerical feeling which only waited to be moved. It seems, moreover, to have served as an occasion for demonstrations of the republicanism that continues to be strong in Spain. Students of the universities were active promoters of the excitement, and set examples of disorder which were followed by rougher mobs. In Madrid, Zaragoza, Valencia, Valladolid, Santandar, Granada, Malaga, Barcelona, and other towns the excitement ran high, and was not quieted by a decision of the High Court on the 19th of February, restoring Señorita Ubao to her friends. At Barcelona, on the last day of March, a meeting of 9,000 citizens, held in the bull-ring, is reported to have passed resolutions in favor of the separation of Church and State, advocating the prohibition of religious orders, and expressing a desire that their property should be taken possession of by the State. The meeting voted messages congratulating France and Portugal on their Anti-Clerical attitude. The meeting was followed by a riotous attack on the Jesuit convent, and by a conflict of the mob with the civil guard, in which blood was shed. From various parts of the country, demands for the expulsion of the religious orders were reported, in April, to be reaching the government.

A royal wedding which occurred in the early days of this anti-clerical agitation added something to the disturbance of the public mind. Doña Maria de las Mercedes, eldest of the children of the late King Alphonso XII. and his second wife, was married on the 14th of February to Prince Charles, of the Neapolitan Bourbon family, son of the Count of Caserta. The Princess was Queen of Spain, in her infancy, for a few months after her father's death, until the posthumous birth of her brother, in 1886, and presumptively she may again inherit the crown. In itself, the marriage does not seem to have been unpopular; but, for some reason, the Count of Caserta was odious to the public of Madrid, and became the object of unpleasant attentions from the mob, while the bride and bridegroom, and other members of the family of the latter, were treated with respect.

SPANISH-AMERICAN CONGRESS, The. See (in this vol.) SPAIN: A. D. 1900 (NOVEMBER).

SPANISH-AMERICAN WAR. See (in this vol.) UNITED STATES OF AM.: A. D. 1898 (FEBRUARY—MARCH), to 1899 (JANUARY—FEBRUARY).

SPANISH SOLDIERS: Letter to American soldiers. See (in this vol.) UNITED STATES OF AM.: A. D. 1898 (AUGUST 21).

SPION KOP, The storming of. See (in this vol.) SOUTH AFRICA (THE FIELD OF WAR): A. D. 1900 (JANUARY—FEBRUARY).

SPITZBERGEN: Claimed by Russia. See (in this vol.) POLAR EXPLORATION, 1898.
    Recent Exploration of. See (in this vol.) POLAR EXPLORATION, 1896, 1897, 1898, 1899, 1900, 1900–.

SPOILS SYSTEM, The: **As** maintained in the service of the U. S. House of Representatives. See (in this vol.) CIVIL SERVICE REFORM: A. D. 1901.

SPOONER AMENDMENT, The. See (in this vol.) PHILIPPINE ISLANDS: A. D. 1901 (FEBRUARY—MARCH).

STAMBOULOFF, M. Stephen, assassi-nation of. See (in this vol.) BALKAN AND DANUBIAN STATES: BULGARIA.

STANDARD OIL COMPANY. See (in this vol.) TRUSTS: UNITED STATES.

STATEN ISLAND: Incorporation **in** Greater New York. See (in this vol.) NEW YORK CITY: A. D. 1896–1897.

STATISTICS: Of the British-Boer **war.** See (in this vol.) ENGLAND: A. D. 1900 (DECEMBER); and SOUTH AFRICA (THE FIELD OF WAR): A. D. 1901 (FEBRUARY), and (APRIL).
    Of Christian Missions. See (in this vol.) MISSIONS, CHRISTIAN.
    Of finances and exports of the United States. See (in this vol.) UNITED STATES OF AM.: A. D. 1900 (JUNE), and (DECEMBER).
    Of the navies of the Sea Powers. See (in this vol.) NAVIES OF THE SEA POWERS.
    Of the shipping of the world. See (in this vol.) SHIPPING OF THE WORLD.
    Of the Spanish-American war. See (in this vol.) UNITED STATES OF AM.: A. D. 1898–1899, STATISTICS; and 1900 (JUNE); also, PHILIPPINE ISLANDS: A. D. 1900 (MAY), and (OCTOBER).
    Of war-making expenditure by the leading Powers. See (in this vol.) WAR BUDGETS.

STEAM TURBINES, The invention of. See (in this vol.) SCIENCE, RECENT: MECHANICS.

STEEL: The Age of. See (in this vol.) NINETEENTH CENTURY: THE AGE OF STEEL.

STEEL PRODUCTION, Combinations in. See (in this vol.) TRUSTS: UNITED STATES.

STEVENSON, Adlai E.: Bi-metallic mission to Europe. See (in this vol.) MONETARY QUESTIONS: A. D. 1897 (APRIL—OCTOBER).

STOCKHOLM, Exposition at.—A Scandinavian industrial exposition, which proved exceedingly attractive, was held with much success at Stockholm, the Swedish capital, in the summer and autumn of 1897.

STONEHENGE: Fall of two stones.— "The last night of the nineteenth century was marked, as a correspondent pointed out in our issue of yesterday, by a serious injury to what remains of the majestic monument of Stonehenge. One of the great uprights of the outer circle of stones, as well as the cross-piece mortised to it on the top, fell to the ground, thus destroying still further the most striking effect of this gigantic temple or sepulchre. The fall was probably caused by the torrents of rain and the violent winds that closed the troubled record of the year 1900. One of the uprights was brought to the ground, where it lies like so many other of the stones that formed this vast megalithic structure, and the capstone has been broken in pieces. The continuous exterior circle of which these formed a part was originally about one hundred feet in diameter, and though the masses were less imposing individually than those of the great tritithons around the centre, the effect of the mighty round of uprights, sixteen feet high, with huge capstones resting on them, must have been wonderful in its noble simplicity . . .

521

" The solicitude of the present age has placed Stonehenge, like other great national monuments, under the permissive protection of the law, but the law itself cannot prevent the ravages of weather and the gradual subsidence of the foundations on which these masses stand. Little, we fear, can be done to keep the remaining uprights standing. They will fall when their time comes and will lie where they fall like those that have already succumbed to their fate. It is better, perhaps, for the dignity of this venerable monument that it is in no serious danger of that restoration which is at work on so many later structures, more splendid as triumphs of art, but less stubborn in their strength."—*London Times, Jan.* 4, 1901.

STORMBERG, Battle of. See (in this vol.) SOUTH AFRICA (THE FIELD OF WAR): A. D. 1899 (OCTOBER—DECEMBER).

STRATHCONA'S HORSE. See (in this vol.) CANADA: A. D. 1899–1900.

STRIKES. See (in this vol.) INDUSTRIAL DISTURBANCES.

SUDAN, The Egyptian: A. D. 1885-1898. — Abandonment to the Dervishes. — Death of the Mahdi. — Reign of the Khalifa. — Anglo-Egyptian re-conquest. See (in this vol.) EGYPT: A. D. 1885–1896; 1897–1898; and 1899–1900.

A. D. 1899.—Anglo-Egyptian condominium established. See (in this vol.) EGYPT: A. D. 1899 (JANUARY).

SUDAN, The French: A. D. 1895. — Under a Governor-General of French West Africa. See (in this vol.) AFRICA: A. D. 1895 (FRENCH WEST AFRICA).

A. D. 1897. — Definition of Tongoland boundary. See (in this vol.) AFRICA: A. D. 1897 (DAHOMEY AND TONGOLAND).

A. D. 1898-1899.—Agreement with Great Britain as to the limits. See (in this vol.) NIGERIA: A. D. 1882–1899.

SUDANESE TROOPS: Mutiny in Uganda. See (in this vol.) UGANDA: A. D. 1897–1898.

SUFFRAGE: Qualifications in the several States of the American Union. See (in this vol.) UNITED STATES OF AM.: A. D. 1901 (JANUARY); also, DELAWARE; LOUISIANA; MARYLAND; MISSISSIPPI; NORTH CAROLINA; and SOUTH CAROLINA.

SUFFRAGE, Woman. See (in this vol.) WOMAN SUFFRAGE.

SUGAR BOUNTIES.—An extremely complicated and irrational state of things, connected with the production and consumption of sugar throughout the world, has been experienced for many years, as a consequence of the system of bounties on exportation, by which a number of European countries have stimulated the production of beet-sugar, in competition with the sugar produced from cane. The system was carried to its extreme development in 1896-7, in consequence of action taken in Germany, for an account of which see (in this vol.) GERMANY: A. D. 1896 (MAY). The legislation in other countries which followed the German measure of 1896 was set forth briefly in a memorial from

the Belgian beet-root sugar makers, in February, 1897, to the Belgian Chamber of Representatives, a translation of which was transmitted at the time to the State Department at Washington by the United States Consul at Ghent. Said that memorial: " The fiscal system applied to sugar factories in force [previously] in the various countries mentioned [was] chiefly established by the following laws: Germany, law of May 31, 1891; Austria, law of May 20, 1888; France, law of July 29, 1884; Russia, law of July 13, 1891; Belgium, law of April 16, 1887; Holland, law of April 15, 1891, and preceding legislation. Since the dates above mentioned, the basis established in these various countries had undergone only secondary modifications, rather local than international, and, generally, of a nature to diminish the fiscal favors instead of increasing them. From the point of view of competition among the countries of Europe, a sort of peaceful stability was thus acquired, resulting in a corresponding equilibrium in the interior relations of each country between the cultivator and owner. This situation, slowly established, has, during the last year, suffered the most serious disturbances. Important modifications have been adopted by all our competitors, Russia excepted; the latter, enjoying a special system, suffices almost entirely for itself without having much to export, it is, therefore, not necessary to give it special consideration.

" The modifications to which we allude are the following : In Germany, the law of May 27, 1896, increased the export bounties in the following proportions : (1) For raw sugar, from 41 cents to 60 cents per 220 pounds; (2) for white sugar, from 41 cents to 72 cents ; (3) for refined sugar, from 48 cents to 89 cents. This is not meant to interfere with other measures, notably the imposition of supplementary taxes, and the provision by which a factory, under the penalty of having its proportion of export bounties reduced, is, so to speak, obliged to increase its output or at least to maintain it at the same level, even under the most unfavorable circumstances. Immediately afterwards, Austria, by the law of July 7, 1896, took corresponding protective and defensive measures, especially increasing from about $2,000,000 to $3,600,000 the amount of public funds destined for export bounties. In France, the Chamber of Deputies has just voted export bounties even more important than those of other countries, amounting to— (1) raw sugar, 68 cents per 220 pounds ; (2) white sugar, 77 cents ; (3) refined sugar, 87 cents. All these export bounties are independent of the interior advantages accorded in Germany and Austria, in various forms less tangible, although not less real, and in France in the form of bonuses upon the manufacture, which, in the official French statistics, appear for sums varying from $1.16 to $1.54½ per 220 pounds, and which may be normally fixed at $1.35 per 220 pounds. Holland, in turn, has just revised its system, giving from the beginning to its producers a bounty of $1.06½ per 220 pounds on raw sugars. It is an economic war to the finish between rival nations, each desiring the ruin of the others, which these measures unchain on the sugar interests of Europe."—*U. S. Consular Reports, June,* 1897, *p.* 304.

The effect of bounty-payments is to enable the

sugars-makers of the country which pays them to sell sugar to foreign buyers at a lower price than to buyers at home. Consumers in such a country as England, where no sugar is produced, and where no duties on imported sugar are levied, reap an enormous gain from them, at the expense of the sugar consumers of the bounty-paying countries. At the same time, the cane-sugar growing colonies of England, especially those in the West Indies, suffer from the competition which is made unnatural by this method of governmental support. England, therefore, has conflicting interests in the matter. The mass of her home population, who are great consumers of "sweets," delight in the continental bounties, which give them cheap sugar; while her West India colonists, and the English sugar refiners, are groaning under the hard competition they maintain.

In the bounty-paying countries the same conflict of interest exists between beet-growers and sugar consumers, and governmental attitudes on the question of adhering to the bounties seem to depend on the relative strength, or political weight, of the two bodies. Repeated attempts have been made to come to an international agreement for their abolition or modification. A general conference on the subject was held without result in London, 1887; and another was undertaken in June, 1898, at Brussels, on the invitation of the Belgian government. The latter made manifest a strong desire to be rid of the bounty-paying system, on the part of Germany, Austria-Hungary, Belgium and the Netherlands. France was willing to withdraw her direct bounties on the exportation of sugar, but insisted on maintaining an internal system of taxes which was said to have the real effect of a bounty. Russia, likewise, would adhere to a domestic system of regulations which had that effect. Great Britain declined to engage herself to impose a duty on what was called "bounty-fed" sugar, for the purpose of neutralizing the bounty, and so placing that commodity on a footing of equality with its rivals in her markets. Hence no agreement of common action could be reached, and the Conference adjourned without result. Continental consumers of sugar continue to pay a high price for the prosperity of their beet-growers and sugar-makers; but Englishmen, who have reveled in cheap "jams" at foreign expense, are probably to lose that privilege, since the exigencies of their Boer war expenditure have forced the Chancellor of the Exchequer, at last, to introduce a duty of 4s. 2d. per cwt. on refined sugar in his budget for 1901. But in his speech on introducing the budget, in the House of Commons (April 18, 1901), the Chancellor expressed hopefulness that the foreign sugar bounty might save England from a rise in price for sugar, notwithstanding the tax. His remarks were as follows : "What is likely to be the effect on the price of sugar of the imposition of a duty? In my opinion that is a very doubtful question, because the price of sugar is not governed solely by the ordinary conditions, but it is governed largely by the bounty system. The great bulk of our imports of sugar come from bounty-giving countries; and what is that system? Why, Sir, it amounts to this, that the country giving the bounty encourages the production of sugar within its borders, and at the same time does its best to restrict the consumption of sugar by its own people by every possible means, so that the result is that there is an enormous surplus of sugar produced which must find a foreign market, and which under present circumstances can only find a market here. Therefore, it is quite conceivable, unless, of course, a bounty-giving country either reduced the area of their sugar production or lowered their own excise duties on sugar for the benefit of their own population—both of which would mean the abolition of the bounty system—it is quite conceivable that the result of the imposition of a tax on sugar here might be that, though at first the price might go up and the consumption of sugar might be consequently decreased, there would be such an influx into this country of bounty-paid sugar that could not go anywhere else that the price might be brought down. I merely put the hypothesis to the Committee, because I think it is one that ought to be considered by any one who looks into this question."—*London Times, April* 19, 1901.

"The geographical poles of the sugar trade are now Great Britain and the United States, and the two great areas of production are the beet-sugar countries of the continent of Europe and the cane-growing countries of the American and the Asiatic tropics. These two areas of production have been in active rivalry for the past thirty years, and out of this rivalry have come some striking results. The first is, that beet sugar controls the world's sugar market ; for of the 8,000,000 tons that constitute the commercial supply of sugar, about 5,000,000 are produced from the beet, and the price of this portion of the supply practically determines the price of the 3,000,000 tons of cane sugar also. Still more significant results are the removal of Great Britain from her once dominant position in tropical sugar production and the elimination of France and Spain from the struggle for leadership in the same line of enterprise, as economic conditions have centered the cane-sugar trade and industry in America. To-day the continental beet-sugar countries supply the United Kingdom with seventy-five per cent. of its annual sugar imports (2,500,000 tons), leaving only one-quarter to come from the tropics. The United States, on the other hand, has become the chief market for tropical sugar. . . .

"India and the United States exclude bounty fed beet sugar ; and the reciprocity treaties with the United States, by favoring tropical sugar with a minimum duty, put a narrower limit to beet-sugar development, now prospering under a protective tariff and state bounties. The general effect of these positive aids to trade, as well as of the negative restraints, has been to encourage tropical enterprise in which sugar plays a leading role. . . .

"As things stand now, Germany continues to control the world's sugar situation—not because of any superiority over the tropics in machinery, nor because of the advantages of fiscal bounties over tropical resources of the soil, but because all the natural advantages under the prevailing slipshod methods of tropical cane cultivation are more than counterbalanced by the scientific methods of European agriculture applied to beet farming. When the tropics apply to the cultivation of canes (which covers half of the cost of producing sugar) the same degree of scientific attention that has been given to the methods of manufacturing the canes into sugar, then—and not until then—need the beet-sugar interests of Europe look to their laurels, under the present conditions of the trade."—J. F. Crowell, *The Sugar Situation in the Tropics* (*Pol. Science Quarterly, Dec.*, 1899).

In the United States, the Dingley Tariff law of 1897 required the Secretary of the Treasury to levy a special countervailing duty on all bounty-fed sugar equal to the benefit derived by the manufacturers of it from the bounty systems under which it was produced. German and French sugars have had to bear such countervailing duty, and it was exacted on Russian sugar for a time after the passage of the Dingley Act; but the Russian government succeeded in bringing about a suspension of it, pending negotiations for a commercial treaty, which came to nothing. It was the Russian contention, that the system operating in that country for the benefit of the sugar producers, by means of internal taxes which are not collected on exported sugar, and by paternal regulations which control prices in the domestic market, is not a bounty system, within the meaning of the American law. (The full text of the Russian law on the subject may be found translated in the "Congressional Record," February 26, 1901, p. 3335.) By these arguments and by protracted negotiations the Russians succeeded in keeping the door of the American market open to their sugar, with no extra levy of duties, until February, 1901, when the Secretary of the Treasury of the United States arrived at the decision that he is required by the law to levy and collect a countervailing duty or tax of 32 cents on each pood (about 36 pounds) of Russian sugar imported into the United States. The order to that effect, issued on the 12th of February, gave great satisfaction to the American sugar-trust, and more than equal dissatisfaction to other important interests in the country, which are threatened by the danger of retaliatory tariffs on the Russian side. The situation produced is thus described in a Washington letter to the "Tribune" of New York: "The iron and steel manufacturers have been clamoring for the continued suspension of the countervailing duty on Russian sugars. They have begun, they say, to build up a market in Russia for American steel products, and that market will be lost to them if Russia in retaliation imposes maximum instead of minimum duties on steel and iron manufactures. The steel industry all over the world is threatened with a glut in production, and the American manufacturers especially are keenly looking about for every possible opportunity to dispose of an increasing surplus. They deplore, therefore, the reimposition of the sugar duty, and will help to fight for a reversal of Secretary Gage's action by the Board of General Appraisers or by the courts. The Secretary contends that the Russian scheme of encouraging the sugar interest should be submitted for judgment to some legal tribunal, and that in such an evident case of doubt it is his duty to favor the Government to the extent of reimposing the disputed duty. The case will go to the Board of General Appraisers in New York, and then to the Federal courts, and a final decision is, perhaps, two years off. Meanwhile the German, French and other Continental governments have been somewhat appeased, and

the Sugar Trust has won a substantial victory at the expense of the iron and steel consolidation. Russia is disposed to resort to retaliatory decrees, and the whole horizon is more or less clouded with threats of commercial warfare."

The immediate consequence of the order of the United States Treasury Department was a retaliatory order by M. De Witte, the Russian Minister of Finance, issued four days later (February 16), directing the collection of an additional tariff of 30 per cent net upon American hardware, iron, steel, boilers, pipes, forgings, castings, tools, gas and water meters, dynamos, sewing machines, when such articles are of American manufacture. This includes motors and machinery of all kinds.

SUGAR TRUST, The. See (in this vol.) TRUSTS: UNITED STATES; UNITED STATES OF AM.: A. D. 1897 (MARCH—JULY); and SUGAR BOUNTIES.

SULU ARCHIPELAGO: Acknowledgment of the sovereignty of the United States. —The Sultan's Government. See (in this vol.) PHILIPPINE ISLANDS: A. D. 1899 (MAY—AUGUST).

SUMER. See (in vol. 1) BABYLONIA, PRIMITIVE; (in vol. 4) SEMITES; and (in this vol.) ARCHÆOLOGICAL RESEARCH: BABYLONIA.

SUPREME COURT OF THE UNITED STATES: A. D. 1895.—Decision against the constitutionality of the Income Tax. See (in this vol.) UNITED STATES OF AM.: A. D. 1895 (APRIL—MAY).

A. D. 1900-1901.—Hearing of cases involving questions concerning the status of the new possessions of the United States. See (in this vol.) UNITED STATES OF AM.: A. D. 1900-1901.

SURGERY, Recent advances in. See (in this vol.) SCIENCE, RECENT: MEDICAL AND SURGICAL, and CHEMISTRY AND PHYSICS (X RAYS).

SUSA, Recent exploration of the ruins of. See (in this vol.) ARCHÆOLOGICAL RESEARCH: PERSIA.

SUWAROFF ISLAND: Proposed annexation to New Zealand. See (in this vol.) NEW ZEALAND: A. D. 1900 (OCTOBER).

SUZERAINTY: The question between Great Britain and the South African Republic. See (in this vol.) SOUTH AFRICA (THE TRANSVAAL): A. D. 1884-1894; 1897 (MAY—OCTOBER); and 1898-1899.

SWAT VALLEY: British India and the tribes of the. See (in this vol.) INDIA: A. D. 1895 (MARCH—SEPTEMBER); 1897-1898; and 1901 (FEBRUARY).

SWAZILAND: Administration assumed by the Transvaal Government. See (in this vol.) AFRICA: A. D. 1895 (THE TRANSVAAL).

SWEDEN AND NORWAY: Norwegian discontent with the union.—"The question of representation in foreign countries has now convulsed Scandinavia for some years. A race of democratic tendencies usually thinks more of its Consular than of its Diplomatic Service, and Norway, in demanding immediate permission to appoint her own Consuls, announces that she is willing to leave for future consideration the subject of separate Ambassadors for the two countries. Professor Harald Hjärne crystallizes the reply of Sweden in the words : ' By granting such a request we run the risk of our foreign policy, and with it also our satisfactory relations with foreign Powers, in fact, the whole external safety of our country, becoming a mere ball for the Norwegian parties during their contests for power.' However, the King, who is ever ready to grant privileges to his Norwegian subjects, even when acting against his better judgment, declared himself willing to accede to the petition as to the Consuls, and to allow the sister country to have the direct voice in the regulation of foreign affairs which she has so long demanded, but only on condition that she would contribute to the defence of the two Kingdoms in proportion to her population. . . . Many leading Norwegians declare that those who shout so loudly for a revision of the Constitution are, after all, in the minority. They argue that claims on Sweden are, for the most part, merely advanced as a party cry, and that if a general appeal were made to the country, the majority would pronounce, without hesitation, in favor of a continuation of the Union to the State which has given Norway, for the first time in her history, a period of nearly a century of peace and uninterrupted prosperity. . . .

"The Left support their plea for separate Consuls by pointing out that the mercantile navy of Norway is far larger than that of Sweden ; they claim for it, in fact, that it is the third largest in the world. A reply to this is that a large proportion of this navy consists of old wooden sailing-boats, unfit for any purpose but that of carrying timber, that Norway has increased her mercantile navy at the expense of her warships, and that in time of war she would have to depend exclusively on the splendid modern battleships of Sweden for the defence both of her harbours and her shipping, since she is not now herself the owner of one single modern ironclad. It may be mentioned, in connection with this matter, that the exports and imports of Sweden are nearly treble those of Norway, the timber trade of the former country alone being the largest in Europe, and that it is in consequence of Sweden leaving so much of her carrying trade in the hands of the sister country, thereby contributing no little to her prosperity, that she has been encouraged and enabled to increase her merchant navy to such an extent. Sweden has throughout the century made enormous sacrifices for her navy, and especially has this been the case since King Oscar came to the throne. She is, therefore, so far as can be foreseen, in a position to defend both her own ports and her merchant vessels. She does not, however, profess to be equal to the task of protecting the long coast-line of Norway and that vast fleet of merchant vessels, of which the land last named is justly proud, without any aid whatever from the sister country, and statistics prove that, however willing in an emergency Norway might be, she would be unable to offer for this purpose help that would be of any practical use. . . .

"In March, 1895, during the Consular crisis, King Oscar went over to Christiania and did his utmost to effect a compromise. Demands were made on him by the Extreme Left, to which he

could not consent, and he referred the Storthing to the Act of Union proving that should be agree to the claim, he would himself be guilty of a violation of the Constitution. Some painful scenes ensued, and the King left Norway almost at once. On his arrival in Stockholm he received an ovation such as few Swedish monarchs can ever have had before. Every distinguished man in the country seemed to have assembled at the railway-station to greet him ; each public body was represented by its leading member, the whole of the Swedish Parliament was present, and the fervour and enthusiasm with which he was saluted is beyond description. The Press, without a single exception, took the King's side, praising His Majesty's action in most lavish terms ; this produced more effect than anything in Norway, where the Left had counted on the support of the Radical Press in Sweden, not realising that, when once there was a question of attacks on the Union and the Constitution, all parties were equally prepared to rally round the King. . . .

"In view of the strained relations between Sweden and Norway, it may be said that Russia's encroachment on the liberties of Finland is extremely ill-timed if, as is probable, she contemplates offering her protection to Norway as she did to the neighbouring country at the beginning of the century. Even if no such extreme step on the part of Russia be in view, should those among Norway's two million inhabitants who demand separation, have their way, the country would be able to offer the Imperial Government a splendid bribe as the price of its non-intervention, for to the north of the territory of Norrland lies the Varanger Fjord, an inlet including several fine harbours, which is practically free from ice throughout the year. This bay, so much coveted by the greater power, is only separated from the Czar's dominions by a narrow strip of Norwegian soil, which has already been crossed by a railway constructed by Russia with the permission of Norway. The value of this fjord to the Empire in time of war would be incalculable, and to have this magnificent gift at its disposal is a perpetual temptation to Norway to win the suffrages of the only European Power she has reason to fear should she ever hoist the flag of revolt she has so long held half-unfurled in her hand."—Constance Sutcliffe, *Scandinavia and her King* (*Fortnightly Review, Oct.*, 1897).

In 1899, an Act directing the removal of the emblem of union from the flag of Norway was passed by the Norwegian Storthing for the third time over the veto of the King, and became law, under the provisions of the Constitution.

A. D. 1899 (May—July).—Representation in the Peace Conference at The Hague. See (in this vol.) PEACE CONFERENCE.

SWITZERLAND: A. D. 1894-1898.—The Initiative and the Referendum in practice.— Three times during the year 1894, with a conservative result in each instance, important questions of legislation were submitted to the vote of the Swiss people. In one instance they were asked to demand that a portion of the federal customs dues should be assigned to the cantons for cantonal use, the avowed aim of the proposition being to weaken the Confederation. They rejected the scheme by a vote of 347,491 against

145,270. A still heavier majority was given against Socialist proposals for a constitutional article guaranteeing the right of every Swiss citizen to remunerated work. This was supported by only 75,880 votes, against 308,289. For another Socialist proposal, of gratuitous medical attendance, the necessary petition (with 50,000 signatures) in order to bring it to a popular vote, could not be obtained. A third, for extending factory regulations to all shops in which manual work is done, and for establishing obligatory trade syndicates, to fix salaries, prices, number of apprentices, was lost by a vote of 135,713 against 158,492.

Again, in 1895, the result of appeals made to the Referendum seemed to show that the disposition of the people was more conservative than that of the government. An Army Reform Bill, which enlarged the federal control of military administration, was rejected by 270,000 votes, against 195,000. Two or three other proposals of less moment were voted down by considerable majorities, and it appeared unmistakably that changes dependent on the popular will were not to be easily made.

In 1896 a proposal from the Federal Council to make the head of the War Office commander-in-chief of the army in time of peace was voted down, on a referendum, by 310,992 against 77,-169. During that year there was much agitation of a project for the establishment of a State Bank, which the Chambers had sanctioned; but, on being submitted to the people, early in 1897, it was defeated by a majority of about 60,000.

Another measure, supported by the Federal Council and adopted in the Chambers, for the purchase of the five principal railways of the republic, was submitted to the decision of the Referendum in February, 1898, and carried by 384,272 votes against 176,002. Accordingly, the five railways known as the Swiss Central, the Union, the Northeastern, the St. Gothard, and the Jura Simplon, about 1,650 miles in total length, became the property of the state. The general plan of the government was to purchase the railways at twenty-five times the average net annual earnings for the past ten years, providing this was not less than the actual cost. The companies to have the privilege of deducting surplus capital, but to turn over the roads in first-class condition.

A. D. 1897.—Constitutional amendments.— Consul Germain wrote from Zurich, July, 1897: "Constitutional amendments were voted on and adopted by the Swiss people on Sunday last, July 11. The first amendment relates to forestry and gives the Federal Government control over and power to enact uniform laws to regulate Swiss forests. The second amendment puts the manufacture, sale, and importation of food products under federal control. These two amendments will relieve the cantons from vexatious legislation, heretofore differing in each of the twenty cantons and four half cantons, and give the whole of Switzerland uniform laws on forestry and the manufacture, sale, and importation of food products."—*U. S. Consular Reports, Oct.,* 1897, *p.* 296.

A. D. 1899 (May—July).—Representation in the Peace Conference at The Hague. See (in this vol.) PEACE CONFERENCE.

A. D. 1900.—Rejection of **new** electoral proposals.—On the 4th of November the Swiss nation gave its decision regarding two important proposals which under the name of the "double initiative" had been causing great excitement among the population of the Confederation. One of these proposals had for its object the election of members of the National Council on the system of proportional representation, the other the election of the Federal Council by the people. Both proposals were rejected, the first by 242,004 popular votes to 163,548, and by 11½ cantonal votes to 10½, and the second by 264,087 popular votes to 134,167 and by 14 cantonal votes to 8.

SYRIA: Exploration of ruined cities of the Roman province. See (in this vol.) ARCHÆOLOGICAL RESEARCH: SYRIA.

SZECHUAN. See (in this vol.) CHUNG-KING.

T.

TA TAO HUI, The. See (in this vol.) CHINA: A. D. 1900 (JANUARY—MARCH).

TACNA, The question concerning. See (in this vol.) CHILE: A. D. 1894-1900.

TAGALOS, or TAGALOGS, The. See (in this vol.) PHILIPPINE ISLANDS : THE NATIVE INHABITANTS.
Revolt against the sovereignty of the United States in the Philippines. See (in this vol.) PHILIPPINE ISLANDS: A. D. 1898 (AUGUST—DECEMBER), and after.

TAKU FORTS, Allied capture of the. See (in this vol.) CHINA: A. D. 1900 (JUNE 10-26).

TALANA HILL, Battle of. See (in this vol.) SOUTH AFRICA (THE FIELD OF WAR): A. D. 1899 (OCTOBER—DECEMBER).

TALIENWAN: A. D. 1895.—Russo-Chinese Treaty. See (in this vol.) CHINA: A. D. 1895.
A. D. 1898.—Lease to Russia. See (in this vol.) CHINA: A. D. 1898 (MARCH—JULY).

A. D. 1899.—Declared a free port. See (in this vol.) CHINA: A. D. 1899 (AUGUST).

TAMMANY HALL. See (in this vol.) NEW YORK CITY: A. D. 1894-1895 ; and 1897 (SEPTEMBER—NOVEMBER).

TARIFF, Chinese. See (in this vol.) LIKIN.

TARIFF LEGISLATION; Australia: A. D. 1894-1895.—Defeat of Protection in New South Wales. See (in this vol.) AUSTRALIA (NEW SOUTH WALES): A. D. 1894-1895.
Australia: A. D. 1901.—Promised **protective** policy for the **new Commonwealth.** See (in this vol.) AUSTRALIA: A. D. 1901 (MAY).
Canada: A. D. 1897.—Revision of tariff, with discriminating duties in favor of Great Britain, and provisions for reciprocity. See (in this vol.) CANADA: A. D. 1896-1897.
Europe and America: A. D. 1896-1901.— The question of sugar bounties and countervailing duties. See (in this vol.) SUGAR BOUNTIES ; and GERMANY: A. D. 1896 (MAY).
Germany: A. D. 1891-1899.—Recent com-

mercial treaties.—Preparations for forthcoming treaties. See (in this vol.) GERMANY : A. D. 1891-1899.

Germany: A. D. 1895-1898.—Demands of the German Agrarian Protectionists. See (in this vol.) GERMANY : A. D. 1895-1898.

Germany: A. D. 1901.—Promised increase of protective duties. See (in this vol.) GERMANY : A. D. 1901 (JANUARY).

Japan: A. D. 1897.—New tariff law. See (in this vol.) JAPAN : A. D. 1897.

Philippines: A. D. 1901.—New tariff for the Islands. See (in this vol.) PHILIPPINE ISLANDS : A. D. 1901 (MARCH).

Porto Rico.—A. D. 1900.—Tariff between Porto Rico and the United States. See (in this vol.) PORTO RICO : A. D. 1899-1900.

United States: A. D. 1897.—The Dingley Tariff. See (in this vol.) UNITED STATES OF AM. : A. D. 1897 (MARCH—JULY) ; and 1899-1901.

United States: A. D. 1899-1901.—Reciprocity treaties. See (in this vol.) UNITED STATES OF AM. : 1899-1901.

United States: A. D. 1900.—Relations of the tariff to steel and tin plate industries. See (in this vol.) TRUSTS : UNITED STATES.

TASMANIA. See (in this vol.) AUSTRALIA; and CONSTITUTION OF AUSTRALIA.

TEHUANTEPEC RAILWAY, The. See (in this vol.) MEXICO : A. D. 1898-1900.

TELEGRAPH, Cape to Cairo.—For the projected line of telegraph from the southern to the northern extremity of Africa, Mr. Cecil Rhodes has undertaken to find most of the needed money. He began construction from the northern terminus of the Cape telegraphic service. In 1899 it was reported : "He has pushed the line northward through Rhodesia to Umtali, in Mashonaland, which is 1,800 miles from the Cape, and is pushing it on through Nyassaland to the southern end of Lake Tanganyika, another 700 miles farther north. The total distance to be covered is 6,600 miles. At the same time the Egyptian government, under British auspices, was pushing its telegraph system southward from Wady Halfa. Its advance was intermittent, the erection of the telegraph poles being necessarily dependent upon the pushing back of the outposts of the Dervishes. Last autumn, however, the destruction of the power of the Khalifa at Omdurman enabled the Anglo-Egyptian authorities to reopen the long-closed telegraph office at Khartoum. Khartoum being 1,300 miles from Cairo, this reduces the distance to be spanned by the telegraph wire to 3,500 miles; or, if we reckon Abercorn, on Lake Tanganyika, as its northern terminus, only 2,800 miles. It is being rapidly eaten into at both ends, more rapidly in the south than in the north. Still nearly one-half of the continent, and that the most difficult part, remains to be crossed."—W. T. Stead (*in McClure's Magazine, August*, 1899).—Soon after this was written, the South African War stopped the progress of the work.

TELEGRAPHS, Submarine.—"The submarine telegraphs of the world number 1,500. Their aggregate length is 170,000 miles; their total cost is estimated at $250,000,000, and the number of messages annually transmitted over them 6,000,000. All the grand divisions of the earth are now connected by their wires, and from country to country and island to island the thoughts and words of mankind are instantaneously transmitted. . . . Adding to the submarine lines the land-telegraph systems by which they are connected and through which they bring interior points of the various continents into instantaneous communication, the total length of telegraph lines of the world is 835,000 miles, the length of their single wires or conductors 3,500,000 miles, and the total number of messages annually sent over them 365,000,000, or an average of 1,000,000 messages each day. In the short half century since the practicability of submarine telegraphy was demonstrated, the electric wires have invaded every ocean except the Pacific. Nearly a score of wires have been laid across the Atlantic, of which no less than thirteen now successfully operate between the United States and Europe, while three others span the comparatively short distance between South America and the African and south European coast lines. Throughout the Indian Ocean, lines connect the far East with Europe and America by way of the Red Sea, the Mediterranean, the western coast of Europe, and the great trans-Atlantic lines. The Mediterranean is crossed and recrossed in its entire length and breadth by numerous cable lines, and the 'Mediterranean of America,' the Gulf of Mexico and the Caribbean Sea, is traversed in all directions by lines which bring its islands and colonies into speaking relations with each other and with South America, Central America, the United States, and thence with Europe, Africa, Asia—the whole world. Along the eastern coast of Asia, cable lines loop from port to port and island to island, receiving messages overland from eastern Europe by way of the Russia-Siberian land lines and forwarding them to Japan, China, Australia, New Zealand, the Straits Settlements, Hongkong, and the Philippines, and receiving others in return. South America is skirted with cable lines along its entire border save the extreme south, where they are brought into inter-communication by land lines. Along the entire coast of Africa, cables loop from place to place and from colony to colony, stretching along the entire circumference and penetrating the interior by land lines at various points. Every body of water lying between the inhabited portions of the earth, with the single exception of the Pacific Ocean, has been crossed and recrossed by submarine telegraph lines. Even that vast expanse of water has been invaded along its margin, submarine wires stretching along its western border from Siberia to Australia, while its eastern borders are skirted with lines which stretch along the western coasts of the two Americas. Several adventurous pioneers in Pacific telegraphy have ventured to considerable distances and depths in that great ocean, one cable line running from Australia to New Zealand, a distance of over 1,000 miles, and another extending from Australia to the French colony of New Caledonia, 800 miles seaward."— *U. S. Bureau of Statistics, Monthly Summary, Jan.*, 1899.

TELEGRAPHY, Wireless. See (in this vol.) SCIENCE, RECENT: ELECTRICAL.

TELEPHONE SYSTEM, Recent development of. See (in this vol.) SCIENCE, RECENT: ELECTRICAL.

TELEPHONY, Dr. Pupin's improvement in long-distance. See (in this vol.) SCIENCE, RECENT: ELECTRICAL.

TEMPERANCE. See (in this vol.) references under LIQUOR SELLING.

TEMPLE LIBRARY, of ancient Nippur, The. See (in this vol.) ARCHÆOLOGICAL RESEARCH: BABYLONIA: AMERICAN EXPLORATION.

TENNESSEE: A. D. 1897.—Centennial Exposition.—The centennial anniversary of the admission of Tennessee to the American Union was celebrated by the holding of a very successful exposition at Nashville, opening May 1, 1897.

TERESA URREA. See (in this vol.) MEXICO: A. D. 1896-1899.

TESLA, Nikola: Electrical inventions and discoveries. See (in this vol.) SCIENCE, RECENT: ELECTRICAL.

THREE AMERICAS RAILWAY, The. See (in this vol.) RAILWAY, INTERCONTINENTAL.

THUTMOSIS I., The tomb of. See (in this vol.) ARCHÆOLOGICAL RESEARCH: EGYPT: NEW DISCOVERIES.

TIENTSIN.—"Tientsin is the most important city of northern China, being located at the head of the Gulf of Pechili and but 80 miles from the capital, Pekin, with which it is connected by water and by a railway line. Another completed railway line runs northeastwardly to Shanhaikwan, and an elaborate railway system is projected southward from this point through the populous provinces of Shantung and Kiangsu to connect Tientsin with Shanghai. In addition to these, the Grand Canal, the most important of the great artificial waterways of China, has for centuries connected Tientsin with the Yangtze-Kiang and Shanghai. Its population is in round numbers 1,000,000."—*United States, Bureau of Statistics, Monthly Summary, March,* 1899, *p.* 2194.

"Tientsin is situated at the junction of the Huei River (sometimes called the Grand Canal) with the Peiho River, in latitude 39° 3′ 55″ north and longtitude 117° 3′ 55″ east. It is distant from Pekin by road about 80 miles. Formerly, it was a military station only, but towards the end of the seventeenth century became a city of great importance. To-day, it is the home of 1,000,000 people, with an annual import and export trade aggregating 65,000,000 taels * ($42,-250,000). . . . The growth of Tientsin within the past few years is most astonishing. The mud holes and swamps of a few years ago have been filled in ; one, two, three, and even four story brick buildings erected ; streets macadamized, trees planted, gas works constructed, and now pipes (from New York) for a very elaborate and perfect water system are being laid—all due to foreign enterprise. On the other hand, the Chinese authorities have been seized with the spirit of progress, and to them is due the building and furnishing of the Imperial Military College, the Imperial University, arsenals for the manufacture of guns and ammunition, a mint for the coinage

* Consul Ragsdale values the haikwan tael at 65 cents ; the estimate of the United States Director of the Mint, July 1, 1898, is 68.8 cents.

of silver, and, last but not least, 320 miles of a splendid railway. . . .

"The Imperial University was established in 1895 by its president, Mr. C. D. Tenney (former United States vice-consul at Tientsin), at the request of His Excellency Sheng Hsuan, with the advice and approval of the Emperor. His Excellency Wu Ting-fang, present Chinese minister at Washington, and Mr. Ts-ai Shao-chin, member of Viceroy Wang's staff, were the first directors. The university is divided into three departments, viz, collegiate, preparatory, and railway. The preparatory course covers four years, after which the students enter the collegiate department, where they remain another four years. At the end of the first year in the collegiate department, the students are drafted into special classes—civil, mining, and mechanical engineering, and law. Each special branch is in charge of foreign professors, assisted by Chinese professors. The railway department was organized for the purpose of providing men for subordinate positions in the railway service—draftsmen, engineers, station masters, etc. The students are admitted to the various departments by competitive examinations. The government of the university is solely in the hands of the president and directors, the former being responsible for the educational work of the institution. Thirty students in each class are supported by the Government and are bound to Government service after their graduation. The present number of students is 250, and the annual expenses are 60,000 taels ($39,000), entirely borne by the Government. The president and four of the five professors are citizens of the United States.

"The Imperial Military College was established by His Excellency Li Hung-Chang, the viceroy of Chihli, in the year 1884. At the beginning, it was simply intended to give employment to the German officers under contract with the Government, but the necessity of training men in the arts of war led the viceroy to memorialize the Throne in behalf of a permanent military college. A suitable building was erected, at a cost of 50,000 taels ($32,500), and the annual expense of maintenance is about the same amount. The students are drafted from the different military camps, and they are supported by the generals under whom they were serving. After a two years' course, they return to their respective commands as instructors. The school is under the directorship of Taotai Yint Chang, a Manchu, who received his military education in Germany, and held a commission of lieutenancy in the Austrian army. All the principal instructors are Germans, most of them being noncommissioned officers."—*U. S. Consular Reports, Dec.,* 1898, *pp.* 550-52.

A. D. 1897.—Extension of British settlement. See (in this vol.) CHINA: A. D. 1897 (MAY—JUNE).

A. D. 1900.—Capture by allied forces. See (in this vol.) CHINA: A. D. 1900 (JULY).

TIGRIS, Valley of the: Recent archæological exploration. See (in this vol.) ARCHÆOLOGICAL RESEARCH: BABYLONIA.

TIN PLATE INDUSTRY, in the United States. See (in this vol.) TRUSTS : UNITED STATES.

TOCHI VALLEY, British-Indian war with

528

the tribes. See (in this vol.) INDIA : A. D. 1897-1898.

Inclusion in a new British Indian province. See (in this vol.) INDIA: A. D. 1901 (FEBRUARY).

TOGOLAND: A. D. 1899.—State of German colony. See (in this vol.) GERMANY: A. D. 1899 (JUNE).

A. D. 1900.—Demarcation of the Hinterland. See (in this vol.) AFRICA: A. D. 1900.

TOLEDO, O.: A. D. 1899-1901.—The election of Mayor Jones.—Importance was given to the municipal election of April, 1899, in Toledo, Ohio, by the character of the chosen Mayor, Samuel M. Jones. He had first made himself known as a manufacturer in the city, by his dealings with his employees. The Golden Rule was posted in his shops, as the law by which he expected his own conduct and that of the men who served him to be governed, and it was found that he consistently obeyed the rule. In 1897, the Republican party, needing a candidate for Mayor, put him forward and elected him. In office, he served the people so well and the politicians and the monopoly interests so little to their satisfaction, that his party, obedient to the latter, cast him aside and nominated to the Mayor's office a more "practical" man. Mr. Jones, thereupon, was induced to present himself as an independent candidate, on a platform denounced as "socialistic," and was elected by more than double the total vote cast against him, for the regular candidates of the Republican and Democratic parties. In the following November, Mr. Jones was put forward as an independent candidate for Governor of Ohio, and was not elected, but received something over 106,000 votes.

On the 1st of April, 1901, Mr. Jones was re-elected Mayor of Toledo for a third term, again as an Independent, and as a champion of municipal ownership for all public utilities.

TONGA ISLANDS, The: Renunciation of German rights to Great Britain. See (in this vol.) SAMOAN ISLANDS.

TORAL, General: The Spanish defense of Santiago de Cuba. See (in this vol.) UNITED STATES OF AM.: A. D. 1898 (JUNE—JULY).

Surrender of Spanish forces in eastern Cuba. See (in this vol.) UNITED STATES OF AM.: A. D. 1898 (JULY 4–17).

TOSKI, Battle of. See (in this vol.) EGYPT: A. D. 1885–1896.

TOWER BRIDGE. See (in this vol.) LONDON: A. D. 1894.

TRANS-MISSISSIPPI EXPOSITION. See (in this vol.) OMAHA: A. D. 1898.

TRANS-SIBERIAN RAILWAY. See (in this vol.) CHINA: A. D. 1895; and RUSSIA IN ASIA: A. D. 1891–1900.

TRANSUBSTANTIATION, English royal declaration against. See (in this vol.) ENGLAND: A. D. 1901 (FEBRUARY).

TRANSVAAL, The. See (in this vol.) SOUTH AFRICA (THE TRANSVAAL).

TRANSVAAL NATIONAL UNION, The. See (in this vol.) SOUTH AFRICA (THE TRANSVAAL): A. D. 1895–1896.

TRIADS, Rebellion of the. See (in this vol.) CHINA: A. D. 1898 (APRIL—JULY).

TRIBUNAL OF ARBITRATION, The Permanent. See (in this vol.) PEACE CONFERENCE.

TRIPLE ALLIANCE, The.—The treaty of the Triple Alliance, or Dreibund, of Germany, Austria-Hungary and Italy, formed in 1882 and renewed in 1887 (see, in vol. 5. TRIPLE ALLIANCE), for common defense against France and Russia, expires in 1903. Rumors of an intention on the part of Italy to withdraw from the Alliance arose in the spring of 1901, and received some color from a marked exchange of friendly courtesies between Italy and France in April, when an Italian squadron was entertained at Toulon, on the occasion of a visit from the President of the French Republic to that city. But there seems to be little reason to believe that any such action has been determined by the Italian government.

TROCHAS.—A Spanish term applied to military entrenchments, or fortified lines. See (in this vol.) CUBA: A. D. 1896–1897; and 1897-1898 (DECEMBER—MARCH).

TROY: Later researches on the site. See (in this vol.) ARCHÆOLOGICAL RESEARCH: TROY.

TRUST, The Sugar, and the Dingley Tariff. See (in this vol.) UNITED STATES OF AM.: A. D. 1897 (MARCH—JULY); and SUGAR BOUNTIES.

TRUSTS.

Industrial combinations in the United States.—An "Industrial Commission," created by Act of Congress in June, 1898—see (in this vol.) UNITED STATES OF AM.: A. D. 1898 (JUNE) —submitted a preliminary report on the 1st of March, 1900, on the subject of "Trusts and Industrial Combinations," from which the following historical information is taken:

"The form of organization that has given them [industrial combinations] their name 'trusts' was the one started by the Standard Oil Trust in 1882, afterwards followed by the Whisky combination —the Distillers and Cattle Feeders' Trust—and by the Sugar Trust—the American Sugar Refineries Company. The plan of that organization

was as follows: The stockholders of the different corporations entering the combination assigned their stock in trust to a board of trustees without the power of revocation. That board of trustees then held the voting power of the stocks of the different companies, and was thus enabled, through the election of directors, to control them absolutely. In place of the stock thus received the trustees issued trust certificates upon which the former holders of the stock drew their dividends, these being paid upon the certificates regardless of what disposition was made of the plants of the different corporations. Owing largely to hostile legislation and to the bitter feeling against the trusts above named, these

6–34   529

trusts, after some adverse decisions of the courts, went out of existence, reorganizing as single corporations in most cases, and none at the present time remain. A somewhat similar form of organization, however—the voting trust—is found at times. In this form of trust the holders of at least a majority of stock of a single corporation put their stock into the hands of trustees for the purpose of voting it, retaining for themselves all the privileges of drawing dividends and making transfers. Such a voting trust has been formed, it is claimed, in the case of the Pure Oil Company —an organization of the independent oil interests —for the sake of protecting a majority of the stock against purchase by the Standard Oil Company. . . . As a form of corporate combination for the sake of securing monopolistic control, the voting trust does not seem to be now in vogue.

"The form of organization that seems most common at the present time is that of the single large corporation, which owns outright the different plants. A combination of this kind is formed by the purchase of all of the plants of the different corporations or individuals who enter into it, the corporations then dissolving as separate corporations. Often payments for the plants are made largely in stock of the new corporation, so that many of the former owners maintain their interest in the business. The affairs are then managed entirely by the stockholders of the one corporation through their board of directors, elected in the ordinary way. It is usual for these larger corporations to choose a very liberal form of charter.

"A third form of organization, which is in many particulars quite like the original trust form, is that which has been taken by the Federal Steel Company, by the Distilling Company of America, and others. In this form the central company, instead of purchasing the plants of the different corporations which it is proposed to unite, simply buys a majority of the stock, or possibly the entire stock of each one of the corporations. The separate corporations keep in separate corporate existence, but a majority of the stock being held by the one larger corporation, its officers, of course, elect the boards of directors of all of the separate corporations, and in this way hold ultimately complete control. It is usually true that the separate corporations manage their own affairs practically independently, although they are furnished information regarding the workings of the other establishments in the combination through the central officers, and are doubtless largely directed in their policy in this way.

"In the case of the Standard Oil Company, when the original trust was dissolved, there were issued to the holders of trust certificates proportional amounts of stocks of each of the constituent companies, and since the trustees themselves had held a majority of the certificates, they retained as individuals a majority of the stock in each one of the companies that had formerly been in the trust. The separate corporations were named as separate corporations, but the majority of the stock of all being held in the same hands, the directors of the different companies were largely the same men, and their affairs were managed in unison in substantially the same way as had been the case before. The new Standard Oil Company of New Jersey has recently been formed with the intention of transferring the stocks of the different corporations into the stock of the new company, so that when the transfer has been finally made, one single corporation, the Standard Oil Company of New Jersey, will own outright the property now owned by the separate companies which are commonly known and mentioned together under the name of the Standard Oil Company. This combination at present has no formal unity. It has a practical unity as great as it will have probably after the complete change into the New Jersey company is effected.

"As most of the larger corporations have, within the last few years, been organized in New Jersey, it will be worth while to note the special advantages given by the corporation laws of that State. The advantages that seem to be brought out most clearly are: First, taxation. The organization tax is considerably lower than that of most of the States, while the annual tax is fixed upon the amount of capital paid in, so that it is an absolutely certain quantity and can be determined by anyone, thus leaving no opportunity for corruption on the part of either the corporation itself or of State officials. The rate of the tax is moderate, and decreases as the amount of capital increases. Second. Perhaps a greater advantage is to be found in the liberal form of the New Jersey charter. The amount of capital is unlimited, the period of organization is unlimited, the amount of indebtedness is not limited, the powers that are granted to corporations are also practically unlimited, with the exception that an ordinary business corporation is forbidden to engage in banking. The Federal Steel Company would have found it impossible to organize for the purpose of engaging in the various enterprises which it has undertaken had it incorporated in the State of Illinois or of Pennsylvania. The same thing holds also with reference to the American Steel and Wire Company. Third. There is less liability on the part of the stockholders than in several other States. Fourth. The directors have also less liability. In case of issuance of stock for property the judgment of the directors is conclusive as to the value of the property taken, unless there is evidence of fraud. Stock issued thus for property is considered fully paid up, and the stockholders can not be held further liable in case the property proves to have been taken at less than its cash value. The directors are not personally liable for the debts of the corporation if they fail to file reports or to conform with certain other requirements. . . .

"During the past few years the total capitalization of the new industrial combinations has reached an enormous sum, well into the billions, and in many cases at least the nominal capitalization of the corporations far exceeds the cash value of their property. . . . Regarding most of the combinations concerning which testimony has been taken the facts appear quite clear. None of the witnesses believe that the Standard Oil Company is on the whole over-capitalized, as compared with the present value of the plants. Its opponents believe that its profits are enormous on the capitalization. The witnesses representing the Standard Oil Company itself, while admitting very large profits and presenting no very definite facts regarding the capitalization, still give the same impression from their testimony. The American Sugar Refining Company seems to be, beyond question, capitalized at a sum twice as large at least as the cost of reconstruction of the plants themselves. The capitalization was shown to be several times the original capitalization of its constituent members. . . .

"Perhaps the clearest testimony on this subject of capitalization came from the witnesses connected with some of the iron and steel companies. The witnesses regarding the tin-plate combination were in substantial agreement in stating that the owners of most of the plants gave an option on their plants at what they considered was the fair cash value, although, owing to the good times and to the fact that, in many cases, the industries were quite prosperous, the prices were high. They were then given, by the promoter, the option of taking this valuation of their property in cash, or of taking instead the same amount in preferred stock with a like amount of common stock added as bonus. . . . One of the witnesses, at least, conceded that the total amount of stock thus paid for the plants, since the cash option was taken in prosperous times and included not merely the value of the plant but also the good will of the running business, probably amounted in some instances to three or four or even five times the cash cost of the plants at that time. . . . Exactly the same system seems to have been followed in the capitalization of the National Biscuit Company, the National Steel Company, and the American Steel Hoop Company. In all these cases there was a clear understanding that the common stock represented simply bonus or anticipated profits. . . .

"In the case of the American Tin Plate Company there was also added ten millions of common stock, which was issued to the promoter for his services and for the cost of organization. It is presumed, of course, that not a little of this ten millions had to be paid out in commissions etc. to those who aided in securing the required amount of capital, including cash furnished for working capital. The amount of extra common stock issued for purposes of promotion in the American Steel Hoop Company and in the National Steel Company was $5,000,000 in each case."—*U. S. Industrial Commission, Preliminary Report* (56th *Cong., 1st Sess., House Doc. No.* 476, *pt.* 1), *pp.* 10–15.

Standard Oil Company.—As the rise of the Standard Oil Company seems to have marked the beginning of the movement towards combination in productive industries, on the great scale of recent times, the following passages from testimony concerning the history of the Company and of the oil business is especially interesting. The first is from the examination of Mr. John D. Rockefeller:

"Q. What was the first combination in which you were interested of different establishments in the oil industry ?—A. The first combination of different establishments in the oil industry in which I was interested was the union of William Rockefeller & Co., Rockefeller & Andrews, Rockefeller & Co., S. V. Harkness, and H. M. Flagler, about the year 1867.

"Q. What were the causes leading to its formation ?—A. The cause leading to its formation was the desire to unite our skill and capital in order to carry on a business of some magnitude and importance in place of the small business that each separately had theretofore carried on. As time elapsed and the possibilities of the business became apparent, we found further capital to

be necessary, obtained the required persons and capital, and organized the Standard Oil Company with a capital of $1,000,000. Later we found more capital could be utilized and found persons with capital to interest themselves with us, and increased our capital to $3,500,000. As the business grew, and markets were obtained at home and abroad, more persons and capital were added to the business, and new corporate agencies were obtained or organized, the object being always the same, to extend our business by furnishing the best and cheapest products.

"Q. Did the Standard Oil Company or other affiliated interests at any time before 1887 receive from the railroads rebates on freight shipped, or other special advantages ?—A. The Standard Oil Company of Ohio, of which I was president, did receive rebates from the railroads prior to 1880, but received no special advantages for which it did not give full compensation. The reason for rebates was that such was the railroads' method of business. A public rate was made and collected by the railway companies, but, so far as my knowledge extends, was never really retained in full, a portion of it was repaid to the shippers as a rebate. . . . The Standard Oil Company of Ohio, being situated at Cleveland, had the advantage of different carrying lines, as well as of water transportation in the summer, and taking advantage of those facilities made the best bargains possible for its freights. All other companies did the same, their success depending largely upon whether they had the choice of more than one route. The Standard sought also to offer advantages to the railways for the purpose of lessening rates of freight. It offered freights in large quantity, car-loads and train loads. It furnished loading facilities and discharging facilities. It exempted railways from liability for fire. For these services it obtained contracts for special allowances on freights. These never exceeded, to the best of my present recollections, 10 per cent. But in almost every instance it was discovered subsequently that our competitors had been obtaining as good, and, in some instances, better rates of freight than ourselves. . . .

"Q. About what percentage of the profits of the Standard Oil Company came from special advantages given by the railroads when these were greatest ?—A. No percentage of the profits of the Standard Oil Company came from advantages given by railroads at any time. Whatever advantage it received in its constant efforts to reduce rates of freight was deducted from the price of oil. The advantages to the Standard from low freight rates consisted solely in the increased volume of its business arising from the low price of its products. . . .

"Q. To what advantages, or favors, or methods of management do you ascribe chiefly the success of the Standard Oil Company ?—A. I ascribe the success of the Standard to its consistent policy to make the volume of its business large through the merits and cheapness of its products. It has spared no expense in finding, securing, and utilizing the best and cheapest methods of manufacture. It has sought for the best superintendents and workmen and paid the best wages. It has not hesitated to sacrifice old machinery and old plants for new and better ones. It has placed its manufactories at the points where they could supply markets at the least expense. It has not only sought markets for its principal products, but for all possible by-products, sparing no expense in introducing them to the public. It has not hesitated to invest millions of dollars in methods for cheapening the gathering and distribution of oils by pipe lines, special cars, tank steamers, and tank wagons. It has erected tank stations at every important railroad station to cheapen the storage and delivery of its products. It has spared no expense in forcing its products into the markets of the world among people civilized and uncivilized. It has had faith in American oil, and has brought together millions of money for the purpose of making it what it is, and holding its markets against the competition of Russia and all the many countries which are producers of oil and competitors against American oil."—*The same, pt. 2, p.* 794.

Against the testimony of Mr. Rockefeller that the Standard Oil Company obtained no exclusive advantages from railway companies, other witnesses contended that such advantages were given to it. On this point, the Commission say in their report: "It was charged by most of the leading opponents of the Standard Oil Company that the chief reason for the rapid growth of the Standard, and its apparent great success in underselling rivals and winning markets, was the special advantages that it had received from the railroads. It was claimed that the company not merely received discriminating rates on its own shipments, but that it was frequently paid rebates on the shipments of its competitors. It was conceded by representatives of the Standard Oil Company that before the passage of the interstate-commerce act special freight rates and rebates were frequently received. It was asserted, however, that this was the usual custom on the part of all railroads with all large shippers, and that competitors of the Standard had received similar favors. . . .

"Much greater differences of opinion exist with reference to the condition of affairs since the passage of the interstate-commerce act. It has been charged as a matter of general belief on the part of almost all of the opponents of the Standard Oil Company that these discriminations in various forms have been continually received even up to date. On the other hand, these charges have been denied in toto and most emphatically by every representative of the Standard Oil Company with reference to all cases excepting one, which they claim was a mistake, the amount of freight due being promptly paid on discovery of the error. . . . Certain opponents of the company claimed that the Standard Oil Company received commissions for shipping freight over railroads, which commissions amounted to rebates. This charge is emphatically denied by the Standard Oil Company and no positive proof on the subject has been offered."—*The same, pt. 1, p.* 25.

Of testimony on the subject of pipe-line consolidations in the oil business, the report says: "Mr. Boyle [publisher of the 'Oil City Derrick'] gives a somewhat detailed history of the development of pipe-line transportation in the oil business. The first successful pipe lines were established in 1864 from Pithole to the Miller farm. Others were soon constructed in the same district. These were usually short, scarcely over 5 miles in length, and at first did not even connect directly with the wells themselves, although

this practice was soon established. Numerous lines soon grew up in different parts of the oil region, but the first more extended systems date from 1869, when the Mutual Pipe Line was laid more or less throughout Clarion County. Vandergrift and Forman later established a system through Butler County which became the nucleus of what is now known as the United Pipe Line System. The original pipe lines were only transporters of oil, but the nature of their work soon led them to purchase oil, although at first it was not in the name of the company itself. . . .

"Mr. Emery [of Bradford] also makes a brief statement of the early history of pipe lines. He states that the first attempt to combine separate pipe lines into a more complex system was made by William H. Abbott and Henry Harley, beginning about 1866. By 1869 they had a capital of nearly $2,000,000, and 500 miles of pipe centering in the Miller farm. The concern was then known as the Pennsylvania Transportation Company.

"Several witnesses describe the process by which the Standard Oil Company gradually secured control of the various pipe lines throughout the oil regions. The opponents of the trust attribute the success of the Standard Oil Company in this movement to the railway discriminations upon oil received from pipe lines controlled by that company. It appears that for a considerable period a rebate of 22 cents per barrel was allowed on oil from pipe lines maintaining the agreed rates of pipage. . . . Other opponents of the combination ascribe its success in driving out competing pipe lines largely to the practice of paying premiums upon oil in the territory of such competing lines.

"Mr. Boyle gives the fullest statement of the growth of the pipe-line consolidation during the seventies and attributes it to the natural advantages arising from large capital and from skill in organizing. He testifies that during the early part of that decade very numerous pipe lines had been established. These were at first constructed on a small scale by separate oil producers, but, having entered the business, many producers were inclined to extend their lines and form a system. There thus arose an excessive number of competing lines, and the solvency and integrity of some of them became a matter of doubt. This excessive competition was the cause of driving the pipe lines into a more complete organization. As early as 1873 or 1874 a pooling arrangement was made by some of the pipe lines, and rebates were paid by railways on oil received from such lines. The United Pipe Line Company was established in 1877, with a capital at first of $3,000,000, and acquired by purchase a large number of lines. The new company included many producers and stockholders of the smaller companies, but it is estimated that the persons controlling the Standard Oil Company had somewhat more than a one-half interest in the United Pipe Lines. The National Transit Company is the present owner of the United Pipe Lines System, and the Standard Oil Company controls the National Transit Company. . . .

"It was pointed out by several witnesses that the almost complete control of the pipe-line system by the Standard Oil Company gives it great power in fixing the prices of crude oil, since producers can dispose of their product only through the pipe lines, especially in view of the further fact, which is alleged, that railway rates on crude oil are by agreement kept at least as high as, if not higher than, the pipe-line charges. The pipe-line system also gives the combination great advantage over other refiners, who must pay the rates of pipage fixed by the Standard, which are claimed to be excessively high, or the high rates of freight."—*The same, pt. 1, p.* 100.

Sugar Trust.—The following is from the testimony of Mr. Henry O. Havemeyer:

"Q. The history and organization of the Sugar Refining Company has been gone over so many times in testimony before that it is not worth while to dwell on it at length, but in order that we may have the record somewhat complete, will you give a brief sketch of its development, going back to the conditions of the old sugar trust? [1887]—A. There were about twenty-five different firms or corporations in the sugar business. I think the evidence before some one of the Congressional committees was that for a period of 5 or 6 years before the formation of the trust, 18 of those failed or went out of business.

"Q. Eighteen out of 25?—A. Not out of 25; 18 out of about 40. It occurred to some one to consolidate the others, and 18 out of 21, I believe, went into the trust, leaving 3 or 4 outside, who represented, I think, 30 per cent. Then Spreckles built a refinery in Philadelphia, and, 2 or 3 years after the formation of the trust, the trust or its successor bought the Philadelphia refineries.

"Q. Will you explain in a word or two the difference between the trust and its successor and the reason for its going into this other form? —A. The trust was attacked, and the courts decided it was illegal, and a company was organized in New Jersey which bought outright and paid for the different companies, which were the constituent companies of the trust. They then represented, I think, over 90 per cent of the output; then other refineries began to be constructed, until now I think they would represent 50 per cent of the consumption. . . .

"Q. The condition before the formation of the trust was about this: When these 18 different companies failed, business was in such a condition, as a whole, that it was considered unprofitable?—A. Very unprofitable—ruinous.

"Q. Now, can you tell what special advantages—if you can give this in some detail I shall be glad—come from this organization, and in what way you make your savings?—A. The greatest advantage is in working the refinery full and uninterruptedly. Of course, if you have a capacity of 140,000,000 and can only melt 100,-000,000 somebody has got to cut down materially. The moment you cut down you increase the cost; by buying up all the refineries . . . and concentrating the meltings in four refineries and working them full, you work at a minimum cost. That enables us to pay a dividend on the common stock.

"Q. So the chief advantage in the combination was in concentrating the production and destroying the poor refineries?—A. Precisely."—*The same, pt. 2, p.* 109.—See, also (in this vol.), UNITED STATES OF AM.: A. D. 1897 (MARCH—JULY).

The earlier combinations in steel production.—Mr. Reis, president of the National Steel Company, states that that company was organized in February, 1899, under the laws of New Jersey, with a capital of $59,000,000, $27,000,000 of 7 per cent cumulative preferred stock and $32,000,000 of common stock. The company includes six steel plants, located at New Castle, Youngstown, Sharon, Mingo Junction, Bellaire, and Columbus. These plants are engaged in producing steel billets and slabs, which are the raw materials for making tin plates and various other products. The plants include 15 blast furnaces. The company also owns iron mines in northern Michigan at Iron Mountain and Ishpeming. These are expected to produce from 1,250,000 to 1,400,000 tons of ore annually, the total amount required for the use of the steel plants in the combination being about 3,000,000 tons. The National Steel Company also owns nine lake boats for transporting ore, capable of carrying about 1,000,000 tons annually. . . . Mr. Reis testifies that the National Steel Company is not a 'trust' in the ordinary sense, since it makes no attempt to secure control of a large proportion of the output of steel. Its economies are sought in the combination of steel plants with sources of raw materials. The National Steel Company produces only about 18 per cent of the Bessemer steel made in this country. The other chief concerns engaged in steel production are the Carnegie Steel Company; Federal Steel Company; the Maryland; Jones & Laughlin Steel Company; Wheeling Steel and Iron Company, and the Lorain Steel Company. . . .

"Mr. Reis states that the tariff, so far as it is placed upon steel billets, bars, and sheets, is no longer necessary for the protection of the industry. No steel is imported, and during the past 8 or 10 years the tariff has cut no figure. But if the tariff should be removed from tin plate or from certain other branches of the iron and steel industry there would be an indirect effect upon the making of steel. . . .

"Mr. Gary states that the Federal Steel Company owns all the capital of the Minnesota Iron Company, the Illinois Steel Company, the Lorain Steel Company, and the Elgin, Joliet and Eastern Railroad Company. The Minnesota Iron Company is the owner of 150,000 acres of iron ore property on the Vermilion and Mesaba ranges. It owns the Duluth and Iron Range Railroad Company, connecting its mines with Lake Superior at Two Harbors and Duluth. It owns large ore docks and also 22 steel lake vessels capable of carrying 2,000,000 tons per annum. The product of the Minnesota Iron Company will probably be 3,500,000 tons in 1900. The Lorain Steel Company manufactures chiefly steel rails for street railways, and to some extent steel billets. It produces about 500,000 tons of pig iron per year. The Illinois Steel Company has plants at North Chicago, West Chicago, South Chicago, Milwaukee, and Joliet. It produces about 1,500,000 tons of pig iron per year, and also manufactures steel rails, billets, plates, etc. It owns the Chicago, Lake Shore and Eastern Railway, which connects its plants in the neighborhood of Chicago. It also owns large tracts of coal property in Pennsylvania and West Virginia, and makes their about 1,500,000 tons of coke per year. This company also owns iron mines in Wisconsin and Michigan. . . .

"Mr. Stetson, a lawyer, who drafted the charter and conducted the legal arrangements in the organization of the Federal Steel Company, testified that it was organized in September, 1898, with an authorized capital of $100,000,000 6 per cent noncumulative preferred stock and $100,-000,000 common stock. Of this, $98,000,000 in all was originally issued. . . . Mr. Gary states that the Federal Steel Company is not a trust in any sense. It has not sought to restrict competition and has not brought together companies which were competing with one another, as is the case with most so-called trusts. The company has bought the stocks of companies doing different lines of business, just as an individual might do. . . .

"The American Steel and Wire Company operates iron mines in the Lake Superior region. It controls, perhaps, one-sixth or one-seventh of the output of that region. It owns and operates coal mines and burns coke. It operates 8 or 9 blast furnaces, 17 open-hearth furnaces, from 22 to 25 rod rolling mills, and from 20 to 30 wire mills. Its finished product is plain wire, barbed wire, wire fencing, rope, etc., wire nails, and all kindred articles. . . . Mr. Gates, chairman of the American Steel and Wire Company of New Jersey, testified concerning the formation of that company. It was organized on January 12, 1899. A gradual process of consolidating wire plants had been going on previously. As early as 1890 companies in which Mr. Gates was interested practically controlled the manufacture of barbed wire in this country. In December, 1897, and January, 1898, J. P. Morgan & Co. investigated the value of the various wire plants throughout the country with a view to further consolidation. The American Steel and Wire Company of Illinois, formed in March, 1898, seems to have resulted from this effort. . . . The combination into the American Steel and Wire Company was not rendered necessary by excessive competition and consequent losses among the wire companies. The Consolidated Steel and Wire Company, for example, made between 27 and 28 per cent during the last three years of its existence. It was believed, however, that more profit would be made through better management under consolidation."—*The same, pt. 1, p.* 190.

Tin Plate Industry.—"The American Tin Plate Company was incorporated under the laws of New Jersey on January 6, 1899. Its authorized capital is $20,000,000 of 7 per cent cumulative preferred stock and $30,000,000 of common stock. Of this, $18,000,000 of preferred and $28,000,000 of common stock has been issued. . . . It is made clear by the evidence of all the witnesses that the tin-plate industry in the United States has been built up practically since the McKinley tariff of 1890, which raised the duty on tin plates from 1 to 2.2 cents per pound. Without the protection, all the witnesses agree, the industry could not have been profitably established. Having once been established, it was able to submit to the reduction of the duty to 1.2 cents by the Wilson tariff of 1894, and is now sufficiently protected by the duty of 1.5 cents under the Dingley tariff of 1897."—*The same, pt. 1, pp.* 174 *and* 187.

The climax of consolidation in steel industries.—Formation of the United States Steel Corporation.—In February, 1901, the climax was reached in movements of industrial combination, so far as concerns the production and greater uses of iron and steel, by the formation

of one gigantic corporation, to embrace not only the companies named above, but to purchase the enormous interests of the Carnegie Company outright, and to take in several organizations of more than considerable magnitude besides. The combination was effected by the firm of J. P. Morgan & Co., New York, as "syndicate managers," and an official statement of its essential terms was published in a circular from that firm, on the 2d of March, addressed to the stockholders of the Federal Steel Company, National Steel Company, National Tube Company, American Steel and Wire Company of New Jersey, American Tin Plate Company, American Steel Hoop Company, American Sheet Steel Company, to whom the following announcement was made: "The United States Steel Corporation has been organized under the laws of the State of New Jersey, with power, among other things, to acquire the outstanding preferred stocks and common stocks of the companies above named, and the outstanding bonds and stock of the Carnegie Company. A syndicate, comprising leading financial interests throughout the United States and Europe, of which the undersigned are managers, has been formed by subscribers to the amount of $200,000,000, (including among such subscribers the undersigned and many large stockholders of the several companies,) to carry out the arrangement hereinafter stated, and to provide the sum in cash and the financial support required for that purpose. Such syndicate, through the undersigned, has made a contract with the United States Steel Corporation, under which the latter is to issue and deliver its preferred stock and its common stock and its five per cent. gold bonds, in consideration for stocks of the above named companies and bonds and stock of the Carnegie Company and the sum of $25,000,000 in cash.

"The syndicate has already arranged for the acquisition of substantially all the bonds and stock of the Carnegie Company, including Mr. Carnegie's holdings. The bonds of the United States Steel Corporation are to be used only to acquire bonds and 60 per cent. of the stock of the Carnegie Company. The undersigned, in behalf of the syndicate, and on the terms and conditions hereinafter stated, offer, in exchange for the preferred stocks and common stocks of the companies above named, respectively, certificates for preferred stock and common stock of the United States Steel Corporation, upon the basis stated."

Details relating to the terms and the procedure of exchange are then given, and several statements of public interest are made, among them these : "The authorized issue of capital stock of the United States Steel Corporation presently provided for in said contract is $850,000,000, of which one-half is to be seven per cent. cumulative preferred stock and one-half is to be common stock. The company will also issue its five per cent. gold bonds to an aggregate amount not exceeding $304,000,000. In case less than all of the bonds and stock of the Carnegie Company or less than all of the stocks of the other companies above referred to shall be acquired, the amounts of bonds and stocks to be issued will be reduced as provided in said contract. The forms of the new bonds and of the indenture securing the same, and of the certificates for the new preferred and common shares, and the entire plan of organization and management of the United States Steel Corporation, shall be determined by J. P. Morgan & Co. Every depositor shall accept in full payment and exchange for his deposited stock the shares of the capital stock of the United States Steel Corporation, to be delivered at the rates above specified, in respect of the stock by him so deposited; and no depositor or holder of any receipt issued hereunder shall have any interest in the disposition of any other of the shares of stock, or of the bonds of the United States Steel Corporation, by it to be issued and delivered to or for account of the syndicate or of any proceeds thereof. All shares of the United States Steel Corporation deliverable to or for account of the syndicate, which shall not be required for the acquisition of the stock of the Carnegie Company or for delivery to depositors under the terms of this circular, are to be retained by and belong to the syndicate. . . . It is proper to state that J. P. Morgan & Co. are to receive no compensation for their services as syndicate managers beyond a share in any sum which ultimately may be realized by the syndicate."

Subsequently the American Bridge Company and the Lake Superior Consolidated Iron Mines were taken into the consolidation, and, on the 1st of April, 1901, the United States Steel Corporation filed with the Secretary of State at Trenton, N. J., amended articles of incorporation increasing its authorized capital stock to $1,100,-000,000. The stock is equally divided into 7 per cent. cumulative preferred stock and common stock. The total is greater by $250,000,000 than the amount stated in the circular issued by J. P. Morgan & Co., on March 2, as "presently provided for," and with the 5 per cent. gold bonds, not exceeding $304,000,000, brings the security issues of the great steel combination up to $1,404,000,000.

Industrial combinations in European countries.—"Trusts of the magnitude and influence of those now so numerous in the United States are as yet rare in the Old World. . . . It is in Germany, . . . of all European countries, that trusts have spread most extensively and have been most successful. . . . The German technical journals for 1897 enumerate about 180 trusts, of which, it is true, only a few would correspond to American ideas, but all of which demonstrate a capacity for wider combination and fuller development. . . . As regards great industrial combinations, the most striking advance has been made in the German coal industry; the most prominent organization in this department being the Rheinisch-Westfälische Kohlensyndikat, which is distinguished by the characteristics of a genuine trust, exercising within its sphere of activity almost unlimited power. Like the American Standard Oil Company, it directly controls the sales, leaving the matter of production entirely to the separate companies. Under the innocent title of 'eines Vereins zum Ankauf und Verkauf von Kohlen' (a society for the buying and selling of coal), this trust has, for the past five years, completely controlled the West German coal industry, and dictated prices. . . .

"In Austria and Hungary trusts have not yet extended so rapidly. Nevertheless, on various occasions several of them have given rise to such unfavorable comment that the sentiment in favor of a legislative restriction of the movement is to-day much more pronounced in the Austrian than in the German Parliament. . . .

"As far as England is concerned, it must be admitted that, notwithstanding her great industrial activity and a competitive warfare not less pronounced than that of other states, the Trust system has as yet found but tardy acceptance in that country. This is doubtless due in some degree to the thorough application of the principle of Free Trade; for it is well known that the largest trusts are powerless unless their interests are secured by a protective tariff excluding from the home market the products of foreign countries. Furthermore, we should remember that in England the principle of individual freedom is regarded as inviolable. There, it still obtains more widely than in most other countries; and the majority of British merchants consider the principle involved in the formation of trusts as a serious menace to the freedom of the individual. . . .

"France is a country in which the Trust system has long flourished and assumed extensive proportions. In the iron trade, great trust companies —local in their character, it is true—have existed for the last twenty years; and the most powerful of these, like those of Germany, limit their activity to the establishment of sales-depots. The chemical industry of France, like that of Germany, is now controlled almost exclusively by combinations. . . . Several international trusts, such as the Zinc Trust, also have their headquarters at Paris. Belgium, like France, is interested in most of the international trusts; and there, as in France, the Trust system has been successful largely in those enterprises which, in other industrial countries, have hitherto maintained a stubborn resistance to the inroads of the Trust. . . .

"In respect to the economic value of trusts in Europe, it may be said that the influence exerted by them, both for good and for evil, is, in its essential features, similar to that exerted by the trusts of America."—W. Berdrow, *Trusts in Europe* (*Forum, May*, 1899).

Industrial combinations in England.— "England no longer enjoys that immunity from monopoly which was the boast of its own economists and the object-lesson of American free-traders. While the position of trusts has not greatly changed in the United States during the past ten years, except to develop on the same lines, a commercial revolution is taking place in England. The country is becoming honey-combed with combinations and trusts; and, what is more and perhaps worse, there is no agitation against the system. No effort is made to check trusts or control them. . . . There are a large number of informal combines in England which give some advantages of monopoly without unity of control or financial association. Thus, the railroad corporations have long ceased to compete as regards rates. It is perfectly well understood, and has been admitted over and over again by railroad men before Parliamentary committees, that the railroad companies combine. They agree in their rates, but compete in facilities, speed, etc. If it were not that the railroad companies are strictly regulated by the Board of Trade, this system of concerted action would be a very serious factor. As it is, the railroads represent the most powerful interest in Parliament. . . . Similarly, the leading shipping companies have fixed rates for freight, to stop under-cutting, competing only in speed and facilities. . . . There are various understandings and agreements in the coal-trade. . . . "Until a few years ago, England was not ripe for trusts. The early efforts failed either through the overcapitalization of the concerns, opposition from outsiders, or defective management. . . . The monopoly that has been most prejudicial to public interests—the National Telephone Company—is now being undermined. . . . The agitation against this monopoly on the part of municipalities became so strong that in 1898 the House of Commons appointed a committee to investigate the question. The result was that last year an act was passed giving municipalities the right to establish telephones, and authorizing the post-office to spend $10,000-000 in creating a competitive system in London. . . .

"During the last three years, there has been a prolific crop of amalgamations—half-way houses

TSUNG-LI-YAMEN, The Chinese. See (in this vol.) CHINA : A. D. 1899 (MARCH).

TUBUAI ISLANDS. See (in this vol.) AUSTRAL ISLANDS.

TUGELA RIVER, Military operations on the. See (in this vol.) SOUTH AFRICA (THE FIELD OF WAR): A. D. 1899 (OCTOBER—DECEMBER) ; and 1900 (JANUARY—FEBRUARY).

TUNIS: A. D. 1881-1898.—During the French Protectorate.—In 1881, under pretexts which were much condemned at the time, the government of France compelled the Bey of Tunis to sign a treaty by which he submitted himself and country to the Protectorate of France (see, in vol. 2, FRANCE: A. D. 1875-1889). This action gave bitter offense to the Italians, who had been intending to lay their own hands on Tunis, and it is to be counted among the causes of the entrance of Italy into the Dreibund or Triple Alliance with Germany and Austria-Hungary in 1882. But time had so far worn away the grievance that the Tunisian protectorate was practically recognized by the Italian government in a treaty with France, signed in September, 1896. In 1898, the general results produced in Tunis by seventeen years of French control were described in an elaborate report to the British government by its representative in the Protectorate, or Regency, Sir H. Johnston. The following is quoted from that report: "The protectorate of Tunis is nominally an Arab Kingdom, ruled by a prince of Turkish descent under the guidance and control of a French Minister Resident-General and a staff of French officials. The present Bey of Tunis, Sidi Ali Pasha-Bey, is, I believe, the most aged ruler living, having been born in the year 1817. He was Heir Apparent at the time of the French treaty of protection, concluded with his elder brother, Sidi Sadok Bey. Sidi Ali at his accession to the throne in 1882 accepted the inevitable with a good grace, and has from the very first lent himself unreservedly to the French efforts for the regeneration of his country. Two of his ministers are Arabs (the Prime Minister and the Minister of the Pen), the remainder of the Council are French officials. M. René Millet, the Resident-General of France, is at the same time Minister for the Foreign Af-

to trusts. . . . There is one kind of amalgamation taking place that deserves special note. Great mining, iron, engineering, and shipbuilding firms have come together. Instead of having between the raw material and the completed ship or engineering work the intermediary profits of the iron-ore miner, the coal-miner, the iron-master, the steel-maker, the iron-founder, the forger, the marine-engine builder, and so forth,—all these middlemen are got rid of, and the whole business placed, as it were, under one roof. . . .

"Consumers in England have not so much to fear from combines regulated by the Companies' Act, and held in check by free trade, as consumers in the United States."—R. Donald, *Trusts in England (Review of Reviews, Nov., 1900)*.

The question in American politics. See (in this vol.) UNITED STATES OF AM. : A. D. 1896 (JUNE—NOVEMBER); and 1900 (MAY—NOVEMBER).

fairs of the Tunisian Government and President of the Council. . . . The personal staff of the Resident-General consists of about nine members. In addition, the French Government is more or less directly represented throughout the Regency by officials corresponding almost exactly to our vice-consuls, collectors and assistant-collectors in our African Protectorates, with this difference, that the collectors are called ' contrôleurs.' . . .

"The whole of Tunisia is now under civil administration, except the Sahara district to the south of Gabes, which still remains under military control. . . . In the districts which I visited, the natives, talking to me freely, said that they would sooner be under the rule of any Frenchman than under that of their own kaids. The French are face to face here with the same problem that we find so difficult in other oriental countries—that of creating amongst the natives a body of public officials who will keep their hands from picking and stealing, and their tongues from evil speaking, lying and slandering. No tyrant is so cruel to an Arab as an Arab; no one is harder on Muhammadans than their co-religionists. Justice is administered to Europeans, and to the protected subjects of European powers, by French tribunals, which equally deal with cases arising between Europeans and Tunisians. . . . Justice is administered to natives, in cases where natives alone are concerned, by Arab courts depending directly on the Tunisian Government, but with a Frenchman at the head of each principal department. At all the centres of population there are Arab courts of justice. The Court of Appeal for the French courts in Tunis is the Supreme Court of Algiers; the appeal from the Arab courts is to the Bey. . . . Public works are entirely under French control, though Tunisians are employed in minor posts. . . .

"Public education is under French and Arab direction. The schools and colleges more or less directly supported by the Government in the city of Tunis are the following :—The Lycée Carnot, the Collége Sadiki, the secondary school for girls, the Alawi College, two lay schools for boys, a school for Jewish children of the Israelite Alliance, a Jewish agricultural school, two schools for Jewish girls, three schools for boys under the direction of friars, **and** a primary school for little girls. There is a Muhammadan university at the Great Mosque in Tunis, and there are 113 primary Muhammadan schools in the same town. In the interior there are about 98 primary schools for boys and girls, supported by the Government, and mainly under French direction. There are also about 500 Muhammadan schools in the interior, either private or assisted by Government funds. In addition to Government-supported schools, a large number of private establishments have sprung up at Tunis and at Sfax, wherein surprisingly good teaching is given, even in such subjects as music. . . . The progress of education is having very marked results on the indigenous population of the coming generation—good results in the dissipation of Muhammadan fanaticism and prejudice, results less pleasing, however, when the recipient of this education is turned out a creature with no particular religion, with no principles, and a contempt for manly labour. . . .

"In 1880 life and property were thoroughly insecure. The property of Europeans, perhaps, was safe, provided they were the subjects of a Power able to coerce the Government of Tunis, and their lives were not in any great danger in the principal towns; but it would have been impossible for any European to have travelled about many parts of the Regency without a considerable escort; impossible, indeed, to penetrate some parts of the Regency at all unless at the head of an army. . . . It was as difficult, and dangerous, and expensive to travel about the Regency 18 years ago as it is now to visit the far interior of Morocco. I spent eight months in Tunisia at that time, but never succeeded in visiting Kairwan, the Holy City. . . . Now, I can go from Tunis to Kairwan in a few hours by railway, see all the sights unhindered, enter the mosques without offence, dine and sleep at an excellent hotel, and be back again at my work in Tunis the next day. I may further add that I have just traversed much of the Tunisian Sahara and a good deal of the Jerid country with no other escort than my servant, and a native cavalryman to act as guide. I should have been equally safe had I been alone. The whole Regency of Tunis is now as safe for tourists as France."—*Great Britain, Parliamentary Publications (Papers by Command, 1898, C. 8649-18, pp. 10–15, and 2–3).*

TUNNELS, New York Rapid Transit and East River. See (in this vol.) NEW YORK CITY: A. D. 1900 (JANUARY—SEPTEMBER).

TURBINES, Steam, The invention of. See (in this vol.) SCIENCE, RECENT: MECHANICS.

TURKEY.

A. D. 1895.—Revolt and massacres in Armenia.—Atrocities on both sides.—A horrible condition of things in Armenia was beginning to cause excitement throughout the world. On one hand, the Armenians were in revolt against the foul Turkish government, and avenging themselves savagely upon their oppressors whenever they found the opportunity; on the other hand the Turks were making the revolt an excuse for the atrocities that are habitual to them in every such case. A special correspondent sent in January by Reuter's news agency to investigate the situation reported his conviction "that both Turk and Armenian are in the wrong, and that, as very often happens, it is the innocent who have suffered for the wrong-doings of the guilty. When it is asserted on behalf of the Turks that they are engaged in suppressing a revolutionary movement in Armenia, the statement is fully justified by the facts of the case. There does exist in Armenia an extremely vigorous revolutionary movement, and it is equally beyond question that the methods of some of the leaders of this movement are no less shocking than the barbarity of the Turk in suppressing it. At every step," he added, "I became more and more convinced that the inhuman ferocity displayed in this terrible struggle for the mastery has not been in the least exaggerated in the reports of the massacres already published in England. At Bitlis I heard the story of a Turkish soldier who boasted, as one who had achieved a glorious feat, that he had taken part in the disembowelling of thirty pregnant women. 'Two lives in one,' was the rallying cry of the armed men who perpetrated this butchery. Another soldier, who had taken part in a massacre in a church, described, gloating upon every ghastly detail, how he had slipped and slid along the blood-washed floor while the inhuman work proceeded. Un-fortunately, something very like a counterpart of these atrocities is presented by the methods of some of the leaders of the Armenian revolutionary movement. I believe there is no doubt of the fact that certain of these Armenian conspirators arranged to murder the Rev. Dr. Edward Riggs and two other American missionaries at Marsovan, and fasten the blame upon the Turks, in order that, as they imagined, the United States might inflict summary punishment upon the Turkish Government, thereby rendering Armenian independence possible. The missionaries only escaped through a timely warning which they received from an Armenian friend. Dr. Riggs has devoted his life to the education of the Armenian youth in the missionary schools, but the conspirators, in their blind fanaticism, gave this fact little heed."

There could be no denial however, that the treatment of Armenia and the Armenians by their Turkish political masters was horribly bad. In May, the governments of Great Britain, France and Russia united in proposing certain reforms for Armenia, over which there were evasive and dilatory negotiations carried on by the Porte for several months. Meantime, the Armenians became more aggressive and threatening, and a secret society called the "Hintchak," which had been in existence among them since 1887, assumed great activity. Connected with the Hintchak there was said to be an organization of spies and "executioners," the latter of whom carried out decrees of assassination, arson, and bomb-explosion which the society had pronounced. Finally, on the 17th of October, an imperial irade (edict, or decree) was issued, approving and adopting the project of reform which the British, French and Russian ambassadors had submitted to the Porte. But the appearance of the sultan's ineffectual irade was speedily followed by fresh reports of frightful massacres of Armenians, at Trebizond, Erzeroum. Bitlis, Zeitoun, and elsewhere, with outraging of women and destruction of property, which increased rather than diminished as time went on. There was no sign that anything had been done towards carrying out the promised reforms; though the sultan wrote personally to Lord Salisbury to remonstrate against an expression of skepticism concerning them, which the latter had let fall in a speech, and to say to the British Premier: "I will execute the reforms. . . . This is my earnest determination, as to which I give my word of honour." But nothing came of it all, and the Powers which had received the Sultan's promises could agree on no steps further, except to demand and obtain permission to bring, each, an additional gunboat into the Bosphorus. —*Annual Register*, 1895, pp. 284–94 and 190–93.

In response to a resolution of the Senate of the United States asking for information relative to the treatment of the Armenian subjects of the Turkish government, the Secretary of State, Mr. Olney, on the 19th of December, 1895, communicated the following, among other statements of fact: Of the massacres at Sassoun, which occurred in August, 1894, "the Department of State has little trustworthy information. . . . Since that time appalling outbreaks against the Armenians have occurred in many other parts of Asia Minor, where these unfortunate people form but a small minority of the population. At first they were scarcely more than local riots, as at Tokat, in the vilayet of Sivas, in March last, where one Armenian was killed outright and more than 30 wounded by the Turkish soldiery. In June last an attempted rising of Armenians in the province of Aleppo in the mountains of Kozar-Dagh and Zeitoun was thwarted without bloodshed by the arrest of the alleged conspirators. . . . In July a band of armed Armenians crossing into the vilayet of Erzerum from Russia was dispersed, several being killed or captured. By August the Moslem feeling against Armenians had become so far aroused that rumors of intended massacres came from several independent quarters, Harpoot, Marsovan, and Bitlis among them, which led to urgent demands by the United States minister for adequate measures looking to the due protection of American citizens in those places.

"On the 30th of September grave disturbances began at Constantinople itself. Several hundred Armenians, who had gathered for the purpose of going in a body to the Sultan's palace and demanding redress for the grievances of their countrymen, were dispersed by the police after a severe conflict in which a number of Turks and Armenians were killed and wounded. Mob violence followed, the Armenians resident in various quarters of the capital being assailed by an excited Turkish rabble, and over 50 were slain. The rioting continued the next day, October 1, in Constantinople and its suburbs. Some 800 or 1,000 Armenians were captured or arrested, many of them being armed with new revolvers of a uniform pattern. By the third day order was restored, and the Armenians who had sought refuge in their churches returned to their homes. The effect of this outbreak at the national capital was most disastrous in the provinces. The danger of a general massacre of Christians in the vilayets of Adana and Aleppo seemed so immi-

nent, that renewed orders for the effective protection of American citizens in those quarters were demanded and obtained. Fears for their safety at Hadjin, Mersine, and Marash were especially felt, and the cruiser Marblehead was promptly ordered to Iskanderoun (Alexandretta), the nearest seaport.

"On October 8 a Turkish uprising occurred at Trebizond, due, it is reported, to an attempt to assassinate the late Vali of Van as he was about to leave for Constantinople, the Turks claiming that the act was done by an Armenian and that they were in danger of a general Armenian attack. On the 9th the disturbance was renewed, many Armenians being killed and their homes and shops looted by the mob. The authorities attempted to quell the riot, but having only some 400 soldiers and policemen at command, were powerless, and murder and pillage ran their course as long as an Armenian was in sight. The official Turkish reports give the number of Armenians slain as 182, of Turks 11, but the general estimate places the total number at some 500. Reinforcements of troops soon arrived, and quiet was restored. No injury to American citizens or property occurred.

"From this time the reports of conflicts between Turks and Armenians, with great loss of life, become frequent and confused. At Akhissar, some 60 miles from Smyrna, 50 Armenians were killed October 9. Koordish raids terrorized many parts of the Armenian provinces. At Bitlis over 500 were reported killed, the Turkish accounts alleging that the Armenians attacked the Moslem mosques during the hour of prayer. At Diarbekir 5,000 are said to have lost their lives, of which 2,300 were Mussulmans—but the Turkish authorities pronounce this estimate exaggerated. From Malatia comes the report of a 'great massacre' early in November, when every adult male Christian is said to have perished. Another sanguinary outbreak, with great slaughter, is reported from Sivas on November 12; some 800 Armenians and 10 Koords are said to have been killed. At Hadjin and Ourfa loss of life is reported, the American missionaries at those places being protected by Turkish guards under orders from the Porte.

"The Kaimakam of Hadjin is credibly said to have announced that he would destroy the town and sow barley on its site. There being an American school at that place, directed by American teachers, the United States minister thereupon notified the Porte that if one of those American ladies received injury from the riotous conduct of the populace, he would demand, in the name of the United States, 'the head of that Kaimakam.' That officer has since been removed. Later reports allege massacres at Marsovan and Amasia. The consular agent at Aleppo telegraphs that a severe conflict had occurred at Aintab, and that great fear prevailed at Aleppo. The burning of the American buildings at Harpoot took place during a bloody riot, and many persons are said to have perished in the province of that name. At Kurun 400 deaths are reported. Particulars of the recent outbreak at Marash, on November 19, in which American missionary property was destroyed, have not yet been received.

"These scattered notices, for the most part received by telegraph, are given, not as official averment of the facts stated, but as showing the alarming degree to which racial prejudices and fanatical passions have been roused throughout Asia Minor. As above said, the Department of State has and can have official knowledge regarding but few of these reported massacres, and though up to the early part of December the United States minister estimated the number of the killed as exceeding 30,000, it is more than likely that the figures are greatly exaggerated. At latest advices mob violence and slaughter appear to have been checked, or at least to have partially subsided. The Turkish Government has been emphatic in assurances of its purpose and ability to restore order in the affected localities; new governors have been appointed in many of the provinces, troops have been sent to the scene of recent or apprehended disorders, and forces have been massed to subdue the Armenians who had gained the ascendant in Zeitoun."

Of the American missionary establishments in Turkey, and of the extent to which they suffered harm during the outbreaks, the same report gave the following account:

"The number of citizens of the United States resident in the Turkish Empire is not accurately known. According to latest advices there are 172 American missionaries, dependents of various mission boards in the United States, scattered over Asia Minor. There are also numbers of our citizens engaged in business or practicing professions in different parts of the Empire. Besides these, more or less persons, originally subjects of Turkey and since naturalized in the United States, have returned to the country of their birth and are temporarily residing there. The whole number of persons comprising these several classes can not be accurately estimated, but, the families of such citizens being considered, can hardly be less than five or six hundred, and may possibly exceed that total.

"Outside of the capital and a few commercial seaport towns, the bulk of this large American element is found in the interior of Asia Minor and Syria, remote from the few consular establishments maintained by this Government in that quarter, inaccessible except by difficult journeys, and isolated from each other by the broken character of the mountain country and the absence of roads. Under these circumstances and in the midst of the alarming agitation which for more than a year past has existed in Asia Minor, it has been no slight task for the representative of the United States to follow the interests of those whose defense necessarily falls to his care, to demand and obtain the measures indispensable to their safety, and to act instantly upon every appeal for help in view of real or apprehended peril. It is, however, gratifying to bear testimony to the energy and promptness of the minister in dealing with every grievance brought to his notice, and his foresight in anticipating complaints and securing timely protection in advance of actual need. The efforts of the minister have had the moral support of the presence of naval vessels of the United States on the Syrian and Adanan coasts from time to time as occasion required. . . .

"While the physical safety of all citizens of the United States appears up to the present date to have been secured, their property has, on at least two recent occasions, been destroyed in the course of local outbursts at Harpoot and Ma-

rash. The details of the Harpoot destruction have so far been only meagerly reported, although it took place about the middle of November. It is stated that the buildings at that place were set on fire separately by Kurds and citizens, in the presence of the Turkish soldiery, during an Armenian riot. Besides the chapel, girls' theological school and seminary building, the ladies' house, boarding house, and residences of three American missionaries were burned, the aggregate loss on the buildings, personal property, stock, fixtures, and apparatus being estimated in the neighborhood of $100,000. The United States minister has notified the Porte that the Turkish Government will be held responsible for the immediate and full satisfaction of all injuries on that score. The American Missionary School of Science at Marash was burned during a sanguinary outbreak on November 19. The value of the property destroyed has not been ascertained, but after prompt investigation the minister will make like demand for adequate indemnity."—*United States, 54th Congress, 1st Session, Senate Document, No.* 33.

"On November 9 one of the Foreign Consuls arrived at Constantinople from Erzeroum on leave, and he reported the scene on his journey as heartrending. 'The whole country between Trebizond and Erzeroum was devastated. He counted 100 dead bodies lying by the road near one town. Nearly all the villages were burnt, and in many cases the male population entirely wiped out.' At last, on December 13, 1895, Lord Salisbury received the following telegraphic despatch from Sir Philip Currie: 'It may be roughly stated that the recent disturbances have devastated, as far as the Armenians are concerned, the whole of the provinces to which the scheme of reforms was intended to apply; that over an extent of territory considerably larger than Great Britain all the large towns, with the exception of Van, Sassun, and Moush, have been the scene of massacres of the Armenian population, while the Armenian villages have been almost entirely destroyed. A modest estimate puts the loss of life at 30,000. The survivors are in a state of absolute destitution, and in many places they are being forced to turn Mussulmans. The charge against the Armenians of having been the first to offer provocation cannot be sustained. Non-Armenian Christians were spared, and the comparatively few Turks who fell were killed in self-defence. The participation of the soldiers in the massacres is in many places established beyond doubt.'

"Of the appalling horror of this account I wish it were needless to speak. . . . [It] would be none the less horrible if the whole of the people massacred and outraged, ruined, and starved, and driven to the snowy mountains in the middle of winter, had been all the rudest villagers of the most rustic village communities. But when we know that many thousands of the victims have been people educated at Christian schools and colleges, and who had acquired there, in addition to the ineradicable virtues of their native and ancient faith, much also of the refinements and activities of civilised life, we may reach some true conception of the agonies which have been inflicted on such a people in the face of Europe and of the world by the cruelty and brutality of the Turks. It is, indeed, right that our first indignation should be directed against the

Infamous Government of Turkey. . . . Let us remember that this is not a Government with which we have had nothing to do, or for which we have had no responsibility, but a Government which the European Powers, and we especially, have been protecting and nursing for half a century. . . . Then we may indeed begin to think, with remorse and shame, of our handiwork, and of its results. In this particular case, indeed, the immediate blame lies almost alone with Russia. By a complete departure from all her previous great traditions she deliberately refused to join the other Powers of Europe for the purpose of compelling the Sultan to act with decent humanity to those of whom she had been the declared defender. She had the physical power and the geographical opportunity which others had not; and there can be no doubt whatever that a joint occupation of the waters of Constantinople by the fleets of the European Powers would have secured the very moderate demands that Europe made upon the Porte."—The Duke of Argyle, *Our Responsibilities for Turkey*, pp. 116-122.

A. D. 1896.—Conflict in Crete between Christians and Mussulmans, and its preceding causes.—In 1868, the Cretans, for the second time, were thrust under the Turkish yoke. "By way of solace the Powers exerted themselves feebly in inducing the Porte to concede the so-called 'Organic Statute' [or 'Organic Regulation,'—see (in vol. 3) GREECE: A. D. 1862–1881]. . . . As the Charter remained a dead letter, the Cretans seized the next favourable opportunity to rise in 1877. Their case was brought before the Congress of Berlin: but the only relief the Powers could extend to them was a fresh promise on the part of the Porte, recorded in the XXIII Article of the Treaty, to observe scrupulously that Organic Statute, which had been proved to be unworkable. Meanwhile, the Cretans had remained under arms during the whole of 1878, the island being again almost completely devastated by the half-naked and famishing troops which had survived the Russo-Turkish War. Ultimately, through the mediation of England, the Porte was induced, in November of that year, to concede the Pact of Halepa, so named after the village near Canea where it was negotiated, and signed under the supervision of the British Consul, Mr. T. B. Sandwith—this fact being expressly recorded in the preamble of the document. The arrangement was accepted by the Cretans as a compromise, in spite of its many and manifest drawbacks. Nevertheless, it brought about, at the outset, certain beneficial results. Political parties were formed in which the Mohammedan Cretans blended, irrespective of religious differences, with their Christian countrymen; and the unprecedented phenomenon of a Christian Vali completing his four years' tenure of governorship was witnessed in the person of Photiades Pasha.

"But this tendency to conciliation of the conflicting elements in the island was by no means to the liking of the Porte. The presence of a Mussulman military governor was therefore discovered to be necessary; and as his grade was usually superior to that of the Vali, and the Mussulman sub-governor was the official whose recommendations were of weight with the Porte, nothing was easier than to create insuperable difficulties for the Christian Vali. Thus succes-

sive Valis were compelled—often by private wire from Constantinople—to tender their resignation; while, at the same time, the Porte took care not to fulfil the financial engagements prescribed by the Pact. By these means an acute crisis was brought about under the Governorship of Sartinski Pasha, a Pole, in 1889, when a preconcerted plan of deception and treachery was carried out by the Porte with consummate skill.

"The Cretans, as it is but natural, are guided in critical contingencies by the advice they seek at Athens. The Porte therefore promised to the Greek Government, as soon as things began to assume a threatening aspect in Crete, to satisfy the demands of the islanders, provided they were prevailed upon to abstain from occupying certain important positions. In spite of the transparent perfidy of the proposal, M. Tricoupis, the then Greek Premier, fell into the snare. While the Cretans were held back, troops were poured into the island, and the strategical points having been seized, the Greek Government and the Cretans were defied. An Imperial firman, issued in November of that year, abrogated the Pact of Halepa, and the British Government, under whose auspices it was concluded, was now powerless to exact respect for what was virtually an international arrangement. There was no longer any question of a Christian Vali with a fixed tenure of office, or of an Assembly of Cretan representatives. Shakir Pasha, the commander of the Turkish troops, was invested with absolute civil and military authority; Mussulman Albanians occupied the Christian villages as gendarmes, and Crete continued to submit to this kind of martial law up to 1894. When, however, Mahmoud Djelaleddin Pasha, the then Mussulman Vali, surpassed even his predecessors in arbitrariness, and actually dictated to the tribunals decisions in favour of Mohammedan litigants, the Cretans began to lose patience and another outbreak appeared imminent. It was only then that the Great Powers moved in the matter and prevailed upon the Porte to revert partly to the pre-existing order of things, by appointing Alexander Karatheodory Pasha, a Christian and a Greek, as Governor. Beyond this, however, the Pact of Halepa was not observed. True to its traditional tactics, the Porte took with one hand what it had given with the other. The Mussulman Deputy Governor and the military commander frustrated every effort of the Vali, the very funds necessary for the maintenance of the gendarmerie being denied him. Karatheodory was consequently forced to resign. Complete anarchy now reigned in the island."—Ypsiloritis, *The Situation in Crete* (*Contemporary Review, Sept.*, 1896).

"Occasional skirmishes between the Christian inhabitants and the soldiers kept the excitement simmering and ushered in the sanguinary scenes that finally followed. Turkhan Pasha, taking time by the forelock, armed the Cretan Moslems for the combat with the approval of the commander of the troops, and the city of Canea prepared for a blood bath. The Mohammedan Lent (Ramazan) was drawing to a close, and the three days of rejoicing which invariably follow (Bairam) were supposed to be fixed for the attack on the Christians. These anticipations were duly realised, and on the 24th May, 1896, at 1 o'clock P. M., the Turks fired the first shots, blowing out the brains of several Christians to make that Moslem holiday. Forearmed, however, is forewarned, and the Christians defended themselves to the best of their ability on that day and the 25th and 26th, during which every house in Canea was barricaded, and neighbours living on opposite sides of the absurdly narrow streets fired at each other from behind stone heaps piled up in the windows of their bedrooms. The streets were deserted, all traffic suspended, and it was not until the 27th that the thirty Christian corpses (including two women and four children) and the twenty lifeless Turks were removed for burial.

"These events provoked a new administrative change of scene: Turkhan Pasha was recalled, and Abdullah Pasha, at the head of four battalions from Salonica, came to take his place. These troops laid waste the villages and fields of the provinces of Apokorona, Cydonia, and Kissamo, burning houses, huts, and churches on the way. The best soldiers in the world, however, run terrible risks in the interior of Crete, and Abdullah was repulsed with the loss of two hundred men at the town of Vamos. The foreign consuls at Canea, having verified these facts, strongly blamed his conduct in a joint verbal note, and the Porte shortly afterwards recalled him, and appointed Berovitch Pasha [Prince of Samos] in his place. This was the beginning of the end. The Christians of the island meanwhile met, and through their delegates formulated certain demands, which the foreign consuls referred to their ambassadors at Constantinople, and the famous 'Modifications of the Convention of Halepa' were framed in consequence. The sultan, too, yielding to tardy pressure, graciously conceded the nomination of a Christian governor-general in the person of Berovitch, the summoning of the National Assembly, and other demands. . . . The questions of the tribunals and the gendarmerie [for the enforcement of peace and order in the island] were to be arranged by international commissions; but weeks and months passed away before they were even appointed. . . . At last the commissions arrived and began their work in December [1896]."—E. J. Dillon, *Crete and the Cretans* (*Fortnightly Rev.*, May, 1897).

A. D. **1896** (January—March).—**Turkish opposition** to English and American measures for relief to Armenian sufferers.—**Work** of Miss Clara Barton and the Red Cross Society.—For some time the distribution of supplies from England and America to the sufferers in Armenia was forbidden by the Turkish government, for reasons stated by the Turkish minister at Washington as follows : "The collections are made on the strength of speeches delivered in public meetings by irreconcilable enemies of the Turkish race and religion, and on the basis of false accusations that Turkey repudiates. Besides, the Sublime Porte is mindful of the true interests of its subjects, and, distinguishing between the real state of things and the calumnies and wild exaggerations of interested or fanatical parties, will under its own legitimate control alleviate the wants of all Turkish subjects, irrespective of creed or race." The Red Cross Society, of which the American branch had prepared to send its President, Miss Clara Barton, with a small corps of assistants, to the scene of the suffering, was especially excluded, by the order of the Porte. Miss Barton and her staff sailed, however, from New York, in January, and Mr. Terrell, the American minister at Constantinople, succeeded in obtaining permission for them to do their humane work as private individuals, not in the name of the obnoxious society, and without displaying its insignia. The single-mindedness, the prudence, the patient energy with which Miss Barton pursued the one object of giving relief to the suffering, overcame all opposition and all obstructions, so that, in April, she was able to report :

"The way is all made clear for sending supplies. The suitable agents all along the route are now known, and have been arranged with for service, so that heavy supplies can be sent at any and all times as they are needed. I feel my breath come lighter as I think of these poor scourged and fever-stricken towns without even one doctor, when our sixteen strong, skilled men, with twenty-five camels' burden of supplies, shall carry some light of hope and help into their night of hopeless woe. I am happy to be able to say for the comfort of contributors, that I hold the written word of the Porte, officially given through the minister of foreign affairs from the grand vizier, that not the slightest interference with any distribution within the province will be had. This official document was addressed and delivered to Sir Philip Currie, the British ambassador, and by him passed to me. The decision is general and final, without question or reservation, and settles all doubt."

In September Miss Barton returned home for rest, and to bear her testimony to America of the immensity of the need still existing in the Armenian provinces and calling for help. Her departure from Constantinople was reported by the newspapers to have been the occasion of a remarkable demonstration, by cheers, flags and salutes, from ship and shore, of the estimate put upon the work she had done.

A. D. **1896** (August).—**Attack of Armenian revolutionists on the Ottoman Bank at Constantinople.—Turkish massacre of Armenians in the city.**—In the spring of 1896, the Armenian revolutionists, encouraged by the outbreak in Crete, made fresh appeals for attention to the sufferings of their country, with threats of some desperate action if no heed was given. In August, the desperate act was undertaken, at Constantinople, by 30 or 40 madly devoted men. This reckless little band of misguided patriots made a sudden attack on the Ottoman Bank, a British institution which controls money in the Turkish empire, gained possession of the building, made prisoners and hostages of two of its directors and some 80 of its clerks, and were fully prepared with dynamite to destroy everything within its walls, including themselves, if certain reforms which they set forth were not instantly decreed. Their theory was, that "the Ambassadors would force the Sultan to grant the reasonable reforms which they demanded for the Armenians, rather than permit the destruction of the Bank and its staff. It was a scheme borrowed from the theatre, absurd in itself, and made ridiculous by the way in which they failed to carry it out. They went in bravely, and nothing hindered their destroying the Bank, but they allowed themselves to be talked out of it by Mr. Maximoff, the Russian dragoman, and would have been the laughing stock of the world if its attention had not been absorbed by the massacre which followed.

"The real heroism of that day **was** displayed

in another quarter of the city, by another small party of Russian Armenians, men and women, who took possession of two stone houses and fought the Turkish troops to the death, the survivors killing themselves when they could fight no longer. There was no serious fighting anywhere else, although dynamite bombs were thrown from the windows of houses and khans upon the troops in a number of places, showing that some preparation had been made for a more extended outbreak. There is nothing to be said in justification of this attempt of the revolutionists. They had provocation enough to justify anything in reason, but there was nothing reasonable in this plan, nothing in it to attract the sympathy of the Powers or to conciliate public opinion ; and if the statements are true which have been made by Armenians as to certain unexecuted parts of the plan, it was diabolical. This only can be said on behalf of these revolutionary committees. They are the natural outcome of the treatment of the Armenians by the Turkish Government during the last twenty years. When oppression passes a certain limit and men become desperate, such revolutionary organisation always appears. They are the fruit and not the cause of the existing state of things in Turkey, and if we can judge by the experience of other countries, the worse things become here, the more violent will be the action of these committees, whether Europe enjoys it or not.

"Revolutionists are the same all the world over, but the Turkish Government is unique, and it is not the attack on the Bank which interests us but the action of the Government which followed it. As we have said, the authorities had full information of what was to be attempted and did nothing to prevent it, but they made every preparation for carrying out their own plan. Bands of ruffians were gathered in Stamboul, Galata, and Pera, made up of Kurds, Lazes, and the lower class of Turks, armed with clubs, knives or firearms ; and care was taken that no one should kill or plunder in the quarter to which he belonged, lest he should be recognised and complaint made afterwards by the Embassies, with a demand for punishment. A large number of carts were in readiness to carry off the dead. The troops and police were in great force to prevent any resistance, and to assist the mob if necessary. It was a beautiful day, the streets were crowded, and few had any idea of what had happened at the Bank, when suddenly, without any warning, the work of slaughter and plunder began, everywhere at once. European ladies on the way to the Bosphorus steamers suddenly found themselves surrounded by assassins, and saw men beaten to death at their feet. Foreign merchants saw their own employés cut to pieces at their doors. The streets in some places literally ran with blood. Every man who was recognised as an Armenian was killed without mercy. In general, the soldiers took no part in the slaughter and behaved well, and this somewhat reassured those in the streets who were not Armenians; but in a few moments the shops were closed and a wild panic spread through the city. The one idea of every one was to get home ; and as the foreigners and better classes live out of the city in summer they had to go to the Galata bridge to take the steamers, which ran as usual all through the three days of massacre. This took them through the streets where the slaughter was going on, and consequently we have the testimony of hundreds of eye-witnesses as to what took place. The work of death and plunder continued unchecked for two days. On Friday there were isolated outbreaks, and occasional assassinations occurred up to Tuesday.

"The number killed will never be known. The Ambassadors put it at 5,000 or 6,000 ; the official report to the palace at 8,750, besides those thrown into the sea. Thousands of houses, shops and offices were plundered, including a number belonging to Greeks and foreigners. Everything was done in the most systematic way, and there was not a moment of anarchy, not a moment when the army and police had not perfect control of the city during all these days. . . . The majority of those massacred belonged to the working class—especially the hamals (porters)—but a large number of gentlemen, merchants and other wealthy men, were killed, together with about fifty women and children. The savage brutality of the Moslem mob was something beyond all imagination, and in many cases the police joined in beating men to death and hacking others to death with knives, in the very face of Europeans. . . . In may cases European officials appealed to the officers in command of the troops, who were looking on at the slaughter of helpless, unarmed men, to interfere and put a stop to it. The reply was ' We have orders.' It was an officer who killed the clerk of the British Post-office on the steps. And some of the most cold-blooded and horrible murders took place in front of the guard house, at the Galata end of the bridge, in the presence of officers of the Sultan's household of the highest rank. They also had their orders.

"Happily for the honour of the Turkish people, there is another side to the story. It was the Government and not the people that conducted this massacre. And although the vile instruments employed were told that they were acting in the name of the Prophet, and freely used his name, and are boasting to-day of what they did for Islam, the Sheik-ul-Islam forbad the Softas taking any part in the slaughter, and many a pious Turk did what he could to protect his neighbours. . . . It is not the people, not even the mob, who are responsible for this great crime. It was deliberately committed by the Government. The Ambassadors of the six Powers have declared this to be an unquestionable fact in the Joint Note addressed to the Porte.

"Since the massacre this same Government has been carrying on a warfare against the Armenians which is hardly less inhuman than beating out their brains with clubs. There were from 150,000 to 200,000 Armenians in Constantinople. They were merchants, shopkeepers, confidential clerks, employés in banks and offices of every kind—the chief business men of the city. They were the bakers of the city, they had charge of the khans and bazaars and the wealth of the city ; they were the porters, house-servants, and navvies. . . . Now the Government has undertaken to ruin this whole population. They are hunted about the city and over the hills, like wild beasts. . . . Thousands have been sent off at once to the Black Sea ports, to find their way as best they can without money or food to their desolated villages in the interior. . . . Thousands have fled to foreign countries."—*The Constantinople Massacre* (*Contemporary Review*, Oct., 1896).

A. D. 1897 (January—February).—Fresh conflicts in Crete.—Attitude of Christians and Mussulmans towards each other.—Reports of the British Consul-General and others.—Early in January, 1897, while proceedings for the organization of the new gendarmerie were under way, and while the discussion of candidates for the National Assembly, to be elected in March, was rife, fresh hostilities between Christians and Mussulmans broke out, and there seems to be good evidence in the following report, by Sir Alfred Biliotti, the British Consul-General at Canea, that responsibility for the state of things in Crete should be charged upon one party hardly more than upon the other. The despatch of the Consul-General to Lord Salisbury, written January 9, 1897, is partly as follows:

"In the afternoon of the 3rd instant a great panic occurred in the town owing to a wounded Christian having been conveyed to the hospital, where he died of his wounds in the night, and to a rumour that two Mussulmans had been killed or wounded at the same time on the road between Canea and Suda Bay. All the shops were shut up as usual, but there was no general 'sauve qui peut,' Christians especially having congregated in the square near the hospital in the hope of finding out further information. Happening to be in the town, I took a carriage and drove towards Suda. When at about a mile distant from Canea I came upon a number of Mussulmans, who told me that four Christians going to Apokorona had, without any provocation whatever, discharged their revolvers on three Mussulmans, two of whom had been severely wounded. I saw one of them in his cottage hard by the road with a bullet wound in the abdomen; the other had been conveyed on horseback to the village of Tsikalaria (south-east of Suda Bay), 2 miles from where he had been wounded, of which he was a native. The four Christians fled across the fields, leaving on the road a horse and an overcoat, and took to the mountains.

"Between half and a quarter of an-hour after this incident another Christian, a native, like the Turk, of Tsikalaria, was passing on the road when he was fired upon by Mussulmans in retaliation for the wounding of their two co-religionists. Not having been hit, the Christian jumped from his mule and ran for his life along the Suda road, being pursued by armed Turks. He was overtaken by three of them about half-a-mile farther down, and was shot at and mortally wounded at 20 paces in front of Commander Shortland, of Her Majesty's ship 'Nile,' who was coming on foot from Suda Bay to Canea. The wounded Christian was taken charge of by the Albanian corporal stationed in a Christian monastery close by, and was subsequently put in a carriage by the Russian Consul, who was returning from Suda Bay at that moment, and sent to the town hospital, where he died. While I was making inquiries on the road a brisk fusillade was heard towards Tsikalaria, and as I was about to return to Halepa a young Turk was seen at a distance running towards us with a letter in his hand. It was a message sent by the Albanian corporal stationed at Tsikalaria asking for assistance.

This messenger had hardly arrived when a gendarme was seen coming down in great haste. He said that the fight between Christians and Mussulmans having become general, and there being only another gendarme with the corporal, armed assistance was immediately required. I took both these messengers and conveyed them to the gate of the town, from whence I drove to Halepa to acquaint the Vali with what was taking place. It was getting dark when I met on the road his Excellency accompanied by the Italian Consul going on foot to Canea, having found no available carriage, and I drove back with them. The position was rather perplexing. There was no available gendarmerie, and no soldiers could be sent out, as they would have been fired upon by the Christians. . . .

"Early on the day following, that is, on the 4th instant, the Governor-General visited the village of Tsikalaria and the villages westward of it in order to ascertain the truth with regard to the numerous reports which were in circulation since the preceding evening. It would seem that on hearing of his son having been killed on the Canea-Suda road, the father of the wounded Mussulman opened fire on the Christians. Other Christians maintain that this wounded Mussulman, after having shot at the Christian on the road, hastened to Tsikalaria, and together with his father, began firing on the Christians. In a very short time all the Christians rushed towards the heights, and the Mussulmans towards the plain. During this evolution a Christian was killed, it is said, by the father of the wounded Mussulman, who had been arrested and is in prison. The same night the women and children took refuge in the villages on the mountains, while a contingent of 150 armed Christians came down from Campos and Keramia in order to assist the male population of Tsikalaria to defend their property. On the other hand, armed Mussulmans flocked from all parts of the plain to defend their co-religionists. The Mussulmans at Perivolia, where they are of nearly equal numerical force, tried to surround the Christians in order to keep them as hostages for the safety of their co-religionists in other villages where the Christians are more numerous. In so doing they shot down a Christian, on whom they also inflicted numerous knife stabs, finally cutting his throat. This was followed by an emigration to, and armed assistance from, the mountain villages as at Tsikalaria.

"In the village of Varipetro the Mayor, assisted by the corporal of gendarmerie, a Mussulman Albanian, was doing his utmost to prevent a conflict between its Christian and Mussulman inhabitants, when a Christian from Lakkos, whose brother had been murdered two years ago by a native Mussulman, stealing behind the corporal, shot him dead. The Christians of Varipetro, with whom the corporal was popular, having tried to arrest his murderer, the Lakkiotes, who had come there in order to defend their co-religionists, turned their arms against them, and prevented them from carrying out their intention. In consequence of this murder all the Christians of Varipetro emigrated to the mountains, and all the Mussulmans to the town of Canea. Nearly 1,000 Christians from the plains of Cydonia and Kissamo came to defend the inhabitants of Galata and Darazzo, and for a time blockaded the Turks in the village of Kirtomado, Aghia, &c. But the inhabitants of Galata, who are all Christians, have so much confidence in the Mussulman Albanian Lieutenant called Islam, who is stationed in their village, that they begged their co-religionists to withdraw, which they did. . . .

"As is always the case, each party claims to have been attacked by the other party, and the truth is not likely to be ever discovered. Be this as it may, both Christians and Mussulmans remain under the unshaken conviction that they are wronged by the other party; this increases the animosity of one sect against the other, and each member of the two races will act on this conviction. This is the inevitable consequence of the absolute want of confidence between the two elements, and there is not the least hope that this feeling will disappear, nor even slightly decrease, so long as they are left to themselves. In the present instance it may be that the Mussulmans, or some of them, may have considered themselves bound to retaliate for recent murders committed on their co-religionists by Christians. . . . The Christians are convinced, and all their proceedings are marked by that conviction, that all the incidents which trouble the public peace are devices of the native Mussulmans to prevent the execution of the promised reforms. I do not deny that the attitude of the authorities at Constantinople may have such an effect on the low class of Cretan Mussulmans; but it is far from being so with the educated class who are as, if not more, anxious than the Christians that the intended reforms should be carried out without delay. In fact, they know that they have nothing to hope from Constantinople, and that the only protection of the minority to which they belong lies in the promised reforms. On the other hand, I have observed with the greatest pleasure that the Christians laid down their arms at the first recommendation of the Consuls to do so, which proves a sincere desire on their part to live in peace. When the Christians were taking up arms in former times they used to remain for weeks, even for months, on the mountains in spite of the entreaties of the Consuls. Therefore, the Christians and the Mussulmans are respectively well disposed, but there is such an insuperable distrust on both sides, that they can never come to a mutual understanding. Whether the incidents which cause disturbances or disorders on the island are the work of the Turks or of the Christians or of both is quite immaterial to me. The important fact to be taken into consideration is that an exchange of a few shots between one or two Christians and as many Mussulmans is sufficient to cause several districts, four in the present instance (Canea, Apokorona, Sphakia, and Kissamo), to take up arms, and also that there can be no doubt that such scenes will be repeated on every recurrence of such incidents."

To the same effect, Captain Custance, of the British ship Bardcur, reported on the 15th to Admiral Hopkins: "The general situation, as I understand it, is, that the Cretan Christian leaders, urged on by certain interested people at Athens, have been preparing for some time to make an attempt to drive the Turkish authorities out of the island in the spring, if a favourable opportunity offers. The Mussulmans would not be sorry to see the last of the Turkish Government if they could only be sure that their lives and property would be safe under the new régime, which, owing to the bitter hatred existing between the Christians and Mussulmans, cannot be expected. The two parties are face to face, armed to the teeth, with long-standing feuds and wrongs, and with no force between them capable of maintaining order."

On the 27th of January the Consul-General reported by telegram to Lord Salisbury: "An outburst of terror, such as has not yet occurred in Candia, has been caused by the commencement of a fresh immigration of Mussulmans into the town, and by the murder, within a week, of two men of that faith, and a few minor outrages." The next day he reported: "Telegraphic news from Candia, dated to-day, reports murder of a Mussulman, and wounding of two others, and murder of seven Christians; murder of further Mussulmans is rumoured. The Mussulman Military Commissioner, and the Austrian Military Attaché, now in Candia, report that they met about 1,000 armed Mussulmans moving inland, and numbers of Mussulman families moving towards the town." Again, on the 2d of February: "Murder of four Mussulmans last night, following on wounding of Christian by Mussulman on the 31st January near Canea. Panic ensued in Canea and Suda Bay this morning. Shops all closed. Shots fired in town and Halepa, which resulted in death of two Mussulmans. Four mixed villages, one large Christian village, and several farms in environs are in flames." On the 4th, Colonel Chermside, of the gendarmerie commission, sent the following statement to Lord Salisbury: " The most that we have been able to attempt to-night is to get a cordon to separate Christian and Moslem quarters. Patrolling was tried, but the fire from the Christians was too heavy to maintain it. Several Turkish soldiers have been killed and wounded."—*Great Britain, Parliamentary Publications (Papers by Command: Turkey, No. 10, 1897, pp. 15–45).*

A. D. 1897 (February—March).—Greek interference in Crete.—Greek forces in the island.—Demands for annexation of Crete to Greece.—Action of the Powers in the " Concert of Europe."—Pacific blockade of Crete.—Early in February, the difficulties of the attempt which the leading European powers, acting in what was known as "the Concert of Europe," were making to settle affairs in Crete by reforming its Turkish government, were complicated by interference from Greece. The Greeks, in ardent sympathy with their Cretan kinsmen, were eager to take up the cause of the Christian inhabitants of the island, and their government was driven into independent action to that end, hoping that Christian sentiment in Europe would constrain the Powers to give it a free hand. A Greek squadron was sent to Crete, to bring away fugitives—women and children especially—and to prevent the landing of Turkish reinforcements. This was quickly followed by an expedition of 2,000 men, Colonel Vassos in command. An instant stimulation of the insurrection occurred, and declarations demanding the annexation of Crete to the kingdom of Greece began to appear; while the Greek government represented in a note to the Powers that no possible solution of the Cretan problem could be found without concession to that demand. The Greek troops, considerably increased in number, were landed on the island, joining the insurgent Cretans, and beginning operations against the Turks.

On the 13th of February the admirals commanding the foreign naval forces at Canea joined in sending a warning to the Greek commodore, requiring him to "desist from all hostile acts and to conform with international law." On the 15th a mixed force of British, French, Russian, Italian and Austrian marines was landed for the protection of the town. On the same day, from Colombari, Colonel Vassos, the Greek commander, issued a proclamation, saying: "In the name of His Majesty, George I., King of the Greeks, I occupy the Island of Crete, and proclaim this to its inhabitants without distinction of sex or nationality. I promise in the name of His Majesty that I will protect the honour, life and property, and will respect the religious convictions, of its inhabitants, bringing them peace and equality rights." On the 17th, the Turkish forces at Canea were attacked by the Greeks and insurgents, and the attack was renewed on the 21st; whereupon, after warnings from the foreign admirals in the harbor, the Russian, German, Austrian and British ships opened fire on the attacking troops. In the meantime, considerable bodies of Mohammedans were being besieged by superior forces at other points in the island, with great danger of massacre if overcome.

On the 2d of March, the representatives of Great Britain, Austria-Hungary, France, Germany, Italy and Russia, at Constantinople, arrived at an agreement of action, and jointly addressed notes to the governments of Turkey and Greece. To the Porte they wrote: "The Great Powers, animated by the desire to assure the maintenance of peace and to see the integrity of the Ottoman Empire respected, have sought for the means of ending the disorders that have led to their armed intervention in Crete, as well as of putting an end to the presence of the Greek forces in the island. They have recognized that in consequence of the delay in applying them, the reforms contemplated in the Arrangement of August 25, 1896, no longer correspond to the requirements of the present situation, and they have agreed upon the following points:—1. Crete can in no case be annexed to Greece in the present circumstances. 2. The island will be endowed by the Powers with an autonomous administration ('régime'). In notifying these decisions to the Sublime Porte by order of their Governments, the Representatives of the Great Powers at Constantinople think it their duty to communicate the resolution which has been taken by their Governments to address to Greece a summons to withdraw her troops and naval forces from Crete."

To the Greek government the same announcement was made, that "Crete can in no case, in the present circumstances, be annexed to Greece," and the communication was more explicit in the further statements, as follows : "In view of the delays caused by Turkey in the application of the reforms agreed upon in concert with the Powers, and which now make it impossible to adapt those reforms to a changed condition of affairs, the Powers are resolved, while maintaining the integrity of the Ottoman Empire, to endow Crete with an absolutely effective autonomous administration (régime), in-

tended to secure to it a separate government, under the high suzerainty of the Sultan. The Cabinets are convinced that these views can only be realized by the withdrawal of the Greek ships and troops now in the waters and on the territory of the island which is occupied by the Powers. We accordingly confidently expect this decision from the wisdom of His Majesty's Government, which cannot wish to persist in a course opposed to the decision of the Powers, who are determined to carry out an early pacification, which is as necessary for Crete as it is for the maintenance of general peace. I will not, however, conceal from your Excellency that I am instructed to warn you that, in case of a refusal of the Royal Government, the Great Powers have arrived at the irrevocable decision not to shrink from any measure of compulsion if, on the expiration of six days, the recall of the Greek ships and troops from Crete has not been effected."

The Turkish government replied on the 6th: "The Sublime Porte has had the honour to receive the note which the Ambassadors of the Great Powers were good enough to address to it on the 2nd of March relative to Crete. The Imperial Government takes note with satisfaction of the assurances which the Great Powers are good enough to give it as to their desire to respect the integrity of the Empire and of the decision which they have taken to obtain the withdrawal of the Greek ships of war and troops from Crete. Relying upon their friendly sentiments, and upon their firm resolve not to impair the Sultan's rights of sovereignty, the Sublime Porte, which is itself desirous of assuring the maintenance of peace, accepts the principle of an autonomy to be accorded to Crete, while reserving to itself liberty to discuss with the Ambassadors the form and the details of the administration ('régime') with which the island is to be endowed."

Two days later, the Greek government replied at greater length, imploring the Great Powers "not to insist upon the system of autonomy decided on, but to give back to Crete what it already possessed at the time of the liberation of the other provinces which form the Hellenic kingdom, and to restore it to Greece, to which it already belonged in the time of the Presidency of Capodistria," and appealing against the demand for the withdrawal of the Greek military forces from the island. "Since, in our opinion," wrote M. Skouses, the Greek minister, "the new autonomous administration ('régime') condition could not fulfil the noble object of the Powers, it is clear what would be the condition of the unfortunate island from now until the establishment of that administration, if the Great Powers decided to persist in their resolve.

"In this connection, and in the name of humanity, as also in the interest of the pacification of the island—a pacification which is the sole object of the solicitude of the Great Powers— we do not hesitate to appeal to them in regard to the other measure, relative to the withdrawal of our military forces. . . . The presence in the island of the Greek army is . . . demanded by the dictates of humanity, and is necessary in the interest of the definitive restoration of order. It is, above all, our duty not to leave the Cretan people at the mercy of Mussulman fanaticism, and of the Turkish army, which has always intentionally, and by connivance, been a party to

6–35

the acts of aggression of the populace against the Christians.

"Above all, if our troops in the island, who are worthy of the full confidence of the Great Powers, were intrusted with the mandate of pacifying the country, their wishes and intentions would at once be completely satisfied. It would then be possible, after order had been restored, to obtain a free expression of the wishes of the Cretan people, with a view to decide their lot. Not only are the horrors which during several decades have occurred periodically in Crete, not committed without profoundly agitating the Hellenic people, but they also interrupt the social activity, and seriously disturb the economy and finances of the State. Even if it were possible for us to forget for a moment that we are co-religionists of the Cretan people, that we are of the same race, and allied by blood, we cannot conceal from the Great Powers that the Hellenic State is unable to resist such shocks any longer. We therefore appeal to the generous sentiments which animate the Great Powers, and beg them to allow the Cretan people to declare how it desires to be governed."—*Great Britain, Parliamentary Publications (Papers by Command : Turkey, Nos. 4 and 5, 1897).*

The position taken by the Greek government in this reply was firmly maintained. Its troops were not withdrawn from Crete, and the Powers of "the Concert," thus practically defied, had difficulty in agreeing upon the next steps they would take. France, England, and Italy would not consent to strong measures of coercion proposed by Russia, Germany and Austria, and the decision reached finally was to establish what is known as a "pacific blockade" of the Cretan coast, to begin on the 21st of March. This was announced on the 18th by the admirals commanding on that coast, who gave notice : "The blockade will be general for all vessels flying the Greek flag. Vessels of the Six Powers or of neutral Powers will be allowed to enter the ports in the occupation of the Powers and land their merchandise there, but only if it is not intended for the Greek troops or for the interior of the island. The ships of the international fleets may visit these vessels." The Greek government was notified to recall its men-of-war still in Cretan waters, with the warning that "they will be retained there by force if they have not left by 8 A. M. on the 21st March."

On the day previous to this announcement of blockade the same admirals had published a proclamation as follows : "The undersigned, Commanders-in-chief of the naval forces of Germany, Austria-Hungary, France, Great Britain, Italy, and Russia, in Cretan waters, acting under instructions from their respective Governments, solemnly proclaim and announce to the people of the island that the Great Powers have arrived at the irrevocable decision to secure the complete autonomy of Crete, under the suzerainty of the Sultan. It is well understood that the Cretans are to be free from all control on the part of the Sublime Porte as regards their internal affairs. The principal aim of the Powers being to provide a remedy for the evils which have afflicted the country, and to prevent their recurrence, they are drawing up in concert a scheme of measures intended to regulate the working of the autonomous régime, to restore peace, to assure to every one, without distinction of race or

religion, liberty and security of property, and to facilitate, by the resumption of agricultural work and trade, the progressive development of the resources of the country. Such is the aim of the Powers. They wish this to be understood by all. A new era is commencing for Crete; let all lay down their arms. The Powers desire peace and order. They will, if it be required, have the necessary authority to make their decisions respected. They count on the co-operation of all the inhabitants of the island, Christian and Mussulman, to assist them in accomplishing a work which promises to secure concord and prosperity to the Cretans."

To the promise of an autonomous government for Crete the insurgent Christians appear to have given no heed; but a great number of the Mohammedan inhabitants of the island united in sending telegrams to the British minister at Constantinople, which were all of the tenor of the following : "Your Excellency knows that the Christians of Crete, forming the numerical majority of the population, but incapable of properly administering the former privileges they enjoyed, have now again been emboldened to massacre, destroy, and ruin, in the same way that in the past they have always made ill-use of their liberties in the country by the treacherous destruction and ruin of their Moslem fellow-countrymen. Therefore, if the people are left irresponsible for the government of the country, which is the very breath of human life, it will facilitate the completion of their bloodthirsty designs, and hasten the ruin of the Mussulmans. We are quite sure that this state of things will not recommend itself to the sympathy of the Great Powers, the propagators of civilization.

"We therefore beg, in the name of the Mussulman population, that the internal affairs of the Christian inhabitants of Crete who have not yet reached even the first step on the path of civilization, and are led away by the seditious designs of Greece, may not be removed from the direction of the Sublime Porte ; if this be impossible, we beg that the internal affairs of the island may be placed under the continual control of the Great Powers in conjunction with the Porte ; and we finally beg that the necessary measures may be taken for the protection of the life, honour, and property, as well as the rights of the 20,000 Mussulman inhabitants now living in Turkey, whose interest in property is greater in value than that of the Christians, and who are occupied with commerce and other pursuits, besides those who live in the island, who, if necessary, are prepared to undergo a census, and who exceed 100,000."

The situation of the Moslem population of the island was represented a little later by Colonel Chermside, in a despatch to Lord Salisbury, as follows : "Over 49,000 Moslems are assembled in Candia and within cordon area, comprising 25 square miles, viz., about two-thirds of Moslem population of Crete. Of these, 29,000 are refugees from central and eastern districts of island. Doles of flour are issued to 39,000 persons ; issue up to date 18 lb. per head ; no other food issued. The mass of the people have no buying power and no work, but since arrival of British troops, armed individuals are rare in streets ; distress is supported with great fortitude, in spite of insufficient food and ravages of small-pox. Population hopes for future for-

eign protection against Christian compatriots."
—*Great Britain, Papers by Command: Turkey,
No.* 10, 1897, *pp.* 153–178.

A. D. 1897 (March—September).—**War
with Greece.—Success of the Turkish arms.
—Peace sought by the Greek Government.**—
Notwithstanding the opposition of the Great
Powers, the Greeks were rashly bent upon war
with the Turks, and, when balked in Crete, began hostile demonstrations along the Turkish
frontier in their own peninsula. The events that
followed have been thus described by an eye-witness, who wrote immediately afterwards: "When
I arrived in Athens," says this writer, "early
last March [1897], although the Cretan insurrection was being openly supported by Greek arms,
war had not been declared against Turkey. It
was what I think was once described in Parliament as 'a condition of war,' but not war. . . .
King George and his advisers rashly decided to
attempt to hasten matters in their own fashion.
Agitation was begun without and within the
Turkish frontier, and the Ethnike Hetairia manufactured alarms and disturbances in Macedonia
and Epirus. Attempts were made in other directions, but though money and emissaries were
sent, nothing came of it. Meanwhile the mobili-
sation of the Greek army was begun, and later
on reserves were called out. Knowing a good
deal about the relative condition of preparedness
for war of both Turkey and Greece, I spoke
without reserve on the subject to the King and,
later on, to the Princes. I told them early
every military intelligence department in Europe
knew that Turkey had been getting her troops
ready for a year past to deal with insurrection
or invasion along the Macedonian frontier. Within the Salonica military district she had nearly
100,000 men under arms, all well trained and
passably equipped. Besides infantry she had
nearly 10,000 cavalry, and within a month could
place a further force of 70,000 infantry in the
field. Against these the Greeks could not bring
more than 60,000 regulars. There no doubt
might be mustered twice that number of men,
but they would be untrained irregulars and volunteers who would take a month at least before
they could be of much use, and Turkey would
have her bands of irregulars out also to offset
their value. It was notorious besides that the
Greek army was indifferently organised, that it
had no transport, no commissariat department,
no medical department, and was without anything like a sufficiency of trained officers. . . .
"Prepared or not, the Greeks clamoured for
war, never doubting latterly but that they would
win. They protested that the Hellenes were
aroused and would fight and die, if need be, to
the last man. Greece would not waive an iota
of her demands. We were told that the Greeks
scattered throughout the Turkish Empire would
spring to arms and paralyze the enemy's hands.
There were to be fearful outbreaks in Macedonia,
Epirus, and Albania, and tumults and burnings
in all the chief cities under Turkish rule where
Greeks dwelt—Smyrna, Constantinople, Salonica,
and so on. I was informed that insurrectionary
bands were being got ready to invade Macedonia
and Epirus, and I was introduced to several of
the leaders of these new expeditions. . . . I saw
many of these Greek filibusters at Kalabaka and
other places. By order from Athens the local
commandants supplied them with stores, trans-

port, and trenching tools, and sent guides to direct them, so that they should slip across into
Macedonia at the most suitable points for conducting their operations. . . .

"The Greeks had a fairly long innings carrying on the war within Turkish territory, whilst
disingenuously disclaiming responsibility for the
acts of their own levies. Finally, in April, the
Sultan declared war and set his forces in motion.
Prior to that date the Greeks had moved up the
whole of their available strength close to the
Thessalian frontier. The army numbered nearer
fifty than sixty thousand, of all ranks. . . . Before war was declared the Crown Prince Constantine arrived in Larissa, and took over the
command of the Greek army in Thessaly. . . .
He had no military experience; and, as events
disclosed, was neither of a martial disposition
nor of a firm temperament. He showed subsequently that he felt keenly his false position, and
he tried to excuse the awful failures made in the
conduct of the campaign of panic and flight. . . .
"Independence Day having passed without
a general invasion of Macedonia by the Greeks,
it is likely that the Turks had thought the danger over, when suddenly firing began in a night
along the frontier from Nezeros to Ravenni.
For a day or two the Greeks carried all before
them, capturing many block-houses and taking
a number of prisoners. They succeeded in penetrating Turkish territory in some places for two
or three miles. . . . The Turks were in immediate danger of being outflanked in one part of the
field of operations, and separated from their main
force at Elassona. It was midday, the 19th of
April, when at a critical moment for the safety of
a portion of Edhem's forces an order arrived from
the Crown Prince to cease firing and retire the
whole Greek army back upon their own side of the
frontier. . . . After an interval of three hours,
during which there was little or no firing, a message arrived from headquarters that a blunder
had been made and the army was to readvance
and engage the enemy. It was a lost opportunity, for the Turks followed up the Greeks and
reoccupied the lines from which they had been
driven. . . . The cost of the blunder was a serious one to the Greeks, for in a futile attempt,
on the following day, to retake Gresovala, General Mavromichali lost 2,000 men. . . .
"On the 21st of April, without any of the pictorial display or reputed hand-to-hand fighting,
some 40,000 Turks, not less, accompanied by
three cavalry regiments and half a score of batteries, quietly streamed down the zigzag paved
way in the steep Melouna pass into Thessaly.
They occupied the village of Legaria and positions among the lowest foot hills at the outlet of
the pass. The Greeks were not able to embarrass
them as they deployed, although an attempt was
made to find the range with artillery. . . . For two
days there was a fierce artillery duel, interspersed
occasionally with sharp rifle fire as the infantry
became engaged on the right and left of the line.
. . . All had ended in favour of the Greeks when
the sun set on the 22nd April, and the battle of
Mati was over. . . . It was the same night that
the Crown Prince ordered the army to retreat
upon Larissa, twenty-five miles distant by road.
About 8 P. M. the men were roused from their
first sleep and commanded to fall in. They did
so very orderly and quietly, thinking it was intended to deliver a surprise attack upon the

Turks. The whole army was on the march, and had got five or six miles from the battle-field, or close to Turnavos, when the unaccountable mad panic seized them. Some say it originated one way, some another. . . . The army broke into pieces and became a furious rabble, which fled by road and fields south as hard as most could run. Arms and ammunition and baggage were cast aside wholesale. The Greek officers, as a rule, behaved worse than the men, for they led the fleeing mob, and many of them never stopped until they reached Pharsala or Volo. . . . The whilom Greek army was a mob convinced that the Turkish cavalry was upon their heels, though it never was near them. It gave them the strength of despair, and so they covered afoot fifty to sixty miles within twenty-four hours. The inhabitants of Larissa and all the surrounding country, terrified at the sudden calamity, were left by the military and civic authorities, without hint or warning, to shift for themselves. . . . The women and children of Larissa had to carry what they wished to save upon their own backs. Thousands of these helpless creatures, together with sick and wounded soldiers, were left around the railway station, whilst officers rode off upon the early or later special trains, to fly, as some of them did, as far as Athens. The troops had gone hours before I left Larissa, and even then there were no signs of the enemy to be seen."—Bennet Burleigh, *The Greek War, as I saw it (Fortnightly Review, July,* 1897).

"Not until several hours after the departure of the last Greek, did a few Turkish cavalrymen cautiously enter the town [Larissa], some distance ahead of the Turkish army. . . . It was the design of the Greeks to save Volo, a wealthy town, and the haven of refuge of many of the peasants. Accordingly, a line was formed from two miles beyond Pharsala to the pass which was the doorway to Volo. About three miles from this pass was the village of Velestino; and on the hills back of it were the headquarters of Col. Smollenske, commander of this, the right wing of the Greek army. The Greek fleet, with decks cleared for action, was in the Bay of Volo; having gone there after the defeat of Mati, hoping that, in case the army failed, its heavy guns would protect the town. After four days, the Turks, having digested their victory with cigarettes and coffee, were ready to renew fighting. Meanwhile, the Greeks had put themselves in a sort of order. Evidently, the first intention of the Turks was to force their way through Smollenske's line and on to Volo. Accordingly, they attempted to storm Smollenske's rifle-pits; but they were driven back for the first time, and with the greatest loss that any such movement had yet encountered in the campaign. . . . The Turks, after a slight resistance, withdrew from the villages in front of Velestino, which they had taken, and were soon moving over to the left. Their plan of cutting the Greek line in two was executed with energy. On the morning of May 7, Edhem Pasha sent his fearless infantry, under heavy fire, up the hollows between the mountain-ridges which ran at right angles to the Turkish line across the plain. They intrepidly sealed the ridges, and forced the Greeks from the position. Smollenske's force was flanked and separated from the Crown Prince's force; and he retreated in an orderly manner to Almyro. The Crown Prince's force had been flanked on its

left; at the same time it was being flanked on its right by the force that had flanked Smollenske. The Crown Prince, therefore, withdrew to the heights of Domoko.

"So apparent was now the hopelessness of the Greek cause that even the new ministry, which had been buoyed up into almost an aggressive spirit by the 'victory' of Velestino, begged for the intervention of the Powers. It was granted in the form of a demand on the Sultan for an armistice. As there are six Powers, each having a formal foreign office, this took some time. The Sultan, as usual, was more deliberate than the six tormentors, whom he in return tormented. Being truly Greek, the Greek Cabinet seemed to believe that articles of peace would be signed the moment the necessity of peace appealed to the ministerial mind. . . . Two days after Pharsala, the Turkish army appeared on the plain some ten miles from Domoko. There it rested quietly for more than a week, leisurely celebrating the important feast of Bairam. This confirmed the belief of the Greek generals that the war was at an end. The morning of May 17 found the Crown Prince's force more than ever convinced of an armistice, and quite unprepared for an attack. At nine o'clock the whole Turkish army began to advance upon the astounded Greeks—most astounded of them all were the Crown Prince and Gen. Macris—in such a manner as to leave no doubt as to its intention.

"The battle of Domoko which followed was the most sanguinary of the campaign. . . . For three hours, that is, until sundown,—the attack having begun at four o'clock, —the Greeks steadily returned the hot fire of the Turks, who soon ceased to advance, and doggedly hung on to the ground that they had gained. . . . During this attack in front the Turks were making a more important movement, strategically, on the right. . . . With amazing intrepidity, during the hot action on the centre, the Turks had fought their way over the mountains at the Greeks' far right. Some reserves were sent around at sunset—but too late. The Turkish left wing was already even with the town of Domoko. Military experts maintain that the Crown Prince, by readjusting his forces over night, could have given the phlegmatic enemy a surprise in the morning, and held him in check for several days. The retreat over the pass to Lamia began at ten o'clock in the evening; and the next morning the battalions covering the retreat were under heavy fire. The Greeks' next stand was to be at Thermopylæ. Should the Turks advance spiritedly, Smollenske's army would be cut off from that of the Crown Prince, and forced to surrender. But the Sultan, being somewhat appeased by more blood-letting, now bowed before a letter from him whom the Greeks called 'a vile enemy,'—the Czar,—who, for this act, saw his influence at Constantinople supplanted by that of Germany, though the fear of Russia was undiminished. At last the armistice came,—none too soon for the demoralized army of Greece. The war had lasted just thirty-one days."—F. Palmer, *How the Greeks were defeated (Forum, November,* 1897).

The preliminary treaty of peace, signed September 18, required Greece to pay to Turkey a war indemnity of nearly eighteen millions of dollars, arrangements for securing the payment of which were to be controlled by an international commission composed of one representative of each of the mediating Powers. The same Powers were likewise to settle with Turkey a rectification of the Greek frontier. Greece, in fact, was helplessly in their hands.

A. D. 1897-1899.—Prolonged anarchy in Crete.—The inharmonious "Concert of Europe."—Final departure of Turkish troops and officials from the island.—Organization of government under Prince George of Greece. —"The autonomous régime promised to this unfortunate island — the Cuba of Europe — is still [at the end of 1897] apparently far from realization. In the meantime a most distressing condition, amounting to practical anarchy, prevails everywhere except at some ports where the international gendarmerie maintain a fair semblance of order. So completely have the houses and property of the Mahometan population been destroyed by the insurgents that the coming of winter has brought no prospect to the former but one of desolation and famine. Considerable pillaging of Christian houses by Mahometan refugees was also reported from Candia, Kydonia, and other points. In Candia the Turkish gendarmerie—recruited from the worst class of Bashi-Bazouks—have proved worse than useless for keeping order; they connive with the marauders and share in the pillage. The British occupation is said to be only nominal. . . .

"A strange satire upon the concert of Europe and the pretenses of Western civilization was the circular letter addressed by the Sultan to the powers, about mid-October, urging upon them 'in firm language' the necessity of promptness in restoring tranquillity to the disordered island, and warning them of the dangers of procrastination in this matter. . . . To accomplish the pacification of Crete, the Sultan, in the letter referred to, suggested that the entire population, Christian and Mahometan, should be disarmed; that the disarmament should be carried out by Ottoman troops; that the international troops should co-operate in the work if the powers so desired; that the entire force should be commanded by a European general in the Turkish service; that an Ottoman garrison should be permanently maintained; that the governor should be a Christian and an Ottoman subject; and that a corps of gendarmerie should be formed. . . . Toward the end of October it was announced that the powers had finally chosen for the post of governor-general of Crete Colonel Charles Schaeffer, a native of the grand duchy of Luxemburg, and a man of extended experience in the Turkish and Egyptian services, . . . related to several of the principal houses of the aristocracy at St. Petersburg, as well as to some of the most influential personages in the entourage of the Sultan. . . . The Porte, however, protested, with the support of Germany, against the appointment of Colonel Schaeffer, who appears to have been suspected of English sympathies. Russia, too, it was said, objected, insisting that the appointee must be of the Orthodox Greek faith. Thus, on the question of selecting a governor-general for Crete, the concert of the powers broke down as it did at other points during the long crisis. At the end of November the name of Prince Francis Joseph of Battenberg was prominently mentioned as a prospective candidate of favor. The Cretan assembly proposed, unless a suitable governor were speedily chosen by the powers, to offer the post to a candidate of its own selection."—*Current History*, 1897, *pp.* 865-6.

Months went on, while the Powers still discussed the Cretan situation and no agreement was reached. In January, 1898, the Turkish government appointed Edhem Pasha governor of Candia; but, in the face of the admirals of the blockading squadrons, who exercised an undefined authority, he seems to have had practically little power. Presently, a new attempt was made to select a Christian Governor-general. France and Russia proposed Prince George of Greece, but Austria and Turkey opposed. In April, Austria and Germany withdrew from the blockade and from the "Concert," leaving Great Britain, Russia, France and Italy to deal with Cretan affairs alone. The admirals of these Powers, acting under instructions, then divided the Cretan coast among themselves, each directing the administration of such government as could be conducted in his own part. The British admiral had Candia, the capital town, and there trouble arose which brought the whole Cretan business to a crisis. He attempted to take possession of the customs house (September 6), and landed for that purpose a small force of 60 men. They were attacked by a Turkish mob, with which they fought desperately for four hours, losing 12 killed and some 40 wounded, before they could make their retreat to the shore and regain their ship. At the same time a general massacre of Christians in the town was begun and some 800 perished before it was stopped. Edhem Pasha, with about 4,000 Turkish troops at his command, was said to have waited long for the mob to do its work before he interfered.

This outbreak brought the four Powers to a decisive agreement. They joined in imperatively demanding the withdrawal of Turkish troops and officials from the island, and enforced the demand. Guarantees for the safety of the Mohammedan population in life and property were given; it was conceded that the Sultan's suzerainty over Crete should be maintained, and he was allowed to hold one military post in the island for a sign of the fact. On those terms the Turkish evacuation of Crete was carried out in November, and Prince George of Greece was appointed, not Governor-general, but High Commissioner of the four Powers, to organize an autonomous government in the island and administer it for a period of three years. The appointment was accepted, and Prince George was received with rejoicing in Crete on the 21st of December. The blockade had been raised on the 5th, and on the 26th the admirals departed.

During the following two years (1899-1900) there seems to have been a generally good condition of order restored and preserved. A constitution was framed by a national assembly, which conferred the executive authority on Prince George, as High Commissioner, with responsible councillors, and created a Chamber of Deputies, elected for the most part by the people, but containing ten members appointed by the High Commissioner. Equal rights for all religious beliefs was made a principle of the constitution.

A. D. 1899 (May—July).—Representation in the Peace Conference at The Hague. See (in this vol.) PEACE CONFERENCE.

A. D. 1899 (October).—Concessions to the Armenians.—In October an irade was published by the Sultan which withdrew restrictions on the movements of Armenians in the provinces, except in the case of suspects; granted pardon or commutation of sentence to a number of Armenian prisoners; ordered payment of sums due to Armenian government officials who had been killed or expelled at the time of the massacres; directed assistance to be given in the repairing and rebuilding of churches, schools, and monasterica which had been injured or destroyed, and also gave direction for the building of an orphanage near Constantinople.

A. D. 1899 (November).—**Railway to the Persian Gulf.**—A German Bank Syndicate obtained from the Sultan, in November, 1899, a concession for the extension of the Anatolian Railway from Konieh in Asia Minor, to Basra, or Bassorah, on the Persian Gulf. The line, which will pass through Bagdad, and along the valleys of the Tigris and Euphrates, is to be completed within eight years from the date of the grant. "The concession is regarded as a startling proof of German influence in Constantinople, and a defeat both for Russian and British diplomacy. It is certainly a defeat for the former, and will greatly increase suspicion at St. Petersburg as to the ultimate ends of Germany in Turkey; but we suspect that Indian statesmen will perceive considerable compensations in the arrangement. Not to mention that all railways which approach India develop Indian trade, the railway may secure us a strong ally in Asia. It is not of much use for Russia to be running a line from the Caspian to Bushire if when she gets there she finds Britain and Germany allied in the Persian Gulf, and able by a railway through Gedrosia to Sind to throw themselves right across her path."—*Spectator* (*London*), *Dec.* 2, 1899.

"The opposition of the French company owning the Smyrna-Kassaba road, which extends east as far as Afiou Karahissar, was removed by granting this company 40 per cent of the shares in the extension, and the local objection was obviated by a provision in the concession giving the Turkish Government the right to purchase the line at any time. Few railroad lines can be of greater prospective importance than this 2,000 miles of railroad uniting the Persian Gulf with Europe, forming a rapid transit to and from the East, opening up large tracts of agricultural country, and paving the way for German commercial supremacy in Asia Minor and Mesopotamia. It is not difficult to see how Germany, with preferential rates for goods on German lines, will be able to control the chief markets of Asia Minor and invade the East. . . . Germans purchased the Constantinople-Ismid Railroad from an English company and extended it to Angora. They also checkmated the French and English by extending their line from Eski-Sher to Konieh, thus preventing extension of both the Smyrna-Afion Karahissar and the Smyrna-Aidin-Dinair roads. The two great distributing points —Constantinople and Smyrna—are thus controlled by Germans, and German goods may enter the interior of Asia Minor and the great valley of the Tigris and Euphrates on German-controlled roads at a decided advantage. Germans have obtained the right to build docks and warehouses at Haida Pasha, the terminus of the Anatolian railroads; and with through rates for German goods on German lines, German freight

cars may be sent across the Bosphorus and travel to Mesopotamia and the confines of India and Persia without change."—*United States Consular Reports, April,* 1900, *p.* 497.

Professor Hilprecht has remarked, in the "Sunday School Times" that "a new era for Babylonian archeology will begin when the railroad from Koniah to Baghdad and Bassorah has been constructed. It will then take about a week from London to the ruins of Babylon, where, doubtless, a railway station (Hillah) will be established. At present the traveler needs at the best six weeks to cover this route. This railroad," says the Professor, "has now become a certainty."

A. D. 1899-1901.—**Impending** outbreak in Macedonia.—The state of things in Macedonia, where the people have long been on the brink of revolt against Turkish rule, excited to it from Bulgaria and encouraged from Greece, but warned otherwise by Russia and Austria, is thus described by the "Economist," in an article quoted in "Littell's Living Age," March, 1899: "It is improbable, for reasons stated below, that Macedonia will rise in insurrection this year [1899], but, nevertheless, there is great danger in that quarter, which is evidently disturbing both Vienna and St. Petersburg, and exciting apprehensions in Constantinople. The Austrian and Russian Foreign Offices are both issuing intimations that if a revolt occurs Turkey will be allowed to put it down by Turkish methods, and the Sultan is raising more troops, sending Asiatic levies to Macedonia, and despatching some of his ablest officers to control the hill districts. Severe warnings have also been sent both to Belgrade and Sofia, and the Greeks are warned that if their active party moves the Government of Athens will not again be saved by Europe from the worst consequences. All these symptoms imply that there is grave fear, among those who watch Macedonia, that the patience of her sorely oppressed people has given way, and that they have resolved to risk everything rather than remain longer under the rule of Pashas from whom no man's life and no woman's honor is safe for twelve hours together. It is known, moreover, that the course of events in Crete and the appearance of the Tsar's Rescript have greatly stirred the population. The former is held by them to show that if a Christian population in Turkey will risk massacre, Europe will not allow them to be exterminated, while the latter has made submission more difficult by putting an end to hope for the next five years. . . .

"Turkish subjects must be driven to despair before they will rise against the Turks, and if they can even hope to be left alone, the Macedonians will wait, rather than encounter so dreadful a risk. They have, it is true, the example of the Cretans to encourage them, but their country is not an island, and they have the fate both of the Armenians and the Thessalians to warn them that on the mainland the Turks cannot be resisted by half-drilled forces.

"It seems almost a truism to say that Europe is foolish to allow such a source of danger as Macedonia presents to continue without a cure; but there is something to be said on the other side. The Powers sincerely desire peace, and the Macedonian magazine cannot be flooded without a war, if it be only a war between Russia and the Sultan. Nobody knows to what such a war would lead, or in what condition Eastern Europe might emerge from it. Moreover, however much the Macedonians may excite the sympathies of philanthropists, they have done a good deal to alienate those of politicians. They decline to be either Austrian or Russian. They asked for years to be aided by Greece, and when Greece declared war on Turkey they refused to rise behind Edhem Pasha, whom they could have cut away from his supports. They now ask aid from Bulgaria, but they are most unwilling to submit to Sofia, and so make of Bulgaria a fairly strong State. They wish, they say, to make of Macedonia a Principality, but if it were so made the Slavo-Macedonians would begin fighting the Græco-Macedonians, until both had been nearly ruined. They must join one party or the other if they wish to be free, and stick to the one they join, and fight for it with a coherence which they have never yet displayed."

On the 7th of January, 1901, a correspondent of the "London Times" wrote on the same subject from Vienna, as follows: "The situation in Macedonia, as described in trustworthy accounts coming from different directions, testifies to the increasing danger of trouble. Things have gone so far that an outbreak may occur this year. In diplomatic circles it is considered impossible that in any case it can be delayed for longer than a twelvemonth. In Constantinople, Athens, and all the capitals of the Balkan States the eventuality of a Macedonian rising has been expected for several years past, and in more than one instance preparations have been made accordingly. To what extent the Macedonia committees have received official patronage in Bulgaria is now of secondary interest. The mischief has been done, and the agitation in Macedonia is at present beyond the control of the Bulgarian authorities, even if they wished to keep it in check, which is not certain. All that can be said with confidence is that last summer Austria and Russia made a vigorous and successful effort to put an end to the almost open encouragement extended to the Macedonian committees at Sofia, which was within an ace of involving the Principality in a war with Rumania. The Austro-Russian 'entente' [an understanding or agreement between Russia and Austria, in 1897, to act together in keeping peace in the Balkan peninsula] has, in fact, done excellent service wherever diplomatic pressure can be brought to bear. But, unfortunately, that does not include Macedonia. If the revolutionary element in that province of the Ottoman Empire sets at defiance the imposing Turkish forces concentrated on the spot, it is not likely that it will be influenced by what is probably regarded as the remote contingency of the direct armed intervention of Austria and Russia. All the warnings and scoldings in the world will not suffice to preserve peace in Macedonia.

"It is difficult to say what foundation there may be for the statement that the Sultan himself seeks to take advantage of the disturbed condition of Macedonia for purposes of his own. It is alleged that he wishes to prevent any change in the existing régime in Crete by exciting the apprehension in Athens and elsewhere that an attempt to modify the status quo in that island would cause a massacre of the Hellenic population in Macedonia. This view of the case finds expression in the following extracts from a letter addressed to the 'Roumanie,' one of the leading organs of Bukharest :—'The thoroughly bad policy pursued by the Sublime Porte in Macedonia, which consists in allowing that unhappy province to remain a prey to Bulgarian agitators so as in case of need to terrify diplomacy by the spectre of a revolution, has contributed to open the eyes of the Powers. On the other hand, the irresistible attraction exercised by the Kingdom of Greece, not only on the Cretans themselves, but also on all the rayahs of the Ottoman Empire, is an indisputable fact.'"— See, also (in this vol.), BALKAN AND DANUBIAN STATES.

A. D. **1900.**—The Zionist movement of **the** Jews to colonize Palestine. See (in this vol.) JEWS : A. D. 1897–1901.

A. D. **1901.**—The Cretan question.—The provisional arrangement of government for Crete, administered by Prince George, of Greece, as High Commissioner for the Powers, expires by limitation in December, 1901. What shall then be done with the island is a question that was referred, by the several Powers of the Concert, in the early part of the year, to their ambassadors at Rome, in conference with the Italian Minister of Foreign Affairs. The administration of Prince George appears to have been quite remarkably satisfactory to all concerned, and its continuation was evidently desired, as much by the Cretans as by the protecting Powers; but the former sought to have it placed on a basis of permanency, in some form that would be practically tantamount to the long craved annexation to Greece. Prince George naturally looks in the same direction, and he is said to have made it known that he would decline to hold his post provisionally beyond the term of three years for which he accepted it in 1898. The ambassadorial conference at Rome decided, however, that the time has not come for a permanent settlement of the Cretan question, and that the provisional arrangement for its government must be renewed. A Press despatch from Athens, on the 22d of March, 1901, announced the decision and indicated the circumstances of the situation, as follows:

"The Cretan Assembly meets at the end of next month, and its probable attitude towards the question of union with Greece is already the subject of speculation here. The decision of the conference of Ambassadors at Rome is embodied in a memorandum which has been handed to Prince George by the Consuls at Canea, while a copy of the document has been unofficially presented to King George 'à titre d'information.' The Ambassadors express their opinion that any manifestation on the part of the Cretans in favour of union with Greece would be inopportune at the present moment, and they propose a prolongation of the present provisional system of government without assigning any definite term to the High Commissioner's mandate.

"Whether Prince George, who is an enthusiastic advocate of union with Greece, will accept the new arrangement unconditionally remains to be seen. Meanwhile the islanders are occupied with preparations for the elections.

"It appears that at a recent sitting of the Prince's Council one of the most prominent of Cretan politicians advocated the institution of an autonomous Principality on the lines already laid down by the existing Constitution. The proposal provoked a violent outburst on the part of the Athenian Press, which denounces its author as a traitor to the cause of Hellenism. The opinion apparently prevails here that the estab-

lishment of a Principality would finally preclude the union of the island with Greece."

A. D. **1901.**—Order regulating the visit **of** Jews to **Palestine.** See (in this vol.) JEWS: A. D. 1901.

TWAIN, Mark: Description of scenes in the Austrian Reichsrath. See (in this vol.)

AUSTRIA-HUNGARY: A. D. 1897 (OCTOBER—DE-CEMBER).

U.

UCHALI, Treaty of. See (in this vol.) ITALY: A. D. 1895-1896.

UGANDA: A. D. **1894.**—Creation of the Protectorate. See (in this vol.) BRITISH EAST AFRICA PROTECTORATE: A. D. 1895-1897.

A. D. **1897-1898.**—Native insurrection and mutiny of Sudanese troops.—A train of serious troubles in the Uganda Protectorate began in May, 1897, with an insurrection of some of the chiefs, instigated by the king, Mwanga, who was restive under British control. The revolt was suppressed after some sharp fighting, especially at Kiango, on the 24th of July, and King Mwanga escaped into German territory. In August he was formally deposed by a council of chiefs, and his infant son, Chua, was elected king in his place, under a regency of three of the chiefs. But a more serious trouble followed, from the mutiny of a part of the Sudanese troops which had been serving in Uganda. These troops were being sent to join an expedition, under Major Macdonald, for the exploration of the districts adjacent to the Italian sphere of influence, and were not permitted to take their women with them. This seems to have been their chief grievance. They also complained of being overworked, underpaid, insufficiently fed, and commanded by young officers who would not listen to their complaints. They seized Fort Lubas, on the frontier between Uganda and Usoga, made prisoners of several of their officers, whom they finally murdered, and held the fort against repeated attacks until early in January, 1898, when they made their escape. They were pursued and attacked (February 24) at Kabagambe, on Lake Kioja, where they had built a fort. Many were killed, the remainder much scattered. A considerable party got away to the eastern side of the Nile and continued to give trouble there throughout the year.

Meantime, the deposed king, Mwanga, had escaped from the Germans and effected a new rising among his late subjects; and another deposed king, Kabarega, of Unyoro, had also reappeared, to make trouble in that region. After the suppression of the Sudanese mutiny these risings were overcome, with the help of some 1,100 troops brought from India for the emergency. In March, there was news of Kabarega's death, and the British Acting Commissioner and Consul General issued the following proclamation: "Whereas Kabarega, the deposed King of Unyoro, is reported to have deceased, and whereas the present disordered state of affairs in that country has proved that, for the maintenance of

good government and good-will, it is expedient to provide for the succession to the kingdom of a member of the Royal House, it is hereby publicly proclaimed that Karukala, son of Kabarega, is now appointed King of Unyoro, under the protection of Her Britannic Majesty. The Kingdom of Unyoro comprises the provinces of— Busindi, Shifalu, Magungu, Kibero, Bugoma, Bugabiaobeire. This appointment is in accordance with the general conditions by which countries in British African Protectorates are guided and regulated, and it secures to the Kingdom of Unyoro all the advantages which accrue from its being an integral part of such a Protectorate. The local government of the country will be administered, under the guidance of Her Majesty's Representative, by a Council of Regency of either two or three Chiefs, to be appointed by Her Majesty's Commissioner. This Council of Regency will, subject to the approval of Her Majesty's Commissioner, select and appoint the Katikiro and the other Chiefs of the first rank required in accordance with local custom. These Chiefs, on their appointment being confirmed, will select and appoint in full Council the lesser grade Chiefs, until the system of local administration is complete."—*Great Britain, Parliamentary Publications (Papers by Command: Africa, No. 7, 1898, p. 42).*

UGANDA RAILWAY, The.—On the 30th of April, 1900, the British Parliament voted £1,930,000 for the completion of the railway under construction from Mombasa, on the Indian Ocean, to Lake Victoria-Nyanza, officially known as the Mombasa-Victoria Railway. Previous expenditure had been about £3,000,000. On the 30th of October it was reported that rails were laid down to the 452d mile from Mombasa, and that advance gangs were working about 40 miles beyond that point.

UITLANDERS. See (in this vol.) SOUTH AFRICA (THE TRANSVAAL): A. D. 1885-1890, and after.

UNGAVA, The district of. See (in this vol.) CANADA: A. D. 1895.

UNITED CHRISTIAN PARTY. See (in this vol.) UNITED STATES OF AM.: A. D. 1900 (MAY—NOVEMBER).

UNITED IRISH LEAGUE, The. See (in this vol.) IRELAND: A. D. 1900-1901.

UNITED STATES OF BRAZIL. See (in this vol.) BRAZIL.

UNITED STATES OF AMERICA.

A. D. 1868-1885.—Cuban questions in controversy with Spain. See (in this vol.) CUBA: A. D. 1868–1885.

A. D. 1894.—Legislation to promote the reclamation of arid lands.—The following measure of legislation to promote the reclamation of arid lands was carried through Congress as an amendment to the appropriation bill for Sundry Civil Expenditures, and became law August 18, 1894 :

"Sec. 4. That to aid the public land States in the reclamation of the desert lands therein, and the settlement, cultivation, and sale thereof in small tracts to actual settlers, the Secretary of the Interior with the approval of the President, be, and hereby is, authorized and empowered, upon proper application of the State to contract and agree, from time to time, with each of the States in which there may be situated desert lands as defined by the Act entitled 'An Act to provide for the sale of desert land in certain States and Territories,' approved March 3d, 1877, and the Act amendatory thereof, approved March 3d, 1891, binding the United States to donate, grant and patent to the State free of cost for survey or price such desert lands, not exceeding one million acres in each State, as the State may cause to be irrigated, reclaimed, occupied, and not less than twenty acres of each one hundred and sixty-acre tract cultivated by actual settlers, within ten years next after the passage of this Act, as thoroughly as is required of citizens who may enter under the said desert land laws.

"Before the application of any State is allowed or any contract or agreement is executed or any segregation of any of the land from the public domain is ordered by the Secretary of the Interior, the State shall file a map of the said land proposed to be irrigated which shall exhibit a plan showing the mode of the contemplated irrigation and which plan shall be sufficient to thoroughly irrigate and reclaim said land and prepare it to raise ordinary agricultural crops and shall also show the source of the water to be used for irrigation and reclamation, and the Secretary of the Interior may make necessary regulations for the reservation of the lands applied for by the States to date from the date of the filing of the map and plan of irrigation, but such reservation shall be of no force whatever if such map and plan of irrigation shall not be adopted. That any State contracting under this section is hereby authorized to make all necessary contracts to cause the said lands to be reclaimed, and to induce their settlement and cultivation in accordance with and subject to the provisions of this section ; but the State shall not be authorized to lease any of said lands or to use or dispose of the same in any way whatever, except to secure their reclamation, cultivation and settlement.

"As fast as any State may furnish satisfactory proof according to such rules and regulations as may be prescribed by the Secretary of the Interior, that any of said lands are irrigated, reclaimed and occupied by actual settlers, patents shall be issued to the State or its assigns for said land so reclaimed and settled : Provided, That said States shall not sell or dispose of more than one hundred and sixty acres of said land to any one person, and any surplus of money derived by any State from the sale of said lands in excess of the cost of their reclamation, shall be held as a trust fund for and be applied to the reclamation of other desert lands in such State. That to enable the Secretary of the Interior to examine any of the lands that may be selected under the provisions of this section, there is hereby appropriated out of any moneys in the Treasury, not otherwise appropriated, one thousand dollars."—*Acts*, 53d *Cong.*, 2d *Sess.*, ch. 301.

A. D. 1895.—Re-survey of Mexican boundary. See (in this vol.) MEXICO : A. D. 1892–1895.

A. D. 1895 (January—February).—The monetary situation.—Contract for replenishing the gold reserve in the Treasury.—The alarming situation of the Treasury of the United States at the beginning of the year 1895 was clearly described by the President in his special Message to Congress, January 28 (see in vol. 5, UNITED STATES OF AM. : A. D. 1895). By the operation of what had been aptly called "the endless chain" of the greenback currency issues of the government (paid out with one hand, to be redeemed with the other in gold, which the declining value of silver brought more and more into demand) the gold reserve in the Treasury was fast being exhausted, and the hour was approaching when, without some effective relief, the obligations of the nation would have to be paid in depreciated silver coin, and its credit lost. The appeal of the President to Congress had no effect. The Senate was controlled by a majority of men who desired precisely the result which he wished to avert. The state of things in that body was described by Senator Sherman, of the Committee on Finance, in the following words : "The Committee on Finance is utterly helpless to deal with this vast question. We are quite divided upon it. We are not allowed to propose a measure to this Senate which all can approve of, unless there is attached to it a provision for free coinage of silver." The attitude of the House was different, but almost equally hostile to the President's views. Its Republican majority was not favorable to the aims of the free silver parties, but held that the relief needed for the Treasury was to be sought in a return to higher import duties, as a means of obtaining increased revenue. Hence, a bill to carry out the recommendations of the President was rejected in the House, on the 7th of February, by a vote of 162 against 135.

On the following day, the Secretary of the Treasury, Mr. Carlisle, exercising authority which he possessed to sell certain four per cent. thirty year bonds, contracted with August Belmont & Co., who represented the Rothschilds of London, and with the house of J. P. Morgan & Co., of New York, on behalf of J. S. Morgan & Co., London, and themselves, for supplying 3,500,000 ounces of standard gold coin of the United States, at the rate of $17.80441 per ounce, in exchange for such bonds. It was a condition of the contract that one half of the coin supplied should be brought from Europe : also that the contracting syndicate should use its influence to protect the Treasury against withdrawals of gold. At the same time, the Secretary of the Treasury reserved the right to substitute three per cent. gold bonds, if Congress would authorize such an issue, to be taken by the syndicate at par, in place of the four per cents to which his existing authority was restricted. It was shown that the consequent saving in interest would be $539,000 per annum, amounting to $16,174,770 in thirty years; but the proposal was rejected in the House of Representatives by 167 votes against 120. The contract was accordingly carried out in its original form, with success so far that the withdrawals of gold from the Treasury dropped for a considerable period to a low point. It appeared that when this emergency break was put upon the working of the "endless chain," the sub-treasury in New York was believed to be within twenty-four hours of a suspension of gold payments. But the contract was loudly condemned, nevertheless, by the opponents of the administration.

A. D. **1895** (February).—**Renewed insurrection** in Cuba. See (in this vol.) CUBA: A. D. 1895.

A. D. **1895** (April—**May**).—Decision of the Supreme Court against the constitutionality of the Income **Tax**.—Cases testing the constitutionality of the income tax which Congress had attached to the Tariff Act of 1894 (see, in vol. 4 of original edition, or in vol. 5 of revised edition, TARIFF LEGISLATION, UNITED STATES: A. D. 1894), were brought to a partial decision in the Supreme Court in April, and finally in May, 1895. The cases in question were "Pollock v. Farmers' Loan and Trust Company," and "Hyde v. Continental Trust Company." On the first hearing, the illness and absence of one of the justices, Mr. Jackson, of Tennessee, left but eight members in attendance, and they divided equally on several points which were vital to the decision of the question of constitutionality in the tax. The appellants accordingly filed a petition for a re-hearing, submitting, among other reasons, the following: "The question involved in these cases was as to the constitutionality of the provisions of the tariff act of August 15, 1894 (sections 27 to 37), purporting to impose a tax on incomes. The Court has held that the same are unconstitutional, so far as they purport to impose a tax upon the rent or income of real estate and income derived from municipal bonds. It has, however, announced that it was equally divided in opinion as to the following questions, and has expressed no opinion in regard to them: (1) Whether the void provisions invalidate the whole act. (2) Whether, as to the income from personal property as such, the act is unconstitutional as laying direct taxes. (3) Whether any part of the tax, if not considered as a direct tax, is invalid for want of uniformity.

"The court has reversed the decree of the Circuit Court and remanded the case, with directions to enter a decree in favor of complainant in respect only of the voluntary payment of the tax on the rents and income of defendant's real estate and that which it holds in trust, and on the income from the municipal bonds owned or so held by it. While, therefore, the two points above stated have been decided, there has been no decision of the remaining questions regarding the constitutionality of the act, and no judgment has been announced authoritatively establishing any principle for interpretation of the statute in those respects."

The re-hearing asked for was granted by the

Court on the 6th of May, when Justice Jackson was able to take his seat on the bench, after which, on the 20th of May, by the opinion of five members of the Court against four, the law was pronounced null, so far as concerned the imposition of a tax on incomes. The opinion of the majority was delivered by Chief Justice Fuller, who said, in part:

"The Constitution divided Federal taxation into two great classes, the class of direct taxes, and the class of duties, imposts and excises; and prescribed two rules which qualified the grant of power as to each class. The power to lay direct taxes apportioned among the several States in proportion to their representation in the popular branch of Congress, a representation based on population as ascertained by the census, was plenary and absolute; but to lay direct taxes without apportionment was forbidden. The power to lay duties, imposts, and excises was subject to the qualification that the imposition must be uniform throughout the United States.

"Our previous decision was confined to the consideration of the validity of the tax on the income from real estate and on the income from municipal bonds. . . . We are now permitted to broaden the field of inquiry, and to determine to which of the two great classes a tax upon a person's entire income, whether derived from rents, or products, or otherwise, of real estate, or from bonds, stocks, or other forms of personal property, belongs; and we are unable to conclude that the enforced subtraction from the yield of all the owner's real or personal property, in the manner prescribed, is so different from a tax upon the property itself, that it is not a direct, but an indirect tax in the meaning of the Constitution.

"The words of the Constitution are to be taken in their obvious sense, and to have a reasonable construction. In Gibbons v. Ogden, Mr. Chief Justice Marshall, with his usual felicity, said: 'As men, whose intentions require no concealment, generally employ the words which most directly and aptly express the ideas they intend to convey, the enlightened patriots who framed our Constitution, and the people who adopted it must be understood to have employed words in their natural sense, and to have intended that they have said.' 9 Wheat. 1, 188. And in Rhode Island v. Massachusetts, where the question was whether a controversy between two States over the boundary between them was within the grant of judicial power, Mr. Justice Baldwin, speaking for the Court, observed: 'The solution of this question must necessarily depend on the words of the Constitution; the meaning and intention of the convention which framed and proposed it for adoption and ratification to the conventions of the people of and in the several States; together with a reference to such sources of judicial information as are resorted to by all courts in construing statutes, and to which this court has always resorted in construing the Constitution.' 12 Pet. 657, 721. We know of no reason for holding otherwise than that the words 'direct taxes,' on the one hand, and 'duties, imposts and excises,' on the other, were used in the Constitution in their natural and obvious sense. Nor in arriving at what those terms embrace do we perceive any ground for enlarging them beyond or narrowing them

554

within their natural and obvious import at the time the Constitution was framed and ratified.

"And passing from the text, we regard the conclusion reached as inevitable, when the circumstances which surrounded the convention and controlled its action and the views of those who framed and those who adopted the Constitution are considered. . . . In the light of the struggle in the convention as to whether or not the new Nation should be empowered to levy taxes directly on the individual until after the States had failed to respond to requisitions—a struggle which did not terminate until the amendment to that effect, proposed by Massachusetts and concurred in by South Carolina, New Hampshire, New York, and Rhode Island, had been rejected —it would seem beyond reasonable question that direct taxation, taking the place as it did of requisitions, was purposely restrained to apportionment according to representation, in order that the former system as to ratio might be retained while the mode of collection was changed. This is forcibly illustrated by a letter of Mr. Madison of January 29, 1789, recently published, written after the ratification of the Constitution, but before the organization of the government and the submission of the proposed amendment to Congress, which, while opposing the amendment as calculated to impair the power only to be exercised in extraordinary emergencies, assigns adequate ground for its rejection as substantially unnecessary, since, he says, 'every State which chooses to collect its own quota may always prevent a Federal collection, by keeping a little beforehand in its finances and making its payment at once into the Federal treasury.'

"The reasons for the clauses of the Constitution in respect of direct taxation are not far to seek. The States, respectively, possessed plenary powers of taxation. They could tax the property of their citizens in such manner and to such extent as they saw fit; they had unrestricted powers to impose duties or imposts on imports from abroad, and excises on manufactures, consumable commodities, or otherwise. They gave up the great sources of revenue derived from commerce; they retained the concurrent power of levying excises, and duties if covering anything other than excises; but in respect of them the range of taxation was narrowed by the power granted over interstate commerce, and by the danger of being put at disadvantage in dealing with excises on manufactures. They retained the power of direct taxation, and to that they looked as their chief resource; but even in respect of that, they granted the concurrent power, and if the tax were placed by both governments on the same subject, the claim of the United States had preference. Therefore, they did not grant the power of direct taxation without regard to their own condition and resources as States; but they granted the power of apportioned direct taxation, a power just as efficacious to serve the needs of the general government, but securing to the States the opportunity to pay the amount apportioned, and to recoup from their own citizens in the most feasible way, and in harmony with their systems of local self-government. If, in the changes of wealth and population in particular States, apportionment produced inequality, it was an inequality stipulated for, just as the equal representation of the States,

however small, in the Senate, was stipulated for. . . .

"Moreover, whatever the reasons for the constitutional provisions, there they are, and they appear to us to speak in plain language. It is said that a tax on the whole income of property is not a direct tax in the meaning of the Constitution, but a duty, and, as a duty, leviable without apportionment, whether direct or indirect. We do not think so. Direct taxation was not restricted in one breath and the restriction blown to the winds in another. Cooley (On Taxation, p. 3) says that the word 'duty' ordinarily 'means an indirect tax imposed on the importation, exportation or consumption of goods'; having 'a broader meaning than "custom," which is a duty imposed on imports or exports'; that 'the term "impost" also signifies any tax, tribute or duty, but it is seldom applied to any but the indirect taxes. An excise duty is an inland impost, levied upon articles of manufacture or sale, and also upon licenses to pursue certain trades or to deal in certain commodities.' In the Constitution the words 'duties, imposts and excises' are put in antithesis to direct taxes. Gouverneur Morris recognized this in his remarks in modifying his celebrated motion, as did Wilson in approving of the motion as modified. . . .

"Our conclusions may therefore be summed up as follows:

"First. We adhere to the opinion already announced, that, taxes on real estate being indisputably direct taxes, taxes on the rents or income of real estate are equally direct taxes.

"Second. We are of opinion that taxes on personal property, or on the income of personal property, are likewise direct taxes.

"Third. The tax imposed by sections twenty-seven to thirty-seven, inclusive, of the act of 1894, so far as it falls on the income of real estate and of personal property, being a direct tax within the meaning of the Constitution, and, therefore, unconstitutional and void because not apportioned according to representation, all those sections, constituting one entire scheme of taxation, are necessarily invalid."

Four dissenting opinions were prepared, by Justices Harlan, Brown, Jackson and White. In that of Mr. Justice Harlan, he said: "What are 'direct taxes' within the meaning of the Constitution? In the convention of 1787, Rufus King asked what was the precise meaning of 'direct' taxation, and no one answered. Madison Papers, 5 Elliott's Debates, 451. The debates of that famous body do not show that any delegate attempted to give a clear, succinct definition of what, in his opinion, was a direct tax. Indeed the report of those debates, upon the question now before us, is very meagre and unsatisfactory. An illustration of this is found in the case of Gouverneur Morris. It is stated that on the 12th of July, 1787, he moved to add to a clause empowering Congress to vary representation according to the principles of 'wealth and numbers of inhabitants,' a proviso 'that taxation shall be in proportion to representation.' And he is reported to have remarked, on that occasion, that while some objections lay against his motion, he supposed 'they would be removed by restraining the rule to direct taxation.' Elliott's Debates, 302. But, on the 8th of August, 1787, the work of the Committee on Detail being before the convention, Mr. Morris is reported to have remarked, 'let it not be said that direct taxation is to be proportioned to representation.' 5 Elliott's Debates, 393. If the question propounded by Rufus King had been answered in accordance with the interpretation now given, it is not at all certain that the Constitution, in its present form, would have been adopted by the convention, nor, if adopted, that it would have been accepted by the requisite number of States."

The following is from the dissenting opinion of Mr. Justice Brown : "In view of the fact that the great burden of taxation among the several States is assessed upon real estate at a valuation, and that a similar tax was apparently an important part of the revenue of such States at the time the Constitution was adopted, it is not unreasonable to suppose that this is the only undefined direct tax the framers of the Constitution had in view when they incorporated this clause into that instrument. The significance of the words ' direct taxes' was not so well understood then as it is now, and it is entirely probable that these words were used with reference to a generally accepted method of raising a revenue by tax upon real estate. . . . But, however this may be, I regard it as very clear that the clause requiring direct taxes to be apportioned to the population has no application to taxes which are not capable of apportionment according to population. It cannot be supposed that the convention could have contemplated a practical inhibition upon the power of Congress to tax in some way all taxable property within the jurisdiction of the Federal government, for the purposes of a national revenue. And if the proposed tax were such that in its nature it could not be apportioned according to population, it naturally follows that it could not have been considered a direct tax, within the meaning of the clause in question."

Mr. Justice Jackson concluded his dissenting opinion as follows: "The practical operation of the decision is not only to disregard the great principles of equality in taxation, but the further principle that in the imposition of taxes for the benefit of the government the burdens thereof should be imposed upon those having the most ability to bear them. This decision, in effect, works out a directly opposite result, in relieving the citizens having the greater ability, while the burdens of taxation are made to fall most heavily and oppressively upon those having the least ability. It lightens the burden upon the larger number in some States subject to the tax, and places it most unequally and disproportionately on the smaller number in other States. Considered in all its bearings, this decision is, in my judgment, the most disastrous blow ever struck at the constitutional power of Congress. It strikes down an important portion of the most vital and essential power of the government in practically excluding any recourse to incomes from real and personal estate for the purpose of raising needed revenue to meet the government's wants and necessities under any circumstances.

"I am therefore compelled to enter my dissent to the judgment of the court."

The opinion delivered by the majority of the Court was criticised with severity by Mr. Justice White, who said : "The injustice of the conclusion points to the error of adopting it. It takes invested wealth and reads it into the Con-

stitution as a favored and protected class of property, which cannot be taxed without apportionment, whilst it leaves the occupation of the minister, the doctor, the professor, the lawyer, the inventor, the author, the merchant, the mechanic, and all other forms of industry upon which the prosperity of a people must depend, subject to taxation without that condition   A rule which works out this result, which, it seems to me, stultifies the Constitution by making it an instrument of the most grievous wrong, should not be adopted, especially when, in order to do so, the decisions of this court, the opinions of the law writers and publicists, tradition, practice, and the settled policy of the government must be overthrown.

"To destroy the fixed interpretation of the Constitution, by which the rule of apportionment according to population, is confined to direct taxes on real estate so as to make that rule include indirect taxes on real estate and taxes, whether direct or indirect, on invested personal property, stocks, bonds, etc., reads into the Constitution the most flagrantly unjust, unequal, and wrongful system of taxation known to any civilized government. This strikes me as too clear for argument. I can conceive of no greater injustice than would result from imposing on one million of people in one State, having only ten millions of invested wealth, the same amount of tax as that imposed on the like number of people in another State having fifty times that amount of invested wealth. The application of the rule of apportionment by population to invested personal wealth would not only work out this wrong, but would ultimately prove a self-destructive process, from the facility with which such property changes its situs. If so taxed, all property of this character would soon be transferred to the States where the sum of accumulated wealth was greatest in proportion to population, and where therefore the burden of taxation would be lightest, and thus the mighty wrong resulting from the very nature of the extension of the rule would be aggravated. It is clear then, I think, that the admission of the power of taxation in regard to invested personal property, coupled with the restriction that the tax must be distributed by population and not by wealth, involves a substantial denial of the power itself, because the condition renders its exercise practically impossible. To say a thing can only be done in a way which must necessarily bring about the grossest wrong, is to delusively admit the existence of the power, while substantially denying it. And the grievous results sure to follow from any attempt to adopt such a system are so obvious that my mind cannot fail to see that if a tax on invested personal property were imposed by the rule of population, and there were no other means of preventing its enforcement, the red spectre of revolution would shake our institutions to their foundation. . . .

"It is, I submit, greatly to be deplored that, after more than one hundred years of our national existence, after the government has withstood the strain of foreign wars and the dread ordeal of civil strife, and its people have become united and powerful, this court should consider itself compelled to go back to a long repudiated and rejected theory of the Constitution, by which the government is deprived of an inherent attribute of its being, a necessary power of taxation."—*U. S. Reports, v.* 158, *pp.* 601–715.

A. D. 1895 (July—November).—Correspondence with the Government of Great Britain on the Venezuela boundary question. See (in this vol.) VENEZUELA: A. D. 1895 (JULY), and (NOVEMBER).

A. D. 1895 (September).—**Executive order for the improvement of the consular service.**—In his annual Message to Congress, December 2, 1895, President Cleveland made the following statement of measures adopted for the improvement of the consular service of the country:

"In view of the growth of our interests in foreign countries and the encouraging prospects for a general expansion of our commerce, the question of an improvement in the consular service has increased in importance and urgency. Though there is no doubt that the great body of consular officers are rendering valuable services to the trade and industries of the country, the need of some plan of appointment and control which would tend to secure a higher average of efficiency can not be denied. The importance of the subject has led the Executive to consider what steps might properly be taken without additional legislation to answer the need of a better system of consular appointments. The matter having been committed to the consideration of the Secretary of State, in pursuance of his recommendations, an Executive order was issued on the 20th of September, 1895, by the terms of which it is provided that after that date any vacancy in a consular or commercial agency with an annual salary or compensation from official fees of not more than $2,500 or less than $1,000 should be filled either by transfer or promotion from some other position under the Department of State of a character tending to qualify the incumbent for the position to be filled, or by the appointment of a person not under the Department of State, but having previously served thereunder and shown his capacity and fitness for consular duty, or by the appointment of a person who, having been selected by the President and sent to a board for examination, is found, upon such examination, to be qualified for the position. Posts which pay less than $1,000 being usually, on account of their small compensation, filled by selection from residents of the locality, it was not deemed practicable to put them under the new system.

"The compensation of $2,500 was adopted as the maximum limit in the classification for the reason that consular officers receiving more than that sum are often charged with functions and duties scarcely inferior in dignity and importance to those of diplomatic agents, and it was therefore thought best to continue their selection in the discretion of the Executive without subjecting them to examination before a board. Excluding seventy-one places with compensation at present less than $1,000, and fifty-three places above the maximum in compensation, the number of positions remaining within the scope of the order is one hundred and ninety-six. This number will undoubtedly be increased by the inclusion of consular officers whose remuneration in fees, now less than $1,000, will be augmented with the growth of our foreign commerce and a return to more favorable business conditions. In execution of the Executive order referred to, the Secretary of State has designated as a board to

conduct the prescribed examinations the Third Assistant Secretary of State, the Solicitor of the Department of State, and the Chief of the Consular Bureau, and has specified the subjects to which such examinations shall relate.

"It is not assumed that this system will prove a full measure of consular reform. It is quite probable that actual experience will show particulars in which the order already issued may be amended, and demonstrate that, for the best results, appropriate legislation by Congress is imperatively required. In any event these efforts to improve the consular service ought to be immediately supplemented by legislation providing for consular inspection. This has frequently been a subject of Executive recommendation, and I again urge such action by Congress as will permit the frequent and thorough inspection of consulates by officers appointed for that purpose or by persons already in the diplomatic or consular service. The expense attending such a plan would be insignificant compared with its usefulness, and I hope the legislation necessary to set it on foot will be speedily forthcoming.

"I am thoroughly convinced that in addition to their salaries our ambassadors and ministers at foreign courts should be provided by the Government with official residences. The salaries of these officers are comparatively small and in most cases insufficient to pay, with other necessary expenses, the cost of maintaining household establishments in keeping with their important and delicate functions. The usefulness of a nation's diplomatic representative undeniably depends upon the appropriateness of his surroundings, and a country like ours, while avoiding unnecessary glitter and show, should be certain that it does not suffer in its relations with foreign nations through parsimony and shabbiness in its diplomatic outfit. These considerations and the other advantages of having fixed and somewhat permanent locations for our embassies, would abundantly justify the moderate expenditure necessary to carry out this suggestion."—*Message of the President (54th Cong., 1st Sess., House Doc., v.* 1).

A. D. 1895 (December).—**Message of President Cleveland on the boundary dispute between Great Britain and Venezuela.—Prompt response from Congress.**—On the 17th of December, 1895, the country was startled and the world at large excited by a message from President Cleveland to Congress, relating to the disputed boundary between British Guiana and Venezuela, and the refusal of the British government to submit the dispute to arbitration—see, in this vol., VENEZUELA: A. D. 1895 (DECEMBER). The tone in which the President recommended the appointment of a commission to ascertain the "true divisional line" between Venezuela and British Guiana, with a view to determining the future action of the United States, was peremptory and threatening enough to awaken all the barbaric passions which wait and watch for signals of war; and Congress, in both branches, met the wishes of the President with the singular alacrity that so often appears in the action of legislative bodies when a question arises which carries the scent of war. The House refused to wait for any reference of the matter to its Committee on Foreign Relations, but framed and passed at once (December 18) without debate or division, an act authorizing

the suggested commission and appropriating $100,000 for the expenses of its work. In the Senate there were some voices raised against needless and unseemly haste in the treatment of so grave a proposition. Senator Teller, of Colorado, was one who spoke to that effect, saying:
"I do not understand that our great competitor in commerce and trade, our great English-speaking relative, has ever denied our right to assert and maintain the Monroe doctrine. What they claim is that the Monroe doctrine does not apply to this case. Whether it applies to this case depends upon the facts, which are unknown to us, it appears. If I knew what the facts were, as an international lawyer I would have no difficulty in applying the law. As a believer in the American doctrine of the right to say that no European power shall invade American soil, either of North or South America, I should have no trouble in coming to a conclusion. Is it an invasion of American soil? I do not know that. I repeat, I thought I did. I have found that I do not.
"If the President of the United States had said that in the Department of State they had determined what was the true line between the British possessions and Venezuela, and if he had said, 'We are confident that the British Government, instead of attempting to arrange a disputed line, is attempting to use this disputed line as a pretense for territorial acquisition,' no matter what may be the character of the Administration, whether Democratic or Republican, I would have stood by that declaration as an American Senator, because there is where we get our information upon these subjects, and not from our own judgment. We must stand by what the Department says upon these great questions when the facts are ascertained by it. The President says that he needs assistance to make this determination. We are going to give it to him. Nobody doubts that. The only question is, how shall we give it to him? I am as firm a believer in the Monroe doctrine as any man who lives. I am as firm a believer as any one in the maintenance of the honor of the American people, and do not believe it can be maintained if we abandon the Monroe doctrine.
"Mr. President, there is no haste in this matter. The dispute is one of long standing. Great Britain is not now taking any extraordinary steps with reference to the control of the territory in dispute. They took, it is said, five months to answer our Secretary's letter of July 20. Mr. President, the time was not excessive. It is not unreasonable in diplomatic affairs that there should be months taken in replying to questions of so much importance. We may properly take months, if we choose, to consider it before we plant ourselves upon what we say are the facts in this case. I repeat, so far as the American people are concerned, the Monroe doctrine is not in dispute, is not in doubt, whatever may be the doubt about the facts in this case. If the facts are not ascertained, we must, before we proceed further, ascertain them.
"This is a very important question. It is not a question of party politics. It is not a question that any political party ought to take advantage of to get votes. The political party that attempts to make capital out of this question will find that it is a loser in the end. The American people will not be trifled with on a

question of this kind. If the other side of the Chamber, or the Administration, or anybody, attempts to make capital out of it they will find that they will lose in the end, as we should lose on our side if we should be foolish enough, as I know we are not, to attempt to make capital out of it in any way. . . . This question is of so much importance that I do not care myself if the bill goes to the Committee on Foreign Relations and lies there a month. You will not impress the world with our solidarity and solidity on this question by any haste in this body. Let this proceeding be a dignified proceeding. Let the bill go to the committee. Let the committee take their time on it. Let them return it here and say what is the best way by which we can strengthen the hands of the President of the United States in his efforts to maintain this American doctrine.
"Mr. President, I am not one of those who want war. I do not believe in war. I believe in this case Great Britain made a great mistake when she said she would not arbitrate, and I have faith enough in the love of justice and right that pervades the people of Great Britain to believe that on second sober thought they will submit this question to arbitration, as many of their representative men have declared they are willing to submit all questions of this character. . . . Let this bill go to the committee. Let it be considered. If the committee wants a week, ten days, or two weeks, or a month, let the committee take it. Nothing will be lost. Great Britain will not misunderstand our attitude. She does not misunderstand it now. She knows just as well how we feel upon these subjects as she will when we pass this bill. She has had it dinned in her ears again and again from nearly every Secretary of State that we were not willing to abandon the Monroe doctrine, nor view with indifference the improper interference of any European power with any existing American Government, whether such interference is a violation of the Monroe doctrine or not."—*Congressional Record, Dec. 19, 1895, p. 246.*
Senator Call made a similar appeal, saying: "As to all this talk about war, in my opinion there is no possibility of war. There can be, and ought to be, no possibility of it. The enlightened sentiment of the nations of the world would forbid that there should be a war between this country and England upon this question. Nevertheless, it would be the duty of this country to maintain by force of arms the proposition that there shall be no forcible establishment of European institutions and European Governments over any portion of this territory. Who can entertain the idea that war can be made with Great Britain, and that the people of the British Empire will permit that Government to engage in war upon a question of boundaries which is not sustained by the facts of the case, but a mere aggression, and that the peace of mankind shall be disturbed by it. . . .
"I agree with the Senator from Ohio [Mr. Sherman] that there is no necessity for haste in this action and that it comports better with the dignity of Congress for the Senate of the United States and the House of Representatives to declare that this Government will firmly maintain, as a definite proposition, that Venezuela shall not be forced to cede any portion of her territory to Great Britain or to recognize a boundary

line which is not based upon the facts of history and upon clear and ascertained proof. It seems to me, Mr. President, that all this discussion about war should not have place here, but that we should make a bold and independent and firm declaration as to the proper policy of this Government, and vote the President of the United States the money necessary, in his judgment, to carry out that declaration so far as obtaining information which may be desired. . . .

"The possibility that war between these two nations will be the result of our defending the right of Venezuela to the integrity of her territory against its forced appropriation by England should not be entertained. These two nations, the United States and Great Britain, are the main pillars of the civilization of the world, neither can afford to demand of the other anything that is wrong or any injustice to the other. Great Britain recognizes the supremacy of the United States in the Western Hemisphere, and it is sufficient for them to know that we will maintain this with all the power of the Republic, and that this is not an idle menace.

"This is my view of the situation. The President has done his duty. He has recommended that the traditional policy of this country to protect all people who establish governments of their choice against forcible intervention by European powers, under whatever pretense, whether by claiming fictitious boundaries and enforcing their claim, or by any other means, and that we will be the judge of this, but that we are ready to submit the facts to the judgment of a fair arbitration. It is sufficient for us to sustain this declaration and for us to provide the means of obtaining the information necessary for an intelligent judgment on the question. It will suffice for the able statesman who represents the Government of Great Britain to know and to inform his Government that the people of the United States are united in the determination to maintain and defend this policy with all their power, and a peaceable settlement of the question will be made."—*Congressional Record, Dec.* 20, 1895, p. 264.

The Senate was persuaded to refer the House Bill to its Committee on Foreign Relations, but the Committee reported it on the following day (December 20), and it was passed without division.

A. D. 1895-1896 (December—January).— The feeling in England and America over the Venezuela boundary dispute.—Happily President Cleveland's Message did not provoke in England the angry and combative temper that is commonly roused by a demand from one nation upon another, made in any peremptory tone. The feeling produced there seemed to have in it more of surprise and regret than of wrath, revealing very plainly that friendliness had been growing of late, much warmer in English sentiment toward the American Republic than in American sentiment toward England. Within the past thirty years there had been what in France would be called a "rapprochement" in feeling going on between the two peoples; but the rate of approach had been greater on one side than on the other, and neither had understood the fact until it was brought home to them by this incident. There seems to be no doubt that the English people were astonished and shocked by the sudden prospect of a serious

quarrel with the United States, and that Americans were generally surprised and moved by the discovery of that state of feeling in the English mind. The first response in the United States to the President's message came noisily from the more thoughtless part of the people, and seemed to show that the whole nation was fairly eager for war with its "kin beyond sea." But that was a short-lived demonstration. The voices that really speak for the country soon made themselves heard in a different tone,—anxious to avert war,—critical of the construction that had been given to the Monroe doctrine by President Cleveland and his Secretary of State,—earnestly responsive to the pacific temper of the English public,—and yet firm in upholding the essential justice of the ground on which their government had addressed itself to that of Great Britain. The feeling in the two countries, respectively, at the beginning of 1896, appears to have been described very accurately by two representative writers in the "North American Review" of February in that year. One was Mr. James Bryce, the well-known English student of American institutions—author of "The American Commonwealth"—who wrote:

"Those Englishmen who have travelled in America have of course been aware of the mischief your school-books do in teaching young people to regard the English as enemies because there was war in the days of George III. Such Englishmen knew that as Britain is almost the only great power with which the United States has had diplomatic controversies, national feeling has sometimes been led to regard her as an adversary, and displays of national feeling often took the form of defiance. Even such travellers, however, were not prepared for the language of the President and its reception in many quarters, while as to Englishmen generally, they could scarcely credit their eyes and ears. 'Why,' they said, 'should we be regarded as enemies by our own kinsfolk? No territorial dispute is pending between us and them, like those we have or have lately had with France and Russia. No explosions of Jingoism have ever been directed against them, like those which Lord Beaconsfield evoked against Russia some twenty years ago. There is very little of that commercial, and none of that colonial, rivalry which we have with France and Germany, for the Americans are still chiefly occupied in developing their internal resources, and have ample occasion for their energy and their capital in doing so. Still less is there that incompatibility of character and temper which sometimes sets us wrong with Frenchmen, or Russians, or even Germans, for we and the Americans come of the same stock, speak the same language, read the same books, think upon similar lines, are connected by a thousand ties of family and friendship. No two nations could be better fitted to understand one another's ideas and institutions. English travellers and writers used no doubt formerly to assume airs of supercilious condescension which must have been offensive to Americans. But those airs were dropped twenty or thirty years ago, and the travellers who return now return full of gratitude for the kindness they have received and full of admiration for the marvellous progress they have witnessed. We know all about the Irish faction; but the Irish faction do not account for this. So we quite understand that resentment was caused in the North and West of America by the attitude of our wealthy class during the Civil War. But that attitude was not the attitude of the British nation. ... Our press, whose tone often exasperates Continental nations, is almost uniformly respectful and friendly to America. What can we have done to provoke in the United States feelings so unlike those which we ourselves cherish?'

"In thus summing up what one has been hearing on all sides in Britain during the last fortnight, I am not exaggerating either the amazement or the regret with which the news of a threatened breach between the two countries was received. The average Englishman 'likes America far better than any foreign nation; he admires the 'go,' as he calls it, of your people, and is soon at home among you. In fact, he does not regard you as a foreign nation, as any one will agree who has noticed how different has been the reception given on all public occasions to your last four envoys, Messrs. Welsh, Lowell, Phelps, and Lincoln (as well as your present ambassador) from that accorded to the ambassadors of any other power. The educated and thoughtful Englishman has looked upon your Republic as the champion of freedom and peace, has held you to be our natural ally, and has even indulged the hope of a permanent alliance with you, under which the citizens of each country should have the rights of citizenship in the other and be aided by the consuls and protected by the fleets of the other all over the world. The sentiments which the news from America evoked were, therefore, common to all classes in England. ... Passion has not yet been aroused, and will not be, except by the language of menace."—J. Bryce, *British Feeling on the Venezuelan Question* (*North American Review*, Feb., 1896).

The writer who described American feeling, or opinion, in the same magazine, was Mr. Andrew Carnegie, who said: "In the United States, East, West, North and South, from which divergent voices were at first heard, there is but one voice now. Public opinion has crystallized into one word—arbitration. In support of that mode of settlement we now know the nation is unanimous. The proofs of this should not fail to carry conviction into the hearts of Britons. The one representative and influential body in the United States which is most closely allied with Britain not only by the ties of trade, but by the friendships which these ties have created, is the Chamber of Commerce of New York. If that body were polled by ballot, probably a greater proportion of its members than of any other body of American citizens would register themselves as friendly to England. So far did the feeling extend in this body, that a movement was on foot to call a meeting to dissent from the President's Message. Fortunately, wiser counsels prevailed, and time was given for an examination of the question, and for members to make up their minds upon the facts. The result was that at the crowded meeting subsequently held, there was passed a resolution, with only one dissenting voice, in favor of a commission for arbitration. In the whole proceedings there was only one sentiment present in the minds of those assembled : 'this is a question for arbitration.' ...

"Every nation has its 'Red Rag,' some nations have more than one, but what the 'Right of Asylum' is to Great Britain, the Monroe Doctrine is to the United States. Each lies very deep in the national heart. Few statesmen of Great Britain do not share the opinion of Lord Salisbury, which he has not feared to express, that the 'Right of Asylum' is abused and should be restricted, but there has not arisen one in Britain sufficiently powerful to deal with it. The United States never had, and has not now, a statesman who could restrain the American people from an outburst of passion and the extreme consequences that national passion is liable to bring, if any European power undertook to extend its territory upon this continent, or to decide in case of dispute just where the boundary of present possessions stand. Such differences must be arbitrated. ...

"In his speech at Manchester Mr. Balfour said he 'trusted and believed the day would come when better statesmen in authority, and more fortunate than even Monroe, would assert a doctrine between the English-speaking peoples under which war would be impossible.' That day has not to come, it has arrived. The British Government has had for years in its archives an invitation from the United States to enter into a treaty of arbitration which realizes this hope, and Mr. Balfour is one of those who, from their great position, seem most responsible for the rejection of the end he so ardently longs for. It is time that the people of Great Britain understood that if war be still possible between the two countries, it is not the fault of the Republic but of their own country, not of President Cleveland and Secretary of State Olney, but of Prime Minister Salisbury, and the leader of the House of Commons, Mr. Balfour, who do not accept the offered treaty which would banish war forever between the two nations of our race. This invitation was sent by the same President Cleveland, who is now denounced as favoring war. ... It was my office to introduce to Mr. Cleveland, then President of the United States, as he is now, the delegation from the British Parliament urging arbitration. In the conferences I had with him previous to his receiving the deputation, I found him as strong a supporter of that policy as I ever met. I do not wonder at his outburst, knowing how deeply this man feels upon that question; it is to him so precious, it constitutes so great an advance over arbitrament by war that—even if we have to fight, that any nation rejecting it may suffer—I believe he feels that it would be our duty to do so, believing that the nation which rejects arbitration in a boundary dispute deserves the execration of mankind." — A. Carnegie, *The Venezuelan Question* (*North American Review*, Feb., 1896).

A. D. 1895-1896 (December—February).— The gold reserve in the Treasury again imperilled.—Refusal of any measures of relief by the Senate.—In his annual Message to Congress, December 2d, 1895, President Cleveland described at length the stress of circumstances under which in the previous February, the Secretary of the Treasury had contracted with certain bankers and financiers to replenish and protect the reserve of gold in the Treasury for redemption of United States notes (see above), and added : "The performance of 'this contract not only restored the reserve, but checked for a time the withdrawals of gold and brought on a period of restored confidence and such peace and quiet in business circles as were of the greatest possible value to every interest that affects our people. I have never had the slightest misgiving concerning the wisdom or propriety of this arrangement, and am quite willing to answer for my full share of responsibility for its promotion. I believe it averted a disaster the imminence of which was, fortunately, not at the time generally understood by our people. Though the contract mentioned stayed for a time the tide of gold withdrawal, its good results could not be permanent. Recent withdrawals have reduced the reserve from $107,571,230 on the 8th day of July, 1895, to $79,333,966. How long it will remain large enough to render its increase unnecessary is only matter of conjecture, though quite large withdrawals for shipment in the immediate future are predicted in well-informed quarters. About $16,000,000 has been withdrawn during the month of November. The foregoing statement of events and conditions develops the fact that after increasing our interest-bearing bonded indebtedness more than $162,000,000 to save our gold reserve we are nearly where we started, having now in such reserve $79,333,966 as against $65,438,377 in February, 1894, when the first bonds were issued.

" Though the amount of gold drawn from the Treasury appears to be very large as gathered from the facts and figures herein presented, it actually was much larger, considerable sums having been acquired by the Treasury within the several periods stated without the issue of bonds. On the 28th of January, 1895, it was reported by the Secretary of the Treasury that more than $172,000,000 of gold had been withdrawn for hoarding or shipment during the year preceding. He now reports that from January 1, 1879, to July 14, 1890, a period of more than eleven years, only a little over $28,000,000 was withdrawn, and that between July 14, 1890, the date of the passage of the law for an increased purchase of silver, and the 1st day of December, 1895, or within less than five and a half years, there was withdrawn nearly $375,000,000, making a total of more than $403,000,000 drawn from the Treasury in gold since January 1, 1879, the date fixed in 1875 for the retirement of the United States notes.

" Nearly $327,000,000 of the gold thus withdrawn has been paid out, on these United States notes, and yet every one of the $346,000,000 is still uncanceled and ready to do service in future gold depletions. More than $76,000,000 in gold has since their creation in 1890 been paid out from the Treasury upon the notes given on the purchase of silver by the Government, and yet the whole, amounting to $155,000,000, except a little more than $16,000,000 which has been retired by exchanges for silver at the request of the holders, remains outstanding and prepared to join their older and more experienced allies in future raids upon the Treasury's gold reserve. In other words, the Government has paid in gold more than nine-tenths of its United States notes and still owes them all. It has paid in gold about one-half of its notes given for silver purchases without extinguishing by such payment one dollar of these notes.

" When, added to all this, we are reminded that to carry on this astounding financial scheme the Government has incurred a bonded indebted-

ness of $95,500,000 in establishing a gold reserve, and of $162,315,400 in efforts to maintain it; that the annual interest charge on such bonded indebtedness is more than $11,000,000; that a continuance of our present course may result in further bond issues, and that we have suffered or are threatened with all this for the sake of supplying gold for foreign shipment or facilitating its hoarding at home, a situation is exhibited which certainly ought to arrest attention and provoke immediate legislative relief.

" I am convinced the only thorough and practicable remedy for our troubles is found in the retirement and cancellation of our United States notes, commonly called greenbacks, and the outstanding Treasury notes issued by the Government in payment of silver purchases under the act of 1890. I believe this could be quite readily accomplished by the exchange of these notes for United States bonds, of small as well as large denominations, bearing a low rate of interest. They should be long-term bonds, thus increasing their desirability as investments, and because their payment could be well postponed to a period far removed from present financial burdens and perplexities, when with increased prosperity and resources they would be more easily met. . . .

" Whatever is attempted should be entered upon fully appreciating the fact that by careless easy descent we have reached a dangerous depth, and that our ascent will not be accomplished without laborious toil and struggle. We shall be wise if we realize that we are financially ill and that our restoration to health may require heroic treatment and unpleasant remedies.

" In the present stage of our difficulty it is not easy to understand how the amount of our revenue receipts directly affects it. The important question is not the quantity of money received in revenue payments, but the kind of money we maintain and our ability to continue in sound financial condition. We are considering the Government's holdings of gold as related to the soundness of our money and as affecting our national credit and monetary strength. If our gold reserve had never been impaired ; if no bonds had ever been issued to replenish it ; if there had been no fear and timidity concerning our ability to continue gold payments; if any part of our revenues were now paid in gold, and if we could look to our gold receipts as a means of maintaining a safe reserve, the amount of our revenues would be an influential factor in the problem. But unfortunately all the circumstances that might lend weight to this consideration are entirely lacking. In our present predicament no gold is received by the Government in payment of revenue charges, nor would there be if the revenues were increased. The receipts of the Treasury, when not in silver certificates, consist of United States notes and Treasury notes issued for silver purchases. These forms of money are only useful to the Government in paying its current ordinary expenses, and its quantity in Government possession does not in the least contribute toward giving us that kind of safe financial standing or condition which is built on gold alone.

" If it is said that these notes if held by the Government can be used to obtain gold for our reserve, the answer is easy. The people draw gold from the Treasury on demand upon United

States notes and Treasury notes, but the proposition that the Treasury can on demand draw gold from the people upon them would be regarded in these days with wonder and amusement; and even if this could be done there is nothing to prevent those thus parting with their gold from regaining it the next day or the next hour by the presentation of the notes they received in exchange for it. The Secretary of the Treasury might use such notes taken from a surplus revenue to buy gold in the market. Of course he could not do this without paying a premium. Private holders of gold, unlike the Government, having no parity to maintain, would not be restrained from making the best bargain possible when they furnished gold to the Treasury; but the moment the Secretary of the Treasury bought gold on any terms above par he would establish a general and universal premium upon it, thus breaking down the parity between gold and silver, which the Government is pledged to maintain, and opening the way to new and serious complications. In the meantime the premium would not remain stationary, and the absurd spectacle might be presented of a dealer selling gold to the Government and with United States notes or Treasury notes in his hand immediately clamoring for its return and a resale at a higher premium.

"It may be claimed that a large revenue and redundant receipts might favorably affect the situation under discussion by affording an opportunity of retaining these notes in the Treasury when received, and thus preventing their presentation for gold. Such retention to be useful ought to be at least measurably permanent; and this is precisely what is prohibited, so far as United States notes are concerned, by the law of 1878, forbidding their further retirement. That statute in so many words provides, that these notes when received into the Treasury and belonging to the United States shall be ' paid out again and kept in circulation.'"—*United States, Message and Documents (Abridgment),* 1895-6, p. 27.

"The difficulty which had been anticipated in keeping gold in the treasury became acute as a result of the president's Venezuelan message of December 17. The ' war scare' which was caused by that document was attended by a panic on the London Exchange, which communicated itself to the Continental exchanges and produced at once serious consequences in New York. Prices fell heavily, some failures were reported, and the withdrawal of gold from the treasury assumed great proportions. On the 20th the reserve had gone down to $69,650,000, ten millions less than three weeks earlier, with future large reductions obviously near at hand. The president accordingly on that day sent to Congress a special message, stating the situation, alluding to the effect of his recently announced foreign policy, and declaring that the result conveyed a ' warning that even the patriotic sentiment of our people is not an adequate substitute for a sound financial policy.' He asked Congress to postpone its holiday recess until something had been done to reassure the apprehensive among the people, but declared that in any case he should use every means in the power of the executive to maintain the country's credit. The suggestion was acted upon. . . .

"On December 26 two bills were introduced

in the House of Representatives by Chairman Dingley of the ways and means committee. Adopting the view maintained by the Republicans, that the chief cause of the difficulty in maintaining the gold reserve was the deficiency in the revenue, he proposed first a bill ' to temporarily increase the revenues.' This provided that until August 1, 1898, the customs duties on most varieties of wool and woolen goods and on lumber, should stand at 60 per cent of those imposed by the McKinley Act of 1890, and that the duties in all the other schedules of the tariff, except sugar, should, with slight exceptions, be increased by 15 per cent over those of the existing law. This bill passed the House on the 27th by a party vote of 205 to 81. On the following day the second bill, ' to maintain and protect the coin redemption fund,' was passed by 170 to 136,—47 Republicans in the minority. This bill authorized the secretary of the treasury to procure coin for redeeming legal-tenders by the sale of three-per-cent five-year bonds, and to provide for temporary deficiencies by the issue of three-year three-per-cent certificates of indebtedness in small denominations. The administration was as little satisfied with this bill as with that changing the tariff, and proceeded with the bond issue. . . .

"The failure of the bills in the Senate was foreseen, but the precise form in which it was manifested excited some surprise. On February 1, [1896], the bond bill was transformed by the adoption of a substitute providing for the free coinage of silver, and this was passed by a vote of 42 to 35. On the 14th the House refused, by 215 to 90, to concur in the Senate's amendment, and the whole subject was dropped. Meanwhile the Senate finance committee had reported a free-coinage substitute for the House tariff bill also. But after this further exhibition of their strength the silver senators refused to go further, and on February 25 joined with the Democrats in rejecting, by 33 to 22, a motion to take up the bill for consideration. This vote was recognized as finally disposing of the measure."—*Political Science Quarterly, June,* 1896.

A. D. 1895-1896 (December—December).— Plans for coast defense.—In his annual report to the President, 1895, the Secretary of War wrote as follows of pending plans for coast defense, and of the progress of work upon them: "In your annual message transmitted to Congress in December, 1886, attention was directed to the urgent necessity for seacoast defense in these words: ' The defenseless condition of our seacoast and lake frontier is perfectly palpable; the examinations made must convince us all that certain of our cities should be fortified and that work on the most important of these fortifications should be commenced at once.' . . . Since that time the condition of these defenses has been under grave consideration by the people and by this Department. Its inadequacy and impotency have been so evident that the intelligence of the country long since ceased to discuss that humiliating phase of the subject, but has addressed itself to the more practical undertaking of urging more rapid progress in the execution of the plan of defense devised by the Endicott Board in 1886, with subsequent slight modifications. That plan contemplated a system of fortifications at 27 ports (to which Puget Sound was subsequently added), requiring 677 guns and 824 mortars of modern construction, at a cost of $97,782,800, excluding $28,595,000 for floating batteries. By an immediate appropriation at that time of $21,500,000 and an annual appropriation of $9,000,000 thereafter, as then recommended, the system of land defenses could have been completed in 1895.

"The original plan contemplated an expenditure of $97,782,800 by the end of the present year. The actual expenditures and appropriations for armament and emplacements have, however, been but $10,631,000. The first appropriation for guns was made only seven years ago and the first appropriation for emplacements was made only five years ago. The average annual appropriations for these two objects has been less than $1,500,000. The work has therefore been conducted at about one-seventh the rate proposed. If future appropriations for the manufacture of guns, mortars, and carriages be no larger than the average authorized for the purpose since 1888, it will require twenty-two years more to supply the armament of the eighteen important ports for which complete projects are approved. If the appropriations for the engineer work are to continue at the rate of the annual appropriations since 1890, it will require seventy years to complete the emplacements and platforms for this armament for the ports referred to."—*Report of the Secretary of War*, 1895, *p. 19 (54th Cong., 1st Sess., House Doc. v. 1).*

In his Message of the following year, the subject was touched upon by the President, as follows: "During the past year rapid progress has been made toward the completion of the scheme adopted for the erection and armament of fortifications along our seacoast, while equal progress has been made in providing the material for submarine defense in connection with these works. . . . We shall soon have complete about one-fifth of the comprehensive system, the first step in which was noted in my message to the Congress of December 4, 1893. When it is understood that a masonry emplacement not only furnishes a platform for the heavy modern high-power gun, but also in every particular serves the purpose and takes the place of the fort of former days, the importance of the work accomplished is better comprehended. In the hope that the work will be prosecuted with no less vigor in the future, the Secretary of War has submitted an estimate by which, if allowed, there will be provided and either built or building by the end of the next fiscal year such additional guns, mortars, gun carriages, and emplacements, as will represent not far from one-third of the total work to be done under the plan adopted for our coast defenses—thus affording a prospect that the entire work will be substantially completed within six years. In less time than that, however, we shall have attained a marked degree of security. The experience and results of the past year demonstrate that with a continuation of present careful methods the cost of the remaining work will be much less than the original estimate. We should always keep in mind that of all forms of military preparation coast defense alone is essentially pacific in its nature."—*Message of the President*, 1896 (*54th Cong., 2d Sess., House Doc., v. 1).*

A. D. 1896 (January).—Admission of Utah to the Union. See (in this vol.) UTAH: A. D. 1895-1896.

A. D. 1896 (January—February).—Appoint-

ment of commission to investigate the Venezuela boundary.—Re-opening of discussion with Great Britain on the arbitration of the dispute. See (in this vol.) VENEZUELA : A. D. 1896-1899.

A. D. 1896 (February).—New treaty with Great Britain for arbitration of Bering Sea claims. See (in this vol.) BERING SEA QUESTIONS.

A. D. 1896 (February).—Weyler made Governor of Cuba.—His Concentration Order. See (in this vol.) CUBA : A. D. 1896-1897.

A. D. 1896 (March).—Removal of Confederate disabilities.—The following enactment of Congress, which may, with propriety, be styled an "Act of Oblivion," was approved by the President on the 31st of March, 1896: "That section twelve hundred and eighteen of the Revised Statutes of the United States, as amended by chapter forty-six of the laws of 1884, which section is as follows : 'No person who held a commission in the Army or Navy of the United States at the beginning of the late rebellion, and afterwards served in any capacity in the military, naval, or civil service of the so-called Confederate States, or of either of the States in insurrection during the late rebellion, shall be appointed to any position in the Army or Navy of the United States,' be, and the same is hereby, repealed."—*United States of Am., Statutes at Large, v. 29, p. 84.*

A. D. 1896 (May).—Extension of civil service rules by President Cleveland. See (in this vol.) CIVIL SERVICE REFORM : A. D. 1893-1896.

A. D. 1896 (June—November.—The Presidential election.—The silver question at issue.—Party Platforms and Nominations.—A national conference held at Washington, in March, 1895, may be looked upon as the beginning of a widely and powerfully organized movement to force the demand for a free and unlimited coinage of silver, on equal terms, as legal tender money, with gold, into the front of the issues of the presidential canvass of 1896. The agitation then projected was carried on with extraordinary ardor and skill and had astonishing success. It was helped by the general depression of business in the country, and especially by the long continued ruling of low prices for the produce of the farms,—for all of which effects the gold standard of values was held to be the one relentless cause. In both political parties the free silver propaganda was pushed with startling effect, and there seemed to be doubt, for a time. whether the controlling politicians in either would take an opposing stand. Southern influences proved decisive of the result in the Democratic party ; eastern influences in that of the Republicans. The ranks of the former were swept rapidly into the movement for free silver, and the party chiefs of the latter were driven to a conflict with it, not wholly by convictions or will of their own. During the spring and early summer of 1896, the Democratic Party in State after State became committed on the question. by declarations for the unlimited free coinage of silver, at the ratio of 16 to 1 ; until there was tolerable certainty, some weeks before the meeting of the national convention, that its nominee for President must be one who represented that demand. How positively the Republican Party would champion the gold monetary standard was somewhat less assured, though its stand on that side had been taken in a general way.

Republican Platform and Nominations.— The Republican national convention was held at St. Louis, on the 16th, 17th and 18th of June. The "platform" reported by the committee on resolutions was adopted without amendment on the last named date. Its declarations were as follows :

"The Republicans of the United States, assembled by their representatives in National Convention, appealing for the popular and historical justification of their claims to the matchless achievements of the thirty years of Republican rule, earnestly and confidently address themselves to the awakened intelligence, experience, and conscience of their countrymen in the following declaration of facts and principles :

"For the first time since the civil war the American people have witnessed the calamitous consequences of full and unrestricted Democratic control of the Government. It has been a record of unparalleled incapacity, dishonor, and disaster. In administrative management it has ruthlessly sacrificed indispensable revenue, entailed an unceasing deficit, eked out ordinary current expenses with borrowed money, piled up the public debt by $262,000,000 in time of peace, forced an adverse balance of trade, kept a perpetual menace hanging over the redemption fund, pawned American credit to alien syndicates, and reversed all the measures and results of successful Republican rule.

"In the broad effect of its policy it has precipitated panic, blighted industry and trade with prolonged depression, closed factories, reduced work and wages, halted enterprise, and crippled American production while stimulating foreign production for the American market. Every consideration of public safety and individual interest demands that the Government shall be rescued from the hands of those who have shown themselves incapable to conduct it without disaster at home and dishonor abroad, and shall be restored to the party which for thirty years administered it with unequalled success and prosperity, and in this connection we heartily endorse the wisdom, patriotism, and the success of the administration of President Harrison.

"We renew and emphasize our allegiance to the policy of protection as the bulwark of American industrial independence and the foundation of American development and prosperity. This true American policy taxes foreign products and encourages home industry ; it puts the burden of revenue on foreign goods ; it secures the American market for the American producer ; it upholds the American standard of wages for the American workingman ; it puts the factory by the side of the farm, and makes the American farmer less dependent on foreign demand and price ; it diffuses general thrift, and founds the strength of all on the strength of each. In its reasonable application it is just, fair, and impartial ; equally opposed to foreign control and domestic monopoly, to sectional discrimination, and individual favoritism.

"We denounce the present Democratic tariff as sectional, injurious to the public credit, and destructive to business enterprise. We demand such an equitable tariff on foreign imports which come into competition with American products as will not only furnish adequate revenue for the necessary expenses of the Government, but will protect American labor from degradation to the wage level of other lands. We are not pledged to any particular schedules. The question of rates is a practical question, to be governed by the conditions of the time and of production ; the ruling and uncompromising principle is the protection and development of American labor and industry. The country demands a right settlement, and then it wants rest.

"We believe the repeal of the reciprocity arrangements negotiated by the last Republican administration [see, in vol. 5, TARIFF LEGISLATION (UNITED STATES): A. D. 1890, and 1894] was a national calamity, and we demand their renewal and extension on such terms as will equalize our trade with other nations, remove the restrictions which now obstruct the sale of American products in the ports of other countries, and secure enlarged markets for the products of our farms, forests, and factories.

"Protection and reciprocity are twin measures of Republican policy and go hand in hand. Democratic rule has recklessly struck down both, and both must be re-established. Protection for what we produce ; free admission for the necessaries of life which we do not produce ; reciprocity agreements of mutual interests which again open markets for us in return for our open markets to others. Protection builds up domestic industry and trade and secures our own market for ourselves ; reciprocity builds up foreign trade and finds an outlet for our surplus. We condemn the present administration for not keeping faith with the sugar producers of this country. The Republican party favors such protection as will lead to the production on American soil of all the sugar which the American people use, and for which they pay other countries more than $100,000,000 annually. To all our products—to those of the mine and the fields as well as to those of the shop and the factory—to hemp, to wool, the product of the great industry of sheep husbandry, as well as to the finished woollens of the mill—we promise the most ample protection.

"We favor restoring the early American policy of discriminating duties for the upbuilding of our merchant marine and the protection of our shipping in the foreign carrying trade, so that American ships—the product of American labor, employed in American shipyards, sailing under the Stars and Stripes, and manned, officered, and owned by Americans—may regain the carrying of our foreign commerce.

"The Republican party is unreservedly for sound money. It caused the enactment of the law providing for the resumption of specie payments in 1879 ; since then every dollar has been as good as gold. We are unalterably opposed to every measure calculated to debase our currency or impair the credit of our country. We are, therefore, opposed to the free coinage of silver except by international agreement with the leading commercial nations of the world, which we pledge ourselves to promote, and until such agreement can be obtained the existing gold standard must be preserved. All our silver and paper currency must be maintained at parity with gold, and we favor all measures designed to maintain inviolably the obligations of the United States and all our money, whether coin or paper, at the present standard, the standard of the most enlightened nations of the earth.

"The veterans of the Union Army deserve and should receive fair treatment and generous recognition. Whenever practicable, they should be given the preference in the matter of employment, and they are entitled to the enactment of such laws as are best calculated to secure the fulfillment of the pledges made to them in the dark days of the country's peril. We denounce the practice in the Pension Bureau, so recklessly and unjustly carried on by the present administration, of reducing pensions and arbitrarily dropping names from the rolls as deserving the severest condemnation of the American people.

"Our foreign policy should be at all times firm, vigorous, and dignified, and all our interests in the Western Hemisphere carefully watched and guarded. The Hawaiian Islands should be controlled by the United States, and no foreign power should be permitted to interfere with them; the Nicaraguan Canal should be built, owned, and operated by the United States; and by the purchase of the Danish Islands we should secure a proper and much needed naval station in the West Indies.

"The massacres in Armenia have aroused the deep sympathy and just indignation of the American people, and we believe that the United States should exercise all the influence it can properly exert to bring these atrocities to an end. In Turkey American residents have been exposed to the gravest dangers and American property destroyed. There and everywhere American citizens and American property must be absolutely protected at all hazards and at any cost.

"We reassert the Monroe doctrine in its full extent, and we reaffirm the right of the United States to give the doctrine effect by responding to the appeal of any American State for friendly intervention in case of European encroachment. We have not interfered with and shall not interfere with the existing possessions of any European power in this hemisphere, but those possessions must not on any pretext be extended. We hopefully look forward to the eventual withdrawal of European powers from this hemisphere and to the ultimate union of all the English-speaking parts of the continent by the free consent of its inhabitants.

"From the hour of achieving their own independence the people of the United States have regarded with sympathy the struggles of other American people to free themselves from European domination. We watch with deep and abiding interest the heroic battle of the Cuban patriots against cruelty and oppression, and our best hopes go out for the full success of their determined contest for liberty. The Government of Spain having lost control of. Cuba, and being unable to protect the property or lives of resident American citizens, or to comply with its treaty obligations, we believe that the Government of the United States should actively use its influence and good offices to restore peace and give independence to the island.

"The peace and security of the Republic and the maintenance of its rightful influence among the nations of the earth demand a naval power commensurate with its position and responsibility. We therefore favor the continued enlargement of the navy and a complete system of harbor and seacoast defenses.

"For the protection of the quality of our American citizenship and of the wages of our workingmen against the fatal competition of low-priced labor, we demand that the immigration laws be thoroughly enforced and so extended as to exclude from entrance to the United States those who can neither read nor write.

"The civil-service law was placed on the statute book by the Republican party, which has always sustained it, and we renew our repeated declarations that it shall be thoroughly and honestly enforced and extended wherever practicable.

"We demand that every citizen of the United States shall be allowed to cast one free and unrestricted ballot, and that such ballot shall be counted and returned as cast.

"We proclaim our unqualified condemnation of the uncivilized and barbarous practice, well known as lynching or killing of human beings suspected or charged with crime, without process of law. We favor the creation of a National board of arbitration to settle and adjust differences which may arise between employers and employed engaged in interstate commerce.

"We believe in an immediate return to the free-homestead policy of the Republican party, and urge the passage by Congress of a satisfactory free-homestead measure such as has already passed the House and is now pending in the Senate.

"We favor the admission of the remaining Territories at the earliest practicable date, having due regard to the interests of the people of the Territories and of the United States. All the Federal officers appointed for the Territories should be selected from bona fide residents thereof, and the right of self-government should be accorded as far as practicable.

"We believe the citizens of Alaska should have representation in the Congress of the United States, to the end that needful legislation may be intelligently enacted.

"We sympathize with all wise and legitimate efforts to lessen and prevent the evils of intemperance and promote morality.

"The Republican party is mindful of the rights and interests of women. Protection of American industries includes equal opportunities, equal pay for equal work, and protection to the home. We favor the admission of women to wider spheres of usefulness, and welcome their co-operation in rescuing the country from Democratic and Populist mismanagement and misrule.

"Such are the principles and policies of the Republican party. By these principles we will abide and these policies we will put into execution. We ask for them the considerate judgment of the American people. Confident alike in the history of our great party and in the justice of our cause, we present our platform and our candidates in the full assurance that the election will bring victory to the Republican party and prosperity to the people of the United States."

Before the adoption of this platform, a motion to amend its currency "plank," by substituting a declaration in favor of "the use of both gold and silver as equal standard money," was laid on the table by a vote of 818½ to 105½. A protest from delegates representing Colorado, Idaho, Nevada, Utah, Montana and South Dakota was then read, and twenty-two withdrew from the convention, as a sign of secession from the party. Immediately following the adoption of the platform, the Hon. William McKinley, ex-Governor of Ohio, and of fame in his connection with the tariff act of 1890, was nominated on the first ballot for President of the United States, by 661½ votes against 240½ divided among several opposing candidates, and the nomination was then made unanimous. For Vice President, the Hon. Garret A. Hobart, of New Jersey, was named, and similarly by the first voting.

Democratic Platform and Nominations.— The Democratic national convention was held in Chicago, July 7–11. The delegates who came to it from the southern States, and from most of the States west of Ohio, were arrayed with a close approach to solid ranks for free silver; while those from New England and the Middle States opposed them in a phalanx almost equally firm. The "Gold Democrats" or "Sound Money Democrats," as the latter were called, ably led by ex-Governor Hill, of New York, fought hard to the end, but without avail. The financial resolution they strove to place in the platform was the following:

"We declare our belief that the experiment on the part of the United States alone of free-silver coinage, and a change in the existing standard of value independently of the action of other great nations, would not only imperil our finances, but would retard or entirely prevent the establishment of international bimetallism, to which the efforts of the government should be steadily directed. It would place this country at once upon a silver basis, impair contracts, disturb business, diminish the purchasing power of the wages of labor, and inflict irreparable evils upon our nation's commerce and industry.

"Until international co-operation among leading nations for the coinage of silver can be secured, we favor the rigid maintenance of the existing gold standard as essential to the preservation of our national credit, the redemption of our public pledges, and the keeping inviolate of our country's honor. We insist that all our paper currency shall be kept at a parity with gold. The democratic party is the party of hard money, and is opposed to legal-tender paper money as a part of our permanent financial system; and we therefore favor the gradual retirement and cancellation of all United States notes and treasury notes, under such legislative provisions as will prevent undue contraction. We demand that the national credit shall be resolutely maintained at all times and under all circumstances."

This resolution was rejected by 626 votes against 303. Another resolution from the same source, commending "the honesty, economy, courage and fidelity" of the "democratic national administration" of President Cleveland, was voted down by 564 to 357. Resolutions to protect existing contracts against a change of monetary standard, and to provide for a suspension of silver free coinage, at the ratio of 16 to 1, after trial for one year, if it failed to maintain parity between silver and gold, were similarly voted down. The declarations then adopted, for the "platform" of the party, were as follows:

"We, the Democrats of the United States, in National Convention assembled, do reaffirm our allegiance to those great essential principles of justice and liberty upon which our institutions are founded, and which the Democratic party

has advocated from Jefferson's time to our own —freedom of speech, freedom of the press, freedom of conscience, the preservation of personal rights, the equality of all citizens before the law, and the faithful observance of constitutional limitations.

"During all these years the Democratic party has resisted the tendency of selfish interests to the centralization of governmental power, and steadfastly maintained the integrity of the dual scheme of government established by the founders of this Republic of republics. Under its guidance and teachings the great principle of local self-government has found its best expression in the maintenance of the rights of the States and in its assertion of the necessity of confining the General Government to the exercise of the powers granted by the Constitution of the United States.

"Recognizing that the money question is paramount to all others at this time, we invite attention to the fact that the Federal Constitution names silver and gold together as the money metals of the United States, and that the first coinage law passed by Congress under the Constitution made the silver dollar the monetary unit, and admitted gold to free coinage at a ratio based upon the silver-dollar unit.

"We declare that the act of 1873 demonetizing silver without the knowledge or approval of the American people has resulted in the appreciation of gold and a corresponding fall in the prices of commodities produced by the people; a heavy increase in the burden of taxation and of all debts, public and private; the enrichment of the money-lending class at home and abroad; prostration of industry and impoverishment of the people.

"We are unalterably opposed to gold monometallism, which has locked fast the prosperity of an industrial people in the paralysis of hard times. Gold monometallism is a British policy, and its adoption has brought other nations into financial servitude to London. It is not only un-American but anti-American, and it can be fastened on the United States only by the stifling of that spirit and love of liberty which proclaimed our political independence in 1776 and won it in the war of the Revolution.

"We demand the free and unlimited coinage of both gold and silver at the present legal ratio of sixteen to one, without waiting for the aid or consent of any other nation. We demand that the standard silver dollar shall be a full legal tender, equally with gold, for all debts, public and private, and we favor such legislation as will prevent for the future the demonetization of any kind of legal-tender money by private contract.

"We are opposed to the policy and practice of surrendering to the holders of the obligations of the United States the option reserved by law to the Government of redeeming such obligations in either silver coin or gold coin.

"We are opposed to the issuing of interest-bearing bonds of the United States in time of peace, and condemn the trafficking with banking syndicates which, in exchange for bonds and at an enormous profit to themselves, supply the Federal Treasury with gold to maintain the policy of gold monometallism.

"Congress alone has the power to coin and issue money, and President Jackson declared that this power could not be delegated to corporations or individuals. We therefore demand that the power to issue notes to circulate as money be taken from the National banks, and that all paper money shall be issued directly by the Treasury Department, be redeemable in coin, and receivable for all debts, public and private.

"We hold that the tariff duties should be levied for purposes of revenue, such duties to be so adjusted as to operate equally throughout the country and not discriminate between class or section, and that taxation should be limited by the needs of the Government honestly and economically administered.

"We denounce, as disturbing to business, the Republican threat to restore the McKinley law, which has been twice condemned by the people in national elections, and which, enacted under the false plea of protection to home industry, proved a prolific breeder of trusts and monopolies, enriched the few at the expense of the many, restricted trade, and deprived the producers of the great American staples of access to their natural markets. Until the money question is settled we are opposed to any agitation for further changes in our tariff laws, except such as are necessary to make the deficit in revenue caused by the adverse decision of the Supreme Court on the income tax.

"There would be no deficit in the revenue but for the annulment by the Supreme Court of a law passed by a Democratic Congress in strict pursuance of the uniform decisions of that court for nearly 100 years, that court having sustained constitutional objections to its enactment which had been overruled by the ablest judges who have ever sat on that bench. We declare that it is the duty of Congress to use all the constitutional power which remains after that decision, or which may come by its reversal by the court, as it may hereafter be constituted, so that the burdens of taxation may be equally and impartially laid, to the end that wealth may bear its due proportion of the expenses of the Government.

"We hold that the most efficient way to protect American labor is to prevent the importation of foreign pauper labor to compete with it in the home market, and that the value of the home market to our American farmers and artisans is greatly reduced by a vicious monetary system, which depresses the prices of their products below the cost of production, and thus deprives them of the means of purchasing the products of our home manufacture.

"We denounce the profligate waste of the money wrung from the people by oppressive taxation and the lavish appropriations of recent Republican Congresses, which have kept taxes high, while the labor that pays them is unemployed, and the products of the people's toil are depressed in price till they no longer repay the cost of production. We demand a return to that simplicity and economy which best befit a Democratic Government and a reduction in the number of useless offices, the salaries of which drain the substance of the people.

"We denounce arbitrary interference by Federal authorities in local affairs as a violation of the Constitution of the United States and a crime against free institutions, and we especially object to government by injunction as a new and highly dangerous form of oppression, by which Federal judges, in contempt of the laws of the States and rights of citizens, become at once legislators, judges, and executioners, and we approve the bill passed at the last session of the United States Senate, and now pending in the House, relative to contempts in Federal courts, and providing for trials by jury in certain cases of contempt.

"No discrimination should be indulged by the Government of the United States in favor of any of its debtors. We approve of the refusal of the Fifty-third Congress to pass the Pacific Railroad funding bill, and denounce the effort of the present Republican Congress to enact a similar measure.

"Recognizing the just claims of deserving Union soldiers, we heartily endorse the rule of the present Commissioner of Pensions that no names shall be arbitrarily dropped from the pension roll, and the fact of an enlistment and service should be deemed conclusive evidence against disease or disability before enlistment.

"We extend our sympathy to the people of Cuba in their heroic struggle for liberty and independence.

"We are opposed to life tenure in the public service. We favor appointments based upon merit, fixed terms of office, and such an administration of the civil-service laws as will afford equal opportunities to all citizens of ascertained fitness.

"We declare it to be the unwritten law of this Republic, established by custom and usage of 100 years, and sanctioned by the examples of the greatest and wisest of those who founded and have maintained our Government, that no man should be eligible for a third term of the Presidential office.

"The absorption of wealth by the few, the consolidation of our leading railroad systems, and formation of trusts and pools require a stricter control by the Federal Government of those arteries of commerce. We demand the enlargement of the powers of the Inter-state Commerce Commission, and such restrictions and guarantees in the control of railroads as will protect the people from robbery and oppression.

"We favor the admission of the Territories of New Mexico and Arizona into the Union as States, and we favor the early admission of all the Territories giving the necessary population and resources to entitle them to Statehood; and while they remain Territories we hold that the officials appointed to administer the government of any Territory, together with the District of Columbia and Alaska, should be bona fide residents of the Territory or District in which their duties are to be performed. The Democratic party believes in home rule, and that all public lands of the United States should be appropriated to the establishment of free homes for American citizens.

"We recommend that the Territory of Alaska be granted a Delegate in Congress, and that the general land and timber laws of the United States be extended to said Territory.

"The Federal Government should care for and improve the Mississippi River and other great waterways of the Republic so as to secure for the interior people easy and cheap transportation to tidewater. When any waterway of the Republic is of sufficient importance to demand aid of the Government, such aid should

567

be extended upon a definite plan of continuous work until permanent improvement is secured.

"Confiding in the justice of our cause and the necessity of its success at the polls, we submit the foregoing declaration of principles and purposes to the considerate judgment of the American people. We invite the support of all citizens who approve them, and who desire to have them made effective through legislation for the relief of the people and the restoration of the country's prosperity."

In the course of the debate upon the silver question, a speech of impassioned eloquence was made by William J. Bryan, of Nebraska, who had represented his district in Congress for two terms, 1891–4, and who was rising to prominence among the leaders of the free-silver Democracy of the west. The speech excited an enthusiasm and an admiration which led to the nomination of Mr. Bryan for the presidency. That unexpected choice was reached after four ballots, in each of which the votes for the Nebraska orator rose steadily in number. At the fifth ballot they had passed the requisite two-thirds, and his nomination was declared to be unanimous, though protests were made. The entire delegation from New York and many delegates from New England and New Jersey cast no votes, refusing to take any part in the nomination of a candidate on the platform laid down. The chosen candidate for Vice President was Arthur Sewall, of Maine.

The National Silver Party.—The considerable body of Republicans who desired an unlimited free coinage of silver, and were prepared to quit their party on that issue, had made efforts to persuade the Democratic convention at Chicago to accept their leader, Senator Teller, of Colorado, for its presidential candidate. Failing in that, they assembled a convention of delegates at St. Louis, July 22–24, and, under the name of the "National Silver Party," took the alternative method of uniting the free-silver Republican vote with that of the free-silver Democracy, by accepting the Democratic nominations as their own. William J. Bryan and Arthur Sewall were duly nominated for President and Vice President, and a "platform" set forth as follows:

"The National Silver Party in Convention assembled hereby adopts the following declaration of principles:

"First. The paramount issue at this time in the United States is indisputably the money question. It is between the gold standard, gold bonds, and bank currency on the one side and the bimetallic standard, no bonds, and Government currency on the other.

"On this issue we declare ourselves to be in favor of a distinctively American financial system. We are unalterably opposed to the single gold standard, and demand the immediate return to the constitutional standard of gold and silver by the restoration by this Government, independently of any foreign power, of the unrestricted coinage of both gold and silver into standard money at the ratio of sixteen to one, and upon terms of exact equality, as they existed prior to 1873; the silver coin to be a full legal tender equally with gold for all debts and dues, private and public, and we favor such legislation as will prevent for the future the demonetization of any kind of legal-tender money by private contract.

"We hold that the power to control and regulate a paper currency is inseparable from the power to coin money, and hence that all currency intended to circulate as money should be issued, and its volume controlled by the General Government only, and should be legal tender.

"We are unalterably opposed to the issue by the United States of interest-bearing bonds in time of peace, and we denounce as a blunder worse than a crime the present Treasury policy, concurred in by a Republican House, of plunging the country in debt by hundreds of millions in the vain attempt to maintain the gold standard by borrowing gold, and we demand the payment of all coin obligations of the United States as provided by existing laws, in either gold or silver coin, at the option of the Government and not at the option of the creditor.

"The demonetization of silver in 1873 enormously increased the demand for gold, enhancing its purchasing power and lowering all prices measured by that standard; and since that unjust and indefensible act the prices of American products have fallen upon an average nearly fifty per cent., carrying down with them proportionably the money value of all other forms of property. Such fall of prices has destroyed the profits of legitimate industry, injuring the producer for the benefit of the non-producer, increasing the burden of the debtor, swelling the gains of the creditor, paralyzing the productive energies of the American people, relegating to idleness vast numbers of willing workers, sending the shadows of despair into the home of the honest toiler, filling the land with tramps and paupers, and building up colossal fortunes at the money centres.

"In the effort to maintain the gold standard the country has, within the last two years, in a time of profound peace and plenty, been loaded down with $262,000,000 of additional interest-bearing debt, under such circumstances as to allow a syndicate of native and foreign bankers to realize a net profit of millions on a single deal.

"It stands confessed that the gold standard can only be upheld by so depleting our paper currency as to force the prices of our product below the European and even below the Asiatic level to enable us to sell in foreign markets, thus aggravating the very evils our people so bitterly complain of, degrading American labor, and striking at the foundations of our civilization itself.

"The advocates of the gold standard persistently claim that the cause of our distress is overproduction; that we have produced so much that it has made us poor—which implies that the true remedy is to close the factory, abandon the farm, and throw a multitude of people out of employment, a doctrine that leaves us unnerved and disheartened, and absolutely without hope for the future.

"We affirm it to be unquestioned that there can be no such economic paradox as over-production, and at the same time tens of thousands of our fellow-citizens remaining half-clothed and half-fed, and who are piteously clamoring for the common necessities of life.

"Second. That over and above all other questions of policy we are in favor of restoring to the people of the United States the time-honored money of the Constitution—gold and silver, not one, but both—the money of Washington and

Hamilton and Jefferson and Monroe and Jackson and Lincoln, to the end that the American people may receive honest pay for an honest product; that the American debtor may pay his just obligations in an honest standard, and not in a standard that has depreciated 100 per cent. above all the great staples of our country, and to the end further that the standard countries may be deprived of the unjust advantage they now enjoy in the difference in exchange between gold and silver—an advantage which tariff legislation alone cannot overcome.

"We therefore confidently appeal to the people of the United States to leave in abeyance for the moment all other questions, however important and even momentous they may appear, to sunder, if need be, all former party ties and affiliations, and unite in one supreme effort to free themselves and their children from the domination of the money power—a power more destructive than any which has ever been fastened upon the civilized men of any race or in any age, and upon the consummation of our desires and efforts we invoke the gracious favor of Divine Providence.

"Inasmuch as the patriotic majority of the Chicago convention embodied in the financial plank of its platform the principles enunciated in the platform of the American Bimetallic party, promulgated at Washington, D. C., January 22, 1896, and herein reiterated, which is not only the paramount but the only real issue in the pending campaign, therefore, recognizing that their nominees embody these patriotic principles, we recommend that this convention nominate William J. Bryan, of Nebraska, for President, and Arthur Sewall, of Maine, for Vice President."

People's or Populist Party Platform and Nominations.—The People's Party, more commonly called the Populist Party, held its national convention at St. Louis on the 22d-25th of July, simultaneously with that of the National Silver Party, and with strong influences urging it to act on the same line. One section of the party strove to bring about a complete endorsement of the Democratic nominations made at Chicago. Another section, styled the "Middle-of-the-Road" Populists, opposed any coalition with other parties; while a third wished to nominate Bryan, with a Populist candidate for Vice President, looking to an arrangement with the Democratic organization for a fusion of electoral tickets in various States. The idea of the latter prevailed, and William J. Bryan was nominated for President, with Thomas E. Watson, of Georgia, for Vice President. The People's Party had little disagreement with the Chicago declarations of the Democratic Party, and none at all on financial questions, concerning which its doctrines were set forth in the following platform:

"The People's Party, assembled in National Convention, reaffirms its allegiance to the principles declared by the founders of the Republic, and also to the fundamental principles of just government as enunciated in the platform of the party in 1892.

"We recognize that through the connivance of the present and preceding administrations the country has reached a crisis in its National life, as predicted in our declaration of four years ago, and that prompt and patriotic action is the supreme duty of the hour.

"We realize that while we have political in-

dependence, our financial and industrial independence is yet to be attained by restoring to our country the constitutional control and exercise of the functions necessary to a people's government, which functions have been basely surrendered by our public servants to corporations and monopolies. The influence of European money-changers has been more potent in shaping legislation than the voice of the American people. Executive power and patronage have been used to corrupt our legislatures and defeat the will of the people, and plutocracy has been enthroned upon the ruins of democracy. To restore the government intended by the fathers, and for the welfare and prosperity of this and future generations, we demand the establishment of an economic and financial system which shall make us masters of our own affairs and independent of European control, by the adoption of the following declaration of principles:

"We demand a National money, safe and sound, issued by the general government only, without the intervention of banks of issue, to be a full legal tender for all debts, public and private, and a just, equitable, and efficient means of distribution direct to the people and through the lawful disbursements of the Government.

"We demand the free and unrestricted coinage of silver and gold at the present legal ratio of sixteen to one, without waiting for the consent of foreign nations.

"We demand that the volume of circulating medium be speedily increased to an amount sufficient to meet the demands of the business population of this country and to restore the just level of prices of labor and production.

"We denounce the sale of bonds and the increase of the public interest-bearing bond debt made by the present administration as unnecessary and without authority of law, and we demand that no more bonds be issued except by specific act of Congress.

"We demand such legislation as will prevent the demonetization of the lawful money of the United States by private contract.

"We demand that the Government, in payment of its obligations, shall use its option as to the kind of lawful money in which they are to be paid, and we denounce the present and preceding administrations for surrendering this option to the holders of government obligations.

"We demand a graduated income tax, to the end that aggregated wealth shall bear its just proportion of taxation, and we denounce the recent decision of the Supreme Court relative to the income-tax law as a misinterpretation of the Constitution and an invasion of the rightful powers of Congress over the subject of taxation.

"We demand that postal savings banks be established by the Government for the safe deposit of the savings of the people and to facilitate exchange.

"Transportation being a means of exchange and a public necessity, the Government should own and operate the railroads in the interest of the people and on non-partisan basis, to the end that all may be accorded the same treatment in transportation, and that the tyranny and political power now exercised by the great railroad corporations, which result in the impairment if not the destruction of the political rights and personal liberties of the citizens, may be destroyed. Such ownership is to be accomplished gradually, in a manner consistent with sound public policy.

"The interest of the United States in the public highways built with public moneys and the proceeds of extensive grants of land to the Pacific railroads should never be alienated, mortgaged, or sold, but guarded and protected for the general welfare as provided by the laws organizing such railroads. The foreclosure of existing liens of the United States on these roads should at once follow default in the payment of the debt of the companies, and at the foreclosure sales of said roads the Government should purchase the same if it becomes necessary to protect its interests therein, or if they can be purchased at a reasonable price; and the Government should operate said railroads as public highways for the benefit of the whole and not in the interest of the few, under suitable provisions for protection of life and property, giving to all transportation interests and privileges and equal rates for fares and freight.

' We denounce the present infamous schemes for refunding those debts and demand that the laws now applicable thereto be executed and administered according to their true intent and spirit.

"The telegraph, like the post-office system, being a necessity for the transmission of news, should be owned and operated by the Government in the interest of the people.

"The true policy demands that the National and State legislation shall be such as will ultimately enable every prudent and industrious citizen to secure a home, and therefore the land should not be monopolized for speculative purposes.

"All land now held by railroads and other corporations in excess of their actual needs should by lawful means be reclaimed by the Government and held for actual settlers only, and private land monopoly, as well as alien ownership, should be prohibited.

"We condemn the frauds by which the land grant to the Pacific Railroad Companies have, through the connivance of the Interior Department, robbed multitudes of bona fide settlers of their homes and miners of their claims, and we demand legislation by Congress which will enforce the exemption of mineral land from such grants after as well as before patent.

"We demand that bona fide settlers on all public lands be granted free homes, as provided in the National homestead law, and that no exception be made in the case of Indian reservations when opened for settlement, and that all lands not now patented come under this demand.

"We favor a system of direct legislation through the initiative and referendum under proper constitutional safeguards.

"We demand the election of President, Vice-President, and United States Senators by a direct vote of the people.

"We tender to the patriotic people of Cuba our deepest sympathy in their heroic struggle for political freedom and independence, and we believe the time has come when the United States, the great Republic of the world, should recognize that Cuba is and of right ought to be a free and independent State.

"We favor home rule in the Territories and the District of Columbia and the early admission of the Territories as States.

"All public salaries should be made to correspond to the price of labor and its products.

"In times of great industrial depression idle labor should be employed on public works as far as practicable.

"The arbitrary course of the courts in assuming to imprison citizens for indirect contempt and ruling by injunction should be prevented by proper legislation.

"We favor just pensions for our disabled Union soldiers.

"Believing that the elective franchise and untrammelled ballot are essential to a government of, for, and by the people, the People's Party condemn the wholesale system of disfranchisement adopted in some States as unrepublican and undemocratic, and we declare it to be the duty of the several State legislatures to take such action as will secure a full, free, and fair ballot and an honest count.

"While the foregoing propositions constitute the platform upon which our party stands, and for the vindication of which its organization will be maintained, we recognize that the great and pressing issue of the pending campaign, upon which the present Presidential election will turn, is the financial question, and upon this great and specific issue between the parties we cordially invite the aid and co-operation of all organizations and citizens agreeing with us upon this vital question."

National Democratic Platform and Nominations.—An extensive revolt in the Democratic Party against the declarations and the action of the party convention at Chicago had been quickly made manifest, and steps were soon taken towards giving it an organized form. These led to the assembling of a convention of delegates at Indianapolis, on the 2d and 3d of September, which, in the name of the "National Democratic Party," repudiated the platform and the candidates put forward at Chicago, and branded them as false to the historic party name which they assumed. General John M. Palmer, of Illinois, was put in nomination for President, and General Simon Bolivar Buckner, of Kentucky, for Vice President, of the United States, and a declaration of Democratic principles adopted, the fundamental passages of which are quoted in the following: "This convention has assembled to uphold the principles upon which depend the honor and welfare of the American people, in order that democrats throughout the Union may unite their patriotic efforts to avert disaster from their country and ruin from their party.

"The democratic party is pledged to equal and exact justice to all men of every creed and condition; to the largest freedom of the individual consistent with good government; to the preservation of the federal government in its constitutional vigor, and to the support of the states in all their just rights; to economy in the public expenditures; to the maintenance of the public faith and sound money; and it is opposed to paternalism and all class legislation. The declarations of the Chicago convention attack individual freedom, the right of private contract, the independence of the judiciary, and the authority of the president to enforce federal laws. They advocate a reckless attempt to increase the price of silver by legislation, to the debasement of our monetary standard; and threaten unlimited issues of paper money by the government. They abandon for republican allies the democratic cause of tariff reform, to court favor of protectionists to their fiscal heresy. In view of these and other grave departures from democratic principles, we cannot support the candidates of that convention, nor be bound by its acts. The democratic party has survived defeats, but could not survive a victory won in behalf of the doctrine and policy proclaimed in its name at Chicago.

"The conditions, however, which made possible such utterances from a national convention, are the direct result of class legislation by the republican party. It still proclaims, as it has for years, the power and duty of government to raise and maintain prices by law, and it proposes no remedy for existing evils except oppressive and unjust taxation. . . . The demand of the republican party for an increase in tariff taxation has its pretext in the deficiency of the revenue, which has its causes in the stagnation of trade and reduced consumption, due entirely to the loss of confidence that has followed the populist threat of free coinage and depreciation of our money, and the republican practice of extravagant appropriations beyond the needs of good government. We arraign and condemn the populistic conventions of Chicago and St. Louis for their coöperation with the republican party in creating these conditions, which are pleaded in justification of a heavy increase of the burdens of the people by a further resort to protection. We therefore denounce protection and its ally, free coinage of silver, as schemes for the personal profit of a few at the expense of the masses ; and oppose the two parties which stand for these schemes as hostile to the people of the republic, whose food and shelter, comfort and prosperity are attacked by higher taxes and depreciated money. In fine, we reaffirm the historic democratic doctrine of tariff for revenue only. . . .

"The experience of mankind has shown that, by reason of their natural qualities, gold is the necessary money of the large affairs of commerce and business, while silver is conveniently adapted to minor transactions, and the most beneficial use of both together can be insured only by the adoption of the former as a standard of monetary measure, and the maintenance of silver at a parity with gold by its limited coinage under suitable safeguards of law. Thus the largest possible employment of both metals is gained with a value universally accepted throughout the world, which constitutes the only practical bimetallic currency, assuring the most stable standard, and especially the best and safest money for all who earn their livelihood by labor or the produce of husbandry. They cannot suffer when paid in the best money known to man, but are the peculiar and most defenceless victims of a debased and fluctuating currency, which offers continual profits to the money changer at their cost.

"Realizing these truths demonstrated by long and public inconvenience and loss, the democratic party, in the interests of the masses and of equal justice to all, practically established by the legislation of 1834 and 1853 the gold standard of monetary measurement, and likewise entirely divorced the government from banking and currency issues. To this long-established democratic policy we adhere, and insist upon the maintenance of the gold standard, and of the parity therewith of every dollar issued by the government, and are firmly opposed to the free and unlimited coinage of silver and to the compulsory purchase of silver bullion. But we denounce also the further maintenance of the present costly patchwork system of national paper currency as a constant source of injury and peril. We assert the necessity of such intelligent currency reform as will confine the government to its legitimate functions, completely separated from the banking business, and afford to all sections of our country uniform, safe, and elastic bank currency under governmental supervision, measured in volume by the needs of business.

"The fidelity, patriotism, and courage with which President Cleveland has fulfilled his great public trust, the high character of his administration, its wisdom and energy in the maintenance of civil order and the enforcement of the laws, its equal regard for the rights of every class and every section, its firm and dignified conduct of foreign affairs, and its sturdy persistence in upholding the credit and honor of the nation are fully recognized by the democratic party, and will secure to him a place in history beside the fathers of the republic. We also commend the administration for the great progress made in the reform of the public service, and we indorse its effort to extend the merit system still further. We demand that no backward step be taken, but that the reform be supported and advanced until the un-democratic spoils system of appointments be eradicated."

Prohibition Platform and Nominations.— The Prohibition Party had been the first to open the presidential campaign with candidates placed in the field. Its national convention was held at Pittsburg, on the 27th and 28th of May, and its nominees for President and Vice President were Joshua Levering, of Maryland, and Hale Johnson, of Illinois. But a split in the convention occurred on attempts made to graft free-silver and kindred doctrines on the one-issue platform which the majority of the party desired. Except in a single particular, the latter prevailed. The platform adopted was as follows :

"The Prohibition Party, in national convention assembled, declares its firm conviction that the manufacture, exportation, importation, and sale of alcoholic beverages has produced such social, commercial, industrial, and political wrongs, and is now so threatening the perpetuity of all our social and political institutions, that the suppression of the same by a national party organized therefor is the greatest object to be accomplished by the voters of our country, and is of such importance that it, of right, ought to control the political actions of all our patriotic citizens until such suppression is accomplished. The urgency of this course demands the union without further delay of all citizens who desire the prohibition of the liquor traffic. Therefore be it

"Resolved, That we favor the legal prohibition by state and national legislation of the manufacture, importation, and sale of alcoholic beverages. That we declare our purpose to organize and unite all the friends of prohibition into one party ; and in order to accomplish this end we deem it of right to leave every prohibitionist the freedom of his own convictions upon all other political questions, and trust our representatives to take such action upon other political questions as the changes occasioned by prohibition and the welfare of the whole people shall demand."

Resolved, " The right of suffrage ought not to be abridged on account of sex."

Those delegates who were dissatisfied with this platform withdrew from the convention, assembled in another hall, assumed the name of " The National Party," adopted the following declarations, and nominated Charles E. Bentley, of Nebraska, and J. H. Southgate, of North Carolina, for the two highest offices in the national government :

" The National Party, recognizing God as the author of all just power in government, presents the following declaration of principles, which it pledges itself to enact into effective legislation when given the power to do so :

" The suppression of the manufacture and sale, importation, exportation, and transportation of intoxicating liquors for beverage purposes. We utterly reject all plans for regulating or compromising with this traffic, whether such plans be called local option, taxation, license, or public control. The sale of liquors for medicinal and other legitimate uses should be conducted by the State, without profit, and with such regulations as will prevent fraud or evasion.

" No citizen should be denied the right to vote on account of sex.

" All money should be issued by the General Government only, and without the intervention of any private citizen, corporation, or banking institution. It should be based upon the wealth, stability, and integrity of the nation. It should be a full legal tender for all debts, public and private, and should be of sufficient volume to meet the demands of the legitimate business interests of the country. For the purpose of honestly liquidating our outstanding coin obligations, we favor the free and unlimited coinage of both silver and gold, at the ratio of sixteen to one, without consulting any other nation.

" Land is the common heritage of the people and should be preserved from monopoly and speculation. All unearned grants of land, subject to forfeiture, should be reclaimed by the Government and no portion of the public domain should hereafter be granted except to actual settlers, continuous use being essential to tenure.

" Railroads, telegraphs, and other natural monopolies should be owned and operated by the Government, giving to the people the benefit of service at actual cost.

" The National Constitution should be so amended as to allow the national revenues to be raised by equitable adjustment of taxation on the properties and incomes of the people, and import duties should be levied as a means of securing equitable commercial relations with other nations.

" The contract convict-labor system, through which speculators are enriched at the expense of the State, should be abolished.

" All citizens should be protected by law in their right to one day of rest in seven, without oppressing any who conscientiously observe any other than the first day of the week.

" American public schools, taught in the English language, should be maintained, and no public funds should be appropriated for sectarian institutions.

" The President, Vice-President, and United States Senators should be elected by direct vote of the people.

" Ex-soldiers and sailors of the United States army and navy, their widows, and minor children, should receive liberal pensions, graded on disability and term of service, not merely as a debt of gratitude, but for service rendered in the preservation of the Union.

" Our immigration laws should be so revised as to exclude paupers and criminals. None but citizens of the United States should be allowed to vote in any State, and naturalized citizens should not vote until one year after naturalization papers have been issued.

" The initiative and referendum and proportional representation should be adopted.

" Having herein presented our principles and purposes, we invite the co-operation and support of all citizens who are with us substantially agreed."

Socialist-Labor Party Nominations.—Still another party which placed candidates for the presidency and vice-presidency in nomination was the Socialist-Labor organization, which held a convention in New York, July 4–10, and named for the two high offices, Charles H. Matchett, of New York, and Mathew Maguire, of New Jersey. Its platform embodied the essential doctrines of socialism, as commonly understood, and was as follows :

" The Socialist Labor Party of the United States, in convention assembled, reasserts the inalienable rights of all men to life, liberty, and the pursuit of happiness.

" With the founders of the American Republic we hold that the purpose of government is to secure every citizen in the enjoyment of this right; but in the right of our conditions we hold, furthermore, that no such right can be exercised under a system of economic inequality, essentially destructive of life, of liberty, and of happiness.

" With the founders of this Republic we hold that the true theory of politics is that the machinery of government must be owned and controlled by the whole people ; but in the light of our industrial development we hold, furthermore, that the true theory of economics is that the machinery of production must likewise belong to the people in common.

" To the obvious fact that our despotic system of economics is the direct opposite of our democratic system of politics, can plainly be traced the existence of a privileged class, the corruption of Government by that class, the alienation of public property, public franchises, and public functions to that class, and the abject dependence of the mightiest of nations upon that class.

" Again, through the perversion of democracy to the ends of plutocracy, labor is robbed of its wealth which it alone produces, is denied the means of self-employment, and by compulsory idleness in wage slavery, is even deprived of the necessaries of life.

" Human power and natural forces are thus wasted, that the plutocracy may rule. Ignorance and misery, with all their concomitant evils, are perpetuated, that the people may be kept in bondage. Science and invention are diverted from their humane purpose to the enslavement of women and children.

" Against such a system the Socialist Labor party once more enters its protest. Once more it reiterates its fundamental declaration that private property in the natural sources of production and in the instruments of labor is the obvious cause of all economic servitude and political dependence.

"The time is fast coming when, in the natural course of social evolution, this system, through the destructive action of its failures and crises on one hand, and the constructive tendencies of its trusts and other capitalistic combinations on the other hand, shall have worked out its own downfall.

" We therefore call upon the wage-workers of the United States, and upon all honest citizens, to organize under the banner of the Socialist Labor party into a class-conscious body, aware of its rights and determined to conquer them by taking possession of the public powers, so that, held together by an indomitable spirit of solidarity under the most trying conditions of the present class struggle, we may put a summary end to that barbarous struggle by the abolition of classes, the restoration of the land and of all the means of production, transportation, and distribution to the people as a collective body, and the substitution of the co-operative commonwealth for the present state of planless production, industrial war, and social disorder, a commonwealth in which every worker shall have the free exercise and full benefit of his faculties, multiplied by all modern factors of civilization.

"With a view to immediate improvement in the condition of labor we present the following demands:

"1. Reduction of the hours of labor in proportion to the progress of production.

"2. The United States shall obtain possession of the railroads, canals, telegraphs, telephones, and all other means of public transportation and communication; the employés to operate the same co-operatively under control of the Federal Government and to elect their own superior officers, but no employé shall be discharged for political reasons.

"3. The municipalities shall obtain possession of the local railroads, ferries, waterworks, gasworks, electric plants, and all industries requiring municipal franchises; the employés to operate the same co-operatively under control of the municipal administration and to elect their own superior officers, but no employé shall be discharged for political reasons.

"4. The public lands declared inalienable. Revocation of all land grants to corporations or individuals the conditions of which have not been complied with.

"5. The United States to have the exclusive right to issue money.

"6. Congressional legislation providing for the scientific management of forests and waterways, and prohibiting the waste of the natural resources of the country.

"7. Inventions to be free to all; the inventors to be remunerated by the nation.

"8. Progressive income tax and tax on inheritances; the smaller incomes to be exempt.

"9. School education of all children under fourteen years of age to be compulsory, gratuitous, and accessible to all by public assistance in meals, clothing, books, etc., where necessary.

"10. Repeal of all pauper, tramp, conspiracy, and sumptuary laws. Unabridged right of combination.

"11. Prohibition of the employment of children of school age and of female labor in occupations detrimental to health or morality. Abolition of the convict-labor contract system.

"12. Employment of the unemployed by the public authorities (county, State, or nation).

"13. All wages to be paid in lawful money of the United States. Equalization of women's wages to those of men where equal service is performed.

"14. Laws for the protection of life and limb in all occupations, and an efficient employers' liability law.

"15. The people to have the right to propose laws and to vote upon all measures of importance according to the referendum principle.

"16. Abolition of the veto power of the Executive (National, State, or municipal), wherever it exists.

"17. Abolition of the United States Senate and all upper legislative chambers.

"18. Municipal self-government.

"19. Direct vote and secret ballots in all elections. Universal and equal right of suffrage without regard to color, creed, or sex. Election days to be legal holidays. The principle of proportional representation to be introduced.

"20. All public officers to be subject to recall by their respective constituencies.

"21. Uniform civil and criminal law throughout the United States. Administration of justice free of charge. Abolition of capital punishment."

The Canvass and Election.—The canvass which occupied the months between party nominations and the election was the most remarkable, in many respects, that the country had ever gone through. On both sides of the silver question intense convictions were burning and intense anxieties being felt. To the defenders of the gold standard of value—the monetary standard of the world at large—an unlimited free coinage of silver legal tender money, at the ratio of 16 to 1, meant both dishonor and ruin—national bankruptcy, the wreck of industry, and chaos in the commercial world. To many of those who strove with desperate eagerness to bring it about it meant, on the contrary, a millennial social state, in which abundance would prevail, the goods of the world be divided more fairly, and labor have a juster reward. So the issue fronted each as one personal, vital, almost as of life and death. Their conflict bore no likeness to those commonly in politics, where consequences seem remote, vague, general to the body politic,—not instantly overhanging the head of the individual citizen, as in this case they did. Not even the patriotic and moral excitements of the canvass of 1860 produced so intense a feeling of personal interest in the election—so painful an anxiety in waiting for its result. And never in any former political contest had the questions involved been debated so earnestly, studied so widely and intently, set forth by every artifice of exposition and illustration with so much ingenious pains. The "campaign literature" distributed by each party was beyond computation in quantity and beyond classification in its kinds. The speeches of the canvass were innumerable. Mr. Bryan contributed some hundreds, in tours which he made through the country, and Mr. McKinley, at his home, in Canton, Ohio, received visiting delegations from all parts of the country and addressed them at more or less length.

With all the excitement of anxiety and the

heated conflict of beliefs there was little violence of any kind, from first to last. The critical election day (November 3) passed with no serious incidents of disorder. The verdict of the people, pronounced for the preservation of the monetary standard which the world at large has established in general use, was accepted with the equanimity to which self-governing citizens are trained. Nearly fourteen millions of votes were cast, of which the Republican presidential electors received 7,104,244; electors representing the various parties which had nominated Mr. Bryan received, in all, 6,506,835; those on the National Democratic ticket received 134,652; those on the Prohibition tickets, 144,606; those on the Social-ist-Labor ticket, 36,416. In the Electoral College, there were 271 votes for McKinley, and 176 for Bryan. The States giving their electoral votes for McKinley were California (excepting 1 vote, cast for Bryan), Connecticut, Delaware, Illinois, Indiana, Iowa, Kentucky (except 1), Maine, Maryland, Massachusetts, Michigan, Minnesota, New Hampshire, New Jersey, New York, North Dakota, Ohio, Oregon, Pennsylvania, Rhode Island, Vermont, West Virginia, Wisconsin. The States which chose electors for Bryan were Alabama, Arkansas, Colorado, Florida, Georgia, Idaho, Kansas, Louisiana, Mississippi, Missouri, Montana, Nebraska, Nevada, North Carolina, South Carolina, South Dakota, Tennessee, Texas, Utah, Virginia, Washington, Wyoming, besides the single votes won in California and Kentucky. For Vice President, Hobart received 271 electoral votes—the same as McKinley; but Sewall received 27 less than Bryan, that number being cast for the Populist candidate, Watson. This was consequent on fusion arrangements between Democrats and Populists in 28 States.

In some States, the majority given against silver free coinage was overwhelming, as for example, in New York, 268,000 plurality for McKinley, besides 19,000 votes cast for the "Gold Democratic" candidate; New Jersey, 87,000 Republican plurality and 6,000 votes for General Palmer; Pennsylvania, 295,000 and 11,000; Massachusetts, 173,000 and 11,000. On the other hand, Texas gave Bryan a plurality of 202,000, and Colorado 135,000.

A. D. 1896 (November).—Agreement with Great Britain for the settlement of the Venezuela dispute. See (in this vol.) VENEZUELA: A. D. 1896–1899.

A. D. 1896 (December).—President Cleveland on affairs in Cuba. See (in this vol.) CUBA: A. D. 1896–1897.

A. D. 1896–1897.—Immigration Bill vetoed by President Cleveland.—On the 17th of December, 1896, a bill to amend the immigration laws, which had passed the House of Representatives during the previous session of Congress, passed the Senate, with amendments which the House refused to accept. By conferences between the two branches of Congress an agreement was finally reached, in which the House concurred on the 9th of February and the Senate on the 17th. But the President disapproved the measure, and returned it to Congress on the 2d of March, with his objections set forth in the following Message:

"I herewith return without approval House bill No. 7864, entitled 'An act to amend the immigration laws of the United States.'

"By the first section of this bill it is proposed to amend section 1 of the act of March 3, 1891, relating to immigration by adding to the classes of aliens thereby excluded from admission to the United States the following: 'All persons physically capable and over 16 years of age who can not read and write the English language or some other language; but a person not so able to read and write who is over 50 years of age and is the parent or grandparent of a qualified immigrant over 21 years of age and capable of supporting such parent or grandparent may accompany such immigrant, or such a parent or grandparent may be sent for and come to join the family of a child or grandchild over 21 years of age similarly qualified and capable, and a wife or minor child not so able to read and write may accompany or be sent for and come and join the husband or parent similarly qualified and capable.'

"A radical departure from our national policy relating to immigration is here presented. Heretofore we have welcomed all who came to us from other lands except those whose moral or physical condition or history threatened danger to our national welfare and safety. Relying upon the zealous watchfulness of our people to prevent injury to our political and social fabric, we have encouraged those coming from foreign countries to cast their lot with us and join in the development of our vast domain, securing in return a share in the blessings of American citizenship. A century's stupendous growth, largely due to the assimilation and thrift of millions of sturdy and patriotic adopted citizens, attests the success of this generous and free-handed policy which, while guarding the people's interests, exacts from our immigrants only physical and moral soundness and a willingness and ability to work. A contemplation of the grand results of this policy can not fail to arouse a sentiment in its defense, for however it might have been regarded as an original proposition and viewed as an experiment its accomplishments are such that if it is to be uprooted at this late day its disadvantages should be plainly apparent and the substitute adopted should be just and adequate, free from uncertainties, and guarded against difficult or oppressive administration.

"It is not claimed, I believe, that the time has come for the further restriction of immigration on the ground that an excess of population overcrowds our land. It is said, however, that the quality of recent immigration is undesirable. The time is quite within recent memory when the same thing was said of immigrants who, with their descendants, are now numbered among our best citizens. It is said that too many immigrants settle in our cities, thus dangerously increasing their idle and vicious population. This is certainly a disadvantage. It can not be shown, however, that it affects all our cities, nor that it is permanent; nor does it appear that this condition where it exists demands as its remedy the reversal of our present immigration policy. The claim is also made that the influx of foreign laborers deprives of the opportunity to work those who are better entitled than they to the privilege of earning their livelihood by daily toil. An unfortunate condition is certainly presented when any who are willing to labor are unemployed, but so far as this condition now exists among our people it must be conceded to be a result of phenomenal business depression and the stagnution of all enterprises in which labor is a factor. With the advent of settled and wholesome financial and economic governmental policies and consequent encouragement to the activity of capital the misfortunes of unemployed labor should, to a great extent at least, be remedied. If it continues, its natural consequences must be to check the further immigration to our cities of foreign laborers and to deplete the ranks of those already there. In the meantime those most willing and best entitled ought to be able to secure the advantages of such work as there is to do.

"It is proposed by the bill under consideration to meet the alleged difficulties of the situation by establishing an educational test by which the right of a foreigner to make his home with us shall be determined. Its general scheme is to prohibit from admission to our country all immigrants 'physically capable and over 16 years of age who can not read and write the English language or some other language,' and it is provided that this test shall be applied by requiring immigrants seeking admission to read and afterwards to write not less than twenty nor more than twenty-five words of the Constitution of the United States in some language, and that any immigrant failing in this shall not be admitted, but shall be returned to the country from whence he came at the expense of the steamship or railroad company which brought him.

"The best reason that could be given for this radical restriction of immigration is the necessity of protecting our population against degeneration and saving our national peace and quiet from imported turbulence and disorder. I can not believe that we would be protected against these evils by limiting immigration to those who can read and write in any language twenty-five words of our Constitution. In my opinion, it is infinitely more safe to admit a hundred thousand immigrants who, though unable to read and write, seek among us only a home and opportunity to work than to admit one of those unruly agitators and enemies of governmental control who can not only read and write, but delights in arousing by inflammatory speech the illiterate and peacefully inclined to discontent and tumult. Violence and disorder do not originate with illiterate laborers. They are, rather, the victims of the educated agitator. The ability to read and write, as required in this bill, in and of itself affords, in my opinion, a misleading test of contented industry and supplies unsatisfactory evidence of desirable citizenship or a proper apprehension of the benefits of our institutions. If any particular element of our illiterate immigration is to be feared for other causes than illiteracy, these causes should be dealt with directly, instead of making illiteracy the pretext for exclusion, to the detriment of other illiterate immigrants against whom the real cause of complaint cannot be alleged.

"The provisions intended to rid that part of the proposed legislation already referred to from obvious hardship appear to me to be indefinite and inadequate. A parent, grandparent, wife, or minor child of a qualified immigrant, though unable to read and write, may accompany the immigrant or be sent for to join his family, provided the immigrant is capable of supporting such relative. These exceptions to the general rule of exclusion contained in the bill were made to prevent the separation of families, and yet

neither brothers nor sisters are provided for. In order that relatives who are provided for may be reunited, those still in foreign lands must be sent for to join the immigrant here. What formality is necessary to constitute this prerequisite, and how are the facts of relationship and that the relative is sent for to be established? Are the illiterate relatives of immigrants who have come here under prior laws entitled to the advantage of these exceptions? A husband who can read and write and who determines to abandon his illiterate wife abroad will find here under this law an absolutely safe retreat. The illiterate relatives mentioned must not only be sent for, but such immigrant must be capable of supporting them when they arrive. This requirement proceeds upon the assumption that the foreign relatives coming here are in every case, by reason of poverty, liable to become a public charge unless the immigrant is capable of their support. The contrary is very often true. And yet if unable to read and write, though quite able and willing to support themselves and their relatives here besides, they could not be admitted under the provisions of this bill if the immigrant was impoverished, though the aid of his fortunate but illiterate relative might be the means of saving him from pauperism.

"The fourth section of this bill provides— 'That it shall be unlawful for any male alien who has not in good faith made his declaration before the proper court of his intention to become a citizen of the United States to be employed on any public works of the United States or to come regularly or habitually into the United States by land or water for the purpose of engaging in any mechanical trade or manual labor for wages or salary, returning from time to time to a foreign country.' The fifth section provides—'That it shall be unlawful for any person, partnership, company, or corporation knowingly to employ any alien coming into the United States in violation of the next preceding section of this act.'

"The prohibition against the employment of aliens upon any public works of the United States is in line with other legislation of a like character. It is quite a different thing, however, to declare it a crime for an alien to come regularly and habitually into the United States for the purpose of obtaining work from private parties, if such alien returns from time to time to a foreign country, and to constitute any employment of such alien a criminal offense. When we consider these provisions of the bill in connection with our long northern frontier and the boundaries of our States and Territories, often but an imaginary line separating them from the British dominions, and recall the friendly intercourse between the people who are neighbors on either side, the provisions of this bill affecting them must be regarded as illiberal, narrow, and un-American. The residents of these States and Territories have separate and especial interests which in many cases make an interchange of labor between their people and their alien neighbors most important, frequently with the advantage largely in favor of our citizens. This suggests the inexpediency of Federal interference with these conditions when not necessary to the correction of a substantial evil, affecting the general welfare. Such unfriendly legislation as is proposed could hardly fail to provoke retaliatory measures, to the injury of many of our citizens who now find employment on adjoining foreign soil. The uncertainty of construction to which the language of these provisions is subject is a serious objection to a statute which describes a crime. An important element in the offense sought to be created by these sections is the coming 'regularly or habitually into the United States.' These words are impossible of definite and certain construction. The same may be said of the equally important words 'returning from time to time to a foreign country.'

"A careful examination of this bill has convinced me that for the reasons given and others not specifically stated its provisions are unnecessarily harsh and oppressive, and its defects in construction would cause vexation and its operation would result in harm to our citizens. GROVER CLEVELAND."

In the House of Representatives, the Bill was passed again, over the veto, by the requisite vote of two-thirds; in the Senate it was referred to the Committee on Immigration, and no further action was taken upon it. Therefore, it did not become a law.

A. D. 1896-1898.—Agitation for monetary reforms.—The Indianapolis Commission.—Secretary Gage's plan.—The Senatorial block in the way.—On November 18, 1896, the Governors of the Indianapolis Board of Trade invited the Boards of Trade of Chicago, St. Louis, Cincinnati, Louisville, Cleveland, Columbus, Toledo, Kansas City, Detroit, Milwaukee, St. Paul, Des Moines, Minneapolis, Grand Rapids, Peoria, and Omaha to a conference on the first of December following, to consider the advisability of calling a larger convention from commercial organizations throughout the country for the purpose of discussing the wisdom of selecting a non-partisan commission to formulate a sound currency system. This preliminary conference issued a call for a non-partisan monetary convention of business men, chosen from boards of trade, chambers of commerce, and commercial clubs, to meet in Indianapolis, on January 12, 1897. At the convention there were assembled, with credentials, 299 delegates, representing business organizations and cities in nearly every State in the Union. The result of its deliberations was expressed in resolutions which opened as follows:

"This convention declares that it has become absolutely necessary that a consistent, straightforward, and deliberately planned monetary system shall be inaugurated, the fundamental basis of which should be: First, that the present gold standard should be maintained. Second, that steps should be taken to insure the ultimate retirement of all classes of United States notes by a gradual and steady process, and so as to avoid the injurious contraction of the currency, or disturbance of the business interests of the country, and that until such retirements provision should be made for a separation of the revenue and note-issue departments of the Treasury. Third, that a banking system be provided, which should furnish credit facilities to every portion of the country and a safe and elastic circulation, and especially with a view of securing such a distribution of the loanable capital of the country as will tend to equalize the rates of interest in all parts thereof."

Recognizing the necessity of committing the formulation of such a plan to a body of men

trained and experienced in these matters, a commission was proposed. In case no commission should be authorized by Congress in the spring of 1897, the Executive Committee of the Convention was authorized to select a commission of eleven members, "to make thorough investigation of the monetary affairs and needs of this country, in all relations and aspects, and to make appropriate suggestions as to any evils found to exist, and the remedies therefor."

Congress did not authorize the appointment of a monetary commission; and the Executive Committee of the Convention selected a commission of eleven members, which began its sittings in Washington, September 22, 1897: . . . The Commission was composed as follows: George F. Edmunds, Vermont, chairman; George E. Leighton, Missouri, vice-chairman; T. G. Bush, Alabama; W. B. Dean, Minnesota; Charles S. Fairchild, New York; Stuyvesant Fish, New York; J. W. Fries, North Carolina; Louis A. Garnett, California; J. Laurence Laughlin, Illinois; C. Stuart Patterson, Pennsylvania; Robert S. Taylor, Indiana; and L. Carroll Root and H. Parker Willis, secretaries. Early in January, 1898, the report of the Monetary Commission was made public, and a second convention of delegates from the boards of trade and other commercial organizations of leading cities in the country was called together at Indianapolis, January 20-26, to consider its recommendations. The measures proposed by the Commission were approved by the convention, and were submitted to Congress by a committee appointed to urge their enactment in law. The Secretary of the Treasury, Mr. Gage, had already, in his first annual report and in the draft of a bill which he laid before the House committee on banking and currency, made recommendations which accorded in principle with those of the Commission, differing somewhat in details. Both plans, with some proposals from other sources, were now taken in hand by the House committee on banking and currency, and a bill was prepared, which the committee reported to the House on the 15th of June. But the other branch of Congress, the Senate, had already declared itself in a way which forbade any hope of success. By a vote of 47 to 32, that body had resolved, on the 28th of January, that "all the bonds of the United States issued, or authorized to be issued, under the said acts of Congress hereinbefore recited, are payable, principal and interest, at the option of the government of the United States, in silver dollars, of the coinage of the United States, containing 412 1-2 grains each of standard silver; and that to restore to its coinage such silver coins as a legal tender in payment of said bonds, principal and interest, is not in violation of the public faith, nor in derogation of the rights of the public creditor." The House, by 182 to 132, had rejected this resolution; but the Senate action had demonstrated the evident uselessness of attempting legislation in the interest of a monetary reform. Accordingly the House bill, after being reported and made public, for discussion outside, was withdrawn by the committee, and the subject rested in Congress, while agitation in the country went on.

A. D. 1897.—The Industrial Revolution.—"In 1865 the problem presented was this: The United States could certainly excel any European nation in economic competition, and possibly the whole Continent combined, if it could utilize its resources. So much was admitted; the doubt touched the capacity of the people to organize a system of transportation and industry adequate to attain that end. Failure meant certain bankruptcy. Unappalled by the magnitude of the speculation, the American people took the risk. What that risk was may be imagined when the fact is grasped that in 1865, with 35,000 miles of road already built, this people entered on the construction of 160,000 miles more, at an outlay, probably, in excess of $10,000,000,000. Such figures convey no impression to the mind, any more than a statement of the distance of a star. It may aid the imagination, perhaps, to say that Mr. Giffen estimated the cost to France of the war of 1870, including the indemnity and Alsace and Lorraine, at less than $3,500,000,000, or about one-third of this portentous mortgage on the future.

"As late as 1870 America remained relatively poor, for America, so far as her export trade went, relied on agriculture alone. To build her roads she had to borrow, and she expected to pay dear; but she did not calculate on having to pay twice the capital she borrowed, estimating that capital in the only merchandise she had to sell. Yet this is very nearly what occurred. Agricultural prices fell so rapidly that between 1890 and 1897, when the sharpest pressure prevailed, it took something like twice the weight of wheat or cotton to repay a dollar borrowed in 1873, that would have sufficed to satisfy the creditor when the debt was contracted. Merchandise enough could not be shipped to meet the emergency, and balances had to be paid in coin. The agony this people endured may be measured by the sacrifice they made. At the moment of severest contraction, in the single year 1893, the United States parted with upwards of $87,000,000 of gold, when to lose gold was like draining a living body of its blood. . . .

"What America owed abroad can never be computed; it is enough that it reached an enormous sum, to refund which, even under favorable circumstances, would have taken years of effort; actually forced payment brought the nation to the brink of a convulsion. Perhaps no people ever faced such an emergency and paid, without recourse to war. America triumphed through her inventive and administrative genius. Brought to a white heat under compression, the industrial system of the Union suddenly fused into a homogeneous mass. One day, without warning, the gigantic mechanism operated, and two hemispheres vibrated with the shock. In March, 1897, the vast consolidation of mines, foundries, railroads, and steamship companies, centralized at Pittsburg, began producing steel rails at $18 the ton, and at a bound America bestrode the world. She had won her great wager with fate. . . . The end seems only a question of time. Europe is doomed not only to buy her raw material abroad, but to pay the cost of transport. And Europe knew this instinctively in March, 1897, and nerved herself for resistance. Her best hope, next to a victorious war, lay in imitating America, and in organizing a system of transportation which would open up the East.

"Carnegie achieved the new industrial revolution in March, 1897. Within a twelvemonth the rival nations had emptied themselves upon the shore of the Yellow Sea. In November Germany seized Kiao-chan, a month later the Russians occupied Port Arthur, and the following April the English appropriated Wei-hai-wei; but the fact to remember is that just 400 miles inland, due west of Kiao-chan, lies Tszechau, the centre, according to Richthofen, of the richest coal and iron deposits in existence. There with the rude methods used by the Chinese, coal actually sells at 13 cents the ton. Thus it has come to pass that the problem now being attacked by all the statesmen, soldiers, scientific men, and engineers of the two eastern continents is whether Russia, Germany, France, England, and Japan, combined or separately, can ever bring these resources on the market in competition with the United States."—B. Adams, *The New Industrial Revolution* (*Atlantic Monthly, Feb.*, 1901).

A. D. 1897 (January—May).—Arbitration Treaty with Great Britain rejected by the Senate.—The correspondence which took place between the governments of the United States and Great Britain, on the subject of an arbitration of the Venezuela Boundary dispute, having led (see, in this vol., VENEZUELA: A. D. 1896-1899) to the revival of a project for the negotiation of a general treaty of arbitration, which the late American Secretary of State, Mr. Gresham, had broached to the British government in the spring of 1895, the terms of such an arrangement were carefully and fully discussed between Secretary Olney and Lord Salisbury, during the year 1896, and an agreement was reached which took form in a solemn compact for the settlement by arbitration of all matters in difference between the two countries, signed at Washington on the 11th of January, 1897. The treaty thus framed was as follows:

"ARTICLE I. The High Contracting Parties agree to submit to Arbitration in accordance with the provisions and subject to the limitations of this Treaty all questions in difference between them which they may fail to adjust by diplomatic negotiation.

"ARTICLE II. All pecuniary claims or groups of pecuniary claims which do not in the aggregate exceed £100,000 in amount, and which do not involve the determination of territorial claims, shall be dealt with and decided by an Arbitral Tribunal constituted as provided in the next following Article. In this Article and in Article IV the words 'groups of pecuniary claims' mean pecuniary claims by one or more persons arising out of the same transactions or involving the same issues of law and fact.

"ARTICLE III. Each of the High Contracting Parties shall nominate one arbitrator who shall be a jurist of repute and the two arbitrators so nominated shall within two months of the date of their nomination select an umpire. In case they shall fail to do so within the limit of time above mentioned, the umpire shall be appointed by agreement between the Members for the time being of the Supreme Court of the United States and the Members for the time being of the Judicial Committee of the Privy Council in Great Britain, each nominating body acting by a majority. In case they shall fail to agree upon an umpire within three months of the date of an application made to them in that behalf by the High Contracting Parties or either of them, the umpire shall be selected in the manner provided for in Article X. The person so selected shall

6–37

be the President of the Tribunal and the award of the majority of the Members thereof shall be final.

"ARTICLE IV. All pecuniary claims or groups of pecuniary claims which shall exceed £100,000 in amount and all other matters in difference, in respect of which either of the High Contracting Parties shall have rights against the other under Treaty or otherwise, provided that such matters in difference do not involve the determination of territorial claims, shall be dealt with and decided by an Arbitral Tribunal, constituted as provided in the next following Article.

"ARTICLE V. Any subject of Arbitration described in Article IV shall be submitted to the Tribunal provided for by Article III, the award of which Tribunal, if unanimous, shall be final. If not unanimous either of the High Contracting Parties may within six months from the date of the award demand a review thereof. In such case the matter in controversy shall be submitted to an Arbitral Tribunal consisting of five jurists of repute, no one of whom shall have been a member of the Tribunal whose award is to be reviewed and who shall be selected as follows, viz :—two by each of the High Contracting Parties, and one, to act as umpire, by the four thus nominated and to be chosen within three months after the date of their nomination. In case they shall fail to choose an umpire within the limit of time above-mentioned, the umpire shall be appointed by agreement between the Nominating Bodies designated in Article III acting in the manner therein provided. In case they shall fail to agree upon an umpire within three months of the date of an application made to them in that behalf by the High Contracting Parties or either of them, the umpire shall be selected in the manner provided for in Article X. The person so selected shall be the President of the Tribunal and the award of the majority of the Members thereof shall be final.

"ARTICLE VI. Any controversy which shall involve the determination of territorial claims shall be submitted to a Tribunal composed of six members, three of whom (subject to the provisions of Article VIII) shall be Judges of the Supreme Court of the United States or Justices of the Circuit Courts to be nominated by the President of the United States, and the other three of whom (subject to the provisions of Article VIII) shall be Judges of the British Supreme Court of Judicature or Members of the Judicial Committee of the Privy Council to be nominated by Her Britannic Majesty, whose award by a majority of not less than five to one shall be final. In case of an award made by less than the prescribed majority, the award shall also be final unless either Power shall, within three months after the award has been reported, protest that the same is erroneous, in which case the award shall be of no validity. In the event of an award made by less than the prescribed majority and protested as above provided, or if the members of the Arbitral Tribunal shall be equally divided, there shall be no recourse to hostile measures of any description until the mediation of one or more friendly Powers has been invited by one or both of the High Contracting Parties.

"ARTICLE VII. Objections to the jurisdiction of an Arbitral Tribunal constituted under this Treaty shall not be taken except as provided in this Article. If before the close of the hearing upon a claim submitted to an Arbitral Tribunal constituted under Article III or Article V either of the High Contracting Parties shall move such Tribunal to decide, and thereupon it shall decide that the determination of such claim necessarily involves the decision of a disputed question of principle of grave general importance affecting the national rights of such party as distinguished from the private rights whereof it is merely the international representative, the jurisdiction of such Arbitral Tribunal over such claim shall cease and the same shall be dealt with by arbitration under Article VI.

"ARTICLE VIII. In cases where the question involved is one which concerns a particular State or Territory of the United States, it shall be open to the President of the United States to appoint a judicial officer of such State or Territory to be one of the Arbitrators under Article III or Article V or Article VI. In like manner in cases where the question involved is one which concerns a British Colony or possession, it shall be open to Her Britannic Majesty to appoint a judicial officer of such Colony or possession to be one of the Arbitrators under Article III or Article V or Article VI.

"ARTICLE IX. Territorial claims in this Treaty shall include all claims to territory and all claims involving questions of servitudes, rights of navigation and of access, fisheries and all rights and interests necessary to the control and enjoyment of the territory claimed by either of the High Contracting Parties.

"ARTICLE X. If in any case the nominating bodies designated in Articles III and V shall fail to agree upon an Umpire in accordance with the provisions of the said Articles, the Umpire shall be appointed by His Majesty the King of Sweden and Norway. Either of the High Contracting Parties, however, may at any time give notice to the other that, by reason of material changes in conditions as existing at the date of this Treaty, it is of opinion that a substitute for His Majesty should be chosen either for all cases to arise under the Treaty or for a particular specified case already arisen, and thereupon the High Contracting Parties shall at once proceed to agree upon such substitute to act either in all cases to arise under the Treaty or in the particular case specified as may be indicated by said notice; provided, however, that such notice shall have no effect upon an Arbitration already begun by the constitution of an Arbitral Tribunal under Article III. The High Contracting Parties shall also at once proceed to nominate a substitute for His Majesty in the event that His Majesty shall at any time notify them of his desire to be relieved from the functions graciously accepted by him under this Treaty either for all cases to arise thereunder or for any particular specified case already arisen.

"ARTICLE XI. In case of the death, absence or incapacity to serve of any Arbitrator or Umpire, or in the event of any Arbitrator or Umpire omitting or declining or ceasing to act as such, another Arbitrator or Umpire shall be forthwith appointed in his place and stead in the manner provided for with regard to the original appointment.

"ARTICLE XII. Each Government shall pay its own agent and provide for the proper remuneration of the counsel employed by it and of the Arbitrators appointed by it and for the expense of preparing and submitting its case to the Arbitral Tribunal. All other expenses connected with any Arbitration shall be defrayed by the two Governments in equal moieties. Provided, however, that, if in any case the essential matter of difference submitted to arbitration is the right of one of the High Contracting Parties to receive disavowals of or apologies for acts or defaults of the other not resulting in substantial pecuniary injury, the Arbitral Tribunal finally disposing of the said matter shall direct whether any of the expenses of the successful party shall be borne by the unsuccessful party, and if so to what extent.

"ARTICLE XIII. The time and place of meeting of an Arbitral Tribunal and all arrangements for the hearing and all questions of procedure shall be decided by the Tribunal itself. Each Arbitral Tribunal shall keep a correct record of its proceedings and may appoint and employ all necessary officers and agents. The decision of the Tribunal shall, if possible, be made within three months from the close of the arguments on both sides. It shall be made in writing and dated and shall be signed by the Arbitrators who may assent to it. The decision shall be in duplicate, one copy whereof shall be delivered to each of the High Contracting Parties through their respective agents.

"ARTICLE XIV. This Treaty shall remain in force for five years from the date at which it shall come into operation, and further until the expiration of twelve months after either of the High Contracting Parties shall have given notice to the other of its wish to terminate the same.

"ARTICLE XV. The present Treaty shall be duly ratified by the President of the United States of America, by and with the advice and consent of the Senate thereof, and by Her Britannic Majesty; and the mutual exchange of ratifications shall take place in Washington or in London within six months of the date hereof or earlier if possible."—*United States, 54th Cong., 2d Sess., Senate Doc. No. 63.*

Public feeling in both countries gave joyful welcome to this nobly conceived treaty when it was announced. All that was best in English sentiment and American sentiment had been shuddering at the thought of possible war between the kindred peoples, and thanked God for what promised some certitude that no dispute would be pushed to that barbarous appeal. Only the mean thought and temper of either country was provoked to opposition; but, unhappily, the meaner temper and the narrower and more ignorant opinion on one side of the sea had been getting so strong a representation in the United States Senate as to prove capable of much mischief there, on this and other matters of most serious public concern. When the great covenant of peace went to that body for approval, there were senators who found it offensive to them because it came from the hands of President Cleveland and Secretary Olney; and there were other senators whose dignity was hurt by the eager impatience with which the public voice cried out for their ratifying vote; and still others there were who looked with official jealousy at the project of an arbitral tribunal which might sometimes take something from senatorial functions in foreign affairs. And the

combination of pitiful motives had strength enough to baffle the high hopes and defeat the will of the American people.

Of the public feeling thus outraged, the following is one expression of the time, among many which it would be possible to quote: Many people "are represented by influential papers like the St. Paul 'Pioneer Press' and the Minneapolis 'Journal,' the latter declaring that it is humiliating to think that, widely as the treaty is favored throughout the country, a few ill-natured men in the Senate have the power to delay ratification. In the Central West the feeling is generally strong for arbitration, if we may judge from the Chicago 'Times-Herald,' the St. Louis 'Republic,' the Indianapolis 'Journal,' and the Cleveland 'Leader.' In the South there are such cheering reports as this from the Memphis 'Scimetar': 'If the treaty now under consideration in the Senate Committee on Foreign Relations should fail of ratification, public opinion in this country would demand that the incoming Administration provide another embodying the same vital principle.' In the East the sentiment in favor of immediate ratification of the original draft has been almost universal, the only two journals of note differing from this being the New York 'Sun' and the Washington 'Post.' The trend of opinion is shown in the adoption by the Massachusetts House of Representatives of an endorsement by a vote of 141 to 11. An important meeting took place last week in Washington in favor of ratification. The speakers were ex-Secretary of State Foster, Mr. G. G. Hubbard, Professor B. L. Whitman, ex-Senator J. B. Henderson, ex-Governor Stanard, and Justice Brewer, of the Supreme Court. The last named said: 'I do not believe in saying to the geptlemen charged with the duty of considering carefully that treaty, that "you must vote for it." There is something in my own nature which, when anybody says to me "you must," causes something to run up my spinal column which says "I won't." It is the Senate's duty to consider that treaty carefully, and when I say that, I say it is no trespass upon their rights for American citizens to express their views of that treaty. What are the errors and losses incidental to arbitration compared to the horrors of war? What are a few million dollars of wrongful damages in comparison to the sacrifice of thousands of human lives?'"—*The Outlook, Feb. 6, 1897.*

"This treaty was greeted with widespread favor in the press, but was antagonized at once in the Senate by the jingo element and by the personal adversaries of the administration. The committee on foreign relations reported the draft favorably, but with certain amendments, on February 1. The ensuing debate soon revealed that a vote on ratification could not be obtained before March 4, and the whole matter was dropped. At the opening of the new Congress the Senate Committee again considered the treaty and reported it, with amendments, on March 18. During two weeks' discussion the Senate adopted the committee's amendments and also others, with the result that the draft was radically transformed. Instead of the general reference of all disputes to the tribunals, it was provided that any difference 'which, in the judgment of either power, materially affects

579

its honor or its domestic or foreign policy,' should be submitted to arbitration only by special agreement ; that no question should be submitted save with the consent of the Senate in its treaty-making capacity ; and that no claim of a British subject against a state or territory of the United States should be submitted under any circumstances. The first of these changes was due mainly to the objection that without it the Monroe Doctrine might be subjected to arbitration ; the second to the sensitiveness of senators as to their constitutional functions in foreign relations ; and the third to a desire to protect states against claims on their defaulted bonds. Other changes modified materially the method of appointing the arbitrators for the United States, and struck out entirely the designation of the King of Sweden as umpire. Even with these amendments, the opposition to the treaty was not overcome ; and the final vote on ratification, taken May 5, resulted in its rejection, the vote standing 43 to 26, less than two-thirds in the affirmative. Thirty Republicans and 13 Democrats voted for the treaty ; 8 Republicans, 12 Democrats and 6 Populists against it."
—*Political Science Quarterly, June,* 1897.

A. D. 1897 (March).—Inauguration of President **McKinley.**— Leading topics of the inaugural address.—The President's Cabinet.— The inauguration of President McKinley was performed with the customary ceremonies on the 4th of March. In his inaugural address, the new President laid somewhat less emphasis than might have been expected on the need of measures for reforming the monetary system of the country, but strongly urged that instant steps be taken to increase the revenues of the government by a return to higher tariff charges. "With adequate revenue secured," he argued, "but not until then, we can enter upon such changes in our fiscal laws as will, while insuring safety and volume to our money, no longer impose upon the government the necessity of maintaining so large a gold reserve, with its attendant and inevitable temptations to speculation. Most of our financial laws are the outgrowth of experience and trial, and should not be amended without investigation and demonstration of the wisdom of the proposed changes. We must be both 'sure we are right' and 'make haste slowly.' . . .

"The question of international bimetallism will have early and earnest attention. It will be my constant endeavor to secure it by coöperation with the other great commercial powers of the world. Until that condition is realized, when the parity between our gold and silver money springs from and is supported by the relative value of the two metals, the value of the silver already coined, and of that which may hereafter be coined, must be kept constantly at par with gold by every resource at our command. The credit of the government, the integrity of its currency, and the inviolability of its obligations must be preserved. This was the commanding verdict of the people, and it will not be unheeded.

"Economy is demanded in every branch of the government at all times, but especially in periods like the present of depression in business and distress among the people. The severest economy must be observed in all public expenditures, and extravagance stopped wherever it is found, and prevented wherever in the future it may be

developed. If the revenues are to remain as now, the only relief that can come must be from decreased expenditures. But the present must not become the permanent condition of the government. It has been our uniform practice to retire, not increase, our outstanding obligations ; and this policy must again be resumed and vigorously enforced. Our revenues should always be large enough to meet with ease and promptness not only our current needs and the principal and interest of the public debt, but to make proper and liberal provision for that most deserving body of public creditors, the soldiers and sailors and the widows and orphans who are the pensioners of the United States. . . .

"A deficiency is inevitable so long as the expenditures of the government exceed its receipts. It can only be met by loans or an increased revenue. While a large annual surplus of revenue may invite waste and extravagance, inadequate revenue creates distrust and undermines public and private credit. Neither should be encouraged. Between more loans and more revenue there ought to be but one opinion. We should have more revenue, and that without delay, hindrance, or postponement. A surplus in the treasury created by loans is not a permanent or safe reliance. It will suffice while it lasts, but it cannot last long while the outlays of the government are greater than its receipts, as has been the case during the last two years. . . . The best way for the government to maintain its credit is to pay as it goes—not by resorting to loans, but by keeping out of debt—through an adequate income secured by a system of taxation, external, or internal, or both. It is the settled policy of the government, pursued from the beginning and practiced by all parties and administrations, to raise the bulk of our revenue from taxes upon foreign productions entering the United States for sale and consumption, and avoiding, for the most part, every form of direct taxation except in time of war.

"The country is clearly opposed to any needless additions to the subjects of internal taxation, and is committed by its latest popular utterance to the system of tariff taxation. There can be no misunderstanding either about the principle upon which this tariff taxation shall be levied. Nothing has ever been made plainer at a general election than that the controlling principle in the raising of revenue from duties on imports is zealous care for American interests and American labor. The people have declared that such legislation should be had as will give ample protection and encouragement to the industries and the development of our country. . . . The paramount duty of congress is to stop deficiencies by the restoration of that protective legislation which has always been the firmest prop of the treasury. The passage of such a law or laws would strengthen the credit of the government both at home and abroad, and go far toward stopping the drain upon the gold reserve held for the redemption of our currency, which has been heavy and well-nigh constant for several years. In the revision of the tariff, especial attention should be given to the re-enactment and extension of the reciprocity principle of the law of 1890, under which so great a stimulus was given to our foreign trade in new and advantageous markets for our surplus agricultural and manufactured products."

Without effect, the incoming President urged the ratification of the treaty of arbitration with Great Britain, negotiated by his predecessor and still pending in the Senate. In concluding his address he announced his intention to convene Congress in extra session, saying: "The condition of the public treasury demands the immediate consideration of congress. It alone has the power to provide revenue for the government. Not to convene it under such circumstances, I can view in no other sense than the neglect of a plain duty."

On the day following his inauguration, the President sent to the Senate the following nominations for his Cabinet, which were confirmed: Secretary of State, John Sherman of Ohio; Secretary of the Treasury, Lyman J. Gage of Illinois; Secretary of War, Russel A. Alger of Michigan; Attorney-General, Joseph McKenna of California; Postmaster-General, James A. Gary of Maryland; Secretary of the Navy, John D. Long of Massachusetts; Secretary of the Interior, Cornelius N. Bliss of New York; Secretary of Agriculture, James Wilson of Iowa.

A. D. 1897 (March—July).—Passage of the Dingley Tariff Act.—Carrying out an intention announced in his Inaugural Address, President McKinley called Congress together in extra session on the 15th of March, asking for immediate action to increase the revenue of the government by increased duties, "so levied upon foreign products as to preserve the home market, so far as possible, to our own producers." In his Inaugural Address the President had expressed the understanding of his party as to the chief meaning of the late election, by saying that "the country is . . . committed by its latest popular utterance to the system of tariff taxation. . . . The people have declared that such legislation should be had as will give ample protection and encouragement to the industries and development of our country. . . . The paramount duty of Congress is to stop deficiencies by the restoration of that protective legislation which has always been the firmest prop of the treasury." To the majority in both Houses of Congress these views were entirely acceptable, and they were acted upon at once. The Ways and Means Committee of the House of Representatives in the previous Congress had already prepared a comprehensive new tariff bill, which it passed on to its successor. This ready-made bill was reported to the House on the first day of the session, by Mr. Dingley, chairman of the newly appointed committee, as he had been of the one before it. Debate on the measure began a week later, and was controlled by a fixed programme, which required it to be ended on the 31st of March. The bill was then passed, by a vote of 205 against 121. Of the action of the Senate upon it, and of the main features of the bill as it was finally shaped and became law, the following is a succinct account:

"The bill, referred at once to the Senate Committee on Finance, was reported after a month, on May 8, with important amendments. There was an attempt to impose some purely revenue duties, and, as to the protective duties, the tendency was towards lower rates than in the House bill, though on certain articles, such as wools of low grade, hides, and others (of which more will be said presently), the drift was the other way. The Senate, however, paid much less respect than the House to the recommendations of the committee in charge. In the course of two months, from May 4 to July 7, it went over the tariff bill item by item, amending without restraint, often in a perfunctory manner, and not infrequently with the outcome settled by the accident of attendance on the particular day ; on the whole, with a tendency to retain the higher rates of the House bill. As passed finally by the Senate on July 7, the bill, though it contained some 872 amendments, followed the plan of the House Committee rather than that of the Senate Committee. As usual, it went to a Conference Committee. In the various compromises and adjustments in the Senate and in the Conference Committee there was little sign of the deliberate plan and method which the House had shown, and the details of the act were settled in no less haphazard fashion than has been the case with other tariff measures. As patched up by the Conference Committee, the bill was promptly passed by both branches of Congress, and became law on July 24. In what manner these political conditions affected the character of the act will appear from a consideration of the more important specific changes.

"First and foremost was the reimposition of the duties on wool. As the repeal of these duties had been the one important change made by the act of 1894, so their restoration was the salient feature in the act of 1897. . . . Clothing wool was subjected once more to a duty of 11 cents a pound, combing wool to one of 12 cents. On carpet wool there were new graded duties, heavier than any ever before levied. If its value was 12 cents a pound or less the duty was 4 cents; if over 12 cents, the duty was 7 cents. . . . The duties on carpet wool, as has already been noted, were made higher than ever before. In the House the rates of the act of 1890 had been retained; but in the Senate new and higher rates were inserted. . . . They were demanded by the Senators from some States in the Far West, especially from Idaho and Montana. . . . They [the Senators in question] needed to be placated; and they succeeded in getting higher duties on the cheap carpet wools, on the plea of encouragement for the comparatively coarse clothing wool of their ranches. . . . The same complications that led to the high duty on carpet wool brought about a duty on hides. This rawest of raw materials had been on the free list for just a quarter of a century, since 1872, when the duty of the war days had been repealed. . . . But here, again, the Senators from the ranching States were able to dictate terms. . . . In the Senate a duty of 20 per cent. was tacked on. The rate was reduced to 15 per cent. in the Conference Committee, and so remains in the act. The restored duties on wool necessarily brought in their train the old system of high compensating duties on woollens. . . . In the main, the result was a restoration of the rates of the act of 1890. There was some upward movement almost all along the line; and the ad valorem duty alone, on the classes of fabrics which are most largely imported, crept up to 55 per cent. . . .

"On cotton goods the general tendency was to impose duties lower than those of 1890. This was indicated by the drag-net rate, on manufactures of cotton not otherwise provided for, which had been 50 per cent. in 1890, and was 45 per cent. in 1897. On two large classes of textile goods new and distinctly higher duties were imposed,—on silks and linens. . . . The mode of gradation was to levy the duties according to the amount of pure silk contained in the goods. The duties were fixed by the pound, being lowest on goods containing a small proportion of pure silk, and rising as that proportion became larger; with the proviso that in no case should the duty be less than 50 per cent. . . . Thus, the duty on certain kinds of silks was $1.30 cents per pound, if they contained 45 per cent in weight of silk; but advanced suddenly to $2.25, if they contained more than 45 per cent. . . . On linens another step of the same kind was taken, specific duties being substituted here also for ad-valorem. . . . Linens were graded somewhat as cottons had been graded since 1861, according to the fineness of the goods as indicated by the number of threads to the square inch. If the number of threads was 60 or less per square inch, the duty was 1¾ cents a square yard; if the threads were between 60 and 120, the duty was 2¾ cents; and so on,—plus 30 per cent. ad-valorem duty in all cases. But finer linen goods, unless otherwise specially provided for, were treated leniently. If the weight was small (less than 4½ ounces per yard), the duty was but 35 per cent. On the other hand, linen laces, or articles trimmed with lace or embroidery, were dutiable at 60 per cent., —an advance at 10 per cent. over the rate of 1890. . . . It was inevitable, under the political conditions of the session, that in this schedule something should again be attempted for the farmer; and, accordingly, we find a substantial duty on flax. The rate of the act of 1890 was restored, —3 cents a pound on prepared flax, in place of the rate of 1¼ cents imposed by the act of 1894. . . .

"On chinaware the rates of 1890 were restored. The duty on the finer qualities which are chiefly imported had been lowered to 35 per cent. in 1894, and was now once more put at 60 per cent. On glassware, also, the general ad-valorem rate, which had been reduced to 35 per cent. in 1894, was again fixed at 45 per cent., as in 1890. Similarly the specific duties on the cheaper grades of window-glass and plate-glass, which had been lowered in 1894, were raised to the figures of 1890. . . . The metal schedules in the act of 1897 showed in the main a striking contrast with the textile schedules. Important advances of duty were made on many textiles, and in some cases rates went considerably higher even than those of 1890. But on most metals, and especially on iron and steel, duties were left very much as they had been in 1894. . . . On steel rails there was even a slight reduction from the rate of 1894— $6.72 per ton instead of $7.84. On coal there was a compromise rate. The duty had been 75 cents a ton in 1890, and 40 cents in 1894; it was now fixed at 67 cents. On the other hand, as to certain manufactures of iron and steel farther advanced beyond the crude stage, there was a return to rates very similar to those of 1890. Thus, on pocket cutlery, razors, guns, we find once more the system of combined ad-valorem and specific duties, graded according to the value of the article. . . . Copper remained on the free list, where it had been put in 1894. . . . For good or ill the copper duty had worked out all its effects years before. On the other hand, the duties on lead and on lead ore went up to the point at which they stood in 1890. Here we have once more the signs of concession to the silver

Republicans of the far West. . . . The duty on tin plate, a bone of contention under the act of 1890, was disposed of, with little debate, by the imposition of a comparatively moderate duty. . . .

" A part of the act which aroused much public attention and which had an important bearing on its financial yield was the sugar schedule—the duties on sugar, raw and refined. . . . The act of 1890 had admitted raw sugar free, while that of 1894 had imposed a duty of 40 per cent. ad valorem. . . . The price of raw sugar had maintained its downward tendency; and the duty of 40 per cent. had been equivalent in 1896 to less than one cent a pound. In the act of 1897 the duty was made specific, and was practically doubled. Beginning with a rate of one cent a pound on sugar tested to contain 75 per cent., it advanced by stages until on sugar testing 95 per cent. (the usual content of commercial raw sugar) it reached 1.65 cents per pound. The higher rate thus imposed was certain to yield a considerable increase of revenue. Much was said also of the protection now afforded to the beet sugar industry of the West. That industry, however, was still of small dimensions and uncertain future. . . . On refined sugar, the duty was made 1.95 cents per pound, which, as compared with raw sugar testing 100 per cent., left a protection for the domestic refiner,—i. e., for the Sugar 'Trust,'—of 1/8 of one cent a pound. Some intricate calculation would be necessary to make out whether this 'differential' for the refining interest was more or less than in the act of 1894; but, having regard to the effect of the substitution of specific for ad-valorem duties, the Trust was no more favored by the act of 1897 than by its predecessor, and even somewhat less favored. The changes which this part of the tariff act underwent in the two Houses are not without significance." In the bill passed by the House, "the so-called differential, or protection to the refiners, was one-eighth of a cent per pound. In the Senate there was an attempt at serious amendment. The influence of the Sugar Trust in the Senate had long been great. How secured, whether through party contributions, entangling alliances, or coarse bribery, the public could not know; but certainly great, as the course of legislation in that body demonstrated." The Senate attempted to make an entire change in the scheme of sugar duties, which would give the Trust a fifth of a cent per pound of protective differential, instead of an eighth; but the House resisted, with more success than in 1894, and the senatorial friends of the Sugar Trust had to give way.— See, also (in this vol.), TRUSTS: UNITED STATES; and SUGAR BOUNTIES.

" The tariff act of 1894 had repealed the provisions as to reciprocity in the act of 1890, and had rendered nugatory such parts of the treaties made under the earlier act as were inconsistent with the provisions of its successor. The act of 1897 now revived the policy of reciprocity, and in some ways even endeavored to enlarge the scope of the reciprocity provisions " (see below: A. D. 1899–1901.)—F. W. Taussig, *Tariff History of the United States*, 4th edition, ch. 7 (*N. Y.: G. P. Putnam's Sons*).

A. D. 1897 (April—October).—Negotiations for an international bi-metallic agreement. See (in this vol.) MONETARY QUESTIONS: A. D 1897 (APRIL—OCTOBER).

A. D. 1897 (June).—Appointment of the Nicaragua Canal Commission. See (in this vol.) CANAL, INTEROCEANIC: A. D. 1889-1899.

A. D. 1897 (November).—Refusal to negotiate with the insurgent republic of the Philippine Islands.—On the 3d of November, 1897, Mr. Rounseville Wildman, the U. S. Consul at Hongkong, addressed the following to the State Department: "Since my arrival in Hongkong I have been called upon several times by Mr. F. Agoncilla, foreign agent and high commissioner, etc., of the new republic of the Philippines. Mr. Agoncilla holds a commission, signed by the president, members of cabinet, and general in chief of the republic of Philippines, empowering him absolutely with power to conclude treaties with foreign governments. Mr. Agoncilla offers on behalf of his government alliance offensive and defensive with the United States when the United States declares war on Spain, which, in Mr. Agoncilla's judgment, will be very soon. In the meantime he wishes the United States to send to some port in the Philippines 20,000 stand of arms and 200,000 rounds of ammunition for the use of his government, to be paid for on the recognition of his government by the United States. He pledges as security two provinces and the custom-house at Manila. He is not particular about the price—is willing the United States should make 25 per cent or 30 per cent profit. He is a very earnest and attentive diplomat and a great admirer of the United States. On his last visit he surprised me with the information that he had written his government that he had hopes of inducing the United States to supply the much-needed guns, etc. In case Señor Agoncilla's dispatch should fall into the hands of an unfriendly power and find its way into the newspapers, I have thought it wise to apprise the State Department of the nature of the high commissioner's proposals. Señor Agoncilla informs me by late mail that he will proceed at once to Washington to conclude the proposed treaty, if I advise. I shall not advise said step until so instructed by the State Department."

To this communication, the Third Assistant Secretary of State, Mr. Cridler, returned the following reply, Dec. 15, 1897: "I have to acknowledge the receipt of your dispatch No. 19 of November 3, 1897, in which you announce the arrival at your post of Mr. F. Agoncilla, whom you describe as foreign agent and high commissioner of the new republic of the Philippines, and who holds full power to negotiate and conclude treaties with foreign powers. Mr. Agoncilla offers an alliance 'offensive and defensive with the United States when the United States declares war on Spain, which, in Mr. Agoncilla's judgment, will be very soon,' and suggests that 20,000 stand of arms and 200,000 rounds of ammunition be supplied to his government by that of the United States. You may briefly advise Mr. Agoncilla, in case he should call upon you, that the Government of the United States does not negotiate such treaties and that it is not possible to forward the desired arms and ammunition. You should not encourage any advances on the part of Mr. Agoncilla, and should courteously decline to communicate with the Department further regarding his alleged mission."—*Treaty of Peace and Accompanying Papers* (*55th Congress, 3d Sess., Senate Doc. No. 62, pt. 1, pp. 333, 334*).

A. D. 1897 (November).—Treaty with Rus-

sia and Japan to suspend pelagic sealing. See (in this vol.) BERING SEA QUESTIONS.

A. D. 1897 (December).—President McKinley on Cuban affairs. See (in this vol.) CUBA: A. D. 1896-1897.

A. D. 1897 (December).—Stringent measures against pelagic sealing. See (in this vol.) BERING SEA QUESTIONS.

A. D. 1897-1898 (December—March).—Reports from Cuba of the suffering condition of the "reconcentrados." See (in this vol.) CUBA: A. D. 1897-1898 (DECEMBER—MARCH).

A. D. 1897-1899.—Agreements with the Choctaw, Chickasaw, Creek, Cherokee, and Seminole tribes of Indians.—Work of the Dawes Commission. See (in this vol.) INDIANS, AMERICAN: A. D. 1893-1899.

A. D. 1897-1900.—Treaty for the annexation of Hawaii.—Its failure of ratification.—Passage of joint resolution to annex, and of an Act for the government of the islands. See (in this vol.) HAWAII.

A. D. 1898 (February—March).—American sympathy with the Cubans and indignation against Spain.—Destruction of the United States battle-ship "Maine" in Havana harbor.—Investigation and findings of the American and Spanish courts of inquiry.—Public feeling in the United States, excited by a terrible state of suffering in Cuba, resulting from Spanish methods of dealing with insurrection in that island (see, in this vol., CUBA: A. D. 1896-1897 and 1897-1898), had been gathering intensity for months past, and threatening a rupture of peaceful relations between the United States and Spain. A sudden crisis in the situation was produced, on the morning of the 15th of February, 1898, by news that the United States battle-ship "Maine," while paying a visit of courtesy to the harbor of Havana, had been totally destroyed, on the previous evening, by an explosion which killed most of her crew. In a subsequent message on the subject to Congress, President McKinley recited the circumstances of the catastrophe, and the proceedings adopted to ascertain its cause, with the conclusions reached, in the following words: "For some time prior to the visit of the 'Maine' to Havana Harbor our consular representatives pointed out the advantages to flow from the visit of national ships to the Cuban waters, in accustoming the people to the presence of our flag as the symbol of good will and of our ships in the fulfillment of the mission of protection to American interests, even though no immediate need therefor might exist. Accordingly on the 24th of January last, after conference with the Spanish minister, in which the renewal of visits of our war vessels to Spanish waters was discussed and accepted, the peninsular authorities at Madrid and Havana were advised of the purpose of this Government to resume friendly naval visits at Cuban ports, and that in that view the 'Maine' would forthwith call at the port of Havana. This announcement was received by the Spanish Government with appreciation of the friendly character of the visit of the 'Maine,' and with notification of intention to return the courtesy by sending Spanish ships to the principal ports of the United States. Meanwhile the 'Maine' entered the port of Havana on the 25th of January, her arrival being marked with no special incident besides the exchange of customary salutes and ceremonial visits.

"The 'Maine' continued in the harbor of Havana during the three weeks following her arrival. No appreciable excitement attended her stay; on the contrary, a feeling of relief and confidence followed the resumption of the long-interrupted friendly intercourse. So noticeable was this immediate effect of her visit that the consul-general strongly urged that the presence of our ships in Cuban waters should be kept up by retaining the 'Maine' at Havana, or, in the event of her recall, by sending another vessel there to take her place. At forty minutes past 9 in the evening of the 15th of February the 'Maine' was destroyed by an explosion, by which the entire forward part of the ship was utterly wrecked. In this catastrophe 2 officers and 264 of her crew perished, those who were not killed outright by her explosion being penned between decks by the tangle of wreckage and drowned by the immediate sinking of the hull. Prompt assistance was rendered by the neighboring vessels anchored in the harbor, aid being especially given by the boats of the Spanish cruiser 'Alfonso XII' and the Ward Line steamer 'City of Washington,' which lay not far distant. The wounded were generously cared for by the authorities of Havana, the hospitals being freely opened to them, while the earliest recovered bodies of the dead were interred by the municipality in a public cemetery in the ity. Tributes of grief and sympathy were offered from all official quarters of the island.

"The appalling calamity fell upon the people of our country with crushing force, and for a brief time an intense excitement prevailed, which in a community less just and self-controlled than ours might have led to hasty acts of blind resentment. This spirit, however, soon gave way to the calmer processes of reason and to the resolve to investigate the facts and await material proof before forming a judgment as to the cause, the responsibility, and, if the facts warranted, the remedy due. This course uecessarily recommended itself from the outset to the Executive, for only in the light of a dispassionately ascertained certainty could it determine the nature and measure of its full duty in the matter. The usual procedure was followed, as in all cases of casualty or disaster to national vessels of any maritime State. A naval court of inquiry was at once organized, composed of officers well qualified by rank and practical experience to discharge the onerous duty imposed upon them. Aided by a strong force of wreckers and divers, the court proceeded to make a thorough investigation on the spot, employing every available means for the impartial and exact determination of the causes of the explosion. Its operations have been conducted with the utmost deliberation and judgment, and while independently pursued no attainable source of information was neglected, and the fullest opportunity was allowed for a simultaneous investigation by the Spanish authorities. The finding of the court of inquiry was reached, after twenty-three days of continuous labor, on the 21st of March, instant, and, having been approved on the 22d by the commander in chief of the United States naval force on the North Atlantic Station, was transmitted to the Executive. It is herewith laid before the Congress, together with the voluminous testimony taken before the court. Its purport is, in brief, as follows:

"When the 'Maine' arrived at Havana she was conducted by the regular Government pilot to buoy No. 4, to which she was moored in from 5½ to 6 fathoms of water. The state of discipline on board and the condition of her magazines, boilers, coal bunkers, and storage compartments are passed in review, with the conclusion that excellent order prevailed and that no indication of any cause for an internal explosion existed in any quarter. At 8 o'clock in the evening of February 15 everything had been reported secure, and all was quiet. At forty minutes past 9 o'clock the vessel was suddenly destroyed. There were two distinct explosions, with a brief interval between them. The first lifted the forward part of the ship very perceptibly. The second, which was more open, prolonged, and of greater volume, is attributed by the court to the partial explosion of two or more of the forward magazines. The evidence of the divers establishes that the after part of the ship was practically intact and sank in that condition a very few moments after the explosion. The forward part was completely demolished. Upon the evidence of a concurrent external cause the finding of the court is as follows:

"'At frame 17 the outer shell of the ship, from a point of 11½ feet from the middle line of the ship and 6 feet above the keel when in its normal position, has been forced up so as to be now about 4 feet above the surface of the water, therefore about 34 feet above where it would be had the ship sunk uninjured. The outside bottom plating is bent into a reversed $\vee$ shape ($\wedge$), the after wing of which, about 15 feet broad and 32 feet in length (from frame 17 to frame 25), is doubled back upon itself against the continuation of the same plating, extending forward. At frame 18 the vertical keel is broken in two and the flat keel bent into an angle similar to the angle formed by the outside bottom plates. This break is now about 6 feet below the surface of the water and about 30 feet above its normal position. In the opinion of the court this effect could have been produced only by the explosion of a mine situated under the bottom of the ship at about frame 18 and somewhat on the port side of the ship.'

"The conclusions of the court are: That the loss of the 'Maine' was not in any respect due to fault or negligence on the part of any of the officers or members of her crew; That the ship was destroyed by the explosion of a submarine mine, which caused the partial explosion of two or more of her forward magazines; and That no evidence has been obtainable fixing the responsibility for the destruction of the 'Maine' upon any person or persons.

"I have directed that the finding of the court of inquiry and the views of this Government thereon be communicated to the Government of Her Majesty the Queen Regent, and I do not permit myself to doubt that the sense of justice of the Spanish nation will dictate a course of action suggested by honor and the friendly relations of the two Governments. It will be the duty of the Executive to advise the Congress of the result, and in the meantime deliberate consideration is invoked."—*Congressional Record,* *March* 28, 1898.

A Spanish naval board of inquiry, convened by the maritime authority at Havana, and investigating the matter with haste, arrived at a conclusion quite opposite to that stated above, reporting on the 22d of March that "an explosion of the first order, in the forward magazine of the American ironclad 'Maine,' caused the destruction of that part of the ship and its total submersion in the same place in this bay at which it was anchored. . . . That the important facts connected with the explosion in its external appearances at every moment of its duration having been described by witnesses, and the absence of all circumstances which necessarily accompany the explosion of a torpedo having been proved by these witnesses and experts, it can only be honestly asserted that the catastrophe was due to internal causes. . . . That the character of the proceedings undertaken and respect for the law which establishes the absolute extraterritoriality of a foreign war vessel have prevented the determination, even by conjecture, of the said internal origin of the disaster, to which also the impossibility of establishing the necessary communication either with the crew of the wrecked vessel or the officials of their Government commissioned to investigate the causes of the said event, or with those subsequently intrusted with the issue, has contributed. . . . That the interior and exterior examination of the bottom of the 'Maine,' whenever it is possible, unless the bottom of the ship and that of the place in the bay where it is sunk are altered by the work which is being carried on for the total or partial recovery of the vessel, will prove the correctness of all that is said in this report; but this must not be understood to mean that the accuracy of these present conclusions requires such proof."—*U. S. Senate Report No. 885, 55th Cong., 2d Sess., p. 635.*

A. D. 1898 (February—December).—In the Chinese "battle of concessions." See (in this vol.) CHINA: A. D. 1898 (FEBRUARY—DECEMBER).

A. D. 1898 (March).—Account by Senator Proctor of the condition of the "reconcentrados" in Cuba. See (in this vol.) CUBA: A. D. 1897–1898 (DECEMBER—MARCH).

A. D. 1898 (March—April).—Continued discussion of Cuban affairs with Spain.—Unsatisfactory results.—Message of the President asking Congress for authority to terminate hostilities in Cuba.—On the 11th of April, President McKinley addressed another special message to Congress, setting forth the unsatisfactory results with which Cuban affairs had been further discussed with the government of Spain, and formally asking to be authorized and empowered to take measures for securing a "full and final termination of hostilities" in the oppressed island. He said:

"Obedient to that precept of the Constitution which commands the President to give from time to time to the Congress information of the state of the Union and to recommend to their consideration such measures as he shall judge necessary and expedient, it becomes my duty now to address your body with regard to the grave crisis that has arisen in the relations of the United States to Spain by reason of the warfare that for more than three years has raged in the neighboring island of Cuba. I do so because of the intimate connection of the Cuban question with the state of our own Union, and the grave relation the course which it is now incumbent upon the nation to adopt must needs bear to the traditional policy of our Government, if it is to accord with the precepts laid down by the founders of the Republic and religiously observed by succeeding Administrations to the present day.

"The present revolution is but the successor of other similar insurrections which have occurred in Cuba against the dominion of Spain, extending over a period of nearly half a century, each of which, during its progress, has subjected the United States to great effort and expense in enforcing its neutrality laws, caused enormous losses to American trade and commerce, caused irritation, annoyance, and disturbance among our citizens, and, by the exercise of cruel, barbarous, and uncivilized practices of warfare, shocked the sensibilities and offended the humane sympathies of our people. Since the present revolution began, in February, 1895, this country has seen the fertile domain at our threshold ravaged by fire and sword in the course of a struggle unequaled in the history of the island and rarely paralleled as to the numbers of the combatants and the bitterness of the contest by any revolution of modern times where a dependent people striving to be free have been opposed by the power of the sovereign state. Our people have beheld a once prosperous community reduced to comparative want, its lucrative commerce virtually paralyzed, its exceptional productiveness diminished, its fields laid waste, its mills in ruins, and its people perishing by tens of thousands from hunger and destitution. We have found ourselves constrained, in the observance of that strict neutrality which our laws enjoin and which the law of nations commands, to police our own waters and to watch our own seaports in prevention of any unlawful act in aid of the Cubans. Our trade has suffered; the capital invested by our citizens in Cuba has been largely lost, and the temper and forbearance of our people have been so sorely tried as to beget a perilous unrest among our own citizens which has inevitably found its expression from time to time in the National Legislature, so that issues wholly external to our own body politic engross attention and stand in the way of that close devotion to domestic advancement that becomes a self-contained commonwealth whose primal maxim has been the avoidance of all foreign entanglements. All this must needs awaken, and has, indeed, aroused the utmost concern on the part of this Government, as well during my predecessor's term as in my own.

"In April, 1896, the evils from which our country suffered through the Cuban war became so onerous that my predecessor made an effort to bring about a peace through the mediation of this Government in any way that might tend to an honorable adjustment of the contest between Spain and her revolted colony, on the basis of some effective scheme of self-government for Cuba under the flag and sovereignty of Spain. It failed through the refusal of the Spanish Government then in power to consider any form of mediation or, indeed, any plan of settlement which did not begin with the actual submission of the insurgents to the mother country, and then only on such terms as Spain herself might see fit to grant. The war continued unabated. The resistance of the insurgents was in no wise diminished. The efforts of Spain were increased, both by the dispatch of fresh levies to Cuba and by the addition to the horrors of the strife of a new and inhuman phase happily unprecedented in the modern history of civilized Christian peoples. The policy of devastation and concentration, inaugurated by the captain-general's bando of October 21, 1896, in the province of Pinar del Rio, was thence extended to embrace all of the island to which the power of the Spanish arms was able to reach by occupation or by military operations. The peasantry, including all dwelling in the open agricultural interior, were driven into the garrison towns or isolated places held by the troops. The raising and movement of provisions of all kinds were interdicted. The fields were laid waste, dwellings unroofed and fired, mills destroyed, and, in short, everything that could desolate the land and render it unfit for human habitation or support was commanded by one or the other of the contending parties and executed by all the powers at their disposal.

"By the time the present Administration took office, a year ago, reconcentration—so called—had been made effective over the better part of the four central and western provinces—Santa Clara, Matanzas, Habana, and Pinar del Rio. The agricultural population to the estimated number of 300,000 or more was herded within the towns and their immediate vicinage, deprived of the means of support, rendered destitute of shelter, left poorly clad, and exposed to the most unsanitary conditions. As the scarcity of food increased with the devastation of the depopulated areas of production, destitution and want became misery and starvation. Month by month the death rate increased in an alarming ratio. By March, 1897, according to conservative estimates from official Spanish sources, the mortality among the reconcentrados, from starvation and the diseases thereto incident, exceeded 50 per centum of their total number. No practical relief was accorded to the destitute. The overburdened towns, already suffering from the general dearth, could give no aid. So-called 'zones of cultivation' established within the immediate areas of effective military control about the cities and fortified camps proved illusory as a remedy for the suffering. The unfortunates, being for the most part women and children, with aged and helpless men, enfeebled by disease and hunger, could not have tilled the soil without tools, seed, or shelter for their own support or for the supply of the cities. Reconcentration, adopted avowedly as a war measure in order to cut off the resources of the insurgents, worked its predestined result. As I said in my message of last December, it was not civilized warfare; it was extermination. The only peace it could beget was that of the wilderness and the grave.

"Meanwhile the military situation in the island had undergone a noticeable change. The extraordinary activity that characterized the second year of the war, when the insurgents invaded even the thitherto unharmed fields of Pinar del Rio and carried havoc and destruction up to the walls of the city of Habana itself, had relapsed into a dogged struggle in the central and eastern provinces. The Spanish arms regained a measure of control in Pinar del Rio and parts of Habana, but, under the existing conditions of the rural country, without immediate improvement of their productive situation. Even thus partially restricted, the revolutionists held their own, and their conquest and submission, put

forward by Spain as the essential and sole basis of peace, seemed as far distant as at the outset. In this state of affairs my Administration found itself confronted with the grave problem of its duty. My message of last December reviewed the situation, and narrated the steps taken with a view to relieving its acuteness and opening the way to some form of honorable settlement. The assassination of the prime minister, Canovas, led to a change of government in Spain. The former administration, pledged to subjugation without concession, gave place to that of a more liberal party, committed long in advance to a policy of reform involving the wider principle of home rule for Cuba and Porto Rico.

"The overtures of this Government, made through its new envoy, General Woodford, and looking to an immediate and effective amelioration of the condition of the island, although not accepted to the extent of admitted mediation in any shape, were met by assurances that home rule, in an advanced phase, would be forthwith offered to Cuba, without waiting for the war to end, and that more humane methods should thenceforth prevail in the conduct of hostilities. Coincidentally with these declarations, the new Government of Spain continued and completed the policy already begun by its predecessor, of testifying friendly regard for this nation by releasing American citizens held under one charge or another connected with the insurrection, so that by the end of November not a single person entitled in any way to our national protection remained in a Spanish prison.

"While these negotiations were in progress the increasing destitution of the unfortunate reconcentrados and the alarming mortality among them claimed earnest attention. The success which had attended the limited measure of relief extended to the suffering American citizens among them by the judicious expenditure through the consular agencies of the money appropriated expressly for their succor by the joint resolution approved May 24, 1897, prompted the humane extension of a similar scheme of aid to the great body of sufferers. A suggestion to this end was acquiesced in by the Spanish authorities. On the 24th of December last I caused to be issued an appeal to the American people, inviting contributions in money or in kind for the succor of the starving sufferers in Cuba, following this on the 8th of January by a similar public announcement of the formation of a central Cuban relief committee, with headquarters in New York City, composed of three members, representing the American National Red Cross and the religious and business elements of the community. The efforts of that committee have been untiring and have accomplished much. Arrangements for free transportation to Cuba have greatly aided the charitable work. The president of the American Red Cross and representatives of other contributory organizations have generously visited Cuba and coöperated with the consul-general and the local authorities to make effective distribution of the relief collected through the efforts of the central committee. Nearly $200,000 in money and supplies has already reached the sufferers, and more is forthcoming. The supplies are admitted duty free, and transportation to the interior has been arranged, so that the relief, at first necessarily confined to Habana and the larger cities, is now extended through most, if not all, of the towns where suffering exists. Thousands of lives have already been saved. The necessity for a change in the condition of the reconcentrados is recognized by the Spanish Government. Within a few days past the orders of General Weyler have been revoked; the reconcentrados, it is said, are to be permitted to return to their homes, and aided to resume the self-supporting pursuits of peace. Public works have been ordered to give them employment, and a sum of $600,000 has been appropriated for their relief.

"The war in Cuba is of such a nature that short of subjugation or extermination a final military victory for either side seems impracticable. The alternative lies in the physical exhaustion of the one or the other party, or perhaps of both—a condition which in effect ended the ten years' war by the truce of Zanjon. The prospect of such a protraction and conclusion of the present strife is a contingency hardly to be contemplated with equanimity by the civilized world, and least of all by the United States, affected and injured as we are, deeply and intimately, by its very existence. Realizing this, it appeared to be my duty, in a spirit of true friendliness, no less to Spain than to the Cubans who have so much to lose by the prolongation of the struggle, to seek to bring about an immediate termination of the war. To this end I submitted on the 27th ultimo, as a result of much representation and correspondence, through the United States minister at Madrid, propositions to the Spanish Government looking to an armistice until October 1 for the negotiation of peace with the good offices of the President. In addition, I asked the immediate revocation of the order of reconcentration, so as to permit the people to return to their farms and the needy to be relieved with provisions and supplies from the United States, coöperating with the Spanish authorities, so as to afford full relief.

"The reply of the Spanish cabinet was received on the night of the 31st ultimo. It offered, as the means to bring about peace in Cuba, to confide the preparation thereof to the insular parliament, inasmuch as the concurrence of that body would be necessary to reach a final result, it being, however, understood that the powers reserved by the constitution to the Central Government are not lessened or diminished. As the Cuban parliament does not meet until the 4th of May next, the Spanish Government would not object, for its part, to accept at once a suspension of hostilities if asked for by the insurgents from the general in chief, to whom it would pertain, in such case, to determine the duration and conditions of the armistice. The propositions submitted by General Woodford and the reply of the Spanish Government were both in the form of brief memoranda, the texts of which are before me, and are substantially in the language above given. The function of the Cuban parliament in the matter of 'preparing' peace and the manner of its doing so are not expressed in the Spanish memorandum; but from General Woodford's explanatory reports of preliminary discussions preceding the final conference it is understood that the Spanish Government stands ready to give the insular congress full powers to settle the terms of peace with the insurgents—whether by direct negotiation or indirectly by means of legislation does not appear.

"With this last overture in the direction of immediate peace, and its disappointing reception by Spain, the Executive is brought to the end of his effort. In my annual message of December last I said: 'Of the untried measures there remain only: Recognition of the insurgents as belligerents; recognition of the independence of Cuba; neutral intervention to end the war by imposing a rational compromise between the contestants, and intervention in favor of one or the other party. I speak not of forcible annexation, for that can not be thought of. That, by our code of morality, would be criminal aggression.' Thereupon I review these alternatives, in the light of President Grant's measured words, uttered in 1875, when after seven years of sanguinary, destructive, and cruel hostilities in Cuba he reached the conclusion that the recognition of the independence of Cuba was impracticable and indefensible; and that the recognition of belligerence was not warranted by the facts according to the tests of public law. I commented especially upon the latter aspect of the question, pointing out the inconveniences and positive dangers of a recognition of belligerence which, while adding to the already onerous burdens of neutrality within our own jurisdiction, could not in any way extend our influence or effective offices in the territory of hostilities. Nothing has since occurred to change my view in this regard; and I recognize as fully now as then that the issuance of a proclamation of neutrality, by which process the so-called recognition of belligerents is published, could, of itself and unattended by other action, accomplish nothing toward the one end for which we labor—the instant pacification of Cuba and the cessation of the misery that afflicts the island.

"Turning to the question of recognizing at this time the independence of the present insurgent government in Cuba, we find safe precedents in our history from an early day. They are well summed up in President Jackson's message to Congress, December 21, 1836, on the subject of the recognition of the independence of Texas. He said: 'In all the contests that have arisen out of the revolutions of France, out of the disputes relating to the Crowns of Portugal and Spain, out of the separation of the American possessions of both from the European Governments, and out of the numerous and constantly occurring struggles for dominion in Spanish America, so wisely consistent with our just principles has been the action of our Government that we have, under the most critical circumstances, avoided all censure, and encountered no other evil than that produced by a transient estrangement of good will in those against whom we have been by force of evidence compelled to decide. It has thus made known to the world that the uniform policy and practice of the United States is to avoid all interference in disputes which merely relate to the internal government of other nations, and eventually to recognize the authority of the prevailing party without reference to our particular interests and views or to the merits of the original controversy. . . . But on this, as on every other trying occasion, safety is to be found in a rigid adherence to principle. In the contest between Spain and the revolted colonies we stood aloof, and waited not only until the ability of the new States to protect themselves was fully established, but until the danger of their being again subjugated had entirely passed away. Then, and not until then, were they recognized. Such was our course in regard to Mexico herself. . . . It is true that with regard to Texas the civil authority of Mexico has been expelled, its invading army defeated, the chief of the Republic himself captured, and all present power to control the newly-organized government of Texas annihilated within its confines; but, on the other hand, there is, in appearance at least, an immense disparity of physical force on the side of Texas. The Mexican Republic, under another Executive, is rallying its forces under a new leader and menacing a fresh invasion to recover its lost dominion. Upon the issue of this threatened invasion the independence of Texas may be considered as suspended; and were there nothing peculiar in the relative situation of the United States and Texas, our acknowledgment of its independence at such a crisis could scarcely be regarded as consistent with that prudent reserve with which we have hitherto held ourselves bound to treat all similar questions.'

"Thereupon Andrew Jackson proceeded to consider the risk that there might be imputed to the United States motives of selfish interest in view of the former claim on our part to the territory of Texas, and of the avowed purpose of the Texans in seeking recognition of independence as an incident to the incorporation of Texas in the Union, concluding thus : ' Prudence, therefore, seems to dictate that we should still stand aloof and maintain our present attitude, if not until Mexico itself or one of the great foreign powers shall recognize the independence of the new government, at least until the lapse of time or the course of events shall have proved beyond cavil or dispute the ability of the people of that country to maintain their separate sovereignty and to uphold the government constituted by them. Neither of the contending parties can justly complain of this course. By pursuing it we are but carrying out the long-established policy of our Government, a policy which has secured to us respect and influence abroad and inspired confidence at home.'

"These are the words of the resolute and patriotic Jackson. They are evidence that the United States, in addition to the test imposed by public law as the condition of the recognition of independence by a neutral state (to wit, that the revolted state shall ' constitute in fact a body politic, having a government in substance as well as in name, possessed of the elements of stability,' and forming de facto, ' if left to itself, a state among the nations, reasonably capable of discharging the duties of a state '), has imposed for its own governance in dealing with cases like these the further condition that recognition of independent statehood is not due to a revolted dependency until the danger of its being again subjugated by the parent state has entirely passed away. This extreme test was, in fact, applied in the case of Texas. The Congress, to whom President Jackson referred the question as one ' probably leading to war,' and therefore a proper subject for ' a previous understanding with that body, by whom war can alone be declared, and by whom all the provisions for sustaining its perils must be furnished,' left the matter of the recognition of Texas to the discretion of the Executive, providing merely for

the sending of a diplomatic agent when the President should be satisfied that the Republic of Texas had become ' an independent State.' It was so recognized by President Van Buren, who commissioned a chargé d'affaires March 7, 1837, after Mexico had abandoned an attempt to reconquer the Texan territory, and when there was at the time no bona fide contest going on between the insurgent province and its former sovereign.

" I said in my message of December last, ' It is to be seriously considered whether the Cuban insurrection possesses beyond dispute the attributes of statehood which alone can demand the recognition of belligerency in its favor.' The same requirement must certainly be no less seriously considered when the graver issue of recognizing independence is in question, for no less positive test can be applied to the greater act than to the lesser, while, on the other hand, the influences and consequences of the struggle upon the internal policy of the recognizing State, which form important factors when the recognition of belligerency is concerned, are secondary, if not rightly eliminable, factors when the real question is whether the community claiming recognition is or is not independent beyond peradventure.

"Nor from the standpoint of expediency do I think it would be wise or prudent for this Government to recognize at the present time the independence of the so-called Cuban republic. Such recognition is not necessary in order to enable the United States to intervene and pacify the island. To commit this country now to the recognition of any particular government in Cuba might subject us to embarrassing conditions of international obligation toward the organization so recognized. In case of intervention our conduct would be subject to the approval or disapproval of such government. We would be required to submit to its direction and to assume to it the mere relation of a friendly ally. When it shall appear hereafter that there is within the island a government capable of performing the duties and discharging the functions of a separate nation, and having, as a matter of fact, the proper forms and attributes of nationality, such government can be promptly and readily recognized and the relations and interests of the United States with such nation adjusted.

"There remain the alternative forms of intervention to end the war, either as an impartial neutral by imposing a rational compromise between the contestants or as the active ally of the one party or the other. As to the first, it is not to be forgotten that during the last few months the relation of the United States has virtually been one of friendly intervention in many ways, each not of itself conclusive, but all tending to the exertion of a potential influence toward an ultimate pacific result just and honorable to all interests concerned. The spirit of all our acts hitherto has been an earnest, unselfish desire for peace and prosperity in Cuba untarnished by differences between us and Spain and unstained by the blood of American citizens. The forcible intervention of the United States as a neutral to stop the war, according to the large dictates of humanity and following many historical precedents where neighboring states have interfered to check the hopeless sacrifices of life by internecine conflicts beyond their borders, is justifiable on rational grounds. It involves, however, hostile constraint upon both the parties to the contest, as well to enforce a truce as to guide the eventual settlement.

"The grounds for such intervention may be briefly summarized as follows: First. In the cause of humanity and to put an end to the barbarities, bloodshed, starvation, and horrible miseries now existing there, and which the parties to the conflict are either unable or unwilling to stop or mitigate. It is no answer to say this is all in another country, belonging to another nation, and is therefore none of our business. It is specially our duty, for it is right at our door. Second. We owe it to our citizens in Cuba to afford them that protection and indemnity for life and property which no government there can or will afford, and to that end to terminate the conditions that deprive them of legal protection. Third. The right to intervene may be justified by the very serious injury to the commerce, trade, and business of our people and by the wanton destruction of property and devastation of the island. Fourth, and which is of the utmost importance. The present condition of affairs in Cuba is a constant menace to our peace, and entails upon this Government an enormous expense. With such a conflict waged for years in an island so near us and with which our people have such trade and business relations—when the lives and liberty of our citizens are in constant danger and their property destroyed and themselves ruined —where our trading vessels are liable to seizure and are seized at our very door by warships of a foreign nation, the expeditions of filibustering that we are powerless to prevent altogether, and the irritating questions and entanglements thus arising—all these and others that I need not mention, with the resulting strained relations, are a constant menace to our peace, and compel us to keep on a semi-war footing with a nation with which we are at peace.

" These elements of danger and disorder already pointed out have been strikingly illustrated by a tragic event which has deeply and justly moved the American people. I have already transmitted to Congress the report of the naval court of inquiry on the destruction of the battleship ' Maine ' in the harbor of Habana during the night of the 15th of February. The destruction of that noble vessel has filled the national heart with inexpressible horror. Two hundred and fifty-eight brave sailors and marines and two officers of our Navy, reposing in the fancied security of a friendly harbor, have been hurled to death, grief and want brought to their homes and sorrow to the nation. The naval court of inquiry, which, it is needless to say, commands the unqualified confidence of the Government, was unanimous in its conclusion that the destruction of the ' Maine ' was caused by an exterior explosion, that of a submarine mine. It did not assume to place the responsibility : that remains to be fixed. In any event the destruction of the ' Maine ' by whatever exterior cause, is a patent and impressive proof of a state of things in Cuba that is intolerable. That condition is thus shown to be such that the Spanish Government cannot assure safety and security to a vessel of the American Navy in the harbor of Habana on a mission of peace, and rightfully there.

" Further referring in this connection to recent diplomatic correspondence, a dispatch from our minister to Spain, of the 26th ultimo, contained the statement that the Spanish minister for foreign affairs assured him positively that Spain will do all that the highest honor and justice require in the matter of the 'Maine.' The reply above referred to of the 31st ultimo, also contained an expression of the readiness of Spain to submit to an arbitration all the differences which can arise in this matter, which is subsequently explained by the note of the Spanish minister at Washington of the 10th instant, as follows : 'As to the question of fact which springs from the diversity of views between the reports of the American and Spanish boards, Spain proposes that the facts be ascertained by an impartial investigation by experts, whose decision Spain accepts in advance.' To this I have made no reply.

"President Grant, in 1875, after discussing the phases of the contest as it then appeared, and its hopeless and apparent indefinite prolongation, said : ' In such an event, I am of opinion that other nations will be compelled to assume the responsibility which devolves upon them, and to seriously consider the only remaining measures possible—mediation and intervention. Owing, perhaps, to the large expanse of water separating the island from the peninsula, . . . the contending parties appear to have within themselves no depository of common confidence, to suggest wisdom when passion and excitement have their sway, and to assume the part of peacemaker. In this view in the earlier days of the contest the good offices of the United States as a mediator were tendered in good faith, without any selfish purpose, in the interest of humanity and in sincere friendship for both parties, but were at the time declined by Spain, with the declaration, nevertheless, that at a future time they would be indispensable. No intimation has been received that in the opinion of Spain that time has been reached. And yet the strife continues with all its dread horrors and all its injuries to the interests of the United States and of other nations. Each party seems quite capable of working great injury and damage to the other, as well as to all the relations and interests dependent on the existence of peace in the island ; but they seem incapable of reaching any adjustment, and both have thus far failed of achieving any success whereby one party shall possess and control the island to the exclusion of the other. Under these circumstances, the agency of others, either by mediation or by intervention, seems to be the only alternative which must sooner or later be invoked for the termination of the strife.'

" In the last annual message of my immediate predecessor during the pending struggle, it was said : ' When the inability of Spain to deal successfully with the insurrection has become manifest, and it is demonstrated that her sovereignty is extinct in Cuba for all purposes of its rightful existence, and when a hopeless struggle for its re-establishment has degenerated into a strife which means nothing more than the useless sacrifice of human life and the utter destruction of the very subject-matter of the conflict, a situation will be presented in which our obligations to the sovereignty of Spain will be superseded by higher obligations, which we can hardly hesitate to recognize and discharge.'

" In my annual message to Congress, December

last, speaking to this question, I said : ' The near future will demonstrate whether the indispensable condition of a righteous peace, just alike to the Cubans and to Spain, as well as equitable to all our interests so intimately involved in the welfare of Cuba, is likely to be attained. If not, the exigency of further and other action by the United States will remain to be taken. When that time comes that action will be determined in the line of indisputable right and duty. It will be faced, without misgiving or hesitancy, in the light of the obligation this Government owes to itself, to the people who have confided to it the protection of their interests and honor, and to humanity. Sure of the right, keeping free from all offense ourselves, actuated only by upright and patriotic considerations, moved neither by passion nor selfishness, the Government will continue its watchful care over the rights and property of American citizens and will abate none of its efforts to bring about by peaceful agencies a peace which shall be honorable and enduring. If it shall hereafter appear to be a duty imposed by our obligations to ourselves, to civilization, and humanity to intervene with force, it shall be without fault on our part, and only because the necessity for such action will be so clear as to command the support and approval of the civilized world.'

" The long trial has proved that the object for which Spain has waged the war cannot be attained. The fire of insurrection may flame or may smoulder with varying seasons, but it has not been and it is plain that it cannot be extinguished by present methods. The only hope of relief and repose from a condition which can no longer be endured is the enforced pacification of Cuba. In the name of humanity, in the name of civilization, in behalf of endangered American interests which give us the right and the duty to speak and act, the war in Cuba must stop.

" In view of these facts and of these considerations, I ask the Congress to authorize and empower the President to take measures to secure a full and final termination of hostilities between the Government of Spain and the people of Cuba, and to secure in the island the establishment of a stable government, capable of maintaining order and observing its international obligations, insuring peace and tranquillity and the security of its citizens as well as our own, and to use the military and naval forces of the United States as may be necessary for these purposes. And in the interest of humanity and to aid in preserving the lives of the starving people of the island I recommend that the distribution of food and supplies be continued, and that an appropriation be made out of the public Treasury to supplement the charity of our citizens.

" The issue is now with the Congress. It is a solemn responsibility. I have exhausted every effort to relieve the intolerable condition of affairs which is at our doors. Prepared to execute every obligation imposed upon me by the Constitution and the law, I await your action.

" Yesterday, and since the preparation of the foregoing message, official information was received by me that the latest decree of the Queen Regent of Spain directs General Blanco, in order to prepare and facilitate peace, to proclaim a suspension of hostilities, the duration and details of which have not yet been communicated to me. This fact with every other pertinent considera-

tion will, I am sure, have your just and careful attention in the solemn deliberations upon which you are about to enter. If this measure attains a successful result, then our aspirations as a Christian, peace-loving people will be realized. If it fails, it will be only another justification for our contemplated action."—*Congressional Record, April* 11, 1898.

A. D. 1898 (April).—Action of Congress empowering the President to expel Spanish authority from the island of Cuba, and its result in a state of **war with Spain.**—On the 13th of April, two days after receiving the President's Message, as above, the House of Representatives adopted the following resolution, by a vote of 324 against 19 : " Resolved, That the President is hereby authorized and directed to intervene at once to stop the war in Cuba, to the end and with the purpose of securing permanent peace and order there and establishing by the free action of the people thereof a stable and independent government of their own in the island of Cuba; and the President is hereby authorized and empowered to use the land and naval forces of the United States to execute the purpose of this resolution."—*Congressional Record, April* 13, 1898, *pp.* 4192–6.

Three days later the Senate adopted the following, by 27 votes against 21 : " Resolved by the Senate and House of Representatives of the United States of America in Congress assembled, First. That the people of the Island of Cuba are, and of right ought to be, free and independent, and that the Government of the United States hereby recognizes the Republic of Cuba as the true and lawful Government of that island.

" Second. That it is the duty of the United States to demand, and the Government of the United States does hereby demand, that the Government of Spain at once relinquish its authority and government in the Island of Cuba and withdraw its land and naval forces from Cuba and Cuban waters.

" Third. That the President of the United States be, and he hereby is, directed and empowered to use the entire land and naval forces of the United States, and to call into the actual service of the United States the militia of the several States, to such extent as may be necessary to carry these resolutions into effect.

" Fourth. That the United States hereby disclaims any disposition or intention to exercise sovereignty, jurisdiction, or control over said island except for the pacification thereof, and asserts its determination when that is accomplished to leave the government and control of the island to its people."—*Congressional Record, April* 16, 1898, *pp.* 4386–7.

The two Houses were in conflict, it will be seen, on the question of the recognition of what claimed to be the government of the Republic of Cuba, organized by the insurgents. A majority of the House shared the doubts expressed by the President in his message, as to the existence of such a government in Cuba as could be recognized without embarrassment ; a majority of the Senate shut its eyes to that doubt. After two days of heated controversy, the Senate gave way, and the following resolution, recommended by conference committees, **was adopted in both** Houses,—in the Senate by 42 yeas to 35 nays (12 not voting) ; in the House by 311 to 6 (39 not voting):

"Resolved, etc.

"First. That the people of the Island of Cuba are and of right ought to be free and independent.

"Second. That it is the duty of the United States to demand, and the Government of the United States does hereby demand, that the Government of Spain at once relinquish its authority and government in the Island of Cuba and withdraw its land and naval forces from Cuba and Cuban waters.

"Third. That the President of the United States be, and he hereby is, directed and empowered to use the entire land and naval forces of the United States, and to call into the actual service of the United States the militia of the several States, to such extent as may be necessary to carry these resolutions into effect.

"Fourth. That the United States hereby disclaims any disposition or intention to exercise sovereignty, jurisdiction, or control over said island, except for the pacification thereof, and asserts its determination when that is accomplished to leave the government and control of the island to its people."—*Congressional Record, April 18, 1898, pp. 4421-22, and 4461-62.*

One week later, on the 25th of April, the President communicated to Congress an account of his action in accordance with this joint resolution, and its result in a state of war between the United States and Spain as follows:

"Upon communicating to the Spanish minister in Washington the demand which it became the duty of the Executive to address to the Government of Spain in obedience to said resolution, the minister asked for his passports and withdrew. The United States minister at Madrid was in turn notified by the Spanish minister for foreign affairs that the withdrawal of the Spanish representative from the United States had terminated diplomatic relations between the two countries, and that all official communications between their respective representatives ceased therewith.

"I commend to your special attention the note addressed to the United States minister at Madrid by the Spanish minister for foreign affairs on the 21st instant, whereby the foregoing notification was conveyed. It will be perceived therefrom that the Government of Spain, having cognizance of the joint resolution of the United States Congress, and in view of the things which the President is thereby required and authorized to do, responds by treating the reasonable demands of this Government as measures of hostility, following with that instant and complete severance of relations by its action which, by the usage of nations, accompanies an existent state of war between sovereign powers.

"The position of Spain being thus made known and the demands of the United States being denied with a complete rupture of intercourse by the act of Spain, I have been constrained, in exercise of the power and authority conferred upon me by the joint resolution aforesaid, to proclaim under date of April 22, 1898, a blockade of certain ports of the north coast of Cuba, lying between Cardenas and Bahia Honda and of the port of Cienfuegos on the south coast of Cuba; and further, in exercise of my constitutional powers and using the authority conferred upon me by the act of Congress approved April 22, 1898, to issue my proclamation dated April 23, 1898, calling forth volunteers in order

to carry into effect the said resolution of April 20, 1898. . . .

"In view of the measures so taken, and with a view to the adoption of such other measures as may be necessary to enable me to carry out the expressed will of the Congress of the United States in the premises, I now recommend to your honorable body the adoption of a joint resolution declaring that a state of war exists between the United States of America and the Kingdom of Spain, and I urge speedy action thereon, to the end that the definition of the international status of the United States as a belligerent power may be made known, and the assertion of all its rights and the maintenance of all its duties in the conduct of a public war may be assured."—*Congressional Record, April 25, 1898, p. 4671.*

The recommendation of the President was carried out, on the same day, by the passage in both Houses, unanimously, of an enactment, "First. That war be, and the same is hereby, declared to exist, and that war has existed since the 21st day of April, A. D. 1898, including said day, between the United States of America and the Kingdom of Spain. Second. That the President of the United States be, and he hereby is, directed and empowered to use the entire land and naval forces of the United States, and to call into the actual service of the United States the militia of the several States, to such extent as may be necessary to carry this act into effect."—*Congressional Record, April 25, pp. 4674 and 4693.*

A. D. 1898 (April).—Cabinet changes.— Two resignations from the President's cabinet occurred in April, both occasioned by failing health. Hon. James A. Gary was succeeded as Postmaster-General by Hon. Charles Emory Smith, and Hon. John Sherman was followed in the Secretaryship of State by his First Assistant in that office, Judge William R. Day.

A. D. 1898 (April—May). — War with Spain.—Military preparations.—Regular and Volunteer armies.—"The Rough Riders."— At the outbreak of the war, the Regular Army of the United States numbered but 28,000 officers and men. Under authority given by acts of Congress it was rapidly increased, and returns for May, 1898, show 2,191 officers and nearly 42,000 men in the ranks. At the same time, a Volunteer Army was being speedily raised and equipped. By proclamation of April 23d, the President called for 125,000 volunteers, to be apportioned, as far as practicable, among the states and territories, according to population. On the 25th of May he called for 75,000 more. Before the end of May, 118,580 enlisted volunteers, with 6,224 officers, were reported to have been mustered in. These were assembled in various camps and prepared for service in a more or less hurried way. At the beginning, six army corps were constituted, embracing both the Regular and Volunteer branches of the army. The First Corps, under Maj. Gen. John R. Brooke, and the Third under Maj. Gen. James F. Wade, were organized at Camp Thomas, Ga. The Second was organized under Maj. Gen. William M. Graham, at Camp Alger, near Falls Church, Va. The organization of the Fourth Corps, Maj. Gen. John J. Coppinger, commanding, was begun at Mobile, Ala. The Fifth Corps was organized at Tampa, Fla., under Maj. Gen. William R. Shafter. A Sixth Corps, which had been provided for, was never organized ; but the Seventh was formed, at Tampa, Fla., under Maj. Gen. Fitzhugh Lee. Subsequently an Eighth Corps was concentrated at San Francisco, and transported to the Philippine Islands. Tampa, Fla., was the port chosen for the shipment of troops to Cuba, and extensive preparations were made for the transport service from that point. The movement waited, first, for the preparation of newly levied troops, and, secondly, for naval operations to make the voyage of transports to Cuba safe from attack.— *Annual Rep't of the Adjutant-General to the Major-General Commanding the Army*, 1898.

Among the Volunteer regiments organized, one known as that of "the Rough Riders" excited public interest in the greatest degree. "The moment that the newspapers sent broadcast the tale that such a regiment was contemplated, excitement began in nearly every State in the Union, and did not end until the announcement was made that the regiment was complete. As it stood, finished, the troops which made it up, theoretically came from the following sections, although men from the East and from other States and Territories were scattered through each troop. Troops A, B, and C, from Arizona. Troop D, from Oklahoma. Troops E, F, G, H, and I, from New Mexico. Troop K, from Eastern colleges and cities. Troops L and M, from Indian Territory.

"Senator Warren, of Iowa, is responsible for the idea of the Rough Riders. He introduced and carried through Congress, aided by Senators Kyle, Carter, and others, a bill authorizing the enrollment of three regiments, to be made up of expert hunters, riflemen, cow-men, frontiersmen, and such other hardy characters as might care to enlist from the Territories. Captain Leonard Wood, of the Medical Corps, was the President's chief medical adviser, and had had much experience in Indian fighting in the West. Theodore Roosevelt was Assistant Secretary of the Navy, and had had some knowledge of men and things on the frontier, through his life on his own and other ranches. It was the President's intention to offer to Wood the colonelcy of one regiment, to Roosevelt the colonelcy of a second, and to Griggsby, of Montana, the colonelcy of a third. Wood and Roosevelt received their offers at about the same moment. Roosevelt promptly declined his, on the theory that he had not had sufficient military experience to warrant him in taking command of a regiment. He asked that he might be given the second place in the regiment commanded by Wood, which was done. Thus the Rough Riders began.

"Alexander Brodie, who afterwards became major of the regiment, was probably the first man to systematically start towards the organization of this particular regiment. . . . It was on the 3d of May that the Arizona men started for San Antonio. It was on the 8th of May that the very last men of all—those of K Troop—left Washington for San Antonio. These were the 'dude warriors,' the 'dandy troopers,' the 'gilded gang.' When their train pulled into San Antonio, and they started stragglingly to march into camp, they encountered a contingent of 340 cowboys from New Mexico. Oil and water are not farther removed than were the everyday natures of these two groups of men.

Yet, instantly they fraternized, and from that moment—through the hardships of it all—these men were brothers. . . . Probably no military organization has ever been made up of men selected from so large a number of applicants, or of men so carefully selected. . . . A large delegation of men from Harvard College called upon Roosevelt one day in Washington and offered their services in a body. Indeed, delegations of that kind from most of the Eastern Colleges went to him, but went to him in vain. His secretary answered more than five thousand individual applications for places in the regiment, and answered ninety-nine per cent. of them with declinations."—E. Marshall, *The Story of the Rough Riders, ch.* 1 (*copyright, G. W. Dillingham & Co., N. Y.*).

A. D. 1898 (April—May : Cuba)—War with Spain.—Blockade of Cuban ports.—On the 21st of April, the following instructions were despatched by the Secretary of the Navy to Rear-Admiral Sampson, appointed that day to the command of the naval force on the Atlantic Station : "You will immediately institute a blockade of the north coast of Cuba, extending from Cardenas on the east to Bahia Honda on the west ; also, if in your opinion your force warrants, the port of Cienfuegos, on the south side of the island. It is considered doubtful if the present force at your command would warrant a more extensive blockade. It should be borne in mind that whenever the Army is ready to embark for Cuba the Navy will be required to furnish the necessary convoy for its transports. For this reason it does not seem desirable that you should undertake at present to blockade any more of the island than has been indicated. It is believed that this blockade will cut off Havana almost entirely from receiving supplies from the outside. The Navy Department is considering the question of occupying the port of Matanzas by a military force large enough to hold it and to open communications with the insurgents, and this may be done at an early date, even before the main party of the Army is ready to embark. If this operation is decided upon, you are directed to co-operate with the Army and assist with such vessels as are necessary to cover and protect such a movement."—*Report of Secretary of Navy*, 1898, *v.* 2, *p.* 175.

In previous confidential orders to the commander of the North Atlantic squadron, issued April 6, in anticipation of hostilities, the Department had directed as follows : "In the event of hostilities with Spain, the Department wishes you to do all in your power to capture or destroy the Spanish war vessels in West Indian waters, including the small gunboats which are stationed along the coast of Cuba.

"2. The Department does not wish the vessels of your squadron to be exposed to the fire of the batteries at Havana, Santiago de Cuba, or other strongly fortified ports in Cuba, unless the more formidable Spanish vessels should take refuge within those harbors. Even in this case the Department would suggest that a rigid blockade and employment of our torpedo boats might accomplish the desired object, viz, the destruction of the enemy's vessels, without subjecting unnecessarily our own men-of-war to the fire of the land batteries. There are two reasons for this : First. There may be no United States troops to occupy any captured stronghold, or to protect from riot and arson, until after the dry season begins, about the first of October. Second. The lack of docking facilities makes it particularly desirable that our vessels should not be crippled before the capture or destruction of Spain's most formidable vessels.

" 3. The Department further desires that, in case of war, you will maintain a strict blockade of Cuba, particularly at the ports of Havana, Matanzas, and, if possible, of Santiago de Cuba, Manzanillo, and Cienfuegos. Such a blockade may cause the Spaniards to yield before the rainy season is over."—*Same Report, p. 171.*

The prudent policy here set forth restricted the action of the fleet to blockading duty so closely, during the early weeks of the war, that no serious demonstrations against the Spanish land batteries were made. Admiral Sampson had been urgent for permission to force the entrance to Havana harbor, before its defenses were strengthened, expressing perfect confidence that he could silence the western batteries, and reach a position from which the city would be at the mercy of his guns; but he was not allowed to make the attempt. The projected occupation of Matanzas was not undertaken.

A. D. 1898 (April—**May :** Philippines).— Statements of the circumstances in which Aguinaldo, the head of the insurrectionary movement in the Philippines, went to Manila, to co-operate with the American forces.—On the 4th of May, 1898, the following was published in the "Singapore Free Press": " Gen. Emilio Aguinaldo, accompanied by his aide-de-camp, Col. Marcelo H. del Pilar, and his private secretary, Mr. J. Leyba, arrived incognito in Singapore from Saigon on April 21, 1898. In Saigon, where Aguinaldo had remained for one week, he had interviews with one or two old Philippino friends now resident there. The special purpose of Aguinaldo's visit to Singapore was to consult other friends here, particularly Mr. Howard W. Bray, an old and intimate English friend, for fifteen years resident in the Philippines, about the state of affairs in the islands generally—particularly as to the possibility of war between the United States and Spain, and whether, in such an event, the United States would eventually recognize the independence of the Philippines, provided he lent his co-operation to the Americans in the conquest of the country. The situation of the moment was this, that the conditions of the honorable peace concluded on December 14, 1897, between President Aguinaldo, on behalf of the Philippine rebels, and H. E. Governor-General Primo di Rivera, on behalf of Spain, had not been carried out, although their immediate execution had been vouched for in that agreement. These reforms would have provided protection to the people against the organized oppression and rapacity of the religious fraternities, would have secured improved civil and criminal procedure in courts, and have guaranteed, in many ways, improvements in the fiscal and social conditions of the people. The repudiation by the Spanish Government of these conditions, made by General Primo di Rivera, now left the rebel leaders, who had for the most part gone to Hongkong, free to act. And it was in pursuance of that freedom of action that Aguinaldo again sought counsel of his friends in Saigon and Singapore, with a view to the immediate resumption of operations in the Philippines.

"Meantime Mr. Bray, whose assistance to this journal on matters connected with the Philippines has been very considerable, as our readers will have seen, was introduced by the editor of the Singapore Free Press to Mr. Spencer Pratt, consul-general of the United States, who was anxious, in view of contingencies, to learn as much as possible about the real condition of the Philippines. It was a few days after this that Aguinaldo arrived incognito in Singapore, when he at once met his friends, including Mr. Bray. Affairs now becoming more warlike, Mr. Bray, after conversation with Mr. Spencer Pratt, eventually arranged an interview between that gentleman and General Aguinaldo, which took place late on the evening of Sunday, the 24th April, at ' The Mansion,' River Valley road. There were present on that occasion Gen. Emilio Aguinaldo y Fami, Mr. E. Spencer Pratt, consul-general United States of America; Mr. Howard W. Bray; Aguinaldo's private secretary, Mr. J. Leyba ; Col. M. H. del Pilar, and Dr. Marcelino Santos.

" During this conference, at which Mr. Bray acted as interpreter, General Aguinaldo explained to the American consul-general, Mr. Pratt, the incidents and objects of the late rebellion, and described the present disturbed state of the country. General Aguinaldo then proceeded to detail the nature of the co-operation he could give, in which he, in the event of the American forces from the squadron landing and taking possession of Manila, would guarantee to maintain order and discipline amongst the native troops and inhabitants in the same humane way in which he had hitherto conducted the war, and prevent them from committing outrages on defenceless Spaniards beyond the inevitable in fair and honorable warfare. He further declared his ability to establish a proper and responsible government on liberal principles, and would be willing to accept the same terms for the country as the United States intend giving to Cuba.

" The consul-general of the United States, coinciding with the general views expressed during the discussion, placed himself at once in telegraphic communication with Admiral Dewey at Hongkong, between whom and Mr. Pratt a frequent interchange of telegrams consequently took place. As a result another private interview was arranged at the American consular residence at the Raffles Hotel between General Aguinaldo, Mr. Spencer Pratt, Mr. Howard Bray, and Mr. Leyba, private secretary to General Aguinaldo. As a sequel to this interview, and in response to the urgent request of Admiral Dewey, General Aguinaldo left Singapore for Hongkong by the first available steamer, the Peninsular and Oriental ' Malacca.' on Tuesday, the 26th April, at noon, accompanied by his aide-de-camp, Captain del Pilar, and Mr. Leyba, his private secretary. . . .

" Throughout the whole stay of General Aguinaldo in Singapore the editor was kept fully informed daily of the progress of affairs. Naturally, however, all statement of what occurred has been withheld by us until what has been deemed the fitting moment has arrived. The substance of the whole incident in its relations to the recent course of affairs in the Philippines has been very fully telegraphed by the editor both to New York and London."

Mr. Pratt, the U. S. Consul-General at Singapore, had already, under date of April 28, given his own official report of the interview with General Aguinaldo, to the Department at Washington, as follows: "I have the honor to report that I sent you on the 27th instant, and confirmed in my dispatch No. 211 of that date, a telegram which deciphered read as follows . . . : 'General Aguinaldo gone my instance Hongkong arrange with Dewey co-operation insurgents Manila. PRATT.'

"The facts are these: On the evening of Saturday the 23d instant, I was confidentially informed of the arrival here, incognito, of the supreme leader of the Philippine insurgents, General Emilio Aguinaldo, by Mr. H. W. Bray, an English gentleman of high standing, who, after fifteen years' residence as a merchant and planter in the Philippines, had been compelled by the disturbed condition of things resulting from Spanish misrule to abandon his property and leave there, and from whom I had previously obtained much valuable information for Commodore Dewey regarding fortifications, coal deposits, etc., at different points in the islands. Being aware of the great prestige of General Aguinaldo with the insurgents, and that no one, either at home or abroad, could exert over them the same influence and control that he could, I determined at once to see him, and, at my request, a secret interview was accordingly arranged for the following morning, Sunday, the 24th, in which, besides General Aguinaldo, were only present the General's trusted advisers and Mr. Bray, who acted as interpreter.

"At this interview, after learning from General Aguinaldo the state of and object sought to be obtained by the present insurrectionary movement, which, though absent from the Philippines, he was still directing, I took it upon myself, whilst explaining that I had no authority to speak for the Government, to point out the danger of continuing independent action at this stage; and, having convinced him of the expediency of co-operating with our fleet, then at Hongkong, and obtained the assurance of his willingness to proceed thither and confer with Commodore Dewey to that end, should the latter so desire, I telegraphed the Commodore the same day as follows, through our consul-general at Hongkong: 'Aguinaldo, insurgent leader, here. Will come Hongkong arrange with Commodore for general cooperation insurgents Manila if desired. Telegraph. PRATT.'

"The Commodore's reply reading thus: 'Tell Aguinaldo come soon as possible. DEWEY.'

"I received it late that night, and at once communicated to General Aguinaldo, who, with his aide-de-camp and private secretary, all under assumed names, I succeeded in getting off by the British steamer 'Malacca,' which left here on Tuesday, the 26th. Just previous to his departure, I had a second and last interview with General Aguinaldo, the particulars of which I shall give you by next mail. The general impressed me as a man of intelligence, ability, and courage, and worthy the confidence that had been placed in him.

"I think that in arranging for his direct co-operation with the commander of our forces, I have prevented possible conflict of action and facilitated the work of occupying and administering the Philippines. If this course of mine meets with the Government's approval, as I trust it may, I shall be fully satisfied; to Mr. Bray, however, I consider there is due some special recognition for most valuable services rendered. How that recognition can best be made I leave to you to decide."

Two days later (April 30), Mr. Pratt reported further, as follows: "Referring to my dispatch No. 212, of the 28th instant, I have the honor to report that in the second and last interview I had with Gen. Emilio Aguinaldo, on the eve of his departure for Hongkong, I enjoined upon him the necessity, under Commodore Dewey's direction, of exerting absolute control over his forces in the Philippines, as no excesses on their part would be tolerated by the American Government, the President having declared that the present hostilities with Spain were to be carried on in strict accord with modern principles of civilized warfare. To this General Aguinaldo fully assented, assuring me that he intended and was perfectly able, once on the field, to hold his followers, the insurgents, in check and lead them as our commander should direct. The general further stated that he hoped the United States would assume protection of the Philippines for at least long enough to allow the inhabitants to establish a government of their own, in the organization of which he would desire American advice and assistance. These questions I told him I had no authority to discuss."

Of the arrival of Aguinaldo at Hongkong and his conveyance thence to Manila, the following account was given by Mr. Wildman, the U. S. Consul at Hongkong, in a communication to the State Department at Washington, which bears date July 18: "On May 2 Aguinaldo arrived in Hongkong and immediately called on me. It was May 16 before I could obtain permission from Admiral Dewey to allow Aguinaldo to go by the United States ship 'McCulloch,' and I put him aboard in the night so as to save any complications with the local Government. Immediately on the arrival of Aguinaldo at Cavite he issued a proclamation, which I had outlined for him before he left, forbidding pillage, and making it a criminal offense to maltreat neutrals. He, of course, organized a government of which he was dictator, an absolutely necessary step if he hoped to maintain control over the natives, and from that date until the present time he has been uninterruptedly successful in the field and dignified and just as the head of his government. According to his own statements to me by letter, he has been approached by both the Spaniards and the Germans, and has had tempting offers made him by the Catholic Church. He has been watched very closely by Admiral Dewey, Consul Williams, and his own junta here in Hongkong, and nothing of moment has occurred which would lead any one to believe that he was not carrying out to the letter the promises made to me in this consulate. The insurgents are fighting for freedom from the Spanish rule, and rely upon the well-known sense of justice that controls all the actions of our Government as to their future."

In reply to Consul Pratt's report of his interviews with General Aguinaldo, and of his proceedings in connection with the departure of that personage from Singapore to Hongkong, the United States Secretary of State, Mr. Day, wrote, June 16, as follows: "The Department observes that you informed General Aguinaldo that you had no authority to speak for the United States ; and, in the absence of the fuller report which you promise, it is assumed that you did not attempt to commit this Government to any alliance with the Philippine insurgents. To obtain the unconditional personal assistance of General Aguinaldo in the expedition to Manila was proper, if in so doing he was not induced to form hopes which it might not be practicable to gratify. This Government has known the Philippine insurgents only as discontented and rebellious subjects of Spain, and is not acquainted with their purposes. While their contest with that power has been a matter of public notoriety, they have neither asked nor received from this Government any recognition. The United States, in entering upon the occupation of the islands, as the result of its military operations in that quarter, will do so in the exercise of the rights which the state of war confers, and will expect from the inhabitants, without regard to their former attitude toward the Spanish Government, that obedience which will be lawfully due from them. If, in the course of your conferences with General Aguinaldo, you acted upon the assumption that this government would coöperate with him for the furtherance of any plan of his own, or that, in accepting his coöperation, it would consider itself pledged to recognize any political claims which he may put forward, your action was unauthorized and cannot be approved."—*Treaty of Peace, and Accompanying Papers* (*55th Congress, 3d Sess.*, *Senate Doc. No. 62, pt. 2, pp. 337–354*).—See, also (in this vol.), PHILIPPINE ISLANDS : A. D. 1896–1898.

A. D. 1898 (April—June).—The War with Spain.—Movements of the Spanish squadron under Admiral Cervera, and the blockading of it in the harbor of Santiago de Cuba.— Lieutenant Hobson's exploit.—The sinking of the collier " Merrimac " in the channel.— The opening of hostilities found a Spanish squadron of four armored cruisers (the " Cristobal Colon," the " Almirante Oquendo," the " Vizcaya," and the " Infanta Maria Teresa,") with three torpedo-boat destroyers (the " Pluton," " Furor " and " Terror ") and some lighter craft, assembled at the Cape Verde islands, under Rear-Admiral Pascual Cervera. They were in Portuguese waters, and Portugal, though friendly to Spain, was forced to issue a proclamation of neutrality, on the 29th of April, which required the Spanish fleet to depart. Some of the vessels then returned to Spain; but the seven named above sailed westward, and their destination became a mystery, very exciting for some time to the American mind. They might attempt to surprise some American coast city ; they might intercept the battle-ship " Oregon," then making her way from the Pacific coast, by the long circuit around Cape Horn ; they might have some plan for breaking the Cuban blockade. Acting on the latter conjecture, and surmising that Porto Rico would be chosen for the Spanish naval base, Admiral Sampson moved in that direction to seek them. He attacked the forts at San Juan (May 12), and satisfied himself that no fleet was in the bay.

The truth was that Cervera was then just entering the Caribbean Sea, considerably to the south of Sampson's search. He touched at the French island of Martinique, and at the Dutch island of Curaçoa, and then slipped across to Santiago de Cuba, where he was to be overtaken by his fate. In the long hill-sheltered bay, with a narrow entrance, which forms this excellent Cuban harbor, the Spanish fleet was so hidden that nearly a fortnight passed before its whereabouts could be fully ascertained. It was not until May 29 that a blockade of Santiago was established by a flying squadron of the American fleet, under Commodore Schley, with certainty that the squadron of Cervera was harbored there. On the 1st of June, Admiral Sampson arrived on the scene, with a stronger naval force, and took command. To attempt to force the narrow entrance of the harbor, strongly fortified and thickly mined as it was, and attack the Spanish fleet in the bay, was not deemed practicable. The course resolved upon was to hold the enemy fast in the shelter he had sought, until Santiago could be taken, by a land attack. In pursuance of this plan, an exploit of splendid daring was performed, in the early morning of June 3, by a young officer, Lieutenant Richmond Pearson Hobson, with a crew of seven volunteers, who placed and sank a huge coaling ship, the " Merrimac," in the channel that leads into Santiago Bay. The following is Admiral Sampson's report of the undertaking and its achievement:

" Before coming here, I decided to make the harbor entrance secure against the possibility of egress of the Spanish ships by obstructing the narrow part of the entrance by sinking a collier at that point. Upon calling upon Mr. Hobson for his professional opinion as to a sure method of sinking the ship, he manifested a most lively interest in the problem. After several days' consideration he presented a solution which he considered would insure the immediate sinking of the ship when she had reached the desired point in the channel. This plan we prepared for before we reached Santiago. This plan included ten electric torpedoes on the outside of the ship, each of 78 pounds of gunpowder, sinking the ship partially before going in, cutting the sea valves, and opening the cargo ports. The plan contemplated a crew of only seven men and Mr. Hobson, who begged that it might be intrusted to him. The anchor chains were ranged upon deck for both the anchors, forward and aft, the plan including the anchoring of the ship almost automatically. As soon as I reached Santiago and had the collier to work upon the details were commenced and diligently prosecuted, hoping to complete them in one day, as the moon and tide served best the first night after our arrival. Notwithstanding every effort, the hour of 4 o'clock in the morning arrived and the preparations were scarcely completed. After a careful inspection of the final preparations I was forced to relinquish the plan for that morning, as dawn was breaking. Mr. Hobson begged to try it at all hazards.

"This morning proved more propitious, as a prompt start could be made. Nothing could have been more gallantly executed. We waited impatiently after the firing by the Spaniards had ceased. When they did not reappear from the harbor at 6 o'clock I feared they had all perished. A steam launch, which had been sent in charge of Naval Cadet Powell to rescue the men, appeared at this time, coming out under a persistent fire from the batteries, but brought none of the crew. A careful inspection of the harbor from this ship showed that the 'Merrimac' had been sunk in the channel somewhat farther in than had been intended. This afternoon the chief of staff of Admiral Cervera came out under a flag of truce with a letter from the Admiral extolling the bravery of the crew in an unusual manner. I can not myself too earnestly express my appreciation of the conduct of Mr. Hobson and his gallant crew. I venture to say that a more brave and daring thing has not been done since Cushing blew up the 'Albemarle.'" The sunken ship did not actually block the channel; but that fact takes nothing from the gallantry of the exploit. Why the intended spot in the channel was missed was explained by Lieutenant Hobson in a statement which he afterwards made: "When the 'Merrimac' poked her nose into the channel," says the Lieutenant, "our troubles commenced. The deadly silence was broken by the swash of a small boat approaching us from the shore. I made her out to be a picket-boat. She ran close up under the stern of the 'Merrimac' and fired several shots from what seemed to be 3-pounder guns. The 'Merrimac's' rudder was carried away by this fire. That is why the collier was not sunk across the channel. We did not discover the loss of the rudder until Murphy [the volunteer assigned to that duty] had east anchor. We then found that the 'Merrimac' would not answer to the helm and were compelled to make the best of the situation. . . . Submarine mines and torpedoes were exploded all around us, adding to the excitement. The mines did no damage, although we could hear the rumbling and feel the ship tremble. We were running without lights, and only the darkness saved us from utter destruction. When the ship was in the desired position and we found that the rudder was gone, I called the men on deck. While they were launching the catamaran I touched off the explosives. At the same time two torpedoes, fired by the 'Reina Mercedes,' struck the 'Merrimac' amidships. I can not say whether our own explosives or the Spanish torpedoes did the work, but the 'Merrimac' was lifted out of the water, and almost rent asunder."

What followed, in the experience of the crew, when their vessel went down, is described as follows by Lieut. Hobson, in a narrative of "The Sinking of the Merrimac," which he published at a later day: "The stricken vessel now reeled to port. Some one said: 'She is going to turn over on us, sir,' to which I replied: 'No; she will right herself in sinking, and we shall be the last spot to go under.' The firing suddenly ceased. The vessel lowered her head like a faithful animal, proudly aware of its sacrifice, bowed below the surface, and plunged forward. The stern rose and heeled heavily: it stood for a moment, shuddering, then started downward, righting as it went. A great rush of water came up the gangway, seething and gurgling out of the deck. The mass was whirling from right to left 'against the sun'; it seized us and threw us against the bulwarks, then over the rail. Two were swept forward as if by a momentary recession, and one was carried down into a coal-bunker—luckless Kelly. In a moment, however, with increased force, the water shot him up out of the same hole and swept him among us. The bulwarks disappeared. A sweeping vortex whirled above. We charged about with casks, cans, and spars, the incomplete stripping

having left quantities on the deck. The life-preservers stood us in good stead, preventing chests from being crushed, as well as buoying us on the surface; for spars came end on like battering-rams, and the sharp corners of tin cans struck us heavily. . . . When we looked for the life-boat we found that it had been carried away. The catamaran was the largest piece of floating debris; we assembled about it. The line suspending it from the cargo-boom held and anchored us to the ship, though barely long enough to reach the surface, causing the raft to turn over and set us scrambling as the line came taut.

"The firing had ceased. It was evident the enemy had not seen us in the general mass of moving objects; but soon the tide began to drift these away, and we were being left alone with the catamaran. The men were directed to cling close in. bodies below and only heads out, close under the edges, and were directed not to speak above a whisper, for the destroyer was near at hand, and boats were passing near. We mustered; all were present, and direction was given to remain as we were till further orders, for I was sure that in due time after daylight a responsible officer would come out to reconnoiter. It was evident that we could not swim against the tide to reach the entrance. Moreover, the shores were lined with troops, and the small boats were looking for victims that might escape from the vessel. The only chance lay in remaining undiscovered until the coming of the reconnoitering boat, to which, perhaps, we might surrender without being fired on. . . . The air was chilly and the water positively cold. In less than five minutes our teeth were chattering; so loud, indeed, did they chatter that it seemed the destroyer or the boats would hear. . . . We remained there probably an hour."

At daylight a steam launch approached, and was hailed by Lieutenant Hobson, who judged that there must be officers on board to whom it would be safe to surrender. He was more than right. The commander of the launch was Admiral Cervera, in person, who took the nearly exhausted men from the water and treated them with great kindness, admiring the bravery of their exploit, and sending a flag of truce to Admiral Sampson to announce their safety. They were taken aboard the 'Reina Mercedes,' and, as prisoners of war, were confined at first in Morro Castle, and afterwards in the city. It so happened that they were locked in the Morro during a bombardment of the Spanish coast defences and fleet by ten of our vessels on June 6th, when about 1,500 projectiles were fired; and much anxiety and indignation were expressed in this country in view of that circumstance; but Mr. Ramsden, British consul at Santiago, explained in a despatch that they were removed as soon as lodgings could be prepared in the barracks—actually on June 7th. They were released on July 6th in exchange for prisoners captured by our forces.

A. D. 1898 (April—July).—**War with** Spain. —Destruction of the Spanish fleet in Manila Bay.—Despatches of Admiral Dewey.—His relations with Aguinaldo, the insurgent chief. —Arrival of American troops for the occupation of the city.—Commodore George Dewey, commanding the Asiatic Squadron, then awaiting orders at Hongkong, received on the 25th of April the following despatch by cable from the Secretary of the Navy: "War has commenced between the United States and Spain. Proceed at once to Philippine Islands. Commence operations at once, particularly against the Spanish fleet. You must capture vessels or destroy. Use utmost endeavors." On the sixth day after receiving these orders (namely on May 1st), he was able to report from Manila, by a telegram sent from Hongkong on the 7th: "The squadron arrived at Manila at daybreak this morning. Immediately engaged enemy and destroyed the following Spanish vessels: 'Reina Christina,' 'Castillia,' 'Don Antonio de Biloa,' 'Don Juan de Austria,' 'Isla de Luzon,' 'Isla de Cuba,' 'General Lezo,' 'Marques del Duaro,' 'El Curreo,' 'Velasco,' one transport, 'Isla de Mandano,' water battery at Cavite. I shall destroy Cavite arsenal dispensatory. The squadron is uninjured. Few men were slightly wounded. I request the Department will send immediately from San Francisco fast steamer with ammunition. The only means of telegraphing is to the American consul at Hongkong."

In due time the post brought particulars of the action, in the following report from Commodore Dewey, dated May 4 : "The squadron left Mirs Bay, [China] on April 27, immediately on the arrival of Mr. O. F. Williams, United States consul at Manila, who brought important information and who accompanies the squadron. Arrived off Bolinao on the morning of April 30 and, finding no vessels there, proceeded down the coast and arrived off the entrance to Manila Bay on the same afternoon. The 'Boston' and 'Concord' were sent to reconnoiter Port Subic, I having been informed that the enemy intended to take position there. A thorough search of the port was made by the 'Boston' and 'Concord,' but the Spanish fleet was not found, although, from a letter afterwards found in the arsenal (inclosed with translation), it appears that it had been their intention to go there. Entered the Boca Grande, or south channel, at 11.30 p. m., steaming in column at distance at 8 knots. After half the squadron had passed, a battery on the south side of the channel opened fire, none of the shots taking effect. The 'Boston' and 'McCulloch' returned the fire. The squadron proceeded across the bay at slow speed, and arrived off Manila at daybreak, and was fired upon at 5.15 a. m. by three batteries at Manila and two at Cavite and by the Spanish fleet anchored in an approximately east and west line across the mouth of Bakor Bay, with their left in shoal water in Canacao Bay. The squadron then proceeded to the attack, the flagship 'Olympia,' under my personal direction, leading, followed at distance by the 'Baltimore,' 'Raleigh,' 'Petrel,' 'Concord,' and 'Boston,' in the order named, which formation was maintained throughout the action. The squadron opened fire at 5.41 a. m. While advancing to the attack, two mines were exploded ahead of the flagship, too far to be effective. The squadron maintained a continuous and precise fire at ranges varying from 5,000 to 2,000 yards, countermarching in a line approximately parallel to that of the Spanish fleet. The enemy's fire was vigorous, but generally ineffective.

"Early in the engagement two launches put out toward the 'Olympia' with the apparent intention of using torpedoes. One was sunk and the other disabled by our fire and beached before an opportunity occurred to fire torpedoes. At 7

a. m. the Spanish flagship 'Reina Christina' made a desperate attempt to leave the line and come out to engage at short range, but was received with such galling fire, the entire battery of the 'Olympia' being concentrated upon her, that she was barely able to return to the shelter of the point. The fires started in her by our shell at this time were not extinguished until she sank. At 7.35 a. m., it having been erroneously reported to me that only 15 rounds per gun remained for the 5-inch rapid-fire battery, I ceased firing and withdrew the squadron for consultation and a redistribution of ammunition, if necessary. The three batteries at Manila had kept up a continuous fire from the beginning of the engagement, which fire was not returned by this squadron. The first of these batteries was situated on the south mole head at the entrance to the Pasig River, the second on the south bastion of the walled city of Manila, and the third at Malate, about one-half mile farther south. At this point I sent a message to the Governor-General to the effect that if the batteries did not cease firing the city would be shelled. This had the effect of silencing them.

"At 11.16 a. m., finding that the report of scarcity of ammunition was incorrect, I returned with the squadron to the attack. By this time the flagship and almost the entire Spanish fleet were in flames, and at 12.30 p. m. the squadron ceased firing, the batteries being silenced and the ships sunk, burnt, and deserted. At 12.40 p. m. the squadron returned and anchored off Manila, the 'Petrel' being left behind to complete the destruction of the smaller gunboats, which were behind the point of Cavite. This duty was performed by Commander E. P. Wood in the most expeditious and complete manner possible. The Spanish lost the following vessels: Sunk—'Reina Christina,' 'Castillia,' 'Don Antonio de Ulloa.' Burnt—'Don Juan de Austria,' 'Isla de Luzon,' 'Isla de Cuba,' 'General Lezo,' 'Marques del Duaro,' 'El Correo,' 'Velasco,' and 'Isla de Mindanao,' (transport). Captured—'Rapido,' and 'Hercules' (tugs), and several small launches. I am unable to obtain complete accounts of the enemy's killed and wounded, but believe their loss to be very heavy. The 'Reina Christina' alone had 150 killed, including the captain, and 90 wounded.

"I am happy to report that the damage done to the squadron under my command was inconsiderable. There were none killed, and only 7 men in the squadron very slightly wounded. As will be seen by the reports of the commanding officers which are herewith inclosed, several of the vessels were struck and even penetrated, but the damage was of the slightest, and the squadron is in as good condition now as before the battle. I beg to state to the Department that I doubt if any commander in chief, under similar circumstances, was ever served by more loyal, efficient, and gallant captains than those of the squadron now under my command. . . . On May 2, the day following the engagement, the squadron again went to Cavite, where it remains. A landing party was sent to destroy the guns and magazines of the batteries there. . . . On the 3d the military forces evacuated the Cavite Arsenal, which was taken possession of by a landing party."

Promptly in response to this report of his victory, a joint resolution of thanks to Commodore Dewey and his officers and men, by the two

Houses of Congress, was despatched to them, with announcement to the former of his promotion to the rank of rear-admiral. The admiral replied, on the 13th, from Cavite, making due acknowledgments, and adding: "I am maintaining strict blockade of Manila by sea, and believe rebels are hemming in by land, although they are inactive and making no demonstrations. Great scarcity of provisions in the city. I believe the Spanish Governor-General will be obliged to surrender soon. I can take Manila at any moment. To retain possession and thus control Philippine Islands would require, in my best judgment, a well equipped force of 5,000 men."

On the 20th he reported, further: "Aguinaldo, the rebel commander in chief, was brought down by the 'McCulloch' [from Hongkong]. Organizing forces near Cavite and may render assistance that will be valuable." On the 27th of June, in reply to inquiries from the Navy Department, he explained his relations with Aguinaldo, as follows: "Aguinaldo, insurgent leader, with thirteen of his staff, arrived May 19, by permission, on 'Nanshan.' Established self Cavite, outside arsenal, under the protection of our guns, and organized his army. I have had several conferences with him, generally of a personal nature. Consistently I have refrained from assisting him in any way with the force under my command, and on several occasions I have declined requests that I should do so, telling him the squadron could not act until the arrival of the United States troops. At the same time I have given him to understand that I consider insurgents as friends, being opposed to a common enemy. He has gone to attend a meeting of insurgent leaders for the purpose of forming a civil government. Aguinaldo has acted independently of the squadron, but has kept me advised of his progress, which has been wonderful. I have allowed to pass by water recruits, arms, and ammunition, and to take such Spanish arms and ammunition from the arsenal as he needed. Have advised frequently to conduct the war humanely, which he has done invariably. My relations with him are cordial, but I am not in his confidence. The United States has not been bound in any way to assist insurgents by any act or promises, and he is not, to my knowledge, committed to assist us. I believe he expects to capture Manila without my assistance, but doubt ability, they not yet having many guns. In my opinion these people are far superior in their intelligence and more capable of self-government than the natives of Cuba, and I am familiar with both races."— *Report of the Secretary of the Navy, 1898, v. 2, pp. 67–72 and 103.*

On the 30th of June, troops sent from San Francisco, to the number of 2,500 officers and men, commanded by Gen. T. M. Anderson, arrived in Manila Bay, to co-operate with the navy in taking Manila and occupying the city, when taken. They were followed by a second expeditionary force, under Gen. F. V. Greene. which arrived July 17, and by a third, July 25 and 31, with which came Gen. Merritt, commanding the corps and the Department of the Pacific. Gen. Merritt's army then numbered nearly 11,000 men, and it was increased during the next few weeks to more than 15,000.—*Reports of the War Dept., 1898, v. 1, pt. 2. p. 499.*

An English officer. Major Younghusband, who visited Manila at this time, remarked: "It may,

perhaps, with some confidence be prophesied that when the cold fit, which will in due course follow the warmth of the present enthusiasm, falls on the nation, America will discover that the true parting of the ways was ... in having allowed Admiral Dewey to do more than defeat the Spanish fleet and exact a heavy indemnity from the city of Manila before sailing away." It would seem to be more true, however, to ·say that the parting of the ways was when a military expedition was sent from San Francisco to Manila, to be landed, for the capture of the city and for the occupation of the islands. It is claimed with reason that Admiral Dewey could not "sail away," after the destruction of the Spanish ships, because he needed the harbor he had seized, his fleet having lost most of the privileges it had formerly been using in neutral ports, when it became the fleet of a belligerent power. To retain possession of Manila Bay while it was needed by the American fleet was clearly a measure connected legitimately with the general conduct of the war against Spain. But it is difficult to see that the landing of soldiers on the island of Luzon and the capture of the city of Manila added anything to the security with which the Bay was held for the purposes of Admiral Dewey's fleet, or that it contributed at all to the weakening of Spain in the war, and to the rescue of Cuba from Spanish misrule. For two months, from the first day of May until the last day of June, before a soldier arrived, and for six weeks longer, before Manila surrendered, Admiral Dewey appears to have been as fully and as conveniently in possession of all the advantages that harborage there could give him, as he was after the Spanish flag had been lowered in the city and on the island. Therefore, the American conquest of the Philippines does not readily connect itself with the war for the liberation of Cuba, as a necessary part of it, but presents itself to the mind as a somewhat supplementary enterprise, undertaken with objects of its own.

A. D. 1898 (May—August).—Conduct of English and German naval officers at Manila.—While Admiral Dewey was holding Manila Bay, before the taking of the city, there were many rumors and exciting stories afloat, of offensive behavior towards the American fleet by commanders of German war ships that were sent to the scene. As far as possible, the facts were officially suppressed, in order to avoid a quarrel between the two countries, and no authoritative account of what occurred can be found. But some incidents obtained publicity which are probably true in the main. The first unpleasant happening appears to have been the arrival in Manila Bay of a German naval vessel, which steamed in with entire disregard of the blockading fleet, as though the port was its own. Thereupon Admiral Dewey sent a forcible reminder to the captain that he was intruding upon a blockade. by firing a shot across his bow, and ordering him to heave to. The German captain, in a rage, is said to have called on the commanding officer of a British squadron that was in the Bay, for advice as to what he should do, and was told that he owed the American Admiral an apology for his violation of naval etiquette, well settled for such circumstances as those existing in Manila Bay. According to the story, the British commander, Captain Sir Edward Chichester, himself on the best of terms with

Admiral Dewey, visited the latter, on behalf of the German officer, and made the matter smooth. But, either through indiscretion of his own, or because he had instructions to interfere as much as possible with the proceedings of the Americans, the German commander continued to pursue an offensive course. According to report, he went so far as to stop a movement which Aguinaldo (then a recognized ally of the United States) was making, to take possession of a certain island, and to capture some Spaniards who were on it. This provoked Admiral Dewey to a demonstration against him so threatening that he drew back in haste, and the island was occupied.

According to all accounts, Admiral Dewey showed unsurpassed wisdom and dignity in meeting and checking these offensive proceedings without allowing them to become a cause of international quarrel; and he was happily aided in doing so by the hearty support of the British naval commander. According to still another report of the time, a German admiral, who had come upon the scene, meditated an interference to forbid the bombarding of Manila, when the city was about to be attacked, and, calling upon Sir Edward Chichester to ascertain what action the latter would take, was significantly told, "That is only known to Admiral Dewey and myself,"—which convinced him that his project was not wise. An English writer has related, with much satisfaction, that when Sir Edward's ship, the "Immortalité," finally steamed out of Manila Bay, returning to Hong Kong, "every ship in the American fleet manned her yards and gave the British man-of-war three cheers as she passed along; and she with the answering signal, 'thank you,' flying at her mast-head, went on her way."

A. D. 1898 (June).—Act creating the United States Industrial Commission.—An Act "authorizing the appointment of a non-partisan Commission to collate information and to consider and recommend legislation to meet the problems presented by labor, agriculture, and capital," was passed by Congress and approved by the President June 18, 1898. It provided: "That a commission is hereby created, to be called the 'Industrial Commission,' to be composed as follows. Five members of the Senate, to be appointed by the presiding officer thereof; five members of the House of Representatives, to be appointed by the Speaker, and nine other persons, who shall fairly represent the different industries and employments, to be appointed by the President, by and with the advice and consent of the Senate. . . . That it shall be the duty of this commission to investigate questions pertaining to immigration, to labor, to agriculture, to manufacturing, and to business, and to report to Congress and to suggest such legislation as it may deem best upon these subjects. . . . That it shall furnish such information and suggest such laws as may be made a basis for uniform legislation by the various States of the Union, in order to harmonize conflicting interests and to be equitable to the laborer, the employer, the producer, and the consumer. . . . That the commission shall give reasonable time for hearings, if deemed necessary, and if necessary it may appoint a subcommission or subcommissions of its own members to make investigation in any part of the United States, and it

shall be allowed actual necessary expenses for the same. It shall have the authority to send for persons and papers and to administer oaths and affirmations. . . . That it may report from time to time to the Congress of the United States, and shall at the conclusion of its labors submit a final report."

The Commission thus contemplated was duly appointed by the President, and organized by the election of Senator Kyle for its chairman. For the scope and plan of its investigations a committee on procedure made the following recommendations, which were adopted by the Commission and which have been followed in what it has done: "The main work of the Commission may . . . be said to be to study and compare existing laws bearing upon industrial conditions, here and elsewhere, to ascertain by competent testimony wherein they are deficient, defective, inoperative, or oppressive, and to recommend such remedial statutes as will tend not only to make the conditions of industry more uniform as between the several States, but to remove such existing sources or causes of discontent, inequality, and injustice as can be reached and regulated through legislation. . . . In order to secure satisfactory results, it appears to your committee imperatively necessary that the work shall be confined strictly to the main purpose, viz, of ascertaining the nature and effects of existing legislation, and the nature of remedial legislation which may be necessary or desirable to equalize conditions in industry and to remove any just grounds of complaint on the part of either labor or capital or of the people at large.

"To facilitate the progress of the work we recommend the division of the Commission into four subcommissions of five members each, to be severally charged with the investigation of present conditions and the formulation of remedial suggestions in the following branches of industry: 1. On agriculture and agricultural labor. 2. On the conditions of labor and capital employed in manufacturing and general business. 3. On the conditions of labor and capital employed in mining. 4. On transportation. In addition, we recommend a fifth subcommission, to be known as the subcommission on statistics, in the membership of which there shall be one representative of each of the above subcommissions. . . .

"The committee also suggests that there are certain subjects of inquiry which appertain equally to all the groups into which it has recommended that the Commission be segregated. The subjects of immigration, of education, of combinations and trusts, and of taxation at once suggest themselves as belonging in this category. It is therefore recommended that these subjects, one or more of them, be examined into by the full Commission pending the organization of the several subcommissions."

The subject to which the Commission gave earliest attention was that of "Trusts and Industrial Combinations," on which it submitted a preliminary report on the 1st of March, 1900. See (in this vol.) TRUSTS.

A. D. 1898 (June).—Act providing for the arbitration of disputes between employers and employees in inter-state commerce.—The following are the main sections of a very important Act of Congress, approved June 1, 1898, which provides for the arbitration of disputes between

railway and other employees engaged in inter-
state commerce and the companies or individuals
employing them:

"That the provisions of this Act shall apply to
any common carrier or carriers and their officers,
agents, and employees, except masters of vessels
and seamen, . . . engaged in the transportation
of passengers or property wholly by railroad, or
partly by railroad and partly by water, for a continuous carriage or shipment, from one State or
Territory of the United States or the District of
Columbia, to any other State or Territory of the
United States, or the District of Columbia, or
from any place in the United States to an adjacent
foreign country, or from any place in the United
States through a foreign country to any other
place in the United States. . . .

"Sec. 2. That whenever a controversy concerning wages, hours of labor, or conditions of
employment shall arise between a carrier subject
to this Act and the employees of such carrier,
seriously interrupting or threatening to interrupt
the business of said carrier, the chairman of the
Interstate Commerce Commission and the Commissioner of Labor shall, upon the request of
either party to the controversy, with all practicable expedition, put themselves in communication with the parties to such controversy, and
shall use their best efforts, by mediation and
conciliation, to amicably settle the same ; and if
such efforts shall be unsuccessful, shall at once
endeavor to bring about an arbitration of said
controversy in accordance with the provisions of
this Act.

"Sec. 3. That whenever a controversy shall
arise between a carrier subject to this Act and
the employees of such carrier which can not be
settled by mediation and conciliation in the manner provided in the preceding section, said controversy may be submitted to the arbitration of
a board of three persons, who shall be chosen in
the manner following : One shall be named by
the carrier or employer directly interested ; the
other shall be named by the labor organization to
which the employees directly interested belong,
or, if they belong to more than one, by that one of
them which specially represents employees of the
same grade and class and engaged in services of
the same nature as said employees so directly interested : Provided, however, That when a controversy involves and affects the interests of two or
more classes and grades of employees belonging to
different labor organizations, such arbitrator shall
be agreed upon and designated by the concurrent action of all such labor organizations ; and
in cases where the majority of such employees
are not members of any labor organization, said
employees may by a majority vote select a committee of their own number, which committee
shall have the right to select the arbitrator on
behalf of said employees.   The two thus chosen
shall select the third commissioner of arbitration ;
but, in the event of their failure to name such
arbitrator within five days after their first meeting, the third arbitrator shall be named by the
commissioners named in the preceding section.
A majority of said arbitrators shall be competent
to make a valid and binding award under the
provisions hereof.   The submission shall be in
writing, shall be signed by the employer and by
the labor organization representing the employees, shall specify the time and place of meeting
of said board of arbitration, shall state the ques-

tions to be decided, and shall contain appropriate
provisions by which the respective parties shall
stipulate, as follows:

"First. That the board of arbitration shall
commence their hearings within ten days from
the date of the appointment of the third arbitrator, and shall find and file their award, as provided in this section, within thirty days from the
date of the appointment of the third arbitrator ;
and that pending the arbitration the status existing immediately prior to the dispute shall not be
changed: Provided, That no employee shall be
compelled to render personal service without his
consent.

"Second. That the award and the papers and
proceedings, including the testimony relating
thereto certified under the hands of the arbitrators and which shall have the force and effect of
a bill of exceptions, shall be filed in the clerk's
office of the circuit court of the United States for
the district wherein the controversy arises or the
arbitration is entered into, and shall be final and
conclusive upon both parties, unless set aside for
error of law apparent on the record.

"Third. That the respective parties to the
award will each faithfully execute the same, and
that the same may be specifically enforced in
equity so far as the powers of a court of equity
permit : Provided, That no injunction or other
legal process shall be issued which shall compel
the performance by any laborer against his will
of a contract for personal labor or service.

"Fourth. That employees dissatisfied with
the award shall not by reason of such dissatisfaction quit the service of the employer before
the expiration of three months from and after the
making of such award without giving thirty
days' notice in writing of their intention so to
quit.   Nor shall the employer dissatisfied with
such award dismiss any employee or employees
on account of such dissatisfaction before the expiration of three months from and after the making of such award without giving thirty days'
notice in writing of his intention so to discharge.

"Fifth. That said award shall continue in
force as between the parties thereto for the period of one year after the same shall go into
practical operation, and no new arbitration upon
the same subject between the same employer and
the same class of employees shall be had until the
expiration of said one year if the award is not set
aside as provided in section four.   That as to
individual employees not belonging to the labor
organization or organizations which shall enter
into the arbitration, the said arbitration and the
award made therein shall not be binding, unless
the said individual employees shall give assent
in writing to become parties to said arbitration. . . .

"Sec. 7. That during the pendency of arbitration under this Act it shall not be lawful for the
employer, party to such arbitration, to discharge
the employees, parties thereto, except for inefficiency, violation of law, or neglect of duty ; nor
for the organization representing such employees
to order, nor for the employees to unite in, aid,
or abet, strikes against said employer ; nor, during a period of three months after an award
under such an arbitration, for such an employer
to discharge any such employees, except for the
causes aforesaid, without giving thirty days'
written notice of an intent so to discharge ; nor
for any of such employees, during a like period, to

quit the service of said employer without just cause, without giving to said employer thirty days' written notice of an intent so to do; nor for such organization representing such employees to order, counsel, or advise otherwise. Any violation of this section shall subject the offending party to liability for damages; Provided, that nothing herein contained shall be construed to prevent any employer, party to such arbitration, from reducing the number of its or his employees whenever in its or his judgment business necessities require such reduction. . . .

"Sec. 10. That any employer subject to the provisions of this Act and any officer, agent, or receiver of such employer who shall require any employee, or any person seeking employment, as a condition of such employment, to enter into an agreement, either written or verbal, not to become or remain a member of any labor corporation, association, or organization; or shall threaten any employee with loss of employment, or shall unjustly discriminate against any employee because of his membership in such a labor corporation, association, or organization; or who shall require any employee or any person seeking employment, as a condition of such employment, to enter into a contract whereby such employee or applicant for employment shall agree to contribute to any fund for charitable, social or beneficial purposes; to release such employer from legal liability for any personal injury by reason of any benefit received from such fund beyond the proportion of the benefit arising from the employer's contribution to such fund; or who shall, after having discharged an employee, attempt or conspire to prevent such employee from obtaining employment, or who shall, after the quitting of an employee, attempt or conspire to prevent such employee from obtaining employment, is hereby declared to be guilty of a misdemeanor, and, upon conviction thereof in any court of the United States of competent jurisdiction in the district in which such offense was committed, shall be punished for each offense by a fine of not less than one hundred dollars and not more than one thousand dollars."—*U. S. Statutes at Large, v.* 30, *p.* 424.

A. D. 1898 (June).—The **War** with Spain. —Seizure of the island of Guam.—The following order, dated May 10, 1898, was addressed by the Secretary of the Navy to the Commander of the U. S. S. 'Charleston': "Upon the receipt of this order, which is forwarded by the steamship 'City of Pekin' to you at Honolulu, you will proceed with the 'Charleston' and 'City of Pekin' in company, to Manila, Philippine Islands. On your way, you are hereby directed to stop at the Spanish Island of Guam. You will use such force as may be necessary to capture the port of Guam, making prisoners of the governor and other officials and any armed force that may be there. You will also destroy any fortifications on said island and any Spanish naval vessels that may be there, or in the immediate vicinity. These operations at the Island of Guam should be very brief, and should not occupy more than one or two days. Should you find any coal at the Island of Guam, you will make such use of it as you consider desirable. It is left to your discretion whether or not you destroy it. From the Island of Guam, proceed to Manila and report to Rear-Admiral George Dewey, U. S. N., for duty in the squadron under his command."

In a despatch dated June 24, Captain Glass, of the "Charleston," reported the execution of these orders as follows: "I have the honor to report that in obedience to the Department's telegraphic order of May 24, 1898, this ship sailed from Honolulu, Hawaiian Islands, on the 4th instant for Manila with the transports 'City of Pekin,' 'Australia,' and 'City of Sydney' under convoy. When clear of land, I opened the confidential order of May 10, 1898, and changed course for the Island of Guam, next day informing Commander Gibson, in charge of transports, and Brigadier-General Anderson, commanding expeditionary force, of the change in my orders and that the transports would accompany the 'Charleston.' Arriving off the north end of the island at daylight, June 20, I first visited the port of Agaña, the capital of Guam, and of the Mariana group, and finding no vessels there of any kind, proceeded to San Luis D'Apra, where it was expected that a Spanish gunboat and a military force would be found, a rumor to that effect having reached me while at Honolulu. Arriving off the port at 8.30 a. m., it was found that Fort Santiago, on Oroté Point, was abandoned and in ruins, and I steamed directly into the harbor, having ordered the transports to take a safe position outside and await instructions. A few shots were fired from the secondary battery at Fort Santa Cruz to get the range and ascertain if it was occupied. Getting no response, ceased firing and came to anchor in a position to control the harbor, and it was then found that this fort also was abandoned. The only vessel in port was a small Japanese trading vessel from Yokohama. An officer had just shoved off from the ship to board the Japanese vessel, and obtain information as to the condition of affairs on shore, when a boat was seen approaching the ship, through the reefs at the head of the harbor, flying the Spanish flag and bringing two officers, the captain of the port, a lieutenant-commander in the Spanish navy, and the health officer, a surgeon of the Spanish army. These officers came on board, and, in answer to my questions, told me they did not know that war had been declared between the United States and Spain, their last news having been from Manila, under date of April 14. I informed them that war existed and that they must consider themselves as prisoners. As they stated that no resistance could be made by the force on the island, I released them on parole for the day, to proceed to Agaña and inform the governor that I desired him to come on board ship at once, they assuring me that he would do so as soon as he could reach the port. While awaiting the return of these officers, an examination was made of the harbor, the only dangers to navigation were buoyed, and the transports came in during the afternoon.

"At 5 p. m. the governor's secretary, a captain in the Spanish army, came on board, bringing me a letter from the governor, in which he stated that he was not allowed by law to go on board a foreign vessel and requested me to meet him on shore for a conference. This letter is appended, marked A. As it was then too late to land a party, from the state of the tide on the reef between the ship and the landing place, I directed the secretary to return and say to the governor that I would send an officer ashore with a communication for him early next day. . . . At

8.30 a. m. on June 21 Lieut. William Braunersreuther was sent ashore, under flag of truce, with a written demand for the immediate surrender of the defenses of the Island of Guam and all officials and persons in the military service of Spain. Mr. Braunersreuther was directed to wait half an hour only for a reply, to bring the governor and other officials on board as prisoners of war in case of surrender, or in case of refusal or delay beyond the time given, to return and take command of the landing force, which he would find in readiness, and proceed to Agaña. At 12.15 p. m. Mr. Braunersreuther returned to the ship, bringing off the governor and three other officers, his staff, and handed me a letter from the governor acceding fully to my demand. Having received the surrender of the Island of Guam, I took formal possession at 2.45 p. m., hoisting the American flag on Fort Santa Cruz and saluting it with 21 guns from the 'Charleston.' From a personal examination of Fort Santa Cruz, I decided that it was entirely useless as a defensive work, with no guns and in a partly ruinous condition, and that it was not necessary to expend any mines in blowing it up. The forts at Agaña, San Luis D'Apra, and Umata are of no value and no guns remain in the island except four small cast-iron guns of obsolete pattern at Agaha, formerly used for saluting, but now condemned as unsafe even for that purpose. No Spanish vessel of war has visited Guam during the last eighteen months. No coal was found on the island."—*Annual Reports of the Navy Dep't*, 1898, *v.* 2, *pp.* 151–3.

A. D. **1898** (June—July).—**War with Spain.**—**Expedition of the army under General Shafter against Santiago de Cuba.**—**Battles of El Caney and San Juan Hill.**—To co-operate with the navy in operations for the capture of Santiago de Cuba, and of the Spanish fleet blockaded in the harbor of that town, orders were issued from Washington on the 31st of May, by Major-General Miles, Commanding the Army, "with the approval of the Secretary of War," which directed General Shafter, commanding the forces assembled at Tampa, Florida, to place them on transports and proceed with them, under convoy of the navy, to Santiago. Owing to an extreme lack of both railway and harbor facilities at Tampa, an entire week was consumed in the embarkation of the troops and supplies. When on shipboard, the expedition was delayed another week by false reports of the appearance of Spanish cruisers on the Cuban coast, which seemed to the Washington authorities to call for a stronger naval convoy to guard the transport fleet. It was not until the 14th of June that the fleet was permitted to sail, with 16,000 men. It arrived off Guantanamo, near Santiago, on the morning of the 20th.

Meantime, the blockading fleet had bombarded the forts at Santiago twice, on the 6th and on the 16th, and had silenced them, for the time being, on both occasions, but apparently with no permanent effect. With more success, two vessels from the fleet had entered the harbor of Guantanamo on the 7th and taken possession of the lower bay, where a marine battalion was landed on the 10th and established in camp, to hold ground until the army arrived. Meantime, also, communication with General Garcia, commanding Cuban forces, had been opened, and arrangements made, the results of which were subsequently acknowledged by General Miles, in his annual report, as follows: "General Garcia regarded my requests as his orders, and promptly took steps to execute the plan of operations. He sent 3,000 men to check any movement of the 12,000 Spaniards stationed at Holguin. A portion of this latter force started to the relief of the garrison at Santiago, but was successfully checked and turned back by the Cuban forces under General Feria. General Garcia also sent 2,000 men, under Pérez, to oppose the 6,000 Spaniards at Guantánamo, and they were successful in their object. He also sent 1,000 men, under General Ríos, against the 6,000 men at Manzanillo. Of this garrison, 3,500 started to reenforce the garrison at Santiago, and were engaged in no less than thirty combats with the Cubans on their way before reaching Santiago. . . . With an additional force of 5,000 men General Garcia besieged the garrison of Santiago, taking up a strong position on the west side and in close proximity to the harbor, and he afterwards received General Shafter and Admiral Sampson at his camp near that place. He had troops in the rear, as well as on both sides of the garrison at Santiago before the arrival of our troops."—*Annual Reports of the War Dept.*, 1898, *v.* 1, *pt.* 2, *p.* 16.

The troops from Tampa, under General Shafter, arriving on the 20th, were disembarked on the 22d, 23d and 24th, at Daiquiri, and advanced to Siboney. The first resistance encountered was at La Guasima, three miles from Siboney, on the Santiago road, where the Spaniards were driven from strong entrenchments by a part of Young's brigade of General Wheeler's cavalry division (dismounted). The brigade thus first in the fighting was composed of the 1st and 10th regiments of regular cavalry and the 1st U. S. Vol. cavalry, commonly called the "Rough Riders." After the engagement at La Guasima, six days were occupied in concentrating the army (including the Cuban auxiliaries of General Garcia), mostly at Sevilla, a short distance beyond La Guasima, on the same road, and in overcoming great difficulties of transportation for supplies.

On June 30, General Shafter reconnoitered the country around Santiago and made his plan of attack. "From a high hill," says his subsequent report, "from which the city was in plain view, I could see the San Juan Hill and the country about El Caney. The roads were very poor, and, indeed, little better than bridlepaths, until the San Juan River and El Caney were reached. The position of El Caney, to the northeast of Santiago, was of great importance to the enemy as holding the Guantanamo road, as well as furnishing shelter for a strong outpost that might be used to assail the right flank and rear of any force operating against San Juan Hill. In view of this I decided to begin the attack next day at El Caney with one division, while sending two divisions on the direct road to Santiago, passing by El Poso House, and, as a diversion, to direct a small force against Aguadores from Siboney along the railroad by the sea, with a view of attracting the attention of the Spaniards in the latter direction and of preventing them from attacking our left flank.

"During the afternoon I assembled the division commanders and explained to them my general plan of battle. Lawton's division [composed of Chaffee's, Miles' and Ludlow's brig-

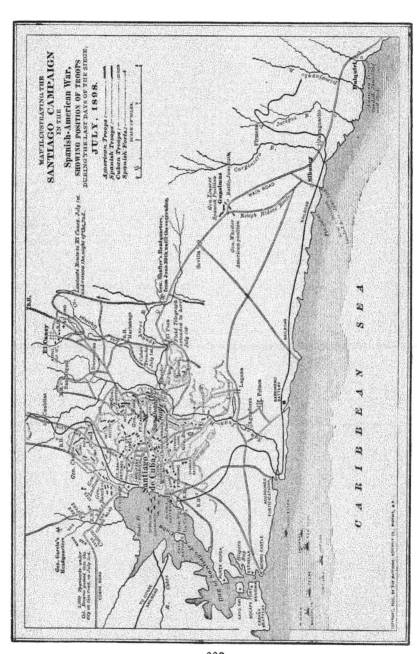

MAP ILLUSTRATING THE
SANTIAGO CAMPAIGN
IN THE
Spanish-American War,
SHOWING POSITION OF TROOPS
DURING THE LAST DAYS OF THE SIEGE,
JULY, 1898.

American Troops :
Spanish Troops :
Cuban Troops :
Spanish Forts :

SCALE OF MILES.

CARIBBEAN SEA

603

ades], assisted by Capron's light battery, was ordered to move out during the afternoon toward El Caney, to begin the attack there early the next morning. After carrying El Caney , Lawton was to move by the Caney road toward Santiago and take position on the right of the line. Wheeler's division of dismounted cavalry [embracing Sumner's brigade—3d, 6th and 9th regular cavalry, and Young's brigade mentioned above] and Kent's division of infantry [Wikoff's, Hawkins's and Pearson's brigades] were directed on the Santiago road, the head of the column resting near El Poso, toward which heights Grimes's battery moved on the afternoon of the 30th, with orders to take position thereon early the next morning and at the proper time prepare the way for the advance of Wheeler and Kent on San Juan Hill. The attack at this point was to be delayed until Lawton's guns were heard at El Caney and his infantry fire showed he had become well engaged.

"The remainder of the afternoon and night was devoted to cutting out and repairing the roads and to other necessary preparations for battle. These preparations were far from what I desired them to be; but we were in a sickly climate ; our supplies had to be brought forward by a narrow wagon road, which the rains might at any time render impassable ; fear was entertained that a storm might drive the vessels containing our stores to sea, thus separating us from our base of supplies ; and lastly, it was reported that General Pando, with 8,000 reenforcements for the enemy, was en route from Manzanillo and might be expected in a few days. Under those conditions I determined to give battle without delay.

" Early on the morning of July 1, Lawton was in position around El Caney, Chaffee's brigade [7th, 12th, and 13th U. S. Infantry] on the right, across the Guantanamo road ; Miles's brigade [1st, 4th, and 25th U. S. Infantry] in the center, and Ludlow's [8th and 22d U. S. Infantry and 2d Mass. Vols.] on the left. The duty of cutting off the enemy's retreat along the Santiago road was assigned to the latter brigade. The artillery opened on the town at 6.15 A. M. The battle here soon became general and was hotly contested. The enemy's position was naturally strong and was rendered more so by blockhouses, a stone fort, and entrenchments cut in solid rock, and the loopholing of a solidly built stone church. The opposition offered by the enemy was greater than had been anticipated, and prevented Lawton from joining the right of the main line during the day, as had been intended.

"After the battle had continued for some time Bates's brigade of two regiments [3d and 20th U. S. Infantry] reached my headquarters from Siboney. I directed him to move near El Caney, to give assistance, if necessary. He did so and was put in position between Miles and Chaffee. The battle continued with varying intensity during most of the day until the place was carried by assault, about 4.30 p. m. As the Spaniards endeavored to retreat along the Santiago road, Ludlow's position enabled him to do very effective work and to practically cut off all retreat in that direction.

" After the battle at El Caney was well opened and the sound of the small-arms fire caused us to believe that Lawton was driving the enemy before him, I directed Grimes's battery to open

fire from the heights of El Poso on the San Juan blockhouse, which could be seen situated in the enemy's entrenchments extending along the crest of San Juan Hill. This fire was effective and the enemy could be seen running away from the vicinity of the blockhouse. The artillery fire from El Poso was soon returned by the enemy's artillery. They evidently had the range of this hill, and their first shells killed and wounded several men. As the Spaniards used smokeless powder it was very difficult to locate the positions of their pieces, while, on the contrary, the smoke caused by our black powder plainly indicated the position of our battery.

" At this time the cavalry division [of General Wheeler] under General Sumner [commanding temporarily in consequence of the illness of General Wheeler, who returned to duty that day], which was lying concealed in the general vicinity of the El Poso House, was ordered forward, with directions to cross the San Juan River and deploy to the right on the Santiago side, while Kent's division was to follow closely in its rear and deploy to the left. These troops moved forward in compliance with orders, but the road was so narrow as to render it impracticable to retain the column of fours formation at all points, while the undergrowth on either side was so dense as to preclude the possibility of deploying skirmishers. It naturally resulted that the progress made was slow, and the long range rifles of the enemy's infantry killed and wounded a number of our men while marching along this road and before there was any opportunity to return this fire. At this time Generals Kent and Sumner were ordered to push forward with all possible haste and place their troops in position to engage the enemy. General Kent, with this end in view, forced the head of his column alongside of the cavalry column as far as the narrow trail permitted, and thus hurried his arrival at the San Juan and the formation beyond that stream. A few hundred yards before reaching the San Juan the road forks, a fact that was discovered by Lieutenant-Colonel Derby, of my staff, who had approached well to the front in a war balloon. This information he furnished to the troops, resulting in Sumner moving on the right-hand road, while Kent was enabled to utilize the road to the left. . . . After crossing the stream, the cavalry moved to the right with a view of connecting with Lawton's left when he should come up, and with their left resting near the Santiago road. In the meanwhile Kent's division, with the exception of two regiments of Hawkins's brigade, being thus uncovered, moved rapidly to the front from the forks previously mentioned in the road, utilizing both trails, but more especially the one to the left, and crossing the creek formed for attack in the front of San Juan Hill."—*Annual Reports of the War Dept.*, 1898, *v.* 1, *pt.* 2, *p.* 147.

" The particulars of this gallant attack, which won the hill and decided the fate of Santiago, are given with more clearness in the report of General Kent, who commanded the division which had most of the fighting to do, than in that of General Shafter. Wikoff's 'heroic brigade,' writes General Kent, 'consisting of the 13th, 9th, and 24th U. S. Infantry, speedily crossed the stream and were quickly deployed to the left of the lower ford. While personally superintending this movement Colonel Wikoff was killed, the command of the brigade then devolving upon Lieutenant-Colonel Worth, 13th Infantry, who immediately fell severely wounded, and then upon Lieutenant-Colonel Liscum, 24th Infantry, who, five minutes later, also fell under the withering fire of the enemy. The command of the brigade then devolved upon Lieutenant-Colonel E. P. Ewers, 9th Infantry. Meanwhile I had again sent a staff officer to hurry forward the second brigade [Pearson's] which was bringing up the rear. The 10th and 2d Infantry, soon arriving at the forks, were deflected to the left to follow the Third Brigade [Wikoff's], while the 21st was directed along the main road to support Hawkins [whose brigade was composed of the 6th and 16th U. S. Infantry and the 71st N. Y. Vols.].

"Crossing the lower ford a few minutes later, the 10th and 2d moved forward in column in good order toward the green knoll . . . on the left. Approaching the knoll the regiments deployed, passed over the knoll, and ascended the high ridge beyond, driving back the enemy in the direction of his trenches. I observed this movement from the Fort San Juan Hill. . . . Prior to this advance of the second brigade, the third, connecting with Hawkins's gallant troops on the right, had moved toward Fort San Juan, sweeping through a zone of most destructive fire, scaling a steep and difficult hill, and assisting in capturing the enemy's strong position (Fort San Juan) at 1.30 p. m. This crest was about 125 feet above the general level and was defended by deep trenches and a loopholed brick fort surrounded by barbed-wire entanglements. General Hawkins, some time after I reached the crest, reported that the 6th and 16th Infantry had captured the hill, which I now consider incorrect. Credit is almost equally due the 6th, 9th, 13th, 16th, and 24th regiments of infantry. . . . The Thirteenth Infantry captured the enemy's colors waving over the fort, but unfortunately destroyed them. . . .

"The greatest credit is due to the officers of my command, whether company, battalion, regimental, or brigade commanders, who so admirably directed the formation of their troops, unavoidably intermixed in the dense thicket, and made the desperate rush for the distant and strongly defended crest. I have already mentioned the circumstances of my third brigade's advance across the ford, where, in the brief space of ten minutes, it lost its brave commander (killed) and the next two ranking officers by disabling wounds; yet in spite of these confusing conditions the formations were effected without hesitation, although under a stinging fire, companies acting singly in some instances and by battalions and regiments in others, rushing through the jungle, across the stream, waist deep, and over the wide bottom thickly set with barbed-wire entanglements. . . .

"The enemy having retired to a second line of rifle pits, I directed my line to hold their positions and intrench. At ten minutes past 3 p. m. I received almost simultaneously two requests— one from Colonel Wood, commanding a cavalry brigade, and one from General Sumner—asking for assistance for the cavalry on my right, 'as they were hard pressed.' I immediately sent to their aid the 13th Infantry, who promptly went on this further mission, despite the heavy losses they had already sustained. Great credit is due

to the gallant officer and gentleman, Brig. Gen. H. S. Hawkins, who, placing himself between the two regiments, leading his brigade, the 6th and 16th Infantry, urged and led them by voice and bugle calls to the attack so successfully accomplished."—*Annual Reports of the War Dept.*, 1898, *v.* 1, *pt.* 2, *p.* 164.

The part borne by the dismounted cavalry division in the capture of the Spanish intrenchments on San Juan Hill is described as follows in the report of General Sumner, temporarily in command : "After crossing the creek with sufficient strength to hold it and protect the crossing, I received verbal orders to move by the right flank to connect with Lawton's left. During the execution of this movement a balloon, under command of Colonel Derby, came up the road, forcing open Wood's Brigade and cutting it in two, thereby delaying the movement. The artillery fire of the enemy opened upon the balloon and continued for more than an hour, thereby subjecting part of my command massed and the rest moving by the flank to long shrapnel fire. Many officers and men were wounded here by exploding shells and small arms' firing of the enemy. After completing the deployment the command was so much committed to battle that it became necessary either to advance or else retreat under fire.

"Lieutenant Miley, representing General Shafter, authorized an advance, which was ordered, Carroll's brigade taking the advance, reinforced on the right by Roosevelt's regiment and supported by the 1st and 10th Cavalry of Wood's Brigade. The advance was made under heavy infantry fire through open flat ground, cut up by wire fences, to the creek, distant about 600 yards. The advance was made in good order, the enemy's fire being returned only under favorable opportunities. In crossing the flat one officer (Captain O'Neil) and several men were killed and several officers and men wounded. Both sides of the creek are heavily wooded for about 200 yards. The creek was swollen, and the crossing through this space and the creek was made with great difficulty. After passing through the thick woods the ground was entirely open and fenced by wire. From this line it was necessary to storm the hill, upon the top of which is a house loopholed, etc., for defense. The slope of the hill is very difficult, but the assault was made with great gallantry and with much loss to the enemy. In this assault Colonel Hamilton, Lieutenants Smith and Shipp were killed ; Colonel Carroll, Lieutenants Thayer and Myer were wounded. A number of casualties occurred among the enlisted men. After taking this hill the front line advanced to take the Fort San Juan Hill under fire from strong force of the enemy in trenches and house known as 'Blockhouse.' . . . The assault was successful, the line storming the trenches and blockhouse with conspicuous gallantry and coolness, capturing three prisoners, wounding and killing many of the enemy. . . . Connected with my left, Hawkins's brigade of Kent's division carried everything in front of it and captured the house and hill known as 'Fort San Juan' proper."—*Annual Reports of the War Dept.*, 1898, *r.* 1, *pt.* 2, *p.* 370.

Lieutenant-Colonel Roosevelt, who commanded the Rough Riders regiment that day, while Colonel Wood commanded the brigade, tells the story of the fight, and what followed, very tersely, in his report : " After crossing the river at the ford," says the Lieutenant-Colonel, " we were moved along and up its right bank under fire, and were held in reserve at a sunken road. Here we lost a good many men, including Captain O'Neil, killed, and Lieutenant Haskell, wounded. We then received your order to advance and support the regular cavalry in the attack on the intrenchments and blockhouses on the hills to the left. The regiment was deployed on both sides of the road, and moved forward until we came to the rearmost lines of the regulars. We continued to move forward until I ordered a charge, and the men rushed the blockhouse and rifle pits on the hill to the right of our advance. They did the work in fine shape, though suffering severely. The guidons of Troops E and G were first planted on the summit, though the first men up were some A and B troopers who were with me.

" We then opened fire on the intrenchments on a hill to our left which some of the other regiments were assailing and which they carried a few minutes later. Meanwhile we were under a heavy rifle fire from the intrenchments along the hills to our front, from whence they also shelled us with a piece of field artillery until some of our marksmen silenced it. When the men got their wind we charged again and carried the second line of intrenchments with a rush. Swinging to the left, we then drove the Spaniards over the brow of the chain of hills fronting Santiago. By this time the regiments were much mixed, and we were under a very heavy fire, both of shrapnel and from rifles from the batteries, intrenchments, and forts immediately in front of the city. On the extreme front I now found myself in command with fragments of the six cavalry regiments of the two brigades under me. The Spaniards made one or two efforts to retake the line, but were promptly driven back.

" Both General Sumner and you sent me word to hold the line at all hazards, and that night we dug a line of intrenchments across our front, using the captured Spaniards' intrenching tools. We had nothing to eat except what we captured from the Spaniards ; but their dinners had fortunately been cooked, and we ate them with relish, having been fighting all day. We had no blankets and coats, and lay by the trenches all night. The Spaniards attacked us once in the night, and at dawn they opened a heavy artillery and rifle fire. Very great assistance was rendered us by Lieutenant Parker's Gatling battery at critical moments ; he fought his guns at the extreme front of the firing line in a way that repeatedly called forth the cheers of my men. One of the Spanish batteries which was used against us was directly in front of the hospital so that the red cross flag flew over the battery, saving it from our fire for a considerable period. The Spanish Mauser bullets made clean wounds ; but they also used a copper-jacketed or brass-jacketed bullet which exploded, making very bad wounds indeed.

" Since then we have continued to hold the ground ; the food has been short ; and until to-day [July 4] we could not get our blankets, coats, or shelter tents, while the men lay all day under the fire from the Spanish batteries, intrenchments, and guerrillas in trees, and worked all night in the trenches, never even taking off their shoes. But they are in excellent spirits, and

ready and anxious to carry out any orders they receive. At the end of the first day the eight troops were commanded, two by captains, three by first lieutenants, two by second lieutenants, and one by the sergeant whom you made acting lieutenant. We went into the fight about 490 strong ; 86 were killed or wounded, and there are about half a dozen missing. The great heat prostrated nearly 40 men, some of them among the best in the regiment."—*Annual Reports of the War Dept.*, 1898, *v.* 1, *pt.* 2, *p.* 684.

There have been much contradiction and controversy concerning some of the orders by which the battle of San Juan was directed. The following are the conclusions on that subject of a civilian observer who seems to have seen and investigated with impartiality : "The orders under which the battle of San Juan was fought were given by Adjutant-General McClernand to General Kent, commanding the Infantry Division—consisting, in addition to the organizations already mentioned (Wikoff's and Pearson's brigades), of the First Brigade, including the Sixth and Sixteenth U. S. Infantry and the Seventy-first New York, under General Hawkins—at about nine o'clock in the morning. There is no question fortunately as to the exact wording of the orders. A little green knoll to the left of the Santiago road and half a mile short of the San Juan Heights was pointed out as the point which was to be the extreme limit of the forward movement of the Infantry Division. Once there, further orders would be given. The orders under which General Sumner advanced from El Pozo would appear to have been more specific, and certainly more clear than the orders which General Kent received for the Infantry Division a few minutes later. At the same time, it is true that these orders were also based upon a complete misconception of the situation and a total ignorance of the Spanish position and the lay of the country beyond El Pozo. General Sumner's orders were to advance along that branch of the Aguadores Creek which runs parallel with the Santiago road from El Pozo, until it joins the main stream of the Aguadores at the angle subsequently known as the ' bloody angle,' where the creek makes a sharp turn to the left, and then runs a general southerly course toward the town of Aguadores and the sea. This creek General Sumner was instructed to hold until the result of Lawton's attack upon Caney became known, and he received further orders. Once the creek was reached, Sumner, under the most unfavorable circumstances of a heavy fire, and the thick and pathless jungles which his men had to penetrate, deployed his whole division, and then sent back word to McClernand, the adjutant-general of the corps, acquainting him with the actual conditions by which he was confronted, and asking whether his orders contemplated an attack upon the enemy's intrenched position, setting forth at the same time the utter impossibility of keeping his men inactive for a long time under such a heavy fire as was being poured in upon them.

" Had it been proposed to carry out the plan, as discussed and agreed upon at General Shafter's headquarters the night before, to advance along the right flank of the Spanish position, keeping in touch with Lawton, obviously these two divisions, or a large part of them, should have been directed to take the direct road which ran north from El Pozo to Marianaje and thence to El Caney, leaving in front of San Juan only force sufficient to retain the Spaniards in their position. But the divisions were ordered to proceed along the Santiago road, and in a very few minutes came under fire. The original plan may have been changed at the last moment, of course; but as every movement that was subsequently made was in the line of carrying this plan out, until finally, on the 12th, General Lawton succeeded in completely investing the town on the north and west, this does not seem likely. The more probable explanation of the movement and of what followed, and the one accepted by general officers, is as follows : That it was still intended to follow Lawton's advance on the right, but that owing to our failure to develop the Spanish position in our front, and our complete ignorance of the lay of the land, the flank movement was not begun until too late—not until the troops had been led into a position from which they could be extricated only by wresting from the Spaniards the block-houses and the trenches from which, unexposed and unseen, they were delivering such a galling fire upon our men, engaged in wandering aimlessly about in an almost trackless tropical jungle. At this moment of great confusion and uncertainty, when the road was choked with the regiments of both the cavalry and infantry divisions, mutually hindering one another in their struggles to advance, and having to sustain a heavy and destructive fire which could not be answered, an ordeal even for the veteran soldier; at this moment, when something might still have been done to mislead the enemy and cover our advance, the war balloon was sent up directly behind our columns. This mistake betrayed the exact location of our advance, and the Spanish fire became heavier and better directed, and our losses more severe."—S. Bonsal, *The Fight for Santiago*, ch. 6 (*N. Y. : Doubleday, Page & Co.*).

The same writer gives a sickening account of the sufferings of the wounded after the battle and the miserable failure of provision for any kind of succor or care of them. " Of course," he says, " in view of the perilous situation which the two divisions now occupied upon the crest of the hill, and the great anxiety which was felt at headquarters for the safety of the whole army, and the preparations which had to be made against the expected night attack of the Spaniards to drive our men back and retake their lost position, the search for the dead and wounded this evening had to be confined to a very limited area, and was only as thorough as the shortness of the time for which men could be spared from the colors permitted. The jungle and the great fields of long grass were not searched, and thus many of the wounded were not discovered until the following day ; and quite a number, indeed, not until the armistice was declared, on the third day after the battle, when the men had time to ransack the hill-side and the valley for the missing. And there were some—those who had the strength when they fell to crawl through the cactus, the Spanish bayonet, and all manner of prickly and trailing plants into the deeper and more protected recesses of the jungle—who were never discovered at all until days, many days, had passed ; and the gathering of the vultures told where some poor fellow had died without care and without food, of his wounds or from starvation. Of such an one, when his place of

hiding was discovered, there was, as a rule, only left a whitened skeleton and pieces of the uniform he had worn. The last resting-place of not a few was never discovered at all.

" I believe I am giving a moderate estimate when I say that at least one-third of the men wounded on July 1st received no attention, and were not brought back to the division hospital until the afternoon of July 3d. This night we knew nothing, and had not even the slightest suspicion, of how numerous the undiscovered wounded were. . . . Only about half of the wounded men who were discovered this evening had been brought back to the dressing station when the moon rose above the dark forest line, and lit up the battlefield and the heights of San Juan as clearly, and, indeed, more clearly than day, for there was now not the dazzling force and the confusing mirage of the pitiless sunlight to blind the sight. The majority of these men had had their wounds dressed where they fell, or soon after falling, with the first-aid bandages. There were very few indeed to whom it had been possible to give any further attention than this, as the regimental surgeons, for want of transportation, had been unable to bring their medical chests, and those who were best provided carried with them only small pocket cases. . . .

" When the first-aid bandages were applied, the wounded man and those who helped him were, as a rule, under fire, which made any but the most summary methods of wound-dressing quite impossible. Fortunately these bandages, so simple and practical, lent themselves excellently well to this procedure. The first thing the soldiers or the hospital attendants would do when they came upon a wounded man was, in the case of a wound in the body, to tear off his shirt, or in the case of a wound in the leg, tear off his trousers, and then wrap around the wound the first-aid bandage. The wound-dressers were generally in such haste, and the wounded men usually so helpless to assist in any way, and their shirts and trousers so rotten from the drenching rains in which they had been worn without change day or night, that the taking off of the clothing was literally what I call it—tearing; and the garment came off so rent as to be quite useless for further wear. Consequently the soldiers were carried half-naked, or, if they had been wounded in both the body and the lower limbs, as was so frequently the case, entirely naked, to the army wagons and so down to the hospital, where there was not a scrap of clothing or bedding forthcoming to cover them with. These who were stripped in this way during the daytime were baked and blistered by the fierce sunlight, only to shiver with the penetrating cold and dampness after the rain had ceased to fall and when the chill night came on.

" Knowing that he was totally unprepared to clothe or cover the wounded that would probably be brought in, the chief surgeon of the corps issued an order, the evening before the battle, that all wounded men should be brought in with their blankets, halves of shelter-tents, and ponchos when possible. This was certainly a step in the right direction, even if it was but a frank confession by the authorities that no preparation had been made by them for the emergency which it cannot be said was suddenly thrust upon them, but which they might have foreseen and should have been preparing against for many weeks previous. While the attending soldiers, realizing how serious for their wounded comrades it would be to have to lie in the hospitals uncovered to wind and weather, made great efforts to find their packs, these efforts were not often successful, and a great majority of the wounded reached the hospital half naked, and had thereafter only the covering and the bedding which their comrades and the hospital attendants were able to ' rustle ' for them, and this was little enough and not seldom nothing at all.

"Had this expedition been provided with a greater number of surgeons and hospital attendants, had the ambulances been at hand which we left in Tampa or upon the transports, ambulances without which it is reasonable to suppose —at least we had supposed—no civilized power would enter upon an aggressive war, much less upon a campaign in which we had the advantage of choosing both our own time and the field of operations, the outrageous treatment which our wounded suffered, and the barbarous scenes which we were called upon to witness upon this and the following days would never have occurred."—S. Bonsal, *The Fight for Santiago, ch. 8 (N. Y. : Doubleday, Page & Co.).*

The troops which had carried San Juan Hill were intrenched, that night, in the positions they had gained, and those which had taken El Caney were brought into connection with them, Lawton's division on the right and Bates's brigade on the left. The battle was renewed by the Spaniards soon after daylight on the morning of the 2d, and raged with more or less fury throughout the day. That evening, about 10 o'clock, a fierce attempt was made to break through the American lines, but without success. Again, on the morning of the third, the Spaniards reopened battle, but with less vigor than before. General Shafter then sent the following letter to General Toral, the Spanish commander: "I shall be obliged, unless you surrender, to shell Santiago de Cuba. Please inform the citizens of foreign countries, and all women and children, that they should leave the city before 10 o'clock to-morrow morning." In reply, General Toral wrote: "It is my duty to say to you that this city will not surrender, and that I will inform the foreign consuls and inhabitants of the contents of your message." Several of the foreign consuls at Santiago then came into the American lines and persuaded General Shafter to delay the shelling of the town until noon of the 5th, provided that the Spanish forces made no demonstration meantime against his own. This established a truce which was renewed, in a series of negotiations until the 10th. "I was of the opinion," reported General Shafter, "that the Spaniards would surrender if given a little time, and I thought this result would be hastened if the men of their army could be made to understand they would be well treated as prisoners of war. Acting upon this presumption I determined to offer to return all the wounded Spanish officers at El Caney who were able to bear transportation, and who were willing to give their paroles not to serve against the forces of the United States until regularly exchanged. This offer was made and accepted. These officers, as well as several of the wounded Spanish privates, 27 in all, were sent to their lines under the escort of some of our mounted cavalry. Our troops were received with honors, and I have every reason to believe the return of

the Spanish prisoners produced a good impression on their comrades. The cessation of firing about noon on the 3d practically terminated the battle of Santiago." General Shafter goes on to say that when the battle was fiercest, on July 1st, he probably had no more than 12,000 men on the firing line, not counting a few Cubans who assisted in the attack on El Caney, and who fought with valor. They were confronted by about equal numbers of the enemy, in strong and intrenched positions. "Our losses in these battles were 22 officers and 208 men killed, and 81 officers and 1,203 men wounded; missing 79. The missing, with few exceptions, reported later." Up to this time, General Shafter had been unable to complete the investment of the town with his own men, and had depended upon General Garcia with his Cubans, placed on the extreme right of the American lines, to watch for and intercept reinforcements. They failed to do so, and 2,800 Spaniards, under General Escario, entered the city on the night of the 2d. The American commander now extended his own lines as rapidly as possible and completed the investment of the town.—*Annual Reports of the War Dept.*, 1898, *v.* 1, *pt.* 2, *p.* 155–7.—As stated above permission was given on the 3d for noncombatants to leave the city. "They did leave in the following days to the number of perhaps 20,000, filling the neighboring villages and roads with destitute people, mostly women and children. It then seemed to fall to our lot to see that these people did not starve in a desolate country, and to be as much our duty to take care of these people, whom our policy had driven from their homes, as it was for Spain to feed the reconcentrados, whom they drove from their homes under their war policy. The task was not insignificant."—*Report of Inspector-General (Annual Reports of the War Dept.*, 1898, *v.* 1, *pt.* 2, *p.* 596).

A. D. 1898 (July).—Annexation of the Hawaiian Islands. See (in this vol.) HAWAIIAN ISLANDS: A. D. 1898.

A. D. 1898 (July 1).—National Bankrupt Law.—After years of effort on the part of its advocates, a national bankrupt law was enacted by both Houses of Congress and received the President's signature on the 1st of July, 1898.

A. D. 1898 (July 3).—Destruction of the Spanish squadron at Santiago.—On the morning of July 3, Admiral Cervera, convinced that Santiago would be taken by the American forces, and acting under orders from the Captain-General at Havana, made a desperate attempt to save his squadron by escaping to sea. The result was a total destruction of the Spanish ships, in an engagement with the blockading fleet, of which Admiral Sampson gave the following account in his official report:

"The enemy's vessels came out of the harbor between 9.35 and 10 a. m., the head of the column appearing around Cay Smith at 9.31 and emerging from the channel five or six minutes later. The positions of the vessels of my command off Santiago at that moment were as follows: The flagship 'New York' was 4 miles east of her blockading station and about 7 miles from the harbor entrance. She had started for Siboney, where I intended to land, accompanied by several of my staff, and go to the front to consult with General Shafter. A discussion of the situation and a more definite understanding between us of the operations proposed had been rendered necessary by the unexpectedly strong resistance of the Spanish garrison of Santiago. I had sent my chief of staff on shore the day before to arrange an interview with General Shafter, who had been suffering from heat prostration. I made arrangements to go to his headquarters, and my flagship was in the position mentioned above when the Spanish squadron appeared in the channel. The remaining vessels were in or near their usual blockading positions, distributed in a semicircle about the harbor entrance, counting from the eastward to the westward, in the following order: The 'Indiana' about a mile and a half from shore, the 'Oregon'—the 'New York's' place being between these two—the 'Iowa,' 'Texas,' and 'Brooklyn,' the latter two miles from the shore west of Santiago. The distance of the vessels from the harbor entrance was from 2½ to 4 miles, the latter being the limit of day blockading distance. The length of the arc formed by the ships was about 8 miles. The 'Massachusetts' had left at 4 a. m., for Guantanamo for coal. Her station was between the 'Iowa' and 'Texas.' The auxiliaries 'Gloucester' and 'Vixen' lay close to the land and nearer the harbor entrance than the large vessels, the 'Gloucester' to the eastward and the 'Vixen' to the westward. The torpedo boat 'Ericsson' was in company with the flagship and remained with her during the chase until ordered to discontinue, when she rendered very efficient service in rescuing prisoners from the burning 'Vizcaya.' . . .

"The Spanish vessels came rapidly out of the harbor, at a speed estimated at from 8 to 10 knots, and in the following order: 'Infanta Maria Teresa' (flagship), 'Vizcaya,' 'Cristobal Colon,' and the 'Almirante Oquendo.' The distance between these ships was about 800 yards, which means that from the time the first one became visible in the upper reach of the channel until the last one was out of the harbor an interval of only about 12 minutes elapsed. Following the 'Oquendo,' at a distance of about 1,200 yards, came the torpedo-boat destroyer 'Pluton,' and after her the 'Furor.' The armored cruisers, as rapidly as they could bring their guns to bear, opened a vigorous fire upon the blockading vessels, and emerged from the channel shrouded in the smoke from their guns. The men of our ships in front of the port were at Sunday 'quarters for inspection.' The signal was made simultaneously from several vessels, 'Enemy ships escaping,' and general quarters was sounded. The men cheered as they sprang to their guns, and fire was opened probably within 8 minutes by the vessels whose guns commanded the entrance. The 'New York' turned about and steamed for the escaping fleet, flying the signal, 'Close in towards harbor entrance and attack vessels,' and gradually increasing speed, until toward the end of the chase she was making 16½ knots, and was rapidly closing on the 'Cristobal Colon.' She was not, at any time, within the range of the heavy Spanish ships, and her only part in the firing was to receive the undivided fire from the forts in passing the harbor entrance, and to fire a few shots at one of the destroyers, thought at the moment to be attempting to escape from the 'Gloucester.'

"The Spanish vessels, upon clearing the harbor, turned to the westward in column, increas-

ing their speed to the full power of their engines. The heavy blockading vessels, which had closed in towards the Morro at the instant of the enemy's appearance, and at their best speed, delivered a rapid fire, well sustained and destructive, which speedily overwhelmed and silenced the Spanish fire. The initial speed of the Spaniards carried them rapidly past the blockading vessels, and the battle developed into a chase in which the 'Brooklyn' and 'Texas' had, at the start, the advantage of position. The 'Brooklyn' maintained this lead. The 'Oregon,' steaming with amazing speed from the commencement of the action, took first place. The 'Iowa' and the 'Indiana' having done good work, and not having the speed of the other ships, were directed by me, in succession, at about the time the 'Vizcaya' was beached, to drop out of the chase and resume blockading stations. These vessels rescued many prisoners. The 'Vixen,' finding that the rush of the Spanish ships would put her between two fires, ran outside of our own column and remained there during the battle and chase.

"The skillful handling and gallant fighting of the 'Gloucester' excited the admiration of every one who witnessed it, and merits the commendation of the Navy Department. She is a fast and entirely unprotected auxiliary vessel — the yacht 'Corsair'—and has a good battery of light rapid-fire guns. She was lying about 2 miles from the harbor entrance, to the southward and eastward, and immediately steamed in, opening fire upon the large ships. Anticipating the appearance of the 'Pluton' and 'Furor,' the 'Gloucester' was slowed, thereby gaining more rapidly a high pressure of steam, and when the destroyers came out she steamed for them at full speed, and was able to close to short range, while her fire was accurate, deadly, and of great volume. During this fight the 'Gloucester' was under the fire of the Socapa Battery. Within twenty minutes from the time they emerged from Santiago Harbor the careers of the 'Furor' and the 'Pluton' were ended, and two-thirds of their people killed. The 'Furor' was beached and sunk in the surf; the 'Pluton' sank in deep water a few minutes later. The destroyers probably suffered much injury from the fire of the secondary batteries of the battle ships 'Iowa,' 'Indiana,' and the 'Texas,' yet I think a very considerable factor in their speedy destruction was the fire, at close range, of the 'Gloucester's' battery. After rescuing the survivors of the destroyers, the 'Gloucester' did excellent service in landing and securing the crew of the 'Infanta Maria Teresa.'

"The method of escape attempted by the Spaniards, all steering in the same direction, and in formation, removed all tactical doubts or difficulties, and made plain the duty of every United States vessel to close in, immediately engage, and pursue. This was promptly and effectively done. As already stated, the first rush of the Spanish squadron carried it past a number of the blockading ships which could not immediately work up to their best speed; but they suffered heavily in passing, and the 'Infanta Maria Teresa' and the 'Oquendo' were probably set on fire by shells fired during the first fifteen minutes of the engagement. It was afterwards learned that the 'Infanta Maria Teresa's' fire main had been cut by one of our first shots, and that she was unable to extingnish fire. With large volumes of smoke rising from their lower decks aft, these vessels gave up both fight and flight and ran in on the beach —the 'Infanta Maria Teresa' at about 10.15 a. m. at Nima Nima, 6½ miles from Santiago Harbor entrance, and the 'Almirante Oquendo' at about 10.30 a. m. at Juan Gonzales, 7 miles from the port.

" The 'Vizcaya' was still under the fire of the leading vessels; the 'Cristobal Colon' had drawn ahead, leading the chase, and soon passed beyond the range of the guns of the leading American ships. The 'Vizcaya' was soon set on fire, and, at 11.15, she turned inshore, and was beached at Aserraderos, 15 miles from Santiago, burning fiercely, and with her reserves of ammunition on deck already beginning to explode. When about 10 miles west of Santiago the 'Indiana' had been signaled to go back to the harbor entrance, and at Aserraderos the 'Iowa' was signaled to 'Resume blockading station.' The 'Iowa' assisted by the 'Ericsson' and the 'Hist,' took off the crew of the 'Vizcaya,' while the 'Harvard' and the 'Gloucester' rescued those of the 'Infanta Maria Teresa' and the 'Almirante Oquendo.' This rescue of prisoners, including the wounded, from the burning Spanish vessels, was the occasion of some of the most daring and gallant conduct of the day. The ships were burning fore and aft, their guns and reserve ammunition were exploding, and it was not known at what moment the fire would reach the main magazines. In addition to this a heavy surf was running just inside of the Spanish ships. But no risk deterred our officers and men until their work of humanity was complete.

"There remained now of the Spanish ships only the 'Cristobal Colon'—but she was their best and fastest vessel. Forced by the situation to hug the Cuban coast, her only chance of escape was by superior and sustained speed. When the 'Vizcaya' went ashore, the 'Colon' was about 6 miles ahead of the 'Brooklyn' and the 'Oregon'; but her spurt was finished, and the American ships were now gaining upon her. Behind the 'Brooklyn' and the 'Oregon' came the 'Texas,' 'Vixen,' and 'New York.' It was evident from the bridge of the 'New York' that all the American ships were gradually overhauling the chase, and that she had no chance of escape. At 12.50 the 'Brooklyn' and the 'Oregon' opened fire and got her range —the 'Oregon's' heavy shell striking beyond her—and at 1.20 she gave up without firing another shot, hauled down her colors, and ran ashore at Rio Torquino, 48 miles from Santiago. Captain Cook, of the 'Brooklyn,' went on board to receive the surrender. While his boat was alongside I came up in the 'New York,' received his report, and placed the 'Oregon' in charge of the wreck to save her, if possible, and directed the prisoners to be transferred to the 'Resolute,' which had followed the chase. Commodore Schley, whose chief of staff had gone on board to receive the surrender, had directed that all their personal effects should be retained by the officers. This order I did not modify. The 'Cristobal Colon' was not injured by our firing, and probably is not much injured by beaching, though she ran ashore at high speed. The beach was so steep that she came off by the working of the sea. But her sea valves were opened and broken, treacherously, I am sure, after her sur-

render, and despite all efforts she sank. When it became evident that she could not be kept afloat, she was pushed by the 'New York' bodily up on the beach, the 'New York's' stem being placed against her for this purpose—the ship being handled by Captain Chadwick with admirable judgment—and sank in shoal water and may be saved. Had this not been done she would have gone down in deep water and would have been, to a certainty, a total loss.

"I regard this complete and important victory over the Spanish forces as the successful finish of several weeks of arduous and close blockade, so stringent and effective during the night that the enemy was deterred from making the attempt to escape at night, and deliberately elected to make the attempt in daylight. The object of the blockade of Cervera's squadron was fully accomplished, and each individual bore well his part in it—the commodore in command on the second division, the captains of ships, their officers, and men. The fire of the battle ships was powerful and destructive, and the resistance of the Spanish squadron was, in great part, broken almost before they had got beyond the range of their own forts. . . . Several of the [American] ships were struck—the 'Brooklyn' more often than the others—but very slight material injury was done, the greatest being aboard the 'Iowa.' Our loss was 1 man killed and 1 wounded, both on the 'Brooklyn.' It is difficult to explain this immunity from loss of life or injury to ships in a combat with modern vessels of the best type, but Spanish gunnery is poor at the best, and the superior weight and accuracy of our fire speedily drove the men from their guns and silenced their fire. This is borne out by the statements of prisoners and by observation."—*Annual Report of Secretary of the Navy*, 1898, v. 2, pp. 506–511.

Some particulars of the destruction of the "Furor," the "Pluton," and the "Infanta Maria Teresa," and of the rescue of surviving Spaniards, including Admiral Cervera, are given in a report by Lieutenant Huse, executive officer of the "Gloucester," as follows: "The 'Pluton' was run on the rocks about 4 miles west of Morro and blew up. Our crew cheered at the sight of the explosion. The 'Furor' soon commenced to describe circles with a starboard helm, her fire ceased, and it became apparent that she was disabled. A white rag was waved from forward and we stopped firing. Lieutenants Wood and Norman and Assistant Engineer Proctor were sent to rescue the crews and to see if the prizes could be saved. These found a horrible state of affairs on the 'Furor.' The vessel was a perfect shambles. As she was on fire and burning rapidly, they took off the living and then rescued all they could find in the water and on the beach. The 'Pluton' was among the rocks in the surf and could not be boarded, but her crew had made their way ashore or were adrift on life buoys and wreckage. These were all taken on board. I have since learned that the 'New York' passed a number of men in the water who had doubtless jumped overboard from the destroyers to escape our fire. All these were probably drowned. While this work was going on several explosions took place on the 'Furor,' and presently—at about 11.30—she threw her bows in the air, and turning to port slowly sank in deep water. . . .

"While one of our boats was still ashore, seeing heavy clouds of smoke behind the next point the ship was moved in that direction, the men being at quarters and everything in readiness for further action. On rounding the point two men-of-war were found on the beach burning fiercely aft, the majority of the crew being crowded on the forecastle and unable apparently to reach land, only 200 yards away. Our boats, under Lieutenant Norman and Ensign Edson, put off to the nearer vessel, which proved to be the flagship 'Infanta Maria Teresa,' and rescued all on board her by landing them on the beach through the surf. Lieutenant Norman formally received the surrender of the commander in chief and all his officers and men present, and as soon as all hands had been transferred ashore, brought on board this ship all the higher officers, including the admiral. Lieutenant Wood meanwhile rescued the remaining survivors on board the 'Oquendo,' the second of the burning vessels. The Spanish officers not feeling that the prisoners on shore were secure from attack by Cuban partisans, by your orders I directed Lieutenant Norman to land with a small force, establish a camp on shore, and hoist the United States flag over it. He took with him all the rations that could be spared from the stores aboard."
—*Annual Report of Secretary of the Navy*, 1898, *v.* 2, *p.* 542.

The following is a translation, from Admiral Cervera's report, as partly published in newspapers at Madrid, giving his description of the destruction of his flagship and his own rescue from death: "The enemy's fire produced terrible damages on board the 'Infanta Maria Teresa,' destroying the elements of defence—among others, the net for protection against fire. In this critical moment the captain of the ship, Señor Concas, fell wounded, and it was necessary to withdraw him, I taking command of the vessel, because it was impossible to find the second commandant of the 'Maria Teresa.' Immediately afterwards they reported to me that my cabin was burning in consequence of an explosion. The fire soon became very great and ignited other parts of the ship. I gave orders to my aid to flood the after magazines, but it was impossible. Dense clouds of smoke impeded walking in the passages and practicing any kind of operations. In this situation I could only think of beaching the ship, and did so, running aground on Punta Cabrera. The contest was impossible on our side, and there was nothing more to be done but to save as much as possible. I thought to lower the flag, but that was not possible on account of the fire, which prevented all operations. In these anxious moments two boats came to the aid of the 'Maria Teresa,' into which a number of us jumped. Those that were not dying were saved with nothing. The 'Teresa' lowered a small boat, which sank before it could be of any service. Subsequently they succeeded in launching a steam launch, but this also sank after making one voyage to the beach. I succeeded in saving myself with nothing, two sailors helping me, one named Andres Sequeros and the officer D. Angel Cervera, all of us arriving on board the American ship 'Gloucester' naked. At this time we were all naked."—*Annual Report of Secretary of the Navy*, 1898, *v.* 2, *pp.* 558–559.

A. D. 1898 (July 4-17).—The surrender of

Santiago and of all the Spanish forces in eastern Cuba.—The following is a continuation of the report made by General Shafter of his operations at Santiago de Cuba, resulting in the surrender of the entire forces of Spain in eastern Cuba: "The information of our naval victory was transmitted under flag of truce to the Spanish commander in Santiago on July 4, and the suggestion again made that he surrender to save needless effusion of blood. On the same date I informed Admiral Sampson that if he would force his way into the harbor the city would surrender without any further sacrifice of life. Commodore Watson replied that Admiral Sampson was temporarily absent, but that in his (Watson's) opinion the navy should not enter the harbor. In the meanwhile letters passing between General Toral and myself caused the cessation of hostilities to continue; each army, however, continued to strengthen its intrenchments. I was still of the opinion the Spaniards would surrender without much more fighting, and on July 6 called General Toral's attention to the changed conditions and at his request gave him time to consult his home Government. This he did, asking that the British consul, with the employees of the cable company, be permitted to return from El Caney to the city. This I granted. The strength of the enemy's position was such I did not wish to assault if it could be avoided. An examination of the enemy's works, made after the surrender, fully justified the wisdom of the course adopted. The intrenchments could only have been carried with very great loss of life, probably with not less than 3,000 killed and wounded.

"On July 8 General Toral offered to march out of the city with arms and baggage, provided he would not be molested before reaching Holguin, and to surrender to the American forces the territory then occupied by him. I replied that while I would submit his proposition to my home Government, I did not think it would be accepted. In the meanwhile arrangements were made with Admiral Sampson that when the army again engaged the enemy the navy would assist by shelling the city from ships stationed off Aguadores, dropping a shell every few minutes. On July 10 the 1st Illinois and the 1st District of Columbia arrived, and were placed on the line to the right of the cavalry division. This enabled me to push Lawton further to the right and to practically command the Cobra road. On the afternoon of the date last mentioned the truce was broken off at 4 p. m., and I determined to open with four batteries of artillery, and went forward in person to the trenches to give the necessary orders; but the enemy anticipated us by opening fire with his artillery a few minutes after the hour stated. His batteries were apparently silenced before night, while ours continued playing upon his trenches until dark. During this firing the navy fired from Aguadores, most of the shells falling in the city. There was also some small-arms firing. On this afternoon and the next morning we lost Capt. Charles W. Rowell, 2d Infantry, and 1 man killed, and Lieutenant Lutz, 2d Infantry, and 10 men wounded. On the morning of July 11 the bombardment by the Navy and my field guns was renewed and continued until nearly noon, and on the same day I reported to the Adjutant-General of the Army that the right of Ludlow's brigade of Lawton's division rested on the bay. Thus our hold upon the enemy was complete.

"At 2 p. m. on this date, the 11th, the surrender of the city was again demanded. The firing ceased and was not again renewed. By this date the sickness in the army was increasing very rapidly as a result of exposure in the trenches to the intense heat of the sun and the heavy rains. Moreover, the dews in Cuba are almost equal to rains. The weakness of the troops was becoming so apparent I was anxious to bring the siege to an end, but in common with most of the officers of the army I did not think an assault would be justifiable, especially as the enemy seemed to be acting in good faith in their preliminary propositions to surrender. On July 11 I wrote General Toral as follows: 'With the largely increased forces which have come to me, and the fact that I have your line of retreat securely in my hands, the time seems fitting that I should again demand of your excellency the surrender of Santiago and of your excellency's army. I am authorized to state that should your excellency so desire the Government of the United States will transport the entire command of your excellency to Spain.' General Toral replied that he had communicated my proposition to his general-in-chief, General Blanco.

"July 12 I informed the Spanish commander that Major-General Miles, commander-in-chief of the American Army, had just arrived in my camp, and requested him to grant us a personal interview on the following day. He replied he would be pleased to meet us. The interview took place on the 13th, and I informed him his surrender only could be considered, and that as he was without hope of escape he had no right to continue the fight. On the 14th another interview took place, during which General Toral agreed to surrender, upon the basis of his army, the Fourth Army Corps, being returned to Spain, the capitulation embracing all of eastern Cuba east of a line passing from Acerraderos on the south to Sagua de Tanamo on the north, via Palma Soriano. It was agreed commissioners should meet during the afternoon to definitely arrange the terms. . . . The terms of surrender finally agreed upon included about 12,000 Spanish troops in the city and as many more in the surrendered district. It was arranged the formal surrender should take place between the lines on the morning of July 17, each army being represented by 100 armed men. At the time appointed, I appeared at the place agreed upon with my general officers, staff, and 100 troopers of the Second Cavalry under Captain Brett. General Toral also arrived with a number of his officers and 100 infantry. We met midway between the representatives of our two armies, and the Spanish commander formally consummated the surrender of the city and the 24,000 troops in Santiago and the surrendered district. After this ceremony I entered the city with my staff and escort, and at 12 o'clock noon the American flag was raised over the governor's palace with appropriate ceremonies."—*Annual Reports of the War Dept.*, 1898, *v. 2, pp.* 157–159.

A. D. 1898 (July—August: Army administration). — Red-tape and politics. — Their working in the campaign.—"The Cuban campaign had been foreseen by intelligent officers for more than a year, but the department which clothes the army had taken no steps

toward providing a suitable uniform for campaigning in the tropics until war was declared. The Fifth Army Corps, a comparatively small body of 17,000 men, was concentrated at Tampa on the railroad within reach of all the appliances for expediting business. Between April 26, when war was declared, and June 6, when the corps embarked for Cuba, sufficient time elapsed to have clothed 1,000,000 men if the matter had been handled in the same manner a wholesale clothing firm would handle similar business. Yet the corps went to Cuba wearing the winter clothing it had brought on its backs from Montana, Wyoming, and Michigan. It endured the heat of the tropics clad in this, and was furnished with light summer clothing by the department to wear for its return to Montauk, where the breezes were so bracing that the teeth chattered even when the men were clad in winter clothing. The only reason for this absolute failure to properly clothe the army was that the methods of the department are too slow and antiquated for the proper performance of business. There was no lack of money. It was a simple case of red-tape delays. There can be no doubt that the intention was that the summer clothing should be worn in Cuba and that there should be warm clothing issued at Montauk. It was issued after the troops had shivered for days in their light clothes. The delays unavoidably connected with an obsolete method caused great suffering that should not have been inflicted upon men expected to do arduous duty. A sensible man would not put a heavy blanket on a horse to do draught work on a hot day ; but the red tape of an antiquated way of doing business caused our soldiers to wear heavy woolen clothes in torrid heat, when every nerve was to be strained to the breaking point in athletic exertion. This is not pointed out in a fault-finding spirit. The men are proud to have been in the Fifth Corps and to have endured these things for the country and the flag ; but these unnecessary sufferings impaired the fighting strength of the army, caused much of the sickness that visited the Fifth Corps, and might have caused the failure of the whole expedition. . . .

"The difficulty here depicted was one which beset the department at every turn in the whole campaign. It is a typical case. Transports, tentage transportation—it was the same in everything. With the most heroic exertions the department was able to meet emergencies only after they had passed. This was caused partly by lack of ready material, but mainly by an inelastic system of doing business which broke down in emergencies. This, in turn, was caused mainly by the illiberal treatment accorded to this, as well as to every other department of the army by Congress. It uniformly cuts mercilessly all estimates of this, as of every other department, and leaves no margin of expenditure or chance of improvement. It dabbles in matters which are purely technical and require the handling of expert executive talent. . . .

"Plans for war should be prepared in advance. This was especially true of the last war, which had been foreseen for years and considered a probability for several months. All details should have been previously worked out, all contingencies foreseen before hostilities began. Such plans would require some modifications, of course, but would form a working basis.

Neither Santiago nor Manila Bay would have been foreseen; but any plans for war would have involved the consideration and solution of the following problems : How to raise, arm, equip, organize, mobilize, clothe, feed, shelter, and transport large bodies of soldiers. The point where the battle might occur would be a mere tactical detail to be worked out at the proper time. The above problems could all be solved in time of peace and should have been solved. The general staff performs this function in foreign armies, but we had no such body in our service and nothing to imperfectly take its place. . . .

"The most urgently needed reform is the absolute divorcement of the army in all of its departments from politics. . . . No department of the army should be more exempt from political influence than the staff. This points at once to the most urgent reform, viz., make the commanding general the real working head of the army, instead of the Secretary of War. No good results have come to the service by the extension of the Secretary's powers in Grant's first administration. Most of the evils of the service can be traced to the fact that the general commanding has since that time been practically deprived of his proper functions, and the real head of the army has been a politician."—Lieut. J. H. Parker, *Our Army Supply Departments and the need of a General Staff* (*Review of Reviews*, Dec., 1898).

A. D. 1898 (July—August : Cuba).—The **War with Spain.**—Sickness in the American army at Santiago.—Its alarming state.— Hurried removal of troops to Montauk Point, Long Island.—"After the surrender of General Toral's army General Shafter urged the War Department from time to time to hasten the shipment of the Spanish prisoners to their homes, in order that the American Army, whose condition was now deplorable, might be transported to the United States. At this time about half the command had been attacked by malarial fever, with a few cases of yellow fever, dysentery, and typhoid fever. The yellow-fever cases were mainly confined to the troops at Siboney, and the few cases found among the troops at the front were at once transferred to that place. . . . There was great fear, and excellent grounds for it, that the yellow fever, now sporadic throughout the command, would become epidemic. With the command weakened by malarial fevers, and its general tone and vitality much reduced by all the circumstances incident to the campaign, the effects of such an epidemic would practically mean its annihilation. The first step taken to check the spread of disease was the removal of all the troops to new camping grounds. . . . It was directed that the command be moved in this way every few days, isolating the cases of yellow fever as they arose, and it was expected that in a short time the yellow fever would be stamped out. . . . But the effect produced on the command by the work necessary to set up the tents and in the removal of the camps increased the number on the sick report to an alarming degree. Convalescents from malarial fever were taken again with the fever, and yellow fever, dysentery, and typhoid increased. It was useless now to attempt to confine the yellow-fever cases to Siboney, and isolation hospitals were established

around Santiago. It was apparent that to keep moving the command every few days simply weakened the troops and increased the fever cases. Any exertion in this heat caused a return of the fever, and it must be remembered that the convalescents now included about 75 per cent. of the command. The Commanding General was now directed to move the entire command into the mountains to the end of the San Luis railroad, where the troops would be above the yellow fever limit ; but this was a physical impossibility. . . .

"The situation was desperate; the yellow-fever cases were increasing in number, and the month of August, the period in which it is epidemic, was at hand. It was with these conditions staring them in the face, that the officers commanding divisions and brigades and the Chief Surgeon were invited by General Shafter to discuss the situation. As a result of this conference the General sent the following telegram giving his views [and those of the General Officers and Medical Officers]. . . . 'In reply to telegram of this date [August 3], stating that it is deemed best that my command be moved to end of railroad, where yellow fever is impossible, I have to say that under the circumstances this move is practically impossible. The railroad is not yet repaired, although it will be in about a week. Its capacity is not to exceed 1,000 men a day, at the best, and it will take until the end of August to make this move, even if the sick-list should not increase. An officer of my staff, Lieutenant Miley, who has looked over the ground, says it is not a good camping ground. . . . In my opinion there is but one course to take, and that is to immediately transport the Fifth Corps and the detached regiments that came with it, and were sent immediately after it, with the least delay possible, to the United States. If this is not done I believe the death-rate will be appalling. I am sustained in this view by every medical officer present. I called together to-day the General Officers and the senior Medical Officers and telegraph you their views.' . . .

"On August 4th instructions were received from the War Department to begin the removal of the command to Montauk Point, Long Island. Some of the immune regiments were on the way to Santiago, and other regiments were at once ordered there to garrison the district as General Shafter's command was withdrawn. The first of the fleet of vessels to return the Spanish troops arrived in time to be loaded and leave August 9th, and by the end of the month nearly all were transported.

"After the surrender the relations between the American and Spanish troops were very cordial. There could be little or no conversation between individuals, but in many ways the respect each had for the other was shown, and there seemed to be no hatred on either side. Most of the Spanish officers remained in their quarters in town, and they shared in the feeling displayed by their men. Salutations were generally exchanged between the officers, and American ways and manners became very popular among the Spaniards. . . .

"By the 25th of the month General Shaffer's entire command, with the exception of a few organizations just ready to embark, had departed, and, turning over the command to General Lawton, he sailed that day with his staff on the 'Mexico,' one of the captured transports, and at noon September 1st went ashore at Montauk Point, Long Island."—J. D. Miley, *In Cuba with Shafter, ch.* 12 (*N. Y. : Chas. Scribner's Sons*).

A. D. 1898 (July—August : Philippines).— Correspondence between the General commanding United States forces at Cavite and Manila, and **Aguinaldo**, the Filipino leader. —On the 4th of July, General Thomas M. Anderson, then commanding the "U. S. Expeditionary Forces" at Cavite Arsenal, addressed the following communication to "Señor Don Emilio Aguinaldo y Famy, Commanding Philippine Forces":

"General : I have the honor to inform you that the United States of America, whose land forces I have the honor to command in this vicinity, being at war with the Kingdom of Spain, has entire sympathy and most friendly sentiments for the native people of the Philippine Islands. For these reasons I desire to have the most amicable relations with you, and to have you and your people co-operate with us in military operations against the Spanish forces. In our operations it has become necessary for us to occupy the town of Cavite as a base of operations. In doing this I do not wish to interfere with your residence here and the exercise by yourself and other native citizens of all functions and privileges not inconsistent with military rule. I would be pleased to be informed at once of any misconduct of soldiers under my command, as it is the intention of my Government to maintain order and to treat all citizens with justice, courtesy, and kindness. I have therefore the honor to ask your excellency to instruct your officials not to interfere with my officers in the performance of their duties and not to assume that they can not visit Cavite without permission."

On the following day Aguinaldo replied: "General : Interpreting the sentiments of the Philippine people, I have the honor to express to your excellency my most profound gratefulness for the sympathy and amicable sentiments with which the natives of these islands inspire the great North American nation and your excellency. I also thank most profoundly your desire of having friendly relations with us, and of treating us with justice, courtesy, and kindness, which is also our constant wish to prove the same, and special satisfaction whenever occasion represents. I have already ordered my people not to interfere in the least with your officers and men, orders which I shall reiterate to prevent their being unfulfilled; hoping that you will inform me of whatever misconduct that may be done by those in my command, so as to reprimand them and correspond with your wishes." . . .

To this communication General Anderson returned the following on the 6th: "General: I am encouraged by the friendly sentiment expressed by your excellency in your welcome letter received on the 5th instant to endeavor to come to a definite understanding, which I hope will be advantageous to both. Very soon we expect a large addition to our forces, and it must be apparent to you as a military officer that we will require much .more room to camp our soldiers, and also storeroom for our supplies. For this I would like to have your excellency's advice and co-operation, as you are best acquainted with the resources of this country. It

must be apparent to you that we do not intend to remain here inactive, but to move promptly against our common enemy. But for a short time we must organize and land supplies, and also retain a place for storing them near our fleet and transports. I am solicitous to avoid any conflict of authority which may result from having two sets of military officers exercising command in the same place. I am also anxious to avoid sickness by taking sanitary precaution. Your own medical officers have been making voluntary inspections with mine, and fear epidemic diseases if the vicinity is not made clean. Would it not be well to have prisoners work to this end under the advice of the surgeons?" . . .

On the 9th of July General Anderson reported to the War Department at Washington : "General Aguinaldo tells me he has about 15,000 fighting men, but only 11,000 armed with guns, which mostly were taken from the Spaniards. He claims to have in all 4,000 prisoners. When we first landed he seemed very suspicious, and not at all friendly, but I have now come to a better understanding with him and he is much more friendly and seems willing to co-operate. But he has declared himself dictator and president, and is trying to take Manila without our assistance. This is not probable, but if he can effect his purpose he will, I apprehend, antagonize any attempt on our part to establish a provisional government."

On the 17th the American commander caused another communication to be addressed to "General Emilio Aguinaldo" as follows : "Sir : General Anderson wishes me to say that, the second expedition having arrived, he expects to encamp in the vicinity of Paranaque from 5,000 to 7,000 men. To do this, supply this army and shelter, will require certain assistance from the Filipinos in this neighborhood. We will want horses, buffaloes, carts, etc., for transportation, bamboo for shelter, wood to cook with, etc. For all this we are willing to pay a fair price, but no more. We find so far that the native population are not willing to give us this assistance as promptly as required. But we must have it, and if it becomes necessary we will be compelled to send out parties to seize what we may need. We would regret very much to do this, as we are here to befriend the Filipinos. Our nation has spent millions of money to send forces here to expel the Spaniards and to give good government to the whole people, and the return we are asking is comparatively slight. General Anderson wishes you to inform your people that we are here for their good, and that they must supply us with labor and material at the current market prices. We are prepared to purchase 500 horses at a fair price, but can not undertake to bargain for horses with each individual owner. I regret very much that I am unable to see you personally, as it is of the utmost importance that these arrangements should be made as soon as possible."

To this communication there seems to have been no written reply until the 24th ; and, on the 20th, the Chief Quartermaster reported to General Anderson "that it is impossible to procure transportation except upon Señor Aguinaldo's order, in this section, who has an inventory of everything. The natives have removed their wheels and hid them." On the 23d General Anderson repeated his request, as follows:

"General : When I came here three weeks ago I requested your excellency to give what assistance you could to procure means of transportation for the American Army, as it was to fight the cause of your people. So far we have received no response. As you represent your people, I now have the honor to make requisition on you for 500 horses and 50 oxen and ox carts. If you can not secure these, I will have to pass you and make requisition directly on the people. I beg leave to request an answer at your earliest convenience."

The next day Aguinaldo replied : " I have the honor to manifest to your excellency that I am surprised beyond measure at that which you say to me in it, lamenting the nonreceipt of any response relative to the needs (or aids) that you have asked of me in the way of horses, buffaloes, and carts, because I replied in a precise manner, through the bearer, that I was disposed to give convenient orders whenever you advised me of the number of these with due anticipation (notice). I have circulated orders in the provinces in the proximity that in the shortest time possible horses be brought for sale, but I cannot assure your excellency that we have the number of 500 that is needed, because horses are not abundant in these vicinities, owing to deaths caused by epizootic diseases in January and March last. Whenever we have them united (or collected), I shall have the pleasure to advise your excellency. I have also ordered to be placed at my disposal 50 carts that I shall place at your disposition whenever necessary, always (premising) that you afford me a previous advice of four days in anticipation."

Meantime, General Anderson had written to the War Department, on the 18th: "Since reading the President's instructions to General Merritt, I think I should state to you that the establishment of a provisional government on our part will probably bring us in conflict with insurgents, now in active hostility to Spain. The insurgent chief, Aguinaldo, has declared himself dictator and self-appointed president. He has declared martial law and promulgated a minute method of rule and administration under it. We have observed all official military courtesies, and he and his followers express great admiration and gratitude to the great American Republic of the north, yet in many ways they obstruct our purposes and are using every effort to take Manila without us. I suspect also that Aguinaldo is secretly negotiating with the Spanish authorities, as his confidential aid is in Manila. The city is strongly fortified and hard to approach in the rainy season. If a bombardment fails we should have the best engineering ability here."

And, again on the 21st, he had written: "Since I wrote last, Aguinaldo has put in operation an elaborate system of military government, under his assumed authority as dictator, and has prohibited any supplies being given us, except by his order. As to this last I have written to him that our requisitions on the country for horses, ox carts, fuel and bamboo (to make scaling ladders) must be filled, and that he must aid in having them filled. His assumption of civil authority I have ignored, and let him know verbally that I could, and would, not recognize it, while I did not recognize him as a military leader. It may seem strange that I have made no formal protest against his proclamation as

dictator, his declaration of martial law, and publication and execution of a despotic form of government. I wrote such a protest, but did not publish it, at Admiral Dewey's request, and also for fear of wounding the susceptibilities of Major-General Merritt, but I have let it be known in every other way that we do not recognize the dictatorship. These people only respect force and firmness. I submit, with all deference, that we have heretofore underrated the natives. They are not ignorant, savage tribes, but have a civilization of their own ; and although insignificant in appearance, are fierce fighters, and for a tropical people they are industrious. A small detail of natives will do more work in a given time than a regiment of volunteers."

On the 24th General Anderson received from the Philippine leader a very clear and definite statement of his attitude towards the "Expeditionary Forces of the United States," and the intentions with which he and the people whom he represented were acting. "I came," he wrote, "from Hong-kong to prevent my countrymen from making common cause with the Spanish against the North Americans, pledging before my word to Admiral Dewey to not give place [to allow] to any internal discord, because, [being] a judge of their desires, I had the strong convictions that I would succeed in both objects, establishing a government according to their desires. Thus it is that in the beginning I proclaimed the dictatorship, and afterwards, when some of the provinces had already liberated themselves from Spanish domination, I established a revolutionary government that to-day exists, giving it a democratic and popular character as far as the abnormal circumstances of war permitted, in order that they [the provinces] might be justly represented, and administered to their satisfaction. It is true that my government has not been acknowledged by any of the foreign powers, but we expected that the great North American nation, which struggled first for its independence, and afterwards for the abolition of slavery, and is now actually struggling for the independence of Cuba, would look upon it with greater benevolence than any other nation. Because of this we have always acknowledged the right of preference to our gratitude.

"Debtor to the generosity of the North Americans, and to the favors we have received through Admiral Dewey, and [being] more desirous than any other person of preventing any conflict which would have as a result foreign intervention, which must be extremely prejudicial, not alone to my nation but also to that of your excellency, I consider it my duty to advise you of the undesirability of disembarking North American troops in the places conquered by the Filipinos from the Spanish, without previous notice to this government, because as no formal agreement yet exists between the two nations the Philippine people might consider the occupation of its territories by North American troops as a violation of its rights.

"I comprehend that without the destruction of the Spanish squadron the Philippine revolution would not have advanced so rapidly. Because of this I take the liberty of indicating to your excellency the necessity that, before disembarking, you should communicate in writing to this government the places that are to be occupied and also the object of the occupation, that the people may be advised in due form and [thus] prevent the commission of any transgression against friendship. I can answer for my people, because they have given me evident proofs of their absolute confidence in my government, but I can not answer for that which another nation whose friendship is not well guaranteed might inspire in it [the people]; and it is certain that I do this not as a menace, but as a further proof of the true and sincere friendship which I have always professed for the North American people, in the complete security that it will find itself completely identified with our cause of liberty."

In the same strain, on the 1st of August, Aguinaldo wrote to U. S. Consul Williams, as to a "distinguished friend:" "I have said always, and I now repeat, that we recognize the right of the North Americans to our gratitude, for we do not forget for a moment the favors which we have received and are now receiving; but however great those favors may be, it is not possible for me to remove the distrust of my compatriots. These say that if the object of the United States is to annex these islands, why not recognize the government established in them, in order in that manner to join with it the same as by annexation? Why do not the American generals operate in conjunction with the Filipino generals and, uniting the forces, render the end more decisive? Is it intended, indeed, to carry out annexation against the wish of these people, distorting the legal sense of that word? If the revolutionary government is the genuine representative by right and deed of the Filipino people, as we have proved when necessary, why is it wished to oppress instead of gaining their confidence and friendship?

"It is useless for me to represent to my compatriots the favors received through Admiral Dewey, for they assert that up to the present the American forces have shown not an active, only a passive, co-operation, from which they suppose that the intentions of these forces are not for the best. They assert, besides, that it is possible to suppose that I was brought from Hongkong to assure those forces by my presence that the Filipinos would not make common cause with the Spaniards, and that they have delivered to the Filipinos the arms abandoned by the former in the Cavite Arsenal, in order to save themselves much labor, fatigue, blood, and treasure that a war with Spain would cost. But I do not believe these unworthy suspicions. I have full confidence in the generosity and philanthropy which shine in characters of gold in the history of the privileged people of the United States, and for that reason, invoking the friendship which you profess for me and the love which you have for my people, I pray you earnestly, as also the distinguished generals who represent your country in these islands, that you entreat the Government at Washington to recognize the revolutionary government of the Filipinos, and I, for my part, will labor with all my power with my people that the United States shall not repent their sentiments of humanity in coming to the aid of an oppressed people.

"Say to the Government at Washington that the Filipino people abominate savagery; that in the midst of their past misfortunes they have learned to love liberty, order, justice, and civil life, and that they are not able to lay aside their own wishes when their future lot and history are under discussion. Say also that I and my leaders know what we owe to our unfortunate country; that we know how to admire and are ready to imitate the disinterestedness, the abnegation, and the patriotism of the grand men of America, among whom stands pre-eminent the immortal General Washington."— *United States, 56th Congress, 1st Sess., Senate Doc. No.* 208.

In an article published in the "North American Review," February, 1900, General Anderson discussed his relations with Aguinaldo very frankly, in part as follows : "On the 1st of July, 1898, I called on Aguinaldo with Admiral Dewey. He asked me at once whether 'the United States of the North' either had recognized or would recognize his government—I am not quite sure as to the form of his question, whether it was 'had' or 'would.' In either form it was embarrassing. My orders were, in substance, to effect a landing, establish a base, not to go beyond the zone of naval co-operation, to consult Admiral Dewey and to wait for Merritt. Aguinaldo had proclaimed his government only a few days before (June 28), and Admiral Dewey had no instructions as to that assumption. The facts as to the situation at that time I believe to be these : Consul Williams states in one of his letters to the State Department that several thousand Tagals were in open insurrection before our declaration of war with Spain. I do not know as to the number, yet I believe the statement has foundation in fact. Whether Admiral Dewey and Consuls Pratt, Wildman and Williams did or did not give Aguinaldo assurances that a Filipino government would be recognized, the Filipinos certainly thought so, probably inferring this from their acts rather than from their statements. If an incipient rebellion was already in progress, what could be inferred from the fact that Aguinaldo and thirteen other banished Tagals were brought down on a naval vessel and landed in Cavite? Admiral Dewey gave them arms and ammunition, as I did subsequently, at his request. They were permitted to gather up a lot of arms which the Spaniards had thrown into the bay; and, with the four thousand rifles taken from Spanish prisoners and two thousand purchased in Hong Kong, they proceeded to organize three brigades and also to arm a small steamer they had captured. I was the first to tell Admiral Dewey that there was any disposition on the part of the American people to hold the Philippines, if they were captured. The current of opinion was setting that way when the first expeditionary force left San Francisco, but this the Admiral had had no reason to surmise.

"But to return to our interview with Aguinaldo. I told him I was acting only in a military capacity; that I had no authority to recognize his government; that we had come to whip the Spaniards, and that, if we were successful, the indirect effect would be to free them from Spanish tyranny. I added that, as we were fighting a common enemy, I hoped we would get along amicably together. He did not seem pleased with this answer. The fact is, he hoped and expected to take Manila with Admiral Dewey's assistance, and he was bitterly disappointed when our soldiers landed at Cavite. . . . A few days thereafter, he made an official call, coming with cabinet and staff and a band of music. On that occasion he handed me an elaborate schedule for an autonomous government which he had received from some Filipinos in Manila, with a statement that they had reason to believe that Spain would grant them such a form of government. With this was an open letter addressed to the Filipino people from Pedro Alexandre Paterno, advising them to put their trust in Spain rather than America. The day before, two German officers had called on Aguinaldo and I believed they had brought him these papers. I asked him if the scheme was agreeable to him. He did not answer, but asked if we, the North Americans, as he called us, intended to hold the Philippines as dependencies. I said I could not answer that, but that in one hundred and twenty years we had established no colonies. He then made this remarkable statement: 'I have studied attentively the Constitution of the United States, and I find in it no authority for colonies and I have no fear.' It may seem that my answer was somewhat evasive, but I was at the time trying to contract with the Filipinos for horses, carts, fuel and forage. . . .

"The origin of our controversies and conflicts with the Filipinos can . . . be traced back to our refusal to recognize the political authority of Aguinaldo. Our first serious break with them arose from our refusal to let them co-operate with us. About nine o'clock on the evening of August 12, I received from General Merritt an order to notify Aguinaldo to forbid the Filipino insurgents under his command from entering Manila. This notification was delivered to him at twenty minutes past ten that night. The Filipinos had made every preparation to assail the Spanish lines in their front. Certainly, they would not have given up part of their line to us unless they thought they were to fight with us. They, therefore, received General Merritt's interdict with anger and indignation. They considered the war as their war, and Manila as their capital, and Luzon as their country. . . . At seven o'clock I received an order from General Merritt to remove the Filipinos from the city. . . . I therefore took the responsibility of telegraphing Aguinaldo, who was at Bacoor, ten miles below, requesting him to withdraw his troops and intimating that serious consequences would follow if he did not do so. I received his answer at eleven, saying that a Commission would come to me the next morning with full powers. Accordingly the next day Señors Buencomeno, Lagarde, Araneto and Sandeco came to Division Headquarters in Manila and stated that they were authorized to order the withdrawal of their troops, if we would promise to reinstate them in their present positions on our making peace with Spain. Thereupon I took them over to General Merritt. Upon their repeating their demands, he told them he could not give such a pledge, but that they could rely on the honor of the American people. The General then read to them the proclamation he intended to issue to the Filipino people. . . .

"There is a great diversity of opinion as to whether a conflict with the Filipinos could not have been avoided if a more conciliatory course had been followed in dealing with them. I believe we came to a parting of the ways when we refused their request to leave their military force in a good strategic position on the contingency of our making peace with Spain without a guarantee of their independence"—T. M.

Anderson, *Our Rule in the Philippines* (*N. Am. Review*, v. 170, p. 275).

A. D. 1898 (July—August: Porto Rico).— Occupation of Porto Rico.—" With the fall of Santiago the occupation of Porto Rico became the next strategic necessity. Gen. Miles had previously been assigned to organize an expedition for that purpose. Fortunately, he was already at Santiago, where he had arrived on the 11th of July with reinforcements for Gen. Shafter's army. With these troops, consisting of 3,415 infantry and artillery, 2 companies of engineers and 1 company of the signal corps, Gen. Miles left Guantanamo on July 21st, having 9 transports, convoyed by the fleet, under Capt. Higginson, with the 'Massachusetts' (flagship), 'Dixie,' 'Gloucester,' 'Columbia' and 'Yale,' the two latter carrying troops. The expedition landed at Guanica on July 25th, which port was entered with little opposition. Here the fleet was joined by the 'Annapolis' and the 'Wasp,' while the 'Puritan' and 'Amphitrite' went to San Juan and joined the 'New Orleans,' which was engaged in blockading that port. The major general commanding was subsequently reinforced by General Schwan's brigade of the Third Army Corps, by Gen. Wilson with a part of his division and also by Gen. Brooke with a part of his corps, numbering in all 16,973 officers and men. On July 27th he entered Ponce, one of the most important ports in the island, from which he thereafter directed operations for the capture of the island. With the exception of encounters with the enemy at Guayama, Hormigueros [the Rio Prieto], Coamo, and Yauco and an attack on a force landed at Cape San Juan, there was no serious resistance. The campaign was prosecuted with great vigor and by the 12th of August much of the island was in our possession and the acquisition of the remainder was only a matter of a short time. At most of the points in the island our troops were enthusiastically welcomed. Protestations of loyalty to the flag and gratitude for delivery from Spanish rule met our commanders at every stage."—*Message of the President of the U. S. to Congress, Dec. 5*, 1898.—"During the nineteen days of active campaign on the Island of Puerto Rico a large portion of the island was captured by the United States forces and brought under our control. Our forces were in such a position as to make the positions of the Spanish forces, outside of the garrison at San Juan, utterly untenable. The Spaniards had been defeated or captured in the six different engagements which took place, and in every position they had occupied up to that time. The volunteers had deserted their colors, and many of them had surrendered to our forces and taken the oath of allegiance. This had a demoralizing effect upon the regular Spanish troops. . . . The loss of the enemy in killed, wounded and captured was nearly ten times our own, which was only 3 killed and 40 wounded."—General Miles, *Report* (*Annual Reports of the War Dep't*, 1898, v. 1, pt. 2, p. 36).

A. D. 1898 (July—September).—The War with Spain.—Capture of Manila.—Relations with the Filipino insurgents.—General Merritt's report.—Aguinaldo declared President of the Philippine Republic.—"Immediately after my arrival [July 25] I visited General Greene's camp and made a reconnaissance of the position held by the Spanish, and also the opposing lines of the insurgent forces, hereafter to be described. I found General Greene's command encamped on a strip of sandy land running parallel to the shore of the bay and not far distant from the beach, but owing to the great difficulties of landing supplies, the greater portion of the force had shelter tents only, and were suffering many discomforts, the camp being situated in a low, flat place, without shelter from the heat of the tropical sun or adequate protection during the terrific downpours of rain so frequent at this season. I was at once struck by the exemplary spirit of patient, even cheerful, endurance shown by the officers and men under such circumstances, and this feeling of admiration for the manner in which the American soldier, volunteer and regular alike, accept the necessary hardships of the work they have undertaken to do, has grown and increased with every phase of the difficult and trying campaign which the troops of the Philippine expedition have brought to such a brilliant and successful conclusion.

"I discovered during my visit to General Greene that the left or north flank of his brigade camp extended to a point on the 'Calle Real' about 3,200 yards from the outer line of Spanish defenses of the city of Manila. This Spanish line began at the powder magazine, or old Fort San Antonio, within a hundred yards of the beach and just south of the Malate suburb of Manila, and stretched away to the Spanish left in more or less detached works, eastward, through swamps and rice fields, covering all the avenues of approach to the town and encircling the city completely. The Filipinos, or insurgent forces at war with Spain, had, prior to the arrival of the American land forces, been waging a desultory warfare with the Spaniards for several months, and were at the time of my arrival in considerable force, variously estimated and never accurately ascertained, but probably not far from 12,000 men. These troops, well supplied with small arms, with plenty of ammunition and several field guns, had obtained positions of investment opposite to the Spanish line of detached works throughout their entire extent; and on the particular road called the 'Calle Real,' passing along the front of General Greene's brigade camp and running through Malate to Manila, the insurgents had established an earthwork or trench within 800 yards of the powder-magazine fort. They also occupied as well the road to the right, leading from the village of Pasay, and the approach by the beach was also in their possession. This anomalous state of affairs, namely, having a line of quasi-hostile native troops between our forces and the Spanish position, was, of course, very objectionable, but it was difficult to deal with, owing to the peculiar condition of our relations with the insurgents, which may be briefly stated as follows :

"Shortly after the naval battle of Manila Bay, the principal leader of the insurgents, Gen. Emilio Aguinaldo, came to Cavite from Hongkong, and, with the consent of our naval authorities, began active work in raising troops and pushing the Spaniards in the direction of the city of Manila. Having met with some success, and the natives flocking to his assistance, he proclaimed an independent government of republican form, with himself as president, and at the time of my arrival in the islands the entire edifice of executive and legislative departments and

subdivision of territory for administrative purposes had been accomplished, at least on paper, and the Filipinos held military possession of many points in the islands other than those in the vicinity of Manila. As General Aguinaldo did not visit me on my arrival nor offer his services as a subordinate military leader, and as my instructions from the President fully contemplated the occupation of the islands by the American land forces, and stated that 'the powers of the military occupant are absolute and supreme and immediately operate upon the political condition of the inhabitants,' I did not consider it wise to hold any direct communication with the insurgent leader until I should be in possession of the city of Manila, especially as I would not until then be in a position to issue a proclamation and enforce my authority, in the event that his pretensions should clash with my designs.

"For these reasons the preparations for the attack on the city were pressed and military operations conducted without reference to the situation of the insurgent forces. The wisdom of this course was subsequently fully established by the fact that when the troops of my command carried the Spanish intrenchments, extending from the sea to the Pasay road on the extreme Spanish right, we were under no obligations, by pre-arranged plans of mutual attack, to turn to the right and clear the front still held against the insurgents, but were able to move forward at once and occupy the city and suburbs.

"To return to the situation of General Greene's brigade as I found it on my arrival, it will be seen that the difficulty in gaining an avenue of approach to the Spanish line lay in the fact of my disinclination to ask General Aguinaldo to withdraw from the beach and the 'Calle Real,' so that Greene could move forward. This was overcome by instructions to General Greene to arrange, if possible, with the insurgent brigade commander in his immediate vicinity to move to the right and allow the American forces unobstructed control of the roads in their immediate front. No objection was made, and accordingly General Greene's brigade threw forward a heavy outpost line on the 'Calle Real' and the beach and constructed a trench, in which a portion of the guns of the Utah batteries was placed. The Spanish, observing this activity on our part, made a very sharp attack with infantry and artillery on the night of July 31. The behavior of our troops during this night attack was all that could be desired, and I have, in cablegrams to the War Department, taken occasion to commend by name those who deserve special mention for good conduct in the affair. Our position was extended and strengthened after this and resisted successfully repeated night attacks, our forces suffering, however, considerable loss in wounded and killed, while the losses of the enemy, owing to the darkness, could not be ascertained.

"The strain of the night fighting and the heavy details for outpost duty made it imperative to re-enforce General Greene's troops with General MacArthur's brigade, which had arrived in transports on the 31st of July. The difficulties of this operation can hardly be overestimated. The transports were at anchor off Cavite, 5 miles from a point on the beach where it was desired to disembark the men. Several squalls, accompanied by floods of rain, raged day after day, and the only way to get the troops and supplies ashore was to load them from the ship's side into native lighters (called 'cascos') or small steamboats, move them to a point opposite the camp, and then disembark them through the surf in small boats, or by running the lighters head on to the beach. The landing was finally accomplished, after days of hard work and hardship; and I desire here to express again my admiration for the fortitude and cheerful willingness of the men of all commands engaged in this operation. Upon the assembly of MacArthur's brigade in support of Greene's, I had about 8,500 men in position to attack, and I deemed the time had come for final action. During the time of the night attacks I had communicated my desire to Admiral Dewey that he would allow his ships to open fire on the right of the Spanish line of intrenchments, believing that such action would stop the night firing and loss of life, but the admiral had declined to order it unless we were in danger of losing our position by the assaults of the Spanish, for the reason that, in his opinion, it would precipitate a general engagement, for which he was not ready. Now, however, the brigade of General MacArthur was in position and the 'Monterey' had arrived, and under date of August 6 Admiral Dewey agreed to my suggestion that we should send a joint letter to the captain-general notifying him that he should remove from the city all non-combatants within forty-eight hours, and that operations against the defenses of Manila might begin at any time after the expiration of that period.

"This letter was sent August 7, and a reply was received the same date, to the effect that the Spanish were without places of refuge for the increased numbers of wounded, sick women, and children now lodged within the walls. On the 9th a formal joint demand for the surrender of the city was sent in. This demand was based upon the hopelessness of the struggle on the part of the Spaniards, and that every consideration of humanity demanded that the city should not be subjected to bombardment under such circumstances. The captain-general's reply, of same date, stated that the council of defense had declared that the demand could not be granted; but the captain-general offered to consult his Government if we would allow him the time strictly necessary for the communications by way of Hongkong. This was declined on our part for the reason that it could, in the opinion of the admiral and myself, lead only to a continuance of the situation, with no immediate result favorable to us, and the necessity was apparent and very urgent that decisive action should be taken at once to compel the enemy to give up the town, in order to relieve our troops from the trenches and from the great exposure to unhealthy conditions which were unavoidable in a bivouac during the rainy season.

"The seacoast batteries in defense of Manila are so situated that it is impossible for ships to engage them without firing into the town, and as the bombardment of a city filled with women and children, sick and wounded, and containing a large amount of neutral property, could only be justified as a last resort, it was agreed between Admiral Dewey and myself that an attempt should be made to carry the extreme right of the Spanish line of intrenchments in front of the positions at that time occupied by our troops, which, with its flank on the seashore, was entirely open to the fire of the navy. It was not my intention to press the assault at this point, in case the enemy should hold it in strong force, until after the navy had made practicable breaches in the works and shaken the troops holding them, which could not be done by the army alone, owing to the absence of siege guns. . . . It was believed, however, as most desirable, and in accordance with the principles of civilized warfare, that the attempt should be made to drive the enemy out of his intrenchments before resorting to the bombardment of the city. . . .

"All the troops were in position on the 13th at an early hour in the morning. About 9 a. m. on that day our fleet steamed forward from Cavite and before 10 a. m. opened a hot and accurate fire of heavy shells and rapid-fire projectiles on the sea flank of the Spanish intrenchments at the powder magazine fort, and at the same time the Utah batteries, in position in our trenches near the 'Calle Real,' began firing with great accuracy. At 10.25, on a prearranged signal from our trenches that it was believed our troops could advance, the navy ceased firing, and immediately a light line of skirmishers from the Colorado regiment of Greene's brigade passed over our trenches and deployed rapidly forward, another line from the same regiment from the left flank of our earthworks advancing swifty up the beach in open order. Both these lines found the powder-magazine fort and the trenches flanking it deserted, but as they passed over the Spanish works they were met by a sharp fire from a second line situated in the streets of Malate, by which a number of men were killed and wounded, among others the soldier who pulled down the Spanish colors still flying on the fort and raised our own.

"The works of the second line soon gave way to the determined advance of Greene's troops, and that officer pushed his brigade rapidly through Malate and over the bridges to occupy Binondo and San Miguel, as contemplated in his instructions. In the meantime the brigade of General MacArthur, advancing simultaneously on the Pasay road, encountered a very sharp fire, coming from the blockhouses, trenches, and woods in his front, positions which it was very difficult to carry, owing to the swampy condition of the ground on both sides of the roads and the heavy undergrowth concealing the enemy. With much gallantry and excellent judgment on the part of the brigade commander and the troops engaged these difficulties were overcome with a minimum loss, and MacArthur advanced and held the bridges and the town of Malate, as was contemplated in his instructions.

"The city of Manila was now in our possession, excepting the walled town, but shortly after the entry of our troops into Malate a white flag was displayed on the walls, whereupon Lieut. Col. C. A. Whittier, United States Volunteers, of my staff, and Lieutenant Brumby, United States Navy, representing Admiral Dewey, were sent ashore to communicate with the Captain-General. I soon personally followed these officers into the town, going at once to the palace of the Governor-General, and there, after a conversation with the Spanish authorities, a preliminary agreement of the terms of capitulation was signed by the Captain-General and myself. This agreement was subsequently incorporated into the formal terms of capitulation, as arranged by the officers representing the two forces, a copy of which is hereto appended and marked. Immediately after the surrender the Spanish colors on the sea front were hauled down and the American flag displayed and saluted by the guns of the navy. The Second Oregon Regiment, which had proceeded by sea from Cavite, was disembarked and entered the walled town as a provost guard, and the colonel was directed to receive the Spanish arms and deposit them in places of security. The town was filled with the troops of the enemy driven in from the intrenchments, regiments formed and standing in line in the streets, but the work of disarming proceeded quietly and nothing unpleasant occurred.

"In leaving the subject of the operations of the 13th, I desire here to record my appreciation of the admirable manner in which the orders for attack and the plan for occupation of the city were carried out by the troops exactly as contemplated. I submit that for troops to enter under fire a town covering a wide area, to rapidly deploy and guard all principal points in the extensive suburbs, to keep out the insurgent forces pressing for admission, to quietly disarm an army of Spaniards more than equal in numbers to the American troops, and finally by all this to prevent entirely all rapine, pillage, and disorder, and gain entire and complete possession of a city of 300,000 people, filled with natives hostile to the European interests, and stirred up by the knowledge that their own people were fighting in the outside trenches, was an act which only the law-abiding, temperate, resolute American soldier, well and skillfully handled by his regimental and brigade commanders, could accomplish. . . .

"The amount of public funds and the numbers of the prisoners of war and small arms taken have been reported in detail by cable. It will be observed that the trophies of Manila were nearly $900,000, 13,000 prisoners, and 22,000 arms. Immediately after the surrender my headquarters were established in the ayuntamiento, or city office of the Governor-General, where steps were at once inaugurated to set up the government of military occupancy. . . . On the 16th a cablegram containing the text of the President's proclamation directing a cessation of hostilities was received by me, and at the same time an order to make the fact known to the Spanish authorities, which was done at once. This resulted in a formal protest from the Governor-General in regard to the transfer of public funds then taking place, on the ground that the proclamation was dated prior to the surrender. To this I replied that the status quo in which we were left with the cessation of hostilities was that existing at the time of the receipt by me of the official notice, and that I must insist upon the delivery of the funds. The delivery was made under protest.

. "After the issue of my proclamation and the establishment of my office as military governor, I had direct written communication with General Aguinaldo on several occasions. He recognized my authority as military governor of the town of Manila and suburbs, and made professions of his willingness to withdraw his troops to a line which I might indicate, but at the same time asking certain favors for himself. The matters in this connection had not been settled at the date of my departure. Doubtless much dissatisfaction is felt by the rank and file of the insur-

gents that they have not been permitted to enjoy the occupancy of Manila, and there is some ground for trouble with them owing to that fact, but, notwithstanding many rumors to the contrary, I am of the opinion that the leaders will be able to prevent serious disturbances, as they are sufficiently intelligent and educated to know that to antagonize the United States would be to destroy their only chance of future political improvement.

"On the 28th instant I received a cablegram directing me to transfer my command to Major-General Otis, United States Volunteers, and to proceed to Paris, France, for conference with the peace commissioners. I embarked on the steamer 'China' on the 30th in obedience to these instructions."—*Report of General Wesley Merritt (Annual Reports of the War Department, 1898, v. 1, pp. 39–45).*

"Aguinaldo. . . retired to Malolos, about 25 miles to the northward, leaving his troops entrenched round Manila, and there with considerable pomp and ceremony on September 29th, 1898, he was declared First President of the Philippine Republic, and the National Congress was opened with Pedro Paterno as President of that assembly."—G. J. Younghusband, *The Philippines and Round About, p.* 27.

A. D. 1898 (July—December).—War with Spain.—Suspension of hostilities.—Negotiation of Treaty of Peace.—Instructions to American Commissioners.—Relinquishment of Spanish sovereignty over Cuba and cession of Porto Rico, the island of Guam and the Philippine Islands to the United States.—In his message to Congress, December 5, 1898, President McKinley gave the following account of his reception of overtures from Spain, for the termination of the war, and of the negotiations which resulted in a treaty of peace: "The annihilation of Admiral Cervera's fleet, followed by the capitulation of Santiago, having brought to the Spanish Government a realizing sense of the hopelessness of continuing a struggle now become wholly unequal, it made overtures of peace through the French Ambassador, who, with the assent of his Government, had acted as the friendly representative of Spanish interests during the war. On the 26th of July M. Cambon presented a communication signed by the Duke of Almodovar, the Spanish Minister of State, inviting the United States to state the terms upon which it would be willing to make peace. On the 30th of July, by a communication addressed to the Duke of Almodovar and handed to M. Cambon, the terms of this Government were announced, substantially as in the protocol afterwards signed. On the 10th of August the Spanish reply, dated August 7th, was handed by M. Cambon to the Secretary of State. It accepted unconditionally the terms imposed as to Cuba, Porto Rico and an island of the Ladrone group, but appeared to seek to introduce inadmissible reservations in regard to our demand as to the Philippine Islands. Conceiving that discussion on this point could neither be practical nor profitable, I directed that, in order to avoid misunderstanding, the matter should be forthwith closed by proposing the embodiment in a formal protocol of the terms upon which the negotiations for peace were to be undertaken. The vague and inexplicit suggestion of the Spanish note could not be accepted, the only reply being to present as a virtual ultimatum a draft of protocol embodying the precise terms tendered to Spain in our note of July 30th, with added stipulations of detail as to the appointment of commissioners to arrange for the evacuation of the Spanish Antilles. On August 12th M. Cambon announced his receipt of full powers to sign the protocol submitted. Accordingly, on the afternoon of August 12th M. Cambon, as the plenipotentiary of Spain, and the Secretary of State, as the plenipotentiary of the United States, signed a protocol providing : Article I—Spain will relinquish all claim of sovereignty over and title to Cuba. Article II—Spain will cede to the United States the island of Porto Rico and other islands now under Spanish sovereignty in the West Indies and also an island in the Ladrones to be selected by the United States. Article III—The United States will occupy and hold the city, bay and harbor of Manila pending the conclusion of a treaty of peace, which shall determine the control, disposition and government of the Philippines. The fourth article provided for the appointment of joint commissions on the part of the United States and Spain, to meet in Havana and San Juan, respectively, for the purpose of arranging and carrying out the details of the stipulated evacuation of Cuba, Porto Rico and other Spanish islands in the West Indies. The fifth article provided for the appointment of not more than five commissioners on each side, to meet at Paris not later than October 1st, and proceed to the negotiation and conclusion of a treaty of peace, subject to ratification according to the respective constitutional forms of the two countries. The sixth and last article provided that upon the signature of the protocol hostilities between the two countries should be suspended and that notice to that effect should be given as soon as possible by each government to the commanders of its military and naval forces. Immediately upon the conclusion of the protocol I issued a proclamation of August 12th, suspending hostilities on the part of the United States. The necessary orders to that end were at once given by telegraph. The blockade of the ports of Cuba and San Juan de Porto Rico was in like manner raised. On the 18th of August the muster-out of 100,000 Volunteers, or as near that number as was found to be practicable, was ordered. On the 1st of December 101,165 officers and men had been mustered out and discharged from the service and 9,002 more will be mustered out by the 10th of this month. Also a corresponding number of general staff officers have been honorably discharged from the service. The military commissions to superintend the evacuation of Cuba, Porto Rico and the adjacent islands were forthwith appointed: For Cuba, Maj.-Gen. James F. Wade, Rear-Admiral William T. Sampson, Maj.-Gen. Matthew C. Butler. For Porto Rico, Maj.-Gen. John R. Brooke, Rear-Admiral Winfield S. Schley and Brig.-Gen. William W. Gordon, who soon afterwards met the Spanish commissioners at Havana and San Juan respectively. . . . Pursuant to the fifth article of the protocol, I appointed William R. Day, late Secretary of State ; Cushman K. Davis, William P. Frye and George Gray, Senators of the United States, and Whitelaw Reid, to be the peace commissioners on the part of the United States. Proceeding in due season to Paris they there met on the first of October five commission-

ers, similarly appointed on the part of Spain."— *Message of the President to Congress, Dec. 5, 1898.*

The instructions given (September 16) by President McKinley to the commissioners appointed to treat for peace with Spain, and the correspondence between the commissioners at Paris and the President and the Secretary of State at Washington during the progress of the negotiations, were communicated confidentially to the U. S. Senate on the 30th of January, 1899, but not published until February, 1901, when the injunction of secrecy was removed and the printing of the papers ordered by vote of the Senate. The chief interest of these papers lies in their disclosure of what passed between the American executive and the peace commissioners on the subject of the Philippine Islands which led to the demand for their entire surrender by Spain.

In his instructions of September 16th to the commissioners, on their departure for the meeting with Spanish commissioners at Paris, the President wrote on this subject: "By article 6 of the protocol it was agreed that hostilities between the two countries should be suspended, and that notice to that effect should be given as soon as possible by each Government to the commanders of its military and naval forces. Such notice was given by the Government of the United States immediately after the signature of the protocol, the forms of the necessary orders having previously been prepared. But before notice could reach the commanders of the military and naval forces of the United States in the Philippines they captured and took possession by conquest of the city of Manila and its suburbs, which are therefore held by the United States by conquest as well as by virtue of the protocol. In view of what has taken place it is necessary now to determine what shall be our future relations to the Philippines. . . .

"Our aim in the adjustment of peace should be directed to lasting results and to the achievement of the common good under the demands of civilization rather than to ambitious designs. The terms of the protocol were framed upon this consideration. The abandonment of the Western Hemisphere by Spain was an imperative necessity. In presenting that requirement we only fulfilled a duty universally acknowledged. It involves no ungenerous reference to our recent foe, but simply a recognition of the plain teachings of history, to say that it was not compatible with the assurance of permanent peace on and near our own territory that the Spanish flag should remain on this side of the sea. This lesson of events and of reason left no alternative as to Cuba, Porto Rico, and the other islands belonging to Spain in this hemisphere. The Philippines stand upon a different basis. It is none the less true, however, that, without any original thought of complete or even partial acquisition, the presence and success of our arms at Manila imposes upon us obligations which we can not disregard. The march of events rules and overrules human action. Avowing unreservedly the purpose which has animated all our effort, and still solicitous to adhere to it, we can not be unmindful that without any desire or design on our part the war has brought us new duties and responsibilities which we must meet and discharge as becomes a great nation on whose growth and career from the beginning the Ruler

of Nations has plainly written the high command
and pledge of civilization.

"Incidental to our tenure in the Philippines
is the commercial opportunity to which American
statesmanship can not be indifferent. It is just
to use every legitimate means for the enlargement
of American trade; but we seek no advantages
in the Orient which are not common to all. Asking only the open door for ourselves, we are ready
to accord the open door to others. The commercial opportunity which is naturally and inevitably
associated with this new opening depends less on
large territorial possessions than upon an adequate
commercial basis and upon broad and equal privileges. It is believed that in the practical application of these guiding principles the present
interests of our country and the proper measure
of its duty, its welfare in the future, and the consideration of its exemption from unknown perils
will be found in full accord with the just, moral,
and humane purpose which was invoked as our
justification in accepting the war.

"In view of what has been stated, the United
States can not accept less than the cession in full
right and sovereignty of the island of Luzon. It
is desirable, however, that the United States
shall acquire the right of entry for vessels and
merchandise belonging to citizens of the United
States into such ports of the Philippines as are
not ceded to the United States upon terms of
equal favor with Spanish ships and merchandise,
both in relation to port and customs charges and
rates of trade and commerce, together with other
rights of protection and trade accorded to citizens
of one country within the territory of another.
You are therefore instructed to demand such
concession, agreeing on your part that Spain
shall have similar rights as to her subjects and
vessels in the ports of any territory in the Philippines ceded to the United States."

On the 7th of October, Mr. Day, on behalf of
the American commissioners, cabled a long communication from Paris to Mr. Hay, his successor in
the U. S. Department of State, summarizing testimony given before the Commission by General
Merritt, lately commanding in the Philippines,
and statements brought by General Merritt from
Admiral Dewey, General Greene, and others. In
part, the telegram was as follows : "General
Anderson, in correspondence with Aguinaldo in
June and July, seemed to treat him and his forces
as allies and native authorities, but subsequently
changed his tone. General Merritt reports that
Admiral Dewey did not approve this correspondence and advised against it. Merritt and Dewey
both kept clear of any compromising communications. Merritt expresses opinion we are in no way
committed to any insurgent programme. Answering questions of Judge Day, General Merritt said
insurrection practically confined to Luzon. Tribal and religious differences between the inhabitants of various islands. United States has
helped rather than injured insurrection. Under
no obligation other than moral to help natives.
Natives of Luzon would not accept Spanish rule,
even with amnesty. Insurgents would be victorious unless Spaniards did better in future than
in past. Insurgents would fight among themselves if they had no common enemy. Think it
feasible for United States to take Luzon and perhaps some adjacent islands and hold them as
England does her colonies. Natives could not
resist 5,000 troops. . . . General Merritt thinks

that if United States attempted to take possession
of Luzon, or all the group as a colony, Aguinaldo
and his immediate followers would resist it, but
his forces are divided and his opposition would
not amount to anything. If the islands were
divided, filibustering expeditions might go from
one island to another, thus exposing us to constant danger of conflict with Spain. In answer
to questions of Senator Frye, Merritt said insurgents would murder Spaniards and priests in
Luzon and destroy their property if the United
States withdrew. United States under moral
obligation to stay there. He did not know
whether the effect of setting up a government
by the United States in Luzon would be to produce revolutions in other islands. It might
cause reforms in their government. . . . Answering questions of Mr. Gray, Merritt said consequences in case of either insurgent or Spanish
triumph made it doubtful whether United States
would be morally justified in withdrawing. Our
acts were ordinary acts of war, as if we had
attacked Barcelona, but present conditions in Philippine Islands were partly brought about by us.
Insurgents not in worse condition by our coming. Spaniards hardly able to defend themselves.
If we restored them to their position and trenches,
they might maintain themselves with the help
of a navy when we withdrew. Did not know
that he could make out a responsibility by argument, but he felt it. It might be sentimental.
He thought it would be an advantage if the
United States would change its policy and keep
the islands. (He) thought our interests in the
East would be helped by the cheap labor in the
Philippines, costing only from 20 to 80 cents a
day, according to skill. . . . Answering questions
of Mr. Reid, Merritt said he considered capture
of Manila practically capture of group. Nothing
left of Spanish sovereignty that was not at mercy
of the United States. Did not think our humanity bounded by geographical lines. After
Dewey's victory we armed insurgents to some
extent, but Dewey says it was over-estimated.
Insurgents bought arms from Hongkong merchants with Dewey's cognizance, but Dewey was
not in favor of allowing this to continue. Spaniards would destroy Aguinaldo and his principal
followers, if allowed to do so."

October 25, Judge Day cabled a message to
Washington, saying: "Differences of opinion
among commissioners concerning Philippine
Islands are set forth in statements transmitted
herewith. On these we request early consideration and explicit instructions. Liable now to be
confronted with this question in joint commission
almost immediately." The differing statements
then transmitted were three in number, the first
of them signed by Messrs. Davis, Frye, and Reid,
who said : "Information gained by commission
in Paris leads to conviction that it would be
naval, political, and commercial mistake to divide
the archipelago. Nearly all expert testimony
taken tends to this effect. As instructions provide for retention at least of Luzon, we do not
consider question of remaining in Philippine
Islands at all as now properly before us. We
therefore ask for extension of instructions. Spain
governed and defended these islands from Manila,
and with destruction of her fleet and the surrender of her army we became as complete masters of the whole group as she had been, with
nothing needed to complete the conquest save to

proceed with the ample forces we had at hand to take unopposed possession. The Ladrones and Carolines were also governed from the same capital by the same governor-general. National boundaries ought to follow natural divisions, but there is no natural place for dividing Philippine Islands. . . . If we do not want the islands ourselves, better to control their disposition; that is, to hold the option on them rather than to abandon it. Could then at least try to protect ourselves by ample treaty stipulations with the acquiring powers. Commercially, division of archipelago would not only needlessly establish dangerous rivals at our door, but would impair value of part we kept."

Disagreeing with this view, Judge Day said: "I am unable to agree that we should peremptorily demand the entire Philippine island group. In the spirit of our instructions, and bearing in mind the often declared disinterestedness of purpose and freedom from designs of conquest with which the war was undertaken, we should be consistent in our demands in making peace. Territory permanently held must be taken as war indemnity and with due regard to our responsibility because of the conduct of our military and naval authorities in dealing with the insurgents. Whether this conduct was wise or unwise is not now important. We cannot leave the insurgents to mere treaty stipulations or to their unaided resources, either to form a government or to battle against a foe which (although) unequal to us, might readily overcome them. On all hands it is agreed that the inhabitants of the islands are unfit for self-government. This is particularly true of Mindanao and the Sulu group. Only experience can determine the success of colonial expansion upon which the United States is entering. It may prove expensive in proportion to the scale upon which it is tried with ignorant and semibarbarous people at the other side of the world. It should therefore be kept within bounds." Judge Day, accordingly, suggested a division of the archipelago that would give to the United States Luzon, Mindoro, and Palawan, and control the entrance to the China Sea.

Senator Gray, in a third statement, dissented from both these views, saying: "The undersigned can not agree that it is wise to take Philippine Islands in whole or in part. To do so would be to reverse accepted continental policy of the country, declared and acted upon throughout our history. Propinquity governs the case of Cuba and Porto Rico. Policy proposed introduces us into European politics and the entangling alliances against which Washington and all American statesmen have protested. It will make necessary a navy equal to largest of powers; a greatly increased military establishment; immense sums for fortifications and harbors; multiply occasions for dangerous complications with foreign nations, and increase burdens of taxation. Will receive in compensation no outlet for American labor in labor market already overcrowded and cheap; no area for homes for American citizens; climate and social conditions demoralizing to character of American youth; new and disturbing questions introduced into our politics; church question menacing. On whole, instead of indemnity—injury. The undersigned can not agree that any obligation incurred to insurgents is paramount to our own manifest interests. . . . No place for colonial administration or government of subject people in American system. So much from standpoint of interest; but even conceding all benefits claimed for annexation, we thereby abandon the infinitely greater benefit to accrue from acting the part of a great, powerful, and Christian nation; we exchange the moral grandeur and strength to be gained by keeping our word to nations of the world and by exhibiting a magnanimity and moderation in the hour of victory that becomes the advanced civilization we claim, for doubtful material advantages and shameful stepping down from high moral position boastfully assumed. We should set example in these respects, not follow in the selfish and vulgar greed for territory which Europe has inherited from medieval times. Our declaration of war upon Spain was accompanied by a solemn and deliberate definition of our purpose. Now that we have achieved all and more than our object, let us simply keep our word. . . . At the very least let us adhere to the President's instructions and if conditions require the keeping of Luzon forego the material advantages claimed in annexing other islands. Above all let us not make a mockery of the injunction contained in those instructions, where, after stating that we took up arms only in obedience to the dictates of humanity and in the fulfillment of high public and moral obligations, and that we had no design of aggrandizement and no ambition of conquest, the President among other things eloquently says: 'It is my earnest wish that the United States in making peace should follow the same high rule of conduct which guided it in facing war. It should be as scrupulous and magnanimous in the concluding settlement as it was just and humane in its original action.' This and more, of which I earnestly ask a re-perusal, binds my conscience and governs my actions."

But the President had now arrived at a different state of mind, and directed Secretary Hay to make the following reply, on the 26th:

"The information which has come to the President since your departure convinces him that the acceptance of the cession of Luzon alone, leaving the rest of the islands subject to Spanish rule, or to be the subject of future contention, can not be justified on political, commercial, or humanitarian grounds. The cession must be of the whole archipelago or none. The latter is wholly inadmissible and the former must therefore be required. The President reaches this conclusion after most thorough consideration of the whole subject, and is deeply sensible of the grave responsibilities it will impose, believing that this course will entail less trouble than any other and besides will best subserve the interests of the people involved, for whose welfare we can not escape responsibility."

Two days later, the moral and political reflections of the President on the subject were expressed still further to the commissioners by Secretary Hay, in the following telegram: "While the Philippines can be justly claimed by conquest, which position must not be yielded, yet their disposition, control, and government the President prefers should be the subject of negotiation as provided in the protocol. It is imperative upon us that as victors we should be governed only by motives which will exalt our nation. Territorial expansion should be our least concern; that we shall not shirk the moral obligations of our victory is of the greatest. It is undisputed that Spain's authority is permanently destroyed in every part of the Philippines. To leave any part in her feeble control now would increase our difficulties and be opposed to the interests of humanity. The sentiment in the United States is almost universal that the people of the Philippines, whatever else is done, must be liberated from Spanish domination. In this sentiment the President fully concurs. Nor can we permit Spain to transfer any of the islands to another power. Nor can we invite another power or powers to join the United States in sovereignty over them. We must either hold them or turn them back to Spain. Consequently, grave as are the responsibilities and unforeseen as are the difficulties which are before us, the President can see but one plain path of duty—the acceptance of the archipelago. Greater difficulties and more serious complications—administrative and international—would follow any other course. The President has given to the views of the commissioners the fullest consideration, and in reaching the conclusion above announced in the light of information communicated to the commission and to the President since your departure, he has been influenced by the single consideration of duty and humanity. The President is not unmindful of the distressed financial condition of Spain, and whatever consideration the United States may show must come from its sense of generosity and benevolence, rather than from any real or technical obligation. The terms upon which the full cession of the Philippines shall be made must be left largely with the commission."

On the 3d of November, Judge Day cabled: "After a careful examination of the authorities, the majority of the commission are clearly of opinion that our demand for the Philippine Islands can not be based on conquest. When the protocol was signed Manila was not captured, siege was in progress and capture made after the execution of the protocol. Captures made after agreement for armistice must be disregarded and status quo restored as far as practicable. We can require cession of Philippine Islands only as indemnity for losses and expenses of the war. Have in view, also, condition of islands, the broken power of Spain, anarchy in which our withdrawal would leave the islands, etc. These are legitimate factors."

On the 4th, Senator Davis added a personal telegram as follows: "I think we can demand cession of entire archipelago on other and more valid grounds than a perfected territorial conquest of the Philippine Islands, such as indemnity or as conditions of peace imposed by our general military success and in view of our future security and general welfare, commercial and otherwise. I think the protocol admits all these grounds, and that the ground alone of perfected territorial conquest of the Philippine Islands is too narrow and untenable under protocol."

Secretary Hay replied, for the President, on the 5th: "The President has no purpose to question the commission's judgment as to the grounds upon which the cession of the archipelago is to be claimed. His only wish in that respect is to hold all the ground upon which we can fairly and justly make the claim. He recognizes fully the soundness of putting forward indemnity as the chief ground, but conquest is a consideration which ought not to be ignored. How our demand shall be presented, and the grounds upon which you will rest it, he confidently leaves with the commissioners. His great concern is that a treaty shall be effected in terms which will not only satisfy the present generation but, what is more important, be justified in the judgment of posterity."

Discussion followed, in which Judge Day and Senator Gray repeated the views they had formerly expressed, in dissent from the policy determined upon by the President and his cabinet, the latter saying: "Believing that the result of a failure to obtain a treaty would be the forcible seizure of the whole Philippine Islands group, an event greatly to be deprecated as inconsistent with the traditions and civilization of the United States, I would be willing to take the islands by the cession of a treaty of peace, and I would, to that end, make such reasonable concessions as would comport with the magnanimity of a great nation dealing with a weak and prostrate foe. I mean that I would prefer the latter alternative to the former, not that I have changed my mind as to the policy of taking the Philippine Islands at all."

So far as concerned the demands of the United States (which Spain was powerless to resist), the question was settled, on the 13th of November, by a telegram from Secretary Hay to Mr. Day, in which he said: "We are clearly entitled to indemnity for the cost of the war. We can not hope to be fully indemnified. We do not expect to be. It would probably be difficult for Spain to pay money. All she has are the archipelagoes of the Philippines and the Carolines. She surely can not expect us to turn the Philippines back and bear the cost of the war and all claims of our citizens for damages to life and property in Cuba without any indemnity but Porto Rico, which we have and which is wholly inadequate. . . . You are therefore instructed to insist upon the cession of the whole of the Philippines, and, if necessary, pay to Spain ten to twenty millions of dollars, and if you can get cession of a naval and telegraph station in the Carolines, and the several concessions and privileges and guaranties, so far as applicable, enumerated in the views of Commissioners Frye and Reid, you can offer more."— *United States, 56th Congress, 2d Sess., Senate Doc. No. 148 (Papers relating to the Treaty with Spain).*

Discussion between the Spanish and American commissioners at Paris was prolonged until the 10th of December, when the former yielded to what they protested against as hard terms, and the following Treaty of Peace was signed:

Treaty of Peace.

ART. I. Spain relinquishes all claim of sovereignty over and title to Cuba. And as the island is, upon its evacuation by Spain, to be occupied by the United States, the United States will, so long as such occupation shall last, assume and discharge the obligations that may under international law result from the fact of its occupation, for the protection of life and property.

ART. II. Spain cedes to the United States the island of Porto Rico and other islands now under Spanish sovereignty in the West Indies, and the island of Guam in the Marianas or Ladrones.

ART. III. Spain cedes to the United States

the archipelago known as the Philippine Islands, and comprehending the islands lying within the following line: A line running from west to east along or near the twentieth parallel of north latitude, and through the middle of the navigable channel of Bachi, from the one hundred and eighteenth (118th) to the one hundred and twenty seventh (127th) degree meridian of longitude east of Greenwich, thence along the one hundred and twenty seventh (127th) degree meridian of longitude east of Greenwich to the parallel of four degrees and forty five minutes (4° 45′) north latitude, thence along the parallel of four degrees and forty five minutes (4° 45′) north latitude to its intersection with the meridian of longitude one hundred and nineteen degrees and thirty five minutes (119° 35′) east of Greenwich, thence along the meridian of longitude one hundred and nineteen degrees and thirty five minutes (119° 35′) east of Greenwich to the parallel of latitude seven degrees and forty minutes (7° 40′) north, thence along the parallel of latitude of seven degrees and forty minutes (7° 40′) north to its intersection with the one hundred and sixteenth (116th) degree meridian of longitude east of Greenwich, thence by a direct line to the intersection of the tenth (10th) degree parallel of north latitude with the one hundred and eighteenth (118th) degree meridian of longitude east of Greenwich, and thence along the one hundred and eighteenth (118th) degree meridian of longitude east of Greenwich to the point of beginning. The United States will pay to Spain the sum of twenty million dollars ($20,000,000) within three months after the exchange of the ratifications of the present treaty.

Art. IV. The United States will, for the term of ten years from the date of the exchange of the ratifications of the present treaty, admit Spanish ships and merchandise to the ports of the Philippine Islands on the same terms as ships and merchandise of the United States.

Art. V. The United States will, upon the signature of the present treaty, send back to Spain, at its own cost, the Spanish soldiers taken as prisoners of war on the capture of Manila by the American forces. The arms of the soldiers in question shall be restored to them. Spain will, upon the exchange of the ratifications of the present treaty, proceed to evacuate the Philippines, as well as the island of Guam, on terms similar to those agreed upon by the Commissioners appointed to arrange for the evacuation of Porto Rico and other islands in the West Indies, under the Protocol of August 12, 1898, which is to continue in force till its provisions are completely executed. The time within which the evacuation of the Philippine Islands and Guam shall be completed shall be fixed by the two Governments. Stands of colors, uncaptured war vessels, small arms, guns of all calibres, with their carriages and accessories, powder, ammunition, livestock, and materials and supplies of all kinds, belonging to the land and naval forces of Spain in the Philippines and Guam, remain the property of Spain. Pieces of heavy ordnance, exclusive of field artillery, in the fortifications and coast defences, shall remain in their emplacements for the term of six months, to be reckoned from the exchange of ratifications of the treaty; and the United States may, in the meantime, purchase such material from Spain, if a satisfactory agreement between

the two Governments on the subject shall be reached.

Art. VI. Spain will, upon the signature of the present treaty, release all prisoners of war, and all persons detained or imprisoned for political offences, in connection with the insurrections in Cuba and the Philippines and the war with the United States. Reciprocally the United States will release all persons made prisoners of war by the American forces, and will undertake to obtain the release of all Spanish prisoners in the hands of the insurgents in Cuba and the Philippines. The Government of the United States will at its own cost return to Spain and the Government of Spain will at its own cost return to the United States, Cuba, Porto Rico, and the Philippines, according to the situation of their respective homes, prisoners released or caused to be released by them, respectively, under this article.

Art. VII. The United States and Spain mutually relinquish all claims for indemnity, national and individual, of every kind, of either Government, or of its citizens or subjects, against the other Government, that may have arisen since the beginning of the late insurrection in Cuba and prior to the exchange of ratifications of the present treaty, including all claims for indemnity for the cost of the war. The United States will adjudicate and settle the claims of its citizens against Spain relinquished in this article.

Art. VIII. In conformity with the provisions of Articles I, II, and III of this treaty, Spain relinquishes in Cuba, and cedes in Porto Rico and other islands in the West Indies, in the island of Guam, and in the Philippine Archipelago, all the buildings, wharves, barracks, forts, structures, public highways and other immovable property which, in conformity with law, belong to the public domain, and as such belong to the Crown of Spain. And it is hereby declared that the relinquishment or cession, as the case may be, to which the preceding paragraph refers, cannot in any respect impair the property or rights which by law belong to the peaceful possession of property of all kinds, of provinces, municipalities, public or private establishments, ecclesiastical or civic bodies, or any other associations having legal capacity to acquire and possess property in the aforesaid territories renounced or ceded, or of private individuals, of whatsoever nationality such individuals may be. The aforesaid relinquishment or cession, as the case may be, includes all documents exclusively referring to the sovereignty relinquished or ceded that may exist in the archives of the Peninsula. Where any document in such archives only in part relates to said sovereignty, a copy of such part will be furnished whenever it shall be requested. Like rules shall be reciprocally observed in favor of Spain in respect of documents in the archives of the islands above referred to. In the aforesaid relinquishment or cession, as the case may be, are also included such rights as the Crown of Spain and its authorities possess in respect of the official archives and records, executive as well as judicial, in the islands above referred to, which relate to said islands or the rights and property of their inhabitants. Such archives and records shall be carefully preserved, and private persons shall without distinction have the right to require, in accordance with law, authenticated copies of the contracts, wills and other instruments forming part of notarial protocols or files, or which may be contained in the executive or judicial archives, be the latter in Spain or in the islands aforesaid.

ART. IX. Spanish subjects, natives of the Peninsula, residing in the territory over which Spain by the present treaty relinquishes or cedes her sovereignty, may remain in such territory or may remove therefrom, retaining in either event all their rights of property, including the right to sell or dispose of such property or of its proceeds; and they shall also have the right to carry on their industry, commerce and professions, being subject in respect thereof to such laws as are applicable to other foreigners. In case they remain in the territory they may preserve their allegiance to the Crown of Spain by making, before a court of record, within a year from the date of the exchange of ratifications of this treaty, a declaration of their decision to preserve such allegiance; in default of which declaration they shall be held to have renounced it and to have adopted the nationality of the territory in which they may reside. The civil rights and political status of the native inhabitants of the territories hereby ceded to the United States shall be determined by the Congress.

ART. X. The inhabitants of the territories over which Spain relinquishes or cedes her sovereignty shall be secured in the free exercise of their religion.

ART. XI. The Spaniards residing in the territories over which Spain by this treaty cedes or relinquishes her sovereignty shall be subject in matters civil as well as criminal to the jurisdiction of the courts of the country wherein they reside, pursuant to the ordinary laws governing the same; and they shall have the right to appear before such courts, and to pursue the same course as citizens of the country to which the courts belong.

ART. XII. Judicial proceedings pending at the time of the exchange of ratifications of this treaty in the territories over which Spain relinquishes or cedes her sovereignty shall be determined according to the following rules: 1. Judgments rendered either in civil suits between private individuals, or in criminal matters, before the date mentioned, and with respect to which there is no recourse or right of review under the Spanish law, shall be deemed to be final, and shall be executed in due form by competent authority in the territory within which such judgments should be carried out. 2. Civil suits between private individuals which may on the date mentioned be undetermined shall be prosecuted to judgment before the court in which they may then be pending or in the court that may be substituted therefor. 3. Criminal actions pending on the date mentioned before the Supreme Court of Spain against citizens of the territory which by this treaty ceases to be Spanish shall continue under its jurisdiction until final judgment; but, such judgment having been rendered, the execution thereof shall be committed to the competent authority of the place in which the case arose.

ART. XIII. The rights of property secured by copyrights and patents acquired by Spaniards in the Island of Cuba and in Porto Rico, the Philippines and other ceded territories, at the time of the exchange of the ratifications of this treaty, shall continue to be respected. Spanish scientific, literary and artistic works, not subversive

of public order in the territories in question, shall continue to be admitted free of duty into such territories, for the period of ten years, to be reckoned from the date of the exchange of the ratifications of this treaty.

ART. XIV. Spain will have the power to establish consular officers in the ports and places of the territories, the sovereignty over which has been either relinquished or ceded by the present treaty.

ART. XV. The Government of each country will, for the term of ten years, accord to the merchant vessels of the other country the same treatment in respect of all port charges, including entrance and clearance dues, light dues, and tonnage duties, as it accords to its own merchant vessels, not engaged in the coastwise trade. This article may at any time be terminated on six months notice given by either Government to the other.

ART. XVI. It is understood that any obligations assumed in this treaty by the United States with respect to Cuba are limited to the time of its occupancy thereof; but it will upon the termination of such occupancy, advise any Government established in the island to assume the same obligations.

ART. XVII. The present treaty shall be ratified by the President of the United States, by and with the advice and consent of the Senate thereof, and by Her Majesty the Queen Regent of Spain; and the ratifications shall be exchanged at Washington within six months from the date hereof, or earlier if possible. In faith whereof, we, the respective Plenipotentiaries, have signed this treaty and have hereunto affixed our seals. Done in duplicate at Paris, the tenth day of December, in the year of Our Lord one thousand eight hundred and ninety-eight. [Signed] William R. Day, Cushman K. Davis, William P. Frye, Geo. Gray, Whitelaw Reid, Eugenio Montero Rios, B. de Abarzuza, J. de Garnica, W. R. de Villa Urrutia, Rafael Cerero.

That the treaty would be ratified by the Senate of the United States was by no means certain when it was signed, and remained questionable for two months. See below: A. D. 1899 (JANUARY—FEBRUARY).

Some time after the conclusion of the treaty, it was discovered that the boundaries defined in it for the cession of the Philippine Islands failed to include the islands of Cagayan, or Kagayan, and Sibutu, in the southern part of the archipelago. Still later, it was found that several small islands (the Bachi or Bashee group, and others) belonging to the Spanish possessions in the East were left lying outside of the northern Philippine boundary, as laid down in the treaty of cession. It is said that the Japanese government called attention to this latter error, desiring to have the islands in question, which are near to Formosa, controlled by the United States, rather than by Spain. By a new treaty with Spain, negotiated in 1900, all these outlying islands were acquired by the United States, for the sum of $100,000.

A. D. 1898 (August).—Losses of the armies at Santiago and in the Philippines. See below: A. D. 1900 (JUNE).

A. D. 1898 (August 21).—The War with Spain.—Letter from departing Spanish soldiers to the soldiers of the American army.— The following letter, addressed, on the eve of their departure for Spain, by the Spanish soldiers at Santiago, to the soldiers of the American army, "is surely," says Lieutenant-Colonel Miley, who quotes it in his book entitled "In Cuba with Shafter"—"is surely the most remarkable letter ever addressed by vanquished soldiers to their conquerors: 'Soldiers of the American Army: We would not be fulfilling our duty as well-born men in whose breasts there lives gratitude and courtesy, should we embark for our beloved Spain without sending you our most cordial and sincere good wishes and farewell. We fought you with ardor and with all our strength, endeavoring to gain the victory, but without the slightest rancor or hate toward the American nation. We have been vanquished by you, so our generals and chiefs ʃ　　in signing the capitulation, but our surrenderged the blood-battles preceding it have left in our souls no place for resentment against the men who fought us nobly and valiantly. You fought and acted in compliance with the same call of duty as we, for we all but represent the power of our respective States. You fought us as men, face to face, and with great courage, as before stated—a quality we had not met with during the three years we have carried on this war against a people without a religion, without morals, without conscience, and of doubtful origin, who could not confront the enemy, but shot their noble victims from ambush and then immediately fled. This was the kind of warfare we had to sustain in this unfortunate land. You have complied exactly with all the laws and usages of war as recognized by the armies of the most civilized nations of the world; have given honorable burial to the dead of the vanquished; have cured their wounded with great humanity; have respected and cared for your prisoners and their comfort; and lastly, to us, whose condition was terrible, you have given freely of food and of your stock of medicines, and have honored us with distinction and courtesy, for after the fighting the two armies mingled with the utmost harmony. With this high sentiment of appreciation from us all, there remains but to express our farewell, and with the greatest sincerity we wish you all happiness and health in this land, which will no longer belong to our dear Spain, but will be yours. You have conquered it by force and watered it with your blood, as your‑conscience called for under the demands of civilization and humanity; but the descendants of the Congos and Guineas, mingled with the blood of unscrupulous Spaniards and of traitors and adventurers —these people are not able to exercise or enjoy their liberty, for they will find it a burden to comply with the laws which govern civilized humanity. From eleven thousand Spanish soldiers. (Signed) Pedro Lopez De Castillo, Soldier of Infantry. Santiago de Cuba, August 21, 1898.'"

A. D. 1898 (August—December).—Situation in the Philippines following the occupation of Manila by American forces.—Growing distrust and unfriendliness of the Tagalos.— Report of General Otis. See (in this vol.) PHILIPPINE ISLANDS: A. D. 1898 (AUGUST—DECEMBER).

A. D. 1898 (December).—Organization of military government in Cuba. See (in this vol.) CUBA: A. D. 1898-1899 (DECEMBER—OCTOBER).

A. D. 1898-1899.—Statistics of the Spanish-American War.—The following military

and naval statistics of the war with Spain, compiled from official sources, were submitted to the House of Representatives, during its debate on the Army Bill, in December, 1900, as part of an appendix to a speech made in support of the Bill by Hon. Charles Dick, of Ohio :

ORGANIZATION AND STRENGTH OF THE ARMY DURING AND AFTER THE WAR.

By an Act of Congress approved April 22, 1898, providing for the temporary increase of the military establishment of the United States, "the organized and active land forces were declared to consist of the Regular Army and of the militia of the several States when called into service, constituting two branches, designated, respectively, as the Regular Army and the Volunteer Army of the United States. And the President was authorized to organize the regular and volunteer troops into divisions of three brigades, each brigade to be composed of three or more regiments, and when three or more divisions are present in the same army, to organize them into army corps, each corps to consist of not more than three divisions. Under the authority conferred upon him by the joint resolution of April 20 and the act of April 22, 1898, the President issued a proclamation, dated April 23, 1898, calling for volunteers to the number of 125,000 men, to be apportioned as far as practicable among the several States, Territories, and the District of Columbia, according to population, to serve for two years unless sooner discharged. Among the several arms of the service the troops were apportioned as follows: Five regiments and 17 troops of cavalry, 16 batteries of light artillery, 1 regiment and 7 batteries of heavy artillery, 119 regiments and 10 battalions of infantry. May 25, 1898, the President issued a proclamation calling for an additional force of 75,000 men. For controlling military reasons, it was determined to utilize so much of this additional force as was necessary to bring up the several State organizations in service to the full legal strength, the remainder to be apportioned among the several States and Territories according to their respective quotas as nearly as possible. The apportionment to the several arms of service under this second call was for 16 batteries of light artillery, 3 battalions of heavy artillery, and 22 regiments, ten battalions, and 46 companies of infantry."

The strength of the Regular Army on the 1st of April, 1898, just before the breaking out of the war, was as follows :

	Officers.	Enlisted Men.
General officers and staff corps	532	2,026
Cavalry..............................	437	6,047
Artillery............................	288	4,486
Infantry.............................	886	12,828
Miscellaneous........................		653
Total.............................	2,143	26,040

The Regular Army was authorized to be increased to 65,000 men as a war footing. The total strength of the armies, Regular and Volunteer, at several later dates, was as follows :

DATE.	Regulars.	Volunteers.	Total.
April 15, 1898.........	28,183	....	28,183
May 31, 1898.........	38,846	124,776	162,592
August 31, 1898......	56,362	216,256	272,618
January 31, 1899......	65,531	90,241	155,772
June 30, 1899.........	63,535	16,550	80,085

Maximum force at any one time during Spanish-American war, 274,717 officers and men. On the 29th of November, 1898, the Army of the United States consisted of 2,324 officers and 61,444 enlisted men of the regular force, and of 5,216 officers and 110,202 enlisted men of the volunteer force, making an aggregate of 7,540 officers and 171,646 enlisted men.

PAY OF ARMY.

Payments made to Regular and Volunteer armies engaged during Spanish-American war, from April 21, 1898, to April 11, 1899, $67,065,-629.56.

CASUALTIES IN ACTION.

In Cuba, Porto Rico, and the Philippines between May 1, 1898, and June 30, 1899.

	In Cuba.	In Porto Rico.	In the Philippines.
Killed :			
Officers..............	21	....	16
Enlisted men.........	223	4	219
Wounded :			
Officers..............	101	....	92
Enlisted men.........	1,344	36	1,349
Died of Wounds:			
Officers..............	10	....	10
Enlisted men.........	64	8	82
Died of Disease :			
Officers..............	34	4	11
Enlisted men.........	888	251	369

Grand total, 5,136.

Casualties in Fifth Army Corps in campaign against Santiago, June 22, 1898, to July 17, 1898.

	Officers.	Enlisted Men.
Killed..........................	21	222
Wounded	101	1,344

At battle of Las Guasimas, June 24, 1898.

	Officers.	Enlisted Men.
Killed..........................	1	15
Wounded......................	6	43

At battle of El Caney, July 1, 1898.

	Officers.	Enlisted Men.
Killed...........................	4	77
Wounded.......................	25	335

At Aguadores, July 1–2, 1898.

		Enlisted Men.
Killed		2
Wounded........................		10

At battle of San Juan, July 1–3, 1898.

	Officers.	Enlisted Men.
Killed...........................	15	127
Wounded.......................	69	945

Casualties around Santiago, July 10–12, 1898.

	Officers.	Enlisted Men.
Killed	1	1
Wounded........................	1	11

Grand total of casualties in killed and wounded during the war with Spain.

WHERE.	KILLED.		WOUNDED.	
	Officers.	Enlisted Men.	Officers.	Enlisted Men.
Cuba	23	237	99	1,332
Porto Rico	....	3	4	36
Manila....	....	17	10	96
Total	23	257	113	1,464

The deaths from all causes (including casualties in action) in the whole Army, regulars and volunteers, for the fourteen months from May, 1898, to June, 1899, inclusive, were 6,619. This is equivalent to an annual rate of 33.03 per thousand of strength. The deaths from disease during the whole period were at an annual rate of but 25.68 per thousand. These were as follows :

STATIONS.	Number of Deaths.	Rate per 1,000.
United States....................	3,577	23.81
Cuba	928	45.14
Porto Rico	238	38.15
Philippines.....................	402	17.20

UNITED STATES, 1898-1899.

Deaths in the armies of the United States, by countries, between May 1, 1898, and June 30, 1899.

COUNTRY.	KILLED.		DIED OF WOUNDS.		DISEASE.		ACCIDENT.	
	Officers.	Enlisted Men.	Officers.	Enlisted Men.	Officers.	Enlisted Men.	Officers.	Enlisted Men.
REGULARS.								
United States	1	5	....	10	32	874	1	51
Cuba	19	184	5	60	8	381	....	7
Porto Rico					3	73	....	3
Hawaiian Islands					....	10	....	1
Philippine Islands	4	81	1	33	4	109	....	10
At sea			1	11	4	77	....	
Total	24	270	7	114	51	1,524	1	72
VOLUNTEERS.								
United States	....	....	....	1	87	2,836	3	111
Cuba	3	39	....	10	16	457	2	12
Porto Rico		3			1	157	....	5
Hawaiian Islands					....	33	....	1
Philippine Islands	14	146	3	67	5	215	....	6
At sea					5	122	....	2
Total	17	188	3	78	114	3,820	5	137
Aggregate	38	458	10	192	165	5,344	6	209

COUNTRY.	DROWNED.		SUICIDE.		MURDER OR HOMICIDE.		TOTAL.	
	Officers.	Enlisted Men.	Officers.	Enlisted Men.	Officers.	Enlisted Men.	Officers.	Enlisted Men.
REGULARS.								
United States	1	16	....	19	....	18	35	993
Cuba	....	7	....	5	....	6	32	650
Porto Rico	....	1	....	3	....	1	3	81
Hawaiian Islands								12
Philippine Islands	....	19	1	3	....	1	10	256
At sea	1	4	1	2	....	....	6	94
Total	2	48	1	32	....	26	86	2,086
VOLUNTEERS.								
United States	....	23	1	15	....	22	91	3,008
Cuba	....	4	....	....	....	3	21	525
Porto Rico	....	2	....	1	....	1	1	169
Hawaiian Islands								34
Philippine Islands	1	9	....	3	....	....	23	446
At sea	....	2	....	1	....	....	5	127
Total	1	40	1	20	....	26	141	4,309
Aggregate	3	88	2	52	....	52	224	6,395

629

Recapitulation of casualties in action in the armies of the United States between May 1, 1898, and June 30, 1899.

COUNTRY.	KILLED.		WOUNDED.		TOTAL.		Aggregate.
	Officers.	Enlisted Men.	Officers.	Enlisted Men.	Officers.	Enlisted Men.	
REGULARS.							
Cuba	18	183	86	1,126	104	1,309	1,413
Porto Rico		1	2	15	2	16	18
United States	1	5		10	1	15	16
Philippines, to Aug. 13, 1898		7	1	25	1	32	33
Philippines, since Feb. 4, 1899	2	74	20	410	22	484	506
Total	21	270	109	1,586	130	1,856	1,986
VOLUNTEERS.							
Cuba	3	39	15	218	18	257	275
Porto Rico		3	2	21	2	24	26
Philippines, to Aug. 13, 1898		11	9	74	9	85	94
Philippines, since Feb. 4, 1899	14	135	62	865	76	1,000	1,076
Total	17	188	88	1,178	105	1,366	1,471
Grand total	38	458	197	2,764	235	3,222	3,457

HOSPITALS.

From the declaration of war with Spain to September 20, 1899, there have been established:

	Beds.
20 field division hospitals, averaging 250 beds each	5,000
31 general hospitals with a total capacity of about	13,800
Railroad ambulance train	270
4 hospital ships	1,000
Total	20,070

In addition to these over 5,000 cases were treated in civil hospitals. It is difficult even to approximate the number of men treated in these hospitals. During that period somewhat over 100,000 cases were admitted on sick report, a number equal to 2,147 per 1,000 of strength during the year, or to 179 per 1,000 per month—the ratio of admissions to hospital cases being 13 to 8. Using these data as a basis, and assuming the mean strength of the Army (Regulars and Volunteers) to have been 154,000, it would appear that from May 1, 1898, to September 20, 1899, about 275,000 cases have been treated in these hospitals.

TRANSPORTATION OF SPANISH PRISONERS OF WAR TO SPAIN.

The following is a statement showing the dates of embarkation, names of vessels, and number of officers, enlisted men, and others who took passage:

Date of embarkation.	NAME OF VESSEL.	Officers.	Enlisted Men.	Women and children over 5 years of age.	Priests and Sisters of Charity.	TOTAL.
Aug. 9	Alicante	38	1,069	6	11	1,124
Aug. 14	Isla de Luzon	137	2,056	40	4	2,237
Aug. 16	Covadonga	109	2,148	79		2,336
Aug. 19	Villaverde	52	565	34		651
Aug. 19	Isla de Panay	99	1,599	26	5	1,729
Aug. 22	P. de Satrustegui	128	2,359	68		2,555
Aug. 25	Montevideo	136	2,108	122	2	2,368
Aug. 27	Cheribon	18	905	37		960
Aug. 28	Colón	100	1,316	59		1,475
Aug. 30	do	23	726	5		754
Sept. 1	Leon XIII	113	2,209	108		2,430
Sept. 3	San Ignacio	59	1,408	20	12	1,499
Sept. 6	Leonora	15	1,118			1,333
Sept. 12	Ciudad de Cadiz	53		19	14	86
Sept. 17	San Augustin	65	800	45		910
Sept. 17	San Francisco	18	588	11		617
	Total	1,163	20,974	679	48	22,864

ARMS AND AMMUNITION CAPTURED AT SANTIAGO.

Mauser rifles, Spanish, 7 mm	16,902
Mauser rifles, Argentine, 7½ mm	872
Remington rifles, 7 mm	6,118
Total rifles	23,892

Mauser carbines, Spanish, 7 mm	833
Mauser carbines, Argentine, 7½ mm	84
Remington carbines, 7½ mm	330
Total carbines	1,247
Revolvers	75

630

Mauser — Spanish — cartridges, 7 mm......... 1,500,000
Mauser — Argentine — cartridges, 7½ mm...... 1,471,200
Remington cartridges, 7½ mm.................. 1,680,000

Total 4,651,200

Nine hundred and seventy-three thousand Remington cartridges, 7½ mm., worthless.

STRENGTH OF THE NAVY, REGULAR AND AUXILIARY.

The number of enlisted men allowed by law prior to the outbreak of hostilities was 12,500. On August 15, when the enlisted force reached its maximum, there were 24,123 men in the service. This great increase was made necessary by the addition of 128 ships to the Navy. The maximum fighting force of the Navy, separated into classes, was as follows:

Battle ships (first class)............................	4
Battle ships (second class)..........................	1
Armored cruisers....................................	2
Coast defense monitors..............................	6
Armored ram..	1
Protected cruisers..................................	12
Unprotected cruisers................................	3
Gunboats...	18
Dynamite cruiser...................................	1
Torpedo boats......................................	11
Vessels of old Navy, including monitors..............	14
Auxiliary Navy:	
Auxiliary cruisers..............................	11
Converted yachts...............................	28
Revenue cutters................................	15
Light-house tenders.............................	4
Converted tugs.................................	27
Converted colliers..............................	19
Miscellaneous..................................	19

NAVAL PRISONERS OF WAR CAPTURED OFF SANTIAGO, JULY 3, 1898.

Officers... 99
Enlisted men.. 1,675

CASUALTIES IN ACTION.

ENGAGEMENT.	Number of casualties.	Killed.	Wounded.	Died subsequently as result of wounds.
Action at Manila Bay, May 1	9	......	9	....
Action off Cienfuegos, May 11....................	12	1	11	1
Action off Cardenas, May 11.	8	5	3	....
Action off San Juan, Porto Rico, May 12..............	8	1	7	....
Engagements at Guantanamo, Cuba, June 11 to 20...	22	*6	16	....
Engagement off Santiago:				
June 22....................	10	1	9	....
July 3.....................	11	1	10	....
Miscellaneous:				
Yankee, June 13.........	1	......	1	....
Eagle, July 12...........	1	......	1	....
Bancroft, August 2......	1	1	......	....
Amphitrite, August 7...	1	......	1	†1
	84	16	68	2

* One accidentally killed.   † Accidentally shot.
—Congressional Record, Feb. 1, 1901, pp. 1941-62.

A. D. 1898-1899.—Investigation of the conduct of the War Department in the war with Spain.—Severe criticism of the conduct of the War Department during the war with Spain, including many charges of inefficiency in its service, produced by improper appointments made for political reasons, and other charges of misdoing in the purchase of supplies, under influences either political or otherwise corrupt, led to the appointment by the President, in September, 1898, of an investigating commission, composed of nine soldier and civilian members, as follows: General Grenville M. Dodge, President, Colonel James A. Sexton, Colonel Charles Denby, Captain Evan P. Howell, Hon. Urban A. Woodbury, Brigadier-General John M. Wilson, U. S. A., General James A. Beaver, Major-General Alexander McD. Cook, U. S. A., Dr. Phineas S. Conner. The report of the Commission, made in the following February, cannot be said to have been a convincing and satisfactory one to the country at large. It was indignantly described as a "whitewashing report," even by many journals and writers of the party in power. Its inquiries did not appear to have been keenly and impartially searching; its conclusions were not thought to be drawn with a rigorous and fearless hand.

The charges against the War Department which excited most feeling and drew most public attention related to the quality of the fresh beef supplied to the army, which was in two forms, refrigerated and canned. Major-General Miles, commanding the Army, had declared that much of the refrigerated beef furnished to the soldiers should be called "embalmed beef," maintaining that it had been "apparently preserved with secret chemicals, which destroy its natural flavor" and which were believed to be "detrimental to the health of the troops." He intimated that hundreds of tons of such beef had been contracted for by the Commissary-General "under pretense of experiment." In repelling this serious accusation, Commissary - General Charles P. Eagan read a statement before the Commission, so violent and unmeasured in its vituperation of the commanding general that it was returned to him for correction; many newspapers declined to publish it, and he was subsequently tried by court-martial in consequence — as related below. The conclusion of the Commission on the subject of the charges relating to refrigerated beef was stated in its report as follows: "The Commission is of the opinion that no refrigerated beef furnished by contractors and issued to the troops during the war with Spain was' subjected to or treated with any chemicals by the contractors or those in their employ."

Concerning the canned beef, which had caused much disgust in the army, the Commission reported: "The result of our own testing and of all the analyses made at our instance. . . is that the canned meat which has been brought to our attention is pure, sound, and nutritive. It has not been found to contain any acids or any deleterious substance, but to be unadulterated meat. The testimony before us is that the canned meat is not, in general, intended to be issued to troops except as an emergency ration. The preponderance of the proof is that meat on the hoof and the refrigerated beef are more acceptable. A number of officers and others have testified that the meat is unpalatable. Its palatability greatly depends upon the mode in which it is cooked. In a tropical climate, carried on the march, exposed to heat, the meat so changes in appearance as to become repulsive. In the Navy, where the meat is properly cared for, there has been no complaint, so far as has appeared in evidence before us. After careful consideration we find that canned meat, as issued to the troops, was generally of good quality, was properly prepared, and contained no deleterious substance.

631

At times probably material of poor quality is issued; in one of the cans sent to us and examined by the chemist a large amount of gristle was found. That it was not issued 'under pretense of an experiment' is indicated by the fact that it has been in use in the Army for more than 20 years."

On the general management of the Quartermaster's Department, with which much fault had been found, the Commission reported: "The conclusions drawn . . . are as follows:

"1. The Quartermaster's Department, a month before war was declared, was neither physically nor financially prepared for the tremendous labor of suddenly equipping and transporting an army over ten times the size of the Regular Army of the United States.

"2. That the department devoted the ability, zeal, and industry of its officers to accomplish the herculean task before it so soon as funds were made available and war was declared.

"3. That it deserves credit for the great work accomplished, for the immense quantity of materials obtained and issued within so short a period, and for its earnest efforts in reference to railroad transportation and in protecting the great interests of the General Government committed to its charge. Its officers, especially those at the headquarters of the department and at its depots, worked earnestly and laboriously day and night, sparing themselves in no possible way.

"4. There appears to have been a lack of system, whereby, even as late as October, troops in camps and in the field were lacking in some articles of clothing, camp and garrison equipage; and hospitals, at least at two important localities in the South — Fort Monroe, Va., and Huntsville, Ala. — lacked stoves, while at Huntsville fuel was wanting.

"5. There appears to have been lack of executive or administrative ability, either on the part of the Quartermaster's Department or the railroad officials, in preventing the great congestion of cars at Tampa and Chickamauga when these camps were first established, which congestion caused delay, annoyance, and discomfort to the large bodies of troops concentrating at those places.

"6. There appears to have been a lack of foresight in preparing and promptly having available at some central locality on the seacoast the necessary fleet of transports which it seemed evident would be required for the movement of troops to a foreign shore, and, finally, when the call came suddenly and the emergency was supreme, the department appears not to have fully comprehended the capacity of the fleet under its command; not to have supplied it with a complete outfit of lighters for the immediate disembarkation of troops and supplies; to have accepted without full investigation the statement that the vessels were capable of transporting 25,000 men, while really they could not and did not transport more than 17,000 with their artillery, equipments, ammunition, and supplies, and lacked sufficient storage room for the necessary amount of wagon transportation — that very important element in the movement of an army in the face of an enemy.

"7. The Quartermaster's Department should maintain on hand at all times a complete supply for at least four months for an army of 100,000 men of all articles of clothing, camp and garrison

equipage, and other quartermaster's supplies which will not deteriorate by storage or which cannot at once be obtained in open market.

"Finally. In the opinion of this commission, there should be a division of the labor now devolving upon the Quartermaster's Department."

In another part of its report, dealing especially with the Santiago campaign, the Commission makes a statement which seems to reflect some additional light on the sixth paragraph of the finding quoted above, relative to the unpreparedness of the quartermaster's department for the landing of the Santiago expedition. It says: "The Navy Department, on the 31st of May, 1898, sent the following communication to the honorable the Secretary of War: 'This Department begs leave to inquire what means are to be employed by the War Department for landing the troops, artillery, horses, siege guns, mortars, and other heavy objects when the pending military expedition arrives on the Cuban coast near Santiago. While the Navy will be prepared to furnish all the assistance that may be in its power, it is obvious that the crews of the armored ships and of such others as will be called upon to remove the Spanish mines and to meet the Spanish fleet in action can not be spared for other purposes, and ought not to be fatigued by the work incident to landing of the troops and stores, etc.' This information, so far as can be ascertained, was never communicated to either General Miles or General Shafter; the expedition therefore left Tampa with no facilities for landing other than were afforded by the boats of the several transports conveying the expedition, with the exception of several lighters and steam tugs of light draft, such as could be hastily secured."

On the conduct of the Medical Department, which was another matter of investigation, the Commission reported: " To sum up, in brief, the evidence submitted shows:

"1. That at the outbreak of the war the Medical Department was, in men and materials, altogether unprepared to meet the necessities of the army called out.

"2. That as a result of the action through a generation of contracted and contracting methods of administration, it was impossible for the Department to operate largely, freely, and without undue regard to cost.

"3. That in the absence of a special corps of inspectors, and the apparent infrequency of inspections by chief surgeons, and of official reports of the state of things in camps and hospitals, there was not such investigation of the sanitary conditions of the army as is the first duty imposed upon the Department by the regulations.

"4. That the nursing force during the months of May, June, and July was neither ample nor efficient, reasons for which may be found in the lack of a proper volunteer hospital corps, due to the failure of Congress to authorize its establishment, and to the nonrecognition in the beginning of the value of women nurses and the extent to which their services could be secured.

"5. That the demand made upon the resources of the Department in the care of sick and wounded was very much greater than had been anticipated, and consequently, in like proportion, these demands were imperfectly met.

"6. That powerless as the Department was to

have supplies transferred from point to point, except through the intermediation of the Quartermaster's Department, it was seriously crippled in its efforts to fulfil the regulation duty of 'furnishing all medical and hospital supplies.'

"7. That the shortcomings in administration and operation may justly be attributed, in large measure, to the hurry and confusion incident to the assembling of an army of untrained officers and men, ten times larger than before, for which no preparations in advance had been or could be made because of existing rules and regulations.

"8. That notwithstanding all the manifest errors, of omission rather than of commission, a vast deal of good work was done by medical officers, high and low, regular and volunteer, and there were unusually few deaths among the wounded and the sick.

"What is needed by the medical department in the future is—

"1. A larger force of commissioned medical officers.

"2. Authority to establish in time of war a proper volunteer hospital corps.

"3. A reserve corps of selected trained women nurses, ready to serve when necessity shall arise, but under ordinary circumstances, owing no duty to the War Department, except to report residence at determined intervals.

"4. A year's supply for an army of at least four times the actual strength, of all such medicines, hospital furniture, and stores as are not materially damaged by keeping, to be held constantly on hand in the medical supply depots.

"5. The charge of transportation to such extent as will secure prompt shipment and ready delivery of all medical supplies.

"6. The simplification of administrative 'paper work,' so that medical officers may be able to more thoroughly discharge their sanitary and strictly medical duties.

"7. The securing of such legislation as will authorize all surgeons in medical charge of troops, hospitals, transports, trains, and independent commands to draw from the Subsistence Department funds for the purchase of such articles of diet as may be necessary to the proper treatment of soldiers too sick to use the army ration. This to take the place of all commutation of rations of the sick now authorized.

"Convalescent soldiers traveling on furlough should be furnished transportation, sleeping berths or staterooms, and $1.50 per diem for subsistence in lieu of rations, the soldier not to be held accountable or chargeable for this amount."—*Report of the Commission, v.* 1.

Public opinion of the report, when divested of partisan prejudice, was probably expressed very fairly in the following comments of "The Nation," of New York : "The two leading conclusions of the court of inquiry as to the quality of the beef supplied to our troops during the war with Spain, are in accordance with the evidence and will be accepted as fairly just by the country. The court finds that so far as the canned roast beef was concerned, the charges which Gen. Miles made against it as an unsuitable ration are sustained, but that as regards the use of chemicals in the treatment of refrigerated beef his charges were not established. If instead of saying 'not established,' the court had said 'not fully sustained,' its verdict would have

been above criticism on these two points. There was evidence of the use of chemicals, but it was not conclusive and was flatly contradicted. There is no doubt whatever that the use of the refrigerated beef was a blunder, but there was very little evidence to sustain a more serious charge than that against it.

"But while the court has found justly on these points, it is difficult to read its report without feeling that its members did so reluctantly, and that, if left to follow their inclinations, they would have censured Gen. Miles and allowed everybody else concerned to go free. Gen. Miles is the one person involved whom they allow no extenuating circumstances to benefit in their report. At every opportunity they take the worst possible view of his conduct, while almost invariably taking the most lenient view possible of nearly everybody else. . . . So far as the findings of the court apply to Eagan's conduct, they are condemnatory in general terms, but they do not seek to go behind him for the reasons for his conduct. . . . No attention whatever is paid to the evidence of several reputable witnesses that Eagan had told them that he had to buy of certain contractors ; none is paid, either, to the evidence of Eagan's subordinates that he himself so altered the refrigerated beef contracts that no one could say whether they called for preservation for seventy-two hours or twenty-four. Leniency of this kind is never shown toward Gen. Miles."—*The Nation, May* 11, 1899.

Perhaps a weightier criticism is represented by the following, which we quote from an article contributed to "The Independent" by General Wingate, President of the National Guard Association of the United States : "So far as the refrigerated beef was concerned, the truth probably is that there was little, if any, 'embalming' about it. Soldiers generally agree that the beef itself was almost universally good. . . . General Miles, on the other hand, was clearly right in asking that the troops might be furnished with beef cattle on the hoof, which could follow the army over any road and which would keep in good condition on the luxuriant grasses of Cuba and Porto Rico. This was the system pursued in our Civil War. No one has yet explained why it was abandoned for the experiment of furnishing this kind of beef to places in the tropics where it had to be hauled in wagons for many hours over muddy roads, and when most of the wagons required to move it promptly had to be left behind for want of water transportation.

"The matter of the refrigerated or so-called 'embalmed' beef is, however, of very slight consequence compared with that of the canned roast beef. The use of that beef as an army ration in this country, at least, was new. Officer after officer has testified before the court of inquiry that they never saw it so issued before the Cuban campaign. It is true that the navy uses it, but the facilities on shipboard for caring for and cooking food are so different and so superior to those of an army in the field that no comparison can justly be made between them. Moreover, as was recently stated in the 'Army and Navy Journal,' the belief is general in the navy that the canned beef it had rejected on inspection was afterward sold to the army and accepted by it without inspection. Be this as it may, the evidence is overwhelming that the canned roast beef which was issued to the army was repulsive in appearance and disagreeable in smell. . . . Governor Roosevelt says in his testimony that 'from generals to privates he never heard any one who did not condemn it as an army ration.' Its defects appeared on the voyage to Santiago, if not before. It was then so bad that the men would not touch it, and as Governor Roosevelt says in his article in 'Scribner's,' his Rough Riders, who certainly were not particular, could not eat it, and as it constituted one-third of the rations, his men had to go hungry. And yet, in spite of these facts, a million pounds of that beef was purchased from Armour & Co. alone, and its issue was continued not only in Cuba but in Porto Rico. What is worse than all, after its defects were fully known it was issued as a traveling ration to the fever-racked men on their homeward voyage to this country ; men who needed and were entitled to receive the most nourishing food and to whom this indigestible stuff was poison. This should never be forgotten or forgiven by the plain people of the country. . . .

"No one in authority has been willing to admit that there was the slightest thing wrong, or the least need for improvement in his department. . . . This is another of the hundreds of examples which have occurred in our past war, and which will continue to take place in the future until the whole staff system of the army has been rectified, of the reign of that hide bound bureaucratic spirit which induces the head of a department in Washington to decide in his office what should be used by the troops in the field without practical experience on the subject, and to stubbornly close his eyes and ears to everything which will tend to show that it is possible that his department has made a mistake. . . .

"It is noticeable that so far not an official in any of the supply or medical departments is known to have been court martialed or even censured. Yet I do not hesitate to say that the summary dismissal from the service, in the beginning, of two or three quartermasters and commissaries, including the gentlemen who were the cause of sending thousands of cars to Tampa without invoices or anything on the outside of them to indicate their contents, would have saved the lives of hundreds of our soldiers. Under these circumstances it is most lamentable to find that the awful experiences which have made so many homes desolate, and so many of our best young men invalids, have borne no practical fruit. Both the army officials and Congress are like the Bourbons, they 'have learned nothing and forgotten nothing.'"—G. W. Wingate, *What the Beef Scandal Teaches* (*Independent, Apr.* 6, 1899).

A. D. 1898-1899.—Joint High Commission for settlement of pending questions with Canada. See (in this vol.) CANADA: A. D. 1898-1899.

A. D. 1898-1899 (October—October).—Military government of Porto Rico. See (in this vol.) PORTO RICO : A. D. 1898-1899 (OCTOBER—OCTOBER).

A. D. 1898-1899 (December—January).—Instructions by the President to General Otis, Military Governor of the Philippines.—Their proclamation by the latter in a modified form.—The effect. See (in this vol.) PHILIPPINE ISLANDS: A. D. 1898-1899 (DECEMBER—JANUARY).

A. D. 1899 (January).—The case of Com-

missary-General Eagan.—A court-martial, sitting in January, 1899, for the trial of Commissary-General Eagan, on the charge that he had been guilty of "conduct unbecoming an officer and a gentleman, and conduct to the prejudice of good order and military discipline," in the abusive language that he had applied to the commanding general of the army, in the course of his testimony before the Commission to investigate the conduct of the War Department (see above : A. D. 1898-1899), found the accused officer guilty, and imposed the inevitable penalty of dismissal from the service, but recommended executive clemency in his case. The sentence was commuted by the President to suspension from rank and duty for six years. This involved no loss of pay, and, at the end of six years, General Eagan will go on the retired list.

A. D. 1899 (January).—Appointment of the First Commission to the Philippines.—The President's instructions to the Commissioners. See (in this vol.) PHILIPPINE ISLANDS: A. D. 1899 (JANUARY).

A. D. 1899 (January—February).—The Treaty of Peace in the Senate.—Its ratification.—The Treaty of Peace with Spain, signed at Paris December 10, 1898, was sent by the President to the Senate on the 4th of January, 1899, and held under debate in that body until the 6th of February following. The opposition to it was very strong, being especially directed against the acquisition of the Philippine Islands, involving, as that acquisition did, the embarkation of the Republic in a colonial or imperial policy, of conquest and of government without the consent of the governed, which seemed to a great number of thoughtful people, not only incongruous with its constitution, but a dangerous violation of the principles on which its republican polity is founded. But even those most opposed to the acquisition of the Philippine Islands were reluctant to reopen the state of war by rejection of the treaty, and directed their efforts mainly towards the securing of a definite declaration from Congress of the intention of the government of the United States to establish independence in the islands.

"Even before the signing of the treaty at Paris, on the 6th of December, when the demand of the American commissioners for cession of the Philippines was known, the opposition expressed itself in the following resolution, introduced by Senator Vest, of Missouri :

"Resolved by the Senate and House of Representatives of the United States of America in Congress assembled, That under the Constitution of the United States no power is given to the Federal Government to acquire territory to be held and governed permanently as colonies. The colonial system of European nations can not be established under our present Constitution, but all territory acquired by the Government, except such small amount as may be necessary for coaling stations, correction of boundaries, and similar governmental purposes, must be acquired and governed with the purpose of ultimately organizing such territory into States suitable for admission into the Union."

This resolution became the ground of much senatorial debate during the following weeks. The arguments opposed to it, and supporting the policy of the administration, are represented fairly by the following passage from a speech made by Senator Platt, of Connecticut, on December 16:

"I propose to maintain that the United States is a nation ; that as a nation it possesses every sovereign power not reserved in its Constitution to the States or the people ; that the right to acquire territory was not reserved, and is therefore an inherent sovereign right ; that is a right upon which there is no limitation, and with regard to which there is no qualification; that in certain instances the right may be inferred from specific clauses in the Constitution, but that it exists independent of these clauses ; that in the right to acquire territory is found the right to govern it; and as the right to acquire is a sovereign and inherent right, the right to govern is a sovereign right not limited in the Constitution, and that these propositions are in accordance with the views of the framers of the Constitution, the decisions of the Supreme Court, and the legislation of Congress.

"Mr. President, this is a nation. It has been called by various names. It has been called a Confederated Republic, a Federal Union, the Union of States, a league of States, a rope of sand ; but during all the time these names have been applied to it it has been a nation. It was so understood by the framers of the Constitution. It was so decided by the great judges of the Supreme Court in the early days of the Constitution. It is too late to deny it, and, Mr. President, it is also too late to admit it, and not have faith in it. Intellectual assent to the doctrines of Christianity does not make a man a Christian. It is saving faith that makes the Christian. And a mere intellectual assent to the doctrine that we are a nation does not make the true patriot. It is high time that we come to believe without qualification, to believe in our hearts, in the exercise of patriotic faith, that the United States is a nation. When we come to believe that, Mr. President, many of the doubts and uncertainties which have troubled men will disappear.

"It is time to be heroic in our faith and to assert all the power that belongs to the nation as a nation. . . . The attempt to shear the United States of a portion of its sovereign power is an attempt which may well be thoroughly and fully discussed. In the right to acquire territory is found the right to govern, and as the right to acquire is sovereign and unlimited, the right to govern is a sovereign right, and I maintain is not limited in the Constitution. If I am right in holding that the power to acquire is the sovereign power without limitation, I think it must be admitted that the right to govern is also sovereign and unlimited. But if it is sought to rest the right to govern upon that clause of the Constitution which gives Congress the power to dispose of or make 'all needful rules and regulations' for the government of the territory of the United States, I submit there is no limitation there. There is no qualification there."

On the 4th of January the Senate received the treaty from the President. On the 7th, Senator Mason, of Illinois, introduced the following resolution, and, subsequently, spoke with earnestness in its support :

"Whereas all just powers of government are derived from the consent of the governed : Therefore, be it

"Resolved by the Senate of the United States, That the Government of the United States of America will not attempt to govern the people of any other country in the world without the consent of the people themselves, or subject them by force to our dominion against their will."

On the 9th an impressive speech was made by Senator Hoar, of Massachusetts, mainly in reply to Senator Platt. He spoke partly as follows:

"Mr. President, I am quite sure that no man who will hear or who will read what I say to-day will doubt that nothing could induce me to say it but a commanding sense of public duty. I think I dislike more than most men to differ from men with whom I have so long and so constantly agreed. I dislike to differ from the President, whose election I hailed with such personal satisfaction and such exulting anticipations for the Republic. I dislike to differ from so many of my party associates in this Chamber, with whom I have for so many years trod the same path and sought the same goal. I am one of those men who believe that little that is great or good or permanent for a free people can be accomplished without the instrumentality of party. And I have believed religiously, and from my soul, for half a century, in the great doctrines and principles of the Republican party. I stood in a humble capacity by its cradle. I do not mean, if I can help it, to follow its hearse. I am sure I render it a service ; I am sure I help to protect and to prolong the life of that great organization, if I can say or can do anything to keep it from forsaking the great principles and doctrines in which alone it must live or bear no life. I must, in this great crisis, discharge the trust my beloved Commonwealth has committed to me according to my sense of duty as I see it. However unpleasant may be that duty, as Martin Luther said, 'God help me. I can do no otherwise.'

"I am to speak for my country, for its whole past and for its whole future. I am to speak to a people whose fate is bound up in the preservation of our great doctrine of constitutional liberty. I am to speak for the dead soldier who gave his life for liberty that his death might set a seal upon his country's historic glory. I am to speak for the Republican party, all of whose great traditions are at stake, and all of whose great achievements are in peril. . . .

"The question with which we now have to deal is whether Congress may conquer and may govern, without their consent and against their will, a foreign nation, a separate, distinct, and numerous people, a territory not hereafter to be populated by Americans, to be formed into American States and to take its part in fulfilling and executing the purposes for which the Constitution was framed, whether it may conquer, control, and govern this people, not for the general welfare, common defense, more perfect union, more blessed liberty of the people of the United States, but for some real or fancied benefit to be conferred against their desire upon the people so governed or in discharge of some fancied obligation to them, and not to the people of the United States.

"Now, Mr. President, the question is whether the men who framed the Constitution, or the people who adopted it, meant to confer that power among the limited and restrained powers of the sovereign nation that they were creating. Upon that question I take issue with my honorable friend from Connecticut. I declare not only that this is not among the express powers conferred upon the sovereignty they created, that it is not among the powers necessarily or reasonably or conveniently implied for the sake of carrying into effect the purposes of that instrument, but that it is a power which it can be demonstrated by the whole contemporaneous history and by our whole history since until within six months they did not mean should exist—a power that our fathers and their descendants have ever loathed and abhorred—and that they believed that no sovereign on earth could rightfully exercise it, and that no people on earth could rightfully confer it. They not only did not mean to confer it, but they would have cut off their right hands, every one of them, sooner than set them to an instrument which should confer it. . . .

"The great contemporaneous exposition of the Constitution is to be found in the Declaration of Independence. Over every clause, syllable, and letter of the Constitution the Declaration of Independence pours its blazing torchlight. The same men framed it. The same States confirmed it. The same people pledged their lives, their fortunes, and their sacred honor to support it. The great characters in the Constitutional Convention were the great characters of the Continental Congress. There are undoubtedly, among its burning and shining truths, one or two which the convention that adopted it were not prepared themselves at once to put into practice. But they placed them before their countrymen as an ideal moral law to which the liberty of the people was to aspire and to ascend as soon as the nature of existing conditions would admit. Doubtless slavery was inconsistent with it, as Jefferson, its great author, has in more than one place left on record. But at last in the strife of a great civil war the truth of the Declaration prevailed and the falsehood of slavery went down, and at last the Constitution of the United States conformed to the Declaration and it has become the law of the land, and its great doctrines of liberty are written upon the American flag wherever the American flag floats. Who shall haul them down?"

Two days later (January 11) the following resolutions were introduced by Senator Bacon, of Georgia:

"Resolved by the Senate and House of Representatives of the United States of America in Congress assembled, First, That the Government and people of the United States have not waged the recent war with Spain for conquest and for the acquisition of foreign territory, but solely for the purposes set forth in the resolution of Congress making the declaration of said war, the acquisition of such small tracts of land or harbors as may be necessary for governmental purposes being not deemed inconsistent with the same.

"Second. That in demanding and in receiving the cession of the Philippine Islands it is not the purpose of the Government of the United States to secure and maintain dominion over the same as a part of the territory of the United States, or to incorporate the inhabitants thereof as citizens of the United States, or to hold said inhabitants as vassals or subjects of this Government.

"Third. That whereas at the time of the declaration of war by the United States against Spain, and prior thereto, the inhabitants of the Philippine Islands were actively engaged in a war with Spain to achieve their independence, and whereas said purpose and the military operations thereunder have not been abandoned, but are still being actively prosecuted thereunder, therefore, in recognition of and in obedience to the vital principle announced in the great declaration that governments derive 'their just powers from the consent of the governed,' the Government of the United States recognizes that the people of the Philippine Islands of a right ought to be free and independent; that, with this view and to give effect to the same, the Government of the United States has required the Government of Spain to relinquish its authority and government in the Philippine Islands and to withdraw its land and naval forces from the Philippine Islands and from the waters thereof.

"Fourth. That the United States hereby disclaim any disposition or intention to exercise sovereignty, jurisdiction, or control over said islands, and assert their determination when an independent government shall have been duly erected therein entitled to recognition as such, to transfer to said government, upon terms which shall be reasonable and just, all rights secured under the cession by Spain, and to thereupon leave the government and control of the islands to their people."

On the 13th, Senator McLaurin, of South Carolina, returned to the question of constitutional power in the government of the United States to hold territory in a permanently subject state, and spoke against the view maintained by Senator Platt, of Connecticut: "To hold," he said, "that there is an inherent power of sovereignty in the nation, outside of the Constitution, to do something not authorized by that instrument is to place this 'inherent sovereignty' above the Constitution and thus destroy the very foundation upon which constitutional government rests. Judge Gray in the Chinese-exclusion case, said: 'The United States are a sovereign and independent nation, and are invested by the Constitution with the entire control of international relations and with all the powers of government necessary to maintain that control and make it effective.' While holding that the United States are a sovereign and independent nation, it will be seen that he also holds that the sovereignty of the nation is vested by the Constitution; and if so, it can only be exercised in the mode pointed out in the Constitution and is controlled by the words of the grant of this sovereignty. There was no nation of the United States until the adoption of the Federal Constitution; hence before that time there could be no sovereignty of the nation. What conferred this sovereignty? Clearly the States, by and through the Federal Constitution. If so, then there can be no inherent right of sovereignty except that conferred by the Constitution.

"The Senator further contends that we are a sovereign nation, and as such have the same inherent right to acquire territory as England, France, Germany, and Mexico. I controvert that proposition. The sovereignty of the nation of Great Britain and the others is vested in the people, and has never been delegated and limited as in our country. These Governments enjoy sovereignty in its elementary form. What the government wills it may do without considering the act or its consequences in the light of an organic law of binding obligation. Our Government is in a very different position. The Federal Constitution is the embodiment of the sovereignty of the United States as a nation, and this sovereignty can only be exercised in accordance with the powers contained in its provisions. Great Britain can do anything as a nation in the way of the exercise of governmental functions. There is nothing to prohibit or restrict the fullest exercise of her sovereignty as a nation. Hence there is no analogy, and the sovereignty of the United States as a nation differs widely from that of Great Britain.

"It is further contended that a sovereign right can not be limited and that all our Constitution can do is to prescribe the manner in which it can be exercised. If, as already shown, the sovereignty of the United States was conferred by the States through the Federal Constitution, it is clear that, in conferring the power and prescribing the manner of its exercise, they did set a limit in the very terms of the instrument itself. I deny, therefore, that the United States as a nation has a sovereign, inherent right and control outside of the grant of such power in the Constitution. This is not an essential element of nationality so far as our nation is concerned, although it may be in England or Russia, where the nationality and sovereignty incident to it are not created and limited by a written constitution."

On the 14th of January, Mr. Hoar submitted the following:

"Resolved, That the people of the Philippine Islands of right ought to be free and independent; that they are absolved from all allegiance to the Spanish Crown, and that all political connection between them and Spain is and ought to be totally dissolved, and that they have, therefore, full power to do all acts and things which independent states may of right do; that it is their right to institute a new government for themselves, laying its foundation on such principles and organizing its powers in such form as to them shall seem most likely to effect their safety and happiness; and that with these rights the people of the United States do not propose to interfere."

On the 18th, Mr. Bacon amended his resolutions, given above, by changing the phrase "an independent government" to "a stable and independent government," and then spoke upon them with force, saying, among other things: "The simple fact that we went to war with Spain did not devolve upon us any obligation with reference to the Philippine Islands. We went to war with Spain not for the purpose of correcting all the evils with which her people were afflicted; we went to war with Spain not to break the chains of tyranny with which she might be binding her different colonies; we did not undertake to be the great universal benefactor and to right all the wrongs of all the world, or even all the wrongs that Spain might be inflicting upon any of her people. We went to war because a particular colony which she was afflicting lay at our doors; we went to war because the disorders of that Government affected the peace of our community and were injurious to our material interest. We said there was a condition of affairs which was unbearable and that we would put an end to it.

"To that extent and to that alone we claimed and avowed the reason for the declaration of war. So it follows that the mere declaration of war did not affect in any manner our relations with the Philippine Islands except to put us in a state of war with them as a part of the Spanish domain, and in no manner laid any obligations upon us as to those islands. We were not charged with the duty of preserving order in Asia. We were not charged with the obligations of seeing that they had a stable and orderly government in any part of that hemisphere. No such duty rested upon us. None such was assumed by us. Therefore the simple declaration of war did not lay any obligation upon us as to the Philippine Islands, and I desire that any Senator will put his finger upon the act which laid us under any obligations to the Philippine Islands outside of the fact that in the war which ensued we took those who were the insurgents in those islands to be our allies and made a common cause with them.

"Now, Mr. President, all that grows out of that—all that grows out of the fact of that cooperation and that alliance—is to impose upon us a single obligation which we must not ignore. How far does that obligation go? Does it require that we shall for all time undertake to be the guardians of the Philippine Islands? Does that particular obligation lay upon us the duty hereafter, not only now but for years to come, to maintain an expensive military establishment, to burden our people with debt, to run the risk of becoming involved in wars in order that we may keep our hands upon the Philippine Islands and keep them in proper condition hereafter? I am unable to see how the obligation growing out of the fact that they were our allies can possibly be extended to that degree. No Senator has yet shown any reason why such an obligation rests upon us, and I venture to say that none which is logical will or can be shown."

The practical considerations, of circumstance and expediency, which probably had more influence than those of law or principle, were strongly urged by Senator Lodge, of Massachusetts, who said, on the 24th: "Suppose we ratify the treaty. The islands pass from the possession of Spain into our possession without committing us to any policy. I believe we can be trusted as a people to deal honestly and justly with the islands and their inhabitants thus given to our care. What our precise policy shall be I do not know, because I for one am not sufficiently informed as to the conditions there to be able to say what it will be best to do, nor, I may add, do I think anyone is. But I believe that we shall have the wisdom not to attempt to incorporate those islands with our body politic, or make their inhabitants part of our citizenship, or set their labor alongside of ours and within our tariff to compete in any industry with American workmen. I believe that we shall have the courage not to depart from those islands fearfully, timidly, and unworthily and leave them to anarchy among themselves, to the brief and bloody domination of some self-constituted dictator, and to the quick conquest of other powers, who will have no such hesitation as we should feel in crushing them into subjection by harsh and repressive methods. It is for us to decide the destiny of the Philippines, not for Europe, and we can do it alone and without assistance. . . .

"During the campaign of last autumn I said in many speeches to the people of my State that I could never assent to hand those islands back to Spain; that I wanted no subject races and no vassal States; but that we had by the fortunes of war assumed a great responsibility in the Philippines; that we ought to meet it, and that we ought to give to those people an opportunity for freedom, for peace, and for self-government; that we ought to protect them from the rapacity of other nations and seek to uplift those whom we had freed. From those views I have never swerved, and I believed then, as I believe now, that they met with the approbation of an overwhelming majority of the people of Massachusetts. . . .

"Take now the other alternative. Suppose we reject the treaty or strike out the clause relating to the Philippines. That will hand the islands back to Spain; and I cannot conceive that any American should be willing to do that. Suppose we reject the treaty; what follows? Let us look at it practically. We continue the state of war, and every sensible man in the country, every business interest, desires the re-establishment of peace in law as well as in fact. At the same time we repudiate the President and his action before the whole world, and the repudiation of the President in such a matter as this is, to my mind, the humiliation of the United States in the eyes of civilized mankind and brands us a people incapable of great affairs or of taking rank where we belong, as one of the greatest of the great world powers.

"The President cannot be sent back across the Atlantic in the person of his commissioners, hat in hand, to say to Spain, with bated breath, 'I am here in obedience to the mandate of a minority of one-third of the Senate to tell you that we have been too victorious, and that you have yielded us too much, and that I am very sorry that I took the Philippines from you.' I do not think that any American President would do that, or that any American would wish him to."

Senator Harris, of Kansas, submitted the following on the 3d of February:

"Resolved by the Senate of the United States of America, That the United States hereby disclaim any disposition or intention to exercise permanent sovereignty, jurisdiction, or control over the Philippine Islands, and assert their determination, when a stable and independent government shall have been erected therein entitled to recognition as such, to transfer to said government, upon terms which shall be reasonable and just, all rights secured under the cession by Spain, and to thereupon leave the government and control of the islands to their people."

The following was offered on the 27th of January by Senator Sullivan, of Mississippi:

"Resolved, That the ratification of the pending treaty of peace with Spain shall in no wise determine the policy to be pursued by the United States in regard to the Philippines, nor shall it commit this Government to a colonial policy; nor is it intended to embarrass the establishment of a stable, independent government by the people of those islands whenever conditions make such a proceeding hopeful of successful and desirable results."

On the same day a joint resolution was proposed by Senator Lindsay, of Kentucky:

"Resolved by the Senate and House of Representatives of the United States of America in Congress assembled, That the acquisition by the United States, through conquest, treaty, or otherwise, of territory, carries with it no constitutional obligation to admit said territory, or any portion thereof, into the Federal Union as a State or States.

"Sec. 2. That it is against the policy, traditions, and interests of the American people to admit states erected out of other than North American territory into our Union of American States.

"Sec. 3. That the United States accept from Spain the cession of the Philippine Islands with the hope that the people of those islands will demonstrate their capacity to establish and maintain a stable government, capable of enforcing law and order at home and of discharging the international obligations resting on separate and independent States, and with no expectation of permanently holding those islands as colonies or provinces after they shall demonstrate their capacity for self-government, the United States to be the judge of such capacity."

None of the resolutions given above obtained favorable consideration in the Senate. On the 6th of February the treaty was ratified, by one vote in excess of the two-thirds which the constitution requires. It received 57 votes against 27, or 61 against 29 if account be taken of senators absent and paired. Of the supporters of the treaty, 42 were Republicans; of its opponents, 24 were Democrats. It was signed by President McKinley on the 10th of February, and by the Queen of Spain on the 17th of March.

After the ratification of the treaty, the Senate, by 26 votes against 22, adopted the following resolution, offered by Mr. McEnery of Louisiana:

"Resolved, That by the ratification of the treaty of peace with Spain it is not intended to incorporate the inhabitants of the Philippine islands into citizenship of the United States, nor is it intended to permanently annex said islands as an integral part of the territory of the United States. But it is the intention of the United States to establish on said islands a government suitable to the wants and conditions of the inhabitants of said islands, to prepare them for local self-government, and in due time to make such disposition of said islands as will best promote the interests of the citizens of the United States and the inhabitants of said islands."—*Congressional Record, Dec. 6, 1898—Feb. 6, 1899.*

A. D. 1899 (January—November).—Attack on Americans at Manila by Aguinaldo's forces.—Continued hostilities.—Progress of American conquest. See (in this vol.) PHILIPPINE ISLANDS: A. D. 1899 (JANUARY—NOVEMBER).

A. D. 1899 (March).—Appointment of the Isthmian Canal Commission. See (in this vol.) CANAL, INTEROCEANIC: A. D. 1889–1899.

A. D. 1899 (May).—Modification of Civil Service Rules by President McKinley. See (in this vol.) CIVIL SERVICE REFORM: A. D. 1899.

A. D. 1899 (May—July).—Representation in the Peace Conference at The Hague. See (in this vol.) PEACE CONFERENCE.

A. D. 1899 (June—October).—Arbitration and settlement of the Venezuela boundary question. See (in this vol.) VENEZUELA: A. D. 1896–1899.

A. D. 1899 (July).—Cabinet change.—General Russel A. Alger resigned his place in the President's Cabinet as Secretary of War, in July, and was succeeded by the Hon. Elihu Root, of New York.

A. D. 1899 (July).—Provisional government established in the island of Negros. See (in this vol.) PHILIPPINE ISLANDS : A. D. 1899 (MARCH—JULY).

A. D. 1899 (October).—Report of conditions in Cuba by the Military Governor. See (in this vol.) CUBA : A. D. 1898–1899 (DECEMBER—OCTOBER).

A. D. 1899 (October).—Modus Vivendi fixing provisional boundary line between Alaska and Canada. See (in this vol.) ALASKA BOUNDARY QUESTION.

A. D. 1899 (November).—Death of Vice-President Hobart.—Hon. Garret A. Hobart, Vice-President of the United States, died November 21. Under the Act provided for this contingency, the Secretary of State then became the successor to the President, in the event of the death of the latter before the expiration of his term.

A. D. 1899 (November).—Re-arrangement of affairs in the Samoan Islands.—Acquisition of the eastern group, with Pago Pago harbor. See (in this vol.) SAMOAN ISLANDS.

A. D. 1899–1900 (September—February).—Arrangement with European Powers of the commercial policy of the "open-door" in China. See (in this vol.) CHINA : A. D. 1899–1900 (SEPTEMBER—FEBRUARY).

A. D. 1899–1900 (November—November).—Continued military operations in the Philippines. See (in this vol.) PHILIPPINE ISLANDS : A. D. 1899–1900.

A. D. 1899–1901. — Reciprocity arrangements under the Dingley Tariff Act, not ratified by the Senate.—The Dingley Tariff Act, which became law on the 24th of July, 1897, authorized the making of tariff concessions to other countries on terms of reciprocity, if negotiated within two years from the above date. At the expiration of two years, such conventions of reciprocity had been arranged with France and Portugal, and with Great Britain for her West Indian colonies of Jamaica, Barbadoes, Trinidad, Bermuda, and British Guiana. With France, a preliminary treaty signed in May, 1898, was superseded in July, 1899, by one of broader scope, which opens the French markets to an extensive list of American commodities at the minimum rates of the French tariff, and cuts the American tariff from 5 to 20 per cent. on many French products, not inclusive of sparkling wines. In the treaty with Portugal, the reduction of American duties on wines is more general. The reciprocal reduction on American products extends to many agricultural and mineral products. The reciprocal agreement with the British West Indies covers sugar, fruits, garden products, coffee and asphalt, on one side, and flour, meat, cotton goods, agricultural machinery, oils, etc., on the other.

None of these treaties was acted upon by the United States Senate during the session of 1899–1900, and it became necessary to extend the time for their ratification, which was done. Some additional reciprocity agreements were then negotiated, of which the following statement was made by the President in his Message to Congress, December 3, 1900 : "Since my last communication to the Congress on this subject special commercial agreements under the third section of the tariff act have been proclaimed with Portugal, with Italy and with Germany. Commercial conventions under the general limitations of the fourth section of the same act have been concluded with Nicaragua, with Ecuador, with the Dominican Republic, with Great Britain on behalf of the island of Trinidad and with Denmark on behalf of the island of St. Croix. These will be early communicated to the Senate. Negotiations with other governments are in progress for the improvement and security of our commercial relations."

The question of the ratification of all these treaties was pending in the Senate when the term of the 56th Congress expired, March 4, 1901. Opposing interests in the United States seemed likely then to defeat their ratification. On the last day of the special session of the Senate, March 5–9, an agreement extending the time for the ratification of the French reciprocity treaty was received and referred to the committee on foreign relations. On the 15th of March, Secretary Hay and Lord Pauncefote signed protocols extending for one year the time of ratification for four of the British West Indian reciprocity treaties, namely, Jamaica, Bermuda, Guiana and Turks and Caicos islands.

A. D. 1900.—Naval strength. See (in this vol.) NAVIES OF THE SEA POWERS.

A. D. 1900.—State of Indian schools.—Recent Indian policy.—Indian population. See (in this vol.) INDIANS, AMERICAN : A. D. 1899–1900.

A. D. 1900 (January).—Report of the First Philippine Commission. See (in this vol.) PHILIPPINE ISLANDS : A. D. 1900 (JANUARY).

A. D. 1900 (January—March).—The outbreak of the "Boxers" in northern China. See (in this vol.) CHINA : A. D. 1900 (JANUARY—MARCH).

A. D. 1900 (February).—Negotiation of the Hay-Pauncefote Convention relative to the Nicaragua Canal. See (in this vol.) CANAL, INTEROCEANIC : A. D. 1900 (DECEMBER).

A. D. 1900 (March—December).—Passage of the Financial Bill.—Settlement of the question of the monetary standard.—The working of the act.—Legislation in the direction sought by the advocates of the gold standard and of a reformed monetary system for the country, whose agitations are referred to above (see above : A. D. 1896–1898), was attained in the spring of 1900, by the passage of an important "Financial Bill" which became law on the 14th of March. The provisions and the effect of the Act were summarized at the time by the Secretary of the Treasury, Mr. Gage, in a published statement, as follows : "The financial bill has for its first object what its title indicates, the fixing of the standard of value and the maintaining at a parity with that standard of all forms of money issued or coined by the United States. It reaffirms that the unit of value is the dollar, consisting of 25.8 grains of gold, nine tenths fine, but from that point it goes on to make it the duty of the Secretary of the Treasury to maintain all forms of money issued or coined at a parity with this standard. It puts into the hands of the Secretary ample power to do that. For that purpose, the bill provides in the Treasury bureaus of issue and redemption and transfers from the general fund of the Treasury's cash $150,000,000 in gold coin and bullion to redemption fund, that gold to be used for the redemption of United States notes and Treasury notes. That fund is henceforth absolutely cut out of and separated from the cash balance in the Treasury and the available cash balance will hereafter show a reduction of $150,000,000 from the figures that have heretofore prevailed. This $150,000,000 redemption fund is to be used for no other purpose than the redemption of United States notes and Treasury notes and those notes so redeemed may be exchanged for the gold in the general fund or with the public, so that the reserve fund is kept full with gold to the $150,-000,000 limit. If redemptions go on so that the gold in this reserve fund is reduced below $100-000,000, and the Secretary is unable to build it up to the $150,000,000 mark by exchange for gold in the general fund or otherwise, he is given power to sell bonds and it is made his duty to replenish the gold to the $150,000,000 mark by such means.

"The 'endless chain' is broken by a provision which prohibits the use of notes so redeemed to meet deficiencies in the current revenues. The act provides for the ultimate retirement of all the Treasury notes issued in payment for silver bullion under the Sherman act. As fast as that bullion is coined into silver dollars Treasury notes are to be retired and replaced with an equal amount of silver certificates. The measure authorizes the issue of gold certificates in exchange for deposits of gold coin, the same as at present, but suspends that authority whenever and so long as the gold in the redemption fund is below $100,000,000 and gives to the Secretary the option to suspend the issue of such certificates whenever the silver certificates and United States notes in the general fund of the Treasury exceed $40,000,000. The bill provides for a larger issue of silver certificates, by declaring that hereafter silver certificates shall be issued only in denominations of $10 and under except as to 10 per cent. of the total volume. Room is made for this larger use of silver certificates in the way of small bills by another provision which makes it necessary as fast as the present silver certificates of high denominations are broken up into small bills to cancel a similar volume of United States notes of small denominations and replace them with notes of denominations of $10 and upward. Further room is made for the circulation of small silver certificates by a clause which permits national banks to have only one third of their capital in denomination under $10.

"One clause of the bill which the public will greatly appreciate is the right it gives to the Secretary to coin any of the 1890 bullion into subsidiary silver coins up to a limit of $100,-000,000. There has for years been a scarcity of subsidiary silver during periods of active retail trade, but this provision will give the Treasury ample opportunity to supply all the subsidiary silver that is needed. Another provision that the public will greatly appreciate is the authority given to the Secretary to recoin worn and uncurrent subsidiary silver now in the Treasury or hereafter received.

"A distinct feature of the bill is in reference to refunding the 3 per cent. Spanish war loan,

the 2 per cent. bonds maturing in 1907 and the 5 per cent. bonds maturing in 1904, a total of $839,000,000, into new 2 per cent. bonds. These new 2 per cent. bonds will not be offered for sale, but will only be issued in exchange for an equal amount, face value, of old bonds. This exchange will save the Government, after deducting the premium paid, nearly $23,000,000, if all the holders of the old bonds exchange them for the new ones. National banks that take out circulation based on the new bonds are to be taxed only one half of 1 per cent. on the average amount of circulation outstanding, while those who have circulation based on a deposit of old bonds will be taxed, as at present, 1 per cent. There are some other changes in the national banking act. The law permits national banks with $25,000 capital to be organized in places of 3,000 inhabitants or less, whereas heretofore the minimum capital has been $50,000. It also permits banks to issue circulation on all classes of bonds deposited up to the par value of the bonds, instead of 90 per cent. of their face, as heretofore. This ought to make an immediate increase in national bank circulation of something like $24,000,000, as the amount of bonds now deposited to secure circulation is about $242,000,000. If the price of the new 2s is not forced so high in the market that there is no profit left to national banks in taking out circulation, we may also look for a material increase in national bank circulation based on additional deposits of bonds. National banks are permitted under the law to issue circulation up to an amount equal to their capital. The total capital of all national banks is $616,000,000. The total circulation outstanding is $253,000,000. There is, therefore, a possibility of an increase in circulation of $363,000,000, although the price of the 2 per cent. bonds, as already foreshadowed by market quotations in advance of their issue, promises to be so high that the profit to the banks in taking out circulation will not be enough to make the increase anything like such a possible total."

Upon the working of the Act, during the first nine months of its operation, Secretary Gage remarked as follows, in his annual report dated December 14, 1900: "The operation of the act of March 14 last with respect to these two important matters of our finances has well exemplified its wisdom. Confidence in the purpose and power of the Government to maintain the gold standard has been greatly strengthened. The result is that gold flows toward the Treasury instead of away from it. At the date of this report the free gold in the Treasury is larger in amount than at any former period in our history. Including the $150,000,000 reserve, the gold in the Treasury belonging to the Government amounts to over $242,000,000, while the Treasury holds, besides, more than $230,000,000, against which certificates have been issued. That provision of the act which liberalized the conditions of bank-note issue was also wise and timely. Under it, . . . there has been an increase of some $77,000,000 in bank-note issues. To this fact may be chiefly attributed the freedom from stress for currency to handle the large harvests of cotton, wheat, and corn. In this respect the year has been an exception to the general rule of stringency which for several years has so plainly marked the autumn season.

640

"Nevertheless, the measures referred to, prolific as they have been in good results, will yet need re-enforcement in some important particulars. Thus, as to the redemption fund provided for in said act, while the powers conferred upon the Secretary are probably ample to enable a zealous and watchful officer to protect fully the gold reserve, there appears to be lacking sufficient mandatory requirement to furnish complete confidence in the continued parity, under all conditions, between our two forms of metallic money, silver and gold. Upon this point further legislation may become desirable. As to the currency, while the liberalizing of conditions has, as previously noted, found response in a necessary increase of bank-note issues, there is under our present system no assurance whatever that the volume of bank currency will be continuously responsive to the country's needs, either by expanding as such needs require or by contracting when superfluous in amount. The truth is that safe and desirable as is our currency system in many respects, it is not properly related. The supply of currency is but remotely, if at all, influenced by the everchanging requirements of trade and industry. It is related most largely, if not entirely, to the price of Government bonds in the market."—*Annual Report of the Secretary of the Treasury*, 1900, *pp.* 72-73.

A. D. 1900 (April).—Speech of Senator Hoar in denial of the right of the government of the United States, under the Constitution, to hold the Philippine Islands as a subject state.—On the 17th of April, the following joint resolution was under consideration in the Senate : "Be it resolved by the Senate and House of Representatives of the United States of America in Congress assembled, that the Philippine Islands are territory belonging to the United States; that it is the intention of the United States to retain them as such and to establish and maintain such governmental control throughout the archipelago as the situation may demand." Senator Hoar, of Massachusetts, spoke in opposition to the resolution, and some passages from his speech are quoted here, because they are notably representative of the ground and spirit of an opposition which existed within the party controlling the government to the war of subjugation in the Philippine Islands, to which the party and the government were finally committed by the adoption of this Congressional declaration. The attitude and argument of parties on the question are set forth below, in the platforms and manifestos of the presidential election. This speech exhibits a feeling on that question which was overridden in the winning party, and it has an importance both forensic and historical :

"The American people, so far as I know, were all agreed that their victory [in the Spanish American war] brought with it the responsibility of protecting the liberated peoples from the cupidity of any other power until they could establish their own independence in freedom and in honor. I stand here to-day to plead with you not to abandon the principles that have brought these things to pass. I implore you to keep to the policy that has made the country great, that has made the Republican party great, that has made the President great. I have nothing new to say. But I ask you to keep in the old chan-

nels, and to keep off the old rocks laid down in the old charts, and to follow the old sailing orders that all the old captains of other days have obeyed, to take your bearings, as of old, from the north star,

Of whose true fixed and resting quality
There is no fellow in the firmament,

and not from this meteoric light of empire.

"Especially, if I could, would I persuade the great Republican party to come back again to its old faith, to its old religion, before it is too late. There is yet time. The President has said again and again that his is only an ad interim policy until Congress shall act. It is not yet too late. Congress has rejected, unwisely, as I think, some declarations for freedom. But the two Houses have not as yet committed themselves to despotism. The old, safe path, the path alike of justice and of freedom, is still easy. It is a path familiar, of old, to the Republican party. If we have diverged from it for the first time, everything in our history, everything in our own nature calls us back. The great preacher of the English church tells you how easy is the return of a great and noble nature from the first departure from rectitude :— ' For so a taper, when its crown of flame is newly blown off, retains a nature so symbolical to light, that it will with greediness reenkindle and snatch a ray from the neighbor fire.'

"I, for one, believed, and still believe that the pathway to prosperity and glory for the country was also the pathway to success and glory for the Republican party. I thought the two things inseparable. If, when we made the treaty of peace, we had adhered to the purpose we declared when we declared war ; if we had dealt with the Philippine Islands as we promised to deal, have dealt, and expect to deal with Cuba, the country would have escaped the loss of 6,000 brave soldiers, other thousands of wrecked and shattered lives, the sickness of many more, the expenditure of hundreds of millions, and, what is far worse than all, the trampling under foot of its cherished ideals. There would have been to-day a noble republic in the East, sitting docile at our feet, receiving from us civilization, laws, manners, and giving in turn everything the gratitude of a free people could give—love, obedience, trade. The Philippine youth would throng our universities ; our Constitution, our Declaration, the lives of Washington and Lincoln, the sayings of Jefferson and Franklin would have been the text-books of their schools. How our orators and poets would have delighted to contrast America liberating and raising up the republic of Asia, with England subduing and trampling under foot the republic of Africa. Nothing at home could have withstood the great party and the great President who had done these things. We should have come from the next election with a solid North and have carried half the South. You would at least have been spared the spectacle of great Republican States rising in revolt against Republican policies. I do not expect to accomplish anything for liberty in the Philippine Islands but through the Republican party. Upon it the fate of these Islands for years to come is to depend. If that party can not be persuaded, the case is in my judgment for the present hopeless. . . .

6-41

"The practical question which divided the American people last year, and which divides them to-day, is this: Whether in protecting the people of the Philippine Islands from the ambition and cupidity of other nations we are bound to protect them from our own. . . . In dealing with this question, Mr. President, I do not mean to enter upon any doubtful ground. I shall advance no proposition ever seriously disputed in this country till within twelve months. . . . If to think as I do in regard to the interpretation of the Constitution ; in regard to the mandates of the moral law or the law of nations, to which all men and all nations must render obedience; in regard to the policies which are wisest for the conduct of the State, or in regard to those facts of recent history in the light of which we have acted or are to act hereafter, be treason, then Washington was a traitor ; then Jefferson was a traitor ; then Jackson was a traitor ; then Franklin was a traitor ; then Sumner was a traitor ; then Lincoln was a traitor ; then Webster was a traitor ; then Clay was a traitor ; then Corwin was a traitor ; then Kent was a traitor ; then Seward was a traitor ; then McKinley, within two years, was a traitor ; then the Supreme Court of the United States has been in the past a nest and hotbed of treason ; then the people of the United States, for more than a century, have been traitors to their own flag and their own Constitution.

"We are presented with an issue that can be clearly and sharply stated as a question of constitutional power, a question of international law, a question of justice and righteousness, or a question of public expediency. This can be stated clearly and sharply in the abstract, and it can be put clearly and sharply by an illustration growing out of existing facts.

"The constitutional question is : Has Congress the power, under our Constitution, to hold in subjection unwilling vassal States ?

"The question of international law is : Can any nation rightfully convey to another sovereignty over an unwilling people who have thrown off its dominion, asserted their independence, established a government of their own, over whom it has at the time no practical control, from whose territory it has been disseized, and which it is beyond its power to deliver ?

"The question of justice and righteousness is : Have we the right to crush and hold under our feet an unwilling and subject people whom we had treated as allies, whose independence we are bound in good faith to respect, who had established their own free government, and who had trusted us ?

"The question of public expediency is : Is it for our advantage to promote our trade at the cannon's mouth and at the point of the bayonet ?

"All these questions can be put in a way of practical illustration by inquiring whether we ought to do what we have done, are doing, and mean to do in the case of Cuba ; or what we have done, are doing, and some of you mean to do in the case of the Philippine Islands.

"It does not seem to me to be worth while to state again at length the constitutional argument which I have addressed to the Senate heretofore. It has been encountered with eloquence, with clearness and beauty of statement, and, I have no doubt, with absolute sincerity by Senators who have spoken upon the other side.

But the issue between them and me can be summed up in a sentence or two, and if, so stated, it can not be made clear to any man's apprehension, I despair of making it clear by any elaboration or amplification. I admit that the United States may acquire and hold property, and may make rules and regulations for its disposition. I admit that, like other property, the United States may acquire and hold land. It may acquire it by purchase. It may acquire it by treaty. It may acquire it by conquest. And it may make rules and regulations for its disposition and government, however it be acquired. When there are inhabitants upon the land so acquired it may make laws for their government. But the question between me and the gentlemen on the other side is this : Is this acquisition of territory, of land or other property, whether gained by purchase, conquest, or treaty, a constitutional end or only a means to a constitutional end ? May you acquire, hold, and govern territory or other property as an end for which our Constitution was framed, or is it only a means toward some other and further end ? May you acquire, hold, and govern property by conquest, treaty, or purchase for the sole object of so holding and governing it, without the consideration of any further constitutional purpose ? Or must you hold it for a constitutional purpose only, such as the making of new States, the national defense and security, the establishment of a seat of government, or the construction of forts, harbors, and like works, which, of course, are themselves for the national defense and security ?

"I hold that this acquisition, holding and governing, can be only a means for a constitutional end—the creation of new States or some other of the constitutional purposes to which I have adverted. And I maintain that you can no more hold and govern territory than you can hold and manage cannon or fleets for any other than a constitutional end ; and I maintain that the holding in subjection an alien people, governing them against their will for any fancied advantage to them, is not only not an end provided for by the Constitution, but is an end prohibited therein. . . . It is an end which the generation which framed the Constitution and the Declaration of Independence declared was unrighteous and abhorrent. So, in my opinion, we have no constitutional power to acquire territory for the purpose of holding it in subjugation, in a state of vassalage or serfdom, against the will of its people.

"It is to be noted just here that we have acquired no territory or other property in the Philippine Islands, save a few public buildings. By every other acquisition of territory the United States became a great land owner. She owned the public lands as she had owned the public lands in the Northwest ceded to her by the old States. But you own nothing in the Philippines. The people own their farms and dwellings and cities. The religious orders own the rest. The Filipinos desire to do what our English ancestors did in the old days when England was Catholic. The laity feared that the Church would engross all the land. So they passed their statute of mortmain. You have either got to let the people of the Philippine Islands settle this matter for themselves, or you must take upon you the delicate duty of settling it for them. Your purchase or conquest is a purchase or conquest of nothing but sovereignty. It is a sovereignty over a people who are never to be admitted to exercise it or to share it. In the present case we have not, I repeat, bought any property. We have undertaken to buy mere sovereignty. There were no public lands in the Philippine Islands, the property of Spain, which we have bought and paid for. The mountains of iron and the nuggets of gold and the hemp-bearing fields—do you purpose to strip the owners of their rightful title? We have undertaken to buy allegiance, pure and simple. And allegiance is just what the law of nations declares you can not buy. . . .

"I have been unable to find a single reputable authority more than twelve months old for the power now claimed for Congress to govern dependent nations or territories not expected to become States. The contrary, until this war broke out, has been taken as too clear for reasonable question. I content myself·with a few authorities. Among them are Daniel Webster, William H. Seward, the Supreme Court of the United States, James Madison.

"Daniel Webster said in the Senate, March 23, 1848: 'Arbitrary governments may have territories and distant possessions, because arbitrary governments may rule them by different laws and different systems. We can do no such thing. They must be of us, part of us, or else strangers. I think I see a course adopted which is likely to turn the Constitution of the land into a deformed monster, into a curse rather than a blessing; in fact, a frame of an unequal government, not founded on popular representation, not founded on equality, but on the grossest inequality; and I think that this process will go on, or that there is danger that it will go on, until this Union shall fall to pieces. I resist it to-day and always! Whoever falters or whoever flies, I continue the contest!'

"James Madison said in the Federalist: 'The object of the Federal Constitution is to secure the union of the thirteen primitive States, which we know to be practicable; and to add to them such other States as may arise in their own bosoms, or in their neighborhood, which we can not doubt will be practicable.'—*James Madison, Federalist, No.* 14.

"William H. Seward said: 'It is a remarkable feature of the Constitution of the United States that its framers never contemplated colonies, or provinces, or territories at all. On the other hand, they contemplated States only, nothing less than States, perfect States, equal States, as they are called here, sovereign States. . . . There is reason—there is sound political wisdom in this provision of the Constitution excluding colonies, which are always subject to oppression, and excluding provinces, which always tend to corrupt and ultimately to break down the parent State.'—*Seward's Works, Volume* 1, *page* 122. 'By the Constitution of the United States, there are no subjects. Every citizen of any one State is a free and equal citizen of the United States. Again, by the Constitution of the United States there are no permanent provinces or dependencies.'—*Seward's Works, Volume* 4, *page* 167.

"The Supreme Court of the United States, in the case of Fleming vs. Page, said: 'The genius and character of our institutions are peaceful; and the power to declare war was not conferred upon Congress for the purposes of aggression or aggrandizement, but to enable the Government to vindicate by arms, if it should become necessary, its own rights and the rights of its citizens. A war, therefore, declared by Congress, can never be presumed to be waged for the purpose of conquest or the acquisition of territory; nor does the law declaring the war imply an authority to the President to enlarge the limits of the United States by subjugating the enemy's country.'

"'Our territories, so far, have all been places where Americans would go to dwell as citizens, to establish American homes, to obtain honorable employment, and to build a State. Will any man go to the Philippine Islands to dwell, except to help govern the people, or to make money by a temporary residence? . . .

"When hostilities broke out, February 5, 1899, we had no occupancy of and no title of any kind to any portion of the Philippine territory, except the town and bay of Manila. Everything else was in the peaceful possession of the inhabitants. In such a condition of things, Mr. President, international law speaks to us with its awful mandate. It pronounces your proposed action sheer usurpation and robbery. You have no better title, according to the law of nations, to reduce this people to subjection than you have to subjugate Mexico or Haiti or Belgium or Switzerland. This is the settled doctrine, as declared by our own great masters of jurisprudence. You have no right, according to the law of nations, to obtain by purchase or acquisition sovereignty over a people which is not actually exercised by the country which undertakes to convey it or yield it. . . . We have not yet completed the acquisition. But at the time we entered upon it, and at the time of this alleged purchase, the people of the Philippine Islands, as appears by General Otis's report, by Admiral Dewey's report, and the reports of officers for whom they vouched, held their entire territory, with the exception of the single town of Manila. They had, as appears from these reports, a full organized government. They had an army fighting for independence, admirably disciplined, according to the statement of zealous advocates of expansion.

"Why, Mr. President, is it credible that any American statesman, that any American Senator, that any intelligent American citizen anywhere, two years ago could have been found to affirm that a proceeding like that of the Paris treaty could give a just and valid title to sovereignty over a people situated as were the people of those islands? A title of Spain, originally by conquest, never submitted to nor admitted by the people of the islands, with frequent insurrections at different times for centuries, and then the yoke all thrown off, a constitutional government, schools, colleges, churches, universities, hospitals, town governments, a legislature, a cabinet, courts, a code of laws, and the whole island occupied and controlled by its people, with the single exception of one city; with taxes lawfully levied and collected, with an army and the beginning of a navy.

"And yet the Senate, the Congress enacted less than two years ago that the people of Cuba—controlling peaceably no part of their island, levying no taxes in any orderly or peaceable way, with no administration of justice, no cabinet—not only of right ought to be, but were, in fact, a free and independent State. I did not give my assent to that declaration of fact. I assented to the doctrine that they of right ought to be. But I thought the statement of fact much calculated to embarrass the Government of the United States, if it were bound by that declaration; and it has been practically disregarded by the Administration ever since. But the question now is a very different one. You not only deny that the Filipinos are, but you deny that they of right ought to be free and independent; and you recognize Spain as entitled to sell to you the sovereignty of an island where she was not at the time occupying a foot of territory, where her soldiers were held captives by the government of the island, a government to which you had delivered over a large number of Spanish prisoners to be held as captives. And yet you come here to-day and say that they not only are not, but they of right ought not to be free and independent; and when you are pressed you answer us by talking about mountains of iron and nuggets of gold, and trade with China.

"I affirm that you can not get by conquest, and you can not get by purchase, according to the modern law of nations, according to the law of nations as accepted and expounded by the United States, sovereignty over a people, or title to a territory, of which the power that undertakes to sell it or the power from whom you undertake to wrest it has not the actual possession and dominion. . . . You cannot buy a war. More than this, you cannot buy a tyrant's claim to subject again an oppressed people who have achieved their freedom. . . .

"Gentlemen tell us that the bill of the Senator from Wisconsin is copied from that introduced in Jefferson's time for the purchase of Louisiana. Do you claim that you propose to deal with these people as Jefferson meant to deal with Louisiana? You talk of Alaska, of Florida, of California; do you mean to deal with the Philippines as we mean to deal with Alaska and dealt with Florida or California?

"I have spoken of the Declaration of Independence as a solemn affirmation of public law, but it is far more than that. It is a solemn pledge of national faith and honor. It is a baptismal vow. It is the bedrock of our republican institutions. It is, as the Supreme Court declared, the soul and spirit of which the Constitution is but the body and letter. It is the light by which the Constitution must be read. . . . There is expansion enough in it, but it is the expansion of freedom and not of despotism; of life, not of death. Never was such growth in all human history as that from the seed Thomas Jefferson planted. The parable of the mustard seed, than which, as Edward Everett said, 'the burning pen of inspiration, ranging heaven and earth for a similitude, can find nothing more appropriate or expressive to which to liken the Kingdom of God,' is repeated again. 'Whereunto shall we liken it, or with what comparison shall we compare it? It is like a grain of mustard seed, which, when it is sown in the earth, is less than all the seeds that be in the earth. But when it is sown, it groweth up, and becometh greater than all herbs, and shooteth out great branches, so that the fowls of the air may lodge under the shadow of it.' This is the expansion of Thomas Jefferson. It has covered

the continent. It is on both the seas. It has saved South America. It is revolutionizing Europe. It is the expansion of freedom. It differs from your tinsel, pinchbeck, pewter expansion as the growth of a healthy youth into a strong man differs from the expansion of an anaconda when he swallows his victim. Ours is the expansion of Thomas Jefferson. Yours is the expansion of Aaron Burr. It is destined to as short a life and to a like fate. . . .

"There are 1,200 islands in the Philippine group. They extend as far as from Maine to Florida. They have a population variously estimated at from 8,000,000 to 12,000,000. There are wild tribes who never heard of Christ, and islands that never heard of Spain. But among them are the people of the island of Luzon, numbering 3,500,000, and the people of the Visayan Islands, numbering 2,500,000 more. They are a Christian and civilized people. They wrested their independence from Spain and established a republic. Their rights are no more to be affected by the few wild tribes in their own mountains or by the dwellers in the other islands than the rights of our old thirteen States were affected by the French in Canada, or the Six Nations of New York, or the Cherokees of Georgia, or the Indians west of the Mississippi. Twice our commanding generals, by their own confession, assured these people of their independence. Clearly and beyond all cavil we formed an alliance with them. We expressly asked them to co-operate with us. We handed over our prisoners to their keeping; we sought their help in caring for our sick and wounded. We were told by them again and again and again that they were fighting for independence. Their purpose was as well known to our generals, to the War Department, and to the President, as the fact that they were in arms. We never undeceived them until the time when hostilities were declared in 1899. The President declared again and again that we had no title and claimed no right to anything beyond the town of Manila. Hostilities were begun by us at a place where we had no right to be, and were continued by us in spite of Aguinaldo's disavowal and regret and offer to withdraw to a line we should prescribe. If we crush that republic, despoil that people of their freedom and independence, and subject them to our rule, it will be a story of shame and dishonor. . . .

"But we are told if we oppose the policy of our imperialistic and expanding friends we are bound to suggest some policy of our own as a substitute for theirs. We are asked what we would do in this difficult emergency. It is a question not difficult to answer. I for one am ready to answer it.

"1. I would declare now that we will not take these islands to govern them against their will.

"2. I would reject a cession of sovereignty which implies that sovereignty may be bought and sold and delivered without the consent of the people. Spain had no rightful sovereignty over the Philippine Islands. She could not rightfully sell it to us. We could not rightfully buy it from her.

"3. I would require all foreign governments to keep out of these islands.

"4. I would offer to the people of the Philippines our help in maintaining order until they have a reasonable opportunity to establish a government of their own.

"5. I would aid them by advice, if they desire it, to set up a free and independent government.

"6. I would invite all the great powers of Europe to unite in an agreement that that independence shall not be interfered with by us, by themselves, or by any one of them with the consent of the others. As to this I am not so sure. I should like quite as well to tell them it is not to be done whether they consent or not.

"7. I would declare that the United States will enforce the same doctrine as applicable to the Philippines that we declared as to Mexico and Haiti and the South American Republics. It is true that the Monroe Doctrine, a doctrine based largely on our regard for our own interests, is not applicable either in terms or in principle to a distant Asiatic territory. But, undoubtedly, having driven out Spain, we are bound, and have the right, to secure to the people we have liberated an opportunity, undisturbed and in peace, to establish a new government for themselves.

"8. I would then, in a not distant future, leave them to work out their own salvation, as every nation on earth, from the beginning of time, has wrought out its own salvation. Let them work out their own salvation, as our own ancestors slowly and in long centuries wrought out theirs; as Germany, as Switzerland, as France, in briefer periods, wrought out theirs; as Mexico and the South American Republics have accomplished theirs, all of them within a century, some of them within the life of a generation. To attempt to confer the gift of freedom from without, or to impose freedom from without, on any people, is to disregard all the lessons of history. It is to attempt

'A gift of that which is not to be given
By all the blended powers of earth and heaven.'

"9. I would strike out of your legislation the oath of allegiance to us and substitute an oath of allegiance to their own country."

A. D. 1900 (April).—Act temporarily to provide revenues and a civil government for Porto Rico. See (in this vol.) PORTO RICO : A. D. 1899-1900 ; and 1900 (APRIL).

A. D. 1900 (April).—Appointment of Second Commission to the Philippines.—The President's instructions.—Steps toward the establishment of civil government and the principles to be observed. See (in this vol.) PHILIPPINE ISLANDS : A. D. 1900 (APRIL).

A. D. 1900 (May—October).—The Twelfth Census of the Republic.—The Twelfth Census of the United States was taken between May 1 and Nov. 1, 1900, with general results reported on the latter date by the Director, William R. Merriam, as follows :—The following statement . . . gives the population of the United States in detail for each State and organized Territory and for Alaska and Hawaii as finally revised. The figures purporting to give the number of "persons in the service of the United States stationed abroad " include an estimated population of 14,-400 for certain military organizations and naval vessels stationed abroad, principally in the Philippines, for which the returns have not yet been received. The total population of the United States in 1900, as shown by the accompanying statement, is 76,304,799, of which 74,610,523

persons are contained in the 45 States, representing the population to be used for apportionment purposes. This statement also shows a total of 134,158 Indians not taxed, of which 44,617 are found in certain of the States and which are to be deducted from the population of such States for the purpose of determining the apportionment of Representatives. The total population in 1890, with which the aggregate population at the present census should be compared, is 63,069,756, comprising 62,622,250 persons enumerated in the States and organized Territories at that census, 32,052 persons in Alaska, 180,182 Indians and other persons in the Indian Territory, 145,282 Indians and other persons on Indian reservations, etc., and 89,990 persons in Hawaii, this last-named figure being derived from the census of the Hawaiian Islands taken as of December 28, 1890. Taking this population for 1890 as a basis, there has been a gain in population of 13,235,043 during the ten years from 1890 to 1900, representing an increase of very nearly 21 per cent. No provision was made by the census act for the enumeration of the inhabitants of Porto Rico, but a census for that island, taken as of October 16, 1899, under the direction of the War Department, showed a population of 953,-243.

STATES AND TERRITORIES.	1900.	1890.	Indians not taxed, 1900.
The United States.....	76,304,799	63,069,756	134,158
STATES.			
Alabama................	1,828,697	1,513,017	....
Arkansas...............	1,311,564	1,128,179	....
California.............	1,485,053	1,208,130	1,549
Colorado	539,700	412,198	597
Connecticut............	908,355	746,258	....
Delaware...............	184,735	168,493	....
Florida................	528,542	391,422	....
Georgia................	2,216,331	1,837,353	....
Idaho..................	161,772	84,385	2,297
Illinois...............	4,821,550	3,826,351	....
Indiana................	2,516,462	2,192,404	....
Iowa...................	2,231,853	1,911,896	....
Kansas.................	1,470,495	1,427,096	....
Kentucky...............	2,147,174	1,858,635	....
Louisiana..............	1,381,625	1,118,587	....
Maine..................	694,466	661,086	....
Maryland...............	1,190,050	1,042,390	....
Massachusetts..........	2,805,346	2,238,943	....
Michigan...............	2,420,982	2,093,889	....
Minnesota..............	1,751,394	1,301,826	1,768
Mississippi............	1,551,270	1,289,600	....
Missouri...............	3,106,665	2,679,184	....
Montana................	243,329	132,159	10,746
Nebraska...............	1,068,539	1,058,910	....
Nevada.................	42,335	45,761	1,665
New Hampshire..........	411,588	376,530	....
New Jersey	1,883,669	1,444,933	....
New York...............	7,268,012	5,997,853	4,711
North Carolina.........	1,893,810	1,617,947	....
North Dakota...........	319,146	182,719	4,692
Ohio...................	4,157,545	3,672,316	....
Oregon.................	413,536	313,767	....
Pennsylvania...........	6,302,115	5,258,014	....
Rhode Island	428,556	345,506	....
South Carolina.........	1,340,316	1,151,149	....
South Dakota...........	401,570	328,808	10,932
Tennessee..............	2,020,616	1,767,518	....
Texas..................	3,048,710	2,235,523	....
Utah...................	276,749	207,905	1,472
Vermont	343,641	332,422	....
Virginia...............	1,854,184	1,655,980	....
Washington.............	518,103	349,390	2,531
West Virginia..........	958,800	762,794	....
Wisconsin..............	2,069,042	1,686,880	1,657
Wyoming	92,531	60,705	....
Total for 45 States...	74,610,523	62,116,811	44,617

STATES AND TERRITORIES.	1900.	1890.	Indians not taxed, 1900.
TERRITORIES.			
Alaska.................	63,441	32,052	....
Arizona...............	122,931	59,620	24,644
District of Columbia..	278,718	230,392	....
Hawaii	154,001	89,990	....
Indian Territory......	391,960	180,182	56,033
New Mexico	195,310	153,593	2,937
Oklahoma	398,245	61,834	5,927
Total	1,604,606	807,663	89,541
Persons in the service of the United States stationed abroad....	89,670	....	....
Indians, etc.,on Indian reservations, except Indian Territory....	....	145,282	....

— *Report of the Director of the Census, Nov. 1, 1900.*

"By the twelfth census the center of population in 1900 was in the following position : Latitude 39° 9′ 36″ ; longitude 85° 48′ 54″. In ten years the center of population has moved westward 16′ 1″, or about fourteen miles, and southward 2′ 20″, or about two and one half miles. It rests now in Southern Indiana, at a point about six miles southeast of Columbus, the county seat of Bartholomew county, Indiana. The center of population is the center of gravity of the country, each individual being assumed to have the same weight. . . . The center of area of the United States, excluding Alaska and Hawaii and other recent accessions, is in northern Kansas, in approximate latitude 39° 55′, and approximate longitude 98° 50′. The center of population is therefore about three-fourths of a degree south and more than 13 degrees east of the center of area."—*United States, Twelfth Census, Bulletin No. 62.*

A. D. 1900 (May—November).—The Presidential election.—Party platforms and nominations.—The issues on which the presidential election of 1900 would naturally and logically have turned were those growing out of the Spanish-American War, relative to principles and policy in dealing with the colonial possessions that were taken from Spain. But circumstances forced those most important political questions into the background of consideration, so far as concerned the opinion of a large part of the American people. The monetary question, which might have been supposed to be settled by the election of 1896 and by the Congressional legislation of March, 1900, was brought forward again with a persistency that caused uneasy feeling in the commercial and industrial world. The party which had fought the battle for a silver monetary standard in 1896, and been beaten, seemed willing to abandon that "lost cause," but the candidate to whose fortunes the party had become commmitted would not consent. His will prevailed, and the old issue came into the canvass again, with such confusing effects that the real meaning of the votes that were cast, as an expression of the judgment and will of the American people, can by no possibility be known. Men dreaded a disturbance of the conditions under which the business of the country was active and prosperous. How far their wish to

preserve those conditions coincided, as a motive in voting, with their judgment on other issues, and how far it overcame dispositions that urged them contrariwise, are puzzling questions which the election of 1900 has left behind.

United Christian Party Platform and Nominations.—The first candidates to be set in the field of the presidential campaign were put forward by a convention held at Rock Island, Illinois, May 1, representing a small combination of voters styled the United Christian Party. It named, in the first instance, the Rev. S. C. Swallow, of Pennsylvania, for President, and John G. Woolley, of Illinois, for Vice President, both of whom declined the nomination. Jonah F. R. Leonard, of Iowa, and David H. Martin, of Pennsylvania, were subsequently made the candidates of the party, and received a few hundred votes at the ensuing election, mostly, it would seem, in Illinois. The "Declarations" of the United Christian Party were as follows :

"We, the United Christian party, in National Convention assembled in the city of Rock Island, Ill., May 1 and 2, 1900, acknowledging Almighty God as the source of all power and authority, the Lord Jesus Christ as the sovereign ruler of nations, and the Bible as the standard by which to decide moral issues in our political life, do make the following declaration :

"We believe the time to have arrived when the eternal principles of justice, mercy, and love, as exemplified in the life and teachings of Jesus Christ should be embodied in the Constitution of our nation, and applied in concrete form to every function of our Government.

"We maintain that this statement is in harmony with the fundamental principles of our National common law ; our Christian usages and customs; the declaration of the Supreme Court of the United States that 'This is a Christian nation,' and the accepted principle in judicial decisions that no law should contravene the Divine law.

"We deprecate certain immoral laws which have grown out of the failure of our nation to recognize these principles, notably such as require the desecration of the Christian Sabbath, authorize unscriptural marriage and divorce, and license the manufacture and sale of intoxicating liquors as a beverage.

"The execution of these immoral laws above mentioned we hold to be neither loyalty to our country nor honoring to God ; therefore it shall be our purpose to administer the Government, so far as it shall be intrusted to us by the suffrages of the people, in accordance with the principles herein set forth, and, until amended, our oath of office shall be to the Constitution and laws as herein explained, and to no other, and we will look to Him who has all power in Heaven and in earth to vindicate our purpose in seeking His glory and the welfare of our beloved land.

"As an expression of consent or allegiance on the part of the governed, in harmony with the above statements, we declare for the adoption and use of the system of legislation known as the 'initiative and referendum,' together with 'proportionate representation' and the 'imperative mandate.'

"We hold that all men and women are created free and with equal rights, and declare for the establishment of such political, industrial, and social conditions as shall guarantee to every person civic equality, the full fruits of his or her honest toil, and opportunity for the righteous enjoyment of the same; and we especially condemn mob violence and outrages against any individual or class of individuals in our country.

"We declare against war, and for the arbitration of all National and international disputes.

"We hold that the legalized liquor traffic is the crowning infamy of civilization, and we declare for the immediate abolition of the manufacture and sale of intoxicating liquors as a beverage.

"We are gratified to note the widespread agitation of the cigarette question, and declare ourselves in favor of the enactment of laws prohibiting the sale of cigarettes or tobacco in any form to minors.

"We declare for the daily reading of the Bible in the public schools and institutions of learning under control of the State.

"We declare for the Government ownership of public utilities.

"We declare for the election of the President and Vice-President and United States Senators by the direct vote of the people.

"We declare for such amendment of the United States Constitution as shall be necessary to give the principles herein set forth an undeniable legal basis in the fundamental law of our land.

"We invite into the United Christian party every honest man and woman who believes in Christ and His golden rule and standard of righteousness. We say especially to the sons of toil:. Jesus, the carpenter's son, is your true friend. In His name and through the practice of His principles you may obtain your rights long withheld and long outraged. You have the votes necessary to enthrone Him. His love and principles, politically applied, will lift you up and give you true civic liberty forever."

People's or Populist Party Platforms and Nominations.—The second of the political parties to appear in the field of the national contest was the People's, known more commonly as the Populist Party, the division in which, shown in 1896, had become separation, complete. The two wings of the party held distinct conventions, in different places, but on the same day, May 10. Those known as the Middle-of-the-Road Populists assembled at Cincinnati and named Wharton Barker, of Pennsylvania, for President, with Ignatius Donnelly, of Minnesota for Vice President. The convention representing those who wished to act in co-operation with the Democratic Party, and known as the Fusion wing, met at Sioux Falls, South Dakota, and anticipated the action of the Democracy by nominating William J. Bryan for President (see, also, in this vol., FARMERS' ALLIANCE), with Charles A. Towne, of Minnesota, for Vice President. The platform declarations of the two wings were substantially the same on main questions ; but those of the Fusionists covered several subjects which the Cincinnati convention passed by. They were as follows:

"The People's party of the United States, in convention assembled, congratulating its supporters on the wide extension of its principles in all directions, does hereby reaffirm its adherence to the fundamental principles proclaimed in its two prior platforms and calls upon all who desire to avert the subversion of free institutions by corporate and imperialistic power to unite with it in bringing the Government back to the

ideals of Washington, Jefferson, Jackson, and Lincoln. It extends to its allies in the struggle for financial and economic freedom, assurances of its loyalty to the principles which animate the allied forces and the promise of honest and hearty coöperation in every effort for their success. To the people of the United States we offer the following platform as the expression of our unalterable convictions:

"Resolved, That we denounce the act of March 14, 1900, as the culmination of a long series of conspiracies to deprive the people of their constitutional rights over the money of the nation and relegate to a gigantic money trust the control of the purse and hence of the people. We denounce this act, first, for making all money obligations, domestic and foreign, payable in gold coin or its equivalent, thus enormously increasing the burdens of the debtors and enriching the creditors. Second—For refunding 'coin bonds' not to mature for years into long-time gold bonds so as to make their payment improbable and our debt perpetual. Third—For taking from the Treasury over $50,000,000 in a time of war and presenting it, as a premium, to bondholders to accomplish the refunding of bonds not due. Fourth—For doubling the capital of bankers by returning to them the face value of their bonds in current money notes so that they may draw one interest from the Government and another from the people. Fifth—For allowing banks to expand and contract their circulation at pleasure, thus controlling prices of all products. Sixth—For authorizing the Secretary of the Treasury to issue new gold bonds to an unlimited amount whenever he deems it necessary to replenish the gold hoard, thus enabling usurers to secure more bonds and more bank currency by drawing gold from the Treasury, thereby creating an 'endless chain' for perpetually adding to a perpetual debt. Seventh—For striking down the greenback in order to force the people to borrow $346,000,000 more from the banks at an annual cost of over $20,000,000. While barring out the money of the Constitution this law opens the printing mints of the Treasury to the free coinage of bank paper money, to enrich the few and impoverish the many.

"We pledge anew the People's party never to cease the agitation until this great financial conspiracy is blotted from the statute books, the Lincoln greenback restored, the bonds all paid, and all corporation money forever retired. We affirm the demand for the reopening of the mints of the United States for the free and unlimited coinage of silver and gold at the present legal ratio of 16 to 1, the immediate increase in the volume of silver coins and certificates thus created to be substituted, dollar for dollar, for the banknotes issued by private corporations under special privilege granted by law of March 14, 1900, and prior National banking laws, the remaining portion of the banknotes to be replaced with full legal-tender Government paper money, and its volume so controlled as to maintain at all times a stable money market and a stable price level.

"We demand a graduated income and inheritance tax, to the end that aggregated wealth shall bear its just proportion of taxation.

"We demand that postal savings banks be established by the Government for the safe deposit of the savings of the people and to facilitate exchange.

"With Thomas Jefferson we declare the land, including all natural sources of wealth, the inalienable heritage of the people. Government should so act as to secure homes for the people and prevent land monopoly. The original homestead policy should be enforced, and future settlers upon the public domain should be entitled to a free homestead, while all who have paid an acreage price to the Government under existing laws should have their homestead rights restored.

"Transportation being a means of exchange and a public necessity, the Government should own and operate the railroads in the interests of the people and on a non-partisan basis, to the end that all may be accorded the same treatment in transportation, and that the extortion, tyranny, and political power now exercised by the great railroad corporations, which result in the impairment, if not the destruction, of the political rights and personal liberties of the citizen, may be destroyed. Such ownership is to be accomplished in a manner consistent with sound public policy.

"Trusts, the overshadowing evil of the age, are the result and culmination of the private ownership and control of the three great instruments of commerce—money, transportation, and the means of transmission of information—which instruments of commerce are public functions, and which our forefathers declared in the Constitution should be controlled by the people through their Congress for the public welfare. The one remedy for the trusts is that the ownership and control be assumed and exercised by the people. We further demand that all tariffs on goods controlled by a trust shall be abolished. To cope with the trust evil, the people must act directly without the intervention of representatives who may be controlled or influenced. We therefore demand direct legislation, giving the people the lawmaking and veto power under the initiative and referendum. A majority of the people can never be corruptly influenced.

"Applauding the valor of our army and navy in the Spanish war, we denounce the conduct of the Administration in changing a war for humanity into a war of conquest. The action of the Administration in the Philippines is in conflict with all the precedents of our National life; at war with the Declaration of Independence, the Constitution, and the plain precepts of humanity. Murder and arson have been our response to the appeals of the people who asked only to establish a free government in their own land. We demand a stoppage of this war of extermination by the assurance to the Philippines of independence and protection under a stable government of their own creation.

"The Declaration of Independence, the Constitution, and the American flag are one and inseparable. The island of Porto Rico is a part of the territory of the United States, and by levying special and extraordinary customs duties on the commerce of that island the Administration has violated the Constitution, abandoned the fundamental principles of American liberty, and has striven to give the lie to the contention of our forefathers that there should be no taxation without representation.

"Out of the imperialism which would force an undesired domination on the people of the Philippines springs the un-American cry for a large standing army. Nothing in the character or purposes of our people justifies us in ignoring the plain lesson of history and putting our liberties in jeopardy by assuming the burden of militarism, which is crushing the people of the Old World. We denounce the Administration for its sinister efforts to substitute a standing army for the citizen soldiery, which is the best safeguard of the Republic.

"We extend to the brave Boers of South Africa our sympathy and moral support in their patriotic struggle for the right of self-government, and we are unalterably opposed to any alliance, open or covert, between the United States and any other nation that will tend to the destruction of liberty.

"And a further manifestation of imperialism is to be found in the mining districts of Idaho. In the Cœur d'Alene soldiers have been used to overawe miners striving for a greater measure of industrial independence. And we denounce the State Government of Idaho and the Federal Government for employing the military arm of the Government to abridge the civil rights of the people, and to enforce an infamous permit system which denies to laborers their inherent liberty and compels them to forswear their manhood and their right before being permitted to seek employment.

"The importation of Japanese and other laborers under contract to serve monopolistic corporations is a notorious and flagrant violation of the immigration laws. We demand that the Federal Government shall take cognizance of this menacing evil and repress it under existing laws. We further pledge ourselves to strive for the enactment of more stringent laws for the exclusion of Mongolian and Malayan immigration.

"We indorse municipal ownership of public utilities, and declare that the advantages which have accrued to the public under that system would be multiplied a hundredfold by its extension to natural interstate monopolies.

"We denounce the practice of issuing injunctions in the cases of dispute between employers and employés, making criminal acts by organizations which are not criminal when performed by individuals, and demand legislation to restrain the evil.

"We demand that United States Senators and all other officials as far as practicable be elected by direct vote of the people, believing that the elective franchise and untrammelled ballot are essential to a government for and by the people.

"The People's party condemns the wholesale system of disfranchisement by coercion and intimidation, adopted in some States, as un-republican and un-democratic. And we declare it to be the duty of the several State Legislatures to take such action as will secure a full, free, and fair ballot, and an honest count.

"We favor home rule in the Territories and the District of Columbia, and the early admission of the Territories as States.

"We denounce the expensive red-tape system, political favoritism, cruel and unnecessary delay and criminal evasion of the statutes in the management of the Pension Office, and demand the simple and honest execution of the law, and the fulfilment by the nation of its pledges of service pension to all its honorably discharged veterans."

Socialist Labor Party Platform and Nominations.—The convention of the Populists was followed next by that of the Socialist Labor Party, which met in New York City, on the 2d of June, and put in nomination Joseph P. Maloney, of Massachusetts, and Valentine Remmel, of Pennsylvania. Its Platform was as follows:

"The Socialist Labor party of the United States, in convention assembled, reasserts the inalienable right of all men to life, liberty, and the pursuit of happiness.

"With the founders of the American Republic we hold that the purpose of government is to secure every citizen in the enjoyment of this right; but in the light of our social conditions we hold, furthermore, that no such right can be exercised under a system of economic inequality, essentially destructive of life, of liberty, and of happiness.

"With the founders of this Republic we hold that the true theory of politics is that the machinery of government must be owned and controlled by the whole people ; but in the light of our industrial development we hold, furthermore, that the true theory of economics is that the machinery of production must likewise belong to the people in common.

"To the obvious fact that our despotic system of economics is the direct opposite of our democratic system of politics can plainly be traced the existence of a privileged class, the corruption of government by that class, the alienation of public property, public franchises, and public functions to that class, and the abject dependence of the mightiest of nations upon that class.

"Again, through the perversion of democracy to the ends of plutocracy, labor is robbed of the wealth which it alone produces, is denied the means of self-employment, and, by compulsory idleness in wage slavery, is even deprived of the necessaries of life. Human power and natural forces are thus wasted, that the plutocracy may rule. Ignorance and misery, with all their concomitant evils, are perpetuated, that the people may be kept in bondage. Science and invention are diverted from their humane purpose to the enslavement of women and children.

"Against such a system the Socialist Labor party once more enters its protest. Once more it reiterates its fundamental declaration that private property in the natural sources of production and in the instruments of labor is the obvious cause of all economic servitude and political dependence.

"The time is fast coming when, in the natural course of social evolution, this system, through the destructive action of its failures and crises on the one hand, and the constructive tendencies of its trusts and other capitalistic combinations on the other hand, shall have worked out its own downfall.

"We, therefore, call upon the wage workers of the United States, and upon all other honest citizens, to organize under the banner of the Socialist Labor party into a class-conscious body, aware of its rights and determined to conquer them by taking possession of the public powers ; so that, held together by an indomitable spirit of solidarity under the most trying conditions of the present class struggle, we may put a summary end to that barbarous struggle by the abolition of classes, the restoration of the land and of all the means of production, transportation, and distribution to the people as a collective body, and the substitution of the Cooperative Commonwealth for the present state of planless production, industrial war, and social disorder— a commonwealth in which every worker shall have the free exercise and full benefit of his faculties, multiplied by all the modern factors of civilization."

Republican Party Platform and Nominations.—On the 19th of June the national convention of the Republican Party began its session at Philadelphia ; adopted its platform on the following day, and nominated President William McKinley for re-election on the 21st, naming Theodore Roosevelt, then Governor of New York, for Vice President, in opposition to his earnestly expressed wish. The adopted platform of principles was as follows:

"The Republicans of the United States, through their chosen representatives, met in National Convention, looking back upon an unsurpassed record of achievement and looking forward to a great field of duty and opportunity, and appealing to the judgment of their countrymen, make these declarations :

"The expectation in which the American people, turning from the Democratic party, intrusted power four years ago to a Republican Chief Magistrate and a Republican Congress, has been met and satisfied. When the people then assembled at the polls, after a term of Democratic legislation and administration, business was dead, industry paralyzed, and the National credit disastrously impaired. The country's capital was hidden away and its labor distressed and unemployed. The Democrats had no other plan with which to improve the ruinous conditions which they had themselves produced than to coin silver at the ratio of 16 to 1. The Republican Party, denouncing this plan as sure to produce conditions even worse than those from which relief was sought, promised to restore prosperity by means of two legislative measures—a protective tariff and a law making gold the standard of value.

"The people, by great majorities, issued to the Republican party a commission to enact these laws. This commission has been executed, and the Republican promise is redeemed. Prosperity more general and more abundant than we have ever known has followed these enactments. There is no longer controversy as to the value of any government obligations. Every American dollar is a gold dollar, or its assured equivalent, and American credit stands higher than that of any nation. Capital is fully employed, and labor everywhere is profitably occupied. No single fact can more strikingly tell the story of what Republican government means to the country than this—that while during the whole period of 107 years from 1790 to 1897 there was an excess of exports over imports of only $383,028,497, there has been in the short three years of the present Republican Administration an excess of exports over imports in the enormous sum of $1,483,537,094.

"And while the American people, sustained by this Republican legislation, have been achieving these splendid triumphs in their business and commerce, they have conducted and in victory concluded a war for liberty and human rights. No thought of National aggrandizement tarnished the high purpose with which American standards were unfurled. It was a war unsought and patiently resisted, but when it came the American Government was ready. Its fleets were cleared for action, its armies were in the field, and the quick and signal triumph of its forces on land and sea bore equal tribute to the courage of American soldiers and sailors and to the skill and foresight of Republican statesmanship. To ten millions of the human race there was given ' a new birth of freedom,' and to the American people a new and noble responsibility.

"We indorse the Administration of William McKinley. Its acts have been established in wisdom and in patriotism, and at home and abroad it has distinctly elevated and extended the influence of the American nation. Walking untried paths and facing unforeseen responsibilities, President McKinley has been in every situation the true American patriot and the upright statesman, clear in vision, strong in judgment, firm in action, always inspiring and deserving the confidence of his countrymen. In asking the American people to indorse this Republican record and to renew their commission to the Republican party, we remind them of the fact that the menace to their prosperity has always resided in Democratic principles, and no less in the general incapacity of the Democratic party to conduct public affairs. The prime essential of business prosperity is public confidence in the good sense of the Government, and in its ability to deal intelligently with each new problem of administration and legislation. That confidence the Democratic party has never earned. It is hopelessly inadequate, and the country's prosperity when Democratic success at the polls is announced halts and ceases in mere anticipation of Democratic blunders and failures.

" We renew our allegiance to the principle of the gold standard, and declare our confidence in the wisdom of the legislation of the Fifty-sixth Congress by which the parity of all our money and the stability of our currency upon a gold basis has been secured.

" We recognize that interest rates are potent factors in production and business activity, and for the purpose of further equalizing and of further lowering the rates of interest, we favor such monetary legislation as will enable the varying needs of the seasons and of all sections to be promptly met in order that trade may be evenly sustained, labor steadily employed, and commerce enlarged. The volume of money in circulation was never so great per capita as it is to-day.

" We declare our steadfast opposition to the free and unlimited coinage of silver. No measure to that end could be considered which was without the support of the leading commercial countries of the world. However firmly Republican legislation may seem to have secured the country against the peril of base and discredited currency, the election of a Democratic President could not fail to impair the country's credit and to bring once more into question the intention of the American people to maintain upon the gold standard the parity of their money circulation. The Democratic party must be convinced that the American people will never tolerate the Chicago platform.

" We recognize the necessity and propriety of the honest coöperation of capital to meet new business conditions, and especially to extend our rapidly increasing foreign trade, but we condemn all conspiracies and combinations intended to restrict business, to create monopolies, to limit production, or to control prices, and favor such legislation as will effectively restrain and prevent all such abuses, protect and promote competition, and secure the rights of producers, laborers, and all who are engaged in industry and commerce.

" We renew our faith in the policy of protection to American labor. In that policy our industries have been established, diversified, and maintained. By protecting the home market competition has been stimulated and production cheapened. Opportunity to the inventive genius of our people has been secured and wages in every department of labor maintained at high rates, higher now than ever before, and always distinguishing our working people in their better conditions of life from those of any competing country. Enjoying the blessings of the American common school, secure in the right of self-government, and protected in the occupancy of their own markets, their constantly increasing knowledge and skill have enabled them finally to enter the markets of the world.

" We favor the associated policy of reciprocity so directed as to open our markets on favorable terms for what we do not ourselves produce in return for free foreign markets.

" In the further interest of American workmen we favor a more effective restriction of the immigration of cheap labor from foreign lands, the extension of opportunities of education for working children, the raising of the age limit for child labor, the protection of free labor as against contract convict labor, and an effective system of labor insurance.

"Our present dependence upon foreign shipping for nine-tenths of our foreign carrying is a great loss to the industry of this country. It is also a serious danger to our trade, for its sudden withdrawal in the event of European war would seriously cripple our expanding foreign commerce. The National defence and naval efficiency of this country, moreover, supply a compelling reason for legislation which will enable us to recover our former place among the trade carrying fleets of the world.

"The nation owes a debt of profound gratitude to the soldiers and sailors who have fought its battles, and it is the Government's duty to provide for the survivors and for the widows and orphans of those who have fallen in the country's wars. The pension laws, founded in this just sentiment, should be liberal, and should be liberally administered, and preference should be given wherever practicable with respect to employment in the public service to soldiers and sailors and to their widows and orphans.

" We commend the policy of the Republican party in maintaining the efficiency of the Civil Service. The Administration has acted wisely in its effort to secure for public service in Cuba, Porto Rico, Hawaii and the Philippine Islands only those whose fitness has been determined by training and experience. We believe that employment in the public service in these territories should be confined as far as practicable to their inhabitants.

"It was the plain purpose of the Fifteenth Amendment to the Constitution to prevent discrimination on account of race or color in regulating the elective franchise. Devices of State governments, whether by statutory or constitutional enactment to avoid the purpose of this amendment are revolutionary and should be condemned.

"Public movements looking to a permanent improvement of the roads and highways of the country meet with our cordial approval and we recommend this subject to the earnest consideration of the people and of the Legislatures of the several States. We favor the extension of the rural free delivery service wherever its extension may be justified.

"In further pursuance of the constant policy of the Republican party to provide free homes on the public domain, we recommend adequate National legislation to reclaim the arid lands of the United States, reserving control of the distribution of water for irrigation to the respective States and Territories.

"We favor home rule for and the early admission to Statehood of the Territories of New Mexico, Arizona and Oklahoma.

"The Dingley act, amended to provide sufficient revenue for the conduct of the war, has so well performed its work that it has been possible to reduce the war debt in the sum of $40,000,000. So ample are the Government's revenues and so great is the public confidence in the integrity of its obligations that its newly funded 2 per cent bonds sell at a premium. The country is now justified in expecting, and it will be the policy of the Republican party to bring about, a reduction of the war taxes.

"We favor the construction, ownership, control and protection of an isthmian canal by the Government of the United States.

"New markets are necessary for the increasing surplus of our farm products. Every effort should be made to open and obtain new markets, especially in the Orient, and the Administration is warmly to be commended for its successful effort to commit all trading and colonizing nations to the policy of the open door in China.

"In the interest of our expanding commerce we recommend that Congress create a department of commerce and industries in the charge of a secretary with a seat in the Cabinet. The United States consular system should be reorganized under the supervision of this new department, upon such a basis of appointment and tenure as will render it still more serviceable to the Nation's increasing trade. The American Government must protect the person and property of every citizen wherever they are wrongfully violated or placed in peril.

"We congratulate the women of America upon their splendid record of public service in the volunteer aid association, and as nurses in camp and hospital during the recent campaigns of our armies in the Eastern and Western Indies, and we appreciate their faithful co-operation in all works of education and industry.

"President McKinley has conducted the foreign affairs of the United States with distinguished credit to the American people. In releasing us from the vexatious conditions of a European alliance for the government of Samoa his course is especially to be commended. By securing to our undivided control the most important island of the Samoan group and the best harbor in the Southern Pacific, every American interest has been safeguarded. We approve the annexation of the Hawaiian Islands to the

United States. We commend the part taken by our Government in the Peace Conference at The Hague. We assert our steadfast adherence to the policy announced in the Monroe Doctrine. The provisions of The Hague Convention were wisely regarded when President McKinley tendered his friendly offices in the interest of peace between Great Britain and the South African republics. While the American Government must continue the policy prescribed by Washington, affirmed by every succeeding President and imposed upon us by The Hague Treaty, of nonintervention in European controversies, the American people earnestly hope that a way may soon be found, honorable alike to both contending parties, to terminate the strife between them.

"In accepting by the Treaty of Paris the just responsibility of our victories in the Spanish war the President and the Senate won the undoubted approval of the American people. No other course was possible than to destroy Spain's sovereignty throughout the West Indies and in the Philippine Islands. That course created our responsibility before the world, and with the unorganized population whom our intervention had freed from Spain, to provide for the maintenance of law and order, and for the establishment of good government and for the performance of international obligations. Our authority could not be less than our responsibility, and wherever sovereign rights were extended it became the high duty of the Government to maintain its authority, to put down armed insurrection and to confer the blessings of liberty and civilization upon all the rescued peoples. The largest measure of self-government consistent with their welfare and our duties shall be secured to them by law.

"To Cuba independence and self-government were assured in the same voice by which war was declared, and to the letter this pledge will be performed.

"The Republican party upon its history, and upon this declaration of its principles and policies, confidently invokes the considerate and approving judgment of the American people."

Prohibition Party Platform and Nominations.—In the next week after the meeting of the Republican national convention, that of the Prohibition Party was held at Chicago, opening on the 27th of June. It chose Mr. John G. Woolley, of Chicago (already named by the United Christian Party for Vice President—see above) to be its candidate for President, with Mr. Henry B. Metcalfe, of Rhode Island, for Vice President. Setting aside all political issues save those connected with the liquor traffic, its declarations were confined to that subject alone, and were as follows:

"The National Prohibition party, in convention represented at Chicago, June 27 and 28, 1900, acknowledged Almighty God as the supreme source of all just government. Realizing that this Republic was founded upon Christian principles, and can endure only as it embodies justice and righteousness, and asserting that all authority should seek the best good of all the governed, to this end wisely prohibiting what is wrong and permitting only what is right, hereby records and proclaims:

"First.—We accept and assert the definition given by Edward Burke, that a party is 'a body of men joined together for the purpose of proteeting by their joint endeavor the National interest upon some particular principle upon which they are all agreed.'

"We declare that there is no principle now advocated, by any other party, which could be made a fact in government with such beneficent moral and material results as the principle of prohibition applied to the beverage liquor traffic ; that the National interest could be promoted in no other way so surely and widely as by its adoption and assertion through a National policy and a coöperation therein by every State, forbidding the manufacture, sale, exportation, importation, and transportation of intoxicating liquors for beverage purposes ; that we stand for this as the only principle proposed by any party anywhere for the settlement of a question greater and graver than any other before the American people, and involving more profoundly than any other their moral future and financial welfare; and that all the patriotic citizenship of this country agreed upon this principle, however much disagreement there may be as to minor considerations and issues, should stand together at the ballot-box from this time forward until prohibition is the established policy of the United States, with a party in power to enforce it and to insure its moral and material benefits.

"We insist that such a party agreed upon this principle and policy, having sober leadership, without any obligation for success to the saloon vote and to those demoralizing political combinations, can successfully cope with all other and lesser problems of government, in legislative halls and in the executive chair, and that it is useless for any party to make declarations in its platform as to any questions concerning which there may be serious differences of opinion in its own membership and as to which, because of such differences, the party could legislate only on a basis of mutual concessions when coming into power.

"We submit that the Democratic and Republican parties are alike insincere in their assumed hostility to trusts and monopolies. They dare not and do not attack the most dangerous of them all, the liquor power. So long as the saloon debauches the citizen and breeds the purchasable voter, money will continue to buy its way to power. Break down this traffic, elevate manhood, and a sober citizenship will find a way to control dangerous combinations of capital. We purpose, as a first step in the financial problem of the nation, to save more than a billion of dollars every year, now annually expended to support the liquor traffic and to demoralize our people. When that is accomplished, conditions will have so improved that with a clearer atmosphere the country can address itself to the questions as to the kind and quantity of currency needed.

"Second.—We reaffirm as true indisputably the declaration of William Windom, when Secretary of the Treasury in the Cabinet of President Arthur, that 'considered socially, financially, politically, or morally, the licensed liquor traffic is or ought to be the overwhelming issue in American politics, and that the destruction of this iniquity stands next on the calendar of the world's progress.' We hold that the existence of our party presents this issue squarely to the American people, and lays upon them the responsibility of choice between liquor parties,

dominated by distillers and brewers, with their policy of saloon perpetuation breeding waste, wickedness, woe, pauperism, taxation, corruption, and crime, and our one party of patriotic and moral principle, with a policy which defends it from domination by corrupt bosses, and which insures it forever against the blighting control of saloon politics.

"We face with sorrow, shame, and fear the awful fact that this liquor traffic has a grip on our Government, municipal, State, and National, through the revenue system and a saloon sovereignty, which no other party dare to dispute ; a grip which dominates the party now in power, from caucus to Congress, from policemen to President, from the rum shop to the White House; a grip which compels the Executive to consent that law shall be nullified in behalf of the brewer, that the canteen shall curse our army and spread intemperance across the seas, and that our flag shall wave as the symbol of partnership, at home and abroad, between this Government and the men who defy and defile it for their unholy gain.

"Third.—We charge upon President McKinley, who was elected to his high office by appeal to Christian sentiment and patriotism almost unprecedented and by a combination of moral influences never before seen in this country, that by his conspicuous example as a wine-drinker at public banquets and as a wine-serving host in the White House, he has done more to encourage the liquor business, to demoralize the temperance habits of young men, and to bring Christian practices and requirements into disrepute than any other President this Republic has had.

"We further charge upon President McKinley responsibility for the Army canteen, with all its dire brood of disease, immorality, sin and death, in this country, in Cuba, in Porto Rico and the Philippines ; and we insist that by his attitude concerning the canteen, and his apparent contempt for the vast number of petitions and petitioners protesting against it, he has outraged and insulted the moral sentiment of this country in such a manner and to such a degree as calls for its righteous uprising and his indignant and effective rebuke. We challenge denial of the fact that our Chief Executive, as commander in chief of the military forces of the United States, at any time prior to or since March 2, 1899, could have closed every Army saloon, called a canteen, by executive order, as President Hayes in effect did before him, and should have closed them, for the same reason that actuated President Hayes; we assert that the act of Congress passed March 2, 1899, forbidding the sale of liquor, 'in any post exchange or canteen,' by any 'officer or private soldier' or by 'any other person on any premises used for military purposes in the United States,' was and is as explicit an act of prohibition as the English language can frame; we declare our solemn belief that the Attorney-General of the United States in his interpretation of that law, and the Secretary of War in his acceptance of that interpretation and his refusal to enforce the law, were and are guilty of treasonable nullification thereof, and that President McKinley, through his assent to and indorsement of such interpretation and refusal on the part of officials appointed by and responsible to him, shares responsibility in their guilt; and we record our conviction that a new and serious peril confronts our country, in the fact that its President, at the behest of the beer power, dare and does abrogate a law of Congress, through subordinates removable at will by him and whose acts become his, and thus virtually confesses that laws are to be administered or to be nullified in the interest of a law-defying business, by an Administration under mortgage to such business for support.

"Fourth.—We deplore the fact that an Administration of this Republic claiming the right and power to carry our flag across seas, and to conquer and annex new territory, should admit its lack of power to prohibit the American saloon on subjugated soil, or should openly confess itself subject to liquor sovereignty under that flag. We are humiliated, exasperated and grieved by the evidence painfully abundant that this Administration's policy of expansion is bearing so rapidly its first fruits of drunkenness, insanity and crime under the hothouse sun of the tropics; and when the president of the first Philippine Commission says 'It was unfortunate that we introduced and established the saloon there, to corrupt the natives and to exhibit the vices of our race,' we charge the inhumanity and un-Christianity of this act upon the Administration of William McKinley and upon the party which elected and would perpetuate the same.

"Fifth.—We declare that the only policy which the Government of the United States can of right uphold as to the liquor traffic under the National Constitution upon any territory under the military or civil control of that Government is the policy of prohibition; that 'to establish justice, insure domestic tranquillity, provide for the common defence, promote the general welfare, and insure the blessings of liberty to ourselves and our posterity,' as the Constitution provides, the liquor traffic must neither be sanctioned nor tolerated, and that the revenue policy, which makes our Government a partner with distillers and brewers and barkeepers, is a disgrace to our civilization, an outrage upon humanity, and a crime against God.

"We condemn the present Administration at Washington because it has repealed the prohibitory law in Alaska, and has given over the partly civilized tribes there to be the prey of the American grogshop, and because it has entered upon a license policy in our new possessions by incorporating the same in the revenue act of Congress in the code of laws for the government of the Hawaiian Islands.

"We call general attention to the fearful fact that exportation of liquors from the United States to the Philippine Islands increased from $337 in 1898 to $167,198 in the first ten months of the fiscal year ended June 30, 1900; and that while our exportations of liquor to Cuba never reached $30,000 a year previous to American occupation of that island, our exports of such liquors to Cuba during the fiscal year of 1899 reached the sum of $629,655.

"Sixth.—One great religious body (the Baptist) having truly declared of the liquor traffic 'that it has no defensible right to exist, that it can never be reformed, that it stands condemned by its unrighteous fruits as a thing unchristian, un-American, and perilous utterly to every interest in life'; another great religious body (the Methodist) having as truly asserted and reiterated that 'no political party has the right to expect, nor should it receive, the votes of Chris-

tian men so long as it stands committed to the license system or refuses to put itself on record in an attitude of open hostility to the saloons'; other great religious bodies having made similar deliverances, in language plain and unequivocal, as to the liquor traffic and the duty of Christian citizenship in opposition thereto, and the fact being plain and undeniable that the Democratic party stands for license, the saloon, and the canteen, while the Republican party, in policy and administration, stands for the canteen, the saloon, and revenue therefrom, we declare ourselves justified in expecting that Christian voters everywhere shall cease their complicity with the liquor curse by refusing to uphold a liquor party, and shall unite themselves with the only party which upholds the prohibition policy, and which for nearly thirty years has been the faithful defender of the church, the State, the home, and the school against the saloon, its expanders and perpetuators, their actual and persistent foes.

"We insist that no differences of belief, as to any other question or concern of government, should stand in the way of such a union of moral and Christian citizenship as we hereby invite for the speedy settlement of this paramount moral, industrial, financial, and political issue which our party presents; and we refrain from declaring ourselves upon all minor matters as to which differences of opinion may exist that hereby we may offer to the American people a platform so broad that all can stand upon it who desire to see sober citizenship actually sovereign over the allied hosts of evil, sin, and crime in a government of the people, by the people, and for the people.

"We declare that there are but two real parties to-day concerning the liquor traffic—Perpetuationists and Prohibitionists—and that patriotism, Christianity, and every interest of genuine republicanism and of pure democracy, besides the loyal demands of our common humanity, require the speedy union, in one solid phalanx at the ballot-box, of all who oppose the liquor traffic's perpetuation, and who covet endurance for this Republic."

Democratic Party Platform and Nominations.—The delegates of the Democratic Party met in national convention at Kansas City, on the Fourth of July. By unanimous vote, on the following day, they again nominated William J. Bryan, of Nebraska, for President, and subsequently associated with him ex-Vice President Adlai E. Stevenson, of Illinois, for Vice President. The platform, adopted on the same day, reiterating the demand of 1896 for a free and unlimited coinage of silver at the ratio of 16 to 1, but emphasizing the question of colonial expansion as the "paramount issue of the campaign," was as follows: "We, the representatives of the Democratic party of the United States, assembled in national convention on the anniversary of the adoption of the Declaration of Independence, do reaffirm our faith in that immortal proclamation of the inalienable rights of man, and our allegiance to the constitution framed in harmony therewith by the fathers of the Republic. We hold with the United States Supreme Court that the Declaration of Independence is the spirit of our government, of which the constitution is the form and letter. We declare again that all governments instituted among men derive their just powers from the consent of the governed; that any government not based upon the consent of the governed is a tyranny; and that to impose upon any people a government of force is to substitute the methods of imperialism for those of a republic. We hold that the constitution follows the flag and denounce the doctrine that an executive or congress, deriving their existence and their powers from the constitution, can exercise lawful authority beyond it, or in violation of it. We assert that no nation can long endure half republic and half empire, and we warn the American people that imperialism abroad will lead quickly and inevitably to despotism at home.

"Believing in these fundamental principles, we denounce the Porto Rico law, enacted by a Republican Congress against the protest and opposition of the Democratic minority, as a bold and open violation of the Nation's organic law and a flagrant breach of National good faith It imposes upon the people of Porto Rico a government without their consent, and taxation without representation. It dishonors the American people by repudiating a solemn pledge made in their behalf by the commanding general of our Army, which the Porto Ricans welcomed to a peaceful and unresisted occupation of their land. It dooms to poverty and distress a people whose helplessness appeals with peculiar force to our justice and magnanimity. In this, the first act of its imperialistic programme, the Republican party seeks to commit the United States to a colonial policy inconsistent with republican institutions and condemned by the Supreme Court in numerous decisions.

"We demand the prompt and honest fulfilment of our pledge to the Cuban people and the world, that the United States has no disposition nor intention to exercise sovereignty, jurisdiction, or control over the island of Cuba, except for its pacification. The war ended nearly two years ago, profound peace reigns over all the island, and still the Administration keeps the government of the island from its people, while Republican carpetbag officials plunder its revenue and exploit the colonial theory to the disgrace of the American people.

"We condemn and denounce the Philippine policy of the present Administration. It has embroiled the Republic in an unnecessary war, sacrificed the lives of many of its noblest sons, and placed the United States, previously known and applauded throughout the world as the champion of freedom, in the false and un-American position of crushing with military force the efforts of our former allies to achieve liberty and self-government. The Filipinos cannot be citizens without endangering our civilization; they cannot be subjects without imperilling our form of government; and as we are not willing to surrender our civilization, or to convert the Republic into an empire, we favor an immediate declaration of the Nation's purpose to give to the Filipinos, first, a stable form of government; second, independence; and third, protection from outside interference such as has been given for nearly a century to the republics of Central and South America. The greedy commercialism which dictated the Philippine policy of the Republican Administration attempts to justify it with the plea that it will pay, but even this sordid and unworthy plea fails when brought to

the test of facts. The war of 'criminal aggression' against the Filipinos, entailing an annual expense of many millions, has already cost more than any possible profit that could accrue from the entire Philippine trade for years to come. Furthermore, when trade is extended at the expense of liberty the price is always too high.

"We are not opposed to territorial expansion, when it takes in desirable territory which can be erected into States in the Union, and whose people are willing and fit to become American citizens. We favor trade expansion by every peaceful and legitimate means. But we are unalterably opposed to the seizing or purchasing of distant islands to be governed outside the Constitution and whose people can never become citizens. We are in favor of extending the Republic's influence among the nations, but believe that influence should be extended not by force and violence, but through the persuasive power of a high and honorable example.

"The importance of other questions now pending before the American people is in nowise diminished and the Democratic party takes no backward step from its position on them; but the burning issue of imperialism, growing out of the Spanish war, involving the very existence of the Republic and the destruction of our free institutions, we regard as the paramount issue of the campaign.

"The declaration of the Republican platform adopted at the Philadelphia Convention, held in June, 1900, that the Republican party 'steadfastly adheres to the policy announced in the Monroe Doctrine,' is manifestly insincere and deceptive. This profession is contradicted by the avowed policy of that party, in opposition to the spirit of the Monroe Doctrine, to acquire and hold sovereignty over large areas of territory and large numbers of people in the Eastern Hemisphere. We insist on the strict maintenance of the Monroe Doctrine in all its integrity, both in letter and in spirit, as necessary to prevent the extension of European authority on these continents and as essential to our supremacy in American affairs. At the same time we declare that no American people shall ever be held by force in unwilling subjection to European authority.

"We oppose militarism. It means conquest abroad and intimidation and oppression at home. It means the strong arm which has ever been fatal to free institutions. It is what millions of our citizens have fled from in Europe. It will impose upon our peace loving people a large standing army, an unnecessary burden of taxation, and would be a constant menace to their liberties. A small standing army and a well disciplined State militia are amply sufficient in time of peace. This Republic has no place for a vast military establishment, a sure forerunner of compulsory military service and conscription. When the Nation is in danger the volunteer soldier is his country's best defender. The National Guard of the United States should ever be cherished in the patriotic hearts of a free people. Such organizations are ever an element of strength and safety. For the first time in our history and coeval with the Philippine conquest has there been a wholesale departure from our time honored and approved system of volunteer organization. We denounce it as un-American, undemocratic and unrepublican and as a subversion of the ancient and fixed principles of a free people.

"Private monopolies are indefensible and intolerable. They destroy competition, control the price of raw material and of the finished product, thus robbing both producer and consumer. They lessen the employment of labor and arbitrarily fix the terms and conditions thereof; and deprive individual energy and small capital of their opportunity for betterment. They are the most efficient means yet devised for appropriating the fruits of industry to the benefit of the few at the expense of the many, and, unless their insatiate greed is checked, all wealth will be aggregated in a few hands and the Republic destroyed. The dishonest paltering with the trust evil by the Republican party in its State and National platforms is conclusive proof of the truth of the charge that trusts are the legitimate product of Republican policies, that they are fostered by Republican laws, and that they are protected by the Republican Administration in return for campaign subscriptions and political support. We pledge the Democratic party to an unceasing warfare in Nation, State and city against private monopoly in every form. Existing laws against trusts must be enforced and more stringent ones must be enacted providing for publicity as to the affairs of corporations engaged in interstate commerce and requiring all corporations to show, before doing business outside of the State of their origin, that they have no water in their stock, and that they have not attempted and are not attempting to monopolize any branch of business or the production of any articles of merchandise; and the whole constitutional power of Congress over interstate commerce, the mails and all modes of interstate communication shall be exercised by the enactment of comprehensive laws upon the subject of trusts.

"Tariff laws should be amended by putting the products of trusts upon the free list, to prevent monopoly under the plea of protection. The failure of the present Republican Administration, with an absolute control over all the branches of the National Government, to enact any legislation designed to prevent or even curtail the absorbing power of trusts and illegal combinations, or to enforce the anti-trust laws already on the statute books, proves the insincerity of the high sounding phrases of the Republican platform. Corporations should be protected in all their rights and their legitimate interests should be respected, but any attempt by corporations to interfere with the public affairs of the people or to control the sovereignty which creates them should be forbidden under such penalties as will make such attempts impossible. We condemn the Dingley tariff law as a trust breeding measure skilfully devised to give to the few favors which they do not deserve, and to place upon the many burdens which they should not bear. We favor such an enlargement of the scope of the Interstate Commerce law as will enable the Commission to protect individuals and communities from discrimination and the public from unjust and unfair transportation rates.

"We reaffirm and indorse the principles of the National Democratic platform adopted at Chicago in 1896 and we reiterate the demand of that platform for an American financial system made by the American people for themselves, which

shall restore and maintain a bimetallic price level, and as part of such system the immediate restoration of the free and unlimited coinage of silver and gold at the present legal ratio of 16 to 1, without waiting for the aid or consent of any other nation.

"We denounce the currency bill enacted at the last session of Congress as a step forward in the Republican policy which aims to discredit the sovereign right of the National Government to issue all money, whether coin or paper, and to bestow upon National banks the power to issue and control the volume of paper money for their own benefit. A permanent National bank currency, secured by Government bonds, must have a permanent debt to rest upon, and, if the bank currency is to increase with population and business, the debt must also increase. The Republican currency scheme is, therefore, a scheme for fastening upon the taxpayers a perpetual and growing debt for the benefit of the banks. We are opposed to this private corporation paper circulated as money, but without legal tender qualities, and demand the retirement of National bank notes as fast as Government paper or silver certificates can be substituted for them. We favor an amendment to the Federal Constitution providing for the election of United States Senators by direct vote of the people, and we favor direct legislation wherever practicable. We are opposed to government by injunction; we denounce the blacklist, and favor arbitration as a means of settling disputes between corporations and their employés.

"In the interest of American labor and the upbuilding of the workingman as the cornerstone of the prosperity of our country, we recommend that Congress create a Department of Labor, in charge of a Secretary, with a seat in the Cabinet, believing that the elevation of the American laborer will bring with it increased production and increased prosperity to our country at home and to our commerce abroad. We are proud of the courage and fidelity of the American soldiers and sailors in all our wars; we favor liberal pensions to them and their dependents; and we reiterate the position taken in the Chicago platform in 1896, that the fact of enlistment and service shall be deemed conclusive evidence against disease and disability before enlistment.

"We favor the immediate construction, ownership and control of the Nicaraguan canal by the United States, and we denounce the insincerity of the plank in the Republican national platform for an Isthmian canal, in the face of the failure of the Republican majority to pass the bill pending in Congress.

"We condemn the Hay-Pauncefote treaty as a surrender of American rights and interests, not to be tolerated by the American people.

"We denounce the failure of the Republican party to carry out its pledges to grant statehood to the territories of Arizona, New Mexico and Oklahoma, and we promise the people of those territories immediate statehood, and home rule during their condition as territories; and we favor home rule and a territorial form of government for Alaska and Porto Rico.

"We favor an intelligent system of improving the arid lands of the West, storing the waters for the purposes of irrigation, and the holding of such lands for actual settlers.

"We favor the continuance and strict enforce-

ment of the Chinese exclusion law and its application to the same classes of all Asiatic races.

"Jefferson said : ' Peace, commerce and honest
friendship with all nations, entangling alliances
with none.' We approve this wholesome doctrine and earnestly protest against the Republican departure which has involved us in so-called
world politics, including the diplomacy of Europe and the intrigue and land-grabbing in Asia,
and we especially condemn the ill-concealed Republican alliance with England, which must
mean discrimination against other friendly nations, and which has already stifled the nation's
voice while liberty is being strangled in Africa.

"Believing in the principles of self-government and rejecting, as did our forefathers, the
claims of monarchy, we view with indignation
the purpose of England to overwhelm with force
the South African Republics. Speaking, as we
believe, for the entire American nation, except
its Republican officeholders, and for all free men
everywhere, we extend our sympathy to the
heroic Burghers in their unequal struggle to
maintain their liberty and independence.

"We denounce the lavish appropriations of
recent Republican congresses, which have kept
taxes high and which threaten the perpetuation
of the oppressive war levies. We oppose the
accumulation of a surplus to be squandered in
such barefaced frauds upon the taxpayers as the
shipping subsidy bill, which, under the false
pretense of fostering American ship-building,
would put unearned millions into the pockets of
favorite contributors to the Republican campaign
fund.

"We favor the reduction and speedy repeal of
the war taxes, and a return to the time-honored
Democratic policy of strict economy in governmental expenditures.

"Believing that our most cherished institutions
are in great peril, that the very existence of our
constitutional Republic is at stake, and that the
decision now to be rendered will determine
whether or not our children are to enjoy those
blessed privileges of free government which have
made the United States great, prosperous and
honored, we earnestly ask for the foregoing declaration of principles the hearty support of the
liberty-loving American people, regardless of
previous party affiliations."

Silver Republican Platform and Nominations.—The Republicans who broke from their
party in 1896 on the silver question, and supported Mr. Bryan for the presidency, were still
in affiliation with him and his party, but preserving a distinct organization, assuming the name
of Lincoln Republicans. Simultaneously with
that of the Democrats (July 6), they held a convention at Kansas City, and named Mr. Bryan as
their candidate for President. The nomination
for Vice President was referred to the national
committee, which ultimately placed Mr. Stevenson's name on the Silver Republican ticket.
The platform adopted differed little in leading
principles from that of the Democratic party,
except in the greater emphasis put on the monetary doctrines that were common to both. It
was as follows:

"We, the Silver Republican party, in National
Convention assembled, declare these as our principles and invite the coöperation of all who
agree therewith:

"We recognize that the principles set forth in

the Declaration of Independence are fundamental
and everlastingly true in their applications of
governments among men. We believe the patriotic words of Washington's farewell to be the
words of soberness and wisdom, inspired by the
spirit of right and truth. We treasure the words
of Jefferson as priceless gems of American statesmanship.

"We hold in sacred remembrance the broad
philanthropy and patriotism of Lincoln, who
was the great interpreter of American history
and the great apostle of human rights and of industrial freedom, and we declare, as was declared
by the convention that nominated the great
emancipator, that the maintenance of the principles promulgated in the Declaration of Independence and embodied in the Federal Constitution,
' that all men are created equal ; that they are
endowed by their Creator with certain inalienable rights ; that among these are life, liberty,
and the pursuit of happiness ; that to secure these
rights governments are instituted among men,
deriving their just powers from the consent of
the governed,' is essential to the preservation of
our republican institutions.

"We declare our adherence to the principle of
bimetallism as the right basis of a monetary
system under our National Constitution, a prin-
cipic that found place repeatedly in Republican
platforms from the demonetization of silver in
1873 to the St. Louis Republican Convention of
1896. Since that convention a Republican Congress and a Republican President, at the dictation of the trusts and money power, have passed
and approved a currency bill which in itself is a
repudiation of the doctrine of bimetallism advocated theretofore by the President and every
great leader of his party.

"This currency law destroys the full money
power of the silver dollar, provides for the payment of all government obligations and the redemption of all forms of paper money in gold
alone ; retires the time-honored and patriotic
greenbacks, constituting one-sixth of the money
in circulation, and surrenders to banking corporations a sovereign function of issuing all paper
money, thus enabling these corporations to control the prices of labor and property by increasing or diminishing the volume of money in circulation, thus giving the banks power to create
panics and bring disaster upon business enterprises. The provisions of this currency law
making the bonded debt of the Republic payable
in gold alone change the contract between the
Government and the bondholders to the advantage of the latter, and is in direct opposition
to the declaration of the Matthews resolution
passed by Congress in 1878, for which resolution the present Republican President, then a
member of Congress, voted, as did also all leading Republicans, both in the House and Senate.
We declare it to be our intention to lend our
efforts to the repeal of this currency law, which
not only repudiates the ancient and time-honored principles of the American people before the
Constitution was adopted, but is violative of the
principles of the Constitution itself, and we shall
not cease our efforts until there has been established in its place a monetary system based upon
the free and unlimited coinage of silver and
gold into money at the present legal ratio of 16
to 1 by the independent action of the United
States, under which system all paper money shall

be issued by the Government and all such money coined or issued shall be a full legal tender in payment of all debts, public and private, without exception.

"We are in favor of a graduated tax upon incomes, and if necessary to accomplish this we favor an amendment to the Constitution.

"We believe that United States Senators ought to be elected by direct vote of the people, and we favor such amendment of the Constitution and such legislation as may be necessary to that end.

"We favor the maintenance and the extension wherever practicable of the merit system in the public service, appointments to be made according to fitness, competitively ascertained, and public servants to be retained in office only so long as shall be compatible with the efficiency of the service.

"Combinations, trusts, and monopolies contrived and arranged for the purpose of controlling the prices and quantity of articles supplied to the public are unjust, unlawful, and oppressive. Not only do these unlawful conspiracies fix the prices of commodities in many cases, but they invade every branch of the State and National Government with their polluting influence and control the actions of their employés and dependents in private life until their influence actually imperils society and the liberty of the citizen. We declare against them. We demand the most stringent laws for their destruction and the most severe punishment of their promoters and maintainers and the energetic enforcement of such laws by the courts.

"We believe the Monroe doctrine to be sound in principle and a wise National policy, and we demand a firm adherence thereto. We condemn acts inconsistent with it and that tend to make us parties to the interests and to involve us in the controversies of European nations and to recognition by pending treaty of the right of England to be considered in the construction of an interoceanic canal. We declare that such canal, when constructed, ought to be controlled by the United States in the interests of American nations.

"We observe with anxiety and regard with disapproval the increasing ownership of American lands by aliens and their growing control over our international transportation, natural resources, and public utilities. We demand legislation to protect our public domain, our natural resources, our franchises, and our internal commerce and to keep them free and maintain their independence of all foreign monopolies, institutions, and influences, and we declare our opposition to the leasing of the public lands of the United States whereby corporations and syndicates will be able to secure control thereof and thus monopolize the public domain, the heritage of the people.

"We are in favor of the principles of direct legislation. In view of the great sacrifice made and patriotic services rendered we are in favor of liberal pensions to deserving soldiers, their widows, orphans, and other dependents. We believe that enlistment and service should be accepted as conclusive proof that the soldier was free from disease and disability at the time of his enlistment. We condemn the present administration of the pension laws.

"We tender to the patriotic people of the South African Republics our sympathy and ex-

press our admiration for them in their heroic attempts to preserve their political freedom and maintain their national independence. We declare the destruction of these republics and the subjugation of their people to be a crime against civilization. We believe this sympathy should have been voiced by the American Congress, as was done in the case of the French, the Greeks, the Hungarians, the Poles, the Armenians, and the Cubans, and as the traditions of this country would have dictated. We declare the Porto Rican Tariff law to be not only a serious but a dangerous departure from the principles of our form of government. We believe in a republican form of government and are opposed to monarchy and to the whole theory of imperialistic control.

"We believe in self-government—a government by the consent of the governed—and are unalterably opposed to a government based upon force. It is clear and certain that the inhabitants of the Philippine Archipelago cannot be made citizens of the United States without endangering our civilization. We are, therefore, in favor of applying to the Philippine Archipelago the principle we are solemnly and publicly pledged to observe in the case of Cuba.

"There no longer being any necessity for collecting war taxes, we demand the repeal of the war taxes levied to carry on the war with Spain.

"We favor the immediate admission into the union of States the Territories of Arizona, New Mexico, and Oklahoma.

"We demand that our nation's promises to Cuba shall be fulfilled in every particular.

"We believe the National Government should lend every aid, encouragement, and assistance toward the reclamation of the arid lands of the United States, and to that end we are in favor of a comprehensive survey thereof and an immediate ascertainment of the water supply available for such reclamation, and we believe it to be the duty of the General Government to provide for the construction of storage reservoirs and irrigation works so that the water supply of the arid region may be utilized to the greatest possible extent in the interests of the people, while preserving all rights of the State.

"Transportation is a public necessity and the means and methods of it are matters of public concern. Railway companies exercise a power over industries, business, and commerce which they ought not to do, and should be made to serve the public interests without making unreasonable charges or unjust discriminations.

"We observe with satisfaction the growing sentiment among the people in favor of the public ownership and operation of public utilities.

"We are in favor of expanding our commerce in the interests of American labor, and to the benefit of all our people by every honest and peaceful means. Our creed and our history justify the nations of the earth in expecting that wherever the American flag is unfurled in authority human liberty and political liberty will be found. We protest against the adoption of any policy that will change in the thought of the world the meaning of our flag.

"We are opposed to the importation of Asiatic laborers in competition with American labor, and favor a more rigid enforcement of the laws relating thereto.

"The Silver Republican party of the United States, in the foregoing principles, seeks to perpetuate the spirit and to adhere to the teachings of Abraham Lincoln."

Platform of the American League of Anti-Imperialists.—Republicans and others opposed to a policy of conquest, and to the government of people, not as citizens, but as subjects of the Republic of the United States, and who wished to make that opposition distinct and emphatic in the presidential canvass, met in convention at Indianapolis, on the 16th of August, as the "Liberty Congress of the American League of Anti-Imperialists." One party among them thought the best demonstration of public opinion on this issue could be obtained by the nomination of a third ticket; while another and larger party deemed it expedient to indorse the candidacy of William J. Bryan, as a pronounced opponent of the imperial policy. The views of the latter prevailed, and the indorsement of Mr. Bryan was carried in the convention; but many of the former refused submission to the vote of the majority, and subsequently held a Third Party convention at New York (see below). The Indianapolis Declaration was as follows:

"This Liberty Congress of Anti-Imperialists recognizes a great National crisis, which menaces the Republic, upon whose future depends in such large measure the hope of freedom throughout the world. For the first time in our country's history the President has undertaken to subjugate a foreign people and to rule them by despotic power. He has thrown the protection of the flag over slavery and polygamy in the Sulu Islands. He has arrogated to himself the power to impose upon the inhabitants of the Philippines government without their consent and taxation without representation. He is waging war upon them for asserting the very principles for the maintenance of which our forefathers pledged their lives, their fortunes and their sacred honor. He claims for himself and Congress authority to govern the territories of the United States without constitutional restraint.

"We believe in the Declaration of Independence. Its truths, not less self-evident to-day than when first announced by our fathers, are of universal application and cannot be abandoned while government by the people endures.

"We believe in the Constitution of the United States. It gives the President and Congress certain limited powers and secures to every man within the jurisdiction of our Government certain essential rights. We deny that either the President or Congress can govern any person anywhere outside the Constitution.

"We are absolutely opposed to the policy of President McKinley, which proposes to govern millions of men without their consent, which in Porto Rico establishes taxation without representation, and government by the arbitrary will of a legislature unfettered by constitutional restraint, and in the Philippines prosecutes a war of conquest and demands unconditional surrender from a people who are of right free and independent. The struggle of men for freedom has ever been a struggle for constitutional liberty. There is no liberty if the citizen has no right which the Legislature may not invade, if he may be taxed by the Legislature in which he is not represented, or if he is not protected by fundamental law against the arbitrary action of executive power. The policy of the President offers the inhabitants of Porto Rico, Hawaii and

the Philippines no hope of independence, no prospect of American citizenship, no constitutional protection, no representation in the Congress which taxes them. This is the government of men by arbitrary power without their consent. This is imperialism. There is no room under the free flag of America for subjects. The President and Congress, who derive all their powers from the Constitution, can govern no man without regard to its limitations.

"We believe the greatest safeguard of liberty is a free press, and we demand that the censorship in the Philippines, which keeps from the American people the knowledge of what is done in their name, be abolished. We are entitled to know the truth, and we insist that the powers which the President holds in trust for us shall not be used to suppress it.

"Because we thus believe, we oppose the re-election of Mr. McKinley. The supreme purpose of the people in this momentous campaign should be to stamp with their final disapproval his attempt to grasp imperial power. A self-governing people can have no more imperative duty than to drive from public life a Chief Magistrate who, whether in weakness or of wicked purpose, has used his temporary authority to subvert the character of their government and to destroy their National ideals.

"We, therefore, in the belief that it is essential at this crisis for the American people again to declare their faith in the universal application of the Declaration of Independence and to reassert their will that their servants shall not have or exercise any powers whatever other than those conferred by the Constitution, earnestly make the following recommendations to our countrymen:

"First, that, without regard to their views on minor questions of domestic policy, they withhold their votes from Mr. McKinley, in order to stamp with their disapproval what he has done.

"Second, that they vote for those candidates for Congress in their respective districts who will oppose the policy of imperialism.

"Third, while we welcome any other method of opposing the re-election of Mr. McKinley we advise direct support of Mr. Bryan as the most effective means of crushing imperialism. We are convinced of Mr. Bryan's sincerity and of his earnest purpose to secure to the Filipinos their independence. His position and the declarations contained in the platform of his party on the vital issue of the campaign meet our unqualified approval.

"We recommend that the Executive committees of the American Anti-Imperialist League and its allied leagues continue and extend their organizations, preserving the independence of the movement; and that they take the most active part possible in the pending political campaign.

"Until now the policy which has turned the Filipinos from warm friends to bitter enemies, which has slaughtered thousands of them and laid waste their country, has been the policy of the President. After the next election it becomes the policy of every man who votes to re-elect him and who thus becomes with him responsible for every drop of blood thereafter shed.

"In declaring that the principles of the Declaration of Independence apply to all men, this Congress means to include the negro race in

America as well as the Filipinos. We deprecate all efforts, whether in the South or in the North, to deprive the negro of his rights as a citizen under the Declaration of Independence and the Constitution of the United States."

The " Third Party " Anti-Imperialist Platform and Nominations.—The Anti-Imperialists who desired a Third Party ticket in the field, called a convention which met in the city of New York, September 5, and put in nomination for President and Vice President Senator Donelson Caffery, of Louisiana, and Archibald Murray Howe, of Massachusetts. The name " National Party " was assumed, and its " aims and purposes " were thus declared :

" We find our country threatened with alternative perils. On the one hand is a public opinion misled by organized forces of commercialism, that have perverted a war intended by the people to be a war of humanity into a war of conquest. On the other is a public opinion swayed by demagogic appeals to factional and class passions, the most fatal of diseases to a republic. We believe that either of these influences, if unchecked, would ultimately compass the downfall of our country, but we also believe that neither represents the sober conviction of our countrymen. Convinced that the extension of the jurisdiction of the United States for the purpose of holding foreign people as colonial dependents is an innovation dangerous to our liberties and repugnant to the principles upon which our Government is founded, we pledge our earnest efforts through all constitutional means:

" First, to procure the renunciation of all imperial or colonial pretensions with regard to foreign countries claimed to have been acquired through or in consequence of military or naval operations of the last two years.

" Second, we further pledge our efforts to secure a single gold standard and a sound banking system.

" Third, to secure a public service based on merit only.

" Fourth, to secure the abolition of all corrupting special privileges, whether under the guise of subsidies, bounties undeserved pensions or trust breeding tariffs.'

Within a few weeks after the holding of this convention, Senator Caffery and Mr. Howe withdrew their names from the canvass, and it was decided to appoint electors-at-large in as many states as possible, to receive the votes of those supporting the movement.

Social Democratic Party Platform and Nominations.—The last distinct movement of organization for the presidential election was that of a " Social Democratic Party," whose convention, at Chicago, September 29, placed Eugene V. Debs, of Illinois, in nomination for President, and Job Harriman, of California, for Vice President, on principles declared as follows :

" The Social Democratic party of America declares that life, liberty, and happiness depend upon equal political and economic rights.

" In our economic development an industrial revolution has taken place, the individual tool of former years having become the social tool of the present. The individual tool was owned by the worker, who employed himself and was master of his product. The social tool, the machine, is owned by the capitalist, and the worker is dependent upon him for employment. The capitalist thus becomes the master of the worker, and is able to appropriate to himself a large share of the product of his labor.

" Capitalism, the private ownership of the means of production, is responsible for the insecurity of subsistence, the poverty, misery, and degradation of the ever-growing majority of our people ; but the same economic forces which have produced and now intensify the capitalist system will necessitate the adoption of Socialism, the collective ownership of the means of production for the common good and welfare.

" The present system of social production and private ownership is rapidly converting society into two antagonistic classes—i. e., the capitalist class and the propertyless class. The middle class, once the most powerful of this great nation, is disappearing in the mill of competition. The issue is now between the two classes first named. Our political liberty is now of little value to the masses unless used to acquire economic liberty. Independent political action and the trade-union movement are the chief emancipating factors of the working class, the one representing its political, the other its economic wing, and both must coöperate to abolish the capitalist system.

" Therefore, the Social Democratic party of America declares its object to be :

" First—The organization of the working class into a political party to conquer the public powers now controlled by capitalists.

" Second—The abolition of wage-slavery by the establishment of a National system of coöperative industry, based upon the social or common ownership of the means of production and distribution, to be administered by society in the common interest of all its members, and the complete emancipation of the socially useful classes from the domination of capitalism.

" The working class and all those in sympathy with their historic mission to realize a higher civilization should sever connection with all capitalist and reform parties and unite with the Social Democratic party of America. The control of political power by the Social Democratic party will be tantamount to the abolition of all class rule. The solidarity of labor connecting the millions of class-conscious fellow-workers throughout the civilized world will lead to international Socialism, the brotherhood of man.

" As steps in that direction, we make the following demands :

" First—Revision of our Federal Constitution, in order to remove the obstacles to complete control of government by the people irrespective of sex.

" Second—The public ownership of all industries controlled by monopolies, trusts, and combines.

" Third—The public ownership of all railroads, telegraphs, and telephones; all means of transportation and communication ; all waterworks, gas and electric plants, and other public utilities.

" Fourth—The public ownership of all gold, silver, copper, lead, iron, coal, and other mines, and all oil and gas wells.

" Fifth—The reduction of the hours of labor in proportion to the increasing facilities of production.

"Sixth—The inauguration of a system of public works and improvements for the employment of the unemployed, the public credit to be utilized for that purpose.

"Seventh—Useful inventions to be free, the inventor to be remunerated by the public.

"Eighth—Labor legislation to be National instead of local, and international when possible.

"Ninth—National insurance of working people against accidents, lack of employment, and want in old age.

"Tenth—Equal civil and political rights for men and women, and the abolition of all laws discriminating against women.

"Eleventh—The adoption of the initiative and referendum, proportional representation, and the right of recall of representatives by the voters.

"Twelfth—Abolition of war and the introduction of international arbitration."

The Canvass and Election.—The canvass preceding the election was much less excited than that of 1896. The confusion of issues greatly lessened the intensity with which they were discussed. Mr. Bryan again took the field in person, travelling widely through all parts of the country, making great numbers of speeches to immense audiences everywhere ; and Governor Roosevelt did the same on the Republican side, to a somewhat less extent.

The election, which occurred on the 6th of November, was conducted with the quiet order that is rarely broken at such times in America. About fourteen millions of votes were cast, of which, according to the returns compiled for the Tribune Almanac, President McKinley received 7,214,027, and Bryan, 6,342,514. For the Prohibition ticket, 197,112 votes were cast ; for the Socialist Labor ticket, 32,433 ; for the Social Democratic ticket, 82,904 ; and 78,444 votes were scattered among other candidates. The States carried for McKinley were: California, giving 9 electoral votes; Connecticut, 6 ; Delaware, 3 ; Illinois, 24 ; Indiana, 15 ; Iowa, 13 ; Kansas, 10 ; Maine, 6 ; Maryland, 8 ; Massachusetts, 15 ; Michigan, 14 ; Minnesota, 9 ; Nebraska, 8 ; New Hampshire, 4 ; New Jersey, 10 ; New York, 36 ; North Dakota, 3 ; Ohio, 23 ; Oregon, 4 ; Pennsylvania, 32 ; Rhode Island, 4 ; South Dakota, 4 ; Utah, 3 ; Vermont, 4 ; Washington, 4 ; West Virginia, 6 ; Wisconsin, 12 ; Wyoming, 3 ; Total, 292. For Bryan, the electoral votes of the following States were given: Alabama, 11 ; Arkansas, 8 ; Colorado, 4 ; Florida, 4 ; Georgia, 13 ; Idaho, 3 ; Kentucky, 13 ; Louisiana, 8 ; Mississippi, 9 ; Missouri, 17 ; Montana, 3 ; Nevada, 3 ; North Carolina, 11 ; South Carolina, 9 ; Tennessee, 12 ; Texas, 15 ; Virginia, 12 ; Total, 155.

President McKinley was re-elected by a majority of 137 votes in the Electoral College, and by a majority of nearly half a million of the popular vote.

"The popular vote for President shows three interesting things :—

"(1) Many men of each party abstained from voting, for the total was only 45,132 greater than in 1896, whereas the increase in population adds about a million to the electorate every four years. The total vote last year was 13,970,234. Mr. McKinley received only about 100,000 more than in 1896, and Mr. Bryan 130,000 less. Many men in each party, then, were dissatisfied with their candidate and platform.

"(2) Mr. Bryan's largest gains were in New England, because of the anti-Imperialistic feeling, and in New York and New Jersey and Illinois, because of a milder fear of financial disturbance ; and his losses were greatest in Utah, in Colorado, and in the Pacific States, an indication of better times and of less faith in free silver.

"(3) Twelve Southern States cast a smaller vote than in 1896, partly because of the elimination of the Negroes, and partly because many Gold Democrats abstained from voting."—*The World's Work, Feb.*, 1901.

The Democratic candidate on "Imperialism."—The issue which ought to have been supreme in the Presidential election, because fundamental principles of government and lasting consequences of policy were bound up in it, but which was unhappily confused by prevailing anxieties in the sensitive region of commercial and industrial affairs, is more broadly and adequately defined in the declarations of the two leading candidates, on their formal acceptance of nominations by the Democratic and Republican parties, than it is in the party platforms quoted above. The first to speak was Mr. Bryan. Responding to the committee which notified him of his nomination, at Indianapolis, on the 8th of August, he devoted the greater part of his remarks to the policy of colonial acquisition on which the government had been embarked. The following passages are fairly representative of the view taken by those who condemned what they termed "imperialism," in the undertaking of the government of the American Republic to impose its sovereignty upon the people of the Philippine Islands, and to hold their country as a "possession : "

"When the president, supported by a practically unanimous vote of the House and Senate, entered upon a war with Spain for the purpose of aiding the struggling patriots of Cuba, the country, without regard to party, applauded. Although the Democrats realized that the administration would necessarily gain a political advantage from the conduct of a war which in the very nature of the case must soon end in a complete victory, they vied with the Republicans in the support which they gave to the President. When the war was over and the Republican leaders began to suggest the propriety of a colonial policy, opposition at once manifested itself.

"When the President finally laid before the Senate a treaty which recognized the independence of Cuba, but provided for the cession of the Philippine Islands to the United States, the menace of imperialism became so apparent that many preferred to reject the treaty and risk the ills that might follow rather than take the chance of correcting the errors of the treaty by the independent action of this country. I was among the number of those who believed it better to ratify the treaty and end the war, release the volunteers, remove the excuse for war expenditures, and then give the Filipinos the independence which might be forced from Spain by a new treaty. . . . The title of Spain being extinguished we were at liberty to deal with the Filipinos according to American principles. The Bacon resolution, introduced a month before hostilities broke out at Manila, promised independence to the Filipinos on the same terms that it was promised to the Cubans. I supported this resolution and believe that its adoption prior to the breaking out of hostilities would have prevented bloodshed, and that its adoption at any subsequent time would have ended hostilities. . . . If the Bacon resolution had been adopted by the Senate and carried out by the President, either at the time of the ratification of the treaty or at any time afterwards, it would have taken the question of imperialism out of politics and left the American people free to deal with their domestic problems. But the resolution was defeated by the vote of the Republican Vice-President, and from that time to this a Republican Congress has refused to take any action whatever in the matter.

"When hostilities broke out at Manila, Republican speakers and Republican editors at once sought to lay the blame upon those who had delayed the ratification of the treaty, and, during the progress of the war, the same Republicans have accused the opponents of imperialism of giving encouragement to the Filipinos. . . .

"The Filipinos do not need any encouragement from Americans now living. Our whole history has been an encouragement, not only · to the Filipinos, but to all who are denied a voice in their own government. If the Republicans are prepared to censure all who have used language calculated to make the Filipinos hate foreign domination, let them condemn the speech of Patrick Henry. When he uttered that passionate appeal, 'Give me liberty or give me death,' he expressed a sentiment which still echoes in the hearts of men. Let them censure Jefferson; of all the statesmen of history none have used words so offensive to those who would hold their fellows in political' bondage. Let them censure Washington, who declared that the colonists must choose between liberty and slavery. Or, if the statute of limitations has run against the sins of Henry and Jefferson and Washington, let them censure Lincoln, whose Gettysburg speech will be quoted in defense of popular government when the present advocates of force and conquest are forgotten. . . . If it were possible to obliterate every word written or spoken in defense of the principles set forth in the Declaration of Independence, a war of conquest would still leave its legacy of perpetual hatred, for it was God himself who placed in every human heart the love of liberty. He never made a race of people so low in the scale of civilization or intelligence that it would welcome a foreign master.

"Those who would have this nation enter upon a career of empire must consider not only the effect of imperialism on the Filipinos, but they must also calculate its effects upon our own nation. We cannot repudiate the principle of self-government in the Philippines without weakening that principle here. . . .

"Our opponents, conscious of the weakness of their cause, seek to confuse imperialism with expansion, and have even dared to claim Jefferson as a supporter of their policy. Jefferson spoke so freely and used language with such precision that no one can be ignorant of his views. On one occasion he declared: 'If there be one principle more deeply rooted than any other in the mind of every American, it is that we should have nothing to do with conquest.' And again he said: 'Conquest is not in our principles; it is inconsistent with our government.' The forcible annexation of territory to be governed by arbitrary power differs as much from the acquisition of territory to be built up into states as a monarchy differs from a democracy. The Democratic party does not oppose expansion when expansion enlarges the area of the Republic and incorporates land which can be settled by American citizens, or adds to our population people who are willing to become citizens and are capable of discharging their duties as such. . . .

"A colonial policy means that we shall send to the Philippine Islands a few traders, a few taskmasters and a few officeholders and an army large enough to support the authority of a small fraction of the people while they rule the natives. If we have an imperial policy we must have a great standing army as its natural and necessary complement. The spirit which will justify the forcible annexation of the Philippine Islands will justify the seizure of other islands and the domination of other people, and with wars of conquest we can expect a certain, if not rapid, growth of our military establishment. . . .

"The Republican platform assumes that the Philippine Islands will be retained under American sovereignty, and we have a right to demand of the Republican leaders a discussion of the future status of the Filipino. Is he to be a citizen or a subject? Are we to bring into the body politic eight or ten million Asiatics, so different from us in race and history that amalgamation is impossible? Are they to share with us in making the laws and shaping the destiny of this nation? No Republican of prominence has been bold enough to advocate such a proposition. The McEnery resolution, adopted by the Senate immediately after the ratification of the treaty, expressly negatives this idea. The Democratic platform describes the situation when it says that the Filipinos cannot be citizens without endangering our civilization. Who will dispute it? And what is the alternative? If the Filipino is not to be a citizen, shall we make him a subject? On that question the Democratic platform speaks with equal emphasis. It declares that the Filipino cannot be a subject without endangering our form of government. A Republic can have no subjects. A subject is possible only in a government resting upon force; he is unknown in a government deriving its just powers from the consent of the governed.

"The Republican platform says that 'the largest measure of self-government consistent with their welfare and our duties shall be secured to them (the Filipinos) by law.' This is a strange doctrine for a government which owes its very existence to the men who offered their lives as a protest against government without consent and taxation without representation. In what respect does the position of the Republican party differ from the position taken by the English government in 1776? Did not the English government promise a good government to the colonists? What king ever promised a bad government to his people? Did not the English government promise that the colonists should have the largest measure of self-government consistent with their welfare and English duties? Did not the Spanish government promise to give to the Cubans the largest measure of self-government consistent with their welfare and Spanish duties? The whole difference between a Monarchy and a Republic may be summed up in one sentence. In a Monarchy the King gives to the people what he believes to be a good government; in a Republic the people secure for themselves what they believe to be a good government. . . .

"The Republican platform promises that some measure of self-government is to be given the Filipinos by law; but even this pledge is not fulfilled. Nearly sixteen months elapsed after the ratification of the treaty before the adjournment of Congress last June, and yet no law was passed dealing with the Philippine situation. The will of the President has been the only law in the Philippine Islands wherever the American authority extends. Why does the Republican party hesitate to legislate upon the Philippine question? Because a law would disclose the radical departure from history and precedent contemplated by those who control the Republican party. The storm of protest which greeted the Porto Rican bill was an indication of what may be expected when the American people are brought face to face with legislation upon this subject. If the Porto Ricans, who welcomed annexation, are to be denied the guarantees of our Constitution, what is to be the lot of the Filipinos, who resisted our authority? If secret influences could compel a disregard of our plain duty toward friendly people, living near our shores, what treatment will those same influences provide for unfriendly people 7,000 miles away? . . .

"Is the sunlight of full citizenship to be enjoyed by the people of the United States, and the twilight of semi-citizenship endured by the people of Porto Rico, while the thick darkness of perpetual vassalage covers the Philippines? The Porto Rico tariff law asserts the doctrine that the operation of the Constitution is confined to the forty-five States. The Democratic party disputes this doctrine and denounces it as repugnant to both the letter and spirit of our organic law. There is no place in our system of government for the deposit of arbitrary and irresponsible power. That the leaders of a great party should claim for any President or Congress the right to treat millions of people as mere 'possessions' and deal with them unrestrained by the Constitution or the bill of rights, shows how far we have already departed from the ancient landmarks and indicates what may be expected if this nation deliberately enters upon a career of empire.

"The territorial form of government is temporary and preparatory, and the chief security a citizen of a territory has is found in the fact that he enjoys the same constitutional guarantees and is subject to the same general laws as the citizen of a state. Take away this security and his rights will be violated and his interests sacrificed at the demand of those who have political influence. This is the evil of the colonial system, no matter by what nation it is applied. . . .

"Let us consider briefly the reasons which have been given in support of an imperialistic policy. Some say that it is our duty to hold the Philippine Islands. But duty is not an argument; it is a conclusion. To ascertain what our duty is, in any emergency, we must apply well settled and generally accepted principles. It is our duty to avoid stealing, no matter whether the thing to be stolen is of great or little value. It is our duty to avoid killing a human being, no

matter where the human being lives or to what race or class he belongs. . . .

"It is said that we have assumed before the world obligations which make it necessary for us to permanently maintain a government in the Philippine Islands. I reply, first, that the highest obligation of this nation is to be true to itself. No obligation to any particular nations, or to all the nations combined, can require the abandonment of our theory of government, and the substitution of doctrines against which our whole national life has been a protest. And, second, that our obligation to the Filipinos, who inhabit the islands, is greater than any obligation which we can owe to foreigners who have a temporary residence in the Philippines or desire to trade there. It is argued by some that the Filipinos are incapable of self-government and that, therefore, we owe it to the world to take control of them. Admiral Dewey, in an official report to the Navy Department, declared the Filipinos more capable of self-government than the Cubans, and said that he based his opinion upon a knowledge of both races. . . .

"Republicans ask, 'Shall we haul down the flag that floats over our dead in the Philippines?' The same question might have been asked when the American flag floated over Chapultepec and waved over the dead who fell there; but the tourist who visits the City of Mexico finds there a national cemetery owned by the United States and cared for by an American citizen. Our flag still floats over our dead, but when the treaty with Mexico was signed American authority withdrew to the Rio Grande, and I venture the opinion that during the last fifty years the people of Mexico have made more progress under the stimulus of independence and self-government than they would have made under a carpet-bag government held in place by bayonets. The United States and Mexico, friendly republics, are each stronger and happier than they would have been had the former been cursed and the latter crushed by an imperialistic policy disguised as 'benevolent assimilation.'

"'Can we not govern colonies?' we are asked. The question is not what we can do, but what we ought to do. This nation can do whatever it desires to do, but it must accept responsibility for what it does. If the Constitution stands in the way, the people can amend the Constitution. I repeat, the nation can do whatever it desires to do, but it cannot avoid the natural and legitimate results of its own conduct. . . .

"Some argue that American rule in the Philippine Islands will result in the better education of the Filipinos. Be not deceived. If we expect to maintain a colonial policy, we shall not find it to our advantage to educate the people. The educated Filipinos are now in revolt against us, and the most ignorant ones have made the least resistance to our domination. If we are to govern them without their consent and give them no voice in determining the taxes which they must pay, we dare not educate them, lest they learn to read the Declaration of Independence and Constitution of the United States and mock us for our inconsistency. The principal arguments, however, advanced by those who enter upon a defense of imperialism are:

"First—That we must improve the present opportunity to become a world power and enter into international politics.

"Second—That our commercial interests in the Philippine Islands and in the Orient make it necessary for us to hold the islands permanently.

"Third—That the spread of the Christian religion will be facilitated by a colonial policy.

"Fourth—That there is no honorable retreat from the position which the nation has taken.

"The first argument is addressed to the nation's pride and the second to the nation's pocket-book. The third is intended for the church member and the fourth for the partisan. It is sufficient answer to the first argument to say that for more than a century this nation has been a world power. For ten decades it has been the most potent influence in the world. Not only has it been a world power, but it has done more to affect the politics of the human race than all the other nations of the world combined. Because our Declaration of Independence was promulgated others have been promulgated. Because the patriots of 1776 fought for liberty, others have fought for it. Because our Constitution was adopted, other constitutions have been adopted. The growth of the principle of self-government, planted on American soil, has been the overshadowing political fact of the nineteenth century. It has made this nation conspicuous among the nations and given it a place in history such as no other nation has ever enjoyed. Nothing has been able to check the onward march of this idea. I am not willing that this nation shall cast aside the omnipotent weapon of truth to seize again the weapons of physical warfare. I would not exchange the glory of this Republic for the glory of all the empires that have risen and fallen since time began.

"The permanent chairman of the last Republican National Convention presented the pecuniary argument in all its baldness when he said : 'We make no hypocritical pretense of being interested in the Philippines solely on account of others. While we regard the welfare of those people as a sacred trust, we regard the welfare of the American people first. We see our duty to ourselves as well as to others. We believe in trade expansion. By every legitimate means within the province of government and constitution we mean to stimulate the expansion of our trade and open new markets.' This is the commercial argument. It is based upon the theory that war can be rightly waged for pecuniary advantage, and that it is profitable to purchase trade by force and violence. . . . The Democratic party is in favor of the expansion of trade. It would extend our trade by every legitimate and peaceful means; but it is not willing to make merchandise of human blood. But a war of conquest is as unwise as it is unrighteous. A harbor and coaling station in the Philippines would answer every trade and military necessity, and such a concession could have been secured at any time without difficulty.

"It is not necessary to own people in order to trade with them. We carry on trade to-day with every part of the world, and our commerce has expanded more rapidly than the commerce of any European empire. We do not own Japan or China, but we trade with their people. We have not absorbed the republics of Central and South America, but we trade with them. It has not been necessary to have any political connection with Canada or the nations of Europe in order to trade with them. Trade cannot be permanently profitable unless it is voluntary. . . .

"Imperialism would be profitable to the army contractors; it would be profitable to the ship-owners, who would carry live soldiers to the Philippines and bring dead soldiers back; it would be profitable to those who would seize upon the franchises, and it would be profitable to the officials whose salaries would be fixed here and paid over there ; but to the farmer, to the laboring man and to the vast majority of those engaged in other occupations it would bring expenditure without return and risk without reward.

"The pecuniary argument, though more effective with certain classes, is not likely to be used so often or presented with so much enthusiasm as the religious argument. If what has been termed the 'gunpowder gospel' were urged against the Filipinos only, it would be a sufficient answer to say that a majority of the Filipinos are now members of one branch of the Christian church; but the principle involved is one of much wider application and challenges serious consideration. The religious argument varies in positiveness, from a passive belief that Providence delivered the Filipinos into our hands for their good and our glory, to the exultation of the minister who said that we ought to 'thrash the natives (Filipinos) until they understand who we are,' and that 'every bullet sent, every cannon shot and every flag waved, means righteousness.' . . . If true Christianity consists in carrying out in our daily lives the teachings of Christ, who will say that we are commanded to civilize with dynamite and proselyte with the sword ? . . .

"Love, not force, was the weapon of the Nazarene; sacrifice for others, not the exploitation of them, was His method of reaching the human heart. A missionary recently told me that the Stars and Stripes once saved his life because his assailant recognized our flag as a flag that had no blood upon it. Let it be known that our missionaries are seeking souls instead of sovereignty ; let it be known that instead of being the advance guard of conquering armies, they are going forth to help and uplift, having their loins girt about with truth and their feet shod with the preparation of the gospel of peace, wearing the breastplate of righteousness and carrying the sword of the spirit ; let it be known that they are citizens of a nation which respects the rights of the citizens of other nations as carefully as it protects the rights of its own citizens, and the welcome given to our missionaries will be more cordial than the welcome extended to the missionaries of any other nation.

"The argument made by some that it was unfortunate for the nation that it had anything to do with the Philippine Islands, but that the naval victory at Manila made the permanent acquisition of those islands necessary, is also unsound. We won a naval victory at Santiago, but that did not compel us to hold Cuba. The shedding of American blood in the Philippine Islands does not make it imperative that we should retain possession forever. American blood was shed at San Juan Hill and El Caney, and yet the President has promised the Cubans independence. The fact that the American flag floats over Manila does not compel us to exercise perpetual sovereignty over the islands ; the American flag waves over Havana to-day, but the

President has promised to haul it down when the flag of the Cuban Republic is ready to rise in its place. Better a thousand times that our flag in the Orient give way to a flag representing the idea of self-government than that the flag of this Republic should become the flag of an empire.

"There is an easy, honest, honorable solution of the Philippine question. It is set forth in the Democratic platform, and it is submitted with confidence to the American people. This plan I unreservedly indorse. If elected, I will convene congress in extraordinary session as soon as inaugurated and recommend an immediate declaration of the nation's purpose, first, to establish a stable form of government in the Philippine Islands, just as we are now establishing a stable form of government in Cuba; second, to give independence to the Cubans; third, to protect the Filipinos from outside interference while they work out their destiny, just as we have protected the republics of Central and South America, and are, by the Monroe doctrine, pledged to protect Cuba."

The Republican candidate on the same subject.—The answer of the party controlling the government to the impeachment of its policy of colonial acquisition, and especially of its conduct in the Philippine Islands, was given by Mr. McKinley, in a letter of acceptance, addressed, September 8, to the committee which gave him formal notice of his renomination by the Republican convention. After rehearsing at considerable length the events which preceded, attended and followed the capture of Manila, he continued:

"Would not our adversaries have sent Dewey's fleet to Manila to capture and destroy the Spanish sea power there, or, dispatching it there, would they have withdrawn it after the destruction of the Spanish fleet; and, if the latter, whither would they have directed it to sail? Where could it have gone? What port in the Orient was opened to it? Do our adversaries condemn the expedition under the command of Gen. Merritt to strengthen Dewey in the distant ocean and assist in our triumph over Spain, with which nation we were at war? Was it not our highest duty to strike Spain at every vulnerable point, that the war might be successfully concluded at the earliest practicable moment? And was it not our duty to protect the lives and property of those who came within our control by the fortunes of war? Could we have come away at any time between May 1, 1898, and the conclusion of peace without a stain upon our good name? Could we have come away without dishonor at any time after the ratification of the peace treaty by the Senate of the United States? There has been no time since the destruction of the enemy's fleet when we could or should have left the Philippine Archipelago. After the treaty of peace was ratified, no power but Congress could surrender our sovereignty or alienate a foot of the territory thus acquired. The Congress has not seen fit to do the one or the other, and the President had no authority to do either, if he had been so inclined, which he was not. So long as the sovereignty remains in us it is the duty of the Executive, whoever he may be, to uphold that sovereignty, and if it be attacked to suppress its assailants. Would our political adversaries do less?

"It has been asserted that there would have been no fighting in the Philippines if Congress had declared its purpose to give independence to the Tagal insurgents. The insurgents did not wait for the action of Congress. They assumed the offensive; they opened fire on our Army. Those who assert our responsibility for the beginning of the conflict have forgotten that, before the treaty was ratified in the Senate, and while it was being debated in that body and while the Bacon resolution was under discussion, on February 4, 1899, the insurgents attacked the American Army, after being previously advised that the American forces were under orders not to fire upon them except in defense. The papers found in the recently captured archives of the insurgents demonstrate that this attack had been carefully planned for weeks before it occurred. This unprovoked assault upon our soldiers at a time when the Senate was deliberating upon the treaty shows that no action on our part, except surrender and abandonment, would have prevented the fighting, and leaves no doubt in any fair mind of where the responsibility rests for the shedding of American blood.

"With all the exaggerated phrase-making of this electoral contest, we are in danger of being diverted from the real contention. We are in agreement with all of those who supported the war with Spain and also with those who counseled the ratification of the treaty of peace. Upon these two great essential steps there can be no issue and out of these came all of our responsibilities. If others would shirk the obligations imposed by the war and the treaty, we must decline to act further with them, and here the issue was made. It is our purpose to establish in the Philippines a government suitable to the wants and conditions of the inhabitants and to prepare them for self-government when they are ready for it and as rapidly as they are ready for it. That I am aiming to do under my Constitutional authority, and will continue to do until Congress shall determine the political status of the inhabitants of the archipelago.

"Are our opponents against the treaty? If so, they must be reminded that it could not have been ratified in the Senate but for their assistance. The Senate which ratified the treaty and the Congress which added its sanction by a large approbation comprised Senators and Representatives of the people of all parties. Would our opponents surrender to the insurgents, abandon our sovereignty or cede it to them? If that be not their purpose, then it should be promptly disclaimed, for only evil can result from the hopes raised by our opponents in the minds of the Filipinos, that with their success at the polls in November there will be a withdrawal of our Army and of American sovereignty over the archipelago; the complete independence of the Tagalog people recognized and the powers of government over all the other people of the archipelago conferred upon the Tagalog leaders. The effect of a belief in the minds of the insurgents that this will be done has already prolonged the rebellion and increases the necessity for the continuance of a large army. It is now delaying full peace in the archipelago and the establishment of civil governments and has influenced many of the insurgents against accepting the liberal terms of amnesty offered by Gen. MacArthur under my direction. But for these false hopes, a considerable reduction could have been had in our military establishment in the Philippines, and the realization of a stable government would be already at hand.

"The American people are asked by our opponents to yield the sovereignty of the United States in the Philippines to a small fraction of the population, a single tribe out of 80 or more inhabiting the archipelago, a faction which wantonly attacked the American troops in Manila while in rightful possession under the protocol with Spain, awaiting the ratification of the treaty of peace by the Senate, and which has since been in active, open rebellion against the United States. We are asked to transfer our sovereignty to a small minority in the islands, without consulting the majority, and to abandon the largest portion of the population, which has been loyal to us, to the cruelties of the guerrilla insurgent bands. More than this, we are asked to protect this minority in establishing a government, and to this end repress all opposition of the majority. We are required to set up a stable government in the interest of those who have assailed our sovereignty and fired upon our soldiers, and then maintain it at any cost or sacrifice against its enemies within and against those having ambitious designs from without. This would require an army and navy far larger than is now maintained in the Philippines and still more in excess of what will be necessary with the full recognition of our sovereignty. A military support of authority not our own, as thus proposed, is the very essence of militarism, which our opponents in their platform oppose, but which by their policy would of necessity be established in its most offensive form.

"The American people will not make the murderers of our soldiers the agents of the Republic to convey the blessings of liberty and order to the Philippines. They will not make them the builders of the new commonwealth. Such a course would be a betrayal of our sacred obligations to the peaceful Filipinos and would place at the mercy of dangerous adventurers the lives and property of the natives and foreigners. It would make possible and easy the commission of such atrocities as were secretly planned to be executed on the 22d of February, 1899, in the city of Manila, when only the vigilance of our Army prevented the attempt to assassinate our soldiers and all foreigners and pillage and destroy the city and its surroundings. In short, the proposition of those opposed to us is to continue all the obligations in the Philippines which now rest upon the Government, only changing the relation from principal, which now exists, to that of surety. Our responsibility is to remain, but our power is to be diminished. Our obligation is to be no less, but our title is to be surrendered to another power, which is without experience or training or the ability to maintain a stable government at home and absolutely helpless to perform its international obligations with the rest of the world. To this we are opposed. We should not yield our title while our obligations last. In the language of our platform, 'Our authority should not be less than our responsibility,' and our present responsibility is to establish our authority in every part of the islands.

"No government can so certainly preserve the peace, restore public order, establish law, justice and stable conditions as ours. Neither Congress nor the Executive can establish a stable government in these islands except under our right of sovereignty, our authority and our flag. And this we are doing. We could not do it as a protectorate power so completely or so successfully as we are doing it now. As the sovereign power, we can initiate action and shape means to ends and guide the Filipinos to self-development and self-government. As a protectorate power we could not initiate action, but would be compelled to follow and uphold a people with no capacity yet to go alone. In the one case we can protect both ourselves and the Filipinos from being involved in dangerous complications: in the other we could not protect even the Filipinos until after their trouble had come. Beside, if we cannot establish any government of our own without the consent of the governed, as our opponents contend, then we could not establish a stable government for them or make ours a protectorate without the like consent, and neither the majority of the people or a minority of the people have invited us to assume it. We could not maintain a protectorate even with the consent of the governed without giving provocation for conflicts and possibly costly wars. Our rights in the Philippines are now free from outside interference and will continue so in our present relation. They would not be thus free in any other relation. We will not give up our own to guarantee another sovereignty.

"Our title is good. Our peace commissioners believed they were receiving a good title when they concluded the treaty. The Executive believed it was a good title when he submitted it to the Senate of the United States for its ratification. The Senate believed it was a good title when they gave it their Constitutional assent, and the Congress seems not to have doubted its completeness when they appropriated $20,000,000 provided by the treaty. If any who favored its ratification believed it gave us a bad title, they were not sincere. Our title is practically identical with that under which we hold our territory acquired since the beginning of the government, and under which we have exercised full sovereignty and established government for the inhabitants. It is worthy of note that no one outside of the United States disputes the fulness and integrity of the cession. What then is the real issue on this subject? Whether it is paramount to any other or not, it is whether we shall be responsible for the government of the Philippines with the sovereignty and authority which enable us to guide them to regulated liberty, law, safety and progress, or whether we shall be responsible for the forcible and arbitrary government of a minority without sovereignty and authority on our part and with only the embarrassment of a protectorate which draws us into their troubles without the power of preventing them. There were those who two years ago were rushing us on to war with Spain who are unwilling now to accept its clear consequence, as there are those among us who advocated the ratification of the treaty of peace, but now protest against its obligations. Nations which go to war must be prepared to accept its resultant obligations, and when they make treaties must keep them.

"Those who profess to distrust the liberal and honorable purposes of the Administration in its treatment of the Philippines are not justified.

Imperialism has no place in its creed or conduct. Freedom is a rock upon which the Republican party was builded and now rests. Liberty is the great Republican doctrine for which the people went to war and for which 1,000,000 lives were offered and billions of dollars expended to make it a lawful legacy of all without the consent of master or slave. There is a strain of ill-conceived hypocrisy in the anxiety to extend the Constitutional guarantees to the people of the Philippines while their nullification is openly advocated at home. Our opponents may distrust themselves, but they have no right to discredit the good faith and patriotism of the majority of the people, who are opposing them; they may fear the worst form of imperialism with the helpless Filipinos in their hands, but if they do, it is because they have parted with the spirit and faith of the fathers and have lost the virility of the founders of the party which they profess to represent.

"The Republican party does not have to assert its devotion to the Declaration of Independence. That immortal instrument of the fathers remained unexecuted until the people under the lead of the Republican party in the awful clash of battle turned its promises into fulfillment. It wrote into the Constitution the amendments guaranteeing political equality to American citizenship and it has never broken them or counseled others in breaking them. It will not be guided in its conduct by one set of principles at home and another set in the new territory belonging to the United States. If our opponents would only practice as well as preach the doctrines of Abraham Lincoln there would be no fear for the safety of our institutions at home or their rightful influence in any territory over which our flag floats.

"Empire has been expelled from Porto Rico and the Philippines by American freemen. The flag of the Republic now floats over these islands as an emblem of rightful sovereignty. Will the Republic stay and dispense to their inhabitants the blessings of liberty, education and free institutions, or steal away, leaving them to anarchy or imperialism? The American question is between duty and desertion—the American verdict will be for duty and against desertion, for the Republic against both anarchy and imperialism."

A. D. 1900 (June).—Revenues and expenditures of the government for the fiscal year ended June 30, 1900.—The revenues of the Government from all sources (by warrants) for the fiscal year ended June 30, 1900, were:

From internal revenue	$295,327,926.76
From customs	233,164,871.16
From profits on coinage, bullion deposits, etc	9,992,374.09
From District of Columbia	4,008,722.77
From fees—consular, letters patent, and land	3,291,716.
From sales of public lands	2,836,882.68
From tax on national banks	1,998,554.06
From navy pension, navy hospital, clothing, and deposit funds	1,621,558.52
From sales of Indian lands	1,384,663.49
From payment of interest by Pacific railways	1,173,466.43
From miscellaneous	997,375.68
From sales of Government property	779,522.78
From customs fees, fines, penalties, etc	675,706.95
From immigrant fund	537,404.81
From deposits for surveying public lands	273,247.19
From sales of ordnance material	257,265.56
From Soldiers' Home, permanent fund	247,926.62
From tax on seal skins, and rent of seal islands	225,676.47

From license fees, Territory of Alaska	157,234.94
From trust funds, Department of State	152,794.56
From depredations on public lands	76,307.54
From Spanish indemnity	57,000.00
From sales of lands and buildings	3,842,737.68
From part payment Central Pacific Railroad indebtedness	3,338,016.49
From dividend received for account of Kansas Pacific Railway	821,897.70
From Postal Service	102,354,579.29
Total receipts	669,595,431.18

The expenditures for the same period were:

For the civil establishment, including foreign intercourse, public buildings, collecting the revenues, District of Columbia, and other miscellaneous expenses	$98,542,411.37
For the military establishment, including rivers and harbors, forts, arsenals, seacoast defenses, and expenses of the war with Spain and in the Philippines	134,774,767.78
For the naval establishment, including construction of new vessels, machinery, armament, equipment, improvement at navy-yards, and expenses of the war with Spain and in the Philippines	55,953,077.72
For Indian Service	10,175,106.76
For pensions	140,877,316.02
For interest on the public debt	40,160,333.27
For deficiency in postal revenues	7,230,778.79
For Postal Service	102,354,579.29
Total expenditures	590,068,371.00
Showing a surplus of	79,527,060.18

"As compared with the fiscal year 1899, the receipts for 1900 increased $58,613,426.83. . . . There was a decrease of $117,358,388.14 in expenditures."—*United States Secretary of the Treasury, Annual Report on the State of the Finances, 1900, pp. 7–9.*

A. D. 1900 (June).—Return of losses from all causes in the armies of the U. S. since May 1, 1898.—In response to a resolution of the Senate, the following return (56th Cong., 1st Sess., Senate Doc. 426) was made by the Secretary of War, June 1, 1900, showing the losses from all causes in the armies of the United States between May 1, 1898, and June 30, 1899; casualties in the Philippines during the war with Spain, and after the close of the war with Spain down to May 20, 1900; and other interesting details:

Statement showing losses, from all causes, in the armies of the United States between May 1, 1898, and June 30, 1899. Average strength.— 1898: Regular Army, 55,853; Volunteers, 163,-103. 1899: Regular Army, 63,370; Volunteers, 45,457.

CAUSES.	REGULAR ARMY.		
	Officers.	Enlisted Men.	Total.
Deaths:			
Killed in action	24	270	294
By wounds	7	114	121
Disease	51	1,524	1,575
Accident	1	72	73
Drowning	2	48	50
Suicide	1	32	33
Murder or homicide		26	26
Total	86	2,086	2,172
Wounded	109	1,586	1,695

CAUSES.	VOLUNTEERS.		
	Officers.	Enlisted Men.	Total.
Deaths:			
Killed in action......	17	188	205
By wounds...........	3	78	81
Disease..............	114	3,820	3,934
Accident.............	5	137	142
Drowning............	1	40	41
Suicide..............	1	20	21
Murder or homicide..	....	26	26
Total..............	141	4,309	4,450
Wounded..............	88	1,178	1,266

CAUSES.	GRAND TOTAL.	
	Officers.	Enlisted Men.
Deaths:		
Killed in action................	38	458
By wounds......................	10	192
Disease........................	165	5,344
Accident.......................	6	209
Drowning......................	3	88
Suicide........................	2	52
Murder or homicide.............	....	52
Total	224	6,395
Wounded........................	197	2,764

Casualties in the Philippines during the war with Spain, June 30, 1898, to August 13, 1898. Average strength, 10,900.

	Officers.	Enlisted Men.	Total.
Killed (no deaths from wounds)................	....	18	18
Wounded..................	10	99	109
Total	10	117	127

In the Philippines, from February 4, 1899, to May 20, 1900. Average strength, 43,232.

	Officers.	Enlisted Men.	Total.
Killed or died of wounds.	43	579	622
Deaths:			
By disease............	19	1,054	1,073
Accident.............	1	43	44
Drowning............	2	94	96
Suicide..............	6	23	29
Murder or homicide..	....	11	11
Total...............	71	1,804	1,875
Wounded..............	132	1,897	2,029
Grand total........	203	3,701	3,904

Casualties in the Fifth Corps in the operations against Santiago, June 22 to July 17, 1898:

ACTIONS.	KILLED.		WOUNDED.	
	Officers.	Men.	Officers.	Men.
Las Guasimas, June 24	1	15	6	43
El Caney, July 1......	4	77	25	335
San Juan, July 1-3....	15	127	69	945
Aguadores, July 1-2 ..	....	2	....	10
Around Santiago, July 10-12.................	1	1	1	11
Total............	21	222	101	1,344

Died of wounds received in the five battles named: Officers, 5; men, 70. Total killed and died of wounds: Officers, 26; men, 292.

Statement of the number of insane soldiers admitted to the Government Hospital for the Insane, Washington, D. C., from the Philippine Islands, May 24, 1900, and the disposition made of them:

	Regulars.	Volunteers.
Admitted	47	15
Discharged recovered.............	16	3
Discharged unimproved..........	1	..
On visit from hospital...........	1	..
Remaining in hospital...........	29	12

A. D. 1900 (June).—Immigration for the year ended June 30.—"The Commissioner-General of Immigration, in the annual report of the operations of his Bureau for the fiscal year ended June 30, 1900, submits tabulated statements showing the arrival in this country during that period of 448,572 alien immigrants, 425,372 through ports of the United States and 23,200 through Canada. Of these, 304,148 were males and 144,424 females; 54,624 were under 14 years of age, 370,382 were from 14 to 45 years old, and 23,566 were 45 and over. As to the literacy of persons 14 years of age and over, there were 93,576 who could neither read nor write, and 2,097 who could read but were unable to write; 54,288 brought each $30 or over, and 271,821 showed sums less than $30, the total amounts displayed to inspectors aggregating $6,657,530. There were returned to their own countries within one year after landing 356, and hospital relief was rendered during the year to 2,417. The total debarred, or refused a landing at the ports, were 4,246, as compared with 3,798 last year. Of these, 1 was excluded for idiocy, 32 for insanity, 2,974 as paupers or persons likely to become public charges, 393 on account of disease, 4 as convicts, 2 as assisted immigrants, 833 as contract laborers, and 7 women upon the ground that they had been imported for immoral purposes. In addition to the foregoing, there were excluded at the Mexican and Canadian borders a total of 1,616 aliens.

"It appears that the Croatian and Slovenian races sent an increase of 99 per cent over those of the same races who came last year; the Hebrew, an increase of 62 per cent; the South Italian (including Sicilian), 28 per cent; the Japanese, 271 per cent; the Finnish, 106 per cent; the Magyar, 181 per cent; the Polish, 64 per cent; the Scandinavian, 41 per cent; the Slovak, 84 per cent. These nine races, of the total of forty-one races represented by immigration, furnished nearly as many immigrants as the total arrivals for the last year, or 310,444, and their aggregate increase represented 85 per cent of the total increase shown for the year. The total immigration reported, 448,572, is in excess of that for the preceding year, 311,715, by 136,-857, or 43.9 per cent. As to countries of origin, 424,700 came from European, 17,946 from Asiatic, 30 from African, and 5,896 from all other sources. The Commissioner-General points out that in addition to the 448,572 immigrants there arrived 65,635 other alien passengers, who, he contends, should be included in conformity to law with those classified as immigrants."—*United States, Secretary of the Treasury, Annual Report, 1900, p. 37.*

A. D. **1900** (June).—**Shipping**, compared with that of **other** countries. See (in this vol.) SHIPPING OF THE WORLD.

A. D. **1900** (June).—**Alaska Act.** See (in this vol.) ALASKA: A. D. 1900.

A. D. **1900** (June).—**Returns of Filipinos killed, wounded** and captured from the beginning of hostilities with them. See (in this vol.) PHILIPPINE ISLANDS : A. D. 1900 (MAY).

A. D. **1900** (June—December).—**Co-operation** with the Powers in China. See (in this vol.) CHINA.

A. D. **1900** (July).—**Appeal of citizens of** Manila to the Congress of the United States. See (in this vol.) PHILIPPINE ISLANDS: A. D. 1900 (JULY).

A. D. **1900** (July).—**Forces sent to China** under General **Chaffee.** See (in this vol.) CHINA: A. D. 1900 (JULY).

A. D. **1900** (August).—**Agreement with Russian proposal** to withdraw troops from **Peking.** See (in this vol.) CHINA: A. D. 1900 (AUGUST—DECEMBER).

A. D. **1900** (September).—**Opposition to** German proposal for dealing with China. See (in this vol.) CHINA: A. D. 1900 (AUGUST—DECEMBER).

A. D. **1900** (September—N o v e m b e r).—Legislative measures of the Philippine Commission. See (in this vol.) PHILIPPINE ISLANDS : A. D. 1900 (SEPTEMBER—NOVEMBER).

A. D. **1900** (October).—**Military forces in** the Philippine Islands. See (in this vol.) PHILIPPINE ISLANDS: A. D. 1900 (OCTOBER).

A. D. **1900** (December).—**Amendment and ratification of the Hay-Pauncefote Convention.** See (in this vol.) CANAL, INTEROCEANIC : A. D. 1900 (DECEMBER).

A. D. **1900** (December).—**Celebration of the** 100th anniversary of the removal of the capital to Washington. See (in this vol.) WASHINGTON.

A. D. **1900** (December).—**Exports for the** calendar year exceeding those of any other nation.—A Press despatch from Washington, dated February 21, 1901, announced the fact that the "complete figures for the calendar year 1900, when compared with those of other nations, show that American exports of domestic products are greater than those of any other country. The total exports of domestic merchandise from the United States in the calendar year 1900 were $1,453,013,659 ; those from the United Kingdom, which has heretofore led in the race for this distinction were $1,418,348,000, and those from Germany $1,050,611,000. Additional interest is given to the first rank which the United States now holds as an exporting nation by the fact that a quarter of a century ago she stood fourth

in that list. In 1875 the domestic exports of the United States were $497,263,737 ; those of Germany, $607,096,000 ; those of France, $747,489,-000, and those of the United Kingdom, $1,087,-497,000. To-day the United States stands at the head of the list, the United Kingdom second, Germany third and France fourth, with the figures as follows: United States, $1,453,013,659 ; United Kingdom, $1,418,348,000 ; Germany, $1,050,611,000 ; France, $787,060,000. All of these figures, it should be remembered, relate to the exports of domestic products. Thus in the quarter century the United States has increased her exports from $497,263,737 to $1.453,013,659, or 192 per cent; Germany, from $607,096,000 to $1,050,611,000, or 73 per cent ; the United Kingdom, from $1,087,497,000 to $1,418,348,000, or 34 per cent, and France, from $747,489,000 to $787,060,000, or 5 per cent.

"The following table, compiled from official reports, shows the exports of domestic merchandise from the United States, the United Kingdom and Germany in each calendar year from 1875 to 1900 :

YEAR.	United States.	United Kingdom.	Germany.
1875.....	$497,263,737	$1,087,497,000	$607,096,000
1876.....	575,735,804	976,410,000	619,919,000
1877.....	607,666,495	967,913,000	672,151,000
1878.....	723,286,821	938,500,000	702,513,000
1879.....	754,656,755	932,000,000	675,397,000
1880.....	875,564,075	1,085,521,000	741,292,000
1881.....	814,162,951	1,138,873,000	724,379,000
1882.....	749,911,309	1,175,099,000	776,228,000
1883.....	777,523,718	1,166,982,000	796,208,000
1884.....	733,768,764	1,134,016,000	779,832,000
1885.....	673,593,506	1,037,124,000	695,892,000
1886.....	699,519,430	1,035,226,000	726,471,000
1887.....	703,319,692	1,079,944,000	762,897,000
1888.....	679,597,477	1,141,365,000	780,076,000
1889.....	814,154,864	1,211,442,000	770,537,000
1890.....	845,999,603	1,282,474,000	809,810,000
1891.....	957,333,551	1,203,160,000	772,679,000
1892.....	923,237,318	1,105,747,000	718,806,000
1893.....	854,729,454	1,062,162,000	753,361,000
1894.....	807,312,116	1,051,193,000	720,607,000
1895.....	807,742,415	1,100,452,000	807,328,000
1896.....	986,830,080	1,168,671,000	857,745,000
1897.....	1,079,834,296	1,139,882,000	884,486,000
1898.....	1,233,564,828	1,135,642,000	894,063,000
1899.....	1,253,466,000	1,287,971,039	1,001,278,000
1900.....	1,453,013,659	1,418,348,000	1,050,611,000

A. D. **1900–1901.**—Questions relating to **the** political status of the **new possessions of the** nation submitted to the Supreme Court.—Questions of surpassing importance, touching the political status of the new possessions which the nation had acquired from Spain, the relations of their inhabitants to the government and laws of the United States, the source and nature of the authority to be exercised over them by the Congress of the United States, whether exercised under the constitution of the United States or independently of it, were taken, in December and January (1900–1901), into the Supreme Court for authoritative decision, by appeals to that tribunal made in several suits which had arisen from disputed exactions of duty on importations from Porto Rico and the Philippine Islands. The questions had been burning ones in American politics, from the moment that the treaty of peace with Spain was signed, and the whole cast, character and consequence of the new policy of over-sea expansion on which the American Republic was then launched depended on the decision of the Court. Soon after the January argument and submission of these cases to the Supreme Court, their extraordinary importance was touched upon with impressive eloquence by the Hon. W. Bourke Cockran, in an address upon "John Marshall," in which he said:

"At this moment the [Supreme Court] is considering the gravest question ever submitted to a judicial tribunal in the history of mankind. Within a few days it must decide whether the government of the United States, or rather whether two of its departments can govern territory anywhere by the sword, or whether authority exercised by officers of the United States must be controlled and limited everywhere by the Constitution of the United States.

"I do not mention this momentous question to express the slightest opinion upon its merits, but merely that this assemblage of judges and of lawyers may realize the part which the judiciary is now required to play in determining the influence which this country must exercise forevermore in the family of nations. The power of Congress to acquire territory is of course unquestioned, but the disposition to exercise that power will always be controlled by the conditions under which newly acquired territory must be held, and these conditions the court must now prescribe. On the one hand it may hold that wherever power is exercised under the constitution there the limitations of the constitution must be obeyed—that wherever the executive undertakes to administer, or Congress to legislate, there the judiciary must enforce upon both respect for the organic law to which they owe their existence. If this doctrine be established it is clear that no scheme of forcible conquest will ever be undertaken by this government, for the simple reason that there can be no profit in such an enterprise. On the other hand the Court may decide that Congress can hold newly annexed territories on any terms that it chooses—that it may govern them according to the constitution or independently of it—that they may be administered to establish justice among the governed or for the glory and profit of the governors. If it be held that government for profit can be maintained under the authority of the United States, conceive the extent to which it may be carried and the consequences which it may portend. If it be possible to maintain two forms of government under our constitution, it is possible to establish twenty in as many different places. Territory may be annexed to the North, to the South, to the East and to the West. The President of the United States may be vested with imperial powers in one place, with royal prerogatives in another and perhaps remain a constitutional magistrate at home. He may be made a military autocrat in some South American State, an anointed emperor in some Northern clime, a turbaned sultan in some Eastern island. Nay, more, Congress can move itself and the seat of government from Washington to some newly annexed territory governed by officers of its own creation, subject to its own unlimited power, and thus take both outside the jurisdiction of the Supreme Court.

"Has the world ever before seen—could the framers of this constitution have conceived—a bench of judges exercising such a power amid the universal submission and approval of the whole people. And more extraordinary than all, this submission remains unanimous though the decision of the court may seriously affect its own position in the structure of our government. For if it be held that the constitution does not extend of itself over newly annexed territory, then clearly the authority of the court cannot extend to it except by the action of Congress and the executive. If the authority, that is to say, the existence of the court in any part of the territory of the United States, depends upon the other departments, then it is idle to contend that it is an independent and coördinate branch of the government. To decide that the executive and legislative departments have the right to govern territory outside the constitution the court must deliberately renounce the importance which it has heretofore enjoyed and accept for itself an inferior place in our political system.

"To me this is the most sublime spectacle ever presented in the history of the world. Think of it! A war has been waged with signal success, vast territory has been exacted from a conquered foe; a great political campaign has been fought and won upon the policy of taking this territory and governing it at the pleasure of Congress and the executive, yet if the court should hold that what the executive has attempted, what Congress has sanctioned, and what the people appear to have approved at the polls is in contravention of the constitution, not one voice would be raised to question the judgment or to resist its enforcement. I have said the spectacle is sublime; my friends, even a few weeks ago it was inconceivable. Before the late election I confess I believed and said that the success of the present administration would be interpreted as a popular endorsement of its foreign policy and that the popular verdict would very probably be made to exercise a strong if not decisive influence on the court. I admit now that I was mistaken. It is evident that this question will be decided on its merits without the slightest attempt to coerce, intimidate or influence the judges, and I say now with all frankness that whatever may be the judgment it will be the very best outcome for the people of this country, for the peace of the world, for the welfare of the human race. I cannot tell what this outcome may be, but I know that whenever a crisis has arisen in the pathway of the republic, the statesmanship of the common people has always met it with justice and solved it with wisdom."—W. Bourke Cockran, *John Marshall: an address before the Erie County Bar Association, Feb. 4, 1901, at Buffalo.*

Argument before the Supreme Court was begun on the 17th of December, 1900, on two cases thus stated in the brief submitted for the government: "On June 6, 1899, Goetze imported from Porto Rico into the port of New York a quantity of leaf or filler tobacco, upon which duty was assessed at 35 cents per pound as filler tobacco not specially provided for, in accordance with the provisions of paragraph 213 of the tariff act of 1897, commonly known as the 'Dingley Act.' The importer protested, claiming that the merchandise was not subject to duty, because Porto Rico at the time of the importation was not a foreign country and because, therefore, the imposition of duties on goods brought from a place within the territory of the United States into a port of the United States is not lawful and valid under the Constitution.

The Board of General Appraisers sustained the assessment of duty imposed by the collector upon the merchandise in question, and thereupon the importer appealed to the United States circuit court for the southern district of New York, by which court the decision of the Board of General Appraisers was affirmed in an opinion rendered by District Judge Townsend. From the judgment of the circuit court this appeal was taken.

"Porto Rico was partially occupied by the war forces of the United States during the months of July and August, 1898. By the protocol of August 12, 1898, between the United States and Spain, Spain agreed to cede Porto Rico to the United States and immediately evacuate. The evacuation was effected and full possession of the island assumed by the United States prior to January 1, 1899. From that date until the 1st of May, 1900, Porto Rico was occupied and governed by the military forces of the United States, under the command of the President, as conquered territory, under the law of belligerent right. The treaty of Paris, made in pursuance of the protocol, was signed December 10, 1898, ratified by the Senate February 6, 1899, and ratifications exchanged April 11, 1899. So that the importation in this case was subsequent to the ratification of the treaty, but prior to the establishment of a civil government in the island under act of Congress. It does not appear that the importers are citizens of the United States or of Porto Rico, nor whether or not the imported tobacco was the product of Porto Rico.

"In the case of Fourteen Diamond Rings, it appears that the claimant, Pepke, is a citizen of the United States and served as a United States soldier in the Island of Luzon; that while there he purchased or acquired the rings in question and brought them into the United States without paying duty thereon some time in the year 1899, between July 31 and September 25. The rings were seized, on May 18, 1900, at Chicago, by a United States customs officer as merchandise liable to duty which should have been invoiced, and was fraudulently imported and brought into the United States contrary to law. An information for the forfeiture of the rings was filed on behalf of the Government, June 1, 1900, to which the claimant pleaded. Setting up that at the time he acquired said property Luzon was a part of the territory of the United States and that the seizure of said goods was contrary to the claimant's right as a citizen of the United States under the Constitution, and particularly under section 2, Article IV, thereof, and he insisted that under Article I, section 8, Congress is required in laying and collecting taxes to see to it that all taxes and duties shall be uniform throughout the United States. To this plea the United States demurred, and upon hearing of the demurrer, the district court gave judgment of forfeiture for the Government. This judgment the claimant has removed into this court by a writ of error."

The contention of the government as set forth in the same brief, and the main contention of the appellants in the case, against which the argument for the government was directed, were partly as follows:

"The Tariff Act of 1897 declares that 'there shall be levied, collected and paid upon all articles imported from foreign countries and mentioned in the schedules herein contained, the rates of duty which are by the schedules and paragraphs respectively prescribed.' (30 Stat., 151.)

"The Government contends, and the circuit court so held, that this act applied to merchandise imported from Porto Rico and the Philippine Islands after their cession to the United States exactly as it did before; that within the meaning of the act these countries are to be regarded as foreign, belonging to but not forming in a domestic sense a part of the United States.

"That it is within the constitutional province of the treaty-making power to accept the cession of foreign territory upon such terms, conditions, and limitations as to its internal status as may best subserve the interests of the United States, and it is not necessary to invest such territory with the full status of an integral part of the Union.

"That this is one of the ordinary and necessary sovereign powers of an independent nation, and nothing in the Federal Constitution or in the fundamental principles that underlie our Republic denies to the nation a right to the full exercise of this usual and common sovereign right.

"That the treaty-making power—the President and the Senate—as evidenced by the language of the treaty of Paris, did not intend to make Porto Rico and the Philippine Islands integral parts of the United States, but intended, in several particulars, to reserve their final status for adjustment by Congress, at the same time making peculiar and special differential provisions for variations and exceptions in customs and port regulations as to Spain and Spanish goods and subjects, which are inconsistent with the intention that the ceded countries became upon the ratification of the treaty a part of the United States in all respects and in the fullest sense.

"The Government contends that the term 'foreign countries' in the act of 1897 is to be regarded as having been understood by Congress to be subject to the rule of interpretation of the phrase given by the Supreme Court in the case of Fleming v. Page, where it was held that under our revenue laws every port is regarded as a foreign one until expressly established as domestic under the authority and control of the statutes of the United States.

"That the clause of the Constitution which declares that duties, imposts, and excises shall be uniform throughout the United States does not apply to nor govern these cases, because the term 'United States,' as there used, means only the territory comprised within the several States of the Union, and was intended only for their benefit and protection, and not for the benefit or protection of outside territory belonging to the nation; that in the latter sense duties on imports from these islands are uniform throughout the United States, because they are uniformly imposed at every port in the United States, so that there is no preference given to the ports of one State over those of another, nor is any inequality between the several States created.

"That the right to bring merchandise into the United States is a right entirely within the regulation of Congress; such right in no wise differs as to either citizens or aliens. Citizenship carries with it no special or peculiar privileges at the custom-house. The American, the Spaniard, the Porto Rican, are treated alike. The basis of the customs laws is not ownership, but (1) the geographical origin of the shipment, and (2) the nature of the goods. The duty is imposed against merchandise, not upon the importer.

"The Government contends, therefore, that in view of the fact that tariff laws are 'in rem,' there is no principle of justice, much less of constitutional restriction, which forbids Congress from taxing in this way the merchandise of outlying possessions of the United States when brought into the ports of the Union. That the limitations of the Constitution as to customs, etc., were intended to secure equality between the States in the geographical sense, and not to forbid Congress from exercising the ordinary sovereign power of taxation as to the products of other sections of country not included within the geographical boundaries of the States; for which we rely upon the opinion of this court in Knowlton v. Moore as decisive and conclusive.

"If the foregoing propositions are sound, then it is established (1) that the tariff act of 1897 was intended by Congress to classify as foreign all countries not a part of or belonging to the United States at the time of its passage, and the subsequent cession of the Spanish islands to the United States did not operate to admit imports from those islands free of duty, under that law; (2) that the tariff act so construed and enforced violates no constitutional rule of uniformity.

"And the case of the plaintiffs in error would seem on these grounds to have no legal foundation.

"The Government might well be content to rest its argument upon these propositions. But counsel for the plaintiffs in error, in the court below as well as in this court, have gone far beyond these limits, and have challenged and denied the constitutionality of certain provisions of the treaty of Paris, contending that the cession of Porto Rico and the Philippine Archipelago effected a complete incorporation of those countries with the United States, so that they have become a part of the United States in the fullest and largest sense, not only internationally, but organically, so completely, indeed, that no difference or distinction can be made by law between imports from those countries and imports from one of the States of the Union.

"They insist that there can be no limited or qualified acquisition of territory by this nation; that when Porto Rico was ceded to the United States it came at once under the obligations of the Constitution and became entitled to the privileges of the Constitution, its inhabitants citizens of the United States, and its territory a part of the United States. They argue, therefore, that the clause of the treaty which says that 'the civil rights and political status of the inhabitants shall be determined by the Congress,' in so far as it is intended to defer the full enjoyment of the rights and privileges of citizenship under the Constitution until Congress shall bestow them hereafter upon the inhabitants, is 'ultra vires' and void. or at least superfluous and ineffective, because the Constitution 'ex proprio vigore' extends at once, as an automatic operation, to all territory ceded to this Govern-

ment, and no treaty or treaty-making power can hinder or even suspend it. . . .

"Counsel have been at great pains to prove that the Government of the United States is one of delegated powers, and that its powers are not absolute and untrammeled, but subject to certain limits never and nowhere to be transcended; that the vague political entity known as The People stands behind the constituted agencies of government, holding in reserve the sources of supreme power, capable and ready to alter or destroy at its pleasure the machinery heretofore set up in its behalf. They call these doctrines truisms, and so they are. They do not help us in this case.

"The Government of the United States has been vested not with all powers but only with certain particular powers. These particular delegated powers are in some respects limited and confined in scope and operation, but in other respects they are entirely unlimited. So that the real and practical question is whether there is any limitation preventing the particular thing here complained of.

"It is worth while, in passing, to allude to the undeniable fact that 'The People' referred to are not the people of the Territories or of the outlying possessions of the United States, but the people of the several States, who ordained and established for themselves and their posterity the Federal Constitution.

"Counsel confuse ideas when they argue that the contention of the Government in these cases implies the possession by Congress of all unlimited and despotic powers in the government of territory. We mean no more than this court meant when it said :

"'The power of Congress over the Territories is general and plenary.

"'Its sovereignty over them is complete.

"'It has full and complete legislative authority over the people of the Territories and all departments of the Territorial governments.

"'The people of the United States, as sovereign owners of the National Territories, have supreme power over them and their inhabitants.

"'In legislating for the Territories Congress would doubtless be subject to those fundamental limitations in favor of personal rights which are formulated in the Constitution and its amendments, but these limitations would exist rather by inference and the general spirit of the Constitution than by any express and direct application of its provisions.'"—*In the Supreme Court of the U. S., October Term, 1900, John H. Goetze, Appellant, &c.; Brief for the United States.*

On the 8th of January, 1901, four other causes, involving substantially the same questions, came before the Supreme Court, and, by order of the Court, were consolidated, to be dealt with virtually as one case. The titles of the cases were respectively as follows : Elias S. A. De Lima et al., plaintiffs in error, agt. George R. Bidwell ; Samuel B. Downes et al., plaintiffs in error, agt. George R. Bidwell ; Henry W. Dooley et al., plaintiffs in error, agt. the United States ; Carlos Armstrong, appellant, agt. the United States, and George W. Crossmon et al., appellants, agt. the United States. For the plaintiffs, in the case of Henry W. Dooley et al., the Hon. John G. Carlisle made an oral argument, in which he said : "What is the Constitution ? In the first place it is not only the supreme law of the States composing the union, but the supreme law of the land; supreme over every branch and department of the Government; supreme over every one exercising authority under the Government; supreme over every other law or order or regulation, and supreme over all the people, wherever they may be, within its jurisdiction, and what we claim is, that so long as this Constitution exists absolute and arbitrary power over the lives, liberties, or property of the people can be exercised nowhere in this Republic. It is now argued that it is supreme only within the boundaries of the several States, unless Congress extends it to the Territories; that it limits the powers of Congress only when legislating for the geographical area embraced in the States; that the inhabitants of the States are the only people who can, as a matter of right, claim the benefit of its guarantees and prohibitions for the protection even of those personal and property rights which have for ages been secured by the common law of England, and that all other people within the jurisdiction of the United States are dependent for the protection of their civil rights substantially upon the will of Congress. The question whether the Constitution should be declared to be the supreme law of the whole land, or only the supreme law of the respective States and their inhabitants or citizens, was presented in the Federal Convention of 1787, and was finally disposed of by the adoption of the clause as it now stands in the Constitution, which declares it to be the supreme law of the land.

"In the plan proposed by Mr. Charles Pinckney, of South Carolina, it was provided that 'all acts made by the legislature of the United States pursuant to this Constitution, and all treaties made under the authority of the United States, shall be the supreme law of the land,' etc. (1 Elliot, page 46). Mr. Patterson's plan proposed 'that all acts of the United States in Congress assembled made by virtue and in pursuance of the powers hereby vested in them, and by the Articles of Confederation and all treaties made and ratified under the authority of the United States, shall be the supreme law of the respective States, so far as those acts or treaties shall relate to such States or their citizens,' etc. (pages 71, 72). These plans and others were referred to the Committee of the Whole House and were reported back without any provision upon this subject. Afterwards the Convention unanimously agreed to the following resolution: 'That the Legislative acts made by virtue and in pursuance of the Articles of Union and all treaties made and ratified under the authority of the United States, shall be the supreme law of the respective States, so far as those acts or treaties shall relate to the said States or their citizens or inhabitants' (page 100). Thus it stood when referred to the committee of five, of which Mr. Rutledge was chairman, and on the 6th of August, 1787, that committee reported back to the Convention a draft of the proposed Constitution, the eighth article of which was the same as the resolution last quoted, except that in the place of the words 'Articles of Union' it contained the words 'this Constitution' (page 120). This report was considered in the Committee of the Whole, and on the 23d of August the eighth article was unanimously amended so as to read: 'This Constitution and all laws of the

United States made in pursuance thereof, and all treaties made under the authority of the United States shall be the supreme law of the several States and of their citizens and inhabitants,' etc. (page 151).

"This was the form in which the article stood when the whole draft was referred to the committee of eleven, but when reported back September 12, it constituted the second clause of the sixth article and declared that the Constitution and laws and the treaties made and to be made should be 'the supreme law of the land,' and so it now stands as part of the Constitution. If the clause had been adopted in the form agreed to in the committee and inserted in the first draft, there would have been at least a certain degree of plausibility in the argument made here for the Government, but even in that case we think the powers of Congress would have been limited whenever and wherever it might attempt to exercise them. But it is argued here that the history of the Constitution and the language employed in the preamble, and in some other places, show that it was intended to establish a government only for such of the States then existing as might ratify it, and such other States as might thereafter be admitted into the Union, and that, therefore, while it confers power upon Congress to govern Territories, it does not require that body to govern them in accordance with the supreme law of the land; that is, in accordance with the instrument from which the power to govern is derived. Even if the premises were true, the conclusion would not follow; but is it true that the Constitution was ordained and established for the government of the States only? If so, how did it happen that the great men who framed that instrument made it confer the power to govern Territories as well as States? It is true that the Constitution was ordained and established by the people of the States, but it created a National Government for national purposes, not a mere league or compact between the States, and jurisdiction was conferred upon that Government over the whole national domain, whatever its boundaries might be. It is not true that the Government was established only for the States, their inhabitants or citizens, but if it were true, then it could exercise no power outside of the States, and this court would have to put a new construction upon that provision which authorizes Congress to dispose of and make all needful rules and regulations respecting the territory, or other property, belonging to the United States. The necessary construction of that clause would be that it conferred power only to dispose of land or other property, and to make necessary rules and regulations respecting land or other property belonging to the United States; that is, belonging to the several States composing the Union. It would confer no power whatever to govern the people outside of the States."—*Supreme Court of the U. S., October Term*, 1900, *Henry W. Dooley [et al.] vs. the United States: Argument of J. G. Carlisle.*

On one point the argument of Mr. Charles H. Aldrich, attorney for the plaintiff in the case of the "Fourteen Diamond Rings," was as follows: In "'the relations of the United States to other nations, our government is a sovereign state, and has the right, and as such 'free and independent State has full power, to levy war, conclude peace, contract alliances, establish commerce, and to do all other acts and things which independent States may of right do.' In this relation it is correct, as I conceive, to speak of the United States of America as a unit and use a singular verb. It is such unit and has this power because there was created a government upon which the people conferred these powers. If war is declared it must be under the constitution; if peace is concluded it is in the exercise of a constitutional power; if commerce is established it is because Congress under the constitution was given power to regulate commerce; if alliances are contracted it can only be done under the constitution. In short, the sovereign nation exists through the adoption of the constitution, and its powers are derived from that instrument and must be found, as this court has often declared, in the language thereof or by necessary implication therefrom. We are in the Philippines and Porto Rico and can be rightfully there only in the exercise of some of these enumerated powers, as in the language of the tenth amendment, 'the powers not delegated to the United States by the Constitution, nor prohibited by it to the States, are reserved to the States respectively, or to the people.' This amendment designates the constitution as the source of the power of the United States and excludes the idea of power free from constitutional restraint derived by implication from powers delegated by the constitution.

"Nor is it true that at the time this declaration was made all independent states or nations claimed and exercised the right to acquire, hold and govern foreign dependencies, and no state or nation then recognized its obligation to confer on the people of such acquired territory the privileges and immunities enjoyed by the people of the home government, except at its own will and discretion. It is true that all independent states claimed and exercised the right to acquire territory, but if it were important in this case I think the arguments of Pitt, Camden and Barré could be used to establish the proposition that under the British Constitution as it then was, that nation had, from the time of King John and the Great Charter until King George, recognized that its subjects had essential rights not dependent upon the 'will and discretion' of the home government. It is unnecessary to follow that subject here. It is sufficient that the Declaration of Independence was brought about by the assertion on the part of King George and his ministers of precisely the present doctrine of this administration' and its representatives in this court. If value is to be attached to contemporary history that fact cannot be lost sight of. The speeches of Grenville and Townshend in favor of unlimited power on the part of Parliament over the American colonists and their affairs have been substantially parodied in Congress by the advocates of unrestrained power over our 'colonics,' as it is now unfortunately fashionable to denominate them. The signers of the Declaration of Independence held that as subjects of the British Constitution there was no right to impose taxes upon them without their consent, to deprive them of trial by jury, to deprive them of their legislatures, and to declare Parliament invested with power to legislate for them 'in all cases whatsoever.' These and other grievances were held denials of rights belonging to every British subject as such and to

justify rebellion and war. It seems impossible that a people who rebelled for such reasons established a State invested with the very power which they had denied to the British government and the assertions of which made rebellion necessary.

"This argument that the power to declare war and conclude peace carries with it, as an auxiliary, power to do whatever other nations are accustomed to do with the people and territory acquired through the exercise of these powers, has a remarkable likeness to the arguments put forward at the beginning of the century with reference to the Alien and Sedition Acts. The supporters of the constitutionality of these acts claimed that the common law had been introduced and become a part of the constitution of the United States, and therefore the powers usually exercisable under the common law could be exercised by the Congress of the United States in the respects involved in those acts. Mr. Madison's letter discussing this contention was answered, so far as it asserted the right of a state to nullify an act of Congress, but was never answered, so far as it denied the existence of the common law as a part of the constitution of the United States. His objections to that contention, succinctly stated, were, that if the common law was a part of the constitution, then there were no constitutional limitations. Congress, like Parliament, could legislate in all cases whatsoever; that the President would be possessed of the royal prerogatives (as is now claimed in this case by the Attorney-General); that the judiciary would have a discretion little short of legislative power; that these powers in the different branches of the government would not be alterable, because, being in the constitution, they could only be repealed by amendment of that instrument; and, lastly, that the constitution would have a different meaning in different States, inasmuch as the common law was different in such States, and that it would lack the certainty which a constitution should have, as the common law was an ever-growing or varying body of law, and, therefore, with reference to the proper action of the government in each instance, the question would be important as to what portion of the common law was in the constitution and what not so embodied.

"Nearly every sentence of Mr. Madison's able argument with reference to the common law as a part of the constitution is applicable to the contention that sovereign powers, so-called, as derived from or defined by international law, became a part of the constitution of the United States through the delegation of the powers to make war, conclude peace, and make all needful rules and regulations respecting the territory and other property belonging to the United States. This court has adopted the view of Mr. Madison. It is hoped that the child of the old error by which again the executive and legislative power is sought to be enlarged through the incorporation into the constitution of 'the sovereign power of other nations' will receive the same answer.

"In fact, we submit that this court has already held that sovereign power in the sense that the words are used in the law of nations as prerogative rights of the King or Emperor, not only is not vested in the United States or in any branch of its government, but cannot be so vested. The sovereign power is with the people. In leaving

6–43

it with the people our government marked a departure from all that had previously existed." —*Supreme Court of the U. S., October Term, 1900, No.* 419: C. H. Aldrich, *Argument in reply.*

A. D. **1901.**—Military and naval expenditure, compared with that of other **Powers.** See (in this vol.) WAR BUDGETS.

A. D. **1901** (January).—Apportionment of Representatives under **the** Twelfth Census.— The question of obedience to the Fourteenth Amendment.—Restrictions of the elective franchise in the States.—Section 3 of Article 1 of the Constitution requires that "Representatives . . . shall be apportioned among the several States which may be included within this Union according to their respective numbers. . . . The actual enumeration shall be made within three years after the first meeting of the Congress of the United States, and within every subsequent term of ten years. . . . The number of Representatives shall not exceed one for every 30,000; but each State shall have at least one." The first meeting of Congress was in 1789; the required first census of the United States was taken in 1790, and, in obedience to the constitutional requirement, the enumeration has been repeated within the closing year of every decade since, to supply the basis for a new apportionment of representatives among the States. The twelfth census, taken in 1900, called for such new distribution, and action upon it was taken in Congress in January, 1901.

As the section quoted above stood in the Constitution until 1868, it contained a further clause, inserted as one of the original compromises made between the slaveholding and the free States, requiring that the determination of numbers to be represented in the several States should be made "by adding to the whole number of free persons, including those bound to service for a term of years, and excluding Indians not taxed, three-fifths of all other persons." This original clause of the Constitution was superseded by the Fourteenth Amendment, adopted in 1868, which introduced this new provision, in its second section: "Representatives shall be apportioned among the several States according to their respective numbers, counting the whole number of persons in each State, except Indians not taxed. But when the right to vote at any election for the choice of electors for President and Vice President of the United States, Representatives in Congress, the executive and judicial officers of a State, or the members of the Legislature thereof, is denied to any of the male inhabitants of such State, being twenty-one years of age, and citizens of the United States, or in any way abridged, except for participation in rebellion, or other crime, the basis of representation therein shall be reduced in the proportion which the number of such male citizens shall bear to the whole number of male citizens twenty-one years of age in such State." To many persons it seemed to be very clear that this provision of the amended Constitution required account to be taken of the qualifications by which a number of States have abridged the suffrage, especially where done for the understood purpose of disfranchising colored citizens (see, in this vol., LOUISIANA, NORTH CAROLINA, SOUTH CAROLINA, MISSISSIPPI, and MARYLAND), and that Congress was left with no discretion to do otherwise.

Those holding this view in the House of Representatives gave support to the following resolution, introduced by Mr. Olmsted, of Pennsylvania:

"Whereas the continued enjoyment of full representation in this House by any State which has, for reasons other than participation in rebellion or other crime, denied to any of the male inhabitants thereof, being 21 years of age and citizens of the United States, the right to vote for Representatives in Congress, Presidential electors, and other specified officers, is in direct violation of the fourteenth amendment to the Constitution of the United States, which declares that in such case 'the basis of representation therein shall be reduced in the proportion which the number of such male citizens shall bear to the whole number of male citizens 21 years of age in such State,' and is an invasion of the rights and dignity of this House and of its members, and an infringement upon the rights and privileges in this House of other States and their representatives; and

"Whereas the States of Massachusetts, Maine, Connecticut, Delaware, California, Louisiana, Mississippi, North Carolina, South Carolina, Wyoming, Oregon, and other States do, by the provisions of the constitutions and statutes of said States, and for reasons other than participation in rebellion or other crime, deny the right to vote for members of Congress and Presidential electors, as well as the executive and judicial officers of such States and members of the legislatures thereof, to male inhabitants 21 years of age and over and citizens of the United States; and such denial in certain of the said States extends to more than one-half of those who prior to the last apportionment of representation were entitled to vote in such States; and

"Whereas in order that the apportionment of membership of the House of Representatives may be determined in a constitutional manner: Therefore, be it

"Resolved by the House of Representatives, That the Director of the Census is hereby directed to furnish this House, at the earliest possible moment, the following information:

"First. The total number of male citizens of the United States over 21 years of age in each of the several States of the Union.

"Second. The total number of male citizens of the United States over 21 years of age who, by reason of State constitutional limitations or State legislation, are denied the right of suffrage, whether such denial exists on account of illiteracy, on account of pauperism, on account of polygamy, or on account of property qualifications, or for any other reason.

"Resolved further, That the Speaker of the House of Representatives is hereby authorized and directed to appoint a select committee of five members from the membership of the Census Committee of the House of Representatives, who shall investigate the question of the alleged abridgment of the elective franchise for any of the causes mentioned in all the States of the Union in which constitutional or legislative restrictions on the right of suffrage are claimed to exist, and that such committee report its findings within twenty days from the date of the adoption of this resolution to the said Census Committee, and that within one week after the said report shall have been received by the Census Committee the Census Committee shall return a bill to the House of Representatives providing for the apportionment of the membership of the House of Representatives based on the provisions of the fourteenth amendment to the Constitution of the United States."

Republicans, hardly less than Democrats, in Congress and outside, were averse to raising what could not fail to be a burning sectional issue, and grounds for ignoring the constitutional mandate were sought with considerable eagerness on both sides. Strict obedience to the requirement of the Constitutional provision was claimed to be impracticable, at least within the time available for proceedings connected with the present apportionment of representatives. Said one speaker, opposing the resolutions in the House: "There is not a State in this Union that has not added to or subtracted from the Federal constitutional requirements—not one. . . . If there is any addition, whether as a matter of police regulation or otherwise, to the constitutional amendments regulating the franchise and the resultant representation in this House—if there is addition or subtraction of one iota—then those who desire to live up to this Constitution, no matter whether they ruin their neighbors, no matter whether they again kindle the fires of sectional strife, those who in their love for the Constitution are so mentally rigid that they would demand its enforcement though they set the Union aflame, must include every State in this Union."

Said another: "How would anybody find out how many people in the State of Mississippi were disfranchised for the reasons stated in this resolution? There is there an educational qualification. How are you to determine how many of the men in the State of Mississippi who did not vote, did not vote because they were disfranchised under the educational qualification? Then there is a qualification in extension and not in limitation of the suffrage, saying that even those who can not read and write may still vote, provided they can give an understanding interpretation of the Constitution or any part of it. How are you going to determine how many are disqualified by that? And then there is a qualification which says that those can not vote who shall not by a certain time have paid their poll tax. Out of the number of people who did not vote, how are you going to determine which of them have not voted because of the educational qualification? Which because of the understanding qualification? Which because of the poll-tax qualification? Which because of the registration qualification? How many because of the pure Australian ballot which exists in the State of Mississippi? . . . There is not a State in the Union which has the Australian ballot which by the very fact and the necessity of voting according to that Australian ballot does not prevent the citizen who can not read and write from voting if he votes a split ticket of any sort."

A third speaker remarked: "To live up to that amendment, 'that no male inhabitant shall be deprived of suffrage except for participation in the rebellion or other crimes,' the male inhabitant, I take it, is he who has acquired domicile in that State, and the moment that he acquires domicile, and is a male, he is a 'male inhabitant' of that State, and entitled at once to suffrage; and yet every State in the Union, I be-

lieve without exception, has requirements as to residence not only in the State, but in the city, in the county, in the precinct and ward and the voting place; and every one of those requirements, as every gentleman on that side must admit, are in direct conflict with and contravention of the fourteenth amendment to the Constitution of the United States literally construed."

But the advocates of obedience to the Constitution, supporting the resolutions of Mr. Olmsted, planted their argument on the very facts brought against it, as demonstrating the need of measures to check a growing tendency in the country to restrict the elective franchise. Said Mr. Shattuck, of Ohio: "We find that in 1870 there were three States that had abridged their electorates—California, Connecticut, and Massachusetts. In these three States there was a constitutional provision for an educational qualification, which disfranchised a certain percentage of the electorate—namely, the illiterates. But, in those States, the percentage of illiteracy is very light, averaging about 6 per cent. The basis of representation would hardly have been affected in those States had the fourteenth amendment been conformed with.

"An examination into the election laws of the various States reveals an astonishing tendency at this time to abridge their electorates. When the Congress which adopted the existing apportionment discussed the matter ten years ago but three States had abridged their electorate by action of the State, and in these the percentage of disfranchised males was but 6 per cent. But since that time similar policies have been adopted by other States, and to-day we face the fact that ten of the forty-five States of this Union have abridged their electorates, and that in these the percentage of males 21 years of age and over, disfranchised, averages over 20 per cent. The constitutions of several other States permit such an abridgment. Besides, there are other States preparing to adopt these policies and to disfranchise thousands of men who to-day hold the right of franchise. In view of this remarkable tendency it is inconceivable that Congress can longer permit the fourteenth amendment to remain a dead letter, and to pass a bill making an apportionment based solely upon the population and neglecting the proviso which applies to all States which have abridged their electorate.

"We will not review the past by any discussion of the question as to whether the provisions of the fourteenth amendment should have been made effective when the last apportionment was made ten years ago. We find to-day conditions existing which make its enforcement imperative. I do not propose to discuss at this time whether the reasons given for these abridgments by the people of the various States are valid or not. . . . I am simply pointing out the conditions as they exist; I am simply pointing out that the time has come when the tendency of the States to abridge their electorates has grown to such proportions as to demand that this Congress shall proceed in a constitutional manner in making the new apportionment. I do not say that States have not the right to establish educational qualifications for their electors, but I do maintain that when they have done so they must pay the penalty prescribed in the Constitution, and have their representation abridged proportionately. I do not say that we shall punish only Louisiana; I do not say that we shall punish only Massachusetts; I do not say that we shall punish only California; but I do say and insist, as the representative of a State in which every male member 21 years of age and over is guaranteed the sacred right of franchise, that there is a constitutional remedy prescribed for their acts, and I do demand that that remedy be applied."

The following interesting table, showing the restrictions of the electorate in the various States of the Union, was appended to the remarks of Mr. Shattuck:

STATES.	REQUIREMENTS AS TO CITIZENSHIP.	PERSONS EXCLUDED FROM SUFFRAGE.
Alabama	Citizen of United States, or alien who has declared intention.	Convicted of treason or other crime punishable by imprisonment, idiots, or insane.
Arkansas	Citizen of United States, or alien who has declared intention.	Idiots, insane, convicted of felony until pardoned, failure to pay poll tax, United States soldiers on duty in state.
California	Citizen by nativity, naturalization, or treaty of Queretaro.	Chinese, insane, embezzlers of public moneys, convicted of infamous crime, person unable to read Constitution in English, and to write his name.
Colorado	Citizen or alien, male or female, who has declared intention 4 months prior to election.	Under guardianship, insane, idiots, or imprisoned.
Connecticut	Citizen of United States	Convicted of felony or theft, unless pardoned. Person unable to read Constitution or statutes.
Delaware	Citizen who has paid registration fee of $1.	Idiots, insane, paupers, felons. Person who can not read the English language and write his name.
Florida	Citizen of United States	Insane, under guardianship, convicted of felony or any infamous crime.
Georgia	Citizen of the United States who has paid all his taxes since 1877.	Idiots, insane, convicted of crime punishable by imprisonment until pardoned, failure to pay taxes.
Idaho	Citizen of the United States, male or female.	Under guardianship, idiots, insane, convicted of felony, treason, or embezzlement of public funds, polygamist or bigamist.
Illinois	Citizen of the United States	Convicted of felony.
Indiana	Citizen of United States, or alien who has declared intention and resided 1 year in United States and 6 months in State.	Convicted of crime and disfranchised by judgment of the court, United States soldiers, Sailors, and marines.
Iowa	Citizen of the United States	Idiots, insane, convicted of infamous crime.
Kansas	Citizen of United States, alien who has declared intention, or [under] treaties with Mexico.	Felons, insane, duelists, rebels, not restored to citizenship, under guardianship, public embezzlers, offering or accepting a bribe.
Kentucky	Citizen of the United States	Treason, felony, bribery at election.
Louisiana	Citizen of United States or alien who has declared intention.	Idiots, insane, convicted of treason, embezzlement of public funds, all crime punishable by imprisonment in penitentiary, persons unable to read and write, and not owning property in the State assessed at $300, or not the son or grandson of a citizen of the United States prior to Jan. 1, 1867, person who has not paid poll tax.
Maine	Citizen of the United States	Paupers, persons under guardianship, Indians not taxed, and in 1893 all new voters who can not read the Constitution or write their own names in English.
Maryland	Citizen of the United States	Convicted of larceny or other infamous crime, unless pardoned, persons convicted of bribery.
Massachusetts	Citizen of the United States	Paupers and persons under guardianship, person who can not read Constitution in English and write his name.
Michigan	Citizen or inhabitant who has declared intention under United States laws 6 months before election and lived in State 2½ years.	Indians, duelists, and accessories.
Minnesota	Citizen of United States or alien who has declared intention, and civilized Indians.	Convicted of treason or felony, unless pardoned, persons under guardianship or insane.
Mississippi	Citizen of the United States	Insane, idiots, Indians not taxed, felons, persons who have not paid taxes, persons who can not read or understand Constitution.
Missouri	Citizen of United States or alien who has declared intention not less than 1 year or more than 5 before offering to vote.	United States soldiers and marines, paupers, criminals convicted once until pardoned, felons and violators of suffrage laws convicted a second time.
Montana	Citizen of the United States	Felons, unless pardoned, idiots, insane, United States Soldiers, seamen, and marines, Indians.
Nebraska	Citizen of United States or alien who has declared intention.	Convicts.
Nevada	Citizen of the United States	Idiots, insane, unpardoned convicts, Indians, Chinese.
New Hampshire	Citizen of United States	Paupers (except honorably discharged United States soldiers and sailors), persons excused from paying taxes at their own request.
New Jersey	Citizen of the United States or alien who has declared intention 30 days prior to election.	Idiots, insane paupers, persons convicted of crimes (unless pardoned) which exclude them from being witnesses.
New York	Citizen who shall have been a citizen for 90 days.	Convicted of bribery or any infamous crime, Indians under tribal relations.
North Carolina	Citizen of the United States	Convicted of felony or other infamous crime, idiots, lunatics, persons unable to read or write, unless lineal descendant of citizen of United States prior to Jan. 1, 1867, nonpayment of poll tax.
North Dakota	Citizen of the United States, alien who has declared intention 1 year, and civilized Indian.	Under guardianship, persons non compos mentis, or convicted of felony and treason, unless restored to civil rights.
Ohio	Citizen of the United States	Felony until pardoned, idiots, insane, United States soldiers and sailors.

676

STATES.	REQUIREMENTS AS TO CITIZENSHIP.	PERSONS EXCLUDED FROM SUFFRAGE.
Oregon............	Citizen of United States or alien who has declared intention 1 year preceding election.	Idiots, insane, convicted of felony, United States soldiers and sailors, Chinese.
Pennsylvania......	Citizen of the United States at least 1 month, and if 22 years old or more, must have paid tax within 2 years.	Convicted of some offense whereby right of suffrage is forfeited, nontaxpayers.
Rhode Island......	Citizen of the United States..........	Paupers, lunatics, persons non compos mentis, convicted of bribery or infamous crime until restored to right to vote under guardianship.
South Carolina....	Citizen of the United States..........	Convicted of treason, murder, or other infamous crime, dueling, paupers, insane, idiots, person who has not paid poll tax, who can not read and write any section of the State constitution, or can show that he has paid all taxes on property within the State assessed at $300.
South Dakota.....	Citizen of the United States or alien who has declared intention.	Under guardianship, idiots, insane, convicted of treason or felony, unless pardoned.
Tennessee.........	Citizen of the United States who has paid poll tax of preceding year.	Convicted of bribery or other infamous offense.
Texas.............	Citizen of the United States or alien who has declared intention.	Idiots, lunatics, paupers, convicted of felony, United States soldiers and seamen.
Utah..............	Citizen, male and female.............	Idiots, insane, convicted of treason or violation of election laws.
Vermont..........	Citizen of the United States..........	Those who have not obtained the approbation of the board of civil authority of the town in which they reside.
Virginia..........	Citizen of the United States..........	Idiots, lunatics, convicted of bribery at election, embezzlement of public funds, treason, felony and petty larceny, duelists and abettors unless pardoned by legislature.
Washington.......	Citizen of the United States..........	Indians not taxed, idiots, insane, persons convicted of infamous crimes.
West Virginia.....	Citizen of the State..................	Paupers, idiots, lunatics, convicted of treason, felony, or bribery at elections.
Wisconsin.........	Citizen of the United States or alien who has declared intention.	Insane, under guardianship, convicted of treason or felony, unless pardoned, Indians having tribal relations.
Wyoming.........	Citizen of the United States, male and female.	Idiots, insane, persons convicted of infamous crimes unless restored to civil rights, unable to read state constitution.

— *Congressional Record, January* 4–5, 1901, *pp.* 618–20, *and* 662–5.

The resolutions of Mr. Olmsted were not adopted. The reapportionment was made on the basis of the totals of the census returns, with no reckoning of any denials of the right to vote. The following is the text of the Act, as passed and approved January 16:

" Be it enacted by the Senate and House of Representatives of the United States of America in Congress assembled, That after the third day of March, nineteen hundred and three, the House of Representatives shall be composed of three hundred and eighty-six members [the existing number being 357] to be apportioned among the several States as follows: Alabama, nine; Arkansas, seven; California, eight; Colorado, three; Connecticut, five; Delaware, one; Florida, three; Georgia, eleven; Idaho, one; Illinois, twenty-five; Indiana, thirteen; Iowa, eleven; Kansas, eight; Kentucky, eleven; Louisiana, seven; Maine, four; Maryland, six; Massachusetts, fourteen; Michigan, twelve; Minnesota, nine; Mississippi, eight; Missouri, sixteen; Montana, one; Nebraska, six; Nevada, one; New Hampshire, two; New Jersey, ten; New York, thirty-seven; North Carolina, ten; North Dakota, two; Ohio, twenty-one; Oregon, two; Pennsylvania, thirty-two; Rhode Island, two; South Carolina, seven; South Dakota, two; Tennessee, ten; Texas, sixteen; Utah, one; Vermont, two; Virginia, ten; Washington, three; West Virginia, five; Wisconsin, eleven; and Wyoming, one.

"SEC. 2. That whenever a new State is admitted to the Union the Representative or Representatives assigned to it shall be in addition to the number three hundred and eighty-six.

"SEC. 3. That in each State entitled under this apportionment, the number to which such State may be entitled in the Fifty-eighth and each subsequent Congress shall be elected by districts composed of contiguous and compact territory and containing as nearly as practicable an equal number of inhabitants. The said districts shall be equal to the number of the Representatives to which such State may be entitled in Congress, no one district electing more than one Representative.

"SEC. 4. That in case of an increase in the number of Representatives which may be given to any State under this apportionment such additional Representative or Representatives shall be elected by the State at large, and the other Representatives by the districts now prescribed by law until the legislature of such State in the manner herein prescribed, shall redistrict such State ; and if there be no increase in the number of Representatives from a State the Representatives thereof shall be elected from the districts now prescribed by law until such State be redistricted as herein prescribed by the legislature of said State ; and if the number hereby provided for shall in any State be less than it was before the change hereby made, then the whole number to such State hereby provided for shall be elected at large, unless the legislatures of said States have provided or shall otherwise provide before the time fixed by law for the next election of Representatives therein.

"SEC. 5. That all Acts and parts of Acts inconsistent with this Act are hereby repealed."

No existing State quota was reduced by the new apportionment, and the gains were as follows: Illinois, New York and Texas, 3 ; Minnesota, New Jersey and Pennsylvania, 2 ; Arkansas, California, Colorado, Connecticut, Florida, Louisiana, Massachusetts, Mississippi, Missouri,

North Carolina, North Dakota, Washington, West Virginia and Wisconsin, 1.

That clause of the third section which requires districts to be " composed of contiguous and compact territory " is intended to be a bar to the partisan trick called " gerrymandering."

The vote on the bill in the House (165 against 102) was singularly non-partisan. The minority was said to be composed of exactly the same number of Republicans and Democrats, 51 of each, and in the majority vote there were included 84 Republicans and 81 Democrats. The vote was also non-sectional, except that New England voted almost solidly for the measure. East, South and West the State delegations were almost equally divided.

A. D. 1901 (February).—Act to increase the standing army of the nation to 100,000 men.— In his annual Message to Congress, December 3, 1900, the President set forth the military needs of the country, created by its new policy of imperial expansion, and recommended that the permanent army be raised to 100,000 in number, from 45,000 to 60,000 of which would be required in the Philippine Islands until their people were made submissive to the authority of the United States. In accord with the executive recommendation, Congress passed " an Act to increase the efficiency of the permanent military establishment of the United States," which became law by the President's signature on the 2d of February, 1901. Its first section provides that " from and after the approval of this Act the Army of the United States, including the existing organizations, shall consist of fifteen regiments of cavalry, a corps of artillery, thirty regiments of infantry, one Lieutenant-General, six major-generals, fifteen brigadier-generals, an Adjutant-General's Department, an Inspector-General's Department, a Judge-Advocate-General's Department, a Quartermaster's Department, a Subsistence Department, a Medical Department, a Pay Department, a Corps of Engineers, an Ordnance Department, a Signal Corps, the officers of the Record and Pension Office, the chaplains, the officers and enlisted men of the Army on the retired list, the professors, corps of cadets, the army detachments and band at the United States Military Academy, Indian scouts as now authorized by law, and such other officers and enlisted men as may hereinafter be provided for." A subsequent section enacts that the total enlisted force of the line of the army shall not exceed at any one time 100,000.

Section 2 provides that " each regiment of cavalry shall consist of one colonel, one lieutenant-colonel, three majors, fifteen captains, fifteen first lieutenants, and fifteen second lieutenants ; two veterinarians, one sergeant-major, one quartermaster-sergeant, one commissary-sergeant, three squadron sergeants-major, two color-sergeants with rank, pay, and allowances of squadron sergeant-major, one band, and twelve troops organized into three squadrons of four troops each. . . . Each troop of cavalry shall consist of one captain, one first lieutenant, one second lieutenant, one first sergeant, one quartermaster-sergeant, six sergeants, six corporals, two cooks, two farriers and blacksmiths, one saddler, one wagoner, two trumpeters, and forty-three privates ; the commissioned officers to be assigned from among those hereinbefore authorized."

Sections 3-9, relating to the Artillery, are, in part, as follows : "That the regimental organiza-

tion of the artillery arm of the United States Army is hereby discontinued, and that arm is constituted and designated as the Artillery Corps. It shall be organized as hereinafter specified and shall belong to the line of the Army. That the Artillery Corps shall comprise two branches— the coast artillery and the field artillery. The coast artillery is defined as that portion charged with the care and use of the fixed and movable elements of land and coast fortifications, including the submarine mine and torpedo defenses ; and the field artillery as that portion accompanying an army in the field, and including field and light artillery proper, horse artillery, siege artillery, mountain artillery, and also machine-gun batteries : Provided, That this shall not be construed to limit the authority of the Secretary of War to order coast artillery to any duty which the public service demands or to prevent the use of machine or other field guns by any other arm of the service under the direction of the Secretary of War. . . . That the Artillery Corps shall consist of a Chief of Artillery, who shall be selected and detailed by the President from the colonels of artillery, to serve on the staff of the general officer commanding the Army, and whose duties shall be prescribed by the Secretary of War ; fourteen colonels, one of whom shall be the Chief of Artillery ; thirteen lieutenant-colonels, thirty-nine majors, one hundred and ninety-five captains, one hundred and ninety-five first lieutenants, one hundred and ninety-five second lieutenants ; and the captains and lieutenants provided for in this section not required for duty with batteries or companies shall be available for duty as staff officers of the various artillery garrisons and such other details as may be authorized by law and regulations ; twenty-one sergeants-major, with the rank, pay, and allowances of regimental sergeants-major of infantry ; twenty-seven sergeants-major, with the rank, pay, and allowances of battalion sergeants-major of infantry ; one electrician sergeant to each coast artillery post having electrical appliances ; thirty batteries of field artillery, one hundred and twenty-six batteries of coast artillery, and ten bands organized as now authorized by law for artillery regiments : Provided, That the aggregate number of enlisted men for the artillery, as provided under this Act, shall not exceed eighteen thousand nine hundred and twenty, exclusive of electrician sergeants."

Concerning the Infantry it is provided, in Section 10, that ' each regiment of infantry shall consist of one colonel, one lieutenant colonel, three majors, fifteen captains, fifteen first lieutenants, and fifteen second lieutenants ; one sergeant-major, one quartermaster-sergeant, one commissary-sergeant, three battalion sergeants-major, two color sergeants, with rank, pay, and allowances of battalion sergeants-major, one band, and twelve companies, organized into three battalions of four companies each. Of the officers herein provided, the captains and lieutenants not required for duty with the companies shall be available for detail as regimental and battalion staff officers and such other details as may be authorized by law or regulations. . . . Each infantry company shall consist of one captain, one first lieutenant, one second lieutenant, one first sergeant, one quartermaster-sergeant, four sergeants, six corporals, two cooks, two musicians, one artificer, and forty-eight privates, the commissioned officers to be assigned from those hereinbefore authorized."

Section 11 provides that "the enlisted force of the Corps of Engineers shall consist of one band and three battalions of engineers. . . . Each battalion of engineers shall consist of one sergeant-major, one quartermaster-sergeant, and four companies. Each company of engineers shall consist of one first sergeant, one quartermaster-sergeant, with the rank, pay, and allowances of sergeant, eight sergeants, ten corporals, two musicians, two cooks, thirty-eight first-class and thirty-eight second-class privates."

Section 12 relates to the appointment of army chaplains—one for each regiment of cavalry and infantry, and twelve for the corps of artillery—no person to be appointed who has passed the age of forty years. The office of post chaplain is abolished. Sections 13 to 27 relate mainly to the organization of the several Departments, of the Adjutant-General, Inspector-General, Judge-Advocate-General, Quartermaster-General, Commissary-General, Surgeon-General, Paymaster-General, Chief of Engineers, Chief of Ordnance, etc.

Section 28, prescribing the rules of promotion and appointment, is as follows: "That vacancies in the grade of field officers and captain, created by this Act, in the cavalry, artillery, and infantry shall be filled by promotion according to seniority in each branch, respectively. Vacancies existing after the promotions have been made shall be provided for as follows: A sufficient number shall be reserved in the grade of second lieutenant for the next graduating class at the United States Military Academy. Persons not over forty years of age who shall have at any time served as volunteers subsequent to April twenty-first, eighteen hundred and ninety-eight, may be ordered before boards of officers for such examination as may be prescribed by the Secretary of War, and those who establish their fitness before these examining boards may be appointed to the grades of first or second lieutenant in the Regular Army, taking rank in the respective grades according to seniority as determined by length of prior commissioned service; but no person appointed under the provisions of this section shall be placed above another in the same grade with longer commissioned service, and nothing herein contained shall change the relative rank of officers heretofore commissioned in the Regular Army. Enlisted men of the Regular Army or volunteers may be appointed second lieutenants in the Regular Army to vacancies created by this Act, provided that they shall have served one year, under the same conditions now authorized by law for enlisted men of the Regular Army."

Important provisions are embodied in Sections 35 and 36, as follows: "SEC. 35. That the Secretary of War be, and he is hereby, authorized and directed to cause preliminary examinations and surveys to be made for the purpose of selecting four sites with a view to the establishment of permanent camp grounds for instruction of troops of the Regular Army and National Guard, with estimates of the cost of the sites and their equipment with all modern appliances, and for this purpose is authorized to detail such officers of the Army as may be necessary to carry on the preliminary work; and the sum of ten thousand dollars is hereby appropriated for the necessary expense of such work, to be disbursed under the direction of the Secretary of War: Provided, That the Secretary of War shall report to Congress the result of such examination and surveys, and no contract for said sites shall be made nor any obligation incurred until Congress shall approve such selections and appropriate the money therefor.

"SEC. 36. That when in his opinion the conditions in the Philippine Islands justify such action the President is authorized to enlist natives of those islands for service in the Army, to be organized as scouts, with such officers as he shall deem necessary for their proper control, or as troops or companies, as authorized by this Act, for the Regular Army. The President is further authorized, in his discretion, to form companies, organized as are companies of the Regular Army, in squadrons or battalions, with officers and non-commissioned officers corresponding to similar organizations in the cavalry and infantry arms. The total number of enlisted men in said native organizations shall not exceed twelve thousand, and the total enlisted force of the line of the Army, together with such native force, shall not exceed at any one time one hundred thousand. . . . When, in the opinion of the President, natives of the Philippine Islands shall, by their services and character, show fitness for command, the President is authorized to make provisional appointments to the grades of second and first lieutenants from such natives, who, when so appointed, shall have the pay and allowances to be fixed by the Secretary of War, not exceeding those of corresponding grades of the Regular Army."

Section 38 abolishes the so-called "Army Canteen," in compliance with strenuous demands from temperance organizations in the country, notwithstanding much testimony favorable to the canteen system from well-informed and conscientious witnesses. The language of the section is as follows: "The sale of or dealing in beer, wine, or any intoxicating liquors, by any person in any post exchange or canteen or army transport, or upon any premises used for military purposes by the United States, is hereby prohibited. The Secretary of War is hereby directed to carry the provisions of this section into full force and effect." Prompt obedience to this command of law was given by the War Department, which issued the required general order February 4th.

The following amendment, proposed by Senator Hoar for addition to the Act, was voted down: "Provided, That no further military force shall be used in the Philippine Islands, except such as may be necessary to keep order in places there now actually under the peaceable control of the United States and to protect persons or property to whom, in the judgment of the President, protection may be due from the United States, until the President shall have first proclaimed an amnesty for all political offenses committed against the United States in the Philippine Islands, and shall have, if in his power, agreed upon an armistice with persons now in hostility to the United States, and shall have invited such number, not less than 10, as he shall think desirable of the leaders or representatives of the persons now hostile to the United States there to come to the United States and state their wishes and the condition. character. and wishes of the people of the Philippine Islands to the

Executive and Congress, and shall have offered to secure to them safe conduct to come, abide, and return, and shall have provided at the public charge for the expenses of their transportation both ways and their stay in this country for a reasonable and sufficient time for such purpose."

A. D. 1901 (February).—The Russian sugar question.—U. S. countervailing duty and Russian retaliation. See (in this vol.) SUGAR BOUNTIES.

A. D. 1901 (February—March).—Adoption of the so-called "Spooner Amendment" to the Army Appropriation Bill empowering the President to establish a civil government in the Philippines. See (in this vol.) PHILIPPINE ISLANDS: A. D. 1901 (FEBRUARY—MARCH).

A. D. 1901 (February—March).—Adoption of the "Platt Amendment," prescribing conditions on which the President is authorized to "leave the government and control of the island of Cuba to its people." See (in this vol.) CUBA: A. D. 1901 (FEBRUARY—MARCH).

A. D. 1901 (March).—Reinauguration of President McKinley for a second term in the executive office.—His inaugural address.—The reinauguration of President McKinley, for the second term of office to which he had been elected, was performed with the customary ceremonies, at the capitol, in Washington, on the 4th of March, 1901. His inaugural address upon the occasion is especially interesting, for the reason that it indicates the understanding with which the President received his re-election, and the interpretation which he has put upon it as an expression of the national will on questions of extraordinary moment. He spoke as follows:

"My Fellow Citizens: When we assembled here on March 4, 1897, there was great anxiety with regard to our currency and credit. None exists now. Then our treasury receipts were inadequate to meet the current obligations of the government. Now they are sufficient for all public needs, and we have a surplus instead of a deficit. Then I felt constrained to convene the Congress in extraordinary session to devise revenues to pay the ordinary expenses of the government. Now I have the satisfaction to announce that the Congress just closed has reduced taxation in the sum of $41,000,000. Then there was deep solicitude because of the long depression in our manufacturing, mining, agricultural and mercantile industries, and the consequent distress of our laboring population. Now every avenue of production is crowded with activity, labor is well employed and American products find good markets at home and abroad. Our diversified productions, however, are increasing in such unprecedented volume as to admonish us of the necessity of still further enlarging our foreign markets by broader commercial relations. For this purpose reciprocal trade arrangements with other nations should in liberal spirit be carefully cultivated and promoted.

"The national verdict of 1896 has for the most part been executed. Whatever remains unfulfilled is a continuing obligation resting with undiminished force upon the Executive and the Congress. But fortunate as our condition is, its permanence can only be assured by sound business methods and strict economy in national administration and legislation. We should not permit our great prosperity to lead us to reckless ventures in business or profligacy in public ex-

penditures. While the Congress determines the objects and the sum of appropriations, the officials of the executive departments are responsible for honest and faithful disbursement, and it should be their constant care to avoid waste and extravagance. Honesty, capacity and industry are nowhere more indispensable than in public employment. These should be fundamental requisites to original appointment and the surest guarantees against removal.

"Four years ago we stood on the brink of war without the people knowing it and without any preparation or effort at preparation for the impending peril. I did all that in honor could be done to avert the war, but without avail. It became inevitable, and the Congress at its first regular session, without party division, provided money in anticipation of the crisis and in preparation to meet it. It came. The result was signally favorable to American arms and in the highest degree honorable to the government. It imposed upon us obligations from which we cannot escape, and from which it would be dishonorable to seek to escape. We are now at peace with the world, and it is my fervent prayer that if differences arise between us and other powers they may be settled by peaceful arbitration, and that hereafter we may be spared the horrors of war.

"Intrusted by the people for a second time with the office of President, I enter upon its administration appreciating the great responsibilities which attach to this renewed honor and commission, promising unreserved devotion on my part to their faithful discharge and reverently invoking for my guidance the direction and favor of Almighty God. I should shrink from the duties this day assumed if I did not feel that in their performance I should have the co-operation of the wise and patriotic men of all parties. It encourages me for the great task which I now undertake to believe that those who voluntarily committed to me the trust imposed upon the chief executive of the republic will give to me generous support in my duties to 'preserve, protect and defend the constitution of the United States,' and to 'care that the laws be faithfully executed.' The national purpose is indicated through a national election. It is the constitutional method of ascertaining the public will. When once it is registered it is a law to us all, and faithful observance should follow its decrees

"Strong hearts and helpful hands are needed, and fortunately we have them in every part of our beloved country. We are reunited. Sectionalism has disappeared. Division on public questions can no longer be traced by the war maps of 1861. These old differences less and less disturb the judgment. Existing problems demand the thought and quicken the conscience of the country, and the responsibility for their presence as well as for their righteous settlement rests upon us all, no more upon me than upon you. There are some national questions in the solution of which patriotism should exclude partisanship. Magnifying their difficulties will not take them off our hands nor facilitate their adjustment. Distrust of the capacity, integrity and high purpose of the American people will not be an inspiring theme for future political contests. Dark pictures and gloomy forebodings are worse than useless. These only becloud, they do not help to point, the way of safety and honor. 'Hope maketh not ashamed.'

"The prophets of evil were not the builders of the republic, nor in its crises have they saved or served it. The faith of the fathers was a mighty force in its creation, and the faith of their descendants has wrought its progress and furnished its defenders. They are obstructionists who despair and who would destroy confidence in the ability of our people to solve wisely and for civilization the mighty problems resting upon them. The American people, intrenched in freedom at home, take their love for it with them wherever they go, and they reject as mistaken and unworthy the doctrine that we lose our own liberties by securing the enduring foundations of liberty to others. Our institutions will not deteriorate by extension, and our sense of justice will not abate under tropic suns in distant seas.

" As heretofore so hereafter will the nation demonstrate its fitness to administer any new estate which events devolve upon it, and in the fear of God will 'take occasion by the hand and make the bounds of freedom wider yet.' If there are those among us who would make our way more difficult we must not be disheartened, but the more earnestly dedicate ourselves to the task upon which we have rightly entered. The path of progress is seldom smooth. New things are often found hard to do. Our fathers found them so. We find them so. They are inconvenient. They cost us something. But are we not made better for the effort and sacrifice, and are not those we serve lifted up and blessed?

"We will be consoled, too, with the fact that opposition has confronted every onward movement of the republic from its opening hour until now, but without success. The republic has marched on and on, and its every step has exalted freedom and humanity. We are undergoing the same ordeal as did our predecessors nearly a century ago. We are following the course they blazed. They triumphed. Will their successors falter and plead organic impotency in the nation? Surely after one hundred and twenty-five years of achievement for mankind we will not now surrender our equality with other Powers on matters fundamental and essential to nationality. With no such purpose was the nation created. In no such spirit has it developed its full and independent sovereignty. We adhere to the principle of equality among ourselves, and by no act of ours will we assign to ourselves a subordinate rank in the family of nations.

"My fellow citizens, the public events of the last four years have gone into history. They are too near to justify recital. Some of them were unforeseen; many of them momentous and far reaching in their consequences to ourselves and our relations with the rest of the world. The part which the United States bore so honorably in the thrilling scenes in China, while new to American life, has been in harmony with its true spirit and best traditions, and in dealing with the results its policy will be that of moderation and fairness.

"We face at this moment a most important question—that of the future relations of the United States and Cuba. With our near neighbors we must remain close friends. The declaration of the purposes of this government in the resolution of April 20, 1898, must be made good. Ever since the evacuation of the island by the army of Spain the Executive with all practicable speed has been assisting its people in the successive steps necessary to the establishment of a free and independent government prepared to assume and perform the obligations of international law, which now rest upon the United States under the Treaty of Paris. The convention elected by the people to frame a constitution is approaching the completion of its labors. The transfer of American control to the new government is of such great importance, involving an obligation resulting from our intervention and the treaty of peace, that I am glad to be advised by the recent act of Congress of the policy which the legislative branch of the government deems essential to the best interests of Cuba and the United States. The principles which led to our intervention require that the fundamental law upon which the new government rests should be adapted to secure a government capable of performing the duties and discharging the functions of a separate nation, of observing its international obligations, of protecting life and property, insuring order, safety and liberty, and conforming to the established and historical policy of the United States in its relation to Cuba.

" The peace which we are pledged to leave to the Cuban people must carry with it the guarantees of permanence. We became sponsors for the pacification of the island, and we remain accountable to the Cubans no less than to our own country and people for the reconstruction of Cuba as a free commonwealth, on abiding foundations of right, justice, liberty and assured order. Our enfranchisement of the people will not be completed until free Cuba shall 'be a reality, not a name—a perfect entity, not a hasty experiment, bearing within itself the elements of failure.'

"While the treaty of peace with Spain was ratified on February 6, 1899, and ratifications were exchanged nearly two years ago, the Congress has indicated no form of government for the Philippine Islands. It has, however, provided an army to enable the Executive to suppress insurrection, restore peace, give security to the inhabitants and establish the authority of the United States throughout the archipelago. It has authorized the organization of native troops as auxiliary to the regular force. It has been advised from time to time of the acts of the military and naval officers in the islands, of my action in appointing civil commissions, of the instructions with which they were charged, of their duties and powers, of their recommendations and of their several acts under Executive commission, together with the very complete general information they have submitted.

"These reports fully set forth the conditions, past and present, in the islands, and the instructions clearly show the principles which will guide the Executive until the Congress shall, as it is required to do by the treaty, determine 'the civil rights and political status of the native inhabitants.' The Congress having added the sanction of its authority to the powers already possessed and exercised by the Executive under the constitution, thereby leaving with the Executive the responsibility for the government of the Philippines, I shall continue the efforts already begun until order shall be restored throughout the islands, and as fast as conditions permit will establish local governments, in the formation of which the full co-operation of the people has been already invited, and when established will encourage the people to administer them.

"The settled purpose, long ago proclaimed, to afford the inhabitants of the islands self-government as fast as they were ready for it will be pursued with earnestness and fidelity. Already something has been accomplished in this direction. The government's representatives, civil and military, are doing faithful and noble work in their mission of emancipation, and merit the approval and support of their countrymen. The most liberal terms of amnesty have already been communicated to the insurgents, and the way is still open for those who have raised their arms against the government for honorable submission to its authority.

"Our countrymen should not be deceived. We are not waging war against the inhabitants of the Philippine Islands. A portion of them are making war against the United States. By far the greater part of the inhabitants recognize American sovereignty, and welcome it as a guarantee of order and security for life, property, liberty, freedom of conscience and the pursuit of happiness. To them full protection will be given. They shall not be abandoned. We will not leave the destiny of the loyal millions in the islands to the disloyal thousands who are in rebellion against the United States. Order under civil institutions will come as soon as those who now break the peace shall keep it. Force will not be needed or used when those who make war against us shall make it no more. May it end without further bloodshed, and there be ushered in the reign of peace, to be made permanent by a government of liberty under law."

A. D. 1901 (March).—Rejection by the British government of the Interoceanic Canal Treaty as amended by the Senate. See(iu this vol.) CANAL, INTEROCEANIC : A. D. 1901 (MARCH).

A. D. 1901 (March).—Death of Ex-President Harrison.—Benjamin Harrison, President of the United States 1889–1893, died at his home in Indianapolis, on the afternoon of March 13, 1901, after an illness of a few days.

A. D. 1901 (March—April).—Capture of Aguinaldo, the Filipino leader.—His oath of allegiance to the United States. See (in this vol.) PHILIPPINE ISLANDS: A. D. 1901 (MARCH—APRIL).

A. D. 1901 (April).—Organization of the enlarged regular army.—Its strength, 76,000 men.—A Press despatch from Washington, April 24, announced that the Secretary of War had approved recommendations of Lieutenant-General Miles for the organization of the army, not raising it to the full strength of 100,000 men authorized by Congress, but providing for a force of 76,787 enlisted men, distributed as follows : "Line of the army, 74.504 ; ordnance department, 700 ; signal corps, 760 : post quartermaster sergeants, 150 ; post commissary sergeants, 200 ; electrician sergeants, 100 ; Military Academy detachment and band, 298 ; Indian scouts, 75. The cavalry is to be organized into fifteen regiments, consisting of 12 troops of 85 enlisted men, which, with the bands, will make a cavalry force of 15,840 men. The infantry is to consist of 38,520 men, divided into 30 regiments of 12 companies each. The artillery corps will have a total of 18,862 men, of which the coast artillery will have

13,734, organized into 126 companies of 109 men each ; and the field artillery, 4,800 men, organized into 30 batteries of 150 men each. The engineer battalions will consist of 12 companies amounting to 1,282 men. This plan makes no provision for the employment of Filipino natives, but this is explained by the fact that the 12,000 authorized for the native military force was made a distinctive feature of the Army bill by Congress and separated from the Regular Army."

A. D. 1901 (April).—Petition from the workingmen of Porto Rico. See (in this vol.) PORTO RICO : A. D. 1901 (APRIL).

A. D. 1901 (May).—Decision of the Supreme Court in the cases involving questions touching the status of the new territorial possessions of the nation.—The opinions of the Supreme Court in the cases before it known as "the insular cases," involving questions touching the relations of the government of the United States to the insular possessions lately acquired (see above: A. D. 1900–1901), were announced on the 27th of May, as these sheets of the present volume were about to go to press.

In the case of Elias S. A. De Lima et al. the opinion of the majority of the Court, delivered by Justice Brown, was against the claim of the government to duties on goods imported into the United States from Porto Rico after the ratification of the treaty of peace with Spain and before the passage of the Porto Rican act of April 12, 1900 (see, in this vol., PORTO RICO : A. D. 1899–1900; and 1900, APRIL). It was held in this decisive opinion that Porto Rico, at the time the duties in question were collected, was not a foreign country, but a territory of the United States. Said Justice Brown: "If an Act of Congress be necessary to convert a foreign country into domestic territory, the question at once suggests itself, What is the character of the legislation demanded for this purpose? Will an act appropriating money for its purchase be sufficient? Apparently not. Will an act appropriating the duties collected upon imports to and from such country for the benefit of its government be sufficient? Apparently not. Will acts making appropriations for its postal service, for the establishment of lighthouses, for the maintenance of quarantine stations, for erecting public buildings, have that effect? Will an act establishing a complete local government, but with the reservation of a right to collect duties upon commerce, be adequate for that purpose? None of these, nor all together, will be sufficient, if the contention of the government be sound, since acts embracing all these provisions have been passed in connection with Porto Rico, and it is insisted that it is still a foreign country within the meaning of the tariff laws. We are unable to acquiesce in this assumption that a territory may be at the same time both foreign and domestic. We are, therefore, of the opinion that at the time these duties were levied Porto Rico was not a foreign country within the meaning of the tariff laws, but a territory of the United States; that the duties were illegally exacted, and that the plaintiffs are entitled to recover them back."

But in the case of Samuel B. Downes et al. a different set of circumstances was dealt with, since the duties in question were on goods imported from Porto Rico after the passage of the Act of April 12 (called "the Foraker Act").

On the question thus presented the majority of the Court sustained the contention of the government, saying, in an opinion delivered by Justice Brown: "We are of opinion that the island of Porto Rico is a territory appurtenant and belonging to the United States, but not a part of the United States within the revenue clause of the Constitution; that the Foraker act is constitutional so far as it imposes duties upon imports from such island and that the plaintiff cannot recover the duties exacted in this case." The following general conclusions were held by Justice Brown to be established:

"First—That the District of Columbia and the Territories are not States, within the judicial clause of the Constitution giving jurisdiction in cases between citizens of different States.

"Second—That Territories are not States, within the meaning of revised statutes, section 709, permitting writs of error from this court in cases where the validity of a State's statute is drawn in question.

"Third—That the District of Columbia and the Territories are States as that word is used in treaties with foreign powers, with respect to the ownership, disposition and inheritance of property.

"Fourth—That the Territories are not within the clause of the Constitution providing for the creation of a Supreme Court and such inferior courts as Congress may see fit to establish.

"Fifth—That the Constitution does not apply to foreign countries or trials therein conducted, and that Congress may lawfully provide for such trials before consular tribunals, without the intervention of a grand or petit jury.

"Sixth—That where the Constitution has been once formally extended by Congress to Territories, neither Congress nor the Territorial Legislature can enact laws inconsistent therewith."

Five of the nine justices of the Court concurred in the decree announced by Justice Brown; but three of them, viz., Justices White, Shiras and McKenna, placed their concurrence on different and quite opposed grounds, in an opinion prepared by Justice White. In their view of the case before the court, "the sole and only issue is, had Porto Rico, at the time of the passage of the Act in question, been incorporated into and become an integral part of the United States?" and their conclusion is reported to have been, that "the question when Porto Rico was to be incorporated was a political question, to be determined by the American people, speaking through Congress, and was not for the courts to determine."

The minority of the Court, consisting of Chief Justice Fuller, Justices Harlan, Brewer and Peckham dissented from the decree rendered by the majority, and from the varying grounds on which the two sections of that majority had rested it. As summarized in press despatches

of the day, their opinion, delivered by the Chief Justice, "absolutely rejected the contention that the rule of uniformity [that is, the constitutional provision that 'all duties, imposts and excises shall be uniform throughout the United States'] was not applicable to Porto Rico because it had not been incorporated into and become an integral part of the United States; the word incorporation had no occult meaning, and whatever its situation before, the Foraker act made Porto Rico an organized Territory of the United States." "The concurring opinion of the majority," said the Chief Justice, "recognized that Congress, in dealing with the people of new territories or possessions, is bound to respect the fundamental guarantees of life, liberty and property, but assumes that Congress is not bound in those territories or possessions to follow the rules of taxation prescribed by the Constitution. And yet the power to tax involves the power to destroy and the levy of duty touches all our people in all places under the jurisdiction of the Government. The logical result is that Congress may prohibit commerce altogether between the States and Territories, and may prescribe one rule of taxation in one Territory, and a different rule in another. That theory assumes that the Constitution created a government empowered to acquire countries throughout the world, to be governed by different rules than those obtaining in the original States and Territories, and substitutes for the present system of republican government, a system of domination over distant provinces in the exercise of unrestricted power. In our judgment, so much of the Porto Rican act as authorized the imposition of these duties is invalid and plaintiffs were entitled to recover."

Justice Harlan announced his concurrence with the dissenting opinion delivered by the Chief Justice. He regarded the Foraker act as unconstitutional in its revenue provisions, and believed that Porto Rico, after the ratification of the treaty with Spain, became a part of the United States. In conclusion, Justice Harlan said: "The addition of Porto Rico to the territory of the United States has been recognized by direct action upon the part of Congress. It has legislated in recognition of the treaty with Spain. If Porto Rico did not by such action become a part of the United States it did become such, at least, when Congress passed the Foraker act. I can not believe that Congress may impose any duty, impost or excise with respect to that territory and its people which is not consistent with the constitutional requirement that all duties, imposts and excises shall be uniform throughout the United States."

No decision was rendered in the case of the Fourteen Diamond Rings, which involved questions relative to the status of the Philippine Islands in their relations to the government of the United States.

UNITED STATES OF CENTRAL AMERICA.—Its formation and dissolution. See (in this vol.) CENTRAL AMERICA: A. D. 1821–1898.

UNITED STATES STEEL CORPORATION. See (in this vol.) TRUSTS: UNITED STATES: THE CLIMAX, &c.

UNIVERSITIES. See EDUCATION.

UNIVERSITY OF PENNSYLVANIA: Expeditions to explore the ruins of Nippur. See (in this vol.) ARCHÆOLOGICAL RESEARCH: BABYLONIA: AMERICAN EXPLORATION.

UNYORO: British regulation of the kingdom. See (in this vol.) UGANDA: A. D. 1897–1898.

UR. See (in vol. 1) BABYLONIA, PRIMITIVE;

(in vol. 4) SEMITES; and (in this vol.) ARCHÆ-
OLOGICAL RESEARCH: BABYLONIA.

URUGUAY: A. D. 1896-1899.—Revolutionary movement.—Assassination of President
Borda.—Blancos and Colorados.—Restoration of tranquil government by the Vice President, Cuestas.—In November, 1896, a movement for the overthrow of President Borda was
begun, with strong assistance from the neighboring Brazilian State of Rio Grande do Sul.
Months of civil war followed, with varying fortunes, but the summer of 1897 found the President parleying with the insurgents, endeavoring
to make terms. His original opponents had
been the party called that of the Blancos, or
Whites; the Colorados, or Reds, had supported
him; but he seemed to be making enemies among
them. By an assassin of his own party he was
shot, on the 25th of August, as he came from a
service in the cathedral at Montevideo which
commemorated the anniversary of Uruguayan
independence. Señor Juan Luis Cuestas, the
President of the Senate and ex-officio Vice President of the Republic, assumed the administration of the government, made peace with the
insurgents, and prepared to deal with a faction
in the Chambers which is said to have made
good government impossible. "The Representatives had made themselves hated by violence,
corruption, and attacks on property. Señor
Cuestas accordingly removed all officials devoted
to the Chambers, called out a thousand National
Guards, and being thus master of the situation,
on February 10th dissolved the Chambers and
declared himself provisional President. He then
appointed a 'Council' of eighty prominent citizens of all parties, invested them with the legislative power, and directed them to elect a new

President, and to settle the method and time of
the next elections. . . . According to the 'Times''
correspondent, the citizens of Monte Video of all
parties approved his action, not a stroke was
struck for the Chambers, and public securities
rose at once by from eight to fourteen points.
Señor Cuestas, in fact, is trusted and competent."
—The Spectator (London), March 26, 1898.—In
due time, the Provisional President had to deal
with a military revolt, which he effectually suppressed. Then, on the 1st of March, 1899, he
was constitutionally elected President, after resigning his dictatorial powers for a fortnight, in
order that the election might be freely held.

UTAH: A. D. 1895-1896.—Prohibition of
polygamous marriages.—Proclamation of admission to the Union.—On the 4th of January,
1896, a proclamation by the President of the
United States, after reciting the provisions of the
Act of Congress approved July 16, 1894, and the
action taken by a convention of the people of
Utah, held in accordance with the said act, in
March, 1895, which convention "did, by ordinance irrevocable without the consent of the
United States and the people of said State, as
required by said act, provide that perfect toleration of religious sentiment shall be secured and
that no inhabitant of said State shall ever be
molested in person or property on account of his
or her mode of religious worship, but that polygamous or plural marriages are forever prohibited," thereupon declared and proclaimed the
creation of the State of Utah and its admission
into the Union to be accomplished. The constitution of the new State has some radical features, providing for an eight-hours labor-day,
and giving to women equal rights with men in
suffrage and in eligibility to public office.

V.

VASSOS, Colonel, in Crete. See (in this
vol.) TURKEY: A. D. 1897 (FEBRUARY—MARCH).

"VEGETARIANS," The. See (in this vol.)
CHINA: A. D. 1895 (AUGUST).

VENEZUELA: A. D. 1895.—Revolt suppressed. An attempted rising, in the interest of
Dr. Rojas Paul, against the government of President Crespo, in the autumn of 1895, was quickly
suppressed.
A. D. 1895 (July).—The question of the
boundary of British Guiana taken up by the
government of the United States.—Despatch
of Secretary Olney to Ambassador Bayard.—
For a number of years the government of the
United States had been exerting itself to bring
about the settlement of a long standing dispute
between Great Britain and Venezuela concerning
the line of boundary between the territory of
Venezuela and that of British Guiana. In 1895
the effort became more resolute, as appeared in
a lengthy despatch addressed, on the 20th of
July, by the American Secretary of State, Mr.
Olney, to the American Ambassador in London,
Mr. Bayard. In this despatch Mr. Olney reviewed the long controversy which had been in
progress, and recalled the communications on the
subject which had passed between the governments of the United States and Great Britain
· since 1886. He then summarised "the important

features of the existing situation" as represented
in his recital, by the following statement:
"1. The title to territory of indefinite but confessedly very large extent is in dispute between Great Britain on the one hand, and the
South American Republic of Venezuela on the
other. 2. The disparity in the strength of the
claimants is such that Venezuela can hope to
establish her claim only through peaceful methods—through an agreement with her adversary
either upon the subject itself or upon an arbitration. 3. The controversy with varying claims
on the part of Great Britain has existed for more
than half-a-century, during which period many
earnest and persistent efforts of Venezuela to
establish a boundary by agreement have proved
unsuccessful. 4. The futility of the endeavour
to obtain a conventional line being recognized,
Venezuela, for a quarter of a century, has asked
and striven for arbitration. 5. Great Britain,
however, has always and continuously refused,
and still refuses, to arbitrate except upon the
condition of a renunciation of a large part of the
Venezuelan claim, and of a concession to herself
of a large share of the territory in controversy.
6. By the frequent interposition of its good
offices at the instance of Venezuela, by constantly
urging and promoting the restoration of diplomatic relations between the two countries, by
pressing for arbitration of the disputed boundary,

by offering to act as Arbitrator, by expressing its grave concern whenever new alleged instances of British aggression upon Venezuelan territory have been brought to its notice, the Government of the United States has made it clear to Great Britain and to the world that the controversy is one in which both its honour and its interests are involved, and the continuance of which it cannot regard with indifference."

Mr. Olney proceeds next to consider the rights, the interests and the duty of the United States in the matter, and to what extent, if any, it "may and should intervene in a controversy between and primarily concerning only Great Britain and Venezuela," and his conclusions on these points are founded on the doctrine set forth by President Monroe, of resistance to European intervention in American affairs. Quoting President Monroe's celebrated Message on the subject, in 1823, Mr. Olney remarks:

" The Message just quoted declared that the American continents were fully occupied, and were not the subjects for future colonization by European Powers. To this spirit and this purpose, also, are to be attributed the passages of the same Message which treat any infringement of the rule against interference in American affairs on the part of the Powers of Europe as an act of unfriendliness to the United States. It was realized that it was futile to lay down such a rule unless its observance could be enforced. It was manifest that the United States was the only Power in this hemisphere capable of enforcing it. It was therefore courageously declared, not merely that Europe ought not to interfere in American affairs, but that any European Power doing so would be regarded as antagonizing the interests and inviting the opposition of the United States.

" That America is in no part open to colonization, though the proposition was not universally admitted at the time of its first enunciation, has long been universally conceded. We are now concerned, therefore, only with that other practical application of the Monroe doctrine the disregard of which by an European Power is to be deemed an act of unfriendliness towards the United States. The precise scope and limitations of this rule cannot be too clearly apprehended. It does not establish any general Protectorate by the United States over other American States. It does not relieve any American State from its obligations as fixed by international law, nor prevent any European Power directly interested from enforcing such obligations or from inflicting merited punishment for the breach of them. It does not contemplate any interference in the internal affairs of any American State, or in the relations between it and other American States. It does not justify any attempt on our part to change the established form of Government of any American State, or to prevent the people of such State from altering that form according to their own will and pleasure. The rule in question has but a single purpose and object. It is that no European Power or combination of European Powers shall forcibly deprive an American State of the right and power of self-government, and of shaping for itself its own political fortunes and destinies. That the rule thus defined has been the accepted public law of this country ever since its promulgation cannot fairly be denied. . . .

"It is manifest that, if a rule has been openly and uniformly declared and acted upon by the Executive Branch of the Government for more than seventy years without express repudiation by Congress, it must be conclusively presumed to have its sanction. Yet it is certainly no more than the exact truth to say that every Administration since President Monroe's has had occasion, and sometimes more occasions than one, to examine and consider the Monroe doctrine, and has in each instance given it emphatic indorsement. . . . A doctrine of American public law thus long and firmly established and supported could not easily be ignored in a proper case for its application, even were the considerations upon which it is founded obscure or questionable. No such objection can be made, however, to the Monroe doctrine understood and defined in the manner already stated. It rests, on the contrary, upon facts and principles that are both intelligible and incontrovertible. That distance and 3,000 miles of intervening ocean make any permanent political union between an European and an American State unnatural and inexpedient will hardly be denied. But physical and geographical considerations are the least of the objections to such a union. Europe, as Washington observed, has a set of primary interests which are peculiar to herself. America is not interested in them, and ought not to be vexed or complicated with them. . . .

"If, . . . for the reasons stated, the forcible intrusion of European Powers into American politics is to be deprecated—if, as it is to be deprecated, it should be resisted and prevented—such resistance and prevention must come from the United States. They would come from it, of course, were it made the point of attack. But, if they come at all, they must also come from it when any other American State is attacked, since only the United States has the strength adequate to the exigency. Is it true, then, that the safety and welfare of the United States are so concerned with the maintenance of the independence of every American State as against any European Power as to justify and require the interposition of the United States whenever that independence is endangered? The question can be candidly answered in but one way. The States of America, South as well as North, by geographical proximity, by natural sympathy, by similarity of Governmental Constitutions, are friends and allies, commercially and politically, of the United States. To allow the subjugation of any of them by an European Power is, of course, to completely reverse that situation, and signifies the loss of all the advantages incident to their natural relations to us. But that is not all. The people of the United States have a vital interest in the cause of popular self-government. . . . To-day the United States is practically Sovereign on this continent, and its fiat is law upon the subjects to which it confines its interposition. Why? It is not because of the pure friendship or goodwill felt for it. It is not simply by reason of its high character as a civilised State, nor because wisdom and justice and equity are the invariable characteristics of the dealings of the United States. It is because, in addition to all other grounds, its infinite resources, combined with its isolated position, render it master of the situation, and practically invulnerable as against any or all other Powers. All the advantages of this superiority are at once imperilled if the principle be admitted that European Powers may convert American States into Colonies or provinces of their own. The principle would be eagerly availed of, and every Power doing so would immediately acquire a base of military operations against us. What one Power was permitted to do could not be denied to another, and it is not inconceivable that the struggle now going on for the acquisition of Africa might be transferred to South America. If it were, the weaker countries would unquestionably be soon absorbed, while the ultimate result might be the partition of all South America between the various European Powers. . . .

"The people of the United States have learned in the school of experience to what extent the relations of States to each other depend not upon sentiment nor principle, but upon selfish interest. They will not soon forget that, in their hour of distress, all their anxieties and burdens were aggravated by the possibility of demonstrations against their national life on the part of Powers with whom they had long maintained the most harmonious relations. They have yet in mind that France seized upon the apparent opportunity of our Civil War to set up a Monarchy in the adjoining State of Mexico. They realize that, had France and Great Britain held important South American possessions to work from and to benefit, the temptation to destroy the predominance of the Great Republic in this hemisphere by furthering its dismemberment might have been irresistible. From that grave peril they have been saved in the past, and may be saved again in the future, through the operation of the sure but silent force of the doctrine proclaimed by President Monroe. . . .

"There is, then, a doctrine of American public law, well founded in principle and abundantly sanctioned by precedent, which entitles and requires the United States to treat as an injury to itself the forcible assumption by an European Power of political control over an American State. The application of the doctrine to the boundary dispute between Great Britain and Venezuela remains to be made, and presents no real difficulty. Though the dispute relates to a boundary-line, yet, as it is between States, it necessarily imports political control to be lost by one party and gained by the other. The political control at stake, too, is of no mean importance, but concerns a domain of great extent—the British claim, it will be remembered, apparently expanding in two years some 33,000 square miles—and, if it also directly involves the command of the mouth of the Orinoco, is of immense consequence in connection with the whole river navigation of the interior of South America. It has been intimated, indeed, that in respect of these South American possessions, Great Britain is herself an American State like any other, so that a controversy between her and Venezuela is to be settled between themselves as if it were between Venezuela and Brazil, or between Venezuela and Colombia, and does not call for or justify United States' intervention. If this view be tenable at all, the logical sequence is plain. Great Britain as a South American State is to be entirely differentiated from Great Britain generally; and if the boundary question cannot be settled otherwise than by force, British Guiana with her own independent resources, and not

those of the British Empire, should be left to settle the matter with Venezuela—an arrangement which very possibly Venezuela might not object to. But the proposition that an European Power with an American dependency is for the purposes of the Monroe doctrine to be classed not as an European but as an American State will not admit of serious discussion. If it were to be adopted, the Monroe doctrine would be too valueless to be worth asserting. . . .

"The declaration of the Monroe Message—that existing Colonies or dependencies of an European Power would not be interfered with by the United States—means Colonies or dependencies then existing with their limits as then existing. So it has been invariably construed, and so it must continue to be construed, unless it is to be deprived of all vital force. Great Britain cannot be deemed a South American State within the purview of the Monroe doctrine, nor, if she is appropriating Venezuelan territory, is it material that she does so by advancing the frontier of an old Colony instead of by the planting of a new Colony. The difference is matter of form, and not of substance, and the doctrine if pertinent in the one case must be in the other also. It is not admitted, however, and therefore cannot be assumed, that Great Britain is in fact usurping dominion over Venezuelan territory. While Venezuela charges such usurpation Great Britain denies it, and the United States, until the merits are authoritatively ascertained, can take sides with neither. But while this is so—while the United States may not, under existing circumstances at least, take upon itself to say which of the two parties is right and which wrong—it is certainly within its right to demand that the truth shall be ascertained. . . .

"It being clear, therefore, that the United States may legitimately insist upon the merits of the boundary question being determined, it is equally clear that there is but one feasible mode of determining them, viz., peaceful arbitration. The impracticability of any conventional adjustment has been often and thoroughly demonstrated. Even more impossible of consideration is an appeal to arms—a mode of settling national pretensions unhappily not yet wholly obsolete. If, however, it were not condemnable as a relic of barbarism and a crime in itself, so one-sided a contest could not be invited nor even accepted by Great Britain without distinct disparagement to her character as a civilized State. Great Britain, however, assumes no such attitude. On the contrary, she both admits that there is a controversy, and that arbitration should be resorted to for its adjustment. But, while up to that point her attitude leaves nothing to be desired, its practical effect is completely nullified by her insistence that the submission shall cover but a part of the controversy—that, as a condition of arbitrating her right to a part of the disputed territory, the remainder shall be turned over to her. If it were possible to point to a boundary which both parties had ever agreed or assumed to be such either expressly or tacitly, the demand that territory conceded by such line to British Guiana should be held not to be in dispute might rest upon a reasonable basis. But there is no such line. The territory which Great Britain insists shall be ceded to her as a condition of arbitrating her claim to other territory has never been admitted to belong to her. It

has always and consistently been claimed by Venezuela. Upon what principle—except her feebleness as a nation—is she to be denied the right of having the claim heard and passed upon by an impartial Tribunal? No reason or shadow of reason appears in all the voluminous literature of the subject. . . .

"In these circumstances, the duty of the President appears to him unmistakable and imperative. Great Britain's assertion of title to the disputed territory, combined with her refusal to have that title investigated, being a substantial appropriation of the territory to her own use, not to protest and give warning that the transaction will be regarded as injurious to the interests of the people of the United States, as well as oppressive in itself, would be to ignore an established policy with which the honour and welfare of this country are closely identified. While the measures necessary or proper for the vindication of that policy are to be determined by another branch of the Government, it is clearly for the Executive to leave nothing undone which may tend to render such determination unnecessary. You are instructed, therefore, to present the foregoing views to Lord Salisbury by reading to him this communication (leaving with him a copy should he so desire), and to reinforce them by such pertinent considerations as will doubtless occur to you. They call for a definite decision upon the point whether Great Britain will consent or will decline to submit the Venezuelan boundary question in its entirety to impartial arbitration. It is the earnest hope of the President that the conclusion will be on the side of arbitration, and that Great Britain will add one more to the conspicuous precedents she has already furnished in favour of that wise and just mode of adjusting international disputes. If he is to be disappointed in that hope, however—a result not to be anticipated, and in his judgment calculated to greatly embarrass the future relations between this country and Great Britain—it is his wish to be made acquainted with the fact at such early date as will enable him to lay the whole subject before Congress in his next Annual Message."— *Great Britain, Parliamentary Publications (Papers by Command: United States No. 1, 1896, pp. 13–21).*

A. D. **1895** (November).—The British Guiana boundary question.—Replies of Lord Salisbury to Secretary Olney.—The reply of Lord Salisbury was not written until the 26th of November. It was then given in two despatches, bearing the same date,—one devoted entirely to a discussion of "the Monroe doctrine" and of the argument founded on it by Mr. Olney; the other to a rehearsal of the Venezuela controversy from the standpoint of the British government. In the communication first mentioned he wrote:

"The contentions set forth by Mr. Olney in this part of his despatch are represented by him as being an application of the political maxims which are well known in American discussion under the name of the Monroe doctrine. As far as I am aware, this doctrine has never been before advanced on behalf of the United States in any written communication addressed to the Government of another nation; but it has been generally adopted and assumed as true by many eminent writers and politicians in the United

States. It is said to have largely influenced the Government of that country in the conduct of its foreign affairs; though Mr. Clayton, who was Secretary of State under President Taylor, expressly stated that that Administration had in no way adopted it. But during the period that has elapsed since the Message of President Monroe was delivered in 1823, the doctrine has undergone a very notable development, and the aspect which it now presents in the hands of Mr. Olney differs widely from its character when it first issued from the pen of its author. The two propositions which in effect President Monroe laid down were, first, that America was no longer to be looked upon as a field for European colonization; and, secondly, that Europe must not attempt to extend its political system to America, or to control the political condition of any of the American communities who had recently declared their independence. The dangers against which President Monroe thought it right to guard were not as imaginary as they would seem at the present day. . . . The system of which he speaks, and of which he so resolutely deprecates the application to the American Continent, was the system then adopted by certain powerful States upon the Continent of Europe of combining to prevent by force of arms the adoption in other countries of political institutions which they disliked, and to uphold by external pressure those which they approved. . . . The dangers which were apprehended by President Monroe have no relation to the state of things in which we live at the present day. . . . It is intelligible that Mr. Olney should invoke, in defence of the views on which he is now insisting, an authority which enjoys so high a popularity with his own fellow-countrymen. But the circumstances with which President Monroe was dealing, and those to which the present American Government is addressing itself, have very few features in common. Great Britain is imposing no 'system' upon Venezuela, and is not concerning herself in any way with the nature of the political institutions under which the Venezuelans may prefer to live. But the British Empire and the Republic of Venezuela are neighbours, and they have differed for some time past, and continue to differ, as to the line by which their dominions are separated. It is a controversy with which the United States have no apparent practical concern. It is difficult, indeed, to see how it can materially affect any State or community outside those primarily interested, except perhaps other parts of Her Majesty's dominions, such as Trinidad. The disputed frontier of Venezuela has nothing to do with any of the questions dealt with by President Monroe. It is not a question of the colonization by a European Power of any portion of America. It is not a question of the imposition upon the communities of South America of any system of government devised in Europe. It is simply the determination of the frontier of a British possession which belonged to the Throne of England long before the Republic of Venezuela came into existence.

"But even if the interests of Venezuela were so far linked to those of the United States as to give to the latter a 'locus standi' in this controversy, their Government apparently have not formed, and certainly do not express, any opinion upon the actual merits of the dispute. The Government of the United States do not say that

Great Britain, or that Venezuela, is in the right in the matters that are in issue. But they lay down that the doctrine of President Monroe, when he opposed the imposition of European systems, or the renewal of European colonization, confers upon them the right of demanding that when a European Power has a frontier difference with a South American community, the European Power shall consent to refer that controversy to arbitration; and Mr. Olney states that unless Her Majesty's Government accede to this demand, it will ' greatly embarrass the future relations between Great Britain and the United States.' Whatever may be the authority of the doctrine laid down by President Monroe, there is nothing in his language to show that he ever thought of claiming this novel prerogative for the United States. . . . I will not now enter into a discussion of the merits of this method of terminating international differences. It has proved itself valuable in many cases; but it is not free from defects, which often operate as a serious drawback on its value. It is not always easy to find an Arbitrator who is competent, and who, at the same time, is wholly free from bias; and the task of insuring compliance with the Award when it is made is not exempt from difficulty. . . .

"In the remarks which I have made, I have argued on the theory that the Monroe doctrine in itself is sound. I must not, however, be understood as expressing any acceptance of it on the part of Her Majesty's Government. It must always be mentioned with respect, on account of the distinguished statesman to whom it is due, and the great nation who have generally adopted it. But international law is founded on the general consent of nations; and no statesman, however eminent, and no nation, however powerful, are competent to insert into the code of international law a novel principle which was never recognized before, and which has not since been accepted by the Government of any other country. . . . Though the language of President Monroe is directed to the attainment of objects which most Englishmen would agree to be salutary, it is impossible to admit that they have been inscribed by any adequate authority in the code of international law; and the danger which such admission would involve is sufficiently exhibited both by the strange development which the doctrine has received at Mr. Olney's hands, and the arguments by which it is supported, in the despatch under reply. In defence of it he says: 'That distance and 3,000 miles of intervening ocean make any permanent political union between a European and an American State unnatural and inexpedient will hardly be denied. But physical and geographical considerations are the least of the objections to such a union. Europe has a set of primary interests which are peculiar to herself; America is not interested in them, and ought not to be vexed or complicated with them.'. . . The necessary meaning of these words is that the union between Great Britain and Canada; between Great Britain and Jamaica and Trinidad; between Great Britain and British Honduras or British Guiana are 'inexpedient and unnatural.' President Monroe disclaims any such inference from his doctrine; but in this, as in other respects, Mr. Olney develops it. He lays down that the inexpedient and unnatural character of the union between a European and an American

State is so obvious that it 'will hardly be denied.' Her Majesty's Government are prepared emphatically to deny it on behalf of both the British and American people who are subject to her Crown."

In his second despatch, Lord Salisbury drew the conclusions of his government from the facts as seen on the English side, and announced its decision, in the following terms: "It will be seen . . . that the Government of Great Britain have from the first held the same view as to the extent of territory which they are entitled to claim as a matter of right. It comprised the coast-line up to the River Amacura, and the whole basin of the Essequibo River and its tributaries. A portion of that claim, however, they have always been willing to waive altogether; in regard to another portion, they have been and continue to be perfectly ready to submit the question of their title to arbitration. As regards the rest, that which lies within the so-called Schomburgk line, they do not consider that the rights of Great Britain are open to question. Even within that line they have, on various occasions, offered to Venezuela considerable concessions as a matter of friendship and conciliation, and for the purpose of securing an amicable settlement of the dispute. If as time has gone on the concessions thus offered diminished in extent, and have now been withdrawn, this has been the necessary consequence of the gradual spread over the country of British settlements, which Her Majesty's Government cannot in j to the inhabitants offer to surrender to foreign rule, and the justice of such withdrawal is amply borne out by the researches in the national archives of Holland and Spain, which have furnished further and more convincing evidence in support of the British claims.

"Her Majesty's Government are sincerely desirous of being in friendly relations with Venezuela, and certainly have no design to seize territory that properly belongs to her, or forcibly to extend sovereignty over any portion of her population. They have, on the contrary, repeatedly expressed their readiness to submit to arbitration the conflicting claims of Great Britain and Venezuela to large tracts of territory which from their auriferous nature are known to be of almost untold value. But they cannot consent to entertain, or to submit to the arbitration of another Power or of foreign jurists, however eminent, claims based on the extravagant pretensions of Spanish officials in the last century, and involving the transfer of large numbers of British subjects, who have for many years enjoyed the settled rule of a British Colony, to a nation of different race and language, whose political system is subject to frequent disturbance, and whose institutions as yet too often afford very inadequate protection to life and property. No issue of this description has ever been involved in the questions which Great Britain and the United States have consented to submit to arbitration, and Her Majesty's Government are convinced that in similar circumstances the Government of the United States would be equally firm in declining to entertain proposals of such a nature."—*Great Britain, Papers by Command: United States No.* 1, 1896, *pp.* 23–31.

A. D. 1895 (December).—Message of President Cleveland to the United States Congress on the Guiana boundary dispute.—As the replies given by Lord Salisbury showed no disposition on the part of the British government to submit its dispute with Venezuela to arbitration, President Cleveland took the subject in hand, and addressed to Congress, on the 17th of December, 1895, a special Message which startled the world by the peremptoriness of its tone. "In my annual message addressed to the Congress on the 3d instant," he said, "I called attention to the pending boundary controversy between Great Britain and the Republic of Venezuela and recited the substance of a representation made by this Government to Her Britannic Majesty's Government suggesting reasons why such dispute should be submitted to arbitration for settlement and inquiring whether it would be so submitted. The answer of the British Government, which was then awaited, has since been received, and, together with the dispatch to which it is a reply, is hereto appended. Such reply is embodied in two communications addressed by the British prime minister to Sir Julian Pauncefote, the British ambassador at this capital. It will be seen that one of these communications is devoted exclusively to observations upon the Monroe doctrine, and claims that in the present instance a new and strange extension and development of this doctrine is insisted on by the United States; that the reasons j i an appeal to the doctrine enunciated by President Monroe are generally inapplicable 'to the state of things in which we live at the present day,' and especially inapplicable to a controversy involving the boundary line between Great Britain and Venezuela.

"Without attempting extended argument in reply to these positions, it may not be amiss to suggest that the doctrine upon which we stand is strong and sound, because its enforcement is important to our peace and safety as a nation and is essential to the integrity of our free institutions and the tranquil maintenance of our distinctive form of government. It was intended to apply to every stage of our national life and can not become obsolete while our Republic endures. If the balance of power is justly a cause for jealous anxiety among the Governments of the Old World and a subject for our absolute non-interference, none the less is an observance of the Monroe doctrine of vital concern to our people and their Government. Assuming, therefore, that we may properly insist upon this doctrine without regard to ' the state of things in which we live' or any changed conditions here or elsewhere, it is not apparent why its application may not be invoked in the present controversy. If a European power by an extension of its boundaries takes possession of the territory of one of our neighboring Republics against its will and in derogation of its rights, it is difficult to see why to that extent such European power does not thereby attempt to extend its system of government to that portion of this continent which is thus taken. This is the precise action which President Monroe declared to be 'dangerous to our peace and safety,' and it can make no difference whether the European system is extended by an advance of frontier or otherwise.

"It is also suggested in the British reply that we should not seek to apply the Monroe doctrine to the pending dispute because it does not em-

body any principle of international law which 'is founded on the general consent of nations,' and that 'no statesman, however eminent, and no nation, however powerful, are competent to insert into the code of international law a novel principle which was never recognized before and which has not since been accepted by the government of any other country.' Practically the principle for which we contend has peculiar, if not exclusive, relation to the United States. It may not have been admitted in so many words to the code of international law, but since in international councils every nation is entitled to the rights belonging to it, if the enforcement of the Monroe doctrine is something we may justly claim, it has its place in the code of international law as certainly and as securely as if it were specifically mentioned; and when the United States is a suitor before the high tribunal that administers international law the question to be determined is whether or not we present claims which the justice of that code of law can find to be right and valid.

"The Monroe doctrine finds its recognition in those principles of international law which are based upon the theory that every nation shall have its rights protected and its just claims enforced. Of course this government is entirely confident that under the sanction of this doctrine we have clear rights and undoubted claims. Nor is this ignored in the British reply. The prime minister, while not admitting that the Monroe doctrine is applicable to present conditions, states: 'In declaring that the United States would resist any such enterprise if it was contemplated, President Monroe adopted a policy which received the entire sympathy of the English Government of that date.'

"He further declares: 'Though the language of President Monroe is directed to the attainment of objects which most Englishmen would agree to be salutary, it is impossible to admit that they have been inscribed by any adequate authority in the code of international law.'

"Again he says: 'They [Her Majesty's Government] fully concur with the view which President Monroe apparently entertained, that any disturbance of the existing territorial distribution in that hemisphere by any fresh acquisitions on the part of any European State would be a highly inexpedient change.'

"In the belief that the doctrine for which we contend was clear and definite, that it was founded upon substantial considerations, and involved our safety and welfare, that it was fully applicable to our present conditions and to the state of the world's progress, and that it was directly related to the pending controversy, and without any conviction as to the final merits of the dispute, but anxious to learn in a satisfactory and conclusive manner whether Great Britain sought under a claim of boundary to extend her possessions on this continent without right, or whether she merely sought possession of territory fairly included within her lines of ownership, this Government proposed to the Government of Great Britain a resort to arbitration as the proper means of settling the question, to the end that a vexatious boundary dispute between the two contestants might be determined and our exact standing and relation in respect to the controversy might be made clear. It will be seen from the correspondence herewith submitted that this proposition has been declined by the British Government upon grounds which in the circumstances seem to me to be far from satisfactory. It is deeply disappointing that such an appeal, actuated by the most friendly feelings toward both nations directly concerned, addressed to the sense of justice and to the magnanimity of one of the great powers of the world, and touching its relations to one comparatively weak and small, should have produced no better result.

"The course to be pursued by this Government in view of the present condition does not appear to admit of serious doubt. Having labored faithfully for many years to induce Great Britain to submit this dispute to impartial arbitration, and having been now finally apprised of her refusal to do so, nothing remains but to accept the situation, to recognize its plain requirements, and deal with it accordingly. Great Britain's present proposition has never thus far been regarded as admissible by Venezuela, though any adjustment of the boundary which that country may deem for her advantage and may enter into of her own free will can not of course be objected to by the United States. Assuming, however, that the attitude of Venezuela will remain unchanged, the dispute has reached such a stage as to make it now incumbent upon the United States to take measures to determine with sufficient certainty for its justification what is the true divisional line between the Republic of Venezuela and British Guiana. The inquiry to that end should of course be conducted carefully and judicially, and due weight should be given to all available evidence, records, and facts in support of the claims of both parties. In order that such an examination should be prosecuted in a thorough and satisfactory manner, I suggest that the Congress make an adequate appropriation for the expenses of a commission, to be appointed by the Executive, who shall make the necessary investigation and report upon the matter with the least possible delay. When such report is made and accepted it will, in my opinion, be the duty of the United States to resist by every means in its power, as a willful aggression upon its rights and interests, the appropriation by Great Britain of any lands or the exercise of governmental jurisdiction over any territory which after investigation we have determined of right belongs to Venezuela.

"In making these recommendations I am fully alive to the responsibility incurred and keenly realize all the consequences that may follow. I am, nevertheless, firm in my conviction that while it is a grievous thing to contemplate the two great English-speaking peoples of the world as being otherwise than friendly competitors in the onward march of civilization and strenuous and worthy rivals in all the arts of peace, there is no calamity which a great nation can invite which equals that which follows a supine submission to wrong and injustice and the consequent loss of national self-respect and honor, beneath which are shielded and defended a people's safety and greatness."— *United States, Message and Documents (Abridgment, 1895-6)*.

The recommendations of the President were acted upon with remarkable unanimity and promptitude in Congress, a bill authorizing the appointment of the proposed commission, and appropriating $100,000 for the necessary expen-

diture, being passed by the House on the day following the Message (December 17), and by the Senate on the 20th. See (in this vol.) UNITED STATES OF AM.: A. D. 1895 (DECEMBER).

A. D. 1895-1896 (December—January).— Feeling in England and the United States over the boundary dispute. See (in this vol.) UNITED STATES OF AM. : A. D. 1895-1896 (DECEMBER—JANUARY).

A. D. 1896-1899.—Appointment of the United States Commission to investigate the boundary question.—Reopening of negotiations between the United States and Great Britain.—The solution of the main difficulty found.—Arbitration and its result.—The Commission authorized by the Congress of the United States to investigate and report on the true divisional line between British Guiana and Venezuela was named by the President of the United States, on the 1st of January, as follows: David J. Brewer, Associate Justice of the Supreme Court of the United States; Richard H. Alvey, Chief Justice of the Court of Appeals in the District of Columbia; Andrew D. White, ex-President of Cornell University, and ex-Minister to Germany and Russia; Daniel C. Gilman, President of Johns Hopkins University ; Frederick R. Coudert, of New York. The Commission was organized on the 4th by the election of Justice Brewer to be its President. Mr. S. Mallet Prevost was subsequently appointed Secretary. One of the first proceedings of the Commission was to address a letter to the Secretary of State, suggesting a friendly intimation to the governments of Great Britain and Venezuela that their assistance to it, in procuring unpublished archives and the like evidence, would be highly acceptable, and that "if either should deem it appropriate to designate an agent or attorney, whose duty it would be to see that no such proofs were omitted or overlooked, the Commission would be grateful for such evidence of good will." This overture was well received in England, and had an excellent effect. It was responded to by Lord Salisbury, with an assurance that Her Majesty's government would readily place at the disposal of the President of the United States any information at their command, and would communicate advance copies of documents soon to be published on the subject of the boundary line. Before the close of January the Commission had organized its work, with several experts engaged to assist on special lines. Professor Justin Winsor, Librarian of Harvard University, had undertaken to report on the early maps of the Guiana-Venezuela country, Professor George L. Burr, of Cornell University, was making ready to examine the Dutch archives in Holland, and Professor J. Franklin Jameson, of Brown University, was enlisted for other investigations.

Before these labors had gone far, however, the two governments, of Great Britain and the United States, were induced to reopen a discussion of the possibility of an arbitration of the dispute. On the 27th of February, Mr. Bayard, the Ambassador of the United States at London, conveyed to Lord Salisbury a proposal from his government "that Her Majesty's Ambassador at Washington should be empowered to discuss the question at that capital with the Secretary of State," and that "a clear definition of the 'settlements' by individuals in the territory in dispute, which it is understood Her Majesty's Government desire should be excluded from the proposed submission to arbitration, should be propounded." Lord Salisbury assented so far as to telegraph, on the same day, to Sir Julian Pauncefote: "I have agreed with the United States' Ambassador that, in principle, the matter may be discussed between the United States Government (acting as the friend of Venezuela) and your Excellency." But, a few days later (March 5), the British Premier and Foreign Secretary gave a broader range to the discussion, by recalling a correspondence that had taken place in the spring of 1895 between the then American Secretary of State, Mr. Gresham, and the British Ambassador, in contemplation of a general system of international arbitration for the adjustment of disputes between the two governments. Reviving that project, Lord Salisbury submitted the heads of a general arbitration treaty between the United States and Great Britain, which became a subject of discussion for some weeks, without offering much promise of providing for the settlement of the Venezuela dispute. In May, the correspondence returned to the latter subject more definitely, Lord Salisbury writing (May 22):

"From the first our objection has been to subject to the decision of an Arbiter, who, in the last resort, must, of necessity, be a foreigner, the rights of British colonists who have settled in territory which they had every ground for believing to be British, and whose careers would be broken, and their fortunes possibly ruined, by a decision that the territory on which they have settled was subject to the Venezuelan Republic. At the same time, we are very conscious that the dispute between ourselves and the Republic of Venezuela affects a large portion of land which is not under settlement, and which could be disposed of without any injustice to any portion of the colonial population. We are very willing that the territory which is comprised within this definition should be subjected to the results of an arbitration, even though some portion of it should be found to fall within the Schomburgk line." He proposed, accordingly, the creation of a commission of four persons, for the determination of the questions of fact involved, on whose report the two governments of Great Britain and Venezuela should endeavor to agree on a boundary line; failing which agreement, a tribunal of arbitration should fix the line, on the basis of facts reported by the Commission. "Provided always that in fixing such line the Tribunal shall not have power to include as the territory of Venezuela any territory which was bonâ fide occupied by subjects of Great Britain on the 1st January, 1887, or as the territory of Great Britain any territory bonâ fide occupied by Venezuelans at the same date."

Objections to this proposal, especially to its final stipulation, were raised by the government of the United States, and the negotiation looked unpromising again for a time; but at length, on the 13th of July, Mr. Olney made a suggestion which happily solved the one difficulty that had been, from the beginning, a bar to agreement between the two governments. "Can it be assumed," he asked, in a letter of that date, "that Her Majesty's Government would submit to unrestricted arbitration the whole of the territory in dispute, provided it be a rule of the arbitration, embodied in the arbitral agreement, that

territory which has been in the exclusive, notorious, and actual use and occupation of either party for even two generations, or say for sixty years, shall be held by the arbitrators to be the territory of such party? In other words, will Her Majesty's Government assent to unrestricted arbitration of all the territory in controversy, with the period for the acquisition of title by prescription fixed by agreement of the parties in advance at sixty years?" Lord Salisbury assented to the principle thus suggested, but proposed a shorter term of occupation than sixty years. Finally the term of fifty years was accepted on both sides, and from that point the arrangement of a Treaty of Arbitration between Great Britain and Venezuela went smoothly on.

The good news that England and America were practically at the end of their dispute was proclaimed by Lord Salisbury, on the 9th of November, in a speech at the Lord Mayor's banquet, in London, when he said : " You are aware that in the discussion had with the United States on behalf of their friends in Venezuela, our question has not been whether there should be arbitration, but whether arbitration should have unrestricted application; and we have always claimed that those who, apart from historic right, had the right which attaches to established settlements, should be excluded from arbitration. Our difficulty for months has been to define the settled districts; and the solution has, I think, come from the suggestion of the government of the United States, that we should treat our colonial empire as we treat individuals; that the same lapse of time which protects the latter in civic life from having their title questioned, should similarly protect an English colony ; but, beyond that, when a lapse could not be claimed, there should be an examination of title, and all the equity demanded in regard thereto should be granted. I do not believe I am using unduly sanguine words when I declare my belief that this has brought the controversy to an end."

On the 10th of November, the Secretary of the United States Commission appointed to investigate the disputed boundary published the following : " The statements of Lord Salisbury, as reported in the morning papers, make it probable that the boundary dispute now pending between Great Britain and Venezuela will be settled by arbitration at an early day. Under the circumstances the Commission, while continuing its deliberations in the preparation and orderly arrangement of many valuable maps, reports, and documents, which have been procured and used in the course of its labors, does not propose to formulate any decision for the present of the matters subject to its examination. It will continue its sessions from time to time, but with the hope and expectation that a friendly and just settlement of all pending differences between the nations interested will make any final decision on its part unnecessary." This hope was substantially realized a few days later, when a convention embodying the agreement of the United States and Great Britain was signed by Secretary Olney and the British Ambassador, Sir Julian Pauncefote. The agreement was carried to its next stage on the 2d of February, 1897, when a treaty between Great Britain and the United States of Venezuela was signed at Washington, which provided as follows :
"Art. I. An Arbitral Tribunal shall be im-

mediately appointed to determine the boundary-line between the Colony of British Guiana and the United States of Venezuela.

" Art. II. The Tribunal shall consist of five Jurists : two on the part of Great Britain, nominated by the Members of the Judicial Committee of Her Majesty's Privy Council, namely, the Right Honourable Baron Herschell, Knight Grand Cross of the Most Honourable Order of the Bath, and the Honourable Sir Richard Henn Collins, Knight, one of the Justices of Her Britannic Majesty's Supreme Court of Judicature ; two on the part of Venezuela, nominated, one by the President of the United States of Venezuela, namely, the Honourable Melville Weston Fuller, Chief Justice of the United States of America, and one nominated by the Justices of the Supreme Court of the United States of America, namely, the Honourable David Josiah Brewer, a Justice of the Supreme Court of the United States of America ; and of a fifth Jurist to be selected by the four persons so nominated, or in the event of their failure to agree within three months from the date of the exchange of ratifications of the present Treaty, to be selected by His Majesty the King of Sweden and Norway. The Jurist so selected shall be President of the Tribunal. In case of the death, absence, or incapacity to serve of any of the four Arbitrators above named, or in the event of any such Arbitrator omitting or declining or ceasing to act as such, another Jurist of repute shall be forthwith substituted in his place. If such vacancy shall occur among those nominated on the part of Great Britain, the substitute shall be appointed by the members for the time being of the Judicial Committee of Her Majesty's Privy Council, acting by a majority, and if among those nominated on the part of Venezuela, he shall be appointed by the Justices of the Supreme Court of the United States, acting by a majority. If such vacancy shall occur in the case of the fifth Arbitrator, a substitute shall be selected in the manner herein provided for with regard to the original appointment.

" Art. III. The Tribunal shall investigate and ascertain the extent of the territories belonging to, or that might lawfully be claimed by, the United Netherlands or by the Kingdom of Spain respectively at the time of the acquisition by Great Britain of the Colony of British Guiana, and shall determine the boundary-line between the Colony of British Guiana and the United States of Venezuela.

" Art. IV. In deciding the matters submitted, the Arbitrators shall ascertain all facts which they deem necessary to a decision of the controversy, and shall be governed by the following Rules, which are agreed upon by the High Contracting Parties as Rules to be taken as applicable to the case, and by such principles of international law not inconsistent therewith as the Arbitrators shall determine to be applicable to the case :—Rules. (a.) Adverse holding or prescription during a period of fifty years shall make a good title. The Arbitrators may deem exclusive political control of a district, as well as actual settlement thereof, sufficient to constitute adverse holding or to make title by prescription. (b.) The Arbitrators may recognize and give effect to rights and claims resting on any other ground whatever valid according to international law, and on any principles of in-

ternational law which the Arbitrators may deem to be applicable to the case, and which are not in contravention of the foregoing rule. (c.) In determining the boundary-line, if territory of one Party be found by the Tribunal to have been at the date of this Treaty in the occupation of the subjects or citizens of the other Party, such effect shall be given to such occupation as reason, justice, the principles of international law, and the equities of the case shall, in the opinion of the Tribunal, require. . . . Art. XIII. The High Contracting Parties engage to consider the result of the proceedings of the Tribunal of Arbitration as a full, perfect, and final settlement of all the questions referred to the Arbitrators."—*Great Britain, Papers by Command: Treaty Series No. 5, 1897.*

Before the Arbitrators named in the treaty had entered on their duties, a vacancy in the tribunal was created by the death of Baron Herschell, and the Lord Chief Justice of England, Lord Russell of Killowen, was appointed in his place. His Excellency, Frederic de Martens, Privy Councillor and Permanent Member of the Council of the Ministry of Foreign Affairs in Russia, was selected to be the fifth Arbitrator. As thus constituted, the Arbitral Tribunal met in Paris on the 15th of June, 1899. In the hearings before it, Venezuela was represented by Benjamin Harrison, ex-President of the United States, and other counsel; the British government by Sir Richard Webster, Attorney-General of Great Britain, and others. The decision of the Tribunal, which is said to have been rendered with unanimity, was announced on the 3d of October, 1899, as follows:

" We the undersigned Arbitrators do hereby make and publish our decision, determination, and Award of, upon, and concerning the questions submitted to us by the said Treaty of Arbitration, and do hereby, conformably to the said Treaty of Arbitration, finally decide, award, and determine that the boundary-line between the Colony of British Guiana and the United States of Venezuela is as follows: —Starting from the coast at Point Playa, the line of boundary shall run in a straight line to the River Barima at its junction with the River Mururuma, and thence along the mid-stream of the latter river to its source, and from that point to the junction of the River Haiowa with the Amakuru, and thence along the mid-stream of the Amakuru to its source in the Imataka Ridge, and thence in a south-westerly direction along the highest ridge of the spur of the Imataka Mountains to the highest point of the main range of such Imataka Mountains opposite to the source of the Barima, and thence along the summit of the main ridge in a south-easterly direction of the Imataka Mountains to the source of the Acarabisi, and thence along the mid-stream of the Acarabisi to the Cuyuni, and thence along the northern bank of the River Cuyuni westward to its junction with the Wenamu, and thence following the mid-stream of the Wenamu to its westernmost source, and thence in a direct line to the summit of Mount Roraima, and from Mount Roraima to the source of the Cotinga, and along the mid-stream of that river to its junction with the Takutu, and thence along the mid-stream of the Takutu to its source, thence in a straight line to the westernmost point of the Akarai Mountains, and thence along the ridge of the Akarai Mountains to the source of the Corentin called the

Cutari River. Provided always that the line of delimitation fixed by this Award shall be subject and without prejudice to any questions now existing, or which may arise, to be determined between the Government of her Britannic Majesty and the Republic of Brazil, or between the latter Republic and the United States of Venezuela.

"In fixing the above delimitation the Arbitrators consider and decide that in times of peace the Rivers Amakuru and Barima shall be open to navigation by the merchant-ships of all nations, subject to all just regulations and to the payment of light or other like dues: Provided that the dues charged by the Republic of Venezuela and the Government of the Colony of British Guiana in respect of the passage of vessels along the portions of such rivers respectively owned by them shall be charged at the same rates upon the vessels of Venezuela and Great Britain, such rates being no higher than those charged to any other nation: Provided also that no customs duties shall be chargeable either by the Republic of Venezuela or by the Colony of British Guiana in respect of goods carried on board ships, vessels, or boats passing along the said rivers, but customs duties shall only be chargeable in respect of goods landed in the territory of Venezuela or Great Britain respectively."—*Great Britain, Papers by Command: Venezuela No. 7, 1899, pp. 6-7.*

A. D. 1898-1900.—Change in the Presidency.—Death of ex-President Crespo.—Revolution.—Rebellion.—General Joaquin Crespo retired from the presidency and was succeeded by General Ignacio Andrade on the 1st of March, 1898. A revolutionary movement was soon started, with General Hernandez at its head, and ex-President Crespo, who led the forces of the government against it, was killed in a charge, on the 16th of April. Hernandez was surprised and captured a few weeks later, and the rebellion then subsided for a time. In the spring of 1899 Hernandez was set at liberty by Andrade, who, meantime, had crushed a minor revolt, undertaken by one General Guerra. August found the harassed President assailed by a fresh rising, started by General Cipriano Castro, and the restless revolutionist, Hernandez, was soon in league with it. This proved to be a revolution in earnest, and, after hard fighting, President Andrade fled from the capital and the country in October; Puerto Cabello, the last town to hold out for him, was bombarded and stormed the following month, and a new government was established, nominally under the Vice President, Rodriguez, but with Castro for its actual head. Before this had been fully accomplished, however, Hernandez was in arms against Castro, with his accustomed ill-success. Before the year closed he had fled the country ; but early in 1900 he was once more in the field, maintaining a troublesome war until May, when he was defeated, and again a prisoner in his opponents' hands.

VICTORIA, Queen: The Diamond Jubilee celebration of her accession to the throne. See (in this vol.) ENGLAND : A. D. 1897 (JUNE).

Her death and funeral.—Tributes to her character. .See (in this vol.) ENGLAND : A. D. 1901 (JANUARY).

VICTORIA. See (in this vol.) AUSTRALIA; and CONSTITUTION OF AUSTRALIA.

VICTORIAN ORDER, The.—A new order of knighthood, to be known as the Victorian Order, and to be conferred as a mark of high distinction, was instituted by Queen Victoria on the 21st of April, 1896.

VIENNA : A. D. 1895-1896.—Anti-Semitic agitation. See (in this vol.) AUSTRIA-HUNGARY: A. D. 1895-1896.

A. D. 1897.—Scenes in the Reichsrath. See (in this vol.) AUSTRIA-HUNGARY : A. D. 1897 (OCTOBER—DECEMBER).

A. D. 1900.—Census.—According to a report from the United States Consul at Vienna, the census taken December 31, 1900, shows a population of 1,635,647, or nearly 63,000 less than that of Chicago, when the recent census of that city was taken. These figures show Vienna to rank next after London, Paris and Berlin among the European capitals, while in this country only New York and Chicago are larger. In the last ten years Vienna has increased 21.9 per cent, or slightly faster than the average for the whole United States. Of the two American cities larger than Vienna New York increased in ten years 37.8 per cent. and Chicago 54.4 per cent.

VIEQUEZ. See (in this vol.) PORTO RICO : AREA AND POPULATION.

VILLIERS, Sir J. H. de : Advice to President Kruger. See (in this vol.) SOUTH AFRICA (THE TRANSVAAL) : A. D. 1899 (MAY—AUGUST).

VIRDEN, Conflict with striking miners at. See (in this vol.) INDUSTRIAL DISTURBANCES : A. D. 1898.

VIRGINIUS AFFAIR, The. See (in this vol.) CUBA : A. D. 1868-1885.

VISAYAN ISLANDS, American occupation of the. See (in this vol.) PHILIPPINE ISLANDS : A. D. 1899 (JANUARY—NOVEMBER).

VISAYANS, The. See (in this vol.) PHILIPPINE ISLANDS : THE NATIVE INHABITANTS.

VOLKSRAAD, South African. See (in this vol.) CONSTITUTION (GRONDWET) OF THE SOUTH AFRICAN REPUBLIC.

VOLUNTARY SCHOOLS, English. See (in this vol.) ENGLAND : A. D. 1896-1897.

VOLUNTEERS OF AMERICA, The. See (in this vol.) SALVATION ARMY.

VOTING, Plural or Cumulative, and **Compulsory.** See (in this vol.) BELGIUM : A. D. 1894-1895.

W.

WADAI. See (in this vol.) NIGERIA, A. D. 1882–1899.

WALDECK-ROUSSEAU, M.: The Ministry of. See (in this vol.) FRANCE: A. D. 1899 (FEBRUARY—JUNE), and after.

WALES, The Prince of.—It has been announced that Prince George, Duke of Cornwall and York, the only living son of King Edward VII., of England, and heir to the British throne, will be created Prince of Wales, by royal patent, after his return from Australia. See (in this vol.) AUSTRALIA: A. D. 1901 (MAY).

WANA: Inclusion in a new British Indian province. See (in this vol.) INDIA: A. D. 1901 (FEBRUARY).

WAR: Measures to prevent its occurrence and to mitigate its barbarities. See (in this vol.) PEACE CONFERENCE.

WAR BUDGETS: Military and naval expenditures of the great Powers.—The following compilation of statistics of the military and naval expenditure of the leading Powers (Great Britain excepted) was submitted to the House of Representatives at Washington by the Hon. George B. McClellan, of New York, in a speech, February 12, 1901, on the bill then pending in Congress, to make appropriations for the support of the Army of the United States. The tabulated statements were introduced with explanations and comments as follows: "For purposes of comparison, I have taken the armies and navies of Austria-Hungary, France, the German Empire, Italy, and Russia. I have not included Great Britain, for its conditions have been abnormal for nearly two years. I have based my estimates on the enlisted strength of the armies referred to, excluding commissioned officers. The figures are the most recent obtainable without direct communication with foreign authorities and are for the most part for the last fiscal year of the several countries, although in some cases they are for 1898–99. The German naval budget does not include the extraordinary expenditures for the new navy authorized by the recent enactment of the Reichstag. This does not begin to be effective until the next fiscal year. In estimating the equivalent in dollars of the Italian budget I have allowed 6 per cent for the depreciation of the present paper currency—a very moderate estimate. The Russian budget will appear abnormally low, for I have recently seen it stated at $159,000,000. This is because the ruble has been assumed to be the gold ruble, worth 52 cents, but the budget is expressed in paper rubles, and is now, under a recent order of M. Witte, uniformly reckoned at two-thirds of the gold ruble. I have therefore called it 34.6 cents."

As to the military expenditure of the United States, "the House has during the present session appropriated, or is about to appropriate, for the support of what may be called the active Army, $152,068,100.84. The appropriations growing out of past wars amount to a total of $154,694,292. I have charged to this account every item that could by any possible construction be assumed to refer to past wars and not to the maintenance of the present Army. The pension appropria-

tion bill carried $145,245,230. The cost of administering the Pension Bureau will amount to $3,352,790. The Record and Pension Office costs $585,170. I have further included appropriations for National and State Homes, back pay, etc., cemeteries, and $712,580 for extra clerks due to the Spanish war. Adding the appropriations due to past wars to the appropriation for the active Army, we find a total of $306,762,392.84, which represents the total of our Army budget. Taking the total cost of our active Army, and assuming the enlisted strength of the Army to be 100,000, we find the cost per annum of each enlisted man to be $1,520. Taking the total Army budget, including appropriations arising from past wars, we find the cost per annum of each enlisted man $3,067.

"Without including appropriations arising from past wars, we find the cost of the Army per capita of population to be $1.99. Including appropriations arising from past wars, we find the cost of the Army per capita of population to be $4.02. The army budget of Austria-Hungary is $67,564,446, the cost of maintaining 1 enlisted man for one year being $183.86, and the cost of the army per capita of population $1.50. The army budget of France is $128,959,064, the cost of maintaining 1 enlisted man is $218.74, and the cost per capita of population is $3.34. The army budget of the German Empire is $156,127,743, the cost per annum of 1 enlisted man is $277.85, the cost per capita of population is $2.98. The army budget of Italy is $43,920,132, the cost of maintaining 1 enlisted man per annum is $202.65, the cost per capita of population is $1.39. The army budget of Russia is $99,927,997, the cost of maintaining 1 enlisted man is $119.65, the cost per capita of population is 77 cents.

"The appropriations for the support of the naval establishment are by no means so widely distributed as are those for the Army. The naval bill carries $77,016,635.60. In the legislative, executive, and judicial bill there are carried appropriations directly chargeable to the support of the Navy, including pay of the clerical force in the Auditor's office, the office of the Secretary, the office of the heads of the bureaus, maintenance of building, and contingent expenses, amounting to $399,150. In the sundry civil bill there are carried, for printing and binding, appropriations amounting to $127,000. Up to the present time the Secretary of the Treasury has submitted to the House a statement of deficiencies for the support of the naval establishment amounting to $2,491,549.64, making a total of $80,034,335.24 that the House has appropriated or is about to appropriate during the present session for the support of the naval establishment. In addition to this the legislative, executive, and judicial bill carries an appropriation of $21,800 for the payment of extra clerks whose employment is necessitated by the Spanish war, making a total naval budget of $80,056,135.24.

"The naval budget of Austria-Hungary is $7,028,167, a cost per capita of population of 15 cents. The naval budget of France is $61,238,478, a cost per capita of population of $1.58. The naval budget of the German Empire is $32,419,602, a cost per capita of population of 62 cents. The naval budget of Italy is $18,455,111, a cost per capita of population of 58 cents. The naval budget of Russia is $48,132,220, a cost per capita of population of 37 cents.

"The combined appropriations for the Army and Navy represent the total war budget, or, as some European countries prefer to call it, the 'defense budget.' The total war budget of the United States, excluding appropriations due to past wars, amounts to $233,102,435, or a cost per capita of population of $3.03. Our total war budget, including appropriations due to past wars, amounts to $386,818,527, a cost per capita of population of $5.06. The total war budget of Austria-Hungary is $74,592,613, a cost per capita of population of $1.66. The total war budget of France is $190,197,542, a cost per capita of population of $4.92. The total war budget of the German Empire is $188,547,345, a cost per capita of population of $3.60. The total war budget of Italy is $62,375,243, a cost per capita of population of $1.97. The total war budget of Russia is $148,060,017, a cost per capita of population of $1.14. The combined total war budgets of France and of the German Empire amount to $378,744,887, or $8,073,640 less than that of the United States.

"The criticism has been made that there can be no comparison between the cost of maintaining our Army and the cost of maintaining those of Europe, for the reason that the European private receives 'no pay' and ours receives $156 a year. As a matter of fact, while service is compulsory on the Continent, the continental private is paid a small sum, amounting on the average to about $56 a year. In other words, our private receives about $100 more than his comrade of Europe. This criticism does not affect comparisons, as will be seen on the consideration of a few figures. The war budget of the German Empire is the largest in Europe. Were the Prussian private to receive the same pay as our private the Prussian army budget would be swelled to $212,354,343. Were the Russian private to receive the same pay as our private the Russian budget would be swelled to about $190,000,000 per annum. The difference in pay does not account for the proportionate difference in the size of the budgets, for were our Army to be increased to the size of that of the German Empire our budget would be increased by $702,644,320, making a total of $854,712,420, without including expenses due to past wars, or, including such expenses, making an Army budget of $1,009,406,712. Were our Army to be increased to the size of Russia's, our budget would be increased by $1,132,120,220, making a total Army budget, without including appropriations due to past wars, of $1,284,188,320, or, including appropriations due to past wars, making a total budget of $1,438,882,612.

"I submit these figures to the consideration of the House without any comment whatsoever. Comment is unnecessary.

"TABLE A. — Analysis of the war budget of the United States as agreed to, or about to be agreed to, by the House of Representatives, first session Fifty-sixth Congress.

1. ARMY.

Appropriations for the active Army.

Army bill...............................	$117,994,649.10
Military Academy bill.....................	700,151.88
Fortification bill.........................	7,227,461.00

Legislative, executive, and judicial bill:

Office of the Secretary of War.....................	$104,150	
Office of the Auditor for the War Department.....	318,300	
Offices of heads of so-called "staff" departments...	653,826	
Maintenance of three-eighths of Department building.................	45,990	
Rent........................	13,500	
Stationery..................	32,500	
Postage....................	1,000	
Contingent expenses......	58,000	
		1,227,266.00

Sundry civil bill:

Arsenals and armories....	281,550	
Military posts............	1,068,960	
Bringing home dead......	150,000	
Maps, etc................	5,100	
Printing and binding......	244,000	
Repairs, three-eighths Department building...	31,500	
		1,721,110.00

Deficiencies submitted:

December 11, 1900........	12,062,223.36	
January 21, 1901............	5,835,239.50	
January 26, 1901..........	5,300,000.00	
		23,197,462.86

Total, active Army....................	152,068,100.84

Appropriations growing out of past wars.

Pensions..............................	$145,245,230.00
Salaries, Pension Bureau, etc..............	3,352,790.00
Record and Pension Office.................	585,170.00
National Homes for Disabled Volunteer Soldiers............................	3,074,142.00
State Homes for Disabled Volunteer Soldiers...........................	950,000.00
Back pay and bounty (civil war)..........	325,000.00
Arrears of pay (Spanish war)..............	200,000.00
National cemeteries......................	191,880.00
Artificial limbs and appliances.............	27,000.00
Headstones and burials....................	28,000.00
Apache prisoners.........................	2,500.00
Secretary of War, extra clerks (Spanish war).................................	600,000.00
Auditor for War Department, extra clerks (Spanish war).........................	112,580.00
Total..............................	154,694,292.00
Appropriations for the active Army......	152,068,100.84
Total Army budget....................	306,762,392.84

2. NAVY.

Naval bill................................	$77,016,635.60

Legislative, executive, and judicial bill:

Office of the Secretary of the Navy...............	$47,900.00	
Office of the Auditor for the Navy Department..	68,080.00	
Offices of heads of bureaus, etc...............	224,430.00	
Maintenance of three-eighths of Department building...............	45,990.00	
Contingent expenses......	12,750.00	
		$399,150.00

Sundry civil bill: Printing and binding....................		127,000.00

Deficiencies submitted:

December 11, 1900.........	74,481.09	
December 17, 1900........	20,000.00	
January 21, 1901..........	2,267,068.55	
January 25, 1901..........	130,000.00	
		2,491,549.64

Total, active Navy....................	80,034,335.24
Auditor for Navy Department, extra clerks (Spanish war)....................	21,800.00
Total Navy budget...................	80,056,135.24

3. RECAPITULATION.

Active Army.................	$152,068,100.84	
Active Navy.................	80,034,335.24	$232,102,436.08
Army (past wars)...........	154,694,292.00	
Navy (past wars)............	21,800.00	154,716,092.00
Total war budget.....................		386,818,528.08

TABLE B. — Analysis of war budgets of various armies.

	Population by last census.	Latest obtainable army budget.	Total enlisted strength, peace footing.	Cost of maintaining one enlisted man for one year.	Cost of army per capita of population.	Latest obtainable naval budget.	Cost of navy per capita of population.	Total war budget.	Cost of army and navy combined per capita of population.
Austria-Hungary	44,901,036	$67,564,446	368,002	$183.86	$1.50	$7,028,167	$0.15	$74,592,613	$1.66
France	38,517,975	128,959,064	589,541	218.74	3.34	61,238,478	1.58	190,197,542	4.92
German Empire..	52,246,589	156,127,743	562,266	277.85	2.98	32,419,602	.62	188,547,345	3.60
Italy	31,479,217	43,920,132	216,720	202.65	1.39	18,455,111	.58	62,375,243	1.97
Russia	129,211,113	99,927,797	835,143	119.65	.77	48,132,220	.37	148,060,017	1.14
United States, not including cost of past wars	76,295,220	152,068,100	100,000	1,520.00	1.99	80,034,335	1.04	233,102,435	3.03
United States, including cost of past wars....	76,295,220	306,762,392	100,000	3,067.00	4.02	80,056,135	1.04	386,818,527	5.06

— *Congressional Record, Feb.* 15, 1901, *pp.* 2707-9.

The following is an abstract of the British Army estimates for 1901–1902, submitted to Parliament in March, 1901, compared with those of the previous year. They cover, of course, the extraordinary expenditure incident to the South African war :

	NET ESTIMATES.	
	1901-1902.	1900-1901.
I. — NUMBERS.	Total Numbers.	Total Numbers.
Number of men on the Home and Colonial Establishments of the Army, exclusive of those serving in India	450,000	430,000
II. — EFFECTIVE SERVICES.	£	£
Pay, &c., of Army (General Staff, Regiments, Reserve, and Departments)	21,657,500	18,450,000
Medical Establishment: Pay, &c.	1,083,600	908,000
Militia: Pay, Bounty, &c.	2,662,000	2,288,000
Yeomanry Cavalry: Pay and Allowances	375,000	141,000
Volunteer Corps: Pay and Allowances	1,230,000	1,730,000
Transport and Remounts	15,977,000	19,800,000
Provisions, Forage and other Supplies	18,782,000	18,200,000
Clothing Establishments and Services	4,825,000	5,530,000
Warlike and other Stores : Supply and Repair	13,450,000	13,200,000
Works, Buildings, and Repairs : Cost, including Staff for Engineer Services	3,281,000	4,730,700
Establishments for Military Education	119,000	113,800
Miscellaneous Effective Services	218,200	206,900
War Office : Salaries and Miscellaneous Charges	305,000	275,000
Total Effective Services	83,970,500	85,573,400
III. — NON-EFFECTIVE SERVICES.		
Non-Effective Charges for Officers, &c.	2,271,000	1,861,000
Non-Effective Charges for Men, &c.	1,485,000	1,379,000
Superannuation, Compensation, and Compassionate Allowances	188,500	186,000
Total Non-Effective Services.	3,944,500	3,426,000
Total Effective and Non-Effective Services	87,915,000	88,999,400

NOTE. — The provision for Ordinary and War Services is as follows : —

	1901–02.	1900–01.
	£	£
For War Services :		
South Africa	56,070,000	61,286,700
China	2,160,000	3,450,000
	58,230,000	64,736,700
For Ordinary Services	29,685,000	24,262,700
Total	87,915,000	88,999,400

The British navy estimates for 1901–1902 amount to a net total of £30,875,500, being an increase of £2,083,600 beyond the amount of £28,791,900 voted for the year 1900–1901. The total number of Officers, Seamen and Boys, Coastguard, and Royal Marines, proposed for the year 1901-1902 is 118,635, being an increase of 3,745.

The following statistics of the numerical strength and ratio to population of the armies of twenty-two nations, compiled in the War Department of the United States, were cited in the debate in the U. S. Senate on the bill to increase the strength of the U. S. Army, January 15, 1901. They differ in some particulars, but not greatly, from the corresponding figures given by Mr. McClellan :

" War Department, Adjutant-General's office, Washington, August 28, 1900. According to the latest available sources, which are considered fairly reliable, the peace and war strength of the armies of the nations mentioned below is stated to be as follows:

NATION.	PEACE STRENGTH.		WAR STRENGTH.
	Officers.	Men.	
Austria-Hungary, 1899.,	26,454	335,239	1,872,178
Belgium, 1899	3,472	48,030	163,000
Brazil, 1897	2,300	25,860	......
China	......	300,000	[1]1,000,000
France, 1900	29,740	586,735	[2]2,500,000

[1] Estimated.
[2] Available men liable to military service.

NATION.	PEACE STRENGTH.		WAR STRENGTH.
	Officers.	Men.	
Germany, 1899..........	23,230	562,266	[1] 3,000,000
Great Britain, 1900.....	11,904	[2] 247,237	503,484
Italy, 1898...............	14,084	310,602	1,304,854
Japan, 1898	6,356	115,673	407,963
Mexico, 1898............	2,068	30,075	151,500
Persia	....	24,500	105,500
Portugal, 1899	1,804	30,000	[3] 157,126
Roumania	3,280	60,000	171,948
Russia, 1900.............	36,000	860,000	[4] 3,500,000
Servia, 1897.............	....	160,751	353,366
Spain, 1899..............	....	98,140	183,972
Sweden, 1899	2,513	37,639	327,000
Switzerland, 1899 [5]......	....	....	509,707
Turkey, 1898.............	....	700,620	900,000
United States, 1900.....	2,587	65,000	100,000

[1] Estimated on present organization to have over 3,-000,000 trained men. War strength not given.
[2] Of this number 74,288 are Indian troops.
[3] In addition there are maintained in the colonies 9,478 officers and men.
[4] Approximately.
[5] No standing army.

"War Department, Adjutant General's office, Washington, December 8, 1900. Peace strength of the armies, population, and percentage of former to latter of the principal countries of the world. This table is not strictly accurate at the present time, because the dates of censuses vary. In preparing this table the latest published census has been taken for population, and the countries are arranged in order of their percentages:

NATION.	Peace Strength.	Population.	Percentage.
France	616,475	38,517,975	1.6
Norway................	30,900	2,000,917	1.54
Germany..............	585,896	52,279,901	1.1
Roumania.............	63,280	5,800,000	1.1
Italy	324,686	31,856,675	1
Greece	25,333	2,433,806	1
Servia	22,448	2,312,484	.97
Austria-Hungary.....	361,693	41,357,184	0.87
Sweden	40,152	5,062,918	.79
Belgium..............	51,502	6,669,732	.77
Russia................	896,000	128,932,173	.69
Great Britain and Ireland	259,141	38,104,975	.68
Turkey	244,000	38,791,000	.63
Portugal	31,804	5,049,729	.62
Spain	98,140	17,565,632	.56
Netherlands	27,696	5,074,632	.54
Denmark	9,769	2,185,335	.45
Japan	122,029	43,745,353	.30
Mexico	32,143	12,630,863	.25
Brazil	28,160	14,333,915	.19
United States	67,587	76,295,220	.089
Switzerland [1]........	....	3,119,635	....

[1] Switzerland has no standing army, but every citizen has to bear arms. The first class (élite), composed of men between the ages of 20 and 32, has from forty to eighty days' training the first year, and every second year thereafter sixteen days. About 18,000 men join the élite annually.

In December, 1900, the British Board of Trade issued a return, for the year 1899 (except as stated otherwise), of the "Naval expenditure and Mercantile Marine" of leading nations, from which the following table is taken:

COUNTRIES.	Aggregate Naval Expenditure on Seagoing Force.	Aggregate Revenue.	Aggregate Tonnage of Mercantile Marine.
	£	£	Tons.
Great Britain (United Kingdom)	26,145,599 (1898-99)	119,839,905 (Year ended 31st March, 1900)	9,164,342
Russian Empire...	8,306,500	165,905,000	554,141 (1898)
Germany...	6,672,788 (1899-1900)	76,309,000	1,639,552 (1898)
Netherlands...	1,133,664 (1899-1900)	10,416,000	302,224 (1898)
France	13,796,033	142,021,000	957,756 (1898)
Portugal...	749,226 (Year ended 30th June, 1900)	11,474,000	129,522 (1898)
Spain...	1,133,664 (Year ended 30th June, 1900)	34,633,000 (1898-99)	657,924 (1897)
Italy...	4,617,034 (Year ended 30th June, 1900)	70,181,000 (Year ended 30th June, 1809)	815,162 (1898)
Austria-Hungary...	1,403,441	Austria, 66,171.000 (1898) Hungary, 42,903,000	Austria. 164,506 (1898) Hungary. 60,072
United States (year ended 30th June).................	9,840,912 (1900)	127,288,000	848,246 (b).
Japan	5,076,294 (1899-1900)	22,017,000 (a)	648,324 (1898)

NOTE.—(a) Includes the Chinese indemnity. (b) Registered for foreign trade only.

WAR DEPARTMENT, The United States: Investigation of its conduct in the **war** with Spain. See (in this vol.) UNITED STATES OF AM.: A. D. 1898–1899.

WASHINGTON, D. C.: A. D. 1897.— Completion of **the building** for **the Library** of Congress. See (in this vol.) LIBRARY OF CONGRESS.

A. D. 1900 (December).—Celebration of the Centennial Anniversary.—The 100th anniversary of the removal of the national capital from Philadelphia to Washington was fittingly celebrated on the 12th of December, 1900, by an imposing military parade and by a notable assemblage in the House of Representatives, where addresses were delivered and the principal exercises took place. The President and the Vice President elect, members of all branches of the public service, the Governors and delegates from all the States and Territories, and various other dignitaries, were present. The day of celebration was not precisely that of the anniversary, but one chosen for convenience to represent it. Under the law in 1800 the two houses of Congress began their regular winter session about two weeks earlier than they do now, and November 17 was set as the date on which the VIth Congress should reassemble at the new seat of Federal power. As neither house could have taken part this year in anniversary ceremonies held on November 17, a day was naturally chosen which should allow the legislative branch its proper share in the centennial celebration. The Executive Departments had, in fact, been partially installed in the new District some time before the members of the VIth Congress found their way to the unfinished Capitol. President Adams, leaving Philadelphia on May 27, and travelling by a circuitous route through Lancaster and Frederick, reached Georgetown on June 3, 1800. He inspected the single wing of the original Capitol, then far from finished, visited Alexandria, at the southern extreme of the District, and after a ten days stay in Georgetown departed for Massachusetts. The President and Mrs. Adams returned to occupy the White House early in November of the same year.

WAZIRIS, British-Indian wars with the. See (in this vol.) INDIA : A. D. 1894, and 1897–1898.

WEI-HAI-WEI, Lease of the harbor of, by Great Britain. See (in this vol.) CHINA : A. D. 1898 (MARCH—JULY).

WELLMAN, Walter: Second Arctic Expedition. See (in this vol.) POLAR EXPLORATION, 1898–1899.

WELSH CHURCH: Failure of Disestablishment Bill. See (in this vol.) ENGLAND : A. D. 1894–1895.

WEST AFRICA: A. D. 1895.—Appointment of a Governor-General of the French possessions. See (in this vol). AFRICA : A. D. 1895 (FRENCH WEST AFRICA).

A. D. 1899.—Definition of British and German boundaries. See (in this vol.) SAMOAN ISLANDS.

WEST INDIES, The British: **A. D. 1897.**—Report of a Royal Commission on the condition and prospects of the sugar-growing colonies.—A state of increasing distress in most of the British West India colonies, caused by the depression of the sugar-growing industry, led to the appointment, in December, 1896, of a Royal Commission "to make an inquiry into the condition and prospects of the colonies of Jamaica, British Guiana, Trinidad and Tobago, Barbados, Grenada, St. Vincent, St. Lucia, and the Leeward Islands, and to suggest such measures as appeared calculated to restore and maintain the prosperity of these colonies and their inhabitants." In the August following the Commission made its report, with the following summary of conclusions:

"a. The sugar industry in the West Indies is in danger of great reduction, which in some colonies may be equivalent or almost equivalent to extinction.

"b. The depression of the industry is due to the competition of other sugar-producing countries and in a special degree to the competition of beet sugar produced under a system of bounties. It is also affected by high protective tariffs, and by the competition of cane sugar, the production of which is specially encouraged by the Governments concerned. The causes of the depression may be described as permanent, inasmuch as they are largely due to the policy of foreign countries, and there is no indication that that policy is likely to be abandoned in the immediate future.

"c. It is not due in any considerable degree to extravagance in management, to imperfection in the process of manufacture, or to inadequate supervision consequent on absentee ownership, and the removal of these causes, wherever they exist, would not enable it, generally, to be profitably carried on under present conditions of competition. . . .

"d. The depression in the industry is causing sugar estates to be abandoned, and will cause more estates to be abandoned, and such abandonment is causing and will cause distress among the labouring population, including a large number of East Indian immigrants, and will seriously affect, for a considerable time, the general prosperity of the sugar-producing Colonies, and will render it impossible for some, and perhaps the greater number of them, to provide, without external aid, for their own government and administration.

"e. If the production of sugar is discontinued or very largely reduced, there is no industry or industries that could completely replace it in such islands as Barbados, Antigua, and St. Kitts, and be profitably carried on and supply employment for the labouring population. In Jamaica, in Trinidad, in British Guiana, in St. Lucia, in St. Vincent, and to some extent in Montserrat and Nevis, the sugar industry may in time be replaced by other industries, but only after the lapse of a considerable period and at the cost of much displacement of labour and consequent suffering. In Dominica the sugar industry is not at the present day of great importance. We think it right to add that in all Colonies where sugar can be completely, or very largely, replaced by other industries, the Colonies in question will be in a much sounder position, both politically and economically, when they have ceased to depend wholly, or to a very great extent, upon the continued prosperity of a single industry.

"f. The total or partial extinction of the sugar industry would, in most places, very seriously affect the condition of the labouring classes for the worse, and would largely reduce the revenue of the Colonies. In some places the loss of revenue could be met to a limited extent by economies, but this could not be done universally nor in a material degree in most of the Colonies. Some of the Colonies could not provide the necessary cost of administration, including the relief of distressed and necessitous persons, or of the support and repatriation (when necessary) of the East Indian immigrants, without subventions from the mother country. Jamaica, Trinidad, and Grenada may be expected to meet from their own resources the whole of the expenditure that is likely to fall on them.

"g. The best immediate remedy for the state

of things which we have shown to exist would be the abandonment of the bounty system by continental nations. This change would in all probability enable a large portion of the sugar-cane cultivation to be carried on successfully, and would certainly reduce the rate at which it will diminish. Looking, however, to what appears to be the policy of the United States of America, to the great cheapening of the cost of production of beet sugar, and the fact that many countries appear to have singled out the sugar industry as one which ought to be artificially stimulated in various ways, it is not clear that, even if the bounties were abolished, another crisis of a similar character might not arise in the West Indies at a future day.

"h. A remedy which was strongly supported by witnesses interested in the West Indian sugar estates was the imposition of countervailing duties on bounty-fed sugar when imported into the United Kingdom. . . .

"i. The special remedies or measures of relief which we unanimously recommend are—(1.) The settlement of the labouring population on small plots of land as peasant proprietors. (2.) The establishment of minor agricultural industries, and the improvement of the system of cultivation, especially in the case of small proprietors. (3.) The improvement of the means of communication between the different islands. (4.) The encouragement of a trade in fruit with New York, and, possibly, at a future time, with London. (5.) The grant of a loan from the Imperial Exchequer for the establishment of Central Factories in Barbados. The subject of emigration from the distressed tracts also requires the careful attention of the various Governments, though we do not find ourselves at the present time in a position to make recommendations in detail.

" j. We estimate the cost of the special remedies recommended in (2) (3) and (4) of i, at 27,-000l. a year for ten years, the expenditure to be borne by the mother country. We estimate the amount of the loan to Barbados for the erection of central factories at 120,000l. This measure no doubt involves the risk of loss. Grants will be required in Dominica and St. Vincent for roads, and to enable the settlement of the labouring population on the land to be carried out, and their amount may be taken at 30,000l. A further grant of about 60,000l. is required to clear off the floating debt in some of the smaller islands. In addition, the smaller islands should receive grants to enable them to meet their ordinary expenditure of an obligatory nature. The amount may be placed at 20,000l. a year for five years, and possibly a reduced amount for a further period of five years. The expenditure which we are able to estimate may be summarized as follows:—(1.) A grant of 27,000l. a year for ten years. (2.) A grant of 20,000l. a year for five years. (3.) Immediate grants of 60,000l. and 30,000l., or 90,000l. in all. (4.) A loan of 120,000l. to Barbados for the establishment of central factories."

On a proposal for the federation of the West India colonies the Commission reported unfavorably, for the reason that the colonies are too widely scattered and differ too greatly in conditions for an efficient or economical common government. " Nor does it seem to us," says the report, "that the very important Island of Jamaica, which is separated by many hundreds of miles of sea from all the other West Indian Colonies, could dispense with a separate Govern-or, even if there should be a Governor-General; whilst the circumstances of British Guiana and Trinidad almost equally demand the constant presence and attention of an Administrator of Governor's rank. It might be possible, without disadvantage, to make some reduction in the number of higher officials in the smaller islands, and we are disposed to think that it would be conducive to efficiency and economy if the islands of the Windward Group, that is, Grenada and the Grenadines, St. Vincent and St. Lucia, were again placed under the Governor of Barbados, as they were for many years previous to 1885. We are also disposed to think that the Island of Dominica, which is not much further than Grenada from Barbados, and which, in its physical, social and industrial conditions partakes more of the character of the Windward Islands than of that of the other Leeward Islands, might be placed under this Government instead of being considered one of the Leeward Group. It might, indeed, be found possible to bring the whole of the Leeward Islands under the same Government as Barbados and the Windward Islands, and thus effect a further economy."—*Great Britain, Parliamentary Publications (Papers by Command: C.—8655, 1897, pp. 69-70, and 23).*

With the sanction of Parliament, most of the recommendations of the Commission were promptly carried out. Provision was made for the construction of roads in the islands; for subsidising steamer lines between the several islands and between Jamaica, Canada and London; for developing the cultivation of fruits and other crops by a botanical department; for establishing model factories for the better and cheaper working of sugar cane; and for wiping off certain debts which were a cause of distress to some of the poorer islands. In these measures the imperial government undertook obligations which might, it was said, involve the payment of £200,-000.

A. D. 1899-1901.—Reciprocity arrangement with the United States. See (in this vol.) UNITED STATES OF AM. : A. D. 1899-1901.

WESTERN AUSTRALIA. See (in this vol.) AUSTRALIA; and CONSTITUTION OF AUSTRALIA.

WEYLER y NICOLAU, General: At Barcelona. See (in this vol.) SPAIN : A. D. 1895-1896.

Administration in Cuba. See (in this vol.) CUBA : A. D. 1896-1897.

Appointed Captain-General of Madrid. See (in this vol.) SPAIN: A. D. 1900 (OCTOBER—NOVEMBER).

WHEATON, General: Military operations in the Philippine Islands. See (in this vol.) PHILIPPINE ISLANDS: A. D. 1899 (JANUARY—NOVEMBER). . . . . .

WHITE, Andrew D.: American Commissioner to the Peace Conference at The Hague. See (in this vol.) PEACE CONFERENCE.

WILDMAN, Rounseville: Report of proposals from Philippine insurgents in 1897. See (in this vol.) UNITED STATES OF AM.: A. D. 1897 (NOVEMBER).

WILHELMINA, Queen of the Netherlands: Enthronement and marriage. See (in this vol.) NETHERLANDS: A. D. 1898, and 1901.

WILLIAM II., German Emperor.—Some of his autocratic speeches against the Social Democrats. See (in this vol.) GERMANY: A. D. 1894-1895.

His claim to kingship by Divine Right. See (in this vol.) GERMANY: A. D. 1894-1899.

His message to President Kruger relative to the Jameson Raid. See (in this vol.) SOUTH AFRICA (THE TRANSVAAL): A. D. 1896 (JANUARY).

His speech to his brother, Prince Henry, at Kiel. See (in this vol.) GERMANY: A. D. 1897 (NOVEMBER—DECEMBER).

His speech to soldiers departing to China. —Punishment of its critics. See (in this vol.) GERMANY: A. D. 1900 (OCTOBER 9).

His system of personal government. See (in this vol.) GERMANY: A. D. 1900 (NOVEMBER—DECEMBER).

WILMINGTON, N. C.: Race war. See (in this vol.) NORTH CAROLINA: A. D. 1898.

WIRELESS TELEGRAPHY. See (in this vol.) SCIENCE, RECENT: ELECTRICAL.

WITU, The State of. See (in this vol.) BRITISH EAST AFRICA PROTECTORATE: A. D. 1895-1897.

WITWATERSRAND, The. See (in this vol.) SOUTH AFRICA (THE TRANSVAAL): A. D. 1885-1890.

WOLCOTT, Senator Edward O.: Bimetallic mission to Europe. See (in this vol.) MONETARY QUESTIONS: A. D. 1897 (APRIL—OCTOBER).

WOMAN SUFFRAGE.—Four States have given to women unlimited political freedom, these States being Colorado, Utah, Wyoming, and Idaho. The women of all these States, except Idaho, had the privilege of voting in the Presidential election of 1896. The women of Idaho voted in the State election of 1898, but their first chance to vote for a Presidential ticket was in 1900. To some extent, in the election of school boards and officers, or on questions of taxation, woman suffrage exists in a limited way in Arizona, Connecticut, Delaware, Illinois, Iowa, Kentucky, Massachusetts, Michigan, Minnesota, Montana, Nebraska, New Hampshire, New York, North Dakota, Ohio, Oklahoma, Oregon, South Dakota, Texas, Vermont, Washington and Wisconsin.

WOMAN'S CENTURY, The. See (in this vol.) NINETEENTH CENTURY. THE WOMAN'S CENTURY.

WOOD, Leonard, Colonel of the Regiment of Rough Riders. See (in this vol.) UNITED STATES OF AM.: A. D. 1898 (APRIL—MAY).

Commanding at Santiago.—Report. See (in this vol.) CUBA: A. D. 1898-1899 (DECEMBER—OCTOBER).

Military Governor of Cuba. See (in this vol.) CUBA: A. D. 1899 (DECEMBER).

WORKINGMEN'S INSURANCE, Compulsory, in Germany. See (in this vol.) GERMANY: A. D. 1897-1900.

WORKMEN'S COMPENSATION ACT, English. See (in this vol.) ENGLAND: A. D. 1897 (MAY—JULY).

WORLD POWERS, The four great. See (in this vol.) NINETEENTH CENTURY: EXPANSION.

X, Y.

X RAYS, The discovery of. See (in this vol.) SCIENCE, RECENT: CHEMISTRY AND PHYSICS.

YAMAGATA, Marquis: Ministry. See (in this vol.) JAPAN: A. D. 1898-1899.

YANG-TSUN, Battle of. See (in this vol.) CHINA: A. D. 1900 (AUGUST 4-16).

YANG-TSZE REGION, Chinese agreement not to alienate. See (in this vol.) CHINA: A. D. 1898 (FEBRUARY).

YAQUIS, Revolts of the. See (in this vol.) MEXICO: A. D. 1896-1899.

YAUCO, Engagement at. See (in this vol.) UNITED STATES OF AM.: A. D. 1898 (JULY—AUGUST: PORTO RICO).

YELLOW FEVER, Detection of the mosquito as a carrier of. See (in this vol.) SCIENCE, RECENT: MEDICAL AND SURGICAL.

YERKES OBSERVATORY, The.—The Yerkes Observatory, built and equipped for the University of Chicago, by Mr. Charles T. Yerkes, of Chicago, at the village of Williams Bay, near Lake Geneva, Wisconsin, was opened and dedicated on the 21st of October, 1897. A remarkable gathering of eminent astronomers gave distinction to the occasion. The Observatory was pronounced to be the most perfectly equipped in the world. The lens of its great telescope—40 inch objective—the last great work of the late Alvan G. Clark, of Cambridge, Massachusetts—was then the largest ever made. Its cost was $66,000; the cost of the equatorial mounting was $55,000.

YOUNG PEOPLE'S SOCIETY OF CHRISTIAN ENDEAVOR. See (in this vol.) CHRISTIAN ENDEAVOR, YOUNG PEOPLE'S SOCIETY OF.

YUKON, The district of. See (in this vol.) CANADA: A. D. 1895.

Z.

ZAMBESIA, Northern. See (in this vol.) SOUTH AFRICA (BRITISH SOUTH AFRICA COMPANY): A. D. 1894–1895.

ZANZIBAR: A. D. 1895.—Mainland divisions of the Sultanate included in British East Africa Protectorate. See (in this vol.) BRITISH EAST AFRICA PROTECTORATE: A. D. 1895–1897.
A. D. 1896.—British suppression of an usurper. See (in this vol.) AFRICA: A. D. 1896 (ZANZIBAR).
A. D. 1897.—Abolition of the legal status of slavery. See (in this vol.) AFRICA: A. D. 1897 (ZANZIBAR).
A. D. 1899.—Renunciation of rights of ex-tra-territoriality by Germany. See (in this vol.) SAMOAN ISLANDS.

ZIONIST MOVEMENT, The. See (in this vol.) JEWS: A. D. 1897–1901.

ZULULAND: Extension of boundary. See (in this vol.) AFRICA: A. D. 1895 (ZULULAND).
Annexation to Natal Colony. See (in this vol.) AFRICA: A. D. 1897 (ZULULAND).

ZOLA, Emile, and the Dreyfus case. See (in this vol.) FRANCE: A. D. 1897–1899, and 1900 (DECEMBER).

ZONA LIBRE. See (in this vol.) MEXICAN FREE ZONE.

CHRONOLOGICAL RECORD OF EVENTS.

1895-1901.

1895.

January 1. Murder of the reigning prince of Chitral, on the northwestern Indian border.
    7. Independence of Korea proclaimed at Seoul.
    13. Death of Sir John Seeley (Professor John Robert Seeley).
    17. Election of M. Felix Faure President of the French Republic.
    21. Agreement between Great Britain and France defining the boundaries of the hinterland of Sierra Leone.
    22-23. Resignation of President Saenz Peña of the Argentine Republic, and election of President Uriburu.
    24. Death of Lord Randolph Churchill.
    26. Death of Arthur Cayley, English mathematician.—Death of Nikolai Karlovich de Giers, Russian statesman.
    28. Death of François Canrobert, Marshal of France.
February 7. Rejection by the United States House of Representatives of the measure asked for by President Cleveland for the relief of the national treasury.
    8. Contract by the United States Secretary of the Treasury with New York and London banking houses for supply of gold to the treasury.—Death of Reginald Stuart Poole, English archæologist.
    12. Death of Charles Etienne Gayarré, historian of Louisiana.
    16. Death of Lady Stanley of Alderley.
    18. Death of Archduke Albrecht of Austria.
    20. Death of Frederick Douglass, the most eminent colored man of his day
    24. Renewal of insurrection in Cuba against Spanish rule.
March 1. Beginning of the siege of a small force of British-Indian troops in the fort at Chitral by surrounding tribes.
    2. Death of the Grand Duke Alexis, brother of the Tzar Alexander III.—Death of Professor John Stuart Blackie.—Death of Ismail Pasha, ex-Khedive of Egypt.
    5. Death of Sir Henry Rawlinson, English archæologist.
    9. Death of Leopold von Sacher-Masoch, German novelist.
    11. Agreement between Great Britain and Russia for fixing the northern frontier of Afghanistan from Zulfikar on the Heri-Rud to the Pamirs.
    17. Bloody battle in the streets of Lima, Peru, ending in the overthrow of the usurping government of Caceres.
    18. Death of Captain Adam Badeau, military biographer of General Grant.
    31. Death of Sir George Chesney, military writer.
April 20. Relief of the beleaguered British garrison at Chitral.
    30. Death of Gustav Freytag, German novelist.
May 1. Proclamation by the British South Africa Company giving the name " Rhodesia " to its territories.
    4. Death of Roundell Palmer, 1st Earl of Selborne.
    5. Death of Karl Vogt, German biologist.
    6. Re-hearing granted by the Supreme Court of the United States on cases testing constitutionality of the income tax.
    10. Relinquishment by Japan of the Fêng-tien peninsula in China.—Census of the Argentine Republic.
    20. Final decision of the Supreme Court of the United States against the constitutionality of the income tax.
    23. Consolidation of the Astor and Lenox libraries with the "Tilden Trust," to form the New York Public Library.
    24. Death of Hugh McCulloch, American statesman and financier.
    28. Death of Walter Quinton Gresham, United States Secretary of State.
    30. Death of Frederick Locker-Lampson, English poet.
    31. Death of Emily Faithfull, philanthropist and author.
June 14. Census of the German Empire.
    17. Celebration of the opening of the Kaiser Wilhelm Ship Canal between the Baltic and North seas.
    21-22. Defeat in the British Parliament and resignation of the Ministry of Lord Rosebery; Lord Salisbury called to form a new government.
    29. Death of Professor Thomas Henry Huxley, English biologist and scientific man of letters.

July 1. Final transfer of the territories of the British East Africa Company to the British government; completed organization of the East Africa Protectorate.
   8. Opening of the railway from Delagoa Bay to Pretoria, in the Transvaal.
  13. Parliamentary elections begun in Great Britain, resulting in a large majority for the Conservatives and Liberal Unionists.
  15. Assassination of M. Stambouloff, late chief Minister in the Bulgarian government, who died of his wounds on the 19th.
  20. Pressing despatch of Mr. Olney, United States Secretary of State, to the American Ambassador to Great Britain, on the question of the Venezuela boundary, asserting the Monroe Doctrine.
  21. Death of Prof. Rudolph von Gneist, German jurist and historian.
  24. Defeat of Protectionist policy in the Parliamentary election, New South Wales.
  31. Death of Heinrich von Sybel, historian, and Director of the Prussian State Archives.—Death of Richard M. Hunt, American architect.

August 1. Massacre of English and American missionaries at Hua Sang in China.
  2. Death of Joseph Thomson, African explorer.
  12. Opening of the first session of the new Parliament in Great Britain.
  13. Death of Christian Bernhard Tauchnitz, Leipzig publisher.

September 2. Government of a young native prince, under British tutelage and protection established at Chitral.
  16-18. Adoption of a constitution and organization of a republican government by the Cuban insurgents.
  18. Opening of the Cotton States and International Exposition at Atlanta.
  20. Executive order by President Cleveland for the improvement of the consular service of the United States.
  28. Death of Louis Pasteur, the father of bacteriology.
  30. Attack by Turkish police in Constantinople on Armenians who had gathered to present their grievances to the Sultan.

October 3. Death of Prof. Hjalmar Hjorth Boyesen, Norwegian-American novelist and poet.
  7. Death of William Wetmore Story, American sculptor and author.
  8-9. Massacre of Armenians at Trebizond by a Turkish mob.
  17. Turkish imperial irade directing reforms in Armenia which were not carried out.
  21. Death of Henry Reeve, English author and editor.

November 4. Revolutionary installation of Aloy Alfaro as executive chief of the Republic of Ecuador.—Death of Eugene Field, American poet and journalist.
  8. Discovery of the X rays by Professor Röntgen.
  9. Death of Col. Benjamin Wait, a leader of the Canadian rebellion of 1837.
  20. Death of Chimeili de Marini, known as Rustem Pasha.
  25. More rigorous anti-slavery law instituted in Egypt.—Death of Jules Barthélemy Saint-Hilaire, French statesman and orientalist.
  26. Reply of Lord Salisbury, for the British government, to the despatch of Mr. Olney, on the Venezuela question.—Death of Henry Seebohm, English naturalist.
  27. Death of Alexandre Dumas, the younger.
  29. Death of Count Edward Taaffe, Austrian statesman.

December 8. Death of George Augustus Sala, English journalist.
  12. Death of Allen G. Thurman, American political leader and statesman.
  17. Message of President Cleveland to the Congress of the United States on the boundary dispute between Great Britain and Venezuela.—Death of Antonio Gallenga (Luigi Mariotti), Italian revolutionist, journalist, and author.
  18-20. Passage by the two branches of the Congress of the United States of an act authorizing the President to appoint a commission to ascertain the true boundary of Venezuela.
  20. Special Message of President Cleveland to the Congress of the United States on the financial situation of the country.
  23. Death of "Stepniak," Russian revolutionist and author.—Death of John Russell Hind, English astronomer.
  27-28. Passage of temporary tariff bill and bill to maintain the coin redemption fund, by the United States House of Representatives.
  29. Raid by Dr. Jameson, Administrator of the British South Africa Company, into the Transvaal, with an armed force of 500 men.

1896.

January 1. Appointment of an United States Commission to investigate the divisional line between Venezuela and British Guiana.—Surrender of Dr. Jameson and his raiders to the Boers.—New constitution for South Carolina brought into effect.
  3. Congratulatory telegram from the German Emperor, William II., to President Kruger, of the South African Republic, on the defeat of the Jameson Raid.
  8. Destructive earthquake shock in Persia.—Death of Paul Verlaine, French poet.
  10. Proclamation of President Kruger to the inhabitants of Johannesburg, promising them a municipal government.
  11. Death of João de Deus, Portuguese poet.

15. Declaration of agreement between Great Britain and France concerning Siam.
17. Occupation of Kumassi, the capital of Ashanti, by British forces, and submission of King Prempeh.
18. Submission by the Queen of Madagascar to a French protectorate of the island.
20. Death of Prince Henry of Battenberg.
24. Death of Lord Leighton, English painter.
29. Death of the Rt. Hon. Hugh Culling Eardley Childers, ex-Chancellor of the Exchequer, Great Britain.

February 1. Substitution, by the United States Senate, of a free silver coinage bill for the House bill to maintain the coin redemption fund.
6. Death of Jean Auguste Barre, French sculptor.
8. Signing of treaty between United States and Great Britain for the arbitration of British claims for seizure of sealing vessels.
10. Arrival of General Weyler at Havana as Governor and Captain-General of Cuba.
11. Notification by the French government to the Powers that it had taken final possession of Madagascar.
14. Rejection by the United States House of Representatives of the Senate substitute for its bill to maintain the coin redemption fund.
16. Promulgation of Weyler's concentration order in Cuba.
25. Defeat of the House tariff bill in the United States Senate.
26. Death of Arsène Houssaye, French author.
27. Reopening of a discussion of the Venezuela boundary question between the governments of the United States and Great Britain.

March 1. Defeat of the Italians by the Abyssinians at Adowa.
5. Suggestion by Lord Salisbury of a general treaty of arbitration between the United States and Great Britain.
10-12. Passage of the Raines Liquor Law by the two branches of the New York Legislature.
21. Beginning of the Anglo-Egyptian movement for the recovery of the Sudan from the Dervishes.
22. Death of Thomas Hughes, author of "Tom Brown's School Days."
24. Death of President Hippolyte of the Haytien Republic.
28. Death of Mrs. Elizabeth Charles, English author.
30. Resumption of the authority of the Pope over the Coptic Church, and re-establishment of the Catholic patriarchate of Alexandria.
31. Reopening of the military and naval service of the United States to persons who had held commissions in the Confederate army or navy during the civil war.

April 6. Revival of Olympic games at Athens.
8. Highest latitude reached by Dr. Nansen, within 261 statute miles of the north pole.
11. Death of Charilaos Trikoupis, Greek statesman.
21. Death of Jean Baptiste Léon Say, French statesman.—Death of Baron Hirsch, financier and millionaire-philanthropist.
24. Promulgation of amendments to the constitution of the Republic of Mexico.
26. Death of Sir Henry Parkes, Australian statesman.

May 1. Opening of German industrial exposition at Berlin.—Assassination of the Shah of Persia.—Promulgation of additional amendments to the Mexican constitution.
2. Opening of the great national exposition and festival at Buda-Pesth to celebrate the millennium of the kingdom of Hungary.
3. Death of Alfred William Hunt, English artist.
4. Opening of the National Electrical Exposition in New York.
6. Promulgation of civil service rules by President Cleveland, adding 29,000 places to the classified service under the government of the United States.
11. The bill to consolidate New York, Brooklyn, and neighboring cities, in the "Greater New York," made law by the Governor's signature.
19. Promulgation of the law of public education in Mexico, establishing a national system.—Publication in England of the manifesto of a New Radical Party, led by Sir Charles Dilke and Mr. Labouchere.—Death of the Archduke Karl Ludwig of Austria.
20. Death of Madame Clara Schumann, pianist.
24. Outbreak of Turks against the Christians in Canea, Crete.—Death of Edward Armitage, English artist.
26. Coronation of the Russian Tzar, Nicholas II.; suffocation of nearly 3,000 people at the feasting.
27. The city of St. Louis struck by a cyclone.
27-28. Meeting of the national convention of the Prohibition Party, at Pittsburgh, to nominate candidates for President and Vice President of the United States.

June 2. Death of Friedrich Gerhard Rohlfs, African explorer.
4. Death of Ernesto Rossi, Italian actor and author.
7. Battle of the British and Egyptian army with the Dervishes at Ferket.
8. Death of Jules Simon, French statesmen and philosopher.
9. Appointment of Commission to draft the "Greater New York" charter.
16-18. Meeeting, at St. Louis, of the Republican national convention, and nomination of William McKinley and Garret A. Hobart for President and Vice President of the United States.

23. Parliamentary elections in Canada, and substantial victory of the Liberal Party.—Death of Sir Joseph Prestwich, English geologist.

26. Resignation of Cecil J. Rhodes from the board of directors of the British South Africa Company.

28. Re-election of President Diaz, of Mexico, for a fifth term.

July 1. Abolition of inter-state taxes in Mexico.—Death of Mrs. Harriet Beecher Stowe.

4-10. Meeting, in New York, of the national convention of the Socialist Labor Party, to nominate candidates for President and Vice President of the United States.

7-11. Meeting, at Chicago, of the Democratic national convention, and nomination of William J. Bryan and Arthur Sewall for President and Vice President of the United States.

8. Retirement of Sir Charles Tupper from and succession of Sir Wilfrid Laurier to the Prime Ministry of the Canadian government.

11. Death of Rt. Hon. Sir Augustus Berkeley Paget, diplomatist.

12. Death of Professor Ernst Curtius, German historian.

14. First international conference in London to plan co-operative work in the preparation of a catalogue of scientific literature.

16. Death of Edmond Huot Goncourt, French novelist.

17. Report of an investigating committee of the Cape Colony House of Assembly declaring Mr. Rhodes to be responsible for the Jameson Raid.

20. Opening of the trial, in England, of Dr. Jameson and other leaders of the raid into the Transvaal.—Death of Charles Dickens, eldest son of the novelist.

22. Meeting of the convention of the National Silver Party, at St. Louis, to endorse the nominations of Bryan and Sewall, for President and Vice President of the United States.

22-25. Meeting of the People's, or Populist Party in national convention at St. Louis; nomination of William J. Bryan and Thomas E. Watson for President and Vice President of the United States.

23. Death of Mary Dickens, eldest daughter of Charles Dickens.

26. Tidal wave on the coast of Kiangsu, China, destroying several thousand people.

28. Conviction of Dr. Jameson and four of his subordinates.

30. Resolution of the British House of Commons to investigate the administration of the British South Africa Company.

August. Discovery of the Klondike gold fields.

1. Death of Rt. Hon. Sir William R. Grove, jurist and man of science.

19. Death of Professor Josiah Dwight Whitney, American geologist.

25. Revolution in the sultanate of Zanzibar suppressed by British forces.—Arrangement of Turkey with the Powers for reforms in Crete.

26-28. Attack of Armenians on the Ottoman Bank at Constantinople; horrible massacre of Armenians by the Turks.

27. Appointment of Monsignor Martinelli to succeed Cardinal Satolli as Papal Delegate to the United States.

30. Death of Prince Alexis Borisovich Lobanof-Rostofski, Russian statesman and diplomatist.

31. Proclamation establishing a British protectorate over the hinterland of Sierra Leone.

September 2-3. Meeting of a convention of the National Democratic Party at Indianapolis; nomination of General John M. Palmer and General Simon B. Buckner for President and Vice President of the United States.

15. Publication in the Paris " Eclair " of the fact that Captain Alfred Dreyfus (degraded and imprisoned in 1894 for alleged betrayal of military secrets to a foreign power) was convicted on the evidence of a document shown secretly to the court martial, and unknown to the prisoner and his counsel.

23. The Dervishes driven from Dongola by the Anglo-Egyptian army.

27. Abolition of slavery in Madagascar by decree of the French Resident-General.

29. Official announcement of bubonic plague at Bombay.

October 3. Death of William Morris, English poet.

8. Death of George Du Maurier, English artist and novelist.

11. Death of Edward White Benson, Archbishop of Canterbury.

20-22. Celebration of the one hundred and fiftieth anniversary of the founding of The College of New Jersey, which then formally assumed the name of Princeton University.

26. Peace made between the government of Italy and King Menelek, of Abyssinia.—Death of Paul Amand Challemel Lacour, French publicist.

November 3. Presidential election in the United States.

9. Announcement by Lord Salisbury of the settlement of the Venezuela question between Great Britain and the United States.

11. Death of Mrs. Mary Frances Scott-Siddons, actress.

16. First transmission of electric power from Niagara Falls to Buffalo.

21. Death of Sir Benjamin Ward Richardson, physician, scientific investigator, and author.

26. Death of Coventry Patmore, English poet.—Death of Mathilde Blind, author.—Death of Benjamin Apthorp Gould, American astronomer.

December 1. Death of Heinrich Gätke, painter and naturalist.

7. Death of Antonio Maceo, leader of Cuban insurgents, killed in a skirmish with the Spaniards.

10. Death of Alfred Noble, Swedish engineer and founder of a great fund for annually rewarding benefactors of humanity.

6-45

11. Political suffrage extended to women in Idaho by an amendment of the constitution.
15. Death of Émile François Chatrousse, French sculptor.

1897.

January 3. Death of Vivien St. Martin, French geographer.
3-4. Outbreak of conflict between Christians and Moslems at Canea in Crete.
5. Death of George Whiting Flagg, American painter.
11. Signing, at Washington, of a general treaty between the United States and Great Britain for the arbitration of all matters of difference.
12. Meeting, at Indianapolis, of a national convention of delegates from commercial organizations to take measures for promoting monetary reform in the United States.
15. Death of Sir Travers Twiss, English jurist.
16. Death of Joel Tyler Headley, American man of letters.
27. Overthrow of the slave-raiding Emir of Nupé by forces of the Royal Niger Company.

February 2. Signing, at Washington, of the treaty of arbitration between Great Britain and Venezuela.
7. Union of Crete with Greece proclaimed by insurgent Christians at Halepa.
9. The taking of the first general census of the Russian Empire.—Death of Eliza Greatorex, American painter.
11. Announcement by the government of Greece to the Powers that it had determined to intervene by force in behalf of the Christians of Crete.
12. Death of Homer Dodge Martin, American artist.
14. Landing of a Greek expedition of 2,000 men in Crete, under Colonel Vassos.
15. Landing of a mixed force at Canea, Crete, by the Powers of the "European Concert," to protect the town; proclamation by the Greek commander, Colonel Vassos, that he had occupied the island in the name of the King of the Greeks.
16. Beginning of the British parliamentary investigation of the Jameson Raid.—Presentation by the South African Republic of its claim for indemnity on account of the Jameson Raid.
17. Attack by the Greeks on the Turkish forces at Canea.
18. Capture of Benin by British forces.
22. Death of Jean François Gravelet Blondin, French acrobat.

March 2. Veto of Immigration Bill by President Cleveland.—Joint note by the Powers of the "Concert" to Greece and Turkey, declaring that Crete cannot be annexed to Greece, but that the island will be endowed by the Powers with an autonomous administration.
4. Inauguration of William McKinley in the office of President of the United States.
6. Death of Rev. Ebenezer Cobham Brewer, English author.
11. Death of Prof. Henry Drummond, Scottish religious writer.
15. Meeting of Congress in extra session called by the President.
21. "Pacific blockade" of the coast of Crete established by the Powers of the European Concert.
25. Passage of the Elementary Education Act by the British House of Commons.
27. Death of William Taylor Adams (Oliver Optic), American writer of fiction for young readers.
30. Opening of debate in the British Parliament on the report of a Royal Commission on the financial relations between Great Britain and Ireland.
31. Passage of the Dingley tariff bill by the United States House of Representatives.

April. Unprecedented floods along the Mississippi river.
3. Death of Johannes Brahms, German composer.
5. Publication in Austria of the language decrees for Bohemia.
6. Edict of the Sultan of Zanzibar terminating the legal status of slavery.
9. Incursion of irregular Greek troops into Turkish territory.
10. Death of Daniel Wolsey Voorhees, United States Senator.
12. Appointment of commissioners from the United States to negotiate in Europe for an international bi-metallic agreement.—Formal delivery to the Governor of Massachusetts of the manuscript of Bradford's History of Plymouth Colony (called "the Log of the Mayflower") as a gift from England.—Death of Edward Drinker Cope, American naturalist.
17. Turkish declaration of a state of war with Greece; beginning of hostilities between regular troops, at Milouna Pass.
22-24. Retreat of the Greek army in panic rout from Tyrnavo.
27. Resignation of the Greek Ministry of M. Delyannis.
30. Repulse by the Greeks of a Turkish attack on positions near Velestino.—Formation of a new Ministry in Greece, under Demetrius Ralli.

May 1. Opening of the Centennial Exposition at Nashville, Tennessee.
2-7. Continued attacks by the Turks on the line held by the Greeks between Pharsala and Volo; withdrawal of the Greeks to Domoko.
4. Fire in a charity bazaar at Paris which was horribly destructive of life.—The "Greater New York" charter becomes law.
5. Rejection by the United States Senate of the arbitration treaty negotiated between the United States and Great Britain.
6. Death of Henri Eugène Philippe Louis, Duc d'Aumale, French prince of the Bourbon-Orleans family, soldier and author.—Death of James Theodore Bent, English traveler and writer.

8. Announcement by the Greek government to the Powers that Colonel Vassos and his forces would be withdrawn from Crete.
11. Proffer by the Powers of the European Concert of mediation between Turkey and Greece.
17. Defeat of the Greeks by the Turks at Domoko.
20. Arrangement of an armistice between the Turks and the Greeks.
23. Withdrawal of the last of the Greek troops from Crete.

June 1. Census taken in Egypt.
2. Opening of the Commercial Museum in Philadelphia.
3. Opening of negotiations for peace between Turkey and Greece at Constantinople.
10. Effect given to a new constitution for the State of Delaware, establishing an educational qualification of the suffrage.—Rising of tribes on the Afghan frontier of India against the British.
14. Convention between France and Great Britain, establishing the boundaries of their respective claims in the Niger region of West Africa.
16. Transmission to Congress of a new treaty for the annexation of the Hawaiian Islands to the United States.
20-22. Celebration in London of the sixtieth anniversary—the "Diamond Jubilee"—of the accession of Queen Victoria to the throne of the United Kingdom.
24. Conference at London of the Premiers of British colonies with the Secretary of State for the Colonies.
25. Death of Mrs. Margaret Oliphant (Wilson) Oliphant, Scottish novelist and writer in many fields.

July 2. Death of Adjutant-General Francis Amasa Walker, American economist.
7. Passage of the Dingley tariff bill by the United States Senate, with many amendments.
8. Death of Isham Green Harris, United States Senator.
10. Death of Daniel Greenleaf Thompson, American author.
11. Adoption of constitutional amendments in Switzerland by popular vote.—The starting of Andrée from Spitzbergen on his attempted balloon voyage to the north pole.
12-15. Conference of American commissioners with Lord Salisbury and other British ministers, on the subject of an international bi-metallic agreement.
13. Report of the British parliamentary committee which investigated the Jameson Raid.—Death of Alfred Marshall Mayer, American physicist.
14. Death of Anthony John Mundella, English statesman.
15. Death of Brigadier-General Philippe Regis de Trobriand, French officer in the American civil war, and writer.
20. Death of Sir John Skelton, Scottish historian.—Death of Sir John Charles Bucknill, English alienist.
24. Final passage of the Dingley tariff bill by both branches of the United States Congres.
26. Attack on British garrisons in the Swat Valley (Afghan frontier of India), excited bys "the mad mullah."
30. Death of Étienne Vacherot, French philosopher.

August 2. Death of Adam Asnyk, Polish poet.
5. Death of James Hammond Trumbull, American philologist.
8. Assassination of Señor Canovas del Castillo, Prime Minister of Spain.
25. Assassination of President Borda, of Uruguay.
29-31. Meeting of the first congress of the Zionists at Basle.
31. Speech by the German Emperor at Coblenz, asserting "kingship by the grace of God," with "responsibility to the Creator alone."—Death of Mrs. Louisa Lane Drew, actress.

September 10. Death of Theodore Lyman, American naturalist.
11. Death of Rev. Abel Stevens, American historian of the Methodist church.
12. Ending of a great strike of coal miners in the United States, which began in July.
16. Death of Edward Austin Sheldon, American educator.
17. Death of Henry Williams Sage, American philanthropist.
18. Signing of a preliminary treaty of peace between Turkey and Greece.
20. Death of Wilhelm Wattenbach, German historian.
22. Meeting at Washington of a commission on monetary reform, appointed by the Indianapolis Convention of January 12.—Death of Charles Denis Sauter Bourbaki, French general.
28. Vote on proposed constitutional amendments in New Jersey.

October 1. Introduction of the gold monetary standard in Japan.
2. Death of Neal Dow, American temperance reformer.
4. Death of Professor Francis William Newman, English scholar and philosopher.
6. The Philippine Islands swept by a typhoon, destroying over 6,000 lives.—Death of Sir John Gilbert, English artist.
18. Death of Rear-Admiral John Lorimer Worden, U. S. N.
19. Death of George Mortimer Pullman, American inventor.
21. Opening and dedication of the Yerkes Observatory, at Williams Bay, Wisconsin.
22. Death of Justin Winsor, American historian and bibliographer.
24. Death of Francis Turner Palgrave, English poet.
25. Death of John Sartain, American artist.—Death of John Stoughton, English church historian.
27. Death of Mary, Duchess of Teck.—Death of Alexander Milton Ross, Canadian naturalist.

28. Stormy session of the Austrian Reichsrath; twelve-hours' speech of Dr. Lecher.—Death of Hercules George Robinson, Baron Rosmead, British colonial administrator.

29. Death of Henry George, American economist.

November 2. Election of the first Mayor of "Greater New York."—Death of Sir Rutherford Alcock, British diplomatist.

4. Seizure by Germany of the port of Kiao-chau on the northeastern coast of China.

6. Signing of treaty between Russia, Japan and the United States, providing for a suspension of pelagic scaling.

10. Adoption of plans for a building for the New York Public Library.

14. Death of Thomas Williams Evans, American dentist in Paris, founder of the Red Cross Society in the Franco-Prussian war.

15. Commandant Esterhazy denounced to the French Minister of War, by M. Matthieu Dreyfus, as the author of the "bordereau" on which Captain Alfred Dreyfus was secretly convicted.

16. The Dreyfus case brought into the French Chamber of Deputies by a question to the Minister of War.

19. Great fire in London, beginning in Aldersgate and spreading over six acres, destroying property estimated at £2,000,000 in value.—Death of Henry Calderwood, Scottish philosopher.

21. Death of Sir Charles Edward Pollock, English jurist.

23. Death of A. Bardoux, French statesman.

25. Promulgation by royal decree at Madrid of a constitution establishing self-government in Cuba and Porto Rico.

29. Death of James Legge, Scotch oriental scholar.

December. Annexation of Zululand to Natal Colony.

5. Death of Mrs. Alice Wellington Rollins, American author.

14. Signing of the treaty of Biac-na-bato, between the Spaniards and the insurgent Filipinos.

29. Approval of Act of Congress forbidding the killing of seals by citizens of the United States, in the Pacific Ocean north of 35° N. lat.—Death of William James Linton, American artist and author.

31. Imperial proclamation, closing the sittings of the Austrian Reichsrath, and continuing the Austro-Hungarian "Ausgleich" provisionally for six months.

1898.

January 2. Death of Sir Edward Augustus Bond, formerly principal librarian of the British museum.

12. Acquittal of Commandant Esterhazy, after a farcical pretense of trial by a military tribunal, on the charge of being the author of the "bordereau" ascribed to Dreyfus.

13. Publication in Paris of a letter by M. Zola, denouncing the conduct of the courts martial in the cases of Dreyfus and Esterhazy.—Death of Mrs. Mary Victoria Cowden Clarke.

16. Death of Charles Pelham Villiers, English statesman.

18. Death of Henry George Liddell, English historian and classical scholar.

20. Second meeting of monetary convention at Indianapolis, to consider the report of its commission.

24. Declaration by Count von Bülow, in the German Reichstag, that no relations or connections of any kind had ever existed between Captain Dreyfus and any German agents.

25. Friendly visit of the United States battle ship "Maine" to Havana, Cuba.

28. End of a great strike and lockout in the British engineering trades, which began in the previous July.

31. Disastrous blizzard in New England.

February 4. Re-election (by voting which began January 3) of President Kruger for a fourth term of five years, in the South African Republic.

7-15. Prosecution of M. Zola for defamation of certain military officers; his scandalous trial and conviction.

14. Destruction of the United States battle ship "Maine," by an explosion, in the harbor of Havana, Cuba.

16. Removal of Chief-Justice Kotze, of the High Court of the South African Republic, by President Kruger.

18. Death of Frances Elizabeth Willard, American social reformer.

19. Death of Dr. Edward Constant Seguin, neurologist, New York.

26. Death of Frederick Tennyson, English poet.—Death of Michael Gregorovich Tchernaieff, Russian soldier and popular hero of the Panslavists.

27. Death of Major-General William Booth Taliaferro, Confederate army.

March 1. Retirement of General Crespo from the Presidency of Venezuela; succession of General Andrade to the office.

6. Death of Felice Cavalotti, Italian statesman and dramatist.

11. Death of Major-General William Starke Rosecrans.

15. Death of Sir Henry Bessemer, English inventor.

16. Death of Aubrey Beardsley, English artist.

17. Speech of Senator Proctor, of Vermont, in the United States Senate, describing the condition of the reconcentrados in Cuba, as he saw them during a recent visit to the island.—Death of Blanche K. Bruce, register of the United States Treasury, born a slave.

21. Report of the United States naval court of inquiry on the destruction of the battle ship "Maine."—Death of Brigadier-General George Washington Rains, Confederate army.

22. Report of Spanish naval board of inquiry on the destruction of the United States battle ship "Maine."

23. Primary election law in New York signed by the Governor.

25. Death of James Payn, English novelist.

27. Proposal by the government of the United States to that of Spain of an armistice and negotiation of peace with the insurgents in Cuba.—Cession by China to Russia of Port Arthur and Talienwan.

28. Message of the President of the United States to Congress on the destruction of the battle ship "Maine."—Death of Anton Seidl, composer and musical conductor.

31. Reply of the Spanish government to the proposals of the United States, for an armistice and negotiation with the Cuban insurgents.—Death of Edward Noyes Westcott, American novelist.

April 2. Quashing of the sentence pronounced on M. Zola, upon his appeal to the Court of Cassation.—Lease by China to Great Britain of the port of Wei-hai Wei with adjacent territory.

7. Death of Margaret Mather, American actress.

8. Great victory of the Anglo-Egyptian army, under the Sirdar, General Kitchener, over the Dervishes, on the Atbara.

10. Passage of bill through the German Reichstag to greatly increase the German navy.

11. Special Message of the President of the United States to Congress on the relations of the country to Spain, consequent on affairs in Cuba.—Lease by China to France of Kwangchow Wan on the southern coast.

13. Adoption by the United States House of Representatives of a joint resolution authorizing and directing the President to "intervene at once to stop the war in Cuba."

16. Adoption by the United States Senate of a joint resolution not only directing intervention to stop the war in Cuba, but recognizing the insurgent government of "the Republic of Cuba."—Death of ex-President Crespo, of Venezuela, killed in battle.

17. Death of Jules Marcou, French geologist.

18. Arrangement of the disagreement between the two branches of the United States Congress respecting the recognition of "the Republic of Cuba," and passage of a joint resolution to intervene for the stopping of the war in the island.

19. Death of George Parsons Lathrop, American author.—Death of Gustave Moreau, French painter.

20. Passports asked for and received by the Spanish Minister at Washington.

21. Appointment of Rear-Admiral Sampson to the command of the U. S. naval force on the Atlantic station.

22. Proclamation by the President of the United States declaring a blockade of certain Cuban ports.

23. Proclamation by the President of the United States calling for 125,000 volunteers.

24. Commodore Dewey, commanding the Asiatic squadron of the United States, ordered to proceed from Hong Kong to the Philippine Islands, to destroy or capture the Spanish fleet in those waters.—Interview, at Singapore, between the leader of the Philippine insurgents, Aguinaldo, and the United States Consul-General, Mr. Spencer Pratt; communication from Mr. Pratt to Commodore Dewey, at Hong Kong; request from Commodore Dewey that Aguinaldo come to Hong Kong.

25. Formal declaration of war with Spain by the Congress of the United States, with authority given to the President to call out the land and naval forces of the nation.—Removal of the American squadron under Commodore Dewey from Hong Kong to Mirs Bay, China.—Signing of protocol between Russia and Japan relative to Korea.

27. Sailing of the American squadron from Mirs Bay to Manila.

29. Proclamation of neutrality by the Portuguese government, which required the Spanish fleet under Admiral Cervera to depart from the Cape Verde islands.

May 1. Destruction of the Spanish squadron in Manila Bay by the American squadron under Commodore Dewey.

2. Arrival of Aguinaldo at Hong Kong.

3. Occupation of Cavite arsenal by American naval forces.

8. General elections for a new Chamber of Deputies in France; first balloting.

9. Serious fighting in Milan, ending bread riots in that city and elsewhere in northern Italy.

12. Attack on the Spanish forts at San Juan, Porto Rico, by Admiral Sampson, then searching for Cervera's fleet.

13. Death of Rev. William Stevens Perry, American church historian.

16. Major-General Wesley Merritt, U. S. A., assigned to the command of the Department of the Pacific.—Conveyance of Aguinaldo from Hong Kong to Cavite by the United States ship "McCulloch."

19. Death of Mr. Gladstone.—Death of Maria Louise Pool, American novelist.

22. Second balloting in French elections, where the first had resulted in no choice.—Death of Spencer Walpole, English historian.—Death of Edward Bellamy, American novelist and social theorist.

25. Proclamation by the President of the United States calling for 75,000 additional volunters.—Departure from San Francisco of the first military expedition from the United States to the Philippine Islands, under General T. M. Anderson.

28. Public funeral of Mr. Gladstone; burial in Westminster Abbey.—Death of Mrs. Madeleine Vinton Dahlgren, American author.

709

29. Blockade of the Spanish squadron under Rear-Admiral Cervera, in the harbor of Santiago de Cuba, by the American flying squadron under Commodore Schley.
30. Agreement between Great Britain, Canada and the United States, creating a Joint High Commission for the adjustment of all existing subjects of controversy between the United States and Canada.

June 1. Arrival of Admiral Sampson and his fleet off the entrance to the harbor of Santiago de Cuba, to perfect the blockade of the Spanish squadron.—Opening of the Trans-Mississippi Exposition at Omaha, Nebraska.—Enactment of law to provide for the arbitration of disputes between employés and companies engaged in interstate commerce in the United States.
2. Death of George Eric Mackay, English poet.
3. Sinking of the collier "Merrimac" in the channel of the harbor-entrance at Santiago de Cuba, by Assistant Naval Constructor Hobson, U. S. N.
6. Bombardment of Spanish forts at Santiago de Cuba by the American blockading fleet.
7-10. Possession of the lower bay at Guantanamo, near Santiago de Cuba, taken by vessels of the American navy, and a marine battalion landed.
11. Reform edict issued by the young Emperor of China.
14. Sailing, from Tampa, Florida, of the military expedition under General Shafter for the capture of Santiago de Cuba.
15. Sailing, from San Francisco, of the second American military expedition to the Philippines. —Adoption by the House of Representatives of a joint resolution to provide for annexing the Hawaiian Islands to the United States.
16. Second bombardment of forts at Santiago de Cuba by the American blockading fleet.
16-24. Elections to the Reichstag of the German Empire.
17. Resignation of the Ministry of Signor Rudini in Italy.—Death of Sir Edward Burne-Jones, English painter.
20. Arrival, off Guantanamo, of the expedition under General Shafter.
21. Capture and occupation of the island of Guam by the U. S. S. "Charleston."
22-24. Landing of General Shafter's army at Daiquiri and Siboney.
24. First engagement between American and Spanish troops in Cuba, at La Guasima.
28. Proclamation by Aguinaldo, assuming the administration of a provisional government of the Philippine Islands.—Approval by the President of the United States of the "Curtis Act," relating to the Five Civilized Tribes of Indians.—Formation of a new Italian Ministry by General Pelloux.

July. Discussion and passage by the British Parliament of a Local Government Act for Ireland.
1. Assault by the American forces, at San Juan Hill and El Caney, on the Spanish lines defending Santiago.
2-3. Continued fighting on the lines around Santiago de Cuba.
3. Demand of General Shafter for the surrender of Santiago, under the threat of bombardment; truce arranged by foreign consuls and negotiations for surrender opened.—Destruction of the Spanish fleet of Admiral Cervera on its attempting to escape from the blockaded port of Santiago de Cuba.
4. Opening of communications between General Anderson, commanding the first expedition of the United States forces landed near Manila, and General Aguinaldo, "commanding the Philippine forces."
6. Destruction of the Spanish cruiser "Alphonso XII.," when attempting to escape from the harbor of Havana.—Adoption by the U. S. Senate of the joint resolution to provide for the annexation of the Hawaiian Islands.—Exchange of Lieutenant Hobson and his fellow captives for prisoners taken from the Spanish forces.
7. Declaration of M. Cavaignac, Minister of War, in the Chamber of Deputies, of his absolute certainty of the guilt of Captain Dreyfus.—Death of Francisco Javier Cisneros, Cuban patriot.—Death of M. Buffet, French statesman.
10. Termination of truce at Santiago; resumption of hostilities; bombardment of the city by the navy.
11. Death of Rear-Admiral Daniel Ammen, U. S. N.
12. Outbreak of yellow fever in the military hospital at Siboney.—Arrival of General Miles at Santiago with reinforcements for General Shafter.
13. Interview of General Miles and General Shafter with General Toral, the Spanish commander at Santiago.
14. Agreement by General Toral to surrender the city of Santiago and the entire district of eastern Cuba with 24,000 Spanish troops.—Death of Mrs. Elizabeth Lynn Linton, English author.
16. Signing of the terms of the Spanish surrender at Santiago.
17. Death of Parker Pillsbury, American abolitionist.—Death of Karl Gehrt, German artist.
18. Opening of second trial of M. Zola, at Versailles.
25. Landing, at Guanica, of the expedition of United States troops, under General Miles, for the conquest of Porto Rico.
26. Overtures for peace addressed by the Spanish government to that of the United States through the French Minister at Washington.
27. Occupation of Ponce, in Porto Rico, by the American forces under General Miles.
28. Death of Dr. William Pepper, of Philadelphia, physician, and extraordinary leader in public enterprise.

30. Terms of peace proposed to Spain by the United States.—Death of Rev. John Caird, Scottish divine and educator.

31. Death of Prince Otto von Bismarck, at the age of 83.

August 3. Urgent message from General Shafter to the U. S. War Department, asking for the instant withdrawal of his forces from Santiago, on account of the deadly ravages of yellow fever, typhoid and dysentery.

4. Orders given for the removal of the American army from Santiago de Cuba to Montauk Point, Long Island.

7. Acceptance by Spain of the terms of peace offered by the United States.—Demand of Admiral Dewey and General Merritt for the surrender of Manila.—Death of James Hall, American geologist.

8. Death of Adolph Heinrich Joseph Sutro, American mining engineer.—Death of Georg Moritz Ebers, German novelist and Egyptologist.

12. Ceremony, at Honolulu, of the transfer of sovereignty over the Hawaiian Islands to the United States.—Order by General Merritt forbidding the Filipino forces under Aguinaldo to enter Manila when the city should be taken.—Signing of the protocol of terms for the negotiation of peace between the United States and Spain; proclamation by the President of the United States suspending hostilities.

13. Attack by American forces on the Spanish lines at Manila and capture of the city.

21. Friendly letter of Spanish soldiers at Santiago, Cuba, before departing for Spain, to their late ememies, the American soldiers.

22. Death of Laupepa Malietoa, King of Samoa.

24. Proposal by the Tzar of Russia of a conference of governments to discuss the means of stopping the progressive increase of military and naval armaments and promote the peace of the world.

25. Transfer of command at Santiago from General Shafter to General Lawton.

28. General Merritt ordered to Paris for consultation with the American Peace Commissioners; command at Manila transferred to General Otis.

31. Termination of the minority of Queen Wilhelmina, of the Kingdom of the Netherlands, and of the regency of her mother, Queen Emma.—Suicide of Colonel Henry, of the Intelligence Department of the French Army, after confessing that he had forged one of the documents on which M. Cavaignac based his certainty of the guilt of Captain Dreyfus.

September 2. Battle of Omdurman; defeat of the Dervishes and occupation of the Khalifa's capital.

3. Death of Wilford Woodruff, president of the Mormon Church.

4. Resignation of M. Cavaignac from the French cabinet, because of his opposition to a revision of the Dreyfus case.

6. Enthronement of Queen Wilhelmina, at Amsterdam.—Turkish outbreak at Candia, Crete, against authority exercised by the British admiral in the name of the concerted Powers.

10. Assassination of Elizabeth, Empress of Austria and Queen of Hungary.

12. Death of Thomas McIntyre Cooley, American jurist.

14. Death of Samuel Eliot, American historian.

19. Death of Sir George Grey, British administrator.

21. Overthrow of the Chinese reformers at Peking; submission of the Emperor to the Empress-Dowager.—Death of Theodor Fontane, German poet.

23. Death of Richard Malcolm Johnston, American author.

26. Decision of the French cabinet to submit the question of a revision of the trial of Captain Dreyfus to the Court of Cassation.

28. Execution of six of the Chinese reformers at Peking.—Death of Thomas Francis Bayard, American statesman and diplomatist.

29. Government of a Philippine Republic organized at Malolos; a national congress convened, and Aguinaldo declared President.—Popular vote in Canada on the question of Prohibition.—Death of Queen Louise of Denmark.

30. Mob attack on foreigners near Peking.

October. Discovery of the Cape Nome mining region in Alaska.—Outbreak of Indians of the Leech Lake Reservation in Northern Minnesota.

1. Call by foreign representatives at Peking for guards of marines to protect their legations.—Meeting of Spanish and American commissioners at Paris to negotiate a Treaty of Peace.

5. Demand of the Powers for the withdrawal of Turkish garrisons from Crete.

6. Decree by the Empress-Dowager of China commanding protection to Christian missionaries and converts.

7. Death of Blanche Willis Howard, Baroness von Teuffel, American novelist.—Death of Abraham Oakey Hall, American lawyer and politician.

12. Inauguration of General Julio Roca President of the Argentine Republic.—Serious conflict at Virden, Illinois, growing out of a strike of coal miners; 14 persons killed and 25 wounded.—Death of Rev. Calvin Fairbank, anti-slavery worker and helper of the freedmen.

19. Death of Harold Frederic, American journalist and novelist.

25. Decision of the Court of Cassation requiring a supplementary investigation of the case of Captain Dreyfus.—Death of Pierre Puvis de Chavannes, French painter.

29. Death of Colonel George Edwin Waring, American sanitary engineer.

31. Death of Helena Faucit, Lady Martin, English actress.

November 1. Establishment of the Constitution of the United States of Central America.

    2. Announcement by Lord Salisbury of the amicable settlement, between France and Great Britain, of "the Fashoda incident."

    5. Death of David Ames Wells, American economist and publicist.

    12. Death of Clara Fisher (Mrs. Clara Fisher Maeder), actress.

    15. Inauguration of Dr. M. F. de Campos Salles, President of United States of Brazil.—Order by the Court of Cassation that Dreyfus be notified by telegraph of the pending revision of his trial.

    19. Death of Brigadier-General Don Carlos Buell.

    20. Death of Sir George S. Baden-Powell, economist.

    25. Dissolution of the United States of Central America by the secession of Salvador.

    26. Appointment of Prince George, of Greece, to be High Commissioner of the Powers in Crete.

    27. Death of Charles Walter Couldock, actor.

    28. Death of Mrs. Mary Eliza (Joy) Haweis, English author and artist.

December 5. Final raising of the "pacific blockade" of Crete by the Powers.

    6. General Guy V. Henry appointed Military Governor of Porto Rico.

    10. Signing, at Paris, of the Treaty of Peace between the United States and Spain.—Death of William Black, English novelist.

    11. Death of Gen. Calixto Garcia, Cuban military leader.

    13. Appointment of General Brooke as commander and military governor of Cuba, by direction of the President of the United States.—Reception by the Empress-Dowager to the wives of foreign representatives at Peking.

    17. Death of Baron Ferdinand James de Rothschild.

    21. Arrival of Prince George of Greece in Crete, to undertake the administration of government as High Commissioner for the Powers.—Instructions of the President of the United States to General Otis, relative to the military government of the Philippine Islands.

    22. Death of Sebastian Bach Mills, composer and pianist.

    23. Decision by the French government to comply with the demand of the Court of Cassation for the secret papers (the "dossier") in the Dreyfus case.

    25. Penny postage to all places in the British Empire except the Australasian colonies and Cape Colony brought into operation.

    28. Death of Justin Smith Morrill, United States Senator.

    30. Death of Don Matias Romero, Mexican ambassador to the United States.

1899.

January 1. Formal relinquishment of the sovereignty of Spain over the island of Cuba, by ceremonies performed at Havana.

    4. The Treaty of Peace between the United States and Spain sent to the United States Senate by the President.—Proclamation of General Otis to the people of the Philippine Islands, amending the instructions of the President.

    5. Proclamation of Aguinaldo to the people of the Philippine Islands, counter to that of General Otis.

    8. Sensational resignation of the President of the civil section of the French Court of Cassation.

    11. Second communication of the Tzar of Russia to other governments on the subject of an International Conference for the promotion of peace.

    13. Death of Representative Nelson Dingley, of Maine.

    17. Death of John Russell Young, librarian of Congress.

    19. Signing of an agreement between the government of Great Britain and that of the Khedive of Egypt, establishing a condominium or joint administration of government over the Sudan.

    20. Appointment of the First Philippine Commission by the President of the United States.

    22. Encyclical letter of Pope Leo XIII. condemning certain opinions called Americanism.

    29. Death of Dr. R. Fruin, Dutch historian.

February 4. First outbreak of hostilities between the American and Filipino forces at Manila.

    6. Ratification by the United States Senate of the Treaty of Peace with Spain.—Death of Gen. Count Georg Leo von Caprivi, formerly chancellor of the German empire.—Death of Irving Browne, American legal writer.

    10. Coup d'état of Señor Cuestas, declaring himself Provisional President of Uruguay.

    11. Occupation of the City of Iloilo, in the Philippine Islands, by the American forces.

    12. Sale of the Caroline and the Marianne or Ladrone Islands (excepting Guam) by Spain to Germany.

    15. Promulgation of a Russian imperial ukase which seriously impairs the constitutional independence of Finland.—Death of Henry Jones ("Cavendish").

    16. Sudden death of François Félix Faure, President of the French Republic.

    18. Election of Émile Loubet to the presidency of the French Republic.

    20. Adjournment of the Joint High Commission appointed to settle questions in dispute between the United States and Canada.

    23. Funeral of the late President Faure, at Paris; attempted revolutionary rising by the "League of Patriots," and others.

    24. Death of Émile Welti, formerly President of the Swiss Confederation.

    25. Death of Paul Julius de Reuter, Baron, founder of a telegraph company and news agency.

712

28. Defeat and resignation of the Spanish Ministry of Señor Sagasta, on the question of the signing of the Treaty of Peace with the United States; formation of the Ministry of Señor Silvela.—Death of Mrs. Emma Waller, English actress.

March. Withdrawal of foreign legation guards from Peking.
  1. Formation of the Visayan Military District in the Philippines under General Marcus P. Miller.—Death of Lord Herschell, English jurist.
  3. Creation of commission to examine and report on all possible routes for an inter-oceanic canal, under the control and ownership of the United States.
  6. Death of Princess Kaiulani, of Hawaii.
  10. Death of Sir Douglas Galton, British sanitary scientist.
  11. The signing of the treaty of peace with the United States by the Queen of Spain, on her own responsibility.
  13. Death of Sir Julius Vogel, British colonial statesman and author.
  14. Death of Émile Erckmann, French novelist.
  18. Modification of the plan of the Bureau of the American Republics, at a conference of the representatives of the American nations.
  21. Completed settlement of boundaries between English and French claims in West Africa and the Western Sudan.

April 2. Death of Baroness Hirsch.
  11. Death of Sir Monier Monier-Williams, English philologist and Oriental scholar.
  15. Death of Ely Thayer, active organizer of " the Kansas crusade."
  28. Agreement between Great Britain and Russia concerning their railway interests in China.

May 1. Death of Professor Karl Christian Ludwig Büchner, German physiologist and philosopher.
  8. General George W. Davis appointed Military Governor of Porto Rico.
  11. Papal proclamation of the " Jubilee of the Holy Year 1900."
  13. Advice from the Netherlands government to President Kruger, of the South African Republic, that he pursue a conciliatory course towards Great Britain.
  15. Death of Francisque Sarcey, French essayist.
  18. Meeting and organization of the International Peace Conference at The Hague. Order by the Tzar of Russia looking to the abolition of transportation to Siberia.
  19. Spanish garrison at Jolo, in the Sulu Archipelago, replaced by American troops.
  25. Death of Emilio Castelar, Spanish orator and statesman.—Death of Rosa Bonheur, French artist.
  27. Death of Dr. Alphonse Charpentier, French physician.
  29. Order by President McKinley seriously modifying the civil service rules.
  31. Conference at Bloemfontein between President Kruger of the South African Republic and the British High Commissioner, Sir Alfred Milner.

June. International Convention respecting the liquor traffic in Africa concluded at Brussels.
  2. Confession of Commandant Esterhazy, a refugee in England, that he wrote the " bordereau" ascribed to Captain Dreyfus.
  3. Decision of the Court of Cassation, quashing and annulling, in certain particulars, the judgment of condemnation pronounced against Captain Dreyfus in 1894 and ordering a new trial by court martial, to be held at Rennes.—Death of Johann Strauss, Austrian composer.
  4. Ruffianly demonstration of young French royalists against President Loubet, at the Auteuil races ; the President struck.
  7. Death of Augustin Daly, American theatrical manager.
  10. Death of John J. Lalor, American writer on political and economic subjects.
  12. Resignation of the Ministry of M. Dupuy, in France ; formation of a "Government of Republican defense," under M. Waldeck-Rousseau.
  15. Meeting at Paris of the tribunal for the arbitration of the Venezuela boundary.—Death of Representative Richard Parks Bland, of Missouri.
  24. Death of the Dowager Queen Kapiolani, widow of King Kalakaua of Hawaii.
  28-30. Political rioting and threatened revolution at Brussels.
  30. Death of Mrs. E. D. E. N. Southworth, Amerian novelist.

July 1. Death of Charles Victor Cherbuliez, French novelist and critic.
  6. Death of Robert Bonner, American publisher.
  7. Death of George W. Julian, American anti-slavery leader.
  10. Death of the Grand Duke George, brother of the Tzar of Russia.
  17. Release of Japan from her old treaties with the Western Powers ; abolition of foreign consular courts.
  18. Death of Horatio Alger, American writer of stories for boys.
  21. Death of Col. Robert G. Ingersoll, American apostle of atheism.
  22. Organization of a half military, half autonomous government in the Philippine island of Negros.
  25. Election to fill municipal offices in Porto Rico, under orders from the Military Governor.
  26. Amendment of its franchise law by the South African Republic.—Assassination of General Heureaux, President of the Dominican Republic.
  29. Adoption and signing of the " Final Act" of the Peace Conference at The Hague, submitting three proposed Conventions, three Declarations, and several other recommendations, to the governments represented in it.
  31. Death of Dr. Daniel Garrison Brinton, American ethnologist.

August 1. Proposal of the British government to that of the South African Republic, that a joint inquiry be made as to the effect, in practical working, of the new franchise law.

4. Renewed counsel of moderation to President Kruger, from the Netherlands government.

7. Destructive cyclone in Porto Rico.—Opening of the new trial of Captain Dreyfus by court martial at Rennes.—A terrific hurricane in the West Indies; loss of life estimated at 5,000.

9. Passage of Act creating a national Board of Education for England and Wales.

11. Death of Dr. Charles Janeway Stillé, American author and educator.

12. Arrest of Déroulède and other pestilential Frenchmen for revolutionary conspiracy.

13. Russian imperial order declaring Talienwan a free port.

14. Attempt, at Rennes, to assassinate M. Labori, one of the counsel for Captain Dreyfus.

16. Death of Prof. Robert Wilhelm Eberhard Bunsen, German chemist.

19. Counter proposals from the government of the South African Republic to that of Great Britain.

20. Rioting in Paris; barricading of M. Guérin and other members of the "Anti-Semitic League" in their headquarters, to defy arrest.

September 4. Death of Jean Ristics, Servian statesman.

6. Proposal by the government of the United States of an "open-door" commercial policy in China.

8. Authorized publication at Berlin of a repeated declaration that the German government had never maintained, either directly or indirectly, any relations with Captain Dreyfus.

9. Verdict of "guilty" pronounced against Dreyfus by five of the seven members of the Rennes court martial.

11. Death of Cornelius Vanderbilt, millionaire.

12. Impassioned protest by M. Zola against the Rennes verdict.

18. Beginning of the trial, at Paris, of Déroulède and his fellow conspirators against the Republic.

19. Pardon of Captain Dreyfus by President Loubet.

22. Ending of the discussion of the Uitlander franchise question between the British and Boer governments.—Death of Major George Edward Pond, military author.

25. Death of Consul Willshire Butterfield, American historical writer.

27. The Orange Free State makes common cause with the Transvaal against the British.—Death of General Henry Heth, Confederate officer and historian.

October. International Commercial Congress and National Export Exposition at Philadelphia.

3. Announcement of the decision of the tribunal of arbitration upon the question of the boundary between Venezuela and British Guiana.—Fall of eleven columns of the great temple at Karnak, Egypt.

9. Ultimatum of the South African Republic to Great Britain.

10. Reply of the British government to the Boer ultimatum.—Contract of the Maritime Canal Company of Nicaragua declared forfeited by the Nicaraguan government.

12. First act in the British-Boer war, in South Africa; Boer invasion of Natal and of Cape Colony.

13. Death of Vice-Admiral Philip Howard Colomb, of the British navy.

14. Death of Charlotte Heine, sister of Heinrich.

15. Death of Lawrence Gronlund, socialist author.

16. Census of Cuba and Porto Rico, taken under the direction of the War Department of the United States.—Death of Professor Edward Orton, American geologist.

20. Battle at Talana Hill, Natal, between British and Boer forces; mortal wounding of General Sir W. Penn Symons.—Agreement between Great Britain and the United States upon a "modus vivendi" pending the settlement of the Alaska boundary.

21. Battle at Elandslaagte, in Natal.

25. Death of Grant Allen, author and naturalist.

27. Death of Brig. Gen. Guy V. Henry, late military governor of Porto Rico.—Death of Florence Marryat (Mrs. Francis Lean), English novelist.

28. Death of John Codman Ropes, American military historian.—Death of Ottmar Mergenthaler, inventor of the linotype printing process.

29. Beginning of the siege of Ladysmith, in Natal.

November 2. Earthquake and tidal wave in the island of Ceram, one of the Moluccas, overwhelming many towns.

3. Death of Col. Henry Inman, American writer on frontier history.

14. Signing of treaties between Great Britain, Germany, and the United States, relative to the Samoan Islands.—Inauguration of Juan Isidro Jiminez, President of the Dominican Republic.

16. Death of Moritz Busch, biographer of Bismarck.

19. Death of Sir John William Dawson, Canadian geologist.

21. Death of Garret A. Hobart, Vice President of the United States.

23. Battle of Belmont, in the South African war.

24. Death of Rev. Samuel May, American abolitionist.

25. Battle at Enslin, or Graspan, in the South African war.

28. Battle at Modder River, in the South African war.

30. Report of Isthmian Canal Commission in favor of the Nicaragua route.

December 6. Appointment of General Leonard Wood to the military command and governorship of Cuba.

10. Repulse of the British by the Boers at Stormberg.
11. Battle at Majesfontein, in the South African war.
12. Inauguration of William S. Taylor, Republican, Governor of Kentucky, his election being disputed by Democratic opponents.
15. First repulse of General Buller in attempting to pass the Tugela River, South Africa.
18. Death of Maj.-Gen. Henry W. Lawton, U. S. V.—Death of Bernard Quaritch, London book dealer.
20. Li Hung-chang appointed Acting Viceroy at Canton.
22. Death of Dwight Lyman Moody, evangelist.
23. Death of Dorman B. Eaton, leader in American civil-service reform.
25. Beginning of the "Jubilee of the Holy Year 1900," proclaimed by Pope Leo XIII.—Death of Elliott Cones, American naturalist.
30. Death of Sir James Paget, British surgeon.
31. Murder of Mr. Brooks, an English missionary, by Chinese "Boxers" in northern Shantung.

1900.

January 1. Abolition of Roman Law and introduction of the Civil Code throughout Germany.—Re-election of President Diaz, of Mexico, for a sixth term.
5. Death of William A. Hammond, American physician.
10. Landing of Field-Marshal Lord Roberts at the Cape, to take the British command in South Africa.
12. Death of Rev. Dr. James Martineau, English divine.
15. Letting of contract for building the Rapid Transit Tunnel in New York.—Death of George W. Steevens, English war correspondent.
17. Beginning of the second movement of General Buller across the Tugela River.
20. Death of John Ruskin.
21. Death of Richard Doddridge Blackmore, English novelist.—Death of the Duke of Teek.
23. Futile storming of the Boer fortifications on Spion Kop by the British troops under General Buller.
24. Decree by the Chinese emperor relating to the succession to the throne.
27. "Identic note" by foreign Ministers at Peking to the Tsung-li Yamên demanding action against the "Boxers" in Shantung and Chihli.
28. Elections to the French Senate; substantial success of the moderate Republicans.
29. Withdrawal of General Buller from beyond the Tugela.
30. Assassination of Senator William Goebel, Democratic claimant of the governorship of Kentucky.
31. Report of First Philippine Commission.
February 5. Third advance of General Buller across the Tugela River.—Signing at Washington of the Hay-Pauncefote Treaty between the United States and Great Britain, to facilitate the construction of an inter-oceanic canal.—Death of William Henry Gilder, arctic explorer.
9. Third retirement of General Buller from the north bank of the Tugela.
11. Beginning of the advance movement of Lord Roberts from the Modder River.
15. The Boer siege of Kimberley raised by General French.
20. Death of William H. Beard, American animal painter.
21. Agreement of Republican and Democratic leaders in Kentucky for a settlement of the gubernatorial question in the courts.—Death of Henry Duff Traill, English man of letters.—Death of Dr. Charles Piazzi Smyth, British astronomer.—Death of Dr. Leslie E. Keeley, originator of the "gold cure" for the liquor habit.
24. Death of Richard Hovey, American poet.
25. Opening of the new ship canal from the sea to Bruges.
27. Surrender of General Cronje and his army to the British, after nine days of battle, near Paardeberg.
27-28. Final passage of the Tugela by General Buller, and relief of Ladysmith.
March 1. Preliminary report of the United States Industrial Commission, on "trusts and industrial combinations."
5. Overtures of peace to Lord Salisbury by Presidents Kruger and Steyn, of the South African republics.
9. Death of Edward John Phelps, American diplomatist.
10. Battle of Driefontein, in the Orange Free State.—Death of Johann Feder E. Hartmann, Danish composer.
11. Reply of Lord Salisbury to the Boer Presidents, declining to assent to the independence of either of the two republics.
12. Occupation of Bloemfontein, capital of the Orange Free State, by the British forces.
13. Death of Père Henri Didon, French Dominican author and preacher.
14. Approval of the Financial Bill, for reforming the monetary system of the United States.
18. Death of Gen. Sir William Stephen Alexander Lockhart, British military commander.
23. Death of Sherman S. Rogers, American lawyer, prominent in civil service reform.
25. Rising of Ashantis and attack on the British in Kumassi.
26. Death of Rabbi M. Wise, American Jewish divine.
27. Death of General Pietrus Jacobus Joubert, Commandant-General and Vice-President of the South African Republic.
29. Order promulgated by the Military Governor of the Philippine Islands providing for the

election and institution of municipal governments.—Death of Archibald Forbes, British war correspondent.

April. Visit of Queen Victoria to Ireland.
1. Death of Professor St. George Mivart, English naturalist and scientific writer.
4. Death of Ghazi Osman Nubar Pasha, Turkish general.
6. Decision of the Kentucky Court of Appeals adverse to the right of William S. Taylor to the Governor's office.
7. The Philippine Islands constituted, by order of the United States Secretary of War, a military division, consisting of four departments.—Appointment of the Second Philippine Commission by the President of the United States.—Death of Frederick E. Church, American landscape painter.
10. Death of Frank H. Cushing, American ethnologist.
12. Act of Congress of the United States to provide revenues and a civil government for Porto Rico.
14. Opening of the Paris Exposition, with unfinished preparations.
17. Cession to the United States by Samoan chiefs of the islands in that group lying east of the 171st degree of west longitude.
19. Death of Robert Alan Mowbray Stevenson, British artist.
21. Meeting of the third Ecumenical Conference on Protestant Foreign Missions, at New York.—Death of Alphonse M. Edwards, French naturalist.
23. Death of George Douglas Campbell, Duke of Argyll, Scottish author.
26. Great fire in the city of Ottawa, Canada, and the town of Hull, on the opposite shore of the river.
30. Approval of an Act of the Congress of the United States "to provide a government for the Territory of Hawaii."

May 1. Meeting, at Rock Island, Illinois, of the national convention of the United Christian Party, to nominate candidates for President and Vice President of the United States.—Inauguration of civil government in Porto Rico; induction into office of Governor Charles H. Allen.—Death of Mihaly (Michael) Munkacsy, Hungarian painter.
10. Meeting of the national conventions of the two wings of the People's Party, at Cincinnati and at Sioux Falls, to nominate candidates for President and Vice President of the United States.
16. Dissolution of the Italian Parliament by the King.
18. Relief of Mafeking, after a siege of seven months by the Boers.
21. Decision of the Supreme Court of the United States that it had no jurisdiction in the matter of the disputed governorship of Kentucky.
23. Passage of the Meat Inspection Bill in the German Reichstag.—Death of Jonas Gilman Clark, founder of Clark University.
24. Proclamation by Lord Roberts of the annexation of the Orange Free State to the dominions of the British Queen.
28. Partial destruction of railway near Peking by "Boxers."—Death of Sir George Grove, English musician.
30. Congress of Cape Colony Afrikanders to protest against the annexation of the Boer republics.
31. Occupation of Johannesburg by the British forces.—Arrival at Peking of British, American, French, Italian, Russian and Japanese guards for the legations.

June 1-3. Fruitless peace parley between British and Boer military commanders.
2. Meeting of the national convention of the Socialist Labor Party, at New York, to nominate candidates for President and Vice President of the United States.—Death of Clarence Cook, American art critic and writer.
3. Election of a new Italian Parliament; resignation of the Pelloux Ministry; formation of a new cabinet under Saracco.
5. Occupation of Pretoria, the capital of the South African Republic, by the British forces.—Death of Rev. Richard Salter Storrs, American divine.—Death of Stephen Crane, author and journalist.—Death of Miss Mary H. Kingsley, African explorer.
6. Approval by the President of the United States of an act providing for the civil government of Alaska.
10. International force of marines from foreign fleets at Taku started for Peking under Vice-Admiral Sir Edward H. Seymour.
11. Murder at Peking of Mr. Sugiyama, the Chancellor of the Japanese Legation.—Counter proclamation of President Steyn, declaring the annexation of the Orange Free State to be null and void.
12. Death of Lucretia Peabody Hale, American author.
12-15. Second fruitless discussion of terms of peace between the British and Boer military leaders.
13. Massacre of native Christians and burning of foreign buildings by "Boxers" in Peking.
16. Opening of the Elbe and Trave Canal.—Election of municipal officers throughout the island of Cuba, under an election law promulgated by the military governor in the previous April.—Death of the Prince de Joinville, son of King Louis Philippe of France.
17. Bombardment and capture of Taku forts by the allied fleets.
19. Meeting, at Philadelphia, of the national convention of the Republican Party, to nominate candidates for President and Vice President of the United States.

716

20. Beginning of the siege of the foreign legations and the Pei-tang Cathedral at Peking.—Murder at Peking of the German Minister, Baron von Ketteler.—Death of Henry Brougham Loch, Baron, British colonial administrator.
21. Imperial Chinese decree proclaiming war upon foreigners and praising the "Boxers" as patriotic soldiers.—Proclamation of amnesty by the Military Governor of the Philippine Islands.—Death of Count Muravieff, Russian statesman.
22. Burning, by the Chinese, of the Hanlin Imperial Academy, at Peking.
25. Death of ex-Judge Mellen Chamberlain, American historical writer.
26. Retreat of Admiral Seymour's expedition to Tientsin, driven back by the Chinese.—Appointment of General Chaffee to command American forces sent to China.
27. Meeting, at Chicago, of the national convention of the Prohibition Party, to nominate candidates for President and Vice President of the United States.
30. Great fire at Hoboken, N. J., destroying the pier system, with three large steamers, of the North German Lloyd steamship line, and with a loss of life estimated at three hundred persons.

July 4. Meeting, at Kansas City, of the national convention of the Democratic Party, to nominate candidates for President and Vice President of the United States.
5. Death of Dr. Henry Barnard, American educator.
6. Meeting of the national convention of Silver Republicans, at Kansas City, to nominate candidates for President and Vice President of the United States.
7. Passage by the British Parliament of the Act to constitute the Commonwealth of Australia.
13. Capture of Tientsin by the allied forces.
14. Opening of Chinese attacks on the Russians in Manchuria.
15. Appeal to Congress by inhabitants of Manila.—Relief of the besieged British in Kumassi.
20. First news from the beleaguered foreigners in Peking received at Washington, in a cipher despatch from the American Minister, Mr. Conger, sent through the Chinese Minister, Mr. Wu Ting Fang.
23. Death of Baron von Manteuffel, German statesman.
27. Speech of the German Emperor to troops departing for China, enjoining them to give no quarter and make no prisoners, but imitate the example of Attila and the Huns.
29. Assassination of King Humbert, of Italy.
31. Death of the Duke of Saxe-Coburg-Gotha and Duke of Edinburgh, second son of Queen Victoria.—Death of John Clark Ridpath, American historian.

August 4. Movement of allied forces from Tientsin, nearly 19,000 strong, for the rescue of foreigners in Peking.—Death of Major-Gen. Jacob D. Cox, American military historian.
6. Capture of Yang-tsun by the allied forces.—Death of Wilhelm Liebknecht, German Socialist leader.
8. Speech of William J. Bryan, at Indianapolis, accepting his nomination for President of the United States.—Death of Cyrus Hamlin, founder of Robert College, Constantinople.
10. Death of Baron Russell of Killowen, Lord Chief Justice of England.
13. International congress of Zionists at London.—Death of Collis P. Huntington, American railway magnate.
14. Rescue of the besieged Legations at Peking ; entrance of the allied forces into the city.
15. Forcing of the gates of the "Forbidden City," at Peking, and expulsion of Chinese troops, by the American forces, under General Chaffee.
16. Meeting, at Indianapolis, of the American League of Anti-Imperialists, to take action with reference to the pending presidential election in the United States.
21. Annexation of Austral Islands to France.
22. Death of Carl Rohl Smith, American sculptor.
25. Death of Friedrich Wilhelm Nietzsche, German philosopher (so-called).
28. March of the allied army through the "Forbidden City," at Peking.
29. Expressions from Russia and the United States in favor of an early withdrawal of troops from Peking.—Death of Prof. Henry Sidgwick, English economist.

September 1. Transfer of all legislative authority from the Military Governor of the Philippine Islands to the Second Philippine Commission.
2. Proclamation by Lord Roberts directing the burning of farms in punishment of guerrilla warfare.
5. Meeting of Anti-Imperialists, at New York, to nominate candidates for President and Vice President of the United States.—Decrees establishing compulsory military service in Chile.
8. Letter of President McKinley, accepting his renomination for a second term as President of the United States.
9. The city of Galveston, Texas, overwhelmed by hurricane and flood.
10. Leave of absence given to President Kruger for departure to Europe.
12. Appropriation of $2,000,000 by the Philippine Commission for improvement of highways and bridges.
15. General election in Cuba of delegates to a convention for framing a constitution.
17. Dissolution of the British Parliament by royal proclamation, and order given for new elections in October.—Proclamation of the Australian Commonwealth by Queen Victoria.—Beginning of a strike of 112,000 anthracite coal miners in Pennsylvania.
19. Adoption by the Philippine Commission of an Act for the establishment and maintenance of an honest and efficient civil service in the islands.

22. Gigantic banquet in Paris to 23,000 representatives of the municipalities of France, in celebration of the centenary of the proclamation of the first French republic.

29. Meeting, at Chicago, of the national convention of the Social Democratic Party, to nominate candidates for President and Vice President of the United States.

October **4.** Points submitted by the government of France as the suggested basis for negotiations with the government of China, accepted subsequently by all the Powers.

10. Annexation of the Cook Islands to New Zealand.

16. Agreement between Great Britain and Germany upon principles to be observed "in regard to their mutual policy in China."

17. Ending of the strike of anthracite coal miners in Pennsylvania.

18. Resignation of Prince Hohenlohe-Schillingsfürst, Chancellor of the German Empire, and appointment of Count von Bülow to succeed him.

20. Death of Charles Dudley Warner, American author.

21. Fall of the Cabinet of Señor Silvela, in Spain; formation of that of General Azcarraga.

22. Death of John Sherman, American statesman.

24. Conclusion of Parliamentary elections in Great Britain; return of an increased majority for the Conservative and Liberal Unionist government of Lord Salisbury.

25. Annexation of the South African Republic to the dominions of the Queen proclaimed by Lord Roberts.

28. Speech of the French premier, M. Waldeck-Rousseau, at Toulouse, foreshadowing a measure against the religious orders in France—the Bill on Associations.—Census of Mexico.—Death of Professor Friedrich Max Müller, Orientalist and philologist.

29. Death of Prince Christian Victor, grandson of Queen Victoria.

31. Union of the Free and the United Presbyterian churches in Scotland.

November **4.** Rejection by popular vote in Switzerland of proposals for proportional representation.

5. Meeting of Cuban constitutional convention at Havana.

6. Presidential election in the United States.—First election in Porto Rico under the Act establishing civil government in the island.

7. Parliamentary elections in Canada, sustaining the Liberal ministry in power.

11. Signing of Russo-Chinese agreement concerning the Manchurian province of Fêng-tien.

12. Closing of the Paris Exposition.

18. Proclamation of Lord Roberts defining the intention of his order concerning farm-burning.—Death of Martin Irons, American labor leader.

22. Death of Sir Arthur Sullivan, British composer.

29. The British command in South Africa delivered to Lord Kitchener by Lord Roberts, lately appointed Commander-in-Chief of the British Army.—Death of Professor Burke A. Hinsdale, American historian and educator.

30. Report of Second Philippine Commission.—Death of Oscar Wilde.

December **3.** Meeting and organization of the first Legislative Assembly in Porto Rico.—Death of Ludwig Jacobowski, German poet and novelist.

5. Death of Mrs. Abby Sage Richardson, dramatist, author, actress.

6. Congress of Cape Colony Afrikanders at Worcester, to appeal for peace and the independence of the defeated republics.—Meeting of the newly elected Parliament in Great Britain.

12. Celebration of the centennial anniversary of the removal of the capital of the United States from Philadelphia to Washington.—Fourth international conference in London on the cataloguing of scientific literature, and final arrangement for beginning the work.

13. Death of Michael G. Mulhall, British statistician.

15. Landing at Sydney of Lord Hopetoun, the first Governor-General of the new Commonwealth of Australia.

17. Opening of the first argument before the Supreme Court of the United States in cases involving questions concerning the status of new colonial possessions.

19. Assumption of the title of Royal Highness by the Prince of Montenegro.

20. A joint note from the plenipotentiaries of the Powers at Peking, setting forth the conditions of settlement with China, formulated, after long discussion, and signed and delivered to the Chinese plenipotentiaries.—Ratification (with amendments) of the Hay-Pauncefote Treaty by the United States Senate.

12. Death of Roger Wolcott, ex-governor of Massachusetts.—Death of Representative Richard A. Wise, of Virginia.

27. Death of Sir William George Armstrong, first Baron Armstrong, English inventor and gun manufacturer.

28. Death of Professor Moses Coit Tyler, historian of American literature.—Death of Major Serpa Pinto, Portuguese explorer of Africa.

30. Death of Hiram Hitchcock, American archæologist.

31. Fall of two stones at Stonehenge.

1901.

January **1.** The beginning of the Twentieth Century.—Organization of the Permanent Court of International Arbitration at The Hague.—Inauguration of the Federal Government of the Commonwealth of Australia.

2. Death of Ignatius Donnelly, Shakespeare-Bacon theorist.

4. Transfer of Sir Alfred Milner from the governorship of Cape Colony to that of the Transvaal, continuing to be British High Commissioner for South Africa at large.
8. Opening of the second argument before the Supreme Court of the United States in cases involving questions concerning the status of new possessions.
12. Submission of the Chinese government to the requirements of the Powers.
14. Defiant proclamation issued by President Steyn and General De Wet.—Death of Right Rev. Mandell Creighton, English historian.—Death of Charles Hermite, French mathematician.
16. Approval of the Act apportioning Representatives in the Congress of the United States, under the census of 1900.
17. Proclamation of martial law throughout most of Cape Colony.
18. Celebration of the bicentenary of the coronation of the first King of Prussia.—Encyclical letter of Pope Leo XIII. concerning Social and Christian Democracy.—Death of Arnold Boecklin, German painter.
19. Death of the Duc de Broglie, French statesman.
21. Death of Professor Elisha Gray, one of the inventors of the telephone.—Death of Col. Frank Frederick Hilder, geographer and ethnologist.
22. Death of Queen Victoria.
24. Formal proclamation of the accession of ¦King Edward VII. to the throne of the United Kingdom of Great Britain and Ireland.
25. Death of Baron Wilhelm von Rothschild, financier.
27. Death of Giuseppe Verdi, Italian composer.
28. Death of Count Joseph V. Gurko, Russian general.
29. Death of Rev. Hugh Reginald Haweis, English clergyman and author.—Death of Vicomte Henri de Bornier, French poet and dramatist.

February 1. Death of Dr. Fitzedward Hall, entomologist.
1-4. Ceremonies of the funeral of Queen Victoria.
2. Act to increase the regular army of the United States to 100,000 men approved by the President.
5. Chinese Imperial decree, commanding new undertakings of reform.
6. Fall of the Saracco Ministry in Italy; formation of a new government under Signor Zanardelli.
7. Marriage of Queen Wilhelmina, of the Kingdom of the Netherlands, to Duke Henry of Mecklenburg.
11. Death of ex-King Milan of Servia.
12. Order by the United States Treasury Department levying a countervailing duty on Russian sugar, as being "bounty-fed."—Death of Don Ramon de Campoamor, Spanish poet, philosopher and statesman.
14. Marriage of the Princess of the Asturias, sister of the young King of Spain, to Prince Charles, of the Neapolitan Bourbon family.—Opening of the British Parliament in state by King Edward VII.
15. Death of Maurice Thompson, American author.
16. Retaliatory order by the Russian Minister of Finance, levying additional duties on American manufactures of iron and steel.
19. Death of Paul Armand Silvestre, French poet and critic.
26. Execution of two high Chinese officials, at Peking, in compliance with the demands of the Powers.—Adoption by the United States Senate of the so-called "Spooner amendment" to the Army Appropriation Bill, authorizing the President to establish civil government in the Philippines.
27. Adoption by the U. S. Senate of the Platt Amendment to the Army Appropriation Bill, defining the conditions under which the President may "leave the government and control of the island of Cuba to its people."—Assassination of the Russian Minister of Public Instruction.
28. Unsuccessful peace parley opened between Lord Kitchener and Commandant Botha.—Death of William Maxwell Evarts, American lawyer and statesman.

March 1. Concurrence of the U. S. House of Representatives in the "Spooner Amendment" and the Platt Amendment of the Senate to the Army Appropriation Bill.
1-14. Census of the Indian Empire, completed in 14 days.
2. Official announcement of the terms of the formation of the United States Steel Corporation.
4. Inauguration of William McKinley for a second term as President of the United States.
6. Death of Canon William Bright, Oxford theologian.
11. Rejection by the British government of the Hay-Pauncefote Treaty, as amended by the United States Senate.
12. Offer, by Mr. Andrew Carnegie, of $5,200,000, for the establishing of branches of the New York Public Library.
13. Death of Benjamin Harrison, ex-President of the United States.
15. Order for withdrawal of American troops from China, excepting a Legation guard.
17. Death of Rev. Elijah Kellogg, American writer of books for boys.
20. Passage of a new election law by the Legislature of Maryland, to exclude the illiterate from the suffrage.
21. Death of Rev. Dr. Frederick A. Muhlenberg, American divine.
22. Attempted assassination of M. Pobiedonostzeff, Procurator of the Holy Synod, in Russia.
23. Capture of the Philippine leader, Aguinaldo, by stratagem.
24. Death of Charlotte Mary Yonge, English novelist and historical writer.

28. Debate in the British Parliament on the peace negotiations between Lord Kitchener and Commandant Botha.

29. Passage of the Bill on Associations by the French Chamber of Deputies.—Death of James Stephens, Irish Fenian leader.

April **1.** Re-election of Mr. Samuel M. Jones for a third term as Mayor of Toledo, Ohio, independently of political parties.—Death of Sir John Stainer, British organist and composer.

2. An oath of allegiance to the government of the United States taken by Aguinaldo.

10. Death of Dr. William Jay Youmans, American scientist.

18. Speech of Sir Michael Hicks-Beach, Chancellor of the Exchequer, in the British House of Commons, introducing the Budget of the year.

19. Address to his countrymen issued by Aguinaldo, counselling submission to the sovereignty of the United States.—Promulgation of a new constitution for the kingdom of Servia.

22. Death of Rt. Rev. William Stubbs, Bishop of Oxford, English constitutional historian.

May 27. Opinions delivered by the Supreme Court of the United States in the so-called "insular cases."